The Wordsworth
Dictionary of Proverbs

The Wordsworth
Dictionary of Proverbs

—

G.L. Apperson

Wordsworth Reference

This edition published 1993 by Wordsworth Editions Ltd,
Cumberland House, Crib Street, Ware, Hertfordshire.

Copyright © Wordsworth Editions Ltd 1993.

ISBN 1-85326-321-4

Printed and bound in Denmark by Nørhaven.

Reprinted 1995

TO
MY DAUGHTERS

PREFACE

THIS book is a humble offshoot from the great parent stock of the *Oxford English Dictionary*. Its purpose is to trace, so far as may be possible, the history of English proverbs and proverbial phrases in English use. A very few sayings which have won proverbial rank, such as "Procrastination is the thief of time" and "Imitation is the sincerest form of flattery," are of definitely literary origin. These can be accurately dated. But the great mass, in most cases, cannot be dated with any precision. Many are translated from or based upon Greek or Latin originals; many have been borrowed, undergoing changes in the process, from those of other countries.

In a few score cases, classical originals and parallels, carefully referenced, have been inserted, in square brackets, before the other references; but no attempt has been made to do this exhaustively.

It is obvious that a proverb or proverbial phrase, a crystallised summary of popular wisdom or fancy, is likely, or, indeed certain, to have been long current in popular speech before it could make any appearance in literature, or even in collections of such lore. Consequently, the historical method of treatment can only give an approximation to accuracy. But I venture to think that the method adopted in this book is sound, and that the results obtained are worth the eight or nine years' labour that its preparation has involved.

Like the great Oxford work, if one may compare small things with great, this book is based upon the independent collection of material. During the leisure of about seven years I made my collections direct from original sources, as detailed in later paragraphs. Until these collections were as complete as I could make them, I refrained from consulting the *Oxford Dictionary*. When, as the actual writing of my *Dictionary* was in progress, I referred to that monumental work, I found that in a few cases examples which I had collected had already been used therein. These I have not marked, as they were the fruits of my own labour, but a small number of other references which I have taken direct from the *Oxford Dictionary*, are carefully marked (O.).

The principal early collections of proverbs and proverbial phrases are Taverner's *Prouerbes or Adagies out of Erasmus*, 1539; Heywood's *Proverbs*, 1546, and *Epigrams*, 1562; Florio's *First Fruites*, 1578, and *Second Frutes*, 1591; a number in Camden's *Remains*, 1605; Draxe's *Bibliotheca Scholastica Instructissima*, 1633; Clarke's *Parœmiologia Anglo-Latina*, 1639; George Herbert's *Jacula Prudentum*, 1640, and second edition, 1651; Howell's *Proverbs*, 1659; Ray's *Proverbs*, 1670, second edition 1678, third 1737, fourth 1768 and fifth 1813; Walker's *Parœmiologia*, 1672; and Fuller's *Gnomologia*, 1732.

The whole of Ray's collections, except a few offensively dirty or indecent sayings, and a considerable part of the examples in the other books, are included in the present *Dictionary*; but I have excluded a very large number of sententious and moral sentences found in such works as Fuller's *Gnomologia*, which certainly can never have been proverbial, and also many sayings which are purely foreign.

Many of the so-called *Proverbs of Alfred, c.* 1270, are not proverbs at all, but I have included a few, and also examples from the *Proverbs of Hendyng, c.* 1320, which have the genuine ring, and indeed, in some cases, afford early authority for some of our most familiar sayings.

Many English sayings have been found in old dictionaries, such as Horman's *Vulgaria,* 1519; Palsgrave's *L'Éclaircissement de la langue Française,* 1530; Withals' *Littel Dictionarie for Children,* 1556, and Lewis's revisal of that work, 1586; Huloet's *Abcedarium,* 1552; Baret's *Alvearie,* 1580; Florio's *Worlde of Wordes,* 1598; Cotgrave's *French-English Dictionary,* 1611; Torriano's *Piazza Universale,* 1666; Robertson's *Phraseologia Generalis,* 1681; and Berthelson's *English and Danish Dictionary,* 1754.

For local sayings all the publications of the English Dialect Society have been searched. I have also examined some thirty other similar works, including such books as Grose's *Provincial Glossary,* second edition 1790; Moor's *Suffolk Words,* 1823; Brockett's *Glossary of North Country Words,* 1825; Carr's *Craven Dialect,* 1828; Forby's *Vocabulary of East Anglia,* 1830; Wilbraham's *Cheshire Glossary,* 1836; Holloway's *Dictionary of Provincialisms,* 1838; Baker's *Northamptonshire Glossary,* 1854; Robinson's *Whitby Glossary,* 1855; *The Dialect of Leeds,* 1862; Brogden's *Provincial Words in Lincolnshire,* 1866; Atkinson's *Cleveland Glossary,* 1868; Parish's *Sussex Dictionary,* 1875; Miss Jackson's *Shropshire Word-Book,* 1879; Mrs. Wright's *Rustic Speech and Folk-Lore,* 1913; Dr. Bridge's *Cheshire Proverbs,* 1917; and Gepp's *Essex Dialect Dictionary,* 1920. One curious point that emerges from an examination of these books is that not a few proverbial sayings and phrases which were current in literature and general speech in the sixteenth and seventeenth centuries, but which have disappeared from more modern literature and from general colloquial speech, are found still to flourish in the dialectal and provincial vocabulary.

Apart from the special sources indicated above, nearly three thousand works in English literature, dating from the twelfth century (and earlier) to the present day, have been read or examined for the purposes of the present work. Shakespeare and Chaucer have been carefully gone through twice. The books of the Early English Text Society, and of other publishing societies, have also been read. This reading has not only provided the illustrative examples and references given, numbering many thousands, of the proverbs brought together in previous collections, but has added a large number of sayings hitherto uncollected.

Wherever possible the illustrative quotations and references have been taken from literature. The various collections are cited only where other references have not been obtained. Reference to the two principal nineteenth-century collections, Bohn's 1855 and Hazlitt's 1869, is made in the few cases only where earlier occurrence in the same form has not been found. Similarly, references to the second, third, fourth and fifth editions of Ray are given only when the saying treated does not appear in an earlier edition. In all cases preference has been given to literary illustration. Details as to the system of reference adopted are given on the page of "Explanations and Abbreviations."

I have been more concerned, from the historical point of view, to find the earliest examples I could of the sayings, than to illustrate their later use. But, where possible, I have tried to supply, roughly speaking, one quotation or reference for each century, with additional examples to illustrate varying forms of a saying.

The omissions, both of sayings and of illustrations, in a work such as this, undertaken and completed by a single hand, must be many; but as it is really the first attempt at a comprehensive Dictionary of the kind, it is hoped that its merits may be found more conspicuous than its deficiencies.

A word must be said as to arrangement. In Ray and other early collections the arrangement is purely fantastic. In more modern books, such as Fuller and Hazlitt, a professedly alphabetical order, under the first word of the form of the proverb adopted, is followed. The result of this is whole pages of sayings beginning with A, He, The, We, and other insignificant words, besides the inclusion of the same proverb in several different forms. Proverbs are used and quoted in very varying forms, and to find what the searcher wants in collections so arranged is often difficult.

In the present *Dictionary*, an attempt has been made to facilitate reference by the adoption of the alphabetical method in a somewhat new way. The arrangement in one alphabet is twofold.

1. All proverbs relating to the Months and Seasons of the year, to the Days of the week, to Saints' Days, Fasts and Festivals, to all Animals, Birds, Insects, etc., are, as a rule, grouped under the Month, Season, Day, etc., to which they refer. Cross-references are supplied to any exceptions. Similarly, sayings relating to God, the Devil, Hell, Heaven, the Sun, the Moon, Rain, Wind, Man, Woman, Child, and to other subjects which naturally suggest themselves as group-headings, such as Fool, Time, Water, Money, Life, War, etc., are, as a rule, grouped under their relative headings, with cross-references to exceptions. Sayings relating to Places are grouped in like manner.

2. Other proverbs, which do not naturally fall into any of the groups just indicated, take their places in the alphabet under either their first word, if that is significant, or under their first significant word—that by which anyone using the book, who was not certain of the saying's precise form, would naturally look for it. Cross-references have been liberally supplied throughout the work.

By this two-fold arrangement, especially by the grouping system, it is hoped that the book may serve the purposes, not only of a dictionary, but to some extent, at least, of a Classified Index of English Proverbs and Proverbial Phrases.

G. L. A.

ABBREVIATIONS AND EXPLANATIONS

ABBREVIATIONS

B. & F., Beaumont and Fletcher.
B.S., Ballad Society.
c., circa.
E.D.S., English Dialect Society.
E.E.T.S., Early English Text Society.
F.L.S., Folk Lore Society.
Hunt. Cl., Hunterian Club.
l., line.
(N.) indicates that the quotation so marked is taken from Nares's *Glossary.*
N. & Q., Notes and Queries.
N. Sh. S., New Shakspere Society.
(O.) indicates that the quotation so marked is taken from the *Oxford English Dictionary.*
P.S., Parker Society.
R. L. S., Robert Louis Stevenson.
Roxb. Cl., Roxburgh Club.
S., Society.
Ser., Series.
Sh. S., Shakespeare Society.
Spens. S., Spenser Society.
Tr., Translations.
T.T., Tudor Translations.
(W.) indicates that the quotation so marked is taken from Dr. Wright's *Dialect Dictionary.*

NOTE.—For some of the Latin and Greek quotations I am indebted to Mr. H. E. P. Platt's *Alia* (Oxford, 1904).

REFERENCES

The reference always precedes the quotation, except in the case of the classical quotations within square brackets.

A reference without a quotation indicates that the example occurs either in precisely the same form, or with trifling difference, as in the heading to the article.

References, other than to plays, are to page, or volume and page, unless otherwise indicated. Plays are referred to by Act and Scene, or by Act alone.

A date or name in brackets indicates the edition to which reference is made.

1530: Palsgrave: Palsgrave's *L'Éclaircissement de la Langue Française*, Ed. Paris, 1852.

1611: Cotgrave: Cotgrave's *French-English Dictionary*, 1611.

1633: Draxe: Thomas Draxe's *Bibliotheca Scholastica Instructissima*, 1633.

1639: Clarke: John Clarke's *Parœmiologia Anglo-Latina*, 1639.

1659: Howell: James Howell's *Proverbs*, 1659.

1670, 1678, etc.: Ray: John Ray's *English Proverbs*, 1670 and subsequent editions. Reference is made to the later editions of Ray only when the saying treated does not occur in an earlier edition.

1732: Fuller: Thomas Fuller's *Gnomologia*, 1732.

1855: Bohn: H. G. Bohn's *A Hand-Book of Proverbs*, 1855.

1869: Hazlitt: W. Carew Hazlitt's *English Proverbs and Proverbial Phrases*, 1869.

A. 1. *A per se*=A paragon. 1475: Henryson, *Test. of Cress.*, l. 78, O fair Cresseid! the flour and A-per-se Of Troy and Grece. 1573: Harvey, *Letter-Book*, 104 (Camden S.), A verie A per se A, not her fellowe in Europe. 1631: Brathwait, *Whimzies*, 123 (1859), Such an one is an a per se a for knavery. 1639: Clarke, 104, A per sea.

2. *To know not A from the gable-end*, or, *from a windmill.* 1401: in T. Wright, *Pol. Poems*, ii. 57 (Rolls Ser., 1861), I know not an a from the wynd-mylne. 1830: Forby, *Vocab. E. Anglia*, 434, He does not know great A from the gable end of a house. Cf. **B** (2).

Aback o' behind like a donkey's tail. 1917: Bridge, *Cheshire Proverbs*, 6.

Abbey to a grange, To bring an. *c.* 1480: *Early Miscell.*, 26 (Warton Cl., 1855), And nowe that abbay is torned to a grange. *c.* 1540: Bale, *Kynge Johan*, 23 (Camden S.), Our changes are soch that an abbeye turneth to a graunge. 1670: Ray, 161.

Above-board. 1608: J. Hall, *Virtues and Vices*, 15, All his dealings are square, and aboue the boord. 1640: Brome, *Antipodes*, III. i., Here's nothing but faire play, and all above boord. 1753: Richardson, *Grandison*, i. 185 (1883), All is fair, all is aboveboard: all is as it was represented. 1891: R. L. S., *Wrecker*, ch. ix., "Oh, everything's open and above board," he cried. 1924: *The Times*, 25 Jan., p. 11, col. 2, The public, which likes dealings to be above board.

Absence is a shrew. *c.* 1480: in Hazlitt, *Early Pop. Poetry*, ii. 13, And therefor it is said in wordes few, how that long absence is a sherew.

Absence sharpens love, presence strengthens it. 1732: Fuller, No. 755.

Absent party is still faulty, The. *c.* 1440: Lydgate, *Fall of Princes*, bk. iii.

l. 3927, For princis ofte, of furious hastynesse, Wil cachche a quarel, causeles in sentence, Ageyn folk absent, thouh ther be non offence. 1612: Shelton, *Quixote*, Pt. I. bk. iii. ch. xi., To him that absent is All things succeed amiss. 1710: S. Palmer, *Moral Essays on Proverbs*, 51, The absent party is always to blame. 1732: Fuller, No. 4390.

Absent without fault. 1633: Draxe, 43, He is neither absent without fault, nor present without excuse.

Abundance depends on sour milk, i.e. thunderstorms aid crops. 1893: Inwards, *Weather Lore*, 119.

Abundance of things ingendereth disdainfulness. 1578: Florio, *First Fruites*, fo. 32, The plenty of things dooth ingender care. 1629: *Book of Meery Riddles*, Prov. 9.

Accidents will happen. 1763: Colman, *Deuce is in Him*, I., Accidents, accidents will happen—No less than seven brought into our infirmary yesterday. 1849: Dickens, *Copperfield*, ch. xxviii., "My dear friend Copperfield," said Mr. Micawber, "accidents will occur in the best-regulated families."

Account not that slavery, That brings in penny savoury. 1678: Ray, 221. 1732: Fuller, No. 6371.

Accusing the times is but excusing our selves. 1732: Fuller, No. 759.

Ace of trumps. *I will not play my ace of trumps yet.* 1732: Fuller, No. 2647.

Aces of allowance. *The best must crave their aces of allowance.* 1672: Walker, *Parœm.*, 23.

Aching teeth. *Who hath aking teeth hath ill tenants.* 1670: Ray, 26.

Aching tooth, To have an. Usually to have a longing or desire for—but *see* 1730 quot. 1590: Lodge, *Rosalynde*, 136 (Hunt. Cl.), I have a longing tooth, a longing tooth that makes me crie. 1667:

L'Estrange, *Quevedo's Visions*, 201
(1904), ".You have still . . . an aching
tooth at those poor varlets." 1730:
Bailey, *Dict.*, s.v. "Ake," To have an
aking tooth at one, to be angry at, to
have a mind to rebuke or chastise one.
1742: North, *Lives of Norths*, ii. 172, He
had an aching tooth, as they say, at the
mill - stones of a water - mill. 1887:
Parish and Shaw, *Dict. of Kent. Dialect*,
I (E.D.S.), Muster Moppett's man's got
a terr'ble aching-tooth for our old sow.
Acorns. *See* Oak (5).

**Acquaintance of the great will I
nought, For first or last dear it will be
bought.** 15th cent.: in *Reliq. Antiquæ*,
i. 205 (1841), Aqueyntanse of lordschip
wyll y noght, For furste or laste dere
hit woll be bowght.

**Acre to keep a peewit, It would take
an.** 1917: Bridge, *Cheshire Proverbs*, 86.
Said of very poor land.

**Action is the proper fruit of know-
ledge.** 1732: Fuller, No. 760.

Adam. 1. *When Adam delved and
Eve span, Who was then the gentleman?*
c. 1330. R. Rolle in *Religious Pieces*,
p. 79 (E.E.T.S. 26), When Adam dalfe
and Eve spane, So spire if thou may
spede, Whare was thon the pride of
man, That now merres his mede.
Before 1500: Hill, *Commonplace-Book*,
131 (E.E.T.S.), Whan Adam delffid and
Eve span, who was than a gentilman?
1592: Greene, *Quip*, in *Works*, xi. 225
(Grosart), I will not forget the old wiues
logick, when Adam delud and Eue
spanne, who was then a gentleman?
1630: T. Adams, *Works*, 872. 1732:
Fuller, No. 6421. Ray, 1670, p. 210,
adds the couplet, *Upstart a churl and
gathered good* [wealth], *And thence did
spring our gentle blood*.

2. *We are all Adam's children, but
silk makes the difference.* 1659: Howell,
Proverbs: Span.-Eng., 13, We are all
Adams sons, silk onely distinguisheth
us. 1732: Fuller, No. 5425. *See also*
Old, D (2).

Add insult to injury. *See* Insult.

Adder. *See* quotations. 1856:
N. & Q., 2nd ser., i. 401, If the adder
could hear and the blindworm could
see, No poor man's children could go

their way free. 1856: Ibid., 2nd ser., i.
331, There is a Kentish proverb: . . . If
I could hear as well as see, No man nor
beast should pass by me. 1875: Parish,
Sussex Dict., 14, The country people
say . . . that on the adder's belly will
be found the words—"If I could hear
as well as see, No man in life could
master me." 1878: *Folk-Lore Record*,
i. 15, I have heard of a labourer
declaring that the "queer marks" on
the belly of the deaf adder could be
made out to be: "If I could hear as
well as see, No mortal man should
master me." *See also* Deaf (6); March
(38); and Snake (1).

Adderbury. *See* Bloxham.

Addled egg. *As good to be an addled
egg as an idle bird.* 1581: Lyly, *Euphues*,
207 (Arber). 1732: Fuller, No. 681.

Adlant. *See* Turn, *verb* (3).

**Advantage is a better soldier than
rashness.** 1855: Bohn, 305.

Adversity flattereth no man. 1732:
Fuller, No. 762.

**Adversity is easier borne than pros-
perity forgot.** Ibid., No. 763.

**Adversity makes a man wise, though
not rich.** 1633: Draxe, 6, In aduersitie
men finde eies. 1678: Ray, 92. 1732:
Fuller, No. 764. *See also* Prosperity.

Advice. 1. *Advice comes too late when
a thing is done.* 1670: Ray, 1. 1748:
Richardson, *Clarissa*, iv. 119 (1785).

2. *Advice to all, security for none.*
1855: Bohn, 305.

3. *Give neither advice nor salt, until
you are asked for it.* 1875: A. B. Cheales,
Proverb. Folk-Lore, 88.

4. *In vain he craves advice that will not
follow it.* 1611: Cotgrave, s.v. "Croire."
1670: Ray, 1.

5. *We may give advice, but we cannot
give conduct.* 1736: Franklin, *Way to
Wealth*, in *Works*, i. 451 (Bigelow).
See also Woman (15) and (60).

**Affairs, like salt fish, ought to be a
good while a soaking.** 1855: Bohn, 305.

Afraid of far enough. 1670: Ray, 161.
1917: Bridge, *Cheshire Proverbs*, 8.

Afraid of grass. c. 1582: G. Harvey,
Marginalia, 192 (1913), He that is
afrayd of euery starting grasse, may not
walke in a meddow. 1710: S. Palmer,

Moral Essays on Proverbs, 195, He that's afraid of every grass must not sleep in a meadow.

Afraid of him that died last year.
1670: Ray, 161. 1732: Fuller, No. 810, Are you afraid of him that dy'd last year? 1917: Bridge, *Cheshire Proverbs*, 6, . . . Of that which is never likely to happen.

Afraid of his own shadow. 1567: G. Fenton, *Bandello*, ii. 285 (Tudor Tr.), He retorned with more fear of his shadow then true reaporte of that he had in charge. 1580: Baret, *Alvearie*, V 92. And as our English prouerbe is, he is afraid of his owne shadowe. 1672: Walker, *Parœm.*, 53.

Afraid of leaves. 1611: Cotgrave, s.v. "Peur," Let him thats skared by leaves keep from the wood. 1651: Herbert, *Jac. Prudentum*, 2nd ed., He that is afraid of leaves goes not to the wood.

Afraid of one's friends when none is near. 1699: in *Harl. Miscell.*, ii. 38 (1744), No girding satyrist can take up the old proverb against you, and say, That you are afraid of your friends, when there is none near you. 1740: Richardson, *Pamela*, i. 222 (1883), You are afraid of your friends, when none are near you.

Afraid of the hatchet, lest the helve stick in his leg. 1917: Bridge, *Cheshire Proverbs*, 7.

Afraid of the wagging of feathers. 1670: Ray, 55, He that's afraid of the wagging of feathers, must keep from among wild fowl.

Afraid of wounds. 1639: Clarke, 310, They that are afraid of wounds, must not come neere a battell. 1670: Ray, 56, He that's afraid of wounds, must not come nigh a battel. 1736: Bailey, *Dict.*, s.v. "Afraid," He that's afraid of wounds must not go to the wars.

Afraid to ask a price. *See* He will never.

After a delay comes a stay. 1732: Fuller, No. 6177.

After a lank comes a bank. 1678: Ray, 343.

After death, the doctor. 1611: Cotgrave, s.v. "Mort," After death drugs. 1681: W. Robertson, *Phraseol. Generalis*,

432. 1732: Fuller, No. 772. 1826: Brady, *Varieties of Lit.*, 39.

After dinner sit awhile; after supper walk a mile. 1588: Cogan, *Haven of Health*, 186 (1612), That old English saying: After dinner sit a while, and after supper walke a mile. 1639: Massinger, *Unnat. Combat*, III. i., As the proverb says, for health sake, after dinner, or rather after supper, willingly then I'll walk a mile to hear thee. 1754: Berthelson, *Eng.-Danish Dict.*, s.v. "Dinner." 1846: Planché, *Extravag.*, iii. 135 (1879), Some tell us after supper walk a mile, But we say, after supper dance a measure.

After drought cometh rain. 15th cent.: in *Reliq. Antiquæ*, i. 323 (1841), After droght commyth rayne. Before 1529: Skelton, *Magnyfycence*, l. 12, Howe after a drought there fallyth a showre of rayne.

After joy comes sorrow. 15th cent.: in *Reliq. Antiquæ*, i. 323 (1841), After plesur commethe payne. 1640: Mabbe, tr. *Exemplary Novels*, i. 59 (1900), For as it is in the proverb, after joy comes sorrow.

After meat, mustard. 1605: Camden, *Remains*, 316 (1870). 1694: Motteux, *Rabelais*, bk. v. ch. xxvii. 1712: Motteux, *Don Quixote*, Pt. I. bk. iii. ch. viii., It is just like the proverb, After meat comes mustard. 1822: Scott, *Nigel*, ch. iii.

After pear. *See* Pear (1).

After wit. 1. *After wit comes ower late.* 1683: Meriton, *Yorkshire Ale*, 83-7 (1697). 1692: L'Estrange, *Æsop*, 144 (3rd ed.), After-wit comes too late when the mischief is done.
2. *After wit is dear bought.* 1709: Dykes, *Eng. Proverbs*, 6, After wit is commonly dear bought.
3. *After wit is not the best.* c. 1605: in Collier, *Roxb. Ballads*, 88 (1847).

After you is manners. 1738: Swift, *Polite Convers.*, Dial. II., Oh! madam; after you is good manners. 1789: O'Keeffe, *Czar Peter*, III. ii., Stop, friend! after me is manners.

After your fling, Watch for the sting. 1917: Bridge, *Cheshire Proverbs*, 7.

Afterthought. *The afterthought is good*

*for nought, except it be to catch blind horses
wi'.* S. Devon. 1869: Hazlitt, 355.

Against the grain. 1670: Ray, 178.
1673: Dryden, *Amboyna*, I. i., But for
this whoreson cutting of throats, it goes
a little against the grain. *c.* 1730:
Swift, *Works*, xiv. 250 (Scott), Hither,
though much against the grain, The
Dean has carried Lady Jane. 1870:
Dickens, *Drood*, ch. xx., Which again,
naturally, rubs against the grain of
Mr. Bazzard.

Against the hair. *c.* 1387: Usk, *Test.
of Love* in Skeat's *Chaucer*, vii. 58,
But ayenst the heer it turneth. 1580:
Lyly, *Euphues*, 394 (Arber), I will goe
against the haire in all things, so I may
please thee in anye thing. 1609: Shakespeare, *Troilus*, I. ii., He is melancholy
without cause, and merry against the
hair. 1696: *Cornish Comedy*, II., *To
have and to hold till us do part, etc.*, goes
against the hair. 1754: Berthelson,
Eng.-Danish Dict., s.v. "Against."

Against the shins. 1678: Ray, 81,
That goes against the shins, i.e. It's to
my prejudice.

Against the wool. 1546: Heywood,
Proverbs, Pt. I. ch. xi., What, should
your face thus agayne the woll be
shorne For one fall? 1576: R.
Peterson, *Galateo*, 25 (1892), For,
fromewarde [froward], signifieth as
muche as Shorne against the wooll.
1693: Urquhart, *Rabelais*, bk. iii. ch.
xxxvi., Let us turn the clean contrary
way, and brush our former words
against the wool.

Age and want. *For age and want
save while you may, No morning sun
lasts a whole day.* 1736: Franklin, *Way
to Wealth*, in *Works*, i. 450 (Bigelow).
1825: Hone, *Ev. Day Book*, i. 1351.
1846: Denham, *Proverbs*, 19 (Percy S.)
[with "summer's" for "morning"].

**Age and wedlock bring a man to his
night-cap.** 1639: Clarke, 279. 1732:
Fuller, No. 778.

Age and wedlock tame man and beast.
1605: Camden, *Remains*, 317 (1870).
1732: Fuller, No. 779.

**Age and wedlock we all desire and
repent of.** 1732: Fuller, No. 780.

Age breeds aches. 1596: Harington,

Metam. of Ajax, 11 (1814), You have
heard the old proverb, "age breeds
aches."

Agree, for the law is costly. 1605:
Camden, *Remains*, 316 (1870). 1692:
L'Estrange, *Æsop*, 383 (3rd ed.), Agree,
agree, says the old saw, the law is costly.
1738: Swift, *Polite Convers.*, Dial. I.,
Come, agree, agree; the law's costly.

Agree like bells. 1630: T. Adams,
Works, 192, They tune like bells, and
want but hanging. 1683: Meriton,
Yorkshire Ale, 83–7 (1697), They agree
like bells, they want neathing but hanging. 1732: Fuller, No. 4948, They agree
like bells; they want nothing but
hanging.

Agreed upon the time. *See* quot.
1855: Bohn, 562, When you are all
agreed upon the time, quoth the vicar,
I'll make it rain.

**Ague in the spring is physic for a
king, An.** 1659: Howell, 20. 1732:
Fuller, No. 6249. 1846: Denham, *Proverbs*, 34 (Percy S.). 1904: *Co. Folk-
Lore : Northumberland*, 175 (F.L.S.).

**Agues come on horseback, but go
away on foot.** 1678: Ray, 33.

Air of a window. *See* Draught (2).

Alciston. *See* Firle Hill.

Alder. *See* quot. 1839: G. C. Lewis,
Herefordsh. Words, 6, When the bud of
the aul [alder] is as big as the trout's
eye, Then that fish is in season in the
River Wye. 1847: Halliwell, *Dict. Prov.
Words*, s.v. "Aul."

Alderman. *See* Paced.

Aldermaston house. *See* quot. 1869:
Hazlitt, 457, When clubs are trumps,
Aldermaston house shakes.

Aldgate. *See* Nick and froth; and
Old, D (3).

Ale. 1. *Ale and history.* I have not
been able to identify the proverb to
which the following quotations refer: Before 1635: Corbet, *Poems*, in Chalmers,
v. 580, Mine host was full of ale and
history. 1654: Gayton, *Pleasant Notes
Don Q.*, 195, That truth be in his ale, as
history. 1676: Etherege, *Man of Mode*,
I., You know the old proverb—ale and
history.

2. *Ale in, wit out.* *See* Drink, *subs.*
(1).

3. *You brew good ale.* c. 1590: Shakespeare, *Two Gent.*, III. i., And thereof comes the proverb: "Blessing of your heart, you brew good ale." 1826: Scott, *Woodstock*, ch. xix., "I will not say blessing on their hearts," said he; "though I must own they drank good ale."

See also Fair, *adv.* (3); Good ale; and Mend (6).

'Aler. *See* Hailer.

Alike every day makes a clout on Sunday. 1732: Fuller, No. 785. 1846: Denham, *Proverbs*, 5 (Percy S.).

All arc good maids, but whence come the bad wives? 1732: Fuller, No. 499.

All are not abed that have ill rest. 1530: Palsgrave, 422, They be nat all in bedde yet that shall have yvell rest to nyght. 1546: Heywood, *Proverbs*, Pt. II. ch. vii. 1670: Ray, 60, All that are in bed must not have quiet rest.

All are not merry. *See* Merry that dance.

All are not saints that go to church. 1687: *Poor Robin Alman.*, July.

All are not turners that are dishthrowers. 1678: Ray, 212. 1732: Fuller, No. 503.

All are presumed good till they are found in a fault. 1640: Herbert, *Jac. Prudentum.*

All asidin as hogs fighten. 1678: Ray, 65.

All blood is alike ancient. 1732: Fuller, No. 505.

All came from and will go to others. 1611: Cotgrave, s.v. "Autruy." 1640: Herbert, *Jac. Prudentum.*

All come to. *You see what we must all come to if we live.* 1678: Ray, 65.

All complain. 1640: Herbert, *Jac. Prudentum.*

All covet all lose. 1297: Robert of Gloucester, 306 (1724) (O.), Wo so coueyteþ al, al leseþ ywys. 1523-5: Berners, *Froissart*, ch. cclix., It is an olde sayenge, He that all coveteth al leseth. 1591: Lodge, *Catharos*, 31 (Hunt. Cl.), The common prouerbe, Hee that coueteth all, often-times looseth much. 1664: J. Wilson, *The Cheats*, IV. i., This is it, when men must manage their business by themselves. All covet and all lose. 1745: *Agreeable Companion*, 19, All covet, all lose [title of story].

All cry and no wool. *See* Much cry.

All cry, fie on the fool. 1659: Howell, *Proverbs: Brit.-Eng.*, 30.

All doors open to courtesy. 1732: Fuller, No. 512.

All draw water. *See* Every man wishes water.

All fear is bondage. 1578: Florio, *First Fruites*, fo. 32, All fearfulnesse is folly. 1629: *Book of Meery Riddles*, Prov. 35.

All feet tread not in one shoe. 1640: Herbert, *Jac. Prudentum.* 1694: D'Urfey, *Quixote*, Pt. I. Act V. sc. ii., Let her bequeath it to the devil, or where she pleases: all shoes fit not all feet.

All fellows at football. 1600: *Sir John Oldcastle*, l. 1487 (Malone S.), Al friends at footebal, fellowes all in field. 1641: in *Harl. Miscell.*, iii. 228 (1744), If we had stayed but a little while longer, we should have been *All fellows at Football.* 1732: Fuller, No. 498.

All fish are not caught with flies. 1580: Lyly, *Euphues*, 350 (Arber), All fyshe are not caught with flyes. 1598: Meres, *Palladis*, leaf 43. 1732: Fuller, No. 514.

All flesh is not venison. 1623: Wodroephe, *Spared Houres*, 519. 1670: Ray, 56. 1732: Fuller, No. 515. 1875: A. B. Cheales, *Proverb. Folk-Lore*, 130.

All fool, or all philosopher. 1732: Fuller, No. 517.

All Fools' Day. *If it thunders on All Fools' Day, It brings good crops of corn and hay.* 1878: Dyer, *Eng. Folk-Lore*, 255. 1882: Mrs. Chamberlain, *W. Worcs. Words*, 37 (E.D.S.). 1893: Inwards, *Weather Lore*, 24.

All fruit fails. *See* Haws (2).

All go we still, etc. c. 1430: Lydgate, *Minor Poems*, 150 (Percy S.), An old proverbe groundid on sapience, Alle goo we stille, the cok hath lowe shoon [this line is the refrain—it ends each stanza].

All griefs with bread are less. 1620: Shelton, *Quixote*, Pt. II. ch. lv., Sancho said to him . . . "Sorrows great are lessened with meat." 1640: Herbert, *Jac. Prudentum.*

All-hallon-tide. *Set trees at Allhallon-*

*tide and command them to grow,
Set them after Candlemas and entreat
them to grow.* 1678: Ray, 52. *c.* 1685:
Aubrey, *Nat. Hist. Wilts,* 105 (1847).
1822: Scott, in Lockhart's *Life,* v. 184,
I hold by the old proverb—plant a tree
before Candlemas, and *command* it to
grow—plant it after Candlemas, and
you must *entreat* it.

All happiness is in the mind. 1855:
Bohn, 307.

All have and naught forego. 1562:
Heywood, *Epigr.,* No. 278. 1639:
Clarke, 40.

All her dishes. *See* **Dish** (1).

All holiday at Peckham. 1825: Hone,
Ev. Day Book, i. 1124. 1848: Forster,
Oliver Goldsmith, bk. i. ch. vi., "Oh, that
is all a holiday at Peckham," said an old
friend . . . in a common proverbial
phrase.

All in a copse. 1863: Wise, *New Forest,*
ch. xvi., Forest proverbs . . . such as . . .
"All in a copse," that is, indistinct.

All in the day's work. 1738: Swift,
Polite Convers., Dial. I., Will you be so
kind to tie this string for me, with
your fair hands? it will go all in your
day's work. 1855: Kingsley, *West. Ho!,*
ch. iv., "It's all in the day's work, as the
huntsman said when the lion ate him."
1908: Lucas, *Over Bemerton's,* ch. xv.

All is fair. *See* **Love,** *subs.* (1).

All is fish that comes to net. *c.* 1520:
in *Ballads from MSS.,* i. 95 (B.S.), Alle
ys ffysshe that commyth to the nett.
1580: Tusser, *Husbandrie,* 87 (E.D.S.),
Alls fish they get that commeth to net.
1664: *Witts Recr.,* Epigr. 644, But Death
is sure to kill all he can get, And all is
fish with him that comes to net. 1769:
Cumberland, *Brothers,* I., Black, brown,
fair, or tawny, 'tis all fish that comes
in your net. 1852: Dickens, *Bleak
House,* ch. v.

All is gone, etc. *When all is gone and
nothing left, What avails the dagger,
with dudgeon haft?* 1583: Melbancke,
Philotinus, sig. D3, When all is gone
and notheinge lefte, farewell dagger
with dudgen haft. 1659: Howell, *Letters,*
ii. 666 (Jacobs) [with "waits" instead
of "avails"]. 1670: Ray, 6. 1732:
Fuller, No. 6393.

All is lost that is put in a riven dish.
1639: Clarke, 169. 1681: W. Robertson,
Phraseol. Generalis, 1280. 1732: Fuller,
No. 546, All's lost that is pour'd into a
crack'd dish. 1880: Spurgeon, *Ploughman's Pictures,* 149 [as in Fuller].

All is not at hand that helps. 1732:
Fuller, No. 526.

All is not gold that glitters. [Non
teneas aurum totum quod splendet ut
aurum, Nec pulchrum pomum quodlibet esse bonum.—Alanus de Insulis
(ob. 1294), *Parabolæ,* c. iii.] *c.* 1220:
Hali Meidenhad, 9 (E.E.T.S.), Nis hit
nower neh gold al þat ter schineþ.
c. 1384: Chaucer, *H. Fame,* bk. i. l. 272,
Hit is not al gold, that glareth. *c.* 1440:
Lydgate, *Fall of Princes,* bk. iv. l. 2944
(E.E.T.S.), Al is not gold that shyneth
briht. 1583: Greene, *Mamillia,* in *Works,*
ii. 26 (Grosart), For al is not gold that
glysters. 1595: Shakespeare, *Merchant of
Venice,* Act II. sc. vii., All that glisters is
not gold. 1703: Ward, *Calves-Head Club,*
5 (1705), We alass see . . . all is not gold
that glisters. 1773: Garrick, Prol. to
Stoops to Conquer, Thus I begin: "All is
not gold that glitters." 1859: Sala,
Twice Round the Clock, 4 p.m. *ad fin.*

All is not lost that is in peril. 1611:
Cotgrave, s.v. "Perdu," All is not lost
that in some danger is. 1700: D. Craufurd, *Courtship à-la-Mode,* IV. ii., All is
not lost that is in hazard, as the saying
is. 1880: Platt, *Money,* 32, To realise
that "all is not lost when much is lost."

All is not won that is put in the purse.
1639: Clarke, 45, 'Tis not all saved that's
put i' th' purse. 1732: Fuller, No. 531.
1758–67: Sterne, *Trist. Shandy,* bk. iii.
ch. xxx., All is not gain that is got into
the purse. 1875: A. B. Cheales, *Proverb. Folk-Lore,* 100.

All is well. *See* **Man** (78).

**All is well save that the worst piece is
in the midst.** Glos. 1639: in *Berkeley
MSS.,* iii. 30 (1885).

All is well that ends well. *c.* 1426:
Audelay, *Poems,* 54 (Percy S.), For al ys
good that hath good ende. 1546: Heywood, *Proverbs,* Pt. I. ch. x. *c.* 1598:
Shakespeare, *All's Well that Ends Well*
[title]. 1757: Murphy, *Upholsterer,* II. i.
1850: Smedley, *Frank Fairlegh,* ch. xlvii.

1901: S. Butler, in *Life*, by H. F. Jones, i. 249 (1919).

All is well with him who is beloved of his neighbours. 1611: Cotgrave, s.v. "Bien," He lives well at home, that is beloved abroad. 1640: Herbert, *Jac. Prudentum.*

All meat is not the same in every man's mouth. 1584: Lodge, *Alarum against Usurers*, 46 (Shakesp. Soc.), Who finding all things meate in the mouth. 1681: W. Robertson, *Phraseol. Generalis*, 597, All meat pleaseth not all mouths. 1732: Fuller, No. 535.

All meats to be eaten, all maids to be wed. 1546: Heywood, *Proverbs*, Pt. II. ch. ii. 1678: Ray, 64.

All men can't be first. 1732: Fuller, No. 536.

All men can't be masters. 1546: Heywood, *Proverbs*, Pt. I. ch. xii., Every man may not syt in the chayre. 1604: Shakespeare, *Othello*, I. i., We cannot all be masters. 1732: Fuller, No. 537.

All men may say that thou art an ass, then bray, If. 1633: Draxe, 11. 1659: Howell, *Proverbs: Span.-Eng.*, 1, When all tell thee thou art an ass, 'tis time for thee to bray.

All men row galley way. 1813: Ray, 16, i.e. Every one draweth towards himself.

All men think all men mortal but themselves. 1924: *Sphere*, 29 March, p. 330, col. 2, That fact is probably explained by the adage, "All men," etc.

All men's friend. *See* Friend (8).

All mouths must be fed. 1710: Ward, *Nuptial Dialogues*, ii. 360.

All my eye and Betty Martin. 1785: Grose, *Class. Dict. Vulgar Tongue*, s.v. "B. M.," That's my eye betty martin, an answer to any one that attempts to impose or humbug. 1828: Carr, *Craven Dialect*, i. 128. 1834-7: Southey, *Doctor*, ch. cxxv., Who was Betty Martin, and wherefore should she so often mentioned in connexion with my precious eye or yours? 1851: Planché, *Extravag.*, iv. 158 (1879), Only your eye and Miss Elizabeth Martin.

All of a dither. *See* quot. 1917: Bridge, *Cheshire Proverbs*, 28, Aw of a

dither-a-wack loike a new-baked custhud. . . . = Trembling or shivering.

All of a heap. 1740: Richardson, *Pamela*, ii. 119 (1883), Mr. Longman, who had struck me of a heap. 1775: Sheridan, *Duenna*, II. ii. 1817: Scott, *Rob Roy*, ch. xxiv. 1842: Planché, *Extravag.*, ii. 167 (1879).

All of a hommock. 1854: Baker, *Northants Gloss.*, s.v. "Hommock," "All of a hommock" . . . is always restricted to a female who, from an excess of ill-made clothing, that sits in heaps or ridges, looks disproportionally stout.

All of a huh. 1886: Elworthy, *West Som. Word-Book*, 357 (E.D.S.), When anything is lopsided, it is said to be "all of a huh."

All of a litter, quoth Lambert. 1709: O. Dykes, *Eng. Proverbs*, 43.

All of a spinning = all alike. Staffs. 1889: *Folk-Lore Journal*, vii. 294.

All on one side. *See* Bridgnorth; Chesterfield; Marton; Parkgate; Smoothey's wedding; and Takeley Street.

All one a hundred years hence. 1611: Cotgrave, s.v. "Fiens," All will be one at the latter day, say we. 1675: in *Bagford Ballads*, ii. 722 (B.S.), For 'tis all one a hundred years hence. 1798: Wolcot, *Works*, v. 260 (1801). 1895: Pinero, *Benefit of the Doubt*, II.

All one, but their meat goes two ways. 1678: Ray, 78.

All our pomp the earth covers. 1640: Herbert, *Jac. Prudentum.* 1666: Torriano, *Piazza Univ.* 285.

All rivers do what they can for the sea. 1633: Draxe, 180, All rivers run into the sea. 1732: Fuller, No. 541.

All roads lead to Rome. *See* Rome (1).

All Saints Summer. 1924: *Observer*, 28 Sept., p. 7, col. 2, "All Saints Summer" occasionally gives us a fine spell before or after All Saints' Day on 1 November.

All shall be well. *See* Jack has his Jill.

All shearers are honest in the harvest field. 1846: Denham, *Proverbs*, 50 (Percy S.).

All sorts to make a world. 1844:

Jerrold, *Story of a Feather*, ch. xxviii., "Well, it takes all sorts to make a world"; and with this worn adage, my new possessor prepared himself to depart. 1901: F. E. Taylor, *Lancs Sayings*, 8, It ta'es o soarts o' folk for t' ma'e a wo'ld.

All that shakes falls out. 1640: Herbert, *Jac. Prudentum.*

All that shines. *See* **All is not gold.**

All the honesty is in the parting. 1678: Ray, 187.

All the levers you can lay will not do it. Somerset. 1678: Ray, 353. 1732: Fuller, No. 554, All the levers you can bring will not heave it up.

All the matter's not in my lord judge's hand. 1678: Ray, 76.

All the water in the sea cannot wash out this stain. 1666: Torriano, *Piazza Univ.*, 143, All the water in the sea cannot wash him. 1732: Fuller, No. 557.

All the world and Bingham. 1863: *N. & Q.*, 3rd ser., iii. 233.

All the world and Little Billing. 1854: Baker, *Northants Gloss.*, s.v. "L. B.," . . . a common mode of expressing that there was a large assemblage of people.

All the world and part of Gateshead. 1846–59: *Denham Tracts*, i. 80 (F.L.S.). 1892: Heslop, *Northumb. Words*, 2 (E.D.S.), "Aall the warld an' pairt o' Gyetside" [Gateshead], a common proverb, used jocularly.

All the world goeth by fair speech. Before 1500: Hill, *Commonplace-Book*, 130 (E.E.T.S.).

All things are not to be granted at all times. 1732: Fuller, No. 562.

All things are soon prepared in a well ordered house. 1611: Cotgrave, s.v. "Apprestée." 1670: Ray, 14. 1732: Fuller, No. 525, All is soon ready in an orderly house.

All things fit not all men. 1539: Taverner, *Proverbs*, fo. 36, All men can not do all thynges. 1639: Clarke, 82.

All things have a beginning. *c.* 1380: Chaucer, *Troylus*, ii. 671, For everything, a ginning hath it mede. 1542: Boorde, *Dyetary*, 240 (E.E.T.S.), Yet euery thynge must haue a begynnynge. 1631: Shirley, *Love Tricks*,

Prol., Nothing so true As all things have beginning.

All things have an end, with later addition, **and a pudding has two.** *c.* 1374: Chaucer, *Troylus*, iii. 615, As every thing hath ende. *c.* 1490: *Partonope*, l. 11144 (E.E.T.S.), Ye wote wele of all thing moste be an ende. 1530: Palsgrave, 527, Every thynge at the laste draweth to his ende. 1593: Nashe, *Strange Newes*, in *Works*, II. 212 (Grosart), Euery thing hath an end, and a pudding hath two. 1613: B. & F., *Burning Pestle*, I. ii., All things have end, And that we call a pudding hath his two. 1738: Swift, *Polite Convers.*, Dial. 1, Well, all things have an end, and a pudding has two. 1826: Scott, *Woodstock*, ch. x. [with the pudding]. 1852: Dickens, *Bleak House*, ch. li., "Well, well!" he cried, shaking it off, "everything has an end. We shall see!"

All things may be suffered saving wealth. *c.* 1390: Gower, *Conf. Amantis*, Prol., l. 787, Bot in proverbe natheles Men sein, ful selden is that welthe Can soffre his oghne astat in helthe. 1611: Cotgrave, s.v. "Aise," We say, all things may be suffered saving wealth.

All things require skill but an appetite. 1640: Herbert, *Jac. Prudentum.*

All thumbs, or, **Tom All thumbs.** 1598: *Servingmans Comfort*, in *Inedited Tracts*, 107 (Hazlitt, 1868): The clowne, the slouen, and Tom althummes. 1886: Elworthy, *West Som. Word-Book*, 395 (E.D.S.), Leave it alone, all thumbs! why thee art as clumsy as a cow handling a musket. Cf. **Finger (2).**

All tongue. 1828: Carr, *Craven Dialect*, ii. 213, "To be all tongue," to be a great talker.

All truths. *See* **Truth (23).**

All weapons. *See* **Weapon (1).**

All women are good, viz. either good for something, or good for nothing. 1678: Ray, 59. 1738: Swift, *Polite Convers.*, Dial. 1, Which of the goods d'ye mean? good for something, or good for nothing? 1869: Spurgeon, *John Ploughman*, ch. xvi.

All work and no play makes Jack a dull boy. 1659: Howell, 12. 1732: Fuller,

No. 6372. 1853: Dickens, in *Letters*, i. 313 (1880,) All work and no play may make Peter a dull boy as well as Jack. 1919: J. A. Bridges, *Victorian Recollections*, 160, No doubt, he got sufficient amusement out of his clients to prevent Jack from becoming a dull boy.

All worse and no better, like Tom Norton's wife. 1869: Spurgeon, *John Ploughman*, ch. xiii.

All's alike at the latter day; a bag of gold and wisp of hay. 1639: Clarke, 215.

All's lost both labour and cost. 1639: Clarke, 153.

All's out is good for prisoners but naught for the eyes. 1678: Ray, 186.

All's over. *See* Burying.

All's well that ends well, as the peacock said when he looked at his tail. 1910: *Devonsh. Assoc. Trans.*, xlii. 90.

Allan a Parson. *See* quot. 1846–59: *Denham Tracts*, i. 69 (F.L.S.), There never was an Allan a Parson. Spoken of the family of Allan of Blackwell . . . and the pedigree of the family fully bears out the saying.

Almond. *See* Parrot.

Almost and hard by save many a lie. 1639: Clarke, 106, Almost and wellnigh saves many a lie. 1662: Fuller, *Worthies*, i. 82 (1840), I approve the plain country by-word: . . . "Almost and very nigh, Have saved many a lie." 1732: Fuller, No. 6188.

Almost was never hanged. 1639: Clarke, 3. 1670: Ray, 56.

Alms. 1. *Alms never make poor.* 1640: Herbert, *Jac. Prudentum*. 1736: Bailey, *Dict.*, s.v. "Alms," Giving alms never lessens the stock. 1855: Bohn, 309, Alms-giving never made any man poor, nor robbery rich, nor prosperity wise.

2. *Alms quencheth sin.* [Water will quench a flaming fire; and almsgiving will make atonement for sin.—*Eccles.* iii. 30.] 10th cent.: Ælfric, *Homilies*, ii. 106 (Thorpe), þæt seo ælmysse ure synna lig adwæsete. *c.* 1175: *Old Eng. Homilies*, 1st ser., 37 (Morris, E.E.T.S.), Al swa thet water acwencheth thet fur swa tha elmesse acwencheth tha sunne. 1303: Robert of Brunne, *Handl. Synne*, l. 7079, Almes fordoth alle wykkednes

And quenchyth synne and makyth hyt les.

3. *It is an alms-deed to punish him.* 1628: Earle, *Microcosm.*, 48 (Arber), No man verifies the prouerbe more, that it is an almes-deed to punish him.

Alsager. 1917: Bridge, *Cheshire Proverbs*, 89, Like Auger [Alsager] wenches —all alike.

Altar. *He that serves at the altar, ought to live by the altar.* 1732: Fuller, No. 2294.

Altringham. 1. *The mayor of Altringham and the mayor of Over, the one is a thatcher, the other a dauber.* 1678: Ray, 301. 1790: Grose, *Prov. Gloss.*, s.v. "Cheshire." 1917: Bridge, *Cheshire Proverbs*, 115.

2. *The mayor of Altringham lies in bed while his breeches are mending.* 1678: Ray, 301. 1790: Grose, *Prov. Gloss.*, s.v. "Cheshire." 1818: Scott, *Heart of Midl.*, ch. xlv., "But, as we say in Cheshire," she added, "I was like the Mayor of Altringham, who lies a bed while his breeches are mending, for the girl did not bring up the right bundle to my room, till she had brought up all the others by mistake." 1917: Bridge, *Cheshire Proverbs*, 116.

Always behind. *See* Miller (7); and Mobberley (1).

Always complains is never pitied, He that. 1732: Fuller, No. 2038.

Always fears danger always feels it, He that. 1732: Fuller, No. 2039.

Always in his saddle, never on his way. 1579: Lyly, *Euphues*, Pt. II. 260 (Bond), Lyke Saint George, who is euer on horse backe yet neuer rideth. 1630: T. Adams, *Works*, 358, He is not like S. Georges statue, euer on horse-backe, and neuer riding. 1788: Franklin, *Autobiog.*, in *Works*, i. 286 (Bigelow), He is like St. George on the signs, always on horseback and never rides on. 1904: *N. & Q.*, 10th ser., ii. 512, I have on several occasions heard the proverb "Always in his saddle, but never on his way," used with reference to equestrian statues generally, especially where the horse's legs express movement.

Always in the lane (or field) when you should be in the field (or lane). *c.* 1791:

Pegge, *Derbicisms*, 138 (E.D.S.), To be in the lane, when you should be in the field. 1883: Burne, *Shropsh. Folk-Lore*, 589, He's al'ays i' the lane when he ought to be i' the leasow [meadow]. 1917: Bridge, *Cheshire Proverbs*, 157, Always in the field when you should be in the lane.

Always taking out of the meal-tub, and never putting in, soon comes to the bottom. 1736: Franklin, *Way to Wealth*, in *Works*, i. 448 (Bigelow). 1880: Spurgeon, *Ploughman's Pictures*, 11, Always taking out and never putting back soon empties the biggest sack.

Amberley. 1. *See* quot. 1870: Lower, *Hist. of Sussex*, i. 8, The local saying, which makes the winter reply to "Where do you belong? "—"Amberley, God help us! ", and the summer— "Amberley, where would you live? " [This kind of saying is current at various other places.]
2. *See* quot. 1884: "Sussex Proverbs," in *N. & Q.*, 6th ser., ix. 341, Amberley—God knows. All among the rooks and crows, Where the good potatoes grows. *See also* Chichester (1).

Amen! Parson Penn, More rogues than honest men. 1886: Elworthy, *West Som. Word-Book*, 24 (E.D.S.), A very common saying is: "Amen," etc.

Amend. 1. *See* quot. 1552: B. Gilpin, *Sermon before Edw. VI.*, 41 (1630), It is a proverbe lately sprung up, *No man amendeth himselfe, but every man seeketh to amend other*; and all that while nothing is amended.
2. *See* quot. 1611: Davies (of Hereford), *Sc. of Folly*, 47, in *Works*, ii. (Grosart), Some do amend when they cannot appaire.

Amendment is repentance. 1546: Heywood, *Proverbs*, Pt. II. ch. vi., Let your amendment amende the matter. 1732: Fuller, No. 789.

Among friends all things are common. 1477: Rivers, *Dictes and Sayings*, 35 (1877), He . . . loued aswele to do good to his frendes as to him self, sayng the goodis of frendes ought to be comyn. 1568: W. Fulwood, *Enemie of Idlenesse*, 91 (1593), The benefites of

fortune are common amongst friendes. 1694: *Terence made English*, 194, The old proverb says, Among friends all things are common.

Amy Florence. *See* quot. 1854: Baker, *Northants Glossary*, s.v., Any female loosely, untidily and tawdrily dressed. "She is quite an Amy Florence."

Ancholme. *See* Witham.

Anfield. *See* Tanfield.

Anger. 1. *Anger and haste hinder good counsel.* 1855: Bohn, 313.
2. *Anger dieth quickly with a good man.* 1670: Ray, 1. 1732: Fuller, No. 796.
3. *Anger edgeth valour.* 1639: Clarke, 178.
4. *Anger is a short madness.* [Ira furor brevis est.—Horace, *Epist.*, I. ii. 62.] Before 1225: *Ancren R.*, 1. 120, Wreththe is a wodschipe. 1477: Rivers, *Dictes and Sayings*, 23 (1877), He that can not refrayne his ire hath no power ouir his witte. *c.* 1568: Wager, *Longer thou livest*, sig. C2, Wrath and madnesse they say be all one. *c.* 1680: L'Estrange, *Seneca's Morals:* "Of Anger," ch. iv., He was much in the right whoever it was that first call'd Anger, a short madness. 1709: R. Kingston, *Apoph. Curiosa*, 36, Anger is a short fit of madness. 1855: Kingsley, *West. Ho!*, ch. xviii., Fear (which, like anger, is a short madness).
5. *Anger is a sworn enemy.* 1732: Fuller, No. 793.
6. *Anger punishes itself.* 1732: Fuller, No. 799.

Anger a wasp. *See* Wasp (4).

Angle, To. 1. *To angle all day, and catch a gudgeon at night.* 1618: Breton, in *Inedited Tracts*, 190 (Hazlitt, 1868).
2. *To angle with a silver (or golden) hook.* 1580: Churchyard, *Charge* 28 (Collier), Although you fishe with golden hookes. 1605: Breton, *Honor of Valour*, in *Works*, i. (Grosart), To fish for honour with a siluer hooke. 1652: Flecknoe, *Miscellanies*, 126, To exchange ones freedome for a little gain . . . I count it fishing with a golden hooke. 1725: Bailey, tr. Erasmus' *Colloq.*, 27, For the way of fishing there is according to the

proverb, with a golden hook. 1754:
Berthelson, *Eng.-Danish Dict.*, s.v.
"Angle," To angle with a golden hook.
Angler. *See* quot. 1658: Franck,
North. Memoirs, 94 (1821), He's an
early angler that angles by moonshine.

Anglesea is the mother of Wales.
1387: Trevisa, tr. Higden, ii. 39 (Rolls
Ser.), A prouerbe and an olde sawe . . .
Mon moder of Wales. *c.* 1440: Anon.,
tr. Higden, ii. 39 (Rolls Ser.), Hit is
wonte to be seide prouerbially . . .
Anglesey is the moder of Wales. 1662:
Fuller, *Worthies*, iii. 508 (1840). 1790:
Grose, *Prov. Gloss.*, s.v. "Anglesey."

Angry. 1. *Angry men make themselves beds of nettles.* 1748: Richardson,
Clarissa, vii. 307 (1785).

2. *Angry men seldom want woe.* 1732:
Fuller, No. 801.

3. *He that cannot be angry.* See
quots. 1604: Dekker, *Honest Whore*,
Pt. I. I. ii., I have heard it often said
that he who cannot be angry is no man.
c. 1615: MS. Proverbs in *N. & Q.*, vol.
154, p. 27, Hee that cannot be angry is
a foole, but hee that will not be angry
is more foole.

4. *He that is angry is not at ease.*
1633: Draxe, 9. 1670: Ray, 1.

5. *He that is angry without a cause,
must be pleased without amends. c.* 1520:
Stanbridge, *Vulgaria*, sig. C2, If ye be
angry with me without a cause thou
shalt be made at one w'out amendes.
1546: Heywood, *Proverbs*, Pt. II. ch. iv.
1642: Fuller, *Holy State*: "Anger," Be
not angry with any without a cause. If
thou beest, thou must not only, as the
proverb saith, be appeased without
amends . . . 1732: Fuller, No. 2277.

6. *If she be angry, beshrew her angry
heart.* 1546: Heywood, *Proverbs*, Pt. I.
ch. xi.

See also **Buckle of belt; Choleric;
Hasty man; and Wasp (1).**

Another man's child. *See* quots.
1670: Ray, 52, Put another man's child
in your bosom, and he'll creep out at
your elbow. *Chesh.* That is, cherish
or love him he'll never be naturally
affected toward you. 1732: Fuller, No.
3982 [with "sleeves" for "elbow"].
1917: Bridge, *Cheshire Proverbs*, 104.

Another man's dog. *He that keeps
another man's dog, shall have nothing
left him but the line.* 1639: Clarke, 20.
1670: Ray, 81. 1710: S. Palmer,
Moral Essays on Proverbs, 275 [with
"string" instead of "line"].

Another threshed what I reaped.
1732: Fuller, No. 802.

Another's bread costs dear. 1640:
Herbert, *Jac. Prudentum.*

**Another's burden, None knows the
weight of.** 1670: Ray, 1. 1732: Fuller, No. 3655.

Ant. 1. *If ants their walls do frequent
build, Rain will from the clouds be
spilled.* 1893: Inwards, *Weather Lore*,
146.

2. *The ant had wings to do her hurt.*
1620: Shelton, *Quixote*, Pt. II. ch. xxxiii.
1694: D'Urfey, *Quixote*, Pt. I. Act IV.
sc. i.

Anthony pig. *See* quots. *c.* 1460:
Good Wyfe wold a pylgremage, l. 16, And
rene [run] thou not fro hous to house
lyke a nantyny gryce [like a St.
Anthony's pig]. 1593: *Passionate
Morrice*, 75 (N. Sh. S.), She followed
him at heeles like a tantinie pigge.
1606: Chapman, *Gent. Usher*, IV. ii.,
I have followed you up and down like
a Tantalus pig. 1700: Congreve, *Way
of the World*, IV. xi., Lead on, little
Tony—I'll follow thee, my Anthony,
my Tantony, sirrah, thou shalt be my
Tantony, and I'll be thy pig. 1738:
Swift, *Polite Convers.*, Dial. I., . . . like
a Tantiny pig. 1762: Bickerstaffe, *Love
in a Village*, I. v., To see you dangling
after me everywhere, like a tantony pig.
1836: Wilbraham, *Cheshire Gloss.*, 2nd
ed., 112, To follow any one like a
Tantony pig. 1917: Bridge, *Cheshire
Proverbs*, 133, To follow one like
t'Anthony's pig.

Anticipates. *That which one most
anticipates, soonest comes to pass.* [Quid
quisque vitet nunquam homini satis
Cautum est in horas.—Horace, *Carm.*,
II. xiii.] 1678: Ray, 71, That which
one most forehets, soonest comes to
pass.

Anvil. 1. *An iron anvil should have
a hammer of feathers.* 1623: Wodroephe,
Spared Houres, 508, For a hard anveld

an hammer of feathers. 1666: Torriano, *Piazza Univ.*, 118, To a hard anvil, a feather hammer. 1710: S. Palmer, *Moral Essays on Proverbs*, 76.
2. *The anvil fears no blows.* 1666: Torriano, *Piazza Univ.*, 118. 1681: W. Robertson, *Phraseol. Generalis*, 102, The great anvil doth not fear noise or stroaks. 1732: Fuller, No. 4395. 1869: Spurgeon, *John Ploughman*, ch. xxi., The anvil is not afraid of the hammer.
3. *When you are an anvil, hold you still; when you are a hammer, strike your fill.* 1591: Florio, *Second Frutes*, 101. 1696: D'Urfey, *Quixote*, Pt. III. Act III. sc. ii. 1732: Fuller, No. 6075.

Any, good Lord, before none. 1886: R. Holland, *Cheshire Gloss.*, 444 (E.D.S.) [supposed exclamation of despairing spinster]. 1917: Bridge, *Cheshire Proverbs*, 8.

Any good. *He that any good would win, at his mouth must first begin.* 1639: Clarke, 136.

Any port in a storm. *c. 1780:* J. Cobb, *First Floor*, II. ii., in Inchbald's *Farces*, vi. 259 (1815), Here is a door open, i' faith—any port in a storm, they say. 1894: R. L. S., *St. Ives*, ch. xxv., "Any port in a storm" was the principle on which I was prepared to act.

Any road leads to the end of the world. 1852: FitzGerald, *Polonius*, 86 (1903).

Any stick to beat a dog with. *See* Stick, *subs.* (1).

Any tooth, good barber. 1659: Howell, 12. 1678: Ray, 91.

Anything for a quiet life. 1624: T. Heywood, *Captives*, III. iii., Anythinge for a quiet lyfe. 1738: Swift, *Polite Convers.*, Dial. I. 1837: Dickens, *Pickwick*, ch. xliii., But anythin' for a quiet life, as the man said wen he took the sitivation at the lighthouse. 1841: Planché, *Extravag.*, ii. 135 (1879).

Ape, and Apes. 1. *An ape is an ape* (or *will be an ape*), *though clad in purple.* 1539: Taverner, *Proverbs*, fo. 21, An ape is an ape, although she weare badges of golde. 1563: Googe, *Eglogs, etc.*, 40 (Arber), An ape wyll euer be an ape, though purple garments hyde. 1683:

White Kennett, tr. Erasmus' *Praise of Folly*, 23 (8th ed.), It is a trite proverb, that An ape will be an ape, though clad in purple. 1732: Fuller, No. 6391, An ape's an ape: a varlet's a varlet, Tho' they be clad in silk or scarlet.
2. *An ape is ne'er so like an ape, As when he wears a doctor's cap.* 1732: Fuller, No. 6382. 1869: Spurgeon, *John Ploughman*, ch. iii. ["popish cape" for "doctor's cap." Spurgeon gives the saying a polemical twist].
3. *An ape may chance to sit amongst the doctors.* 1732: Fuller, No. 580.
4. *An old ape has an old eye.* 1605: Camden, *Remains*, 317 (1870). 1653: R. Brome, *Damoiselle*, III. ii. 1738: Swift, *Polite Convers.*, Dial. I.
5. *Ape and whip.* *See* quots. 1588: *Mar-Prelate's Epitome*, 7 (1843), Reader cannot chuse but have as great delight therein as a Jack an Apes hath in a whip. 1639: in *Berkeley MSS.*, iii. 33 (1885), As proud as an ape of a whip, viz. not proud at all. 1659: Howell, 12, I love it as an ape loves a whipp. 1703: Ward, *Writings*, ii. 358, Which every wiseman dreads, as much as an ape does a whip.
6. *Apes are never more beasts than when they wear men's clothes.* 1732: Fuller, No. 807.
7. *As fine as an ape in purple.* 1596: Harington, *Ulysses upon Ajax*, 18 (1814), Howsoever clothed like an ape in purple. 1639: Clarke, 7.
8. *As free as an ape is of his tail.* 1670: Ray, 205.
9. *It is like nuts to an ape.* 1732: Fuller, No. 2970.
10. *The ape kills her young with kindness.* 1580: Lyly, *Euphues*, 215 (Arber), I should resemble the ape, and kill it by cullyng it. 1586: Whitney, *Emblems*, 188, With kindeness, lo, the ape doth kill her whelpe. 1607: Topsell, *Four-footed Beasts*, 5, She [the ape] killeth that which she loueth, by pressing it to hard. 1732: Fuller, No. 4396, The ape hugs her darling, till she kills it.
11. *The higher the ape goes, the more he shows his tail.* *c.* 1594: Bacon, *Promus*, No. 924, He doth like the ape that the higher he clymbes the more he

shows his ars. 1640: Herbert, *Jac. Prudentum.* 1710: S. Palmer, *Moral Essays on Proverbs,* 218. 1860: Reade, *Cloister and Hearth,* ch. lii., Your speech betrays you. 'Tis not till the ape hath mounted the tree that she shows her tail so plain. 1901: F. E. Taylor, *Lancs Sayings,* 20, Th' heegher a monkey climbs an' th' mooar he shows his tail.

12. *To lead apes in hell.* 1575: Gascoigne, *Posies,* in *Works,* i. 430 (Cunliffe), I am afrayde my marryage will bee marred, and I may go lead apes in hell. 1599: Shakespeare, *Much Ado,* II. i. 1658: Cowley, *Cutter of Coleman St.,* II. viii., I do not intend to die the whining way, like a girl that's afraid to lead apes in hell. 1738: Swift, *Polite Convers.,* Dial. I., Miss, you may say what you please; but faith you'll never lead apes in hell. 1842: Barham, *Ing. Leg.,* 2nd ser., "Bloudie Jackie," I'm sadly afraid That she died an old maid. . . . So they say she is now leading apes.

13. *To say an ape's Paternoster.* 1611: Cotgrave, s.v. "Barboter," To chatter, or didder for cold; to say an apes Paternoster. 1846: Denham, *Proverbs,* 4 (Percy S.), You're saying the ape's Paternoster [said to one whose teeth are chattering with cold].

See also Bit (1); and Wise (3).

Apothecary. 1. *As fit as a thump with a stone in an apothecary's eye.* 1732: Fuller, No. 679.

2. *Apothecaries would not give pills in sugar unless they were bitter.* 1670: Ray, 2.

See also Broken (1); Proud; and Talk (9).

Apparel makes the man. 1591: Florio, *Second Frutes,* 115, Though manners makes, yet apparell shapes. 1602: Shakespeare, *Hamlet,* I. iii., For the apparel oft proclaims the man. 1617: Greene, *Works,* ix. 19 (Grosart), Thy estate may bee great, for the hood makes not the monke, nor the apparrell the man.

Appearances are deceitful. 1666: Torriano, *Piazza Univ.,* 12, Appearance oft deceives. 1750: Smollett, *Gil Blas,* iii. 7, Egad, appearances are very deceitful. 1880: Spurgeon, *Ploughman's Pictures,* 27. 1922: A. Bennett, *Prohack,* ch. xx. iii., I think there is a proverb to the effect that appearances are deceptive.

Apple and **Apples.** 1. *A rotten apple.* See quots. 1340: *Ayenbite,* 205 (E.E.T.S.), A roted eppel amang þe holen makeþ rotie þe yzounde yef he is longe ther amang. *c.* 1386: Chaucer, *Cook's Tale,* l. 42, A proverbe that seith this same word "Wel bet is roten appel out of hord Than that it rotie al the remenaunt."

2. *A wink-a-pip* [imperfect] *blow Brings apples enow.* 1882: Mrs. Chamberlain, *W. Worcs. Words,* 39 (E.D.S.).

3. *An apple a day keeps the doctor away.* 1913: E. M. Wright, *Rustic Speech, etc.,* 238, Ait a happle avore gwain to bed, An' you'll make the doctor beg his bread (Devon); or as the more popular version runs: An apple a day keeps the doctor away. 1921: F. E. Baily, in *Royal Mag.,* Aug., p. 310.

4. *An apple may happen to be better given than eaten. c.* 1300: *Prov. of Hending,* st. 13 (ed. Berlin, 1878), Betere is appel y-yeue then y-ete. 1732: Fuller, No. 581.

5. *Apple and oyster* (or *lobster*). See quots. 1532: More, *Works,* 724 (1557), No more lyke then an apple to an oyster. 1565: Calfhill, *Answer to Marshall,* 99 (P.S.), Which have learned to make *quidlibet ex quodlibet*; an apple of an oyster. 1594: Shakespeare, *Tam. of Shrew,* IV. ii. 1667: L'Estrange, *Quevedo's Visions,* 34 (1904), You are no more like . . . than an apple's like an oyster. 1732: Fuller, No. 707, As like as an apple is to a lobster.

6. *Apples, eggs, and nuts, one may eat after sluts.* 1586: L. Evans, *Revised Withals Dict.,* sig. A7, Apples, egges and nuttes, a man may eate thoughe they be dressed by a slute. *c.* 1640: in *Roxb. Ballads,* ii. 186 (B.S.), My wife is such a beastly slut, Unlesse it be an egge or a nut, I in the house dare nothing eat. 1681: W. Robertson, *Phraseol. Generalis,* 113. 1732: Fuller, No. 6250, An apple, an egg, and a nut, You may eat after a slut. 1875: A. B. Cheales, *Proverb.*

Folk-Lore, 84 [as in Fuller]. 1913: *Folk-Lore*, xxiv. 76 [Oxfordsh.], You can eat apples and nuts, after any sluts.

7. *Apples, pears, and nuts spoil the voice.* 1659: Howell, *Proverbs: Ital.-Eng.*, 15. 1678: Ray, 41.

8. *Eat an apple on going to bed, And you'll keep the doctor from earning his bread.* Pembrokeshire and Cornwall. 1866: *N. & Q.*, 3rd ser., ix. 153.

9. *How we apples swim.* 1639: Clarke, 32. 1678: Ray, 253. 1852: FitzGerald, *Polonius*, 51 (1903).

10. *If apples bloom in March, etc.* 1883: *N. & Q.*, 6th ser., vii. 447, In East Sussex the rustics have the following rhyme anent the blooming: If apples bloom in March, In vain for 'um you'll sarch; If apples bloom in April, Why, then they'll be plentiful; If apples bloom in May, You may eat 'um night and day.

11. *If good apples you would have, etc.* 1883: *N. & Q.*, 6th ser., vii. 496, In South Devon the people say: If good apples you would have, The leaves must be in the grave; i.e. the trees should be planted after the fall of the leaf.

12. *To give an apple where there's an orchard;* i.e. coals to Newcastle. 1821: Clare, *Rural Life*, 114, Old Fortune, like sly Farmer Dapple, Where there's an orchard, flings an apple. 1854: Baker, *Northants Glossary*, s.v. "Orchard," Giving an apple where there's an orchard. 1883: Burne, *Shropsh. Folk-Lore*, 590, Those who have an orchard shall have an apple sent them, And those who have a horse shall have another lent them.

13. *Won with an apple and lost with a nut;* or vice versa. 1546: Heywood, *Proverbs*, Pt. I. ch. x., She is lost with an apple, and woon with a nut. 1573: G. Harvey, *Letter-Book*, 121 (Camden S.), Woone with a napple and loste with a nutt. 1630: *Tinker of Turvey*, 73 (Halliwell), Marian, thinking she had lost her lover with a nut, sent him a present of apples to winne him againe. 1732: Fuller, No. 2201, He that is won with a nut, may be lost with an apple.

See also Egg (8); Michaelmas (1); St. Swithin (2); Small choice; and Two apples.

Apple-cart, To upset one's. [ὅλην τὴν a ἅμαξαν ἐπεσπάσω.—Lucian, *Pseudol.*, 32. Plaustrum perculit. — Plautus, *Epid.*, 592.] 1854: E. A. Andrews, *Latin-Eng. Lex.*, s.v. "Plaustrum," I have upset my apple cart ! I am done for ! 1880: Courtney, *W. Cornwall Words*, 18 (E.D.S.), In Cornwall "Down with your dresser," or, "Over goes your apple-cart." 1928: Heslop, *Northumb. Words*, 16 (E.D.S.), "That's upset his apple-cairt for him, sa think,"—that has completely stopped his project. 1926: *Church Times*, 8 Jan., p. 46, col. 4, Should he attempt to do anything which in their opinion might upset the ecclesiastical apple-cart.

Appleby. *See* quot. 1690: *New Dict. Canting Crew*, sig. G7, "Who has any lands in Appleby? " a question askt the man at whose door the glass stands long.

April. 1. *A cold April the barn will fill.* 1659: Howell, *Proverbs: Span.-Eng.*, 21, A cold April, much bread, and little wine. 1732: Fuller, No. 6356. 1882: Mrs. Chamberlain, *W. Worcs. Words*, 37 (E.D.S.).

2. *A dry April Not the farmer's will: April wet Is what he would get.* 1893: Inwards, *Weather Lore*, 22.

3. *A flood in April, a flood in May, And a flood to take away the hay.* 1917: Bridge, *Cheshire Proverbs*, 162.

4. *A raggy [frosty] April an' a groo [cold, raw] May, Gars eydent [prudent] farmers ettle out their hay.* 1899: Dickinson, *Cumberland Gloss.*, 112.

5. *A sharp April kills the pig.* 1893: Inwards, *Weather Lore*, 23.

6. *After a wet April a dry June.* Ibid., 24.

7. *An April cling is good for nothing.* Somerset. 1678: Ray, 345. 1846: Denham, *Proverbs*, 43 (Percy S.).

8. *An April flood carries away the frog and her brood.* 1639: Clarke, 307. 1744: Claridge, in Mills' *Essay on Weather*, 101 (1773). 1893: Inwards, *Weather Lore*, 22.

9. *April and May the keys of the year.* 1659: Howell, *Proverbs: Span.-Eng.*, 21. 1732: Fuller, No. 809, April and May are the key of all the year. 1893: Inwards, *Weather Lore*, 23.

10. *April cold and wet fills barn and barrel.* 1893: Inwards, *Weather Lore*, 23.

11. *April comes in with his hack and his bill, And sets a flower on every hill.* 1846: Denham, *Proverbs*, 41 (Percy S.). 1879: Henderson, *Folk-Lore of N. Counties*, 95 (F.L.S.).

12. *April rains for men* [corn], *May for beasts* [grass]. 1893: Inwards, *Weather Lore*, 24.

13. *April showers bring May flowers.* c. 1560: in Wright, *Songs, etc., Philip and Mary*, 213 (Roxb. Cl.), When Aprell sylver showers so sweet Can make May flowers to sprynge. 1580: Tusser, *Husbandrie*, 103 (E.D.S.), Sweete April showers, Doo spring Maie flowers. 1611: Barry, *Ram-Alley*, V., I'll show you how April showers bring May flowers. 1732: Fuller, No. 6126. 1921: *Sphere*, 14 May, p. 152, If there was anybody left to believe in the saying that "April showers bring forth May flowers" . . .

14. *April snow breeds grass.* 1893: Inwards, *Weather Lore*, 23.

15. *April wears a white hat.* Ibid., 23.

16. *April weather, Rain and sunshine, both together.* Ibid., 23.

17. *Betwixt April and May if there be rain, 'Tis worth more than oxen and wain.* Ibid., 23.

18. *He is like an April shower.* 1639: in *Berkeley MSS.*, iii. 26 (1885), [Of an unconstant man] Hee's like an Aprill shoure, that wets the stone nine times (Glos.).

19. *If the first three days, etc.* 1861: *N. & Q.*, 2nd ser., xii. 303, "If the first three days in April be foggy, there will be a flood in June," said a Huntingdonshire woman the other day. 1912: R. L. Gales, *Studies in Arcady*, 2nd ser., 105, Fogs in April, floods in June.

20. *Moist April, clear June.* 1893: Inwards, *Weather Lore*, 24.

21. *On the third day of April come in the cuckoo and the nightingale.* 1732: Fuller, No. 6136. 1846: Denham, *Proverbs*, 41 (Percy S.).

22. *Snow in April is manure; snow in March devours.* 1893: Inwards, *Weather Lore*, 23.

23. *The first day of April, you may send a fool whither you will.* 1732: Fuller, No. 6135. 1846: Denham, *Proverbs*, 41 (Percy S.), On the first of April hunt the gowke another mile.

24. *Thunderstorm in April is the end of hoar-frost.* 1893: Inwards, *Weather Lore*, 24.

25. *Till April's dead Change not a thread.* Ibid., 23.

26. *When April blows his horn* [thunder], *It's good for hay and corn.* 1670: Ray, 41. 1744: Claridge, in Mills' *Essay on Weather*, 100 (1773). 1882: *N. & Q.*, 6th ser., v. 327.

See also **Cherry** (3); **Cuckoo**; **Dove's Flood**; **Frosty winter**; **January** (14); **March** (6), (13), (21), (24), (27), (34), (39), and (47); and **Potatoes** (2).

Apron-strings. *See* quot. 1678: Ray, 226, To hold by the apron-strings, i.e. in right of his wife.

Apt to promise is apt to forget, A man. 1732: Fuller, No. 271.

Archer is not known by his arrows, but his aim, A good. Ibid., No. 135.

Architect of one's own fortune. *See* Every man is the architect.

Arden, He is the black bear of. 1662: Fuller, *Worthies*, iii. 270 (1840). 1790: Grose, *Prov. Gloss.*, s.v. "Warwickshire," . . . Guy Beauchamp, Earl of Warwick, was so called. . . . This saying was used to express that the person . . . so denominated, was really an object of terror.

Argus at home, but a mole abroad. 1732: Fuller, No. 582. 1813: Ray, 78.

Arm. 1. *Don't stretch thy arm farther than thy sleeve will reach.* 1541: Coverdale, *Christ. State Matrimony*, sig. I3, Strech out thine arme no farther then thy sleue wyll retche. 1549: Latimer, *Seven Sermons*, 51 (Arber). 1683: Meriton, *Yorkshire Ale*, 83–7 (1697). 1817: Scott, *Rob Roy*, ch. xxii., "Nick," said he, "never put out your arm farther than ye can draw it easily back again." 1901: F. E. Taylor, *Lancs Sayings*, 9, Never put thi arm eawt furr nor thi sleeve'll cover.

2. *He's arm i' link wi' him.* 1917: Bridge, *Cheshire Proverbs*, 69, . . . Very familiar.

Armour is light at table. 1640: Herbert, *Jac. Prudentum.*

Army. *See* quot. 1911: Hackwood, *Good Cheer*, 313, "An army marches on its stomach," says the old proverb.

Aroint thee, witch. *c.* 1605: Shakespeare, *Lear*, III. iv. 1606: Shakespeare, *Macbeth*, I. iii. 1670: Ray, *Coll. of Eng. Words*, s.v. "Rynt ye," By your leave, stand handsomely, as *Rynt you witch*, quoth Besse Locket to her mother. — Proverb — Cheshire. 1816: Scott, *Antiquary*, ch. vi., The Antiquary interposed. "Aroint thee, witch ! wouldst thou poison my guests with thy infernal decoctions? " 1834: W. Toone, *Glossary*, s.v. "Aroint." 1917: Bridge, *Cheshire Proverbs*, 106. [In both Toone and Bridge with the "Bessie Locket" addition.]

Arrow. 1. *He makes arrows of all sorts of wood.* 1732: Fuller, No. 1983.

2. *The arrow often hits the shooter.* Before 1500: Hill, *Commonplace-Book*, 129 (E.E.T.S.), Often times the arow hitteth the shoter. 1709: R. Kingston, *Apoph. Curiosa*, 15, Like arrows shot against Heaven, fall upon their own heads.

3. *This arrow cometh never out of thine own bow.* Before 1500: Hill, *Commonplace-Book*, 129 (E.E.T.S.).

Art. 1. *Art hath no enemy but ignorance.* 1644: Taylor (Water-Poet), "To John Booker," 5, in *Works*, 2nd coll. (Spens. S., 1873).

2. *Art improves nature.* 1587: Underdowne, *Heliodorus*, bk. iii. p. 94 (T.T.), Arte can breake nature. 1732: Fuller, No. 814, Art helps nature, and experience art. 1827: Hone, *Ev. Day Book*, ii. 310, "Art improves nature," is an old proverb which our forefathers adopted without reflection.

3. *Art is long, life short.* [ὁ βίος βραχὺς ἡ δὲ τέχνη μακρή.—Hippocrates, Aph. 1. Inde illa maximi medicorum exclamatio est, "vitam brevem esse, longam artem."—Seneca, *De Brevit. Vit.*, c. i.] *c.* 1380: Chaucer, *Parl. of Foules*, l. 1, The lyf so short, the craft so long to lerne. 1630: Brathwait, *Eng. Gent., etc.*, 74 (1641), Art is long, life short, Experi-

ence deceiving. 1710: S. Palmer, *Moral Essays on Proverbs*, 380. 1850: Dickens, *Chuzzlewit*, ch. v. 1912: Lucas, *London Lav.*, ch. xx., And then there's not time . . . Life is short you know, Art can be too long.

4. *Art must be deluded by art.* 1583: Melbancke, *Philotinus*, sig. G1, It is a chiefe point of art to dissemble art. 1637: Breton, in *Works*, ii. *h* 11 (Grosart), I haue heard schollers say, that it is art to conceale art. 1732: Fuller, No. 815.

Artful fellow. *See* Devil (1).

Arthur, King. 1. *Arthur could not tame a woman's tongue.* 1659: Howell, *Proverbs : Brit.-Eng.*, 23.

2. *Arthur was not but whilst he was.* 1659: Howell, *Proverbs : Brit.-Eng.*, 35, Arthur himself had but his time. 1662: Fuller, *Worthies*, iii. 519 (1840), "Bu Arthur ond tra fu." That is, "Arthur was not, but whilst he was." 1790: Grose, *Prov. Gloss.*, s.v. "Cardiganshire," . . . spoken of a great family reduced to indigence.

3. *King Arthur did not violate the refuge of a woman.* 1662: Fuller, *Worthies*, iii. 519 (1840), . . . By the woman's refuge, many understand her tongue. 1790: Grose, *Prov. Gloss.*, s.v. "Cardiganshire."

Artist lives everywhere, An. 1560: Becon, *Catechism*, 355 (P.S.), According to this common proverb: *Artem quævis terra alit*; that is to say, "A man having an occupation shall be able to live wheresoever he become." 1725: Bailey, tr. Erasmus' *Colloq.*, 238, But you know the old proverb ; *a Man of Art will live anywhere.* 1823: D'Israeli, *Cur. of Lit.*, 2nd ser., i. 429 (1824), Nero . . . replied to his censurers by the Greek proverb, "An artist lives every where."

Arundel. *See* quot. 1894: A. J. C. Hare, *Sussex*, 221, A proverb says— Since William rose and Harold fell, There have been Earls of Arundel, And Earls old Arundel shall have While rivers flow and forests wave. *See also* Chichester (1).

As ever water wet. 1591: Harington, *Orl. Furioso*, bk. xvi. st. 15, Vnchast and false, as ever water wet. *See also* Good as ever.

As far. 1. *I have seen as far come as nigh.* 1546: Heywood, *Proverbs*, Pt. I. ch. xi. *c.* 1594: Bacon, *Promus*, No. 638.

2. *I've been as far south, as ye've been north.* A Wooler saying. 1846–59: *Denham Tracts*, i. 26 (F.L.S.).

As good a man. *See* Honest (9) and (10).

As good as. *See* Good.

As good beat your heels against the ground. 1639: Clarke, 154.

As good do it at first, as at last. 1593: G. Harvey, *Pierces Superer.*, in *Works*, ii. 247 (Grosart). 1632: Jonson, *Magnetic Lady*, V. vi., Well, you must have it; As good at first as last.

As good do nothing as to no purpose. 1732: Fuller, No. 684.

As good lost as found. 1605: Camden, *Remains*, 316 (1870).

As good never a whit. *See* Never a whit.

As good undone. *See* Undone (1).

As good water. *See* Mill (1).

As long as I am riche reputed, With solem vyce I am saluted; But wealthe away once woorne, Not one wyll say good morne. 16th cent.: in *Reliq. Antiquæ*, i. 207 (1841).

As much need on't, as he hath of the pip, or of a cough. 1670: Ray, 187.

As please the painter. *c.* 1594: Bacon, *Promus*, Nos. 159 and 1396. 1690: *New Dict. Canting Crew*, sig. I2, *What pleases the painter*, when any representation in the productions of his or any art is unaccountable, and so is to be resolv'd purely into the good pleasure of the artist. 1737: Ray, 61, As it pleases the painter.

As the goodman saith, so say we; But as the goodwife saith, so it must be. 1639: in *Berkeley MSS.*, iii. 33 (1885) [with "so it should be" instead of "so say we"]. 1670: Ray, 51 [with "good woman" instead of "goodwife"]. 1732: Fuller, No. 6408. 1875: A. B. Cheales, *Proverb. Folk-Lore*, 7.

Ascension Day. 1. *As the weather on Ascension Day, so may be the entire autumn.* 1893: Inwards, *Weather Lore*, 41.

2. *See* quot. 1669: *New Help to Discourse*, 284, If it rain upon Ascension Day . . . it doth betoken scarcity of all kinde of food for cattel, but being fair it signifieth plenty.

Ash. 1. *Burn ash-wood green, 'Tis fire for a queen; Burn ash-wood sear, 'Twill make a man swear.* 1851: Borrow, *Lavengro*, iii. 334, That makes good the old rhyme . . . "Ash, when green, is fire for a queen." 1884: H. Friend, *Flowers and Flower Lore*, 219.

2. *If the ash is out before the oak, You may expect a thorough soak; If the oak is out before the ash, You'll hardly get a single splash.* *c.* 1870: Smith, *Isle of Wight Words*, 62 (E.D.S.) [slightly varied from the foregoing]. 1893: Inwards, *Weather Lore*, 151.

3. *Oak, smoke* [summer hot]: *Ash, squash* [summer wet]. 1893: Inwards, *Weather Lore*, 151.

4. *When the ash is out before the oak, Then we may expect a choke* [drought]; *When the oak is out before the ash, Then we may expect a splash.* Shropshire. Ibid., 151.

It will be noted that 4 is the precise reverse of 2. There are variants of both 2 and 4 which may be found in Inwards.

See also Oak (3).

Ashford. *See* quots. 1735: Pegge, *Kentish Proverbs*, in E.D.S., No. 12, p. 67, Naughty Ashford, surly Wye, Poor Kennington hard by. 1899: J. W. Ebsworth, in *Roxb. Ballads*, viii. 640 (B.S.), Proud is Ashford, surly is Wye; Lousy Kennington stands hard by.

Ashton. *See* quot. 1869: Hazlitt, 320, Proud Ashton, poor people, ten bells and an old crack't steeple.

Ash Wednesday. 1. *As Ash Wednesday, so the fasting time.* 1893: Inwards, *Weather Lore*, 40.

2. *Wherever the wind lies on Ash Wednesday, it continues during the whole of Lent.* 1830: Forby, *Vocab. E. Anglia*, 414. 1893: Inwards, *Weather Lore*, 40.

Ask. 1. *Ask but enough, and you may lower the price as you list.* 1813: Ray, 2.

2. *Ask much to have a little.* *c.* 1582: G. Harvey, *Marginalia*, 191 (1913), Craue

and haue. 1640: Herbert, *Jac. Prudentum.*

3. *Ask my fellow whether I be a thief.*
1546: Heywood, *Proverbs*, Pt. II. ch. v.
1630: T. Adams, *Works*, 316, This is
somewhat to the prouerbe, Aske the
sons if the father be a theefe. 1692:
L'Estrange, *Æsop*, 355 (3rd ed.), Ask
my brother if I'm a thief. 1732: Fuller,
No. 817.

4. *Ask the mother if the child be like
his father.* 1732: Fuller, No. 818.

5. *Ask the seller if his ware be bad.*
1666: Torriano, *Piazza Univ.*, 73, Ask
mine host whether he have good wine.
1732: Fuller, No. 819. 1774: C. Dibdin, *The Quaker*, II. iii., Ask the vintner
if the wine be good.

6. *He that asketh a courtesy promiseth
a kindness.* 1732: Fuller, No. 2041.

7. *He that asketh faintly beggeth a
denial.* Ibid., No. 2042.

8. *He that cannot ask cannot live.*
1633: Draxe, 20. 1639: Clarke, 41.
See also Ax.

Aspen leaf. 1. *To tremble like an
aspen leaf.* c. 1374: Chaucer, *Troylus,*
iii. 1200, Right as an aspes leef she gan
to quake. 1449: J. Metham, *Works,*
61 (E.E.T.S.), Than euyn as an espys
lef doth schake Ayens the wynd, ryght
so than dyd he, Dyd qwake for fere.
1567: Golding, *Ovid,* iii. 46, Stoode
trembling like an aspen leafe. c. 1591:
Shakespeare, *Titus Andr.*, II. iv. 1675:
C. Cotton, *Burl. upon Burlesque*, 247
(1765), But like an aspen-leaf I shook.
1740: Richardson, *Pamela*, i. 228 (1883),
She came into bed, but trembled like an
aspen-leaf. 1780: Walpole, *Letters*, vii.
376 (Cunningham), Lord Mansfield . . .
quivered on the wool-sack like an aspen.
1828: Scott, *Fair Maid*, ch. xxxii.
1920: A. A. Milne, *Second Plays*, 186
(1921), I was shaking like an aspen
leaf.

2. *When the aspen leaves are no bigger
than your nail, Is the time to look out for
truff and peel.* 1850: *N. & Q.*, 1st ser.,
ii. 511.

Ass and Asses. 1. *A dull ass near
home needs no spur.* 1732: Fuller,
No. 83.

2. *An ass is but an ass, though laden*
with gold. 1660: Howell, *Parly of
Beasts*, 17, The asse often times carries
gold on his back, yet feeds on thistles.
1666: Torriano, *Piazza Univ.*, 15, An
asse, though loaded with gold, eats
but nettles and thistles. 1732: Fuller,
No. 585.

3. *An ass is the gravest beast, the owl
the gravest bird.* 1732: Fuller, No. 586.
1886: Swainson, *Folk-Lore of British
Birds*, 125 (F.L.S.).

4. *An ass laden with gold. See* quots.
1620: Shelton, *Quixote*, Pt. II. ch. xxxv.,
The usual proverbs are: "An ass laden
with gold will go lightly uphill" . . .
1630: T. Adams, *Works*, 863, Philip was
wont to say, that an asse laden with
golde would enter the gates of any
citie. 1631: Mabbe, *Celestina*, 72 (T.T.),
There is not any place so high, whereunto an asse laden with gold will not
get up. 1645: Howell, *Letters*, bk. i.
§ ii. ch. ix., There's no fence or fortress
against an ass laden with gold. 1732:
Fuller, No. 587, An ass laden with
gold overtakes every thing. Ibid.,
No. 588, An ass loaded with gold
climbs to the top of a castle.

5. *An ass must be tied where the
master will have him.* 1732: Fuller,
No. 589.

6. *An ass pricked must needs trot.*
1629: *Book of Meery Riddles*, Prov. 58.

7. *An ass was never cut out for a
lap-dog.* 1732: Fuller, No. 592.

8. *As proud as an ass of a new packsaddle.* 1823: Scott, *Q. Durward*,
ch. xxvii.

9. *Asses die and wolves bury them.*
1732: Fuller, No. 821.

10. *Better ride an ass that carries me,
than a horse that throws me.* 1633:
Draxe, 223. 1732: Fuller, No. 920.
1880: Spurgeon, *Ploughman's Pictures*,
35. 1929: *Times*, 17 Jan., p. 9, col. 1.

11. *Better strive with an ill ass, than
carry the wood one's self.* 1732: Fuller,
No. 930.

12. *Did you ever hear an ass play on a
lute?* 1556: G. Colvile, tr. Boethius, 18
(1897), Art thou no more apt to vnderstand them then an asse to play on the
harpe? 1732: Fuller, No. 1282. 1781:
T. Francklin, *Lucian's Works*, ii. 109,

What, indeed, as the proverb says, has the ass to do with a lyre?

13. *Every ass loves to hear himself bray.* 1732: Fuller, No. 1404.

14. *Every ass thinks himself worthy to stand with the king's horses.* 1639: Clarke, 254. 1670: Ray, 58. 1732: Fuller, No. 1405.

15. *Hark! I hear the asses bray; We shall have some rain to-day.* Rutland. 1893: Inwards, *Weather Lore*, 127.

16. *He that makes himself an ass, must not take it ill if men ride him.* 1732: Fuller, No. 2232. 1869: Spurgeon, *John Ploughman*, ch. iv., We may make ourselves asses, and then everybody will ride us.

17. *It is good to hold the ass by the bridle, and a scoffing foole by his wits end.* 1647: Countrym. *New Commonwealth*, 32. 1651: Herbert, *Jac. Prudentum*, 2nd ed. [the first half of the saying only].

18. *Jest with an ass, and he will flap you in the face with his tail.* 1855: Bohn, 436.

19. *Never went out an ass and came home horse.* 1732: Fuller, No. 2668, If an ass goes a travelling, he'll not come home an horse. 1852: FitzGerald, *Polonius*, 48 (1903).

20. *Put not an embroidered crupper on an ass.* 1732: Fuller, No. 3984.

21. *The ass brays when he pleases.* Ibid., No. 4399.

22. *The ass that brays most eats least.* 1611: Cotgrave, s.v. "Asne." 1670: Ray, 3. 1732: Fuller, No. 822.

23. *'Tis a sorry ass that will not bear his own burden.* 1659: Howell, 4.

24. *'Tis time to cock your hay and corn, When the old donkey blows his horn.* 1836: *Farmer's Mag.*, vol. iv. pt. i, p. 447. 1893: Inwards, *Weather Lore*, 127.

25. *To a rude ass a rude keeper.* 1623: Wodroephe, *Spared Houres*, 475.

26. *What good can it do an ass to be called a lion?* 1732: Fuller, No. 5490.

27. *What would you have an ass chop logic?* Ibid., No. 5527.

28. *When an ass climbeth a ladder, you may find wisdom in women.* Ibid., No. 5546.

29. *Where-ever an ass falleth, there will he never fall again.* Ibid., No. 5643.

30. *Who drives an ass, and leads a whore, hath pain and sorrow evermore.* 1639: Clarke, 259. 1670: Ray, 52. 1687: *Poor Robin Almanac*, July. 1736: Bailey, *Dict.*, s.v. "Ass."

31. *You will make me believe that an ass's ears are made of horns.* 1659: Howell, 8.

See also All men; Beat, *verb* (3); Honey (8); Horse (51) and (75); Lawyer (9); and One mule.

Ass's head, To wash the. 1578: Florio, *First Fruites*, fo. 34, Who washeth an asses head loseth both labour and sope. 1593: G. Harvey, *Works*, i. 276 (Grosart), I . . . take small pleasure in washing the asses head. 1660: Howell, *Parly of Beasts*, 28, The old proverb . . . He who washeth an assc's head doth lose both time and sope. 1732: Fuller, No. 5193, To lather an asse's head, is but spoiling of soap.

Assail who will, the valiant attends. 1640: Herbert, *Jac. Prudentum.*

Assfordby Bridge. *He has gone over Assfordby Bridge backwards.* Spoken of one that is past learning. 1678: Ray, 317. 1790: Grose, *Prov. Gloss.*, s.v. "Leicestershire." 1881: Evans, *Leics. Words, etc.*, 299 (E.D.S.), . . . In modern usage [the saying] is applied to one who "sets the cart before the horse," in word or deed.

Astrology is true, but the astrologers cannot find it. 1640: Herbert, *Jac. Prudentum.*

Atheist is got one point beyond the devil, An. 1732: Fuller, No. 593. 1875: A. B. Cheales, *Proverb. Folk-Lore*, 124.

Attorney. *See* Bawds; and Lawyer.

Auger. *See* Alsager.

August. 1. *As August so the next February.* 1893: Inwards, *Weather Lore*, 32.

2. *Dry August and warm Doth harvest no harm.* 1732: Fuller, No. 6209. 1893: Inwards, *Weather Lore*, 32.

3. *If the first week in August is unusually warm, the winter will be white and long.* 1893: Inwards, 33.

4. *If the twenty-fourth of August be fair and clear, Then hope for a prosperous autumn that year.* 1732: Fuller, No. 6470. 1893: Inwards, 33.

5. *None in August should over the land, In December none over the sea.* 1893: Inwards, 32.

6. *So many August fogs, so many winter mists.* Ibid., 32.

See also Cuckoo (8), (11), and (12); March (15); Merry be the first; July (6) and (10); and Thistle (2).

Autumn. 1. *Clear autumn, windy winter; Warm autumn, long winter.* 1893: Inwards, 8.

2. *Of fair things the autumn is fair.* 1640: Herbert, *Jac. Prudentum.*

See also Ascension Day (1); August (4); Blossom; St. Bartholomew (2); and Spring (7).

Autumnal agues are long or mortal. 1640: Herbert, *Jac. Prudentum.*

Avarice. *See* Covetousness.

Avoidance is the only remedy. *c.* 1380: Chaucer, *Minor Poems,* in *Works,* i. 340 (Skeat), Theschewing is only the remedye. Before 1542: Sir T. Wyatt, *Song:* "From these hie hilles," The first eschue is remedy alone.

Aw makes Dun draw. 1639: Clarke, 93. 1670: Ray, 58. 1881: Evans, *Leics. Words, etc.,* 95 (E.D.S.), Au, au! an exclamation to horses to bid them turn to the left or near side. "Aw makes Dun draw" is a punning proverb quoted by Ray.

Away the mare. Before 1529: Skelton, *Magnyfycence,* l. 1342, Nowe then goo we hens, away the mare! *c.* 1550: in Hazlitt, *Early Pop. Poetry,* iii. 62 (1866), Of no man he had no care, But sung, hey howe, awaye the mare, And made ioye ynough. 1611: Ravenscroft, *Melismata,* No. 6, Heigh ho, away the mare, Let vs set aside all care.

Awls, To pack up one's. 1681: W. Robertson, *Phraseol. Generalis,* 971, To pack up his awls; Colligere vasa. 1694: Motteux, *Rabelais,* Prol. to bk. iv., The enemy, who were already packing up their awls . . . 1762: Bickerstaffe, *Love in a Village,* II. iii., So pack up your alls, and be trudging away. 1849: F. T. Dinsdale, *Teesdale Gloss.,* 5, To pack up his awls, is spoken of a person departing in haste. 1881: Evans, *Leics. Words, etc.,* 229 (E.D.S.), Whenever the employer gave a workman his sack, it was an obvious hint to him to pack up his "alls" and be off.

Ax near, sell dear. 1881: *N. & Q.,* 6th ser., iii. 326, [A Lincolnshire J.P.] well versed in rural matters, repeated a short time ago in my hearing this proverb: "Ax near, sell dear." That is, if you have corn, cattle, or other matters to sell, you are more likely to get their full market value if you do not ask too much. 1889: Peacock, *Manley, etc., Gloss.,* 366 (E.D.S.).

Axe after the helve. *See* Throw (7).

Axe goes to the wood where it borrowed its helve, The. 1732: Fuller, No. 4401.

Axle-tree. *A pretty fellow to make an axle-tree for an oven.* Cheshire. 1670: Ray, 162. 1732: Fuller, No. 362. 1917: Bridge, *Cheshire Proverbs,* 5.

Axwell Park. *See* quot. 1846–59: *Denham Tracts,* i. 91 (F.L.S.), From Axwell Park to Shotley, A squirrel could leap from tree to tree. [Axwell Park is in the township of Winlaton and parish of Ryton, Durham.]

Ay be as merry as be can, For love ne're delights in a sorrowful man. 1678: Ray, 55.

Aylsham treat. 1890: P. H. Emerson, *Wild Life,* 108 *n.,* An Aylsham treat is treat yourself.

B

B. 1. *To know not B from a battledore.*
1565: J. Hall, *Hist. Expostulation*, 16
(Percy S.), He . . . knewe not a letter,
or a b from a bateldore. 1593: Harvey,
Works, ii. 208 (Grosart), The learnedest
of them could not say . . . B to a
battledore. 1630: Taylor (Water-Poet),
Works, pagin. 2, 59, To the Gentlemen
Readers, that vnderstand A. B. from a
battledore. 1681: Robertson, *Phraseol.
Generalis*, 757, He is as ignorant, he
knows not a B from a battle-door.
    2. *To know not B from a bull's foot.*
1401: in Wright, *Pol. Poems*, ii. 57
(Rolls Ser., 1861), I know not . . . a b
from a bole foot. 1800: Colman Jr.,
Review, II. ii., Fie upon you!—not to
know a B from a bull's foot. 1886:
Elworthy, *West Som. Word-Book*, 36
(E.D.S.), The common description of a
dolt or ignoramus is . . . he does not
know B from a bull's foot. Cf. **A** (2).
    Babies in the eyes, To look. 1618:
B. & F., *Loyal Subject*, III. ii., Can ye
look babies, sisters, In the young
gallants' eyes? *c.* 1685: in *Roxb.
Ballads*, vii. 445 (B.S.), 'Tis the babes
in thine eyes that set my poor heart
all on fire. 1709: T. Baker, *Fine
Lady's Airs*, I. i., Sweeten her again
with ogling smiles, look babies in her
eyes.
    Bachelor and **Bachelors.** 1. *A lewd
bachelor makes a jealous husband.* 1855:
Bohn, 292.
    2. *Bachelor's fare: bread and cheese
and kisses.* 1738: Swift, *Polite Convers.*,
Dial. I.
    3. *Bachelors' wives and maids' chil-
dren be well taught.* 1546: Heywood,
Proverbs, Pt. II. ch. vi. 1549: Latimer,
Seven Sermons, 138 (Arber), The maydes
chylde is euer best taughte. 1637:
Breton, in *Works*, ii. *h* 18 (Grosart),
For bachelors wiues, and maidens children are pretty things to play withall.
1738: Swift, *Polite Convers.*, Dial. I.
1761: Colman, *Jealous Wife*, IV. i.,
What a pity it is that nobody knows
how to manage a wife, but a batchelor.

1920: *Sphere*, 30 March, p. 316, col. 1,
But then there is a saying, "Old maids'
children and bachelors' wives are
always perfection."
    4. *We bachelors grin, but you married
men laugh till your hearts ache.* 1670:
Ray, 48. 1732: Fuller, No. 5433.
    Back and edge=entirely, completely.
1639: Clarke, 26, Sticke to him back
and edge. 1866: Brogden, *Lincs Words*,
17, He stuck up for me back-and-edge.
1899: Dickinson, *Cumberland Gloss.*, 10.
Cf. **Fall**, *verb* (1).
    Backdoor robs the house, The. 1732:
Fuller, No. 4402. 1854: J. W. Warter,
Last of the Old Squires, 53. *See also*
Fair, *adj.* (9); and cf. **Postern door.**
    Back is broad enough, His. 1639:
Clarke, 86, His back's broad enough to
beare jests. 1670: Ray, 163. 1738:
Swift, *Polite Convers.*, Dial. I., I suppose
you think my back's broad enough to
bear everything.
    Back may trust but belly won't.
1855: Robinson, *Whitby Gloss.*, 8,
. . . dress may be deferred, but hunger
cannot.
    Back with that leg. 1678: Ray, 65.
    Backare! quoth Mortimer to his sow.
1546: Heywood, *Proverbs*, Pt. I. ch. xi.
c. 1550: Udall, *Roister Doister*, I. ii.
1594: Shakespeare, *Tam. of Shrew*, II. i.,
Let us, that are poor petitioners, speak
too: Baccare! you are marvellous forward. 1659: Howell, 20.
    Backing. *He's allus backing i' th'
breech bent* [breechband]. 1917: Bridge,
Cheshire Proverbs, 69, . . . Said of one
who is not very "go-ahead," or
energetic.
    Bacon. *Where you think there is
bacon, there is no chimney.* 1640: Herbert, *Jac. Prudentum*. *See also* **Save.**
    Bad as Jeffreys. 1863: Wise, *New
Forest*, ch. xvi., "As bad as Jeffreys"
preserves, as throughout the West of
England, the memory of one who,
instead of being the judge, should have
been the hangman.
    Bad as Swath Hoome. Staffs. 1889:

Folk-Lore Journal, vii. 294, As bad as Swath Hoome [Hulme], who was two hours getting his shirt on, and then he didna do it right.

Bad bargain. 1685: Meriton, *Yorkshire Ale*, 66, It's an ill made bargain, where beath parties rue. 1732: Fuller, No. 2839, It is a bad bargain, where both are losers.

Bad broom [slovenly servant] **leaves a dirty room, A.** 1917: Bridge, *Cheshire Proverbs*, 1.

Bad bush. *See* Bush (1).

Bad cause that none dare speak in, It is a. 1639: Clarke, 199. 1670: Ray, 4. 1732: Fuller, No. 2840.

Bad choice where the whole stock is bad, There's but. 1732: Fuller, No. 4889.

Bad cloth that will take no colour, It is a. 1546: Heywood, *Proverbs*, Pt. II. ch. ix. 1592: Lyly, *Gallathea*, IV. i. 1670: Ray, 71. 1732: Fuller, No. 2841.

Bad cook. *See* Ill cook.

Bad custom. *A bad custom is like a good cake, better broken than kept.* 1611: Cotgrave, s.v. "Gasteau." 1670: Ray, 76. 1732: Fuller, No. 832, Bad customs are better broke than kept up.

Bad day. 1. *A bad day has a good night.* 1893: Inwards, *Weather Lore*, 43. 2. *It is never a bad day that hath a good night.* 1639: in *Berkeley MSS.*, iii. 32 (1885), Hee never hath a bad day that hath a good night. 1670: Ray, 6.

Bad excuse (or shift) ·is **better than none, A.** *c.* 1550: Udall, *Roister Doister*, V. ii. 1579: Gosson, *Sch. of Abuse*, 42 (Arber). 1599: Porter, *Two Angry Women*, in *Old Plays*, vii. 360 (Hazlitt), A bad shift is better than none at all. 1692: L'Estrange, *Æsop*, 112 (3rd ed.), And at the worst, a bad shift is better than none. 1732: Fuller, No. 4.

Bad for a worse, To change a. 1678: Bunyan, *Pilgr. Progress*, Pt. I. p. 56 (1849), Thou hast done in this according to the proverb, changed a Bad for a Worse.

Bad for the rider. *See* Worse (4).

Bad guides may soon mislead. 1639: Clarke, 1.

Bad is a bad servant, but worse being without him. 1659: Howell, *Proverbs·Brit.-Eng.*, 3.

Bad is the best. 1564: Bullein, *Dialogue*, 77 (E.E.T.S.). 1579: Spenser, *Sheph. Calendar*, Sept., l. 117, Bad is the best (this English is flat). 1606: Day, *Ile of Gulls*, II. v., Badd's the best. *c.* 1630: B. & F., *Bloody Brother*, IV. ii. 1753: Richardson, *Grandison*, iii. 110 (1883), Bad is my best. 1852: Planché, *Extravag.*, iv. 228 (1879), I've no doubt bad enough she'll prove at best. 1905: H. A. Evans, *H. and B. in Oxfordsh. and Cotswolds*, 218, The reader will exclaim that bad is the best.

Bad Jack may have as bad a Jill, A. 1754: Berthelson, *Eng.-Danish Dict.*, s.v. "Jack," There is not so bad a jack but there is as bad a gill.

Bad lease. *He never hath a bad lease, that hath a good landlord.* Glos. 1639: in *Berkeley MSS.*, iii. 32 (1885).

Bad luck often brings good luck. 1732: Fuller, No. 834.

Bad luck top end. 1917: Bridge, Cheshire Proverbs, 29. [Of one not very bright mentally.]

Bad market. *He that cannot abide a bad market, deserves not a good one.* 1678: Ray, 173. 1732: Fuller, No. 2058.

Bad news. *See* Ill news.

Bad padlock invites a picklock, A. 1732: Fuller, No. 2.

Bad paymaster. *From a bad paymaster get what you can.* 1855: Bohn, 359.

Bad ploughman beats the boy, A. 1917: Bridge, *Cheshire Proverbs*, 1. Cf. Ill workman.

Bad priests bring the devil into the church. 1732: Fuller, No. 835.

Bad sack. *See* Ill sack.

Bad shearer never had a good sickle, A. 1846: Denham, *Proverbs*, 50 (Percy S.).

Bad stake. *See* Ill stake.

Bad thing never dies, A. 1732: Fuller, No. 3.

Bad to do evil, but worse to boast of it, It is. 1606: T. Heywood, *If you know not me*, Pt. II., in *Dram. Works*, i. 275 (1874).

Bad wintering will tame both man and beast. 1846: Denham, *Proverbs*, 6 (Percy S.). Cf. Wedding.

Bad words find bad acceptance. 1611: Cotgrave, s.v. "Meschant."

Bad words make a woman worse.
1659: Howell, *Proverbs: Brit.-Eng.*, 8.

Bad workman. See **Ill workman.**

Badger. See **Brock; Greasy; Grizzling;** and **Grey.**

Badger-like, one leg shorter than another. 1659: Howell, 20.

Bag [meal] **and pump** [water] **don't pay like bag and milk.** 1877: E. Leigh, *Cheshire Gloss.*, 11. 1886: R. Holland, *Cheshire Gloss.*, 447 (E.D.S.). 1917: Bridge, *Cheshire Proverbs*, 29.

Bag=sack. 1. *The bag mouth was open.* 1877: E. Leigh, *Cheshire Gloss.*, 11, "The bag mouth was open" is a Cheshire expression to show that everything that was unknown has become public. 1917: Bridge, *Cheshire Proverbs*, 111.

2. *To give the bag*=originally, to go off, or abandon a thing or person. Later, to dismiss—*see* 1883 quot. 1576: *Common Conditions*, in Brandl's *Quellen*, 599, This tinkerly trade, wee giue it the bagge. 1592: Greene, *Quip*, in *Works*, xi. 263 (Grosart), Lighte witted vpon euery small occasion to geue your maister the bagge. 1607: Dekker and Webster, *Westward Hoe*, IV. ii., I fear our oars have giuen us the bag. 1823: Scott, *Peveril*, ch. vii., She gave me the bag to hold, and was smuggling in a corner with a rich old Puritan. 1883: A. Easther, *Almond-bury Gloss.*, 7 (E.D.S.), "To give the bag," which is to dismiss; or "to get the bag," i.e. to be dismissed.

Bagpipe. *He's like a bag-pipe, he never talks till his belly be full.* 1623: Wodroephe, *Spared Houres*, 249, Sir, I am like vnto the bagpipes of Bolonia, which can not blow vnlesse they be full of wind. 1678: Ray, 291. 1732: Fuller, No. 2459.

Bagshot. The sayings in the two following quotations are clearly akin. 1575: R. Laneham, *Letter*, in *Capt. Cox*, 31 (B.S.), Hee . . . can talk az much without book, az ony inholder betwixt Brainford [Brentford] and Bagshot. 1670: Ray, 205, As good as any between Bagshot and Baw-waw. There's but the breadth of a street between these two.

Bait hides the hook, The. 1732: Fuller, No. 4403.

Bake. *As one bakes so one may brew* (or *eat*). Cf. **Brew,** *verb* (1). [Tute hoc intristi; tibi omne est exedendum.—Terence, *Phormio*, II. ii. 4.] 1548: Hall, *Chronicle*, 431 (1809), Such breade as they bake, suche muste they eate. 1577: *Misogonus*, III. i., As thou bakst, so shat [shalt] brewe. 1664: Pepys, *Diary*, 15 August, But I will have no more to do with her, let her brew as she has baked. 1775: Garrick, *May-Day*, sc. ii., As they bake they must brew, Old Nick and his crew. 1840: Barham, *Ing. Legends:* "St. Odille." 1849: C. Brontë, *Shirley*, ch. xxi., "What would Moore have done if nobody had helped him?" asked Shirley. "Drunk as he'd brewed—eaten as he'd baked." 1909: De Morgan, *Never can Happen Again*, ch. v., "As they bake, so they will brew," philosophized Mr. Challis to himself.

Baker. 1. *Be not a baker if your head be of butter.* 1640: Herbert, *Jac. Prudentum.* 1732: Fuller, No. 1321, Don't turn baker, if your head be made of butter.

2. *He should be a baker by his bow-legs.* 1607: Dekker and Webster, *Westward Hoe*, II. ii., Will women's tongues, like bakers' legs, never go straight! 1678: Ray, 91.

3. *Quoth the baker to the pillory.* See quots. 1546: Heywood, *Proverbs*, Pt. II. ch. ii., We be new kneet, And so late met, that I feare we parte not yeet, Quoth the baker to the pylorie. 1659: Howell, 7, Ile take no leave of you, quoth the baker to the pillory.

Baker's wife. See quot. 1598: *Servingman's Comfort*, in *Inedited Tracts*, 166 (Hazlitt), Mee thinkes he myght remember the olde saying: A bakers wyfe may byte of a bunne, a brewers wyfe may drinke of a tunne, and a fysh-mongers wyfe may feede of a cunger, but a seruingmans wyfe may starue for hunger.

Balance distinguisheth not between gold and lead, The. 1640: Herbert, *Jac. Prudentum.* 1670: Ray, 2.

Bald. 1. *A bald head is soon shaven.*

c. 1450: in *Reliq. Antiquæ*, i. 75 (1841), A bare berd wyl sone be shave. 1678: Ray, 96. 1732: Fuller, No. 836.

2. *As bald as a bladder of lard.* 1886: Elworthy, *West Som. Word-Book*, 41 (E.D.S.). 1894: R. L. S., *St. Ives*, ch. xv., His head as bald as a bladder of lard. 1901: Raymond, *Idler Out of Doors*, 219.

3. *As bald as a coot. c.* 1290: *Treatise of Walter de Biblesworth*, in Wright's *Early Vocab.*, i. 165, A balled coote. 1412–20: Lydgate, *Troy-Book*, bk. ii. l. 4673, He was ballid as a cote. 1566: Adlington, tr. Apuleius, bk. v., Older than my father, more bald than a coot. 1604: Breton, in *Works*, ii. *k* 13 (Grosart), And left her [head] as bare as a balde coote. *c.* 1770: Hall-Stevenson, in *Works*, i. 238 (1795), As bare as a coot. 1881: Evans, *Leics. Words, etc.*, 128 (E.D.S.), "As bald as a coot" is a common simile for baldness.

4. *You'll not believe he's bald till you see his brains.* 1580: Lyly, *Euphues*, 267 (Arber), As incredulous as those, who thinke none balde, till they see his braynes. 1670: Ray, 163. 1732: Fuller, No. 6032.

Bale. *See* **Boot.**

Balks of good ground, Make not. 1605: Camden, *Remains*, 328 (1870). 1670: Ray, 58. 1732: Fuller, No. 3316, Make no baulks in good ground. 1846: Denham, *Proverbs*, 6 (Percy S.), Make not a balk of good ground.

Ball. 1. *Ball on the bat.* 1893: G. L. Gower, *Gloss. of Surrey Words*, 4 (E.D.S.), [Surrey witness *loq.*] "He'd a mind to make me the ball on the bat between him and the police."

2. *To strike the ball under the line* = To fail. 1546: Heywood, *Proverbs*, Pt. I. ch. xi., Thou hast striken the ball vnder the lyne. 1634: S. Rowley, *Noble Soldier*, II. ii., She has been strucke under line, master souldier. 1907: Hackwood, *Old English Sports*, 151, Hence [at tennis] came the old proverb, "Thou hast stricken the ball under the line," meaning one had failed in his purpose.

Baltic. *See* **Drunk as the Baltic.**

Bambroughshire Laird. *See* quot.

1846–59: *Denham Tracts*, i. 258 (F.L.S.), He rides like a Bambroughshire Laird. That is, with one spur, and a stick or whip in his opposite hand.

Banbury. 1. *As thin as Banbury cheese.* 1562: Heywood, *Epigr.*, 6th hundred, No. 24, I neuer saw Banbery cheese thicke enough. 1575: G. Harvey, *Letter-Book*, 91 (Camden S.), More fine then any Banberry cheese. 1600: Shakespeare, *Merry Wives*, I. i., Bardolph. [*to Slender.*] You Banbury cheese! 1664: Bp. Griffith Williams, *Sad Condn. of the Clergy in Ossory*, 26, Our lands and glebes are clipped and pared to become as thin as Banbury cheese. 1790: Grose, *Prov. Gloss.*, s.v. "Oxfordshire," Banbury cheese. 1911: Hackwood, *Good Cheer*, 214, A local saying was of similar significance—"As thin as a Banbury cheese, nothing but paring."

2. *Banbury ale, a half-yard pot.* 1658: *Wit Restor'd*, 159. *c.* 1660: in *Roxb. Ballads*, ii. 130 (B.S.), Banbury-ale, a two-yard pot.

3. *Banbury zeal, cheese and cakes.* 1596: Harington, *Anat. of Metam. Ajax*, liiijb, O that I were at Oxenford to eate some Banberie cakes. 1662: Fuller, *Worthies*, iii. 5 (1840), Banbury zeal, cheese, and cakes. 1790: Grose, *Prov. Gloss.*, s.v. "Oxfordshire," Banbury veal [query misprint for "zeal"], cheese and cakes.

4. *Like Banbury tinkers, that in mending one hole make three.* 1647: Miles Corbet, *Speech*, in *Harl. Miscell.*, i. 274, The malignants do compare this commonwealth to an old kettle with here and there a fault or hole, a crack or flaw in it; and that we (in imitation of our worthy brethren of Banbury) were instructed to mend the said kettle; but, like deceitful and cheating knaves, we have, instead of stopping one hole, made them three or four score. 1790: Grose, *Prov. Gloss.*, s.v. "Oxfordshire." Cf. **Tinker** (3).

Banquets every day, never makes a good meal, He that. 1732: Fuller, No. 2043.

Bapchild. *See* quot. 1735: Pegge, *Kent. Proverbs*, in E.D.S., No. 12, p. 67,

If you'd live a little while, Go to Bapchild; If you'd live long, Go to Tenham
or Tong.

Bar light law, 'Tis sure to blaw.
1891: R. P. Chope, *Hartland Dialect*,
20 (E.D.S.).

Barber and Barbers. 1. *Barbers are
correctors of capital crimes.* 1659:
Howell, 11.
2. *Barbers learn to shave by shaving
fools.* 1611: Cotgrave, s.v. "Fol," By
shaving a foole one learnes to shave.
1654: Whitlock, *Zootomia*, 46, The fools
beard teacheth the young barber his
trade. 1792: Wolcot, *Works*, ii. 446
(1795), Accept a proverb out of Wisdom's schools—"Barbers first learn to
shave by shaving fools!"
3. *Common as a barber's chair*, or,
Like a barber's chair fit for every one.
1579: Gosson, *Apol. of Schoole of Abuse*,
66 (Arber), Venus . . . that made her
self as common as a barbar's chayre.
c. 1598: Shakespeare, *All's Well*, II. ii.,
It Is like a barber's chair, that fits all
buttocks. 1651: Burton, *Melancholy*,
III. iv. 1, 3, p. 688 (1836), Venus, a
notorious strumpet, as common as a
barber's chair. 1732: Fuller, No. 3218,
Like a barber's chair, fit for every one.
1825: Hone, *Ev. Day Book*, i. 1269, In a
newspaper report . . . 1825, a person
deposing against the prisoner, used the
phrase, "as common as a barber's
chair."
4. *No barber shaves so close but another
finds work.* 1640: Herbert, *Jac. Prudentum.* 1732: Fuller, No. 3737, One
barber shaves not so close but another
finds work. 1869: Spurgeon, *John
Ploughman*, ch. xxii.

Bardney, Lincs. *See* quot. 1905:
N. & Q., 10th ser., iii. 145, "I see you
come from Bardney" is said to a person
who has the habit of leaving doors open
when he could shut them.

Bardon Hill. *See* quot. 1894: *Leics.
N. & Q.*, iii. 160, When Bardon Hill has
a cap, Hay and grass will suffer for
that.

Bare as a bird's tail. c. 1470: *Mankind*, l. 475, Yt [his purse] ys as clene as
a byrdes ars. 1528: Sir T. More, in
Works, p. 238, col. 1 (1557), And some-

tyme as bare as a byrdes arse. 1661:
Stevenson, *Twelve Moneths*, 35, Bare as
birds britch. 1709: Ward, *Account of
Clubs*, 209 (1756). 1889: Peacock,
Manley, etc., Gloss., 29 (E.D.S.), Bare
as a bo'ds [bird's] tail. Said of a person
who has lost everything which he
possessed.

Bare as a bone. c. 1460: *Erthe upon
Erthe*, 22 (E.E.T.S.), As bare as any bon.

Bare as January. *See* January (6).

Bare as Job. Cf. **Poor as Job.** 1530:
Palsgrave, 620, I shall make hym as
bare as ever was Job. 1542: Udall, tr.
Erasmus' *Apoph.*, 236 (1877), Hauing
been afore in soch wyse pilled, and left
as bare as Job. 1633: Draxe, 137.

Bare as my nail. *See* **Naked as my
nail.**

Bare as the back of my hand. 1678:
Ray, 281. 1880: Spurgeon, *Ploughman's Pictures*, 21.

Bare as the birch at Yule even 1822:
Scott, *Nigel*, ch. xxi., His gentle beggarly kindred . . . keep him as bare as
a birch at Christmas 1823: Scott,
Q. Durward, ch. vi., It is ill going to
Oliver empty-handed, and I am as bare
as the birch in December. 1846: Denham, *Proverbs*, 63 (Percy S.).

Bare as the Bishop of Chester. A
sarcastic allusion to the wealth of the
bishopric. c. 1470: in *Reliq. Antiquæ*,
i. 85 (1841), I wolde I wore as bart as
the beschope of Chester. 1917: Bridge,
Cheshire Proverbs, 9.

Bare foot is better than none, A.
1611: Cotgrave, s.v. "Nud." 1694:
D'Urfey, *Quixote*, Pt. I. Act I. sc. i.,
Better a bare foot than no foot at all.
1748: Richardson, *Clarissa*, ii. 111
(1785), And hence a third proverb . . .
Better a bare foot than none at all.

Bare legs, Four. *See* **Marriage** (9).

Bare of a suit. *See* **Lie**, *verb* (1).

Bare walls make giddy housewives.
1605: Camden, *Remains*, 319 (1870).
1670: Ray, 59. 1723: Defoe, *Col. Jack*,
ch. x., But, as we say, bare walls make
giddy hussies. 1732: Fuller, No. 839,
Bare walls make gadding housewives.

Bare words are no good bargain.
1639: Clarke, 85. 1669: *Politeuphuia*,
183, Bare words are no lawful bargain.

Bare words buy no barley. 1732:
Fuller, No. 838.

Barefoot and **Barefooted.** *See* **Thorn.**

Bargain. 1. *A bargain is a bargain.*
1560: Wilson, *Rhetorique*, 34 (1909),
Resting vpon this point, that a bargaine is a bargaine, and must stande
without all exception. 1592: Lyly,
Mother Bombie, III. iii. 1692: L'Estrange, *Æsop*, 328 (3rd ed.). 1721:
C. Cibber, *Refusal*, III. 1860: Reade,
Cloister and Hearth, ch. xxxvi., However . . . 'tis ill luck to go back upon
a bargain. 1891: Q.-Couch, *Noughts
and Crosses,* 77.

2. *The bargain is ill made where
neither party gains.* c. 1597: A. Douglas, quoted in *N. & Q.*, 10th ser., ii. 23,
There is a proverb that says, the bargain is ill made where neither of the
parties doth gain. 1732: Fuller, No.
2878, It is a silly bargain, where no
body gets.

See also **Bare words.**

Bark, *verb.* 1. *To bark against the
moon.* 1401: in T. Wright, *Political
Poems,* ii. 53 (Rolls Ser., 1861), But
thou, as blynde Bayarde, berkest at the
mone. 1530: Palsgrave, 443, This
dogge barketh agaynste the moone.
1629: Davenant, *Albovine,* V., Thou
bark'st against the moon! 1655: Heywood and Rowley, *Fortune by Land and
Sea,* I. i., We should in that but bark
against the moon. 1736: Bailey, *Dict.*,
s.v. "Bark," To bark at the moon.

2. *To bark false.* 1639: Clarke, 2,
He never barkes false.

Bark, *subs. His* (or *her*) *bark is
worse than his* (or *her*) *bite.* [Canis
timidus vehementius latrat quam mor-
det.—Quintus Curtius, *De rebus gestis
Alexandri Magni,* vii. 14.] 1655: Fuller, *Church History,* bk. viii. § ii. (22),
Because politicly presumed to bark the
more that he might bite the less. 1860:
Reade, *Cloister and Hearth,* ch. lxvi.,
The weakness of her nerves would have
balanced the violence of her passions,
and her bark been worse than her bite.
1912: Pinero, "*Mind the Paint*" *Girl,*
Act II., p. 89.

Bark and tree. *See* quots. The
saying is usually applied as in last

quotation. 1546: Heywood, *Proverbs,*
Pt. II. ch. ii., But it were a foly for mee,
To put my hande betweene the barke
and the tree. 1580: Tusser, *Husbandrie,*
22 (E.D.S.). 1642: D. Rogers, *Naaman,*
sig. Cc1, Being so audacious as to go
between barke and tree, breeding sus-
pitions . . . betweene man and wife.
1714: Ozell, *Molière,* iii. 185, Cicero
says, that between the tree and the
finger you must not put the rind.
1820: Scott, *Abbot,* ch. iv., Is it for me
to stir up strife betwixt them, and put
as 'twere my finger betwixt the bark
and the tree? 1901: F. E. Taylor,
Lancs Sayings, 8, It's ill meddlin'
between th' bark an' th' tree (It is
unwise to interfere between man and
wife). Cf. **Oak** (7).

Bark and wood. *Between the bark and
the wood.* 1847: Halliwell, *Dict.*, s.v.
"Bark," A well adjusted bargain, where
neither party has the advantage.
Suffolk. 1866: J. G. Nall, *Great Yarmouth, etc.,* 510 [as in Halliwell].

Bark-year. *See* quot. 1863: Wise,
New Forest, ch. xvi., Forest proverbs
. . . such as . . . "A good bark-year"
makes a good wheat-year."

Barker's knee. *See* **Stiff.**

Barking dogs. *See* **Dog** (2).

Barley. 1. *Barley makes the heape, but
wheat the cheape.* Glos. 1639: *Berkeley MSS.,* iii. 32 (1885).

2. *Sow barley in dree, and wheat in pul*
[mud]. 1865: Hunt, *Pop. Romances W.
of England,* 436 (1896).

See also **Cotswold** (2); **Cuckoo** (3);
Good elm; Oak (8); **October** (1); **St.
David** (3); **St. John** (4); **St. Vitus** (2);
and **Wheat** (6).

**Barley-corn is better than a diamond
to a cock, A.** 1732: Fuller, No. 7.

Barley-corn is the heart's key, The.
1659: Howell, *Proverbs : Brit.-Eng.,* 5.

Barley-corn. *See also* **John Barley-
corn.**

**Barley-straw's good fodder when the
cow gives water.** 1678: Ray, 51.

Barn. 1. *Better a barn filled than a
bed.* 1716: Ward, *Female Policy,* 82.
1732: Fuller, No. 858.

2. *When the barn is full, you may
thresh before the door.* 1647: Howell

Letters, Bk. II. No. xxiv., When the barn was full any one might thrash in the haggard. 1732: Fuller, No. 5570. 1846: Denham, *Proverbs*, 5 (Percy S.).

3. *You have a barn for all grain.* 1732: Fuller, No. 5910.

Barnaby bright, the longest day and shortest night. 1659: Howell, 20. 1672: *Westm. Drollery*, Pt. II., p. 100 (Ebsworth), It was in June, and 'twas on Barnaby Bright too, A time when the days are long, and nights are short. 1732: Fuller, No. 6206. 1901: *N. & Q.*, 9th ser., vii. 445, The old saying as preserved in this part of England [Hants] is Barnaby bright, All day and no night.

Barnard Castle. 1. *A coward! a coward! o' Barney Castle, Dare na come out to fight a battle!* 1846–59: *Denham Tracts*, i. 98 (F.L.S.). *c.* 1860: Longstaffe, *Richmondshire*, 132. 1913: E. M. Wright, *Rustic Speech, etc.*, 183 [after quoting the saying], In all probability this refers to the holding of Barnard Castle by Sir George Bowes during the Rising of the North in 1569.

2. *Barney Cassel the last place that God made.* 1846–59: *Denham Tracts*, i. 83 (F.L.S.). *c.* 1860: Longstaffe, *Richmondshire*, 132.

3. *Come! come! that's Barney Castle!* 1846–59: *Denham Tracts*, i. 83 (F.L.S.). . . . an expression often uttered when a person is heard making a bad excuse in a still worse cause.

4. *See* quot. Ibid., i. 81, [He] carries his coals round by Richmond to sell at Barnard Castle. This saying is peculiar to the central and mid-southern portions of the county of Durham. It is spoken of a person who is guilty of a circumlocutory act.

See also **Lartington.**

Barnstaple Fair weather = Cold and wet weather. 1893: *Daily Graphic*, 21 April (W.), Throughout all this period —and particularly in September—what Devonians out of their experience call "Barnstaple fair weather" is to prevail in England.

Barnwell ague, A = Venereal disease. 1678: Ray, 88. 1790: Grose, *Prov. Gloss.*, s.v. "Cambridgeshire."

Barometer. 1. *First rise after low Foretells stronger blow.* 1893: Inwards, *Weather Lore*, 123.

2. *When the glass falls low, Prepare for a blow; When it rises high, Let all your kites fly.* Nautical. Ibid.

Barrel the better herring, Never a = Not a pin to choose between them. *c.* 1540: Bale, *Kynge Johan*, in Manby's *Spec. of Pre-Shaksp. Drama*, i. 591 (1903), Lyke lorde, lyke chaplayne; neyther barrell better herynge. 1566: Gascoigne, *Supposes*, IV. vi. 1633: Jonson, *Tale of a Tub*, II., One bad, there's ne'er a good; And not a barrel the better herring among you. 1736: Fielding, *Pasquin*, III., Nor like our misses, about bribing quarrel, When better herring is in neither barrel. 1826: Scott, *Woodstock*, ch. xxx., After bestowing a mental curse both on Sectaries and Presbyterians, as being, in his opinion, never a barrel the better herring. 1852: FitzGerald, *Polonius*, 51 (1903).

Barren places. *See* quot. 1610: Holland, tr. Camden's *Britannia*, 692, And haue proved the saying to bee true, That *barrain places giue a good edge to industry.*

Barsen's miller, always behind, Like. 1920: J. H. Bloom, in *N. & Q.*, 12th ser., vii. 67. [Said to have been heard in Warwickshire within the last ten years.]

Bartholomew baby, Dressed like a. 1670: Brooks, *Works*, vi. 51 (1867) (O.), Men . . . were dressed up like fantastical antics, and women like Bartholomew - babies. 1790: Grose, *Prov. Gloss.*, s.v. "London."

Barton, etc. *See* quot. 1869: Hazlitt, 80, Barton under Needwood, Dunstall in the Dale; Sitenhill for a pretty girl, and Burton for good ale.

Bashful. 1. *As bashful as a Lentel lover.* 1846: Denham, *Proverbs*, 32 (Percy S.).

2. *His bashful mind hinders his good intent.* 1737: Ray, 51.

Bashfulness is an enemy to poverty. 1670: Ray, 2.

Basket, You shall have the. Taunton. 1678: Ray, 344.

Basket-Justice will do Justice, right or

wrong, A. An ironical saying—*see* 1860 quot. 1678: Ray, 74, A basket Justice; a jyll Justice; a good forenoon Justice. He'll do Justice right or wrong. 1732: Fuller, No. 8. 1860: Wynter, *Curios. Civiliz.*, 493 (O.), The basket-justices were so called because they allowed themselves to be bought over by presents of game.

Basket of chips. *See* Smile, *verb* (1).

Bastard brood is always proud. 1736: Bailey, *Dict.*, s.v. "Bastard."

Bate me an ace, quoth Bolton. 1571: Edwards, *Damon, etc.*, in Hazlitt, *Old Plays*, iv. 77. 1578: Whetstone, *Promos and Cassandra*, sig. E3. 1651: Randolph, *Hey for Honesty*, II. v. 1681: W. Robertson, *Phraseol. Generalis*, 213. 1732: Fuller, No. 845.

Bath, The beggars of. 1662: Fuller, *Worthies*, iii. 92 (1840). 1790: Grose, *Prov. Gloss.*, s.v. "Somerset."

Bathing. *See* May, F. (26).

Bats in the belfry=Of unsound mind. 1926: Phillpotts, *Peacock House*, 219, His father's sister had bats in the belfry and was put away.

Battersea. *Go to Battersea to be cut for the simples.* 1785: Grose, *Dict. of Vulgar Tongue*, s.v. "Simples." 1790: Grose, *Prov. Gloss.*, s.v. "Surrey." 1847: Halliwell, *Dict.*, s.v. "Simples." 1925: J. G. Taylor, *Our Lady of Batersey*, 93, [Simples, or medicinal herbs, were cultivated at B.] Hence was derived the now forgotten proverb, addressed to one not overburdened with wits, "You must go to Battersea to get your simples cut!" Cf. Cut, *verb* (10).

Battle, Sussex. *See* quot. 1894: A. J. C. Hare, *Sussex*, 103, The capture in 1377 of John de Cariloes, Prior of Lewes, on Rottingdean Hill, by the French, gave rise to the proverb, "Ware the Abbot of Battel, when the Prior of Lewes is taken prisoner," meaning when one man falls into trouble, his neighbours had better beware.

Bawds and attorneys are like andirons, the one holds the wood, the other their clients till they consume. 1659: Howell, 10.

Bawtry. *The saddler of Bawtry was hanged for leaving his liquor behind him.* 1790: Grose, *Prov. Gloss.*, s.v. "Yorkshire." 1878: *Folk-Lore Record*, i. 172, There is a Yorkshire saying applied to a man who quits his friends too early at a convivial meeting, that "He will be hanged for leaving his liquor, like the saddler of Bawtry." *See also* Hang, *verb* (7).

Bayard. 1. *As bold as blind Bayard.* c. 1350: *Cleanness*, l. 886, in *Allit. Poems*, 64 (E.E.T.S.), Thay blustered as blynde as bayard watz euer. c. 1386: Chaucer, *Canon's Yeoman's Tale*, l. 860, Ye been as bolde as is Bayard the blinde. 1412–20: Lydgate, *Troy-Book*, bk. ii. l. 4731, But ben as bolde as Baiard is, the blynde. c. 1475: Caxton, *Hist. of Troy*, Prol., And began boldly to run forth as blind Bayard. 1575: *Appius, etc.*, in Hazlitt, *Old Plays*, iv. 118, As bold as blind bayard, as wise as a woodcock. 1681: W. Robertson, *Phraseol. Generalis*, 270, Who so bold as blind Bayard? 1825: Scott, *Talisman*, ch. xvii., I am no blind Bayard, to take a leap in the dark.

2. *Bayard bites on the bridle.* c. 1426: Audelay, *Poems*, 15 (Percy S.).

3. *Bayard of ten toes.* 1597: *Discouerie of Knights of the Poste*, sig. A3, As I trauelled . . . upon my well approued hacney (old Bayard of ten toes) [travelled afoot]. 1616: Breton, *Good and Badde*, 35 (O.), The walke of the wofull and his Horse, Bayard of ten-toes. 1866: Brogden, *Lincs Words*, 20, Bayard-of-ten-toes. To walk on foot, a man doing horses' work.

4. *To keep Bayard in the stable.* c. 1400: *Beryn*, l. 3183 (E.E.T.S.), fful trewe is that byword, "a man to serues-abill, Ledith offt beyard [Bayard] from his owne stabill." 1546: Heywood, *Proverbs*, Pt. I. ch. xii., To haue kept Bayard in the stable. 1605: Camden, *Remains*, 327 (1870). 1639: Clarke, 278.

Bayton-bargh. *See* Brayton-bargh.

Be as be may is no banning. c. 1475: *Mankind*, sc. ii. st. 86, Be as be may, I xall do a-nother. 1546: Heywood, *Proverbs*, Pt. II. ch. i. 1592: Lyly, *Mother Bombie*, II. ii., Well, bee as bee may is no banning. 1670: Ray, 59.

Be as you would seem to be. 1640:
Herbert, *Jac. Prudentum*, Be what thou
wouldst seem to be. 1732: Fuller,
No. 849.

**Be it better, be it worse, do after him
that beareth the purse.** Before 1500:
R. Hill, *Commonplace - Book*, 130
(E.E.T.S.). *c.* 1600: T. Deloney, *Thos.
of Reading*, ch. 8, in *Works*, 244 (Mann),
For it is an old prouerbe, Be it better,
or be it worse, Please you the man that
beares the purse. 1642: D. Rogers,
Matrim. Honour, 85, And as the prouerb
saith, Be it better or worse, we must be
ruled by him that beares the purse.
1732: Fuller, No. 6387, Be it better, be
it worse, Be ruled by him that bears the
purse. 1817: Scott, *Rob Roy*, ch. xxvii.
[as in 1732, with "has" for "bears"].

Beacon Hill, near Halifax, Yorks.
See quot. 1855: *N. & Q.*, 1st ser., xi.
223, You might as well try to bore a
hole through Beacon Hill. 1878: *Folk-
Lore Record*, i. 174.

**Beads about the neck and the devil in
the heart.** 1659: Howell, *Proverbs:
Span.-Eng.*, 15, Beads about his neck,
and the devil in his body. 1732: Fuller,
No. 944.

Bean and **Beans.** 1. *A bean in liberty
is better than a comfit in prison.* 1670:
Ray, 15. 1732: Fuller, No. 9.

2. *A good year of kidney beans, a good
year of hops.* 1882: Mrs. Chamberlain,
W. Worcs. Words, 38 (E.D.S.).

3. *Every bean hath its black.* 1639:
Clarke, 211. 1709: O. Dykes, *Eng.
Proverbs*, 103. 1754: Berthelson, *Eng.-
Danish Dict.*, s.v. "Bean." 1817: Scott,
Rob Roy, ch. xxxviii., Ye hae had your
ain time o't, Mr. Syddall; but ilka bean
has its black. 1878: *Folk-Lore Record*,
i. 166, Which is equivalent to every
bean hath its black.

4. *Like a bean in a monk's hood.*
1546: Heywood, *Proverbs*, Pt. II. ch. vi.,
Like a beane in a moonkis hood. 1611:
Cotgrave, s.v. "Febve."

5. *Plant the bean when the moon is
light; Plant potatoes when the moon is
dark.* 1893: Inwards, *Weather Lore*, 154.

6. *Sow beans in the mud and they'll
grow like wood.* 1639: Clarke, 307.
1647: Fuller, *Good Thoughts in Worse*

Times, 112 (1830), His answer was
returned me in their country rhyme:
Sow beans in the mud, And they'll
come up like a wood. 1732: Fuller,
No. 6143. 1893: Inwards, *Weather
Lore*, 154.

7. *Sow* (or *set*) *beans in Candlemas
waddle*, i.e. the wane of the moon.
Somerset. 1678: Ray, 343.

8. *The bigger eateth the bean.* 1525:
Wydow Edyth: Mery Gestes, 89 (1864),
And yet alway I stand in great doubt,
Least that the bigger wyll eate the
been. 1546: Heywood, *Proverbs*, Pt. II.
ch. v. 1611: Davies (of Hereford), *Sc.
of Folly*, 45, in *Works*, ii. (Grosart),
Euer the bigger eateth the beane.

9. *The more beans the fewer for a
penny.* Glos. 1639: *Berkeley MSS.*,
iii. 31 (1885).

10. *To know how many beans make
five.* 1612: Shelton, *Quixote*, Pt. I.
bk. iv. ch. v., As though I know not
how many numbers are five. 1830:
Galt, *Lawrie Todd*, II. i. 42 (1849) (O.),
Few men who better knew how many
blue beans it takes to make five. 1889:
Daily News, 4 Nov., p. 6, col. 5, It is as
simple as how many blue beans make
five.

11. *See* quot. 1905: E. G. Hayden,
Travels round our Village, 75, "When
parson 'gins the Bible, 'tis time to sow
the beans "—thus runs the ancient
proverb. [Genesis i. is read on Septua-
gesima Sunday.]

See also **Blue** (6); **Elm-leaves; May,
F.** (4); **Pea** (2) and (4); **St. David** (1);
and **St. Valentine** (2).

Bean-belly Leicestershire. *See* Leicestershire.

Bear and **Bears,** *subs.* 1. *Are you
there with your bears?* 1592: Lyly,
Mother Bombie, II. iii. 1642: Howell,
Forreine Trauell, 20 (Arber). 1740:
North, *Examen*, 220. 1822: Scott,
Nigel, ch. xxxii. "Ay, man, are you
there with your bears?" said the King.

2. *As handsomely as a bear picketh
muscles.* 1546: Heywood, *Proverbs*, Pt.
II. ch. v.

3. *If it were a bear it would bite him*
(or *you*). 1633: Draxe, 4. 1690: *New
Dict. Canting Crew*, sig. B4, If it had

been a bear it would have bit you.
1738: Swift, *Polite Convers.*, Dial. I.

4. *Like a bear with a sore head. See*
Cross, *adj.* (1).

5. *One thing thinketh the bear, but
another thinketh his leader.* c. 1374:
Chaucer, *Troylus*, bk. iv., l. 1453.

6. *The bear wants a tail and cannot be
a lion.* 1662: Fuller, *Worthies*, iii. 271
(1840). 1790: Grose, *Prov. Gloss.*, s.v.
"Warwickshire."

7. *To go like a bear to the stake.*
c. 1430: Lydgate, *Churl and Bird*, st. 19,
To goo at large but as a bere at a stake
To passe his boundes but yf he leue
take. 1591: Florio, *Second Frutes*, 89,
I am as loath to goe to it, as a beare is
to goe to the stake. 1642: D. Rogers,
Naaman, sig. D5, If he goes, yet it is as
a beare to the stake. 1722: Defoe,
Moll Flanders, in *Works*, iii. 42 (Bohn),
It was easy to see I should go to church
like a bear to the stake. 1823: Scott,
Q. Durward, ch. xxi., Pavillon and his
lieutenant . . . faced their fate like
bears bound to a stake.

8. *To sell the bear's skin. See* **Sell.**

9. *You dare as well take a bear by the
tooth.* 1601: Dent, *Pathw. Heauen*, 62
(O.), To . . . take the beare by the
tooth. 1639: Clarke, 209. 1690: *New
Dict. Canting Crew*, sig. B4, As good
take a bear by the tooth, [spoken] of a
bold desperate undertaking. 1732:
Fuller, No. 5895.

See also **Cross,** *adj.* (1); **Dancing bear;
Guts; Iron nails; King** (8); **Like a young
bear;** and **Mastiff** (3).

Bear-garden, To talk. 1678: Ray, 66,
He speaks Bear-garden. 1698: Collier,
Short View, 232, This is brave Bear-
Garden language! 1707: Ward, *Lon-
don Terræfilius*, No. III. p. 29, He's as
great a master of ill language as ever
was bred at a Bear-Garden. 1732:
Fuller, No. 2033, He talks in the Bear-
Garden tongue.

Bear-pie. *He that hath eaten a bear-
pie, will always smell of the garden,* i.e.
the Bear-garden. 1659: Howell, 18.
1670: Ray, 216.

Bear, *verb.* 1. *Bear wealth, poverty
will bear itself.* 1853: Trench, *Proverbs*,
84 (1905).

2. *Bear with evil and expect good.*
1640: Herbert, *Jac. Prudentum.* 1670:
Ray, 8. 1732: Fuller, No. 945.

3. *Bear with me and I'll bear with thee.*
1546: Heywood, *Proverbs*, Pt. II.
ch. viii. 1639: Clarke, 63.

4. *He bears misery best that hides it
most.* c. 1590: G. Harvey, *Marginalia*,
95 (1913), He bearith his misery best
that hydeth it most. 1732: Fuller,
No. 1810.

5. *I bear him on my back.* 1639:
Clarke, 303, I bore him all the while on
my back. 1670: Ray, 164.

6. *To bear the bell.* c. 1374: Chaucer,
Troylus, bk. iii. l. 198, And lat see which
of yow shal bere the belle To speke of
love a-right! 1468: *Coventry Mysteries*,
161 (Sh. S.), Of bewte and of boldnes
I bere evermore the belle. Before
1529: Skelton, in *Works*, i. 127 (Dyce),
Of all prowde knauys thow beryst the
belle. 1575: Gascoigne, *Glasse of Govt.*,
III. vi., So vices brag, but vertue beares
the bell. 1633: Herbert, *Temple:*
"Church Porch," st. xxxii., In clothes,
cheap handsomenesse doth bear the bell.
1713: Gay, *Wife of Bath*, IV. i.,
Appearance, Sir, bears away the bell,
almost in everything. 1812: Combe,
Syntax: Picturesque Tour, can. xix.,
That e'en her merchants bore the bell
In eating and in drinking well. 1912:
Lucas, *London Lav.*, ch. iii., But for
human features . . . the capuchin . . .
bears away the bell.

See also **Born.**

Beard. 1. *The beard will* (or *will not*)
pay for the shaving. 1830: Forby,
Vocab. E. Anglia, 431, The beard will
pay for the shaving. 1879: G. F.
Jackson, *Shropsh. Word-Book*, 28, "The
beard won't pay for the shaving" is a
proverbial saying analogous to the
French—*Le jeu ne vaut pas la chandelle.*
1883: Burne, *Shropsh. Folk-Lore*, 590
[will not pay]. 1917: Bridge, *Cheshire
Proverbs*, 111 [will not pay].

2. *'Tis not the beard that makes the
philosopher.* 1732: Fuller, No. 5102.

Beast. 1. *Better a beast sold than
bought.* 1659: Howell, *Proverbs: Brit.-
Eng.*, 16.

2. *The beast that goes always never*

wants blows. 1640: Herbert, *Jac. Prudentum.*

Beast of many heads. See **Many-
headed beast.**

Beat. 1. *Beat a bush and start a
thief.* 1622: Drayton, *Polyol.*, xxiii.,
Where if you beat a bush, 'tis odds you
start a thief. 1662: Fuller, *Worthies*,
i. 194 (1840). 1790: Grose, *Prov.
Gloss.*, s.v. "Bucks."

2. *Better to be beaten than be in bad
company.* 1670: Ray, 2.

3. *He that cannot beat his horse, beats
the saddle.* 1578: Florio, *First Fruites*,
fo. 29, Who cannot beat the horse, let
hym beat the saddle. 1629: *Book of
Meery Riddles*, Prov. 82. 1732: Fuller,
No. 4174, Since he cannot be reveng'd
on the ass, he falls upon the pack-saddle.

4. *To beat* (or *go*) *about the bush.* 1560:
Wilson, *Rhetorique*, 2 (1909), If he . . .
tell it orderly, without going about the
bush. 1611: Cotgrave, s.v. "Aller,"
To use many circumstances, to goe
about the bush. 1696: *Cornish Comedy*,
IV. ii., He doth not beat about the
bush, but falls immediately upon the
point. 1884: *Punch*, 29 Nov., p. 256,
col. 2, Excuse me . . . but no good
beating about the bush.

5. *To beat the bush while others catch
the birds.* c. 1390: Gower, *Conf. Amantis*, ii. 2355, And takth the bridd to his
beyete, Wher othre men the buisshes
bete. 1472: *Paston Letters*, iii. 44
(Gairdner, 1900), We bette the busschysse
and have the losse and the diswor-
schuppe and ether men have the byrds.
1580: G. Harvey, in *Works*, i. 93
(Grosart), I beate the bushe, the birdes
to them doe flye. 1606: *Ret. from
Parnassus*, II. v., It hath been my luck
always to beat the bush, while another
killed the hare. 1732: Fuller, No. 3738,
One beateth the bush, and another
catcheth the bird. 1828: Scott, letter
to Mrs. Hughes, in her *Letters, etc., of
Scott*, ch. xi., Your active benevolence
starts the game while others beat the
bush.

6. *You may beat the devil into your
wife, but you'll never bang him out again.*
1732: Fuller, No. 5940.

Beauchamp, As bold as. 1608:

Middleton, *Mad World*, V. ii., Being
every man well hors'd like a bold
Beacham. 1612: Drayton, *Polyol.*,
xviii. 1662: Fuller, *Worthies*, iii. 271
(1840). 1790: Grose, *Prov. Gloss.*, s.v.
"Warwickshire." 1834: W. Toone,
Glossary, 112, Bold Beauchamp. This
person was said to be Thomas Beauchamp, Earl of Warwick, whose prowess
[*c.* 1350] became proverbial, "as bold
as Beauchamp."

Beaulieu Fair. See **Cuckoo** (17).

Beauty. 1. *An enemy to beauty is a
foe to nature.* 1855: Bohn, 311.

2. *Beauty draws more than oxen.*
1640: Herbert, *Jac. Prudentum.* 1670:
Ray, 2. 1732: Fuller, No. 948.

3. *Beauty is but a blossom.* 1633:
Draxe, 15. 1670: Ray, 2. 1681: W.
Robertson, *Phraseol. Generalis*, 223.
1732: Fuller, No. 947, Beauty's a
blossom.

4. *Beauty is but skin-deep.* 1606:
Davies (of Hereford), *Select Sec. Husb.*,
6, in *Works*, ii. (Grosart), Beauty's but
skin deepe. 1730: Lillo, *Silvia*, I. ix.,
She was the handsomest woman in all
our parish. But beauty is but skin
deep, as the saying is. 1829: Cobbett,
Advice to Young Men, Lett. III. 1881:
Evans, *Leics. Words, etc.*, 101 (E.D.S.),
A very common proverb on the lips of
the Midland pessimist is: "Beauty's
only skin-deep, but ugly goes to the
bone." 1921: W. H. Hudson, *Traveller
in Little Things*, 12.

5. *Beauty is no inheritance.* 1633:
Draxe, 15, Beauty is no heritage.
1670: Ray, 2. 1732: Fuller, No. 951.

6. *Beauty is potent, but money is
omnipotent.* 1670: Ray, 122. 1732:
Fuller, No. 952, Beauty is potent; but
money is more potent.

7. *Beauty is soon blasted.* 1732:
Fuller, No. 953.

8. *Beauty is the subject of a blemish.*
Ibid., No. 954.

9. *Beauty may have fair leaves, yet
bitter fruit.* Ibid., No. 955.

10. *Beauty provoketh thieves sooner
than gold.* 1599: Shakespeare, *As You
Like It*, I. iii.

11. *Beauty will buy no beef.* 1732:
Fuller, No. 956.

12. *Beauty without bounty avails
nought.* 1580: Lyly, *Euphues*, 295
(Arber), Beautie without riches, goeth
a begging. 1869: Hazlitt, s.v.

**Beccles for a puritan, Bungey for the
poor, Halesworth for a drunkard, and
Bliborough for a whore.** 1670: Ray,
253. 1790: Grose, *Prov. Gloss.*, s.v.
"Suffolk" ["Bilborough" for "Bliborough"].

Beck is as good as a Dieu-garde, A.
1546: Heywood, *Proverbs*, Pt. I. ch. x.,
And thus with a becke as good as a dieu
garde, She flang fro me. 1583: Melbancke, *Philotinus*, sig. F4, A becke of
yours is as good as a Dieugarde. 1611:
Davies (of Hereford), *Sc. of Folly*, 48, in
Works, ii. (Grosart).

Bed. *If the bed would tell all it knows,
it would put many to the blush.* 1659:
Howell, 4. 1732: Fuller, No. 2702.

Bed-time for berriers [threshers] **and
supper-time for carriers.** Old Cumberland proverb. 1895: T. Ellwood, *Lake-
land, etc., Gloss.*, 6 (E.D.S.).

Beddingham. *When Beddingham hills
wear a cap, Ripe and Chalvington gets a
drap.* 1884: "Sussex Proverbs," in
N. & Q., 6th ser., ix. 342.

Bede's chair. *See* quot. 1846–59:
Denham Tracts, i. 67 (F.L.S.), *Has a
Chip of Bede's chair in her pouch.* It
has been a custom from time immemorial for the ladies, immediately after the
conclusion of the marriage ceremony
(before Hymen's altar in Jarrow
church), to proceed to the vestry and
cut a chip off Bede's chair, to ensure
their fruitfulness. The saying is generally applied to those females who show
signs of fecundity rather early after
entering into the happy state of
matrimony.

Bedford. 1. *Bedford malt-horses.* 1622:
Drayton, *Polyol.*, xxiii., Of malt-horse,
Bedfordshire long since the blazon wan.
1911: Hackwood, *Good Cheer*, 163, As
Hampshire men were dubbed "hogs"
in allusion to their pig-breeding, so
Bedford folk were nicknamed "malt-
horses" because of the high quality of
malt they produced from their barley.

2. *The Bailiff of Bedford is coming.*
1662: Fuller, *Worthies*, i. 167 (1840).

1790: Grose, *Prov. Gloss.*, s.v. "Bedfordshire." 1874: Smiles, *Lives of Engineers*, i. 15, After a heavy fall of rain, or
after a thaw in winter, when the river
[Ouse] swelled suddenly, the alarm
spread abroad, "the bailiff of Bedford
is coming!" the Ouse passing by that
town. 1904: *N. & Q.*, 10th ser., i. 391.

Bedfordshire=Bed. 1608: Middleton,
Mad World, II. v., You come rather out
of Bedfordshire; we cannot lie quiet
in our beds for you. 1670: Cotton,
Scarronides, bk. iv., Each one departs
to Bedfordshire; And pillows all
securely snort on. 1738: Swift, *Polite
Convers.*, Dial. III. 1818: Scott, *Heart
of Midl.*, ch. xxx., Jeanie heard the
highwayman say, to her no small relief,
"She's as fast [asleep] as if she were in
Bedfordshire." 1841: Hood, *Miss Kilmansegg:* "Her Dream," And there was
the bed, so soft, so vast, Quite a field of
Bedfordshire clover. 1927: Lucas, in
Punch, 30 Nov., p. 613, I hear the Dust-
man drawing near To take you into
Bedfordshire; It's time you went to bed.
See also **Cheshire** (6).

Bedlam broke loose. *c.* 1635: Davenant, *News from Plymouth*, IV. ii.,
What's here? Kent Street, Or bedlam
broke loose? 1864: "Cornish Proverbs," in *N. & Q.*, 3rd ser., vi. 494,
Bedlam broke loose: What a clapper-
house!

Bedminster. *See* **Sold.**

Bedpost and **Bedstaff.** *See* **Twinkling.**

Bedworth beggars. 1678: Ray, 317.
1790: Grose, *Prov. Gloss.*, s.v. "Leicestershire."

Bee and **Bees.** 1. *A bee was never
caught in a shower.* 1893: Inwards,
Weather Lore, 146.

2. *A dead bee will make no honey.*
1578: Florio, *First Fruites*, fo. 25, A
dead bee wil make no hony. 1651:
Herbert, *Jac. Prudentum*, 2nd ed., A
dead bee maketh no honey. 1894:
Northall, *Folk Phrases of Four Counties*,
7 (E.D.S.), A still bee gathers no honey.
Glos.

3. *A swarm of bees in May, etc. See*
quots. 1655: *Reformed Commonwealth
of Bees*, 26, It being a proverb, that a
swarm of bees in May is worth a cow

and a bottle of hay, whereas a swarm
in July is not worth a fly. 1676: W.
Lawson, *New Orchard and Garden*, 77,
A May's swarm is worth a mares foal.
1710: *Tusser Redivivus*, The proverb
says, "A swarm in May is worth a load
of hay." 1744: Claridge, in Mills' *Essay
on Weather*, 101 (1773), A swarm of bees
in May Is worth a load of hay; But a
swarm in July Is not worth a fly. 1850:
N. & Q., 1st ser., ii. 512, If they swarm
in May, They're worth a pound next
day; If they swarm in July, They're not
worth a fly. Devon. 1883: Burne,
Shropsh. Folk-Lore, 234, In the retired
villages among the Clee Hills the following much more curious version may
sometimes be heard: A play o' bees in
May's wuth a noble the same day, A
play in June's purty soon, A play in
July's nod with a butterfly. [N.B.—
The gold noble, worth 6s. 8d., was first
coined 1344.] 1921: *Times*, 7 Oct.,
p. 8, col. 4, An old rhyme . . . which
says: "A swarm of bees in May Is
worth a load of hay; A swarm of bees
in June Is worth a silver spoon: A
swarm of bees in July Isn't worth a fly."

4. *As big as a bee's knee.* 1797:
quoted in *N. & Q.*, 8th ser., x. 260, It
cannot be as big as a bee's knee. 1894:
Northall, *Folk Phrases of Four Counties*,
7 (E.D.S.). 1896: *N. & Q.*, 8th ser.,
x. 199, " As big as a bee's knee " is a
phrase I have frequently heard in South
Notts to indicate a very small piece of
anything. 1896: Locker-Lampson, *Con-
fidences*, 98 *n.*, It isn't so big as a
bee's knee.

5. *Bees that have honey in their
mouths, have stings in their tails.* 1579:
Lyly, *Euphues*, 79 (Arber), The bee
that hath hunny in hir mouth, hath a
sting in hir tayle. 1732: Fuller, No. 959.

6. *Bees will not swarm Before a near
storm.* 1893: Inwards, *Weather Lore*,
146.

7. *Every bee's honey is sweet.* 1640:
Herbert, *Jac. Prudentum.*

8. *He's like the master bee that leads
forth the swarm.* Glos. 1639: in *Berkeley
MSS.*, iii. 28 (1885).

9. *His head is full of bees*=cares,
fancies, or, he is restless. 1546: Hey-

wood, *Proverbs*, Pt. I. ch. xii., Their
hartes full heauy, their heades be full of
bees. 1575: Churchyard, *Chippes*, 55
(Collier), About he flees, As though his
hed wear full of bees. 1614: Jonson,
Bart. Fair, I., He will whistle him and
all his tunes over at night in his sleep !
he has a head full of bees ! 1745:
Franklin, *Drinker's Dict.*, in *Works*,
ii. 23 (Bigelow), His head is full of bees
[=he is drunk]. 1814: Scott, *Waverley*,
ch. lxvi., This word had somewhat a
sedative effect, but the baillie's head, as
he expressed himself, was still "in the
bees." Cf. No. 13.

10. *If bees stay at home, Rain will
soon come ; If they fly away, Fine will be
the day.* 1878: Dyer, *Eng. Folk-Lore*,
131. 1893: Inwards, *Weather Lore*, 146.

11. *See* quot. 1863: Wise, *New
Forest*, ch. xvi., Forest proverbs . . .
such as . . . "Like a swarm of bees all
in a charm " [or *churm*=noise].

12. *To bumble like a bee in a tar-tub.*
Ibid., ch. xvi.

13. *To have a bee in one's bonnet.* Cf.
No. 9. 1553: *Respublica*, I. i., Ye
muste perdonne my wyttes, for I tell
you plaine, I have a hive of humble
bees swarmynge in my braine. 1648:
Herrick, *Mad Maid's Song*, Ah ! woe is
mee, woe, woe is me, Alack and well-a-
day ! For pitty, Sir, find out that bee,
Which bore my love away I'le seek
him in your bonnet brave, I'le seek him
in your eyes. 1682: A. Behn, *False
Count*, II. iii., What means he, sure he
has a gad-bee in his brain. 1860:
Reade, *Cloister and Hearth*, ch. xcvii.,
He may have a bee in his bonnet, but
he is not a hypocrite. 1922: Weyman,
Ovington's Bank, ch. xxxii., What
mare's nest, what bee in the bonnet
was this?

14. *When bees are old they yield no
honey.* 1633: Draxe, 146. 1670: Ray,
19. 1732: Fuller, No. 3706, Old bees
yield no honey.

15. *When bees to distance wing their
flight, Days are warm and skies are
bright; But when their flight ends near
their home, Stormy weather is sure to
come.* 1893: Inwards, *Weather Lore*,
146.

16. *Where bees are there is honey.*
1633: Draxe, 77. 1670: Ray, 60.
1732: Fuller, No. 5636.

17. *Where the bee sucks honey, the
spider sucks poison.* 1633: Draxe, 123.
1732: Fuller, No. 5661. 1853: Trench,
Proverbs, 114 (1905).

See also Better feed; Brisk; Busy;
February (9); Honey (9); Quick; St.
Matthew (2); Sheep (5); and Swine (2).

Beech in summer and oak in winter.
1884: H. Friend, *Flowers and Fl. Lore*,
220, "Beech in summer and Oak in
winter " [for felling] has now become a
common saying.

Beelzebub's Bower. *See* quots. 1362:
Langland, *Plowman*, A, ii. 100, A
bastard i-boren of Belsabubbes kunne.
1546: Heywood, *Proverbs*, Pt. II. ch. iv.,
But ye be a baby of Belsabubs bowre.

Beer. 1. *Beer a bumble, 'twill kill you,
afore 'twill make ye tumble.* 1869:
Hazlitt, 82.

2. *What's better than the beer that's
made of malt?* 1659: Howell, 14.

3. *See* quot. 1913: *Devonshire Assoc.
Trans.*, xlv. 90, Yu can't 'ave better
beer'n wat's putt in the barrow (barrel).

See also Ale; Cider; Cloth (2); and
July (3).

Beetle. *See* Blind, *adj.* (12); and
Deaf (1).

Beg. 1. *Beg from beggars and you'll
never be rich.* 1736: Bailey, *Dict.*, s.v.
"Beg."

2. *To be begged for a fool.* 1591:
Florio, *Second Frutes*, 187, Euen the
vulgar would begge him for a foole
that thinks a bungling-stainers dawbing
better than the polisht Helen of Zeuxes.
1592: Lyly, *Mother Bombie*, I. i., He
needs not, sir, Ile beg him for a fool.
1649: in *Somers Tracts*, vii. 88 (1811),
If there should be a king again, I shall,
perhaps, be begg'd for a fool. 1653:
Middleton and Rowley, *Spanish Gipsy*,
II. ii., You are my guardian, best beg
me for a fool now. 1707: *Spanish
Bawd*, III. iii., If he continues so a
week longer, his friends will beg him
for a fool. 1736: Hervey, *Mem.*, ii. 143
(O.), Moyle either deserved to be . . .
begged for a fool, or hanged for a knave.

3. *To beg at the wrong door.* 1546:

Heywood, *Proverbs*, Pt. I. ch. ix., Then
of trouth ye beg at a wrong mans dur.
1596: Jonson, *Ev. Man in his Humour*,
II. vii., He . . . claps his dish at the
wrong man's door. 1659: Howell, 5.

4. *To beg like a cripple at a cross.*
1812: Brady, *Clavis Cal.*, i. 334. We
have yet in common usage the old
saying of "He begs like a cripple at
a cross." 1855: Robinson, *Whitby
Gloss.*, 40, "He begged like a cripple
at a cross," very urgently. 1917:
Bridge, *Cheshire Proverbs*, 125.

Beggar and Beggars. 1. *A beggar
pays a benefit with a louse.* 1678: Ray,
98. 1732: Fuller, No. 10.

2. *A beggar's purse is bottomless.*
1539: Taverner, *Proverbs*, fo. 39, A
beggers scryppe is neuer fylled. 1639:
Clarke, 38. 1670: Ray, 60, A begger
can never be bankrupt. 1681: W.
Robertson, *Phraseol. Generalis*, 229, A
beggers purse is always empty. Cf.
Lady's heart; and **Proud heart**.

3. *A shameless beggar must have a
shameful denial.* 1639: Clarke, 37.
1732: Fuller, No. 392 [with "short"
for "shameful "].

4. *Beggars breed and rich men feed.*
1639: Clarke, 98. 1670: Ray, 60.
1754: Berthelson, *Eng.-Danish Dict.*,
s.v. "Beggar."

5. *Beggars cannot be choosers.* 1546:
Heywood, *Proverbs*, Pt. I. ch. x.,
Beggers should be no choosers. 1616:
B. & F., *Scornful Lady*, V. iii., Beggars
must be no choosers. 1635: Glapthorne, *Hollander*, I., Beggars are no
chusers my friend. Before 1726: Vanbrugh, *Journey to London*, III., My
lord, says I, beggars must not be
choosers. 1819: Scott, *Familiar Letters*,
ii. 62 (1894), But beggars must not be
chusers. 1889: R. L. S., *Ballantrae*,
ch. iii., For all this we were to pay
at a high rate; but beggars cannot
be choosers. 1920: Barbellion, *Last
Diary*, 13.

6. *Beggars make a free company.*
Before 1658: Cleveland, *Works*, 76
(1742), There was a time when such
cattle would hardly have been taken
upon suspicion for men in office, unless
the old proverb were renewed, That the

beggars make a free company, and those their wardens.

7. *Better to die a beggar than live a beggar.* 1670: Ray, 2. 1732: Fuller, No. 888.

8. *It is better to be a beggar than a fool.* 1813: Ray, 81.

9. *It would make a beggar beat his bag.* 1678: Ray, 228.

10. *Much ado to bring beggars to the stocks.* 1633: Draxe, 14. 1639: Clarke, 19. 1670: Ray, 60, [with the addition] and when they come there, they'll not put in their legs.

11. *One beggar is enough at a door.* 1639: Clarke, 187.

12. *One beggar is woe that another by the door should go.* 1539: Taverner, *Erasm. Prov.*, 9 (1552) (O.), One begger byddeth wo that another by the dore shuld go. 1608: Armin, *Nest of Ninnies*, 47 (Sh. S.). 1681: W. Robertson, *Phraseol. Generalis*, 229, It's one beggers wo to see another by the door go. 1736: Bailey, *Dict.*, s.v. "Beggar" [as in 1681].

13. *Puling, like a beggar at Hallowmas.* c. 1590: Shakespeare, *Two Gent.*, II. i.

14. *Set a beggar on horseback and he'll* (a) *never alight;* (b) *ride a gallop;* (c) *ride to the devil;* (d) *ride to the gallows;* (e) *run his horse out of breath;* (f) *run his horse to death.* [Asperius nihil est humili, cum surgit in altum.—Claudian, xviii. 181.] (a) 1576: Pettie, *Petite Pallace*, ii. 100 (Gollancz, 1908). 1599: Greene, *Orpharion*, in *Works*, xii. 36 (Grosart), Set a begger on horsebacke, and they say he will neuer light. 1620: Rowlands, *Night Raven*, 30 (Hunt. Cl.). (b) 1605: Camden, *Remains*, 330 (1870), Set a begger on horseback, and he will gallop. 1651: Burton, *Melancholy*, II. iii. 2. 1670: Ray, 60. (c) 1616: B. & F., *Scornful Lady*, IV. ii., Such beggars Once set o' horseback, you have heard, will ride—How far, you had best to look to. 1709: O. Dykes, *Eng. Proverbs*, 98, Set a beggar on horseback, and he'll ride . . . Whither, but to the devil? 1855: Mrs. Gaskell, *North and South*, ch. x. (d) c. 1626: in *A Pepysian Garland*, 241 (Rollins, 1922), There is

an old prouerbe, that oft hath bin try'd, Set a beggar on horse-back, to th' gallowes heel ride. (e) 1633: Draxe, 163. (f) 1594: *Second Part Contention*, 132 (Sh. S.), Beggers mounted run their horse to death.

15. *Small invitation will serve a beggar.* 1855: Bohn, 487.

16. *Sue a beggar and catch a louse.* 1594: R. Wilson, *Coblers Proph.*, l. 836 (Malone S.), I intreat yee be not ouer nice, What thinke ye as the prouerb goes that beggers haue no lice? 1654: Gayton, *Pleasant Notes Don Q.*, 83, Sue a begger and get a louse. 1681: W. Robertson, *Phraseol. Generalis*, 229. 1721: Bailey, *Eng. Dict.*, s.v. "Louse." 1819: Scott, *Bride of L.*, ch. ii., I guess it is some law phrase—but sue a beggar, and—your honour knows what follows.

17. *The beggar is never out of his way.* 1630: T. Adams, *Works*, 120, Vagrant rogues . . . are neuer out of their way. 1650: Fuller, *Pisgah-Sight*, bk. iii. ch. ii. § 7, Fancy is never at a loss, like a beggar never out of his way. 1732: Fuller, No. 965, Beggars are never out of their way.

18. *The beggar may sing before the thief.* 1546: Heywood, *Proverbs*, Pt. I. ch. xii., The begger maie syng before the theefe. 1670: Ray, 2. 1732: Fuller, No. 964. 1829: Scott, in Lockhart's *Life*, vii. 173, The last prerogative of beggary, which entitled him to laugh at the risk of robbery.

19. *To know one as well as a beggar knows his dish.* 1546: Heywood, *Proverbs*, Pt. I. ch. xi., And my selfe knowth him, I dare boldly brag, Euen as well as the begger knowth his bag. 1579: Gosson, *Apol. of Schoole of Abuse*, 74 (Arber), Such as he knew as well as the begger his dishe. 1638: T. Heywood, *Wise W. of Hogsdon*, II. i. 1779: Mrs. Cowley, *Who's the Dupe*, II. ii. 1822: Scott, *Nigel*, ch. xxi.

See also **Merry as beggars; Misery may be;** and **Wish (1) to (4).**

Beggars' Bush. 1564: Bullein, *Dialogue*, 78 (E.E.T.S.), In the ende thei go home . . . by weepyng cross, by beggers barne, and by knaues acre. 1599:

Porter, *Two Angry Women*, in Hazlitt, *Old Plays*, vii. 335, They have danc'd a galliard at beggars'-bush for it. 1662: Fuller, *Worthies*, ii. 98 (1840), " This is the way to Beggar's-bush." It is spoken of such who use dissolute and improvident courses, which tend to poverty; Beggar's-bush being a tree notoriously known, on the left hand of London road from Huntingdon to Caxton. 1790: Grose, *Prov. Gloss.*, s.v. " Hunts."

Begin. 1. *As you begin the year so you'll end it.* 1767: Garrick, Prol. to *Cymon*, There is a good old saying . . . As you begin the year, you'll surely end it.

2. *Good to begin well, better to end well.* 1670: Ray, 8.

3. *He beginneth to build too soon that hath not money to finish it.* 1633: Draxe, 1.

4. *He begins to die that quits his desires.* 1611: Cotgrave, s.v. " Abandonner," He truly begins to dye that quits his chiefe desires. 1640: Herbert, *Jac. Prudentum.*

5. *Let him that beginneth the song make an end.* 1633: Draxe, 12.

Beginning. 1. *It is better coming to the beginning of a feast than to the end of a fray.* [1546: Heywood, *Proverbs*, Pt. II. ch. vii., It is yll commyng . . . To thend of a shot [feast], and begynnyng of a fray.] *c.* 1590: *Plaine Percevall*, Dedication, I would it had bin Percevals hap, to haue com to the beginning of a friendly feast, or to the latter ending of so dangerous a fraye. 1597: Shakespeare, I *Henry IV.*, IV. ii. 1636: Massinger, *Bashful Lover*, III., Our grandsires . . . said, Haste to the beginning of a feast . . . but to the end of a fray. 1672: Marvell, *Rehearsal Transpr.*, Pt. I., in *Works*, iii. 119 (Grosart).

2. *It is better coming to the end of a feast than to the beginning of a fray.* *c.* 1594: Bacon, *Promus*, No. 977. 1670: Ray, 90. 1769: Colman, *Man and Wife*, III. ii., I arrived just at the conclusion of the ceremony; but the latter end of a feast is better than the beginning of a fray, they say. 1821: Scott,

Kenilworth, ch. xii. 1855: Robinson, *Whitby Gloss.*, 54, " It is better to come at the far end of a feast than at the fore end of a fray," better late at a feast than early at a fight.

Behappen! [perhaps] says Jack Dallow. 1883: Burne, *Shropsh. Folk-Lore*, 591.

Behind before. See **Horse** (25).

Behind the door to mend old breeches, You must go. 1864: " Cornish Proverbs," in *N. & Q.*, 3rd ser., vi. 495.

Believe. 1. *Believe not all you hear.* 1205: Layamon, *Brut*, 8015, Ful so[t]h seide the seg þe þeos saye talda: Yif þu ileuest æhcne mon, Selde þu sælt wel don (Very truth said the man who told this saw: If thou believest each man, seldom shalt thou do well). Before 1562: Lord Vaux, *Poems*, 37 (Grosart), Beleve not euery speache. Before 1640: Massinger, *Believe as You List* [title].

2. *Believe well and have well.* 1546: Heywood, *Proverbs*, Pt. II. ch. ix. 1670: Ray, 61. 1732: Fuller, No. 968.

3. *He that believes all, misseth; He that believeth nothing, hits not.* 1640: Herbert, *Jac. Prudentum.*

4. *We soon believe what we desire.* 1581: tr. Seneca's *Tragedies*, 15 (Spens. S.), What wretches doe most chiefly wishe of all, They soone beleue. 1591: Harington, *Orl. Furioso*, bk. i. st. 56, It is a proverbe used long ago, We soone beleeve the thing we would have so. 1696: *Cornish Comedy*, Act II., p. 16, What we desire we easily believe. 1709: Manley, *New Atlantis*, ii. 77 (1736). 1732: Fuller, No. 5426, We are apt to believe what we wish for.

Bell and Bells. 1. *A crackt bell can never sound well.* 1732: Fuller, No. 6358.

2. *Bells call others to church, but go not themselves.* 1557: North, *Diall of Princes*, fo. 138 vᵒ, For men yᵗ reade much, and worke litle, are as belles, the which do sound to cal others, and they themselues neuer enter into the church. 1670: Ray, 3. 1732: Fuller, No. 969.

3. *Bells on one horse.* See **Hang** (9).

4. *He is like a bell that will go for every one that pulls it.* 1732: Fuller, No. 1923.

5. *He who cannot bear the clapper, should not pull the bell.* 1732: Fuller, No. 2767, If you love not the noise of the bells, why do you pull the ropes? 1875: A. B. Cheales, *Proverb. Folk-Lore*, 10. 1917: Bridge, *Cheshire Proverbs*, 71.

6. *They are like bells; every one in a several note.* 1732: Fuller, No. 4954.

7. *To curse with bell, book and candle.* Before 1300: *Cursor Mundi*, l. 17110 (E.E.T.S.), Curced in kirc pan sal pai be wid candil, boke, and bell. *c.* 1394: in Wright, *Political Poems*, i. 341 (Rolls Ser., 1859), Thou shalt be cursed with bookc and bell. 1485: Malory, *Morte d'Arthur*, bk. xxi. ch. i., I shall curse you wyth book and belle and candell. 1593: Nashe, *Strange Newes*, in *Works*, ii. 185 (Grosart), The blind vicar would needs . . . curse me with bel, book and candle. 1610: Rowlands, *Martin Mark-all*, 6 (Hunt. Cl.). 1715: Cent-livre, *Gotham Election*, sc vi. 1840: Barham, *Ing. Legends:* "Jackdaw of Rheims." 1920: Barbellion, *Last Diary*, 138, The *Saturday Review* I cursed with bell, book, and candle.

8. *When the bell begins to toll, Lord have mercy on the soul.* 1813: Brand, *Pop. Antiq.*, ii. 205 (Bohn). 1888: Gilbert, *Yeomen of Guard*, I., The funeral bell begins to toll—May Heaven have mercy on his soul!

See also Agree like bells.

Bell the cat *See* Cat (65).

Bellesdon. *In and out like Bellesdon I wot.* 1678: Ray, 317. 1790: Grose, *Prov. Gloss.*, s.v. "Leicestershire." 1881: Evans, *Leics. Words, etc.*, 300 (E.D.S.), "In and out, like Billesdon I wote" . . . Billesdon being, or having been, noted for the crookedness of its main thoroughfare.

Bell-grave. *The same again, quoth Mark of Bell-grave.* 1644: J. Taylor (Water-Poet), in *Works*, 2nd coll., 22 (Spens. S.). 1790: Grose, *Prov. Gloss.*, s.v. "Leicestershire." 1818: Scott, *Heart of Midl.*, ch. xxix.

Belly. 1. *A belly full of gluttony will never study willingly.* 1678: Ray, 146. 1732: Fuller, No. 6115.

2. *Better belly burst than good drink* lost. 1659: Howell, 17. 1738: Swift, *Polite Convers.*, Dial. II., Come miss; better belly burst than good liquor be lost. 1917: Bridge, *Cheshire Proverbs*, 30, Better belly burst, than good meat lost.

3. *He whose belly is full believes not him that is fasting.* 1578: Florio, *First Fruites*, fo. 29, He that is fed beleeueth not the fasting. 1611: Cotgrave, s.v. "Pance," He that hath gorged himselfe thinkes all mens mawes be full. 1732: Fuller, No. 2399.

4. *If it were not for the belly, the back might wear gold.* 1732: Fuller, No. 2690. Cf. Nos. 11 and 16.

5. *My belly cries cupboard.* 1678: Ray, 237, His belly cries cupboard. 1694: *Terence made English*, 88, My belly chym'd cupboard above half an hour ago. 1738: Swift, *Polite Convers.*, Dial. II. 1826: Scott, *Woodstock*, ch. xx., Whose belly sings cupboard too? 1855: Kingsley, *West. Ho!*, ch. iii., So now away home. My inside cries cupboard. 1901: F. E. Taylor, *Lancs Sayings*, 24, Mi bally's cryin' cubbort. Cf. No. 15.

6. *My belly thinks my throat cut.* 1540: Palsgrave, *Acolastus*, sig. H2, I am so soore forhungered, that my bealy weneth my thiote is cutte. 1575: Churchyard, *Chippes*, 127 (Collier), When hongry mawe thinks throat is cut in deed. *c.* 1630: B. & F., *Love's Pilgrimage*, II. ii., Let's walk apace; hunger will cut their throats else. 1738: Swift, *Polite Convers.*, Dial. II., You are in great haste; I believe your belly thinks your throat's cut. 1901: F. E. Taylor, *Lancs Sayings*, 24, Mi bally's beginnin' for t'think 'at mi throoat's cut (I am hungry).

7. *The belly carries the legs, and not the legs the belly.* 1620: Shelton, *Quixote*, Pt. II. ch. xxxiv. 1694: D'Urfey, *Quixote*, Pt. I. Act IV. sc. i. 1732: Fuller, No. 3194, Let the guts be full, for it's they that carry the legs.

8. *The belly hates a long sermon.* 1732: Fuller, No. 4407.

9. *The belly hath no ears.* 1539: Taverner, *Proverbs*, fo. 47, The bely hath no eares. *c.* 1560: Becon, in

Catechism, etc., 601 (P.S.). 1609: Dekker, *Guls Horne-Booke*, in *Works*, ii. 245
(Grosart). 1721: Bailey, *Eng. Dict.*,
s.v. " Belly." 1853: Trench, *Proverbs*,
29 (1905), We have on one side the
English, Hungry bellies have no ears.
10. *The belly is not filled with fair
words.* 1639: Clarke, 113. 1670: Ray,
61. 1748: *Gent. Mag.*, 21. 1880:
Spurgeon, *Ploughman's Pictures*, 18,
Promises don't fill the belly.
11. *The belly robs the back.* 1619:
W. Hornby, *Scourge of Drunkennes*,
sig. B3, That by his paunch his backe
should fare the worse. 1659: Howell,
Proverbs: Brit.-Eng., 33. Cf. Nos. 4
and 16.
12. *The belly teaches all arts.* 1855:
Bohn, 498.
13. *When the belly is full, the bones
would be at rest.* Before 1500: in Hill,
Commonplace - Book, 129 (E.E.T.S.),
Whan the beli is fwll, the bonis wold
haue rest. 1553: *Respublica*, III. iv.
1669: *Politeuphuia*, 182. 1738: Swift,
Polite Convers., Dial. II.
14. *When the belly is full the mind is
amongst the maids.* c. 1645: MS. Proverbs, in *N. & Q.*, vol. 154, p. 27.
15. *Your belly chimes, it's time to go
to dinner.* 1678: Ray, 66. Cf. No. 5.
16. *Your belly will never let your back
be warm.* 1732: Fuller, No. 6043.
Cf. Nos. 4 and 11.
See also **Back** may trust; **Empty** (1)
and (2); **Eye** (5); **Full**; **Hard**, *adj.* (8);
and **Rule** (3).
Bellyfull is a bellyfull, A. 1666:
Torriano, *Piazza Univ.*, 321. 1694:
Motteux, *Rabelais*, bk. v. ch. xxiii.
1738: Swift, *Polite Convers.*, Dial. II.
1823: Scott, *St. Ronan's*, ch. x., " A
wamefou is a wamefou," said the writer,
swabbing his greasy chops.
**Bellyfull is one of meat, drink, or
sorrow, A.** 1864: " Cornish Proverbs,"
in *N. & Q.*, 3rd ser., vi. 495.
Belvoir. *See* **Bever.**
Benacre. *See* **Cowhithe.**
Bench-whistler, He is a. c. 1430:
Lydgate, *Minor Poems*, 170 (Percy S.),
Al suche benche whistelers, God late
hem never the! [thrive]. 1546: Heywood, *Proverbs*, Pt. I. ch. xi., That

benchwhistler (quoth I) is a pinchpeny.
1632: T. Heywood, *Iron Age*, Pt. I.
Act V., A very bench-whistler.
Bend. 1. *Best to bend while 'tis a
twig.* c. 1560: T. Ingelend, *Disobedient
Child*, 56 (Percy S.), For as longe as the
twygge is gentell and plyent, . . . With
small force and strength it may be bent.
1590: Lodge, *Rosalynde*, 18 (Hunt. Cl.),
I will bende the tree while it is a wand.
1667: *Roxb. Ballads*, vii. 696 (B.S.), A
twig will bend when it is young and
weak. 1732: Fuller, No. 971. 1841:
Hood, *Miss Kilmansegg*, As the twig is
bent, the tree's inclined.
2. *When you bend the elbow, the mouth
opens.* Kentish saying. 1882: *N. & Q.*,
6th ser., v. 266.
**Benefits please like flowers while they
are fresh.** 1640: Herbert, *Jac. Prudentum.*
**Benfieldside, where the Devil stole the
key of the Quakers' Meeting - house.**
1846–59: *Denham Tracts*, i. 92 (F.L.S.),
Benfieldside, in the parish of Lanches-
ter, is celebrated as the site of one of
the earliest Quaker meeting-houses in
England.
Bent of one's bow, The. 1546:
Heywood, *Proverbs*, Pt. I. ch. xi.,
I, hauyng the bent of your vncles bow.
1579: Lyly, *Euphues*, 75 (Arber), Do
you therefore thinke me easely entised
to the bent of your bow? 1670: Ray,
164, To have the bent of one's bow.
Berkshire. *See* quot. 1790: Grose,
Prov. Gloss., s.v. " Barkshire," He is a
representative of Barkshire [applied to
one who coughs]. *See also* **Cheshire** (6).
Berry's wife. *Just the thing, like old
Berry's wife.* 1920: J. H. Bloom, in
N. & Q., 12th ser., vii. 67 [said to have
been heard in Warwickshire within the
last ten years].
Berwick. 1. *From Berwick to Dover;*
later with addition, *three hundred miles
over.* c. 1300: R. Brunne, tr. Langtoft's
Chron., 305 (Hearne), Alle Inglond fro
Berwick vnto Kent. 1560: Wilson,
Rhetorique, 105 (1909), Whereas oftentimes they [preachers] beginne as much
from the matter, as it is betwixt Douer
and Berwicke. 1642: D. Rogers, *Naaman*, sig. Hh3, Though you should

runne from Barwicke to Dover. 1662:
Fuller, *Worthies*, ii. 542 (1840), From
Berwick to Dover, three hundred miles
over. 1790: Grose, *Prov. Gloss.*, s.v.
" Northumberland " [as in 1662]. 1846–
59: *Denham Tracts*, i. 283 (F.L.S.) [as
in 1662].

2. *Once going through Berwick maketh
not a man of war.* 1846–59: *Denham
Tracts*, i. 287 (F.L.S.).

Beside the book, To be. 1672: Walker,
Parœm., 32, He is quite beside the book ;
mightily mistaken.

Beside the cushion, To be. 1546:
Heywood, *Proverbs*, Pt. II. ch. ix.,
I may set you besyde the cushyn yit.
1654: Gayton, *Pleasant Notes Don Q.*,
36, He let fly at the Biscaine . . . and
as we say in our poor English proverb,
put him clean beside the cushion. 1681:
W. Robertson, *Phraseol. Generalis*, 247,
Beside the cushion ; Nihil ad rhombum.
1778: II. Brooke, *Female Officer*, I. xii ,
The man did not speak much beside the
cushion of common sense.

Besom. *They have need of a besom
that sweep the house with a turf.* 1678:
Ray, 101. 1683: Meriton, *Yorkshire
Ale*, 83–7 (1697).

Best. 1. *Best among them.* See **Fox-
cubs.**

2. *Best by yourself like Lowd's tup*
[ram]. 1886: R. Holland, *Cheshire
Gloss.*, 447 (E.D.S.), Best by hissel like
Lowndes's tup Said of a disagreeable,
quarrelsome fellow. 1917: Bridge,
Cheshire Proverbs, 29.

3. *Best cart.* See **Cart** (2).

4. *Best friends.* See **Friend** (7).

5. *He's one o' th' best eend o' th' worser
sort o' folks.* 1917: Bridge, *Cheshire
Proverbs*, 70.

6. *In the deepest water is the best
fishing.* 1633: Draxe, 66. 1670: Ray,
9. Cf. No. 14.

7. *It is best to take half in hand and the
rest by and by.* 1678: Ray, 354. 1732:
Fuller, No. 2921.

8. *Living at the best end of the pig-
trough.* 1856: E. Hinchliffe, *Barthom-
ley*, 135, The Shropshire farmers, more
accustomed to the delicacies of beef and
beer, charge ours, in Cheshire, with
" living at the best end of the pig

trough." 1917: Bridge, *Cheshire Proverbs*, 93.

9. *Men are best loved furthest off.*
1639: Clarke, 71.

10. *Sometimes the best gain is to lose.*
1640: Herbert, *Jac. Prudentum*.

11. *That is the best gown that goes up
and down the house.* Ibid.

12. *The best bred have the best portion.*
Ibid.

13. *The best cloth may have a moth in
it.* 1732: Fuller, No. 4411.

14. *The best fish swim near the bottom.*
1639: Clarke, 212. 1670: Ray, 90.
1732: Fuller, No. 4412, The best fish
swim deep. 1754: Berthelson, *Eng.-
Danish Dict.*, s.v. " Fish." Cf. No. 6.

15. *The best go first, the bad remain to
mend.* 1855: Bohn, 498.

16. *The best ground is the dirtiest.*
c. 1393: Langland, *Plowman*, C, xiii.
224, On fat londe and ful of donge
foulest wedes groweth. 1598. Shakespeare, *2 Henry IV.*, IV. iv., Most
subject is the fattest soil to weeds.
1633: Donne, *Poems*, i. 81 (Grierson),
There is best land, where there is
foulest way. 1676: Cotton, *Walton's
Angler*, Pt. II. ch. i., According to the
proverb, " there is good land where
there is foul way." 1846: Denham,
Proverbs, 3 (Percy S.) [as in 1676].
1904: Co. *Folk-Lore: Northumberland*,
173 (F.L.S.) [as in 1676]. Cf. **Worse** (4).

17. *The best horse needs breaking.*
1639: Clarke, 100. 1670: Ray, 105,
The best horse needs breaking, and the
aptest child needs teaching. 1732:
Fuller, No. 6441 [as in 1670]. 1868:
Quart. Review, cxxv. 253, The best
horse needs breeching, And the aptest
child needs teaching.

18. *The best is as good as stark naught.*
1639: Clarke, 14.

19. *The best is best cheap.* 1546:
Heywood, *Proverbs*, Pt. II. ch. vii.
1580: Tusser, *Husbandrie*, 104 (E.D.S.),
Count best the best cheape, wheresoeuer
ye dwell. 1655: Gurnall, *Christian in
Armour*, Verse 11, ch. iii., p. 41 (1679),
He that sells cheapest shall have most
customers, though at last best will be
best cheap. 1785–95: Wolcot, *Lousiad*,

can. v., " Best is best cheap "—you
very wisely cry.

20. *The best is best to speak to.* 1683:
Meriton, *Yorkshire Ale*, 83-7 (1697).

21. *The best mirror is an old friend.*
1611: Cotgrave, s.v. " Miroir," An old
friend an excellent looking - glasse.
1670: Ray, 10. 1732: Fuller, No. 4905,
There is no better looking-glass than an
old friend.

22. *The best of men are but men at the
best.* 1885: Harley, *Moon Lore*, 191.

23. *The best of the sport is to do the
deed and say nothing.* 1639: Clarke,
326, Sport is sweetest when there be
no spectators. 1670: Ray, 25.

24. *The best part is still behind.*
Before 1529: Skelton, *Works*, i. 17
(Dyce), Take thys in worth, the best
is behynde. 1630: Randolph, in *Works*,
i. 49 (Hazlitt), For now the proverb
true I find, That the best part is still
behind. 1659: Howell, 6, The best is
behind.

25. *The best patch is off the same
cloth.* 1732: Fuller, No. 4417.

26. *The best remedy against an ill
man is much ground between both.* 1640:
Herbert, *Jac. Prudentum.* 1670: Ray,
14.

27. *The best things are worst (or hard)
to come by.* 1635: Swan, *Spec. Mundi*,
465, Excellent things are hard to come
by. 1670: Ray, 61. 1732: Fuller,
No. 4420.

28. *The best things may be abused.*
1639: Clarke, 5.

29. *To make the best of a bad bargain*
(or *game*, or *market*). 1663: Pepys,
Diary, 14 Aug., I . . . therefore am
resolved to make the best of a bad
market. *c.* 1680: L'Estrange, *Seneca's
Morals:* " Happy Life," ch. xvi., It is an
equal prudence to make the best of a
bad game and to manage a good one.
1714: Ozell, *Molière*, ii. 142, All the art
lies in making the best of a bad market.
1765: Bickerstaff, *Maid of the Mill*,
III. iv. [bad market]. 1823: Scott,
Q. Durward, ch. xxxvi., Her aunt
seemed determined to make the best
of a bad bargain. 1836: Dickens,
Sketches by Boz: " Scenes," ch. xiii.,
. . . a bad bargain. 1923: J. S.

Fletcher, *The Diamonds*, ch. xxviii.,
Resolved to . . . make the best of an
undeniably bad job.

30. *To put the best* (*a*) *foot*, (*b*) *leg*,
foremost. (*a*) *c.* 1591: Shakespeare,
Titus Andr., II. iii., Come on, my lords,
the better foot before. 1626: Overbury,
Characters: " A Footman," His legs are
not matches, for he is still setting the
best foot forward. 1700: Congreve,
Way of the World, IV. x., You should
commence an amour, and put your
best foot foremost. 1886: R. L. S.,
Kidnapped, ch. xviii., I set my best
foot forward. 1901: Raymond, *Idler
Out of Doors*, 61, Then he must hurry
up best foot afore. (*b*) *c.* 1500: Medwall, *Nature*, l. 825 (Brandl's *Quellen*,
99), Com behynd and folow me Set out
the better leg I warne the. 1633:
Jonson, *Tale of a Tub*, II. i., Cheer up,
the better leg avore. 1742: Fielding,
Andrews, bk. i. ch. xi., Lovers do not
march like horse-guards . . . they put
the best leg foremost. 1838: Dickens,
Twist, ch. v., Now, you must put your
best leg foremost, old lady! 1886:
Elworthy, *West Som. Word-Book*, 428
(E.D.S.), To put the best leg before is
to hasten briskly, not necessarily in
walking, but in whatever is in hand.

31. *We are usually the best men when
in the worst health.* 1855: Bohn, 551.

32. *You are always best when asleep.*
Ibid., 575.

Betshanger. *See* quot. 1735: Pegge,
Kent. Proverbs, in E.D.S., No. 12, p. 75,
At Betshanger a gentleman, at Fredvile a squire, at Bonington a noble
knight, at . . . a lawyer [pron. *lyer*].

**Better a blush in the face, than a spot
in the heart.** 1620: Shelton, *Quixote*,
Pt. II. ch. xliv., Better shame in the
face than spot in the heart. 1732:
Fuller, No. 859.

Better a clout than a hole out. 1605:
Camden, *Remains*, 325 (1870), It is
better to see a clout [patch] than a
hole out. 1732: Fuller, No. 6310.
1864: " Cornish Proverbs," in *N. & Q.*,
3rd ser., v. 208.

**Better a fair pair of heels than a
halter.** 1620: Shelton, *Quixote*, Pt. II.
ch. lxvii., Better a fair pair of heels

than die at the gallows. 1694: D'Urfey, *Quixote*, Pt. II. Act II. sc. ii. [as in 1620]. 1732: Fuller, No. 861.

Better a finger off than always aching. Before 1225: *Ancren Riwle*, 360, Betere is finker offe þen he eke euer. 1681: W. Robertson, *Phraseol. Generalis*, 252. 1825: Scott, *Fam. Letters*, ii. 384 (1894), As to our losing them a few days sooner, one must piece it out with the old proverb, " Better a finger off than aye wagging."

Better a good keeper than a good winner. 1611: Cotgrave, s.v. " Amasseur," A warie keeper is better than a carefull getter. 1623: Wodroephe, *Spared Houres*, 503.

Better a lean jade than an empty halter. 1678: Ray, 166. 1732: Fuller, No. 863.

Better a lean peace than a fat victory. 1578: Florio, *First Fruites*, fo. 32, Better is a leane agreement then a fat sentence. 1700: in *Thoresby's Correspondence*, i. 396 (1832), You will all find the old adage verified, that " a lean arbitration is better then a fat judgment." 1732: Fuller, No. 864. Cf. **Ill agreement.**

Better a lean purse than a lere [empty] **stomach.** 1860: Reade, *Cloister and Hearth*, ch. xxv.

Better a little fire to warm us, than a great one to burn us. *c.* 1510: A. Barclay, *Egloges*, 9 (Spens. S.), Then better is small fire one easyly to warme Then is a great fire to do one hurt or harme. 1732: Fuller, No. 865.

Better a loss at sea than a bad debt at land. 1742: North, *Lives of Norths*, ii. 50 (Bohn), The merchants have a proverb, " Better," etc.

Better a mischief than an inconvenience. The saying was also reversed, see the first two quotations. 1583: Melbancke, *Philotinus*, sig. Z1, Yet must I commit an inconuenience to preuent a mischiefe. 1593: G. Harvey, in *Works*, i. 284 (Grosart), So in many priuate cases, better an inconuenience then a mischief. 1642: D. Rogers, *Matrim. Honour*, 117, Better admit a mischiefe then an inconuenience. 1681: W. Robertson, *Phraseol. Generalis*, 252,

Better once a mischief, then always inconuenience. 1714: *Spectator*, No. 564. 1740: North, *Examen*, 330, Littleton's rule, better a mischief than an inconvenience, sounds oddly, but hath this very meaning.

Better a mouse in the pot than no flesh at all. 1605: Camden, *Remains*, 319 (1870) [has " louse " for " mouse "]. 1670: Ray, 117 [has " louse," but adds,] The Scotch proverb saith a mouse, which is better sence, for a mouse is flesh and edible. 1696: D'Urfey, *Quixote*, Pt. III. Act V. sc. i. ["mouse"]. 1732: Fuller, No. 867 [" mouse "]. Cf. **Louse** (1).

Better a new friend than an old foe. 1590: Spenser, *F. Q.*, I. ii. 243, Better new friend then an old foe is said. 1600: Bodenham, *Belvedere*, 94 (Spens. S.).

Better a portion. *See* **Wife** (6).

Better a quick penny than a dallying shilling. 1894: Northall, *Folk Phrases of Four Counties*, 11 (E.D.S.).

Better a witty fool than a foolish wit. 1601: Shakespeare, *Twelfth Night*, I. v.

Better alone than have a false friend for company. 1825: Scott, *Betrothed*, ch. xiv. Cf. **Better be alone**, *infra*.

Better an egg in peace than an ox in War. 1611: Cotgrave, s.v. " Oeuf."

Better are meals many than one too merry. 1546: Heywood, *Proverbs*, Pt. II. ch. vii. *c.* 1594: Bacon, *Promus*, No. 494. 1678: Ray, 40.

Better bad than 'bout [without]. 1826: Wilbraham, *Cheshire Gloss.*, s.v. Said by a woman urged to quit a bad husband. 1917: Bridge, *Cheshire Proverbs*, 29.

Better be a fool than a knave. 1616: *Rich Cabinet*, fo. 44, Yet better to bee a foole then a knaue. 1659: Howell, 18. 1875: A. B. Cheales, *Proverb Folk Lore*, 164.

Better be alone than in bad company. 1477: Rivers, *Dictes and Sayings*, 8 (1877), It is better a man . . . to be a lone than to be acompayned with euill people. 1586: B. Young, tr. Guazzo's *Civil Convers.*, fo. 180. 1648: Fuller, *Holy State:* " Of Company," Better therefore ride alone than have a thief's

company. 1732: Fuller, No. 872. Cf.
Better alone, *supra*.

Better be drunk than drowned. 1830:
Forby, *Vocab. E. Anglia*, 430.

Better be envied than pitied. 1546:
Heywood, *Proverbs*, Pt. I. ch. xi. 1584:
Lodge, *Alarum against usurers*, 57 (Sh.
S.). 1670: Ray, 86. 1754: Berthelson,
Eng.-Danish Dict., s.v. "Envyed."

Better be half blind than have both
eyes out. 1639: Clarke, 86. 1670:
Ray, 64.

Better be half hanged than ill wed.
1670: Ray, 48.

Better be half hanged than lose estate.
1681: Otway, *Soldier's Fortune*, V. iii.

Better be ill spoken of by one before
all, than by all before one. 1659:
Howell, *Proverbs*, "To Philologers."
1670: Ray, 14.

Better be out of the world. *See* Out
of the world.

Better be over-manned than over-
tooled. 1886: Elworthy, *West Som.
Word-Book*, 547 (E.D.S.), A common
saying is,—"'Tis better to be . . .,"
i.e. that the tool should be rather light
than heavy in comparison with the
man's strength.

Better be the head of a lizard than the
tail of a lion. 1640: Herbert, *Jac.
Prudentum*.

Better be the head of a pike (or dog)
than the tail of a sturgeon (or lion).
1670: Ray, 101. 1736: Bailey, *Dict.*,
s.v. "Head." 1823: D'Israeli, *Cur. of
Lit.*, *ut infra*.

Better be the head of an ass than the
tail of a horse. 1639: Clarke, 105.
1670: Ray, 101. 1732: Fuller, No. 928.

Better be the head of the yeomanry
than the tail of the gentry. 1639:
Clarke, 22. 1670: Ray, 101. 1732:
Fuller, No. 933. 1823: D'Israeli, *Cur.
of Lit.*, 2nd ser., i. 447 (1824), The
ancient . . . spirit of Englishmen was
once expressed by our proverb, "Better
be the head of a dog than the tail of a
lion"; i.e. the first of the yeomanry
rather than the last of the gentry.

Better be the tail of a horse than the
head of an ass. 1639: Clarke, 91.

Better be unmannerly than troublesome. 1659: Howell, 5. 1670: Ray,

153. 1732: Fuller, No. 880. Cf. Unmannerliness.

Better be up to the ankles, than quite
to over head and ears. 1732: Fuller,
No. 879.

Better believe it than go where it was
done to prove it. 1670: Ray, 164.

Better blue clothes, He's in his, i.e. He
thinks himself very fine. 1678: Ray,
66.

Better bow than break. *c.* 1374:
Chaucer, *Troylus*, i. 257, The yerde
[twig, branch] is bet that bowen wole
and winde Than that that brest
[breaks]. 1413: in *Twenty-six Poems*,
No. 124, p. 54 (E.E.T.S.), Beter bowe
than brest. 1530: Palsgrave, 660,
Better plye than breake. 1560: Wilson, *Rhetorique*, 189 (1909). 1611:
Davies (of Hereford), *Sc. of Folly*, 44,
in *Works*, ii. (Grosart). 1732: Fuller,
No. 882.

Better bread than is made of wheat,
No. 1546: Heywood, *Proverbs*, Pt. II.
ch. vii., Lyke one . . . That would
haue better bread than is made of
wheate. 1592: Lyly, *Mother Bombie*,
I. iii. 1611: Cotgrave, s.v. "Frou-
ment," Would you have better bread
then's made of wheat. 1712: Motteux,
Quixote, Pt. I. bk. i. ch. vii., Rambling
up and down like a vagabond, and seeking for better bread than is made of
wheat. 1853: Trench, *Proverbs*, 83
(1905), We note very well the folly of
one addicted to this, saying: He expects
better bread than can be made of wheat.

Better buy than borrow. 1539:
Taverner, *Proverbs*, fo. 13, I had leuer
bye then begge. 1633: Draxe, 18.
1732: Fuller, No. 884.

Better children weep than old men.
1541: Coverdale, *Christ. State Matrimony*, sig. I8, Better it is that children
wepe then old men. *c.* 1594: Bacon,
Promus, No. 481. 1650: Fuller, *Pisgah
Sight*, bk. iii. ch. iv. § 1.

Better cut the shoe than pinch the foot.
1732: Fuller, No. 887.

Better direct well than work hard.
Ibid., No. 889.

Better do it than wish it done. 1546:
Heywood, *Proverbs*, Pt. II. ch. v.,
Better it be doone than wishe it had

been doone. 1670: Ray, 29 [as in
1546]. 1732: Fuller, No. 890.

Better dule than dawkin. 1883: A.
Easther, *Almondbury Gloss.*, 40 (E.D.S.),
The proverb is well known, " Better
have a dule nor a dawkin," i.e. an evil
spirit than a fool.

Better early than late. *c.* 1225:
Ancren Riwle, p. 340 (Morton), Better
is er þen to lete (Better is early, or too
soon, than too late). *c.* 1520: *Hickscorner*, in Hazlitt, *Old Plays*, i. 193, It
is better betime than too late. 1560:
Nice Wanton, in ibid., ii. 168, Better
in time than too late. 1817: Scott,
Rob Roy, ch. xviii., Better sune as syne.

Better end of the staff. 1567: Pickering, *Horestes*, l. 168 (Brandl, *Quellen*,
499), By godes ge, iche had not the best
end of the staffe. 1667: L'Estrange,
Quevedo's Visions, 38 (1904), The devil
of money has the better end of the staff.
1753: Richardson, *Grandison*, i. 360
(1883), Miss Byron, I have had the
better end of the staff, I believe. 1924:
Shaw, *Saint Joan*, sc. v., She does not
know everything; but she has got hold
of the right end of the stick.

Better eye out than always ache.
1546: Heywood, *Proverbs*, Pt. I. ch. viii.
1597: Bacon, *Coulers of good and euill*,
10. 1670: Ray, 86.

Better fed than taught. 1530: Palsgrave, 557, He is better fostred
[nourished] than taught. 1548: Hall,
Chron., 15 (1809), These monasticall
persones . . . better fed then taught.
1636: Taylor (Water-Poet), *Travels*, 19,
in *Works*, 3rd coll. (Spens. S.). 1820:
Scott, *Monastery*, ch. i.

**Better feed five drones than starve one
bee.** 1732: Fuller, No. 935, Better two
drones be preserv'd, than one good bee
perish. 1875: A. B. Cheales, *Proverb.
Folk-Lore*, 126.

**Better fill a glutton's belly than his
eye.** 1590: Greene, in *Works*, ix. 167
(Grosart), Now gentlewomen, do I finde
the olde prouerbe true: Better fill a
mans belly then his eye. 1670: Ray,
96.

Better give a shilling than lend . . .
1659: Howell, *Proverbs: Ital.-Eng.*, 14,
Better give a penny then lend twenty.

1732: Fuller, No. 895, Better give a
shilling than lend and lose half a crown.
1875: A. B. Cheales, *Proverb. Folk-Lore*,
101, Give a shilling sooner than lend
half a crown.

Better give than take. 1493: *Dives
and Pauper*, fo. 2 (1536), It is . . . more
blyssful to giue than to take. 1546:
Heywood, *Proverbs*, Pt. I. ch. v. 1611:
Davies (of Hereford), *Sc. of Folly*, 44, in
Works, ii. (Grosart). 1710: S. Palmer,
Moral Essays on Proverbs, 351, 'Tis
better to give than to receive.

**Better go about than fall into the
ditch.** 1659: Howell, *Proverbs: Span.-
Eng.*, 5. 1670: Ray, 1. 1732: Fuller,
No. 897, Better go back than lose your
self.

Better go to bed supperless. *See*
Supperless.

Better good afar off than evil at hand.
1640: Herbert, *Jac. Prudentum*.

Better have it than hear of it. 1639:
Clarke, 256, Better to have than to
heare of a good thing. 1670: Ray, 215.

**Better have one plough going than
two cradles.** 1580: Lyly, *Euphues*, 229
(Arber), It is better to haue one plough
going, then two cradells. 1716: Ward,
Female Policy, 82, Therefore it's better
to have two ploughs going, than one
cradle. 1732: Fuller, No. 905. 1846:
Denham, *Proverbs*, 5 (Percy S.).

**Better hazard once than be always in
fear.** 1732: Fuller, No. 906.

Better is art than strength. *c.* 1205:
Layamon, *Brut*, ii. 297 (Madden), Hit
wes yare i-queðen: þat betere is liste
þene ufel strenþe (It was said of yore,
that better is art than evil strength).

**Better is cost upon something worth
than expense on nothing worth.** 1545:
Ascham, *Toxoph.*, 122 (Arber).

**Better is the last smile than the first
laughter.** 1546: Heywood, *Proverbs*,
Pt. II. ch. ix. *c.* 1594: Bacon, *Promus*,
No. 501. 1611: Davies (of Hereford),
Sc. of Folly, 47, in *Works*, ii. (Grosart).
1732: Fuller, No. 929.

Better keep now than seek anon.
1659: Howell, *Proverbs: Brit.-Eng.*, 16.

**Better kiss a knave than be troubled
with him.** 1605: Camden, *Remains*,
326 (1870). 1670: Ray, 110. 1738:

Swift, *Polite Convers.*, Dial. I., I had rather give a knave a kiss, for once, than be troubled with him.

Better known than trusted. *c.* 1560: in Huth, *Ancient Ballads, etc.*, 228 (1867), They are not so wel trust as knowne. 1592: Chettle, *Kind-Hearts Dream*, 10 (Percy S.), Better knowne than lou'd. 1670: Ray, 183. 1732: Fuller, No. 909. 1817: Scott, *Rob Roy*, ch. xxvi., Rashleigh Osbaldistone is better kend than trusted in Glasgow.

Better late ripe and bear, than early blossom and blast. 1732: Fuller, No. 910.

Better late than never. [κρεῖττον ἐστὶν ἀρξασθαι ὀψὲ τὰ δέοντα πράττειν ἢ μηδέποτε. —Dionysius of Halicarnassus, ix. 9.] *c.* 1386: Chaucer, *Canon's Yeoman's Tale*, l. 857, For bet than never is late. *c.* 1420: Lydgate, *Assembly of Gods*, st. 172, p. 36 (E.E.T.S.), He seyde vyce to forsake ys bettyr late than neuer. 1579: Gosson, *Sch. of Abuse*, 41 (Arber). 1667: Pepys, *Diary*, 17 March, I have been . . . much ashamed of our not visiting her sooner, but better now than never. 1669: *Politeuphuia*, 183, Better late thrive than never. 1767: Murphy, *Sch. for Guardians*, I. iv. 1790: M. P. Andrews, [farce] *Better Late than Never* [title]. 1868: Robertson, *Play*, IV.

Better leave than lack. 1546: Heywood, *Proverbs*, Pt. I. ch. v. 1681: W. Robertson, *Phraseol. Generalis*, 475, At dinner 'tis better to leave then to lack. 1725: Bailey, tr. Erasmus' *Colloquies*, 71, We had better leave than lack.

Better lose a jest than a friend. 1593: G. Harvey, in *Works*, ii. 125 (Grosart), And Papp-hatchet, it is better to loose a new iest, then an old frend. 1670: Ray, 109. 1732: Fuller, No. 915.

Better lose cloth than bread. Before 1500: Hill, *Commonplace-Book*, 129 (E.E.T.S.), Better it is, to lese cloth than brede.

Better lost than found. 1584: Robinson, *Handf. Pleas. Delights*, 14 (Arber), For you are better lost than found. 1586: Whitney, *Emblems*, 158, For such a wife is better loste then founde. 1692: L'Estrange, *Æsop*, 121 (3rd ed.). 1821:

Scott, *Kenilworth*, ch. i., I have one wild slip of a kinsman . . . but he is better lost than found.

Better luck still, quoth Rowley Burdon. 1846-59: *Denham Tracts*, i. 68 (F.L.S.), . . . An extremely popular toast and saying through nearly the whole of the North of England.

Better my hog dirty home than no hog at all. 1670: Ray, 13. 1712: Motteux, *Quixote*, Pt. II. ch. lxv. 1732: Fuller, No. 927, Better's a dirty hog than no hog at all.

Better never to begin than never to make an end. 1633: Draxe, 51. 1639: Clarke, 247. 1736: Bailey, *Dict.*, s.v. "Better," Better never begun than never ended.

Better one house filled than two spilled. 1670: Ray, 51. 1735: Pegge, *Kenticisms*, in E.D.S., No. 12, p. 48. 1887: Parish and Shaw, *Dict. Kent. Dialect*, 157 (E.D.S.), Spilled. Spoilt. And so the proverb, "Better one house filled than two spill'd."

Better one house troubled than two. 1587: Greene, *Penelope's Web*, in *Works*, v. 162 (Grosart), Where the old prouerb is fulfild, better one house troubled then two. 1924: *Folk-Lore*, xxxv. 358 [Suffolk], Better one house spoilt than two [said when a witless man marries a foolish woman].

Better one's house. *See* House (5).

Better pay the butcher than the doctor. 1875: A. B. Cheales, *Proverb. Folk-Lore*, 82.

Better play a card too much than too little. 1620: Shelton, *Quixote*, Pt. II. ch. xxxvii. 1694: D'Urfey, *Quixote*, Pt. I. Act IV. sc. i.

Better ride safe, etc. *See* quot. 1821: Scott, *Kenilworth*, ch. viii., "Better ride safe in the dark," says the proverb, "than in daylight with a cut-throat at your elbow."

Better riding on a pad than on a horse's bare back. 1792: Wolcot, in *Works*, ii. 403 (1795).

Better rule than be ruled by the rout. 1546: Heywood, *Proverbs*, Pt. I. ch. v., And better to rule, than be ruled by the rout. 1605: Camden, *Remains*, 320 (1870). 1670: Ray, 23.

Better say here it is, than here it was.
1683: Meriton, *Yorkshire Ale*, 83–7
(1697). 1732: Fuller, No. 931.

Better sell than live poorly. 1732:
Fuller, No. 941.

Better shelter under an old hedge, than
a young furze-bush. 1639: Clarke, 25,
Better to keep under an old hedge than
creepe under a new furs-bush. 1732:
Fuller, No. 922.

Better sit still. *See* Sit (2).

Better so than worse. 1732: Fuller,
No. 925.

Better sold than bought. 1546: Heywood, *Proverbs*, Pt. I. ch. x., But, for a
farthyng, who euer did sell you Myght
bost you to be better solde then bought.

Better some of a pudding than none of
a pie. 1670: Ray, 135. 1732: Fuller,
No. 924.

Better spare at brim than at bottom.
1523: Fitzherbert, *Husbandry*, 100
(E.D.S.), Thou husbande and huswife,
that intend to . . . kepe measure, you
must spare at the brynke, and not at
the bottom. 1580: Tusser, *Husbandrie*,
23 (E.D.S.), Some spareth too late, and
a number with him, the foole at the
bottom, the wise at the brim. 1681:
W. Robertson, *Phraseol. Generalis*, 275.
1732: Fuller, No. 4237. 1869: Spurgeon, *John Ploughman*, ch. xvi., He
never spares at the brim, but he means,
he says, to save at the bottom.

Better spare to have of thine own
than ask of other men. 1640: Herbert,
Jac. Prudentum.

Better spared than ill spent. 1633:
Draxe, 196. 1670: Ray, 144.

Better speak to the master, than the
man. 1661: Gurnall, *Christian in
Armour*, 498 (1679).

Better spent than spared. 1530:
Palsgrave, 726, It is better somtyme to
spende than to spaare. 1560: Wilson,
Rhetorique, 189 (1909), It were better
sometimes wastefully to spende, then
warely to keepe. 1732: Fuller, No. 926.

Better suffer ill than do ill. 1639:
Clarke, 15, Better to suffer wrong than
doe wrong. 1640: Herbert, *Jac. Prudentum.* 1875: A. B. Cheales, *Proverb.
Folk-Lore*, 164.

Better the day, better the deed. 1607:

Middleton, *Mich. Term*, III. i. 1612:
Rowlands, *Knave of Hearts*, 46 (Hunt.
Cl.), They say, The better day, the
better deede. 1738: Swift, *Polite Convers.*, Dial. I. 1775: Garrick, *May-Day*,
sc. ii. 1870: Dickens, *Drood*, ch. x.,
Ask Mr. Landless to dinner on Christmas Eve (the better the day the better
the deed).

Better the feet slip than the tongue.
1586: Pettie, tr. Guazzo's *Civil Convers.*,
fo. 55, It is better to slip with the foote,
then with the tongue. 1611: Cotgrave,
s.v. " Glisser." 1670: Ray, 26. 1732:
Fuller, No. 932. 1875: A. B. Cheales,
Proverb. Folk-Lore, 88. Cf. Slip of
the foot.

Better the harm I know than that
I know not. 1586: D. Rowland, tr.
Lazarillo, 73 (1924), Remembring the
olde proverbe: Better is the evill
knowne, than the good which is yet
to knowe.

Better to be a-cold than a cuckold.
1678: Ray, 69.

Better to be born lucky than rich.
1639: Clarke, 49, Better to have good
fortune then be a rich man's child.
1784: *New Foundl. Hosp. for Wit*,
iv. 128, Better be fortunate than rich.
1846–59, *Denham Tracts*, i. 224 (F.L.S.)

Better to be happy than wise. 1546:
Heywood, *Proverbs*, Pt. II. ch. vi.
1581: B. Rich, *Farewell*, 7 (Sh. S.),
There is an old proverbe . . . " It is
better to be happie than wise." 1670:
Ray, 99.

Better to be idle than ill occupied.
1560: E. More, *Defence of Women*,
Dedication, Better had it bene for hym
(as Erasmus sayth) to haue bene ydle
then euyll occupyed. 1601: Lyly,
Love's Metam., I. ii., Yet better idle
then ill employed. 1681: W. Robertson, *Phraseol. Generalis*, 252, Better be
idle then not well employed. 1725:
Bailey, tr. Erasmus' *Colloquies*, 210,
Thence comes the proverb, It is better
to be idle, than to be doing, but to no
purpose.

Better to be stung by a nettle, than
prickt by a rose. That is, better be
wronged by a foe than a friend. 1659:
Howell, 18.

Better to cry over your goods than after them. 1855: Bohn, 532.

Better to give the fleece than the sheep. 1578: Florio, *First Fruites*, fo. 32. 1605: Camden, *Remains*, 326 (1870). 1732: Fuller, No. 896, Better give the wool than the whole sheep.

Better to hang. *See* Hang (2).

Better to have than wish. 1546: Heywood, *Proverbs*, Pt. II. ch. iv. 1670: Ray, 29.

Better to knit (or knot) than blossom. 1670: Ray, 111 [" knit "]. 1732: Fuller, No. 2917 [" knot "].

Better to leave than to maintain folly. *c.* 1477: Caxton, *Jason*, 116 (E.E.T.S.), For as it is said communly, hit is better to leue folie thenne to mayntene folie.

Better to live in low degree than high disdain. 1589: L. Wright, *Display of Dutie*, 17, It is a true saying, better to liue in lowe degree then high disdaine. 1647: *Countrym. New Commonwealth*, 25, It is better for him to live in low content then in high infamy.

Better to play with the ears than with the tongue. 1611: Davies (of Hereford), *Sc. of Folly*, 46, in *Works*, ii. (Grosart). 1633: Draxe, 172.

Better to wear out than to rust out. 1770: G. Whitefield, in Southey, *Wesley*, ii. 170 (1858), I had rather wear out than rust out. 1830: Forby, *Vocab. E. Anglia*, 434, It is better to wear up with work, than with rust. 1865: A. K. H. Boyd, *Crit. Essays of Co. Parson*, 40, " It is better," said Bishop Cumberland, " to wear out than to rust out." 1924: *Folk-Lore*, xxxv. 358, It is better to wear up than rust up. Suffolk.

Better tooth out than always ache. 1659: Howell, 7. 1732: Fuller, No. 869.

Better unborn than untaught. *c.* 1270: *Prov. of Alfred*, in *O. E. Miscell.*, 128 (E.E.T.S.), For betere is child vnbore þan vnbuhsum [unbuxom=disobedient]. *c.* 1460: *How the Goode Wyfe*, l. 203, For a chyld vn-borne wer better Than be vn-taught, thus seys the letter. *c.* 1555: in Wright, *Songs, etc.*, *Reign of Philip and Mary*, 6 (Roxb. Cl.), Unborne ys better than untought. 1662: Fuller, *Worthies*, i. 44 (1840), Our

English proverb, " It is as good to be unborn as unbred." 1732: Fuller, No. 937, Better unborn than unbred.

Better unfed than untaught. 1557: Seager, *Sch. of Vertue*, in *Babees Book, etc.*, 348 (E.E.T.S.), The common prouerbe remember ye oughte, " Better vnfedde then vn-taughte." 1580: Lyly, *Euphues*, 420 (Arber), I haue beene better taught then fedde.

Better untaught than ill taught. 1678: Ray, 345. 1732: Fuller, No. 938. 1780: K. O'Hara, *Tom Thumb*, I. iii., in Inchbald, *Farces*, vi. 174 (1815), Better quite ignorant, than half instructed.

Better wear out shoes than sheets. 1732: Fuller, No. 940. 1875: A. B. Cheales, *Proverb. Folk-Lore*, 82.

Better wed over the mixen than over the moor. 1662: Fuller, *Worthies*, i. 266 (1840). 1790: Grose, *Prov. Gloss.*, s.v. " Cheshire." 1818: Scott, *Heart of Midl.*, ch. xxxi. 1874: Hardy, *Madding Crowd*, ch. xxii. 1917: Bridge, *Cheshire Proverbs*, 30.

Better were within, better would come out, If. 1732: Fuller, No. 2672.

Better workman, the worse husband, The. 1633: Draxe, 62. 1670: Ray, 158. 1754: Berthelson, *Eng.-Danish Dict.*, s.v. " Workman." 1901: F. E. Taylor, *Lancs Sayings*, 32, Better workmon—wo'se husbant.

Between promising and performing a man may marry his daughter. 1611: Cotgrave, s.v. " Donner," *Entre promettre et donner doit on la fille marier;* Betweene promising, and giving the maid ought to be married. 1670: Ray, 22. 1732: Fuller, No. 974.

Between the anvil (or beetle) and the hammer (or block). 1583: Melbancke, *Philotinus*, sig. Cc2, My spirite was betwixt the anvile and hammer. *c.* 1594: Bacon, *Promus*, No. 741, Between the hammer and the anvill. 1613: Hayward, *Norm. Kings*, 274 (O.), Earle William being thus set as it were betweene the beetle and the block— was nothing deiected. 1633: Draxe, 37, Betweene the anuill and the hammer. 1902: in *N. & Q.*, 9th ser., ix. 12, The frequency with which the word " beetle " occurs in proverbial phrases, like . . . " Between the beetle and the block " . . .

Between twelve and two. See **Hours.**

Between you and me and the post (or bed - post, door - post, etc.). 1838: Dickens, in *Letters*, i. 11 (1880), Between you and me and the general post. 1839: Dickens, *Nickleby*, ch. x., Between you and me and the post, sir, it will be a very nice portrait. 1843: Planché, *Extravag.*, ii. 245 (1879), I fancy between you and me and the post . . .

Bever. *If Bever have a cap, You churls of the vale look to that.* 1662: Fuller, *Worthies*, ii. 226 (1840). 1790: Grose, *Prov. Gloss.*, s.v. " Leicestershire." 1881: Evans, *Leics. Words, etc.*, 300 (E.D.S.), I have heard the proverb repeatedly, but always in the form: When Belvoir wears his cap, You churls of the Vale look to that.

Bewails. *He that bewails himself hath the cure in his hands.* 1640: Herbert, *Jac. Prudentum.*

Beware beginnings. 1639: Clarke, 259.

Beware by other men's harms. See **Warn** (1).

Beware of breed, i.e. ill breed. Cheshire. 1670: Ray, 65. 1917: Bridge, *Cheshire Proverbs*, 31.

Beware of little expense. 1855: Bohn, 331.

Beware of the forepart of a woman, the hind part of a mule, and all sides of a priest. 1591: Florio, *Second Frutes*, 99, To womens forepartes dou not aspire, From a mules hinder parte retire, And shun all partes of monke or frire. 1623: Wodroephe, *Spared Houres*, 276 [with " asses " for " mule "]. 1732: Fuller, No. 978. 1880: Spurgeon, *Ploughman's Pictures*, 118, Beware of a mule's hind foot, a dog's tooth, and a woman's tongue.

Beware the buyer. See **Buyer.**

Bewcastler, He's a. 1846-59, *Denham Tracts*, i. 72 (F.L.S.), The parallel saying of Cumberland, " He's a Bewcastler "—i.e. a bad one.

Bibble-babble. See **Tittle-tattle.**

Bible and a stone do well together, The. 1672: Marvell, *Rehearsal Transpr.*, in *Works*, iii. 151 (Grosart), The Welch

have a proverb, that the Bible and a stone do well together; meaning, perhaps, that if one miss, the other will hit.

Bid me and do it yourself. 1639: Clarke, 232.

Big a liar as Tom Pepper, As. 1862: *Dialect of Leeds*, 405, A noted propagator of untruths is " as big a liar as Tom Pepper."

Big as a Dorchester butt. 1838: Holloway, *Provincialisms*, 23, The old saying, you are as big as a Dorchester butt. 1851: *Dorset Gloss.*, 4, As big as a Dorchester butt, i.e. very fat.

Big as a parson's barn. Dorset. 1869: Hazlitt, 58.

Big as bull beef; or, To look as if one had eaten bull beef. 1580: Baret, *Alvearie*, T 270, Such as . . . looke as though they had eaten bulbeefe. 1681: W. Robertson, *Phraseol. Generalis*, 257, He looks as big as bull beef. 1712: Motteux, *Quixote*, Pt. II. ch. v., You may go, and be a governor, or an islander, and look as big as bull-beef an you will. 1881: Evans, *Leics. Words, etc.*, 112 (E.D.S.), " As big as bull-beef " is a phrase equivalent to " as proud as a pump wi' two spouts." 1901: F. E. Taylor, *Folk-Speech of S. Lancs*, s.v. " Bull-beef."

Big in the mouth. 1917: Bridge, *Cheshire Proverbs*, 32, Big i' th' maith [given to boasting].

Dilberry. See **Blue** (2).

Bilbrough. See **Beccles.**

Bill after helve. Apparently equivalent to " Helve after hatchet." 1670: Ray, 164.

Billing Hill, between the valleys of Wharfe and Aire. *When Billing Hill puts on its cap, Calverley Mill will get a slap.* 1878: *Folk-Lore Record*, i. 169.

Billingsgate. 1. *Billingsgate language.* 1654: Gayton, *Pleasant Notes Don Q.*, 60, Most bitter Billingsgate rhetorick. 1687: A. Behn, *Lucky Chance*, I. ii., She . . . did so rail at him, that what with her Billinsgate . . . 1740: North, *Lives of Norths*, i. 288 (Bohn), Such Billingsgate language as should not come out of the mouth of any man. 1822: Byron, in *Letters and Journals*, vi. 4 (Prothero), I'll work the Laureate before I have done with him, as soon as I can muster Billingsgate therefor. 1918: Muirhead, *Blue Guide to London*, 389, The word " Billingsgate " as a synonym for coarse language is an aspersion on the fish-porters that is alleged to have passed long since into the domain of pointless slander.

2. *You shall have as much favour as at Billingsgate, for a box on the ear.* 1659: Howell, 15. 1670: Ray, 215.

Billingshurst. *See* Rudgwick.

Billy has found a pin. 1694: Ld. Delamere, *Speech on Arbitrary and Illegal Imprisonments* [quoted in Bridge, below], In our county [Cheshire] when a man makes a great stir about a matter and it ends in nothing that is significant, we say—" Billy has found a pin ! " 1917: Bridge, *Cheshire Proverbs*, 32.

Bind so as you may unbind. 1732: Fuller, 980.

Bingham. *See* All the world.

Birch. *See* Bare as the birch.

Birchen twigs break no ribs. 1639: Clarke, 75. 1670: Ray, 61. 1732: Fuller, No. 6380. Cf. Rod.

Bird and Birds. 1. *A bird in the hand is worth two in the bush.* [τὰν παρεοῖσαν ἀμέλγε. τὶ τὸν φεύγοντα διώκεις;—Theocritus, xi. 75.] Before 1500: in Hill, *Commonplace-Book*, 128 (E.E.T.S.), A birde in hond is better than thre in the wode. *c.* 1530: J. Heywood, *Witty and Witless*, 213 (Farmer), Better one bird in hand than ten in the wood. *c.* 1550: *Parl. of Byrdes*, l. 196, in Hazlitt, *Early Pop. Poetry*, iii. 177, A byrde in hande is worth two in the wood. 1581: Woodes, *Confl. of Conscience*, iv., One bird in the hand is worth two in the bush. *c.* 1660: in *Roxb. Ballads*, ii. 44 (Hindley). 1696: T. Brown, in *Works*, iv. 276 (1696). 1736: Fielding, *Pasquin*, II. 1855: Gaskell, *North and South*, ch. xvii.

2. *A bird may be caught with a snare that will not be shot.* 1732: Fuller, No. 13.

3. *A bird of the air shall carry it; or, A bird told me.* [Eccles. x. 20, For a bird of the air shall carry the voice, and that which hath wings shall tell the matter.] 1546: Heywood, *Proverbs*, Pt. II. ch. v.,

I did lately heere . . . by one byrd that in mine eare was late chauntyng. 1583: Melbancke, *Philotinus*, sig. F3, I had a little bird, that brought me newes of it. 1598: Shakespeare, 2 *Henry IV.*, V. v. 1652: Shirley, *Cardinal*, I. i., Take heed; the Cardinal holds Intelligence with every bird i' th' air. 1736: Fielding, *Pasquin*, IV., But I have also heard a sweet bird sing . . . 1822: Scott, *Nigel*, ch. vi. 1840: Barham, *Ing. Legends:* " St. Dunstan." 1919: A. A. Milne, *Camb. Triangle*, in *Sec. Plays*, 149 (1921), How did you know my name? *Dennis.* A little bird told me about you.

4. *As the bird is, such is the nest.* 1611: Cotgrave, s.v. " Nid," Such bird, such neast. 1666: Torriano, *Piazza Univ.*, 296.

5. *Birds are entangled by their feet, and men by their tongues.* 1732: Fuller, No. 981.

6. *Birds of a feather flock (or fly) together.* [ὡς αἰεὶ τὸν ὁμοῖον ἄγει θεὸς ὡς τὸν ὁμοῖον.—Homer, *Od.*, xvii. 218. Pares vetere proverbio cum paribus facillime congregantur. — Cicero, *Sen.*, iii. 7.] 1578: Whetstone, *Promos and Cassandra*, sig. C1, Byrds of a fether, best flye together. 1607: Rowlands, *Diog. Lanthorne*, 43 (Hunt. Cl.), Birds of a feather and a kinde, Will still together flocke. 1665: Head and Kirkman, *English Rogue*, i. 197. 1729: Fielding, *Author's Farce*, III., Men of a side Like birds of a feather Will flock together. 1850: Dickens, *Chuzzlewit*, ch. iii., He has conspired against me, like the rest, and they are but birds of one feather.

7. *Each bird loves to hear himself sing.* 1659: Howell, *Proverbs: Brit.-Eng.*, 11.

8. *He hath brought up a bird to pick out his own eyes.* 1639: Clarke, 157. 1672: Walker, *Parœm.*, 53, You bring up a bird to pick out your own eye. 1732: Fuller, No. 1864.

9. *He's in great want of a bird, that will give a groat for an owl.* 1678: Ray, 101. 1732: Fuller, No. 2458.

10. *If every bird take back its own feathers, you'll be naked.* 1633: Draxe, 18, If euery birde had his owne, he

should be as rich as a new shorne sheepe.
1732: Fuller, No. 2675.

11. *Ill fare that bird that picks out the
dam's eye.* 1639: Clarke, 169.

12. *Of all birds give me mutton.* 1732:
Fuller, No. 3695.

13. *Old birds are not caught with chaff.*
1481: Caxton, *Reynard*, 110 (Arber),
Wenest thou thus to deceyue me . . .
I am no byrde to be locked ne take by
chaf. 1640: R. Brome, *Sparagus Garden*, IV. xi., Teach 'hem to licke hony,
catch birds with chaffe . . . 1668:
Shadwell, *Sullen Lovers*, V. iii., There's
no catching old birds with chaff. 1713:
Gay, *Wife of Bath*, I. 1852: Dickens,
Bleak House, ch. xlix., He has bought
two specimens of poultry, which, if
there be any truth in adages, were
certainly not caught with chaff.

14. *That is the bird that I would catch.*
1732: Fuller, No. 4358.

15. *The bird is known by his note, the
man by his words.* 1659: Howell, *Proverbs: Ital.-Eng.*, 10. 1732: Fuller,
No. 12.

16. *The bird that can sing and won't
sing, must be made to sing* 1678: Ray,
343. 1681: W. Robertson, *Phraseol.
Generalis*, 1133. 1888: Q.-Couch, *Troy
Town*, ch. i., Remember the proverb
about little birds that can sing and
won't sing.

17. *The birds are flown.* 1562: Heywood, *Three Hund. Epigr.*, No. 280.

18. *There are no birds of this year in
last year's nests.* 1620: Shelton, *Quixote*,
Pt. II. ch. lxxiv. 1732: Fuller, No. 4863.
1841: Longfellow, *It is not always May*,
There are no birds in last year's nest.
1906: Q.-Couch, *Cornish Window*, 5, He
bade his friends look not for this year's
birds in last year's nests.

19. *To take the bird by its feet.* 1678:
Ray, 354.

20. *We shall catch birds to-morrow.*
1546: Heywood, *Proverbs*, Pt. II.
ch. viii. 1633: Draxe, 2.

See also Addled egg; Build (1); Child
(3); Early (7) and (8); Every bird; Fine
(12); Fright a bird; Ill bird; Lion (10);
Little and little; March (20), (21), and
(23); Rough net; St. Valentine (1); and
Small birds.

Birkenhead. *See* **Blacon Point.**

Birmingham. *See* **Sutton.**

**Birstal for ringers, Heckmondwike for
singers, Dewsbury for peddlers, Cleckheaton for sheddlers** [swindlers]. 1878:
Folk-Lore Record, i. 174.

Birth is much but breeding more.
1639: Clarke, 103. 1670: Ray, 63. 1712:
Motteux, *Quixote*, Pt. II. ch. lxviii.
1732: Fuller, No. 983.

Bishop. 1. *The bishop hath blessed it.*
1528: Tyndale, *Obed. of Chryst. Man*,
166, When a thynge speadeth not well
we borowe speach and say "the
byshope hath blessed it," because that
nothynge speadeth well that they
medyll withall.

2. *The bishop has put his foot in it.*
1528: Ibid., 166, If the podech be
burned to, or the meate over rosted, we
say, "the byshope has put his fote in
the potte," or "the byshope hath
played the coke," because the byshopes
burn who they lust, and whosoever displeaseth them. 1634: T. Heywood, *Lancs
Witches*, II., . . . till it [burnt milk]
stinke worse than the proverbe of the
bishops foot. 1790: Grose, *Prov. Gloss.*,
s.v. "Bishop," The bishop has set his
foot in it, a saying in the North, used
for milk that is burnt-to in boiling.
1825: Brockett, *Gloss. N. Country
Words*, 16. 1888: S. O. Addy, *Sheffield
Gloss.*, 18 (E.D.S.). 1917: Bridge,
Cheshire Proverbs, 112.

3. *What, a bishop's wife? eat and
drink in your gloves?* This is a cryptic
saying. 1678: Ray, 229.

**Bishop Auckland i' Bisho' brigg, God
help me!** 1846–59: *Denham Tracts*,
i. 93 (F.L.S.).

Bisho' Brigg into Yorkshire, Out o' =
Out of the frying pan into the fire.
Ibid., i. 77.

**Bishop-Middleham; where Might rules
Right.** Ibid., i. 93.

Bishop's Nympton. *See* quot. 1889:
N. & Q., 7th ser., vii. 274, The local
saying runs in North Devon . . .
Bishop's Nympton for length, South
Molton for strength, And Chittlehampton for beauty [the reference is
to the respective churches].

Bit. 1. *A bit and a blow;* sometimes

with the addition, *as they feed apes.*
1638: D. Turvill, *Vade Mecum*, 81
(3rd ed.), Some againe that doe feed
them, but alas! it is as the proverbe
saith, with a bit and a knocke. 1672:
Walker, *Parœm.*, 10, You feed me like
an ape, with a bit and a knock. 1738:
Swift, *Polite Convers.*, Dial. I., Why,
miss, I find there is nothing but a bit
and a blow with you. 1855: Robinson,
Whitby Gloss., 14, A bite and a buffet, a
maxim, never do a good deed and then
upbraid with the obligation. " Ne'er
give a bit And a buffet wi' 't."

2. *A bit in the morning is better than
nothing all day;* or, *than a thump on the
back with a stone.* 1639: in *Berkeley
MSS.*, iii. 33 (1885), Better a bit then
noe bread. 1670: Ray, 33. 1736:
Bailey, *Dict.*, s.v. " Bit."

Bitch that I mean is not a dog, The.
1732: Fuller, No. 4426.

Bite, *verb.* 1. *He bites the ear, yet
seems to cry for fear.* Glos. To bite
the ear, was a caress; see *Romeo and
Juliet*, II. iv. 1639: in *Berkeley MSS.*,
iii. 32 (1885).

2. *He that bites on every weed, must
needs light on poison.* 1639: Clarke,
211. 1669: *Politeuphuia*, 185. 1710:
S. Palmer, *Moral Essays on Proverbs*,
24. 1732: Fuller, No. 2046 [with
" may " for " must needs "].

3. *If you cannot bite, never show your
teeth.* 1670: Ray, 63. 1736: Bailey,
Dict., s.v. " Bite."

4. *Though I am bitten, I am not all
eaten.* 1639: Clarke, 32, Though he be
bitten, he's not all eaten. 1670: Ray,
164. 1732: Fuller, No. 6170.

5. *To bite the mare by the thumb*=?
1546: Heywood, *Proverbs*, Pt. II. ch. vi.,
This biteth the mare by the thumbe, as
they sey. 1611: Davies (of Hereford),
Sc. of Folly, 43, in *Works*, ii. (Grosart),
Thus bitt the mare by the thumbe.

6. *To bite upon the bridle.* See
Bridle (2).

Bite, *subs.* *You have taken a bite out of
your own arm.* 1732: Fuller, No. 5925.

Biter is sometimes bit, The. [ὸ
νεβρὸς τὸν λέοντα.—Lucian, *Dial. Mort.*,
viii.] 1693: D'Urfey, *Richmond Heiress*,
Epil., Once in an age the biter

should be bit. 1710: Ward, *Nuptial
Dialogues*, ii. 179, I think she merits
equal praise That has the wit to bite
the biter. 1880: Spurgeon, *Ploughman's Pictures*, 16, Biters deserve to
be bitten.

Biting and scratching. *See* **Cat** (14).

Bitter. 1. *Bitter as gall.* *c.* 1305: in
Wright's *Pol. Songs John to Edw. II.*,
193 (Camden S.), Ther hi habbeth
dronke bittrere then the galle. 1468:
Cov. Mysteries, 233 (Sh. S.), My mowthe
is byttyr as galle. 1581: B. Rich,
Farewell, 38 (Sh. S.), Whose taste
I finde more bitter now then gall.
1623: Webster, *Devil's Law-Case*, I. ii.,
Iol. Bitter as gall. 1716: Ward, *Female
Policy*, 30. 1892: Heslop, *Northumb.
Words*, 311, As bitter as gaa [gall].

2. *Bitter as soot.* *c.* 1305: in Wright's
Pol. Songs John to Edw. II., 195
(Camden S.), Hit falleth the Kyng of
Fraunce bittrore then the sote. *c.* 1374:
Chaucer, *Troylus*, iii. 1194, To whom
this tale sucre be or soot [i.e. sweet or
bitter]. 1758–67: Sterne, *Trist. Shandy*,
Vol. IV. ch. xiii. (1788), And now thy
mouth . . . is as bitter, I dare say, as
soot. 1857–72: Buckland, *Curios. of
Nat. Hist.*, iii. 29, They are as bitter
as soot, if you eats 'em raw.

3. *Bitter pills may have wholesome
effects.* [*c.* 1374: Chaucer, *Troylus*,
iii. 1215, And for to han gladnesse, Men
drinken often peyne and greet dis-
tresse.] 1732: Fuller, No. 985.

4. *He who hath bitter in his mouth,
spits not all sweet.* 1640: Herbert, *Jac.
Prudentum*. 1670: Ray, 3. 1732:
Fuller, No. 2387 [with " breast "
instead of " mouth "].

5. *That which was bitter to endure, may
be sweet to remember.* 1732: Fuller,
No. 4385.

Bittern. 1. *A bittern makes no good
hawk.* 1611: Davies (of Hereford), *Sc.
of Folly*, 42, in *Works*, ii. (Grosart).

2. *To roar like a bittern at a seg-root*
[sedge]. 1883: Burne, *Shropsh. Folk-
Lore*, 594.

Blab, *subs.* *He that is a blab is a scab.*
1639: Clarke, 132. 1670: Ray, 63.
1732: Fuller, No. 6296, He that is a
blab is a meer scab.

Blab, *verb.* *Blab it wist and out it must.* 15th cent.: *Harl. MS.* 3362 (V. Lean), Labbe hyt whyste, and owt yt must. 1546: Heywood, *Proverbs*, Pt. I. ch. x. 1633: Draxe, 16, He cannot hold, but all must out.

Black, *adj.* 1. *A black plum is as sweet as a white.* 1633: Draxe, 15, A blacke raisin as good as a white. 1670: Ray, 63. 1732: Fuller, No. 986, Black plums may eat as sweet as white.

2. *A black shoe makes a merry heart.* 1659: Howell, 18. 1670: Ray, 216.

3. *A black woman hath turpentine in her.* 1659: Howell, *Letters*, ii. 666 (Jacobs).

4. *Although I am black, I am not the devil.* 1595: Peele, *Old Wives Tale*, sig. D3.

5. *Black as a coal.* c. 1000: *Sax. Leechd.*, ii. 332 (O.), And swa sweart swa col. c. 1260: *King Horn* (Camb.), l. 590 (Hall), Also blak so eny cole. Before 1300: *Cursor M.*, l. 22489. c. 1386: Chaucer, *Knight's Tale*, l. 1834, As blak he lay as any cole. c. 1450: *Partonope*, l. 3918 (E.E.T.S.), Blak as cole than was his hois. 1599: Breton, in *Works*, ii. c 14 (Grosart), The other as blacke as a coale. 1640: Tatham, in *Dram. Works*, 20 (1879). 1819: Byron, *Don Juan*, can. iv. st. 94, With eyes . . . black and burning as a coal. 1860: Reade, *Cloister and Hearth*, ch. liv., Else our hearts were black as coal.

6. *Black as a crow* (or *crake*). c. 1320: *Horn Childe*, l. 1049, in Hall's *King Horn* (1901), Blac as ani crawe. c. 1386: Chaucer, *Knight's Tale*, l. 1834, Blak he lay as any . . . crowe. c. 1540: Bale, *King Johan*, Act I. l. 88, I shall cawse the Pope to curse the as blacke as a crowe. 1610: Shakespeare, *Wint. Tale*, IV. iv., Cypress black as e'er was crowe. 1716: Ward, *Female Policy*, 86, If brown, think her as black as a crow. 1828: Carr, *Craven Dialect*, i. 91, Crake, a crow, as black as a crake. 1876: C. C. Robinson, *Mid-Yorks Gloss.*, 26 (E.D.S.), As black as a crake.

7. *Black as a raven.* c. 1300: Robert of Brunne, tr. Langtoft's *Chron.*, 295 (Hearne), His stede was blak as rauen. 1663: Killigrew, *Thomaso*, Pt. II. Act I.

sc. ii., It keeps him as black as a raven. 1720: Gay, *Trivia*, bk. ii. l. 198, Black as the . . . glossy raven's back.

8. *Black as a sloe.* 14th cent.: *Guy of Warwick*, l. 506 (E.E.T.S.), Guy they fonde as blak as sloo. c. 1386: Chaucer, *Miller's Tale*, l. 60. 15th cent.: *Torrent of Portyngale*, 17 (E.E.T.S.), Ys fytte [his feet] blac ase slon. 1567: Golding, *Ovid*, bk. ii. l. 315, His wares as blacke as any slo. 1685: *Roxb. Ballads*, viii. 418 (B.S.), Hair black as a sloe. 1727: Gay, *Fables*, 1st ser., No. 3, l. 16, The mother's eyes as black as sloes. 1823: Moor, *Suffolk Words*, 363, Her eyes are as black as sloons [sloes]. 1894: R. L. S., *St. Ives*, ch. xxx.

9. *Black as hell.* 1506: Guylforde, *Pylgrymage*, 53 (Camden S.), It is comenly derke as hell. 1590: Spenser, *F. Q.*, I. viii. 355, But all a deepe descent, as dark as hell. 1600: in *Lyrical Poems*, 66 (Percy S.), Aire, made to shine, as blacke as hell shall prove. 1825: Scott, *Talisman*, ch. xv., If his treachery be as black as hell.

10. *Black as ink.* c. 1510: A. Barclay, *Egloges*, 30 (Spens. S.), At euery tempest they be as blacke as inke. 1590: Spenser, *F. Q.*, I. i. 201, Deformed monsters, fowle, and blacke as inke. c. 1685: Aubrey, *Nat. Hist. Wilts*, 21 (1847), Which . . . became immediately as black as inke. 1721: D'Urfey, *Two Queens of Brentford*, IV., Whose sordid soul, as black as ink. . . . 1893: R. L. S., *Ebb-Tide*, ch. i., Clouds . . . black as ink-stains. 1901: Raymond, *Idler Out of Doors*, 7, The tall elm-top that draws, as black as ink, its tracery of naked limbs.

11. *Black as jet.* 1412–20: Lydgate, *Troy Book*, bk. ii. l. 987, It cometh out of Ethiope and Ynde, Blak as is get. 1590: Marlowe, *Tamburlaine*, Pt. II. Act I. sc. iii. 1682: Evelyn, *Diary*, 19 June, Their nails and teeth as black as jet. 1705: Philips, *Splendid Shilling*, l. 20. 1872: A. Dobson, in *Poet. Works*, 109 (1923), Circling a silky curl as black as jet.

12. *Black as Newgate knocker.* See **Newgate.**

13. *Black as soot.* 1678: Ray, 281.

14. *Black as the devil.* c. 1580:
Spelman, *Dialogue*, 42 (Roxb. Cl.), His
face was as black as a devill in a playe.
1670: Ray, 203. 1754: Berthelson,
Eng.-Danish Dict., s.v. " As."

15. *Black as the devil's nutting-bag.*
1866: Gilpin, *Songs* (Cumberland), 393
(W.), Her smock's leyke auld Nick's
nuttin' bag. 1879: Henderson, *Folk-
Lore N. Counties*, 96, A proverb is current there [Sussex], " As black as the
de'il's nutting-bag." 1899: *N. & Q.*,
9th ser., iv. 478 [saying common in N.
Lincs]. 1900: *N. & Q.*, 9th ser., v. 38
and 197 [saying common in Berks,
Somerset, and Suffolk].

16. *Black as thunder.* 1839: Planché,
Extravag., ii. 56 (1879), He looks as
black as thunder. 1922: Weyman,
Ovington's Bank, ch. iii., He's in his
room and as black as thunder.

17. *Black fleet of Norway.* See
Boston's Bay; and **England** (11).

18. *Black hen.* See **Hen** (1).

19. *Black Jack rides a good horse* =
Zinc ore gives good promise for copper.
1865: Hunt, *Pop. Romances W. of Eng.*,
194 (1896). 1902: Wright, *Eng. Dial.
Dict.*, iii. 239.

20. *Black lad Monday* = Monday in
Easter - week. 1846: Denham, *Proverbs*, 32 (Percy S.).

21. *Black man.* See **Red hair**.

22. *Black men are pearls in ladies'
eyes;* or, *A black man is a jewel, etc.*
1599: Chapman, *Hum. Day's Mirth*,
sc. viii., Oh, sir, black is a pearl in a
woman's eye. c. 1623: B. & F., *Love's
Cure*, III. iv., The fairest ladies like
the blackest men. 1623: Shakespeare,
Two Gent., V. ii. 1670: Ray, 51.
1732: Fuller, No. 16.

23. *No one can say black is my* (or
his, or *your*) *eye* (or *nail*). 1402: Hoccleve, in *Minor Poems*, 76 (E.E.T.S.),
That when thow twynnest 'fro hir
companye, another cometh and blered
ys thyn ye! 1412: Hoccleve, *Regement*, st. 404, l. 2823 (E.E.T.S.), No man
seith onës that blak is his eye. 1583:
Stubbes, *Anat. of Abuses*, 88 (N. Sh. S.),
And yet maie no man saie blacke is
their eye. 1625: Jonson, *Staple of
News*, I. ii., He . . . can commit whom

he will, and what he will . . . and no
man say black is his eye, but laugh at
him. 1711: Steele, *Spectator*, No. 79,
The most insolent of all creatures to her
friends and domesticks, upon no other
pretence in nature but that . . . no
one can say blacke is her eye. 1761:
J. Reed, *Reg. Office*, I., in Inchbald's
Farces, iii. 145 (1815), I defy ony body
. . . to say black's my nail. 1771:
Smollett, *Clinker*, in *Works*, vi. 125
(1817), I challenge you to say black is
the white of my eye. 1828: Carr,
Craven Dialect, i. 136, " Black's my
eye," no one can impute blame to me.
1889: Peacock, *Manley, etc., Gloss.*, 52
(E.D.S.), Noäbody niver so much as
said black's my naail to me [said
anything evil], when I liv'd at
Burringham.

24. *The black ox treads on one's foot.*
1546: Heywood, *Proverbs*, Pt. I., ch. vii.,
It was yet but hony moone ; The blacke
oxe had not trode on his nor hir foote.
1584: Lyly, *Sapho and Phao*, I. 199
(1858), Now crowes foote is on her eye,
and the black oxe hath trod on her
foot. 1633: Jonson, *Tale of a Tub*,
IV. v., Well, young squire, The black
ox never trod yet on your foot. 1738:
Swift, *Polite Convers.*, Dial. I., Poor
creature ! the black ox has set his foot
upon her already. 1822: Scott, *Nigel*,
ch. ii. 1883: Burne, *Shropsh. Folk-
Lore*, 209, " The black ox has not
trodden on you "—i.e. care has not
come near you—is an old Shropshire
saying.

25. *Those that eat black pudding will
dream of the devil.* 1738: Swift, *Polite
Convers.*, Dial. II.

26. *To have the black dog on one's
back.* 1778: Mrs. Thrale, in *Piozzi
Letters*, ii. 32, I have lost what made my
happiness . . . but the black dog shall
not make prey of both my master and
myself. 1816: Scott, *Antiquary*, ch. vi.,
Sir Arthur has got the black dog on his
back again. 1889: Peacock, *Manley,
etc., Gloss.*, 51 (E.D.S.), " He's gotten
th' black dog on his back this mornin',"
that is, he is in a bad temper.

See also **Dark**.

Black, *subs.* 1. *Above black there is no*

colour, and above salt no savour. 1578:
Florio, *First Fruites*, fo. 33. 1629:
Booke of Meery Riddles, Prov. 120.
1659: Howell, *Proverbs: Ital.-Eng.*, 7.

2. *Black will take no other hue.* 1546:
Heywood, *Proverbs*, Pt. II. ch. ix. 1593:
Peele, *Edward I.*, sc. viii. 1681: W.
Robertson, *Phraseol. Generalis*, 262.
1754: Berthelson, *Eng.-Danish Dict.*,
s.v. " Black."

3. *In black and white.* c. 1440:
Lydgate, *Fall of Princes*, bk. i. l. 465,
Hauyng no colours but onli whit and
blak, To the tragedies which that I shal
write. 1596: Jonson, *Ev. Man in his
Humour*, IV. iii., I have it here in black
and white [pulls out the warrant].
1658: Cowley, *Cutter of Coleman Street*,
I. v., I saw it from a good hand beyond
sea, under black and white. 1678:
Bunyan, *Pilgr. Progress*, Author's
Apology. 1740: North, *Examen*, 404,
A wicked paragraph it is, as ever was
put in black and white. 1823: Scott,
St. Ronan's, ch. xxiii. 1886: Hardy,
Casterbridge, ch. ix.

Blackamoor. *To wash (or make) the
blackamoor white.* [Laterem lavare.—
Terence, *Phorm.*, 186.] 1543: Becon,
in *Early Works*, 49 (P.S.), Here, therefore, do ye nothing else than, as the
common proverb is, go about to make
an Ethiop white. 1604: Dekker, *Honest
Whore*, Pt. II. Act I. sc. i., This is the
blackamoor that by washing was turned
white. 1673: Wycherley, *Gent. Danc.-
Master*, IV. i., You wash the blackamoor white, in endeavouring to make a
Spaniard of a monsieur. 1748: Richardson, *Clarissa*, ii. 160 (1785), I should
suspect the whole to be a plot set on
foot to wash a blackamoor white. 1853:
Planché, *Extravag.*, iv. 280 (1879), If
any one could wash a blackamoor white
It would be Mrs. Beecher Stowe.

Blackberries, Plentiful as. 1596:
Shakespeare, 1 *Henry IV.*, II. iv., If
reasons were as plentie as black-berries.
1690: *Reason of Mr. Bays changing his
Religion*, Pt. II., p. 35, Were reasons as
cheap as black-berries. 1868: *Quart.
Review*, cxxv. 231, Parallels are " as
plentiful as blackberries." 1886: Hardy,
Casterbridge, ch. xvi., Earthworks . . .

were as common as blackberries here-
about. *See also* **Devil** (82).

Blackberry summer. 1846: Denham,
Proverbs, 57 (Percy S.). 1883: Cope,
Hants Words, 8 (E.D.S.), Blackberry-
summer. Fine weather experienced at
the end of September and the beginning
of October when blackberries are ripe.

Blacksmith. *It is much like a blacksmith with a white silk apron.* 1732:
Fuller, No. 2980.

Blackthorn winter. 1789: White,
Selborne, ii. 292 (1813) (O.), The harsh
rugged weather obtaining at this season,
is called by the country people black-
thorn-winter. 1838: Holloway, *Provincialisms*, 13, Blackthorn winter.
The cold which is generally experienced
at the latter end of April and beginning
of May, when the black-thorn is in
blossom. 1884: H. Friend, *Flowers and
Fl. Lore*, 214.

Blacon Point. *See* quot. 1917:
Bridge, *Cheshire Proverbs*, 59, From
Blacon Point to Hilbre, A squirrel
might leap from tree to tree. [In
N. & Q., 4th ser., xi. 13 (1873), is the
variant, " From Birkenhead to far
Hilbree A squirrel could leap from tree
to tree."]

Blade to haft, True as. 1823: Scott,
Q. Durward, ch. xxiii., I will be true to
you as blade to haft, as our cutlers say.

Blake [yellow] **as a paigle** [cowslip
or marigold]. [1530: Palsgrave, s.v.,
Blake, wan of colour.] 1678: Ray, 355.
1683: Meriton, *Yorkshire Ale*, 83 (1697).
1834: Toone, *Glossary*, s.v. " Paigle."
1866: Mrs. Lynn Linton, *Lizzie Lorton*,
ii. 217, As blake as marygowds. 1884:
H. Friend, *Flowers and Fl. Lore*, 210.

Blake as butter. 1876: C. C. Robinson, *Mid-Yorks Gloss.*, 10 (E.D.S.).

Blames. *He that blames would buy.*
1640: Herbert, *Jac. Prudentum*. 1732:
Fuller, No. 2383, He who findeth fault,
meaneth to buy.

Bledlow, Bucks. *See* quot. 1869:
Hazlitt, 400, They who live and do
abide, Shall see Bledlow church fall
into the Lyde.

Bless the king and all his men. A
common exclamation when surprised
and startled. 1862: *Dialect of Leeds*, 251.

Blessed is the corpse. *See* Happy.

Blessing, *subs.* 1. *Blessings are not valued till they are gone.* 1732: Fuller, No. 989.

2. *They have need of a blessing that kneel to a thistle.* 1639: Clarke, 13. 1670: Ray, 63. 1732: Fuller, No. 4964.

Blessing of your heart. *See* Ale (3).

Blest is the bride. *See* Happy.·

Blind, *adj.* 1. *A blind man cannot* (or *should not) judge colours. c.* 1374: Chaucer, *Troylus,* bk. ii. l. 21, A blind man can nat iuggen wel in hewis. 1412: Hoccleve, *Regement,* 36 (E.E.T.S.), The blynde man of coloures al wrong deemeth. 1530: Palsgrave, 511, A blynde man can nat deme no coulours. 1637: Breton, in *Works,* ii. *h* 44 (Grosart). 1759: Warburton, in *Garrick Corresp.,* i. 93 (1831), Proposing an emendation to the generality of those they call scholars, was desiring a blind man to judge of colours.

2. *A blind man will not thank you for a looking-glass.* 1732: Fuller, No. 18.

3. *A blind man would be glad to see it.* 1738: Swift, *Polite Convers.,* Dial. I., A blind man would be glad to see that. 1894: Northall, *Folk Phrases of Four Counties* (E.D.S.), A blind man on a galloping horse would be glad to see it. Cf. Nos. 15 and 18.

4. *A man's blind side.* 1606: Chapman, *Gent. Usher,* I. i., We'll follow the blind side of him. 1681: A. Behn, *Rover,* Pt. II. I. i., The rascals have a blind side as all conceited coxcombs have. 1742: Fielding, *Andrews,* bk. iii. ch. v., If this good man had an enthusiasm, or what the vulgar call a blind side, it was this. 1869: Spurgeon, *John Ploughman,* ch. xxi., In the hope of getting on the parson's blind side when the blankets were given away at Christmas.

5. *A pebble and a diamond are alike to a blind man.* 1732: Fuller, No. 340.

6. *As one blind man said to another, let's behold ourselves.* 1612: Shelton, *Quixote,* Pt. I. bk. iv. ch. xxiii. 1694: D'Urfey, *Quixote,* Pt. I. Act V. sc. ii. 1869: Hazlitt, 258, Let me see, as the blind man said.

7. *As the blind man catcheth the hare.*

1638: Taylor (Water-Poet), *Bull, Beare,* 10, in *Works,* 3rd coll. (Spens. S.), A blinde man may be taken with a hare [purposely reversed]. 1659: W. Cole, in *Harl. Miscell.,* iv. 309 (1745), And so they are as capable to do equity therein, as a blind man to shoot a hare.

8. *As the blind man shot the crow.* 1546: Heywood, *Proverbs,* Pt. II. ch. ix., As the blind man casts his staffe, or shootes the crow. 1605: Armin, *Foole vpon Foole,* 11 (Grosart), Yet now and then a blinde man may hit a crow. 1732: Fuller, No. 1393. 1830: Forby, *Vocab. E. Anglia,* 428, Hitty-missy, as the blind man shot the crow.

9. *As wary as a blind horse.* 1732: Fuller, No. 745.

10. *Better to be blind than to see ill* 1640: Herbert, *Jac. Prudentum.*

11. *Blind as a bat.* 1639: Clarke, 52, As blind as a bat at noone. *c.* 1780: in *Poems on Costume,* 262 (Percy S.), Which makes her as blind as a bat. 1889: J. Nicholson, *Folk Speech E. Yorks,* 16.

12. *Blind as a beetle.* 1549: Latimer, *Seven Sermons,* 90 (Arber), In this wysdome he is as blynd as a beatel. 1647: in *Polit. Ballads,* 47 (Percy S.), Jack Maynard is a loyall blade, yet blind as any beetle. Before 1704: T. Brown, *Works,* i. 236 (1760). 1786: Mrs. Cowley, *Sch. for Greybeards,* V. ii., Oh, what a beetle, what a blind bat I have been ! 1860: Reade, *Cloister and Hearth,* ch. l. 1881: Evans, *Leics. Words,* 102 (E.D.S.), " As blind as a beetle " is a very common simile, the cockchafer being the beetle referred to. 1892: Heslop, *Northumb. Words,* 60 (E.D.S.), Bittle, a beetle, or wooden beater for beating flax or linen clothes. " As blind as a bittle," a very common expression.

13. *Blind as a buzzard.* [1377: Langland, *Plowman,* B, x. 267, I rede eche a blynde bosarde.] 1577: Kendall, *Flow. of Epigr.,* 143 (Spens. S.), When buzzard blynd thou canst not see what is before thy feete. 1681: Otway, *Soldier's Fortune,* IV. iii., I'll . . . weep till blind as buzzard. 1730: Bailey, *Eng. Dict.,* s.v. " Buzzard," A stupid

senseless fellow; as a blind buzzard.
1823: Moor, *Suffolk Words*, 61, We have
the phrase "as blind as a buzzard."
1886: Swainson, *Folk-Lore of Brit.
Birds*, 133 (F.L.S.), The saying . . .
" as blind as a buzzard " does not refer
to the bird of that name, which is
extremely quick-sighted, but rather to
the beetle, from the buzzing sound of
its flight.

14. *Blind as a mole.* 1584: B. R.,
Euterpe, 68 (Lang), In the water as
blinde as a moale. 1658: Willsford,
Natures Secrets, 2, When they are as
blind as moles. 1785: Wolcot, in
Works, i. 84 (1795). 1823: Scott,
Peveril, ch. xxxii.

15. *Blind George. See* quots. 1633:
Jonson, *Tale of a Tub*, II. i., That
I would fain zee, quoth the blind George
of Holloway. 1678: Ray, 268, That
would I fain see, said blind George of
Hollowee. Cf. Nos. 3 and 18.

16. *Blind harpers. See* **Have among
you.**

17. *Blind horse. See* Nos. 9 and 26;
also **Afterthought.**

18. *Blind Hugh. See* quots. 1533:
J. Heywood, *Pardoner and Friar*, in
Hazlitt, *Old Plays*, i. 232 (1874), Marry
that I would see, quod blind Hew.
1639: in *Berkeley MSS.*, iii. 30 (1885),
I w'ud I c'ud see't, ka' blind Hugh.
1738: Swift, *Polite Convers.*, Dial. I.,
Would I could see it, quoth blind Hugh.
Cf. Nos. 3 and **15.**

19. *Blind man's holiday.* 1599:
Nashe, *Lenten Stuffe*, in *Works*, v. 263
(Grosart), What will not blinde Cupid
doe in the night which is his blindmans
holiday? 1690: *New Dict. Canting
Crew*, sig. B6, Blind-man's-holiday,
when it is too dark to see to work.
1738: Swift, *Polite Convers.*, Dial. III.
1828: Carr, *Craven Dialect*, i. 38. 1891:
Q.-Couch, *Noughts and Crosses*, 109,
Day was breakin'—a sort of blind man's
holiday.

20. *Blind whelps. See* **Hasty bitch.**

21. *He's so blind he can't see a hole
through a ladder*, or, *the holes of a sieve.*
1620: Shelton, *Quixote*, Pt. II. ch. i.,
How blind is he that sees not light
through the bottom of a meal-sieve!

1694: D'Urfey, *Quixote*, Pt. I. Act I.
sc. i. [the holes of a sieve]. 1864:
" Cornish Proverbs," in *N. & Q.*, 3rd
ser., vi. 494, He's so blind he can't see
a hole through a nine-foot ladder.

22. *It is a blind man's question to ask,
why those things are loved which are
beautiful.* 1855: Bohn, 426.

23. *Men are blind in their own cause.*
1546: Heywood, *Proverbs*, Pt. II. ch. v.,
Folk oft tymes are most blind in their
owne cause. 1683: Meriton, *Yorkshire
Alo*, 85 (1697), Men are blind in their
awn cause.

24. *None are so blind as those that
will not see.* 1547: Borde, *Brev. of
Helthe*, bk. ii. fo. vi v°, Who is blynder
than he y^t wyl nat se. 1670: Ray, 64,
Who so blind as he that will not see?
1671: *Westm. Drollery*, 20 (Ebsworth),
Ther's none so blind As those that will
not see. 1738: Swift, *Polite Convers.*,
Dial. III. 1859: Sala, *Twice Round the
Clock*, 3 a.m., Homer not unfrequently
nods in Scotland Yard. " None are so
blind as those that won't see," whisper
the wicked.

25. *The blind man's wife needs no
painting.* 1659: Howell, *Proverbs:
Span.-Eng.*, 4. 1670: Ray, 3. 1732:
Fuller, No. 992.

26. *To a blind horse a nod is as good as
a wink.* 1802: in Dor. Wordsworth's
Journal, i. 129 (Knight), A wink's as
good as a nod with some folks. 1822:
Scott, *Nigel*, ch. xxv., Let me hear from
you to-morrow. Good night, good
night—a nod is as good as a wink.
1842: Barham, *Ing. Legends*, 2nd ser.:
" Old Woman Clothed in Grey." 1894:
Northall, *Folk Phrases of Four Counties*,
6 (E.D.S.). 1926: Phillpotts, *Peacock
House*, 147, So a nod's as good as a
wink, Joe.

27. *What matters it to a blind man,
that his father could see?* 1855: Bohn,
555.

Blind, *subs.* 1. *The blind eat many
a fly.* c. 1430: Lydgate, *Ballade*, in
Skeat's *Chaucer*, vii. 295, The blind et
many a fly. Before 1529: Skelton, in
Works, i. 213 (Dyce), But, as the man
sayes, The blynde eteth many a flye.
1609: Rowlands, *Whole Crew of Kind*

Gossips, 19 (Hunt. Cl.). 1671: Head and Kirkman, *English Rogue*, ii. 88. 1732: Fuller, No. 4428. 1881: Evans, *Leics. Words*, 300 (E.D.S.), Blind i' th' eye Eats many a fly.

2. *When the blind leads the blind, both fall into the ditch.* [Luke vi. 39.] *c.* 1450: in *Reliq. Antiquæ*, ii. 238 (1843), For now the bysom [blind] ledys the blynde. 1583: Melbancke, *Philotinus*, sig. Y1, In the ditch falls the blind that is led by the blind. 1699: Farquhar, *Love and a Bottle*, V. i., When the blind leads the blind, no wonder they both fall into—matrimony. 1712: Motteux, *Quixote*, Pt. II. ch. xiii.

See also Kingdom (2).

Blindworm. *See* **Adder.**

Blister on one's tongue, A. 1732: Fuller, No. 1127, Common fame [=liar] hath a blister on its tongue. 1738: Swift, *Polite Convers.*, Dial. I., I have a blister on my tongue; yet I don't remember I told a lye.

Blood. 1. *Blood is thicker than water.* [1412–20: Lydgate, *Troy Book*, bk. iii. l. 2071, For naturelly blod will ay of kynde Draw vn-to blod, wher he may it fynde.] 1857: Hughes, *Tom Brown*, Pt. I. ch. i., With them there is nothing like the Browns, to the third and fourth generation. " Blood is thicker than water," is one of their pet sayings. 1871: G. Eliot, *Middlemarch*, ch. xxxii.

2. *Blood without groats is nothing.* 1665: J. Wilson, *Projectors*, II., He . . . compares 'em [great matches] to an ill pudding—all blood and no fat. 1670: Ray, 166, He hath good bloud if he had but groats to him. Cheshire. Good parentage if he had but wealth. 1732: Fuller, No. 1703, Good blood makes poor pudding without suet. 1825: Brockett, *Gloss. of N. Country Words*, 87, Hence the northern proverb, " blood without groats is nothing," meaning that family without fortune is of no consequence. 1828: Carr, *Craven Dialect*, i. 200. 1917: Bridge, *Cheshire Proverbs*, 68 [as in 1670].

3. *Human blood is all of a colour.* 1732: Fuller, No. 2560.

4. *The blood of the martyrs is the seed of the church.* [Semen est sanguis Christianorum.—Tertullian,*Apologet.*,l.] 1630: T. Adams, *Works*, 205, So the bloud of martyrs seedes the church. Before 1680: Butler, *Remains*, i. 135 (1759), The ancient churches, and the best, By their own martyrs blood increas'd. 1746: *Foundl. Hosp. for Wit*, No. III., p. 41.

5. *You can't get blood* (or *water*) *out of a stone.* [Nam tu aquam a pumice nunc postulas, Qui ipsus sitiat.—Plautus, *Pers.*, I. i. 42.] 1599: J. Weever, *Epigrammes*, 17 (1911), For who'le wrest water from a flintie stone? 1666: Torriano, *Piazza Univ.*, 161, There's no getting of bloud out of that wall. 1836: Marryat, *Japhet*, ch. iv., I have often heard it said, there's no getting blood out of a turnip. 1865: Dickens, *Mutual Friend*, bk. iv. ch. xv. 1917: Bridge, *Cheshire Proverbs*, 158, You cannot whip blood out of a post.

Blossom. *That which doth blossom in the spring, will bring forth fruit in the autumn.* 1633: Draxe, 13. 1670: Ray, 3. 1732: Fuller, No. 3544, No autumn-fruit without spring-blossoms.

Blot. 1. *A blot is no blot till it be hit.* A " blot " in backgammon is an exposed piece which is liable to capture. 1664: J. Wilson, *The Cheats*, V. iii., I will join with you in anything, provided always you carry it prudently, for fear of scandal. A blot is no blot till it be hit. 1712: Motteux, *Quixote*, Pt. II. ch. xliii. 1820: Scott, *Fam. Letters*, ii. 97 (1894), But then a blot is not a blot till hit.

2. *Cleaning a blot with blotted fingers maketh a greater blur.* 1732: Fuller, No. 1112.

Blow, verb. 1. *Blow devil, the more wind the better boat.* 1724: Defoe, *Tour*, Lett. II., p. 13 [cited as " a rude sailor's proverb "].

2. *Blow first and sip afterwards.* 1678: Ray, 103. 1732: Fuller, No. 995.

3. *Blow out the marrow and throw the bone to the dogs.* 1678: Ray, 343.

4. *Blow, Smith, and you'll get money.* 1732: Fuller, No. 997.

5. *Blow the wind high, or blow the wind low, It bloweth good to Hawley's hoe.* Plymouth. 1849: Halliwell, *Pop.*

Rhymes, 194. 1897: Norway, *H. and B. in Devon, etc.*, 115 [with " still " for " good," and " hawe " for " hoe "].

6. *Blow thy own pottage and not mine.* 1732: Fuller, No. 998.

7. *He can't neither blow nor strike.* A blacksmith's description of a useless person. 1926: *Devonsh. Assoc. Trans.*, lvii. 152.

8. *He that blows in the dust fills his eyes with it.* 1640: Herbert, *Jac. Prudentum.* 1694: D'Urfey, *Quixote*, Pt. I. Act IV. sc. i., He that blows in the dust will make himself blind. 1732: Fuller, No. 2048.

9. *To blow at the coal.* c. 1350: Rolle de Hampole, *Prose Treatises*, No. xi., p. 33 (E.E.T.S.), Bot habyde and suffire a while, and go blawe at the fyre, that es, first do thi werkes, and go than allane to thi prayers and thi meditacyons. c. 1380: *Sir Ferumbras*, 74 (E.E.T.S.), We haue a game in this contray to blowen atte glede [tho " game " is described in the text, ll. 2236–43]. 1485: Caxton, *Charles the Grete*, 119 (E.E.T.S.), By my fayth, syr duc, ye can wel playe and blowe atte cole. c. 1530: *Detection . . . of Dice Play*, 6 (Percy S.), Let them that be acold blow the coals, for I am already on the sure side. 1633: Draxe, 29, Let him that is cold blow at the coale. 1694: *Terence made English*, 11, Were it not much better to try if ye can put that love out of your head, than to indulge your passion thus, stand blowing o' the cole, and to no purpose neither. 1732: Fuller, No. 3184, Let him that is cold blow the fire. 1837: Mrs. Palmer, *Devonsh. Dialect*, 31, To blow a coal, is to make mischief or sow dissension between neighbours.

10. *To blow hot and cold.* [Simul flare sorbereque haud factu facilest.— Plautus, *Most.*, 791.] 1577: Grange, *Golden Aphroditis*, sig. D2, Out of one mouthe commeth bothe hotte and colde. 1619: H. Hutton, *Follies Anat.*, 12 (Percy S.), Which, Gnato like, doth blowe both hot and cold. 1692: L'Estrange, *Æsop*, 219 (3rd ed.), The old adage of blowing hot and cold; which is taken for the mark and

character of a dissembler. 1740: North, *Examen*, 115, So apt are ill men to blow hot and cold. 1853: Dickens, in *Letters*, iii. 139 (1882).

11. *To blow one's own trumpet.* 1799: T. Knight, *Turnpike Gate*, I. i., in Inchbald, *Farces*, iii. 72 (1815), Or I should not blush so often as I do, by blowing the trumpet of my own praise. 1844: Planché, *Extravag.*, ii. 287 (1879), The fellow Blows his own trumpet. 1920: W. H. Hudson, *Dead Man's Plack*, ch. ii., The people of her own country, who were great . . . at blowing their own trumpets.

12. *To go blow one's flute.* See **Pipe** in an ivy leaf.

Blow, *subs. A blow with a reed makes a noise, but hurts not.* 1732: Fuller, No. 20.

Bloxham for length, Adderbury for strength, but King's Sutton for beauty. Warwickshire church spires. 1878: *N. & Q.*, 5th ser., ix. 175.

Bloxwich Bull. See quot. 1867: Timbs, *Nooks and Corners*, 261, [The bull to be baited was stolen by a joker, and the expectant crowd were disappointed.] This circumstance gave rise to a local proverb still in use. When great expectations are baffled, the circumstance is instinctively likened to " the Bloxwich bull."

Blue, *adj.* 1. *Blue as a mazzard.* W. Cornwall, 19th cent. (Mr. C. Lee).

2. *Blue as a wimberry* (bilberry). 1600: Shakespeare, *Merry Wives*, V. v., There pinch the maids as blue as bilberry. 1901: F. E. Taylor, *Lancs Sayings*, 1, As blue as a wimberry. 1917: Bridge, *Cheshire Proverbs*, 10.

3. *Blue veins in the nose.* 1865: Hunt, *Pop. Romances W. of Eng.*, 431 (1896), The old lady of the house had just told her that the child could not live long, because he had a blue vein across his nose. 1889: *N. & Q.*, 7th ser., vii. 216, If he has blue veins on the nose, He'll never wear his wedding clothes (Somerset). Born with a blue mark over her nose, She never will live to wear wedding clothes (Worcs.).

4. *Once in a blue moon.* 1528: Roy and Barlowe, *Rede me, etc.*, 114 (Arber),

Yf they saye the mone is belewe, We must beleve that it is true. 1607: Dekker, *Knight's Conjuring*, 25 (Percy S.), She would have trickes (once in a moone) to put the diuell out of his wits. 1880: Braddon, *Barbara*, iii. 8, I suppose you would have sent ma a tenpound note once in a blue moon. 1920: A. G. Bradley, *Book of the Severn*, 18.

5. *There may be blue and better blue.* 1732: Fuller, No. 4940.

6. *Three blue beans in a blue bladder.* 1595: Peele, *Old Wives Tale*, sig. Diii, Three blue beanes in a blue bladder, rattle, bladder, rattle. 1600: Dekker, *Old Fortunatus*, I. ii. [as in 1595]. 1652: in *Catch that Catch can*, As there be three blew beans in a blew bladder, And thrice three rounds in a long ladder . . . 1687: Aubrey, *Gentilisme*, 12 (F.L.S.) [as in 1595]. 1715: Prior, *Alma*, can. i. l. 29, They say . . . That, putting all his words together, 'Tis three blue beans in one blue bladder. 1823: Moor, *Suffolk Words*, 23, [as in 1595]—thrice repeated, is as old a frolicsome sort of Suffolk shibboleth as I can recollect; and is still frequently heard.

Blunt wedge will do it, where sometimes a sharp ax will not, A. 1732: Fuller, No. 19.

Blurt, master constable. 1602: Middleton, *Blurt, Master Constable* [title]. 1659: Howell, 14, Blurt, Mr. Constable: spoken in derision. 1855: Kingsley, *West. Ho!*, ch. xxx., Blurt for him, sneak-up! say I.

Blush like a black dog, To. 1579: Gosson, *Apol. of Sch. of Abuse*, 75 (Arber), You shall see we will make him to blush like a blacke dogge, when he is graveled. *c.* 1590: *Plaine Percevall*, 13 (1860), He is given to blush no more then my black dog. *c.* 1591: Shakespeare, *Titus Andr.*, V. i. 1694: Motteux, *Rabelais*, bk. v. ch. xxviii. 1738: Swift, *Polite Convers.*, Dial. I. [with "blue" for "black"].

Blushing is a sign of grace. 1595: *A Quest of Enquirie*, 4 (Grosart), Margaret blushing (for she hath a little grace yet left her). 1605: R. T., *Sch. of Slovenrie*, 96, When guiltie men beginne to blush, it is a signe of grace. 1670:

Ray, 64, Blushing is vertues colour. 1738: Swift, *Polite Convers.*, Dial. I., Well, however, blushing is some sign of grace.

Blustering night, a fair day, A. 1640: Herbert, *Jac. Prudentum*.

Bo to a goose (or **mouse**), **To say.** 1588: *Mar-Prelate's Epistle*, 60 (1843), He is not able to say bo to a goose. 1610: Rowlands, *Martin Mark-all*, 15 (Hunt. Cl.), He neuer durst say so much as boh to a mouse. 1664: *Wits Recr.*, Epigr. 749, You see, I can cry Bo unto a goose. 1748: Smollett, *Rod. Random*, ch. liv. 1885: Pinero, *Magistrate*, I., He is too good-natured to say "Bo!" to a goose. 1920: Galsworthy, *Tatterdemalion*, 189, We are accustomed to exalt those who can say "bo" to a goose.

Boar. *See* quot. 1863: Wise, *New Forest*, ch. xvi., "To rattle like a boar in a holme bush," is a thorough proverb of the Forest district, where a "holme" bush means an old holly. *See also* **Feed** (3).

Boaster and a liar are all one (or **cousins**), **A.** *c.* 1374: Chaucer, *Troylus*, bk. iii. l. 309, Avantour [a boaster] and a lyere, al is on. 1683: Meriton, *Yorkshire Ale*, 83–7 (1697), A vaunter and a lyar is baith yay thing. 1732: Fuller, No. 21, A boaster and a lyar are cousingermans. 1869: Spurgeon, *John Ploughman*, ch. viii., You will soon find out that a boaster and a liar are first cousins.

Boat. *Ill goes the boat without oars.* 1578: Florio, *First Fruites*, fo. 28. 1629: *Book of Meery Riddles*, Prov. 64. 1659: Howell, *Proverbs: Fr.-Eng.*, 3. *See also* **Oar**; and **Same boat**.

Bocking. *See* **Braintree**.

Bode. *Boad a bagg, and bearn,* i.e. An ill hap falles where it is feared. Glos. 1639: in *Berkeley MSS.*, iii. 32 (1885).

Bodkin, To ride. 1638: Ford, *Fancies*, IV. i. (O.), Where but two lie in a bed, you must be—bodkin, bitch-baby— must ye? 1816: Scott, *Antiquary*, ch. xvii., Between the two massive figures . . . was stuck, by way of bodkin, the slim form of Mary M'Intyre. 1849: Mrs. Trollope, *Lottery of Marriage*, ch. xiii., Her position as bodkin between her father and mother.

Bodmin. 1. *I'll send you to Bodmin* = gaol. 1869: Hazlitt, 216.

2. *Into Bodmin and out of the world.* 1897: A. H. Norway, *H. and B. in Devon, etc.*, 253, The kind of feeling thrown by other Cornishmen into the saying, "Into Bodmin and out of the world." Indeed, Bodmin has a very sleepy aspect.

Body. 1. *The body is more dressed than the soul.* 1633: Draxe, 10, His body is better clothed then his soule. 1640: Herbert, *Jac. Prudentum.*

2. *The body is sooner dressed than the soul.* 1640: Herbert, *Jac. Prudentum.*

3. *The body is the socket of the soul.* 1670: Ray, 3.

Body-louse. *Brisk* (with variants) *as a body-louse.* c. 1570: *Marr. of Wit and Science*, II. i., As brag as a body-louse. 1651: Randolph, *Hey for Honesty*, III. iii., She is skimming her milk-bowls . . an busy as a body louse. 1670: Cotton, *Scarronides*, bk. iv., At last she sallies from the house, As fine and brisk as body-louse. 1720: Gay, *Poems*, ii. 279 (Underhill), Brisk as a body-louse she trips. 1812: Colman, jr., *Poet. Vagaries*, in *Hum. Works*, 141 (Hotten, 1869), Brisk as a flea.

Boil stones in butter, and you may sip the broth. 1732: Fuller, No. 1003.

Bolas. *Cold and chilly, like Bolas.* 1883: Burne, *Shropsh. Folk-Lore*, 592.

Bold. 1. *Be not too bold with your betters.* 1659: Howell, 3. 1855: Bohn, 324, Be bold but not too bold.

2. *Bold as a lion.* Before 1225: *Ancren R.*, 274, Vor þi beoþ euer agean him herdi ase leun ine treowe bileaue. 14th cent.: *Guy of Warwick*, l. 9587 (E.E.T.S.), As stowte as a lyon. c. 1430: Lydgate, *Minor Poems*, 198 (Percy S.), Force of juventus, hardy as lioun. 1597: Shakespeare, *1 Henry IV.*, III. i., Valiant as a lion. 1694: *Terence made English*, 84, I cowhearted? I'm as bold as a lion. 1710: Ward, *Eng. Reform.*, 136 (1716). 1819: Scott, *Bride of L.*, ch. xi. 1893: R. L. S., *Catriona*, ch. xxx.

3. *Bold as blind Bayard.* See **Bayard** (1).

4. *Bold as brass.* 1789: G. Parker, *Life's Painter*, 162, He died . . . as bold as brass. 1849: Lytton, *Caxtons*, Pt. I. ch. iv., Master Sisty . . . as bold as brass. 1922: Weyman, *Ovington's Bank*, ch. xvii.

5. *Bold as Hector.* 1684: *Great Frost*, 20 (Percy S.), Some bold as Hector.

Boldness in business is the first, second and third thing. 1732: Fuller, No. 1006.

Boldness is blind. Ibid., No. 1005.

Bolney. *Merry Bolney, rich Twineham, Proud Cowfold, and silly Shermanbury.* 1884: "Sussex Proverbs," in *N. & Q.*, 6th ser., ix. 403.

Bolsover. See quot. c. 1791: Pegge, *Derbicisms*, 136 (E.D.S.), Bowser [Bolsover] for bacco-pipes; Tre[e]lton for trenchers; Laughton for a pretty lass, Whiston for wenches.

Bolt. 1. *A bolt from the blue.* [Homer, *Od.*, v. 102. Horace, *Carm.*, I. xxxiv. Virgil, *Georg.*, i. 487–8.] 1898: II. James, in *Letters*, i. 285 (1920), Such an inspiration was your charming note—out of the blue!—of a couple of days ago. 1901: W. James, in *Letters*, ii. 142 (1920), In general I don't see how an epigram, being a pure bolt from the blue, with no introduction or cue, ever gets itself writ.

2. *A bolt lost is not a bow broken.* 1821: Scott, *Kenilworth*, ch. xvi.

3. *This bolt never came out of your quiver.* 1683: Meriton, *Yorkshire Ale*, 83–7 (1697), This bolt com never out of your bag. 1732: Fuller, No. 4334.

4. *To make a bolt or a shaft* = To take the risk. 1600: Shakespeare, *Merry Wives*, III. iv. 1608: Middleton, *Trick to Catch, etc.*, II. i. 1694: *Terence made English*, 12, Since my life's at stake, I'm resolved to make a bolt or a shaft on't. 1732: Fuller, No. 5201.

See also **Fool** (24).

Bone. 1. *A bone to pick* (or *bite*) *on.* 1565: Calfhill, *Answ. to Martiall*, 277 (P.S.), Only therefore will I add this, which may be a bone for you to pick on. 1583: Melbancke, *Philotinus*, sig. C1, I cast the[e] a bone to bite on. 1612:

Chapman, *Widow's Tears*, II. i., [He] has given me a bone to tire on, with a pestilence. 1681: L'Estrange, *Observator*, i., No. 64, But here's a bone for ye to pick. 1795: Cobbett, *A Bone to Gnaw for the Democrats* [title]. 1830: Scott, in Lockhart's *Life*, vii. 215, A dish unknown elsewhere, so there is a bone for the gastronomers to pick.

2. *Bones bring meat to town.* 1639: in *Berkeley MSS.*, iii. 31 (1885), . . . meaninge, Difficult and hard things are not altogether to bee reiected, or things of small consequence. 1642: Fuller, *Profane State:* " Andronicus," We have an English proverb that *bones bring meat to town.*

3. *To have a bone in one's arm, leg, etc.* A humorous excuse. 1542: Udall, tr. Erasmus' *Apoph.*, 375 (1877), Demosthenes [having been bribed not to speak] . . . refused to speake, allegeing that he had a bone in his throte and could not speake. 1666: Torriano, *Piazza Univ.*, 276, The English say; He hath a bone in his arm and cannot work. 1738: Swift, *Polite Convers.*, Dial. III., I can't go, for I have a bone in my leg. 1877: E. Leigh, *Cheshire Gloss.*, 25, When a person has a shooting pain in the arm or leg, it is common to say, " I've a bone i' th' arm or leg." 1920: E. F. Benson, *Our Family Affairs*, 15, Panting and bright-eyed she would stop and say, " Eh, dear, I can't run any more: I've got a bone in my leg."

See also **Make** (19).

Bonington. *See* **Betshanger.**

Book that is shut is but a block, A. 1732: Fuller, No. 23.

Boot after bale=Help or relief after woe or distress. Before 1300: *Cursor M.*, l. 21621 (E.E.T.S.), þate wiþ beting was bote of bale For sek’nes sere to mac þaim hale. *c.* 1320: in *Reliq. Antiquæ*, i. 113 (1841), When the bale is hest [highest], Thenne is the bote nest, quoth Hendyng. *c.* 1380: *Gamelyn*, l. 631, in Skeat's *Chaucer*, iv. 660, After bale cometh boote thurgh grace of God almight. *c.* 1400: *Beryn*, l. 3956 (E.E.T.S.), So " aftir bale comyth bote." *c.* 1450: *Boke of Nurture*, in

Babees Book, 119 (E.E.T.S.), " When bale is hext [highest] than bote is next [nighest] " good sone, lerne welle this. 1567: Golding, *Ovid*, bk. xiv. l. 557, When that bale is hyghest growne, then boote must next ensew. 1607: *Chester Plays*, 431 (E.E.T.S.), After bale boot thar bringes. 1875: A. B. Cheales, *Proverb. Folk-Lore*, 125, But how often When bale is hext, Boot is next.

Booted. *They that are booted are not always ready.* 1640: Herbert, *Jac. Prudentium.*

Borage. *A leaf of borage might buy all the substance that they can sell.* 1546: Heywood, *Proverbs*, Pt. I. ch. x.

Born. 1. *Born in a mill*=Deaf. 1578: Whetstone, *Promos and Cassandra*, sig. B3, Were you borne in a myll, curtole? you prate so hye. 1678: Ray, 76.

2. *Born on Monday. See* **Monday** (5).

3. *He's born in a good hour who gets a good name.* 1732: Fuller, No. 2455.

4. *He that is born to be hanged will never be drowned.* 1605: Camden, *Remains*, 324 (1870). 1670: Cotton, *Scarronides*, bk. iv., Since as the proverb old 'tis found, *Who's born to hang, will ne'er be drown'd.* 1732: Fielding, *Cov. Garden Tragedy*, I. iii., If born to swing, I never shall be drown'd. 1850: Smedley, *Frank Fairlegh*, ch. xi.

5. *He that's born under a threepenny planet. See* **Threepenny.**

6. *I was not born in a wood to be scared by an owl.* 1738: Swift, *Polite Convers.*, Dial. III., Do you think I was born in a wood, to be afraid of an owl? 1830: Forby, *Vocab. E. Anglia*, 429. 1872: J. Glyde, jr., *Norfolk Garland*, 148.

7. *She that is born a beauty is half married.* 1633: Draxe, 15, Shee that is faire hath halfe her portion. 1732: Fuller, No. 4141.

8. *To be born in a frost*=To be blockheaded, dull of apprehension. 1828: Carr, *Craven Dialect*, i. 166.

9. *We are born crying, live complaining, and die disappointed.* 1732: Fuller, No. 5427.

Borough Hill. *See* quot. 1854: Baker, *Northants Gloss.*, s.v. " Jackson's pig,"

" It's gone over Borough Hill (. . . near
Daventry) after Jackson's pig." A
common phrase in that neighbourhood
when anything is lost.

Borough-men, Bread for. 1639:
Clarke, 113, Burrough men merry,
more bread than drink. 1678: Ray,
317. 1790: Grose, *Prov. Gloss.*, s.v.
" Leicestershire."

Borrow. 1. *Borrow or flatter.* See
Contented (2) ; and **Rich**, *adj.* (8).

2. *He that borrows must pay again
with shame or loss.* 1639: Clarke, 246,
He that will borrow must pay. 1678:
Ray, 104.

3. *He that goes a-borrowing goes a-
sorrowing.* 1539: Taverner, *Proverbs*,
46 (O.). 1580: Tusser, *Husbandrie*, 31
(E.D.S.), Who goeth a borrowing, goeth
a sorrowing. 1669: *Politeuphuia*, 184.
1714: Ozell, *Molière*, iv. 19. 1736:
Franklin, *Way to Wealth*, in *Works*,
i. 448 (Bigelow). 1836: Marryat, *Easy*,
ch. viii.

4. *To borrow on usury brings sudden
beggary.* 1639: Clarke, 327. 1670: Ray,
153. 1732: Fuller, No. 6089, To borrow upon usury, bringeth on beggary.

5. *Who would borrow when he hath
not, let him borrow when he hath.* 1855:
Bohn, 567.

See also **Swear** (2).

Borrowed. 1. *A borrowed loan.* See
Loan.

2. *Borrowed garments never sit well.*
1732: Fuller, No. 1008.

3. *Borrowed things will home.* 1400:
in *Twenty-six Poems*, 2 (E.E.T.S.), And
borwed thyng mot home ful nede.
c. 1460: *Prov. of Good Counsel*, in
E.E.T.S., Extra Ser., No. 8, p. 68, For
borowurd thynge wyll home agayne.
c. 1550: *Parl. of Byrdes*, l. 224, in
Hazlitt, *Early Pop. Poetry*, iii. 179,
Borowed ware wyll home agayne.

4. *He that trusts to borrowed ploughs,
will have his land lie fallow.* 1732:
Fuller, No. 2337.

Boscastle Fair (or **Market**). *See* quots.
1864: " Cornish Proverbs," in *N. & Q.*,
3rd ser., v. 276, Backwards and forwards like Boscastle Fair. All play and
no play, like Boscastle Fair, which
begins at twelve o'clock and ends at

noon. 1880: Courtney, *W. Cornwall
Words*, xiii. (E.D.S.), All play, etc.
[as in 1864, but with " Market " for
" Fair "] 1888: Q.-Couch, *Troy Town*,
chaps. xiii. and xix. [as in 1864].

Bosom-friend. *No friend like to a
bosom friend, as the man said when he
pulled out a louse.* 1732: Fuller,
No. 3571. 1738: Swift, *Polite Convers.*,
Dial. I., I'm afraid your bosom friends
are become your backbiters.

Boston's Bay. *See* quot. 1869:
Hazlitt, 88, Between Boston's Bay and
the Pile of Fouldray, shall be seen the
black navy of Norway.

Botch and sit, build and flit. 1618:
W. Lawson, *New Orchard and Garden*,
9 (1676), Tenants who have taken up
this proverb, *Botch and sit, Build and
flit.* 1639: in *Berkeley MSS.*, iii. 33
(1885).

Both together do best of all. 1639:
Clarke, 10.

Bottom of the bag, To bring out the.
1399: in Wright, *Pol. Poems*, i. 363
(Rolls Ser., 1859), The grete bagge,
that is so mykille, Hit schal be kettord
[diminished], and maked litelle ; the
bothom is ny ougt. 1546: Heywood,
Proverbs, Pt. II. ch. x., He brought the
bottome of the bag cleane out.

**Boughs that bear most, hang lowest,
The.** 1732: Fuller, No. 4430.

Bought. 1. *Bought wit.* See **Wit**
(2) and (12).

2. *To be bought and sold.* 1639:
Clarke, 86, You are bought and sold
like sheepe in a market. 1670: Ray,
166, To be bought and sold in a company. 1738: Swift, *Polite Convers.*,
Dial. III. 1792: *Looker-on*, No. 11,
He was bought and sold by people
in power.

**Bounce buckram, velvet's dear, Christ-
mas comes but once a year** ; **And when it
comes it brings good cheer, But when
it's gone it's never the near.** 1639:
Clarke, 71 [first line only]. 1670: Ray,
211. 1843: Halliwell, *Nursery Rhymes*,
121 [first two lines only]. 1846: Denham, *Proverbs*, 64 (Percy S.) [four lines,
but in first " buckler " for " buckram,"
and for last line, " So farewell Christmas
once a year "].

Bound is he that takes gifts. *c.* 1460: *How the Good Wife*, l. 70, Bounden he is that gifte takithe.

Bound must obey, The. 1205: Layamon, *Brut*, 1051, Ah heo mot nede beien, þe mon þe ibunden bith (But he needs must bow, the man that is bounden). *c.* 1390: Gower, *Conf. Amantis*, ii. 540, For who is bounden, he mot bowe. *c.* 1410: *Towneley Plays*, 118 (E.E.T.S.), Wo is hym that is bun, ffor he must abyde. *c.* 1520: in Hazlitt, *Early Pop. Poetry*, iv. 92 (1866), The bounde must euer obaye. 1615: T. Heywood, *Foure Prentises*, I., Bound must obey. 1653: R. Brome, *Mad Couple*, II. 1732: Fuller, No. 4972, They that are bound must obey.

Bounty being free itself, thinks all others so. 1855: Bohn, 332.

Bourd. *It is a good bourd to drink of a gourd. c.* 1400: *Towneley Plays*, xii. p. 115 (E.E.T.S.), It an is old by-worde, It is a good bowrde, for to drynk of a gowrde,—It holdys a mett potell. [Bourd=jest.]

Bourne. *See* Chichester (1).

Bout as Barrow was. Cheshire. 1670: Ray, 217. 1691: Ray, *Words not generally Used*, 34 (E.D.S.). 1917: Bridge, *Cheshire Proverbs*, 125, . . . The meaning is lost. [Bout=without.]

Bout's [Without's] bare but it's easy. 1873: Harland and Wilkinson, *Lancs Leg.*, 202. 1917: Bridge, *Cheshire Proverbs*, 32, . . . Common in Lancashire.

Bow, *subs.* 1. *A bow long bent grows weak.* 1541: Coverdale, *Christ. State Matrimony*, sig. I1, The bowe will breake yf it be to sore bent. *c.* 1577, Northbrooke, *Against Dicing, etc.*, 44 (Sh. S.), Euen as too much bending breketh a bow. 1669: Dudley North, *Obs. and Adv. Œconom.*, 123, A bow that stands alwayes bent looseth its strength in the end. 1732: Fuller, No. 1013, Bows too long bent, grow weake. 1741: *Tom King's: or The Paphian Grove*, 10, The bow, if always bent, will lose It's spring elastic.

2. *Draw not thy bow before thy arrow be fixed.* 1732: Fuller, No. 1326.

See also Robin Hood (2) and (5).

Bow than break, Better. *See* Better bow.

Bow-bell. *To be born within sound of Bow-bell.* 1662: Fuller, *Worthies*, ii. 344 (1840). 1753: in *Stukeley Memoirs*, i. 404 (Surtees S.), Interest is such a prevailing principle within the sound of Bow bell. 1793: Grose, *Olio*, 24 (2nd ed.), Born within the sound of Bow-bell, he rarely ventured out of it. 1918: Muirhead, *Blue Guide to London*, 351, Any one born within the sound of Bow Bells is a "cockney," i.e. a Londoner pure and simple.

Bow-hand. *See* Wide at the bow-hand.

Bow-wow. *See* July (3).

Bowdon. *Every man cannot be vicar of Bowden.* 1678: Ray, 300. 1790: Grose, *Prov. Gloss.*, s.v. "Cheshire." 1917: Bridge, *Cheshire Proverbs*, 54, Every man was not born to be Vicar of Bowdon.

Bowdon Wakes. *See* quot. 1886: R. Holland, *Cheshire Gloss.*, 456 (E.D.S.), When Bowdon Wakes is at Bowdon, winter's at Newbridge Hollow. 1917: Bridge, *Cheshire Proverbs*, 151.

Bowling green. *See* Three things are thrown away.

Bowls. *They that play at bowls must expect* (or *meet with*) *rubbers.* 1762: Smollett, *Sir L. Greaves*, ch. x. [title], Which sheweth that he who plays at bowls will sometimes meet with rubbers. 1824: Scott, *Redgauntlet*, ch. xx. 1854: Baker, *Northants Gloss.*, s.v. "Rubbers." 1907: Hackwood, *Old Eng. Sports*, 180, For "he who plays at bowls must look out for rubs." *See also* Easy to bowl.

Boy and Boys. 1. *Boys to bed, dogs to doors, and maidens to clean up the ashes.* Cornwall. 1895: J. Thomas, *Randigal Rhymes*, 60.

2. *Boys will be boys.* 1681: W. Robertson, *Phraseol. Generalis*, 330, Children will do like children. 1849: Lytton, *Caxtons*, Pt. XV. ch. i., "Well," said I to myself, "I will save for him; boys will be boys." 1911: G. B. Shaw, *Fanny's First Play*, I.

3. *Boys will be men.* 1611: Cotgrave, s.v. "Enfant," Or, (as we say)

boyes will be men one day. 1732:
Fuller, No. 1014.

4. *The boy has gone by with the cows* =
has missed opportunities. Oxfordsh.
1913: *Folk-Lore*, xxiv. 77.

5. *To leave boys' play and go to blow
point.* 1639: Clarke, 197. 1681: W.
Robertson, *Phraseol. Generalis*, 997, To
leave boys-play, and fall to blow point;
Relinquere nuces. 1738: Swift, *Polite
Convers.*, Dial. I., Come, let us leave
off children's play, and come to push-
pin.

Brabling curs. *See* **Brawling curs.**

**Brackley breed, better to hang than
feed.** 1636: in *Somers Tracts*, vii. 212
(1811), Heer's the full summe of the
reckoning and a pottle over; though we
be Leicestershire fed, yet we be not
Brackley bred, I assure you. 1670:
Ray, 246. 1790: Grose, *Prov. Gloss.*,
s.v. "Northamptonshire." 1851: Sternberg, *Dialect, etc., of Northants*, 191.

**Bradshaw's windmill, What have I to
do with?** i.e. What have I to do with
another man's business? 1678: Ray,
317. 1790: Grose, *Prov. Gloss.*, s.v.
"Leicestershire." 1869: Spurgeon,
John Ploughman, ch. ii.

Brag, *subs.* 1. *Brag's a good dog but
dares not bite.* 1685: Meriton, *Yorkshire Ale*, 58, Braggs a good dog . . .
But he was hang'd for biting that was
ill. 1732: Fuller, No. 1015.

2. *Brag is a good dog but Holdfast is a
better.* c. 1598: Deloney, *Gentle Craft*,
Pt. II. ch. v., Brag is a good dog (quoth
Stutely), but tell vs, hast thou made thy
Will? 1599: Shakespeare, *Henry V.*,
II. iii., Men's faiths are wafer-cakes
And holdfast is the only dog, my duck.
1709: Dykes, *Eng. Proverbs*, 123. 1748:
Gent. Mag., 21. 1861: Dickens, *Great
Expect.*, ch. xviii. 1924: *Devonsh. Assoc.
Trans.*, lv. 112.

3. *Brag's a good dog but that he hath
lost his tail.* 1678: Ray, 105.

4. *Brag's a good dog if he be well set on.*
1670: Ray, 65. 1736: Bailey, *Dict.*,
s.v. "Brag."

Brag, *verb.* 1. *They brag most that can
do least.* c. 1598: Deloney, *Gentle Craft*,
Pt. II. ch. vi., It is an old saying, they
brag most that can doe least.

2. *To brag of many goodmorrows.*
1670: Ray, 178.

Brain and Brains. 1. *He carries his
brains in his breeches-pocket.* 1883:
Burne, *Shropsh. Folk-Lore*, 589.

2. *He hath no more brains than a
burbolt* (bird-bolt). c. 1550: Udall,
Roister Doister, III. ii., He hath in
his head . . . As much braine as a
burbolt. 1672: Walker, *Parœm.*, 11.

3. *His brain is not big enough for his
skull.* 1732: Fuller, No. 2504.

4. *His brains are addle.* 1670: Ray,
165.

5. *His brains crow.* 1678: Ray, 230.

6. *His brains will work without barm.*
Yorks. 1670: Ray, 166. 1732: Fuller,
No. 2505, His brains want no barm to
make them work.

7. *If the brain sows not corn, it plants
thistles.* 1640: Herbert, *Jac. Prudentum.* 1659: Howell, 6. 1732: Fuller,
No. 4437.

8. *The brains don't lie in the beard.*
1732: Fuller, No. 4431.

**Braintree boys, brave boys; Bocking
boys, rats; Church Street, puppy dogs;
High Garret, cats.** 1813: Ray, 246.

**Braintree for the pure, and Bocking
for the poor, Cogshall for the jeering
town, and Kelvedon for the whore.**
1670: Ray, 228.

Brandy is Latin for a goose. 1588:
Mar-Prelate's Epitome, 25 (1843), Can
you tell your brother Marprelat with
all your learning, howe to decline whut
is Latine for a goose? 1738: Swift,
Polite Convers., Dial. II. 1847: Halliwell, *Dict.*, s.v. "Pig," *Brandy is Latin
for pig and goose*, an apology for drinking a dram after either.

Brass farthing = No value. 1660:
Andromana, I. i., in Hazlitt, *Old Plays*,
xiv. 197, Some wench, my life to a
brass farthing! 1740: North, *Lives of
Norths*, i. 229 (Bohn), He would not
give one brass farthing to buy all the
Presbyterians in England. 1801: Colman, jr., *Poor Gent.*, II. i., It doesn't
signify a brass farthing what they are
called. 1911: Shaw, *Fanny's First Play*,
Induction, Vaughan is honest, and don't
care a brass farthing what he says.

Brass knocker on a barn-door. *See*

quot. 1886: Elworthy, *West Som. Word-Book*, 44 (E.D.S.), A very common saying expressive of inconsistency is . . . may as well put a brass knocker on a barn-door.

Brave, *adj.* 1. *A brave retreat is a brave exploit.* 1732: Fuller, No. 24.

2. *Brave actions never want a trumpet.* Ibid., No. 1016.

3. *Brave man at arms, but weak to Balthasar.* 1659: Howell, 5.

4. *Some have been thought brave, because they were afraid to run away.* 1732: Fuller, No. 4214.

Brawling curs never want sore ears. 1611: Cotgrave, s.v. " Hargneux," A brabling curre is never without torne eares. 1694: D'Urfey, *Quixote*, Pt. I. Act IV. sc. i., Come, come, sir, babling curs never want sore ears. 1709: R. Kingston, *Apoph. Curiosa*, 9, Barking currs commonly go with bitten ears. 1732: Fuller, No. 6231. 1865: " Lancs Proverbs," in *N. & Q.*, 3rd ser., viii. 494.

Bray. *The Vicar of Bray will be Vicar of Bray still.* 1662: Fuller, *Worthies*, i. 113 (1840). 1707: Dunton, *Athenian Sport*, 400, The Vicar of Bray; or, a paradox in praise of the Turncoat Clergy. 1869: Spurgeon, *John Ploughman*, ch. xviii., They admire the Vicar of Bray, whose principle was to be Vicar of Bray, whether the Church was Protestant or Popish.

Brayton-bargh. *If Brayton-bargh and Hambleton hough, and Burton bream, Were all in thy belly 't would never be team* (full). 1670: Ray, 257. 1683: Meriton, *Yorkshire Ale*, 83–7 (1697). 1790: Grose, *Prov. Gloss.*, s.v. " Yorkshire." 1878: *Folk-Lore Record*, i. 172.

Brazen-nose College, You were bred in. 1732: Fuller, No. 6011.

Bread. 1. *Be fair conditioned and eat bread with your pudding.* 1678: Ray, 79.

2. *Bread and cheese be two targets against death.* 1655: T. Muffett, *Healths Improvement*, 236. 1666: Torriano, *Piazza Univ.*, 92, Cheese and bread is physick to such as are in health.

3. *Bread is the staff of life, but beer's life itself.* Oxfordsh. 1913. *Folk-Lore*, xxiv. 76.

4. *Bread of a day.* See **Egg** (3).

5. *Bread with eyes and cheese without eyes, and wine that leaps to the eyes.* 1666: Torriano, *Piazza Univ.*, 41. 1670: Ray, 3 [without the " wine " part]. 1732: Fuller, No. 1017.

6. *He has got a piece of bread and cheese in his head*=He is drunk. 1678: Ray, 87.

7. *He that hath store of bread may beg his milk merrily.* 1659: Howell, *Proverbs: Brit.-Eng.*, 5.

8. *His* (or *your*) *bread is buttered on both sides.* 1678: Ray, 232. 1732: Fuller, No. 6044. 1837: Lockhart, *Scott*, i. 206 *n.* (1839) (O.), Wherever Walter goes he is pretty sure to find his bread buttered on both sides.

9. *It is a good thing to eat your brown bread first.* 1830: Forby, *Vocab. E. Anglia*, 429. 1872: J. Glyde, jr., *Norfolk Garland*, 148.

10. *It's no use my leaving off eating bread, because you were choked with a crust.* 1883: Burne, *Shropsh. Folk-Lore*, 589.

11. *They that have no other meat, bread and butter are glad to eat.* 1639: Clarke, 113. 1670: Ray, 66. 1732: Fuller, No. 6128.

12. *To know on which side one's bread is buttered.* 1546: Heywood, *Proverbs*, Pt. II. ch. vii. 1564: Bullein, *Dialogue*, 112 (E.E.T.S.), He knoweth vpon whiche side his breade is buttered well enough, I warrante you. 1638: Ford, *Lady's Trial*, II. i. 1721: C. Cibber, *Refusal*, I., Does his Grace think I don't know which side my bread's butter'd on? 1822: Scott, *Nigel*, ch. xxiii. 1914: H. A. Vachell, *Quinney's*, bk. ii. ch. xvi. (ii.), James is a bit of a knave, but he knows which side his bread is buttered.

13. *What bread men break is broke to them again.* 1630: Taylor (Water-Poet), *Works*, 2nd pagin., 186, In this the prouerb is approued plaine, What bread men breake is broke to them againe.

14. *Who hath no more bread than need, must not keep a dog.* 1640: Herbert, *Jac. Prudentium.*

15. *You show bread in one hand, and*

a stone in the other. 1732: Fuller,
No. 5994.

See also **Better bread; Better lose;
Borough men; Buying of bread; Eaten;
Half a loaf; Loaf;** and **Wine** (10).

Breage and Germoe. *God keep us
from rocks and shelving sands, And save
us from Breage and Germoe men's hands.*
Cornwall. 1887: M. A. Courtney, in
Folk-Lore Journal, v. 18. 1897: Norway, *H. and B. in Devon, etc.*, 282,
Verse said to have been current in old
days about the two seaboard parishes
just mentioned . . . God keep us, etc.

Break, *verb.* 1. *A man shall as soon
break his neck as his fast there.* 1546:
Heywood, *Proverbs*, Pt. I. ch. xi. 1670:
Ray, 165. 1732: Fuller, No. 3770.

2. *A man that breaks his word, bids
others be false to him.* 1548: Hall,
Chron., 184 (1809), But (as the common proverbe saieth) he whiche is a
promise breaker, escapeth not alway
free. 1732: Fuller, No. 311.

3. *Break coals; cut candle; set brand
an end, Neither good housewifery nor good
housewife's friend.* 1666: Torriano,
Piazza Univ., 242. 1732: Fuller,
No. 6424.

4. *Break the legs of an evil custom.*
1659: Howell, *Proverbs: Span.-Eng.*, 8,
Cut off the leg of an ill custome. 1855:
Bohn, 333.

5. *To break a flint upon a feather-bed.*
1659: Gayton, *Art of Longevity*, 20, Just
as a feather-bed the flint doth break.
1666: Torriano, *Piazza Univ.*, 123, As
the English say, To break, etc.

6. *To break a man's back.* 1613:
Shakespeare, *Henry VIII.*, I. i., Many
Have broke their backs with laying
manors on 'em For this great journey.
1632: Rowley, *A New Wonder*, IV., Oh,
my poor father! this loss will break his
back. 1894: Northall, *Folk Phrases*,
26 (E.D.S.), To break a man's back=To
ruin him.

7. *To break my head and then give me
a plaster.* c. 1430: Lydgate, *Minor
Poems*, 56 (Percy S.), To breke myn
hede, and yeve me an houffe. 1573:
G. Harvey, *Letter-Book*, 52 (Camden S.),
To break a mans hed . . . and at his
laisure, give him a plaster. 1631:

Mabbe, *Celestina*, 283 (T.T.), Thou
breakest our head, and givest us a
plaister. 1738: Swift, *Polite Convers.*,
Dial. I. 1818: J. Austen, *Persuasion*,
ch. xiii., A new sort of way this, for a
young fellow to be making love, by
breaking his mistress's head! is not it,
Miss Elliot? This is breaking a head
and giving a plaster truly!

8. *To break no squares*=To do no
harm, to make no difference. 1562:
Heywood, *Three Hund. Epigr.*, No. 4,
An inch breaketh no square. 1593:
Nashe, *Strange Newes*, in *Works*, ii. 281
(Grosart), For calling me calfe, it
breakes no square. 1675: Crowne,
Country Wit, I. i., Two or three days
can break no square. 1707: Cibber,
Comical Lovers, III., One minute will
break no squares, I'll warrant you.
1798: T. Morton, *Speed the Plough*, I. ii.,
I do hope, zur, breaking your head will
break noa squares. 1823: Byron, *Don
Juan*, can. xiii. st. 25, At Blank-Blank
Square;—for we will break no squares
By naming streets. 1850: Dickens,
Copperfield, ch. xxxix., There are no
squares broke between us. I've been
into his room already, and we've made
it all smooth. 1923: [at a Surrey C.C.
Committee meeting, I heard a member
(a builder), referring to a small difference between two estimates of cost, say,
" This will break no squares."]

9. *To break the ice.* 1592: Nashe,
P. Penilesse, in *Works*, ii. 5 (Grosart),
He that hath once broke the ice of his
impudence, neede not care how deepe
he wade in discredite. 1631: Shirley,
Love Tricks, III. i., When I had but
broke the ice of my affection, she fell
over head and ears in love with me.
1708: tr. Aleman's *Guzman*, i. 173, To
break the ice in making the first over-
ture. 1848: Dickens, *Dombey*, ch. lxi.,
" If he would have the goodness to
break the—in point of fact, the ice,"
said Cousin Feenix.

See also **Broke;** and **Broken.**

Breath. *Keep (save,* etc.*) one's breath
to cool one's porridge.* c. 1598: Deloney,
Gentle Craft, Pt. II. ch. iii., I was about
to tell you of a matter, but I see it is
to small purpose, and therefore Ile keep

my breath to coole my pottage. 1633:
Machin, *Dumb Knight*, II., My lord,
save your breath for your broth. 1725:
Bailey, tr. Erasmus' *Colloq.*, 441, He
had as good keep his breath to cool his
porridge. 1813: J. Austen, *Pride and
Prejudice*, ch. vi. 1886: R. L. S.,
Kidnapped, ch. vii., Instead of asking
riddles . . . ye would keep your breath
to cool your porridge. 1924: Shaw,
Saint Joan, sc. ii.

**Bred in the bone will not out of the
flesh, What is.** [*c.* 1290: in Wright's
Pol. Songs John to Edw. II., 167
(Camden S.), Osse radicatum raro de
carne recedit.] 1481: Caxton, *Reynard*,
29 (Arber), That whiche cleuid by the
bone myght not out of the flesshe.
1485: Malory, *Morte d'Arthur*, bk. ix.
ch. 39, Sir launcelot smyled and said
hard hit is to take oute of the flesshe
that is bred in the bone. 1546: Heywood, *Proverbs*, Pt. II. ch. viii. 1596:
Jonson, *Ev. Man in his Humour*, II. i.
1632: Massinger, *City Madam*, II. iii.,
What's bred in the bone, Admits no
hope of cure. 1694: *Terence made
English*, 5. 1713: Gay, *Wife of Bath*,
III. ii. 1842: Barham, *Ing. Legends*,
2nd ser.: " Lay of St. Aloysius."

Bredon Hill. *When Bredon Hill puts
on its hat, Ye men of the vale, beware of
that.* Worcs. 1882: Mrs. Chamberlain, *W. Worcs. Words*, 39 (E.D.S.).
1893: Inwards, *Weather Lore*, 101.

Breech makes buttons, His (or **My**) =
To be in great fear. *c.* 1550: *Jacke
Jugeler*, 46 (Grosart, 1873), His arse
maketh buttens now. *c.* 1618: B. & F.,
Bonduca, II. iii. 1653: Middleton and
Rowley, *Span. Gipsy*, IV. iii., O Soto,
I make buttons! 1736: Bailey, *Dict.*,
s.v. " Breech." 1808: Ainsworth, *Lat.
Dict.*, i., s.v. " Button," His tail maketh
buttons, *valde trepidat* (O.).

Breeches, To wear the. 15th cent.:
Songs and Carols of 15th Cent., 65
(Percy S.), Nova, Nova, sawe you euer
such, The most mayster of the hows
weryth no brych. 1592: Greene, *Quip*,
in *Works*, xi. 219 (Grosart), I saw a
great many of women vsing high wordes
to their husbandes: some striuing for
the breeches . . . 1596: Harington,

Metam. of Ajax, 63 (1814), I am sure
his wife wore the breeches. 1653: R.
Brome, *City Wit, or the Woman wears
the Breeches* [title]. 1712: Addison,
Spectator, No. 482, Since you have given
us the character of a wife who wears
the breeches, pray say something of
a husband that wears the petticoat.
1927: *Observer*, 27 March, p. 15, col. 3,
Mrs. Scally wore the breeches, and her
word went in the Scally household.

Breed in the mud are not eels, All that.
1732: Fuller, No. 549.

Breed is stronger than pasture. 1917:
Bridge, *Cheshire Proverbs*, 31.

Breeks off a Highlander, To take the.
[Vis nudo vestimenta detrahere?—
Plautus, *Asin.*, I. i. 79.] 1546: Heywood, *Proverbs*, Pt. I. ch. ix., There is
nothing more vain . . . Than to beg a
breeche of a bare arst man. 1580:
Baret, *Alvearie*, B, 150, To pull a
breeche from a bare arst man. 1630:
Taylor (Water-Poet), in *Works*, 2nd
pagin., 37, To seek a breech from
breechlesse men 'twere vain. 1817:
Scott, *Rob Roy*, ch. xxvii., It's ill
taking the breeks off a Hielandman.

Breeze in one's breech, To have a.
Breeze=gadfly. *c.* 1630: B. & F.,
Monsieur Thomas, IV. vi., What, is the
breeze in your breech? 1678: Ray,
232.

Brent Hill. *See* quot. 1893: in
N. & Q., 8th ser., iii. 209, " Looking
from under Brent Hill " . . . used to
be very popular [saying] in Devonshire
fifty or sixty years ago. It is said of a
sullen, frowning person in an ill humour,
Brent Hill indicating the eyebrows.

Brentford. *See* quot. 1790: Grose,
Prov. Gloss., s.v. " Middlesex," His face
was like the red lion of Brentford.
That is, exceeding red.

Brevity is the soul of wit. 1602:
Shakespeare, *Hamlet*, II. ii. 1802:
Lamb, *John Woodvil*, III., Brevity is
the soul of drinking, as of wit. 1851:
Borrow, *Lavengro*, i. 311.

Brew, *verb.* 1. *As one brews so bake.*
c. 1560: T. Ingelend, *Disob. Child*, in
Hazlitt, *Old Plays*, ii. 294 (1874), But
as he had brewed, that so he should
bake. *c.* 1626: in *Pepysian Garland*,

241 (Rollins, 1922), For some that are
fond, as they brew let them bake. 1670:
Cotton, *Scarronides*, bk. iv. 1766:
Garrick and Colman, *Clandest. Marriage*, I. i. 1847: Planché, *Extravag.*,
iii. 187 (1879). 1922: Weyman, *Ovington's Bank*, ch. xxiii., No, you may go, my
lad. As you ha' brewed you may bake!
    2. *As one brews so drink.* *c.* 1264: in
Ritson, *Songs and Ballads*, 11 (Hazlitt),
Let him habbe ase he brew, bale to
dryng. Before 1300: *Cursor M.*,
l. 2848, Suche as þai brew such haue
þai dronkyn. *c.* 1390: Gower, *Conf.
Amantis*, bk. iii. l. 1626, And who so
wicked alë breweth Ful ofte he mot
[must] the wersë drinke. *c.* 1425:
Castle of Persev., sc. viii. st. 271, in
Macro Plays, 171 (E.E.T.S.), As he hath
browyn, lete hym drynke. 1596: Jonson, *Ev. Man in his Humour*, II. i.,
Well, as he brews, so shall he drink.
1605: Chapman, etc., *Eastw. Hoe*, IV. i.
1762: Smollett, *Sir L. Greaves*, ch. x.
1849: Brontë, *Shirley*, ch. xxi. 1883:
R. L. S., *Treasure I.*, ch. xxx.
    3. *To brew in a bottle and bake in
a bag.* 1542: Boorde, *Dyetary*, 240
(E.E.T.S.), For these men the which
do brew in a botyl and bake in a
walet, it wyll be long or he can by Iacke
a salet. 1678: Ray, 91.
    Brewer's horse. *One whom the
brewer's horse hath bit* = A drunkard.
1597: Shakespeare, 1 *Henry IV.*, III.
iii., [Falstaff *log.*] I am a peppercorn, a
brewer's horse. 1635: 1. Heywood,
Philocothonista, 45, One whom brewer's
horse hath bit. 1847: Halliwell, *Dict.*,
s.v. "Brewer's horse." 1907: Hackwood, *Inns, Ales, etc.*, 167. 1917:
Bridge, *Cheshire Proverbs*, 100.
    Briars. 1. *It is good to cut the briars
in the sere month* [August]. *c.* 1686:
Aubrey, *Gentilisme*, 123 (F.L.S.).
    2. *In the briars.* See **Leave**, *verb* (8).
    Bribe, *subs.* 1. *A bribe I know is
a juggling knave.* 1659: Howell, *Proverbs: Brit.-Eng.*, 33.
    2. *A bribe will enter without knocking.*
1619: B. Rich, *Irish Hubbub*, 9 (margin), Honesty stands at the gate and
knockes, and bribery enters in. 1633:
Draxe, 18, A bribe entreth euery where

without knocking. 1670: Ray, 65.
1732: Fuller, No. 1019.
    Bribe, *verb.* *Neither bribe nor lose thy
right.* 1640: Herbert, *Jac. Prudentum.*
    Bridge and Bridges. 1. *Bridges were
made for wise men to walk over, and fools
to ride over.* 1678: Ray, 106.
    2. *He is building a bridge over the sea.*
1813: Ray, 75.
    3. *Praise the bridge.* See **Praise the
bridge.**
    4. *To make a bridge of one's nose.*
1678: Ray, 231. 1690: *New Dict.
Canting Crew*, sig. H8, You make a
bridge of his nose, when you pass your
next neighbour in drinking, or one is
preferr'd over another's head. 1738:
Swift, *Polite Convers.*, Dial. II., Pray,
my lord, don't make a bridge of my
nose. 1828: Carr, *Craven Dialect*, ii. 12,
"To mak a brigg o' yans nose," to pass
by him in drinking. 1847: Halliwell,
Dict., s.v. "Nose."
    5. *To make* (or *build*) *a bridge of gold*
(or *silver*) *for a flying enemy.* [1535:
Rabelais (*c.* 1490–1533), *Gargantua*,
liv. i. ch. 43, Ouurez tousiours a voz
ennemys toutes les portes et chemins,
et plustost leur faictes ung pont
d'argent, affin de les renvoyer.] 1576:
Lambarde, *Peramb. of Kent*, 371 (1826),
It was well saide of one . . . If thine
enemie will flie, make him a bridge of
golde. 1634: Massinger, *Guardian*, I. i.,
For a flying foe Discreet and provident
conquerors build up A bridge of gold.
1732: Fuller, No. 3312, Make a silver
bridge for your enemy to go over.
1889: R. L. S., *Ballantrae*, ch. iv., You
may have heard of a military proverb:
that it is a good thing to make a bridge
of gold to a flying enemy.
    **Bridgnorth Election, All on one side
like.** 1841: Hartshorne, *Salopia Ant.*,
336. 1861: in *N. & Q.*, 2nd scr., xi. 219,
In 1835 I heard a boy say "all on one
side, like Bridgnorth election," in the
town of Stone, in Staffordshire. 1883:
Burne, *Shropsh. Folk-Lore*, 592 [full
explanation of saying]. 1920: A. G.
Bradley, *Book of Severn*, 195.
    Bridle. 1. *A bridle for the tongue is
a necessary piece of furniture.* 1732:
Fuller, No. 25.

2. *To bite upon the bridle.* *c.* 1390:
Gower, *Conf. Amantis*, bk. vi. l. 929,
And as who seith, upon the bridel
I chiewe. 1552: Latimer, *Works*, ii. 57
(P.S.), Though it goeth hard with us,
though we must bite on the bridle.
1605: Chapman, etc., *Eastw. Hoe*,
IV. ii., They are like to bite o' the
bridle [i.e. to fast]. 1642: D. Rogers,
Matrim. Honour, 300, Be quiet, my
soule, bite not upon the bridle. 1750:
Smollett, *Gil Blas*, iv. 248, The minister
was going to retire into his closet, to
bite upon the bridle at liberty. *c.* 1791:
Pegge, *Derbicisms*, 91 (E.D.S.), " To
bite on the bridle," to suffer or fare
hard. 1828: Carr, *Craven Dialect*, i. 52,
To bite on the bridle, to suffer great
hardship, to be driven to straits.

Bridport dagger, Stabbed with a =
Hanged, hemp being manufactured at
Bridport. 1662: Fuller, *Worthies*, i.
453 (1840). 1716: Browne Willis,
Notitia Parl., quoted in *N. & Q.*, 9th
ser., iii. 365. 1790: Grose, *Prov. Gloss.*,
s.v. " Dorset."

Bright. 1. *Bright as the sun on a
summer's day.* *c.* 1440: Lydgate, *Lyf
of our Lady*, sig. F2 (Caxton), That
shone as bright as ony somers day.
1846: Denham, *Proverbs*, 51 (Percy S.).

2. *He is only bright that shines by
himself.* 1640: Herbert, *Jac. Prudentium.*

Brighton. *See* quot. 1884: " Sussex
Proverbs," in *N. & Q.*, 6th ser., ix. 342,
When the Island's [Wight] seen above
the line Brighthelmstone loses weather
fine. *See also* **Lewes.**

Brim. *See* **Better spare.**

Brisk as a bee. 1732: Fuller, No. 666,
As brisk as a bee in a tar-pot. 1742:
Fielding, *Andrews*, bk. iii. ch. ii.,
Joseph immediately prevailed with
parson Adams, who was as brisk as
a bee, to stop. *c.* 1770: Hall-Stevenson, *Works*, i. 23 (1795), Away skipp'd
the urchin, as brisk as a bee. 1901:
F. E. Taylor, *Lancs Sayings*, 1.

Brisk as bottled ale. 1720: Gay,
Poems, ii. 278 (Underhill), And merry
as a grig is grown, And brisk as bottled
ale. 1745: *Agreeable Companion*, 351,
Brisk as bottled beer.

Bristol. 1. *A Jew cannot live in
Bristol.* 1790: Grose, *Prov. Gloss.*, s.v.
" Somerset."

2. *Bristol men sleep with one eye open.*
Ibid., s.v. " Somerset." 1868: *Quart.
Review*, cxxv. 231, Bristol men, who
are currently reported to " sleep with
one eye open." 1906: Q.-Couch, *Mayor
of Troy*, Prol., We slept Bristol fashion,
with one eye open.

3. *Bristol milk.* *See* 1848 quot.
1661: *Antid. against Melanch.*, 156
(Ebsworth), Merrily now let's sing,
carouse, and tiple, Here's Bristow
milk, come suck this niple. 1668:
Pepys, *Diary*, 13 June, Plenty of brave
wine, and above all Bristol milk. 1785:
Grose, *Class. Dict. of Vulgar Tongue*,
s.v., . . . A Spanish wine called sherry,
much drank at that place, particularly
in the morning. 1848: Macaulay, *Hist.
Eng.*, i. 335. The repast was . . . accompanied by a rich brewage made of
the best Spanish wine, and celebrated
over the whole kingdom as Bristol milk.

4. *The Bristol hogs have built a sty,
but cannot find their way into it.* 1752:
Journey through England, 144, quoted in
Hazlitt, *Proverbs*, 1869.

See also **Sold.**

Britain. *See* quot. 1580: Lyly,
Euphues, 439 (Arber), Whereof there
was an olde saying, all countries stande
in neede of Britaine, and Britaine of
none.

Brittle as glass. 1412–20: Lydgate,
Troy Book, bk. v. l. 854, Brotel as glas.
c. 1550: Becon, in *Catechism, etc.*, 437
(P.S.), It is more brittle than glass.
1639: Fuller, *Holy War*, bk. ii. ch. xii.,
Her fortune being as brittle as her
glasses. 1927: J. B. Priestley, *Open
House:* " Midsummer Day's Dream,"
All this beauty . . . is as brittle as
glass.

Broad. 1. *A broad hat does not always
cover a venerable head.* 1732: Fuller,
No. 26.

2. *As broad as narrow like Paddy's
plank* = " Much of a muchness." 1917:
Bridge, *Cheshire Proverbs*, 10.

3. *It's as broad as it's long.* 1678:
Ray, 67, As broad as long. Before
1680: Butler, *Remains*, i. 110 (1759).

1732: Fuller, No. 2933.   1821: Byron,
Letters, etc., v. 379 (Prothero), So that
the thing is as broad as it is long.
1907: De Morgan, *Alice-for-Short*, ch. xl.
  Brock=A badger.   1. *To stink like a
brock.*   1892: Heslop, *Northumb. Words*,
101 (E.D.S.).
  2. *To sweat like a brock.*   1788: in
Reprinted Gloss., 23 (E.D.S., No. 1), He
sweats like a brock [E. Yorks].   1892:
Heslop, *Northumb. Words*, 101 (E.D.S.).
  Brockley Hill.   *See* quot.   1724:
Stukeley, *Itin. Cur.*, 111, They have a
proverb here, no heart can think nor
tongue can tell, what lys between
Brockley-hill and Pennywell.   1849:
Halliwell, *Pop. Rhymes and Nursery
Tales*, 198 [as in 1724].
  **Broke his hour that kept his day, He
never.**   1678: Ray, 122.
  Broken, *part. adj.*   1. *A broken apothe-
cary, a new doctor.*   1659: Howell, 13.
1670: Ray, 2.
  2. *A broken glass can't be hurt.*   1732:
Fuller, No. 28.
  3. *A broken latch* (or what not) *lasts
longer than a good one.*   1883: Burne,
Shropsh. Folk-Lore, 588.
  4. *A broken leg is not healed by a silk
stocking.*   1875: A. B. Cheales, *Proverb.
Folk-Lore*, 122.
  5. *A broken sack will hold no corn.*
1629: *Book of Meery Riddles*, Prov. 114,
A broken bag can hold no meale.   1633:
Draxe, 15.   1670: Ray, 65.   1732:
Fuller, No. 1022.
  6. *A broken sleeve holdeth* (or *keepeth*)
the arm back.   Before 1500: in Hill,
Commonplace-Book, 132 (E.E.T.S.), For
my brokyn sleve, men me refuce, Pro
manica fracta, manus est mea sepe
retracta.   *c.* 1550: *Parl. of Byrdes*,
l. 164, in Hazlitt, *Early Pop. Poetry*, iii.
175 (1866), It is a terme with John
and Jacke, Broken sleue draweth arme
a backe.   1625: Jonson, *Staple of News*,
I. i., And therefore you've another
answering proverb, *A broken sleeve keeps
the arm back.*   1670: Ray, 66.
  7. *As broken a ship.   See* **Ship** (1).
  8. *Trust not to a broken staff.*   1580:
H. Gifford, *Posie*, 71 (Grosart), To trust
her lookes . . . Is nothing els but trust
a broken staffe.   1622: in *Pepysian*

Garland, 167 (Rollins, 1922), 'Tis bad
to trust a broaken staffe.   1732: Fuller,
No. 5290.
  Broken, *part.*   1. *He has broken his
leg.*   1828: Carr, *Craven Dialect*, i. 285,
" He's broke his leg," said of a dissolute
person on whom a child has been
filiated.   1847: Halliwell, *Dict.*, s.v.
" Leg."
  2. *She hath broken her leg at the
church-door.*   Cheshire.   *See* 1877 quot.
1670: Ray, 166.   1710: Ward, *Nuptial
Dialogues*, i. 313, You crown the proverb, *That the nicest maid Becomes the
greatest slattern when she's wed.*   1732:
Fuller, No. 4119, She broke her elbow
on her wedding-day.   1877: Leigh,
Cheshire Gloss. (W.), . . . said of a
woman who, as a daughter, was a hard
worker and did not spare her elbow
grease, but who, after marriage, became
lazy and indolent.   1917: Bridge,
Cheshire Proverbs, 108.
  3. *She hath broken her leg* (or *elbow*)
above the knee = has had a bastard.
1618: B. & F., *Loyal Subject*, III. v.,
If her foot slip, and down fall she, And
break her leg above the knee.   Before
1625: B. & F., *Wild-Goose Chase*, IV. i.
1650: R. Heath, *Epigrams*, 64, And so
she broke her elboe 'gainst the bed.
1709: Cibber, *Rival Fools*, V., *Gov.* . . .
Your niece ! your niece ! sir.   *Sir Ol.*
What ! broke her leg?   1785: Grose,
Class. Dict. of Vulgar Tongue, s.v.
" Leg."   Cf. **Sprained her ankle.**
  Broom.   *He bestows his gifts as
broom yields honey.*   1586: L. Evans,
Revised Withals Dict., sig. D4.   1639:
Clarke, 38.   1670: Ray, 177.   *See also*
Lads' love ; **May** (10) ; and **Under the
furze.**
  Broom.   *To hang out the broom.   See*
quots.   1773: in *Garrick Corresp.*, i. 516
(1831), She [his wife] is gone to fleece my
flock at St. Mary's; . . . and I hang
out the broom in her absence.   *c.* 1791:
Pegge, *Derbicisms*, 91 (E.D.S.), " To
hang about the broom." This means, to
signify that the wife is from home, and
that the goodman's friends may come
freely to visit him.   1862: *N. & Q.*,
3rd ser., ii. 484 [a proverbial expression
in Lancs].

Broth. 1. *See* quot. 1913: *Devonsh.
Assoc. Trans.*, xlv. 286, "When they'm
wit (white), they'm fit; When they'm
boil'd, they'm spoil'd." Meaning that
broth should be warmed until a white
scum appears on the surface, but should
not be boiled or raised to boiling
point.

2. *Many esteem more of the broth, than
of the meat sod therein.* 1577: Stanihurst, *Descrip. of Ireland*, fo. 4, Setteth
hymselfe forth to the gaper, by making
more of the broth then yᵉ flesh is
worth. 1639: in *Berkeley MSS.*, iii. 32
(1885).

3. *Owd* [old] *broth's a jell sooner
warmt up tan new made.* 1917: Bridge,
Cheshire Proverbs, 103. Cf. **Old pottage.**

**Brother had rather see the sister rich
than make her so, The.** 1611: Cotgrave,
s.v. "Frere," The brother would have
his sister rich any way, but at his
charges. 1678: Ray, 203. 1732: Fuller,
No. 4435.

Brough Hill weather is stormy weather, which often occurs at Fair time.
Durham.' 1909: *Folk Lore*, xx. 75.

Brown as a berry. *c.* 1386: Chaucer,
Prol., l. 207, His palfrey was as brown
as is a berye. 1640: Tatham, *Love
Crowns the End*, in *Dram. Works*, 20
(1879), Thy nose is as brown as a berry.
1777: Sheridan, *Sch. for Scandal*, III. iii.
1843: Dickens, *Letters*, iii. 54 (1882).
1874: R. L. S., *Letters*, i. 173 (Tusitala
ed.), I am back again here, as brown as
a berry with sun.

Brown study, To be in a. Originally
simply "in a study," and this form persisted for centuries after the inexplicable
"brown" had been introduced. (*a*) *In a
study*, simply. *c.* 1300: Robert of Brunne,
tr. Langtoft's *Chron.*, 58 (Hearne),
Whan Edward perceyued, his herte was
in studie. *c.* 1386: Chaucer, *Knight's Tale*,
l. 672, Into a studie he fil sodeynly.
1485: Malory, *Morte d'Arthur*, bk. i.
ch. 20, The kyng sat in a study. 1576:
Pettie, *Petite Pallace* i. 72 (1908), This
youth stood staring in her face in a great
study. 1685: *Mother Bunch's Closet*,
5 (Gomme), I am persuaded you are in
a study. 1791: Boswell, *Johnson*, ii.
34 (Hill), Dr. Johnson, who was still in

a profound study. 1875: Parish, *Sussex
Dict.*, 116, He seems all in a stud as he
walks along. (*b*) *In a brown study.*
c. 1530: *Dice Play*, 6 (Percy S.), Lack of
company will soon lead a man into a
brown study. 1591: Greene, in *Works*,
x. 17 (Grosart), Halfe in a browne study
at this strange salutation. 1646:
Quarles, *Shep. Oracles*, egl. xi., In a
browne studie? . . . Speechlesse? 1778:
Burney, *Evelina*, Lett. xxxiii., He stood
some time quite in a brown study, a-
thinking what he should do. 1841:
Dickens, *Barn. Rudge*, ch. lxxii., Sitting
by the hour together in a brown study.
1908: Lucas, *Over Bemerton's*, ch. xxiii.,
I walked home in a brown study.

**Brown wench in face shows that
nature gives her grace, A.** 1623:
Wodroephe, *Spared Houres*, 485.

Brush at his back. *See* **Wear** (2).

Brush, He has bought a = has run
away. 1813: Ray, 56.

Buck of the first head, He's like a =
brisk, pert, forward. 1678: Ray, 67.
1846–59: *Denham Tracts*, ii. 109 (F.L.S.).

Buckets in a well, Like. *c.* 1386:
Chaucer, *Knight's Tale*, l. 675, Now in
the croppë, now doun in the breres,
Now up, now doun, as boket in a welle.
1596: Shakespeare, *Rich. II.*, IV. i.
c. 1620: in *Roxb. Ballads*, i. 76 (Hindley), In Bath a wanton wife did dwell,
She had two buckets to a well. *c.* 1705:
in *Bagford Ballads*, ii. 835 (B.S.), Then
be not like buckets, one up, t'other
down. 1743: T. Sheridan, in *Garrick
Corresp.*, i. 15 (1831), I don't know
whether the old simile of the two
buckets would not do as well. 1893:
R. L. S., *Ebb-Tide*, ch. viii., The three
lives went up and down before him like
buckets in a well.

Buckingham. *See* **Old**, A (*b*) (6).

Buckinghamshire bread and beef.
1622: Drayton, *Polyol.*, xxiii., Rich
Buckingham doth bear the term of
Bread and Beef. 1662: Fuller, *Worthies*,
i. 194 (1840). 1790: Grose, *Prov.
Gloss.*, s.v. "Buckinghamshire."

Buckle and thong. 1. *See* quot.
1631: Mabbe, *Celestina*, 71 (T.T.), His
mother and I were nayle and flesh,
buckle and thong.

2. *He'll bring buckle and thong together.*
1678: Ray, 232. 1732: Fuller, No. 2422.

3. *To be held to it, buckle and thong.*
1658: *Wit Restor'd*, in *Mus. Deliciæ*,
i. 280 (Hotten), When one is held
to it hard, buckle and thong. 1678:
Ray, 73.

4. *To come* (or *be brought*) *to bare
buckle and thong.* 1546: Heywood,
Proverbs, Pt. II. ch. viii. 1600: *Weakest
to the Wall*, l. 1053 (Malone S.), My
benefice doth bring me in no more But
what will hold bare buckle and thong
together. Before 1746: *Exmoor Courtship*, sc. iii., in *Gent. Mag.*, 297–300
(1746). 1886: Elworthy, *West Som.
Word-Book*, 96 (E.D.S.), Poor old blid,
her's a'most come to nothin'—can't call
her nort but nere buckle-n thongs.

Buckle of belt. *If you be angry, turn
the buckle of your girdle* (or *belt*) *behind
you.* 1599: Shakespeare, *Much Ado*,
V. i., *D. Pedro.* . . . I think he be
angry indeed. *Claud.* If he be, he
knows how to turn his girdle. 1637:
Breton: *Poste with Packet Mad Letters*
(N.), If you be angry, turne the buckle
of your girdle behind you. *c.* 1663:
Davenant, *Play-House to be Let*, V.
1738: Swift, *Polite Convers.*, Dial. I.,
If miss will be angry for nothing, take
my counsel, and bid her turn the buckle
of her girdle behind her. 1817: Scott,
Rob Roy, ch. xxv., If ye're angry, ye
ken how to turn the buckle o' your belt
behind you. 1917: *Devonsh. Assoc.
Trans.*, xlix. 335, " He may turn his
buckle behind his back," meaning,
apparently, he may prepare to fight.

Buckley panmug, A face like a. 1917:
Bridge, *Cheshire Proverbs*, 2, Buckley in
Flintshire . . . produces a good deal
of coarse red earthenware.

Bucknall, Staffs. *Booked for Bucknall* = Going to be married. 1889:
Folk-Lore Journal, vii. 294.

Build. 1. *He builds cages fit for oxen,
to keep birds in.* 1678: Ray, 352.
1732: Fuller, No. 1815.

2. *He that builds on the people, builds
on the dirt.* 1633: Draxe, 154. 1641:
Jonson, *Timber:* " Principum Varia,"
Nor let the common proverb (of he that
builds on the people, builds on the dirt)

discredit my opinion. 1666: Torriano,
Piazza Univ., 212.

3. *Who-so that buildeth his house all of
sallows, And pricketh his blind horse over
the fallows, And suffereth his wife to seek
many hallows, Is worthy to be hanged on
the gallows!* *c.* 1386: Chaucer, *Wife of
Bath's Prol.*, ll. 655–8. 1417: in *Reliq.
Antiquæ*, i. 233 (1841) [with last line,
" God sende hym the blisse of everlasting galos "]. 1486: *Boke of St. Albans*,
sig. f4 [as in 1417]. 1717: Pope, *Wife
of Bath*, 347, Oft would he say, who
builds his house on sands, Pricks his
blind horse across the fallow lands, Or
lets his wife abroad with pilgrims roam,
Deserves a fool's cap, and long ears at
home.

**Building and marrying of children are
great wasters.** 1611: Cotgrave, s.v.
" Abandon," The building of houses
and making of feasts, are unlimited
wasters of a mans substance. 1640:
Herbert, *Jac. Prudentum*. 1670: Ray,
3. 1875: A. B. Cheales, *Proverb. Folk-
Lore*, 43.

Building is a sweet impoverishing.
1602–3: Manningham, *Diary*, 9 (Camden S.), The proverbe is that building
is a theife, because it makes us lay out
more money then wee thought on. 1640:
Herbert, *Jac. Prudentum*. 1670: Ray, 3.

Bull, *subs.* 1. *A mad bull is not to
be tied up with a packthread.* 1732:
Fuller, No. 266.

2. *As sulky as a bull.* 1917: Bridge,
Cheshire Proverbs, 22.

3. *He bellows like a bull, but is as
weak as a bulrush.* 1639: Clarke, 142.

4. *He wears the bull's feather*=He is
a cuckold. 1533: in *Ballads from MSS.*,
i. 199 (B.S.), Lyke cokold foles to-gether
. . . we wer an oxes fether. *c.* 1680: in
Roxb. Ballads, iii. 418 (B.S.), And to all
merry cuckolds who think it no scorn
To wear the bull's feather, though made
of a horn. 1707: Dunton, *Athen. Sport*,
p. 118, col. 2, Pompey, Cæsar . . .
were not the less esteem'd for having
the bull's feather given 'em by their
wives. 1737: Ray, 53.

5. *Let him take the bull that stole the
calf.* 1548: Hall, *Chron.*, 406 (1809),
Accordyng to the old prouerbe, let him

take, etc. 1569: Grafton, *Chron.*, ii. 142 (1809).

6. *Like a bull in a china-shop.* 1850: Smedley, *Frank Fairlegh*, ch. xli., Stigmatising himself as an awkward dog, and comparing himself to a bull in a china-shop. 1899: H. James, in *Letters*, i. 349 (1920), Floundering and romping through the arts, both literary and plastic, very much as a bull through a china-shop. 1913: R. E. Francillon, *Mid-Vict. Memories*, 149.

7. *No further than you can throw a bull by the tail.* 1869: Hazlitt, 293.

8. *To take the bull by the horns.* 1816: Scott, *Old Mortality*, ch. xxv. 1849: Lytton, *Caxtons*, Pt. II. ch. i. 1869: Spurgeon, *John Ploughman*, ch. xi., I have often been told to be bold, and take the bull by the horns.

9. *You may play with a bull, till you get his horn in your eye*=Don't play with edged tools. 1886: R. Holland, *Cheshire Gloss.*, 457 (E.D.S.). 1917: Bridge, *Cheshire Proverbs*, 158.

See also Lawless; No law; and Town bull.

Bull, *verb. See* 1659 quot. 1612: *Cornucopiæ*, 78 (Grosart), Yours is the cow, and you shall keepe the calfe. 1659: Howell, *Proverbs*, "To Philologers," That [proverb] which began in Henrie the Fourth's time, He that bulls the cow must keep the calf. *c.* 1670: in *Roxb. Ballads*, iii. 368 (B.S.), Said they "The calf must with the cow." 1691: Southerne, *Sir Ant. Love*, IV. ii., I had the reputation of it indeed [a bastard]; and should have had the cow with the calf. 1732: Fuller, No. 5695, Who bulls the cow must keep the calf.

Bullet has its billet, Every. 1575: Gascoigne, *Fruites of Warre*, st. 67, in *Works*, i. 154 (Cunliffe), Every bullet hath a lighting place. 1757: Smollett, *Reprisal*, II. viii., Every shot has its commission, d'ye see. 1765: Wesley, *Journal*, 6 June, He never received one wound. So true is the odd saying of King William, that "every bullet has its billet." 1826–44: Hood, *Comic Poems:* "Waterloo Ballad," Its billet every bullet has. 1837: Dickens, *Pickwick*, ch. xix.

Bungay. *Go to Bungay, to get new-bottomed.* 1830: Forby, *Vocab. E. Anglia*, 434. 1872: J. Glyde, jr., *Norfolk Garland*, 150. *See also* Beccles.

Burford bait, A=Drink. 1636: Taylor (Water-Poet), *Cat. of Taverns*, 58, in *Works*, 4th coll. (Spens. S.), Beware of a Burfourd bayt, for it may brew the staggers. 1662: Fuller, *Worthies*, iii. 5 (1840), To take a Burford bait. 1790: Grose, *Prov. Gloss.*, s.v. "Oxfordshire."

Buried under the gallows. *See* quots. 1678: Ray, 221, He that kills himself with working must be buried under the gallows. 1828: Carr, *Craven Dialect*, i. 174, . . . This is said to be the doom of a man who kills himself with hard working. 1889: Peacock, *Manley, etc., Gloss.*, 227 (E.D.S.), Thaay bury them as kills ther'sens wi' hard wark aneän th' galla's.

Burn, *verb.* 1. *Burn not your house to fright away the mice.* 1732: Fuller, No. 1024.

2. *He is burnt to the socket*=is dying, is at his last gasp. 1813: Ray, 57.

3. *He that burns his house warms himself for once.* 1640: Herbert, *Jac. Prudentum.*

4. *He that burns most shines most.* 1640: Herbert, *Jac. Prudentum.* 1852: FitzGerald, *Polonius*, 92 (1903).

5. *He will burn his house to warm his hands.* 1481: Caxton, *Reynard*, 78 (Arber), They retche not whos hows brenneth, so that they may warme them by the coles. 1640: Herbert, *Jac. Prudentum.*

6. *They that burn you for a witch lose all their coals.* 1732: Fuller, No. 4974. 1846–59: *Denham Tracts*, ii. 84 (F.L.S.).

7. *To burn daylight.* 1587: Churchyard, *Worth. of Wales*, 84 (Spens. S.), Tyme rouleth on, I doe but daylight burne. 1592: Lyly, *Mother Bombie*, II. i., Wee burne time. 1692: L'Estrange, *Æsop*, 298 (3rd ed.), Talk does but burn daylight. 1707: Cibber, *Comical Lovers*, II., We burn day-light, lose time, and love. 1828: Carr, *Craven Dialect*, i. 58, Burn day-light, To light candles before dark.

8. *To burn the house, and run away by the light of it.* 1530: Palsgrave, 710,

I can set a house a fyre and ronne awaye
by the lyght. *c.* 1720: J. Smedley, in
Somers Tracts, xiii. 824 (1811), The following English proverbs . . . Burn
the house, and run away by the light
of it.

Burnt child dreads the fire, A. [Cui
dolet, meminit.—Cicero, *Pro Mur.*, 42.]
c. 1300: in *Reliq. Antiquæ*, i. 113 (1841),
Brend child fur dredeth; Quoth Hendyng. *c.* 1400: *Rom. Rose*, l. 1820:
Brent child of fyr hath muche drede.
1580: Lyly, *Euphues*, 319 (Arber), A
burnt childe dreadeth the fire. 1616:
Jonson, *Devil an Ass*, I. ii. 1725:
Bailey, tr. Erasmus' *Colloq.*, 157.
c. 1760: Foote, *Cozeners*, I. 1820:
Scott, *Fam. Letters*, ii. 73 (1894).

Burroughs end of sheep, Some one =?
1678: Ray, 68.

Burst at the broadside, To. A drinking phrase. 1670: Ray, 217.

**Burthen of one's own choice is not
felt, A.** 1855: Bohn, 282.

Burton. *See* Barton.

Burton-bream. *See* Brayton-bargh.

Bury the hatchet, To. *See* Hatchet.

Burying a wife. *See* quots. 1847:
Halliwell, *Dict.*, s.v. "Burying-a-wife,"
A feast given by an apprentice at the
expiration of his articles. 1899: Dickinson, *Cumberland Gloss.*, 23, Berryin'
t'ould wife. The treat given by an apprentice on obtaining his freedom.

Burying is gone by, The. *See* quots.
c. 1791: Pegge, *Derbicisms*, 92 (E.D.S.),
"The burying's gone by," i.e. you are
too late. 1891: *N. & Q.*, 7th ser., xi.
148, " Th' berrin's gone by, and t'child's
called Anthony." This saying used to
be current in Lancashire fifty years ago,
when any one appeared just too late for
the event he had come to witness.

Bush. 1. *A bad (thin, etc.) bush is
better than no shelter.* *c.* 1300: *Prov. of
Hendyng*, st 22 (Berlin, 1878), Under
boske shal men weder abide. 1670:
Ray, 58, A bad bush is better then the
open field. 1732: Fuller, No. 432, A
thin bush is better than no shelter.
1820: Scott, *Monastery*, ch. iii., These
evil showers make the low bush better
than no bield.

2. *Bush natural.* *See* Hair (3).

3. *He thinks every bush a boggard.*
1678: Ray, 232.

Bushel. 1. *A whole bushel of wheat is
made up of single grains.* 1732: Fuller,
No. 456.

2. *In a bushel of winning is not a
handful of cunning.* Before 1500: Hill,
Commonplace-Book, 131 (E.E.T.S.).

3. *You should eat a bushel of salt with
a man before you trust him.* [Aristotle,
Ethics, viii. 4. Multos modios salis
simul edisse.—Cicero, *Læl.*, 19.] 1539:
Taverner, *Proverbs*, fo. 30, Trust no man
onles thou hast fyrst eaten a bushel of
salte wyth hym. 1579: Lyly, *Euphues*,
48 (Arber), One should eate a bushel of
salt with him whom he meaneth to
make his friend. 1637: Shirley, *Hyde
Park*, III. i., If you allow a bushel of
salt to acquaintance . . . 1707: Dunton, *Athen. Sport*, 452. 1716: Ward,
Female Policy, 83. 1875: A. B. Cheales,
Proverb. Folk-Lore, 95.

Business. 1. *Business is business.*
1857: Thackeray, *Virginians*, ch. i.,
Business is business, my dear young
sir. 1876: Blackmore, *Cripps*, ch. iii.
1922: Weyman, *Ovington's Bank*,
ch. xxvi.

2. *Business is the salt of life.* 1732:
Fuller, No. 1026.

3. *Business makes a man as well as
tries him.* 1855: Bohn, 334.

4. *He that thinks his business below
him, will always be above his business.*
1732: Fuller, No. 2333.

Busy as a bee. *c.* 1386: Chaucer,
Merch. Tale, Epil., l. 4, For ay as bisy
as bees Ben they. 1580: Lyly, *Euphues*,
252 (Arber). 1655: Fuller, *Church
Hist.*, bk. ix. § vii. (24). 1709: Cibber,
Rival Fools, I. 1792: Wolcot, in
Works, ii. 405 (1795). 1834-7: Southey,
Doctor, ch. lxxix. 1901: Raymond,
Idler Out of Doors, 35, The place is busy
as a swarm of bees. Cf. **Busy as bees
in a basin.**

Busy as a cat. *See* Cat (9).

Busy as a dog. *See* Dog (17).

Busy as a good wife at oven. 1670:
Ray, 203.

Busy as a hen. *See* Hen (2).

Busy as Batty. 1850: *N. & Q.*, 1st
ser., i. 475, In Devonshire they say

"Busy as Batty," but no one knows who "Batty" was.

Busy as bees in a basin. 1834: Toone, *Gloss.*, s.v. "Bees." There is a proverb in Leicestershire . . . "as busy as bees in a basin." Cf. Busy as a bee.

Busy folks are always meddling. 1736: Bailey, *Dict.*, s.v. "Busy."

Busy will have bands (or bonds). 1633: Draxe, 19. 1670: Ray, 66.

Busy. Who more busy than he that hath least to do? 1633: Draxe, 20. 1670: Ray, 66. 1753: Richardson, *Grandison*, i. 294 (1883), I tell the ladies here,. that those who have least to do, are generally the most busy people in the world.

Busy-bodies never want a bad day. 1732: Fuller, No. 1029.

"But," says Parson Lasky. 1864: "Cornish Proverbs," in *N. & Q.*, 3rd ser., vi. 5. 1888: Q.-Couch, *Troy Town*, ch. iv.

But when, quoth Kettle to his mare. Cheshire. 1678: Ray, 276. 1852: in *N. & Q.*, 1st ser., vi. 386. 1917: Bridge, *Cheshire Proverbs*, 33.

Butcher. 1. *He would have made a good butcher, but for the by-blow.* 1639: Clarke, 77.

2. *I think this is a butchers horse, he carries a calf so well.* 1678: Ray, 232.

3. *The butcher looked for his knife and it was in his mouth.* 1639: Clarke, 75. c. 1640: in *Roxb. Ballads*, iii. 321 (B.S.), [Kit the butcher] Hee'd with his candell looke his knife, When hee had it in his mouth. 1692: L'Estrange, *Æsop*, 340 (3rd ed.). 1738: Swift, *Polite Convers.*, Dial. I.

4. *The butcher looked for the candle, and 'twas in his hat.* 1639: Clarke, 75.

Butler's grace = ? 1609: Melton, *Sixfold Politician*, 33, Fidlers, who are regarded but for a baudy song, at a merry meeting, and when they have done, are commonly sent away with butler's grace.

Butter. 1. *Butter is gold in the morning, silver at noon, and lead at night.* 1588: Cogan, *Haven of Health*, 156 (1612), According to the old English prouerbe: Butter is gold, etc. c. 1653: in *Somers Tracts*, vii. 69 (1811), This

butter-print parliament was gold in the morning and lead at night. 1738: Swift: *Polite Convers.*, Dial. I.

2. *Butter is good for anything but to stop an oven.* 1659: Howell, 6.

3. *Butter is in the cow's horn once a year.* Ibid., 14. 1670: Ray, 44. 1846: Denham, *Proverbs*, 5 (Percy S.), When the cow is *dried* for calving it is usual to say, "All the butter is gone into the cow's horn."

4. *Butter is mad twice a year*, i.e. when very hard, and very soft. 1625: Jonson, *Staple of News*, II., So butter answer my expectation, and be not mad butter; "if it be, It shall both July and December see!" 1626: B. & F., *Noble Gent.*, I. ii., Mad as Maybutter. 1738: Swift, *Polite Convers.*, Dial. I. 1921: in *N. & Q.*, 12th ser., ix. 330, A Hertford servant girl, some forty-five years ago, when experiencing any difficulty in spreading butter on the bread, used to remark, "Butter goes mad twice a year, as my grandmother says."

5. *No butter will cleave on my bread.* 1546: Heywood, *Proverbs*, Pt. II. ch. vii. 1591: Greene, in *Works*, x. 22 (Grosart), Well, saith the setter, no butter will cleave on my bread. 1656: Flecknoe, *Diarium*, 38, No butter'd stick upon my bread. 1727: Swift, *Works*, xiv. 203 (Scott), But now I fear it will be said, No butter sticks upon his bread. 1824: Scott, *Redgauntlet*, ch. xv., The devil a crumb of butter was ever churned that would stick upon my bread.

6. *That which will not be butter must be made into cheese.* 1678: Ray, 107. 1732: Fuller, No. 4387.

7. *They that have good store of butter may lay it thick on their bread.* 1639: Clarke, 49. 1681: W. Robertson, *Phraseol. Generalis*, 1302. 1732: Fuller, No. 4980.

8. *To look as if butter would not melt in one's mouth.* 1530: Palsgrave, 620, He maketh as thoughe butter wolde nat melte in his mouthe. 1583: Stubbes, *Anat. of Abuses*, 89 (N. Sh. S.). 1641: Cowley, *Guardian*, III. viii. 1687: Sedley, *Bellamira*, IV., in *Works*, ii. 163

(1778). 1714: Ozell, *Molière*, iv. 122.
1850: Dickens, *Chuzzlewit*, ch. iii.
1922: Weyman, *Ovington's Bank*, ch. ix.

9. *To take butter out of a dog's mouth.*
1732: Fuller, No. 699, As irrecoverable
as a lump of butter in a greyhound's
mouth. 1886: Elworthy, *West Som.
Word-Book*, 202 (E.D.S.), We have an
old saying, as easy to get butter out of
a dog's mouth, as money out of a lawyer.
1908: T. Ratcliffe, in *N. & Q.*, 10th ser.,
x. 387.

Butter one's bread, To. *See* **Bread**
(8) and (12).

Butterbump. *See* **Foot** (3).

Buttermilk wedding, A. A poor affair.
1917: Bridge, *Cheshire Proverbs*, 2.

Button-hole. *See* **Take** (27).

Buy. 1. *Buy at a fair but sell at
home.* 1633: Draxe, 21, A man must
buie at the faire, and sell at home.
1670: Ray, 4, Buy at a market, but
sell at home. 1732: Fuller, No. 1034
[as in 1670].

2. *He is able to buy an Abbey*=He is a
spendthrift. 1678: Ray, 352.

3. *He that buyeth magistracy, must
sell justice.* 1642: Fuller, *Holy State:*
"The Good Judge," They that buy
justice by wholesale, to make themselves savers must sell it by retail.
1732: Fuller, No. 2055. Cf. No. 11.

4. *He that buys a house.* *See* **House**
(7).

5. *He that buys and lies shall feel it in
his purse.* 1612: Shelton, *Quixote*, Pt. I.
bk. iii. ch. xi. 1712: Motteux, *Quixote*,
Pt. I. bk. iii. ch. xi. 1732: Fuller,
No. 2056.

6. *He that buys dearly must sell dearly.*
c. 1538: Starkey, *England*, II. i. 175
(O.), He that byth dere may sel dere.
1681: Yarranton, *Eng. Improvement*,
Pt. II., p. 183, The old saying is, *He
that buys dear, must sell dear.*

7. *He that buys land buys many
stones; He that buys flesh buys many
bones; He that buys eggs buys many
shells; But he that buys good ale buys
nothing else.* 1670: Ray, 211. 1732:
Fuller, No. 6422. 1865: in *N. & Q.*,
3rd ser., viii. 494. 1901: F. E. Taylor,
Lancs Sayings, 42, Thoose 'at buy'n
beef buy'n booans; Thoose 'at buy'n

lond buy'n stooans; Thoose 'at buy'n
eggs buy'n shells; Thoose 'at buy'n good
ale buy'n nout elze !

8. *He that refuseth to buy counsel
cheap, shall buy repentance dear.* 1647:
Countrym. *New Commonwealth*, 39.
1669: *Politeuphuia*, 98. *c.* 1670: *Sir
Richard Whittington*, 5 (Villon S., 1885).

9. *It is good to buy wit with other
men's money.* 1672: Walker, *Parœm.*,
30. 1681: W. Robertson, *Phraseol.
Generalis*, 297.

10. *One may buy gold too dear.* 1546:
Heywood, *Proverbs*, Pt. II. ch. vii., A
man may by gold to deere. 1579:
Spenser, *Shep. Cal.*, August, l. 123, So
you may buye golde too deare. 1692:
L'Estrange, *Æsop*, 167 (3rd ed.). 1844:
Thackeray, *Barry Lyndon*, ch. xiii., The
fact is, in my opinion, that we often
buy money very much too dear.

11. *They that buy an office must sell
something.* 1650: Taylor, *Holy Living*,
ch. iii. § 2, For they that buy the office
will sell the act. 1732: Fuller, No. 4975.
Cf. No. 3.

12. *To buy and sell and live by the loss.*
1633: Draxe, 20. 1660: Fuller, *Mixt
Contempl.*, 347 (1830), Merchandizing is
a ticklish matter, seeing many buy and
sell and live by the loss. 1732: Fuller,
No. 1033.

13. *To buy dear is not bounty.* 1640:
Herbert, *Jac. Prudentum.* 1670: Ray, 4.

14. *Who always buys and sells, feels
not what he spends.* 1659: Howell,
Proverbs: Span.-Eng., 1. 1732: Fuller,
No. 5693.

15. *Who buyeth dear and taketh up on
credit, shall ever sell to his loss.* 1578:
Florio, *First Fruites*, fo. 28, Who buyeth
deere, and taketh of credit, consumeth
the body and looseth the seede. 1629:
Book of Meery Riddles, Prov. 70.

Buyer. 1. *Beware the buyer.* 1607:
E. Sharpham, *Fleire*, II., in Bang,
Materialien, B. 36, p. 19, Beware the
buyer say they, you shall haue enough
for your money. 1672: Walker, *Parœm.*,
41, Let the buyer look to himself.

2. *The buyer needs a hundred eyes, the
seller but one.* 1640: Herbert, *Jac.
Prudentum.* 1732: Fuller, No. 1035
[with " none " for " but one "]. 1869:

Spurgeon, *John Ploughman*, ch. xvi., Buyers ought to have a hundred eyes. 1928: *Sporting and Dramatic News*, 7 Jan., p. 27.

Buying and selling is but winning and losing. 1678: Ray, 107. 1732: Fuller, No. 1036.

Buying of bread undoes us, This. 1678: Ray, 67. 1748: *Gent. Mag.*, 21.

Buzzard. *See* Blind, *adj.* (13); Hawk (1); Sparrow-hawk; and Too low.

By and by is easily said. 1855: Bohn, 334.

By chance, as the man killed the devil. 1738: Swift, *Polite Convers.*, Dial. I.

By fits and starts (or girds). 1620: Sanderson, *Serm. ad Pop.*, i. 145 (1681) (O.), If thou hast these things only by fits and starts. 1650: Fuller, *Pisgah Sight*, bk. i. ch. ii., That froward people worshipped Him by fits and girds. 1709: Ward, *Acc. of Clubs*, 69 (1756), Yet still, by fits and starts, he'll jadish be. 1732: Fuller, No. 1039, By fits and girts, as an ague takes a goose. 1748: Richardson, *Clarissa*, iv. 318 (1785), . . . by fits and starts. 1825: Jennings, *Somersetsh. Words*, 42, By fits and gurds. 1840: Dickens, *Curiosity Shop*, ch. xxvii. *ad fin.*, . . . by fits and starts all night. 1847: Halliwell, *Dict.*, s.v. "Gurds," Gurds. Fits; starts. *Var. dial.*

By one and one spindles are made. 1578: Florio, *First Fruites*, fo. 25. 1629: *Book of Meery Riddles*, Prov. 62.

By the ears. 1539: Taverner, *Garden of Wysdome*, ch. iv., He set a yonge lyon and a very eger dogge togither by the eares. *c.* 1580: Spelman, *Dialogue*, 74 (Roxb. Cl.), One euyll tonge may sette a nomber of men to gether by the eares. *c.* 1630: *Dicke of Devonsh.*, I. iii., in Bullen, *Old Plays*, ii. 21. 1742: Fielding, *Andrews*, bk. ii. ch. xi. 1819: Byron, *Letters, etc.*, iv. 295 (Prothero).

By the great. *See* Work (4).

Bygones be bygones, Let. [τὰ μέχρι νῦν ἀφῶμεν.—Epictetus, *Disc.*, II. xix. 34.] 1546: Heywood, *Proverbs*, Pt. II. ch. ix., Let all thinges past pas. 1648: Nethersole, *Parables*, 5 (O.), Let bygans be bygans.' 1710: S. Palmer, *Moral Essays on Proverbs*, 292, By-gones be by-gones, and fair play for time to come. 1857: Borrow, *Rom. Rye*, ch. xliv. 1909: De Morgan, *Never can happen Again*, ch. xxviii.

C

Ca me, ca thee. *See* Ka me, ka thee.

Cackle, *verb.* 1. *I would not have your cackling for your eggs.* 1732: Fuller, No. 2658.

2. *She can cackle like a cadowe* [jackdaw]. 1579: *Marr. of Wit and Wisdom,* sc. iii., p. 26 (Sh. S.), Ah, that drabe, she can cacklel like a cadowe. 1886: Swainson, *Folk-Lore of Brit. Birds,* 82 (F.L.S.).

3. *You cackle often but never lay an egg.* 1732: Fuller, No. 5867.

Cadbury castle. *See* quot. 1790: Grose, *Prov. Gloss.,* s.v. " Devonshire," If Cadburye-castle and Dolbury-hill dolven wer, All England might ploughe with a golden sheere.

Cæsar's wife must be above suspicion. [Tum Cæsar . . . respondit: Quia suam uxorem etiam suspicione vacare vellet. —Plutarch, *Julius Cæsar,* x. (4).] 1740: North, *Examen,* 59, A judge should be, like Cæsar's wife, neither false nor suspected. 1748: Richardson, *Clarissa,* iii. 85 (1785). 1895: Shaw, *Man of Destiny, Lady* [*humbly*] I beg your pardon. Cæsar's wife is above suspicion.

Caistor was city when Norwich was none, And Norwich was built of Caistor stone. 1840: *Penny Cyclop.,* xvi. 327. 1865: W. White, *Eastern England,* i. 64.

Cake. 1. *I had rather my cake burn than you should turn it.* 1732: Fuller, No. 2598.

2. *One's cake is dough.* 1559: Becon, in *Prayers, etc.,* 277 (P.S.), Or else your cake is dough, and all my fat lie in the fire. *c.* 1598: Jonson, *Case is Altered,* V. iv. 1665: Pepys, *Diary,* 27 April, Which puts . . . me into a great fear, that all my cake will be doe still. 1720: C. Shadwell, *Hasty Wedding,* IV. i. 1854: Baker, *Northants. Gloss.,* s.v. " Cake," " All our cakes are dough." A proverbial expression, indicating the failure of any undertaking or project. Nares says, obsolete; not so with us.

1886: Hardy, *Casterbridge,* ch. xiii., She'll wish her cake dough afore she's done of him.

3. *That cake came out of my oven.* 1732: Fuller, No. 4335.

4. *There is no cake but there is the like of the same make.* 1659: Howell, 5. 1670: Ray, 4. 1762: Smollett, *Sir L. Greaves,* ch. x., Crabshaw replied, " There's no cake but there's another of the same make."

Calais. *See* quot. 1528: Tyndale, *Obed. of Christ. Men,* 239 (P.S.), He shall be cast out of the court, or, as the saying is, conveyed to Calais, and made a captain or an ambassador.

Calder. *See* Hodder.

Calenick. *The Mayor of Calenick, who walked two miles to ride one.* 1891: Q.-Couch, *Noughts and Crosses,* 185. 1906: Ibid., *Mayor of Troy,* Prol.

Cales. *See* Knight.

Calf and Calves. 1. *A calf's head will feed a huntsman and his hounds.* 1678: Ray, 108. 1846–59: *Denham Tracts,* ii. 108 (F.L.S.).

2. *As good luck as the lousy calf, that lived all winter and died in the summer.* 1678: Ray, 287.

3. *As many calves' skins come to market as of bulls or kine.* 1552: Latimer, *Sermons,* 416 (P.S.), It is a common saying, " There do come, etc."

4. *As wanton as a calf with two dams.* 1670: Ray, 208.

5. *He who will steal a calf will steal a cow.* 1736: Bailey, *Dict.,* s.v. " Calf."

6. *His calves are gone down to grass.* 1678: Ray, 232.

7. *That calf never heard church-bell.* 1917: Bridge, *Cheshire Proverbs,* 110, A calf born and killed between two Sundays.

8. *The largest calves are not the sweetest veal.* 1605: Camden, *Remains,* 332 (1870), The greatest calf is not the sweetest veal. 1790: Wolcot, *Works,* ii. 111 (1795).

9. *To eat the calf in the cow's belly* =
To reckon one's chickens before they
are hatched. 1642: Fuller, *Holy State:*
" Of Expecting Preferment," The law of
good husbandry forbids us to eat a kid
in the mother's belly, spending our
pregnant hopes before they be delivered.
1748: Richardson, *Clarissa*, iii. 122
(1785), I ever made shift to avoid
anticipations: *I never would eat the calf
in the cow's belly*, as Lord M's phrase is.
1792: Wolcot, *Works*, ii. 388 (1795).
1875: Smiles, *Thrift*, 264.   1886:
Elworthy, *West Som. Word-Book*, 58
(E.D.S.), A very common bucolic
saying, precisely expressive of what
is called " discounting " in commercial
talk, is eating the calf in the cow's belly.
See also Bull, *subs.* (5) ; Change, *subs.*
(3) ; **Cow** (3), (20), and (31) ; Eat (43) ;
Essex ; and Like cow.

Call.   1. *Call one a thief and he will
steal.*   1838: Carlyle, *Sartor*, bk. ii.
ch. i., In a very plain sense the proverb
says, Call one a thief, and he will steal.
2. *Call over the coals.   See* **Over the
coals.**
3. *It is too late to call again yesterday.*
Before 1529: Skelton, *Magnyfycence*,
l. 2057, Yesterday wyll not be callyd
agayne.   1538: Latimer, *Works*, ii. 398
(P.S.).   1639: Davenport, *Too Late to
call back Yesterday* [title of dialogue].
1676: Dryden, *Aureng-Zebe*, V. i., To
love, once past, I cannot backward
move ; Call yesterday again, and I may
love.   1707: Dunton, *Athen. Sport*,
p. 14, col. 2., So can we no more
recommend them, than call back
yesterday.
4. *To call one sir and something else*,
i.e. sirrah.   1678: Ray, 269.

Calm.   1. *Calm after a storm.   See*
Storm (1) and (2).
2. *Calm as a clock.*   1831: Hone,
Year-Book, 622, " As calm as a clock "
has long been a favourite proverb with
me.
3. *In a calm sea every man is a pilot.*
[Seneca, Epist. LXXXV.   1639: Clarke,
313 [with " passenger " for " man "].
1670: Ray, 4.   1732: Fuller, No. 2808,
In a calm every one can steer.

Calmest husbands.   See Husband (4).

Calverley Mill.   See Billing Hill.
Camberwell.   See quots.   1588: A.
Fraunce, *Lawiers Logike*, fo. 27, All the
maydes in Camberwell may daunce in an
egge shell.   1861: *N. & Q.*, 2nd ser.,
xi. 449, [as in 1588+] For there are noe
maydes in that well.   Cf. **Wanswell.**
Cambridge.   1. *A Royston horse and a
Cambridge Master of Arts are a couple of
creatures that will give way to nobody.*
1662: Fuller, *Worthies*, i. 226 (1840)
[with " boisten " for " Royston "].
1790: Grose, *Prov. Gloss.*, s.v. " Cambridgeshire " [as in 1662].   1885: *Folk-
Lore Journal*, iii. 85, The proverb, " A
Royston horse and a Cambridge M.A.
will give way to no one," refers to the
stolid way in which the malt-laden
horses of the Hertfordshire town bore
their burdens to the London market.
2. *Cambridge requires all to be equal.*
1662: Fuller, *Worthies*, i. 226 (1840).
1790: Grose, *Prov. Gloss.*, s.v. " Cambridgeshire."
Cambridgeshire Camels.   1662: Fuller
—as before.   1790: Grose—as before.
1874: Smiles, *Lives of Engineers*, i. 14,
The proverb of " Cambridgeshire
Camels " doubtless originated in this
old practice of stilt-walking in the Fens.
Cambridgeshire Oaks = Willows.
1785: Grose, *Class. Dict. Vulgar Tongue*,
s.v.   1790: Grose—as before.
Candle.   1. *A candle lights others and
consumes itself.*   1855: Bohn, 283.
2. *Candle ate the cat.   See* **True** (6).
3. *His candle burns within the socket.*
1639: Clarke, 279.   1681: W. Robertson, *Phraseol. Generalis*, 307, His candle
burns within the socket ; Homo depon-
tanus est.   1736: Bailey, *Dict.*, s.v.
" Candle."
4. *Not worth the candle.   See* **Game.**
5. *To burn the candle at both ends.*
1658: Flecknoe, *Enigm. Characters*, 64,
He consuming just like a candle on both
ends, betwixt wine and women.   1750:
Smollett, *Gil Blas*, iii. 116, The butler
and steward were in a confederacy, and
burnt the candle at both ends.   1842:
Barham, *Ing. Legends*, 2nd ser.: " St.
Cuthbert."   1889: Peacock, *Manley,
etc., Gloss.*, 81 (E.D.S.), Burn candles at
both ends.—To be very wasteful.

6. *To hold (or set) a candle before the
devil.* 1461: *Paston Lett.*, ii. 73 (Gairdner, 1900), For it is a comon proverbe,
"A man must sumtyme set a candel
befor the Devyle." *c.* 1540: *Thersites*,
in Hazlitt, *Old Plays*, i. 427, It is good to
set a candle before the devil. 1672:
Wycherley, *Love in a Wood*, I. i., You
cannot hold a candle to the devil.
1705: Ward, *Hud. Rediv.*, Pt. III.
can. iv., p. 16. 1828: Scott, *Fair
Maid*, ch. xxix. 1871: G. Eliot, *Middlemarch*, ch. xvi., Their impression that
the general scheme of things . . . required you to hold a candle to the
devil.

7. *To waste a candle and find a flea* (or
farthing). 1623: Wodroephe, *Spared
Houres*, 504, . . . find a flea. 1880:
Spurgeon, *Ploughman's Pictures*, 19,
They are like Pedley, who burnt a
penny candle in looking for a farthing.
See also Sun (13).

Candlemas Day. 2 Feb. The Feast
of the Purification of the B.V.M.
[Before 1529: Skelton, *Garl. of Laurell*,
l. 1442, How men were wont for to
discerne By candelmas day, what
wether shoulde holde.]

A. A FINE CANDLEMAS DAY. *c.* 1576:
G. Harvey, *Marginalia*, 175 (1913), A
faire Candlemas, a fowle Lent. 1584:
R. Scot, *Witchcraft*, bk. xi. ch. xv., If
Maries purifying day Be cleare and
bright with sunny raie, Then frost and
cold shall be much more, After the
feast than was before. 1640: *Countrym.
Counsellor*, in *Helpe to Discourse*, 224,
When on the Purification sun hath
shin'd, The greatest part of winter
comes behind. 1646: Browne, *Pseudo.
Epi.*, bk. vi. ch. iv. [cites the old distich:
Si Sol splendescat Maria purificante,
Major erit glacies post festum quam
fuit ante]. 1678: Ray, 51, If Candlemas day be fair and bright Winter will
have another flight. 1732: Fuller,
No. 6486 [as in 1678]. 1799: *Gent.
Mag.*, Pt. I., p. 203, If the sun shines
i' th' forenoon [of Candlemas Day],
Winter is not half done. 1846: Denham, *Proverbs*, 29 (Percy S.), If Candlemas-day be dry and fair, The half of
winter's to come and mair. 1879:

Henderson, *Folk-Lore N. Counties*, 76
(F.L.S.), If the sun shines bright on
Candlemas Day, The half of the winter's
not yet away. 1893: Inwards, *Weather
Lore*, 15, If Candlemas Day be fine and
clear, Corn and fruits will then be dear
[also as in 1640 and 1678]. Ibid., 16,
After Candlemas Day the frost will be
more keen, If the sun then shines bright,
than before it has been. 1904: *Co.
Folk-Lore: Northumb.*, 175 (F.L.S.), If
Candlemas day is fair and clear, There'll
be two winters in the year.

B. A FOUL CANDLEMAS DAY. 1678:
Ray, 51, If on Candlemas day it be
showre and rain, Winter is gone and
will not come again. 1732: Fuller,
No. 6486 [as in 1678]. 1855: *N. & Q.*,
1st ser., xi. 421, On Candlemas Day if
the thorns hang a-drop, Then you are
sure of a good pea-crop. 1893: Inwards, *Weather Lore*, 16 [as in 1678,
with slight variation, and as in 1855].
1917: Bridge, *Cheshire Proverbs*, 164, If
Candlemas Day be damp and black, It
will carry cold winter away on its back.

C. CANDLEMAS DAY AND CANDLES.
1678: Ray, 344, On Candlemas day,
throw candle and candlestick away.
1732: Fuller, No. 6152 [as in 1678].
1855: *N. & Q.*, 1st ser., xi. 239 [as in
1678]. 1893: Inwards, *Weather Lore*,
15 [as in 1678].

D. CANDLEMAS DAY AND FORAGE.
1639: in *Berkeley MSS.*, iii. 30 (1885),
At Candlemas a provident husbandman
should have halfe his fodder, and all his
corne remaininge. 1732: Fuller, No.
6487, On Candlemas-day, You must
have half your straw, and half your hay.
1855: [a Norfolk correspondent] in
N. & Q., 1st ser., xi. 239, The farmer
should have on Candlemas Day, Half
his stover [winter forage], and half his
hay. 1881: C. W. Empson, in *Folk-
Lore Record*, iv. 127, If it neither rains
nor snows on Candlemas Day, You may
striddle your horse and go buy hay.
Lincs. 1893: Inwards, *Weather Lore*,
15 [as in 1732]. 1916: in *N. & Q.*, 12th
ser., ii. 118, Rime . . . known in
several North-Midland counties runs :—
"If Candlemas Day comes blithe and
gay, You may saddle your horse and

buy some hay; But if Candlemas Day comes rugged and rough, You may fodder away — you'll have fodder enough." Which means that if there be hard weather at the beginning of February it bodes well for the hay and corn crops later on.

E. CANDLEMAS DAY AND GOOSE-LAYING. 1846. Denham, *Proverbs*, 31 (Percy S.), On Candlemas-day a good goose will lay; But on Valentine's day, any goose will lay. 1883: Burne, *Shropsh. Folk-Lore*, 578, At Candlemas Day A good goose should lay; But at St. Chad Both good and bad. 1913: E. M. Wright, *Rustic Speech, etc.*, 289, At this date, according to a common proverb: gooid geese all lay; New Candlemas Day, good goose will lay, Old Candlemas Day any goose will lay.

F. CANDLEMAS DAY AND SHEEP. 1732: Fuller, No. 6485, The shepherd had as live see his wife on the bier, As that Candlemas-day should be pleasant and clear. 1830: Forby, *Vocab. E. Anglia*, 416, On Candlemas Day, if the sun shines clear, The shepherd had rather see his wife on the bier. 1846: Denham, *Proverbs*, 28 (Percy S.) [as in 1732, with "hind" for "shepherd"]. 1879: Henderson, *Folk - Lore N. Counties*, 76 [as in 1830].

G. CANDLEMAS DAY AND SNOW. 1678: Ray, 43, When Candlemas day is come and gone The snow lies on a hot stone. 1825: Hone, *Ev. Day Book*, i. 2 Feb., *ad fin.* [as in 1678]. 1855: *N. & Q.*, 1st ser., xi. 239, (1) When Candlemas Day is come and gone, The snow won't lay on a hot stone. [Also] (2) As far as the sun shines in on Candlemas Day, So far will the snow blow in afore old May. 1872: J. Glyde, jr., *Norfolk Garland*, 153 [as in 1855 (1)—"won't lie"]. 1873: *N. & Q.*, 4th ser., xi. 275, Snow at Candlemas, Stops to handle us [Rutland].

H. CANDLEMAS DAY: MISCELLANEOUS. 1. *A Candlemas crack.* 1877: F. Ross, etc., *Holderness Gloss.*, 37 (E.D.S.), A Cannlemas-crack [storm] Lays monny a sailor on his back. 2. *As long as the bird sings before Candlemas, it will greet after it.* 1846. Denham,

Proverbs, 27 (Percy S.). 3. *At Candlemas, the cold comes to us.* 1732: Fuller, No. 6381. 1893: Inwards, *Weather Lore*, 15. 4. *February 2nd, bright and clear, Gives a good flax year.* Ibid., 16. 5. *See* quot. 1910: *Devonsh. Assoc. Trans.*, xlii. 81, "Green Candlemas, barren Redmas"; proverb used by an old Ashwater man, when a cold May followed a warm early spring [" Redmas" probably=Festival of Invention of Cross, 3 May]. 6. *When the wind's in the east on Candlemas day, There it will stick till the second of May.* 1852: *N. & Q.*, 1st ser., v. 462. 1893: Inwards, *Weather Lore*, 16 [as in 1852].

See also **All-hallon-tide**; and **Bean** (7).

Candlemas Eve Wind. 1839: G. C. Lewis, *Herefs. Words*, 122, When the wind blows on Candlemas-eve, it will continue till May - eve. 1858: *N. & Q.*, 2nd ser., v. 391, [An old farmer said] it had been observed by him, and by his father before him, that in whatever quarter the wind might be on Candlemas Eve, it "mainly" remained in that quarter for forty days.

Can't you hit the door? 1639: Clarke, 1.

Canterbury. 1. *A Canterbury gallop.* 1675: in *Harl. Miscell.*, vii. 598 (1746), For his grace at meat, what can I better compare it to, than a Canterbury rack, half-pace, gallop? 1759: Rider, *Dict.*, s.v., In horsemanship, the hard gallop of an ambling horse; probably derived from the monks riding to Canterbury upon ambling horses. 1830: Galt, *Lawrie Todd*, VI. vii. 280 (1849) (O.), On horse-back, and off at a Canterbury trot.

2. *A Canterbury tale.* 1549: Latimer, *Seven Sermons*, 49 (Arber), We myghte as well spende that tyme in reading of prophane hystories, of cantorburye tales, or fit of Robyn Hode. 1663: *Roxb. Ballads*, vii. 230 (B.S.), A sad relation, a strange Canterbury tale. 1724: Defoe, *Roxana*, in *Works*, xiii. 151 (Boston, 1903), That foolish young girl held us all in a Canterbury story; I thought she would never have done with it. 1774: Colman, *Man of Business*, V. ii. 1785:

Grose, *Class. Dict. Vulgar Tongue*, s.v., Canterbury Story, a long roundabout tale.

3. *Canterbury is the higher rack, but Winchester is the better manger.* 1608: in Harington, *Nugæ Antiquæ*, ii. 87 (1804), A bishop of Winchester [said to have been W. Edington, *ob.* 1366] one day in pleasant talke, comparing his revenew with the archbishops of Canterburie should say—"Your Graces will shew better in the racke, but mine will be found more in the maunger." 1662: Fuller, *Worthies*, ii. 5 (1840). 1790: Grose, *Prov. Gloss.*, s.v. "Hampshire." 1908: Read, *H. and B. in Hants*, 74, To Edington . . . is credited the origin of one of Hampshire's proverbs— "Though Canterbury is the highest rack, Winchester has the deepest manger."

See also **Deal** (2).

Canting. *See* **Courting.**

Cap, *subs.* 1. *If his cap be made of wool* = As sure as his cap is made of wool. 1633: Jonson, *Tale of a Tub*, II. ii., Slip, you will answer it, an if your cap be of wool. 1662: Fuller, *Worthies*, ii. 68 (1840), Our English garments from head to foot were formerly made thereof [of wool], till the beginning of the reign of King Henry the Eighth, when velvet caps becoming fashionable for persons of prime quality, discomposed the proverb, "If his cap be made of wool," as formerly comprising all conditions of people how high and haughty soever. 1670: Ray, 167. 1736: Bailey, *Dict.*, s.v. "Cap."

2. *If the cap fits—wear it.* 1714: Ozell, *Molière*, iv. 10, If the fool's cap fits any body, let 'em put it on. 1748: Richardson, *Clarissa*, vii. 59 (1785), If indeed . . . the cap fits thy own head . . . e'en take and clap it on. 1854: Dickens, *Hard Times*, bk. ii. ch. vii.

3. *My* (or *thy*) *cap is better at ease than my* (or *thy*) *head.* 1546: Heywood, *Proverbs*, Pt. II. ch. vii. 1659: Howell, 5.

4. *She's cap and button too.* Said of a lady who "wears the breeches." 1887: Croston, *Enoch Crump*, 8 (W.), Th' owd lass were cap and button too i'

that house. 1917: Bridge, *Cheshire Proverbs*, 100, Oo's cap and button too.

5. *To throw one's cap after a thing.* 1607: Shakespeare, *Timon*, III. iv., I perceive our masters may throw their caps at their money. 1690: *New Dict. Canting Crew*, sig. C4, He may fling up his cap after it, when a thing or business is past hope.

See also **Considering cap.**

Cap, *verb. See* quot. 1892: Heslop, *Northumb. Words*, 132 (E.D.S.), "This caps the stack "—is a proverb, meaning something overtopping.

Capel rides a good horse. Cornwall. 1887: M. A. Courtney, *Folk-Lore Journal*, v. 187, "Capel rides a good horse." Capel is schorl, and indicates the presence of tin.

Capon. 1. *Capons were at first but chickens.* 1732: Fuller, No. 1056.

2. *If you have not a capon, feed on an onion.* 1611: Cotgrave, s.v. "Chapon." 1710: S. Palmer, *Moral Essays on Proverbs*, 201.

3. *Who gives thee a capon, give him the leg and the wing.* 1640: Herbert, *Jac. Prudentum.* 1670: Ray, 11.

See also **Chickens** (1).

Car and Pen, Pol and Tre, Would make the devil run away. Cornwall. 1887: M. A. Courtney, *Folk-Lore Journal*, v. 106.

Carcase. *Where the carcase is, the ravens will gather.* 1855: Bohn, 563.

Card of ten. *See* **Outface.**

Cards. 1. *Cards are the devil's books.* 1676: *Poor Robin Alman. Prognost.*, sig. C4, Cards and dice . . . the devil's books and the devil's bones. 1745: *Agreeable Companion*, 73, Time out of mind, they [cards] are and have been call'd the devil's books. 1840: Lytton, *Money*, IV. ii.

2. *Many can pack* (or *shuffle*) *the cards, that cannot play well.* 1659: Howell, 10 (8). 1670: Ray, 20. 1694: D'Urfey, *Quixote*, Pt. II. Act III. sc. ii., There's many will shuffle the cards that won't play. 1732: Fuller, No. 3341.

3. *When you have told your cards, you'll find you have gained but little.* 1546: Heywood, *Proverbs*, Pt. I. ch. xi., Tell thy cardes, and than tell me what

thou hast wonne. *c.* 1594: Bacon,
Promus, No. 641 [as in 1546]. 1633:
Draxe, 116, Let him count his cardes
and see his winnings. 1678: Ray, 68.
1732 : Fuller, No. 5628, When you have
counted your cards, you'll find you have
little left.
See also Cooling card.

Care and diligence bring luck. 1732:
Fuller, No. 1057.

Care is no cure. *c.* 1591: Shakespeare, 1 *Henry VI.*, III. iii. 1678:
Ray, 108. 1732 : Fuller, No. 1060.

Care killed a cat. 1585–1618 : *Shirburn Ballads*, 91 (1907), Let care kill a
catte, Wee'le laugh and be fatte. 1599:
Shakespeare, *Much Ado*, V. i., What,
courage, man! What though care
killed a cat. *c.* 1630 : in *Roxb. Ballads*,
ii. 103 (Hindley). 1726: Swift, *Poems*,
in *Works*, xiv. 542 (Scott), Then who
says care will kill a cat? 1816 : Scott,
Antiquary, ch. xiv. 1871 : Planché,
Extravag., v. 287 (1879).

Care never paid a pound of debt.
c. 1640 : in *Roxb. Ballads*, i. 416 (B.S.).

Care not would have it. 1670 :
Ray, 67.

Care Sunday, care away, Palm Sunday
and Easter-day! 1812 : Brady, *Clavis
Cal.*, i. 242. 1904: *Co. Folk-Lore:
Northumb.*, 175 (F.L.S).

Cares not whose child cries, so his
laugh, He. 1732 : Fuller, No. 1823.

Careless hussy makes many thieves,
A. 1683 : Meriton, *Yorkshire Ale*, 83–7
(1697).

Carleton wharlers. *See* 1700 quot.
1622 : W. Burton, *Descrip. of Leics.*,
67–8. 1650: Fuller, *Pisgah Sight*,
bk. ii. ch. ix., It is observed in a
village at Charleton in Leicestershire
that the people therein are troubled
with wharling in their utterance. 1700 :
J. Brome, *Travels*, 77, Not far from
hence is Carleton, of which we were
told, that most persons that are born
there . . . have an ill favoured, un-
tunable, and harsh manner of speech,
fetching their words with very much
ado, deep from out of the throat, with
a certain kind of wharling, the letter
R being very irksome and troublesome
to them to pronounce. 1790 : Grose,

Prov. Gloss., s.v. " Leicestershire,"
Carleton warlers.

Carlisle, a seaport without ships, merchants or trade; and, Nearer God's
blessing than Carlisle Fair. Both in
1846–59 : *Denham Tracts*, i. 180, 181
(F.L.S.).

Carpenter is known by his chips, A.
1611 : Coryat, *Crudities*, i. 407 (1905),
For, according to the old proverbe the
best carpenters make the fewest chips.
1653 : R. Brome, *Novella*, III. i., The
best carpenters make fewest chips.
1738 : Swift, *Polite Convers.*, Dial. II.,
They say a carpenter's known by his
chips. 1830 : Forby, *Vocab. E. Anglia*,
430, You may know a carpenter by his
chips. *See also* Such carpenter.

Carper can cavil at anything, A.
1732: Fuller, No. 33.

Carrion kite will never make good
hawk, A. 1567 : Painter, *Pal. of
Pleasure*, iii. 68 (Jacobs), It is impossible of a kyte or cormerant to make
a good sparhauk. 1605 : Camden,
Remains, 316 (1870). 1669: *Politeuphuia*, 183. 1732: Fuller, No. 1063.
1820 : Scott, *Monastery*, ch. xix., For
seldom doth a good hawk come out of
a kite's egg.

Carry. 1. *He carrieth all his wardrobe
about him.* 1659 : Howell, 16.

2. *He carries well to whom it weighs
not.* 1640 : Herbert, *Jac. Prudentum.*

3. *To carry an M* [for " Master "]
under one's girdle. c. 1550 : Udall,
Roister Doister, III. iii., Neare [never]
an M by your girdle? 1605 : Chapman,
Eastw. Hoe, IV. ii., You might carry an
M under your girdle to Maister Deputis
worship. 1640 : Shirley, *Arcadia*, I. ii.
1738 : Swift, *Polite Convers.*, Dial. I.
1816 : Scott, *Old Mortality*, ch. xxxix.,
Ye might hae had an M under your belt
for *Mistress* Wilson of Milnwood.

4. *To carry coals.* Before 1529 :
Skelton, in *Works*, ii. 34 (Dyce), Wyll
ye bere no coles? 1575 : Churchyard,
Chippes, 37 (Collier), He carryed coales
that could abide no geast. 1581 : B.
Rich, *Farewell*, 112 (Sh. S.), He had
offended one that would beare no coales.
c. 1602 : Chapman, *May-Day*, I., Above
all things you must carry no coals.

1631 : Mabbe, *Celestina*, 127 (T.T.), He
is chollericke, and I can carrie no coles.
1821 : Scott, *Kenilworth*, ch. xxviii.,
I am no dog in the manger—but I will
not carry coals neither.

5. *To carry one's cup even between two
parties*=To be impartial. 1690 : *New
Dict. Canting Crew*, sig. D4.

6. *To carry one's dish upright*. Before
1680 : Butler, *Remains*, ii. 334 (1759),
An affected man carries himself like
his dish (as the proverb says) very
uprightly. 1725 : Defoe, *Everybody's
Business*, You must carry your dish
very upright, or miss, [the servant]
forsooth, gives you warning.

Carshalton. *See* Sutton.

Cart. 1. *An old cart, well used, may
last out a new one abused*. 1732 : Fuller,
No. 6287.

2. *The best cart may overthrow*. 1546 :
Heywood, *Proverbs*, Pt. I. ch. xi. 1611 :
Cotgrave, s.v. " Chartier." 1670 : Ray,
67. 1732 : Fuller, No. 4410.

3. *To keep cart on wheels*=To be in a
state to carry on business, etc., as usual.
1639 : Clarke, 242. 1662 : Newcome,
Diary, 56 (1849) (O.), I must walke
closer with God or I cannot keep cart
on wheeles. 1828 : Carr, *Craven Dialect*, ii. 251 [explained as above].

4. *To put the cart before the horse*.
[ή άμαξα τὸν βοῦν.—Lucian, *Dial. Mort*,
vi. 2.] 1528 : More, *Works*, p. 154,
col. 1 (1557), Muche like as if we
woulde go make the carte to drawe
the horse. 1542 : Udall, tr. Erasmus'
Apoph., 359 (1877), The tale . . . also
setteth the carte before the horses.
1630 : Taylor (Water-Poet), *Works*,
pagin. 1, 15. 1705 : Ward, *Hudibras
Rediv.*, Pt. II. can. iii., p. 27, Excuse
me, that the Muses force The cart to
stand before the horse. 1893 : R. L. S.,
Catriona, ch. ix.

Case is altered, The; sometimes with
the addition, **quoth Plowden**. (*a*) With
the addition. 1603 : Dekker,*Batch.Banq.*,
in *Works*, i. 235 (Grosart), Then is their
long warre come to an end, and the
case (as Ployden sayth) cleane altered.
c. 1620 : in *Roxb. Ballads*, i. 77 (Hindley), Your case is altered in the law
quoth Ployden. 1662 : Fuller, *Worthies*,

iii. 54 (1840). 1714 : Ozell, *Molière*,
vi. 8. 1809 : Pegge, *Anonym.*, cent. ii.
8. 1841 : Hartshorne, *Salopia Antiqua*
[said to be still in use in Shropshire].
1883 : Burne, *Shropsh. Folk-Lore*, 591.
(*b*) Without the addition. 1594 :
Greene, in *Works*, xiv. 38 (Grosart),
Faith sir, the case is altered ; you told
me it before in an other manner.
c. 1598 : Jonson, *The Case is Altered*
[title]. 1634 : T. Heywood, *Mayden
Head Well Lost*, III. 1714 : Ozell,
Molière, iii. 184. 1824 : Scott, *Redgauntlet*, ch. xii., But when you are
out of your canonicals the case is
altered.

**Cask and an ill custom must be broken,
A.** 1640 : Herbert, *Jac. Prudentum*.

Cask savours of the first fill, The.
[Quo semel est imbuta recens servabit
odorem Testa diu.—Horace, *Epist.*,
II. ii. 69.] *c*. 1230 : in Wright's *Pol.
Songs John to Edw. II.*, 31 (Camden S.)
[the Horatian line borrowed]. 1509 :
Barclay, *Ship of Fools*, i. 47 (1874), But
fyll an erthen pot first with yll lycoure
And euer after it shall smell somwhat
soure. *c*. 1577 : Northbrooke, *Against
Dicing, etc.*, 11 (Sh. S.), The vessel will
conserve the tast Of lycour very long,
With which it was first seasoned.
Before 1615 : B. & F., *Custom of Country*,
I. i., With what the maiden vessel
Is season'd first—you understand the
proverb. 1655 . Howell, *Letters*, bk. iv.,
No. 14, The cask savours still of the
liquor it first took in. 1820 : Colton,
Lacon, Pt. II., No. 203, The new cask
takes its odour from the first wine that
it receives.

Cast of his office, To give one a.
1577 : Grange, *Golden Aphroditis*, sig.
N1, Here Boreas with his swelling
cheekes shewed a caste of his office.
1666 : Torriano, *Piazza Univ.*, 79, The
devil gives him a cast of his office.
1690 : *New Dict. Canting Crew*, sig. H8,
A cast of your office, or a touch of your
employment. 1718 : W. Taverner, *Artful Wife*, V. ii., My chaplain shall give
you a cast of his office presently.
1754 : Berthelson, *Eng.-Danish Dict.*,
s.v. " Cast."

Cast, *verb*. 1. *To be cast at cart's arse*.

1546 : Heywood, *Proverbs*, Pt. I. ch. ix.
1611 : Davies (of Hereford), *Sc. of Folly*,
50, in *Works*, ii. (Grosart).

2. *To cast a sheep's eye. See* **Sheep**
(17).

3. *To cast beyond the moon.* 1546 :
Heywood, *Proverbs*, Pt. I. ch. iv., Feare
may force a man to cast beyonde the
moone. 1579 : Lyly, *Euphues*, 78
(Arber), Pardon me, Euphues, if in
loue I cast beyond the moone. 1607 :
T. Heywood, *Woman Killed with Kindness*, IV. v., I talk of things impossible,
And cast beyond the moon. 1638 :
Ford, *Lady's Trial*, I. ii., He casts
Beyond the moon, and will be greater
yet, In spight of Don. 1847 : Halliwell,
Dict., s.v. " Moon," To cast . . ., to be
very ambitious, to calculate deeply, to
make an extravagant conjecture.

4. *To cast dust. See* **Dust**.

5. *To cast in one's dish. See* **Lay a
thing**.

6. *To cast up accounts*=To vomit.
1607 : Dekker and Webster, *West. Hoe*,
V. i., I would not have 'em cast up
their accounts here, for more than they
mean to be drunk this twelvemonth.
1612 : W. Parkes, *Curtain-drawer of the
World*, 17 (Grosart). 1745 : Franklin,
Drinker's Dict., in *Works*, ii. 22 (Bigelow), He's casting up his accounts.
c. 1791 : Pegge, *Derbicisms*, 93 (E.D.S.).

7. *To cast up old scores.* 1659 :
Howell, 2. 1670 : Ray, 214. 1732 :
Fuller, No. 6145.

8. *To cast water into* (*a*) *the sea*,
(*b*) *the Thames*. (*a*) [His qui contentus
non est, in mare fundat aquas.—Ovid,
Tr., V. vi. 44.] 1509 : Barclay, *Ship of
Fools*, i. 166 (Jamieson), Or in the se
cast water, thynkynge it to augment.
1585 : Sir E. Dyer, in *Writings*, 103
(Grosart, 1872), Vnless the casters of
water into the sea are to be praised for
their charitie. 1600 : F. Thynne, *Embl.
and Epigr.*, 3 (E.E.T.S.), In vaine for
mee to . . . add water to the large sea
of your rare lerning. 1654 : Gayton,
Pleasant Notes Don Q., 127, To doe good
to men unthankfull is to cast water
into the sea. (*b*) 1377 : Langland,
Plowman, B, xv. 332, And went forth
with that water to woke with Themese

[to moisten or dilute therewith the
Thames]. 1611 : Davies (of Hereford),
Sc. of Folly, 45, in *Works*, ii. (Grosart),
To cast water in Thames is superfluous.
1662 : Fuller, *Worthies*, ii. 347 (1840).
1790 : Grose, *Prov. Gloss.*, s.v.
" London."

Castle and **Castles**. 1. *A castle of
comfort*. *c.* 1560 : Becon, *A Castell of
Comfort* [title]. 1599 : Peele, *Sir Clyomon, etc.*, sc. xiii., You have a castle of
comfort brought in that you have me
told. *c.* 1630 : *Dicke of Devonsh.*, I. iii.,
in Bullen, *Old Plays*, ii. 23, I think long
till I be at home in our Castle of comfort.

2. *A castle that speaketh is near a
surrender.* 1580 : Lyly, *Euphues*, 334
(Arber), Castles that come to parlue,
and woemen that delight in courting,
are willing to yeelde. 1660 : Howell,
Parly of Beasts, 66, The female and
fortress which begins to parly is half-
gain'd. 1666 : Torriano, *Piazza Univ.*,
93, A fortress that comes to parley, is
neer a surrender. Cf. **City**.

3. *It is easy to keep a castle that was
never assaulted.* [1591 : Harington, *Orl.
Furioso*, bk. xliii. st. 25, 'Tis easie to
resist where none invade.] 1732 :
Fuller, No. 2924. 1883 : Burne,
Shropsh. Folk-Lore, 588, A castle's
easy kept as is never stormed.

4. *To build castles in Spain.* *c.* 1400 :
Rom. Rose, l. 2573, Thou shalt make
castels than in Spayne, And dreme of
Ioye, al but in vayne. *c.* 1477 : Caxton,
Jason, 25 (E.E.T.S.), He began to make
castellis in Spaygne as louers doo.
1567 : G. Fenton, *Bandello*, ii. 249
(T.T.), He began to sighe and build
castels in Spaine. 1685-6 : Cotton,
Montaigne, bk. iii. ch. iv., Let me think
of building castles in Spain. 1750 :
Smollett, *Gil Blas*, iii. 76, I . . . fell
asleep, in the very act of building
castles in Spain. 1853 : G. W. Curtis,
" Castles in Spain," in *Putnam's Mag.*,
ii. 657.

5. *To build castles in the air.* 1566 :
Painter, *Pal. of Pleasure*, i. 266 (Jacobs),
Alerand . . . was a building of castels
in the ayre. 1595 : Sidney, *Apol. for
Poetrie*, par. 12, As we are wont to say
by them that build castles in the air.

1651 : Randolph, *Hey for Honesty*, I. ii.,
Castles in the air are very impregnable.
1787 : D'Arblay, *Diary*, ii. 424 (1876),
'Tis best to build no castles in the air.
1852 : Dickens, *Bleak House*, ch. xiv.,
Richard . . . began, on no other foun-
dation, to build as many castles in the
air as would man the great wall of China.
Castleford women. *See* quot. 1868 :
Quart. Review, cxxv. 492, The old
rhyme may have been true enough—
" Castleford women must needs be fair,
Because they wash both in Calder and
Aire." 1878 : *Folk-Lore Record*, i. 172
[as in 1868].

Castleton. *See* **Hope, Derbyshire.**

Cat. 1. *A baited cat may grow as
fierce as a lion.* 1620 : Shelton, *Quixote*,
Pt. II. ch. xiv., If a cat shut into a
room, much baited and straitened, turn
to be a lion . . . 1710 : S. Palmer, *Moral
Essays on Proverbs*, 305.

2. *A cat has nine lives.* 1546 : Heywood, *Proverbs*, Pt. II. ch. iv., A woman
hath nyne lyues like a cat. 1592 :
Shakespeare, *Romeo*, III. i., Good king
of cats, nothing but one of your nine
lives. 1605 : Marston, *Dutch Courtezan*,
III. i., Thou hast nine lives like a cat.
1678 : Butler, *Hudibras*, Pt. III. can. ii.
l. 1629, With new reversions of nine
lives Starts up, and like a cat revives.
1709 : Ward, *Acc. of Clubs*, 9 (1756),
Assert the same, in spite of her nine
lives, to be rank poison to a cat. 1862 :
Borrow, *Wild Wales*, ch. vii., Even a
cat, an animal known to have nine
lives, cannot live without food.

3. *A cat may look at a king.* 1546 :
Heywood, *Proverbs*, Pt. II. ch. v., A cat
maie looke on a king, ye know. 1590 :
Greene, in *Works*, viii. 181 (Grosart).
1638 : T. Heywood, *Wise Woman*, II.
1714 : *A Cat may Look upon a King*
[title], in *Somers Tracts*, xiii. 509.
1793 : Wolcot, in *Works*, ii. 475 (1795).
1868 : *Quart. Review*, cxxv. 231, " A cat
may look at a king " is but a modern
way of putting the Greek adage,
" You're nothing sacred." 1893 :
R. L. S., *Catriona*, ch. i.

4. *A cat's walk : a little way and back.*
Cornwall. 1869 : Hazlitt, 5.

5. *A muzzled cat was never good*

mouser. 1605 : Camden, *Remains*, 317
(1870). Cf. No. 49.

6. *All cats are grey in the dark.*
1546 : Heywood, *Proverbs*, Pt. I. ch. v.,
When all candels be out all cats be grey.
1596 : Lodge, *Marg. of America*, 56
(Hunt. Cl.). Before 1634 : Chapman,
Alphonsus, III. i., By night all cats are
grey. 1730 : Lillo, *Silvia*, I. ix., For,
in the night, Sure ev'ry cat is grey.
1880 : R. L. S. and Henley, *Deacon
Brodie*, I. i. ix., The grimy cynical night
that makes all cats grey.

7. *An old cat laps as much milk as a
young.* 1605 : Camden, *Remains*, 318
(1870). 1670 : Ray, 68.

8. *An old cat sports not with her prey.*
1640 : Herbert, *Jac. Prudentum.*

9. *As busy as a cat in a tripe shop.*
1890 : J. D. Robertson, *Gloucester
Gloss.*, 186 (E.D.S.). 1894 : Northall,
Folk Phrases of Four Counties, 7
(E.D.S.).

10. *As nimble as a blind cat in a barn.*
Glos. 1639 : in *Berkeley MSS.*, iii. 30
(1885).

11. *As the cat licks* (or *loves*) *mustard.*
1639 : Clarke, 235, He loves me as the
cat doth mustard. 1659 : Howell, 2, As
the catt licks mustard. 1754 : Berthelson, *Eng.-Danish Dict.*, s.v. " Love " [as
in 1639].

12. *As the cat plays with* (or *watches*) *a
mouse.* 1340 : *Ayenbite*, 179 (E.E.T.S.),
The dyeuel playth ofte . . . ase deth
the cat mid the mous. 1566 : J. Stud-
ley, tr. Seneca's *Agam.*, in Bang's
Material., B. 38, p. 22, With whom (as
the cat with the mouse) it liketh her to
daly. 1579 : Gosson, *Sch. of Abuse*, 25
(Sh. S.), To watch their conceates, as
the catte for the mouse. 1645 : Howell,
Letters, bk. i. § iii. No. 18, He watch'd
her as a cat doth a mouse. 1710 : C.
Shadwell, *Fair Quaker*, II. ii., You play
with him as a cat plays with a mouse.
1821 : Scott, *Kenilworth*, ch. viii., My
hang-dog kinsman watching you as
close as ever cat watched a mouse.
1886 : R. L. S., *Kidnapped*, ch. iv., We
sat at table like a cat and a mouse, each
stealthily observing the other.

13. *Before the cat can lick her ear.*
1670 : Ray, 168. 1732 : Fuller, No. 960.

14. *By biting and scratching cats and dogs come together.* 1546: Heywood, *Proverbs*, Pt. II. ch. i. 1605 : Camden, *Remains*, 320 (1870). 1670: Ray, 68. 1732: Fuller, No. 984, Biting and scratching gets the cat with kitten.

15. *Cat will after kind. c.* 1275: *Prov. of Alfred*, A 296, For ofte museth the kat after hire moder. 1546: Heywood, *Proverbs*, Pt. I. ch. xi., Cat after kynde good mouse hunt. 1583 : Greene, *Mamillia*, in *Works*, ii. 119 (Grosart), Shewing yt the cat wil to kinde. 1601 : Shakespeare, *As You Like It*, III. ii., If the cat will after kind, So be sure will Rosalind. 1668: Shadwell, *Sullen Lovers*, IV. i. 1697: Vanbrugh, *Esop*, III. 1716: Ward, *Female Policy*, 93. 1732 : Fuller, No. 1070.

16. *Cats eat what hussies spare.* 1683 : Meriton, *Yorkshire Ale*, 83–7 (1697).

17. *Cats hide their claws.* 1732: Fuller, No. 1072.

18. *Good liquor will make a cat speak.* 1585–1618 : *Shirburn Ballads*, 93 (1907), Who is it but loues good liquor? 'Twill make a catte speake. 1611 : Shakespeare, *Tempest*, II. ii., Open your mouth ; here is that which will give language to you, cat. 1661 : *Antid. against Melanch.*, 126 (Ebsworth), Old liquor able to make a cat speak, and a wise man dumb. 1720: *Vade Mecum for Maltworms*, Pt. I., p. 35, There . . . is drink will almost make a cat to speak. 1838 : Dickens, *Nickleby*, ch. xii., Talk, miss ! It's enough to make a Tom cat talk French grammar.

19. *He's sure of a cat that hath her skin.* 1611 : Cotgrave, s.v. " Chat."

20. *He lives under the sign of the cat's foot*=He is henpecked. 1678 : Ray, 68. 1880 : Spurgeon, *Ploughman's Pictures*, 87.

21. *He signifies no more than a blind cat in a barn.* 1732 : Fuller, No. 2020.

22. *He stands in great need that borrows the cat-dish.* 1639 : Clarke, 225.

23. *He that will play with cats, must expect to be scratched.* 1710 : S. Palmer, *Moral Essays on Proverbs*, 249.

24. *Honest as the cat when the . . .* (*see* quots.). 1732 : Fuller, No. 2524, . . . meat is upon the hook. 1875 :

A. B. Cheales, *Proverb. Folk-Lore*, 129, . . . milk's away. 1880 : Spurgeon, *Ploughman's Pictures*, 20, . . . meat is out of reach.

25. *How can the cat help it, if the maid be a fool?* 1591 : Florio, *Second Frutes*, 41, Is the catt to blame, if maides be fooles with shame? 1623 : Wodroephe, *Spared Houres*, 243, What faulte makes the cat when the maidseruant is full of folie and carelessnesse ? 1670 : Ray, 67. 1732 : Fuller, No. 5595, When the maid leaves open the door blame not the cat.

26. *I know a cat from a cowl staff.* 1696 : T. Dilke, *Lover's Luck*, III. i.

27. *I will keep no cats that will not catch mice.* Somerset. 1678 : Ray, 350. 1710 : S. Palmer, *Moral Essays on Proverbs*, 358, Keep no more cats than will catch mice. 1732 : Fuller, No. 2638.

28. *It would make a cat laugh.* 1851 : Planché, *Extravag.*, iv. 148 (1879), It would have made a cat laugh, or a dog. 1898 : Weyman, *Shrewsbury*, ch. xxxv., You three all mixed up ! It would make a cat laugh, my lad.

29. *Kiss the black cat, An' 'twill make ye fat; Kiss the white ane, 'Twill make ye lean.* 1878 : Dyer, *Eng. Folk-Lore*, 108.

30. *Let the cat wink, and let the mouse run.* 1522 : *World and the Child*, in Hazlitt, *Old Plays*, i. 265 (1874), Ah, ah, sirs, let the cat wink. Before 1529 : Skelton, *Elynor Runnyng*, l. 306, But drynke, styll drynke, And let the cat wynke. 1546 : Heywood, *Proverbs*, Pt. II. ch. iv., Let the cat winke, and leat the mouse ronne. 1659 : Howell, 7. 1709 : Dykes, *Eng. Proverbs*, 45, And so let the cat be winking.

31. *Like a cat he'll still fall upon his legs.* 1678 : Ray, 282, He's like a cat, fling him which way you will he'll light on's legs. 1732 : Fuller, No. 3220. 1820 : Colton, *Lacon*, Pt. I. No. 348, There are some men who are fortune's favourites, and who, like cats, light for ever upon their legs.

32. *Like a cat in a bonfire, don't know which way to turn.* Cornwall. 1895 : Jos. Thomas, *Randigal Rhymes*, 60.

33. *Like a cat in pattens.* Oxfordsh.

1913: *Folk-Lore*, xxiv. 77, Slipping about like a cat in pattens. 1914: R. L. Gales, *Vanished Country Folk*, 193, " Like a cat in pattens " was said of an awkward person.

34. *Like a cat round hot milk.* 1855: Bohn, 442.

35. *Little by little as the cat ate the flickle.* Before 1500 : in Hill, *Commonplace-Book*, 130 (E.E.T.S.), A litill and a litill, the cat etith vp the bacon flicke. 1546: Heywood, *Proverbs*, Pt. II. ch. vii., Yet littell and littell the cat eateth the flickell. 1897: C. Lee, *Widow Woman*, ch. vii. [with " candle " for " flickle "]. 1898: E. Peacock, in *N. & Q.*, 9th ser., i. 390, " Do it by degrees, as the cat ate the pestle [pig's foot]," is a proverbial saying in these parts [Kirton-in-Lindsey, Lincs].

36. *My cat hath no such ears.* 1659: Howell, 11.

37. *My cat is a good mouse-hunt.* Glos. 1639: in *Berkeley MSS.*, iii. 27 (1885), My catt is a good moushunt. An vsuall speach when wee husbands commend the diligence of our wives . . . hee that somtimes flattereth not his wife cannot alwaies please her.

38. *Never was cat or dog drowned that could see the shore.* c. 1594: Bacon, *Promus*, No. 590, A catt will never drowne if she sees the shore. 1666: Torriano, *Piazza Univ.*, 36, Neither dog nor cat ever drown, so long as they can discern the shore. 1732: Fuller, No. 3532.

39. *No playing with a straw before an old cat.* 1546: Heywood, *Proverbs*, Pt. II. ch. viii. 1611: Davies (of Hereford), *Sc. of Folly*, 47, in *Works*, ii. (Grosart). 1792: Wolcot, in *Works*, ii. 318 (1795), May stun thee with two proverbs all so pat—" What, what, Pitt—' play a jig to an old cat?' " 1817: Scott, *Rob Roy*, ch. xxvi., They were ower auld cats to draw that strae afore them.

40. *None but cats and dogs are allowed to quarrel in my house.* 1732: Fuller, No. 3643.

41. *Send not a cat for lard.* 1640: Herbert, *Jac. Prudentum*.

42. *She paid en like the cat paid the*

owl—*cross the face.* Newlyn, W. Cornwall, 19th cent. (Mr. C. Lee).

43. *That cat is out of kind* [nature] *that sweet milk will not lap.* 1678: Ray, 108.

44. *That that comes of a cat will catch mice.* 1678 : Ray, 109.

45. *The cat and dog may kiss, yet are none the better friends.* 1855: Bohn, 499.

46. *The cat has kittened*=Something has happened. 1883: Burne, *Shropsh. Folk-Lore*, 596.

47. *The cat has kittened in your mouth.* 1618 : Field, *Amends for Ladies*, II. i., *Grace.* Your mother's cat has kittened in your mouth, sure.

48. *The cat hath eaten her count.* 1678 : Ray, 68.

49. *The cat in gloves catches no mice.* 1578 : Florio, *First Fruites*, fo. 30, A cat gloued catcheth no mice. 1623: Wodroephe, *Spared Houres*, 287, A mufeld cat is not meete to take mice. 1681: Rycaut, tr. Gracian's *Critick*, 122, The proverb says, the mousing cat preys not with mittens. 1736: Franklin, *Way to Wealth*, in *Works*, i. 444 (Bigelow). 1869: Spurgeon, *John Ploughman*, ch. iii., Do not preach in gloves, for cats in mittens catch no mice. Cf. No. 5.

50. *The cat invites the mouse to a feast.* 1732 : Fuller, No. 4441.

51. *The cat is hungry when a crust contents her.* 1611 : Cotgrave, s.v. " Chat." 1670 : Ray, 4.

52. *The cat is in the cream-pot.* 1678 : Ray, 233.

53. *The cat knows whose lips she licks.* c. 1210 : in Wright's *Essays on Middle Ages*, i. 149 (1846), Wel wot hure cat whas berd he licket. Before 1529: Skelton, *Garl. of Laurell*, l. 1438, And wele wotith the cat whos berde she likkith. 1670 : Ray, 68. 1732 : Fuller, No. 4442.

54. *The cat sees not the mouse, ever.* 1640 : Herbert, *Jac. Prudentum.* 1670 : Ray, 67. 1732 : Fuller, No. 4443, The cat sees not every mouse.

55. *The cat, the rat, and Lovel the dog, Rule all England under the hog.* 1542 : Fabyan, *Chron.*, fo. 468, The catte, the ratte, and louel our dogge, Ruleth all

Englande vnder a hogge. The whyche
was mente that Catysby, Ratclyffe, and
the lorde Louell ruled the lande vnder
the kynge [Richard III.], whyche bare
the whyte bore for his conysaunce.
1669: *New Help to Discourse*, 201.
1814: Byron, *Letters, etc.*, iii. 29 *n.*
(Prothero). 1816: Scott, *Antiquary*,
ch. ii., His name, the young gentleman
said, was Lovel. " What ! the cat, the
rat, and Lovel our dog? Was he
descended   from   King   Richard's
favourite? "

56. *The cat winked when her eye was*
(or *both her eyes were*) *out.* 1528: More,
in *Works*, p. 241, col. 1 (1557), It was
alway that yͤ cat winked whan her eye
was oute. *c.* 1550: *Jacke Jugeler*, 80
(Grosart), The prouerbe olde That the
catte winkid when here eye was out.
1670: Ray, 67, . . . both her eyes.
1738: Swift, *Polite Convers.*, Dial. I., No
wonder the cat wink'd, when both her
eyes were out.

57. *The cat would eat fish but would
not wet her feet. c.* 1250: MS., Trin.
Coll., Camb., quoted in Farmer's ed. of
Heywood's *Proverbs*, 340 (1906), Cat
lufat visch, ac he nele his feth wete.
c. 1384: Chaucer, *H. Fame*, bk. iii.
ll. 693-5. *c.* 1390: Gower, *Conf.
Amantis*, iv. 1108, And as a cat wolde
ete fisshes Withoute wetinge of his cles
[claws]. 1583: Melbancke, *Philotinus*,
sig. O1, The cat would licke milke, but
she will not wette her feete. 1606:
Shakespeare, *Macbeth*, I. vii., Letting
" I dare not " wait upon " I would,"
Like the poor cat i' the adage. 1732:
Fuller, No. 6130, Fain would the cat
fish eat, But she's loth her feet to wet.
1928: *Sphere*, 7 Jan., p. 36.

58. *The liquorish cat gets many a rap.*
1611: Cotgrave, s.v. " Chat," The
lickorous cat hath many a rap. 1670:
Ray, 4. 1732: Fuller, No. 6228.

59. *The more you rub a cat on the
rump, the higher she sets up her tail.*
1678: Ray, 109.

60. *The scalded cat fears cold water.*
1611: Cotgrave, s.v. " Chat." 1694:
D'Urfey, *Quixote*, Pt. I. Act V. sc. ii.
1709: O. Dykes, *Eng. Proverbs*, 147-8.

61. *There are more ways of killing*
a cat than choking her with cream.
1855: Kingsley, *West. Ho!*, ch. xx.
1926: *Devonsh. Assoc. Trans.*, lvii. 152,
There's more ways o' killin' a cat 'n
chuckin' o' en wi' craim.

62. *They want to know the ins and outs
of the cat's tale.* Said of people who
desire full particulars of anything.
1919: *Devonsh. Assoc. Trans.*, li. 77.

63. *Though the cat winks she is not
blind.* 1576: *Parad. of Dainty Devices*,
in *Brit. Bibliog.*, iii. 59 (1812), I am not
blinde although I winke. 1609: Rowlands, *Whole Crew of Kind Gossips*, 20
(Hunt. Cl.), The cat ofte winkes, and
yet she is not blinde.

64. *To agree like cat and dog.* 1566:
Drant, *Horace: Satires*, sig. D7, Lyke
dogge and catte these two did then
agree. 1579: Gosson, *Sch. of Abuse*,
27 (Arber), He . . . shall see them
agree like dogges and cattes. 1629: in
Pepysian Garland, 301 (Rollins, 1922),
Like cat and dog they still agree'd;
Each small offence did anger breed.
1727: Gay, *Fables*, 1st ser., No. 12,
l. 33, If they like cat and dog agree . . .
1878: *Folk-Lore Record*, i. 13, You and
your wife will lead a cat-and-dog life.

65. *To bell the cat.* 1377: Langland,
Plowman, B, Prol., ll. 165-81 [the fable
of " belling the cat " related]. 1388:
in Wright, *Pol. Poems*, i. 274, (Rolls Ser.,
1859), The cattys nec to bylle [bell].
Before 1529: Skelton, *Col. Clout*, l. 163,
They are . . . loth to hang the bell
Aboute the cattes necke, For drede to
haue a checke. 1623: Taylor (Water-
Poet), in *Works*, pagin. 2, p. 28 (1630),
Not one will aduenture to hang the bell
about the cats necke. 1712: Motteux,
Quixote, Pt. II. ch. 43, Who shall hang
the bell about the cat's neck? 1830:
Scott, *Journal*, 17 July, A fine manly
fellow, who has belled the cat with
fortune, and held her at bay as a man
of mould may.

66. *To go like a cat on a hot backstone.*
1683: Meriton, *Yorkshire Ale*, 83-7
(1697), As nimble as a cat on a haite
back-stane. 1737: Ray, 222. 1892:
S. Hewett, *Peasant Speech of Devon*,
13, Her 'opp'th like a cat 'pon 'ot
bricks.

67. *To keep the cat from the tongs*=To stay idly at home. 1598 : *Servingmans Comfort*, in *Inedited Tracts*, 161 (Hazlitt, 1868), Because his sonne shalbe sure to keep the catte from the tonges at home, when other his neighbours children shall trudge into Fraunce, Flaunders, and other nations.

68. *To let the cat out of the bag.* 1760 : *Lond. Mag.*, xxix. 224 (O.), We could have wished that the author . . . had not let the cat out of the bag. 1849 : Brontë, *Shirley*, ch. xxxvii., This last epithet I choose to suppress, because it would let the cat out of the bag. 1922 : *Evening Standard*, 1 July, p. 5, col. 1, The man himself lets the embarrassed cat out of the bag when the spirit moves him.

69. *To turn cat in pan.* Before 1384 : Wiclif, *Works*, iii. 332 (1871), Many men of lawe . . . bi here suteltes turnen the cat in the panne. 1543 : Becon, *Against Swearing*, Preface, God saith, " Cry, cease not " ; but they turn cat in the pan, and say " Cease, cry not." 1625 : Bacon, *Essays.* " Of Cunning," There is a cunning, which we in England call, The turning of the cat in the pan ; which is, when that which a man sayes to another, he laies it, as if another had said 't to him. 1688 : Crowne, *City Polit.*, II., You are a villain, have turn'd cat in pan, and are a Tory. 1740 : North, *Examen*, 55, Can his lordship's high flying entrance, huffing speeches, and then turning cat in the pan, be unknown or ever forgot ? 1816 : Scott, *Old Mortality*, ch. xxxv., O, this precious Basil will turn cat in pan with any man !

70. *When the cat's away the mice will play.* 1578 : Florio, *First Fruites*, fo. 33, When the cat is abroade the mise play. 1603 : Dekker, *Batch. Banq.*, in *Works*, i. 169 (Grosart). 1732 : Fuller, No. 5572, When the cat's gone, the mice grow sawcy. 1852 : Dickens, *Bleak House*, ch. liv., So it is, and such is life. The cat's away, and the mice they play.

71. *When the cat winketh little wots the mouse what the cat thinketh.* 1678 : Ray, 109. 1732 : Fuller, No. 6453.

72. *Whenever the cat of the house is*

black, *The lasses of lovers will have no lack.* 1878 : Dyer, *Eng. Folk-Lore*, 108.

73. *Which way the cat jumps.* 1826 : Scott, *Journal*, 7 Oct., I would like to be there, were it but to see how the cat jumps. 1907 : De Morgan, *Alice-for-Short*, ch. xxvii., " Easy enough to see which way the cat would jump," or, " Are you surprised ? I'm not."

74. *You can have no more of a cat than her skin.* 1570 : in H. G. Wright's *Arthur Hall of Grantham*, 88 (1919). 1637 : Heywood, *Royal King*, II., Thou canst have no more of the cat but his skinne. 1738 : Swift, *Polite Convers.*, Dial. II. 1894 : Northall, *Folk Phrases*, 32 (E.D.S.), What's a cat but its skin ? 1901 : F. E. Taylor, *Lancs Sayings*, 11, Yo' conno ma'e mooar o' th' cat nor th' skin.

75. *You shall have what the cat left in the malt-heap.* 1639 : Clarke, 71. *c.* 1660 : in Marchant, *Praise of Ale*, 138 (1888), The brewer at last made him to halt ; And gave them what the cat left in the malt. 1670 : Ray, 168.

See also Care ; Chestnuts ; Cry (1) ; February (18) ; Full of sin ; Good wife ; Kid ; Lame ; Long and slender ; Melancholy ; Rat (4) and (5) ; Two cats ; Two women.

Catch, *verb.* 1. *Catch that catch can.* *c.* 1390 : Gower, *Conf. Amantis*, bk. vii. l. 4422, Bot cacche who that cacche myghte. Before 1529 : Skelton, *Magnyfycence*, l. 1773, They catche that catch may, kepe and holde fast. 1614 : Jonson, *Bart. Fair*, II., Let him catch this that catch can. 1652 : J. Hilton, *Catch that Catch can* [title]. 1761 : O'Hara, *Midas*, II. viii., There's catch as catch can, hit or miss, luck is all. 1855 : Kingsley, *West. Ho!*, ch. v., Each shall slay his man, catch who catch can. 1919 : A. A. Milne, *Camb. Triangle*, in *Sec. Plays*, 153 (1921), Swords, pistols, fists, catch-as-catch-can—what would you like ?

2. *He that can catch and hold, he is the man of gold.* 1654 : Gayton, *Pleasant Notes Don Q.*, 243.

3. *To catch a Tartar.* 1679 : A. Behn, *Feign'd Courtezans*, IV. ii., Ha—what the devil have I caught—a

Tartar? 1708: Cibber, *Lady's Last Stake*, II. i., I'm sure catching a husband is catching a Tartar. 1841: Dickens, *Barn. Rudge*, ch. lxxx., A poor goodnatur'd mean-spirited creetur, as went out fishing for a wife one day, and caught a Tartar.

4. *To catch cold by lying in bed barefoot.* Said of one who is extremely careful of himself. 1828: Carr, *Craven Dialect*, i. 82.

Cater-cousins, They are not. 1519: Horman, *Vulgaria*, fo. 223, They be cater cosyns and almoste neuer a sonder. *c.* 1580: Lodge, *Defence of Plays, etc.*, 29 (Sh. S.), We should find you cater-cosens with a (but hush) you know my meaning. 1670: Ray, 168. 1759: Smollett, in Hill's *Boswell*, i. 349, He was humble enough to desire my assistance on this occasion, though he and I were never cater-cousins. 1866: Brogden, *Lincs Words*, 37, We had a chip [tiff], but are now cater-cousins.

Catty put down thy feet. 1917: Bridge, *Cheshire Proverbs*, 35, . . . used to denote surprise or annoyance at an interruption.

Cavil will enter in at any hole, and if it find none it will make one. 1633: Draxe, 22.

Ceremonious friends are so, as far as a compliment will go. 1732: Fuller, No. 1078.

Certain as death. *See* **Sure as death.**

Certainty. *He that leaves certainty and sticks to chance, when fools pipe he may dance.* 1546: Heywood, *Proverbs*, Pt. II. ch. xi., Who that leaveth surety and leaneth vnto chance, When fools pipe, by authority he may dance. 1633: Draxe, 22 [as in 1546]. 1670: Ray, 68. 1732: Fuller, No. 6439.

Chains of gold are stronger than chains of iron. 1732: Fuller, No. 1079.

Chairs at home, He has none of his, = He is wrong (*or* weak) in his head. The 1582 passage is a curious anticipation of the Lancashire saying. 1582: R. Robinson, tr. *Assertion of Arthur*, 89 (E.E.T.S.), Whether with like eloquence, grace, and good successe I haue done this, let that by the iudgement of honest and learned persons bee determined. For I knowe very well, *How slender furniture I have at home.* 1864: Ormerod, *Felley fro Rachde*, ch. ii. (W.), Foke met get it hinto ther yeds us aw'd noane sure cheers owhomme. 1865: "Lancs Proverbs," in *N. & Q.*, 3rd ser., viii. 494.

Chalk and Cheese. 1. *I talk of chalk and you of cheese.* 1631: Mabbe, *Celestina*, 212 (T.T.), You talke of chalke, and we of cheese. 1681: W. Robertson, *Phraseol. Generalis*, 752. 1721: Bailey, *Eng. Dict.*, s.v. "Chalk."

2. *To take chalk for cheese;* or, *To know one from* (or *compare one with*) *the other. c.* 1390: Gower, *Conf. Amantis*, ii. 2346, And thus fulofte chalk for chese He changeth with ful litel cost. *c.* 1550: *John Bon and Mast Person*, in Hazlitt, *Early Pop. Poetry*, iv. 15 (1866), For thoughe I have no learning, yet I know chese from chalke. 1586: Pettie, tr. Guazzo's *Civil Convers.*, fo. 144, They know not chaffe from corne, or chalke from cheese. *c.* 1615: R. C., *Times Whistle*, 28 (E.E.T.S.), A verier foole Dame Nature never bred, That scarce knowes chalke from cheese, or blew from red. 1849: Brontë, *Shirley*, ch. v., "You think yourself a clever fellow, I know, Scott." "Ay! I'm fairish; I can tell cheese fro' chalk." 1926: Phillpotts, *Marylebone Miser*, ch. vi., Though we're as different as chalk from cheese.

Chalked land makes a rich father but a poor son. 1677: Plot, *Nat. Hist. Oxfordsh.*, 243.

Chalvington. *See* **Beddingham.**

Chamber of sickness. *See* **Sickness.**

Chance is a dicer. 1732: Fuller, No. 1080.

Chance the ducks, To. 1894: Northall, *Folk Phrases*, 12 (E.D.S.), To do a thing and "chance the ducks" is to do it, come what may. 1917: Bridge, *Cheshire Proverbs*, 149, We mun chance the ducks.

Chancery. *See* **Hell** (2).

Chances in an hour. *See* **Happeth.**

Chanctonbury. *See* quot. 1894: A. J. C. Hare, *Sussex*, 161, The proverb "Old Mother Goring's got her cap on,

We shall soon have wet "—refers to Chanctonbury.

Change, *subs.* 1. *Change is no robbery.* *See* **Fair,** *adj.* (19).

2. *Change of fortune is the lot of life.* 1855 : Bohn, 336.

3. *Change of pasture makes fat calves.* 1546 : Heywood, Pt. II. ch. iv. 1575 : Gascoigne, *Glasse of Govt.,* IV. iii. 1696 : D'Urfey, *Quixote,* Pt. III. Act IV. sc. i. 1732 : Fuller, No. 1081. 1846 : Denham, *Proverbs,* 6 (Percy S.).

4. *Change of weather is the discourse of fools.* 1659 : Howell, *Proverbs : Span.- Eng.,* 2. 1670 : Ray, 28. 1732 : Fuller, No. 1082. 1846 : Denham, *Proverbs,* 3 (Percy S.).

5. *Change of women makes bald knaves.* 1605 : Camden, *Remains,* 320 (1870). 1685 : Meriton, *Yorkshire Ale,* 50, But change of women macks lean knaves Ise flaid.

6. *Change of work is as good as touch-pipe* [short interval of rest], *A.* Cornwall. 1895 : Jos. Thomas, *Randigal Rhymes,* 59.

7. *Changes never answer tho end.* 1740 : North, *Examen,* 352, Short sentences, commonly called proverbs . . . such as, *Honesty is the best policy* . . . *Changes never answer the end.*

Change, *verb.* 1. *I am loath to change my mill.* Somerset. 1678 : Ray, 349.

2. *To change copy.* See **Copy** (2).

3. *To change the name and not the letter, Is a change for the worse, and not for the better.* 1862 : Chambers, *Book of Days,* i. 723. 1878 : Dyer, *Eng. Folk-Lore,* 200. 1901 : F. E. Taylor, *Lancs Sayings,* 41, Iv yo' choange yore name beawt choangin' th' letter, youe choange for th' wo'se i'stid o' for th' better.

4. *See* quot. 1853 : *N. & Q.,* 1st ser., vii. 156, I have frequently in youth heard the proverb, "You may change *Norman* for a worsei (worse) horse."

Changeable as a weather-cock. 1548 : Hall, *Chron.,* 38 (1809), Which be more variable then the wethercocke. 1615 : R. Tofte, tr. *Blazon of Iealousy,* 81, Since thou as weather-cocke dost change.

Changeful as the moon. Before 1599 : Spenser, *Mutabilitie,* can. ii. st. 50, So

that as changefull as the moone men use to say.

Changing [exchanging] **of words is the lighting of hearts.** 1855 : Bohn, 336.

Chap as married Hannah, The. 1900 : *N. & Q.,* 9th ser., vi. 346, " The chap as married Hannah " . . . is a very common phrase in South Notts. "That's the chap as married Hannah " means that is the person or thing I am seeking or that I need. 1900 : Ibid., 434, This common here [Worksop], and in many other localities. It is a women's saying, though men occasionally use it. When something has been successfully done, comes out, " There ! That's the chap as married Hannah."

Char is charred, This (or That) = That business (*or* job) is done. *c.* 1400 : *Seven Sages,* 88 (Percy S.), " Sire," scho sayed, " this char hys heved." 1593 : Peele, *Edward I.,* sc. vi., Why, so, this chare is chared. 1670 : Ray, 168, That char is char'd (as the good wife said when she had hang'd her husband). 1917 : Bridge, *Cheshire Proverbs,* 111, " That char's charred," as the boy said when he'd killed his father.

Chare-folks are never paid enough. 1678 : Ray, 112 [without " enough "]. 1732 : Fuller, No. 1083.

Charing, Smoky. 1735 : Pegge, *Kent. Proverbs,* in E.D.S., No. 12, 69.

Charing-Cross, *See* **Old** (D), (5).

Charitable. 1. *He is not charitable that will not be so privately.* 1732 : Fuller, No. 1932.

2. *The charitable gives out at door, and God puts in at the window.* 1678 : Ray, 353.

Charity and Pride do both feed the poor. 1669 : *Politeuphuia,* 243. 1732 : Fuller, No. 1084, Charity and Pride have different aims, yet both feed the poor.

Charity begins at home. [ἀπωτέρω ἢ γόνυ κνάμα. — Theocritus, xvi. 18. Proximus sum egomet mihi.—Terence, *Andr.,* IV. i. 12.] *c.* 1380 : Wiclif, in *Eng. Works,* 76 (E.E.T.S.), Whanne charite schuld bigyne at hem-self. 1509 : Barclay, *Ship of Fools,* i. 277 (1874), For perfyte loue and also charite Begynneth with hym selfe for

to be charitable. 1572: T. Wilson,
Disc. upon Usury, 235 (1925), Charity
beginneth first at it selfe. 1641: R.
Brome, *Joviall Crew*, II., Good sister
Meriel, Charity begins at home. 1763:
Murphy, *Citizen*, I. ii. 1850: Dickens,
Chuzzlewit, ch. xxvii., But charity
begins at home, and justice begins
next door.

Charterhouse, Sister of the. *See* quot.
1528: Tyndale, *Obed. of Christ. Man*,
305 (P.S.), Of her that answereth her
husband six words for one, we say,
" She is a sister of the Charterhouse " :
as who should say, " She thinketh that
she is not bound to keep silence; their
silence shall be a satisfaction for her."

Chaste. 1. *Although thou be not
chaste, yet be chary.* 1576: Pettie,
Petite Pallace, i. 32 (Gollancz), Do not
some men say that women always live
chastely enough, so that they live
charily enough? 1612: *Cornucopiæ*, 25
(Grosart). 1630: *Tinker of Turvey*, 36
(Halliwell), I learned this old saying in
Latin, *Caute, si non caste*. Live charily,
if not chastely.

2. *She is chaste who was never asked
the question.* 1695: Congreve, *Love for
Love*, III. iii.

**Chastiseth one, amendeth many, He
that.** 1633: Draxe, 32. 1670: Ray, 4.
1732: Fuller, No. 2065.

**Chatting to chiding is not worth a
chuet.** 1546: Heywood, *Proverbs*, Pt. II.
ch. v.

Chawbent. *See* Cheshire (8).

Cheap. 1. *It is as cheap sitting as
standing.* 1666: Torriano, *Piazza
Univ.*, 277, The English say, It is as
cheap sitting as standing, my masters.
1738: Swift, *Polite Convers.*, Dial. I.
1776: O'Keeffe, *Tony Lumpkin in
Town*, I. iii. 1854: Surtees, *Handley
Cross*, ch. lxiv. 1901: F. E. Taylor,
Lancs Sayings, 18.

2. *It is cheap enough to say, God help
you.* 1732: Fuller,. No. 2922.

Cheapside, He got it by way of = for
less than its value. 1790: Grose, *Prov.
Gloss.*, s.v. "London."

Cheat, *verb.* 1. *Cheat and the cheese
will show.* 1917: Bridge, *Cheshire Proverbs*, 35.

2. *Cheat me in the price but not in the
goods.* 1732: Fuller, No. 1090.

3. *He that cheateth in small things is
a fool; but in great things is a rogue.*
Ibid., No. 2066.

4. *He that will cheat at play, Will cheat
you any way.* Ibid., No. 6302.

Cheek by jowl. *c.* 1300: R. Brunne,
tr. Langtoft's *Chron.*, i. 223 (Hearne),
Vmwhile cheke bi cheke. *c.* 1534:
Berners, *Huon*, ch. lv., p. 189 (E.E.T.S.),
Rydynge cheke by cheke by kynge
yuoryn. 1599: *Sir Clyomon, etc.*, sig.
F2, She went euen cheke by ioule With
our head controms wife. 1682: Dryden, Prol. to Southerne's *Loyal Brother*,
The devil . . . Sits cheek by jowl, in
black, to chear his heart : Like thief and
parson in a Tyburn cart. 1709: Ward,
Clubs, 252 (1756), Those two sat
cheek-by-jole. 1822: Byron, *Vis. of
Judg.*, st. 20. 1851: FitzGerald,
Euphranor, 68 (1855), Victor and
vanquisht having to settle down cheek
by jowl again. 1922: Weyman, *Ovington's Bank*, ch. xxiii.

Cheer up. *See* God is where he was.

Cheerful look makes a dish a feast, A.
1640: Herbert, *Jac. Prudentum*.

Cheese. 1. *After cheese comes nothing.*
1639: Clarke, 136. 1655: Fuller, *Church
Hist.*, bk. vi. § v. (ii. 20), As after cheese,
nothing to be expected. 1700: Ward,
London Spy, 5 (1924). 1732: Fuller,
No. 769.

2. *Cheese and money should always
sleep together one night.* 1917: Bridge,
Cheshire Proverbs, 35 [said of old when
payment was demanded before de-
livery].

3. *Cheese, it is a peevish elf, it digests
all things but itself.* 1584: Lyly, *Sapho
and Phao*, III. ii., Cheese . . . digesteth
all things except. itselfe. 1630: T.
Adams, *Works*, 170, As cheese to digest
all the rest, yet it selfe neuer digested.
1678: Ray, 40. 1738: Swift, *Polite
Convers.*, Dial. II., They say, cheese
digests everything but itself. 1846–59:
Denham Tracts, ii. 215 (F.L.S.), The
moral taught was, " Cheese digests
everything but itself."

4. *Cheese of three halfpence a pound
won't choke her.* 1696: D'Urfey,

Quixote, Pt. III. Act III. sc. i., The
jade simpers as if butter would not
melt in her mouth; but cheese of three
half pence a pound won't choak her,
as the old saying is.

5. *If you will have a good cheese, and
have'n old, You must turn'n seven times
before he is cold.* Somerset. 1678 : Ray,
352. *c.* 1685 : Aubrey, *Nat. Hist.
Wilts*, 105 (1847). 1732 : Fuller, No.
6477.

6. *You can't hang soft cheese on a
hook.* 1852 : FitzGerald, *Polonius*, 39
(1903).

See also Bread (2), (5), and (6) ; Chalk ;
Cheat (1) ; Eat (37) ; Green (11) ; King
(17) ; Suffolk cheese ; and Toasted cheese.

Chelsea. *See* Dead (6) ; and Safe as
Chelsea.

**Chepstow born and Chepstow bred,
Strong in the arm and weak in the head.**
Mon. 1905 : *Folk-Lore*, xvi. 67.

Cherry and Cherries. 1. *A cherry
year A merry year.* 1678 : Ray, 52.
1732 : Fuller, No. 6139. 1893 : Inwards,
Weather Lore, 5.

2. *Eat not cherries with the great.*
c. 1530, *Dialogues of Creatures*, xx., As it
is sayde in a commune prouerbe. I
counsell not seruauntis to ete churyes
with ther bettyrs. Fer they wyl haue
the rype and leue them the harde.
1611 : Cotgrave, s.v. " Manger," Mean
men are not to eat cherries . . . with
great lords; least the stones of the best
flie faster at their eyes then . . . the
worst into their mouths. 1662 : Fuller,
Worthies, ii. 112 (1840), As for the
outlandish proverb, " He that eateth
cherries with noblemen, shall have his
eyes spurted out with the stones," it
fixeth no fault in the fruit. 1732 :
Fuller, No. 5026 [as in 1662]. 1854 :
Doran, *Table Traits*, 209, There is a
German proverb which says that " it
is unadvisable to eat cherries with
potentates."

3. *If they blow in April, You'll have
your fill ; But if in May, They'll all go
away.* 1735 : Pegge, *Kent. Proverbs*, in
E.D.S., No. 12, p. 75.

4. *One cherry-tree sufficeth not two
jays.* 1576 : Lambarde, *Peramb. of
Kent*, 269 (1826).

5. *What is a tree of cherries worth to
four in a company?* 1568 : in *Loseley
MSS.*, 208 (Kempe).

See also Disgraces ; Pea (1) ; Red ;
Two bites ; Woman (6).

Cherry's Boose. *See* quots. *c.* 1791 :
Pegge, *Derbicisms*, 90 (E.D.S.), When a
man weds a second wife, older and
perhaps not so handsome as the first,
they say, " he has put Browney into
Cherry's boose" [stall]. 1836 : Wilbraham, *Cheshire Gloss.*, 2nd ed., 20,
Any person who is got into a comfortable situation is said to be " put into
Cherry's boose." 1917 : Bridge, *Cheshire
Proverbs*, 67.

Cheshire. 1. *By waif, soc, and theam,
You may know Cheshire men.* 1917 :
Bridge, *Cheshire Proverbs*, 33, . . .
Powerful in their legal rights and
tenacious of them.

2. *Cheshire bred, beef down to th'
heels.* Said of any very stout person.
1886 : R. Holland, *Cheshire Gloss.*, 447
(E.D.S.). 1917 : Bridge, *Cheshire Proverbs*, 36.

3. *Cheshire born and Cheshire bred,
Strong i' th' arm and weak i' th' head;* or,
All strong i' th' arm and thick i' th' yed.
1917 : Bridge, *Cheshire Proverbs*, 36.

4. *Cheshire chief of men.* 1608 : in
Harington, *Nugæ Antiquæ*, ii. 276
(1804), He was translated to Chester,
the chiefe city of that shire, that some
call chiefe of men. 1612 : Drayton,
Polyol., xi. l. 8, For which, our proverb
calls her, Cheshire chief of men. 1644 :
Taylor (Water-Poet), *Crop-eare Curried*, 10, in *Works*, 2nd coll. (Spens. S.),
The Cheshire men . . . tendred themselves as a guard for the person of King
Richard the Second, in a time of
rebellion, for which they are honoured
ever since with the proverbe of *Cheshire
chiefs of men.* 1790 : Grose, *Prov. Gloss.*,
s.v. " Cheshire." 1917 : Bridge, *Cheshire
Proverbs*, 36.

5. *Cheshire for choice of lads.* 1895 :
C. F. Lawrence, *Hist. Middlewich*, 50,
" Cheshire for choice of lads." Old
Cheshire proverb.

6. *Cheshire for men, Berkshire for
dogs, Bedfordshire for naked flesh, And
Lincolnshire for bogs.* *c.* 1809, in

N. & Q., 9th ser., xi. 266. 1917:
Bridge, *Cheshire Proverbs*, 37.

7. *In Cheshire* . . . (*see* quots.).
1790: Grose, *Prov. Gloss.*, s.v.
"Cheshire," In Cheshire there are
Lees as plenty as fleas, and as many
Davenports as dogs-tails. 1917 : Bridge,
Cheshire Proverbs, 18, As many Leighs
as fleas, Massies as asses, Crewes as
crows, and Davenports as dogs' tails.

8. *Neither in Cheshire nor Chawbent.*
= Neither in Kent nor Christendom.
Chawbent is a town in Lancashire.
1678 : Ray, 301. 1917 : Bridge, *Cheshire
Proverbs*, 96.

9. *To grin like a Cheshire cat.* 1792 :
Wolcot, in *Works*, ii. 424 (1795), Yet, if
successful, thou wilt be ador'd—Lo,
like a Cheshire cat our Court will grin !
1806 : A. Ferguson, in Scott's *Fam.
Letters*, i. 66 (1894), Ever since the
Polts have grinned at me like so many
Cheshire cats. 1855 : Thackeray, *New-
comes*, ch. xxiv. 1917 : Bridge, *Cheshire
Proverbs*, 135.

Chester. 1. *The sweet Rood of Chester.*
1575 : Gascoigne, *Glasse of Govt.*, They
are as much a kynne to the Markgrave
as Robyn Fletcher and the Sweet Roode
of Chester. 1917 : Bridge, *Cheshire
Proverbs*, 120.

2. *There is more than one yew-bow in
Chester.* 1662 : Fuller, *Worthies*, iii.
537 (1840). 1790 : Grose, *Prov. Gloss.*,
s.v. "Flintshire." 1917 : Bridge, 118.

3. *To kill the Mayor of Chester, on
Cevn Cerwyni.* 1917 : Bridge, 138.

4. *Up before the dogs of Chester.*
1917 : Ibid., 46 [N. Wales saying].

See also **Bare as the Bishop**; **Easter**
(4) ; and **West Chester.**

**Chesterfield steeple, All on one side,
like.** Derby. 1889 : *Folk-Lore Journal*,
vii. 293.

Chestnuts. *To take the chestnuts out
of the fire with the cat's paw.* The story
of the ape using the whelp's foot to get
chestnuts out of the fire, is told in 1586 :
G. Whitney, *Emblems*, 58. 1664 : J.
Wilson, *The Cheats*, V. iv., Some few
that . . . make use of us, as the
monkey did of the cat's paw, to scrape
the nuts out of the fire. 1753 :
Richardson, *Grandison*, iii. 31 (1883),

He makes her . . . become herself the
cat's paw to help him to the ready
roasted chesnuts. 1855 : Kingsley,
West. Ho!, ch. ix., Ready to make a
cat's-paw of him or any man, if there
be a chestnut in the fire.

Chet. *See* **May** (19).

Chevin. *See* quot. 1678 : Ray, 52,
Said the chevin to the trout, My head's
worth all thy bouk.

Cheviot. *See* quot. 1846–59 : *Denham Tracts*, i. 317 (F.L.S.), When
Cheeyut [Cheviot] ye see put on his
cap, Of rain yelle have a wee bit drap.
[Variants are given.]

Chew the cud, To. 1382 : Wiclif,
Hosea, vii. 14 (O.), Thei chewiden cud
vpon whete, and wyne, and departiden
fro me. 1596 : Spenser, *F. Q.*, bk. v.
can. vi. st. 19, Chawing the cud of
griefe and inward paine. *c.* 1617 :
B. & F., *Queen of Corinth*, IV. i.,
Revenge is now the cud That I do
chew. 1665 : R. Howard, *Surprisal*, I.,
How he mumbles to himself ! sure he
does chew the cud of some set speech.
1774 : in *Garrick Corresp.*, ii. 33 (1832),
People are for ever chewing the cud, and
ruminating on the unsuccessful passages
of their lives. 1827 : Southey, *Letter
to C. Bowles*, 10 July, Upon this plain
statement he is now chewing the cud.

Chichester. 1. *A Chichester lobster,
a Selsey cockle, an Arundel mullet, a
Pulborough eel, an Amberley trout, a Rye
herring, a Bourne wheat-ear.* 1610 :
P. Holland, tr. Camden's *Britannia*,
308, Selsey . . . is most famous for
good cockles, and full lobsters. 1653 :
Walton, *Angler*, Pt. I. ch. viii., Just so
doth Sussex boast of four sorts of fish ;
namely an Arundel mullet, a Chichester
lobster, a Shelsey cockle, and an
Amerley trout. 1790 : Grose, *Prov.
Gloss.*, s.v. "Sussex."

2. *If Chichester church steeple fall, In
England there's no king at all.* 1861 :
Lower, in *Sussex Arch. Coll.*, xiii. 233.

Chickens. 1. *Chickens feed capons.*
1678 : Ray, 111.

2. *The chickens are the country's, but
the city eats them.* 1640 : Herbert, *Jac.
Prudentum.* 1670 : Ray, 4. 1732 :
Fuller, No. 4447.

3. *To reckon one's chickens before they are hatched.* [ἀεὶ γεωργὸς εἰς νέωτα πλούσιος.— Philemon, 4 (Mein., 29).] 1577 : *Misogonus*, IV. i., My chickings are not hatcht ; I nil to counte of him as yet. 1583 : Melbancke, *Philotinus*, sig. G2, Why doe we reckon our chickens before they be hatcht. 1674 : J. Howard, *Eng. Mounsieur*, III. iii., Take heed we don't reckon our chicken before they are hatcht. 1725 : Bailey, tr. Erasmus' *Colloq.*, 39, You are a little too hasty ; you reckon your chickens before they are hatch'd. 1829 : Scott, *Journal*, 20 May, But we must not reckon our chickens before they are hatched, though they are chipping the shell now.

See also **Capon** (1) ; **Children** (1) ; **Fox** (31) ; and **July** (7).

Chiddingly. *See* **Hellingly.**

Child. 1. *A child may have too much of his mother's blessing.* 1639 : Clarke, 161 [with " man " for " child "]. 1659 : Howell, 11 (9). 1853 : Trench, *Proverbs*, 86 (1905).

2. *A child . . . (see* quot.). 1886 : Elworthy, *West Som. Word-Book*, 290 (E.D.S.), A very common proverb is : A cheel that can tell [talk] avore he can go [walk], 'll sure t' ha nort but zorrow and wo.

3. *A child's birds and a boy's wife are well used. c.* 1430 : Lydgate, *Churl and Bird*, st. 52, A childes birde and a knaues wyff Haue ofte sithe grete sorrwe and meschaunce. Before 1529 : Skelton, *Garl. of Laurell*, l. 1452, But who may haue a more vngracyous lyfe Than a chyldes birde and a knaues wyfe ? 1678 : Ray, 351. 1732 : Fuller, No. 37.

4. *" Child my dear," says Mrs. Chapman.* 1864 : " Cornish Proverbs," in *N. & Q.*, 3rd ser., vi. 6.

5. *Child's pig and daddy's bacon.* 1678 : Ray, 111, Childs pig, but fathers bacon. 1732 : Fuller, No. 1101, Child's pig, but father's hog. 1883 : Burne, *Shropsh. Folk-Lore*, 589, Child's pig, and daddy's bacon = nominal ownership.

6. *Even a child may beat a man that's bound.* 1732 : Fuller, No. 1387.

7. *Give a child all he shall crave, And a dog while his tail doth wave ; And you'll have a fair dog and foul knave.* 1303 : Brunne, *Handlyng Synne*, l. 7240, Gyue thy ˏchylde when he wyl kraue, And thy whelpe whyl hyt wyl haue,—than mayst thou make you a stounde A foulë chylde and a feyrë hounde. 1670 : Ray, 82. 1732 : Fuller, No. 6456. 1880 : Spurgeon, *Ploughman's Pictures*, 70, Yet remember if you give a child his will and a whelp his fill, both will surely turn out ill.

8. *He that wipes the child's nose, kisseth the mother's cheek.* 1640 : Herbert, *Jac. Prudentum.* 1659 : Howell, *Proverbs : Span.-Eng.*, 18.

9. *Let not a child sleep upon bones,* i.e. the nurse's lap. Somerset 1678 : Ray, 351.

10. *The child hath a red tongue like its father.* 1678 : Ray, 234.

11. *The child says nothing but what it heard by the fire.* 1640 : Herbert, *Jac. Prudentum.* 1732 : Fuller, No. 4449.

12. *The child that's born must bo kept.* 1605 : R. F., *Sch. of Slovenrie*, The Epistle, 'Tis a proverb, The child thats borne must be kept.

13. *The child was born ˏ . . (see* quot.). 1605 : *London Prodigal*, I. i., According to the old proverb, The child was born, and cried, Became a man, after fell sick, and died.

14. *To a child all weather is cold.* 1640 : Herbert, *Jac. Prudentum.* 1670 : Ray, 4.

15. *When the child is christened you may have godfathers enough.* 1639 : Clarke, 283, When the child is christ'ned, every man will be god father. 1670 : Ray, 69. 1732 : Fuller, No. 5573. *c.* 1800 : Trusler, *Prov. in Verse*, 29. 1826 : Brady, *Varieties of Lit.*, 39.

See also **Another** man's child ; **Ask** (4) ; **Burnt** child ; **Cares** not ; **Children** ; **Good** child ; **Happy** is the child ; **Innocent** ; **Kiss**, *verb* (6) ; **Nurse** (3) and (4) ; **Old, A** (1) ; **One** child ; **One** pretty ; **Pap** ; **Praise** the child ; **Quick** child ; **Spare** the rod ; and **Wise** (7), (31), and (32).

Children. 1. *Children and chicken must be always picking.* 1573 : Tusser, *Huswiferie*, 178 (E.D.S.), Yong children

and chickens would euer be eating.
1670 : Ray, 33. 1732 : Fuller, No. 6078.
1893 : *Co. Folk-Lore: Suffolk*, 156
(F.L.S.), Children and chicken are
always a - picking. 1917 : Bridge,
Cheshire Proverbs, 52.

2. *Children and fools have merry lives.*
1639 : Clarke, 298. 1681 : W. Robertson, *Phraseol. Generalis*, 330. *c.* 1800 :
Trusler, *Prov. in Verse*, 41.

3. *Children and fools speak the truth.*
1546 : Heywood, *Proverbs*, Pt. I. ch. xi.,
Children and fooles can not ly. 1591 :
Lyly, *Endymion*, IV. ii., 'Tis an old said
saw, " Children and fools speak true."
c. 1610 : Rowlands, *More Knaues Yet?*,
36 (Hunt. Cl.), Fooles and babes tell
true. 1652 : Tatham, *Scots Figgaries*,
III., I am but a fool, 'tis confest,—but
children and fools tell truth sometimes,
you know. 1769 : Colman, *Man and
Wife*, III., Fools and children always
speak truth, they say. 1805 : Scott, in
Lockhart's *Life*, ii. 22. 1921 : *Evening
Standard*, 21 Oct., p. 9, col. 2, *Solicitor*
(to a witness in the Bow County Court
to-day) :—" Are you telling the truth
in this case? " *Witness:*—" Only children and fools tell the truth."

4. *Children are certain cares, uncertain comforts. c.* 1460 : *How the Good
Wife*, l. 145, Care he hathe that childryn
schalle kepe. 1641 : Brathwaite, *Eng.
Gent., etc.*, Suppl., p. 27, Children reflect
constant cares, but uncertaine comforts.
1707 : Dunton, *Athen. Sport*, 389, I shall
not be in danger of the certain troubles,
but uncertain comforts of children.
1732 : Fuller, No. 1095. 1854 : Surtees,
Handley Cross, ch. xxxix.

5. *Children are poor men's riches.*
1611 : Cotgrave, s.v. " Enfant." 1670 :
Ray, 4. 1732 : Fuller, No. 1094. 1875 :
A. B. Cheales, *Proverb. Folk-Lore*, 47.

6. *Children be first a yearm-ache* [arm-
ache] *and a'terwards a heart-ache.* S.W.
Wilts. 1901 : *Folk-Lore*, xii. 82.

7. *Children have wide ears and long
tongues.* 1732 : Fuller, No. 1097.

8. *Children in Holland . . . (see
quot.).* 1822 : Scott, *Nigel*, Introd.
Epist., As the nursery proverb goes—
" The children in Holland take pleasure
in making What the children in England

take pleasure in breaking" [i.e. toys].
1849 : Halliwell, *Pop. Rhymes and Nurs.
Tales*, 187.

9. *Children pick up words as pigeons
pease, And utter them again as God shall
please.* 1670 : Ray, 213.

10. *Children should be seen and not
heard.* 1914 : Shaw, " Parents and Children," in *Misalliance, etc.*, p. xxi, And
impudently proclaim the monstrous
principle that little children should be
seen and not heard. Cf. **Maid** (9) and
(12).

11. *Children suck the mother when they
are young, and the father when they are
old.* 1678 : Ray, 112. 1732 : Fuller,
No. 1099 [with " grown up " for " old "].

12. *Children to bed and the goose to
the fire.* 1670 : Ray, 168. 1675 : W.
Churchill, *Divi Britannici*, 278, It was
high time (as the vulgar proverb hath
it) to put the children to bed, and lay
the goose to the fire.

13. *Children when they are little make
parents fools, when great, mad.* 1670 :
Ray, 4. 1748 : Richardson, *Clarissa*,
iv. 120 (1785).

14. *He that has no children knows not
what is love.* 1666 : Torriano, *Piazza
Univ.*, 89. 1875 : A. B. Cheales, *Proverb. Folk-Lore*, 47.

15. *He that hath children, all his
morsels are not his own.* 1640 : Herbert,
Jac. Prudentum. 1666 : Torriano, *Piazza
Univ.*, 89.

16. *He that hath no children feedeth
them fat.* 1611 : Davies (of Hereford),
Sc. of Folly, 46, in *Works*, ii. (Grosart),
Who hath no children feedes them fatt.
1633 : Draxe, 58.

17. *What children hear at home soon
flies abroad.* 1611 : Cotgrave, s.v.
" Enfant." 1670 : Ray, 4. 1732 :
Fuller, No. 5482. 1875 : A. B. Cheales,
Proverb. Folk-Lore, 47.

18. *When children stand still, They
have done some ill.* 1640 : Herbert, *Jac.
Prudentum* [with " quiet " for " still "].
1749 : Fielding, *Tom Jones*, bk. xv.
ch. ii., I remember a wise old gentleman
who used to say, " When children are
doing nothing, they are doing mischief."
1875 : A. B. Cheales, *Proverb. Folk-Lore*,
47.

.19. See quot. 1913 : Folk-Lore, xxiv.
76, When you've got one, you may run,
When you've got two, you may goo,
But when you've got three, you must
stop where you be. Oxfordsh.
See also Better children; Boy (2);
Kindness; Offspring; Old, A (b) (15);
and Woman (48)

Children's play. See Boy (5).

Childwall. See Preston.

Chimney. 1. It is easier to build two
chimneys, than to maintain one. 1640 :
Herbert, Jac. Prudentum. 1736 :
Franklin, Way to Wealth, in Works,
i. 450 (Bigelow), It is easier to build
two chimneys than to keep one in fuel.
1869 : Spurgeon, John Ploughman,
ch. xix.

2. There is not always good cheer
where the chimney smokes. 1620 : Shelton, Quixote, Pt. II. ch. lxv. 1694 :
D'Urfey, Quixote, Pt. I. Act I. sc. i.
1732 : Fuller, No. 4930.

Chink. So we have the chink, we will
bear with the stink. 1596 : Harington,
Metam. of Ajax, 68 (1814), So we get
the chinks, We will bear with the stinks.
1670 : Ray, 4. 1681 : W. Robertson,
Phraseol. Generalis, 332, So we may
have the chink, we will away with the
stink. 1732 : Fuller, No. 6277, We will
bear with the stink, If it bring but in
chink. Cf. Money (16).

Chip. 1. A chip of the old block.
1633 : Rowley, Match at Midnight, I.,
He's a chip o' th' old block. 1644 :
Quarles, in Works, i. 166 (Grosart), A
true chip of the old block. 1709 :
Dykes, Eng. Proverbs, 30, A chip of the
old block, is the vulgar nick-name of a
father-like boy. 1762 : Colman, Musical
Lady, II. 1824 : Scott, Redgauntlet,
ch. xv., There was my father . . . a
true chip of the old Presbyterian
block. 1850 : Dickens, Chuzzlewit, ch.
xviii. 1921 : Hutchinson, If Winter
Comes, Pt. III. ch. iii. (iii.).

2. Chip in one's eye. See Hews too
high.

3. Like a chip in porridge. 1666 :
Torriano, Piazza Univ., 182, The English say, like a chip in pottage. 1678 :
Dryden, Limberham, IV. i., A note
under his hand ! that is a chip in

porridge; it is just nothing. 1754 :
Berthelson, Eng.-Danish Dict., s.v.
" Chip," It tastes just like chips in a
porridge. 1872 : Hardy, Greenwood
Tree, Pt. II. ch. iv., " Very well; we'll
let en come in," said the tranter feel-
ingly. " You'll be like chips in porridge, Leaf—neither good nor hurt."

Chippenham. See quot. c. 1685 :
Aubrey, Nat. Hist. Wilts, 58 (1847),
When Chipnam stood in Pewsham's
wood, Before it was destroy'd, A cow
might have gone for a groat a yeare—
But now it is denyed.

Chittlehampton. See Bishop's Nympton.

Choice of a wife. See Wife (7).

Choke up—in various phrases. See
quots. 1605 : R. F., Sch. of Slovenrie, 6,
Say not, God blesse him, but choake vp,
or some such matter, rather. 1678 :
Ray, 343, Choak up, the churchyard's
nigh. 1732 : Fuller, No. 1102 [as in
1678]. 1738 : Swift, Polite Convers.,
Dial. I., Choke, chicken; there's more
a-hatching. 1871 : " Shropshire Sayings," in N. & Q., 4th ser., vii. 9, Choke
chicken more hatching. 1883 : Burne,
Shropsh. Folk-Lore, 598, Choke up,
Chicken ! said to a child choking.
1894 : Northall, Folk Phrases, 12
(E.D.S.), Choke up, chicken, more
a-hatching. Glos. [=There's as good
fish in the sea, etc.]

Choleric. 1. From a choleric man,
withdraw a little; from him that says
nothing, for ever. 1631 : Mabbe, Celestina, 99 (T.T.), That ancient adage;
from an angry man, get the gone but
for a while; but from an enemy, for
ever. 1640 : Herbert, Jac. Prudentum.

2. The choleric drinks, the melancholic
eats, the phlegmatic sleeps. 1670 : Ray, 5.

3. The choleric man never wants woe.
1633 : Draxe, 9, The angry man neuer
wanted woe. 1659 : Howell, 11 (9).
Cf. Hasty man.

Choose a wife. See Wife (7).

Choose for yourself and use for yourself. 1639 : Clarke, 230.

Choose thy company before thy drink.
Ibid., 24.

Chop logic, To. 1528 : More, Workes,
p. 153, col. 2 (1557), She will then waxe

copious and chop logicke with her maistres. 1560 : Awdeley, *Vacabondes*, 15 (E.E.T.S.), Choplogyke is he that when his mayster rebuketh him of hys fault he wyll geue hym xx wordes for one. 1682 : A. Behn, *City Heiress*, I. i., Send him to chop logick in an University. 1771 : Smollett, *Clinker*, in *Works*, vi. 21 (1817), A man must not presume to use his reason, unless he has studied the categories, and can chop logic by mode and figure.

Chopt hay, It goes down like. 1678 : Ray, 235.

Chrisom child, To die like a. 1599 : Shakespeare, *Henry V.*, II. iii., A' made a finer end and went away an it had been any Christom child. *c.* 1620 : A. Cooke, in Hunter's *New Ill. of Shakesp.*, ii. 60 (1845), He who dieth quietly, without ravings or cursings, much like a chrysom child, as the saying is. 1680 : Bunyan, *Badman*, 566 (O.), Mr. Badman died . . . as they call it, like a chrisom-child, quietly and without fear.

Christ's Cross. *See* quot. 1593 : *Tell Trothes N. Yeares Gift*, 33 (N. Sh. S.), Suppose the worst that can happe, imagine shee will neuer be good, building vpon the old sayinge : *Shee that knowes where Christes crosse standes, will neuer forget where great A dwels* . . .

Christen. 1. *He was christened with pump-water*=He has a red face. 1678 : Ray, 79.

2. *To christen one's own child first.* 1659 : Howell, 5, Ile christen my own child first. 1694 : D'Urfey, *Quixote*, Pt. II. Act III. sc. ii., Charity . . . begins at home, you know ; and ever, while you live, christen your own child first. 1738 : Swift, *Polite Convers.*, Dial. I., You know, the parson always christens his own child first. 1864 : "Cornish Proverbs," in *N. & Q.*, 3rd ser., vi. 494, They'll christen their own child first. 1893 : G. L. Gower, *Gloss. Surrey Words*, 9 (E.D.S.), "Christen your own child first" [said by a Surrey man].

Christmas. It is noticeable how curiously some of the following sayings contradict one another. 1. *A black Christmas makes a fat churchyard.* 1846 : Denham, *Proverbs*, 62 (Percy S.).

2. *A dark Christmas makes a heavy wheatsheaf.* 1878 : Dyer, *Eng. Folk-Lore*, 54, In Huntingdonshire it is a common saying that " a dark Christmas sends a fine harvest." 1878 : *N. & Q.*, 5th ser., x. 467, [Surrey woman *loq.*] "They always say a dark Christmas makes a heavy wheatsheaf."

3. *A green Christmas brings a heavy harvest.* 1873 : *N. & Q.*, 4th ser., xi. 212 [Rutland labourer *loq.*].

4. *A green Christmas makes a fat churchyard.* 1635 : Swan, *Spec. Mundi*, 161, They also say, that a hot Christmas makes a fat church-yard. 1642 : Fuller, *Holy State :* " Of Time-Serving," A green Christmas is neither handsome nor healthful. 1710 : *British Apollo*, vol. iii. No. 106, col. 3. 1830 : Forby, *Vocab. E. Anglia*, 418. 1879 : Henderson, *Folk-Lore of N. Counties*, 75.

5. *A kiss at Christmas and an egg at Easter.* 1846-59 : *Denham Tracts*, II. 92 (F.L.S.).

6. *A light Christmas makes a full sheaf.* 1659 : Howell, 12, A light Christmas, a heavy sheaf. 1670 : Ray, 4 [as in 1659]. 1881 : *N. & Q.*, 6th ser., iv. 535, " A light Christmas makes a full sheaf " . . . I heard it the other day in Surrey.

7. *A windy Christmas and a calm Candlemas are signs of a good year.* 1846 : Denham, *Proverbs*, 27 (Percy S.). 1893 : Inwards, *Weather Lore*, 39.

8. *After Christmas comes Lent.* 1611 : Cotgrave, s.v. " Banquet," After feasting, fasting. 1678 : Ray, 113, After a Christmas comes a Lent. 1732 : Fuller, No. 770. 1846-59 : *Denham Tracts*, ii. 92 (F.L.S.) [as in 1678].

9. *As many mince pies as you taste at Christmas, so many happy months you will have.* 1846-59 : *Denham Tracts*, ii. 91 (F.L.S.).

10. *At Christmas great loafs, at Easter clean souls, at Whitsuntide new clothes.* 1659 : Howell, 11 (9).

11. *At Christmas meadows green, at Easter covered with frost.* 1893 : Inwards, *Weather Lore*, 38. 1912 : R. L. Gales, *Studies in Arcady*, 2nd ser., 108, A green Christmas, a white Easter.

12. *At old Christmas the days are*

longer by a cock's stride. 1830 : Forby, *Vocab. E. Anglia,* 418. Cf. No. 17 ; and New Year (2).

13. *Better have a new-laid egg at Christmas than a calf at Easter.* 1882 : Mrs. Chamberlain, *W. Worcs. Words,* 38 (E.D.S.).

14. *Christmas comes but once a year.* 1580 : Tusser, *Husb.,* 28 (E.D.S.), At Christmas play and make good cheere, for Christmas comes but once a yeere. 1652 : Taylor (Water-Poet), *Christmas In and Out,* 16, in *Works,* 1st coll. (Spens. S.). 1834 : Planché, *Extravag.,* i. 204 (1879). 1892 : S. Hewett, *Peasant Speech of Devon,* 68, Cursemas com'th but wance a year.

15. *Christmas wet, empty granary and barrel.* 1893 : Inwards, *Weather Lore,* 38.

16. *Coming—like Christmas.* 1738 : Swift, *Polite Convers.,* Dial. I., Coming ! ay, so is Christmas. *c.* 1760 : Foote, *Maid of Bath,* I., Coming ! ay, zo be Christmas. 1839 : Planché, *Extravag.,* ii. 60 (1879).

17. *From Christmas-tide to New'us-tide, The days do get a cock's stride.* 1890 : J. D. Robertson, *Gloucester Gloss.* (E.D.S.). Cf. No. 12 ; and New Year (2).

18. *He has more business than English ovens at Christmas.* c. 1594 : Bacon, *Promus,* No. 912, He hath moe to doe than the ovens in Christmas. 1659 : Howell, *Proverbs : Ital.-Eng.,* 1. 1846 : Denham, *Proverbs,* 63 (Percy S.), Busy as an oven at Christmas.

19. *If Christmas day on a Sunday fall, A troublous winter we shall have all.* 15th cent. : Song, in Denham, *Proverbs,* 69, (Percy S. 1846), Yf Crystmas day on the Son day be, A trobolus wynter ye shall see. 1882 : *N. & Q.,* 6th ser., v. 7.

20. *If Christmas day on Monday be, A wintry winter you shall see.* 15th cent. : Song, in Denham, *Proverbs,* 70 (Percy S., 1846), Yf Crystemas day on Monday be, A grete wynter that yere have shall ye. 1893 : *N. & Q.,* 8th ser., iv. 505.

21. *If Christmas finds a bridge, he'll break it ; if he finds none he'll make one.* 1893 : Inwards, *Weather Lore,* 38.

22. *If the sun shines . . . See* quots.

1839 : G. C. Lewis, *Herefs. Words,* 122, The following are old sayings current . . . If the sun shines on Christmas-day, there will be accidents by fire all the year after. 1878 : Dyer, *Eng. Folk-Lore,* 249, If the sun shine through the apple-tree on Christmas Day there will be an abundant crop in the following year.

23. *Light Christmas ; light wheatsheaf : Dark Christmas ; heavy wheatsheaf.* 1855 : *N. & Q.,* 1st ser., xii. 490 [current in Kent, and firmly believed]. 1872 : *ibid.,* 4th ser., ix. 13, I have heard the following saying referred to the neighbourhood of Ledbury, Herefordshire : " A light Christmas, a light harvest."

24. *The twelve days of Christmas.* 1846 : Denham, *Proverbs,* 62 (Percy S.).

25. *They keep Christmas all the year.* 1672 : Walker, *Parœm.,* 25. 1681 : W. Robertson, *Phraseol. Generalis,* 783.

26. *They talk of Christmas so long that it comes.* 1611 : Cotgrave, s.v. " Noel," So long is Christmas cryed that at length it comes. 1670 : Ray, 26. 1846–59 : Denham *Tracts,* ii. 92 (F.L.S.).

See also **Bounce buckram** ; **Easter** (1) and (5) ; **Ice** (1), (2), and (3) ; **Michaelmas** (1) ; **Monday** (5) ; **St. Michael** (2) ; **Simpers** ; **Three things that never** ; and **Whitsuntide** (7).

Christmas-Eve. *See* **Ghosts.**

Christmas-pies. *See* **Devil** (71) ; and **Eat** (17).

Christmas play. *See* **Good as.**

Chuck under the chin, A. *See* quot. 1738 : Swift, *Polite Convers.,* Dial. I., Well said, girl ! [giving her a chuck]. Take that : they say a chuck under the chin is worth two kisses.

Chue. *See* **Stanton Drew.**

Church have leave to stand in the churchyard, Let the. 1678 : Ray, 113. 1732 : Fuller, No. 3192.

Church Street. *See* **Braintree.**

Church Stretton, where they eaten more nor they getten. 1883 : Burne, *Shropsh. Folk-Lore,* 583.

Church work goes on slowly. 1639 : Fuller, *Holy War,* bk. i. ch. xiii., So that, contrary to the proverb, church

work went on the most speedily. 1655:
Fuller, *Church Hist.*, bk. i. § v. (iii. 4),
Church work is a cripple in going up
[building], but rides post in coming
down! [destroying a church]. 1732:
Fuller, No. 1106.   1875: A. B. Cheales,
Proverb. Folk-Lore, 79.

Churchman. *Though you see a
Churchman ill, yet continue in the
church still.* 1640: Herbert, *Jac. Prudentum.*

Churchyard. *A piece of a churchyard
fits everybody.* Ibid.

Churl and **Churls.** 1. *A churl's churl
is often woebegone.* c. 1430: Lydgate,
Churl and Bird, st. 40, Fcr hit was said
of folkes yeres agoon A chorles chorle is
ofte woo begoon.

2. *A churl's feast is better than none
at all.* 1594: Lodge and Greene,
Looking Glass, l. 1191, We must feed
vpon prouerbes now, as . . . "A
churles feast is better than none at
all."

3. *Give a churl rule. See* quot. 1485:
Malory, *Morte d'Arthur*, bk. x. ch. 61,
Hit is an old sawe gyue a chorle rule
and there by he wylle not be suffysed.

4. *Of churls may no good come.*
c. 1489: Caxton, *Blanchardyn, etc.*, 173
(E.E.T.S.), Of churles, bothe man and
wyff, can departe noo goode fruyte.
Ibid., 173, Men sayen that "of a kerle
may nought come but poyson and
fylth, that maketh the place to stynke
where he haunted ynne."

See also Claw (1); and Put (7).

Churning days, I'll make him know.
1678: Ray, 235.

**Cider is treacherous because it smiles
in the face, and then cuts the throat.**
1653: T. Adams,*Works*, iii. 267 (V. Lean)
Those bottled windy drinks that laugh
in a man's face and then cut his throat.
1738: Swift, *Polite Convers.*, Dial. II.,
Pray, my lord, how is it [cider] treacherous? *Ld. Sparkish.* Because it
smiles in my face, and cuts my throat.

**Cider on beer is very good cheer,
But beer upon cider's a rider** [doesn't
mix well]. 1888: Marchant, *Praise of
Ale*, 462.

Cipher among numbers, He is a.
1633: Draxe, 29.   1639: Clarke, 70.

Circumstances alter cases. 1870:
Dickens, *Drood*, ch. ix. 1923: J. S.
Fletcher, *The Diamonds*, ch. ii., Is it
not one of your proverbs that circumstances alter cases?

**Citizen is at his business before he
rise, The.** 1640: Herbert, *Jac. Prudentum.*

**City which comes to parle is half won,
The.** 1567: Painter, *Pal. of Pleasure*,
iii. 48 (Jacobs), For a city is halfe won
when they within demaunde for parle.
1651: Herbert, *Jac. Prudentum*, 2nd
ed., A city that parleys is half gotten.

**Civil denial is better than a rude
grant, A.** 1732: Fuller, No. 38.

**Claps his dish at the wrong man's
door, He.** 1596: Jonson, *Ev. Man in
his Humour*, II. i.   1678: Ray, 239.

Claw, *verb.* 1. *Claw a churl by the
tail, and he will defile your hand.* 1546:
Heywood, *Proverbs*, Pt. II. ch. vii.
1568: *Jacob and Esau*, II. iii., in Hazlitt,
Old Plays, ii. 216 (1874), This proverb
in Esau may be understand: Claw a
churl by the tail, and he will file your
hand.   1621: Jonson, *Gyps. Metam.*
1670: Ray, 70.

2. *Claw me and I'll claw you.* 1530:
Palsgrave, 486, Clawe my backe, and
I wyll clawe thy toe. 1619: H.
Hutton, *Follies Anat.*, 31 (Percy S.),
Let coxcombs curry favour with a
fee, Extoll their braines, with Claw me,
I'l claw thee.   1754: Berthelson, *Eng.-
Danish Dict.*, s.v. "Claw." Cf. **Ka me,
ka thee;** and **Scratch me.**

3. *He claws it as Clayton claw' the
pudding, when he ate bag and all.* 1678:
Ray, 282. 1732: Fuller, No. 1826.
Cf. **Eat** (38).

Clay and sand. *See* **England** (12).

Clean as a clock. 1669: H. More,
Antid. against Idolatry, To Reader, Who
will be ready to wipe you as clean as a
clock, before you come to the castle.
1874: *N. & Q.*, 5th ser., i. 454, "As
clean as a clock."—A common phrase
in Yorkshire, referring to the shining
and clean-looking black beetles (always
called *clocks* in the North) which are to
be found under every piece of cow-dung
which has been dropped a few hours.

Clean as a new pin. *See* **New pin.**

Clean as a penny. 1681 : W. Robertson, *Phraseol. Generalis*, 338. 1720 :
Gay, *Poems*, ii. 279 (Underhill), Clean
as a penny drest. 1828 : Carr, *Craven
Dialect*, 40, I've lost my knife as clean
as a penny. 1854 : Baker, *Northants
Gloss.*, s.v. " Penny," " Clean as a
penny " is a common simile for any one
that is neatly and cleanly dressed.

Clean as a whistle. 1828 : Carr,
Craven Dialect, ii. 256, " As clean as a
whistle," a proverbial simile, signifying
completely, entirely. 1851 : Planché,
Extravag., iv. 164 (1879), Or else his
head cut off, clean as a whistle. 1925 :
Observer, 14 June, p. 11, col. 3, " Hay
Fever " [a play] is as clean as a whistle
—if this matters to anybody.

Clean (or white) as nip. 1838 :
Holloway, *Provincialisms*, 116, Nepeta
cataria, the herb cat-mint, which is
covered with a white down ; hence the
saying " as white as nep." 1890 :
P. H. Emerson, *Wild Life*, 96, Where
that have been on the skin that turn
as white as nip. 1899 : Dickinson,
Cumberland Gloss., 378, Clean as a nip.
—Smart, very tidy ; free from dirt.
1917 : Bridge, *Cheshire Proverbs*, 11.
Cf. **Nice as nip.**

**Clean-fingered huswife, and an idle,
folk say, A.** 1546 : Heywood, *Proverbs*,
Pt. I. ch. x.

Clean hands want no washball. 1732 :
Fuller, No. 1111.

Clean heels, light meals. This " refers
to the superiority of clay land over sand
land for yielding milk." 1886 : R.
Holland, *Cheshire Gloss.*, 447 (E.D.S.).
1917 : Bridge, *Cheshire Proverbs*, 38.

**Clean linen only that makes the feast,
'Tis not.** 1732 : Fuller, No. 5093.

Clean man when dirty-washed, I'm a.
1917 : Bridge, *Cheshire Proverbs*, 99,
Oi'm a clane mon when dirty-weshed. =
Straightforward man even though I may
be dirty.

Clean pair of heels. *See* **Show.**

Cleanliness is next to godliness. 1605 :
Bacon, *Adv. of Learning*, bk. ii., Cleanness of body was ever deemed to proceed from a due reverence to God.
c. 1790 : quoted in Wesley, *Sermon* 93,
" On Dress," Cleanliness is, indeed, next

to godliness. 1861 : Dickens, *Great
Expect.*, ch. iv.

Clear as a bell. 1670 : Ray, 203.
1838 : Dickens, *Twist*, ch. xxiii., Fresh,
genuine port wine . . . clear as a bell ;
and no sediment !

Clear as crystal. Before 1300 : *Cursor
M.*, l. 376, The lift [sky] wit sternes
[stars] grete and small wit water clere
als cristale. *c.* 1350 : *Alexander*, l. 2541,
It was clerir than cristalle. *c.* 1430 :
Lydgate, *Minor Poems*, 343 (E.E.T.S.),
Shewe out in chyldhode as ony crystall
clere. 1584 : R. Scot, *Witchcraft*,
bk. xiii. ch. vi., A stone about the
bignesse of a bean, as clear as the
crystall. 1605 : Sylvester, *Du Bartas*,
Week I. Day iii. l. 141, And, cleer as
crystall, in the glasse doth hop. 1700 :
J. Brome, *Travels*, 36. 1870 : Dickens,
Drood, ch. xiv. 1884 : R. L. S., *Letters*,
ii. 298 (Tusitala ed.), The weather I
have —cloudless, clear as crystal. 1909 :
Lucas, *Wand. in Paris*, ch. i., My duty
is clear as crystal.

Clear as the day. 1541 : Coverdale,
Christ. State Matrimony, sig. D8, Euy-
dent it is and as cleare as the daye.
1565 : Shacklock, *Hatch. of Heresies*,
fo. 76, It is as clear as the daye. 1692 :
L'Estrange, *Æsop*, Life, p. 28 (3rd ed.).
1740 : North, *Examen*, 190, The plot
was as clear as noon day. 1883 :
R. L. S., *Treasure I.*, ch. vi., " The
thing is as clear as noonday," cried the
squire. 1922 : A. Bennett, *Prohack*,
ch. xx. (iv.), She *must* be. It's as clear
as day-light !

Clear as the sun. *c.* 1579 : Harvey,
Letter-Book, 66 (Camden S.), Is it not
cleerer then the sonne at noone dayes ?
1680 : in North, *Lives of Norths*, i. 159
(Bohn), Who would make the plot as
clear as the sun. 1709 : Mandeville,
Virgin Unmask'd, 133 (1724). 1749 :
Fielding, *Tom Jones*, bk. xii. ch. vii.

Clear conscience. *See* **Conscience** (1),
(2), and (3).

**Clear gain that remains by honest
gettings, 'Tis.** 1659 : Howell, 11.

Clear. *See also* **Innocent as a new-
born babe.**

Cleave. 1. *He cleaves the clouds.*
1813 : Ray, 75.

2. *They cleave together like burs.*
1546: Heywood, *Proverbs*, Pt. II.
ch. v. 1580: Churchyard, *Charge*, 30
(Collier), Ye cleave together so like
burres.

Cleckheaton. *See* **Birstal.**

Clent. *See* quot. 1894: Northall,
Folk Phrases, 24 (E.D.S.), The people of
Clent are all Hills, Waldrons, or devils.

Clerk makes the justice, The. 1660:
A. Brome, *Poems*: " The Leveller," 'Tis
we commons make the lords, and the
clerk makes the justice. 1691: *Merry
Drollery*, 37 (Ebsworth) [as in 1660].
1729: Defoe, *Compl. Gent.*, Pt. I. ch. vi.,
p. 239 (1890), So makeing good the
old proverb that the clark makes the
justice, while the master does just
nothing. 1732: Fuller, No. 3024, It is
the Justice's clerk that makes the
Justice.

**Cleveland in the clay, Bring in two
soles and carry one away.** 1670: Ray,
257. 1790: Grose, *Prov. Gloss.*, s.v.
" Yorkshire." 1878: *Folk-Lore Record*,
i. 168.

Cleveland. *See* **Rosebery-Topping.**

**Client twixt his attorney and coun-
sellor is like a goose twixt two foxes, A.**
1659: Howell, 11 (9).

Climb. 1. *He that never climbed
never fell.* 1546: Heywood, *Proverbs*,
Pt. I. ch. xii. *c.* 1594: Bacon, *Promus*,
No. 484. 1762: Smollett, *Sir L. Greaves*,
ch. x., Crabshaw replied " . . . who
never climbed, never fell."

2. *Who climbs high his fall is great.*
c. 1430: Lydgate, *Minor Poems*, 120
(Percy S.), Who clymbythe hyest most
dredfulle is his falle. *c.* 1460: *Wisdom*,
sc. iii., in *Macro Plays*, 50 (E.E.T.S.),
Who clymyt hye, hys fall gret ys. 1513:
Bradshaw, *St. Werburge*, 40 (E.E.T.S.),
Who clymbed to hye often hath a fall.
c. 1580: Spelman, *Dialogue*, 96 (Roxb.
Cl.), The ould saynge (the higher thou
clymeste, and thy foote slyppe, the
greater is thy fall). 1631: Mabbe,
Celestina, 221 (T.T.), It is an ancient
proverbe: That the higher a man
climbes, the greater is his fall. 1884:
Gilbert, *Princess Ida*, II., Pray you
bear in mind Who highest soar fall
farthest.

Cloak. 1. *A cloak for the rain* = An
expedient for every turn of fortune.
Before 1529: Skelton, *Magnyfycence*,
l. 618, Ye, for your wyt is cloked for
the rayne. 1548: Hall, *Chron.*, 701
(1809), Whatsoeuer was saied by the
Recorder in his excuse was taken as
a cloke for the rain, and a dissimula-
cion or a mocke. 1601: Munday, etc.,
Death of Robert, E. of Hunt., III. i.,
Bruce, I tell you plain, Is no sound
cloak to keep John from the rain.
1633: Rowley, *Match at Midnight*, III.
Cf. **Hypocrisy.**

2. *Don't have thy cloak to make when
it begins to rain.* 1639: Clarke, 267,
Hee that provides not a cloak before
the raine, may chance to be wet to his
coste. 1732: Fuller, No. 1808. 1846:
Denham, *Proverbs*, 4 (Percy S.).

3. *He hath a cloak for his knavery.*
1678: Ray, 235.

4. *You may as soon make a cloak for
the moon.* 1732: Fuller, No. 6158.

Clock goes as it pleases the clerk, The.
1678: Ray, 114. 1732: Fuller, No. 4451.

Clocks of London. *See* **London** (6).

**Clogs to clogs is only three genera-
tions, From;** or, **There's nobbut three
generations between clog and clog.**
1871: *N. & Q.*, 4th ser., vii. 472,
. . . A Lancashire proverb, implying
that, however rich a poor man may
eventually become, his great-grandson
will certainly fall back to poverty and
clogs. 1875: Smiles, *Thrift*, 292, Hence
the Lancashire proverb, " Twice clogs,
once boots." 1924: *Clogs to Clogs*
[title of play produced at Everyman
Theatre, London, 10 Nov.].

Close as oak. *See* **Oak** (2).

Close as wax. 1772: Cumberland,
Fash. Lover, III. ii., You mun be as
close as wax, d'ye see. 1828: in
Brasenose Ale, 24 (1878), Sleep seals
my eyes as close as wax. 1891: Doyle,
White Company, ch. xx., " Good lad ! "
whispered Ford. " Stick to it close
as wax ! "

Close is my shirt. *See* **Near.**

Close mouth catches no flies, A.
1605: Camden, *Remains*, 316 (1870).
1670: Ray, 71. 1745: *Agreeable Companion*, 51.

Close mouth makes a wise head, A.
1703: Ward, *Writings*, ii. 112.

Close pasture where he can't nibble,
It must be a. 1887: *N. & Q.*, 7th ser.,
iii. 514, . . . This is a common saying
in the Midlands, and is probably well
known through the country.

Cloth. 1. *See* quot. 1570: Googe,
tr. *Popish Kingdome*, 41 (1880), According to the proverbe thus, the cloth must
still be shorne, Least it should hap to
be consumde with mothes, and all to
torne.

2. *See* quot. 1825: Scott, *Betrothed*,
ch. x., You know the good old saw,—
"Cloth must we wear, Eat beef and
drink beer, Though the dead go to
bier."

Clothe thee in war, arm thee in peace.
1640: Herbert, *Jac. Prudentum*.

Clothe thee warm, eat little, drink
enough, and thou shalt live. 1578:
Florio, *First Fruites*, fo. 34, Cloathe
warme, eate little, drink wel, so shalt
thou lyue. 1629: *Book of Meery
Riddles*, Prov. 129.

Clothes. *He is making clothes for
fishes*. 1813: Ray, 75.

Clothmarket, In the = In bed. 1678:
Ray, 235. 1738: Swift, *Polite Convers.*,
Dial. I.

Cloud and Clouds. 1. *A round-topped
cloud, with flattened base, Carries rainfall
in its face*. 1893: Inwards, *Weather
Lore*, 96.

2. *After clouds* (or *black clouds*), *clear
weather*. c. 1400: *Beryn*, l. 3955
(E.E.T.S.), ffor "aftir mysty cloudis
there comyth a cler sonne." 1546:
Heywood, *Proverbs*, Pt. I. ch. xi.,
After cloudes blacke, we shall haue
weather cleere. 1685: Meriton, *Yorkshire Ale*, 72, After fowl weather
followes a fair day. 1762: Smollett,
Sir L. Greaves, ch. x., Crabshaw replied
". . . after clouds comes clear weather." 1893: Inwards, *Weather Lore*, 88.

3. *At sunset with a cloud so black, A
westerly wind you shall not lack*. Ibid.,
86.

4. *Clouds that the sun builds up,
darken him*. 1732: Fuller, No. 1115.
1893: Inwards, 85.

5. *He that pryeth into every cloud,*

may be struck with a thunderbolt. 1639:
Clarke, 31. 1670: Ray, 134. 1732:
Fuller, No. 2255.

6. *Hen's scarts* [scratchings] *and filly
tails Make lofty ships carry low sails;*
also, *If clouds look as if scratched by a
hen, Get ready to reef your topsails then.*
Nautical. 1893: Inwards, *Weather
Lore*, 92.

7. *If clouds be bright, 'Twill clear
to-night; If clouds be dark, 'Twill rain—
do you hark?* Ibid., 88.

8. *North and south, the sign of
drought; East and west, the sign of blast.*
Ibid., 93.

9. *Red clouds in the east, rain the next
day*. Ibid., 88.

10. *The higher the clouds, the finer the
weather*. Ibid., 85.

11. *Trace in the sky the painter's
brush, Then winds around you soon will
rush*. Ibid., 92.

12. *When clouds appear like rocks and
towers, The earth's refreshed by frequent
showers*. 1831, Hone, *Year-Book*, 300.
1893: Inwards, 96.

13. *When mountains and cliffs in the
clouds appear, Some sudden and violent
showers are near*. 1893: Inwards, 96.

14. *When the clouds are upon* (or *go
up*) *the hills, they'll come down by the
mills*. 1678: Ray, 49. 1846: Denham, *Proverbs*, 19 (Percy S.). 1893:
Inwards, 99, [as in 1846 *plus*] When it
gangs up i' fops [small clouds on hills],
It'll fa' down i' drops. . . . North
Country. When the clouds go up the
hill, They'll send down water to turn
a mill. Hants.

15. *When the clouds of the morn to
the west fly away, You may conclude on
a settled, fair day*. 1893: Inwards, 86.

See also Curdly; Flea (2); Mackerel;
Moon (16); and Woolly fleeces.

Cloudy mornings turn to clear even-
ings. 1546: Heywood, *Proverbs*, Pt. II.
ch. ix., Cloudy mornynges turne to
cleere after noones. 1681: W. Robertson, *Phraseol. Generalis*, 341. 1732:
Fuller, No. 1116, . . . may turn . . .
1846: Denham, *Proverbs*, 6 (Percy S.).

Clout is better than a hole out, A.
Corn. 1895: Jos. Thomas, *Randigal
Rhymes*, 59.

Clover, To be in. 1813 : Ray, 57.

Clown. *See* quots. 1586 : Pettie, tr.
Guazzo's *Civil Convers.*, fo. 171, You
know well the prouerbe—Claw a clown
he will thee scratch, Scratch a clown
he will thee claw. 1623 : Wodroephe,
Spared Houres, 520, Anoynt a clowne,
and hee will grip you, grip a clowne
and hee will anoynt you. 1659.:
Howell, *Proverbs: Fr.-Eng.*, 9, Anoint
a clown, and he will prick you.

Clowns are best in their own company,
but gentlemen are best everywhere.
1732 : Fuller, No. 1117.

Clowns kill [each] other, and gentles
cleave together. 1623 : Wodroephe,
Spared Houres, 520.

Clubs are trumps. Glos. 1639 : in
Berkeley MSS., iii. 29 (1885), Beware,
Clubs are trumps; or clubs will prove
trumps.

Clude. *To escape Clude and be
drowned in Conway.* Two Welsh rivers.
1662 : Fuller, *Worthies*, iii. 527 (1840).
1790 : Grose, *Prov. Gloss.*, s.v. " Caer-
narvonshire."

Clunton and Clunbury, Clungunford
and Clun, are the . . . (*see* quots.).
1883 : Burne, *Shropsh. Folk-Lore*, 583,
. . . drunkenest (*or* dirtiest, *or* quietest)
places under the sun. 1896 : Housman,
Shropsh. Lad, 1., . . . quietest places
under the sun.

Coaches won't run over him, The =
He is in gaol. 1813 : Ray, 186.

Coal-pit cale = First come, first served.
1917 : Bridge, *Cheshire Proverbs*, 38.

Coals to Newcastle, To send. [In
silvam non ligna feras insanius ac si
Magnas Græcorum malis implere cater-
vas.—Horace, *Sat.*, I. x. 34–5.] 1583 :
Melville, *Autobiog.*, i. 163 (Wodrow S.),
Salt to Dysart, or colles to Newcastle !
1650 : Fuller, *Pisgah Sight*, 128, So far
from being needless pains it may bring
considerable profit to carry Char-coals
to New-castle. 1682 : in *Thoresby Corresp.*, i. 16 (1832), To send you our news
from England, were to carry coals to
Newcastle. 1709: *Labour in Vain; or,
Coals to Newcastle* [title of sermon
advertised in *Daily Courant*, 6 Oct.,
1709]. 1874 : R. L. S., *Letters*, i. 134
(Tusitala ed.), It seems rather like

sending coals to Newcastle to write a
lecture to a subsidised professor. 1920 :
Galsworthy, *Tatterdemalion*, 9, However much she carried coals to Newcastle, or tobacco pouches to those who
did not smoke. Cf. Owl (9).

Coals. *See* Over the coals.

Coarse. *See* Rough as gorse.

Coats change with countries. 1659 :
Howell, 17.

Cob = Mud. *See* quot. 1869 : Hazlitt, 142, Give cob a hat and pair of
shoes, and he'll last for ever. S. Devon.
Provide a stone foundation and a slate
coping for a cob [mud] wall.—*Shelly.*

Cobble. *They that cobble and clout
shall have work when others go without.*
1670 : Ray, 72. 1732 : Fuller, No. 6454.

Cobbler. 1. *Cobbler's law, he that
takes money must pay the shot.* 1678 :
Ray, 90.

2. *Cobbler's Monday.* 1825 : Brockett,
Gloss. N. Country Words, 44, Cobbler's-
Monday, every Monday throughout
the year is a regular holiday among
the "gentle craft." 1862 : *Dialect of
Leeds*, 270, . . . A day to do nothing in.

3. *Cobblers and tinkers are the best ale-
drinkers.* 1659 : Howell, 17. 1670 :
Ray, 5. 1732 : Fuller, No. 6229. 1886 :
Bickerdyke, *Curios. of Ale and Beer*,
172, Cobblers and tinkers are your true
ale drinkers. 1909 : Hackwood, *Inns,
Ales, etc.*, 98 [as in 1886].

4. *Let not the cobbler go beyond his
last.* [Denuntiantem ne supra crepidam
sutor judicaret.—Pliny, *Nat. Hist.*,
xxxv. 85.] 1539 : Taverner, *Proverbs*,
fo. 17, Let not the shoemaker go beyond
hys shoe. 1613 : Wither, *Abuses Stript,
etc.*, To Reader, You will be counted but
saucy cobblers to goe beyond your lasts.
1692 : L'Estrange, *Æsop*, 205 (3rd ed.).
1754 : *World*, No. 55, Extinguished him
at once with the famous proverb in use
at this day, " The shoemaker must not
go beyond his last."

5. *The cobbler deals with all* [awl]. A
verbal quibble. 1639 : Clarke, 32.

6. *The richer the cobbler the blacker his
thumb.* 1710 : *Brit. Apollo*, vol. iii.,
No. 111, col. 6.

7. *Without all* [awl] *the cobbler's
nobody.* 1639 : Clarke, 71.

Cobwebs. *Where cobwebs are plenty,
kisses are scarce.* 1864 : " Cornish Proverbs," in *N. & Q.*, 3rd ser., vi. 6. 1906 :
Cornish N. & Q., 266.

Cock. 1. *A cock and bull tale.* 1608 :
Day, *Law Trickes*, IV. ii., What a tale
of a cock and a bull he tolde my father.
c. 1625 : B. & F., *Chances*, II. iv., Thou
talk'st of cocks and bulls. 1702 : T.
Brown, in *Works*, ii. 94 (1760), Things
which some call a cock and a bull, and
others the product of a lively imagination. 1762 : Hall-Stevenson, *Crazy
Tales*, 16, My Cousin's Tale of a Cock
and a Bull [title]. 1823 : Byron, *Don
Juan*, can. vi. st. 80. 1858 : O. W.
Holmes, *Autocrat*, v.

2. *A good cock may come out of a bad
bag.* 1883 : Burne, *Shropsh. Folk-Lore*,
590, There'll come a good cock out of
a ragged bag. 1917 : Bridge, *Cheshire
Proverbs*, 3.

3. *Better be a cock for a day, than a hen
for a year.* 1659 : Howell, 13.

4. *Every cock is brave on his own
dunghill.* [Gallum in suo sterquilinio
plurimum posse.—Seneca, *Apocol.*, 7.]
Before 1225 : *Ancren R.*, 140, Ase me
seið " þet coc is kene on his owune
mixenne." 1546 : Heywood, *Proverbs*,
Pt. I. ch. xi. [with " proude " for
" brave "]. 1580 : Spenser, *Shep. Cal.*,
Sept., l. 47, As cocke on his dunghill
crowing cranck. 1692 : Congreve, *Old
Bachelor*, II. ii., For every cock will
fight upon his own dunghill. 1869 :
Spurgeon, *John Ploughman*, ch. xiii.,
Every cock may crow on his own
dunghill. 1917 : Bridge, *Cheshire Proverbs*, 2, A cock fights best on his own
bouk.

5. *If the cock goes crowing to bed, He's
sure to rise with a watery head.* 1846 :
Denham, *Proverbs*, 18 (Percy S.). 1893 :
Inwards, *Weather Lore*, 133. 1920 :
N. & Q., 12th ser., vii. 67, If the cock
crows when he goes to bed, He gets up
in the morn with a wet head [heard in
Warwickshire within the last ten years].

6. *If the cock moult before the hen, We
shall have weather thick and thin : But if
the hen moult before the cock, We shall
have weather hard as a block.* 1670 :
Ray, 43. *c.* 1685 : Aubrey, *Nat. Hist.*

Wilts, 16 (1847), When the hen doth
moult before the cock, The winter will
be as hard as a rock ; But if the cock
moults before the hen, The winter
will not wett your shoes seame. 1825 :
Hone, *Ev. Day Book*, i. 669. 1893 :
Inwards, *Weather Lore*, 133.

7. *It is a very ill cock that will not
crow before he be old.* 1580 : Lyly,
Euphues, 366 (Arber).

8. *The cock crows but the hen goes.*
1659 : Howell, 19. 1670 : Ray, 5.

9. *The cock does crow, To let us know,
If we be wise, 'Tis time to rise.* 1846 :
Denham, *Proverbs*, 19 (Percy S.).

10. *There is chance in the cock's spur.*
1678 : Ray, 111. 1732 : Fuller, No.
4890.

11. *To leap like a cock at a blackberry.*
1670 : Ray, 209. . . . Spoken of one
that endeavours, but can do no harm.

Cock's stride. *See* **Christmas** (12) ;
and **New Year** (2).

Cock on hoop, To set=To be prodigal.
Origin unknown—*see* discussion, s.v., in
Oxford English Dict. 1519 : Horman,
Vulgaria, fo. 301, He setteth al thyngs
at cocke in the hope. 1540 : Palsgrave,
Acolastus, sig. G3, Let us sette the
cocke on the hope, and make good
chere. *c.* 1568 : Wager, *Longer thou
livest*, sig. B2, Make mery, daunce and
sing, Set cocke a whope, and play care
away. 1606 : T. Heywood, *If you
know not me*, Pt. II., These knaues
Sit cock-a-hope, but Hobson pays for
all. 1730 : Bailey, *Eng. Dict.*, s.v.,
Cock on hoop [i.e. the cock or spiggot
being laid upon the hoop, and the barrel
of ale stunn'd, i.e. drank out without
intermission] at the height of mirth
and jollity.

Cock the little finger, To. Said of
one given to drinking. 1917 : Bridge,
Cheshire Proverbs, 131.

Cockatrice in the shell, Kill the.
1659 : Howell, 17 [" Crush " for " Kill "].
1669 : N. Smith, *Quakers Spirit. Court*,
15, I thought it was best to kill the
cockatrice in the egg. 1732 : Fuller,
No. 3124 [" egg " for " shell "].

Cocking, Sussex. *See* quot. 1870 :
Lower, *Hist. Sussex*, i. 119, When
Foxes brewings [mist among trees] go

to Cocking Foxes brewings come back
dropping.

Cockles of the heart. 1685: S.
Wesley, *Maggots*, 126, It terrifies the
cocales of my heart. 1690: *Reason of
Mr. Bays changing his Religion*, Pt. II.,
p. 33, Now you rejoyce the cockles of
my heart. 1792: Scott, in Lockhart's
Life, i. 191, Which would have delighted
the very cockles of your heart. 1858:
Darwin, in *Life, etc.*, ii. 112 (1888) (O.),
I have just had the innermost cockles
of my heart rejoiced by a letter from
Lyell.

Cockloft is unfurnished, His = Brain-
less. 1646: Fuller, *Andronicus*, § vi.
par. 18, Often the cockloft is empty in
those whom Nature hath built many
stories high. 1678: Ray, 235.

Codnor's Pond. *See* quot. 1884:
Folk-Lore Journal, ii. 279, When Codnor's Pond runs dry, The Lords may
say good-bye. Derby.

Coggeshall, Essex. 1. *A Coggeshall
job.* 1880: *N. & Q.*, 6th ser., ii. 307,
This name is generally shortened into
Coxall. . . . It is the Essex phrase for
any blundering or awkward contrivance.
1913: E. M. Wright, *Rustic Speech, etc.*,
182. 1920: E. Gepp, *Essex Dialect Dict.*,
8, A "Coxall job" means a foolish act.
2. *Jeering Coxhall.* 1662: Fuller,
Worthies, i. 498 (1840). 1790: Grose,
Prov. Gloss., s.v. "Essex," Jeering
Cogshall.
See also **Braintree.**

Coin. *Where coin is not common,
commons must be scant.* 1546: Heywood, *Proverbs*, Pt. II. ch. i. 1633:
Draxe, 1. 1670: Ray, 74.

Colchester, The Weavers' Beef of =
Sprats. 1662: Fuller, *Worthies*, i. 498
(1840). 1790: Grose, *Prov. Gloss.*, s.v.
"Essex." 1865: W. White, *Eastern
England*, i. 145, She had never heard
sprats described as "weavers' beef,"
as they are (or were) at Colchester. 1866:
J. G. Nall, *Great Yarmouth, etc.*, 683.

Cold as a clock. 1579: Lyly, *Euphues*,
106 (Arber), Though Curio bee as hot as
a toast, yet Euphues is as colde as [a]
clocke. 1583: Melbancke, *Philotinus*,
sig. H3. 1592: T. Lodge, *Euphues
Shadow*, sig. G2, As coole as a clock.

Cold as a cucumber. *See* **Cool** (2).

Cold as a key. 1501: Douglas, *Pal.
Honor*, Pt. I. st. 61., With quaikand
voce and hart cald as a key. 1587:
Turbervile, *Trag. Tales, etc.*, 276 (1837),
As colde as any kaye. 1702: Farquhar,
Inconstant, IV. iii., Till they be as cold
as a key.

Cold as a stone. *c.* 1300: Brunne, tr.
Langtoft's *Chron.*, 56 (Hearne), He felle
dede doun colde as ony stone. 1506:
A. Barclay, *Cast. of Labour*, sig. A6, My
herte was colde as ony stone. 1697:
Dilke, *City Lady*, III. iii., In the morning he may find him self as cold as
a stone. 1889: R. L. S., *Ballantrae*,
ch. xi.

Cold as charity. 1640: Shirley, *St.
Pat. for Ireland*, III. i., Would I were a
whale in the frozen sea ! charity is not
cold enough to relieve me. 1675: *Poor
Robin Alman.*, Nov., Weather cold as
charity. 1909: De Morgan, *Never can
happen again*, ch. liii.

Cold as clay. 1468: *Coventry Myst.*,
227 (Sh. S.), My hert is colde as clay.
c. 1680: in *Roxb. Ballads*, iii. 480 (B.S.),
Will find the world as cold as clay.
1681: Rycaut, tr. Gracian's *Critick*, 228,
His hands were as cold as clay. 1894:
W. Raymond, *Love and Quiet Life*, 168,
But the old man was as cold as clay.

Cold as ice. 1552: Huloet, *Abced.*,
sig. F1, Colde as yse. 1672: Walker,
Parœm., 23. 1845: Jerrold, *Mrs.
Caudle*, v., As cold, too, as any ice.
1889: J. Nicholson, *Folk Speech E.
Yorks*, 17, As cawd as ice. 1923: G.
Sturt (Bourne), *Wheelwright's Shop*, 13,
Feeling my feet cold as ice.

Cold as mutton. Said of weather.
Glos. 1911: *Folk-Lore*, xxii. 239.

**Cold broth hot again, that loved I
never; Old love renew'd again, that loved
I ever.** 1732: Fuller, No. 6429.

Cold of complexion good of condition.
1678: Ray, 116. 1732: Fuller, No. 1119.

Cold pudding settles love. 1685: S.
Wesley, *Maggots*, 41, Settle the wit, as
pudding settles love. 1709: Ward,
Works, iv. verse 30, Pudding cold, Is
said you know in proverb old, To
settle love. 1738: Swift, *Polite Convers.*, Dial. II., Cold pudden will settle

your love. 1848 : Albert Smith, *Chris. Tadpole*, ch. lx., The cold plum pudding, too, was a wonder . . . when Tom Baker said that . . . there was enough of it to settle everybody's love . . . they laughed. 1917 : Bridge, *Cheshire Proverbs*, 110, Take a little cold pudding to settle your love.

Cold weather and crafty knaves come out of the North. 1659 : Howell, 10 (8). 1670 : Ray, 19 [omitting " crafty."]. Cf. **Three great evils.**

Coldest flint there is hot fire, In the. 1598 : Meres, *Palladis*, fo. 321. 1647 : A. Brewer, *Countrie Girle*, sig. C2, The coldest flint has fire, I see. 1670 : Ray, 72. 1732 : Fuller, No. 2822.

Cole under candlestick, To play. Nares says, s.v. " Coal," that Coal-under-candlestick was a Christmas game mentioned in the *Declaration of Popish Impostures* (1603) ; but the quotations below suggest the sense of— to be secretly deceitful. 1546 : Heywood, *Proverbs*, Pt. I. ch. x., Coll vnder canstyk, she can plaie on bothe handis. 1559 : Becon, *Display of Popish Mass*, in *Prayers, etc.*, 260 (P.S.), Therefore can ye not play cole under candlestick cleanly. 1659 : Howell, 4 [as in 1546, with " he " for " she " and " with " for " on "].

Coleford. *I've been to Coleford—got both eyes open!* Mon. 1905 : *Folk-Lore*, xvi. 67.

Cole-prophet, To play. 1546 : Heywood, *Proverbs*, Pt. I. ch. ix., Ye plaie coleprophet (quoth I), who takth in hande To knowe his answere before he do his erraunde. 1560 : Awdeley, *Vacabondes*, 15 (E.E.T.S.), Cole Prophet is he, that when his maister sendeth him on his errand, he wyl tel his answer therof to his maister or he depart from hym. 1584 : R. Scot, *Witchcraft*, bk. ix. ch. iii., To play the cold prophet, is to recount it good or bad luck, when salt or wine falleth on the table, or is shed, etc.

Coleshill. *See* **Sutton.**

Colewort twice sodden=Crambe bis cocta. 1580 : Lyly, *Euphues*, 391 (Arber), Who left out nothing that before I put in, which I must omitte,

least I set before you, colewortes twice sodden. 1611 : Coryat, *Coryats Crambe, or his Colwort twise sodden, etc.* [title]. 1647 : Stapylton, *Juvenal*, 126, The same verses i' th' same tune instills, Poore school-masters this twice boil'd lettuce kills.

Collier. 1. *As freely as the collier that called my Lord Mayor knave, when he got on Bristow causey* [causeway]. 1869 : Hazlitt, 63.

2. *If you wrestle with a collier, you will get a blotch.* 1618 : Harington, *Epigrams*, bk. ii. No. 36, The proverb says, Who fights with durty foes, Must needs be soyl'd, admit they win or lose. 1732 : Fuller, No. 2802.

3. *Like a collier's sack ; bad without but worse within.* Ibid., No. 3221.

Collins' cow, Troubled in mind like. 1906 : *Cornish N. & Q.*, 263.

Colly Weston. *See* quots. 1587 : Harrison, *Descrip. of Eng.*, Pt. I. 168 (Furnivall), The Morisco gowns, the Barbarian sleeues, the mandilion worne to Collie weston ward. 1841 : Hartshorne, *Salopia Ant.*, 366, Colly Weston . . . implies anything awry, or on one side. 1854 : Baker, *Northants Gloss.*, s.v., When any thing goes wrong, it is said, " It is all along o' Colly Weston." 1917 : Bridge, *Cheshire Proverbs*, 82, It's aw along o' Colly Wes(t)on. Cf. **Cotton's neck.**

Coloquintida for Herb-John, You give me. 1732 : Fuller, No. 5905.

Coloquintida spoils all the broth, A little. 1630 : T. Adams, *Works*, 711.

Color upon color is false heraldry. 1659 : Howell, *Proverbs*, "To Philologers." 1738 : Swift, *Polite Convers.*, Dial. II., [burlesque version] I have heard that goose upon goose is false heraldry.

Colt. 1. *A colt you may break, but an old horse you never can.* 1732 : Fuller, No. 45.

2. *Cut the colt, he's sure to draw*— " not being so cunning as the ' old stagers.' " 1883 : Burne, *Shropsh. Folk-Lore*, 589.

3. *To have a colt's tooth.* c. 1386 : Chaucer, *Reeve's Tale*, l. 34, And yet ik have alwey a coltes tooth. 1588 : Greene, *Perimedes*, in *Works*, vii. 91

(Grosart), Hee hath beene a wag, but
nowe age hath pluckt out all his coltes
teeth. *c.* 1620 : B. & F., *Elder Brother*,
II. iii., If he should love her now, As
he hath a colt's tooth yet . . . 1674 :
Head and Kirkman, *Eng. Rogue*, iii. 7,
I myself have been good in my time ;
and still have a colt's tooth in my head.
1770 : Colman, *Portrait*, Pt. II., in
Dram. Works, iv. 215 (1777), Tho' not
in the bloom of my youth, Yet still
I have left a colt's tooth. 1841 : J. T.
Hewlett, *Parish Clerk*, i. 81 (O.), They
not shedding their colt's teeth yet.

4. *When you ride a young colt, see your
saddle be well girt.* 1659 : Howell, 6.
1670 : Ray, 5. 1736 : Bailey, *Dict.*,
s.v. " Colt."

See also Horse (21) ; Ragged as a colt ;
and Ragged colt.

Comb one's head with a stool, To.
1594 : Shakespeare, *Tam. of Shrew*, I. i.,
Doubt not her care should be To comb
your noddle with a three-legg'd stool.
1671 : *Westm. Drollery*, 38 (Ebsworth),
She flew in my face, and call'd me fool,
And comb'd my head with a three-
legg'd stool. 1785 : Grose, *Class. Dict.
of Vulgar Tongue*, s.v. " Comb," She
combed his head with a joint stool ;
she threw a stool at him. 1886 :
Elworthy, *West Som. Word-Book*, 150
(E.D.S.), It is very usual now . . . to
say of a termagant wife who beats
her husband : she will comb out his
head with a three-legged stool. 1901 :
F. E. Taylor, *Lancs Sayings*, 17, Hoo'll
comb thi yed wi' a three-leg't stoo'.

Come. 1. *As good comes behind as
goes before.* 1683 : Meriton, *Yorkshire
Ale*, 83–7 (1697).

2. *Come and welcome, go by and no
quarrel.* 1670 : Ray, 169. 1738 : Swift,
Polite Convers., Dial. II., Faith, colonel,
come and welcome ; and stay away, and
heartily welcome.

3. *Come, but come stooping,* i.e. well
loaded. 1813 : Ray, 93.

4. *Come day, go day.* 1633 : Draxe,
98, Come day, goe day, the day is long
enough. 1854 : Baker, *Northants Gloss.*,
s.v. " Day," " Come day, go day." An
expression applied to an improvident
person . . . " It's come day, go day,

with him." 1876 : Robinson, *Whitby
Gloss.*, s.v. (E.D.S.). 1893 : J. Salisbury, *S.E. Worcs. Gloss.*, 77 (E.D.S.),
It is said of a careless person, " It's
all Come day, go day, God send Sunday with him " (or " her "). 1921 :
N. & Q., 12th ser., viii. 36, A Leicestershire woman . . . would often speak of
an idle shiftless person as " a poor
come day, go day, God send Sunday
creature."

5. *Come dog, come devil.* 1600 :
Weakest to the Wall, l. 400 (Malone S.),
Come dogge, come diuell, he that scapes
best Let him take all.

6. *Come every one heave a pound.*
Somerset. 1678 : Ray, 355.

7. *Come in if you're fat.* 1738 :
Swift, *Polite Convers.*, Dial. I., Who's
there? . . . come in, if you be fat.

8. *Come Sunday, come se'night =*
Next Sunday but one. 1917 : Bridge,
Cheshire Proverbs, 38.

9. *Come what come would.* 1546 :
Heywood, *Proverbs*, Pt. I. ch. xi.
1606 : Shakespeare, *Macbeth*, I. iii.,
Come what come may, Time and the
hour runs through the roughest day.
1639 : Clarke, 122, Come what come
may.

10. *Come wind come weather. c.* 1630 :
in *Pepysian Garland*, 368 (Rollins,
1922), We needs must drinke come
wind come wether.

11. *Cometh last to the pot. See* Last
to the pot.

12. *He that comes after, sees with
more eyes than his own.* 1732 : Fuller,
No. 2067.

13. *He that comes every day shall have
a cockney and he that comes but now and
then shall have a fat hen.* 1546 : Heywood, *Proverbs*, Pt. I. ch. xi. 1633 :
Draxe, 84.

14. *He that cometh last maketh all
fast.* 1562 : Heywood, *Three Hund.
Epigr.*, No. 202. 1611 : Cotgrave, s.v.
" Porte," The last commer latches the
door, maketh all sure. 1670 : Ray, 112.
1732 : Fuller, No. 6308. Cf. Last makes
fast.

15. *He who comes uncalled sits un-
served.* 1597 : A. Montgomery, *Poems*,
42 (1821), Quha cum uncallt, unservd

suld sit. 1732 : Fuller, No. 1123, Come uncall'd; sit unserv'd.

16. *If they come, they come not; and if they come not, they come.* 1662 : Fuller, *Worthies*, ii. 543 (1840). 1790 : Grose, *Prov. Gloss.*, s.v. " Northumberland." 1846–59 : *Denham Tracts*, i. 243 (F.L.S.).

17. *If thou wilt come with me, bring with thee.* 1578 : Florio, *First Fruites*, fo. 33, If thou wilt go with me bryng with thee. 1629 : *Book of Meery Riddles*, Prov. 115. 1732 : Fuller, No. 6286, Bring something, lass, along with thee, If thou intend to live with me.

18. *It comes by kind, it costs nothing.* 1605 : Camden, *Remains*, 325 (1870), It cometh by kind [nature], it cost them nothing. 1670 : Ray, 182. 1732 : Fuller, No. 5484, What cometh by kind, costeth nothing.

19. *To come bluely off.* 1678 : Ray, 230.

20. *To come to fetch fire.* c. 1380 : Chaucer, *Troylus*, bk. v. l. 484, Be we comen hider To fecchë fyr, and rennen hoom ayeyn? 1670 : Ray, 175. 1738 : Swift, *Polite Convers.*, Dial. I., Where are you going so soon? I hope you did not come to fetch fire.

21. *Who cometh late lodgeth ill.* 1578 : Florio, *First Fruites*, fo. 5. 1732 : Fuller, No. 2381, He who cometh in late, has an ill lodging.

Comfortable as matrimony, As. A two-edged saying. 1736 : Bailey, *Dict.*, s.v. " Comfortable."

Comforter's head never aches, The. 1640 : Herbert, *Jac. Prudentum.* 1670 : Ray, 5. 1732 : Fuller, No. 4454.

Coming events cast their shadows before. 1802 : Campbell, *Lochiel's Warning* (O.).

Command of custom is great, The. 1640 : Herbert, *Jac. Prudentum.*

Command, *verb.* 1. *Command your man, and do it yourself.* 1666 : Torriano, *Piazza Univ.*, 60 [plus " As the English say "]. 1692 : L'Estrange, *Æsop*, 53 (3rd ed.), Which is all but according to the old saying, *Command your man and do't yourself.* 1732 : Fuller, No. 1124.

2. *Command your wealth, else that will command you.* 1732 : Fuller, No. 1125.

3. *He commands enough that obeys a wise man.* 1640 : Herbert, *Jac. Prudentum.* 1670 : Ray, 5. 1732 : Fuller, No. 1827.

4. *He that commandeth well shall be obeyed well.* 1732 : Fuller, No. 2068.

Commend. 1. *Commend not your wife, wine, nor house.* Ibid., No. 1126.

2. *Commend or amend.* c. 1449 : R. Pecock, *Repressor*, Pt. I. ch. ix. p. 48 (Rolls Ser.), And bi the oolde wijs prouerbe, *A man schulde blame or commende as he fyndeth.* 1868 : W. C. Hazlitt, in *N. & Q.*, 4th ser., i. 201, Mr. Corney ought to bear in mind the old maxim, " Commend or amend."

3. *Who commends himself.* See **Neighbour** (2).

Commit. *He that commits a fault thinks every one speaks of it.* 1640 : Herbert, *Jac. Prudentum.*

Common, *adj.* 1. *A common servant is no man's servant.* 1629 : *Book of Meery Riddles*, Prov. 85.

2. *Common as a barber's chair.* See **Barber** (3).

3. *Common as a cart-way.* 1362 : Langland, *Plowman*, A, iii. 127, [She is] as comuyn as the cart-wei to knaues and to alle. 1493 : *Dives and Pauper*, fo. 1 (1536), Other wickednesses ben as common as the carte way. 1566 : Drant, *Horace: Sat.*, sig. D6, As common as the carts way. 1678 : Ray, 90, As common as the highway.

4. *Common as Coleman-hedge.* 1639 : Clarke, 191. 1670 : Ray, 202.

5. *Common as Get out.* Corn. 1869 : Hazlitt, 60.

6. *Common as Ratcliff Highway.* 1667 : L'Estrange, *Quevedo's Visions*, 80 (1904).

7. *Common fame is a common liar.* 1606 : B. Rich, *Faultes*, fo. 46, But Report is a lier. 1710 : Ward, *Nuptial Dialogues*, i. 214, Since common Fame is but a common lyar. 1821 : Scott, *Pirate*, ch. xxxix., But common fame, Magnus considered, was a common liar. Cf. **Blister.**

8. *Common fame is seldom to blame.* 1597 : H. Lok, *Poems*, 299 (Grosart),

Though prouerbe truely say, by fame's
affect, God's iudgement lightly doth a
truth detect. 1694: D'Urfey, *Quixote*,
Pt. II. Act I. sc. i. 1732: Fuller,
No. 6120, Common fame Is mostly
to blame [another opinion !]. 1853:
Trench, *Proverbs*, 13 (1905), *Common
fame is seldom to blame . . .* is the
baser proverb.

9. *Keep the common road, and thou'rt
safe.* 1732: Fuller, No. 3118.

10. *The common people look at the
steeple.* 1639: Clarke, 148.

11. *To be common Jack.* 1546: Heywood, *Proverbs*, Pt. I. ch. xi., I haue
bene common Iacke to all that hole
flocke. 1611: Davies (of Hereford),
Sc. of Folly, 45, in *Works*, ii. (Grosart),
Some Iackes are common to all that
will play.

Companion. 1. *A man knows his
companion in a long journey and a little
inn.* 1732: Fuller, No. 284.

2. *He is an ill companion that has a
good memory.* 1683: White Kennett,
tr. Erasmus' *Praise of Folly*, 167 (8th
ed.), It is an old proverb, *I hate a
pot-companion with a good memory.*
1710: S. Palmer, *Moral Essays on
Proverbs*, 78.

3. *It is good to have companions in
misery.* c. 1374: Chaucer, *Troylus*,
bk. i. l. 708, Men seyn, "to wrecche is
consolacioun To have an-other felawe
in his peyne." c. 1390: Gower, *Conf.
Amantis*, bk. ii. l. 261. 1579: Lyly,
Euphues, 96 (Arber), In misery Euphues
it is great comfort to haue a companion.
1681: W. Robertson, *Phraseol. Generalis*, 348, 'Tis a comfort to have
companions in misery. 1709: Centlivre, *Busy Body*, III. v., 'Tis some
comfort to have a companion in our
sufferings. 1850: Planché, *Extravag.*,
iv. 72 (1879), Well, really, when one's
heart is breaking with vexation, To see
one's friend in the same distress, is a
wond'rous consolation !

Company. 1. *Company makes cuckolds.* 1639: Clarke, 152. 1678: Ray,
116. 1732: Fuller, No. 1132.

2. *Company's good if you are going
to be hanged.* 1864: "Cornish Proverbs," in *N. & Q.*, 3rd ser., vi. 495.

3. *For company, as Kit went to
Canterbury.* 1735: Pegge, *Kent. Proverbs*, in E.D.S., No. 12, p. 69.

4. *The company makes the feast.*
1911: Hackwood, *Good Cheer*, 361,
This has been crystallized into the
terse English proverb, "The company
makes the feast."

Comparison. *See* Nothing (14).

Comparisons are odious. c. 1440:
Lydgate, in *Pol., Relig., and Love
Poems*, 22 (E.E.T.S.), Odyous of olde
been comparisonis. 1583: Greene,
Mamillia, in *Works*, ii. 52 (Grosart),
I will not make comparisons, because
they be odious. 1607: T. Heywood,
Woman Killed with Kindness, I. ii.
1742: Fielding, *Andrews*, bk. i. ch. xvi.,
But comparisons are odious; another
man may write as well as he. 1872:
H. James, *Letters*, i. 32 (1920), Nürem-
burg is excellent—and comparisons are
odious; but I would give a thousand
N's for one ray of Verona !

**Complains wrongfully on the sea that
twice suffers shipwreck, He.** 1640:
Herbert, *Jac. Prudentum.* 1670: Ray,
23.

Complimenting is lying. 1738: Swift,
Polite Convers., Dial. I., I have heard
say that complimenting is lying.

**Compliments fly when gentlefolk
meet.** 1894: R. L. S., *St. Ives*, ch.
xxviii. 1894: Northall, *Folk Phrases*,
12 (E.D.S.), [ironical version] Compliments pass when beggars meet.

Conceal. *See* Hide nothing.

Conceited as a churchwarden. 1917:
Bridge, *Cheshire Proverbs*, 11.

**Conceited [ingenious] goods are
quickly spent.** 1678: Ray, 116.

Coney-catching. *See* Rabbit-hunting.

Confess and be hanged. 1594: A.
Copley, *Wits, Fits, etc.*, 148 (1614),
Confesse and be hang'd, and so he was.
1612: Dekker, *If it be not Good, etc.*, in
Dram. Works, iii. 345 (1873), I haue
confest, and shal be hangd. 1672:
Marvell, *Rehearsal Transpr.*, Pt. I., in
Works, iii. 55 (Grosart), After so simple
a confession as he hath made, must
he now be hang'd too to make good
the proverb? 1710: S. Palmer, *Moral
Essays on Proverbs*, 199, That unlucky

proverb, *Confess and be hang'd.* 1821 :
Scott, *Pirate*, ch. xxxix.

Confess debt and beg days. 1732 :
Fuller, No. 1139.

Confessing a fault makes half amends.
1618 : Harington, *Epigrams*, bk. iii.
No. 25, A fault confest were half
amended. 1670 : Ray, 5. 1732 : Fuller,
No. 1140.

Confession disarms slander, A generous. 1732 : Fuller, No. 126.

Confession is the first step to repentance. 1654 : Gayton, *Pleasant Notes
Don Q.*, 66.

Confine your tongue lest it confine you.
1855 : Bohn, 338.

Congleton rare. *See* 1862 quot. 1813 :
Ray, 242, Congleton bears [the clerk
of C. is said to have sold the church
Bible, to buy a bear for baiting].
1862 : *N. & Q.*, 3rd ser., ii. 166, Passing
through Congleton some time since, a
gentleman heard some tailors, singing,
—Congleton rare, Congleton rare, Sold
the Bible to pay for a bear. 1917 :
Bridge, *Cheshire Proverbs*, 39, [*plus* the
variant] Like Congleton Bear Town
where they sold the Bible to buy a
bear. [Similar stories are told of
Ecclesfield, and Clifton, a village near
Rugby, *N. & Q.*, 3rd ser., ii. 236.]

Conies love roast meat. *c.* 1685 :
Aubrey, *Nat. Hist. Wilts*, 59 (1847),
'Tis a saying, that conies doe love
rost-meat.

Conquer. *He that will conquer must
fight.* 1732 : Fuller, No. 2346.

Conscience. 1. *A clear conscience can
bear any trouble.* Ibid., No. 40.

2. *A clear conscience is a sure card.*
1581 : Lyly, *Euphues*, 207 (Arber).
1659 : Howell, *Proverbs: Brit.-Eng.*, 3.
1732 : Fuller, No. 41.

3. *A clear conscience laughs at false
accusations.* 1580 : Lyly, *Euphues*, 256
(Arber), A cleere conscience needeth no
excuse, nor feareth any accusation.
1669 : *Politeuphuia*, 12 [as in 1580].
1732 : Fuller, No. 42.

4. *A conscience as large as a ship-
man's hose.* 1639 : Clarke, 66. 1670 :
Ray, 205.

5. *A good conscience is a continual
feast.* 1633 : Draxe, 28. Before 1680 :

Butler, *Remains*, ii. 273 (1759), For
a good conscience being a perpetual
feast . . . *c.* 1736 : Franklin, in *Works*,
i. 456 (Bigelow), A good conscience is
a continual Christmas.

6. *A good conscience is the best
divinity.* 1732 : Fuller, No. 141.

7. *A guilty conscience is a self-
accuser* (or *feels continual fear*). [1580 :
Sidney, *Arcadia*, bk. ii. p. 121 (1893),
She felt the terrors of her own conscience.] 1598 : *Servingmans Comfort*,
in *Inedited Tracts*, 99 (Hazlitt), The
guyltie conscience thinkes what as is
sayd, is alwayes spoken himselfe to
vpbrayde. 1604 : Drayton, *The Owl*,
A guilty conscience feels continual fear.
1679 : Crowne, *Ambitious Statesman*,
V. iii., No hell like a bad conscience.
1732 : Fuller, No. 208, A guilty conscience never thinketh itself safe.
c. 1800 : Trusler, *Prov. in Verse*, 112,
Conscience is a self-accuser.

8. *A quiet conscience causes a quiet
sleep.* 1732 : Fuller, No. 374, [*plus*, on
p. 375] A quiet conscience sleeps in
thunder. 1827 : Wilson, *Noctes*, in
Blackw. Mag., April, 476 (O.), That
sweet sound sleep that is the lot o'
a gude conscience.

9. *An evil conscience breaks many a
man's neck.* 1678 : Ray, 116. 1732 :
Fuller, No. 602.

10. *Conscience is a cut-throat.* 1639 :
Clarke, 66.

11. *Conscience serveth for a thousand
witnesses.* 1539 : Taverner, *Proverbs*,
fo. 29, The conscience is a thousande
wytnesses. 1629 : *Book of Meery
Riddles*, Prov. 33. 1633 : Draxe, 27
[as in 1539]. 1639 : Clarke, 66, Conscience is witness enough.

12. *His conscience is made of stretching
leather.* 1597 : *Discouerie of Knights of
the Poste*, sig. B4, Their consciences are
like chiuerell skins, that will stretch
euery way. 1613 : Shakespeare, *Henry
VIII.*, II. iii. 1737 : Ray, 274, He
hath a conscience like a cheverel's
skin (That will stretch). A cheverel is
a wild goat. Somerset. 1830 : Forby,
Vocab. E. Anglia, 430, Your conscience
is made of stretching leather.

13. *See* quot. I do not know to

what proverb allusion is made. 1638:
Randolph, *Works*, ii. 633 (Hazlitt), And
since large conscience (as the proverb
shows) In the same sense with bad
one goes.

14. *Whos conscience is combred and
stondith nott clene, Of another mans
dedis the wursse woll he deme.* 15th cent. :
in *Reliq. Antiquæ*, i. 205 (1841).

See also Friend (1).

Consideration is half conversion, and
Consideration is the parent of wisdom.
1732 : Fuller, Nos. 1146 and 1147.

Considering cap, To put on (or off)
one's. 1605 : Armin, *Foole vpon Foole*,
40 (Grosart), The cobler puts off his
considering cap. 1618 : B. & F.,
Loyal Subject, II. i., And now I'll put
on my considering cap. 1738 : Swift,
Polite Convers., Dial. I., Guess who it
was that told me; come, put on your
considering cap. 1861 : Dickens, *Great
Expect.*, ch. xxxvii., I'll put on my considering cap, and I think all you want to
do may be done by degrees.

Constable for your wit, You might
be a. 1599 : Jonson, *Ev. Man out of
Humour*, I., *Sog.* Why, for my wealth
I might be a justice of peace. *Car.* Ay,
and a constable for your wit. 1678 :
Ray, 236.

Constant dropping will wear away a
stone. [Mr. E. Marshall, in *N. & Q.*,
5th ser., viii. 513, says : " The first
place in which this proverb, expressing
a metaphor which occurs several times
in early writers, is found is the
fragment of Chœrilus, *c.* A.C. 440
(p. 169, ed. Naëke, Lips., 1817):
— πέτρην κοιλαίνει ῥανὶς ὕδατος ἐνδελεχείη."
Gutta cavat lapidem.—Ovid, *Epp. ex
Ponto*, IV. x. 5.] Before 1225, *Ancren
R.*, 220 (Morton), Lutle dropen purleð
þene ulint þet ofte ualleð þeron.
c. 1387 : Usk, *Test. of Love*, in Skeat's
Chaucer, vii. 135, So ofte falleth the
lethy water on the harde rocke, til it
have thorow persed it. *c.* 1477 : Caxton, *Jason*, 26 (E.E.T.S.), How well the
stone is myned and holowed by cer-
tynuell droppyng of water. 1581 :
Lyly, *Euphues*, 127 (Arber), The lyttle
droppes of rayne pearceth hard marble.
1591 : Spenser, *Sonnets*, 18. 1631 :

Mabbe, *Celestina*, 150 (T.T.), Often
dropping makes stones hollow. 1736 :
Franklin, *Way to Wealth*, in *Works*,
i. 444 (Bigelow). 1852 : Dickens, *Bleak
House*, ch. l.

Consult your pillow. *See* Take (25).

Contemplates. *He that contemplates
hath a day without night.* 1640 : Herbert,
Jac. Prudentum. 1670 : Ray, 5. 1732 :
Fuller, No. 2069 [with " on his bed "
before " hath "].

Contempt will sooner kill an injury
than revenge. 1855 : Bohn, 339.

Content, *subs.* 1. *Content is all.*
1639 : Clarke, 38.

2. *Content is happiness.* 1666 : Torriano, *Piazza Univ.*, 52, Who is contented, enjoys. 1732 : Fuller, No. 1152.

3. *Content is more than kingdom.*
1639 : Clarke, 213, Content is a kingdome. 1732 : Fuller, No. 1153.

4. *Content is the philosopher's stone,
that turns all it touches into gold.* 1732 :
Fuller, No. 1154.

5. *Content is worth a crown.* 1630 :
Brathwaite, *Eng. Gent.*, 203 (1641).

6. *Content lodges oftener in cottages
than palaces.* 1732 : Fuller, No. 1155.

7. *He who wants content, can't find
an easy chair.* Ibid., No. 2408.

Content, *adj. He who is content in
his poverty, is wonderfully rich.* 1623 :
Wodroephe, *Spared Houres*, 480.

Contented. 1. *A contented mind is a
continual feast.* 1535 : Coverdale, *Bible*,
Prov. xv. 15, A quiet heart is a continual feast. 1592 : Warner, *Alb. England*, bk. vii. ch. 37, It is a sweete
continuall feast To liue content I see.
1611 : Cotgrave, s.v. " Contenter," We
say, a contented minde is a great
treasure ; or, is worth all. 1681 : W.
Robertson, *Phraseol. Generalis*, 381.
1725 : Bailey, tr. Erasmus' *Colloq.*, 576.

2. *He may well be contented who needs
neither borrow nor flatter.* 1477 : Rivers,
Dictes and Sayings, 69 (1877), Some
axed him of howe moche goode[s] a man
ought to be content, and he answered
to haue so moche as he neded nat to
flatre nor borowe of other. 1670 : Ray,
5. 1748 : Richardson, *Clarissa*, iv. 119
(1785), The man was above control who
wanted not either to borrow or flatter.

Contentment is the greatest wealth.
1633 : Draxe, 31, Contentment is a
great riches. 1754 : Berthelson, *Eng.-
Danish Dict.*, s.v. " Wealth."

Contrary way. *He that goes the contrary way must go over it twice.* 1732 :
Fuller, No. 2120.

Controller. *See* quot. 1591 : Lodge,
Catharos, 14 (Hunt. Cl.), It is an olde
saying and a true, *A controller is not
without contempt.*

Converses. *He that converses not,
knows nothing.* 1670 : Ray, 5. 1732 :
Fuller, No. 2070.

Conway. *See* Clude.

Cook. 1. *A cook is known by his
knife.* 1732 : Fuller, No. 50.

2. *Cooks are not to be taught in their
own kitchen.* Ibid., No. 1160. 1911 :
Hackwood, *Good Cheer*, 234.

3. *Every cook praises his own broth.*
1663 : Gerbier, *Counsel* (1664), Every
cook commends his own sauce. 1855 :
Bohn, 349.

See also **Ill cook; and Too many.**

**Cook-ruffian, able to scald the devil
out of his feathers.** 1670 : Ray, 169
[with " in his " for " out of his "].
1690 : *New Dict. Canting Crew*, sig. D1,
Cook-ruffian, the devil of a cook, or a
very bad one. 1732 : Fuller, No. 1159.

Cool. 1. *A cool mouth and warm feet
live long.* 1611 : Cotgrave, s.v. " Pied,"
A coole mouth, and a dry foot preserve
a man long time alive. 1640 : Herbert,
Jac. Prudentium. 1672 : R. Codrington,
Proverbs, 4.

2. *Cool as a cucumber.* 1615 :
Fletcher, *Cupid's Revenge*, I. i., Young
maids were as cold as cucumbers.
1720 : Gay, *Poems*, ii. 278 (Underhill),
Cool as a cucumber could see The rest
of womankind. 1829 : Scott, *Journal*,
7 July, I rose as cool as a cucumber.
1909 : De Morgan, *Never can happen
again*, ch. xxxiv.

3. *Cool enough to shave a Jew.* 1864 :
" Cornish Proverbs," in *N. & Q.*, 3rd
ser., vi. 495.

4. *Cool words scald not the tongue.*
1732 : Fuller, No. 1161.

Cooling card, A. 1577 : *Misogonus*,
III. ii., Heavy newes for yow, I can tell
yow, of a cowlinge carde. 1584 :

Greene, *Myrr. of Modestie*, in *Works*,
iii. 24 (Grosart), Hir godly counsel was
a cooling carde to their inordinate
desires. 1671 : Head and Kirkman,
Eng. Rogue, ii. 104, This was a shrewd
cooling card to my high hopes.

Cooper's ducks. *See* quot. 1902 :
N. & Q., 9th ser., ix. 127, A short time
ago I heard a respectable young master-
butcher in London use the following
curious saying, viz. " It would soon
have been all Cooper's ducks with me,"
meaning that death would have resulted
had he not quickly recovered from a
recent attack of influenza.

Coot. *See* **Bald** (3).

**Copplestone, Crewys and Crocker were
home when the Conqueror came.** A
Devon saying. 1850 : *N. & Q.*, 1st ser.,
ii. 511. 1876 : *ibid.*, 5th ser., vi. 476.

Copy, subs. 1. *A copy of one's countenance.* c. 1568 : Wager, *Longer thou
livest*, sig. C2, It is but a coppie of his
countenaunce. 1673 : Dryden, *Assignation*, III. i., Sure this is but a copy of
her countenance ; for my heart . . .
whispers to me, she loves me still.
Before 1704 : T. Brown, in *Works*,
iv. 232 (1760), All the while he devours
you, he cants of moderation, and
pretends he does it unwillingly ; but
this is only a copy of his countenance.
1783 : Mrs. Brooke, *Rosina*, II., in
Inchbald's *Farces*, iii. 295 (1815). 1865 :
Editor, *N. & Q.*, 3rd ser., viii. 30, The
phrase, " That is a copy of your countenance," which we have occasionally
heard, but which is not of frequent use,
civilly implies, " That is not spoken
sincerely."

2. *To change* (or *turn*) *one's copy.*
1523 : Berners, *Froissart*, I. ccxlix. (O.),
Thus the knyghtes and squyers turned
theyr copies on both partes. 1553 :
Respublica, II. ii., We must now
chaunge our coppie. 1584 : Lodge,
Alarum against Venus, 39 (Sh. S.),
Whereupon, altering his coppie . . .
the king concluded thus . . . 1606 :
A. Craig, *Amorose Songes*, 21 (Hunt.
Cl.), But being old, hee chaunged copie,
and writ as violently against it. 1632 :
W. Rowley, *New Wonder*, III., Then
did my father change his copy, and set

up a brewhouse. 1706: *George-a-
Greene*, in Thoms, *Early Prose Rom.*,
ii. 18 (1828), He began to alter his
phrases, and changed the copy of his
countenance.

Cormorant. See **Wet** (2).

Corn. 1. *Corn and horn go together.*
1678: Ray, 116. 1846: Denham, *Proverbs*, 2 (Percy S.). 1893: Inwards,
Weather Lore, 5.

2. *Corn in good years is hay, in ill
years straw is corn.* 1640: Herbert,
Jac. Prudentum. 1670: Ray, 5. 1732:
Fuller, No. 1162.

3. *Corn is cleansed with the wind, and
the soul with chastening.* 1670: Ray, 5.

4. *Corn is not to be gathered in the
blade but the ear.* 1580: Lyly, *Euphues*,
360 (Arber) [with "budde" for
"blade"]. 1732: Fuller, No. 1163.

5. *Much corn lies under the straw that
is not seen.* 1639: Clarke, 145. 1670:
Ray, 73. 1732: Fuller, No. 3480,
Much corn lies in the chaff unseen.

6. *The corn hides itself in the snow as
an old man in furs.* 1640: Herbert,
Jac. Prudentum.

7. *When the corn is in the shock, Then
the fish are on the rock.* Old Cornish
rhyme. 1865: Hunt, *Pop. Romances
W. of England*, 428 (1896).

See also **Candlemas**, D; **Cuckoo** (3),
(7), (16), and (22); **Famine; Fog** (3);
Good seed; July (1) and (8); **June** (4);
March (3), (11), and (21); **May**, A (2)
and (3), E (1) and (5), and F (12); **Nut**
(1); **Old**, E (23); **Up horn; Weeds;** and
Wind, A (*b*) (1).

Cornish gentlemen are cousins, All.
1602: Carew, *Surv. of Cornwall*, 179
(1811) [cited as "the proverb"]. 1724:
Defoe, *Tour*, Lett. III. 102. 1880:
Courtney, *W. Cornwall Words*, 14
(E.D.S.).

Cornish hug, A. 1638: Nabbes,
Tott. Court, III. iii., You are so taken
with your Cornish prentice . . . hearing him talke the other day of the
hugge . . . 1705: in *Harl. Miscell.*,
ii. 338 (1744), His St. Maw's Muse
has given the French troops a Cornish
hug, and flung them all upon their
backs. 1796: Wolcot, *Works*, iv. 131
(1796), Give, to black blasphemy, a

Cornish hug. 1818: *Gent. Mag.*, i. 310,
Cornwall is celebrated for athletic
exercises, particularly wrestling. A
"Cornish hug" has been long proverbial. 1907: Hackwood, *Old Eng.
Sports*, 189, To give a Cornish hug is
a proverbial expression.

Corns in the head, To have = To be
drunk. 1745: Franklin, in *Works*,
ii. 23 (Bigelow).

Cornwall. 1. *Cornwall will bear a
shower every day, and two on Sunday.*
1864: "Cornish Proverbs," in *N. & Q.*,
3rd ser., v. 208. 1887: M. A. Courtney,
in *Folk-Lore Journal*, v. 219.

2. *In Cornwall are the best gentlemen.*
1851: Borrow, *Lavengro*, ch. i. *n.* 1864:
"Cornish Proverbs," in *N. & Q.*,
3rd ser., vi. 6.

3. *There are more saints in Cornwall
than in heaven.* Ibid., 3rd ser., v. 275.
1880: Courtney, *W. Cornwall Words*,
xiv. (E.D.S.). 1927: J. M. Bulloch, in
Sunday Times, 15 May, It is a common
saying in the West of England that
"there are more saints in Cornwall
than in heaven."

4. *See* quot. 1906: *Cornish N. & Q.*,
293, We all know the old proverb "'Tis
a bad wind that blows no good to
Cornwall."

5. *To send a husband into Cornwall
without a boat.* See 1847 quot. 1567:
Painter, *Pal. of Pleasure*, iii. 128
(Jacobs), They seemed . . . to be
iealous ouer their wyues. But . . .
eyther of them without shipping,
sought to send other into Cornouale.
1591: Florio, *Second Frutes*, 143, She
spins crooked spindles for her husband,
and sends him into Cornwall without
ship or boate. 1670: Ray, 223, He
doth sail into Cornwall without a bark.
1790: Grose, *Prov. Gloss.*, s.v. "Cornwall" [as in 1670]. 1847: Halliwell,
Dict., s.v., A woman who cuckolds her
husband was said to send him into
Cornwall without a boat.

See also **Devil** (87).

Cornwallis Family. *See* **Paston Family.**

**Corpus Christi Day clear Gives a good
year.** 1893: Inwards, *Weather Lore*, 41.

Corrat as Crocker's mare. 1879:
Folk-Lore Record, 203. 1882: Jago,

Gloss. of Cornish Dialect, 144, Corrat.
Pert, impudent, sharp in rejoinder.
" As corrat as Crocker's mare." East
Cornwall Proverb. 1888: Q.-Couch,
Troy Town, ch. v. Cf. **Coy.**

Correction gives understanding. 1552:
Latimer, *Sermons*, 501 (P.S.), It is a
common saying, *Vexatio dat intellectum*,
" Correction giveth understanding."

Corruption of best is worst, The.
1642 : D. Rogers, *Matrim. Honour*, 34.
1702 : Penn, *Fruits of Solitude*, Pt. II.
No. 160, The proverb is verified, The
corruption of the best things is the
worst and most offensive. 1732 :
Fuller, No. 1166.

**Corruption of one is the generation
of another, The.** 1576 : Lambarde,
Peramb. of Kent, 244 (1826), The olde
maxime of Philosophie, *Corruptio unius,
generatio alterius:* The corruption of one
is the generation of another. 1583 :
Melbancke, *Philotinus*, sig. Y3. *c.* 1602 :
Chapman, *May-Day*, III. iii., The corruption of a bawd is the generation of
a witch. 1738 : Swift, *Polite Convers.*,
Dial. II., [a burlesque version] They
say that the corruption of pipes is the
generation of stoppers.

Cossingland. *See* **Cowhithe.**

Costs little is little esteemed, What.
1612 : Shelton, *Quixote*, Pt. I. bk. iv.
ch. vii. 1732 : Fuller, No. 5485, What
costs little is less esteemed.

**Cotherston cheeses will cover a
multitude of sins, and Cotherston, where
they christen calves, hopple lops [fleas],
and kneeband spiders.** Both—1863 :
N. & Q., 3rd ser., iii. 233.

Cotswold. 1. *A Cotswold lion* = A
sheep. *c.* 1440 : Satirical rhymes on
Siege of Calais, in *Archæologia*, xxxiii.
130, Com rennyng on him fersly as
lyons of Cotteswold. 1546 : Heywood,
Proverbs, Pt. I. ch. xi., She is as fierce
as a lyon of Cotsolde. 1600 : *Sir John
Oldcastle*, l. 700 (Malone S.), You old
stale ruffin, you lion of Cotswold. 1785 :
Grose, *Class. Dict. Vulgar Tongue*, s.v.,
Cotswould Lion, a sheep.

2. *It is as long in coming as Cotswold
barley.* 1662 : Fuller, *Worthies*, i. 552
(1840). 1790 : Grose, *Prov. Gloss.*, s.v.
" Gloucestershire." 1898 : Gibbs, *Cots-*

wold Village, ch. iv., p. 85 (3rd ed.), Two
proverbs that are in constant use
amongst all classes are, . . . and " 'Tis
as long in coming as Cotswold berle "
(barley).

**Cottage in possession for a kingdom
in hope, I'll not change a.** 1639 :
Clarke, 256. 1670: Ray, 3 [with
" reversion " for " hope "]. 1732 :
Fuller, No. 2643 [as in 1670].

Cotton's neck. 1841 : Hartshorne,
Salopia Ant., 375, " All awry like
Cotton's neck." A simile applied to
any thing that is warped or twisted.
1883 : Burne, *Shropsh. Folk-Lore*, 592.
Cf. **Colly Weston.**

**Cough will stick longer by a horse
than a peck (or half a peck) of oats, A.**
1678 : Ray, 117. 1732 : Fuller, No. 54.

Counsel, *subs.* 1. *Counsel breaks not
the head.* 1640: Herbert, *Jac. Prudentum.*

2. *Counsel is no command.* 1732 :
Fuller, No. 1182.

3. *Counsel is to be given by the wise,
the remedy by the rich.* 1855 : Bohn,
339.

4. *Counsel must be followed, not
praised.* 1732 : Fuller, No. 1183.

5. *Counsel of fools. See* **Fool** (12).

6. *Counsel over cups is crazy.* 1670 :
Ray, 5, Counsels in wine seldom
prosper. 1732 : Fuller, No. 1184.

7. *Good counsel does no harm.* 1633 :
Draxe, 33. 1639 : Clarke, 67.

8. *Good counsel is lacking when most
needed.* *c.* 1386 : Chaucer, *Tale of
Melibeus*, § 13, " I see wel," quod this
wyse man, " that the commune proverbe is sooth ; that 'good conseil
wanteth whan it is most nede.' "

9. *Good counsel never comes amiss.*
1732 : Fuller, No. 1708.

10. *If the counsel be good, no matter
who gave it.* Ibid., No. 2704.

11. *Ill counsel hurts the counsellor.*
1539 : Taverner, *Proverbs*, fo. 4, Euyll
counsayle is worst to the counseylour.
1639 : Clarke, 21.

12. *The counsel thou wouldest have
another keep, first keep thyself.* 1605 :
Camden, *Remains*, 334 (1870).

Counsel, *verb.* He that will not be
counselled, cannot be helped. 1639 :

Clarke, 22. 1670: Ray, 6. 1732:
Fuller, No. 2350. 1875: A. B. Cheales,
Proverb. Folk-Lore, 103.

Counterfeit. *See* quot. *c.* 1645:
"MS. Proverbs," in *N. & Q.*, vol. cliv.,
p. 27, Hee is a counterfett who is
afraid of the touchstone.

Count every step. *See* **Tell (5).**

Counting the pothooks. 1917: Bridge,
Cheshire Proverbs, 44, Said of servants,
when in a new place they sit quietly
at first and don't quite know what to
do or say.

Country. 1. *A country man may be
as warm in kersey, as a king in velvet.*
1732: Fuller, No. 55. 1869: Spurgeon,
John Ploughman, ch. ii. [with " fustian "
for " kersey "].

2. *The country for a wounded heart.*
1906: A. C. Benson, *College Window*,
107, " The country for a wounded
heart," says the old proverb.

3. *You must go into the country to
hear what news at London.* 1678: Ray,
345. 1732: Fuller, No. 1664 [with
" town " for " London "].

County. *See* **Hundred.**

Couple are newly married. *See* quot.
1670: Ray, 53, When a couple are
newly married, the first moneth is
honey-moon or smick smack; the
second is, hither and thither: the third
is, thwick thwack: the fourth, the Devil
take them that brought thee and I
together. 1754: Berthelson, *Eng.-
Danish Dict.*, s.v. " Thwack " [with
" me and thee " for " thee and I "].

Courage mounteth with occasion.
1855: Bohn, 340.

**Courage ought to have eyes as well
as arms.** 1732: Fuller, No. 1188.

**Courageous foe is better than a
cowardly friend, A.** Ibid., No. 56.

Course. 1. *If that course be fair,
again and again quoth Bunny to his bear.*
1639: Clarke, 179. 1670: Ray, 163.

2. *The course of true love never did
run smooth.* 1857: Reade, *The Course
of True Love, etc.* [title]. 1872: Trollope,
Golden Lion, ch. i., He . . . feels it to
be a sort of duty to take care that the
course of love shall not run altogether
smooth.

Court. 1. *At court, every one for*
himself. 1611: Cotgrave, s.v. " Court,"
In court men study only their owne
fortunes. 1640: Herbert, *Jac. Prudentum.* 1732: Fuller, No. 825.

2. *Court holy water*=Flattery. 1519:
Horman, *Vulgaria*, fo. 231, I haue many
feyre promessis and haly water of court.
1565: Shacklock, *Hatch. of Heresies*,
quoted in *N. & Q.*, 2nd ser., v. 411,
Therefore were we so wone with courte
holy water, that is, fayre and flattring
wordes. 1614: B. Rich, *Honestie of
This Age*, 52 (Percy S.), Shee may bee
rewarded with some *court holy water*
wordes. 1692: L'Estrange, *Æsop*, 14
(3rd ed.), A little court holy water
washes off all stains. 1740: North,
Examen, 136, Some words slipt, as it
were, from his pen, a drop of mere
court holy water. 1785: Grose, *Class.
Dict. Vulgar Tongue*, s.v., Court holy
water, fair speeches and promises
without performance.

3. *Courts keep no almanacs.* 1640:
Herbert, *Jac. Prudentum*, The court
hath no almanack. 1670: Ray, 6.
1710: S. Palmer, *Moral Essays on
Proverbs*, 318, All Europe has consented
to the proverb, that in a Prince's Court
there is no almanack. 1732: Fuller,
No. 1192.

4. *One of the court, but none of the
counsel.* 1546: Heywood, *Proverbs*,
Pt. I. ch. xi., I was neyther of court
nor of counsayle made. 1670: Ray,
170.

Courtesy. 1. *A courtesy much en-
treated is half recompensed.* 1732:
Fuller, No. 57.

2. *Courtesy on one side only lasts not
long.* 1640: Herbert, *Jac. Prudentum.*
1670: Ray, 6. 1732: Fuller, No. 1191.

3. *Full of courtesy and full of craft.*
1594: Nashe, *Unfort. Trav.*, in *Works*,
v. 14 (Grosart), Much companie, much
knauerie, as true as that olde adage,
Much curtesie, much subtiltie. 1639:
Clarke, 13. 1670: Ray, 73. 1732:
Fuller, No. 1635.

4. *He may freely receive courtesies,
that knows how to requite them.* 1670:
Ray, 22.

Courtier young, beggar old. *c.* 1510:
A. Barclay, *Egloges*, 20 (Spens. S.), Oft

yonge courters be beggers in their age.
1579: Lyly, *Euphues*, 185 (Arber),
Certes it is an olde saying that who so
liueth in the court, shall dye in the
strawe. 1613: *Vncasing of Machivils
Instr. to his Sonne*, 7, And than do
proue the prouerbe often tolde, "A
careless courtier young, a begger olde."
1732: Fuller, No. 642, [the converse]
An old courtier, a young beggar.
Cf. Live (15).

**Courting and wooing bring dallying
and doing.** 1605: Camden, *Remains*,
320 (1870). 1670: Ray, 48. 1732:
Fuller, No. 6264 [with "canting" for
"courting"].

Cousin. 1. *Call me cousin, but cozen
me not.* 1678: Ray, 118. 1732:
Fuller, No. 1046. *c.* 1800: J. Trusler,
Prov. in Verse, 47.

2. *Cousin germans quite removed.*
1678: Ray, 69. 1732: Fuller, No. 1193.

3. *First cousins may marry, second
cousins can't; third cousins will marry,
fourth cousins won't.* S. Devon. 1869:
Hazlitt, 132.

See also Marry! come up.

Covent Garden ague, The = Venereal
disease. 1678: Ray, 88. 1790: Grose,
Prov. Gloss., s.v. "Westminster."

Covent Garden is the best garden.
1790: Ibid.

Coventry blue, He is true. 1662:
Fuller, *Worthies*, iii. 272 (1840). 1790:
Grose, *Prov. Gloss.*, s.v. "Warwickshire."

Coventry, To send to. 1777: Garrick,
in *Garrick Corresp.*, ii. 237 (1832), I
seemed to be the person marked for
displeasure, and was almost literally
sent to Coventry. 1787: D'Arblay,
Diary, ii. 427 (1876), This again sent
me to Coventry for the rest of the
dinner. 1850: Dickens, *Copperfield*,
ch. v. 1874: Smiles, *Lives of Engineers*,
ii. 239, They thwarted him at every
turn, out-voted him, snubbed him, and
"sent him to Coventry."

Cover your head. *See* Head (2).

**Cover yourself with your shield, and
care not for cries.** 1640: Herbert, *Jac.
Prudentum*.

**Covers me with his wings, and bites
me with his bill, He.** 1633: Draxe, 97.
1670: Ray, 5. 1732: Fuller, No. 1829.

Covers thee, discovers thee, He that.
1620: Shelton, *Quixote*, Pt. II. ch. v.

Covet. *He that covets all. See* All
covet.

Covetous, *adj.* 1. *A covetous man
does nothing well till he dies.* 1539:
Taverner, *Proverbs*, fo. 51, A couetous
man doth noman good but whan he
dyeth. 1572: T. Wilson, *Disc. upon
Usury*, 230 (1925). 1732: Fuller, No. 51.

2. *A covetous man is good to none,
but worst to himself.* 1614: Lodge, tr.
Seneca, 443, The couetous man is good
to no man, and worst to himselfe. 1669:
Politeuphuia, 287. 1732: Fuller, No. 53.

3. *A covetous man is like a dog in a
wheel that roasts meat for others.* 1659:
Howell, 10 (8). 1670: Ray, 5. 1732:
Fuller, No. 52.

4. *A covetous man makes a halfpenny
of a farthing, and a liberal man makes
sixpence of it.* 1855: Bohn, 284.

5. *Covetous men live like drudges to
die wretches.* 1732: Fuller, No. 1171.

6. *The covetous spends more than the
liberal.* 1640: Herbert, *Jac. Prudentum*.

Covetousness. 1. *Covetousness, as
well as prodigality, brings a man to a
morsel of bread.* 1732: Fuller, No. 1173.

2. *Covetousness breaks the sack.*
c. 1594: Bacon, *Promus*, No. 616.
1612: Shelton, *Quixote*, Pt. I. bk. iii.
ch. vi. 1710: S. Palmer, *Moral Essays
on Proverbs*, 34, Covetousness breaks
the Jack. Antiquity appears in the
face of this proverb; for without doubt
'tis the old black leathern Jack that
was in use in the time of our forefathers,
that is here designed. [This explanation may well be doubted. Why
should "Jack" have become uniformly
"sack"?] 1712: Motteux, *Quixote*,
Pt. I. bk. iii. ch. vi. 1821: Scott,
Kenilworth, ch. iv., Be not over-greedy,
Anthony. Covetousness bursts the sack.

3. *Covetousness brings nothing home.*
1639: Clarke, 37. 1732: Fuller,
No. 1175.

4. *Covetousness is always filling a
bottomless vessel.* 1732: Fuller, No. 1176.

5. *Covetousness is the mother of ruin
and mischief.* 1387: Trevisa, tr. Higden, iii. 475 (Rolls Ser.), Covetise is
moder of povert. *c.* 1440: Anon., tr.

Higden, iii. 475 (Rolls Ser.), Covetise
is the moder of pouerte. 1533: in
Ballads from MSS., i. 202 (B.S.), Be
ware of covetyse, The rote of all ill
vice. 1589: L. Wright, *Display of
Dutie*, 10, Couetousnesse is the roote
of all euill : the ground of all vice.
c. 1670: *Sir Rich. Whittington*, 26
(Villon S.), It is an old and true saying,
Covetousness is the mother of ruine
and mischief.

6. *Covetousness often starves other
vices.* 1732: Fuller, No. 1178.

7. *When all sins grow old, covetousness is young.* 1560 : Becon, *Catechism*,
373 (P.S.), Covetousness is a vice appro-
priated as it may seem to old men,
according to this old saying : *Cum
omnia vitia senescunt, sola avaritia
juvenescit :* " When all vices wax old,
covetousness alone waxeth young."
c. 1570: in Collmann, *Ballads, etc.*, 130
(Roxb. Cl.). 1611 : Cotgrave, s.v.
" Peché," When all sinnes else be old
is avarice young. 1666 : Torriano,
Piazza Univ., 17.

Cow. 1. *A collier's cow and an alewife's sow are always well fed.* 1678 :
Ray, 119.

2. *A cow will not clem [starve], if there
are three blades of pink grass in the field.*
1877 : E. Leigh, *Cheshire Gloss.*, 155
[" an old saying "]. 1917: Bridge,
Cheshire Proverbs, 2.

3. *A lowing cow soon forgets her calf.*
c. 1330 : in Wright's *Pol. Songs*, 332
(Camden S., 6), Hit nis noht al for the
calf that kow louweth, Ac hit is for the
grene gras that in the medewe grouweth.
1882 : Mrs. Chamberlain, *W. Worcs.
Words*, 39 (E.D.S.). 1894: Northall,
Folk Phrases, 6 (E.D.S.). 1913: *Folk-
Lore*, xxiv. 77, A bellowing cow soon
forgets her calf. Oxfordsh. 1928 : in
London Mercury, Feb., 439, Common
proverb in the West Country is " A
belving cow soon forgets her calf."

4. *A red cow gives good milk.* 1917 :
Bridge, *Cheshire Proverbs*, 5.

5. *As comely (or as nimble) as a cow
in a cage.* 1399 : Langland, *Rich. the
Redeless*, iii. 262, As be-cometh a kow
to hoppe in a cage ! 1546 : Heywood,
Proverbs, Pt. II. ch. i., As comely as is

a cowe in a cage. 1577 : J. Grange,
Golden Aphroditis, sig. F1, As seemely
as a cowe in a cage. 1678 : Ray, 287,
As nimble . . . 1732 : Fuller, No. 718,
As nimble . . .

6. *As cows come to town, some good
some bad.* 1639 : Clarke, 219.

7. *As good luck as had the cow that
stuck herself with her own horn.* 1678 :
Ray, 287.

8. *As much use as a cow has for side
pockets.* 1917 : Bridge, *Cheshire Proverbs*, 18. Cf. **Toad** (1).

9. *Cow's horn.* See **Butter** (3) ; and
Milk (5).

10. *Curst cows have short horns.*
1509: Barclay, *Ship of Fools*, i. 182
(1874), To a wylde cowe god doth
short hornys sende. 1588 : Greene,
Pandosto, in *Works*, iv. 247 (Grosart),
A curst cow hath oftentimes short
hornes, and a willing minde but a
weake arme. 1599: Shakespeare,
Much Ado, II. i. 1721 : Centlivre,
Artifice, III. i. 1793 : Grose, *Olio*,
281 (2nd ed.), Having thus shown the
futility of your criticism, and thereby
the truth of that proverb which says,
God sends curst cows short horns . . .
1880 : Courtney, *W. Cornwall Words*,
xiii. (E.D.S.), 'Tis well that wild cows
have short horns.

11. *He becomes it as well as a cow
doth a cart-saddle.* [Bovi clitellas im-
ponere:—*ap.* Cicero, *Att.*, V. xv. 3.]
1530 : Palsgrave, 427, As mete to be a
great mans keever as a kowe to bear
a saddle. 1639 : Clarke, 5.

12. *He knows no more what to do with
it than a cow does with a holiday.* Devon.
1882 : *Folk-Lore Record*, v. 159.

13. *His cow has calved.* 1596: Jonson, *Ev. Man in his Humour*, IV. ii.,
How now ! whose cow has calv'd?
1678: Ray, 70. 1828 : Scott, *Fair Maid*,
ch. xxii., How now—what's the matter?
. . . whose cow has calved?

14. *If you buy the cow, take the tail
into the bargain.* 1732 : Fuller, No. 2743.

15. *If you sell the cow, you sell her milk
too.* Ibid., No. 2786.

16. *It is not all butter that comes from
the cow.* 1546 : Heywood, *Proverbs*,
Pt. II. ch. ix., It is not all butter that

the coow s—. 1666: Torriano, *Piazza Univ.*, 294, All is not butter that the cow makes. 1732: Fuller, No. 527.

17. *Let him that owns the cow take her by the tail.* 1611: Cotgrave, s.v. "Queue" [with "asse" for "cow"]. 1694: D'Urfey, *Quixote*, Pt. II. Act III. sc. ii. 1732: Fuller, No. 3185.

18. *Like a crab in a cow's mouth.* 1732: Fuller, No. 2990, It is no more to him than a crab in a cow's mouth. 1913: *Folk-Lore*, xxiv. 77, Like a crab in a cow's mouth (Oxfordsh.).

19. *Look to the cow and the sow, and the wheat-mow, and [all] will be well enow.* Somerset. 1678: Ray, 347. 1846: Denham, *Proverbs*, 19 (Percy S.).

20. *Many a good cow hath an evil calf.* 1546: Heywood, *Proverbs*, Pt. I. ch. x. 1580: Baret, *Alvearie*, H 406. 1605: Chapman, etc., *Eastw. Hoe*, IV. ii., Thou art not the first good cow hast had an ill calf. 1681: W. Robertson, *Phraseol. Generalis*, 404, Many a good cow has but a bad calf. 1732: Fuller, No. 3337. 1846: Denham, *Proverbs*, 3 (Percy S.).

21. *Milk the cow that standeth still.* c. 1594: Bacon, *Promus*, No. 553, Milk the standing cowe. Why follow you the flying? 1688: *Gesta Grayorum*, 38 (Malone S.), The proverb is a countrey-proverb, but significative, Milk the cow that standeth still; why follow you her that flieth away?

22. *Steal my cow and give away the hide.* 1869: Hazlitt, 345.

23. *The cow gives good milk, but kicks over the pail.* 1599: Porter, *Two Angry Women*, sc. xi., Be not you like the cowe, that gives a good sope of milke, and casts it downe with her heeles. 1659: Howell, 14, Like a curst cow that gives a paile of milk, and then kicks it down. 1716: Ward, *Female Policy*, 84, A cow that gives good milk, but kicks it to the ground. 1753: Richardson, *Grandison*, iv. 148 (1883), You are a pretty cow, my love; you give good store of milk, but you have a very careless heel.

24. *The cow knows not what her tail is worth till she has lost it.* 1640: Herbert, *Jac. Prudentum.*

25. *The cow little giveth, that hardly liveth.* 1732: Fuller, No. 6325.

26. *The old brown cow laid an egg.* 1917: Bridge, *Cheshire. Proverbs*, 117, . . . used as an answer to importunate questions.

27. *The tune the old cow died of.* 1732: Fuller, No. 4360, That is the old tune upon the bag-pipe. 1836: Marryat, *Japhet*, ch. lxviii., This tune, "which the old cow died of," as the saying is, used to be their horror.

28. *Till the cows come home.* 1625: in *Harl. Miscell.*, iv. 125 (1745), Drinking, eating, feasting, and revelling, till the cow come home, as the saying is. 1738: Swift, *Polite Convers.*, Dial. II., I warrant you lay abed till the cows came home. 1836: Marryat, *Easy*, ch. vii., Which receipt . . . was, in point of law, about as valuable as if he had agreed to pay as soon "as the cows came home." c. 1873: John Hay, *Little Breeches*, etc., 22, You may nezo-loot till the cows come home. 1924: M. Kennedy, *Constant Nymph*, 320, You can keep on guessing till the cows come home.

29. *To grow down like a cow's tail.* [Haec colonia retroversus crescit tanquam coda vituli.—Petr., 44.] 1649: in *Somers Tracts*, vii. 87 (1811), I would still be growing, though it be downwards. Why should not old lords, as well as old men, be cows-tails? 1653: Urquhart, *Rabelais*, bk. ii. ch. xxvii., Which never grow but like cowes tailes downwards. 1710: Ward, *Nuptial Dialogues*, ii. 76, You're growing downwards now, Like tail of heifer or of cow. 1894: Northall, *Folk Phrases*, 19 (E.D.S.), Like a cow's tail, [he *or* she] grows down hill.

30. *To have a cow's tongue.* 1750: W. Ellis, *Housewife's Companion*, vii., The gossiping sort . . . have a cow's tongue (as we call it in the country), a smooth side and a rough side.

31. *To look on one as a cow on a bastard calf.* Somerset. 1678: Ray, 353. 1883: Burne, *Shropsh. Folk-Lore*, 594, To look like a cow at a bastard calf=to look coldly, suspiciously at one.

32. *To set a cow to get a hare.* 1611:

Cotgrave, s.v. "Vache," A cow may catch a hare. 1683: Meriton, *Yorkshire Ale*, 83–7 (1697), Sett a cow to git a hare. 1883: Burne, *Shropsh. Folk-Lore*, 588, We don't go by size, or a cow would catch a hare.

33. *To tip the cow's horn with silver*. 1917: Bridge, *Cheshire Proverbs*, 144, When a butcher pays for the cow he has bought, he expects a "luckpenny" to be returned to him which, in the case of a cow, is usually a shilling, and is technically called "tipping the cow's horn with silver."

34. *What should a cow do with a nutmeg?* 1732: Fuller, No. 5502.

35. *Who will sell the cow must say the word*. 1640: Herbert, *Jac. Prudentum*.

36. *Who would keep a cow when he may have a quart of milk for a penny?* 1659: Howell, *Letters*, ii. 666 (Jacobs), In this case it is better to buy a quart of milk by the penny than keep a cow. *c.* 1680: in *Roxb. Ballads*, viii. 859 (B.S.), What need I keep a cow, or at such charges to be, When I can have a quart of milk for a penny? 1732: Fuller, No. 5697. 1917: Bridge, *Cheshire Proverbs*, 155 [with "pottle" for "quart"].

See also Calf (3), (5), and (9); Horse (72); Like cow; Lincolnshire where; Margery; Milk (5); Parson's cow; and Slender.

Coward and **Cowards**. 1. *A coward, a coward*. *See* Barnard Castle (1).

2. *A coward's fear can make a coward valiant*. 1732: Fuller, No. 58.

3. *Cowards are cruel*. 1485: Malory, *Morte d'Arthur*, bk. xviii. ch. 24, Euer wylle a coward shewe no mercy. 1591: Harington, *Orl. Furioso*, bk. xxxvi., Notes, Cruelty ever proceeds from a vile minde, and often from a cowardly heart. 1639: Clarke, 76, Cruell people are fearefull. 1727: Gay, *Fables*, 1st ser., No. 1, l. 33, Cowards are cruel. 1891: R. L. S., *Wrecker*, ch. xxii., For once the proverb was right, cruelty was coupled with cowardice.

4. *Cowards die often*. 1927: *Sphere*, 3 Dec., p. 414, col. 1, It is true that cowards die many times before their death.

5. *If he be a coward he is a murderer*. 1595: *Polimanteia*, sig. N1, Alleadging an olde prouerbe to that ende, *If he be*, etc.

6. *Make a coward fight and he will kill the devil*. 1669: *New Help to Discourse*, 151. 1732: Fuller, No. 3980, Put a coward to his mettle, and he'll fight the devil.

7. *Many would be cowards, if they had courage enough*. 1732: Fuller, No. 3366.

Cowardly is unlucky. *c.* 1386: Chaucer, *Reeve's Tale*, l. 290, "Unhardy is unsely," thus men sayth.

Cowfold. *See* Bolney.

Cowhithe. *See* quot. 1670: Ray, 253, Between Cowhithe and merry Cossingland, The devil s— Benacre, look where it stands. 1790: Grose, *Prov. Gloss.*, s.v. "Suffolk."

Cowl. *See* Hood.

Cowling moon. *See* quot. 1827: Hone, *Table-Book*, 775, In the vulgar vocabulary of Craven a silly fellow is called a "Cowling moon."

Cox's pig. *He thought a lie, like Cox's pig*. War. 1920: *N. & Q.*, 12th ser., vii. 67.

Coy as a croker's mare. 1546: Heywood, *Proverbs*, Pt. II. ch. i. 1670: Ray, 202. Cf. **Corrat**.

Crab. *See* Cow (18); and Devil (122).

Crab of the wood. *See* quot. 1659: Howell, 6, A crabb of the wood is sawce very good for a crabb of the sea, The wood of a crabb is good for a drabb that will not her husband obey. 1670: Ray, 210. 1736: Bailey, *Dict.*, s.v. "Crab" [very slightly varied].

Crabbed knot must have a crabbed wedge, A. 1611: Davies (of Hereford), *Sc. of Folly*, 24, in *Works*, ii. (Grosart).

Crabs. *The greatest crabs are not always the best meate*. 1546: Heywood, *Proverbs*, Pt. I. ch. xi. 1611: Cotgrave, s.v. "Bœuf." 1670: Ray, 75.

Crab-tree. *Plant the crab-tree where you will, it will never bear pippins*. 1732: Fuller, No. 3880.

Crack me that nut. *See* Nut (2).

Crack the nut. *See* Eat (25).

Crack was a good dog. *See* quot. 1891: S. O. Addy, *Sheffield Gloss. Supp.*, 14 (E.D.S.), There is a proverb which

says that " Crack was a good dog, but
he got hung for barking." It is
intended to show that a swaggerer
comes to a bad end.

Cradle over thy head, Cast not thy.
1678 : Ray, 347.

**Cradle straws are scarce out of his
breech.** 1678 : Ray, 346. 1683 : Meriton, *Yorkshire Ale*, 83–7 (1697), Credle
streays are scarce out of his breech.

Craft. 1. *All the craft is in the
catching.* 1631 : Mabbe, *Celestina*, 163
(T.T.). Before 1680 : Butler, *Remains*,
ii. 279 (1759), For all the craft is not in
the catching (as the proverb says) but
the better half at least is being catched.

2. *Craft against craft makes no living.*
1640 : Herbert, *Jac. Prudentum.*

3. *Craft bringeth nothing home.* 1633 :
Draxe, 35. 1670 : Ray, 6. 1732 : Fuller,
No. 1199.

4. *Craft is found in clouted shoes.*
c. 1600 : in *Roxb. Ballads*, ii. 574 (B.S.),
Craft lies under clowted shoone. 1618 :
Harington, *Epigrams*, bk. i. No. 11,
I heare some say, and some believe it
too, That craft is found ev'n in the
clouted shoo.

5. *Craft must have clothes, but truth
loves to go naked.* 1732 : Fuller,
No. 1200.

6. *He that hath not craft, let him shut
up shop.* 1640 : Herbert, *Jac. Prudentum.*

7. *There's craft in daubing.* c. 1454 :
in *Paston Letters*, i. 269 (1900), For her
moder . . . seyth to her that ther is
gode crafte in dawbyng. c. 1520 :
Hickscorner, in Hazlitt, *Old Plays*, i.
159, For ye know well, there is craft
in daubing : I can look in a man's face
and pick his purse. 1670 : Ray, 75.
1732 : Fuller, No. 4892. 1901 : F. E.
Taylor, *Lancs Sayings*, 22, Ther's
cunnin' i' dobin' beside layin' it on.

Crafthole. *See* quot. 1602 : Carew,
Surv. of Cornwall, 256–7 (1811), In this
parish [Sheviock] standeth Crafthole
. . . a poor village . . . somewhat in-
famous, not upon any present desert,
but through an inveterate by-word,
viz. that it is peopled with twelve
dwellings and thirteen cuckolds. Cf.
Strand-on-the-Green.

Crafty. 1. *A crafty fellow never has
any peace.* 1732 : Fuller, No. 59.

2. *A crafty knave needs no broker.*
1592 : Greene, in *Works*, x. 185 (Grosart). 1596 : Jonson, *Ev. Man in
Humour*, III. ii. 1639 : Breton, in
Works, ii. 11 (Grosart). 1659 : Howell,
5 [with " cunning " for " crafty "].

3. *To a crafty man, a crafty and a
half.* 1640 : Herbert, *Jac. Prudentum.*

Crane's dirt. *See* quots. 1530 :
Palsgrave, 719, You sayd treuthe,
you can well skyll of cranes dyrte,
your father was a poulter. 1592 :
Lyly, *Mother Bombie*, II. iii., You
are well seene in crane's dirt, your
father was a poulter.

Crave in hope, and have in hap, " oft
hast thou heard it." 1583 : Melbancke,
Philotinus, sig. Ff2.

Crawley, Beds. 1. *As crooked as
Crawley brook.* 1662 : Fuller, *Worthies*,
i. 167 (1840). 1790 : Grose, *Prov.
Gloss.*, s.v. " Beds." 1878 : *N. & Q.*,
5th ser., ix. 345, As crooked as Crawley.

2. *Crawley! God help us.* 1878 :
Ibid., 345.

Crawley, Sussex. *It always rains on
Crawley Fair day.* 1884 : " Sussex
Proverbs," in *N. & Q.*, 6th ser., ix.
342.

Crazy ship. *To a crazy ship all winds
are contrary.* 1640 : Herbert, *Jac. Prudentum.* 1670 : Ray, 6. 1732 : Fuller,
No. 5126.

Creaking cart goes long, A. 1900 :
N. & Q., 9th ser., vi. 298, A creaking
cart goes long on the wheels [quoted
as a common proverb].

Creaking gate (or door) **hangs long, A.**
1776 : T. Cogan, *John Buncle, Junior*,
i. 239, But they say a creaking gate
goes the longest upon its hinges; that's
my comfort. 1854 : Baker, *Northants
Gloss.*, s.v. " Gate," " A creaking gate
hangs longest on the hinges." Used
figuratively of an invalid, who outlives
an apparently healthier person. 1901 :
F. E. Taylor, *Lancs Sayings*, 7, A
creakin' dur 'll hong a good while on
it' hinges. 1913 : *Folk-Lore*, xxiv. 76,
Oxfordsh. A creaking door hangs long
on its hinges.

Cream of the jest, That's the. 1678 :

Ray, 69. 1754: Berthelson, *Eng.-Danish Dict.*, s.v. " Cream."

Cream - pot love = Cupboard love. 1678: Ray, 69.

Credit. 1. *Credit keeps the crown of the causeway.* 1875: A. B. Cheales, *Proverb. Folk-Lore*, 101.

2. *Credit lost is like a Venice glass broke.* 1670: Ray, 6. 1732: Fuller, No. 4021, Reputation crackt, is a Venice-glass broke.

3. *He that has cracked his credit is half hanged.* 1519: Horman, *Vulgaria*, fo. 77, Yf a man haue lost his credence, he is halfe vndon. 1590: Greene, in *Works*, viii. 154 (Grosart).

4. *He that has lost his credit is dead to the world.* 1639: Clarke, 87, To lose a mans credit is the greatest losse. 1640: Herbert, *Jac. Prudentum.* 1670: Ray, 6. 1732: Fuller, No. 2142.

5. *No man ever lost his credit, but he who had it not.* 1670: Ray, 6.

Crediton, Devon. 1. *As fine as Kerton spinning.* 1790: Grose, *Prov. Gloss.*, s.v. " Devon."

2. *That's extra. See* quot. 1901: *Devon N. & Q.*, i. 120, Many years ago it was frequently said in Devonshire, " ' That's extra,' as the old woman said when she saw ' Kirton ' " [Créditon].

3. *When Kirton, etc.* 1876: *N. & Q.*, 5th ser., vi. 364, When Ex'ter was a furzy down, Kirton was a mayor-town. 1892: S. Hewett, *Peasant Speech of Devon*, 145, When Kirton wuz a borough town, Ex'ter wuz a vuzzy-down.

Creditors have better memories than debtors. 1659: Howell, *Proverbs: Span.-Eng.*, 8. 1736: Franklin, *Way to Wealth*, in *Works*, i. 450 (Bigelow). *c.* 1800: Trusler, *Prov. in Verse*, 53. 1880: Spurgeon, *Ploughman's Pictures*, 18.

Creep before we can go. *See* **First creep.**

Creep up one's sleeve, To. 1821: Clare, *Rural Life*, 161, For there's none apter, I believe, at " creeping up a mistress' sleeve." 1854: Baker, *Northants Gloss.*, s.v. " Creep," Creep up your sleeve. A colloquial phrase for endeavouring to obtain a favour by coaxing or wheedling. 1889: Peacock,

Manley, etc., Gloss., 144 (E.D.S.), He's crept up her sleäve till he can do anything wi' her he likes. 1926: Phillpotts, *Yellow Sands*, I., I ain't going to creep up her sleeve because there's money hid there. Cf. **Speak** (20).

Cringing is a gainful accomplishment. 1710: S. Palmer, *Moral Essays on Proverbs*, 266, A man's hat in his hand never did him any harm. 1732: Fuller, No. 1206.

Cripple. *He that dwells near a cripple will soon learn to halt.* 1579: Lyly, *Euphues*, 131 (Arber), It is an olde prouerbe that if one dwell the next doore to a creeple he will learne to hault. 1647: *Countrym. New Commonwealth*, 12.

Critics are like brushers of noblemen's clothes. 1651: Herbert, *Jac. Prudentum*, 2nd ed.

Crock as the porridge, She will as soon part with the. Somerset. 1678: Ray, 352.

Crocker. *See* **Copplestone.**

Crooked as a cammock [a bent piece of wood; a cambrel]. Before 1529: Skelton, in *Works*, i. 117 (Dyce), Your longe lothy legges, Crokyd as a camoke. 1592: Lyly, *Mother Bombie*, I. iii., They study twentie yeares together to make us grow as straight as a wand, and in the end, by bowing us, as crooked as a cammocke.

Crooked as a dog's hind leg. 1886: Elworthy, *West Som. Word-Book*, 170 (E.D.S.), So crooked's a dog's hind-leg . . . are the superlative absolutes in constant use. 1886: R. Holland, *Cheshire Gloss.*, 445 (E.D.S.), As crookit as a dog's elbow. 1889: Peacock, *Manley, etc., Gloss.*, 146 (E.D.S.). 1926: *Tatler*, 10 Nov., p. 280, He was also as crooked as a dog's hind leg on the turf.

Crooked as a ram's horn. 1658: *Wit Restor'd*, 102, [Ironical] Straight as a rams horne is thy nose. 1820: Colton, *Lacon*, Pt. II. No. 130, The dolphin, which is always painted more crooked than a ram's horn. 1923: *Folk-Lore*, xxxiv. 329 [Oxfordsh.].

Crooked as S. 1917: Bridge, *Cheshire Proverbs*, 12.

Crooked logs make straight fires.
1611 : Cotgrave, s.v. " Busche." 1694 :
D'Urfey, *Quixote*, Pt. I. Act I. sc. ii.,
Crooked logs make good fires. 1875 :
A. B. Cheales, *Proverb. Folk-Lore*, 132.
**Crooked stick will have a crooked
shadow, A.** 1732 : Fuller, No. 61.
Crooked without, crabbed within.
1593 : *Passionate Morrice*, 86 (N. Sh. S.).
Crooked. *See also* **Crawley;** and
Wembury.
Cross, *adj.* 1. *As cross as a bear with
a sore head.* 1830 : Marryat, *King's
Own*, ch. xxvi., The captain was as
savage as a bear with a sore head.
1870 : *N. & Q.*, 4th ser., vi. 321, Thus
we say " As sulky as a bear with a
sore head." 1922 : Weyman, *Ovington's
Bank*, ch. v., But I assure you, sir, he's
like a bear with a sore head.
2. *As cross as nine highways.* 1855 :
Bohn, 316.
3. *As cross as two sticks.* 1831 :
Scott, *Journal*, 2 Nov., Wind as cross
as two sticks. 1854 : Baker, *Northants
Gloss.*, s.v. " Cross," . . . A common
comparison for an irritable person.
1855 : Thackeray, *Newcomes*, ch. xxxiii.,
She scolded her maid and was as cross
as two sticks. 1909 : Pinero, *Mid-
Channel*, III.
Cross and **Crosses,** *subs.* 1. *Cross or
(and) pile.* [Capita aut navia.—Macro-
bius, *Sat.*, i. 7.] [*c.* 1320 : in Grose's
Antiq. Repertory, ii. 406 (1808), Item
paie a Roi mesmes pour lewer a Cros et
pil . . . les Deniers xij.] *c.* 1390 :
Gower, *Conf. Amantis.*, ii. 390, Whos
tunge neither pyl ne crouche Mai hyre.
1552 : Huloet, *Abced.*, sig. E2, Cast
lottes or crosse and pyle. 1665 : J.
Wilson, *Projectors*, Prol., That, in
effect, 'tis but a cross or pile, In all
that's written, whether well or ill.
1673 : A. Behn, *Dutch Lover*, I. i.,
Cross or pile who shall go. 1707 :
Ward, *London Terræfilius*, No. IV.,
p. 18, He is ready to toss up cross
or pile. *c.* 1770 : Pegge, *Derbicisms*,
15 (E.D.S.), When boys turn up a
halfpenny at play, the head side they
call cross, and the Britannia pile.
2. *Crosses are ladders to heaven.*
1633 : Draxe, 36, The crosse is the

ladder of heauen. 1670 : Ray, 6.
1732 : Fuller, No. 1208. 1859 : Smiles,
Self-Help, 341 (1869), " Crosses," says
the old proverb, " are the ladders that
lead to heaven."
3. *He has not a cross* [coin] *to bless
himself with.* 1540 : Palsgrave, *Acolastus*, sig. T4, That hath neuer a crosse
left him to blesse him with. 1579 :
Marr. of Wit and Wisdom, sc. iii., p. 31
(Sh. S.), I have neuer a crose to blesse
me. 1632 : Rowley, *New Wonder*, III.,
Your good husband will leave you ne'er
a cross i' th' house to bless you with.
1708 : tr. Aleman's *Guzman*, i. 318,
I . . . had not a penny left to bless
myself with. 1819 : Scott, *Bride of L.*,
ch. iv., The Lord Keeper has got all his
estates—he has not a cross to bless
himself with.
4. *The cross on the breast, and the devil
in the heart.* 1633 : Draxe, 97, The
crosse in his breast and the deuill in
his actions. 1732 : Fuller, No. 4462.
5. *To have neither cross nor coin.*
1768 : Goldsmith, *Vicar*, ch. xxi., You
trumpery, to come and take up an
honest house without cross or coin to
bless yourself with ! 1828 : Carr,
Craven Dialect, i. 94, " I've neither
cross nor coin," that is, no money at
all. 1855 : Robinson, *Whitby Gloss.*,
" I'm blest wi' nowther cross nor coin,"
or as we have otherwise heard it said,
" nowther brass nor benediction."
6. *To make a cross upon anything*
=Mark with a white stone. 1546 :
Heywood, *Proverbs*, Pt. I. ch. xi., And
now will I make a cross on this gate.
**Cross a bridge till you come to it,
Never.** 1921 : R. L. Gales, *Old-World
Essays*, 242.
**Cross a stile, and a gate hard by,
You'll be a widow before you die.**
1864 : " Cornish Proverbs," in *N. & Q.*,
3rd ser., v. 208.
Cross the stream where it is ebbest
[shallowest]. 1603 : Holland, tr. Plu-
tarch's *Morals*, 747, There is still a
Lancashire proverb, " Cross the stream
where it is ebbest."
**Crotchets in the head (or brain), To
have.** 1592 : G. Harvey, *Works*, i. 189
(Grosart), A wilde head ful of mad

braine and a thousande crotchets.
1611: Cotgrave, s.v. "Moucheron,"
Avoir des moucherons en teste. To . . .
have many . . . crotchets in the head.
1660: Howell, *Parly of Beasts*, 49, When
a crochet hath got once into his
noddle . . . 1690: *New Dict. Canting
Crew*, sig. D3, Crochets in the crown,
whimsies, maggots. 1807: Crabbe,
Par. Reg., iii. 930 (O.), And gloomy
crotchets fill'd his wandering head.

Crouse as a lop [flea] **(or a louse).**
1670: Ray, 203, Crouse as a new
washen louse. 1825: Brockett, *Gloss.
N. Country Words*, 51 [as in 1670].
1855: Robinson, *Whitby Gloss.*, 40, "As
crowse as a lop," as brisk as a flea.
1868: Atkinson, *Cleveland Gloss.*, 321,
Peert as a lopp, used of a person nimble
and active in his movements. 1889:
J. Nicholson, *Folk Speech E. Yorks*, 17,
As croose (lively) as a loose or lopp.

Crow and Crows. 1. *As good land as
any the crow flies over.* 1684: Bunyan,
Pilgr. Progr., Pt. II., p. 98 (O.), As
fruitful a place, as any the crow flies
over. 1690: *New Dict. Canting Crew*,
sig. D4.

2. *Crows are never the whiter for
washing themselves.* 1678: Ray, 121.
1732: Fuller, No. 1210.

3. *Crows do not pick out crows' eyes.*
1578: Florio, *First Fruites*, fo. 29, One
crow wil neuer put out an other crowes
eyes. 1629: *Book of Meery Riddles*,
Prov. 93. 1732: Fuller, No. 3744.
1815: Scott, *Mannering*, ch. xl., Na,
na! hawks shouldna pike out hawks'
een.

4. *Hoarse as a crow.* 1883: R. L. S.,
Treasure I., ch. xiv., He was not only
red in the face, but spoke as hoarse as
a crow. 1911: T. Edwardes, *Neighbourhood*, 116, Tired as a navigator,
and hoarse as a crow.

5. *It is ill killing a crow with an empty
sling.* 1678: Ray, 120. 1732: Fuller,
No. 2960.

6. *'Tis long of your eyes, the crows
might have helped it when you were young.*
1678: Ray, 345.

7. *The crow bewails the sheep, and then
eats it.* 1640: Herbert, *Jac. Prudentum.*
1670: Ray, 6, Carrion crows bewail the

dead sheep, and then eat them. 1732:
Fuller, No. 1211.

8. *The crow thinks her own birds
fairest.* 1513: Douglas, *Æneis*, ix.,
Prol., 78 (O.), The blak crawe thinkis
hir awin byrdis quhite. 1580: H.
Gifford, *Posie*, 32 (Grosart), Not vnlike
the crow, who alwaies thinkes her owne
byrdes fayrest. 1639: Massinger, *Unnat. Combat*, III. ii., I . . . like the
foolish crow Believe my black brood
swans. 1732: Fuller, No. 4463. 1855:
Gaskell, *North and South*, ch. xv., You
think you never heard of this wonderful
son of mine, Miss Hale. You think I'm
an old woman whose . . . own crow is
the whitest ever seen.

9. *To have a crow to pluck* (or *pull*)
with one. c. 1410: *Towneley Plays*, 18
(E.E.T.S.), Na, na, abide, we haue a
craw to pull. 1546: Heywood, *Proverbs*, Pt. II. ch. v., We haue a crow to
pul. 1592: Lyly, *Mother Bombie*, II. i.,
If I thought thou meanest so . . . thou
shouldst have a crow to pull. 1665:
J. Wilson, *Projectors*, V., I've a crow to
pluck w' ye. 1754: Berthelson, *Eng.-
Danish Dict.*, s.v. "Crow." 1841:
Dickens, *Barn. Rudge*, ch. xiii., Tell
him that whenever he comes here
I have a crow to pluck with him.
1865: *N. & Q.*, 3rd ser., vii. 104, "I've
a crow to pluck with you, and a poke
to put the feathers in," is I think the
usual North country proverb, the poke
for the feathers being rather an important part of the threat, judging from
the stress the speaker lays upon it.

10. *To make the crow a pudding.*
c. 1598: Deloney, *Gentle Craft*, Pt. II.
ch. iii., Plucke up a good heart woman,
let no man . . . say thou gauest the
crow a pudding, because loue would
let thee liue no longer. 1599: Shakespeare, *Henry V.*, II. i., By my troth,
he'll yield the crow a pudding one of
these days. 1767: Hall - Stevenson,
Works, i. 208 (1795), But if he drops
him, down he goes, And makes a
pudding for the crows. 1889: *Folk-
Lore Journal*, vii. 292, Derby. He's
nowt good-for till he gies crows a
pudden [is dead].

11. *To say the crow is white.* 1528.:

More, *Works*, p. 207, col. 1 (1557), As
he that would say the crowe were white.
1579 : *Marr. of Wit and Wisdom*, sc. i.,
p. 10 (Sh. S.), Say as she sayeth,
although that she Doe say the crowe
is white. 1649 : in *Somers Tracts*,
vi. 52 (1811), If they say the crow is
white, so must the souldier.

12. *To strut like a crow in a gutter.*
1579 : Fulke, *Confut. Sanders*, 675 (O.),
He triumpheth like a crow in a gutter.
1690 : *New Dict. Canting Crew*, sig. D4,
Strut like a crow in a gutter, said in
jeer of the stalking of a proud fellow.
Before 1729 : in *Roxb. Ballads*, viii. 812
(B.S.), I used for to vaunt, as if I would
fly, And strut like a crow in a gutter.
1880 : Spurgeon, *Ploughman's Pictures*,
48, He struts like a crow in a gutter,
and thinks himself cock of the walk.

13. *When the crow begins to build
then sheepe begin to yeald.* Glos. 1639 :
in *Berkeley MSS.*, iii. 31 (1885).

See also Black, *adj.* (6) ; Hungry as a
June crow ; Like crow ; March (20) and
(42) ; No carrion ; and Safe as a crow.

Crowd is not company, A. 1732 :
Fuller, No. 62.

Crowland. *See* quots. 1662 : Fuller,
Worthies, ii. 268 (1840), All the carts
that come to Crowland are shod with
silver. 1790 : Grose, *Prov. Gloss.*, s.v.
" Lincs " [as in 1662]. 1865 : W. White,
Eastern England, i. 281, " Every cart
that comes to Crowland is shod with
silver " is a saying that carries us back
to days when there was no gravel.

Crown. 1. *A crown in pocket doth
you more credit than an angel spent.*
1732 : Fuller, No. 63.

2. *From the crown of the head to the
sole of the foot.* [Usque ab unguiculo
ad capillum summum.—Plautus, *Epid.*,
623.] *c.* 1300 : *Havelok*, l. 1847
(E.E.T.S.), Fro the croune til the to.
1468 : *Coventry Myst.*, 241 (Sh. S.), ffro
the sool of the ffoot to the hyest asen-
cion. 1547 : Borde, *Brev. of Helthe*,
fo. vi., Which may be frõ the crowne of
the heede to the sole of the foote.
1599 : Shakespeare, *Much Ado*, III. ii.
1607 : *Chester Plays*, x. 439 (E.E.T.S.),
From the crowne of the head to the
right toe I leave no wholl fell. 1741 :

Arbuthnot, *Mart. Scriblerus*, bk. i.
ch. viii., From the crown of my head
to the sole of my foot, I shall ever
acknowledge myself your worship's
humble servant. 1857 : Dickens, *Dorrit*, bk. ii. ch. xxxiii., Mr. Merdle was
found out from the crown of his head
to the sole of his foot the moment he
was found out in his pocket.

Crowson's mare. *See* quot. 1841 :
Hartshorne, *Salopia Ant.*, 381, Here a
comes, limping along like owd Crowson's mare. 1883 : Burne, *Shropsh.
Folk-Lore*, 593 [as in 1841].

Crow-trodden, You look as if you were.
1678 : Ray, 237.

**Cruelty is a tyrant that's always
attended with fear.** 1670 : Ray, 6.
1732 : Fuller, No. 1213. *c.* 1800 :
Trusler, *Prov. in Verse*, 103.

Cruelty is God's enemy, A man of.
1732 : Fuller, No. 303.

**Crumb not your bread before you taste
your porridge.** 1594 : A. Copley, *Wits,
Fits, etc.*, 116 (1614), Tast your pottage
before you crumb in your bread *c.* 1630 :
B. & F., *Monsieur Thomas*, IV. iv.

Crumbs. *See* Pick up.

Crusty. *See* quots. 1592 : Lyly,
Mother Bombie, II. iii., You need not
bee crustie, you are not so hard backt
[baked]. 1678 : Ray, 237 [as in 1592].
Ibid., 352, She is as crousty as that is
hard bak'd. *Somerset.*

Cry. 1. *Cry you mercy killed my cat.*
1639 : Clarke, 281. 1670 : Ray, 68.

2. *I cry you mercy I killed your
cushion.* 1530 : Palsgrave, 501, I kry
you mercy, I kylled your cussheyn.
1592 : Lyly, *Mother Bombie*, IV. ii.

3. *I cry you mercy, I took you for a
joint stool.* Ibid., IV. ii. 1608 : Shakespeare, *Lear*, III. vi., *Fool.* Cry you
mercy, I took you for a joint-stool.
1670 : Ray, 186.

4. *To cry notch. See* Notch.

5. *To cry out before one is hurt.* 1548 :
in *Reliq. Antiquæ*, ii. 16 (1843), Ye may
the better understand that I cry not
before I am pricked. 1611 : Cotgrave,
s.v. " Anguille," Such as . . . crye
before their paine approach them.
1818 : Byron, *Don Juan*, can. i. st. 207,
They will not cry out before they're

hurt. 1848 : Dickens, *Dombey*, ch. xxv.,
My lad . . . don't you sing out afore
you're hurt.

6. *To cry over spilt milk.* In the first
quotation the proverb is in solution.
1484 : Caxton, *Æsope, etc.*, ii. 270
(Jacobs), The thyrd [doctrine] is that
thow take no sorowe of the thynge lost
whiche may not be recouered. 1681 :
Yarranton, *Englands Improvement*,
Pt. II., p. 107, Sir, there is no crying
for shed milk, that which is past cannot
be recall'd. 1741 : *True Anti-Pamela*,
131, Well, my dear, said I, it is needless crying after shed milk. *c.* 1890 :
Gilbert, *Foggarty's Fairy*, I., However,
it's no use crying over spilt milk.
1923 : J. S. Fletcher, *The Diamonds*,
ch. xxviii., She was one of those
women who do not believe in crying
over spilled milk.

7. *To cry roast meat. See* **Roast
meat** (3).

8. *To cry whore.* 1676 : A. Behn,
Town Fop, IV. iii., She cries whore
first, brings him upon his knees for
her fault ; and a piece of plate, or a
new petticoat, makes his peace again.
1738 : Swift, *Polite Convers.*, Dial. I.,
Nay, miss, you cried whore first, when
you talked of the knapsack.

9. *To cry with one eye and laugh with
the other. c.* 1500 : quoted in Collier's
Bibliogr. Cat., ii. 482, Full harde it is
to fynde a woman stedfast, For yf
one eye wepe, the other dothe contrary.
1667 : L'Estrange, *Quevedo's Visions*,
106 (1904), One of them I saw crying
with one eye . . . and laughing with
t'other. 1732 : Fuller, No. 4737, The
rich widow cries with one eye and laughs
with the other.

Cuckold. 1. *A discontented cuckold
has not wit.* 1612 : *Cornucopiæ*, 92
(Grosart), Well doth their folly this
old saying fit, *A male-contented cuckold
hath no wit.*

2. *Cuckolds are Christians.* 1678 :
Ray, 69. 1732 : Fuller, No. 1215,
Cuckolds are Christians all the world
over.

3. *Cuckolds are going to heaven.*
1659 : Howell, 12, In rain and sunshine
cuckolds go to heaven. 1670 : Ray, 6

[as in 1659]. 1681 : Otway, *Soldier's
Fortune*, IV. i., For all cuckolds go to
Heaven, that's most certain. 1699 :
Farquhar, *Love and a Bottle*, V. i. 1870 :
N. & Q., 4th ser., v. 366, In the West
of England it was in my childhood, and
probably is still, a saying, when the sun
shines, and it rains at the same time
. . . that the " Cuckolds are going to
heaven."

4. *Cuckolds are kind.* 1620 : *Westw.
for Smelts*, 40 (Percy S.), Which made
her to beleeve that the proverbe is true
(cuckolds are kinde men). 1696 : Mrs.
Manley, *Lost Lover*, V. i., Vain hopes of
having the proverb of your side, *That
cuckolds are kind to those who make
them so.*

5. *If a cuckold come he'll take away
the meat.* 1678 : Ray, 69, . . . viz. If
there be no salt on the table. 1738 :
Swift, *Polite Convers.*, Dial. II., Here's
no salt ; cuckolds will run away with
the meat. Cf. No. 9.

6. *It is better to be a cuckold and not
know it, than be none, and everybody say
so.* 1659 : Howell, *Proverbs: Span.-
Eng.*, 14, Better to be a cuckold and
none know it, then to be none, and
yet to be thought so. 1732 : Fuller,
No. 871.

7. *Let every cuckold wear his own
horns.* 1659 : Howell, 3. 1670 : Ray,
6. 1762 : Smollett, *Sir L. Greaves*,
ch. xiii., Growling within himself, that
thenceforward he should let every
cuckold wear his own horns.

8. *The cuckold is the last that knows
of it.* 1605 : Camden, *Remains*, 332
(1870). 1693 : Dryden, *Juvenal*, Sat. x.
l. 528, For cuckolds hear the last.
1758–67 : Sterne, *Trist. Shandy*, ix. 4,
It is with love as with cuckoldom, the
suffering party is generally the last who
knows anything about the matter.

9. *Think of a cuckold.* 1709 : *Brit.
Apollo*, vol. ii. No. 59, col. 3, *Q.* When
a person is joynting a piece of meat, if
he finds it difficult to joynt, he is bid
to think of a cuckold. I desire to know
whence the proverb? *A.* Thomas Webb,
a carver to a Lord Mayor of London in
King Charles the First's reign, was as
famous for his being a cuckold as for

his dexterity in carving; therefore what became a proverb was used first as an invocation, when any took upon him to carve. Cf. No. 5.

10. *To be a cuckold and know it not, is no more than to drink with a fly in the cup and see it not.* 1580 : Lyly, *Euphues*, 284 (Arber), To weare a horne and not knowe it, will do me no more harme then to eate a flye, and not see it. 1593 : *Tell-Trothes N. Years Gift*, 20 (N. Sh. S.). 1732 : Fuller, No. 5250 [as in 1580].

11. *Who is a cuckold and conceals it, carries coals in his bosom.* 1659 : Howell, *Proverbs: Span.-Eng.*, 14. 1670 : Ray, 6. 1732 : Fuller, No. 2332, He that thinks himself a cuckold, carries live coals in his heart.

See also Company (1); and To-day a man.

Cuckoo. 1. *A cuckoo for one!* An expression of contempt or derision. 1633 : Rowley, *Match at Midnight*, V., You, a new-fangled fowler, came to show your art i' th' dark; but take this truth, you catched in truth à cuckoo for 't.

2. *As scabbed as a cuckoo.* 1659 : Howell, 5. 1670 : Ray, 207. 1797 : *Gent. Mag.*, Pt. I., p. 456, " As scabbed as a cuckoo " is a common saying in the North of England. 1828 : Carr, *Craven Dialect*, ii. 99. 1866 : *Science Gossip*, ii. 184, " As scabbed as a cuckoo " is a common saying in Yorkshire.

3. *Bad for the barley, and good for the corn, When the cuckoo comes to an empty thorn.* 1883 : Burne, *Shropsh. Folk-Lore*, 221. 1893 : Inwards, *Weather Lore*, 136.

4. *Comes in mid March, Sings in mid April, Stuts in mid May, And in mid June flies away.* North country. 1797 : *Gent. Mag.*, Pt. I., p. 456.

5. *Cuckoo oats and woodcock hay, Make a farmer run away.* 1864 : *N. & Q.*, 3rd ser., v. 394. 1891 : ibid., 7th ser., xii. 486 [with " Michaelmas " for " woodcock " — Staffs]. 1893 : G. L. Gower, *Gloss. of Surrey Words*, 12 (E.D.S.), Cuckoo oats are late-sown oats, and are never supposed to yield much. " There'll be nothing but cuckoo oats this year," said a man in the wet spring of 1889.

6. *Hoarse as a cuckoo.* 1917 : Bridge, *Cheshire Proverbs*, 15.

7. *If the cuckoo sings when the hedge is brown, Sell thy horse and buy thy corn.* Welsh [You will not be able to afford horse corn]. *If the cuckoo sings when the hedge is green, Keep thy horse and sell thy corn.* Salop [It will be so plentiful that you will have enough and to spare]. 1893 : Inwards, *Weather Lore*, 136.

8. *In April, come he will; In May, he sings all day; In June he alters his tune; In July, he prepares to fly; In August, go he must; If he stay till September, 'Tis as much as the oldest man can ever remember.* Ibid., 24.

9. *In April, cuckoo sings her lay; In May, she sings both night and day; In June, she loses her sweet strain; In July, she flies off again.* N. Yorks. Ibid., 25.

10. *In April the cuckoo can sing her song by rote; In June, out of tune, she cannot sing a note.* 1562 : Heywood, *Epigr.*, 6th Hund., No. 95.

11. *In April the cuckoo shows his bill; In May he sings both night and day; In June he altereth his tune; In July away he'll fly; In August go he must.* 1838 : Mrs. Bray, *Trad. of Devon*, i. 326 [slightly varied]. 1846 : Denham, *Proverbs*, 42 (Percy S.). 1893 : Inwards, *Weather Lore*, 25 [slightly varied].

12. *In March The cuckoo starts. In April 'A tune his bill. In May 'A sing all day. In June 'A change his tune. In July Away 'a fly. In August Away's must. In September you'll ollers remember. In October 'A'll never get over.* East Anglia. 1869 : *N. & Q.*, 4th ser., iii. 94.

13. *March he sits upon his perch; April he soundeth his bell; May he sings both night and day; June he altereth his tune, And July—away to fly.* Derby. 1869 : *N. & Q.*, 4th ser., iii. 94.

14. *On the third of April Comes in the cuckoo and nightingale.* 1879 : J. Hardy, in *Folk-Lore Record*, ii. 54, It is a popular saw that . . .

15. *The cuckoo comes in April, Sings a song in May; Then in June another tune, And then she flies away.* Glos.

1878 : Dyer, *Eng. Folk-Lore*, 56. 1869 : Hazlitt, 363, The cuckoo comes in Aperill, and stays the month of May ; sings a song at Midsummer, and then goes away. Wilts.

16. *The cuckoo comes of mid March, And cucks of mid Aperill ; And gauns away of Midsummer month, When the corn begins to fill.* 1846 : Denham, *Proverbs*, 38 (Percy S.). 1893 : Inwards, *Weather Lore*, 20 [with " Lammas-tide " for " Midsummer month "].

17. *The cuckoo goes to Beaulieu Fair to buy him a petticoat.* 1863 : Wise, *New Forest*, ch. xvi., " The cuckoo . . .," referring to the arrival of the cuckoo about the 15th of April.

18. *The cuckoo singeth all the year.* 1541 : *Sch. House of Women*, l. 321, All beit that few men doo him hear, The cucko singeth all the yeer.

19. *The cuckoo sings in April, The cuckoo sings in May, The cuckoo sings at Midsummer, But not upon the day.* 1883 : Burne, *Shropsh. Folk-Lore*, 222.

20. *The first cock of hay Frights the cuckoo away.* 1846 : Denham, *Proverbs*, 52 (Percy S.). 1879 : *Folk-Lore Record*, ii. 50. 1924 : *Folk-Lore*, xxxv. 358.

21. *Turn your money when you hear the cuckoo, and you'll never be without it during the year.* 1879 : *Folk-Lore Record*, ii. 90. 1883 : Burne, *Shropsh. Folk-Lore*, 219.

22. *When the cuckoo comes to the bare thorn, Sell your cow and buy you corn : But when she comes to the full bit, Sell your corn and buy you sheep.* 1659 : Howell, 16, When the cuckow sitteth on a dry thorn, Sell thy cow, and sow thy corn. 1670 : Ray, 43. 1825 : Hone, *Ev. Day Book*, i. 669. 1893 : Inwards, *Weather Lore*, 6.

23. *When the cuckoo has pecked up the dirt*=Spring. 1830 : Forby, *Vocab. E. Anglia*, 430, I will come when the cuckoo, etc. 1893 : J. Salisbury, *S.E. Worcs. Gloss.*, 75, In April it is said that the cuckoo comes and picks up all the dirt. 1904 : *Co. Folk-Lore : Northumb.*, 176 (F.L.S.).

24. *When the cuckoo . . .* (see quot.). 1879 : J. Hardy, in *Folk-Lore Record*, ii. 58, " When the cuckoo purls its

feathers, the housewife should become chary of her eggs," is a popular saying in many parts of the country.

25. *You are like a cuckoo, you have but one song.* c. 1430 : Lydgate, *Minor Poems*, 192 (Percy S.), The cokkowe syng can than but oon lay. c. 1535 : *Dialogues of Creatures*, C (1816), Many folkes . . . synge allwaye oon songe lyke the cuckowe. 1630 : T. Adams, *Works*, 219, He is like the cuckoe, alwaies in one tune. 1681 : W. Robertson, *Phraseol. Generalis*, 12, To be still cuckow ; or to have always the same song. 1732 : Fuller, No. 5850. 1899 : Dickinson, *Cumberland Gloss.*, 144, Ye breed o' the gowk, ye've nae rhyme but ane.

See also **Naked** ; **Nightingale** ; **Ragged** ; **Weirling** ; and **Welsh ambassador.**

Cuckstone. *See* quot. 1735 : Pegge, *Kent. Proverbs*, in E.D.S., No. 12, p. 69, If you would goe to a church mis-went, You must go to Cuckstone in Kent. 1849 : Halliwell, *Pop. Rhymes, etc.*, 193.

Cucumbers. *See* quot. 1738 : Swift, *Polite Convers.*, Dial. II., Madam, I dare not touch it : for they say cucumbers are cold in the third degree. See also **Cool** (2).

Culmstock Fair. *See* quot. 1886 : Elworthy, *West Som. Word-Book*, 191 (E.D.S.), Till Culmstock Fair be come and gone, There mid be apples, and mid be none. Cf. **Devil** (43).

Cumberland Jwohny. A satirical appellation for a Cumberland man. 1846–59 : *Denham Tracts*, i. 166 (F.L.S.).

Cumberland. *See* **Shrewsbury.**

Cunning as a dead pig. 1738 : Swift, *Polite Convers.*, Dial. III.

Cunning as Captain Drake. 1678 : Ray, 353.

Cunning as Craddock. 1678 : Ray, 280. 1846–59 : *Denham Tracts*, i. 45 (F.L.S.), As cunning as a crafty Cradock. [It is suggested that the saying refers to John Cradock, vicar of Gainford, 1594, who was a high commissioner for Durham, and J.P., etc. He is alleged to have taken bribes and to have been guilty of other underhand practices.]

Cunning as crowder. 1754 : *Gent.*

Mag., 211, One saying we have in the Northern parts . . . *as cunning as Crowder* . . . and a crowder is a fidler. 1841 : Hartshorne, *Salopia Ant.*, 381. 1883 : Burne, *Shropsh. Folk-Lore*, 594.

Cunning. *See* **Fox** (4).

Cunning is no burden. 1539 : Taverner, *Proverbs*, fo. 22, Cunnynge (they say) is no burthen. 1573 : G. Harvey, *Letter-Book*, 121 (Camden S.). 1642 : Fuller, *Holy State:* " The True Gentleman," He knows well that cunning is no burthen to carry. 1732 : Fuller, No. 4182, Skill is no burthen.

Cup. 1. *A cup in the pate is a mile in the gait.* 1694 : Motteux, *Rabelais*, bk. iv. ch. lxv. 1738 : Swift, *Polite Convers.*, Dial. II. *c.* 1791 : Pegge, *Derbicisms*, 135 (E.D.S.) [with " pot " for " cup "].

2. *As merry as cup and can.* 1546 : Heywood, *Proverbs*, Pt. II. ch. iii., Mery we were as cup and can could holde. 1577 : *Misogonus*, II. ii., The merye man, with cupp and cann. 1610 : Rowlands, *Martin Mark-all*, 49 (Hunt. Cl.), Where they, as merry as pot and can passe their time in villany and robbery. 1678 : Ray, 287.

3. *He has got a cup too much.* 1678 : Ray, 87.

4. *There's many a slip between cup and lip.* [Saepe audivi inter os atque offam multa intervenire posse.—M. Cato, in Gellius, xiii. 17.] 1539 : Taverner, *Proverbs*, fo. 15, Many thynges fall betwene the cuppe and the mouth. 1576 : Lambarde, *Peramb. of Kent*, 422 (1826), Even as many things happen (according to the proverbe) betweene the cup and the lippe. 1633 : Jonson, *Tale of a Tub*, III. iv., Many things fall between the cup and lip. 1712 : Arbuthnot, *Law a Bott. Pit*, Pt. III. App. ch. iii., Many things happen between the cup and the lip. 1769 : Colman, *Man and Wife*, III. [as in 1712]. 1840 : Barham, *Ing. Legends:* " Lady Rohesia," There's many a slip 'Twixt the cup and the lip. 1922 : Weyman, *Ovington's Bank*, ch. vii.

5. *To be cup and can*=To be " pals." 1690 : *New Dict. Canting Crew*, sig. C3, As great as cup and can. 1712 : Ward,

Poet. Entertainer, No. 2, p. 18, Who was as great as cup and kan With the new-marry'd gentleman. 1788 : O'Keeffe, *Tantara-rara*, I. i., My colonel and he are as great as cup and can.

6. *When the cup is fullest, then carry it most carefully.* c. 1320 : in *Reliq. Antiquæ*, i. 112 (1841), " When the coppe is follest, thenne ber hire feyrest," Quoth Hendyng. 1736 : Bailey, *Dict.*, s.v. " Cup," When the cup's full carry it even.

See also **Such cup.**

Curdly sky will not leave the earth long dry, A; or, will not be twenty-four hours dry. [1736 : Bailey, *Dict.*, s.v. " Curdled," A curdled sky and a painted woman are not of long duration.] 1893 : Inwards, *Weather Lore*, 94.

Cure. *See* **Remedy.**

Cured. 1. *I have cur'd her from laying* [sic] *in the hedge, quoth the goodman when he had wed his daughter.* 1678 : Ray, 56. 1732 : Fuller, No. 2604.

2. *What can't be cured must be endured.* 1377 : Langland, *Plowman*, B, x. 439, For qant OPORTET vyent en place yl ny ad que PATI. *c.* 1460 : *How the Goode Wyfe*, Thynge that may be tyde is for to dowre, my lere childe. 1579 : Spenser, *Shep. Cal.*, Sept., ll. 150-2, Better it were, a little to faigne, And clenly couer that cannot be cured, Such ill, as is forced, mought needes be endured. 1639 : Massinger, *Unnat. Combat*, II. i., What's past help, is Beyond prevention. 1706 : Ward, *Hudibras Rediv.*, Pt. IX. can. xiv., p. 5, 'Tis our prudence to endure With patience what we cannot cure. 1771 : Smollett, *Clinker*, in *Works*, iii. 191 (1817). 1837 : Dickens, *Pickwick*, ch. xlviii., What was over couldn't be begun, and what couldn't be cured must be endured. 1851 : Borrow, *Lavengro*, ii. 54.

Curiosity is endless, restless, and useless, and Curiosity is ill manners in another's house. 1732 : Fuller, Nos. 1219 and 1220.

Curlew. *See* quots. 1866 : *N. & Q.*, 3rd ser., x. 235, A curlew lean, or a curlew fat, Carries twelve pence upon his back, as they say in North Lincoln-

shire. [Variant at same reference,] Be
it lean, or be it fat, It bears tenpence on
its back. 1886 : Swainson, *Folk-Lore
of Brit. Birds*, 201 (F.L.S.), Be she
white or be she black, The curlew has
tenpence on her back (Lincolnshire).
  Curses come home to roost. *c.* 1275 :
Prov. of Alfred, A 84, Eueryches
monnes dom to his owere dure churreth
(Every man's judgment returns to his
own door). *c.* 1386 : Chaucer, *Parson's
Tale*, 41, And ofte tyme swich cursinge
wrongfully retorneth agayn to him that
curseth, as a brid that retorneth agayn
to his owene nest. 1816 : Scott, *Old
Mortality*, ch. xlii., I have heard a good
man say, that a curse was like a stone
flung up to the heavens, and maist like
to return on the head that sent it.
1894 : Northall, *Folk Phrases*, 12
(E.D.S.), Curses, like chickens, come
home to roost.
  Cursing the weather is bad farming.
1917 : Bridge, *Cheshire Proverbs*, 46.
  Curst cow. *See* **Cow** (10).
  Curst cur must be tied short, A.
1605 : Camden, *Remains*, 317 (1870)
[with " dog " for " cur "]. 1670 : Ray,
76. 1732 : Fuller, No. 65 [with
" should " for " must "].
  Curtain lectures. [Semper habet lites
alternaque jurgia lectus In quo nupta
jacet : minimum dormitur in illo.—
Juvenal, *Sat.*, vi. 267-8.] 1638 : *A
Curtaine Lecture : as it is read by a
Country Farmer's Wife to her Good
Man, etc.* [title]. 1649 : Quarles, *Virgin
Widow*, II., For which I have had
already two curtaine-lectures, and a
black and blue eye. 1717 : Pope, *Wife
of Bath*, 165, Or curtain-lectures made
a restless night. 1821 : Combe, *Syntax
in Search of Wife*, can. xxxiv., p. 19,
Yes, she may toss her head and hector,
But she shall have a curtain lecture.
1846 : Jerrold, *Mrs. Caudle's Curtain
Lectures* [title].
  Cushions. *See* quot. I can't identify
the proverb to which allusion is made.
1609 : Rowlands, *Whole Crew of Kind
Gossips*, 12 (Hunt. Cl.), Go to (quoth
I) y'are best beat out my braines
With cushions now, to make the prouerbe true.

Custom is second nature. *c.* 1390 :
Gower, *Conf. Amantis*, bk. vi. l. 664,
For in phisique this I finde, Usage is
the seconde kinde. 1422 : J. Yonge,
Tr. of Govt. of Prynces, 238 (E.E.T.S.),
For as ypocras sayth, " costome is the
seconde nature or kynde." 1558 :
Bullein, *Govt. of Health*, fo. 98, Custome
is like vnto another nature. 1607 :
Marston, *What You Will*, III. 1712 :
Addison, *Spectator*, No. 447. 1774 :
C. Dibdin, *Quaker*, II. iii. 1817 : Scott,
Rob Roy, ch. x., Habit has become a
second nature. 1864 : Mrs. H. Wood,
Trevlyn Hold, ch. xxiv., Habit and use,
as we read, are second nature.
  Custom makes all things easy.
c. 1598 : Deloney, *Gentle Craft*, Pt. II.
ch. vi., Labour by custome becommeth
easie. *c.* 1680 : L'Estrange, *Seneca :
Epistles*, x., There is nothing so hard,
but custom makes it easie to us. 1703 :
T. Baker, *Tunbridge Walks*, II., Custom
. . . makes every thing familiar. 1732 :
Fuller, No. 1225.
  **Custom without reason is but ancient
error.** 1647 : *Countrym. New Commonwealth*, 29, Custome (though never so
ancient) without truth, is but an old
errour. 1732 : Fuller, No. 1226.
  Cut, *verb.* 1. *Cut and come again.*
1738 : Swift, *Polite Convers.*, Dial. II.,
I vow, 'tis a noble sirloin, *Neverout.*
Ay ; here's cut and come again. 1772 :
Garrick, *Irish Widow*, I. i., Give me a
slice of a good English surloin ; cut and
come again. 1848 : in Marchant, *Praise
of Ale*, 418 (1888), For the boys that
can cut and come again Must quaff
whole butts of ale.
  2. *Cut and long tail.* *See* **Tag, rag, etc.**
  3. *Cut down an oak.* *See* **Oak** (1)
and (4).
  4. *Cut loaf.* *See* **Shive.**
  5. *Cut not the bough.* *See* quot.
1528 : Tyndale, *Obed. of Christian Men*,
304 (P.S.), " Cut not the bough that
thou standest upon " : whose literal
sense is, " Oppress not the commons."
  6. *Cut off the head and tail and throw
the rest away.* 1678 : Ray, 346. 1732 :
Fuller, No. 1227.
  7. *Cut or give me the bill.* 1732 :
Fuller, No. 1228.

8. *See* quot. 1880: Spurgeon, *Ploughman's Pictures*, 36, The old saying is
"Don't cut off your head because it
aches."

9. *He has cut his leg* = is drunk.
1678: Ray, 87.

10. *To be cut for the simples.* 1650:
in Simpson, *Documents St. Paul's*, 148
(Camden S.), The witts of Pauls, or a
catalogue of those book-sellers appren-
tices . . . which are to be cut of the
simples the next spring. 1690: *New
Dict. Canting Crew*, sig. L2, He must
be cut of the simples, Care must be
taken to cure him of his folly. 1738:
Swift, *Polite Convers.*, Dial. I., Indeed,
Mr. Neverout, you should be cut for the
simples. 1881: Evans, *Leics. Words*,
239 (E.D.S.), " A'd ought to be coot
for the simples "; a phrase implying
that the person spoken of is a fool.
Cf. Battersea.

11. *To cut broad* (or *large*) *thongs of
another's leather.* c. 1320: in *Reliq.
Antiquæ*, i. 114 (1841), "Of un boht hude
men kerveth brod thong," Quoth
Hendyng. 1484: Caxton, *Æsope*, ii.
220 (Jacobs), Ne also it is not honeste
to make large thonges of other mennes
leder. 1595: *Maroccus Extaticus*, 8
(Percy S.), To cut such large thonges
of another mans lether. 1667: L'Estrange, *Quevedo's Visions*, 8 (1904),
Those that were in for detraction and
calumny, and for cutting large thongs
out of other men's leather. 1721:
Bailey, *Eng. Dict.*, s.v. "Thong."
1853: Trench, *Proverbs*, 100 (1905), On
the comparative wastefulness where-
with that which is another's is too
often used: *Men cut broad thongs from
other men's leather.*

12. *To cut large shives of another's
loaf.* 1630: *Tinker of Turvey*, 31
(Halliwell), By this, the prior perceived
that the scull [scullion] had cut a shive
[slice] on his loafe. 1670: Ray, 162.

13. *To cut off one's nose to spite one's
face.* [Stultum est vicinum velle ulcisci
incendio.—*Publ. Syr.*, 611. Henri iv
conçut fort bien que détruire Paris,
c'étoit, comme on dit, se couper le nez
pour faire dépit à son visage.—*c.* 1658:
Tallemant des Réaux, *Historiettes*, i. 17

(1834).] 1889: R. L. S., *Ballantrae*,
ch. x., He was in that humour when a
man—in the words of the old adage—
will cut off his nose to spite his face.
1924: *Times*, 20 Nov., p. 13, col. 1,
Continual harassing of the railways, in
payment for real or fancied grievances,
is much like cutting off one's nose to
spite one's face.

14. *To cut one's coat according to one's
cloth.* 1546: Heywood, *Proverbs*, Pt. I.
ch. viii., I shall Cut my cote after my
cloth when I haue her. 1594: Nashe,
Unfort. Trav., in *Works*, v. 54 (Grosart),
They must shape their cotes good men
according to their cloth. 1669: Dryden, *Wild Gallant*, I. ii., I love your
wit well, sir; but I must cut my coat
according to my cloth. 1720: C.
Shadwell, *Sham Prince*, II. i., I am a
plain dealing man, and am fain to cut
my coate according to my cloath.
1869: Spurgeon, *John Ploughman*,
ch. xii. 1926: Inge, *Lay Thoughts*,
187, We must cut our coat according
to our cloth and adapt ourselves to
changing circumstances.

15. *To cut one's comb.* 1542: Becon,
in *Early Works*, 205 (P.S.), This shall
pluck down your comb, as they use to
say. 1548: Hall, *Chron.*, 17 (1809),
My life stood in ieopardie and my combe
was clerely cut. 1584: R. Scot, *Witchcraft*, bk. viii. ch. iii., Since the preaching thereof their combes are cut, and
few that are wise regard them. 1642:
D. Rogers, *Matrim. Honour*, 45, God
cuts their combe, fils their new hopes
with new sorrow. 1826: Scott, *Journal*,
13 May, *Malachi* might clap his wings
upon this, but, alas! domestic anxiety
has cut his comb.

16. *To cut one's thong according to
one's leather.* 1637: R. Whitford, *Werke
for Housholders*, sig. F5, Than (atter
the commune prouerbe) cute your thong
after or accordynge vnto your ledder.

17. *To cut the grass* (or *ground*) *from
under the feet.* 1567: Fenton, *Bandello*,
ii. 10 (T.T.), I find a greater falt in my
self in suffring an other to cut the earthe
frome under my feete. 1576: Pettie,
Petite Pallace, i. 121 (Gollancz), Seeing
this young gentleman, as he thought, in

great favour . . . thought the grass had
been cut from under his feet. 1672 :
Marvell, *Rehearsal Transpr.*, Pt. I., in
Works, iii. 195 (Grosart), While you are
all this while cutting the grass under
his feet, and animating the people
against the exercise of his ecclesiastical
supremacy. 1760 : Murphy, *Way to
keep him*, II. ii., The grass is cut under
my feet if she ever hears a word of it.

1891 : Gilbert, *Rosenc. and Guildenstern*,
Tabl. II., Thus will you cut the ground
from 'neath his feet.

18. *To cut the hair. See* Split hairs.

Cutpurse. *A cut-purse is a sure
trade, for he hath ready money when his
work is done.* 1659 : Howell, 8. 1670 :
Ray, 16.

Cutting out well is better than sewing
up well. 1732 : Fuller, No. 1230.

D

Dacre was slain in North Acre, The Lord—at the Battle of Towton, 1461. 1849 : Halliwell, *Pop. Rhymes, etc.*, 200. 1868 : *Quart. Review*, cxxv. 518, In Saxton churchyard, where is also the tomb of " The Lord of Dacres Slain in the North Acres," according to the local rhyme.

Daft as a yat [gate] 'at swings beath ways, As. 1899 : Dickinson, *Cumberland Gloss.*, 372.

Daggers drawn, To be at. 1540 : Palsgrave, *Acolastus*, sig. F1, We neuer mete togyther, but we be at daggers drawynge. 1618 : Harington, *Epigrams*, bk. i. No. 91, From spightfull words they fell to daggers drawing. 1694 : *Terence made English*, 82, The captain and she were almost at daggers drawing when I left 'em. 1736 : Bailey, *Dict.*, s.v. "Dagger," To be at dagger's drawing. 1840 : Dickens, *Curiosity Shop*, ch. vii., The old man and I will remain at daggers-drawn to the end of our lives. 1867 : Mrs. H. Wood, *Life's Secret*, Pt. I. ch. ii., I am sure there's no love lost between him and me ; we should be at daggers drawn.

Daily cost, and all of it lost, There's a. 1855 : Bohn, 524.

Daimport's dog. *See* quots. 1883 : Burne, *Shropsh. Folk-Lore*, 595, He talks as Dutch [speaks as unintelligibly] as Darnford's dog. 1917 : Bridge, *Cheshire Proverbs*, 144, To talk as Dutch as Daimport's dog.

Dainties. *Who dainties love shall beggars prove.* 1580 : Tusser, *Husb.*, 72 (E.D.S.), Who dainties loue, a begger shall proue. 1736 : Franklin, *Way to Wealth*, in *Works*, i. 447 (Bigelow). 1783 : Mrs. Cowley, *More Ways than One*, II. iv., You know the proverb— those that are dainty . . .

Dainty makes dearth. 1590 : Spenser, *F.Q.*, I. ii. 248, So dainty they say maketh derth.

Dainty thing would have a dainty dish, The. 1672 : Walker, *Parœm.*, 29 [with "bit" for "dish"]. 1681 : W. Robertson, *Phraseol. Generalis*, 418.

Daisies. *See* Spring (8).

Daisy year. *See* quot. 1901 : F. E. Taylor, *Lancs Sayings*, 7, A daisy year's awlus a lazy year (A farmer's saying).

Dally not with money or women. 1640 : Herbert, *Jac. Prudentum*. 1669 : *New Help to Discourse*, 310.

Dalmanazar, As bright as. 1880 : Courtney, *W. Cornwall Words*, xiii. (E.D.S.).

Dalton bell-rope, Like. 1846-59 : *Denham Tracts*, i. 86 (F.L.S.), Like Dalton bell-rope. That is, a deed half-done. A story is told how, after many vestry meetings holden by the principal inhabitants of this place to take into consideration the propriety of purchasing a new rope for the one bell of their parish church, the church-wardens and ratepayers at last came to the conclusion that the old one should be spliced.

Dam. 1. *The dam of that was whisker.* Said of a great lie. 1678 : Ray, 89.

2. *Where the dam leaps over, the kid follows.* 1732 : Fuller, No. 5662.

Dame Hockaday's hen, As disconsolate as. Corn. 1869 : Hazlitt, 61.

Dance, *verb.* 1. *He dances well to whom fortune pipes.* 1578 : Florio, *First Fruites*, fo. 25, He daunseth wel, vnto whom fortune pipeth. 1605 : Camden, *Remains*, 323 (1870). 1670 : Ray, 77. 1732 : Fuller, No. 1832 [with "merrily" for "well"].

2. *He'll dance to nothing but his own pipe.* 1732 : Fuller, No. 2423.

3. *If you dance you must pay the fiddler.* 1681 : in *Roxb. Ballads*, v. 67 (B.S.).

4. *I'll make him dance without a pipe.* =I'll do him an injury, and he shall not know how. 1678 : Ray, 71. 1732 : Fuller, No. 2639.

5. *They who dance are thought mad by those who hear not the music.* Spoken

of as an " old proverb." 1927 : *Times*,
16 Feb., p. 15, col. 4.

6. *To dance as another pipes.* c. 1480 :
Early Miscellanies, 25 (Warton Cl.,
1855), I wylle dance whylle the world
wylle pype. 1546 : Heywood, *Proverbs*,
Pt. II. ch. xi., Whan fooles pype, by
auctoritee he maie daunce. 1593 :
Giffard, *Dial. on Witches, etc.*, 65
(Percy S.), Ignorant people, which are
ready to beleeve all that he telleth, and
to dance after his pipe. 1642 : D.
Rogers, *Matrim. Honour*, 357, If they
moove, must not all inferior ones dance
after their pipe?

7. *To dance attendance on one.* Before
1529 : Skelton, *Why come ye not*,
ll. 625-6, And syr ye must daunce
attendaunce And take pacient sufferaunce. 1594 : Shakespeare, *Rich. III.*,
III. vii., Welcome, my lord : I dance
attendance here. 1645 : Howell, *Letters*,
bk. i. § iii. No. xiii., Going one morning
to speak with the Duke, and having
danc'd attendance a long time. 1742 :
Fielding, *Andrews*, bk. ii. ch. xvi., The
man hath danced attendance for about
a month. 1923 : Lucas, *Advisory Ben*,
§ vi. p. 24, The young men . . . were
dancing attendance upon creatures
more capricious.

8. *To dance Barnaby.* 1664 : Cotton,
Scarronides, bk. i. l. 189, Bounce, cries
the port-hole ; out they fly, And make
the world dance Barnaby. 1727 : in
Roxb. Ballads, viii. 270 (B.S.), Speak,
and we'll let your thunder fly, And make
the world dance Barnaby.

9. *To dance in a net.* 1532 : More,
Confut. of Tyndale, cxxvii., I go so bare
dawnsyng naked in a net. 1587 :
Greene, in *Works*, vi. 181 (Grosart), At
last being Venus scholler, and therefore
daring with hir to dance in a net. 1605 :
Chapman, *All Fools*, II., Think not you
dance in nets [think not you are un-
detected]. 1670 : Ray, 6. 1821 : Scott,
Kenilworth, ch. iv., Thou canst not
dance in a net, and they not see thee.

10. *To dance to every man's pipe*
(or *whistle*). 1670 : Ray, 170. 1732 :
Fuller, No. 2644, I will not dance to
every fool's pipe. 1880 : Spurgeon,
Ploughman's Pictures, 25, If we dance

to every fiddle we shall soon be lame
in both legs.

11. *When you go to dance, take heed
whom you take by the hand.* 1639 :
Clarke, 24. 1670 : Ray, 77. 1732 :
Fuller, No. 5614.

12. *You'll dance at the end of a rope
without teaching.* 1732 : Fuller, No. 6022.

13. *You will neither dance nor hold
the candle.* Ibid., No. 6013.

Dancing bear. *As many tricks* (*antics,*
etc.) *as a dancing bear.* 1670 : Ray,
163, He hath as many tricks as a
dancing bear. 1732 : Fuller, No. 1862
[as in 1670]. 1738 : Swift, *Polite
Convers.*, Dial. I., I wish you would be
quiet, you have more tricks than a
dancing bear. 1886 : Elworthy, *West
Som. Word-Book*, 374 (E.D.S.), He has
got more antics than a dancing bear.
This is one of the commonest of sayings.
1894 : Northall, *Folk Phrases*, 8
(E.D.S.), As full of megrims as a
dancing bear.

Dancing days are done, His (or **My**).
1658 : Flecknoe, *Enigm. Characters*, 60,
His dancing dayes are never done.
1738 : Swift, *Polite Convers.*, Dial. I.,
I doubt her dancing days are over.
1816 : Austen, *Emma*, ch. xxxviii., My
dancing days are over.

Dancing. *They love dancing well
that dance among thorns.* 1639 : Clarke,
326. 1670 : Ray, 77. 1732 : Fuller,
No. 4966 [with " barefoot upon thorns "
instead of " among thorns "].

Danger and **Dangers.** 1. *A danger
foreseen is half avoided.* 1658 : R.
Franck, *Northern Memoirs*, 95 (1821),
Dangers foreseen are the sooner prevented. 1732 : Fuller, No. 67.

2. *Better pass a danger once, than be
always in fear.* 1670 : Ray, 9.

3. *Danger and delight grow on one
stock.* 1580 : Lyly, *Euphues*, 226
(Arber) [with " stalke " for " stock "].
1732 : Fuller, No. 1231.

4. *Danger is next neighbour to security.*
Ibid., No. 1233.

5. *Dangers are overcome by dangers.*
1651 : Herbert, *Jac. Prudentum*, 2nd ed.,
Danger itself the best remedy for
danger. 1732 : Fuller, No. 1232.

6. *He that fears danger in time*

seldom feels it. 1611 : Cotgrave, s.v.
"Asseur," He that feares, is assured.
1732 : Fuller, No. 2099.

7. *The danger past God is forgotten.*
1670 : Ray, 6, The danger past and
God forgotten. 1732 : Fuller, No. 1234.

Dare not for his (or my) ears, He (or I).
1607 : Topsell, *Serpents*, 640 (O.), The
yonger not daring for their ears to
break into their fathers lands. 1678 :
Ray, 240 (He). 1754 : Berthelson,
Eng.-Danish Dict., s.v. "Ears" (I).

Dark as a wolf's mouth. 1823 :
Scott, *St. Ronan's*, ch. xxxvi. 1828 :
Scott, *Fair Maid*, ch. xxiv., The moon
is quite obscured, and the road as
black as a wolf's mouth. 1901 : F. E.
Taylor, *Lancs Sayings*, 1, As dark as a
fox's meawth. 1926 : Phillpotts, *Peacock House*, 222, 'Twas blowing and
raining that night and dark as a wolf's
mouth.

**Dark as a Yule (or Martinmas) mid-
night.** 1814 : Scott, *Waverley*, ch. xlviii.,
He may look as black as midnight
at Martinmas. 1846 : Denham, *Proverbs*, 62 (Percy S.), As dark as a
Yule midnight. 1904 : *Co. Folk-lore:
Northumb.*, 179 (F.L.S.) [as in 1846].

Dark as black hogs. 1869 : Fitz-
Gerald, *Sea Words and Phrases*, 2.

Dark as Newgate knocker. *See* Newgate.

Dark (or Black) as pitch. *c.* 1300 :
in *Vernon MS.*, 354 (E.E.T.S.), As blac
as eny pich he was. *c.* 1380 : *Sir
Ferumbras*, 81 (E.E.T.S.), Than lai he
thar so blac so pych. 1485 : Caxton,
Charles the Grete, 165 (E.E.T.S.), He
is as blacke as pytche boylled. 1598 :
R. Tofte, *Alba*, 39 (Grosart), And darke
as pitch shall shew the glistering sunne.
1666 : Pepys, *Diary*, 18 Jan., Got home
well by coach, though as dark as pitch.
1714 : Ozell, *Molière*, iii. 217, 'Tis as
dark as pitch. 1824 : Scott, *Redgauntlet*, ch. xvi., All the windows were dark
as pitch. 1890 : P. H. Emerson, *Wild
Life*, 42, The wind roared . . . It was
as dark as pitch.

Dark as the devil's mouth. 1826 :
Scott, *Woodstock*, ch. xii., It is dark as
the devil's mouth.

Dark. *See also* Black.

Darkest hour is before the dawn, The.
1650 : Fuller, *Pisgah Sight*, bk. ii.
ch. xi., It is always darkest just before
the day dawneth. 1889 : R. L. S.,
Letters, iii. 245 (Tusitala ed.), It is
always darkest before dawn. 1912 :
Lucas, *London Lav.*, ch. xvi., I'll pull
this round safe enough. Things look
blackest before the dawn, don't you
know.

Darlington. 1. *Darnton, where the
wind once blew a dog's tongue out.*
1846-59 : *Denham Tracts*, i. 80 (F.L.S.).

2. *Dirty Darlington.* 1658 : R. Franck,
North. Memoirs, 264 (1821), One course
directs us to dirty Darlington. 1846-59 :
Denham Tracts, i. 80, Dirty Darnton or
Darnton-in-the-dirt.

3. *To take Darnton Trod*, or *May take
Darnton Trod.* Ibid., i. 78.

Darnell for dim sight. 1597 : Gerarde,
Herbal, Darnell hurteth the eyes and
maketh them dim . . . and hereupon
it seemeth that the old proverbe came,
that such as are dim sighted should be
said to eate of darnell, 1917 : Bridge,
Cheshire Proverbs, 49 [spelt "Darnall"
and referred to Cheshire village of
Darnhall].

Darnford's dog. *See* Daimport's dog.

Darnton. *See* Darlington.

Dart, River. *See* quots. 1850 :
N. & Q., 1st ser., ii. 511, River of
Dart, oh, river of Dart, Every year
thou claim'st a heart. 1897 : Norway,
H. and B. in Devon, etc., 85 [as in 1850].
1908 : *Folk-Lore*, xix. 171, "The river
Dart every year claims its heart" is a
South of England saying. Cf. **Don,
River.**

Dartford. *See* Sutton.

**Dasnell dawcock sits among the
doctors, The.** 1634 : Withals, *Dict.*, 558,
The dosnell dawcock comes dropping
in among the doctors [given as translation of *Graculus inter musas, anser
strepit inter olores*]. 1659 : Howell, 15
[as in 1634]. 1670 : Ray, 217.

Daughter. 1. *Daughters and dead
fish are no keeping wares.* 1732 : Fuller,
No. 1235.

2. *He that would the daughter win,
Must with the mother first begin.* 1670 :
Ray, 49. 1732 : Fuller, No. 6266.

3. *When the daughter is stolen, shut Pepper-gate.* 1662: Fuller, *Worthies*, i. 291 (1840). 1790: Grose, *Prov. Gloss.*, s.v. " Cheshire." 1825: Hone, *Ev. Day Book*, i. 430. 1917: Bridge, *Cheshire Proverbs*, 151.

Dava, As ancient as the floods of. 1880: Courtney, *W. Cornwall Words*, xiii. (E.D.S.).

Davenham steeple the centre of Cheshire within three barley - corns. 1917: Bridge, *Cheshire Proverbs*, 49.

Davenports. *See* Cheshire (7).

Davie Debet=Debt personified, or a bailiff. 1575: Gascoigne, *Posies*, in *Works*, i. 65 (Cunliffe), Till Davie Debet in thy parler stand. 1583: Melbancke, *Philotinus*, sig. Q3, Dauie debte stoode watching with a mace at the doore.

Dawes Cross. 1579: *Marr. of Wit and Wisdom*, 28 (Sh. S.), Hold heare ! thou shalt not lease all ; thy purse shall not come home weeping for lose ; and as for the, thou shalt be commist to Dawes crosse. 1583: Melbancke, *Philotinus*, sig. Y1, You may sooner be doctors at Dawes crosse. 1596: Nashe, *Haue with you*, in *Works*, iii. 16 (Grosart), To grant them their absolute graces, to commence at Dawes Crosse.

Daws. *See* Norwich.

Day. 1. *A day after Doomsday=* Greek kalends. 1540: Palsgrave, *Acolastus*, sig. V1, At the Grekish calendes . . . or a daye after domesday.

2. *A day to come shows longer than a year that's gone.* 1732: Fuller, No. 68.

3. *As the day lengthens so the cold strengthens.* 1639: in *Berkeley MSS.*, iii. 30 (1885), When the daies begin to lengthen the cold begins to strengthen. 1646: Browne, *Pseudo. Epi.*, bk. iv. ch. xiii., We observe the cold to augment, when the daies begin to increase. 1732: Fuller, No. 6140. 1893: Inwards, *Weather Lore*, 11. *See also* New Year.

4. *As the days begin to shorten, The heat begins to scorch them.* 1893: Inwards, 8.

5. *As the days grow longer, The storms grow stronger.* 1827: Hone, *Table-Book*, 667. 1893: Inwards, 7.

6. *Be the day never so long, at length cometh even-song.* c. 1390: Gower, *Conf. Amantis*, bk. vi. l. 578, Bot hou so that the dai be long, The derke nyht comth ate laste. 1555: Hawes, *Past. of Pleasure*, 207 (Percy S.), For though the day be never so longe, At last the belles ringeth to evensonge. 1563: Foxe, *Actes, etc.*, vii. 346 (1828), His saying was that, although the day was never so long, yet at the last it ringeth to evensong. 1670: Ray, 77. 1732: Fuller, No. 6132.

7. *Day and night ; sun and moon ; air and light ; every one must have, and none can buy.* 1732: Fuller, No. 1237. 1846: Denham, *Proverbs*, 5 (Percy S.).

8. *No day passeth without some grief.* 1670: Ray, 6.

9. *The day is short and the work is long.* c. 1400: *Beryn*, l. 3631 (E.E.T.S.).

10. *The day that you do a good thing, there will be seven new moons.* 1732: Fuller, No. 4468.

11. *'Tis day still while the sun shines.* 1639: Clarke, 294. 1670: Ray, 77.

12. *To come a day after the fair.* 1546: Heywood, *Proverbs*, Pt. I. ch. viii., A daie after the fayre comth this remors. 1596: Nashe, *Haue with you*, in *Works*, iii. 205 (Grosart), A day after the faire when he is hangd Haruey takes him in hand. 1676: Etheredge, *Man of Mode*, III. i., I must confess, madam, you came a day after the fair. 1864: Mrs. H. Wood, *Trevlyn Hold*, ch. xxxiv., They must make good speed, unless they would be " a day too late for the fair." 1910: H. James, *Letters*, ii. 164 (1920). 1913: E. M. Wright, *Rustic Speech, etc.*, 79, There is an old English proverb : He's a fond chapman that comes the day after the fair.

13. *To see day at a little hole.* 1546: Heywood, *Proverbs*, Pt. I. ch. x., I see daie at this little hole. c. 1598: Deloney, *Gentle Craft*, Pt. II. ch. ii., I perceiue you can spie day at a little hole. 1691: J. Wilson, *Belphegor*, IV. ii., Men of my station can see day at a little hole—letters make words, and circumstances things ! 1714: Ozell, *Molière*, v. 153, In love, everything speaks, and in this case daylight is to be spy'd thro' a little hole. 1859:

Smiles, *Self-Help*, 391 (1869), As day-light can be seen through very small holes, so little things will illustrate a person's character.

14. *What a day may bring, a day may take away.* 1732 : Fuller, No. 5475.

Dead, *adj.* 1. *A dead wife's the best goods in a man's house.* 1678 : Ray, 58. 1738 : Swift, *Polite Convers.*, Dial. I., a dead wife under the table is the best goods in a man's house.

2. *A dead woman will have four to carry her forth.* 1678 : Ray, 354.

3. *As dead as a door-nail* (or *door-tree*). *c.* 1350 : *Will. Palerne*, 29 (E.E.T.S.), I am ded as dore-nail. 1596 : Nashe, *Haue with you*, in *Works*, iii. 182 (Grosart), Wee'l strike it as dead as a doore-naile. 1598 : Shakespeare, *2 Henry IV.*, V. iii. 1700 : Farquhar, *Constant Couple*, IV. ii., I can't tell whether he be dead in law : but he's dead as a door-nail. 1801 : Lamb, *Letters*, i. 223 (1908), " The Albion " is dead—dead as nail in door. 1843 : Dickens, *Carol*, Stave I. 1907 : De Morgan, *Alice-for-Short*, ch. xii., She may be as dead as a door-nail.

4. *As dead as a herring.* 1600 : Shakespeare, *Merry Wives*, II. iii., By gar, de herring is no dead so as I vill kill him. 1638 : Nabbes, *Tott. Court*, I. v., Is shee quite dead? Dead as a herring, sir. 1748 : Smollett, *Rod. Random*, ch. iv., Ay, ay, I'll warrant him as dead as a herring. 1834 : Marryat, *P. Simple*, ch. xxix. 1880 : R. L. S. and Henley, *Deacon Brodie*, IV. vii. iv., Stabbed to the heart and dead as a herring !

5. *As dead as a nit.* 1883 : Burne, *Shropsh. Folk-Lore*, 594. 1887 : Parish and Shaw, *Dict. Kent. Dialect*, 108 (E.D.S.), " Dead as a nit " is a common expression. 1890 : P. H. Emerson, *Wild Life*, 13 n., *Dead as nits*, a common Norfolk expression. 1923 : *Folk-Lore*, xxxiv. 329 (Oxfordsh.).

6. *As dead as Chelsea.* 1823 : Egan's Grose's *Class. Dict. of Vulgar Tongue*, s.v. " Chelsea," To get Chelsea ; to obtain the benefit of [Chelsea] hospital. " Dead Chelsea, by God ! " An exclama-tion uttered by a grenadier at Fontenoy,

on having his leg carried away by a cannon ball. [The phrase is not in 1st ed. of Grose, 1785.] 1833 : *National Mag.*, quoted in *N. & Q.*, 5th ser., xii. 29, Dead as Chelsea.

7. *As dead as ditchwater. See* **Flat** as ditchwater.

8. *As dead as mutton.* c. 1770 : Bickerstaffe, *Spoiled Child*, II. ii., Thus let me seize my tender bit of lamb—(*aside*) there I think I had her as dead as mutton. *c.* 1816 : in Farmer's *Musa Pedestris*, 80, Your Larry will be dead as mutton. 1860 : Reade, *Cl. and Hearth*, ch. xxiv. 1914 : Shaw, " Parents and Children," in *Misalliance, etc.*, p. vii, The old Bernard Shaw is as dead as mutton.

9. *At a dead lift.* 1551 : R. Robinson, tr. More's *Utopia*, 76 (Arber), Whiche they graunte to be not so good as horses at a sodeyne brunte, and (as we saye) at a deade lifte. 1614 : B. Rich, *Honestie of This Age*, 43 (Percy S.), Shee . . . hath . . . twenty companions at a becke, that will stick to her at a dead lift. 1640 : Shirley, *St. Pat. for Ireland*, IV. ii., They talk of woman's wit at a dead lift. 1712 : Motteux, *Quixote*, Pt. I. bk. iii. ch. iv. 1881 : Evans, *Leics. Words, etc.*, 136 (E.D.S.), A dead-lift is a lift or effort that will raise a weight by sheer strength without the intervention of any artificial means.

10. *Dead bee. See* **Bee** (2).

11. *Dead dog. See* **Dog** (25).

12. *Dead folks are past fooling.* 1732 : Fuller, No. 1238.

13. *Dead men bite not* (or *do no harm*). 1548 : Hall, *Chron.*, 128 (1809), A prouerbe, whiche saith, a dead man doth no harme. 1596 : Harington, *Metam. of Ajax*, 64 (1814), I care not, seeing thou art dead, *Mortui non mordent*. 1613 : B. & F., *Coxcomb*, II. ii., Knock out her brains ! And then she'll never bite. 1732 : Fuller, No. 1239, Dead folks can't bite. 1816 : Scott, *Old Mortality*, ch. xxxiv., Take him [dead man] away now, then, you gaping idiot, and see that he does not bite you, to put an old proverb to shame. 1883 : R. L. S., *Treasure I.*, ch. xi., " Dead men don't bite," says he.

14. *Dead men tell no tales.* 1664:
J. Wilson, *Andron. Commenius*, I. iv.,
'Twere best To knock them i' th' head
. . . The dead can tell no tales. 1681:
Dryden, *Span. Friar*, IV. i. 1795:
Mrs. Cowley, *The Town*, I. ii., The dead
do tell no tales! 1860: Reade, *Cl. and
Hearth*, ch. xxv. 1901: W. James, in
Letters, ii. 154 (1920), We never know
what ends may have been kept from
realization, for the dead tell no tales.

15. *Dead mice feel no cold.* 1678:
Ray, 123, A dead mouse feels no cold.
1732: Fuller, No. 1241.

16. *He demands tribute of the dead.*

17. *He chastises the dead.*

18. *He paints the dead.* All three—
1813: Ray, 75.

19. *It's a sad burden to carry a dead
man's child.* 1655: Fuller, *Church
Hist.*, bk. ii. § v. (29), Our women have
a proverb, " It is a sad burden . . ."
1670: Ray, 53. 1732: Fuller, No. 2873
[with " for a woman " after " burden "].

20. *Speak not of a dead man at the
table.* 1640: Herbert, *Jac. Prudentum*.

21. *The dead, and only they, should
do nothing.* 1732: Fuller, No. 4469.

22. *The dead have few friends.* 1303:
Brunne, *Handl. Synne*, l. 6302, For the
dedë hath few frendys. *c.* 1320: in
Reliq. Antiquæ, i. 116 (1841), " Frendles
ys the dede "; Quoth Hendyng. 1611:
Cotgrave, s.v. " Ami," The dead have
no friends, the sick but faint ones.
Before 1701: Sedley, *Ballad*, in *Works*,
i. 92 (1778), Justice has hid the world
adieu, And dead men have no friends.

23. *To get a f—t of a dead man.* 1546:
Heywood, *Proverbs*, Pt. I. ch. xi.,
I shall . . . as soone as a farthyng of
him. 1605: Chapman, etc., *Eastw.
Hoe*, IV. ii. 1611: Cotgrave, s.v.
" Pet." 1681: W. Robertson, *Phraseol.
Generalis*, 471.

24. *To wait for dead men's shoes.*
1530: Palsgrave, 644, Thou lookest
after deed mens shoes. 1597: Hall,
Satires, bk. ii. sat. v., Or if thee list
not waite for dead men's shoon.
1631: Mabbe, *Celestina*, 24 (T.T.), He
that lookes after dead-mens shooes,
may chance to goe barefoote. 1714:
Ozell, *Molière*, iii. 194. 1757: Murphy,

Upholsterer, I. ii., You have very good
pretensions; but then its waiting for
dead men's shoes. 1912: Lucas, *London Lav.*, ch. iv., " It's ill waiting for
dead men's shoes," Naomi quoted.

25. *To work for a dead horse.* 1659:
in *Harl. Miscell.*, v. 299 (1745), I shall
be content to play at any game, but
shall be unwilling to play for a dead
horse. 1712: Motteux, *Quixote*, Pt. II.
ch. lxxi., It shall never be said of me
. . . that I thought it working for a
dead horse, because I am paid beforehand. 1785: Grose, *Class. Dict. Vulgar
Tongue*, s.v. " Dead Horse," . . . to
work for wages already paid. 1853:
Cooper, *Sussex Provincialisms*, 41, To
work out a dead horse is to work out
an old debt. 1886: Elworthy, *West
Som. Word-Book*, 186 (E.D.S.), Work
done in redemption of debt is called
working out the dead-horse.

26. *When I am dead make me a
caudle.* 1732: Fuller, No. 5558.

27. *You'll not believe a man is dead,
till you see his brains out.* 1678: Ray,
67. 1732: Fuller, No. 6031.

**Deadly disease neither physician nor
physic can ease, A.** 1629: *Book of
Meery Riddles*, Prov. 56.

Deaf. 1. *As deaf as a beetle.* 1867:
N. & Q., 3rd ser., xi. 34. 1876:
Leveson-Gower, *Surrey Provincialisms*,
86 (E.D.S.), That there horse is as deaf
as a beetle. 1887: Parish and Shaw,
Dict. of Kent. Dialect, 11 (E.D.S.),
Beetle. A wooden mallet. . . . The
phrase—" as death [deaf] as a beetle,"
refers to this mallet, and is equivalent
to . . . " as deaf as a post." 1923:
Folk-Lore, xxxiv. 329 (Oxfordsh.).

2. *As deaf as a door.* 1599: Breton,
in *Works*, ii. *c* 49 (Grosart), Hee is as
deafe as a doore.

3. *As deaf as a door-nail.* 1572: T.
Wilson, *Disc. upon Usury*, 224 (1925),
The userer is as deafe as a doore nayle.
1589: L. Wright, *Display of Dutie*, 10.
1633: Draxe, 38. 1837: Mrs. Palmer,
Devonsh. Dialect, 42, As deave [deaf] as
a door-nail. 1901: F. E. Taylor, *Lancs
Sayings*, 25, He's as deeof as a dur nail.

4. *As deaf as a haddock.* 1882: Jago,
Gloss. of Cornish Dialect, 151, There is

a term also, "defe as a haddock," meaning very deaf. 1886 : Elworthy, *West Som. Word-Book*, 310 (E.D.S.), We seldom hear . . . any other than "so deef's a 'addick."

5. *As deaf as a post.* 1575 : Churchyard, *Chippes*, 136 (Collier), I thereat seemde dumme and deaffe as post. 1720 : Gay, *Poems*, ii. 280 (Underhill), Till you grow tender as a chick, I'm dull as any post. 1777 : Sheridan, *Sch. for Scandal*, I. i., Who you know is as deaf as a post. 1849 : Brontë, *Shirley*, ch. i.

6. *As deaf as an adder.* 1605 : Chapman, etc., *Eastw. Hoe*, V. ii., I will be deafe as an adder. 1618 : Minshull, *Essayes, etc.*, 37 (1821). 1702 : T. Brown, in *Works*, ii. 246 (1760), I would rather chuse to be as deaf as an adder. 1821 : Scott, *Pirate*, ch. xxviii., As deaf as the adder to the voice of the charmer. 1839 : Dickens, *Nickleby*, ch. xlvii.

7. *Deaf nuts*=Nuts without kernels. [1648 : Herrick, *Hesp.*, No. 670, As deaf as nuts. 1686 : G. Stuart, *Joco-Serious Discourse*, 42, Twou'd vex a man to th' very guts, To sit seaven year cracking deaf nuts.] (*a*) *No deaf nuts.* See quots. 1808 : Scott, in Lockhart's *Life*, ii. 231, The appointments of our historian are £300 a year—no deaf nuts. 1825 : Scott, *Journal*, 5 Dec., I received . . . a bill for £750, *no deaf nuts*. 1868 : Atkinson, *Cleveland Gloss.*, 138, He does not look as if he lived upon deeaf nuts. 1899 : Dickinson, *Cumberland Gloss.*, 95, "He cracks nea deef-nuts"—said of a well-fed person or animal. 1917 : Bridge, *Cheshire Proverbs*, 65, He doesna crack many deaf nuts. (*b*) *To give a ha'porth of deaf nuts*=A worthless gift. Shropsh. saying. 1917 : Bridge, *Cheshire Proverbs*, 65.

8. *Deaf men are quick-eyed and distrustful.* 1732 : Fuller, No. 1242.

9. *Deaf men go away with the blame.* 1670 : Ray, 6 [with "injury" for "blame"]. 1732 : Fuller, No. 1243.

10. *None so deaf as those that won't hear.* 1546 : Heywood, *Proverbs*, Pt. II. ch. ix., Who is so deafe or so blynde, as is hee That wilfully will nother here nor see? 1611 : Cotgrave, s.v. "Sourd,"

No man's worse deafe then he that will not heare. 1714 : Ozell, *Molière*, iii. 91, 'Tis a true saying, that none are so deaf as those that won't hear. 1869 : Spurgeon, *John Ploughman*, ch. ii. 1905 : E. G. Hayden, *Travels round our Village*, 268, "He! he!" cackled Joane . . . "ther be none sa deaf as them who wun't hear!"

11. *To be deaf of that ear.* 1598 : Chamberlain, *Letters*, 12 (Camden S.), I feare we are deafe on that side. 1654 : Gayton, *Pleasant Notes Don Q.*, 141, The Don hearing but of one eare. 1754 : Berthelson, *Eng.-Danish Dict.*, s.v. "Deaf," He is deaf of that ear. 1814 : Scott, *Waverley*, ch. xxxvi., Ye are deaf as adders upon that side of the head.

Deal, Kent. 1. *Deal, Dover and Harwich, The devil gave with his daughter in marriage; And by a codicil to his will, He added Helvoet and the Brill.* 1785 : Grose, *Class. Dict. Vulgar Tongue*, s.v. "Devil's Daughter's Portion."

2. *Deal savages, Canterbury parrots, Dover sharps, and Sandwich carrots.* 1735 : Pegge, *Kent. Proverbs*, in E.D.S., No. 12, p. 69.

See also **Dover** (1).

Deals in the world, needs four sieves, He that. 1640 : Herbert, *Jac. Prudentum.*

Deansgate, As long as. Manchester. 1869 : Hazlitt, 66.

Dear. 1. *As dear as cinnamon.* Derby. 1889 : *Folk-Lore Journal*, vii. 291.

2. *As dear as saffron.* Newlyn, W. Corn., 19th cent. (Mr. C. Lee).

3. *As dear as two eggs a penny.* 1678 : Ray, 282.

4. *Dear bought.* See **Far** fetched.

5. *Dear child it behoveth to learn.* c. 1320 : in *Reliq. Antiquæ*, i. 110 (1841), "Luef child lore byhoveth"; Quoth Hendyng. 1377 : Langland, *Plowman*, B, v. 38, That the leuere childe the more lore bihoueth. c. 1460 : *Good Wyfe wold a Pylgremage*, l. 11, That lothe chylde lore be-howytt, and leve chyld moche more.

6. *It's a dear collop that is cut out of*

Dearth 140 **Deceive**

one's own flesh. 1546: Heywood, *Proverbs*, Pt. I. ch. x., For I haue heard saie, it is a deere colup That is cut out of thowne fleshe. 1639: Clarke, 240, It's a deare collop that's taken out of the flesh.

Dearth always begins. *See* England (1).
Dearths foreseen come not. 1640: Herbert, *Jac. Prudentum.*

Death. 1. *Death dealeth doubtfully.* 1669: *Politeuphuia*, 183.

2. *Death devours lambs as well as sheep.* 1620: Shelton, *Quixote*, Pt. II. ch. xx. 1732: Fuller, No. 1245.

3. *Death is the grand leveller.* Ibid., No. 1250.

4. *Death keeps no calendar.* 1640: Herbert, *Jac. Prudentum.* 1670: Ray, 6. 1732: Fuller, No. 1251.

5. *Death squares all accounts.* 1653: Shirley, *Cupid and Death*, in *Works*, vi. 357 (Dyce), Death quits all scores. 1685-6: Cotton, *Montaigne*, bk. i. ch. vii., 'Tis a saying, "That death discharges us of all our obligations." 1714: Ozell, *Molière*, iii. 87, But Death settles all things. 1815: Scott, *Mannering*, ch. xxiii., The Laird's dead—aweel, death pays a' scores. 1860: Reade, *Cl. and Hearth*, ch. xcii., Death squares all accounts. Cf. **Die** (3).

6. *Death when it comes will have no denial.* 1611: Cotgrave, s.v. "Appel," Death admits no appeale. 1681: W. Robertson, *Phraseol. Generalis*, 432.

7. *Death's day is Doomsday.* 1579: Lyly, *Euphues*, 181 (Arber), Euery ones deathes daye is his doomes daye. 1732: Fuller, No. 1255.

8. *Men fear death as children do to go in the dark.* 1659: Howell, 10 (8). 1670: Ray, 7. 1732: Fuller, No. 3392.

9. *Thou hast death in thy house, and dost bewail another's.* 1640: Herbert, *Jac. Prudentum.*

Debt. 1. *Debt is an evil conscience.* 1732: Fuller, No. 1257.

2. *Debt is better than death.* 1659: Howell, 6.

3. *Debt is the worst poverty.* 1732: Fuller, No. 1258. 1880: Spurgeon, *Ploughman's Pictures*, 19, Too often debt is the worst kind of poverty, because it breeds deceit.

4. *Speak not of my debts unless you mean to pay them.* 1640: Herbert, *Jac. Prudentum.* 1875: A. B. Cheales, *Proverb. Folk-lore*, 88, Don't talk of my debts unless you mean to pay them.

5. *To pay the debt to nature.* [1289: in *Lanercost Chron.*, 131 (Maitland Cl.), Quo dicto, debitum naturæ statim exsolvit et in Christo quievit.] 1494: Fabyan, *Chron.*, II. xli. 28 (O.), Fynally he payde the dette of nature. 1563: Becon, *Reliques of Rome*, fo. 51, When he was an hundred yeare olde, he payed nature her dutye. 1606: Shakespeare, *Macbeth*, V. viii., Your son, my Lord, has paid a soldier's debt. 1758-67: Sterne, *Trist. Shandy*, vol. v. ch. iii., To die, is the great debt and tribute due unto nature. 1783: Johnson, *Letters*, ii. 331 (Hill), Mrs. Williams, from mere inanition, has at length paid the great debt to nature. 1845: Planché, *Extravag.*, iii. 26 (1879), In peace to pass, with Jason, all her days, Till he or she the debt o' natur' pays.

See also **Sin**, *subs.* (3).

Debtors are liars. 1640: Herbert, *Jac. Prudentum.* 1869: Spurgeon, *John Ploughman*, ch. xii., Debtors can hardly help being liars.

Deceit. 1. *Deceit, weeping, spinning, God hath give to women kindly, while they may live.* 1869: Hazlitt, 109, . . . This is a paraphrase of the old leonine verse—Fallere, flere, nere dedit Deus in muliere.

2. *There's no deceit in a bag pudding.* 1678: Ray, 193.

3. *There's no deceit in a brimmer.* 1660: A. Brome, *Poems*, in Chalmers, vi. 653 (1810), Then quaff it round, No deceit in a brimmer is found. 1738: Swift, *Polite Convers.*, Dial. II. 1750: R. Heath, *Account of Scilly*, 443, Upon the silver mugs in the town of Liskerd it is written, *Qui fallit in poculis, fallit in omnibus*, there is no deceit in a bumper.

Deceive. 1. *If a man deceive me once, shame on him; but if he deceive me twice, shame on me.* 1736: Bailey, *Dict.*, s.v.

2. *To deceive a deceiver is no deceit.* c. 1580: Fulwell, *Ars Adulandi*, sig. G3.

1631 : Mabbe, *Celestina*, 264 (T.T.), For he that deceives the deceiver, you know what I meane. 1669 : *Politeuphuia*, 293. 1732 : Fuller, No. 1261, Deceiving of a deceiver is no knavery.

Deceiver. *See* Guiler.

December. 1. *December cold with snow, good for rye; 2. December's frost and January's flood Never boded the husbandman's good;* and 3. *Thunder in December presages fine weather*—all in 1893, Inwards, *Weather Lore*, 38. *See also* August; May, F (16); and October (5).

Deed well done pleaseth the heart, A. *c.* 1460 : *How the Good Wife*, l. 110, A dede wele done, herte it whemyth [pleaseth].

Deeds are fruits, words are but leaves. 1633 : Draxe, 40. 1670 : Ray, 7. 1732 : Fuller, No. 1263.

Deeds are males, words are females. 1578 : Florio, *First Fruites*, fo. 32. 1581 : T. Howell, *Devises*, 31 (1906), Women are wordes, men are deedes. 1645 : Howell, *Letters*, bk. i. § i. No. xxxix. 1732 : Fuller, No. 5814, Words are for women ; actions for men. 1894 : Northall, *Folk Phrases*, 12 (E.D.S.), Deeds are Johns, and words Nans. *Worcs.* A local version of the proverb—" Deeds are males, but words females."

Deeds not words. 1546 : Heywood, *Proverbs*, Pt. II. ch. v., Deede without woords shall driue him to the wall. Before 1681. J. Lacy, *Sawny the Scot*, II.

Dee-mills. *If thou hadst the rent of Dee mills, thou wouldst spend it.* Cheshire. 1670 : Ray, 171. 1790 : Grose, *Prov. Gloss.*, s.v. "Cheshire." 1917 : Bridge, *Cheshire Proverbs*, 77.

Deem [Judge] **not my deeds.** *See* quot. 15th cent. : in *Reliq. Antiquæ*, i. 205 (1841), Deme nott my dedis, thogh thyne be noght ; Say whate thow wilte, knowyst noth my thowght.

Deem the best till the truth be tried out. *c.* 1387 : Usk, *Test. of Love*, in Skeat's *Chaucer*, vii. 26, Thou shalt not juge ne deme toforn thou knowest. 15th cent. : in *Reliq. Antiquæ*, i. 92 (1841), Deme the best of every doute,

Tyl the truthe be tryed out. Before 1500 : in Hill, *Commonplace Book*, 131 (E.E.T.S.), Deme no thyng that is in dowt till the trowth be tred owt. 1546 : Heywood, *Proverbs*, Pt. II. ch. v., Deeme the best, till time hath tryde the trouth out. 1591 : Florio, *Second Frutes*, 105, Judge nothing till the end be seene.

Deep as the North. 1869 : Fitz-Gerald, *Sea Words and Phrases*, 4, Deep as the North star, said . . . of a very wide-a-wake babe four months old. 1883 : Burne, *Shropsh. Folk-Lore*, 594, As dip [deep=crafty] as the North.

Deeper the sweeter, The. 1596 : Jonson, *Ev. Man in Humour*, II. iv., My poesy was, " The deeper, the sweeter." 1611 : Barry, *Ram-Alley*, I. 1661 : Davenport, *City Nightcap*, I. 1738 : Swift, *Polite Convers.*, Dial. I., Stir it up with the spoon, miss ; for the deeper the sweeter.

Deep in the mud. *See* quot. 1914 : R. L. Gales, *Vanished Country Folk*, 205, " One's as deep in the mud as the other in the mire " is a proverb I still sometimes hear.

Deer. *Where the deer is slain, there will some of his blood lie.* 1732 : Fuller, No. 5663.

Defend me and spend me. *c.* 1595 : Spenser, *State of Ireland*, 624 (Globe ed.), The Irish . . . saying commonly, " Spend me and defend me." 1645 : Howell, *Fam. Letters*, bk. i. § i. No. vii., So that the saying is truly verify'd here, *Defend me, and spend me*. 1737 : Ray, 274, Defend me and spend me. (Saith the Irish churl.) 1853 : Trench, *Proverbs*, 59 (1905).

Delay. *After a delay comes a let.* 1736 : Bailey, *Dict.*, s.v. "Delay." *See also* Wise, *adj.* (35).

Delays are dangerous. *c.* 1300 : *Havelok*, l. 1352, Dwelling [delay] haueth ofte scathe [injury] wrouht. *c.* 1384 : Chaucer, *Troylus*, bk. iii. l. 853, That peril is with dreeching in y-drawe. 1457 : *Paston Lett.*, i. 414 (Gairdner, 1900), Taryeng drawyth parell. 1579 : Lyly, *Euphues*, 65 (Arber), Delayes breede daungers. 1655 : Shirley, *Gent. of Venice*, V. i.,

Shall we go presently? delays are
dangerous. 1691: Southerne, *Sir
Antony Love*, V. iv. 1725: Bailey,
tr. Erasmus' *Colloq.*, 200, Why not to
day rather than to morrow, if delays
are dangerous. 1888: R. L. S., *Black
Arrow*, bk. i. ch. i., Delay, they say,
begetteth peril.

Deliberating is not delaying. 1732:
Fuller, No. 1266.

Demand. *When the demand is a jest,
the answer is a scoff.* 1639: Clarke, 86.
1732: Fuller, No. 5575.

Denshire. *See* **Devonshire.**

Denton. *See* **Heighton.**

Denying a fault doubles it. 1669:
Politeuphuia, 163, Denials make little
faults great. 1732: Fuller, No. 1267.

Dependence is a poor trade. Ibid.,
No. 1268.

**Depends on another, dines ill and sups
worse, He who.** 1813: Ray, 164, Who
depends upon another man's table often
dines late. 1855: Bohn, 399.

Derby ale and London beer. 1614:
Cooke, *Greene's Tu Quoque*, in Hazlitt,
Old Plays, xi. 234, I have sent my
daughter this morning as far as Pimlico
to fetch a draught of Derby ale. 1659:
Howell, 14. 1670: Ray, 258. 1703:
Ward, *Writings*, ii. 122, Two or three
gallons of Derby ale had one day set
my wits a wooll-gathering.

Derby's bands. 1576: Gascoigne,
Steel Glas, 71 (Arber), To binde such
babes in father Derbies bands. 1592:
Greene, *Quip*, in *Works*, xi. 244
(Grosart), They tie the poore soule in
such Darbies bands. 1602: Carew,
Surv. of Cornwall, 49 (1811), For which
the poor wretch is bound in Darby's
bonds to deliver him two hundred
weight of tin at the next coinage.

**Derbyshire born and Derbyshire bred,
Strong i' th' arm and weak i' th' head.**
1852: *N. & Q.*, 1st ser., v. 573. 1884:
Folk - Lore Journal, ii. 279 [with
" thick " instead of " weak "].

**Derbyshire for lead, Devonshire for
tin, Wiltshire for hunting plains, And
Middlesex for tin.** 1669: *New Help to
Discourse*, 113, Darbyshire for wooll
and lead. *c.* 1809: quoted in *N. & Q.*,
9th ser., xi. 266.

**Desert and reward seldom keep com-
pany.** 1611: Davies (of Hereford), *Sc.
of Folly*, 42, in *Works*, ii. (Grosart),
Desart and reward be euer farre od.
1670: Ray, 7. 1748: Richardson,
Clarissa, iv. 120 (1785), Desert and
reward, I can assure her, seldom keep
company together.

Deserve. *See* **First deserve.**

Deserved a cushion, He has. That
is, he hath gotten a boy. 1678:
Ray, 69.

**Deserves no pity that chooseth to do
amiss twice, He.** 1637: T. Heywood,
Dialogues, etc., in Bang's *Materialien*,
B. 3, p. 218 [cited as a proverb].

Desire hath no rest. *c.* 1582: G.
Harvey, *Marginalia*, 201 (1913), Desier
sufferith no delay. 1621: Burton,
Melanch., I. ii. 3, 11, A true saying it is,
desire hath no rest.

Desires are nourished by delays.
1633: Draxe, 41. 1670: Ray, 7.

**Desires but little, has no need of
much, He that.** 1614: Lodge, tr.
Seneca, 443, He that coueteth little,
hath not need of much. 1732: Fuller,
No. 2077.

Despair gives courage to a coward.
Ibid., No. 1272.

**Desperate diseases must have des-
perate cures.** 1539: Taverner, *Proverbs*, fo. 4, Stronge disease requyreth
a stronge medicine. 1602: Shakespeare,
Hamlet, IV. iii. 1670: Shadwell,
Humourists, IV., Well, a desperate
disease must have a desperate cure.
1748: Richardson, *Clarissa*, vii. 61
(1785), For desperate diseases must
have desperate remedies. 1831: Hone,
Year-Book, 1416, Desperate cuts must
have desperate cures.

**Desperate that thinks himself so, He
is.** 1732: Fuller, No. 1913.

Devil. 1. *An artful fellow is a devil
in a doublet.* 1732: Fuller, No. 583.

2. *As bad as marrying the devil's
daughter, and living with the old folks.*
1830: Forby, *Vocab. E. Anglia*, 434.

3. *As busy as the devil in a high wind.*
1811: *Gent. Mag.*, lxxxi. 505, That
adage, so common among the vulgar,
" as busy as the devil in a high gale
of wind." 1821: Scott, *Pirate*, ch. viii.,

They are as busy as the devil in a gale of wind.

4. *As great* [intimate] *as the Devil and the Earl of Kent.* 1703 : Ward, *Writings*, ii. 90, As great as old Nick, and the old Earl of Kent. 1738 : Swift, *Polite Convers.*, Dial. III. [Scott, in a note to this, says : " The villainous character given by history to the celebrated Goodwin, Earl of Kent, in the time of Edward the Confessor, occasioned this proverb"].

5. *As the devil looks over Lincoln.* 1546 : Heywood, *Proverbs*, Pt. II. ch. ix. 1662 : Fuller, *Worthies*, ii. 268 (1840), He looks as the devil over Lincoln. 1738 : Swift, *Polite Convers.*, Dial. I. 1822 : Scott, *Nigel*, ch. xxi., When I offer you gold for the winning, you look on me as the devil looks over Lincoln. 1827 : Hone, *Ev. Day Book*, ii. 1238, The origin of the statue of the devil at Oxford [Lincoln College] is not so certain as that the effigy was popular, and gave rise to the saying of " the devil looking over Lincoln " [it was taken down in 1731].

6. *As the devil loves apple-dumplings.* 1858 : *Gent. Mag.*, Pt. II., p. 401, . . . This is a not uncommon saying, but to all appearance a very silly one.

7. *As the devil loves holy water.* c. 1500 : in Hazlitt, *Early Pop. Poetry*, i. 227 (1864), They dyd flee fro hym, as the deuyll fro holy water. 1576 : Lambarde, *Peramb. of Kent*, 301 (1826), You remember the olde prouerbe, how well the divell loveth holy water. 1679 : *Roxb. Ballads*, iv. 141 (B.S.). 1715 : Centlivre, *Wife well Managed*, sc. iv., Nothing frights the devil like holy water,—thence comes the proverb, you know. 1828 : Carr, *Craven Dialect*, i. 232, " He likes him as the devil likes holy water "; i.e. he mortally hates him. 1913 : E. M. Wright, *Rustic Speech, etc.*, 205.

8. *As the devil mended his dame's leg.* c. 1542 : Brinklow, *Complaynt*, 34 (E.E.T.S.), It is amended, euen as the deuel mendyd his damys legg (as it is in the prouerbe) : whan he shuld haue set it right, he bracke it quyte in pecys !

9. *Away goes the devil when he finds*

the door shut against him. 1659 : Howell, *Proverbs : Ital.-Eng.*, 4, The devil turns his back at a gate shut up. 1855 : Bohn, 323.

10. *Better keep the devil at the door, than turn him out of the house.* 1732 : Fuller, No. 907.

11. *Between the devil and the deep sea.* [Hac urget lupus, hac canis, aiunt.— Horace, *Sat.*, II. ii. 64.] 1637 : quoted in *N. & Q.*, 7th ser., i. 453, Betwixt the devill and the deepe sea. 1672 : Walker, *Parœm.*, 11, I am in a twittering case ; betwixt the devil and the deep sea. 1762 : Smollett, *Sir L. Greaves*, ch. last. 1820 : Byron, *Letters*, v. 4 (Prothero), Between the devil and deep sea, Between the lawyer and trustee—it is difficult to decide. 1902 : Sir H. Lucy, *Diary of Journalist*, 170 (1920).

12. *Bring you the devil and I'll bring out his dam.* 1639 : Clarke, 209.

13. *Down the lane to the devil.* 1546 : Heywood, *Proverbs*, Pt. II. ch. vii., The deuel go with the doune the lane. 1619 : Chapman, *Two Wise Men*, VII. iii., *Her.* By that meanes thou wilt accompanie him to hell. *Sim.* Downe the lane to the divell.

14. *Every devil has not a cloven foot.* 1726 : Defoe, *Hist. of Devil*, Pt. II. ch. vi., p. 242 (4th ed.).

15. *Give the devil his due.* 1589 : *Pap with a Hatchet*, 31 (1844), Giue them their due though they were diuels. 1597 : Shakespeare, 1 *Henry IV.*, I. ii. 1669 : Dryden, *Wild Gallant*, II. ii., Let every man speak as he finds, and give the devil his due. 1709 : Mandeville, *Virgin Unmask'd*, 28 (1724), Tho' I give the devil his due, I still defy him. 1825 : Planché, *Extravag.*, i. 25 (1879), You certainly have great merit. I will give the devil his due.

16. *He does the devil's work for nothing.* 1742 : Fielding, *Andrews*, bk. ii. ch. xvi., What a silly fellow must he be who would do the devil's work for nothing ! 1830 : Forby, *Vocab. E. Anglia*, 433 [said of a common swearer].

17. *He is like the devil, always in mischief.* 1659 : Howell, 13.

18. *He that sups with the devil needs a*

long spoon. c. 1386: Chaucer, *Squire's Tale,* l. 594, "Therfor bihoveth him a ful long spoone That shal ete with a feend," thus herde I seye. 16th cent.: in *Reliq. Antiquæ,* i. 208 (1841), He hath need of a long spoone that eateth with the devill. 1626: Overbury, *Characters:* "A Jesuit," A Jesuit is a larger spoon for a traytor to feed with the devil, than any other order. 1633: Marlowe, *Jew of Malta,* III. iv. 1840: Barham, *Ing. Legends:* "St. Nicholas." 1893: R. L. S., *Catriona,* ch. xxix.

19. *He that (a) takes the devil into his boat,* or *(b) that hath shipped the devil must (c) carry him over the Sound,* or *(d) make the best of him.* 1678: Ray, 125 [(*a*) and (*c*), also (*b*) and (*d*)]. 1732: Fuller, No. 2326 [(*a*) and (*c*)], and No. 2152, He that has purchas'd the devil, must make the most of him. 1853: Trench, *Proverbs,* 143 (1905), He who has shipped the devil, must carry him over the water.

20. *He that the devil drives, feels no lead at his heels.* 1732: Fuller, No. 2331.

21. *If the devil be a vicar, thou shalt be his clerk.* 1670: Ray, 171. 1738: *Gent. Mag.,* 475.

22. *If the devil catch a man idle, he'll set him at work.* 1732: Fuller, No. 2705.

23. *If you buy the devil you must sell the devil.* 1775: Grose, *Antiq. Repertory,* ii. 395 (1808), Buying and selling the devil has long been a proverbial expression. 1820: Colton, *Lacon,* Pt. II. No. 167 *n.,* Booksellers are like horse-dealers in one respect, and if they buy the devil, they must also sell the devil.

24. *Ill doth the devil preserve his servant.* 1659: Howell, *Proverbs: Brit.-Eng.,* 3.

25. *It is a sin to belie the devil.* 1548: Hall, *Chron.,* 363 (1809), It wer synne to lye on the deuil. 1607: Dekker, *Knights Coniuring,* 21 (Percy S.), 'Tis sinne to belye the diuell. 1712: Motteux, *Quixote,* Pt. I. bk. iii. ch. 11. 1732: Fuller, No. 2884.

26. *It is an ill army where the devil carries the colours.* 1639: Clarke, 70, 'Tis an ill company where the devil beares the banner. 1670: Ray, 7 [with

"battel" for "army"]. 1732: Fuller, No. 2896.

27. *It is an ill procession where the devil (a) bears the cross,* or (*b*) *holds the candle.* 1633: Draxe, 86 [(*a*)]. 1641: in *Harl. Miscell.,* iii. 222 (1744), There is an old saying, There can be no holy procession where the divel carryes the crosse. 1694: D'Urfey, *Quixote,* Pt. I. Act IV. sc. i. [(*b*)]. 1732: Fuller, No. 2902 [(*b*)].

28. *More like the devil than St. Lawrence.* 1678: Ray, 256.

29. *Much about a pitch, Quoth the devil to the witch.* 1846-59: *Denham Tracts,* ii. 81 (F.L.S.).

30. *Never go to the devil with a dishclout in your hand.* 1738: *Gent. Mag.,* 475.

31. *One devil is like another.* 1612: Shelton, *Quixote,* Pt. I. bk. iv. ch. iv. 1732: Fuller, No. 3747.

32. *One might as well eat the devil as the broth he's boiled in.* 1545: Brinklow, *Lamentacyon,* 89 (E.E.T.S.), Yf it be so that God, through the kynge, hath caste out the deuell out of this realme, and yet both he and we soppe of the broth in which the deuell was soden. 1660: T. Hall, *Funebriæ Floræ,* 12, Wee must not so much as tast of the devils broth, lest at last hee bring us to eat of his beef. 1696: D'Urfey, *Quixote,* Pt. III. Act I., One had as good eat the devil, as the broth he's boiled in. 1738: Swift, *Polite Convers.,* Dial. II. 1834: Taylor, *Philip v. Art.,* III. i. part 2, Hast courage but for half a sin? As good To eat the devil as the broth he's boil'd in. 1865: "Lancs Proverbs," in *N. & Q.,* 3rd ser., viii. 494. 1901: F. E. Taylor, *Lancs Sayings,* 13, Aw'd as lief eyt the divvle as sup th' broth 'at he's boil't in.

33. *Seldom lies the devil dead by the gate* (or *in the ditch*). *c.* 1400: *Towneley Plays,* xiii., p. 123 (E.E.T.S.), Seldom lys the dewyll dede by the gate. 1670: Ray, 79 [ditch]. 1758-67: Sterne, *Trist. Shandy,* vol. viii. ch. xxviii., Which the devil, who never lies dead in a ditch, had put into her head.

34. *She will scold the devil out of a haunted house.* 1732: Fuller, No. 4149.

35. *Strike Dawkin! the devil is in the hemp.* 1678: Ray, 70. 1889: *Folk-Lore Journal*, vii. 293. Derby saying. Strike, Dakeyne! the devil's i' th' hemp.

36. *Talk of the devil and he'll appear.* [Lupus in fabula.—Terence, *Ad.*, 537. de Varrone loquebamur; lupus in fabula : venit enim ad me.—Cicero, *Att.*, 13, 33, 4.] 1666: Torriano, *Piazza Univ.*, 134, The English say, " Talk of the devil, and he's presently at your elbow." 1697: Vanbrugh, *Esop*, II. i., Talk of the devil, and he's at your elbow." 1725: Bailey, tr. Erasmus' *Colloq.*, 17, Rather it is according to the old proverb ; *talk of the devil and he'll appear* ; for we were just now speaking of you. 1799: T. Knight, *Turnpike Gate*, II. i., Speak o' th' devil and behold his horns ! 1822 : Scott, *Nigel*, ch. xv., They are the very men we spoke of—talk of the devil, and—humph?

37. *The devil always tips at the biggest ruck* [heap]. 1886 : R. Holland, *Cheshire Gloss.*, 454 (E.D.S.). 1917 : Bridge, *Cheshire Proverbs*, 113.

38. *The devil and (or) Dick Senhouse.* 1826 : Brady, *Varieties of Lit.*, 13, A common saying [in Cumberland], " It will do in spite of the Devil and Dick Senhouse." 1846–59 : *Denham Tracts*, i. 167 (F.L.S.), " I will do it in spite of the Devil and Dick Senhouse " ; also " Either the devil or Dick Senhouse."

39. *The devil and Dr. Faustus.* 1726 : Defoe, *Hist. of Devil*, 326 (4th ed.), It is become a proverb, *as great as the devil and Dr. Foster* [Faustus]. 1749 : Fielding, *Tom Jones*, bk. xviii. ch. viii., What the devil and Doctor Faustus ! shan't I do what I will with my own daughter? 1848 : Carleton, *Fardorougha*, 233 (W.), You'd beat the divil an' Docthor Fosther.

40. *The devil and his dam(e).* c. 1440 : *York Plays*, 300 (L. T. Smith), What the deuyll and his dame schall y now doo? 1550 : R. Crowley, *Works*, 49 (E.E.T.S.), But they saye that ye purchase the deuill, his dame, and all. c. 1615 : *Times Whistle*, 97 (E.E.T.S.), Me thought as both their heades together came, I saw the devill kissing of his

dam. 1657 : *Lust's Dominion*, IV. v., The devil and his dam, The Moor and my mother. 1830 : Scott, *Doom of Devorgoil*, III. ii., I have heard of the devil's dam before, But never of his child.

41. *The devil and John of Cumber.* 1659 : Howell, 20.

42. *The devil and ninepence go with her.* Before 1704 : T. Brown, *Works*, iii. 245 (1760), The devil and ninepence go with her, that's money and company, according to the laudable adage of the sage mobility ! 1738 : Swift, *Polite Convers.*, Dial. II., The devil go with him and sixpence ; and there's money and company too.

43. *The devil and the malster.* 1886 : Elworthy, *West Som. Word-Book*, 191 (E.D.S.), It is always said that on Culmstock Fair-day, May 21, " 'tis a fight twixt the devil and the malster "—to decide if there shall be cider to drink, or whether it must be beer. Cf. **Culmstock Fair.**

44. *The devil can quote Scripture.* 1595 : Shakespeare, *Merchant of Venice*, I. iii., The devil can cite Scripture for his purpose. 1609 : Armin, *Maids of More-clacke*, sig. E3, The diuell has scripture for his damned ill. 1821 : Scott, *Kenilworth*, ch. iv. 1850 : Dickens, *Chuzzlewit*, ch. xi., Does any one doubt the old saw, that the Devil (being a layman) quotes Scripture for his own ends?

45. *The devil danceth in a woman's placket.* 1659 : Howell, 15.

46. *The devil dares not peep under a maid's coat.* 1675 : *Mistaken Husband*, V. v., Good Mrs. Isbel hide me under your petticoats that the divel may not find me, they say he dares not peep under a maids coat.

47. *The devil gets up to the belfry by the vicar's skirts.* 1659 : Howell, *Proverbs: Span.-Eng.*, 20. 1732 : Fuller, No. 4476.

48. *The devil goes a nutting on Holy-rood Day.* 1689 : *Poor Robin Alman.*, Sept., The 14th day [of September], for then, they say, the devil goes a nutting.

49. *The devil goes share in gaming.* 1855 : Bohn, 501.

50. *The devil has a chapel wherever God has a church.* 1560 : Becon, *Catechism*, 361 (P.S.), For commonly, wheresoever God buildeth a church, the devil will build a chapel just by. 1609 : Dekker, in *Works*, iv. 220 (Grosart), And where God hath a church, the deuill hath a chappell. 1701 : Defoe, *True Born Eng.*, Pt. I. ll. 1-2, Wherever God erects a House of Prayer, The devil always builds a chapel there. 1748 : Richardson, *Clarissa*, vii. 327 (1785), It is an old proverb . . . God never had a House of Pray'r, But Satan had a chapel there.

51. *The devil has no power over a drunkard.* 1635 : Glapthorne, *Lady Mother*, III. ii., in Bullen, *Old Plays*, ii. 160, They say the divell has . . .

52. *The devil hath cast a bone to set strife.* 1546 : Heywood, *Proverbs*, Pt. II. ch. ii. *c.* 1594 : Bacon, *Promus*, No. 654. 1633 : Draxe, 197.

53. *The devil is a busy bishop in his own diocese.* 1549 : Latimer, *Sermon on Ploughers*, 29 (Arber), Who is the most diligent bishoppe and prelate in al England . . .? I wyl tel you. It is the deuyl. He is the moste dylygent preacher of al others, he is neuer out of his dioces. 1732 : Fuller, No. 4479. 1910 : *N. & Q.*, 11th ser., i. 34, The sanctity of the day became violated by the devil, who is " a busy bishop in his own diocese," the proverb says.

54. *The devil is a knave.* 1553 : *Respublica*, I. iii., The devyll ys a knave. 1571 : in *Ballads*, 85 (Percy S., No. 1). 1639 : Davenport, *New Trick to cheat Devil*, IV. i.

55. *The devil is an ass.* 1616 : Jonson, *Devil is an Ass* [title]. 1681 : Otway, *Soldier's Fortune*, IV. i., The devil's an ass, sir. 1745 : *Agreeable Companion*, 304, She found a trick she thought would pass, And prove the devil but an ass.

56. *The devil is at home.* 1620 : Middleton, in *Works*, vii. 185 (Bullen), Why, will he have it in's house, when the proverb says, The devil's at home? 1753 : Richardson, *Grandison*, i. 231 (1883), The devil's at home, is a phrase ; and our modern ladies live as if they thought so. 1810 : Crabbe, *Borough*, xix. 56, A foolish proverb says, " The devil's at home."

57. *The devil is dead. c.* 1470 : *Mankind*, in Manly's *Spec. of Pre-Shakesp. Drama*, i. 337, Qwyst, pesse ! The deull ys dede ! Before 1529 : Skelton, *Col. Clout*, l. 36, The deuyll, they say, is dede, The deuell is dede. 1661 : Davenport, *City Nightcap*, III., He thinks the devil's dead too. 1671 : *Westm. Drollery*, 109 (Ebsworth), The night is our own, for the devil is dead. 1860 : Reade, *Cl. and Hearth*, ch. lii., Courage, brave wife ; the divell is dead.

58. *The devil is easier to raise than to lay.* 1725 : Bailey, tr. Erasmus' *Colloq.*, 202, 'Tis an old saying and a true, 'Tis an easier matter to raise the devil, than 'tis to lay him.

59. *The devil is God's ape.* 1595 : *Polimanteia*, sig. B1, Satan desiring in this to bee Gods ape. 1639 : Fuller, *Holy War*, bk. iv. ch. xxi., As the devil is God's ape. 1666 : Torriano, *Piazza Univ.*, 67. 1904 : J. C. Wall, *Devils*, 22, " Satan," says Tertullian, " is God's ape "—a term which in those days (third century and after) became very general among Christians.

60. *The devil is good* (or *kind*) *to his own* (or *to some*). 1606 : Day, *Isle of Gulls*, II. iv., You were not worse then the devil els, for they say hee helps his . . . seruants. 1660 : A. Brome, *Poems* : " New Montebank," The devil's ever kind to his own. 1738 : Swift, *Polite Convers.*, Dial. III., They say, the devil is kind to his own.

61. *The devil is good when he is pleased.* 1581 : Woodes, *Conflict of Conscience*, III. iii., The devil is a good fellow, if one can him please. *c.* 1600 : *Grim the Collier*, II. 1677 : *Poor Robin Alman.*, Dec., The devil's good when he is pleased. 1738 : Swift, *Polite Convers.*, Dial. II. 1813 : Byron, *Letters, etc.*, ii. 257 (Prothero), But they say the devil is amusing when pleased.

62. *The devil is in the dice.* 1678 : Ray, 70. 1904 : J. C. Wall, *Devils*, 121, Dice are known as the Devil's Bones.

63. *The devil is not always at one door.* 1611 : Cotgrave, s.v. " Diable." 1694 :

D'Urfey, *Quixote*, Pt. I. Act IV. sc. i.
1732 : Fuller, No. 4482.

64. *The devil is not so black as he
is painted.* 1596 : Lodge, *Marg. of
America*, 57 (Hunt. Cl.), Wel . . .
diuels are not so blacke as they be
painted. 1642 : Howell, *Forreine Travell*, 65 (Arber). 1726 : Defoe, *Hist. of
Devil*, Pt. II. ch. vi., p. 232 (4th ed.),
As if the devil was not so black as he
was painted. *c.* 1770 : Foote, *Devil
upon Two Sticks*, I. 1860 : Reade, *Cl.
and Hearth*, ch. xxxvii.

65. *The devil is seldom outshot in his
own bow.* 1642 : D. Rogers, *Matrim.
Honour*, 42.

66. *The devil laughs when one thief
robs another.* 1819 : Scott, *Ivanhoe*,
ch. xxi., The fiend laughs, they say,
when one thief robs another.

67. *The devil lies brooding in the
miser's chest.* 1732 : Fuller, No. 4484.
1904 : J. C. Wall, *Devils*, 127.

68. *The devil loves all colliers.* 1583 :
Melbancke, *Philotimus*, sig. L1.

69. *The devil lurks behind the cross.*
1612 : Shelton, *Quixote*, Pt. I. bk. i.
ch. vi. 1712 : Motteux, *Quixote*, Pt. II.
ch. xlvii., Your honour ought not to eat
any of the things that stand here before
you, for they were sent in by some of the
convents ; and it is a common saying,
"The devil lurks behind the cross."

70. *The devil made askers.* 1738 :
Swift, *Polite Convers.*, Dial. II., Sir
John, will you taste my October? . . .
Sir John. My lord, I beg your pardon ;
but they say, the devil made askers.
Ld. Smart [to the butler]. Here, bring
up the great tankard, full of October,
for Sir John.

71. *The devil makes his Christmas pies
of clerks' fingers and lawyers' tongues.*
1591 : Florio, *Second Frutes*, 179, Of
three things the deuill makes his messe,
Of lawyers tongues, of scriueners fingers,
you the third may gesse. 1630 : T.
Adams, *Works*, 145, An euill tongue is
meate for the deuill, according to the
Italian prouerbe : the deuill makes his
Christmasse pie of lewd tongues. 1659 :
Howell, 11 (9).

72. *The devil may dance in his pocket*
—because it contains no *cross* (coin).

1411 : Hoccleve, *Reg. of Princes*, 25
(E.E.T.S.), The feende men seyn may
hoppen in a pouche Whan that no
croys there-inne may a-pere. *c.* 1470 :
Mankind, l. 474, The deull may daunce
in my purse for ony peny. 1567 :
Drant, *Horace*, I. iii., The deuille may
daunce in crosslesse purse. 1623 :
New and Merrie Prognos., 24 (Halliwell),
Some wanting money shall both ban and
curse That the devill hath roome to
dance in their purse. 1785 : Grose,
Class. Dict. Vulgar Tongue, s.v. "Devil."
1826 : Scott, *Woodstock*, ch. iii., No devil
so frightful as that which dances in the
pocket where there is no cross to keep
him out.

73. *The devil on Dun's back.* 1639 :
Clarke, 197. 1677 : *Poor Robin's
Visions*, 25, In term-time the divel
upon Dun rides to and frow.

74. *The devil owed a cake and paid a
loaf.* 1690 : *New Dict. Canting Crew*,
sig. C3, The devil ow'd her a cake, and
has pai'd her a loaf, when instead of a
small, a very great disaster, or misfortune has happen'd to a woman. 1732 :
Fuller, No. 4477, The devil hath owed
me a cake of a long time, and now hath
paid me a loaf.

75. *The devil owed him a shame.*
1542 : *Sch. House of Women*, l. 245,
The deuil, gossip, ought me a shame.
1679 : D'Urfey, *Squire Oldsapp*, V. ii.
The devil I think ow'd me a shame,
and sought to pay it this way. 1753 :
Richardson, *Grandison*, i. 320 (1883),
The devil has long, continued he, owed
me a shame. 1823 : Scott, in Lockhart's *Life*, v. 259, I hope the devil
does not owe me such a shame.

76. *The devil pay the maltman.*
c. 1532 : R. Copland, *Spyttal Hous*,
l. 682, Make we mery as longe as we
can, And drynke a pace : the deuill pay
the malt man ! 1559 : Becon, *Prayers,
etc.*, 282 (P.S.), To drinke them all out,
to set cock on the hoop, let the devil
pay the maltman. 1573 : Bullein,
Dialogue, 123 (E.E.T.S.), A dogge hath
but a daie. Let the deuill paie the
malt manne.

77. *The devil rebukes sin.* 1666 :
Torriano, *Piazza Univ.*, 60, The devil

corrects sin. 1682 : A. Behn, *Round-heads*, V. ii., How the devil rebukes sin ! 1754 : Berthelson, *Eng.-Danish Dict.*, s.v. " Devil." 1822 : Scott, *Nigel*, ch. xxxii., " I am afraid," said George Heriot, more hastily than prudently, " I might have thought of the old proverb of Satan reproving sin." 1894 : R. L. S., *St. Ives*, ch. x., " Now, really," said I, " is not this Satan reproving sin ? " 1922 : Ramsay Macdonald in Parl., in *Times*, 24 Nov., p. 7, col. 3, That incident is one of the most deplorable examples I have ever known of Satan reproving sin.

78. *The devil rides upon a fiddlestick* =Much ado about nothing. 1597 : Shakespeare, 1 *Henry IV.*, II. iv., Heigh, heigh ! the devil rides upon a fiddlestick : what's the matter ? *c.* 1620 : B. & F., *Hum. Lieut.*, IV. iv., The fiend rides on a fiddle-stick.

79. *The devil run through thee booted and spurred, with a scythe at his back.* Called the Sedgeley curse, I know not why. Sedgeley is in Staffordshire. *c.* 1620 : B. & F., *Woman's Prize*, V. ii., A Sedgly curse light on him ; which is, Pedro, " The fiend ride throgh him [as above]." 1659 : Howell, 2. 1726 : Defoe, *Hist. of Devil*, Pt. II. ch. ix., p. 297 (4th ed.), And make the devil, as the Scots express it, ride through them booted and spurred. 1790 : Grose, *Prov. Gloss.*, s.v. " Staffs." 1829 : Scott, *Gen. Preface to Waverley*, app. ii., " May the foul fiend, booted and spurred, ride down his bawling throat, with a scythe at his girdle," quoth Albert Drawslot.

80. *The devil s— upon a great heap.* 1659 : Howell, 6 [with " the usurers heaps " for " a great heap "]. 1670 : Ray, 80.

81. *The devil sometimes speaks the truth.* 1635 : Glapthorne, *Lady Mother*, I. iii., in Bullen, *Old Plays*, ii. 123. 1732 : Fuller, No. 5308, Truth may sometimes come out of the devil's mouth.

82. *The devil spits on the blackberries,* or *puts his foot on them,* or *casts his club over them,* on Michaelmas Day. 1727 : Threlkeld, quoted in *Folk-Lore*

Record, i. 155, After Michaelmas the d—l casts his club over them [black-berries]. 1900 : Hudson, *Nature in Downland*, ch. xii., In early October the devil flies abroad, as some believe, to spit on the bramble-bushes, and make its berries uneatable.

83. *The devil take the hindmost.* [Occupet extremum scabies.—Horace, *A. P.*, 417. *c.* 1470 : *Mankind*, l. 709, Hens wyth yowur stuff ! fast we were gone I be-schrew the last, xall come to hys home !] *c.* 1618 : B. & F., *Bonduca*, IV. ii. 1671 : Dryden, *An Evening's Love*, IV. iii., If it be come to that once, the devil take the hindmost ! 1850 : Planché, *Extravag.*, iv. 83 (1879).

84. *The devil tempts some, but an idle man tempts the devil.* 1709 : R. Kingston, *Apoph. Curiosa*, 57, An idle person tempts the devil to tempt him. 1820 : Colton, *Lacon*, Pt. I. No. 70, The Turks have a proverb, which says, that *The devil tempts all other men, but that idle men tempt the devil.* 1875 : A. B. Cheales, *Proverb. Folk-Lore*, 110.

85. *The devil to pay.* *c.* 1400 ; in *Reliq. Antiquæ*, i. 257 (1841), Beit wer be at tome for ay, Than her to serve the devil to pay. 1738 : Swift, *Polite Convers.*, Dial. II., I must be with my wife on Tuesday, or there will be the devil and all to pay. 1748 : Richard-son, *Clarissa*, vi. 87 (1785), Here's the devil to pay. 1821 : Scott, *Pirate*, ch. xxxvi., If they hurt but one hair of Cleveland's head, there will be the devil to pay, and no pitch hot. 1922 : Weyman, *Ovington's Bank*, ch. xxvi.

86. *The devil was sick, the devil a monk would be ; The devil was well, the devil a monk was he.* [*c.* 1450 : W. Bower, *Scotichronicon*, ii. 292 (Goodall), quoted in *N. & Q.*, 8th ser., xii. 331, Lupus languebat monachus tunc esse volebat, Sed cum convaluit lupus ut ante fuit.] 1586 : L. Evans, *Withals Dict. Revised*, sig. K8, The diuell was sicke and crasie ; Good woulde the monke bee that was lasie. 1692 : L'Estrange, *Æsop*, 104 (3rd ed.). 1757 : Garrick, *Gamesters*, III. *ad fin.* 1875 : Smiles, *Thrift*, 314 [with " saint " for " monk "]. 1875 : R. L. S., *Letters,*

i. 210 (Tusitala ed.), The story shall be called, I think, *When the Devil was well*, in allusion to the old proverb.

87. *The devil will not come into Corn-wall for fear of being put into a pie.* 1790: Grose, *Prov. Gloss.*, s.v. "Corn-wall." 1891: *N. & Q.*, 7th ser., xii. 216.

88. *The devil will take his own.* 1846: T. Wright, *Essays on Middle Ages*, i. 146, We say, "The devil will take his own."

89. *The devil wipes his tail with the poor man's pride.* 1659: Howell, 12 (10). 1670: Ray, 21.

90. *The devil would have been a weaver but for the Temples.* 1678: Ray, 91.

91. *The devil's behind the glass.* 1855: Bohn, 502. 1904: J. C. Wall, *Devils*, 128.

92. *The devil's children have the devil's luck.* 1678: Ray, 126, The devils child the devils luck. 1776: T. Cogan, *John Buncle, Junior*, i. 240, I wish the devil's children devil's luck, that's all. 1865: "Lancs Proverbs," in *N. & Q.*, 3rd ser., viii. 494. 1901: F. E. Taylor, *Lancs Sayings*, 9, The divvle's childer awlus han the divvle's luck.

93. *The devil's guts*=The surveyor's chain. 1678: Ray, 72.

94. *The devil's martyr.* 1639: Fuller, *Holy War*, bk. ii. ch. xxix., The unhappy Dutch proverb, "He that bringeth him-self into needless dangers, dieth the devil's martyr." 1670: Ray, 18 [as in 1748]. 1748: Richardson, *Clarissa*, iv. 121 (1785), Then that other fine saying, He who perishes in needless danger, is the Devil's martyr.

95. *The devil's meal is half bran.* 1611: Cotgrave, s.v. "Diable," Halfe of the devils meale turns unto branne. 1732: Fuller, No. 4487, The devil's flour is half bran. 1865: "Lancs Proverbs," in *N. & Q.*, 3rd ser., viii. 494, One half of the devil's meal runs to bran.

96. *The devil's mouth is a miser's purse.* 1600: Bodenham, *Belvedere*, 128 (Spens. S.), The deuils mouth is tearm'd a misers purse. 1669: *Poli-teuphuia*, 288, A covetous mans purse is called the divels mouth.

97. *The devil's run over Jock Wabster* —an allusion to one whose affairs are said to be going back in the world. N. of England. 1876: *N. & Q.*, 5th ser., vi. 64.

98. *There is a devil in every berry of the grape.* 1647: Howell, *Letters*, bk. ii. No. iii., He rails bitterly against Bacchus, and swears there's a devil in every berry of his grape. 1884: H. Friend, *Flowers and Fl. Lore*, 54, Perhaps every one has not heard the proverb, "There is a devil in every berry of the grape." This proverb is in use in some parts of England, and is said to have strayed hither from Turkey.

99. *To beat the devil round the goose-berry-bush*=To be wordy, roundabout. 1875: Parish, *Dict. Sussex Dialect*, He did not think the new curate was much of a hand in the pulpit, he did beat the devil round the gooseberry-bush so.

100. *To drink the devil dry.* 1594: R. Wilson, *Coblers Prophecy*, l. 106 (Malone S.), Ile looke in thy purse by and by: And if thou haue any money in it, Wele drinke the diuell dry, diuell dry.

101. *To hug as the devil hugged the witch.* 1678: Ray, 286. 1715: *Poli-tical Merriment*, Pt. III., p. 20, And hug and kiss, and are so great, as the devil and witch of Endor. 1738: Swift, *Polite Convers.*, Dial. I., I've seen her hug you as the devil hugg'd the witch. 1745: *Agreeable Companion*, 251. 1846-59: *Denham Tracts*, ii. 84 (F.L.S.), To hug one, as the devil hugs a witch.

102. *To lie in the devil's mouth*=To be wide open. 1609: in *Roxb. Ballads*, vii. 437 (B.S.), He could not find a priuy place, for all lay in the diuel's mouth.

103. *To patter the devil's Paternoster.* c. 1386: Chaucer, *Parson's Tale*, 506-7, They . . . grucche and murmure priuely for verray despyt, whiche wordes men clepen the deuelles pater noster. 1552: Latimer, *Sermons*, 350 (P.S.), Go not away with the devil's Paternoster, as some do. Do all things with a good mind. 1567: Golding, *Ovid*, bk. ii. l. 984, Began to mumble with hir selfe the divels Paternoster. 1641: Jonson, *Sad Shepherd*, II. ii., What devil's

pater noster mumbles she? 1847:
Halliwell, *Dict.*, s.v., To say the devil's
pater-noster, to mutter or grumble.

104. *To play the devil for God's sake.*
c. 1640 : in *Harl. Miscell.*, iv. 155 (1745),
To play the devil for God's sake hath
been a common proverb, but was never
entered for an article in a sober belief.
1681 : L'Estrange, *Dissenters Sayings*,
50 (1685), Which is no more, in short,
than playing the devil in God's name.
1820 : Scott, *Abbot*, ch. xxiv., That
would be a serving, as they say, the
devil for God's sake.

105. *To play the devil in the bulmong.*
1670 : Ray, 171.

106. *To play the devil in the horologe.*
1519 : Horman, *Vulgaria*, fo. 231, Some
for a tryfull play the deuyll in the
orlege. *c.* 1550 : Udall, *Roister Doister*,
III. iii., *C.C.* What will he? *M.M.*
Play the devill in the horologe. 1593 :
Harvey, in *Works*, i. 276 (Grosart),
Finding nothing in all those pestilent
and virulent sheetes of wast-paper, but
meere—meere forgeryes, and the diuell
in the horologe. 1659 : Howell, 6, The
devil's in the orologe.

107. *To put out the devil's eye. See*
long story in 1303 : Brunne, *Handlyng*
Synne, ll. 12165–12252 (Roxb. Cl.). 1710:
S. Palmer, *Moral Essays on Proverbs*,
81, Come, let's be friends and put out
the devil's eye.

108. *To set the devil on sale.* 1546 :
Heywood, *Proverbs*, Pt. II. ch. vii.,
Here is a tale, For honestie, meete to
set the diuell on sale.

109. *'Twas surely the devil that taught*
women to dance, and asses to bray. 1732 :
Fuller, No. 5319.

110. *What's got over the devil's back*
is spent under his belly. 1607 : Middleton, *Mich. Term*, IV. i., What's got
over the devil's back (that's by knavery)
must be spent under his belly (that's by
lechery). 1671 : Head and Kirkman,
English Rogue, ii. 97. 1725 : Bailey,
tr. Erasmus' *Colloq.*, 30. *c.* 1800 :
Trusler, *Prov. in Verse*, 85. 1889 : Peacock, *Manley, etc., Gloss.*, 167 (E.D.S.),
What's gotten o' th' divil's back goäs
oot under his ḷbelly. 1917 : Bridge,
Cheshire Proverbs, 150.

111. *When it rains and the sun shines*
at the same time the devil is beating his
wife. 1666 : Torriano, *Piazza Univ.*,
79 [quoted as "the French say"].
1703 : Ward, *Writings*, ii. 299, To go
and thrash him round the church-yard,
as the devil does his wife in rainy
weather when the sun shines. 1738 :
Swift, *Polite Convers.*, Dial. I., [in
mingled rain and sunshine] the devil
was beating his wife behind the door
with a shoulder of mutton. 1846 : T.
Wright, *Essays on Middle Ages*, i. 130
[saying credited to the Normans].
1893 : Inwards, *Weather Lore*, 110, If
it rains while the sun is shining the
devil is beating his grandmother. He
is laughing and she is crying.

112. *When the devil is a hog, you shall*
eat bacon. 1670 : Ray, 217. 1732 :
Fuller, No. 5578.

113. *When the devil is blind*=Never.
1659 : Howell, 12. *c.* 1670 : in *Bagford*
Ballads, i. 7 (B.S.), They'l pay me again
when the devil is blind. 1709 : Ward,
Works, iv., *Verse* 35, They pay for
when the devil's blind. 1815 : Scott,
Mannering, ch. xxii., Ay, Tib, that will
be when the devil's blind,—and his
een's no sair yet. 1847 : Halliwell,
Dict., s.v., ' Horn.''

114. *When the devil is dead . . .*
1678 : Ray, 84, When the devil's dead,
there's a wife for Humphrey. 1732 :
Fuller, No. 5580 [as in 1678, but with
" widow " for " wife "]. 1853 : Trench,
Proverbs, 72 (1905), When the devil is
dead, he never wants a chief mourner.

115. *When the devil prays, he has a*
booty in his eye. 1732 : Fuller, No. 5576.

116. *When the devil preaches, the*
world's near an end. 1667 : L'Estrange,
Quevedo's Visions, 21 (1904).

117. *When the devil quotes Latin, the*
priests go to prayers. 1863 : *N. & Q.*,
3rd ser., iii. 492.

118. *Where had the devil the friar, but*
where he was? 1639 : Davenport, *New*
Trick to cheat Devil, IV. ii. 1738 :
Swift, *Polite Convers.*, Dial. I., Why,
where 'twas to be had ; where the devil
got the friar.

119. *Where none else will, the devil*
must bear the cross. 1579 : Lyly,

Euphues, 53 (Arber). 1732 : Fuller,
No. 5652.

120. *You can't stand between the oak
an' the rain* [rind], *where the devil can't
go.* Torquay. 1910 : *Devonsh. Assoc.
Trans.*, xlii. 88. Cf. Oak (7).

121. *You have daily to do with the
devil, and pretend to be frightened at a
mouse.* 1855 : Bohn, 577.

122. *You look like a runner, quoth the
devil to the crab.* 1732 : Fuller, No. 5934.

See also **Bad priests**; **Beads**; **Benfield-
side**; **Black**, *adj.* (4), (14), and (15);
Blow, *verb* (1); **Candle** (6); **Cards** (1);
Dark as the devil's mouth; **Deal** (1);
Flatterer (4); **Friday** (10); **Give** (17);
Go (8); **God for money**; **God hath few
friends**; **God sends corn**; **God sends meat**;
Happy is the child; **Harrow**; **Idle** (2) and
(7); **Innocent** as a devil; **Leave**, *verb* (5);
Marriage (2); **Needs must**; **No sin**; **Play
at small game**; **Pull devil**; **Rake hell**;
Rise (2); **Saint**; **Sloth** is the devil's
cushion; **Sure** as the devil; **Truth** (3)
and (22); **Ugly**; **Up** with it; and
Woman (4), (9), and (33).

Devonshire. *See* **Derbyshire.**

Devonshire ground, To. 1607 : Nor-
den, *Surv. Dial.*, 228 (O.), They . . .
call it in the west parts, burning of
beate, and in the south-east parts,
Devonshiring. 1681 : Worlidge, *Dict.
Rusticum*, s.v., To Denshire, is to cut
off the turf of land ; and when it is dry,
to lay it in heaps and burn it. *c.* 1770 :
Pegge, *Derbicisms*, 16 (E.D.S.), Den-
chering, *sb.* Devonshiring ; it being a
practice brought from Devonshire. 'Tis
when they pare off the sword [sward]
and burn it. 1837 : Mrs. Palmer,
Devonsh. Dialect, 29, Peat- or sod-
burning ; an agricultural operation,
which appears to have originated in
Devonshire, and hence is called Den-
shiring in many parts.

**Devonshire lawyer, To know as much
as a.** W. Corn., 19th cent. (Mr. C. Lee).

Dew. *If nights three dewless there be,
'Twill rain you're sure to see;* and *With
dew before midnight, The next day will
sure be bright*—both in 1893 : Inwards,
Weather Lore, 103.

Dewsbury. *See* **Birstal.**

Diamond. 1. *A diamond is valuable,*

tho' *it lie on a dunghill.* 1732 : Fuller,
No. 74.

2. *A fine diamond may be ill set.*
Ibid., No. 97.

3. *Diamond cut diamond.* 1604 :
Webster and Marston, *Malcontent*, IV.
iii., 'Tis found None cuttes a diamond
but a diamond. 1693 : Congreve,
Double Dealer, I. v., Wit must be
foiled by wit ; cut a diamond with
a diamond. 1738 : Swift, *Polite Convers.*, Dial. III., Sharp's the word with
her ; diamonds cut diamonds. 1844 :
Thackeray, *Barry Lyndon*, ch. x.,
Among such fellows it was diamond
cut diamond. What you call fair play
would have been a folly.

Dick's as dapper as a cock-wren.
1732 : Fuller, No. 1281.

Dick's hatband. *See* quots. 1834-7 :
Southey, *Doctor*, ch. cxxv., Who was
that other Dick who wore so queer a
hat-band that it has ever since served
as a standing comparison for all queer
things ? 1841 : Hartshorne, *Salopia
Ant.*, 393, As curst as [also " as fause
as," " as contrary as," " as cruckit
as," " all across like," " as queer as,"
etc.] Dick's hatband, which will come
nineteen times round and won't tie at
last. 1854 : Baker, *Northants Gloss.*,
s.v. " Dick," As queer as Dick's hatband, made of pea-straw, that went
nine times round, and would not meet
at last. 1917 : Bridge, *Cheshire Proverbs*, 25, As queer as Dick's hatband,
that went nine times round but was
too short to tie. [The saying is
used all over the country in differing
forms.]

Dick Smith. *See* **Dish-clout.**

Dickson. *See* quot. 1670 : Ray, 171,
To get a thing as Dickson did by his
distress. That is, over the shoulders,
as the vulgar usually say.

Die, *verb.* 1. *He dies like a beast who
has done no good while he lived.* 1855 :
Bohn, 370.

2. *He that died half a year ago is as
dead as Adam.* 1732 : Fuller, No. 2079.

3. *He that dies pays all debts.* 1611 :
Shakespeare, *Tempest*, III. ii. Cf.
Death (5).

4. *To die in a fog.* 1917 : Bridge,

Cheshire Proverbs, 132, . . . To give up a task in despair.

5. *To die in one's shoes*=usually, To be hanged. 1725 : *Matchless Rogue*, 87, I have been told by a fortune-teller, that I should die in my shoes. 1725 : Gay, *Newgate's Garland*, l. 4, Ye honester poor rogues, who die in your shoes. 1840 : Barham, *Ing. Legends*, 1st ser.: "Sucklethumbkin's Story," And there is . . . all come to see a man "die in his shoes"! 1917 : Bridge, *Cheshire Proverbs*, 68, He'll die in his shoon.

6. *When you die of old age, I shall quake for fear.* 1738 : Swift, *Polite Convers.*, Dial. I., Why, my Lord, when I die for age, she may quake for fear. 1919 : *N. & Q.*, 12th ser., v. 235, . . . This was a common saying among peasants and workpeople, when speaking to some one rather older than themselves. Ibid., 325, A common Warwickshire saying round Stratford-on-Avon.

Diet cures more than doctors. 1875 : A. B. Cheales, *Proverb. Folk-Lore*, 82.

Dieted bodies. *See* quot. 1655 : T. Muffett, *Healths Improvement*, 8, These addle proverbs, 1. Dieted bodies are but bridges to physicians mindes.

Difference. 1. *The difference is wide that the sheets will not decide.* 1678 : Ray, 201. 1732 : Fuller, No. 6155 [with " very " before " wide "].

2. *There is difference between living long and suffering long.* 1732 : Fuller, No. 4893.

3. *There is difference between staring and stark blind.* 1546 : Heywood, *Proverbs*, Pt. II. ch. vii., The difference betwene staryng and starke blynde The wise man at all tymes to folow can fynde. 1593 : G. Harvey, in *Works*, ii. 235 (Grosart), Hee mought haue spied a difference betweene staring, and starke-blinde.

4. *There is difference between staring and stark mad.* 1633 : Draxe, 44. 1681 : W. Robertson, *Phraseol. Generalis*, 471. 1787 : Wolcot, *Works*, i. 351 (1795), Peter, there's odds 'twixt staring and stark mad . . .

5. *There is difference in servants.*

1725 : Bailey, tr. Erasmus' *Colloq.*, 507, The old proverb, There is difference in servants. .

6. *There is no difference of bloods in a bason.* 1580 : Lyly, *Euphues*, 289 (Arber), You talke of your birth, when I knowe there is no difference of blouds in a basen. 1732 : Fuller, No. 4907.

7. *There is some difference between Peter and Peter.* 1612 : Shelton, *Quixote*, Pt. I. bk. iv. ch. xx. 1631 : Mabbe, *Celestina*, 130 (T.T.), Know you not, the proverbe tels us : That there is a great deale of difference betwixt Peter and Peter? 1732 : Fuller, No. 4937.

Different sores must have different salves. 1732 : Fuller, No. 1283.

Difficult before they are easy, All things are. Ibid., No. 560.

Difficulty makes desire. Ibid., No. 1284.

Diffidence is the (*a*) mother of safety, (*b*) right eye of prudence. (*a*) 1754 : Berthelson, *Eng.-Danish Dict.*, s.v. " Mother." (*b*) 1732 : Fuller, No. 1286.

Dig one's grave with one's teeth, To. 1630 : T. Adams, *Works*, 108, They have digged their graue with their teeth. 1655 : Fuller, *Church Hist.*, bk. iv. § iii. (42), Who by intemperance in his diet, in some sort, digged his grave with his own teeth. 1709 : Dykes, *Eng. Proverbs*, 173, How many people daily dig their own graves, either with their teeth, their tongues, or their tails. 1880 : Smiles, *Duty*, 418, We each day dig our graves with our teeth. 1923 : *Observer*, 25 Feb., p. 11, col. 6.

Digs the well at the river, He. 1813 : Ray, 75.

Dighton. *When Dighton is pulled down, Hull shall become a great town.* 1670 : Ray, 257. 1790 : Grose, *Prov. Gloss.*, s.v. " Yorkshire." 1878 : *Folk-Lore Record*, i. 162.

Diligence is the mother of good luck (or **success**). 1612 : Shelton, *Quixote*, Pt. I. bk. iv. ch. xix., It is a common proverb, beautiful lady, that diligence is the mother of good hap. 1712 : Motteux, *Quixote*, Pt. I. bk. iv. ch. xix. [" success "]. 1736 : Franklin, *Way to Wealth*, in *Works*, i. 444 (Bigelow)

["good luck"]. 1875 : Smiles, *Thrift*,
160 [" good luck "].

**Diligent scholar, and the master's
paid, A.** 1640 : Herbert, *Jac. Prudentum.*

Diligent spinner has a large shift, The.
1736 : Franklin, *Way to Wealth*, in
Works, i. 445 (Bigelow).

**Dilly-dally brings night as soon as
Hurry-scurry.** 1882 : Mrs. Chamberlain, *W. Worcs. Words*, 39 (E.D.S.).

**Dim Sarsnick [Dym Sassenach] with
him, It's=**None so deaf as those who
won't hear. 1917 : Bridge, *Cheshire
Proverbs*, 84.

Dine with Duke Humphrey, To.
1592 : G. Harvey, in *Works*, i. 206
(Grosart), To seek his dinner in poules
with Duke humfrey. 1632 : Nabbes,
Covent Garden, IV. iv., Some breake
their fasts with Duke Humphrey.
1753 : *World*, No. 37, Sometimes I eat
as little as those who dine with Duke
Humphrey. 1794 : *Gent. Mag.*, Pt. I.,
p. 529. 1815 : D'Arblay, *Diary*, iv.
344 (1876), Or else the whole party
. . . must have made interest to dine
with Duke Humphrey. 1850 : Dickens,
Chuzzlewit, ch. i., One Diggory Chuzzlewit was in the habit of perpetually
dining with Duke Humphrey.

**Dines and leaves, lays the cloth twice,
He that.** 1640 : Herbert, *Jac. Prudentum.*

Dinner. *See* quot. 1605 : *Fair Maid
of Bristow*, sig. C1, For as the old saying
is, He that hath a good dinner, knowes
better the way To supper.

**Dinners cannot be long where dainties
want.** 1546 : Heywood, *Proverbs*, Pt.
II. ch. i. 1670 : Ray, 79.

Dirt. 1. *Cast no dirt into the well that
hath given you water.* 1732 : Fuller,
No. 1067.

2. *He that flings dirt at another,
dirtieth himself most.* Ibid., No. 2107.

3. *That dirt made this dust.* Ibid.,
No. 4337.

4. *Throw dirt enough and some will
stick.* 1660 : T. Hall, *Funebria Floræ*,
38, Lye lustily, some filth will stick.
1705 : Ward, *Hudibras Rediv.*, Pt. II.
1769: Colman, *Man and Wife*, Prel., The
scandal of others is mere dirt—throw

a great deal, and some of it will stick.
1857 : Hughes, *Tom Brown*, Pt. I. ch.
ix., Only throw dirt enough, and some
of it is sure to stick.

Dirt-bird (or **Dirt-owl**) **sings, we shall
have rain, The.** 1678 : Ray, 80.

Dirty. 1. *Dirty grate makes dinner
late.* Derby. 1884 : *Folk-Lore Journal*, ii. 279.

2. *Dirty hands make clean money.*
1869 : Hazlitt, 110.

3. *Dirty troughs will serve dirty sows.*
1732 : Fuller, No. 1292.

4. *Don't throw away dirty water till
you have got clean.* 1710 : S. Palmer,
Moral Essays on Proverbs, 89. 1738 :
Swift, *Polite Convers.*, Dial. III., Why,
the fellow's rich ; and I think she was a
fool to throw out her dirty water before
she got clean. 1869 : Spurgeon, *John
Ploughman*, ch. viii.

Discreet. *While the discreet advise,
the fool doth his business.* 1640 : Herbert, *Jac. Prudentum.*

**Discreet women have neither eyes
nor ears.** 1640 : Herbert, *Jac. Prudentum.* 1670 : Ray, 7. 1732 : Fuller,
No. 1295, Discreet wives have sometimes neither eyes nor ears.

Discretion is the better part of valour.
c. 1477 : Caxton, *Jason*, 23 (E.E.T.S.),
Than as wyse and discrete he with-
drewe him sayng that more is worth
a good retrayte than a folisshe abyd-
inge. 1597 : Shakespeare, 1 *Henry IV.*,
V. iv., The better part of valour is discretion. 1611 : B. & F., *King and No
King*, IV. iii. 1830 : Marryat, *King's
Own*, ch. xxxi. 1914 : E. V. Lucas,
Landmarks, 37, Mrs. Sergison here chose
the better part of valour and urged
Rudd to go to sleep. *See also* **Valour.**

Disdainful as ditch water. c. 1386 :
Chaucer, *Reeve's Tale*, l. 44, Sche was
as deyne as water in a dich As ful of
hokir and of bissemare. c. 1394 : *Piers
P. Crede*, l. 375, They ben digne
[haughty, disdainful] as dich water
that dogges in bayteth.

Disease known is half cured, A. 1725 :
Bailey, tr. Erasmus' *Colloq.*, 9, When
the disease is known, it is half cured.
1732 : Fuller, No. 75.

Disease will have its course. 1655 :

T. Muffett, *Healths Improvement*, 8,
These addle proverbs . . . 3. Every
disease will have its course.

Diseases are the price of ill pleasures.
1670 : Ray, 7, Diseases are the interests
of pleasures. 1732 : Fuller, No. 1297.
See also Sickness.

Disgraces are like cherries, one draws
another. 1640: Herbert, *Jac. Prudentum*.

Dish and Dishes. 1. *All her dishes are
chafing dishes.* 1562 : Heywood, *Epigr.*,
6th Hund., No. 38, Wyfe, all thy disshes
be chaffyng disshes plast; For thou
chafest at sight of euery dishe thou
hast. 1639 : Clarke, 34, All his meat
is in chafing dishes. 1670 : Ray, 7.

2. *He has got a dish* =is drunk. 1678 :
Ray, 87.

3. *The dish wears its own cover.* 1680 :
L'Estrange, *Select Coll. Erasmus*, 135,
The dish (as we say) wears its own
cover. 1754 : Berthelson, *Eng.-Danish
Dict.*, s.v. " Dish."

Dish-clout. 1. *I will not make my
dish-clout my table-cloth.* 1678 : Ray,
125. 1732 : Fuller, No. 2646.

2. *There's a thing in it quoth the
fellow when he drank the dish-clout.*
1639 : Clarke, 8. 1670 : Ray, 196.
1732 : Fuller, No. 4884, . . . when he
drunk dish-clout and all. 1883 : Burne,
Shropsh. Folk-Lore, 591, Ahem ! as Dick
Smith said when he swallowed the dish-
clout.

Diss, Norfolk. *See* quot. Before
1852 : S. W. Rix, in *Norfolk Arch.
Papers*, ii. 18 (quoted in *N. & Q.*, 1st
ser., vi. 303), [Diss] was formerly so
little frequented by travellers that it
became a proverb at Cambridge to
express indifference respecting trivial
matters, " He knows nothing about
Diss."

Dissembled sin is double wickedness.
1633 : Draxe, 46, Pretended holiness is
double iniquity. 1647 : *Countrym. New
Commonwealth*, 12 [as in 1633, but with
" Dissembled " for " Pretended "].
1732 : Fuller, No. 1299.

Distrust. *See* quot. 1645 : Howell,
Letters, bk. i. § v. No. xx., It is a rule in
friendship, *When distrust enters in at
the fore-gate, love goes out at the postern.*

Ditch. *See* Hedge (5).

Ditton. *See* Hutton.

Diurnal-maker is the sub-amner to
an historian, A. 1659 : Howell, 2.

Diversity of humors breedeth tumors.
Ibid., 17. 1670: Ray, 7. 1732: Fuller,
No. 6230.

Divide. *See* quot. 1551 : T. Wilson,
Rule of Reason, sig. D8, It is an old
saying . . . he y^t doth well diuide, doth
teache well.

Dizzy (or Giddy) as a goose. " Dizzy "
was probably used in the old sense of
foolish or stupid. 1639 : Clarke, 286,
As dizzie as a goose. 1670 : Ray, 204.
1745 : Franklin, *Drinker's Dict.*, in
Works, ii. 24 (Bigelow), He's as dizzy
as a gooze. 1774 : Burgoyne, *Maid of
the Oaks*, IV. ii., I am as giddy as a
goose, yet I have not touched a drop
of liquor to-day. 1788 : Colman, jr.,
Ways and Means, III. ii.; Giddy as a
goose.

Do and Doing. 1. *By doing nothing
we learn to do ill.* 1567 : Fenton, *Bandello*, ii. 63 (T.T.), Plato, who affirmeth
that in doynge nothyng men lerne to
do evill. 1669: *Politeuphuia*, 307.
1732 : Fuller, No. 1038.

2. *Do and undo, the day is long enough.*
1639: Clarke, 156. 1672: Walker,
Parœm., 50. 1736: Bailey, *Dict.*, s.v.
" Do."

3. *Do as I say, not as I do.* [Faites
ce que nous disons et ne faites pas ce
que nous faisons.—Tr. of Boccaccio
(3rd day, 7th novel) by A. Sabatier de
Castres (1801).] 1546: Heywood, *Proverbs*, Pt. II. ch. v., It is as folke dooe,
and not as folke saie. 1631: Mabbe,
Celestina, 27 (T.T.), Do you that good
which I say, but not that ill which
I do. 1859: Smiles, *Self-Help*, 360
(1869), The common saying of " Do as
I say, not as I do," is usually reversed
in the actual experience of life. 1881:
Evans, *Leics. Words, etc.*, 300 (E.D.S.),
" Do as I say an' not as I do " says
the paa'son. A *var.* of this which
I have heard more than once runs :
" as the paa'son said when they whelt
'im hum in a wheel-barra.''

4. *Do as most men do, and men will
speak well of you.* 1546: Heywood,

Proverbs, Pt. II. ch. ii., He that dooth as most men doo, shalbe least wondred on. 1670 : Ray, 122, Do as the most do, and fewest will speak evil of thee. 1732 : Fuller, No. 1303.

5. *Do as you're bidden and you'll never bear blame.* 1678 : Ray, 101.

6. *Do evil and look for the like.* 1569 : Grafton, *Chron.,* i. 482 (1809), So the common prouerbe was verified, as you have done, so shall you feele. 1633 : Draxe, 179, Doe euill and euill will come of it. 1732 : Fuller, No. 1305.

7. *Do good and then do it again.* 1659 : Howell, *Proverbs : Brit.-Eng.,* 12, Do it good, or do it again. 1855 : Bohn, 269.

8. *Do good : thou dost it for thyself.* 1732 : Fuller, No. 1306, Do good, if you expect to receive it. 1864 : "Cornish Proverbs," in *N. & Q.,* 3rd ser., vi. 495.

9. *Do it by degrees.* See **Cat** (35).

10. *Do it well that thou may'st not do it twice.* 1732 : Fuller, No. 1308.

11. *Do-little good, do-little evil, etc.* See **Come** (4).

12. *Do man for thyself, etc.* See quot. 15th cent. : in *Reliq. Antiquæ,* i. 314 (1841), Do mon for thiselffe, Wyl thou art alyve ; For he that dose after thu dethe, God let him never thryve. Quod Tucket.

13. *Do not all you can ; spend not all you have ; believe not all you hear ; and tell not all you know.* 1855 : Bohn, 344.

14. *Do nothing hastily but catching of fleas.* 1678 : Ray, 151, Nothing must be done hastily but killing of fleas. 1732 : Fuller, No. 1309. *c.* 1791 : Pegge, *Derbicisms,* 136 (E.D.S.), Do nothing rashly, but kill fleas. 1881 : Mrs. Parker, *Oxfordsh. Words : Suppl.,* 87 (E.D.S.), "You shouldn do nothun in a 'urry but ketch flaes [fleas]." A saying.

15. *Do the likeliest and hope the best.* 1732 : Fuller, No. 1310.

16. *Do well and have well.* 1362 : Langland, *Plowman,* A, viii. 97, I con no pardoun fynde, Bote "dowel, and haue wel and god schal haue thi soule." *c.* 1483 : Caxton, *Dialogues,* 47 (E.E.T.S.), I say atte begynnyng, Who doth well shall well haue. 1546 :

Heywood, *Proverbs,* Pt. II. ch. ix. 1611 : Cotgrave, s.v. "Bien," He that does well shall. speed well. 1732 : Fuller, No. 1311.

17. *Do what thou oughtest and come what can come.* 1659 : Howell, 6. 1670 : Ray, 7.

18. *Doing is better than saying.* 1633 : Draxe, 41.

19. *He does well, but none knows but himself.* 1639 : Clarke, 145.

20. *He doeth much that doeth a thing well.* 1732 : Fuller, No. 1839.

21. *He may do much ill ere he can do much worse.* 1546 : Heywood, *Proverbs,* Pt. I. ch. xi. 1594 : Bacon, *Promus,* No. 956. 1639 : Clarke, 150.

22. *He that does not love a woman.* See **Hate** (1).

23. *He that does you an ill turn.* See **Ill turn** (2).

24. *He that doth amiss may do well.* 1629 : *Book of Meery Riddles,* Prov. 76.

25. *He that doth his own business hurteth not his hand.* 1591 : Florio, *Second Frutes,* 11 [with "doth not defile" for "hurteth"]. 1640 : Herbert, *Jac. Prudentum* [with "fouls" for "hurteth"]. 1732 : Fuller, No. 2086.

26. *He that doth ill hatch the light.* 1629 : *Book of Meery Riddles,* Prov. 77.

27. *He that doth most at once doth least.* 1855 : Bohn, 385.

28. *He that doth nothing doth ever amiss.* 1629 : *Book of Meery Riddles,* Prov. 75. 1865 : "Lancs Proverbs," in *N. & Q.,* 3rd ser., viii. 494, Those who are doing nothing are doing ill. 1901 : F. E. Taylor, *Lancs Sayings,* 10, Thoose 'at are doin' nowt are doin' ill.

29. *He that doth well wearieth not himself.* 1633 : Draxe, 32. 1732 : Fuller, No. 2090.

30. *He that doth what he will, doth not what he ought.* 1640 : Herbert, *Jac. Prudentum.* 1748 : Richardson, *Clarissa,* iv. 121 (1785), I am sure he has proved the truth of a hundred times, That he who does what he will seldom does what he ought.

31. *He that hath done ill once will do it again.* 1855 : Bohn, 400.

32. *He that hath done so much hurt that he can do no more may sit down*

and rest him. 1633 : Draxe, 43. 1639 :
Clarke, 150.

33. *He that would do no ill must do
all good, or sit still.* 1855 : Bohn, 396.

34. *I do what I can, quoth the fellow
when he thresht in his cloake.* 1639 :
Clarke, 155.

35. *If thou thyself canst do it, rely
not on another.* 1541 : Coverdale, *Christ.
State Matrimony*, sig. I3, That whych
thou cannest do conueniently thy selfe
commytte it not to another. 1611 :
Cotgrave, s.v. " Faire." 1670 : Ray, 1.
1710 : S. Palmer, *Moral Essays on Proverbs*, 152, For what you can do your
self don't depend on another. 1831 :
Hone, *Year-Book*, col. 1612, Never
trouble another for what you can do
yourself. 1880 : Spurgeon, *Ploughman's
Pictures*, 33, If you want a thing well
done, do it yourself.

36. *In doing we learn.* 1640 : Herbert, *Jac. Prudentum.*

37. *That may be done in an hour,
which we may repent all our life after.*
1658 : *Wit Restor'd*, 151.

38. *We must do as we may, if we can't
do as we would.* 1633 : Draxe, 32, A
man must doe as he can, when hee
cannot as he would. 1698 : *Terence
made English*, 43, They that can't do
as they wou'd, must e'en do as they
may, as the saying is. 1732 : Fuller,
No. 4988.

39. *We'll do as they do at . . .* (see
quots.). 1678 : Ray, 80, We'll do as
they do at Quern, What we do not do
to-day, we must do i' th' morn. 1830 :
Forby, *Vocab. E. Anglia*, 427, You
must do as they do at Hoo, What you
can't do in one day, you must do in
two. 1919 : *Devonsh. Assoc. Trans.*, II.
77, Oh, my dear love ! 'e must do same's
they doo's in France, the best 'e can.

40. *What is done by night appears by
day. c.* 1390 : Gower, *Conf. Amantis*,
bk. v. l. 4599, Thing don upon the
derke nyht Is after knowe on daies
liht. 1666 : Torriano, *Piazza Univ.*,
263, That which is done in the dark,
appears in the sun shine. 1732 : Fuller,
No. 5495.

41. *What's done can't be undone. See
Once done.*

42. *What we do willingly is easy.*
1630 : T. Adams, *Works*, 422. 1831 :
Hone, *Year-Book*, col. 1612, Nothing is
troublesome that we do willingly.

43. *Who would do ill, ne'er wants occasion.* 1640 : Herbert, *Jac. Prudentum.*

Dock to a daisy, As like as a. 1639 :
Clarke, 96, An odious comparison ! a
dock to a dazie. 1670 : Ray, 204, As
like as a dock to a daisie. That is very
unlike.

Dock. *See* In dock.

Doctor Diet, etc. *See* quots. 1558 :
Bullein, *Govt. of Health*, fo. 51, The first
was called doctor diet, the seconde
doctor quiet, the thirde doctor mery-
man. 1596 : Harington, *Metam. of
Ajax*, 99 (1814), Doctor Diet, Doctor
Quiet, and Doctor Merryman. 1660 :
Howell, *Parly of Beasts*, 23, After these
two, Doctor Diet and Doctor Quiet,
Doctor Merriman is requisit to preserve
health. 1738 : Swift, *Polite Convers.*,
Dial. II., The best doctors in the world
are [as in 1596]. 1869 : Spurgeon, *John
Ploughman*, ch. v. [as in 1738]. 1920 :
Times, 5 Oct., p. 6, col. 1 [as in 1738].

Doctor Dodipoll. A proverbial name
for a simpleton. *c.* 1410 : *Towneley
Plays*, 173 (E.E.T.S.), ffy, dotty-pols,
with your bookys ! 1550 : Latimer,
Sermons, 245 (P.S.), They, like dodi-
poles laughed their godly father to
scorn. 1600 : *The Wisedome of Dr.
Dodypoll* [title], in Bullen, *Old Plays*,
vol. iii. 1639 : Clarke, 137, Doctor
Dodipoll is more honoured then a good
divine. 1881 : Evans, *Leics. Words*,
etc., 139 (E.D.S.), Doddipole, a simpleton; noodle. 1889 : Peacock, *Manley*,
etc., *Gloss.*, 169 (E.D.S.), Dodipoll—a
blockhead.

Doctors differ (or disagree). 1677 :
Wycherley, *Plain Dealer*, I. i., Well,
doctors differ. 1735 : Pope, *Moral
Essays*, Epist. iii., Who shall decide
when Doctors disagree? 1813 : *Gent.
Mag.*, Pt. I., p. 627, I shall stand pro-
tected by the rhyming adage : " When
Doctors disagree, Disciples then are
free." 1830 : Colman, jr., in *Hum.
Works*, 429 (Hotten).

Doe in the month of May. *See* quot.
c. 1676 : in *Roxb. Ballads*, vii. 558 (B.S.),

If it be true, as old wives say, "Take a doe in the month of May, And a forester's courage she soon will allay."
Doff one's shoes. *See* Put (1).
Dog and Dogs. 1. *A bad dog never sees the wolf.* 1611: Cotgrave, s.v. "Loup," A bad dog hates to looke upon a wolfe. 1640: Herbert, *Jac. Prudentum.*
2. *A barking dog bites little.* c. 1350: Alexander, l. 1805, Bot as bremely as he [a "curre"] baies he bitis never the faster. 1387: Trevisa, tr. Higden, iii. 427 (Rolls Ser.), Hit is þe manere of þe feblest houndes for to berke most. 1581: T. Howell, *Devises*, 30 (1906), Those dogs byte least, that greatest barkings keepe. 1669: *Politeuphuia*, 198, A dog that barketh much will bite but little. 1736: Bailey, *Dict.*, s.v. "Barking," Barking dogs seldom bite.
3. *A dog in a doublet.* 1577: J. Grange, *Golden Aphroditis*, sig. F1, As seemely as . . . a dogge in a dublet. 1600: Dekker, *Shoem. Hol.*, III. i., My maister will be as proud as a dogge in a dublet, al in beaten damaske and velvet. 1639: in *Berkeley MSS.*, iii. 33 (1885), As proud as a dog in a doublett, i.e. very proud. 1754: Berthelson, *Eng.-Danish Dict.*, s.v. "Dog," A meer dog in a doublet. 1894: Northall, *Folk Phrases*, 6 (E.D.S.), A mere dog in a doublet=A mean pitiful creature. Cf. No. 62.
4. *A dog in a halter.* 1639: Clarke, 274, To take a man up as short as a dog in a halter. 1660: *Roxb. Ballads*, vii. 648 (B.S.), For the pence hee's your dog in a halter.
5. *A dog is made fat in two meals.* 1863: Wise, *New Forest*, ch. xvi., "A dog is made fat in two meals," is applied to upstart or purse-proud people.
6. *A dog will not cry if you beat him with a bone.* 1659: Howell, *Proverbs: Brit.-Eng.*, 24, The dog will not bite, for being struck with a bone. 1732: Fuller, No. 79.
7. *A dog's life; hunger and ease.* 1666: Torriano, *Piazza Univ.*, 276, The English say, Hunger and ease is a dogs life. 1670: Ray, 172.

8. *A dog's nose and a maid's knees are always cold.* 1639: Clarke, 72, A dog's nose is ever cold. 1659: Howell, 9 (7), A womans knee and a doggs snowt are alwayes cold. 1670: Ray, 51. 1870: "C. Bede," in *N. & Q.*, 4th ser., vi. 495, [Old Hunts cottager *loq.*] Why, that's a very old saying, "A maid's knee and a dog's nose are the two coldest things in creation." ["Knee" is sometimes "elbow." See a long story of Noah's ark and the leak therein in Lowsley's *Gloss. of Berkshire Words* (1888), quoted in Mrs. Wright's *Rustic Speech, etc.*, p. 227 (1913).]
9. *A good dog deserves a good bone.* 1611: Cotgrave, s.v. "Bon." 1633: Jonson, *Tale of a Tub*, II. i., A good dog Deserves, sir, a good bone. 1732: Fuller, No. 144. 1875: A. B. Cheales, *Proverb. Folk-Lore*, 35.
10. *A man may provoke his own dog to bite him.* 1546: Heywood, *Proverbs*, Pt. II. ch. vii., A man maie handle his dog so That he maie make him byte him, though he would not. 1670: Ray, 7 [with "cause" for "provoke"]. 1732: Fuller, No. 298.
11. *A still dog bites sore.* c. 1270: *Prov. of Alfred*, in *Old Eng. Miscell.*, 137 (Morris, E.E.T.S.), þe bicche bitit ille þan he berke still. 1593: *Tell-Trothes N. Yeares Gift*, 15 (N. Sh. S.), A stille dogge bites sore, but the barking cur feares [frightens] more. 1638: D. Tuvill, *Vade Mecum*, 130 (3rd ed.), The slowest barker is the surest biter. 1906: A. C. Doyle, *Sir Nigel*, ch. xiv., "Good!" said he. "It is the mute hound which bites the hardest."
12. *A toiling dog comes halting home.* 1732: Fuller, No. 441.
13. *All the dogs follow the salt bitch.* 1639: Clarke, 13. 1670: Ray, 80.
14. *An old dog barks not in vain.* 1578: Florio, *First Fruites*, fo. 28. 1651: Herbert, *Jac. Prudentum*, 2nd ed. 1732: Fuller, No. 3711, Old dogs bark not for nothing.
15. *An old dog bites sore.* 1546: Heywood, *Proverbs*, Pt. II. ch. vi., It is saide of olde: an olde dog byteth sore. 1605: Breton, in *Works*, ii. *l* 15 (Grosart). 1716: Ward, *Female Policy*,

46, 'Tis a certain truth that an old dog and . . . bite sore.

16. *An old dog will learn no new tricks.* 1605: Camden, *Remains*, 326 (1870), It is hard to teach an old dog tricks. 1694: D'Urfey, *Quixote*, Pt. I. Act II. sc. i. 1758–67: Sterne, *Trist. Shandy*, vol. iii. ch. xxxiv., It is a singular blessing, that nature has formed the mind of man with the same happy backwardness and renitency against conviction, which is observed in old dogs,—" of not learning new tricks." 1823: Scott, *Peveril*, Introd., par. 2. 1924: I. Hay, *The Shallow End*, 5, We are an ancient and dignified people, and you cannot teach an old dog new tricks.

17. *As busy as a dog in dough.* 1879: G. F. Jackson, *Shropsh. Word-Book*, 128, " As busy as a dog in duff [dough] " is a proverbial saying heard in some parts of Shropshire. 1894: Northall, *Folk Phrases*, 19 (E.D.S.), Like dogs in dough, i.e. unable to make headway. 1917: Bridge, *Cheshire Proverbs*, 11, As busy (as thrunk) as a dog in dough.

18. *As courteous as a dog in a kitchen.* Ironical. 1377: Langland, *Plowman*, B, v. 261, " I am holden," quod he, " as hende as hounde is in kychyne."

19. *As the old dog barks, so the young one.* c. 1470: G. Ashby, *Poems*, 32 (E.E.T.S.), Aftur the oolde dogge the yonge whelp barkes.

20. *As vain as a dog with two tails.* 1889: J. Nicholson, *Folk Speech E. Yorks*, 17.

21. *At every dog's bark seem not to awake.* 1546: Heywood, *Proverbs*, Pt. II. ch. v. *c.* 1594: Bacon, *Promus*, No. 662, At every dogges bark to awake. 1633: Draxe, 48, Wake not at euery dogges barke.

22. *At open doors, dogs come in.* 1820: Scott, *Monastery*, ch. xxxiii.

23. *Better have a dog fawn upon you than bite you.* 1639: Clarke, 219. 1678: Ray, 128. 1732: Fuller, No. 902.

24. *Cut off a dog's tail and he will be a dog still.* 1578: Florio, *First Fruites*, ·fo. 33. 1629: *Book of Meery Riddles*, Prov. 122.

25. *Dead dogs bark not.* 1596: A.

Copley, *Fig for Fortune*, 23 (Spens. S.), Dead dogges barke not. 1667: L'Estrange, *Quevedo's Visions*, 252 (1904), A dead dog will never bite.

26. *Dog and side pockets. See* Toad (1).

27. *Dog does not eat dog.* [. . . parcit Cognatis maculis similis fera.—Juvenal, *Sat.* xv. 160.] 1651: Herbert, *Jac. Prudentum*, 2nd ed., A wolf will never make war against another wolf. 1790: Wolcot, in *Works*, ii. 203 (1795), Dog should not prey on dog, the proverb says. 1809: Pegge, *Anonym.* cent. vi. 26, It is a common observation that dog will not eat dog. 1869: Spurgeon, *John Ploughman*, ch. xiv., Dog won't eat dog, but men will eat each other up like cannibals.

28. *Dogs bark as they are bred.* 1732: Fuller, No. 1313. 1875: A. B. Cheales, *Proverb. Folk-Lore*, 140, Dogs bark as they are bred, and fawn as they are fed.

29. *Dogs bark before they bite.* 1546: Heywood, *Proverbs*, Pt. II. ch. vii., A dog will barke er he bite. 1670: Ray, 81. 1732: Fuller, No. 1316, Dogs ought to bark before they bite. [Camden (1605, *Remains*, 316 (1870)) reverses the saying—A dog will bite ere he bark.]

30. *Dogs bark more from custom than fierceness.* 1631: Mabbe, *Celestina*, Epist. Ded., Like dogges that barke by custome. 1647: Wharton, *Merlini Anglici*, Pref., It is a common proverb, " Dogs bark more for custome than fiercenesse."

31. *Dogs bark not at him.* 1546: Heywood, *Proverbs*, Pt. II. ch. v., All dogs barke not at him. 1607: Dekker, *Knight's Conjuring*, 30 (Percy S.), He car'de not what dogges bark'd at him. 1650: Fuller, *Pisgah Sight*, bk. iii. ch. iv. § 1, In his peaceable country, where no dog durst bark against him.

32. *Dogs begin in jest and end in earnest.* 1855: Bohn, 345.

33. *Dogs gnaw bones because they cannot swallow them.* 1670: Ray, 7.

34. *Dogs run away with whole shoulders.* 1670: Ray, 172.

35. *Dogs that bark at a distance never bite.* 1605: Camden, *Remains*, 321 (1870), Dogs barking aloof bite not at hand. 1732: Fuller, No. 1317.

36. *Dogs that put up many hares kill none.* 1732 : Fuller, No. 1319. 1846–59 : *Denham Tracts*, ii. 108 (F.L.S.).

37. *Dogs wag their tails not so much in love to you as to your bread.* 1611 : Cotgrave, s.v. " Amour," Dogs fawne on a man no longer then he feeds them. 1633 : Draxe, 21, The dog waggeth his taile, not for you, but for your bread. 1670 : Ray, 7. 1732 : Fuller, No. 1320.

38. *Dogs will run away with the meat but not with the work.* 1864 : " Cornish Proverbs," in *N. & Q.*, 3rd ser., vi. 494.

39. *Enough to make a dog laugh.* c. 1603 : in Collier, *Roxb. Ballads*, 158 (1847), 'Two'd make a dog laugh. 1664 : Pepys, *Diary*, 8 Jan., To hear how W. Symons do commend and look sadly . . . would make a dogg laugh. 1794 : Wolcot, *Works*, ii. 528 (1795), Enough to make the sourest cynic smile, Or, as the proverb says, " make a dog laugh."

40. *Every dog considers himself a lion at home.* 1666 : Torriano, *Piazza Univ.*, 36, Every dog is a lion at home. 1732 : Fuller, No. 1414, Every dog is stout at his own door. 1865 : " Lancs Proverbs," in *N. & Q.*, 3rd ser., viii. 494. 1869 : Spurgeon, *John Ploughman*, ch. xiii., A dog is a lion when he is at home.

41. *Every dog has his day.* 1546 : Heywood, *Proverbs*, Pt. I. ch. xi., A dog hath a daie. 1573 : *New Custom*, II. iii., Well, if it chance that a dog hath a day. c. 1630 : in *Roxb. Ballads*, i. 184 (Hindley), Let's spend while we may; Each dog hath his day. 1705 : Ward, *Hudibras Rediv.*, Pt. 2, can. iii., p. 18, I've heard a good old proverb say, That ev'ry dog has got his day. 1860 : Reade, *Cl. and Hearth*, ch. xxxvi. 1864 : *N. & Q.*, 3rd ser., v. 97, They say in this county [Essex] " Every dog has his day, and a cat has two Sundays." 1896 : F. M. T. Palgrave, *Hetton-le-Hole Word List*, 3 (E.D.S.), A saying sometimes heard is " Every dog has its day, and a bitch two afternoons."

42. *For fashion's sake, as dogs go to church.* 1732 : Fuller, No. 1590.

43. *Give a dog an ill name and hang him.* 1760 : Colman, *Polly Honeycombe*, sc. iv. 1815 : Scott, *Mannering*, ch.

xxiii. 1922 : E. Hutton, in *Sphere*, 8 April, p. 40, " Give a dog a bad name and hang him " has proved too often to be a true proverb. Cf. Ill name.

44. *Hang a dog on a crab-tree and he'll never love verjuice.* 1659 : Howell, 5, He that is hang'd in a crabb tree will never love verjuyce. 1670 : Ray, 81. 1692 : L'Estrange, *Æsop*, 59 (3rd ed.). 1753 : *World*, No. 32, It is true to a proverb, that if you hang a dog upon a crab-tree, he will never love verjuice.

45. *He is a good dog which goes to church.* 1826 : Scott, *Woodstock*, ch. i., Bevis, indeed, fell under the proverb which avers " He is a good dog which goes to church."

46. *He looks like a dog under a door.* 1678 : Ray, 70.

47. *He that would hang his dog gives out first that he is mad.* 1530 : Palsgrave, 450, He that wyll kyll his neyghbours dogge beareth folkes in hande he is madde. 1670 : Ray, 81. 1732 : Fuller, No. 2362.

48. *He went as willingly as a dog to a whip.* 1654 : Gayton, *Pleasant Notes Don Q.*, 188.

49. *He who lies down with dogs will rise with fleas.* 1578 : Florio, *First Fruites*, fo. 29, Who sleepeth with dogges, shal rise with fleas. 1612 : Webster, *White Devil*, V. i. 1791 : Wolcot, *Works*, ii. 232 (1795). 1853 : Trench, *Proverbs*, 82 (1905).

50. *I am not every body's dog that whistles.* 1633 : Draxe, 18, Hee is ready to runne at euery mans whistle. 1659 : Howell, 16, I am not like a dogg that cometh at every ones whisling. 1826 : Scott, *Woodstock*, ch. ix., You are sure he will come, like a dog at a whistle.

51. *I will never keep a dog to bite me.* 1732 : Fuller, No. 2640.

52. *I'll give you no more quarter than a dog does a wolf.* 1725 : Bailey, tr. Erasmus' *Colloq.*, 555, So that it is grown into a proverb, *I'll give you, etc.*

53. *If the old dog bark, he gives counsel.* 1640 : Herbert, *Jac. Prudentum.* 1670 : Ray, 19. 1732 : Fuller, No. 2709.

54. *If you would wish the dog to follow you, feed him.* 1855 : Bohn, 422.

55. *Into the mouth of a bad dog, often falls a good bone.* 1639: Clarke, 45. 1670: Ray, 82. 1732: Fuller, No. 2832.

56. *It is a good dog that can catch anything.* 1678: Ray, 70. 1732: Fuller, No. 2854.

57. *It is a hard winter when dogs eat dogs.* 1732: Fuller, No. 2894.

58. *It is a poor dog that does not know "come out."* 1830: Forby, *Vocab. E. Anglia*, 428.

59. *It is a poor dog that is not worth whistling for.* 1546: Heywood, *Proverbs*, Pt. I. ch. xi., A poore dogge that is not woorth whystlyng. 1605: Camden, *Remains*, 318 (1870). 1670: Ray, 81 [with "ill" for "poor"]. 1738: Swift, *Polite Convers.*, Dial. I. *c.* 1770: Murphy, in *Garrick Corresp.*, ii. 335 (1832), If they are determined to think me a dog not worth whistling for. 1881: Evans, *Leics. Words*, 139 (E.D.S.), "It's a surry doog as een't woo'th a whistle," used by an old man, who, though infirm, would have helped a neighbour in getting in his corn if he had been applied to. The saying is very common.

60. *It is hard to make an old dog stoop.* 1523: Fitzherbert, *Husbandry*, 45 (E.D.S.), The dogge must lerne it, whan he is a whelpe, or els it wyl not be: for it is harde to make an olde dogge to stoupe. 1611: Davies (of Hereford), *Sc. of Folly*, 47, in *Works*, ii. (Grosart), Its hard to make an olde dogge lye low. 1725: Bailey, tr. Erasmus' *Colloq.*, 75, It is a hard matter to mend the manners of an old sinner. An old dog won't be easily brought to wear a collar.

61. *It's an ill dog that deserves not a crust.* 1639: Clarke, 91 [with "bad" for "ill"]. 1670: Ray, 81. 1732: Fuller, No. 2899.

62. *It would make a dog doff his doublet.* Cheshire. 1678: Ray, 239. 1917: Bridge, *Cheshire Proverbs*, 86. Cf. No. 3.

63. *It would make a dog forget his dinner.* *c.* 1630: B. & F., *Love's Pilgrimage*, II. ii.

64. *Let every dog carry his own tail.* 1666: Torriano, *Piazza Univ.*, 36, Euery dog values his tail. 1880: Spurgeon, *Ploughman's Pictures*, 47.

65. *Let the dog worry the hog.* 1659: Howell, 13.

66. *Like a dog in a fair.* *c.* 1520: in Skelton, *Works*, ii. 445 (Dyce), Ye come among vs plenty By coples in a peire, As sprites in the haire, Or dogges in the ffayre. 1840: Barham, *Ing. Legends:* "Jackdaw of Rheims," That little jackdaw kept hopping about; Here and there Like a dog in a fair. 1893: G. L. Gower, *Gloss. Surrey Words*, vii. (E.D.S.), They didn't keep nothing reg'lar, it was all over the place like a dog at a fair.

67. *Like a dog in a wheel.* *c.* 1653: in *Somers Tracts*, vii. 73 (1811), But I durst undertake to pose him with a riddle, and stand his intelligence in a dog in a wheel. 1748: Richardson, *Clarissa*, iv. 120 (1785), [Like] a dog in a wheel, which roasts meat for others. 1827: Scott, *Journal*, 22 March, It . . . makes me feel like a dog in a wheel, always moving and never advancing.

68. *Like a dog in the manger.* [καθάπερ τὴν ἐν τῇ φάτνῃ κύνα μήτε αὐτὴν ἐσθίουσαν τῶν κριθῶν μήτε τῷ ἵππῳ πεινῶντι ἐπιτρέπουσαν.— Lucian, *Timon.*] *c.* 1390: Gower, *Conf. Amantis*, bk. ii. l. 84, Thogh it be noght the houndes kinde To ete chaf, yit wol he werne An oxe which comth to the berne, Therof to taken eny fode. 1484: Caxton, *Æsope* [Caxton has the fable of the Dog, but does not give the proverb or phrase "dog in a manger" in any form]. 1546: *Supplication of Poore Commons*, 65 (E.E.T.S.), They are lyke to a curre dogge lying in a cocke of haye. For he wyll eate none of the hey hym selfe, nother suffer any other beast that commeth to eate therof. 1580: Tusser, *Husbandrie*, 69 (E.D.S.), To dog in the manger some liken I could. 1663: Pepys, *Diary*, 25 Nov., He wittily replied that there was nothing in the world so hateful as a dog in the manger. 1760: Foote, *Minor*, I., Dead to pleasure themselves, and the blasters of it in others —mere dogs in a manger. 1836: Marryat, *Japhet*, ch. lxxii., Why what a dog in the manger you must be—

you can't marry them both. 1923 :
Lucas, *Advisory Ben*, 179, But we
mustn't be dogs in the manger : old
men like us.

69. *Like dogs, if one bark, all bark.*
1639 : Clarke, 148.

70. *Like dogs that snarl about a bone ;
And play together when they've none.*
1732 : Fuller, No. 6431.

71. *Many a dog is hanged for his
skin, and many a man is killed for his
purse.* 1639 : Clarke, 97.

72. *Many a dog's dead since you were
a whelp.* 1732 : Fuller, No. 3336.

73. *The best dog leap the stile first,*
i.e. let the worthiest person take place.
1678 : Ray, 76.

74. *The dog that licks ashes trust not
with meal.* 1640 : Herbert, *Jac. Prudentum.* 1670 : Ray, 82.

75. *The dog that fetches will carry.*
1830 : Forby, *Vocab. E. Anglia*, 429.
1872 : J. Glyde, jr., *Norfolk Garland*,
148.

76. *The dog who hunts foulest hits at
most faults.* 1659 : Howell, 1. 1670 :
Ray, 7. 1732 : Fuller, No. 1318, Dogs
that hunt foulest hit off most faults.

77. *The foremost dog catcheth the hare.*
1670 : Ray, 10.

78. *The hindmost dog may catch the
hare.* 1580 : Lyly, *Euphues*, 419 (Arber),
The last dogge oftentimes catcheth the
hare. 1681 : W. Robertson, *Phraseol.
Generalis*, 728. 1732 : Fuller, No. 4597
[with " catcheth " for " may catch "].

79. *The mad dog bites his master.*
1732 : Fuller, No. 4644.

80. *The scalded dog fears cold water.*
1561 : Hoby, *Courtier*, 191 (T.T.), As
dogges, after they have bine once
scaulded with hott water, are aferd
of the colde. 1611 : Cotgrave, s.v.
" Chien," The scaulded dog feares
even cold water. 1853 : Trench, *Proverbs*, 66 (1905).

81. *The worst dog that is will wag
his tail.* 1578 : Florio, *First Fruites*,
fo. 33, The worst dog waggeth his tayl.
1666 : Torriano, *Piazza Univ.*, 36, The
pittyfull'st dog that is will wag his tail.

82. *There are more ways to kill a dog
than hanging.* 1678 : Ray, 127. 1725 :
in Swift, *Works*, vi. 478 (Scott), I know

that very homely proverb, More ways
of killing a dog than hanging him.
1762 : Smollett, *Sir L. Greaves*, ch. xii.
[title]. 1836 : Marryat, *Easy*, ch. v.

83. *To beat the dog before the lion.*
c. 1386 : Chaucer, *Squire's Tale*, l. 491,
And for to maken other be war by me,
As by the whelp chasted is the leoun.
1602 : Chamberlain, *Letters*, 148 (Camden S.), It was so well and cunningly
convayed to beate the whelp before
the lion, and reade her her lesson in
her fellowes booke. 1611 : Cotgrave,
s.v. " Batre," *Batre le chien devant le
lyon.* To punishe a meane person in
the presence, and to the terror, of a
great one. 1604 : Shakespeare, *Othello*,
II. iii., As one would beat his offenceless
dog to affright an imperious lion. 1892 :
D. G. Rossetti, *Dante and his Circle*,
314, Since a dog scourged can bid the
lion fear.

84. *To behave as dogs in a bag.*
c. 1380 : Wiclif, *Works*, ii. 358 (Arnold),
Than shulde pees be in the chirche
withouten strif of doggis in a poke.
c. 1386 : Chaucer, *C. Tales*, A, 4278
(Skeat), They walwe [wallow, roll
about, struggle] as doon two piggës in
a poke.

85. *To give one the dog to hold*—To
serve one a dog-trick. 1678 : Ray, 70.

86. *To have a dog in one's sleeve.*
This seems to mean the same as " a
flea in one's ear." 1577 : J. Grange,
Golden Aphroditis, sig. Ll, Some of
the company departed with a dogge
in their sleeve.

87. *To scorn a thing as a dog scorns
tripe.* 1670 : Ray, 207.

88. *To sit where the dog was hanged* =
" A succession of petty mischances."
1830 : Forby, *Vocab. E. Anglia*, 409.

89. *To sleep a dog's sleep.* 1660 :
Fuller, *Mixt Contempl.*, 269 (1830), He
sleepeth not, but only shutteth his eyes
in dogsleep. 1669–96 : Aubrey, *Lives*,
ii. 46 (Clark), He was wont to sleep
much in the house [of Commons] (at
least dog-sleepe). 1773 : in *Garrick
Corresp.*, i. 571 (1831), Mr. Willmot
. . . fell asleep. Dr. B— thought it
dog sleep. 1820 : Colton, *Lacon*, Pt. II.
No. 122 *n.*, A Greek quotation . . .

roused our slumbering professor, from a kind of dog sleep, in a snug corner of the vehicle.

90. *What! keep a dog and bark myself.* 1583 : Melbancke, *Philotinus,* sig. Q2, It is smal reason you should kepe a dog, and barke yourselfe. 1670 : Ray, 81. 1738 : Swift, *Polite Convers.,* Dial. I., But I won't keep a dog, and bark myself. 1924 : Austen Chamberlain, reported in *Times,* 16 Dec., p. 8, col. 3, I said to those with whom I talked : " We have an English proverb, ' Why bark yourself when you keep a dog? ' "

91. *When a dog is drowning every one offers him water* (or *drink*). 1611 : Cotgrave, s.v. " Chien." 1670 : Ray, 7. 1736 : Bailey, *Dict.,* s.v. " Dog." 1875 : A. B. Cheales, *Proverb. Folk-Lore,* 69.

92. *When the dog is beaten out of the room, where will they lay their stink?* 1732 : Fuller, No. 5581.

93. *When the whelp plays the old dog grins.* Before 1500 : Hill, *Commonplace-Book,* 132 (E.E.T.S.), Whan the whelpe gameth, the old dogge grenneth.

94. *While the dog* (or *hound*) *gnaweth a bone, he loveth no company. c.* 1210 : in T. Wright, *Essays on Middle Ages,* i. 149 (1846), Wil the hund gnagh bon, i-fere neld he non. 1586 : L. Evans, *Revised Withals Dict.,* sig. C3, Whiles a dog gnawes a bone, he hateth his fellowe, whom otherwise he loues.

95. *See* quot. 1417 : in *Reliq. Antiquæ,* i. 233 (1841), Who that maketh in Christemas a dogge to his larder, And in Marche a sowe to his gardyner, And in Maye a fole of a wise mannes councell, He shall never have good larder, faire gardeyn, nor wele kepte councell. 1486 : *Boke of St. Albans,* sig. F4 [as in 1417].

96. *Who regards not his dog, will make him a choke-sheep.* 1864 : " Cornish Proverbs," in *N. & Q.,* 3rd ser., vi. 494.

97. *You may choke a dog with pudding.* 1875 : A. B. Cheales, *Proverb. Folk-Lore,* 117.

See also **Another man's dog; Brag; Brawling curs; Butter** (9)**; Cat** (14)**, (38), (40), (45),** and (64)**; Covetous** (3)**; Crack; Curst cur; Eat** (29)**; Fight** (2) and (3)**; Fit as a pudding; Flesh; Greedy;**

Greyhound; Hare (7)**; Horse** (66)**; Hungry; Lame; Lean dog; Lie,** *verb* (3) and (4)**; Living; Look** (19)**; Love,** *verb* (10) and (20)**; Man** (1)**; Many dogs; Mastiff; Musk; One dog; Pleased; Plough,** *verb* (3)**; Pudding** (4)**; Rise** (5)**; Scornful; Silent** (4)**; Sleeping dogs; Stick,** *subs.* (1)**; Two dogs; Waking; We dogs; Wolf** (18)**;** and **Woman** (8) and (38).

Dog-days. 1. *As the dog days commence, so they end;* 2. *Dog days bright and clear Indicate a happy year; But when accompanied by rain, For better times our hopes are vain;* 3. *If it rains on first dog day, it will rain for forty days after* —all three in 1893: Inwards, *Weather Lore,* 31.

Dogmatical tone, a pragmatical pate, A. 1732 : Fuller, No. 77.

Dog-trick, To play or serve one a. *c.* 1540 : tr. Polydore Vergil's *Eng. Hist.,* 284 (Camden S., No. 36) (O.), I will heere in the way of mirthe, declare a prettie dog tricke or gibe as concerninge this mayden. 1667 : Flecknoe, *Tomaso the Wand.,* 11 (1925), By which dog-trick of his . . . he made every one an enemy to him. 1690 : *New Dict. Canting Crew,* sig. D7, He play'd me a dog-trick, he did basely and dirtily by me.

Dole. *Ye deal this dole out at a wrong door* = Your charity is ill bestowed. 1546 : Heywood, *Proverbs,* Pt. I. ch. iii. *See also* **Happy man.**

Don, River. *See* quot. 1828 : J. Hunter, *South Yorks,* i. 2, The shelving shining river Don Each year a daughter or a son, is an old saw often too fatally verified in modern experience. Cf. **Dart, River.**

Doncaster cuts = Horses. Before 1529 : Skelton, *Magnyfycence,* l. 296, In fayth, I set not by the worlde two Dauncaster cuttys.

Donkey. *See* **Aback o' behind;** and **Ass.**

Door. 1. *Make not the door wider than the house.* 1639 : Clarke, 11.

2. *Who will make a door of gold, must knock a nail every day.* 1640 : Herbert, *Jac. Prudentum.*

Dorsetshire dorsers. 1662 : Fuller,

Worthies, i. 453 (1840). 1790: Grose,
Prov. Gloss., s.v. " Dorset."

Dotterel. 1. *See* quot. 1878: Dyer,
Eng. Folk-Lore, 96, The appearance of
the dotterel . . . is regarded by shepherds as a sign of coming winter, and
hence the adage :—" When dotterel do
first appear, it shows that frost is very
near ; But when the dotterel do go, then
you may look for heavy snow."

2. *A dish of dottrells.* 1639: Clarke,
220.

Doublet. *See* Put (1).

Doubt, do nowt, When in. 1917:
Bridge, *Cheshire Proverbs,* 155.

Doubts. *He that casteth all doubts
shall never be resolved.* 1732: Fuller,
No. 2063.

Dove's flood. *In April* (or *spring*)
Dove's flood Is worth a king's good
[ransom]. 1610: P. Holland, tr. Cam-
den's *Britannia,* 587. 1662: Fuller,
Worthies, iii. 127 (1840). *c.* 1791:
Pegge, *Derbicisms,* 137 (E.D.S.). 1812:
Brady, *Clavis Cal.,* i. 69. 1852: *N. & Q.,*
1st ser., vi. 184.

Dover. 1. *A Dover shark and a Deal
savage.* 1790: Grose, *Prov. Gloss.,* s.v.
" Kent."

2. *A Jack of Dover*=A sole. *c.* 1386:
Chaucer, *Cook's Prol.,* l. 23, For many
a pastee hastow laten blood, And many
a Iakke of Dover hastow sold. 1604:
Jacke of Dover [title] (Percy S.). 1790:
Grose, *Prov. Gloss.,* s.v. " Kent."

3. *As sure as there's a dog in Dover.*
1735: Pegge, *Kent. Proverbs,* in E.D.S.,
No. 12, p. 69.

4. *Dover, a den of thieves.* 1735:
Ibid., 70. 1766: Smollett, *Travels,* in
Works, viii. 4 (1872).

5. *From Dover to Dunbar*; and
6. *When it's dark in Dover, 'Tis dark
all the world over* — both in 1735:
Pegge, *Kent. Proverbs,* in E.D.S., No. 12,
p. 70.

See also **Berwick**; and **Deal.**

**Dover-court : all speakers and no
hearers.** Essex. North in 1740 quot.
misunderstands the saying. 1662:
Fuller, *Worthies,* ii. 124 (1840). 1700:
T. Brown, in *Works,* iii. 66 (1760), The
whole room was a perfect resemblance
of Dover-court, where all speak, but

no body heard or answer'd. 1740:
North, *Examen,* 517, As in the proverbial court at Dover, *all speakers
and no hearers.* 1851: *Essex Gloss.,* 6,
Dovercourt, a great noise. (Said to
have arisen from Dovercourt being
famous for its scolds.) 1888: Q.-Couch,
Troy Town, ch. xix., For up ten minutes
'twas Dover to pay, all talkers an' no
listeners.

Down, *adv.* 1. *Down came Tit, and
away tumbled she arsy-varsy.* 1813:
Ray, 274.

2. *Down the hill goes merrily.* 1639:
Clarke, 260.

3. *Going down the brewe* [short, steep
declivity]=Failing in health. 1917:
Bridge, *Cheshire Proverbs,* 61.

4. *He that's down, down with him.*
1678: Ray, 129. 1732: Fuller, No.
2282 [*plus* " cries the world "]. 1875:
A. B. Cheales, *Proverb. Folk-Lore,* 154,
He that is down, down with him, is an
expression of some of the basest feelings
of human nature.

5. *To go down the wind* — To be
unfortunate. Cf. **Up the weather.**
1604: Breton, in *Works,* ii. *k* 8 (Grosart),
My purse grew so bare . . . two or
three yeares brought me so doune the
winde . . . 1663: Pepys, *Diary,* 25
Jan., I perceive he goes down the
wind in honour as well as everything
else, every day. *c.* 1680: L'Estrange,
Seneca's Morals : Happy Life, ch. xviii.,
When a man goes down the wind, no
body comes near him. 1754: Berthelson, *Eng.-Danish Dict.,* s.v. " Down."
1827: Scott, *Journal,* 25 April, It is
certain the old Tory party is down the
wind. 1865: J. Sleigh, *Derbysh. Gloss.,*
Down in the wind, bankrupt.

Down, *subs.* *There's no down without
eyes, no hedge without ears.* 1864:
" Cornish Proverbs," in *N. & Q.,* 3rd
ser., vi. 494.

Draff is good enough for swine.
c. 1535: *Gentleness and Nobility,* sig. C1,
Thou sayst trew drafe is good inough
for swyne. 1591: Harington, *Orl.
Furioso,* bk. xx. st. 83, Tis fit (quoth
he) that swine should feed on draffe.
1683: Meriton, *Yorkshire Ale,* 83–7
(1697). 1732: Fuller, No. 1324.

Draff was his errand, but drink he would have. 1546 : Heywood, *Proverbs*, Pt. I. ch. xi., That draffe is your errand, but drinke ye wolde. 1619 : Chapman, *Two Wise Men*, VII. i. 1670 : Ray, 83. 1732 : Fuller, No. 1325.

Draughts. 1. *If cold wind reach you through a hole, Say your prayers, and mind your soul.* 1846 : Denham, *Proverbs*, 16 (Percy S.). 1872 : *N. & Q.*, 4th ser., x. 83, If draught comes to you through a hole, Go make your will, and mind your soul.

2. *The air of a window is as the stroke of a cross-bow.* 1678 : Ray, 41. 1732 : Fuller, No. 6257.

Draw in one's horns, To. 1577 : *Misogonus*, III. ii., It will make yow plucke in your hornes, an yow were near [never] so wilde. 1642 : D. Rogers, *Naaman*, sig. S1, Let them cause you to be ashamed, or to shrinke in your hornes ever the more. 1672 : Walker, *Parœm.*, 15, To pull in his horns ; make a retreate. 1776 : in *Garrick Corresp.*, ii. 140 (1832), Give me your assurance *not*, and I will draw in my horns with great pleasure. 1817 : Scott, *Rob Roy*, ch. xxvii., He " drew in his horns," to use the Bailie's phrase, on the instant.

Draw the nail, To. 1917 : Bridge, *Cheshire Proverbs*, 132.

Drawn wells are seldom dry. 1639 : Clarke, 107. 1670 : Ray, 83. 1732 : Fuller, No. 1327. 1853 : Trench, *Proverbs*, 104 *n.* (1905), In the sense of the latter half of this proverb we say, *Drawn wells are seldom dry.*

Drawn wells have sweetest water. 1639 : Clarke, 107. 1681 : W. Robertson, *Phraseol. Generalis*, 1196.

Drayton. See **Hodnet.**

Dream of a dry summer. See **Summer** (8).

Dream, To. See quots. 1639 : Clarke, 236, After a dreame of weddings comes a corse. 1670 : Ray, 83 [as in 1639]. 1883 : Burne, *Shropsh. Folk-Lore*, 263, We have the sayings, " To dream of the dead, good news of the living " ; " Dream of a funeral, hear of a wedding " ; " Dream of a death, hear of a birth," and vice versa. Ibid., 264, As they say at Welshampton, To dream of things out of season Is trouble without reason.

Dreams go by contraries. *c.* 1400 : *Beryn*, Prol.,l. 108, ffor comynly of these swevenys [dreams] the contrary men shul fynde. 1566 : W. Adlington, tr. Apuleius, bk. iv., So the visions of the night do often chance contrary. 1633 : Rowley, *Match at Midnight*, IV., O, strange ! to see how dreams fall by contraries. 1673 : Wycherley, *Gent. Danc.-Master*, IV. i., Dreams go by the contraries. 1731 : Fielding, *Grub-Street Opera*, I. xi., Oh ! the perjury of men ! I find dreams do not always go by contraries. 1851 : Planché, *Extravag.*, iv. 179 (1879), You know That dreams by their contraries always go. 1922 : *Punch*, 7 June, p. 441, col. 2, " Dreams go by contraries," declares a contemporary. That must be how our Derby-tipster got his information.

Drift is as bad as unthrift. 1659 : Howell, 6. 1678 : Ray, 71.

Drink, subs. 1. *Drink in wit out.* [In proverbium cessit sapientiam vino obumbrari. — Pliny, XXIII. i. 23.] *c.* 1390 : Gower, *Conf. Amantis*, bk. vi. l. 555, For wher that wyn doth wit aweie, Wisdom hath lost the rihte weie. 1560 : Becon, *Catechism*, 375 (P.S.), For when the wine is in, the wit is out. 1599 : Shakespeare, *Much Ado*, III. v., *Dogb.* A good old man, sir ; he will be talking : as they say, When the age [ale] is in, the wit is out. 1642 : D. Rogers, *Naaman*, sig. Ee2, Next day when wine was out, and wit in. 1712 : Swift, *Journal to Stella*, Lett. xlii., But after dinner is after dinner—an old saying and a true, " much drinking, little thinking." 1854 : J. W. Warter, *Last of Old Squires*, 53, When the drink goes in, then the wit goes out.

2. *Drink and drought come not always together.* 1732 : Fuller, No. 1329.

3. *Drink washes off the dawb, and discovers the man.* Ibid., No. 1330.

4. *Of all the meat in the world, drink goes down the best.* 1855 : Bohn, 466.

Drink, verb. 1. *Don't say, I'll never drink of this water, how dirty soever it be.* 1710 : S. Palmer, *Moral Essays on Proverbs*, 236. 1732 : Fuller, No. 5016.

2. *Drink as much after an egg as after
an ox.* 1608: Harington, *Sch. of
Salerne*, sig. A7, Remember . . . For
euery egge you eate you drink as oft.
1659: Howell, 13. 1670: Ray, 36.
1738: Swift, *Polite Convers.*, Dial. II.,
And, faith, one should drink as much
after an egg as after an ox.

3. *Drink in the morning staring, then
all the day be sparing.* 1659: Howell, 1.
1670: Ray, 39. 1846: Denham, *Proverbs*, 14 (Percy S.).

4. *Drink less and go home by day-
light.* c. 1320: in *Reliq. Antiquæ*, i. 116
(1841), "Drynk eft lasse, and go by lyhte
hom"; Quoth Hendyng.

5. *Drink off your drink, and steal no
lambs.* 1659: Howell, 20. 1670: Ray,
216.

6. *Drink only with the duck*=Drink
water only. 1377: Langland, *Plowman*,
B, v. 75, Drynke but myd [with] the
doke and dyne but ones.

7. *Drink the devil. See* Devil (100).

8. *Drink wine and have tho gout;
drink no wine and have the gout.* 1588:
Cogan, *Haven of Health*, Epist. Ded.,
As I haue heard many gentlemen say
ere now: Drinke wine and hauc the
gowte: drink none and haue the gowt.
1655: T. Muffett, *Health's Improvement*,
5. 1699: in *Harl. Miscell.*, ii. 49
(1744) [with "claret" instead of
"wine"]. 1732: Fuller, No. 1331.

9. *He drank till he gave up his halfpenny*=vomited. 1678: Ray, 87. 1745:
Franklin, *Drinker's Dict.*, in *Works*, ii.
25 (Bigelow).

10. *He drinks like a hen, with head
held up.* 1675: in *Roxb. Ballads*, iv. 45
(B.S.), Though he drinks like a chick,
with his eye-balls lift up. 1810: Mary
Allen, *Poems for Youth*, The little
chickens, as they dip Their beaks into
the river, Hold up their heads at every
dip, And thank the Giver. 1880:
Spurgeon, *Ploughman's Pictures*, 28,
There's Solomon Braggs holding up
his head like a hen drinking water, but
there's nothing in it.

11. *He is drinking at the Harrow when
he should be at the plough.* 1639:
Clarke, 47. 1670: Ray, 180. 1732:
Fuller, No. 2456.

12. *He that drinketh well sleepeth well,
and he that sleepeth well thinketh no
harm.* 1530: Palsgrave, 721. 1551:
T. Wilson, *Rule of Reason*, sig. H8, He
that drynkes wel, slepes wel. 1609:
Lithgow, *Rare Adventures*, 69 (1906),
He that eateth well, drinketh well, he
that drinketh well, sleepeth well, he
that sleepeth well sinneth not, and he
that sinneth not goeth straight through
Purgatory to Paradise.

13. *If you drink with your porridge,
you'll cough in your grave.* 1670: Ray,
133. 1738: Swift, *Polite Convers.*,
Dial. II.

14. *The more one drinks the more one
may.* 1633: Draxe, 49. 1666: Torriano,
Piazza Univ., 25 [with "would" for
"may"].

15. *To drink like a fish.* 1646:
Shirley, in *Works*, vi. 321 (Dyce),
I can drink like a fish. 1701: Farquhar, *Sir H. Wildair*, II., Where I
may . . . drink like a fish, and swear
like a devil. 1778: H. More, in *Garrick
Corresp.*, ii. 320 (1832), I shall have
nothing to do but to go to Bath and
drink like a fish. 1885: A. Dobson, in
Poet. Works, 297 (1923), Thou drink'st
as fishes do. 1894: R. L. S., *St. Ives*,
ch. xiii., He drank like a fish or an
Englishman.

16. *To drink like a funnel.* 1813:
Ray, 191.

17. *When thou dost drink, beware the
toast, for therein lies the danger most.*
Glos. 1639: in *Berkeley MSS.*, iii.
31 (1885).

18. *You drink out of the broad end
of the funnel, and hold the little one to
me.* 1732: Fuller, No. 5898.

19. *You drink vinegar when you have
wine at your elbow.* Ibid., No. 5899.

**Drinking kindness is drunken friend-
ship.** Ibid., No. 1333.

Drive, verb. 1. *Drive the nail that
will go.* 1655: Fuller, *Church Hist.*,
bk. ii. § iv. (12), Thus he drave that
nail . . . which would go best for the
present. 1737: Gay, *Fables*, 2nd ser.,
No. 9, l. 14, Hence politicians, you
suggest, Should drive the nail that
goes the best. 1857: Hughes, *Tom
Brown*, Pt. II. ch. ii., How often have

I told you, Tom, that you must drive a nail where it'll go.

2. *Drive the nail to the head.* 1639: Clarke, 3.

3. *Drive thy business, let not that drive thee.* 1736: Franklin, *Way to Wealth*, in *Works*, i. 443 (Bigelow).

4. *He drives a subtle trade.* 1678: Ray, 91.

5. *It is ill to drive black hogs in the dark.* 1678: Ray, 103. 1732: Fuller, No. 2963.

Drive a top. *See* Top.

Droppings. *See* Save (2).

Drought never bred dearth in England. 1533: Heywood, *Play of Weather*, l. 634, And it is sayd syns afore we were borne That drought doth neuer make derth of corne. 1640: Herbert, *Jac. Prudentum*, Drought never brought dearth. 1732: Fuller, No. 1338. 1825: Hone, *Ev. Day Book*, i. 669. 1875: Parish, *Sussex Dict.*, 38, Drythe never yet bred dëarth. 1917: Bridge, *Cheshire Proverbs*, 52.

Drown not thyself to save a drowning man. 1732: Fuller, No. 1340.

Drown the miller, To. 1889: J. Nicholson, *Folk Speech E. Yorks*, 5, If, in making dough, the good wife should put too much water, she has "dhroondid minler" (drowned the miller). 1899: Dickinson, *Cumb. Gloss.*, 105, One whose liquor has been diluted too much, will say that the miller has been drowned. Cf. Miller (14).

Drowning men catch at straws. 1614: C. Brooke, *Rich. the Third*, 105 (Grosart), And now like to a man (ready to drowne) Catch at a helplesse thing. *c.* 1640: in *Harl. Miscell.*, iv. 153 (1745), Sinking she will take hold of reeds. *c.* 1680: L'Estrange, *Seneca's Epistles*, xviii., We catch hold of hopes . . . as drowning men do upon thorns, or straws. 1748: Richardson, *Clarissa*, vi. 5 (1785), The dear implacable, like a drowning man, catches at a straw to save herself! 1860: Reade, *Cl. and Hearth*, ch. xciii. 1875: R. L. S., *Letters*, i. 229 (Tusitala ed.), I cling to you as a drowning man to a straw. 1926: Phillpotts, *Marylebone Miser*, ch. ix.

Drum's entertainment = A rough

reception. 1583: Melbancke, *Philotinus*, sig. D1, Hee had scarce Jacke Drummes enterteynement. 1592: Greene, *Groatsworth*, in *Works*, xii. 129 (Grosart), And so giuing him Jacke Drums entertainment, shut him out of doores. 1634: C. Butler, *Feminine Monarchie*, 64, They gently give them Tom Drums enterteinment. *c.* 1685: in *Roxb. Ballads*, viii. 869 (B.S.), Thy entertainment shall be like Jack Drums. 1834-7: Southey, *Doctor*, ch. cxxv., It is at this day doubtful whether it was Jack Drum or Tom Drum, whose mode of entertainment no one wishes to receive.

Drunk as a beggar. 1622: Massinger, *Virgin Martyr*, III. iii., Be drunk as a beggar, he helps you home. 1670: Ray, 204. 1745: Franklin, *Drinker's Dict.*, in *Works*, ii. 23 (Bigelow). 1909: Hackwood, *Inns, Ales, etc.*, 169, He may be as . . . drunk as a beggar or . . . as a lord.

Drunk as a besom. 1888: S. O. Addy, *Sheffield Gloss.*, 13 (E.D.S.), There is a saying "as drunk as a beesom."

Drunk as a boiled owl. 1889: Peacock, *Manley, etc., Gloss.*, 182 (E.D.S.).

Drunk as a fiddler. 1884: R. L. S. and Henley, *Adm. Guinea*, II. vi., I'm as drunk as a Plymouth fiddler, Pew.

Drunk as a fiddler's bitch. 1362: Langland, *Plowman*, A, v. 197, Thenne gon he for to go lyk a gleo-monnes bicche, Sum tyme asyde and sum tyme arere. 1830: Forby, *Vocab. E. Anglia*, 27. 1894: Northall, *Folk Phrases*, 8 (E.D.S.). 1901: F. E. Taylor, *Lancs Sayings*, 2.

Drunk as a fish. 1704: Congreve, *Way of World*, IV. ix., Thou art both as drunk and as mute as a fish. 1864: T. W. Robertson, *David Garrick*, II., He's drunk as a fish.

Drunk as a lord. 1659: in *Somers Tracts*, vii. 184 (1811), Yet the proverb goes, "As drunk as a lord." 1670: Cotton, *Scarronides*, bk. iv. 1731: Coffey, *Devil to Pay*, I. ii. 1872: Hardy, *Greenwood Tree*, Pt. I. ch. i., Time enough to get as drunk as lords!

Drunk as a mouse. *c.* 1307: in *Lyric Poetry*, 111 (Percy S.), When that he is dronke ase a dreynt mous. *c.* 1386 : Chaucer, *Wife of Bath's Prol.*, l. 246, Thou comest hoom as dronken as a mous. *c.* 1470 : *Songs and Carols*, 90 (Percy S.). Before 1529 : Skelton, *Col. Clout*, l. 803, Dronken as a mouse, At the ale house. *c.* 1580 : *Tom Tyler*, l. 300, p. 9 (Malone S.). 1889 : Peacock, *Manley, etc., Gloss.*, 182 (E.D.S.), Drunk as . . . mice.

Drunk as a piper. 1720 : Gay, *Poems*, ii. 277 (Underhill), Drunk as a piper all day long. 1772 : Graves, *Spirit. Quixote*, bk. x. ch. xxix., He became as drunk as a piper.

Drunk as a rat. 1542 : Boorde, *Introduction*, 147 (E.E.T.S.), Although I wyll be dronken other whyles as a rat. 1583 : Stubbes, *Anat. of Abuses*, 113 (N. Sh. S.), Till thei were bothe as dronke as rattes. 1691 : *Merry Drollery*, 28 (Ebsworth). 1880 : Spurgeon, *Ploughman's Pictures*, 41.

Drunk as a swine (or hog, pig, sow). *c.* 1440 : Lydgate, *Fall of Princes*, bk. iii. l. 2369, Thei lai and slepte lik as dronke swyn. *c.* 1500 : in Hazlitt, *Early Pop. Poetry*, i. 100 (1864), To be as dronke as any swyne. 1681 : *Poor Robin Alman.*, June, Well may they say men drunk as hogs I think. 1700 : Ward, *London Spy*, 264 (1924), Both were as drunk as swine. 1744 : *Foundl. Hosp. for Wit*, No. II., p. 52 (1749), A man for his health to get drunk— as a sow. *c.* 1795 : Wolcot, *Works*, v. 71 (1801), And Dundas gets as drunk as a pig. 1803 : Colman, jr., *John Bull*, III. ii., There's a hog; — for he's as drunk as one, I know, by his beastly bawling. 1889 : Peacock, *Manley, etc., Gloss.*, 182 (E.D.S.), Drunk as a pig.

Drunk as a tinker. 1701 : Cibber, *Love Makes a Man*, I., I sent young Louis back again to Marli, as drunk as a tinker. 1909 : Hackwood, *Inns, Ales, etc.*, 169, He may be . . . as drunk as a tinker.

Drunk as a wheelbarrow. 1678 : Ray, 87. 1697 : T. Dilke, *City Lady*, I. i., To have made a German general as drunk as a wheel-barrow. 1745 : Franklin, *Drinker's Dict.*, in *Works*, ii. 23 (Bigelow).

Drunk as an ape. *c.* 1500 : in Hazlitt, *Early Pop. Poetry*, i. 104 (1864), Such as wilbe as drongen as an ape. 1583 : Stubbes, *Anat. of Abuses*, 151 (N. Sh. S.), Swilling and gulling, night and day, till they be as drunke as apes. 1633 : Draxe, 49. 1762 : Hall-Stevenson, *Crazy Tales*, p. vii, They'll make you drunker than an ape. 1909 : Hackwood, *Inns, Ales, etc.*, 169, He may be . . . as fuddled as an ape.

Drunk as an emperor. 1697 : T. Dilke, *City Lady*, III. ii., Here's my brother as drunk as an emperor.

Drunk as an owl. 1883 : R. L. S., *Treasure I.*, ch. xxiv., " Clumsy fellows," said I; " they must still be drunk as owls." 1886 : Elworthy, *West Som. Word-Book*, 549 (E.D.S.), Com. simile is " Drunk's a owl." Why the solemn bird should be taken as the ideal drunkard I know not.

Drunk as Chloe. 1906 : Q.-Couch, *Mayor of Troy*, ch. ix.

Drunk as David's sow. 1671 : Shadwell, *Miser*, IV., I am as drunk . . . as David's sow, as the saying is. 1711 : *Brit. Apollo*, i. 572 [gives the story which is said to have originated the saying. It is quoted in *Gent. Mag.*, 1811, Pt. I., pp. 634-5]. 1725 : Bailey, tr. Erasmus' *Colloq.*, 160, He comes home . . . as drunk as David's sow. 1834 : Marryat, *P. Simple*, ch. iii. 1901 : F. E. Taylor, *Lancs Sayings*, 2, As drunk as David's soo.

Drunk as muck, and **Drunk as soot**, —both in 1889 : Peacock, *Manley, etc., Gloss.*, 182 (E.D.S.).

Drunk as the Baltic. 1823 : Scott, *Peveril*, ch. xxvii., Fill him as drunk as the Baltic sea. 1824 : Scott, *Redgauntlet*, ch. xiv. 1899 : *N. & Q.*, 9th ser., iv. 336, The phrase is still in use among the seafaring population of the East of Scotland in this homely form of " as fou's the Baltic."

Drunk as the devil. *c.* 1350 : in *Allit. Poems*, 82 (Morris, E.E.T.S.), Now a boster on benche bibbes ther-of Tyl he be dronkken as the deuel. 1709 : Ward, *Account of Clubs*, 272 (1756), Madam Bibbington, in a chair, as drunk as the devil. 1864 : T. W. Robertson,

David Garrick, II., He's as d-d-drunk
as the very de-de-devil!

Drunk is as great as a king, He that is.
1672: *Westm. Drollery*, Pt. II. 77
(Ebsworth). 1696: D'Urfey, *Quixote*,
Pt. III. Act III. sc. ii.

Drunk. *See also* **Ever drunk.**

Drunkard. *As the drunkard goes, is
knowne by his nose.* 1623: Wodroephe,
Spared Houres, 491.

Drunkard's purse is a bottle, A. 1640:
Herbert, *Jac. Prudentum.*

**Drunkards have a fool's tongue and a
knave's heart.** 1732: Fuller, No. 1342.

Drunken and drowsy. *See* quot.
1596: *Knack to Know an Honest Man*,
l. 657 (Malone S.), The prouerbe is true
that I tell to you, Tis better to be
dronken and drowsie. Than hunger
starued and lousie.

**Drunken days have all their to-
morrows,** "as the old proverb says."
1875: Smiles, *Thrift*, 167.

**Drunken general is a bad commander,
A**—"an old proverb." Before 1704:
T. Brown, in *Works*, iii. 256 (1760).

Drunken men never take harm.
1591: Harington, *Orl. Furioso*, bk. xxx.
st. 13, If fortune that helps frantike
men and drunke Had not him safe
conveyd. 1604: *Meeting of Gallants*,
26 (Percy S.), But there is an oulde
prouerbe, and now confirmed true, a
druncken man neuer takes harme.
1605: Chapman, etc., *Eastw. Hoe*, III.
ii. 1714: Gay, *Shep. Week*, Sat., l. 127,
The power that guards the drunk, his
sleep attends. 1894: R. L. S., *St. Ives*,
ch. xiii., I am well aware there is a
Providence for drunken men.

**Drunken night makes a cloudy morn-
ing, A.** 1601: Cornwallis, *Essayes*,
Pt. II. sig. Dd8 (1610) [with "mistie"
for "cloudy"]. 1732: Fuller, No. 81.

**Drunkenness reveals what soberness
conceals.** [Quid non ebrietas designat?
Operta recludit.—Horace, *Epist.*, I. v.
16.] *c.* 1386: Chaucer, *C. Tales*, B 776
(Skeat), Ther dronkënessë regneth in
any route, Ther is no conseil hid,
withouten doute. 1539: Taverner,
Proverbs, fo. 30, The thynge that lyeth
in a sobre mans hart is in the tongue of
the dronkarde. 1579: Lyly, *Euphues*,

146 (Arber), It is an old prouerbe,
Whatsoeuer is in the heart of the sober
man, is in the mouth of the drunkarde.
1681: W. Robertson, *Phraseol. Generalis*, 508. 1732: Fuller, No. 6117.

Dry. 1. *A dry cough is the trumpeter
of death.* 1655: Howell, *Letters*, bk. iv.
No. ix. 1670: Ray, 5. 1736: Bailey,
Dict., s.v. "Trumpeter."

2. *A dry year never starves itself.*
c. 1685: Aubrey, *Nat. Hist. Wilts*, 33
(1847), 'Tis a saying in the West, that
a dry yeare does never cause a dearth.
1893: Inwards, *Weather Lore*, 4.

3. *As dry as a bone. c.* 1555: in
Wright, *Songs, etc., Philip and Mary*,
14 (Roxb. Cl.), Also the congars, as dry
as a bonne. 1678: Ray, 283. 1834:
Marryat, *P. Simple*, ch. i., Here, Peter,
take mine, it's as dry as a bone. 1886:
Elworthy, *West Som. Word-Book*, 219
(E.D.S.), Dry as a bone. This is the
almost invariable simile to express the
superlative of dryness.

4. *As dry as a chip.* 1630: Jonson,
New Inn, IV. i. 1725: Bailey, tr.
Erasmus' *Colloq.*, 533, By that time it
came to me it was as dry as a chip, and
no more taste in it than a foot of a
joint-stool. 1850: Dickens, *Copperfield*, ch. xxxi., "It's quite dry." "So
'tis! . . . as a chip!" 1877: Ross,
Holderness Gloss. (E.D.S.), Ah's as dry
as a chip.

5. *As dry as a fish.* 1862: *Dialect
of Leeds*, 405. 1889: Peacock, *Manley,
etc., Gloss.*, 182 (E.D.S.), I'm as dry
as a fish, do gie us a drink o' aale.

6. *As dry as a kex.* 1553: *Respublica*, V. x. (E.E.T.S.), An ye bydde
mee, chill [I will] squease hym as drie as
a kyxe. 1566: Drant, *Horace: Satires*,
sig. A4, Whose lippes as drye as any
kykkes. 1684: L'Estrange, *Observator*,
ii. No. 118, The Covenant . . . squeez'd
as dry as a kex. 1725: Bailey, tr.
Erasmus' *Colloq.*, 7, You're as thin a
body may see through you, and as dry
as a kecks. 1842: Akerman, *Wilts
Gloss.*, 30, As dry as kecks. 1887:
Hardy, *Woodlanders*, ch. xlviii,, My
throat's as dry as a kex. 1891: Hardy,
Tess, ch. xvii.

7. *As dry as dust.* 1669: *New Help*

to Discourse, 248, Who is by drinking
drunk as dry as dust. 1679 : D'Urfey,
Squire Oldsapp, I. i., My Westwhap-
hallan at dinner has made me as dry
as dust.

8. *Be it dry or be it wet, The weather'll
always pay its debt.* 1875 : A. B.
Cheales, *Proverb. Folk-Lore*, 18.

9 *Dry bread at home is better than
roast meat abroad.* 1640 : Herbert, *Jac.
Prudentum.* 1670 : Ray, 13.

10. *Dry over head happy.* 1659 :
Howell, *Proverbs : Brit.-Eng.*, 4, A house
dry over head is happy. 1855 : Bohn,
267.

11. *It is got into dry cock.* A haying
simile. 1639 : Clarke, 234, You have it
in dry cocke. 1672 : Walker, *Parœm.*,
13, It is got into dry cock; out of
harms way. 1681 : W. Robertson,
Phraseol. Generalis, 678, It is got in a
dry cock; Res est jam in vado salutis.

Duck and **Ducks.** 1. *A duck will
not always dabble in the same gutter.*
1732 : Fuller, No. 82.

2. *Ducks fare well in the Thames.*
1670 : Ray, 83. 1735 : Pegge, *Kent.
Proverbs*, in E.D.S., No. 12, p. 78.

3. *Ducks will not lay till they have
drunk March water.* 1879 : *Folk-Lore
Record*, ii. 202, There is a saying in
Luxulyan [Cornwall] that " ducks will
not lay till they have drunk Lide
[March] water."

4. *Fine weather for ducks* = Wet.
[1546 : Heywood, *Proverbs*, Pt. I.
ch. xiii., Weather meete to sette pad-
dockes (frogs) abroode in.] 1840 :
Dickens, *Curiosity Shop*, ch. ii., From
which appearance he augured that
another fine week for the ducks was
approaching, and that rain would certainly ensue.

5. *Like a duck in thunder.* 1823 :
Scott, *Peveril*, ch. xi., Till she had . . .
closed her eyes like a dying fowl—
turned them up like a duck in a
thunderstorm. 1863 : Kingsley, *Water
Babies*, ch. v. 1917 : Bridge, *Cheshire
Proverbs*, 72, He winks and thinks like
a duck i' thunner.

6. *Like water off a duck's back.* 1824 :
Maginn, *O'Doherty's Maxims*, 128
(1849), The thing passed off like water

from a duck's back. 1916 : B. Duffy,
The Old Lady, 12, To let his attentions
run off me like water off a duck's back.

7. *They follow each other like ducks
in a gutter.* 1855 : Bohn, 525.

8. *To make ducks and drakes of money*
=To squander it. [1585 : *Nomenclator*,
299, A stone throwne into the water,
and making circles yer it sinke, . . . it
is called a ducke and a drake, and a
halfe penie cake.] 1605 : Chapman,
etc., *Eastw. Hoe*, I. i., Why, do nothing,
be like a gentleman, be idle . . . make
duckes and drakes with shillings. 1653 :
Shirley, *Cupid and Death*, in *Works*, vi.,
349 (Dyce), And play'd at duck and
drake with gold, like pebbles. 1765 :
in *Garrick Corresp.*, i. 207 (1831), I had
rather make ducks and drakes of my
money, than buy his book. 1850 :
Dickens, *Copperfield*, ch. xlvii., He soon
made ducks and drakes of what I gave
him. 1859 : Sala, *Twice Round Clock*,
3 p.m., It is but very rarely indeed
that they make ducks and drakes of
their customers' money.

9. *When ducks are driving through
the burn, That night the weather takes a
turn.* 1893 : Inwards, *Weather Lore*,
133.

10. *When the ducks eat up the dirt.*
1738 : Swift, *Polite Convers.*, Dial. II.,
But, Sir John, when may we hope to
see you again in London? *Sir John.*
Why, Madam, not till the ducks have
eat up the dirt, as the children say.
1910 : *N. & Q.*, 11th ser., i. 316, Some
time in the early sixties I was told in
North Lincolnshire that I might go out
to play " when the ducks had picked
up [or " had eaten "] the mud."

See also **Drink** (6) ; and **Prate.**

Dudleston. *See* quot. 1883 : Burne,
Shropsh. Folk-Lore, 583, The longer
you live the more you see, Dudleston
Chapel-bell hung on a tree.

Dudman and Ramhead meet, When.
1602 : Carew, *Surv. of Cornwall*, 330
(1811), Amongst sundry proverbs, allot-
ting an impossible time of performance,
the Cornishmen have this one, " When
Ram Head and Dudman meet." 1662 :
Fuller, *Worthies*, i. 307 (1840). 1790 :
Grose, *Prov. Gloss.*, s.v. " Cornwall."

1821 : Scott, *Kenilworth*, ch. iv., Depart
—vanish—or we'll have you summoned
before the Mayor of Halgaver, and that
before Dudman and Ramhead meet.
1865 : Hunt, *Pop. Romances W. of Eng.*,
182 (1896), Merlyn is said to have pronounced the following prophecy, standing near St. German's Grotto on the
shores of Whitsand Bay :—" When the
Rame Head and Dodman meet, Men
and women will have cause to greet."
    Dufton. *See* quot. 1846–59 : *Den-
ham Tracts*, i. 165 (F.L.S.), "'How's
that?' says Dufton." This saying is
very common in Cumberland, and
originated with the notorious thief of
the name. [He stole corn from farmers'
granaries, by boring a hole with an
auger through the floor of the granary
and holding a sack under it. One
farmer had nailed sheet-iron over his
boards. When Dufton failed to pene-
trate this with his auger he said, " How's
that? "]
    Duke Humphrey. *See* **Dine.**
    Dulcarnon, At=At one's wits' end.
c. 1374 : Chaucer, *Troylus*, bk. iii.
ll. 930–3, " I am, til god me bettre
minde sende, At dulcarnon, right at
my wittes ende." Quod Pandarus,
" ye, nece, wol ye here? Dulcarnon
called is ' fleminge of wrecches.' "
c. 1584 : Stanihurst, *Descrip. of Ireland*,
28, These sealie soules were (as all
dulcarnanes for the most part are)
more to be terrified from infidelitie
. . . than allured to Christianitie. 1736 :
Bailey, *Dict.*, s.v., To be at Dulcarnon,
to be non-plussed, to be at one's wits'
end. 1852 : *N. & Q.*, 1st ser., v. 180,
I heard it used the other day by a
person who, declaring he was at his
wits' end, exclaimed, " Yes, indeed,
I am at Dulcarnon."
    Dule and dawkin. *See* **Better dule.**
    Dull as a beetle. 1670 : Ray, 204.
1753 : *World*, No. 45, " As dull as a
beetle," is a term I have no dislike to.
    Dull as a Dutchman. 1639 : Clarke,
296. 1681 : W. Robertson, *Phraseol.
Generalis*, 510.
    Dumb as a door. 1362 : Langland,
Plowman, A, xi. 94, As doumbe as a
dore. *c.* 1440 : *York Plays*, 322 (L. T.

Smith), Bot domme as a dore gon he
dwell.
    Dumb as a fish. *See* **Mute.**
    Dumb man gets no land, The. *c.* 1390 :
Gower, *Conf. Amantis*, bk. vi. l. 447,
For selden get a domb man lond. Tak
that proverbe, and understond That
wordes ben of vertu grete. 1406 :
Hoccleve, in *Minor Poems*, 38
(E.E.T.S.), The prouerbe is " the
doumb man no lond getith." 1670 :
Ray, 83, Dumb folks get no lands.
1732 : Fuller, No. 84, A dumb man
never gets land. 1899 : Dickinson,
Cumb. Gloss., 106, " Dumb folk heirs
nae lan' "—said when anything is to
be or has been obtained by speaking.
    Dun as a mouse. 1678 : Ray, 283.
    Dun cow, To stand like the. 1663 :
Killigrew, *Parson's Wedding*, II. vi.,
I'll make him jostle like the miller's
mare [q.v.] and stand like the dun cow,
till thou may'st milk him.
    Dun is in the mire. *c.* 1386 :
Chaucer, *Manciple's Prol.*, l. 5, Ther
gan our hoste for to iape and pleye,
And seyde, " sirs, what! Dun is in the
myre!" 1412 : Hoccleve, *Regement*,
86 (E.E.T.S.), Be his day kept, he
rekketh nat a bene, But elles, siker,
" don is in the myre." Before 1529 :
Skelton, in *Works*, i. 418 (Dyce), Dun
is in the myre, dame, reche me my
spur. 1592 : Shakespeare, *Romeo*, I. iv.,
If thou art Dun, we'll draw thee from
the mire. 1694 : Motteux, *Rabelais*,
bk. iv. ch. lxiii., We were all out of
sorts, moping, drooping . . . as dull as
Dun in the mire. 1905 : *N. & Q.*, 10th
ser., iii. 11, An old proverb " Dun's
in the mire " . . . " Dun " is evidently
the name of a horse, and the saying no
doubt had its origin in the dreadful
state of the roads in early times.
    Dun out of the mire. [To draw Dun
out of the mire was an old game,
described by Gifford in his edition of
Ben Jonson, vii. 283.] 1607 : Dekker
and Webster, *Westw. Hoe*, II. iii., I see
I'm borne still to draw Dun out oth
mire for you : that wise beast will I be.
1663 : Butler, *Hudibras*, III. iii. 110,
Who has dragged your dunship out
o' th' mire.

Dun's the mouse=Keep still. 1592 :
Shakespeare, *Romeo*, I. iv., Tut, dun's
the mouse. 1609 : *Ev. Woman in her
Humor*, IV. i., in Bullen, *Old Plays*, iv.
352, I will see and say little ; what I say
duns the mouse, and welcome my
bullies. *c.* 1630 : in *Roxb. Ballads*, i. 69
(Hindley), I'le say no more but duns
the mouse.

Dunder [Thunder] **clo gally** [affright]
the beans, The. Somerset. 1678 : Ray,
347.

Dunghill gentleman. *See* **Gentleman**
(2).

Dunmow. 1. *Dunmow bacon, Doncaster daggers.* 1659 : Howell, 21. 1670 :
Ray, 258. 1878 : *Folk-Lore Record,* i.
172, We hear as a local [Yorks]
proverb of " Dunmow bacon and
Doncaster daggers."

2. *They may claim the flitch at Dunmow.* 1362 : Langland, *Plowman,* A,
x. 188, Thaugh thei don hem to Don-
mowe but the deuel helpe To folewen
attur the flucchen fecche thei hit
neuere. *c.* 1386 : Chaucer, *Wife of
Bath's Prol.,* l. 217, The bacoun was
nat fet for hem, I trowe, That som
men han in Essex at Dunmowe.
c. 1580 : *Tom Tyler*, l. 760, p. 21
(Malone S.), But you may now go for
bacon to Dunmo. 1662 : Fuller,
Worthies, i. 498 (1840), He may fetch
a flitch of bacon from Dunmow.
1790 : Grose, *Prov. Gloss.*, s.v. " Essex."
1821 : Combe, *Syntax in Search of Wife*,
can xxxiv., p. 57, While I, though
I have married been So many years, at
least sixteen ; Yes, I with honest heart
and hand, Can now the *Dunmow
Flitch* demand.

3. *Who fetcheth a wife from Dunmow,
Carrieth home two sides of a sow.* 1659 :
Howell, 21.

Dunstable. *As plain as Dunstable
highway,* or *Plain* (or *Downright*) *Dunstable.* 1546 : Heywood, *Proverbs*, Pt.
II. ch. v., As plaine as dunstable by
waie. *c.* 1560 : in Huth, *Ancient
Ballads, etc.*, 1 (1867), As playne . . .
as Donstable waye. 1599 : Breton, in
Works, ii. *c* 48 (Grosart), Alas ! to use
glosing speeches gives suspicion of little
good meaning . . . plaine Dunstable

is the high way, and yet there are
many holes in it. 1658 : Dekker,
Witch of Edmonton, I. ii., What must
it be, Master Frank? or son Frank?
I am plain Dunstable. 1718 : Dennis,
Works, ii. 344, Look you, my Lord,
I am downright, I am dunstable, Gads-
bud, and must speak the truth. 1754 :
Richardson, *Clarissa*, i. 217 (1785),
That's the plain Dunstable of the
matter, Miss ! 1790 : Grose, *Prov.
Gloss.*, s.v. " Beds," As plain as Dunstable road. Downright Dunstable.
1824 : Scott, *Redgauntlet*, ch. xviii., If
this is not plain speaking, there is no
such place as downright Dunstable in
being ! 1852 : M. A. Keltie, *Reminisc.
of Thought, etc.*, 101, It was mapped out
according to square and rule, and I was
not to be substituting any heresies of
my own in the room of such good old
Dunstable doings.

Dunstall. *See* **Barton.**

Durham. 1. *As peppery as Durham
mustard.* 1846–59 : *Denham Tracts*, i.
39 (F.L.S.).

2. *Durham folks are troubled with
afterwit.* 1909 : *Folk-Lore*, xx. 73.

3. *He's a Durham man : he's knocker
kneed.* 1823 : Grose, *Class. Dict.*, ed.
Egan, s.v. " Durham man," Durham
man. Knocker kneed, he grinds mustard with his knees : Durham is famous
for its mustard. 1846–59 : *Denham
Tracts*, i. 48 (F.L.S.).

4. *Like a Durham heifer, beef to the
heels.* 1846–59 : Ibid., i. 64.

5. *See* quot. 1892 : J. Hardy, editor,
Denham Tracts, i. 52, " There's not
much law at Durham for a happeny."
This is spoken of the heavy expenses
attending the Probate Court at Durham,
and the obtaining of extracts from wills
which are deposited there. It is a
common saying at Newcastle.

6. *Too dear for the Bishop of Durham.*
1846–59 : *Denham Tracts*, i. 39 (F.L.S.),
It would appear from the above that
the bishops of Durham have been proverbial for their riches from a very
early period.

See also **York** (4).

Dursley, You are a man of=one who
breaks his word. 1639 : in *Berkeley*

MSS., iii. 26 (1885), Hee'l proove, I thinke, a man of Durseley. 1662 : Fuller, *Worthies*, i. 551 (1840). 1790 : Grose, *Prov. Gloss.*, s.v. " Gloucest." 1851 : *Gloucestershire Gloss.*, 14.

Dust in a man's eyes, To cast. [Tenebras offudisse indicibus.—Quintil., II. xvii. 21.] 1581 : Pettie, tr. Guazzo's *Civil Convers.*, i. 276 (1586) (O.), They doe nothing else but raise a dust to doe out their owne eies. 1633 : Draxe, 18. 1690 : *New Dict. Canting Crew*, sig. B2. 1718 : W. Taverner, *Artful Wife*, I., To throw dust in the eyes of censure is proper. 1928 : *Times*, 9 March, p. 14, col. 3, He said that the speech was . . . designed to throw dust in the eyes of the public.

Dutchman drinketh pure wine in the morning, at noon wine without water, in the evening as it comes from the butt, The. 1659 : Howell, 20.

Dutchman drinks his buttons off, the English doublet and all away, The.

1640 : Glapthorne, *Ladies Priv.*, III., As is the common proverb, The Dutchman, etc.

Dutchman saith that segging is good cope, The. 1546 : Heywood, *Proverbs*, Pt. II. ch. ix.

Dutchman's headache, The = Drunkenness. 1869 : Hazlitt, 366.

Dwarf on a giant's shoulder sees farther of the two, A. 1640 : Herbert, *Jac. Prudentum*. 1654 : Whitlock, *Zootomia*, 218, A proverb . . . that a child on a giant's shoulder, may see farther than the giant.

Dwarf threatens Hercules, A. *c.* 1440 : Lydgate, *Fall of Princes*, bk. iii. l. 531 (E.E.T.S.), But it may falle a dwery [dwarf] in his riht Toutraie a geaunt, for al his grete myht. 1732 : Fuller, No. 85.

Dwells far from neighbours. *See* Neighbour (2).

Dying is as natural as living. 1732 : Fuller, No. 1348.

E

Each cross. *See* Every cross.

Each man for one. *See* Every man for himself.

Eagle and Eagles. 1. *Eagles fly alone.*
1639 : Clarke, 291. 1669 : *Politeuphuia*,
185, Eagles flie alone, and they are but
sheep that always flock together.

2. *The eagle does not catch flies.*
1573 : G. Harvey, *Letter-Book*, 50
(Camden S.), Now I se Aquila non
capit muscas. 1607 : Rowlands, *Guy,
E. of Warwick*, 12 (Hunt. Cl.), That
proverb in this point might make thee
wise, *That princely eagles scorn the
catching flies.* 1640 : Shirley, *Opportunity*, V. ii., Eagles stoop not to flies.
1924 : *Sphere*, 27 Sept., p. 386, col. 2,
More subtle is the insult in the saying
that "the eagle does not catch flies."

3. *You cannot fly like an eagle with
the wings of a wren.* 1909 : Hudson,
Afoot in England, ch. vi., As the
proverb says, "You cannot," etc.

Eagle-eyed. *He is eagle-eyed in other
mens matters, but as blind as a buzzard in
his own.* 1633 : Draxe, 26.

Ear. *If your ear burns* (*or glows*),
some one is talking about you. [Quin et
absentes [tinnitu] aurium praesentire
sermones de se?—Pliny, *Hist. Nat.*,
xxviii. 2.] *c.* 1374 : Chaucer, *Troylus*,
bk. ii. l. 1022, And we shal speke of
thee som-what, I trowe, Whan thou
art goon, to do thyne eres glowe !
1546 : Heywood, *Proverbs*, Pt. II. ch. i.,
I suppose that daie hir eares might well
glow, For all the towne talkt of hir,
hy and low. 1599 : Shakespeare, *Much
Ado*, III. i., What fire is in my ears?
Can this be true? 1687 : Aubrey,
Gentilisme, 110 (F.L.S.), When our
cheek burneth, or eare tingleth, we
usually say that some body is talking
of us. 1755 : *Connoisseur*, No. 59, If
your right ear or cheek burns, your
left friends are talking of you. 1868 :
Dickens, *Letters*, iii. 257 (1882), I dine
with Dolby . . . and if your ears do not

burn from six to nine this evening,
then the Atlantic is a non-conductor.

Early. 1. *Early ripe. See* Soon ripe.

2. *Early riser. See* Name (1).

3. *Early sow, early mow.* 1639 :
Clarke, 233. 1670 : Ray, 84. 1732 :
Fuller, No. 1350.

4. *Early to bed and early to rise,
makes a man healthy and wealthy and
wise.* 1523 : Fitzherbert, *Husbandry*,
101 (E.D.S.), At grammer-scole I
lerned a verse, that is this, *Sanat,
sanctificat et ditat surgere mane.* That
is to say, Erly rysyng maketh a man
hole in body, holer in soule, and rycher
in goodes. 1577 : Rhodes, *Boke of
Nurture*, in *Babees Book*, 72 (E.E.T.S.),
Ryse you earely in the morning, for
it hath propertyes three : Holynesse,
health, and happy welth, as my father
taught mee. 1670 : Ray, 38. 1736 :
Franklin, *Way to Wealth*, in *Works*, i.
443 (Bigelow). 1854 : J. W. Warter,
Last of Old Squires, 60.

5. *Early up and never the nearer.* 1546 :
Heywood, *Proverbs*, Pt. I. ch. ii., And
than, their timely weddyng doth clere
appere, That they were carely vp, and
neuer the nere. 1594 : Greene, *Frier
Bacon*, sc. vi., Your [You are] early
up, pray God it be the neere [nearer].
1633 : Jonson, *Tale of a Tub*, Epil.,
Wherein the poet's fortune is, I fear,
Still to be early up, but ne'er the near.
1732 : Fuller, No. 1351. 1881 : Evans,
Leics. Words, etc., 200 (E.D.S.), Never-
the-near, or Never-the-nigh, *adv.* none
the nearer ; no forwarder.

6. *Early wed, early dead.* 1895 :
N. & Q., 8th ser., viii. 516, The old
English proverb which says, Early
wed, early dead.

7. *The early bird catches the worm.*
1605 : Camden, *Remains*, 333 (1870).
1670 : Ray, 84. 1732 : Fuller, No.
5118. 1883 : R. L. S., *Treasure I.*,
ch. xxx., And it's the early bird, as
the saying goes, that gets the rations.

8. *The early bird gets the late one's breakfast.* 1882 : Mrs. Chamberlain, *W. Worcs. Words*, 39 (E.D.S.).

9. *The early sower never borrows of the late.* 1659 : Howell, 17, The rath sower never borroweth of the late. 1670 : Ray, 22 [as in 1659]. 1732 : Fuller, No. 4492.

Earth must to earth. *c.* 1480 : *Early Miscell.*, 40 (Warton Cl., 1855), How erth schal to erthe he thinkes nothinge. 1593 : Peele, *Edward I.*, sc. xxiv., An old said saw, earth must to earth.

Earth produces all things and receives all again, The. 1732 : Fuller, No. 4493.

Earthen pot must keep clear of the brass kettle, The. Ibid., No. 4494.

Earth's the best shelter. 1659 : Howell, *Proverbs : Brit.-Eng.*, 38.

Ease. 1. *Ease and success are fellows. c.* 1300 : *Havelok the Dane*, l. 1338 (Skeat), Lith and selthe felawes are.

2. *He is at ease who has enough. c.* 1460 : *Wisdom*, sc. iv. st. 70, Farewell, cousyens ! I know not yow ; I am at eas, hade I inow. 1493 : *Dives and Pauper*, fo. 1 (1536), It is an olde prouerbe, He is wel at ease that hath inough, and can say ho.

3. *He may not have all his ease that shall thrive. c.* 1460 : *How the Good Wife*, l. 130.

4. *He that is at ease seeks dainties.* 1640 : Herbert, *Jac. Prudentum*.

Easier said than done. *See* Said.

Easier to fall (or descend) **than rise** (or ascend)**, It is.** 1605 : Camden, *Remains*, 326 (1870), It is easier to descend than to ascend. 1633 : Draxe, 54, A man may sooner fall then rise. 1684 : Bunyan, *Pilgr. Progr.*, Pt. II., p. 239 (1849), Then said *Mercy*, But the proverb is, *To go down the hill is easy.* 1732 : Fuller, No. 1353, Easier it is fall, than rise.

Easier to pull down than to build up, It is. 1587 : J. Bridges, *Defence of Govt. in Church of Eng.*, 518, We may quicklier pull downe with one hande, than wee can easilie builde againe with both. 1732 : Fuller, Nos. 2930 and 1354.

Easier to spy two faults than mend one, It is. *c.* 1555 : Starkey, *Life and Lett.*, I. iii. 2 (E.E.T.S.), Much easyar hyt ys to spy ii fautes then amend one.

Easily done is soon believed, That which is. 1670 : Ray, 8. 1732 : Fuller, No. 4379.

Easily led but dour to drive. Derby. 1889 : *Folk-Lore Journal*, vii. 292.

Easily won. *See* Lightly gained.

East Cheap. *See* quot. *c.* 1430 : in *Reliq. Antiquæ*, i. 3 (1841), He that wyll in Eschepe ete a goose so fat, With harpe, pype, and song ; He must slepe in Newgate on a mat, Be the nyght never so long.

East Grinstead. *See* quot. 1894 : A. J. C. Hare, *Sussex*, 10, A Sussex proverb says [of E. G.]—Large parish, poor people, Large new church, no steeple.

East Looe. *The Mayor of East Looe, who called the King of England " Brother."* 1906 : Q.-Couch, *Mayor of Troy*, Prol.

East, West, Home's best. 1869 : Spurgeon, *John Ploughman*, ch. xiii., East and West, Home is best. 1920 : Lucas, *Verena in the Midst*, ch. xiii., p. 176, None the less I don't envy the traveller. " East, west, home's best."

East Wind. *See* Wind, B.

Easter. 1. *A kiss at Christmas and an egg at Easter.* 1846-59 : *Denham Tracts*, ii. 92 (F.L.S.).

2. *As hard as an egg at Easter.* 1846 : Denham, *Proverbs*, 32 (Percy S.).

3. *At Easter let your clothes be new, or else be sure you will it rue.* 1592 : Shakespeare, *Romeo*, III. i., Didst thou not fall out with a tailor for wearing his new doublet before Easter ? 1902 : Lean, *Collectanea*, i. 378.

4. *At Easter the wind is at Chester.* 1611 : in Coryat, *Crudities*, i. 93 (1905), And as about the time of Easter,* [*(Note) Prov. At Easter the winde is at Chester. Because it is good for Ireland.] T'enrich the towne and trade of shipping, The winde which evermore is skipping, Is said to come and dwell at Chester . . .

5. *Easter in snow, Christmas in mud ; Christmas in snow, Easter in mud.* 1893 : Inwards, *Weather Lore*, 38.

6. *Easter so longed for is gone in a day.* 1659 : Howell, 20.

7. *If the sun shines on Easter Day, it shines on Whit Sunday.* 1640 : *Countryman's Coms.*, in *Helpe to Discourse*, 224, If the sunne shine on Easter day, it shines on Whit Sonday likewise. 1893 : Inwards, *Weather Lore*, 41.

8. *I'll warrant you for an egg at Easter.* 1659 : Howell, 2. 1666 : Torriano, *Piazza Univ.*, 323, The English tradition was Hai for an egg at Easter. 1738 : Swift, *Polite Convers.*, Dial. III., I suppose her ladyship plays sometimes for an egg at Easter.

9. *Late Easter, long, cold spring.* Sussex. 1893 : Inwards, *Weather Lore*, 40.

10. *Past Easter frost, Fruit not lost.* Ibid., 41.

11. *Such weather as there is on Easter Day there will be at harvest.* Ibid., 41.

12. *When Easter falls in our Lady's lap, Then let England beware of a rap.* 1648 : in Rollins, *Cavalier and Puritan*, 216 (1923), When Easter-day sitteth in Lady-dayes lap, The proverbe bids England beware of a clap. 1659 : Howell, 16, When Christ falleth in our Ladies lapp, Then lett England look for a clapp. 1846 : Denham, *Proverbs*, 36 (Percy S.). 1904 : *Co. Folk-Lore: Northumb.*, 176 (F.L.S.). 1921 : *Sphere*, 2 April, p. 2, Only the very superstitious had their Easter holiday a little dimmed by the ominous falling together of Lady Day and Good Friday [*sic* in 1921], for as the old rhyme runs—When our Lord falls into our Lady's lap, England shall meet with great mishap.

13. *When rain falls on Easter Day, We get no grass and little hay.* 1851 : Sternberg, *Dialect, etc., of Northants*, 189, Rain on Easter-day, Plenty of grass, but little good hay. 1893 : Inwards, *Weather Lore*, 41, A good deal of rain upon Easter Day Gives a good crop of grass, but little good hay. Hertfordshire. 1917 : Bridge, *Cheshire Proverbs*, 163.

14. *You keep Easter, when I keep Lent.* 1732 : Fuller, No. 5927.

See also **Christmas** (5), (10), (11),

and (13) ; **Good Friday** ; **Jews** ; **Lady Day** ; and **Michaelmas** (5).

Easy as an old shoe. 1894 : Northall, *Folk Phrases*, 8 (E.D.S.).

Easy as falling off . . . 1917 : Bridge, *Cheshire Proverbs*, 27, As aisy as fawin off a chair when yo're drunk. 1924 : M. Kennedy, *Constant Nymph*, 307, They'd find it as easy as falling off a log, you see !

Easy as kiss my hand. 1670 : Cotton, *Scarronides*, bk. iv., But you may make 'em, at command, As cas'ly stay as kiss your hand. 1754 : Berthelson, *Eng.-Danish Dict.*, s.v. " Easy." 1878 : Sketchley, *Mrs. Brown at Paris Exhib.*, 30, It's as easy as kiss my 'and a-goin' to Paris now-a-days. 1921 : *Punch*, 7 Sept., p. 200, I bet if you only liked you could put me on to the winner of the St. Leger as easy as kiss me 'and !

Easy as lying. 1602 : Shakespeare, *Hamlet*, III. ii., It is as easy as lying. 1823 : Scott, *St. Ronan's*, ch. xxvi., Which to me seemed as easy and natural as lying. 1913 : L. P. Jacks, *All Men are Ghosts*, 117, Next morning Piecraft bought the book. As no patients came that day he had ample leisure to read it. " Easy as lying," he said to himself when he had finished.

Easy as to lick a dish. 1678 : Ray, 283.

Easy fool is a knave's tool, An. 1732 : Fuller, No. 6189.

Easy that are done willingly, All things are. 1596 : Lodge, *Wits Miserie*, 102 (Hunt. Cl.), A good will winneth all things. 1732 : Fuller, No. 561.

Easy to bowl down hill, It is. 1639 : Clarke, 151. 1670 : Ray, 3. 1732 : Fuller, No. 1352.

Easy to fall into a trap, but hard to get out again, 'Tis. 1732 : Fuller, No. 5072.

Easy to find a stick, etc. *See* **Stick**, *subs.* (1).

Easy to hold the latch, etc. *See* quot. 1917 : Bridge, *Cheshire Proverbs*, 81, It's aizy howdin dain th' latch when nobody poos at th' string.

Easy to rob an orchard when no man keeps it, 'Tis. 1639 : Clarke, 55. 1670 : Ray, 23. 1732 : Fuller, No. 2925.

Easy to wade the stream, etc. *See*
quot. 1615 : Brathwait, *Strappado*,
222 (1878), (Its easie saies the Prouerb) to wade the streame, Where th'
foord's at lowest.

Easy to wed a widow as to catch a
dead horse, It's as. 1917 : Bridge,
Cheshire Proverbs, 82, [Shropsh. vari-
ant] It's as easy to marry a widow as
to put a halter on a dead horse.

Eat. 1. *Eat a good dinner. See*
Good dinner.

2. *Eat and welcome, fast and heartily
welcome.* 1678 : Ray, 84. 1732 : Fuller,
No. 1355.

3. *Eat at pleasure drink by measure.*
1611 : Cotgrave, s.v. " Pain." 1670 :
Ray, 38. 1732 ; Fuller, No. 6079.
1875 : A. B. Cheales, *Proverb. Folk-
Lore*, 84, Bread at pleasure Drink by
measure is also a maxim much to be
commended.

4. *Eat enough and it will make you
wise.* 1592 : Lyly, *Mydas*, IV. iii.
[quoted as " an old proverb "].

5. *Eat less and drink less, and buy a
knife at Michaelmas.* 1659 : Howell, 6.

6. *Eat peas. See* Pea (1).

7. *Eat the devil. See* Devil (32).

8. *Eat thy meat and drink thy drink,
and stand thy ground, old Harry.* Somerset. 1678 : Ray, 343.

9. *Eat to live not live to eat.* [Non
vivas ut edas, sed edas ut vivere posses.
—Dionysius *in Rom.*, cap. 13.] *c.* 1410 :
tr. of *Secreta Secret.*, 67 (E.E.T.S.),
And ypocraas answerde, " ffair sone,
I will ete so that y leue, and noght
lyf that y ete." *c.* 1577 : Northbrooke,
Dicing, etc., 40 (Sh. S.), Thou lyuest
not to eate, butte eat as thou mayest
lyue. 1671 : Shadwell, *Miser*, III. ii.,
People should eat to live, not live to
eat ; as the proverb says. 1733 : Fielding, *Miser*, III. iii. 1911 : Pinero,
Preserving Mr. Panmure, II., p. 85.

10. *Eat-well is drink-well's brother.*
1732 : Fuller, No. 1357.

11. *Eat well of the cresses.* 1577 :
J. Grange, *Golden Aphrodites*, sig. F3,
Remember the prouerbe, *Eate well of
the cresses* [cress was supposed to help
the memory].

12. *Eat when you're hungry and drink*

when you're dry. 1917 : Bridge, *Cheshire
Proverbs*, 52.

13. *Eat your own side, speckle-back.*
1863 : Wise, *New Forest*, ch. xvi., " Eat
your own side, speckle-back," is a
common Forest expression, and is used
in reference to greedy people. It is
said to have taken its origin from a
girl who shared her breakfast with a
snake, and thus reproved her favourite
when he took too much.

14. *He could eat me without salt* (or
with garlic). 1596 : Harington, *Metam.
of Ajax*, 3 (1814), The poor sheep still,
for an old grudge, would eat him without salt (as they say). 1639 : Clarke,
71, You must not think to eat me up
without salt. 1670 : Ray, 173, He
could eat my heart with garlick. That
is, he hates me mortally. 1693 :
D'Urfey, *Richmond Heiress*, V. iv., Now
could I eat that satyrical devil without
salt for my breakfast. 1748 : Richardson, *Clarissa*, vii. 59 (1785), Yet I can
tell thee I could . . . eat him up without
a corn of salt, when I think of his
impudence.

15. *He eats in plate, but will die in
irons.* 1732 : Fuller, No. 1842.

16. *He has eat up the pot, and asks
for the pipkin.* Ibid., No. 1868.

17. *He has eaten many a Christmas
pie.* 1639 : Clarke, 189.

18. *He hath eaten his roast meat first.*
Glos. 1639 : in *Berkeley MSS.*, iii. 32,
(1885).

19. *He is so hungry he could eat a
horse behind the saddle.* 1678 : Ray,
253. 1826 : Scott, *Woodstock*, ch. xx.,
I think he could eat a horse, as the
Yorkshireman says, behind the saddle.

20. *He that eats least eats most.*
c. 1645 : MS. Proverbs, in *N. & Q.*,
vol. cliv., p. 27.

21. *He that eats most porridge shall
have most meat.* 1732 : Fuller, No. 2092.

22. *He that eats the hard shall eat the
ripe.* 1640 : Herbert, *Jac. Prudentum.*

23. *He that eats till he is sick must
fast till he is well.* 1732 : Fuller,
No. 2094.

24. *He that eats well and drinks well
should do his duty well.* 1654 : Gayton,
Pleasant Notes Don Q., 13, He that

eates well does his worke well. 1732 :
Fuller, No. 2095.

25. *He that will eat the kernel must
crack the nut.* c. 1500 : in *Antiq.
Repertory*, iv. 416 (1809), And yf ye
wolde the swetnes haue of the kyrnell,
Be content to byte vpon the harde
shell. 1577 : J. Grange, *Golden Aphroditis*, sig. I3, I see the prouerbe is true,
*who wil the curnell of the nut must
breake the shell.* 1635 : Swan, *Spec.
Mundi*, 465, For be it so that we
desire the sweetnesse of the well relisht
kernell, then must we likewise crack
the hard shell. 1729 : Coffey, *Beggar's
Wedding*, II. iii., He that wou'd obtain
a kernel, must first hazard his teeth in
breaking the shell. 1901 : F. E. Taylor,
Lancs Sayings, 9, Theaw mun crack th'
nut afore theaw con eyt th' krindle.

26. *He'll as soon eat sand as do a good
turn.* 1732 : Fuller, No. 2421.

27. *He'll eat till he sweats, and work
till he freezes.* Ibid., No. 2424.

28. *If she would eat gold he would give
it her.* 1708 : Centlivre, *Busie Body*,
III. iv., If . . eating gold, as the old
saying is, can make thee happy, thou
shalt be so. 1738 : Swift, *Polite Convers.*, Dial. II. 1845 : Jerrold, *Mrs.
Caudle*, xxi., You'd have given me
pearls and diamonds to eat, if I could
have swallowed 'em.

29. *If you eat a pudding at home, the
dog shall have the skin.* 1605 : Camden,
Remains, 325 (1870). 1732 : Fuller,
No. 2751.

30. *If you eat till you are cold, you
will live to be old, and every one will be
tired of you.* Oxfordsh. 1923 : *Folk-
Lore*, xxxiv. 328. 1925 : *N. & Q.*, cxlviii.
134 [with last eight words omitted].

31. *To eat a stake. See* quots. 1530 :
Palsgrave, 461, Haste thou eaten a
stake, I shall make the[e] bowe. 1667 :
L'Estrange, *Quevedo's Visions*, 140
(1904), He sat stiff and upright, as
if he had swallowed a stake. 1732 :
Fuller, No. 1901, He hath swallow'd
a stake; he cannot bow.

32. *To eat bullbeef.* 1583 : Melbancke,
Philotinus, sig. Y2, Thou hast eaten
bulbeefe, and braggest highlie.

33. *To eat one's heart out.* 1539 :

Taverner, *Proverbs*, fo. 54, Eate not
thy harte (that is to saye) consume
not thy selfe wyth cares. 1587 : Underdowne, *Heliodorus*, bk. i., p. 23 (T.T.),
And there lived eating (as the proverbe
saith) his owne harte out. 1633 : Draxe,
123, He eateth his owne heart. 1890 :
W. A. Wallace, *Only a Sister?*, xviii.
155 (O.), Why, there's poor Aikone
. . . eating his heart out and getting
no further.

34. *To eat one's words.* 1577 : Stanihurst, *Descrip. of Ireland*, fo. 20, Before
I eate these wordes, I will make thee
eate a piece of my blade. 1670 : Ray,
173. 1710 : E. Ward, *Nuptial Dialogues*, i. 353, I'll make you eat your
words before I've done. 1838 : Hood,
Hood's Own, 1st ser., 486 (1865), The
Marine Society must despise me for it
. . . but I cannot eat my words.

35. *To eat out of house and home.*
c. 1400 : *Towneley Plays*, xiii. 124
(E.E.T.S.), Bot were I not more gracyus
and rychere befar, I were eten outt of
howse and of harbar 1469 : *Paston
Lett.*, ii. 348 (Gairdner), For I eete
lyek an horse, of purpose to eete yow
owte at the dorys. 1509 : Barclay,
Ship of Fools, ii. 93 (1874), They wast
and ete theyr mayster out of hous
Deuourynge his good, tyll he be pore
and bare. 1600 : Day, *Blind Beggar*,
IV. i., Till we haue eat him out of house
and home in diet. 1668 : Shadwell,
Sullen Lovers, V. iii., They would eat
me out of house and home, as the
saying is. 1734 : Fielding, *Intrig.
Chambermaid*, II. vii., So generously
condescend to eat a poor citizen out of
house and home. 1909 : De Morgan,
Never can happen Again, i. 17, Who
was he, that he was to eat his sister
out of house and home?

36. *To eat sauce.* Before 1529 : Skelton, *Magnyfycence*, l. 1421, What, wyll
ye waste wynde, and prate thus in
vayne? Ye haue eten sauce, I trowe,
at the Taylers Hall. Before 1529 :
Skelton, *Bowge of Courte*, l. 72.

37. *To eat the cheese in the trap.*
1813 : Ray, 186.

38. *To eat the pudding and the bag.*
1659 : Howell, 6, You are he that did

eat the pudding and the bagg. 1732:
Fuller, No. 1826, He claws it as
Clayton claw'd the pudding, when he
eat bag and all.

39. *We must all eat a peck of dirt
before we die.* 1639: Clarke, 165, You
must eat a peck of ashes ere you die.
1670: Ray, 57, Every man must eat a
peck of ashes before he dies. 1709:
O. Dykes, *Eng. Proverbs*, 11, So that
if we must eat a peck of dirt before we
die, it must certainly go down when
we are a hungry. 1738: Swift, *Polite
Convers.*, Dial. I. 1881: Evans, *Leics.
Words*, 209 (E.D.S.), Here, as elsewhere,
" way mut all ate a peck-o'-dut afore
way doy" is very commonly current,
and almost equally common is the
rider, " but non on us wants it all at
woonst." 1922: *Observer*, 10 Dec.,
p. 11, col. 7, I suppose a little garbage
is necessary in newspapers, just as we
must all eat a peck of dirt before we die.

40. *Who eats and leaves, has another
meal good.* 1732: Fuller, No. 5700.

41. *Who eats his cock alone, must
saddle his horse alone.* 1640: Herbert,
Jac. Prudentum. 1670: Ray, 8 [with
" dinner " for " cock "]. 1732: Fuller,
No. 5701, Who eats his dinner alone,
must saddle his horse.

42. *You cannot eat your cake and
have it.* 1546: Heywood, *Proverbs*,
Pt. II. ch. ix., Wolde ye bothe eate
your cake and haue your cake? 1650:
R. Heath, *Occasional Poems*, 19, I can't
I tro Both eat my cake and have it
too. 1738: Swift, *Polite Convers.*, Dial.
I., She was handsome in her time; but
she cannot eat her cake and have her
cake. 1871: Planché, *Extravag.*, v.
307 (1879), 'Tis to point to the moral
the proverb implies, " You can't have
your cake if you eat it." 1922: *Punch*,
7 June, p. 441, col. 2, " You cannot eat
your cake and have it," says a physical
culture journal. This of course is the
distressing experience of many people
at sea.

43. *You eat above the tongue like a
calf.* 1678: Ray, 348.

44. *You eat and eat but you do not
drink to fill you.* 1670: Ray, 33.

45. *You had as good eat your nails.*

c. 1660: in *Roxb. Ballads*, ii. 130 (B.S.),
Your roaring-boy . . . Could never yet
make the smith eat his nails. 1738:
Swift, *Polite Convers.*, Dial. I., Say a
word more, and you had as good eat
your nails. 1784: *New Foundl. Hosp.
for Wit*, i. 287, Jove would not sooner
eat his nails, Than break with us, to
humour Juno. 1827: Scott, in Lockhart's *Life*, vii. 62, I shall only revenge
myself by publishing the whole extracts
. . . in which he will find enough to
make him bite his nails.

46. *You must eat another yard of
pudding first =* grow older. 1830:
Forby, *Vocab. E. Anglia*, 428. 1886:
Elworthy, *West Som. Word-Book*, 374
(E.D.S.), You must eat some more beef
and potatoes first, i.e. wait till you are
older—a very common phrase.

Eaten bread is forgotten. 1605:
Camden, *Remains*, 321 (1870), Eaten
bread is forgot. 1670: Ray, 84. 1732:
Fuller, No. 1358. 1869: Spurgeon,
John Ploughman, ch. xiv., Eaten bread
is forgotten, and the hand that gave
it is despised. 1913: E. M. Wright,
Rustic Speech, etc., 110, Etten cake's
sooin forgotten is a proverbial saying
[*cake* (Yorks)=bread].

Eating and drinking. See quots.
1611: Cotgrave, s.v. " Mangeant,"
Eating and drinking will take away
any mans stomack. 1738: Swift, *Polite
Convers.*, Dial. II., Well; this eating and
drinking takes away a body's stomach.
1785: Grose, *Class. Dict. Vulgar Tongue*,
s.v. " Damper," Eating and drinking
being, as the proverb wisely observes,
apt to take away the appetite.

Eating and scratching. See quots.
1732: Fuller, No. 5158, To eat and to
scratch, a man need but begin. 1738:
Swift, *Polite Convers.*, Dial. II., They
say, eating and scratching wants but
a beginning.

Eccles Wakes. See **Thrunk**.

Economy. See **Frugality**.

Eden, River. See quots. 1659:
Howell, 20, Let Uter Pendragon doe
what he can, Eden will run the same
way she ran. 1766: MS. Tour, quoted
in *Denham Tracts*, i. 207 (1846–59)
(F.L.S.), Let sly Pendragon do all he

can, Old Eden will run where first he
ran. 1790 : Grose, *Prov. Gloss.*, s.v.
" Westmoreland," Let Uter Pendragon
do what he can, The river Eden will
run as it ran.

Edged tools, It is ill jesting with.
c. 1568 : Wager, *Longer thou Livest*,
sig. D1, It is a prouerbe wise and
auncient, Beware how you geue any
edge toole, Unto madmen that be
insipient, Unto a yonge childe, and
unto a foole. 1579 : Gosson, *Sch. of
Abuse*, 57 (Arber), Some say that it is
not good iesting with edge toles. 1652 :
Tatham, *Scots Figgaries*, III., I say
again, 'tis dangerous meddling with
edge-tools. 1728 : Fielding, *Love in
several Masques*, IV. vii., Sir Apish,
jesting with matrimony is playing with
edged tools. 1839 : Planché, *Extravag.*,
ii. 58 (1879), To play with edge tools
is held unwise.

**Education begins a gentleman, con-
versation completes him.** 1732 : Fuller,
No. 1359.

Eel and Eels. 1. *See* quot. 1879 :
G. F. Jackson, *Shropsh. Word-Book*, 16,
" Eels are in season when oats are in
aw [ear]." Proverbial saying heard
about Aston Botterell.

2. *He is as much out of his element as
an eel in a sand-bag.* 1732 : Fuller,
No. 1912.

3. *He that will catch eels must disturb
the flood.* 1607 : *Lingua*, I. i.

4. *To have an eel by the tail.* 1546 :
Heywood, *Proverbs*, Pt. I. ch. x., Her
promise of freendship for any auayle,
Is as sure to holde as an ele by the
tayle. 1616 : B. & F., *Scornful Lady*,
II. i., I will end with the wise man, and
say, " He that hath a woman has an
eel by the tail." 1640 : Shirley, *Arcadia*,
V. i., But I see a woman and a wet
eel have both slippery tails. 1696 : T.
Dilke, *Lover's Luck*, V. i., He that has
holt on a young woman has got a
slippery eel by the tail. 1754 : Berthelson, *Eng.-Danish Dict.*, s.v. " Eel,"
There is as much hold of his words as
a wet eel by the tail.

5. *You cannot hide an eel in a sack.*
1640 : Herbert, *Jac. Prudentum.* 1670 :
Ray, 8. 1732 : Fuller, No. 5875.

See also Breed ; Mud ; Nimble ; Slippery ; and Wriggle.

**Effect speaks, the tongue needs not,
The.** 1640 : Herbert, *Jac. Prudentum.*

Egg and Eggs. 1. *All your eggs have
two yolks apiece, I warrant you.* 1732 :
Fuller, No. 573.

2. *An egg and to bed.* 1639 : Clarke,
113. 1670 : Ray, 36. 1732 : Fuller,
No. 594.

3. *An egg of an hour, etc. See* quots.
1623 : Wodroephe, *Spared Houres*, 253–
4, An eg of one houre old, bread of
one day, a goat of one moneth, wine
of six moneths, flesh of a yeare, fish of
ten yeares, a wife of twentie yeares, a
friend among a hundred, are the best
of all number. 1666 : Torriano, *Piazza
Univ.*, 181, An egg of an hour's
laying, bread of a daies, flesh of one
year's growth, fish of ten, a woman of
fifteen, and a friend of a hundred years
standing.

4. *An egg will be in three bellies in
twenty-four hours.* 1678 : Ray, 131.
1732 : Fuller, No. 1361, Eggs will be, etc.

5. *As full as an egg is of meat.*
c. 1565 : Still, *Gammer Gurton*, V. ii.,
An egge is not so ful of meate, as she
is ful of lyes. 1592 : Shakespeare,
Romeo, III. i. 1641 : Cowley, *Guardian*,
I. i., The Colonel's as full of waggery as
an egge's full of meat. 1696 : Vanbrugh, *Relapse*, III. 1758-67 : Sterne,
Trist. Shandy, vol. vii. ch. xxxvii.,
My remarks through France, which
were as full of wit as an egg is full of
meat. 1854 : Doran, *Table Traits*, 190,
An egg is proverbially " full of meat."

6. *As sure as eggs are eggs.* In
N. & Q., 3rd ser., vi. 203, A. de
Morgan suggested that "as sure as
eggs is eggs "=" corruption of the
logician's announcement of identity,
' X is X.' " 1680 : Otway, *Caius
Marius*, IV. ii., 'Twas to seek for lord
Marius, as sure as eggs be eggs. 1720 :
Vade Mecum for Malt-worms, Pt. II.,
p. 48, Certainly, as eggs are eggs. 1772 :
Graves, *Spirit. Quixote*, bk. vii. ch. xi.,
If she lives to Lammas-day next she
will be but fourteen years old, as sure
as eggs is eggs. 1837 : Dickens, *Pick-
wick*, ch. xliii., And the Bishop says,

" Sure as eggs is eggs, This here's the bold Turpin ! " 1857 : Hughes, *Tom Brown*, Pt. II. ch. vi.

7. *But one egg and that addled too.* 1732 : Fuller, No. 1031.

8. *From the eggs to the apples.* [Ab ovo Usque ad mala citaret, Io Bacche ! —Horace, *Sat.*, I. iii. 6.] 1639 : Clarke, 3, From th' egges to th' apples. 1655 : T. Muffett, *Health's Improvement*, 295, The most nourishing meat is first to be eaten that ancient proverb ratifieth *Ab ovo ad mala*; from the eg to the apples. 1736 : Bailey, *Dict.*, s.v. "End," From the beginning to the end . . . from the egg to the apples.

9. *He has brought his eggs to a fine market.* 1883 : Burne, *Shropsh. Folk-Lore*, 589, He has brought his eggs to a nice (or fine, or pretty) market; said in irony of a spendthrift or bankrupt trader.

10. *He'll dress an egg and give the offal to the poor.* 1678 : Ray, 90.

11. *He'll never be good egg nor bird.* 1630 : T. Adams, *Works*, 178, Sinne of it selfe is good neither egge nor bird. 1670 : Ray, 173, Neither good egg nor bird. 1784 : O'Keeffe, *Fontainebleau*, III. iv., She was never good, egg, or bird. 1868 : Atkinson, *Cleveland Gloss.*, 151, He'll never dow [thrive], egg nor bird.

12. *To come in with five* (or *two*) *eggs.* 1542 : Udall, tr. Erasmus' *Apoph.*, 303 (1877), To certain persones comyng in with their fiue egges, how that Sylla ·had geuen ouer his office of Dictature, as he shuld do . . . he aunswered that Sylla was not bokishe, nor halfe a good clerke, and therefore gaue vp his Dictature. [In the Appendix to this edition, R. Roberts, editor and publisher, says : " This was rather a common proverb in the sixteenth century, and has never been explained, but it evidently means a silly rumour, equivalent to ' mare's nest.' ' Will you take eggs for money? ' (*see* 15 below) belongs to the same family."] 1551 : R. Robinson, tr. More's *Utopia*, 56 (Arber). 1639 : Clarke, 19, He comes in with his five egges and foure be rotten. 1683 : Meriton, *Yorkshire Ale*, 83–7

(3rd ed., 1697), You come with your five eggs a penny and four of them be rotten. 1711 : Swift, *Journal to Stella*, Lett. 34, The Whigs are still crying down our peace, but we will have it, I hope, in spite of them : the Emperor comes now with his two eggs a penny, and promises wonders to continue the war ; but it is too late. 1738 : Swift, *Polite Convers.*, Dial. I., What ! and you must come in with your two eggs a penny, and three of them rotten. 1869 : Spurgeon, *John Ploughman*, ch. xvi., When there's five eggs a penny, four of them are rotten.

13. *To have both the egg and the hen.* 1578 : Florio, *First Fruites*, fo. 33, There be many that wyl haue both the egge and the hen. 1629 : *Book of Meery Riddles*, Prov. 118, In the world there be men That will have the egge and the henne.

14. *To have eggs on the spit.* 1596 : Jonson, *Ev. Man in Humour*, III. vi., I have eggs on the spit ; I cannot go yet. 1614 : Jonson, *Bart. Fair*, I., I have both eggs on the spit, and iron in the fire. 1670 : Cotton, *Scarronides*, bk. iv., Half-frighted out on's little wit, He now has eggs (i' faith) o' th' spit. 1713 : Swift, *Journal to Stella*, 23 April, I write short journals now. I have eggs on the spit. 1827 : Scott, *Journal*, 18 May, I have other eggs on the spit.

15. *To take eggs for money.* 1610 : Shakespeare, *Wint. Tale*, I. ii., *Leon.* . . . Mine honest friend, Will you take eggs for money? *Mam.* No, my lord, I'll fight. 1666 : Pepys, *Diary*, 27 June, By the next fight, if we beat, the Dutch will certainly be content to take eggs for their money (that was his [Sir W. Coventry's] expression). 1720 : *New Dict. Canting Crew*, He will be glad to take eggs for his money, i.e. compound the matter with loss. 1847 : Halliwell, *Dict.*, s.v., A proverbial expression, used when a person was awed by threats, or had been overreached into giving money for comparatively worthless things.

16. *Too many eggs in one basket.* 1710 : S. Palmer, *Moral Essays on Pro-*

verbs, 344, Don't venture all your eggs in one basket. 1763 : Murphy, *Citizen*, I. ii., George, too many eggs in one basket.

17. *Won with the egg and lost with the shell*. 1575 : Gascoigne, *Posies*, in *Works*, i. 450 (Cunliffe), Nor woman true, but even as stories tell, Wonne with an egge, and lost againe with shell. 1633 : Draxe, 75.

See also Addled egg ; Apple (6) ; Better an egg ; Christmas (5) and (13) ; Dear (2) ; Drink, *verb* (2) ; Easter (2) and (8) ; Fool (93) ; Half an egg ; Hard (19) ; Hen (1), (8), (10), and (14) ; Like as one egg ; Omelets ; and Reason (7).

Elbow itches, I must change my bed-fellow, My. 1659 : Howell, 12.

Elbow-grease gives the best polish. 1672 : Marvell, *Rehearsal Transpr.*, i. 5 (O.), Two or three brawny fellows in a corner with meer ink and elbow-grease, do more harm than . . . 1690 : *New Dict. Canting Crew*, sig. E1, It will cost nothing but a little elbow-grease. 1830 : Forby, *Vocab. E. Anglia*, 431, Elbow grease gives the best polish. 1872 : J. Glyde, jr., *Norfolk Garland*, 149.

Elbow-grease, It smells of. 1639 : Clarke, 92. 1670 : Ray, 173.

Elden Hole wants filling. Derby. 1670 : Ray, 173 [with " needs " for " wants "]. 1790 : Grose, *Prov. Gloss.*, s.v. " Derbyshire." 1889 : *Folk-Lore Journal*, vii. 292 [Derby sayings], Eldon Hole wants filling up.

Elder. *When elder is white brew and bake a peck, When elder is black brew and bake a sack.* 1678 : Ray, 352 [Somerset]. 1732 : Fuller, No. 6478. 1904 : *Co. Folk-Lore: Northumb.*, 177 (F.L.S.). *See also* Sheep (20).

Eldern stake. *See* quot. 1842 : Akerman, *Wilts Gloss.*, 19, They have a rhyme in Wiltshire on the formation of a " stake and ether hedge "—" An eldern stake and black-thorn ether [hedge] Will make a hedge to last for ever." 1875 : Parish, *Sussex Dict.*

Elm. 1928 : *Times*, 29 Nov., p. 10, col. 5, " Every elm has its man " is an old country saying. *See also* Good elm.

Elm-leaves. *See* quots. 1856 : *N. & Q.*, 2nd ser., i. 429, Here is

another Worcestershire saying . . . When elm leaves are as big as a shilling, Plant kidney-beans, if to plant 'em you're willing. When elm leaves are as big as a penny, You *must* plant kidney-beans, if you mean to have any. 1866 : *Field*, 28 April, When the elmen leaf is as big as a mouse's ear, Then to sow barley never fear. When the elmen leaf is as big as an ox's eye, Then says I, " Hie, boys ! hie ! " 1881 : C. W. Empson, in *Folk-Lore Record*, iv. 131 [as in 1856 and 1866]. 1893 : Inwards, *Weather Lore*, 152 [as in 1856].

Elm-tree for pears, You ask an. 1732 : Fuller, No. 5862.

Elstow Fair, 3 May, O.S., now 15. *See* quot. 1831 : Hone, *Year-Book*, 1595, It is a common saying in many parts of Bedfordshire, when flies first begin to be troublesome on meat, fish, etc., that " the flies have been to Elstow Fair to buy their bellows."

Embrace too much. *See* Grasp.

Empty, *adj.* 1. *An empty belly hears no body.* 1732 : Fuller, No. 596. 1880 : Spurgeon, *Ploughman's Pictures*, 52, An empty belly makes no compliments.

2. *An empty belly makes a lazy back.* 1846–59 : *Denham Tracts*, i. 42 (F.L.S.), There is much truth contained in the good old northern proverb—A tume [empty] belly makes a lazy back.

3. *An empty purse and a new house make a man wise, but too late.* 1813 : Ray, 20.

4. *An empty purse causes a full heart.* 1734 : Fielding, *Don Quix. in England*, I. vi.

5. *An empty purse fills the face with wrinkles.* 1633 : Draxe, 161. 1670 : Ray, 22. 1736 : Bailey, *Dict.*, s.v. " Purse."

6. *An empty purse frights away friends.* 1732 : Fuller, No. 597.

7. *An empty purse is the devil.* 1882 : *N. & Q.*, 6th ser., vi. 17.

8. *Better an empty house than an ill tenant.* 1732 : Fuller, No. 870.

9. *Empty bags cannot stand upright.* 1666 : Torriano, *Piazza Univ.*, 245, An empty sack cannot stand upright. 1736 : Franklin, *Way to Wealth*, in *Works*, i. 449 (Bigelow), It is hard for

an empty bag to stand upright. 1849:
Lytton, *Caxtons*, Pt. VIII. ch. iii., You
have found it more difficult, I fear,
than you imagined, to make the empty
sack stand upright. Considering that
at least one-third of those born to work
cannot find it, why should I? 1880:
Platt, *Money*, 199, As empty bags
cannot stand upright.

10. *Empty barns need no thatch.*
Suffolk. 1924: *Folk-Lore*, xxxv. 358.

11. *Empty chambers make foolish maids.*
1611 : Cotgrave, s.v. "Chambre," Empty
chambers make women play the wan-
tons. 1640: Herbert, *Jac. Prudentum.*

12. *Empty hands. See* **Hawk** (11).

13. *Empty vessels make the most sound.*
1579: Lyly, *Euphues*, 45 (Arber), The
emptie vessell giueth a greater sound
then the full barrell. 1612: *Cornucopiæ*, 90 (Grosart), An emptie vessell
giues a mighty sound. 1754: Berthelson, *Eng.-Danish Dict.*, s.v. "Empty,"
Empty vessels make the greatest noise.
1913 : E. M. Wright, *Rustic Speech, etc.*,
171, Empty barrels make the most
noise.

14. *That is but an empty purse that is
full of other men's money.* 1678 : Ray,
194. 1732 : Fuller, No. 4352 [with
"folks" for "men's"].

15. *The empty leech sucks sore.* 1672 :
Walker, *Parœm.*, 36. 1681 : W. Robertson, *Phraseol. Generalis*, 528.

End, *subs.* 1. *In the end things will
mend.* 1659: Howell, 9. 1670: Ray,
8. 1736 : Bailey, *Dict.*, s.v. "End."

2. *Next the ende of sorowe, anon
entreth joy.* c. 1387: Usk, *Test. of
Love*, in Skeat's *Chaucer*, vii. 82.

3. *The end crowns all* (or *the work*).
c. 1390: Gower, *Conf. Amantis*, bk. vi.
l. 2383, An ende proveth euery thing.
1478: Rivers, tr. C. de Pisa's *Moral
Proverbs*, Thende dooth shewe euery
werk as hit is. 1578: Florio, *First
Fruites*, fo. 29, The end maketh al.
1592: Shakespeare, 2 *Henry VI.*, V. ii.,
O. Clif. La fin couronne les œuvres.
1658: R. Brome, *Weeding of Covent
Garden*, III. i., Was ever good patriot
so rudely handled? but the end crowns
all. 1820: Scott, *Abbot*, ch. xiii., But
as the end crowns the work . . .

1870 : Dickens, *Drood*, ch. xviii., Proof
must be built up stone by stone . . .
As I say, the end crowns the work.

4. *The end makes all equal.* 1578 :
Florio, *First Fruites*, fo. 31, The end
maketh al men equal. 1605 : Camden,
Remains, 332 (1870). 1732 : Fuller,
No. 4496.

5. *The end of our good begins our evil.*
1611 : Davies (of Hereford), *Sc. of
Folly*, 50, in *Works*, ii. (Grosart).
1633 : Draxe, 117, The end of his good
is the beginning of his woe.

6. *The end trieth all.* 1639 : Clarke,
117. 1669 : *Politeuphuia*, 183.

Endure, *verb.* 1. *He that endures is
not overcome.* 1640 : Herbert, *Jac.
Prudentum.* 1670 : Ray, 8.

2. *He that can quietly endure overcometh. c.* 1393 : Langland, *Plowman*,
C, xvi. 138, Quoth Peers the Plouhman
"*pacientes uincunt.*" 1629 : *Book of
Meery Riddles*, Prov. 28.

3. *He that will not endure labour in
this world, let him not be born.* 1578 :
Florio, *First Fruites*, fo. 28, Who wil
not suffer labor in this world, let him
not be borne. 1629 : *Book of Meery
Riddles*, Prov. 7.

Enemy and **Enemies.** 1. *An enemy
may chance to give good counsel.* 1732 :
Fuller, No. 600.

2. *An enemy's mouth seldom says well.*
1481 : Caxton, *Reynard*, I. iiii., p. 7
(Arber), Sir Isegrym that is euyl sayd
it is a comyn prouerbe An enemyes
mouth saith seeld wel.

3. *He is no one's enemy but his own.*
1600 : Cornwallis, *Essayes*, sig. E7
(1610), It smarts not halfe so ill as the
phrase, *Euery bodies friend but his owne.*
1664 : in *Musarum Deliciæ, etc.*, ii. 237
(Hotten, 1874), How ere he fail'd in's
life, 'tis like Jack Friend, Was no man's
foe but's own, and there's an end.
1749: Fielding, *Tom Jones*, bk. iv.
ch. v., Tom, though an idle, thoughtless, rattling rascal, was nobody's
enemy but his own. 1850: Dickens,
Copperfield, ch. xxv., He is quite a
good fellow—nobody's enemy but his
own.

4. *He that has no enemies has no
friends.* 1725 : Bailey, tr. Erasmus'

Colloq., 131, There is this old saying: He that has no enemies has no friends.

5. *Take heed of reconciled enemies.* c. 1600 : in *Roxb. Ballads*, i. 432 (B.S.), Trust not a reconciled friend more than an open foe. 1618 : Harington, *Epigrams*, bk. i. No. 87, Dicke said, beware a reconciled foe. 1656 : F. Osborne, *Advice to Son*, 89 (Parry), A reconciled enemy is not safely to be trusted. 1670 : Ray, 22, Take heed of enemies reconcil'd, and of meat twice boil'd.

England. 1. *A famine in England begins at the horse-manger.* 1605 : Camden, *Remains*, 329 (1870), No dearth but breeds in the horse-manger. 1662 : Fuller, *Worthies*, i. 117 (1840). 1790 : Grose, *Prov. Gloss.*, s.v. "England." 1893 : Inwards, *Weather Lore*, 7.

2. *England is a little garden full of very sour weeds.* 1790 : Grose, *Prov. Gloss.*, s.v. "England," This is said to have been an observation frequently in the mouth of Louis XIV. during the victorious Duke of Marlborough's campaigns.

3. *England is a ringing island.* 1655 : Fuller, *Church Hist.*, bk. vi. § ii. (iii.), This, in England, (commonly called the "ringing-island") was done with tolling a bell. 1790 : Grose, *Prov. Gloss.*, s.v. "England." 1827 : Hone, *Ev. Day Book*, ii. 509, England is proverbially called "the ringing island."

4. *England is the paradise of women, hell of horses, and purgatory of servants* —with variant. 1591 : Florio, *Second Frutes*, 205, England is the paradise of women, the purgatory of men, and the hell of horses. c. 1593 : Deloney, in *Works*, 377 (Mann, 1912), The wife of euery Englishman is counted blest. 1619 : *New Help to Discourse*, 51, England is termed by foreigners the paradise of women, as it is by some accounted the hell of horses, and purgatory of servants. 1642 : Howell, *Forreine Travel*, 69 (Arber), Which makes them call England the hell of horses. 1790 : Grose, *Prov. Gloss.*, s.v. "England."

5. *England were but a fling, Save for the crooked stick and the gray-goose wing.* 1662 : Fuller, *Worthies*, i. 116

(1840). 1790 : Grose, *Prov. Gloss.*, s.v. "England."

6. *He that England will win must with Ireland begin.* 1567 : Diego Ortiz, quoted in Froude, *Hist. of Eng.*, x. 480, There is an English proverb in use among them which says—He who would England win, In Ireland must begin. 1592 : Warner, *Alb. Eng.*, ch. liv. st. 4, It is a saying auncient (not Autenticall, I win) That who-so England will subdew, With Ireland must begin. 1617 : Fynes Moryson, *Itin.*, Pt. II., p. 3. 1658 : Howell, *Lexicon Tetraglotton*, App., p. 2, Get Ireland to-day and England may be thine to-morrow. 1790 : Grose, *Prov. Gloss.*, s.v. "England." 1868, *N. & Q.*, 4th ser., i. 437, A speaker on the Irish Church question lately quoted as an old proverb :—"He that would England win, Must with Ireland first begin."

Here is a variant 1918 : *N. & Q.*, 12th ser., iv. 78, A correspondent, writing to the *Times* under the heading "Perils of the Coast" on January 3, quoted as an East Anglian proverb of immemorial antiquity :—He who would Old England win Must at Weybourne Hoop begin.

7. *Long beards heartless, painted hoods witless, Gay coats graceless, make England thriftless.* 1662 : Fuller, *Worthies*, i. 119 (1840). 1790 : Grose, *Prov. Gloss.*, s.v. "England," A saying said to have been made by the Scotch in the reign of Edward II., when elated with their victory at Stirling.

8. *There is more good victuals in England than in seven other kingdoms.* 1639 : Clarke, 74.

9. *When all England is aloft, etc.* See quots. 1636 : R. James, *Iter Lancast.* (Chetham S.), When all England is aloft, Then happy they whose dwellings in God's Crofte ; And where thinke you this crofte of Christ should be, But midst Ribchester's Ribble and the Dee. 1669 : *New Help to Discourse*, 114, When as wars are aloft Safe is he that's at Christs croft; And where should this Christs croft be, But betwixt Rible and Mersie.

10. *When hemp is spun England is done.*

1625: Bacon, *Essays:* "Prophecies," The triuiall prophecie, which I heard, when I was a childe, and Queene Elizabeth was in the flower of her yeares, was; *When hempe is sponne; England's done.* 1662, Fuller, *Worthies,* i. 114 (1840). 1790: Grose, *Prov. Gloss.,* s.v. "England." 1812: Brady, *Clavis Cal.,* ii. 31.

11. *When the black fleet of Norway,* etc. See quots. These sayings are very obscure. I cannot suggest an interpretation. *c.* 1500: in *Thos. of Erceldoune,* App., ii. 59 (E.E.T.S.), Then the blake flett of Norwaye is commyn and gone, And drenchid in the flode truly; Mekelle ware hath bene beforne, but after shall none be. [Also] Ibid., 61, Thomas of Asheldon sayeth the egle of the trewe brute shall see all inglond in peas and rest both spirituall and temporall; and euery estate of in thaire degre and the maydens of englonde bylde your howses of lyme and stone. 1625: Bacon, *Essays:* "Prophecies," There was also another prophecie, before the year of 88, which I doe not well vnderstand. *There shall be seene upon a day, Betweene the Baugh, and the May, The Blacke Fleet of Norway. When that that is come and gone, England build Houses of Lime and Stone For after Warres shall you haue None.* 1662: Fuller, *Worthies,* i. 115 (1840), When the black fleet of Norway is come and gone, England build houses of lime and stone, For after wars you shall have none. 1790: Grose, *Prov. Gloss.,* s.v. "England" [as in 1662].

12. *When the sand feeds the clay* [wet summer], *England cries well-a-day; But when the clay feeds the sand* [dry summer] *it is merry with England.* 1662: Fuller, *Worthies,* i. 116 (1840). 1790: Grose, *Prov. Gloss.,* s.v. "England." 1893: Inwards, *Weather Lore,* 7.

See also Drought; Hallamshire; Hops; King (14); Lady-day; Mouth (7); Oxford (5); and Sheffield Park.

English are the Frenchmen's apes, The. 1605: Sylvester, *Du Bartas,* Week I. Day ii. l. 231, Much like the French (or like our selves, their apes). 1662: Fuller, *Worthies,* i. 118

1840). 1790: Grose, *Prov. Gloss.,* s.v. "England." 1826: Brady, *Varieties of Lit.,* 43.

English glutton, The. *c.* 1540: in *Reliq. Antiquæ,* i. 326 (1841), He sayd that Englysshemen ar callyd the grettyste fedours in the worlde. 1662: Fuller, *Worthies,* i. 118 (1840). 1790: Grose, *Prov. Antiq.,* s.v. "England."

English poke-pudding, The. Ibid., s.v. "England."

Englishman. 1. *A right Englishman.* See quots. 1639: Clarke, 78, A right Englishman. 1659: Howell, 10 (8), You are a right Englishman, you cannot tell when you are well. 1670: Ray, 85, A right Englishman knows not when a thing is well.

2. *An Englishman Italianate is a devil incarnate.* 1586: J. Overton, *Jacobs Troublesome Journey,* 8, As manie of our countrimen haue doone from the other side of the sea . . . and are therefore become a by-word vnto the worlde to bee called Deuils incarnate. 1630: T. Adams, *Works,* 12. 1645: Howell, *Letters,* bk. i. § iii. No. ii., There is an ill-favour'd saying, That . . . an Englishman Italianate is a devil incarnate. 1823: D'Israeli, *Cur. of Lit.,* 2nd ser., i. 468 (1824).

3. *In settling an island.* See quot. 1790: Grose, *Prov. Gloss.,* s.v. "England," In settling an island, the first building erected by a Spaniard will be a church; by a Frenchman, a fort; by a Dutchman, a warehouse; and by an Englishman, an alehouse.

4. *The Englishman greets.* See quot. 1846–59: *Denham Tracts,* i. 302 (F.L.S.), The prosperity of our northern neighbours is further celebrated in proverb lore by the following:—the Englishman greets, the Irishman sleeps, but the Scotchman gangs till he gets it.

See also Scottish mist.

Enjoy. *If you would enjoy the fruit, pluck not the flower.* 1855: Bohn, 422.

Enough and no more, like Mrs. Milton's feast. 1917: Bridge, *Cheshire Proverbs,* 54.

Enough is as good as a feast. [ἐπεὶ τά γ' ἀρκοῦνθ' ἱκανὰ τοῖσι σώφροσιν. — Euripides, *Phœn.,* 554.] *c.* 1420: Lydgate,

Assembly of Gods, 59 (E.E.T.S.), As good ys ynowgh as a gret feste. 1546 : Heywood, *Proverbs*, Pt. II. ch. xi. 1590 : Greene, *Franc. Fortune*, in *Works*, viii. 168 (Grosart), Die not indebted to thy bellie, but enough is a feast. 1605 : Chapman, etc., *Eastw. Hoe*, III. ii. 1696 : Vanbrugh, *Relapse*, V., O, enough's as good as a feast. 1732 : Fielding, *Cov. Garden Tragedy*, II. vi., A little dish oft furnishes enough : And sure enough is equal to a feast. 1826 : Lamb, *Pop. Fallacies*, vi. 1855 : Kingsley, *West. Ho!*, ch. xxv. 1922 : Weyman, *Ovington's Bank*, ch. xix.

Enough is enough. 1546 : Heywood, *Proverbs*, Pt. II. ch. xi. 1834–7 : Southey, *Doctor*, ch. xx. p.i., As for money, enough is enough ; no man can enjoy more. 1924 : Shaw, *Saint Joan*, sc. vi.

Enough one day. *See* quots. 1639 : Clarke, 38, Ilee'l have enough one day, when his mouth is full of moulds. 1670 : Ray, 173 [as in 1639]. 1732 : Fuller, No. 2428, He'll ne'er have enough, till his mouth is full of mould. 1903 : Wright, *Eng. Dial. Dict.*, s.v. "Mould," Thou'l niver be satisfied til thoo gets thi mooth ful a moud. Yorksh.

Enough who is contented with a little, He hath. 1666 : Torriano, *Piazza Univ.*, 52.

Envious heart fretteth itself, An. *c.* 1460 : *How the Good Wyfe*, l. 109, Enuyos hert hym-selue fretys. 1597 : *North. Mothers Blessing*, in *Plasidas, etc.*, 167 (Roxb. Cl.), For an enuious hert Procures mickle smert.

Envious man is a squint-eyed fool, An. 1732 : Fuller, No. 601.

Envious man shall never want woe, The. 1605 : Camden, *Remains*, 333 (1870).

Envious man waxes lean with the fatness of his neighbour, An. 1855 : Bohn, 311.

Envy never dies. 1523–5 : Berners, *Froissart*, ch. 428, There is a comune proverbe, the whiche is true, and that is, howe envy never dyeth.

Envy never enriched any man. 1633 : Draxe, 52, A man shall never bee enriched by enuie. 1670 : Ray, 8.

1732 : Fuller, No. 1380 [with "yet" after "never"].

Envy, Nothing sharpens sight like. Ibid., No. 3674.

Envy shoots at others and wounds herself. *c.* 1590 : G. Harvey, *Marginalia*, 103 (1913), Enuy shootith at other ; but hittith and woundith herself. 1669 : *Politeuphuia*, 25. 1732 : Fuller, No. 1381.

Epsom. *See* Sutton.

Erith. *See* quot. 1588 : A. Fraunce, *Lawiers Logike*, fo. 27, The mayre of Earith is the best mayre next to the mayre of London.

Error is always in haste. 1732 : Fuller, No. 1382.

Errs and mends. *See* quots. 1620 : Shelton, *Quixote*, Pt. II. ch. xxviii., Who errs and mends, to God himself commends. 1732 : Fuller, No. 2037, He that after sinning mends, recommends himself to God.

Escape a scouring, To. 1588 : *Mar-Prelate's Epitome*, 31 (1843), His grace shall on [one] day answer me this point or very narrowly escape me a scouringe. 1639 : Clarke, 80, He scap'd a scouring. 1753 : Richardson, *Grandison*, i. 318 (1883), 'Fore God, Sir Hargrave, somebody has escaped a scouring, as the saying is.

Escape the rocks and perish in the sands, To. 1732 : Fuller, No. 5169.

Escape the thunder and fall into the lightning, To. 1651 : Herbert, *Jac. Prudentum*, 2nd ed.

Eschewing. *See* Avoidance.

Essex calves. 1573 : G. Harvey, *Letter-Book*, 135 (Camden S.), Foes mustbe frende, quoth an Essex kalfe. 1599 : Buttes, *Dyets Dry Dinner*, sig. I1, Essex calfes the prouerb praiseth. 1605 : Chapman, etc., *Eastw. Hoe*, II. iv., These women, sir, are like Essex calves. 1677 : A. Behn, *Rover*, Pt. I. II. i., Tho' this Essex calf believe them persons of quality. 1704 : T. Baker, *An Act at Oxford*, V., Thou art an Essex calf. 1869 : Hazlitt, 216, If a man beats a bush in Essex, out jumps a calf.

Essex lions = Calves. 1630 : Taylor (Water-Poet), *Wit and Mirth*, 79, Essex calves, called lions. 1672 : *Poor Robin*

Alman., March, Essex lyons there might
live, Which some name of calves do
give. 1785 : Grose, *Class. Dict. Vulgar
Tongue*, s.v., Essex Lion, a calf, Essex
being famous for calves.

Essex man. Proverbial for a simpleton. Cf. **Essex calves**, (1573, 1677,
and 1704). 1663 : Killigrew, *Parson's
Wedding*, III. v., *Jolly*. Have you no
friends in the close committee? *Capt.*
Yes, yes, I am an Essex man.

Essex miles. 1662 : Fuller, *Worthies*,
i. 497 (1840).

Essex stiles [ditches], **Kentish miles,
Norfolk wiles, many men beguiles—**
with variants. 15th cent. : in *Reliq.
Antiquæ*, i. 269 (1841), Suffolk, full of
wiles ; Norffolk, full of giles. 1580 : Tusser, *Husbandrie* 209 (E.D.S.), For Norfolk wiles, so full of giles, Haue caught
my toe. 1605 : Camden, *Remains*, 321
(1870), Essex stiles, Kentish miles,
Norfolk wiles, many men beguiles.
1622 : Drayton, *Polyol.*, xxiii., As Essex
hath of old been named, Calves and
Stiles . . . Norfolk many wiles. 1735 :
Pegge, *Kent. Proverbs*, in E.D.S., No. 12,
p. 66 [as in 1605]. 1790 : Grose, *Prov.
Gloss.*, s.v. " Essex " [as in 1605].

**Estate in two parishes is bread in two
wallets.** 1640 : Herbert, *Jac. Prudentum.*

Este bueth owne brondes = Pleasant
is one's own fireside. *c.* 1320 : in *Reliq.
Antiquæ*, i. 111 (1841).

Even reckoning makes long friends.
1546 : Heywood, *Proverbs*, Pt. II. ch. iv.,
Euen recknyng maketh longe freendis.
1658 : *Wit Restor'd*, 151. 1732 : Fuller,
No. 1399, Even reckonings keep long
friends. 1754 : Berthelson, *Eng.-Danish
Dict.*, s.v. " Even."

Evening. 1. *A joyful evening may
follow a sorrowful morning.* 1732 :
Fuller, No. 230.

2. *Evening grey and morning red.
See* quots. 1830 : Forby, *Vocab. E.
Anglia*, 416, Evening gray, and morning
red, Send the poor shepherd home wet
to his bed. 1846 : Denham, *Proverbs*,
9 (Percy S.), But if the evening's grey,
and the morning red, Put on your hat
or you'll wet your head. 1893 : Inwards, *Weather Lore*, 53, An evening

grey and a morning red Will send the
shepherd wet to bed; [or] Evening grey
and morning red Make the shepherd
hang his head.

3. *Evening oats are good morning
fodder.* 1639 : Clarke, 114 [with " orts "
for " oats "]. 1670 : Ray, 86 [as in
1639]. 1732 : Fuller, No. 1401. 1846 :
Denham, *Proverbs*, 3 (Percy S.).

4. *Evening red and morning grey. See*
quots. 1586 : L. Evans, *Withals Dict.
Revised*, sig. N7, The euening red, the
morning gray, Foreshewes a cleare and
summers day. 1611 : Cotgrave, s.v.
" Matin," The evening red and morning
gray presage a faire succeeding day.
1772 : Mills, *Essay on Weather*, 34
(1773), The evening red, and the morning grey, is a sign of a fair day. 1830 :
Forby, *Vocab. E. Anglia*, 416, Evening
red and morning gray Are sure signs of
a fair day. 1846 : Denham, *Proverbs*,
8 (Percy S.), An evening red and
morning grey, Will set the traveller on
his way. 1893 : Inwards, *Weather Lore*,
53. . . . Two sure signs of one fine day.

5. *Evening words are not like to morning.* 1611 : Cotgrave, s.v. " Parole,"
The evening chat is not like the
mornings tattle. 1640 : Herbert, *Jac.
Prudentum.*

6. *The evening crowns the day.* 1605 :
Chapman, *All Fools*, II., Well, th' evening crowns the day. 1633 : Ford, *'Tis
Pity, etc.*, II. vi. *ad fin.*, Welcome sweet
night ! the evening crowns the day.
1692 : L'Estrange, *Æsop*, 264 (3rd ed.).
1754 : Berthelson, *Eng.-Danish Dict.*,
s.v. " Evening."

7. *The evening praises the day.* 1616 :
Breton, *Cross. of Proverbs*, 5 (Grosart).
1640 : Herbert, *Jac. Prudentum*, [with
addition] and the morning a frost.

Evenwood, Co. Durham. *See* quots.
1846–59 : *Denham Tracts*, i. 84 (F.L.S.),
Evenwood, Where never straight tree
stood; [or] You've been at Evenwood,
where never A straight tree grew; [or]
You've been to Evenwood, Where
straight tree never stood.

Ever drunk ever dry. 1562 : Pilking-
ton, *Works*, 51 (P.S.) (O.), " A drunken
man is always dry," according to the
proverb. 1605 : Camden, *Remains*, 321

(1870). 1681 : W. Robertson, *Phraseol.
Generalis*, 508. 1754 : Berthelson, *Eng.-
Danish Dict.*, s.v. " Drunk."

Ever lack evil name. *c.* 1460 : *How
the Good Wife*, l. 45.

Ever out cometh evil spun web.
c. 1320 : in *Reliq. Antiquæ*, i. 115 (1841),
" Ever out cometh evel spoune web " ;
Quoth Hendyng.

Ever spare and ever bare. 1546 :
Heywood, *Proverbs*, Pt. II. ch. v.
1670 : Ray, 144. 1732 : Fuller, No. 6168.

Ever the higher. *See* quot. 15th
cent. : in *Reliq. Antiquæ*, i. 92 (1841),
Ever the hiere that thou art, Ever the
lower be thy hert.

**Every art, In, it is good to have a
master.** 1640 : Herbert, *Jac. Prudentum.*

Every ass. *See* **Ass** (13) and (14).

Every bean. *See* **Bean** (3).

Every beginning is difficult. 1537 :
R. Whitford, *Werke for Housholders*,
sig. A8, Euery begynnynge is harde
and of greate diffyculte. 1666 : Torriano, *Piazza Univ.*, 219.

Every bird is known by its feathers.
1616 : Breton, in *Works*, ii. e 5 (Grosart).
1732 : Fuller, No. 1407.

Every bird likes its own nest. 1611 :
Cotgrave, s.v. " Nid." 1640 : Herbert,
Jac. Prudentum, The bird loves her nest.
1732 : Fuller, No. 1408. Every bird likes
its own nest best. 1846 : T. Wright,
Essays on Middle Ages, i. 146, We say
" every bird likes its own nest," a
saying which runs thus in the old
French :—" A chescun oysel Son nye li
semble bel."

Every bird must hatch its own eggs.
1616 : Breton, in *Works*, ii. e 6 (Grosart).
1683 : Meriton, *Yorkshire Ale*, 83–7
(1697). 1732 : Fuller, No. 1409.

Every body loves his own likeness.
1730 : T. Saldkeld, tr. Gracian's *Compl.
Gentleman*, 79.

**Everybody's business is nobody's
business.** 1611 : Cotgrave, s.v. " Ouvrage," Every bodies work is no bodies
work. 1653 : Walton, *Compl. Angler*,
Pt. I. c. ii., I remember that a wise
friend of mine did usually say, " That
which is everybody's business is nobody's business." 1725 : Defoe, *Everybody's Business is Nobody's Business*

[title]. 1910 : G. B. Shaw, *Misalliance*,
p. 10 (ed. 1914).

Everybody's friend. *See* **Friend** (8).

**Every commodity hath its discom-
modity.** 1583 : Melbancke, *Philotimus*,
sig. E1. 1598 : Meres, *Palladis*, fo. 159.
1633 : Draxe, 24. 1672 : Walker, *Pa-
ræm.*, 36, No convenience without
its inconveniency. 1748 : Richardson,
Clarissa, ii. 110 (1785), *There's no inconvenience but has its convenience*, said
Betty, giving me proverb for proverb.
1877 : L. J. Jennings, *Field Paths*,
ch. xxi., Sometimes I have thought of
taking a missis, but there never was
conweniency without an ill conweniency, and so I don't do it.

Every country dogs bite, In. 1640 :
Herbert, *Jac. Prudentum.* 1666 : Torriano, *Piazza Univ.*, 36.

**Every country the sun rises in the
morning, In.** 1640 : Herbert, *Jac.
Prudentum.* 1670 : Ray, 25.

Every couple is not a pair. 1875 :
A. B. Cheales, *Proverb. Folk-Lore*, 37.

Every cross hath its inscription.
1639 : Clarke, 16, Each cross has its
inscription. 1670 : Ray, 75. *c.* 1800 :
Trusler, *Prov. in Verse*, 62. 1853 :
Trench, *Proverbs*, 132 (1905), This of
ours is Christian both in form and in
spirit : *Every cross hath its inscription*
—the name, that is, inscribed upon it,
of the person for whom it was shaped.

Every day brings a new light. 1732 :
Fuller, No. 1413.

Every day brings its bread with it.
1640 : Herbert, *Jac. Prudentum.* 1666 :
Torriano, *Piazza Univ.*, 73, There's no
to morrow but brings its bread with it.

Every day cometh night. 1578 :
Florio, *First Fruites*, fo. 33.

**Every day in the week a shower of
rain, and on Sunday twain.** 1659 :
Howell, 11, . . . a proverb in many
shires of England. 1670 : Ray, 257.

Every day is holiday with sluggards.
1542 : Udall, tr. Erasmus' *Apoph.*, 174
(1877), To this matter he wrested the
prouerbe, in whiche it is saied : That
with the slouthfull and idle lubbers
that loue not to do any werke, euery
day is holidaye. 1611 : Davies (of
Hereford), *Sc. of Folly*, Epigr. 142, in

Works, ii. (Grosart), " With sluggards
eu'ry day is holy day "; And so it is
with some that seldome sleepes.

Every day is not Sunday. 1611 :
Cotgrave, s.v. " Feste," Feasts last
not alwayes . . . every day is not
Sunday (say we). 1666 : Torriano,
Piazza Univ., 88, Every day is not
holy day.

Every day is not yesterday. 1639 :
Clarke, 124.

Every day's no Yule-day— cast the cat
a castock [stump of a cabbage]. 1846 :
Denham, *Proverbs*, 62 (Percy S.). 1904 :
Co. Folk-Lore : Northumb., 179 (F.L.S.).

Every dog has his day. *See* Dog (41).

**Every door may be shut but death's
door.** 1666 : Torriano, *Piazza Univ.*,
317. 1853 : Trench, *Proverbs*, 18 (1905),
What were " All men are mortal," as
compared with the proverb : *Every
door may be shut but death's door?*

Every evil under the sun, For, there
is a remedy, or there is none; if there
be one, try and find it, if there be none,
never mind it. 1869 : Hazlitt, 135.

Every extremity is a fault. 1629 :
Book of Meery Riddles, Prov. 30.

Every eye forms its own beauty.
1906 : Harper, *Brighton Road*, 249, It
is not true that it is the prettiest place,
but, of course (as the proverb truly
says), " every eye forms its own
beauty."

Every fault there is folly, In. 1878 :
J. Platt, *Morality*, 34.

Every fool. *See* Fool (36) and (37).

Every fox. *See* Fox (8).

Every gap hath its bush. 1678 : Ray,
354.

**Every gracious man is also a grateful
man.** 1875 : A. B. Cheales, *Proverb.
Folk-Lore*, 94.

Every grain hath its bran. 1826 :
Brady, *Varieties of Lit.*, 37.

Every groom. *See* Every man is a
king at home.

Every hand fleeceth, Where, the sheep
goes naked. 1639 : Clarke, 187. 1647 :
Countrym. New Commonwealth, 19.
1670 : Ray, 91. 1732 : Fuller, No.
5645.

Every hill. *See* Hill (6).

Every hog his own apple. 1748 :

Smollett, *Rod. Random*, ch. xli., It
was soon spent, because I let them
have share and share while it lasted.
Howsomever, I should have remembered the old saying, *Every hog his
own apple.*

Every horse. *See* Horse (28).

Every ill man hath his ill day. 1640 :
Herbert, *Jac. Prudentum.* 1710 : S.
Palmer, *Moral Essays on Proverbs*, 123,
Every ill man will have an ill time.

Every Jack. *See* Jack has his Jill.

Every knave has a fool in his sleeve.
1710 : S. Palmer, *Moral Essays on
Proverbs*, 55.

Every light hath its shadow. 1669 :
Politeuphuia, 262.

Every light is not the sun. 1659 :
Howell, 13. 1670 : Ray, 15.

Every little helps. 1791 : O'Keeffe,
Wild Oats, V. iii., Here—it's not much !
but every little helps. 1854 : *N. & Q.*,
1st ser., ix. 409, On the principle that
every little helps . . . I would offer
the following suggestions. 1869 : Spurgeon, *John Ploughman*, ch. xix., Every
little helps, as the sow said when she
snapped at a gnat.

Every man a knave till found honest.
1720 : C. Shadwell, *Irish Hospitality*, I.,
Besides my maxim is, I think every man
a knave, till I find him honest.

**Every man a little beyond himself is a
fool.** 1732 : Fuller, No. 1421.

Every man after the fashion. *See*
Every one.

Every man as he loves. 1639 :
Clarke, 16.

Every man as his business lies. 1678 :
Ray, 107.

Every man basteth the fat hog. 1546 :
Heywood, *Proverbs*, Pt. I. ch. xi. 1639 :
Clarke, 10. 1869 : Spurgeon, *John
Ploughman*, ch. xiv., All the cooks
baste the fat pig, and the lean one
gets burned.

**Every man before he dies shall see
the devil.** *c.* 1560 : Becon, *Catechism*,
etc., 624 (P.S.), The common people
have a saying among them, that
" every man before he dieth shall see
the devil."

Every man born to be rich? Is,
1659 : Howell, 9.

Every man can rule (or tame) a shrew.
See **Shrew** (3).

Every man cannot hit the nail on the head. 1605 : Camden, *Remains*, 321 (1870). 1659 : Howell, 8.

Every man cannot speak with the king. 1611 : Cotgrave, s.v. " Parler," Everie one hath not the kings eare at command. 1681 : W. Robertson, *Phraseol. Generalis*, 788, Every man cannot come at the king.

Every man (or one) for himself— (*a*) without addition ; (*b*) *plus* and the devil for all ; (*c*) *plus* and God for us all. (*a*) *c*. 1386 : Chaucer, *C. Tales*, A 1181 (Skeat), At the kingës court, my brother, Ech man for himself. 1478 : *Paston Lett.*, iii. 228 (Gairdner, 1900), The wyche ye shall understond more when I come, for ther is eury man for hym selff. 1550 : R. Crowley, *Works*, 11 (E.E.T.S.), Where euerye man is for him selfe, And no manne for all. 1615 : Brathwait, *Strappado*, 206 (1878), Th' old prouerbe's in request, *each man for one.* 1729 : Gay, *Polly*, II. iii., Every man for himself, say I. 1869 : M. Arnold, *Culture and Anarchy :* " Sweetness and Light," Our hatred to all limits to the unrestrained swing of the individual's personality, our maxim of " Every man for himself." (*b*) 1578 : Florio, *First Fruites*, fo. 33, Euery one for him selfe and the diuel for al. (*c*) 1546 : Heywood, *Proverbs*, Pt. II. ch. ix., Euery man for him sclfe and god for us all. 1641 : Cowley, *Guardian*, III. vi. [as in 1546, but with " one " for " man "]. 1712 : Motteux, *Quixote*, Pt. I. bk. iii. ch. ii., Every man for himself, and God for us all, say I. 1836 : Marryat, *Easy*, ch. ix., At certain times, on board ship, it is every man for himself, and God for us all.

Every man gnaw on his own bone, Let. *c*. 1430 : Lydgate, *Minor Poems*, 160 (Percy S.).

Every man has his faults. 1607 : Shakespeare, *Timon*, III. i., Every man has his faults, and honesty is his. 1670 : Ray, 89. 1732 : Fuller, No. 1427, Every man hath his weak side.

Every man has his humour. 1598 :

Jonson, *Every Man in his Humour* [title]. 1639 : Clarke, 17. 1681 : W. Robertson, *Phraseol. Generalis*, 554.

Every man hath a fool in his sleeve. 1640 : Herbert, *Jac. Prudentum* [with " one " for " man "]. 1732 : Fuller, No. 1424. 1754 : Berthelson, *Eng.-Danish Dict.*, s.v. " Fool."

Every man hath his proper gift. 1639 : Clarke, 89.

Every man in his way. 1677 : Yarranton, *Englands Improvement*, 105, Now I see the old saying is true, Every man is a fool when he is out of his own way. 1678 : Ray, 84. 1753 : Richardson, *Grandison*, iii. 72 (1883), I understand you . . . you need not speak out —every one in their way.

Every man is a king at home. 1611 : Davies (of Hereford), *Sc. of Folly*, 42, in *Works*, ii. (Grosart), Euery groome is a king at home. 1611 : Cotgrave, s.v. " Roy," Every one is a king in his own house.

Every man is best known to himself. 1633 : Draxe, 27. 1670 : Ray, 13. 1732 : Fuller, No. 1429.

Every man is not born to be a boatswain. 1817 : Scott, in Lockhart's *Life*, iv. 76, There is an old saying of the seamen's, " every man is not born to be a boatswain."

Every man is the architect of his own fortune—with variants. [Nullum numen abest, si sit Prudentia : nos te, Nos facimus, Fortuna, Deam coeloque locamus.—Juvenal, x. 365. Sallust (*De Repub. Ordin.*) attributes the saying to Appius Claudius Cæcus, the Censor, 312 B.C.] 1539 : Taverner, *Proverbs*, fo. 37, A mans owne maners do shape hym hys fortune. 1612 : Shelton, *Quixote*, Pt. I. bk. i. ch. iv., And, what is more, every one is son of his works. *c*. 1680 : L'Estrange, *Seneca's Epistles*, xiii., Every man is the artificer of his own fortune. 1707 : Dunton, *Athen. Sport*, 454, It is a highway saying, that we are architects of our own fortune. 1800 : Coleridge, *Wallenstein*, Man is made great or little by his own will. 1873 : E. Tew, in *N. & Q.*, 4th ser. xii. 515, We have not a commoner saying among us than " Every man is the architect of his own fortune," and we have very few much older.

Every man Jack. 1841: Dickens, *Barn. Rudge*, ch. xxxix., " Every one of 'em," replied Dennis. " Every man Jack!" 1883: R. L. S., *Treasure I.*, ch. ix., I am responsible for the ship's safety and the life of every man Jack aboard of her. Cf. **Every mother's son.**

Every man knows his own business best. 1616: Breton, in *Works*, ii. *e* 5 (Grosart), Euery man knowes what is best for himselfe. 1742: Fielding, *Andrews*, bk. ii. ch. v., The gentleman stared . . . and, turning hastily about, said, " Every man knew his own business." 1837: J. S. Knowles, *Love-Chase*, V. i., But every man, As they say, to his own business.

Every man may not wear a furred hood. 1578: T. Lupton, *All for Money*, sig. C2, By the olde prouerbe euerie man may not weare a fourde hood.

Every man mend one, all shall be mended, If. 1562 : Heywood,*Three Hund. Epigr.*, No. 1. 1579: Lyly, *Euphues*, 142 (Arber), Let vs endeaour euery one to amend one, and we shall all soone be amended. 1604 : Terilo, *Friar Bakon's Proph.*, 27 (Percy S.), Let every man mend one, And I will not be out. 1740: Richardson, *Pamela*, ii. 4 (1883), At least, it will be . . . answering the good lesson I learned at school, *Every one mend one.* 1793 : D'Arblay, *Diary*, etc., iii. 477 (1876), " Let every one mend one," as Will Chip says [*Will Chip, or Village Politics*, by Hannah More]; and then states, as well as families, may be safely reformed. 1880 : Spurgeon, *Ploughman's Pictures*, 47, Mend your own manners, and if every man does the same all will be . . . mended.

Every man must bear his own burden. 1611 : Cotgrave, s.v. " Chasque," Every one must look to his owne charge; or beare his owne burthen. 1855 : Kingsley, *Westw. Ho!*, ch. xxvi., It was Heaven's will . . . and to be borne as such. Every man must bear his own burden.

Every man must row with such oars

as he has. 1875 : A. B. Cheales, *Proverb. Folk-Lore*, 131.

Every man to his trade (or craft, or business). 1539: Taverner, *Proverbs*, fo. 33, Let euerye man exercise hym selfe in the facultie that he knoweth. 1597 : Shakespeare, 1 *Henry IV.*, II. ii., *Fal.* . . . every man to his business. 1682 : A. Behn, *False Count*, I. ii., Father mine, every man to his business, I say. 1732 : Fuller, No. 1435, Every man to his trade, quoth the boy to the bishop. 1821 : Scott, *Kenilworth*, ch. xi., Every man to his craft, says the proverb, the parson to the prayer-book, and the groom to his curry-comb. 1895 : Shaw, *Man of Destiny, Giuseppe*. . . . Every man to his trade, excellency.

Every man will shoot at the enemy, but few will gather the shafts. 1678 : Ray, 202 [with " go to fetch " for " gather "]. 1732 : Fuller, No. 1436.

Every man wishes water to his own mill. 1578 : Florio, *First Fruites*, fo. 14, Euery man draweth water to hym selfe. 1593 : G. Harvey, in *Works*, ii. 181 (Grosart), Euery miller is ready to conuey the water to his owne mill. 1670: Ray, 121, Every miller draws water to his own mill. 1740 : North, *Lives of Norths*, i. 133 (Bohn), The serjeants . . . would have no water go by their mill. 1823 : Scott, *Peveril*, ch. xxi., I hears on nought, except this Plot, as they call it, that they are pursuing the Papishers about; but it brings water to my mill, as the saying is.

Every man's nose will not make a shoeing-horn. [c. 1520: Stanbridge, *Vulgaria*, sig. B5, His nose is lyke a shoynge horne.] 1659: Howell, 4, Every one cannot have a nose like a shooing-horn. 1670 : Ray, 125. 1732 : Fuller, No. 1434.

Every may be hath a may not be. 1678 : Ray, 174. 1932 : Fuller, No. 1437.

Every mile is two in winter. 1640 : Herbert, *Jac. Prudentum.*

Every miller. *See* **Every man wishes.**

Every mother's son. [c. 1310 : in Wright's *Pol. Songs*, 312 (Camden S., 6), Sur le sollempnement escomege e maldie Trestuz le fiz de mere . . . (Upon it he solemnly excommunicates and curses

—every son of a mother . . .).] *c.* 1350 :
Alexander, l. 2098, For mekely ilka
modir sonn. 1485 : Malory, *Morte
d'Arthur,* bk. ii. ch. 10, And there were
slayn mony moders sones. 1560 : T. Wilson, *Rhetorique,* 72 (1909), Die we must
euery mothers sonne of vs. 1595 :
Shakespeare, *Mids. N. Dream,* I. ii.,
That would hang us, every mother's
son. 1694 : *Terence made English,* 260,
Ay ev'ry mothers son of 'em. 1710 : T.
Ward, *Eng. Reform.,* 27 (1716), Convict
them every mother's son. 1814 : Scott,
Fam. Letters, i. 334 (1894), Fire was
maintained at the mouth of the cavern,
until every man and mother's son were
suffocated. 1883 : R. L. S., *Treasure I.,*
ch. xxix., That's about where we are,
every mother's son of us. Cf. **Every
man Jack.**

Every new thing has a silver tail.
1864 : " Cornish Proverbs," in *N. & Q.,*
3rd ser., vi. 495.

Every one after his fashion. 1546 :
Heywood, *Proverbs,* Pt. I. ch. xi.
c. 1594 : Bacon, *Promus,* No. 955,
Every man after his fashen. 1605 :
Camden, *Remains,* 321 (1870). 1659 :
Howell, 8.

**Every one can keep house better than
her mother till she trieth.** 1732 :
Fuller, No. 1443. 1875 : A. B. Cheales,
Proverb. Folk Lore, 49.

**Every one tastens where there is
gain.** 1640 : Herbert, *Jac. Prudentum.*
1666 : Torriano, *Piazza Univ.,* 109.

**Every one gets his own, you'll get
the gallows, When.** 1732 : Fuller, No.
5550.

Every one is a master and servant.
1640 : Herbert, *Jac. Prudentum.*

Every one is kin to the rich man.
1666 : Torriano, *Piazza Univ.,* 235.

**Every one is (or should be) master in
his own house.** 1611 : Cotgrave, s.v.
" Maison," . . . master within his own
doores. Ibid., s.v. " Maistre," Every
one rules in his own house.

Every one is not born a poet. 1659 :
Howell, 13.

**Every one is weary : the poor in
seeking, the rich in keeping, the good
in learning.** 1640 : Herbert, *Jac. Prudentum.* 1666 : Torriano, *Piazza Univ.,*

4, Every one will labour, the poor man
in seeking what he wants, and the rich
man in preserving what he hath.

Every one knows how to find fault.
1732 : Fuller, No. 1447.

**Every one puts his fault on the
times.** 1640 : Herbert, *Jac. Prudentum.*
1670 : Ray, 26. 1732 : Fuller, No.
1448, Every one lays his faults upon
the time.

Every one says. *See* True (15).

Every one swale [sell] **his own wuts**
[oats], **Let.** 1917 : Bridge, *Cheshire
Proverbs,* 89.

**Every one takes care of himself, care
is taken of all, When.** 1855 : Bohn, 558.

Every one talks of what he loves.
1732 : Fuller, No. 1450.

Every one that can lick a dish. 1678 :
Ray, 76.

Every one thinks he knows much.
1732 : Fuller, No. 1451.

Every one thinks his sack heaviest.
1611 : Cotgrave, s.v. " Fardeau," Every
one finds his owne burthen heavy
enough. 1640 : Herbert, *Jac. Prudentum.*

**Every one to catch a salmon, 'Tis
not for.** 1732 : Fuller, No. 5095.

Every one to his taste—(*a*) *plus* as
. . . said when he (or she) kissed the cow ;
(*b*) without the cow. (*a*) 1546 : Heywood, *Proverbs,* Pt. II. ch. i., Euery
man as he loueth Quoth the good man
whan that he kyst his coowe. 1630 :
Davenant, *Just Italian,* III., Th' old
amorous deacon that embrac'd his cow
Was not so destitute. 1675 : Cotton,
Burl. upon Burlesque, 189 (1765), Why
each one as he likes (you know), Quo'
th' good man when he kiss'd his cow.
1694 : Motteux, *Rabelais,* bk. v. ch.
xxix., Every one as they like, as the
woman said when she kiss'd her cow.
1738 : Swift, *Polite Convers.,* Dial. I.
[as in 1694, *plus* " good " before
" woman "]. 1823 : Scott, *Peveril,* ch.
vii., She hath a right to follow her
fancy, as the dame said who kissed
her cow. 1883 : Burne, *Shropsh. Folk-
Lore,* 591, Every one to his liking, as
the old woman said when she kissed
her cow. (*b*) 1611 : Cotgrave, s.v.
" Chascun," Every one as hee likes.

1656 : Middleton, *Old Law*, II. ii., Every one to their liking. 1714 : Ozell, *Molière*, ii. 110, Every one to his mind. 1759 : Sterne, *Trist. Shandy*, bk. i. ch. vii., I never could envy Didius in these kinds of fancies of his :— But every man to his own taste.

Every one's censure is first moulded in his own nature. 1855 : Bohn, 351.

Every one's faults are not written in their foreheads. 1678 : Ray, 9.

Every path. *See* Path.

Every pease hath its veaze—and variant. 1599 : Buttes, *Dyets Dry Dinner*, Our common proverb accordeth, speaking somewhat homely : Euery pease wil haue a fease, but euerie beane, fifteene. 1608 : Armin, *Nest of Ninnies*, 51 (Sh. S.), It was in Lent, when pease pottage bare great sway, and euery pease must have his ease. 1670 : Ray, 214, Every pease hath its veaze, and a bean fifteen.

Every peddler thinks well of his pack. 1611 : Cotgrave, s.v. "Panier." 1631 : Mabbe, *Celestina*, 161 (T.T.), Every pedler prayseth his owne needles.

Every penny that is taken is not clear gain. 1732 : Fuller, No. 1454.

Every pleasure hath a pain. 1598 : Chapman, *Blind Beggar of Alex.*, sc. v. 1631 : Mabbe, *Celestina*, 149 (T.T.), There is no pleasure without sorrow.

Every plummet is not for every sound. 1732 : Fuller, No. 1455.

Every pot has two handles. 1650 : Taylor, *Holy Living*, ch. ii. § 6, There is nothing but hath a double handle, or at least we have two hands to apprehend it. 1827 : Hone, *Ev. Day Book*, ii. 649, "Every pot has two handles." This means "that one story's good till another story's told," or "there is no evil without its advantages."

Every question requireth not an answer. 1578 : Florio, *First Fruites*, fo. 32 [with "woorde" for "question"]. 1629 : *Book of Meery Riddles*, Prov. 31. 1875 : A. B. Cheales, *Proverb. Folk-Lore*, 118, It is not every question that deserves answer.

Every reed will not make a pipe. 1732 : Fuller, No. 1457.

Every river. *See* All rivers.

Every scale hath its counterpoise. 1666 : Torriano, *Piazza Univ.*, 53 [with "balance" for "scale"]. 1732 : Fuller, No. 1458.

Every shoe fits not every foot. 1616 : B. Rich, *Ladies Looking Glasse*, 21, As euery shooe is not fit for euery foote. 1670 : Ray, 142. 1754 : Berthelson, *Eng.-Danish Dict.*, s.v. "Shoe."

Every slip is not a fall. 1732 : Fuller, No. 1461.

Every spot is not the leprosy. 1875 : A. B. Cheales, *Proverb, Folk-Lore*, 117.

Every thing has an end. *See* All things have an end.

Every thing hath a beginning. 1566 : Gascoigne, *Supposes*, V. v. 1661 : Middleton, *Mayor of Q.*, IV. iii., Everything has beginning.

Every thing hath an ear, and a pitcher has two. 1639 : Clarke, 237.

Every thing hath his seed. 1633 : Draxe, 12.

Every thing hath its time. 1509 : Barclay, *Ship of Fooles*, ii. 46 (1874), For euery thynge God hath a tyme puruayde. 1578 : *Gorgeous Gallery*, 47 (Rollins), Eche thing must haue a time. 1666 : Torriano, *Piazza Univ.*, 283. 1732 : Fuller, No. 1466, Every thing hath its time, and that time must be watch'd. 1875 : A. B. Cheales, *Proverb. Folk-Lore*, 12, As another proverb reminds us, Every thing will come into use if you only keep it long enough.

Every thing is as it is taken. 1552 : Latimer, *Works*, ii. 150 (P.S.), We have a common saying amongst us, "Every thing is as it is taken." *c.* 1597 : in Harington, *Nugæ Antiquæ*, i. 223 (1804), We must say as is oft sayd, "it was as it was taken." 1632 : Jonson, *Magnetic Lady*, III. iii., All counsel's as 'tis taken.

Every thing is good in its season. 1633 : Draxe, 184. 1670 : Ray, 23. 1732 : Fuller, No. 1467. 1851 : Borrow, *Lavengro*, iii. 261, He had no objection to tea; but he used to say, "Every thing in its season."

Every thing is of use to a housekeeper. 1640 : Herbert, *Jac. Prudentum*.

Every thing is the worse for wearing. Before 1529 : Skelton, *Magnyfycence*,

l. 456, All thynge is worse whan it is worne. 1560: T. Wilson, *Rhetorique*, 151 (1909), Your witte is good enough, if you keepe it still and vse it not, for euery thing, as you knowe, is the worse for the wearing. 1694: Southerne, *Fatal Marriage*, III. ii. 1754: Berthelson, *Eng.-Danish Dict.*, s.v. " Worse."

Every thing new is fine. 1639: Clarke, 228, Every thing's pretty, when 'tis new. 1666: Torriano, *Piazza Univ.*, 171, A new, every thing is handsome.

Every thing would live. 1670: Ray, 116. 1732: Fuller, No. 1469.

Every tide will have an ebb. 1583: Melbancke, *Philotinus*, sig. U2, Euerie tide [hath] his eb. 1732: Fuller, No. 1470.

Every time the sheep bleats. See Sheep (3).

Every tub must stand on its own bottom. 1564: Bullein, *Dialogue*, 65 (E.E.T.S.), Let euerie fatte [vat] stande vpon his owne bottome. 1678: Bunyan, *Pilgr. Progr.*, Pt. I. p. 35 (1849), *Sloth* said, *Yet a little more sleep*; and *Presumption* said, *Every tub must stand upon his own bottom.* 1721: C. Cibber, *Refusal*, V. 1781: Macklin, *Man of the World*, I. 1857: Borrow, *Rom. Rye*, ch. xxix., " Every vessel must stand on its own bottom," said I; " they take pleasure in receiving obligations, I take pleasure in being independent." 1901: F. E. Taylor, *Lancs Sayings*, 8, Let ev'ry tub stond on it' own bothum.

Every where is no where, He that is. 1586: Pettie, tr. Guazzo's *Civil Convers.*, fo. 63, The prouerbe, That he is not any where, who is euerie where. 1669: *Politeuphuia*, 131, He is no-where that is every-where. 1732: Fuller, No. 2176.

Every wind bloweth not down the corn. 1546: Heywood, *Proverbs*, Pt. II. ch. ix. 1633: Draxe, 234.

Every wind is ill to a broken ship. 1633: Ibid., 171. 1869: Spurgeon, *John Ploughman*, ch. vii., Every wind is foul for a crazy ship.

Every woman. See quot. 1612: Field, *Woman a Weathercock*, IV. ii., They say every woman has a springe to catch a woodcock [gull, or silly fellow].

Evil, *adj.* 1. *An evil lesson is soon learned.* 1670: Ray, 8, That which is evil is soon learn't.

2. *An evil suspicion has a worse condition.* 1886: R. Holland, *Cheshire Gloss.*, 444 (E.D.S.). 1917: Bridge, *Cheshire Proverbs*, 8.

3. *Evil beginning hath evil end.* c. 1400: *Mirk's Festial*, 120 (E.E.T.S.), For hyt ys oft sene, all euell bygynnyng hathe a foule endyng. c. 1440: Lydgate, *Fall of Princes*, bk. viii. l. 2241, Ther gynnyng cursid hadde a wengable fyn.

4. *Evil crow.* See Like crow.

5. *Evil doers.* See Ill doers.

6. *Evil guise.* See Sluggards guise.

7. *Evil name is evil fame.* c. 1430: in *Babees Book, etc.*, 39 (E.E.T.S.), For he that cacchith to him an yuel name, It is to him a foule fame.

8. *Evil news.* See Ill news.

9. *Evil will.* See Ill will.

10. *Evil words corrupt good manners.* 1530: Palsgrave, 499, Foule wordes corupte good maners. 1596: Harington, *Ulysses upon Ajax*, 23 (1814), Evil words corrupt good manners (saith both Paul and Menander). 1631: Brathwait, *Eng. Gentlewoman*, 293 (1641), As by good words evill manners are corrected, so by evill words are good ones corrupted. 1749: Fielding, *Tom Jones*, bk. xii. ch. iii., Evil communication corrupts good manners. 1821: Scott, *Pirate*, ch. xxx., Gude forgie me for swearing—but evil communication corrupteth good manners.

11. *Of evil grain no good seed can come.* 1633: Draxe, 13 [without last two words]. 1670: Ray, 8.

12. *Of evil life comes evil end.* c. 1300: *King Alisaunder*, l. 753, Soth hit is, in al thyng, Of eovel lif comuth eovel eyndyng. c. 1440: *La Tour-Landry*, 72 (E.E.T.S.), For gladly euelle lyff hathe euelle ende.

13. *The evil wound is cured, but not the evil name.* 1670: Ray, 18.

Evil, *adv. Evil gotten, evil* (or *worse*) *kept* (or *spent*). 1481: Caxton, *Reynard*, 8 (Arber), Therof hym had be better to haue holde his pees for he had stolen it Male quesisti et male perdidisti hit is ryght that it be euil loste that is euil wonne. 1541 : Coverdale, *Christ. State Matrimony*, sig. I2, Euyll geten, worse kept. 1579 : *Marr. of Wit and Wisdom*, sc. iii. p. 28 (Sh. S.), Euell gotten worse spent. 1670 : Ray, 8, Evil gotten evil spent. 1754 : Berthelson, *Eng.-Danish Dict.*, s.v. " Evil," Evil got evil spent.

Evil, *subs.* 1. *Evil is soon believed.* 1732 : Fuller, No. 1474.

2. *Evil to him that evil thinks* (or *seeks*). *c.* 1386 : Chaucer, *Prioress's Tale*, l. 180, Yvel shal have, that yvel wol deserve. 1484 : Caxton, *Æsope*, ii. 207 (Jacobs), Now the euyl which men wysshe to other cometh to hym whiche wyssheth hit. 1666 : Torriano, *Piazza Univ.*, 200, To who thinks evil, evil befalls him. 1712 : Motteux, *Quixote*, Pt. I. bk. iii. ch. vi, Good betide us all, and evil to him that evil seeks.

3. *He that evil does never good weens.* *c.* 1386 : Chaucer, *C. Tales*, A 4320 (Skeat), Him thar nat wenë wel that yvel doth.

4. *He that helpeth the evil hurteth the good.* *c.* 1615 : *Time's Whistle*, 45 (E.E.T.S.), For true's the saying . . . " He harmes the good that doth the evill spare." 1669 : *Politeuphuia*, 186, He that helpeth an evil man hurteth him that is good. 1732 : Fuller, No. 2163.

5. *No evil without its advantages.* 1827 : Hone, *Ev. Day Book*, ii. 649.

6. *The evil that cometh out of thy mouth, flyeth into thy bosom.* 1633 : Draxe, 192 [with "returneth (or falleth) " for " flyeth "]. 1670 : Ray, 8. 1732 : Fuller, No. 4505.

7. *Whoso will no evil do.* See quots. 1537 : R. Whitford, *Werke for Housholders*, sig. D7, The olde prouerbe sayth, who so wyll none euyll do, shulde do nothynge that longeth therto. 1639 : Clarke, 202, He that would no evills doe, must shun all things that longs thereto.

Evils. See **Misfortunes**; and **Two evils.**

Ewell. See **Sutton.**

Example. 1. *Example is better than precept.* *c.* 1400 : *Mirk's Festial*, 216

(E.E.T.S.), Then saythe Seynt Austeyn that an ensampull yn doyng ys mor commendabull then ys techyng other prechyng. 1570 : Ascham, *Scholemaster*, 61 (Mayor), One example is more valiable . . . than twenty preceptes written in bookes. 1656 : F. Osborne, *Advice to Son*, 34 (Parry), Example prevails more than precept. 1742 : Fielding, *Andrews*, bk. i. ch. i., It is a trite but true observation, that examples work more forcibly on the mind than precepts. 1868 : W. C. Hazlitt, in *N. & Q.*, 4th ser., i. 201, The copy-book says that " Example is better than Precept."

2. *He is in ill case that gives example to another.* 1629 : *Book of Meery Riddles*, Prov. 125.

Excellent soldier, he lacks nothing but a heart and a feather, An. 1639 : Clarke, 310.

Excellent tale and 'twere told in Greek, An. Ibid., 231.

Exceptions prove the rule. 1664 : J. Wilson, *The Cheats*, To Reader, For if I have shown the odd practices of two vain persons pretending to what they were not, I think I have sufficiently justified the brave man even by this reason, that the exception proves the rule. 1771 : Smollett, *Clinker*, in *Works*, vi. 82 (1817), They serve only as exceptions ; which, in the grammarian's phrase, confirm and prove a general canon. 1808 : Byron, *Letters and Journals*, i. 204 (Prothero), You will recollect that " *exceptions only prove the Rule*." 1883 : Trollope, *Autob.*, ch. xii., But the exceptions are not more than enough to prove the rule. 1909 : W. H. Helm, *Jane Austen*, 169, The retort . . . is that they are the exceptions that " prove " the rule. Cf. **Rule.**

Exchange. See **Fair,** *adj.* (19).

Experience is good, if not bought too dear. 1732 : Fuller, No. 1479.

Experience is sometimes dangerous. 1578 : Florio, *First Fruites*, fo. 30, Experience sometymes is perilous. 1629 : *Book of Meery Riddles*, Prov. 110.

Experience is the father of wisdom, and memory the mother. 1732 : Fuller, No. 1480.

Experience is the mistress of fools.

1579: Lyly, *Euphues*, 123 (Arber), It is commonly said . . . that experience is the mistresse of fooles. 1618: Breton, in *Inedited Tracts*, 187 (Hazlitt). 1692: L'Estrange, *Æsop*, 185 (3rd ed.), Experience is the mistress of knaves as well as of fools. 1710: S. Palmer, *Moral Essays on Proverbs*, 33, As experience is the school-mistress of fools. *c.* 1800: J. Trusler, *Prov. in Verse*, 25.

Experience is the mother of knowledge. 1578: Florio, *First Fruites*, fo. 32, Experience is the mother of al things. 1637: Breton, in *Works*, ii. *l* 8 (Grosart), Reading makes a scholler by rule . . . but experience is the mother of knowledge. 1700: D. Craufurd, *Courtship à-la-Mode*, I. ii.

Experience keeps a dear school, but fools will learn in no other. 1736: Franklin, *Way to Wealth*, in *Works*, i. 451 (Bigelow). 1875: A. B. Cheales, *Proverb. Folk Lore*, 115.

Experience teacheth fools. 1732: Fuller, No. 1484, Experience teacheth fools, and he is a great one that will not learn by it. 1884: *Folk-Lore Journal*, ii. 279, Experience makes fools wise. *Derbysh.*

Experience without learning is better than learning without experience. 1855: Bohn, 352.

Extreme right. *See* **Greater the right.**

Extremes meet. 1589: *Triumph of Love and Fortune*, IV., in Hazlitt, *Old Plays*, vi. 214, A right woman—either love like an angel, Or hate like a devil —in extremes so to dwell. 1780: Walpole, *Letters*, vii. 395 (Cunningham), We seem to be plunging into the horrors of France . . . yet, as extremes meet, there is at this moment amazing insensibility. 1822: Lamb, *Elia:* "Chimney-Sweepers," That dead time of the dawn, when (as extremes meet) the rake . . . and the hard-handed artizan . . . jostle . . . for the honours of the pavement. 1900: Lucas, *Domesticities*, 24, Oatmeal marks not only the child's breakfast, it is the favourite food of Edinburgh Reviewers. Thus do extremes meet.

Eye and Eyes. 1. *A small hurt in*

the eye is a great one. 1732: Fuller, No. 406.

2. *Better eye sore than all blind.* *c.* 1320: in *Reliq. Antiquæ*, i, 110 (1841), "Betere is eye sor, then al blynd "; Quoth Hendyng. 1846: T. Wright, *Essays on Middle Ages*, i. 141, Thus we have the saying "A sore eye is better than all blind."

3. *He has an eye behind him.* *c.* 1565: Still, *Gammer Gurton*, II. ii., Take hede of Sim Glovers wife, she hath an eie behind her! 1681: W. Robertson, *Phraseol. Generalis*, 1032, He hath an eye behind; a wary man. 1869: P. Fitzgerald, *Comediettas*, 111, Watch every look, every gesture. She has eyes in the back of her head.

4. *He shuts his eyes and thinks none see.* 1852: FitzGerald, *Polonius*, 28 (1903).

5. *His eye is bigger than his belly.* 1640: Herbert, *Jac. Prudentum* [with "the" for "his"]. 1738: Swift, *Polite Convers.*, Dial. II., I thought I could have eaten this wing of a chicken; but my eye's bigger than my belly. 1828: Carr, *Craven Dialect*, i. 137, "His eyes are bigger than his belly"; spoken of a glutton. 1889: Peacock, *Manley, etc., Gloss.*, 193 (E.D.S.), A person is said to have his "eyes bigger than his belly" who takes more food upon his plate than he can eat. 1901: F. E. Taylor, *Lancs Sayings*, 24, His een are bigger nor his bally.

6. *His* (or *her*) *eyes draw straws.* 1709: Mandeville, *Virgin Unmask'd*, 98 (1724), My eyes begin to draw straws . . . I wish ye a good repose. 1790: *Gent. Mag.*, Pt. II. 978, It is a current expression, in a great part of the kingdom, to say of a person, when his eyes are heavy, and he is much inclined to sleep, *that his eyes draw straws.* 1830: Forby, *Vocab. E. Anglia*, 430. 1883: Burne, *Shropsh. Folk-Lore*, 596, The eyes are drawing straws=the person is becoming drowsy.

7. *Neither eyes on letters nor hands in coffers.* 1578: Florio, *First Fruites*, fo. 33, Neither eyes, nor handes in other mens writings or purses. 1640: Herbert, *Jac. Prudentum.*

8. *Neither my eye nor my elbow.*
1894: Northall, *Folk Phrases,* 20
(E.D.S.), Neither . . ., i.e. neither one
thing nor the other. 1907: T. Ratcliffe, in *N. & Q.,* 10th ser., viii. 7,
I have never heard this phrase except
from Derbyshire folks. It is used as
a comment on an unsatisfactory answer,
promise, or arrangement, as "It's
neither my eye nor my elbow"—
neither the one thing nor the other.

9. *One eye of the master's sees more
than ten of the servant's.* 1640: Herbert, *Jac. Prudentum.* 1670: Ray, 17.
1732: Fuller, No. 3749. Cf. Nos. 13
and 17.

10. *The eye and religion can bear no
jesting.* 1630: T. Adams, *Works,* 14,
We say . . . it is no safe jesting
with holy things. 1640: Herbert, *Jac.
Prudentum.* 1710: S. Palmer, *Moral
Essays on Proverbs,* 322, 'Tis ill jesting
with your eye and religion.

11. *The eye is a shrew.* 1678: Ray,
354.

12. *The eye is the pearl of the face.*
1580: Lyly, *Euphues,* 406 (Arber), As
the eye hath euer bene thought the
pearle of the face. 1732: Fuller, No.
4506.

13. *The eye of a master will do more
work than both his hands.* 1736: Franklin, *Way to Wealth,* in *Works,* i. 445
(Bigelow). 1843: Carlyle, *Past and
Present,* bk. ii. ch. x., But continual
vigilance, rigorous method, what we
call "the eye of the master," work
wonders. Cf. Nos. 9 and 17.

14. *The eye that sees all things else,
sees not itself.* 1732: Fuller, No.
4507.

15. *The eye will have his part.* 1640:
Herbert, *Jac. Prudentum.*

16. *The eyes have one language everywhere.* Ibid.

17. *The master's eye fats the horse.*
[ἐρωτηθεὶς τί μάλιστα ἵππον πιαίνει; Ὁ τοῦ
δεσπότου ὀφθαλμός, ἔφη.—Aristotle, *Œcum.,*
I. vi. 4.] 1537: R. Whitford, *Werke for
Housholders,* sig. F5, The eye of the
mayster[maketh] a fatte horse. 1552:
Latimer, *Sermons,* 395 (P.S.). 1579:
Lyly,*Euphues,*144 (Arber),That notable
saying of the horse-keeper—nothing did

so fatte the horse as the eye of the king.
1631: Brathwait, *Whimzies,* 69 (1859),
The proverbe is, The masters eye
feedes his horse. 1709: O. Dykes, *Eng.
Proverbs,* 281. 1869: Austen Leigh,
Memoir of Jane Austen, 35, Two homely
proverbs were held in higher estima-
tion in my early days than they are
now—"The master's eye makes the
horse fat," and . . . Cf. Nos. 9 and 13.

18. *To whirl the eyes too much shows
a kite's brain.* 1640: Herbert, *Jac.
Prudentum.*

19. *What the eye sees not, the heart
rues not. c.* 1477: Caxton, *Jason,* 83
(E.E.T.S.), Men saye communely that
ferre ys from the eye is ferre from
the herte. 1546: Heywood, *Proverbs,*
Pt. II. ch. vii. 1592: Greene, in
Works, xi. 140 (Grosart), What the
eie sees not Phylomela neuer hurteth
the heart. *c.* 1613: Rowlands, *Paire
of Spy-Knaues,* 7 (Hunt. Cl.), For what
the eye ne're sees, the heart ne're rues.
1653: R. Brome, *City Wit,* III. iii.
1712: Motteux, *Quixote,* Pt. II. ch. 67.
1883: Burne, *Shropsh. Folk-Lore,* 588,
What the eye doesn't see, the heart
doesn't grieve. Cf. **Out of sight out of
mind**; and **Seldom seen.**

20. *You may put it in the eye and see
none the worse.* 1530: Palsgrave, 478,
I maye put my wynnyng in myn eye.
1545: Ascham, *Toxoph.,* 151 (Arber),
So that shoter whiche putteth no
difference, but shooteth in all lyke, in
rough weather and fayre, shall alwayes
put his wynninges in his eyes. 1641:
Cowley, *Guardian,* I. i., What you get
by him you may e'en put i' your eye,
and ne'er see the worse for 't. 1738:
Swift, *Polite Convers.,* Dial. I.

21. *You should never touch your eye
but with your elbow,* i.e. you should not
touch your eye at all. 1640: Herbert,
Jac. Prudentum, Diseases of the eye
are to be cured with the elbow. 1670:
Ray, 39. 1732: Fuller, No. 3529,
Never rub your eye but with your
elbow. 1894: Northall, *Folk Phrases,*
21 (E.D.S.), Rub your sore eye with
your elbow, i.e. not at all.

See also **Every eye; Four eyes;
Mistress (3); and Two eyes.**

Eyelet-holes. *See* quots. 1599 : Porter, *Two Angry Women*, in Hazlitt, *Old Plays*, vii. 381, 'Twill be a good while, ere you wish your skin full of eyelet-holes. 1678 : Ray, 219, It will be long enough ere you wish your skin full of holes. 1738 : Swift, *Polite Convers.*, Dial. I., You'll be long enough before you wish your skin full of eyelet holes. 1855 : Kingsley, *West. Ho!*, ch. iii., I expected to be full of eyelet holes ere I could close with him.

Eye-servant is never good for his master, The. 1659 : Howell, 10.

Eye-teeth, To have one's. 1730 : Morier, in Atterbury, *Misc. Works*, v. 147 (O.), There is no dealing with him without having one's eye teeth. 1778 : T. Cogan, *John Buncle, Junior*, ii. 148, My ladies have all *their eye teeth about them*, as the saying is. 1870 : Emerson, *Works*, ii. 7 (Bohn) (O.), Progress that is made by a boy " when he cuts his eye-teeth."

F

Face. 1. *A face of brass.* 1578 :
Whetstone, *Promos and Cassandra,*
Pt. II. III. i., Well, I wyll set a face
of brasse on it. 1647 : in *Somers
Tracts,* v. 490 (1811), Had he not had
more brass in his face than in his
kitchen . . . 1718 : in *Roxb. Ballads,*
viii. 633 (B.S.), Then, with a face of
brass, he ask'd poor Betty more.

2. *Face to face the truth comes out.*
1732 : Fuller, No. 1485. 1852 : Fitz-
Gerald, *Polonius,* 59 (1903), Face to
face truth comes out apace.

3. *I think his face is made of a fiddle,
every one that looks on him loves him.*
1678 : Ray, 243. 1762 : Smollett, *Sir
L. Greaves,* ch. viii., We may see your
honour's face is made of a fiddle ; every
one that looks on you, loves you. 1816 :
Scott, *Old Mortality,* ch. xxxvii., How
could I help it? His face was made of
a fiddle, as they say, for a' body that
looked on him liked him.

4. *The face is index of the heart.*
1586 : L. Evans, *Withals Dict. Revised,*
sig. L7, Your face doth testifie what you
be inwardly. *c.* 1615 : *Times Whistle,*
23 (E.E.T.S.), That olde saying is
vntrue, " the face Is index of the
heart." 1645 : Howell, *Letters,* bk. i.
§ iii. No. xv., The face is oftentimes
a true index of the heart. 1713 :
Ward, *Hist. Grand Rebellion,* i. 8, For
in the face judicious eyes may find
The symptoms of a good or evil mind.
1864 : Mrs. H. Wood, *Trevlyn Hold,*
ch. i., You have not to learn that the
face is the outward index of the mind
within.

Face with a card of ten. *See* Outface.

Facts are stubborn things. 1749 :
Smollett, *Gil Blas,* bk. x. ch. i. 1925 :
E. Lyttelton, *Memories and Hopes,* 228,
These are facts ; and after all, facts are
stubborn things.

Fail at a pinch. *See* Pinch.

Fails, He who never, will never grow

rich. 1869 : Spurgeon, *John Ploughman,* ch. xii. [cited " as the proverb
is "].

Fain as a fowl. *See* Fowl.

Faint at the smell of a wall-flower,
He will. 1790 : Grose, *Prov. Gloss.,*
s.v. " London."

Faint heart never won fair lady.
[*c.* 1390 : Gower, *Conf. Amantis,* bk. v.
l. 6573, Bot as men sein, wher herte
is failed, Ther schal no castell ben
assailed.] *c.* 1570 : in *Black Letter
Ballads, etc.,* 16 (Lilly, 1867), Faint
harts faire ladies neuer win. 1580 :
Lyly, *Euphues,* 364 (Arber), Faint
heart . . . neither winneth castell nor
lady. 1664 : Cotton, *Scarronides,* bk. i.,
Faint heart, you know, ne'er wins fair
lady. 1702 : Vanbrugh, *False Friend,*
III. *c.* 1750 : Foote, *Knights,* II.
1846 : Planché, *Extravag.,* iii. 130
(1879), And faint heart ne'er fair lady
wins, I'll venture—come what may !

Faint praise is disparagement. 1813 :
Ray, 106.

Fair, *adj.* 1. *A fair booty makes
many a thief.* 1732 : Fuller, No. 86.

2. *A fair day in winter is the mother
of a storm.* 1639 : Clarke, 171, A faire
day is mother of a storme. 1651 :
Herbert, *Jac. Prudentum,* 2nd ed.

3. *A fair face cannot have a crabbed
heart.* 1593 : *Passionate Morrice,* 92
(N. Sh. S.), Building vpon the prouerbe,
A faire face, etc.

4. *A fair face is half a portion.* 1633 :
Draxe, 15, Shee that is faire hath halfe
her portion. 1732 : Fuller, No. 89.

5. *A fair face may be a foul bargain.*
1590 : Greene, in *Works,* viii. 36 (Grosart), Such as marie but to a faire
face, tie themselues oft to a foule
bargain. 1732 : Fuller, No. 87, A fair
face and a foul bargain. 1875 : A. B.
Cheales, *Proverb. Folk-Lore,* 35 [as in
1732]. *See also* Good face.

6. *A fair field and no favour.* 1883 :

E. Pennell-Elmhirst, *Cream Leics.*, 202
(O.), He . . . asked only for a fair field
and a clear course. 1927 : *Sphere*,
27 March, p. 492, col. 3, What our small
body of genuine talent needs is a fair
field and no favour.

7. *A fair pawn never shamed his
master.* 1639 : Clarke, 109. 1670 :
Ray, 130.

8. *A fair shop and little gain.* 1629 :
Book of Meery Riddles, Prov. 69.

9. *A fair wife, a wide house, and a
back-door, Will quickly make a rich man
poor.* c. 1460 : *Prov. of Good Counsel*,
in E.E.T.S., Ext. Ser., No. 8, p. 69,
A nyse wyfe, and a backe dore, Makyth
oftyn tymes a ryche man pore. 1647 :
Countrym. New Commonwealth, 43.

10. *A fair wife and a frontier castle
breed quarrels.* 1640 : Herbert, *Jac.
Prudentum.*

11. *A fair wife.* See **Horse** (34).

12. *A fair woman and a slasht gown
find always some nail in the way.* 1659 :
Howell, *Proverbs : Ital.-Eng.*, 10. 1670 :
Ray, 9.

13. *A fair woman with foul conditions
is like a sumptuous sepulchre full of
rotten bones.* 1647 : *Countrym. New
Commonwealth*, 11 [with " painted "
for " sumptuous "]. 1669 : *Politeuphuia*, 31.

14. *A fair woman without virtue is
like palled wine.* 1855 : Bohn, 285.

15. *As fair as Lady Done.* Cheshire.
1670 : Ray, 208. 1790 : Grose, *Prov.
Gloss.*, s.v. " Cheshire." 1917 : Bridge,
Cheshire Proverbs, 12, As fair as Lady
Done, or, There's Lady Done for you.
The wife of Sir John Done (d. 1629)
of Utkinton.

16. *Expect not fair weather in winter
on one night's ice.* 1670 : Ray, 28.

17. *Fair and far off.* Wide of the
mark. 1690 : *New Dict. Canting Crew*,
sig. E3.

18. *Fair and foolish.* See quots.
1600 : W. Vaughan, *Directions for
Health*, Faire and foolish, little and
loud, Long and lazie, blacke and proud ;
Fat and merry, leane and sad, Pale
and peevish, red and bad. 1615 :
R. Tofte, *Blazon of Iealousie*, 34 [as
in 1600 but with " lusty " for " lazie "

and " pettish " for " peevish "]. Before
1658 : Cleveland, *Works*, 268 (1742),
Foolish (the proverb says) if fair. 1732 :
Fuller, No. 6409 : Fair and foolish,
black and proud ; Long and lazy ; little
and loud. Cf. **Long and lazy.**

19. *Fair exchange is no robbery.*
1546 : Heywood, *Proverbs*, Pt. II. ch. iv.,
Chaunge be no robbry. 1628 : J. Clavell,
Recantation, 13, Then chop your horses
most familiarly, Exchange you tell
them is no roberie. 1771 : Smollett,
Clinker, in *Works*, vi. 339 (1817), " No
mistake at all," cried the baronet ; " a
fair exchange is no robbery." 1852 :
Planché, *Extravag.*, iv. 253 (1879), The
proverb of " Exchange no robbery ! "
1922 : Weyman, *Ovington's Bank*, ch.
xvii., Exchange is no robbery and I
ain't afeard.

20. **Fair feathers.** See **Fine** (12).

21. *Fair gainings make fair spendings.*
1629 : *Book of Meery Riddles*, Prov. 99.

22. *Fair in the cradle and foul in
the saddle.* 1639 : Clarke, 83. 1670 :
Ray, 87. 1709 : R. Kingston, *Apoph.
Curiosa*, 50, The proverb says, Fair,
etc. 1732 : Fuller, No. 6119. Cf.
Foul in the cradle.

23. *Faire is the weather where cup
and cover doe hold together*, i.e. where
husband and wife agree. Glos. 1639 :
Berkeley MSS., iii. 32 (1885).

24. *Fair pair of heels.* See **Show.**

25. *Fair play is a jewel.* 1824 : Scott,
Redgauntlet, ch. xxi., No, no, friend
—fair play's a jewel—time about, if
you please. 1832 : Planché, *Extravag.*,
i. 104 (1879), Fair play's a jewel, then
—let go my hair. 1865 : in *N. & Q.*,
3rd ser., viii. 317, This saying is or was
to be found in Kent, as part of a longer
formula—" Fair play is a jewel ! Lucy,
let go my hair." 1898 : Weyman,
Shrewsbury, ch. xx., But fair-play is a
jewel, my lord. . . . If you would see
my face, show me yours !

26. *Fair play is good play.* 1827 :
Hone, *Ev. Day Book*, ii. 1008, A
wooden ball . . . covered with a plate
of silver, which . . . has commonly a
motto—" Fair play is good play."
1864 : " Cornish Proverbs," in *N. & Q.*,
3rd ser., vi. 495.

27. *Fair water makes all clean.* 1639 : Clarke, 66.

28. *Fair without but foul within.* 1633 : Draxe, 10. 1732 : Fuller, No. 88, A fair face and a foul heart.

29. *Fair words and foul deeds cheat wise men as well as fools.* 1578 : Florio, *First Fruites*, fo. 25, Fayre words and yl deedes deceive both wise and fooles. 1633 : Draxe, 46, Faire words and foul deedes deceive many. 1710 : S. Palmer, *Moral Essays on Proverbs,* 154.

30. *Fair words and foul play cheat both young and old.* 1855 : Bohn, 353.

31. *Fair words break no bones.* c. 1460 : *How the Goode Wyfe*, l. 43, Ne fayre wordis brake neuer bone. 1611 : Davies (of Hereford), *Sc. of Folly*, 42, in *Works,* ii. (Grosart), Faire wordes breake no bones. 1670 : Ray, 158, Soft words break no bones. 1732 : Fuller, No. 6183, Fair words never break a bone, Foul words have broke many a one.

32. *Fair words* (or *Fine words*) *butter no parsnips.* [ἀλλ' οὐ λόγων λάρ, φασίν, ἡ ἀγορὴ δεῖται.—Herodas, vii. 49.] 1639 : Clarke, 12. 1680 : L'Estrange, *Select Coll. of Erasmus*, 131, *Co.* Your charity upon earth will be rewarded in heaven. *Pan.* Those words butter no parsnips. 1714 : Ozell, *Molière,* iv. 222, Meer praise butters no turnips. 1763 : Murphy, *Citizen,* I. ii., Fine words butter no parsnips. 1826 : Scott, *Journal,* 15 April. 1843 : Planché, *Extravag.,* ii. 205 (1879), Fine words, I grant . . . But sure, the proverb says, " No parsnips butter."

33. *Fair words cost nothing.* 1712 : Gay, *Mohocks*, sc. ii., Mr. Constable is . . . a great man, neighbour, and fair words cost nothing.

34. *Fair words fill not the belly.* 1580 : Lyly, *Euphues,* 476 (Arber), Fayre words fatte few. 1732 : Fuller, No. 1491.

35. *Fair words foul deeds.* 1581 : T. Howell, *Devises,* 16 (1906).

36. *Fair words hurt not the tongue.* 1546 : Heywood, *Proverbs,* Pt. I. ch. ix., It hurteth not the tounge to geue fayre wurdis. 1605 : Chapman, etc., *Eastw.*

Hoe, IV. i., O, madam, " Faire words never hurt the tongue." 1640 : Herbert, *Jac. Prudentum,* Fair language grates not the tongue. 1670 : Ray, 158, Soft words hurt not the mouth. 1732 : Fuller, No. 4205 [as in 1670].

37. *Fair words make fools fain.* c. 1480 : *Early Miscell.,* 25 (Warton Cl., 1855), Fayre promese ofte makyth foollis fayne. c. 1530 : *Everyman,* in Hazlitt, *Old Plays,* i. 117, Lo, fair words maketh fools fain. c. 1600 : Deloney, *Thos. of Reading,* ch. 14, Hold thy peace, faire words make fooles faine. 1732 : Fuller, No. 1492, Fair words please fools. 1820 : Scott, *Abbot,* ch. xxx., I have on my side put him off with fair words, which make fools fain.

38. *Fair words make me look to my purse.* 1640 : Herbert, *Jac. Prudentum.*

39. *Fair words slake wrath.* 1421 : in *Twenty-six Poems,* 83 (E.E.T.S., No. 124), For fayre speche doth wraththe breke. c. 1460 : *How the Goode Wyfe,* l. 30, Fayre wordes wratthe slakithe. 1597 : *North. Mothers Blessing,* in *Plasidas,* 164 (Roxb. Cl.), Faire words slaken yre. 1630 : Brathwait, *Eng. Gent.,* 236 (1641), As soft words pacifie wrath.

40. *Fair words will not make the pot boil.* 1736 : Bailey, *Dict.,* s.v. " Fair."

41. *He has a fair forehead to graft on.* An allusion no doubt to cuckolding. 1678 : Ray, 245. 1732 : Fuller, No. 1855.

42. *He who gives fair words feeds you with an empty spoon.* 1855 : Bohn, 399.

43. *In fair weather prepare for foul.* 1732 : Fuller, No. 2818.

44. *It's a pity fair weather should do any harm.* 1633 : Draxe, 45. 1665 : R. Howard, *Committee,* I., 'Tis a thousand pities that fair weather should do any hurt. 1738 : Swift, *Polite Convers.,* Dial. II., 'Tis a pity that fair weather should ever do any harm. 1846 : Denham, *Proverbs,* 6 (Percy S.). 1872 : J. Glyde, jr., *Norfolk Garland,* 151 [with " fine " for " fair "].

45. *Neay, faire words in flighting.* 1683 : Meriton, *Yorkshire Ale,* 83-7 (1697).

46. *Some to hide faire faults can make*

faire weather. 1611 : Davies (of Hereford), *Sc. of Folly*, 44, in *Works*, ii. (Grosart).

47. *To a fair day open the window, but make you ready as to a foul.* 1640 : Herbert, *Jac. Prudentum.* 1669 : *New Help to Discourse*, 310, To a fair day open your window.

48. *There was never fair prison nor love with foul face.* 1611 : Davies (of Hereford), *Sc. of Folly*, 46, in *Works*, ii. (Grosart). 1611 : Cotgrave, s.v. " Prison " [omitting " love with "].

49. *Who hath a fair wife needs more than two eyes.* 1670 : Ray, 9.

Fair, *adv.* 1. *Fair and softly.* See **Lawyer** (4) ; and **Soft and fair.**

2. *Fair chieve all where love trucks.* 1670 : Ray, 47.

3. *Fair chieve good ale, it makes many folks speak as they think.* 1678 : Ray, 93. 1886 : Bickerdyke, *Curios. of Ale and Beer*, 404, The old proverb, " Fair chieve good ale, it makes folk speak what they think."

4. *Fair fall nothing once a year.* Glos. 1639 : in *Berkeley MSS.*, iii. 30 (1885). 1678 : Ray, 182. Cf. **Well** (9).

Fair, *subs.* 1. *Fair is fair, work or play.* 1710 : S. Palmer, *Moral Essays on Proverbs*, 31. 1926 : *Humorist*, 20 Nov., p. 409, Fair is fair, when all is said.

2. *Fair is not fair, but that which pleaseth.* 1640 : Herbert, *Jac. Prudentum.* 1670 : Ray, 9.

3. *Men speak of the fair as things went with them there.* 1631 : Mabbe, *Celestina*, 84 (T.T.), And as you find your penniworths, so you speake of the faire. 1640 : Herbert, *Jac. Prudentum.* 1759 : Sterne, *Trist. Shandy*, bk. i. ch. v., For every man will speak of the fair as his own market has gone in it.

4. *The fair is done.* c. 1380 : *Gamelyn*, l. 270, in Skeat's *Chaucer*, iv. 652, For sothe at this tyme this feire is y-doon.

5. *The fair lasts all the year.* 1541 : *Sch. House of Women*, l. 348, in Hazlitt, *Early Pop. Poetry*, iv. 118, He need go no farther, the fair is heer ; Bye when ye list, it lasteth ouer yeer. 1546 : Heywood, *Proverbs*, Pt. II. ch. ii. 1618 : Harington, *Epigrams*, bk. i.

No. 72, Her fayre lasts all the yeare. 1633 : Draxe, 120.

Fairer the hostess, the fouler the reckoning, The. Before 1635 : Corbet, *Poems*, in Chalmers, v. 579, A handsome hostesse makes the reckoning deare. 1696 : D'Urfey, *Quixote*, Pt. III. Act IV. sc. i. 1754 : Berthelson, *Eng.-Danish Dict.*, s.v. " Hostess."

Fairer the paper the fouler the blot, The. 1732 : Fuller, No. 4513.

Fairest looking shoe may pinch the foot, The. Ibid., No. 4514. Cf. **Finest shoe.**

Fairest rose at last is withered, The. 1591 : Florio, *Second Frutes*, 105, The fairest and the sweetest rose In time must fade and beauty lose. 1605 : Camden, *Remains*, 333 (1870) [with " in the end " for " at last "]. c. 1630 : *Roxb. Ballads*, i. 296 (B.S.), The fairest flower will wither. 1670 : Ray, 138. 1732 : Fuller, No. 4515. Cf. **Finest flower.**

Fairest silk is soonest stained, The. 1633 : Draxe, 63, The fairest silke will soonest be soiled. 1670 : Ray, 88. 1732 : Fuller, No. 4516. Cf. **Finest lawn.**

Fairlight Down. *See* quot. 1884 : " Sussex Proverbs," in *N. & Q.*, 6th ser., ix. 403, When Fairlie Down puts on his cap, Romney Marsh will have its sap.

Faith sees by the ears. 1732 : Fuller, No. 1493.

Fall, *verb.* 1. *Fall back fall edge—* Whatever may happen. In many English dialects " back and edge "= thoroughly, entirely—*see* Wright, *Eng. Dial. Dict.*, s.v. " Back." 1553 : *Respublica*, V. v., Fall backe, fall edge, I am ons at a pointe . . . taduenture a joyncte. 1618 : Minshull, *Essayes, etc.*, 68 (1821), Yet fall back, fall edge, thus trauerse wee our ground. c. 1680 : L'Estrange, *Seneca's Morals:* "Benefits," ch. xvii., And, fall back, fall edge, we must be grateful still. 1712 : Motteux, *Quixote*, Pt. II. ch. 29, But for all that, fall back fall edge, I must and will discharge my conscience. 1825 : Scott, *Journal*, 18 Dec., I will yield to no delusive hopes, and fall back fall edge, my resolutions hold. 1828 : Carr,

Craven Dialect, i. 140, "Fall back,"
"fall edge," at all adventures, let what
will happen.

2. *Fall not out with a friend for a
trifle.* 1639: Clarke, 25. 1670: Ray, 9.

3. *Fall than rise. See* Easier.

4. *He falls low that cannot rise again.*
1685 : Meriton, *Yorkshire Ale,* 72.

5. *He that falls into the dirt, the longer
he lies the dirtier he is.* 1640 : Herbert,
Jac. Prudentum. 1732 : Fuller, No.
2096.

6. *He that falls to-day may be up again
to - morrow.* 1620: Shelton, *Quixote,*
Pt. II. ch. lxv. 1732 : Fuller, No. 2097.

7. *He that is fallen cannot help him
that is down.* 1640: Herbert, *Jac.
Prudentum.*

8. *It falls not under one's cap.* 1740 :
North, *Lives of Norths,* i. 62 (Bohn), It
fell not under every one's cap to give
so good advice.

**Falling out of friends is the renewal
of love, The.** [Amantium iræ amoris
integratio est.—Terence, *Andr.,* III. iii.
23.] 1576: *Parad. of Dainty Devices,*
No. 42, The fallyng out of faithfull
frends is the renuyng of loue. *c.* 1610 :
in *Roxb. Ballads,* i. 21 (B.S.), Though
falling out of faithfull friends renewing
be of loue. 1748 : Richardson, *Clarissa,*
iv. 48 (1785), Old Terence has taken
notice of that ; and observes upon it,
That lovers falling-out occasions lovers
falling-in. 1847 : Tennyson, *Princess,*
i. 251, Blessings on the falling out That
all the more endears.

Falmouth. *See* quot. 1891 : Q.-Couch,
Noughts and Crosses, 185, The Mayor of
Falmouth, who thanked God when the
town gaol was enlarged.

False, *adj.* 1. *A false abstract comes
from a false concrete.* Before 1529 :
Skelton, *Bowge of Courte,* l. 439.

2. *A false knave. See* Crafty.

3. *A false report rides post.* 1659 :
Howell, *Proverbs: Brit.-Eng.,* 14.

4. *A false tongue will hardly speak
truth.* 1633 : Draxe, 11.

5. *As false as a fox.* 1886 : R.
Holland, *Cheshire Gloss.,* 445 (E.D.S.),
As fause as a fox.

6. *As false as a Scot.* 1670 : Ray,
204. 1825 : Scott, *Talisman,* ch. xv.,

It is enough of folly . . . to have in-
trusted your banner to a Scot—said
I not they were ever fair and false?

7. *As false as fair.* 1546 : Heywood,
Proverbs, Pt. II. ch. ix. 1825 : Scott
[as under No. 6].

8. *As false as God is true.* 1546 :
Heywood, *Proverbs,* Pt. II. ch. vii., She
is, of trouth, as fals as God is trew.
1633 : Draxe, 61.

9. *As false as hell.* 1680 : D'Urfey,
Virtuous Wife, IV. iii., Ye are false
as hell. 1720 : Gay, *Poems,* ii. 280
(Underhill), But false as hell, she,
like the wind, Changed. 1872 : Trollope, *Golden Lion,* ch. xi., His passion
told him every hour . . . that she was
as false as hell.

10. *As false as the devil.* 1546 : Heywood, *Proverbs,* Pt. II. ch. v., The
deuill is no falser then is hee. 1639 :
Clarke, 139.

11. *In a false quarrel there is no true
valour.* 1855 : Bohn, 423.

Falsehood in fellowship, There is.
c. 1470 : G. Ashby, *Poems,* 26 (E.E.T.S.),
Be wele ware of falsehode in felawship.
Before 1529 : Skelton, *Magnyfycence,*
l. 723, Falshode in felowshyp is my
sworne brother. 1599 : Porter, *Two
Angry Women,* in Hazlitt, *Old Plays,*
vii. 356, I see all is not gold, that
glitters ; there's falsehood in fellowship.
1653 : Naunton, *Frag. Regalia,* 204
(1694), That there might be (as the
adage hath it) falsity in friendship.
1732 : Fuller, No. 4894.

Falsehood in packing, There is. 1574 :
R. Scot, *Hoppe Garden,* 49, There is,
according to the prouerbe, much fals-
hoode in packing.

Fame is a magnifying glass. 1732 :
Fuller : No. 1495.

Fame is but the breath of the people.
1611 : in Coryat, *Crudities,* i. 60 (1905),
Fame is but winde. 1732 : Fuller, No.
1497, Fame is but the breath of the
people ; and that often unwholesome.

**Fame is dangerous, All : good, bringeth
envy ; bad, shame.** 1732 : Fuller, No.
513.

**Fame, like a river, is narrowed at its
source and broadest afar off.** 1855 :
Bohn, 353.

**Fame to infamy is a beaten road,
From.** 1732 : Fuller, No. 1628.

Fame (River). *See* Yoke.

Familiarity breeds contempt. [Assiduus in oculis hominum, quae res minus verendos magnos homines ipsa satietate facit.—Livy, xxxv. 10. Parit enim conversatio contemptum, raritas conciliat ipsis rebus admirationem.— Apuleius, *De Deo Socratis.*] 12th cent. : Alanus de Insulis, in Wright, *Minor Anglo-Latin Satirists*, Record Ser., ii. 454. *c.* 1386 : Chaucer, *Melibeus,* § 55, For right as men seyn, that "over-greet homlinesse engendreth dispreysinge," so fareth it by to greet humylitee or mekenesse. 1593 : G. Harvey, in *Works*, i. 293 (Grosart), Truth begetteth hatred ; Vertue Enuy, Familiaritie cõtempt. 1600 : Shakespeare, *Merry Wives*, I. i., I hope upon familiarity will grow more contempt. 1689 : Shadwell, *Bury Fair*, II. i. 1769 : Smollett, *Adv. of Atom*, 148 (Cooke, 1795), Greater familiarity on his side might have bred contempt. 1852 : M. A. Keltic, *Reminisc. of Thought, etc.*, 67, The familiarity which reigns there, and which, according to the old proverb, engenders contempt.

Famine in England. *See* England (1).

Famine in the stall [bad hay crop], **After a, comes a famine in the hall** [bad corn crop]. 1678 : Ray, 353. 1825 : Hone, *Ev. Day Book*, i. 1669. 1893 : Inwards, *Weather Lore*, 7.

Fan, *verb. He fans with a feather.* 1813 : Ray, 75.

Fancy is a fool. 1633 : Draxe, 6. 1639 : Clarke, 28.

Fancy may bolt bran and think it flour. 1546 : Heywood, *Proverbs*, Pt. II. ch. iv., Fancy may boult bran and make ye take it floure. 1670 : Ray, 88. 1732 : Fuller, No. 1499.

Fancy may kill or cure. 1732 : Fuller, No. 1500.

Fancy surpasses beauty. 1678 : Ray, 136, Fancy passes beauty. 1732 : Fuller, No. 1501.

Far-fetched and dear bought is good for ladies. Before 1500 : in Hill, *Commonplace-Book*, 132 (E.E.T.S.), A thynge ferre fett is good for ladyes.

1546 : Heywood, *Proverbs*, Pt. I. ch. xi., Dere bought and far fet Are deinties for ladies. 1583 : Stubbes, *Anat. of Abuses*, 33 (N. Sh. S.), But "farre fetched and deare boughte" is good for ladyes, they say. 1608 : Day, *Law Trickes*, IV. i., Fare fech'd and deere bought, is good for you know who. 1696 : Vanbrugh, *Relapse*, IV. 1738 : Swift, *Polite Convers.*, Dial. I. 1886 : Elworthy, *West Som. Word-Book*, 799 (E.D.S.), The very common alliterative proverb—far-fetched, dearly bought. 1917 : Bridge, *Cheshire Proverbs*, 56.

Far folks fare well. 1633 : Draxe, 45, Farre folks fare best. 1678 : Ray, 136, Far folks fare well, and fair children die.

Far from Court far from care. 1639 : Clarke, 205. 1670 : Ray, 73. 1732 : Fuller, No. 1503.

Far from eye. *See* Eye (19) ; Out of sight ; and Seldom seen.

Far from his good is nigh his harm, A man. 1546 : Heywood, *Proverbs*, Pt. II. ch. ix. 1611 : Cotgrave, s.v. "Plat," We say (more generally) a man thats far from his good is neere his harme. 1670 : Ray, 89.

Far from Jupiter, far from thunder. 1692 : L'Estrange, *Æsop*, 11 (3rd ed.).

Far from thy kin. *See* quot. 1417 : in *Reliq. Antiquæ*, i. 233 (1841), Far from thy kyn cast the, Wreth not thy neighber next the, In a good corne contrey rest the, And sit downe, Robyn, and rest the.

Far goeth the pilgrim as the post, As. *c.* 1594 : Bacon, *Promus*, No. 508.

Far shooting never killed bird. 1640 : Herbert, *Jac. Prudentum.*

Fare, *verb.* 1. *Better fare hard with good men, than feast it with bad.* 1732 : Fuller, No. 893.

2. *See* quot. *c.* 1645 : MS. Proverbs, in *N. & Q.*, vol. 154, p. 27, He feares [fares] like a commissioner for fish and flesh.

3. *I never fared worse than when I wished for my supper.* 1639 : Clarke, 114. 1670 : Ray, 157. 1732 : Fuller, No. 2622.

Farewell and be hanged. 1575 : G. Harvey, *Letter-Book*, 95 (Camden S.),

Farewell and be hanged, goodman cowe.
1634 : S. Rowley, *Noble Soldier*, IV. ii.,
Fa ? why, farewell and be hang'd. 1668 :
Davenant, *Rivals*, III.   1707 : Dunton,
Athen. Sport, 108, To say, Farewell, be
hang'd, that's twice goodbwy.   1732 :
Fuller, No. 1504, Farewel and be
hang'd ; friends must part.

Farewell fieldfare! This and the
three following sayings all seem to have
much the same half-contemptuous import as " Farewell and be hanged."
c. 1374 : Chaucer, *Troylus*, bk. iii. l. 861,
The harm is doon, and fare-wel feldefare ! *c.* 1400 : *Rom. Rose*, l. 5510, Go,
farewel feldefare !   1825 : Jennings,
Somersetsh. Words, 37, . . . This expression is occasionally heard.   It
means, I apprehend, that as fieldfares
disappear at a particular season, *the
season is over ; the bird is flown.*

Farewell forty pence! 1583 : Melbancke, *Philotinus*, sig. T4, Farewell
fortie pence, too deare of [=by] three
shillings.   1599 : *Sir Clyomon, etc.*, sig.
F2, Nay varewell vorty pence, ye are a
knaue.   1600 : Day, *Blind Beggar*, V.,
Why, farewell forty pence ! I ha fight
fair and caught a frog.   1639 : Clarke,
68, Farewell fortie pence, Jack Noble
is dead.

Farewell frost! 1564 : Bullein, *Dialogue*, 72 (E.E.T.S.), Farewell Frost !
[said here sardonically].   1592 : Lyly,
Mother Bombie, II. iii., And so farewell
frost, my fortune naught me cost.
1631 : *Faire Em*, III.   1637 : T. Heywood, *Royal King*, III.   1670 : Ray,
174, Farewel frost, nothing got nor
nothing lost.   1732 : Fuller, No. 6156
[as in 1670].

Farewell, gentle Geoffrey! 1546 :
Heywood, *Proverbs*, Pt. I. ch. xi.

**Farewell my good days! they will be
soon gone.** Ibid., Pt. II. ch. ii.

**Farmer's care that makes the field
bear, 'Tis the.** 1732 : Fuller, No. 6350.

Farther from stone. *See* quot. 1865 :
W. White, *Eastern England*, i. 4, We
. . . find the old proverb realized,
" The farther from stone, the better
the church."

Farther. *See also* **Further.**

Farthest way. *See* **Longest way.**

Farthing good silver, To think one's.
1546 : Heywood, *Proverbs*, Pt. I. ch. x.,
She thinkth her farthyng good syluer.
c. 1594 : Bacon, *Promus*, No. 636. 1659 :
Howell, 4, She thinks her farthing as
good silver as anothers. Cf. **Halfpenny** ;
and **Penny** (26).

**Farthing is good that makes the penny
bud, The.** 1623 : Wodroephe, *Spared
Houres*, 477.

Fashion's sake. *See* **Dog** (42).

Fast and loose is no possession. 1639 :
Clarke, 159.

Fast and loose. *See also* **Play.**

Fast [asleep] as a church. 1708 : tr.
Aleman's *Guzman*, i. 284, I went . . .
to see if he slept still, and found both
him and my mistress as fast as a church.
1788 : Colman, jr., *Ways and Means*,
III. iii., All's snug.   The baronet's as
fast as a church.   1845 : Jerrold, *Mrs.
Caudle*, xxvii., No sooner in bed than
you're fast as a church.   1883 : Burne,
Shropsh. Folk-Lore, 594.   Cf. **Sleep,
verb** (6).

Fast as a thief. *See* **Safe as a thief.**

Fast as hops. *See* **Thick as hops.**

Fast bind fast find. 1484 : Caxton,
Æsope, V. iv. (Jacobs), For who
that wel byndeth well can he
vnbynd.   *c.* 1540 : Bale, *Kynge Johan*,
in Manly, *Spec. of Pre-Shakesp. Drama*,
i. 592, As the saynge is, he fyndeth that
surely bynde.   1622 : B. & F., *Span.
Curate*, II. ii.   1768 : Bickerstaffe, *Padlock*, I. iii., " Fast bind, safe find," is
an excellent proverb.   I'll e'en lock
her up with the rest.   1824 : Scott,
Redgauntlet, ch. xiii.

Fast, verb. 1. *He fasts enough that
has a bad meal.* 1611 : Cotgrave, s.v.
" Assez," He that feeds barely fasts
sufficiently.   1732 : Fuller, No. 1844.

2. *He fasts enough whose wife scolds
all dinner-time.* Ibid., No. 1845.

3. *If I were to fast for my life, I would
eat a good breakfast in the morning.*
1678 : Ray, 67.

4. *Is there no mean but fast or feast?*
1732 : Fuller, No. 3113.

Fasting belly may never be merry, A.
Before 1500 : in Hill, *Commonplace-
Book*, 131 (E.E.T.S.).

Fat as a fool. 1579 : Lyly, *Euphues*,

118 (Arber), That feedeth a louer as
fat as a foole. 1630 : *Tinker of Turvey*,
59 (Halliwell), To feed him with her
faire speeches, till she made him as fat
as a foole. 1678 : Ray, 283.

Fat as a hen in the forehead. 1611 :
Cotgrave, s.v. " Pie," *Maigre comme
vne pie*, We say (to the same purpose)
as fat as a henne's on the forehead.
c. 1618 : B. & F., *Bonduca*, I. ii., As
fat as hens i' th' foreheads. 1670 :
Ray, 204. 1738 : Swift, *Polite Convers.*,
Dial. III., Fat ! ay, fat as a hen in the
forehead.

Fat as a hog (or pig, or bacon-pig).
1485 : Malory, *Morte d'Arthur*, bk. vii.
ch. i., He shall be as fatte . . . as
a porke hog. 1611 : Cotgrave, s.v.
" Cochon," *Gras comme vn cochon*,
(Wee say the same) as fat as a pigge.
1653 : Walton, *Angler*, Pt. I. ch. x.,
He will grow not only to be very large,
but as fat as a hog. 1767 : Garrick, in
Garrick Corresp., i. 252 (1831), I am
grown as fat as a hog. 1846 : Denham,
Proverbs, 60 (Percy S.), Fat as a bacon-
pig at Martlemas.

Fat as a porpoise. 1738 : Swift,
Polite Convers., Dial. II., I shall grow
as fat as a porpoise. 1872 : Hardy,
Greenwood Tree, Pt. I. ch. vii., There's
your brother Bob—as fat as a porpoise.

Fat as Big Ben. 1862 : *Dialect of
Leeds*, 247, " As fat as Big Ben," is yet
a household phrase. A former bellman
in great repute upon account of his
huge proportions.

Fat as butter. 1678 : Ray, 283. 1720 :
Gay, *Poems*, ii. 278 (Underhill), My
cheeks as fat as butter grown.

Fat commodity hath no fellow, A.
1659 : Howell, 3.

Fat drops fall from fat flesh. 1678 :
Ray, 137.

Fat, fair, and forty. 1795 : O'Keeffe,
Irish Minnie, II. iii., Fat, fair, and forty
were all the toast of the young men.

Fat housekeeper (or **kitchen**) **makes
lean executors** (or **will**), A. 1611 :
Cotgrave, s.v. " Testament," A fat
kitchin a leane will. Ibid., s.v. " Cui-
sine," Great house-keepers leave poor
executors. 1670 : Ray, 9, A fat housekeeper makes lean executors. 1732 :

Fuller, No. 1505 [as in 1670]. 1736 :
Franklin, *Way to Wealth*, in *Works*, i.
446 (Bigelow), A fat kitchin makes a
lean will. 1880 : Spurgeon, *Ploughman's Pictures*, 11 [as in 1736].

Fat is in the fire, The. *c.* 1374 :
Chaucer, *Troylus*, bk. iii. st. 95, Or
caste al the grewel in the fire. 1559 :
Becon, in *Prayers, etc.*, 277 (P.S.), Or
else your cake is dough, and all your
fat lie in the fire. 1603 : Dekker, in
Works, i. 174 (Grosart), Then must he
trudge to get gossips, such as shee will
appoint, or else all the fatte is in the
fire. 1633 : Jonson, *Love's Welcome*.
1740 : North, *Examen*, 506, They might
fall in with the King . . . and then all
the fat was in the fire. 1898 : H. James,
in *Letters*, i. 287 (1920), It is this morning precisely that one feels the fat at
last fairly in the fire. 1910 : Shaw,
Misalliance, 15 (1914), I said I was
sure I knew nothing about such things,
and hadn't we better change the subject. Then the fat was in the fire,
I can tell you.

**Fat man knoweth not what the lean
thinketh, The.** 1640 : Herbert, *Jac.
Prudentum*.

Fat (or **Fattest**) **land** (or **soil**). See
Best (16).

Fat paunches make lean pates. 1586 :
B. Young, tr. Guazzo's *Civil Convers.*,
fo. 190, The prouerbe is as true as
common. That a fat bellie doth not
engender a subtill witte. 1592 : Shakespeare, *L. L. L.*, I. i., Fat paunches
have lean pates. 1681 : W. Robertson,
Phraseol. Generalis, 587. 1732 : Fuller,
No. 1506.

Fat soil. See Worse for the rider.

Fat sorrow is better than lean sorrow.
1678 : Ray, 137. 1732 : Fuller, No. 1507.

Fat sow. See Sow (2), (10), and (14).

Fat with the lean, To take the. 1850 :
Dickens, *Copperfield*, ch. li., A man must
take the fat with the lean; that's what
he must make up his mind to, in this
life.

**Fate leads the willing but drives the
stubborn.** 1732 : Fuller, No. 1508.

Father and Fathers. 1. *Father Derby*.
See **Derby's bands**.

    2. *He whose father is judge goes safe*

to his trial. 1620 : Shelton, *Quixote*, Pt. II. ch. xliii., For according to the proverb, " He that hath the judge to his father, etc.," and I am governor, which is more than judge. 1712 : Motteux, *Quixote*, Pt. II. ch. xliii. 1732 : Fuller, No. 2400.

3. *His father will never be dead while he is alive.* 1672 : Walker, *Parœm.*, 50.

4. *Our fathers who were wondrous wise, Did wash their throats before their eyes.* 1613 : Wither, *Abuses Stript, etc.*, bk. ii. Sat. 1, Prethee let me intreat thee now to drinke Before thou wash ; Our fathers that were wise, Were wont to say 'twas wholesome for the eyes. 1670 : Ray, 212. 1732 : Fuller, No. 6423.

5. *The father to the bough, the son to the plough. See* 1730 quot. 1576 : Lambarde, *Peramb. of Kent*, 497 (1826). 1659 : W. Cole, in *Harl. Miscell.*, iv. 306 (1745), And therefore it is the saying in Kent, The father, etc. 1730 : Bailey, *Eng. Dict.*, s.v. " Gavel-kind," In Gavel-kind, tho' the father be hang'd, the son shall inherit ; for their custom is, *the Father to the bough, the son to the plough.* 1790 : Grose, *Prov. Gloss.*, s.v. " Kent."

6. *Thou art thy father's own son.* 1672 : Walker, *Parœm.*, 30. 1681 : W. Robertson, *Phraseol. Generalis*, 587.

Fault and **Faults.** 1. *A fault is sooner found than mended.* c. 1580 : Fulwell, *Ars Adulandi*, sig. H4.

2. *A fault once denied* (or *excused*) *is twice committed.* c. 1590 : G. Harvey, *Marginalia*, 100 (1913) [with " excused "]. 1669 : *Politeuphuia*, 166 [" excused "]. 1732 : Fuller, No. 93 [" denied "]. 1875 : A. B. Cheales, *Proverb. Folk-Lore*, 165 [as in 1732].

3. *Fault confessed. See* **Confessing.**

4. *Faults are thick where love is thin.* 1659 : Howell, *Proverbs : Brit.-Eng.*, 2. 1670 : Ray, 16, Where love fails, we espy all faults. 1732 : Fuller, No. 5676, Where there is no love, all are faults. 1869 : Spurgeon, *John Ploughman*, ch. x.

5. *Faults that are rich are fair.* 1855 : Bohn, 354.

6. *He hath but one fault—he is naught.* 1546 : Heywood, *Proverbs*, Pt. I. ch. xi.

1560 : T. Wilson, *Rhetorique*, 153 (1909), Such a man hath no fault but one, and if that were amended, all were well : what is that? (quoth an other). In good faith he is naught. 1633 : Draxe, 43 [with " starke " before " naught "]. 1732 : Fuller, No. 6054, Your main fault is, you are good for nothing.

7. *The first faults are theirs that commit them, the second theirs that permit them.* 1732 : Fuller, No. 4528.

Faulty stands on his guard, The. 1578 : Florio, *First Fruites*, fo. 28, Who is faultie is suspected. 1640 : Herbert, *Jac. Prudentum.* 1670 : Ray, 9.

Faustus, Dr. *See* Devil (39).

Favour will as surely perish as life. 1651 : Herbert, *Jac. Prudentum*, 2nd ed.

Favour, Without, none will know you, and with it you will not know yourself. 1640 : Herbert, *Jac. Prudentum.*

Fawn peckles [Brown freckles] once made a vow, They never would come on a face that was fou [foul or ugly]. 1877 : E. Leigh, *Cheshire Gloss.*, 152. 1917 : Bridge, *Cheshire Proverbs*, 56.

Fear and **Fears,** *subs.* 1. *Fear and shame much sin doth tame.* c. 1550 : in Hazlitt, *Early Pop. Poetry*, iii. 246.

2. *Fear causeth a man to cast beyond the moon.* 1546 : Heywood, *Proverbs*, Pt. I. ch. iv., Feare may force a man to cast beyonde the moone. 1633 : Draxe, 63.

3. *Fear gives* (or *lends*) *wings.* 1580 : Sidney, *Arcadia*, bk. ii. p. 195 (1893), They all cried, " O ! see how fear gives him wings." 1590 : Spenser, *F. Q.*, III. vii. 26, Therto fear gave her wings. 1666 : Torriano, *Piazza Univ.*, 60, Fear hath wings.

4. *Fear hath a quick ear.* 1654 : Gayton, *Pleasant Notes Don Q.*, 65.

5. *Fear is one part of prudence.* 1732 : Fuller, No. 1512.

6. *Fear is stronger than love.* Ibid., No. 1513.

7. *Fear keeps the garden better than the gardener.* 1640 : Herbert, *Jac. Prudentum.*

8. *Fear, the beadle of the law.* 1651 : Ibid., 2nd ed.

9. *Fears are divided in the midst.* 1640 : Ibid.

10. *'Twas fear that first put on arms.*
1732 : Fuller, No. 5317.

Fear, *verb.* 1. *He that feareth every
bush must never go a-birding.* 1580 :
Lyly, *Euphues,* 354 (Arber). 1732 :
Fuller, No. 2098.

2. *He that fears death lives not.* 1640 :
Herbert, *Jac. Prudentum.* 1708 : tr.
Aleman's *Guzman,* i. 432, I comforted
myself with this saying, *That he that
fears death, does not deserve to live.*

3. *It is good to fear the worst; the best
will save itself.* 1633 : Draxe, 65. 1639 :
Clarke, 66, Tis good to fear the worst.
1670 : Ray, 89.

4. *To fear no colours*=To fear no
enemy. 1594 : *True Trag. Rich. Third,*
15 (Sh. S.), I will neuer feare colours.
1601 : Yarington, *Two Trag. in One,*
I. iv., I'le fear no coulours. 1679 :
Dryden, *Troilus,* II. ii., Take a good
heart, man . . . and fear no colours,
and speak your mind. 1704 : Swift,
Tale of a Tub, § xi., He was a person
that feared no colours.

Feared men be fearful. 1639 : Clarke,
208.

**Feast and a belly-ful, Little difference
between a.** 1659 : Howell, 13. 1670 :
Ray, 215. 1732 : Fuller, No. 3253.

**Feast is not made of mushrooms
only, A.** 1732 : Fuller, No. 96.

Feasting makes no friendship. Ibid.,
No. 1515.

Feastings are the physicians' harvest,
Christmas. 1639 : Clarke, 174.

Feather, *subs.* 1. *A feather in one's
cap.* 1714 : Mandeville, *Fable of Bees,*
197, Men . . . then put feathers in their
caps . . . talk of publick-spiritedness.
1754 : Berthelson, *Eng.-Danish Dict.,*
s.v. " Feather," That is but feather in
his cap. 1803 : Colman, jr., *John Bull,*
I. i., Who . . . fancy female ruin a
feather in your caps of vanity. 1821 :
Byron, *Letters and Journals,* v. 472
(Prothero). 1922 : Weyman, *Ovington's
Bank,* ch. xvi., It would be a feather
in the bank's cap if the money . . .
were recovered through the bank's
exertions.

2. *A feather of the same wing.* 1639 :
Clarke, 14.

3. *Feather by feather.* 1653 : Middle-

ton and Rowley, *Span. Gipsy,* II. i.,
Feather by feather birds build nests.
1666 : Torriano, *Piazza Univ.,* 174,
Quill by quill is a goose pluck'd. 1732 :
Fuller, No. 1514, Feather by feather
the goose is pluck'd.

4. *Let not him that fears feathers come
among wild fowl.* 1640 : Herbert, *Jac.
Prudentum.*

5. *The feather makes not the bird.*
1572 : G. Fenton, *Monophylo,* sig. T4,
Seing (with the olde prouerbe) as the
feather makes not the byrde.

Feather one's nest, To. 1553 : *Respublica,* I. i., And nowe ys the tyme
come . . . to make vp my mouth, and
to feather my neste. 1590 : Greene, in
Works, viii. 138 (Grosart), She sees
thou hast fethred thy nest, and hast
crowns in thy purse. 1653 : Urquhart,
Rabelais, bk. ii. ch. xvii., If thou didst
know what advantage I made, and how
well I feathered my nest . . . 1709 :
Ward, *Acc. of Clubs,* 77 (1756), Who, as
yet, have not had the lucky opportunity of feathering their nests. 1834-7 :
Southey, *Doctor,* ch. lxiv., He feathered
his nest with the spoils of the Loyalists.
1915 : Pinero, *Big Drum,* II. p. 98.

February. 1. *A February spring is
not worth a pin.* Corn. 1893 : Inwards,
Weather Lore, 13.

2. *A Welshman had rather see his dam
on her bier than see a fair Februeer.*
1678 : Ray, 44. 1744 : Claridge, in
Mills, *Essay on Weather,* 100 (1773).
1846 : Denham, *Proverbs,* 31 (Percy S.).
1917 : Bridge, *Cheshire Proverbs,* 164.

3. *All the months in the year curse a
fair Februeer.* 1670 : Ray, 40. 1732 :
Fuller, No. 6151. 1893 : Inwards,
Weather Lore, 13.

4. *Double-faced February,* Ibid., 13.

5. *February fill-dyke.* 1557 : Tusser,
Hund. Points, in *British Bibliog.,* iii. 20
(1812), And feuerell fill dyke, doth good
with his snowe. 1577 : Tusser, *Husb.,*
ch. 34, Feb, fill the dike with what
ye like. 1630 : Taylor (Water-Poet),
Workes, 2nd pagin., 257, If foulefac'd
February keepe true touch . . . By
night, by day, by little and by much,
It fills the ditch, with either blacke
or white. 1799 : *Gent. Mag.,* Pt. I.

p. 203, February fill dike Either black
or white. 1893: Inwards, *Weather Lore*,
13, February fill the dyke Weather
either black or white. Ibid., 14, February fill dyke; March lick it out.
February fill dyke, be it black or be it
white; But if it be white, it's better to
like. 1900: *N. & Q.*, 9th ser., v. 384,
[Northants] February fills the dykes;
March winds blow the organ pipes.
1922: Lucas, *Genevra's Money*, 4, February was filling the dykes to the very
margin.

6. *February fire lang, March tide to
bed gang*—"a Craven proverb." 1828:
Carr, *Craven Dialect*, i. 144.

7. *February, if ye be fair, The sheep
will mend, and nothing mair; February,
if ye be foul* [rainy], *The sheep will die
in every pool.* 1846: Denham, *Proverbs*,
29 (Percy S.).

8. *February makes a bridge, and
March breaks it.* 1640: Herbert, *Jac.
Prudentum*. 1732: Fuller, No. 1516.
1846: Denham, *Proverbs*, 27 (Percy S.),
February builds a bridge, and March
breaks it down.

9. *February singing, Never stints
stinging.* " If bees get out in February,
the next day will be windy and rainy.
Surrey." 1893: Inwards, *Weather Lore*,
13.

10. *February's rain fills the barn.*
1611: Cotgrave, s.v. " Pluye," February
rain is the husbandmans gaine. 1666:
Torriano, *Piazza Univ.*, 86.

11. *Februeer doth cut and shear.*
1633: Jonson, *Tale of a Tub*, I. i., Old
bishop Valentine, You have brought
us nipping weather—*Februere doth cut
and shear.* 1678: Ray, 44. 1893: Inwards, *Weather Lore*, 13 [with " both "
for " doth "].

12. *If February calends be summerly
gay, 'Twill be winterly weather in the
calends of May.* 1882: Mrs. Chamberlain, *W. Worcs. Words*, 37 (E.D.S.).

13. *If February give much snow, A
fine summer it doth foreshow.* 1878:
Dyer, *Eng. Folk-Lore*, 251.

14. *If in February there be no rain,
The hay won't goody, nor the grain.*
1913: E. M. Wright, *Rustic Speech,
etc.*, 317.

15. *In February if thou hearest thunder, Thou wilt see a summer's wonder.*
1893: Inwards, *Weather Lore*, 14.

16. *Reckon right, and February hath
one and thirty days.* 1640: Herbert,
Jac. Prudentum. 1670: Ray, 9.

17. *When gnats dance in February the
husbandman becomes a beggar.* 1878:
Dyer, *Eng. Folk-Lore*, 251.

18. *When the cat lies in the sun in
February, she will creep behind the
stove in March.* 1905: *N. & Q.*, 10th
ser., iii. 314.

See also August (1); Candlemas,
H (4); January (1); October (7);
St. Matthias; St. Valentine; and Snow
(4).

Feed, *verb.* 1. *Feed by measure and
defy the physician.* 1546: Heywood,
Proverbs, Pt. II. ch. vii. 1670: Ray, 39
[with " sparingly " for " by measure "].

2. *He that feeds the poor hath treasure.*
c. 1460: *How the Good Wife*, l. 15,
Tresour he hathe that pouere fedithe.

3. *To feed like a boar in a frank.*
1598: Shakespeare, 2 *Henry IV.*, II. ii.,
Where sups he? doth the old boar feed
in the old frank? 1631: F. Lenton,
Characters, sig. C12 (1663), And then
feed at ease like a boar in a frank.
1825: Scott, in Lockhart's *Life*, vi. 81,
From Lowther we reached Abbotsford
in one day, and now doth the old *bore*
feed in the old frank.

4. *To feed like a farmer.* 1655:
Fuller, *Church Hist.*, bk. vi. § ii. (v. 13),
On which the abbot feed as the farmer
of his grange. *c.* 1680: in *Roxb.
Ballads*, vii. 278 (B.S.), And if he to a
pudding gets, he farmer-like doth feed.
1754: Berthelson, *Eng.-Danish Dict.*,
s.v. " Feed," He feeds like a farmer.

Feeling hath no fellow. 1678: Ray,
138. 1725: *Matchless Rogue*, 56, Tho'
seeing is believing, and feeling has no
fellow. 1732: Fuller, No. 1518.

Feet. *See* Foot.

Fellow-ruler. *He that hath a fellow-
ruler, hath an over-ruler.* 1611: Cotgrave, s.v. " Avoir." 1670: Ray, 9.

**Fencer hath one trick in his budget
more than ever he taught his scholar, A.**
1639: Clarke, 127.

Fennel. *See* quot. 1884: Friend,

Flowers and Fl. Lore, 208, An old proverb says: "Sowing fennel is sowing
sorrow."

**Fern begins to look red, When, then
milk is good with brown bread.** 1588:
Cogan, *Haven of Health*, 152-3 (1612),
According to that old saying; when
fearne waxeth red, then is milke good
with bread. 1659: Howell, 11. 1670:
Ray, 35.

**Fern is as high as a ladle, When the,
You may sleep as long as you are able.**
1670: Ray, 35.

**Fern is as high as a spoon, When the,
You may sleep an hour at noon.** Ibid.,
34 1732: Fuller, No. 6186. 1846:
Denham, *Proverbs*, 50 (Percy S.). 1904:
Co. Folk-Lore: Northumb., 178 (F.L.S.).

Festival. *See* quot. 1660: T. Hall,
Funebria Floræ, 10, Insomuch that 'tis
a common saying, That 'tis *no festival
unless there boe some fightings.*

Fetters. *See* **Love**, *verb* (13).

Fever lurden=Laziness. *See* quots.
c. 1500: in Hazlitt, *Early Pop. Poetry*,
i. 93 (O.), I trow he was infecte certeyn
With the faitour, or the fever lordeyn.
1568: W. Fulwood, *Enem. of Idlenesse*,
132 (1593), You have the palsey or
eke the feuer lurden. 1606: B. Rich,
Faultes Faults, sig. F2, One of them
growing a little sicke of a feuer lordan.
1678: Ray, 172, He that's sick of a
feaver lurden must be cured by the
hasel gelding.

Fever of lurk. *See* **Two stomachs.**

**Few arc fit to be entrusted with them-
selves.** 1732: Fuller, No. 1523.

Few days pass without some clouds.
1846: Denham, *Proverbs*, 4 (Percy S.).

Few friends. *See* **Friend** (13) and (19).

Few lawyers. *See* **Lawyer** (5).

Few leaves and bad fruit. 1732:
Fuller, No. 1526.

**Few men and much meat make a
feast.** 1639: Clarke, 74.

Few physicians live well. 1605:
Camden, *Remains*, 322 (1870).

Few words and many deeds. 1633:
Draxe, 40.

Few words are best. *c.* 1600: in
Roxb. Ballads, i. 157 (Hindley), It is an
old saying, that few words are best.
1660: Tatham, *The Rump*, II., Well,

I know what I know; few words are
best. 1771: Smollett, *Clinker*, in *Works*,
vi. 70 (1817), I wonder what the devil
possessed me—but few words are best.
1828: Scott, *Fair Maid*, ch. xxv.,
Wherefore, few words are best, wench.

Few words the wise suffice. 1546:
Heywood, *Proverbs*, Pt. II. ch. vii.,
Fewe woordis to the wise suffice to be
spoken. 1605: Camden, *Remains*, 322
(1870). Before 1680: Butler, *Remains*,
i. 379 (1759), Few words do best with
the wise. 1730: T. Saldkeld, tr.
Gracian's *Compl. Gent.*, 60, 'Tis a
common saying that few words are
sufficient to make a thing intelligible
to a man of sense.

**Fewer his years, the fewer his tears,
The.** 1732: Fuller, No. 6233.

Fewer the better cheer. *See* **More the
merrier.**

Fiddle, *subs.* 1. *As well try to borrow a
fiddle at a wakes.* 1917: Bridge, *Cheshire
Proverbs*, 26.

2. *He has got the fiddle but not the
stick.* 1678: Ray, 86. 1732: Fuller,
No. 1871. 1820: Colton, *Lacon*, Pt. II.
No. 231, Those who attempted to
imitate them, would find that they had
got the fiddle, but not the fiddle-stick.

3. *To hang the fiddle at the door.*
c. 1791: Pegge, *Derbicisms*, 100 (E.D.S.),
"To hang the fiddle at the door"
[said] of a person who is merry and
cheerful abroad, but surly and ill-
tempered in his family. 1883: Burne,
Shropsh. Folk-Lore, 597, To hang up
the fiddle at the house-door=to be
merry abroad and morose at home.

See also **Face** (3); and **Fine** (3).

Fiddle for shives [slices of bread]
among old wives, Go. 1639: Clarke,
68 [with "good" for "old"]. 1670:
Ray, 175. 1877: E. Leigh, *Cheshire
Gloss.*, 184. 1917: Bridge, *Cheshire
Proverbs*, 61.

Fiddler and Fiddlers. 1. *Fiddler's
fare.* 1608: *Dumb Knight*, III., in
Hazlitt, *Old Plays*, x. 169, You have
had more than fidler's fare, for you
have meat, money, and cloth. 1660:
Howell, *Parly of Beasts*, 128, He was
dismissed fidler-like, with meat, drink,
and money. 1738: Swift, *Polite*

Convers., Dial. III., Fiddler's fare, meat, drink, and money. 1828 : Carr, *Craven Dialect*, i. 149 [as in 1738].

2. *Fiddlers' dogs and flies come to feasts uncalled.* 1683 : Meriton, *Yorkshire Ale*, 83–7 (1697).

3. *Fiddlers' money* = Small change. 1785 : Grose, *Class. Dict. Vulgar Tongue*, s.v., Fiddlers' money: all six pences. 1877 : *N. & Q.*, 5th ser., vii. 138, In Oxfordshire threepenny and fourpenny pieces are called " fiddler's money." 1889 : Peacock, *Manley, etc., Gloss.*, 203 (E.D.S.), Fiddlers' money. Groats, threepenny pieces, pennies. [The expression is common in many parts of the country.]

4. *Fiddlers' pay. See* quots. 1597 : 1st part *Return from Parnassus*, I. i. (O.), He . . . gave me fidler's wages, and dismiste me. 1690 : *New Dict. Canting Crew*, sig. E4, Fidlers-pay, Thanks and wine.

5. *In a fiddler's house. See* quots. 1640 : Herbert, *Jac. Prudentum*, In the house of a fiddler, all fiddle. 1732 : Fuller, No. 2809, In a fidler's house, all are dancers.

6. *Like a fiddler's elbow.* 1887 : T. Darlington, *S. Cheshire Folk Speech*, 187 (E.D.S.). 1917 : Bridge, *Cheshire Proverbs*, 79, In and out like a fiddler's elbow. 1926 : *Devonsh. Assoc. Trans.*, lvii. 152, " Too much play, like a fiddler's elbow." Said of something which had worked loose.

Field, Always in the. *See* **Always in the lane.**

Field requires three things; fair weather, sound seed, and a good husbandman, A. 1846 : Denham, *Proverbs*, 3 (Percy S.).

Fields have eyes and woods have ears. 13th cent. : quoted in Wright, *Essays on Middle Ages*, i. 168, Wode has erys, felde has sight. *c.* 1386 : Chaucer, *Knight's Tale*, l. 664, Feeld hath eyen, and the wode hath eres. 1564 : Bullein, *Dialogue*, 13 (E.E.T.S.), The fielde haue eyes and the wood haue eares. Therefore we must comen closelie, and beware of blabbes. 1611 : Cotgrave, s.v. " Bois." 1670 : Ray, 95. 1732 : Fuller, No. 1532, Fields have eyes, and

hedges ears. 1924 : I was told by a Wiltshire woman that a very common saying in that county is, " Hedges have eyes and walls have ears."

Fierce as a dig [duck]—" a Lancashire and probably a Cheshire proverb." 1877 : E. Leigh, *Cheshire Gloss.*, 61.

Fierce as a goose. 1670 : Ray, 204.

Fierce as a ratten [rat]. 1862 : *Dialect of Leeds*, 406.

Fifth wheel to a coach, A=A hindering superfluity. [1531 : C. B. Bouelles, *Proverb. Vulg.*, fo. 36, La cinquiesme roue au chariot, ne faict qu'empescher.] 1631 : Dekker, *Match me in London*, I. *ad fin.*, Thou tyest but wings to a swift gray hounds heele, And add'st to a running charriot a fift wheele. 1644 : Taylor (Water-Poet), *Crop-eare Curried*, 32, in *Works*, 2nd coll. (Spens. S.), As much pertinent as the fift wheele in a coach. 1921 : *Observer*, 11 Dec., p. 13, col. 2, Asquithian Liberalism by itself is the fifth wheel to the coach.

Fig for thy friend, and a peach for thine enemy, Provide a. 1629 : *Book of Meery Riddles*, Prov. 53. 1678 : Ray, 53.

Fight, verb. 1. *A man that will fight may find a cudgel in every hedge.* 1639 : Clarke, 324.

2. *Fight dog fight bear.* 1583 : Stubbes, *Anat. of Abuses*, 178 (N. Sh. S.), Some . . . will not make anie bones of xx. xl. c. pound at once to hazard at a bait [bear-baiting], with " fight dog, feight beare (say they), the deuill part all ! " 1632 : R. Brome, *Northern Lasse*, II. v., We shall have a foul house on't I fear. But since it is too late, fight dog, fight bear, I'le turn my master loose to her. 1687 : A. Behn, *Lucky Chance*, III. ii., Why, let 'em fight dog, fight bear ; mun, I'll to bed. 1716 : E. Ward, *St. Paul's Church*, 21, But cry halloo, fight dog, fight bear. 1821 : Scott, *Kenilworth*, ch. xvii. 1831 : Scott, *Journal*, 5 March.

3. *Fight dog, fight devil.* 1656 : T. Ady, *Candle in the Dark*, 62. 1873 : Spilling, *Molly Miggs*, 5 (W.), I had had a pratty gude spell o' work morning and night, pull dawg pull devil, as the saying is.

*4. He that fights and runs away may
live to fight another day.* [Post inde
aliquanto tempore Philippus apud
Chaeroneam proelio magno Athenienses
vicit. Tum Demosthenes orator ex eo
proelio salutem fuga quaesivit : quum-
que id ei, quod fugerat, probrose
objiceretur; versu illo notissimo elusit,
ἀνὴρ ὁ φεύγων, inquit, καὶ πάλιν μαχήσεται.
—Aulus Gellius, *Noct. Att.*, xvii. 21.]
c. 1320 : in *Reliq. Antiquæ*, i. 111.
(1841), " Wel fytht, that wel
flyth "; Quoth Hendyng. *c.* 1350 :
Owl and Nightingale, l. 174, " Wel fi3t
that wel fli3t," seith the wise. *c.* 1440 :
Gesta Rom., 374 (E.E.T.S.), It is
an olde sawe, he feghtith wele that
fleith faste. 1542 : Udall, tr. Erasmus'
Apoph., 372 (1877), That same man,
that renneth awaie, Maie again fight,
an other daie. 1663 : Butler, *Hudibras*,
Pt. III. can. iii., For those that fly may
fight again, Which he can never do
that's slain. 1761 : *Art of Poetry on a
New Plan*, ii. 147, For he who fights
and runs away May live to fight another day. 1849 : Planché, *Extravag.*,
iii. 334 (1879).

5. To fight with one's own shadow.
1595 : Shakespeare, *M. of Venice*, I.
ii., He will fence with his own shadow.
1670 : Ray, 175. 1736 : Bailey, *Dict.*,
s.v. " Shadow."

Fill the mouth with empty spoons, To.
1639 : Clarke, 314. 1670 : Ray, 175.

*Fill what you will and drink what you
fill.* 1678 : Ray, 88. 1732 : Fuller,
No. 6180.

Find, *verb.* 1. *Take heed you find not
what you do not seek.* 1596 : Harington,
Metam. of Ajax, 122 (1814), Yet he
would feel, to seek that he would not
find, for fear lest they should find that
they did not seek. 1670 : Ray, 9.
1732 : Fuller, No. 4309.

2. To find fault. See **Blames.**

3. To find things before they are lost.
1546 : Heywood, *Proverbs*, Pt. I. ch. xi.,
If ye seeke to foule thynges er they be
lost, Ye shall fynde one daie you come
to your cost. 1633 : Draxe, 203, He
findeth things before they are lost.
1732 : Fuller, No. 5918, You have found
what was never lost.

Fine, *adj.* 1. *A fine new nothing.*
1678 : Ray, 342.

2. All is fine that is fit. 1732 :
Fuller, No. 523.

3. As fine as a fiddle. 1862 : *Dialect
of Leeds*, 407.

4. As fine as a horse. 1838 : Mrs.
Bray, *Trad. of Devon*, i. 328, This
Hobby was very gay and gorgeous,
and hence have we, in all probability,
the common saying of " as fine as the
horse." 1883 : Burne, *Shropsh. Folk-
Lore*, 595, As fine (or proud) as a horse
in bells.

5. As fine as a new scraped carrot.
1886 : R. Holland, *Cheshire Gloss.*, 445
(E.D.S.). 1917 : Bridge, *Cheshire Proverbs*, 13.

6. As fine as Filliloo. 1917 : Ibid., 13,
. . . The word [Filliloo] has no particular meaning in Cheshire.

7. As fine as fivepence. 1564 : Bullcin,
Dialogue, 62 (E.E.T.S.), Out of the
countree . . . as fine as fippence!
c. 1600 : *Grim the Collier*, II., As a
man would say, finer than fivepence,
or more proud than a peacock. 1685 :
S. Wesley, *Maggots*, 109, All finer than
fippence, they dazzl'd my eye. 1738 :
Swift, *Polite Convers.*, Dial. III., She
was as fine as fi'pence. 1854 : Baker,
Northants Gloss., s.v. " Fippence,"
" As fine as fippence," is a common
proverbial simile. 1901 : F. E. Taylor,
Lancs Sayings, 2, As fine as fippence.

8. As fine as flying pigs. 1883 :
Burne, *Shropsh. Folk-Lore*, 595.

*9. As fine (or proud) as a lord's
bastard.* 1678 : Ray, 284.

10. Fine cloth is never out of fashion.
1732 : Fuller, No. 1537.

*11. Fine dressing is a foul house swept
before the doors.* 1640 : Herbert, *Jac.
Prudentum.* 1670 : Ray, 8 [with " windows " for " doors "]. 1732 : Fuller,
No. 1538.

12. Fine feathers make fine birds.
1611 : Davies (of Hereford), *Sc. of
Folly*, 46, in *Works*, ii. (Grosart), The
faire feathers still make the faire fowles.
1678 : Bunyan, *Pilgr. Progr.*, Pt. I. p. 35
(1849), Strange! He's another man,
upon my word; They be fine feathers,
that make a fine bird. *c.* 1760 : Foote,

Author, I. 1891 : Hardy, *Tess*, ch.
xxxiv., As everybody knows, fine
feathers make fine birds. 1917 : Bridge,
Cheshire Proverbs, 57, Fine feathers
make fine birds, but they don't make
lady-birds.

13. *Fine words. See* Fair (32).

14. *To fine folks a little ill finely wrapt.*
1640 : Herbert, *Jac. Prudentum.*

Finest flower will soonest fade, The.
c. 1570 : in Huth, *Ancient Ballads, etc.*,
374 (1867). Cf. **Fairest rose.**

Finest lawn soonest stains, The.
1556 : Withals, *Dict.*, sig. A2, The
finest colours will sonest be staigned.
1600 : Bodenham, *Belvedere*, 44 (Spens.
S.), The purest lawne is apt for euery
staine. 1670 : Ray, 90. 1875 : A. B.
Cheales, *Proverb. Folk-Lore*, 164, The
finest silks are soonest stained. Cf.
Fairest silk.

Finest shoe often hurts the foot, The.
1639 : Clarke, 82, The finest shooe fits
not every foot. 1670 : Ray, 90. Cf.
Fairest looking.

Finger and **Fingers.** 1. *At one's
fingers' ends.* 1561 : Hoby, *Courtier*, 42
(T.T.), Ye are so good a courtyer that
you have at your fingers endes that
belongeth thereto. 1596 : *Knack to
Know Honest Man*, l. 625 (Malone S.),
A begger hath fiue of the seuen liberall
sciences at his fingers ends. *c.* 1630 :
Dicke of Devonsh., III. i., Who is more
expert in any quality than he that
hath it at his fingers ends. 1748 :
Richardson, *Clarissa*, viii. 57 (1785),
An hundred more wise adages, which
I have always at my fingers end? 1852 :
M. A. Keltie, *Reminisc. of Thought, etc.*,
171, She had the Bible at her fingers'
ends. 1906 : Lucas, *Listener's Lure*,
156, One has so many thoughts about
it all at one's fingers' end.

2. *Each finger is a thumb,* or *All his
fingers are thumbs.* 1546 : Heywood,
Proverbs, Pt. II. ch. v., Whan he should
get ought, eche fynger is a thumbe.
c. 1594 : Bacon, *Promus*, No. 660, Ech
finger is thumb. 1642 : D. Rogers,
Matrim. Honour, 141, Though each
finger were a thumbe. 1659 : Howell,
5, When he should work all his fingers
are thumbs. 1732 : Fuller, No. 5556,

When he should work every finger is
a thumb. 1866 : Brogden, *Lincs Words*,
207, His fingers are all thumbs, i.e.
he is very awkward. 1920 : *Times Lit.
Suppl.*, 3 Feb., p. 73, col. 2, Except on
metaphysics (a keyboard upon which
his fingers are all thumbs) he has usually
disguised sound sense under his purple
panache.

3. *Finger in dish, finger in pouch.*
1654 : Gayton, *Pleasant Notes Don Q.*,
83.

4. *Fingers for fish, prongs for meat.*
Newlyn, W. Corn. 19th cent. (Mr. C. Lee,
who says cf. Boswell, *Tour to Hebrides*,
13 Sept.).

5. *Fingers were made before forks.*
1567 : in *Loseley MSS.*, 212 (Kempe), As
God made hands before knives . . .
1738 : Swift, *Polite Convers.*, Dial. II.,
They say fingers were made before
forks, and hands before knives. 1914 :
Lucas, *Landmarks*, 19, Certain crusted
scraps of nursery wisdom were in
Sarah's repertory, such as . . . " Fingers
were made before forks."

6. *His fingers are lime-twigs.* 1596 :
Harington, *Metam. of Ajax*, 65 (1814)
(O.), A certain gentleman that had his
fingers made of lime-twigs, stole a piece
of plate. 1633 : Draxe, 203, His fingers
are made of lime-twigs. 1672 : Walker,
Parœm., 14. 1736 : Bailey, *Dict.*, s.v.
" Finger."

7. *If I am a fool, put you your finger
in my mouth.* 1694 : D'Urfey, *Quixote*,
Pt. I. Act IV., If you meddle with my
mouth, I shall snap at your fingers.
1732 : Fuller, No. 2682.

8. *My hand. See* quot. 1842 : Pul-
man, *Sketches*, 95 (1871) (W.), My
hand's all vingers-an-thums [Devon].

9. *The finger next the thumb.* 1579 :
Lyly, *Euphues*, 68 (Arber), I will be
the finger next thy thombe. Cf. No. 12.

10. *To have a finger in the pie.* 1553 :
Respublica, I. iii., And first speake for
me, bring me in credyte that my hande
be in the pye. 1613 : Shakespeare,
Henry VIII., I. i., The devil speed him !
no man's pie is freed From his ambitious
finger. 1694 : Southerne, *Fatal Marriage*, I. iii., By your good will you
would have a finger in every bodies

pie. 1798 : B. Thompson, *The Stranger*,
II. iii., The world will be astonished
when it comes to light; and not a soul
will suppose that Old Solomon had a
finger in the pye. 1860 : Reade, *Cl.
and Hearth*, ch. lvi., Their law thrusteth
its nose into every platter, and its finger
into every pie. 1909 : Lucas, *Wand. in
Paris*, ch. xviii., All the best French
Royal Academicians (so to speak) . . .
had a finger in this pie.

11. *To put one's finger in the fire.*
1546 : Heywood, *Proverbs*, Pt. II. ch. ii.,
To put my finger to far in the fyre.
1633 : Draxe, 29, Let him put his finger
in the fire that needeth. 1670 : Ray,
175. 1732 : Fuller, No. 3986, Put your
finger into the fire, and say 'twas your
ill fortune.

12. *You two are finger and thumb.*
1659 : Howell, 13. 1670 : Ray, 215.
1736 : Bailey, *Dict.*, s.v. "Thumb,"
They are finger and thumb. Cf. No. 9.
See also Better a finger.

Finglesham Church. *See* quot. 1735 :
Pegge, *Kent. Proverbs*, in E.D.S., No. 12,
p. 71, To be married at Finglesham
Church. There is no church at Finglesham; but a chalk-pit celebrated for
casual amours; of which kind of
rencounters the saying is us'd.

Fire. 1. *A fire of straw.* *See* quots.
1578 : Florio, *First Fruites*, fo. 28, Who
makes a fire of straw, hath much smoke
and nought els. 1629 : *Book of Meery
Riddles*, Prov. 71, A fire of straw yeelds
naught but smoake. 1666 : Torriano,
Piazza Univ., 97 [as in 1578]. 1732 :
Fuller, No. 2236, He that maketh a
fire of straw, hath much smoke and but
little warmth.

2. *As fire kindled by bellows, so is
anger by words.* 1732 : Fuller, No. 677.

3. *Fire and flax* (or *tow*). This untoward combination has suggested
several sayings. *See* quots. *c.* 1386 :
Chaucer, *C. Tales*, D 89 (Skeat), For
peril is bothe fyr and tow t'assemble.
c. 1460 : *Good Wyfe wold a Pylgr.*, l. 79
(E.E.T.S.), Feyre and towe I-leyde
to-gedore, kyndoll hit woll, be resson.
1530 : Palsgrave, 417, Adde fyre to
towe and you shal sone have a flame.
1578 : Florio, *First Fruites*, fo. 30,

Fire and flaxe agree not. 1633 : Draxe,
141, There is no quenching of fire with
towe. 1637 : B. & F., *Elder Brother*,
I. ii., For he is fire and flax. 1666 :
Torriano, *Piazza Univ.*, 97 [as in 1578].
1670 : Ray, 175, All fire and tough
[tow]. 1717 : Pope, *Wife of Bath*, 30,
There's danger in assembling fire and
tow. 1732 : Fuller, No. 1541, Fire in
flax will smoke. 1822 : Scott, *Nigel*,
ch. xxx., " I know his Majesty's wisdom
well," said Heriot ; " yet there is an old
proverb about fire and flax—well, let
it pass."

4. *Fire and pride cannot be hid.*
c. 1375 : Barbour, *Bruce*, bk. iv. l. 119,
For men sais [oft], that fire, na pryd,
But discoueryng, may no man hyd.

5. *Fire and water are good servants
but bad masters.* 1562 : Bullein, *Bulwarke of Defence*, fo. 12, Water is a
very good seruaunt, but it is a cruell
maister. 1630 : T. Adams, *Works*, 178,
We say of water, it is a good seruant,
though an ill master. 1659 : Howell, 5
[with "ill" for "bad"]. 1692 :
L'Estrange, *Æsop*, 38 (3rd ed.), It is
with our passions, as it is with fire and
water, they are good servants, but bad
masters. 1738 : Swift, *Polite Convers.*,
Dial. II. 1841 : Dickens, *Barn. Rudge*,
ch. liii., Fire, the saying goes, is a good
servant but a bad master.

6. *Fire drives out fire.* 1592 : Shakespeare, *Romeo*, I. ii., Tut, man, one fire
burns out another's burning. 1629 :
Quarles, in *Works*, iii. 267 (Grosart),
Whose desire Was all this while, by fire,
to draw out fire ; And by a well advised
course to smother The fury of one
passion with another. 1706 : Vanbrugh,
Mistake, III. i., Come ! courage, my
dear Lopez ; fire will fetch out fire.
1732 : Fuller, No. 4523, The fire that
burneth, taketh out the heat of a burn.

7. *Fire in the one hand and water
in the other.* 1412–20 : Lydgate, *Troy
Book*, bk. iv. l. 4988, On swiche folke,
platly, is no trist, that fire and water
holden in her fist. 1546 : Heywood,
Proverbs, Pt. I. ch. x. 1593 : G. Harvey,
in *Works*, ii. 317 (Grosart), Water in the
one hand, fier in the other. 1681 : W.
Robertson, *Phraseol. Generalis*, 314, He

carries fire in one hand, and water in the other. 1732: Fuller, No. 5886.

8. *Fire is as hurtful as healthful.* 1669 : *Politeuphuia,* 184.

9. *Fire is love and water sorrow.* 1590: Greene, in *Works,* viii. 51 (Grosart), If th' old saw did not borrow, Fier is loue, and water sorrow.

10. *Fire of chats. See* **Love** (31).

11. *Fire, quoth the fox, when he p—on the ice.* 1639: Clarke, 5. 1670: Ray, 93. 1732: Fuller, No. 1542.

12. *If the fire blows. See* quot. 1839: G. C. Lewis, *Herefs. Words,* 122, The following are old sayings current . . . If the fire blows (i.e. makes a flaring noise from the escape of gas), wind will soon follow.

13. *If you light your fire at both ends, the middle will shift for itself.* 1712: Addison, *Spectator,* No. 265 [called "the old kitchen proverb"]. 1732: Fuller, No. 2765.

14. *Make no fire, raise no smoke.* 1546: Heywood, *Proverbs,* Pt. II. ch. v.

15. *The closer the fire the hotter.* c. 1380: Chaucer, *Leg. of Good Women,* l. 735, Wry [Cover] the gleed [glowing coal], and hotter is the fyr. 1566: L. Wager, *Mary Magdalene,* sig. C2, The more closely that we kepe fyre, no doubt The more feruent it is when it breaketh out. c. 1591 : Shakespeare, *Two Gent.,* I. ii., Fire that's closest kept burns most of all.

16. *The fire in the flint shows not till it's struck.* 1855 : Bohn, 504.

17. *The fire that does not warm me shall never scorch me.* Ibid., 504.

18. *The fire which lighteth us at a distance, will burn us when near.* Ibid., 504.

19. *To get fire out of a pumice-stone.* 1658 : Willsford, *Natures Secrets,* 21, From whence the old adagie is derived, *To strike fire out of a pumice-stone,* is to expect an impossibility.

20. *To go through fire and water.* c. 825: *Vesp. Psalter,* lxv(i.), 12 (O.), We leordun ðorh fy and weter. 1530: Palsgrave, 653, He shall passe thorowe fyre and water or he get it. 1600: Shakespeare, *Merry Wives,* III. iv., A woman would run through fire and

water for such a kind heart. *c.* 1660 : in *Bagford Ballads,* i. 291 (B.S.), Through fire and water I would go I swear. 1708 : *Brit. Apollo,* i. No. 113, col. 3, That common saying may expound it ; I will go thro' fire and water to serve you. 1797: Colman, jr., *Heir at Law,* I. ii. 1884: R. L. S. and Henley, *Adm. Guinea,* II. vi., I'll go through fire and water.

See also **London** (5); and **Smoke** (3) and (5).

Firle Hill. *See* quot. 1884: "Sussex Proverbs," in *N. & Q.,* 6th ser., ix. 341, When Firle Hill and Long Man has a cap, We at A'ston [Alciston] gets a drap.

First and last frosts are the worst, The. 1640: Herbert, *Jac. Prudentum.*

First blow is half the battle, The. Ibid., The first blow is as much as two. 1773: Goldsmith, *She Stoops,* II., I fancy, Charles, you're right : the first blow is half the battle. 1790: Burns, *Prol. for Dumfries Theatre,* The first blow is ever half the battle.

First born, first fed. 1633: Draxe, 142. 1659: Howell, *Proverbs: Fr.-Eng.,* 4.

First breath is the beginning of death, The. 1732: Fuller, No. 4524.

First come first served. *c.* 1386: Chaucer, *Wife of Bath's Prol.,* l. 389, Who-so that first to mille comth, first grint. *c.* 1475 : *Paston Lett.,* iii. 133 (Gairdner, 1900), For who comyth fyrst to the mylle, fyrst must grynd. 1593: *Pass. Morrice,* 91 (N. Sh. S.), The drift whereof is, that first commers should be first serued. 1614: Jonson, *Bart. Fair,* III., Pardon me, sir, first come first serv'd. *c.* 1663 : Davenant, *Play-House to be Let,* I. 1720: C. Shadwell, *Irish Hospit.,* II., I was first come, and therefore ought to be first serv'd. 1825 : Planché, *Extravag.,* i. 24 (1879).

First creep then go. *c.* 1400: *Towneley Plays,* 103 (E.E.T.S.), ffyrst must vs crepe and sythen go. 1540 : Palsgrave, *Acolastus,* sig. b 3, They shoulde soner be able to go, then they coulde afore tymes be able to creepe. 1606: *Wily Beguiled,* in Hazlitt, *Old Plays,* ix. 266. 1622 : Hornby, *Horn-*

book, sig. B3, And as the prouerbe old doth teach vs, so We first must creepe, before we well can goe. 1662 · Fuller, *Worthies*, iii. 210 (1840), We did first creep, then run, then fly into preferment. 1754 : Berthelson, *Eng.-Danish Dict.*, s.v. " Creep," You must learn to creep before you can go. 1823 : Scott, *St. Ronan's*, ch. iii., Folk maun creep before they gang. 1901 : F. E. Taylor, *Lancs Sayings*, 11, Yo' mun creep first, an' then goo.

First cut and all the loaf besides, The. 1732 : Fuller, No. 4526.

First deserve and then desire. 1605 : Camden, *Remains*, 322 (1870). 1670 : Ray, 7. 1736 : Bailey, *Dict.*, s.v. " Deserve."

First dish pleaseth all, The. 1640 : Herbert, *Jac. Prudentum.* 1670 : Ray, 9. 1732 : Fuller, No. 4527.

First hand buy, At the; At the third let lie. 1732 : Fuller, No. 6337.

First learn then discern. 1568 : in *Loseley MSS.*, 207 (Kempe).

First men in the world were a gardener, a ploughman, a grasier, The. 1732 : Fuller, No. 4529.

First of the nine orders of knaves is he that tells his errand before he goes it, The. 1855 : Bohn, 504.

First pig, but the last whelp of the litter is the best, The. 1678 : Ray, 53. 1732 : Fuller, No. 4530.

First point, The. *See* **Hawk**, *verb* (2).

First step is the only difficulty, The. 1639 : Clarke, 171, The first step is as good as halfe over. 1659 : Howell, *Proverbs: Ital.-Eng.*, 7, The hardest step is that over the threshold, viz. the beginning.

First tale, The. *See* **One tale.**

First year of wedlock. *See* quot. *c.* 1430 : Lydgate, *Minor Poems*, 45 (Percy S.), And ever thynk wel on this prouerb trewe . . . That the first yere wedlokk is called pleye, The second dreye, and the third yere deye.

Fish, *subs.* 1. *Fish and company stink in three days.* 1580 : Lyly, *Euphues*, 307 (Arber), Fishe and gesse [guests] in three dayes are stale. 1586 : L. Evans, *Withals Dict. Revised*, sig. B2, After three dayes fish is vnsauoury,

and so is an ill guest. 1678 : *Poor Robin Alman.*, As the proverb saies, Guests and fish stink in three days. *c.* 1736 : Franklin, in *Works*, i. 455 (Bigelow), Fish and visitors smell in three days. 1869 : *N. & Q.*, 4th ser., iv. 272, " See that you wear not out your welcome." This is an elegant rendering of the vulgar saying that " Fish and company stink in three days."

2. *Fish bite the least with wind in the east.* 1893 : Inwards, *Weather Lore*, 141.

3. *Fish bred up in dirty pools will taste of mud.* 1563 : Googe, *Eglogs, etc.*, 40 (Arber) [with " stynke " for " taste "]. 1576 : Pettie, *Petite Pall.* ii. 100 (Gollancz, 1908).

4. *Fish, flesh, etc.* See **Flesh nor fish, etc.**

5. *Fish is cast away that is cast in, dry pools.* 1546 : Heywood, *Proverbs.* Pt. I. ch. xi. 1605 : Chapman, etc., *Eastw. Hoe*, V. ii. 1670 : Ray, 90, Fishes are cast away, that are cast into dry ponds.

6. *Fish make no broth.* 1732 : Fuller, No. 1546.

7. *Fish marreth water and · flesh mendeth it.* 1578 : Florio, *First Fruites*, fo. 29, Fish marreth the water, and flesh doth dresse it. 1629 : *Book of Meery Riddles*, Prov. 104. 1678 : Ray, 41, Fish spoils water, but flesh mends it.

8. *Fish should swim thrice.* 1611 : Cotgrave, s.v. " Poisson," We say, fish must ever swimme twice [water, wine]. 1620 : *Westw. for Smelts*, 6 (Percy S.), Fish . . . never doth digest well . . . except it swimme twice after it comes forth the water : that is, first in butter, so to be eaten : then in wine or beere after it is eaten. 1738 : Swift, *Polite Convers.*, Dial. II., They say fish should swim thrice . . . first it should swim in the sea . . . then it should swim in butter; and at last, sirrah, it should swim in good claret. 1787 : O'Keeffe, *Little Hunchback*, II. ii., Fish should swim three times; water, sauce, and wine.

9. *Fish will not enter the net, but rather turn back.* 1623 : Wodroephe, *Spared Houres*, 508.

10. *Here is fish for catching, etc. See* quot. 1723 : in Bliss, *Reliquiæ Hearn.*, ii. 154, The people there [Great Marlow] commonly say, Here is fish for catching, corn for snatching, and wood for fetching.

11. *I have other fish to fry.* 1660 : Evelyn, *Mem.*, iii. 132 (1857) (O.), I fear he hath other fish to fry. 1670 : Ray, 176. 1710 : Swift, *Journal to Stella*, 3 Nov., Which I shall not answer tonight . . . No, faith, I have other fish to fry. 1849 : Brontë, *Shirley*, ch. xx., Your uncle will not return yet, he has other fish to fry. 1910 : Lucas, *Mr. Ingleside*, ch. xv., Most women will continue to be unmoved—they will have other and more primitive fish to fry.

12. *It is a silly fish that is caught twice with the same bait.* 1732 : Fuller, No. 2879.

13. *It is ill catching of fish when the hook is bare.* 1583 : Greene, in *Works*, ii. 63 (Grosart).

14. *Like a fish out of water.* [Mus in matella.—Petr., 58. Sicut piscis sine aqua caret vita, ita sine monasterio monachus.—Attributed to a Pope Eugenius ; but it is adapted from the Greek. It occurs in Sozomen, *Eccl. Hist.*, bk. i. c. 13 ; and still earlier, in a *Life of St. Anthony* (c. 85) attributed to St. Athanasius, and not later than A.D. 373. Skeat, *Early Eng. Proverbs*, 89.] *c.* 1380 : Wiclif, *Gospel Sermons*, cxxxi., in *Works*, ii. 15 (Arnold), And how thei weren out of ther cloistre as fishis withouten water. *c.* 1386 : Chaucer, *Prol.*, l. 180, Ne that a monk whan he is cloysterles Is likned til a fissh that is waterles. 1655 : Gurnall, *Christian in Armour*, 117 (1679), You may possibly find a tradesman out of his shop now and then, but he is as a fish out of the water. 1679 : Shadwell, *True Widow*, III. i. 1724 : Defoe, *Roxana*, in *Works*, xiii. 37 (Boston, 1903), I was like a fish out of water. 1860 : Reade, *Cl. and Hearth*, ch. xxxi., I have been like a fish out of water in all those great dungeons. 1916 : B. Duffy, *The Old Lady*, 17, I feel like a fish out of water here.

15. *Like fish that live in salt-water,*

and yet are fresh. 1732 : Fuller, No. 3228.

16. *Sweet is that fish, etc. See* quot. 1607 : E. Topsell, *Four-footed Beasts*, 46, Whence came the prouerbe, *That sweet is that fish, which is not fishe at all* [beaver].

17. *That fish will soon be caught that nibbles at every bait.* 1732 : Fuller, No. 4342.

18. *The fish adores the bait.* 1640 : Herbert, *Jac. Prudentum.* 1670 : Ray, 9, The fish follow the bait. 1754 : Berthelson, *Eng.-Danish Dict.*, s.v. " Bait " [as in 1670].

19. *The fish may be caught in a net that will not come to a hook.* 1732 : Fuller, No. 4535.

20. *There are as good fish in the sea as ever came out of it.* [*c.* 1380 : Chaucer, *Parl. of Foules*, in *Works*, i. 356 (Skeat), There been mo sterres, god wot, than a paire !] 1822 : Scott, *Nigel*, ch. xxxv. 1881 : Gilbert, *Patience*, I., There's fish in the sea, no doubt of it, As good as ever came out of it. 1904 : H. James, in *Letters*, ii. 10 (1920), I still cling to the belief that there are as good fish in the sea —that is, my sea ! . . .

21. *To find fish on one's fingers.* 1587 : Greene, in *Works*, iv. 140 (Grosart), Who (as the nature of women is, desirous to see and bee seene) thought she should both heare the *parle* and view the person of this young embassadour, and therefore found fish on her fingers, that she might staye still in the chamber of presence. 1590 : Lodge, *Rosalynde*, 122 (Hunt. Cl.), Ganimede rose as one that would suffer no fish to hang on his fingers.

22. *To make fish of one and flesh of another.* 1639 : Clarke, 182, I will not make fleshe of one, and fish of the other. 1709 : O. Dykes, *Eng. Proverbs*, 137, If the father proves such a partial fool . . . as to make fish of one [child], and flesh of another. 1738 : Swift, *Polite Convers.*, Dial. II. 1828 : Carr, *Craven Dialect*, i. 151, " I will not make fish o' yan and fowl of another," an expression by which a person declares that he will shew no partiality.

See also All fish; All is fish; Best (14);
Daughter (1); Great fish; Little fish;
Old, E (10) and (11); Sauce; Sea hath
fish; Sole; Some fish; Swear (6); and
Wind, C (3) and D (4).

Fish, *verb.* 1. *He has well fished and
caught a frog.* 1546: Heywood, *Proverbs*, Pt. I. ch. xi. *c.* 1548: Latimer,
in *Works*, ii. 419 (P.S.), As the common
saying is, "Well I have fished and
caught a frog." 1595: Churchyard,
Charitie, 9 (1816), We angle in the reeds
And catch a frog. 1629: in *Pepysian
Garland*, 318 (Rollins, 1922), The man
that wedds for greedy wealth, he goes
a fishing faire, But often times he gets
a frog, or very little share. 1732:
Fuller, No. 5903, You fish fair, and
catch a frog.

2. *It is no sure rule to fish with a
cross-bow.* 1640: Herbert, *Jac. Prudentum.*

3. *Still he fishes that catches one.*
1611; Cotgrave, s.v. "Pescher," And
yet he fishes who catcheth one. 1670:
Ray, 91. 1732: Fuller, No. 4262.

4. *To fish before the net.* *c.* 1400:
Towneley Plays, 104 (E.E.T.S.), Ye fysh
before the nett. 1460: Lydgate, *Order
of Fools*, l. 131 (E.E.T.S., E.S. 8, p. 83),
And he ys a fole afore the nette that
fysshes. 1596: Harington, *Metam. of
Ajax*, 20 (1814), Which either we miss
(fishing before the net, as the proverb
is) . . . 1683: Meriton, *Yorkshire Ale*,
83-7 (1697), He that fishes afore the net,
laug fish or he fish get.

5. *To fish for* (or *with*) *a herring and
catch a sprat.* 1639: Clarke, 2, I fish't
for a herring and catcht a sprat. 1670:
Ray, 180 [" for "]. 1732: Fuller, No.
5165 [" with "].

6. *To fish in troubled waters.* 1569:
Grafton, *Chron.*, i. 283 (1809), Which
alwayes desyre your vnquietnesse,
whereby they may the better fishe in
the water when it is troubled. 1591:
Harington, *Orl. Furioso*, bk. xli., Notes,
Thinking it (as the prouerb saith) best
fishing in troubled waters. 1630:
Pathomachia, sc. i., It is good fishing
in troubled waters. 1660: Tatham,
The Rump, III. [as in 1630]. 1756:
Murphy, *Apprentice*, I. ii., We had

better get away from this house; all
fishing in troubled waters here.

Fisherman. *See* quot. 1868: *N. & Q.*,
4th ser., ii. 94, Never a fisherman need
there be, If fishes could hear as well as
see (West Kent).

Fisherman's walk, A : three steps and
overboard. 1867: Smyth, *Sailor's Word-
Book*, s.v.

Fisher's folly. *See* Kirbie's castle.

Fishing, *verb. subs.* 1. *No fishing like
fishing in the sea.* 1575: Churchyard,
Chippes, 41 (Collier), Some say there is
no fishing to the seas. 1605: Camden,
Remains, 334 (1870), There is no fishing
to the sea. 1609: Melton, *Sixfold
Politician*, 94 [as in 1605]. 1670:
Ray, 90, No fishing to fishing in the
sea.

2. *The end of fishing is catching.*
1580: Lyly, *Euphues*, 396 (Arber).
1732: Fuller, No. 4497. The end of
fishing is not angling, but catching.

Fishing-net. *See* quots. 1528: More,
Works, 224 (1557), It were as soone done
to weue a newe web of clothe as to soue
up euery hole in a net. 19th cent. :
Newlyn, W. Corn., saying, Like a fishing-net—the more you mend it, the
more holes there are in it (Mr. C. Lee).

Fit as a fan for a forehorse. 1619:
Chapman, *Two Wise Men*, IV. iii.

Fit as a fiddle. 1616: Haughton,
Eng. for my Money, IV. i., This is
excellent, i' faith; as fit as a fiddle!
c. 1625: B. & F., *Women Pleased*, IV.
iii. 1883: R. L. S., *Treasure I.*, ch.
xxx., Looking fit and taut as a fiddle.
1922: Lucas, *Genevra's Money*, 86, He
hasn't been really sober for years and
he's as fit as a fiddle.

Fit as a pudding. 1600: Dekker,
Shoem. Hol., IV. v., Tis a very brave
shooe, and as fit as a pudding.

Fit as a pudding for (*a*) a dog's mouth;
(*b*) a friar's mouth. (*a*) 1592: Lyly,
Mother Bombie, II. i., But looke where
Prisius' boy comes, as fit as a pudding
for a dogges mouth. (*b*) 1578: Whetstone, *Promos and Cassandra*, sig. D3,
Your answeare then in sooth, Fyts me
as iumpe as a pudding a friars mouth.
1593: Peele, *Edward I.*, sc. ii. 1605:
Camden, *Remains*, 318 (1870). 1670:

Ray, 204. 1732 : Fuller, No. 678 [with
" fritter " for " pudding "].

Fit for the chapel. *See* quot. 1579 :
G. Gates, *Defence of Mil. Profession*, 37,
The prouerbe (no lesse wise then it is
olde) is also profitable, as it is moste
true, He that is fitte for the chappell,
is meete for the fielde.

Fitting. *He that is suffered to do
more than is fitting, will do more than
is lawful.* 1670 : Ray, 9.

Five score. *See* Six score.

Flanders mare. *See* quots. 1717 : in
Six N. Count. Diaries, 82 (Surtees S.),
Uncle told me now we are to see yon
damsel of Mr. Collingwood's. She's like
a Flanders mare. 1732 : Fuller, No.
3229, Like Flanders mares, fairest
afar off.

Flanders reckoning, A. 1606 : T. Heywood, *If You Know Not Me*, Pt. II., in
Dram. Works, i. 271 (1874), God send
me but once to finger it, and if I doe
not make a Flanders reckoning on't
—and that is, as I have heard mad
wagges say, receiue it here, and reuell
it away in another place . . .

Flap with a fox-tail, To give one a.
1530 : Palsgrave, 563, I flatter hym to
begyle hym, or I gyve one a slappe
with a foxe tayle. 1565 : Calfhill, *Answ.
to Martiall*, 292 (P.S.), Break God's
[works], and they either look through
their fingers, or else give a flap with
a fox-tail, for a little money. 1581 :
B. Rich, *Farewell*, 4 (Sh. S.), And
when a souldier hath thus served in
many a bloudie broile, a flappe with a
foxe taile shall bee his beste reward.
1640 : *King and Poore North. Man*,
l. 368, in Hazlitt, *Early Pop. Poetry*,
iv. 307, Where they with brave claret
and brave old canary, they with a foxe
tale him soundly did pay. 1762 :
Smollett, *Sir L. Greaves*, ch. viii., Your
honour has a mortal good hand at
giving a flap with a fox's tail, as the
saying is. 1808 : Scott, in Lockhart's
Life, ii. 218, I owe Jeffrey a flap with
a fox-tail on account of his review of
Marmion. 1847 : Halliwell, *Dict.*, s.v.
" Fox-tail," Fox-tail. Anciently one
of the badges of a fool. Hence perhaps the phrase *to give one a flap with

a fox-tail*, to deceive or make a fool
of him.

Flat as a cake (or pancake). 1542 :
Udall, tr. Erasmus' *Apoph.*, 250 (1877),
His nose as flat as a cake, bruised or
beaten to his face. 1580 : Baret,
Alvearie, F 649, A nose as flat as a
cake. 1631 : Mabbe, *Celestina*, 209
(T.T.), My caske strangely bruised,
beaten as flat as a cake. 1758–67,
Sterne, *Trist. Shandy*, vol. iii. ch. xxvii.,
He has crushed his nose . . . as flat as a
pancake to his face. 1786 : R. Twining,
in *Twining Fam. Papers*, 139 (1887),
The Gâtinois . . . is extremely fertile,
but as flat as a pancake. 1830 :
Marryat, *King's Own*, ch. xvii., Under
which it had lain, jammed as flat as a
pancake.

Flat as a dab. 1869 : FitzGerald, *Sea
Words and Phrases*, 3.

Flat as a flawn, i.e. a custard. 1678 :
Ray, 355. 1775 : Watson, *Hist. of
Halifax*, quoted in Hunter's *Hallamsh.
Gloss.*, 145, As flat as a flawn (custard),
is a proverb. 1887 : *Brighouse News*,
23 July (W.), As flat as a flawn.

Flat as a flounder. *c.* 1625 : B. & F.,
Women Pleased, II. iv. 1671 : E.
Howard, *Six Days Adventure*, I., Who
lay as flat as flounders. Before 1704 :
T. Brown, *Works*, i. 313, and ii. 137
(1760). 1788 : O'Keeffe, *Highland
Reel*, III. i., This instant say in plain,
audible English, " How do you do, Mr.
McGilpin "—or down you go as flat as
a fluke [flounder]. *c.* 1800 : *Irishman
in London*, I. ii., in Inchbald, *Farces*,
ii. 95 (1815).

Flat as ditchwater. 1772 : in *Garrick
Corresp.*, i. 465 (1831), " The Grecian
Daughter's " being dead as dish-water
after the first act. 1854 : Baker,
Northants Gloss., s.v. " Ditchwater,"
" As flat," or, " as dead as ditch-
water," said of anything tasteless and
insipid. 1862 : *Dialect of Leeds*, 406,
As dull as ditch-watter. 1865 : Dickens,
Mutual Friend, bk. iii. ch. x., He'd be
sharper than a serpent's tooth, if he
wasn't as dull as ditch water. 1888 :
Lowsley, *Berks Gloss.*, 70 (E.D.S.),
" Dead as ditch water " is said of beer
that is flat to the taste.

Flatterer. 1. *A flatterer's throat is an open sepulchre.* 1640 : Herbert, *Jac. Prudentum.*

2. *Flatterers haunt not cottages.* 1732 : Fuller, No. 1550. 1869 : Spurgeon, *John Ploughman*, ch. xiv.

3. *There is no such flatterer as a man's self.* 1732 : Fuller, No. 4922.

4. *When flatterers meet, the Devil goes to dinner.* 1678 : Ray, 139. 1799 : Wolcot, in *Works*, v. 196 (1801), Porteus, there is a proverb thou should'st read, " When flatt'rers meet, the *Devil goes to dinner.*"

Flattering as a spaniel. 1639 : Clarke, 285. 1670 : Ray, 204.

Flattery. 1. *He that rewards flattery begs it.* 1732 : Fuller, No. 2269.

2. *Flattery sits in the parlour, when plain dealing is kicked out of doors.* Ibid., No. 1552.

3. *The coin that is most current among us is flattery.* Ibid., No. 4452.

4. *There is flattery in friendship.* 1600 : Shakespeare, *Henry V.*, III. vii., Con. I will cap that proverb with " There is flattery in friendship."

Flax. *At leisure, as flax groweth.* 1639 : Clarke, 304. *See also* **Candlemas,** H (4) ; *Fire* (3) ; and **God will send thee flax.**

Flay a flint (or stone). *See* **Skin a flint.**

Flea and Fleas. 1. *A flea in one's ear.* [Comment Panurge auoyt la pulce en l'oreille.—Rabelais, *Pantagruel*, bk. iii. ch. vii., part of title.] *c.* 1430 : *Pilgr. Lyf. Manhode*, II. xxxix. 91 (1869) (O.), And manye oothere grete wundres . . . whiche ben fleen in myne eres. 1546 : Heywood, *Proverbs*, Pt. I. ch. xi., He standth now as he had a flea in his eare. 1602 : Middleton, *Blurt, Master Const.*, II. ii., I will send him hence with a flea in's ear. 1656 : *Musarum Deliciæ*, i. 65 (Hotten, 1874), Some, telling how they vexed another, say I sent him with a flea in's eare away. 1709 : Cibber, *Rival Fools*, III., So, he's gone with this flea in his ear to my uncle, I suppose. 1871 : G. Eliot, *Middlemarch*, ch. lvi., The best way would be to . . . send 'em away with a flea in their ear, when they came spying and measuring. 1922 : Weyman, *Ovington's Bank*, ch. ix., On which he dismissed her with a flea in her ear.

2. *When eager bites the thirsty flea, Clouds and rain you sure shall see.* 1639 : Clarke, 263, We shall have raine, the fleas bite. 1893 : Inwards, *Weather Lore*, 148.

3. *When fleas do very many grow, Then 'twill surely rain or snow.* 1893 : Inwards, *Weather Lore*, 148.

See also **Do** (14) ; and **Dog** (49).

Flea-bitten horse never tires, A. 1577 : Googe, *Heresbach.'s Husb.*, ii. 116b (1586) (O.), The fleabitten horse prooveth alwaies good in travell. 1696 : D'Urfey, *Quixote*, Pt. III. Act I., Take this proverb with you by way of advice : If you an old flea-bitten ride, you need not fear the dirt ; But when you back a young colt, see your saddle be well girt. 1922 : *N. & Q.*, 12th ser., xi. 169.

Fleece and fell, To have both. 1639 : Clarke, 39, Will you have both fleece and fell. 1642 : D. Rogers, *Naaman*, sig. Dd2, Thy servant is for thee to use, not tire or teare out : Thou must not take both fleece and flesh too.

Fleet, The. *He may whet his knife on the threshold of the Fleet.* 1662 : Fuller, *Worthies*, ii. 348 (1840). 1790 : Grose, *Prov. Gloss.*, s.v. " London," Said of persons who are not in debt [and therefore not in danger of arrest].

Flesh never stands so high but a dog will venture his legs. 1678 : Ray, 139. 1732 : Fuller, No. 1553.

Flesh nor fish nor good red herring, Neither. 1528 : *Rede Me and be not Wrothe*, I. iii. *b*, Wone that is nether flesshe nor fisshe. 1546 : Heywood, *Proverbs*, Pt. I. ch. x., She is nother fyshe, nor fleshe, nor good red hearyng. 1599 : Nashe, *Lenten Stuffe*, in *Works*, v. 302 (Grosart). 1630 : Taylor (Water-Poet), *Workes*, pagin. 1, 34. Before 1704 : T. Brown, *Works*, iii. 240 (1760), They . . . marry their wives, before they know whether they are fish, flesh, or good red herring. 1711 : Addison, *Spectator*, No. 165. 1824 : Scott, *Redgauntlet*, ch. xii., I never thought twice about it, Mr. Fairford ; it was neither fish, nor flesh, nor salt herring of mine. 1921 : *Times*, 7 Oct., p. 8, col. 4, Its compromise with sentiment and the proprieties leaves it neither fish, flesh, nor good red-herring.

Flesh upon horses and money with women hide a many faults. 1917: Bridge, *Cheshire Proverbs*, 57.

Fletching. *See* quot. 1884: " Sussex Proverbs," in *N. & Q.*, 6th ser., ix. 342, The people of Fletching Live by snapping and ketching.

Flies. *See* **Fly.**

Flitting of farms makes mailings dear. 1846: Denham, *Proverbs*, 3 (Percy S.).

Float is rotten, What does not. 1813: Ray, 194.

Flow will have an ebb, A. 1412–20 ; Lydgate, *Troy Book*, bk. ii. l. 2013, After a flowe, an ebbe folweth ay. 1626: *Scoggins Jests*, 158 (1864), There was never so great a flood, but there may bee as lowe an ebbe. 1670: Ray, 91. 1754: Berthelson, *Eng.-Danish Dict.*, s.v. "Flow."

Flower in his garden, It is the finest. 1659: Howell, 15, 'Tis the fairest flower in your garden. 1732 : Fuller, No. 3023.

Flowers in May. *See* **Fresh**; and **Welcome.**

Fly and Flies. 1. *A fly and eke a friar.* See quot. *c.* 1386 : Chaucer, *Wife of Bath's Prol.*, 835, Lo, gode men, a fiye and eek a frere Wol falle in every dish and eek matere.

2. *A fly hath its spleen.* 1580: Lyly, *Euphues*, 316 (Arber), Low trees haue their tops . . . the flye his splene. 1590: Lodge, *Rosalynde*, 70 (Hunt. Cl.), I tell thee, flies haue their spleene. 1605: Camden, *Remains*, 317 (1870). 1646: Browne, *Pseudo. Epi.*, bk. iii. ch. iii., So is it proverbially said *Formicæ sua bilis inest, habet et musca splenem.* 1732 : Fuller, No. 1388, Even a fly hath its spleen. 1924: *Sphere*, 27 Sept., p. 386, col. 2, A Latin tag declares that " even a fly hath its spleen."

3. *A fly on your nose. See* quot. 1893 : Inwards, *Weather Lore*, 148, A fly on your nose, you slap, and it goes ; If it comes back again, it will bring a good rain.

4. *Flies come to feasts unasked.* 1683: *See* **Fiddler** (2). 1924: *Sphere*, 27 Sept.,

p. 386, col. 2, Another proverb of un-impeachable veracity proclaims that " Flies come to feasts unasked."

5. *Flies go to lean horses.* 1578: Florio, *First Fruites*, fo. 25, Vnto the leane horses, alwayes resort the flyes. 1631: Mabbe, *Celestina*, 214 (T.T.), Flyes bite none but leane and feeble oxen. 1666 : Torriano, *Piazza Univ.*, 43, Flyes do rest upon lean horses.

6. *Flies will tickle lions being dead.* 1610: Marston, *Histrio-Mastix*, VI.

7. *He changes a fly into an elephant.* 1736 : Bailey, *Dict.*, s.v. "Elephant," To make of a fly an elephant. 1813 : Ray, 75.

8. *He takes a spear to kill a fly.* Ibid., 75.

9. *Into a shut mouth flies fly not.* 1640 : Herbert, *Jac. Prudentum*. 1869: Spurgeon, *John Ploughman*, ch. vi., No flies will go down your throat if you keep your mouth shut.

10. *Like a fly in a tar-box* (or *glue-pot*). 1659 : Howell, 19, He capers like a flie in a tar-box. 1670 : Ray, 216 [as in 1659]. 1886: Elworthy, *West Som. Word-Book*, 437 (E.D.S.), Like a fly in a glue-pot. Com[mon] expression, to express nervous excitement.

11. *More flies are taken with a drop of honey than a tun of vinegar.* 1732 : Fuller, No. 3454. 1821 : Combe, *Syntax in Search of Wife*, can. xxxiv. p. 24, Madam, the ancient proverb says . . . That one rich drop of honey sweet, As an alluring, luscious treat, Is known to tempt more flies, by far, Than a whole tun of vinegar. 1830 : Forby, *Vocab. E. Anglia*, 433, You will catch more flies with a spoonful of honey, than with a gallon of vinegar. 1865 : " Lancs Proverbs," in *N. & Q.*, 3rd ser., viii. 494, There's more flies caught with honey than alegar.

12. *One cannot catch a fly when he will.* 1659 : Howell, 11.

13. *The fly on the wheel.* 1586 : Pettie, tr. Guazzo's *Civil Convers.*, fo. 71, The flye, which sitting vppon a cart that was driuen on the waye, sayde he had raysed a very great dust. 1612: Bacon, *Essays*: " Vainglory," It was pretily deuised of

Æsop, *The flie sate vpon the axletree of the chariot wheele, and said, What a dust doe I raise!* 1661 : Gurnall, *Christian in Armour*, 299 (1679), Yet these are no more than the flie on the wheel. 1732 : Fuller, No. 5476, What a dust have I rais'd! quoth the fly upon the coach. 1814 : Byron, in *Letters and Journals*, ii. 401 (Prothero), Like the fly in the fable, I seem to have got upon a wheel which makes much dust ; but, unlike the said fly, I do not take it all for my own raising. 1922 : *Observer*, 5 March, p. 12, col. 5, The fly on the cart-wheel might as well have claimed not only that it was raising all the dust, but that it had built the cart.

14. *To a boiling pot flies come not.* 1640 : Herbert, *Jac. Prudentum.*

15. *'Twould make even a fly laugh.* 1732 : Fuller, No. 5340.

16. *You must lose a fly to catch a trout.* 1640 : Herbert, *Jac. Prudentum.*

See also **Eagle** (2) ; **Elstow** ; **Honey** (3) ; **Hungry flies** ; and **Lion** (5).

Fly, verb. 1. *Fly, and you will catch the swallow.* 1659 : Howell, 13.

2. *Fly brass, thy father's a tinker.* Ibid., 12.

3. *Fly the pleasure that bites to-morrow.* 1591 : Florio, *Second Frutes*, 99, Flie that present ioye, Which in time will breede annoy. 1623 : Wodroephe, *Spared Houres*, 277, Flee all present pleasure that gives the future payne. 1629 : *Book of Meery Riddles*, Prov. 29, Fly that pleasure which paineth afterward. 1640 : Herbert, *Jac. Prudentum.* 1710 : S. Palmer, *Moral Essays on Proverbs*, 347.

4. *He has flown high and let in a cow-clap at last.* 1917 : Bridge, *Cheshire Proverbs*, 66, . . . Said of one very particular in choosing a wife, but who has made an ill-assorted marriage after all.

5. *He would fain fly, but wanted feathers.* 1546 : Heywood, *Proverbs*, Pt. I. ch. xi. 1681 : W. Robertson, *Phraseol. Generalis*, 614, He would flie, but he wants feathers. 1732 : Fuller, No. 2415.

6. *To fly at all game.* 1670 : Ray,

176. 1846–59 : *Denham Tracts*, ii. 108 (F.L.S.).

Fly-catcher. *See* quot. 1886 : Swainson, *Folk-Lore of Brit. Birds*, 49 (F.L.S.), In Somerset these birds are supposed to bring good luck to the homestead they frequent, hence the rhyme :—" If you scare the fly-catcher away, No good luck will with you stay."

Flying enemy. *See* **Bridge** (5).

Flying without wings, No. 1633 : Draxe, 124. 1670 : Ray, 91. 1732 : Fuller, No. 3569.

Foal. *How can the foal amble, if the horse and mare trot?* 1546 : Heywood, *Proverbs*, Pt. I. ch. xi. 1614 : B. Rich, *Honestie of This Age*, 32 (Percy S.), The olde proverbe is : *If the mother trot how should the daughter amble?* 1670 : Ray, 91. 1732 : Fuller, No. 2554. *See also* **Rugged** ; and **Trot sire.**

Foe is better than a dissembling friend, A. 1548 : Briant, *Dispraise of Life of Courtier*, sig. D3, Alexander sayd assure me my frende Parmeno of those that be dissemblyng frendes, for I wil be ware of them that be my open enemies. 1589 : L. Wright, *Display of Dutie*, 19, As good a foe that hurts not, as a friend that helpes not. 1600 : Bodenham, *Belvedere*, 176 (Spens. S.). 1647 : *Countrym. New Commonwealth*, 13, It is better to have an open foe, then a dissembling friend.

Fog. 1. *See* quot. 1874 : W. Pengelly, in *N. & Q.*, 5th ser., ii. 184, I often heard the following weather-rhymes in Cornwall in my boyhood :— . . . A fog and a small moon Bring an easterly wind soon. 1893 : Inwards, *Weather Lore*, 58.

2. *A fog cannot be dispelled with a fan.* 1846 : Denham, *Proverbs*, 1 (Percy S.).

3. *A fog from the sea, Brings honey to the bee ; A fog from the hills Brings corn to the mills.* Pembrokesh. 1889 : *N. & Q.*, 7th ser., viii. 204.

4. *Fog on the hill, water to the mill ; Fog in the hollow, fine day to follow.* Oxfordsh. 1928 : *Spectator*, 3 Nov., p. 640, col. 2.

See also **March** (15), (16), (18), (43).

Folkestone. *See* quots. 1735 : Pegge, *Kent. Proverbs*, in E.D.S., No. 12, p. 71,

Folkstone Washerwomen. These are the white clouds which commonly bring rain. 1887 : Parish and Shaw, *Dict. Kent. Dialect*, 57 (E.D.S.), Folkestone Girls; the name given to heavy rain clouds. Also Folkestone Lasses and Folkestone Washerwomen.

Follow, *verb.* 1. *Follow love and it will flee; Flee love and it will follow thee.* 1581 : T. Howell, *Devises*, 64 (1906), Flee it [love], and it will flee thee, Follow it, and it will follow thee. 1678 : Ray, 55. 1732 : Fuller, No. 6258. 1875 : A. B. Cheales, *Proverb. Folk-Lore*, 29.

2. *Follow the river and you'll get to the sea.* 1732 : Fuller, No. 1556.

3. *He that follows Nature is never out of his way.* Ibid., No. 2108.

4. *He that follows truth too closely, etc.* See quots. 1651 : Herbert, *Jac. Prudentum*, 2nd ed., Follow not truth too near the heels, lest it dash out thy teeth. 1681 : W. Robertson, *Phraseol. Generalis*, 619, He that follows truth too near the heels, shall have dust thrown in his face. 1820 : Colton, *Lacon*, Pt. I. No. 558, He that follows truth too closely, must take care that she does not strike out his teeth.

5. *To follow one's nose.* c. 1350 : *Cleanness*, l. 978, in *Allit. Poems*, 67 (Morris, E.E.T.S.), Loth and tho luly-whit his lefly two deȝter, Ay folȝed here face [followed their face] bifore her bothe yȝen. c. 1520 : Stanbridge, *Vulgaria*, sig. C2, Ryght forthe on thy nose. Recta via incede. 1637 : Heywood, *Royal King*, I., Follow thy nose, and thou wilt be there presently. 1742 : Fielding, *Andrews*, bk. ii. ch. ii., The fellow . . . bade him follow his nose and be d—n'd. 1917 : D. Grayson, *Great Possessions*, ch. iii., One has only to step out into the open country . . . and follow his nose.

6. *You may follow him long e're a shilling drop from him.* 1732 : Fuller, No. 5944.

Folly. 1. *Folly grows without watering.* 1640 : Herbert, *Jac. Prudentum*. 1854 : J. W. Warter, *Last of the Old Squires*, ch. v. p. 53.

2. *Folly is never long pleased with it self.* 1732 : Fuller, No. 1560.

3. *Folly is often sick of itself.* Ibid., No. 1559.

4. *Folly is wise in her own eyes.* 1629 : *Book of Meery Riddles*, Prov. 95.

5. *Folly may hinder a man of many a good turn.* 1694 : D'Urfey, *Quixote*, Pt. II. Act II. sc. ii.

6. *Folly without faults is as reddish* [radish] *without salt.* 1608 : Armin, *Nest of Ninnies*, 40 (Sh. S.).

7. *If folly were grief, every house would weep.* 1640 : Herbert, *Jac. Prudentum.*

8. *It is folly to run to the foot when one may run to the head.* 1546 : Heywood, *Proverbs*, Pt. II. ch. v., Folke show much foly, when things should be sped, To ren to the foote that maie go to the hed. 1633 : Draxe, 72.

9. *Many for folly themselves fordo.* c. 1460 : *How the Good Wife*, l. 140, Many for folye hem self for-doothe.

10. *The chief disease that reigns this year is folly.* 1640 : Herbert, *Jac. Prudentum.*

11. *The folly of one man is the fortune of another.* 1607 : Bacon, *Essays*: "Fortune."

12 *'Tis a folly to fret; grief's no comfort.* 1813 : Ray, 195.

See also **Zeal.**

Fond as a besom. 1855 : Robinson, *Whitby Gloss.*, 13, He's as fond as a bezom . . . very foolish indeed. 1889 : Peacock, *Manley, etc., Gloss.*, 44 (E.D.S.), " He's as fond as a beäsom " signifies that the person spoken of is very foolish. [The phrase is proverbial in other dialects also.]

Fond pride of dress is sure a very curse; Ere fancy you consult, consult your purse. 1736 : Franklin, *Way to Wealth*, in *Works*, i. 448 (Bigelow).

Fool and **Fools.** 1. *A fool always comes short of his reckoning.* 1611 : Cotgrave, s.v. " Fol," A foole oft finds himselfe short of his reckonings.

2. *A fool and his money are soon parted.* 1580 : Tusser, *Husb.*, 19 (E.D.S.), A foole and his monie be soone at debate. c. 1640 : in *Roxb. Ballads*, iii. 550 (B.S.). 1763 : Murphy, *Citizen*, I. ii. 1894 : Shaw, *Arms and the Man*, III.

3. *A fool at forty is a fool indeed.*
c. 1670: Cotton, *Visions*, No. 1, He
who at fifty is a fool, Is far too stubborn
grown for school. 1725 : Young, *Satires*,
No. ii. *ad fin.*, Be wise with speed ; A fool
at forty is a fool indeed. 1820 : Colton,
Lacon, Pt. I. No. 352 [quotes Young].

4. *A fool believes everything.* 1625 :
in *Harl. Miscell.*, iv. 130 (1745), Flori-
mundus justified the proverb, A fool
believeth every thing.

5. *A fool believes the thing he would
have so.* 1681 : W. Robertson, *Phraseol.
Generalis*, 620.

6. *A fool can dance without a fiddle.*
1732 : Fuller, No. 99.

7. *A fool is fulsome.* 1659 : Howell,
10. 1670 : Ray, 10. 1686 : in *Roxb.
Ballads*, viii. 604 (B.S.), Prating like a
fool is fulsome.

8. *A fool knows more in his own house
than a wise man in another's.* 1620 :
Shelton, *Quixote*, Pt. II. ch. xliii. 1694 :
D'Urfey, *Quixote*, Pt. II. Act V. sc. i.
[with " sees " for " knows "]. 1732 :
Fuller, No. 103.

9. *A fool looks to the beginning, a
wise man regards the end.* c. 1535 :
Dialogues of Creatures, ccvii. (1816),
A foole beholdith but onely the begynnynge of his workys, but a wiseman
takyth hede to the ende.

10. *A fool loseth his estate before he
finds his folly.* [c. 1489 : Caxton, *Sonnes
of Aymon*, 485 (E.E.T.S.), For a fole
never byleveth tyll he fele sore.] 1732 :
Fuller, No. 104.

11. *A fool may make money, but it
needs a wise man to spend it.* 1869 :
Spurgeon, *John Ploughman*, ch. xix.
1875 : A. B. Cheales, *Proverb. Folk-
Lore*, 100.

12. *A fool may sometimes give a
wise man counsel* — with variants.
[πολλάκα γὰρ καὶ μωρὸς ἀνὴρ μάλα καίριον εἶπεν.—
Aulus Gellius, ii. 6.] c. 1374 : Chaucer,
Troylus, bk. i. l. 630, A fool may eek
a wys man ofte gyde. c. 1450 : *Partonope*, l. 7982, p. 321 (E.E.T.S.), Yet
an old proverbe sayd ys all day : Of a
foole a wyse man may Take wytt.
1581 : Stafford, *Exam. of Complaints*, 11
(N. Sh. S.), Yet fooles (as the prouerbe
is) sometimes speake to the purpose.

1678 : Ray, 140, A fool may put somewhat in a wise bodies head. 1693 :
Urquhart, *Rabelais*, bk. iii. ch. 37,
I have often heard it said in a vulgar
proverb, The wise may be instructed
by a fool. 1732 : Fuller, No. 105, A
fool may chance to put something into
a wise man's head. 1818 : Scott, *Heart
of Midl.*, ch. xlv., And if a fule may gie
a wise man a counsel . . . 1926 : Phillpotts, *Marylebone Miser*, ch. i., Listen
to everybody, for the biggest fool may
come out with a bit of sense when you
least expect it.

13. *A fool may throw a stone into a
well, which a hundred wise men cannot
pull out.* 1640 : Herbert, *Jac. Prudentum.* 1854 : J. W. Warter, *Last of
Old Squires*, 53.

14. *A fool on a bridge soundeth like
a drum.* 1611 : Cotgrave, s.v. " Pont,"
A foole on a bridge is a drumme in
a river. 1623 : Wodroephe, *Spared
Houres*, 485.

15. *A fool or a physician.* An associa-
tion or alternative in various proverbial
forms. *See* quots. [Sed gravescente
valetudine nihil e libidinibus omitte-
bat, in patientia firmitudinem simulans
solitusque eludere medicorum artes
atque eos, qui post tricesimum ætatis
annus ad internoscenda corpori suo
utilia vel noxia alieni consilii indigerunt.
—Tacitus, *Annals*, VI. xlvi.] 1607 :
B. Barnes, *Divils Charter*, sig. L3,
Eyther mere fooles or good phisitions
all. 1634 : T. Heywood, *Ma.-Head
Well Lost*, III., No matter whether I
bee a foole or a phisitian, if I loose,
Ile pay. c. 1645 : MS. Proverbs, in
N. & Q., vol. cliv., p. 27, Every man is
either a foole or a physitian. 1678 :
*The Quacks Academy . . . A New Art to
cross the Old Proverb, and make a Man
a Fool and Physician both at a Time*
[title], in *Harl. Miscell.*, ii. (1744).
1707 : Dunton, *Athen. Sport*, p. 13,
col. 1, Remember, Every man is a fool,
or physician to himself at least. 1732 :
Fuller, No. 1428, Every man is a fool,
or a physician, at forty. 1777 : in
Garrick Corresp., ii. 219 (1832) [as in
1732]. 1793 : O'Keeffe, *World in a
Village*, III. i. [as in 1732].

16. *A fool thinketh himself wise.* 1557 :
North, *Diall of Princes*, fo. 91 v°, He
may be called a foole that . . . auaunceth
him selfe to be wise. 1601 : Shakespeare, *As You Like It*, V. i., I do
now remember a saying, "The fool
doth think he is wise, but the wise man
knows himself to be a fool."

17. *A fool wants* [lacks] *his cloak on
a rainy day.* 1732 : Fuller, No. 110.

18. *A fool when he hath spoke hath
done all*, or, *A fool is known by his speech.*
1303 : R. Brunne, *Handl. Synne*, l. 2970,
By foly wurdys mow men a foyle kenne.
1412–20 : Lydgate, *Troy Book*, bk. ii.
l. 7022, For be his tonge a fole is ofte
knowe. 1570 : Barclay, *Mirrour of
Good Manners*, 73 (Spens. S.), A foole
is knowen by speche negligent. 1611 :
Cotgrave, s.v. "Fol," Fools are wise
untill they speake. 1732 : Fuller, No.
111, A fool, when he hath spoke, hath
done all.

19. *A fool will ask more questions
than the wisest can answer.* 1666 : Torriano, *Piazza Univ.*, 69, A fool may
ask more than seven wise men can
answer. 1670 : Ray, 91, A fool may
ask more questions in an hour, then a
wise man can answer in seven years.
1738 : Swift, *Polite Convers.*, Dial. II.
1821 : Scott, *Pirate*, ch. xviii., He
knows a fool may ask more questions
than a wise man cares to answer.
1901 : F. E. Taylor, *Lancs Sayings*, 7,
A foo' con ax mooar questions i' five
minits nor a wise mon con answer i'
a month.

20. *A fool will laugh when he is
drowning.* 1577 : *Misogonus*, I. ii., A
foole in laughture puttethe all his
pleasure. 1616 : Breton, in *Works*, ii.
e 6 (Grosart), A foole is euer laughing.
1659 : Howell, *Proverbs : Brit.-Eng.*, 2.

21. *A fool will not be foiled.* 1659 :
Ibid., 22. 1710 : S. Palmer, *Moral Essays
on Proverbs*, 127.

22. *A fool will not part with his
bauble for the Tower of London.* Before
1500 : in Hill, *Commonplace-Book*, 130
(E.E.T.S.) [with "geve" for "part
with"]. 1509 : Barclay, *Ship of Fools*,
i. 256 (1874), For it is sayd of men
both yonge and olde A foole wyll nat

gyue his babyll for any golde. 1599 :
Porter, *Two Angry Women*, in Hazlitt, *Old Plays*, vii. 359 [with "leave"
for "part with"]. 1630 : T. Adams,
Works, 774, The foole will not giue
his bable for the Kings Exchequer.
1662 : Fuller, *Worthies*, ii. 342 (1840).
1716 : E. Ward, *Female Policy*, 86,
Some would not give their babel for
the Tower of London. 1790 : Grose,
Prov. Gloss., s.v. "London."

23. *A fool's bell is soon rung.* c. 1400 :
Rom. Rose, l. 5266, And fooles can not
holde hir tunge; A fooles belle is sone
runge.

24. *A fool's bolt is soon shot.* c. 1270 :
Prov. of Alfred, in *O. E. Miscell.*,
128 (Morris), And sottes bolt is sone
i-schotte. c. 1320 : in *Reliq. Antiquæ*,
i. 111 (1841), "Sottes bolt is sone
shote"; Quoth Hendyng. c. 1460 :
Good Wyfe wold a Pylgr., l. 95, A
follis bolt ys son I-schot. 1583 :
Greene, in *Works*, ii. 79 (Grosart).
1600 : Shakespeare, *Henry V.*, III. vii.
1667 : Lord Bristol, *Elvira*, V., How
soon a fool's bolt's shot without distinction. 1748 : Smollett, *Rod. Random*, ch. liii., "Zounds, I have done,"
said he. "Your bolt is soon shot,
according to the old proverb," said
she. 1826 : Brady, *Varieties of Lit.*, 21,
The implement shot from the cross-bow
is called . . . by the English a bolt.
Hence the saying . . . "the fool's bolt
is soonest shot." 1847 : Planché, *Extravag.*, iii. 198 (1879).

25. *A fool's bolt may sometimes hit
the white.* 1732 : Fuller, No. 107.

26. *A fool's handsel is lucky.* 1614 :
Jonson, *Bart. Fair*, II., Bring him a
sixpenny bottle of ale : they say, a
fool's handsel is lucky. 1668 : Dryden,
Sir Martin Mar-all, V. iii., A fool's plot
may be as lucky as a fool's handsel.

27. *A fool's heart is in his tongue.*
1566 : Drant, *Horace : Satires*, Sat. 2,
That sillye foole . . . His harte is euer
in his toungue. 1622 : P. Hannay,
Poet. Works, 184 (Hunt. Cl.), The wise
man's tongue is euer in his heart ; The
fooles heart's in his tongue. 1641 :
Quarles, *Enchyridion*, Cent. III. cap.
lv. 1669 : *Politeuphuia*, 37, The heart

of a fool is in his mouth. Cf. **Wise**,
adj. (50).

28. *A fool's paper.* See **White** (11).

29. *A fool's paradise.* 1462 : *Paston
Lett.*, ii. 109 (Gairdner, 1900), But I
wold not be in a folis paradyce. 1549 :
Mathew's Bible, 2 Kings, ch. iv., Dyd
I desyre a sonne of my Lorde? Dyd
I not say that thou shouldest not brynge
me in a foles paradyse. 1604 : Webster
and Marston, *Malcontent*, V. iii., Promise of matrimony by a yong gallant,
to bring a virgin lady into a fooles
paradise ! 1632 : R. Brome, *Northern
Lasse*, V. viii., Why I am fubdoodled
thus. In I protest and vow a kind of
fools Paradise. 1732 : Fielding, *Mod.
Husband*, I. ix., A levee is the paradise
of fools. 1894 : R. L. S., *St. Ives*,
ch. xxvi., The next moment I had
recognised the inanity of that fool's
paradise. 1914 : Shaw, "Parents and
Children," in *Misalliance, etc.*, p. cxiii,
A means of pleasing himself and be-
guiling tedious hours with romances
and fairy tales and fools' paradises.

30. *A fool's speech is a bubble of air.*
1732 : Fuller, No. 109.

31. *A fool's tongue is long enough to
cut his own throat.* Ibid., No. 108.

32. *Answer a fool according to his
folly.* [Answer a fool according to his
folly lest he be wise in his own conceit.
—*Prov.* xxvi. 5.] 1484 : Caxton, *Æsope*,
ii. 175 (Jacobs), To foolish demui
[question] behoveth a foolish answer.
1589 : Nashe, in *Works*, i. 166 (Grosart),
It is therefore thought the best way
. . . to answere the fooles, according
to their foolishness. 1692 : L'Estrange,
Æsop, 10 (3rd ed.), It does not yet
become a man of honour . . . to
answer every fool in his folly. 1740 :
North, *Lives of Norths*, i. 332 (Bohn),
And so fools are often answered in
their folly.

33. *As the fool thinks, so the bell
clinks.* 1607 : *Lingua*, III. vii., As the
fool thinketh, so the bell clinketh.
I protest I hear no more than a post.
1673 : Marvell, *Rehearsal Transpr.*,
Pt. II., in *Works*, iii. 387 (Grosart),
I understand, sir, what you mean;
" as the fool thinks, so the conscience

tinks." 1738 : Swift, *Polite Convers.*,
Dial. I., *Miss*. Peace ! I think I hear
the church-clock. *Neverout*. Why, you
know, as the fool thinks . . . 1831 :
Hone, *Year-Book*, 455, As the bell
tinks, so the fool thinks; As the fool
thinks, so the bell tinks.

34. *Bray a fool in a mortar, etc.*
[Though thou shouldest bray a fool in
a mortar among wheat with a pestle,
yet will not his foolishness depart
from him.—*Prov.* xxvii. 22.] *c.* 1568 :
Wager, *Longer thou Livest*, sig. D2,
Beate a foole in a morter saith the
wise man, and thou shalt not make
him leaue his folly. 1694 : D'Urfey,
Quixote, Pt. I. Act V. sc. ii., Bray a
fool in a mortar, and you'll find all
of him but his brains. 1855 : Kingsley,
West. Ho!, ch. v.

35. *By their words we know fools, and
asses by their ears.* 1586 : L. Evans,
Revised Withals Dict., sig. C4.

36. *Every fool can find faults that a
great many wise men can't remedy.*
1732 : Fuller, No. 1416.

37. *Every fool is a fiddle to the company.* 1616 : Sharpham, *Cupid's Whirligig*, IV., They say, euery foole is a fiddle
to the companie.

38. *Fool's haste is no speed.* 1732 :
Fuller, No. 1575. 1827 : Scott, *Journal*,
12 Jan., I wish it may not prove fool's
haste, yet I take as much pains too as
is in my nature.

39. *Fools and foumarts* [polecats].
See quot. 1898 : *N. & Q.*, 9th ser., ii.
88, " Fools and foumards can't see by
day-leet." I heard this near here
[Epworth] the other day.

40. *Fools and little dogs are ladies'
play-fellows.* 1583 : Melbancke, *Philotinus*, sig. T3.

41. *Fools and madmen speak the
truth.* 1621 : Burton, *Melancholy*, II.
III. viii. 429 (1836), For fools and
mad men tell commonly truth. 1634 :
Massinger, *Very Woman*, III. i., Wilt
thou be my fool? for fools, they say,
will tell truth. 1791 : Mrs. Thrale, in
Hayward, *Mrs. Piozzi*, i. 342 (2nd ed.),
He is quite light-headed, yet madmen,
drunkards, and fools tell truth, they say.

42. *Fools are all the world over, as he*

said that shod the goose. 1732 : Fuller, No. 1567. 1880 : Spurgeon, *Ploughman's Pictures*, 141.

43. *Fools are known by their babbling.* 1477 : Rivers, *Dictes and Sayings*, 57 (1877), A man may knowe a fole by his moche clatering. 1597 : H. Lok, *Ecclesiastes*, 98, Fooles if they once begin, can neuer end. 1641 : Jonson, *Timber :* "Homeri Ulysses," For too much talking is ever the indice of a fool. 1647 : *Countrym. New Commonwealth*, 10, Fooles are known by their bablings.

44. *Fools are of all sizes.* 1901 : F. E. Taylor, *Lancs Sayings*, 9, Ther's foo's ov o sizes.

45. *Fools are pleased with their own blunders.* 1732 : Fuller, No. 1570.

46. *Fools are weatherwise.* 1887 : M. A. Courtney, *Folk-Lore Journal*, v. 192, Here [Cornwall] it is well known that " fools are weatherwise," and that " those that are weatherwise are rarely otherwise." 1906 : *Cornish N. & Q.*, 271.

47. *Fools are wise men in the affairs of women.* 1732 : Fuller, No. 1571.

48. *Fools build houses and wise men buy them.* 1670 : Ray, 91. 1732 : Fuller, No. 1573 [with " enjoy " for " buy "]. *c.* 1860 : R. S. Hawker, in Byles, *Life, etc.*, 82 (1905) [with " inhabit " for " buy "]. 1875 : A. B. Cheales, *Proverb. Folk-Lore*, 43 [with " live in " for " buy "].

49. *Fools give, to please all but their own.* 1640 : Herbert, *Jac. Prudentum.*

50. *Fools grow without watering.* 1732 : Fuller, No. 1574. 1853 : Trench, *Proverbs*, 73 (1905).

51. *Fools have fortune. c.* 1568 : Wager, *Longer thou Livest*, sig. E2, They say that fooles are fortunable. 1639 : Glapthorne, *Wit in a Constable*, III., The old proverbe, of fooles have fortune. 1720 : *Vade Mecum for Maltworms*, Pt. II. p. 22, Dick . . . fulfills the proverb which says, Fools have fortune. *c.* 1760 : Garrick, *Lying Valet*, II. Cf. **Fortune favours fools**; and **God sends fortune.**

52. *Fools lade the water and wise men catch the fish.* 15th cent. : in *Babees Book*, 332 (Furnivall), Folus [Fools] lade polys [pools] ; wisemenn ete þe fysshe.

1605 : Camden, *Remains*, 322 (1870). 1670 : Ray, 92. 1732 : Fuller, No. 1581, Fools lade out all the water, and wise men take the fish.

53. *Fools laugh at their own sport.* 1855 : Bohn, 356.

54. *Fools live poor to die rich.* Ibid., 356.

55. *Fools love all that is good.* 1738 : Swift, *Polite Convers.*, Dial. I., I'm like all fools ; I love everything that's good. Cf. **Lord Mayor's fool.**

56. *Fools make feasts and wise men eat them.* 1578 : Florio, *First Fruites*, fo. 30, Fooles make the banquets, and wise men enjoy them. 1683 : Meriton, *Yorkshire Ale*, 83–7 (1697). 1736 : Franklin, *Way to Wealth*, in *Works*, i. 447 (Bigelow). 1823 : D'Israeli, *Cur. of Lit.*, 2nd ser., i. 449 (1824), A great man in Scotland, who, having given a splendid entertainment, was harshly told that " Fools make feasts, and wise men eat them . . ."

57. *Fools may invent fashions that wise men will wear.* 1732 : Fuller, No. 1579.

58. *Fools never know when they are well.* 1519 : Horman, *Vulgaria*, fo. 67, He is a foole that can nat holde hym selfe content whan he is well at ease. 1794 : Wolcot, in *Works*, ii. 528 (1795), Fools never know when they are well. 1822 : Scott, *Nigel*, ch. xxi., 'Tis always thus—fools and children never know when they are well.

59. *Fools no Latin know.* 1869 : Hazlitt, 134.

60. *Fools refuse favours.* 1659 : Howell, *Proverbs : Brit.-Eng.*, 22.

61. *Fools set stools for wise men to stumble at.* 1605 : Camden, *Remains*, 322 (1870). 1613 : S. Rowley, *When You See Me*, sig. F3, Yee know what the old prouerbe saies, . . . When fooles set stocks, and wise men breake their shinnes. 1670 : Ray, 91. 1754 : Berthelson, *Eng.-Danish Dict.*, s.v. "Fool." 1880 : Spurgeon, *Ploughman's Pictures*, 141.

62. *Fools should not see half done work.* I am not sure that this is not a purely Scottish saying. 1818 : Scott, in Lockhart's *Life*, iv. 216, It is not

fit to be shown to " bairns and fools,"
who,˙ according to our old canny
proverb, should never see half done
work.

63. *Fools tie knots and wise men loose
them.* 1639 : Clarke, 88. 1670 : Ray,
10. 1732 : Fuller, No. 1583.

64. *Fools will be fools.* 1650 : R.
Heath, *Satyrs*, 9, Fools will still be
fools. 1784 : *New Foundl. Hosp. for
Wit*, ii. 201, Fools will be fools, say
what we will.

65. *Fools will be meddling.* c. 1380 :
Chaucer, *Parl. of Foules*, l. 574,
But sooth is seyd, " a fool can noght
be stille." 1670 : Ray, 91. 1738 :
Swift, *Polite Convers.*, Dial. I., Why,
madam, fools will be meddling. 1822 :
Scott, *Nigel*, ch. xxiii., Beasts and fools
will be meddling, my lord.

66. *Fools' paradises are wise men's
purgatories.* 1763 : Colman, *Deuce is
in Him*, I. i., A fool's paradise is better
than a wiseacre's purgatory. 1922 :
Saintsbury, *Scrap-Book*, 254.

67. *Fools' thoughts often fail.* c. 1374 :
Chaucer, *Troylus*, bk. i. l. 217, But
alday fayleth thing that foolës wenden
[imagined]. c. 1387 : Usk, *Test. of
Love*, ii. 8, 122, Thus alday fayleth
thinges that fooles wende. c. 1534 :
Berners, *Huon*, 502 (E.E.T.S.), It is
a comune sayng that many thingis
lackethe of folysshe thoughtis. ˙

68. *Give a fool a candle to tind* [light],
He will light it at the ind. 1883 : Burne,
Shropsh. Folk-Lore, 588.

69. *He hath great need of a fool that
plays the fool himself.* 1640 : Herbert,
Jac. Prudentum.

70. *He is a fool that deals with fools.*
c. 1350 : *Parlement of Three Ages*, l. 264
(Gollancz), Fole es that with foles delys.

71. *He is a fool that forgets himself.*
c. 1270 : in *Old Eng. Miscell.*, 59 (Morris,
E.E.T.S.), Sot is þat is oþer mannes
freond more þan his owe. c. 1374 :
Chaucer, *Troylus*, bk. v. l. 98, I have
herd seyd, eek tymes twyës twelve,
" He is a fool that wol for-yete him-
selve." 1611 : Cotgrave, s.v. " Fol,"
Hee is a right foole that forgets himselfe.
1683 : Meriton, *Yorkshire Ale*, 83-7
(1697).

72. *He is a fool that is not melancholy
once a day.* 1678 : Ray, 346. 1683 :
Meriton, *Yorkshire Ale*, 83-7 (1697), He
is a feaul that is not mallancholy yance
a day. 1732 : Fuller, No. 2434.

73. *He is a fool that makes a wedge of
his fist.* 1611 : Cotgrave, s.v. " Coing."
1666 : Torriano, *Piazza Univ.*, 221.

74. *He is a fool that thinks not that
another thinks.* 1640 : Herbert, *Jac.
Prudentum.*

75. *He is fool enough himself, who
will bray against another ass.* 1855 :
Bohn, 375.

76. *He is not the fool that the fool is,
but he that with the fool deals.* 1683 :
Meriton, *Yorkshire Ale*, 83-7 (1697).

77. *He's a fool that is wiser abroad
than at home.* 1732 : Fuller, No. 2435.

78. *He's a fool.* See quot. 1846 :
Denham, *Proverbs*, 65 (Percy S.), He's
a fule that marries at Yule ; For when
the bairn's to bear, The corn's to shear.
1904 : Co. *Folk-Lore : Northumb.*, 179
(F.L.S.) [as in 1846].

79. *He that sends a fool means to
follow him.* 1640 : Herbert, *Jac. Prudentum.* 1659 : Howell, 3, Who sendeth
a fool upon an errand, must goe himself
after.

80. *He who is born a fool is never cured.*
1732 : Fuller, No. 2391.

81. *If all fools had baubles we should
want fuel.* 1611 : Cotgrave, s.v. " Ma-
rotte," If all that fooles arc bables
wore, of wood we should have but
small store. 1670 : Ray, 10, If all
fools ware bables fewel would be
dear. 1732 : Fuller, No. 2676, If
every fool were to wear a bauble,
they would grow dear.

82. *If all fools wore white caps, we
should seem a flock of geese.* 1640 :
Herbert, *Jac. Prudentum.*

83. *If fools should not fool it, they
shall lose their reason.* Ibid.

84. *It is the property of fools to be
always judging.* 1732 : Fuller, No. 3027.

85. *Much abides behind what a fool
thinks.* c. 1489 : Caxton, *Blanchardyn,
etc.*, 181 (E.E.T.S.), It ys said often in
a comyn langage that " moche abydeth
behynde that a fole thynketh."

86. *No one is a fool always, every one*

sometimes. 1640: Herbert, *Jac. Prudentum.* 1694: D'Urfey, *Quixote*, Pt. I. Act I. sc. i., None are fools always, tho every one sometimes. 1748: Richardson, *Clarissa*, iv. 237 (1785). 1854: J. W. Warter, *Last of Old Squires*, 53.

87. *One fool in a play is more than enough.* Derby. 1889: *Folk-Lore Journal*, vii. 293.

88. *One fool makes many.* 1640: Herbert, *Jac. Prudentum*, One fool makes a hundred. 1654: Gayton, *Pleasant Notes Don Q.*, 140. 1769: Brooke, *Fool of Quality*, iv. 228. 1821: Byron, *The Blues*, Ecl. i. l. 57. 1860: Reade, *Cl. and Hearth*, ch. lxxiv., Loose tongue found credulous ears, and so one fool made many.

89. *Only fools and fiddlers sing at meals.* 1813: Ray, 9, None but fools and fiddlers sing at their meat. 1889: *Folk-Lore Journal*, vii. 293 (Derbyshire).

90. *Play with a fool at home, and he will play with you in the market.* 1640: Herbert, *Jac. Prudentum.* 1670: Ray, 10. 1732: Fuller, No. 2763.

91. *Send a fool to the market, and a fool he'll return.* 1586: G. Whitney, *Emblems*, 178, The foole, that farre is sente some wisedome to attaine; Returnes an ideot, as he wente, and bringes the foole againe. 1604: *Pasquils Jests*, 38 (1864), You may all depart like fooles as you came. 1666: Torriano, *Piazza Univ.*, 147, Who sends a fool expects the same back again. 1732: Fuller, No. 4096. 1738: Swift, *Polite Convers.*, Dial. I., You may go back again, like a fool as you came.

92. *Set a fool to catch a fool.* 1654: Gayton, *Pleasant Notes Don Q.*, 178, As they say, set a fool, etc.

93. *Set a fool to roast eggs, and a wise man to eat them.* 1678: Ray, 241.

94. *That which a fool doth at last, a wise man doth at first.* 1666: Torriano, *Piazza Univ.*, 197. 1880: Spurgeon, *Ploughman's Pictures*, 20, A wise man does at first what a fool does at last.

95. *The first chapter of fools is to esteem themselves wise.* 1578: Florio, *First Fruites*, fo. 29 [with " count " for " esteem "]. 1586: Pettie, tr. Guazzo's *Civil Convers.*, fo. 40. 1659: Howell,

1 [with " hold " for " esteem "]. 1732: Fuller, No. 4525.

96. *The fool asks much, but he is more fool that grants it.* 1633: Draxe, 21. 1670: Ray, 10. 1732: Fuller, No. 100, A fool demands much; but he's a greater that gives it.

97. *The fool is busy in every one's business but his own.* 1732: Fuller, No. 4537.

98. *The fool runs away while his house is burning down.* Ibid., No. 4538.

99. *The fool saith, who would have thought it?* 1633: Draxe, 13, It is the part of a foole to say, I had not thought. 1732: Fuller, No. 4539.

100. *The fool wanders, the wise man travels.* Ibid., No. 4540.

101. *The higher the fool, the greater the fall.* 1878: J. Platt, *Morality*, 34.

102. *The more riches a fool hath, the greater fool he is.* 1732: Fuller, No. 4666.

103. *The praise of fools is censure in disguise.* 1855: Bohn, 513.

104. *There is no fool like the old fool.* 1546: Heywood, *Proverbs*, Pt. II. ch. ii., There is no foole to the olde foole, folke say. 1592: Lyly, *Mother Bombie*, IV. ii. 1616: Breton, in *Works*, ii. *e*6 (Grosart). 1712: Gay, *Mohocks*, sc. ii., Oh Peter, Peter! an old fool of all fools is the worst. 1856: Planché, *Extravag.*, v. 157 (1879), In love there's no fool, madam, like an old fool. 1922: Weyman, *Ovington's Bank*, ch. viii.

105. *To deal fool's dole.* 1670: Ray, 171.

106. *To the counsel of fools, a wooden bell.* 1640: Herbert, *Jac. Prudentum.*

107. *We are fools one to another.* Ibid.

108. *Were there no fools bad ware would not be sold.* 1611: Cotgrave, s.v. " Marché," If fooles went not to markets bad wares would not be sold. 1696: D'Urfey, *Quixote*, Pt. III. Act I. [as in 1611, with " coxcombs " for " fooles "]. 1732: Fuller, No. 2677 [as in 1611]. 1869: Spurgeon, *John Ploughman*, ch. xvi. [as in 1611].

109. *When a fool hath bethought himself, the market's over.* 1732: Fuller, No. 5530.

110. *When the fool finds a horse-shoe,
He thinks always so to do.* Ibid., No.
6415.

See also **April** (23); **Certainty**; **Children** (2) and (3); **Experience**; **Fortune favours**; **God** sends fortune; **Honour** (4); **Many a one**; **None but fools**; **None is so wise**; **Robin Hood** (9); **Wise,** *passim*; **Wit** (4); **Woman** (5); and **World** (7) and (10).

Foolish fear doubleth danger. 1732:
Fuller, No. 1563.

Foolish pity spoils a city. 1556:
Heywood, *Spider and Flie,* cap. 70,
p. 307 (Farmer), This . . . Is either not
pity, or peevish pity, Which (as th' old
saying saith) marreth the city. 1613:
Wither, *Abuses Stript, etc.,* bk. i. sat. 13,
A foolish pitty quickly ouerthrowes, In
warre an army, and in peace a state.
1670: Ray, 131. 1732: Fuller, No.
6216 [" ruins " for " spoils "].

Foolish tongues talk by the dozen.
1640: Herbert, *Jac. Prudentum.*

Foot and Feet. 1. *He thinks his feet
be where his head shall never come.*
1546: Heywood, *Proverbs,* Pt. I., ch. xi.
1611: Davies (of Hereford), *Sc. of
Folly,* 49, in *Works,* ii. (Grosart), Some
thinke their feete be where their head
shall neuer come.

2. *The foot on the cradle, the hand on
the distaff.* 1659: Howell, *Proverbs:
Span.-Eng.,* 2, [*plus*] a sign of a good
housewife. 1670: Ray, 14 [as in 1659].
1732: Fuller, No. 4541.

3. *Thy foot is longer than thy leg.*
1917: Bridge, *Cheshire Proverbs,* 124,
Thou'rt like a butterbump [bittern],
thy foot's longer than thy leg.

4. *To have* (or *know*) *the length of
one's foot.* 1580: Lyly, *Euphues,* 290
(Arber), You shal not know the length
of my foote, vntill by your cunning
you get commendation. 1603: Dekker,
in *Works,* i. 263 (Grosart), Having now
the full length of his foot, then shewes
she herselfe what she is. *c.* 1663:
Davenant, *Play-House to be Let,* V.,
Well, gossip, I know too the length of
your foote. 1720: C. Shadwell, *Irish
Hospit.,* II., What I speak is in my own
praise, 'tis a very easy matter to get
the length of my foot. 1858: Hughes,

White Horse, ch. iii., I have got the
length of his foot, and he has asked
me to luncheon. 1922: Weyman,
Ovington's Bank, ch. xix., He had taken
the length of the Squire's foot.

5. *To thrust one's feet under another
man's table.* 1678: Ray, 272. 1732:
Fuller, No. 5247.

See also **Leg** (4) and (5); and **One
Foot.**

Football. *See* **All fellows**; and **Two
to one.**

For ill do well, then fear not hell.
1855: Bohn, 357.

For mad words deaf ears. 1633:
Draxe, 69, For foolish talke deafe
eares. 1732: Fuller, No. 1593.

For my part. *See* **Kiln** (1).

Forbearance is no acquittance. 1546:
Heywood, *Proverbs,* Pt. II. ch. iv.,
Sufferaunce is no quittance. 1578:
Florio, *First Fruites,* fo. 33, Forbearance
is no payment. 1605: T. Heywood,
If You Know Not Me, in *Works,* i. 332
(1874). 1670: Ray, 92. 1732: Fuller,
No. 1587.

Forbidden fruit is sweet. 1855:
Bohn, 357.

**Force without fore-cast is of little
avail.** 1732: Fuller, No. 1589.

Forced kindness deserves no thanks, A.
Ibid., No. 113.

Forced put. *See* quots. 1657: G.
Starkey, *Helmont's Vind.,* 328 (O.), To
give poysons to purge, in expectation
that Nature being forced to play a
desperate game, and reduced to a
forc't put, may . . . 1678: Ray, 79,
He's at a forc't put. 1754: Berthelson,
Eng.-Danish Dict., s.v. " Put," 'Tis a
forced put. 1880: Courtney, *W. Cornwall Words,* 23 (E.D.S.), A fo'ced put is
no choice.

Ford. 1. *Never praise a ford till you
get over.* 1633: Draxe, 51, It is not
good praysing of a foord, vntill a man
be ouer. 1670: Ray, 92 [as in 1633].
1754: Berthelson, *Eng.-Danish Dict.,*
s.v. " Ford."

2. *To take the ford as one finds it.*
1575: Gascoigne, *Posies,* 6 (Cunliffe),
Yet is it true that I must take the
foord as I finde it: sometimes not as
I woulde, but as I may. 1817: Scott,

Rob Roy, ch. xxvii., Let ilka ane roose the ford as they find it.

Forecast is better than work hard. 1612 : Chapman, *Widow's Tears,* II. iv. [with " labour " for " work hard "]. 1670 : Ray, 92. 1732 : Fuller, No. 1588.

Forehand pay. *See* quots. 1886 : Elworthy, *West Som. Word-Book,* 186 (E.D.S.), Hence the old saying " Vore-hand-pay and never-pay's the wist [worst] of all pay." 1894 : Northall, *Folk Phrases,* 13 (E.D.S.), Forehanded pay is the worst pay as is. Cf. **Pay** (4).

Forehead and the eye, In the, the lecture of the mind doth lie. 1633 : Draxe, 60 [" heart is read " for last three words]. 1670 : Ray, 92. 1754 : Berthelson, *Eng.-Danish Dict.,* s.v. " Lecture." Cf. **Face** (4).

Foreheet [Predetermine] **nothing but building churches and louping over them, I'll.** 1678 : Ray, 355. 1683 : Meriton, *Yorkshire Ale,* 83–7 (1697) [with " Fore-sheet " for " Foreheet "]. 1691 : Ray, *Words not Generally Used,* 43 (E.D.S.).

Fore-horse by the head. *See* quots. 1875 : Parish, *Sussex Dict.,* 45, " He has got the fore-horse by the head " is a Sussex expression for " he has got matters well in hand." 1894 : Northall, *Folk Phrases,* 28 (E.D.S.), To get the forehorse by the head=To get out of debt : to see one's way clear, etc.

Fore-warned fore-armed, or in some early examples, **half-armed.** [Egon' ut cavere nequeam, cui praedicitur?—Plautus, *Pseudol.,* I. v. 101.] Before 1500 : in Hill, *Commonplace-Book,* 132 (E.E.T.S.), He that is warned ys half armed. *c.* 1569 : in Collmann, *Ballads and Broadsides,* 194 (Roxb. Cl.), But they that warned are in tyme, Halfe armed are gainst daungerous crime. 1587 : Greene, in *Works,* iv. 154 (Grosart), By his fore-warning, thou hadst bene fore-armed. 1620 : Shelton, *Quixote,* Pt. II. ch. xvii., He that is warned is half armed. 1673 : Wycherley, *Gent. Danc.-Master,* V. i. 1712 : *Spectator,* No. 395. 1834 : Marryat, *P. Simple,* ch. liv., I now knew the ground which I stood upon ; and fore-warned was being forearmed. Cf. **Once warned.**

Forget, *verb.* 1. *To forget a wrong is the best revenge.* 1639 : Clarke, 324. 1670 : Ray, 92. *c.* 1800 : Trusler, *Prov. in Verse,* 101, To forget an injury is the best revenge. Cf. **Forgive** (4).

2. *We have all forgot more than we remember.* 1732 : Fuller, No. 5442.

Forgetful head makes a weary pair of heels, A. 1869 : Hazlitt, 12.

Forgive, *verb.* 1. *Forgive and forget.* Before 1225 : *Ancren R.,* 124 (O.), Al ꝥet hurt and al ꝥet sore were uorȝiten and forȝiuen uor glednesse. 1546 : Heywood, *Proverbs,* Pt. II. ch. iii., All our great fraie . . . Is forgeuen and for-gotten betwene vs quight. *c.* 1605 : Shakespeare, *Lear,* IV. vii., Pray you now, forget and forgive. 1696 : Southerne, *Oroonoko,* V. ii., Endeavour to forget, sir, and forgive. 1792 : Holcroft, *Road to Ruin,* V. iii., We ought all to forget and forgive. 1823 : Scott, *Peveril,* ch. xxv., Years had taught Deborah to forget and forgive. 1921 : 22 June, King George V., *Speech* at Belfast, opening Ulster Parl., I appeal to all Irishmen to pause, to stretch out the hand of forbearance and concilia-tion, to forgive and to forget.

2. *Forgive any sooner than thyself.* 1670 : Ray, 10.

3. *If we are bound to forgive an enemy, we are not bound to trust him.* 1732 : Fuller, No. 2728.

4. *Revenge a wrong by forgiving it.* 1710 : S. Palmer, *Moral Essays on Proverbs,* 81, Forgiveness and a smile is the best revenge. 1831 : Hone, *Year-Book,* col. 1417. 1853 : Trench, *Proverbs,* 13 (1905), *The noblest ven-geance is to forgive:* here is the godlike proverb. Cf. **Forget** (1).

Fork. *I ask you for a fork and you bring me a rake.* 1732 : Fuller, No. 2587. *See also* **Rake.**

Forkle-end. *See* quot. " Forkle-end " is not in Wright's *Eng. Dialect Dict.* 1869 : Hazlitt, 201, He's standing on his forkle-end. S. Devon : i.e. he's well and on his legs, able to get about.—Shelly.

Forms keep fools at a distance. *c.* 1750 : Foote, *Englishm. returned from Paris,* II., They say forms keep fools at a distance.

Fort. *See* Castle (2).

Fortunate boor needs but be born, A.
1659 : Howell, *Proverbs : Brit.-Eng.*, 26.

Fortunate man may be any where, A.
1732 : Fuller, No. 114.

Fortune and love. *See* quot. Before
1704 : T. Brown, in *Works*, iii. 167
(1760), The ancient proverb, which
says, that fortune and love don't
always favour the most deserving.

Fortune can take from us nothing
but what she gave us. 1732 : Fuller,
No. 1598.

Fortune favour, If. *See* quot. 1670 :
Ray, 212, If fortune favour I may have
her, for I go about her ; If fortune fail you
may kiss her tail, and go without her.

Fortune favours fools. 1563 : Googe,
Eglogs, etc., 74 (Arber), But Fortune
favours fooles as old men saye. 1599 :
Jonson, *Ev. Man out of Humour*, I. i.,
M. One of those that fortune favours.
C. The periphrasis of a fool. 1687 :
Sedley, *Bellamira*, II., Does my patron
lose? fortune favours fools. 1737 : Gay,
Fables, 2nd ser., No. 12, l. 119, 'Tis a
gross error, held in schools, That For-
tune always favours fools. Cf. Fool
(51) ; and God sends fortune.

Fortune favours the bold. [Fortes
fortuna adjuvat.—Terence, *Phorm.*, I.
iv. 26. Audentes fortuna juvat.—
Virgil, *Æn.*, x. 284. Audentes deus
ipse juvat. — Ovid, *Met.*, x. 586.]
c. 1385 : Chaucer, *Leg. Good Women*, V.,
Lucretia, l. 94, " Hap helpeth hardy
man alday," quod he. *c.* 1390 : Gower,
Conf. Amantis, bk. vii. l. 4902, And
seith " Fortune unto the bolde Is
favorable forto helpe." 1481 : Caxton,
Reynard, 66 (Arber), Who that is hardy
the auenture helpeth him. 1594 : Drayton, *Ideas*, lix., Fortune assists the
boldest, I reply. 1674 : Head and
Kirkman, *Eng. Rogue*, iii. 142, Fortune
helps the bold. 1731 : Swift, *Strephon
and Chloe*, l. 148, Who had been often
told That fortune still assists the bold.
1840 : Barham, *Ing. Legends*, 1st ser. :
" Grey Dolphin," Fortune . . . delights
to favour the bold.

Fortune helps him that is willing to
help himself. 1611 : Cotgrave, s.v.
" Aider."

Fortune is variant. *See* quots.
c. 1420 : Lydgate, *Assembly of Gods*,
st. 46, p. 10 (E.E.T.S.), Varyaunt she
[Fortune] was ; ay in short space Hyr
whele was redy to turne without let.
c. 1490 : *Partonope*, l. 4389 (E.E.T.S.),
Lo, thus ffortune can turne hur dyse
Nowe vp, nowe doune ; here whele ys
vnstabelle. 1509 : Barclay, *Ship of
Fools*, i. 126 (1874), Fortune euer hath
an incertayne end. 1692 : L'Estrange,
Æsop, 15 (3rd ed.), The wheel of time,
and of fortune is still rolling. 1712 :
Motteux, *Quixote*, Pt. I. bk. iv. ch. xx.,
The old proverb is true again, fortune
turns round like a mill-wheel, and he
that was yesterday at the top, lies
to-day at the bottom. *c.* 1824 : in
Farmer, *Musa Pedestris*, 91, But fortune fickle, ever on the wheel . . .

Fortune knocks once at least at every
man's gate. 1567 : Fenton, *Bandello*,
ii. 148 (T.T.), Fortune once in the course
of our life dothe put into our handes
the offer of a good torne. 1869 :
Hazlitt, 136.

Fortune rarely brings good or evil
singly. 1732 : Fuller, No. 1605.

Fortune smiles, When, embrace her.
1670 : Ray, 10, When fortune smiles
on thee, take the advantage. 1732 :
Fuller, No. 5553. 1736 : Bailey, *Dict.*,
s.v. " Fortune," When fortune knocks
be sure to open the door.

Fortune to one is mother, to another
is stepmother. 1651 : Herbert, *Jac.
Prudentum*, 2nd ed.

Forty save one. *See* quots. 1841 :
Hartshorne, *Salopia Ant.*, 520 [with
long explanatory legend, pp. 520–2],
Forty sa [save] one like Obitch's
[? Holbeach's] cowt. 1883 : Burne,
Shropsh. Folk-Lore, 593, Forty save
one, like Rhoden's colt . . . some-
times " like Obitch's colt," but not,
I think, correctly. " Obitch's" colt was
a spectre.

Foul in the cradle and fair in the
saddle. 1605 : Camden, *Remains*, 322
(1870), Foul in the cradle proveth fair
in the saddle. 1659 : Howell, 8. 1754 :
Berthelson, *Eng.-Danish Dict.*, s.v.
" Foul." 1889 : *Folk-Lore Journal*, vii.
292, [Derby sayings] Fou' i' th'

cradle, fair i' th' saddle. Cf. **Fair in
the cradle.**

Foul water is thrown down the sink.
1683: White Kennett, tr. Erasmus'
Praise of Folly, 142 (8th ed.), I will
take the proverb for a satisfactory
reply; namely, *Foul water is thrown
down the sink*; which saying, that no
person may slight it, may be convenient
to advertise that it comes from no
meaner an author than that oracle of
truth, Aristotle himself.

**Foul water will quench fire as well as
fair.** 1546: Heywood, *Proverbs*, Pt. I.
ch. v. 1592: Lyly, *Mother Bombie*,
III. iv., Yet I hope foule water will
quench hot fire as soone as faire. 1616:
Jack Drum, I., in Simpson, *Sch. of
Shakesp.*, ii. 144, Foule water quencheth
fire well enough. 1670: Ray, 154,
Foul water will quench fire. 1732:
Fuller, No. 1607 [as in 1670].

Four bare legs. *See* **Marriage** (9).

Four eyes see more than two. 1666:
Torriano, *Piazza Univ.*, 175, Four eyes
see better than two. 1732: Fuller,
No. 1606.

**Four farthings and a thimble, Make
a tailor's pocket jingle.** 1659: Howell,
15. 1670: Ray, 215. 1732: Fuller,
No. 6328.

Four things drive a man. *See* **Three
things drive a man.**

Four things, it is said. *See* quot.
1809: Pegge, *Anonymiana*, cent. ix. 45,
Four things, it is said, are most to be
desired: a good neighbour; a window
to every man's heart; that men's
tongues and hearts should go together;
and an house upon wheels.

**Four-pence for that advice, If I had
given, I had bought it a groat too dear.**
1732: Fuller, No. 2685.

Four-pence to a groat. *See* **Near as.**

Fowey, The gallants of. Corn. 1602:
Carew, *Surv. of Cornwall*, 315 (1811),
The merit of which exploit afterwards entitled them Gallants of Foy.
1790: Grose, *Prov. Gloss.*, s.v. " Cornwall," The gallants of Foy. 1864:
" Cornish Proverbs," in *N. & Q.*, 3rd
ser., v. 275, . . . Gallants of Foy.
1904: *Morning Post*, 11 April, quoted
in *N. & Q.*, 10th ser., i. 505, It was

stated that though no charter was in
the possession of the parish [Fowey],
their rights were traditionally inherited
by a grant from the Black Prince, as
Duke of Cornwall, in reward for ser-
vices rendered at sea by " the Gallants
of Fowey," from which the village
takes its name.

Fowl of a fair day, As glad as a.
1362: Langland, *Plowman*, A, xi. 109,
Thenne was I as fayn as foul on feir
morwen. *c.* 1386: Chaucer, *Canon's
Yeoman's Tale*, l. 789, This sotted
preest, who was gladder than he?
Was never brid gladder agayn the
day. *c.* 1430: Lydgate, *Minor Poems*,
111 (Percy S.), Sir John was as glad of
thys as ever was fowle of daye. 1598:
Servingm. Comfort, in *Inedited Tracts*,
133 (Hazlitt), Who restes no lesse glad
of his place, then the foule of a fayre
day. 1639: Clarke, 185.

Fox and Foxes. 1. *A fox should not
be of the jury at a goose's trial.* 1732:
Fuller, No. 116.

2. *An old fox need learn no craft.*
1639: Clarke, 267. 1670: Ray, 127.
1732: Fuller, No. 644, An old fox needs
not be taught tricks. Cf. Nos. 3 and 19.

3. *An old fox understands a trap.*
1539: Taverner, *Proverbs*, fo. 27, An
olde foxe is not taken in a snare. 1540:
Palsgrave, *Acolastus*, sig. Q3 [as in
1539]. 1732: Fuller, No. 645. 1880:
Spurgeon, *Ploughman's Pictures*, 116,
An old fox is shy of a trap. Cf. Nos. 2
and 19.

4. *As cunning as a klyket* [fox]. 1846–
59: *Denham Tracts*, ii. 107 (F.L.S.).

5. *As long as you are in the fox's
service, you must hold up his tail.*
1738: *Gent. Mag.*, 475.

6. *At length the fox is brought to the
furrier.* 1640: Herbert, *Jac. Prudentum.* 1666: Torriano, *Piazza Univ.*,
199, All foxes are found at the furriers
shop. 1880: Spurgeon, *Ploughman's
Pictures*, 18, They think it is time that
the fox went to the furrier, and they
had their share of his skin.

7. *At length the fox turns monk.*
1611: Cotgrave, s.v. " Moine." 1640:
Herbert, *Jac. Prudentum.*

8. *Every fox must pay his own skin*

to the flayer. 1639 : Clarke, 215. 1670 :
Ray, 93. 1710 : S. Palmer, *Moral
Essays on Proverbs*, 123. 1846–59:
Denham Tracts, ii. 107 (F.L.S.).

9. *Fie upon heps* [query, misprint
for "hens"] (*quoth the fox*) *because he
could not reach them.* 1678 : Ray, 142.

10. *Foxes dig not their own holes.*
1732 : Fuller, No. 1608. 1846–59 :
Denham Tracts, ii. 107 (F.L.S.).

11. *Foxes when sleeping have nothing
fall into their mouths.* 1611 : Cotgrave,
s.v. "Emplumé," The sleepy fox hath
seldome feathered breakfasts. 1633 :
Draxe, 98, When the foxe sleepeth,
nothing falleth into his mouth. 1670 :
Ray, 10. 1736 : Franklin, *Way to
Wealth*, in *Works*, i. 443 (Bigelow),
The sleeping fox catches no poultry.

12. *Foxes are all tail and women all
tongue.* 1869 : Spurgeon, *John Ploughman*, ch. vi. 1917 : Bridge, *Cheshire
Proverbs*, 58.

13. *Good following the way where the
old fox goes.* 1639 : Clarke, 146.

14. *He does not know a fox from a
fern-bush.* 1587 : Bridges, *Def. of Govt.
in Church of Eng.*, 99, It seemed (as
the saying is) either a foxe or a fearne
brake. 1639 : in *Berkeley MSS.*, iii. 33
(1885), Beware the fox in a fearne
bush. . . . Hypocrisy often clokes a
knave. 1639 : Clarke, 143, He spoke
of a fox, but when all came to all, it
was but a ferne brake. 1659 : Howell,
16 [as in 1639]. 1846–59: *Denham
Tracts*, ii. 107 (F.L.S.), Does not know
a fox from a fern-bush. Cf. **Goose** (20).

15. *He has caught a fox* = is drunk.
c. 1600 : *Fryer Bacon*, in Thoms, *Early
Prose Rom.*, i. 52 (1848), They kindly
thanked Miles for his song, and so sent
him home with a foxe at his tayle.
1690 : *New Dict. Canting Crew*, sig. E7,
He has caught a fox, he is very drunk.

16. *He that hath a fox for his mate
hath need of a net at his girdle.* 1640 :
Herbert, *Jac. Prudentum.*

17. *He that will deceive the fox must
rise betimes.* 1640: Ibid. 1670 : Ray, 10.
1732 : Fuller, No. 2357.

18. *It is an ill sign to see a fox lick
a lamb.* 1678 : Ray, 142. 1748 : *Gent.
Mag.*, 21.

19. *Old foxes want no tutors.* 1732 :
Fuller, No. 3712. 1792 : Wolcot, in
Works, ii. 318 (1795). Cf. Nos. 2 and 3.

20. *The fox had a wound, etc.*, or *The
fox was sick.* 1659 : Howell, 12 [wound].
1678 : Ray, 71, The fox was sick, and
he knew not where : He clap't his hand
on his tail, and swore it was there.
1738 : Swift, *Polite Convers.*, Dial. II.,
Ay ; the fox had a wound, and he could
not tell where, etc.

21. *The fox is taken when he comes to
take.* *c.* 1610 : Rowlands, *More Knaues
Yet?*, 10 (Hunt. Cl.), And the old
ancient prouerbe true did make, Some
fox is taken, when he comes to take.

22. *The fox is the finder.* 1738 :
Swift, *Polite Convers.*, Dial. I., *Col.* . . .
Here's a very bad smell. *Miss.* Per-
haps, Colonel, the fox is the finder.
1846–59 : *Denham Tracts*, ii. 107
(E.D.S.), The foxe the finder.

23. *The fox kills the lambs, and the
hounds the old sheep.* 1619 : Chapman,
Two Wise Men, III. i. [quoted as a
proverb].

24. *The fox knows much, but more he
that catcheth him.* 1631 : Mabbe, *Celestina*, 264 (T.T.), If the foxe be crafty,
more crafty is hee that catches him.
1732 : Fuller, No. 4544. 1846–59:
Denham Tracts, ii. 107 (F.L.S.).

25. *The fox may grow grey but never
good.* 1631 : Mabbe, *Celestina*, 207
(T.T.), Though the fox change his haire,
yet he never changeth his nature. 1671 :
E. Howard, *Six Days Adv.*, III.
p. 41, The fox is gray before he's good.
1732 : Fuller, No. 4545. [1892 : Wilde,
Lady W.'s Fan, I., Men become old,
but they never become good.]

26. *The fox praiseth the meat out of the
crow's mouth.* 1732 : Fuller, No. 4546.

27. *The fox preys furthest from his
hole.* 1639 : Clarke, 127, A crafty fox
never preyeth neare his den. 1642 :
Fuller, *Holy State:* "Constant Virgin,"
This they do . . . to divert suspicion,
that they may prey the furthest from
their holes. 1670 : Ray, 92. 1732 :
Fuller, No. 1610 [in the plural].
1846 – 59: *Denham Tracts*, ii. 107
(F.L.S.), Foxes prey furthest from
their earths.

28. *The fox that having lost his tail.*
See quots. 1658: Flecknoe, *Enigm.*
Characters, 78, Like the fox, who having
lost his own taile, would needs per-
swade all others out of theirs. 1779:
Boswell, *Letters*, ii. 299 (Tinker), A
Scotchman might preach on union to
them [the Irish], as a fox who has lost
his tail. 1824: Scott, *Redgauntlet*,
ch. xxiii., " They that took my land the
last time, may take my life this; and
that is all I care about it." The English gentlemen, who were still in possession of their paternal estates . . .
whispered among them of the fox which
had lost his tail. 1922: Weyman,
Ovington's Bank, ch. xxxi., Foxes who
had lost their tails, they felt themselves
marked men until others followed their
example.

29. *The more the fox is cursed, the
better he fares.* c. 1580: Spelman,
Dialogue, 109 (Roxb. Cl.), The fox
fareth beste when he is moste careste
[cursed]. 1594: Greene, *Friar Bacon*,
etc., sc. xi. 1660: Tatham, *The Rump*,
II., The fox fares best when he is curst.
1712: Motteux, *Quixote*, Pt. II. ch. l.,
Let them laugh that win; the cursed
fox thrives the better. 1853: Trench,
Proverbs, 79 (1905), For *The fox thrives
best when he is most cursed*; the very
loudness of the clamour was itself rather
an evidence how well they were faring.

30. *The tail doth oft catch the fox.*
1576: Lambarde, *Peramb. of Kent*, 362
(1826), For as the proverbe is . . . the
taile is ynough to bewray the foxe.
1633: Draxe, 72.

31. *Though the fox run, the chicken
hath wings.* 1640: Herbert, *Jac. Prudentum*. 1670: Ray, 4. 1732: Fuller,
No. 5008.

32. *To be in a fox's sleep.* 1672:
Walker, *Parœm.*, 25. 1681: W. Robertson, *Phraseol. Generalis*, 639, To be in a
foxes sleep; Somnum mentiri. 1796:
O'Keeffe, *The Doldrum*, II. i., He sleeps
. . . aye like a fox. 1875: *N. & Q.*,
5th ser., iv. 286, A few days ago I heard
a working-man say, " I was in a fox's
sleep."

33. *To set the fox to keep the geese.*
1639: Clarke, 9. 1709: O. Dykes, *Eng.*

Proverbs, 45, He sets the fox to keep
his geese. 1721: Bailey, *Eng. Dict.*,
s.v. " Fox " [as in 1709].

34. *What is the fox but his case?*
1637: A. Warwick, *Spare Minutes*, 84
(1829), Methinks the proverbe sutes
those sutes [gallants in brave attire],
what is the fox but his case? Cf. No. 37.

35. *When the fox preaches, beware
the geese.* c. 1410: *Towneley Plays*, 12
(E.E.T.S.), How ! let furth youre geyse,
the fox will preche. 1546: Heywood,
Proverbs, Pt. II. ch. vii. 1609: Rowlands, *Whole Crew, etc.*, 14 (Hunt. Cl.),
Take in your geese, the fox begins to
preach. 1692: L'Estrange, *Æsop*, 319
(3rd ed.). 1754: Berthelson, *Eng.-
Danish Dict.*, s.v. " Fox."

36. *With foxes we must play the fox.*
1732: Fuller, No. 5797.

37. *You can have no more of the fox
than his skin.* 1546: Heywood, *Proverbs*, Pt. II. ch. ix., He can haue no
more of the foxe but the skyn. 1659:
Howell, 4. Cf. No. 34.

See also **False** (5); **Fire** (11); **Flap;
Grapes; Lion** (7); **Quietness; Ram;
Reynard;** and **Wily.**

Fox-cubs. *See* quot. 1678: Ray,
228, There's ne'er a best among them,
as the fellow said by the fox-cubs.

Foxes brewings. *See* **Cocking.**

France. 1. *France is a meadow that
cuts thrice a year.* 1640: Herbert, *Jac.
Prudentum.*

2. *If that you will France win, Then
with Scotland first begin.* 1548: Hall,
Chron., 55 (1809), The old auncient
prouerbe . . . whiche saieth he that
will Fraunce wynne, muste with Scot-
lande firste beginne. 1599: Shakespeare, *Henry V.*, I. ii.

Fraud and deceit are always in haste.
1732: Fuller, No. 1611.

Fredvile. *See* **Betshanger.**

Free as a bird in air. 1635: in
Somers Tracts, vii. 204 (1811), He may
trade as free as a bird in ayre.

Free as the wind. 1609: Shakespeare, *Coriolanus*, I. ix., Were he
the butcher of my son, he should Be
free as is the wind. c. 1625: B. & F.,
Double Marriage, IV. iii., I am free,
free as air. 1822: Peacock, *Maid*

Marian, ch. xvi., But he roamed where he listed, as free as the wind.

Free of another man's pottage, You are very. 1732 : Fuller, No. 5861.

Free of her lips free of her hips. 1576 : Pettie, *Petite Pall.*, ii. 32 (Gollancz), They are as loose of their lips and as free of their flesh as may be. 1678 : Ray, 62. 1732 : Fuller, No. 6269.

Free of his gifts as a blind man of his eye, As. 1546 : Heywood, *Proverbs*, Pt. I. ch. xi., As free of gyft as a poore man of his eie. 1580 : Baret, *Alvearie*, D 994, As we say, he is as true of his promise, as a poore man of his eie. 1633 : Draxe, 92, As free of his guift, as a Iewe of his eye. 1670 : Ray, 205, As free as a blindman is of his eye.

Freedom. See quot. *c.* 1430 : Lydgate, *Minor Poems*, 183 (Percy S.), I remember a proverbe said of olde, Who lesethe his fredam, in faith ! he loseth all.

Freer than a gift, What is ? 1583 : Fulke, *Defence*, xv. 403 (O.), A gift that is freely giuen . . . wherof the prouerbe is, what is so free as gift ? 1633 : Draxe, 80, What is freer than gift? 1670 : Ray, 93. 1732 : Fuller, No. 5510.

French leave, To take. 1782 : D'Arblay, *Diary*, i. 476 (1876), I felt myself extremely awkward about going away, not choosing, as it was my first visit, to take French leave. 1788 : Colman, jr., *Ways and Means*, III. ii., You'd have taken leave without asking— French leave—if I had not been here. 1824 : Scott, *Redgauntlet*, ch. xv., I took French leave, and . . . so I am free of all that business. 1883 : R. L. S., *Treasure I.*, ch. xxii., As I was certain I should not be allowed to leave the enclosure, my only plan was to take French leave, and slip out when nobody was watching.

Frenchmen. See quot. 1303 : Brunne, *Handl. Synne*, l. 4154, A forbyseyn ys toldë þys, Seyde on Frenshe men and on Englys, "That Frenche men synne yn lecherye, And Englys men yn enuye."

Frenzy, heresy, and jealousy. See quots. Before 1529 : Skelton, *Replycacion*, l. 406, For be ye wele assured

That frensy nor ielousy Nor heresy wyll neuer dye. 1562 : Bullein, *Bulw. of Defence:* "Soreness and Chir.," fo. 75, The old proverb is, that heresy, fransie, and jealousie be so bred by the bone that they will neuer out of the fleshe. 1591 : Harington, *Orl. Furioso*, bk. xxxi., Notes, Our old English proverb : From heresie, phrenesie, and Iealousie, good Lord deliver me. 1666 : Torriano, *Piazza Univ.*, 95, Frensie, jealousy and heresie are never to be cur'd any way.

Fresh as a daisy. 1815 : E. S. Barrett, *Heroine*, iii. 155 (O.), As fresh as a daisy. 1845 : Dickens, *Cricket*, Chirp 2, She presently came bouncing back— the saying is, as fresh as any daisy; *I* say fresher. 1925 : I. and C. I. Gordon, *Two Vagabonds in Languedoc*, 41, Here he comes swinging in from his fifteen kilometres fresh as a daisy.

Fresh as a rose. 1412–20 : Lydgate, *Troy Book*, bk. v. l. 2897, With swetenes freshe as any rose. 1468 : *Coventry Mys.*, 154 (Sh. S.), Fayr and fresche, as rose on thorn. 1590 : Spenser, *F. Q.*, bk. ll. can. ix. st. 36, That was right faire and fresh as morning rose. 1615 : in *Roxb. Ballads*, vi. 166 (B.S.), Cheeks as fresh as rose in June. 1700 : T. Brown, etc., tr. Scarron, ii. 182 (1892), The duke . . . found her as gay and fresh as a rose upon the stalk. 1906 : J. M. Rigg, tr. *Decameron*, i. 122, A brother, twenty-five years of age, fair and fresh as a rose.

Fresh as an eel. *c.* 1410 : *Towneley Plays*, 127 (E.E.T.S.), As fresh as an eyll.

Fresh as flowers in May. *c.* 1440 : Lydgate, *Lyf of our Lady*, sig. G2 (Caxton), Fayrer than floure in maye. 1566 : L. Wager, *Mary Magdalene*, sig. B1, Freshe and flourishyng as the floures in May. 1592 : Warner, *Alb. England*, ch. xxxi. st. 4, As peart as bird, as straite as boulte, as freshe as flowers in May. 1631 : Heywood, *Fair Maid of West*, Pt. II. Act I., You shall meete some of them sometimes as fresh as flowers in May. 1714 : Gay, *Shep. Week*, Prol., l. 55, But Lansdown fresh as flower of May. 1868 : A. Dobson, in *Poet. Works*, 6 (1923), The artless,

ageless things you say Are fresh as
May's own flowers.

Fresh as paint. 1850 : Smedley, *Frank
Fairlegh*, ch. xli., You are looking as
fresh as paint ; getting round again,
wind and limb, eh ? 1859 : Sala, *Twice
Round Clock*, 8 p.m. 1912 : Pinero,
" *Mind the Paint* " *Girl*, III. p. 146,
I feel as fresh as paint.

Fresh fish. *See* Fish (1).

Fret like gummed taffety, To. 1605 :
R. F., *Sch. of Slovenrie*, The Epistle,
The translator vowes to conclude that
either Signior Malevola his sute of
gumme is fretted out at elbowes, or . . .
1732 : Fuller, No. 1846, He frets like
gum'd taffety. 1738 : Swift, *Polite
Convers.*, Dial. II., You have made him
fret like gum taffety.

Friar and Friars. 1. *Friar's mouth.
See* Fit as a pudding.

2. *Friars observant spare their own
and eat other men's.* 1578 : Florio,
First Fruites, fo. 30, Obseruant friers
spare theyr owne, and eate that which
is other mens. 1629 : *Book of Meery
Riddles*, Prov. 112.

3. *Never friar forgot feud.* 1820 :
Scott, *Monastery*, ch. x., I might have
remembered the proverb, " Never Friar
forgot feud."

4. *The friar preached against stealing
and had a goose* (or *pudding*) *in his
sleeve.* 1526 : *Hundred Mery Talys*,
No. lxx. p. 120 (Oesterley, 1866) [the
story of the stolen pudding falling out of
the friar's sleeve]. 1640 : Herbert, *Jac.
Prudentum* [goose]. 1670 : Ray, 95
[pudding]. 1732 : Fuller, No. 4548
[goose]. 1871 : Smiles, *Character*, 36,
The teaching of the friar was not worth
much, who preached the virtue of
honesty with a stolen goose in his sleeve.

5. *What was good the friar never loved.*
1670 : Ray, 94.

6. *When the friar's beaten, then comes
James.* 1639 : Clarke, 282. 1670 :
Ray, 94. 1672 : Walker, *Parœm.*, 10.
See also Devil (118) ; and Fly, *subs.* (1).

Friday. 1. *A Friday look* (or *face*).
1592 : Greene, in *Works*, xii. 120
(Grosart), The foxe made a Friday
face, counterfeiting sorrow.   1667 :
L'Estrange, *Quevedo's Visions*, 152

(1904), Look what a Friday-face that
fellow makes ! 1846 : Denham, *Proverbs*, 6 (Percy S.), Has a Friday look
(sulky, downcast). 1872 : J. Glyde, jr.,
Norfolk Garland, 150, He has a Friday
look.

2. *A Friday night's dream on the
Saturday told, is sure to come true be it
never so old.* 1626 : Overbury, *Characters:* " Milkmaid," Only a Fridaies
dreame is all her superstition : that she
conceales for feare of anger. 1831 :
Hone, *Year-Book*, 252, It is a common
saying, and popular belief, that, Friday
night's dreams, etc. 1879 : Henderson, *Folk-Lore N. Counties*, 101. 1883 :
Burne, *Shropsh. Folk-Lore*, 261. 1884 :
Folk-Lore Journal, ii. 279 [with " Sunday" for " Saturday "—Derby].

3. *A Friday's feast.* 1639 : Davenport, *New Trick, etc.*, III. i., I'de make
you both make but a Fridayes feast.
1640 : in Rollins, *Cavalier and Puritan*,
103 (1923), But now, at last the greedy
Scot, Hath a friday's breakefast got,
few of such feasts will pull their courage
down.

4. *A Friday's flit will not long sit.*
1868 : Atkinson, *Cleveland Gloss.* [with
" never " for " not long "]. 1917 :
Bridge, *Cheshire Proverbs*, 107 [Lancs].
Cf. Saturday.

5. *A Friday's sail always fail.* 1875 :
A. B. Cheales, *Proverb. Folk-Lore*, 19.
1924 : *Folk-Lore*, xxxv. 347, The
[Suffolk] fishermen say : " A Friday's
sail Always fail."

6. *As the Friday, so the Sunday.*
1853 : *N. & Q.*, 1st ser., viii. 512, Fine
on Friday, fine on Sunday, Wet on
Friday, wet on Sunday (Northants).
1875 : A. B. Cheales, *Proverb. Folk-
Lore*, 19, As the Friday, so the Sunday,
As the Sunday so the week. 1886 :
Elworthy, *West Som. Word-Book*, 271
(E.D.S.), As Friday so Sunday. 1893 :
Inwards, *Weather Lore*, 43, If on Friday
it rain, 'Twill on Sunday again ; If
Friday be clear, Have for Sunday no
fear. Ibid., 42, As the Friday so the
Sunday.

7. *Friday is the best or the worst day
of the week. c.* 1386 : Chaucer, *Knight's
Tale*, l. 676, Right as the Friday, soothly

for to telle, Now it shyneth, now it
reyneth faste. 16th cent.: in *Reliq.
Antiquæ*, ii. 10 (1843), Vendredy de la
semaine est Le plus beau jour, ou le
plus laid. 1830: Forby, *Vocab. E.
Anglia*, 415, Friday is either a very
fine or a very wet day. 1851: in
N. & Q., 1st ser., iii. 153, A Shropshire
lady tells me that her mother (who was
born in 1760) used to say Friday was
always the fairest, or the foulest, day
of the week. 1893: Inwards, *Weather
Lore*, 43. Cf. Nos. 8 and 9.

8. *Friday will be either king or under-
ling.* Wilts. This seems to be a
fanciful version of No. 7. 1875: A. B.
Cheales, *Proverb. Folk-Lore*, 19.

9. *Friday's a day as'll have his trick
The fairest or foulest day o' the wik.*
Another version of No. 7. 1883:
Burne, *Shropsh. Folk-Lore*, 261.

10. *Friday's hair and Sunday's horn
Go to the Devil on Monday morn.* It is
considered wrong to cut the hair
on Friday or the nails on Sunday.
1678: Ray, 294. 1851: *N. & Q.*, 1st
ser., iii. 462, The legend that I have
heard in Devonshire . . . ran thus:
Friday cut hair, Sunday cut horn,
Better that man had never been born.
1878: *N. & Q.*, 9th ser., ii. 436.

11. *Friday's morn come when it will
it comes too soon.* [1656: Flecknoe,
Diarium, 38, Now Friday came, your
old wives say, Of all the week's the
unluckiest day.] 1825: Brockett, *Gloss.
N. Country Words*, 77. 1878: Dyer,
Eng. Folk-Lore, 243.

12. *Friday's noon is Sunday's doom.*
Corn. 1887: M. A. Courtney, in
Folk-Lore Journal, v. 191.

13. *Fridays in the week are never
aleek* [alike]. c. 1386: Chaucer, *Knight's
Tale*, l. 681, Selde is the Fryday at the
wyke i-like. 1850: *N. & Q.*, 1st ser.,
i. 303, The following meteorological proverb is frequently repeated in Devonshire, to denote the variability of the
weather on Fridays:—Fridays in the
week Are never aleek. 1874: W.
Pengelly, in *N. & Q.*, 5th ser., ii. 184,
[Corn.] Friday and the week Are
seldom aleek. 1886: Elworthy, *West
Som. Word-Book*, 271 (E.D.S.), On

Friday's weather we have . . . Friday
in the week Is seldom alike.
See also Sing (4); and **Thursday** (1).
Friend and Friends. 1. *A friend as
far as conscience permits.* 1736: Bailey,
Dict., s.v. " Conscience."

2. *A friend in a corner.* c. 1579:
Harvey, *Letter-Book*, 80 (Camden S.),
Particular contentement of mynde that
I have sutch an odd frende in a corner.
1607: Dekker, etc., *Westw. Hoe*, II. ii.,
Had it not been for a friend in a corner
[*Takes aqua-vitæ*], I had kicked up my
heels. c. 1663: Davenant, *Play-House
to be Let*, V., And Cæsar, you shall find
—a friend in corner. 1681: W. Robertson, *Phraseol. Generalis*, 1056, A friend
in a corner for a refuge. 1740: North,
Examen, 611, For it might . . . happen
that a friend in a corner had been of
great service to them.

3. *A friend in court is better than a
penny in purse.* c. 1400: *Rom. Rose*,
ll. 5541-2, For freend in court ay better
is Than peny in purs, certis. 1509:
Barclay, *Ship of Fools*, i. 70 (1874).
1580: Lyly, *Euphues*, 476 (Arber).
1641: Peacham, *Worth of Penny*, in
Arber, *Garner*, vi. 256 (1883). 1738:
Gent. Mag., 475, A friend at court is
worth a penny in the purse. 1848:
Dickens, *Dombey*, ch. xxxviii., I
shouldn't wonder—friends at court
you know . . . Cf. **Penny** (6).

4. *A friend in need is a friend indeed.*
c. 1270: *Prov. of Alfred*, in Kemble,
Salomon and Sat., 247 (Ælfric S.), A
sug fere þe his help in mod (A safe fere
[companion] is he that helps at need).
1484: Caxton, *Æsope*, ii. 251 (Jacobs),
The very and trewe frend is fond in
the xtreme nede. 1581: T. Howell,
Devises, 58 (1906), A friend thou art
in deede, That helps thy friend in time
of nipping neede. 1618: Harington,
Epigrams, bk. ii. No. 101, Behold, how
much it stands a man in steed, To have
a friend answer in time of need. 1772:
Graves, *Spirit. Quixote*, bk. viii. ch.
xxii. [heading].

5. *A friend in the market is better
than money in the chest.* 1732: Fuller,
No. 119.

6. *A friend is never known till a man*

have need. 1303 : Brunne, *Handl.
Synne*, l. 2251, At nedë shul men proue
here frendys. *c.* 1470 : G. Ashby,
Poems, 67 (E.E.T.S.), A freende is
knowen in necessite. 1546 : Heywood,
Proverbs, Pt. I. ch. xi. 1683 : Meriton,
Yorkshire Ale, 83–7 (1697), A friend is
not knawn but in need. 1732 : Fuller,
No. 118, A friend is never known till
needed.

7. *A friend is not so soon gotten as
lost.* 1567 : Painter, *Pal. of Pleasure*, ii.
177 (Jacobs), As the common prouerbe
and wise sayinge reporteth, that the
vertve is no lesse to conserue frendship
gotten, than the wisedome was great
to get and win the same. 1580 : Lyly,
Euphues, 324 (Arber), A friend is long
a getting, and soone lost. 1661 :
Webster and Rowley, *Cure for a
Cuckold*, III. i., They that study man
say of a friend, There's nothing in the
world that's harder found, Nor sooner
lost. 1732 : Fuller, No. 1612.

8. *A friend to all is a friend to
none.* [ᾧ φίλοι οὐδεὶς φίλος. — Diogenes
Laertius, V. i. Attributed to Aristotle.]
1623 : Wodroephe, *Spared Houres*, 475,
All men's friend, no man's friend.
1666 : Torriano, *Piazza Univ.*, 8, Every
bodies friend is nobodies friend. 1732 :
Fuller, No. 120. 1779 : Johnson, in
Boswell's *Life*, 24 April, I believe he
is right, Sir . . . He had friends, but no
friend. Cf. **Many friends.**

9. *A friend's frown. See* quots. 1570 :
A. Barclay, *Mirr. of Good Manners*, 21
(Spens. S.), For much better it is, To
bide a frendes anger then a foes kisse.
1659 : Howell, *Proverbs : Brit.-Eng.*, 3,
A friends frown is better then a fools
smiles.

10. *A good friend never offends.* 1659 :
Howell, *Proverbs : Brit.-Eng.*, 23.

11. *All are not friends that speak us
fair.* 1639 : Clarke, 128. 1670 : Ray,
93. 1732 : Fuller, No. 500.

12. *Be a friend to thyself, and others
will be so too.* Ibid., No. 847.

13. *Choose thy friends like thy books,
few but choice.* 1659 : Howell, 10 (8).

14. *Friends are like fiddle-strings,
they must not be screwed too tight.* 1855 :
Bohn, 358.

15. *Friends fail flyers.* 1548 : Hall,
Chron., 361 (1809), Frendes fayle fliers.
1605 : Camden, *Remains*, 322 (1870).
1639 : Clarke, 25.

16. *Friends may meet but mountains
never.* 1530 : Palsgrave, 635, Hylles do
never mete, but acquayntaunce dothe
often. 1653 : Wither, *Dark Lantern*,
29, Friends possibly may meet (our
proverb sayes) But mountains never.
1754 : Berthelson, *Eng.-Danish Dict.*,
s.v. " Friend," Friends may meet but
mountains never greet.

17. *Friends must part.* *c.* 1620 : in
Roxb. Ballads, i. 253 (B.S.), For friends,
you know, must part. 1727 : Gay,
Fables, 1st ser., No. 50, But dearest
friends, alas ! must part. 1821 : Scott,
Kenilworth, ch. xi., The best friends
must part.

18. *Friends through fortune become
enemies through mishap.* *c.* 1386 :
Chaucer, *Monk's Tale*, l. 254, For
what man that hath freendes thurgh
fortune, Mishap wol make hem enemys,
I gesse : This proverbe is ful sooth and
ful commune.

19. *Have but few friends though much
acquaintance.* 1659 : Howell, 5. 1670 :
Ray, 11. 1732 : Fuller, No. 1807.

20. *He is my friend that grindeth at
my mill.* 1633 : Draxe, 74. 1670 : Ray,
93. 1732 : Fuller, No. 2464.

21. *He is my friend that succoureth
me.* 1477 : Rivers, *Dictes and Sayings*,
57 (1877), He is a good frende that
doth the[e] good. *c.* 1640 : in *Roxb.
Ballads*, iii. 288 (B.S.), But he is my
friend, That helps me i' th' end. 1732 :
Fuller, No. 1926, He is my friend that
succoureth me, not he that pitieth me.

22. *He's a friend that speaks well
on's behind our backs.* 1678 : Ray, 143.
1732 : Fuller, No. 2465.

23. *Here's to our friends and hang up
the rest of our kindred.* 1678 : Ray, 347.

24. *If you have one true friend, you
have more than your share.* 1732 :
Fuller, No. 2760.

25. *It is good to have friends but bad
to need them.* 1669 : *New Help to
Discourse*, 15.

26. *Make not thy friend too cheap to
thee, nor thy self to thy friend.* 1659 :

Howell, 18 [with "too dear to him" after "thy self"]. 1670: Ray, 10.

27. *No man has a worse friend than he brings with him from home*=himself. 1605: Camden, *Remains*, 335 (1870), Where shall a man have a worse friend than he brings from home? 1670: Ray, 94 [as in 1605]. 1738: Swift, *Polite Convers.*, Dial. I., I see there's no worse friend than one brings from home with one. 1831: Hone, *Year-Book*, col. 1417, You may find your worst enemy, or best friend, in yourself. 1853: Trench, *Proverbs*, 139 (1905).

28. *One friend watcheth for another.* 1611: Cotgrave, s.v. "Ami," One friend ever watches, or cares for another. 1666: Torriano, *Piazza Univ.*, 8.

29. *Save a man from his friends, and leave him to struggle with his enemies.* 1869: Hazlitt, 328.

30. *The friend that faints is a foe.* 1611: Davies (of Hereford), *Sc. of Folly*, 46, in *Works*, ii. (Grosart).

31. *When a friend asks there is no to-morrow.* 1640: Herbert, *Jac. Prudentum.* 1710: S. Palmer, *Moral Essays on Proverbs*, 367.

32. *Wherever you see your friend trust yourself.* 1639: Clarke, 26. 1670: Ray, 94.

33. *Who hath too many friends, eats too much salt.* 1659: Howell, 10 (8). Cf. Bushel (3).

See also Afraid of one's friends; Among; Best (21); Falling out; God defend me; God hath few; God send me; Good cheer; Kindred; Live (37); Lose (8); Many humble; Many kinsfolk; Merry when friends; Near friend; New friend; Old, C; Prove; Servant (7); True (10) and (13); Try (3); Two friends; and Write (1).

Friendship. 1. *A broken friendship may be soder'd, but will never be sound.* 1732: Fuller, No. 27.

2. *Friendship is not to be bought at a fair.* Ibid., No. 1619.

3. *Friendship that flames goes out in a flash.* Ibid., No. 1623. Cf. Sudden friendship.

4. *While the pot boils friendship blooms.* 1875: A. B. Cheales, *Proverb. Folk-Lore*, 95.

Fright a bird is not the way to catch her, To. 1633: Draxe, 2. 1670: Ray, 95. 1732: Fuller, No. 1627, Frightning of a bird is not the way to catch it. 1875: A. B. Cheales, *Proverb. Folk-Lore*, 127 [as in 1732].

Frog. 1. *Frog and feathers. See* quots. 1823: Lockhart, *Reg. Dalton*, VI. i. 345 (1842) (O.), Whose coat was as bare of nap as a frog's is of feathers. 1873: *N. & Q.*, 4th ser., xi. 63, I well remember a farmer in my parish, saying when describing to me an impoverished house, twenty - five years ago,—" It was as bare of furniture as a frog is of feathers." [Another version at the same reference:] "I'm as bare of brass as a toad is of feathers."

2. *Frog and harrow. See* **Toad.**

3. *If frogs make a noise in the time of cold rain, warm dry weather will follow.* 1846: Denham, *Proverbs*, 3 (Percy S.).

4. *Like a frog on a chopping-block.* 1678: Ray, 289. 1732: Fuller, No. 723, As pert as a frog upon a washing-block.

5. *The frog cannot out of her bog.* 1670: Ray, 95. 1732: Fuller, No. 6113.

6. *When the frog and mouse would take up the quarrel, the kite decided it.* 1732: Fuller, No. 5586.

See also April (8); Gossips; Thunder (3); and Toad.

Frost. 1. *A white frost never lasts more than three days.* 1893: Inwards, *Weather Lore*, 114.

2. *Bearded frost, forerunner of snow.* Ibid., 114.

3. *Frost and falsehood have both a dirty gangway.* 1846: Denham, *Proverbs*, 5 (Percy S.).

4. *Frost and fraud both end in foul.* 1605: Camden, *Remains*, 322 (1870), Frost and fraud have always foul ends. 1657: Gurnall, *Christ. in Armour*, Pt. II. V. 14, ch. xvii. p. 66 (1679), So true is that proverb, that *frost and fraud have dirty ends.* 1709: R. Kingston, *Apoph. Curiosa*, 80 [as in 1657]. 1853: Trench, *Proverbs*, 21 (1905). 1904: *Co. Folk-Lore : Northumb.*, 172 (F.L.S.). 1917: Bridge, *Cheshire Proverbs*, 60.

5. *Hoar-frost and gipsies never stay*

nine days in a place. 1893: Inwards, *Weather Lore,* 114.

6. *If hoar-frost come on mornings twain, The third day surely will have rain.* Ibid., 114.

7. *The frost hurts not weeds.* 1732: Fuller, No. 4550.

8. *Three white frosts bring rain.* 1881: C. W. Empson, in *Folk-Lore Record,* iv. 131. 1893: Inwards, *Weather Lore,* 114, Three white frosts and then a storm. 1917: Bridge, *Cheshire Proverbs,* 163, Three yarry [hoary] frosts are sure to end in rain.

See also Hail (1); and March (43) and (44).

Frosty nights and hot sunny days Set the corn fields all in a blaze. 1893: Inwards, *Weather Lore,* 43.

Frosty winter, A. *See* quot. 1846: Denham, *Proverbs,* 68 (Percy S.), A frosty winter, and a dusty March, And a rain about Aperill; And another about the Lammas time, When the corn begins to fill; Is worth a plough of gold, And all her pins theretill. 1893: Inwards, *Weather Lore,* 42.

Frugality is an income. 1542: Udall, tr. Erasmus' *Apoph.,* 44 (1877), Accordyng to the prouerbe: good husbandrie, and sparyng in an hous, is a great penie rent of yerely reuenues. 1681: W. Robertson, *Phraseol. Generalis,* 650, Frugality and good husbandry makes things go far; is great incomes. 1725: Bailey, tr. Erasmus' *Colloq.,* 491, Frugality is a handsome income. 1875: A. B. Cheales, *Proverb. Folk-Lore,* 102, Economy is a good income.

Fruit. 1. *Fruit is gold in the morning, etc. See* quots. 1904: *N. & Q.,* 10th ser., i. 251, About fifty years ago a farmer in the county of Durham said in my hearing, " The late Bishop Barrington used to say, ' Fruit is gold in the morning, silver in the afternoon, and lead at night.' " 1922: *Punch,* 20 Sept., p. 279, col. 3, The old adage tells us that " fruit is gold in the morning, silver at noon and lead at night."

2. *Fruit out of season, sorrow out of reason.* 1884: H. Friend, *Flowers and Fl. Lore,* 207, " Fruit . . . reason," say

the old folk of Sussex; and the same notion is found from Land's End to John o' Groats.

3. *He that would have the fruit must climb the tree.* 1732: Fuller, No. 2366.

4. *If you would have fruit, you must bring the leaf to the grave,* i.e. transplant in autumn. 1678: Ray, 53. 1893: Inwards, *Weather Lore,* 8.

5. *No tree bears fruit in autumn that does not blossom in the spring.* 1846: Denham, *Proverbs,* 57 (Percy S.).

Fry in one's own grease. *See* Grease.

Fry me for a fool and you'll lose your fat in frying. 1864: " Cornish Proverbs," in *N. & Q.,* 3rd ser., vi. 495.

Frying-pan into the fire, Out of the. [Plato, *De Rep.,* viii. ἐς αὐτό, φασί, τὸ πῦρ ἐκ τοῦ καπνοῦ βιαζόμενος.—Lucian, *Necyom.,* 4. Pervenimus igitur de calcaria (quod dici solet) in carbonariam.—Tertullian, *De Carne Christi,* vi.] 1528: More, *Works,* p. 179, col. 2 (1557), Lepe they lyke a flounder out of a frying-panne into the fyre. 1591: Harington, *Orl. Furioso,* bk. xiii. st. 28, But I was sav'd, as is the flounder, when He leapeth from the dish into the fire. 1621: Burton, *Melancholy,* I. iv. i. 286 (1836), Though, many times, as Æsops fishes, they leap from the frying pan into the fire itself. 1671: Head and Kirkman, *Eng. Rogue,* ii. 53. 1772: Garrick, *Irish Widow,* II., Out of the pan into the fire ! there's no putting him off. 1842: Barham, *Ing. Legends,* 2nd ser.: " M. of Venice." 1921: *Times Lit. Suppl.,* 8 Sept., p. 582, col. 2, One is left with an uncomfortable suspicion that Virginia's future may not impossibly exemplify the old saying about the frying-pan into the fire.

See also Pot (6).

Fuel to the fire, To add. [οὐ γὰρ χρῆ πῦρ ἐπὶ πῦρ ὀχετεύειν.—Plato, *Legg.,* 666A. Velut materiam igni praebentes.—Livy, xxi. 10.] *c.* 1380: Chaucer, *Troylus,* bk. ii. l. 1332, Through morë wode or col, the morë fyr. 1592: Warner, *Alb. England,* ch. lix. st. 27, All adding fewel to the fire. 1632: Massinger, *Maid of Honour,* II. i., 'Tis far From me, sir, to add fuel to your anger, That . . . burns Too hot already. 1671: A. Behn, *Amorous Prince,* I. iv., Every look adds fuel to my flame. 1712: Motteux, *Quixote*, Pt. I. bk. iv. ch. vii., Anselmo . . . so added new fuel to the fire that was to consume his reputation. 1843: Planché, *Extravag.*, ii. 248 (1879), Each look is fuel added to my fire.

Full as a jade, quoth the bride. 1678: Ray, 285. 1732: Fuller, No. 2584.

Full as a piper's bag. 1678: Ray, 284.

Full as a tick. Ibid., 284. 1854: Baker, *Northants Gloss.*, s.v. "Tick," "As full as a tick": a state of repletion. 1886: Elworthy, *West Som. Word-Book*, 272 (E.D.S.), . . . Said of any animal, whether man or beast, which has eaten its fill. 1889: J. Nicholson, *Folk-Speech E. Yorks*, 19, . . . A tick is a sheep-louse, which has always a full bloated appearance.

Full as a toad of poison. 1678: Ray, 284.

Full as a tun. 1546: Heywood, *Proverbs*, Pt. I. ch. xi., As fulle as a tunne. 1633: Draxe, 79 *bis*, He is fed as full as a tun.

Full as an egg. See Egg (5).

Full bellies make empty skulls. 1732: Fuller, No. 1633.

Full belly neither fights nor flies well, A. 1640: Herbert, *Jac. Prudentum*. 1732: Fuller, No. 1634, Full guts neither run away, nor fight well.

Full bowls make empty brains. 1632: T. Heywood, *Iron Age*, Pt. I. Act I.

Full cup must be carried steadily, A. c. 1300: *Prov. of Hending*, st. 16 (ed. Berlin, 1878), When the coppe is follest, thenne ber hire feyrest. 1732: Fuller, No. 122.

Full nor fasting. See Never well.

Full of courtesy. See Courtesy (3).

Full of himself that he is quite empty, He's so. 1732: Fuller, No. 2472.

Full of items. 1886: Elworthy, *West Som. Word-Book*, 374 (E.D.S.), One of the commonest of sayings . . . is "All full of his items," to describe a restless fidgety person. 1920: *Devonsh. Assoc. Trans.*, lii. 70, "He's vull o' items," meaning he is very fidgety about things.

Full of sin. See quot. 1924: *Devonsh. Assoc. Trans.*, lv. 112, "Her's zo vull o' sin's a cat is of hairs."

Full of unbelief. Said of a cow that will not stay in her pasture. 1917: Bridge, *Cheshire Proverbs*, 60.

Full purse makes the mouth to speak, A. 1602: Carew, *Surv. of Cornwall*, 315 (1811), A full purse begetting a stout stomach. 1670: Ray, 22. 1732: Fuller, No. 123, A full purse makes the mouth run over.

Further East, the shorter West. 1846: Denham, *Proverbs*, 1 (Percy S.). Cf. Longer East.

Further off the better looked upon, The. Glos. 1911: *Folk-Lore*, xxii. 239.

Further than the wall we cannot go. 1528: More, *Works*, p. 187, col. 1 (1557), I am in this matter euen at the harde walle, and se not how to go further. 1546: Heywood, *Proverbs*, Pt. II. ch. v. [with "he" for "we"]. 1659: Howell, 5.

Further you go, the further behind, The. 1477: Rivers, *Dictes and Sayings*, 144 (1877), He that goth owte of his weye, the more he goth, the ferther he is behinde. 1530: Palsgrave, 852, The farder I go, the more I am behynde. 1670: Ray, 11, The further we go the further behind. 1732: Fuller, No. 4552, The further you run, the further you are behind.

Furze is out of bloom [=never], kissing is out of fashion, When the. 1752: *Poor Robin Alman.*, August, Joan says: "Furze in bloom is still," and she'll be kiss'd if she's her will. 1855: *N. & Q.*, 1st ser., xi. 416, When the gorse is out of blossom, kissing is out of fashion. 1899: Dickinson, *Cumb. Gloss.*, 363, When t' whins is oot o' blossom kissin's oot o' fashion.

Furze. See also Under the furze.

G

Gabriel blows his horn, When, this question will be decided. 1659 : Howell, *Proverbs*, To Philologers.

Gadding gossips shall dine on the potlid. 1732 : Fuller, No. 1637.

Gain, *verb.* 1. *He gaineth enough whom fortune loseth.* 1611 : Cotgrave, s.v. " Gaigner," Assez gaigne qui malheur perd ; He gets enough that misses an ill turn. 1629 : *Book of Meery Riddles*, Prov. 60.

2. *He that gains time gains all things.* 1710 : S. Palmer, *Moral Essays on Proverbs*, 380.

3. *To gain teacheth how to spend.* 1640 : Herbert, *Jac. Prudentum.*

Gain, *subs.* 1. *No gains without pains.* 1577 : J. Grange, *Golden Aphroditis*, sig. M1, Who will the fruyte that haruest yeeldes, must take the payne. 1589 : L. Wright, *Display of Dutie*, 4, No gaine without pain. 1670 : Ray, 129, Without pains, no gains. 1736 : Franklin, *Way to Wealth*, in *Works*, i. 443 (Bigelow). 1775 : O'Hara, *Two Misers*, II. 1853 : Trench, *Proverbs*, 106 (1905), They consequently accept the law of labour, *No gains, no pains.*

2. *Who heeds not gain, must expect loss.* 1864 : " Cornish Proverbs," in *N. & Q.*, 3rd ser., vi. 494.

Gainsborough. *See* quot. 1865 : W. White, *East. England*, ii. 41, Poor Gainsburgh, proud people, Built a new church to an old steeple. 1889 : Peacock, *Manley, etc., Gloss.*, 226 (E.D.S.) [without " Poor "].

Galled horse, Touch a, and he'll kick (or **wince**). Before 1384 : Wiclif, *Works*, iii. 231 (Arnold), As a horce unrubbed, that haues a sore back, wynses when he is oght touched or rubbed on his rugge. *c.* 1483 : *Quatuor Sermones*, 27 (Roxb. Cl.), A gallyd horse that is touchyd on the sore wynseth and wryeth. 1566 : L. Wager, *Mary Magdalene*, Prol., A horse will kick if you touche where he is galled. 1602 : Shakespeare, *Hamlet*, III. ii., Let the galled jade wince, our

withers are unwrung. 1621 : Burton, *Melancholy*, Dem. to Reader, 74 (1836), It is not my freeness of speech, but a guilty conscience, a gauled back of his own, that makes him winch. 1697 : Vanbrugh, *Prov. Wife*, V., How the gall'd horse kicks ! 1738 : Swift, *Polite Convers.*, Dial. I., Touch a gall'd horse, and he'll wince. 1784 : *New Foundl. Hosp. for Wit*, ii. 32, Like a gall'd jade he winces.

See also **Scabbed horse.**

Gallows groans for you, The. 1577 : *Misogonus*, I. iv., The gallowes grones for this wage as iust rype ripe. 1585 : *Nomenclator*, 525, One for whom ye gallowes grones. 1611 : Cotgrave, s.v. " Pendard," A rake-hell, crack-rope, gallow-clapper, one for whom the gallows longeth. 1738 : Swift, *Polite Convers.*, Dial. I. 1754 : Berthelson, *Eng.-Danish Dict.*, s.v. " Gallows," The gallows groans for him.

Gallows will have its own at last, The. 1855 : Bohn, 506.

Galtey's cat. *See* quot. 1925 : *Devon and Corn. N1 & Q.*, xiii. 206, His race is jis rin, like Galtey's cat (Mid Cornwall).

Game is not worth the candle, The. 1640 : Herbert, *Jac. Prudentum*, It is a poor sport that is not worth the candle. 1668 : Cowley, *Essays*, No. 10, Yet when the light of life is so near going out, and ought to be so precious, *Le jeu ne vaut pas la Chandele*, The play is not worth the expence of the candle. 1704 : *Gent. Instructed*, 556 (1732), After all, these discoveries are not worth the candle. 1883 : Trollope, *Autobiog.*, ch. x., To do all this thoroughly was in my heart from first to last ; but I do not know that the game has been worth the candle. 1919 : J. A. Bridges, *Vict. Recollections*, 163, If he occasionally doubted whether the game was worth the candle, he was generally one of the happiest of men.

Game's end we shall see, who gains, At the. 1640 : Herbert, *Jac. Prudentum.*

1732 : Fuller, No. 826, At the end of the game you'll see who's the winner.

Gamesters and race-horses never last long. 1640 : Herbert, *Jac. Prudentum.*

Gaming, women and wine, while they laugh, they make men pine. Ibid.

Gander. *See* **Goose.**

Gangs up. *See* quot. 1828 : Carr, *Craven Dialect*, ii. 147, When it gangs up i' sops, It'll fau down i' drops.

Gape, *verb.* 1. *He that gapeth till he be fed, Well may he gape until he be dead.* 1546 : Heywood, *Proverbs*, Pt. I. ch. ix., He that gapeth till he be fed, Maie fortune to fast and famishe for hounger. 1732 : Fuller, No. 6459. 1869 : Spurgeon, *John Ploughman*, ch. vii., He that gapes till he be fed, will gape till he be dead.

2. *No gaping against an oven.* 1577-87, Holinshed, *Chron.*, ii. 389 (1807), The legat blushed, and said . . . " A man ought not to chide with a foole, nor gape ouer an ouen." 1623 : Wodroephe, *Spared Houres*, 485, To gape against an ouen. 1670 : Ray, 96. 1732 : Fuller, No. 3575.

3. *You gape for gudgeons.* 1659 : Howell, 15.

4. *You may gape long enough ere a bird fall in your mouth.* 1639 : Clarke, 153. 1670 : Ray, 96. 1732 : Fuller, No. 5945.

Gape-seed, She is fond of. 1830 : Forby, *Vocab. E. Anglia*, 431. 1872 : J. Glyde, jr., *Norfolk Garland*, 149.

Gaping is catching. 1736 : Bailey, *Dict.*, s.v.

Gardener, As is the, so is the garden. 1732 : Fuller, No. 701.

Garlands are not for every brow. Ibid., No. 1642.

Garlic. 1. *Garlic makes a man wink, drink, and stink.* 1594 : Nashe, *Unfort. Trav.*, in *Works*, v. 71 (Grosart). 1608 : Harington, *Sch. of Salerne*, sig A8. [1754 : Berthelson, *Eng.-Danish Dict.*, s.v. " Wink," Onions make a man stink and wink.]

2. *See* quot. 1609 : J. Melton, *Sixfold Politician*, 35, (according to the prouerbe) : the smel of Garlicke takes away the stink of dunghills.

See also **Eat** (14); and **White** (17).

Garrick, As deep as. 1880 : Courtney, *W. Cornwall Words*, xiii. (E.D.S.). 1889 : Peacock, *Manley, etc., Gloss.*, 162 (E.D.S.). 1907 : *N. & Q.*, 10th ser., viii. 251, Seventy years ago a common expression in Cornwall and Devon, in description of a specially acute or clever man, was that he was " as deep as Garrick." [See an article by A. Smythe Palmer in *Nineteenth Century*, Sept. 1910, pp. 550-2.]

Gaunt as a greyhound. 1678 : Ray, 285, As gant as a greyhound. 1848 : Thackeray, *Van. Fair*, ch. lvii., He was quite well (though as gaunt as a greyhound).

Gauntlet of a hedging-glove, Make not a. 1639 : Clarke, 5. 1670 : Ray, 96. 1732 : Fuller, No. 3318.

Gay as a goldfinch. 1821 : Scott, *Kenilworth*, ch. v., Thou art gay as a goldfinch.

Geese. *See* **Goose.**

Gelt. *See* quot. Gelt is the last peak of the Helvellyn Mountains. 1846-59 : *Denham Tracts*, i. 160 (F.L.S.), When Gelt puts on his night-cap, 'tis sure to rain.

Gentility without ability is worse than plain beggery. 1670 : Ray, 96. 1831 : Hone, *Year-Book*, 1416 [with " plain " omitted].

Gentle as a falcon. [1412-20 : Lydgate, *Troy Book*, bk. ii. l. 6605, Ageyn the faukon—gentil of nature . . .] Before 1529 : Skelton, *Garl. of Laurell*, Gentyll as faucoun. 1579 : *Marr. of Wit and Wisdom*, sc. ii. p. 14 (Sh. S.), You shall find him as gentell as a faulcon.

Gentle Craft, The, i.e. shoemaking. 1594 : R. Wilson, *Coblers Proph.*, l. 1677 (Malone S.), Ile . . . fall to my old trade of the gentle craft the cobler. 1637 : L. Price, in *Pepysian Garland*, 447 (1922), The gentle craft doth beare good will to all kind hearted tradesmen still. 1713 : Ward, *Hist. Grand Rebellion*, iii. 464, When young, of Crispin's gentle craft by trade. 1834-7 : Southey, *Doctor*, ch. liii., St. Crispin is of the Gentle Craft. 1921 : *Times Lit. Suppl.*, 29 Dec., p. 868, col. 3, There must have been some reason, in times gone by, for the term of the " gentle craft," applied only to the shoemaker's occupation.

Gentle heart is tied with an easy thread, A. 1640 : Herbert, *Jac. Prudentum.*

Gentle hound should never play the cur, A. Before 1529 : Skelton, *Garl. of Laurell*, l. 1436.

Gentle housewife mars the household, A. 1611 : Cotgrave, s.v. "Femme," The over gentle houswife marres her houshold. 1640 : Herbert, *Jac. Prudentum.*

Gentle is that gentle does. 1854 : J. W. Warter, *Last of Old Squires*, 43, His common saying was "Gentle is that gentle does."

Gentleman. 1. *A gentleman may make a king and a clerk may prove a pope.* 1591 : Harington, *Orl. Furioso*, bk. v., Annot., According to the old proverb, A gentleman, etc.

2. *A gentleman of the first head*, or, *A dunghill gentleman.* 1552 : Huloet, *Abced.*, sig. N5, Gentlemen of the first head, or *ironice* to be applyed to such as would be estemed a gentleman, hauing no poynt or qualitie of a gentleman, nor gentleman borne. 1583 : Stubbes, *Anat. of Abuses*, 122 (N. Sh. S.), Notwithstanding he be a dunghill gentleman, or a gentleman of the first head, as they vse to term them. 1606 : *Choice Chance, etc.*, 69 (Grosart), A gull, that for a little wealth was made a gentleman of the first head. 1681 : W. Robertson, *Phraseol. Generalis*, 710, A gentleman of the first head; Novus homo.

3. *A gentleman ought to travel abroad, but dwell at home.* 1732 : Fuller, No. 127.

4. *A gentleman should have more in his pocket than on his back.* 1732 : Ibid., No. 128. 1869 : Spurgeon, *John Ploughman*, ch. iii.

5. *A gentleman will do like a gentleman.* 1630 : Brathwait, *Eng. Gent.*, 148 (1641) [quoted as "a common saying amongst us "].

6. *A gentleman without an estate is a pudding without suet.* 1659 : Howell, 12 [with " money " for " an estate "]. 1732 : Fuller, No. 129.

7. *A gentleman's greyhound and a salt-box, seek them at the fire.* 1640 : Herbert, *Jac. Prudentum.*

8. *Gentlemen and rich men are venison in heaven;* that is, " very rare and daintie to haue them come thither." *c.* 1577 : Northbrooke, *Against Dicing, etc.*, 22 (Sh. S.).

9. *He was meant for a gentleman but was spoiled in making.* 1738 : Swift, *Polite Convers.*, Dial. I., I think she was cut out for a gentlewoman, but she was spoiled in the making. 1830 : Forby, *Vocab. E. Anglia*, 434. 1872 : J. Glyde, jr., *Norfolk Garland*, 150.

10. *It is not the gay coat that makes the gentleman.* 1639 : Clarke, 124. 1670 : Ray, 11. 1732 : Fuller, No. 3002 [with " fine " for " gay " and " fine " before " gentleman "].

11. *Knowledge begins a gentleman, but 'tis conversation that completes him.* 1732 : Fuller, No. 3136.

12. *What's a gentleman but his pleasure?* 1573 : G. Harvey, *Letter-Book*, 15 (Camden S.). 1595 : *Maroccus Extat.*, 10 (Percy S.), You shall find in an old tracte printed by Winkin de Woorde, this olde sayde sawe : Whats a gentleman but his pleasure? 1670 : Ray, 96. 1732 : Fuller, No. 5506.

13. *Who would be a gentleman, let him storm a town.* 1670 : Ray, 11.

See also **Adam.**

Gentry by blood is bodily gentry. 1732 : Fuller, No. 1647.

Gentry sent to market will not buy one bushel of corn. Before 1598 : Lord Burghley, in Peck, *Desid. Curiosa*, 47 (1779), For a man can buy nothing in the market with gentility. 1662 : Fuller, *Worthies*, iii. 441 (1840) [quoted as " the plain proverb "]. 1670 : Ray, 96.

Geordy Potter. *See* quot. 1846–59 : *Denham Tracts*, i. 76 (F.L.S.), Lost in a wood, like Geordy Potter o' Sadberge [there is a rather long explanatory story].

George of Green. *See* **Good as.**

Gerards Bailiff. *See* quot. 1678 : Ray, 355, Here is Gerards Bailiff, work or you must die with cold. *Somerset.*

Germain's lips. *See* quots. 1546 : Heywood, *Proverbs*, Pt. II. ch. ii., Iust (quoth she), As Iermans lips. 1579 :

Gosson, *Sch. of Abuse*, 27 (Arber), He
. . . shall see them agree like dogges
and cattes, and meete as iump as Germans lippes. 1596: Harington, *Ajax:*
"Apology," 41 (1814), Just as Jermin's
lips. 1659: Howell, 3, As just as
Jermans lipps; spoken in derision.
1869: *N. & Q.*, 4th ser., iii. 468, [Refer-
ring to the Gosson extract, a correspondent says:] Is not this an allusion
to the proverb respecting "Germain's
lips, which came not together by nine
mile"? [I have not met with this
proverb.]

German's wit is in his fingers, The.
1605: Sylvester, *Du Bartas*, Week II.
Day ii. Pt. 3, l. 616, The Northern-man,
whose wit is in's fingers settles. 1611:
Coryat, *Crudities*, ii. 81 (1905), In so
much that they say, the Germanes have
their wit at their fingers ends. 1659:
Howell, *Proverbs: Ital.-Eng.*, 17, The
Germanes have their wits at their fingers
ends. viz. good artificers.

Germoe. *See* Breage.

Get, *verb.* 1. *Get up early. See* Rise.

2. *Get what you can, and what you get
hold; 'Tis the stone that will turn all
your lead into gold.* 1736: Franklin,
Way to Wealth, in *Works*, i. 451
(Bigelow).

3. *Getting out well is a quarter of the
journey.* 1732: Fuller, No. 1648.

4. *He gets by that as Dickens did by
his distress.* 1639: Clarke, 82.

5. *He who gets doth much, but he who
keeps doth more.* 1855: Bohn, 399.

6. *To get out of the way of the waggon*
=To go one's way. Dorset. 1869:
Hazlitt, 416.

7. *What he gets, he gets out of the fire.*
1678: Ray, 246.

Ghosts never appear on Christmas Eve.
1846: Denham, *Proverbs*, 63 (Percy S.).

Giant loves the dwarf, The. 1869:
Blackmore, *Lorna Doone*, ch. 1., And
verified the proverb that the giant loves
the dwarf.

Giant will starve with what will surfeit
a dwarf, A. 1732: Fuller, No. 209.

Giddy. *See* Dizzy.

Giff-gaff was a good fellow. 1549:
Latimer, *Seven Sermons*, 84 (Arber).
1598: *Servingm. Comfort*, in *Inedited*

Tracts, 130 (Hazlitt), The giffe gaffe
promise he repentes. 1605: Camden,
Remains, 322 (1870), Give gave is a
good fellow. 1670: Ray, 96, Giff gaff
was a good man, but he is soon weary.
1824: Scott, *Redgauntlet*, ch. xiii., I
have pledged my word for your safety,
and you must give me yours to be
private in the matter—giff-gaff, you
know. 1868: Atkinson, *Cleveland
Gloss.*, 217, Giff-gaff, *sb.* The inter-
change of familiar or unstudied conversation on cursory topics. 1913:
E. M. Wright, *Rustic Speech, etc.*, 121,
Giff-gaff . . . mutual obligation, reci-
procity, used especially in the proverbial
saying: giff-gaff makes good friends.

Gift and Gifts. 1. *A gift long waited
for is sold not given.* 1732: Fuller,
No. 130.

2. *Gifts break a rock.* 1640: Mabbe,
Exemplary Novels, ii. 169 (1900), Gifts
will break through stone walls. 1732:
Fuller, No. 1649.

3. *Gifts enter without knocking.* 1633:
Draxe, 19. 1640: Herbert, *Jac. Prudentum*, Gifts enter everywhere without
a wimble.

4. *Gifts from enemies are dangerous.*
1732: Fuller, No. 1650.

5. *Gifts make beggars bold.* 1669:
Politeuphuia, 86. 1732: Fuller, No.
1651.

6. *Gifts on nails. See* Nails (3).

7. *He has a gift. See* quot. 1828:
Carr, *Craven Dialect*, i. 182, "He's a
gift at God nivver gave him," i.e. he
is a notorious liar.

8. *Look not a gift horse in the mouth.*
[Equi donati dentes non inspiciuntur.—
Hier., *Ep. ad Ephes.*, Proem (quoted
"ut vulgare proverbium est").] *c.* 1520,
Stanbridge, *Vulgaria*, sig. C4, A gyuen
hors may not be loked in the tethe.
1539: Taverner, *Proverbs*, fo. 49, A
gyuen horse (we saye) maye not be
loked in the mouth. 1674: Head and
Kirkman, *Eng. Rogue*, iii. 158, I am
resolved to ride this way [facing the
horse's tail], to make good the proverb,
that I may not look a gift horse in the
mouth. 1712: Motteux, *Quixote*, Pt. II.
ch. lxii. 1826: Lamb, *Pop. Fallacies*,
xi. 1871: G. Eliot, *Middlemarch*, ch.

xiv., I thought I was not to look a gift-horse in the mouth, sir.

9. *Throw no gift again at the giver's head.* 1546 : Heywood, *Proverbs*, Pt. I. ch. xi. 1633 : Draxe, 80, A man must not throw a gift at the giuers head.

Gilt off the gingerbread, To take the. 1830 : Forby, *Vocab. E. Anglia*, 432, It will take the gilding off the gingerbread. 1927 : *Observer*, 27 Feb., p. 22, col. 3, It was happy news that our income had increased by £76,000, and that the new year had started with a surplus of £26,000. But Mr. Jenkinson quickly removed the gilt from our gingerbread.

Gilt spurs do not make the knight. 1572 : J. Bossewell, *Workes of Armorie*, fo. 90, Chaucer sayeth that habite maketh no mŏcke, ne wearing of gylte spurres maketh no knyghte.

Gimmingham, Trimmingham, Knapton and Trunch, North Repps and South Repps are all of a bunch. 1670 : Ray, 245. 1790 : Grose, *Prov. Gloss.*, s.v. " Norfolk." 1865 : W. White, *East. England*, i. 188.

Gip. *See* quots. 1659 : Howell, 4, Gip quoth Gilbert when his mare f—. 1678 : Ray, 85, Gip with an ill rubbing, quoth Badger when his mare kickt. This is a ridiculous expression, used to people that are pertish and froward.

Gipsies. *See* Frost (5).

Girdle will not gird me, That. 1732 : Fuller, No. 4343.

Give. 1. *A given bite is soon put out of sight.* 1855 : Robinson, *Whitby Gloss.*, 71.

2. *Give a clown your finger, and he will take your hand.* 1640 : Herbert, *Jac. Prudentum.* 1670 : Ray, 5 [with " whole " before " hand "].

3. *Give a loaf and beg a shive* [slice]. 1678 : Ray, 247. 1879 : G. F. Jackson, *Shropsh. Word-Book*, 376, 'Er wuz too good-natured ; 'er gid the loaf an' 'as to beg the shive.

4. *Give advice. See* **Advice.**

5. *Give and be blessed.* 1548 : Hall, *Chron.*, 16 (1809), Wherof the prouerbe began, geue and be blessed, take awaie and bee accursed.

6. *Give her the bells and let her fly.* 1603 : Dekker, *Pat. Grissil*, I., Ile be

hangd if he do not . . . geue her the belles, let her flye. 1847 : Halliwell, *Dict.*, s.v. " Bells," . . . an old proverb taken from hawking, . . . applied to the dismissal of any one that the owner has no longer occasion for.

7. *Giving is dead and restoring very sick.* 1578 : Florio, *First Fruites*, fo. 30, Geuyng is dead and restoring is yl at ease. 1670 : Ray, 11 [with " now a days " after " dead "]. 1732 : Fuller, No. 1661, . . . deadly sick. 1880 : Spurgeon, *Ploughman's Pictures*, 154, They used to say that " Give " is dead, and " Restore " is buried, but I do not believe it.

8. *Giving much to the poor doth enrich a man's store.* 1640 : Herbert, *Jac. Prudentum.* 1732 : Fuller, No. 6114. 1880 : Spurgeon, *Ploughman's Pictures*, 7.

9. *Giving to God is no loss.* 1875 : A. B. Cheales, *Proverb. Folk-Lore*, 126.

10. *He can give little to his servant that licks his knife.* 1640 : Herbert, *Jac. Prudentum.*

11. *He gives twice that gives quickly.* [Duplex fit bonitas, simul accessit celeritas.—Pub. Syr., 141.] *c.* 1385 : Chaucer, *Leg. Good Women*, Prol., l. 441, For who-so yeveth a yift, or doth a grace, Do hit by tyme, his thank is wel the more. 1539 : Taverner, *Proverbs*, fo. 25, He gyueth twyse yᵗ gyueth quyckely. 1560 : T. Wilson, *Rhetorique*, 119 (1909), He giueth twise that giueth sone and cherefully. 1631 : F. Lenton, *Characters*, sig. H2 (1663), He that gives timely gives twice. 1712 : Motteux, *Quixote*, Pt. I. bk. iv. ch. vii. 1846 : Wright, *Essays on Middle Ages*, i. 146.

12. *He that gives his goods before he be dead. See* quots. 1640 : Herbert, *Jac. Prudentum*, He that gives all before he dies provides to suffer. 1683 : Meriton, *Yorkshire Ale*, 83-7 (1697), He that gives all his geir to his bairns may tack a mell and knock out his harnes [brains]. 1710 : S. Palmer, *Moral Essays on Proverbs*, 27, Give away all before I am dead, And take a beetle and knock me o' th' head. 1735 : Inscription on front wall of Hospital at Leominster, founded 1735, He that gives away all Before he is

dead, Let 'em take this hatchet And
knock him on yᵉ head.

13. *He that gives me small gifts would
have me live.* c. 1320 : in *Reliq. Antiquæ*,
i. 112 (1841), " That me lutel geveth, he
my lyf ys on " ; Quoth Hendyng. 1640 :
Herbert, *Jac. Prudentum.*

14. *He who gives to another bestows
on himself.* 1681 : Rycaut, tr. Gracian's
Critick, 240. 1732 : Fuller, No. 2114,
He that gives to a worthy person,
bestows a benefit upon himself.

15. *I thought I would give him one,
and lend him another,* " i.e. I would be
quit with him." 1670 : Ray, 177.

16. *They that give are ever welcome.*
Quoted as " a sayenge." c. 1534 :
Berners, *Huon*, 235 (E.E.T.S.).

17. *To give a thing and take a thing,
is to wear the devil's gold ring*—with
variants. 1611 : Cotgrave, s.v. " Re-
tirer," To weare the devills gold-ring
(say we in a triviall proverb). 1663 :
Killigrew, *Parson's Wedding*, III. v.,
Fie ! give a thing and take a thing ?
1666 : Torriano, *Piazza Univ.*, 79, As
the English say, to give a thing, and
take it again is the devil's gold ring.
1678 : Ray, 146, Give a thing and take
again, And you shall ride in hell's wain.
1816 : Byron, *Letters and Journals*, iv.
11 (Prothero), It is so like these fellows,
to do by it as they did by their sovereigns—abandon both ; to parody the
old rhymes, " Take a thing and give
a thing "—" Take a king and give a
king." 1894 : *N. & Q.*, 8th ser., vi.
155, Another saying among boys is—
Give a thing and take a thing, To wear
the devil's gold ring. 1901 : F. E.
Taylor, *Lancs Sayings*, 43, Give a
thing—tak' a thing ; God's gowd ring !

18. *To give always, there is never no
end.* [Largitio fundum non habet.—
Cicero, *Off.*, II. xv. 55.] 1623 : Wodroephe, *Spared Houres*, 475.

19. *To give and keep there is need of
wit.* 1620 : Shelton, *Quixote*, Pt. II.
ch. lviii. [as in 1732]. 1670 : Ray, 11.
1712 : Motteux, *Quixote*, Pt. II. ch. lviii.,
I guess he stuck to the proverb, To give
and keep what is fit, requires a share of
wit. 1732 : Fuller, No. 6353, To give
and to have, Doth a brain crave.

20. *To give one as good as one brings.*
1542 : Udall, tr. Erasmus' *Apoph.*, i.
139 (1877), Plato paied Diogenes home
againe well enough, and gaue as good as
he brought. 1676 : Etherege, *Man of
Mode*, I., To him ! give him as good as
he brings. 1709 : O. Dykes, *Eng. Proverbs*, 230, You shall have as good as you
bring, at Billingsgate ; not to say, worse.
1843 : Carlyle, *Past and Present*, bk. ii.
ch. xii., Everywhere we try at least to
give the adversary as good as he brings.

21. *To give one's head for the washing*
(or *for nought*). c. 1500 : Medwall,
Nature, l. 721, A well drawen man ys
he and a well taught That wyll not
gyue hys hed for nought. 1596 : Nashe,
Haue with You, in *Works*, iii. 106
(Grosart), The time was when he would
not haue giuen his head for the washing.
1602 : Chettle, *Hoffman*, III. ii. 1615 :
B. & F., *Cupid's Revenge*, IV. iii., And
so am I, and forty more good fellows,
That will not give their heads for the
washing, I take it. 1738 : Swift, *Polite
Convers.*, Dial. I. 1847 : Halliwell,
Dict., s.v. " Head," *To give . . . washing*,
to submit to be imposed upon.

22. *To give or to forbear requires
judgment.* 1736 : Bailey, *Dict.*, s.v.
" Give."

23. *To give up the girdle*=To submit.
c. 1350 : *Alexander*, l. 181, Bot gefe
thaim up the girdill. 1655 : Howell,
Letters, bk. iv. No. xix., The other
[French] proverb is, *Il a quitté sa
ceinture*, he hath given up his girdle ;
which intimated as much as if he had
become bankrupt, or had all his estate
forfeited.

24. *What thou sparest from giving for
God's sake, the devil will carry another
way.* 1541 : Coverdale, *Christ. State
Matrimony*, sig. I4 [cited as " the
common prouerbe "].

25. *Who gives to all denies all.* 1611 :
Cotgrave, s.v. " Donner," He that gives
me all denies me all : viz. He that offers
me all, meanes to give me nothing.
1640 : Herbert, *Jac. Prudentum.*

26. *You give me roast and beat me with
the spit.* 1560 : T. Wilson, *Rhetorique*,
131 (1909), Such are not to bee liked
that giue a man a shoulder of mutton,

and breake his head with the spitte
when they haue done. 1658 : in *Musarum Deliciæ*, i. 280 (Hotten). 1716 :
E. Ward, *Female Policy*, 53, She will
give thee roast - meat, but beat thee
with the spit. 1855 : Robinson, *Whitby
Gloss.*, 165, Never invite a friend to a
roast and then beat him with the spit.
1913 : E. M. Wright, *Rustic Speech,
etc.*, 172 [as in 1855].

Glad as a fowl. *See* **Fowl.**

**Gladness, A man of, seldom falls into
madness.** 1659 : Howell, 17. 1670 :
Ray, 11. 1732 : Fuller, No. 6235.

Glass houses. *See* quots. 1640 : Herbert, *Jac. Prudentum*, Whose house is
of glass, must not throw stones at
another. 1720 : C. Shadwell, *Sham
Prince*, I. ii., Ay cousen, no body
should throw stones, whose house is
made of glass. 1793 : Grose, *Olio*, 281
(2nd ed.), One who has a head of glass
should never engage in throwing stones.
1842 : Barham, *Ing. Legends*, 2nd ser.:
"St. Medard," If you've any glass
windows never throw stones! 1892 :
Shaw, *Widowers' Houses*, II., People
who live in glass houses have no right
to throw stones. 1909 : De Morgan,
Never can happen Again, i. 159, Why
condemn him? No!—Lizarann lived in
a glass house, and wouldn't throw
stones.

**Glass tells you, What your, will not
be told by counsel.** 1640 : Herbert, *Jac.
Prudentum*. 1670: Ray, 11.

Glasses and lasses are brittle ware.
1666 : Torriano, *Piazza Univ.*, 304,
Glass and a maid ever in danger. 1736 :
Bailey, *Dict.*, s.v. 1875 : A. B. Cheales,
Proverb. Folk-Lore, 4.

Glastonbury. *See* **Old, D** (7) ; and
Shaftesbury.

Glean before the cart has carried, To.
1546 : Heywood, *Proverbs*, Pt. I. ch. xi.,
Thou goest a glenyng er the cart haue
caried. 1633 : Draxe, 175, Hee goeth
a gleaning before that the cart haue
carried.

Glorious Sixth of May, The. 1917 :
Bridge, *Cheshire Proverbs*, 114 [6 May,
1807—see a long story at the reference
given].

Gloucester. *See* **Worcester.**

Gloucestershire, As sure as God's in.
1655 : Fuller, *Church Hist.*, bk. vi.
§ ii. (iv. 15), Hence the topical
wicked proverb . . . " As sure as God
is in Gloucestershire," as if so many
convents had certainly fastened His
gracious presence to that place. 1724 :
Stukeley, *Itin. Cur.*, 64, The old proverb, as sure as God's at Glocester.
1858 : P. J. Bailey, *The Age*, 44.
1898 : Gibbs, *Cotswold Village*, ch. iv.
1920 : Ditchfield, *Byways in Berkshire,
etc.*, 276.

**Gloucestershire kindness, giving away
what you don't want yourself.** 1894 :
Northall, *Folk Phrases*, 14 (E.D.S.).

Glowing coals will be sparkling.
1633 : Draxe, 84, Glowing coales sparkle
often. 1732 : Fuller, No. 1662.

**Glow-worm lights her lamp, When
the, the air is always damp.** 1893 :
Inwards, *Weather Lore*, 145.

Glue did not hold, The, "i.e. You were
baulked in your wishes : you missed
your aim." 1813 : Ray, 196.

Glutton. 1. *A glutton is never generous.*
1855 : Bohn, 287.

2. *A glutton young, a beggar old.*
Cited as " the old saying." 1880 :
Spurgeon, *Ploughman's Pictures*, 11.

3. *Non sigheth so sore as the gloton
that mai no more.* Before 1500 : Hill,
Commonplace-Book, 129 (E.E.T.S.).

4. *Who hastens a glutton chokes him.*
1640 : Herbert, *Jac. Prudentum.*

Gluttony kills more than the sword.
c. 1535 : *Dialogues of Creatures*, ccxxviii.
(1816), Many moo people be glotonye
is slayne, Then in batell or in fight,
with other peyne. 1580 : Lyly, *Euphues*,
275 (Arber), More perish by a surfet
then the sword. *c.* 1625 : B. & F.,
Women Pleased, I. ii., Surfeits destroy
more than the sword. 1669 : *Politeuphuia*, 302, By gluttony more die
then perish by the sword. 1736 :
Bailey, *Dict.*, s.v. " Surfeit," Surfeits
slay more than swords. Cf. **More die.**

Go, *verb.* 1. *Do not say go, but gaw.*
" viz. go thy self along." 1659 : Howell,
4. 1669 : Dudley North, *Obs. and Adv.
Œconom.*, 50, In small families especially in the country, the master may
say *Gow* (as we phrase it in East

England) or go we, implying that he
will accompany them. 1670 : Ray, 11.
1823 : Moor, *Suffolk Words and Phrases,*
A farmer observed, that when his
mother called the maids at " milking
time," she never said " go " but "gow."

2. *Go forward and fall, go backward
and mar all.* 1639 : Clarke, 102. 1670 :
Ray, 177. 1738 : *Gent. Mag.*, 475, Go
back and fall ; go forward and mar all.

3. *Go here away, go there away, quoth
Madge Whitworth, when she rode the
mare i' th' tedder.* 1678 : Ray, 85.

4. *Go in God's name, so you ride no
witches.* 1678 : Ray, 247. 1846–59 :
Denham Tracts, ii. 83 (F.L.S.).

5. *Go it cripples, crutches are cheap.*
1869 : Hazlitt, 143.

6. *Go shake your ears. See* **Shake
your ears.**

7. *Go to bed and sleep for wit, and
buy land when you have more money.*
1886 : R. Holland, *Cheshire Gloss.*, 448
(E.D.S.). 1917 : Bridge, *Cheshire Proverbs*, 62.

8. *Go to the devil and shake yourself.*
c. 1816 : T. Wilson, *Companion to Ball-
room*, 86 [an Irish jig so entitled].
1846–59 : *Denham Tracts*, i. 46 (F.L.S.),
We have also, in the south of England,
" Go to Bath ! " and . . . the whole of
which are pretty much on a par with
the still more impious one of " Go to
the devil and shake yourself." 1862 :
Borrow, *Wild Wales*, ch. xxv., And
when I persisted, [he] bade me to go
to the Divil and shake myself. Cf.
Shake your ears.

9. *He goes not out of his way that goes
to a good inn.* 1611 : Cotgrave, s.v.
" Fourvoyer." 1670 : Ray, 14. 1732 :
Fuller, No. 1851. 1909 : Hackwood,
Inns, Ales, etc., 189.

10. *He goes* (or *runs) far that never
turns.* 1546 : Heywood, *Proverbs*, Pt.
II. ch. ix., He runneth far that never
turneth again. 1577 : *Misogonus*, I. i.,
He goeth farr that never tournes
agayne, as folke say. 1606 : T. Heywood, *If You Know Not Me*, Pt. II., in
Dram. Works, i. 329 (1874), But he goes
far that neuer turns. 1633 : in *Pepysian
Garland*, 420 (1922), He runs farre that
ne'r returneth, is a prouerbe still in vse.

1732 : Fuller, No. 2012, He runneth far
indeed that never returneth.

11. *He goes upright that never halts.*
c. 1592 : *Sir T. More*, 23 (Malone S.).

12. *He is going to grass with his teeth
upwards* = He is going to be buried.
1813 : Ray, 196.

13. *He that goes and comes maketh a
good voyage.* 1578 : Florio, *First Fruites*,
fo. 29 [with " returneth " for " comes "].
1629 : *Book of Meery Riddles*, Prov. 90.

14. *He that goes barefoot. See* **Thorn**
(1).

15. *He that goes softly, goes safely.*
1549 : Latimer, *Seven Sermons*, 28
(Arber), For as they say commonly
Qui vadit plane, vadit sane, that is, He
that walketh playnly, walketh safely.
1681 : W. Robertson, *Phraseol. Generalis*, 672.

16. *He that goes to bed sober. See*
Often drunk.

17. *He that goes to bed thirsty riseth
healthy.* 1640 : Herbert, *Jac. Prudentum*. 1670 : Ray, 36. 1754 : Berthelson, *Eng.-Danish Dict.*, s.v. " Bed."

18. *How does he go through dirt?*
1917 : Bridge, *Cheshire Proverbs*, 75,
. . . How does he bear suffering or
temptation?

19. *To go a high lone.* 1586 : Pettie,
tr. Guazzo's *Civil Convers.*, fo. 12, All
beastes so soone as they are deliuered
from their dam get vpon there feete,
and are able to stand a high alone.
1672 : Walker, *Parœm.*, 37, To go a
high lone ; by himself.

20. *To go about the bush. See* **Beat** (4).

21. *To go as if dead lice dropped off
you.* 1672 : Walker, *Parœm.*, 20. 1678 :
Ray, 75. 1893 : J. Salisbury, *S.E.
Worcs. Gloss.*, 36 (E.D.S.), Look at
'im, 'e creeps along as ef dyud lice
wus a drappin' off 'im.

22. *To go round land—*To die. 1888 :
Q.-Couch, *Troy Town*, ch. xi., He went
round land at las', and was foun' dead
in his bed. 1926 : *Devonsh. Assoc.
Trans.*, lvii. 152, " 'E's a gone round
land," i.e. died.

23. *To go the whole hog.* 1836 :
Marryat, *Japhet*, ch. liv., As you are
not prepared, as the Americans say,
to go the whole hog, we will part good

friends. 1846: *Bentley Ballads*, 20
(1876), Each a democrat dog, That
will go the whole hog.

24. *To go to heaven on a feather-bed.*
1630: Brathwait, *Eng. Gent.*, 152
(1641), Wee cannot goe to heaven on
beds of down. 1681: W. Robertson,
Phraseol. Generalis, 718, None go to
heaven on a feather-bed. 1736: Bailey,
Dict., s.v. " Way."

25. *To go to heaven in a string*=To be
hanged. Before 1635: Corbet, *Poems*,
in Chalmers, v. 582, Thou shortly shalt
to Heaven in a string. . . . We'll all be
glad, Great Tom, to see thee hang'd.
1679: in *Roxb. Ballads*, iv. 141 (B.S.),
But some are gone to heaven in a string.
1710: T. Ward, *Eng. Reform.*, 178
(1716), And go to heaven in a string.
1778: T. Cogan, *John Buncle, Jr.*, ii. 251.

26. *To go to pot. See* Pot (7).

27. *Who goes a borrowing.   See*
Borrow (3).

28. *Who goes to bed supperless, all
night tumbles and tosses.* 1567: Painter,
Pal. of Pleasure, iii. 215 (Jacobs),
Accordynge to the prouerbe : He that
goeth to bed supperlesse, lyeth in his
bed restlesse. 1670: Ray, 37. 1906:
J. M. Rigg, tr. *Decameron*, i. 201, I have
heard you say a thousand times ; " Who
fasting goes to bed, uneasy lies his
head."

29. *You go as if nine men held you.*
1546 : Heywood, *Proverbs*, Pt. I. ch. xi.,
Ye ren to woorke in haste as nine men
helde ye. 1672: Walker, *Parœm.*, 20,
To go . . . as if nine men pull'd you
and ten men held you. 1678 : Ray, 348.

30. *You may go farther and fare
worse.* [Nota mala res optumast.—
Plautus, *Trin.*, 63.] 1546: Heywood,
Proverbs, Pt. II. ch. iv., You . . .
might haue gone further and haue
faren wurs. 1632: Shirley, *Love in
a Maze*, II. ii., I may go farther, and
fare worse. 1738 : Swift, *Polite Convers.*, Dial. II. 1834–7: Southey, *Doctor*, ch. viii. p.i., Because if there be
no Purgatory, the Dean may have gone
farther and fared worse. 1905 : E. G.
Hayden, *Travels Round our Village*, 95, I
reckon them two's a-thinkin' o' gettin'
wed . . . an' he med go furder an'

fare wuss, fur she's a swate purty
cratur.

Goat and Goats. 1. *An old goat is
never the more reverend for his beard.*
1732 : Fuller, No. 646. 1901 : *N. & Q.*,
9th ser., viii. 510.

2. *Contend not about a goat's beard.*
1732 : Fuller, No. 1151.

3. *Goats are not sold at every fair.*
Ibid., No. 1667.

4. *The goat must browse where she is
tied.* 1611 : Cotgrave, s.v. " Chevre."
1640 : Herbert, *Jac. Prudentum.* 1714 :
Ozell, *Molière*, iii. 207. 1852 : Fitz-
Gerald, *Polonius*, 66 (1903).

5. *You have no goats, and yet you sell
kids.* 1732 : Fuller, No. 5922.

God above gets all men's love, Not.
1639: Clarke, 147. 1670: Ray, 97.
1732 : Fuller, No. 6105.

God Almighty by the toe (or foot),
To have. 1548: Hall, *Chron.*, 462
(1809), The duches thinkyng to haue
gotten God by the foote, when she had
the deuell by the tayle. 1591 : Harington, *Orl. Furioso*, bk. xliv., Notes, For
if they may match their daughters so
as they may say, my lord my sonne,
they thinke they haue God almightie
by the toe (as the prouerbe saith).
1639: Clarke, 125, He hath got God
Almighty by the toe.

God bade ho, One of them to whom.
1546 : Heywood, *Proverbs*, Pt. I. ch. xi.,
She is one of them to whom God bad
who ; She will all haue, and will right
nought forgo. *c.* 1594: Bacon, *Promus*,
No. 646, He is one of them to whom
God bidd how. 1659 : Howell, 7.

**God comes at last when we think he
is furthest off.** 1659 : Howell, *Proverbs :
Ital.-Eng.*, 7. 1670: Ray, 11.

God comes to see without a bell.
1640 : Herbert, *Jac. Prudentum.* 1659 :
Howell, *Proverbs : Span.-Eng.*, 2, God
comes to visit us without a bell, viz.
without noise.

**God comes with leaden feet but strikes
with iron hands.** 1579 : Lyly, *Euphues*,
172 (Arber), Though God haue leaden
handes which when they strike pay
home, yet hath he leaden feete whiche
are as slow to ouertake a sinner. 1630 :
T. Adams, *Works*, 777, He will strike

with yron hands, that came to strike
with leaden feet. 1670: Ray, 11.
1853: Trench, *Proverbs*, 140 (1905).
Cf. **God stays long.**

**God complains not, but does what is
fitting.** 1640: Herbert, *Jac. Prudentum.*

**God defend me from my friends, I'll
keep myself from my enemies.** 1477:
Rivers, *Dictes and Sayings*, 127 (1877),
Ther was one that praied god to kepe
him from the daunger of his frendis.
1594: A. Copley, *Wits, Fits, etc.*, 50
(1614), A fained friend God shield me
from his danger, For well I'le saue my
selfe from foe and stranger. 1647:
Howell, *Letters*, bk. ii. No. 75, There is
a saying that carrieth with it a great
deal of caution ; *From him whom I trust,
God defend me; for from him whom I
trust not, I will defend myself.* 1710:
S. Palmer, *Moral Essays on Proverbs*,
311. 1821: Scott, in Lockhart's *Life*,
v. 58. 1890: *N. & Q.*, 7th ser., x. 428,
" God save me from my friends, I can
take care of my enemies myself " . . .
is generally given as the saying of
Maréchal Villars on taking leave of
Louis XIV. [It is obviously older.]

**God defend me from the still water,
and I'll keep myself from the rough.**
1666: Torriano, *Piazza Univ.*, 2. 1732:
Fuller, No. 1668.

**God deliver me from a man of one
book.** 1659: Howell, *Proverbs: Ital.-
Eng.*, 7, From one that reads but one
book . . . the Lord deliver us. 1855:
Bohn, 362.

**God deprives him of bread who likes
not his drink.** 1670: Ray, 11.

**God for money, He that serves, will
serve the devil for better wages.** 1692:
L'Estrange, *Æsop*, 100 (3rd ed.] [cited
as " the old saying "].

**God grant your early rising do you no
harm.** " Spoken jeeringly." 1659:
Howell, 11.

God has a church. *See* **Devil** (50).

God hath done his part. 1556: Heywood, *Spider and Flie*, 4 (1908), God
hath done his part : she hath a good face.
1567: Harman, *Caveat*, 48 (E.E.T.S.),
But as the prouerbe is " God hath done
his part." 1605: Chapman, etc., *Eastw.
Hoe*, IV. ii., (God hath done his part

in thee), but thou haste made too much,
and beene to proud of that face.

**God hath few friends, the devil hath
many.** *c.* 1610: Drayton, *Mooncalf*, in
Works, ii. 483 (1753).

**God hath marked, Beware of him
whom.** 1678: Ray, 347. 1710: S.
Palmer, *Moral Essays on Proverbs*,
113, Take heed of him that God has
mark'd.

**God hath often a great share in a little
house.** 1611: Cotgrave, s.v. " Maison."
1670: Ray, 11. 1880: Spurgeon, *Ploughman's Pictures*, 154.

**God, He who serves, hath a good
master.** 1611: Cotgrave, s.v. "Maistre,"
The servant of God hath a good master.
1666: Torriano, *Piazza Univ.*, 69. 1853:
Trench, *Proverbs*, 138 (1905).

**God heals, and the physician hath
the thanks.** 1640: Herbert, *Jac. Prudentum.* 1660: Howell, *Parly of Beasts*,
77, Though God heals, yet the physitian
carries away the fees. *c.* 1736: Franklin,
in *Works*, i. 456 (Bigelow), God heals,
the doctor takes the fee. 1861: O. W.
Holmes, *Elsie Venner*, ch. xxii., " I
dressed his wound and God healed
him." That was an old surgeon's saying.

God help the fool, quoth Pedley.
1678: Ray, 72. 1732: Fuller, No. 1674.

God help the rich, the poor can beg.
1659: Howell, 16. 1670: Ray, 22.
1732: Fuller, No. 1675.

**God helps them that help them-
selves.** [τὸν 'Αθηνᾷ καὶ χεῖρα κίνει.—Zeno-
bius, v. 93.] 1580: Baret, *Alvearie*,
I. 136, God doth helpe those in their
affaires, which are industrious. 1611:
Cotgrave, s.v. " Ourdi," Begin to helpe
thy selfe, and God will helpe thee.
1736: Franklin, *Way to Wealth*, in
Works, i. 442 (Bigelow). 1875: Smiles,
Thrift, 177.

God helps, Where, nought harms.
c. 1300: *Havelok*, l. 648, Ther God wile
helpen, nouht ne dereth. *c.* 1460: *How
the Good Wife*, l. 14, Seldam is the
house pore there God is stywarde.
c. 1534: Berners, *Huon*, 480 (E.E.T.S),
It is a comune prouerbe sayde, whome
that god wyll ayde no man can hurte.
c. 1555: in Wright, *Songs, etc.*, *Philip
and Mary*, 161 (Roxb. Cl.), Whom Gode

wolde have holpen he shall never
waunte.

**God in thy calling, Serve, it is better
than praying.** 1659 : Howell, 9 (7).

God is a good man. 1526 : *Hund.
Mery Talys*, No. 85, p. 140 (Oesterley),
There came one which sayde y^t god
was a good man. 1599 : Shakespeare,
Much Ado, III. v. 1646 : Quarles, in
Works, i. 79 (Grosart), It is enough
for mee to know, that God is a good
man.

**God is at the end when we think he
is farthest off it.** 1640 : Herbert, *Jac.
Prudentum.*

**God is better pleased with adverbs
than with nouns.** 1570 : in *Complete
Hist. of England*, ii. 502 (1706), That
evil was not to be done that good might
come of it : that God was better pleased
with adverbs than with nouns ; and
more approved what was done *well* and
lawfully than what was otherwise good.
1607 : Bp. Hall, *Holy Observations*,
§ 14, God loveth adverbs ; and cares
not how good, but how well. 1620 :
Ford, *Line of Life*, 64 (Sh. S.), This
man not only liues, but liues well,
remembring alwayes the old adage,
that God is the rewarder of aduerbes,
not of nownes. 1860 : Motley, *United
Netherlands*, i. 2 (1876), Fortunately
that member of Parliament had made
the discovery in time . . . that " The
Lord was better pleased with adverbs
than nouns."

God is in the ambry. 1546 : Hey-
wood, *Proverbs*, Pt. II. ch. iv. 1633 :
Draxe, 159. 1659 : Howell, 6, There is
God in the almery.

God is no botcher. 1562 : Heywood,
Three Hund. Epigr., No. 62. 1659 :
Howell, 5.

God is where he was. 1530 : Palsgrave, 519, Never dispayre, man, God
is there as he was. 1602 : Breton, in
Works, ii. g 12 (Grosart), God is where
he was, he hath called me home, follow
me to him. 1678 : Ray, 147.

**God kills, That which, is better than
that killed by man.** 1869 : Hazlitt, 354.

**God knows well which are the
best pilgrims.** 1611 : Cotgrave, s.v.
"Pelerin," God knowes who's a good

pilgrim. 1678 : Ray, 147. 1732 : Fuller,
No. 1678.

**God loves, Whom, his house is savoury
to him.** 1620 : Shelton, *Quixote*, Pt. II.
ch. xliii. 1732 : Fuller, No. 5724.

God made, What, he never mars.
1659 : Howell, *Proverbs : Brit.-Eng.*, 24.

**God make you an honester man than
your father.** 1678 : Ray, 347.

**God makes and apparel shapes, but it
is money that finishes the man.** 1650 :
Bulwer, *Anthropomet.*, 256, I shall a
little explain this proverb ; *God makes
and the tailor shapes*. 1670 : Ray, 122
[with " makes " for " finishes "]. 1732 :
Fuller, No. 1680. 1926 : *Evening Standard*, 11 Dec., p. 5, col. 2.

God never pays his debts with money.
Said of any bad person who falls ill,
or meets with misfortunes. 1893 : *Co.
Folk-Lore : Suffolk*, 150 (F.L.S.).

**God never sends mouths but he sends
meat.** 1377 : Langland, *Plowman*, B,
xiv. 39, For lente neuere was lyf but
lyflode were shapen. *c.* 1560 : Becon,
Catechism, etc., 602 (P.S.), There is a
proverb no less true than common :
" God never made mouth but he made
meat." 1658 : R. Brome, *New Academy*, IV., There comes not a mouth
into the world, but there's meat for't.
1732 : Fuller, No. 1681. 1829 : Cobbett,
Advice to Young Men, Lett. III., " I do
not care how many " [children I have],
said the man, " God never sends mouths
without sending meat."

God only makes heirs. 1669 : Dudley
North, *Obs. and Adv. Œconom.*, 25, Our
lawyers have this saying, that God
onely makes heirs.

**God or a painter, He is either a, for
he makes faces.** 1592 : Shakespeare,
L. L. L., V. ii. 1732 : Fuller, No. 1914.

**God, our parents and our master can
never be requited.** 1670 : Ray, 12.

**God send me a friend that may tell me
of my faults ; if not, an enemy, and he
will.** 1678 : Ray, 346 [very slight
variation]. 1732 : Fuller, No. 1686
[ending with " faults "] 1748 : Richardson, *Clarissa*, iv. 238 (1785).

**God send us of our own when rich
men go to dinner.** 1639 : Clarke, 37.
1670 : Ray, 129.

God send you joy, for sorrow will come fast enough. 1633 : Draxe, 119.

God send you more wit and me more money. 1659 : Howell, 15. 1670 : Ray, 199. 1732 : Fuller, No. 1689.

God sends cold after clothes. 1546 : Heywood, *Proverbs*, Pt. I. ch. iv. 1611 : Cotgrave, s.v. " Dieu," God sends men cold according to their cloath ; viz. afflictions according to their faith. 1732 : Fuller, No. 1687. 1853 : Trench, *Proverbs*, 66 (1905), Many languages have this proverb : *God gives the cold according to the cloth.*

God sends corn and the devil mars the sack. 1633 : Draxe, 4 [with " asketh " for " sends "]. 1670 : Ray, 97.

God sends fortune to fools. 1546 : Heywood, *Proverbs*, Pt. II. ch. vi. *c.* 1594 : Bacon, *Promus*, No. 493. 1601 : Shakespeare, *As You Like It*, II. vii., Call me not fool till heaven hath sent me fortune. 1659 : Howell, 8. Cf. **Fool** (51) ; and **Fortune favours fools.**

God sends good luck and God sends bad. 1639 : Clarke, 165.

God sends meat and the devil sends cooks. 1542 : Boorde, *Dyetary*, 260 (E.E.T.S.), It is a common prouerbe, " God may sende a man good meate, but the deuyll may sende an euyll coke to dystrue it." *c.* 1600 : Deloney, in *Works*, 221 (1912), God sends meate, and the diuell sends cookes. 1674 : Head and Kirkman, *Eng. Rogue*, iii. 271. 1738 : Swift, *Polite Convers.*, Dial. II. 1822 : Scott, *Nigel*, ch. xxvii. 1904 : J. C. Wall, *Devils*, 127, " God sends meat, but the devil sends cooks," is an old adage which Giraldus Cambrensis, in his caustic criticisms on the greed of the monastic Orders, thus revised—" God sent the abbeys, but the devil sent the kitchens and the cellars."

" **God speed you well,**" quo' clerk of Hope. 1889 : *Folk-Lore Journal*, vii. 292.

God stays long but strikes at last. 1659 : Howell, *Proverbs : Brit.-Eng.*, 19. 1878 : J. Platt, *Morality*, 34. Cf. **God comes with leaden feet.**

God strikes not with both hands. [1600 : Bodenham, *Belvedere*, 1 (Spens.

S.), God with his finger strikes, and not his arme.] 1640 : Herbert, *Jac. Prudentum*, God strikes not with both hands, for to the sea He made havens, and to rivers fords. 1853 : Trench, *Proverbs*, 132 (1905), Nor otherwise with the Spanish : *God never wounds with both hands* ; . . . for He ever reserves one with which to bind up and to heal.

God tempers the wind to the shorn lamb. [1594 : H. Estienne, *Prémices*, 47, Ces termes, Dieu mesure le froid à la brebis tondue, sont les propres termes du proverbe.] 1640 : Herbert, *Jac. Prudentum*, To a close shorn sheep, God gives wind by measure. 1768 : Sterne, *Sent. Journey*, 162 (1794), How she had borne it, and how she had got supported, she could not tell—but God tempers the wind, said Maria, to the shorn lamb. 1835 : Lytton, *Rienzi*, bk. iii. ch. iii., God help her, and temper the rough wind to the lamb ! 1921 : *Punch*, 9 Nov., p. 366, col. 2, It was an advertisement of the Only Infallible Hair Producer. Even so is the wind tempered to shorn lambs.

God than gold, Better. 1659 : Howell, *Proverbs : Brit.-Eng.*, 16.

God that helps a man, He is a. 1725 : Bailey, tr. Erasmus' *Colloq.*, 517, If the proverb be true, *That he is a God that helps a man*, then you are a God to me.

God, The grace of, is worth a fair. *c.* 1400 : *Mirks Festial*, 86 (E.E.T.S.), Ye haue a comyn sayng among you, and sayn that Godys grace ys worth a new fayre. 1546 : Heywood, *Proverbs*, Pt. I. ch. xii. *c.* 1594 : Bacon, *Promus*, No. 37. 1595 : Shakespeare, *M. of Venice*, II. ii., The old proverb is very well parted between my master Shylock and you, sir : you have the grace of God, sir, and he hath enough. 1659 : Howell, 3. 1868 : *Quart. Review*, cxxv. 248, Our old and beautiful adage, " The grace of God is gear enough."

God white [require] you. 1653 : Walton, *Angler*, Pt. I. ch. iv., Marry, God requite you, Sir, and we'll eat it cheerfully. 1917 : Bridge, *Cheshire Proverbs*, 61.

God will send thee flax, Get thy spindle

and thy distaff ready, and. 1670 : Ray,
11.

God will, What, no frost can kill.
1670 : Ray, 97. 1732 : Fuller, No. 6106.

God will, When, all winds bring rain.
1633 : Draxe, 81, When God will, at all
windes it will raine. 1681 : W. Robertson, *Phraseol. Generalis*, 674. 1732 :
Fuller, No. 5554. 1875 : A. B. Cheales,
Proverb. Folk-Lore, 25.

God's blessing, Out of. *See* Out of.

God's grace. *See* Pilling Moss; and
God, The grace of.

God's help is better than early rising.
1620 : Shelton, *Quixote*, Pt. II. ch.
xxxiv. 1732 : Fuller, No. 1685.

**God's help, Who hopeth in, his help
cannot start.** 1546 : Heywood, *Proverbs*,
Pt. I. ch. iv.

God's mill grinds slow but sure.
[ὀψὲ θεῶν ἀλέουσι μύλοι, ἀλέουσι δὲ λεπτά.—
Proverbia e Cod. Coisl., No. 396,
in Gaisford, *Parœm. Grœc.*, 164
(1836).] 1640 : Herbert, *Jac. Prudentum.* 1853 : Trench, *Proverbs*, 140
(1905), The ancient Greek one : *The
mill of God grinds late, but grinds to
powder.*

**God's name, That never ends ill which
begins in.** 1639 : Clarke, 109. Cf. the
reverse, s.v. In the name of the Lord.

God. *See also* Charitable (2) ; Danger
(7) ; Devil (50), (59), and (104) ; Gift (7) ;
Give (9) and (24) ; Gloucestershire ; Good
spender ; In time ; Man (54), (56), (59),
and (77) ; Means ; One God ; Out of God's
blessing ; Owe (3) ; Pains ; Please (7) ;
Poor (35) ; Sow, *verb* (9) ; Speed the
plough ; Spend (6) ; Sure as God ; and
True (4).

Godalming. 1. *Godalmin cats*; and
2. *Godalmin rabbits.* 1790 : Grose, *Prov.
Gloss.*, s.v. " Surrey" [Old taunts—the
latter based on the story of Mrs. Tofts].

3. *See* quot. 1904 : Jekyll, *Old West
Surrey*, 243, The local saying has it
that " If the sun shines before noon on
Godalming fair-day [13 Feb.], the winter
isn't half over."

Godamercy, horse! An almost meaningless proverbial exclamation. 1546 :
Heywood, *Proverbs*, Pt. II. ch. vii., God
haue mercy, hors. 1579 : *Marr. of Wit
and Wisdom*, sc. iii., p. 27 (Sh. S.).

1611 : *Tarltons Jests*, 24 (Sh. S.), But
ever after it was a by word thorow
London, God a mercy horse, and is to
this day. 1647 : in *Polit. Ballads*, 51
(Percy S.), Oh, God-a-mercy, parliament. 1664 : in *Musarum Deliciæ*, ii.
232 (Hotten), A taylor is a theef, a
sergeant is worse, Who here lyes dead,
god-a-mercy horse. 1681 : in *Harl.
Miscell.*, ii. 100 (1744), God-a-mercy
horse, this rogue Will was tugging up
stream . . . 1710 : *Brit. Apollo*, iii.
No. 118, p. 3, col. 1, I find I'm whole,
God a mercy horse. Cf. Gramercy.

**God-fathers oft give their blessings in
a clout.** 1611 : Davies (of Hereford),
Sc. of Folly, 47, in *Works*, ii. (Grosart).

Gods love die young, Whom the.
[Quem Di diligunt Adolescens moritur.
—Plautus, *Bacchides*, IV. vi.] 1560 :
T. Wilson, *Rhetorique*, 73 (1909), Whom
God loueth best, those he taketh
sonest. 1651 : Herbert, *Jac. Prudentum*,
2nd ed., Those that God loves, do not
live long. 1819 : Byron, *Don Juan*,
can. iv. st. 12. 1894 : R. L. S., *Letters*,
v. 125 (Tusitala ed.), I was meant to
die young, and the gods do not love me.
1923 : Lucas, *Advisory Ben*, § x. p. 48,
It has never been satisfactorily determined whether the saying about the
darlings of the gods dying young means
young in years or young in heart.

Gold. 1. *Gold dust blinds all eyes.*
1875 : A. B. Cheales, *Proverb. Folk-
Lore*, 98.

2. *Gold goes in at any gate except
heaven's.* 1630 : T. Adams, *Works*, 24,
The prouerbe saith, There is no earthly
gate, but an asse laden with gold can
enter. 1670 : Ray, 97. 1736 : Bailey,
Dict., s.v. 1875 : A. B. Cheales, *Proverb. Folk-Lore*, 98.

3. *Gold is an orator.* 1594 : Barnfield,
Affect. Shep., 48 (Percy S.), Gold is a
deepe-perswading orator. Cf. **Money**
(38) ; and also No. 12 *infra.*

4. *Gold is but muck.* *c.* 1598 : Jonson, *Case is Altered*, IV. iv. [cited as
" the old proverb "].

5. *Gold makes a woman penny-white.*
1754 : Berthelson, *Eng.-Danish Dict.*,
s.v. " Penny." 1894 : Northall, *Folk
Phrases*, 14 (E.D.S.).

6. *Gold maketh an honest man an ill man.* 1579 : Lyly, *Euphues*, 63 (Arber) [cited. as " a by word amongst vs "].

7. *He that has gold may buy land.* 1683 : Meriton, *Yorkshire Ale*, 83–7 (1697).

8. *If gold knew what gold is, gold would get gold, I wis.* 1640 : Herbert, *Jac. Prudentum.*

9. *Pour gold on him, he'll never thrive.* 1639 : Clarke, 220.

10. *That is gold that is worth gold.* 1611 : Cotgrave, s.v. " Or." 1667 : Gurnall, *Christian in Armour*, Pt. II. v. 15, ch. ix. p. 144 (1679), We say, *that is gold which is worth gold*, which we may anywhere exchange for gold. 1853 : Trench, *Proverbs*, 87 (1905), Which the brief Italian proverb long ago announced : *Gold's worth is gold.*

11. *What words won't do, gold will.* 1700 : Ward, *London Spy*, 400 (1924) [called an " old saying "].

12. *When gold speaks you may e'en hold your tongue.* 1666 : Torriano, *Piazza Univ.*, 179, Where gold speaks, every tongue is silent. 1670 : Ray, 12, You may speak with your gold and make other tongues dumb. 1732 : Fuller, No. 5555. Cf. No 3, *supra*; and Money (38).

13. *When we have gold we are in fear, when we have none we are in danger.* 1670 : Ray, 12.

See also **All is not gold**; **Money**; and **Touchstone**.

Golden. 1. *A golden dart kills where it pleases.* 1732 : Fuller, No. 132.

2. *A golden shield is of great defence.* Ibid., No. 133.

3. *Golden dreams make men awake hungry.* 1678 : Ray, 129. 1732 : Fuller, No. 1695.

4. *Golden hook.* See **Angle** (2).

5. *The golden age never was the present age.* 1732 : Fuller, No. 4556.

6. *The golden ball never goes up but once.* Oxfordsh. 1913 : *Folk-Lore*, xxiv. 77. [No explanation is given.]

7. *The golden mean.* Before 1225 : *Ancren R.*, 336, Þe middel weie of mesure is euer guldene. 1596 : Gosson, *Pleasant Quips*, 14 (Percy S.), The golden meane is free from trips. 1611 : Coryat,

Crudities, ii. 150 (1905), To keepe the golden meane in the levell of their thoughts. 1687 : Norris of Bemerton, *Poems*, 94 (Grosart). 1754 : *World*, No. 95, The golden mean, or middle track of life. 1826 : Scott, in Lockhart's *Life*, vi. 341, They . . . are too desirous to make a show, to preserve the golden mean.

8. *We must not look for a golden life in an iron age.* 1633 : Draxe, 242, A man must not . . . yron world. 1639 : Clarke, 124, Expect not a golden life in an iron world. 1670 : Ray, 14. 1732 : Fuller, No. 5450.

Good a maid as her mother, A. 1659 : Howell, 11.

Good a will as ever I came from school, With as. 1594 : Shakespeare, *Tam. of Shrew*, III. ii., As willingly as e'er I came from school. 1659 : Howell, *Letters*, ii. 666 (Jacobs). 1732 : Fuller, No. 5794.

Good action always finds its recompence, A. 1750 : Smollett, *Gil Blas*, iv. 101 [quoted " as the proverb says "].

Good against evil, Set. 1640 : Herbert, *Jac. Prudentum.*

Good ale is meat, drink, and cloth. 1602 : Carew, *Surv. of Cornwall*, 189 (1811), The liquor [ale] itself is the Englishman's ancientest and wholesomest drink, and serveth many for meat and cloth too. *c.* 1620 : in *Roxb. Ballads*, ii. 588 (B.S.), Were't not for this barley broth (Which is meat, drinke, and cloth). 1697 : in Marchant, *Praise of Ale*, 403, On the rare virtues of this barley broth ! To rich and poor it's meat and drink and cloth. 1738 : Swift, *Polite Convers.*, Dial. II. 1815 : Scott, *Mannering*, ch. xxxix., Sheer ale supports him under everything. It is meat, drink, and cloth, bed, board, and washing.

Good and all, For. 1519 : Horman, *Vulgaria*, fo. 208, We begen a newe counte for good and all. 1663 : Pepys, *Diary*, 23 June, I do resolve even to let him go away for good and all. 1710 : Swift, *Journal to Stella*, 13 Sept., She is broke for good and all, and is gone to the country. 1850 : Dickens, *Chuzzlewit*, ch. ii., Mr. Westlock, sir, going away for good and all, wishes to leave none but friends behind him. 1892: Pinero, *Lady Bountiful*, I. p. 45, I've sold my business . . . and I've cleared out of Baverstoke for good and all.

Good and evil are chiefly in the imagination. 1732: Fuller, No. 1699.

Good and quickly seldom meet. 1640: Herbert, *Jac. Prudentum*. 1670: Ray, 12. 1736: Bailey, *Dict.*, s.v. "Soon."

Good as a Christmas play, As. 1880: Courtney, *W. Cornwall Words*, 24 (E.D.S.), . . . is said of anything very funny.

Good as a play, As. 1638: Taylor (Water-Poet), *Bull, Beare, etc.*, 43, in *Works*, 3rd coll. (Spens. S.), It was as good as a comedy to him to see the trees fall. 1672: Marvell, *Rehearsal Transpr.*, Pt. I. in *Works*, iii. 41 (Grosart), It was grown almost as good as a play. 1845: Dickens, *Cricket*, Chirp 2, John had such a lively interest in all the parcels, that it was as good as a play. 1915: A. Machen, *Far-off Things*, 130 (1922), The naughty prints and books of Holywell Street were as good as a play.

Good as ever drew sword, As. 1599: Porter, *Two Angry Women*, sc. xi., You are as good a man as ever drew sword.

Good as ever flew in the air, As. 1678: Ray, 285.

Good as ever struck, As. c. 1660: in *Roxb. Ballads*, ii. 131 (B.S.), Yet is he as good as ever strooke.

Good as ever the ground went upon, As—with variants. 1599: Porter, *Two Angry Women*, sc. xi., You are as good a man . . . as ere trode on Gods earth. 1678: Ray, 285, As good as ever the ground went upon. c. 1890: Gilbert, *Foggerty's Fairy*, II., I know you're as good a girl as ever stepped.

Good as ever twanged, As. 1577: *Misogonus*, II. ii., I must nedes loue the, i faithe, thart as good as ere twangde. 1667: L'Estrange, *Quevedo's Visions*, 205 (1904), As good a wench as ever twanged. 1678: Ray, 285.

Good as ever water wet, As. 1670: Ray, 205. 1736: Bailey, *Dict.*, s.v. "Wet." *See also* As ever.

Good as ever went endways, As. 1678: Ray, 285.

Good as George of Green, As. 1670: Ray, 205. 1721: Bailey, *Eng. Dict.*, s.v. "Greenwich."

Good as gold, As. 1843: Dickens, *Carol*, Stave 3, "And how did little Tim behave?" asked Mrs. Cratchit . . . "As good as gold," said Bob. 1876: Blackmore, *Cripps*, ch. xxxvii., My mother is as good as gold, and much better. 1926: Phillpotts, *Yellow Sands*, II., Him and Emma are both so good as gold.

Good as good for nothing, So. 1639: Clarke, 78.

Good as goose skins that never man had enough of, As. Cheshire. 1670: Ray, 208. 1917: Bridge, *Cheshire Proverbs*, 13, . . . impossible to explain. The meaning has died out.

Good as one shall see in a summer's day, As. 1599: Porter, *Two Angry Women*, sc. xi. [with "upon" for "in"]. 1595: Shakespeare, *Mids. N. Dream*, I. ii., A proper man, as one shall see in a summer's day. 1742: Fielding, *Andrews*, bk. iv. ch. xv., As fine a fat thriving child as you shall see in a summer's day.

Good at a distance is better than evil at hand. 1732: Fuller, No. 1700.

Good bargain is a pick-purse, A. 1611: Cotgrave, s.v. "Argent," Good cheap commodities are notable pick-purses. 1640: Herbert, *Jac. Prudentum*. 1732: Fuller, No. 1701, Good bargains are pick-pockets.

Good bargain, On a, think twice. 1640: Herbert, *Jac. Prudentum*. 1710: S. Palmer, *Moral Essays on Proverbs*, 29. Cf. Great bargain.

Good be good, Though, yet better is better (or better carries it). 1639: Clarke, 105. 1655: Fuller, *Church Hist.*, bk. xi. § iii., Ded., Good is not good, where better is expected. 1670: Ray, 97. 1736: Bailey, *Dict.*, s.v. "Good," Good is good, but better is better.

Good be still is worth a groat, A. c. 1430: Lydgate, *Minor Poems*, 152 (Percy S.), [from a poem in praise of Silence] A good be still is well worth a groote. 1546: Heywood, *Proverbs*, Pt. II. ch. v., A good bestyll is woorth a grote. 1633: Draxe, 190 [in the section on "Silence"].

Good bearing. *See* quot. *c.* 1460:
How the Good Wife, l. 20, In thi gode
berynge begynnythe thy worschipe.

Good beef that costs nothing, It is.
1732: Fuller, No. 2935.

Good beginning makes a good ending,
A. [Non possum togam praetextam
sperare, cum exordium pullum videam.
—Quint., V. x. 71.] *c.* 1320: in *Reliq.
Antiquæ*, i. 109 (1841), "God biginning
maketh god endyng," quoth Hendyng.
1477: Rivers, *Dictes and Sayings*, in
Brit. Bibliog., iv. 239 (1814), And sayd
the lokyng vpon the begynnyng of the
werke yf it be goode yeueth hope to
the endyng. 1546: Heywood, *Proverbs*, Pt. I. ch. x., Of a good begynnyng
comth a good end. 1637: Breton, in
Works, ii. *h* 22 (Grosart), A good beginning, with a better proceeding, promiseth a blessed ending. 1710: S.
Palmer, *Moral Essays on Proverbs*, 1.
1825: Hone, *Ev. Day Book*, i., 1 Jan.
1854: J. W. Warter, *Last of Old Squires*,
48 [a variant], There was regularly the
full service and a good plain sermon,
and parson and squire both held to the
old saw—Good onset bodes good end!
Cf. Well (8).

Good blood, You come of, and so does
a black pudding. 1855: Bohn, 576.

Good blood. *See* Blood (2).

Good bourd [jest] to drink of a gourd,
It is a. *c.* 1410: *Towneley Plays*, 115
(E.E.T.S.), It is an old by-worde, It is
a good bowrde for to drynk of a gowrde.

Good broth may be made in an old pot.
1666: Torriano, *Piazza Univ.*, 111 [with
"sops" for "broth"]. 1880: Spurgeon, *Ploughman's Pictures*, 84, Many a
drop of good broth is made in an old
pot.

Good building without a good foundation, No. 1732: Fuller, No. 3578.

Good cake. *See* Bad custom.

Good candle-holder proves a good
gamester, A. 1659: Howell, 13. 1670:
Ray, 4.

Good cards to show for it, He hath.
1678: Ray, 354. 1732: Fuller, No.
1887.

Good cause makes a stout heart and
a strong arm, A. 1732: Fuller, No. 140.

Good cheap is dear. 1640: Herbert,

Jac. Prudentum. 1659: Howell, 8, [as
in 1640, *plus*] for it tempts one to buy
what he needs not. 1732: Fuller,
No. 1704, [as in 1640, *plus*] at long run.

Good cheer. *See* quots. *c.* 1477: Caxton, *Book of Curteseye*, 27 (E.E.T.S.), The
poete saith hou that a poure borde Men
may enriche with cheerful wil and
worde. Before 1500: in Hill, *Commonplace-Book*, 131 (E.E.T.S.), In a
thyn table, good chere is best sawse.
1639: Clarke, 12, When good cheare is
lacking, our friends will be packing.
1670: Ray, 69 [as in 1639]. 1732:
Fuller, No. 6299 [as in 1639]. 1869:
Spurgeon, *John Ploughman*, ch. xviii.
[as in 1639, but with "such" for
"our"].

Good child soon learns, A. *c.* 1280:
Prov. of Hendyng, Sely chyld is sone
ylered. *c.* 1386: Chaucer, *Prioress's
Tale*, l. 60, For sely child wol alday
some lere.

Good cloak, I have a, but 'tis in
France. 1732: Fuller, No. 2602.

Good clothes open all doors. *Ibid.*,
No. 1705.

Good company. *See* quots. 1639:
Clarke, 291, Good company is a good
coach. 1768: Goldsmith, *Vicar*, ch.
xviii., "Good company upon the road,"
says the proverb, "is the shortest cut."
1853: Trench, *Proverbs*, 28 (1905), Our
own proverb, *Good company on a journey is worth a coach*, has come down to
us from the ancient world (Comes
facundus in viâ pro vehiculo est).

Good conscience. *See* Conscience.

Good contriver is better than a big
eater, A. 1906: *Cornish N. & Q.*, 267
[with "little" for "big"]. 1909:
Folk-Lore, xx. 73 (Durham).

Good cook. *See* Ill cook.

Good corn, He that hath, may be
content with some thistles. 1732:
Fuller, No. 2159.

Good cow. *See* Cow (20).

Good day will not mend him, nor a
bad day impair him, A. 1678: Ray, 71.
1732: Fuller, No. 143.

Good deed is never lost, A. 1633:
Draxe, 40. 1732: Fuller, No. 1710,
Good deeds remain; all things else
perish.

Good dinner, He that would eat a, let
him eat a good breakfast. 1678 : Ray, 124.

Good divine that follows his own
instructions, It is a. 1595 : Shakespeare,
M. of Venice, I. ii.

Good eating. *See* quot. 1840 : Barham, *Ing. Legends:* "Bagman's Dog,"
I've seen an old saw, which is well
worth repeating, That says, "Good
Eatynge Deserveth good Drynkynge."

Good edge is good for nothing, if it
has nothing to cut, A. 1732 : Fuller,
No. 145.

Good elm, good barley ; good oak, good
wheat. 1865 : W. White, *East. England*,
i. 38.

Good enough for the parson unless the
paint were better, It's. 1678 : Ray, 187.

Good enough is never ought. 1678 :
Ray, 148.

Good estate. *See* quot. 1678 : Ray,
78, He has a good estate, but that the
right owner keeps it from him.

Good example is the best sermon, A.
1732 : Fuller, No. 146.

Good face is a letter of recommendation, A. 1751 : Fielding, *Amelia*, bk. ix.
ch. v.

Good face needs no band, A. 1639 :
Clarke, 131. 1670 : Ray, 59. 1709 :
O. Dykes, *Eng. Proverbs*, 175, In opposition to the fantastical humour of
emulating butter-flies in the glory of
external dress, we commonly say, A
good face needs no band. 1738 : Swift,
Polite Convers., Dial. I.

Good face needs no paint, A. 1581 :
Lyly, *Euphues*, 204 (Arber), Where the
countenaunce is faire, there neede no
colours. 1612 : T. Heywood, in *Somers
Tracts*, iii. 575 (1811), A good face
needes no painting, and a good cause
no abetting. 1732 : Fuller, No. 148.

Good face on a thing, To set a. 1387 :
Trevisa, tr. Higden, vii. 25 (Rolls Ser.),
And made good face to þe eorle and
semblant. 1412–20 : Lydgate, *Troy
Book*, bk. ii. l. 4366, And wher thou
hast most mater to compleyne, Make
ther good face and glad in port the[e]
feine. *c.* 1540 : Bale, *Kynge Johan*,
l. 1991, Though it be a foule lye, set
upon it a good face. 1580 : H. Gifford,
Posie, 44 (Grosart), But — as the

fashione of the worlde is now a dayes
—set a good face on a bad matter.
1621 : Brathwait, *Natures Embassie*,
107 (1877), Making a good face of an
euill matter. 1740 : North, *Examen*,
49, His Lordship was not surprised,
but . . . set a good face upon the
matter. 1866 : G. Eliot, *Felix Holt*,
ch. i., Well, madam, put a good face
on it.

Good fame is better than a good face,
A. 1732 : Fuller, No. 150.

Good finds good. 1640 : Herbert, *Jac.
Prudentum*.

Good fire and clean grate, Just as
good as half your meat. Newlyn, W.
Corn., 19th cent. (Mr. C. Lee).

Good fish if it were caught, It is.
1659 : Howell, 12, Good fish, but all
the craft is in the catching. 1690 :
New Dict. Canting Crew, sig. E4, Good
fish when it is caught. 1732 : Fuller,
No. 2936. 1883 : Burne, *Shropsh. Folk-
Lore*, 589.

Good for something. *See* All women.

Good for the back (or head). *See*
quots. 1604 : James I., *Counterblaste*,
107 (Arber), According to the olde
prouerbe, That which is good for the
head, is euill for the necke and the
shoulders. 1670 : Ray, 58, That which
is good for the back is bad for the head.

Good Friday. 1. *He may eat his part.*
See quots. 1546 : Heywood, *Proverbs*,
Pt. I. ch. xi., He maie his parte on
good fridaie eate, And faste neuer the
wurs, for ought he shall geat [get].
1596 : Shakespeare, *King John*, I. i.,
Sir Robert might have eat his part in
me Upon Good Friday and ne'er broke
his fast.

2. *Rain on Good Friday. See* quots.
1882 : Mrs. Chamberlain, *W. Worcs.
Words*, 37 (E.D.S.), If it rain on Good
Friday or Easter Day, 'Twill be a good
year of grass, but a sorrowful year of
hay. 1890 : J. D. Robertson, *Gloucester Gloss.*, 187 (E.D.S.), Rain on
Good Friday and Easter Day Brings
plenty of grass but little good hay.
1893 : Inwards, *Weather Lore*, 40 [to
same effect as 1890 quot.]. [Also:]
Rain on Good Friday foreshows a
fruitful year.

Good friend is my nearest relation, A. 1611 : Cotgrave, s.v. " Parenté," A sound friend is a second kinsman. 1732 : Fuller, No. 151.

Good garden may have some weeds, A. Ibid., No. 152.

Good goose don't bite. 1592 : Shakespeare, *Romeo*, II. iv., Nay, good goose bite not. 1599 : Porter, *Two Angry Women*, in Hazlitt, *Old Plays*, vii. 359, Good goose, bite not. 1678 : Ray, 72. 1732 : Fuller, No. 1712.

Good hand good hire. 1639 : Clarke, 45. 1788 : *Town's Book of Pownall Fee*, quoted in Bridge, *Cheshire Proverbs*, 62, He . . . worked sometimes on weekly wages and sometimes good hand good hire, but was never hired for twelve months. 1917 : Bridge, *Cheshire Proverbs*, 62, . . . Piece-work.

Good harvest, He that hath a, may be content with some thistles. 1639 : Clarke, 198. 1670 : Ray, 13. 1846 : Denham, *Proverbs*, 57 (Percy S.).

Good harvests make men prodigal, bad ones provident. 1611 : Cotgrave, s.v. " Année." 1670 : Ray, 13. 1754 : Berthelson, *Eng.-Danish Dict.*, s.v. " Harvest." 1846 : Denham, *Proverbs*, 54 (Percy S.). 1904 : *Co. Folk-Lore : Northumb.*, 178 (F.L.S.).

Good health. *See* quot. 1855 : Bohn, 400, He who hath good health is young; and he is rich who owes nothing.

Good heed hath good hap. 1681 : W. Robertson, *Phraseol. Generalis*, 719. 1736 : Bailey, *Dict.*, s.v. " Heed," Take good heed will surely speed.

Good hope is better than a bad possession, A. 1620 : Shelton, *Quixote*, Pt. II. ch. lxv. 1732 : Fuller, No. 154.

Good house, all things are quickly ready, In a. 1611 : Cotgrave, s.v. " Maison." 1631 : Mabbe, *Celestina*, 152 (T.T.), In a plentifull house a supper is soone provided. 1640 : Herbert, *Jac. Prudentum*.

Good housewife. *See* quot. 1678 : Ray, 88, She's not a good house-wife that will not wind up her bottom, i.e. take off her drink.

Good husband, Be a=Be thrifty. *See* quot. 1813 : Ray, 13, Be a good hus-band, and you will soon get a penny to spend, a penny to lend, and a penny for a friend.

Good husband makes a good wife, A. 1621 : Burton, *Melancholy*, III. iii. 4, 1, p. 648 (1836), For as the old saying is, a good husband makes a good wife. 1702 : Farquhar, *Inconstant*, II., i., A good husband makes a good wife at any time. 1753 : *World*, No. 21. 1869 : Spurgeon, *John Ploughman*, ch. xvii. Cf. Good Jack ; and Good wife.

Good husbandry is good divinity. 1846 : Denham, *Proverbs*, 2 (Percy S.). 1904 : *Co. Folk-Lore : Northumb.*, 173 (F.L.S.).

Good husbandry. *See also* Frugality.

Good ill that comes alone, 'Tis a. 1620 : Shelton, *Quixote*, Pt. II. ch. lv. 1732 : Fuller, No. 5059.

Good in the mouth and bad in the maw [stomach]. 1669 : *Politeuphuia*, 172, What is sweet in the mouth is bitter in the stomach. 1732 : Fuller, No. 5511. 1855 : Kingsley, *West. Ho!*, ch. xi., Do I not know that it is sweet in the mouth but bitter in the belly? 1925 : E. F. Benson, in *London Mercury*, July, 279 [the converse], That crisp little roll which may be bitter to the mouth, but is sweet to the belly.

Good is to be sought out, and evil attended [awaited]. 1640 : Herbert, *Jac. Prudentum*.

Good Jack makes a good Jill, A. 1605 : Camden, *Remains*, 317 (1870). 1670 : Ray, 108. 1828 : Carr, *Craven Dialect*, i. 250. Cf. Good husband.

Good Jill may mend the bad Jack, A. 1669 : Brathwait, *Hist. of Moderation*, 15, See by experience, what may not a wise woman bring a bad husband to in time? *The good Gill may mend the bad Jack*.

Good judge conceives quickly, judges slowly, A. 1640 : Herbert, *Jac. Prudentum*.

Good judgment that relieth not wholly on his own, He hath a. 1710 : S. Palmer, *Moral Essays on Proverbs*, 330. 1732 : Fuller, No. 1882.

Good kail is half a meal. 1670 : Ray, 36. 1732 : Fuller, No. 6252. [In both " keal " for " kail ".]

Good kin that none do amiss in, 'Tis a.
1639 : Clarke, 160.

Good knife. See quots. 1678 : Ray,
255, It's a good knife, it will cut butter
when 'tis melted. A good knife, it was
made five miles beyond Cutwell. 1732 :
Fuller, No. 2857, It is a good knife,
'twas made at Dull-edge.

Good land. See Best (16).

Good language -that all understand
not, That's not. 1640 : Herbert, *Jac.
Prudentum.* 1670 : Ray, 27.

Good lather is half the shave, A. 1732 :
Fuller, No. 5472, Well lather'd is half
shaven. 1825 : Hone, *Ev. Day Book,*
i. 1269, He also says, that " a good
lather is half the shave," is a very old
remark among the trade [barbers].

Good laws. See quots. 1659 : Howell,
Proverbs : Fr.-Eng., 9, Good laws come
from lewd lives. 1855 : Bohn, 364, Good
laws often proceed from bad manners.

Good life. See quots. 1629 : *Book of
Meery Riddles,* Prov. 27, A good life
makes a good death. 1633 : Draxe,
113, A good life hath a good death.
Ibid., 39, A good life will have a good
end. *See also* Handful.

Good liquor. *See* Cat (18).

Good looks are good cheap. 1639 :
Clarke, 34.

Good luck comes by cuffing. 1813 :
Ray, 136.

Good luck for a grey horse. 1862 :
Dialect of Leeds, 316, " Good luck for
a grey horse ! "—a common expression
of children, accompanied by the act of
spitting over their little finger, at the
sight of a grey horse. 1922 : *N. & Q.,*
12th ser., xi. 169.

Good luck in cards bad luck in
marriage. 1755 : *Connoisseur,* No. 59,
She is no less sure of a good one
[husband] because she generally has
ill luck at cards. 1887 : M. A. Courtney, *Folk-Lore Journal,* v. 219, Good
luck in cards, bad luck in a husband
(or wife). (Cornish.)

Good luck lurks under a black deuce.
Cornish card saying. 1887 : M. A.
Courtney, *Folk-Lore Journal,* v. 219.

Good luck never comes too late.
c. 1610 : Drayton, *Mooncalf,* in *Works,*
ii. 511 (1753).

Good luck reaches farther than long
arms. 1732 : Fuller, No. 1717.

Good luck. *See also* Calf (2) ; and
Cow (7).

Good maid but for thought, word,
and deed, She's a. 1678 : Ray, 258.

Good man, A. In a general sense.
1. *A good man can no more harm than
a sheep.* The first example seems to
be a humorous perversion of the saying.
1546 : Heywood, *Proverbs,* Pt. I. ch. x.,
But she can no more harme than can
a she ape. 1605 : Camden, *Remains,*
316 (1870). 1670 : Ray, 98. 1732 :
Fuller, No. 160, A good man is no
more to be fear'd than a sheep.

2. *See* quot. 1485 : Malory, *Morte
d'Arthur,* bk. xix. ch. 4, Hit is an old
sawe a good man is neuer in daunger but
whan he is in the daunger of a coward.

3. *He's a good man whom fortune
makes better.* 1732 : Fuller, No. 2438.

4. *If a good man thrive, all thrive with
him.* 1640 : Herbert, *Jac. Prudentum.*

B.=The master of the house. 1. *The
goodman's the last that knows what's
amiss at home.* 1670 : Ray, 52. 1732 :
Fuller, No. 4558. Cf. **Cuckold** (8)

2. *When the good man is abroad,
the good woman's table is soon spread.*
1678 : Ray, 61 [with " from home "
for " abroad," and " wives " for
" woman's "]. 1732 : Fuller, No. 5587.
See also As the goodman.

Good manners, You know, but you
use but a few. 1639 : Clarke, 2. 1670 :
Ray, 185. 1732 : Fuller, No. 5919, You
have good manners, but never carry
them about you.

Good manners. *See* Lord Mayor (1).

Good marksman may miss, A. 1732 :
Fuller, No. 163.

Good master. *See* quot. c. 1530 :
Rhodes, *Boke of Nurture,* 108
(E.E.T.S.), He that hath a good
mayster and cannot keepe him, He
that hath a good servaunt and not
content with hym, He that hath such
condicions that no man loueth hym,
May well know other, but few men
wyll knowe him. 1578 : Florio, *First
Fruites,* fo. 105.

Good masters make good servants.
1888 : Q.-Couch, *Troy Town,* ch. xix.

Good maxim is never out of season, A.
1855 : Bohn, 288.

Good men are a public good. 1732 :
Fuller, No. 1718.

Good men are scarce. 1638 : D.
Tuvill, *Vade Mecum*, 96 (3rd ed.).
1668 : *Poor Robin Alman.*, Sept., Pretending this reason for it, *That good
people are scarce.* 1732 : Fuller, No.
3307, Maids, make much of one; good
men are scarce. 1738 : Swift, *Polite
Convers.*, Dial. I., Good folks are scarce.

Good men company, Keep, and you
shall be of the number. 1477 : Rivers,
Dictes, etc., 26 (1877), Acompanye
the[e] with good people, and thou
shalt be on of them. 1560 : T. Wilson,
Rhetorique, 5 (1909), According to
the prouerbe, by companying with
the wise, a man shall learne wisedome.
1640 : Herbert, *Jac. Prudentum*. 1748 :
Richardson, *Clarissa*, iv. 242 (1785).

Good mind, good find. 1853 : Trench,
Proverbs, 19 (1905).

Good mother says not "Will you?"
but gives, The. 1640 : Herbert, *Jac.
Prudentum*, 1670 : Ray, 18. 1852 :
FitzGerald, *Polonius*, 74 (1903), The
wise mother says not " Will you? "
but gives.

Good name for-winneth, A. *c.* 1460 :
How the Good Wife, l. 35.

Good name is better than riches.
1477 : Rivers, *Dictes, etc.*, 64 (1877),
Good renomme is bettir than richesse.
1506 : A. Barclay, *Castell of Labour*,
sig. E7, Good name is better than
rychesse.

Good name is worth gold, A. *c.* 1460 :
How the Good Wife, l. 75, Gode name is
golde worthe. 1597 : in *Plasidas, etc.*,
166 (Roxb. Cl.), For wise men and old
Seyne good name is worth gold. 1611 :
Cotgrave, s.v. " Assez," A good name
is wealth sufficient. 1754 : Berthelson,
Eng. Danish Dict., s.v. " Above," A
good name is above the wealth.

Good name keeps its lustre in the
dark, A. 1670 : Ray, 18.

Good name, Take away my, and take
away my life. Ibid., 124. 1732 : Fuller, No. 4306. *c.* 1800 : Trusler, *Prov.
in Verse*, 75.

Good neighbour. *See* Neighbour.

Good news, He that brings, knocks
boldly. 1611 : Cotgrave, s.v. " Hardi-
ment." 1659 : Howell, *Proverbs : Span.-
Eng.*, 18. 1666 : Torriano, *Piazza
Univ.*, 213.

Good news may be told at any time,
but ill in the morning. 1640 : Herbert,
Jac. Prudentum.

Good night, Nicholas, the moon is in
the flock-bed. 1659 : Howell, 11.

Good office, He hath a, he must needs
thrive. 1678 : Ray, 263.

Good often fare the worse for the bad,
The. 1712 : Motteux, *Quixote*, Pt. I.
bk. i. ch. vii.

Good or ill hap. *See* quot. 1732 :
Fuller, No. 6413, The good or ill hap of
a good or ill life, Is the good or ill choice
of a good or ill wife.

Good orator who convinces himself,
He is a. 1855 : Bohn, 374.

Good painter can draw a devil as well
as an angel, A. 1639 : Clarke, 311.

Good palliate a bad action, The. 1855 :
Bohn, 506.

Good pawn never shames the master,
A. 1631 : Brathwait, *Whimzies*, 104
(1859). 1639 : Glapthorne, *Wit in a
Constable*, V. 1659 : Howell, 11.

Good paymaster is lord of another
man's purse, The. 1640 : Herbert, *Jac.
Prudentum*, A good payer is master of
another's purse. 1748 : Franklin, in
Works, ii. 119 (Bigelow).

Good paymaster may build Paul's, A.
1732 : Fuller, No. 167.

Good paymaster needs no surety, A.
1620 : Shelton, *Quixote*, Pt. II. ch. xiv.
1694 : D'Urfey, *Quixote*, Pt. I. Act IV.
sc. i. 1732 : Fuller, Nos. 1726-7, Good
paymasters need no surety. Good paymasters need not bring a pawn.

Good paymaster never wants workmen, A. 1732 : Fuller, No. 168.

Good physician who cures himself,
He is a. *c.* 1430 : Lydgate, *Daunce of
Machabree*, l. 424, Good leche is he that
can himself recure. 1666 : Torriano,
Piazza Univ., 148.

Good presence is letters of recommendation, A. 1732 : Fuller, No. 170.

Good reasons. *See* quot. 1623 : Wodroephe, *Spared Houres*, 477, Good
reasons said, and euill vnderstood, are

rozes strawen to hogges, and not so good.

Good recorder sets all in order, A. 1659: Howell, 11. 1670: Ray, 22. 1732: Fuller, No. 6245.

Good reputation is a fair estate, A. 1732: Fuller, No. 172.

Good riding at two anchors. [ἀγαθαὶ δὲ πέλοντ', ἐν χειμερίᾳ νυκτὶ θοᾶς ἐκ ναὸς ἀπεσκίμφθαι, δύ᾽ ἄγκυραι.—Pindar, Olymp., Ode VI. 170.] 1546: Heywood, Proverbs, Pt. II. ch. ix., Good riding at two anchors, men haue told, For if the tone fail, the tother may hold. 1579: Lyly, Euphues, 116 (Arber), Haue more strings to thy bow then one, it is safe riding at two ankers. 1670: Ray, 151 [as in 1546]. 1716: E. Ward, Female Policy, 85, It's safe riding with two anchors. 1732: Fuller, No. 6450 [as in 1546]. Cf. **Two strings.**

Good riding. See also **Safe riding.**

Good roller, A, a good rider. 1869: FitzGerald, Sea Words and Phrases, 9, " A good roller a good rider "; that is to say, the breadth of beam and bottom that will make a vessel roll, will also make her ride comfortably at anchor.

Good rye thrives high. 1884: Egerton, Sussex Folks and Ways, 82, When I was a growing lad . . . a kindly old far- mer's wife . . . would [say] " and good rye thrives high."

Good sailor may mistake in a dark night, A. 1732: Fuller, No. 173.

Good saver is a good server, A. Somerset. 1678: Ray, 350.

Good scholar is not a good school- master, Every. 1732: Fuller, No. 1417.

Good seed, Of, proceedeth good corn. c. 1568: Wager, Longer thou Livest, sig. A2.

Good servant must come, A. See quots. 1645: Howell, Letters, bk. i. § v. No. xiii., He [a footman] will come when you call him, go when you bid him, and shut the door after him. 1738: Swift, Polite Convers., Dial. I., Remember, that a good servant must always come when he's called, do what he's bid, and shut the door after him.

Good servant must have good wages, A. c. 1555: in Wright, Songs, etc., Philip and Mary, 173 (Roxb. Cl.), A

goode sarvaunte hopes for to be well rewardyde. 1611: Cotgrave, s.v. " Ser- vir," Good service, of itself, demands reward. 1732: Fuller, No. 176.

Good service is a great enchantment. 1640: Herbert, Jac. Prudentum.

Good shape is in the shears' mouth, A. 1855: Bohn, 289.

Good shift may serve long, but it will not serve ever, A. 1678: Ray, 201. 1732: Fuller, No. 177.

Good skill in horseflesh. See quots. 1670: Ray, 181, He hath good skill in horseflesh to buy a goose to ride on. 1738: Swift, Polite Convers., Dial. I., She had good skill in horse flesh that could choose a goose to ride on.

Good small beer. See quot. 1738: Swift, Polite Convers., Dial. II., They say, there is no such thing as good small beer, good brown bread, or a good old woman. Cf. **Good things.**

Good spear, He that hath a, let him try it. 1578: Florio, First Fruites, fo. 28 [with " proue it against a wal " for " try it "]. 1629: Book of Meery Riddles, Prov. 74.

Good spender, To a, God is the trea- surer. 1640: Herbert, Jac. Prudentum. 1670: Ray, 24. 1732: Fuller, No. 5127.

Good sport that fills the belly, That is. Ibid., No. 4354.

Good steward abroad when there is a wind frost, There is a. 1830: Forby, Vocab. E. Anglia, 431. 1872: J. Glyde, jr., Norfolk Garland, 149.

Good stomach is the best sauce, A. Cf. **Hunger.**

Good surgeon. See **Surgeon.**

Good swimmers are oftenest drowned. 1611: Cotgrave, s.v. " Nageur," Good swimmers at the length feed haddocks. 1640: Herbert, Jac. Prudentum, Good swimmers at length are drowned. 1732: Fuller, No. 1729.

Good table, At a, we may go to school. Ibid., No. 823.

Good take-heed doth surely speed. 1639: Clarke, 266. 1670: Ray, 147. 1732: Fuller, No. 6093.

Good tale ill told is marred in the telling, A. 1546: Heywood, Proverbs, Pt. II. ch. vii. 1670: Ray, 147. 1732:

Fuller, No. 178, A good tale ill told is
a bad one.

Good tale is none the worse for being
twice told, A. 1816 : Scott, *Old Mortality*, ch. vii.

Good that causeth so many good deeds,
Needs must it be. *c.* 1387 : Usk, *Test.
of Love*, in Skeat's *Chaucer*, vii. 79,
Nedes mot it be good that causeth so
many good dedes.

Good that does me good, That's my.
1639 : Clarke, 109, That's good that
doth us good. 1678 : Ray, 148. 1732 :
Fuller, No. 276, A man has no more
goods than he gets good by.

Good that knows not why he is good,
He cannot be. 1602 : Carew, *Surv. of
Cornwall*, 219 (1811), It hath been well
said, " He cannot long be good, that
knows not why he is good." 1732 :
Fuller, No. 1819.

Good thing is soon caught up, A.
1670 : Ray, 13 [with " snatch't " for
" caught "]. 1732 : Fuller, No. 181.

Good things I do not love. *See* quot.
1678 : Ray, 148, Some good things I do
not love, a good long mile, good small
beer, and a good old woman. Cf. Good
small beer.

Good, though long stayed for, is good.
1659 : Howell, *Proverbs : Brit.-Eng.*, 3.

Good tither a good thriver, A. Somerset. 1678 : Ray, 352.

Good to be in the dark, as without
light, It's as. 1670 : Ray, 77.

Good to be near of kin. *See* quots.
1662 : Fuller, *Worthies*, ii. 227 (1840),
Indeed our English proverb, " It is
good to be near a-kin to land," holdeth
in private patrimonies, not titles to
crowns. 1748 : Richardson, *Clarissa*,
i. 81 (1785), My sister says, in the words
of an old saw, *It is good to be related to
an estate.*

Good to fetch a sick man sorrow, or
a dead man woe. 1670 : Ray, 194,
. . . *Cheshire*. 1738 : Swift, *Polite Convers.*, Dial. I., You are fit to be sent for
sorrow, you stay so long by the way.
1917 : Bridge, *Cheshire Proverbs*, 70.

Good to have some friends both in
heaven and hell, It's. 1639 : Clarke, 232,
It's good having a friend both in heaven
and hell. 1670 : Ray, 93.

Good to learn at other men's cost, It is.
1546 : Heywood, *Proverbs*, Pt. I. ch. xi.,
It is good to beware by other men's
harmes. Before 1651 : in Peck, *Desid.
Curiosa*, 443 (1779), It is good learning
by another's book. 1736 : Bailey, *Dict.*,
s.v. " Cost."

Good to send on a dead man's errand.
1670 : Ray, 171 [with " bodies " for
" man's "]. 1738 : Swift, *Polite Convers.*, Dial. I., Well, have you been with
my Lady Club? You are good to send
of a dead man's errand.

Good tongue, Who has not a, ought to
have good hands. 1813 : Ray, 166.

Good trade. *See* quots. 1659 : Howell,
Proverbs : Fr.-Eng., 23, He that hath a
good trade will have his share. 1732 :
Fuller, No. 2386, He who hath a trade,
hath a share every where. 1855 : Bohn,
566, Who hath a good trade, through all
waters may wade.

Good tree brings forth good fruit, A.
c. 1534 : Berners, *Huon*, 13 (E.E.T.S.),
Alwayes I haue harde say that a good
impe [tree] bryngethe forth good frcute.
1586 : Pettie, tr. Guazzo's *Civil Convers.*, fo. 127, It is seldome seene that a
good tree bringeth foorth ill fruites.
Cf. Such tree.

Good tune played on an old fiddle,
There's many a. 1917 : Bridge, *Cheshire
Proverbs*, 117.

Good turns, One never loseth by doing.
1670 : Ray, 12.

Good voice to beg bacon, He hath a.
1659 : Howell, 6.

Good walking with a horse in one's
hand, It's. 1591 : Lyly, *Endymion*, IV.
ii., Is it not said, " It is good walking
when one hath his horse in his hand."
1653 : Taylor (Water-Poet), *Short Relation*, 5, in *Works*, 1st coll. (Spens. S.),
'Tis merry walking with a horse in hand.
1685-6 : Cotton, *Montaigne*, bk. iii.
ch. iii., He may well go a foot, they
say, who leads his horse in his hand.
1738 : Swift, *Polite Convers.*, Dial. II.,
I always love to walk with a horse in
my hand.

Good ware. *See* quots. 1611 : Cotgrave, s.v. " Marchand," Good chaffer
cannot want a chapman. 1616 : Breton, in *Works*, ii. *e* 5 (Grosart), Good

ware makes quick markets. 1659:
Howell, *Proverbs: Fr.-Eng.*, 8, Good
ware will never want a chapman. 1681:
W. Robertson, *Phraseol. Generalis*, 677,
Good ware will off. 1754: Berthelson,
Eng.-Danish Dict., s.v. "Market" [as
in 1616].

Good watch prevents misfortune.
1670: Ray, 28.

**Good weight and measure is heaven's
treasure.** 1732: Fuller, No. 6161.

Good wheat. *See* Wheat.

**Good wife and a good cat are best at
home, A.** 1894: Northall, *Folk Phrases*,
6 (E.D.S.).

**Good wife and good name hath no
make** [mate] **in goods nor fame, A.**
1623: Wodroephe, *Spared Houres*, 478.

**Good wife and health Is a man's best
wealth, A.** 1732: Fuller, No. 6313.
1869: Spurgeon, *John Ploughman*,
ch. xvi.

Good wife mækes a good husband, A.
1546: Heywood, *Proverbs*, Pt. II.
ch. viii. 1659: Howell, 7. 1759:
Johnson, in Hill's *Boswell*, i. 324, We
tell the ladies that good wives make
good husbands. Cf. **Good husband**; and
Good Jack.

Good wife must be bespoke, A; for
there's none ready made. 1738: Swift,
Polite Convers., Dial. I.

**Good wife spares, What the, the cat
eats.** 1639: Clarke, 242. 1670: Ray,
144. 1732: Fuller, No. 5520.

**Good will, I'll do my, as he said that
thresh't in his cloak.** 1602–3: Manningham, *Diary*, 131 (Camden S.), "I will
doe myne endeavor," quoth he that
thrasht in his cloke. 1670: Ray, 178.
1732: Fuller, No. 2634.

Good wind. *See* quot. 1592: Lyly,
Mother Bombie, II. v., I have heard my
great grandfather tell how his great
grandfather should say, that it was an
old proverbe, when his great grandfather was a childe, that it was a good
wind that blew a man to the wine.

Good wine needs no bush. 1539:
Taverner, *Proverbs*, fo. 42, Wyne that is
saleable and good nedeth no bushe or
garland of yuye to be hanged before.
1575: Gascoigne, *Glasse of Govt.*, I. i.,
The good wyne needeth none iuye

garland. 1608: Day, *Law Trickes*, IV. i.
1638: Brathwait, *Barn. Journal*, Pt. I.
ad fin., Good wine no bush it needs, as
I suppose. 1711: Addison, *Spectator*,
No. 221. 1831: Peacock, *Crotchet Castle*,
ch. xv.

**Good wit, Such a one hath a, if a wise
man had the keeping it.** 1605: Camden,
Remains, 331 (1870).

Good wits jump, i.e. agree. 1620:
Shelton, *Quixote*, Pt. II. ch. xxxvii.,
I have heard you say . . . "Good wits
will soon meet." 1664: in *Musarum
Deliciæ*, ii. 85 (Hotten), Like will to
like: Good wits will jump (quoth he).
1710: Centlivre, *Man's Bewitch'd*, IV.
ii., Good wits jump—I resolve to marry
too. 1775: in *Garrick Corresp.*, ii. 94
(1832), See how good wits jump. *See
also* Great wits.

Good woman. *See* Woman (2), (28).

**Good word is as soon said as a bad
one, A.** *c.* 1615: R. C., *Times Whistle*,
111 (E.E.T.S.). 1736: Bailey, *Dict.*,
s.v. "Word."

**Good words and ill deeds deceive wise
and fools.** 1611: Davies (of Hereford),
Sc. of Folly, 46, in *Works*, ii. (Grosart).

**Good words anoint us, and ill do
unjoint us.** 1578: Florio, *First Fruites*,
fo. 31, Good woords annoynt a man,
the yl woordes kyl a man. 1611:
Davies (of Hereford), *Sc. of Folly*, 43,
in *Works*, ii. (Grosart).

**Good words are worth much and cost
little.** 1640: Herbert, *Jac. Prudentum*.
1732: Fuller, No. 1736, Good words
cost nothing, but are worth much.

Good words cost no more than bad.
1692: L'Estrange, *Æsop*, 249 (3rd ed.),
A good word, they say, costs no more
than a bad. 1732: Fuller, No. 1735.

Good words cost nought. 1599:
Porter, *Two Angry Women*, in Hazlitt,
Old Plays, vii. 356, Good words cost
nought: ill words corrupt good manners,
Richard. 1670: Ray, 158.

Good words fill not a sack. 1678:
Ray, 220. 1732: Fuller, No. 1737.

**Good words make amends for mis-
deeds.** 1604: *Wit of a Woman*, sc. i.
l. 20 (Malone S.) [cited as "an olde
saying"].

Good words quench more than a

bucket of water. 1640 : Herbert, *Jac.
Prudentum.* 1670 : Ray, 158, Good
words cool more then cold water.

**Good words without deeds are rushes
and reeds.** 1659 : Howell, 17. 1670 :
Ray, 30. 1732 : Fuller, No. 6247.
1875 : A. B. Cheales, *Proverb. Folk-
Lore,* 86.

**Good workman is known by his chips,
A.** 1869 : Hazlitt, 16.

Goodly. *See* Handsome (3).

Goodness coming out. *See* quot.
1738 : Swift, *Polite Convers., Dial. I.,
Miss feels a pimple on her face;* Lord !
I think my goodness is coming out.
[In my boyhood, 1863–73, I heard this
expression similarly used.—G. L. A.]

Goodness is not tied to greatness.
1639 : Clarke, 226, Greatnesse and goodnesse goe not alwey together. 1655 :
T. Muffett, *Healths Improvement,* 161,
As the Greek proverb saith, Goodnesse
is not tied to greatness, but greatness
to goodness.

Goods are theirs who enjoy them.
1578 : Florio, *First Fruites,* fo. 31, The
ware is not his that gathers it, but his
that enjoyes it. 1670 : Ray, 12. 1732 :
Fuller, No. 1739. Cf. Wealth (6).

Goodwin Sands, To set up shop on=
To be shipwrecked. 1546 : Heywood,
Proverbs, Pt. II. ch. ix., And so set vp
shop vpon Goodwins sands. 1670 :
Ray, 215, Let him set up shop on
Goodwins Sands. 1735 : Pegge, *Kent,
Proverbs,* in E.D.S., No. 12, p. 72 [as in
1670]. *See also* Tenterden steeple.

**Goodyer's pig, Like, never well but
when he is doing mischief.** Cheshire
1670 : Ray, 209. 1852 : " Cheshire Proverbs," in *N. & Q.,* 1st ser., vi. 386.
1917 : Bridge, *Cheshire Proverbs,* 89.

Goodyer's pigs. *See* quot. 1678 :
Ray, 235, They'll come again, as
Goodyers pigs did, i.e. never.

Goose and Geese. 1. *A goose cannot
graze after him. c.* 1602 : Chapman,
May-Day, III. i., What should he do
to him, sir ? The pasture is so bare
with him that a goose cannot graze
upon't. 1639 : Clarke, 36. 1670 : Ray,
178.

2. *A goose go barefoot. See* Woman (3).

3. *A goose is a silly bird. See* quots.

1872 : *N. & Q.,* 4th ser., ix. 104, That
" a goose is a very silly bird, too much
for one but not enough for two," is
scarcely a local saying. I have heard
it in several widely separated parts of
England. 1880 : Poole, *Archaic, etc.,
Words of Staffs,* 25, The presumed
foundation for this proverb is, that a
Walsall man, when asked if he and his
wife were going to have a goose for
their Christmas dinner, replied " No " ;
for said he, " the goose was a silly bird
— too much for one to eat, and not
enough for two." 1894 : Northall,
Folk Phrases, 31 (E.D.S.), Too much for
one, and not enough for two, like the
Walsall man's goose.

4. *All his geese are swans.* Before
1529 : Skelton, *Magnyyfcence,* l. 302,
In faythe, els had I gone to longe to
scole, But yf I coulde knowe a gose
from a swanne. 1615 : J. Andrews,
Anat. of Baseness, 30 (Grosart), That
by this art, can make a goose a swanne.
1621 : Burton, *Melancholy,* Dem. to
Reader, 40 (1836), All their geese are
swans. 1725 : Bailey, tr. Erasmus's
Colloq., 445, For every man's own geese
are swans. 1864 : Newman, *Apologia,*
68, He was particularly loyal to his
friends, and, to use the common phrase,
" all his geese were swans."

5. *As deep drinketh the goose as the
gander.* 1546 : Heywood, *Proverbs,* Pt.
II. ch. vii. 1580 : Lyly, *Euphues,* 275
(Arber). 1659 : Howell, *Letters,* ii. 666
(Jacobs), The goose will drink as deep
as the gander. 1732 : Fuller, No. 671.
1880 : Spurgeon, *Ploughman's Pictures,*
136, When the goose drinks as deep as
the gander, pots are soon empty, and
the cupboard is bare.

6. *As great as a goose's egg. c.* 1394 :
Piers P. Crede, l. 225.

7. *As is the gander so is the goose.*
1732 : Fuller, No. 700.

8. *As open as a goose's eye. c.* 1500 :
Medwall, *Nature,* Pt. II. l. 130 (Brandl,
Quellen, 120), Nay all ys open that
they do there As open as a gose eye.

9. *Geese with geese and women with
women.* 1732 : Fuller, No. 1645.

10. *Give the goose more hay. See*
Tittle-tattle.

11. *Go flay the geese.* 1683 : Meriton, *Yorkshire Ale*, 83–7 (1697).

12. *Gone is the goose that the great egg did lay.* 1732 : Fuller, No. 1696.

13. *Goose, gander, and gosling are three sounds, but one thing.* 1659 : Howell, *Proverbs: Span.-Eng.*, 20. 1670 : Ray, 98.

14. *Goslins lead the geese to water.* 1732 : Fuller, No. 1740.

15. *Have a goose and get a goose.* 1869 : Spurgeon, *John Ploughman*, ch. xiv.

16. *He hopes to see a goose graze on your head.* 1583 : Melbancke, *Philotinus*, sig. Ee2, I hope thou shalt eat of the goose that shall tread on her graue. 1670 : Ray, 178, He hopes to eat of the goose shall graze on your grave.

17. *He that turneth the goose should have the neck.* Before 1500 : Hill, *Commonplace-Book*, 131 (E.E.T.S.).

18. *I have a goose to pluck with you.* 1659 : Howell, 2. Cf. **Crow** (9).

19. *If you eat goose on Michaelmas Day you will never want money all the year round.* 1708 : *Brit. Apollo*, i. No. 74, The custom'd proverb . . . That who eats goose on Michael's-day, Shan't money lack, his debts to pay. 1825 : Hone, *Ev. Day Book*, i. 1339 [cited as "a popular saying"]. 1830 : Forby, *Vocab. E. Anglia*, 414, If you do not baste the goose on Michaelmas-day, you'll want money all the year. 1904 : *Co. Folk-Lore: Northumb.*, 178 (F.L.S.).

20. *It is a blind goose that knows not a fox from a fern-bush.* 1580 : Lyly, *Euphues*, 319 (Arber). 1732 : Fuller, No. 2848.

21. *It is a silly goose that comes to a fox's sermon.* Ibid., No. 2881.

22. *It is a sorry goose that will not baste herself.* 1670 : Ray, 218. 1732 : Fuller, No. 2886.

23. *It is an old goose that will eat no oats.* 1591 : Lyly, *Endymion*, V. ii. Cf. No. 36.

24. *Sauce for the goose is sauce for the gander.* [Idem Accio quod Titio jus esto. —Varro, *ap.* Aul. Gell., *Noct. Att.*, III. xvi. 13.] 1671 : Head and Kirkman, *Eng. Rogue*, ii. 120, I could not justly complain, seeing what was sause for a goose was sause for a gander. 1710 :

Swift, *Journal to Stella*, 24 Jan. 1785–95 : Wolcot, *Lousiad*, can. v. 1823 : Byron, *Don Juan*, can. xiv. st. 83. 1853 : Planché, *Extravag.*, iv. 364 (1879).

25. *Shall the goslins teach the goose to swim?* 1732 : Fuller, No. 4115.

26. *Steal a goose.* See **Steal** (6), (7).

27. *There's meat in a goose's eye.* 1621 : Taylor (Water-Poet), *Works*, pagin. 1, 105 (1630), For the old pro-uerbe I must here apply, Good meate men may picke from a gooses eye. 1678 : Ray, 148.

28. *To as much purpose as the geese slurr* [slide] *on the ice.* Cheshire. 1670 : Ray, 190. 1877 : E. Leigh, *Cheshire Gloss.*, 191. 1917 : Bridge, *Cheshire Proverbs*, 125.

29. *To as much purpose as to give a goose hay.* Cheshire. 1670 : Ray, 190. 1917 : Bridge, *Cheshire Proverbs*, 125.

30. *To give a goose and charge for the garlic.* c. 1380 : Wiclif, in *Eng. Works*, 82 (E.E.T.S.), For thei sillen a faat goos for litel or nought, but the garlek costith many shillyngis.

31. *To kill the goose that laid the golden eggs.* 1484 : Caxton, *Æsope*, ii. 245 (Jacobs) [story told in a fable of Avian]. 1855 : Gaskell, *North and South*, ch. xvii., And now they come to us, and say we're to take less. And we won't. . . . They'll have killed the goose that laid 'em the golden eggs, I reckon. 1922 : Weyman, *Ovington's Bank*, ch. xl., They had cooked their goose with a vengeance—no more golden eggs for them !

32. *We desire but one feather out of your goose.* 1732 : Fuller, No. 5439.

33. *You're a man among the geese when the gander's away.* 1670 : Ray, 177. 1732 : Fuller, No. 5842. 1917 : Bridge, *Cheshire Proverbs*, 157.

34. *You are a pretty fellow to ride a goose a gallop.* 1678 : Ray, 248, [*plus*] through a dirty lane. 1732 : Fuller, No. 5843.

35. *You find fault with a fat goose.* 1678 : Ray, 248. 1732 : Fuller, No. 5902.

36. *Young is the goose that will eat no oats.* 1580 : Lyly, *Euphues*, 366 (Arber). 1732 : Fuller, No. 6037. Cf. No. 23.

See also **Bo**; **Candlemas, E**; **Children**
(12); **Dizzy**; **Fierce**; **Fool** (82); **Fox** (1),
(33), and (35); **Good goose**; **Harborough
Field**; **Hare** (16); **Ice** (2); **St. Chad**;
St. Martin (1); **St. Valentine** (3); **Shoe**
(2); **Snow** (6); **Steal** (6) and (7);
Tittle-tattle; **Wild** (3); **Wise** (2); and
Wolf (4).

Goose-quill gentleman, A. 1639:
Clarke, 226.

**Goose-quill is more dangerous than
a lion's claw, A.** 1732: Fuller, No.
184. 1868: *Quart. Review*, cxxv. 252,
There is . . . strong testimony to the
superiority of letters to arms, or to
the danger of law, in this other, "A
goose quill is more dangerous than a
lion's claw."

Gorse. *See* **Furze**; and **Under the
furze.**

Goshawk beats not at a bunting, A.
1639: Clarke, 69. 1670: Ray, 98.
1732: Fuller, No. 185. 1846–59:
Denham Tracts, ii. 108 (F.L.S.), A
goss-hawk strikes not at a bunting.

Gospel, All is (or **is not**), **that one
speaks**; or, more recently, **To take for
Gospel** = To accept as true; or, **To be
Gospel** = to be true. [Credite me vobis
folium recitare Sibyllae.—Juvenal, viii.
126.] Before 1250: *Owl and Nightingale*,
1268 (O.), For-thi seide Alfred swithe
wel And his worde was goddspel.
c. 1374: Chaucer, *Troylus*, bk. v. l. 1265,
Every word was gospel that ye seyde!
c. 1400: *Rom. Rose*, l. 7609, Al is not
gospel, out of doute, That men seyn in
the towne aboute. 1593: Nashe, in
Works, iv. 142 (Grosart), His creditors
(thinking all is Gospell he speakes . . .).
1691: *Merry Drollery*, 238 (Ebsworth),
Now all is Gospel that she saith. 1771:
Smollett, *Clinker*, in *Works*, vi. 291
(1817), As for Jenkins, she affects to
take all her mistress's reveries for
gospel. 1883: Trollope, *Autobiog.*, ch.
v., I merely showed the letter to my
wife, declaring my conviction that it
must be taken as gospel. 1910: Lucas,
Mr. Ingleside, ch. xxii., " No, no, . . .
I'm too old to be caught like that."
" It's gospel, I assure you."

**Gossip speaks ill of all, and all of her,
A.** 1732: Fuller, No. 186.

Gossiping and lying go together. 1732:
Fuller, No. 1741.

**Gossips are frogs—they drink and
talk.** 1640: Herbert, *Jac. Prudentum*.
1670: Ray, 12.

Gotham—in various sayings. *See*
quots. *c.* 1400: *Towneley Plays*, 106
(E.E.T.S.), Now god gyf you care foles
all sam; Sagh I neuer none so fare bot
the foles of Gotham. 1526: *Hund.
Mery Talys*, No. xxiv., " Of the iii wyse
men of gotam " [title], p. 45 (Oesterley). 1597: Hall, *Satires*, bk. ii. sat.
v., Saint Fooles of Gotam mought thy
parish be. 1639: Taylor (Water-Poet),
Summ. Trav., 16, in *Works*, 1st coll.
(Spens. S.), I saw the ancient towne of
Gotham, famous for the seven sages (or
wise men) who are fabulously reported
to live there in former ages. 1662:
Fuller, *Worthies*, ii. 569 (1840), As wise
as a man of Gotham. 1703: E. Ward,
Writings, ii. 316, I happen'd to be a
hopeful branch of that ancient and
renown'd family of the wise-men of
Gotham. 1754: Berthelson, *Eng.-Dan-
ish Dict.*, s.v. " Wise," A wise man of
Gotham. 1842: Halliwell, *Nursery
Rhymes*, 19 (Percy S.), Three wise men
of Gotham, Went to sea in a bowl:
And if the bowl had been stronger, My
song would have been longer. [Date of
" song " unknown.] 1863: Kingsley,
Water Babies, ch. viii., On the borders
of that island he found Gotham, where
the wise men live; the same who
dragged the pond because the moon had
fallen into it. 1894: A. J. C. Hare,
Sussex, 74, The proverb, " As wise as
the wise men of Gotham " . . . is
believed to refer to Gotham, a manor
partly in the parish of Hailsham, partly
in that of Pevensey. [The seat of
wisdom is more usually identified with
the Notts village of Gotham.]

Gout. *See* **Drink**, *verb* (8).

**Gown is his that wears it, The, and
the world his that enjoys it.** 1640:
Herbert, *Jac. Prudentum*. 1670: Ray,
28 [with " hers " for the first " his "].
1732: Fuller, No. 4560 [as in 1670].

Grace groweth after governance, "Is
an old said saw in each place." 1566:
Becon, in *Early Works*, 395 (P.S.).

Grace of God = Shipwreck. 1659:
Howell, 12, O Master Vier, we cannot
pay you your rent, for we had no
Grace of God this year; No ship-
wrack upon our coast : a saying of the
Cornish.

Grace of God. *See* God, The grace of.

Grace will last, beauty will blast.
1639: Clarke, 119 [with " favour " for
" beauty "]. 1670: Ray, 98 [as in
1639]. 1732 : Fuller, No. 6292.

Graft good fruit all, Or graft not at all.
Ibid., No. 6335.

Grafting on a good stock, 'Tis good.
1678 : Ray, 354. 1732 : Fuller, No.
5082.

Grafts be very good, Let the, or the
knife be where it stood. 1855 : Bohn,
441.

Grain by grain the hen fills her belly.
1653 : Middleton and Rowley, *Span.
Gipsy*, II. i., Grain pecked up after
grain makes pullen fat. 1732 : Fuller,
No. 1744.

Grain of prudence is worth a pound of
craft, A. Ibid., No. 187.

Graith and grout. *See* quot. 1917 :
Bridge, *Cheshire Proverbs*, 78, If you've
graith [riches] and grout [good breed],
You'll never be without.

Gramercy forty pence, Jack Noble's
dead. 1659: Howell, 13. 1670 : Ray,
215.

Gramercy horse. *c.* 1600 : in Collier,
Roxb. Ballads, 29 (1847), The hostler,
to maintaine himselfe with money in's
purse, Approves the proverbe true, and
sayes, gramercy horse. 1631 : Brathwait, *Whimzies*, 71 (1859), If he [an
ostler] rise to any preferment, he may
say, *Gramercy, horse*. 1659: Howell,
14. Cf. Godamercy horse.

Grandfather's servants are never good.
1732 : Fuller, No. 1745.

Grant all that is asked, To. *See* quot.
1593: Peele, *Edward I.*, sc. x., Glocester,
an old said saying,—He that grants all
is ask'd, Is much harder than Hercules
task'd.

Grantham gruel, nine grits and a
gallon of water. 1662 : Fuller, *Worthies*,
ii. 269 (1840). Before 1674 : in *Roxb.
Ballads*, viii. 427 (B.S.), Some gruel of
Grantham, boyl'd for the nonce. 1790 :

Grose, *Prov. Gloss.*, s.v. " Lincs." 1818 :
Scott, *Heart of Midl.*, ch. xxix., [Newark
man *loq.*] Thou wilt get naething at
night save Grantham gruel, nine grots
and a gallon of water. 1869 : Spurgeon,
John Ploughman, ch. xxi.

Grantham steeple stand awry, 'Tis
height makes. 1596: Lodge, *Wits
Miserie*, 14 (Hunt. Cl.), His beard is
cut like the spier of Grantham steeple.
1604: Middleton, *Works*, viii. 21 (Bullen), Wresting them quite awry, like
Grantham steeple. Before 1659 : Cleveland, *Poems*, 63 (1742), Few churchmen
can be innocent and high; 'Tis height
makes Grantham steeple stand awry.
1732 : Fuller, No. 5086.

Grapes are sour, The. *c.* 1580: U.
Fulwell, *Ars Adulandi*, sig. E3, I see
full well the fox will eate no grapes
because he cannot reache them. 1630 :
T. Adams, *Works*, 69, The foxe dis-
praiseth the grapes he cannot reach.
1691 : *Wit for Money*, 4, And like the
fox, to cry the grapes are sowre. 1721 :
Cibber, *Refusal*, IV., Poor Tom ! What
are the grapes sour, my dear ! 1760 :
Murphy, *Way to Keep Him*, I., You
would be glad to have me : but sour
grapes, my dear. 1876 : Blackmore,
Cripps, ch. iii., Ah, poor Mary, the
grapes are sour.

Grasp all, lose all. *c.* 1800 : J.
Trusler, *Prov. in Verse*, 77. 1880 :
Spurgeon, *Ploughman's Pictures*, 152.

Grasp no more than thy hand will hold.
1732 : Fuller, No. 1747.

Grasps at too much, He that, holds
nothing fast. *c.* 1205 : Layamon, *Brut*,
i. 278 (Madden), For the mon is muchel
sot The nimeth to him-seoluen Mare
thonne he mayen walden (For the man is
a great fool who taketh upon himself
more than he can manage). *c.* 1386 :
Chaucer, *Melibeus*, § 24, For the proverbe seith : " he that to muche embraceth, distreyneth litel." 1578 :
Florio, *First Fruites*, fo. 6, Who
imbraceth much, litle closeth. 1653 :
Urquhart, *Rabelais*, bk. i. ch. xlvi., It
is too great an undertaking . . . and
(as the proverb is), He that gripes too
much, holds fast but little. 1732 :
Fuller, No. 2123.

Grass. 1. *Grass and hay, we are all mortal.* 1631 : Brathwait, *Whimzies*, 73 (1859), Which makes him conclude in his owne element; *Grasse and hay, we are all mortall.* 1666 : Torriano, *Piazza Univ.*, 277, Good fellows . . . who say, grass and hay, we are mortal, let's live till we dye.

2. *Grass grows not upon the highway*, nor *in the market-place.* 1659 : Howell, *Proverbs : Brit.-Eng.*, 24, In market growes no grass nor grain. 1678 : Ray, 149, Grass grows not upon the highway.

3. *Grass never grows when the wind blows.* 1846 : Denham, *Proverbs*, 7 (Percy S.).

4. *No grass grows where the Turk's horse has trod.* 1639 : Fuller, *Holy War*, bk. v. ch. xxx., According to the old proverb, Grass springeth not where the grand signior's horse setteth his foot. Before 1658 : Cleveland, *Works*, 77 (1742), Of whom you may say, as of the Great Sultan's horse, where he treads the grass grows no more. 1732 : Fuller, No. 5664, Where the great Turk's horse treads, grass never grows.

5. *To let the grass grow under one's feet.* 1550 : Udall, *Roister Doister*, III. iii., There hath grown no grass on my heel, since I went hence. 1707 : *Spanish Bawd*, IV. iii., I have not been idle— I have not let grass grow under my feet. 1864 : Mrs. H. Wood, *Trevlyn Hold*, ch. xlvi., Nora never let the grass grow under her feet, or under any one else's feet, when there was work to do. 1923 : Lucas, *Advisory Ben*, 1, Her disapproval of the pastoral process known as letting the grass grow under your feet was intense.

6. *While the grass grows the steed starves.* c. 1440 : Capgrave, *Life of St. Kath.*, ii. 253 (O.), The gray hors, whyl his gras growyth, May sterue for hunger, þus seyth þe prouerbe. 1546 : Heywood, *Proverbs*, Pt. I. ch. xi. 1593 : *Pass. Morrice*, 89 (N. Sh. S.). 1602 : Shakespeare, *Hamlet*, III. ii., Ay, sir, but " while the grass grows,"— the proverb is something musty. 1621 : Burton, *Melancholy*, II. iii. 3, p. 404 (1836). c. 1760 : Foote, *Commissary*, III., And while the grass grows—you

know the proverb . . . 1869 : Spurgeon, *John Ploughman*, ch. xv.

7. *You must look for grass on the top of the oak tree*, i.e. " the grass seldom springs well till the oak comes out."— Inwards. 1670 : Ray, 44. 1893 : Inwards, *Weather Lore*, 151. 1917 : Bridge, *Cheshire Proverbs*, 159.

See also Cut (17).

Grateful man. *See* quots. 1640 : Herbert, *Jac. Prudentum*, To a grateful man, give money when he asks. 1732 : Fuller, No. 2113, He that gives to a grateful man, puts out to usury.

Grave as a judge. 1685 : S. Wesley, *Maggots*, 2, As grave as judge that's giving charge. 1753 : *World*, No. 45, Nor have I any great objection to " as grave as a judge." 1836 : Marryat, *Easy*, ch. xxxii., Mesty sat on the chest between them, looking as grave as a judge. 1907 : De Morgan, *Alice-for-Short*, ch. viii., " What a funny little tot it is ! " he cried. " As grave as a judge ! "

Grave as an old gate-post. 1678 : Ray, 280. 1732 : Fuller, No. 692.

Grave as an owl. 1702 : Farquhar, *Inconstant*, III. ii., Why, then, look grave as an owl in a barn. 1828 : Scott, *Fair Maid*, ch. v., What has befallen you, that makes you look as grave as an owl?

Grave, *subs.*, and **Graves, r** *Graves are of all sizes.* 1732 : Fuller, No. 1751.

2. *The grave is the general meeting-place.* Ibid., No. 4563.

3. *The grave's good rest.* 1632 : Rowley, *Woman never Vexed*, v., But I must go before him ; and 'tis said, The grave's good rest when women go first to bed.

4. *To the grave with the dead, and them that live to the bread.* 1612 : Shelton, *Quixote*, Pt. I. bk. iii. ch. v, 1710 : S. Palmer, *Moral Essays on Proverbs*, 247. 1732 : Fuller, No. 6347.

Grays Inn for walks, Lincoln's Inn for a wall, The Inner Temple for a garden, and the Middle for a hall. 1659 : Howell, 21. 1670 : Ray, 258. 1790 : Grose, *Prov. Gloss.*, s.v. " London."

Graze on the plain, To=To be turned out of doors. 1869 : Hazlitt, 418.

Grease, To fry in one's own. [Quasi

quom caletur cochleae in occulto latent,
Suo sibi suco vivont, ros si non cadit;
Item parasiti rebus prolatis latent In
occulto, miseri victitant suco suo, Dum
ruri rurant homines quos ligurriant.—
Plautus, *Capt.*, i. 80–4.] *c.* 1386:
Chaucer, *Wife of Bath's Prol.*, l. 487,
But certeinly, I made folk swich chere,
That in his owene grece I made him
frye For angre. *c.* 1400: Lydgate,
Temple of Glas, 14 (E.E.T.S.), Thus
is he fryed in his owene gres, To-rent
and torn with his owene rage. 1540:
Palsgrave, *Acolastus*, sig. T3, He lyeth
and fryeth in his owne grease for anger.
Before 1577: Gascoigne, *Works*, i. 474
(Hazlitt), The sisters being thus on all
sides reiected . . . began to melt in
their owne grease. 1681: in *Roxb.
Ballads*, vi. 2 (B.S.), And lie like abbey-
lubbers stew'd in their own greases.
1898: Weyman, *Shrewsbury*, ch. xxiv.,
If they impeach me, I return to Loo;
and they may stew in their own juice!
  Grease, *verb.* 1. *Grease a fat sow*.
See **Every man basteth**; and **Sow** (14).
  2. *He who greases his wheels, helps his
oxen.* 1732: Fuller, No. 2384.
  3. *If you grease a cause well it will
stretch.* Ibid., No. 2753.
  4. *To grease in the fist* = To bribe.
1387: Trevisa, tr. Higden, vii. 7 (Rolls
Ser.), Elsinus . . . groped here hondes,
and gat slyliche a maundmente of þe
kyng, and was i-put in at Caunterbury.
1569: E. Fenton, *Wonders of Nature*,
135, Annointing their clarkes in the
hand with double fee. 1576: Wapull,
Tide tarrieth no Man, sig. C1, Wherefore he will largely grease me in the
hand. 1606: *Ret. from Parnassus*, Pt. II.
II. ii., Ought his gowty fists then first
with gold to be greased? 1681: W.
Robertson, *Phraseol. Generalis*, 281,
You must grease him in the fist with
a new fee, for a bribe. 1789: in
Farmer, *Musa Pedestris*, 72, Cease
greasing their fist and they'll soon
cease their jaw. 1881: Evans, *Leics.
Words*, 159 (E.D.S.), A farmer said to
me in reference to a douceur which
his landlord's agent appeared to expect,
". . . but this 'ere giff-gaff grease i'
fist sort o' woo'k doon't dew for may."

  5. *To grease one's boots* = To cajole or
flatter. 1813: Ray, 198.
  Greasy as a badger. 1917: Bridge,
Cheshire Proverbs, 14.
  **Great and good are seldom the same
man.** 1732: Fuller, No. 1752.
  **Great and the little have need of one
another, The.** Ibid., No. 4564.
  Great as the devil and Doctor Faustus.
See **Devil** (39).
  Great bargain, At a, pause. 1736:
Franklin, *Way to Wealth*, in *Works*, i.
447 (Bigelow), At a great pennyworth
pause a while. 1875: A. B. Cheales,
Proverb. Folk-Lore, 101, At a great
pennyworth pause. Cf. **Good bargain.**
  Great barkers are no biters. 1605:
Camden, *Remains*, 322 (1870). 1659:
Howell, 8.
  Great birth is a very poor dish at table.
1855: Bohn, 365.
  Great boast small roast. *c.* 1532:
R. Copland, *Spyttel House*, l. 978, Grete
boost and small roost. 1591: Haring-
ton, *Orl. Furioso*, bk. xxv. st. 66, As if
there were great boast and little rost.
c. 1660: in *Roxb. Ballads*, ii. 409 (Hind-
ley). 1732: Fuller, No. 6297. 1869:
Spurgeon, *John Ploughman*, ch. xv.,
Such hopes lead to great boast and
small roast.
  Great bodies move slowly. 1855:
Bohn, 365.
  Great braggers little doers. 1539:
Taverner, *Proverbs*, fo. 49, Great brag-
gers commonly be least fyghters. 1732:
Fuller, No. 1753. Cf. **Greatest talkers.**
  Great businesses turn on a little pin.
1640: Herbert, *Jac. Prudentum.* Cf.
Great engines.
  Great ceremony for a small saint, A.
1732: Fuller, No. 190.
  Great city, A, a great solitude. 1625:
Bacon, *Essays:* "Friendship," The
Latine adage meeteth with it a little;
Magna civitas, magna solitudo. 1732:
Fuller, No. 191.
  Great cry. *See* **Much cry.**
  **Great doings at Gregory's, heat the
oven twice for a custard.** 1678: Ray,
72. 1732: Fuller, No. 1755.
  **Great doings in the North when they
bar their doors with tailors, There's.**
1678: Ray, 341. 1683: Meriton,

Yorkshire Ale, 83–7 (1697). 1846–59,
Denham Tracts, ii. 75 (F.L.S.) [with
" steek " for " bar "].

Great dowry is a bed full of brambles,
A. 1640 : Herbert, *Jac. Prudentum.*
1670 : Ray, 8 [with " brabbles " for
" brambles "]. 1732 : Fuller, No. 193.

Great engines turn on small pivots.
1855 : Bohn, 366. Cf. Great businesses.

Great fish eateth the little, The. 1575 :
Churchyard, *Chippes*, 145 (Collier), The
whales, you see, eates up the little fishe.
1578 : Florio, *First Fruites*, fo. 29.
1633 : Draxe, 141.

Great force hidden in a sweet command, There is. 1640 : Herbert, *Jac.
Prudentum.*

Great fortune, in the hands of a fool,
is a great misfortune, A. 1732 : Fuller,
No. 194.

Great fortune is a great slavery, A.
Ibid., No. 195.

Great gain makes work easy. Ibid.,
No. 1756.

Great gifts are for great men. 1639 :
Clarke, 188. 1670 : Ray, 98 [with
" from " for " for "].

Great Glen. *See* quot. 1678 : Ray,
317, At Great Glen there are more great
dogs then honest men.

Great harvest. *See* Harvest (7).

Great head and little wit. 1562 : Heywood, *Epigr.*, 6th Hund., No. 56, Thy
head is great . . . and without wit
within. 1633 : Draxe, 17. 1670 : Ray,
101. 1732 : Fuller, No. 196. 1813 :
Brand, *Pop. Antiq.*, iii. 176 (Bohn).

Great head and small necke is the
beginning of a gecke [fool]. 1623 :
Wodroephe, *Spared Houres*, 518.

Great honours are great burdens.
1670 : Flecknoe, *Epigrams*, 53, If that
saying be true, Great honours are
great burthens.

Great hopes make great men. 1732 :
Fuller, No. 1759.

Great journey to the world's end, It
is a. 1639 : Clarke, 3. 1670 : Ray, 158.
1732 : Fuller, No. 2859 [with "life's "
for " world's "].

Great light a great lanthorn, To a.
1640 : Herbert, *Jac. Prudentum.*

Great man, A, and a great river are
often ill neighbours. 1732 : Fuller,

No. 198. 1813 : Ray, 117, A great
lord is a bad neighbour.

Great marks are soonest hit. 1732 :
Fuller, No. 1760.

Great men have great faults. 1633 :
Draxe, 127. 1639 : Clarke, 160, Great
mens faults are never small.

Great men's favours are uncertain.
1736 : Bailey, *Dict.*, s.v. " Favour."

Great men would have care of little
ones, If, both would last long. 1640 :
Herbert, *Jac. Prudentum.*

Great need of a wife that marries
mamma's darling, He has. 1732 : Fuller, No. 1872.

Great oaks. *See* Oak (5).

Great ones, There would be no, if
there were no little. 1670 : Ray, 12.
1732 : Fuller, No. 4868.

Great pain and little gain make a man
soon weary. 1633 : Draxe, 221. 1670 :
Ray, 129.

Great pains quickly find ease. 1640 :
Herbert, *Jac. Prudentum.*

Great pan. *See* quot. 1913 : *Devonsh.
Assoc. Trans.*, xlv. 90, If yu've a got a
gurt pan an' little to cook, the pan aits
the lot, as the zayin' is.

Great promise small performance.
1562 : Heywood, *Epigr.*, 5th Hund.,
No. 10. 1611 : Cotgrave, s.v. " Fai-
seur," Great promisers, weak per-
formers. 1880 : Spurgeon, *Ploughman's
Pictures*, 18, Those who are quick to
promise are generally slow to perform.

Great put the little on the hook, The.
1640 : Herbert, *Jac. Prudentum.*

Great river. *See* quot. Ibid., In a
great river great fish are found ; but
take heed lest you be drowned. 1869 :
Spurgeon, *John Ploughman*, ch. xix.

Great ship asks deep waters, A. 1640 :
Herbert, *Jac. Prudentum.* 1670 : Ray,
24. 1732 : Fuller, No. 203, A great
ship must have deep water.

Great shoe fits not a little foot, A.
1633 : Draxe, 3. 1639 : Clarke, 138.

Great spenders are bad lenders. 1639 :
Clarke, 262. 1670 : Ray, 145. 1732 :
Fuller, No 6169.

Great stirring in the North when old
wives ride scout, There's. 1678 : Ray,
341. 1846–59 : *Denham Tracts*, ii. 75
(F.L.S.).

Great strokes make not sweet music.
1640 : Herbert, *Jac. Prudentum.* 1670 :
Ray, 12, The greatest strokes make not
the best musick.

Great talkers are great liars. 1736 :
Bailey, *Dict.*, s.v. " Talker."

Great talkers are like leaky pitchers,
everything runs out of them. 1855 :
Bohn, 366.

Great torch may be lighted at a little
candle, A. 1583 : Melbancke, *Philotinus*,
sig. A3.

Great tree hath a great fall, A. *c.* 1380:
Chaucer, *Troylus*, bk. ii. ll. 1380–6,
Whan that the sturdy ook, On which
men hakken oftë, for the nones,
Receyvëd hath the happy falling strook,
The gretë sweigh doth it come al at
ones, As doon these rokkës or these
milnë-stones. For swifter cours com'th
thing that is of wighte, Whan it de-
scendeth, than don thingës lighte.
1732 : Fuller, No. 204.

Great trees keep under the little ones.
Ibid., No. 1769.

Great way to the bottom of the sea,
'Tis a. 1639 : Clarke, 4. 1670 : Ray,
154. 1732 : Fuller, No. 1850, He goes
a great voyage, that goes to the bottom
of the sea.

Great wealth and content seldom live
together. 1732 : Fuller, No. 1771.

Great weights hang on small wires.
1639 : Clarke, 109. 1670 : Ray, 154.
1732 : Fuller, No. 1773 [with " may "
before " hang "].

Great wits have short memories.
1668 : Dryden, *Sir M. Mar-all*, IV. i.,
He has forgot it, sir; good wits, you
know, have bad memories. 1720 :
Swift, in *Works*, ix. 191 (Scott, 1883),
A common-place book is what a
provident poet cannot subsist without,
for this proverbial reason, that " great
wits have short memories." 1763 :
Murphy, *Citizen*, II., *George.* . . . do
you remember what you read, Miss?
Maria. Not so well as I could wish.
Wits have short memories.

Great wits jump. 1691 : *Wit for
Money*, 14, 'Tis much like it, I must
confess, but wits jump. 1758–67 :
Sterne, *Trist. Shandy*, vol. iii. ch. ix.,
Great wits jump :—for the moment

Dr. Slop cast his eyes upon his bag . . .
the very same thought occurred. 1826–
44 : Hood, *Comic Poems:* " To Gri-
maldi," Ah, where thy legs—that witty
pair ! For " great wits jump "—and so
did they ! 1884 : *N. & Q.*, 6th ser., x.
216, " Les beaux esprits rencontrent "
is, of course, the same as our " Great
wits jump together." 1922 : *Punch*,
27 Dec., p. 601, col. 3, Lord Riddell
considers that Mr. H. G. Wells is one
of the world's greatest minds. Great
minds, as the saying is, think alike.
Cf. Good wits.

Great would have none great, The,
and the little all little. 1640 : Herbert,
Jac. Prudentum.

Greater state, the more wisdom, The.
Before 1500 : in Hill, *Commonplace-
Book*, 130 (E.E.T.S.), The grettir state,
the more wisedom.

Greater the right, The, the greater the
wrong. 1569 : Grafton, *Chron.*, ii. 228
(1809), According to the adage, the ex-
tremitie of iustice is extreme iniustice.
1639 : Clarke, 182, Extremity of law is
extremity of wrong. 1680 : L'Estrange,
Tully's Offices, 18, From whence comes
that saying, *Extreme right is extreme
wrong.* 1820 : Colton, *Lacon*, Pt. II.
No. 139, There is one motto that ought
to be put at the head of our penal code,
" *Summum jus, summa injuria.*"

Greater the sinner, The, the greater
the saint. 1856 : E. Hinchliffe, *Bar-
thomley*, 29, How well is the old proverb
illustrated . . . The greater the sinner,
the greater the saint. 1913 : *Folk-Lore*,
xxiv. 76 (Oxon).

Greatest barkers bite not sorest, The.
1587 : Greene, in *Works*, iv. 152 (Grosart), Orlanio . . . thought the greatest
barkers were not alwayes the sorest
biters. 1639 : Clarke, 153. 1670 : Ray,
59. 1732 : Fuller, No. 4567, The
greatest barkers are not the greatest
biters.

Greatest boasters are not the boldest
men, The. 1509 : Barclay, *Ship of
Fools*, i. 198 (1874), For greattist
crakers ar nat ay boldest men. 1570 :
Barclay, *Mirrour of Good Manners*, 76
(Spens. S.), The greatest crakers are
not the boldest men.

Greatest burdens are not the gain-fullest, The.   1611 : Cotgrave, s.v. "Acquests." 1670 : Ray, 4.

Greatest calf.   See Calf (8).

Greatest clerks are not the wisest men, The.   c. 1386 : Chaucer, Reeve's Tale, l. 134, "The gretteste clerkes been noght the wysest men," As whylom to the wolf thus spak the mare.   1476 : Paston Letters, iii. 153 (Gairdner, 1900), Wherffor, late men deme what they wylle, grettest clerkys are nott alweye wysest men.   1580 : Lyly, Euphues, 237 (Arber).   1633 : Jonson, Tale of a Tub, I. ii.   1732 : Fuller, No. 4570.   1821 : Scott, Kenilworth, ch. xxxi., He . . . may be one of those whom Geoffrey Chaucer says wittily, the wisest clerks are not the wisest men.

Greatest hate springs from the greatest love, The.   1732 : Fuller, No. 4573.

Greatest step is that out of doors, The. 1640 : Herbert, Jac. Prudentum.

Greatest talkers are always the least doers, The.   1594 : Shakespeare, Rich. III., I. iii., Talkers are no good doers. 1607 : Marston, What You Will, III., Ther's an old fustie proverbe, these great talkers are never good dooers. 1681 : W. Robertson, Phraseol. Generalis, 1203.   1692 : L'Estrange, Æsop, 360 (3rd ed.), The boldest talkers are not always the greatest doers.   1754 : Berthelson, Eng.-Danish Dict., s.v. "Talk."   Cf. Great braggers.

Greatest vessel hath but its measure, The.   1732 : Fuller, No. 4580.

Greatest wealth is contentment with a little, The.   1659 : Howell, 6.   1670 : Ray, 28.   1732 : Fuller, No. 4581.

Greedy as a dog.   1639 : Clarke, 285. 1670 : Ray, 205.   1714 : Mandeville, Fable of Bees, 187, Dogs, tho' become domestick animals, are ravenous to a proverb.

Greedy is the godless.   c. 1320 : in Reliq. Antiquæ, i. 111 (1841), "Gredy is the godles"; Quoth Hendyng.

Greek Kalends, At the = Never.   [In literis cum aliquos nunquam soluturos significare vult Ad Kalendas Graecas soluturos ait. — Suetonius, Ost., 87.] 1540 : Palsgrave, Acolastus, sig. V1, At

the Grekish calendes . . . or a daye after domesday.   1595 : Lodge, Fig for Momus, Epist. vii., Yea, when the Grecian Calends come (quoth I).   1653 : Urquhart, Rabelais, bk. i. ch. xx., The judgment or decree shall be given out and pronounced at the next Greek Calends, that is, never.   1740 : North, Examen, 477, It must be dated ad Græcas Calendas.   1880 : World, 13 Oct., p. 6, Any prospects of earning a dividend on which must be relegated to the Greek kalends.   1922 : Observer, 5 March, p. 7, col. 5, The policy . . . which seemed to postpone to the Greek Kalends the concessions now freely granted to Egypt.

Greek to one, To be.   1603 : Shakespeare, Cæsar, I. ii., But for mine own part, it was Greek to me.   1620 : Shelton, Quixote, Pt. II. ch. xix., All this to the husbandmen was heathen Greek.   1821 : Scott, Kenilworth, ch. xxix., But this is Greek to you now, honest Lawrence, and in sooth learning is dry work.

Green, adj.   1. A green shear is an ill shake.   1846 : Denham, Proverbs, 51 (Percy S.).

2. A green wound is soon healed. 1639 : Clarke, 283.   1670 : Ray, 31. 1732 : Fuller, No. 206.

3. A green Yule.   See Christmas (3) and (4).

4. All green things are gay.   1546 : Heywood, Proverbs, Pt. II. ch. i., All thing is gay that is greene.   1611 : Davies (of Hereford), Sc. of Folly, 48, in Works, ii. (Grosart).

5. As green as a leek.   1585 : Nomenclator, 180, A colour as greene as a leeke.   1595 : Shakespeare, Mids. N. Dream, V. i., His eyes were green as leeks. 1745 : Agreeable Companion, 141, If ladies cheek Be green as leek.   1886 : Elworthy, West Som. Word-Book, 426 (E.D.S.), So green's a leek is the usual simile.

6. As green as grass.   1387 : Trevisa, tr. Higden, i. 123 (Rolls Ser.), þe þridde [third] þre monþes grene as gras.   c. 1420 : Lydgate, Assem. of Gods, st. 48, p. 11 (E.E.T.S.), Grene as any gresse in the somertyde.   1593 : G. Harvey,

in *Works*, i. 271 (Grosart), As greene as the greenest grasse. *c.* 1660: in *Roxb. Ballads*, ii. 444 (B.S.), Her gown was of velvet as green as the grass. 1869: Spurgeon, *John Ploughman*, ch. iv., Poor soft Tommy, as green as grass, and as ready to bend as a willow.

7. *Green wood makes a hot fire.* 1477: Rivers, *Dictes, etc.*, 65 (1877), The grene wode is hotter than the other whan it is wel kyndeled. 1586: G. Whitney, *Emblems*, 173, Greenest wood, though kindlinge longe, yet whottest most it burnes. 1670: Ray, 30. 1732: Fuller, No. 1774.

8. *King Green.* See quot. 1887: Parish and Shaw, *Dict. Kent. Dialect*, 155 (E.D.S.), The use of green meat as a purge gives rise to this old East Kent saying—" King Grin [i.e. Green], Better than all medcin."

9. *Strew green rushes for the stranger.* 1546: Heywood, *Proverbs*, Pt. II. ch. iii., Greene rushes for this straunger. *c.* 1594: Bacon, *Promus*, No. 118, Ceremonies and green rushes are for strangers. *c.* 1618: B. & F., *Valentinian*, II. iv., Where is this stranger? Rushes, ladies, rushes, Rushes as green as summer for this stranger. 1738: Swift, *Polite Convers.*, Dial. I., If we had known of your coming, we would have strewn rushes for you.

10. *When there's a green frost=* Never. 1883: Burne, *Shropsh. Folk-Lore*, 595.

11. *You see no green cheese but your teeth must water.* 1546: Heywood, *Proverbs*, Pt. II. ch. ix. 1553: *Respublica*, III. iv., Ye can see no grene cheese but your teethe wyll watier. 1670: Ray, 198.

Grenvile family. See quot. 1897: Norway, *H. and B. in Devon, etc.*, 183, "Never a Grenvile wanted loyalty," so say the Cornish still.

Grey and green make the worst medley. 1678: Ray, 149 ["Gray"].

Grey as a badger. 1720: Swift, in *Works*, xiv. 134 (Scott), Though she lives till she's grey as a badger all over. 1786: Wolcot, in *Works*, i. 140 (1795). 1823: Moor, *Suffolk Words*, 45, We say " as grey as a badger " of one whose head is " silvered o'er with age." 1862: *Dialect of Leeds*, 406. 1880: Courtney, *W. Cornwall Words*, 26 (E.D.S.), " Grey as a badger " is a Cornish proverb.

Grey as grannum's cat. 1732: Fuller, No. 693. 1880: Spurgeon, *Ploughman's Pictures*, 48, He will be as grey as grannum's cat before he improves.

Grey before he is good, He's. 1678: Ray, 249.

Grey hairs are death's blossoms. Ibid., 149 [" Gray "]. 1853: Trench, *Proverbs*, 70 (1905) [" Gray "].

Grey mare is the better horse, The. 1546: Heywood, *Proverbs*, Pt. II. ch. iv. *c.* 1570: *Marr. of Wit and Science*, II. i., Break her betimes, and bring her under by force, Or else the grey mare will be the better horse. 1626: Charles I., in Ellis, *Orig. Letters*, iii. 249 (1824), My sister and brother (I place them so, becaus I thinke the gray meare is the best horse). 1723: Steele, *Conscious Lovers*, I. i. *c.* 1740: Fielding, *Eurydice*. 1849: Macaulay, *Hist. Eng.*, i. ch. iii. *n.*, The vulgar proverb, that the grey mare is the better horse, originated, I suspect, in the preference generally given to the grey mares of Flanders over the finest coach horses of England. 1926: Phillpotts, *Yellow Sands*, II., And when the grey mare's the better hoss, that's no marriage neither.

Grey-hound. Proverbial descriptions of the shape of a good grey-hound. 1486: *Boke of St. Albans*, sig. Fiiii. v., The propreteis of a goode grehound. A grehounde shulde be heded like a snake, and necked like a drake. Foted like a kat. Tayled like a rat. Syded lyke a terne. Chyned like a berne. 1611: Markham, *Country Contentments*, 39 (1675), An old rime left by your fore fathers, from which you shall understand the true shapes of a perfect grey-hound, and this it is, If you will have a good tike, Of which there are few like, He must be headed like a snake, Neckt like a drake, Backt like a beam, Sided like a bream, Tayled like a rat, And footed like a cat. 1670: Ray, 212, A head like a snake, a neck

like a drake, A back like a beam, a
belly like a bream, A foot like a cat, a
tail like a rat. 1736 : Bailey, *Dict.*, s.v.
" Grey-hound " [as in 1670].

Grind or find, I'll either. 1670 : Ray,
178.

Grind with every wind, To. 1736 :
Bailey, *Dict.*, s.v. " Grind."

Grist to the mill, To bring. 1583 :
Golding, *Calvin on Deut.*, 755 (O.),
There is no lykelihoode that those
thinges will bring gryst to the mill.
1661 : Gurnal, *Christian in Armour*,
Pt. III. v. 18, ch. xxi. p. 481 (1679),
'Tis a pick-purse doctrine, contrived
to bring grist to the Popes mill. 1720 :
Vade Mecum for Malt - worms, Pt. I.
p. 21, No writs have we, to draw
Grist to your mill. 1767 : Murphy,
Sch. for Guardians, I. iv., (*A rap at
the door*) More grist to the mill. Go
and open the door, Peter. 1871 : G.
Eliot, *Middlemarch*, ch. x., Some people
make fat, some blood, and some bile—
that's my view of the matter; and
whatever they take is a sort of grist
to the mill.

Grizzling like a badger. Corn. 1895 :
Jos. Thomas, *Randigal Rhymes*, 60.

Groaning horse and a groaning wife
never fail their master, A. 1546 : Heywood, *Proverbs*, Pt. II. ch. iv. 1611 :
T. Heywood, *Golden Age*, I., You know
the prouerbe : A grunting horse and a
groning wife neuer deceiue their maister.
1670 : Ray, 51, A grunting horse . . .
seldom fail their master. 1732 : Fuller,
No 207 [as in 1670, *minus* " their
master "].

Groat is ill saved that shames the
master, The. 1605 : Camden, *Remains*,
332 (1870). 1670 : Ray, 23. 1732 :
Fuller, No. 4345. 1853 : Trench, *Proverbs*, 103 (1905).

Groats. *See* Blood (2).

Groby pool, Leics. 1. *See* quots.
1678 : Ray, 317, For his death there is
many a wet eye in Groby pool. 1790 :
Grose, *Prov. Gloss.*, s.v. " Leicestershire " [as in 1678]. 1881 : Evans,
Leics. Words, 301 (E.D.S.), This is
generally used in the form of a prophecy : " When a doys, thee'll ba wet
oys i' Grewby Pule."

2. *See* quots. 1678 : Ray, 317, Then
I'll thatch Groby pool with pancakes.
1790 : Grose, *Prov. Gloss.*, s.v. " Leicestershire " [as in 1678]. 1818 : Scott,
Heart of Midl., ch. xxix., [Newark man
loq.] Why, when [there's no bad company on the road] . . . I'll thatch
Groby pool wi' pancakes. 1843 : Carlyle, *Past and Present*, bk. iii. ch. i.,
Think of that. " Groby Pool *is*
thatched with pancakes,"—as Jeanie
Deans's Innkeeper defied it to be !

Gropes in the dark, He that, finds that
he would not. 1659 : Howell, 13. 1670 :
Ray, 12. 1732 : Fuller, No. 2124.

Groundsel, The = Sill or threshold.
See quots. 1640 : Herbert, *Jac. Prudentum*, The groundsel speaks not, save
what it heard at the hinges. 1670 :
Ray, 12 [" grounsel," and " of " for
" at "]. 1732 : Fuller, No. 4583, The
groundsel speaketh but what it heard
of the hinges.

Ground-sweat cures all disorders, A.
c. 1816 : in Farmer, *Musa Pedestris*, 81,
We . . . sent him to take a ground-
sweat [buried him]. 1830 : Forby,
Vocab. E. Anglia, 434. 1872 : J. Glyde,
jr., *Norfolk Garland*, 150.

Grout [Good breed] afore brass for me.
1917 : Bridge, *Cheshire Proverbs*, 63.

Grow, *verb.* 1. *He grows warm in his
harness.* 1623 : Wodroephe, *Spared
Houres*, 487.

2. *See* quot. 1678 : Ray, 72, This
grow'd by night. Spoken of a crooked
stick or tree, it could not see to grow.

Growing youth. *See* Wolf (1).

Grunting horse. *See* Groaning.

Guest is never welcome, A constant.
1732 : Fuller, No. 48.

Guildford. 1. *Guildford bulls.* 1790 :
Grose, *Prov. Gloss.*, s.v. " Surrey." [A
Godalming retort in answer to the
taunts against the Godalming folk of
cats and rabbits. *See* Godalming.]

2. *Poor Guildford, proud people, three
churches, no steeple.* 1886 : Hissey, *On
the Box Seat*, 42.

Guiler is beguiled, The. 1377 : Langland, *Plowman*, B, xviii. 337, The olde
lawe graunteth, That gylours be bigiled.
c. 1386 : Chaucer, *Reeve's Tale*, l. 401,
A gylour shal himself bigyled be.

c. 1390 : Gower, *Conf. Amantis*, bk. vi. l. 1381. 1484 : Caxton, *Æsope*, ii. 50 (Jacobs), As men saye it is meryte to begyle the begylers . . . And therfore he that begyleth other is oftyme begyled hym self. 1598 : Bernard, *Terence in English*, 111 (1607), *Frustratur ipse sibi*, he deceiues himselfe, he playeth wilie beguile himselfe. 1606 : *Wily Beguiled*, in Hazlitt, *Old Plays*, ix.

Guilt is always jealous. 1732 : Fuller, No. 1779.

Guilty Gilbert. *See* quot. 1608 : Armin, *Nest of Ninnies*, 39 (Sh. S.), By her cheeks you might find guilty Gilbert, where he had hid the brush.

Gull comes against the rain, The. 1633 : Draxe, 189, The gull commeth not, but against a tempest. 1670 : Ray, 98.

Gup quean, gup. " Gup " probably = Go up. 1525 : *Wydow Edyth : Mery Gestys*, 36 (1864), Than her lemman cast her vp, Go where she wold : gup quean gup. 1546 : Heywood, *Proverbs*, Pt. II. ch. iv., Walke drab, walke ! Nay (quoth she), walke knaue walke ! 1573 : G. Harvey, *Letter-Book*, 118 (Camden S.), Marry gupp, hore, gupp, all the day longe. Cf. **Hop, whore.**

Guts in his brains, He has. 1663 : Butler, *Hudibras*, Pt. I. can. iii. l. 1091, Hard matter for a man to do That has but any guts in 's brains. 1697 : T. Dilke, *City Lady*, III. ii., They have no guts in their brains. 1720 : Swift, *Right of Precedence*, par. 23, Our vulgar saying, " that men have guts in their brains," is a vulgar error. 1828 : Carr, *Craven Dialect*, i. 47, " You have no guts in your brains "; you are completely ignorant, you are quite destitute of skill or cunning. 1889 : *Longman's Mag.*, April, 619 (W.), Maurie has good guts i' her brain.

Guts to a bear, Not fit to carry. 1659 : Howell, 17, He is not worthy to carry gutts to a bear. 1670 : Ray, 200, Not worthy to carry guts after a bear. 1785–95 : Wolcot, in *Works*, i. 198 (1795), George thinks us scarcely fit ('tis very clear) To carry guts, my brethren, to a bear. 1826 : in Mrs. Hughes, *Letters, etc., of Scott*, ch. vi., " So, Sir, I hear you have had the impudence to assert that I am not fit to carry guts to a bear." " Oh no !— I defended you : I said you were."

Gutter Lane, All goeth down. 1631 : Brathwait, *Whimzies*, 145 (1859), Whatsoever hee draines from the four corners of the citty, goes in muddy taplash downe Gutter-lane. 1662 : Fuller, *Worthies*, ii. 348 (1840). 1721 : Bailey, *Eng. Dict.*, s.v., All goes down Guttur Lane. 1880 : Spurgeon, *Ploughman's Pictures*, 40.

H

Hab or nab. 1542: Udall, tr.
Erasmus' *Apoph.*, 209 (1877), To be
put to the plounge of making or
marring, and of habbe or nhabbe to
wynne all, or to lese all. 1595:
Pedlars Prophecy, l. 1174 (Malone S.),
Sing and be mery, hab or nab; away
the mare. 1693: Urquhart, *Rabelais*,
bk. iii. ch. xliv., The chance and hazard
of a throw of the dice, hab nab, or luck
as it will. 1754: Berthelson, *Eng.-
Danish Dict.*, s.v., 'Tis meer hab-nab
whether it succeeds or not. 1828:
Carr, *Craven Dialect*, i. 204, To obtain
a thing by hab and by nab, i.e. by fair
means or foul. 1886: Elworthy, *West
Som. Word-Book*, 307 (E.D.S.), Hab
or nab=" get or lose "—" hit or miss."

Habit. *See* **Custom.**

Hackney mistress, hackney maid.
1639: Clarke, 217. 1670: Ray, 99.
1732: Fuller, No. 1780. Cf. **Like
mistress like maid.**

Had I fish, is good without mustard.
1639: Clarke, 114. 1670: Ray, 99.

Had I wist, Beware of. *c.* 1400:
Beryn, l. 2348 (E.E.T.S.), But nowe it
is to late to spekc of had-I-wist !
c. 1460: *Good Wyfe wold a Pylgr.*,
l. 120, When dede is doun, hit ys to
lat; be ware of hady-wyst. Before
1529: Skelton, *Mugnyfycence*, l. 213,
Hem, syr, yet beware of Had I wyste !
1587: Greene, in *Works*, iv. 110 (Grosart), But alas, had I wist now comes
too late. 1651: Taylor (Water-Poet),
Epigr., 11, in *Works*, 2nd coll. (Spens.
S.), Beware of, had I wist, before thou
wed. 1732: Fuller, No. 976. 1825:
Brockett, *Gloss. N. Country Words*, 2,
Addiwissen, had I known it. An expression nearly obsolete, though still
retained by some old persons. 1868:
Atkinson, *Cleveland Gloss.*, 577, Had
I wist. Had I known. 1892: Heslop,
Northumb. Words, 7 (E.D.S.), Addiwissen . . . that is, " Had I but known."

Had what he hath not. *See* quot.
1546: Heywood, *Proverbs*, Pt. II.
ch. ix., Ye, (quoth she), who had
that he hath not, woulde Doo that
he dooth not, as olde men haue tolde.
1611: Davies (of Hereford), *Sc. of
Folly*, 47, in *Works*, ii. (Grosart) [as
in 1546].

Haddock to paddock, To bring = To
lose everything. 1546: Heywood, *Proverbs*, Pt. II. ch. x., And thus had he
brought haddocke to paddocke. 1577:
Stanihurst, *Descrip. of Ireland*, fo. 10,
I had been like to haue brought
haddocke to paddocke.

Haddock. *See* **Deaf** (4); and **May,**
E (9).

Haft on an old blade, Fresh. *See* quot.
1877: E. Leigh, *Cheshire Gloss.*, 96,
" Dunna waste a fresh haft on an oud
blade," Don't throw good money after
bad. 1917: Bridge, *Cheshire Proverbs*,
51 [as in 1877].

Hail, *subs.* 1. *Hail brings frost in
the tail.* 1639: Clarke, 197. 1670: Ray,
42. 1825: Hone, *Ev. Day Book*, i. 670.
1893: Inwards, *Weather Lore*, 115.

2. *He skips like hail on a pack-saddle.*
1732: Fuller, No. 2022.

Hail fellow well met. 1519: Horman, *Vulgaria*, fo. 148, He made so
moche of his scrvaunt that he waxed
hayle felowe with hym. *c.* 1550:
Becon, *Catechism, etc.*, 561 (P.S.), They
would be " hail fellow well-met " with
him. *c.* 1630: *Dicke of Devonsh.*, IV.
ii., in Bullen, *Old Plays*, ii. 72, The
hangman and you had bene " hayle
fellow ! well met." 1748: Richardson,
Clarissa, v. 146 (1785), Who, being no
proud woman, is hail fellow, well met,
as the saying is, with all her aunt's
servants. 1838: Carlyle, *Sartor*, bk. i.
ch. x. 1857: Hughes, *Tom Brown*,
Pt. II. ch. iii., The ease with which he
himself became hail - fellow - well - met
with anybody, and blundered into and
out of twenty friendships a half year . . .

Hailer is as bad as the stailer, The =
The receiver is as bad as the thief.
1825: Jennings, *Somersetsh. Words*, 43,

Hence the very common expression, The heeler is as bad as the stealer. 1879: *Folk-Lore Record*, ii. 203, The healer is as bad as the stealer [Corn.]. 1883: Burne, *Shropsh. Folk-Lore*, 588, The heler is as bad as the heaver. 1886: Elworthy, *West Som. Word-Book*, 335 (E.D.S.), Heler . . . one who covers up or conceals—hence . . . in the every-day saying: the heler's so bad as the stealer. 1892: S. Hewett, *Peasant Speech of Devon*, 8.

Hailstorm by day denotes a frost at night, A. 1893: Inwards, *Weather Lore*, 115.

Hair. 1. *A hair of the dog that bit you.* 1546: Heywood, *Proverbs*, Pt. I. ch. xi., I pray the leat me and my felow haue A heare of the dog that bote vs last night—And bitten were we both to the braine aright. 1614: Jonson, *Bart. Fair*, I., 'Twas a hot night with some of us, last night, John: shall we pluck a hair of the same wolf to-day, proctor John? 1674: Head and Kirkman, *Eng. Rogue*, iii. 91, If they, in the morning, did fall to drinking again, taking a hair of the old dog . . . 1717: E. Ward, *Brit. Wonders*, 17, A hair of the same dog next morning, Is best to quench our fev'rish burning. 1817: Scott, *Rob Roy*, ch. xii., He poured out a large bumper of brandy, exhorting me to swallow " a hair of the dog that had bit me." 1841: Dickens, *Barn. Rudge*, ch. lii.

2. *His hair grows through his hood*= He is on the road to ruin. *c.* 1450: in *Reliq. Antiquæ*, ii. 67 (1843), He that lovyth welle to fare, Ever to spend and never spare, But he have the more good, His here wol grow throw his hood. Before 1529: Skelton, *Bowge of Courte*, l. 350, [of Riot] His here was growen thoroweoute his hat. *c.* 1600: Deloney, *Thos. of Reading*, ch. v., Out you durty heeles, you will make your husbands haire grow through his hood I doubt. 1694: Motteux, *Rabelais*, bk. iv. ch. lii., In so much that Snip was condemn'd to make good the stuffs to all his customers; and to this day poor Cabbidge's hair grows through his hood.

3. *More hair than wit*—often with *Bush natural* prefixed. 1546: Heywood, *Proverbs*, Pt. II. ch. vii., Thy tales (quoth he) shew long heare, and short wit, wife. 1589: L. Wright, *Display of Dutie*, 38, According to the old prouerbe, bush naturall, more hayre than wit. 1608: Middleton, *Mad World*, II. i., There's great hope of his wit, his hair's so long a-coming. 1670: Ray, 166, Bush natural, more hair then wit. 1732: Fuller, No. 1025 [as in 1670]. 1880: *N. & Q.*, 6th ser., i. 403, There was formerly a vague notion that abundance of hair denoted a lack of brains, and from this idea arose a proverb, " Bush natural, more hair than wit."

4. *Pull hair and hair and you'll make the carle bald.* 1639: Clarke, 10. 1670: Ray, 134.

Hake. *See* Lose (16).

Haldon, Devon. *See* quots. 1838: Holloway, *Provincialisms*, 147, In Devonshire they say, " When Haledown has a hat, Let Kenton beware of a skatt [shower of rain]." 1850: *N. & Q.*, 1st ser., ii. 511, When Haldon hath a hat, Kenton may beware a skat. 1893: Inwards, *Weather Lore*, 101 [as in 1838].

Halesworth. *See* Beccles.

Half a loaf is better than no bread. 1546: Heywood, *Proverbs*, Pt. I. ch. xi. 1605: Camden, *Remains*, 319 (1870). 1642: D. Rogers, *Naaman*, To Reader, He is a foole who counts not halfe a loafe better then no bread. 1681: A. Behn, *Rover*, Pt. II. II. ii., You know the proverb of the half loaf, Ariadne. *c.* 1720: in *Somers Tracts*, xiii. 824 (1811). 1793: Grose, *Olio*, 123 (2nd ed.). 1857: Hughes, *Tom Brown*, Pt. II. ch. ii., Yes, he's a whole-hog man, is Tom . . . Sooner have no bread any day than half the loaf.

Half an acre is good land. 1659: Howell, 4. 1670: Ray, 99. 1732: Fuller, No. 1782.

Half an egg is better than an empty shell. 1639: Clarke, 86. 1670: Ray, 84. 1732: Fuller, No. 901. 1855: Robinson, *Whitby Gloss.*, 176, Half an egg is better than a team'd [empty] shell.

Half an eye, To see with. 1531 : in *State Papers :* " Henry VIII.," v. 266, As with half an eye ye may perceive. 1584 : B. R., *Euterpe*, 58 (Lang), Whych any man with halfe an eye may easily discerne. *c.* 1660 : Jer. Taylor, in *Works*, ix. 386 (Edinb. ed.), But half an eye may see the different accounts. 1715 : Prior, *Alma*, can. i. 1. 238. 1876 : Blackmore, *Cripps*, ch. xl., Anybody with half an eye could see through that conspiracy.

Half an hour is soon lost at dinner. 1738 : Swift, *Polite Convers.*, Dial. II.

Half an hour past three quarters, and ready to strike again. 1639 : Clarke, 72.

Half an hour's hanging hinders five miles' riding. 1678 : Ray, 150.

Half-baked. *See* quot. 1864 : " Cornish Proverbs," in *N. & Q.*, 3rd ser., vi. 494, He is only half-baked ; he would take a brush more. Cf. **Loaf** (1).

Half-egg, Give him the other, and burst him. 1678 : Ray, 241.

Half hanged. *See* **Ill name.**

Half is better than the whole, The. [πλέον ἥμισυ παντός.—Hesiod, *Works and Days*.] There seems to be an allusion to the saying in the first quotation. 1546 : Heywood, *Proverbs*, Pt. I. ch. xiii., Thats iust, if the halfe shall iudge the whole (quoth I). 1550 : Latimer, *Sermons*, 277 (P.S.), There is a proverb which I read many years ago, *Dimidium plus toto :* " The half sometimes more than the whole." 1726 : tr. Gracian's *Hero*, 4, That seemingly strange paradox of the wise man of Mitilene, That the half is better than the whole. 1782 : T. Twining, in *Twining Fam. Papers*, 104 (1887), The famous saying of old Hesiod, that " half is more than the whole " . . . is to nothing more applicable than to a numerous party.

Half sheweth what the whole meaneth, The. 1546 : Heywood, *Proverbs*, Pt. II. ch. vii., This halfe showth what the hole meaneth. 1633 : Draxe, 79.

Half the truth is often a whole lie. 1875 : A. B. Cheales, *Proverb. Folk-Lore*, 166.

Half the world knows not how the other half lives. 1640 : Herbert, *Jac. Prudentum. c.* 1750 : *Low Life ; or One Half of the World knows not how the Other*

Half Live [title]. 1830 : Marryat, *King's Own*, ch. x. 1925 : C. K. S., in *Sphere*, 27 June, p. 392, col. 3, One half the world, we are told, does not know how the other half lives.

Half warned, half armed. 1546 : Heywood, *Proverbs*, Pt. II. ch. vi. 1605 : Camden, *Remains*, 323 (1870). *c.* 1625 : B. & F., *Women Pleased*, III. iii., Since you're so high and hot, sir, you have half arm'd us. 1659 : Howell, 8.

Halfpenny good silver, To think one's. 1575 : Gascoigne, *Glasse of Govt.*, I. v., I thought my halfpeny good siluer within these few yeares past, and now no man esteemeth me vnlesse it be for counsell. 1586 : Pettie, tr. Guazzo's *Civil Convers.*, fo. 115, Shee hath great cause . . . to thinke her halfe penie better siluer than other womens. 1633 : Draxe, 26, He thinketh his halfpeny good siluer. Cf. **Farthing** ; and **Penny** (26).

Halfpenny. *See* **Hand** (8).

Halgaver Court. *See* quots. 1602 : Carew, *Surv. of Cornwall*, 296 (1811), Hence is sprung the proverb, when we see one slovenly apparelled, to say " He shall be presented in Halgaver Court." 1662 : Fuller, *Worthies* (Cornwall), i. 307 (1840), He is to be summoned before the Mayor of Halgaver. 1790 : Grose, *Prov. Gloss.*, s.v. " Cornwall " [as in 1662]. 1821 : Scott, *Kenilworth*, ch. iv., Depart—vanish—or we'll have you summoned before the Mayor of Halgaver. 1880 : Courtney, *W. Cornwall Words*, xiii. (E.D.S.), To be presented in Halgaver Court.

Halifax. 1. *Go to Halifax.* 1878 : *Folk - Lore Record*, i. 165, We have also the expression, " Go to Halifax." 1920 : L. J. Jennings, *Chestnuts and Small Beer*, 140, I refused to admit that I had made a *faux pas*, and told my critics to go to Halifax.

2. *Gooide brade, etc. See* quot. 1878 : *Folk-Lore Record*, i. 165, A similarity is also said to exist between the local dialect [Halifax] and that of Friesland and the low countries, whence the following distich :—Gooide brade, botter, and cheese, Is gooid Halifax and gooid Friese.

3. *Halifax Law.* *See* quots. 1586:
Leicester, in Motley, *United Neth.*, i.
444 (1860), Under correction, my good
Lord, I have had Halifax law—to be
condemned first and inquired upon
after. 1609: Quoted in *N. & Q.*, 5th
ser., iv. 154, First executing the
prisoner, then enquiring of his demerits,
as men say they doe at Halifax. 1708:
*Hallifax and its Gibbet-Law placed in a
True Light* [title]. 1922: in *N. & Q.*,
12th ser., xi. 102, This was the celebrated Halifax Gibbet Law, which gave
rise to the well-known proverb:—
From Hell, Hull, and Halifax, Good
Lord deliver us [q.v. s.v. "Hell"].

Hallamshire. *When all the world
shall be aloft, Then Hallamshire shall be
God's croft.* 1678: Ray, 340. 1790:
Grose, *Prov. Gloss.*, s.v. "Yorkshire."
1878: *Folk-Lore Record*, i. 166.

Halloo before you are out of the wood.
See Out of the wood.

Hallowmas. *See* Beggar (13).

Halt before a cripple, Don't. *c.* 1374:
Chaucer, *Troylus*, bk. iv. l. 1457, It is
ful hard to halten unespyed Bifore a
crepul, for he can the craft. 1592:
Lyly, *Gallathea*, IV. i., Hee must halt
cunningly that will deceive a cripple.
1630: Jonson, *New Inn*, III. i., It is ill
halting afore cripples. 1653: Urquhart, *Rabelais*, bk. i. ch. xx., Halt not
before the lame. 1732: Fuller, No.
1784, Halt not before a cripple.

Halt before you are lame, You. 1670:
Ray, 179. 1754: Berthelson, *Eng.-
Danish Dict.*, s.v. "Halt."

Halter. 1. *A halter and a rope for
him that will be Pope, Without all right
and reason.* 1659: Howell, 11. 1670:
Ray, 212.

2. *He hath made a halter to hang
himself.* 1639: Clarke, 200.

3. *It is ill talking of a halter in the
house of a man that was hanged.* 1612:
Shelton, *Quixote*, Pt. I. bk. iii. ch. xi.,
One should not make mention of a
rope in one's house that was hanged.
1710: S. Palmer, *Moral Essays on
Proverbs*, 96, Don't talk of a halter in
the company of him whose father was
hang'd. 1814: Scott, *Waverley*, ch.
lxxi., "There were mony good folk

at Derby, and it's ill speaking of
halters," with a sly cast of his eye
toward the Baron.

Halterburn. *See* quot. 1913: E. M.
Wright, *Rustic Speech, etc.*, 123, A
Northumbrian proverbial saying is:
Like the butter of Halterburn, it
would neither rug nor rive [be pulled
nor torn] nor cut with a knife—it was
confounded.

Hambleton-bough. *See* Bayton.

Hamilton. *See* Hood-hill.

Hampshire ground requires every day
of the week a shower of rain, and on
Sunday twain. 1790: Grose, *Prov.
Gloss.*, s.v. "Hants."

Hampshire hog, A = A native of
Hampshire. 1622: Drayton, *Polyol.*,
xxiii., As Hampshire, long for her, hath
had the term of Hogs. 1720: *Vade
Mecum for Maltworms*, Pt. I. 50, Now
to the sign of fish let's jog, There to
find out a Hampshire Hog, A man
whom none can lay a fault on, The
pink of courtesie at Alton. 1910: in
N. & Q., 11th ser., ii. 57, To the
circumstance of this county [Hants]
having been proverbially famous for
its breed of hogs is owing the fact that
a native bears the county nickname of
"Hampshire Hog."

Hand. 1. *A hand like a foot.* 1732:
Fuller, No. 5921, You have made a
hand of it like a foot. 1738: Swift,
Polite Convers., Dial. I., Whoe'er writ
it, writes a hand like a foot.

2. *Don't put or stretch thy hand. See*
Arm (1).

3. *From hand to mouth.* 1605: Sylvester, *Du Bartas*, Week II. Day i.
Pt. 4, l. 122, Living from hand to
mouth, soon satisfi'd. 1631: Brathwait, *Whimzies*, 143 (1859), All the
meanes of his gettings is but from
hand to mouth. 1712: Arbuthnot,
John Bull, Pt. II. ch. iii., He has a
numerous family, and lives from hand
to mouth. 1790: Cowper, *Letter to
Newton*, 5 Feb. 1869: Spurgeon, *John
Ploughman*, ch. xii., His poor creditors
cannot get more than enough to live
from hand to mouth.

4. *Hand over head. c.* 1440: *Bone
Flor.*, 475 (O.), Than they faght hand

ovyr hedd. 1530: Palsgrave, 836,
Hande over heed, confusedly. 1555:
Latimer, *Sermons*, 284 (P.S.), And
again sent other servants to bid
guests to his bridal, hand-over-head,
come who would. 1627: Drayton,
Agincourt, st. 204, Hand over head
pell mell upon them run. 1681: W.
Robertson, *Phraseol. Generalis*, 75, Give
not your almes hand over head; Do
good with discretion. 1769: Bickerstaffe and Foote, *Dr. Last in his Chariot*,
II., Nor endure to see you run hand
over head into all the snares she lays
for you. 1823: D'Israeli, *Cur. of Lit.*,
2nd ser., i. 462 (1824), Among our own
proverbs a remarkable incident has
been commemorated; *Hand over head,
as men took the Covenant!* [D'Israeli
seems to have misunderstood the saying, and taken " hand over head " as
descriptive of a physical attitude. It
simply meant, as the other illustrations
show—hurriedly, confusedly, unthink-
ingly.] 1863: Reade, *Hard Cash*, ch. i.,
He laid out all his powers, and went at
the leading skiffs hand over head.
1886: Elworthy, *West Som. Word-Book*,
316 (E.D.S.), Hand-over-head. In a
reckless thoughtless manner.

5. *The hand that gives gathers.* 1659:
Howell, *Proverbs: Brit.-Eng.*, 34.

6. *Thy hand* [is] *never* [the] *worse for
doing thy own work.* Ibid., 35.

7. *To be hand and glove.* 1678: Ray,
347, They two are hand and glove.
Somerset 1732: Fuller, No. 4960,
They both put their hands in one glove.
1748: Smollett, *Rod. Random*, ch. li.,
Who was hand and glove with a certain
person who ruled the roast. 1824:
Scott, *Redgauntlet*, ch. xii., Poor Harry
Redgauntlet, that suffered at Carlisle,
was hand and glove with me. 1883:
R. L. S., *Treasure I.*, ch. xxxiv., I'm
on your side now, hand and glove.
1922: Weyman, *Ovington's Bank*, ch.
xxxvi., He ought to know. Wasn't
he hand in glove with them?

8. *To have one's hand* (or *heart*) *on
one's halfpenny* = To have an eye to the
main chance, or to any particular
object. 1546: Heywood, *Proverbs*, Pt.
I. ch. vi., So harde is your hande set

on your halfpeny, That my reasonyng
your reason setteth nought by. 1583:
Greene, in *Works*, ii. 45 (Grosart), She
stood as though her heart had bin on
her halfepeny. 1639: Clarke, 231, His
heart is on his halfpenny. 1681: W.
Robertson, *Phraseol. Generalis*, 885,
His mind is on his halfpenny. 1707:
in *Thoresby's Correspondence*, ii. 62
(1832), I quickly found they had their
hand too much upon their halfpenny.
1828: Carr, *Craven Dialect*, i. 216, " To
have his hand on his hawpny," a proverbial phrase for being ever attentive
to his own interest.

**Handful of good life is better than a
bushel of learning, A.** 1640: Herbert,
Jac. Prudentum. 1748: Richardson,
Clarissa, iv. 120 (1785).

**Handful of trade is an handful of gold,
An.** 1732: Fuller, No. 603.

Handle thorns, To. *See* **Thorn** (2).

Handle without mittens, To. 1659:
Howell, *Proverbs: Fr.-Eng.*, 16, They
will not be caught without mittains.
1670: Ray, 216.

**Handsaw is a good thing, but not to
shave with, A.** 1732: Fuller, No. 210.
1880: Spurgeon, *Ploughman's Pictures*,
31.

Handsel. *See* quot. 1867: Harland,
etc., *Lancs Folk-Lore*, 70, Hansell (they
[market folk] say) is always lucky when
well wet. [First money received is spit
upon.]

Handsel Monday. *See* **New Year** (1).

Handsome. 1. *A handsome bodied
man in the face.* 1678: Ray, 73.

2. *A handsome woman.* *See* quot.
1650: Bulwer, *Anthropomet.*, 228, The
vote of the proverb, for a handsome
woman, would have been English to
the neck, French to the waste, and
Dutch below.

3. *Handsome is that handsome does.*
1580: Munday, *Sundry Examples*, 78
(Sh. S.), But as the auncient adage is,
goodly is he that goodly dooth. 1600:
Dekker, *Shoem. Hol.*, II. i., By my
troth, he is a proper man; but he is
proper that proper doth. 1713: Gay,
Wife of Bath, III. i., He is handsome
that handsome does. 1768: Goldsmith, *Vicar*, ch. i. 1826: Lamb, *Pop.*

Fallacies, x. 1829: Cobbett, *Advice to Young Men*, Lett. III., " Handsome is that handsome does," used to say to me an old man, who had marked me out for his not over-handsome daughter.

4. *He that is not handsome at* 20, etc. *See* quots. 1640: Herbert, *Jac. Prudentum*, He that is not handsome at 20, nor strong at 30, nor rich at 40, nor wise at 50, will never be handsome, strong, rich, or wise. 1732: Fuller, No. 2287 [as in 1640, except " wise " for " rich at 40," and " rich " for " wise at 50 "]. 1822: Southey, *Letter to Bedford*, 20 Dec., You know the proverb, that he who is not handsome at twenty, wise at forty, and rich at fifty, will never be rich, wise, or handsome.

5. *You have a handsome head of hair, pray give me a tester* [sixpence]. 1678: Ray, 73.

Handsomest flower is not the sweetest, The. 1855: Bohn, 507.

Hang, *verb.* 1. *As good be hanged. See* Sheep (2).

2. *Better to hang than to hold.* 1639: Clarke, 86. 1685: Meriton, *Yorkshire Ale*, 48, Sike fowkes are fitter to hang than hawd.

3. *Hang him that hath no shifts.* 1639: Clarke, 42. 1670: Ray, 141. 1732: Fuller, No. 1785, Hang him that has no shifts; and hang him that has one too many.

4. *Hang saving. See* quots. c. 1630: *Hang Pinching* [title of ballad], in *Roxb. Ballads*, iii. (B.S.). 1666: Torriano, *Piazza Univ.*, 276, As one would say, Hang pinching, let's be mery. 1738: Swift, *Polite Convers.*, Dial. II., Come, hang saving; bring us up a half-p'orth of cheese.

5. *Hang yourself for a pastime.* 1678: Ray, 73.

6. *He may go hang himself in his own garters.* 1597: Shakespeare, 1 *Henry IV.*, II. ii., Go hang thyself in thine own heir-apparent garters! 1678: Ray, 246.

7. *He was hanged that left his drink behind.* c. 1640: in *Roxb. Ballads*, i. 416 (B.S.), He was hang'd that left his drinke behinde. 1672: *Westm. Drollery*, Pt. II. 86 (Ebsworth), Yet he was bang'd, nay some say hang'd, That

left his drink behind. 1738: Swift, *Polite Convers.*, Dial. II., Stay till this bottle's out; you know, the man was hang'd that left his liquor behind him. 1830: Forby, *Vocab. E. Anglia*, 433, The man was hanged, that left his liquor. *See also* Bawtry.

8. *I have hanged up my hatchet. See* Hatchet.

9. *I'll not hang all my bells on one horse*, i.e. give all to one son. 1659: Howell, 14. 1670: Ray, 215. 1732: Fuller, No. 1786, Hang not all your bells upon one horse. 1913: *Folk-Lore*, xxiv. 77, To put all the bells on one horse [Oxfordsh.].

10. *If I be hanged, I'll choose my gallows.* 1659: Howell, 16. 1670: Ray, 216. 1738: Swift, *Polite Convers.*, Dial. II., If I must be hanged, I won't go far to choose my gallows.

11. *It hangs together as pebbles in a wyth.* 1639: Clarke, 155.

12. *Let him hang by the heels.* Somerset. Said of a man that dies in debt. 1678: Ray, 353.

13. *To hang in the bell-ropes.* c. 1750: in *N. & Q.*, 3rd ser., xii. 91, So what so long has been hanging in the bell-ropes will at last be brought to a happy period. 1867: *N. & Q.*, 3rd ser., xii. 139, This is a common phrase in Cumberland at the present day. A couple are said to be " hingin' i' t' bell reaps " during the period which transpires between the first publication of banns and marriage. . . . In Worcestershire, if marriage does not come off, the deserted one is said to be " hung in the bell ropes." [Also common in Leicestershire.] 1884–6: Holland, *Cheshire Words* (E.D.S.), From the time the banns of a couple are completed asking in church, to the time they marry, they are said to " hing i' th' bell ropes." 1917: Bridge, *Cheshire Proverbs*, 138.

14. *To hang one's ears.* 1670: Ray, 179.

Hanged hay never dōes [fattens] cattle, 1836: Wilbraham, *Cheshire Gloss.*, 33 (2nd ed.). 1917: Bridge, *Cheshire Proverbs*, 64, Hanged hay is hay that has been weighed or hung on the steel-yard [i.e. bought hay].

Hanging. *See* **Marriage** (3).

Hangman is a good trade, A, he doth his work by daylight. 1678 : Ray, 91.

Hangman leades the dance, The. 1615 : Stephens, *Essays, etc.*, bk. ii. No. 28, He [the hangman] hath many dependant followers : for (as the proverb saith) hangman leades the dance.

Hap and a half-penny are world's gear enough. 1639 : Clarke, 126, Hap and half-penny goods enough. 1670 : Ray, 100, [as in 1639, *plus*] i.e. good luck is enough, though a man have not a penny left him. 1846-59 : *Denham Tracts*, i. 296 (F.L.S.). 1907 : *Introd.* to A. Brewer, *Love-Sick King*, in Bang's *Materialien*, B. 18, p. xii [quoted as " a very ancient proverb "].

Hap good hap ill. *c.* 1489 : Caxton, *Sonnes of Aymon*, 332 (E.E.T.S.), " I care not," sayd Rychard, " hap as it hap wyll." 1530 : Palsgrave, 578, Happe what happe shal. 1587 : Greene, in *Works*, iv. 149 (Grosart), He was so puffed vp with wrath and choller, as hap what hap would, he fell into these tearmes. 1599 : Breton, in *Works*, ii. *c* 7 (Grosart), Therefore hap good, or hap ill, I will walke on still.

Happeth in one hour, It, that happeth not in seven years. Before 1500 : in Hill, *Commonplace-Book*, 128 (E.E.T.S.), Hit fallith in a dai, that fallith not all the iere after. 1546 : Heywood, *Proverbs*, Pt. I. ch. xi. 1606 : T. Heywood, *If You Know Not Me*, Pt. II., in *Dram. Works*, i. 327 (1874), They say, that may happen in one hour that happens not againe in 7 yeare. 1681 : W. Robertson, *Phraseol. Generalis*, 322, It chances in an hour, that happens not in seven years. 1732 : Fuller, No. 2836, It happens in an hour that comes not in an age. 1846 : Denham, *Proverbs*, 6 (Percy S.) [as in 1681].

Happy as a king, or, earlier, **Merry as a king.** *c.* 1554 : *Enterlude of Youth*, in Bang, *Materialien*, B. 12, p. 8, I wyll make as mery as a kynge. 1595 : Peele, *Old Wiues Tale*, sig. A3, This Smith leads a life as merrie as a king. 1618 : B. Holyday, *Technogamia*, III. v., Be as merry as a king. 1661 : *Trag. Hist. of Guy, E. of Warwick*, V., . . . have

thought ourselves as happy as a king. 1781 : D'Arblay, *Diary*, i. 359 (1876), Who again stayed dinner, and was as happy as a prince. 1861 : Dickens, *Great Expect.*, ch. xxxvii., Only tip him a nod every now and then . . . and he'll be as happy as a king.

Happy as the day is long. 1631 : Mabbe, *Celestina*, 54 (T.T.), Even as merry as the day is long. 1772 : Graves, *Spirit. Quixote*, bk. xi. ch. viii., They were married in a fortnight's time ; and are now as happy as the day is long. 1851 : Borrow, *Lavengro*, iii. 12, I sat there hard at work, happy as the day's long. 1889 : Nicholson, *Folk Speech E. Yorks*, 19, As happy as days is long.

Happy as the parson's wife during her husband's life. Query meaning. 1663 : Killigrew, *Parson's Wedding*, I. i. [cited as a proverb].

Happy is he that chastens himself. 1640 : Herbert, *Jac. Prudentum.*

Happy is he that is happy in his children. 1732 : Fuller, No. 1787.

Happy is he who knows his follies in his youth. 1659 : Howell, 3. 1670 : Ray, 12. 1748 : Richardson, *Clarissa*, iv. 121 (1785) [with " the man " for " he "].

Happy is he whose friends were born before him. 1670 : Ray, 99. 1732 : Fuller, No. 1790.

Happy is the bride the sun shines on, and happy the corpse the rain rains on. 1607 : *The Puritan*, I. i., If blessed be the corse the rain rains upon, he had it pouring down. 1632 : Randolph, *Jealous Lovers*, V. iii., A fair sun Shine on the happy bridegroom. 1827 : Hone, *Table-Book*, 667, Blessed is the corpse that rain falls on. Blessed is the bride that the sun shines on. 1859 : E. Peacock, in *N. & Q.*, 2nd ser., viii. 319, A superstition prevalent in many parts of Britain . . . Happy is the wedding that the sun shines on ; Blessed is the corpse that the rain rains on. Otherwise thus :—Sad is the burying in the sun shine ; But blessed is the corpse that goeth home in rain. 1879 : Henderson, *Folk-Lore of N. Counties*, 34, Here, in fact, as all Christendom over—Blest is

the bride that the sun shines on ! 1922 :
Lucas, *Genevra's Money*, 4, " Happy,"
said some foolish proverbialist, " are
the dead that the rain rains on."

**Happy is the child whose father goes
to the devil.** 1549 : Latimer, *Third Sermon*, 97 (Arber) [cited as " the old
sayinge "]. 1590 : Greene, in *Works*,
vii. 235 (Grosart). 1593 : Shakespeare,
3 *Henry VI.*, II. ii., And happy always
was it for that son Whose father for his
hoarding went to hell. 1655 : Howell,
Letters, bk. iv. No. ix. [cited as " the
City proverb "]. 1708 : tr. Aleman's
Guzman, i. 405. 1827 : Hone, *Table-
Book*, 430.

Happy man happy dole. 1546 : Heywood, *Proverbs*, Pt. I. ch. iii. 1660 :
Tatham, *The Rump*, I., A short life and
a merry life, I cry. Happy man be his
dole. 1671 : Crowne, *Juliana*, I. i.,
Here's five thousand crowns bid for his
head, Happy man be his dole that
catches him. 1796 : White, *Falstaff's
Letters*, Preface, A man renown'd among
his cotemporaries, famous through succeeding centuries, happy be his dole.
1840 : Barham, *Ing. Legends:* " Leech
of Folkestone," par. 1, These are
genuine and undoubted marks of
possession ; and if you never experienced any of them,—why, " happy
man be his dole ! " 1924 : *Punch*, 28
May, p. 573, col. 3, " The Unemployment Committee are compiling an
insular register of persons likely to
desire unemployment at the end of
the summer season." *Manx Paper*.
Hence the expression, " Happy Man
be his dole ! "

Happy than wise, Better be. *c.* 1594 :
Bacon, *Promus*, No. 970. 1605 : Cam-
den, *Remains*, 319 (1870). 1736 : Bailey,
Dict., s.v. " Better."

**Happy that knoweth not himself
happy, He is not.** 1539 : Taverner,
Proverbs, fo. 51. 1586 : Pettie, tr.
Guazzo's *Civil Convers.*, fo. 58. 1732 :
Fuller, No. 1918, He is happy that
knoweth not himself to be otherwise.

Happy the wooing. *See* **Wooing.**

Harborne. *See* quot. 1894 : Northall,
Folk Phrases, 16 (E.D.S.), Hungry
Harborne, poor and proud. *Staffs.*

Harborough Field. 1. *A goose will
eat all the grass that grows in Harborough
Field.* 1622 : W. Burton, *Descrip. of
Leics.*, 128. 1895 : Billson, *Co. Folk-
Lore: Leics.*, 151 (F.L.S.).

2. *I'll throw you into Harborough
Field.* 1678 : Ray, 317. 1790 : Grose,
Prov. Gloss., s.v. " Leicestershire."

Hard, *adj.* 1. *A hard beginning hath
a good ending.* 1546 : Heywood, *Proverbs*, Pt. I. ch. iv.; A hard beginnyng
makth a good endyng. 1605 : Camden,
Remains, 317 (1870). 1659 : Howell, 7.

2. *A hard thing it is. See* quot. 15th
cent. : in *Reliq. Antiquæ*, i. 205 (1841),
A harde thynge hit is, y-wys, To deme
a thynge that unknowen is.

3. *As hard as a flint* (or *stone*).
c. 1440 : Lydgate, *Fall of Princes*,
bk. iii. l. 63 (E.E.T.S.), But, hard as
ston, Pierides and Meduse. *c.* 1489 :
Caxton, *Sonnes of Aymon*, 347
(E.E.T.S.), A lord that hath no pite
in him, hath a hert as harde as a stone.
c. 1510 : A. Barclay, *Egloges*, 18 (Spens.
S.), Thy bread is . . . harde as a flint.
1587 : Churchyard, *Worth. of Wales*, 104
(Spens. S.), A mightie cragge, as hard
as flint or steele. 1675 : *Poor Robin
Alman.*, May, A heart as hard as flint.
1720 : Gay, *Poems*, ii. 278 (Underhill),
Hard is her heart as flint or stone.
1789 : Boswell, *Letters*, ii. 364 (Tinker),
I should have a heart as hard as a
stone were I to remain here. 1823 :
Scott, *St. Ronan's*, ch. xxii., A selfish,
spiteful heart, that is as hard as a
flint. 1908 : Hudson, *Land's End*,
ch. xv., It was not ice but something
as hard as stone.

4. *As hard as a north toad*=tod=fox.
1917 : Bridge, *Cheshire Proverbs*, 14.

5. *As hard as brazil.* 1867 : Waugh,
Owd Bl., 85, " Aw'm as hard as brazill,"
said Tip. 1879 : Jackson, *Shropsh.
Word-Book*, 48, Brazil [Iron pyrites] is
so extremely hard as to have given rise
to a common proverbial saying, " As
hard as brazil." 1917 : Bridge, *Cheshire
Proverbs*, 15, As hard as brazzil.

6. *As hard as horn* (or *bone*). *c.* 1420 :
Lydgate, *Assem. of Gods*, st. 89, p. 19
(E.E.T.S.), Hard as any horn. 1545 :
Ascham, *Toxoph.*, 113 (Arber), This

wood is as harde as horne and very fit
for shaftes. 1631 : Brathwait, *Eng.
Gentlewoman*, 196 (1641), . . . was found
to have her elbowes as hard as horne.
1670 : Ray, 202. 1824 : in Lockhart's
Scott, v. 326, The remainder of the wood
was as hard as a bone.

7. *As hard as nails.* 1838 : Dickens,
Twist, ch. ix., " Hard," replied the
Dodger. " As nails," added Charley
Bates. 1896 : Shaw, *You Never Can
Tell*, I., My landlord is as rich as a Jew
and as hard as nails. 1922 : Weyman,
Ovington's Bank, ch. xxxv., Hard and
sharp as nails ! I take off my hat to
him !

8. *Hard fare makes hungry bellies.*
1616 : Breton, in *Works*, ii. *e* 6 (Grosart),
Hard fare makes hungry stomackes.
1670 : Ray, 100. 1732 : Fuller, No. 1796.

9. *Hard winter. See* **Dog** (57); and
Wolf (6).

10. *Hard with hard never made good
wall.* 1578 : Florio, *First Fruites*, fo.
29. 1655 : Fuller, *Church Hist.*, bk. ii.
§ ii. (69), " Hard with hard," saith the
proverb, " makes no wall." 1732 :
Fuller, No. 1797, Hard with hard makes
not the stone wall.

11. *It is hard for any man all faults
to mend.* 1546 : Heywood, *Proverbs*,
Pt. I. ch. xi. 1611 : Davies (of Hereford), *Sc. of Folly*, 49, in *Works*, ii.
(Grosart).

12. *It is hard to be high and humble.*
1732 : Fuller, No. 2948.

13. *It is hard to be wretched, but worse
to be known so.* 1640 : Herbert, *Jac.
Prudentum.*

14. *It is hard to carry a full cup
without spilling.* 1875 : A. B. Cheales,
Proverb. Folk-Lore, 117.

15. *It is hard to make a good web of
a bottle of hay.* 1670 : Ray, 154. 1732 :
Fuller, No. 2950.

16. *It is as hard to please a knave as a
knight.* 1639 : Clarke, 275. 1670 : Ray,
111. 1732 : Fuller, No. 2907.

17. *It is hard to please all.* c. 1430 :
Lydgate, *Minor Poems*, 60 (Percy S.),
To please al folk it is ful hard. 1519 :
Horman, *Vulgaria*, fo. 93, It is harde
to content all menys myndis.

18. *It is hard to sail over the sea in an*

egg-shell. 1639 : Clarke, 5. 1670 : Ray,
139. 1732 : Fuller, No. 2906. 1880 :
Spurgeon, *Ploughman's Pictures*, 20.

19. *It is hard to shave an egg.* 1639 :
Clarke, 243. 1732 : Fuller, No: 2952.
1869 : Spurgeon, *John Ploughman*,
ch. xii.

20. *It is hard to sup and blow with one
breath.* 1672 : Walker, *Parœm.*, 8 [with
" a wind " for " one breath "]. 1681 :
W. Robertson, *Phraseol. Generalis*, 1190.
1736 : Bailey, *Dict.*, s.v. " Sup," 'Tis
hard to sup and blow at the same time.
Cf. **Whistle**.

21. *Set hard heart against hard hap.*
1639 : Clarke, 15. 1670 : Ray, 100.
1732 : Fuller, No. 4108.

22. *The hard gives no more than he
that hath nothing.* 1640 : Herbert, *Jac.
Prudentum* [with omission of " no "].
1670 : Ray, 12.

**Hard-fought field where none escapes,
It is a.** 1546 : Heywood, *Proverbs*,
Pt. I. ch. xi., A hard foughten feeld
where no man skapth vnkyld. 1670 :
Ray, 59, It's a hard battel where none
escapes. 1732 : Fuller, No. 2861.

**Hard-hearted as a Scot of Scotland,
As.** 1678 : Ray, 285.

**Hardly attained, Things, are long
retained.** 1639 : Clarke, 101. 1670 :
Ray, 12. 1754 : Berthelson, *Eng.-
Danish Dict.*, s.v. " Hardly."

**Hardwick Hall, More window than
wall.** Derby. 1884 : *Folk-Lore
Journal*, ii. 279.

Hare and Hares. 1. *Hare is melancholy meat.* 1558 : Bullein, *Govt. of
Health*, fo. 90, The fleshe of hares be
hoote and drye, ingenderers of melan-
cholye. 1666 : Torriano, *Piazza Univ.*,
133, A hare being a melancholy meat.
1738 : Swift, *Polite Convers.*, Dial. II.,
They say [hare] 'tis melancholy meat.
Cf. No. 3.

2. *Hares may pull dead lions by the
beard.* 1586 : Pettie, tr. Guazzo's *Civil
Convers.*, fo. 31, Of these this saying
rose, That the lion being dead, the verie
hares triumph ouer him. 1593 : Nashe,
in *Works*, ii. 198 (Grosart), Strike a man
when he is dead? So hares may pull
dead lions by the beards. 1596 : Shakespeare, *King John*, II. i., You are the

hare of whom the proverb goes, Whose valour plucks dead lions by the beard. 1639 : Clarke, 216.

3. *He hath devoured a hare.* 1600 : W. Vaughan, *Directions for Health*, 17, Hare . . . maketh a man to look amiably, according to the prouerb : He hath deuoured a hare. But it is vnwholesome for lazie and melancholick men. Cf. No. 1.

4. *He that hunts two hares loses both.* 1578 : Florio, *First Fruites*, fo. 28, Who hunteth two hares, loseth the one and leaueth the other. 1630 : T. Adams, *Works*, 232, The hound that follows two hares, will catch neither. 1640 : Shirley, *Opportunity*, III. iii. 1732 : Fuller, No. 2782, If you run after two hares, you will catch neither. 1880 : Spurgeon, *Ploughman's Pictures*, 24, We shall be like the man who hunted many hares at once and caught none.

5. *If a man wants a hare for his breakfast* (or *dinner*) *he must hunt overnight.* 1605 : Camden, *Remains*, 323 (1870), He that will have a hare to breakfast must hunt overnight. 1670 : Ray, 13 [as in 1605]. 1732 : Fuller, No. 2365 [as in 1605]. 1846–59 : *Denham Tracts*, ii. 107 (F.L.S.) [as in 1605]. 1883 : Burne, *Shropsh. Folk-Lore*, 589, If a man wants a hare for his Sunday dinner, he had best catch it over night.

6. *It's either a hare or a brake-bush.* 1659 : T. Pecke, *Parnassi Puerp.*, 143, He can't discern a hare from a brake-bush. 1670 : Ray, 179, It's either a hare or a brake - bush. Πλοῖον ἤ κυνῆ. Aut navis aut galerus. Something if you knew what.

7. *Little dogs start the hare but great ones catch it.* 1640 : Herbert, *Jac. Prudentum.* 1670 : Ray, 16. 1732 : Fuller, No. 3254. 1846–59 : *Denham Tracts*, ii. 108 (F.L.S.).

8. *The hare starts when a man least expects it.* *c.* 1384 : Chaucer, *H. Fame*, bk. ii. l. 173, That been betid, no man wot why, But as a blind man stert an hare. 1712 : Motteux, *Quixote*, Pt. II. ch. xxx., But, where we least think, there starts the hare. 1869 : Spurgeon, *John Ploughman*, ch. x., For hares pop

out of the ditch just when you are not looking for them. Cf. No. 9.

9. *There goes the hare away.* *c.* 1500 : Medwall, *Nature*, Pt. II. l. 589 (Brandl, *Quellen*, 134), There went the hare away. Before 1529 : Skelton, *Works*, ii. 30 (Dyce) [as in 1500]. 1594 : Kyd, *Span. Tragedy*, sig. G3 (1618), There goes the hare away. 1670 : Ray, 100, Where we least think, there goeth the hare away. 1846–59 : *Denham Tracts*, ii. 108 (F.L.S.), There goes the hare away. Cf. No. 8.

10. *'Tis as hard to find a hare without a muse, as a woman* (or *knave*) *without a 'scuse.* 1576 : Pettie, *Petite Pall.*, ii. 157 (Gollancz), We ourselves have a common saying amongst us, that women are never without an excuse. 1592 : Greene, in *Works*, x. 217 (Grosart) [" woman "]. 1659 : Howell, 12, Take a hare without a muse, and a knave without an excuse, and hang them up. 1732 : Fuller, No. 6081, Find you without excuse, And find an hare without a muse. 1913 : E. M. Wright, *Rustic Speech, etc.*, 102, The old English proverbial saying :— [as in 1659].

11. *To catch* (or *hunt*) *the hare with a taber* [drum]. 1399 : Langland, *Rich. the Redeless*, i. 58, Men my3tten as well haue huntyd an hare with a tabre. 1546 : Heywood, *Proverbs*, Pt. I. ch. ix. 1579 : Lyly, *Euphues*, 44 (Arber), You shal assoone catch a hare with a taber. 1611 : Cotgrave, s.v. " Lievre," Hares are not to be caught by drumming. 1642 : D. Rogers, *Naaman*, sig. S5 [as in 1579]. 1732 : Fuller, No. 1341, Drumming is not the way to catch an hare. 1901 : F. E. Taylor, *Lancs Sayings*, 23, Yo' met as weel try for t' catch a hare wi' thumpin' on a drum. Cf. No. 12.

12. *To fright the hare is not the way to catch her.* 1846–59 : *Denham Tracts*, ii. 108 (F.L.S.). Cf. No. 11.

13. *To know both hare and hare-gate.* 1882 : Nodal and Milner, *Lancs Gloss.*, 154 (E.D.S.), " He knows both th' hare an' th' hare-gate," i.e. he knows both the hare, and the way the hare runs.

14. *To run with the hare.* See **Run** (18).

15. *To seek a hare in a hen's nest.*
1599 : Porter, *Two Angry Women*, in
Hazlitt, *Old Plays*, vii. 355, He is gone
to seek a hare in a hen's nest, a needle
in a bottle of hay.

16. *To set the hare's head against the
goose giblets.* 1546 : Heywood, *Proverbs*, Pt. II. ch. iv. 1607 : Dekker,
etc., *Westw. Hoe*, V. 1618 : Field,
Amends for Ladies, I. 1670 : Ray, 179.
1732 : Fuller, No. 4109.

See also Blind,¯ *adj.* (7) ; Cow (32) ;
Dog (36), (77), and (78) ; Kiss, *verb* (13) ;
Run (18) ; and We dogs.

Harlow Hill. *See* Heddon.

Harm watch harm catch. 1481 :
Caxton, *Reynard*, 50 (Arber), Yf he wil
seche harm he shal fynde harme. 1614 :
Jonson, *Bart. Fair*, V. iii. 1721 :
Bailey, *Eng. Dict.*, s.v. 1826–44 : Hood,
Comic Poems : " Hints to Paul Pry,"
Harm-watching, harm thou still dost
catch—That rule should save thee
many a sore.

Harms the good, He. *See* Evil,
subs. (4).

Harp and harrow, To agree like.
1559 : Becon, *Prayers, etc.*, 283 (P.S.),
Agree together like God and the devil
. . . as the common proverb is, " Like
harp and harrow." 1589 : L. Wright,
Display of Dutie, 24, Agreeing like
harpe and harrowe. 1659 : Howell, 12
(10), They agree like harp and harrow.
Before 1704 : T. Brown, *Works*, iii. 29
(1760), Whether the name and thing
be not as disagreeable as harp and
harrow?

Harp on a string, To (or on the same
string). [Cantilenam eandem canere.—
Terence, *Phorm.*, III. ii. 10. Chorda
qui semper oberrat eadem.—Horace,
Ars Poetica, 356.] *c.* 1513 : More, *Works*,
p. 49, col. 2 (1557), He should harp no
more vpon that string. 1594 : Shakespeare, *Rich. III.*, IV. iv., Harp not on
that string, madam ; that is past. 1644 :
Quarles, in *Works*, i. 176 (Grosart),
Doctor, you still harp upon the same
string. 1753 : Richardson, *Grandison*,
i. 478 (1883), The poor girl has been
harping upon this string ever since you
have been gone. 1821 : Scott, in Lockhart's *Life*, v. 72, All this is extremely

like prosing, so I will harp on that
string no longer.

**Harp on the string that gives no
melody, To.** 1546 : Heywood, *Proverbs*,
Pt. II. ch. iv. 1633 : Draxe, 222, Hee
harpeth on that string that will make
no good musicke.

Harrow: the visible church. 1725 :
Defoe, *Tour*, ii. 20, They tell us King
Charles II. . . . us'd to say of it [Har-
row church] that if there was e'er a
visible church upon earth, he believed
this was one. 1790 : Grose, *Prov.
Gloss.*, s.v. " Middx." The visible
church ; i.e. Harrow on the Hill.

**Harrow (or Rake) hell and scum the
devil.** 1670 : Ray, 180. 1732 : Fuller,
No. 1798, Harrow hell, and rake up
the devil.

Harry Sophister. *See* Henry Sophister.

**Harry's children of Leigh, never an
one like another.** Cheshire. 1670 : Ray,
217. 1917 : Bridge, *Cheshire Proverbs*, 63.

Hartland Light. *See* Padstow Point.

Hartlepool. *Like the Mayor of
Hartlepool, you cannot do that.* 1678 :
Ray, 317. 1790 : Grose, *Prov. Gloss.*,
s.v. " Leicestershire." 1846–59 : *Denham Tracts*, i. 55 (F.L.S.), . . . The sense
of this saying is, you cannot work
impossibilities. A certain mayor of
this (at that time) poor but ancient
corporation, desirous to show his old
companions that he was not too much
elated by his high office, told them that,
though he was Mayor of Hart-le-pool,
he was still but a man ! there being many
things he could not do.

Harvest. 1. *A fine harvest a wet
hopping.* Kent. 1887 : Parish and Shaw,
Dict. Kent. Dialect, 78 (E.D.S.).

2. *Harvest comes not every day, tho' it
come every year.* 1732 : Fuller, No.
1799.

3. *Harvest ears, thick of hearing.*
1546 : Heywood, *Proverbs*, Pt. II.
ch. ix., You had on your haruest eares,
thicke of hearyng. *c.* 1594 : Bacon,
Promus, No. 674, Harvest ears. 1681 :
W. Robertson, *Phraseol. Generalis*, 715,
You hearken not at all ; you have
on your harvest ears. 1854 : Baker,
Northants Gloss., s.v., You've got your
harvest ears on, I can't make you hear.

4. *Harvest will come, and then every farmer's rich.* 1732 : Fuller, No. 1800.

5. *Short harvests make short addlings* [earnings]. 1846 : Denham, *Proverbs*, 54 (Percy S.). 1893 : Inwards, *Weather Lore*, 8.

6. *The harvest moon.* 1812 : Brady, *Clavis Cal.*, i. 55, The Harvest-moon is also used to denote that month in which harvest is usually collected. 1923 : *Observer*, 23 Sept., p. 14, col. 1, The feature that distinguishes it from other full moons, and has earned for it the name of harvest moon, is the short interval that separates two successive risings.

7. *To make a long harvest of a little corn.* 1546 : Heywood, *Proverbs*, Pt. I. ch. xii., Ye haue . . . Made a long haruest for a little corne. 1587 : Greene, in *Works*, v. 208 (Grosart), I will not make a long haruest for a small crop. 1604 : Breton, in *Works*, ii. *k* 12 (Grosart), Yee two . . . haue made a long haruest of a little corne, and haue spent a great deale of money about a little matter. 1681 : W. Robertson, *Phraseol. Generalis*, 1207, Not to make a long harvest of so little corn ; not to be tedious in a trifle. 1748 : Richardson, *Clarissa*, iv. 175 (1785), But why . . . should I make so long a harvest of so little corn? 1893 : Inwards, *Weather Lore*, 8, A long harvest, a little corn.

8. *When harvest flies hum, Warm weather to come.* 1893 : Ibid., 148.

See also Christmas (2), (3), and (6); Good harvest; Ill sowers; and May, C, and E (2).

Harwich. *See* Deal.

Haste, *subs.* 1. *Haste and wisdom are things far odd.* 1546 : Heywood, *Proverbs*, Pt. I. ch. ii.

2. *Haste comes not alone.* 1611 : Cotgrave, s.v. " Haste," Haste never comes alone, viz. hath ever some trouble or other t'accompany it. 1640 : Herbert, *Jac. Prudentum.*

3. *Haste makes waste.* 1546 : Heywood, *Proverbs*, Pt. I. ch. ii. 1583 : Greene, in *Works*, ii. 28 (Grosart). 1663 : Butler, *Hudibras*, Pt. I. can. iii. l. 1254. 1678 : Ray, 151, Haste makes

waste, and waste makes want, and want makes strife between the good man and his wife. 1864 : " Cornish Proverbs," in *N. & Q.*, 3rd ser., vi. 495, Haste makes waste, and waste makes a rich man poor.

4. *Haste often rues.* c. 1280 : *Prov. of Hendyng*, l. 256, Ofte rap reweth. c. 1386 : Chaucer, *Melibeus*, § 11, The commune proverbe seith thus : " he that sone demeth, sone shall repente." 1477 : Rivers, *Dictes, etc.*, 62 (1877), Hastynesse engendreth repentaunce. c. 1580 : Spelman, *Dialogue*, 2 (Roxb. Cl.), Thinges dunne in haste bringeth spedye repentance.

5. *Haste trips up its own heels.* 1732 : Fuller, No. 1801. 1869 : Spurgeon, *John Ploughman*, ch. xix.

6. *Make no more haste when you come down than when you went up.* 1604 : *Pasquils Jests*, 42 (1864), Take heed that you never get faster downe then you go up. 1678 : Ray, 151, . . . as the man said to him on the tree top. 1692 : L'Estrange, *Æsop*, 337 (3rd ed.), You must take care for the future, whenever you climb another tree ; that you come no faster down than you went up.

7. *There is no haste to hang true men.* c. 1550 : *Jacke Juggeler*, in Hazlitt, *Old Plays*, ii. 120, I fear hanging, whereunto no man is hasty. 1599 : Porter, *Two Angry Women*, in Ibid., vii. 301, There's no haste to hang true [honest] men. 1670 : Ray, 101. *See also* No haste.

Haste, *verb.* *He hasteth well that wisely can abide.* c. 1374 : Chaucer, *Troylus*, bk. i. l. 956. c. 1386 : Chaucer, *Melibeus*, § 13. c. 1430 : Lydgate, *Minor Poems*, 121 (Percy S.).

Hastings, He is none of the. *See* quots. 1546 : Heywood, *Proverbs*, Pt. I. ch. xi., Ye make such tastingis, As approue you to be none of the hastingis. 1577 : *Misogonus*, I. iv., Youil come when yow list, sir . . . yow are none of ye hastlinges. 1658 : Flecknoe, *Enigm. Characters*, 124, A low spirited man . . . he is none of the Hastings'es. 1662 : Fuller, *Worthies*, iii. 243 (1840), Now men commonly say, They are none of the Hastings, who being slow and slack, go about business with no agility. 1681 : W. Robertson, *Phraseol. Generalis*, 1114, You are none of the Hastings; you'll not break your shins for hast. 1790 : Grose, *Prov. Gloss.*, s.v. " Sussex."

Hasty bitch bringeth forth blind whelps, The. [Festinatio improvida est, et caeca.—Livy, xxii. 39.] 1556 : R. Robinson, tr. More's *Utopia*, 2nd ed., To Reader, 19 (Arber), But as the latin prouerbe sayeth : The hastye bitche bringeth furth blind whelpes. For when this my worke was finished, the rudenes therof shewed it to be done in poste haste. 1559 : Bercher, *Nobil. of Women*, 97 (Roxb. Cl.). 1642 : D. Rogers, *Matrim. Honour*, 234, They perceive their haste to have brought foorth blind whelpes. 1681 : W. Robertson, *Phraseol. Generalis*, 705.

Hasty climbers have sudden falls. c. 1480 : *Digby Plays*, 154 (E.E.T.S.), Who clymyth high, his ffalle grett is. 1592 : Greene, in *Works*, xii. 158 (Grosart), Hee foreseath not that such as clime hastely fall sodainely 1616 : Breton, in *Works*, ii. e 9 (Grosart). 1754 : Berthelson, *Eng.-Danish Dict.*, s.v. " Climber." 1869 : Spurgeon, *John Ploughman*, ch. xix.

Hasty gamesters oversee themselves. 1678 : Ray, 151 [without " themselves "]. 1732 : Fuller, No. 1803.

Hasty glory goes out in a snuff. Ibid., No. 1804.

Hasty love. *See* Soon hot.

Hasty (or Angry) man never wants woe, The. c. 1374 : Chaucer, *Troylus*, bk. iv. l. 1568, For hasty man ne wanteth never care. 1449 : Metham, *Works*, 36 (E.E.T.S.), Trwe that prouerbe than preuyd so, That ouer-hasty man wantyd neuer woo. 1587 : Greene, in *Works*, iv. 77 (Grosart). 1605 : Chapman, etc., *Eastw. Hoe*, V. i., " The hastie person never wants woe," they say. 1712 : *Spectator*, No. 438, You are of an impatient spirit, and an impatient spirit is never without woe. 1875 : A. B. Cheales, *Proverb. Folk-Lore*, 106. Cf. **Choleric** (3).

Hasty meeting, a hasty parting, A. 1736 : Bailey, *Dict.*, s.v. " Woo."

Hasty people will never make good midwives. 1659 : Howell, 3. 1670 : Ray, 101.

Hasty to outbid another, Be not too. 1670 : Ray, 3. 1732 : Fuller, No. 853.

Hat is not made for one shower, A. 1640 : Herbert, *Jac. Prudentum*.

Hat on the wind's side, Pull down your. 1640 : Ibid. 1670 : Ray, 29. 1732 : Fuller, No. 3978 [with " windy " for " wind's "].

Hatch before the door, It is good to have a=to keep silence. 1546 : Heywood, *Proverbs*, Pt. I. ch. xi. 1607 : Deloney, *Strange Histories*, 70 (Percy S.), A wise man, then, sets hatch before the dore, And, whilst he may, doth square his speech with heed. 1670 : Ray, 101. 1732 : Fuller, No. 2941.

Hatchet, To hang up (or bury) the. Before 1327 : *Pol. Songs*, 223 (Camden) (O.), Hang up thyn hachet ant thi knyf. c. 1440 : Hoccleve, *Minor Poems*, 136 (E.E.T.S.), Hange vp his hachet and sette him adoun. 1546 : Heywood, *Proverbs*, Pt. I. ch. xi., I haue hangd vp my hatchet, God speede him well! 1659 : Howell, 6, I have hang'd up my hatchet and scap'd my self. 1794 : Wolcot, *Works*, iv. 485 (1796), Gentle Reader, wouldst thou not have imagined that the war hatchet was buried for ever? 1897 : W. E. Norris, *Clarissa Furiosa*, ch. xliii., She neither affirmed nor denied that she and her husband had buried the hatchet.

Hate, *verb.* 1. *He that hates woman sucked a sow.* 1667 : L'Estrange, *Quevedo's Visions*, 144 (1904), " My officious friend," said I, " he that does not love a woman sucked a sow." 1732 : Fuller, No. 2083 [as in 1667]. 1738 : Swift, *Polite Convers.*, Dial. I.

2. *If you hate a man, eat his bread ; and if you love him, do the same.* 1732 : Fuller, No. 2756.

Hatfield, Yorks. *See* quot. 1878 : *Folk-Lore Record*, i. 173, There are no rats at Hatfield, nor sparrows at Lindholme.

Hatherleigh, Devon. *See* quot. 1869 : Hazlitt, 382, The people are poor at Hatherleigh moor, and so they have been, for ever and ever.

Hatred is blind as well as love. 1732:
Fuller, No. 1805.

Hatred with friends is succour to foes.
1578: Florio, *First Fruites*, fo. 33,
Hatred among friendes is succour vnto
strangers. 1633: Draxe, 30.

Have a little. *See* quot. 1917:
Bridge, *Cheshire Proverbs*, 64, Have a
little, give a little, let neighbour lick
the mundle [piece of wood for stirring
porridge, cream, etc.] [=Charity begins
at home].

Have all, He that will, loseth all.
1481: Caxton, *Reynard*, 95 (Arber), It
falleth ofte who that wold haue all
leseth alle Ouer couetous was neuer
good. 1629: *Book of Meery Riddles*,
Prov. 87. Cf. All covet.

Have among you blind harpers! 1546:
Heywood, *Proverbs*, Pt. II. ch. vii. 1593:
G. Harvey, *Works*, ii. 123 (Grosart),
But now there is no remedie, haue
amongest you, blind harpers of the
printing house. *c.* 1663: Davenant,
Play-House to be Let, V., Have w'ee
[with you], quoth the blind harper,
When he wisht to be as little seen as
he saw others. 1785: Grose, *Class.
Dict. Vulgar Tongue*, s.v. "Harp,"
Have among you, my blind harpers,
an expression used in throwing or
shooting at random among a crowd.

Have at it, and have it. 1852: Fitz-
Gerald, *Polonius*, 123 (1903).

Have in a string, To. 1580: Lyly,
Euphues, 319 (Arber), Thou hast not
loue in a string, affection is not thy
slaue. 1631: Shirley, *Love Tricks*, I.,
They have their conscience in a string,
and can stifle it at their pleasure. 1693:
Dryden, *Juvenal*, Sat. III. l. 72, Since
such as they have fortune in a string.
1748: Richardson, *Clarissa*, v. 33
(1785), Led us both on—like fools, like
tame fools, in a string.

Have one in the wind, To. 1546:
Heywood, *Proverbs*, Pt. I. ch. xi.,
I smelde hir out, and had hir streight
in the wynde. 1587: Churchyard,
Worth. of Wales, 26 (Spens. S.), That
hardly we shall haue them in the winde,
To smell them forth. 1670: Ray, 199.

Hawk and Hawks. 1. *Between hawk
and buzzard.* 1639: Clarke, 70. 1670:
Ray, 164. 1692: L'Estrange, *Æsop*,
318 (3rd ed.), A fantastical levity that
holds us off and on, betwixt hawk and
buzzard, as we say, to keep us from
bringing the matter in question to a
final issue. 1745: *Agreeable Companion*,
56, At which, the priest, being driven
between hawk and buzzard, told them,
he did not know what would please
them. 1854: Baker, *Northants Gloss.*,
s.v. "Buzzard," "Between a hawk and
a buzzard"; in a state of perplexity and
indecision. 1878: *N. & Q.*, 5th ser., ix.
46, "Neither hawk nor buzzard" . . .
is used in North and East Derbyshire,
and in parts of Notts, and is thus
applied:—Persons on being asked how
they are will reply, "Oh! I'm neither
hawk nor buzzard," which means a
state of being "rather out of sorts."

2. *By hawk and by hound Small profit
is found.* 1732: Fuller, No. 6339.

3. *Hawks don't pike* [poke] *out hawks'
e'en.* 1846–59: *Denham Tracts*, ii. 107
(F.L.S.).

4. *He's a hawk of the right nest.* 1732:
Fuller, No. 2439.

5. *High flying hawks are fit for princes.*
1639: Clarke, 41. 1670: Ray, 101.
1732: Fuller, No. 2500. 1846–59:
Denham Tracts, ii. 108 (F.L.S.) [with
"good" for "fit"].

6. *It is easy to reclaim a hawk that
has lost its prey. c.* 1300: *Cursor M.*,
3529, For hauk es eth—als i here say—
To reclaym þat has tint his pray.

7. *She hath one point of a good hawk;
she is hardy.* 1546: Heywood, *Proverbs*, Pt. II. ch. iv.

8. *The gentle hawk half mans herself.*
1611: Cotgrave, s.v. "Debonnaire."
1670: Ray, 13 [omitting "half"].
1846–59: *Denham Tracts*, ii. 107
F.L.S.) [as in 1670].

9. *To know a hawk from a handsaw.*
1602: Shakespeare, *Hamlet*, II. ii.,
When the wind is southerly I know a
hawk from a handsaw. 1703: Centlivre, *Stolen Heiress*, III. iv., He knows
not a hawk from a handsaw. 1912:
R. L. Gales, *Studies in Arcady*, 2nd
ser., 241, I have heard the proverb
"He doesn't know a hawk from a
handsaw." 1920: Barbellion, *Last Diary*,

54, I suspect " Charlie " . . . could not
tell a hawk from a handsaw, even when
the wind was southerly.

10. *Unmanned hawks forsake the lure.*
1577 : J. Grange, *Golden Aphroditis*, sig.
G3 [cited as a " prouerbe "].

11. *With empty hands men may no
hawks lure.* Before 1180 : John of
Salisbury, *Polycraticus*, lib. v. cap. x.,
Veteri celebratur proverbio : Quia va-
cuae manus temeraria petitio est.
c. 1386 : Chaucer, *Wife of Bath's Prol.*,
l. 415, With empty hand men may none
hawkes lure. *c.* 1430 : Lydgate, in *Pol.,
Relig., and Love Poems*, 25 (E.E.T.S.).
1575 : Gascoigne, *Posies*, 65 (Cunliffe),
For haggard hawkes mislike an emptie
hand. 1612 : Webster, *White Devil*,
III. ii., With empty fist no man doth
falcons lure. 1717 : Pope, *Wife of Bath*,
172, With empty hands no tassels you
can lure. 1829 : Scott, *Geierstein*, ch.
xxv., Men lure no hawks with empty
hands.

See also Carrion ; Crow (3) ; Goshawk ;
Hungry as a hawk ; Too low ; Wild (2).

Hawk, *verb*. 1. *He has been out a
hawking for butterflies.* 1732 : Fuller,
No. 1863.

2. *The first point of hawking is hold
fast. c.* 1450 : in *Reliq. Antiquæ*, i. 296
(1841), Termes of hawkyng . . . The
first is holde fast when abatith. 1579 :
Lyly, *Euphues*, 93 (Arber), If thou
haddest learned the first point of hauk-
ing, thou wouldst haue learned to haue
held fast. 1665 : J. Wilson, *Projectors*,
II., 'Tis the first part of falconry to
hold fast. 1748 : *Gent. Mag.*, 21.
1846–59 ; *Denham Tracts*, ii. 108 (F.L.S.).

Hawley's Hoe. *See* Blow, *verb* (5).

Haws. 1. *Many haws, cold toes.*
1855 : Robinson, *Whitby Gloss.*, 22,
As many haws, So many cold toes.
1879 : *N. & Q.*, 5th ser., xii. 327, A
North Riding saying, " Many haws,
cold toes." *See also* Many hips.

2. *When all fruit fails welcome haws.*
1732 : Fuller, No. 5544.

Hay. 1. *A good hay year a bad fog
year.* " Fog "=the aftermath. 1846 :
Denham, *Proverbs*, 49 (Percy S.). 1893 :
Inwards, *Weather Lore*, 5.

2. *He has hay on his horn.* [Foenum

habet in cornu.—Horace, *Sat.*, I. iv. 34.]
1648 : Herrick, *Hesp.*, No. 444, He's
sharp as thorn And fretful, carries hay
in's horn.

3. *To make hay while the sun shines.*
1509 : Barclay, *Ship of Fools*, ii. 46
(1874), Who that in July whyle Phebus
is shynynge About his hay is not besy
labourynge . . . Shall in the wynter
his negligence bewayle. 1546 : Heywood, *Proverbs*, Pt. I. ch. iii., Whan the
sunne shinth make hay. 1625 : Dekker, *Works*, iv. 308 (Grosart), He, drawing out one handfull of gold, and
another of siluer, cryed . . . I haue
made hay whilst my sunne shined.
1702 : T. Brown, *Works*, ii. 63 (1760).
1860 : Reade, *Cl. and Hearth*, ch. lxiii.,
We must lose no time ; we must make
our hay while shines the sun. 1915 :
Pinero, *Big Drum*, I., Some day it'll
turn and rend you? Perhaps. Still,
if you make hay while the sun shines . . .

See also Candlemas, D ; Cuckoo (5) and
(20) ; Famine ; Hanged hay ; and May, A
(2) and (3), E (1), (5), and (6), and
F (2) and (5).

He claws it. *See* Eat (38).

He hath but one fault. *See* Fault (6).

He is in his own clothes=Let him do
as he pleases. 1830 : Forby, *Vocab. E.
Anglia*, 427.

**He that doth what he should not shall
feel what he would not.** *c.* 1386 :
Chaucer, *C. Tales*, iv. 125 (Skeat), And
therfore this prouerbe is seyd ful sooth,
" Him thar nat wene wel that yvel
dooth " [He must not expect good that
does evil]. 1591 : Florio, *Second
Frutes*, 97, Who dooth what he ought
not, Shall finde what he thought not.
1640 : Herbert, *Jac. Prudentum*. 1732 :
Fuller, No. 2089, He that doth not as
he ought, must not look to be done to
as he would.

**He that has but four and spends five,
has no need of a purse.** 1623 : Wodroephe, *Spared Houres*, 278, Who hath
but four and spendeth seauen, Needeth
no purse to put his money in. 1732 :
Fuller, No. 2134.

He that hath a good neighbour. *See*
Neighbour (4).

He that hath it, and will not keep it,

He that wanteth it and will not seek it,
He that drinketh and is not dry, Shall
want money as well as I. 1659 : Howell,
21. 1670 : Ray, 211. 1869 : Spurgeon,
John Ploughman, ch. xix.

He that hath plenty of goods shall have
more; He that hath but little he shall
have less; And he that hath right
nought, right nought shall possess.
1546 : Heywood, *Proverbs*, Pt. I. ch. xi.
1605 : Camden, *Remains*, 324 (1870)
[first line only]. 1670 : Ray, 212.

He that in youth. *See* quot. 15th
cent. : in *Reliq. Antiquæ*, i. 92 (1841),
He that in youthe no vertu usit, In
age alle honure hym refusit.

He that is in is half way over. 1694 :
D'Urfey, *Quixote*, Pt. I. Act IV. sc. i.

He that is thought to rise betime.
See Name (1).

He that speaks. *See* quot. 1683 :
Meriton, *Yorkshire Ale*, 83–7 (1697),
He that speaks the things he sud not,
hears the things he wad not.

He that will no evil do, must do nothing
that belongs thereto. 1546 : Heywood,
Proverbs, Pt. II. ch. v. 1660 : T. Hall,
Funebria Floræ, 12. 1732 : Fuller,
No. 6305, He that would no evil do,
Must do nought that's like thereto.

He that will not be ruled by his own
dame shall be ruled by his stepdame.
[14th cent. : *Guy of Warwick*, l. 1593
(E.E.T.S.), For often ichaue herd it
say, and y me self it sigge may, " Who
that nil nought leue his fader, He schel
leue his steffader."] 1546 : Heywood,
Proverbs, Pt. II. ch. ix. 1670 : Ray, 77.

He that will not when he may, when
he will he shall have nay. [Corrigant
se, qui tales sunt, dum vivunt, ne
postea velint et non possint.—St.
Augustine, *Opera*, xxxviii. 1095 (Migne).
Cf. Isaiah lv. 6.] 10th cent. : *A.-S.
Homily*, quoted in Skeat, *Early
Eng. Proverbs*, vi., þe læs, gif he nu
nelle þa hwile þe he mæge, eft þonne
he late wille, þæt he ne mæge [Lest, if
he will not now (do so) while he may,
afterwards, when he at last will, he
may not]. *c.* 1150 : John of Salisbury,
Policraticus, lib. viii. c. xvii., Nam et
proverbio dici solet, quia qui non vult
cum potest, non utique poterit cum

volet. Before 1225 : *Ancren R.*, 296,
hwo ne deþ hwon he mei, he ne schal
nout hwon he wolde. 1303 : Brunne,
Handl. Synne, l. 4799, He þat wyl nat
whan he may, He shal nat when he wyl.
1422 : J. Yonge, tr. *Gouernance of
Prynces*, 161 (E.E.T.S.), That is to say,
" Who so will not whan he may, he
shal not when he wille." 1546 : Heywood, *Proverbs*, Pt. I. ch. iii. *c.* 1590 :
Greene, *Alphonsus*, V. iii., No, damsel;
he that will not when he may, When he
desires, shall surely purchase nay.
1621 : Burton, *Melancholy*, III. ii. vi.
5, p. 612 (1836). 1709 : O. Dykes, *Eng.
Proverbs*, 188. 1880 : Mrs. Oliphant,
*He Who Will Not When He May, When
He Wills He Shall Have Nay* [title of
novel].

He whom God will have kept. *See*
quot. *c.* 1489 : Caxton, *Blanchardyn*, 155
(E.E.T.S.), Men sayen comynly, that he
whome god wyll haue kept, may not be
peryshed.

He will never have a thing good cheap
that is afraid to ask the price. 1633 :
Draxe, 4. 1639 : Clarke, 41. 1732 :
Fuller, No. 2427, He'll ne'er get a
pennyworth, that is afraid to ask a
price.

He's a fond chapman. *See* Day (12).

Head. 1. *An head that's white to
maids brings no delight.* Glos. 1639 :
in *Berkeley MSS.*, iii. 30 (1885).

2. *Cover your head by day as much as
you will, by night as much as you can.*
1678 : Ray, 41.

3. *He that has no head needs no hat.*
1611 : Cotgrave, s.v. " Chaperon," He
that hath no head needs no hood. 1670 :
Ray, 101. 1732 : Fuller, No. 2145, He
that has no head, deserves not a laced
hat.

4. *He that hath a head of wax must
not walk in the sun.* 1640 : Herbert, *Jac.
Prudentum*. 1732 : Fuller, No. 2155.
1854 : J. W. Warter, *Last of Old Squires*,
53. 1864 : " Cornish Proverbs," in
N. & Q., 3rd ser., vi. 495, People with
wax heads shouldn't walk in the sun.

5. *He that will be a head, let him be a
bridge.* 1790 : Grose, *Prov. Gloss.*, s.v.
" Cardiganshire."

6. *Head and feet kept warm, the rest*

will take no harm. 1611 : Cotgrave, s.v. " Demeurant," The foot and head kept warme, no matter for the rest. 1640 : Herbert, *Jac. Prudentum,* Dry feet, warm head, bring safe to bed. 1678 : Ray, 41, Keep your feet dry and your head hot, and for the rest live like a beast. 1732 : Fuller, No. 6255.

7. *Head full of bees. See* Bee (9).

8. *Heads I win, tails you lose.* 1672 : Shadwell, *Epsom Wells,* II. i., The cheat . . . worse than *Cross I win, Pile you lose* : but there are some left, that can lose upon the square. 1846 : in *Croker Papers,* iii. 59 (1884), A game which a sharper once played with a dupe, intituled, " Heads I win, and tails you lose." 1909 : De Morgan, *Never can happen Again,* ch. xxxviii., Women's claims are not allowed in law-courts. It's heads Law wins, tails they lose.

9. *Let your head be not higher than your hat.* 1580 : Lyly, *Euphues,* 284 (Arber), When you match, God send you such a one as you like best : but be sure alwaies, that your head be not higher then your hat. Cf. Hair (2).

10. *The grief of the head is the grief of griefs.* 1659 : Howell, 10.

11. *The head grey, and no brains yet.* 1732 : Fuller, No. 4587.

12. *To have a head full of proclamations.* 1567 : Fenton, *Bandello,* ii. 146 (T.T.), At last, beinge past the misterye of his traunce, he repaired to his house with his head full of proclamacions. 1611 : Cotgrave, s.v. " Moucheron," *Avoir des moucherons en teste.* To be humorous, moodie, giddie-headed ; or to have many proclamations or crotchets in the head. 1631 : Brathwait, *Whimzies,* 97 (1859). 1690 : *New Dict. Canting Crew,* sig. I8, His head is full of proclamations, much taken up to little purpose. 1754 : Berthelson, *Eng.-Danish Dict.,* s.v. " Proclamations."

13. *To have a man's head under one's girdle =* To have him at one's mercy. 1546 : Heywood, *Proverbs,* Pt. II. ch. v., Then haue ye his head fast vnder your gyrdell. 1605 : Chapman, etc., *Eastw. Hoe,* IV. ii., I list not ha' my head fastened under my child's

girdle. 1642 : D. Rogers, *Naaman,* sig. Qq3, I will not doe so meane a fellow such honour, as to subdue my spirit, or put my neck under his girdle. 1754 : Berthelson, *Eng.-Danish Dict.,* s.v. " Girdle." 1829 : Scott, *Geierstein,* ch. xxv., I am a man little inclined to put my head under my wife's girdle.

14. *When the head acheth all the body is the worse. c.* 1230 : in Wright, *Pol. Songs John to Edw. II.,* 31 (Camden S.), Cui caput infirmum cetera membra dolent. *c.* 1399 : Gower, *Pr. of Peace,* l. 260, in Skeat's, *Chaucer,* vii. 212, Of that the heed is syk, the limmes aken. 1546 : Heywood, *Proverbs,* Pt. II. ch. vii. 1620 : Shelton, *Quixote,* Pt. II. ch. ii., I mean . . . that when the head aches all the body is out of tune. 1670 : Ray, 13. 1732 : Fuller, No. 5588 [with " feels it " for " is the worse "].

15. *You have a head and so has a pin.* 1738 : Swift, *Polite Convers.,* Dial. I., Thou hast a head, and so has a pin. 1797 : Colman, jr., *Heir at Law,* V. iii.

16. *Your head will never fill your pocket.* 1855 : Bohn, 582.

17. *Your head will never save your legs.* 1828 : Carr, *Craven Dialect,* i. 216, Thy heod'll nivver saav thy legs. 1895 : S. O. Jewett, *Life of Nancy,* 253, You'd ought to set her to work, and learnt her head to save her heels.

18. *Your head's running upon Jolly Robins =* Your wits are wool-gathering. 1917 : Bridge, *Cheshire Proverbs,* 159. [Jolly Robin used to figure in old ballads.]

19. *Your head's so hot that your brains bubble over.* 1732 : Fuller, No. 6050.

Headlam hens lay twice a day. " A gentle hint in the place of one more discourteous : to wit, that of telling a person he's a liar. Headlam, a small village in the extensive Saxon parish of Gainford." Durham. 1846–59 : *Denham Tracts,* i. 89 (F.L.S.). 1909 : *Folk-Lore,* xx. 73.

Heady is ruled by a fool, He that is. 1732 : Fuller, No. 2178.

Heady man and a fool, may wear the same cap, A. Ibid., No. 212.

Healed as hurt, One is not so soon. 1670 : Ray, 13.

Health and money go far. 1640 : Herbert, *Jac. Prudentum.*

Health and wealth create beauty. 1855 : Bohn, 405.

Health is better than wealth. 1678 : Ray, 153. 1736 : Bailey, *Dict.*, s.v. " Health," Health surpasses riches. 1812 : Scott, *Fam. Letters*, i. 255 (1894), As health is better than wealth, I trust you will hasten the period of your return.

Health is great riches. 1639 : Clarke, 314, Health is a jewell. 1672 : Walker, *Parœm.*, 45 [as in 1639]. 1732 : Fuller, No. 2477.

Health is not valued till sickness comes. 1666 : Torriano, *Piazza Univ.*, 119, In sickness health is known. 1732 : Fuller, No. 2478.

Health without money is half an ague. 1640 : Herbert, *Jac. Prudentum.* 1732 : Fuller, No. 2479, Health without wealth is half a sickness.

Healthful man can give counsel to the sick, The. 1651 : Herbert, *Jac. Prudentum,* 2nd ed.

Hear, *verb.* 1. *He hears not on that side.* 1546 : Heywood, *Proverbs*, Pt. II. ch. ix., Than were ye deafe ; ye could not here on that syde. 1632 : Jonson, *Magnetic Lady*, I., He will not hear of it. *Rut.* Not of that ear. 1681 : W. Robertson, *Phraseol. Generalis*, 713, He cannot hear on that ear. 1736 : Bailey, *Dict.*, s.v. " Ear " [as in 1681].

2. *He may be heard where he is not seen.* 1639 : Clarke, 58. 1670 : Ray, 180.

3. *He that hears much and speaks not at all, shall be welcome both in bower and hall.* 1586 : G. Whitney, *Emblems*, 191, Heare much ; but little speake. 1670 : Ray, 102. 1694 : D'Urfey, *Quixote*, Pt. I. Act III. sc. ii. 1732 : Fuller, No. 6461.

4. *He who hears one side only, hears nothing.* 1546 : Heywood, *Proverbs*, Pt. I. ch. xiii., A man should here all partis, er he judge any. 1750 : Smollett, *Gil Blas*, iv. 105.

5. *Hear all, see all. See* quots. 1578 : Florio, *First Fruites*, fo. 10, Who heares, sees and holds his peace, may alway live in peace. 1623 : Wodroephe, *Spared*

Houres, 276, Heare all, see all, and hold thee still If peace desirest with thy will. 1925 : Yorkshire " motto " in *N. & Q.*, vol. 149, p. 411, Hear all, see all, say now't, tak' all, keep all, gie now't, and if tha ever does ow't for now't do it for thysen." [There are several variants of this compendium of selfishness.]

6. *Hear twice before you speak once.* 1855 : Bohn, 405.

7. *To hear as hogs do in harvest.* 1670 : G. Firmin, *Real Christian,* 11, quoted in *N. & Q.*, 2nd ser., viii. 17, The country proverb is Hear as hogs in harvest. . . . When they are gotten into good shack, when they at home call them or knock at the trough, the hogs will lift up their heads out of the stubble and listen, but fall to their shack again.

Hearers, Were there no, there would be no backbiters. 1640 : Herbert, *Jac. Prudentum.*

Hearing. *From hearing comes wisdom ; from speaking, repentance.* 1855: Bohn, 359.

Heart. 1. *Every heart hath its own ache.* 1732 : Fuller, No. 1418.

2. *He is heart of oak.* 1609 : *Old Meg of Herefs.* (Nares, s.v. " Heart "), Here is a doozen of yonkers that have hearts of oake at fourescore yeares. 1672 : Walker, *Parœm.*, 24, He was heart of oak ; he wore like iron. 1694 : *Terence made English*, 125, Marry, I think, you're heart of oak. 1870 : Dickens, *Drood*, ch. xii., So small a nation of hearts of oak.

3. *Heart of the sober man. See* Drunkenness.

4. *Heart on halfpenny. See* Hand (8).

5. *Hearts may agree though heads differ.* 1732 : Fuller, No. 2480.

6. *His heart is in his hose* (or, later, *boots*). *c.* 1410 : *Towneley Plays*, 113 (E.E.T.S.), A, thy hart is in thy hose ! Before 1529 : Skelton, in *Works*, ii. 35 (Dyce), Their hertes be in theyr hose. 1616 : Breton, *Works*, ii. *r* 9 (Grosart), Hanging doune his head as if his heart were in his hose. 1694 : Motteux, *Rabelais*, bk. v. ch. xxxvi., If I be not half dead with fear, my heart's sunk down into my hose. 1767 : in *Garrick*

Corresp., i. 271 (1831), Whose soul and spirit . . . are now even in her shoes. 1883 : R. L. S., *Treasure I.*, ch. xiii., My heart sank, as the saying is, into my boots. 1900 : Lucas, *Domesticities*, 39, My head was adamant, but, as the saying is, my heart was in my boots.

7. *His heart is in his mouth.* [Mihi animam in naso esse.—Petr., 62.] 1548: Udall, tr. Erasmus' *Par. Luke*, xxiii. 199 (O.), Hauyng their herte at their verai mouth for feare. 1618 : B. Holyday, *Technogamia*, V. v., My heart's almost at my mouth with feare. 1694 : Dryden, *Love Triumphant*, I. i., He's come on again ; my heart was almost at my mouth. 1740 : Richardson, *Pamela*, i. 136 (1883), My heart was at my mouth ; for I feared . . . 1876 : Blackmore, *Cripps*, ch. ii., She . . . glided along with her heart in her mouth. 1883 : R. L. S., *Treasure I.*, ch. iv., A sound that brought my heart into my mouth,

8. *Never set at thy heart what others set at their heel.* 1546 Heywood, *Proverbs*, Pt. I. ch. xi., Nor suche foly feele, To set at my hert that thou settest at thy heele. *c.* 1580 : *Tom Tyler*, l. 807, p. 23 (Malone S.), Never set at thy heart, thy wives churlish part, That she sets at her heel. 1659 : Howell, 13, I will not sett at my heart what I should sett at my heel. 1871 : *N. & Q.*, 4th ser., viii. 506, [A common Lancashire proverb] Never lay sorrow to your heart, when others lay it to their heels.

9. *The joy of the heart makes the face merry.* 1611 : Davies (of Hereford), *Sc. of Folly*, 46, in *Works*, ii. (Grosart), The ioy of the heart fairly coulors the face. 1629 : *Book of Meery Riddles*, Prov. 54, The heart's mirth doth make the face fayre. 1633 : Draxe, 128.

10. *To take heart of grace.* 1530 : Palsgrave, 748, They lyved a great whyle lyke cowardes, but at the laste they toke herte a gresse to them. 1560 : Becon, *Catechism*, 345 (P.S.), It is now high time to take hart of grease unto them. 1593 : *Tell-Trothes New-yeares Gift*, 23 (N. Sh. S.), She . . . tooke harte at grasse, and woulde needes trie a newe conclusion. 1630 : *Tinker of Turvey*, 58 (Halliwell), Rowland, at this

taking heart of grasse, stept to her. 1687 : A. Behn, *Emp. of the Moon*, II. ii., Come, come, take heart of grace. 1712 : Motteux, *Quixote*, Pt. I. bk. iii. ch. vi., He took heart of grace, and made shift to carry over one goat, then another. 1826 : Scott, *Journal*, 15 Sept., I e'en took heart of grace and finished my task. 1922 : Weyman, *Ovington's Bank*, ch. v., He took heart of grace.

11. *To wear one's heart upon one's sleeve.* 1604 : Shakespeare, *Othello*, I. i., I will wear my heart upon my sleeve For daws to peck at. 1909 : Lucas, *Wand. in Paris*, ch. xix., Had he too . . . carried in his breast or even on his sleeve a great heart . . . like Hugo's.

12. *What the heart thinks the tongue clinks* (or *speaks*). 1477 : Rivers, *Dictes, etc.* 26 (1877), The mouth sheweth often what the hert thinketh. 1583 : Greene, in *Works*, ii. 116 (Grosart), Gonzaga . . . thought, what the heart did think, the tongue would clinck. 1670 : Ray, 13, What the heart thinketh, the tongue speaketh. 1754 : Berthelson, *Eng.-Danish Dict.*, s.v. " Heart " [as in 1670].

13. *Whatever comes from the heart goes to the heart.* 1878 : J. Platt, *Morality*, 10 [cited as " an old proverb "].

14. *When the heart is a fire, some sparks will fly out of the mouth.* 1732 : Fuller, No. 5589.

15. *Where hearts are true, Few words will do.* 1875 : A. B. Cheales, *Proverb. Folk-Lore*, 86.

16. *Where the heart is past hope, the face is past shame.* 1580 : Lyly, *Euphues*, 341 (Arber) [with " minde " for " heart "]. 1732 : Fuller, No. 5665.

17. *With all one's heart and a piece of one's liver.* 1598 : *Mucedorus*, sig. F4, Weele waite on you with all our hearts. *Clo.* And with a pecce of my liuer to [too]. 1738 : Swift, *Polite Convers.*, Dial. I., With all my heart, and a piece of my liver.

Heat nor cold abides always in the sky, Neither. 1678 : Ray, 47. 1846 : Denham, *Proverbs*, 6 (Percy S.).

Heave and theave, To. Somerset. 1678 : Ray, 354.

Heaven upon earth, A. 1618 : Breton,

Court and Country, 5 (Grosart), If
there may be a similie of heauen vpon
earth . . . *See also* Hell (6) and (8).

Heavy as lead. *c.* 1300: Brunne,
Langtoft's Chron., 252 (Hearne), And
wex heuy als lede. *c.* 1320: in *Reliq.*
Antiquæ, i. 121 (1841), Myn herte is
hevy so led. 1414: T. Brampton,
Seven Penit. Psalms, 13 (Percy S.), My
synnes ben hevy as hevy leed. 1592:
Shakespeare, *Romeo*, III. v., Unwieldy,
slow, heavy and pale as lead. 1694:
Dryden, *Love Triumphant*, I. i., Try
his wit, senor, you'll find it as heavy
as lead. 1714: Mandeville, *Fable of
Bees*, 54, He is heavy as lead; the head
is hung down . . . 1850: Dickens,
Copperfield, ch. vii., My head is as
heavy as so much lead.

Heavy purse makes a light heart, A.
c. 1510: A. Barclay, *Egloges*, 29 (Spens.
S.), When purse is heauy oftetime the
heart is light. 1595: *Pedlar's Prophecy*,
l. 1591 (Malone S.), An heauie purse
maketh a mans heart light. 1630:
Jonson, *New Inn*, I. i. 1670: Ray, 114.
1754: Berthelson, *Eng.-Danish Dict.*,
s.v. " Light."

Heckmondwike. *See* Birstal.

Hector's Cloak, To take =To deceive
a friend who confides in one's fidelity.
1662: Fuller, *Worthies*, ii. 542 (1840).
1709: Grose, *Prov. Gloss.*, s.v. " Northumberland." 1846–59: *Denham Tracts*,
i. 242 (F.L.S.).

Heddon. *See* quot. 1892: Heslop,
Northumb. Words, 33 (E.D.S.), East
Heddon, West Heddon, Heddon on the
Waall, Harlow Hill, an' Horsley, an'
Wylam bangs them aall. Old saying.

Hedge and **Hedges.** 1. *A hedge
between keeps friendship green.* [*See*
Prov. xxv. 17.] 1710: S. Palmer,
Moral Essays on Proverbs, 168, A wall
between preserves love. 1875: A. B.
Cheales, *Proverb. Folk-Lore*, 93. 1917:
Bridge, *Cheshire Proverbs*, 3.

2. *Hedge abides that fields divides.*
1130: *A.-S. Chron.*, in Skeat, *Early
Eng. Proverbs*, vi., Man seið to biworde,
hæge sitteð þa aceres dæleth.

3. *Hedges have eyes* (or *ears*). 1650:
Fuller, *Pisgah Sight*, bk. iii. ch. i. § 7, If
policy be jealous, that hedges may have

ears . . . 1738: Swift, *Polite Convers.*,
Dial. III., Ay, madam; but they say
hedges have eyes, and walls have ears.
c. 1800: J. Trusler, *Prov. in Verse*, 18.

4. *If you would a good hedge have,
carry the leaves to the grave.* 1678: Ray,
350. 1732: Fuller, No. 6141.

5. *Where the hedge is lowest men may
soonest over.* 1546: Heywood, *Proverbs*,
Pt. II. ch. v. 1564: Bullein, *Dialogue*,
65 (E.E.T.S.), Where the hedge is lowest that commonlie is sonest cast to
grounde. 1610: Rowlands, *Martin
Mark-all*, 14 (Hunt. Cl.), You will
verifie the old saying, where the ditch
is lowest, there men goe over thicke and
three-fold. 1685: Meriton, *Yorkshire
Ale*, 62, Where th' hedge is law, its
eath [easy] gitting ore there. 1732:
Fuller, No. 5666 [with " leap over " for
" may soonest over "].

6. *You seek a brack where the hedge
is whole.* 1639: Clarke, 80, You'd break
a gap where the hedge is whole. 1670:
Ray, 165.

Hedgehog. *See* quots. 1623: Wodroephe, *Spared Houres*, 487, Decke a
hedgehog, and he will seeme a baron.
1659: Howell, *Proverbs: Fr.-Eng.*, 9,
Trim up a hedge-hog, and he will look
like a lord. 1895: Jos. Thomas, *Randigal Rhymes*, 62, Cornwall. Scrumped
up like a hedgehog.

Heeler. *See* Hailer.

**Heighton, Denton and Tarring All
begins with A.** 1861: Lower, in *Sussex
Arch. Coll.*, xiii. 210.

Heler. *See* Hailer.

Hell. 1. *From Hell, Hull, and Halifax,
Good Lord deliver us.* 1594: A. Copley,
Wits, Fits, etc., 112 (1614), It is prouerbiall in our countrie; From Hull, Hell,
and Halifax, Good Lord deliuer vs.
1599: Nashe, in *Works*, v. 284 (Grosart),
Let them seek him, and neither in
Hull, Hell, nor Halifax. 1622: Taylor
(Water-Poet), in *Works*, pagin. 2, p. 12
(1630). 1662: Fuller, *Worthies*, iii.
398 (1840). 1790: Grose, *Prov. Gloss.*,
s.v. " Yorkshire." 1875: E. Peacock,
in *N. & Q.*, 5th ser., iv. 154, From Hull,
Hell, and Halifax, Good Lord, deliver
us, is a saying well known in these
parts [Lincs]. 1922: in *N. & Q.*, 12th

ser., xi. 102, This was the celebrated
Halifax Gibbet Law [*see* **Halifax**], which
gave rise to the well-known proverb :—
From Hell, Hull, etc.

2. *Hell and Chancery are always open.*
1732 : Fuller, No. 2486.

3. *Hell, Hull, and Halifax all begin
with a letter; Brag is a good dog, but
hold-fast is better.   c.* 1791 : Pegge,
Derbicisms, 137 (E.D.S.).

4. *Hell is broken loose.*   1577 :
Misogonus, II. v., I thinke, hell breake
louse, when thou gatst ye this porte.
1596 : Jonson, *Ev. Man in Humour*,
IV. i., They should say, and swear,
hell were broken loose, ere they went
hence.   1667 : Milton, *Par. Lost*, iv.
918, Wherefore with thee Came not all
Hell broke loose?   1694 : D'Urfey,
Quixote, Pt. II. Act II. sc. ii., All hell
is broke loose yonder!   1738 : Swift,
Polite Convers., Dial. I., Hey! what a
clattering is here; one would think,
hell was broke loose.   1822 : Byron,
Vis. of Judg., st. 58, And realised the
phrase of " Hell broke loose."

5. *Hell is paved with good intentions.*
1574 : E. Hellowes, *Guevara's Epistles*,
205, Hell is full of good desires.   1654 :
Whitlock, *Zootomia*, 203, It is a saying
among Divines, that hell is full of good
intentions, and meanings.   1775 : Johnson, in Boswell, ii. 360 (Hill), He said
one day, talking to an acquaintance on
this subject, " Sir, Hell is paved with
good intentions."   1825 : Scott, in
Lockhart's *Life*, vi. 82.   1865 : Dickens,
Mutual Friend, bk. iv. ch. x., You
recollect what pavement is said to be
made of good intentions.

6. *Hell is wherever heaven is not.*
1669 : *Politeuphuia*, 320.   1732 : Fuller,
No. 2489.

7. *There is no redemption from hell.*
1468 : *Coventry Mys.*, 240 (Sh. S.),
Quia in inferno nulla est redemptio!
1619 : Chapman, *Two Wise Men*, I. i.,
It is so deep . . . that it reacheth to
hell, and ther's no redemption.   1662 :
Fuller, *Worthies*, ii. 413 (1840).   1790 :
Grose, *Prov. Gloss.*, s.v. " Westminster."
[In the last two examples the saying is
applied to a prison at Westminster for
the King's debtors.]

8. *They that be in hell ween there is
no other heaven.*   1546 : Heywood, *Proverbs*, Pt. I. ch. xi.   1605 : Camden,
Remains, 334 (1870).   1621 : Wither,
Motto, in *Juvenilia*, iii. 681 (Spens. S.),
For, those the proverb saith, that liue
in hell, Can ne'er conceive what 'tis in
heauen to dwell.   1670 : Ray, 102, They
that be in hell, think there's no better
heaven.

See also **Harrow**.

Hellingly, Sussex.   *See* quot.   1861 :
Lower, in *Sussex Arch. Coll.*, xiii. 210,
Herrin*ly*, Chiddn*ly* and Hoäd*ly*, Three
lies and all true.

Hell-kettles, Deep as the.   [1577 :
Harrison, *England*, I. xxiv. iii. 164
(1881) (O.), There are certeine pits, or
rather three little pooles, a mile from
Darlington . . . which the people call
the kettles of hell, or the diuels kettles.
1727 : Defoe, *Tour*, iii. 188, As to the
Hell Kettles . . . which are to be seen
as we ride from the Tees to Darlington.]
1846–59 : *Denham Tracts*, i. 79 (F.L.S.),
Deep as the hell-kettles . . . the name
of three deep pits at Oxen-le-Hall, in
the parish of Darlington.

Help a lame dog.   *See* **Lame dog**.

Help at a pinch.   *See* **Pinch**.

Help hands! for I have no lands.
1567 : Golding, *Ovid*, bk. iii. l. 745, [An
allusion] His handes did serve in steade
of landes.   1605 : Armin, *Foole vpon
Foole*, 36 (Grosart).   *c.* 1630 : in *Roxb.
Ballads*, i. 305 (B.S.), He passeth some
with house and lands ; when that decays,
he cryes " Helpe, hands!"   1670 : Ray,
99.   1736 : Franklin, *Way to Wealth*, in
Works, i. 444 (Bigelow).

Help to salt.   *See* **Salt** (1).

Help yourself.   *See* quots.   *c.* 1460 :
How the Goode Wife, in Hazlitt, *Early
Pop. Poetry*, i. 191, Thi thrifte is thi
frendis myrthe, my dere childe.   1738 :
Swift, *Polite Convers.*, Dial. II., Come,
Colonel ; help yourself, and your friends
will love you the better.

**Helps little that helpeth not himself,
He.**   1629 : *Book of Meery Riddles*,
Prov. 16.

Helsby (Hill) **wears a hood, As long
as, The weather's never very good.**
1886 : R. Holland, *Cheshire Gloss.*, 445

(E.D.S.). 1917: Bridge, *Cheshire Proverbs*, 161.

Helve after hatchet. *See* **Throw** (7).
Hemp. *See* **England** (10).
Hen. 1. *A black hen will lay a white egg.* 1633: Draxe, 50, A blacke hen may bring foorth white egges. 1670: Ray, 63. 1738: Swift, *Polite Convers.*, Dial. I., Oh! the wonderful works of nature : That a black hen should have a white egg!

2. *Busy as a hen with one chick.* 1632: Shirley, *Witty Fair One*, II. ii., It has been a proverb, as busy as a hen with one chicken. 1659: Howell, 6, . . . with ten chickins. 1732: Fuller, No. 669. 1857: Hughes, *Tom Brown*, Pt. II. ch. ii., In short, as East remarked, cackled after him like a hen with one chick. 1888: Lowsley, *Berks Gloss.*, 30 (E.D.S.), As proud as a hen wi' one chick. 1923: *Folk-Lore*, xxxiv. 329 (Oxfordsh.).

3. *He has swopped his hen for a hooter* [owl]=A bad exchange. 1917: Bridge, *Cheshire Proverbs*, 67.

4. *He puts a hat on a hen.* 1813: Ray, 75.

5. *He that comes of a hen must scrape.* 1591: Florio, *Second Frutes*, 179, What is hatcht by a hen, will scrape like a hen. 1611: Cotgrave, s.v. "Grater," He thats borne of a henne loves to be scraping. 1640: Herbert, *Jac. Prudentum.* 1852: FitzGerald, *Polonius*, 102 (1903). 1880: Spurgeon, *Ploughman's Pictures*, 111, That which is born of a hen will be sure to scratch in the dust.

6. *If the hen does not prate she will not lay.* 1666: Torriano, *Piazza Univ.*, 100, The hen that cakels is she that hath laid. 1732: Fuller, No. 2799, If you would have a hen lay, you must bear with her cackling. 1830: Forby, *Vocab. E. Anglia*, 427 [Scolding wives make the best housewives]. 1872: J. Glyde, jr., *Norfolk Garland*, 148. Cf. No. 10.

7. *It is a sad house where the hen crows louder than the cock.* 1578: Florio, *First Fruites*, fo. 33, They are sory houses, where the hennes crowe, and the cock holdes his peace. 1633: Ford, *'Tis Pity, etc.*, IV. iii., Then I

remembered the proverb, that "where hens crow, and cocks hold their peace, there are sorry houses." 1678: Ray, 64. 1732: Fuller, No. 2842 [with "bad" for "sad"].

8. *It is better to have a hen to-morrow than an egg to-day*—but the first reference gives the reverse. 1659: Howell, *Proverbs: Ital.-Eng.*, 1, 'Tis better to have an egg to-day, then a hen to-morrow. 1732: Fuller, No. 2916.

9. *It is no good hen that cackles in your house, and lays in another's.* Ibid., No. 2987.

10. *It is not the hen that cackles most which lays most eggs.* 1865: "Lancs Proverbs," in *N. & Q.*, 3rd ser., viii. 494. 1901: F. E. Taylor, *Lancs Sayings*, 8, It's no' th' hen 'at cackles th' mooest · 'at lays th' mooest eggs. Cf. No. 6.

11. *It's a poor hen that can't scrat for one chick.* 1882: Mrs. Chamberlain, *W. Worcs. Words*, 39 (E.D.S.). 1894: Northall, *Folk Phrases*, 17 (E.D.S.).

12. *Never offer your hen for sale on a rainy day.* 1768: Goldsmith, *Vicar*, ch. xii., I'll warrant we'll never see him sell his hen on a rainy day. 1846: Denham, *Proverbs*, 3 (Percy S.). 1872: J. Glyde, jr., *Norfolk Garland*, 151.

13. *The hen discovers her nest by cackling.* Before 1225: *Ancren R.*, 66, The hen hwon heo haueth ileid, ne con buten kakelen. And hwat bigit heo perof? Kumeð þe coue [chough] anon-riht and reueð hire hire eiren. 1694: D'Urfey, *Quixote*, Pt. II. Act IV. sc. ii.

14. *The hen lays as well upon one egg as many.* 1620: Shelton, *Quixote*, Pt. II. ch. vii. 1694: D'Urfey, *Quixote*, Pt. I. Act IV. sc. i.

See also **Cock** (3), (6), and (8); **Drink** (10); **Fat as a hen**; **Grain**; **January** (10); **Son** (1); and **Woman** (39).

Hengsten Down, well ywrought, Is worth London Town dear ybought. 1602: Carew, *Surv. of Cornwall*, 272 (1811). 1610: Holland, tr. Camden's *Britannia*, 196. 1659: Howell, 21 ["Hinkeson Down"]. 1662: Fuller, *Worthies*, i. 306 (1840). 1790: Grose, *Prov. Gloss.*, s.v. "Cornwall." 1864: "Cornish Proverbs," in *N. & Q.*, 3rd ser., v. 276, Kingston down, well wrought, Is worth London Town, dear bought. 1880 : Courtney, *W. Cornwall Words*, xiii. (E.D.S.) [as in 1864].

Hen-pen. *See* quot. 1825 : Jennings, *Somersetsh. Words*, xiv. [as in 1838]. 1838 : Holloway, *Provincialisms*, 50, Boys use these words at the game [ducks and drakes] in Somersetshire :— Hen-pen, Duck and mallard, Amen.

Henry Sophister, A, shortened to **Harry - Soph.** Sophista Henricanus. The expression originated in Henry VIII.'s time. 1662 : Fuller, *Worthies*, i. 227 (1840). 1720 : Stukeley, *Memoirs*, i. 40 (Surtees S.), I . . . threw off my ragged Sophs gown . . . and commenced Harry Soph as its there [Cambridge] styled, and took the habit accordingly. 1790 : Grose, *Prov. Gloss.*, s.v. " Cambs." 1859 : *N. & Q.*, 2nd ser., viii. 239, A student at Cambridge, who has declared for Law or Physic, may put on a full-sleeved gown, when those of the same year, who go out at the regular time, have taken their degree of Bachelor of Arts. He is then styled a *Harry-Soph*, i.e. ἐρισοφός. [This Greek reference is a University joke.]

Herb John. *See* quots. Two contradictory sayings. 1614 : T. Adams, *Devil's Banquet*, 307 (O.), Balme, with the destitution of Gods blessing, doth as much good as a branch of hearb-John in our pottage. 1633 : Draxe, 30, He is Iohn herbe in the pottage, that will doe neither good nor harme. 1659 : Howell, 13, Without Herb-John, no good pottage. 1679 : *Hist. Jetzer*, 33 (O.), The Bishop of Lausanne, being a flegmatick and heavy piece, moved slowly, and was herb John in the whole proceeding.

Hercules against two. [*See* Plato, *Euthyd.*, 297B ; *Phædo*, 89C.] 1539 : Taverner, *Proverbs*, fo. 17, Not Hercules against two, that is to say. 1576 : Gascoigne, in *Works*, ii. 540 (Cunliffe), But two to one, can be no equall lott For why? the latten proverbe saith you wott, . . . *Ne Hercules enim contra duos.* 1630 : T. Adams, *Works*, 372, But *ne Hercules contra duos*, two is odds though against Hercules. 1647 :

A. Brewer, *Countrie Girle*, sig. G3. 1693 : Urquhart, *Rabelais*, bk. iii. ch. xii., And two in fight against Hercules are too strong.

Here a little and there a little. 1633 : Draxe, 13.

Here is the door and there is the way. 1546 : Heywood, *Proverbs*, Pt. I. ch. xi. 1633 : Draxe, 29. 1639 : Clarke, 70.

Hereafter comes not yet. 1546 : Heywood, *Proverbs*, Pt. II. ch. vii., Though hereafter come not yit. 1577 : J. Grange, *Golden Aphrodilis*, sig. D4, Here after commeth not yet. 1611 : Davies (of Hereford), *Sc. of Folly*, 43, in *Works*, ii. (Grosart).

Heresy. *See* **Frenzy**; and **Hops** (1).

Hero to his valet, No man is a. [ὅθεν Ἀντίγονος ὁ γέρων Ἑρμοδότου τινος ἐν ποιήμασιν αὐτὸν Ἡλίου παῖδα καὶ θεὸν ἀναγορεύοντος οὐ τοιαῦτά μοι, εἶπεν, ὁ λασανοφόρος σύνοιδεν —Plutarch, *De Iside et Osiride*, c. xxiv.] 1685-6 : Cotton, *Montaigne*, III. ii., Few men have been admired by their own domestics. 1764 : Foote, *Patron*, II. i., It has been said, and I believe with some shadow of truth, that no man is a hero to his *valet de chambre*. 1899 : Wheatley, *Pepysiana*, 240 [as in 1764]. 1924 : *Sphere*, 9 Feb., p. 137, col. 2, I referred in these columns to the well-known statement that " no man was a hero to his valet."

Herring. 1. *Every herring must hang by its own gills.* 1639 : Clarke, 20. 1670 : Ray, 102. 1694 : D'Urfey, *Quixote*, Pt. I. Act III. sc. ii. 1817 : Scott, *Rob Roy*, ch. xxvi., Na, na ! let every herring hang by its ain head. 1865 : " Lancs Proverbs," in *N. & Q.*, 3rd ser., viii. 494 [with " should " for " must "]. 1901 : F. E. Taylor, *Lancs Sayings*, 7, Every yerrin' should hong bi it' own gills.

2. *Gentleman Jack Herring.* *See* quot. 1599 : Nashe, *Lenten Stuffe*, in *Works*, v. 302 (Grosart), He . . . raised this prouerbe of him, *Gentleman Iacke Herring that puttes his breeches on his head for want of wearing*.

3. *Of all the fish in the sea, herring is the king.* 1659 : Howell, 21.

4. *Set a herring to catch a whale.* 1869 : Hazlitt, 331. Cf. **Sprats.**

5. *The herring-man hates the fisher-man.* [1633: Ames, *Against Cerem.*, Preface, 28 (O.), Its a hard world, when heerring men revile fishermen.] 1869: Hazlitt, 373.

See also Barrel; Dead (4); Fish, *verb* (5); Lean; Lose; Red herring; Straight; and Wet (7).

Hertfordshire. 1. *Hertfordshire clubs and clouted shoon.* 1662: Fuller, *Worthies*, ii. 39 (1840). 1790: Grose, *Prov. Gloss.*, s.v. " Herts," . . . A gibe at the rusticity of the honest Hertford-shire yeomen and farmers.

2. *Hertfordshire hedgehogs.* 1662: Fuller, ii. 39. 1790: Grose, *Prov. Gloss.*, s.v. " Herts."

3. *Hertfordshire kindness.* 1662: Fuller, ii. 40. 1703: Ward, *Writings*, ii. 61, For want of a third in our mess, we were fain To use Hertfordshire kindness, *Here's to you again.* 1738: Swift, *Polite Convers.*, Dial. II. 1785: Grose, *Class. Dict. Vulgar Tongue*, s.v., Hertfordshire kindness, drinking twice to the same person.

4. *If you wish to go into Hertfordshire, Hitch a little nearer the fire.* A rather childish play on the word " hearth " and the name of the county. 1806: Lysons, *Magna Brit.*, i. 117 (Bedford). 1854: Baker, *Northants Gloss.*, s.v. " Hitch," The distich on the old beam which separated Bedfordshire from an insulated portion of Hertfordshire in the dining-room of the late parsonage house, at Mappershall, near Shefford: *If you wish, etc.*

Hesky's library, Like—all outside. 1917: Bridge, *Cheshire Proverbs*, 90.

Hewin or Dick, Be oather=Be either one thing or the other. 1917: Bridge, *Cheshire Proverbs*, 160.

Hews too high may get a chip in his eye, He that. *c.* 1300: Brunne, tr. Langtoft's *Chron.*, i. 91 (Hearne), Sorow þan is his pyne, þat he wis ouer his heued, þe chip falles in his ine. *c.* 1310: in Wright, *Pol. Songs*, 323 (Camden S.), It falles in his eghe, That hackes ovre heghe. *c.* 1390: Gower, *Conf. Amantis*, bk. i. l. 1918: Fulofte he heweth up so hihe, That chippes fallen in his yhe. 1546: Heywood,

Proverbs, Pt. II. ch. vii., Hewe not to hye lest the chips fall in thine iye. 1589: Peele, in *Works*, ii. 270 (Bullen), Thou art too crank, and crowdest all too high; Beware a chip fall not into thine eye. 1659: Howell, 4 [as in 1546]. 1732: Fuller, No. 2164.

Hexham. Eight sayings. 1846–59: *Denham Tracts*, i. 278–81 (F.L.S.), (1) Hexham, the heart of all England. (2) Hexham measure; up heaped, pressed down, and running over. (3) He comes fra' Hexham green, and that's ten miles ayont Hell. (4) Every one for their ain hand, like the pipers o' Hexham. (5) Hexham, where they knee-band lops [fleas], and put spectacles upon blind spiders. (6) Silly—good-natured, like a Hexham goose; bid him sit down, and he will lie down. (7) A Hexham sixpence-worth. (8) Go to Hexham [a Newcastle malediction]. (2) 1892–4: Heslop, *Northumb. Words* (E.D.S.), " Hexham measure, heaped full an' runnin' over," was a proverb, which . . . originated in the circum-stance that the " beatment " [quarter-peck measure] at Hexham had twice the capacity of the Newcastle " beat-ment."

Heyden family. *See* **Paston.**

Heytor. *See* quot. 1869: Hazlitt, 458, When Heytor rock wears a hood, Manxton folk may expect no good. *S. Devon.*

Hickup. *See* quot. 1825: Brockett, *N. Country Words*, s.v., Hickup, snick-up, stand up, straight up, One drop, two drops—good for the hiccup. [There are variants.]

Hide can find, They that. *c.* 1400: *Seven Sages*, 68 (Percy S.), He may wel fynde that hyde hym selven. 1671: *Westm. Drollery*, 21 (Ebsworth), But now I'm lost, and here am crost, 'Tis they that hide must find. 1740: North, *Examen*, 172, As they say, he that hides can find. 1816: Scott, *Antiquary*, ch. xxi., Trust him for that—they that hide ken best where to find. 1855: Bohn, 406, Hiders are good finders. 1917: Bridge, *Cheshire Proverbs*, 71, He that feals [hides slyly] can find.

Hide nothing from thy minister,

physician and lawyer. 1578: Florio,
First Fruites, fo. 27, From the phisition
and attorney keepe not the truth hidden. 1596: Harington, *Metam. of Ajax*,
98 (1814), From your confessor, lawyer,
and physician, Hide not your case on
no condition. 1670: Ray, 103. 1736:
Bailey, *Dict.*, s.v. " Hide," Hide nothing
from thy priest, physician .or lawyer;
Lest thou wrong thy soul, body, or estate.

Higgledy-piggledy, Malpas shot=All
share alike. *See* story of " Two Rec-
tors," in Leigh's *Ballads and Legends of
Cheshire*, 133 (1867). 1869: *N. & Q.*,
4th ser., iii. 194. 1913: E. M. Wright,
Rustic Speech, etc., 186, The kernel of
the story . . . is the refusal of the then
Rector of Malpas [either *temp.* James I.
or William III.] to treat the monarch to
his share of a dinner at the village inn.
In spite of the remonstrances of the
Curate, who was also present, the shot
was equally divided between the three :
higgledy-piggledy all pay alike. Later
the monarch caused the same rule to
be applied to the benefice, and hence-
forth the Curate received a moiety of
the glebe and tithes. 1917: Bridge,
Cheshire Proverbs, 73.

High, *adj.* 1. *A high building, a low
foundation.* 1605: Camden, *Remains*,
316 (1870). 1670: Ray, 103. 1732:
Fuller, No. 2499, High buildings have
a low foundation.

2. *As high as three horse loaves.* 1546:
Heywood, *Proverbs*, Pt. I. ch. x., As
high as twoo horsen loues hir person is.
1639: Clarke, 73. 1670: Ray, 202.

3. *High as a hog. See* Hog (3).

4. *High days and holidays.* 1653:
The Queen, I., in Bang's *Materialien*,
B. 13, p. 2, col. 1, Or at a feast upon
high holy dayes. 1857: Hughes, *Tom
Brown*, Pt. I. ch. i., The Pusey horn,
which . . . the gallant old squire . . .
used to bring out on high days, holidays,
and bonfire nights. 1859: Sala, *Twice
Round Clock*, One p.m., Who consume
an orthodox dinner of meat, vegetables,
and cheese—and on high days and
holidays pudding—at one p.m. 1907:
Hackwood, *Old Eng. Sports*, 2, Popular
games and diversions on all " high days
and holy days."

5. *High places have their precipices.*
1616: Haughton, *Englishm. for my
Money*, IV. ii., They say high climbers
have the greatest falls. 1732: Fuller,
No. 2501. Cf. *Higher standing*.

6. *High words break no bones.* 1584:
Greene, in *Works*, iii. 231 (Grosart),
Wordes breake no bones, so we cared
the lesse for hir scolding. 1683: Meriton, *Yorkshire Ale*, 83–7 (1697), Foul
words break neay banes. 1734: Fielding, *Don Quix. in England*, II. vi.,
High words break no bones. 1774:
C. Dibdin, *Quaker*, I. viii.

7. *To be high in the instep* = To be
proud. 1542: Boorde, *Introd.*, ch. xxvi.
p. 189 (E.E.T.S.), They be hyghe in the
instep, and stondeth in theyr owne con-
sayte. 1546: Heywood, *Proverbs*, Pt.
I., ch. xi., He is so hy in thinstep, and
so streight laste [laced]. 1655: Fuller,
Church Hist., bk. x. § vi. (16), Too high
in the instep . . . to bow to beg a
kindness. 1754: Berthelson, *Eng.-
Danish Dict.*, s.v. " Instep." 1854:
Baker, *Northants Gloss.*, s.v. " Instep,"
" She's high in the instep," i.e. proud
and haughty.

8. *To be on the high ropes.* 1690:
New Dict. Canting Crew, sig. K5, Upon
the high ropes, Cock-a-hoop. 1771:
in *Garrick Corresp.*, i. 433 (1831), Who,
as I hear, were always upon the high
ropes with her. 1864: Mrs. H. Wood,
Trevlyn Hold, ch. xxii., Nora was rather
on the high ropes just then, and would
not notice him.

**Higham on the Hill, Stoke in the Vale,
Wykin for buttermilk, Hinckley for ale.**
1795–1811: Nichols, *Hist. of Leics.*, iv.
677. 1849: Halliwell, *Pop. Rhymes and
Nursery Tales*, 197.

Higher standing the lower fall, The.
1633: Draxe, 7, The higher that
I climbe, the greater is my fall. 1658:
Franck, *North. Memories*, 39 (1821),
The higher any man rises, the greater
is his fall expected. 1670: Ray, 102.
1709: O. Dykes, *Eng. Proverbs*, 248,
The highest standing, the lowest fall.

Higher the ape goes. *See* Ape (10).

Higher the tree. *See* Plum-tree.

**Highest branch is not the safest roost,
The.** 1855: Bohn, 507.

Highest flood has the lowest ebb, The. *c.* 1555: in Wright, *Songs, etc., Philip and Mary,* 59 (Roxb. Cl.), Thoughe that the flude be great, the ebe as lowe doth rone. 1598: J. Dickenson, *Greene in Conceipt,* 32 (Grosart). 1658: Franck, *North. Memories,* 39 (1821), High tides have their low ebbs. 1709: O. Dykes, *Eng. Proverbs,* 248.

Highest spoke in Fortune's wheel may soon turn lowest, The. 1732: Fuller, No. 4595.

Highest tree. *See* Tree (5).

High Garret. *See* Braintree.

Highgate. 1. *I'll make him water his horse at Highgate.* 1678: Ray, 86. 1790: Grose, *Prov. Gloss.,* s.v. " Middx."

2. *To be sworn at Highgate. See* long accounts in Hone, *Ev. Day Book,* ii. 79–87. *c.* 1720: J. Smedley, in *Somers Tracts,* xiii. 825 (1811), Dined, and was sworn at Highgate. 1769: Colman, *Man and Wife,* III. ii., I have been sworn at Highgate, Mrs. Lettice, and never take the maid instead of the mistress. 1812: Byron, *Childe Harold,* can. i. st. 70. 1826: G. Daniel, *Sworn at Highgate* [title]. 1902: Wright, *Dialect Dict.,* s.v. " Highgate," He has been sworn in at Highgate, used of a man who is very sharp or clever.

Highway is never about, The. 1670: Ray, 13. 1732: Fuller, No. 4596.

Hill and Hills. 1. *A hill an' a fill an' an o'er-neet.* 1917: Bridge, *Cheshire Proverbs,* 3, Hill=Bed (covering). Fill =A meal. O'er-neet=A place to pass the night in. The whole=A night's lodging.

2. *Do on hill as you would do in hall.* 1570: A. Barclay, *Mirrour of Good Manners,* 25, Liue thou vpon hill as thou would liue in hall. 1732: Fuller, No. 1307, Do in the hole as thou would'st do in the hall. 1853: Trench, *Proverbs,* 21 (1905), In the proverb you will find it [alliteration] of continual recurrence . . . Thus . . . Do on hill as you would do in hall.

3. *Hills are green afar off.* 1904: *N. & Q.,* 10th ser., i. 434.

4. *The higher the hill the lower the grass.* 1732: Fuller, No. 4593.

5. *There's always a hill against a*

slack [hollow]. 1828: Carr, *Craven Dialect,* Ollas a hill anenst a slack. 1899: Dickinson, *Cumb. Gloss.,* 165, To set hills against slacks is to equalise matters by giving and taking. Cf. No. 6.

6. *There's no hill without his valley.* 1583: Melbancke, *Philotinus,* sig. U2, Euerie hill hath his dale. 1633: Draxe, 5. Cf. No. 5.

Hinckley. *See* Higham.

Hinckley field. *See* quots. 1678: Ray, 317, The last man that he kill'd keeps hogs in Hinckley field. Spoken of a coward that never durst fight. 1790: Grose, *Prov. Gloss.,* s.v. " Leicestershire." 1881: Evans, *Leics. Words,* 301 (E.D.S.), " The last man . . . Hinckley Field," . . . is now, and I imagine always was, applied rather to a boaster of the " Ancient Pistol " type.

Hires the horse must ride before, He that. 1639: Clarke, 99. 1670: Ray, 106. 1875: A. B. Cheales, *Proverb. Folk-Lore,* 99. 1917: Bridge, *Cheshire Proverbs,* 71, He who hires the horse should ride first.

Hit, *verb.* 1. *He that once hits will be ever shooting.* 1640: Herbert, *Jac. Prudentum,* He that once hits, is ever bending [his bow]. 1710: S. Palmer, *Moral Essays on Proverbs,* 378.

2. *Hit or miss.* 1560: T. Wilson, *Rhetorique,* 87 (1909), Which shot in the open and plaine fieldes at all aduentures hittie missie. 1656: *Choyce Drollery,* 21 (Ebsworth), But hit or misse I will declare The speeches at London and elsewhere. 1678: Ray, 73, Hit or misse for a cow-heel. 1709: O. Dykes, *Eng. Proverbs,* 272, For we haue a smart saying to this effect, Hit or miss, luck is all. 1823: Byron, *Don Juan,* can. vii. st. 33, Renown's all hit or miss. 1872: J. Glyde, jr., *Norfolk Garland,* 148, Hitty missy, as the blind man shot the crow.

3. *Hit the nail. See* Nail (5).

4. *To hit over the thumbs*=To rebuke. 1540: Palsgrave, *Acolastus,* sig. B4, Haue men hytte the[e] vpon the thombes? 1560: T. Wilson, *Rhetorique,* 3 (1909), Phanorinus . . . did hit a young man ouer the thumbes very handsomely, for vsing ouer old, and ouer

straunge wordes. 1607 : Dekker, etc.,
Westw. Hoe, V. i., And he, bristling up
his beard to rail at her too, I cut him
over the thumbs thus . . . 1678 : Ray,
349.

5. *To hit the bird o' th' eye.* 1670 :
Ray, 181.

Ho (or **whooping**), **Out of all**=Out of
all bounds. *c.* 1374: Chaucer, *Troylus*,
bk. ii. l. 1034 (1083) (O.), þan gan he
telle his wo, But þat was endlees withouten ho. 1577: *Misogonus*, II. iii.,
Though you thinke him past whoo, He
may yet reduce him. *c.* 1592: *Sir T.
More*, 67 (Sh. S.), Would not my lord
make a rare player? Oh, he would vp-
holde a companie beyond all hoe. 1599:
Shakespeare, *As You Like It, III.* ii.,
O wonderful . . . out of all whooping.
1631: Mabbe, *Celestina*, 108 (T.T.), You
will hold your peace, will you not? . . .
What? Is there no ho with you?
1711 : Swift, *Journal to Stella*, Lett. xx.
When your tongue runs there's no ho
with you. 1855 : Kingsley, *Westw. Ho!*,
ch. xxiii., Wonderful, past all whooping.
1894 : Northall, *Folk Phrases*, 20
(E.D.S.), Out of all ho, i.e. immoderately.

**Hoardeth up money, He that, taketh
pains for other men.** 1669 : *Politeuphuia*,
130. 1732: Fuller, No. 2165.

Hoar-frost. *See* Frost.

Hoarse. *See* Crow (4) ; and Cuckoo (6).

Hoathly. *See* Hellingly.

Hobbledehoy. 1540: Palsgrave,
Acolastus, sig. D4, Theyr hobledehoye
tyme, the yeares that one is neyther a
man nor a boye. 1670 : Ray, 216, A
hoberdehoy, half a man and half a
boy. 1738: Swift, *Polite Convers.*,
Dial I. *c.* 1791: Pegge, *Derbicisms*,
105 (E.D.S.), A hobblety-hoy, neither
man nor boy. 1879 : Jackson, *Shropsh.
Word-Book*, 209, Yo' dunna think I'd
tak' up ooth a 'obbety-'oy like that fur
a sweet'eart ! 1894: W. Raymond, *Love
and Quiet Life*, 103, No rascally Upton
hobbledehoy, half man and half boy.

Hobson's choice=No choice at all.
1649: in *Somers Tracts*, vii. 87 (1811),
I had Hobson's choice, either be a
Hobson or nothing. 1660 : *Bradshaw's
Ultimum Vale*, quoted in *N. & Q.*, 6th

ser., ii. 426, I know no other remedy
[for death] ; 'tis Hobson's choice. 1712 :
Spectator, No. 509 [the story of Hobson,
the Cambridge carrier]. 1718 : Cibber,
Non-Juror, I., Can any woman think
herself happy, that's obliged to marry
only with Hobson's choice? 1867 :
Dutton Cook, *Hobson's Choice* [title].

**Hockin's duck, Neither mate nor
fella, like.** Mid-Corn. 1888 : Q.-Couch,
Troy Town, ch. xxiv. 1925 : *Devon and
Corn. N. & Q.*, xiii. 206.

Hodder, The. *See* quot. 1869 : Haz-
litt, 374, The Hodder, the Calder, the
Ribble and rain, all meet in a point on
Milton's domain.

Hodnet, Shropsh. *See* quot. 1883 :
Burne, *Shropsh. Folk-Lore*, 579, As sure
as Hodnet sends the wind, A rainy day
will Drayton find.

Hog. 1. *A hog that's bemired endca-
vours to bemire others.* 1732 : Fuller,
No. 214.

2. *A hog upon trust grunts till he's paid
for.* Ibid., No. 215.

3. *As high as a hog all but the bristles.*
1670 : Ray, 202.

4. *It is hard to break a hog of an ill
custom.* 1678 : Ray, 154. 1732 : Fuller, No. 2949, It is hard to break an old
hog off a custom.

5. *Like a hog in armour.* 1659 :
Howell, 19, He looketh like a hogg in
armour. 1708 : Ward, *London Terræfilius*, No. v. p. 26. 1740 : North,
Examen, 572, So ridiculous was the
figure, as they say, of hogs in armour.
1820: Scott, *Monastery*, ch. x. 1847 :
Halliwell, *Dict.*, s.v., *A hog in armour*,
a person finely but very awkwardly
dressed. 1867 : Larwood and Hotten,
Signboards, 440, " Hog in armour "
. . . a favourite epithet applied to rifle
volunteers by costermongers, street fish-
mongers and such like.

6. *Lose not a hog.* *See* Sheep (18).

7. *The hog is got into the honey-pot.*
1678 : Ray, 354, The hogs to the honey
pots. 1732 : Fuller, No. 4598.

8. *The hog never looks up to him that
threshes down the acorns.* Ibid., No.
4599.

9. *To make a hog or a dog of a thing.*
1670 : Ray, 217. 1712 : Motteux,

Quixote, Pt. II. ch. xxii., He will go
through stitch with it : he will make a
hog or a dog of it, I will warrant you.

10. *What can you expect of a hog but
his bristles?* 1813 : Ray, 201.

See also **Better my hog; Draff; Drive**
(5); **Every hog; Every man basteth;
Go** (23); **Hear** (7); **Lincolnshire; October**
(2); **One hog; Pig; Swarston Bridge;**
and **Swine.**

Hoghton, near Blackburn, Lancs. *See*
quot. 1869 : Hazlitt, 196, He who would
see old Hoghton right, must view it by
the pale moonlight.

Hogs Norton. *To be born* (or *brought
up*) *at Hogs Norton, where the pigs play
on the organs.* It is said that this saying
refers to the village of Hock-Norton,
Leicestershire, where the organist once
upon a time was named Piggs ! *c.* 1554 :
Enterlude of Youth, in Bang's *Materialien*, B. 12, p. 19, I shall laye the
on the eare were thou borne in trump-
ington and brought vp at Hogges
norton. 1593 : Nashe, in *Works*, ii.
273 (Grosart), I was brought vp at
Hoggenorton, where pigges play on the
organs. 1615 : Armin, *Val. Welshman*,
II. iii., This fellow was porne at hogs
Norton, where pigges play on the organ.
1670 : Ray, 249, You were born at Hogs
Norton. 1670 : Cotton, *Scarronides*,
bk. iv., And pillows all securely snort
on, Like organists of fam'd Hog's-Nor-
ton. 1725 : Bailey, tr. Erasmus' *Colloq.*,
317, He being in a violent passion, says
to him, out you saucy fellow, where was
you drag'd up, *at Hogs Norton*? 1729 :
Fielding, *Author's Farce*, III., Though
his voice be only fit to warble at Hog's
Norton, where the pigs would accompany it with organs. 1738 : Swift,
Polite Convers., Dial. II. 1821 : Scott,
Kenilworth, ch. ix., He was born at
Hogsnorton, where, according to popular saying, the pigs play upon the organ.

Holbeach, Lincs. *See* quot. 1869 :
Hazlitt, 206, Holbeach pots, Whaplode
pans, Houltan organs, Weston ting-
tangs. Higson's *MSS. Coll.*, No. 214,
These are four places in South Lincolnshire, and the lines are satirical of
the Church bells at each town.

Holborn-hill, He will ride backwards

up=He will be hanged. 1790 : Grose,
Prov. Gloss., s.v. " London."

Hold fast when you have it. 1546 :
Heywood, *Proverbs*, Pt. I. ch. x. 1583 :
Melbancke, *Philotinus*, sig. F1, As to
haue is good happ, so to hould fast is a
great vertue. 1605 : Camden, *Remains*,
324 (1870). 1659 : Howell, 8.

Hold him to it. *See* **Buckle** (3).

Hold one's tongue in an ill time, One
may. 1633 : Draxe, 5, A man may holde
his peace in an ill time. 1670 : Ray,
103. 1754 : Berthelson, *Eng.-Danish
Dict.*, s.v. " Hold " [as in 1633].

Hold or cut codpiece point. 1678 :
Ray, 73.

Hold the dish while I shed my pottage.
1670 : Ray, 218.

Hold up your dagger-hand. A drinking
phrase. 1639 : Clarke, 46. 1670 : Ray,
216.

**Hold up your head: there's money bid
for you.** 1738 : Swift, *Polite Convers.*,
Dial. I., Well, methinks here's a silent
meeting. Come, miss, hold up your
head, girl; there's money bid for you.
1836 : Marryat, *Japhet*, ch. iv., As the
saying is, there's money bid for you.

**Hold your tongue, husband, and let
me talk that have all the wit.** 1678 :
Ray, 84. 1732 : Fuller, No. 2521.

Hole. 1. *He has a hole under his
nose, that all his money runs into.* 1659 :
Howell, *Proverbs: Fr.-Eng.*, 10, The
hole too ope under the nose, breeds
ragged shoes and tattered hose. 1732 :
Fuller, No. 1858. 1880 : Spurgeon,
Ploughman's Pictures, 39, He has a
hole under his nose, and his money
runs into it.

2. *The hole calls the thief.* 1640 : Herbert, *Jac. Prudentum.*

3. *To make a hole in the water* = To
drown oneself. 1813 : Ray, 201. 1926 :
Phillpotts, *Yellow Sands*, I., I'll make a
hole in the water—I'll drown to-night
sure as death !

4. *You tell how many holes be in a
scummer.* 1639 : Clarke, 146.

Holiday dame, She's an. 1678 : Ray,
73.

Hollow as a kex, As. 1678 : Ray, 284.
1883 : A. Easther, *Almondbury Gloss.*,
73 (E.D.S.), " He is as hollow as a

kex," said of a deceitful man. 1917 :
Bridge, *Cheshire Proverbs*, 15.

**Hollow as a shoe when the foot's
out, As.** Said of a deceitful person.
1886 : R. Holland, *Cheshire Gloss.*, 445
(E.D.S.). 1917 : Bridge, *Cheshire Proverbs*, 17.

Holly. *See* quot. 1846 : Denham,
Proverbs, 6 (Percy S.), He never lies
but when the hollin's green.

Holmby, It shines like. 1854 : Baker,
Northants Gloss., s.v. " Holmby."

Holme. *See* quot. 1846-59 : *Denham
Tracts*, i. 169 (F.L.S.), . . . saying,
which is prevalent in the north-west
part of the county [Cumberland], is
valuable as characteristic of the dour
and satirical disposition of the natives.
When they wish to say a particularly
severe thing against any of the gentry,
they remark, " When he dies there will
be dry eyes at Holme." [Holme is
pronounced as " home."]

**Holmsdale, The Vale of, Never won
nor never shall.** Surrey. 1576 : Lambarde, *Peramb. of Kent*, 469 (1826).
1662 : Fuller, *Worthies*, iii. 204 (1840).
1724 : Defoe, *Tour*, Lett. II. 104
[" conquered " for " won "]. 1902 : G.
Thompson, *Picturesque Surrey*, 271.
1906 : Harper, *Brighton Road*, § xxix.,
p. 276, It is . . . that Vale of Holmes-
dale Never wonne, ne never shall, as the
braggart old couplet has it, in allusion
to the defeat and slaughter of the
invading Danes at Ockley, A.D. 851.

Holt, Cheshire. 1. *Go to Holt to see
Farne Races* = You are going the wrong
way to work. 1917 : Bridge, *Cheshire
Proverbs*, 62.

2. *Holt lions.* Ibid., 73 [Bridge has
a long discussion of the meaning of the
phrase].

Holy, I'll be, I, marry will I. 1639 :
Clarke, 139.

Holyrood, 14 Sept. *See* quot. 1893 :
Inwards, *Weather Lore*, 34, If dry be
the buck's horn On Holyrood morn,
'Tis worth a kist of gold ; But if wet
it be seen Ere Holyrood e'en, Bad harvest is foretold. Yorkshire. *See also*
Devil (48).

Holy Thursday. *See* **Whitsuntide** (2).

Home, He that lives always at, sees

nothing but home. 1618 : Breton, in
Works, ii. *u* 7 (Grosart) [cited as a
" prouerbe "].

**Home is home though never so
homely** (or poor). *c.* 1300 : *Prov. of
Hending*, st. 14 (Berlin, 1878), Este
bueth oune brondes (Pleasant are one's
own brands—i.e. one's own fireside).
1546 : Heywood, *Proverbs*, Pt. I. ch. iv.,
Home is homely, though it be poore in
syght. 1591 : Harington, *Orl. Furioso*,
bk. xxxix. st. 61, For home though
homely twere, yet is it sweet. 1605 :
Camden, *Remains*, 324 (1870), Home is
homely. Before 1680 : Butler, *Remains*,
ii. 285 (1759), Though *home be homely*, it
is more delightful than finer things
abroad. 1712 : Arbuthnot, *Law a Bott.
Pit*, Pt. III. ch. iv., The little I have
is free, and I can call it my own !
" Hame's hame, be it never so hamely !"
1776 : Colman, *Spleen*, I. 1826 : Lamb,
Pop. Fallacies, xii. 1848 : Dickens,
Dombey, ch. xxxv., The saying is, that
home is home, be it never so homely.

**Home - keeping youths have ever
homely wits.** *c.* 1591 : Shakespeare,
Two Gent., I. i. 1822 : Scott, *Fam.
Letters*, ii. 134 (1894), I hold by the true
saying " untravelled youths have ever
homely wits." 1830 : Marryat, *King's
Own*, ch. xxxvii.

Homer sometimes nods. [Quandoque
bonus dormitat Homerus.—Horace, *Ars
Poet.*, 359.] 1530 : Palsgrave, 897, And
ther where they shall se the good Homer
have ben aslepe to be wyllyng by good
maner to wake him, in correctyng the
fautes in the whiche by cause of the
same he is fallin. 1648 : Herrick, *Hesp.*,
No. 95, Homer himself, in a long work,
may sleep. 1820 : Byron, *Don Juan*,
can. v. st. 159, Meanwhile, as Homer
sometimes sleeps, perhaps You'll pardon
to my muse a few short naps.

Honest, *adj.* 1. *An honest good look
covereth many faults.* 1732 : Fuller,
No. 609.

2. *An honest man.* *See* **Wind**, E (2)
and F (1).

3. *An honest man and a good bowler.*
1592 : Shakespeare, *L. L. L.*, V. ii., An
honest man, look you . . . a marvellous good neighbour, faith, and a

very good bowler. 1635: Quarles,
Emblemes, bk. i. No. x., The vulgar
proverb's crost: He hardly can Be a
good bowler and an honest man. 1670:
Ray, 181.

4. *An honest man's word is as good
as his bond.* 1670: Ray, 103. 1730:
Lillo, *Silvia*, I. ix., And every honest
man is as good as his word.

5. *An honest plain man, without
pleats.* 1546: Heywood, *Proverbs*, Pt.
II. ch. v., Be plaine without pletes.
1659: Howell, 15.

6. *An honest shilling is better than a
knavish sovereign.* Surrey. 1875: A. B.
Cheales, *Proverb. Folk-Lore*, 100.

7. *An honest woman dwells at the
sign of an honest countenance.* 1615:
in *Harl. Miscell.*, ii. 147 (1744) [cited
as " the common saying "].

8. *As honest a man as any in the
cards when the kings are out.* 1639:
Clarke, 286. 1678: Ray, 291. 1732:
Fuller, No. 697.

9. *As honest a man as ever broke
bread.* 1599: Porter, *Two Angry
Women*, sc. xi., You are as good a
man . . . as ere broke bread. 1600:
Shakespeare, *Much Ado*, III. v. 1696:
J. Harris, *City Bride*, IV. ii. 1793:
O'Keeffe, *World in a Village*, I. i., As
good natur'd a man as ever broke
bread.

10. *As honest* (or *good*) *a man as ever
trod on shoe leather.* 1599: Porter, *Two
Angry Women*, sc. xi., You are as good
a man as . . . ere went on neats
leather. 1670: Ray, 181. 1754: Berthelson, *Eng.-Danish Dict.*, s.v. " Shoe."
1889: J. Nicholson, *Folk Speech E.
Yorks*, 19, As good as ivver stepped
upo' shoe leather. 1901: F. E. Taylor,
Lancs Sayings, 33, He were as bonny a
lad as ever step't i' shoe-leather.

11. *As honest a man as the sun ever
shone on.* 1789: G. Parker, *Life's
Painter*, 26.

12. *As honest a woman as ever burnt
malt.* 1589: *Pap with a Hatchet*, 23
(1844).

13. *Honest men do marry but wise
men not.* 1659: Howell, *Letters*, ii. 666
(Jacobs), Honest men use to marry but
wise men not. 1696: D'Urfey, *Quixote*,

Pt. III. Act III. sc. ii., A pure proverb,
that says, Honest men marry quickly,
but wise men not at all.

14. *Nobody so like an honest man as
an arrant knave.* 1732: Fuller, No.
2525, Honest men and knaves may
possibly wear the same cloth. 1855:
Bohn, 463.

15. *Of all crafts, to be an honest man
is the master craft.* 1678: Ray, 13. 1732:
Fuller, No. 3696, Of all crafts to an
honest man, downright is the only craft.

16. *The honester man the worse luck.*
1611: Cotgrave, s.v. " Mescheoir."
1670: Ray, 117.

Honesty. 1. *A man never surfeits of
too much honesty.* 1639: Clarke, 213,
Too much honesty did never man harm.
1670: Ray, 13.

2. *Honesty is a fine jewel, but much out
of fashion.* 1732: Fuller, No. 2533.

3. *Honesty is ill to thrive by.* 1639:
Clarke, 30.

4. *Honesty is plain, but no good fellow.*
1594: *Knack to Know a Knave*, in
Hazlitt, *Old Plays*, vi. 509.

5. *Honesty is the best policy.* 1599:
Sandys, *Europæ Spec.*, 102 (1632) (O.),
Our grosse conceipts, who think hones-
tie the best policie. 1622: P. Hannay,
Poet. Works, 166 (Hunt. Cl.), Honestie
In shew, not deed, is policie. 1638:
D. Tuvill, *Vade Mecum*, 27 (3rd ed.),
He would ever say that *Honesty is the
best policy.* 1671: Head and Kirkman,
Eng. Rogue, ii. 92. 1788: Colman, jr.,
Ways and Means, I. ii., My policy was
chosen from the proverb, Random;
I thought honesty the best. 1850:
Dickens, *Copperfield*, ch. iv.

6. *Honesty may be dear bought, but can
never be a dear pennyworth.* 1732: Fuller, No. 2535. 1736: Bailey, *Dict.*, s.v.

7. *If honesty cannot knavery should
not.* 1732: Fuller, No. 2680.

Honey. 1. *A honey tongue, a heart of
gall.* 1583: Melbancke, *Philotinus*, sig.
D3, With honye in her mouth, and a
sting in her tayle. *c.* 1590: in *Roxb.
Ballads*, ii. 5 (B.S.). 1670: Ray, 104.
1732: Fuller, No. 610.

2. *Being anointed with honey live
sweetly.* 1725: Bailey, tr. Erasmus'
Colloq., 571 [cited as " the old saying "].

3. *Cover yourself with honey and the flies will eat you.* 1620: Shelton, *Quixote*, Pt. II. ch. xlix. 1712: Motteux, *Quixote*, Pt. II. ch. xliii, It is so, daub yourself with honey, and you will never want flies. 1853: Trench, *Proverbs*, 65 (1905), We say: *Daub yourself with honey, and you'll be covered with flies.*

4. *He guides the honey ill, that may not lick his fill.* 1623: Wodroephe, *Spared Houres*, 503.

5. *He that handles honey shall feel it cling to his fingers.* 1481: Caxton, *Reynard*, 64 (Arber), How shold ony man handle hony, but yf he lycked his fyngres. 1631: Mabbe, *Celestina*, 158 (T.T.). 1707: *Spanish Bawd*, IV. i.

6. *He that hath no honey in his pot, let him have it in his mouth.* 1633: Draxe, 161, He that hath no honie in his pot, hath none in his mouth. 1640: Herbert, *Jac. Prudentum.* 1659: Howell, *Proverbs: Fr.-Eng.*, 3. 1736: Bailey, *Dict.*, s.v. "Honey."

7. *Honey is dear bought if licked off thorns.* c. 1175: *Old Eng. Homilies*, i. 185 (Morris), Nis nan blisse sothes in an thing thet is utewith, thet ne beo to bitter aboht; thet et huni ther-in, beoth licked of thornes (There is no true bliss in anything external that is not too dearly bought; he that eats honey therein, it is licked off thorns). c. 1320: in *Reliq. Antiquæ*, i. 114 (1841), " Dere is botht the hony that is licked of the thorne "; Quoth Hendyng. 1611: Cotgrave, s.v. "Acheter," He that licks honey of thornes paies too deare for it. 1732: Fuller, No. 2215, He that licks honey from a nettle, pays too dear for it. 1827: Hone, *Table-Book*, 686, One who marries an ill-tempered person attempts to lick honey from off a thorn. 1869: Spurgeon, *John Ploughman*, ch. xix., Never try dirty dodges to make money. It will never pay you to lick honey off of thorns.

8. *Honey is not for the ass's mouth.* 1732: Fuller, No. 2537.

9. *Honey is sweet, but the bee stings.* 1640: Herbert, *Jac. Prudentum.* 1670: Ray, 13. 1732: Fuller, No. 2538.

10. *Honey is too good for a bear.* Ibid., No. 2530.

11. *Lick honey with your little finger.* 1586: Pettie, tr. Guazzo's *Civil Convers.*, fo. 118, That olde saying, that we must tast honie but with our fingers end. 1670: Ray, 13. 1672: Walker, *Parœm.*, 58.

12. *No honey without gall.* 1611: Cotgrave, s.v. "Nul." 1666: Torriano, *Piazza Univ.*, 313.

13. *The best honey. See* quot. 1924: *Devonsh. Assoc. Trans.*, lv. 111, " The best honey idd'n got by squeezin'." Meaning that what is given spontaneously is better than what is gained by pressure.

14. *To lick honey through a cleft stick.* 1670: Ray, 184. 1732: Fuller, No. 5197.

See also **Bee**; **Broom**; **Fly** (11); **Fog** (3); **Sweet as honey**; and **Wine** (3).

Honeymoon, It will not always be. 1639: Clarke, 123.

Honeymoon with them, It is but. 1546: Heywood, *Proverbs*, Pt. I. ch. vii., It was yet but hony moone. 1633: Draxe, 118. 1659: Howell, 4.

Honour and **Honours.** 1. *Honour and ease are seldom bedfellows.* 1640: Herbert, *Jac. Prudentum*, Honour and profit lie not in one sack. 1670: Ray, 13. 1732: Fuller, No. 2540.

2. *Honour bought, temporal simony.* 1659: Howell, 9 (7).

3. *Honour is but ancient riches.* Before 1598: Ld. Burghley, in Peck, *Desid. Curiosa*, 48 (1779), For gentility is nothing else but antient riches. 1618: Breton, *Court and Country*, in *Inedited Tracts*, 190 (Hazlitt), Honour was but ancient riches. 1623: Webster, *Devil's Law-Case*, I. i., What tell you me of gentry? 'tis nought else . . . But ancient riches. 1737: Ray, 52, Nobility is nothing but ancient riches.

4. *Honour is unseemly for a fool.* 1598: Meres, *Palladis*, fo. 211. 1633: Draxe, 3.

5. *Honour will buy no beef.* 1668: Shadwell, *Sullen Lovers*, V. iii. [cited as " the excellent proverb "].

6. *Honour without profit is a ring on the finger.* 1611: Cotgrave, s.v. " Seigneurie," Honour without profit is like a six-penny rent to one that hath nothing else to live on. 1631: Mabbe,

Celestina, 140 (T.T.). 1659: Howell, *Proverbs: Span.-Eng.*, 19.

7. Honours change manners. [Honores mutant mores. — Polydore Vergil, *Adagia*, Prov. ccii. p. 89 (Basel, 1541).] *c.* 1430: Lydgate, in Skeat's *Chaucer*, vii. 297, Ther beth four thinges that maketh a man a fool, Honour first putteth him in outrage [extravagant self-importance]. 1552: Latimer, *Sermons*, 437 (P.S.), So they verify that saying *Honores mutant mores*, " Honours change manners." 1590: Greene, in *Works*, vii. 294 (Grosart), Honours chaungeth manners. 1616: Haughton, *Englishm. for my Money*, IV. i. [cited as " an old said saw "]. 1711: *Spectator*, No. 259, This good creature is resolved to show the world, that great honour cannot at all change his manners, he is the same civil person he ever was. 1748: Richardson, *Clarissa*, vii. 325 (1785). 1820: Scott, *Abbot*, ch. xxii., How I have offended the Lord of Lindesay I know not, unless honours have changed manners.

8. Honours nourish arts. *c.* 1570: F. Thynn, *Pride and Lowliness*, 22 (Sh. S.), Sayeth not the proverbe, honors norishe artes?

9. There is honour among thieves. [Cum igitur tanta vis iustitiae sit, ut ea etiam latronum opes firmet atque augeat.—Cicero, *Off.*, II. xi. 39.] 1712: Motteux, *Quixote*, Pt. II. ch. lx., The old proverb still holds good, Thieves are never rogues among themselves. 1723: Defoe, *Col. Jack*, ch. i., Which is what other thieves make a point of honour of; I mean that of being honest to one another. 1824: Scott, *Redgauntlet*, ch. x. 1840: Dickens, *Curiosity Shop*, ch. xlii., " Honour among— among gentlemen, sir," returned the other, who seemed to have been very near giving an awkward termination to the sentence.

10. We cannot come to honour under coverlet. 1640: Herbert, *Jac. Prudentum*.

11. Where honour ceaseth, there knowledge decreaseth. 1639: Clarke, 137. 1681: W. Robertson, *Phraseol. Generalis*, 737. 1736: Bailey, *Dict.*, s.v.

12. Where there is no honour, there is no grief. 1633: Draxe, 91, He that hath no honour hath no soroow. 1640: Herbert, *Jac. Prudentum*.

Hoo. See Do (39).

Hoo, Kent. See quot. 1735: Pegge, *Kent. Proverbs*, in E.D.S., No. 12, p. 73, He that rideth into the Hundred of Hoo, Besides pilfering seamen, shall find dirt enow.

Hood does not make the monk, The. *c.* 1387: Usk, *Test. of Love*, in Skeat's *Chaucer*, vii. 91, For habit maketh no monk. *c.* 1400: *Rom. Rose*, l. 6192, Habit ne maketh monk ne frere. 1617: Greene, in *Works*, ix. 19 (Grosart), The hood makes not the monke, nor the apparrell the man. 1673: Wycherley, *Gent. Danc.-Master*, IV. i. 1754: *Connoisseur*, No. 10, Mere regimentals no more create a soldier, than the cowl makes a monk. 1820: Scott, *Abbot*, ch. xxvi., The cowl makes not the monk, neither the cord the friar.

Hood for this fool, A. *c.* 1566: in Collmann, *Ball. and Broadsides*, 93 (Roxb. Cl.), A hood, a hood, for such a foole. 1570: in Huth, *Ancient Ballads, etc.*, 128 (1867), And, as the prouerbe doth show very playne, A hood for this foole, to kepe him from the rayne.

Hood-hill [Cleveland, Yorks] **has on his cap, When, Hamilton's sure to come down with a clap.** 1846–59: *Denham Tracts*, ii. 14 (F.L.S.). 1878: *Folk-Lore Record*, i. 169.

Hook or by crook, By. *c.* 1380: Wiclif, in *Eng. Works*, 250 (E.E.T.S.), Comynly thei schulle bie hem with pore mennes goodis with hook or with crook. *c.* 1390: Gower, *Conf. Amantis*, bk. v. l. 2872, So what with hepe [hook] and what with crok Thei make here maister ofte winne. 1546: Heywood, *Proverbs*, Pt. I. ch. xi., By hooke or crooke nought could I wyn there. 1583: Stubbes, *Anat. of Abuses*, 75 (N. Sh. S.), Yet will they haue it . . . eyther by hooke or crooke, by right or wrong, as they say. 1694: Motteux, *Rabelais*, bk. v. ch. xiv., Well, by hook or by crook we must have something out of you. 1761: K. O'Hara, *Midas*, II. ii. 1860: Reade, *Cl. and Hearth*, ch. i., The

Church could always maintain her children by hook or by crook in those days.

Hook well lost to catch a salmon, A.
1633 : Draxe, 5. 1670 : Ray, 104. 1736 : Bailey, *Dict.*, s.v.

Hool. *See* **Hutton.**

Hop, *verb.* 1. *Hop whore! pipe thief!*
1546 : Heywood, *Proverbs*, Pt. II. ch. vii., Where all thy pleasure is, hop hoore, pipe theefe. 1611 : Davies (of Hereford), *Sc. of Folly*, 47, in *Works*, ii. (Grosart), Hop whoore, pipe theefe, hangman lead the dance.

2. *To hop against the hill. See* quots.
1575 : Gascoigne, *Posies*, in *Works*, i. 335 (Cunliffe), So strive I now to shewe, my feeble formed will, Although I know my labour lost, to hop against the hill. 1576 : Pettie, *Petite Pall.*, i. 27 (Gollancz), For to hop against the hill and strike [? strive] against the stream, hath ever been counted extreme folly. 1597 : Bacon, *Col. of Good and Evil*, 10, Running against the hill : Rowing against the streame, etc.

3. *To hop in a person's neck.* 1917 : Bridge, *Cheshire Proverbs*, 138, . . . To have one's revenge on him.

Hop o' my thumb = a dwarf. 1530 : Palsgrave, p. 232, col. 1 (O.), Hoppe upon my thombe, *fretillon*. 1546 : Heywood, *Proverbs*, Pt. I. ch. xi., It is a small hop on my thombe. 1630 : *Wine, Beere, Ale, etc.*, 27 (Hanford, 1915), Away hop of my thumbe . . . I am asham'd of thee. 1888 : S. O. Addy, *Sheffield Gloss.*, 112 (E.D.S.), He's a little hop-o'-my-thumb, and stands no higher than nine penn'orth of brass.

Hope, Derby. *See* quot. 1889 : *Folk-Lore Journal*, vii. 293, [Derby sayings] Mony a one lives in Hope as ne'er saw Castleton [one and a half miles away].

Hope, *subs.* 1. *He that liveth in hope, danceth without a fiddle.* 1670 : Ray, 13 [with " minstrel " for " fiddle "]. 1732 : Fuller, No. 2224.

2. *He that lives on hope will die fasting.* 1623 : Wodroephe, *Spared Houres*, 302, Hee who liues of hope makes a thinne belly. 1725 : Bailey, tr. Erasmus' *Colloq.*, 12, They that feed upon Hope, may be said to hang but not to live. 1736 : Franklin, *Way to*

Wealth, in *Works*, i. 443 (Bigelow). 1869 : Spurgeon, *John Ploughman*, ch. xv., He who. lives on hope has a slim diet.

3. *He that wants hope is the poorest man alive.* 1732 : Fuller, No. 2342.

4. *Hope deferred makes the heart sick.* 1631 : Mabbe, *Celestina*, 38 (T.T.), For (as it is in the proverbe) delayed hope afflicteth the heart. 1633 : Draxe, 42, Long hope is the fainting of the soule. 1768 : Sterne, *Sent. Journey*, 102 (1794), And felt what kind of sickness of the heart it was which arises from hope deferred. 1836 : Marryat, *Easy*, ch. xxix.

5. *Hope is a good breakfast but a bad supper.* Before 1626 : Bacon, in Aubrey, *Lives*, i. 74 (Clark), " But," sayd his lordship, " Hope is a good breakfast, but an ill supper." 1732 : Fuller, No. 2541. 1817 : Mrs. Piozzi, in Hayward, *Autobiog., etc., of Mrs. P.*, ii. 358 (1861), Ah ! he was a wise man who said Hope is a good breakfast but a bad dinner. It shall be my supper, however, when all's said and done.

6. *Hope is a lover's staff.* 1855 : Bohn, 408.

7. *Hope is as cheap as despair.* 1732 : Fuller, No. 2542.

8. *Hope is grief's best music.* 1855 : Bohn, 408.

9. *Hope is the poor man's bread.* 1640 : Herbert, *Jac. Prudentum.*

10. *Hope is worth any money.* 1732 : Fuller, No. 2543.

11. *Hope of long life beguileth many a good wife.* c. 1320, in *Reliq. Antiquæ*, i. 116 (1841), " Hope of long lyf Gyleth mony god wyf " ; Quoth Hendyng.

12. *Hope often blinks at a fool.* c. 1300 : *Havelok*, l. 307, Hope maketh fol man ofte blenkes.

13. *If hope were not heart would break.* Before 1225 : *Ancren R.*, 80, Ase me seith, gif hope nere, heorte to breke. c. 1340 : Hampole, *Pricke of Con.*, l. 7266 (Morris), And men saye, warn hope ware it [the " hert "] suld brest. c. 1440 : *Gesta Rom.*, 228 (E.E.T.S.), He made thes wordes to be wreten, " yf hope wer not, hert shulde breke." c. 1590 : Harvey, *Marginalia*, 95 (1913), But for hope y[e] hart woold brust. 1655 : A.

Brewer, *Love-sick King*, II., in Bang's *Materialien*, B. 18, p. 13, Hope keeps the heart whole. 1748 : Richardson, *Clarissa*, vi. 200 (1785). 1893 : *Co. Folk-Lore : Suffolk*, 150 (F.L.S.), If it warn't for hope, the heart 'ud die.

14. *Too much hope deceiveth.* 1578 : Florio, *First Fruites*, fo. 33. 1629 : *Book of Meery Riddles*, Prov. 126.

Hope, *verb*. 1. *He that hopes not for good, fears not evil.* 1640 : Herbert, *Jac. Prudentum.* 1732 : Fuller, No. 2166, He that hopes no good, fears no ill. 1854 : Surtees, *Handley Cross*, ch. lxxii., Where no hope is left, is left no fear.

2. *I hope better, quoth Benson, when his wife bade him come in cuckold.* 1678 : Ray, 86. 1732 : Fuller, No. 2608.

3. *Hope for the best and prepare for the worst.* 1587 : J. Bridges, *Defence of Govt. of Church of Eng.*, 74, I wishe the best, and therefore if I feare the worst I hope I am the easier to bee pardoned. 1590 : Spenser, *F. Q.*, IV. vi. 37, Its best to hope the best, though of the worst affrayd. *c.* 1680 : L'Estrange, *Seneca's Morals :* " Happy Life," ch. x., I'le hope the best, and provide for the worst. 1706 : Ward, *Works*, iii. 337 [as in 1680].

4. *Hope helpeth.* 1568 : in *Loseley MSS.*, 209 (Kempe).

5. *Hope well and have well.* 1583 : Melbancke, *Philotinus*, sig. H2. 1647 : A. Brewer, *Countrie Girle*, sig. G2. 1712 : Motteux, *Quixote*, Pt. II. ch. lxv. 1732 : Fuller, No. 2545, Hope well and have well, quoth Hickwell.

Hopkins. *See* quots. 1678 : Ray, 290, As well come as Hopkin, that came to jayl over night, and was hang'd the next morning. 1732 : Fuller, No. 695 [with " hasty " for " well come " and " Hopkins " for " Hopkin "]. 1869 : Hazlitt, 113, Don't hurry, Hopkins. This seems to be an Americanism [clearly not].

Hops. 1. *Hops and turkeys, carp and beer, Came into England all in one year.* As the examples which follow show, there are several versions of this saying. They are brought together here, with cross-references from the various objects named. The year referred to is sup-

posed to be 1520. 1599 : Buttes, *Dyets Dry Dinner*, sig. G4, Heresie and beere came hopping into England both in a yeere. 1643 : Sir R. Baker, *Chron.*, 298 (1730), About his [Henry VIII.'s] fifteenth year it happen'd that diverse things were newly brought into England, whereupon this rhime was made : Turkeys, Carps, Hopps, Piccarel, and Beer, Came into England all in one year. *c.* 1685 : Aubrey, *Nat. Hist. Wilts*, 62 (1847), Greeke, carps, turkeycocks, and beere, Came into England all in a yeare. 1714 : Ward, *Hudib. Brewer*, 21, To the same year's produce, we see, Ascribe both hops and heresy. 1724 : Defoe, *Tour*, Lett. II. p. 34, Hops, Reformation, bays [baize], and beer, Came, etc. 1809 : Pegge, *Anonym.*, Cent. V. 88 [as in 1643]. 1826 : Brady, *Varieties of Lit.*, 264 [as in 1724]. 1834-7 : Southey, *Doctor*, inter-chap. xvi. 1886 : Bickerdyke, *Curios. of Ale and Beer*, 67 [as in 1724]. 1909 : Hackwood, *Inns, Ales, etc.*, 44.

2. *Hops make or break.* Referring to the speculative nature of the hop harvest. 1869 : Hazlitt, 208.

3. *Plenty of lady-birds, plenty of hops.* Ibid., 317.

See also **Bean** (2) ; **St. James's Day** ; and **Thick as hops.**

Hopton. *See* **Horner.**

Horestone. *See* **Padwell.**

Horn and **Horns.** 1. *A horn heard soon though hardly seen.* 1659 : Howell, *Proverbs : Brit.-Eng.*, 9.

2. *He cannot hold a horn in his mouth, but must blow it. c.* 1470 : *Songs and Carols*, 23 (Percy S.), I hold hym wyse and wel i-taught, Can bar an horn and blow it naught. 1571 : Edwards, *Damon, etc.*, in Hazlitt, *Old Plays*, iv. 77, I can wear a horn and blow it not. 1681 : W. Robertson, *Phraseol. Generalis*, 733.

3. *He had better put his horns in his pocket than wind them.* 1678 : Ray, 74. 1732 : Fuller, No. 1852.

4. *He that hath horns in his bosom, let him not put them on his head.* 1640 : Herbert, *Jac. Prudentum.* 1670 : Ray, 104. 1732 : Fuller, No. 5704 [with " forehead " for " head "].

5. *Horns and grey hairs do not come by years.* 1678 : Ray, 156.

6. *Let the horns go with the hide.* 1855 : Bohn, 441.

7. *Your horns hang in your eyes.* 1583 : Melbancke, *Philotinus*, sig. F2, Her mothers husband . . . could not see for hornes growing ouer his eyes. 1631 : Lenton, *Characters*, No. 32 (N.), A cuckold is a harmelesse horned creature, but they [his horns] hang not in his eies, as your wittals doe. 1709 : Ward, *Works*, iv. *Verse* 132, To improve your old horns till they hang in your light. 1732 : Fuller, No. 6051. Cf. Jealous.

Horn Fair, All is fair at. 1813 : Brand, *Pop. Antiq.*, ii. 195 (Bohn), So many indecencies were committed upon this occasion on Blackheath . . . that it gave rise to the proverb of " All is fair at Horn fair." 1862 : Chambers, *Book of Days*, i. 645 (1869).

Horner, Popham, Wyndham, and Thynne, When the abbot[s] went out, then they came in. 1669–96 : Aubrey, *Lives*, i. 279 (Clark), Hopton, Horner, Smyth, and Thynne, When abbots went out, they came in. 1790 : Grose, *Prov. Gloss.*, s.v. " Somerset."

Hornet, He is as mild as a. An ironical Glos. saying. 1639 : in *Berkeley MSS.*, iii. 30 (1885).

Horse and Horses. 1. *A boisterous horse must have a rough bridle.* 1633 : Draxe, 171. 1639 : Clarke, 200 [with " boystrous " for " rough "].

2. *A free horse is soon tired.* 1593 : *Pass. Morrice*, 93 (N. Sh. S.), How easie is a free horse tired.

3. *A good horse cannot be of a bad colour.* 1653 : Walton, *Angler*, Pt. I. ch. v., It is observed by some that " there is no good horse of a bad colour." 1710 : S. Palmer, *Moral Essays on Proverbs*, 297, A good horse is never of an ill colour. 1838 : Hood, *Hood's Own*, 1st ser., 146 (1865). 1922 : *N. & Q.*, 12th ser., xi. 169.

4. *A good horse oft needs a good spur.* 1639 : Clarke, 93. 1670 : Ray, 105.

5. *A good horse should be seldom spurred.* 1732 : Fuller, No. 156.

6. *A hired horse tired never.* 1683 : Meriton, *Yorkshire Ale*, 83–7 (1697).

7. *A horse foaled of an acorn* = the gallows. 1678 : Ray, 253, You'll ride on a horse that was foal'd of an acorn. 1762 : Smollett, *Sir L. Greaves*, ch. viii. 1827 : Lytton, *Pelham*, ch. lxxxii.

8. *A horse is neither better nor worse for his trapping.* 1732 : Fuller, No. 217.

9. *A horse kiss.* 1678 : Ray, 74, An horse-kiss. A rude kiss, able to beat one's teeth out. 1732 : Fuller, No. 611 [as in 1678].

10. *A horse of another colour.* 1840 : Barham, *Ing. Legends:* " Leech of Folkestone," They are manifest asses ; but you, good Leech, you are a horse of another colour. 1880 : Spurgeon, *Ploughman's Pictures*, 51, Farmer Gripper thinks we can live upon nothing, which is a horse of another colour.

11. *A horse stumbles that hath four legs.* 1640 : Herbert, *Jac. Prudentum.* 1683 : Meriton, *Yorkshire Ale*, 83–7 (1697), A horse may stumble on four feet.

12. *A horse that will not carry a saddle must have no oats.* 1732 : Fuller, No. 218.

13. *A horse that will travel well, a hawk that will fly well, a servant that will wait well and a knife that will cut well.* 16th cent. : in *N. & Q.*, 4th ser., iii. 10.

14. *A horse will not void oats.* See quot. 1745 : Franklin, in *Works*, ii. 35–6 (Bigelow), If, as the proverb says, it is unreasonable to expect a horse should void oats, which never eat any.

15. *A horse with a wame.* See quots. 1670 : Ray, 44, A nagg with a weamb and a mare with nean. 1828 : Carr, *Craven Dialect*, ii. 233, " A horse wi' a waam And a meear in naan." This Craven distich denotes that a horse should have a large paunch and a mare a small one.

16. *A hungry horse makes a clean manger.* 1659 : Howell, 5. 1670 : Ray, 107. 1754 : Berthelson, *Eng.-Danish Dict.*, s.v. " Hungry."

17. *A pair of good spurs to a borrowed horse is better than a peck of haver* [oats]. 1683 : Meriton, *Yorkshire Ale*, 83–7 (1697).

18. *A resty horse must have a sharp*

spur. 1639 : Clarke, 167. 1670 : Ray, 105.

19. *A spur and a whip for a dull horse.* 1639 : Clarke, 76.

20. *All lay the load on the willing horse.* 1546 : Heywood, *Proverbs*, Pt. I. ch. xi., Folke call on the horse that will cary alwey. 1611 : Cotgrave, s.v. "Cheval," [as in 1546, *plus*] the willingest are sorest laid unto. 1670 : Ray, 116. 1732 : Fuller, No. 532.

21. *An inch of a horse is worth a span of a colt.* Ibid., No. 636.

22. *As holy as a horse.* 1530 : Palsgrave, 620, He maketh as thoughe he were as holy as a horse.

23. *As shortly as a horse will lick his ear.* 1546 : Heywood, *Proverbs*, Pt. II. ch. ix.

24. *As strong as a horse.* 1703 : Ward, *Writings*, ii. 81. 1845 : Jerrold, *Mrs. Caudle*, xxix., You're not as strong as a horse.

25. *Behind before, before behind, a horse is in danger to be prick't.* 1670 : Ray, 44.

26. *Choose a horse made and a wife (or man) to make.* 1611 : Cotgrave, s.v. "Cheval," A made horse, and a man unarm'd are fittest for use. 1640 : Herbert, *Jac. Prudentum* [has two sayings, one "man," the other "wife"]. 1736 : Bailey, *Dict.*, s.v. "Wife," A horse broken and a wife to break.

27. *Do not spur a free horse.* [Addere calcaria sponte currenti.—Pliny, *Ep.*, I. viii. 1.] 1477 : *Paston Lett.*, iii. 200 (Gairdner), It shall never neede to prykk nor threte a free horse. I shall do whatt I can. 1633 : Jonson, *Tale of a Tub*, III. iv., Spur a free horse, he'll run himself to death. 1712 : Motteux, *Quixote*, Pt. II. ch. lxxi., Ride not a free horse to death. 1820 : Scott, *Monastery*, ch. xxv., Be advised, therefore, by me—Spur not an unbroken horse.

28. *Every horse thinks his own pack heaviest.* 1732 : Fuller, No. 1420. 1875 : A. B. Cheales, *Proverb. Folk-Lore*, 120.

29. *Good horses make short miles.* 1640 : Herbert, *Jac. Prudentum.*

30. *Have a horse of your own, and then you can borrow one.* 1869 : Spurgeon, *John Ploughman*, ch. xiv.

31. *He hath eaten a horse, and the tail hangs out at his mouth.* 1678 : Ray, 74.

32. *He hath taken my horse and left me the tether.* 1672 : Walker, *Parœm.*, 17.

33. *He is ready to lend a horse who never had one.* c. 1320 : in *Reliq. Antiquæ*, i. 114 (1841), "He is fre of hors that ner nade non"; Quoth Hendyng.

34. *He that hath a white horse and a fair wife is never without trouble.* 1586 : Pettie, tr. Guazzo's *Civil Convers.*, fo. 124 [with "woman" for "wife" —cited as "an ordinary saying"]. 1591 : Florio, *Second Frutes*, 191, He that a white horse and a fayre wife keepeth, For feare, for care, for ielousie scarce sleepeth. 1716 : Ward, *Female Policy*, 33. 1732 : Fuller, No. 2156.

35. *He that hath neither horse nor cart, cannot always load.* 1611 : Cotgrave, s.v. "Charger," Hee loads not when he lists that wants both horse and cart. 1623 : Wodroephe, *Spared Houres*, 480.

36. *He that lets his horse drink at every lake, And his wife go to every wake; Shall never have a good horse, Nor a good wife which is worse.* 1640 : Herbert, *Jac. Prudentum*, Who lets his wife go to every feast, and his horse drink at every water, shall neither have good wife nor good horse. 1670 : Ray, 28 [as in 1640]. 1696 : D'Urfey, *Quixote*, Pt. III. Act IV. sc. i., He that lets his wife drink of every cup, ugh, and his horse at every water, shall be sure to have neither of 'em good for any thing. 1732 : Fuller, No. 6187.

37. *His horse's head is swollen so big, that he cannot come out of the stable =* He owes the ostler so much. 1659 : Howell, 6.

38. *Horse and man =* Completely. 1639 : Clarke, 86, He's undone horse and man. 1666 : Torriano, *Piazza Univ.*, 134, As much as to say, Undone, horse and man. 1740 : Walpole, *Letters*, i. 87 (1820) (O.), She cheats horse and foot.

39. *Horse in hand. See* **Good walking.**

40. *It is a good horse that never stumbles.* 1530 : Palsgrave, 742, He is a good horse that stumbleth nat sometyme. 1579 : G. Harvey, in *Works*, i. 23

(Grosart), A good horse that trippeth
not once in a iourney. 1616 : Breton, in
Works, ii. *e* 6 (Grosart). 1709 : O. Dykes,
Eng. Proverbs, 19. 1869: Spurgeon,
John Ploughman, ch. x., It is a good
horse that never stumbles, And a good
wife that never grumbles.

41. *It is the bridle and spur that makes
a good horse.* 1732 : Fuller, No. 3021.

42. *It would make a horse break his
bridle, or a dog his halter.* 1577 : Stanihurst, *Descrip. of Ireland*, fo. 6, It would
make a horse breake hys halter, to see
so dronken a pageant. 1659 : Howell,
10, It would make a horse break his
halter. 1670 : Ray, 165.

43. *It's an ill horse can neither
whinny nor wag his tail.* 1595 : *Maroccus
Extaticus*, 6 (Percy S.) [" a jade "].
1639 : Clarke, 70. 1670 : Ray, 105.
1732 : Fuller, No. 2882 [" a silly horse "].

44. *Lend thy horse for a long journey,
thou mayest have him again with his
skin.* 1659 : Howell, 4. 1670 : Ray, 14.

45. *Let a horse drink when he will, not
what he will.* 1678 : Ray, 157.

46. *Let the best horse leap the hedge
first.* 1732 : Fuller, No. 3191.

47. *Let the quick horse. See* quot.
1573 : Bullein, *Dialogue*, 123 (E.E.T.S.),
Mingle the good with the bad, as men
saie, lette the quicke horse drawe the
deade horse out of the myre.

48. *Live, horse! and thou shalt have
grass.* 1738 : Swift, *Polite Convers.*,
Dial. I. 1901: F. E. Taylor, *Lancs
Sayings*, 8, Live, hawse [horse], an'
theawst ha' graiss.

49. *One white foot. See* quots. 1659 :
Howell, *Proverbs : Ital.-Eng.*, 13, A four
white-foot horse is a horse for a fool, a
three white-foot horse is a horse for a
King, and if he hath but one Ile give
him to none. 1666 : Torriano, *Piazza
Univ.*, 59, A horse with one white foot
is suppos'd to be best. 1851 : Fitz-
Gerald, *Euphranor*, 84 (1855), One
[white foot], I have heard say, is as
good a sign, as all four white are a bad.
1877 : *N. & Q.*, 5th ser., vii. 64, One
white foot, buy a horse; Two white
feet, try a horse : Three white feet,
look well about him; Four white feet,
do without him. 1922 : *N. & Q.*, 12th

ser., xi. 169, One white leg, ride him
for your life ; Two white legs, give him
to your wife ; Three white legs, give
him to your man ; Four white legs, sell
him if you can. Ibid., 212, Four white
feet and a white nose, Strip off his hide,
and give him to the crows. [There is
more than one variant of these rhymes.]

50. *Put no more on an old horse than
he can bear.* 1775 : Garrick, *May-Day*,
sc. i. [cited as " an excellent saying "].

51. *Ride a horse and a mare on the
shoulders, an ass and mule on the
buttocks.* 1659: Howell, *Proverbs : Ital.-
Eng.*, 2 [with "towards" for each
"on"]. 1678 : Ray, 53.

52. *Steal the horse and carry home
the bridle.* 1678 : Ray, 342. 1732 :
Fuller, No. 4173, Sim steals the horse,
and carries home the bridle honestly.

53. *That horse is troubled with corns*
= is foundered. 1678 : Ray, 74.

54. *The biggest horses are not the best
travellers.* 1732 : Fuller, No. 4425.

55. *The blind horse is fittest for the
mill.* 1692 : Southerne, *Maid's Last
Prayer*, III. i.

56. *The common horse is worst shod.*
1546 : Heywood, *Proverbs*, Pt. I. ch. xi.
1670 : Ray, 105.

57. *The fault of the horse is put on the
saddle.* 1620 : Shelton, *Quixote*, Pt. II.
ch. lxvi., According to the opinion of
wise men, the fault of the ass must not
be laid upon the pack-saddle. 1640 :
Herbert, *Jac. Prudentum*. 1732 : Fuller,
No. 4519 [as in 1620].

58. *The good horse must carry drink.*
S. Devon. 1869 : Hazlitt, 370.

59. *The good horse must not cocky to
a gally-whacker* [start at a scarecrow].
S. Devon. Ibid.

60. *The good horse must smell to a
pixy* [know where the bog is]. S.
Devon. Ibid.

61. *The horse may starve. See* **Grass**
(6).

62. *The horse next the mill carries all
the grist.* 1605 : Camden, *Remains*, 334
(1870). 1670 : Ray, 121. 1694 : D'Urfey,
Quixote, Pt. I. Act II. sc. i. 1732 : Fuller,
No. 4601.

63. *The horse that draws his halter is
not quite escaped.* 1639 : Clarke, 250.

1732 : Fuller, No. 4602. 1853 : Trench, *Proverbs,* 139 (1905).

64. *The horse thinks one thing, and he that saddles him another.* 1631 : Mabbe, *Celestina,* 264 (T.T.). 1696 : D'Urfey, *Quixote,* Pt. III. Act III. sc. ii., D'ye hear, friend of mine, the ass thinks one thing, and he that rides him another. 1732 : Fuller, No. 3799, One thing thinketh the horse, and another he that saddles him.

65. *The willing horse is always most ridden.* 1546 : Heywood, *Proverbs,* Pt. I. ch. xi., Folke call on the horse that will cary alwey.

66. *They are scarce of horses where two ride on a dog.* 1678 : Ray, 157, They are scarce of horse-flesh who two and two ride on a dog. 1732 : Fuller, No. 4958.

67. *They cannot set their horses together* = cannot agree. 1639 : Clarke, 94, They cannot set their horses i' th' same stable. 1670 : Ray, 181. *c.* 1710 : Swift, in *Works,* xiv. 109 (Scott), And since we're so near, like birds of a feather, Let's e'en, as they say, set our horses together. 1776 : in *Garrick Corresp.,* ii. 171 (1832), We do not quite set our horses together, though I have done a piece of service lately he knows nothing of, nor ever shall. 1887 : Parish and Shaw, *Dict. Kent. Dialect,* 79 (E.D.S.), Muster Nidgett and his old 'ooman can't set their horses together at all.

68. *To make a horse's meal,* i.e. to eat without drinking. 1793 : Grose, *Olio,* 91 (2nd ed.).

69. *Trust not a horse's heel nor a dog's tooth.* 1678 : Ray, 158.

70. *When the horse is starved, you bring him oats.* 1732 : Fuller, No. 5591.

71. *Where the horse lies down, there some hairs will be found.* Before 1500 : in Hill, *Commonplace - Book,* 129 (E.E.T.S.), Whan the hors waloweth, som heris be loste. 1602 : Carew, *Surv. of Cornwall,* 9 (1811), Where the horse walloweth, some hairs will still remain. 1662 : Fuller, *Worthies,* i. 299 (1840). 1732 : Fuller, No. 6331. 1864 : " Cornish Proverbs," in *N. & Q.,* 3rd ser., vi. 494.

72. *You may beat a horse till he be sad, and a cow till she be mad.* 1678 : Ray, 98.

73. *You may know the horse by his harness.* 1670 : Ray, 105. 1732 : Fuller, No. 5883, [a contradiction] You can't judge of the horse by the harness.

74. *You may take a horse to the water, but you can't make him drink. c.* 1175 : *Old Eng. Homilies,* 1st ser., p. 9 (Morris), Hwa is thet mei thet hors wettrien the him-self nule drinken? (Who is he that may water the horse and not drink himself?). 1546 : Heywood, *Proverbs,* Pt. I. ch. xi., A man maie well bring a horse to the water, But he cannot make him drinke without he will. 1616 : *Jack Drum,* I., in Simpson, *Sch. of Shakesp.,* ii. 143, What ! a man may lead a horse to the water, but heele chuse to drinke. 1763 : Johnson, in Hill's *Boswell,* i. 427, As the proverb says, " One man may lead a horse to the water, but twenty cannot make him drink." 1830 : Marryat, *King's Own,* ch. xxxiv. 1884 : J. Platt, *Poverty,* 62.

75. *You'll ride a horse that was foaled of an ass.* 1855 : Bohn, 581.

76. *Your horse cast a shoe.* 1678 : Ray, 349.

See also **Afterthought ; Ass** (10) and (14) ; **Beat** (3) ; **Better be the tail ; Better riding ; Blind,** *adj.* (9) and (26) ; **Change,** *verb* (4) ; **Colt** (1) ; **Cough ; Eat** (19) ; **Fine** (4) ; **Flea-bitten ; Flesh ; Fly** (5) ; **Foal ; Galled ; Gift** (8) ; **Good luck ; Grey mare ; Groaning ; Hang** (9) ; **Hires ; Lazy groom ; Like a horse ; Like a loader's horse ; Mad horse ; Man** (1), (55), and (78) ; **One saddle ; Ox** (7) ; **Proud horse ; Saddle ; Scabbed ; Scald ; Short ; Shoulder of mutton ; Sick** (4) ; **Stable-door ; Steal** (1) and (5) ; **Throw** (4) ; **Two ride ; Up the hill ; Wife** (12) ; **Wild** (9) ; **Willow ; Win** (4) ; and **Young** (9).

Horse-load to a cart-load, To fall away from a. 1678 : Ray, 243. 1690 : *New Dict. Canting Crew,* sig. G1, Fallen away from a horse-load to a cart-load, spoken ironically of one considerably improved in flesh on a sudden. 1738 : Swift, *Polite Convers.,* Dial. I.

Horse-nest. *See* **Mare** (6).

Horsham. *See* **Rudgwick.**

Horsley. *See* **Heddon.**

Horton town. See **Wotton hill.**

Hosed and shod, He came in = He was
born to a good estate. 1678 : Ray, 74.

Host. See **Reckon.**

Host's invitation is expensive, An.
1732 : Fuller, No. 612.

Hot as a toast. c. 1430 : Two Cookery-
Books, 12 (O.), Seene forth alle hote as
tostes. c. 1520 : in Skelton, Works, ii.
415 (Dyce), Chafyng lyke myne hoste,
As hott as any toste. c. 1580 : in Roxb.
Ballads, i. 94 (Hindley), Six pelican
chickens as hote as a toast. 1696 :
D'Urfey, Quixote, Pt. III. Act II. sc. i.,
She makes me as hot as a toast. 1714 :
Ozell, Molière, ii. 9, You'll have it as
hot as a toast, monster ! 1860 : Reade,
Cl. and Hearth, ch. xxv., They were
soon as warm as toast, and fast asleep.
1901 : F. E. Taylor, Lancs Sayings, 4,
As waarm as a toast.

Hot as coals. 1551 : T. Wilson, Rule
of Reason, sig. U4, You shalbe as whote
as coles by and by. 1563 : Foxe, Actes,
etc., v. 19 (1846), The bishop and all
his doctors were as hot as coals.

Hot as fire. c. 1350 : Will. Palerne, 36
(E.E.T.S.), Sum-time it hentis me with
hete as hot as ani fure. c. 1440 : Gesta
Rom., 46 (E.E.T.S.), For he woll . . .
make me foryete my anger, though I
wer as hote as fire. 1579 : Spenser,
Shep. Cal., March, l. 48, A stepdame
eke as hote as fyre. 1634 : Fletcher,
Two Noble Kins., V. vi., The hot
horse, hot as fire. 1786 : D'Arblay,
Diary, ii. 212 (1876), I was as hot as
fire at this question. 1855 : Gaskell,
North and South, ch. xiv., My cheeks
were as hot as fire. 1872 : Hardy,
Greenwood Tree, Pt. I. ch. viii., You
dance and get hot as fire.

**Hot as if he had a bellyful of wasps
and salamanders, He is as.** 1732 : Fuller,
No. 1911.

Hot love hasty vengeance. 1736 :
Bailey, Dict., s.v. " Vengeance."

Hot love is soon cold. 1537 : R.
Whitford, Werke for Housholders, sig.
D7, Hote loue is sone colde. 1587 :
Greene, in Works, v. 210 (Grosart).
1620 : Two Merry Milkmaids, II. i.,
The old [adage]. Hot loue's soone cold.
1670 : Ray, 46. 1732 : Fuller, No. 2549.

1889 : Folk-Lore Journal, vii. 292
(Derbyshire).

Hot needle. See **Put** (11).

Hot porridge (or **worts**) **will soak old
crusts.** 15th cent. : in Reliq. Antiquæ,
i. 82 (1841), This is to saye to your
lewde undurstandyng, that hoote wortes
erased crusstes makeyn sofft hard
wortes. Before 1500 : in Hill, Commonplace-Book, 132 (E.E.T.S.), Whote wor-
tis make softe crustis. 1917 : Bridge,
Cheshire Proverbs, 75, Hot porridge will
soak old crusts.

Hot shot indeed, You are a, " spoken
in a slighting derision." 1659 : Howell,
4. 1678 : Ray, 86, He's a hot shot in a
mustard pot, when both his heels stand
right up. 1732 : Fuller, No. 2440 [as
in 1678].

Hot sup, hot swallow. 1639 : Clarke,
200. 1670 : Ray, 106. 1732 : Fuller,
No. 2551.

Hot water. See quot. 1654 : Gayton,
Pleasant Notes Don Q., 79, This same
search hath not cost me hot water (as
they say).

Hotspurs, You are none of the. 1732 :
Fuller, No. 5855, You are none of the
hastings, nor hotspurs. 1846–59 : Denham Tracts, i. 228 (F.L.S.), You're none
of the hotspurs. Made use of when
accusing a noisy braggadocio, be he
soldier or civilian, of cowardice.

Houltan. See **Holbeach.**

Hound gnaweth bone. See **Dog** (94).

**Hour in a day between a good house-
wife and a bad, There's but an.** 1678 :
Ray, 74.

**Hour in the morning, before break-
fast, is worth two all the rest of the day,
An.** 1827 : Hone, Ev. Day Book, ii. 477
[cited as " an old and a true saying "].
1846 : Denham, Proverbs, 3 (Percy S.).

**Hour may destroy what an age was a
building, An.** 1732 : Fuller, No. 613.

**Hour of pain is as long as a day of
pleasure, An.** Ibid., No. 614.

**Hour's cold will suck out seven years'
heat, An.** 1846 : Denham, Proverbs, 3
(Percy S.).

Hours Sayings. See quots. 1891 :
R. P. Chope, Hartland Dialect, 21
(E.D.S.), 'Twixt twelve an' two You'd
zee 'ot the day'll do. 1893 : Inwards,

Weather Lore, 44, Between the hours of ten and two Will show you what the day will do [also as in 1891].

House. 1. *A house built by the wayside is either too high or too low.* 1666: Torriano, *Piazza Univ.*, 40, Who buildeth a house in the street, either it is too high or too low. 1670: Ray, 106. 1732: Fuller, No. 220.

2. *A house filled with guests is eaten up and ill spoken of.* 1855: Bohn, 291.

3. *A house ready made and a wife to make.* 1611: Cotgrave, s.v. "Acheter," Buy a house made, and a wife unman'd. 1732: Fuller, No. 222.

4. *After the house is finished, leave it.* 1640: Herbert, *Jac. Prudentum.*

5. *Better one's house too little one day, than too big all the year after.* 1670: Ray, 106. 1732: Fuller, No. 919. 1852: FitzGerald, *Polonius*, 30 (1903). 1868: *Quart. Review*, cxxv. 252 [with last words, "too large all the year"].

6. *Choose not a house near an inn* [for noise], *or in a corner* [for filth]. 1640: Herbert, *Jac. Prudentum.*

7. *He that buys a house ready wrought hath many a pin and nail for nought.* 1605: Camden, *Remains*, 324 (1870). 1670: Ray, 106. 1732: Fuller, No. 6442.

8. *He that hath no house must lie in the yard.* 1591: Lyly, *Endymion*, IV. ii.

9. *His house stands on my lady's ground.* 1678: Ray, 75.

10. *Much it behoveth him to do that house shall hold.* c. 1460: *How the Good Wife*, l. 120, Mykelle mote hym be-houethe to don that house schall holden.

11. *One's house one's castle.* 1602–3: Manningham, *Diary*, 21 (Camden S.), His house . . . is his castle. 1669: Dudley North, *Obs. and Adv. Œconom.*, 72, Masters of families are much favoured in our law, for their houses are termed their castles. 1767: Murphy, *Sch. for Guardians*, III. v., My house is my castle, gentlemen, and nobody must offer violence here. 1848: Dickens, *Dombey*, ch. ix., Mrs. MacStinger immediately demanded whether an Englishwoman's house was her castle or not.

12. *Set not your house on fire to be revenged of the moon.* 1732: Fuller,

No. 4111. 1880: Spurgeon, *Ploughman's Pictures*, 36, . . . to spite the moon.

13. *The house goes mad when women gad.* 1822: Scott, *Nigel*, ch. iv.

14. *The house shows the owner.* 1611: Cotgrave, s.v. "Maison," The house discovers the owner. 1640: Herbert, *Jac. Prudentum.*

15. *To eat out of house and home.* See **Eat** (35).

16. *To throw the house out of the windows.* 1562: Bullein, *Bulwarke of Defence*, fo. 28, Haue at all . . . caste the house out at the window. 1659: in *Pol. Ballads*, 161 (Wright, Percy S.), If we take them there any more, wee'l throw the house out of the window. 1714: Ozell, *Molière*, i. 180, I'll have a virtuous wife, or I'll throw the house out o' th' window. 1836: Dickens, *Sketches by Boz*, 248 (C. D. ed.), The whole family was infected with the mania for Private Theatricals; the house, usually so clean and tidy, was, to use Mr. Gattleton's expressive description, "regularly turned out o' windows." 1889: Peacock, *Manley, etc., Gloss.*, 563 (E.D.S.), To throw the house out of the windows, To make a great noise, disturbance, or tumult in a house.

17. *When house and land are gone and spent, Then learning is most excellent.* 1753: Foote, *Taste*, I. [cited as "the old saying"]. 1773: Garrick, *Prol.* to Goldsmith's *She Stoops*, When ign'rance enters, folly is at hand; Learning is better far than house and land. 1805: Scott, *Fam. Letters*, i. 31 (1894), I am at pains with her education, because you know "learning is better than house or land." 1859: Planché, *Extravag.*, v. 206 (1879) [as in 1805].

18. *When my house burns, it is not good playing at chess.* 1640: Herbert, *Jac. Prudentum.* 1670: Ray, 106. 1732: Fuller, No. 5539, When a man's house is on fire, it's time to break off chess.

19. *When the house is burned down you bring water.* 1732: Fuller, No. 5592.

20. *Who would hold his house very clean, Ought lodge no priest nor pigeon therein.* 1611: Cotgrave, s.v. "Pigeon," He that in a neat house will dwell, must

priest and pigeon thence expell. 1666 :
Torriano, *Piazza Univ.*, 48, Who means
to have a clean house, let him not keep
pidgeons. 1886 : Swainson, *Folk-Lore
of Brit. Birds*, 169 (F.L.S.).
See also **Commend** (1) ; and **Eat** (35).

Housekeeping is a privy thief. 1542 :
Udall, tr. Erasmus' *Apoph.*, 44 (1877),
And (as our Englishe prouerbe saieth)
Hous kepyng is a priuie theef. *See also*
Marriage (5).

Housetop, to be at the = in anger.
1546 : Heywood, *Proverbs*, Pt. II. ch. v.,
He is at three woordis vp in the house
roufe. 1626 : *Scoggins Jests*, 92 (1864),
I defie thee, said Scogins wife (and was
up in the house top). 1633 : Draxe, 10,
At three words he is at the top of the
house. 1828 : Carr, *Craven Dialect*, i.
236, To be at t' house - top, to be in
a great rage. 1875 : Parish, *Sussex
Dialect*, 123, If you says anything to
him, he's up-a-top-of-the-house drackly
minut.

Housewifery is a great revenue, Good.
1725 : Bailey, tr. Erasmus' *Colloq.*, 144.
1869 : Spurgeon, *John Ploughman*, ch.
xvi., A thrifty housewife is better than
a great income. Cf. **Frugality**.

How doth your whither go you? =
your wife. 1678 : Ray, 346.

**Howick Hole, No good ever came out
of.** 1846–59 : *Denham Tracts*, ii. 364
(F.L.S.).

Hulch and stulch, By=By hook or
by crook. 1541 : *Schoolhouse of Women*,
By huch or by cruch. 1913 : E. M.
Wright, *Rustic Speech, etc.*, 125. 1917 :
Bridge, *Cheshire Proverbs*, 33.

Hull cheese, You have eaten some =
You are drunk. 1678 : Ray, 340. 1790 :
Grose, *Prov. Gloss.*, s.v. " Yorkshire."
1878 : *Folk-Lore Record*, i. 162.

Hull. *See also* **Dighton**; **Hell** (3) ;
and **Oxford** (1).

Humble-bee in a cow-t—d thinks himself a king, An. 1659 : Howell, 1.
1670 : Ray, 14.

Humble hearts have humble desires.
1640 : Herbert, *Jac. Prudentum.* 1854 :
J. W. Warter, *Last of Old Squires*, 53.

**Humphrey Hambly's ducks, as is said
to look larger than they be.** 1888 :
Q.-Couch, *Troy Town*, ch. viii.

Hundred and County (or **Shire**).
There are two contradictory sayings ;
or rather, two ways of expressing the
same idea. (*a*) *What is won in the
hundred is lost in the shire* (or *county*).
1546 : Heywood, *Proverbs*, Pt. II. ch.
ix., What ye wan in the hundred, ye
lost in the sheere. 1605 : Camden,
Remains, 335 (1870), What some win
in the hundred, they lose in the shire.
1625 : Bacon, *Essays :* " Of Empire,"
Taxes and imposts vpon them, doe
seldome good to the Kings reuenew,
for that he winnes in the Hundred, he
leeseth in the Shire. 1682 : Bunyan,
Holy War, ch. xv., [Lucifer names two
agents] They are Mr. Penny-wise-pound-
foolish, and Mr. Get-i'-the-hundred-
and-lose-i'-th'-shire. (*b*) *What is won in
the shire* (or *county*) *is lost in the hundred.*
1662 : Fuller, *Worthies*, ii. 538 (1840), As
our English proverb saith, " What is
lost in the hundred will be found in the
shire." 1732 : Fuller, No. 5522, What
they lose in the Hundred they gain in
the County. 1917 : Bridge, *Cheshire
Proverbs*, 151, What is got in the
County is lost in the Hundred.

**Hundred pounds of sorrow pays not
one ounce of debt,** An. Before 1704 :
T. Brown, *Works*, iii. 247 (1760) [cited
as " the country proverb "]. 1869 :
Spurgeon, *John Ploughman*, ch. xii.,
A hundred years of regret Pay not a
farthing of debt.

**Hundred tailors, A, a hundred millers,
and a hundred weavers make three
hundred thieves.** 1659 : Howell, *Proverbs : Span.-Eng.*, 11. 1672 : R. Codrington, *Proverbs*, 4. 1732 : Fuller,
No. 615. Cf. **Miller** (10).

**Hunger and cold deliver a man up to
his enemy.** 1813 : Ray, 126.

Hunger and ease. *See* **Dog** (7).

Hunger breaks through stone walls.
1546 : Heywood, *Proverbs*, Pt. I. ch.
xii., Some saie, and I feele hunger
perseth stone wall. *c.* 1580 : Spelman,
Dialogue, 121 (Roxb. Cl.), As the oulde
saynge is, honger breketh stone walles.
1605 : Chapman, etc., *Eastw. Hoe*, V. i.
1651 : Cartwright, *Ordinary*, II. i.,
Hunger may break stone walls, it ne'er
hurts men. 1759 : Colman, *Rolliad*,

can. i., Hunger, they say, thro' stony
walls will break. 1821 : W. Combe,
Syntax in Search of Wife, can. xxxiv.
p. 53, Hunger, by you know whom, 'tis
said, Will break through walls to get
its bread.

Hunger droppeth out of his nose.
Before 1529 : Skelton, *Magnyfycence*,
l. 2288, I gyue hym Crystys curse,
With neuer a peny in his purse . . .
Ye, for *requiem æternam* groweth forth
of his nose. 1546 : Heywood, *Proverbs*,
Pt. I. ch. xi., Hunger droppeth euen out
of bothe their noses. 1611 : Cotgrave,
s.v. " Chiche-face," A . . . wretched
fellow ; one out of whose nose hunger
drops. 1659 : Howell, *Letters*, ii. 666
(Jacobs), She will in a short time make
hunger to dropp out at your nose.

**Hunger fetcheth the wolf out of the
woods.** 1567 : Painter, *Pal. of Pleasure*,
iii. 216 (Jacobs), I well perceiue that
hunger forceth the woulf oute of hir
denne. 1611 : Cotgrave, s.v. " Bois,"
Hunger drives woolves out of the wood.
1750 : Smollett, *Gil Blas*, iv. 245,
Hunger, thou knowest, brings the wolf
out of the wood.

**Hunger finds no fault with the
cookery.** 1732 : Fuller, No. 2566. 1869 :
Spurgeon, *John Ploughman*, ch. v. with
[" cook " for " cookery "].

**Hunger in frost that will not work in
heat,** They must. 1546 : Heywood,
Proverbs, Pt. I. ch. xi. 1605 : Camden,
Remains, 333 (1870). 1670 : Ray, 30.
1754 : Berthelson, *Eng.-Danish Dict.*,
s.v. " Hunger."

Hunger is not dainty. 1732 : Fuller,
No. 2567.

Hunger is sharper than thorn.
c. 1560 ; Becon, *Catechism, etc.*, 601
(P.S.), Ye know the common proverbs . . . " Hunger is sharper than
thorn." 1884 : Cudworth, *Dialect
Sketches*, 15 (W.), Hunger, they say, is
a sharp thorn, an' begow it's true.

Hunger is the best sauce. [Optimum
cibi condimentum fames, sitis potus.—
Cicero, *De Finibus*, lib. 2. Cf. Horace,
Sat., II. ii. 38]. *c.* 1375 : Barbour,
Bruce, iii. 540, That soucht nan othir
salso thartill Bot appetyt, that oft
men takys (That sought for no other

sauce thereto except appetite, such as
often seizes men). 1542 : Udall, tr.
Erasmus' *Apoph.*, 2 (1877), Socrates
said, the best sauce in the world for
meates, is to bee houngrie. 1639 :
Massinger, *Unnat. Combat*, III. i., Nor
do you Find fault with the sauce, keen
hunger being the best. 1709 : O. Dykes,
Eng. Proverbs, 11, Hunger is sawce for
an emperor. 1827 : Hone, *Table-Book*,
139, That " a sharp stomach is the best
sauce," is a saying as true as it is
common.

**Hunger makes dinners, pastime sup-
pers.** 1640 : Herbert, *Jac. Prudentum*.

Hunger makes hard beans sweet.
Before 1500 : Hill, *Commonplace-Book*,
133 (E.E.T.S.), Hungre maketh harde
bones softe. 1546 : Heywood, *Proverbs*,
Pt. I. ch. x. 1670 : Ray, 107, Hunger
makes hard bones sweet beans. 1732 :
Fuller, No. 2570, Hunger makes raw
beans relish well.

Hungry as a church-mouse. 1670 :
Ray, 205. 1901 : F. E. Taylor, *Lancs
Sayings*, 3.

Hungry as a dog. 1862 : *Dialect of
Leeds*, 405.

Hungry as a hawk. 1652 : Taylor
(Water-Poet), *Works*, 1st coll., *Christmas In and Out* (Spens. S.), I and my
men were as hungry as hawks. 1681 :
W. Robertson, *Phraseol. Generalis*, 749.
1703 : Ward, *Writings*, ii. 105, Hungry
as hawks, having food to delight 'em.
1883 : R. L. S., *Treasure I.*, ch. vi., I
made a hearty supper, for I was as
hungry as a hawk.

Hungry as a hunter. 1800 : Lamb,
Letters, i. 162 (Lucas), I came home . . .
hungry as a hunter. 1834 : Marryat,
P. Simple, ch. ii. 1864 : Mrs. H. Wood,
Trevlyn Hold, ch. xix., I am as hungry
as a hunter. Get me something to eat.

Hungry as a June crow. 1886 : C.
Swainson, *Folk-Lore of Brit. Birds*, 87
(F.L.S.), About June and July, should
there be a drought of long duration,
rooks suffer terribly ; hence the proverb
" As hungry as a June crow."

Hungry as a kite. *c.* 1555 : in Wright,
Songs, etc., Philip and Mary, 17 (Roxb.
Cl.), When Lent cummys to the towene
as hongré as a glede [kite]. 1855 :

Robinson, *Whitby Gloss.*, 71, "As hungry as a glead," ravenous.

Hungry as a wolf. 1540: Palsgrave, *Acolastus*, sig. L1, I am more hungry than any wolfe is. 1611: Cotgrave, s.v. "Allouvi," As hungry as a woolfe. 1858: Lytton, *What Will He Do?* I. iii., I have the hunger of a wolf.

Hungry as the grave. 1880: Courtney, *W. Country Words*, 29 (E.D.S.).

Hungry bellies. *See* Belly.

Hungry dogs will eat dirty puddings. [Jejunus raro stomachus vulgaria temnit. Horace, *Sat.*, II. ii. 38.] 1546: Heywood, *Proverbs*, Pt. I. ch. v. 1553: *Respublica*, III. vi., Suche hongrye doggs will slabbe vp sluttishe puddinges. 1600: Dekker, *Old Fortunatus*, II. ii., A hungry dog eats dirty puddings. 1721: Bailey, *Eng. Dict.*, s.v. "Hungry." 1830: Colman, jr., in *Hum. Works*, 421 (Hotten). 1893: J. Salisbury, *S.E. Worcs. Gloss.*, 55 (E.D.S.), A 'ongry dog'll yut dirty puddin'. — *Proverb.* 1901: F. E. Taylor, *Lancs Sayings*, 7, A hungry dog's fain o' dirty puddin', Cf. Scornful dogs.

Hungry flies bite sore. 1546: Heywood, *Proverbs*, Pt. II. ch. ix. 1670: Ray, 107. 1736: Bailey, *Dict.*, s.v.

Hungry, If thou be, I am angry, let us go fight. 1678: Ray, 65.

Hungry man is an angry man, A. 1659: Howell, 13. 1670: Ray, 14. 1880: Spurgeon, *Ploughman's Pictures*, 52. 1911: Hackwood, *Good Cheer*, 345, A hungry man is an angry man, and an empty stomach has no conscience.

Hungry man smells meat afar off, A. 1732: Fuller, No. 224.

Hungry men think the cook lazy. Ibid., No. 2574.

Hunt's dog, that will neither go to church nor stay at home, Like. 1678: Ray, 291. 1708: *Brit. Apollo*, i. No. 105, col. 3. 1785: Grose, *Class. Dict. Vulgar Tongue*, s.v. [a Shropshire story told]. 1883: Burne, *Shropsh. Folk-Lore*, 593. 1917: Bridge, *Cheshire Proverbs*, 90. 1920: in *N. & Q.*, 12th ser., vii. 67 [the correspondent says he had heard the saying in Warwickshire within the last ten years]. Cf. Wood's dog.

Hunter's moon, The. 1710: *Brit.*

Apollo, iii. No. 70, p. 2, col. 1 (O.), The country people call this the Hunters-Moon. 1846: Denham, *Proverbs*, 58 (Percy S.), An October moon is called the "hunter's moon." 1855: Kingsley, *West. Ho!*, ch. v., The broad, bright hunter's moon. 1873: in *N. & Q.*, 4th ser., xi. 45, The Hunter's Moon in October, and the Harvest Moon in September, are not called so simply because hunting begins and harvest is being got in in these months.

Hunters that blow the horn, All are not. 1586: L. Evans, *Withals Dict. Revised*, sig. E6, Euery horne blower is not a hunter. 1678: Ray, 158. 1869: Spurgeon, *John Ploughman*, ch. i., All are not hunters that wear red coats, and all are not working men who call themselves so.

Huntingdon sturgeon, A. *See* quot. 1667: Pepys, *Diary*, 22 May, This day coming from Westminster . . . we saw at White Hall stairs a fisher-boat, with a sturgeon that he had newly catched in the River; which I saw, but it was but a little one; but big enough to prevent my mistake of that for a colt, if ever I become Mayor of Huntingdon. [Lord Braybrooke's note on this is: "During a very high flood in the meadows between Huntingdon and Godmanchester, something was seen floating, which the Godmanchester people thought was a black pig, and the Huntingdon folk declared it was a sturgeon; when rescued from the waters, it proved to be a *young donkey*. This mistake led to the one party being styled 'Godmanchester black pigs,' and the other 'Huntingdon sturgeons,' terms not altogether forgotten at this day. Pepys's *colt* must be taken to be the *colt of an ass*."] 1790: Grose, *Prov. Gloss.*, s.v. "Hunts."

Huntingdonshire. *See* quot. 1865: W. White, *East. England*, ii. 95, Huntingdonshire . . . where, in the words of the proverb, "they have churches for mile-stones."

Hurstpierpoint. *See* Wolstonbury.

Hurts another hurts himself, He that. 1578: Florio, *First Fruites*, fo. 29. 1629: *Book of Meery Riddles*, Prov. 84.

Husband and **Husbands.** I. *A husband must be deaf, and the wife blind, to
have quietness.* 1666 : Torriano, *Piazza
Univ.*, 144. Cf. **Wife** (24).

2. *A husband ofttimes makes the best
physician.* 1840 : Barham, *Ing. Legends :*
" Lady Rohesia."

3. *Husbands are in heaven whose
wives scold not.* 1546 : Heywood, *Proverbs*, Pt. II. ch. vii. 1670 : Ray, 14
[with " chide " for " scold "]. 1732 :
Fuller, No. 2579 [as in 1670].

4. *The calmest husbands make the
stormiest wives.* 1823 : D'Israeli, *Cur.
of Lit.*, 2nd ser., i. 423 (1824), The
husband was reminded of his lordly
authority when he only looked into his
trencher [*temp.* Elizabeth], one of its
learned aphorisms having descended to
us,—" The calmest husbands make the
stormyest wives."

5. *When the husband drinks to the
wife, all would be well : When the wife
drinks to the husband, all is well.* 1659 :
Howell, 9 (7), When the good wife
drinketh to the husband all is well in
the house. 1670 : Ray, 53. 1732 :
Fuller, No. 5593.

6. *When the husband is fire and the
wife tow, the devil easily sets all in a
flame.* 1732 : Fuller, No. 5594.

See also **Bachelor** (1) ; **Good husband** ;
Hold your tongue ; **Ill husband** ; **Maid**
(13) ; **Sorrow for a husband** ; and **Wife**
(3), (21), and (24).

Husbandman. *See* quot. 1569 :
Grafton, *Chron.*, ii. 5 (1809), The olde
auncient adage which sayeth, that the
husbandman ought first to taste off the
newe growen fruite.

**Husk, By the, you may guess at the
nut.** 1732 : Fuller, No. 1044.

**Hustings (or Hoistings), You are all
for the.** 1662 : Fuller, *Worthies*, ii. 349
(1840). 1670 : Ray, 244.

Hutton. *See* quot. 1869 : Hazlitt, 210,
Hutton an' Huyton, Ditton an' Hoo
[Hool in Cheshire] are three [? four] of
the merriest towns that ever a man rode
through. Higson's *MSS. Coll.*, No. 37.

Huyton. *See* **Hutton** ; and **Preston.**

**Hypocrisy can find out a cloak for
every rain.** 1573 : *New Custom*, II. ii.
c. 1580 : Spelman, *Dialogue*, 56 (Roxb.
Cl.), [speaking of hypocrites] Such a
cloke use they for the rayne.

**Hypocrisy is a sort of homage that vice
pays to virtue.** 1732 : Fuller, No. 2580.

I

I know what I do when I drink. 1639 :
Clarke, 85. 1670 : Ray, 216.

I made of my friend my foe. *See* quot.
15th cent. : in *Reliq. Antiquæ*, i. 316
(1841), I made of my frend my foo,
I will beware I do no more soo.

I stout. *See* Stout.

I was by (quoth Pedley) when my eye
was put out. 1678 : Ray, 242.

I'll make one (quoth Kirkham) when
he danced in his clogs. Cheshire. 1670 :
Ray, 182. 1917 : Bridge, *Cheshire
Proverbs*, 78.

I'll tent [prevent] thee, quoth Wood,
If I can't rule my daughter, I'll rule my
good. Cheshire. 1670 : Ray, 52. 1877 :
E. Leigh, *Cheshire Gloss.*, 208. 1917 :
Bridge, *Cheshire Proverbs*, 78.

I'm very wheamow [nimble], said the
old woman, when she stept into the
milk-bowl. 1670 : Ray, 217. 1877 : E.
Leigh, *Cheshire Gloss.*, 225 [with " bitt-
len " for " milk-bowl "]. 1917 : Bridge,
Cheshire Proverbs, 79 [with " middle of
the bittlin " for " milk-bowl "].

Ice. 1. *If at Christmas ice hangs on
the willow, clover may be cut at Easter.*
1893 : Inwards, *Weather Lore*, 39.

2. *If the ice will bear a goose before
Christmas, it will not bear a duck after.*
1846 : Denham, *Proverbs*, 62 (Percy S.).
1893 : Inwards, *Weather Lore*, 9.

3. *If the ice will bear a man before
Christmas, it will not bear a goose* (or
duck, or *mouse*) *after.* c. 1870 : Smith,
Isle of Wight Words, 62 (E.D.S.). 1881 :
Folk-Lore Record, iv. 126 [" duck."
Notts]. 1893 : Inwards, *Weather Lore*,
39 ["mouse"]. 1902 : *N. & Q.*, 9th ser.,
x. 506 [" goose "].

4. *Trust not one night's ice.* 1640 :
Herbert, *Jac. Prudentum*. 1875 : A. B.
Cheales, *Proverb. Folk-Lore*, 114.

See also Martinmas (2) ; November
(3) ; and St. Matthias (3).

Idle, *adj.* 1. *An idle head is a box
for the wind.* 1640 : Herbert, *Jac.
Prudentum.*

2. *An idle person is the devil's cushion*
(or *playfellow*). 1630 : T. Adams, *Works*,

197, The idle man is the deuils cushion,
whereupon he sits and takes his ease.
1660 : Howell, *Parly of Beasts*, 134, To
avoid idlenes, which is the devills couch.
1732 : Fuller, No. 620 ["playfellow"].
1859 : Smiles, *Self-Help*, 273 (1869), A
lazy man [is] the devil's bolster.

3. *An idle youth a needy age.* 1611 :
Cotgrave, s.v. " Jeunesse." 1651 :
Herbert, *Jac. Prudentum*, 2nd ed.

4. *As idle as Dain's* [Dean's] *dog as
laid 't deaun t' bark.* 1917 : Bridge,
Cheshire Proverbs, 17. Cf. Lazy as
Ludlam's dog.

5. *Be not idle and you shall not be longing.* 1640 : Herbert, *Jac. Prudentum.*

6. *He is idle that might be better
employed.* 1732 : Fuller, No. 1919.

7. *Idle brains are the devil's workshop.*
1678 : Ray, 161, An idle brain is the
devils shop. 1732 : Fuller, No. 3053
[" workhouses "]. 1875 : A. B. Cheales,
Proverb. Folk-Lore, 110. 1901 : F. E.
Taylor, *Lancs Sayings*, 7, An idle mon's
yed's the divvle's smithy.

8. *Idle folks have the least leisure.*
1869 : Spurgeon, *John Ploughman*, ch. i.

9. *Idle folks lack no excuses.* 1639 :
Clarke, 234. 1670 : Ray, 109.

10. *Idle folks take the most pains.*
1678 : Ray, 161, Idle folks have the most
labour. 1732 : Fuller, No. 3056. 1831 :
Hone, *Year-Book*, 1416. Cf. Lazy folks.

11. *Idle men are dead all their life
long.* 1732 : Fuller, No. 3055.

See also Devil (22) and (84).

Idle, *subs. You'll soon learn to shape
Idle a coat.* 1602 : Carew, *Surv. of Cornwall*, fo. 56 (1769), To reproue one of
lazines, they will say, Doest thou make
Idle a coate? 1678 : Ray, 254.

Idleness is the greatest prodigality in
the world. 1650 : Taylor, *Holy Living*,
ch. i. § 1. 1732 : Fuller, No. 3060.

Idleness is the key of beggary (or
mother of poverty). 1616 : *Rich Cabinet*,
fo. 73, Idlenesse is the mother of
pouerty. 1670 : Ray, 14, Idleness is
the key of beggery. 1754 : Berthelson,
Eng.-Danish Dict., s.v. [as in 1670].

1869 : Spurgeon, *John Ploughman*, ch. i.
[as in 1670].

Idleness is the parent of all vice.
c. 1440 : Lydgate, *Fall of Princes*,
bk. ii. l. 2249 (E.E.T.S.), Mooder off
vices, callid idilnesse. *c.* 1483 : *Quatuor
Sermones*, 35 (Roxb. Cl.), Fle ydelnesse
for it is . . . the key of all vyces. *c.* 1568 :
W. Wager, *Longer thou Livest*, sig. C2,
Idlenes the parent of all vice. 1630 :
Brathwait, *Eng. Gent.*, etc., 61 (1641),
Idlenesse . . . being the mother of all
vices. 1851 : Borrow, *Lavengro*, i. 189,
It has been said that idleness is the
parent of mischief.

Idleness is the root of all evil. 1566 :
Becon, in *Early Works*, 444 (P.S.), Idleness, which is the well-spring and root
of all vice. 1598 : *Servingmans Comfort*, in *Inedited Tracts*, 158 (Hazlitt),
Idlenesse is the roote of all mischiefe.
1760 : Foote, *Minor*, I. 1850 : Dickens,
Copperfield, ch. x.

**Idleness makes the wit rust (or turns
the edge of wit).** 1600 : Bodenham,
Belvedere, 131 (Spens. S.), Idlenes is
the canker of the mind. 1650 : Taylor,
Holy Living, I. i. 14, Idleness is the
rust of time. 1670 : Ray, 14, Idleness
turns the edge of wit. 1732 : Fuller,
No. 3061, Idleness makes the wit rust.

Idleness, Of, comes no goodness.
1611 : Cotgrave, s.v. " Gueule." 1678 :
Ray, 161. 1732 : Fuller, No. 3698, Of
idleness never comes any good.

If it be not true here's my elbow.
1659 : Howell, 17.

**If my aunt had been a man, she'd
have been my uncle.** 1813 : Ray, 202.

**If you want clear water, you must go
to the head of the well.** S. Cornwall,
19th cent. (Mr. C. Lee).

**If thou won't have me old Shenton
will.** 1917 : Bridge, *Cheshire Proverbs*,
77, [Two men courting a farm-house
servant came the same evening] She
put one in the brick oven, and being
somewhat piqued at the slowness of
the other, she said, " If thou won't
have me old Shenton will." " Will
he? " said Shenton from the oven; and
ever since then it has been a saying in
that neighbourhood.

If you wish a thing done, go; if not,

send. 1566 : Painter, *Pal. of Pleasure*,
i. 87 (Jacobs), Alwayes fixe fast in
breast, in prompt and ready wise :
This prouerbe olde and true, a sentence
of the wise : The thing do not expect, by
frends for to atchieue : Which thou
thyselfe canst doe, thy selfe for to
relieue. 1692 : L'Estrange, *Æsop*, 53
(3rd ed.), He that would be sure to have
his business well done, must either do it
himself, or see the doing of it. 1736 :
Franklin, *Way to Wealth*, in *Works*, i.
445 (Bigelow), If you would have your
business done, go; if not, send. 1842 :
Barham, *Ing. Legends*, 2nd ser. : " In-
goldsby Penance." 1859 : Smiles, *Self-
Help*, 272 (1869), " If you want your
business done," says the proverb, " go
and do it; if you don't want it done,
send some one else."

Ifs and Ands. *c.* 1513 : More, *Works*,
p. 54, col. 2 (1557), What quod the
protectour thou seruest me I wene with
iffes and with andes. 1589 : Nashe,
Introd. to Greene's *Menaphon*, 10
(Arber), Sufficeth them to bodge vp a
blanke verse with ifs and ands. *c.* 1624 :
Davenport, *King John*, I. ii., Well, well,
with *ifs* and *ands* Mad men leave rocks
and leap into the sands. 1681 : W.
Robertson, *Phraseol. Generalis*, 90,
Without Ifs and Ands ; plane, absolute.
1748 : Richardson, *Clarissa*, v. 237
(1785), Then he came with his If's and
And's. 1828 : Carr, *Craven Dialect*, i.
241, " Let's hev naan o' yower ifs an'
ans," let us have no hesitation, be
decisive. 1889 : Peacock, *Manley, etc.*,
Gloss., 286 (E.D.S.), If ifs and ands was
pots and pans There'd be noä wark for
th' tinkers. 1924 : Sir R. Horne, in
Times, 30 May, p. 9, col. 4, If he might
vary an old saw he would say, " If ' ifs
and ands ' could create employment,
then there would be little use for the
Minister of Labour to tinker at it."

Ignorance is a voluntary misfortune.
1669 : *Politeuphuia*, 63.

Ignorance is the mother of devotion.
1559 : Bp. Jewell, *Works*, iii. pt. ii.,
1202 (P.S.), Ignorantia enim, inquit,
mater est verae pietatis, quam ille appel-
lavit devotionem. 1573 : *New Custom*,
I. i. 1593 : G. Harvey, *Works*, ii. 138

(Grosart), Ignorance . . . was wont to
be termed the moother of deuotion.
1621 : Burton, *Melancholy*, III. iv. 1, 2,
p. 678 (1836). 1668 : Dryden, *Secret
Love*, I. ii., Your ignorance is the
mother of your devotion to me. 1700 :
T. Brown, *Works*, iii. 67-8 (1760).

Ignorance is the mother of impudence.
1666 : Torriano, *Piazza Univ.*, 116,
Ignorance the mother of presumption
and of errors. Before 1680 : Butler,
Remains, ii. 213 (1759), Impudence is
the bastard of ignorance. 1732 : Fuller, No. 3067. 1869 : Spurgeon, *John
Ploughman*, ch. ii., His ignorance is the
mother of his impudence, and the nurse
of his obstinacy.

Ignorance. *See also* **Knowledge.**

**Ignorant hath an eagle's wings and an
owl's eyes, The.** 1640 : Herbert, *Jac.
Prudentum.*

Ilchester. *See* quots. 1670 : Ray, 342,
All Ilchester is gaol, say prisoners there.
1790 : Grose, *Prov. Gloss.*, s.v. " Somerset," All Ilchester is gaol.

**Ill agreement is better than a good
judgment, An.** 1640 : Herbert, *Jac.
Prudentum.* 1666 : Torriano, *Piazza
Univ.*, 1, A sorry agreement is better
than a good sute in law. Cf. **Better a
lean peace.**

Ill air where we gain nothing, It is an.
1640 : Herbert, *Jac. Prudentum.* 1670 :
Ray, 1. 1732 : Fuller, No. 2895.

Ill bird lays an ill egg, An. 1586 :
Pettie, tr. Guazzo's *Civil Convers.*,
fo. 127, An ill byrde layeth an ill egge.
1617: *Arraignment of Lewd, etc., Women*,
44. 1716 : Ward, *Female Policy*, 93
[cited as " the old proverb "].

Ill bird that fouls its own nest, It is an.
c. 1250 : *Owl and Nightingale*, 99, Dahet
habbe that ilkë best That fuleth his owë
nest (A curse be upon that beast [creature, bird] that defiles his own nest).
1402 : Hoccleve, *Minor Poems*, 80
(E.E.T.S.), An olde proverbe seyde ys
in englyssh : men seyn " that brid or
foule ys dyshonest, what that he be and
holden ful chirlyssh, that vseth to defoule his oone neste." 1509 : Barclay,
Ship of Fools, i. 173 (1874), It is a lewde
byrde that fyleth his owne nest. 1583 :
Greene, in *Works*, ii. 31 (Grosart), It is

a fowle bird defiles the own neast.
1685 : *Mother Bunch's Closet, etc.*, 6
(Gomme, 1885), An ill bird befoules its
own nest. 1817 : Scott, *Rob Roy*, ch.
xxvi. 1851 : FitzGerald, *Euphranor*, 13
(1855), You . . . must not, like a bad
bird, foul your own nest.

**Ill boy that goes like a top, no longer
than 'tis whipt, He's an.** 1732 : Fuller,
No. 2449.

Ill cause. *See* quot. 1855 : Bohn, 399,
He who hath an ill cause, let him sell
it cheap.

**Ill comes in by ells and goes out by
inches.** 1640 : Herbert, *Jac. Prudentum.*
1666 : Torriano, *Piazza Univ.*, 138, Evil
cometh by cartloads, and goes away by
ounces, cometh on horseback and goes
away on foot.

**Ill cook that can't lick his own fingers,
He's an.** *c.* 1520 : Stanbridge, *Vulgaria*,
sig. C4, He is an euyll coke y^t can not
lycke his owne lyppes. 1592 : Shakespeare, *Romeo*, IV. ii. 1646 : Quarles,
Works, iii. 222 (Grosart), He's but a
silly cook that wists not how To lick
his fingers. 1738 : Swift, *Polite Convers.*, Dial. I. 1822 : Scott, *Nigel*,
ch. vi., They say, a good cook knows
how to lick his own fingers.

Ill doers are ill deemers. [Tuo ex
ingenio mores alienos probas.—Plautus,
Truc., ii. 47.] 1738 : Swift, *Polite
Convers.*, Dial. I., They say ill doers are
ill deemers. 1828 : Scott, *Fair Maid*,
ch. xvii., Put me not to quote the old
saw, that evil doers are evil dreaders.
1853 : Trench, *Proverbs*, 115 (1905).

Ill done must be done twice, A work.
1659 : Howell, *Proverbs: Brit.-Eng.*, 3.

Ill egging makes ill begging. 1605 :
Camden, *Remains*, 325 (1870). 1670 :
Ray, 84, Ill egging makes ill begging. Evil
persons by enticing and flattery, draw
on others to be as bad as themselves.

**Ill fortune, He that hath no, is troubled
with good.** 1640 : Herbert, *Jac. Prudentum.* 1670 : Ray, 10 [with " cloy'd "
for " troubled "].

**Ill game that hath not one trump, It
is an.** 1740 : North, *Lives of Norths*, i.
357 (Bohn).

**Ill gathering of stones where the sea
is bottomless, 'Tis.** 1659, Howell, 11.

Ill gotten ˈgoods (a) thrive not; (b) thrive not to the third heir. (a) 1519: Horman, *Vulgaria*, fo. 77, Euyll goten ryches wyll neuer proue longe. 1591: Spenser, *Moth. Hubb. Tale*, l. 1149, Ill might it prosper, that ill gotten was. *c.* 1630: in *Roxb. Ballads*, i. 184 (Hindley), Ill gotten goods never doe thrive. 1732: Fuller, No. 3070, Ill gotten goods seldom prosper. 1826: Lamb, *Pop. Fallacies*, II. 1842: Barham, *Ing. Legends*, 2nd ser.: "Babes in Wood." (b) 1303: Brunne, *Handl. Synne*, l. 9436, Here mayst thou se, euyl-wunne thyng Wyth eyre shal neuer make gode endyng. Ibid., l. 9479, For thys men se, and sey alday, "The threde eyre selleth alle away." *c.* 1430: in *Twenty-six Poems*, 149 (E.E.T.S.), Men seyen "good geten vntrewly, The iij^de eyre browke hit ne may." 1493: *Dives et Pauper*, It is a common prouerbe . . . Of euyll gotten goods the thyrde heyre vnneth hath ioy. 1593: Nashe, in *Works*, iv. 146 (Grosart), Ill gotten goods neuer touche the third heyre. 1619: *Helpe to Discourse*, 70 (1640), Of piles of wealth, rais'd by unjust extortion, The third heir seldom doth injoy his portion. 1708: tr. Aleman's *Guzman*, i. 405, It being next to impossible that ill-got wealth should descend to the third heir. 1875: A. B. Cheales, *Proverb. Folk-Lore*, 101, Ill gotten gear Wilna enrich the third heir.

Ill gotten ill spent. [Male partum male disperit.—Plautus, *Poen.*, IV. ii. 22.] 1539: Taverner, *Proverbs*, fo. 24, Euyll gotten good go euyll away. 1564: Bullein, *Dialogue*, 72 (E.E.T.S.), For euill gotten goodes are euill spent, saied our curate vpon Sondaie. 1603: Breton, in *Works*, ii. *i* 11 (Grosart). 1680: L'Estrange, *Select Colloq. of Erasmus*, 55, It is but reasonable that what's *Ill got* should be *Worse spent*. 1763: Murphy, *Citizen*, I. ii., The moment young master comes to possession, "Ill got, ill gone," I warrant me.

Ill guest that never drinks to his host, It's an. 1678: Ray, 86.

Ill healing of an old sore, It is. 1546: Heywood, *Proverbs*, Pt. II. ch. viii. 1659: Howell, 4.

Ill husband. 1. *He is an ill husband that is not missed.* 1633: Draxe, 2.

2. *She that has an ill husband shews it in her dress.* 1732: Fuller, No. 4139.

Ill language, There were no, if it were not ill taken. 1640: Herbert, *Jac. Prudentum.* 1699: Farquhar, *Love and a Bottle*, IV. ii., For as nothing's ill said, but what's ill taken. 1732: Fuller, No. 4945.

Ill look among lambs, ˈHe has an. Ibid., No. 1861.

Ill luck. 1. *Ill luck is good for something.* 1605: Camden, *Remains*, 326 (1870). 1732: Fuller, No. 3074.

2. *Ill luck is worse than found money.* 1670: Ray, 110.

3. *What's worse than ill luck?* 1639: Clarke, 166. 1641: *Roxb. Ballads*, vii. 613 (B.S.), The prouerbe sayes, "What's worse than ill-luck?" 1685: Meriton, *Yorkshire Ale*, 47. 1736: Bailey, *Dict.*, s.v. "Worse."

4. *When ill luck falls asleep, let nobody wake her.* 1659: Howell, *Proverbs: Span.-Eng.*, 1, When ill fortune lies asleep, let none awake her. 1869: Hazlitt, 458.

Ill man lie in thy straw, Let an, and he looks to be thy heir. 1640: Herbert, *Jac. Prudentum.*

Ill marriage is a spring of ill fortune, An. 1633: Draxe, 229.

Ill master makes an ill servant, An. 1666: Torriano, *Piazza Univ.*, 258.

Ill master makes bad scholars, An. 1639: Clarke, 238.

Ill name is half hanged, He that hath an. 1546: Heywood, *Proverbs*, Pt. II. ch. vi. 1560: T. Wilson, *Rhetorique*, 186 (1909). 1613: T. Heywood, *Silver Age*, II., I am halfe hang'd already, for my good name is lost. 1732: Fuller, No. 2133. 1822: Peacock, *Maid Marian*, ch. xviii., Your hero makes laws to get rid of your thief, and gives him an ill name that he may hang him. Cf. **Dog** (43).

Ill natures never want a tutor. 1732: Fuller, No. 3076.

Ill natures, the more you ask them, the more they stick. 1640: Herbert, *Jac. Prudentum.*

Ill neighbour. *See* Neighbour (2) and (3).

Ill news are commonly true. 1611: Davies (of Hereford), *Sc. of Folly*, 42, in *Works*, ii. (Grosart). 1633: Draxe, 139.

Ill news flies apace. 1574: E. Hellowes, *Guevara's Epistles*, 91, Euill newes neuer commeth to late. 1629: Massinger, *Picture*, II. i., Ill news, madam, Are swallow-wing'd, but what's good walks on crutches. 1694: *Terence made English*, 46, Bad news always fly faster than good. 1792: Holcroft, *Road to Ruin*, II. i., Ill news travels fast. 1850: Dickens, *Chuzzlewit*, ch. xxxi., There's a true saying that nothing travels so fast as ill news. 1922: Weyman, *Ovington's Bank*, ch. xxxviii., Ill news has many feet. Rides apace and needs no spurs.

Ill paymaster never wants excuse, An. 1732: Fuller, No. 627.

Ill pipe that wants his upper lip, He can. 1546: Heywood, *Proverbs*, Pt. II. ch. ix. [with " lacketh " for " wants "]. 1670: Ray, 131. 1732: Fuller, No. 6374. 1819: Scott, *Ivanhoe*, ch. xxxii., I had mumbled but a lame mass an thou hadst broken my jaw, for the piper plays ill that wants the nether chops.

Ill playing with short daggers, It be. 1546: Heywood, *Proverbs*, Pt. I. ch. xii.

Ill plea should be well pleaded, An. 1855: Bohn, 312.

Ill putting a naked sword in a madman's hand, It is. 1546: Heywood, *Proverbs*, Pt. II. ch. viii. 1670: Ray, 147. 1672: Walker, *Parœm.*, 48. 1736: Bailey, *Dict.*, s.v. " Sword," Don't put a sword into a madman's hands.

Ill run that cannot go, He may. 1468: *Coventry Mys.*, 97 (Sh. S.), He may evyl go that is ner lame; In sothe I com as fast as I may. 1546: Heywood, *Proverbs*, Pt. II. ch. ix. 1670: Ray, 138.

Ill sack that will abide no clouting, It is an. 1546: Heywood, *Proverbs*, Pt. II. ch. iv. 1670: Ray, 23. 1732: Fuller, No. 2843.

Ill seed ill weed. *c.* 1440: Lydgate, *Fall of Princes*, bk. v. l. 116 (E.E.T.S.),

Of froward seed may growe no good corn. 1611: Cotgrave, s.v. " Moisson."

Ill servant will never be a good master, An. 1683: Meriton, *Yorkshire Ale*, 83–7 (1697). 1887: *Brighouse News*, 23 July (W.).

Ill shaving against the wool, It's. 1670: Ray, 141.

Ill song who has ne'er a tongue, He makes an. 1855: Bohn, 379.

Ill sowers make ill harvest. 1732: Fuller, No. 3078.

Ill spun web. *See* quots. *c.* 1300: *Prov. of Hending*, st. 35 (Berlin, 1878), Euer out cometh euel sponne web. *c.* 1410: *Towneley Plays*, 21 (E.E.T.S.), Ill spon weft ay comes foule out. *c.* 1460: *Wyse Man taught hys Sone*, l. 7 (E.E.T.S.), For zerne that is euylle spone Euylle it comes out at the laste. 1670: Ray, 154, An ill-spun weft [web] will out either now or eft. . . . This is a Yorkshire proverb.

Ill stake standeth longest, An. 1659: Howell, 3. 1670: Ray, 14.

Ill stake that can't stand one year in a hedge, It's an. 1546: Heywood, *Proverbs*, Pt. II. ch. iv. 1670: Ray, 145. 1732: Fuller, No. 2845.

Ill talking between a full man and a fasting, It is. 1823: Scott, *Q. Durward*, ch. x. 1828: Scott, *Fair Maid*, ch. xx. 1875: A. B. Cheales, *Proverb. Folk-Lore*, 107.

Ill to himself will be good to nobody, He that's. 1732: Fuller, No. 2284.

Ill to trust who will trust nobody, He is. 1644: Taylor (Water-Poet), *Crop-eare Curried*, 19, in *Works*, 2nd coll. (Spens. S.).

Ill turn. 1. *An ill turn is soon done.* 1732: Fuller, No. 631.

2. *He that does you a very ill turn, will never forgive you.* 1710: S. Palmer, *Moral Essays on Proverbs*, 263 [with " an injury " for " a very ill turn "]. 1732: Fuller, No. 2085.

Ill vessels seldom miscarry. 1640: Herbert, *Jac. Prudentum*.

Ill ware is never cheap. Ibid. 1659: Howell, *Proverbs: Fr.-Eng.*, 8, Bad ware is never too cheap.

Ill weather comes unsent for. 1583: Melbancke, *Philotinus*, sig. F3, Though

I come like ill weather, vnsent for.
1846 : Denham, *Proverbs*, 3 (Percy S.),
Ill weather and sorrow come unsent
for. Cf. Sorrow.

Ill weather is seen soon enough when
it comes. Ibid., 1.

Ill weeds grow apace. *c.* 1490 : *Harl.
MS.*, quoted in Hulme, *Proverb Lore*, 12,
Euyl weed ys sone y-growe. 1546 :
Heywood, *Proverbs*, Pt. I. ch. x., Ill
weede growth fast. 1594 : Shakespeare,
Rich. III., II. iv., Small herbs have
grace, great weeds do grow apace.
1660 : Tatham, *The Rump*, I. 1733 :
Fielding, *Miser*, III. v. *c.* 1750 : Foote,
Knights, I. 1846 : Denham, *Proverbs*, I
(Percy S.).

Ill will never speaks well. 1566 : L.
Wager, *Mary Magdalene*, Prol., For euill
will neuer said well, they do say. 1599 :
Shakespeare, *Henry V.*, III. vii. 1660 :
Fuller, *Mixt Contempl.*, 300 (1830).
1732 : Fuller, No. 3081.

Ill wind that blows nobody good, It's
an. *c.* 1540 : J. Heywood, *Song against
Idleness.* 1580 : Tusser, *Husbandrie*, 29
(E.D.S.). *c.* 1640 : *Capt. Underwit*, II.,
in Bullen, *Old Plays*, ii. 347. 1692 :
Congreve, *Old Bachelor*, II. i. 1769 :
Smollett, *Adv. of Atom*, 113 (Cooke,
1795). 1837 : Dickens, *Pickwick*, ch.
xxxii. 1917 : Bridge, *Cheshire Proverbs*,
81, It's an ill wind that blows no-one
any good, but it's well-a-day to them
as lost it.

Ill words are bellows to a slackening
fire. 1732 : Fuller, No. 3082.

Ill workman quarrels with his tools,
An. 1611 : Cotgrave, s.v. " Outil," A
bungler cannot find (or fit himselfe
with) good tooles. 1696 : D'Urfey,
Quixote, Pt. III. Act I. sc. i., 'Tis an ill
workman that quarrels with his own
tools. 1738 : Swift, *Polite Convers.*,
Dial. II., They say an ill workman never
had good tools. 1818 : Byron, *Don
Juan*, can. i. st. 201, Good workmen
never quarrel with their tools. 1859 :
Smiles, *Self-Help*, 124 (1869), It is
proverbial that the bad workman never
yet had a good tool.

Ill wound is cured, not an ill name,
An. 1640 : Herbert, *Jac. Prudentum.*

Ill youth. *See also* Untoward.

Image of rye-dough. *See* quot. 1687 :
Aubrey, *Gentilisme, etc.*, 107 (F.L.S.),
We have a saying, She lookes (*or* He
stands) like an image of rye-dough.
Mdm. In the old time the little images
that did adorn the altars were made of
rye-dough.

Imitation is the sincerest form of
flattery. 1820 : Colton, *Lacon*, Pt. I.
No. 217 [omitting " form "]. 1892 :
B. Pain, *Playthings and Parodies*, § i.
[title], The Sincerest Form of Flattery.

Impressions soon fade, Slight. *c.* 1374 :
Chaucer, *Troylus*, bk. ii. l. 1238, For-
why men seyth, " impressiounes lighte
Ful lightly been ay redy to the flighte."

Impudence to show himself a fool,
He hath. 1732 : Fuller, No. 1888.

Impudence. *See also* Ignorance.

In a quandary. 1577 : *Misogonus*, III.
i., Thou makest me in a greater quandary. 1577 : J. Grange, *Golden Aphroditis*, sig. D3, The captaine . . . standeth
in a quandare, not knowing what to
doe. 1694 : *Terence made English*, 61,
I'm in a strange quandary. 1742 :
Fielding, *Andrews*, bk. ii. ch. iv., " Poor
woman ! " says Mrs. Slipslop, " what a
terrible quandary she must be in ! "
1816 : Scott, *Old Mortality*, ch. viii.
1894 : R. L. S., *St. Ives*, ch. xxvii., This
put me in a quandary. It was a degree
of risk I was scarce prepared for.

In dock out nettle, or In nettle dock out
= unstable, fickle. *c.* 1374 : Chaucer,
Troylus, bk. iv. l. 461, But canstow
pleyen raket, to and fro, Netle in, dokke
out, now this, now that, Pandare?
1546 : Heywood, *Proverbs*, Pt. II. ch. i.,
Waueryng as the wynde, in docke out
nettle. 1586 : L. Evans, *Withals Dict.
Revised*, sig. E2, Oute nettle, in docke.
1655 : Fuller, *Church Hist.*, bk. ii. § v.
(47–8), Thus was it often, " in dock,
out nettle," as they could strengthen
their parties. 1732 : Fuller, No. 3831,
Out, nettle; in, dock. 1882 : Jago,
Gloss. of Cornish Dialect, 225. 1917 :
Bridge, *Cheshire Proverbs*, 80.

In for a penny. *See* Penny (13).

In the name of the Lord begins all
mischief. 1703 : Ward, *Writings*, ii.
193 [cited as an " old saying "]. Cf.
the reverse, s.v. God's name.

In the nick; now usually In the nick
of time. 1577 : *Misogonus*, II. iv., That
came ith nicke. 1577 : Stanihurst, *Descrip. of Ireland*, fo. 1, He was so crost
in the nycke of thys determination.
1603 : Chamberlain, *Letters*, 173 (Camden S.), Mr. Gent comming in the
nicke. *c.* 1620 : *Barnavelt*, V. iii., in
Bullen, *Old Plays*, ii. 307, The Prince
strikes iust i' th' nick. 1740 : North,
Examen, 255, Why not before or after,
but just in the nick of one judge being
absent. 1821 : Scott, *Pirate*, ch. xi.,
The fortunate arrival of Mordaunt, in
the very nick of time. 1866 : G. Eliot,
Felix Holt, ch. vii., Our lucky youngster
is come in the nick of time.

In time comes he whom God sends.
1640 : Herbert, *Jac. Prudentum*. 1670 :
Ray, 51 [with " she " for " he "]. 1732 :
Fuller, No. 2831.

Ince, Go to=Go to Jericho. 1917 :
Bridge, *Cheshire Proverbs*, 63.

Inch. 1. *An inch in a miss is as
good as an ell.* 1605 : Camden, *Remains*,
318 (1870). 1670 : Ray, 109. 1732 :
Fuller, No. 635, An inch in missing is
as bad as an ell. Cf. A miss is as good
as a mile, s.v. " Miss "—a less intelligible saying.

2. *An inch in a man's nose is much.*
1732 : Fuller, No. 634.

3. *An inch in an hour is a foot a day.*
1678 : Ray, 74. 1732 : Fuller, No. 633.

4. *Give an inch you'll take an ell.*
1546 : Heywood, *Proverbs*, Pt. II. ch. ix.,
Whan I gaue you an ynche ye tooke an
ell. 1599 : Porter, *Two Angry Women*,
in Hazlitt, *Old Plays*, vii. 357. 1630 :
Taylor (Water-Poet), *Works*, 2nd pagin.,
168, Giue a knaue an inch, hee'l take
an ell. 1660 : Tatham, *The Rump*, IV.
1720 : C. Shadwell, *Sham Prince*, Epil.,
If they encourage him, he thinks if's
well, For, give him but an inch, he'll
take an ell. 1822 : Scott, *Nigel*, ch.
xxvii. 1865 : Dickens, *Mutual Friend*,
bk. iii. ch. xiv., Give him an inch, and
he'll take an ell. Let him alone this
time, and what'll he do with our
property next?

5. *To see an inch before one's nose.*
1683 : Meriton, *Yorkshire Ale*, 83–7
(1697), He sees an inch before his nose.

1853 : Planché, *Extravag.*, iv. 272
(1879), The stupid painters fancied,
I suppose, That I might see an inch
beyond my nose.
See also Break (8).

Inconvenience. *See* Every commodity.

Indentures. *See* Make (18).

Industry is fortune's right hand and
frugality her left. [*c.* 1300 : *Havelok*,
l. 1338, p. 49 (Skeat), Lith and selthe
felawes are (Helpfulness and success
companions are).] 1670 : Ray, 14. 1732 :
Fuller, No. 3092.

Ingleborough. *See* Pendle.

Ingratitude drieth up wells, and the
time bridges fells. 1623 : Wodroephe,
Spared Houres, 490.

Ingratitude is the daughter of pride.
1620 : Shelton, *Quixote*, Pt. II. ch. li.
1732 : Fuller, No. 3094.

Ingratitude is worse than witchcraft.
1846–59 : *Denham Tracts*, ii. 83 (F.L.S.).

Ink in his pen. *See* quots. 1540 :
Palsgrave, *Acolastus*, sig. H3, Is there
no more of thynge and is there noo
more ynke lefte in thy penne, or
nothynge yet left the? *Pant.* Nothynge
at all. 1678 : Ray, 254, He hath no
ink in's pen, i.e. no money in his purse,
or no wit in his head.

Ink. *See also* Milk (3).

Inkle-weavers. *See* Thick as.

Inn diversely, but end alike, We.
1639 : Clarke, 13.

Inner Temple. *See* Gray's Inn.

Innocence is no protection. 1732 :
Fuller, No. 3100.

Innocence itself sometimes hath need
of a mask. Ibid., No. 3101.

Innocent actions carry their warrant
with them. 1578 : Florio, *First Fruites*,
fo. 31, Innocencie beareth her defence
with her. 1732 : Fuller, No. 3102.

Innocent as a devil of two years old,
As. 1678 : Ray, 286. 1738 : Swift,
Polite Convers., Dial. I., No, to be sure,
my lord ! you are as innocent as a devil
of two years old.

Innocent as a new-born babe (or as
child unborn). 1609 : Armin, *Maids of
More-clacke*, sig. D3, I . . . am now as
cleare as is the babe new borne.
c. 1679 : in *Somers Tracts*, viii. 131
(1811), Though they died as innocent

as the child unborn. 1745: Swift,
Direct. to Servants: "Chambermaid,"
Offering to take her oath . . . that she
was innocent as the child unborn. 1777:
in *Garrick Corresp.*, ii. 250 (1832), I am
as ignorant of it as the child unborn.
1816: Scott, *Old Mortality*, ch. x., If
he were as innocent as the new-born
infant, they would find some way of
making him guilty. 1888: R. L. S.,
Black Arrow, Prol., I am as innocent
. . . as the babe unchristened.

Insult to injury, To add. [Iniuriae qui
addideris contumeliam.—Phaedrus, V.
iii. 5.] 1748: E. Moore, *The Foundling*,
V. ii., This is adding insult to injuries.
1831: Peacock, *Crotchet Castle*, ch. ii.,
To offer me a sandwich, when I am
looking for a supper, is to add insult
to injury. 1837: Dickens, *Pickwick*,
ch. xxxv.

Interest will not lie. 1709: R. Kingston, *Apoph. Curiosa*, 80, 'Tis a common
proverb, that interest will not lie.

**Inward sore puts out the physician's
eye, An.** 1587: Greene, in *Works*, iii.
114 (Grosart).

Ipswich. *See* quot. 1790: Grose,
Prov. Gloss., s.v. "Suffolk," Ipswich,
a town without inhabitants, a river
without water, streets without names,
where asses wear boots.

**Iron nails that scratcheth with a bear,
He must have.** 1678: Ray, 98 [omit-
ting "with"]. 1732: Fuller, No. 1991.
1801: Wolcot, *Works*, v. 124, A man
must have, the proverb says, Good
iron nails that scratches with a bear.

Iron to swim, He is teaching. 1813:
Ray, 75.

Iron windfall, An. *See* quot. 1863:
Wise, *New Forest*, ch. xvi., Forest proverbs . . . such as . . . "An iron windfall," for anything unfairly taken.

Irons in the fire, To have other (or
many). Before 1549: Sir W. Paget,
Lett. to Somerset (P.R.O. St. Pap. Dom.
Edw. VI., viii. No. 4) (O.), Put no
more so many yrons in the fyre at
ones. 1576: Lambarde, *Peramb. of
Kent*, 336 (1826), To the ende that the
King should have at once many yrons
(as the saying is) in the fire to attend
upon. *c.* 1590: G. Harvey, *Marginalia*,

94 (1913), On[e] iron in yᵉ fyer at once.
1612: Chapman, *Widow's Tears*, II. i.,
But you know, brother, I have other
irons on th' anvil. 1639: Clarke, 78,
He that hath many irons in the fire,
some will coole. 1671: Dryden, *An
Evening's Love*, IV. i., Make haste,
then; for I have more irons in the fire.
c. 1750: Foote, *Englishm. in Paris*, I.,
Leave her to my management, and
consider we have more irons in the
fire than one. 1849: Lytton, *Caxtons*,
Pt. VII. ch. ii., Uncle Jack . . . had
other irons in the fire. 1883: R. L. S.,
Letters, ii. 273 (Tusitala ed.), I have
many irons in the fire.

Irwell. *See* **Yoke.**

It comes with a fear. 1598: Guilpin,
Skialetheia, 24 (Grosart), Thou fear'st
I am in loue with thee (my deare), I
prethy feare not, *It comes with a feare.*
1748: Richardson, *Clarissa*, vi. 205
(1785), For they seldom enquire, but
when they fear—And the proverb, as
my lord has it, says, *It comes with a
fear.* That is, I suppose, what they
fear generally happens, because there
is generally occasion for the fear.

**Italians are wise before the deed, the
Germans in the deed, the French after
the deed, The.** 1640: Herbert, *Jac.
Prudentum.* 1669: *New Help to Discourse*, 56, The Italian is wise before
hand, The German wise in the action,
And the French after it is done.

Itch and ease can no man please.
1546: Heywood, *Proverbs*, Pt. II. ch. iv.
c. 1594: Bacon, *Promus*, No. 486. 1670:
Ray, 14. 1732: Fuller, No. 6237.

Itch is worse than a smart, An—but
the first quotation says the reverse.
1530: Palsgrave, 594, It is better to
ytche than to smarte. 1670: Ray, 14.
1732: Fuller, No. 3114, Itch is more
intolerable than smart.

**Itch, He that will not bear the, must
endure the smart.** 1546: Heywood,
Proverbs, Pt. I. ch. x., And he, Whom in
itching no scratchyng will forbere, He
must beare the smartyng that shall
folow there. 1678: Ray, 162. 1732:
Fuller, No. 2349.

Iveston (Iceton). *See* **Tanfield.**

Ivinghoe. *See* **Tring.**

J

Jack-a-lent, A. *See* 1827 quot.
c. 1560: in Wright, *Songs, etc., Philip
and Mary*, 191 (Roxb. Cl.), Then Jacke-
a-lent comes justlynge in, With the
hedpeece of a herynge. 1575: Churchyard, *Chippes*, 50 (Collier), He was
dressed up like Jack a Lent. 1626:
Breton, in *Works*, ii. *t* 12 (Grosart), It
is now Easter, and Jacke of Lent is
turned out of doores. 1646: Quarles,
Works, iii. 223 (Grosart), How like a
Jack-a-lent He stands, for boys to
spend their shrovetide throws. 1742:
Fielding, *Andrews*, bk. i. ch. ii., His
office was to perform the part the
ancients assigned to the god Priapus,
which deity the moderns call by the
name of Jack o' Lent. 1821: Scott,
Pirate, ch. xxxvi. 1827: Hone, *Table-
Book*, 135, Jack o' Lent. This was a
puppet, formerly thrown at, in our own
country, during Lent, like Shrove-cocks.

Jack-a-thrum. *See* Wise (5).

Jack-an-apes. 1. *Can Jack an apes
be merry when his clog is at his heels?*
1605: Camden, *Remains*, 321 (1870).
1670: Ray, 71. 1732: Fuller, No. 1052.
2. *There is more ado with one Jack
an apes than all the bears.* 1633: Draxe,
69. 1694: D'Urfey, *Quixote*, Pt. II.
Act I. sc. ii. 1732: Fuller, No. 3464.

Jack and Jill. *See* Bad Jack.

Jack at a pinch. *See* quots. 1622:
Mabbe, tr. Aleman's *Guzman*, i. 130
(O.), When there was neede of my
seruice . . . I was seldome or neuer
wanting; I was Iacke at a pinch. 1690:
New Dict. Canting Crew, sig. G2, Jack
at a pinch, a poor hackney parson.
1754: Berthelson, *Eng.-Danish Dict.*,
s.v. "Jack." 1847: Halliwell, *Dict.*,
s.v., *Jack-at-a-pinch*, a sudden unex-
pected call to do anything. Also, a
poor parson.

Jack but there's a Jill, Never a. 1611:
Cotgrave, s.v. "Demander," Like will
to like; a Jacke lookes for a Gill. 1735:
Pegge, *Kenticisms*, in E.D.S., No. 12,
p. 51, According to the proverb, "never

a Jack but there's a Gill." 1738: Swift,
Polite Convers., Dial. I. 1912: R. L.
Gales, *Studies in Arcady*, 2nd ser., 241,
"For every Jack there's a Jill" was a
thoroughly Elizabethan bit of English.

Jack Drum. *See* Drum's entertainment.

**Jack has his Jill, Every, or Jack shall
have Jill.** Before 1529: Skelton, *Magnyfycence*, l. 290, What auayleth lord-
shyp, yourselfe for to kyll With care
and with thought howe Jacke shall
haue Gyl? 1595: Shakespeare, *Mids.
N. Dream*, III. ii. *ad fin.*, Jack shall
have Jill; Nought shall go ill. 1639:
Clarke, 63, All shall be well and Jack
shall have Jill. 1725: Defoe, *Everybody's Business*, in *Works*, ii. 511(Bohn),
For not a Jack among them but must
have his Gill. 1823: Scott, *St. Ronan's*,
ch. ii., Every Jack will find a Jill, gang
the world as it may. 1886: Bickerdyke, *Curios. of Ale and Beer*, 168, As
every Jack will have his Jill, so . . .
1911: T. Edwardes, *Neighbourhood*, 10,
After much water-spilling and cracking
of crowns, Jack has got his Jill, and the
wedding-bells are lin-lan-loning.

Jack in a box. 1592: Chettle, *Kind-
Hart's Dreame*, 45 (Percy S.), As cunningly . . . as euer poore cuckoe coulde
commend his Iacke in a boxe. *c.* 1623:
B. & F., *Love's Cure*, III. i., My Lord
Vitelli's love, and maintenance, Deserves no other Jack i' th' box but
he. 1690: *New Dict. Canting Crew*,
sig. G2, Jack in a box, a sharper or
cheat.

Jack in office. 1670: Ray, 214, To
be Jack in an office. 1709: O. Dykes,
Eng. Proverbs, 117, How uppish and
sawcy soever such a Jack-in-an-Office
may be . . . 1732: Fuller, No. 3050,
Jack in an office is a great man. 1785-
95: Wolcot, *Lousiad*, can. iv., Some
folks are Jacks-in-office, fond of power.
1857: Dickens, *Dorrit*, bk. i. ch. ii., A
type of Jack-in-office insolence and
absurdity . . . a beadle.

Jack of all trades. 1618: Minshull, *Essayes, etc.*, 50 (1821), Some broken citizen, who hath plaid Jack-of-all-trades. 1639: Mayne, *City Match*, II. v., Why, you mongrel, You John-of-all-trades. 1690: Dryden, *Amphitryon*, I. i., Yet I am still in my vocation; for you know I am a jack of all trades. 1776: Colman, *Spleen*, I., The town Jack of all trades, a mere Jack o' lanthern! half bookseller, half apothecary! 1836: Dickens, *Sketches by Boz:* "Parish," ch. ii., He is a bit of a Jack of all trades, or to use his own words, "a regular Robinson Crusoe." 1923: Lucas, *Advisory Ben*, 66, You might have chosen something better to do than to be . . . . a Jack-of-all-trades at the command of anyone with the money to pay your fee.

Jack of both sides. 1557: Grindal, *Lett. to Foxe*, 28 Dec., 233 (P.S.), Nam qui in tota vita praeposterissimus (ut ita dicam) fuit, omnium rerum humanarum et divinarum inversor, consentaneum est ut in scribendo etiam praeposterum sese ostentet, et, ut vulgo dici solet Joannem ad oppositum. 1609: Dekker, in *Works*, iv. 158 (Grosart), Who plaid yᵉ iackes on both sides, and were indeede Neuters. 1671: *Westm. Drollery*, 89 (Ebsworth), She'l play Jack a both sides in war, And cares not a pin for her foes. 1729: Defoe, *Compl. Gent.*, Pt. I. ch. i. p. 30 (1890), How often have those men of honour . . . play'd Jack a both sides, to-day for and to-morrow against . . . as the money could be got or the party was strongest. 1869: Spurgeon, *John Ploughman*, ch. xviii., They try to be Jack-o'-both-sides, and deserve to be kicked like a football by both parties.

Jack out of office. 1546: Heywood, *Proverbs*, Pt. II. ch. iii., And Jack out of office she maie bid me walke. *c.* 1591: Shakespeare, *1 Henry VI.*, I. i. 1598: *Servingmans Comfort*, in *Inedited Tracts*, 166 (Hazlitt), In good credite with his maister at noone, and Jacke out of office before night. 1735: Pegge, *Kenticisms*, in E.D.S., No. 12, p. 51.

Jack roast beef. 1855: Bohn, 436.

Jack Robinson, Before one can say.
1778: Burney, *Evelina*, Lett. lxxxii., "Will you?" returned he; "why, then, 'fore George, I'd do it as soon as say Jack Robinson." 1812: Miss Edgeworth, *Absentee*, ch. ii., I'd get her off before you could say Jack Robinson. 1843: Dickens, *Carol*, Stave 2, Let's have the shutters up . . . before a man cán say Jack Robinson. 1872: Hardy, *Greenwood Tree*, Pt. III. ch. iii., You've got him before you can say . . . Jack Robinson! 1911: T. Edwardes, *Neighbourhood*, 277, Afore I could s-s-say Jack Robinson.

Jack Sprat could eat no fat. *See* quots. The single appearance — in 1659 — of Jack as an ecclesiastical dignitary is very surprising. 1639: Clarke, 17, Jack will eat no fat, and Jill doth love no leane, Yet betwixt them both, they lick the dishes cleane. 1659: Howell, 20, Archdeacon Pratt would eat no fatt, His wife would eat no lean; Twixt Archdeacon Pratt and Joan his wife, The meat was eat up clean. 1670: Ray, 211, Jack Sprat he loved no fat, and his wife she lov'd no lean : And yet betwixt them both, they lick't the platters clean. 1843: Halliwell, *Nursery Rhymes*, 34, Jack Sprat could eat no fat, His wife could eat no lean ; And so, betwixt them both, you see, They lick'd the platter clean.

Jack Sprat would teach his grandame.
1639: Clarke, 4, Jack-Sprat teacheth his grandame. 1670: Ray, 108. 1754: Berthelson, *Eng.-Danish Dict.*, s.v. "Jack."

Jack will never make a gentleman.
1681: W. Robertson, *Phraseol. Generalis*, 659. 1721: Bailey, *Eng. Dict.*, s.v. "Gentleman."

Jack would be a gentleman. Before 1529: Skelton, *Works*, i. 15 (Dyce), Lo, Jack wold be a jentylman! 1546: Heywood, *Proverbs*, Pt. I. ch. xi., Iacke would be a gentleman, if he coulde speake frenche. 1599: Breton, in *Works*, ii. *c* 42 (Grosart), And nowe Jacke will bee gentleman, no longer a sheepheard. 1662: Fuller, *Worthies*, i. 118 (1840), We ape the French chiefly in two particulars: First, in their language (" which if Jack could speak,

he would be a gentleman "). 1732:
Fuller, No. 3052 [as in 1546].

**Jack would wipe his nose if he had
one.** 1659: Howell, 8. 1670: Ray,
108.

**Jackasses never can sing well, because
they pitch their notes too high.** Said of
a foolish person. 1865: "Lancs Proverbs," in *N. & Q.*, 3rd ser., viii. 494.
1901: F. E. Taylor, *Lancs Sayings*, 8.

Jackdaw. See quot. 1886: Swainson,
Folk-Lore of Brit. Birds, 81 (F.L.S.), At
Norwich there is an old rhyme—" When
three daws are seen on St. Peter's vane
together, Then we're sure to have bad
weather." 1893: Inwards, *Weather
Lore*, 137 [as in 1886].

Jackson's end. See quot. 1889:
Folk-Lore Journal, vii. 294, [Staffs
sayings] Fly round by Jackson's end
[= to make haste].

Jackson's hens, To fly up with—To
become bankrupt. 1577: *Misogonus*,
IV. ii., Ye may fly vp toth roust with
Iacksons hens. 1678: Ray, 86, I'll
make him fly up with Jacksons hens;
i.e. undo him. 1917: Bridge, *Cheshire
Proverbs*, 132.

Jackson's pig. *See* Borough Hill.

Jacob Dawson's wife died, We live as.
1777: Nicolson and Burn, *Hist. and
Antiq. of Westmore. and Cumb.*, i. 78, On
the third pillar in the south ile of the
church [of Kendal] is the following
inscription :—Here lyes Frances late
wife of Jacob Dawson Gent. who
departed this life 19th June 1700, in
the 25th year of her age : Who by a
free and chearful resignation of herself,
even *in the midst of this world's affluence*,
has left us just grounds to hope she is
now happy.—This epitaph we only take
notice of, as it hath occasioned a display
of the droll humour of the people, who
upon any particular occasion of festivity
have from hence framed a proverb,
" We live as Jacob Dawson's wife died."
1918: A Durham correspondent, in
N. & Q., 12th ser., iv. 214, I have
frequently heard this proverb or saying.

Jade eats as much as a good horse, A.
1640: Herbert, *Jac. Prudentum*. 1854:
J. W. Warter, *Last of Old Squires*, 53.

Jailor's conscience and his fetters

[are] made both of one metal, A.
1659: Howell, 18.

January. 1. *A January haddock, A
February bannock, And a March pint
of ale* [are better than those of any
other month]. 1846: Denham, *Proverbs*,
25 (Percy S.).

2. *A January spring Is worth naething.* Ibid., 25. 1913: E. M. Wright,
Rustic Speech, etc., 317.

3. *A summerish January, a winterish
spring.* 1893 : Inwards, *Weather Lore*, 10.

4. *A warm January, a cold May.*
1878: Dyer, *Eng. Folk-Lore*, 247. 1893:
Inwards, *Weather Lore*, 11. Cf. No. 8.

5. *A wet January, a wet spring,*
1893: Ibid., 10.

6. *As bare as January.* 1609: Armin,
Maids of More-clacke, sig. A1, I will not
say as poore as Iob, but as bare as
Ianuary.

7. *If grain grows in January, there
will be a year of great need.* 1893:
Inwards, *Weather Lore*, 10.

8. *If Janiveer's calends be summerly
gay, 'Twill be winterly weather till the
calends of May.* 1732: Fuller, No. 6483.
1879: Henderson, *Folk-Lore N. Counties*, 75. 1893: Inwards, *Weather Lore*,
10. Cf. No. 4.

9. *If January calends fall on Thursday. See* quot. 1493: *Dives and Pauper*, fo. 66 (1536), The kalendas of
Ianuarie fell on the thursday, whan
(as they saye) shulde fall plentie of all
good and peace also.

10. *If one knew how good it were To
eat a hen in Janivere; Had he twenty
in the flock, Ho'd leave but one to go with
the cock.* 1659: Howell, 21 [with slight
variations in third and fourth lines].
1670: Ray, 213. 1732: Fuller, No. 6389.
1846: Denham, *Proverbs*, 26 (Percy S.).

11. *If the grass grow in Janiveer, It
grows the worse for't all the year.* 1670:
Ray, 40. 1744: Claridge, in Mills,
Essay on Weather, 100 (1773). 1830:
Forby, *Vocab. E. Anglia*, 418, The grass
that grows in Janiveer Grows no more
all the year. 1893: Inwards, *Weather
Lore*, 10 [as in 1744]. 1912: R. L.
Gales, *Studies in Arcady*, 2nd ser., 101.

12. *If the sun shine the 12th of
January, there shall be store of wind*

that year. 1669 : *New Help to Discourse*,
283.

13. *If you see grass in January, Lock
your grain in your granary.* 1893 :
Inwards, *Weather Lore*, 10.

14. *In January if the sun appear,
March and April pay full dear.* Ibid., 10.

15. *Jack Frost in Janiveer, Nips the
nose of the nascent year.* 1878 : Dyer,
Eng. Folk-Lore, 247. 1893 : Inwards,
Weather Lore, 11.

16. *Janiveer freeze the pot by the fire.*
1557 : Tusser, *Husbandrie*, in *Brit.
Bibliog.*, iii. 20 (1812), As Janeuer fryse
pot, bidth corne kepe hym lowe. 1670 :
Ray, 40. 1744 : Claridge, in Mills, *Essay
on Weather*, 100 (1773). 1879 : Jackson,
Shropsh. Word-Book, 224, Janniwerry-
freeze-the-pot-by-the-fire, *sb.* the month
of January.

17. *January and May.* c. 1400 :
Lydgate, *Temple of Glas*, 7 (E.E.T.S.),
For it ne sit not vnto fresshe May Forto
be coupled to colde Januari. c. 1580 :
Spelman, *Dialogue*, 94 (Roxb. Cl.),
When I loked apon her husbond with
his white hedde and horye berde I
judged Janiary and May to be copled
together. 1604 : *Wit of a Woman*, sc.
xi. (Malone S.), Is not this a prettie
world? Ianuary and May make a
match? 1656 : *Musarum Deliciæ*, i. 103
(Hotten), Lustfull he was, at forty
needs must wed, Old January will have
May in bed. 1717 : Pope, *January and
May* [title]. 1855 : Kingsley, *West. Ho!*,
ch. vii., If they had never allowed that
fresh and fair young May to be forced
into marrying that old January . . .

18. *January commits the fault and
May bears the blame.* 1893 : Inwards,
Weather Lore, 11.

19. *January never lies dead in a dyke
gutter.* 1846 : Denham, *Proverbs*, 23
(Percy S.).

20. *January warm, the Lord have
mercy!* 1893 : Inwards, *Weather Lore*, 10.

21. *March in Janiveer, Janiveer in
March, I fear.* 1678 : Ray, 44. 1732 :
Fuller, No. 6148. 1893 : Inwards, 11.
1912 : R. L. Gales, *Studies in Arcady*,
2nd ser., 102.

22. *The blackest month in all the year,
Is the month of Janiveer.* 1846 : Denham,

Proverbs, 26 (Percy S.). 1893 : Inwards,
10.

23. *The first three days of January
rule the coming three months.* Ibid., 11.

24. *To have January chickens* = To
have children in old age. 1813 : Ray,
202.

25. *Who in Janiveer sows oats Gets
gold and groats; Who sows in May Gets
little that way.* 1732 : Fuller, No. 6149.
1893 : Inwards, 11.

See also December; and July (2).

Jape with me. *See* Play with me.

Jarrow. 1. *Bump against Jarrow.*
1825 : Brockett, *Gloss. of N. Country
Words*, 32, . . . is a common expression among the keelmen when they
run foul of any thing. 1846–59 : *Denham Tracts*, i. 88 (F.L.S.).

2. *It's never dark in Jarrow Church.*
Ibid., i. 89.

Jaws. *See* quot. 1887 : T. Darlington,
S. Cheshire Folk Speech, 280 (E.D.S.),
"Dunna let yur jaws o'errun your
claws" . . . is a proverbial saying
equivalent to "Do not live beyond
your means." 1917 : Bridge, *Cheshire
Proverbs*, 50.

Jays. *See* Cherry (4).

Jealous head is soon broken, A. 1732 :
Fuller, No. 225.

**Jealous man's horns hang in his eyes,
A.** 1666 : Torriano, *Piazza Univ.*, 174,
A jealouse man hath his horns in his
eyes. 1732 : Fuller, No. 226. Cf.
Horn (7).

**Jealousy shuts one door and opens
two.** 1710 : S. Palmer, *Moral Essays
on Proverbs*, 370.

Jealousy. *See also* Frenzy.

Jemmy Rule's larks, Gone—like.
1888 : Q.-Couch, *Troy Town*, ch. viii.

**Jenny Kemp, who had an occasion
for all things, Like.** 1864 : "Cornish
Proverbs," in *N. & Q.*, 3rd ser., vi. 6.

Jericho, Go to. 1648 : *Mercurius
Aulicus*, 23–30 March, If the Upper
House, and the Lower House Were in
a ship together, And all the base
Committées, they were in another; And
both the ships were botomlesse, And
sayling on the mayne, Let them all goe
to Jericho, And ne'ere be seen againe.
1694 : *Terence made English*, 146, Ay,

let him be jogging to Jericho for me.
1778 : Mrs Thrale, in D'Arblay, *Diary*,
i. 31 (1876), They wish the poor children
at Jericho when they accept it. 1849 :
C. Brontë, *Shirley*, ch. vii., Her habit
was to . . . come forward hurriedly,
yet hesitatingly, wishing herself mean-
time at Jericho.

Jericho, He has been to = is drunk.
1745 : Franklin, *Drinker's Dict.*, in
Works, ii. 24 (Bigelow).

Jerusalem, He's going to = is drunk.
Ibid., ii. 24.

Jest breaks no bones, A. 1781 :
Johnson, in Boswell's *Life*, iv. 129
(Hill), It is a certain thing, it is proverbially known, that *a jest breaks
no bones*.

Jesters do oft prove prophets. 1855 :
Bohn, 436.

Jesting lies bring serious sorrows.
Ibid., 436.

**Jesting while it pleaseth, Leave, lest
it turn to earnest.** 1640 : Herbert, *Jac.
Prudentum*.

**Jests are never good till they're
broken.** 1869 : Hazlitt, 250.

Jewel. *See* quot. 1639 : Fuller, *Holy
War*, bk. iii. ch. iv., So true it is, none
can guess the jewel by the casket.

Jew's eye, Worth a. 1593 : G. Harvey,
in *Works*, ii. 146 (Grosart), As deare as
a Iewes eye. 1595 : Shakespeare, *M.
of Venice*, II. v., There will come a
Christian by, Will be worth a Jewess'
eye. 1842 : Barham, *Ing. Legends*, 2nd
ser. : " Old Woman in Grey," Hence the
late Mr. Froude, and the live Dr. Pusey,
We moderns consider as each worth a
Jew's eye. 1886 : Elworthy, *West Som.
Word-Book*, 382 (E.D.S.), Take care of
it, and put it away, it will be worth a
Jew's eye some day.

**Jews, The, spend at Easter, the Moors
at marriages, the Christians in suits.**
1640 : Herbert, *Jac. Prudentum.* 1670 :
Ray, 24 [with " of law " added at end].

Jill. *See* quots. 1678 : Ray, 146,
There's not so bad a Gill but there's as
bad a Will. 1690 : *New Dict. Canting
Crew*, sig. F2, There's not so ord'nary a
Gill, but there's as sorry a Jack. 1732 :
Fuller, No. 6112 [as in 1678]. *See also*
Jack.

Joan Blunt. *See* quot. 1854 : Baker,
Northants Gloss., s.v., Joan - Blunt.
One in the habit of speaking her mind
freely, without ceremony.

**Joan is a good contriver, My wife;
and a good contriver is better than a
little eater.** 1864 : " Cornish Proverbs,"
in *N. & Q.*, 3rd ser., vi. 6.

**Joan is as good as my lady in the
dark.** 1601 : Munday, *Downfall of Earl
of Hunt.*, III. ii., *Prior*. . . . He is our
lady's chaplain, but serves Joan. *Don.*
Then, from the friar's fault, perchance,
it may be The proverb grew, Joan's
taken for my lady. *c.* 1640 : in *Roxb.
Ballads*, i. 390 (Hindley). 1720 : C.
Shadwell, *Irish Hospitality*, I. i. 1838 :
Carlyle, *Sartor*, bk. i. ch. x., Much also
we shall omit about confusion of Ranks,
and Joan and My Lady [" Society in a
state of Nakedness "].

Job, Poor as. *See* **Poor** (11).

Job's comforter, A. 1630 : Brathwait,
Eng. Gent., 132 (1641), Iob called his
friends miserable comforters. 1724 :
Defoe, *Roxana*, in *Works*, xii. 20 (Boston,
1903), They sat down, like Job's three
comforters, and said not one word to
me for a great while. 1748 : Richardson, *Clarissa*, vii. 230 (1785), He called
her Small Hopes, and Job's comforter.
1824 : Scott, *Redgauntlet*, ch. xv., O,
this was a new theme for my Job's
comforter. 1864 : Mrs. H. Wood,
Trevlyn Hold, ch. li., " You are a
pretty Job's comforter," gasped Mr.
Chattaway.

Jock Wabster. *See* **Devil** (97).

John at night. *See* quot. 1883 :
Burne, *Shropsh. Folk-Lore*, 596, To be
John at night and Jack in the morning
= to boast of one's intentions overnight and leave them unfulfilled next
day.

**John Barley-corn is no body with him,
Sir.** 1639 : Clarke, 306.

**John Barley - corn's the strongest
knight, Sir.** 1670 : Ray, 59.

John Dod about him, He has a deal o'.
1917 : Bridge, *Cheshire Proverbs*, 68,
. . . Conceited, arrogant. *Dodd* or
Dod is a well-known Cheshire name.

John Drawlatch. *See* quot. 1546 :
Heywood, *Proverbs*, Pt. II. ch. viii.,

Why will ye (quoth he) I shall folow
hir will? To make me Iohn drawlache,
or such a snekebill.

John Drum. *See* **Drum's entertainment.**

John Gray's bird. *See* quots. *c.* 1575 :
Gascoigne, *Fruites of Warre*, cxxxi., The
greene knight was amongst the rest
Like John Greyes birde that ventured
withe the best. 1579: *Quarrell between
Hall and Mallerie*, 6, in *Misc. Ant.
Angl.* (1816), Maister Robert Audeley
. . . perceiving them to cluster together
like John Grayes birde, *ut
dicitur*, who always loved company.

John Lively. *See* **Kelloe.**

John Long, the carrier. 1546 : Heywood,
Proverbs, Pt. I. ch. xi., I will
send it him by Iohn Longe the carier.
1611 : Cotgrave, s.v. " Attendre," To
stay for John Long the Carrier; to
tarry long for that which comes but
slowly. 1681 : W. Robertson, *Phraseol.
Generalis*, 839, Whether all things are
carried by Tom Long the Carrier;
Quo tardissime omnia perferuntur.
1785 : Grose, *Class. Dict. Vulgar Tongue*,
s.v. " Tom Long," It is coming by Tom
Long the carrier, said of anything that
has been long expected. *c.* 1791 : Pegge,
Derbicisms, 129 (E.D.S.), Tom Long,
carrier, [said] of a person that loiters
and is long in coming or returning.
1830 : Scott, *Doom of Devorgoil*, II. i.,
A limping sonnet Which he had
fashion'd to my cousin's glory, And
forwarded by blind Tom Long the
carrier. 1883 : Burne, *Shropsh. Folk-
Lore*, 597, To send by John the long
carrier=by a roundabout route.

John of Cumber. *See* **Devil** (41).

John o' Groats. *See* **Land's End.**

John Platt. *See* quot. 1886 : R.
Holland, *Cheshire Gloss.*, 456 (E.D.S.),
Very likely co [quoth] John Platt. A
common saying about Wilmslow. 1917 :
Bridge, *Cheshire Proverbs*, 148.

John Toy. *See* quots. 1864 : " Cornish
Proverbs," in *N. & Q.*, 3rd ser., vi. 6,
Like lucky John Toy. 1880 : Spurgeon,
Ploughman's Pictures, 20, The luck that
comes to them is like Johnny Toy's, who
lost a shilling and found a two-penny
loaf. 1883 : Burne, *Shropsh. Folk-Lore*,

598, O lucky Tom Hodges! lost five
pund an' fund a pig's yok'!

Johnny Middleton's hints, Like. Durham.
1909: *Folk-Lore*, xx. 73.

Johnny tuth' Bellas. *See* quot. 1849 :
Halliwell, *Pop. Rhymes and Nursery
Tales*, 200, Johnny tuth' Bellas daft
was thy poll, When thou changed
Bellas for Henknoll. [Said to date
from 1386. Halliwell says we can only
account for the saying by supposing
that at some former period Bellasyse
had been exchanged for lands, but not
the manor of Henknoll. He gives an
account of the tradition on which the
saying is said to be founded.]

Johnson's End. *See* quot. 1860 : in
N. & Q., 2nd ser., x. 249, I have
frequently heard it said, in Worcestershire,
when a man has become very
poor : " He is gone up Johnson's end."

**Joke never gains over an enemy, but
often loseth a friend, A.** 1732 : Fuller,
No. 228.

**Jokes are as bad coin to all but the
jocular.** 1831 : Hone, *Year-Book*, col.
1416.

Jolly as a sandboy. 1863 : Kingsley,
Water Babies, ch. viii., She would send
them a lot of tops, and balls, and
marbles, and ninepins, and make them
all as jolly as sandboys. 1894 : Northall,
Folk Phrases, 9 (E.D.S.).

Jone's ale is new. 1594 : *Jones Ale is
Newe* [title of ballad]. 1630 : *Wine,
Beere, Ale, etc.*, 30 (Hanford, 1915), Tis
growne to a prouerbe Iones ale's new.

Jove laughs at lovers' lies. [Perjuria
ridet amantum Juppiter et ventos irrita
ferre jubet.—Tibullus, III. vi. 49. Cf.
Horace, *Carm.*, II. viii. 13.] 1567 : *Lady
Lucres*, in *Plasidas, etc.*, 143 (Roxb. Cl.),
Jupiter rather laughethe then takethe
angerlye the periurynge of louers.
1592 : Shakespeare, *Romeo*, II. ii., At
lovers' perjuries, They say, Jove laughs.
1627 : Massinger, *Great Duke of Florence*,
II. iii., For the queen of love, As they
hold constantly, does never punish, But
smile at lovers' perjuries. 1700 : Dryden,
Pal. and Arcite, ii. 149, And
Jove but laughs at lovers' perjury!
1829 : Cobbett, *Advice to Young Men*,
Lett. III., Though I do not approve of

the saying, "At lovers' lies Jove laughs." 1922 : Judge Parry, in *Evening Standard*, 17 Oct., p. 5, col. 1, Perjury in the Divorce Court has been openly permitted to the upper classes for many years, following the maxim, perhaps, which our poets have borrowed from Tibullus, that "Jove but laughs at lovers' perjury."

Joy go with you. *See* quot. 1854 : Baker, *Northants Gloss.*, s.v., "Joy go with you, and sixpence; and then you'll want neither love nor money," is a common familiar phrase.

Joy of the heart. *See* **Heart** (9).

Judas kiss, A. *c.* 1540 : Bale, *Kynge Johan*, l. 2109, A false Judas kysse he hath gyven and is gone. 1570 : Barclay, *Mirrour of Good Manners*, 75, Of a flattering foe to haue a Iudas kisse. 1684 : in *Roxb. Ballads*, vii. 473 (B.S.), They'l giue to you a Judas kisse. 1708 : *Brit. Apollo*, i. No. 116, col. 5, They once with Judas - kiss With artful smiles . . . 1838 : Hood, *Hood's Own*, 1st ser., 323 (1865), Her lips were glued on his, in a close "Judas' kiss." 1925 : *Punch*, 2 Sept., p. 237, col. 1, 'Twas ever thus with misses, They leave the ancient home To plant their Judas kisses Upon some manly dome.

Judge, *subs.* *He who will have no judge but himself, condemns himself.* 1855 : Bohn, 401.

Judge, *verb.* *He who judges hastily.* See quots. *c.* 1450 : *Partonope*, l. 9975 (E.E.T.S.), Full yor now hit ys a-goo I haue herd sey, and other moo, That who so yeveth hasty jugegyment Must be the fyrst that shall repent. 1666 : Torriano, *Piazza Univ.*, 105, Who suddenly will judge, hastens himself to repentance. 1732 : Fuller, No. 2244, He that passeth a judgment as he runs, overtaketh repentance.

July. 1. *A shower in July, when the corn begins to fill, Is worth a plow of oxen, and all belongs there till.* 1732 : Fuller, No. 6468. 1893 : Inwards, *Weather Lore*, 30.

2. *As July so the next January.* Ibid., 30.

3. *Bow-wow dandy fly, Brew no beer in July.* 1846 : Denham, *Proverbs*, 54

(Percy S.). 1886 : Bickerdyke, *Curios. of Ale and Beer*, 58 [cited as "the old saying"].

4. *If it rains on July 10th, it will rain for seven weeks.* 1893 : Inwards, *Weather Lore*, 31.

5. *If the first of July, it be rainy weather, 'Twill rain, more or less, for four weeks together.* 1732 : Fuller, No. 6467. 1893 : Inwards, 30.

6. *In July, some reap rye, In August, if one will not, the other must.* 1831 : Hone, *Year Book*, 1595. 1846 : Denham, *Proverbs*, 51 (Percy S.), In July, shear your rye. 1893 : Inwards, 30 [both 1831 and 1846 versions].

7. *July chickens.* *See* quot. 1921 : *Observer*, 20 March, p. 5, col. 5, An old saying, which used to be current in my youth, grouped clergymen's sons and doctors' daughters in the same category as July chickens, and declared that, with some exceptions, of course, none of the three ever came to good.

8. *No tempest, good July, Lest corn come off bluely.* 1732 : Fuller, No. 6208. 1825 : Hone, *Ev. Day Book*, i. 670 [with "blue by" [mildew] for "bluely"]. 1893 : Inwards, 30 [as in 1825, and also] No tempest, good July, Lest the corn look ruely.

9. *To the 12th of July from the 12th of May All is day.* 1732 : Fuller, No. 6201, 'Tis said from the twelfth of May To the twelfth of July, all is day. 1893 : Inwards, 31.

10. *Whatever July and August do not boil, September cannot fry.* Ibid., 30.

See also **Bee** (3) ; **Cuckoo** ; **March** (18) ; and **Thistle** (2).

June. 1. *A cold and wet June spoils the rest of the year.* 1893 : Inwards, *Weather Lore*, 29.

2. *A good leak in June Sets all in tune.* 1846 : Denham, *Proverbs*, 50 (Percy S.). 1893 : Inwards, 29, [as in 1846, with, in addition] A dripping June Brings all things in tune. 1920 : *Times*, 21 June, p. 9, col. 2, "A dripping June puts all things in tune," runs the old adage.

3. *A wet June makes a dry September.* Corn. 1893 : Inwards, 29.

4. *Calm weather in June Sets corn in*

tune. 1732 : Fuller, No. 6207. 1893 : Inwards, 28.

5. *If it rains on June 27th, it will rain seven weeks.* Ibid., 30.

6. *If it rain the twenty-fourth day of June, hazel-nuts will not prosper.* 1669 : *New Help to Discourse,* 284.

7. *If on the 8th of June it rain, It foretells a wet harvest, men sain.* 1732 : Fuller, No. 6204. Cf. St. Medard.

8. *June damp and warm Does the farmer no harm.* 1893 : Inwards, 29.

See also **April** (6) and (20) ; **Bee** (3) ; **Cuckoo,** *passim* ; **March** (14) ; **May,** B,

C, E (2), F (11), (12), (17), and (26) ; and **Thistle** (2).

Just before you are generous, Be. 1744–6 : Mrs. Haywood, *Fem. Spectator,* ii. 27 (1771), There is, I think, an old saying, that we " ought to be just before we are generous." 1777 : Sheridan, *Sch. for Scandal,* IV. i. 1850 : Dickens, *Copperfield,* ch. xiii.

Just to all, but trust not all, Be. 1855 : Bohn, 325.

Justice pleaseth few in their own house. 1640 : Herbert, *Jac. Prudentum.*

Justice. *See also* **Basket Justice.**

K

Ka' me, ka' thee. 1546: Heywood, *Proverbs*, Pt. I. ch. xi., Ka me, ka the, one good tourne askth an other. *c.* 1570: in Skelton's *Works*, I. lxv. (Dyce), Yea, sayde the hostler, ka me, ka thee; yf she dooe hurte me, I wyll displease her. Before 1627: Middleton, *More Diss. besides Women*, I. iv., Ka me, ka thee; if you will ease the melancholy of my mind with singing, I will deliver you from the calamity of boots-haling. 1821: Scott, *Kenilworth*, ch. v., Ka me, ka thee—it is a proverb all over the world. 1823: Byron, *Don Juan*, can. xi. st. 78. Cf. **Claw** (2); and **Scratch me**.

Kail [Broth] in a riven dish, He gat his. 1873: A. C. Gibson, *Folk Speech of Cumb.*, 184.

Kate Mullet. *See* quot. 1888: Q.-Couch, *Troy Town*, ch. xi., As knowing as Kate Mullet . . . they say she was hanged for a fool.

Keep, *verb.* 1. *He keepeth a fair castle that keepeth well his mouth. c.* 1300: in *Vernon MS.*, 340 (E.E.T.S.).

2. *He keeps a stir but is no constable.* 1639: Clarke, 20.

3. *He keeps his road well enough who gets rid of bad company.* 1855: Bohn, 378.

4. *It is no less praise to keep than to get.* 1559: Bercher, *Nobil. of Women*, 97 (Roxb. Cl.) [cited as "the owlde vers"].

5. *Keep a thing seven years. See* quots. 1663: Killigrew, *Parson's Wedding*, II. vii., According to the proverb, keep a thing seven years, and then if thou hast no use on't, throw't away. 1816: Scott, *Antiquary*, ch. xxi., They say, keep a thing seven year, an' ye'll aye find a use for't. 1826: Scott, *Woodstock*, ch. xxviii.

6. *Keep bad men company, and you'll soon be of their number.* 1640: Herbert, *Jac. Prudentum*, Keep not ill men company, lest you increase the number. 1875: A. B. Cheales, *Proverb. Folk-Lore*, 96.

7. *Keep counsel thyself first.* 1639: Clarke, 67. 1670: Ray, 5. 1732: Fuller, No. 3117.

8. *Keep some till furthermore come.* 1670: Ray, 110. 1736: Bailey, *Dict.*, s.v. "Keep."

9. *Keep touch in small things.* 1732: Fuller, No. 3120.

10. *Keep your feet. See* **Head** (6).

11. *Keep your house and your house will keep you.* 1776: Colman, *Spleen*, I. [cited as "the old proverb"]. Cf. No. 13.

12. *Keep your mouth shut and your eyes open.* 1710: S. Palmer, *Moral Essays on Proverbs*, 143.

13. *Keep your shop and your shop will keep you.* 1605: Chapman, etc., *Eastw. Hoe*, I. i., I . . . garnished my shop . . . with good wholesome thriftie sentences; as "Touchstone, keep thy shoppe, and thy shoppe will keepe thee." 1642: D. Rogers, *Matrim. Honour*, 224. 1712: *Spectator*, No. 509. 1759: Goldsmith, *The Bee*, No. vii. 1905: Wells, *Kipps*, bk. iii. ch. iii. § 7, "Shop!" said Kipps. "That's right. Keep a shop and the shop'll keep you." Cf. No. 11.

14. *Keep your thanks to feed your chickens.* 1681: W. Robertson, *Phraseol. Generalis*, 784. 1709: O. Dykes, *Eng. Proverbs*, iii. 1732: Bailey, *Dict.*, s.v. "Thanks."

15. *Keep yourself from the anger of a great man, from the tumult of a mob, from a man of ill fame, from a widow that has been thrice married, from a wind that comes in at a hole, and from a reconciled enemy.* 1855: Bohn, 437.

16. *To keep band in the nick*=To make things meet. *c.* 1791: Pegge, *Derbicisms*, 88 (E.D.S.).

17. *To keep it in Pimlico. See* Pimlico.

18. *You'll keep it no longer than you can a cat in a wheel-barrow.* 1732: Fuller, No. 6025.

Kelloe. *See* quot. 1849: Halliwell, *Pop. Rhymes and Nursery Tales*, 202,

John Lively, Vicar of Kelloe, Had seven daughters and never a fellow.

Kelvedon. *See* **Braintree.**

Kenchester. *See* **Sutton-Well.**

Kendale fox, As craftie as a. 1659 : Howell, 20. 1670 : Ray, 254.

Kennel of hounds. *See* **Pound of butter.**

Kennington. *See* **Ashford.**

Kenspeckle [Conspicuous] **as a cock on a church broach** [spire], **As.** 1855 : Robinson, *Whitby Gloss.*, 95.

Kent. 1. *A man of Kent.* 1662 : Fuller, *Worthies*, ii. 122 (1840). *c.* 1750 : C. Smart, *Fables*, No. ii., Are all to idle discord bent, These Kentish men— those men of Kent. 1887 : Parish and Shaw, *Dict. Kent. Dialect*, 98 (E.D.S.), Man of Kent. A title claimed by the inhabitants of the Weald as their peculiar designation ; all others they regard as Kentish men.

2. *Kent and Christendom.* Various proverbial uses. *See* quots. 1579 : Spenser, *Shep. Cal.*, Sept., l. 168, Neuer was woolfe seene, many nor some, Nor in all Kent, nor in Christendome. 1592 : Lyly, *Mother Bombie*, III. iv., I care not . . . I can live in Christendome as well as in Kent. 1599 : Nashe, in *Works*, v. 221 (Grosart), How William the Conquerour hauing heard the prouerb of Kent and Christendome, thought he had woone a countrey as goode as all Christendome when he was enfeofed of Kent. 1651 : Randolph, *Hey for Honesty*, I. i., All the cudgels in Christendom, Kent, or New England, shall never make me quiet. 1662 : Fuller, *Worthies*, ii. 122 (1840), Neither in Kent nor Christendom. 1790 : Grose, *Prov. Gloss.*, s.v. " Kent " [as in 1662].

3. *Kent is divided into three parts.* *See* quots. 1576 : Lambarde, *Peramb. of Kent*, 181 (1826), Very reasonable is their conceite, which doe imagine that Kent hath three steps, or degrees, of which the first (say they) offereth wealth without health : the second, giveth both wealth and health ; and the thirde affoordeth health onely, and little or no wealth. 1670 : Ray, 234, Some part of Kent hath health and no wealth, viz. East Kent. Some wealth

and no health, viz. The weald of Kent. Some both health and wealth, viz. the middle of the countrey and parts near London. 1735 : Pegge, *Kent. Proverbs*, in E.D.S., No. 12, p. 76, Health and no wealth ; Wealth and no health ; Health and Wealth. 1790 : Grose, *Prov. Gloss.*, s.v. " Kent " [abbreviated version of 1670].

4. *Kent ; red veal and white bacon.* 1735 : Pegge, *Kent. Proverbs*, in E.D.S., No. 12, p. 61.

See also **Knight of Cales.**

Kentish Jury. *See* **London** (1).

Kentish Long-tails. Versions of the legend or story may be found in 1205 : Layamon, *Brut*, ll. 29555–86 ; also in Polydore Vergil, *Angl. Hist.*, lib. xiii. 218 (ed. Basel, 1546). There is a version in Lambarde, *Peramb. of Kent*, 356–62 (1826). *See also* Matthew Paris, 785, 790. 1551 : Bale, *Eng. Votaryes*, 30, For castynge of fyshe tayles atthys Augustyne, Dorsett shyre men had tales euer after. But Polydorus applyeth yt vnto Kentysh men at Stroude by Rochester, for cuttynge of Thomas Beckettes horses tayle. *c.* 1600 : Deloney, in *Works*, 383 (Mann), The valiant courage and policie of the Kentishmen with long tayles. 1639–61 : in *Rump Songs*, Pt. II. 47 (1662, repr. 1874), I shall not dispute whether Long-tails of Kent, Or papist, this name of disgrace did invent. 1701 : T. Brown, *Works*, i. 134 (1760), Advice to the Kentish Long-tails, by the Wise Men of Gotham. 1887 : Parish and Shaw, *Dict. Kent. Dialect*, 95 (E.D.S.), Long-tails. An old nickname for the natives of Kent.

Kentish miles. *See* **Essex stiles.**

Kentish yeoman. *See* **Knight of Cales.**

Kenton. *See* **Haldon.**

Kentshire, hot as fire. 1735 : Pegge, *Kent. Proverbs*, in E.D.S., No. 12, p. 61.

Kent-street distress, A. 1790 : Grose, *Prov. Gloss.*, s.v. " Surrey."

Kerdon. *See* **Crediton.**

Kernel. *See* **Eat** (25).

Kerton. *See* **Crediton.**

Kettle. *See* **Pot** (6).

Kettle of fish, A pretty! 1742 : Fielding, *Andrews*, bk. i. ch. xii.,

" Here's a pretty kettle of fish," cries
Mrs. Tow-wouse, " you have brought
upon us ! " 1767 : Brooke, *Fool of
Quality*, ii. 249, If matters come to this
pass, I shall have made a fine kettle of
fish on't. 1850 : Dickens, *Copperfield*,
ch. xix., And then it will go in, you
know—and then . . . there'll be a pretty
kettle of fish ! 1872 : Hardy, *Greenwood
Tree*, Pt. II. ch. viii., Here's another
pretty kettle o' fish for thee.

Kex. See *Dry* (6); **Hollow**; and
Light as a kex.

Key fits not that lock, Your. Before
1529 : Skelton, *Works*, i. 20 (Dyce),
Youre key is mete for euery lok. 1732 :
Fuller, No. 6052.

Key under the door, To leave the =
To become bankrupt. 1602 : Chamberlain, *Letters*, 156 (Camden S.), The
mercer of Temple Barre . . . hath laide
the key under the doore and is become
banckrupt. 1670 : Ray, 182, To lay
the key under the threshold. 1677 :
Yarranton, *Eng. Improvement*, 126, If
it hold cheap for three or four years,
the tenant lays the key under the door.
1724 : Swift, *Drapier Letters*, Lett. I.,
The shopkeeper . . . must break, and
leave the key under the door.

**Keys hang not at one man's girdle,
All.** Before 1500 : Hill, *Commonplace-
Book*, 129 (E.E.T.S.). 1546 : Heywood,
Proverbs, Pt. I. ch. xi. 1670 : Ray, 110.
1732 : Fuller, No. 553.

Keystone. See quot. 1863 : Wise,
New Forest, ch. xv., The smuggler's
local proverb, " Keystone under the
hearth, keystone under the horse's
belly." [The smuggled spirits were concealed either below the fireplace or in
the stable.]

Kick, *verb*. 1. *To kick against the
pricks*. [πρὸς κέντρα μὴ λάκτιζε μὴ πταίσας
μογῇς. — Æschylus, *Agam.*, 1624. Ad-
uorsum stimulum calcas. — Terence,
Phorm., I. ii. 28.] 1382 : Wiclif, *Acts*,
ix. 5 (O.), It is hard to thee, for to
kyke aȝens the pricke. 1539 : Taverner,
Proverbs, fo. 14, It is harde kyckynge
against the gode. 1567 : Pickering,
Horestes, l. 977. c. 1594 : Bacon,
Promus, No. 962, Folly it is to spurn
against the pricke. 1605 : Camden,

Remains, 322 (1870) [as in 1594]. 1638 :
D. Tuvill, *Vade Mecum*, 46 (3rd ed.), It
is madnesse in a man to kick against a
thorne, to strive against a streame.
1842 : Marryat, *P. Keene*, ch. iii., It's
folly to kick against tenpenny nails.

2. *To kick the beam*. 1838 : Hood,
Hood's Own, 1st ser., 5 (1865), Despon-
dency . . . may make you kick the beam
and the bucket both at once.

3. *To kick the bucket*. 1796 : Wolcot,
Works, v. 242 (1812), Pitt kicked the
bucket. 1828 : Carr, *Craven Dialect*,
i. 55, To kick the bucket, an unfeeling
phrase for to die. 1890 : G. Allen, *Tents
of Shem*, ch. x. (Farmer), Sir Arthur
. . . will do the right thing in the end
before he kicks the bucket.

4. *To kick the wind*. 1598 : Florio,
Worlde of Wordes, s.v. " Dar de' calci
a Rouaio," To be hang'd, to kicke the
wind. 1813 : Ray, 203.

Kick, *subs*. 1. *I'll give him a kick
for a culp* = a Rowland for an Oliver.
1830 : Forby, *Vocab. E. Anglia*, 427.
1872 : J. Glyde, jr., *Norfolk Garland*,
148.

2. *The kick of the dam hurts not the
colt*. 1732 : Fuller, No. 4611.

Kid. *A piece of a kid is worth two
of a cat*. 1546 : Heywood, *Proverbs*,
Pt. II. ch. vii. 1670 : Ray, 110. 1732 :
Fuller, No. 348.

**Kidney, All of a; or Of such and
such a kidney.** Before 1555 : Latimer,
Sermons and Rem., 312 (P.S.) (O.), To
pronounce all to be thieves to a man,
except myself, of course, and those
men . . . that are of my own kidney.
1658 : R. Franck, *North. Memoirs*, 39
(1821), Such Furiosos, I must confess,
are of an odd kidney. 1694 : *Terence
made English*, 6, If any such has got
a tutor of his own kidney, he shall be
sure to be ply'd o' the weak side.
1742 : Fielding, *Andrews*, bk. ii. ch. viii.,
I am heartily glad to meet with a man
of your kidney. 1854 : Baker, *Northants
Gloss.*, s.v. " Kidney," " All of a kidney." A common expression when
children inherit the bad qualities of
their parents ; also applied to a number
of dissolute associates, " such young
men are all of a kidney."

Kill, *verb.* 1. *He often kills.* See
quot. *c.* 1645 : MS. Proverbs, in
N. & Q., vol. 154, p. 27, Hee often
kills that thinks but to hurt that
which is worth the restoringe.

2. *He that killeth a man when he is
drunk shall be hanged when he is sober.*
1546 : Heywood, *Proverbs,* Pt. I. ch. x.
1605 : Camden, *Remains,* 324 (1870).
1641 : in Marchant, *Praise of Ale,* 154
(1888), Suppose you should kill a man
whan you are drunk, you shall never
be hanged for it until you are sober.
1732 : Fuller, No. 2204.

3. *He that kills himself.* See **Buried.**

4. *He will kill a man for a mess
of mustard.* 1562 : Heywood, *Three
Hund. Epigr.,* No. 207. 1659 : Howell, 7.

5. *I killed her for good will, said Scot,
when he killed his neighbour's mare.*
1678 : Ray, 85.

6. *To kill a man with a cushion.* 1639 :
Clarke, 310. 1670 : Ray, 218.

7. *To kill one with kindness.* 1594 :
Shakespeare, *Tam. of Shrew,* IV. i.,
This is a way to kill a wife with kindness. 1607 : T. Heywood, *A Woman
Kilde with Kindnesse* [title]. 1699 :
Farquhar, *Love and a Bottle,* III. i., I
bear her an amorous grudge still . . .
I could kill her with kindness. 1761 :
Colman, *Jealous Wife,* IV. i., You
absolutely kill him with kindness.
1815 : Byron, *Letters and Journals,* iii.
205 (Prothero), Don't let them kill
you with claret and kindness at the
national dinner in your honour. 1876 :
in *N. & Q.*, 5th ser., vi. 246, They say
here [Worksop] of a man who . . .
shortened his days by . . . excess of
any kind, that he has " killed himself
with kindness."

8. *To kill two birds with one stone.*
[Iam ego uno in saltu lepide apros
capiam duos.—Plautus, *Cas.,* II. viii.
40. Una mercede duas res adsequi.—
Cicero, *Rosc. Am.,* xxix. 80.] 1611 :
Cotgrave, s.v. " Coup." 1671 : T.
Shadwell, *Miser,* II., And (if you can
bring this lady) I should kill two birds
with one stone, as that excellent thrifty
proverb says. 1734 : Fielding, *Univ.
Gallant,* V. ii., This is better than my
hopes ! This is killing two birds with

one stone. 1850 : Dickens, *Chuzzlewit,*
ch. viii.

9. *To kill two flies with one flap.*
1678 : Ray, 275.

10. *We will not kill but whoave* [cover].
Cheshire. 1691 : Ray, *Words not Generally Used,* 74 (E.D.S.). 1917 : Bridge,
Cheshire Proverbs, 150, . . . Spoken of a
pig or fowl which has been covered by
some utensil in readiness to kill.

11. *Who was killed by a cannon bullet
was curst in his mother's belly.* 1659 :
Howell, 6. 1670 : Ray, 110. 1738 :
Swift, *Polite Convers.,* Dial. I.

Kiln. 1. *For my part burn the kiln
boldly.* 1639 : Clarke, 77.

2. *For my peck of malt set the kiln
on fire.* Ibid., 254. 1666 : Torriano,
Piazza Univ., 164, The English say,
For my peck of malt, set the keel on
fire. 1681 : W. Robertson, *Phraseol.
Generalis,* 982. 1917 : Bridge, *Cheshire
Proverbs,* 58.

3. *Kill's-a-fire.* See quot. 1851 :
Sternberg, *Dialect, etc., of Northants,*
58, Kill's-a-fire. A proverbial expression intimating the existence of enmity.
" Kill's-a-fire 'tween they two."

4. *My kiln of malt is on fire.* 1605 :
Camden, *Remains,* 328 (1870).

5. *The kiln calls the oven burnt house.*
1603 : Florio, *Montaigne,* 503 (1634)
(O.), Which some say prouerbially, " Ill
may the kill call the ouen ' burnt
taïle ' ! " 1639 : Clarke, 196 (with
" hearth " for " house "]. 1670 : Ray,
110. 1853 : Trench, *Proverbs,* 63 (1905).

Kim-kam. See quots. 1611 : Cotgrave, s.v. " Anguille," To doe a thing
cleane kamme, out of order, the wrong
way. 1609 : Shakespeare, *Coriol.,* III.
i., *Sic.* This is clean kam. *Bru.* Merely
awry. 1637 : Clarke, 7, Kim kam arsie
versie. 1740 : North, *Examen,* 151,
The reason of all this chim-cham stuff
is . . . 1879 : Jackson, *Shropsh. Word-
Book,* 235, Let's 'a none o' yore kim-kam
ways.

Kind [Soft] **as a glove.** 1828 : Carr,
Craven Dialect, i. 264.

Kind as a kite. 1639 : Clarke, 287.
1670 : Ray, 202, As kind as a kite, all
you cannot eat you'll hide.

Kind as Cockburn. 1600 : *Weakest*

Goeth to the Wall, II. iii., Faith, as kind as Cockburn; I'll break my heart to do them good. [A note on this in Hazlitt's Webster's *Dram. Works*, iv. 252, says "An old proverb"; but I have not met it elsewhere.]

Kind heart loseth nought at last, A. 1639: Clarke, 45.

Kind to-day, cross to-morrow. Ibid., 159.

Kind, *subs.* *See* Love; and Nature.

Kinder scout. *See* quot. 1869: Hazlitt, 253, Kinder scout, the cowdest [coldest] place areawt. *Derbyshire.* Higson's *MSS. Coll.*

Kinder than he was wont. *See* Use (1).

Kindle not a fire that you cannot extinguish. 1584: B. R., *Euterpe*, 136 (Lang), I will kindle no moe coales then I may well quenche. 1869: Hazlitt, 253.

Kindness is lost that's bestowed on children and old folks. 1639: Clarke, 45.

Kindnesses, like grain, increase by sowing. 1855: Bohn, 437.

Kindred, Wheresoever you see your, make much of your friends. 1659: Howell, 5, For all your kindred make much of your friends. 1670: Ray, 15. 1732: Fuller, No. 5660.

King and Kings. 1. *A king promises, but observes only what he pleases.* 1855: Bohn, 292.

2. *A king without learning is but a crowned ass.* c. 1534: Berners, *Huon*, 730 (E.E.T.S.), For comonly it is said that a kyng without letter or conynge is compared to an asse crowned. c. 1535: *Dialogues of Creatures*, lv. (1816). 1868: Freeman, *Norman Conquest*, II. viii. 277 (O.), An unlettered king is a crowned ass.

3. *A king's face should give grace.* 1831: Croker, Note to *Boswell*, Johnson's letter of 20 June, 1777, The Royal prerogative of mercy, expressed by the old adage, "The King's face gives grace." 1853: Trench, *Proverbs*, 19 (1905).

4. *A king's favour is no inheritance.* 1678: Ray, 163. 1732: Fuller, No. 4618.

5. *He clips the King's English*=He is drunk. 1745: Franklin, *Drinker's Dict.*, in *Works*, ii. 24 (Bigelow).

6. *He shall have the king's horse*=He is a liar. 1678: Ray, 89.

7. *He that eats the king's goose.* *See* quots. 1611: Cotgrave, s.v. "Oye," He that eats the king's goose doth void fethers an hundred yeares after. 1748: Richardson, *Clarissa*, iv. 243 (1785), Often have I thought of that excellent old adage; He that eats the King's goose shall be choaked with his feathers.

8. *Kings and bears often worry their keepers.* 1738: *Gent. Mag.*, 475.

9. *Kings have long arms.* 1539: Taverner, *Prov. out of Erasmus*, fo. 4, Kynges haue longe handes.. 1581: Lyly, *Euphues*, 76 (Arber). 1669: *Politeuphuia*, 78, Kings have long arms, and rulers large reaches. 1736: Bailey, *Dict.*, s.v. "King," Kings have long hands.

10. *The king and his staff Be a man and a half.* 1869: Blackmore, *Lorna Doone*, ch. liv. [cited as "an ancient saying"].

11. *The King and Pope.* *See* quot. 1659: Howell, 12, The King and Pope, the lion and the wolf: a proverb used in King John's time, in regard of the great exactions.

12. *The king can make a serjeant, but not a lawyer.* 1732: Fuller, No. 4613.

13. *The king must wait while his beer's drawing.* 1869: Hazlitt, 375. 1888: Q.-Couch, *Troy Town*, ch. xix., They do say as the Queen must wait while her beer's a-drawin'.

14. *The King of England is the king of devils.* c. 1645: Taylor (Water-Poet), *Generall Complaint*, 4, in *Works*, 4th coll. (Spens. S.). 1662: Fuller, *Worthies*, i. 118 (1840). 1785-95: Wolcot, *Lousiad*, can. iii., A king of Englis be a king of defils.

15. *The king of good fellows is appointed for the queen of beggars.* 1605: Camden, *Remains*, 333 (1870). 1732: Fuller, No. 4616.

16. *The king's chaff is better than other people's corn.* 1612: Shelton, *Quixote*, Pt. I. bk. iv. ch. xii., Men say that a king's crumb is more worth than a lord's loaf. 1738: *Gent. Mag.*, 474. 1825: Scott, *Fam. Letters*, ii. 318 (1894),

" King's chaff being better than other folk's corn," his Excellency's lunch served me for my dinner.

17. *The king's cheese goes half away in parings.* 1659 : Howell, 3. 1660 : Howell, *Parly of Beasts*, 19, Whence grew the proverb, that the King's cheese goes away three parts in parings? 1709 : O. Dykes, *Eng. Proverbs*, 299. 1738 : *Gent. Mag.*, 474.

18. *The King's English.* It will be observed that in 1560, 1600, and 1602, when a queen was on the throne, the phrase used was still " The King's English." *c.* 1380 : Chaucer, *Astrolabe*, Prol., And preye, god save the king, that is lord of this langage. 1560 : T. Wilson, *Rhetorique*, 162 (1909), If a man should charge them for counterfeiting the Kings English. 1593 : Nashe, *Works*, ii. 184 (Grosart), Still he must be . . . abusing the Queenes English. 1600 : *Look About You*, sc. ix., in Hazlitt, *Old Plays*, vii. 412, Marry, here's a stammerer taken clipping the king's English. 1600 : Shakespeare, *Merry Wives*, I. iv. 1603 : Dekker, *Works*, i. 136 (Grosart). Before 1681 : Lacy, *Sir Hercules Buffoon*, V. iv., That is not shorthand, 'tis called clipping the King's English. 1714 : *Spectator*, No. 616. 1787 : O'Keeffe, *The Farmer*, I. iii., My dear ma'am how do you clack away, King George's English hack away. 1864 : Alford, *The Queen's English* [title]. 1886 : R. L. S., *Kidnapped*, ch. x., I have translated it here, not in verse . . . but at least in the king's English.

19. *The king's errand may lie in the cadger's gate.* 1826 : Scott, *Journal*, 22 Feb.

20. *The king's word is more than another man's oath.* 1554 : Princess Elizabeth, in Ellis, *Orig. Letters*, 2nd ser., ii. 255 [cited as " this olde saynge "].

21. *The king's word must stand.* 1509 : Bp. Fisher, *Eng. Works*, 230 (E.E.T.S.), It is a comyn prouerbe. Verbum regis stet oportet A kynges worde must stande.

See also **Kingdom; Nothing** (36); **Subject;** and **Two Kings.**

King Arthur. *See* **Arthur.**

King Harry. 1. *A King Harry's face.* 1678 : Ray, 73.

2. *King Harry loved a man.* 1605 : Camden, *Remains*, 327 (1870). 1613 : S. Rowley, *When You See Me*, sig. D3, King Harry loves a man, I can tell yee. 1653 : Naunton, *Frag. Regalia*, 182 (1694), The people hath it to this day in proverb, King Harry loved a man. 1670 : Ray, 100, King Harry lov'd a man, i.e. valiant men love such as are so, hate cowards. 1825 : Scott, *Talisman*, ch. xx., The King of England, who, as it was emphatically said of his successor Henry the Eighth, loved to look upon A MAN . . .

3. *King Harry robbed the Church and died a beggar.* 1678 : Ray, 354.

4. *This was a hill in King Harry's days.* Ibid., 73.

King Log, If you despise, you shall fear King Crane. 1732 : Fuller, No. 2749.

King's Sutton. *See* **Bloxham.**

Kingdom. 1. *In the kingdom of a cheater, the wallet is carried before.* 1640 : Herbert, *Jac. Prudentum.*

2. *In the kingdom of the blind, the one-eyed is king.* Before 1529 : Skelton, in *Works*, ii. 43 (Dyce), But haue ye nat harde this, How an one eyed man is Well syghted when He is amonge blynde men? 1540 : Palsgrave, *Acolastus*, Amongst xx blynde an one-eyed man may be a kynge. 1640 : Herbert, *Jac. Prudentum.* 1696 : Sir W. Temple, *Miscellanea*, 2nd part, 342 (4th ed.), For among the blind, he that has one eye is a Prince. 1732 : Fuller, No. 2137, He that has but one eye is a prince among those that have none. 1822 : Scott, *Fam. Letters*, ii. 147 (1894), The *purblind* is a king you know among the blind.

3. *Woe to the kingdom whose king is a child.* *c.* 1513 : More, *Works*, p. 63, col. 2 (1557), That the greate wise manne well perceiued, when hee sayde : *Veh regno cujus rex puer est*, Woe is that realme that hathe a chylde to theyr kynge. 1596 : Lodge, *Divel Coniured*, 80 (Hunt. Cl.). 1594 : Shakespeare, *Rich. III.*, II. iii., Woe to that land

that's govern'd by a child! 1642:
Fuller, *Holy State:* " Gust. Adolphus."

Kingston Down. See **Hengsten Down.**

**Kinsman helps kinsman, but woe to
him that hath nothing.** 1578: Florio,
First Fruites, fo. 32, Kinsfolkes with
kinsfolke, wo to hym that hath nothing.
1629: *Book of Meery Riddles*, Prov. 19.

Kinsman. See also **Servant** (7).

Kinsman's ear will hear it, The.
1659: Howell, *Proverbs: Brit.-Eng.*, 4.

**Kirbie's castle and Megse's glory,
Spinola's pleasure, and Fisher's folly.**
1662: Fuller, *Worthies*, ii. 343 (1840).
1790: Grose, *Prov. Gloss.*, s.v. " London."

Kirby. See **Sutton.**

Kiss, *subs.* 1. *A kiss of the mouth
often touches not the heart.* 1855: Bohn,
292.

2. *Kisses are keyes,* and *Wanton
kisses are keyes of sin.* 1639: Clarke, 28.
See also **Christmas** (5).

Kiss, *verb.* 1. *Do not make me kiss,
and you will not make me sin.* 1855:
Bohn, 345.

2. *He that doth kiss and do no more,
may kiss behind and not before.* 1659:
Howell, 9 (7).

3. *He that kisseth his wife in the
market-place, shall have enough to teach
him.* 1605: Camden, *Remains*, 323
(1870) [with " many teachers " for
" enough to teach him "]. 1670: Ray,
110. 1732: Fuller, No. 2205.

4. *If you can kiss the mistress, never
kiss the maid.* 1670: Ray, 111. 1742:
in Hone, *Ev. Day Book*, ii. 377, To kiss
with the maid when the mistress is
kind, A gentleman ought to be loth, sir.

5. *Kiss and be friends.* c. 1300:
R. Brunne, tr. Langtoft's *Chron.*, 64
(Hearne), Kisse and be gode frende in
luf and in a wille. 1419: in *Twenty-
six Poems*, 69 (E.E.T.S.), Make hem
kyssen and be frende. 1672: Lacy,
Dumb Lady, IV., Weep not, Nurse! I
am satisfied. Come, kiss and be friends.
1740: Richardson, *Pamela*, ii. 73 (1883),
Dear aunt, said her kinsman, let's see
you buss and be friends. 1775: Franklin, in *Works*, v. 450 (Bigelow), " They
should kiss and be friends," said I.
1847: Tennyson, *Princess*, vi. 271.

6. *Many kiss the child for the nurse's
sake.* 13th cent.: MS. quoted in 1846:
Wright, *Essays on Middle Ages*, i. 150,
Osculor hunc ore natum nutricis amore.
1546: Heywood, *Proverbs*, Pt. II. ch.
vii. 1590: Lodge, *Rosalynde*, 98 (Hunt.
Cl.), Aliena . . . thoght she kist the
childe for the nurses sake. 1683:
Meriton, *Yorkshire Ale*, 83–7 (1697),
For love of the nurse the bairn gets
mony a cuss. 1732: Fuller, No. 3351.
1823: Scott, *Peveril*, ch. viii., But
among men, dame, many one caresses
the infant that he may kiss the child's
maid.

7. *Many kiss the hand they wish cut
off.* 1640: Herbert, *Jac. Prudentum.*
1670: Ray, 15. 1754: Berthelson,
Eng.-Danish Dict., s.v. " Kiss," Many
do kiss the hands they wish to see
cut off.

8. *She had rather kiss than spin.*
1732: Fuller, No. 4123.

9. *To kiss a man's wife, or wipe his
knife, is a thankless office.* 1639:
Clarke, 45. 1670: Ray, 111.

10. *To kiss and tell.* 1616: Jonson,
Forest, V., 'Tis no sin love's fruit to
steal, But the sweet theft to reveal.
1675: Cotton, *Burl. upon Burlesque*,
200 (1765), And if he needs must kiss
and tell, I'll kick him headlong into
Hell. 1695: Congreve, *Love for Love*,
II. x., Oh fie, Miss, you must not kiss
and tell. 1757: Murphy, *Upholsterer*,
II., Why must they kiss and tell?
1816: Byron, in *Letters and Journals*, iii.
339 (Prothero), The old reproach against
their admirers of " Kiss and tell."
1910: Shaw, *Misalliance*, 88 (1914),
As a gentleman, I do not kiss and tell.

11. *To kiss one where he sat on Sunday.* 1583: Melbancke, *Philotimus*, sig.
Y1, When a mans hose be doune, it is
easie to kisse him where he sat on
Saterday. c. 1685: in *Roxb. Ballads*,
viii. 869 (B.S.), Thou shalt kiss me
where I sat on Sunday.

12. *To kiss the Counter.* c. 1560: in
Huth, *Ancient Ballads, etc.*, 227 (1867),
Then some the Counter oft doo kisse,
If that the money be not paid.

13. *To kiss the hare's foot. See* quots.
1598: *Servingmans Comfort*, in *Inedited*

Tracts, 112 (Hazlitt, 1868), Vpon payne to dyne with Duke Humfrie, or kisse the Hares foote. 1616 : Browne, *Brit. Past.*, II. ii., 'Tis supper time with all, and we had need Make haste away, unless we mean to speed With those that kiss the hare's foot. 1738 : Swift, *Polite Convers.*, Dial. II., Well, I am the worst in the world at making apologies; it was my lord's fault : I doubt you must kiss the hare's foot. 1818 : Scott, in Lockhart's *Life*, iv. 118, The poor clergyman [got] nothing whatever, or, as we say, *the hare's foot to lick.* 1847 : Halliwell, *Dict.*, s.v. " Kiss," *To kiss the hare's foot, to kiss the post*, to be too late for any thing.

14. *To kiss the post.* Before 1529 : Skelton, *Philip Sparrow*, l. 716, Troylus also hath lost On her moch loue and cost, And now must kys the post. 1595 : Churchyard, *Charitie*, 10 (1816), But some that lost their blood in countries right May kisse the post. 1623 : *New and Merrie Prognos.*, 19 (Halliwell), That such as come late must kisse the post. 1847 : *See* No. 13.

15. *You must kiss a parson's wife.* 1678 : Ray, 86, He that would have good luck in horses, must kiss the parsons wife. 1738 : Swift, *Polite Convers.*, Dial. II., *Sir John.* . . . I have had devilish bad luck in horse flesh of late. *Ld. Smart.* Why, then, Sir John, you must kiss a parson's wife.

Kissing, *verb. subs.* 1. *After kissing comes more kindness.* 1484 : Caxton, *La Tour-Landry*, ch. xxxiii. p. 185 (E.E.T.S.), The kyssynge is nyghe parente and cosyn vnto the fowle faytte or dede. 1639 : Clarke, 28. 1661 : Davenport, *City Nightcap*, I., She that will kiss, they say, will do worse.

2. *Kissing goes by favour.* 1605 : Camden, *Remains*, 327 (1870). 1649 : Quarles, *Virgin Widow*, I. 1725 : Bailey, tr. Erasmus' *Colloq.*, 239. 1871 : Planché, *Extravag.*, v. 300 (1879), And kissing more than ever now is found to go by favour.

See also **Furze.**

Kit after kind = A chip of the old block. 1599 : *Life of Sir T. More*, in

Wordsworth, *Eccl. Biog.*, ii. 112 (1853) (O.), She would now and then show herself to be her mother's daughter, kitt after kinde. 1670 : Ray, 183.

Kit to watch your chickens, Never put the. Corn. 1869 : Hazlitt, 290.

Kitchen. 1. *By a kitchen fat and good makes the poor most neighbourhood.* 1623 : Wodroephe, *Spared Houres*, 481.

2. *Kitchen physic is the best physic.* 1562 : Bullein, *Bulwarke of Defence*, According with kitchen physic, which kitchen, I assure you, is a good potecary's shop. *c.* 1670 : *Roxb. Ballads*, vii. 238 (B.S.), Good kitchen-physick is the best. 1738 : Swift, *Polite Convers.*, Dial. II.

3. *The smallness of the kitchen makes the house the bigger.* 1732 : Fuller, No. 4753.

4. *The taste of the kitchen is better than the smell.* 1633 : Draxe, 41. 1670 : Ray, 26. 1732 : Fuller, No. 4784.

Kite sees a dead horse afar off, An hungry. 1732 : Fuller, No. 616.

Kite. *See also* **Carrion**; **Hungry**; **Kind**; **Lark** (1); and **Yellow** (2).

Kitling. 1. *Did you ever know a killing bring a mouse to the old cat?* 1917 : Bridge, *Cheshire Proverbs*, 50, . . . Children are not always ready to support their aged parents.

2. *Wanton kitlins may make sober old cats.* 1732 : Fuller, No. 5415. Cf. **Untoward girl or boy.**

See also **Kit**; and **Mouse** (10).

Knack me that nut. *See* **Nut** (2).

Knapton. *See* **Gimmingham.**

Knave and **Knaves.** 1. *A knave discovered is a great fool.* 1732 : Fuller, No. 232.

2. *A knave (or rogue) in grain.* 1540 : Palsgrave, *Acolastus*, sig. S2, Whan knaues in graine mete. 1593 : *Tell-Trothes New-yeares Gift*, 18 (N. Sh. S.), But these of the sixt kinde are knaues in graine. 1640 : *The Knave in Grain New Vampt* [title of comedy]. 1728 : Swift, in *Works*, xiv. 241 (Scott), Among his crew of rogues in grain. 1785 : Grose, *Class. Dict. Vulgar Tongue*, s.v., Knave in grain, a knave of the first rate. 1855 : Bohn, 299, A rogue in grain is a rogue amain. 1869 : Spur-

geon, *John Ploughman*, ch. xviii., Like corndealers, they are rogues in-grain.

3. *As good a knave I know as a knave I know not.* 1678 : Ray, 74.

4. *I'd rather have a knave than a fool.* Oxfordsh. 1913 : *Folk-Lore*, xxiv. 77.

5. *If ye would know a knave, give him a staff.* 1640 : Herbert, *Jac. Prudentum.*

6. *Knaves and fools divide the world.* 1670 : Ray, 111. 1690 : *New Dict. Canting Crew*, sig. G6, Knaves and fools are the composition of the whole world. 1732 : Fuller, No. 2133.

7. *Knaves and whores go by the clock.* 1659 : Howell, 19.

8. *Knaves imagine nothing can be done without knavery.* 1732 : Fuller, No. 3135.

9. *One of the four and twenty politics of a knave is to stay long at his errand.* 1659 : Howell, 2.

10. *There I caught a knave in a purse-net.* 1639 : Clarke, 127. 1670 : Ray, 216. 1732 : Fuller, No. 4870.

11. *When a knave is in a plum-tree, he hath neither friend nor kin.* 1640 : Herbert, *Jac. Prudentum.*

Knavery in all trades, There is. 1671 : Head and Kirkman, *Eng. Rogue*, ii. 115. 1692 : L'Estrange, *Æsop*, 161 (3rd ed.), Hence comes the old saying ; *There's knavery in all trades, but most in taylors.*

Knavery is in credit, Where, honesty is sure to be a drug. 1754 : Berthelson, *Eng.-Danish Dict.*, s.v. " Drug."

Knavery may serve a turn, but honesty never fails. 1678 : Ray, 164 [with " is best at long run " for " never fails "]. 1732 : Fuller, No. 3131.

Knavish wit, a knavish will, A. 1736 : Bailey, *Dict.*, s.v.

Knife. 1. *Carry your knife even, between the paring and the apple.* 1732 : Fuller, No. 1065.

2. *Every knife. See* quot. 1877 : E. Leigh, *Cheshire Gloss.*, 96, " Every knife of his'n has a golden haft," i.e. everything he undertakes turns out well. 1917 : Bridge, *Cheshire Proverbs*, 55.

Knight of Cales [Cadiz], A, and a gentleman of Wales, and a laird of the North countree, A yeoman of Kent, with his yearly rent, will buy them

out all three. 1659 : Howell, 17. 1662 : Fuller, *Worthies*, ii. 121 (1840). 1790 : Grose, *Prov. Gloss.*, s.v. " Kent." 1840 : Barham, *Ing. Legends :* " Leech of Folkestone." 1887 : Parish and Shaw, *Dict. Kent. Dialect*, 193 (E.D.S.).

Knight or a knitter of caps, A. 1580 : Lyly, *Euphues*, 285 (Arber), Determining either to be a knight as we saye, or a knitter of cappes.

Knights. *See* quot. 1606 : B. Rich, *Faultes*, fo. 28, The prouerbe is olde, and it may be true, that as knights grow poor, ladies grow prowd.

Knipe-scar. *See* quot. 1846–59 : *Denham Tracts*, ii. 14 (F.L.S.), When Knipe-scar gets a hood, Sackworth may expect a flood. Westmoreland.

Knock at a deaf man's door, To (or at the wrong door). 1616 : B. Rich, *Ladies Looking Glasse*, 3, Therefore it is but to knocke at a deafe mans doore. 1639 : Clarke, 7, You knock at a deafe man's doore, *or* wrong doore.

Knock in the cradle, He got a. 1678 : Ray, 255.

Knock under the board, To =To yield. 1678 : Ray, 74, Knock under the board. He must do so that will not drink his cup.

Knock Cross, As old as. 1846–59 : *Denham Tracts*, i. 207 (F.L.S.).

Knot. 1. *To find* (or *seek*) *a knot in a rush.* 1340 : *Ayenbite*, 253, þet zekþ þet uel ine þe aye oþer þane knotte inc þe resse. 1532 : More, *Works*, 778 (1557). 1567 : Jewel, *Defence of Apol.*, Pt. IV. 733 (P.S.), It is a childish labour to seek a knot in a rush, and to imagine doubts where the case is clear. 1579 : Gosson, *Sch. of Abuse*, 46 (Arber), They thinke themselues no scholers, if they bee not able to finde out a knotte in euery rushe. 1661 : Davenport, *City Nightcap*, III., The trick's come out, And here's the knot i' th' rush. 1740 : North, *Lives of Norths*, i. 206 (Bohn), To cavil at every step, and raise moot points, like finding knots in bulrushes.

2. *To tie a knot with the tongue not to be undone with the teeth.* 1580 : Lyly, *Euphues*, 468 (Arber), We might knit that knot with our tongues, that we shall neuer vndoe with our teeth. 1617 :

Greene, *Works*, ix. 76 (Grosart), A woman may knit a knot with her tongue, that shee cannot vntie with all her teeth. 1738: Swift, *Polite Convers.*, Dial. I., He has tied a knot with his tongue, that he can never untie with his teeth. 1831: Scott, *Journal*, 6–7 May, I cannot conceive that I should have tied a knot with my tongue which my teeth cannot untie. 1913: -E. M. Wright, *Rustic Speech, etc.*, 272, To get married is : to tie a knot wi' the tongue, 'at yan cannot louze wi' yan's teeth (Yorkshire and Northamptonshire).

3. *Where the knot is loose the string slippeth.* 1639: Clarke, 248. 1670: Ray, 111. 1732: Fuller, No. 5667.

Knott Mill Fair, As throng [busy] **as.** Manchester. 1869: Hazlitt, 74.

Knotty timber. *See* quots. 1670: Ray, 15, A knotty piece of timber must have smooth wedges. 1855: Bohn, 438, Knotty timber requires sharp wedges.

Know, verb. 1. *He knows best what good is that has endured evil.* 1855: Bohn, 378.

2. *He knows enough that can live and hold his peace.* 1586: Pettie, tr. Guazzo's *Civil Convers.*, fo. 55, It is likewise saide, That he knoweth ynough who knoweth nothing if he know how to holde his peace. 1611: Cotgrave, s.v. "Sçavoir," He is cunning enough that can live and hold his peace. 1629: *Book of Meery Riddles*, Prov. 21 [as in 1586].

3. *He knows no end of his wealth.* 1546: Heywood, *Proverbs*, Pt. I. ch. xi., They know no ende of their good. 1639: Clarke, 97.

4. *He knows not whether his shoe goes awry.* 1678: Ray, 81.

5. *He knows one point more than the devil.* Spoken of a cunning fellow. 1620: Shelton, *Quixote*, Pt. II. ch. xxviii., I know that you know an ace more than the devil in all you speak or think. 1659: Howell, *Proverbs: Span.- Eng.*, 2.

6. *He knows tin.* Corn. 1864: " Cornish Proverbs," in *N. & Q.*, 3rd ser., vi. 495, One who seems to know tin [a cunning fellow]. 1887: M. A. Courtney, *Folk-Lore Journal*, v. 187,

" It's a wise man that knows tin " alludes to the various forms it takes.

7. *He that knoweth himself best, esteemeth himself least.* 1647 : *Countrym. New Commonwealth*, 26.

8. *He that knoweth when he hath enough is no fool.* 1546: Heywood, *Proverbs*, Pt. II. ch. vii.

9. *He that knows little often repeats it.* 1732 : Fuller, No. 2209.

10. *He that knows not how to hold his tongue, knows not how to talk.* 1669: *Politeuphuia*, 157, He that knows not when to hold his peace, knows not when to speak. 1732: Fuller, No. 2210.

11. *He that knows nothing doubts nothing.* 1611: Cotgrave, s.v. " Rien." 1640: Herbert, *Jac. Prudentum*. 1869: Spurgeon, *John Ploughman*, ch. ii., He who knows nothing is confident in everything.

12. *He that knows thee will never buy thee.* 1667: L'Estrange, *Quevedo's Visions*, 28 (1904) [cited as " the old proverb "].

13. *I know enough to hold my tongue, but not to speak.* 1732: Fuller, No. 2609.

14. *I know him as well as if I had gone through him with a lighted link.* 1732: Fuller, No. 2611. 1880: Spurgeon, *Ploughman's Pictures*, 97 [with " candle " for " link "].

15. *I know him not though I should meet him in my dish.* 1672: Walker, *Parœm.*, 13. 1732: Fuller, No. 2513 [with " porridge " for " dish "].

16. *I know no more than the man in the moon.* 1805: Scott, in Lockhart's *Life*, ii. 28, So on I wrote, knowing no more than the man in the moon how I was to end. 1828: Carr, *Craven Dialect*, i. 329, " I kna naa maar nar man ith moon," I am totally ignorant of it. 1878: R. L. S., *Inland Voyage:* " Down the Oise," I knew no more than the man in the moon about my only occupation.

17. *I know no more than the Pope of Rome.* 1663: Butler, *Hudibras*, Pt. II. can. iii. l. 894, He knew no more than the Pope of Rome. 1706: *Oxford Jests*, 93, " Read ! truly, my lord," says he, " I can read no more than the Pope of Rome." 1793: *Looker-on*, No. 73,

He . . . assured the gentleman . . . that he knew no more of Italy than the Pope of Rome. 1863 : *N. & Q.*, 3rd ser., iii. 470, I have often heard persons, when professing entire ignorance of any subject, exclaim " I know no more than the Pope of Rome about it."

18. *In the world who knows not to swim, goes to the bottom.* 1640 : Herbert, *Jac. Prudentum.*

19. *Know yourself and your neighbours will not mistake you.* 1899 : Dickinson, *Cumb. Gloss.*, 184.

20. *One may know by his nose what porridge he loves.* 1590 : Lodge, *Rosalynde*, 91 (Hunt. Cl.), Your nose bewrayes what porredge you loue. 1631 : Mabbe, *Celestina*, 104 (T.T.), I know by your nose what porridge you love. 1732 : Fuller, No. 3775.

21. *One may know your meaning by your gaping, (etc.).* 1639 : Clarke, 64, I know your meaning by your winking. 1659 : Howell, 21, You may know his meaning by his gaping. 1667 : L'Estrange, *Quevedo's Visions*, 112 (1904), They might have known their meaning by their mumping. 1670 : Ray, 186. 1738 : Swift, *Polite Convers.*, Dial. II., I can tell your meaning by your mumping. 1753 : Richardson, *Grandison*, iv. 226 (1883), You know my meaning by my gaping.

22. *They that know one another, salute afar off.* 1640 : Herbert, *Jac. Prudentum.*

23. *To know one from a black sheep.* 1670 : Ray, 183.

24. *To know what's what. See* What's what.

25. *To know when one is well.* 1553 : *Respublica*, IV. iv., Thou canst not see, thow wretch, canst thow, whan thow art well? 1576 : Wapull, *Tide tarrieth no Man*, Prol., Neyther of them know when they are well. 1692 : Southerne, *Wives Excuse*, III. ii., You are very happy in the discretion of a good lady, if you know when you're well. 1738 : Swift, *Polite Convers.*, Dial. I., I won't quarrel with my bread and butter for all that : I know when I'm well. 1855 : Kingsley, *West. Ho!*, ch. xix., " Overboard with you ! " quoth Amyas.

" Don't you know when you are well off ? "

26. *With all thy knowledge know thyself.* 1659 : Howell, 11 (9).

27. *You know not where a blessing may light.* 1869 : Hazlitt, 486.

28. *You may know by a handful the whole sack.* 1732 : Fuller, No. 5949.

29. *You never know what you can do till you try.* 1837 : Dickens, *Pickwick*, ch. xlix.

Knowledge hath no enemy but ignorance. 1559 : W. Cunningham, *Cosmogr. Glasse*, 46 (O.). 1613 : Wither, *Abuses Stript, etc.*, bk. ii. sat. 1, For thus the saying goes, and I hold so; *Ignorance onely is true wisedomes foe.* 1654 : Whitlock, *Zootomia*, 160.

Knowledge is a treasure, but practice is the key to it. [*c.* 1460 : *Prov. of Good Counsel*, in E.E.T.S., Ext. Ser. No. 8, p. 69, For of all tresure connynge ys flowur.] 1732 : Fuller, No. 3139. Cf. **Knowledge without practice.**

Knowledge is no burden. 1640 : Herbert, *Jac. Prudentum.* 1690 : *New Dict. Canting Crew*, sig. G7.

Knowledge is power. [Nam et ipsa scientia potestas est.—Bacon, *De Heresibus.* A wise man is strong.— *Prov.* xxiv. 5.] 1620 : Bacon, *Novum Organum*, 1, Knowledge and human power are synonymous, since the ignorance of the cause frustrates the effect. 1822 : Byron, *Letters and Journals*, vi. 11 (Prothero), They say that " Knowledge is Power " : I used to think so. 1878 : Platt, *Business*, 2, To commercial men knowledge is power. 1923 : *Sphere*, 29 Dec., p. 368, col. 1, The old copybook maxim, " Knowledge is power."

Knowledge makes one laugh, but wealth makes one dance. 1640 : Herbert, *Jac. Prudentum.* 1690 : *New Dict. Canting Crew*, sig. G7.

Knowledge without practice makes but half an artist. 1732 : Fuller, No. 3141. 1885 : *N. & Q.*, 6th ser., xii. 450 [cited as " The English proverb "]. Cf. **Knowledge is a treasure.**

Knowledge. *See also* **Gentleman** (11) ; and **Zeal.**

Kype. *See* **Scrape.**

L

Labour for one's pains, To have one's.
1589 : Nashe : in Greene's *Works*, vi. 13
(Grosart), They haue nought but . . .
(to bring it to our English prouerbe)
their labour for their trauaile. 1609 :
Shakespeare, *Troilus*, I. i., I have had
my labour for my travail. 1675 : Cotton,
Burl. upon Burlesque, 186 (1765), And
all that I by that should gain Would be
my labour for my pain. 1709 : Mandeville, *Virgin Unmask'd*, 59 (1724),
You'll get nothing but your labour
for your pains. 1778 : Burney, *Evelina*,
Lett. xxxiii., I'm glad the villain got
nothing but his trouble for his pains.

Labour in vain is loss of time. 1639 :
Clarke, 61.

Labour is light where love doth pay.
1594 : Drayton, *Ideas*, lix.

Labour to be as you would be thought.
c. 1597 : in Harington, *Nugæ Antiquæ*,
i. 210 (1804).

Labour. *See also* Past labour.

**Labours and thrives, spins gold, He
that.** 1640 : Herbert, *Jac. Prudentum*.
1670 : Ray, 15. 1732 : Fuller, No. 2211.

Lack a tile, lack a sheaf. 1639 :
Clarke, 10.

**Lacketh a stock, Whoso, his gain is
not worth a chip.** 1546 : Heywood,
Proverbs, Pt. II. ch. ix. 1605 : Camden, *Remains*, 335 (1870). 1670 : Ray,
146. 1732 : Fuller, No. 5731.

Lad to wed a lady. *See* quot. 1513 :
Bradshaw, *St. Werburge*, 43 (E.E.T.S.),
By a prouerbe auncyent " A lad [lout]
to wedde a lady is an inconuenyent."

Ladder to bed, You'll go up the = be
hanged. 1678 : Ray, 256.

Laden with iron, laden with fear.
1631 : Mabbe, *Celestina*, 204 (T.T.), It
is not saide in vaine ; Laden with iron,
laden with feare. 1666 : Torriano,
Piazza Univ., 88 [" loaded " for
" laden "].

Ladie Lift. *See* quot. Ladie Lift
Clump is a clump of trees on the
top of a high hill near Bredwardine,

Herefordshire. 1881 : C. W. Empson,
in *Folk-Lore Record*, iv. 130, When Ladie
Lift Puts on her shift, She feares a
downright raine ; But when she doffs
it, you will finde The rain is o'er and
still the winde, And Phœbus shine
againe.—*Herefordshire.*

**Lads' love's a busk of broom, hot
awhile and soon done.** Cheshire. 1670 :
Ray, 46. 1877 : E. Leigh, *Cheshire
Gloss.*, 34. 1917 : Bridge, *Cheshire
Proverbs*, 87. Cf. **Love**, *subs.* (31).

**Lads' love is lassies' delight, And if
lads don't love, lassies will flite.** 1828 :
Carr, *Craven Dialect*, i. 273. 1917 :
Bridge, *Cheshire Proverbs*, 87.

Lady-birds. *See* **Hops** (3).

Lady-day. 1. *On Lady-day the latter,
The cold comes on the water.* 1732 :
Fuller, No. 6217.

2. *When our Lady.* See first quot.
1662 : Fuller, *Worthies*, i. 113 (1840),
"When our Lady falls in our Lord's lap,
Then let England beware a sad clap
(*or* mishap)." *Alias* " Then let the
clergyman look to his cap." I behold
this proverbial prophecy, or this pro-
phetical menace, to be not above six
score years old, and of Popish extrac-
tion since the Reformation. 1790 :
Grose, *Prov. Gloss.*, s.v. " England "
[as in 1662]. 1812 : Brady, *Clavis Cal.*,
i. 261 [as in 1662]. Cf. **Easter**.

Lady Done. *See* **Fair** (15).

**Lady's heart and a beggar's purse,
Nothing agreeth worse than a.** 1546 :
Heywood, *Proverbs*, Pt. I. ch. x. Cf.
Lord (1).

Lag puts all in his bag. 1666 : Torriano, *Piazza Univ.*, 322, The English
say, Lagg puts all in his bagg.

Lamb. 1. *A lamb in the house a lion
in the field.* c. 1387 : Usk, *Test. of
Love*, in Skeat's *Chaucer*, vii. 24, Lyons
in the felde and lambes in chambre.
1589 : Puttenham, *Eng. Poesie*, 299
(Arber), We say it is comely for a
man to be a lambe in the house, and

a lyon in the field. 1593 : G. Harvey,
Works, i. 277 (Grosart), A lion in the
field, a lamme in the towne.

2. *A lamb is as dear to a poor man,
as an ox to the rich.* [1611 : Cotgrave,
s.v. " Povre," An egge's as much to a
poor man as an oxe.] 1732 : Fuller,
No. 234.

3. *Every lamb knows its dam.* Ibid.,
No. 6490.

4. *Go to bed with the lamb.* See **Rise**
(12).

5. *The first lamb. See* quot. 1862 :
R. S. Hawker, in Byles, *Life, etc.*, 357
(1905), Did you ever hear the saying
that if the first lamb be a lady the
Mistress of the house will govern for
that year, and if *versa vice* the first be
a gentleman then the Master?

See also **Fox** (18) and (23); **God
tempers ; Mild ;** and **Quiet.**

Lamb's skin. *See* **Soon goes.**

Lambeth Doctor, A. 1790 : Grose,
Prov. Gloss., s.v. " Surrey."

Lambskin, To lap in a. 1546 : Heywood, *Proverbs*, Pt. II. ch. vi., She
must obey those lambs, or els a lambs
skyn Ye wlll prouyde for hir, to lap
her in. Cf. *The Wyfe lapped in Morels
Skyn* (c. 1570), in Hazlitt, *Early Pop.
Poetry*, iv.

Lambtons. *See* quot. 1846–59 : *Denham Tracts*, i. 106 (F.L.S.), In the
northern portion of the bishoprick [of
Durham], and southern border of
Northumberland, they have an old saw,
when speaking of a dashing, flashing,
stylish fellow, " Oh ! he's fit to keep
company with the Lambtons."

Lame as a cat, As. 1889 : Peacock,
Manley, etc., Gloss., 98 (E.D.S.) [a
" proverb "].

Lame as a dog, As. 1886 : Elworthy,
West Som. Word-Book, 202 (E.D.S.),
" Lame as a dog " is the constantly
used expression to denote severe lame-
ness, whether in man or beast.

Lame as a tree, As. 1869 : Hazlitt,
65.

Lame dog over a stile, To help a.
1546 : Heywood, *Proverbs*, Pt. I. ch. xi.,
As good a deede As it is to helpe
a dogge ouer a style. 1630 : Taylor
(Water-Poet), *Works*, 2nd pagin., 249,

My wit should be so crippled with the
gowt, That it must haue assistance to
compile, Like a lame dog, that's limping o'r a stile. 1720 : C. Shadwell,
Hasty Wedding, II., You're a clever
fellow to lead a lame dog over a stile.
1788 : Wolcot, *Works*, i. 509 (1795), Let
me display a Christian spirit, And try
to lift a lame dog o'er a style. 1901 :
S. Butler, in H. F. Jones's *Life*, i. 344
(1919), When my nightly game of
patience goes amiss . . . I sometimes
help a lame dog over a style [*sic*] by a
little cheating rather than waste the
game.

Lame Giles has played the man. 1639 :
Clarke, 17.

Lame goes as far as the staggerer, The.
1640 : Herbert, *Jac. Prudentium.* 1670 :
Ray, 15.

Lame hares are ill to help. 1732 :
Fuller, No. 3143.

Lame post brings the truest news, The.
Ibid., No. 4620.

**Lame returns sooner than his servant,
The.** 1659 : Howell, *Proverbs ; Brit -
Eng.*, 40.

Lame tongue gets nothing, The.
1605 : Camden, *Remains*, 333 (1870).
1732 : Fuller, No. 4619. 1830 : Forby,
Vocab. E. Anglia, 434.

**Lame traveller should get out betimes,
A.** 1732 : Fuller, No. 235.

**Lammas, After, corn ripens as much
by night as by day.** 1678 : Ray, 352.
1893 : Inwards, *Weather Lore*, 33.

Lammas-tide. *See* **Cuckoo** (16).

Lancashire fair women. 1622 : Drayton, *Polyol.*, xxiii., Fair women doth
belong to Lancashire again. 1662 :
Fuller, *Worthies*, ii. 191 (1840). 1710 :
Brit. Apollo, iii. No. 30, col. 4, Lancashire fair women is past into a proverb.
1790 : Grose, *Prov. Gloss.*, s.v. " Lancs."

Lancashire law, no stakes, no draw.
1828 : Carr, *Craven Dialect*, i. 274.
1847 : Halliwell, *Dict.*, s.v., . . . a
saying to avoid payment of a bet when
verbally made. 1901 : F. E. Taylor,
Lancs Sayings, 41. Cf. **Stopford law.**

Lancashire man. *See* quots. 1599 :
Buttes, *Dyets Dry Dinner*, sig. A2, Here
are neither eg-pies for the Lancashire-
man, nor . . . 1622 : Drayton, *Polyol.*,

xxvii. 68, Ye lusty lasses then, in Lancashire that dwell . . . As ye the egg-pye love, and apple cherry-red. 1655 : T. Muffett, *Healths Improvement*, 36, As our Welshmen esteem of cheese, Lancashire men of egg-pies. 1711 : Hearne, *Collections*, iii. 156 (Oxford Hist. S.), He yᵗ will fish for a Lancashire Lad At any time or tide Must bait his hook with a good egg py or an apple wᵗʰ a red side. 1911 : Hackwood, *Good Cheer*, 163 [as in 1711].

Land and **Lands.** 1. *He that hath lands, hath quarrels.* 1640 : Herbert, *Jac. Prudentum.* 1855 : Bohn, 566, Who has land has war.

2. *He that hath some land, must have some labour.* 1639 : Clarke, 59. 1670 : Ray, 112. 1732 : Fuller, No. 2161.

3. *Land was never lost for want of an heir.* 1678 : Ray, 165.

See also **House** (17).

Land's End. *See* quots. 1546 : Heywood, *Proverbs*, Pt. II. ch. vii., Thou gossepst at home to meete me at landis ende. 1560 : T. Wilson, *Rhetorique*, 148 (1909), Some newe fellowes when they thinke yee a papist, they will call him streight a catholique, and bee euen with him at the lands end.

Land's End to John o' Groats, From. 1823 : Scott, *St. Ronan's*, ch. x., I can beat Wolverine from the Land's-End to Johnnie Groat's. 1831 : Peacock, *Crotchet Castle*, ch. iv., Who forages for articles in all quarters, from John o' Groat's House to the Land's End.

Landlords. *See* **Quick landlord.**

Land-mark stones. *See* **Stone** (4).

Lane, In the. *See* **Always in the lane.**

Lansallos treat, A, everybody pay for hisself. 1906 : *Cornish N. & Q.*, 265.

Lapped. *See* **Wrapped.**

Lapwing cries most farthest from her nest, The. 1584 : Lyly, *Campaspe*, II. i., Wherein you resemble the lapwing, who crieth most where her nest is not. *c.* 1620 : Massinger, *Old Law*, IV. ii., He has the lapwing's cunning, I am afraid, That cries most when she's furthest from the nest. 1732 : Fuller, No. 4621.

Lareovers. *See* **Layers.**

Lark and **Larks.** 1. *A leg of a lark is better than the body of a kite.* 1546 :

Heywood, *Proverbs*, Pt. I. ch. iv. 1605 : Chapman, etc., *Eastw. Hoe*, V. i., The legge of a larke is better then the body of a kight. 1732 : Fuller, No. 3765.

2. *It were better to hear the lark sing than the mouse cheep.* 1855 : Bohn, 435.

3. *Larks fall there ready roasted.* 1659 : Howell, *Proverbs : Fr.-Eng.*, 3, He thinks that roasted larks will fall into his mouth ; spoken of a sluggard.

See also **Lovers** ; **Rise** (12) ; and **Sky falls.**

Lartington. *See* quot. 1846–59 : *Denham Tracts*, i. 81 (F.L.S.), Lartington for frogs, And Barney Castle for butchers' dogs ; or, Lartington frogs, And Barney Castle butcher-dogs. 1852 : Longstaffe, *Richmondshire*, 133.

Lass in the red petticoat shall pay for all, The. 1664 : J. Wilson, *The Cheats*, I. ii., That estate Which you believe so fair . . . is at present At that low ebb, that if I don't look to't In time, it will be past recovery. Come ; the red petticoat must piece up all. 1678 : Ray, 80.

Lassies are lads' leavings. Cheshire. 1670 : Ray, 217. 1917 : Bridge, *Cheshire Proverbs*, 88.

Last benefit is most remembered, The. 1732 : Fuller, No. 4622.

Last but not least. 1580 : Lyly, *Euphues*, 343 (Arber), Of these three but one can stand me in steede, the last, but not the least. 1676 : Shadwell, *Virtuoso*, IV. iv., These are the last, but not the least. 1782 : in *Twining Fam. Papers*, 103 (1887), Upon my word, a goodly party, and the rear well brought up by Mr. George T., though " last, but not least."

Last dog. *See* **Dog** (78).

Last drop makes the cup run over, The. 1855 : Bohn, 509.

Last evil smarts most, The. 1732 : Fuller, No. 4623.

Last for his shoe, He has found a. Ibid., No. 1869.

Last has luck : Finds a penny in the muck. Worcs. 1904 : Lean, *Collectanea*, iv. 27.

Last legs, To be on one's. 1599 : Massinger, etc., *Old Law*, V. i. (O.), *Eugenia*. My husband goes upon his last hour now. *1st Courtier*. On his last legs, I am sure. 1678 : Ray, 89, He goes on's last legs. 1753 : Richardson, *Grandison*, iv. 50 (1883), What would poor battered rakes and younger brothers do, when on their last legs, were it not for good-natured widows? 1827 : Hone, *Ev. Day Book*, ii. 1013, The " regular drama " is on its last legs. 1857 : Trollope, *Barch. Towers*, ch. i., The bishop was quite on his last legs.

Last makes fast. 1659 : Howell, 6, Last makes fast, viz. Shut the door. 1881 : Evans, *Leics. Words*, 302 (E.D.S.), " Last makes fast " . . . is a recognised rule in passing through a gate that has been opened. Cf. Come (14).

Last prayers, She is at her. 1678 : Ray, 79. 1690 : *New Dict. Canting Crew*, sig. L5, Stale maid, at her last prayers. 1698 : *Terence made English*, 157 (2nd ed.), S'death ! I'm at my last prayers.

Last race-horse brings snow on his tail, The. 1884 : " Sussex Proverbs," in *N. & Q.*, 6th ser., ix. 402.

Last straw breaks the camel's back, The. [Quemadmodum clepsydram non extremum stillicidium exhaurit, sed quidquid ante defluxit ; sic ultima hora qua esse desinimus, non sola mortem facit, sed sola consummat. — Seneca, *Ep.*, xxiv. 19.] 1677 : Archbp. Bramhall, *Works*, iv. 59, It is the last feather that breaks the horse's back. 1732 : Fuller, No. 5120 [as in 1677]. 1848 : Dickens, *Dombey*, ch. ii., As the last straw breaks the laden camel's back . . . 1869 : P. Fitzgerald, *Comediettas*, It is the Last Straw that breaks the Camel's Back [title of play].

Last suitor wins the maid, The. 1611 : Cotgrave, s.v. " Aimé " [with " wench " for " maid "]. 1670 : Ray, 15. 1732 : Fuller, No. 4624.

Last to the pot is soonest wroth, He that cometh. *c.* 1400 : *Beryn*, l. 3366, p. 101 (E.E.T.S.), fful soth is that by-word, " to pot, who comyth last ! He worst is servid " ; and so it farith by me. 1546 : Heywood, *Proverbs*, Pt. II. ch. x. 1659 : Howell, 8.

Last word though he talk bilk for it, He 'll have the. 1678 : Ray, 228.

Late repentance is seldom true. 1552 :

Latimer, *Works*, ii. 193 (P.S.), It is a common saying, *Pœnitentia sera raro vera.* 1639 : Clarke, 255. 1732 : Fuller, No. 3145.

Lathom and Knowsley. *See* quot. 1858 : *N. & Q.*, 2nd ser., v. 211, It is a very common expression [Lancashire] to say of a person having two houses, even if temporarily, that he has " Lathom and Knowsley " . . . Though separate possessions for above 150 years, the expression " Lathom and Knowsley " still survives.

Latter Lammas = never. 1553 : *Respublica*, III. v., Faith youer Marsship will thrive att the latter Lammas. *c.* 1566 : in Collmann, *Ballads, etc.*, 92 (Roxb. Cl.). 1672 : Walker, *Parœm.*, 52, At latter Lammas ; at Nevermass. 1709 : O. Dykes, *Eng. Proverbs*, xxxvi. 1754 : *Gent. Mag.*, 416. 1885 : W. L. Birkbeck, *Hist. Sketch Distrib. of Land in Eng.*, Pt. I. ch. v., Hence " Latter Lammas," a later month than Lammas, became proverbial, as an equivalent to the Greek Calends.

Laugh, verb. 1. *He can laugh and cry both in a wind.* 1670 : Ray, 184. 1732 : Fuller, No. 4120 [with " she " for " he "].

2. *He is not laughed at that laughs at himself first.* Ibid., No. 1936.

3. *He laughs best that laughs last.* 1706 : Vanbrugh, *Country House*, II. v. 1823 : Scott, *Peveril*, ch. xxxviii., Your Grace knows the French proverb, " He laughs best who laughs last." But I hear you. 1920 : O. Onions, *A Case in Camera*, 147, Very well, young-fellow-me-lad ; you watch it ! They laugh best that laugh last. It isn't over yet !

4. *He laughs ill that laughs himself to death.* 1639 : Clarke, 201. 1670 : Ray, 15. 1732 : Fuller, No. 1962.

5. *Laugh and grow fat.* 1596 : Harington, *Metam. of Ajax*, 68 (1814), Many of the worshipful of the city, that make sweet gains of stinking wares ; and will laugh and be fat. *c.* 1610 : in *Roxb. Ballads*, i. 476 (B.S.), Ile laugh and be fatte, for care kils a catte. 1765 : Garrick, in *Garrick Corresp.*, i. 201 (1831), Laugh and be fat

all the world over. 1823: Scott,
Peveril, ch. xxxiii., He seems to have
reversed the old proverb of "laugh and
be fat." 1926: *Humorist*, 9 Oct., p. 237,
col. 3, I was told, by my excellent
daddy, To laugh and grow fat.

6. *Laugh and lie down.* Before 1529:
Skelton, *Works*, ii. 55 (Dyce), Now
nothynge but pay, pay, With, laugh
and lay downe, Borowgh, cyte, and
towne. 1596: A. Copley, *Fig for
Fortune*, 24 (Spens. S.), Tis faire lie
downe and laugh. 1641: R. Brome,
Joviall Crew, III. 1671: *Westm. Drollery*, 28 (Ebsworth), And when we have
done These innocent sports, we'l laugh
and lie down. 1825: Jennings, *Somerset
Words*, 52, Laugh-and-lie-down. A
common game at cards.

7. *Let them laugh that win.* 1546:
Heywood, *Proverbs*, Pt. I. ch. v., He
laughth that wynth. 1599: *Sir Clyomon, etc.*, sig. F1, Wel let them laugh
that win. 1604: Shakespeare, *Othello*,
IV. i., So, so: they laugh that win.
1674: Head and Kirkman, *Eng. Rogue*,
iii. 132, If the proverb be true, *Let them
laugh that win.* 1767: Garrick, *Epil.* to
Colman's *Eng. Merchant.* 1844: Thackeray, *Barry Lyndon*, ch. xiii., Let those
laugh that win. 1862: Borrow, *Wild
Wales*, ch. lxiv.

8. *Shut your eyes when you laugh, and
you'll never see a merry day.* W. Corn.
(Mr. C. Lee).

9. *To laugh from the teeth outwards.*
1532: More, *Confut. of Tyndale*, cxlviii.,
He lawgheth but from the lyppes for-
warde. 1611: Cotgrave, s.v. "Rire,"
Rire à grosses dents. From the teeth
outwards, say we. 1754: Berthelson,
Eng.-Danish Dict., s.v. "Laugh."

10. *To laugh in one's face and cut
one's throat.* 1670: Ray, 184. 1716:
E. Ward, *Female Policy*, 53, A woman
will . . . laugh in your face, and cut
your throat. 1732: Fuller, No. 5194.

11. *To laugh in one's sleeve.* [Tu
videlicet tecum ipse rides.—Cicero,
De Fin., II. xxiii. 76.] 1546: Heywood,
Proverbs, Pt. II. ch. v. 1567: Harman,
Caveat, 46 (E.E.T.S.), Hee laughed in
his sleue. 1683: Chalkhill, *Thealma,
etc.*, 89 (1820), Now Orandra laugh

within her sleeve. 1744-6: Mrs. Haywood, *Fem. Spectator*, ii. 95 (1771), A
certain gentleman . . . may be laughing in his sleeve at me. 1849: C.
Brontë, *Shirley*, ch. viii., There was a
kind of leer about his lips; he seemed
laughing in his sleeve at some person
or thing.

12. *To laugh like a piskie.* 1865:
Hunt, *Pop. Romances W. of Eng.*, 82
(1896), They [the fairies] must have
been a merry lot, since to "laugh like
a Piskie" is a popular saying.

13. *To laugh on the wrong side of
one's mouth.* 1666: Torriano, *Piazza
Univ.*, 173, Now you can laugh but on
one side of your mouth, friend. 1714:
Ozell, *Molière*, iv. 36, If you provoke
me, I'll make you laugh on the wrong
side o' your mouth. 1849: C. Brontë,
Shirley, ch. xxx., I see, however, you
laugh at the wrong side of your mouth;
you have as sour a look at this moment
as one need wish to see. 1925: *Times*,
6 March, p. 12, col. 2, You laugh
immoderately, and end by laughing on
the wrong side of the mouth.

Laughton. *See* Bolsover.

**Laundress washeth her own smock
first, The.** 1732: Fuller, No. 4626.

Lavants, The. *See* quot. 1789: White,
Selborne: " Letters to Barrington," xix.,
The land springs which we call lavants,
break out much on the Downs of Sussex,
Hampshire, and Wiltshire. The country people say " When the lavants rise,
corn will always be dear."

Lavishness is not generosity. 1732:
Fuller, No. 3147.

Law and **Laws.** 1. *A suit at law and
a urinal bring a man to the hospital.*
1670: Ray, 15. 1732: Fuller, No. 6238.

2. *He is a crust of the law; he will
never know a crumb of it.* 1830: Forby,
Vocab. E. Anglia, 430.

3. *He that goes to law holds a wolf by
the ears.* 1621: Burton, *Melancholy*,
Dem. to Reader, 48 (1836), He that goes
to law (as the proverb is) holds a wolf
by the ears. Cf. **Wolf** (15).

4. *He will go to law for the wagging of
a straw.* 1615: W. Goddard, *Nest of
Wasps*, No. 16, Thou knowst a barlie
strawe Will make a parish parson

goe to lawe. 1670: Ray, 184. Cf.
Wagging.

5. *In a thousand pounds of law there's
not an ounce of love.* 1611: Cotgrave,
s.v. " Amour," In a hundred pound of
law ther's not a half-peny weight of
love. 1670: Ray, 15. 1732: Fuller,
No. 2811, In a thousand pounds worth
of law, there is not a shilling's worth
of pleasure.

6. *Law governs man, and reason the
law.* 1732: Fuller, No. 3149.

7. *Law, Logic and Switzers may be
hired to fight for anybody.* 1593: Nashe,
Christs Teares, in *Works*, iv. 148 (Grosart). 1630: Brathwait, *Eng. Gent., etc.*,
7 (1641), It is commonly said that Law,
etc. . . . *c.* 1640: Davenport, in *Works*,
327 (Bullen), Law, logick, Switzers,
fight on any side.

8. *Laws catch flies, but let the hornets
go free.* 1591: Harington, *Orl. Furioso*,
bk. xxxii., Notes, For the most part
lawes are but like spiders webs, taking
the small gnats, or perhaps sometime
the fat flesh flies, but hornets that have
sharpe stings and greater strength,
breake through them. 1625: Bacon,
Apoph, No. 181, One of the Seven was
wont to say, " That laws were like
cobwebs: where the small flies were
caught, and the great brake thorough."
1732: Fuller, No. 3150.

9. *The law groweth of sin and doth
punish it.* 1578: Florio, *First Fruites*,
fo. 32. 1629: *Book of Meery Riddles*,
Prov. 39 [with " chastiseth " for " doth
punish "].

10. *The law is not the same at morning
and at night.* 1640: Herbert, *Jac.
Prudentum*. 1670: Ray, 15.

11. *The worst of law is that one suit
breeds twenty.* 1640: Herbert, *Jac.
Prudentum*. 1670: Ray, 15.

See also **Agree.**

Lawless as a town-bull, As. 1678:
Ray, 286. 1732: Fuller, No. 706. Cf.
No law.

Law-makers. *See* **Make** (13).

Lawn. *See* quots. 1546: Heywood,
Proverbs, Pt. I. ch. viii., He that will
sell lawne before he can folde it, He
shall repent him before he haue solde
it. 1580: Lyly, *Euphues*, 290 (Arber),

He that will sell lawne must learne to
folde it. *c.* 1594: Bacon, *Promus*, No.
474 (as in 1546]. 1670: Ray, 112, He
that buyes lawn before, etc. . . . 1732:
Fuller, No. 6443 [as in 1670].

Lawrence. *See* **Lazy Lawrence.**

Lawton-gate a clap, She hath given.
1678: Ray, 300. 1710: *Brit. Apollo*,
iii. No. 26, col. 7. 1877: E. Leigh,
Cheshire Gloss., 43, They say of a girl
who from misconduct finds it convenient to leave the county, " She has
given Lawton Gate a clap "—Lawton
being the boundary of Cheshire towards
Staffordshire. 1917: Bridge, *Cheshire
Proverbs*, 109.

Lawyer and **Lawyers.** 1. *A good
lawyer, an evil neighbour.* 1611: Cotgrave, s.v. " Advocat." 1670: Ray, 15.
1754: Berthelson, *Eng.-Danish Dict.*,
s.v. " Neighbour," A good lawyer is
an ill neighbour. 1831: Hone, *Year-
Book*, 125 [quoted as an old French
saying].

2. *A good lawyer must be a great liar.*
1703: E. Ward, *Writings*, ii. 319 [cited
as " a common saying "].

3. *A wise lawyer never goes to law
himself.* 1855: Bohn, 303.

4. *Fair and softly as lawyers go to
Heaven.* 1670: Ray, 193. 1694:
Motteux, *Rabelais*, bk. v. ch. xxviii.,
Come, let's now talk with deliberation,
fair and softly, as lawyers go to Heaven.
1856: *N. & Q.*, 2nd ser., i. 267, The
following was related to me the other
day by a Salopian: " An inch every
Good Friday, the rate lawyers go to
Heaven." 1894: Northall, *Folk Phrases*,
11 (E.D.S.), By degrees, as lawyers go
to Heaven. 1901: F. E. Taylor, *Lancs
Sayings*, 15 [as in 1894].

5. *Few lawyers die well.* 1605: Camden, *Remains*, 321 (1870).

6. *He hath as many tricks as a lawyer.*
1672: Walker, *Parœm.*, 51.

7. *He who is his own lawyer, has a
fool for his client.* 1875: A. B. Cheales,
Proverb. Folk-Lore, 76.

8. *Kick an attorney downstairs and
he'll stick to you for life.* " A Bar
proverb." 1904: Lean, *Collectanea*,
iv. 24.

9. *Lawyers and asses always die in*

their shoes. 1867 : Harland, etc., *Lancs Folk-Lore*, 20, The proverb that " lawyers . . . shoes " is invariably quoted.

10. *Lawyers' gowns are lined with the wilfulness of their clients.* 1855 : Bohn, 439.

11. *Lawyers' houses are built on the heads of fools.* 1640 : Herbert, *Jac. Prudentium.* 1660 : Howell, *Parly of Beasts*, 17, The lawyer replied . . . this house [his own] is made of asses heads and fools sculls. 1865 : " Lancs Proverbs," in *N. & Q.*, 3rd ser., viii. 494 [" Attorneys' " for " Lawyers' "].

12. *You are one of those lawyers that never heard of Littleton.* 1732 : Fuller, No. 5858.

See also Hide nothing ; and Part three things.

Lay a stone at one's door, To=To " cut " one. 1872 : J. Glyde, jr., *Norfolk Garland*, 150, He has laid a stone at my door.

Lay a straw, To=To make a stop, or mark a stopping-place. *c.* 1510 : A. Barclay, *Egloges*, 47 (Spens. S.), Haue done nowe Faustus, lay here a straw. 1562 : Bullein, *Bulwarke of Defence*, fo. 21, But here will I stoppe, and laie a strawe, and fall into my bias againe. 1619 : B. Rich, *Irish Hubbub*, 54, But I will here stop and lay a straw.

Lay a thing in one's dish, To=To accuse, or to charge against, one. 1559 : Becon, *Prayers, etc.*, 390 (P.S.), Let no man object and lay in my dish old custom. 1560 : T. Wilson, *Rhetorique*, Prol. (1909), That it be not yet once again cast in my dish. 1609 : in Halliwell, *Books of Characters*, 96 (1857), Your former follies shall be laide in your dish. 1681 : W. Robertson, *Phraseol. Generalis*, 806, To lay in ones dish ; Aliquid alieni, ut crimen, objicere. 1740 : North, *Lives of Norths*, i. 191 (Bohn), He found that, when they were pressed, they laid a fresh story in his dish. 1816 : Scott, *Old Mortality*, ch. x., If I had thought I was to have had him cast in my dish . . . 1894 : Northall, *Folk Phrases*, 31 (E.D.S.), To throw a thing in one's teeth, *or* dish = to reproach.

Lay a water, To=To defer judgment.

1401 : in Wright, *Pol. Poems*, ii. 43 (Rolls Ser., 1861), But, Jack, thoug thi questions semen to thee wyse, yit lightly a lewid [unlearned] man maye leyen hem a water. 1533 : *Ballads from MSS.*, i. 228 (B.S.), And care not thoughe the matter were clerely layde a watter. 1546 : Heywood, *Proverbs*, Pt. I. ch. iii., The triall therof we will lay a water Till we trie more. 1592 : Lyly, *Mydas*, IV. iii., I see all his expeditions for warres are laid in water ; for now when he should execute, he begins to consult.

Lay it on with a trowel, To. 1601 : Shakespeare, *As You Like It*, I. ii., Well said : that was laid on with a trowel. 1693 : Congreve, *Double Dealer*, III. x., Paints, d'ye say ? Why, she lays it on with a trowel. 1732 : Fuller, No. 5930, You lay on your butter as with a trowel. 1784: *New Foundl. Hosp. for Wit*, iii. 81, They also lay on praise with a trowel. 1860 : Reade, *Cl. and Hearth*, ch. l., The old hand laying the court butter on his back with a trowel. 1921 : J. C. Squire, in *Observer*, 10 April, p. 4, col. 3, And Disraeli, actor in his own play, who laid the flattery on with a trowel.

Lay on more wood, ashes give money. [1611 : Cotgrave, s.v. " Bois," All wood is worth logs.] 1678 : Ray, 65. 1732 : Fuller, No. 3152, Lay on more wood : the ashes will yield money.

Lay things by, they may come to use. Ibid., No. 3154.

Lay thy hand on thy heart and speak the truth. 1659 : Howell, 21.

Layers for meddlers. *See* quots. 1690 : *New Dict. Canting Crew*, sig. G7, Lareover, said when the true name of the thing must (in decency) be concealed. 1785 : Grose, *Class. Dict. Vulgar Tongue*, s.v. " Lareovers," Lareovers for medlers, an answer frequently given to children . . . as a rebuke for their impertinent curiosity. 1854 : Baker, *Northants Gloss.*, s.v. " Lay-o'ers," Lay-o'ers-for-meddlers. An expression used to repress childish or impertinent curiosity. A contraction of *lay-overs*, i.e. things laid over, covered up, or protected from meddlers. 1879 : Jackson, *Shropsh. Word-Book*, 249, Lay-

o'ers-for-meddlers. 1902 : *N. & Q.*, 9th
ser., x. 475, Almost every county has
its variation probably of this phrase.
The most common form in which it
survives, however, is "Layers for
meddlers," and it is generally, though
not exclusively so, addressed to over-
inquisitive children.

**Laziness is not worth a pin unless
it is well followed.** 1864 : "Cornish
Proverbs," in *N. & Q.*, 3rd ser., vi. 495.

**Laziness travels so slowly that Poverty
soon overtakes him.** 1736 : Franklin,
Way to Wealth, in *Works*, i. 443
(Bigelow).

**Lazy as Ludlam's dog, that leant his
head against a wall to bark.** The
quotations show variations in the name
of the dog's owner. 1670 : Ray, 202.
c. 1791 : Pegge, *Derbicisms*, 135 (E.D.S.),
. . . who laid himself down to bark.
1801 : Wolcot, *Works*, v. 118 (1801),
. . . that held his head against the
wall to bark. 1850 : *N. & Q.*, 1st ser.,
i. 382, As lazy as Ludlum's dog, as laid
him down to bark. 1883 : Burne,
Shropsh. Folk-Lore, 595, As lazy as
Kittenhallet's dog; 'e laned 'is yed
agen a wall to bark. 1886 : Elworthy,
West Som. Word-Book, 420 (E.D.S.),
He's like lazy Lawrence's dog, that
lied his head agin the wall to bark.
1886 : R. Holland, *Cheshire Gloss.*, 445
(E.D.S.), As lazy as Larriman's dog.
1917 : Bridge, *Cheshire Proverbs*, 17 [as
in 1886, Holland]. Ibid., 91 [as in
1670, with very slight variation]. 1921 :
Hudson, *Trav. in Little Things*, ch. ix.
56, Until I knew Dandy I had always
supposed that the story of Ludlam's
dog was pure invention . . . but Dandy
made me reconsider the subject; and
eventually I came to believe that
Ludlam's dog did exist once upon a
time, centuries ago perhaps, and that
if he had been the laziest dog in the
world, Dandy was not far behind him
in that respect. Cf. Idle (4).

Lazy folk take the most pains. 1734 :
Franklin, in *Works*, i. 416 (Bigelow).
1869 : Spurgeon, *John Ploughman*, ch. i.,
It is not much ease that lazy people get
by all their scheming, for they always
take the most pains in the end.

**Lazy groom never loves a grey horse,
A.** Yorks. 1922 : *N. & Q.*, 12th ser.,
xi. 212.

Lazy Lawrence. Several sayings are
grouped under this head. In all, Lawrence is the embodiment of laziness.
1784 : *Gent. Mag.*, Pt. II. 349, When
a person in hot weather seems lazy, it
is a common saying, that Lawrence
bids him high wages. [St. Lawrence's
Day is 10 August.] 1809 : Pegge,
Anonymiana, cent. viii. 19, *Laurence
bids wages*; a proverbial saying for to
be lazy. 1828 : Carr, *Craven Dialect*,
i. 280, When a person is remarkably
idle, he is often thus addressed. "I
see lang Lawrence hes gitten hod on
thee." 1830 : Forby, *Vocab. E. Anglia*
427, Laurence has got hold of him.
1880 : Courtney, *W. Cornwall Words*,
33 (E.D.S.), He's as lazy as Lawrence.
One would think that Lawrence had
got hold of him. 1882 : Jago, *Gloss. of
Cornish Dialect*, 205, He is as lazy as
Larrence. 1882 : *N. & Q.*, 6th ser., v.
266, He's got St. Lawrence on the
shoulder [Kent]. 1886 : Elworthy, *West
Som. Word-Book*, 420 (E.D.S.), "So
lazy as Lawrence" is a common saying.

Lazy man. *See* Idle (2).

Lazy man's guise, The. 1828 : Carr,
Craven Dialect, i. 294, T' lither man's
guise, Is nivver to bed And nivver to
rise. Cf. Sluggard's guise.

Lazy sheep thinks its wool heavy, A.
1732 : Fuller, No. 237. 1869 : Spurgeon,
John Ploughman, ch. i., Like lazy
sheep, it is too much trouble for them
to carry their own wool.

Lead by the nose, To. [τῆς ῥινὸς
φασίν, ἕλκων.— Lucian, *Dial. Deorum*,
vi. 3.] 1583 : Golding, *Calvin on
Deut.*, cxxi. 745 (O.), Men . . . suffer
themselues to bee led by the noses
like brute beasts. 1598 : Florio, *Worlde
of Wordes*, s.v. "Mener," To leade by
the nose. 1625 : Bacon, *Essays:*
"Suitors," Let him chuse well his
Referendaries, for else he may be led
by the nose. 1714 : Ozell, *Molière*,
iii. 92, Go, go, you must not suffer your
self to be led by the nose. 1766 :
Garrick, *Neck or Nothing*, II. i., I heard
her say myself that she could lead you

by the nose. 1830: Marryat, *King's
Own*, ch. xxviii., Seven-eighths of the
town are led by the nose by this or
that periodical work.

Leaden sword. *See* quots. 1562:
Heywood, *Three Hund. Epigr.*, No. 71,
Thou makst much of thy peynted
sheathe. 1568: W. Fulwood, *Enemie
of Idlenesse*, 244 (1593), Drawe not (as
the prouerbe saith) a leaden sword out
of a golden scabbard. 1579: Lyly,
Euphues, 69 (Arber), Heere you may
see . . . the paynted sheath with the
leaden dagger, the faire wordes that
make fooles faine. 1611: Cotgrave,
s.v. "Cousteau," A leaden sword in a
golden sheath; a foule heart in a faire
body. 1630: Brathwait, *Eng. Gent.,
etc.*, 47 (1641), The first sort generally,
are so miserably enamoured of words,
as they care little for substance. These
are ever drawing a leaden sword out of
a gilded sheath. 1732: Fuller, No. 238,
A leaden sword in an ivory scabbard.

Lean arbitration. *See* Ill agreement.

Lean as a rake. *c.* 1386: Chaucer,
Prol., l. 287, As leene was his hors as
is a rake. *c.* 1480: *Early Miscell.*, 8
(Warton Cl.), I waxe as leyne as anny
rake. 1567: Golding, *Ovid*, bk. ii.
l. 967, Hir bodie leane as any rake.
1653: Urquhart, *Rabelais*, bk. ii. ch.
xiv., He was . . . as lean as a rake.
1754: Berthelson, *Eng.-Danish Dict.*,
s.v. "Lean." 1823: Moor, *Suffolk
Words*, 305, " Thin as a rake " is not an
infrequent comparison with us. 1875:
Parish, *Sussex Dict.*, 93, . . . a common
proverb among Sussex people.

Lean as a shotten herring. 1659:
Howell, *Proverbs: Fr.-Eng.*, 18. 1754:
Berthelson, *Eng.-Danish Dict.*, s.v.
"Shotten," He looks like a shotten
herring. 1889: *Folk-Lore Journal*, vii.
291 (Derbyshire).

Lean dog for a hard road, A. 1917:
Bridge, *Cheshire Proverbs*, 4.

**Lean fee is a fit reward for a lazy
clerk, A.** 1583: Melbancke, *Philotinus*,
sig. E3, In deede a leane fee befits a
lazye clarke. 1669: *Politeuphuia*, 182.

Lean liberty is better than fat slavery.
1732: Fuller, No. 3158.

Lean not on a reed. *c.* 1586: Deloney,

Garl. of Goodwill, 13 (Percy S.), But,
senseless man, what do I mean Upon a
broken reed to lean? 1732: Fuller,
No. 3157.

Lean sorrow is hardest to bear, A.
1895: S. O. Jewett, *Life of Nancy*, 278
[quoted as " the ancient proverb "].

Leap, *subs. A leap in the dark.*
1697: Vanbrugh, *Prov. Wife*, V. v.,
So, now, I am in for Hobbes's voyage;
a great leap in the dark. [Hobbes is said
to have used the expression when dying,
1680.] *c.* 1716: *The Merry Musician*,
i. 238, All you that will take a leap in
the dark, Think of the fate of Lawson
and Clark [both executed]. 1826:
Disraeli, *Vivian Grey*, bk. ii. ch. xvi.,
I saw the feeble fools were wavering,
and, to save all, made a leap in the dark.

Leap, *verb.* 1. *He is ready to leap over
nine hedges.* 1678: Ray, 353.

2. *He leaps into a deep river to avoid
a shallow brook.* 1732: Fuller, No. 1963.

3. *If you leap into a well, Providence
is not bound to fetch you out.* Ibid.,
No. 2795.

4. *Leap over the stile. See* Stile.

5. *She cannot leap an inch from a
slut.* 1678: Ray, 256 [with " doth "
for " can " and " shrew " for " slut "].
1732: Fuller, No. 4121.

6. *To leap at a crust.* 1633: Draxe,
94, Hee will leape at a crust. 1738:
Swift, *Polite Convers.*, Dial. I., I believe,
Colonel, Mr. Neverout can leap at a
crust better than you.

7. *To leap at a daisy*=To be hanged.
1553: *Respublica*, V. ii., Some of vs
erelong maie happe leape at a daisie.
1592: Greene, *Black Book's Messenger*,
To Reader, At last hee leapt at a
daysie . . . with a halter about his
necke. 1604: *Pasquils Jests*, 48 (1864),
He sayd : Haue at yon dasie that growes
yonder; and so leaped off the gallows.

8. *To let leap a whiting*=To miss an
opportunity. 1546: Heywood, *Proverbs*, Pt. II. ch. vii., There lepte a
whityng, (quoth she). 1597: Breton,
in *Works*, ii. *b* 8 (Grosart), There are
many such misfortunes in the world,
a man may . . . leape a whiting, whilst
he is looking on a codshead. 1670: Ray,
199. 1754: Berthelson, *Eng.-Danish*

Dict., s.v. "Whiting," To let go a whiting.

Leap year is never a good sheep year, A. 1846 : Denham, *Proverbs*, 17 (Percy S.). 1920 : *Sphere*, 3 April, p. 10, Whether it be true to say that—" A leap year Is never a good sheep year " remains to be proved so far as this season goes.

Learn not and know not. 1659 : Howell, *Proverbs: Brit.-Eng.*, 26.

Learn to lick betimes, you know not whose tail you may go by. 1670 : Ray, 117.

Learn to pray, He that will, let him go to sea. 1611 : Cotgrave, s.v. "Mer." 1640 : Herbert, *Jac. Prudentum.* 1732 : Fuller, No. 2368.

Learn to say before you sing. 1639 : Clarke, 116. 1670 : Ray, 139. 1732 : Fuller, No. 3165.

Learn weeping and thou shalt laugh gaining. 1640: Herbert, *Jac. Prudentum.*

Learning and law, To, there's no greater foe, than they that nothing know. 1592 : Greene, *Works*, xii. 103–4 (Grosart) [cited as " an olde said saw "].

Learning in a prince is like a knife in the hand of a madman. 1591 : Harington, *Orl. Furioso:* " Allegory," 413 (1634), The chiefe fault commonly is, in those counsellors that put a sword into a mad-mans hand, by putting such conceits into Princes heads. 1638 : D. Tuvill, *Vade Mecum*, 16 (3rd ed.) [with " dangerous " before " knife "].

Learning is the eye of the mind. 1633 : Draxe, 111.

Learning makes a good man better and an ill man worse. 1732 : Fuller, No. 3162.

Learning. *See also* House (17).

Learnt young is hard to lose, What is. *c.* 1275 : *Prov. of Alfred*, A, 100–5, The mon the on his youhthe yeorne leorneth Wit and wisdom, and iwriten reden, He may beon on elde wenliche lortheu [good teacher]. *c.* 1320 : in *Reliq. Antiquæ*, i. 110 (1841), " Whose yong lerneth, olt he ne leseth "; Quoth Hendyng. *c.* 1400 : *Beryn*, 938, For thing i-take in [youthe, is] hard to put away.

Least boy always carries the biggest fiddle, The. 1670 : Ray, 112. 1732 : Fuller, No. 4629 [" always " omitted]. 1880 : Spurgeon, *Ploughman's Pictures*, 28, As a rule, the smallest boy carries the biggest fiddle.

Least foolish is wise, The. 1640 : Herbert, *Jac. Prudentum.*

Least room. *See* quot. 1913 : E. M. Wright, *Rustic Speech, etc.*, 17, A proverbial saying applied to any one who has a great deal to say about the conduct or characters of other people, and is not above suspicion himself, runs : Where there's leeost reawm, there's moast thrutchin' [crowding].

Least said soonest mended. 1776 : T. Cogan, *John Buncle, Junior*, i. 237–8, But mum's the word; least said is soonest mended. 1818 : Scott, *Heart of Midl.*, ch. vi. 1837 : Dickens, *Pickwick*, ch. xlviii. 1917 : Bridge, *Cheshire Proverbs*, 89, Least said soonest mended, but nout said needs no mending. Cf. Little meddling; and Little said.

Least talk most work. 1611 : Cotgrave, s.v. " Besongner," The fewer words the more worke. 1666 : Torriano, *Piazza Univ.*, 189, Where there is least talk there is most work.

Leave, *subs.* 1. *He must have leave to speak who cannot hold his tongue.* 1683 : Meriton, *Yorkshire Ale*, 83–7 (1697). 1732 : Fuller, No. 1992.

2. *Leave is light.* 1546 : Heywood, *Proverbs*, Pt. I. ch. x., Ye might hauc knokt er ye came in; leaue is light. *c.* 1598 : Deloney, *Gentle Craft*, Pt. II. ch. ii., Leaue is light, which being obtained a man may be bold without offence. 1633 : Jonson, *Love's Welcome*, Our English proverb, *Leave is light.* 1757 : Franklin, in *Works*, ii. 518 (Bigelow), I am sorry, however, that he took it without leave . . . Leave, they say, is light. 1827 : Hone, *Ev. Day Book*, ii. 248.

Leave, *verb.* 1. *He has left off work to go and make bricks.* 1864 : " Cornish Proverbs," in *N. & Q.*, 3rd ser., vi. 494.

2. *He that leaves the highway, to cut short, commonly goes about.* 1732 : Fuller, No. 2213.

3. *Leave a jest when it pleases you best.* Ibid., No. 6357.

4. *Leave boys' play. See* **Boy** (5).

5. *Leave her on a ley. See* quots. 1599: Porter, *Two Angry Women*, in Hazlitt, *Old Plays*, vii. 355, They should set her on the lee-land, and bid the devil split her. 1659: Howell, 16, Leave her on a ley, and lett the devil flitt her ; A Lincolnshire proverb spoken of a scolding wife; viz.. tye her to a plow-ridge, and lett the devill remove her to a better pasture. 1847 : Halliwell, *Dict.*, s.v. " Flitten " [as in 1659].

6. *Leave off with an appetite.* 1558 : Bullein, *Govt. of Health*, fo. 37, And so leue with an appetite. 1588 : Cogan, *Haven of Health*, 167 (1612), The surest way in feeding is to leaue with an appetite, according to the old saying. 1648 : Herrick, *Hesp.*, i. 236 (Hazlitt), Go to your banquet then, but use delight, So as to rise still with an appetite. 1693: Penn, *Fruits of Solitude*, No. 64, If thou rise with an appetite, thou art sure never to sit down without one.

7. *Leave the Court ere the Court leave thee.* 1710 : S. Palmer, *Moral Essays on Proverbs*, 61. 1738 : *Gent. Mag.*, 475.

8. *To leave in the briers* (or *suds*). 1533: Udall, *Flowers out of Terence*, fo. 18, Doest thou not se me brought in the briers through thy devise. 1577 : *Misogonus*, III. i., Leaue me not now ith breares, yow haue told me thus much of my sonne. *c.* 1590: G. Harvey, *Marginalia*, 87 (1913), Lett not any necessary or expedient action lye in the suddes. 1631: Mabbe, *Celestina*, 280 (T.T.), Out alas ! . . . Our solace is in the suds. 1670: Ray, 166, To leave one in the briers (or suds). 1690 : *New Dict. Canting Crew*, sig. B8, In the briers, in trouble. 1753 : Richardson, *Grandison*, i. 86 (1883), How, madam !—Why, we are all in the *suds*, then ! 1784-1815 : *Annals of Agric.*, xxxix. 83, Very favourable weather must occur, or the farmer is in the suds.

9. *To leave in the lurch.* 1576 : G. Harvey, *Letter-Book*, 163 (Camden S.), Lest he fail in his reckning . . . and so leave himself in the lurch. 1611 :

Tarlton's Jests, 37 (Sh. S.), Ile leave him in the lurch, and shift for my selfe. Before 1680 : Butler, *Remains*, i. 255 (1759), And leaves the true ones in the lurch. 1768 : Brooke, *Fool of Quality*, iii. 240, But here the Master in whom he trusted, happened to leave him in the lurch. 1823 : Scott, *Fam. Letters*, ii. 182 (1894), It will be an eternal shame if they leave the poor fellow in the lurch after all he has done. 1923 : Lucas, *Advisory Ben*, 234, She doesn't like to leave me in the lurch, she says.

10. *To leave no stone unturned.* [πάντα κινῆσαι πέτρον. — Eur., *Heracl.*, 1002.] *c.* 1548 : Latimer, in *Works*, ii. 427 (P.S.), I will leave no one stone unmoved to have both you and your brother saved. 1560 : Becon, *Catechism, etc.*, 313 (P.S.), I would wish that according to the common proverb, every stone should be moved . . . to win them unto the truth. 1642 : D. Rogers, *Matrim. Honour*, 163, Therfore roll each stone to find this grace. 1709 : Mandeville, *Virgin Unmask'd*, 144 (1724), I find, Aunt, you leave no stone unturned. 1839 : Dickens, *Nickleby*, ch. lii., Don't leave a stone unturned. It's always something, to know you've done the most you could. 1925 : *Sphere*, 6 June, p. 298, col. 1, No stone should be left unturned in the endeavour to make the piece a success.

11. *To leave the meal and take the bran.* 1639 : Clarke, 5.

12. *Who leaveth the old way for the new, will find himself deceived.* 1578 : Florio, *First Fruites*, fo. 28. 1623 : Wodroephe, *Spared Houres*, 278, Who leaues ye old way for to seeke a newe, Is intangled with dangers not a fewe. 1666 : Torriano, *Piazza Univ.*, 271. 1862 : Borrow, *Wild Wales*, ch. xv., " There is a proverb in the Gerniweg," said I, " . . . saying, ' ne'er leave the old way for the new.' "

Leaves, The. 1. *He that fears leaves. See* **Afraid of leaves**.

2. *If on the trees the leaves still hold, The coming winter will be cold.* 1661 : M. Stevenson, *Twelve Moneths*, 48, They say if leaves now [October] hang on the tree, it portends a cold winter, or many

caterpillars. 1893 : Inwards, *Weather Lore*, 150.

3. *Leaves enough but few grapes* = Many words and few deeds. 1659 : Howell, *Proverbs : Ital.-Eng.*, 1.

4. *When the leaves show their undersides, Be very sure that rain betides.* 1893 : Inwards, *Weather Lore*, 150.

Lechery and covetousness go together. 1653 : *The Queen*, IV., in Bang's *Materialien*, B. 13, p. 30, col. 1 [cited as " an old proverbe "].

Leek. *See* Green (5).

Leeks. *See* Lovers live.

Leeks in March. *See* quots. [1558 : Bullein, *Govt. of Health*, fo. 64, Leekes purgeth the bloud in march.] *c.* 1685 : Aubrey, *Nat. Hist. Wilts* 51 (1847), Eate leekes in Lide [March], and ramsins [wild garlic] in May, And all the yeare after physitians may play. 1875 : A. B. Cheales, *Proverb. Folk-Lore*, 85, Eat leeks in March, Garlick in May, All the rest of the year The doctors may play. *Sussex.* 1913 : E. M. Wright, *Rustic Speech, etc.*, 238 [as in 1685].

Lees. *See* Cheshire (7).

Left hand luck. 1540 : Palsgrave, *Acolastus*, sig. X2, A lefte hande lucke, this is yll lucke.

Left or right Brings good at night. 1831 : Hone, *Year Book*, 252. 1849 : Halliwell, *Pop. Rhymes and Nursery Tales*, 183 [with " and " for " or "].

Left shoulder. *See* Over the shoulder.

Left side, To rise on one's. 1579 : Marr. *of Wit and Wisdom*, sc. iii. p. 30 (Sh. S.), I rose on my lift side [i.e. wrong side] to day. Cf. **Right side.**

Leg and **Legs.** 1. *Leg of a lark. See* Lark (1).

2. *Stretch your legs according to your coverlet.* 1640 : Herbert, *Jac. Prudentum*, Every one stretcheth his legs according to his coverlet. 1670 : Ray, 25. 1880 : Spurgeon, *Ploughman's Pictures*, 136, Stretch your legs according to the length of your blanket, and never spend all you have.

3. *To lay one's legs on one's neck* (or *to ground*) = To be off. 1611 : *Tarlton's Jests*, 41 (Sh. S.), The fellow . . . laid his legges on his neck, and got him gone. 1913 : *Devonsh. Assoc. Trans.*,

xlv. 290, In phrase " lay legs to groun," a curious but common idiom, implying speed.

4. *To see which leg one is lame of.* 1586 : D. Rouland, *Lazarillo*, 40 (1924), As for me, when I perceiued upon which foot hee halted, I made hast to eat. 1631 : Mabbe, *Celestina*, 212 (T.T.), I now perceive on which foot you halt. 1732 : Fuller, No. 2623, I now see which leg you are lame of. 1823 : Scott, *Q. Durward*, ch. xxix., 'Tis a sure sign what foot the patient halts upon.

5. *While the leg warmeth the boot harmeth.* Before 1500 : Hill, *Commonplace-Book*, 128 (E.E.T.S.), While the fote warmith, the sho harmith. 1546 : Heywood, *Proverbs*, Pt. II. ch. ii. *c.* 1594 : Bacon, *Promus*, No. 385. 1670 : Ray, 113. 1732 : Fuller, No. 6309.

Leg-bail, To give. 1774 : Fergusson, *Poems*, 234 (1807) (O.), They took leg-bail and ran awa. 1784 : O'Keeffe, *Positive Man*, II. ii., I'll give him leg-bail for my honesty (*runs off*). 1819 : Scott, *Ivanhoe*, ch. xix., Shall we stand fast . . . or shall we e'en give him leg-bail ? 1876 : Blackmore, *Cripps*, ch. xlii., Two Sundays, when even an attorney may give leg-bail to the Power under whose " Ca. ad sa." he lives.

Leicestershire, Bean-belly. 15th cent. : in *Reliq. Antiquæ*, i. 269 (1841), Leicesterschir, full of benys. 1622 : Drayton, *Polyol.*, xxiii., Bean belly Le'stershire, her attribute doth bear. 1662 : Fuller, *Worthies*, ii. 225 (1840), Those in the neighbouring counties used to say merrily, " Shake a Leicestershire yeoman by the collar, and you shall hear the beans rattle in his belly." 1732 : Fuller, No. 4114 [as in 1662]. 1762 : *St. James Magazine*, ii. 13, Shake a Leicestershire woman by the petticoat, and the beans will rattle in her throat. 1790 : Grose, *Prov. Gloss.*, s.v. " Leicestershire." 1818 : Scott, *Heart of Midl.*, ch. xxix., An ye touch her, I'll give ye a shake by the collar shall make the Leicester beans rattle in thy guts.

Leicestershire plover, A = A bag-pudding. 1678 : Ray, 317. 1790 : Grose, *Prov. Gloss.*, s.v. " Leicestershire."

Leighs. *See* **Cheshire** (7).

Leighton Buzzard. *See* **Tring** (2).

Leisure. *He hath no leisure who useth it not.* 1640 : Herbert, *Jac. Prudentum.*

Lemster. *See* **Leominster.**

Lend, *verb.* 1. *He that doth lend doth lose his money and friend.* 1602 : Shakespeare, *Hamlet*, I. iii., For loan oft loses both itself and friend. 1666 : Torriano, *Piazza Univ.*, 217, Who lends loseth double. 1708 : tr. Aleman's *Guzman*, i. 240, How much money has been lent and borrowed on the score of friendship, and yet both money and friend have been lost at last. 1869 : Spurgeon, *John Ploughman*, ch. iv., Very often he that his money lends, loses both his gold and his friends.

2. *He that lends, gives.* 1640 : Herbert, *Jac. Prudentum.*

3. *Lend and lose, so play fools.* 1737 : Ray, 271.

4. *Lend never that thing thou needest most.* Before 1500 : Hill, *Commonplace-Book*, 131 (E.E.T.S.).

5. *Lend not horse, nor wife, nor sword.* 1574 : E. Hellowes, *Guevara's Epistles*, 509, It is an old prouerb that the wife and the sword may bee shewed, but not lent. 1575 : Fenton, *Golden Epistles*, 300 (1582), A wife being the dearest of the two things (according to the common saying) which we ought not to lende. 1577 : Kendall, *Flow. of Epigr.*, 284 (Spens. S.), Three thinges a man not lendeth rife, His horse, his fighting sword, his wife. 1605 : Camden, *Remains*, 332 (1870) [as in 1574]. 1647 : *Countrym. New Commonwealth*, 43, Thy sword, thy horse, and eke thy wife, Lend not at all, lest it breed strife. 1922 : *N. & Q.*, 12th ser., xi. 499, The Yorkshire version of this is " Lend neither your horse nor your wife." I fear in ancient Yorkshire the horse would come first as being the most valued.

Length of one's foot. *See* **Foot** (4).

Lenson-hill to Pilsen-pen, As much akin as. 1662 : Fuller, *Worthies*, i. 453 (1840). 1790 : Grose, *Prov. Gloss.*, s.v. " Dorset."

Lent. 1. *Dry Lent, fertile year.* 1893 : Inwards, *Weather Lore*, 40.

2. *He has but a short Lent. See* quots. 1659 : Howell, *Proverbs: Ital.-Eng.*, 11, Who desires a short Lent, let him make a debt to be paid at Easter. 1736 : Franklin, *Way to Wealth*, in *Works*, i. 450 (Bigelow), Those have a short Lent who owe money to be paid at Easter. 1846 : Denham, *Proverbs*, 32 (Percy S.), Lent seems short to him that borrows money to be paid at Easter.

See also **Ash Wednesday; Christmas** (8) ; and **Shrovetide.**

Leominster bread and Weobley ale. 1610 : P. Holland, tr. Camden's *Britannia*, 620, Lemster bread and Weabley Ale . . . are growne unto a common proverbe. 1619 : Jonson, *For the Honour of Wales*, 4th song, And what you say to ale of Webley. 1662 : Fuller, *Worthies*, ii. 70 (1840), Lemster bread, and Weabley ale. 1700 : J. Brome, *Travels*, 102, Hence it is grown proverbial among the inhabitants, for Lempster bread and Weobley beer, none can come near. 1725 : Defoe, *Tour*, ii. 72. 1886 : Bickerdyke, *Curios. of Ale and Beer*, 171, " Lemster bread and Weobley ale " had passed into a proverb before the seventeenth century. 1905 : A. G. Bradley, *March and Borderland of Wales*, 156.

Leominster wool. Before 1530 : Barclay, *Egloges*, iv., Cornewall hath tynne and lymster woole fine. 1593 : Drayton, *Shep. Garland*, Ecl. iv., Her skin as soft as Lemster wool. 1648 : Herrick, *Hesp.*, No. 444, And far more Soft than the finest Lemster ore [wool]. 1670 : Ray, 258, Monmouth caps and Lemster wooll. 1725 : Defoe, *Tour*, ii. 72, This town [Leominster], besides the fine wool, is noted for . . .

Leopard, In a, the spots are not observed. 1640 : Herbert, *Jac. Prudentum.*

Less of your courtesy and more of your purse. 1639 : Clarke, 43. 1670 : Ray, 74. 1732 : Fuller, No. 3172, Less of your courtship, I pray, and more of your coin.

Less wit a man has, The, the less he knows that he wants it. Ibid., No. 4630.

Let him alone with the saint's bell, and give him rope enough. 1737 : Ray, 63.

Let the world pass (or slide, or wag, etc.). *c.* 1400 : *Towneley Plays*, 201

(E.E.T.S.), Whoso couthe take hede
and lett the warld pas. 1519: *Four
Elements*, in Hazlitt, *Old Plays*, i. 20,
With huffa gallant, sing tirl on the
berry, And let the wide world wind !
Before 1529 : Skelton, *Works*, ii. 6
(Dyce), Let the world wag. 1546 :
Heywood, *Proverbs*, Pt. I. ch. v., To
let the world wag, and take mine ease
in mine in. 1550 : Udall, *Roister
Doister*, III. iii., Let the world pass.
1594 : Shakespeare, *Tam. of Shrew*,
Ind. i., Let the world slide. 1678 :
Dryden, *Limberham*, V. i., Let the
world pass. 1848 : Planché, *Extravag.*,
iii. 258 (1879), Let the world wag.

Let well alone. [Actum, aiunt, ne
agas.—Terence, *Phorm.*, II. iii. 72.]
c. 1386 : Chaucer, *Minor Poems*, in
Works, i. 399 (Skeat), Unwys is he that
can no wele endure. 1829 : Peacock,
Misfor. of Elphin, ch. ii., It is well :
it works well : let well alone. 1863 :
Kingsley, *Water Babies*, ch. i., Let well
alone, lad, and ill too at times. 1913 :
Hankin and Calderon, *Thompson*, III.,
Why the devil can people never let
well alone.

**Letter stay for the post, Let your, not
the post for the letter.** 1666 : Torriano,
Piazza Univ., 127, Let a letter expect
the messenger, not the messenger the
letter. 1670 : Ray, 15.

Lettuce. *See* Like lips.

**Lewes, Proud, and poor Brighthelm-
stone.** 1827 : Horsfield, *Hist.*, etc., *of
Sussex*, ii. 34. 1894 : A. J. C. Hare,
Sussex, 99, " Proud Lewes and poor
Brighthelmstone " is a proverb of the
days when letters were addressed,
" Brighthelmstone, near Lewes."

Lewisham, Long, lazy, lousy. 1790 :
Grose, *Prov. Gloss.*, s.v. " Kent."

Liar and Liars. 1. *A liar is not
believed when he speaks truth.* 1477 :
Rivers, *Dictes, etc.*, 117 (1877), The
reward of a lyar is that he be not
beleuid of that he reherseth. 1586 :
Pettie, tr. Guazzo's *Civil Convers.*, fo.
42, The liar neuer is beleeued, although
an oath he take. 1645 : Howell, *Letters*,
bk. i. § v. No. xi., It being one of the
punishments . . . of a lyar, not to be
believ'd when he speaks truth. 1681 :

in *Somers Tracts*, viii. 290 (1811), Do
not be deceived by an old saying, That
when one usually tells lyes, he is not
trusted when he speaks truth. 1820 :
Colton, *Lacon*, Pt. I. No. 553.

2. *A liar is worse than a thief.* 1630 :
Taylor (Water-Poet), *Works*, 2nd pagin.,
123, But sure the prouerbe is as true
as briefe, A lyer's euer worser then a
thiefe. 1639 : Clarke, 150.

3. *Liar, liar, lick spit.* 1602 : Chettle,
Hoffman, V. i. p. 75 (1852), Liar, liar !
—Lick-dish ! 1843 : Halliwell, *Nur-
sery Rhymes*, 164, Liar, liar, lick spit,
Turn about the candlestick. What's
good for liar ? Brimstone and fire.

4. *Liars should have good memories.*
[Verumque est illud, quod vulgo dicitur,
mendacem memorem esse oportere.—
Quintilian, *Instit. Oratoria*, IV. ii. § 91.]
c. 1531 : Latimer, *Works*, ii. 312 (P.S.),
You may learn how necessary it is for
a liar to have a good memory. 1565 :
Calfhill, *Answ. to Martiall*, 88 (P.S.), I
see it is true . . . " a liar had need
have a good remembrance." 1673 :
Marvell, *in Works*, iii. 367 (Grosart),
There is one sort of men, for whose
sake there is a common maxime estab-
lish'd, that there is an absolute necessity they should have good memories.
1738 : Swift, *Polite Convers.*, Dial. I.,
Here's a pin for that lie ; I'm sure liars
had need of good memories.

5. *Show me a liar and I'll show you a
thief.* 1607 : R. West, *Court of Conscience*, sig. F1, He that will lie will
steale. 1630 : T. Adams, *Works*, 505.
1725 : Bailey, tr. Erasmus' *Colloq.*, 178,
It is sometimes for a man's advantage
to have pilfering hands ; and the old
proverb is a witness, that that is a
vice that is cousin-german to yours
of lying.

Lick honey, To. *See* Honey (7), (11),
and (14).

Lick one's cauf [calf] over again, To.
1917 : Bridge, *Cheshire Proverbs*, 140,
. . . To do one's work a second time.

Lick one's self whole again, To. 1670 :
Ray, 184.

Lick the mundle, To. *See* quots. 1879 :
Jackson, *Shropsh. Word-Book*, 254, [To]
lick the crame-mundle [=to live well].

1883 : Burne, *Shropsh. Folk-Lore*, 597,
To lick the crame-mundle=to live well,
as in a dairy or farm-house. [The
" mundle " is a piece of wood used for
stirring porridge, cream, etc.]   1917 :
Bridge, *Cheshire Proverbs*, 64 [as in
1883]. Ibid., 64, That's th' lad as
licked the mundle [curried favour].
  Lid worthy of the kettle, A.   A correspondent of *N. & Q.* (12th ser., ii. 7)
refers to the story of Crassus laughing
at an ass eating thistles, instead of
lettuces, finding that they matched his
mouth (whence the saying, *Similes
habent labra lactucas — see* Like lips),
and adds : " Jerome illustrates the story
by another proverb, ' *Patellæ dignum
operculum,*' a lid to match the kettle."
1540 : Palsgrave, *Acolastus*, sig. M2, He
shall gyue a lydde or couer worthy for
. . . the lyttell panne. 1586 : L. Evans,
Withals Dict. Revised, sig. G7, Like
pot, lyke potlid.   1611 : Cotgrave, s.v.
" Couvercle," Such pot, such pot-lid,
like master like man.   1653 : Urquhart,
Rabelais, Prol. to bk. i., If perhaps he
had met with as very fools as himself,
(and as the proverb saies) a lid worthy
of such a kettle.   1732 : Fuller, No.
4276, Such a pot must have such a lid.
  Lide [March].   *See* quot.   1639 : in
Berkeley MSS., iii. 30 (1885), Lide
pilles the hide : meaninge that March
. . . pinches the poare man's beast
(Glouc.).
  Lidford.   *See* Lydford.
  Lie, *subs.*   1. *A lie begets a lie.*   1732 :
Fuller, No. 262, A lye begets a lye, till
they come to generations.
  2. *A lie has no legs.*   1666 : Torriano,
Piazza Univ., 30, A lye hath no feet.
1732 : Fuller, No. 263, A lye has no leg,
but a scandal has wings. 1853 : Trench,
Proverbs, 120 (1905).
  3. *A lie made out of the whole stuff=*
without foundation.   1830 : Forby,
Vocab. E. Anglia, 427.
  4. *A lie stands on one leg, and truth
on two.*   1659 : Howell, 10 (8).
  5. *His lies are latticed lies; and you
may see through them.*   1830 : Forby,
Vocab. E. Anglia, 429.
  6. *If a lie could have choked him, that
would have done it.*   1678 : Ray, 89.

  7. *Lies have short wings* (or *legs*).
1578 : Florio, *First Fruites*, fo. 31, Lyes
haue short legges.   1611 : Davies (of
Hereford), *Sc. of Folly*, 43, in *Works*,
ii. (Grosart), Lyes haue short wings.
1666 : Torriano, *Piazza Univ.*, 30,
. . . legs.
  8. *Tell a lie and find out the truth.*
1678 : Ray, 75. 1732 : Fuller, No. 4324.
  9. *That's a lie and a loud one.*   1678 :
Ray, 89, That's a loud one.   1819 :
Scott, *Ivanhoe*, ch. xliii., " That's a lie,
and a loud one," said the Friar.
  10. *That's a lie with a latchet.*   1678 :
Ray, 89. 1732 : Fuller, No. 6157, [as
in 1678, *plus*] All the dogs in the town
cannot match it.   1828 : Carr, *Craven
Dialect*, i. 283, Lee-with-a-latchet.   A
notorious lie. 1849 : Halliwell, *Pop.
Rhymes and Nursery Tales*, 182, " A
lee with a latchet," as they say in the
North, of a circumstantial self-evident
falsehood.
  11. *That's a lie with a lid on.*   1880 :
Spurgeon, *Ploughman's Pictures*, 99.
1901 : F. E. Taylor, *Lancs Sayings*, 28,
That's a lie wi' a lid on—an' a brass
hondle for t' lift it wi'.
  12. *Though a lie be well drest, it is
ever overcome.*   1640 : Herbert, *Jac.
Prudentum.*
  13. *To tell a man a lie, and give him
a reason for it.*   1678 : Ray, 257.
  Lie, *verb.*   To tell a falsehood.   1. *He'll
not let anybody lie by him*=He is a liar.
1678 : Ray, 89.
  2. *Thou'lt lie all manner of colours but
blue, and that is gone to the litting,* i.e.
dyeing.   Ibid., 75.
  3. *To lie as fast as a dog can lick a
dish.*   1546 : Heywood, *Proverbs*, Pt. II.
ch. vii., She will lie as fast as a dogge
will licke a dishe.   1670 : Ray, 184.
  4. *To lie as fast as a dog* (or *horse*) *will
trot.*   1530 : Palsgrave, 610, He wyll lye
as fast as a dogge wyll trotte.   1589 :
Hay any Worke for Cooper, 65 (1845),
Thou canst cog, face and lye, as fast
as a dog can trot. 1607 : Dekker, etc.,
Westw. Hoe, IV. i. [dog].   1694 :
Motteux, *Rabelais*, bk. v. ch. xxx.
[dog]. 1737 : Ray, 70 [dog]. 1845 :
J. Petheram, Note to 1589 quotation,
p. 83, " To lie as fast as a dog can

trot " is still in use in Somersetshire.
1869 : Spurgeon, *John Ploughman*,
ch. xii. [horse].

5. *You licked not your lips since you
lied last.* 1732 : Fuller, No. 5931.
See also **Swear** (3) and (4).

Lie, *verb.* To be in a recumbent
position. 1. *He lies bare of a suit=*
He has no money. 1830 : Forby,
Vocab. E. Anglia, 434. 1872 : J. Glyde,
jr., *Norfolk Garland*, 150.

2. *He that lies long abed, his estate
feels it.* 1640 : Herbert, *Jac. Prudentum*.
1763 : Murphy, *Citizen*, I. ii., He that
lies in bed, his estate feels it.

3. *He that lies on the ground can fall
no lower.* 1570 : A. Barclay, *Mirrour of
Good Manners*, 46 (Spens. S.), A man
on grounde resting can not much lower
fall. 1648 : Wither, *Single Si Quis*,
1 (Spens. S.), He that is prostrate on
the floor, Lies there, whence he can
fall no lower. 1732 : Fuller, No. 2217.

4. *Lie not in the mire and say " God
help me."* c. 1602 : Chapman, *May-Day*,
I., Do not lie in a ditch, and say " God
help me ! " 1710 : S. Palmer, *Moral
Essays on Proverbs*, 94, Don't lie still
and cry God help you. 1869 : Spurgeon,
John Ploughman, ch. vii., There's no
good in lying down and crying " God
help us ! "

5. *She lies backward and lets out her
fore-rooms.* 1639 : *Conceits, Clinches,
etc.*, No. 278, One asked a gentlewoman
in which part of the house she did use
to lye. It was answer'd, that she lay
backwards and did let out her fore-
roomes. 1694 : Motteux, *Rabelais*, bk.
iv. ch. lxiv. 1785 : Grose, *Class. Dict.
Vulgar Tongue*, s.v. " Rooms," She lets
out her fore-room and lies backwards,
saying of a woman suspected of
prostitution.

6. *To lie by the wall=*To be dead.
c. 1430 : Lydgate, *Minor Poems*, 230
(Percy S.), To day thawgh thou be
stowt and gay, A-morow thou lyyst
by the walle. 1823 : Moor, *Suffolk
Words*, 62, By the walls. An unburied
corpse. " Poor John Smith ! he lie
by the walls." 1847 : Halliwell, *Dict.*,
s.v. " Laid," Laid. Killed, dead.
Suffolk. The common phrase is, *laid*

by the wall. 1913 : *Devonsh. Assoc.
Trans.*, xlv. 290, Lied by the wall.
The interval between death and burial
is always expressed by this phrase.
1920 : E. Gepp, *Essex Dialect Dict.*, 21,
" To lay by the wall " is used of a
corpse lying in a house awaiting burial.

7. *To lie in bed and forecast.* 1678 :
Ray, 75.

8. *To lie like a lapwing.* 1606 : Sir
Giles Goosecappe, I. i., As fearefull as a
haire, and will lye like a lapwing.

9. *We shall lie all alike in our graves.*
1639 : Clarke, 13. 1670 : Ray, 56.
1732 : Fuller, No. 5455.

Life. 1. *A life of leisure and a life of
laziness are two things.* 1732 : Fuller,
No. 240. 1736 : Franklin, *Way to
Wealth*, in *Works*, i. 445 (Bigelow).

2. *Life is a shuttle.* 1855 : Bohn, 442.

3. *Life is half spent before we know
what it is.* 1600 : Cornwallis, *Essayes*,
sig. B3 (1610), We begin not to liue
before we are ready to die. 1640 :
Herbert, *Jac. Prudentum*. 1670 : Ray,
16. 1732 : Fuller, No. 3208.

4. *Life is sweet.* c. 1350 : *Patience*,
l. 156, in *Allit. Poems*, 96 (E.E.T.S.),
For be monnes lode neuer so luther, the
lyf is ay swete. c. 1390 : Gower, *Conf.
Amantis*, v. 1861, Bot nou our feerfull
prelat seith " The lif is swete." c. 1440 :
York Plays, 65 (L. T. Smith), A ! dere
fadir lyff is full swete. 1576 : Pettie,
Petite Pall., ii. 45 (Gollancz), Life is
sweet to every one. 1664 : Dryden,
Rival Ladies, IV. iii., Well, life is sweet.
1743 : Fielding, *Jon. Wild*, bk. iv.
ch. xiii., All this is very true; but life
is sweet for all that. 1851 : Borrow,
Lavengro, i. 325, Life is sweet, brother.

5. *Life lies not in living but in liking.*
1639 : Clarke, 322. 1670 : Ray, 113.
1732 : Fuller, No. 3209 [with " by "
for " but in." ? misprint].

6. *Life without a friend is death without a witness.* 1640 : Herbert, *Jac.
Prudentum.* 1670 : Ray, 10 [with
" with " for second " without "]. 1732 :
Fuller, No. 3211, Life without a friend
is death with a vengeance.

7. *Life would be too smooth if it had
no rubs in it.* Ibid., No. 3212.

8. *The life of man is a winter way.*

1640 : Herbert, *Jac. Prudentum.* 1670 :
Ray, 16, The life of man is a winters
day and a winters way. 1694 : D'Urfey, *Quixote*, Pt. I. Act V. sc. ii. [as in
1670]. 1732 : Fuller, No. 6239 [as in
1670].

9. *What is life where living is extinct?*
1546 : Heywood, *Proverbs*, Pt. II. ch. ix.
1633 : Draxe, 160 [with " wanting " for
" extinct "].

10. *While there's life there's hope.*
[Modo liceat vivere, est spes.—Terence,
Haut., V. ii. 28. Ut aegroto, dum
anima est, spes esse dicitur.—Cicero,
Ad. Att., IX. x. 3.] 1539 : Taverner,
Proverbs, fo. 36, The sycke person whyle
he hath lyfe, hath hope. 1671 : Crowne,
Juliana, V., Madam, he breathes, and
whilst there's life There's hope. 1707 :
C. Cibber, *Double Gallant*, V. ii. 1761 :
Murphy, *Old Maid*, II. 1888 : R. L. S.,
Black Arrow, bk. iv. ch. ii., But while
there is life, Joanna, there is hope !

Lifeless that is faultless, He is. 1546 :
Heywood, *Proverbs*, Pt. I. ch. xi. 1681 :
W. Robertson, *Phraseol. Generalis*, 825.
1732 : Fuller, No. 1922. 1869 : Spurgeon, *John Ploughman*, ch. x., The old
saying is, " Lifeless, faultless."

Light. *See* Sore eyes.

Light as a feather. 1548 : Hall,
Chron., 474 (1809). 1567 : Golding,
Ovid, bk. iv. l. 765, Now here, now
there, as light as any feather. 1629 :
Shirley, *Wedding*, II. iii., Light as a
feather, hanging will ne'er kill you.
1778 : Johnson, *Letters*, ii. 73 (Hill),
I hope he will soon shake off the black
dog, and come home as light as a
feather. 1813 : Austen, *Pride and
Prejudice*, ch. xl. 1906 : Doyle, *Sir
Nigel*, ch. ix.

Light as a fly. 1670 : Ray, 206.

Light as a kex. 1562 : Heywood,
Epigr., 1st Hund., No. 47, Ye make my
heart light as a kyx.

Light as leaf. *See* Lind.

Light as the Queen's groat. 1639 :
Clarke, 159.

Light beginning, a heavy ending, A.
1593 : G. Harvey,*Works*,ii. 196 (Grosart).

Light burden far heavy. 1546 : Heywood, *Proverbs*, Pt. II. ch. ix., A sir
light burdeine far heauy (quoth she).

1594 : Drayton, *Ideas*, lix., (Saith he)
Light burdens heavy, if far borne.
1670 : Ray, 114.

Light cheap lither yield. *c.* 1320 : in
Reliq. Antiquæ, i. 114 (1841), " Lyht
chep luthere yeldes " ; Quoth Hendyng.
c. 1400 : *Towneley Mys.*, xiii. 171.
1670 : Ray, 114. Cf. Good cheap.

Light come. *See* Lightly.

Light fare begets light dreams. 1851 :
Borrow, *Lavengro*, ii. 79. Cf. Light
suppers.

Light gains make heavy purses. 1546 :
Heywood, *Proverbs*, Pt. I. ch. xi. 1597 :
Bacon, *Essays :* " Ceremonies, etc."
1605 : Chapman, etc., *Eastw. Hoe*, I. i.
c. 1685 : Aubrey, *Nat. Hist. Wilts*, 95
(1847), Perhaps they did not consider
the proverb, that " light gaines with
quick returnes make heavy purses."
1754 : Berthelson, *Eng.-Danish Dict.*,
s.v. " Light."

Light hand makes a heavy wound, A.
1602-3 : Manningham, *Diary*, 52 (Camden S.).

Light heart. *See* quots. 1733 : C.
Coffey, *Boarding-School*, sc. i., A light
heart and thin pair of breeches, Go
thro' the world, brave boys. *c.* 1742 :
Merry Companion, 175 [as in 1733].
1748 : Smollett, *Rod. Random*, ch. v.
[as in 1733]. 1778 : in Doran's *Lady
of Last Century*, 243 (1873), He will be
in better spirits as a light heart and a
thin pair of breeches is a conjunction he
has little notion of.

Light heeled mother makes a heavy
heeled daughter, A. 1670 : Ray, 53.
1732 : Fuller, No. 3214 [in the plural].

Light load. *See* Light burden.

Light love will change. 1575 : G.
Fenton, *Golden Epistles*, 321 (1582),
Light loue is an affection great and
vehement, and yet lasteth not long.
1576 : *Parad. of Dainty Devices*, in *Brit.
Bibliog.*, iii. 63 (1812), Light love will
chaunge.

Light purse is a heavy curse, A. 1732 :
Fuller, No. 6493.

Light purse makes a heavy heart, A.
1600 : F. Thynne, *Embl. and Epigr.*, 59
(E.E.T.S.). 1716 : E. Ward, *Female
Policy*, 36, When thy purse is light,
then will thy heart be heavy. 1732 :

Fuller, No. 241. 1880: Spurgeon, *Ploughman's Pictures*, 12.

Light suppers make clean sheets. 1616: Breton, *Crossing of Proverbs*, 8 (Grosart). 1670: Ray, 36. 1732: Fuller, No. 3216. Cf. Light fare.

Lightening before death, A. 1588: Cogan, *Haven of Health*, 135 (1612), Whereof is growen a Latin prouerbe, *Cygnea cantio*, which among the common people is termed, a lightning before death. 1592: Shakespeare, *Romeo*, V. iii. 1641: R. Brome, *Joviall Crew*, V. 1748: Richardson, *Clarissa*, viii. 65 (1785), Her late tranquillity and freedom from pain seemed but a *lightening*, as Mrs. Lovick and Mrs. Smith call it. 1847: Halliwell, *Dict.*, s.v., . . . a proverbial phrase, alluding to the resuscitation of the spirits which frequently occurs before dissolution. 1901: F. E. Taylor, *Lancs Sayings*, 31, He'd a bit of a leetenin' like afore he dee'd.

Lightly come lightly go. *c.* 1374: Chaucer, *Troylus*, bk. ii. l. 1239, For-why men seyth, " impressiounes lighte Ful lightly been ay redy to the flighte." 1412–20: Lydgate, *Troy Book*, bk. ii. l. 4635, Lightly it cam and lightly went a-way. 1546: Heywood, *Proverbs*, Pt. II. ch. ix., Light come, light go. *c.* 1615: *Times Whistle*, 89 (E.E.T.S.). 1765: Garrick, *Sick Monkey, ad fin.*, What lightly comes, as lightly goes, With all such pretty fellows. 1826: Lamb, *Pop. Fallacies*, II. 1860: Reade, *Cl. and Hearth*, ch. xxxvii. 1909: R. Nevill, *Light Come, Light Go* [title].

Lightly gained quickly lost. *c.* 1580: Fulwell, *Ars Adulandi*, sig. E2, Experience taught me that easely wonne was lightly loste. 1583: Greene, *Works*, ii. 25 (Grosart), He wil iudge that is lightly to bee gained, is as quickly lost. 1898: Besant, *Orange Girl*, II. iv. (O.), Lightly got, lightly spent.

Lightning. 1. *Forked lightning at night, The next day clear and bright.* 1893: Inwards, *Weather Lore*, 119.

2. *Lightning brings heat.* Ibid., 117.

3. *There's lightning lightly before thunder.* 1633: Draxe, 226, Lightly before thunder, lightning. 1670: Ray, 114.

4. *When caught by the tempest, wherever it be, If it lightens and thunders beware of a tree!* 1846: Denham, *Proverbs*, 19 (Percy S.).

Like a cat. *See* Cat.

Like a feather on a hill, He's. Glos. Applied to an inconstant man. 1639: in *Berkeley MSS.*, iii. 26 (1885).

Like a fiddler's elbow. *See* Fiddler (6).

Like a horse in a mill. *c.* 1540: J. Heywood, *Wit and Folly*, 22 (Percy S.), Evyn lyke the myll hors, they be whyppyd amayne. 1607: Dekker, etc., *Northw. Hoe*, I. iii., I that like a horse Ran blind-fold in a mill, all in one circle. 1654: Whitlock, *Zootomia*, 432, Carefull men, like horses in a mill, run round in a competency. 1720: Stukeley, *Memoirs*, iii. 461 (Surtees S.), The same circle must be observed every day of one's life, like a horse in a mill. 1825: Lamb, *Superann. Man*, par. 11, Like horses in a mill, drudging on in the same eternal round. 1839: Dickens, *Nickleby*, ch. lxiv., I am perpetually turning, like a demd old horse in a demnition mill.

Like a house on fire=rapidly. 1857: Dickens, *Dorrit*, bk. ii. ch. xxxiv., I assure you he is making out his case like a house a-fire.

Like a loader's horse, that lives among thieves. Somerset. 1678: Ray, 350. 1732: Fuller, No. 3223.

Like a ribbon double-dyed, Never worn and never tried. 1864: " Cornish Proverbs," in *N. & Q.*, 3rd ser., v. 209.

Like a silver pin. 1869: Spurgeon, *John Ploughman*, ch. xviii., They are like a silver pin, Fair without but foul within.

Like a threeha'penny chick in a wheaten arish [stubble]. Corn. 1895: Jos. Thomas, *Randigal Rhymes*, 60.

Like a young bear with all your sorrows to come. 1870: in *N. & Q.*, 4th ser., vi. 321.

Like as one egg to another. [Tam similem quam lacte lacti est.—Plautus, *Mil. Glor.*, II. ii. 85.] 1542: Becon, *Early Works*, 90 (P.S.), Our houses . . . are so like one to another, that ye can less discern an egg from an egg . . . as they say. 1654: Gayton, *Pleasant*

Notes Don Q., 23, Not eggs to eggs are liker. 1738: Swift, *Polite Convers.*, Dial. III. *c.* 1783: in *Roxb. Ballads*, vii. 94 (B.S.).

Like as two peas. [σῦκον εἰκάσαι σύκῳ. —Herodas, vi. 60.] 1580: Lyly, *Euphues*, 215 (Arber), Who wer as lyke as one pease is to an other. *c.* 1680: in *Roxb. Ballads*, vii. 77 (B.S.), And will be as like her as one pea's like another. 1725: Bailey, tr. Erasmus' *Colloq.*, 40. 1846: Planché, *Extravag.*, iii. 139 (1879), They are as like each other as two peas! 1884: R. L. S. and Henley, *Adm. Guinea*, II. vi. 1925: E. Lyttelton, *Memories and Hopes*, 322, He and his twin brother . . . were as like as two peas.

Like author like book. 1670: Ray, 15.

Like Benjamin's mess. 1628: Earle, *Microcos.*, 124 (1811), His talk at the table is like Benjamin's mess, five times to his part.

Like blood, like goods, and like age, make the happiest marriage. 1639: Clarke, 28. 1681: W. Robertson, *Phraseol. Generalis*, 266. 1732: Fuller, No. 6184.

Like carpenter. *See* Such carpenter.

Like carver like cook. 1673: *Vinegar and Mustard*, 23, in Hindley, *Old Book Coll. Miscell.*, iii.

Like cow like calf. 1573: Bullein, *Dialogue*, 21 (E.E.T.S.), Her sonne is like the mother as seemeth by one in the house, like cowe like calfe.

Like crow like egg. 1536: Latimer, *Sermons*, 42 (P.S.), Ye know this is a proverb much used : " An evil crow an evil egg." 1611: Cotgrave, s.v. " Corbeau," Of an ill bird, an ill brood. 1655: T. Muffett, *Healths Improvement*, 135, As the Greek proverb saith, Like crow, like egg.

Like cup. *See* Such cup.

Like father like son. 1377: Langland, *Plowman*, B, ii. 28, Qualis pater, talis filius. 1509: Barclay, *Ship of Fools*, i. 236 (1874), An olde prouerbe hath longe agone be sayde That oft the sone in maners lyke wyll be Vnto the father. 1605: Camden, *Remains*, 331 (1870), Such a father, such a son. 1721: Bailey, *Eng. Dict.*, s.v. " Father."

1860: Reade, *Cl. and Hearth*, ch. lxxix. 1907: De Morgan, *Alice-for-Short*, ch. xxx., " ' Like father, like son '—so people say," says Alice.

Like fault like punishment. 1542: Becon, *Early Works*, 243 (P.S.) [cited as " the common proverb "].

Like host like guest. 1540: Palsgrave, *Acolastus*, sig. M2, Such a geste, such an hoste. 1586: L. Evans, *Withals Dict. Revised*, sig. H2, Lyke hoste, lyke guest. *c.* 1613: Rowlands, *Paire of Spy-Knaues*, 21 (Hunt. Cl.), Such oast, such ghest, the prouerbe sayes. 1654: Gayton, *Pleasant Notes Don Q.*, 9, Like guest like landlord.

Like it or lump it. 1880: Courtney, *W. Cornwall Words*, 36 (E.D.S.), If you don't like it you must lump it. 1901: F. E. Taylor, *Lancs Sayings*, 10, They con like it or lump it, as beggars done pot-bo'.

Like John Gray's bird. *See* John Gray.

Like lips like lettuce. [Similem habent labra lactucam (a saying of M. Crassus when he saw an ass eating thistles).—Hieronymus, *Ep.*, vii. 5.] 1546: Heywood, *Proverbs*, Pt. II. ch. vii., Suche lips, suche lettice. 1587: Greene, *Works*, iii. 60 (Grosart), As you said before, like lips like lettice, as the man is so is his manners. 1634: Massinger, *Guardian*, II. iii., There's other lettuce For your coarse lips. 1681: W. Robertson, *Phraseol. Generalis*, 830. 1732: Fuller, No. 3231. 1853: Trench, *Proverbs*, 21 (1905), In the proverb you will find it [alliteration] of continual recurrence . . . Thus . . . *Like lips, like lettuce.*

Like lord like chaplain. *c.* 1540: Bale, *Kynge Johan*, 73 (Camden S.), Lyke lorde, lyke chaplayne; neyther barrell better herynge.

Like master like man. [Plane qualis dominus talis et servus.—Petr., 58.] *c.* 1390: Gower, *Conf. Amantis*, iii. 2421, Such capitein such retenue. 1568: Fulwell, *Like will to Like*, in Hazlitt, *Old Plays*, iii. 330, Like master, like man. 1584: Lyly, *Sapho and Phao*, II. iii. 1641: Marmion, *Antiquary*, IV. 1750: Smollett, *Gil Blas*, iii. 189, Scipio, on his side, (for it was like master, like man) kept

table also, in the buttery. 1830:
Marryat, *King's Own*, ch. xix., She
call me d—d nigger, and say like
massa like man. 1855 : Gaskell, *North
and South*, ch. xv., What the master
is, that will the men be, without
overmuch taking thought on his part.
See also Trim-tram.

Like me, God bless the example.
1670 : Ray, 184.

Like mistress like maid. 1557 : Tusser, *Husbandrie*, in *Brit. Bibliog.*, iii. 15
(1812), Such mistres suche mayde.
1620 : Rowlands, *Night Raven*, 17
(Hunt. Cl.), Like mistris like maide.
1699 : Farquhar, *Love and a Bottle*,
II. i. 1849 : Planché, *Extravag.*, iv.
19 (1879). Cf. **Hackney mistress.**

Like mother like daughter. 1509 :
Barclay, *Ship of Fools*, i. 236 (1874),
An olde prouerbe hath long agone be
sayde That oft . . . the mayde Or
doughter, ynto the mother wyll agre.
1611 : *Bible*, Ezek. xvi. 44, Every one
that useth proverbs shall use this
proverb against thee, saying, As is the
mother, so is her daughter. 1860 :
Reade, *Cl. and Hearth*, ch. xlvii.

Like priest like people. 1382 : Wiclif,
Bible, Hos. iv. 9, As the peple so the
prest. 1589 : Nashe, *Works*, i. 121
(Grosart), Like people, like priest begins
now to be verified. 1611 : *Bible*, Hos.
iv. 9, Like people, like priest. 1681 :
Yarranton, *Eng. Improvement*, Pt. II.
183, In most places, it is at this day,
like parson, like people. 1725 : Bailey,
tr. Erasmus' *Colloq.*, 246, Like people,
like priest.

**Like punishment and equal pain, both
key and key-hole do sustain.** 1639 :
Clarke, 239. 1670 : Ray, 135.

Like saint. *See* **Such saint.**

Like the boose, To. *See* quot. 1877 :
E. Leigh, *Cheshire Gloss.*, 170, When
men or women marry for fortune they
are said . . . " To like the boose [stall
for cattle] but not the ring-stake," i.e.
they like the plenty round but fret at
the confinement and chains, with which
plenty has been purchased. 1917 :
Bridge, *Cheshire Proverbs*, 140.

Like the Irishman's pig. *See* quot.
1901 : F. E. Taylor, *Lancs Sayings*, 5,

He's like th' Oirishmon's pig—he'll
noather leeod nor droive.

**Like the old woman's dish-cloth, looks
better dry than wet.** Oxfordsh. 1913 :
Folk-Lore, xxiv. 76.

Like to one as if spit out of his mouth.
c. 1400 : *Beryn*, l. 3232 (E.E.T.S.), Behold thy sone ! it semeth crope out of
thy mowith. 1602 : Breton, in *Works*, ii.
g 8 (Grosart), The one as like an owle, the
other as like an urchin, as if they had
beene spitte out of the mouthes of them.
1616 : Haughton, *Englishm. for my
Money*, IV. i., Now look I as like the
Dutchman as if I were spit out of his
mouth. 1668 : Dryden, *Sir Martin
Mar-all*, V. i. 1703 : Centlivre, *Stolen
Heiress*, III. iv. 1738 : Swift, *Polite
Convers.*, Dial. III. 1828 : Carr, *Craven
Dialect*, ii. 155, " That barn's as like his
fadder, as an he'd been spit out of his
mouth," i.e. he very much resembles
him. 1887 : Parish and Shaw, *Dict.
Kent. Dialect*, 158 (E.D.S.), Spit. A
double or counterpart. " He's the very
spit of his brother."

Like water. *See* **Duck** (6).

Like will to like—with varied addi-
tions. [Pares autem vetere proverbio
cum paribus facillime congregantur.—
Cicero, *De Senect.*, 7.] *c.* 1375 : Sc.
Leg. Saints, i. 543 (Petrus) (O.), Lyk to
lyk accordis welc. *c.* 1430 : Lydgate,
Churl and Bird, st. 38, Eche thinge
draweth to his semblable. *c.* 1460 :
Prov. of Good Counsel, in E.E.T.S.,
Ext. Ser., No. 8, p. 70, As for this
proverbe dothe specify, " lyke wyll to
lyke in eche company." 1509 : Barclay, *Ship of Fools*, ii. 35 (1874), For
it is a prouerbe, and an olde sayd sawe
That in euery place lyke to lyke wyll
drawe. 1546 : Heywood, *Proverbs*, Pt.
I. ch. iv. 1568 : Fulwell, *Like will to
Like* [title]. 1580 : Baret, *Alvearie*, A
589, Lyke will to lyke, quoth the deuill
to the colliar. 1614 : B. Rich, *Honestie
of This Age*, 48 (Percy S.) [as in 1580].
1664 : *Poor Robin Alman. Prognost.*, sig.
C5 [as in 1580]. 1670 : Ray, 15, Like to
like, and Nan for Nicholas. 1679 : A.
Behn, *Feign'd Curtezans*, V. i. [as in
1580]. 1732 : Fuller, No. 3239 [as in
1670]; and No. 3240 [as in 1580].

1823 : Scott, *Peveril*, ch. xiv., How
could I help it ? like will to like—the boy
would come—the girl would see him.
1922 : Weyman, *Ovington's Bank*, ch.
xxxi., He's learned this at your d—d
counter, sir ! That's where it is. It's
like to like.

Like wood like arrows. 1633 : Draxe,
113.

Like word like deed. *c.* 1386 : Chaucer,
C. Tales, A 741 (Skeat), Eek Plato
seith, who-so that can him rede, The
wordës mote be cosin to the dede.

Like workman. *See* **Workman** (1).

**Likely lies in the mire when Unlikely
gets over.** 1732 : Fuller, No. 3242.

Likeness causeth liking. 1639 : Clarke,
27. 1732 : Fuller, No. 3243, Likeness
begets love ; yet proud men hate one
another.

Likes not his business, Who. *See* quot.
1846 : T. Wright, *Essays on Middle
Ages*, i. 140, We have the saying, " Who
likes not his business, his business likes
not him."

**Lilies are whitest in a blackmoor's
hand.** 1732 : Fuller, No. 3244.

Lill for loll. *See* quot. 1639 : in
Berkeley MSS., iii. 33 (1885), Lill for
loll : id est, one for another : as good
as hee brought. (Glouc:).

Lily. *See* **White** (2).

Lim hay, To lick it up like. 1670 :
Ray, 206. 1790 : Grose, *Prov. Gloss.*,
s.v. " Cheshire." 1917 : Bridge, *Cheshire
Proverbs*, 139. [Lymm is a village on the
Mersey where the best hay is got.]

**Lime enriches the father and beggars
the son.** 1846 : Denham, *Proverbs*, 6
(Percy S.), Lime makes a rich father
and a poor son. 1917 : Bridge, *Cheshire
Proverbs*, 92.

Lincoln. *See* **Devil** (5).

Lincoln, As loud as Tom of. 1662 :
Fuller, *Worthies*, ii. 267 (1840). 1790 :
Grose, *Prov. Gloss.*, s.v. " Lincs."

**Lincoln shall be hanged for London's
sake.** *c.* 1592 : *Sir T. More*, 21 (Malone
S.), This the olde prouerbe now com-
pleate dooth make, that Lincolne should
be hangd for Londons sake.

**Lincoln was, London is, and York
shall be.** 1603 : Dekker, *Wond. Yeare*,
in *Works*, i. 101 (Grosart) [cited as

" that worme-eaten prouerbe "]. 1662 :
Fuller, *Worthies*, iii. 413 (1840). 1700 :
J. Brome, *Travels*, 148, Lincoln was,
and London is, And York shall be, The
fairest city of the three. 1724 : Stukeley, *Itin. Cur.*, 85 [as in 1700]. 1725 :
Defoe, *Tour*, ii. 140 [as in 1603]. 1865 :
W. White, *East. England*, ii. 45 [as
in 1700].

Lincolnshire. *See* **Cheshire** (6).

Lincolnshire bagpipes. 1590 : *Three
Lords, etc.*, in Hazlitt, *Old Plays*, vi. 393,
The sweet ballad of the Lincolnshire
bagpipes. 1598 : Shakespeare, 1 *Henry
IV.*, I. ii., I am as melancholy as . . .
the drone of a Lincolnshire bagpipe.
1622 : Drayton, *Polyol.*, xxiii., And bells
and bagpipes next, belong to Lincolnshire. 1790 : Grose, *Prov. Gloss.*, s.v.
" Lincs," Lincolnshire bagpipers.

**Lincolnshire where the hogs sh—
soap, and the cows fire.** 1659 : Howell,
21. 1670 : Ray, 236. 1790 : Grose,
Prov. Gloss., s.v. " Lincs." 1889 : Peacock, *Manley, etc., Gloss.*, 324 (E.D.S.).

Lincoln's Inn. *See* **Gray's Inn.**

Lind [Linden or Lime-tree], **As light
as leaf on.** *c.* 1310 : in Ritson, *Songs
and Ballads*, 56 (Hazlitt), And lef is
lyht on lynde. 1377 : Langland, *Plowman*, B, i. 154, Was neuere leef vpon
lynde lighter ther-after. *c.* 1386 :
Chaucer, *Clerk's Tale*, l. 1155. 1457 :
in *Reliq. Antiquæ*, ii. 70 (1843), Be ay
of chere as lighte as lefe on lynde.
1520 : in *Ballads from MSS.*, i. 450
(B.S.), As lyght as lefe on lynde.

Lindholme. *See* **Hatfield.**

**Line to the wall, Bring your, not the
wall to the line.** 1732 : Fuller, No. 1021.

Lingering love breeds mislike. 1593 :
Pass. Morrice, 87 (N. Sh. S.).

Lion. 1. *A lion among sheep and a
sheep among lions.* 1589 : Puttenham,
Eng. Poesie, 299 (Arber), As the prouerbe goeth . . . a lyon, etc.

2. *A lion may be beholden to a mouse.*
1639 : Fuller, *Holy War*, bk. iii. ch. viii.,
As the fable telleth us . . . the mouse
[may] befriend the lion. 1732 : Fuller,
No. 264, A lyon may come to be
beholding to a mouse.

3. *A lion's skin is never cheap.* 1611 :
Cotgrave, s.v. " Lion," A lyons skinne

was never bought good cheape. 1670:
Ray, 16. 1732: Fuller, No. 4643.

4. *Destroy the lion while he is yet but
a whelp.* Ibid., No. 1276. 1869: Spurgeon, *John Ploughman*, ch. i., You know
it is best to kill the lion while it is a cub.

5. *Even the lion must defend itself
against flies.* 1924: *Sphere*, 27 Sept.,
p. 386, col. 2.

6. *He is a lion in a good cause.* 1732:
Fuller, No. 1907.

7. (a) *If the lion's skin cannot do it,
the fox's shall,* or (b) *To patch a fox's tail
to a lion's skin*=to supplement strength
by craft. 1605: Camden, *Remains*, 326
(1870) [(a)]. Before 1634: Chapman,
Alphonsus, I. i., And where the
lion's hide is thin and scant, I'll
firmly patch it with the fox's fell.
1645: Howell, *Letters*, bk. i. § 1, No.
xlii. [(b)]. 1664: J. Wilson, *Andron.
Commenius*, IV. iv., Craft, where
strength doth fail, And piece the lion
with the fox's tail! 1670: Ray, 184
[(a)]. 1736: Bailey, *Dict.*, s.v. "Lion,"
If the lion's skin cannot the fox's shall.
1745: *Agreeable Companion*, 182, The
lion's skin too short, you know . . . Was
lengthen'd by the fox's tail; And art
supplies, where strength may fail. 1754:
Berthelson, *Eng.-Danish Dict.*, s.v.
"Lion" [(b)].

8. *If thy hand be in a lion's mouth,
get it out as fast as thou canst.* 1696:
Cornish Comedy, V., My hand is in the
lion's mouth; I must agree with him.
1732: Fuller, No. 2724. 1819: Scott,
Ivanhoe, ch. xix., "Our heads are in
the lion's mouth," said Wamba . . .
"get them out how we can."

9. *It is a base thing to tear a dead lion's
beard off.* 1596: Shakespeare, *King
John*, II. i., You are the hare of whom
the proverb goes, Whose valour plucks
dead lions by the beard. 1632: Randolph, *Jealous Lovers*, IV. iii., Do not,
live hare, pull the dead lion's beard.
1656: R. Fletcher, *Ex Otio Negotium*,
95, Be afear'd To pull a deceas'd lyon
by the beard. 1732: Fuller, No. 2846.

10. *Little birds may pick a dead lion.*
Ibid., No. 3250.

11. *The lion is not so fierce as he is
painted.* 1633: Draxe, 64 [with

"furious" for "fierce"]. 1640: Herbert, *Jac. Prudentum.* 1670: Ray,
114 [with "half" before "so"]. 1732:
Fuller, No. 4642 [as in 1670].

12. *To see the lions.* Originally the
lions in the Tower of London, and, by
extension, sights generally. 1590:
Greene, *Works*, viii. 68 (Grosart), This
countrey Francesco was no other but
a meere nouice, and that so newly,
that to vse the old prouerb, he had
scarce seene the lions. 1595: *Maroccus
Extaticus*, 8 (Percy S.), Indeed those
be the young men that never sawe
the lyons. 1765: Mrs. Cibber, in *Garrick Corresp.*, i. 200 (1831), This is not
the right season of the year to show
the lions. 1785: Grose, *Class. Dict.
Vulgar Tongue*, s.v. "Lion," To shew
the lions and tombs, to point out the
particular curiosities of any place.
1843: Dickens, *Letters*, iii. 46 (1882),
He . . . has been in London too, and
seeing all the lions under my escort.

13. *Wake not a sleeping lion.* 1580:
Sidney, *Arcadia*, bk. iv. 416 (1893),
Dametas, thinking it not good to awake
a sleeping lion. 1611: Cotgrave, s.v.
"Esveiller," To awake the sleeping
lyon (say we). 1693: Urquhart, *Rabelais*, bk. iii. ch. xiv., As when we say
proverbially to incense hornets, to move
a stinking puddle, and to awake a
sleeping lyon.

See also Better be the head; Dog (40)
and (83); Fly (6); Hare (2); Lamb (1);
Living dog; and Waking dog.

**Lip-honour costs little, yet may bring
in much.** 1659: Howell, *Proverbs:
Ital.-Eng.*, 13, The honor one doth with
the mouth avails much and costs little.
1732: Fuller, No. 3245.

**Lip-wisdom that wants experience,
All is but.** 1580: Sidney, *Arcadia*,
bk. i. 92 (1893). 1647: *Countrym.
New Commonwealth*, 22. 1732: Fuller,
No. 522.

Lips hang in your light, Your. Before
1529: Skelton, *Magnyfycence*, l. 1061,
Tusshe, thy lyppes hange in thyne eye.
1546: Heywood, *Proverbs*, Pt. II. ch.
iv. 1611: Davies (of Hereford), *Sc.
of Folly*, 49, in *Works*, ii. (Grosart),
Some lasses lips hang in their light.

1681 : W. Robertson, *Phraseol. Generalis*, 621, A born fool; his lips hang in's light.

Lips however rosy must be fed. 1875 : A. B. Cheales, *Proverb. Folk-Lore*, 29.

Liquorish. *See* quot. 1668 : Davenant, *Man's the Master*, IV., That baggage carries her purse in her bosom; and, according to the Northern proverb, is as liquorish at a penny as at a posset.

Liquorish tongue, A, a lecherous tail. *c.* 1386 : Chaucer, *Wife of Bath's Prol.*, l. 466, A likerous mouth moste han a likerous tayl. 1560 : T. Wilson, *Rhetorique*, 119 (1909), Likerish of tongue, light of taile. 1670 : Ray, 16. 1717 : Pope, *Wife of Bath*, l. 218, A liquorish mouth must have a lecherous tail. 1732 : Fuller, No. 3205.

Liquorish tongue is the purse's canker, A. 1678 : Ray, 169.

Lisping lass is good to kiss, A. 1638 : Ford, *Lady's Trial*, IV. ii., No, sweet madam, Your lips are destined to a better use, Or else the proverb fails of lisping maids. 1737 : Ray, 273. 1917 : Bridge, *Cheshire Proverbs*, 4.

Listeners hear no good of themselves. 1678 : Ray, 75. 1748 : Richardson, *Clarissa*, v. 116 (1785), The event . . . justified the old observation, that listners seldom hear good of themselves. 1822 : Scott, *Nigel*, ch. xxxiii., They say that hearkeners hear ill tales of themselves. 1857 : Borrow, *Rom. Rye*, ch. xi.

Lith and selthe. *See* Ease and success.

Lithe as lass of Kent. 1579 : Spenser, *Shep. Cal.*, Feb., His dewelap as lythe as lasse of Kent. 1735 : Pegge, *Kent. Proverbs*, in E.D.S., No. 12, p. 61, Lythe as lass of Kent, i.e. gentle, lithsom, etc.

Lither. *See* Lazy man's guise; and Long as he is lither.

Lither look. *See* Wanton look.

Little and good fills the trencher. 1640 : Herbert, *Jac. Prudentum.* 1666 : Torriano, *Piazza Univ.*, 211. 1670 : Ray, 16 [with " which is " for " and "].

Little and little. *See* Cat (35).

Little and little, By, the bird makes his nest. 1846 : T. Wright, *Essays on Middle Ages*, i. 130, We have in Eng-land a proverb, " Little and little make mickle," which appears again under the shape, " By little and little the bird makes his nest."

Little and little, By, the poor whore sinks her barn. 1678 : Ray, 170.

Little and often fills the purse. 1666 : Torriano, *Piazza Univ.*, 211. 1685 : L'Estrange, *Observator*, iii. No. 2, But a little and often is a good rule. 1732 : Fuller, No. 3249.

Little barrel can give but a little meal, A. 1732 : Fuller, No. 243.

Little betwixt right and wrong. 1659 : Howell, *Proverbs: Brit.-Eng.*, 38.

Little Billing. *See* All the world.

Little bird is content with a little nest, A. 1633 : Draxe, 115, For a little bird, a little nest. 1732 : Fuller, No. 244.

Little body doth often harbour a great soul, A. 1611 : Cotgrave, s.v. " Lievre," A little bush may hold a great hare; a little body a great heart. 1670 : Ray, 16. 1732 : Fuller, No. 3252, Little bodies have commonly great souls. 1875 : A. B. Cheales, *Proverb. Folk-Lore*, 9, Little bodies have large souls.

Little, By the, is known the much. 1541 : *Sch. House of Women*, l. 846, in Hazlitt, *Early Pop. Poetry*, iv. 138.

Little cannot be great unless he devour many, The. 1640 : Herbert, *Jac. Prudentum.* 1670 : Ray, 16.

Little cattle little care. 1917 : Bridge, *Cheshire Proverbs*, 92. Cf. **Little goods.**

Little debt makes a debtor, but a great one an enemy, A. 1732 : Fuller, No. 245.

Little dogs. *See* Hare (7).

Little drops. *See* Constant dropping.

Little end of the horn. Pictures of the " horn of suretyship " used to be common—" I had the horn of suretiship ever before my eyes. You all know the device of the horne where the young fellow slippes in at the butts-end and comes squeezed out at the buckall."—1605 : Jonson, etc., *Eastw. Hoe*, I. i. *See also* 1624 : B. & F., *Wife for a Month*, III. iii. The horn also represented prison — the wide mouth indicating ease of entrance, the small opening at the other end indicating difficulty of exit. Larwood and Hotten, in *Hist. of Signboards*, 339 (1867),

say : " Among the Roxburghe Ballads
(ii. 138) there is one entitled ' The
Extravagant Youth, or an Emblem of
Prodigality,' with a woodcut repre-
senting a youth jumping into the
mouth of a large horn. On one side
stands the father, seemingly in distress; on the other is a mad-house,
with the sign of THE FOOL, two of the
inmates looking out from behind the
bars. The extravagant youth . . . says :

But now all my glory is clearly decay'd,
And into the horn myself have betray'd
  .   .   .   .   .
All comforts now from us are flown,
My father in Bedlam makes his moan,
And I in the *Counter* a prisoner thrown,
This Horn is a figure by which it is known.

1639-61 : in *Rump Songs*, Pt. I., 127
(1662, repr. 1874), So that a poor de-
linquent fleec'd and torn Seems like a
man that's creeping through a horn,
Finds a smooth entrance, wide, and fit,
but when Hee's squeez'd and forc'd up
through the smaller end, He looks as
gaunt and pin'd, as he that spent A
tedious twelve years in an eager Lent,
1887 : J. Eliot Hodgkin, in *N. & Q.*,
7th ser., iv. 323, " Coming out of the
little end of the horn." This expression . . . I first heard it used many
years ago by a Warwickshire man.
  Little England beyond Wales=Pem-
brokeshire. 1586 : Camden, *Britannia*,
373. 1603 : G. Owen, *Descrip. of Pembrokeshire.* 1670 : Ray, 258. 1888 :
E. Laws, *Hist. of Little England beyond
Wales* [title]. 1925 : *Observer*, 31 May,
p. 9, col. 4.
  **Little fellow, He's a; but every bit
of that little is bad.** 1732 : Fuller,
No. 2441.
  Little field. *See* **Little house.**
  Little finger. *See* quots. [Cuius pluris
erat unguis, quam tu totus es.—Petr.,
57.] 1618 : B. Holyday, *Technogamia*,
I. iv., H'as more loue in's little finger,
then both they in their whole bodyes.
1670 : Ray, 175, He hath more in's little
finger, then thou in thy whole body.
1738 : Swift, *Polite Convers.*, Dial. II.,
She has more goodness in her little
finger, than he has in his whole body.
  Little fish are sweet. 1830 : Forby,

Vocab. E. Anglia, 434. 1872 : J. Glyde,
jr., *Norfolk Garland*, 149.
  **Little fishes slip through nets, but
great fishes are taken.** 1598 : Meres,
Palladis, fo. 246.
  Little good is soon spent, A. 1605 :
Camden, *Remains*, 327 (1870). 1670 :
Ray, 116. 1732 : Fuller, No. 3255,
Little goods are soon spent.
  **Little good to stark naught, To come
from.** 1639 : Clarke, 83. 1670 : Ray,
178.
  Little goods little care. [*c.* 1300 : *King
Alisaunder*, l. 7365, Beter is, lyte to
have in ese Then muche to have[n]
in malese.] 1633 : Draxe, 161. 1640 :
Herbert, *Jac. Prudentum*, Little wealth,
little care. 1732 : Fuller, No. 3256.
1875 : A. B. Cheales, *Proverb. Folk-Lore*,
101, Little wealth, little woe. Cf.
Little cattle.
  Little, He that hath, is the less dirty.
1640 : Herbert, *Jac. Prudentum.*
  Little house has a wide mouth, A.
1883 : Burne, *Shropsh. Folk-Lore*, 589.
  Little house well filled. *See* quots.
16th cent. : in *N. & Q.*, 4th ser., iii. 10,
A littile grounde well tilled, A litel
house well filled, A litel wife well willed,
Would make him live that weare halfe
killed. *c.* 1582 : G. Harvey, *Marginalia*,
200 (1913), A lyttle house well filled :
a lyttle land well tilled. 1670 : Ray,
53, [as in 1582, *plus*] and a little wife
well will'd. 1738 : Swift, *Polite Convers.*, Dial. II. [as in 1670]. 1880 :
Spurgeon, *Ploughman's Pictures*, 156
[as in 1670, but with " field " for
" land "].
  Little in the morning. *See* quots.
16th cent. : in *Reliq. Antiquæ*, i. 208
(1841), A little in the morning, nothing
at noone, And a light supper doth
make to live longe. 1619 : *Helpe to
Discourse*, 125 (1640), A little in the
morning is enough, enough at dinner
is but a little; a little at night is too
much.
  Little John. *See* quot. 1605 : Camden,
Remains, 328 (1870), Many a man talks
of Little John that never did him know.
  **Little journeys and good cost bring
safe home.** 1640 : Herbert, *Jac.
Prudentum.*

Little kitchen makes a large house, A.
Ibid. 1666 : Torriano, *Piazza Univ.*, 57.

Little knocks Rive great blocks. 1830 :
Forby, *Vocab. E. Anglia*, 430. 1872 :
J. Glyde, jr., *Norfolk Garland*, 148.

Little knows the fat sow. *See* Sow (10).

Little labour, much health, A. 1640 :
Herbert, *Jac. Prudentum*.

Little leak will sink a great ship, A.
1642 : Fuller, *Holy State:* "Good Servant," Many little leaks may sink a
ship. 1736 : Franklin, *Way to Wealth*,
in *Works*, i. 447 (Bigelow) [with "small"
for "little"]. 1875 : A. B. Cheales,
Proverb. Folk-Lore, 165 (as in 1736].

Little let [hindrance] lets an ill workman, A. 1640 : Herbert, *Jac. Prudentum*.

Little London=Penrith. 1846–59 :
Denham Tracts, i. 182 (F.L.S.).

Little London beyond Wales=Beau-
maris. 1670 : Ray, 258.

Little losses amaze, great tame. 1640 :
Herbert, *Jac. Prudentum*.

Little love and a little money, A.
Before 1704 : T. Brown, in *Works*, i.
293 (1760) [cited as "a good old
proverb"].

Little love, little trust. Before 1500 :
Hill, *Commonplace-Book*, 47 (E.E.T.S.),
An old said sawe . . . "Wher is lytill
love ther is lytill tryste."

Little man. *See* quot. 1921 : *Times*,
10 Sept., p. 9, col. 4, We are ready to
join in the general welcome [to C.
Chaplin]. "A little man may," as
the adage truly says, "cast a great
shadow."

Little mead, little need. Somerset. A
mild winter hoped for after a bad
summer. 1678 : Ray, 352.

Little meddling, Of, cometh great rest
(or ease). *c.* 1386 : Chaucer, *Manciple's
Tale*, l. 350, That litel jangling causeth
muchel rest. 1546 : Heywood, *Proverbs*,
Pt. II. ch. ii., . . . reste. 1599 : Porter,
Two Angry Women, in Hazlitt, *Old
Plays*, vii. 337, . . . rest. 1669 : *Politeuphuia*, 166, . . . much rest. 1694 :
D'Urfey, *Quixote*, Pt. I. Act II. sc. ii.,
. . . ease. 1902 : in *N. & Q.*, 9th ser.,
x. 475, In chastising a child for undue
curiosity, with a view to impress the
young mind with the truth of the

proverb that "of little meddling comes
great ease."

Little minds like weak liquors are
soonest soured. 1855 : Bohn, 444.

Little mischief too much. 1659 :
Howell, *Proverbs: Brit.-Eng.*, 31.

Little money little law. *c.* 1550 : *Parl.
of Byrdes*, l. 146, in Hazlitt, *Early Pop.
Poetry*, iii. 174, Than sayde the Cornysh
daw, Lytle money lytle lawe.

Little neglect may breed great mischief, A. 1736 : Franklin, *Way to
Wealth*, in *Works*, i. 446 (Bigelow).

Little, Of a, a little. 1611 : Cotgrave,
s.v. "Petit," Of a little take a little, of
a mickle, mickle. 1631 : Mabbe, *Celestina*, 212 (T.T.), That common saying
of your little children : Of a little, a
little ; of much, nothing.

Little of everything is nothing in the
main, A. 1732 : Fuller, No. 247.

Little pitchers have wide ears. 1546 :
Heywood, *Proverbs*, Pt. II. ch. v.,
Auoyd your children : small pitchers
haue wide eares. 1594 : Shakespeare,
Rich. III., II. iv., Pitchers have ears.
1617 : Jonson, *Vis. of Delight* [as in
1594]. Before 1681 : J. Lacy, *Sauny
the Scot*, IV., I would have it private.
Pitchers have ears, and I have many
servants. 1721 : Bailey, *Eng. Dict.*,
s.v. "Pitchfork" [with "great" for
"wide"]. 1852 : Dickens, *Bleak House*,
ch. xxxvii., Charley verified the adage
about little pitchers, I am sure ; for she
heard of more sayings and doings, in a
day, than would have come to my ears
in a month. 1914 : Lucas, *Landmarks*,
ch. iv., Certain crusted scraps of nursery
wisdom . . . such as . . . "Little Pitchers
have long ears." 1917 : Bridge, *Cheshire
Proverbs*, 92, Little pigs have long ears.

Little pot is soon hot, A. 1546 :
Heywood, *Proverbs*, Pt. I. ch. xi.
1606 : J. Day, *Ile of Gulls*, II. iv., Nay,
tho I be but a little pot, I shall be as
soone hote as another. 1659 : Howell,
Letters, ii. 665 (Jacobs). 1732 : Fuller,
No. 6173.

Little rain. *See* Rain, *subs.* (3), (22).

Little said soon amended. *c.* 1555 : in
Wright, *Songs, etc., Philip and Mary*,
31 (Roxb. Cl.), Therfor lyttell sayd ys
sowne amended. 1577 : J. Grange,

Golden Aphroditis, sig. B1. 1603 : Dekker, *Pat. Grissil*, III. 1664 : in *Musarum Deliciæ, etc.*, ii. 162 (Hotten), Little
or nothing said, soon mended is. 1748 :
Richardson, *Clarissa*, V. iii. (1785), I
should be angry if I proceed in my
guesses — and little said is soon
amended. Cf. Least said.

Little saving is no sin, A. 1792 : Wolcot, *Works*, ii. 313 (1795) [cited as a
proverb " that economic souls revere "].

Little spark. *See* Spark.

**Little sticks kindle the fire, great ones
put it out.** 1303 : Brunne, *Handlyng
Synne*, l. 12438, Thou seest stykkës
that are smale, They brenne fyrst
feyre. 1640 : Herbert, *Jac. Prudentum*.
1670 : Ray, 16. 1732 : Fuller, No. 3261.

**Little stone may overturn a great
wagon, A.** *c.* 1375 : Barbour, *Bruce*, bk.
xi. l. 24, A litell stane, as men sayis, May
ger weltir ane mekill wane.

**Little stream may quench thirst as
well as a great river, A.** 1732 : Fuller,
No. 249.

Little stream will drive a light mill, A.
1639 : Clarke, 88, A little stream serveth
to drive a light milne. 1670 : Ray, 116.
1732 : Fuller, No. 250.

Little string will tie up a little bird, A.
Ibid., No. 251.

Little strokes fell great oaks. 1539 :
Taverner, *Proverbs*, fo. 26, Wyth many
strokes is an oke ouerthrowne. 1579 :
Lyly, *Euphues*, 81 (Arber), Many
strokes ouerthrow the tallest oke. 1607 :
J. Day, *Trav. of Three Eng. Brothers*, 69
(Bullen), By many strokes the tallest
okes are shaken. 1736 : Franklin, *Way
to Wealth*, in *Works*, i. 444 (Bigelow).
c. 1800 : Trusler, *Prov. in Verse*, 83.
1869 : Spurgeon, *John Ploughman*, ch.
xxii., By little strokes Men fell great
oaks.

Little thing, Of a, a little displeaseth.
1640 : Herbert, *Jac. Prudentum*.

Little things are good. 1666 : Torriano, *Piazza Univ.*, 215, That which is
good is ever little.

Little things are great to little men.
1827 : Hone, *Table-Book*, 110.

Little things are pretty. 1539 :
Taverner, *Proverbs*, fo. 50, Vnto lyttle
thynges is a certayne grace annexed.

1678 : Ray, 169. 1754 : *World*, No. 65,
Recollecting the proverb, that " every
thing that is little is pretty."

Little things please little minds. 1584 :
Lyly, *Sapho and Phao*, II. iv. [with
" catch " for " please "]. 1880 : Spurgeon, *Ploughman's Pictures*, 81.

Little tit, all tail. 1546 : Heywood,
Proverbs, Pt. I. ch. x., Little titte all
tayle, I haue heard er this. *c.* 1570 :
G. Harvey, *Marginalia*, 139.

Little wealth. *See* Little goods.

**Little wimble will let in the great
auger, The.** 1732 : Fuller, No. 4632.

**Little wind kindles, much puts out the
fire, A.** 1586 : B. Young, tr. Guazzo's
Civil Convers., fo. 193. 1640 : Herbert,
Jac. Prudentum. 1732 : Fuller, No. 253.

**Little wit in the head makes much
work for the feet.** 1855 : Bohn, 445.
Cf. Head (17).

**Little wit will serve a fortunate man,
A.** Ibid., 293.

**Little wit, You have a, and it doth you
good sometimes.** 1670 : Ray, 30. 1732 :
Fuller, No. 5911.

**Little with honesty is better than a
great deal with knavery, A.** 1659 :
London Chanticleers, sc. i., in Hazlitt,
Old Plays, xii. 325 [cited as " that
precise axiom "].

Little with quiet. *See* quots. 1611 :
Cotgrave, s.v. " Peu," A little with
quietnesse is Gods owne gift. Ibid.,
s.v. " Paix," A little with peace is a
great blessing. 1640 : Herbert, *Jac.
Prudentum*, A little with quiet is the
only diet.

Little Witham. Used in punning
references to lack of wit. 1589 : Nashe,
in *Works*, i. 192 (Grosart), I giue and
bequeath . . . to each of them an
aduouson : To the former of small
Witam : and to the other of little
Brainford. 1595 : *Pedlars Prophecy*,
l. 481 (Malone S.), At Little Wytham
seuen years I went to schoole. 1662 :
Fuller, *Worthies*, ii. 269, He was born
at Little Witham. 1790 : Grose, *Prov.
Gloss.*, s.v. " Essex " and " Lincs "
[as in 1662]. 1818 : Scott, *Heart of
Midl.*, ch. xxxii., " Has she the capacity
of taking care of herself ? " " Why,
your Reverence, . . . I cannot just say

—I will be sworn she was not born at
Witt-ham."

Little wood will heat a little oven, A.
1732 : Fuller, No. 254. 1869 : Spurgeon,
John Ploughman, ch. v.

**Little worm will lie under a great
stone, A.** 1666 : Torriano, *Piazza Univ.*,
243, The English say, A little worm,
etc.

Live, verb. 1. *A man may live upon
little, but he cannot live upon nothing.*
1855 : Bohn, 295.

2. *Better to live well than long.*
Ibid., 330.

3. *He lives long that lives till all are
weary of him.* 1732 : Fuller, No. 1966.
1738 : Swift, *Polite Convers.*, Dial. II.,
I believe I shall live till all my friends
are weary of me.

4. *He lives long that lives well.* 1560 :
T. Wilson, *Rhetorique*, 83 (1909), For they
liued long enough, that haue liued well
enough. 1642 : Fuller, *Holy State* :
" Good Child," If he chance to die
young, yet he lives long that lives
well. 1748 : Richardson, *Clarissa*, iv.
121 (1785), He that lives well, lives long.

5. *He lives unsafely that looks too near
on things.* 1611 : Cotgrave, s.v. " Esplu-
cher " [with " to matters " for " on
things "]. 1640 : Herbert, *Jac. Prudentum.*

6. *He that lives always at home sees
nothing but the same.* 1618 : Breton, in
Inedited Tracts, 184 (Hazlitt, 1868)
[quoted as a proverb].

7. *He that lives ill, fear follows him.*
1640 : Herbert, *Jac. Prudentum.* 1666 :
Torriano, *Piazza Univ.*, 286, Who lives
ill, fear attends him.

8. *He that lives in hope danceth
without music.* 1591 : Florio, *Second
Frutes*, 149, He that dooth liue in
hope, dooth dance in narrowe scope.
1640 : Herbert, *Jac. Prudentum.* 1659 :
Howell, *Proverbs: Span.-Eng.*, 18.

9. *He that lives long suffers much.*
1620 : Shelton, *Quixote*, Pt. II. ch.
xxxii. 1732 : Fuller, No. 2220.

10. *He that lives most, dies most.*
1640 : Herbert, *Jac. Prudentum.*

11. *He that lives not well one year,
sorrows seven after.* 1640 : Ibid. 1748 :
Richardson, *Clarissa*, iv. 121 (1785), He

that lives ill one year, will sorrow for
it seven.

12. *He that lives well is learned
enough.* 1611 : Cotgrave, s.v. " Vivre,"
He that lives well enough hath skill
enough. 1640 : Herbert, *Jac. Prudentum.*

13. *He that lives well sees afar off.*
1640 : Ibid. 1748 : Richardson, *Clarissa*,
iv. 121 (1785).

14. *He that lives with the muses shall
die in the straw.* 1732 : Fuller, No. 2223.

15. *He that liveth in Court dieth upon
straw.* 1578 : Florio, *First Fruites*, fo. 29.
1579 : Lyly, *Euphues*, 185 (Arber).
1629 : *Book of Meery Riddles*, Prov. 91.
Cf. **Courtier young.**

16. *He that liveth overcometh.* 1578 :
Florio, *First Fruites*, fo. 33, Who lyueth
vanquisheth. 1629 : *Book of Meery
Riddles*, Prov. 131.

17. *He that liveth wickedly, can hardly
die honestly.* 1670 : Ray, 16.

18. *He that will live in peace and rest,
Must hear and see and speak the best.*
c. 1450 : *Prov. of Good Counsel*, l. 52
(E.E.T.S.), Yf thou wylte leve in peas
and reste, here, and see, and sey the
beste. 1591 : Florio, *Second Frutes*, 101,
If you wil stil liue at ease, heare and
see, and hold your pease. 1605 : Camden, *Remains*, 323 (1870) [with " say "
for " speak "]. 1710 : S. Palmer, *Moral
Essays on Proverbs*, 143, He that means
to live at rest, Must hear and see,
and say the best. 1732 : Fuller, No.
6182.

19. *He would live even in a gravel-pit.*
" Spoken of a wary, sparing, niggardly
person." 1678 : Ray, 72. 1732 : Fuller,
No. 2417.

20. *I live, and lords do no more.* 1599 :
Porter, *Two Angry Women*, in Hazlitt,
Old Plays, vii. 307, *Fran.* Well, how doth
thy master? *Nich.* Forsooth, live, and
the best doth no better. 1732 : Fuller,
No. 2616.

21. *If you would live for ever. See*
Wash (3).

22. *If you would live well for a week,
etc. See* 1809 quot. 1666 : Torriano,
Piazza Univ., 151, Who intends to have
a good month, let him to the bath, a
good year, let him marry, a good week,
let him kill a hog, who will be happy

alwaies, let him turn priest. 1809:
Pegge, *Anonym.*, cent. ii. 19, " If you
would live well for a week, kill a hog;
if you would live well for a month,
marry; if you would live well all your
life, turn priest " [i.e. never marry].
This is an old proverb. 1827 : Hone,
Table-Book, 430 [as in 1809].

23. *If you would not live to be old, you
must be hanged when you are young.*
1670 : Ray, 126.

24. *Live and learn.* c. 1620 : in *Roxb.
Ballads*, i. 80 (Hindley), A man may
live and learne. 1663 : Killigrew, *Parson's Wedding*, II. iii. 1747 : Garrick, *Miss in her Teens*, I. ii., I was
innocent myself once, but *live and
learn* is an old saying, and a true one.
1837 : Dickens, *Pickwick*, ch. xix.
1885 : M. Twain, in *Letters*, 256 (ed.
Paine), One lives and learns. I find
it takes 7 binderies four months to
bind 325,000 books. 1922 : Weyman,
Ovington's Bank, ch. xix.

25. *Live and let live.* 1622 : Malynes,
Anc. Law-Merch., 229 (O.), According
to the Dutch prouerbe . . . Leuen ende
laeten leuen, to liue and to let others
liue. 1678 : Ray, 170. 1692 : L'Estrange,
Æsop, 127 (3rd ed.), Live and let live
is the rule of common justice. 1762 :
Smollett, *Sir L. Greaves*, ch. xvi., You
knows, meester, one must live and let
live, as the saying is. 1852 : Dickens,
Bleak House, ch. xliii. 1909 : Lucas,
Wand. in Paris, ch. xiv., Liberty is the
very air of the Boulevards. Live and
let live.

26. *Live well. See* Man (47).

27. *Living upon trust is the way to
pay double.* 1732 : Fuller, No. 3265.

28. *Living well is the best revenge.*
1640 : Herbert, *Jac. Prudentum.*

29. *One cannot live by selling ware
for words.* 1639 : Clarke, 156 [with
" I " for " One "]. 1670 : Ray, 154.
1732 : Fuller, No. 3741 [with " goods "
for " wares "].

30. *One must live long to learn much.*
c. 1568 : W. Wager, *The longer thou
livest, the more foole thou art* [title].
1633 : Draxe, 58, The longer that one
liueth, the more he knoweth. 1666 :
Torriano, *Piazza Univ.*, 313.

31. *She lives by love and lumps in
corners.* 1678 : Ray, 75.

32. *They live but ill who always think
to live.* 1600 : Bodenham, *Belvedere*,
228 (Spens. S.). 1732 : Fuller, No.
4971, They seldom live well, who think
they shall live long.

33. *They live not most at ease that have
the world at will.* 1577 : J. Grange,
Golden Aphroditis, sig. H2.

34. *They that live longest must die at
last.* 1670 : Ray, 116. 1732 : Fuller,
No. 4982.

35. *They that live longest must go
farthest for wood.* 1639 : Clarke, 190,
He that lives longest must fetch his
wood furthest. 1670 : Ray, 116. 1732 :
Fuller, No. 4983.

36. *They who live longest will see most.*
1620 : Shelton, *Quixote*, Pt. II. ch. lii.,
My mother was used to say that it was
needful to live long to see much. 1869 :
Spurgeon, *John Ploughman*, ch. xx.,
But now they have left they say there's
a screw loose, and they who live longest
will see most.

37. *We can live without our friends,
but not without our neighbours.* 1732 :
Fuller, No. 5435.

38. *We must live by the quick and not
by the dead.* 1578 : Florio, *First Fruites*,
fo. 34, Quicke with the quicke and dead
with the dead. 1605 : T. Heywood,
If You Know Not Me, in *Dram. Works*,
i. 243 (1874) [quoted as " the old
prouerb "]. 1626 : Overbury, *Characters:* " Sexton." 1694 : Southerne,
Fatal Marriage, IV. i., We must live
by the living, you know. 1738 : Swift,
Polite Convers., Dial. II. [with " living "
for " quick "].

39. *We shall live till we die.* 1600 :
Dekker, *Shoem. Hol.*, IV. iii., Hereof
am I sure, I shall live till I die. 1655 :
T. Muffett, *Healths Improvement*, 8, We
shall live till we dye, in despight of diet.
1889 : Jefferies, *Hedgerow*, 65 (W.),
The old country proverb, " Ah, well, we
shall live till we die if the pigs don't eat
us, and then we shall go acorning."
1901 : F. E. Taylor, *Lancs Sayings*, 10,
We shan o live till we dee'n—iv th'
dogs dunno wory us. 1917 : Bridge,
Cheshire Proverbs, 149, We . . . die

if the pigs don't eat us. Cf. **Tantera Bobus.**

40. *Who lives well dies well.* 1506: Pynson, *Kal. of Shepherds*, 169 (1892), He that leuyth well maye not dye amys. 1537: R. Whitford, *Werke for Housholders*, sig. G4, The moste sure way to dye well is well to lyue. 1578: Florio, *First Fruites*, fo. 28. 1639: Clarke, 215, They die well that live well. 1732: Fuller, No. 1890, He hath liv'd ill that knows not how to die well.

Lively as a cricket. *See* **Merry.**

Lively as a maggot. 1883: Burne, *Shropsh. Folk-Lore*, 595.

Living dog is better than a dead lion, A. 1382: Wiclif, *Bible*, Eccles. ix. 4 (O)., Betere is a quyc dogge thanne a leoun dead. 1558: When Queen Mary died, one preacher of a funeral sermon comforted his audience on the virtues of her successor by observing that " a living dog was better than a dead lion " — *see* Johnson, *Letters*, ii. 437 (Hill). 1697: Vanbrugh, *Prov. Wife*, V. 1798: Wolcot, *Works*, v. 252 (1801). 1855: Gaskell, *North and South*, ch. xlvi., " I like you twenty times better than Hamlet." " On the principle that a living ass is better than a dead lion? " 1909: Lucas, *Wand. in Paris*, ch. xii. 1924: Phillpotts, *Human Boy's Diary*, Term 3, 18 April, " True," admitted Briggs, " Better be a live ass than a dead lion."

Lizard. *See* **Better to be.**

Lizard, The. *See* **Rain,** *subs.* (27).

Loaded. *See* **Laden.**

Loaf and Loaves. 1. *He went in with the loaves and came out with the cakes=* He is "half-baked." 1864: " Cornish Proverbs," in *N. & Q.*, 3rd ser., vi. 494, He is only half-baked ; put in with the bread and taken out with the cakes. 1896: Northall, *Warwicksh. Word-Book* (E.D.S.), Put in with the bread and pull'd out with the cakes. 1917: Bridge, *Cheshire Proverbs*, 70.

2. *Set not your loaf in till the oven's hot.* 1732: Fuller, No. 4110.

3. *The loaves and fishes*—of office. 1614: Bp. Hall, *Recoll. Treat.*, 954 (O.), If it were not for the loaves and fishes, the traine of Christ would bee lesse.

1789: Wolcot, *Works*, ii. 59 (1795), What pity 'tis, in this our goodly land, Amongst the apostolic band, So ill divided are the loaves and fishes ! 1816: Scott, *Old Mortality*, ch. xxvii., Thou art one of those that follow the Gospel for the loaves and for the fishes. 1880: Spurgeon, *Ploughman's Pictures*, 122, They go to the church for the loaves, and then go over to the Baptist Chapel for the fishes.

See also **Half a loaf.**

Loan should come laughing home, A borrowed. *c.* 1300: *Prov. of Hendyng*, st. 25 (Berlin, 1878), Selde cometh lone lahynde hom. 1732: Fuller, No. 6314.

Lob's pound. Described by A. H. Bullen as " the thraldom of the henpecked married man " : also=a prison. 1595: Peele, *Old Wives Tale*, sig. E1, Lobb be your comfort, and cuckold bee your destenie. 1612: *Cornucopiæ*, 64 (Grosart), Thus is the woodcocke fall'n into the gin, And in Lobs-pound intangled by a wile. 1623: Massinger, *Duke of Milan*, III. ii. 1671: Crowne, *Juliana*, I. i., And so there's a heavy bustle, the Cardinal on one side, and the Princess on the t'other, and between 'um both he's got into Lobb's pound. Before 1704: T. Brown, *Works*, iv. 323 (1760), Instead of paradise, they have got into lob's pound. 1785: Grose, *Class. Dict. Vulgar Tongue*, s.v. Lob's pound, a prison. 1823: Moor, *Suffolk Words*, 215, Lob's-pound. The bridewell. 1866: J. G. Nall, *Great Yarmouth, etc.*, 595 [as in 1823].

Lobster. *See* **Apple** (5).

Lock and key, To have under. Before 1250: *Owl and Nightingale*, l. 1557 (O.), He hire bi-lukþ myd keye and loke. *c.* 1390: Gower, *Conf. Amantis*, bk. v. l. 6621, Which under lock and under keie . . . Hath al the Tresor . . . *c.* 1440: Lydgate, *Fall of Princes*, bk. i. l. 4886, The brond reseruyng vnder lok and keie. 1584: Robinson, *Handf. Pleas. Delights*, 42 (Arber), Some are as sure as lock and key. 1630: *Wine, Beere, Ale, etc.*, 27 (Hanford, 1915), Art not thou kept vnder locke and key, confinde to some corner of a cellar? 1693: Dryden, *Juvenal*, Sat. vi. l. 464, Keep

close your women under lock and key.
1740 : North, *Examen*, 112, There was
a paper found under his lordship's lock
and key in his closet. 1894 : R. L. S.,
St. Ives, ch. xii., The great thing is to
have me under lock and key. 1925 :
Bodleian Quart. Record, iv. 192, Books
of the smaller sizes, which were kept
under lock and key.

Lock, stock and barrel. 1817 : Scott,
in Lockhart's *Life*, iv. 102, She wants
stock, lock, and barrel to put her into
repair. 1914 : H. A. Vachell, *Quinney's*,
bk. ii. ch. xxiii. (i.), I'd sooner be ruined,
lock, stock, and barrel, than give my
daughter to that man !

**Lock will hold against the power of
gold, No.** 1640 : Herbert, *Jac. Prudentum.* 1670 : Ray, 12. 1732 : Fuller,
No. 6236. 1875 : A. B. Cheales, *Proverb.
Folk-Lore*, 99.

Lockington Wakes, Put up your pipes
and go to. 1678 : Ray, 317. 1790 : Grose,
Prov. Gloss., s.v. " Leicestershire."

Lombard Street to a china orange, All
—with variants for the orange. 1752 :
Murphy, *Gray's Inn Journal*, No. xi.,
30 Dec., I'll lay all Lombard-street to
an egg-shell that it is true. 1819 :
Moore, *Tom Cribb's Mem.*, 38, All
Lombard Street to ninepence. 1826 :
G. Daniel, *Sworn at Highgate*, I. iv.,
I'd bet Lombard Street to a Brumma-
gem sixpence. 1849 : Lytton, *Caxtons*,
Pt. IV. ch. iii., " It is Lombard Street
to a China orange," quoth Uncle Jack.
1898 : *Sun*, 7 June, Lombard Street to
a china orange did not represent the
odds against Horsford. 1918 : Muirhead, *Blue Guide to London*, 375, Lombard Street, the proverbial wealth of
which is indicated in the phrase " All
. . . China orange." 1921 : A. Dobson, *Later Essays*, i. 11, The eighteenth-
century " All . . . China orange."

London. 1. *A London jury ; hang
half and save half.* Said also of Kentish
and Middlesex juries—*see* quots. 1608 :
Middleton, *Trick to Catch Old One*, IV. v.,
Thou that goest upon Middlesex juries,
and wilt make haste to give up thy
verdict, because thou wilt not lose thy
dinner. 1662 : Fuller, *Worthies*, ii. 340
(1840). 1732 : Fuller, No. 231, A

Kentish jury ; hang half and save half.
1790 : Grose, *Prov. Gloss.*, s.v. "London."

2. *London Beer. See* **Derby ale.**

3. *London lickpenny. c.* 1440 : attrib.
to Lydgate, *London Lyckpeny* [title].
1600 : J. Day, *Blind Beggar*, II. ii.,
London lickpenny call ye it,—t'as
lick'd me with a witness. 1641 : in
Harl. Miscell., i. 484 (1744), Do as you
please, but you will find the old proverb
true, *London Lickpenny.* 1710–11 :
Swift, *Journal to Stella*, 15 Jan., It has
cost me three guineas to-day, for a
periwig . . . Well, London lickpenny ;
I find it true. 1790 : Grose, *Prov.
Gloss.*, s.v. " London."

4 *She hath been at London to call a
strea a straw, and a waw a wall.* Cheshire.
1670 : Ray, 218. 1790 : Grose, *Prov.
Gloss.*, s.v. " Cheshire." 1913 : E. M.
Wright, *Rustic Speech, etc.*, 1, There is
a very old proverb in Cheshire, applied
to any one who goes out of the county
for improvement, and returns without
having gained much ; such a one is said
to have " been at London to learn to
call a streea a straw." 1917 : Bridge,
Cheshire Proverbs, 108.

5. *The Fire of London was a punishment for gluttony.* 1790 : Grose, *Prov.
Gloss.*, s.v. " London."

6. *They agree like the clocks o/
London.* 1589 : Nashe, in *Works*, i. 111
(Grosart), The preachers of England
begin to strike and agree like the clocks
of England, that neuer meete iumpe on
a point together. 1678 : Ray, 325.
1823 : D'Israeli, *Cur. of Lit.*, 2nd ser.,
i. 469 (1824), It was probably some
sarcastic Italian, and perhaps, horo-
loger, who, to describe the disagreement
of persons, proverbed our nation—
" They agree like the clocks of London ! "

See also **Country** (3) ; **Lincoln** ; **Lord
Mayor** ; **Oxford** (1) and (2) ; **Ware** ; and
Which way.

**London Bridge was built upon wool-
packs.** *c.* 1685 : Aubrey, *Nat. Hist.
Wilts*, 98 (1847), There is a saying also
that London-Bridge . . . 1708 : *Brit.
Apollo*, i. No. 43, col. 3, Is the
receiv'd report of London-Bridge's
being founded upon wool, true? 1812 :
Brady, *Clavis Cal.*, i. 194, The very

common [saying] " that London Bridge
was built upon wool-sacks." 1913 :
W. Whitten, *Londoner's London*, 308,
The saying that the bridge is " built
upon wool-packs," refers to the impost
on wool which helped to defray its cost.

**London Bridge was made for wise
men to go over and fools to go under.**
This refers to the danger incurred by
boats in " shooting " the arches of the
old bridge. 1639 : Clarke, 249. 1670 :
Ray, 16. 1874 : Smiles, *Lives of
Engineers*, ii. 64. 1913 : W. Whitten,
Londoner's London, 308.

**Londoner-like ask as much more as
you will take.** 1678 : Ray, 349.

Lone sheep. *See* **Sheep** (15).

Long=Longdon, Staffs. 1883 : Burne,
Shropsh. Folk-Lore, 583, The stoutest
beggar that goes by the way, Can't
beg through Long on a midsummer's
day.

Long absent soon forgotten. 1611 :
Cotgrave, s.v. " Ami," Long absence
alters affection. 1670 : Ray, 55. 1736 :
Bailey, *Dict.*, s.v. " Absent." Cf. **Out
of sight**; and **Seldom seen.**

Long and lazy. 1591 : Florio, *Second
Frutes*, 189, If long, she is lazy, if little,
she is lowde, If fayre, she is slutish, if
foule, she is proud. 1648 : Herrick,
Hesp., No. 357, Long and lazy.
That was the proverb. 1732 : Fuller,
No. 3267.

Long and slender, like a cat's elbow.
Ibid., No. 3268.

Long and the short of it, The. " The
short and the long " was common earlier
than the now more usual form, and is
still used. *c.* 1330 : Brunne, tr. Langtoft's *Chron.*, 222 (Hearne), To say longly
or schorte, alle [that] armes bare. 1571 :
Edwards, *Damon, etc.*, in Hazlitt, *Old
Plays*, iv. 47, Howsover it be, this is
the short and long. 1589 : Nashe, in
Works, i. 185 (Grosart), This is the
short and the long, and the somme of
all. 1599 : Shakespeare, *Henry V.*, III.
ii., . . . the breff and the long. 1622 :
Taylor (Water-Poet), in *Works*, 2nd
pagin., 3 (1630), Here's the long and
short on't. 1676 : Shadwell, *Libertine*,
II., The short and the long on't is . . .
1681 : W. Robertson, *Phraseol. Gener-*

alis, 837, The long and the short of
a business; Summa rei. 1748 : Richardson, *Clarissa*, i. 289 (1785), The short
and the long was . . . *c.* 1760 : Foote,
Lame Lover, II., And that, Mr. John,
is the long and the short on't. 1838 :
Dickens, *Twist*, ch. xx., " The short
and the long of what you mean," said
Nancy. 1849 : C. Brontë, *Shirley*, ch.
ix., The short and the long of it is . . .
1850 : Dickens, *Chuzzlewit*, ch. xxvii.,
The long and the short of it is . . .
1886 : R. L. S., *Kidnapped*, ch. xviii.,
The short and the long of it is . . .

**Long as he is lither [lazy], If he were
as, he might thatch a house without a
ladder.** 1678 : Ray, 257. 1828 : Carr,
Craven Dialect, i. 294. 1890 : P. H.
Emerson, *Wild Life*, 72, You are as
long as you are lazy. 1917 : Bridge,
Cheshire Proverbs, 76.

**Long as I live, I'll spit in my parlour,
As.** 1732 : Fuller, No. 710.

**Long be thy legs, and short be thy
life.** 1546 : Heywood, *Proverbs*, Pt. II.
ch. vii.

Long beards heartless, etc. *See* quot.
1589 : Puttenham, *Eng. Poesie*, 184
(Arber), The craking Scotts as the
Cronicle reportes at a certaine time
made this bald rime vpon the Englishman. Long beards hartlesse, Painted
hoodes witlesse : Gay coates gracelesse,
Make all England thriftlesse. 1602–3 :
Manningham, *Diary*, 116 (Camden S.).
1605 : Camden, *Remains*, 211 (1870),
As in the time of King Edward the
third . . . " Long beards . . ."

Long-Compton. *See* quot. 1719 : R.
Gale, in *Stukeley Mem.*, iii. 155 (Surtees
S.), The country tradition joyning them
together in a rhyme they all have—If
Long Compton thou can'st see, Then
King of England thou shalt be. 1743 :
Stukeley, *Abury*, 83 [as in 1719]. 1849 :
Halliwell, *Pop. Rhymes and Nursery
Tales*, 193 [as in 1719].

Long - Crown. *See* quot. 1847 :
Halliwell, *Dict.*, s.v., " That caps Long-
Crown, and he capped the Devil," a
Lincolnshire saying in reference to a
great falsehood.

**Long day, Not a, but a good heart rids
work.** 1611 : Cotgrave, s.v. " Grand,"

Not long dayes, but strong hearts, dis-
patch a worke. 1640: Herbert, *Jac.
Prudentum*.

Long day that never pay, They take a.
1678 : Ray, 188.

Longer east, the shorter west, The.
1546 : Heywood, *Proverbs*, Pt. I. ch.
xiii. 1605 : Camden, *Remains*, 333
(1870). 1670 : Ray, 84. 1732 : Fuller,
No. 6108, The longer east, the longer
[*sic*] west. 1899 : Dickinson, *Cumb.
Gloss.*, 192, Longer east shorter west.
A deficiency in one part is compensated
by abundance in another.

Longer forenoon, the shorter afternoon, The. 1546 : Heywood, *Proverbs*,
Pt. I. ch. xiii.

Longer lives a good fellow than a dear
year. 1678 : Ray, 170.

Longest day must have an end, The.
1580 : Lyly, *Euphues*, 250 (Arber), The
longest summers day hath his euening.
1694 : Southerne, *Fatal Marriage*, IV.
ii. [with " will " for " must "]. 1732 :
Fuller, No. 4633.

Longest way round, nearest way
home, The. 1635 : Quarles, *Emblemes*,
bk. iv. No. ii., The next way home's the
farthest way about. 1681 : W. Robertson, *Phraseol. Generalis*, 1300, The
farthest way about is the nearest way
home. 1734 : Fielding, *Intrig. Chambermaid*, I. i., The young fellow finds,
though he go round about, It's only to
come The nearest way home. 1776 :
Colman, *Spleen*, II., The longest way
about is the shortest way home, you
know.

Long foretold Long last. Short notice
Soon past. 1875 : A. B. Cheales, *Proverb.
Folk-Lore*, 26.

Long harvest. *See* Harvest (7).

Long home = the grave. 1303 :
Brunne, *Handlyng Synne*, l. 9195, And
thy traueyle shalt thou sone ende, For
to thy long home sone shalt thou wende.
c. 1400 : Mirk's *Festial*, 295 (E.E.T.S.),
Ther is also a mete-yorde leyde be hym
[the corpse] instede of a staf, in token-
yng that he goth to hys long home.
1598 : *Servingmans Comfort*, in *Inedited
Tracts*, 128 (Hazlitt), Yet would I, at
my owne charges, haue seene him
honestly brought foorth to his' long

home (as the saying is). 1611 : *Bible,
Eccles.* xii. 5. Before 1681 : J. Lacy,
Sauny the Scot, V. 1762 : Smollett, *Sir
L. Greaves*, ch. iv., A fever, which, in a
few days, brought Sir Everhard to his
long home. 1843 : Dickens, *Chuzzlewit*,
ch. xxv., Playing at berryins down in
the shop, and follerin' the order-book
to its long home in the iron safe !

Longing than loathing, Better go
away. 1732 : Fuller, No. 942.

Long jesting was never good. 1640 :
Herbert, *Jac. Prudentum*.

Long journey, In a, straw weighs.
Ibid.

Long lane and a fair wind, and always
thy heels here away, A. 1678 : Ray, 75.

Long lane that has no turning, It is a.
1670 : Ray, 117, It's a long run that
never turns. 1748 : Richardson, *Clarissa*, iv. 237 (1785). 1774 : C. Dibdin,
Quaker, II. iii. 1849 : Lytton, *Caxtons*,
Pt. XVII. ch. i. 1880 : A. Dobson,
Old-world Idylls: "Dead Letter," II.

Long life hath long misery. 1611 :
Cotgrave, s.v. " Vivre," The longer life
the greater griefe. 1669 : *Politeuphuia*,
203, A long life hath commonly long
cares annexed with it. 1732 : Fuller,
No. 3270.

Long liveth. *See* Merry man.

Long looked for comes at last. *c.* 1483 :
Quatuor Sermones, 53 (Roxb. Cl.), A
thynge that is long desyred at the last
it comyth. 1605 : Armin, *Foole vpon
Foole*, 11 (Grosart), Though long looke
for comes at last. 1658 : in *Musarum
Deliicæ, etc.*, i. 261 (Hotten). 1740 :
Richardson, *Pamela*, i. 179 (1883),
Here's a letter for you : long looked for
is come at last.

Long spoon. *See* Devil (18).

Long standers. *See* quot. 1600 : J. Day,
Blind Beggar, IV. iii., 'Tis an old saying in our country [Norfolk], " Long
standers are but short doers."

Long standing and small offering
maketh poor parsons. 1546 : Heywood,
Proverbs, Pt. II. ch. ix. 1659 : Howell,
4 [with " poor " for " small " and
" priests " for " parsons "].

Long time to know the world's pulse,
There needs a. 1640 : Herbert, *Jac.
Prudentum*. 1670 : Ray, 30.

Long tongue is a sign of a short hand, **A.** 1640 : Herbert, *Jac. Prudentum*. 1670 : Ray, 26. 1880 : Spurgeon, *Ploughman's Pictures*, 28, A long tongue generally goes with a short hand.

Long-tongued wives go long with bairn. 1670 : Ray, 49.

Look, *subs. Looks breed love.* 1639 : Clarke, 28.

Look, *verb.* 1. *A man need not look in your mouth to know how old you are.* 1639 : Clarke, 280. 1670 : Ray, 188.

2. *He looks as if he had eaten live birds.* 1868 : *Quart. Review*, cxxv. 231, In modern parlance a person unwontedly animated is told he looks as if " he had eaten live birds."

3. *He looks as if he had neither won nor lost.* 1590 : Lodge, *Rosalynde*, 120 (Hunt. Cl.), The shepheard stoode as though hee had neither wonne nor lost. 1594 : Greene, *Frier Bacon*, sc. xiii. 1678 : Ray, 257. 1738 : Swift, *Polite Convers.*, Dial. I., What's the matter? You look as if you had neither won nor lost. 1828 : Carr, *Craven Dialect*, i. 299, He looks as an heed neyther won nor lost.

4. *He looks as if he had sold all and took nothing for it.* 1659 : Howell, 13.

5. *He looks like a tooth-drawer,* i.e. thin and meagre. 1620 : B. & F., *Philaster*, I. i., The outlandish prince looks like a toothdrawer. 1678 : Ray, 83.

6. *He looks not well to himself that looks not ever.* 1611 : Cotgrave, s.v. " Garder," He lookes not, that still lookes not, to himselfe. 1640 : Herbert, *Jac. Prudentum.*

7. *He looks one way and rows another.* 1583 : Melbancke, *Philotinus*, sig. P1, And so imitate the waterman, which looketh one waye, and roweth another. 1636 : Dekker, *Wond. of a Kingdom,* V. ii., She has but us'd you As watermen use their fares, for she look'd one way And row'd another. 1694 : D'Urfey, *Quixote*, Pt. II. Act III. sc. i., Like rowers we look one way—move another. 1740 : North, *Examen*, Pref., v, The opposers . . . bore a false face, looking one way and rowing another. 1869 : Spurgeon, *John Ploughman*, ch. xviii.

8. *He that looks not before finds himself*

behind. 1640 : Herbert, *Jac. Prudentum*. 1670 : Ray, 3. 1736 : Bailey, *Dict.*, s.v. " Before."

9. *Look before you leap.* 1528 : Tyndale, *Obed. of Chryst. Man*, 304 (P.S.), " Look ere thou leap "; whose literal sense is, " Do nothing suddenly, or without advisement." 1567 : Painter, *Pal. of Pleasure*, iii. 53 (Jacobs), According to the common saying : He that loketh not before he leapeth, may chaunce to stumble before he sleepeth. 1621 : Burton, *Melancholy*, II. iii. 7, p. 427 (1836). 1705 : Steele, *Tender Husband*, III. ii., I love to look before I leap. 1849 : C. Brontë, *Shirley*, ch. ix., When you feel tempted to marry, think of our four sons and two daughters, and look twice before you leap. 1920 : Hudson, *Dead Man's Plack*, 41, Let me . . . exercise caution and look before I leap.

10. *Look behind thee and consider what thou wast.* 1659 : Howell, 21.

11. *Look high and fall low.* 1670 : Ray, 13, Look high and fall into a cowturd. 1732 : Fuller, No. 3272.

12. *Look like a runner. See* **Devil** (122).

13. *Look not too high lest a chip fall in your eye.* 1584 : Robinson, *Handf. Pleas. Delights*, 39 (Arber). 1696 : D'Urfey, *Quixote*, Pt. III. Act II. sc. ii. 1732 : Fuller, No. 6316.

14. *Look on the wall and it will not bite you.* 1678 : Ray, 83 [" spoken in jeer to such as are bitten with mustard." —Ray, 65 (1737)].

15. *Look to him, jailor, there's a frog in the stocks.* 1678 : Ray, 72. 1732 : Fuller, No. 3274.

16. *To look as if he had eaten his bedstraw.* 1678 : Ray, 286.

17. *To look as though he had sucked his dam through a hurdle.* 1670 : Ray, 170. 1732 : Fuller, No. 1971.

18. *To look both ways for Sunday.* 1828 : Carr, *Craven Dialect*, ii. 180, " He was born in the middle of the week, and looked baath ways for Sunday "—a burlesque expression for a person who squints. 1854 : Baker, *Northants Gloss.*, s.v. " Sunday " [as in 1828]. 1920 : E. Gepp, *Essex Dialect Dict.*, 35, The phrase " to look all ways for Sunday "

is used of a bewildered person failing
to see the obvious. The similar phrase
" to look two ways for Easter " is used
in some parts. Cf. No. 24.

19. *To look like a dog that hath lost his
tail.* 1678 : Ray, 286.

20. *To look like a drowned mouse.*
c. 1591 : Shakespeare, 1 *Henry VI.*, I.
ii., Or piteous they will look, like
drowned mice. 1678 : Ray, 286.

21. *To look like a Jew.* 1611 : Coryat,
Crudities, i. 372 (1905), Our English
proverbe : To looke like a Jewe (whereby
is meant sometimes a weather beaten
wasp-faced fellow, sometimes a phren-
ticke and lunaticke person, sometimes
one discontented).

22. *To look like a strained hair in a
can.* 1670 : Ray, 206. 1917 : Bridge,
Cheshire Proverbs, 140.

23. *To look like the picture of ill luck.*
1639 : Clarke, 119. 1670 : Ray, 206.

24. *To look nine ways.* 1542 : Udall,
tr. Erasmus' *Apoph.*, 203 (1877),
Squyntyied he was, and looked nyne
wayes. Before 1680 : Butler, *Remains*,
ii. 213 (1759), Which commonly is
squint-ey'd, and looks nine ways at
once. 1688 : Crowne, *City Politiques*,
I. i., He looks ten ways at once. 1696 :
D'Urfey, *Quixote*, Pt. III. Act III. sc. ii.,
I'll make her look nine ways at once
before I have done with her. Cf. No. 18.

25. *To look through the fingers.* 1532 :
Tyndale, *Expos. St. Mathew*, 127 (P.S.),
They either look through the fingers, or
else give thee a flap with a fox-tail, for a
little money. 1535 : Coverdale, *Bible*,
Lev. xx. 4, The people of the londe loke
thorowe the fyngers upon that man
which hath geuen his sede vnto Moloch.
1583 : Stubbes, *Anat. of Abuses*, 100
(N. Sh. S.), The magistrates wincke at it,
or els, as looking thorowe their fingers,
they see it, and will not see it. 1691 :
J. Wilson, *Belphegor*, III. i., Enough to
make a modest woman look through
her fingers.

26. *To look to one's water.* 1546 :
Heywood, *Proverbs*, Pt. I. ch. xi., By
my faith, you come to look in my
water. 1621 : B. & F., *Pilgrim*, III.
iv., Yes still I'll watch his water, he
shall pay for it. 1709 : Manley, *New*

Atlantis, i. 132 (1736), He would have
watched his waters for him to some
purpose. 1894 : Northall, *Folk Phrases*,
31 (E.D.S.), To watch one's waters=To
keep an eye on a person ; to follow his
movements.

27. *You look for hot water under the
ice.* 1732 : Fuller, No. 5933.

28. *You must look where it is not, as
well as where it is.* Ibid., No. 5964.

Lookers on see most of the game.
[Aiunt homines plus in alieno negotio
videre quam in suo.—Seneca, *Ep.*, cix.
16.] 1597 : Bacon, *Essays: "* Followers, etc.," To take aduise of friends
is euer honorable : *For lookers on many
times see more then gamesters.* 1640 : R.
Brome, *Sparagus Garden*, Epil., For we
know lookers on more then the gamsters
see. 1706 : Vanbrugh, *Mistake*, I. i., A
stander-by, sir, sees more than a gamester. 1850 : Smedley, *Frank Fairlegh*,
ch. xlvii. 1909 : Pinero, *Mid-Channel*,
I. p. 43.

Loon in a wash, A, Is as good as a
shilling in a poor man's purse. 1886 :
Swainson, *Folk-Lore of Brit. Birds*, 215
(F.L.S.).

Loose in the haft=unreliable. c. 1325 :
in *Pol. Songs*, 339 (Camden) (O.), Un-
nethe is nu eny man that can eny craft
That he nis a party los in the haft.
c. 1555 : in Wright, *Songs, etc., Philip
and Mary*, 68 (Roxb. Cl.), For, alas !
she was nat sur in the hafte. 1888–90 :
Addy, *Sheffield Gloss.* (E.D.S.), He's a
bit loose i' t' heft. 1889 : Peacock,
Manley, etc., Gloss., 329 (E.D.S.), Lohse
i' th' heft. That is, loose in the handle.
A person of a wild, profligate or wasteful
disposition is called " a lohse i' th' heft."
1917 : Bridge, *Cheshire Proverbs*, 70.

Loose in the hilts=*usually*, unfaithful
in marriage, or loose in life. 1623 :
Webster, *Duchess of Malfi*, II. v., She's
loose i' th' hilts ; grown a notorious
strumpet. 1650 : Howell, *Epist. Ded.*
to Cotgrave's *Dict.*, So in French *cocu*
is taken for one whose wife is loose in
the hilts. 1712 : Motteux, *Quixote*, Pt.
I. bk. iii. ch. vi., The shepherd thought
her no better than she should be, a little
loose in the hilts, and free of her hips.
1745 : Franklin, *Drinker's Dict.*, in

Works, ii. 24 (Bigelow), He's loose in the hilts [drunk]. 1847 : Halliwell, *Dict.*, s.v. " Hilts," She is loose in the hilts, i.e. frail ; a common phrase.

Loose stake may stand long, A. 1639 : Clarke, 44. Cf. **Low Stake.**

Lopp. *See* **Crouse.**

Lord. 1. *A lord's heart and a beggar's purse agree not.* *c.* 1430 : Lydgate, *Minor Poems*, 160 (Percy S.), A lordis herte, a purs that peiseth lihte [are not commendable]. *c.* 1510 : A. Barclay, *Egloges*, 39 (Spens. S.), A lordes stomake and a beggers pouche Full ill accordeth. 1592 : G. Harvey, *Works*, i. 207 (Grosart), The two vnmeete companions, a lordes heart, and a beggers purse. 1659 : Howell, 5, A lords heart and a beggars purse. Cf. **Lady's heart.**

2. *He is a lord for a year and a day, etc.* 1869 : Hazlitt, 164, He is a lord for a year and a day, and she is a lady for ever and aye. This is said of the Lord Mayor of York and his spouse ; the latter, it is suggested, never renounces at heart the fugitive dignity conferred on her husband for the year of his mayoralty. Higson's *MSS. Coll.*, No. 24.

Lord Mayor. 1. *Good manners to except my Lord Mayor.* [1655 : Fuller, *Church Hist.*, bk. iii. § vi. (14), The richest and proudest (always good manners to except Cardinal Wolsey).] 1662 : Fuller, *Worthies*, ii. 346 (1840), Good manners to except my Lord Mayor of London. 1670 : Ray, 242. 1790 : Grose, *Prov. Gloss.*, s.v. " London."

2. *I have dined as well as my Lord Mayor of London.* 1580 : Lyly, *Euphues*, 437 (Arber), Hauing halfe dyned, they say as it were in a prouerbe, y^{at} they are as well satisfied as the Lorde Maior of London whom they think to fare best, though he eate not most. 1633 : Rowley, *Match at Midnight*, I. 1659 : Gayton, *Art of Longevity*, 12, Shall find a satisfaction in his fare, As great as if h' had din'd with my Lord May'r. 1738 : Swift, *Polite Convers.*, Dial. II. 1807 : Sir R. Wilson, *Journal*, in *Life*, II. viii. 253 (1862) (O.), I . . . would not have exchanged meals with the Lord Mayor of London.

3. *Like my Lord Mayor's fool, full of business, and nothing to do.* 1738 : Swift, *Polite Convers.*, Dial. I.

4. *Like my Lord Mayor's fool, I like everything that is good.* 1678 : Ray, 247, I am a fool, I love everything that is good. 1812 : Brady, *Clavis Cal.*, ii. 252, " The Lord Mayor's Fool, who likes everything that is good," is yet a common expression. 1895 : J. R. Robinson, *Old Q.*, 123, In drinking as in eating, March was a veritable Lord Mayor's fool ; " the best of everything did for him."

Lose, *verb.* 1. *A man loseth his time that comes early to a bad bargain.* 1732 : Fuller, No. 286.

2. *A man may lose his goods for want of demanding them.* 1633 : Draxe, 17. 1670 : Ray, 7.

3. *He has lost his leease*=He has broken down. 1917 : Bridge, *Cheshire Proverbs*, 67, . . . The *leease* is the crossing of the yarn up and down over the warp in regular order. If by chance the warp is divided, the leease is then lost and weaving at a standstill.

4. *He has not lost all who has one cast left.* 1670 : Ray, 16 [with "throw to cast" for "cast left"]. 1732 : Fuller, No. 1876.

5. *He loseth his thanks who promiseth and delayeth.* 1633 : Draxe, 42. 1681 : W. Robertson, *Phraseol. Generalis*, 844. 1732 : Fuller, No. 1977.

6. *He loseth many a good bit that striveth with his betters.* 1659 : Howell, *Proverbs : Brit.-Eng.*, 9.

7. *He loseth nothing that loseth not God.* 1640 : Herbert, *Jac. Prudentium.* 1732 : Fuller, No. 1976, He loseth nothing that keepeth God for his friend.

8. *He would rather lose his friend than his jest.* Before 1598 : Ld. Burghley, in Peck, *Desid. Curiosa*, 49 (1779), They would rather leese their friend then their jest. 1630 : Brathwait, *Eng. Gent.*, *etc.*, 137 (1641), These many times . . . will not sticke to lose their friend rather than their jest. 1709 : Cibber, *Rival Fools*, I. [with " dinner " for " friend "]. 1744–6 : Mrs. Haywood, *Fem. Spectator*, bk. 21, iv. 135.

9. *He'll not lose his jest for his guest, if he be a Jew.* 1639 : Clarke, 255.

10. *I have lost all and found myself.*
Ibid., 198.

11. *Lose a leg rather than life.* 1732 :
Fuller, No. 3278.

12. *Lose a wife. See* Wife (13).

13. *Lose an hour in the morning and
you'll be all day hunting for it.* 1859 :
Smiles, *Self-Help*, 275 (1869), It was
wittily said by Lord Chesterfield of the
old Duke of Newcastle—" His Grace
loses an hour in the morning, and is looking for it all the rest of the day." 1875 :
A. B. Cheales, *Proverb. Folk-Lore*, 18.

14. *Lose nothing for (want of) asking.*
1586 : B. Young, tr. Guazzo's *Civil
Convers.*, fo. 218, Nothing is lost for
asking. 1639 : Clarke, 38, Hee'l not
lose it for asking. 1665 : R. Howard,
Committee, I., I see thou wouldst not
lose any thing for want of asking.
1670 : Ray, 58.

15. *Lose with a nut. See* Apple (13).

16. *What we lose in hake, we shall
have in herring.* Corn. 1602 : Carew,
Surv. of Cornwall, 105 (1811). 1639 :
Clarke, 17, What I lost i' th' salt fish
I gained i' th' red herrings. 1750 :
R. Heath, *Account of Scilly*, 324. 1864 :
" Cornish Proverbs," in *N. & Q.*, 3rd
ser., vi. 494.

17. *Who loseth his due getteth no
thanks.* 1640 : Herbert, *Jac. Prudentum.*
1670 : Ray, 8. 1732 : Fuller, No. 5709.

Losers leave to speak, Give. 1533 :
More, in *Works*, 1018 (1557), Hit
is an olde curtesye at the cardes
perdy, to let the leser haue hys
wordes.' 1594 : *First Part Content.*,
36 (Sh. S.), I can giue the loser
leaue to speake. 1630 : Taylor (Water-
Poet), *Works*, 2nd pagin., 233. 1673 :
Wycherley, *Gent. Danc.-Master*, V. i.
1769 : Colman, *Man and Wife*, III., We
must give losers leave to talk, you
know. 1818 : Scott, *Heart of Midl.*,
ch. xlviii., The Captain . . . was in the
pouting mood not unusual to losers,
and which, says the proverb, must be
allowed to them.

Loss embraceth shame. 1640 : Herbert, *Jac. Prudentum.*

**Loss of one is a gain for two and a
chance for twenty more, The.** Corn.
19th cent. (Mr. C. Lee).

**Loss of the bell more than the loss of
the steeple, To fear the.** 1678 : Ray, 351.

Lost, *part. adj.* 1. *As good lost as found.*
1639 : Clarke, 68. 1670 : Ray, 184.

2. *It is lost that is unsought.* 1546 :
Heywood, *Proverbs*, Pt. I. ch. xi. 1659 :
Howell, 14.

3. *Lost in the hundred. See* Hundred
and County.

4. *Lost time is never found again.*
1736 : Franklin, *Way to Wealth*, in
Works, i. 443 (Bigelow).

" **Loth to drink and loth to leave off**,"
they say. 1880 : Spurgeon, *Ploughman's
Pictures*, 40.

Loud as a horn, As. 1659 : Howell, 19.
1670 : Ray, 206.

Louse. 1. *A louse is better than no
meat.* 1639 : Clarke, 241, Better a louse
i' the pot than no flesh at all. 1656 :
Musarum Deliciæ, i. 31 (Hotten). Cf.
Better a mouse.

2. *As sure as louse in bosom.* 1659 :
Howell, 5. 1670 : Ray, 208. 1917 :
Bridge, *Cheshire Proverbs*, 22.

3. *He'd drive a louse a mile for the
skin and tallow of 'en.* S. Devon. 1869 :
Hazlitt, 198.

4. *He'd skin a louse for the sake of
its hide.* 1591 : Florio, *Second Frutes*,
117, He was such a couetous miser, that
he would haue fleade a louse to saue
the skin of it. 1623 : Wodroephe,
Spared Houres, 285, He would haue
flayed a louse for her skin, he was so
couetous. 1916 : B. Duffy, *The Coiner*,
7, Thrifty ! Man, she'd skin a flea for
his hide.

5. *If a louse miss its footing on his
coat, 'twill be sure to break its neck.* 1362 :
Langland, *Plowman*, A, v. 112, But yif
a lous couthe lepe I con hit not i-leue
Heo scholde wandre on that walk hit
was so thred-bare. 1530 : Palsgrave,
620, He hath made my gowne so bare
that a lowse can get no holde on it.
c. 1580 : Spelman, *Dialogue*, 116 (Roxb.
Cl.), Truth among clothyers hath lesse
harborowe then the lowce upon a thryd-
bare clothe. *c.* 1610 : *Ballad*, quoted in
Wright, *Essays on Middle Ages*, ii. 277
(1846), Thy doublet and breech that
were so playne, On which a louse could
scarse remayne. 1732 : Fuller, No. 2661.

6. *Louse in Pomfret. See* Pomfret.

See also **Beggar** (1) and (16) ; **Crouse**; and **Three skips.**

Love, *subs.* 1. *All is fair in love and war. c.* 1630 : B. & F., *Lovers' Progress,* V. ii., All stratagems In love, and that the sharpest war, are lawful. 1687 : A. Behn, *Emp. of the Moon,* I. iii., Advantages are lawful in love and war. 1710 : Centlivre, *Man's Bewitch'd,* V. i., Stratagems ever were allow'd of in love and war. 1850 : Smedley, *Frank Fairlegh,* ch. 1. 1906 : Lucas, *Listener's Lure,* 196.

2. *He that hath love in his breast, hath spurs in his sides.* 1640 : Herbert, *Jac. Prudentum.* 1732 : Fuller, No. 2160 [with " at his heels " for " in his sides "].

3. *Mirk's Festial,* 165 (E.E.T.S.), For loue hath no lake. 1546 : Heywood, *Proverbs,* Pt. I. ch. iv. 1592 : Lyly, *Mother Bombie,* I. iii. 1641 : R. Brome, *Joviall Crew,* III., Where love is, there's no lack. 1670 : Ray, 117.

4. *In love's wars he who flyeth is conqueror.* 1732 : Fuller, No. 2819.

5. *Love and a cough cannot be hid. c.* 1300 : *Cursor Mundi,* l. 4276, Luken luue at þe end wil kiþ (Concealed love will show itself at last). 1590 : Greene, in *Works,* vii. 294 (Grosart), There are foure things cannot be hydden. 1 The cough. 2 Loue. 3 Anger. 4 And sorrow. 1640 : Herbert, *Jac. Prudentum.* 1709 : Mandeville, *Virgin Unmask'd,* 196 (1724). 1732 : Fuller, No. 3298, Love, the itch, and a cough cannot be hid.

6. *Love and business teach eloquence.* 1640 : Herbert, *Jac. Prudentum.*

7. *Love and knowledge live not together.* 1611 : Cotgrave, s.v. " Aimer." 1658 : Flecknoe, *Enigm. Characters,* 134, He is bound by the proverb; 'Tis impossible to love and to be wise. 1666 : Torriano, *Piazza Univ.,* 7, Knowledge and love, altogether cotten not.

8. *Love and lordship like no fellowship.* [Non bene conveniunt, nec in una sede morantur Maiestas et Amor.— Ovid, *Met.,* ii. 846.] *c.* 1386 : Chaucer, *Knight's Tale,* l. 767, Ful sooth is seyd that love ne lordshipe Wol noght, his thankes, have no felaweshipe. *c.* 1440 : Lydgate, *Fall of Princes,* bk. vi. l. 2221,

Vnto purpos was saide ful yore agon, How that loue nouther hih lordshippe . . . Nowther of hem wolde haue no felashipe. 1587 : Greene, in *Works,* vi. 251 (Grosart), Ambition . . . not suffring loue or lordship to brooke any fellowship. 1658 : R. Brome, *Love-sick Court,* I. ii., Love, and ambition (I have heard men say) admit no fellowship. 1681 : W. Robertson, *Phraseol. Generalis,* 846. 1736 : Bailey, *Dict.,* s.v. " Love," Love and lordship never like fellowship.

9. *Love and pease porridge will make their way.* 1674 : Head and Kirkman, *Eng. Rogue,* iii. 176, You know the old proverb, that sad are the effects of love and pease porridge. 1738 : Swift, *Polite Convers.,* Dial. I., Ay ; they say love and pease porridge are two dangerous things ; one breaks the heart ; and the other the belly.

10. *Love and pride stock Bedlam.* 1732 : Fuller, No. 3284.

11. *Love asks faith, and faith asks firmness.* 1670 : Ray, 16.

12. *Love comes in at the window and goes out at the door.* 1605 : Camden, *Remains,* 327 (1870). 1670 : Ray, 47. 1732 : Fuller, No. 3285 [with " flies " for " goes "].

13. *Love does much but money does all.* 1587 : Greene, in *Works,* iii. 61 (Grosart). 1611 : Cotgrave, s.v. " Amour." 1667 : L'Estrange, *Quevedo's Visions,* 38 (1904). 1732 : Fuller, No. 3286 [with " more " for " all "].

14. *Love is a sweet torment.* 1633 : Draxe, 119.

15. *Love is above King or Kaiser, lord or laws.* 1583 : Greene, in *Works,* ii. 122 (Grosart).

16. *Love is blind. c.* 1386 : Chaucer, *Merch. Tale,* l. 354, For love is blind al day, and may nat see. *c.* 1490 : *Partonope,* l. 10796, In this case love is blynde. 1566 : Painter, *Pal. of Pleasure,* ii. 43 (Jacobs). 1621 : Burton, *Melancholy,* III. ii. 4, 1, p. 564 (1836), Love is blind, as the saying is. 1733 : Gay, *Achilles,* III. 1837 : Dickens, *Pickwick,* ch. xvii. 1893 : Gilbert, *Utopia,* I.

17. *Love is full of busy fear. c.* 1374 : Chaucer, *Troylus,* bk. iv. l. 1645, For

I am ever a-gast, for why men rede,
That "love is thing ay ful of bisy
drede." 1506: A. Barclay, *Cast. of
Labour*, sig. D2, This prouerbe that I
the lere . . . Loue goth neuer without
fere. 1595 : Munday, *John a Kent*, 50
(Sh. S.), Loove is full of feare. 1654 :
Flecknoe, *Loves Dominion*, II. i., Love's
a solicitous thing, and full of fears.
1736 : Bailey, *Dict.*, s.v. "Love," Love
is never without jealousy.

18. *Love is liberal.* 1639 : Clarke, 28.

19. *Love is not found in the market.*
1640 : Herbert, *Jac. Prudentum*.

20. *Love is the loadstone of love.* 1732 :
Fuller, No. 3288. 1870 : Hawker, *Footprints of Former Men*, 77, No man ever
more fully realised the truth of the
saying that "Love makes love."

21. *Love is the true price of love.*
c. 1420 : in *Twenty-six Poems*, 76
(E.E.T.S.), Loue for loue is euenest
boughte. 1569 : E. Fenton, *Wonders of
Nature*, 66 v⁰, Al things . . . be priced
at a certaine rate, except Loue, which
can not be payed but wyth loue. 1631 :
Mabbe, *Celestina*, 138 (T.T.), Love is
never pay'd but with pure love. 1696 :
Mrs. Manley, *Lost Lover*, V. iii., What
can pay love but love? 1700 : Dryden,
Pal. and Arcite, ii. 373, For 'tis their
maxim,—Love is love's reward. 1837 :
J. S. Knowles, *Love Chase*, I. ii., But
love's the coin to market with for love.
1852 : FitzGerald, *Polonius*, 122 (1903).

22. *Love is without law.* 1581 : B. Rich,
Farewell, 191 (Sh. S.). 1639 : Clarke, 27,
Love is lawlesse. 1700 : Dryden, *Pal.
and Arcite*, i. 326, Know'st thou not, no
law is made for love? Cf. **Lover.**

23. *Love lasteth as long as the money
endureth.* 1474 : Caxton, *Chesse*, III.
iii. [cited as "a comyn proverbe in
Englond"].

24. *Love laughs at locksmiths.* 1803 :
Colman, jr., *Love Laughs at Locksmiths*
[title]. 1898 : W. J. Locke, *Idols*, ch. vi.
1923 : Lucas, *Advisory Ben*, 4, We know
how Love treats locksmiths.

25. *Love lives in cottages as well as
in courts.* 1590 : Lodge, *Rosalynde*, 95
(Hunt. Cl.), Loue lurkes assoone about
a sheepcoate as a pallaice. 1611 :
Cotgrave, s.v. "Amourettes" [with

"bides" for "lives"]. 1670 : Ray, 16.
1732 : Fuller, No. 3290, Love lives
more in cottages than courts.

26. *Love locks no cupboards.* 1639 :
Clarke, 26.

27. *Love looks for love again.* 1570 :
Barclay, *Mirrour of Good Manners*, 74
(Spens. S.), Shewe thou loue to win loue
in worde, heart and dede. 1591 : Harington, *Orl. Furioso*, bk. xxviii. st. 80,
And sure love craveth love, like asketh
like. 1639 : Clarke, 27. 1751 : Fielding,
Amelia, bk. v. ch. ix., But the devil take
me, if I think anything but love to be
the object of love.

28. *Love makes a good eye squint.*
1640 : Herbert, *Jac. Prudentum*. 1670 :
Ray, 16.

29. *Love makes a wit of the fool.* 1774 :
C. Dibdin, *Quaker*, I. viii., According
unto the proverb, love maketh a wit
of the fool.

30. *Love makes men orators.* 1583 :
Greene, in *Works*, ii. 57 (Grosart), It
hath byn a saying more common then
true, that loue makes al men orators.
1630 : *Tinker of Turvey*, 63 (Halliwell)
[cited as an "old said saw"].

31. *Love of lads and fire of chats
[chips] is soon in and soon out.* c. 1460 :
Good Wyfe wold a Pylgr., l. 83 (E.E.T.S.),
A fyre of sponys [wood-shavings], and
lowe of gromis, Full soun woll be att a
nende. 1670 : Ray, 46. Cf. **Lads' love.**

32. *Love rules his kingdom without a
sword.* 1640 : Herbert, *Jac. Prudentum*.
1666 : Torriano, *Piazza Univ.*, 9. 1853 :
Trench, *Proverbs*, 130 (1905).

33. *Love sees no faults.* 1732 : Fuller,
No. 3297.

34. *Love will creep where it can not
(or may not) go.* c. 1400 : *Towneley
Plays*, 135 (E.E.T.S.), I trow, kynde
will crepe where it may not go. 1481 :
Caxton, *Reynard*, 70 (Arber), Blood
must krepe where it can not goo.
c. 1530 : *Everyman*, in Hazlitt, *Old
Plays*, i. 113 [with "Kind" for "Love"].
1569 : Grafton, *Chron.*, ii. 2 (1809) [with
"Kinne" for "Love"]. 1602 : Rowlands, *Merrie when Goss. meete*, 20
(Hunt. Cl.), They say loue creepeth
where it cannot go. 1658 : *Musarum
Deliciæ*, i. 172 (Hotten) ["can not"].

1753 : Richardson, *Grandison*, i. 403
(1883) ["can not"].   1917 : Bridge,
Cheshire Proverbs, 93 ["can not"].

35. *Love will find a way.* c. 1597 :
Deloney, *Gentle Craft*, ch. xv., Thus loue
you see, can find a way To make both
men and maids obey. c. 1600 : in
Roxb. Ballads, ii. 639 (B.S.) [with
" out " after " find "]. 1662 : Fuller,
Worthies, ii. 227 (1840), But love and
money will find or force a passage.

36. *Neither for love nor money.* 971 :
Blickl. Hom., 43 (O.), Ne for feo, ne for
nanes mannes lufon. *c.* 1310 : in Wright,
Pol. Songs, 302 (Camden S.), Pur amy
ne pur dener Ray ne dait esparnier
(For love nor for pence—A King ought
not to spare). 1595 : *Pedlars Proph.*,
l. 578 (Malone S.), Neither for loue nor
mony they will worke. 1669 : Shadwell, *Royal Shep.*, Prol., If it were to
be had For love or money. 1771 :
Smollett, *Clinker*, in *Works*, vi. 45
(1817), It can't be had for love nor
money. 1894 : Shaw, *Arms and the
Man*, II., You shall never get that out
of me, for love or money.

37. *The love of a woman, etc.* See
quots. 1578 : Florio, *First Fruites*, fo.
25, The loue of a whore and the wine
of a bottle at night is good, in the
mornyng naught. 1629 : *Book of Meery
Riddles*, Prov. 57, The love of a harlot,
and wine of a flagon, is good in the
morning and nought in the evening.
1666 : Torriano, *Piazza Univ.*, 9 [as
in 1578, with " woman " for " whore,"
" evening " for " night," and " spoyl'd "
for " naught "]. 1678 : Ray, 55, The
love of a woman, and a bottle of wine,
Are sweet for a season, but last for a
time. 1732 : Fuller, No. 6401 [as in
1678].

38. *The love of money and the love of
learning rarely meet.* 1651 : Herbert,
Jac. Prudentum, 2nd ed.

39. *There's love in a budget.* 1678 :
Ray, 258.

40. *Though love is blind, yet 'tis not
for want of eyes.* 1732 : Fuller, No. 5004.

41. *When love puts in, friendship is
gone. c.* 1630 : B. & F., *Lovers' Progress*, I. i. [quoted—" as the proverb
says "].

42. *Where love fails.* See Fault (4).

43. *Where love's in the case, the doctor
is an ass.* 1667 : L'Estrange, *Quevedo's
Visions*, 111 (1904) [quoted as " the old
rhyme "]. 1678 : Ray, 50. 1722 : Defoe,
Moll Flanders, in *Works*, iii. 35 (Bohn).
See also **One love.**

Love, verb. 1. *He loves bacon well
that licks the swine-sty door.* 1678 : Ray,
96. 1732 : Fuller, No. 1978 [with " sow's
breech " for " swine-sty door "].

2. *He that does not love a woman.* See
Hate (1).

3. *He that loves Glass without G, Take
away L and that is he.* 1669 : *New Help
to Discourse*, 265. 1678 : Ray, 55. 1732 :
Fuller, No. 6260.

4. *He that loves the tree loves the
branch.* 1639 : Clarke, 285, If you love
the boll, you cannot hate the braunches.
1640 : Herbert, *Jac. Prudentum.*

5. *I love thee like pudding, if thou
wert pie I'd eat thee.* 1678 : Ray, 349.
1685 : S. Wesley, *Maggots*, 24, I love
you so that I could eat ye. 1711 :
Spectator, No. 47, Whom the common
people of all countries admire, and seem
to love so well, that they could eat
them, according to the old proverb.
1738 : Swift, *Polite Convers.*, Dial. II.,
I love him like pye, I'd rather the devil
had him than I.

6. *I love you well but touch not my
pocket.* 1732 : Fuller, No. 2618.

7. *I must love you and leave you.*
1917 : Bridge, *Cheshire Proverbs*, 79,
. . . Often said on taking leave of a
person.

8. *If you love not the noise of bells.*
See **Bell** (5).

9. *Love me little love me long.* 1546 :
Heywood, *Proverbs*, Pt. II. ch. ii. 1580 :
Munday, *Sundry Examples*, 73 (Sh. S.).
1633 : Marlowe, *Jew of Malta*, IV. vi.
1711 : Steele, *Spectator*, No. 140, My
mother says, As he is slow he is sure;
He will love me long, if he love me little.
1859 : Reade, *Love me Little, Love me
Long* [title].

10. *Love me love my dog.* [Qui me
amat, amat et canem meum.—12th
cent. : St. Bernard, *Fest. S. Mich.*,
Ser. i. § 3.] *c.* 1480 : *Early Miscell.*, 62
(Warton Cl.), He that lovythe me

lovythe my hound. 1527 : Tyndale, in
Treatises, 84 (P.S.), We say also, He
that loveth not my dog, loveth not
me. 1583 : Stubbes, *Anat. of Abuses*,
178 (N. Sh. S.). 1664 : in *Musarum
Deliciæ, etc.*, ii. 77 (Hotten). 1714 :
Spectator, No. 579. 1826 : Lamb, *Pop.
Fallacies*, xiii. 1920 : W. H. Mallock,
Memoirs, 42.

11. *Love to live and live to love.* 1576 :
Pettie, *Petite Pall.*, i. 133 (Gollancz),
Whatsoever be your common saying,
that you must as well love to live as
live to love.

12. *Love your neighbour yet pull not
down your hedge.* 1640 : Herbert, *Jac.
Prudentum.* 1763 : Murphy, *Citizen*,
I. ii. 1875 : A. B. Cheales, *Proverb.
Folk-Lore*, 93.

13. *No man loves his fetters, though
they be made of gold.* 1546 : Heywood,
Proverbs, Pt. I. ch. viii. *c.* 1594 :
Bacon, *Promus*, No. 475. 1607 :
Webster, *Sir T. Wyatt*, in *Works*, i. 9
(1857), Who would weave fetters though
they were all of gold? 1670 : Ray, 89.
1732 : Fuller, No. 1522, Fetters of gold
are still fetters ; and silken cords pinch.

14. *One cannot love and be wise.* 1631 :
Eng. Gentlewoman, 288 (1641).

15. *She loves the poor well, but cannot
abide beggars.* Somerset. 1678 : Ray,
350.

16. *They love like chick.* Somerset.
Ibid., 347.

17. *They love too much that die for
love.* 1611 : Cotgrave, s.v. " Mourir "
[with " He " for " They "]. 1670 :
Ray, 16.

18. *They who love most are least set by.*
1659 : Howell, 12. 1670 : Ray, 16.
1748 : Richardson, *Clarissa*, iv. 119
(1785), Those, Mr. Belford, who most
love, are least set by.

19. *To love at the door and leave at the
hatch.* 1678 : Ray, 258. 1732 : Fuller,
No. 5200 [omitting each " at "].

20. *To love it as a dog loves a whip.*
1678 : Ray, 287.

21. *Whom we love best, to them we can
say least.* 1670 : Ray, 47. 1732 : Fuller,
No. 6259.

22. *You love to make much of naught*,
i.e. yourself. 1678 : Ray, 347.

Lover, Who may give law to a ?
[Quis legem dat amantibus? Maior lex
amor est sibi.—6th cent. : Boethius, *De
Consol. Philos.*, bk. iii. metre xii.]
c. 1386 : Chaucer, *Knight's Tale*, l. 306,
Wostow nat wel the olde clerkes sawe,
That who shal yeve a lovere any lawe?
c. 1450 : *Partonope*, l. 8710 (E.E.T.S.),
Ther-for this ys a full old sawe : Who
may gyfe to a louer lawe? 1581 : B.
Rich, *Farewell*, 131 (Sh. S.), What is
he, I praie you, that is able to prescribe
lawes to love? Cf. **Love**, *subs.* (15), (22).

**Lovers live by love as larks live by
leeks.** Desire for alliteration seems to be
the only explanation of the absurd
comparison. 1546 : Heywood, *Proverbs*,
Pt. I. ch. x. 1596 : Churchyard, *Pleas.
Disc. of Court, etc.*, sig. B4 (Boswell,
1816), All one we liue . . . By loue as
larks do liue by leekes. 1623 : Wodroephe, *Spared Houres*, 313, They bee
some that do liue of loue, Well yea, as
larkes do of leekes. 1670 : Ray, 46.
1833 : T. Hook, *Parson's Daughter*, vol.
i. ch. xi , One of those sighing swains
who, the proverb says—why, nobody
has ever exactly ascertained—" live on
love, as larks on leeks." 1884 : H.
Friend, *Flowers and Fl. Lore*, Notes,
641.

Loving comes by looking. 1639 :
Clarke, 28.

Low hedge is easily leapt over, A.
1605 : Camden, *Remains*, 317 (1870).
1670 : Ray, 16. 1732 : Fuller, No. 259.

Low stake standeth long, The. 1546 :
Heywood, *Proverbs*, Pt. II. ch. iv., The
lothe stake standeth longe. *c.* 1594 :
Bacon, *Promus*, No. 485. 1732 : Fuller,
No. 4637 [in the plural]. Cf. **Loose stake.**

**Lower mill-stone grinds as well as
the upper, The.** 1519 : Horman,
Vulgaria, fo. 153, The lower stone can
do no good without the hyar. 1678 :
Ray, 172. 1732 : Fuller, No. 4638
[with " much " for " well "].

Lowly sit, richly warm. 1670 : Ray,
117.

Lubberland. *See* quots. Nares
(*Glossary*, s.v.) says : " There was an
old proverbial saying about ' Lubberland, where the pigs run about ready
roasted, and cry Come eat me.' " 1598 :

Florio, *Worlde of Wordes, Cocagna*, as
we say Lubberland. 1614 : Jonson, *Bart.
Fair*, III. ii.; Will it run off o' the
spit into our mouths, think you, as in
Lubberland, and cry, *we, we?* 1813 :
Ray, 64, You'd do well in Lubberland,
where they have half a crown a day
for sleeping.

Luck. 1. *Give a man luck and throw
him in the sea.* 1576 : *Parad. of Dainty
Devices*, No. 27, She [Fortune] vseth
neuer partiall hands for to offend, or
please, Geve me good Fortune all men
sayes, and throw me in the seas. 1580 :
Churchyard, *Charge*, 28 (Collier), Our
old proverbe is, given me hap and cast
me in the sea. 1632 : Rowley, *Woman
never Vexed*, I. [with " woman " for
" man "]. 1671 : Head and Kirkman,
Eng. Rogue, ii. 202. 1709 : O. Dykes,
Eng. Proverbs, 271. 1837 : Planché,
Extravag., i. 268 (1879), Give a man
but luck they say, sir, In the sea fling
him you may, sir.

2. *Luck for the fools and chance for the
ugly.* 1754 : Berthelson, *Eng.-Danish
Dict.*, s.v. " Luck."

3. *Luck is a lord.* 1564 : Bullein,
Dialogue, 101 (E.E.T.S.), If good lucke
had been our good lord. 1709 : O.
Dykes, *Eng. Proverbs*, 272, Luck is a
lord, we say. 1848 : Planché, *Extravag.*,
iii. 272 (1879).

4. *There is luck in leisure.* 1855 :
Bohn, 522.

5. *There is luck in odd numbers.*
1600 : Shakespeare, *Merry Wives*, V. i.,
This is the third time ; I hope good luck
lies in odd numbers. 1672 : *Dream of the
Cabal*, quoted in Wheatley's *Pepys*, vii.
229 *n.*, Methought there met the grand
Cabal of Seven, (Odd numbers, some
men say, do best please Heaven). 1784 :
New Foundl. Hosp. for Wit, ii. 118, Odd
numbers are lucky. 1883 : Burne,
Shropsh. Folk-Lore, 262, We say now,
" There's luck in odd numbers."

See also **Good luck; Hit** (2) ; and **Ill
luck.**

Lucky men need no counsel. 1855 :
Bohn, 447.

**Lucy light, the shortest day and the
longest night.** [1633 : Donne, *Poems*,
i. 254 (Grierson), Laies thee to sleepe

but a Saint Lucies night.] 1659 : Howell,
Proverbs : Span.-Eng., 13, San Lucy
bright, the shortest . . . 1678 : Ray,
52. 1732 : Fuller, No. 6222. 1881 :
C. W. Empson, in *Folk-Lore Record*,
iv. 129, Lucy light ! Lucy light !
Longest day and shortest night !

Luddington. *See* quot. 1889 : Peacock,
Manley, etc., Gloss., 333 (E.D.S.), Luddington poor people, With a stoän
chech an' a wooden steeple.

Ludgate bird, A. 1639 : Clarke, 245.

Ludlam's dog. *See* **Lazy.**

**Lundy high, Sign of dry ; Lundy plain,
Sign of rain.** 1891 : R. P. Chope, *Hartland Dialect*, 20 (E.D.S.).

Lust. *See* **Pleasure** (4).

**Lust is as young as his limbs are old,
His.** 1659 : Howell, 10.

Lydford Law. *See* quots. 1399 :
Langland, *Richard Redeless*, iii. 145,
Be the lawe of Lydfford. 1644 :
Browne, *Lydford Castle*, st. 1, I oft
have heard of Lydford Law, How in
the morn they hang and draw, And
sit in judgment after. 1662 : Fuller,
Worthies, i. 399 (1840), First hang and
draw, Then hear the cause by Lidford
law. 1714 : Ozell, *Molière*, iv. 215, Hang
a man first, and try him afterwards ;
Lidford law you know ! 1838 : Mrs.
Bray, *Trad. of Devon*, iii. 12, The old
saying of Lydford Law, to express an
arbitrary procedure in judgment. 1855 :
Kingsley, *West. Ho!*, ch. xiv., And by
Lydfor' law if they will, hang first and
try after. 1887 : *Cornhill Mag.*, Nov.,
523, " Hang first and try afterwards "
was the fundamental maxim of Lydford
Law.

Lying rides on Death's back. 1736 :
Franklin, *Way to Wealth*, in *Works*, i.
449 (Bigelow). 1875 : Smiles, *Thrift*,
242.

Lymm from Warburton, To tear.
1901 : F. E. Taylor, *Folk-Speech of
S. Lancs*, s.v. " Limb," Limb-fro'-War-
button. A term used to denote the
division or pulling to pieces of anything. 1917 : Bridge, *Cheshire Proverbs*,
144, . . . Lymm-cum-Warburton were
two medieties of one parish on the
Chester side of the Mersey.

Lythe. *See* **Lithe.**

M

M under one's girdle. *See* **Carry** (3).

Macclesfield. *To feed like a free-holder of Macclesfield, who hath neither corn nor hay at Michaelmas.* 1670 : Ray, 208. 1790 : Grose, *Prov. Gloss.*, s.v. "Cheshire." 1917 : Bridge, *Cheshire Proverbs*, 65 [with "Christmas" for "Michaelmas"]. *See also* **Maxfield;** and **Treacle town.**

Mackerel sky, A. *See* quots. [1669 : Worlidge, *Syst. Agric.*, 295 (1681) (O.), In a fair day, if the sky seem to be dapled with white clouds (which they usually term a mackarel-sky) it usually predicts rain.] 1854 : Baker, *Northants Gloss.*, s.v. A mackarel sky, Never holds three days dry. *c.* 1870 : Smith, *Isle of Wight Words*, 62 (E.D.S.), (*a*) Mares'·tails and a mackarel sky, Not four and twenty hours dry. (*b*) A mackarel sky and mares' tails Make lofty ships carry low sails. 1886 : Elworthy, *West Som. Word-Book*, 453 (E.D.S.), Mackerel-sky! not much wet, not much dry. 1891 : Addy, *Sheffield Gloss. Suppl.*, 36 (E.D.S.), In this district it is said that A mackerel sky Is never long dry. 1893 : Inwards, *Weather Lore*, 94, [as in 1870 (*b*), *plus*] (*a*) Mackerel sky, mackerel sky, Never long wet and never long dry. (*b*) Mackerel clouds in sky, Expect more wet than dry. (*c*) Mackerel scales, Furl your sails. (*d*) A mackerel sky, Not twenty-four hours dry.

Mad as a hatter. 1849 : Thackeray, *Pendennis*, ch. x. 1857 : Hughes, *Tom Brown*, Pt. II. ch. iii., He's a very good fellow, but as mad as a hatter. 1863 : F. A. Marshall, *Mad as a Hatter* [title of farce].

Mad as a March hare. *c.* 1386 : Chaucer, *Friar's Tale*, l. 29, For thogh this Sommour wood [mad] were as an hare. *c.* 1450 : *Partonope*, l. 7934 (E.E.T.S.), There he rennyth wode [mad] as ony hare. *c.* 1500 : in Hazlitt, *Early Pop. Poetry*, i. 105, And be as braynles as a Marshe hare. 1546 :

Heywood, *Proverbs*, Pt. II. ch. v., As mad as a marche hare. 1577 : Stanihurst, *Descrip. of Ireland*, fo. 14. *c.* 1620 : Fletcher, *Wild-Goose Chase*, IV. iii., They are all, all mad. I came from a world of mad women, Mad as March hares. 1678 : Dryden, *Limberham*, V. i. 1749 : Fielding, *Tom Jones*, bk. xii. ch. vii. 1850 : Dickens, *Chuzzlewit*, ch. xlvi. 1917 : Bridge, *Cheshire Proverbs*, 26, As wyndy [wild] as a March hare.

Mad as a tup. 1883 : Burne, *Shropsh. Folk-Lore*, 595, As mad as a tup [ram] in a halter. 1901 : in *N. & Q.*, 9th ser., viii. 501, In Derbyshire . . . there is no commoner saying to express anger shown by any one than to say that he or she was "as mad as a tup." "A tup" is a ram.

Mad as a weaver. 1609 : *Ev. Woman in Humor*, I., in Bullen, *Old Plays*, iv. 314, If he were as madde as a weaver.

Mad as Ajax. 1592 : Shakespeare, *L. L. L.*, IV. iii., By the Lord, this love is as mad as Ajax. 1607 : Chapman, *Bussy d'Ambois*, III., And run as mad as Ajax. 1732 : Fuller, No. 3287, Love is as mad as Ajax.

Mad horse. *See* quot. 1685 : Meriton, *Yorkshire Ale*, 66, A weand [mad] horse I've heard it oft reported And a rotten harrow are seaun parted.

Mad world, my masters, A. 1603 : Breton, *A Mad World my Masters* [title], in *Works*, (Grosart), ii. 1608 : Middleton, *A Mad World my Masters* [title]. 1649 : Taylor (Water - Poet), *Western Voyage*, l. 1, 'Tis a mad world, my masters.

Mad, You'll never be, you are of so many minds. 1670 : Ray, 118. 1738 : Swift, *Polite Convers.*, Dial. I.

Madam Parnell, crack the nut and eat the kernel. Howell says that this saying alludes to a woman's labour. It may be noted that "Pernel" in the seventeenth century and earlier was a name for a woman of loose life. 1659 : Howell, 1. 1670 : Ray, 84.

Madge. *See* **Margery.**

Madman and a fool are no witnesses, A.
1732 : Fuller, No. 267.

Mad parish must have a mad priest, A.
Ibid., No. 268.

Maggot bites, When the‽ = When the
whim takes one. 1683 : L'Estrange,
Observator, i. No. 470, Prethee, where
bites the magot to-day, Trimmer ?
1709 : E. Ward, *Works*, iv., *Verse*, 21,
So touchy when the maggot.takes him.
1754 : Berthelson, *Eng.-Danish Dict.*,
s.v. " Maggot," I shall do it when the
maggot bites.

Maggots in the brain, To have = To
have whimsies. *c.* 1625 : B. & F.,
Women Pleased, III. iv., Have not you
maggots in your brains ? 1675 : in
Harl. Miscell. vii. 597 (1746), He puts
off . . . the maggots of his own brain
for divine inspiration. 1704 : D'Urfey,
Tales Trag. and Comical, 51, The maggots in the brain With novelty possess'd his pate.

Magistracy. *See* quot. 1642 : D.
Rogers, *Matrim. Honour*, 45, The old
speech is, Magistracy makes not the
man, but discovers what mettell is in
him.

Magnificat, The. 1. *To correct Magnificat* = To find fault unreasonably,
and presumptuously. 1540 : Palsgrave, *Acolastus*, sig. B3, Thou . . .
whiche takest vppon the to correct
Magnificat. 1583 : Melbancke, *Philotinus*, sig. E1, That correcteth Magnificat before he can sing Te Deum.
1589 : Nashe, *Works*, i. 152 (Grosart),
They would correct Magnificat, not
knowing *Quid significat*. 1681 : W.
Robertson, *Phraseol. Generalis*, 388, To
correct the Magnificat ; Nodum in scirpo
quærere. Ibid., 856, . . . Lumen soli
mutuare. 1694 : L'Estrange, *Æsop*, 283
(3rd ed.). 'Tis the same case where
subjects take upon them to correct
Magnificat, and to prescribe to their
superiors. 1736 : Bailey, *Dict.*, s.v.
" Correct."

2. *See* quots. 1588 : Bp. Andrewes,
Serm. at Spital, 24 (1629) (O.), The note
is heere all out of place . . . and so,
their note comes in like Magnificat at
Matins. 1611 : Cotgrave, s.v. " Magni-

ficat," *Chanter Magnificat à matines*, To
doe things disorderly, or use a thing un-
seasonably. 1653 : Urquhart, *Rabelais*,
bk. i. ch. xi., He . . . made a mock at
the gods, would cause sing Magnificat
at Matines.

Magpie. 1. Query the proverb
alluded to. 1576 : G. Harvey,
Letter - Book, 163 (Camden S.), Mai
perhaps fli at a pie, as yᵉ proverb is,
but he is most likeli to catch a dawe.

2. *Omens and sayings.* 1849 : Dinsdale, *Teesdale Gloss.*, 95, One's sorrow,
Two's good luck, Three's a wedding,
Four's death. 1867 : Harland, in
Lancs Folk-Lore, 144, In Lancashire
they say :—" One for anger, Two for
mirth, Three for a wedding, Four for a
birth, Five for rich, Six for poor, Seven
for a witch, I can tell you no more."
1878 : *Folk-Lore Record*, i. 8, In speaking of the magpie they confidently tell
you that—" One is for sorrow, two for
mirth, Three for a wedding, Four for a
birth." 1883 : Burne, *Shropsh. Folk-
Lore*, 224, [as in 1878, *plus*] " Four for
a death," say some ; and from Church
Stretton we have another variation,
" One for anger, two for luck," etc.
1886 : Elworthy, *West Som. Word-Book*,
454 (E.D.S.), One, sign of anger ; two,
sign o' muth ; Dree, sign o' wedding-
day ; vower, sign o' death ; Vive, sign o'
zorrow ; zix, sign o' joy ; Zebm, sign
o' maid ; an' eight sign o' boy. 1892 :
S. Hewett, *Peasant Speech of Devon*, 26,
Wan is vur zorrow, Tü is vur mirth,
Dree is vur a wedding, Vowr is vur
death. 1901 : F. E. Taylor, *Lancs
Sayings*, 41, One for cryin'—two for
mirth—Three for a weddin'—four for a
d'yeth.

3. *Worth one's weight in magpies.*
Corn. 1869 : Hazlitt, 481.

Mahomet and the mountain. 1625 :
Bacon, *Essays :* "Boldness," Mahomet
cald the hill to come to him, againe, and
againe ; and when the hill stood still,
he was neuer a whit abashed, but said ;
*If the hill will not come to Mahomet,
Mahomet wil go to the hil.* Before 1704 :
T. Brown, in *Works*, iv. 259 (1760), And
then 'twas with us in the case of drink,
what it was formerly between Mahomet

and the mountain. 1874 : R. L. S.,
Letters, i. 163 (Tusitala ed.).

Maid, Maids, and **Maidens.** 1. *A
maid and a virgin is not all one.* 1639 :
Clarke, 152.

2. *A maid oft seen, and a gown oft
worn, Are disesteem'd, and held in scorn.*
1611 : Cotgrave, s.v. " Fille." 1670 :
Ray, 17. 1732 : Fuller, No. 6395.

3. *A maid that giveth yieldeth.* 1611 :
Cotgrave, s.v. "Abandonner." 1670 :
Ray, 16. 1736 : Bailey, *Dict.*, s.v.
" Maid."

4. *A maid that laughs is half taken.*
1670 : Ray, 16. 1732 : Fuller, No. 269.

5. *A maid's knee. See* **Dog** (8).

6. *Every maid is undone.* 1678 : Ray,
172.

7. *If the maid be a fool. See* **Cat** (25).

8. *Maidens must be mild and meek;
Swift to hear, and slow to speak.* 1732 :
Fuller, No. 6410. 1736 : Bailey, *Dict.*,
s.v.

9. *Maidens should be mim* [silent] *till
they're married.* 1917 : Bridge, *Cheshire
Proverbs*, 93.

10. *Maids' children. See* **Bachelor** (3).

11. *Maids say nay and take.* 1562 :
Heywood, *Three Hund. Epigr.*, No. 223,
Say nay, and take it. 1594 : Shake-
speare, *Rich. III.*, III. vii., Play the
maid's part, still answer nay, and take
it. 1609 : W. Rowley, *Search for
Money*, 32 (Percy S.). 1694 : Motteux,
Rabelais, bk. v. ch. xxviii. 1738 : Swift,
Polite Convers., Dial. I.

12. *Maids should be seen and not
heard. c.* 1400 : *Mirk's Festial*, 20
(E.E.T.S.), For hyt ys an old Englysch
sawe : " A mayde schuld be seen, but
not herd." 1560 : Becon, *Catechism, etc.*,
369 [as in 1400]. Before 1627 :
Middleton, *More Diss. besides Women*,
III. i., Virgins should be seen more
than they're heard. 1675 : Cotton,
Burl. upon Burlesque, 252 (1765).
1738 : Swift, *Polite Convers.*, Dial. I.
1858 : G. Eliot, *Clerical Life :* " Janet's
Rep.," ch. viii., "Hush, Lizzie, little gells
must be seen and not heard." 1907 :
De Morgan, *Alice-for-Short*, ch. ix.,
These [maxims] were the old-fashioned
sort, such as—" Little girls should be
seen not heard." Cf. **Children** (10).

13. *Maids want nothing but husbands.*
1678 : Ray, 347, . . . *Somerset.* 1732 :
Fuller, No. 3309, [as in 1678, *plus*] and
then they want every thing.

14. *The worst store* [is] *a maid un-
bestowed.* 1659 : Howell, *Proverbs :
Brit.-Eng.*, 15.

15. *There are never the fewer maids
for her.* 1678 : Ray, 258.

16. *This maid was born old.* Ibid.,
77.

17. *When maidens sue, men live like
gods.* 1855 : Bohn, 559.

18. *Who knows who's a good maid ?*
1678 : Ray, 172.

See also **All** meats ; **Good** a maid ;
Meeterly ; and **Wife** (25).

Main chance, Have an eye to the.
1580 : Lyly, *Euphues*, 430 (Arber),
Always haue an eye to the mayne,
what soeuer thou art chaunced at the
buy. *c.* 1610 : in *Roxb. Ballads*, i. 454
(B.S.), She had a care of the main-
chance. 1681 : W. Robertson, *Phraseol.
Generalis*, 322, Have a care of the main
chance. 1722 : Defoe, *Moll Flanders*,
in *Works*, iii. 40 (Bohn), A man . . .
getting money, seldom at home,
thoughtful of the main chance. 1924 :
Sphere, 29 March, p. 344, col. 1, Ernest
Stanton, M.P., has a suave manner and
an eye for the main chance.

Main lost, cast the by away, The.
1594 : Drayton, *Ideas*, lix. (Proverbs).

Maisemore. *See* quot. 1894 :
Northall, *Folk Phrases*, 7 (E.D.S.), All
together like the men of Maisemore,
and they went one at a time.

Make, *verb.* 1. *As you make your bed
so you must lie on it.* [Tute hoc intristi :
tibi omne est exedendum.—Terence,
Phorm., 318]. *c.* 1590 : G. Harvey,
Marginalia, 88 (1913), Lett them . . .
go to there bedd, as themselves shall
make it. 1640 : Herbert, *Jac. Prudentum.* He that makes his bed ill, lies
there. 1670 : Ray, 3 [as in 1640]. 1732 :
Fuller, No. 2233 [as in 1640, but ending
" must be contented to lie ill "]. 1842 :
Barham, *Ing. Legends*, 2nd ser. : " Aunt
Fanny," She could not prevent her—
'twas no use in trying it—Oh, no—she
had made her own bed, and might lie in
it. 1922 : Weyman, *Ovington's Bank*, ch.

xxxi., He has . . . disgraced our blood
. . . he has done it! He has made his
bed and must lie on it!

2. *He that can make a fire well can
end a quarrel.* 1640: Herbert, *Jac.
Prudentum.*

3. *He that makes his mistress a goldfinch, may perhaps find her a wagtail.*
1647 : *Countrym. New Commonwealth,*
8–9.

4. *He that makes the shoe can't tan
the leather.* 1580: Lyly, *Euphues,* 224
(Arber), You know that it is not for
him that fashioneth the shoe, to make
the graine of the leather. 1732 : Fuller,
No. 2235.

5. *I'll make you know your driver.*
1678 : Ray, 345, . . . *Somerset.*

6. *I will not make my dish-clout my
table-cloth.* 1732 : Fuller, No. 2646.
1737 : Ray, 96.

7. *Make a-do and have a-do.* 1678 :
Ray, 70.

8. *Make haste and leave nothing to
waste.* 1827: Hone, *Ev. Day Book,* ii.
927 [quoted as " the old proverb "].

9. *Make hay. See* **Hay** (3).

10. *Make me a diviner and I will make
thee rich.* 1578: Florio, *First Fruites,*
fo. 30. 1623: Wodroephe, *Spared
Houres,* 172, Make me a guesser, and I
shall make you rich of it. 1629: *Book
of Meery Riddles,* Prov. III. 1732 :
Fuller, No. 3315 [with " sooth-sayer "
for " diviner "].

11. *Make nor meddle. See* **Meddle.**

12. *That which will not make a pot,
may make a pot-lid.* 1732 : Fuller, No.
4388.

13. *They that make laws should not
break them.* c. 1386 : Chaucer, *Introd.*
to *Man of Law's Prol.,* l. 434, For swich
lawe as man yeveth another wight, He
sholde him-selven usen it by right.
1598: *Servingmans Comfort,* in *Inedited
Tracts,* 154 (Hazlitt), It is a shame for
the lawgiuer to break and violate his
owne institutions. 1669: *Politeuphuia,*
95, It becometh a law-maker not to be
a law-breaker. 1739 : *Gent. Mag.,* 427,
The old proverb . . . that law-makers
ought not to be law-breakers. 1830 :
Marryat, *King's Own,* ch. xi. [as in
1739].

14. *They who make the best use of
their time have none to spare.* 1855 :
Bohn, 527.

15. *To make a wry mouth* = To be
hanged. 1611 : Cotgrave, s.v. "Moue,"
We say of one that's hanged, he makes
a wry mouth.

16. *To make both ends meet.* 1639 :
Clarke, 242, I cannot make, etc. 1662 :
Fuller, *Worthies:* "Cumb.," Worldly
wealth he cared not for, desiring
onely to make both ends meet. 1748 :
Richardson, *Clarissa,* iv. 137 (1785),
Tho' he had a good estate, hardly
making both ends meet. 1864 : Mrs.
H. Wood, *Trevlyn Hold,* ch. xx., If you
have the pleasure of making both ends
to meet . . . upon the moderate sum
of one hundred pounds sterling. 1913 :
E. M. Wright, *Rustic Speech, etc.,* 14,
The sort of life where it is hard to make
both ends meet.

17. *To make buttons. See* **Breech.**

18. *To make indentures* = To walk
unsteadily, as when drunk. 1605 :
R. F., *Sch. of Slovenrie,* 35, Before he
with his feete do seeme indentures for
to make. 1615 : Stephens, *Essays, etc.,*
bk. ii. No. 11, If he bee drunken you
must say hee staggers, to avoide
æquivocation; for when he is sober
hee makes indentures [character of a
lawyer's clerk]. 1681 : in *Roxb. Ballads,* vi. 3 (B.S.), Being so drunk that
he cutteth indentures. 1745 : Franklin, *Drinker's Dict.,* in *Works,* ii. 25
(Bigelow), He makes indentures with
his leggs.

19. *To make no bones about a thing.*
1565 : Shacklock, *Hatch. of Heresies,* fo.
14, They haue made no bones at it to
say. 1608 : Armin, *Nest of Ninnies,*
27 (Sh. S.), Which, making no bones of,
the sweete youth gaue his doings thus.
1633 : T. May, tr. Barclay's *Mirr. of
Minds,* 196, Which [dinner] . . . they
make no bones many times to prolong
till supper time. 1740 : North, *Examen,* 604, He . . . made no bones of
telling this passage in all companies.
1894 : R. L. S., *St. Ives,* ch. xxv.,
" O, don't make any bones about it ! "
he interrupted.

20. *To make orts of good hay.* 1639 :

in *Berkeley MSS.*, iii. 29 (1885), Hee's well served, for hee hath oft made orts of better hay. 1670: Ray, 188. 1732: Fuller, No. 3317, Make no orts of good hay.

21. *To make up one's mouth.* This bears more than one meaning. *See* quots. 1546: Heywood, *Proverbs*, Pt. I. ch. xi., His wife to make vp my mouthe, Not onely hir husbandes tauntyng tale auouthe, But therto deuiseth to cast in my teeth,' Checks and chokyng oysters. *c.* 1570: T. Preston, *Cambysses*, in Hazlitt, *Old Plays*, iv. 175, According to the proverb old, My mouth I will up make. 1669: Shadwell, *Royal Shep.*, III. i., My mother . . . would have made a hard shift to have sat the upper end of my Lord Neander's table, to have had occasion to have made up a fine mouth, and have said . . . Before 1704: T. Brown, in *Works*, iv. 202 (1760), All the while she was at church, she made up her mouth as demurely as the best of the congregation. 1888: *N. & Q.*, 7th ser., vi. 38, " A snack of bread and cheese to make up your mouth " is often the goodwife's suggestion to her farmer lord [Shropsh.].

22. *You make the better side the worse.* 1678: Ray, 355 . . . *Somerset.*

Malachi's child, choke full of sense, Like. 1906: *Cornish N. & Q.*, 266.

Malice hath a sharp sight and strong memory. 1650: Fuller, *Pisgah Sight*, bk. ii. ch. iii., Yet we know malice hath a strong memory. 1732: Fuller, No. 3328.

Malice hurts itself most. 1639: Clarke, 197. 1732: Fuller, No. 3327, Malice drinketh up the greatest part of its own poison.

Malice is mindful. 1639: Clarke, 196. 1670: Ray, 118. 1732: Fuller, No. 3329.

Malice never spoke well. 1574: E. Hellowes, *Guevara's Epistles*, 492, Mallice findes manie faultes. 1605: Camden, *Remains*, 328 (1870).

Malice seldom wants a mark to shoot at. 1855: Bohn, 448.

Malpas ales and Malpas gales [S.W. winds] **Cheer the farmer, fill his**

pails. 1917: Bridge, *Cheshire Proverbs*, 164.

Malpas shot. *See* Higgledy-piggledy.

Malt is above the water, The = He is drunk. 1678: Ray, 87. 1745: Franklin, *Drinker's Dict.*, in *Works*, ii. 26 (Bigelow).

Malt is above wheat with him = He is drunk. 1546: Heywood, *Proverbs*, Pt. I. ch. xi. 1588: Cogan, *Haven of Health*, 217 (1612), Take good heede that malt be not aboue wheate before you parte. *c.* 1640: in *Roxb. Ballads*, ii. 95 (Hindley), Men will call for it [tobacco] when malt's above wheat. 1824: Scott, *Redgauntlet*, ch. xii., " Come, come, Provost," said the lady, rising, " if the maut gets abune the meal with you, it is time for me to take myself away."

Malt to sell, They may sit in the chair that have. 1639: Clarke, 99. 1670: Ray, 68. 1732: Fuller, No. 4967.

Maltman comes on Monday, The. 1659: Howell, 9.

Malvern Hill. 1. *All about Malvern Hill, A man may live as long as he will.* 1882: Mrs. Chamberlain, *W. Worcs. Words*, 39 (E.D.S.).

2. *Go dig at Mavern Hill.* Spoken of one whose wife " wears the breeches." 1659: Howell, 20. 1790: Grose, *Prov. Gloss.*, s.v. " Worcestershire."

Malvern measure, full and running over. 1894: Northall, *Folk Phrases*, 19 (E.D.S.).

Malvern. *See also* Severn.

Mamma's milk is scarce out of your nose yet, Your. 1732: Fuller, No. 6055.

Man and Men. 1. *A man, a horse, and a dog are never weary of each other's company.* 1749: W. Ellis, *Shep. Sure Guide*, etc., 9 [quoted as a proverb].

2. *A man among children will be long a child, a child among men will be soon a man.* 1732: Fuller, No. 270.

3. *A man assaulted is half taken.* 1629: *Book of Meery Riddles*, Prov. 22.

4. *A man at five may be a fool at fifteen.* 1736: Bailey, *Dict.*, s.v. " Five." 1875: A. B. Cheales, *Proverb. Folk-Lore*, 48.

5. *A man at sixteen will prove a child at sixty.* 1732: Fuller, No. 273.

6. *A man can do no more than he can.*
1530: Palsgrave, 474, No man can
do aboue his power. 1626: *Scoggins
Jests*, 158 (1864), No man can aske
more of a man than hee is able to
doe. 1670: Ray, 67. 1814: Scott, in
Lockhart's *Life*, iii. 152, The islanders
retort, that a man can do no more than
he can. 1901: F. E. Taylor, *Lancs
Sayings*, 11, A body conno' do mooar
nor he con, con he?

7. *A man cannot live by the air.* 1633:
Draxe, 180, A man cannot liue by
thankes. 1670: Ray, 56. 1748: *Gent.
Mag.*, xviii. 21.

8. *A man every inch of him.* 1639:
Clarke, 247. 1678: Ray, 76. 1698:
Terence made English, 64 (2nd ed.),
Thou'rt a man every inch of thee.
1870: Carlyle, in Forster's *Dickens*, iii.
475, The good, the gentle, high-gifted,
ever-friendly noble Dickens,—every inch
of him an Honest Man.

9. *A man has choice to begin love, but
not to end it.* 1855: Bohn, 294.

10. *A man has often more trouble to
digest meat than to get it.* Ibid., 294.

11. *A man hath many enemies when
his back is to the wall.* 1639: Clarke,
166.

12. *A man in distress or despair does
as much as ten.* 1732: Fuller, No. 282.

13. *A man is a lion in his own cause.*
1738: *Gent. Mag.*, 476.

14. *A man is a man if he have but
a nose on his face.* 1612: Shelton,
Quixote, Pt. I. bk. iii. ch. xi., A man
is but a man though he have a nose on
his head. 1738: Swift, *Polite Convers.*,
Dial. II.

15. *A man is a man though he have
but a hose on his head.* This saying was
popular in the 16th and 17th centuries,
but its meaning is not clear. It may
mean that a man is not to be judged
by his apparel, however grotesque that
may be. [c. 1386: Chaucer, *Canon's
Yeoman's Tale*, l. 171, Ther I was wont to
be right fresh and gay Of clothing and
of other good array, Now may I were
an hose upon myn heed, And wher my
colour was bothe fresh and reed, Now
is it wan and of a leden hewe.] 1593:
Nashe, in *Works*, ii. 249 (Grosart).

1652: Tatham, *Scots Figgaries*, IV.
1664: Cotton, *Scarronides*, bk. i. 1709:
O. Dykes, *Eng. Proverbs*, 255 (2nd ed.),
A man is a man still, if he hath but
a hose on his head. 1732: Fuller,
No. 277.

16. *A man is as old* (or *young*) *as he
feels.* [Tam miser est quisque, quam
credit.—Seneca, *Epist.*, 78.] 1921:
R. L. Gales, *Old-World Essays*, 243,
" You are always as young as you feel "
is a saying quoted in this book. I have
heard it all my life. 1926: *Times*,
25 March, p. 14, col. 2, A fine figure of a
man is Owen Keegan. " A man is only
as old as he feels," he says.

17. *A man is known by his company.*
1620: Shelton, *Quixote*, Pt. II. ch.
lxviii., You may know the man by
the conversation he keeps. 1672:
Wycherley, *Love in a Wood*, I. i., There
is a proverb, Mrs. Joyner, " You may
know him by his company." 1748:
Richardson, *Clarissa*, vi. 362 (1785),
Men are known by their companions.
1829: Cobbett, *Advice to Young Men*,
Lett. 1, " Show me a man's companions," says the proverb, " and I
will tell you what the man is." 1871:
Smiles, *Character*, 65, It is a common
saying that men are known by the
company they keep.

18. *A man is not so soon healed as
hurt.* 1599: Porter, *Two Angry Women*,
in Hazlitt, *Old Plays*, vii. 357 [with
" whole " for " healed "]. 1670: Ray,
102. 1732: Fuller, No. 281.

19. *A man is weal or woe, As he thinks
himself so.* [There is a base proverb,
thou shalt bee so much esteemed by
others, as thou esteemest thy selfe.—
1642: D. Rogers, *Naaman*, sig. E5.]
1732: Fuller, No. 6312.

20. *A man may be an artist tho' he
have not his tools about him.* Ibid.,
No. 288.

21. *A man may bear till his back
break.* 1611: Cotgrave, s.v. " Sommer," *Tant travaille et tracasse l'homme,
qu'en fin il se rompt, ou somme* ; A man
so long doth toile and swink, till under
his own charge he sink. 1639: Clarke,
15. 1670: Ray, 59. 1732: Fuller,
No. 3397 [in the plural].

22. *A man may come soon enough to an ill bargain.* 1633 : Draxe, 54. 1639 : Clarke, 157.

23. *A man may hold his tongue.* See **Hold one's tongue.**

24. *A man may lose.* See **Lose** (1) and (2).

25. *A man may love his house well, though he ride not on the ridge.* 1546 : Heywood, *Proverbs*, Pt. II. ch. iv. 1560 : T. Wilson, *Rhetorique*, 189 (1909). 1685 : Meriton, *Yorkshire Ale*, 52, He can love the house well that hes [has] Tibb in, And not be alwayes rideing o' th' riggin. 1738 : Swift, *Polite Convers.*, Dial. II., A man may love his house very well, without riding on the ridge. 1824 : Scott, *Redgauntlet*, ch. xiii., Well, now, you see one may love the Kirk, and yet not ride on the rigging of it.

26. *A man must go old to the Court, and young to a cloister, that would go from thence to heaven.* 1678 : Ray, 117.

27. *A man of courage never wants weapons.* 1732 : Fuller, No. 302.

28. *A man of many trades begs his bread on Sundays.* [1642 : Fuller, *Holy State:* "Lady Paula," I know two trades together are too much for one man to thrive upon.] 1732 : Fuller, No. 304.

29. *A man of straw is worth a woman of gold.* 1591 : Florio, *Second Frutes*, 173 [with "more worth than" for "worth"]. 1647 : Howell, *Letters*, bk. ii. No. iv. 1869 : Spurgeon, *John Ploughman*, ch. xvii., They say a man of straw is worth a woman of gold, but I cannot swallow it.

30. *A man of words and not of deeds, Is like a garden full of weeds.* 1659 : Howell, 20. 1670 : Ray, 211. 1706 : Ward, *Hudibras Rediv.*, Pt. 5, can. vii. p. 9 [in the plural]. 1758 : Franklin, in *Works*, iii. 36 (Bigelow). 1869 : Spurgeon, *John Ploughman*, ch. xiv.

31. *A man or a mouse.* 1541 : Sch. House of Women, l. 386, Fear not, she saith vnto her spouse, A man or a mouse whether be ye. 1590 : *Tarltons Newes out of Purg.*, 54 (Sh. S.), What, old acquaintance, a man or a mouse ? c. 1623 : B. & F., *Love's Cure*, II. ii., I will make a man or a mouse on you.

1681: W. Robertson, *Phraseol. Generalis*, 863. 1709: O. Dykes, *Eng. Proverbs*, 113 (2nd ed.), His . . . final resolution to make himself either a man or a mouse. 1843: Carlyle, *Past and Present*, bk. ii. ch. vii., To see how Monks elect their Abbot in the Twelfth Century ; how the St. Edmundsbury mountain manages its midwifery ; and what mouse or man the outcome is. 1901 : F. E. Taylor, *Lancs Sayings*, 13, Aw'd oather be a mon or a meawse if aw were thee.

32. *A man should keep from the blind.* See quot. 1461 : *Paston Lett.*, ii. 73 (Gairdner), And also understondyng that he was kynnyes man to my master, and it is a comon proverbe, "A man xuld kepe fro the blynde and gevyt to is kyn."

33. *A man surprised is half beaten.* 1732 : Fuller, No. 310.

34. *A man that cannot sit still.* See quot. 1662 : Pepys, *Diary*, 8 Aug., Another rule is a proverb that he hath been taught, which is that a man that cannot sit still in his chamber . . . and he that cannot say no . . . is not fit for business.

35. *A man that does what no other man does, is wondered at by all.* 1387 : Trevisa, tr. Higden, viii. 19 (Rolls Ser.), þat proverbe is ofte had in his mouþ . . . "Alle men wondreþ of hym þat doþ as noon oþer doþ." c. 1440 : Anon., tr. Higden, viii. 19 (Rolls Ser.), This proverbe : "A man that doothe a thynge whiche noon other man usethe, causethe alle men to mervayle."

36. *A man that keeps riches and enjoys them not is like an ass that carries gold and eats thistles.* 1732: Fuller, No. 312.

37. *A man under no restraint is a bear without a ring.* Ibid., No. 313.

38. *A man will rather hurt his body than displease his palate.* 1659 : Howell, 1.

39. *A man without money is a bow without an arrow.* 1732 : Fuller, No. 316.

40. *A man without money is no man at all.* Ibid., No. 317.

41. *A man without reason is a beast in season.* 1659: Howell, 11. 1670 : Ray, 22. 1732 : Fuller, No. 6244.

42. *A man's best fortune, or his worst,*

is a wife. 1659 : Howell, 5. 1732 :
Fuller, No. 306.

43. *A man's country is where he does
well.* 1576 : Pettie, *Petite Pall.*, i. 40
(Gollancz), I count any place my
country where I may live well and
wealthily. 1599 : Kyd, *Sol. and Per-
seda*, IV., And where a man lives well,
there is his country. 1659 : T. Pecke,
Parnassi Puerp., 94, My countrey is
where ever I am well. 1732 : Fuller,
No. 5659, Wheresoever we live well,
that is our country.

44. *A man's praise in his own mouth
doth stink.* c. 1615 : *Times Whistle*,
37 (E.E.T.S.), Hast thou that auncient,
true saide sawe forgot, That " a mans
praise in his owne mouth doth stinke " ?

45. *A man's wealth is his enemy.*
1659 : Howell, *Proverbs : Brit.-Eng.*, 3.

46. *As a man is friended so the law
is ended.* 1538 : Latimer, in *Works*,
ii. 399 (P.S.), The assize, where as men
be friended, so (they say) things be
ended. c. 1542 : Brinklow, *Complaynt*,
25 (E.E.T.S.). 1600 : Day, *Blind Beggar*, III. ii., Remember this old law
" As men are friended, So either right
or wrong their sutes are ended." 1681 :
W. Robertson, *Phraseol. Generalis*, 470,
As a man is friended, so is his difference,
or cause ended. 1738 : *Gent. Mag.*, 475.

47. *As a man lives, so shall he die; As
a tree falls so shall it lie.* 1678 : Ray, 296.

48. *Every man thinks he may live
another year.* [Nemo enim est tam
senex, qui se annum non putet posse
vivere.—Cicero, *De Senect.*, vii. 24.] c.
1577 : Northbrooke, *Dicing, etc.*, 14
(Sh. S.), As Cicero saith, no man is so
old and aged, that he perswadeth not
him selfe that he may liue a whole yeare.
1669 : *Politeuphuia*, 203, No man is so
old, but thinketh he may yet live
another year. 1784 : Johnson, in Boswell's *Life*, iv. 270 (Hill), Yet we hope
and hope, and fancy that he who has
lived to-day may live to-morrow. Cf.
None so old.

49. *Give a man luck.* See **Luck** (1).

50. *He'll be a man among the geese.*
1690 : *New Dict. Canting Crew*, sig. F3,
He'll be a man among the geese when
the gander is gone.

51. *If a man once fall, all will tread
on him.* 1530 : Palsgrave, 757, Whan
a man is throwen under the foote ones.
[once], than every man gothe upon
hym. 1618 : B. Holyday, *Technogamia*, V. iv., When a man's once downe,
I perceiue he shall be trod vpon. 1681 :
W. Robertson, *Phraseol. Generalis*, 574.
1754 : Berthelson, *Eng.-Danish Dict.*, s.v.
" Fall."

52. *If men become sheep, the wolf will
devour them.* 1611 : Davies (of Hereford), *Sc. of Folly*, 42, in *Works*, ii.
(Grosart).

53. *It is meet that a man be at his own
bridal.* 1546 : Heywood, *Proverbs*, Pt.
I. ch. vi. 1633 : Draxe, 230 [with
" euery " for " a "].

54. *Man doth what he can and God
what He will.* 1633 : Draxe, 80 *bis.*
1670 : Ray, 97. 1736 : Bailey, *Dict.*,
s.v. " Man."

55. *Man hath as many diseases as a
horse.* 1660 : Howell, *Parly of Beasts*,
77.

56. *Man is a God to man.* 1548 :
Hall, *Chron.*, 324 (1809), The olde Greke
prouerbe to bee very trew, which is that
a man to a man shall sometyme be as
a God. 1566 : L. Wager, *Mary Magd.*,
sig. C3. 1630 : T. Adams, *Works*, 190.
Before 1680 : Butler, *Remains*, ii. 378
(1759), The philosopher said—Man to
man is a God and a wolf.

57. *Man is a wolf to man.* [Lupus
homo homini.—Plautus, *As.*, II. iv. 88.]
c. 1577 : Northbrooke, *Dicing, etc.*, 57
(Sh. S.), A man is a wolfe to a man,
that is, a devourer one of another.
1585 : Sir E. Dyer, in *Writings*, 90
(Grosart), We are (by our owne censures)
iudged wolues one to another. 1620 :
Ford, *Line of Life*, 50 (Sh. S.), The old
proverbe was . . . that a man is a
beast to a man. 1707 : Dunton, *Athen.
Sport*, 251, 'Tis enmity makes one man
a wolf to another.

58. *Man is the head but woman turns
it.* 1875 : A. B. Cheales, *Proverb. Folk-
Lore*, 12. 1913 : *Folk-Lore*, xxiv. 76,
[Oxfordsh.] The man's the head, and
the woman's the neck, and the neck
turns the head. 1917 : Bridge, *Cheshire
Proverbs*, 93.

59. *Man proposes but God disposes.*
[A man's heart deviseth his way ; but
the Lord directeth his steps. — *Prov.*
xvi. 9. Sed sicut scriptum esse, Homo
cogitat, Deus ordinat. — Ord. Vitalis,
Eccles. Hist., bk. iii. Nam homo proponit, sed Deus disponit.—A'Kempis,
De Imit., lib. i. cap. xix.] 1377 :
Langland, *Plowman*, B, xi. 36, " Homo
proponit," quod a poete and Plato
he hyght, "And Deus disponit," quod
he. 1509 : Bp. Fisher, *Eng. Works*, 222
(E.E.T.S.), It is a comyn prouerbe . . .
Man purposeth and god dysposeth.
1576 : Pettie, *Petite Pall.*, ii. 44 (Gollancz)
[as in 1509]. 1640 : Herbert, *Jac. Prudentum.* 1700 : T. Brown, tr. Scarron, ii.
64 (1892). 1854 : J. W. Warter, *Last of
Old Squires*, 53.

60. *Man, remember thy end, And thou
shalt never be shend.* 15th cent.: in
Reliq. Antiquæ, i. 316 (1841).

61. *Man's best candle* [is his] *under-
sanding.* 1659 : Howell, *Proverbs: Brit.-
Eng.*, 14.

62. *Man's extremity. See* **Need** (6).

63. *Man's life is filed by his foe.*
1659 : Howell, *Proverbs : Brit.-Eng.*, 19.

64. *May the man be damned and never
grow fat, who wears two faces under one
hat.* 1855 : Bohn, 451.

65. *Men are April when they woo,
December when they wed.* Ibid., 451.

66. *Men are never wise but returning
from law.* 1623 : Wodroephe, *Spared
Houres*, 501.

67. *Men are not to be measured by
inches.* 1732 : Fuller, No. 3390.

68. *Men dream in courtship but in
wedlock wake.* 1875 : A. B. Cheales,
Proverb. Folk-Lore, 38.

69. *Men fear death. See* **Death** (8).

70. *Men may meet but mountains
never. c.* 1541 : *Mellynge of Dr. Barnes
and Dr. Powell*, It is sene often That
men mete now and than, But so do
hylles never. 1590 : *Three Lords, etc.*,
in Hazlitt, *Old Plays*, vi. 410, Men may
meet, though mountains cannot. 1611 :
Cotgrave, s.v. " Montaigne," Men meet
often, mountaines never. 1681 : W.
Robertson, *Phraseol. Generalis*, 760.
1736 : Bailey, *Dict.*, s.v. " Men," Men
meet but mountains never greet. 1823 :

Scott, *Q. Durward*, ch. xxxi., Mountains,
it is said, may meet, and why not mortal
creatures . . . ?

71. *Men muse as they use.* 1583 :
Melbancke, *Philotinus*, sig. G3, Use not,
as you muse. 1639 : Clarke, 64, You
muse as you use. 1670 : Ray, 123.
1685 : Meriton, *Yorkshire Ale*, 71,
You meause wife as ye use. 1710 : S.
Palmer, *Moral Essays on Proverbs*, 39.

72. *Men of principle. See* quot. 1820:
Colton, *Lacon*, Pref., The old adage may
be verified, that " the men of principle
may be the principal men."

73. *Men shut their doors against a
setting sun.* 1607 : Shakespeare, *Timon*,
I. ii.

74. *Men use to worship the rising sun.*
Before 1634 : Chapman, *Alphonsus*, I.
i., Men rather honour the sun rising than
the sun going down. 1639 : Clarke, 12.
1670 : Ray, 137. 1732 : Fuller, No.
3470, Most men worship the rising sun.

75. *Men's vows are women's traitors.*
1855 : Bohn, 452.

76. *Men's years and their faults are
always more than they are willing to own.*
Ibid., 452.

77. *The man of God is better by having
his bows and arrows about him.* 1659 :
Howell, 4.

78. *The man shall have his mare
again.* 1595 : Shakespeare, *Mids. N.
Dream*, III. ii., The man shall have his
mare again, and all shall be well.
1653 : R. Brome, *Damoiselle*, IV. ii.
[as in 1595]. 1694 : Dryden, *Love
Triumphant*, III. ii., Then all shall be
set right, and the man, etc. 1712 :
Addison, *Spectator*, No. 481, Honest
Sampson . . . solves it very judiciously,
by the old proverb, that if his first
master be still living, *The man must
have his mare again.* 1738 : Swift, *Polite
Convers.*, Dial. I., *Col.* . . . but her
parents forced her to take the old fellow
for a good settlement. *Ld. Sparkish.*
So the man got his mare again. 1827 :
Creevey, in *C. Papers*, ii. 123 (1904) (O.),
No tidings of the Beau yet ! but he must
have his mare again.

79. *Those, or that which, a man knows
best, he must use most.* [c. 1384 :
Chaucer, *H. Fame*, bk. i. l. 290, Therfor

I wol seye a proverbe, That "he that
fully knoweth therbe May saufly leye
hit to his yë."] 1611 : Cotgrave, s.v.
"Herbe."
80. *What's a man but his mind?*
1639 : Clarke, 16.
81. *When a man grows angry his
reason rides out.* 1732 : Fuller, No.
5533.
82. *You'll needs be a man before your
time.* 1639 : Clarke, 267.
See also Every man ; No man ; and
Wise man.
Man, verb. *He that is manned with
boys and horsed with colts shall have his
meat eaten and his work undone.* 1605 :
Camden, *Remains*, 323 (1870). 1670 :
Ray, 118. 1732 : Fuller, No. 2286.
1846 : Denham, *Proverbs*, 6 (Percy S.).
**Manchester bred : long in the arms,
and short in the head.** 1869 : Hazlitt,
273.
**Manners and money make a gentle-
man.** 1732 : Fuller, No. 3333.
Manners make often fortunes. 1670 :
Ray, 17.
Manners make the man. *c.* 1460 : in
Babees Book, etc., 14 (E.E.T.S.), Nurtur
and good maners maketh man. 1513 :
Bradshaw, *St. Werburge*, 131 (E.E.T.S.),
Good maners and conynge maken a
man. 1602 : Rowlands, *Merrie when
Goss. meete*, 44 (Hunt. Cl.), The prouerbe
sayes 'tis manners that doth make.
1659 : Howell, 16, Manners make a man,
quoth William of Wickham. 1694 :
D'Urfey, *Quixote*, Pt. II. Act I. sc. i. [as
in 1659, but with "the" for "a"].
1729 : Defoe, *Compl. Gent.*, Pt. I. ch. i.
p. 18 (1890), The manners make the
man. 1732 : Fuller, No. 3334 [as in
1659]. 1887 : E. J. Hardy, *Manners
makyth Man* [title]. 1922 : in *Sphere*,
5 Aug., 142, "Manners," they say,
"make the man." I maintain also that
a climate makes manners.
Manners. *See also* Unmannerliness.
Manxton. *See* Heytor.
Many a little makes a mickle. [εἰ γάρ
κεν καὶ σμικρὸν ἐπὶ σμικρῷ καταθεῖο, καὶ θαμὰ τοῦτ'
ἔρδοις, τάχα κεν μέγα καὶ τὸ γένοιτο.—Hesiod,
Works and Days, 359–60.] Before 1225 :
Ancren R., 54, þus ofte, ase me seith, of
lutel wacseþ muchel. 1303 : Brunne,

Handl. Synne, l. 2366, For many smale
makeþ a grete. *c.* 1386 : Chaucer,
Parson's Tale, § 21, Manye smale maken
a greet. 1546 : Heywood, *Proverbs*, Pt.
I. ch. xi. [as in 1386]. 1593 : G. Harvey,
Works, ii. 311 (Grosart), Many a little,
by little and little maketh a mickle.
1616 : *Jack Drum*, I., in Simpson, *Sch. of
Shakesp.*, ii. 137, Oh, sir, many a small
make a great. 1680 : L'Estrange, *Select
Colloq. of Erasmus*, 19. 1712 : *Spectator*,
No. 509. 1758 : Franklin, *Poor Rich.
Imp.*, in Arber, *Garner*, v. 582 (1882).
1869 : Spurgeon, *John Ploughman*, ch.
ix., Many littles make a mickle.
Many a man singeth. *See* quots.
c. 1300 : *Prov. of Alfred*, in *Reliq.
Antiquæ*, i. 178 (1841), Monymon
singeth, that wif hom bryngeth ; wiste
he hwat he brouhte, wepen he myhte.
c. 1320 : in Ibid., i. 112, "Moni mon
syngeth When he hom bringeth Is
yonge wyf ; Wyste wot he brohte,
Wepen he mohte, Er his lyf syth" ;
Quoth Hendyng.
Many a miller. *See* Miller (8).
**Many a one for land takes a fool by
the hand.** *c.* 1320 : in *Reliq. Antiquæ*,
i. 115 (1841), "Moni mon for londe
wyveth to shonde" ; quoth Hendyng.
1639 : Clarke, 99, For a little land,
take a fool by the hand. 1670 : Ray,
116 [as in 1639]. 1678 : Ray, 56.
1732 : Fuller, No. 6263.
Many a one says well that thinks ill.
1738 : Swift, *Polite Convers.*, Dial. I.
**Many by wit purchase wealth, but
none by wealth purchase wit.** 1647 :
Countrym. New Commonwealth, 15.
**Many can bear adversity, but few
contempt.** 1732 : Fuller, No. 3340.
**Many can brook the weather that
love not the wind.** 1592 : Shakespeare,
L. L. L., IV. ii.
Many dishes make many diseases.
1655 : T. Muffett, *Healths Improve-
ment*, 272 [quoted as a proverb].
Many dogs may easily worry one.
1639 : Clarke, 56.
Many drops make a shower. 1616 :
Honest Lawyer, sig. G2, Many drops
make a floud. 1736 : Bailey, *Dict.*, s.v.
"Drop." 1846 : Denham, *Proverbs*, 1
(Percy S.).

Many drops of water will sink a ship.
1732 : Fuller, No. 3345.

Many estates are spent in the getting,
Since women for tea forsook spinning
and knitting, And men for punch forsook
hewing and splitting. 1736 : Franklin,
Way to Wealth, in *Works*, i. 446 (Bigelow). 1883 : Burne, *Shropsh. Folk-
Lore*, 578 [as in 1736, but with " their
beer" for " punch." Given as a
Chirbury saying].

Many friends no friend. 1875 : A.
B. Cheales, *Proverb. Folk-Lore*, 96. Cf.
Friend (8).

Many frosts and many thowes, Make
many rotten yowes [ewes]. 1846 : Denham, *Proverbs*, 62 (Percy S.). 1872 :
J. Glyde, jr., *Norfolk Garland*, 157.

Many hands make light work. 1401 :
in Wright, *Pol. Poems*, ii. 106 (Rolls
Ser., 1861), Yit many hondis togider
maken ligt werk. *c.* 1460 : *How the Goode
Wife*, in Hazlitt, *Early Pop. Poetry*, i.
188, Many handys make light werke,
my leue childe. *c.* 1550 : *Parl. of
Byrdes*, l. 192, in Ibid., iii. 177. 1634 :
G. Markham, *Art of Archerie*, 20. 1665 :
Head and Kirkman, *Eng. Rogue*, i. 164.
1732 : Fuller, No. 3347. 1923 : *Observer*, 11 Feb., p. 9, col. 7, What is the
use of saying that " Many hands make
light work " when the same copy-book
tells you that " Too many cooks spoil
the broth " ?

Many hands will carry off much
plunder. 1725 : Bailey, tr. Erasmus'
Colloq., 342 [cited as " the old saying "].

Many have been ruined by buying good
pennyworths. 1732 : Fuller, No. 3349.
1736 : Franklin, *Way to Wealth*, in
Works, i. 447 (Bigelow).

Many haws. See Haws.

Many-headed beast, The=The multitude. [Bellua multorum es capitum.—
Horace, *Epist.*, I. i.] 1542 : Udall, tr.
Erasmus' *Apoph.*, 122 (1877), The multitude of the grosse people, being a
beaste of many heades. 1580 : Sidney,
Arcadia, 226 (1893), O weak trust of
the many-headed multitude. 1604 :
Webster, etc., *Malcontent*, III. iii., That
beast with many heads, The staggering
multitude. 1664 : J. Wilson, *Andron.
Commenius*, III. ii., What is this giddy

multitude ?—this beast Of many heads ?
1734 : Pope, *Imit. Horace, Epist.* I. i.
l. 121, The people are a many-headed
beast. 1773 : in *Garrick Corresp.*,
i. 527 (1831), The public is a many-
headed monster and hard to please.
1810 : Scott, *Lady of Lake*, can. v. st. 30,
Thou many-headed monster-thing, Oh,
who would wish to be thy king ! 1834-7 :
Southey, *Doctor*, interch. xxi., I will
tell you [the public] what you are ;
you are a great, ugly, many-headed
beast.

Many hips and haws, Many frosts and
snaws. 1846 : Denham, *Proverbs*, 24
(Percy S.). 1913 : E. M. Wright,
Rustic Speech, etc., 318, Many hips,
many haas, Many frosts, many snaas.
Cf. Haws.

Many humble servants, but not one
true friend. 1732 : Fuller, No. 3350.

Many kinsfolk and few friends. 1546 :
Heywood, *Proverbs*, Pt. I. ch. xi. 1616 :
Rich Cabinet, fo. 50, A man may haue
many kinsfolks, but few friends. 1639 :
Clarke, 26. 1710 : S. Palmer, *Moral
Essays on Proverbs*, 252, Many relations,
few friends.

Many knacks in his budget, He hath.
1659 : Howell, 14.

Many lords many laws. 1633 : Draxe,
7.

Many masters. See Toad (2).

Many men have many minds, But
women have but two : Everything would
they have, And nothing would they do.
Lancs. 1865 : *N. & Q.*, 3rd ser., viii.
494. 1891 : *N. & Q.*, 7th ser., xii. 373.

Many nuts (or nits). See Nut (3).

Many rains, many rowans [mountain-
ash berries] ; Many rowans, many
yawns. 1846 : Denham, *Proverbs*, 54
(Percy S.).

Many relations. See Many kinsfolk.

Many sands will sink a ship. 1630 :
T. Adams, *Works*, 708, Many little sands
gather'd to an heape, faile not to swallow a greet vessell. 1639 : Clarke, 11.
1670 : Ray, 118.

Many seames many beanes. Glos.
1639 : in *Berkeley MSS.*, iii. 33 (1885).

Many slones [sloes] many groans.
1850 : *N. & Q.*, 1st ser., ii. 511. 1884 :
H. Friend, *Flowers and Fl. Lore*, 207,

In Cornwall they have a proverb . . .
" Many slones, many groans."

**Many speak much who cannot speak
well.** 1633 : Draxe, 11. 1670 : Ray, 17.

**Many strike on an anvil, When, they
must strike by measure.** 1670 : Ray, 17.
1732 : Fuller, No. 5561 [with " observe
order " for " strike by measure "].

Many strokes. See Little strokes.

**Many things are lost for want of ask-
ing.** 1640 : Herbert, *Jac. Prudentum.*

**Many things grow in the garden which
were never sowed.** 1659 : Howell, *Proverbs : Span.-Eng.*, 6. 1670 : Ray, 12.
1732 : Fuller, No. 3363.

Many things lawful are not expedient.
1855 : Bohn, 450.

Many ventures make a full freight.
1633 : Draxe, 5. 1670 : Ray, 17. 1694 :
D'Urfey, *Quixote*, Pt. II. Act IV. sc. ii.

Many wells, many buckets. 1546 :
Heywood, *Proverbs*, Pt. II. ch. vii.
1633 : Draxe, 237.

**Many without punishment, but none
without fault.** 1633 : Draxe, 62.
1670 : Ray, 17 [with " sin " for " fault "].

Many women. See Woman (30).

Many words hurt. See Word (16).

Many words, In. See quots. 1548 :
Hall, *Chron.*, Dedn., I haue redde an
olde prouerbe, whiche saithe, that in
many woordes, a lye or twayne sone
maie scape. 1633 : Draxe, 11, Where
many words are the truth often goeth
by.

Many words will not fill a bucket.
1659 : Howell, 9. 1712 : Motteux,
Quixote, Pt. I. bk. iii. ch. iv. [with
" bushel " for " bucket "]. 1732 : Fuller,
No. 3365 [as in 1712].

**Marazion to learn manners, You must
go to.** 1864 : " Cornish Proverbs," in
N. & Q., 3rd ser., v. 275.

Marazion. See also Market-Jew.

Marbles. See quot. 1880 : Courtney, *W. Cornwall Words*, xiii. (E.D.S.),
Those that have marbles may play,
but those that have none must look on.

March, subs. 1. *A bushel of March
dust is worth a king's ransom.* 1533 :
Heywood, *Play of Weather*, 114
(Farmer). 1580 : Tusser, *Husbandrie*,
97 (E.D.S.), March dust to be sold,
Worth ransome of gold. 1662: Fuller,

Worthies, i. 120 (1840), In England a
bushel, etc. 1732 : Fuller, No. 30.
1753 : *Gent. Mag.*, 267 [with " peck " for
" bushel." Midland Counties]. 1812 :
Brady, *Clavis Cal.*, i. 66. 1893 : Inwards, *Weather Lore*, 18 [both " bushel "
and " peck "].

2. *A damp rotten March gives pain
to farmers.* Ibid., 19, March damp and
warm Will do farmer much harm.

3. *A dry March and a wet May Fill
barns and bays with corn and hay.*
1886 : Holland, *Cheshire Gloss.*, 443
(E.D.S.). 1917 : Bridge, *Cheshire Proverbs*, 162.

4. *A dry March, an' a windy; A full
barn an' a findy.* 1876 : C. C. Robinson, *Mid-Yorks Gloss.*, 40 (E.D.S.).

5. *A dry March never begs its bread.*
1846 : Denham, *Proverbs*, 31 (Percy S.).
1893 : Inwards, *Weather Lore*, 18 [with
" and cold " after " dry "].

6. *A dry March, wet April, and cool
May, Fill barn, cellar, and bring much
hay.* Ibid., 20.

7. *A fair March is worth a king's
ransom.* c. 1598 : Jonson, *Case is
Altered*, V. iv.

8. *A March sun sticks like a lock of
wool.* 1893 : Inwards, *Weather Lore*, 19.

9. *A March wind is salt which
seasoneth all pulse.* c. 1620 : Markham,
Farew. to Husbandry, 95 (1676) [quoted
as " an old saying among the best "
farmers].

10. *A March wisher (or whisker) Is
never a good fisher.* 1732 : Fuller, No.
6127 [" whisker "]. 1893 : Inwards,
Weather Lore, 19 [" wisher "].

11. *A peck of March dust and a
shower in May, Makes the corn green
and the fields gay.* 1732 : Fuller, No.
6476. 1893 : Inwards, 18.

12. *A wet March makes a sad harvest.* 1878 : Dyer, *Eng. Folk-Lore*, 252.
1893 : Inwards, 19.

13. *A windy March and a rainy April
make May beautiful.* 1659 : Howell,
Proverbs: Span.-Eng., 21. 1732 : Fuller,
No. 468. 1893 : Inwards, 20.

14. *As it rains in March, so it rains
in June.* Ibid., 20.

15. *As much dew in March, so much
fog rises in August.* Ibid., 19.

16. *As much fog in March, so much rain in summer.* Ibid., 19.

17. *Dust in March brings grass and foliage.* Ibid., 18.

18. *Fog in March, thunder in July.* Ibid., 19.

19. *In beginning or in end, March its gifts will send.* Ibid., 18.

20. *In March, kill crow, pie and cadow* [jackdaw], *Rook, buzzard, and raven; Or else go desire them To seek a new haven.* 1846: Denham, *Proverbs*, 35 (Percy S.).

21. *In March, the birds begin to search; in April, the corn begins to fill; in May, the birds begin to lay.* 1869: Hazlitt, 233.

22. *In Valentine March lays her line.* Ibid., 235.

23. *March birds are best.* 1678: Ray, 344. 1732: Fuller, No. 3368. 1846: Denham, *Proverbs*, 31 (Percy S.). 1904: Co. *Folk-Lore: Northumb.*, 176 (F.L.S.).

24. *March borrows.* See quots. 1646: Browne, *Pseudo. Epi.*, bk. vi. ch. iv., So is it usual among us . . . to ascribe unto March certain borrowed days from April. 1670: Ray, 41, April borrows three days of March and they are ill. 1687: Aubrey, *Gentilisme, etc.*, 95 (F.L.S.) [as in 1670]. 1710: *Brit. Apollo*, iii. No. 18, col. 4, March borrows of April Three days, and they are ill; April returns them back again Three days, and they are rain. 1732: Fuller, Nos. 6133, 6134, March borrows of April Three days, and they be ill. April borrows of March again Three days of wind and rain. 1893: Inwards, 22, [as in 1732, *plus*] March borrowed of April, April borrowed of May, Three days, they say; One rained, and one snew, And the other was the worst day that ever blew. Staffs. March borrowed from April Three days, and they were ill: The first of them is wan and weet, The second it is snaw and sleet, The third of them is peel-a-bane, And freezes the wee bird's neb to the stane. 1921: R. L. Gales, *Old-World Essays*, 250, March borrowed a cloak from his father and pawned it after three days. Cf. **Borrowing days.**

25. *March comes in like a lion and goes out like a lamb*—very occasionally reversed. 1624: B. & F., *Wife for a Month*, II. i., *Men.* I would choose March, for I would come in like a lion. *Tony.* But you'd go out like a lamb, when you went to hanging. 1670: Ray, 41, March hackham comes in, etc. 1740: North, *Lives of Norths*, i. 259 (Bohn), Then came my Lord Shaftesbury, like the month of March, as they say, " in like a lion, and out like a lamb." 1849: Brontë, *Shirley*, ch. xv., Like March, having come in like a lion, he purposed to go out like a lamb. 1893: Inwards, 19, March, black ram Comes in, etc. Ibid., 20, March comes in like a lamb and goes out like a lion. 1921: *Sphere*, 12 March, p. 254, col. 1, In all proper well-regulated years March comes in like a lion and goes out like a lamb.

26. *March comes in with an adder's head, and goes out with a peacock's tail.* 1846: Denham, *Proverbs*, 32 (Percy S.). 1921: R. L. Gales, *Old-World Essays*, 250.

27. *March dry, good rye; April wet, good wheat.* 1893: Co. *Folk-Lore: Suffolk*, 162 (F.L.S.).

28. *March dust on an apple-leaf brings all kinds of fruit to grief.* 1876: Bull, *Pomona Hereford.*, 50.

29. *March flowers Make no summer bowers.* 1893: Inwards, 18.

30. *March grass never did good.* 1678: Ray, 44. 1732: Fuller, No. 6475. 1846: Denham, *Proverbs*, 31 (Percy S.). 1904: Co. *Folk-Lore: Northumb.*, 175 (F.L.S.).

31. *March grows never dows* [flourishes]. 1855: Robinson, *Whitby Gloss.*, 48, " March grows Never dows." March blossom, being premature, is often blighted.

32. *March many weathers.* 1678: Ray, 44. 1732: Fuller, No. 6475, March many-weathers rain'd and blow'd. 1893: Inwards, *Weather Lore*, 18. 1912: R. L. Gales, *Studies in Arcady*, 2nd ser., 104.

33. *March rain spoils more than clothes.* 1659: Howell, *Proverbs: Span.-Eng.*, 21, March water is worse than a

stain in cloath. 1882 : Mrs. Chamberlain, *W. Worcs. Words*, 37 (E.D.S.).
1893 : Inwards, 19 [as in 1659 and
1882].

34. *March, search; April, try; May
will prove if you live or die.* 1855 :
N. & Q., 1st ser., xi. 416. 1893 : Inwards, 20.

35. *March sun lets snow stand on a
stone.* Ibid., 18.

36. *March thunder makes all the world
wonder.* 1895 : Rye, *E. Anglian Words*,
228 (E.D.S.).

37. *March wind and May sun Makes
clothes white and maids dun.* 1670 :
Ray, 41. 1744 : Claridge, in Mills,
Essay on Weather, 100 (1773). 1882 :
N. & Q., 6th ser., vi. 14. 1893 : In-
wards, 20.

38. *March wind kindles the ether
[adder] and blooms the whin.* 1846 :
Denham, *Proverbs*, 39 (Percy S.).

39. *March winds and April showers
Bring forth May flowers.* 1886 : El-
worthy, *West Som. Word-Book*, 461
(E.D.S.). 1893 : Inwards, 20.

40. *March yeans the lammie And buds
the thorn, And blows through the flint Of
an ox's horn.* Northumb. Ibid., 18.

41. *Never come March, never come
winter.* 1882 : Mrs. Chamberlain, *W.
Worcs. Words*, 37 (E.D.S.).

42. *On the first of March, The crows
begin to search.* 1846 : Denham, *Proverbs,* 39 (Percy S.).

43. *So many fogs in March, so many
frosts in May.* 1669 : *New Help to
Discourse*, 284, So many mists as there
be in March, so many hoar frosts there
will be after Easter. 1732 : Fuller, No.
6474, So many mists as in March you
see, So many frosts in May will be.
1823 : Moor, *Suffolk Words*, 510. 1830 :
Forby, *Vocab. E. Anglia*, 416. 1879 :
N. & Q., 5th ser., xi. 327, " Fogs in
March, frosties in May " is a common
proverb in this part of Surrey [Limps-
field]. 1893 : Inwards, 19, [as in 1732,
plus] As many mistises in March, So
many frostises in May.—Wilts. Ibid.,
20, Mists in March bring rain, Or in
May frosts again.

44. *So many frosts in March so many
in May.* 1659 : Howell, 16, If frost in

March, there will be some in May.
1737 : Ray, 269. 1893 : Inwards, 19.

45. *The March sun causeth dust, and
the wind blows it about.* 1670 : Ray, 17.

46. *The March sun raises but dissolves
not.* 1640 : Herbert, *Jac. Prudentum.*

47. *Whatever March does not want,
April brings along.* 1893 : Inwards, 23.

48. *When it thunders in March, it
brings sorrow.* Ibid., 19.

See also **April** (22) ; **Borrowing days** ;
Cuckoo (4), (12), (13), and (16) ; **Febru-
ary** (6), (8), and (18) ; **Frosty winter** ;
January (1), (14), and (21) ; **Leeks** ;
Nettles (3); **September** (2); and **Wheat** (2).

Mare. 1. *A mare's shoe and a horse's
shoe are both alike.* 1732 : Fuller, No.
318.

2. *If the mare have a bald [white] face,
the filly will have a blaze.* 1659 :
Howell, 2. 1696 : D'Urfey, *Quixote,*
Pt. III. Act I. 1732 : Fuller, No. 5596.
1828 : Carr, *Craven Dialect*, i. 21.

3. *I'll not go before my mare to the
market.* 1678 : Ray, 259.

4. *Mares' tails. See* **Mackerel sky.**

5. *There are more mares in the wood
than Grisell.* 1678 : Ray, 173.

6. *To find a mare's nest.* 1576 : R.
Peterson, *Galateo*, 111 (1892), Nor stare
in a mans face, as if he had spied
a mares nest. 1582 : Breton, *Works*,
i. *a* 6 (Grosart), To laughe at a horse
nest, and whine too like a boy. 1619 :
B. & F., *Bonduca*, V. ii., Why dost
thou laugh ? What mare's nest hast
thou found ? 1704 : D'Urfey, *Tales
Trag. and Comical*, 216 n., An old wife's
saw . . . He has found a mare's nest,
and laughs at the eggs. 1864 : " Cornish Proverbs," in *N. & Q.*, 3rd ser., vi.
494, They have found a wee's nest
[mare's nest], and are laughing over
the eggs. 1922 : Weyman, *Ovington's
Bank*, ch. xxxii.

7. *Whose mare is dead?* = What's
the trouble ? 1595 : *Maroccus Extaticus*, 5 (Percy S.), Whose mare is
dead, that you are thus melancoly ?
c. 1598 : Deloney, *Gentle Craft*, Pt. II.
ch. iii. 1598 : Shakespeare, 2 *Henry IV.*,
II. i., How now ! whose mare's dead ?
What's the matter ? 1738 : Swift, *Polite
Convers.*, Dial. I.

See also **Horse** (51) ; **Man** (78) ; **Money** (33) ; **Ride** ; **Simper as a mare; and Tale** (7).

Margaret's flood [Devon] = heavy rain about St. Margaret's Day—20 July. 1850 : *N. & Q.*, 1st ser., ii. 512.

Margery, good cow. *See* quots. 1546 : Heywood, *Proverbs*, Pt. II. ch. vii., Margery good coowe, (quoth he), gaue a good meele, But than she cast it downe again with hir heele. 1639 : Clarke, 83 [" gives " for " gave," and " kicks " for " cast "]. 1670 : Ray, 185, Madge, good cow, gives a good pail of milk, and then kicks it down with her foot.

Mariners' craft is the grossest, yet of handicrafts the subtillest. 1629 : *Book of Meery Riddles*, Prov. 101.

Mark after her mother, She hath a. 1678 : Ray, 259.

Market. 1. *As the market goes wives must sell.* 1732 : Fuller, No. 734.

2. *Forsake not the market for* [because of] *the toll.* 1605 : Camden, *Remains*, 322 (1870). 1670 : Ray, 119. 1736 : Bailey, *Dict.*, s.v. " Toll."

3. *My market's made.* 1590 : Lodge, *Rosalynde*, 104 (Hunt. Cl.), Well, sir, if your market may be made no where els, home again. 1649 : Quarles, *Virgin Widow*, I., Is it even so ? Quack's thread is fairly spun, Quack may go home again, his market's done. 1724 : Defoe, *Roxana*, in *Works*, xiii. 143 (Boston, 1903), " In her coach ! " said I ; " upon my word, she had made her market then ; I suppose she made hay while the sun shone."

4. *No man makes haste to the market where there's nothing to be bought but blows.* 1670 : Ray, 119. 1732 : Fuller, No. 3651.

5. *The market is the best garden.* 1640 : Herbert, *Jac. Prudentum.* 1670 : Ray, 17, [as in 1640, *plus*] At London they are wont to say, Cheapside is the best garden.

6. *You may know by the market folks how the market goes.* 1546 : Heywood, *Proverbs*, Pt. I. ch. xi., Men know . . . How the market goth by the market men. *c.* 1594 : Bacon, *Promus*, No. 642. 1600 : Day, *Blind Beggar*, IV. iii.

1670 : Ray, 119. 1716 : Ward, *Female Policy*, 94. 1732 : Fuller, No. 5952.

Market - Jew = Marazion, Corn. *In your own light like the Mayor of Market-Jew.* 1859 : *N. & Q.*, 2nd ser., viii. 451. 1906 : Q.-Couch, *Mayor of Troy*, Prol. *See also* **Marazion.**

Mark Lane. *See* quot. 1591 : Greene, *Works*, x. 99 (Grosart), Perceiued he was bitten [cheated] of all the bite [money] in his bung [purse], and turned to walke penylesse in Marke lane, as the old prouerbe is.

Marls sand, He that. *See* quots. 1753 : *Gent. Mag.*, 120, We have an old saying [Lancs] : He that marls sand, may buy land ; He that marls moss, suffers no loss ; But he that marls clay, throws his money away. 1815 : W. Peck, *Topog. Acc. of Isle of Axholme*, 47, If you marle sand, you may buy land ; If you marle moss, you shall have no loss ; But if you marle clay, you throw all away. 1889 : Peacock, *Manley, etc., Gloss.*, 341 (E.D.S.) [as in 1815, but with " there is " for " you shall have," and " fling " for " throw "]. 1908 : W. Johnson, *Folk Memory*, 220 [as in 1889]. 1917 : Bridge, *Cheshire Proverbs*, 72, He who marls sand may buy the land.

Marriage. 1. *At marriages and funerals friends are discerned from kinsfolk.* 1578 : Florio, *First Fruites*, fo. 25, At mariages and burials friends and kinrede is known. 1629 : *Book of Meery Riddles*, Prov. 55 [as in 1578]. 1732 : Fuller, No. 829.

2. *He has a great fancy to marriage that goes to the devil for a wife.* Ibid., No. 1856.

3. *Marriage and hanging go by destiny.* 1519 : Horman, *Vulgaria*, fo. 19, It is my destenye to be hanged. 1546 : Heywood, *Proverbs*, Pt. I. ch. iii., Wedding is destiny And hanging likewise, saith that proverb. 1595 : Shakespeare, *M. of Venice*, II. ix., The ancient saying is no heresy, Hanging and wiving goes by destiny. 1624 : B. & F., *Wife for a Month*, II. i. 1664 : Butler, *Hudibras*, Pt. II. can. i. l. 839, If matrimony and hanging go By dest'ny, why not whipping too ?

1784 : *New Foundl. Hosp. for Wit*, v.
106.

4. *Marriage is a lottery.* 1875 :
Smiles, *Thrift*, 252, The maxim is
current, that " marriage is a lottery."

5. *Marriage is honourable but housekeeping is a shrew.* 1616 : Breton,
Works, ii. *e* 8 (Grosart), Marriage is
honourable. 1670 : Ray, 48. 1780 :
Mother Bunch, 2nd Pt., 28 (Gomme,
1885), For although housekeeping is
chargeable, yet marriage is honourable.

6. *Marriage leapeth up upon the
saddle, and repentance upon the crupper.*
1669 : *Politeuphuia*, 35. 1732 : Fuller,
No. 3372.

7. *Marriage with peace is this world's
Paradise; with strife, this life's Purgatory.* 1669 : *Politeuphuia*, 227.

8. *Marriages are made in heaven.* [A
prudent wife is from the Lord.—*Prov.*
xix. 14.] 1567 : Painter, *Pal. of
Pleasure*, iii. 24 (Jacobs), True it is,
that mariages be don in heauen and
performed in earth. 1663 : Killigrew,
Parson's Wedding, II. vii., Were not
those marriages made in heaven ?
1738 : Swift, *Polite Convers.*, Dial. I.
1850 : Smedley, *Frank Fairlegh*, ch. xlvii.
1922 : Lucas, *Genevra's Money*, ch. xi.

9. *More belongs to marriage than four
bare legs in a bed.* 1546 : Heywood,
Proverbs, Pt. I. ch. viii. *c.* 1630 : in
Roxb. Ballads, i. 166 (Hindley). 1738 :
Swift, *Polite Convers.*, Dial. I. 1822 :
Scott, *Nigel*, ch. xxxvii., A sort of
penny-wedding it will prove, where all
men contribute to the young folks'
maintenance, that they may not have
just four bare legs in a bed thegether.

See also **Age and wedlock ; May**, F (14)
and (15) ; **Wedding ;** and **Wedlock**.

**Married man must turn his staff into
a stake, The.** 1640 : Herbert, *Jac. Prudentum* [with " turns " for " must turn "].
1670 : Ray, 17.

Marrow to the patch = well suited.
1917 : Bridge, *Cheshire Proverbs*, 94.

Marry, *verb.* 1. *Before thou marry
Make sure of an house wherein to tarry.*
1666 : Torriano, *Piazza Univ.*, 144,
Before thou marry, get thy habitation
ready. 1670 : Ray, 17. 1732 : Fuller,
No. 6396.

2. *He that goes to marry likes to know
whether he shall have a chimney to his
house.* Corn. 1869 : Hazlitt, 178.

3. *He that marries a slut eats mickle
dirt.* 1683 : Meriton, *Yorkshire Ale*,
83–7 (1697).

4. *He that marries late marries ill.*
1589 : Nashe, *Works*, i. 17 (Grosart),
Thys common prouerbe, he that marrieth late marrieth euill. 1666 : Torriano, *Piazza Univ.*, 143, Who marries
late marries amiss.

5. *He that marrieth for wealth sells his
liberty.* 1670 : Ray, 17. 1732 : Fuller,
No. 2238.

6. *He who is about to marry should
consider how it is with his neighbours.*
1855 : Bohn, 400.

7. *If you marry in Lent you will live
to repent.* 1850 : *N. & Q.*, 1st ser., ii.
259. 1879 : Henderson, *Folk-Lore N.
Counties*, 34.

8. *It is better to marry a quiet fool
than a witty scold.* 1647 : *Countrym.
New Commonwealth*, 34. 1669 : *Politeuphuia*, 227.

9. *It's good to marry late or never.*
1670 : Ray, 47.

10. *Marry and thrive.* See **Wive and
thrive**.

11. *Marry first and love will follow.*
1714 : *Spectator*, No. 605, The old
family maxim, that If she marries first,
love will come after. 1780 : Mrs.
Cowley, *Belle's Stratagem*, III. i.

12. *Marry in haste, repent at leisure.*
1566 : Painter, *Pal. of Pleasure*, i. 115
(Jacobs) . . . leaste in making hastie
choise, leasure for repentaunce shuld
folow. 1592 : Greene, *Works*, xi. 86
(Grosart), She was afrayde to match in
haste least shee might repent at ley-
sure. 1632 : Randolph, *Jealous Lovers*,
V. ii., Marry too soon, and you'll repent too late. 1692 Congreve, *Old
Batchelor*, V. viii. 1713 : Gay, *Wife of
Bath*, I. 1842 : Barham, *Ing. Legends*,
2nd ser.: " Aunt Fanny," They " repent
at leisure who marry at random."

13. *Marry your daughters betimes,
lest they marry themselves.* 1651 : Herbert, *Jac. Prudentum*, 2nd ed. 1670 :
Ray, 47. 1732 : Fuller, No. 3373.

14. *Marry your son when you will ;*

your daughter when you can. 1640 : Herbert, *Jac. Prudentum.* 1696: D'Urfey, *Quixote*, Pt. III. Act I. 1736 : Bailey, *Dict.*, s.v. "Daughter." 1875 : A. B. Cheales, *Proverb. Folk-Lore*, 48 [with "may" for "can"].

15. *To marry the mixen for the sake of the muck=*" to marry an undesirable person for money." 1737 : Ray, 202, You'd marry a midden for muck. 1883 : Burne, *Shropsh. Folk-Lore*, 597.

16. *Who marries between the sickle and the scythe, Will never thrive.* 1678 : Ray, 352. 1846: Denham, *Proverbs*, 49 (Percy S.). 1872 : J. Glyde, jr., *Norfolk Garland*, 16, They that wive Between sickle and scythe Shall never thrive. Cf. **Sickle** (1).

17. *Who marries does well, who marries not does better.* 1659 : Howell, *Letters*, ii. 666 (Jacobs). 1666 : Torriano, *Piazza Univ.*, 143.

18. *Who marrieth for love without money, hath merry nights and sorry days.* 1666 : Ibid., 10, He who marries for love, in the night-time hath pleasure, in the day-time sorrow. 1670 : Ray, 17. 1732 : Fuller, No. 5710.

See also **May, F** (14) and (15) ; **Wed** ; **Wife** ; and **Widow**.

Marry! come up, my dirty cousin. 1678 : Ray, 68. 1700 : Ward, *London Spy*, 416 (1924). 1738 : Swift, *Polite Convers.*, Dial. II. 1847 ; Halliwell, *Dict.*, s.v., . . . a saying addressed to any one who affects excessive delicacy. 1917 : Bridge, *Cheshire Proverbs*, 94.

Marsham, Lincs. *See* quots. 1662 : Fuller, *Worthies*, ii. 269 (1840), They held together as the men of Mar[s]ham when they lost their common. 1790 : Grose, *Prov. Gloss.*, s.v. "Lincs" [as in 1662]. 1818 : Scott, *Heart of Midl.*, ch. xxix. [Newark man *loq.*] They hold together no better than the men of Marsham when they lost their common.

Marshland, He is arrested by the bailiff of. 1662 : Fuller, *Worthies*, ii. 447 (1840). 1790 : Grose, *Prov. Gloss.*, s.v. "Norfolk." 1874 : Smiles, *Lives of Engineers*, i. 15, When a man was stricken down by the ague, it was said of him, " he is arrested by the bailiff of Marshland."

Martin. *See* **Robin** (5).

Martin Harvey's duck, Weak in paarts, Like. 1906 : *Cornish N. & Q.*, 262.

Martin's hammer. *See* quot. 1847 : Halliwell, *Dict.*, s.v., "She has had Martin's-hammer knocking at her wicket," said of a woman who has twins.

Martinmas. 1. *Between Martinmas and Yule, Water's worth wine in any pule.* 1846–59 : Denham *Tracts*, ii. 96 (F.L.S.). 1878 : Dyer, *Eng. Folk-Lore*, 261, In the North of England, there is a curious rhyme descriptive of the value of rain in the latter part of the year— " 'Tween Martinmas and Yule, Water's wine in every pool."

2. *When the ice before Martlemas bears a duck, Then look for a winter o' mire and muck.* 1881 : Evans, *Leics. Words*, 191 (E.D.S.) [cited as "a common weather proverb"].

3. *Where the wind is on Martinmas Eve, there it will be the rest of the winter.* 1893 : Inwards, *Weather Lore*, 37 [" an old saying with the people round "— Atherstone].

4. *Wind north-west at Martinmas, severe winter to come.* Hunts. Ibid., 37.

See also **St. Martin.**

Marton Chapel, All on one side like. 1886 : Holland, *Cheshire Gloss.*, 444 (E.D.S.). 1917 : Bridge, *Cheshire Proverbs*, 9, . . . The meaning is lost.

Marvel. *See* **Wonder.**

Mass and meat never hindered work. 1817 : Scott, *Rob Roy*, ch. xxix. 1823 : Scott, *St. Ronan's*, ch. xiv. 1863 : *N. & Q.*, 3rd ser., iii. 258, Mass and meat never marred work. Ibid., 439, Mass and meat take up nobody's time. Cf. **Meals and matins; Meat** (5); and **Prayers and provender.**

Master, *subs.* 1. *A master of straw eats a servant of steel.* 1640 : Herbert, *Jac. Prudentum.*

2. *He can ill be master that never was scholar.* 1639 : Clarke, 149.

3. *He that is a master must serve (another).* 1640 : Herbert, *Jac. Prudentum.*

4. *He that is master of himself will soon be master of others.* 1732 : Fuller, No. 2182.

5. *He that teaches himself has a fool to his master.* 1641: Jonson, *Timber:* "Consilia," For he that was only taught by himself, had a fool to his master. 1692 : L'Estrange, *Æsop*, 283 (3rd ed.). 1710 : S. Palmer, *Moral Essays on Proverbs*, 32. 1867: F. C. H., in *N. & Q.*, 3rd ser., xi. 192, [as to origin of the saying] I believe it has arisen from the following sentence of St. Bernard :— " Qui se sibi magistrum constituit, stulto se discipulum subdit." Ep. 83— which may be thus rendered in English : He that will teach himself in school, Becomes a scholar to a fool.

6. *If the master say the crow is white, the servant must not say 'tis black.* 1672 : Walker, *Parœm.*, 10. 1681: W. Robertson, *Phraseol. Generalis*, 871.

7. *Masters should be sometimes blind, and sometimes deaf.* 1732 : Fuller, No. 3376.

8. *The master's eye. See* Eye (9), (13), and (17).

9. *The master's footsteps fatten the soil.* 1537 : R. Whitford, *Werke for Housholders*, sig. F5, The steppe of the husbande [farmer] maketh a fatte donghyll. 1659: Howell, 10. 1666 : Torriano, *Piazza Univ.*, 206 [with " field " for " soil "].

Master, *verb. Better master one than engage with ten.* 1732: Fuller, No. 916.

Master Hogge. *See* quots. 1857 : *Archæologia*, xxxvii. 483, " Master Hogge and his man John, they did cast the first can-non." [No date given for original.] 1894 : A. J. C. Hare, *Sussex*, 125, The Hog House, with a hog and 1581 carved over the door [near Buxted]. It was the residence of the Hogge or Huggett family, of whom Ralf Hogge, in 1543, cast the first iron cannon made in England :—" Master Huggett and his man John, They did cast the first cannon. "

Mastiff. 1. *A mastiff groweth the fiercer for being tied up.* 1732 : Fuller, No. 320.

2. *The mastiff never loveth the greyhound.* 1576 : Pettie, *Petite Pall.*, ii. 85 (Gollancz) [quoted—" as the saying is "].

3. *Though the mastiff be gentle, yet bite him not by the lip.* 1640 : Herbert, *Jac.Prudentum.* 1696: D'Urfey,*Quixote*, Pt. III. Act I. sc. i., As the proverb says, tho' the bear be gentle, don't bite him by the nose. 1732 : Fuller, No. 5011.

Match, A. *See* quots. 1670 : Ray, 216, A match quoth Hatch, when he got his wife by the breech. 1678 : Ray, 76, A match quoth Jack, when he kist his dame. 1732 : Fuller, No. 321 [as in 1678, but with " John " for " Jack "].

Matter but the mind, 'Tis not. Ibid., No. 5105.

Matter lieth a bleeding, His. 1562 : Heywood, *Epigr.*, No. 209, Here lieth all and bleedeth. 1633 : Draxe, 198 [section on " Ill success "].

Matty Tasker's jarlers, Like one o' owd. " Jarler "=anything out of the common. 1917: Bridge, *Cheshire Proverbs*, 91.

Mavern Hill. *See* Malvern Hill.

Maxfield measure, heap and thrutch= very good measure. 1670 : Ray, 217, Macklesfield measure, heap and thrust. *Cheshire.* 1790: Grose, *Prov. Gloss.*, s.v. " Cheshire." 1877 : E. Leigh, *Cheshire Gloss.*, 132. 1917 : Bridge, *Cheshire Proverbs*, 94, Maxfield measure, hĕăp and thrutch ; or, Maxfilt mizzer, up-yepped and thrutched [pressed down].

May, *subs.* A. COLD MAY. 1. *A cold May and a windy makes a fat barn and findy.* 1659: Howell, 21. 1744: Claridge, in Mills, *Essay on Weather*, 101 (1773) [with " full " for " fat "]. 1825 : Hone, *Ev. Day Book*, i. 669. 1893 : Inwards, *Weather Lore*, 26 [as in 1744].

2. *A cold May is good for corn and bad for hay.* 1891 : C. Wordsworth, *Rutland Words*, 22 (E.D.S.).

3. *A cold May is good for corn and hay.* 1893 : Inwards, *Weather Lore*, 26.

4. *A cold May is kind.* 1882 : Mrs. Chamberlain, *W. Worcs. Words*, 17 (E.D.S.), Local proverb [" kind "= favourable].

5. *A cold May is kindly, And fills the barn finely.* 1893 : Inwards, 26.

6. *Cold May brings many things.* Ibid., 26.

7. *Cold May enriches no one.* Ibid., 26.

8. *For an east wind in May 'tis your
duty to pray.* Ibid., 26.

B. DRY MAY. 1. *A dry May and a
dripping June Bring all things into tune.*
Beds. Ibid., 28.

2. *A dry May and a leaking June
Make the farmer whistle a merry tune.*
Ibid., 27.

3. *A dry May is followed by a wet
June.* Ibid., 27.

4. *Dry May brings nothing gay.*
Ibid., 25.

C. MISTY MAY. *Mist in May and
heat in June, Make the harvest come
right soon.* 1846: Denham, *Proverbs,*
47 (Percy S.). 1882: Mrs. Chamberlain, *W. Worcs. Words,* 37 (E.D.S.).
1893: Inwards, 27, [also] A misty
May and a hot June Bring cheap meal
and harvest soon.

D. WARM MAY. 1. *A hot May makes
a fat church-yard.* 1659: Howell, 11.
1670: Ray, 42. 1825: Hone, *Ev. Day
Book,* i. 669. 1869: *N. & Q.,* 4th ser.,
iv. 174, A hot May makes a fat church-
hay [yard]. Cornwall. 1893: Inwards,
25.

2. *For a warm May the parsons pray.*
1893: Inwards, 25.

E. WET MAY. 1. *A dropping May
Fills the barns with corn and hay.* 1917:
Bridge, *Cheshire Proverbs,* 162.

2. *A leaky May and a warm June,
Bring on the harvest very soon.* 1878:
Dyer, *Eng. Folk-Lore,* 256.

3. *A May flood never did good.* 1639:
Clarke, 307. 1670: Ray, 41. 1744:
Claridge, in Mills, *Essay on Weather,* 101
(1773). 1893: Inwards, 26.

4. *A May wet was never kind yet.*
Ibid., 25.

5. *A wet and windy May, Fills the
barn with corn and hay.* 1917: Bridge,
Cheshire Proverbs, 162.

6. *A wet May brings plenty of hay.*
1846: Denham, *Proverbs,* 44 (Percy
S.), A wet May Will fill a byre full
of hay. 1889: Peacock, *Manley, etc.,
Gloss.,* 345 (E.D.S.), A weet May Brings
plenty o' corn, An' plenty o' haay.
1893: Inwards, 26, [as in 1846, *plus*]
A wet May makes a big load of
hay. West Shropshire. 1917: Bridge,
Cheshire Proverbs, 162.

7. *May damp and cool fills the barns
and wine vats.* 1893: Inwards, 25.

8. *May rain kills lice.* 1846: Denham, *Proverbs,* 43 (Percy S.).

9. *The haddocks are good When dipped
in May flood.* 1862: Chambers, *Book of
Days,* i. 569 (1869). 1893: Inwards, 25.

10. *Water in May is bread all the
year.* 1666: Torriano, *Piazza Univ.,*
135. 1878: Dyer, *Eng. Folk-Lore,* 256.

F. UNCLASSIFIED. 1. *A red gay May.*
See quot. 1623: Wodroephe, *Spared
Houres,* 475, A red gay May is best in
any yeare; Februare full snow is to
ye ground most deare; A whistling
March (that makes the ploughman
blithe); and moistie April that fits him
for the sithe.

2. *A snow-storm in May Is worth a
waggon-load of hay.* 1893: Inwards, 27.

3. *As fine as a May-pole on May-day.*
1846: Denham, *Proverbs,* 43 (Percy S.).

4. *Be it weal or be it woe, Beans
blow before May doth go.* 1678: Ray,
351. 1732: Fuller, No. 6202 [with
"should" before "blow"]. 1893:
Inwards, 27 [as in 1678].

5. *Be sure of hay Till the end of May.*
1732: Fuller, No. 6197.

6. *Blossoms in May Are not good
some say.* 1893: Inwards, 25.

7. *Come it early or come it late, In
May comes the cow-quake* [tremulous
grass]. 1670: Ray, 41, May come she
early or come she late, she'll make the
cow to quake. 1732: Fuller, No. 6191,
May come early, come late, 'Twill make
the cow to quake. 1893: Inwards, 26.

8. *He who sows oats in May, Gets little
that way.* 1846: Denham, *Proverbs,* 47
(Percy S.). 1893: Inwards, 27.

9. *If May will be a gardener, he will
not fill the granaries.* Ibid., 25.

10. *If you sweep the house with broom
in May, You'll sweep the head of that
house away.* 1878: *Folk-Lore Record,*
i. 52. 1879: Henderson, *Folk-Lore
N. Counties,* 50 [heard in Sussex].
1887: Zincke, *Hist. of Wherstead,* 179,
I used to hear the rhymes:—"Sweep
with a broom that is cut in May, And
you will sweep the head of the house
away."

11. *In May an east-lying field is*

*worth wain and oxen; in June, the oxen
and the yoke.* 1893: Inwards, 27.

12. *Look at your corn in May, and
you'll come weeping away: Look at the
same in June, and you'll come home in
another tune.* 1639: Clarke, 307 [a
little varied]. 1670: Ray, 41. 1827:
Hone, *Table-Book*, 667, He that goes to
see his wheat in May Comes weeping
away. 1883: Burne, *Shropsh. Folk-
Lore*, 579, Of green corn: Go in the
May, And come weeping away: Go in
the June, And come home another tune.
1893: Inwards, 27, . . . a proverb alluding to the magical way in which
unpromising crops sometimes recover.

13. *Many thunderstorms in May, And
the farmer sings "Hey! hey!"* Ibid.,
27.

14. *Married in May will soon decay.*
1846: Denham, *Proverbs*, 48 (Percy S.),
From the marriages in May All the
bairns die and decay. 1872: J. Glyde,
jr., *Norfolk Garland*, 16 [as in 1846].
1917: Bridge, *Cheshire Proverbs*, 93.

15. *Marry in May, you'll rue it for
aye.* 1675: *Poor Robin Alman.*, May,
The proverb saies . . . Of all the
moneths 'tis worst to wed in May.
1879: Henderson, *Folk-Lore N. Counties*,
34, The ancient proverb still lives on
the lips of the people of Scotland and
the Borders—Marry in May Rue for aye.
1913: E. M. Wright, *Rustic Speech, etc.*,
218, Marry in May, you'll rue it for aye,
is a Devonshire saying.

16. *May and December* (or *January*).
c. 1386: Chaucer, *Merch. Tale*, l. 449,
That she, this mayden, which that
May us highte . . . should wedded be
vnto this Ianuarie. 1606: Dekker,
Works, ii. 71 (Grosart), You doe wrong
to Time, enforcing May to embrace
December. *c.* 1613: Rowlands, *Paire
of Spy-Knaues*, 7 (Hunt. Cl.), Yonder
goes cold December match'd with May.
1634: Massinger, *Guardian*, I. i., I am
in the May of my abilities, And you in
your December. 1891: R. Buchanan,
Coming Terror, 267 (O.), When asthmatic
January weds buxom May.

17. *May and June are twin sisters.*
1846: Denham, *Proverbs*, 49 (Percy S.).

18. *May-bees don't fly this month.*

A punning saying. 1738: Swift, *Polite
Convers.*, Dial. I., *Miss.* Maybe there is
colonel. *Col.* Ay; but May bees don't
fly now, miss.

19. *May chets bad luck begets.* "Chets"
=children in Cornwall, and, hence,
kittens also. 1690: Dryden, *Amphitryon*, III., Blear-ey'd, like a May-
kitten. 1865: Hunt, *Pop. Romances
W. of Eng.*, 430 (1896). 1878: Dyer,
Eng. Folk-Lore, 176. 1879: Henderson, *Folk-Lore N. Counties*, 115, A
certain unluckiness is held all England
over to attend a May kitten as well as
a May baby. 1882: Jago, *Gloss. of
Cornish Dialect*, 131. 1902: *N. & Q.*,
9th ser., x. 77, In Huntingdonshire it
is a common saying that a "May
kitten makes a dirty cat." 1913:
E. M. Wright, *Rustic Speech, etc.*, 218.

20. *May never goes out without a wheat-
ear.* 1830: Forby, *Vocab. E. Anglia*,
417. 1893: *Co. Folk-Lore: Suffolk*, 163
(F.L.S.).

21. *May-day has come and gone, thou
art a gosling and I am none.* 1846:
Denham, *Proverbs*, 44 (Percy S.). 1904:
Co. Folk-Lore: Northumb., 177 (F.L.S.).

22. *Never cast a clout till May be out.*
1732: Fuller, No. 6193 [with "Leave not
off" for "Never cast"]. 1886: Elworthy, *West Som. Word - Book*, 467
(E.D.S.), If you would the doctor pay
Leave your flannels off in May. 1887:
Parish and Shaw, *Dict. Kent. Dialect*,
99 (E.D.S.). 1893: Inwards, *Weather
Lore*, 26, Till May be out Leave not
off a clout: or, Change not a clout
Till May be out. 1906: *N. & Q.*, 10th
ser., v. 433, Never change a thing Till
May comes in. Never cast, etc. Ibid.,
474, Button to chin Till May be in;
Cast not a clout till May be out.

23. *No grass first of May, Fetch
another cow to the ley.* 1917: Bridge,
Cheshire Proverbs, 98.

24. *The first of May is Robin Hood's
day.* 1846: Denham, *Proverbs*, 47
(Percy S.).

25. *The more thunder in May, the
less in August and September.* 1893:
Inwards, *Weather Lore*, 27.

26. *They who bathe in May will soon
be laid in clay; They who bathe in June*

Will sing a merry tune. 1827 : Hone, *Table-Book,* 315 [quoted as an " old saying . . . very prevalent in Skipton," Yorks]. 1893 : Inwards, 27, [as in 1827, *plus*] They who bathe in July Will dance like a fly.

27. *To get up* (or *over*) *May hill.* 1825 : Hone, *Ev. Day Book,* i. 652, The month of May is called a " trying " month, to persons' long ailing with critical complaints. It is common to say " Ah, he'll never get up May-hill ! " or, " If he can climb over May-hill he'll do." 1863 : Wise, *New Forest,* ch. xvi., " He won't climb up May Hill," that is, he will not live through the cold spring. 1887 : Parish and Shaw, *Dict. Kent. Dialect,* 99 (E.D.S.), I don't think he'll ever get up May hill.

28. *To wed in May is to wed poverty.* 1878 : Dyer, *Eng. Folk-Lore,* 257. 1893 : Inwards, *Weather Lore,* 27.

29. *Twenty-ninth of May Royal-oak day* (or *oaken-apple day*). 1846 : Denham, *Proverbs,* 48 (Percy S.).

30. *You must not count your yearlings till Muy-day.* 1823 : D'Israeli, *Cur. of Lit.,* 2nd ser., i. 441 (1824), The state of an agricultural people appears in such proverbs as " You must not," etc.

See also April (3), (4), (9), (12), (13), and (17) ; Bee (3) ; Cuckoo, *passim* ; Doe ; Fresh as flowers ; January (4), (8), (17), and (18) ; July (9) ; Leeks ; March, *passim* ; Merry month ; Sage ; Sheep (13) ; and Thistle (2).

May, *verb.* 1. *That one may not another may.* 1546 : Heywood, *Proverbs,* Pt. II. ch. ii.

2. *That which may fall out at any time, may fall out to-day.* 1732 : Fuller, No. 4383.

3. *What may be done at any time will be done at no time.* Ibid., No. 5500.

4. *Who that may not as they will, must will as they may.* 1546 : Heywood, *Proverbs,* Pt. II. ch. v. 1633 : Draxe, 1.

5. *You may if you list, but do if you dare.* 1678 : Ray, 350.

Mayors. *See* Altringham ; Calenick ; East Looe ; Falmouth ; Halgaver ; Hartlepool ; Lord-Mayor ; Market-Jew ; Northampton ; Over ; Tregoney ; and Wigan.

Mazed. *See* quots. 1895 : J. Thomas, *Randigal Rhymes,* 61, Mazed as a curley [Corn.]. 1926 : *Devonsh. Assoc. Trans.,* lvii. 144, " Mazed as a brish" [brush] is a common saying about Newton Abbot . . . Still commoner, " mazed as a sheep." I have also heard " mazed as a broom-stick."

Meal make before sail take. Corn. 1869 : Hazlitt, 279.

Meals. *See* Better are meals.

Meals and matins minish never. 1853 : Trench, *Proverbs,* 21 (1905), Meal and matins minish no way. 1863 : *N. & Q.,* 3rd ser., iii. 209. Cf. Mass and meat ; Meat (5) ; and Prayers and provender.

Mean as an higgler, As. 1917 : Bridge, *Cheshire Proverbs,* 18, Higgler = Huckster or hawker.

Mean as tongs, As. 1899 : S. O. Addy, in *N. & Q.,* 9th ser., iv. 206, . . . I have occasionally heard this phrase in Sheffield.

Means, Use the, and God will give the blessing. 1633 : Draxe, 109. 1670 : Ray, 17. 1732 : Fuller, No. 5413, Use the means, and trust to God for the blessing.

Measure, *subs.* 1. *He that loves measure and skill, oft hath his will.* c. 1460 : *How the Good Wife,* l. 55, That mesure louethe, and skille, ofte hathe his wille.

2. *Measure for measure.* 1595 : *True Trag. Rich. Duke of York,* 151 (Sh. S.), Measure for measure must be answered. 1603 : Shakespeare, *Measure for Measure* [title]. 1834-7 : Southey, *Doctor,* interch. xxi. [title].

3. *Measure is a merry mean.* c. 1380 : Langland, *Dep. of Rich. II.,* 12 (Camden S.), Mesure is a meri mene. c. 1450 : Russell, *Book of Nurture,* in *Babees Book,* 124 (E.E.T.S.). Before 1529 : Skelton, *Magnyfycence,* l. 385. 1590 : Greene, *Works,* ix. 209 (Grosart). 1670 : Ray, 17.

4. *Measure is medicine.* 1362 : Langland, *Plowman,* A, i. 33.

5. *Measure is treasure.* c. 1225 : *Ancren R.,* 336 (Morton), The middel weie of mesure is euer guldene [golden]. c. 1420 : Lydgate, *Minor Poems,* 82 (Percy S.), An olde proverbe—" mesour is tresoure." Before 1529 : Skelton,

Magnyfycence, l. 126. 1639 : Clarke,
206. 1732 : Fuller, No. 6321.

6. *There is a measure in all things.*
[*c.* 1450 : *Abce of Aristotill*, in E.E.T.S.,
Ext. Ser., 67 (1869), For a mesurable
mene is best for vs alle.] 1633 : Draxe,
129.

Measure, *verb.* 1. *He measures a
twig.* 1813 : Ray, 75.

2. *He that measures not himself is measured.* 1640 : Herbert, *Jac. Prudentum.*

3. *Measure thrice and cut once.* 1591 :
Florio, *Second Frutes*, 97, Alwaies
measure manie, Before you cut anie.
1623 : Wodroephe, *Spared Houres*, 275,
Measure thrice, before thou shapest
once. 1670 : Ray, 17, Measure thrice
what thou buyest, and cut it but once.
1732 : Fuller, No. 3381.

4. *To measure another by your own
yard.* 1589 : *Pap with a Hatchet*, To
Reader, They measure conscience by
their owne yard. 1659 : Howell, 12,
You measure every one by your own
yard. 1883 : Burne, *Shropsh. Folk-
Lore*, 597, To measure your neighbours
cloth by your own yard.

5. *To measure another's corn by one's
own bushel.* 1631 : W. Saltonstall,
Picturæ Loquentes, sig. F1, Her corne
stands not long for the sellers sake, and
she crosses the proverbe, for shee
measures it out by anothers bushell.
1670 : Ray, 186, You measure every
ones corn by your own bushel. 1713 :
Gay, *Wife of Bath*, I., Pray do not
measure my corn with your bushel, old
Drybones! 1828 : Carr, *Craven Dialect*, i. 58, " You measure me a peck out
of your own bushel " ; you judge of
my disposition by your own. 1920 :
L. J. Jennings, *Chestnuts and Small
Beer*, 138, No man is inclined to measure
his own corn by another man's bushel.

Meat, *subs.* 1. *A man is not sure of
his meat till it is in his mouth.* 1684 :
Great Frost, 14 (Percy S.) [cited as an
old proverb].

2. *If 'twasn't for meat and good drink
the women might gnaw the sheets.* 1698 :
Terence made English, 96 (2nd ed.)
[quoted as " the old saying "].

3. *Look not on the meat but on the
man.* 1533 : Heywood, *Play of Love*,

l. 1230 (Brandl, *Quellen*, 198). 1639 :
Clarke, 84, Shew me not the meat, but
shew me the man. 1678 : Ray, 354,
To measure the meat by the man.

4. *Meat and drink to one, To be.*
1533 : Frith, *Answ. More*, E*j* (O.),
It ys meate and drinke to this childe
to plaie. 1573 : G. Harvey, *Letter-Book*,
51 (Camden S.), Whitch were sutch
matter . . . as would be meat and
drink to M. Proctor. 1642 : Fuller, *Profane State:* " Hypocrite," Even fasting
itself is meat and drink to him, whilst
others behold it. 1681 : Robertson,
Phraseol. Generalis, 876, It is meat and
drink to me.

5. *Meat and mass* (or *matins*) *hinder
no man's journey* (or *work*). 1639 :
Clarke, 273, Meat and mattens hinder
no mans journey. 1670 : Ray, 120
[as in 1639]. 1732 : Fuller, No. 3382
[as in 1639, but " not a " for " no
mans "]. 1823 : Scott, *Q. Durward*,
ch. xi., " Meat and mass " (crossing
himself) " never hindered the work of a
good Christian man." 1893 : R. L. S.,
Catriona, ch. xix., I beg to remind
you of an old musty saw, that meat
and mass never hindered man. Cf.
Mass and meat ; **Meals and matins** ;
and **Prayers and provender.**

6. *Meat is much but manners is more.*
1639 : Clarke, 93. 1685 : Meriton,
Yorkshire Ale, 54, For meat is mickle
but mence [credit] is more. 1732 :
Fuller, No. 3383 [with " malice " for
" manners," but this must surely be
a misprint].

7. *Meat must be had, but work may
stay.* 1687 : *Poor Robin Alman. Prognost.*, sig. C8 [quoted as " ancient
proverb "].

8. *Meat was made for mouths.* 1609 :
Shakespeare, *Coriolanus*, I. i.

9. *One man's meat is another man's
poison.* [Tantaque in his rebus dis-
tantia, differitasque est, Ut quod aliis
cibus est, aliis fuat acre venenum.—
Lucretius, iv. 638.] 1546 : Heywood,
Proverbs, Pt. II. ch. ii., That one loueth
not, an other doth. 1630 : Taylor (Water-
Poet), *Works*, 2nd pagin., 254, And one
mans meat, anothers poyson is. 1709 :
O. Dykes, *Eng. Proverbs*, iv. (2nd ed.).

1759: Townley, *High Life below Stairs*,
I. i., Alas, Sir! what is one man's
poison is another man's meat. 1883:
Trollope, *Autobiog.*, ch. x. [with " food "
for " meat "]. 1914 : Lucas, *Landmarks*,
197.

10. *To be meat for another's mouth.*
[Non ego sum pollucta pago.—Plautus,
Rud., 425.] 1598 : Shakespeare, 2 *Henry
IV.*, II. iv., I am meat for your master.
1616 : Haughton, *Englishm. for my
Money*, II. i., I am no meat for his mow-
ing [mouthing], nor yours neither. 1681:
Otway, *Soldier's Fortune*, II. i., Let my
doxy rest in peace, she's meat for thy
master. 1738 : Swift, *Polite Convers.*,
Dial. I., That's meat for your master.
1855 : Kingsley, *West. Ho!*, ch. viii.,
And that you can't have, for it's meat
for your masters.

11. *To bring meat in the mouth.*
1580 : G. Harvey, *Works*, i. 92 (Grosart),
Those studies and practizes, that carrie
as they saye, meate in their mouth.
1639 : Clarke, 43, It brings meat i' th'
mouth. 1670 : Ray, 186.

12. *When meat is in anger is out.*
1639 : Clarke, 178.

Meddle, verb. 1. *He that will meddle
with all things may go shoe the goslings.*
c. 1434: inscrip. in Whalley Church,
cited in Farmer's *Heywood's Proverbs*,
377 (1906), Whoso melles of wat men
doo, Let hym cum hier and shoo the
ghos 1546 : Heywood, *Proverbs*, Pt.
II. ch. iii., Who medleth in all thyng
maie shooe the goslyng. 1670 : Ray,
120. 1732 : Fuller, No. 6445.

2. *I will neither meddle nor make*,
1593 : Nashe, *Works*, iv. 151 (Grosart).
If in speech you neither meddle nor
make with hym. 1609 : Shakespeare,
Troilus, I. i., For my part, I'll not
meddle nor make no further. 1675: Cotton, *Burl. upon Burlesque*, 259 (1765), I
should do very imprudently . . . Either
to meddle or to make. 1730 : Lillo,
Silvia, III. v., They are ticklish things,
and I don't much care to meddle or
make with 'em. 1849 : Brontë, *Shirley*,
ch. xxi., Moore may settle his own
matters henceforward for me ; I'll
neither meddle nor make with them
further. 1920 : E. Gepp, *Essex Dialect*

Dict., 22, " I 'on't nuther meddle nor
make," I won't interfere.

3. *Meddle with your old shoes.* 1577 :
Misogonus, II. v., What, are you his
spoksman ? meddle you with your old
showes. 1639 : Clarke, 18, Meddle
with what you have to doe. 1670 :
Ray, 186. 1681 : Robertson, *Phraseol.
Generalis*, 877, Meddle with your old
shoes ; Tuâ quod nihil refert, ne cures.

Medgelly's cow. *See* quot. 1753: in
Stukeley Memoirs, iii. 179 (Surtees S.),
A proverb in this country [Shropsh.],
" Medgelly's cow, for one that gives a
deal of milk."

Medicines be not meat to live by.
1669 : *Politeuphuia*, 175.

Medlars are never good till rotten.
1599: J. Weever, *Epigr.*, 19 (1911),
Medlers are neuer ripe before that they
be rotten. 1674 : Head and Kirkman,
Eng. Rogue, iii. 259, A medlar, which is
never good till rotten. 1678 : Ray, 52.

Medlock. *See* Yoke.

Meet with one's match, To. c. 1305 :
Miracle of St. James, 48, in E.E.P.,
59 (1862) (O.), þe schrewe fond his
macche þo. c. 1400 : *Beryn*, 4 (E.E.T.S.),
Lo! howe þe clowdis worchyn,
eche man to mete his mach. 1485 :
Malory, *Morte d'Arthur*, bk. x. ch. 54,
Goo feche sire launcelot or sir Tristram
and there shalle ye fynde your matche.
1594 : Greene, *Frier Bacon*, sc. ix.,
How now . . . have you met with your
match ? 1632 : Shirley, *Witty Fair
One*, I. iii., *Clare*. I am married, sir.
Bra. Then I hope you have met with
your match already. 1700 : Congreve,
Way of World, III. vii., Well, Mr.
Fainall, you have met with your match.
1874 : *N. & Q.*, 5th ser., i. 205, Nor
insult any one, lest you meet with your
match.

Meeterly [Tolerably, Indifferently] as
maids are in fairness. 1678 : Ray, 355.
1683 : Meriton, *Yorkshire Ale*, 83–7
(1697).

Meg of Westminster, As long as.
1582 : *The Life and Pranks of Long
Meg of Westminster* [title]. 1662 :
Fuller, *Worthies*, ii. 413 (1840). 1785 :
Grose, *Class. Dict. Vulgar Tongue*, s.v.
" Long Meg," A jeering name for a

very tall woman, from one famous in
story, called Long Meg of Westminster.
Melancholy as a cat, As. 1592 :
Lyly, *Midas*, V. ii. 1597 : Shakespeare,
1 *Henry IV.*, I. ii., I am as melancholy as a gib cat. 1599 : Chapman,
Hum. Day's Mirth, sc. xi. 1609 : in Halliwell, *Books of Characters*, 115 (1857).
1694 : D'Urfey, *Quixote*, Pt. II. Act I.
sc. i., Yonder he lies, and as melancholy
as a cat in a church-steeple, expecting
my return. 1720 : Gay, *Poems*, ii. 278,
(Underhill), I melancholy as a cat, Am
kept awake to weep. 1785 : Grose,
Class. Dict. Vulgar Tongue, s.v. " Gib
cat," As melancholy as a gib cat ; as
melancholy as a he-cat who has been
catterwauling, whence they always
return scratched, hungry, and out of
spirits. 1820 : Lamb, *South-Sea House*,
Melancholy as a gib-cat over his counter
all the forenoon.

Melancholy as a collier's horse, As.
1659 : Howell, 10.

Melancholy as a sick monkey, As.
1836 : Marryat, *Easy*, ch. xxi.

Melancholy as a sick parrot, As.
1682 : A. Behn, *False Count*, I. ii.

Melverley, Shropsh. 1841 : Hartshorne, *Salopian Ant.*, 504, Its remote-
ness, perhaps, and the frequency of
inundations to which it is subject, has
occasioned the place to pass into a bye
word, and its inhabitants to be called
Melverly God helps. [Also, after good
crops] Melverly where do you think?
1913 : E. M. Wright, *Rustic Speech*,
etc., 181, To direct a person to go to a
place not to be named to ears polite is
to tell him, to go to Melverley, a saying
which has arisen from the fact that
this village is continually flooded by
the irruptions of the Severn, and is
therefore a place where ills and misfortunes befall the inhabitants. 1928 :
Truth, 12 Sept., p. 454, col. 2, Melverley
God help us ! . . . Melverley, where
else?

Memory is the treasure of the mind.
1560 : T. Wilson, *Rhetorique*, 209 (1909),
The memorie called the threasure of
the minde. 1642 : Fuller, *Holy State*:
"Memory," Memory . . . is the
treasure-house of the mind.

**Memory of happiness makes misery
woeful, The.** *c.* 1440 : Lydgate, *Fall
of Princes*, bk. i. l. 650, Nor nothyng
more may hertis disauaunce Than off
old ioie newe remembraunce. 1669 :
Politeuphuia, 102, The consideration of
pleasures past greatly augments the
pain present. 1732 : Fuller, No. 4650.

Men. *See* **Man.**

Mend, *verb.* 1. *He may mend but
not grow worse.* 1633 : Draxe, 43,
Some doe mend, when they cannot
appaire. 1659 : Howell, 7.

2. *If you mend things on your back,
you'm sure to lack,* i.e. to want. 1919:
Devonsh. Assoc. Trans., li. 77.

3. *Let him mend his manners, 'twill
be his own another day.* 1678 : Ray, 76.

4. *Mend one. See* **Every man mend
one.**

5. *Mend your clothes and you may
hold out this year.* 1640 : Herbert, *Jac.
Prudentum.* 1854 : J. W. Warter, *Last
of Old Squires*, 53.

6. *To mend as sour ale mends in
summer* = To become worse. 1546 :
Heywood, *Proverbs*, Pt. II. ch. ix.,
Than wolde ye mend . . . as sowre ale
mendth in summer. 1564 : Bullein,
Dialogue, 77 (E.E.T.S.), The worlde
amendes like sower ale in sommer.
1647 : Wither, *Amygdala Brit.*, 6
(Spens. S.), And, like sowre ale in
summer, mend. 1738 : Swift, *Polite
Convers.*, Dial. III. 1823 : Moor, *Suffolk Words*, 377, " 'A mend like sour
ale in summer "—that is, gets worse
and worse.

7. *To mend as the fletcher does his
bolt.* 1530 : Palsgrave, 634, He mendeth as the fletcher dothe his bolte.
1633 : Draxe, 242.

Merchandize. *See* quot. 1593 :
Nashe, *Works*, iv. 139 (Grosart), It is
nowe growne a prouerbe *That there is
no merchandize but vsury.*

Merchant. 1. *A merchant of eel-
skins* = of refuse, or of nothing. 1545 :
Ascham, *Toxoph.*, 151 (Arber), He that
wyll at all aduentures vse the seas
knowinge no more what is to be done
in a tempest than in a caulme, shall
soone becumme a marchaunt of eele
skinnes. 1624 : T. Heywood, *Captives,*

IV. i., *Fisher.* . . . who knowes but I
In tyme may proove a noble marchant ?
Clowne. Yes, of eele skinnes. 1655 :
A. Brewer, *Love-sick King*, II., in Bang,
Materialien, B. 18, p. 13, Then am I a
merchant, not of eels-skins, but lamb-
skins.

2. *A merchant that gains not loses.*
1611 : Cotgrave, s.v. " Gaigner," The
marchant loses when he gaines not.
1640 : Herbert, *Jac. Prudentum.*

3. *A merchant without either money
or ware.* 1546 : Heywood, *Proverbs*,
Pt. II. ch. v. 1659 : Howell, 7.

4. *He is not a merchant bare that hath
money-worth or ware.* 1670 : Ray, 17.
1732 : Fuller, No. 6240.

5. *He that could know what would be
dear, need be a merchant but one year.*
1546 : Heywood, *Proverbs*, Pt. I. ch. i.
1611 : Cotgrave, s.v. " Adventure,"
We say, he that did know what would be
he deare, might grow full rich within
a yeare. 1670 : Ray, 78. 1732 : Fuller,
No. 6077.

6. *He that loseth is a merchant as well
as he that gains.* 1640 : Herbert, *Jac.
Prudentum.* 1666 : Torriano, *Piazza
Univ.*, 150.

7. *Merchant May's little summer.*
= St. Martin's little summer. Corn.
1869 : Hazlitt, 280.

8. *To play the merchant* = To rob or
cheat. 1593 : Nashe, *Works*, iv. 240
(Grosart), Is it not a common prouerbe
amongst vs when any man hath cosend
or gone beyonde vs, to say, Hee hath
playde the merchant with us ? 1611 :
Cotgrave, s.v. " Larron," Either a
merchant or a theefe. 1632 : Rowley,
New Wonder, IV., I doubt, sir, he will
play the merchant with us.

Mercury. *See* quot. 1588 : Cogan,
Haven of Health, 45 (1612), It is a
common prouerbe among the people,
Be thou sicke or whole, put Mercurie
in thy koale.

Mere scholar. *See* **Scholar.**

Mere wishes are silly fishes. 1732 :
Fuller, No. 6290.

Merry and wise. 1546 : Heywood,
Proverbs, Pt. I. ch. ii., Good to be mery
and wise, they thinke and feele. 1593 :
G. Harvey, *Works*, ii. 247 (Grosart), It is

good, they say, to be merry, and wise.
1668 : Davenant, *Man's the Master*,
Prol., The proverb says, " Be merry
and be wise." 1774 : Colman, *Man of
Business*, I. 1779 : Johnson, in *Letters*,
ii. 114 (Hill), Old Times have be-
queathed us a precept, *to be merry and
wise*, but who has been able to observe
it ? 1840 : Dickens, *Curiosity Shop*,
ch. vii.

Merry as a cricket. 1546 : Heywood,
Proverbs, Pt. I. ch. xi. 1597 : Shake-
speare, 1 *Henry IV.*, II. iv. 1653 :
Urquhart, *Rabelais*, bk. i. ch. xxix.,
And send them home as merry as
crickets unto their own houses. 1787 :
O'Keeffe, *The Farmer*, I. ii. 1834 :
Marryat, *Peter Simple*, ch. i. 1918 :
Walpole, *Green Mirror*, bk. i. ch. i.,
Healthy, happy, . . . lively as crickets
—not a happier family in England.

Merry as a Greek. *c.* 1551 : Udall,
Roister Doister, I. i. [one of the characters
is Mathew Merygreeke]. 1611 : Jon-
son, in Coryat, *Crudities*, i. 17 (1905),
Hce is a mad Greeke, no lesse than a
merry. 1655 : Fuller, *Church Hist.*, bk.
ii. § iii. (22), We know the modern
proverb, of *a merry Greek.* 1670 :
Cotton, *Scarronides*, bk. iv., Merry as
Greeks, and drunk as Lords. 1784 :
New Foundl. Hosp. for Wit, iii. 176,
Make me as merry as a Greek.

Merry as a grig. 1566 : Drant,
Horace : Sat., I. iii., A merry grigge, a
iocande frende. 1675 : Cotton, *Burl. upon
Burlesque*, 195 (1765), A merry grig, and
a true toper. Before 1704 : T. Brown, in
Works, ii. 188 (1760), They drank till they
all were as merry as grigs. 1713 : Gay,
Wife of Bath, V. iii., Ah ! friend, we
were merry grigs in times past. 1775 :
Jos. Wedgwood, in *Letters* (priv. printed
1903), We have a housefull of children,
all as merry as Griggs. 1859 : Sala,
Twice Round Clock, 3 p.m., They can
be as merry as grigs among themselves
when they so choose. 1886 : Elworthy,
West Som. Word-Book, 301 (E.D.S.),
" So merry's a grig" and " So merry's
a cricket " are equally common.

Merry as a king. *See* **Happy.**

Merry as a pie. *c.* 1386 : Chaucer,
Shipm. Tale, l. 209, And forth she gooth,

as iolif as a pye. 1546: Heywood,
Proverbs, Pt. II. ch. iii. 1590: *Tarltons
Newes out of Purg.*, 68 (Sh. S.), Home
went Lysetta, as merry as a pye.
1600: Dekker, *Shoem. Holiday*, V. v.,
Ile be as merrie as a pie. 1613: S.
Rowley, *When You See Me*, sig. C3, Hele
lafe and be as merry as a mag-pie.
c. 1630: B. & F., *Mons. Thomas*, IV.
ii., At Valentine's house so merry?
As a pie, sir.

Merry as beggars. 1659: Howell,
11, As merry as fourty beggars. 1700:
Ward, *London Spy*, 264 (1924), Both
were . . . as merry as beggars. 1724:
Swift, *Drapier*, Lett. IV., We should
live together as merry and sociable as
beggars.

**Merry as he that hath nought to lose,
Who so?** 1672: Walker, *Parœm.*,
39.

Merry as mice in malt. 1639: Clarke,
185. 1659: Howell, 3. 1869: Spurgeon, *John Ploughman*, ch. xvi., Some
families are as merry as mice in malt
on very small wages.

Merry as the maids. c. 1630: in
Roxb. Ballads, i. 448 (B.S.), For with
joviall blades I'm as mery as the maids.
17th cent.: in Marchant, *Praise of Ale*,
249 (1888), We will be as merry as the
maides. 1670: Ray, 202.

Merry as three chips. 1546: Heywood, *Proverbs*, Pt. I. ch. vii.

Merry as tinkers. 1659: Howell, 3.

Merry at meat, It is good to be. 1633:
Draxe, 66. 1670: Ray, 18.

**Merry be the first, and merry be the
last, and merry be the first of August.**
1869: Hazlitt, 280.

Merry but unlooked-for guest. See
quot. 1819: Combe, *Syntax Consol.
Tour*, can. xxix., And if the proverb
says what's true, Which those old saws
are apt to do, The merry, but unlook'd
for guest, Full often proves to be the
best.

Merry companion, A. See quots.
1597: Lyly, *Woman in Moone*, IV., A
merry companion is as good as a wagon.
1616: Breton, in *Works*, ii. e 8 (Grosart),
A merry companion is a wagon in the
way. 1666: Torriano, *Piazza Univ.*, 49,
A merry companion on the way is as

good as a nag. 1732: Fuller, No. 324,
. . . is musick in a journey.

Merry-go-down=good ale. c. 1470:
in *Songs and Carols*, 92 (Percy S.), I
know a drawght off mery-go-downe.
1567: Golding, *Ovid*, bk. v. l. 556, Out
she brought hir by and by a draught
of merrie go downe. 1591: Lodge,
Cattaros, 21 (Hunt. Cl.). c. 1791:
Pegge, *Derbicisms*, 111 (E.D.S.). 1886:
Bickerdyke, *Curios. of Ale and Beer*,
120, Used by those ancient worthies in
compounding their "merrie-go-downe."

Merry in hall when beards wag all,
'Tis. c. 1310: *King Alisaunder*, l. 1163,
Swithe mury hit is in halle, When
the burdes wawen alle. 1546: Hey-
wood, *Proverbs*, Pt. II. ch. vii.
Shakespeare, 2 *Henry IV.*, V. iii. 1616:
Jonson, *Masque of Christmas*. 1712:
Addison, *Spectator*, No. 371. 1846:
Wright, *Essays on Middle Ages*, i. 43,
The object at which they now aimed be-
ing to make "beards wag merry in hall."

**Merry is the company till the reckon-
ing comes.** 1678: Ray, 175, Merry is
the feast-making till we come to the
reckoning. 1732: Fuller, No. 3409.

**Merry man as the sad, As long liveth
the.** c. 1300: in *Vernon MS.*, 347
(E.E.T.S.), Lengor liueth a glad mon
then a sori. c. 1550: Udall, *Roister
Doister*, I. i., As long liveth the merry
man (they say), As doth the sorry man,
and longer by a day. 1599: Porter,
Two Angry Women, in Hazlitt, *Old
Plays*, vii. 308. 1630: *Tinker of Turvey*-
p. iv (Halliwell), Lives not a merry-man
longer than a sad? 1732: Fuller, No.
711 ["heart" for "man"]. 1861: Peacock, *Gryll Grange*, ch. xxxii. [as in
1550].

Merry meet merry part. 1678: Ray,
175. 1732: Fuller, No. 3410.

Merry month of May, The. [1412–
20: Lydgate, *Troy Book*, bk. i. l. 1293,
And May was come, the monyth of
gladnes.] 1577: J. Grange, *Golden
Aphroditis*, sig. K4, It might be the
merry moneth of May. 1594: Barnfield, *Affect. Sheph.*, 41 (Percy S.).
c. 1610: in *Roxb. Ballads*, iii. 42 (B.S.).
c. 1680: in Ibid., iii. 434 (B.S.). 1700:
Dryden, *Pal. and Arcite*, ii. 44,

Observance to the month of merry May.
1889: Gilbert, *Gondoliers*, I., All the
year is merry May!

Merry nights make sorry days. Staffs.
1896: *Folk-Lore*, vii. 377.

Merry pin, On. *c.* 1386: Chaucer,
Merch. Tale, l. 272, Your herte hangeth
on a ioly pin. *c.* 1480: *Digby Plays*, 156
(E.E.T.S.), I wyll no more row a-geyn
the fflode, I wyll sett my soule on a
mery pynne. 1553: *Respublica*, II. iii.,
Canne Avarice harte bee sett on a merie
pynne . . .? 1639: Davenport, *New
Trick to cheat Devil*, I. ii., Faith I was
never on a merrier pinn, Nor my breast
lighter hearted. 1710: Matt. Henry,
Commentary (Dan. v. 4), The cups
going round apace, and all upon the
merry pin. 1818: *Gent. Mag.*, Pt. II.
13–17, When a person is much elated,
we say he is *in a merry pin*, which no
doubt originally meant he had reached
that *mark* [in a pegged tankard] which
had deprived him of his usual sedate-
ness and sobriety. 1909: Hackwood,
Inns, Ales, etc., 146, By which time he
was in merry mood, or, as the phrase
ran, "in merry pin."

Merry that dance, All are not. *c.* 1430:
Lydgate, *Daunce of Machabree*, l. 392,
Al be not merye which that men seen
daunce. 1611: Cotgrave, s.v. "Aise,"
Every one is not merry that dances.
1640: Herbert, *Jac. Prudentum*, All are
not merry that dance lightly.

Merry to keep one's own, It is.
c. 1460: *How the Good Wife*, l. 60,
Mery is owne thinge to kepe.

Merry when friends meet, It's. 1639:
Clarke, 26.

Merry when gentle-folks meet, 'Tis.
1647: A. Brewer, *Countrie Girl*, sig.
H3, And soe—as the proverbe is, tis
merry when gentle folkes meete.

Merry when gossips meet, It is.
1616: Breton, in *Works*, ii. *e* 6 (Grosart).
1625: Jonson, *Staple of News*, Induction. 1639: Clarke, 184.

Merry when knaves meet, It is.
c. 1520: *Cock Lorells Bote*, 14 (Percy
S.), But mery it is whan knaues done
mete. 1590: *Three Lords and Three
Ladies*, in Hazlitt, *Old Plays*, vi. 410.
1639: Clarke, 290.

Merry when maltmen meet, It is.
c. 1630: in *Roxb. Ballads*, i. 59 (B.S.),
'Tis merry when kinde maltmen meet.
1631: Brathwait, *Whimzies*, 145
(1859).

Mersey. *See* Yoke.

Mettle is dangerous in a blind horse.
1670: Ray, 18, Metal is, etc. 1696:
D'Urfey, *Quixote*, Pt. III. Act I., Too
much mettle is, etc. 1732: Fuller, No.
3411.

Mettle to the back, He is. *c.* 1591:
Shakespeare, *Titus Andr.*, IV. iii., But
metal, Marcus, steel to the very back.
1733: Coffey, *Boarding-School*, sc. v.,
The girl is mettle to the back. 1745:
Agreeable Companion, 105, A notable
fellow of his inches, and metal to the
back. Cf. **Steel.**

Mice. *See* Dead (15); **Mouse**; No
larder; and Rat (1) and (6).

Michaelmas. 1. *At Michaelmas time,
or a little before, half an apple goes to the
core; at Christmas time, or a little after,
a crab in the hedge, and thanks to the
grafter.* 1869: Hazlitt, 77.

2. *He spent Michaelmas rent in Midsummer moon.* 1605: Camden, *Remains*, 323 (1870). 1665: J. Wilson,
Projectors, II., A good honest man's
daughter, that shall bring him no
charge . . . One that shall not spend
his Michaelmas rents in Midsummer
moon. 1732: Fuller, No. 2026. 1846:
Denham, *Proverbs*, 6 (Percy S.).

3. *Michaelmas chickens and parsons'
daughters never come to good.* 1894:
Northall, *Folk Phrases*, 19 (E.D.S.).

4. *The Michaelmas moon.* *See* **Moon**
(17).

5. *'Tis good to have a Michaelmas-
groat at Easter.* 1710: S. Palmer,
Moral Essays on Proverbs, 280, . . .
The . . . proverb is vulgar and peculiar
to the watermen, whose business is
brisk only in the summer.

See also **Eat** (5); **Goose** (19); **Moon**
(13) and (17); **St. Michael**; and **Three
things that never.**

Mickle ado and little help. 1670:
Ray, 120.

Middle Temple. *See* **Gray's Inn.**

Middlesex clowns. 1662: Fuller,
Worthies, ii. 313 (1840) [in the singular].

1790 : Grose, *Prov. Gloss.*, s.v. " Middlesex."

Middlesex jury. *See* **London** (1).

Middlesex. *See also* **Derbyshire.**

Midsummer Eve. *See* quot. 1878 : Dyer, *Eng. Folk-Lore*, 257, According to an old saying, " If it rains on Midsummer Eve, the filberts will be spoilt." 1893 : Inwards, *Weather Lore*, 29.

Midsummer moon. *See* quots. 1596 : Nashe, *Works*, iii. 55 (Grosart), Ere hee bee come to the full Midsommer Moone and raging Calentura of his wretchednes. 1601 : Shakespeare, *Twelfth N.*, III. iv., Why, this is very midsummer madness. 1670 : Ray, 214, 'Tis Midsummer moon with you, i.e. you are mad. 1732 : Fuller, No. 2974 [as in 1670]. 1846 : Denham, *Proverbs*, 51 (Percy S.) [as in 1670].

Midsummer rain spoils hay and grain. 1893 : Inwards, *Weather Lore*, 7.

Midsummer. *See also* **St. John.**

Might is (or overcometh) right. [Plus potest, qui plus valet.—Plautus, *Trucul.*, IV. iii. 30.] *c.* 1311 : in Wright, *Pol. Songs John to Edw. II.*, 254 (Camden S.), For might is riht. 1546 : Heywood, *Proverbs*, Pt. II. ch. v., Might ouercomth right. 1591 : Greene, *Works*, x. 60 (Grosart), Might ouercomes right. 1638 : D. Tuvill, *Vade Mecum*, 182 (3rd ed.), It is an old country proverbe, that Might overcomes right. 1742 : North, *Lives of Norths*, ii. 66 (Bohn) [as in 1591]. 1836 : Marryat, *Easy*, ch. vi., This is the age of iron, in which might has become right. 1846 : *Bentley Ballads*, 22 (1876), That often Might has vanquished Right, Is now a thrice-told tale.

Might or slight, Either by. 1639 : Clarke, 127. 1670 : Ray, 186.

Mild as a lamb. 1530 : Palsgrave, 626, I can make hym as mylde as a lambe. 1596 : Shakespeare, *Rich. II.*, II. i., In peace was never gentle lamb more mild. 1670 : Ray, 206. 1707 : tr. Aleman's *Guzman*, ii. 62, From a tygress she became as mild as a lamb. 1883 : R. L. S., *Treasure I.*, ch. xiii.

Mile from an ess-midden, He'll never get a. 1886 : R. Holland, *Cheshire Gloss.*, 449 (E.D.S.). 1917 : Bridge, *Cheshire Proverbs*, 69, . . . He hasn't the pluck or energy to go far or do much.

Mile of an oak, Within a. 1599 : Porter, *Two Angry Women*, sc. xi., *Coo*. Where be your tooles ? *Nic*. Within a mile of an oake, sir. 1678 : A. Behn, *Sir Patient Fancy*, III. i., Sir Credulous, where's your mistress ? *Sir Cred*. Within a mile of an oak, dear madam, I'll warrant you. 1696 : D'Urfey, *Quixote*, Pt. III. Act V. sc. i., Your worship can tell within a mile of an oak where he is. 1738 : Swift, *Polite Convers.*, Dial. I.

Milk, *subs*. 1. *His milk boiled over.* 1732 : Fuller, No. 2510.

2. *I'll have none of your flat milk.* 1659 : Howell, 11.

3. *Mylke . . . is white And lieth not in the dike, But all men know it good meate Inke is all blacke And hath an ill smacke No man will it drink nor eat.* 1546 : Heywood, *Proverbs*, Pt. II. ch. iv.

4. *Milk says to wine, "Welcome friend."* 1640 : Herbert, *Jac. Prudentum.*

5. *My milk.* *See* quot. 1639 : in *Berkeley MSS.*, iii. 31 (1885), My milke is in the cowes horne, now the zunne is 'ryv'd at Capricorne [Glos.].

See also **Nothing** (29).

Mill, *subs*. 1. *As good water goes by the mill as drives it.* 1732 : Fuller, No. 691.

2. *From mill and market.* *See* quots. Before 1225 : *Ancren R.*, 88, Vrom mulne and from cheping, from smiðe and from ancre huse, me tiðinge bringeð. 1611 : Cotgrave, s.v. " Moulin," An oven and mill are nurseries of news. 1659 : Howell, *Proverbs: Fr.-Eng.*, 11, If you will learn news, you must go to the oven or the mill.

3. *His mill will go with all winds.* 1732 : Fuller, No. 2511.

4. *In vain does the mill clack, if the miller his hearing lack.* 1631 : Mabbe, *Celestina*, 244 (T.T.), To what use serves the clapper in the mil, if the miller be deafe ? 1640 : Herbert, *Jac. Prudentum.* 1670 : Ray, 121. 1732 : Fuller, No. 6388.

5. *Mills and wives ever want.* 1586 : Pettie, tr. Guazzo's *Civil Convers.*, fo. 137, Wherevpon it is said that mils and

women euer want something. 1640 :
Herbert, *Jac. Prudentum.* 1670 : Ray,
18.

6. *Mills will not grind if you give
them not water.* 1732 : Fuller, No.
3414.

7. *The mill cannot grind with water
that's passed.* 1633 : Draxe, 151, The
water that is past cannot make the
mill goe. 1640 : Herbert, *Jac. Prudentum.* 1712 : Motteux, *Quixote,* Pt. II. ch.
lxxi., Delay breeds danger. It is best
grinding at the mill before the water
is past. *c.* 1890 : S. Doudney, *Lesson
of the Watermill,* And a proverb haunts
my mind As a spell is cast ; " The
mill cannot grind With the water that
is passed."

8. *The mill gets by going.* 1640 :
Herbert, *Jac. Prudentum.*

9. *You had rather go to mill than to
mass.* 1605 : Camden, *Remains,* 336
(1870), Ye had as lief go to mill as to
mass. 1732 : Fuller, No. 5909.

See also **Born in a mill** ; **Change,** *verb*
(1) ; **First come** ; **Friend** (20) ; **Horse**
(55) and (62) ; and **No mill.**

Miller. 1. *A miller is never dry*=
never waits to be thirsty before drinking. 1894 : Northall, *Folk Phrases,* 6
(E.D.S.).

2. *An honest miller hath a golden
thumb*—with some variations. *c.* 1386 :
Chaucer, *Prol.,* l. 563. [The Miller]
Wel koude he stelen corn and tollen
thries, And yet he hadde a thombe of
gold, pardee. *c.* 1520 : *Cock Lorells
Bote,* 3 (Percy S.), A myller dusty poll
than dyde corne, A Ioly felowe with
a golden thome. 1526 : *Hund. Mery
Tales,* No. xii. p. 22 (Oesterley), I haue
hard say that euery trew mylner that
tollythe trewlye hath a gyldeyn thombe.
1612 : in *Pepysian Garland,* 32 (Rollins),
The miller with his golden thumbe . . .
he needs must steale a pecke. 1732 :
Fuller, No. 2531, Honest millers have
golden thumbs. 1846 : Jerrold, *Chron.
of Clovernook,* 94, The miller—the
prosperous fellow with the golden
thumb.

3. *As stout as a miller's waistcoat,
that takes a thief by the neck every day.*
1732 : Fuller, No. 731.

4. *It is good to be sure, toll it again,
quoth the miller. c.* 1386 : Chaucer
[*See* the allusion to "tollen thries "
in the first quotation under No. 2].
1678 : Ray, 91.° 1820 : Scott, *Monastery,* ch. xxxvii., " It will not be the
worse of another bolting," said the
Miller ; " it is always best to be sure,
as I say when I chance to take multure
twice from the same meal-sack."

5. *Like a miller he can set to every
wind.* 1732 : Fuller, No. 3224.

6. *Like a miller's mare* = clumsily.
1606 : *Choice Chance and Change,* 68
(Grosart), Can seeme as sober as a
millers mare. *c.* 1620 : B. & F.,
Little Fr. Lawyer, IV. v., *Nurse.* . . .
I can jump yet or tread a measure.
Lam. Like a miller's mare. 1663 :
Killigrew, *Parson's Wedding,* II. vi.,
I'll make him jostle like the miller's
mare, and stand like the dun cow, till
thou may'st milk him.

7. *Like the miller's filler. See* quot.
1869 : Hazlitt, 199, He's always behind
hand, like the miller's filler. *Northampt.*

8. *Many a miller many a thief.*
1673 : *Vinegar and Mustard,* 19, in
Hindley, *Old Book-Coll. Miscell.,* iii.

9. *No bigger than a miller's thumb.*
1675 : Cotton, *Burl. upon Burlesque,*
163 (1765). 1847 : Halliwell, *Dict.,* s.v.
" Miller's thumb," . . . a common
simile.

10. *Put a miller, a tailor and a weaver
into one bag, and shake them, the first
that comes out will be a thief.* 1659 :
Howell, 8. 1670 : Ray, 217. Cf. **Hundred tailors.**

11. *The miller grinds more men's corn
than one.* 1596 : Nashe, *Works,* iii. 25
(Grosart).

12. *The miller sees not all the water
that goes by his mill.* 1546 : Heywood,
Proverbs, Pt. II. ch. v., Muche water
goeth by the myll That the miller
knowth not of. 1583 : Melbancke,
Philotinus, sig. Ee3, Muche water
passeth besides the mill that the milner
seeth not. 1616 : *Rich Cabinet,* fo. 31
[as in 1546]. 1670 : Ray, 121 [as in
1546]. 1825 : Scott, *Betrothed,* ch.
xxvii., Much water slides past the
mill that Hob Miller never wots of.

13. *The miller's boy said so*=It was
a matter of common report. 1872 :
J. Glyde, jr., *Norfolk Garland*, 149.

14. *To put out the miller's eye. See*
quots. 1678 : Ray, 343. 1783 : *Gent.
Mag.*, 675, The phrase of putting the
miller's eye out, when too much liquid
is put to any dry or powdery substance.
1854 : Baker, *Northants Gloss.*, s.v.
" You've put the miller's eye out."
A general phrase when any liquid is
too much diluted with an excess of
water. 1887 : Parish and Shaw, *Dict.
Kent. Dialect.*, 101 (E.D.S.), To put the
miller's eye out is when a person, in
mixing mortar or dough, pours too
much water into the hole made to
receive it. 1920 : E. Gepp, *Essex Dialect Dict.*, 23, . . . to overdo the water
in a mixture.

15. *Ye braide of the millers dogg, Ye
lick your mouth or the poke be open.*
1683 : Meriton, *Yorkshire Ale*, 83–7
(1697).

See also **Drown the miller.**

**Mill-post to a pudding-prick, He hath
thwitten** [whittled] **a.** 1528 : More, in
Works, p. 236, col. 2 (1557), Thys processe
came to a wise purpose, here was a
gret post wel thuyted to a pudding
pricke. 1611 : Cotgrave, s.v. " Arbre,"
Wee say of one that hath squandered
away great wealth hee hath, etc.
1660 : Howell, *Parly of Beasts*, 59, She
will bring her poor husband quickly to
thwitten a mill-post into a pudding-
prick. 1691 : Ray, *Words not Generally
Used*, 70 (E.D.S.).

Mince-pies. *See* **Christmas** (9).

Mind to me a kingdom is, My. [Mens
regnum bona possidet.—Seneca, *Thy-
estes*, II. 380.] 1588 : Sir E. Dyer,
in Byrd, *Psalmes, etc.*, My minde to
me a kingdome is, Such perfect joy
therein I finde. *c.* 1598 : Jonson, *Case
is Altered*, I. i. 1618 : Breton, in *Works*,
ii. *u* 9 (Grosart). 1775 : in *Roxb.
Ballads*, vii. 520 (B.S.), My mind is a
kingdom to me, there's danger in being
too great. 1871 : Smiles, *Character*,
371, " . . . " applies alike to the peasant
as to the monarch. 1912 : H. James,
in *Letters*, ii. 253 (1920).

Mind. *See also* **Hand** (8).

Mine ease. *See* **Take** (28).

Mirth and mischief are two things.
1732 : Fuller, No. 3415.

**Mirth of the world dureth but a while,
The.** 1629 : *Book of Meery Riddles*,
Prov. 11.

Mischief. 1. *He that mischief hatch-
eth, mischief catcheth.* 1605 : Camden,
Remains, 324 (1870). 1732 : Fuller,
No. 6348.

2. *Mischief comes by the pound and
goes away by the ounce.* 1578 : Florio,
First Fruites, fo. 29, The yll commeth
by poundes and goeth away by ounces.
1670 : Ray, 121 [in the plural]. 1732 :
Fuller, No. 3417.

3. *Mischief has swift wings.* 1609 :
J. Melton, *Six-fold Politician*, 13, Mischiefe is well saide to haue swift winges.

4. *Mischief is ever too bold. c.* 1604 :
in *Ballads from MSS.*, ii. 47 (B.S.)
[quoted as a familiar saying].

5. *There is no mischief done. See*
quots. 1577 : *Misogonus*, II. v., Thers
no mischiefe, as they say commenly,
but a preist at one end. 1658 : *Wit
Restor'd*, 150, There is no mischiefe, but
a woman is at one end of it. 1670 : Ray,
50, There's no mischief in the world
done, But a woman is always one.
1732 : Fuller, No. 6405 [as in 1670].
1875 : Cheales, *Proverb. Folk-Lore*, 5,
There's no mischief done, But a woman's
one.

See also **Better a mischief.**

Miser spares. *See* quot. 1611 : Cotgrave, s.v. " Despendre," That which
the wretch [miser] doth spare the
waster spends.

Miserly father has a thriftless son, A.
1612 : W. Parkes, *Curtaine-Drawer of
the World*, 30 (Grosart), Conferme the
proverbe, that it currant runne, A
miser father finds a thriftlesse sonne.

**Misery acquaints a man with strange
bed-fellows.** 1611 : Shakespeare, *Tempest*, II. ii. 1837 : Lockhart, *Life of
Scott*, i. 411, Literature, like misery,
makes men acquainted with strange
bed-fellows. Cf. **Poverty.**

**Misery enough to have once been
happy, It is.** 1639 : Clarke, 166.

**Misery may be the mother when
one beggar begs of another.** 1546 :

Heywood, *Proverbs*, Pt. II. ch. x.
1633 : Draxe, 14.

Misfortunes come on wings and depart
on foot. 1855 : Bohn, 452.

Misfortunes never come singly. *c.* 1300 :
King Alisaunder, l. 1281, Men tellen,
in oldë mone [remembrance], The qued
commth nowher alone. *c.* 1490 : *Partonope*, l. 5542 (E.E.T.S.), For efter won
euylle comythe mony mo. 1509 : Barclay, *Ship of Fools*, ii. 251 (1874),
For wyse men sayth . . . That one
myshap fortuneth neuer alone. *c.* 1580 :
Spelman, *Dialogue*, 3 (Roxb. Cl.), A
man cannot have one losse, but more
will ffolowe. 1602 : Shakespeare, *Hamlet*, IV. v., When sorrows come, they
come not single spies, But in bat-
talions. 1694 : *Terence made English*,
30, My misfortunes come one upo'
th' neck of another. 1711 : Addison,
Spectator, No. 7. 1743 : Fielding, *Jon.
Wild*, bk. i. ch. viii., One misfortune
never comes alone. 1826 : Lamb, *Pop.
Fallacies*, xiii., Misfortunes seldom come
alone. 1841 : Dickens, *Barn. Rudge*, ch.
xxxii. 1914 : Lucas, *Landmarks*, 262.

Misfortunes tell us what fortune is.
1732 : Fuller, No. 3420.

Misfortunes, when asleep, are not to
be awakened. Ibid., No. 3422.

Misreckoning is no payment. 1546 :
Heywood, *Proverbs*, Pt. II. ch. iv.
1670 : Ray, 121. 1732 : Fuller, No.
3423.

Miss is as good as a mile, A. Cf.
Inch in a miss is as good as an ell—the
earlier form of the saying. 1825 :
Scott, *Journal*, 3 .Dec., He was very
near being a poet—but a miss is as
good as a mile, and he always fell short
of the mark. 1869 : Spurgeon, *John
Ploughman*, ch. vii., A little too late is
much too late; and a miss is as good
as a mile. 1894 : Shaw, *Arms and the
Man*, I., A narrow shave ; but a miss
is as good as a mile.

Miss one's mark, To. 1530 : Palsgrave, 638, If I mysse nat my marke,
he is a busy felowe. 1639 : Clarke, 1,
To misse of his marke. 1690 : *New
Dict. Canting Crew*, sig. B1, He has
mist his aim or end. 1754 : Berthelson,
Eng.-Danish Dict., s.v. " Mark."

Miss the cushion, To. Before 1529 :
Skelton, *Colin Clout*, l. 998, And whan
he weneth to syt, Yet may he mysse the
quysshon. 1533 : Latimer, in *Works*, ii.
366 (P.S.), No doubt he did miss the
cushion in many things. 1585 : Greene,
in *Works*, v. 124 (Grosart), Euery one
yeelded his verdicte but all mist the
cushion. 1639 : Clarke, 2, You mist
the cushion.

Mist. *See* quots. 1846 : Denham,
Proverbs, 18 (Percy S.), When the
mist comes from the hill, Then good
weather it doth spill ; When the mist
comes from the sea, Then good weather
it will be. 1891 : R. P. Chope, *Hartland Dialect*, 20 (E.D.S.), Mist vrom
the say Bring'th vore a dry day ; Mist
vrom the 'ills, Bring'th watter to the
mills. 1893 : Inwards, *Weather Lore*,
98 [as in 1846]. Cf. Fog (3) and (4).

Mistress. 1. *All is well when the
mistress smiles.* 1659 : Howell, 17.

2. *The mistress of the mill May say
and do what she will.* 1864 ; " Cornish
Proverbs," in *N. & Q.*, 3rd ser., v. 208.

3. *The mistress's eye feeds the capon.*
1616 : Breton, in *Works*, ii. *e* 8 (Grosart),
The mistris eye makes the capon fatt.
1639 : Clarke, 163.

4. *When the mistress is the master,
The parsley grows the faster.* Mon.
1905 : *Folk-Lore*, xvi. 67.

See also Hackney mistress; and Like
mistress.

Misty morning may have a fine day,
A. 1732 : Fuller, No. 327.

Misunderstanding brings lies to town.
1639 : Clarke, 2. 1670 : Ray, 121.
1712 : Motteux, *Quixote*, Pt. I. bk. iii.
ch. xi. 1732 : Fuller, No. 3424.

Misunderstandings are best prevented
by pen and ink. 1831 : Hone, *Year-
Book*, col. 1416.

Mitcham whisper, A=A shout. 1880 :
Spurgeon, *Ploughman's Pictures*, 80,
They generally speak four or five at a
time, and every one in a Mitcham
whisper, which is very like a shout.
1881 : *N. & Q.*, 6th ser., iii. 336, In
this town [Leigh, Lancs] an unearthly
yell, given at the close of a convivial
evening and as a sequel to a popular
toast, is called a " Leigh whisper."

**Mob has many heads but no brains,
The.** 1732 : Fuller, No. 4653.

Mobberley, Cheshire. 1. *Always behind, like Mobberley clock.* 1886 : R.
Holland, *Cheshire Gloss.*, 444 (E.D.S.).
1917 : Bridge, *Cheshire Proverbs*, 7.

2. *It rains, it pains. See* quot.
1917 : Ibid., 163, It rains, it pains, it
patters i' th' docks, Mobberley wenches
are weshin their smocks.

3. *The rain always comes out of Mobberley hole.* Ibid., 117.

4. *Thou'rt like. See* quot. Ibid., 124,
Thou'rt like old Mode o' Mobberley that
seed th' new moon i' th' morning.

5. *You may know a Mobberley man
by his breeches.* Ibid., 158.

**Mock no panyer-men, your father was
a fisher.** 1678 : Ray, 78. 1732 : Fuller,
No. 3425 [with " if " before " your "].

**Mock not, quoth Mumford, when his
wife called him cuckold.** 1659 : Howell,
9. 1670 : Ray, 186. 1732 : Fuller, No.
3426.

**Mock the lame you will go so your-
self, If you.** *c.* 1577 : Northbrooke,
Dicing, etc., 80 (Sh. S.), According to
the old saying—If thou with him that
haltes doest dwell, To learne to halt
thou shalt full well. 1732 : Fuller,
No. 2774.

Mocking is catching. 1533 : Heywood, *Play of Love*, l. 568 (Brandl,
Quellen, 177), For who so that mocketh
shall surely stur This olde prouerbe
mockum moccabitur. 1710 : S. Palmer,
Moral Essays on Proverbs, 319. 1738 :
Swift, *Polite Convers.*, Dial. I. 1880 :
Spurgeon, *Ploughman's Pictures*, 15, The
old saying is, " Hanging's stretching,
and mocking's catching."

Modest words. *See* quot. *c.* 1645 :
MS. Proverbs, in *N. & Q.*, vol. cliv,
p. 27, It is good to find modest words
to express immodest things.

Mole—the animal. 1. *A mole wants
no lanthorn.* 1732 : Fuller, No. 329.

2. *He holds a looking-glass to a mole.*
1813 : Ray, 75.

See also Blind (14).

Mole—a growth on the body. 1. *A
mole on the neck. See* quots. 1883 :
Burne, *Shropsh. Folk-Lore*, 267, A mole
on the neck You shall have money by

the peck. 1923 : *Folk-Lore*, xxxiv. 156,
Mole on the neck, trouble by the peck
(Gloucest.).

2. *Five moles in a span, You shall
have houses and land.* 1883 : Burne,
Shropsh. Folk-Lore, 267.

3. *If you've got a mole above your chin
You'll never be beholden to any of your
kin.* Ibid., 267.

Molehill. *See* **Mountain** (3).

Monday. 1. *A stranger on Monday
means a stranger all the week.* Suffolk.
1924 : *Folk-Lore*, xxxv. 358.

2. *Monday flit, never sit.* 1641 : Best,
Farming Book, 135 (Surtees S.), As for
Munday, they account it ominous, for
they say, Munday flitte, Neaver sitte.
Cf. **Saturday** (2).

3. *Monday for wealth, etc. See* quot.
1879 : Henderson, *Folk-Lore N. Counties*, 33, [Marriage] Monday for wealth,
Tuesday for health, Wednesday the
best day of all ; Thursday for losses,
Friday for crosses, And Saturday no
luck at all. *Durham.*

4. *Monday is Sunday's brother.*
1611 : *Tarltons Jests*, 41 (Sh. S.), One
asked Tarlton why Munday was called
Sundaies fellow. 1637 : in *Pepysian
Garland*, 445 (Rollins), Tho Munday
Sundayes fellow be, when tuesday
comes to worke fall we. 1846 : Denham, *Proverbs*, 15 (Percy S.), Monday is
Sunday's brother ; Tuesday is such
another. Wednesday you must go to
church and pray ; Thursday is half-
holiday. On Friday it is too late to
begin to spin ; The Saturday is half-
holiday agen. 1890 : J. D. Robertson,
Gloucest. Gloss., 187 (E.D.S.), [Cobbler's
Creed] Monday is a Saint's day ;
Tuesday's just another such a day ;
Wednesday's the middle pin ; Thursday's too late to begin ; Friday we
must fast and pray ; Saturday never
was but half a day.

5. *Monday's child. See* quots. 1838 :
Mrs. Bray, *Trad. of Devon*, ii. 288, Monday's child is fair of face, Tuesday's
child is full of grace, Wednesday's child
is full of woe, Thursday's child has far
to go, Friday's child is loving and
giving, Saturday's child works hard for
its living ; And a child that's born on

Christmas Day Is fair and wise, good and gay. 1877 : *N. & Q.*, 5th ser., vii. 424, Born on Monday, fair in the face ; Born on Tuesday, full of God's grace ; Born on Wednesday, sour and sad ; Born on Thursday, merry and glad ; Born on Friday, worthily given ; Born on Saturday, work hard for your living ; Born on Sunday you will never know want [there is a variant at 5th ser., viii. 45]. 1879 : Henderson, *Folk-Lore N. Counties*, 9 [as in 1838, but with " Sabbath day " for " Christmas Day," and " blithe and bonny " for " fair and wise "]. Cf. **Sunday** (4).

Money. 1. *All things are obedient to money.* [Omnis enim res, virtus, fama, decus, divina humanaque pulchris divitiis parent.—Horace, *Sat.*, II. iii. 94–6.] 1539 : Taverner, *Proverbs*, fo. 14, Vnto money be all thynges obedient. 1542 : Becon, *Early Works*, 222 (P.S.). 1611: Cotgrave, s.v. " Argent," All (earthly) things are commanded, and compassed, by it. 1692 : L'Estrange, *Æsop*, 359 (3rd ed.), The old saying, that money does all things, is not much wide of the truth. 1775 : Grose, *Antiq. Repertory*, ii. 395 (1808), That " every thing may be had for money," is . . . no less ancient than true. Cf. No. 31.

2. *He that gets money before he gets wit, Will be but a short while master of it.* 1732 : Fuller, No. 6432.

3. *He that hath money in his purse, cannot want a head for his shoulders.* 1659: Howell, 13. 1763: Murphy, *Citizen*, I. ii.

4. *He that hath no money needeth no purse.* 1633: Draxe, 138. 1666: Torriano, *Piazza Univ.*, 63.

5. *He that wants money wants all things.* 1542 : Becon, in *Early Works*, 223 (P.S.), He is a wretch that hath no money. 1611: Cotgrave, s.v. " Argent." 1633 : Draxe, 24, When wee want mony, we want all. 1772 : Cumberland, *Fash. Lover*, II. i., In England, he that wants money wants everything.

6. *He would get money in a desert.* 1813 : Ray, 196.

7. *He'll find money for mischief, when he can find none for corn.* 1732 : Fuller, No. 2425.

8. *His money burns in his pocket.* c. 1530: More, in *Works*, 195 (1557), A little wanton money, which . . . burned out the bottom of his purse. 1601 : Cornwallis, *Essayes*, Pt. II. sig. P4 (1610), Like an vnthrifts money that burnes in his purse. 1637 : Shirley, *Hyde Park*, IV. iii., My gold has burnt this twelve months in my pocket. 1702 : Farquhar, *Inconstant*, V. iii., Time lies heavy on my hands, and my money burns in my pocket. 1857 : Hughes, *Tom Brown*, Pt. I. ch. vi., Tom's new purse and money burnt in his pocket.

9. *His money comes from him like drops of blood.* 1678 : Ray, 90.

10. *If money go before, all ways lie open.* 1542 : Becon, in *Early Works*, 223 (P.S.), Whosoever hath money may go where he list . . . at his own pleasure. 1600 : Shakespeare, *Merry Wives*, II. ii. 1666 : Torriano, *Piazza Univ.*, 163, Money makes all gates to fly open.

11. *If thou wouldest keep money, save money; If thou wouldest reap money, sow money.* 1732 : Fuller, Nos. 2721 and 2722.

12. *If you would know the value of money, try to borrow some.* 1640 : Herbert, *Jac. Prudentum*, Would you know what money is, go borrow some. 1732 : Fuller, No. 2801 [" a ducat " for " money," and " one " for " some "]. 1736 : Franklin, *Way to Wealth*, in *Works*, i. 448 (Bigelow). 1875 : Cheales, *Proverb. Folk-Lore*, 101 [as in 1640].

13. *Money answers all things.* 1667 : L'Estrange, *Quevedo's Visions*, 38 (1904). 1700 : Ward, *London Spy*, 400 (1924).

14. *Money begets money.* 1587 : Turbervile, *Trag. Tales, etc.*, 22 (1837), But, where wealth is, there lightlie follows more. 1625 : Bacon, *Essays:* " Usurie," They say . . . that it is against Nature for money to beget money. 1748 : Franklin, in *Works*, ii. 119 (Bigelow), Money can beget money, and its offspring can beget more. 1865 : Dickens, *Mutual Friend*, bk. iii. ch. v., We have got to recollect that money makes money, as well as makes everything else.

15. *Money governs the world.* 1754 :
Berthelson, *Eng.-Danish Dict.*, s.v.
" Money."

16. *Money has no smell.* 1922 : A.
Bennett, *Prohack*, ch. iii. (i.), He understood in a flash the deep wisdom of
that old proverb . . . that money has
no smell. Cf. **Chink.**

17. *Money in purse will be always
in fashion.* 1633 : Draxe, 82, Money
neuer commeth out of season. 1639 :
Clarke, 220 [as in 1633]. 1732 : Fuller,
No. 3435.

18. *Money is a good servant but a bad
master.* 1855 : Bohn, 453.

19. *Money is a great traveller in the
world.* 1616 : Breton, in *Works*, ii. *e* 5
(Grosart) [" continuall " for " great "].
1639 : Clarke, 98.

20. *Money is ace of trumps.* 1732 :
Fuller, No. 3438.

21. *Money is no fool, if a wise man
have it in keeping.* Glos. 1639 : in
Berkeley MSS., iii. 27 (1885).

22. *Money is oft lost for want of money.*
1633 : Draxe, 69.

23. *Money is round. See* quots.
1619 : *Helpe to Discourse*, 120 (1640),
Why is the forme of money round ?
Because it is to runne from every man.
1666 : Torriano, *Piazza Univ.*, 64,
Moneys are round, and that makes
them rowl away. 1869 : Spurgeon,
John Ploughman, ch. xii., Money is
round, and rolls away easily.

24. *Money is that which art hath
turned up trump.* 1659 : Howell, 18.
1670 : Ray, 18.

25. *Money is the sinew of love as well
as of war.* 1732 : Fuller, No. 3442.

26. *Money is welcome though it come
in a dirty clout.* 1542 : Becon, in
Early Works, 222 (P.S.), The savour of
lucre is good, howsoever a man come
by it. 1647 : Howell, *Letters*, bk. ii.
No. xxv. 1670 : Ray, 18. 1723 :
Defoe, *Col. Jack*, ch. ii., I have often
since heard people say, when they could
not get in, I wish I had it in a foul
clout.

27. *Money is wise, it knows its way.*
Somerset. 1678 : Ray, 352.

28. *Money, like dung, does not good
till it's spread.* 1625 : Bacon, *Essays :*
"Seditions, etc.," Money is like muck,
not good except it be spread. 1659 :
Howell, 19, Riches like muck which
stinks in a heap, but spread abroad,
maketh the earth fruitful. 1670 : Ray,
22 [as in 1659]. 1732 : Fuller, No.
3444.

29. *Money makes friends enemies.*
1616 : Breton, *Crossing of Proverbs*, 6
(Grosart). 1732 : Fuller, No. 3446,
Money makes not so many true friends
as real enemies.

30. *Money makes marriage.* Ibid.,
No. 3445.

31. *Money makes mastery.* 1602 :
Liberality and Prodig., I. v. 1686 :
Loyal Garland, 42 (Percy S.), This
masters money, though money masters
all things. Cf. No. 1.

32. *Money makes the man.* [Cf. Pindar,
Isth. Ode, ii. 15.] 1542 : Becon, in *Early
Works*, 222 (P.S.). 1564 : Bullein, *Dialogue*, 102 (E.E.T.S.), That will make
readie money, and money maketh a
man. *c.* 1630 : in *Pepysian Garland*,
362 (Rollins), They say tis money makes
a man. 1681 : Robertson, *Phraseol.
Generalis*, 892. 1840 : Lytton, *Money*,
II. i. 1926 : *Evening Standard*, 11 Dec.,
p. 5, col. 2.

33. *Money makes the mare to go.*
1578 : Florio, *First Fruites*, fo. 30,
Money maketh horses runne. 1605 :
Breton, in *Works*, ii. *l* 7 (Grosart), For
money . . . makes . . . the olde mare
trot, and the young tit amble. 1691 :
Merry Drollery, 117 (Ebsworth), 'Tis
money makes . . . the mare to go.
c. 1760 : Foote, *Author*, I. 1857 :
Kingsley, *Two Years Ago*, Introd., I'm
making the mare go here . . . without
the money too sometimes.

34. *Money makes the merchant.* 1468 :
Coventry Mys., 268 (Sh. S.), In old
termys I have herd seyde, That mony
makyth schapman.

35. *Money makes the old wife trot.*
1691 : *Merry Drollery*, 117 (Ebsworth).
1700 : Ward, *London Spy*, 400 (1924).
1732 : Fuller, No. 3433.

36. *Money paid and arms broken.*
1620 : Shelton, *Quixote*, Pt. II. ch. lxxi.,
It shall never be said of me, " Money

well paid, and the arms broken."
1631 : Mabbe, *Celestina*, 67 (T.T.), How
softly she goes! How one leg comes
drawling after another! Now she has
her money, her armes are broken.
1666 : Torriano, *Piazza Univ.*, 257, A
servant paid, his arm broke.

37. *Money refused loseth its brightness.*
1640 : Herbert, *Jac. Prudentum.*

38. *Money talks.* 1586 : Pettie, tr.
Guazzo's *Civil Convers.*, fo. 88, It is sayd
that . . . the tongue hath no force when
golde speaketh. 1666 : Torriano, *Piazza
Univ.*, 179, Man prates, but gold speaks.
1915 : P. G. Wodehouse, *Something
Fresh*, ch. iii. (vi.), The whole story
took on a different complexion for Joan.
Money talks. 1925 : A. Palmer, in
Sphere, 19 Dec., p. 364, col. 3, " Money
talks," I reminded myself, " So why not
listen to it ? "

39. *Money will do more than my lord's
letter.* 1678 : Ray, 177. 1732 : Fuller,
No. 3447.

40. *Money will make the pot boil.*
1692 : L'Estrange, *Æsop*, 305 (3rd ed.),
'Tis that [Money] which makes the pot
boyl (as the proverb says). 1732 :
Fuller, No. 3449.

41. *Money without love is like salt
without pilchers.* 1880 : Courtney, *W.
Cornwall Words*, 42 (E.D.S.).

42. *Of money, wit, and virtue, believe
one-fourth of what you hear.* 1855 :
Bohn, 466.

43. *The abundance of money ruins
youth.* 1670 : Ray, 18.

44. *The money you refuse will never
do you good.* 1855 : Bohn, 510.

45. *The skilfullest wanting money is
scorned.* 1670 : Ray, 18.

46. *They that take money. See* quot.
c. 1640 : in *Roxb. Ballads*, iii. 253 (B.S.),
The proverb observing—" They that
money take Must pay all the charges."

47. *What will not money do?* 1581 :
T. Howell, *Devises*, 54 (1906), But briefe
to bee, what can you craue, That now
for golde you may not haue ? 1623 :
Webster, *Devil's Law-Case*, IV. i., Lord,
lord, To see what money can do!
1681 : Robertson, *Phraseol. Generalis*,
892. 1708 : tr. Aleman's *Guzman*, i. 13,
What is not to be done with money ?

See also Beauty (6) ; Fool (2) and (11) ;
Little money ; Love, *subs.* (13), (23), (36),
and (38) ; My son; Pretty things ; Ready
money ; and Sinews of war.

**Moneyless man goes fast through the
market**, A. 1732 : Fuller, No. 330.

**Mongst many chapmen there are few
that buyes.** 1606 : Heywood, *If You
Know Not Me*, Pt. II., in *Works*, i. 263
(1874).

Monkey. *See* **Melancholy.**

Monkey on the chimney, A = A
mortgage or debt on a house. 1877 :
N. & Q., 5th ser., viii. 289, A monkey
on the house. 1887 : T. Darlington,
S. Cheshire Folk Speech., 264 (E.D.S.).
1917 : Bridge, *Cheshire Proverbs*, 4.

Monkey's grease, As useless as. 1732 :
Fuller, No. 744.

Monmouth caps. *See* **Leominster
wool.**

Month of Sundays, A = A prolonged
but indefinite period. 1832 : Marryat,
N. Forster, v. (O.), It may last a month
of Sundays. 1850 : Kingsley, *Alton
Locke*, ch. xxvii., I haven't heard more
fluent or passionate English this month
of Sundays. 1898 : Gibbs, *Cotswold
Village*, ch. iv. 71 (3rd ed.), A joint of
mutton is not seen by the peasants
more than " once in a month of
Sundays." 1923 : *Punch*, 20 June, p. 582,
col. 3, I will engage to talk at that
level for a month of Sundays.

**Month that comes in good, will go
out bad, The.** 1893 : Inwards, *Weather
Lore*, 42.

Month's mind, A = An eager desire.
1575 : Gascoigne, *Glasse of Govt.*, II. v.,
She hath a monethes minde vnto
Phylosarchus. 1605 : *London Prodigal*, I. ii., He hath a month's mind
here to mistress Frances. 1631 : Brathwait, *Eng. Gentlewoman*, 355 (1641), I
have a moneth's mind to see the man !
1731 : in Peck, *Desid. Curiosa*, 229
(1779), When people earnestly desire a
thing, they frequently say, they have
a month's mind to it. 1766 : Garrick
and Colman, *Clandest. Marriage*, I. i.,
Persuading a silly girl to do what she
has more than a month's mind to do.
1824 : Scott, *Redgauntlet*, Lett. III.,
I have a month's mind . . . to give

thee the history of a little adventure which befell me yesterday. 1877 : E. Leigh, *Cheshire Gloss.*, 136, " To have a month's mind " is to have a strong inclination to do something. 1913 : E. M. Wright, *Rustic Speech, etc.*, 282, To have a month's mind to anything [in general dialectal use]. This alludes to a pre-Reformation practice of repeating one or more masses at the end of a month after death for the repose of a departed soul.

Moon. 1. *A dry moon is far north and soon seen.* 1893 : Inwards, *Weather Lore*, 59.

2. *A new moon soon seen is long thought of.* 1846 : Denham, *Proverbs*, 2 (Percy S.). 1904 : *Co. Folk-Lore: Northumb.*, 171 (F.L.S.).

3. *A Saturday's moon. See* quots. 1732 : Fuller, No. 6491, A Saturday's moon If it comes once in seven years, it comes too soon. 1818 : Mrs. Piozzi, in Hayward, *Mrs. Piozzi*, ii. 391 (1861), St. David's Day has been a rough one, and your brother Dorset forces me on the reflection that it was a Saturday's moon. 1830 : Forby, *Vocab. E. Anglia*, 417, On Saturday new, on Sunday full, Was never good, and never wooll. 1846 : Denham, *Proverbs*, 9 (Percy S.), A Saturday's moon, Come when it will it comes too soon. Ibid., 18, A Saturday's change brings the boat to the door ; But a Sunday's change brings it upon t' mid floor. 1864 : " Cornish Proverbs," in *N. & Q.*, 3rd ser., v. 209, A Saturday or a Sunday moon, Comes once in seven years too soon. *c.* 1870 : Smith, *Isle of Wight Words*, 62 (E.D.S.) [essentially as in 1830]. 1879 : Henderson, *Folk-Lore N. Counties*, 114, Throughout Northumberland this couplet is said and believed in : A Saturday's moon and a Sunday's prime Never brought good in any man's time. 1887 : M. A. Courtney, *Folk-Lore Journal*, v. 191, A Saturday's moon is a sailor's curse. *Cornwall*. 1893 : *Co. Folk-Lore: Suffolk*, 161 (F.L.S.) [as in 1830]. 1893 : Inwards, *Weather Lore*, 59 [as in 1732, 1830, etc.].

4. *An old moon in a mist Is worth gold in a kist* [chest] *; But a new moon's*

mist Will never lack thirst. 1878 : Dyer, *Eng. Folk-Lore*, 41. 1893 : Inwards, *Weather Lore*, 65. Cf. No. 23.

5. *Auld moon mist Ne'er died of thirst.* Ibid., 65.

6. *Have a care, etc. See* quot. 1846–59 : *Denham Tracts*, ii. 57 (F.L.S.), We have, however, an old, very old proverb . . . to wit ; " Have a care lest the churl fall out o' the moon."

7. *If the full moon rise red expect wind.* 1588 : A. Fraunce, *Lawiers Logike*, fo. 43, When the moone is red, shee betokeneth wind. 1893 : Inwards, 64.

8. *If the moon show a silver shield, Be not afraid to reap your field; But if she rises haloed round, Soon we'll tread on deluged ground.* 1893 : Ibid., 64.

9. *In the old of the moon a cloudy morning bodes a fair afternoon.* 1639 : in *Berkeley MSS.*, iii. 31 (1885), A misty morne in th' old o' th' moone doth alwaies bring a faire post - noone. An hilly proverbe about Simondsall (Glouc.). 1678 : Ray, 48. 1831 : Hone, *Year-Book*, 300, In the waning of the moon, A cloudy morn—fair afternoon. 1893 : Inwards, 59, In the decay of the moon A cloudy morning bodes a fair afternoon. Ibid., 64, Near full moon, a misty sunrise Bodes fair weather and cloudless skies.

10. *It is a fine moon, God bless her!* 1678 : Aubrey, in *Antiq. Repertory*, i. 73 (1807), Some of them sitting astride on a gate or stile the first evening the new moon appears, and say, *A fine moon, God bless her!* 1846 : Denham, *Proverbs*, 4 (Percy S.).

11. *No moon, no man. See* quot. 1878 : Dyer, *Eng. Folk-Lore*, 41, In Cornwall, when a child is born in the interval between an old moon and the first appearance of a new one, it is said that it will never live to reach the age of puberty. Hence the saying, " No moon, no man."

12. *Pale moon doth rain, red moon doth blow, White moon doth neither rain nor snow.* 1639 : Clarke, 263.

13. *So many days old the moon is on Michaelmas Day, so many floods after.* 1661 : M. Stevenson, *Twelve Moneths*,

44. 1819 : Henderson, *Folk-Lore N. Counties*, 96. 1885 : Harley, *Moon Lore*, 185.

14. *Sunday's moon.* See quots. 1851 : Sternberg, *Dialect, etc., of Northants*, 110, Thus the proverb, "Sunday's moon floods 'for 'ts out." 1893 : Inwards, 59, If the moon change on a Sunday, there will be a flood before the month is out. Worcestershire. *See also* No. 3.

15. *The full moon brings fine weather.* Ibid., 64.

16. *The full moon eats clouds.* Nautical. And, *The moon grows fat on clouds.* Ibid., 64.

17. *The Michaelmas moon Rises nine nights alike soon.* 1878 : Dyer, *Eng. Folk-Lore*, 259.

18. *The moon does not heed the barking of dogs.* 1813 : Ray, 208.

19. *The moon is a moon still, whether it shine or not.* 1732 : Fuller, No. 4654.

20. *The moon is made of green cheese, To believe* (or *To tell one*) *that.* This is one of the most frequently found sayings in 16th and 17th-century literature. 1529 : Frith, *Antith. Works*, p. 105, col. 1 (1573) (O.), They woulde make men beleue . . . that yᵉ moone is made of grene chese. 1542 : Udall, tr. Erasmus' *Apoph.*, 193 (1877), With this pleasaunt mery toye, he . . . made his frendes beleue the moone to be made of a grene chese. 1584 : R. Scot, *Witchcraft*, bk. xv. ch. v. 1658 : in *Musarum Deliciæ, etc.*, i. 199 (Hotten), The moon is made of nothing but green cheese. 1696 : *Cornish Comedy*, IV. i. 1754 : Berthelson, *Eng.-Danish Dict.*, s.v. "Believe."

21. *The moon is not seen where the sun shines.* 1670 : Ray, 122. 1826 : Brady, *Varieties of Lit.*, 38.

22. *The moon on her back holds water* = a sign of rain. 1893 : Inwards, *Weather Lore*, 82, The bonnie moon is on her back ; Mend your shoes and sort your thack [thatch]. When the new moon lies on her back, She sucks the wet into her lap. Ellesmere. 1895 : Rye, *E. Anglia Words*, 143 (E.D.S.).

23. *The new moon's mist Is better than gold in a kist* [chest]. 1879 : Henderson, *Folk-Lore N. Counties*, 115 [quoted as "A Yorkshire rhyme"]. Cf. No. 4.

24. *Two full moons in a month bring on a flood.* Beds. 1855 : *N. & Q.*, 1st ser., xi. 416, It will be a wet month when there are two full moons in it. 1893 : Inwards, 64.

25. *When early seen, 'Tis seldom seen.* 1872 : J. Glyde, jr., *Norfolk Garland*, 157. 1893 : *Co. Folk-Lore: Suffolk*, 163 (F.L.S.).

26. *When round the moon there is a burr* [halo], *The weather will be cold and rough.* 1631 : Brathwait, *Whimzies*, 104 (1859), A burre about the moone is not halfe so certaine a presage of a tempest, as . . . 1659 : Howell, *Proverbs: Span.-Eng.*, 21, The moon with a circle brings water in her beak. 1690 : *New Dict. Canting Crew*, sig. C2, *Bur*, a cloud or dark circle about the moon, boding wind and rain. 1830 : Forby, *Vocab. E. Anglia*, 417, Near bur, far rain. 1846 : Denham, *Proverbs*, 17 (Percy S.). 1887 : Parish and Shaw, *Dict. Kent. Dialect*, 23 (E.D.S.), The weatherwise in East Kent will tell you, "The larger the burr the nearer the rain." 1893 : *Co. Folk-Lore: Suffolk*, 162 (F.L.S.), If it [the halo] is large, the proverb is :— Far burr, near rain ; Near burr, far rain. 1893 : Inwards, 56 [as in 1659]. 1899 : Dickinson, *Cumb. Gloss.*, 48, A far-off burgh tells of a near-hand storm. When t' burrs far t' rains nar.

27. *When the moon lies on her back, Then the sou'-west wind will crack; When she rises up and nods, Then north-easters dry the sods.* 1867 : *Symons' Meteorological Mag.*, Sept., quoted in Inwards, *Weather Lore*, 62.

28. *When the moon's in the full, then wit's in the wane.* 1846 : Denham, *Proverbs*, 4 (Percy S.).

29. *You gazed at the moon and fell in the gutter.* 1732 : Fuller, No. 5904. 1846 : Denham, 5.

See also **Bean** (5) ; **Changeful** ; and **Fog** (1).

Mooney's goose, Like. 1850 : *N. & Q.*, 1st ser., ii. 153, Full of fun and fooster, like Mooney's goose.

Moonshine in a can. 1639 : Clarke, 154, The moone shine i' th' water-pot.

1828 : Carr, *Craven Dialect*, i. 329, " To run about moonshine in a can," to be employed in no useful purpose.

Moonshine in the mustard-pot for it, Thou shalt have, i.e. nothing. 1639 : Clarke, 68, Moonshine i' th' mustard pot. 1678 : Ray, 76.

Moonshine in the water = Nothing. 1468 : *Paston Letters*, ii. 326 (O.), If Sir Thomas Howys wer . . . made byleve and put in hope of the moone shone in the water and I wot nat what. 1530 : Palsgrave, 865, For moone shyne in the water, *pour une chose de riens*. 1565 : Shacklock, *Hatch. of Heresies*, quoted in *N. & Q.*, 2nd ser., v. 411. 1592 : Shakespeare, *L. L. L.*, V. ii. 1659 : Howell, 15, He waits for moonshine in the water. 1817 : Scott, *Rob Roy*, ch. xxvi., I care little about that nonsense—it's a' moonshine in water— waste threads and thrums, as we say. 1861 : Peacock, *Gryll Grange*, ch. iv., He will not break his heart for any moon in the water, if his cooks are as good as his waiting-maids.

Mope-eyed by living so long a maid, You are. 1678 : Ray, 346.

More acquaintance the more danger, The. 1732 : Fuller, No. 4656.

More balks. *See* quot. "Balk"=a strip of unploughed land, also little ridges left in ploughing. 1888 : *N. & Q.*, 7th ser., v. 194, We have here [Lincs] a proverb, " More balks, more barley ; more seams, more beans."

More bold than wise (or welcome). 1591 : Florio, *Second Frutes*, 53, You are not so bold as welcome. 1633 : Draxe, 17, He is more bolde than wise. 1738 : Swift, *Polite Convers.*, Dial. I., You are more bold than welcome.

More brass than pash=More money than brains. 1877 : E. Leigh, *Cheshire Gloss.*, 152. 1917 : Bridge, *Cheshire Proverbs*, 160.

More clout than dinner=More show than substance. 1828 : Carr, *Craven Dialect*, i. 78. Cf. **More poke.**

More cost more worship. 1591 : Harington, *Orl. Furioso*, Adv. to Reader, At least (by the old proverbe) the more cost, the more worship. 1615 : Markham, *Eng. House-wife*, 163

(1675), According to the old proverb (*Most cost, most worship*). 1670 : Ray, 73. 1821 : Scott, *Pirate*, ch. xi., The mair cost the mair honour.

More cost than worship. 1732 : Fuller, No. 3451. 1738 : Swift, *Polite Convers.*, Dial. III., She was as fine as fi'pence ; but, truly, I thought there was more cost than worship. 1828 : Carr, *Craven Dialect*, i. 86, " More cost than worship," i.e. more expense and trouble than the acquisition is worth. 1877 : F. Ross, etc., *Holderness Gloss.*, 45 (E.D.S.), " It's mair cost-an-worship," it is more trouble than it is worth. 1917 : Bridge, *Cheshire Proverbs*, 95, More cost nor worship. Cf. **More trouble.**

More danger, the more honour, The. *c.* 1534 : Berners, *Huon*, 56 (E.E.T.S.), Where as lyeth grete parelles [perils] there lieth grete honour. *c.* 1625 : B. & F., *Women Pleased*, III. ii., Where the most danger is, there's the most honour. 1671 : E. Howard, *Six Days Adventure*, I. 1710 : S. Palmer, *Moral Essays on Proverbs*, 85. 1772 : Garrick, *Irish Widow*, I. iii.

More die by food than famine. 1588 : Cogan, *Haven of Health*, 219 (1612), The Greeke poet Theognis most truely hath written, that surfet hath destroied mo than famin. 1732 : Fuller, No. 3453. Cf. **Gluttony.**

More faults than hairs, and more wealth than faults, He hath. Ibid., No. 1892.

More folks are wed than keep good houses. 1685 : Meriton, *Yorkshire Ale*, 67.

More fool than fiddler. 1678 : Ray, 245.

More frightened than hurt — originally, **More afraid** . . . 1530 : Palsgrave, 558, He was sorer frayed than hurt. 1579 : Lyly, *Euphues*, 189 (Arber), Certeinly thou art more afraide then hurte. 1628 : J. Clavell, *Recantation*, 12, Thus more afraid than hurt you often are. Before 1704 : T. Brown, *Works*, i. 74 (1760), Thou art more afraid than hurt. 1768 : Sterne, *Sent. Journey*, 34. (1794), All of us . . . being ten times more frighten'd than hurt by the very

report. 1872 : Butler, *Erewhon*, ch.
xiii., The Erewhonians, therefore, hold
that death, like life, is an affair of being
more frightened than hurt. 1883 :
R. L. S., *Treasure I.*, ch. xxi.

More good victuals. *See* England (8).

More guts than brains, He has. 1678 :
Ray, 249. 1732 : Fuller, No. 1873.

More haste, worse speed, The. 1542 :
Udall, tr. Erasmus' *Apoph.*, 41 (1877),
Soche persones, as do make moste hast
in the beginning, haue commonly
(accordyng to our Englishe prouerbe)
worst spede toward the endyng. *c.* 1560 :
Jacke Jugeler, in Hazlitt, *Old Plays*, ii.
121, When a man hath most haste, he
speedeth worst. 1633 : Rowley, *Match
at Midnight*, I. 1705 : Ward, *Hudibras
Rediv.*, Pt. I. can. i. p. 23, The greater
hurry, the worst speed. 1776: Colman,
The Spleen, I. 1829 : Scott, *Journal*, 15
Feb., Unhappily there is such a thing
as more haste and less speed. 1919 :
Weyman, *Great House*, ch. xxvii., More
haste, less speed, you know.

**More have repented speech than
silence.** 1640 : Herbert, *Jac. Prudentum*.
1875 : Cheales, *Proverb. Folk-Lore*, 86.

More he hath, The. *See* Much would
have more.

**More hope of a fool than of him that
is wise in his own eyes, There is.** 1629 :
Book of Meery Riddles, Prov. 23.

More knave than fool. *c.* 1630 : in
Roxb. Ballads, i. 72 (Hindley), This
man's more knaue than foole. 1634 :
Strange Metam. of Man, sig. G4. 1738 :
Swift, *Polite Convers.*, Dial. II.

More knave, the better luck, The.
1550 : Latimer, *Sermons*, 280 (P.S.), It
is an old proverb, " the more wicked,
the more fortunate." 1611 : Cotgrave,
s.v. " Escheoir," The verier knave the
better lucke, say we. 1670 : Ray, 111.
1732 : Fuller, No. 6332, He's like
Marten ; The more knave, the better
fortune. 1917 : *Devonsh. Assoc. Trans.*,
xlix. 68, The greater the rogue, the
better the luck.

More knave, the worse company, The.
1546 : Heywood, *Proverbs*, Pt. I. ch. xi.

**More know Tom Fool than Tom Fool
knows.** 1723 : Defoe, *Col. Jack*, ch.
xvii. [quoted as " the old English

proverb "]. 1754 : Berthelson, *Eng.-
Danish Dict.*, s.v. " Jack " [with " jack-
pudding " for " Tom Fool "]. 1830 :
Forby,*Vocab. E. Anglia*, 431. 1922: A.B.
Walkley, in *Times*, 15 Nov., p. 10, col. 2.

More laws, the more offenders, The.
1732 · Fuller, No. 4663.

**More light a torch gives, the less
while it lasts, The.** Ibid., No. 4664.

More maids than Malkin, There are.
[*c.* 1377 : Langland, *Plowman*, B, i.
181, Ye ne haue na more mcryte in
masse ne in houres [church-services]
Than Malkyn of hire maydenhode that
no man desireth.] 1546 : Heywood,
Proverbs, Pt. I. ch. xi., [If] there was
no mo maydes but malkyn tho Ye had
been lost. *c.* 1598 : Deloney, *Gentle
Craft*, Pt. II. ch. iii. 1659 : Howell,
Letters, ii. 666 (Jacobs). 1732 : Fuller,
No. 4859, There are more maids than
Moggy, and more men than Jockey.

More malice than matter. Somerset.
1678: Ray, 352. 1732: Fuller, No. 3458.

**More men threatened than struck,
There are.** 1640 : Herbert, *Jac. Pru-
dentum*. 1670: Ray, 26. 1732: Fuller,
No. 4860.

More mischief, the better sport, The.
1750 : Smollett, *Gil Blas*, i. 136. 1816 :
Scott, *Black Dwarf*, ch. xii.

More nice than wise. 1581 : B.
Rich, *Farewell*, 139 (Sh. S.), I warrant
you, thei can make it more nice than
wise. 1599 : Buttes, *Dyets Dry Dinner*,
Epist. Ded. 1670: Ray, 187. 1754: Berthelson, *Eng.-Danish Dict.*, s.v. " Nice."

**More noble that deserves than he that
confers benefits, He is.** 1732 : Fuller,
No. 1925.

More noble, the more humble, The.
1633 : Draxe, 140. 1670 : Ray, 19.
1748 : Richardson, *Clarissa*, iv. 238
(1785), The more noble any one is, the
more humble.

**More painful to do nothing than some-
thing, It is.** 1659 : Howell, 6. 1732 :
Fuller, No. 2978.

More pigs and less parsons. Derby.
1889 : *Folk-Lore Journal*, vii. 293.

**More places than the parish church,
There are.** 1579 : Gosson, *School of
Abuse*, 37 (Arber), There are more
houses then parishe churches. 1725 :

Defoe, *Everybody's Business*. 1760 :
Colman, *Polly Honeycombe*, sc. iv.
1864 : ." Cornish Proverbs," in *N. & Q.*,
3rd ser., v. 276.

**More pleasure in loving than in being
beloved, There is.** 1732 : Fuller, No.
4900.

More poke [bag] **than pudding**=More
show than substance. 1828: Carr, *Craven
Dialect*, ii. 52. 1892 : Heslop, *Northumb.
Words*, 546 (E.D.S.). Cf. **More clout.**

More riches. *See* **Fool** (102).

More sacks to the mill. 1590 : Nashe,
Works, i. 238 (Grosart), To the next,
to the next, more sacks to the myll.
1607 : Dekker and Webster, *Westw. Hoe*,
IV. i. 1661: in *Harl. Miscell.*, ii. 503
(1744), Come, sirs, more sacks unto the
mill, More taxes, more free-quarter.
1738 : Swift, *Polite Convers.*, Dial. I.,
[Neverout, as Miss is standing, pulls
her suddenly on his lap, and then says]
Now, colonel, come sit down on my
lap ; more sacks upon the mill. 1748 :
Richardson, *Clarissa*, vii. 310 (1785).
1913 : E. M. Wright, *Rustic Speech,
etc.*, 60, *More sacks to the mill* is a
game played in Oxfordshire and Berkshire. It is a rough-and-tumble boys'
game, in which as many boys as possible
are heaped together, one above another.
As each successive boy is added to the
heap—the boys shout : More sacks to
the mill !

More said the less done, The. 1760 :
Colman, *Polly Honeycombe*, sc. i., It's
an old saying and a true one, The more
there's said the less there's done.

More sauce than pig. 1671 : *Poor
Robin Alman. Prognost.*, sig. C7. 1690 :
New Dict. Canting Crew, sig. K8.
1738 : Swift, *Polite Convers.*, Dial. II.

**More spends the niggard than the
liberal.** 1557 : North, *Diall of Princes*,
fo. 199, recto, So sayth the common
prouerbe, yᵗ the nigard spendeth
asmuche as the liberall. 1639 : Clarke,
39. 1666 : Torriano, *Piazza Univ.*, 17,
A covetous man out-spends a liberal
man. Cf. **No feast to a miser's.**

More squeak than wool. 1740 : North,
Lives of Norths, i. 220 (Bohn), And for
matter of title, he thought there was
more squeak than wool. Cf. **Much cry.**

More stars than a pair. *c.* 1380:
Chaucer, *Parl. of Foules*, l. 595, There
been mo sterres, god wot, than a paire !

More store more stink. S.W. Wilts.
1901 : *Folk-Lore*, xii. 82.

More talk than trouble, There is.
1640 : Herbert, *Jac. Prudentum*.

More than enough is too much.
1629 : *Book of Meery Riddles*, Prov.
107, More than enough breaks the
cover. 1732 : Fuller, No. 3461.

More than nits in *his* **head, There's.**
1917 : Bridge, *Cheshire Proverbs*, 118;
[also] There's more in his yed nor a smo'
tooth comb con fot eawt (Lancashire!)

**More than we use is more than we
want.** 1732 : Fuller, No. 3462.

**More the merrier, The; the fewer
the better fare.** (*a*) *The full saying.*
1530 : Palsgrave, 885, The mo the
meryer ; the fewer, the better fare.
1546: Heywood, *Proverbs*, Pt. II. ch.
vii. 1681: Robertson, *Phraseol. Generalis*, 598 ["cheer" for "fare"].
1738 : Swift, *Polite Convers.*, Dial. II.
["cheer"]. 1769 : Colman, *Man and
Wife*, II. ["cheer"]. 1855: Kingsley,
West. Ho!, ch. v. 1863 : Kingsley,
Water Babies, ch. vi. 1917 : Bridge,
Cheshire Proverbs, 95, More and merrier:
less and better fare, like Meg o' Wood's
merry meal. (*b*) *The first part only.* 1553:
Respublica, III. v., Come nere, on
Goddes halfe, the mo knaves the merrier.
c. 1570: *Marr. of Wit and Science*, III. ii.,
The more company the merrier. 1629 :
Ford, *Lover's Melancholy*, II. ii. 1696 :
Vanbrugh, *Relapse*, IV. 1727 : Vanbrugh and Cibber, *Prov. Husband*, II.
1772 : Garrick, *Irish Widow*, I. iii., The
more the merrier, I say—who's afraid ?
1841 : Dickens, *Barn. Rudge*, ch. lix.,
Who's afraid ? Let 'em come, I say,
let 'em come. The more, the merrier.
1918 : A. A. Milne, *Make-Believe*, Prol.,
in *Second Plays*, 6 (1921). (*c*) *The second
part only.* 1605 : Camden, *Remains*, 332
(1870). 1704 : Steele, *Lying Lover*, II.
ii., The fewer the better cheer.

**More thy years, the nearer thy grave,
The.** 1605 : Camden, *Remains*, 333
(1870) ["nigher" for "nearer"]. 1670 :
Ray, 31. 1732 : Fuller, No. 6248.

More tongue. *See* quot. 1864 :

"Cornish Proverbs," in *N. & Q.*, 3rd ser., vi. 494, He has more tongue than teeth; better keep a heps [hapse, or hatch] before his mouth. 1880: Courtney, *W. Cornwall Words*, 28 (E.D.S.) ["She" for "He" and "her" for "his"].

More trouble than worship = More trouble than it is worth. 1854: Baker, *Northants Gloss.*, s.v. "Worship." Cf. **More cost.**

More ways to kill a dog. *See* Dog (82).

More ways to the wood than one, There are. 1546: Heywood, *Proverbs*, Pt. II. ch. ix. 1579: Gosson, *Sch. of Abuse*, 37 (Arber), There are . . . more wayes to the woode then one, and more causes in nature then efficients. 1608: Middleton, *Family of Love*, III. iv. 1664: Falkland, *Marriage Night*, III., Destiny has many ways to the wood. 1732: Fuller, No. 4861.

More wit the less courage, The. Ibid., No. 4668.

More witty than wise. 1714: *Spectator*, No. 568, Ay, says he, more witty than wise I am afraid.

More words than one go to a bargain. 1670: Ray, 58. 1732: Fuller, No. 3465. Cf. **Two words to a bargain.**

More you heap, the worse you cheap, The. 1670: Ray, 102. 1732: Fuller, No. 6101.

More you stir, the worse it will stink, The. 1546: Heywood, *Proverbs*, Pt. II. ch. vi. 1596: Harington, *Metam. of Ajax*, 105 (1814), As the proverb is, "'Tis noted as the nature of a sink, Ever the more it is stirred, the more to stink." 1632: Jonson, *Magn. Lady*, IV. ii. 1664: J. Wilson, *Cheats*, V. ii., 'Tis a foul business—the more you stir, the worse 'twill be. 1710: S. Palmer, *Moral Essays on Proverbs*, 150, A stink is still worse for the stirring. 1752: Fielding, *Cov. Garden Journal*, No. 7, Pray let Grub-street alone, for the more you stir the more it will stink. 1924: *Folk-Lore*, xxxv. 358, The more you stir, the more it stinks (Suffolk).

Morley's black, Like, born without a notion. 1878: *N. & Q.*, 5th ser., x. 10, This was . . . a Nottinghamshire saying, but a very common one—

spoken of some one on the occasion of his committing a stupid action.

Morning. 1. *A foul morn may turn to a fair day.* [1586: Pettie, tr. Guazzo's *Civil Convers.*, fo. 142, As the prouerbe is, That by the morning it may be gathered how all the day will proue after.] 1732: Fuller, No. 115.

2. *A gaudy morning bodes a wet afternoon.* 1893: Inwards, *Weather Lore*, 50.

3. *In the morning mountains, in the evening fountains.* 1640: Herbert, *Jac. Prudentum.* 1846: Denham, *Proverbs*, 13 (Percy S.), The morn to the mountain, The evening to the fountain.

4. *Morning dreams are true.* [Post mediam noctem visus quum somnia vera.—Horace, *Sat.*, I. x. 33.] 1540: Palsgrave, *Acolastus*, sig. I1, After mydnyght men saye, that dreames be true. 1584: R. Scot, *Witchcraft*, bk. x. ch. vii., In the morning . . . there happen more pleasant and certain dreames. 1611: Jonson, *Love Restored*, last line, And all the morning dreams are true. 1681: Dryden, *Span. Friar*, III. iii., At break of day, when dreams, they say, are true. 1713: Gay, *Wife of Bath*, IV. ii., Morning dreams, I learned . . . are most to be relied upon. *c.* 1820: Shelley, *Boat on the Serchio*, If morning dreams are true . . . 1867: Harland, etc., *Lancs Folk-Lore*, 147, Morning dreams are more to be relied on than those of any other time. *See also* Evening.

Morning sun, or, Morning without clouds. *See* Sun (1).

Moroah Downs, Like, hard and never ploughed. 1864: "Cornish Proverbs," in *N. & Q.*, 3rd ser., v. 275.

Morpeth compliment, A. 1834: Service, *Metrical Leg. of Northumb.*, 140, She gav' me nout i' plenty but her tongue, O' that a Morpeth compliment she flung.

Morsel eaten gains no friend, A. 1813: Ray, 140.

Mortar on head. *See* Rome (3).

Mortar, To have one's finger in = To dabble in the proverbial. 1639: in *Berkeley MSS.*, iii. 28 (1885), Dip not thy finger in the morter, nor seeke thy penny in the water. 1662: Gerbier, *Disc. of*

Building, 3, Those who say, That a wise-man never ought to put his finger into morter. 1738 : Swift, *Polite Convers.*, Dial. II., You are come to a sad, dirty house . . . but we have had our hands in mortar.

Mort-stone, He may remove. 1662 : Fuller, *Worthies*, i. 399 (1840). 1790 : Grose, *Prov. Gloss.*, s.v. " Devonshire."

Morvah Downs—ploughed, not harrowed, Like. Corn. 1895 : Jos. Thomas, *Randigal Rhymes*, 61. 1906 : *Cornish N. & Q.*, 264, Like Morvah Downs, harved and never ploughed.

Morvah Fair. *See* quot. 1870 : Bottrell, *Traditions of W. Cornwall*, 42, The old saying of " riding three on one horse, like going to Morvah fair."

Moss and his mare. *See* Napping.

Most take all. 1678 : Ray, 347.

Most things have two handles ; and a wise man takes hold of the best. 1732 : Fuller, No. 3472.

Most time. *See* Time.

Most wild. *See* quot. 1630 : T. Adams, *Works*, 498, The prouerbe saith, that the most wilde are in least danger to be starke madde.

Mote is a beam, Every. 1615 : R. Tofte, *Blazon of Iealousie*, 29, Hee will then quickly take occasion to be angry with her, and euery mote (as the prouerbe goeth) is a beame in his eye.

Mote may choke a man, A. 1670 : Ray, 122.

Mother. 1. *It is not as thy mother sayeth, but as thy neighbours say.* 1732 : Fuller, No. 2995.

2. *Mother's cheek.* *See* Child (8).

3. *Mothers' darlings make but milk-sop heroes.* 1732 : Fuller, No. 3474.

4. *The mother's side is the surest.* 1548 : Hall, *Chron.*, 101 (1809), If the old and trite prouerbe be true that the woman's side is the surer side, and that the childe foloweth the wombe. Before 1627 : Middleton, *More Diss. besides Women*, I. iii., Only death comes by the mother's side, and that's the surest.

See also Ask (4) ; and Oven (1).

Mother-in-law and daughter-in-law are a tempest and hailstorm. 1855 : Bohn, 455.

Mother-in-law remembers not that she was a daughter-in-law, The. 1659 : Howell, *Proverbs: Brit.-Eng.*, 36. 1732 : Fuller, No. 4675.

Mother-in-law, There is but one good, and she is dead. A New Forest proverb. 1863 : Wise, *New Forest*, ch. xvi.

Motions are not marriages. 1678 : Ray, 56.

Mountain. 1. *A mountain and a river are good neighbours.* 1640 : Herbert, *Jac. Prudentum.*

2. *The mountain was in labour and produced a mouse.* [Parturiunt montes, nascetur ridiculus mus.—Horace, *Ars Poetica*, 139.] *c.* 1390 : Gower, *Conf. Amantis*, bk. vii., ll. 3553-75 [the story of the mountain and mouse]. 1579 : Gosson, *Sch. of Abuse*, 21 (Arber), It is a pageant woorth the sight, to beholde how he labors with mountaines to bring foorth mise. 1599 : Greene, *Works*, xii. 7 (Grosart), Then might you thinke I had sweld with the mountaines, and brought foorth a mouce. 1624 : Massinger, *Bondman*, IV. iii., *Cleo.* Why do you laugh ? *Leost.* To hear the labouring mountain of your praise Deliver'd of a mouse. 1709 : O. Dykes, *Eng. Proverbs*, 304 (2nd ed.). 1853 : Planché, *Extravag.*, iv. 291 (1879), Oft of the mountain in labour you've heard, Which but gave birth to a mouse so absurd.

3. *To make a mountain of a mole-hill.* [ἐλέφαντα ἐκ μυίας ποιεῖν.—Lucian, *Musc. Enc., ad fin.*] 1560 : Becon, *Catechism*, 338 (P.S.), They make of a fly an elephant, and of a mole-hill a mountain. 1573 : G. Harvey, *Letter-Book*, 14 (Camden S.), To make huge mountains of smal low molhils. 1653 : R. Brome, *City Wit*, IV. i., She takes me for a mountaine, that am but a mole-hill. *c.* 1760 : Foote, *Lame Lover*, II., Those people are ever swelling mole hills to mountains. 1834: Marryat, *Peter Simple*, ch. xxxvii. 1909 : De Morgan, *Never can happen Again*, ch. xxxviii.

See also Man (70) ; and Morning (3).

Mountsorrel. *See* quot. 1790 : Grose, *Prov. Gloss.*, s.v. " Leicestershire," He leaps like the Bell-giant, or devil of Mountsorrel.

Mouse and Mice. 1. *A mouse in time*

may bite in two a cable. 1546 : Heywood, *Proverbs*, Pt. II. ch. vii. 1736 : Franklin, *Way to Wealth*, in *Works*, i. 444 (Bigelow), By diligence and patience the mouse ate in two the cable. 1754 : Berthelson, *Eng. - Danish Dict.*, s.v. " Time."

2. *A mouse must not think to cast a shadow like an elephant.* 1732 : Fuller, No. 332.

3. *As sure as a mouse tied with a thread.* 1546 : Heywood, *Proverbs*, Pt. II. ch. vii.

4. *As warm as a mouse in a churn.* 1678 : Ray, 290.

5. *Can a mouse fall in love with a cat?* 1732 : Fuller, No. 1051.

6. *Don't make yourself a mouse, or the cat will eat you.* 1875 : Cheales, *Proverb. Folk-Lore*, 105.

7. *I gave the mouse a hole, and she is become my heir.* 1640 : Herbert, *Jac. Prudentum.*

8. *It must be a bold* (or *wily*) *mouse that can breed in the cat's ear.* c. 1430 : Lydgate, *Minor Poems*, 167 (Percy S), An hardy mowse that is bold to breede In cattis eeris. Before 1529: Skelton, *Why Come Ye Not?*, l. 753, Yet it is a wyly mouse That can bylde his dwellinge house Within the cattes eare Withouten drede or feare. 1579 : Lyly, *Euphues*, 63 (Arber) [" wily "]. 1623 : Webster, *Duchess of Malfi*, IV. ii., Thou sleepist worse than if a mouse should be forc'd to take up her lodging in a cat's ear. 1732 : Fuller, No. 3040 [" wilely "]. 1894 : R. L. S., *St. Ives*, ch. xiv., We ate like mice in a cat's ear.

9. *Like a mouse in a cheese.* 1658 : Flecknoe, *Enigm. Characters*, 16, She is like a mouse in a Holland cheese, her house and diet all the same. 1736 : Ainsworth, *Lat. Dict.*, s.v. (O.), He speaketh like a mouse in a cheese.

10. *Mice care not to play with kittens.* 1732 : Fuller, No. 3412.

11. *The escaped mouse ever feels the taste of the bait.* 1640 : Herbert, *Jac. Prudentum.*

12. *The mouse goes abroad where the cat is not lord.* Before 1500 : in Hill, *Commonplace-Book*, 132 (E.E.T.S.).

13. *The mouse that has only one hole*

is easily taken. c. 1386 : Chaucer, *Wife of Bath's Prol.*, l. 572, I holde a mouses herte not worth a leek, That hath but oon hole for to sterte to. 1586 : L. Evans, *Withals Dict. Revised*, sig. C3, That mouse is in an ill case that hath but one hole to lurke in. 1631 : Mabbe, *Celestina*, 139 (T.T.), It goes hard (daughter) with that mouse that hath but one hole to trust to. 1717 : Pope, *Wife of Bath*, 298, The mouse that always trusts to one poor hole, Can never be a mouse of any soul. 1865 : " Lancs Proverbs," in *N. & Q.*, 3rd ser., viii. 494. 1901 : F. E. Taylor, *Lancs Sayings*, 7, A meawse 'at's nob-but getten one hole's soon takken.

See also Better a mouse ; Cat, *passim* ; Dead (15) ; Dun ; Frog (6) ; Lark (2) ; Lion (2) ; Mountain (2) ; No larder ; Plough, *subs.* (3) ; Quiet ; Rat (1) and (6) ; Safe as a mouse ; and Water (4).

Mousehole, where they eat their beef before they sup their broth. Corn., 19th cent. Mr. C. Lee says, " The story is that when the Spaniards raided Mount's Bay, they landed at Mousehole just as the inhabitants were sitting down to their Sunday dinner—broth, duff (dumplings), and beef. Broth and duff had been consumed when the alarm was given, and the diners fled, leaving the Spaniards to eat the beef. Ever since, they have made sure of the beef first. Cf. Scott, *Peveril*, Note P, ' Cutlar Mac-Culloch.' "

Mouse-trap smell of cheese, You must not let your. 1659 : Howell, 11. 1670 : Ray, 18. 1732 : Fuller, No. 3189 [with " blood " for " cheese "].

Mouth. 1. *A mouth like a Low-country loop-hole* = A wide mouth. 1888 : *Yorkshire N. & Q.*, ii. 73 (W.).

2. *Between the mouth and the morsel.* c. 1594 : Bacon, *Promus*, No. 791. Cf. Cup (4).

3. *He has a mouth for every matter.* 1732 : Fuller, No. 1859.

4. *He that hath a mouth of his own must not say to another, Blow.* 1640 : *Jac. Prudentum.* 1732 : Fuller, No. 2130 [" should " for " must "].

5. *Mouth full of mould. See* Enough one day.

6. *Mouth in the heart.* *See* Wise (50).

7. *Whoso hath but a mouth Will ne'er in England suffer drought.* 1670 : Ray, 42. 1893 : Inwards, *Weather Lore*, 4. 1904 : *Co. Folk-Lore: Northumb.*, 171 (F.L.S.).

8. *Your mouth hath beguiled your hands.* 1678 : Ray, 260. 1732 : Fuller, No. 6057.

Mouthful of moonshine, To give one a. 1813 : Ray, 208.

Mow breeze. *See* quot. 1917 : Bridge, *Cheshire Proverbs*, 164, It's always dull when there's a Mow breeze [=when wind blows from Mow Cop= east wind].

Much ado about nothing. 1599 : Shakespeare, *Much Ado, etc.* [title]. 1692 : L'Estrange, *Æsop*, 24 (3rd ed.), [Mountain in labour fable] Moral. Much ado about nothing. 1748 : Richardson, *Clarissa*, v. 12 (1785), It were better for herself . . . that she had • not made so much ado about nothing. 1863 : Kingsley, *Water Babies*, ch. vi., I know some people will only laugh at it, and call it much ado about nothing.

Much bran and little meal. 1633 : Draxe, 17. 1670 : Ray, 65. 1732 : Fuller, No. 3477 [" flour " for " meal "].

Much bruit little fruit. 1639 : Fuller, *Holy War*, bk. ii. ch. xxix. 1670 : Ray, 66. 1732 : Fuller, No. 6122.

Much business much pardon. 1750 : Franklin, in *Works*, ii. 208 (Bigelow), Remember in my favor the old saying, They who have much business must have much pardon.

Much coin much care. [Crescentem sequitur cura pecuniam.—Horace, *Carm.*, III. xvi.] 1639 : Clarke, 98. 1647 : *Countrym. New Commonwealth*, 22. 1732 : Fuller, No. 3478.

Much corn. *See* Corn (5).

Much courtesy. *See* Courtesy (3).

Much cry and little wool. *c.* 1475 : Fortescue, *Govern. of England*, ch. x. 132 (Plummer), And so his hyghnes shal haue theroff, but as hadd the man that sherid is hogge, muche crye and litill woll. 1579 : Gosson, *Sch. of Abuse*, 28 (Arber), Or as one said at the shearing of hogs, great cry and little wool. 1663 : Butler, *Hudibras*, Pt. I.

can. i. l. 852, Thou wilt at best but suck a bull, Or shear swine, all cry and no wool. 1711 : *Spectator*, No. 251. 1827 : Scott, *Journal*, 24 Feb., As to the collection, it was much cry and like woo', as the deil said when he shore the sow. 1871 : S. Butler, in H. F. Jones's *Life*, i. 143 (1919), So I fought shy of Taine, who, too—for I did read some of him rapidly—seemed to me to be much cry and little wool. 1922 : *Punch*, 29 Nov., p. 520, col. 2, Ministers have taken good care that the adage, " Much cry and little wool," shall not apply to them. Cf. **More squeak.**

Much hath, much behoveth, He that. 1493 : *Dives et Pauper*, fo. 4 (1536).

Much heed doth no harm. 1639 : Clarke, 66.

Much law but little justice. 1694 : *Terence made English*, 139, The old saying's true, You may have much law o' your side, and but little equity. 1732 : Fuller, No. 3482.

Much learning much sorrow. 1639 : Clarke, 101 [" science " for " learning "]. 1669 : *Politeuphuia*, 183.

Much matter of a wooden platter = Much fuss about nothing in particular. 1639 : Clarke, 133. 1670 : Ray, 185. 1732 : Fuller, No. 6159.

Much meat much malady. 1639 : Clarke, 98. 1670 : Ray, 120. 1732 : Fuller, No. 3483. *c.* 1800 : J. Trusler, *Prov. in Verse*, 22.

Much meddling, Of, comes no sound sleeping. Glos. 1639 : in *Berkeley MSS.*, iii. 30 (1885).

Much of a muchness. 1727 : Vanbrugh and Cibber, *Prov. Husband*, I., *Man.* I hope at least, you and your good woman agree still. *John M.* Ay! ay! much of a muchness. Bridget sticks to me. 1857 : Reade, *Never too Late*, ch. xviii., Why they are all pretty much of a muchness for that. 1905 : E. G. Hayden, *Travels Round our Village*, 24, Folks is folks all the world over—much of a muchness, I reckon, when you gets inside 'um, so to spake.

Much power makes many enemies. 1736 : Bailey, *Dict.*, s.v. " Much."

Much smoke little fire. Glos. 1639 : in *Berkeley MSS.*, iii. 32 (1885).

Much spending. *See* quot. 1541 : Coverdale, *Christ. State Matrimony*, sig. I3, Mich spendinge and many gyftes make bar[e] celars and empty thystes.

Much wit as three folks, As — two fools and a madman. Cheshire. 1670 : Ray, 209. 1732 : Fuller, No. 716. 1828 : Lytton, *Pelham*, ch. lxxvii., " No, no, my fine fellow," said Thornton with a coarse chuckle, " you have as much wit as three folks—two fools and a madman, but you won't *do* me for all that." 1917 : Bridge, *Cheshire Proverbs*, 19.

Much would have more. [Multa petentibus desunt multa.—Horace, *Carm.*, III. xvi.] *c.* 1350 : *Alexander*, l. 4398, Bot ay mekill wald have mare. 1578 : Florio, *First Fruites*, fo. 32, The more a man hath, the more he desireth. 1618 : W. Lawson, *New Orchard and Garden*, 5 (1676), 'Tis with grounds in this case, as it is with men . . . Much will have more. 1732 : Fuller, No. 3487, Much would have more ; but often meets with less. 1828 : Carr, *Craven Dialect*, i. 323, Mickle wad hev maar. 1901 : F. E. Taylor, *Lancs Sayings*, 9, Mitch would ha' mooar, an' mooar would have o [all].

Muck, *subs.* = manure. 1. *Where there's muck there's money*—with variants. 1678 : Ray, 179, Muck and money go together. 1865 : W. White, *Eastern England*, i. 127, " The more muck the more money," is an East Anglian proverb. 1866 : J. G. Nall, *Gt. Yarmouth, etc.*, 605, Where there's muck, there's money. Norfolk Proverb. 1901 : F. E. Taylor, *Lancs Sayings*, 11, Wheer ther's muck — ther's luck. 1917 : Bridge, *Cheshire Proverbs*, 95, Muck's the mother of money.

2. *You'll have his muck for his meat.* 1639 : Clarke, 170. 1670 : Ray, 186.

Muckhill at his door, He hath a good =He is rich. 1678 : Ray, 261.

Muckhill on my trencher, You make a, quoth the bride=You carve me a great heap. 1678 : Ray, 77. 1732 : Fuller, No. 5936.

Muck-midden. *See* quot. 1846–59 : *Denham Tracts*, ii. 97 (F.L.S.), There is an old proverb which says " The muck-midden is the mother of the meal-ark [chest]."

Muckson up to the buckson=Dirty up to the knuckles. Derby. 1889 : *Folk-Lore Journal*, vii. 293.

Mud chokes no eels. 1732 : Fuller, No. 3488.

Muddy springs will have muddy streams. Ibid., No. 3489.

Mulberry leaf. *See* quots. 1659 : Howell, *Proverbs: New Sayings*, 3, With time and art, the mulberry leafs grow to be sattin. 1852 : M. A. Keltie, *Reminiscences of Thought and Feeling*, 36, I would also say, value greatly, and exercise as often as possible, *small* efforts of self-denial. " By little and little the mulberry leaf becomes satin."

Mule, As dummel as a. Oxfordsh. 1923 : *Folk-Lore*, xxxiv. 329.

Mule. *See also* Beware ; Horse (51) ; and One mule.

Mulfra, Cornwall. *See* quot. 1864 : " Cornish Proverbs," in *N. & Q.*, 3rd ser., v. 275, All of a motion, like a Mulfra toad on a hot showl [shovel]. Blown about like a Mulfra toad in a gale of wind.

Mum. *See* Silence.

Mumchance. *See* quots. 1690 : *New Dict. Canting Crew*, sig. H5, He looks like Mumchance that was hang'd for saying of nothing. 1694 : *Terence made English*, 150, What an unreasonable thing 'tis to make me stand like mum-chance at such a time as this. 1738 : Swift, *Polite Convers.*, Dial. I. [as in 1690]. 1785 : Grose, *Class. Dict. Vulgar Tongue*, s.v. " Mum," You sit like mumchance who was hanged for saying nothing. 1881 : Mrs. Parker, *Oxfordsh. Words : Suppl.*, 90 (E.D.S.), Mumchance, to sit quietly thinking. Cf. Mumphazard.

Mumphazard. *See* quot. 1670 : Ray, 209, He stands like Mumphazard, who was hang'd for saying nothing. *Cheshire.* 1917 : Bridge, *Cheshire Proverbs*, 71 [as in 1670]. Cf. Mumchance.

Murder will out. Before 1300 : *Cursor Mundi*, l. 1084, For-þi men sais into þis tyde, Is no man þat murthir may hide. *c.* 1386 : Chaucer, *Prioress's Tale*, l. 124, Mordre wol out, certein it wol not faille. *c.* 1400: *Beryn*, l. 2293 (E.E.T.S.), þer may no man hele murdir, þat it woll out atte last. *c.* 1440 : Lydgate, *Fall of Princes*, bk. iii. l. 2741 (E.E.T.S.). Before 1529: Skelton, *Bowge of Courte*, l. 524, I drede mordre wolde come oute. 1641: Marmion, *Antiquary*, V. 1676: Shadwell, *Libertine*, II. 1760: Murphy, *Way to Keep Him*, V. 1780: Mrs. Cowley, *Belle's Strat.*, I. iv., Like murder—Vanity will out. 1840 : Barham, *Ing. Legends*, 1st ser.: "Hand of Glory," *ad fin.*

Muse as they use. *See* Man (71).

Muses love the morning, The. 1732 : Fuller, No. 4681.

Music as a wheel-barrow, You make as good. Ibid., No. 5938.

Music helps not the toothache. 1640 : Herbert, *Jac. Prudentum.* 1670: Ray, 18. 1732 : Fuller, No. 3493.

Musician has forgot his note, When a, he makes as though a crumb stuck in his throat. 1639 : Clarke, 108. 1670 : Ray, 123. 1732 : Fuller, No. 6471.

Musk in a dog's kennel, Look not for. 1611 : Cotgrave, s.v. "Chien" [" civet " for " musk "]. 1640 : Herbert, *Jac. Prudentum.* 1854: J. W. Warter, *Last of Old Squires*, 53. 1894: Northall, *Folk Phrases*, 34 (E.D.S.), You must not expect perfumes in a pigsty.

Must be if we brew, This. 1678 : Ray, 87. 1738 : Swift, *Polite Convers.*, Dial. III., Well, thus it must be, if we sell ale.

Must fly, If you, fly well. 1640 : Herbert, *Jac. Prudentum.*

Must is a king's word. *c.* 1600 : Queen Elizabeth, in Lingard, *Hist. of England*, vi. 310, " Must she ? " exclaimed she, " is must a word to be used to princes ? " 1738 : Swift, *Polite Convers.*, Dial. I., Must ? Why, colonel, must's for the King.

Mustard is very uncivil because it takes one by the nose. 1634 : *Strange Metam. of Man*, sig. D8, Hee [mustard] is very snappish, for if you meddle with him, he will strait take you by the nose. 1738 : Swift, *Polite Convers.*, Dial. II.

Mustard. *See also* After meat; Cat (11) ; Pity ; Strong ; and Tewkesbury.

Muston, Kent. *See* quot. 1576 : Lambarde, *Peramb. of Kent*, 224 (1826), The common rythme of the countrie . . . He that will not live long, Let him dwell at Muston, Tenham, or Tong. 1735 : Pegge, *Kent. Proverbs*, in E.D.S., No. 12, p. 73 [as in 1576].

Mute as a fish. [καὶ πολὺ ἀφωνότερος ἔσομαι τῶν ἰχθύων.—Lucian, *The Dream, or The Cock*.] *c.* 1450 : Burgh (and Lydgate), *Secrees*, st. 330, p. 73 (E.E.T.S.), Dowmbe as þe ffysh. 1620 : J. Melton, *Astrologaster*, 38, She shall be as mute as a fish. 1693 : Urquhart, *Rabelais*, bk. iii. ch. xxiv., They are all of them become as dumb as so many fishes. 1704: Congreve, *Way of World*, IV. ix., Thou art both as drunk and as mute as a fish. 1788 : Wolcot, *Works*, i. 477 (1795), The handsome bar-maids stare, as mute as fishes. 1844 : Thackeray, *Barry Lyndon*, ch. xvi. 1915 : Galsworthy, *Bit o' Love*, II. ii., Round which are gathered five or six sturdy fellows, dumb as fishes.

Mutton is meat for a glutton. 1611 : Cotgrave, s.v. "Mouton," Flesh of a mutton is food for a glutton. 1623 : Wodroephe, *Spared Houres*, 514, Flesh of mutton is cheere of glutton. 1666 : Torriano, *Piazza Univ.*, 42.

Mutton's going, When the. *See* quot. 1678 : Ray, 350, When the shoulder of mutton is going 'tis good to take a slice. 1732 : Fuller, No. 5598 [omitting " shoulder of "].

Mutton. *See also* Sheep.

Muxy. *See* quots. 1633 : Draxe, 54, He is gotten out of the myre and is fallen into the riuer. 1849 : Halliwell, *Pop. Rhymes, etc.*, 183, He got out of the muxy [dunghill], And fell into the pucksy [quagmire].

My house, my house, though thou art small, thou art to me the Escurial. 1640 : Herbert, *Jac. Prudentum.*

My Lord Baldwin's dead. Sussex. 1670 : Ray, 163.

My son, put money in thy purse. 1654 : Gayton, *Pleasant Notes Don Q.*, 9.

My wife. *See* Wife (16).

N

Nab me, I'll nab thee. 1678 : Ray, 351.

Nail, *subs.* 1. *Another nail in one's coffin.* 1789: Wolcot, *Works*, ii. 100 (1795), Care to our coffin adds a nail, no doubt. 1824 : Scott, *Redgauntlet*, ch. xvi., Every minute he lies here is a nail in his coffin.

2. *Drive not a second nail, till the first be clinched.* 1732 : Fuller, No. 1334.

3. *Nail of wax. See* quot. 1852 : FitzGerald, *Polonius*, 39 (1903), You can't . . . drive a nail of wax.

4. *Nail that will go. See* **Drive** (1).

5. *To hit the nail on the head.* [Acu rem tangere.—Plautus, *Rud.*, V. ii. 19.] *c.* 1520 : Stanbridge, *Vulgaria*, sig. B5, Thou hyttest the nayle on the head. *c.* 1580 : Spelman, *Dialogue*, 115 (Roxb. Cl.), How saye you . . . to this discourse of this husbondman, I thinke he hath hitte the nayle on the heade. 1656 : *Choyce Drollery*, 11 (Ebsworth), Tis true what we have sed, In this we hit the naile o' th' head. 1728 : Fielding, *Love in Several Masques*, II. vi., You have hit the nail on the head, my dear uncle. 1834 : Marryat, *P. Simple*, ch. xii., He has hit the right nail on the head.

6. *Upon the nail.* 1596 : Nashe, *Works*, iii. 59 (Grosart), Speake the word, and I will help you to it vpon the naile. 1637 : T. Heywood, *Pleas. Dialogues, etc.*, Dial. 4, in Bang's *Materialien*, B. 3, p. 69, That could not pay One single halfpenny downe vpon the naile. 1692 : L'Estrange, *Æsop*, Life, 13 (3rd ed.), Lay down the mony upon the nail, and the business is done. 1729 : Gay, *Polly*, I., I'll have her. I'll pay you down upon the nail. 1859 : Sala, *Twice Round Clock*, 6 a.m., We would drink brown ale, and pay the reckoning on the nail. 1922 : *Punch*, 20 Dec., p. 598, col. 1, I paid for them on the nail—a little over fifteen pounds.

See also **One nail.**

Nails of fingers, etc. 1. *Cutting them.* 1596 : Lodge, *Wits Miserie*, 18 (Hunt. Cl.), He will not . . . paire his nailes while Munday, to be fortunat in his loue. 1618 : B. Holyday, *Technogamia*, II. vi., That you may neuer pare your nailes vpon a Friday. Before 1627 : Middleton, *Anything for Quiet Life*, IV. ii., What a cursed wretch was I to pare my nails to-day! a Friday too; I looked for some mischief. 1695 : Congreve, *Love for Love*, III. ix., As melancholie as if thou hadst . . . pared thy nails on a Sunday. 1830 : Forby, *Vocab. E. Anglia*, 411, Cut them on Monday, you cut them for health ; Cut them on Tuesday, you cut them for wealth ; Cut them on Wednesday, you cut them for news ; Cut them on Thursday, a new pair of shoes ; Cut them on Friday, you cut them for sorrow ; Cut them on Saturday, see your true-love to-morrow ; Cut them on Sunday, the devil will be with you all the week. 1879 : Henderson, *Folk-Lore N. Counties*, 18, [as in 1830, except that the last three lines read] Cut them on Saturday, a present to-morrow ; But he that on Sunday cuts his horn, Better that he had never been born! Ibid., 17, Better a child had ne'er been born Than cut his nails on a Sunday morn! [Also] Friday hair, Sunday horn, Better that child had ne'er been born! [There are other variants of these sayings—see *N. & Q.*, 9th ser., vi. 93, and 12th ser., vii. 67.]

2. *See* quot. 1869 : Hazlitt, 482, Ye've nails at wad scrat your granny out of her grave. *Leeds.*

3. *Specks on nails*—commonly called " gifts." 1620 : J. Melton, *Astrologaster*, 45, That to haue yellow speckles on the nailes of one's hand's a great signe of death. 1646 : Browne, *Pseudo. Epi.*, bk. v. ch. xxiii., That temperamental dignotions, and conjecture of prevalent humours, may be collected

from spots in our nails, we are not averse to concede . . . that white specks presage our felicity, blew ones our misfortunes. 1755 : *Connoisseur,* No. 59, A white speck upon the nails made them as sure of a gift, as if they had it already in their pockets. 1854 : Baker, *Northants Gloss.*, s.v. " Gifts," (*a*) A gift, a friend, a foe, A lover to come, a journey to go. (*b*) A gift on the thumb is sure to come, A gift on the finger is sure to linger. 1879 : Jackson, *Shropsh. Wood-Book*, 173 [as in 1854 (*b*)]. 1882 : Jago, *Gloss. of Cornish Dialect*, 176 [as in 1854 (*b*)]. 1884–6 : Holland, *Chesh. Gloss.* (E.D.S.), The popular belief is that they [white specks on finger-nails] betoken a present, and children say—beginning with the thumb, and ending with the little finger: " A gift, a friend, a foe, a sweetheart, a journey to go." The event to happen is indicated by the word which corresponds to the finger on which the white spot is seen. 1886 : Elworthy, *West Som. Word-Book*, 284 (E.D.S.) [as in 1854 (*b*), but in plural].

Naked as a cuckoo. 1609 : Dekker, *Guls Horne-Booke*, 20 (Hindley), As naked as the cuckoo in Christmas. 1879 : J. Hardy, in *Folk-Lore Record*, ii. 66, It is from the reported deplumed condition of the cuckoo in winter that the proverb originates, " As naked as a cuckoo," which I have heard in Northumberland applied to a prodigal.

Naked as a needle. *c.* 1350 : *Alexander*, l. 4027, And ay is naked a nedill as natour tham schapis. 1377 : Langland, *Plowman*, B, xii. 162, Bothe naked as a nedle. 1485 : Malory, *Morte d'Arthur*, bk. xi. ch. i., She was naked as a nedel. 1858 : P. J. Bailey, *The Age*, 75, Nude as a needle.

Naked as a robin. •1883 : Burne, *Shropsh. Folk-Lore*, 595.

Naked as a shorn sheep. 1654 : Gayton, *Pleasant Notes Don Q.*, 88, As naked and bare as a shorne sheep, as we say in our English proverb.

Naked as a stone. 14th cent.: in Wright, *Songs and Carols*, 3 (1856), He stod as nakyd as a ston.

Naked as a worm. *c.* 1400 : *Rom.*

Rose, l. 454, For naked as a worm was she.

Naked as my nail. 1533 : Heywood, *Play of Wether*, l. 922, Thou myghtest go as naked as my nayle. 1600 : Day, *Blind Beggar*, V., Yet would I had her as naked as my nayl. 1629 : Massinger, *Renegado*, I. i. 1681 : Robertson, *Phraseol. Generalis*, 905, As naked as ones nail.

Naked as truth. 1647 : in *Somers Tracts*, v. 491 (1811), Lest it strip him as naked as truth.

Naked sword. *See* Ill putting.

Name, *subs.* 1. *When your name is up you may lie abed.* 1611 : Cotgrave, s.v. " Bruit," Hee that is thought to rise betime, may lie abed till noon. 1659 : Howell, 11 (9), He that hath the name to be an early riser may sleep till noon. 1714 : *Spectator*, No. 602, So that to use the old proverb, When his name is up he may lye a-bed. *c.* 1730 : Swift, in *Works*, xiv. 423 (Scott), His name is up, he may in bed lie. . 1772 : Graves, *Spirit. Quixote*, bk. i. ch. viii., If our name were thus once up . . . we might lie a-bed.

2. *You had not your name for nothing.* 1633 : Draxe, 135, He hath not his name for naught. 1678 : Ray, 261.

Napping, as Moss caught his mare. The allusions to this saying and song in 16th- and 17th-century literature are very numerous. 1569–70: in Arber, *Stat. Registers*, i. 193, Recevyd of William Greffeth for his lycense for the pryntinge of a ballett intituled *taken nappynge as Mosse toke his meare*, iiii[d]. 1597 : *Discouerie of Knights of Poste*, sig. C4, Fortune feeding them, as Mosse did his mare, through a hurdle, which made him take her so soone napping. 1641 : J. Taylor, *Swarme of Sectaries, etc.* [motto], The cobler preaches and his audience are As wise as Mosse was, when he caught his mare. 1658 : *Wit Restored*, 304 (reprint). 1672 : *Westminster Drollery*, Pt. II. 74 (Ebsworth), Her cresses that were wrought Most like the golden snare, My loving heart has caught, As *Mos* did catch the mare. 1785 : Grose, *Class. Dict. Vulgar Tongue*, s.v. " Nap "

["morse" for "Moss"]. 1850: in
N. & Q., 1st ser., i. 320, There is also
a song sung among the farmers of
South Devon, of which the last line
of each verse is "As Morse caught the
mare." [There is a version of a song
about Moss and his mare in Halliwell's
Nursery Rhymes (Percy S., No. 17).]
1917: Bridge, *Cheshire Proverbs*, 127.

Natural to him as milk to a calf, As.
1678 : Ray, 287.

Nature draws more than ten oxen.
1640: Herbert, *Jac. Prudentum* ["teams"
for "oxen"]. 1670: Ray, 18.

**Nature gives what no man can take
away.** Before 1500: in Hill, *Commonplace-Book*, 129 (E.E.T.S.).

Nature is the true law. 1578: Florio,
First Fruites, fo. 32, Nature is the right
law. 1629: *Book of Meery Riddles*,
Prov. 34.

Nature out of the door, Shut. *See*
quot. 1692: L'Estrange, *Æsop*, 61
(3rd ed.), How impossible it is to make
Nature change her biass, and that if
we shut her out of the door, she'll
come in at the window.

Nature passes nurture. Cf. Nurture
for a contrary statement. 1647:
Stapylton, *Juvenal*, 189, Nature can
do more then breeding can. 1732:
Fuller, No. 3505, Nature is beyond all
teaching. 1880: Spurgeon, *Ploughman's
Pictures*, 70, Nature does sometimes
overcome nurture.

Nature requires five. *See* Sleep, *subs.*
(1).

**Nature, time, and patience are the
three great physicians.** 1855: Bohn, 457.

Nature will have her course. *c.* 1400:
Beryn, 105 (E.E.T.S.), ffor "kynde
woll have his cours." 1580: Lyly,
Euphues, 326 (Arber). *c.* 1647: Wither,
Doubtfull Almanack, 6 (Spens. S.), It
is a true saying, Nature will not be
hid.

Naught is never in danger. 1639:
Clarke, 126. 1678: Ray, 180. 1738:
Swift, *Polite Convers.*, Dial. I. 1889:
Peacock, *Manley, etc., Gloss.*, 373
(E.D.S.), "That that's noht's niver e'
daanger," a proverb used when a worth-
less person is prosperous, or a worth-
less thing escapes destruction. 1889:

Folk-Lore Journal, vii. 293, Nowght's
niver i' danger (Derbyshire saying).

**Naught is that muse that finds no
excuse.** 1629: *Book of Meery Riddles*,
Prov. 123.

Naught. *See also* Nothing; and
Nought.

**Nay, stay, quoth Stringer, when his
neck was in the halter.** 1678: Ray,
82. 1732: Fuller, No. 3512.

Near as fourpence to a groat, As.
c. 1550: *Jacke Jugeler*, 75 (Grosart),
And in cueri thing as just as iiii pens to
a grot. 1670: Ray, 205 ["like" for
"near"]. 1886: Elworthy, *West Som.
Word-Book*, 302 (E.D.S.), The usual
simile for exactness is "'Tis as near's
fowerpence is to a groat." 1894:
Northall, *Folk Phrases*, 9 (E.D.S.).

Near burr. *See* Moon (26).

**Near friend is better than a far-
dwelling kinsman, A.** 1669: Politeuphuia, 184.

**Near is my kirtle (or petticoat), but
nearer is my smock.** [Tunica propior
pallio est.—Plautus, *Trin.*, V. ii. 30.]
1461: *Paston Letters*, i. 542 (Gairdner),
He answered a geyn in these wordes,
"Nere is my kyrtyl, but nerre [nearer]
is my smok." 1546: Heywood, *Proverbs*, Pt. I. ch. x. 1611: Cotgrave,
s.v. "Chair" ["petticoat"]. *c.* 1685:
in *Roxb. Ballads*, viii. 869 (B.S.)
["petticoat"]. 1860: Reade, *Cl. and
Hearth*, ch. xcviii. 1894: Northall, *Folk
Phrases*, 25 (E.D.S.), The smock is
nearer than the petticoat.

**Near is my purse, but nearer is my
soul.** 1860: Reade, *Cl. and Hearth*,
ch. lxxvi.

**Near is my shirt, but nearer is my
skin.** [1539: Taverner, *Proverbs*, fo. 15,
My cote is nerer me than my robe or
gowne.] *c.* 1570: in *Ballads* (Percy
S., No. 1), 99, Neerer is my skin then
shirte. 1593: G. Harvey, *Works*, ii.
311 (Grosart), That euery man was
neerest to himselfe, and the skinne
neerer then the shirt. 1685: Meriton, *Yorkshire Ale*, 66 ["sarke" for
"shirt"]. 1712: Arbuthnot, *Law a
Bott. Pit*, Pt. IV. ch. v., "My shirt,"
quoth he, "is near me, but my skin is
nearer!" 1792: Wolcot, *Works*, ii.

313 (1795). 1883 : A. Easther, *Al-mondbury Gloss.*, 113 (E.D.S.), A local saying here . . . was "Nar [Near] is mi sark, but narrer's mi skin." 1890 : Caine, *Bondman*, II. x. (O.).

Near love by craft maketh the far love loathed, The. *c.* 1386 : Chaucer, *Miller's Tale*, l. 206, Ful sooth is this proverbe, it is no lye, Men seyn right thus, alwey the nye slye Maketh the ferre leve to be looth. *c.* 1390: Gower, *Conf. Amantis*, bk. iii. l. 1899, An old sawe is, "Who that is slyh In place where he mai be nyh, He makth the ferre lieve loth."

Nearer the bone the sweeter the flesh, The. 1559 : in *Ballads* (Percy S., No. 1), 21, The nigher the bone, the flesh is much sweeter. 1614 : Cook, *City Gallant*, in Hazlitt, *Old Plays*, xi. 207. 1661: Davenport, *City Nightcap*, I. 1819 : Scott, *Bride of L.*, ch. vi., The nearer the bane the sweeter, as your honours weel ken.

Nearer the church the farther from God, The. 1303 : Brunne, *Handl. Synne*, l. 9243, The nerë the cherche, the fyrther fro Gode. Before 1500: in Hill, *Commonplace - Book*, 130 (E.E.T.S.). 1579: Spenser, *Shep. Cal.*, July, l. 104, To kirke the narre, to God more farre, has bene an old said saw. 1611 : Tourneur, *Atheist's Tragedy*, I. iv. 1662 : Fuller, *Worthies*, ii. 266 (1840). 1784 : *New Foundl. Hosp. for Wit*, iv. 166, The old proverb . . . That the nearest the church are the farthest from God. 1824 : Scott, *Redgauntlet*, ch. xix., For the nearer the church —the proverb is somewhat musty.

Nearer the kin the further in, The. 1591 : Harington, *Orl. Furioso*, bk. xvi., Moral, The nearer of kin, the sooner in. 1615 : R. Tofte, tr. *Blazon of Iealousie*, 28, The nigher kinne the farther in. 1639 : Clarke, 26.

Nearest to the well. *See* quot. 1639 : in *Berkeley MSS.*, iii. 32 (1885), Neerest to the well furthest from the water, Like nearest to 'the church furthest from God (Gloucest.).

Neat as a new pin. *See* New pin.

Neat as ninepence, As. 1659 : Howell, 11. 1857 : *Blackw. Mag.*, lxxxi. 397

(O.), If I didn't see him whip a picture out of its frame, as neat as ninepence. 1911 : *Devonsh. Assoc. Trans.*, xliii. 94, "So neat as ninepence " is the common superlative absolute of neatness.

Neat but not gaudy. 1631 : Brathwait, *Eng. Gentlewoman*, 399 (1641), Making this her impreze : *Comely, not gaudy*. 1806 : Lamb, *Letters*, i. 354 (Lucas), A little thin flowery border round, neat not gaudy . . . 1838: Ruskin, in *Archit. Mag.*, Nov., 483, That admiration of the " neat but not gaudy," which is commonly reported to have influenced the devil when he painted his tail pea green.

Necessary. *See* Sow, *subs.* (4).

Necessary and opportunity may make a coward valiant. 1732 : Fuller, No. 3514. 1783 : Day, *Sandf. and Merton*, 44 (1891), Necessity makes even cowards brave.

Necessity has no law. In the earlier examples it is always **Need** . . . [Necessitas dat legem, non ipse accipit.—Publ. Syrus. Feriis caret necessitas.—Palladius, I. vi. 7. Legem non habet necessitas.—St. Augustine, *Solil. animæ ad Deum*, c. 2.] 1377 : Langland, *Plowman*, B, xx. 10, Nede ne hath no lawe. *c.* 1390: Gower, *Conf. Amantis*, bk. iv. l. 1167, For as men sein, nede hath no lawe. *c.* 1450: *Partonope*, l. 8268, But this ys a full olde sawe : Nede had no maner of lawe. 1493 : *Dives et Pauper*, fo. 123 (1536) [as in 1390]. Before 1529: Skelton, *Colin Clout*, l. 865 [as in 1390]. 1577 : Kendall, *Flow. of Epigrams*, 292 (Spens. S.) [as in 1390]. 1608 : Rowlands, *Hum. Look. Glasse*, 9 (Hunt. Cl.), Necessitie it hath no law, I must my gelding sell. 1678: Dryden, *Limberham*, III. ii., Necessity has no law; I must be patient. 1713 : C. Shadwell, *Hum. of the Army* V. ii. [as in 1678]. *c.* 1800: J. Trusler, *Prov. in Verse*, 79 [as in 1678]. 1864 : Mrs. H. Wood, *Trevlyn Hold*, ch. xxxiv., But necessity has no law, and he was obliged to rise.

Necessity is a hard dart. 1560: Becon, in *Catechism, etc.*, 601 (P.S.) [quoted as " the common proverb"].

Necessity is coal-black. 1678 : Ray, 180.

Necessity is the mother of invention.
1519 : Horman, *Vulgaria*, fo. 52, Nede
taught hym wytte. 1587 : Underdowne, *Heliodorus*, 201 (T.T.), Surely
necessitie is the deviser of all manner
of shiftes. 1602 : Rowlands, *Greenes
Ghost*, 32 (Hunt. Cl.), As necessitie
is neuer without stratagems. 1672 :
Wycherley, *Love in a Wood*, III. iii.,
Necessity, mother of invention ! 1703 :
Farquhar, *Twin-Rivals*, I. i., If necessity
be the mother of invention, she was
never more pregnant than with me.
1830 : Scott, *Journal*, 11 July. 1860 :
C. Reade, *Cl. and Hearth*, ch. xxxiii.

Neck and crop. 1816 : in Hone, *Ev.
Day Book*, i. 461, Explain the terms
milling—fibbing—cross buttock—neck
and crop — bang up — and — prime.
1872 : Hardy, *Greenwood Tree*, Pt. II.
ch. ii., " Now 'tis to turn us out of the
quire neck and crop," said the tranter.
1894 : Caine, *Manxman*, ch. xxii.

Neck and heels. 1740 : North, *Examen*, 72, The liberty of the subject is
brought in neck and heels, as they say,
that the Earl might be popular.

**Neck as long as my arm, I'll first see
thy.** 1678 : Ray, 261.

Neck of another, One trouble in the.
1533 : Udall, *Flowers out of Terence*, fo.
103, One myschiefe on an others necke.
1567 : G. Fenton, *Bandello*, i. 232 (T.T.),
Other straung mischiefes . . . one in
the necke of another. *c.* 1640 : in
Roxb. Ballads, i. 370 (P.S.), One vice
on the neck of another pursues. 1708 :
tr. Aleman's *Guzman*, i. 80, My misfortunes came so upon the neck of
one another. 1889 : Peacock, *Manley,
etc., Gloss.*, 367 (E.D.S.), " One bad job
alus falls on th' neck of anuther," is a
common saying when misfortunes follow
each other quickly.

Neck or nothing. 1678 : Ray, 347.
1708 : Cibber, *Lady's Last Stake*, III.,
But to scamper, neck or nothing, after
a mad galloping jade of a hind. 1766 :
Garrick, *Neck or Nothing* [title]. 1823 :
Byron, *Don Juan*, can. viii. st. 45.
1884 : R. L. S. and Henley, *Adm.
Guinea*, I. ii., By George, it's neck or
nothing now. Stand by to back me up.

Need *subs.* 1. *Need and night make*

the lame to trot. Glos. 1639 : in *Berkeley
MSS.*, iii. 32 (1885).

2. *Need makes the naked man run.*
1639 : Clarke, 225. 1670 : Ray, 124.
1754 : Berthelson, *Eng.-Danish Dict.*,
s.v. " Need."

3. *Need makes the naked quean spin.*
1670 : Ray, 124. 1754 : Berthelson,
s.v. " Need."

4. *Need makes the old wife trot.*
c. 1210 : in Wright, *Essays on Middle
Ages*, i. 149 (1846), Neode makath heald
wif eorne. Before 1500 : in Hill, *Commonplace-Book*, 128 (E.E.T.S.), Nede makith
the old wiff to trotte. 1573 : *New
Custom*, III. i., For need (they say)
maketh the old wife and man both to
trudge. 1602 : *Liberality and Prod.*,
III. v. 1681 : Robertson, *Phraseol.
Generalis*, 911. 1712 : *Spectator*, No.
509. 1816 : Scott, *Old Mortality*, ch.
viii., Just what gars the auld wives trot
—neshessity.

5. *Need will have its course.* 1678 :
Ray, 180.

6. *When the need is highest, the help
is nighest.* 1630 : T. Adams, *Works*,
619, Mans extremity is Gods oppor-
tunitie. 1822 : Scott, *Nigel*, ch. xxi.
1853 : Trench, *Proverbs*, 61 (1905),
Our own proverb, *Man's extremity,
God's opportunity*, or as we sometimes
have it, *When need is highest, help is
nighest.* Cf. Boot after bale.
See also Necessity.

Need, *verb.* 1. *I may see him need,
but I'll not see him bleed.* Spoken by
father of erring son. 1639 : Clarke,
42. 1670 : Ray, 187. 1754 : Berthelson, *Eng.-Danish Dict.*, s.v. " Need."

2. *They need much whom nothing will
content.* 1639 : Clarke, 38. 1670 : Ray,
124. 1732 : Fuller, No. 4969.

3. *You need not doubt, you are no
doctor.* 1670 : Ray, 172.

Needham. *See* quots. 1580 : Tusser,
Husb., 188 (E.D.S.), Soone sets thine
host at needams shore, to craue the
beggers bone. 1662 : Fuller, *Worthies*,
iii. 161 (1840), They are said to be in
the highway to Needham who hasten
to poverty. 1790 : Grose, *Prov. Gloss.*,
s.v. " Suffolk," You are in the highway
to Needham. 1869 : Spurgeon, *John*

Ploughman, ch. vii., They will find out their mistake when want finds *them* out . . . they are already a long way on the road to Needham.

Needingworth, It comes from. 1639 : Clarke, 68.

Needle in a bottle of hay, Like a. 1532 : More, *Works*, 837 (1557), To seke out one lyne in all hys workes wer to go looke a nedle in a medow. 1592 : Greene, *Works*, xi. 252 (Grosart), The poore man . . : gropeth in the darke to find a needle in a bottle of hay. 1608 : Day, *Law Trickes*, I. ii., My father . . . is gone to seeke a needle in a bottle of hay. 1691 : *Merry Drollery*, 79 (Ebsworth), You'd as soon find a needle in a bottle of hay. 1720 : C. Shadwell, *Sham Prince*, II. i. 1772 : Graves, *Spirit. Quixote*, bk. iii. ch. x. [with "bundle" for "bottle"]. 1834 : Marryat, *P. Simple*, ch. xxii. ["bundle"]. 1886 : R. L. S., *Kidnapped*, ch. xx. 1913 : R. E. Francillon, *Mid-Vict. Memories*, I discovered what had hitherto been the proverbial needle in the pottle of hay.

Needles and pins, needles and pins, When a man marries his trouble begins. 1843 : Halliwell, *Nursery Rhymes*, 122. 1876 : Blackmore, *Cripps*, ch. lii. 1880 : *N. & Q.*, 6th ser., ii. 205 [with "girl" for "man"].

Needs must go when the devil drives. *c.* 1420 : Lydgate, *Assem. of Gods*, st. 3, p. 2 (E.E.T.S.), For hit ys oft seyde by hem that yet lyues He must nedys go that the deuell dryues. 1533 : Heywood, *John, Tyb, etc.*, 77 (Farmer, 1905), He must needs go that the devil driveth. 1594 : Kyd, *Span. Trag.*, III. xii., Needs must he go that the devils drive. 1633 : Jonson, *Tale of a Tub*, III. v., Wife, I must go, needs, whom the devil drives. 1672 : J. Lacy, *Old Troop*, II. *c.* 1750 : Foote, *Orators*, II. 1822 : Scott, *Nigel*, Introd. Epistle. 1840 : Barham, *Ing. Legends*: "St. Odille," Needs must when a certain old gentleman drives.

Needs must trot afoot, that tires his horse, He. 1607 : T. Heywood, *Woman Killed with Kindness*, IV. v.

Needy when he is married, shall be rich when he is buried, He that is. 1633 : Draxe, 229. 1670 : Ray, 48. 1732 : Fuller, No. 2183 [with "scarce" after "shall"].

Neighbour and Neighbours. 1. *Every man's neighbour is his looking-glass.* 1659 : Howell, *Proverbs: Brit.-Eng.*, 3.

2. *He hath ill neighbours (or dwells far from neighbours) that is fain to praise himself.* 1548 : Hall, *Chron.*, 70 (1809), He that praiseth him self lacketh louyng neighbors. 1599 : Porter, *Two Angry Women*, sc. xi., You dwell by ill neighbours, Richard ; that makes yee praise your selfe. 1631 : Brathwait, *Eng. Gentlewoman*, 320 (1641), Beware of self-prayse ; it argues you have slow neighbours, or few deserts. 1670 : Ray, 125. 1754 : Berthelson, *Eng.-Danish Dict.*, s. v. "Fain."

3. *He's an ill neighbour that is not missed.* 1639 : Clarke, 75.

4. *He that hath a good neighbour hath a good morrow.* 15th cent.: in *Reliq. Antiquæ*, i. 316 (1841), He that hath a good neyghboure hath a good morowe ; He that hath a schrewyd wyfe hath much sorowe ; He that fast spendyth must nede borowe ; But when he schal paye agen, then ys al the sorowe. 1591 : Florio, *Second Frutes*, 57, You have a good neighbour then And by consequence a good morrow. 1611 : Cotgrave, s.v. "Matin," . . . morrow ; viz. good words next his heart a mornings. 1633 : Draxe, 138. 1670 : Ray, 124, A good neighbour, a goodmorrow. 1732 : Fuller, No. 165 [as in 1670].

5. *Here's talk of the Turk and the Pope, but it's my next neighbour that does me the harm.* 1659 : Howell, 4 ["hurt" for "harm"]. 1670 : Ray, 125. 1732 : Fuller, No. 2497.

6. *Hold him not for a good neighbour that's at table and wine at every hour.* 1623 : Wodroephe, *Spared Houres*, 521.

7. *Neighbour's fare. See* quots. 1678 : Ray, 180, Neighbour-quart is good quart, i.e. giffe gaffe [q.v.] is a good fellow. *c.* 1680 : in *Roxb. Ballads*, iii. 419 (B.S.), Since neighbour's fare always is counted the best. 1869 : FitzGerald, *Sea Words and Phrases*, 8, I mayn't make a fortune, but I look

for neighbour's fare nevertheless. 1901 :
F. E. Taylor, *Lancs Sayings*, 19,
Neighbour's fare's no ill-fare.

8. *When thy neighbour's house doth
burn, then look to your own.* [Nam tua
res agitur paries cum proximo ardet.
—Horace, *Epist.*, I. xviii. 84.] 1519 :
Horman, *Vulgaria*, fo. 126, Whan my
neybours house is a fyre, I can nat be
out of thought for myn owne. 1548 :
Hall, *Chron.*, 438 (1809), He remem-
bred the prouerbe that sayth, when
thy neighboures house is a fyer, thy
staffe standeth nexte the doore. 1593 :
Pass. Morrice, 75 (N. Sh. S.), When our
neighbours house is on fier, we haue
neede to bestirre vs. 1681 : Robertson,
Phraseol. Generalis, 744. 1732 : Fuller,
No. 5399 : When the next house is a
fire it's high time to look to thy own.

9. *Who more ready to call her neighbour scold, than the arrantest scold in all
the street?* 1639 : Clarke, 79 [with
" i' th' parish " for " in all the street "].
1732 : Fuller, No. 5712.

10. *You must ask your neighbour if
you shall live in peace.* 1639 : Clarke,
203. 1670 : Ray, 125. 1732 : Fuller,
No. 5961. 1855 : Bohn, 463, Nobody
can live longer in peace than his neighbour pleases.
See also All is well.

Neither ashore nor afloat. Corn. 1895:
Jos. Thomas, *Randigal Rhymes*, 61.

Neither borrow nor flatter. *See* Rich
(8).

Neither do right nor suffer wrong,
He'll. 1678 : Ray, 266. 1732 : Fuller,
No. 2426 [with " ne'er " for " neither "].

Neither end nor side to it, There's.
1917 : Bridge, *Cheshire Proverbs*, 119,
There's noather eend nor side to 't.

Neither fish nor flesh, etc. *See* Flesh
nor fish.

**Neither give to all nor contend with
fools.** 1855 : Bohn, 458.

**Neither great poverty nor great riches
will hear reason.** 1855 : Bohn, 458.

Neither idle nor well occupied. 1567 :
Harman, *Caveat*, 33 (E.E.T.S.), In the
night they be not idle,—nether, as the
common saying is, " well occupyed."
c. 1570 : *Marr. of Wit and Science*, IV.
iv., The proverb is verified, I am neither

idle, nor yet well-occupied. 1611 : W.
Goddard, *A Satirycall Dialogve . . .
Imprinted . . . for all such gentlewomen
as are not altogether idle nor yet well
ocvpyed.* 1662 : Fuller, *Worthies*, ii.
513 (1840), He had an excellent wit,
which, the back friends to stage-plays
will say, was neither idle nor well employed.

Neither lead nor drive. 1667 : L'Estrange, *Quevedo's Visions*, 80 (1904),
Another . . . would neither lead nor
drive. 1678 : Ray, 75.

Neither maid, wife, nor widow, She is.
1678 : Ray, 90, She is neither wife,
widow nor maid. 1732 : Fuller, No.
4132.

Neither seeds nor meal. 1892 : Heslop, *Northumb. Words*, 471 (E.D.S.),
" Nowther seeds nor meal "—neither
one thing nor another—is a common
proverb.

Neither sugar nor salt. 1738 : Swift,
Polite Convers., Dial. I., We were
neither sugar nor salt, we were not
afraid the rain would melt us. 1880 :
Banks, *Wooers*, iii. 7 (W.), Bless the
bairn, shoo's noather sugar nor saut,
schoo'l noan melt.

Nene and Welland, The Rivers. *See*
quots. 1596 : Spenser, *F. Q.*, IV. xi.
35, And after him the fatal Welland
went, That, if old sawes prove true,
(which God forbid !) Shall drowne all
Holland with his excrement. 1865 :
W. White,⁎ *Eastern England*, i. 273,
Nene and Welland Shall drown all
Holland, recites the ancient saying
upon the district . . . between the two
rivers.

Nertown. *See* quot. 1851 : in *N.
& Q.*, 1st ser., iv. 149, At Taunton, in
Somersetshire, there is a similar tradi-
tion current : Nertown was a market
town When Taunton was a furzy down.
This Nertown is a village adjoining
Taunton, and lying on the north side
of it.

**Net fills though the fisherman sleeps,
The.** 1683 : White-Kennett, tr. Erasmus' *Praise of Folly*, 135 (8th ed.),
Thus Timotheus, the Athenian commander, in all his expeditions was a
mirror of good luck, because he was

a little under-witted; from him was
occasioned the proverb, *The net fills
though the fisherman sleeps.*

Nettle. 1. *Better be stung by a nettle
than pricked by a rose.* 1670 : Ray, 25.
1732 : Fuller, No. 878.

2. *He that handles a nettle tenderly is
soonest stung.* 1579 : Lyly, *Euphues,*
65 (Arber), Hee which toucheth the
nettle tenderly, is soonest stoung.
1732 : Fuller, No. 2126.

3. *Nettles in March. See* quots.
1846 : Denham, *Proverbs,* 38 (Percy S.),
If they would drink nettles in March,
And eat mugwort in May, So many
fine maidens Wouldn't go to the clay.
1882 : *N. & Q.,* 6th ser., v. 408, If they
wad drink nettles in March, And eat
muggins in May, Sae mony braw
maidens Wad not go to clay. 1913 :
E. M. Wright, *Rustic Speech, etc.,* 241,
As the old rhyme says : [as in 1882].

4. *Nip a nettle hard, and it will not
sting you.* 1830 : Forby, *Vocab. E.
Anglia,* 430. 1872 : J. Glyde, jr., *Norfolk Garland,* 149.

See also In dock.

**Never a fou' face, but there's a fou'
fancy, There's.** 1917 : Bridge, *Cheshire
Proverbs,* 119.

**Never a whit, As good, as never the
better.** 1546 : Heywood, *Proverbs,* Pt.
II. ch. xi. 1553 : *Respublica,* IV. iii.
1597 : Bacon, *Coulers of Good and Euill,*
10. 1639 : Fuller, *Holy War,* bk. iv.
ch. viii. 1670 : Ray, 125. 1709 : R.
Kingston, *Apoph. Curiosa,* 72, We say,
as good never a whit at all, as never a
whit the nearer. 1732 : Fuller, No. 687.

Never be ashamed to eat your meat.
1639 : Clarke, 269. 1670 : Ray, 57.

Never be weary of well doing. 1633 :
Draxe, 32, Neuer wearie of that which
is good. 1670 : Ray, 154.

Never climbed. *See* Climb (1).

Never drank was never athirst, He
that. 1659 : Howell, 13.

**Never enough where nothing left,
There was.** 1639 : Clarke, 38. 1670 :
Ray, 85, Ther's never enough where
nought leaves. 1736 : Bailey, *Dict.,*
s.v. " Enough."

Never go home. *See* quot. 1888 :
Lowsley, *Berks Gloss.,* 31 (E.D.S.),

Never go whoam Wi'out stick or stwun
[stone].

**Never good that mind their belly so
much.** 1678 : Ray, 347.

Never is a long day. *c.* 1386 : Chaucer,
Canon's Yeoman's Tale, l. 858, Never
to thryve were to long a date. 1736 :
Bailey, *Dict.,* s.v. " Term," Never
is a long term. 1839 : Dickens,
Nickleby, ch. lxi., Never, though
never is a long day. 1841 : Dickens,
Barn. Rudge, ch. last. 1886 : El-
worthy, *West Som. Word - Book,* 508
(E.D.S.), Stap cheel ! never's a long day.

Never less alone than when alone.
1586 : Pettie, tr. Guazzo's *Civil Convers.,*
fo. 19, Scipio sayd, yᵗ he was neuer lesse
alone, then when he was alone. 1596 :
Lodge, *Divel Coniured,* 9 (Hunt. Cl.), A
good man is neuer lesse alone then when
alone (as Themistocles said). 1669 :
Politeuphuia, 45, A wise man is never,
etc. 1680 : L'Estrange, *Tully's Offices,*
141, It was the saying . . . of Scipio
Affricanus the Elder . . . that he was
never less idle, or alone, then when he
most appeared so to be. 1816 : Scott,
Black Dwarf, ch. iv.

Never - mass, At = never. 1639 :
Clarke, 229.

**Never quiet but when she is sleeping,
She is.** 1631 : Brathwait, *Whimzies,*
104 (1859).

Never quit certainty for hope. 1855 :
Bohn, 459.

Never sigh but send. 1678 : Ray, 81,
Sigh not but send, he'll come if he be
unhang'd. 1738 : Swift, *Polite Convers.,* Dial. I., Come, miss, never sigh,
but send for him. 1852 : FitzGerald,
Polonius, 78 (1903).

**Never tell thy foe that thy foot
acheth.** *c.* 1320 : in *Reliq. Antiquæ,*
i. 111 (1841), . . . Quoth Hendyng.

Never the nearer. *See* Early (5).

Never too late to learn. 1670 : Ray,
112 [" old " for " late "]. *c.* 1680 :
L'Estrange, *Seneca's Epistles,* xx., It
is never too late to learn what it
is always necessary to know. 1726 :
Southerne, *Money the Mistress,* V. iii.
1752 : Fielding, *Cov. Garden Journal,*
No. 72, An old proverb, which says,
It is never too late to grow wise.

Never too late to mend. [ἀκεσταί τοι
φρένες ἐσθλῶν.—Homer, *Iliad*, xiii. 115.]
1590: Greene, *Neuer too Late* [title].
1655: Howell, *Letters*, bk. iv. No. 38,
It is never over-late to mend. 1856:
Reade, *It is Never too Late to Mend*
[title]. 1891: R. L. S., *Letters*, iv. 54
(Tusitala ed.).

Never too late to repent. 1670: Ray,
112. 1736: Bailey, *Dict.*, s.v. "Late."

Never trust a Little. 1846–59: *Denham Tracts*, i. 65 (F.L.S.), Never trust
a Little. Although this saying is
nearly universally used under another
name in the bishoprick [Durham], and
elsewhere in the North of England, I
have reason to believe that the above
is the correct form, and the other a
mere adaptation. A family of this
name (Little) were celebrated rievers,
or . . . thieves.

Never was bad woman fair. 1640:
Herbert, *Jac. Prudentum.*

Never well, full nor fasting. 1639:
Clarke, 34, Neither pleased full nor fasting. 1659: Howell, 2. 1670: Ray,
176. 1692: L'Estrange, *Æsop*, 265
(3rd ed.). 1738: Swift, *Polite Convers.*,
Dial. II., You don't know your own
mind; you are neither well, full nor
fasting. 1896: *Folk-Lore*, vii. 377,
He'll neither be satisfied, full nor fasting (Staffs).

New bread. *See* quot. 1888: Lowsley, *Berks Gloss.*, 30 (E.D.S.), New
bread, new beer, an' gre-an 'ood, 'ull
bring ruin to any man's house.

Newbridge Hollow. *See* **Bowdon
Wakes.**

New brooms sweep clean. 1546:
Heywood, *Proverbs*, Pt. II. ch. i., The
greene new brome sweepth cleene.
1579: Lyly, *Euphues*, 88 (Arber), Ah
well I wot that a new broome sweep-
eth cleane. 1659: *Lady Alimony*, II. i.
c. 1760: Foote, *Cozeners*, I., New acts,
like new brooms, make a little bustle
at first; but the dirt will return, never
fear. 1815: Scott, *Mannering*, ch. vi.
1905: E. G. Hayden, *Travels Round
our Village*, 97, A noo broom swapes
clane; but when it's a scrub ther's a
job.

Newcastle. 1. *Canny Newcastle.* 1790:

Grose, *Prov. Gloss.*, s.v. "Northumberland." 1825: Brockett, *Gloss. N.
Country Words*, 37, Canny, a genuine
Newcastle word, applied to anything
superior or of the best kind. . . .
"Canny Newcassel," *par excellence*, is
proverbial. 1846–59: *Denham Tracts*,
i. 309 (F.L.S.).

2. *Coals to Newcastle.* *See* **Coals.**

3. *He has the Newcastle bur in his
throat.* 1790: Grose, *Prov. Gloss.*, s.v.
"Northumberland." 1846–59: *Denham
Tracts*, i. 292 (F.L.S.).

4. *Newcastle grindstone.* *See* **Scot** (1).

5. *Newcastle hospitality.* *See* quot.
1892: Heslop, *Northumb. Words*, 498
(E.D.S.), Newcastle hospitality—that is,
roasting a friend to death; or, according to a more popular colloquial phrase,
"killing a person with kindness."

6. *Newcastle Scots are the worst of
all Scots.* 1846–59: *Denham Tracts*, i.
298 (F.L.S.).

7. *That is going round by Newcastle
to get to Shields.* Ibid., ii. 364.

New College. *See* quot. 1659:
Howell, 20, They thrive as New
Colledge students, who are golden
schollers, silver batchelors and leaden
masters.

**New friend makes the old forgotten,
A.** 1611: Cotgrave, s.v. "Aimé."
1800: Lamb, *Letters*, i. 159 (Lucas),
But ever the new friend driveth out
the old, as the ballad sings. [Mr. Lucas
notes: "The ballad I have not found."]

Newgate. *See* quot. 1662: Fuller,
Worthies, ii. 314 (1840), He that is [at]
a low ebb at Newgate, may soon be
afloat at Tyburn. 1790: Grose, *Prov.
Gloss.*, s.v. "London" [as in 1662].

Newgate Knocker. *See* quots. 1881:
in *N. & Q.*, 6th ser., iii. 248, "As black
as Newgate Knocker"—I heard this
expressive phrase used the other day
by a servant. 1893: G. L. Gower,
Gloss. of Surrey Words, 12 (E.D.S.),
Coming from Croydon on a very dark
night the driver remarked "Ay! it
is a dark night, dark as Newgate
Knocker."

New grief awakens the old. 1732:
Fuller, No. 3535.

New honours. *See* **Honour** (7).

New lords, new laws. 1548 : Hall, *Chron.*, 233 (1809). *c.* 1597 : in Harington, *Nugæ Antiquæ*, i. 201 (1804), To such reprovers I answer, *new lords, new laws.* 1605 : Sylvester, *Du Bartas*, Week I. Day ii. l. 97. 1659 : R. Brome, *Queen and Concubine*, II. v. 1712 : Motteux, *Quixote*, Pt. II. ch. xliii. 1823 : Scott, *St. Ronan's*, ch. xiv., But new lords new laws—naething but fine and imprisonment.

Newmarket heath, A fine morning to catch herrings on. 1639 : Clarke, 308.

New meat begets a new appetite. 1633 : Draxe, 23, New meats prouoke the appetite. 1670 : Ray, 18. 1732 : Fuller, No. 3534, New dishes beget new appetites.

New pin, Clean (or Neat) as a. 1829 : Scott, *Journal*, 19 April, It is a great thing to have a certainty to be clear as a new pin of every penny of debt. R. L. S., *Treasure I.*, ch. x., Always glad to see me in the galley, which he kept as clean as a new pin. 1886 : Elworthy, *West Som. Word-Book*, 504 (E.D.S.), Her was a-dressed off so fine and so nate's a new pin. 1889 : Peacock, *Manley, etc., Gloss.*, 366 (E.D.S.), Neat as a new pin. 1923 : Alice Brown, *Old Crow*, ch. vi., Charlotte told me . . . he was neat as a new pin.

News. *See* **Country** (3).

New things are fair. [1412–20 : Lydgate, *Troy Book*, bk. iv. l. 301, It is a natural Men to delite in thing that is newe.] 1611 : Cotgrave, s.v. "Nouveau," Every new thing lookes faire. 1651 : Herbert, *Jac. Prudentum*, 2nd ed. 1700 : T. Brown, *Scarron*, ii. 248 (1892), As all new things are apt to please. 1732 : Fuller, No. 3537, New things are most look'd at.

New Year. 1. *A good new year and a merry Handsel Monday.* 1846 : Denham, *Proverbs*, 23 (Percy S.).

2. *At New Year's tide The days lengthen a cock's stride.* 1710 : *Brit. Apollo*, ii. No. 90, col. 3, That old saying, that the days lengthen a cock stride. 1759 : *Gent. Mag.*, 16, The countryman . . . has a saying that I believe is very general all over England —At New Year's tide, etc. 1846 :

Denham, *Proverbs*, 30 (Percy S.), At new-year's day, a cock's stride, At Candlemas, an hour wide. 1904 : *Co. Folk-Lore: Northumb.*, 174 (F.L.S.).

3. *If New Year's eve.* *See* quot. 1846 : Denham, *Proverbs*, 23 (Percy S.), If new-year's eve night wind blow South, It betokeneth warmth and growth ; If West, much milk, and fish in the sea ; If North, much cold, and storms there will be ; If East, the trees will bear much fruit—If north-east, flee it man and brute.

4. *Pay away money on New Year's day, And all the year through you'll have money to pay.* Worcs. and Herefs. 1882 : *N. & Q.*, 6th ser., vi. 186.

Next to love quietness. 1678 : Ray, 104.

Next to no wife. *See* **Wife** (17).

Next way, round about, is at the far door. 1639 : Clarke, 8.

Nice as a ha'porth of silver spoons. 1546 : Heywood, *Proverbs*, Pt. II. ch. ix., Sodeinly waxen as nyse As it had bene a halporth of syluer spoones. *c.* 1550 : *Jacke Jugeler*, 40 (Grosart), As denty and nice, as an halpeny worth of siluer spoons.

Nice as a nun's hen. 15th cent.: in *Reliq. Antiquæ*, i. 248 (1841), Some [women] be nyse as a nanne hene. 1546 : Heywood, *Proverbs*, Pt. II. ch. i. 1670 : Ray, 202. 1847 : Halliwell, *Dict.*, s.v. "Nanny," As nice as a nanny hen, i.e. very affected or delicate. [Halliwell follows the 15th - century example in rendering "nanne" as "nanny," but the other references give "nun's," as also does Wilson in his *Rhetorique*, 1560, p. 219 (1909).]

Nice as nip. 1854 : Baker, *Northants Gloss.*, s.v. Nice as nip. Just the thing ; to a nicety. A very common colloquial expression. 1901 : F. E. Taylor, *Lancs Sayings*, 3. Cf. **Clean as nip.**

Nice wife and a back door Do often make a rich man poor, A. *c.* 1450 : *Prov. of Good Counsel*, l. 33 (E.E.T.S.), For a nyse wyfe and a backe dore Makyth oftyn tymus a ryche man pore. 1639 : Clarke, 218. 1732 : Fuller, No. 6268.

Nichils in nine holes = Nothing at

all. Variants of "holes" are "pokes,"
"nooks," etc. 1584: R. Scot, *Witchcraft*, bk. xvi. ch. vi., And their bodies
to the hangman to be trussed on the
gallowes, for nichels in a bag. 1662:
Fuller, *Worthies*, ch. xxv., There is an
officer in the Exchequer, called Clericus
Nihilorum, or the Clerk of the Nichills,
who maketh a Roll of all such sums as
are nichill'd by the Sheriff upon their
estreats of the Green Wax, when such
sums are set on persons, either not
found, or not found solvible. 1670:
Ray, 188. 1730: Bailey, *Eng. Dict.*,
s.v., Nichils (in Common Law) are issues
or debts, which the sheriff being op-
posed, says are worth nothing, by reason
that the parties that should pay them
are nothing worth. 1852: "Cheshire
Proverbs," in *N. & Q.*, 1st ser., vi. 386,
Nichils in nine nooks. 1917: Bridge,
Cheshire Proverbs, 97.

Nicholas Kemp. *See* quot. 1888:
Q.-Couch, *Troy Town*, ch. xi., Like
Nicholas Kemp, he'd occasion for all.

Nick and froth. A proverbial expression for tapsters' tricks. 1600–12:
Rowlands, *Four Knaves*, 48 (Percy S.),
With cannes of beere . . . And those
they say are fil'd with nick and froth.
1656: R. Fletcher, *Ex Otio Negotium*,
133, From the nick and froth of a penny
pot-house. 1674: *Poor Robin Alman.*,
August, What with nick and froth, by
filling Cans half full for fear of spilling.
1690: *New Dict. Canting Crew*, sig.
H7, Nick and froth built the Pye at
Aldgate.

Nick in the post. *See* quot. 1847:
Halliwell, *Dict.*, s.v. "Nick," The
proverbial expression "to knock a nick
in the post," i.e. to make a record of
any remarkable event.

Niggard. *See* More spends.

Niggard never hath enough, The.
1493: *Dives et Pauper*, fo. 8 (1536).

Night brings the crows home. 1901:
F. E. Taylor, *Lancs Sayings*, 9, Neet
brings th' crows whoam.

Night is the mother of counsel. 1578:
Florio, *First Fruites*, fo. 31, The nyght
is the mother of thoughts. 1611:
Cotgrave, s.v. "Conseil," Night gives
advice; we say, take counsell of your

pillow. 1640: Herbert, *Jac. Prudentum*.
1707: Dunton, *Athenian Sport*, 527,
Whence came the saying, *That the night
gives counsels?* 1884: R. L. S. and
Henley, *Adm. Guinea*, III. iv., The
night brings counsel: to-morrow shall
decide. 1925: Locke, *Great Pandolfo*,
ch. ii., The night brings counsel. Cf.
Take (25).

**Night to run away with another man's
wife, A fine.** 1591: Florio, *Second
Frutes*, 165, It were euen a fine night,
etc. *c.* 1630: B. & F., *Lovers' Progress*,
III. ii., Here were a night to choose to
run away, etc. 1633: Rowley, *Match
at Midnight*, IV., They say a moonshine
night is good to run, etc. 1659:
Howell, 6, A fit night to steal away
a fair lady, viz. A cleer moonshine. 1738: Swift, *Polite Convers.*,
Dial. I., Oh! 'twas a delicate night
to run, etc.

**Nightingale and cuckoo sing both in
one month, The.** 1639: Clarke, 106.
1696: D'Urfey, *Quixote*, Pt. III. Act V.
sc. i., D'ye hear, sir, as great as you are,
remember this, the nightingale and
cuckoo sing both in a month.

Nightingale cannot sing in a cage, A.
1732: Fuller, No. 335.

Nightingale. *See also* **Cuckoo** (14).

**Nightingales can sing their own song
best.** 1732: Fuller, No. 3542.

Nimble as an eel, As. *c.* 1620: B. &
F., *Woman's Prize*, IV. i. 1675: *The
Mistaken Husband*, I. iii., As nimble as
an eele riggling in the mud. 1710:
T. Ward, *Eng. Reform.*, 88 (1716), As
glib and nimble As tail of eell. 1732:
Fuller, No. 719, As nimble as an eel
in a sand-bag. 1889: Peacock, *Manley*,
etc., *Gloss.*, 611 (E.D.S.), Wick [Quick]
as an eel.

Nimble as ninepence, As. 1882: Mrs.
Chamberlain, *W. Worcs. Words*, 13
(E.D.S.), 'E gamboled over the yat
[gate] as nimble as ninepence.

**Nimble ninepence is better than a slow
shilling, A.** 1851: *N. & Q.*, 1st ser.,
iv. 234 [cited as an "old proverb"].
1886: Elworthy, *West Som. Word-
Book*, 513 (E.D.S.) [with "dead" for
"slow"]. 1913: E. M. Wright, *Rustic
Speech, etc.*, 173.

Nimble penny is worth a slow six-pence, A. Glos. 1911 : Folk - Lore, xxii. 239.

Nimblest footman is a false tale, The. 1659 : Howell, Proverbs: Brit.-Eng., 3.

Nine crabs high, Ever since I was. Yorks. 1861 : N. & Q., 2nd ser., xii. 309, . . . That is, I suppose, since I was a mere child.

Nine days wonder, A. [Romanis quoque ab eodem prodigio novendiale sacrum publice susceptum est, seu voce caelesti ex Albano monte missa—nam id quoque traditur—seu aruspicum monitu.—Livy, i. 31.] c. 1374 : Chaucer, Troylus, bk. iv. l. 588, A wonder last but nyne night never in toune. 1546 : Heywood, Proverbs, Pt. II. ch. i., This wonder, (as wonders last,) lasted nine daies. 1600 : Kemp, Nine Days Wonder [title]. 1621: Burton, Melancholy, II. iii. 7, p. 424 (1836), Be content ; 'tis but a nine dayes wonder. 1633 : Massinger, New Way, etc., IV. ii. 1767 : Murphy, Sch. for Guardians, I. ii., And when the nine days wonder is over, I shall pack off. 1818 : Byron, Don Juan, can. i. st. 188, The nine days' wonder which was brought to light. 1898 : Shaw, Plays Pleasant, etc., I. Pref., xii, The volume . . . is a curious relic of that nine days wonder. 1926: Phill-potts, Peacock House, 221.

Ninepence to nothing, As like as. 1670 : Ray, 206.

Ninepence to nothing, To bring. Before 1729 : in Roxb. Ballads, viii. 812 (B.S.), A brace of as delicate jades As ever brought ninepence to nothing. 1883 : Burne, Shropsh. Folk-Lore, 596, To bring one's ninepence to nothing=to lose property by neglect and waste.

Nine tailors make a man. The earlier examples show an uncertainty as to the number required for the composition. Before 1603 : Q. Elizabeth—see 1838 quotation. 1607 : Dekker and Web-ster, Northw. Hoe, II., They say three taylors go to the making vp of a man. 1611 : Tarltons Jests, 20 (Sh. S.), Two tailors goe to a man. 1630 : Taylor (Water-Poet), Works, 3rd pagin., 73, Some foolish knaue (I thinke) at first began The slander that three taylers are

one man. 1639–61 : Rump Songs, Pt. I. 159 (1662, repr. 1874), Like to nine taylors, who if rightly spell'd, Into one man are monosyllabel'd. 1663 : Butler, Hudibras, Pt. I. can. ii. l. 22, Just like the manhood of nine tailors. 1720 : C. Shadwell, Sham Prince, II. i. 1771 : Smollett, Clinker, in Works, vi. 236 (1817), Who . . . made her believe I was a tailor, and that she was going to marry the ninth part of a man. 1838 : Carlyle, Sartor, bk. iii. ch. xi., Does it not stand on record that the English Queen Elizabeth, receiving a deputation of Eighteen Tailors, addressed them with a " Good morning, gentlemen both ! "

Nineteen bits of a bilberry, He'll make. 1678 : Ray, 229.

Nine words at once, To talk. 1611 : Cotgrave, s.v. "Tost," To speak thick, or fast, or (as we say) nine words at once.

Nip the briar in the bud. 1732 : Fuller, No. 3543.

Nippence, no pence, half a groat wanting twopence. 1659 : Howell, 12. 1670 : Ray, 215, Nipence nopence, etc.

Nits will be lice. 1690 : New Dict. Canting Crew, sig. H7. 1823: D'Israeli, Cur. of Lit., 2nd ser., i. 431 (1824), Oliver Cromwell's coarse, but descrip-tive proverb . . . . " Nits will be lice."

No alchemy to saving. 1640 : Her-bert, Jac. Prudentum. 1710: S. Palmer, Moral Essays on Proverbs, 162, No alchymy like to thrift. 1736 : Bailey, Dict., s.v. "Alchymy." 1928 : Times, 11 May, p. 17, col. 3.

No better than she should be. 1604 : Pasquils Jests, 35 (1864), A man whose wife was no better then she should be. 1666 : Torriano, Piazza Univ., 172, As much as to say, she is no saint, she is no better, etc. 1738 : Swift, Polite Convers., Dial. I. 1781 : Macklin, Man of the World, V. 1875 : Griffiths, Mem. of Millbank, 281 (1884), These daughters were not a bit better than they should have been. 1925 : Punch, 11 Nov., p. 506, col. 3, We're working now on a screen version of the Iliad . . . and Helen no better than she should be.

No bishop no king. 1641 : Smectym-nuus, Vind. Answ., §16, 208 (O.), King James of blessed memory said, *no Bishop, no King.* 1653 : Chetwynd, Dedn. to Harington's *Briefe View of the Church*, Who held that prophetick axiom as a sure truth, and we see it fulfilled, No Bishop, No King. 1709 : O. Dykes, *Eng. Proverbs*, 278 (2nd ed). Cf. **No mitre.**

Noble as the race of Shenkin and line of Harry Tudor. An old Shropshire saying. 1871 : *N. & Q.*, 4th ser., vii. 9.

Noble blood to market, and see what it will bring, Send your. 1732 : Fuller, No. 4099.

Noble housekeeper needs no doors, A. 1640 : Herbert, *Jac. Prudentum* [in the plural]. 1670 : Ray, 7.

Noble plant suits not with a stubborn ground, A. 1640 : Herbert, *Jac. Prudentum.* 1670 : Ray, 21, Noble plants suit not a stubborn soil.

Noble to ninepence, To bring a. A proverbial expression for idle dissipation of money. 1568 : Fulwell, *Like will to Like*, in Hazlitt, *Old Plays*, iii. 344, For why Tom Tosspot, since he went hence, Hath increased a noble just unto ninepence. 1681 : Robertson, *Phraseol. Generalis*, 922, A noble quickly brought to ninepence. 1725 : Bailey, tr. Erasmus' *Colloq.*, 235, I have brought a noble to nine pence, and of a master of seven arts I am become a workman of but one art. 1854 : Baker, *Northants Gloss.*, s.v. "Noble," It is said of a person who is thoughtless and wasteful in expenditure, "He'll soon bring his noble to ninepence." 1886 : Elworthy, *West Som. Word-Book*, 516 (E.D.S.), To spend lavishly or to live extravagantly is said to be the way to bring the noble to ninepence. 1914 : R. L. Gales, *Vanished Country Folk*, 199, As a child I remember "Their noble has come to a ninepence" as the commonest of sayings.

Nobody calls himself rogue. 1855 : Bohn, 463.

Nobody hath too much prudence or virtue. Ibid., 463.

Nobody is fond of fading flowers. Ibid., 463.

No carrion will kill a crow. 1670 : Ray, 76. 1685 : Meriton, *Yorkshire Ale*,

49. 1732 : Fuller, No. 3553 [" poison " for "kill "]. 1890 : J. D. Robertson, *Gloucester Gloss.*, 186 (E.D.S.).

No chink, no drink. 1659 : T. Pecke, *Parnassi Puerp.*, 64.

Nocke anew, nocke anew, i.e. Try again. Glos. 1639 : in *Berkeley MSS.*, iii. 32 (1885).

No cross, no crown. [1587 : Greene, *Works*, iv. 48 (Grosart), He deserueth not to haue the crowne of victorie, which hath not abidde the brunt of the battaile.] 1660 : W. Penn, *No Cross No Crown* [title]. 1709 : O. Dykes, *Eng. Proverbs*, 278 (2nd ed.). 1853 : Trench, *Proverbs*, 21 (1905).

No cut to unkindness. 1659 : Howell, 13. 1670 : Ray, 27. 1732 : Fuller, No. 3557.

Nod as good as a wink. *See* **Blind,** *adj.* (26).

No day so clear but hath dark clouds. 1651 : Herbert, *Jac. Prudentum*, 2nd ed.

No deceit in a brimmer. *See* **Deceit** (3).

Nod for a wise man, and a rod for a fool, A. 1732 : Fuller, No. 337.

Nod from a lord is a breakfast for a fool, A. Ibid., No. 338. 1901 : F. E. Taylor, *Lancs Sayings*, 7, A nod fro' a lord's a breakfast for a foo'.

Nod, Land of=Sleep. 1738 : Swift, *Polite Convers.*, Dial. III., I'm going to the land of Nod. 1818 : Scott, *Heart of Midl.*, ch. xxx.

Nod of an honest man is enough, A. 1732 : Fuller, No. 336.

No fault is, Where, there needs no pardon. *c.* 1617 : *Machivels Dogge*, fo. 8 [" excuse " for " pardon "]. 1631 : Mabbe, *Celestina*, 83 (T.T.), There is no neede of pardon, where there is no fault committed. 1633 : Draxe, 28. 1670 : Ray, 89. 1732 : Fuller, No. 5651 [" punishment " for " pardon "].

No feast to a miser's. 1611 : Cotgrave, s.v. " Chiche." 1670 : Ray, 90. 1753 : Richardson, *Grandison*, iii. 175 (1883), It is an observation that the miser's feast is often the most splendid.

No fee, no law. 1597 : G. Harvey, *Works*, iii. 26 (Grosart). 1618 : B. Holyday, *Technogamia*, II. v., A man may as well open an oister without a knife, as a lawyers mouth without a fee.

No fence against a flail. 1670 : Ray, 89. 1685 : S. Wesley, *Maggots*, 96. 1707 : Dunton, *Athenian Sport*, 317, The common old proverb here meant ; is that—There's no fence against a flail. 1730 : Swift, *Works*, xiv. 256 (Scott). 1830 : Forby, *Vocab. E. Anglia*, 428.

No fence against ill fortune. 1605 : Camden, *Remains*, 329 (1870) [" for " for " against "]. 1670 : Ray, 89. 1732 : Fuller, No. 3566.

No fishing. *See* Fishing (1).

No foe to a flatterer. 1576 : *Parad. Dainty Devices*, 59 (1810). 1630 : T. Adams, *Works*, 194, There is no foe to the flatterer.

No folly to being in love. 1659 : Howell, *Proverbs: Brit.-Eng.*, 27, No folly to love. 1678 : Ray, 50. 1710 : S. Palmer, *Moral Essays on Proverbs*, 137.

No foolery to falling out. 1659 : Howell, *Proverbs: Brit. - Eng.*, 27. 1875 : Cheales, *Proverb. Folk-Lore*, 106 [" like " for " to "].

No further. *See* Bull (7).

No gains. *See* Gain (1).

No garden without its weeds. 1716 : E. Ward, *Female Policy*, 89, The finest garden is not free from weeds. 1732 : Fuller, No. 3576.

No going to heaven in a sedan, There is. Ibid., No. 4910.

No gold. *See* No silver.

No good accord where every man would be a lord, There is. 1546 : Heywood, *Proverbs*, Pt. II. ch. vi. *c.* 1594 : Bacon, *Promus*, No. 968 [" jack " for " man "]. 1633 : Draxe, 8 [omitting " good "].

No grass grows in the market-place. 1855 : Bohn, 461.

No great banquet but none fares ill, There is. 1640 : Herbert, *Jac. Prudentum*. 1670 : Ray, 2.

No great loss but some small profit. Ibid., 117.

No harm, no force [matter]. 1604 : *Pasquils Jests*, 21 (1864), Why then, no harme, no force (quoth the fellow), and so went his wayes.

No haste but good. *c.* 1534 : Berners, *Huon*, 320 (E.E.T.S.), It is a saynge that an yll haste is not good. 1546 : Heywood, *Proverbs*, Pt. II. ch. ix. 1576 : Wapull, *Tide tarrieth no Man*, sig. F2, No haste but good, stay yet a while. *c.* 1640 : in *Roxb. Ballads*, ii. 104 (B.S.), No haste but good I hope there be.

No heart. *See* quots. 1578 : Florio, *First Fruites*, fo. 28, Who hath not a hart let hym haue legges. 1629 : *Book of Meery Riddles*, Prov. 78, He that hath no heart, hath legs. 1732 : Fuller, No. 2146, He that has no heart, ought to have heels.

No hell like a troubled conscience. 1590 : Lodge, *Rosalynde*, 60 (Hunt. Cl.), There is no stinge to the worme of conscience, no hell to a minde toucht with guilt. 1754 : *Connoisseur*, No. 28, A dreadful instance of the truth of that maxim, *There is no hell like a troubled conscience.*

No heralds in the grave. 1732 : Fuller, No. 3581.

No joy without annoy. 1576 : *Parad. Dainty Devices*, 64 (1810), No pleasure without some paine. 1587 : Greene, *Works*, iii. 101 (Grosart), No blisse without bale. 1670 : Ray, 109. 1732 : Fuller, No. 6322.

No knaves and fools, If there were, all the world would be alike. Ibid., No. 2715.

No lack to lack a wife. 1546 : Heywood, *Proverbs*, Pt. II. ch. xi. 1639 : Clarke, 329, No lack to a wife.

No land without stones, Or meat without bones. 1875 : Cheales, *Proverb. Folk-Lore*, 120.

No larder but hath its mice. 1732 : Fuller, No. 3587.

No law for a town's bull. 1886 : R. Holland, *Cheshire Gloss.*, 454 (E.D.S.). 1917 : Bridge, *Cheshire Proverbs*, 119. Cf. Lawless.

No law for lying = A man may lie without danger of the law. 1678 : Ray, 172.

No living man all things can. [Non omnia possumus omnes.—Virgil.] 1639 : Clarke, 147. 1670 : Ray, 56.

No longer foster, no longer friend.

"Foster" = food, nourishment. 1412 : Hoccleve, *Regement*, st. 238, l. 1661, p. 60 (E.E.T.S.), Styntynge the cause, the effect styntith eek ; No lenger forster, no lenger lemman. 1546 : Heywood, *Proverbs*, Pt. II. ch. ix., No longer foster, no longer lemman. 1639 : Clarke, 12. 1681 : Robertson, *Phraseol. Generalis*, 638. 1754 : Berthelson, *Eng.-Danish Dict.*, s.v. "Foster."

No longer pipe. *See* Pipe.

No love is foul nor prison fair. 1651 : Herbert, *Jac. Prudentum*, 2nd ed.

No love to a father's. 1640 : Herbert, *Jac. Prudentum*.

No man. *See* Call (3).

No man. *See* quots. 1577 : Kendall, *Flow. of Epigrams*, 264 (Spens. S.), No man can doe twoo thyngs at once, the prouerbe old doeth tell. 1611 : Cotgrave, s.v. "Moulin," One cannot be in two places, or follow two businesses at once.

No man can master his own mind. 1764 : Garrick, in *Garrick Corresp.*, i. 171 (1831) [quoted as "the old saying"].

No man can please all. Before 1500 : in Hill, *Commonplace-Book*, 132 (E.E.T.S.), Ther may no man all men please. 1633 : Draxe, 45, One can hardly please all men. 1666 : Torriano, *Piazza Univ.*, 204, One cannot please all people.

No man can serve two masters. *c.* 1330 : in Wright, *Pol. Songs*, 325 (Camden S.), That no man may wel serve tweie lordes to queme. *c.* 1477 : Caxton, *Jason*, 57 (E.E.T.S.), For no man may wel serue two maistres for that one corumpeth that other. 1649 : T. Forde, *Lusus Fort.*, Epistle, We cannot serve two masters with a single heart. 1924 : Shaw, *Saint Joan*, sc. iv., Men cannot serve two masters.

No man can stand always upon his guard. 1732 : Fuller, No. 3592.

No man comes to heaven with dry eyes. 1630 : T. Adams, *Works*, 180, The prouerbe is too true for many ; No man, etc.

No man is born wise. 1620 : Shelton, *Quixote*, Pt. II. ch. xxxiii., For no man is born wise, and bishops are made of men and not of stones. 1710 : S.

Palmer, *Moral Essays on Proverbs*, 285, No man is born a Master of Arts. 1732 : Fuller, No. 3599, No man is born wise or learned.

No man is his craft's master the first day. 1639 : Clarke, 35. 1670 : Ray, 75. 1754 : Berthelson, *Eng.-Danish Dict.*, s.v. "Crafts-master."

No man knows what is good except he hath endured evil. 1600 : Bodenham, *Belvedere*, 6 (Spens. S.), We neuer know what 'tis in heaven to dwell, Till wee haue had some feeling of grim hell. 1633 : Draxe, 59. 1670 : Ray, 8, No man better knows what good is, then he who hath endured evil. 1736 : Bailey, *Dict.*, s.v. "Endure" [as in 1670].

No man lives so poor as he was born. 1732 : Fuller, No. 3604.

No man liveth without a fault. 1659 : Howell, 9.

No man so good. *See* quot. 1662 : Fuller, *Worthies*, i. 265 (1840), And some will oppose to this narrow county-proverb, an English one of greater latitude, viz. "No man so good, but another may be as good as he."

No marvel if water be lue. 1678 : Ray, 215.

No mill no meal. 1639 : Clarke, 163. 1670 : Ray, 120. 1732 : Fuller, No. 3613. 1853 : Trench, *Proverbs*, 106 (1905), They courageously accept the law of labour . . . *No mill, no meal.*

No mitre no crown. 1639–61 : in *Rump Songs*, 121 (1662, repr. 1874), The proverb proves true *No miter no crown.* Cf. **No bishop.**

No money, no Swiss. [1687 : Dryden, *Hind and Panther*, iii. 177, Those Swisses fight on any side for pay.] Before 1704 : T. Brown, *Works*, iii. 162 (1760), After long observation, I find it to hold truer *no money, no mistress*, than *no money, no Swiss.* 1737 : Gay, *Fables*, 2nd ser., No. 9, l. 61, For these, like Swiss, attend ; No longer pay, no longer friend. 1829 : Cobbett, *Advice to Young Men*, Lett. V., "No money, no Swiss," is a proverb throughout the world.

No more mortar no more brick, A cunning knave has a cunning trick.

1678 : Ray, 296. 1732 : Fuller, No. 291. 1880 : Spurgeon, *Ploughman's Pictures*, 83.

No more purpose, To, than to beat your heels against the ground (or wind). 1670 : Ray, 190. 1732 : Fuller, No. 5209.

No more sib. *See* Sieve and riddle.

No more water than the ship drew, There was. 1546 : Heywood, *Proverbs*, Pt. II. ch. viii. *c.* 1594 : Bacon, *Promus*, No. 672. 1659: Howell, 14.

No more wit than a coot. *c.* 1540 : Bale, *Kynge Johan*, I. l. 176, Thou semyste by thy wordes to have no more wytt than a coote.

None are so wise as those who know nothing. 1875 : Cheales, *Proverb. Folk-Lore*, 103.

None but fools lay wagers. 1677 : *Poor Robin's Visions*, 16, Your actions verifie a proverb among you ; *none but fools lay wagers.* 1711 : *Brit. Apollo*, iii. No. 146, col. 4, Its an old saying (and I think a true one) That none but knaves or fools lay wagers. 1732 : Fuller, No. 452, A wager is a fool's argument.

None is born master. 1640 : Herbert, *Jac. Prudentum.*

None is offended but by himself. Ibid.

None is so wise but the fool overtakes him. *c.* 1205 : Layamon, *Brut*, i. 32 (Madden), Nis nawer nan so wis mon That me ne mai bi-swiken. *c.* 1275 : Ibid., ii. 211, Thar nis no man so wis That me ne mai bi-swike. 1640 : Herbert, *Jac. Prudentum.* 1670 : Ray, 29. 1732 : Fuller, No. 3654 [with " sometimes " after " fool "].

None knows the weight of another's burden. 1640 : Herbert, *Jac. Prudentum.*

None plays the fool well without wit. 1611 : Davies (of Hereford), *Sc. of Folly*, 42, in *Works*, ii. (Grosart).

None says his garner is full. 1640 : Herbert, *Jac. Prudentum.*

None so blind. *See* Blind, *adj.* (24).

None so deaf. *See* Deaf (10).

None so good that's good to all. 1639 : Clarke, 16.

None so old that he hopes not for a year of life. *c.* 1520 : *Calisto and Mel.*,

in Hazlitt, *Old Plays*, i. 78, None so old but may live a year ; And there is none so young, but, ye wot well, May die in a day. 1631 : Brathwait, *Whimzies*, 45 (1859), Hee seemes to verifie the proverbe : *There is none so desperately old, but he hopes to live one yeare longer.* 1732 : Fuller, No. 3653. Cf. **Man** (48).

No news is good news. 1616 : James I., in *Loseley MSS.*, 403 (Kempe), No newis is bettir then evill newis. 1632 : Lupton, *Lond. and Country*: "Country," No. 12, The best newes is when we heare no newes. 1776 : Colman, *Spleen*, I., No news is good news sometimes, as the proverb goes. 1850 : Dickens, *Copperfield*, ch. xxxvi. 1921 : S. Gwynn, in *Observer*, 31 July, p. 5, col. 2, People not unnaturally grow a little impatient under the delays here. But it was never truer that no news is good news.

No one is always wise. 1539 : Taverner, *Proverbs*, fo. 37, No man in the worlde is wyse at all houres. 1666 : Torriano, *Piazza Univ.*, 249, No body is wise at all times. 1714 : Ozell, *Molière*, i. 113, If none is wise at all times, yet the shortest errors are the best.

No pains. *See* Gain (1).

No penny, no pardon. 1531 : Tyndale, *Expos.* 1 *John*, in *Works*, p. 395, col. 1 (1573) (O.), O Popishe forgiuenesse with whom it goeth after the comon prouerbe, no peny no pardon. 1732 : Fuller, No. 3616.

No penny, no Paternoster. 1528 : Tyndale, *Obed. of Christ. Man.*, 245 (P.S.), After the common saying, " No peny, no Paternoster." 1546 : *Suppl. of Poore Commons*, 87 (E.E.T.S.). *c.* 1598 : Deloney, *Gentle Craft*, Pt. II. ch. vii. 1651 : Randolph, *Hey for Honesty*, I. ii. 1709 : O. Dykes, *Eng. Proverbs*, 200 (2nd ed.), Whence came this comical saying, *No peny, no Paternoster*, but from pecuniary Indulgences ? 1754 : Berthelson, *Eng.-Danish Dict.*, s.v. " Penny."

No pipe, no pudding. Glos. 1639 : in *Berkeley MSS.*, iii. 27 (1885).

No play without a fool in it. 1650 : *Newes from New Exchange*, 14, 'Tis an

old proverb, there can be no play without a foole in it.

No priest, no mass. 1732 : Fuller,
No. 3618.

**No raillery is worse than that which
is true.** 1855 : Bohn, 462.

No remedy but patience. 1633 :
Draxe, 151. 1670 : Ray, 190. 1694 :
Cibber, *Love's Last Shift*, II. 1723 :
Defoe, *Col. Jack*, ch. xviii., I had no
remedy but the old insignificant thing,
called patience. 1824 : Scott, *Redgauntlet*, ch. xv. Cf. Patience.

Norfolk capon, A = A red herring.
1785 : Grose, *Class. Dict. Vulgar
Tongue*, s.v. 1836 : in Farmer's *Musa
Pedestris*, 121, A Norfolk capon is jolly
grub. Cf. Yarmouth capon.

Norfolk dumpling, A = A Norfolk
man. 1600 : Day, *Blind Beggar*, I. iii.,
Make me your cheat, your gull . . .
your Norfolk dumpling. 1608 : Armin,
Nest of Ninnies, 17 (Sh. S.), He lookt
like a Norfolke dumpling, thicke and
short. 1662 : Fuller, *Worthies*, ii. 446
(1840), Norfolk dumplings . . . This
. . . relates to the fare they commonly
feed on. 1790 : Grose, *Prov. Gloss.*,
s.v. " Norfolk."

Norfolk wiles. *See* Essex stiles.

No rogue like to the godly rogue.
1732 : Fuller, No. 3624.

No rose without a thorn. [Nulla est
sincera voluptas.—Ovid, *Met.*, vii. 453.]
c. 1440 : Lydgate, *Fall of Princes*, bk. i.
l. 57, As there is no rose Spryngyng in
gardeyns, but ther be sum thorn.
1579 : Lyly, *Euphues*, 33 (Arber), The
sweetest rose hath his prickell. 1681 :
Robertson, *Phraseol. Generalis*, 1084,
No rose without its prickle. 1754 :
Berthelson, *Eng.-Danish Dict.*, s.v.
" Rose." 1855 : Kingsley, *West. Ho!*,
ch. viii., True, the rose has its thorn.

North, The. *See* quot. *c.* 1670 :
Aubrey, *Wilts MS. Collect.*, quoted in
Halliwell, *Dict.*, s.v. " North," The
North for largeness, The East for
health ; The South for buildings, The
West for wealth.

Northampton. 1. *He that must eat a
buttered fagot, let him go to Northampton.* 1662 : Fuller, *Worthies*, ii. 501
(1840). 1790 : Grose, *Prov. Gloss.*, s.v.

" Northants" [" would " for " must "].
1851 : Sternberg, *Dialect, etc., of
Northants*, 191.

2. *The mayor of Northampton opens
oysters with his dagger.* 1662 : Fuller,
Worthies, ii. 500 (1840). 1790: Grose,
s.v. " Northants." 1851 : Sternberg,
191. Cf. Oyster (1).

**Northamptonshire for spires and
squires.** 1869 : Hazlitt, 297.

North country. *See* Knight of Cales.

North-Crawley. *See* quot. 1854 :
Baker, *Northants Gloss.*, s.v., How
North-Crawley her bonnet stands ; i.e.
not straight, all on one side.

**Northerly wind and blubber Brings
home the Greenland lubber.** 1846 : Denham, *Proverbs*, 20 (Percy S.).

Northern air brings weather fair, A.
Ibid., 15.

Northern har [mist] **brings drought
from far, A.** 1849 : Halliwell, *Pop.
Rhymes*, 156.

North Repps. *See* Gimmingham.

North wind. *See* Wind.

Norwich. *See* Caistor.

Norwich, St. Peter's. *See* quot.
1869 : Hazlitt, 464, When three daws
are seen on St. Peter's vane together,
then we are sure to have bad weather.

Nose. 1. *A nose of wax.* *See* quots.
1533 : in *Ballads from MSS.*, i. 206
(B.S.), The text to turne and glose,
like a welshe manes hose, or lyk a
waxen nose. 1596 : Lodge, *Marg. of
America*, 40 (Hunt. Cl.), Where-through
iustice is made a nose of waxe warmed.
1609 : J. Melton, *Six-fold Politician*,
77, They meete with no such noses
of waxe as will be so iested withall.
1611 : Cotgrave, s.v. " Tordre," To
make a nose of wax of ; to wrest, wrie,
manage, turne, at pleasure. 1740 :
North, *Lives of Norths*, i. 366 (Bohn),
To treat plain words and expressions
as a nose of wax to bend one way or
other to gratify parties. 1815 : Scott,
Mannering, ch. v., Because I let . . .
the constable draw the warrants, and
manage the business his ain gate, as if
I had been a nose o' wax. 1847 :
Halliwell, *Dict.*, s.v. " Nose," . . . a
proverbial phrase for anything very
pliable.

2. *As plain as the nose on a man's face.* 1639: Clarke, 188. 1683: White-Kennett, tr. Erasmus' *Praise of Folly*, 25 (8th ed.), I . . . can make it (as the proverb goes) *as plain as the nose on your face.* 1773: Graves, *Spirit. Quixote*, bk. v. ch. xviii., The gentleman talks main-well, and has made it as plain as the nose in one's face. 1906: Q.-Couch, *Mayor of Troy*, ch. iii.

3. *Doth your nose swell* (or *eek*, i.e. itch) *at that?* 1678: Ray, 77.

4. *He can't tell where to turn his nose.* c. 1565: in Huth, *Ancient Ballads, etc.*, 211 (1867) [cited as a " prouerbe "].

5. *He that has a great nose thinks everybody is speaking of it.* 1732: Fuller, No. 2129. 1826: Scott, *Journal*, 24 Jan., I went to the Court for the first time to-day, and, like the man with the large nose, thought everybody was thinking of me and my mishaps.

6. *His nose will abide no jests.* 1588: *Mar-Prelate Epit.*, 9 (1843), I am sure their noses can abide no iest. 1592: Lodge, *Euphues Shadow*, sig. H3, My nose loues no iesting. 1659: Howell, 6. 1678: Ray, 77.

7. *If your nose itches, you will shake hands with* (or *kiss*) *a fool.* 1738: Swift, *Polite Convers.*, Dial. I., My nose itched, and I knew I should drink wine or kiss a fool. 1755: *Connoisseur*, No. 59.

8. *To hold one's nose to the grindstone.* 1546: Heywood, *Proverbs*, Pt. I. ch. v., I shall, to reuenge former hurtis, Hold their noses to grinstone. 1653: Middleton and Rowley, *Span. Gipsy*, IV. iii., Hold his nose to the grin'stone, my lord. 1732: Fuller, No. 5187. 1865: Dickens, *Mutual Friend*, bk. iii. ch. xiv.

9. *To put one's nose out of joint.* 1581: Rich, *Apolonius and Silla*, 71 (1912), It could be no other than his own man that had thrust his nose so far out of joint. 1607: *The Puritan*, V. i., Now all the knights' noses are put out of joint. 1663: Pepys, *Diary*, 22 July, As soon as the King can get a husband for Mrs. Stewart, however, my

Lady Castlemaine's nose will be out of joynt. 1754: Berthelson, *Eng.-Danish Dict.*, s.v. "Nose." 1848: Planché, *Extravag.*, iii. 247 (1879), Your lovely eyes Out of joint have put her nose. 1912: Lucas, *London Lav.*, ch. xxxvi., Every baby puts some one's nose out of joint.

10. *You make his nose warp.* 1737: Ray, 204. [Query = the same as 9.]

See also Follow (5) ; Know (20) ; and Lead.

Nosegay to him as long as he lives, It will be a. 1678: Ray, 262.

No service to the King's. 1484: Caxton, tr. Chartier's *Curial*, 19 (E.E.T.S.), Ne seruyse lyke to the kyng souerayn. c. 1580: G. Harvey, *Marginalia*, 142 (1913), No fishing to yᵉ sea, nor service to a king. 1618: Breton, *Court and Country*, in *Inedited Tracts*, 190 (Hazlitt). 1659: Howell, 14.

No silver no servant. 1633: Draxe, 179. 1670: Ray, 143. 1732: Fuller, No. 3629, No silver, no service.

No silver (or gold) without dross. 1611: Cotgrave, s.v. " Or," No gold without some drosse. 1633: Draxe, 62, No siluer without his drosse. 1639: Clarke, 80 [as in 1633].

No sin to cheat the devil. 1726: Defoe, *Hist. of Devil*, Pt. II. ch. x., 304 (4th ed.), The old Latin proverb, *Fallere fallentem non est fraus* . . . 'tis no sin to cheat the devil.

No song no supper. 1613: B. & F., *Burning Pestle*, II. ii., Let thy father go snick-up . . . let him stay at home, and sing for his supper, boy. 1893: R. L. S., *Ebb-Tide*, ch. vii., If you're not there by the time named, there will be no banquet; no song, no supper, Mr. Whish !

No sooner up but head in the ambry, and nose in the cup. 1639: Clarke, 136. 1670: Ray, 198. 1736: Bailey, *Dict.*, s.v. " Aumbry " [ending with " aumbry "].

No sport, no pie. c. 1620: B. & F., *Woman's Prize*, I. iii., I'll bring it to th' old proverb, " No sport, no pie." 1670: Ray, 147.

No sure dungeon but the grave. 1825: Scott, *Talisman*, ch. xix., It is an

ancient saying,—no sure dungeon but
the grave.

No sweat. *See* **Sweet** (3).

Notch (or **Notchel**), **To cry.** 1681 :
Dialogue, in *Harl. Miscell.*, ii. 114, *Will.*
The first I think on is the king's majesty
(God bless him !), him they cried nochell.
Sam. What, as Gaffer block of our town
cried his wife ? *Will.* I do not know
what he did ; but they voted that
nobody should either borrow or lend,
nor sell nor buy with him, under pain
of their displeasure. 1859 : *Blackburn
Standard*, quoted in *N. & Q.*, 3rd ser.,
x. 108, On Wednesday there was at
Accrington an extraordinary instance
of the disgraceful practice of "notchel
crying." [Bellman sent round first by
husband disclaiming responsibility for
wife's debts, and then by wife doing
the same as regards her husband and
also making scandalous charges against
him.] 1892 : *N. & Q.*, 8th ser., ii., 526,
A short time ago, at St. Helens County
Court, the defendant in an action dis-
claimed his responsibility on the ground
that he had " cried the notchel," an
expression which meant, as explained
to the judge, that he had published a
notice in the journals that he would
not be held responsible for debts con-
tracted by his wife. 1917 : Bridge,
Cheshire Proverbs, 131, To cry notch or
nichil (or notchel).

Not free that draws his chain, He is.
1640 : Herbert, *Jac. Prudentum.*

No, thank you. *See* quots. 1883 : A.
Easther, *Almondbury Gloss.*, 20 (E.D.S.),
No thank ye has lost mony a gooid
butterchauv. 1901 : F. E. Taylor,
Lancs Sayings, 9, " Nowe, thank yo' "
has lost monny a good butter-cake.

Nothing. 1. *He has nothing to eat
and yet invites guests.* 1732 : Fuller,
No. 1877.

2. *He that has nothing is frighted at
nothing.* 1639 : Clarke, 41, They that
have nothing, need feare to lose nothing.
1732 : Fuller, No. 2150.

3. *He that hath nothing is not contented.* 1670 : Ray, 19.

4. *If you put nothing into your purse,
you can take nothing out.* 1732 : Fuller,
No. 2781.

5. *It's more painful to do nothing than
something.* 1670 : Ray, 19.

6. *Nothing but up and ride?* 1639
Clarke, 116, What ? no more but up
and ride. 1670 : Ray, 198. 1732 :
Fuller, No. 5497.

7. *Nothing down, nothing up.* 1659 :
Howell, 3. 1670 : Ray, 19. Cf.
Nought (4).

8. *Nothing dries sooner than a tear.*
[Cito arescit lacrima, praesertim in
alienis malis.—Cicero, *Part. Or.*, 17.]
1560 : T. Wilson, *Rhetorique*, 134 (1909),
For as Cicero doth say, nothing drieth
soner then teares. 1640 : Herbert, *Jac.
Prudentum.* 1681 : Robertson, *Phraseol.
Generalis*, 927, Nothing dries up sooner
than tears. 1732 : Fuller, No. 3661
[" woman's tears " after " a "].

9. *Nothing for nothing.* Before 1704 :
T. Brown, in *Works*, i. 131 (1760), Thou
know'st the proverb, *nothing due for
nought.* 1714 : Ozell, *Molière*, ii. 129,
She must refuse all presents offer'd her
by men ; for now-a-days nothing is
given for nothing. 1800 : Miss Edgeworth, *Castle Rackrent*, 61 (Everyman),
Nothing for nothing, or I'm under a
mistake with you, Jason. 1864 : Mrs.
H. Wood, *Trevlyn Hold*, ch. xxii., I
might have knowed a lawyer wouldn't
give nothing for nothing.

10. *Nothing hath no savour.* 1546 :
Heywood, *Proverbs*, Pt. I. ch. viii.
1559 : Becon, in *Prayers, etc.*, 365
(P.S.), Nought hath no savour. 1659 :
Howell, *Letters*, ii. 666 (Jacobs). 1738 :
Swift, *Polite Convers.*, Dial. I., They say,
Something has some savour, but nothing
has no flavour.

11. *Nothing have, nothing crave.*
1670 : Ray, 19. 1732 : Fuller, No.
6242.

12. *Nothing is a man's truly, that he
cometh not by duly.* Ibid., No. 6280.

13. *Nothing is easy to the unwilling.*
Ibid., No. 3663.

14. *Nothing is good or ill but by comparison.* 1676 : Shadwell, *Virtuoso*, II.,
No man is happy but by comparison.
1763 : Mrs. F. Sheridan, *Discovery*,
IV. i.

15. *Nothing is impossible.* *See* quot.
1917 : Bridge, *Cheshire Proverbs*, 96,

Naught's impossible, as t'auld woman said when they told her cauf had swallowed grindlestone.

16. *Nothing is impossible to a willing heart.* 1546 : Heywood, *Proverbs,* Pt. I. ch. iv. 1555 : S. Hawes, *Past. of Pleasure,* 7 (Percy S.), To a willyng harte is nought impossible. 1631 : Mabbe, *Celestina,* 183 (T.T.) [" minde " for " heart "]. 1707 : *Spanish Bawd,* IV. ii. [as in 1631].

17. *Nothing is lost in a good market.* 1827 : Hone, *Table-Book,* 8.

18. *Nothing is more easily blotted out than a good turn.* 1647 : *Countrym. New Commonwealth,* 26, Nothing sooner waxeth old then a good turne or benefit. 1732 : Fuller, No. 3669.

19. *Nothing is stolen without hands.* 1639 : Clarke, 149.

20. *Nothing is to be bought in the market without a penny.* Before 1704 : T. Brown, *Works,* i. 293 (1760) [quoted as a proverb].

21. *Nothing kindles sooner than fire.* 1560 : T. Wilson, *Rhetorique,* 133 (1909) [cited as " a common saying "].

22. *Nothing like leather.* 1692 : L'Estrange, *Æsop,* 421 (3rd ed.), Up starts a currier. Gentlemen, says he, when y'ave said all that can be said, there's nothing in the world like leather. 1855 : Gaskell, *North and South,* ch. x., " I dare say, my remark came from the professional feeling of there being nothing like leather," replied Mr. Hale.

23. *Nothing more proud. See* quot. 1642 : in *Harl. Miscell.,* ii. 65 (1744), By his carriage the proverb is verified, *Nothing more proud than basest blood, when it doth rise aloft.*

24. *Nothing more smooth than glass, yet nothing more brittle; Nothing more fine than wit, yet nothing more fickle.* 1732 : Fuller, No. 6472.

25. *Nothing new. See* quots. 1850 : Emerson, *Repr. Men :* "Montaigne," " Ah," said my languid gentleman at Oxford, " there's nothing new or true—and no matter." 1887 : *N. & Q.,* 7th ser., iv. 257, The Cornish version of this proverb has been known to me for many years : " There's nothing new,

and there's nothing true, and it don't sinnify [signify]."

26. *Nothing stake. See* **Nought** (4).

27. *Nothing succeeds like success.* 1882 : Sir Stafford Northcote, quoted in *N. & Q.,* 6th ser., v. 189. Cf. **Success.**

28. *Nothing to be got without pains.* 1594 : Churchyard, *Mirror of Man,* sig. A4 (Boswell, 1816), Nothing is gotten without toyle and labor. 1611 : Cotgrave, s.v. " Peine," Nor bread, nor ought is gotten without paines. 1732 : Fuller, No. 3677, Nothing to be got without pains, but poverty. 1869 : Spurgeon, *John Ploughman,* ch. vii. [as in 1732, *plus* " and dirt "]. Cf. No. 32.

29. *Nothing turns sourer than milk.* 1830 : Forby, *Vocab. E. Anglia,* 428.

30. *Nothing venture, nothing have.* [Necesse est facere sumptum qui quaerit lucrum.—Plautus, *Asin.,* I. iii. 65.] *c.* 1374 : Chaucer, *Troylus,* bk. ii. l. 807, And seyde, he which that no-thing under-taketh, No-thing ne acheveth, be him looth or dere. *c.* 1390 : Gower, *Conf. Amantis,* bk. iv. l. 2694, For he which dar nothing beginne, I not what thing he scholde achieve. 1481: Caxton, *Reynard,* 27 (Arber), He that wil wynne he muste laboure and auenture. 1546 : Heywood, *Proverbs,* Pt. I. ch. xi., Nought venter, nought haue. 1580 : Tusser, *Husb.,* 44 (E.D.S.) [as in 1546]. 1624 : T. Heywood, *Captives,* IV. i., I see here that nought venters, nothinge gaynes. 1674 : Head and Kirkman, *Eng. Rogue,* iii. 142. 1709 : O. Dykes, *Eng. Proverbs,* 113 (2nd ed.). 1791 : Boswell, *Johnson,* iii. 189 (Hill). 1840 : Lytton, *Money,* III. vi.

31. *Nothing will come of nothing.* *c.* 1374 : Chaucer, *Boeth.,* bk. v. pr. 1, For this sentence is verray and sooth, that " nothing ne hath his beinge of naught." 1599 : Breton, in *Works,* ii. *c* 23 (Grosart), Then of nothing growes nothing, but nothing. *c.* 1605 : Shakespeare, *Lear,* I. i. 1652 : Flecknoe, *Miscell.,* 73, Of nothing, nothing's made (they say). *c.* 1750 : Fielding, *Essay on Nothing,* Sect. 1, There is nothing falser than that old proverb which . . . is in every one's mouth :

" *Ex nihilo nihil fit.*" Thus translated by Shakespeare in Lear's " Nothing can come of nothing." 1818 : Scott, *Heart of Midl.*, ch. i. [" can " for " will "]. 1846 : Planché, *Extravag.*, iii. 117 (1879) [as in 1818].

32. *There is nothing done without trouble, only loosing the fire out.* 1883 : Burne, *Shropsh. Folk-Lore*, 588. Cf. No. 28.

33. *There's nothing but is good for something.* 1639 : Clarke, 72.

34. *Where nothing is, a little doth ease.* 1546 : Heywood, *Proverbs*, Pt. I. ch. x. 1639 : Clarke, 10. 1694 : D'Urfey, *Quixote*, Pt. I. Act II. sc. i., Where nothing is, a little goes a great way.

35. *Where nothing is, nothing can be had.* 1630 : Taylor (Water-Poet), *Works*, 2nd pagin., 38, Where nought is, there's nothing to be got. 1675 : *Poor Robin Alman.*, Sept., He who hath nothing, nothing can he pay. 1734 : Fielding, *Don Quix. in England*, I. iii., Where nothing is, nothing can come on't. 1774 : Colman, *Man of Business*, Epil., Where nothing's in, there's nothing can come out.

36. *Where nothing is, the King must lose his right.* 1546 : Heywood, *Proverbs*, Pt. I. ch. xii. 1594 : *True Trag. Rich. Third*, 12–13 (Sh. S.), Where nothing is to be had, the King looseth his right they say. 1664 : *Wits Recr.*, in *Mus. Deliciæ, etc.*, ii. 54 (Hotten). 1709 : O. Dykes, *Eng. Proverbs*, 127 (2nd ed.). 1817 : Scott, *Rob Roy*, ch. ix.

37. *Who nothing save shall nothing have.* 1732 : Fuller, No. 6338.

38. *Who practiseth nothing shall have nothing.* 1580 : Tusser, *Husb.*, 48 (E.D.S.).

See also **Naught**; and **Nought**.

No time like the present. 1696 : Mrs. Manley, *Lost Lover*, IV. i. 1828 ; Scott, *Fair Maid*, ch. ii. 1839 : Dickens, *Nickleby*, ch. xxxvi.

Not Jack out of doors nor yet gentleman. 1639 : Clarke, 206.

Not lost that a friend gets, It is. 1642 : Taylor, *Answer to Tale of a Tub* (Lean), It is no tint that a friend gets. 1816 : Scott, *Old Mortality*, ch. xli.

Not lost that comes at last, It is.

1612 : Shelton, *Quixote*, Pt. I. bk. iv. ch. iv. 1670 : Ray, 117. 1732 : Fuller, No. 2999 [" if it " for " that "]. 1754 : Berthelson, *Eng.-Danish Dict.*, s.v. " Lost."

Not so good to borrow as be able to lend. 1546 : Heywood, *Proverbs*, Pt. I. ch. x.

Not so old. 1738 : Swift, *Polite Convers.*, Dial. I., Col. Not so old nor yet so cold—You know the rest, miss. [I hope " Miss " did know the rest—I do not].

Nottingham ale. 1622 : Drayton, *Polyol.*, xxiii., Little Rutlandshire is termed raddleman. As Nottingham's, of old (is common) ale and bread. 1708 : in *Bagford Ballads*, i. 389 (B.S.), With Nottingham ale At every meal. 1763 : in Hackwood, *Inns, Ales, etc.*, 99 (1909), I grant that fair Nottingham once bore the bell For our grand sires that tasted the sweets of good ale.

Nottingham, The little smith of, Who doeth the work that no man can. 1634 : C. Butler, *Feminine Monarchie*, 17. 1662 : Fuller, *Worthies*, ii. 570 (1840). 1790 : Grose, *Prov. Gloss.*, s.v. " Notts."

Not too fast for [fear of] falling. 1580 : Baret, *Alvearie*, C 59, As we say, not too fast for breaking your shinnes. 1599 : Porter, *Two Angry Women*, in Hazlitt, *Old Plays*, vii. 301.

Not too high for the pie, nor too low for the crow. 1546 : Heywood, *Proverbs*, Pt. II. ch. vii. 1577 : *Misogonus*, II. ii. 1670 : Ray, 189.

Not worth a (1) band's end ; (2) bean ; blue point—*see* No. 29 ; (3) button ; (4) cherry ; (5) chip ; (6) cobbler's curse ; (7) cress ; (8) curse ; (9) dodkin ; (10) farthing ; (11) fig ; (12) flea ; (13) fly ; (14) gnat ; (15) gooseberry ; (16) groat ; (17) haddock ; (18) hair ; (19) haw ; (20) hen ; (21) herring ; (22) leek ; (23) louse ; (24) needle ; (25) nut ; (26) pea ; (27) pear : (28) pin ; (29) point and blue-point [a tagged lace or cord] ; (30) potato ; (31) rush ; (32) sloe ; (33) straw ; (34) tinker's curse ; (35) an apple ; (36) egg ; (37) ivy leaf ; (38) onion ; (39) hiring, who talks of tiring ; (40) shoe-buckles ; (41) three halfpence.

(1) 1855 : Robinson, *Whitby Gloss.*,

10, " It is not worth a band's end "—
valueless.

(2) 1297 : R. Glouc., 497 (O.), Al
nas wurth a bene. *c.* 1374 : Chaucer,
Troylus, bk. iii. l. 1167, Swich arguments ne been not worth a bene.
c. 1430 : in *Twenty-six Poems*, 131
(E.E.T.S.), I am nat worthe a bene.
Before 1529 : Skelton, *Bowge of Courte*,
l. 95. 1595 : *Pedlars Prophecy*, l. 1002
(Malone S.), All is not worthe a beane.
1620 : Shelton, *Quixote*, Pt. II. ch.
xlvii., An office that will not afford a
man his victuals is not worth two beans.
1823 : Scott, *Peveril*, ch. xxiii.

(3) 14th cent.: *Guy of Warwick*, l.
2216 (E.E.T.S.), His scheld [shield] nas
nought worth a botoun. 1532 : More,
Confut. of Tyndale, Pref., sig. Ee1, All
hys welbeloued boke is not worth a
boton. 1590 : Nashe, *Almond for a
Parrot*, 37 (1846), All is not worth a
button, if it be too stale. 1609 : in Halliwell, *Books of Characters*, 119 (1857).
1776 : T. Cogan, *John Buncle, Junior*,
i. 9. 1857 : Hughes, *Tom Brown*, Pt.
II. ch. ii., He'll never be worth a button,
if you go on keeping him under your
skirts.

(4) *c.* 1390 : *Chevelere Assigne*, l. 329
(E.E.T.S.), I charde not thy croyse
[cross] . . . the valwe of a cherye.

(5) 1672 : Walker, *Parœm.*, 15.

(6) 1886 : Elworthy, *West Som. Word-
Book*, 146 (E.D.S.), Cobler's curse.
The extreme of valuelessness . . .
Why ! he idn a-wo'th a cobbler's cuss.
1897 : *N. & Q.*, 8th ser., xi. 452, Our
every-day appraisement is "not wo'th
a cobbler's cuss " [Somerset].

(7) *c.* 1350 : *Pearl*, l. 343, For anger
gayne3 the not a cresse [not a mite].
c. 1387 : Usk, *Test. of Love*, in Skeat's
Chaucer, vii. 73, Their might is not
worth a cresse. *c.* 1390 : Gower, *Conf.
Amantis*, bk. iii. l. 588, And so to me
nys worth a kerse. *c.* 1400 : *Beryn*,
l. 971 (E.E.T.S.), ffor [ne] to body, ne
to soule this vaylith nat a karse.

(8) 1820 : Byron, in *Letters, etc.*,
v. 57 (Prothero), The Neapolitans are
not worth a curse, and will be beaten.

(9) 1660 : B. & F., *Faithful Friends*,
IV. v., If my trade then prove not

worth a dodkin. 1672 : Cowell, *In-
terpreter*, s.v. " Doitkin " (O.), Hence
probably we retain that phrase when
we would undervalue a man, to say,
He is not worth a doit or doitkin. 1881 :
Duffield, *Don Quix.*, III. xxvii. 206 (O.),
I did not care two dotkins.

(10) 1613 : S. Rowley, *When You See
Me*, sig. D2, As for the Popes faith
(good faith's) not worth a farthing.
1633 : *Dux Grammaticus*, quoted in *N. &
Q.*, 5th ser., viii. 165, All the gaine that
thou shalt get by this bargain is not
worth a farthing. 1786 : Wolcot, *Works*,
i. 118 (1795). 1824 : Scott, *Redgauntlet*,
Lett. III. 1876 : C. Loftus, *My Youth*,
i. 87, He was never " worth a farthing "
afterwards ; his heart and his spirit
were broken.

(11) [Non tressis agaso.—Persius, v.
76.] 1528 : More, *Works*, 241 (1557).
1596 : Harington, *Metam. of Ajax*, 68
(1814), It had not been worth a fig, if
they had not . . . 1667 : *Poor Robin
Alman.*, July, For what is out of date,
is not worth a fig. 1750 : Smollett, *Gil
Blas*, iii. 98, Although it was not worth
a fig, it met with great success. 1880 :
Spurgeon, *Ploughman's Pictures*, 56,
Some pretty nothing, not worth a fig.

(12) *c.* 1450 : Henryson, *Moral Fables*,
195 (O.), For it is said in proverb, But
lawté all other vertewis ar nocht worth
ane fle. *c.* 1640 : in *Roxb. Ballads*, i.
527 (B.S.), All your warrants are not
worth a flee.

(13) 1297 : R. Glouc., 428 (1724) (O.),
Wat was þy strengþe worþ ? . . . ywys
no3t worþ a flye. *c.* 1352 : in Wright,
Pol. Poems, i. 59 (Rolls Ser., 1859),
And all thaire fare noght wurth a
flye. *c.* 1380 : *Sir Ferumbras*, l. 4930
(E.E.T.S.). *c.* 1386 : Chaucer, *Frank-
lin's Tale*, l. 404. 1412 : Hoccleve,
Regement, st. 88, l. 613, By that sette
I naght the worth of a flye. 1489 :
Skelton, in *Works*, i. 10 (Dyce), Of whos
[life] they counted not a flye. *c.* 1550 :
in Heywood, *Spider and Flie*, 440
(Farmer). *c.* 1640 : in *Roxb. Ballads*,
ii. 160 (B.S.), Your speeches are not
worth a fly. 1744 : Claridge, in Mills,
Essay on Weather, 101 (1773), But a
swarm [of bees] in July Is not worth

a fly. 1906 : Doyle, *Sir Nigel*, ch. xii., Mistress Edith told me that she counted him not a fly.

(14) *c.* 1395 : *Plowman's Tale*, in Skeat's *Chaucer*, vii. 161, Such maters be nat worth a gnat. *c.* 1565 : Still, *Gammer Gurton*, V. ii., Al is not worth a gnat—thou canst sweare till to morow.

(15) 1598 : Shakespeare, 2 *Henry IV.*, I. ii., All the other gifts . . . are not worth a gooseberry.

(16) 1530 : Palsgrave, 657, He pyncheth as though he were nat worthe a grote. 1587 : Turbervile, *Trag. Tales, etc.*, 309 (1837), He that feares caliuer shot, Can neuer . . . skirmish woorth a grote. 1694 : *Terence made English*, 189, And the woman's not worth a groat. 1709 : Ward, *Acc. of Clubs*, 257 (1756), In all its bloom not worth a groat, It does so quickly die. 1784 : *New Foundl. Hosp. for Wit*, iv. 30, Notions to you not worth a groat.

(17) 1546 : Heywood, *Proverbs*, Pt. II. ch. x., Till they both were not woorth a haddocke.

(18) 1613 : Wither, *Abuses Stript, etc.*, Epigr. 10, To call you best, or the most faire, . . . Is now not commendations worth a haire. 1639 : *Conceits, Clinches, etc.*, No. 18, Give me a man's face : a boyes face is not worth a haire.

(19) *c.* 1280 : *Castle of Loue*, in *Vernon MS.*, 368 (E.E.T.S.), Ne wisdam nis not worth an hawe. *c.* 1300 : in Ibid., 336, Hit is not worth an hawe. 1412–20 : Lydgate, *Troy Book*, bk. ii. l. 4043. 1468 : *Coventry Mys.*, 190 (Sh. S.). 1583 : Melbancke, *Philotimus*, sig. G1, A whelpe that firste doth misse of his game, doth neuer after proue woorth an haw.

(20) *c.* 1386 : Chaucer, *Wife of Bath's Tale*, l. 256, Swich arrogance is nat worth an hen. 1508 : Dunbar, *Tua Mariit Wemen*, 269 (O.), That hurtis 3ow nought worth a hen.

(21) *c.* 1270 : in *Old Eng. Miscell.*, 95 (Morris, E.E.T.S.), Al were sone his prute [pride] agon hit nere on ende wrth on heryng.

(22) *c.* 1350 : *Alexander*, l. 4229, And your lare of a leke suld nevir the les worth. *c.* 1370 : Chaucer, *Rom. of*

Rose, in *Works*, fo. 130 (1602), Such loue I preise not at a leke. *c.* 1400 : *Sowdone of Babylone*, 50 (E.E.T.S.), His witte was not worth a leke. *c.* 1480 : in Hazlitt, *Early Pop. Poetry*, ii. 2. Before 1529 : Skelton, *Colin Clout*, l. 183. 1594 : Greene, *Works*, xiv. 203 (Grosart). 1612 : *Cornucopiæ*, 79 (Grosart), This opinion is not worth two leekes.

(23) *c.* 1380 : *Sir Ferumbras*, l. 439 (E.E.T.S.), Him semede it nas noght worth a lous batayl with him to wage. *c.* 1540 : in Hazlitt, *Early Pop. Poetry*, iii. 308, Then seke an other house ; This is not worth a louse. 1595–6 : Gosson, in Ibid., iv. 253, All this new pelfe now sold in shops, In value true not worth a louse. 1639–61 : *Rump Songs*, Pt. II. 168 (1662, repr. 1874). 1698 : in *Harl. Miscell.*, ii. 276 (1744), But, faith, I'm scarce worth a louse. 1720 : *Vade Mecum for Malt-worms*, Pt. I. 21. 1801 : Wolcot, *Works*, v. 380 (1801), Life was never worth a louse To the man who ne'er was mellow. 1886 : Elworthy, *West Som. Word-Book*, 840 (E.D.S.), An equally common depreciatory saying is, " He idn a-wo'th a louse."

(24) Before 1225 : *Ancren R.*, 400, And alle þeos þinges somed, aȝean mine bode, ne beoð nout wurð a nelde [needle]. *c.* 1395 : *Plowman's Tale*, in Skeat's *Chaucer*, vii. 172, Such willers wit is nat worth a neld. *c.* 1450 : *Towneley Plays*, 13 (E.E.T.S.), When all mens corn was fayre in feld Then was myne not worth a neld.

(25) *c.* 1300 : *Havelok*, l. 1332 (E.E.T.S.), Nouth the worth of one nouthe [nut].

(26) *c.* 1393 : Langland, *Plowman*, C, x. 345, Ich sette by pardon nat a peese. *c.* 1430 : *Roland and Otuel*, l. 1157 (E.E.T.S.), Your lawes are noghte worthe a pye [pea]. 1561 : *Queene Hester*, 21 (Grosart), It is not worth a pease. 1587 : Turbervile, *Trag. Tales, etc.*, 393 (1837), With idle words not woorth a parched pease.

(27) 1303 : Brunne, *Handl. Synne*, l. 769, For euery gadling nat wurth a pere. *c.* 1420 : Lydgate, *Assembly of Gods*, 18 (E.E.T.S.), Without myn

helpe, be nat worth a peere. 1485 :
Malory, *Morte d'Arthur*, bk. xv. ch. vi.,
Vayne glory of the world, the whiche
is not worth a pere. *c.* 1540 : Bale,
Kynge Johan, 38 (Camden S.), And that
is not worth a rottyn wardon [pear].

(28) 1533 : Heywood, *Play of Wether*,
l. 750, And all our other gere not worth
a pyn. 1589 : Greene, *Works*, vi. 39
(Grosart), Cupide must be . . . blinde
(or all were not worth a pinne). 1685–
6 : Cotton, *Montaigne*, bk. ii. ch. xvii.,
I cannot . . . carve at table worth a
pin. 1782 : Wolcot, *Works*, i. 36 (1795).
1865: Planché, *Extravag.*, v. 243 (1879),
Your violin Not worth a pin.

(29) 1542 : Udall, tr. Erasmus' *Apoph.*,
187 (1877), He was for the respect of
his qualitees not to be esteemed worth
a blewe point or a good lous. 1547 :
Borde, *Brev. of Helthe*, fo. lxix. vᵒ,
All is nat worthe a blewe poynt. 1570 :
Googe, *Popish Kingdome*, 14 vᵒ (1880),
That now he is not worth a poynt, in
any kinde of place. 1666 : Torriano,
Piazza Univ., 128, A head without
tongue is not worth a point. 1672 :
Walker, *Parœm.*, 59, Not worth a point.

(30) 1823 : Byron, *Don Juan*, can. vii.
st. 4, Who knew this life was not worth
a potato.

(31) 1362 : Langland, *Plowman*, A,
xi. 17, Wisdam and wit nou is not worth
a russche. *c.* 1470 : G. Ashby, *Poems*,
39 (E.E.T.S.), Suche maner reule is nat
worthe two russhes. 1594 : *Willobie's
Avisa*, 76 (Grosart), Yet this is all not
worth a rush. 1653 : Walton, *Angler*,
Pt. I. ch. iii., If this chub that you ete
of had been kept till to-morrow, he had
not been worth a rush. 1713 : Arbuthnot, *John Bull*, Pt. V. ch. vii., His
friendship is not worth a rush. 1838 :
Dickens, *Twist*, ch. xxxviii., Don't
move a step forward, or your life is not
worth a bulrush. 1878 : R. L. S., *Letters*,
ii. 49 (Tusitala ed.), It is a rotten
book, and not worth a rush at best.

(32) *c.* 1250 : *Orison our Lady*, 28,
in *Old Eng. Miscell.*, 160 (O.), þis liues
blisse nis wurð a slo. *c.* 1300 : *Havelok*, l. 849, Of me ne is me nouth a
slo. *c.* 1380 : *Sir Ferumbras*, l. 4338
(E.E.T.S.), Hit were noght worth a

slo. 14th cent. : *Guy of Warwick*,
l. 2936 (E.E.T.S.), Scheld no hauberk
nas him worth a slo.

(33) *c.* 1300 : *Havelok*, l. 315, He let
his oth al ouer-ga [entirely be dis-
regarded], Therof ne gaf he nouht a
stra [Thereof he gave not a straw].
c. 1386 : Chaucer, *Tale of Melibeus*,
§ 34, And whan that they been accom-
pliced, yet be they nat worth a stree.
c. 1470 : G. Ashby, *Poems*, 74 (E.E.T.S.),
His wyt is not worth a strawe. Before
1529 : Skelton, *Magnyfycence*, l. 1394,
Yet lyberte without rule is not worth
a strawe. Before 1635 : Corbet, *Poems*,
20 (1807), The doctors of the civil law
Urg'd ne're a reason worth a straw.
1740 : North, *Examen*, 439, Their co-
gency is not worth a straw. 1863 :
Reade, *Hard Cash*, ch. i., When he has
got a headache, Hardie of Exeter is not
worth a straw in a boat.

(34) 1894 : Northall, *Folk Phrases*,
20 (E.D.S.), Not worth a tinker's curse.

(35) *c.* 1489 : Caxton, *Sonnes of
Aymon*, 544 (E.E.T.S.), The sones of a
traytour whiche ben not worthe a roten
apple.

(36) *c.* 1430 : *Roland and Otuel*,
l. 222 (E.E.T.S.), That the lawes of
Cristyante ne are noghte worthe ane
aye [egg]. *c.* 1500 : More, in *Works*
(1557), "Juvenile Poems," And all not
worth an egge. 1659 : Howell, 14,
Tis not worth an egg-shel. 1883 :
R. L. S., *Letters*, ii. 260 (Tusitala ed.),
Pouring words upon him by the hour
about some truck not worth an egg
that had befallen me.

(37) *c.* 1390 : Gower, *Conf. Amantis*,
iv. 586, That all nys worth an yvy lef.

(38) 1509 : Barclay, *Ship of Fools*,
i. 63 (1874), A yonge boy that is nat
worth an onyon. 1556 : Heywood, *Spider
and Flie*, cap. 23, p. 103 (Farmer), Your
case in law is not worth an inion.

(39) 1883 : Burne, *Shropsh. Folk-
Lore*, 588, He's not worth hiring, who
talks of tiring.

(40) 1670 : Ray, 192, Not worth
shooe-buckles.

(41) 1672 : Walker, *Parœm.*, 26, Not
worth three halfpence.

Not worthy to carry books, to loose

the latchet of shoes, to wipe one's shoes, etc., etc. *See* quots. *c.* 1410: *Towneley Plays*, 196 ,(E.E.T.S.), I am not worthy for to lawse The leste thwong that longys to his shoyne. 1569: in Huth, *Ancient Ballads, etc.*, 21 (1867), For I with all that I can dooe, Vnworthie . . . To undoe the lachet of her shooe. 1611: Coryat, *Crudities*, Epist. to Reader, i. 15 (1905), Travellers of that learning, that I am not worthy to loose their shoe-lachet. 1620: Shelton, *Quixote*, Pt. II. ch. iii., I have seen . . . of your governors . . . that are not worthy to wipe my shoes. 1631: Mabbe, *Celestina*, 147 (T.T.), She is not worthy to carry her shooes after her. 1670: Ray, 200, Not worthy to carry his books after him . . . to be named the same day ; . . . to wipe his shoes. 1672: Walker, *Parœm.*, 54, Not worthy to . . . hold him water to wash his hands. 1709: Mandeville, *Virgin Unmask'd*, 30 (1724), Treats him . . . as if he was not worthy to wipe her shoes. 1748: Richardson, *Clarissa*, ii. 201 (1785), . . . not worthy to buckle his shoes. 1821: Scott, *Pirate*, ch. xiv., Not fit to tie the latchets of John's shoes. 1909: Hudson, *Afoot in England*, ch. xxiv., As a poet he was not worthy to unloose the buckles of their shoes. 1926: Phillpotts, *Yellow Sands*, I., You hold your tongue about Arthur. You ain't worthy to black Arthur's boots. *See also* Guts to a bear.

Nought. 1. *He that hath nought is nought set by.* Before 1500 : in Hill, *Commonplace-Book*, 132 (E.E.T.S.).

2. *He that hath nought shall have nought.* *c.* 1550: *Parl. of Byrdes*, l. 221, in Hazlitt, *Early Pop. Poetry*, iii. 179.

3. *Nought can restrain consent of twain.* [Non caret effectu, quod voluere duo. — Ovid, *Amores*, II iii. 16.] 1591 : Harington, *Orl. Furioso*, bk. xxviii. Notes. *c.* 1596: Marlowe, *Ovid's Elegies*, bk. ii. el. 3, What two determine never wants effect. 1740: Richardson, *Pamela*, i. 162 (1883), I should have had a hard task to prevent you, I find ; for, as the saying is, *Nought can restrain consent of twain.*

4. *Nought lay down nought take up.* *c.* 1374 : Chaucer, *Troylus*, bk. iv. l. 1585, Men seyn . . . "who-so wol have leef, he leef mot lete" [He who will have what he wants must give up what he likes]. 1546: Heywood, *Proverbs*, Pt. I. ch. vi. 1577: *Misogonus*, II. iv., Nought stake, nought drawe. 1678: Ray, 206, Nothing stake nothing draw. Cf. **Nothing** (7).

5. *Nought won by the one, nought won by the other.* 1546 : Heywood, *Proverbs*, Pt. I. ch. xi.

6. *Where nought is to wed with, wise men flee the clog.* Ibid., Pt. I. ch. xi. 1605 : Camden, *Remains*, 335 (1870). 1659 : Howell, 10.

See also **Naught**; and **Nothing.**

November. 1. *As November so the following March.* 1893: Inwards, *Weather Lore*, 36.

2. *As November 21 so is the winter.* Ibid., 37.

3. *If there's ice in November that will bear a duck, There'll be nothing after but sludge and muck.* 1878: Dyer, *Eng. Folk-Lore*, 260. 1891: R. P. Chope, *Hartland Dialect*, 20 (E.D.S.), Vrost in November to carr' a duck, The rest o' the winter'll be a muck. 1893: Inwards, *Weather Lore*, 36.

4. *November and flail.* *See* **Thresher.**

5. *November 10. See* quot. 1669 : *New Help to Discourse*, 285, If on the 10th of November the heavens be cloudy, it prognosticates a wet winter ; if clear and dry, a sharp winter.

6. *On the 1st of November, if the weather hold clear, An end of wheat sowing do make for the year.* 1580 : Tusser, *Husb.*, 181 (E.D.S.), Wife, some time this weeke, if the wether hold cleere, an end of wheat sowing we make for this yeere. 1893 : Inwards, *Weather Lore*, 36.

7. *The third of November. See* quot. 1659 : Howell, 6, The third of November the Duke of Vandosm was under water, The fourth of November the Queen was delivered of a daughter, The fifth of November we were like to have a great slaughter, And the sixth of November was the next day after.

8. *Thunder in November a fertile*

year to come. 1893 : Inwards, *Weather Lore*, 36.

No venom to that of the tongue. 1659 : Howell, 11.

No vice goes alone. 1732 : Fuller, No. 3637.

No vice like avarice. Ibid., No. 6171.

No weal without woe. 1578 : Florio, *First Fruites*, fo. 33.

No wheat without its chaff. *c.* 1440 : Lydgate, *Fall of Princes*, bk. i. l. 6732 (E.E.T.S.), Out off good corn men may sum darnel weede. 1611 : Cotgrave, s.v. " Paille," No corne without some chaffe. 1681 : Robertson, *Phraseol. Generalis*, 1312. 1736 : Bailey, *Dict.*, s.v. " Wheat."

Now I have got. *See* quots. 1732 : Fuller, No. 3691, Now I have got an ewe and a lamb, every one cries, Welcome, Peter. 1736 : Franklin, *Way to Wealth*, in *Works*, i. 445 (Bigelow), Now I have a sheep and a cow, everybody bids me good morrow.

No wisdom to silence. 1659 : Howell, *Proverbs : Brit.-Eng.*, 27.

Now's now. 1631 : Mabbe, *Celestina*, 144 (T.T.), Now is now ; and then is then. 1707 : *Spanish Bawd*, III. ii. [as in 1631]. 1846 : Denham, *Proverbs*, 6 (Percy S.), Now's now, but Yule's in winter.

No-where. *See* **Every-where.**

Number. *See* **One is no number.**

Numbers the waves, He. 1813 : Ray, 75.

Nurse and Nurses. 1. *A nurse spoils a good huswife.* 1659 : Howell, 3.

2. *A nurse's tongue is privileged to talk.* 1659 : Howell, *Proverbs : Brit.-Eng.*, 4. 1670 : Ray, 19.

3. *Nurses put one bit in the child's mouth and two in their own.* 1639 : Clarke, 39.

4. *The nurse is valued till the child is done sucking.* 1732 : Fuller, No. 4688. *See also* Kiss, *verb* (6).

Nursed in cotton, To be = To be brought up very tenderly. 1813 : Ray, 209.

Nurture passes nature. [1579 : Joubert, *Erreurs Populaires*, I. v. 9 (Lean), Nourriture passe nature.] 1611 : Cotgrave, s.v. " Nourriture," Nurture

surpasseth nature. 1633 : Draxe, 50, Nurture is above nature. 1754 : Berthelson, *Eng.-Danish Dict.*, s.v. " Nurture," Nurture goes beyond nature. Cf. **Nature.**

Nut and Nuts. 1. *A good nut year, a good corn year.* 1846 : Denham, *Proverbs*, 55 (Percy S.). 1893 : Inwards, *Weather Lore*, 5.

2. *Crack me that nut.* 1546 : Heywood, *Proverbs*, Pt. II. ch. vii., Knak me that nut. 1564 : Bullein, *Dialogue*, 62 (E.E.T.S.), Ha, ha, ha, how cracke you this nutte ? 1600 : Dekker, *Old Fortunatus*, I. i., My tongue speaks no language but an almond for a parrot, and crack me this nut. 1670 : Ray, 214, Crack me that nut, quoth Bumsted. 1732 : Fuller, No. 1121 [as in 1670]. 1828 : Scott, *Fair Maid*, ch. xvi., While this prince of revellers exhorted him,—" Crack me this nut, and do it handsomely."

3. *Many nits* [nuts], *many pits* [graves] = If hazel nuts be plentiful, the season will be unhealthy. [1672 : Howard, *All Mistaken*, I., A very hopeful generation ! sure, This was great nut year !] 1850 : in *N. & Q.*, 1st ser., ii. 510, Many nits Many pits. A common saying hereabouts [locality not indicated], meaning that if hazel nuts, haws, hips, etc., are plentiful, many deaths will occur. 1884 : H. Friend, *Flowers and Fl. Lore*, 207, . . . still in use in Devon . . . 1891 : R. P. Chope, *Hartland Dialect*, 71 (E.D.S.), Many nits, Many pits ; Many slones, Many groans.

4. *To be nuts to one.* 1589 : *Hay any Worke for Cooper*, 33 (1845), Like you any of these nuts Iohn Canterbury ? [The context shows that " nuts " is used in this No. 4 sense.] 1674 : Head and Kirkman, *Eng. Rogue*, iii. 102, It was honey and nuts to him to tell the guests. 1740 : North, *Lives of Norths*, i. 33 (Bohn), This was nuts to the old lord who thought he had outwitted Frank. 1819 : Byron, *Letters, etc.*, iv. 294 (Prothero), It will be nuts to all of them : they never had such an opportunity.

See also **Ape** (9) ; **Apple** (6) and (13) ; and **Deaf** (7).

O

Oak and Oaks. 1. *An oak is not felled
at one stroke.* c. 1440 : Lydgate, *Fall
of Princes*, bk. i. l. 96, These ookis grete
be nat doun ihewe First at a strok.
1477 : *Paston Letters*, iii. 169 (Gairdner),
It is but a sympill oke, That [is] cut
down at the first stroke. 1611 : Cotgrave, s.v. "Arbre," Though a little
man can fell a great oke, yet fals it not
at the first blow. 1732 : Fuller, No.
639 ["chop" for "stroke"]. 1880 :
Spurgeon, *Ploughman's Pictures*, 127,
One stroke fells not an oak.

2. *As close as oak* = Close as the
grain of oak. 1604 : Shakespeare,
Othello, III. iii., To seel her father's
eyes up close as oak. 1763 : Colman,
Deuce is in Him, II., I am close as oak,
an absolute free-mason for secresy.
1764 : Murphy, *The Choice*, I., I never
repeat a word ; I am as close as oak.

3. *Beware of an oak, It draws the
stroke ; Avoid an ash, It counts the flash ;
Creep under the thorn, It can save you
from harm.* 1878 : *Folk-Lore Record*,
i. 43.

4. *Cut down an oak and set up a
strawberry.* 1662 : Fuller, *Worthies*, i.
396 (1840), I would not wish this
county [Devon] the increase of these
berries, according to the proverb ;
"Cut down," etc. 1670 : Ray, 188.

5. *Great oaks from little acorns grow.*
Before 1635: Corbet, *Poems*, in Chalmers,
v. 584, An acorn one day proves an
oke. 1732 : Fuller, No. 4576, The
greatest oaks have been little acorns.
1852 : FitzGerald, *Polonius*, 6 (1903),
Every oak must be an acorn. 1923 :
Mackenzie King, *Speech*, in *Times*,
13 Oct., p. 7, col. 2, Here in England,
as nowhere else in the world, "great
oaks from little acorns grow."

6. *Oaks may fall when reeds stand the
storm.* 1732 : Fuller, No. 3692.

7. *To go between the oak and the rind.*
1886 : Elworthy, *West Som. Word-
Book*, 528 (E.D.S.), "To go 'twixt th'

oak and the rind " expresses the making
of very fine distinctions—hair splitting ;
hence the phrase has come to mean
the quibbling by which a trimmer
agrees with both sides. 1917 : *Devonsh.
Assoc. Trans.*, xlix. 338, To creep between the oak and the rind. Cf. **Bark
and tree**; and **Devil** (120).

8. *When the oak puts on his gosling
grey, 'Tis time to sow barley, night
and day.* 1846 : Denham, *Proverbs*,
46 (Percy S.). 1893 : Inwards, *Weather
Lore*, 152. 1904 : *Co. Folk-Lore :
Northumb.*, 177 (F.L.S.).

See also **Ash** ; **Beech** ; **Good elm** ;
and **Grass** (7).

Oar in another's boat, To have (or
put) **an.** 1542 : Udall, tr. Erasmus'
Apoph., 203 (1877), Whatsoeuer came
in his foolyshe brain, Out it should,
wer it neuer so vain. In eche mans
bote would he haue an ore, But no
woorde, to good purpose, lesse or
more. 1551 : R. Crowley, *Works*, 120
(E.E.T.S.), You had an owre in echmans
barge. 1597: G. Harvey, *Works*, iii. 33
(Grosart), Those . . . that will . . . haue
an oare (as we say) in euerie mans
boate. 1630 : Brathwait, *Eng. Gent.*,
etc. 6 (1641), Youth . . . putting his
oare in every mans boat. 1712 : Motteux, *Quixote*, Pt. II. ch. xxii., He has
an oar in every man's boat, and a
finger in every pye. 1731 : Coffey,
Devil to Pay, I. ii., I will govern my
own house without your putting in an
oar. 1922 : Weyman, *Ovington's Bank*,
ch. xxxv., Then a pretty fool you
were to put your oar in !

Oath is better broken than kept, An
unlawful. 1670 : Ray, 126. 1672:
Walker, *Parœm.*, 46.

Oatmeal. *See* quot. 1678 : Ray, 352,
Where there is store of oatmeal, you
may put enough in the crock. *Somerset.*

Oats. *See* **Eel** (1) ; **Horse** (14) ; **January** (25) ; **May**, F (8) ; **St. David** (3) ;
Water (21) ; and **Wild** (7).

Occasion is bald behind. [Fronte capillata, post est occasio calva.— Cato, *Disticha*, ii. 26.] 1553 : *Respublica*, III. vi., The goddesse occasyon . . . behinde hathe not one heare. 1566 : Painter, *Pal. of Pleasure*, i. 266 (Jacobs), Occasion . . . being balde can not easely be gotten againe if she be once let slip. 1629 : Quarles, *Arg. and Parth.*, bk. i., in *Works*, iii. 246 (Grosart). 1634 : Massinger, *Guardian*, IV. i. 1655 : Heywood and Rowley, *Fortune by Land and Sea*, IV. i., Occasions head is bald behind.

Occasion lost cannot be redeemed, An. 1813 : Ray, 144.

October. 1. *Dry your barley land in October, Or you'll always be sober.* If not, there will be no malt. 1846 : Denham, *Proverbs*, 60 (Percy S.). 1893 : Inwards, *Weather Lore*, 35.

2. *Good October, a good blast, To blow the hog acorn and mast.* 1732 : Fuller, No. 6218. 1893 : Inwards, 35.

3. *In October dung your field, And your land its wealth shall yield.* Ibid., 36.

4. *Leaves in October. See* quots. c. 1630 : B. & F., *Bloody Brother*, II. ii., And he that will to bed go sober, Falls with the leaf, still in October. 1652 : in *Festive Songs*, 60 (Percy S.), Let him drink his small beer and be sober, Whilst we drink sack, and sing as if it were Spring, He shall drop like the leaves in October. 1854 : Doran, *Table Traits*, 335, There was an old adage that—He who goes to bed and goes to bed sober, Falls as the leaves do, and dies in October ; But he who goes to bed, and goes to bed mellow, Lives as he ought to do, and dies a good fellow. Cf. **Often drunk.**

5. *Much rain in October, much wind in December.* 1893 : Inwards, 35.

6. *There are always twenty-one fine days in October.* But the number appears to be variable. 1855 : Gaskell, *North and South*, ch. ii., And when the brilliant fourteen fine days of October came on, her cares were all blown away. 1871 : *N. & Q.*, 4th ser., viii. 505, It is an old saying that October always gives us twenty-one fine

days. 1881 : *Folk-Lore Record*, iv. 128, October always has twenty-one fine days. 1893 : Inwards, *Weather Lore*, 35, There are always nineteen fine days in October.—Kent.

7. *Warm October, cold February.* Ibid., 35.

Odd numbers. *See* **Luck** (5).

Odds in all things, There are. 1864 : " Cornish Proverbs," in *N. & Q.*, 3rd ser., vi. 494.

Odds in evil. 1633 : Draxe, 55, In euill there is ods. 1639 : Clarke, 197 [as in 1633].

Odds in gossips. 1797 : Wolcot, in *Works*, v. 44 (1801), " *There's odds in Gossips*," says an old adage.

Odds will beat anybody. 1666 : Torriano, *Piazza Univ.*, 320, The English say that odds will beat anybody.

Offender never pardons, The. 1640 : Herbert, *Jac. Prudentum.* Before 1680 : Butler, *Remains*, ii. 39 (1759), Bad men never use to forgive those whom they have injured, or received any extraordinary obligation from. 1732 : Fuller, No. 2393, He who is the offender, is never the forgiver.

Offer much, To. *See* quots. 1631 : Mabbe, *Celestina*, 116 (T.T.), It is a common saying ; To offer much to him that asketh but a little, is a kinde of deniall. 1666 : Torriano, *Piazza Univ.*, 176, To proffer much is a kind of denyal.

Offices may well be given, but not discretion. 1578 : Florio, *First Fruites*, fo. 33 [" are " for " may well be "]. 1629 : *Book of Meery Riddles*, Prov. 116.

Offspring of those that are very young or very old, lasts not, The. 1640 : Herbert, *Jac. Prudentum.* 1670: Ray, 19. 1748 : Richardson, *Clarissa*, iv. 121 (1785), The children of very young and very old men . . . last not long.

Off the hinges. 1611 : Cotgrave, s.v. " Hallebrené," Off the hindges, cleane out of heart. 1645 : Howell, *Letters*, bk. i. § iii. No. xxxi., All businesses here are off the hinges. 1661 : Webster and Rowley, *Cure for a Cuckold*, V. i., Bear with him, sir, he's strangely off o' th' hinges. 1828 : Carr, *Craven Dialect*, s.v. " Hinges," *To be off t' hinges*, to be out of health. 1894 : Northall,

Folk Phrases, 26 (E.D.S.), . . . = To be out of temper, or in bad spirits.

Off the hooks—used with various significations. *See* quots. 1621 : B. & F., *Pilgrim*, III. vi., What fit's this ? The pilgrim's off the hooks too! [mad, " off his head "]. 1635 : in *Somers Tracts*, vii. 188 (1811), If debts . . . fling not all off the hooks. 1639 : Davenport, *New Trick to cheat Devil*, I. ii., What, Roger, al amort, me thinkes th'art off o' th' hookes [crestfallen]. 1681 : Robertson, *Phraseol. Generalis*, 739, To be off the hooks, or out of humour. 1692 : L'Estrange, *Æsop*, Life, 8 (3rd ed.), Easily put off the hooks, and monstrous hard to be pleased again. 1740 : North, *Lives of Norths*, i. 377 (Bohn), He was continued in his office by King James II., but then he was soon off the hooks. 1824 : Scott, *Redgauntlet*, ch. i., Then this smart young hopeful is off the hooks with too hard study. 1881 : Evans, *Leics. Words*, 205 (E.D.S.), Off-the-hooks, or Off-of-the-hooks . . . shabby; " seedy "; worn-out; ailing. 1889 : Peacock, *Manley, etc., Gloss.*, 277 (E.D.S.), Maaster seems clear off th' hooks to-daay [ill, or in bad temper].

Oft craving makes soon forgetting. 1869 : Hazlitt, 301.

Often and little eating makes a man fat. 1670 : Ray, 38.

Often drunk, and seldom sober, Falls like the leaves in October. 1732 : Fuller, No. 6219. Cf. October (4).

Often happeth evil for a good turne. *c.* 1489 : Caxton, *Sonnes of Aymon*, 265 (E.E.T.S.) [quoted as a proverb].

Often to the water often to the tatter. Said of linen. 1678 : Ray, 347. 1732 : Fuller, No. 6378, Linnen often to water, Soon to tatter.

Oil, *subs.* 1. *He that measureth oil shall anoint his fingers.* 1611 : Cotgrave, s.v. " Huile " [" besmeares " for " shall anoint "]. 1670 : Ray, 126.

2. *The oil-bottle. See* quot. 1827 : Hone, *Table-Book*, 775, "He's got t' oil bottle in his pocket." *Craven*=he is double-faced.

3. *To bring* (or *add*) *oil to fire.* [Oleum adde camino.—Horace, *Sat.*,

II. iii. 321.] *c.* 1386 : Chaucer, *C. Tales*, C. 60 (Skeat), For wyne and youthë doon Venus encrese, As men in fyr wol casten oile or grece. *c.* 1560 : Ingelend, *Disob. Child*, in Hazlitt, *Old Plays*, ii. 280, And, after the proverb, we put oil to the fire. *c.* 1605 : Shakespeare, *Lear*, II. ii., Bring oil to fire, snow to their colder moods. 1647 : Cowley, *The Mistress:* " The Incurable, " st. 4, But wine, alas ! was oil to th' fire.

4. *To cast oil in the fire is not the way to quench it.* 1639 : Clarke, 167. 1670 : Ray, 126. 1732 : Fuller, No. 5142.

5. *To hold up oil*=To aid and abet, or consent flatteringly. [Narratur belle quidam dixisse, Marulle, Qui te ferre oleum dixit in auriculam.—Martial, *Epigr.*, V. lxxviii.] 1387 : Trevisa, tr. Higden, iii. 447 (Rolls Ser.), Alisaundre gan to boste and make him self more worthy than his fader, and a greet deel of hem [them] that were at the feste hilde up the kynges oyl. *c.* 1390 : Gower, *Conf. Amantis*, bk. vii. vol. iii. 159 (Pauli), For, when he doth extorcion, Men shall not finden one of tho To grueche or speke there agein, But holden up his oile and sain, That all is well that ever he doth.

6. *To pour oil on troubled waters.* 1855 : Kingsley, *West. Ho !*, ch. iv., Campion . . . the sweetest-natured of men, trying to pour oil on the troubled waters.

See also Truth (4).

Old, *adj.* Classification: A. Sayings relating to human life: (*a*) General, (*b*) Man, (*c*) Woman. B. Sayings relating to other living creatures. C. Sayings relating to books, friends, etc. D. Similes. E. Unclassified.

A. Sayings relating to Human Life.

(*a*) General. 1. *An old child sucks hard.* 1602–3: Manningham, *Diary*, 12 (Camden S.), . . . i.e. children when they growe to age proue chargeable.

2. *An old thief desires a new halter.* 1639 : Clarke, 299. 1670 : Ray, 127.

3. *Old age is sickness enough of itself.* 1672 : Walker, *Parœm.*, 33.

4. *Old and tough, young and tender.* 1678 : Ray, 85.

5. *Old be or young die.* Ibid., 182.
6. *Old heads and young hands.*
Somerset. Ibid., 347.

7. *Old heads on young shoulders.*
1639: Clarke, 7, You set .an old
mans head on a yong mans shoulders.
c. 1780: *First Floor*, II. i., in Inchbald's
Farces, vi. 243 (1815), Ah, sir, there
is no putting an old head on young
shoulders. 1850: Dickens, *Chuzzlewit*,
ch. xi., We should not expect to find
old heads upon young shoulders. 1906:
Lucas, *Listener's Lure*, 154.

8. *Though old and wise, yet still advise.*
1640: Herbert, *Jac. Prudentum*. 1670:
Ray, 1. 1732: Fuller, No. 6227. 1875:
Cheales, *Proverb. Folk-Lore*, 49.

9. *Where old age is evil, youth can
learn no good.* 1633: Draxe, 145
[" faultie " for " evil," and " goodnesse " for " good "]. 1670: Ray, 20.
1736: Bailey, *Dict.*, s.v. " Youth."

(*b*) **Man.** 1. *An old knave is no babe.*
1528: More, *Works*, p. 242, col. 1
(1557), They shal for al that well fynde
in some of us yt an olde knaue is no
chylde. 1546: Heywood, *Proverbs*, Pt.
II. ch. ii. [" childe " for " babe "].
1670: Ray, 20.

2. *An old man is a bed full of bones.*
1678: Ray, 184. 1732: Fuller, No.
648.

3. *An old man never wants a tale to
tell.* Ibid., No. 649.

4. *An old man's end is to keep sheep.*
1659: Howell, *Proverbs: Brit.-Eng.*, 2.
1823: D'Israeli, *Cur. of Lit.*, 2nd ser.,
i. 441 (1824), The state of our agricultural people appears in such proverbs as . . . " An old man's end is to
keep sheep " !

5. *An old man's staff is the rapper
at death's door.* 1640: Herbert, *Jac.
Prudentum* [" of " for " at "]. 1670:
Ray, 19. 1732: Fuller, No. 4690.

6. *An old man who weds a buxom
young maiden, biddeth fair to become a
freeman of Buckingham.* 1790: Grose,
Prov. Gloss., s.v. " Bucks."

7. *An old physician and a young
lawyer.* 1640: Herbert, *Jac. Prudentum.* 1670: Ray, 36. 1732: Fuller,
No. 652. 1875: Cheales, *Proverb. Folk-
Lore*, 75, An old physician and a young

lawyer, and confide in both with equal
frankness.

8. *An old soldier.* *See* quot. 1894:
R. L. S., *St. Ives*, ch. xx., I own
myself an idiot. Well do they say, *an
old soldier, an old innocent* !

9. *An old wise man's shadow is better
than a young buzzard's sword.* 1640:
Herbert, *Jac. Prudentum.*

10. *Better be an old man's darling
than a young man's warling.* 1546:
Heywood, *Proverbs*, Pt. II. ch. vii.
1602: Breton, *Works*, ii. g 12 (Grosart)
[" worldling " for " warling "]. 1611:
Barry, *Ram-Alley*, II. 1738: Swift,
Polite Convers., Dial. I. 1842: Harr.
Ainsworth, *Miser's Daughter*, bk. iii. ch.
xv. 1859: Planché, *Extravag.*, v. 206
(1879), Better be an old man's darling,
Than become a young man's slave.

11. *He that would be well old must be
old betimes.* [Nec enim unquam sum
assensus illi veteri laudatoque proverbio,
quod monet, mature fieri senem, si diu
velis esse senex.—P. Vergil, *Adag. Op.*,
67 (1541).] 1539: Taverner, *Proverbs*,
fo. 10, Become an olde man betyme yf
thou wylt be an olde man longe. 1583:
Melbancke, *Philotinus*, sig. C1, He that
will be an old man long, must bee an
old man soone. 1640: Herbert, *Jac.
Prudentum.* 1670: Ray, 34, (*a*) They
who would be young when they are
old must be old when they are young.
[Also] (*b*) Old young and old long.
1711: Steele, *Spectator*, No. 153, It
was prettily said, " He that would be
long an old man must begin early to
be one." 1732: Fuller, No. 6179 [as
in 1670 (*b*)]. Ibid., No. 854, Be old
betimes ; that thou may'st long be so.

12. *He wrongs not an old man that
steals his supper from him.* 1640:
Herbert, *Jac. Prudentum.* 1670: Ray,
19. 1732: Fuller, No. 2420.

13. *Old man, when thou diest give me
thy doublet.* 1678: Ray, 77.

14. *Old men and travellers may lie by
authority.* 1605: Camden, *Remains*, 330
(1870). 1681: Robertson, *Phraseol.
Generalis*, 947. 1732: Fuller, No. 3715.
Cf. **Painters and Poets**; and **Traveller**.

15. *Old men are twice children.* 1539:
Taverner, *Proverbs*, fo. 16, Olde folke

are twyse chyldren. 1549: Latimer, *Sec. Sermon*, 56 (Arber). 1588: Cogan, *Haven of Health*, 182 (1612). 1631: W. Saltonstall, *Picturæ Loquentes*, sig. B9, Though the proverbe be, once a man and twice a child. 1632: Randolph, *Jealous Lovers*, III. vi. 1707: Dunton, *Athenian Sport*, 389, Old men are said to be a second time children. 1825: Hone, *Ev. Day Book*, i., 19 Jan. [as in 1631].

16. *Old men go to death; death comes to young men.* 1640: Herbert, *Jac. Prudentum*. 1732: Fuller, No. 3719.

17. *Old men.* See these two quotations. The first is not very intelligible. 1640: Herbert, *Jac. Prudentum*, Old men, when they scorn young, make much of death. 1748: Richardson, *Clarissa*, iv. 121 (1785), Old men, when they marry young women, are said to make much of death.

18. *Old men will die and children soon forget.* c. 1567: in *Black Letter Ballads*, etc., 53 (Lilly, 1867), Bot as the prouerbe speikis, it plaine appeiris, Auld men will die and barnes will sone forget.

19. *When an old man will not drink, look for him in another world.* 1666: Torriano, *Piazza Univ.*, 298. 1670: Ray, 20 [" go to see " for " look for "]. 1732: Fuller, No. 5548, When an old man will not drink, you may safely promise him a visit in the next world. *See also* Young, *passim*.

(c) **Woman.** 1. *An old woman in a wooden ruff* [in an antique dress]. 1678: Ray, 77.

2. *He is teaching an old woman to dance.* 1813: Ray, 75.

3. *Old maids. See* Ape (12).

4. *Old maids' children. See* Bachelors (3).

5. *Old wife. See* Wife (15).

6. *Old wife's fair. Craven.* The second day of the fair. 1869: Hazlitt, 303.

7. *Old wives' tales.* 1387: Trevisa, tr. Higden, iii. 265 (Rolls Ser.), And vseþ telynges as olde wifes dooþ. 1509: Barclay, *Ship of Fools*, i. 72 (1874), A fole he is for his moste felycyte Is to byleue the tales of an olde wyfe. 1580: Lyly, *Euphues*, 347 (Arber),

Thinking euery olde wiues tale to be a truth. 1604: Marlowe, *Faustus*, sc. v., Tush; these are trifles, and mere old wives' tales. 1614: Rowlands, *Fooles Bolt*, 12 (Hunt. Cl.). 1672: Marvell, *Works*, iii. 39 (Grosart), Who will . . . tax up an old-wife's fable to the particularity of history. 1720: C. Shadwell, *Irish Hosp.*, Dram. Pers., *Lady Peevish* . . . a mighty observer of cross days, foolish superstitions, and old wives' sayings. 1860: Reade, *Cl. and Hearth*, ch. lxxiv., "These be old wives' fables," said Jerome contemptuously. 1921: Locke, *Mountebank*, ch. iv., Mine differed only in brevity from an old wife's tale.

8. *The old wives' Paternoster.* Query = the devil's Paternoster — *see* **Devil** (103). 1580: in H. G. Wright, *Arthur Hall of Grantham*, 63 (1919), He plucking his hatte about his cares, mumbling the olde wiues Paternoster, departed.

B. SAYINGS RELATING TO OTHER LIVING CREATURES.

1. *My old mare would have a new crupper.* 1546: Heywood, *Proverbs*, Pt. II. ch. i. 1578: Lupton, *All for Money*, sig. E1, Gylle my olde mare must haue a newe crupper. 1670: Ray, 19, Old mares lust after new cruppers.

2. *Old ape. See* Ape (4).

3. *Old birds and chaff. See* Bird (13).

4. *Old cat. See* Cat (7), (8), and (39).

5. *Old cattle breed not.* 1639: Clarke, 169. 1670: Ray, 127.

6. *Old cock. See* Young (17).

7. *Old dog. See* Dog (14)–(16), (19), (53), (60), and (93).

8. *Old foxes. See* Fox (2), (3), (13), and (19).

C. SAYINGS RELATING TO BOOKS, FRIENDS, ETC.

1. *An old friend is a new house.* 1640: Herbert, *Jac. Prudentum*.

2. *Old friends and old wine are best.* 1589: see quot. under No. 3. 1633: Draxe, 75. 1670: Ray, 19. 1736: Bailey, *Dict.*, s.v. " Old." 1884: A. Dobson, in *Poet. Works*, 387 (1923), All these I prize, but (*entre nous*) Old friends are best!

3. *Old wood to burn. See* quots. 1589: L. Wright, *Display of Dutie*,

19-20, As olde wood is best to burne ;
old horse to ride ; old bookes to reade ;
and old wine to drinke ; so are old
friends alwayes most trusty to vse.
1594: A. Copley, *Wits, Fits, etc.*, 4
(1614), Olde wood for fewell; an olde
horse for easie riding ; wine of a yeare
olde ; olde friendes, and olde bookes.
1773: Goldsmith, *She Stoops*, I. i., I
love everything that's old ! old friends,
old times, old manners, old books, old
wine. 1816: Scott, *Antiquary*, ch. vi.,
One who professes the maxim of King
Alphonso of Castile—old wood to burn
—old books to read—old wine to drink
—and old friends . . . to converse
with. Cf. E (11).

D. SIMILES. 1. *An old ewe dressed
lamb fashion.* 1777: *Gent. Mag.*, xlvii.
187, Here antique maids of sixty three
Drest out lamb-fashion you might
see. 1785: Grose, *Class. Dict. Vulgar
Tongue*, s.v. " Ewe," An old ewe drest
lamb fashion, an old woman drest like
a young girl. 1909: *N. & Q.*, 10th
ser., xii. 189.

2. *As old as Adam. c.* 1579: G.
Harvey, *Letter-Book*, 82 (Camden S.),
Yower newe complaynte . . . is nye as
owlde as Adam and Eve. 1662: in
Roxb. Ballads, iii. 578 (B.S.), If I had
as many lives I should be as old as
Adam. 1888: Lowsley, *Berks Gloss.*, 38
(E.D.S.), " As awld as Adam " is the
common phrase to denote great age
or antiquity.

3. *As old as Aldgate.* 1725: Defoe,
Tour, ii. 153, Aldgate was very ancient
and decay'd, so that *as old as Aldgate*
was a city proverb for many years.

4. *As old as Cale-hill.* 1639: Clarke,
171.

5. *As old as Charing Cross.* 1678:
Ray, 287.

6. *As old as Eggerton.* 1709: in
Stukeley Memoirs, ii. 124 (Surtees S.),
'Tis proverbial [Dorset] when they
would express what has a long time
been, to say, *'tis as old as Eggerton.*

7. *As old as Glastonbury tor.* Somerset. 1678: Ray, 344.

8. *As old as my tongue. See* quots.
1738: Swift, *Polite Convers.*, Dial. I.,
I am as old as my tongue, and a little

older than my teeth. 1828: Carr,
Craven Dialect, ii. 213, " As oud as my
tongue and ouder ner my teeth," a
saucy answer given to the question,
" how oud isto ? " 1862: *Dialect of
Leeds*, 379 [as in 1828]. 1889: J.
Nicholson, *Folk Speech E. Yorks*, 16, As
awd as mi tongue, an' a bit awdher
then mi teeth.

9. *As old as Pandon Gate.* 1649:
Grey, *Chorographia*, As old as Pandon.
1776: Stukeley, *Itin. Cur.*, cent. ii. 65,
It is an old proverb in this country
[Northumberland], " As old as Pandon
gate." 1847: Halliwell, *Dict.*, s.v.
" As old as Panton-Gates," a very
common proverb. There is a gate
called Pandon Gate at Newcastle on
Tyne. 1846-59: *Denham Tracts*, i. 300
(F.L.S.), As old as Pandon. As old as
Pandon Yatts. . . . The latter is used
in the southern portions of the Bishopric
[Durham] and the county of York. . . .
Nothing is more general than the above
saying, when any one would describe
the great antiquity of anything. Pan-
don Gate is believed to have been of
Roman workmanship.

10. *As old as Paul's. See* Paul's.

11. *As old as the hills.* 1820: Scott,
Monastery, ch. ix. 1850: Dickens,
Copperfield, ch. xv. 1924: *Sphere*,
30 Aug., p. 264, col. 1, The capital city,
Luxembourg . . . old as the hills.

12. *As old as the itch.* 1732: Fuller,
No. 722.

13. *To come the old soldier.* 1823:
Scott, *St. Ronan's*, ch. xviii., I should
think he was coming the old soldier
over me, and keeping up the game.

E. UNCLASSIFIED. 1. *An old band
is a captain's honour.* 1578: Florio,
First Fruites, fo. 28, An old ensigne is
the honor of a captaine. 1629: *Book
of Meery Riddles*, Prov. 65.

2. *An old nought will never be ought.*
1678: Ray, 184. 1732: Fuller, No.
6342.

3. *An old sack asketh much patching.*
1546: Heywood, *Proverbs*, Pt. II. ch.
ii. 1578: Lupton, *All for Money*, sig.
E1, When I was a boye it was an olde
saying, That an olde sacke would lacke
much clouting and patching. 1670:

Ray, 127. 1732 : Fuller, No. 3726, Old
sacks want much patching.

4. *An old thing and a young thing
both of an age.* 1917 : Bridge, *Cheshire
Proverbs*, 8, . . . Things must be considered old or young by comparison.

5. *An old wrinkle never wears out.*
1732 : Fuller, No. 654.

6. *Be off with the old love before you
are on with the new.* 1571 : R. Edwards, *Damon and Pithias*, in Hazlitt,
Old Plays, iv. 447, 'Tis good to be off
wi' the old love Before you are on wi'
the new. 1861 : Peacock, *Gryll Grange*,
ch. xxx. 1923 : Lucas, *Advisory Ben*,
§ xxxix. p. 210, That proverb about
being off with the old love is a very
sound one.

7. *Better keep under an old hedge,
than creep under a new furze-bush.*
1670 : Ray, 127. Cf. **Sheltering.**

8. *If the old year goes out like a lion,
the new year will come in like a lamb.*
1893 : Inwards, *Weather Lore*, 4.

9. *Old enough to lie without doors.*
1678 : Ray, 77.

10. *Old fish and young flesh do feed
men best.* 1546 : Heywood, *Proverbs*,
Pt. II. ch. iv. 1588 : Cogan, *Haven of
Health*, 118 (1612) [quoted as " that
English prouerbe "]. 1611 : Cotgrave,
s.v. " Chair," Young flesh and old
fish (are daintiest). 1666 : Torriano,
Piazza Univ., 39, Young flesh and old
fish. 1717 : Pope, *Jan. and May*, 102,
There goes a saying, and 'twas shrewdly
said, Old fish at table, but young flesh
in bed.

11. *Old fish, old oil and an old friend
are the best.* 1678 : Ray, 41. Cf. C.

12. *Old Johnny.* 1911 : A. S. Cooke,
Off Beaten Track in Sussex, 285, Ague
is also referred to in the phrase, " Old
Johnny has been running his fingers
down my back."

13. *Old lad. See* **Devil.**

14. *Old muckhills will bloom.* 1678 :
Ray, 77.

15. *Old porridge is sooner heated than
new made.* 1670: Ray, 47, Old pottage,
etc. 1732 : Fuller, No. 3724 [" warmed "
for " heated "]. Cf. **Broth** (3).

16. *Old praise dies unless you feed it.*
1640 : Herbert, *Jac. Prudentum.*

17. *Old reckonings make new quarrels.*
1611 : Cotgrave, s.v. " Dispute," Old
accompts breed new differences. 1732 :
Fuller, No. 3725.

18. *Old sin makes new shame.* c. 1300 :
Havelok, l. 2461. c. 1390 : Gower, *Conf.
Amantis*, bk. iii. l. 2033, Men sein,
" Old senne newe schame." c. 1470 :
Hardyng, *Chron.*, can. 114, st. 18, Thus
synnes olde make shames come ful
newe. 1578 : Florio, *First Fruites*, fo.
32, Old sinne and new penaunce. 1611 :
Cotgrave, s.v. " Honte," Old sinne
inflicts new shame. 1666 : Torriano,
Piazza Univ., 197, An old sin, new
repentance.

19. *Old sores are hardly cured.* 1509 :
Barclay, *Ship of Fools*, i. 164 (1874),
In olde sores is grettest ieopardye.
1670 : Ray, 19, It's ill healing an old
sore. 1732 : Fuller, No. 3727.

20. *Old thanks pay not for a new debt.*
Ibid., No. 3728.

21. *Old tree. See* **Remove.**

22. *Old vessels must leak.* 1666 :
Torriano, *Piazza Univ.*, 163. 1732 :
Fuller, No. 3729.

23. *Out of old fields comes new corn.*
c. 1390 : Chaucer, *Parl. of Foules*, l. 22,
For out of olde feldes, as men seith,
Cometh al this newe corn fro yeer to
yere.

24. *The old withy-tree would have a
new gate hung at it.* 1732 : Fuller, No.
4691.

25. *To bring an old house over one's
head* = To get into trouble. 1576 :
Gascoigne, in *Works*, ii. 548 (Cunliffe),
My boye (q⁴ he) who badd the be so
bolde, As for to plucke an olde house on
thy hedd ? 1607 : Dekker and Webster,
Westw. Hoe, V., Well do so . . . and
bring an old house ouer your heads if
you do. 1687 : Sedley, *Bellamira*, II.,
She may be a person of quality, and
you may bring an old house upon your
head. 1758–67 : Sterne, *Trist. Shandy*,
ii. ch. xvii., If, in our communion, sir, a
man was to insult an apostle . . . he
would have an old house over his head.
1907 : De Morgan, *Alice-for-Short*, ch.
xxxviii., Papa observes in an undertone
to Dr. Fludyer that he has brought an
old house about his ears.

26. *To throw an old shoe after one—*
for luck. 1546 : Heywood, *Proverbs*,
Pt. I. ch. ix., Nowe for good lucke, cast
an olde shoe after mee.   1621 : Brathwait, *Natures Embassie*, 204 (1877),
One should haue throwne an old shoo
after thee. 1665 : R. Howard, *Surprisal*, III. vii., I shall need nothing
now but an old shoe cast after me.
1754 : Berthelson, *Eng.-Danish Dict.*,
s.v. "Shoe." 1842 : Tennyson, *Will
Waterproof*, And, wheresoe'er thou
move, good luck Shall fling her old
shoe after.

Older the more covetous, The. 1655 :
Fuller, *Church Hist.*, bk. iv. § iii. (42).
1659 : in *Harl. Miscell.*, iv. 311 (1745).

Older the wiser, The. 1639 : Clarke,
267. 1683: White-Kennett, tr. Erasmus'
Praise of Folly, 17 (8th ed.), Contrary
to the proverb of *older and wiser*, the
more ancient they grow, the more fools
they are. 1707 : tr. Aleman's *Guzman*,
ii. 339, If I did not grow wiser as I grew
older.

Older the worse, The. 1639 : Clarke,
84, The older the worse, like my old
shooes. 1732 : Fuller, No. 4693, The
older a fool is, the worse he is.

Oldham. *See* quot. 1869: Hazlitt,
233, In Oldham brewis wet and warm,
and Rochdale puddings there's no
harm. Higson's *MSS. Coll.*, 212.

Olive. *Call me not an olive till thou
see me gathered.* 1640 : Herbert, *Jac.
Prudentum*.

Oliver's Mount. *See* quot. 1878 :
Folk-Lore Record, i. 169, When Oliver's
Mount puts on his hat, Scarborough
town will pay for that.

**Omelets are not made without
breaking of eggs.** Mr. A. B. Cheales,
in his *Proverbial Folk - Lore*, p. 131
(1875), fathers this saying on Robes-
pierre. 1859: Gen. P. Thompson, *Audi
Alt.*, II. xc. 65 (O.), We are walking
upon eggs, and whether we tread East
or tread West, the omelet will not be
made without the breaking of some.
1894 : R. L. S., *St. Ives*, ch. viii., " My
dear Miss Flora, you cannot make an
omelette without breaking eggs," said
I. 1922 : Weyman, *Ovington's Bank*,
ch. xix., But it could not be helped.

Without breaking eggs one could not
make omelettes.

Once a captain always a captain.
1831 : Peacock, *Crotchet Castle*, ch. ix.
1838 : Mrs. Bray, *Trad. of Devon*, iii.
239 [cited as " the old proverb "].

Once a knave and ever a knave. 1659 :
Howell, 6. 1672 : Walker, *Parœm.*, 49,
Once a knave and never an honest man.

Once a man twice a child. *See* Old,
A (*b*) (15).

Once a whore and ever a whore.
1613 : H. Parrot, *Laquei Ridiculosi*, bk.
ii. epi. 121. 1659 : Howell, 15. 1663 :
Killigrew, *Thomaso*, Pt. I. II. iv. 1670 :
Ray, 155. 1703 : in *Harl. Miscell.*,
v. 432 (1745). 1754 : *World*, No. 57.

Once a wood. *See* Pilling Moss.

**Once a year a man may say, On
his conscience.** 1640 : Herbert, *Jac.
Prudentum*.

Once an use and ever a custom.
1605 : Camden, *Remains*, 330 (1870).
1670: Ray, 153. 1732 : Fuller, No. 3733,
Once in use, and ever after a custom.

Once and use it not. 1678 : Ray, 263.

Once at a Coronation. Ibid., 263.

Once at a wedding. Ibid., 263 and
346, I never see't but once and that
was at a wedding.

Once bit twice shy. [1484 : Caxton,
Æsope, ii. 203 (Jacobs), And therfore he
that hath ben ones begyled by somme
other ought to kepe hym wel fro the
same.] 1894 : Northall, *Folk Phrases*,
20 (E.D.S.), Once bitten, twice shy.
1920 : Conrad, *The Rescue*, Pt. III.
ch. ix. 168.

**Once deceives is ever suspected, He
that.** 1640 : Herbert, *Jac. Prudentum*.

**Once done is never to be undone,
What is.** 1601: Yarington, *Two Trag. in
One*, I. iii., in Bullen, *Old Plays*, iv. 23,
Whats done already cannot be undone.
1609 : *Man in the Moone*, 41 (Percy S.),
That which is done cannot be undone. Before 1704 : T. Brown, *Works*,
i. 238 (1760). 1836: Marryat, *Easy*,
ch. xxxii., I felt much the same; but
what's done cannot be undone. Cf.
Thing (5).

Once in seven years. *See* quot.
1733 : Tull, *Horse-hoing Husb.*, Pref.,
v, Contrary to the proverb that says,

That once in seven years, the worst
husbands [farmers] have the best corn.
Once in ten years one man hath need
of another. 1578 : Florio, *First Fruites*,
fo. 33. 1666 : Torriano, *Piazza Univ.*,
26, Every ten years, one hath need of
another. 1732 : Fuller, No. 3732.
Once nought twice somewhat = A
first offence counts for nothing. 1889 :
Folk-Lore Journal, vii. 295, Once nowt,
twice summat.
Once out and always out. 1678 :
Ray, 77.
Once paid never craved. 1639 :
Clarke, 182. 1678 : Ray, 188.
Once poor. *See* quot. 1618 : W.
Lawson, *New Orchard and Garden*, 5
(1676), 'Tis with grounds in this case,
as it is with men . . . Much will have
more : and, *Once poor, seldome or never
rich*.
Once warned twice armed. 1581 :
T. Howell, *Devises*, 15 (1906). Cf.
Forewarned.
One and none is all one. 1670 : Ray,
20. Cf. One is no number.
One and thirty, He is = He is drunk.
1678 : Ray, 87.
One beats the bush. *See* Beat (5).
One beggar. *See* Beggar (11) and (12).
One body is no body. 1639 : Clarke,
44. Cf. One is no number.
One bush. *See* quots. 1583 : Melbancke, *Philotinus*, sig. L4, One bushe,
saith the prouerbe, can not harbour
two Robin redbreasts. 1586 : G. Whit-
ney, *Emblems*, 55, One groaue maie not
two redbreastes serue. Before 1634 :
Chapman, *Alphonsus*, I. i., Una arbusta
non alit duos erithraeos.
One business begets another. 1528 :
More, *Works*, p. 105, col. 1 (1557), It is
an olde said saw, that one busynes
begetteth and bryngeth forth another.
One cannot, another can, What.
1630 : Davenant, *Cruel Brother*, I.
One can't help many, but many can
help one. 1917 : Bridge, *Cheshire Proverbs*, 99.
One cherry tree. *See* Cherry (4).
One child. *See* quot. 1864: "Cornish Proverbs," in *N. & Q.*, 3rd ser.,
v. 209, With one child you may walk,
with two you may ride ; When you

have three at home you must bide. Cf.
Children (19).
One cloud is enough to eclipse all the
sun. 1732 : Fuller, No. 3743.
One coat, He that has, cannot lend it.
Ibid., No. 2135.
One day is sometimes better than
a whole year. [*c.* 1290: in Wright,
Pol. Songs John to Edw. II., 176
(Camden S.), Saepe dat una dies quod
totus denegat annus.] 1481 : Caxton,
Reynard, 66 (Arber), Oftymes one day
is better than somtyme an hole yere.
1631 : Mabbe, *Celestina*, 248 (T.T.), Of
more worth is one day of a wise man
then the whole life of a foole. 1846 :
Denham, *Proverbs*, 4 (Percy S.).
One day of pleasure is worth two of
sorrow. 1732 : Fuller, No. 3746.
One day of respite. *See* quot. *c.*
1534 : Berners, *Huon*, 128 (E.E.T.S.),
It is a common sayeng, one day of
respite is worth c. yere [of endurance].
One devil. *See* Devil (31).
One dog, one bull=fair play. 1879 :
Jackson, *Shropsh. Word-Book*, 309.
1883 : Burne, *Shropsh. Folk-Lore*, 447,
Only one dog was allowed to be
" loosed " on the bull at a time ; hence
arose a proverbial saying, " One dog,
one bull," i.e. fair play : now applied
in the Collieries to any kind of fight
or fray.
One door shuts, another opens, When.
1586 : D. Rowland, tr. *Lazarillo*, 32
(1924), This proverbe was fulfild, when
one doore is shut the other openeth.
1612 : Shelton, *Quixote*, Pt. I. bk. iii.
ch. vii., Where one door is shut another
is opened. 1710 : S. Palmer, *Moral
Essays on Proverbs*, 49. 1869 : Spurgeon, *John Ploughman*, ch. v., If one
door should be shut, God will open
another. 1921 : R. L. Gales, *Old-World
Essays*, 244.
One doth the scathe [harm], and
another hath the scorn. 1611 : Cotgrave, s.v. " Faire." 1670 : Ray, 20.
1732 : Fuller, No. 6344, One doth harm,
and another bears the blame.
One ear and out at the other, In at.
[Nec quae dicentur superfluent aures.—
Quintilian, II. v. 13.] *c.* 1374 : Chaucer,
Troylus, bk. iv. l. 434, But Troilus

. . . Tok litel hede of al that ever he
mente ; Oon ere it herde, at the other
out it wente. *c.* 1500: in Hazlitt, *Early
Pop. Poetry*, i. 229. 1552 : Latimer,
Works, ii. 87 (P.S.). *c.* 1610 : Harington, *Briefe View of Church*, 145 (1653).
1640 : *Ar't asleepe Husband?*, Frontis-
piece, But she might full as well her
lecture smother, For ent'ring one eare,
it goes out at t'other. 1750 : Smollett,
Gil Blas, iii. 182, A world of thanks,
which would only have entered at one
ear and gone out at the other, had he
not assured me . . . 1855 : Gaskell,
North and South, ch. xxviii. 1909 :
Hudson, *Afoot in England*, ch. xxii.

One enemy is too much. 1640 :
Herbert, *Jac. Prudentum*. 1855 : Bohn,
468, One enemy is too much for a man
in a great post, and a hundred friends
are too few.

One extreme produces another. 1748 :
Richardson, *Clarissa*, vi. 213 (1785).

One eye. 1. *Better to have one eye
than be blind altogether.* 1670 : Ray, 8.
1736 : Bailey, *Dict.*, s.v. " Better,"
Better one eye than quite blind.

2. *He that has but one eye, had need
look well to that.* 1611 : Cotgrave, s.v.
" Garder," He that hath but one eye
had need make much of it, had best
looke well to it. 1732 : Fuller, No.
2136.

3. *He that hath but one eye, sees the
better for it.* 1639 : Clarke, 44. 1639 :
Conceits, Clinches, etc., No. 113, Hee
that hath but one eye is more like to
hit the marke he aimes at then another,
because he hath a monstrous sight.
[This is a lame explanation of an absurd
saying.] 1678 : Ray, 134, . . . a ridiculous saying.

**One eye-witness is better than ten
ear - witnesses.** [Pluris est oculatus
testis unus quam auriti decem.—
Plautus, *Truc.*, II. vi. 8.] 1539 : Taverner, *Proverbs*, No. 43 [with " of more
value " for " better "]. 1582 : Robinson, tr. *Assertion of K. Arthur*, 39
(E.E.T.S.), Of more force standes eye
witnesse one, Than ten eare witnesses
among. 1681 : Robertson, *Phraseol.
Generalis*, 567. 1732 : Fuller, No. 3750
[" hearsays " for " ear-witnesses "].

**One fair day assureth not a good
summer.** 1548 : Hall, *Chron.*, 42 (1809).

**One fair day in winter makes not birds
merry.** 1640 : Herbert, *Jac. Prudentum*.

One false knave accuseth another.
1639 : Clarke, 79.

**One father is more than a hundred
schoolmasters.** 1640 : Herbert, *Jac.
Prudentum*.

**One fault (they say) doth but one
pardon need.** 1615 : Wither, *A Satyre*,
l. 720.

One favour qualifies for another.
1732 : Fuller, No. 3751. Cf. One kindness.

One flower makes no garland. 1640 :
Herbert, *Jac. Prudentum*. 1670 : Ray,
10.

One fool. *See* Fool (87) and (88).

One foot in the grave. [One foot
in Charon's boat.—Lucian, *Apol.*, i.]
1566 : Painter, *Pal. of Pleasure*, ii. 109
(Jacobs), To visite him, who hath one
of his feet alreadie within the graue.
1592 : Warner, *Albion's Eng.*, bk. ix.
ch. 47, Old doting foole, one foote in
graue. *c.* 1620 : B. & F., *Little Fr.
Lawyer*, I. i., You that already Have
one foot in the grave. 1694 : *Terence
made English*, 196. 1707 : *Spanish
Bawd*, III. i. 1822 : Peacock, *Maid
Marian*, ch. xiii., What, in the devil's
name, can you want with a young wife,
who have one foot in flannels, and the
other in the grave ?

**One foot in the straw, He that hath,
hath another in the spittle** [hospital].
1640 : Herbert, *Jac. Prudentum*.

One foot is better than two crutches.
Ibid.

One gate. *See* One Yate.

**One God, no more, but friends good
store.** 1639 : Clarke, 26. 1670 : Ray,
94. 1732 : Fuller, No. 6104.

**One good forewit is worth two after-
wits.** 1546 : Heywood, *Proverbs*, Pt. I.
ch. viii. 1633 : Draxe, 169.

**One good head is better than an
hundred strong hands.** 1732 : Fuller,
No. 3753.

**One good turn asks (or deserves,
or requires) another.** 1546 : Heywood,
Proverbs, Pt. I. ch. xi. [" asketh "].
c. 1610 : Rowlands, *More Knaues Yet?*,

17 (Hunt. Cl.) [" asketh "]. 1638 : Randolph, *Amyntas*, V. vi. [" deserves "].
1670 : Cotton, *Scarronides*, bk. iv.
[" requires "]. 1703 : Farquhar, *Twin-Rivals*, V. iii. 1777 : Murphy, *Know your own Mind*, I. 1818 : Scott, *Heart of Midl.*, ch. xxx. 1894 : R. L. S., *St. Ives*, ch. i. [the last four all have " deserves "]. Cf. **One shrewd turn.**

One good wife. *See* quots. 1620 : Shelton, *Quixote*, Pt. II. ch. xxii., It was an opinion of I know not what sage man, that there was but one good woman in the world, and his advice was, that every man should think, that was married, that his wife was she.
1707 : Dunton, *Athenian Sport*, 333, 'Tis a saying, there is but one good wife in the world, and every man enjoys her.
1738 : Swift, *Polite Convers.*, Dial. I., They say, that every married man should believe there's but one good wife in the world, and that's his own.
1869 : Spurgeon, *John Ploughman*, ch. xvii., If there is only one good wife in England, I am the man who put the ring on her finger. Cf. **One shrew;** and **One pretty child.**

One grain fills not a sack, but helps his fellows. 1640 : Herbert, *Jac. Prudentum.* 1659 : Howell, *Proverbs : Span.-Eng.*, 17.

One grief drives out another; and sorrow expelleth sorrow. 1631 : Mabbe, *Celestina*, 280 (T.T.).

One had as good be nibbled to death by ducks, or pecked to death by a hen. 1678 : Ray, 240.

One hair of a woman draws more than a team of oxen. 1591 : Florio, *Second Frutes*, 183, Ten teemes of oxen draw much lesse, Than doth one haire of Helens tresse. 1647 : Howell, *Letters*, bk. ii. No. iv., One hair of a woman can draw more than a hundred pair of oxen. 1712 : Pope, *Rape of Lock*, ii. 28, And beauty draws us with a single hair. 1732 : Fuller, No. 3757. 1928 : *Bystander*, 28 March, p. 624, col. 1, One hair of a woman can draw more than a hundred pair of oxen. Cf. **Beauty** (2).

One hand claweth another. 1567 : Jewel, *Defence of Apol.*, Pt. IV. 692 (P.S.), The proverb is common : " One hand claweth another." The Pope was advanced by Pipine ; and Pipine was likewise advanced by the Pope.

One hand washeth the other, and both the face. [Manus manum lavat.— Seneca, *Apoc.*, 9, *fin.*] 1578 : Florio, *First Fruites*, fo. 34. 1580 : Lyly, *Euphues*, 221 (Arber). 1607 : Middleton, *Phœnix*, I. i., 'Tis through the world, this hand will rub the other.
1640 : Herbert, *Jac. Prudentum.* 1732 : Fuller, No. 3759, One hand may wash the other, but both the face.

One hand will not clasp. 1875 : A. B. Cheales, *Proverb. Folk-Lore*, 91.

One head for the reckoning. *See* quot.
1573 : *New Custom*, III. i., I could have tarried longer there [at the tavern] with a good will, But, as the proverb saith, it is good to keep still One head for the reckoning, both sober and wise.

One hog. *See* quot. 1670 : Ray, 20, He who hath but one hog, makes him fat, and he who hath but one son makes him a fool. 1732 : Fuller, No. 2138 [as in 1670].

One honest man is worth two rogues. 1855 : Kingsley, *West. Ho !*, ch. xx.

One honest man scares twenty thieves.
c. 1770 : in *Roxb. Ballads*, vii. 645 (B.S.) [quoted as a " saying of old "].

One hour to-day is worth two to-morrow. 1732 : Fuller, No. 3761.

One hour's sleep. *See* Sleep, *subs.* (2).

One ill turn. *See* One shrewd turn.

One ill weed mars a whole pot of pottage. 1579 : Lyly, *Euphues*, 39 (Arber), One leafe of Colloquintida marreth and spoyleth the whole pot of porredge. 1605 : Camden, *Remains*, 329 (1870). 1606 : in *Antiq. Repertory*, i. 193 (1807), But last of all, to marre all the pottage with one filthy weede, to mar this good prayers with an il conclusion . . . 1670 : Ray, 154.

One ill word asks another. 1546 : Heywood, *Proverbs*, Pt. I. ch. ix. 1591 : Harington, *Orl. Furioso*, bk. xxvi. st. 77, Thus one ill word another doth draw on.
1670 : Ray, 30. 1685 : *Mother Bunch's Closet, etc.*, 15 (Gomme, 1885), One evil word brings in another.

One is a play, and two is a gay [toy].
1864 : " Cornish Proverbs," in *N. & Q.*,

3rd ser., v. 208. 1880 : Courtney, *W. Cornwall Words*, 24 (E.D.S.).

· **One is no number.** 1539 : Taverner, *Proverbs*, fo. 17, One man no man. 1586 : G. Whitney, *Emblems*, 66, The prouerbe saieth, one man is deemed none. 1598 : Marlowe, *Hero and L.*, sest. v., For one no number is. 1621 : Brathwait, *Natures Embassie*, 268 (1877), Number can ne're consist of lesse then two. 1681 : Robertson, *Phraseol. Generalis*, 953, One's as good as none. 1823 : Moor, *Suffolk Words*, 236, An old Norfolk and Suffolk saw may be given here—" One is none— tew is some—three is a sort—four is a mort [lot]." 1843 : Halliwell, *Nursery Rhymes*, 162, One's none ; Two's some, etc. Cf. **One and none;** and **One body.**

One is wise, two are happy, Where. 1710 : S. Palmer, *Moral Essays on Proverbs*, 338.

One kindness is the price of another. 1645 : Howell, *Letters*, bk. i. § ii. No. ix., Sir, Thanks for one courtesy is a good usher to bring on another. 1732 : Fuller, No. 3764. Cf. **One favour.**

One knock on the iron, and two on the anvil, He gives. Ibid., No. 1849.

One lie makes many. 1533 : Udall, *Flowers out of Terence*, fo. 25, One falshode or subtiltie bringeth in an other. 1732 : Fuller, No. 3766, One lie calls for many.

One lordship is worth all his manners. A punning saying—" manors." 1670 : Ray, 185.

One love expels another. 1666 : Torriano, *Piazza Univ.*, 10.

One man is worth a hundred and a hundred is not worth one. 1578 : Florio, *First Fruites*, fo. 32. 1629 : *Book of Meery Riddles*, Prov. 42.

One man's breath, another's death. 1639 : Clarke, 253. 1670 : Ray, 128. 1732 : Fuller, No. 6343 [with " is " after " breath "].

One man's fault is another man's lesson. 1855 : Bohn, 469.

One man's meat. *See* **Meat** (9).

One man's will is another man's wit. 1647 : *Countrym. New Commonwealth*, 14.

One mend - fault is worth twenty

spy-faults. 1882 : Mrs. Chamberlain, *W. Worcs. Words*, 39 (E.D.S.). 1901 : F. E. Taylor, *Lancs Sayings*, 9, One mend-fawt's wo'th a score o' find-fawts.

One month's cheer is better than a churl's whole life. 1546 : Heywood, *Proverbs*, Pt. II. ch. vii. 1633 : Draxe, 129.

One mouth doth nothing without another. 1640 : Herbert, *Jac. Prudentum.*

One mule scrubs another. [Mutuum muli scabant. — Auson., *Idyll.*, xii. Praef. monos.] 1638 : Randolph, *Muses' Looking-Glass*, III. iv. 1666 : Torriano, *Piazza Univ.*, 15, Asses scratch one another. 1738 : Swift, *Polite Convers.*, Dial. III., It looked like two asses scrubbing one another.

One nail drives out another. Before 1225 : *Ancren R.*, 404 (Morton), Vor, al so as on neil driueð ut þen oðerne . . . 1387 : Trevisa, tr. Higden (Rolls Ser.), vii. 25, þanne þe kyng drof out on nayle wiþ anoþer. *c.* 1570 : *Marr. of Wit and Science*, I., Much like the nail, that last came in, and drives the former out. 1607 : Tourneur, *Revenger's Trag.*, IV. i., Slaves are but nails to drive out one another. 1658 : R. Brome, *Love-sick Court*, V. i., Variety of objects Like nails abandon one another. 1725 : Bailey, tr. Erasmus' *Colloq.*, 492. 1781 : T. Francklin, *Lucian's Works*, ii. 136, And thus, according to the old adage, drive out one nail by another. 1852 : FitzGerald, *Polonius*, 129 (1903).

One of his hands is unwilling to wash the other for nothing. 1732 : Fuller, No. 3787.

One of these days is none of these days. 1855 : Bohn, 470.

One of those gentle ones, that will use the devil himself with courtesy. Ibid., 470.

One pair of ears draws dry a hundred tongues. 1640 : Herbert, *Jac. Prudentum.*

One pair of legs is worth two pairs of hands. *c.* 1565 : Still, *Gammer Gurton*, IV. ii., If one pair of legs had not bene worth two paire of hands . . . 1597 : Harvey, *Works*, iii. 52 (Grosart). 1600 : *Weakest goeth to the Wall*, I. ii. [" running " before "legs," and " working "

One   473   One

before "hands"]. 1611: Coryat, *Cru-
dities*, i. 35 (1905). 1688: in *Bagford
Ballads*, i. 375 (B.S.) ["heels" for
"legs"]. 1712: Motteux, *Quixote*, Pt.
II. ch. lxvii. [as in 1688]. 1817: Scott,
Rob Roy, ch. xxv., Take the bent, Mr.
Rashleigh. Make ae pair o' legs worth
twa pair o' hands.

One poison drives out another. 1567:
G. Fenton, *Bandello*, ii. 218 (T.T.).
1591: Harington, *Orl. Furioso*, bk.
xxv. st. 1, Ev'n as one poyson doth
another heale. 1659: Howell, *Proverbs: Brit.-Eng.*, 34, One poyson
expels another.

One pretty child. *See* quot. 1917:
Bridge, *Cheshire Proverbs*, 119, There's
only one pretty child in the world,
and every mother has it. *Cf.* **One good
wife; and One shrew.**

One saddle is enough for one horse.
1732: Fuller, No. 3791.

One shoe will not fit all feet. 1672:
Walker, *Parœm.*, 47, To make one shoe
serve for all feet. 1690: *New Dict.
Canting Crew*, sig. L2.

**One shoulder of mutton drives down
another.** 1611: Cotgrave, s.v. "Appe-
tit" ["drawes" for "drives"]. 1738:
Swift, *Polite Convers.*, Dial. II. 1811:
J. Austen, *Sense and Sens.*, ch. xxx.
1840: Barham, *Ing. Legends*, Introd.
to "Look at the Clock."

One shrew. *See* quots. 1528: More,
in *Works*, p. 233, col. 1 (1557), He sayth
plainly yt there is but one shrewde
wyfe in the worlde; but he sayth in
dede that eueri man weneth he hath
her. 1588: Cogan, *Haven of Health*,
252 (1612), Howbeit (as I haue heard
say) there is but one shrew in all the
world, but euery man thinketh he hath
yᵗ one. *Cf.* **One good wife; and One
pretty child.**

One shrewd turn asks another. 1509:
Barclay, *Ship of Fools*, ii. 38 (1874), One
yll turne requyreth another be thou
sure. 1591: Harington, *Orl. Furioso*,
bk. viii. st. 45, For one ill turne alone
is seldome done. 1602: Chamberlain,
Letters, 126 (Camden S.), One shrewd
turne seldome comes alone. 1732:
Fuller, No. 3794. *Cf.* **One good turn.**

One slumber invites another. 1611:

Cotgrave, s.v. "Attraire" ["drawes
on" for "invites"]. 1640: Herbert,
Jac. Prudentum ["finds" for "invites"]. 1670: Ray, 20.

One sows. *See* Sow, *verb* (10).

One's too few, three too many. 1678:
Ray, 342.

One stroke. *See* Oak (1).

One swallow. *See* Swallow.

**One sword keeps another in the
sheath.** 1640: Herbert, *Jac. Prudentum*. 1747: Franklin, in *Works*, ii. 57
(Bigelow), It is a wise and true saying,
that one sword often keeps another in
the scabbard. 1853: Trench, *Proverbs*,
88 (1905) [as in 1747].

One tainted sheep. *See* Sheep (10).

One tale is good till another is told.
[μηδὲ δίκην δικάσῃς πρὶν ἂν ἀμφοῖν μῦθον ἀκούσῃς.
—Cicero, *ad Att.*, vii. 18.] 1593: Greene,
Works, ii. 222 (Grosart), Tush syr quoth
the Marquesse, one tale is alwayes good
vntil another is heard. 1617: Taylor
(Water-Poet), *Works*, 3rd pagin., 83.
1662: Fuller, *Worthies*, ii. 125 (1840),
One story is good till another is heard.
1748: Richardson, *Clarissa*, vii. 314
(1785) [as in 1662]. 1827: Hone, *Ev.
Day Book*, ii. 649, "Every pot has two
handles." This means "that one story's
good till another story's told."

One thief robs another. *c.* 1510: A.
Barclay, *Egloges*, 46 (Spens. S.), It is
ill stealing from a thiefe. 1600: *Sir
John Oldcastle*, l. 1382 (Malone S.), Just
the prouerb, one thiefe robs another.
1681: Robertson, *Phraseol. Generalis*,
s.v. "Thief," One thief accuseth
another.

One to-day is worth two to-morrows.
1641: Quarles, *Enchyridion*, Cent. IV.,
C. xcv. 1736: Franklin, *Way to
Wealth*, in *Works*, i. 444 (Bigelow).
1875: Cheales, *Proverb. Folk-Lore*, 134,
One to-day is better than ten to-
morrows.

One tongue. *See* Woman (31).

One tongue and two ears (or eyes).
c. 1535: *Dialogues of Creatures*, cclvi.
(1816), To euery creature longith but
oon tonge and two erys; and so a man
shulde suffir more with his tway erys
than any man myght speke with oon
tonge. 1572: T. Wilson, *Disc. upon*

Usury, 211 (1925), You have twoe eares
and one tongue, because you shoulde
heare more than you speake. 1820 :
Colton, *Lacon*, Pt. I. No. 112, Men are
born with *two* eyes, but with *one* tongue,
in order that they should see twice as
much as they say.

**One trick needs another trick to back
it up.** 1732 : Fuller, No. 3801, One
trick needs a great many more to make
it good. 1880 : Spurgeon, *Ploughman's
Pictures*, 19.

**One, two, or three tell you, you are
an ass, put on a tail, If.** 1732 : Fuller,
No. 2697.

**One, two, three, four, are just half a
score.** 1678 : Ray, 86.

One vice. *See* quots. 1581 : B.
Rich, *Farewell*, 197 (Sh. S.), Like as we
saie, one vice spilles a greate noumber
of vertues. 1736 : Franklin, *Way to
Wealth*, in *Works*, i. 446 (Bigelow), What
maintains one vice, would bring up two
children.

One wedding begets another. *c.* 1640 :
in *Roxb. Ballads*, iii. 54 (B.S.), 'Tis said
that one wedding produceth another.
1713 : Gay, *Wife of Bath*, I.

One woodcock. *See* **Woodcock.**

One word for me and two for yourself.
1854 : Baker, *Northants Gloss.*, s.v.
" Word," . . . Said to one who is
selfish under an appearance of dis-
interestedness.

**One word in time than two after-
wards, Better.** 1659 : Howell, *Proverbs :
Brit.-Eng.*, 17. 1736 : Bailey, *Dict.*,
s.v. " Better."

**One yate [gate] for another, good
fellow.** 1678 : Ray, 263, They father
the original of this upon a passage between one of the earls of Rutland and
a country fellow. The earl, riding by
himself one day, overtook a countryman, who very civilly opened him the
first gate they came to, not knowing
who the earl was. When they came
to the next gate, the earl expecting
he should have done the same again,
Nay, soft, saith the countryman ; one
yate for another, good fellow.

**One year a nurse and seven years the
worse.** 1678 : Ray, 182. 1732 : Fuller, No. 6377.

One year of joy. *See* quot. 1678 :
Ray, 63, One year of joy, another of comfort, and all the rest of content. A marriage wish. 1732 : Fuller, No. 3806
[after " content "].—" make the married
life happy "]. 1869 : Spurgeon, *John
Ploughman*, ch. xvii. [as in 1678].

One year's seed seven years' weed.
1884 : H. Friend, *Flowers and Fl.
Lore*, 230, If we would keep our gardens
free from weeds . . . let us bear in
mind what a Northamptonshire peasant
recently told me in the following homely
but expressive rhyme, which still passes
current as a proverb :—" One year's
seed, Seven years' weed." Or, as they
give it in Oxfordshire : " One year's
seeding makes seven years' weeding."
1917 : Bridge, *Cheshire Proverbs*, 100.

Onion, It may serve with an. An
ironical saying. 1659 : Howell, 1.
1670 : Ray, 214.

**Onion's skin very thin, Mild winter
coming in ; Onion's skin thick and
tough, Coming winter cold and rough.**
A gardener's rhyme. 1893 : Inwards,
Weather Lore, 155.

Onion. *See also* **Capon** (2) ; **Garlic** (1) ;
and **Spruce.**

On the hip, To have one. *c.* 1400 :
Beryn, l. 1781, p. 55 (E.E.T.S.), So
within an houre or to, Beryn he had
i-caughte Somwhat oppon the hipp,
that Beryn had the wers. 1591 :
Harington, *Orl. Furioso*, bk. xlvi. st.
117, In fine he doth applie one speciall
drift, Which was to get the pagan
on the hippe. 1604 : Shakespeare,
Othello, II. i., I'll have our Michael
Cassio on the hip. 1681 : Robertson,
Phraseol. Generalis, 805, He has him
on the hip, at an advantage in Law.
1865 : Planché, *Extravag.*, v. 262
(1879), Now, infidel, I have thee on
the hip.

Open door may tempt a saint, An.
1659 : Howell, *Proverbs : Span.-Eng.*,
16, An open gate tempts a saint. 1732 :
Fuller, No. 655.

Opens the door with an ax, He. 1813 :
Ray, 75.

Opinion rules the world. 1615 : Markham, *Eng. House-wife*, 70 (1675), Yet
it is but opinion, and that must be

the worlds master alwayes. 1647 :
Howell, *Letters*, bk. ii. No. xxxix.,
Opinion can do much, and indeed she
is that great lady which rules the world.
Before 1680 : Butler, *Remains*, i. 241
(1759), Opinion governs all mankind.

Oppenshaw. *The constable of Oppenshaw sets beggars in stocks at Manchester.* 1678 : Ray, 301. 1790 : Grose,
Prov. Gloss., s.v. " Cheshire." 1917 :
Bridge, *Cheshire Proverbs*, 113.

Opportunity. *See* quot. 1660 :
Howell, *Parly of Beasts*, 72, Opportunity is the best moment in the whole
extension of time. 1869 : Hazlitt, 311,
Opportunity is the cream of time.

Opportunity is whoredom's bawd.
1605 : Camden, *Remains*, 329 (1870).

Opportunity makes the thief. *c.* 1220 :
Hali Meidenhad, 17 (E.E.T.S.), Man
seið þat eise makeð þeof. 1387 :
Trevisa, tr. Higden, vii. 379 (Rolls Ser.),
I see wel þat ese makeþ þe to synne.
c. 1440 : Anon., tr. Higden, vii. 379
(Rolls Ser.), Me thenke that oportunite
maketh a thefe. 1591 : Florio, *Second
Frutes*, 169, Opportunity makes a man
committ larcenie. 1611 : Cotgrave,
s.v. " Coffre." 1700 : T. Brown, etc.,
Scarron, ii. 182 (1892), Yet do I know
full well that opportunity makes a thief.
1754 : Berthelson, *Eng.-Danish Dict.*,
s.v. " Opportunity." 1834 7 : Southey,
Doctor, ch. cv., Opportunity, which
makes thieves, makes lovers also. 1925 :
Sphere, 14 Nov., p. 197, col. 1.

Orchard is his shambles, His. 1639 :
Clarke, 50.

Orts. *See* Make (20).

Ossing comes to bossing = Effort
leads to success. 15th cent. MS., Digby,
52, lf. 28, quoted in *N. & Q.*, 10th
ser., vii. 69, Ossyng comys to bossyng :
Vulgus opinatur quod postmodum veri-
ficatur. 1691 : Ray, *Words not Generally Used*, 58 (E.D.S.) [Cheshire].
1917 : Bridge, *Cheshire Proverbs*, 101.

Other people's fires. *See* quot. 1692 :
L'Estrange, *Æsop*, Life, 13 (3rd ed.),
There's an old saying ; *What have we
to do to quench other peoples fires?*
And I'll e'en keep myself clear of other
peoples matters.

Other side of the road always looks

cleanest, The. 1852 : FitzGerald, *Polonius*, 20 (1903).

**Ounce of debt will not pay a pound of
care, An.** 1599 : Porter, *Two Angry
Women*, in Hazlitt, *Old Plays*, vii. 308.

**Ounce of discretion is worth a pound
of learning, An.** 1630 : T. Adams,
Works, 91. 1670 : Ray, 79 [" wit "
for " learning "].

**Ounce of fortune is worth a pound
of forecast, An.** 1611 : Cotgrave, s.v.
" Sagesse," An ounce of luck excels a
pound of wit. 1732 : Fuller, No. 657.

**Ounce of good fortune is worth a
pound of discretion, An.** 1672 : Walker,
Parœm., 42.

**Ounce of mirth is worth a pound of
sorrow, An.** 1619 : B. Rich, *Irish
Hubbub*, 4, A little mirth (they say) is
worth a great deale of sorrow. 1734 :
Carey, *Chronon.*, II. iv.

**Ounce of mother-wit is worth a
pound of clergy [learning], An.** 1690 :
New Dict. Canting Crew, sig. C7. 1712 :
Addison, *Spectator*, No. 464, There is a
saying among the Scotch, that an ounce
of mother is worth a pound of clergy.
1827 : Hone, *Table-Book*, 285 [" learning " for " clergy "]. 1880 : A. Dobson, in *Poet. Works*, 444 (1923), This
was, as Hamlet says, " a hit " ; Clergy
was posed by Mother-wit.

**Ounce of prudence is worth a pound
of gold, An.** 1748 : Smollett, *Rod.
Random*, ch. xv.

**Ounce of state requires a pound of
gold, An.** 1629 : *Book of Meery Riddles*,
Prov. 26.

**Ounce of wit that's bought is worth a
pound that's taught, An.** 1732 : Fuller,
No. 6495. Cf. Wit (2) and (12).

Out at elbows. 1590 : Nashe, *Almond for a Parrot*, 26 (1846), Your witte
wilbe welny worn thredbare, and your
banquerout inuention cleane out at the
elbowes. 1685 : S. Wesley, *Maggots*,
To the Reader, Who knows but . . .
my stockings happen to be a little out
at elbows. 1700 : Ward, *London Spy*,
163 (1924), They are one day very
richly drest, and perhaps out at elbows
the next. 1828 : Carr, *Craven Dialect*,
i. 129, " Hee's gitten his land out
at elbows " ; that is, his estate is

mortgaged. 1875: Smiles, *Thrift*, 273,
He [Steele] died out at elbows on his
wife's little property in Wales.

Outface with a card of ten, To. *See*
1847 quot. Before 1529: Skelton,
Bowge of Courte, l. 315, Fyrste pycke a
quarell, and fall oute with hym then,
And soo outface hym with a carde of
ten. *c*. 1542: Brinklow, *Complaynt*,
45 (E.E.T.S.), Eyther he shal haue
fauor for his masters sake, or els bragg
it out with a carde of x. 1594:
Shakespeare, *Tam. of Shrew*, II., Yet I
have faced it with a card of ten. 1633:
Dux Grammaticus, quoted in *N. & Q.*, 5th
ser., viii. 165, I set very little or nought
by him that cannot face out his ware
with a card of ten. 1847: Halliwell,
Dict., s.v. "Face," Face. A term at
the game of Primero, to stand boldly
upon a card . . . Whence came the
phrase *to face it with a card of ten*, to
face anything out by sheer impudence.

**Out of debt grows rich, He that
gets.** 1611: Cotgrave, s.v. "Acquiter."
1657: Gurnall, *Christian in Armour*, Pt.
II. V. 15, ch. v. p. 129 (1679).

Out of debt out of danger. 1639:
Clarke, 82, Out of debt and deadly
danger. 1667: Peacham, *Worth of
Penny*, in Arber, *Garner*, vi. 256
(1883). 1710: S. Palmer, *Moral Essays
on Proverbs*, 132. 1869: Spurgeon,
John Ploughman, ch. xii.

Out of debt out of deadly sin. 1605:
Camden, *Remains*, 330 (1870).

Out of door out of debt. Somerset.
1678: Ray, 354, . . . Spoken of one
that pays not when once gone.

**Out of God's blessing into the warm
sun** = From better to worse. 1540:
Palsgrave, *Acolastus*, sig. H3, To leappe
out of the halle into the kytchyn, or out
of Chryst's blessynge in to a warme
sonné. 1546: Heywood, *Proverbs*, Pt.
II. ch. v. 1579: Lyly, *Euphues*, 196
(Arber), Therefore if thou wilt follow
my advice . . . than thou shalt come
out of a warme sunne into Gods blessing.
1593: G. Harvey, in *Works*, ii. 207
(Grosart), What reason hath Zeale to
fly from God's blessing into a warm
sunne. *c*. 1605: Shakespeare, *Lear*, II.
ii. [The editor of the "Temple" Shake-

speare notes on this passage: "Prof.
Skeat suggests to me that the proverb
refers to the haste of the congregation
to leave the shelter of the church, immediately after the priest's benediction,
running from God's blessing into the
warm sun. This explanation seems by
far the best that has been suggested."]
1642: Howell, *Forreine Travell*, 37
(Arber). 1712: Motteux, *Quixote*, Pt.
I. bk. iii. ch. iv. [Motteux takes the
saying to mean "out of the frying pan
into the fire"—but the earlier quotations show clearly that this is wrong.]
1846–59: *Denham Tracts*, i. 77 (F.L.S.).
[This gives the same misinterpretation
as in the 1712 reference.]

Out of gunshot. 1551: Robinson,
tr. *Utopia*, 26 (Arber),. Beyng them
selues in the meane season sauffe,
and as sayeth the prouerbe, oute of
all daunger of gonneshotte. 1672:
Walker, *Parœm.*, 25, Out of reach of
gunshot. 1678: Ray, 249.

Out of sight out of mind. *c*. 1270:
Prov. of Alfred, in *Old Eng. Miscell.* 134
(Morris, E.E.T.S.), For he that is ute
bi-loken [shut out = absent] he is inne
sone for-geten. *c*. 1320: in *Reliq.
Antiquæ*, i. 114 (1841), " Fer from eye,
fer from herte," Quoth Hendyng.
c. 1386: Chaucer, *Miller's Tale*, l. 206,
Ful sooth is this proverbe, it is no lye,
Men seyn right thus, " alwey the nye
slye Maketh the ferre leve to be looth."
1546: Heywood, *Proverbs*, Pt. I.
ch. iii. *c*. 1570: *Marr. of Wit and
Science*, V. i. 1697: Vanbrugh, *Esop*,
I. i. 1711: *Spectator*, No. 77. 1791:
Boswell, *Letters*, ii. 434 (Tinker). 1863:
Kingsley, *Water Babies*, ch. i. Cf.
Eye (19) ; **Long absent; and Seldom seen.**

Out of the North an ill comes forth.
1649: in *Harl. Miscell.*, vii. 199 (1746)
[quoted as " the old saying "].

**Out of the wood, Don't shout till you
are.** [μήπω μέγ' εἴπῃς πρὶν τελευτήσαντ' ἴδῃς.
—Sophocles, in Cicero, *ad Att.*, iv.
8 *a* 1.] 1792: D'Arblay, *Diary*, iii.
473 (1876), Mr. Windham says we
are not yet out of the wood, though
we see the path through it. 1840:
Barham, *Ing. Legends*, 1st ser.: "Spectre
of Tappington," There is a rustic

adage, which warns us against self-gratulation before we are quite "out of the wood." 1897: W. E. Norris, *Clarissa Furiosa,* ch. xliii., I should have told you so before this, only it was better not to shout until we were out of the wood. 1909: De Morgan, *Never can happen Again,* ch. xxviii., Marianne is greatly relieved. But we must not halloa before we are out of the wood.

Out of the world, as out of the fashion, As good. 1639: Clarke, 171. 1671: Head and Kirkman, *Eng. Rogue,* ii. 111, For out of the fashion, out of the world. 1694: Cibber, *Love's Last Shift,* II. 1752: Fielding, *Cov. Garden Journal,* No. 30. 1903: Ella F. Maitland, *Window in Chelsea,* 31, Better be out of the world than out of the fashion.

Outrun the constable, To. The quotations show the progress from a literal meaning of the phrase to the now current one = to run into debt. 1600: Kemp, *Nine Daies Wonder,* 15, I far'd like one that had . . . tride the use of his legs to out-run the constable. 1635: in *Somers Tracts,* vii. 204 (1811), If the gentleman be predominant, his running nagge will outrun the constable. 1694: *Terence made English,* 241, But we shou'dn't have out run the constable as the saying is. 1748: Smollett, *Rod. Random,* ch. xxiii., "How far have you over run the constable?" I told him that the debt amounted to eleven pounds. 1843: Planché, *Extravag.,* ii. 197 (1879), *Light (whispering),* Outran the constable; lived *fast,* you know.

Outshoot a man in his own bow, To. 1605: Bacon, *Adv. of Learning,* II. xxiii. 88 *b* (O.), I doubt not but learned men with meane experience, woulde . . . outshoote them in their owne bowe. 1639: Fuller, *Holy War,* bk. iv. ch. vi., Let us see if the Greek church may not outshoot her in her own bow. 1670: Ray, 188. 1732: Fuller, No. 5212.

Oven. 1. *He* (or *she*) *that has been in the oven knows where to look for son, daughter, etc.* This was a very common 16th- and 17th-century saying,

and was most frequently said of mother and daughter. 1520: W. de Worde, *Seven Wise Masters,* 40 (Gomme, 1885), But it appereth by a comyn proucrbe, he yᵗ is defectyve or culpable hymself in a synne, he iugeth euery man to be in the same, or elles yᵗ fader soughte neuer his sone in yᵉ ouen: but yf he had bin therin hymselfe. 1583: Greene, *Works,* ii. 16 (Grosart), They seeke others, where they have been hidde them selues. 1596: Nashe, *Works,* iii. 191 (Grosart), That meazild inuention of the good-wife my mothers finding her daughter in the ouen, where she would neuer have sought her, if she had not been there first her selfe: (a hackney prouerb in mens mouths euer since K. Lud was a little boy). 1605: Camden, *Remains,* 329 (1870), No woman seeks another in the oven which hath not before been there. 1678: Dryden, *Limberham,* III. ii. [an allusion to the saying in a passage too long to quote]. 1740: North, *Lives of Norths,* i. 146 (Bohn), For he, as they say, had been in the oven himself, and knew where to look for the pasty. 1785: Grose, *Class. Dict. Vulgar Tongue,* s.v. "Oven," The old woman would never have looked for her daughter in the oven, had she not been there herself. 1854: Baker, *Northants Gloss.,* s.v. "Oven," [as in 1785, *plus*] This proverb . . . is still in common use.

2. *It is time to set in when the oven comes to the dough.* 1678: Ray, 186. 1714: Ozell, *Molière,* iv. 206, Ho, ho! a coming girl! truly—It's time, etc. 1732: Fuller, No. 3020 [" bread " for " dough "].

3. *Like stopping an oven with butter.* 1917: Bridge, *Cheshire Proverbs,* 91.

See also Christmas (18).

Over, Cheshire. *See* quot. 1917: Bridge, *Cheshire Proverbs,* 57, For honours great and profits small The Mayor of Over beats them all. *See also* Altringham.

Over head and ears. [Ire praecipitem in lutum, per caputque pedesque.— Catullus, xvii. 9.] *c.* 1565: Still, *Gam. Gurton,* I. iii., And Gyb, our cat, in the milke pan she spied over head and eares. 1630: *Wine, Beere, Ale, etc.,* 36 (Hanford, 1915), Ouer head and eares in ale. 1679: Crowne, *Ambitious Statesman,* IV. ii., Must plunge his soul O'er head and ears betimes in wickedness. 1681: Robertson, *Phraseol. Generalis,* 434, He is in debt over head and ears. 1738: Swift, *Polite Convers.,* Dial. I., Over head and ears in love with some lady. 1831: Peacock, *Crotchet Castle,* ch. xvi., The plunge [into love] must have been very sudden, if you are already over head and ears. 1889: Gilbert, *Gondoliers,* II., I am over head and ears in love with somebody else. Cf. **Over shoes.**

Over-niceness may be under-niceness. 1748: Richardson, *Clarissa,* vi. 213 (1785).

Oversee workmen, Not to, is to leave them your purse open. 1732: Fuller, No. 3685. 1736: Franklin, *Way to Wealth,* in *Works,* i. 446 (Bigelow).

Over shoes, over boots. 1616: Breton, in *Works,* ii. *e* 6 (Grosart). 1616: Sharpham, *Cupid's Whirligig,* II., Ouer-shooes, ouer-bootes . . . now goe deeper euen. 1726: L. Welsted, *Dissemb. Wanton,* IV. i., Ho ! ho ! since she has heard of me, I'll over shoes, over boots. 1740: North, *Examen,* 218, The faction was engaged, over shoes, over boots, and must flounce through. 1824: Scott, *Redgauntlet,* Lett. XIII., Never mind the Court of the Gentiles, man . . . we will have you into the Sanctuary at once . . . over shoes, over boots. Cf. **Over head and ears.**

Overtakes at last who tires not, He. 1736: Bailey, *Dict.,* s.v. "Overtake."

Over the coals, To fetch (or **haul**) = To rebuke. 1580: *The Bee Hive of the Romish Church . . . wherein the Catholike Religion is substantially confirmed, and the Heretikes finely fetch'd ouer the coales* [title]. 1639: Fuller, *Holy War,* bk. v. ch. ii., If they should say the Templars were burned wrongfully, they may be fetched over the coals themselves for charging his Holinesse so deeply. 1691: *Merry Drollery,* 228 (Ebsworth). 1818: Byron, *Beppo,* st. iv., They'd haul you o'er the coals. 1825: Brockett, *Gloss. of N.-Country*

Words, 43, To call over the coals, is to give a severe reprimand. Supposed to refer to the ordeal by fire. 1834: Marryat, *P. Simple,* ch. xiii., The captain had been hauling him over the coals for not carrying on the duty according to his satisfaction.

Over the fire-stones. S. Devon. i.e. to prison. 1869: Hazlitt, 312.

Over the shoulder, or **Over the left shoulder.** 1611: Cotgrave, s.v. "Espaule," Over the shoulder, or the wrong way. 1659: Howell, 17, I have gott it ore the left shoulder. 1670: Ray, 177, To get over the shoulders. 1681: Robertson, *Phraseol. Generalis,* 655, He gains over the left shoulder ; i.e. his gain is mischief. *c.* 1750: in Peck, *Desid. Curiosa* 233 (1779), The face of Bacchus, as I have been informed, is very like a certain, *quondam* dean ; for whom Verrio [the painter of the Bacchus], they say, had a respect over the left shoulder. 1841: Hartshorne, *Salopia Ant.,* 525, Over the left . . . a metaphor by which one who speaks by figure is reproved . . . "Ah ! that's over the left." 1889: Peacock, *Manley, etc., Gloss.,* 384 (E.D.S.), Over the left. In debt.

Ovington Edge. *See* quot. 1846–59: *Denham Tracts,* i. 86 (F.L.S.), Ovington Edge and Cockfield Fell Are the coldest spots 'twixt Heaven and Hell. Ovington is a village near Greta Bridge, in Yorkshire. Cockfield is near Staindrop, in the bishoprick of Durham. They are both lofty and extremely exposed places.

Owe, verb. 1. *He that owes nothing, if he makes not mouths at us, is courteous.* 1640: Herbert, *Jac. Prudentum.*

2. *He who oweth is in all* [? all in] *the wrong.* 1732: Fuller, No. 2398.

3. *I owe God a death.* 1597: Shakespeare, 1 *Henry IV.,* V. i., Why, thou owest God a death. 1655: Heywood and W. Rowley, *Fortune by Land and Sea,* I. i., He owed a death, and he hath payed that debt. 1681: Robertson, *Phraseol. Generalis,* 969.

Owl and Owls. 1. *An owl is the king of the night.* 1633: Draxe, 69. 1639: Clarke, 1.

2. *He lives too close to the wood to be frightened by owls.* 1864 : " Cornish Proverbs," in *N. & Q.*, 3rd ser., vi. 494. 1883 : Burne, *Shropsh. Folk-Lore*, 589. 1886 : Elworthy, *West Som. Word-Book*, 549 (E.D.S.), Another very common saying now become literary is . . . I live too near the wood to be frightened by an owl.

3. *Like an owl in an ivy bush.* 1606 : Day, *Ile of Gulls*, V., How say you, my lady ? what oule sings out of that ivy bush ? 1700 : T. Brown, in *Works*, iii. 2 (1760), You know that man was made for business, and not to set amusing himself like an owl in an ivy-bush. 1738 : Swift, *Polite Convers.*, Dial. I. c. 1780 : in *Poems on Costume*, 245 (Percy S.), When your hair's finely dress'd, I plainly do see, You look like an owl in an old ivy-tree. 1891 : Q.-Couch, *Noughts and Crosses*, 76. 1900 : *N. & Q.*, 9th ser., vi. 397, " Like an owl in an ivy bush " is a proverbial saying in North Lincolnshire.

4. *The owl flies.* See quot. 1683 : White-Kennett, tr. Erasmus' *Praise of Folly*, 135 (8th ed.), There is also another favourable proverb, *The owl flies, an omen of success.*

5. *The owl is not accounted the wiser for living retiredly.* 1732 : Fuller, No. 4697. 1886 : Swainson, *Folk-Lore of Brit. Birds*, 125 (F.L.S.).

6. *The owl thinks all her young ones beauties.* c. 1580 : U. Fulwell, *Ars Adulandi*, sig. D3, The oule thought her owne birdes fairest. 1732 : Fuller, No. 4698. 1886 : Swainson, *Folk-Lore of Brit. Birds*, 125 (F.L.S.).

7. *The owl was a baker's daughter.* 1602 : Shakespeare, *Hamlet*, IV. v., They say the, etc.

8. *They have need of a bird, that will give a groat for an owl.* c. 1685 : in *Roxb. Ballads*, iv. 72 (B.S.).

9. *To bring owls to Athens*=" Coals to Newcastle." [γλαῦκ' εἰς 'Αθήνας.— Aristophanes, *Av.*, 301.] 1583 : Melbancke, *Philotinus*, sig. L3, Thy exhortation . . . is as if thou shouldest bring owles to Athens. 1591 : Harington, *Orl. Furioso*, bk. xl. st. 1, To beare pots (as they say) to Samos Ile. . . . Or owls to Athens, crocodils to Nyle. 1600 : F. Thynne, *Embl. and Epigr.*, 3 (E.E.T.S.), Therfore in vaine for mee to bring owles to Athens, or add water to the large sea of your rare lerning. 1693 : Hacket, *Life of Williams*, i. 217. 1704 : *Gent. Instructed*, 545 (1732). 1732 : Fuller, No. 5866.

10. *To walk by owl-light* = To fear arrest. 1659 : Howell, 10. 1670 : Ray, 214.

11. *When owls whoop much at night, expect a fair morrow.* 1886 : Swainson, *Folk-Lore of Brit. Birds*, 123 (F.L.S.) [cited as a Sussex saying].

See also Ass (3); **Drunk ; Grave ;** and **Poor** (12).

Own is own. c. 1320 : in *Reliq. Antiquæ*, i. 114 (1841), " Owen ys owen, and other mennes edneth," Quoth Hendyng. 1546 : Heywood, *Proverbs*, Pt. II. ch. iv , For alwaie owne is owne, at the recknynges eend. 1602 : Marston, *Antonios Revenge*, II. ii., Loose fortunes rags are lost ; my owne's my owne. 1646 : Quarles, *Works*, i. 72 (Grosart). 1659 : Howell, 7.

Ox and Oxen. 1. *A lazy ox is little better for the goad.* 1732 : Fuller, No. 236.

2. *A long ox and a short horse.* Ibid., No. 257.

3. *An old ox makes a straight furrow.* 1659 : Howell, *Proverbs: Span.-Eng.*, 9, The old ox makes the streightest furrow. 1732 : Fuller, No. 650.

4. *An old ox will find a shelter for himself.* Ibid., No. 651.

5. *An ox is taken by the horns, and a man by the tongue.* 1611 : Cotgrave, s.v. " Homme," An oxe (is bound) by the horne, a man by his word. 1640 : Herbert, *Jac. Prudentum.* 1659 : Howell, *Proverbs: Span.-Eng.*, 5, Take a bull by the horn, and a man by his word.

6. *Seldom dieth the ox that weepeth for the cock.* Before 1500 : in Hill, *Commonplace-Book*, 133 (E.E.T.S.).

7. *Take heed of an ox before, of a horse behind, of a monk on all sides.* 1640 : Herbert, *Jac. Prudentum.* 1670 : Ray, 20 [" asse " for " horse "]. 1736 : Bailey, *Dict.*, s.v. " Ox " [as in 1670].

1875 : Cheales, *Proverb. Folk - Lore*, 77.

8. *The ox is never wo till he to the harrow go.* 1523 : Fitzherbert, *Husb.*, 24 (E.D.S.) [quoted as " an olde saying "].

9. *The ox when weariest treads surest.* 1539 : Taverner, *Proverbs*, fo. 3, An olde beaten oxe fastenethe hys fote the stronger. 1611 : Cotgrave, s.v. " Bœuf," The weary oxe goes slowly. 1650 : Taylor, *Holy Living*, ch. ii. § 6, The ox, when he is weary, treads surest. 1678 : Ray, 186. 1732 : Fuller, No. 4699.

10. *To swallow an ox and be choked with the tail.* 1659 : Howell, 6. 1670 : Ray, 194. 1732 : Fuller, No. 5238.

11. *Where shall the ox go but he must labour?* 1631 : Mabbe, *Celestina*, 78 (T.T.), Which way shall the oxe goe, but he must needs plough ? 1670 : Ray, 20. 1732 : Fuller, No. 5657.

See also **Black** (24) ; **Build** (1) ; **Lamb** (2) ; **Plough**, *subs.* (5), *verb* (8) and (9) ; **St. Jude** ; and **Sow**, *subs.* (5), *verb* (7).

Oxford. 1. *Oxford for learning, London for wit, Hull for women, and York for a tit.* 1869 : Hazlitt, 312.

2. *Oxford knives, London wives.* 1659 : Howell, 21. 1670 : Ray, 257. 1790 : Grose, *Prov. Gloss.*, s.v. " Oxfordshire."

3. *Send verdingales* [farthingales] *to Broad-gates, Oxford.* 1562 : Heywood, *Epigr.*, 5th hund., No. 55, Alas poore verdingales must lie in the streete : To house them, no doore the citee made meete Syns at our narow doores they in can not win, Send them to Oxforde, at Brodegates to get in. 1662 : Fuller, *Worthies*, iii. 7 (1840). 1790 : Grose, *Prov. Gloss.*, s.v. " Oxfordshire." 1834 : W. Toone, *Gloss.*, s.v. " Farthingale," They [farthingales, *c.* 1600] were so preposterously large, as to give rise to a proverb—" send fardingales to Broadgates (in Oxford)," for the wearers could not enter an ordinary sized doorway except sideways.

4. *Testons are gone to Oxford, to study in Brazen-nose.* 1562 : Heywood, *Epigr.*, 5th hund., No. 63. 1662 : Fuller, *Worthies*, iii. 6 (1840), . . . This proverb began about the end of the

reign of King Henry the Eighth, and happily ended about the middle of the reign of Queen Elizabeth. [A teston= a shilling of Henry VIII.] 1790 : Grose, *Prov. Gloss.*, s.v. " Oxfordshire." 1823 : D'Israeli, *Cur. of Lit.*, 2nd ser., i. 462 (1824).

5. *When Oxford scholars fall to fight.* See quot. 1662 : Fuller, *Worthies*, iii. 8 (1840), Mark the chronicles aright, When Oxford scholars fall to fight, Before many months expir'd, England will with war be fir'd. 1790 : Grose, *Prov. Gloss.*, s.v. " Oxfordshire."

Oyster. 1. *He opens an oyster with a dagger.* 1732 : Fuller, No. 2001. Cf. **Northampton** (2).

2. *Oysters are a cruel meat.* See quots. 1611 : *Tarltons Jests*, 6 (Sh. S.), They [oysters] are ungodly, because they are eaten without grace ; uncharitable, because they leave nought but shells ; and unprofitable, because they must swim in wine. 1738 : Swift, *Polite Convers.*, Dial. II., They say, oysters are a cruel meat, because we eat them alive. Then they are an uncharitable meat, for we leave nothing to the poor ; and they are an ungodly meat, because we never say grace.

3. *Oysters are not good in the month that has not an R in it.* 1599 : Buttes, *Dyets Dry Dinner*, sig. N1, The oyster . . . is vnseasonable and vnwholesome in all moneths that haue not the letter R in their name. 1600 : W. Vaughan, *Directions for Health*, 22, Oisters . . . must not bee eaten in those monethes, which in pronouncing wante the letter R. 1655 : T. Muffett, *Healths Improvement*, 46, Oisters in all months in whose name an R is found. 1737 : Ray, 273, Oysters are not good in a month that hath not an R in it. 1868 : *Quart. Review*, cxxv. 251, What epicure would act in contravention of the adage that " Oysters [as in 1737] ? "

4. *Oysters would be profitable food if the servants could eat the orts* [shells]. 1883 : Burne, *Shropsh. Folk-Lore*, 590.

5. *The oyster is a gentle thing, and will not come unless you sing.* 1869 : Hazlitt, 381.

See also **Apple** (5) ; and **St. James** (3).

P

P's and Q's, To mind one's. 1602 :
Dekker, *Satiro-mastix*, in *Works*, i. 211,
(1873), For now thou art in thy Pee
and Kue. 1612 : Rowlands, *Knave of
Hearts*, 20 (Hunt. Cl.), Bring in a quart
of Maligo right true : And looke, you
rogue, that it be *Pee* and *Kew*. 1779 :
Mrs. Cowley, *Who's the Dupe?*, I. ii., You
must mind your P's and your Q's with
him, I can tell you. 1801 : Mrs. Piozzi,
in Hayward *Autobiog.*, *etc.*, *of Mrs.
Piozzi*, ii. 253 (2nd ed.), I used to tell
the borough folks who kept our books,
they must *mind their p's and q's*. 1825 :
Brockett, *Gloss. of N. Country Words*,
167, P's and Q's . . . perhaps from a
French injunction to make proper
obeisances, " Soyez attentifs à vos pies
et vos cues." 1842 : Barham, *Ing.
Legends*, 2nd ser.: " Lay of St. Aloys."
1885 : Pinero, *Magistrate*, I. 1909 : De
Morgan, *Never can happen Again*, ch.
xxxii., And then the Rector had to
mind his *p's* and *q's*. For he hadn't so
much as thought of the text he should
preach on.

Paced like an alderman, He is. 1583 :
Melbancke, *Philotinus*, sig. I4, Vsing an
aldermans pace before he can wel gauge.
1611 : Cotgrave, s.v. " Abbé," Alderman's pace, a leasurely walking, slow
gate. 1639 : Clarke, 32. 1685 : S.
Wesley, *Maggots*, 1, And struts . . . as
goodly as any alderman. 1754 : Berthelson, *Eng.-Danish Dict.*, s.v. " Alderman," To walk an Aldermans pace.

Pad in the straw, A. 1530 : Palsgrave, 595, There is a padde in the
strawe. 1575 : Still, *Gam. Gurton*, V.
ii., Ye perceive by this lingering there
is a pad in the straw. 1616 : Haughton,
Englishm. for my Money, V. ii., Yet take
heed, wench, there lies a pad in straw.
1650 : Fuller, *Pisgah Sight*, bk. iii. ch.
iv. § 8, *Latet anguis in herba*, " there is
a pad in the straw." 1737 : Ray, 61.
1847 : Halliwell, *Dict.*, s.v. *A pad in*

the straw, something wrong, a screw
loose. . . . Still in use.

Paddington Fair. *See* quots. 1690 :
New Dict. Canting Crew, sig. I2, Paddington Fair, an execution of malefac-
tors at Tyburn. 1793 : Grose, *Olio*, 232
(2nd ed.), Of those advent'rous youths,
who make their exit At fair of Paddington. 1898 : Weyman, *Shrewsbury*, ch.
xlii., Send her packing, and see she
takes naught of mine, not a pinner or
a sleeve, or she goes to Paddington fair
for it !

Padstow, The Good Fellowship of.
1602 : Carew, *Surv. of Cornwall*, 220
(1811), Some of the idle disposed
Cornishmen nick their towns with by-
words, as " The good fellowship of Padstow." 1864 : " Cornish Proverbs," in
N. & Q., 3rd ser., v. 275.

Padstow Point. *See* quot. 1870 :
Hawker, *Footprints of Former Men*, 213,
From Padstow Point to Lundy Light,
Is a watery grave by day or night.
1897 : Norway, *H. and B. in Devon*, *etc.*,
342 [" Hartland " for " Lundy "].

Padwell. *See* quot. 1851 : Stern-
berg, *Dialect*, *etc.*, *of Northants*, 190, If
we can Padwell overgoe, and Horestone
we can see, Then Lords of England we
shall be.

Page of your own age, Make a = Do
it yourself. 1633 : Draxe, 30, Let him
make a page of his age. 1670 : Ray,
189. 1738 : Swift, *Polite Convers.*,
Dial. I.

Pain is forgotten where gain follows.
1605 : Camden, *Remains*, 330 (1870).
1670 : Ray, 129. 1732 : Fuller, No.
3836.

Pain past is pleasure. 1567 : G.
Fenton, *Bandello*, i. 4 (T.T.), The remembrance of the paine that is past
is sweete. 1732 : Fuller, No. 3838.
1869 : Spurgeon, *John Ploughman*, ch.
v., Pain past is pleasure, and experience
comes by it.

Pains are the wages of ill pleasures.
1732 : Fuller, No. 3839.

Pains be a pleasure to you, If, profit
will follow. Ibid., No. 2699.

Pains is the price that God putteth
upon all things. 1659 : Howell, 19.

Pains to get, care to keep, fear to lose.
1633 : Draxe, 181, There is paine in
getting, care in keeping, and griefe in
losing riches. 1640 : Herbert, *Jac.
Prudentum.* 1763 : Murphy, *Citizen*,
I. ii.

Painted pictures are dead speakers.
1616 : Breton, in *Works* ii. *e* 5 (Grosart).
1670 : Ray, 131.

Painted sheath. *See* Leaden sword.

Painters and Poets may lie by authority. 1591 : Harington, *Apol. of Poetrie*,
par. 3, According to that old verse . . .
Astronomers, painters, and poets may
lye by authoritie. 1618 : Harington,
Epigrams, bk. ii. No. 88, Besides, we
poets lie by good authoritie. 1650 :
R. Heath, *Epigrams*, 35, Poets and
painters by authoritie As wel as travellers we say may lie. 1681 : Robertson, *Phraseol. Generalis*, 1003. 1736 :
Bailey, *Dict.*, s.v. "Poets," Poets and
painters lye with license. Cf. Old, A (*b*)
(14) ; and **Traveller** (1).

Painting and fighting, On, look aloof.
1640 : Herbert, *Jac. Prudentum.* 1670 :
Ray, 20.

Pair of shears. *See* Shears.

Paises its pasture, It = It does credit
to its food. Said of a child. 1917 :
Bridge, *Cheshire Proverbs*, 80.

Pale as ashes. *c.* 1385 : Chaucer, *Leg.
Good Women*, ix. l. 88, Deed wex her
hewe, and lyk as ash to sene. *c.* 1386 :
Chaucer, *Knight's Tale*, l. 506, His
hewe salow, and pale as asshen colde.
c. 1477 : Caxton, *Jason*, 156 (E.E.T.S.),
He . . . after becam pale and dede as
asshes. *c.* 1490 : *Partonope*, l. 10166
(E.E.T.S.). 1567 : *Merry Tales, etc.*,
No. 48, p. 64 (Hazlitt). 1607 : *Conceits of Old Hobson*, 30 (Percy S.), As
pale as ashes for feare. 1758–67 :
Sterne, *Trist. Shandy*, ii. ch. xix., Seeing her turn as pale as ashes at the
very mention of it. 1817 : Byron,
Letters, etc., iv. 51 (Prothero). 1870 :
Dickens, *Drood*, ch. x., He was still

as pale as gentlemanly ashes at what
had taken place in his rooms.

Pale as clay. *c.* 1600 : in Collier,
Roxb. Ballads, 328 (1847), His face was
pale as any clay. 1813 : Scott, *Rokeby*,
V. xxvii., He looks pale as clay. 1893 :
R. L. S., *Letters*, v. 11 (Tusitala ed.),
He was . . . as pale as clay, and
walked leaning on a stick.

Pale as death. 1567 : Painter, *Pal.
of Pleasure*, iii. 9 (Jacobs), The colour
whereof is more pale than death. 1602 :
Chettle, *Hoffman*, I. i., Desert looks
pale as death. 1700 : T. Brown, etc.,
Scarron, i. 214 (1892), He gave a great
shriek, turned pale as death . . . 1751 :
Fielding, *Amelia*, bk. vii. ch. i. 1815 :
Scott, *Mannering*, ch. xxxv., Lucy . . .
turned as pale as death. 1886 : Hardy,
Casterbridge, ch. xxxix., "'Tis me !" she
said, with a face pale as death.

Palm Sunday. *See* quot. 1846 :
Denham, *Proverbs*, 33 (Percy S.), He
that hath not a palm in his hand on
Palm Sunday must have his hand cut
off. 1904 : *Co. Folk-Lore : Northumb.*,
176 (F.L.S.).

Pancake Tuesday. *See* Shrove-tide.

Pancridge parson, A. 1612 : Field,
Woman a Weathercock, II., Thou Pancridge parson ! 1847 : Halliwell, *Dict.*,
s.v., . . . a term of contempt.

Pandon. *See* Old, D (9).

Pantofles. *See* Stand (7).

Pap before the child be born, Boil not
the. 1732 : Fuller, No. 1002.

Pap with a hatchet. 1589 : *Pap
with a Hatchet* [title of pamphlet].
1592 : Lyly, *Mother Bombie*, I. iii.,
They give us . . . pap with a hatchet.
1719 : D'Urfey, *Pills*, iv. 329 (O.), A
custard was to him pap with a hatchet.
1847 : Halliwell, *Dict.*, s.v. " To give
pap with a hatchet," a proverbial
phrase, meaning to do any kind action
in an unkind manner.

Paradise, He that will enter into,
must have a good key. 1640 : Herbert, *Jac. Prudentum.* 1670 : Ray, 20.
1732 : Fuller, No. 2347 [" come with a
right key "].

Pardon all but thyself. 1611 : Cotgrave, s.v. " Pardonner." 1640 : Herbert, *Jac. Prudentum.*

Parings of a pippin are better than a whole crab, The. 1732 : Fuller, No. 4701. 1869 : Spurgeon, *John Plough-man*, ch. v.

Parings of his nails, He'll not lose the = He is a miser. 1546 : Heywood, *Proverbs*, Pt. I. ch. xi., She will not part with the paryng of hir nayles. *c.* 1598 : Deloney, *Gentle Craft*, Pt. II. ch. i., Such penny fathers and pinch-fistes, that will not part, etc. 1631 : Mabbe, *Celestina*, 212 (T.T.), She will not part with anything, no, not so much as the parings of her nailes. 1681 : Robertson, *Phraseol. Generalis*, 843. 1894 : Northall, *Folk Phrases*, 15 (E.D.S.), He would not give anyone the parings of his nails.

Parkgate, All on one side like. 1886 : R. Holland, *Cheshire Gloss.*, 444 (E.D.S.). 1917 : Bridge, *Cheshire Proverbs*, 9, . . . Parkgate consists of a row of houses facing the Dee.

Parrot must have an almond, The. This expression was proverbial in the 16th and 17th centuries, but its meaning is not apparent. Before 1529 : Skelton, in *Works*, ii. 2 (Dyce), Then Parot must haue an almon or a date. 1590 : Nashe, *Almond for a Parrot* [title]. 1609 : Shakespeare, *Troilus*, V. ii., The parrot will not do more for an almond than he for a com-modious drab. 1616 : Haughton, *En-glishm. for my Money*, IV. ii., An almond for parrot ! a rope for parrot ! 1632 : Jonson, *Magnetic Lady*, V. v., Almond for parrot. 1635 : Taylor (Water-Poet), *A Bawd*, 25, in *Works*, 3rd coll. (Spens. S.), Shee knowes a bribe to a catchpole is as sufficient as an almond for a parrot.

Parrot. *See also* Melancholy.

Parsley. 1. *Parsley fried will bring a man to his saddle, and a woman to her grave.* This seems a meaningless say-ing. 1678 : Ray, 345. 1884 : Friend, *Flowers and Fl. Lore*, 209.

2. *Parsley must be sown nine times.* See quots. 1658 : R. Barnsley, in *Wit Restored*, 152 (Hotten), Or else the weed, which still before it's born Nine times the devill sees. 1883 : Burne, *Shropsh. Folk-Lore*, 248, Parsley must be sown

nine times, for the devil takes all but the last. 1885 : *N. & Q.*, 6th ser., xi. 467, There is a saying in the North Riding of Yorkshire that "parsley seed (when it has been sown) goes nine times to the devil," a phrase which seems to have originated in the fact that it remains some time in the earth before it begins to germinate.

3. *The baby comes out of the parsley-bed.* 1640 : R. Brome, *Antipodes*, I. iv., For I am past a child My selfe to thinke they are found in parsley beds. 1659 : *London Chanticleers*, sc. ii., My mother indeed used to say that I was born to be a gardener's wife, as soon as ever I was taken out of her pars-ley bed. *c.* 1730 : Swift, *Receipt for Stewing Veal*, Some sprigs of that bed Where children are bred. 1883 : Burne, *Shropsh. Folk-Lore*, 249, We have the common English saying that the baby, etc. 1886 : Elworthy, *West Som. Word-Book*, 557 (E.D.S.), Parsley-bed . . . the source whence children are told that the little girls come. 1918 : *N. & Q.*, 12th ser., iv. 256.

See also Mistress (4).

Parson gets the children, The. 1663 : Killigrew, *Parson's Wedding*, II. iii. [quoted as a proverb].

Parson of Saddlewick. *See* Saddle-wick.

Parson Palmer. *See* 1785 quot. 1682 : A. Behn, *Roundheads*, IV. iii., Bread, my Lord, no preaching o'er yar liquer. 1709 : O. Dykes, *Eng. Pro-verbs*, 295 (2nd ed.), Dangerous to preach over your liquor. 1738 : Swift, *Polite Convers.*, Dial. II., *Ld. Smart* [*interrupting*]. Pray, Sir John, did you ever hear of parson Palmer ? *Sir John.* No, my lord ; what of him ? *Ld. Smart.* Why, he used to preach over his liquor. 1754 : Berthelson, *Eng.-Danish Dict.*, s.v. "Liquor," To preach over ones liquor. 1785 : Grose, *Class. Dict. Vulgar Tongue*, s.v. "Parson Palmer," Parson Palmer, a jocular name or term of reproach, to one who stops the circulation of the glass by preaching over his liquor, as it is said was done by a parson of that name, whose cellar was under his pulpit.

Parson's cow with a calf at her foot,
To come home like the. Cheshire. 1670:
Ray, 209. 1917: Bridge, *Cheshire Pro-
verbs*, 131.

Parson's side, To pinch on the.
1579: Lyly, *Euphues*, 87 (Arber),
Lucilla perceiuing the drift of the olde
foxe hir father . . . shaped him an
aunswere which . . . pinched Philautus
on the persons syde . . . . *c.* 1580:
Fulwell, *Ars Adulandi*, sig. H1, Pinch
on the parsons side, my lorde, the
whorsons haue to much. 1630: T.
Adams, *Works*, 77, This is a common
slander, when the . . . couetous wretch
pincheth on the priest's side. 1690:
New Dict. Canting Crew, To pinch on
the parson's side, or sharp him of his
tithes. 1737: Ray, 268.

Parsons are souls' waggoners. 1640:
Herbert, *Jac. Prudentum*.

Parsons pay for the clerks. 1812:
Combe, *Syntax: Pict. Tour*, can. iv.,
And there's a proverb, as they say,
That for the clerks the parsons pay.

Part three things, To. *See* quot.
1659: Howell, 17, It is pitie to part
three things—the lawyer and his client,
the physician and his patient, and a
pot of good ale and a toast.

Partridge. 1. *If the partridge had
the woodcock's thigh, 'Twould be the
best bird that ever did fly.* 1670: Ray,
44. 1732: Fuller, No. 6400. 1854:
Doran, *Table Traits*, 176, [with the
addition] If the woodcock had but
the partridge's breast, 'Twould be the
best bird that ever was dress'd. 1888:
S. O. Addy, *Sheffield Gloss.*, 255 (E.D.S.),
If a partridge had but a woodcock's
thee [thigh] 'Twere the finest bird that
ever did flee.

2. *If you had not aimed at the partridge, you had not missed the snipe.*
1846–59: *Denham Tracts*, ii. 108
(F.L.S.).

See also Plump.

Pass the pikes, To = To get out of
danger. 1567: G. Fenton, *Bandello*,
i. 239 (T.T.), Hee wolde graunte him
dispence and saffe conduit to passe
thorow the pikes of his infortunat
dangers. 1581: Pettie, tr. Guazzo's
Civil Convers., Pref., Hauing alreadie

past the pikes in a daungerous conflict, without wound of honour. 1626:
Breton in *Works*, i. e6 (Grosart), To
passe the pikes of Danger's deadly
smart. 1682: A. Behn, *Roundheads*,
V. iv., With much ado . . . I have
pass'd the pikes, my house being sur-
rounded. 1690: *New Dict. Canting
Crew*, sig. I5. 1785: Cowper, *Lett. to
Lady Hesketh*, 30 Nov. (O.), So far,
therefore, have I passed the pikes.
The Monthly Critics have not yet
noticed me.

Passion entereth at the fore-gate,
wisdom goeth out of the postern, When.
1732: Fuller, No. 5564.

Passion will master you, if you do
not master your passion. 1831: Hone,
Year-Book, col. 1417.

Passionate men. *See* quots. 1692:
Sir T. P. Blount, *Essays*, 141, 'Twas the
usual saying of a very ingenuous person
that passionate men, Like Yorkshire
hounds, are apt to overrun the scent.
1732: Fuller, No. 283: A man in
passion rides a horse that runs away
with him. 1880: Spurgeon, *Ploughman's Pictures*, 143 [as in 1732].

Past cure past care. 1593: Greene,
Works, ii. 154 (Grosart), Remember the
olde prouerbe . . . past cure, past care,
without remedie, without remembrance.
1592: Shakespeare, *L. L. L.*, V. ii.
c. 1625: B. & F., *Double Marriage*, I. i.,
But what is past my help is past my
care.

Past dying of her first child, She is =
She hath had a bastard. 1678: Ray,
240.

Past labour is pleasant. 1539:
Taverner, *Proverbs*, fo. 34, Labours
ones [once] done be swete. 1732:
Fuller, No. 3845.

Paston Family. 1678: Ray, 327,
There never was a Paston poor, a
Heyden a coward, nor a Cornwallis a
fool. 1790: Grose, *Prov. Gloss.*, s.v.
" Norfolk."

Pastor Sunday. *See* Whitsuntide (3).

Patch and long sit, build and soon
flit. 1670: Ray, 21.

Patch by patch. *See* quots. 1639:
in *Berkeley MSS.*, iii. 33 (1885), Patch
by patch is yeomanly ; but patch vpon

patch is beggerly. 1670 : Ray, 129,
Patch by patch is good husbandry, but
patch upon patch is plain beggery.
1732 : Fuller, No. 6181 [as in 1670,
but "housewifery" for "husbandry"].
1909 : *Folk-Lore*, xx. 73, [Durham say-
ing] Patch neighbourly, patch on patch
beggarly.

Paternoster. 1. *A man may say even
his Pater-noster out of time.* 1732 :
Fuller, No. 299.

2. *A paternoster while* = A little while,
a time in which one might say a Paternoster. 1362 : Langland, *Plowman*, A,
v. 192, In a paternoster-while. 1536 :
Latimer, *Sermons*, 37 (P.S.), Though
it be but a Pater-noster while. 1584 :
R. Scot, *Witchcraft*, To Readers, And
yet they last not pater noster while
the longer. 1888 : R. L. S., *Black
Arrow*, Prol., And think ever a paternoster-while on Bennet Hatch.

3. *He may be in my Pater-noster, but
never in my Creed.* 1546 : Heywood,
Proverbs, Pt. II. ch. ix., He maie be in
my Pater noster in deede. But be sure,
he shall neuer come in my Creede.
c. 1590 : in *Roxb. Ballads*, iii. 92 (B.S.).
c. 1594 : Bacon, *Promus*, No. 270.
1659 : Howell, 5.

4. *Paternoster built churches, and Our
Father pulls them down.* 1630 : T.
Adams, in *Works*, 16. 1662 : Fuller,
Worthies, i. 44 (1840), There is a generation of people who, to prevent the
verifying of the old proverb, " *Pater
noster* built churches, and *Our Father*
plucks them down," endeavour to
pluck down both churches and our
Father together, neglecting, yea despis-
ing the use both of the one and the
other. 1670 : Ray, 70. 1732 : Fuller,
No. 3851.

Path hath a puddle, Every. 1640 :
Herbert, *Jac. Prudentum*. 1732 : Fuller, No. 1453. 1817 : Scott, *Rob Roy*,
ch. xxxviii., But ilka bean has its black,
and ilka path has its puddle. 1852 :
FitzGerald, *Polonius*, 153 (1903). 1854 :
Warter, *Last of Old Squires*, 53.

Patience. 1. *He preacheth patience
that never knew pain.* 1855 : Bohn,
381.

2. *He that hath no patience hath no-*

thing. 1611 : Cotgrave, s.v. " Patience."
1666 : Torriano, *Piazza Univ.*, 194.

3. *He that hath patience, hath fat
thrushes for a farthing.* 1640 : Herbert,
Jac. Prudentum.

4. *Let patience grow in your garden.*
1546 : Heywood, *Proverbs*, Pt. I. ch. xi.
1633 : Draxe, 152.

5. *Patience carries with it half a
release.* 1642 : D. Rogers, *Matrim.
Honour*, 196.

6. *Patience conquers.* c. 1374 : Chaucer, *Troylus*, bk. iv. l. 1584, Men seyn,
" the suffraunt overcometh," pardee.
1611 : Davies (of Hereford), *Sc. of Folly*,
46, in *Works*, ii. (Grosart), Who suffers
orecomes. 1639 : Clarke, 242, Patient
men win the day.

7. *Patience is a flower that grows not
in every garden.* 1645 : Howell, *Letters*,
bk. i. § vi. No. 58. 1694 : D'Urfey,
Quixote, Pt. I. Act I. sc. i. 1732 : Fuller,
No. 3854, Patience grows not in every
garden. 1869 : Spurgeon, *John Ploughman*, ch. v., It is not every garden
that grows the herbs to make it
[patience] with.

8. *Patience is a good nag, but she'll
bolt.* 1875 : Cheales, *Proverb. Folk-
Lore*, 121.

9. *Patience is a plaister for all sores.*
c. 1390 : Gower, *Conf. Amantis*, bk. iii.
l. 614, And tak into thi remembrance If
thou miht gete pacience, Which is the
leche of alle offence, As tellen ons these
olde wise. c. 1393 : Langland, *Plowman*, C, xx. 89, And yet be plastred
with pacience. 1560: Wilson, *Rhetorique*,
206 (1909), Pacience is a remedie for
euery disease. 1605 : Breton, in *Works*,
ii. *m* 4 (Grosart) [" paine " for " sores "].
1694: D'Urfey, *Quixote*, Pt. II. Act I.
sc. i. 1901: F. E. Taylor, *Lancs Sayings*,
9, Payshunce is a plister for o maks
o' sores.

10. *Patience is a virtue.* 1377 : Langland, *Plowman*, B, xi. 370, Suffraunce
is a souereygne vertue. c. 1386,
Chaucer, *C. Tales*, F, 773 (Skeat):
Patience is an heigh vertu, certéyn.
1599 : Breton, in *Works*, ii. *c* 7 (Grosart).
1614 : R. Tailor, *Hog hath lost his
Pearl*, V. 1706 : Vanbrugh, *Confederacy*,
III. ii. 1729 : Gay, *Polly*, I. 1798 :

Morton, *Speed the Plough*, IV. iii., There is a point when patience ceases to be virtue. 1821 : Byron, *Letters, etc.*, v. 287 (Prothero).

11. *Patience is the best remedy.* 1578 : Florio, *First Fruites*, fo. 44, Pacience is the best medicine that is, for a sicke man. 1761 : Colman, *Jealous Wife*, IV. i. Cf. **No remedy**.

12. *Patience, money, and time, bring all things to pass.* 1640 : Herbert, *Jac. Prudentum*, Patience, time, and money accommodate all things. 1732 : Fuller, No. 3858.

13. *Patience perforce. See* 1847 quot. 1575 : Gascoigne, *Patience Perforce* [title of poem]. 1590 : Spenser, *F. Q.*, III. x. 3, But patience perforce ; he must abie What future and his fate on him will lay. 1659 : Howell, 11 (9), Patience perforce is medicine for a mad horse. 1694 : Motteux, *Rabelais*, bk. v. ch. i., Patience per force is a remedy for a mad-dog. 1702 : Penn, *Fruits of Solitude*, Pt. II. No. 188, According to the proverb, *Patience per force*, and *thank you for nothing*. 1837 : Southey, *Lett. to Mrs. Hughes*, 7 Dec., " Patience perforce " was what I heard of every day in Portugal. 1847 : Halliwell, *Dict.*, s.v. " Perforce," *Patience perforce*, a phrase when some evil must be endured which cannot by any means be remedied.

14. *Patience with poverty is all a poor man's remedy.* 1639 : Clarke, 15. 1656 : Flecknoe, *Diarium*, 6, Patience, vertue of the poor. 1670 : Ray, 130. 1732 : Fuller, No. 6361 [omitting " all "].

See also **Nature ; Time ; and No remedy**.

Patient, and you shall have patient children, Be. 1678 : Ray, 346.

Patient is not like to recover who makes the doctor his heir, That. 1659 : Howell, *Proverbs: Fr.-Eng.*, 11, He is a fool that makes his physitian his heir. 1732 : Fuller, No. 4368.

Paull, a village on the Humber. *See* quot. 1878 : *Folk-Lore Record*, i. 167, High Paull, and low Paull, and Paull Holme, There never was a fair maid married at Paull town.

Paul's, Old as. 1662 : in *Roxb. Ballads*, iii. 577 (B.S.), I can call 'um pritty souls, though they be as old as Pouls.

1667 : L'Estrange, *Quevedo's Visions*, 184 (1904), Let her be as old as Paul's. 1738 : Swift, *Polite Convers.*, Dial. I. 1752 : Fielding, *Cov. Garden Journal*, No. 28, And told me that my secret was not only a lye, but as old as Paul's. 1888 : Lowsley, *Berks Gloss.*, 124 (E.D.S.), The expression as " awld as St. Paul's" is used to denote great antiquity.

Paul's steeple, Old as. 1659 : Howell, *Proverbs*, Dedn., Some of them may be said to be as old as Pauls steeple. 1670 : Ray, 242. 1790 : Grose, *Prov. Gloss.*, s.v. " London."

Paul's will not always stand. 1593 : G. Harvey, in *Works*, i. 297 (Grosart), Powles steeple, and a hugyer thing is doune. 1659 : Howell, *Proverbs*, Dedn., A very ancient proverb . . . viz. Pauls cant alwayes stand. 1670 : Ray, 130. 1732 : Fuller, No. 3861.

Paul's. *See also* **Westminster**.

Paves the meadow, He. 1813 : Ray, 75.

Pay, verb. 1. *He pays him with penpowder.* 1639 : Clarke, 58.

2. *He that cannot pay let him pray.* 1611 : Cotgrave, s.v. " Argent." 1670 : Ray, 130. 1732 : Fuller, No. 6362.

3. *He that payeth another remembereth himself.* Ibid., No. 2247.

4. *He that payeth beforehand shall have his work ill done.* 1591 : Florio, *Second Frutes*, 39, He that paieth afore hand, hath neuer his worke well done. 1611 : Cotgrave, s.v. " Bras," . . . lames his workeman ; or, hath it but lamely done. 1732 : Fuller, No. 2245.

5. *He that pays last never pays twice.* 1659 : Howell, 4, Who payeth last, payeth but once. 1670 : Ray, 130. 1732 : Fuller, No. 2246.

6. *It is hard to pay and pray too.* 1631 : F. Lenton, *Characters*, sig. D11 (1663), In his trade, above all others, you must both pray and pay. 1642 : D. Rogers, *Matrim. Honour*, 53, And now I adde, pray for it, pay and pray too. 1725 : Defoe, *Everybody's Business*, Nor would I be so unchristian to put more upon any one than they can bear ; but to pray and pay too is the devil. 1732 : Fuller, No. 2951.

7. *Pay what you owe, And what you're worth you'll know.* Ibid., No. 6352. 1869 : Spurgeon, *John Ploughman*, ch. xii. 1875 : Smiles, *Thrift*, 89, Who pays what he owes enriches himself.

8. *Pay with the same dish you borrow.* 1639 : Clarke, 14.

9. *To pay it with thinking.* See **Say,** *verb* (9).

10. *To pay one in his own coin.* 1589 : Greene, *Works*, vii. 133 (Grosart), Glad that he had giuen hir a soppe of the same sauce, and paide hir his debt in hir owne coine. 1612 : Chapman, *Widow's Tears*, II. iii., I did but pay him in's own coine. 1687 : A. Behn, *Lucky Chance*, I. ii., I would make use of Sir Cautious's cash : pay him in his own coin. 1748 : Richardson, *Clarissa*, i. 71 (1785), They had best take care he did not pay them in their own coin. 1821 : Byron, *Blues*, Ecl. i. l. 132, Or he'll pay you back in your own coin. 1851 : Borrow, *Lavengro*, iii. 353, If you attempt to lay hands on me, I'll try to pay you in your own coin.

11. *To pay the debt to Nature.* See **Debt** (5).

12. *To pay the piper.* 1638 : J. Taylor (Water-Poet), *Taylors Feast*, 98, in *Works*, 3rd coll. (Spens. S.), Alwayes those that dance must pay the musicke. 1695 : Congreve, *Love for Love*, II. v., I warrant you, if he danced till doomsday, he thought I was to pay the piper. *c.* 1791 : Pegge, *Derbicisms*, 115 (E.D.S.), " To pay the piper," to bear the expense. 1923 : *Evening Standard*, 14 Feb., p. 5, col. 1, The old adage of " He who pays the piper can call the tune " has held good.

13. *To pay the shot* = To pay the reckoning or bill. 1519 : Horman, *Vulgaria*, fo. 165, He loueth well to be at good fare but he wyll pay no scotte. *c.* 1534 : Berners, *Huon*, 704 (E.E.T.S.), Yf it may please you to let me eat and drynke with you I wyll pay for my scot [" shotte " in 1601 ed.]. 1587 : Churchyard, *Worth. of Wales*, 15 (Spens. S.), The shot is great, when each man paies his groate. 1607 : Dekker and Webster, *Northw. Hoe*, II. i., Did thy father pay the shot ? 1611 : Cotgrave,

s.v. " Escorter," Every one to pay his shot, or to contribute somewhat towards it. 1842 : in Crawhall, *Fishers Garlands*, 109 (1864), Yet still while I have got Enough to pay the shot Of Boniface . . . 1907: Hackwood, *Old Eng. Sports*, 222, The customers called for their ale . . . and . . . expected the losers " to pay the shot."

14. *You pay more for your schooling than your learning is worth.* 1639 : Clarke, 59. 1732 : Fuller, No. 5955.

Pea and **Pease.** 1. *Eat peas with the king, and cherries with the beggar.* 1732 : Fuller, No. 1356.

2. *Sow peas and beans in the wane of the moon, Who soweth them sooner, he soweth too soon.* 1846 : Denham, *Proverbs*, 42 (Percy S.).

3. *The smaller the peas.* See quots. 15th cent. : in *Reliq. Antiquæ*, ii. 40 (1843), Tho smallere pese tho mo to the pott ; Tho fayrere woman tho more gyglott. 1541 : *Sch. House of Women*, l. 558, in Hazlitt, *Early Pop. Poetry*, iv. 126, The smaller pease, the mo to the pot, The fairer woman the more gillot.

4. *To give a pea for a bean* = To give a present with an eye to future return. Staffs. 1896 : *Folk-Lore*, vii. 377.

5. *Who hath many peas may put the more in the pot.* 1546 : Heywood, *Proverbs*, Pt. I. ch. v. 1670 : Ray, 21.

See also **Candlemas,** B ; **St. Benedict ;** and **St. David** (1).

Peace. 1. *Peace and catch a mouse.* 1659 : Howell, 11.

2. *Peace maketh plenty.* 15th cent. : in *Reliq. Antiquæ*, ii. 315 (1841), Pees maketh plenté, Plenté maketh pride, Pride maketh plee, Plee maketh poverté, Povert maketh pees. And therefore, grace growith after governaunce. 1589 : Puttenham, *Eng. Poesie*, 217 (Arber), Peace makes plentie, plentie makes pride, Pride breeds quarrell, and quarrell brings warre : Warre brings spoile, and spoile pouertie, Pouertie pacience, and pacience peace : So peace brings warre and warre brings peace. [Puttenham attributes the lines to " Ihean de Mehune the French Poet."] 1619 : B. Rich, *Irish Hubbub*, 49, An old obseruation, Peace brings plenty, Plenty brings

pride, and Pride in the end is it that brings in penury. 1659: Howell, 19, Through peace cometh plenty.

3. *'Tis safest making peace with sword in hand.* 1699: Farquhar, *Love and a Bottle*, V. iii.

4. *Where there is peace, God is.* 1640: Herbert, *Jac. Prudentum.*

Peach will have wine, and the fig water, The. 1577: J. Grange, *Golden Aphroditis*, sig. E1. 1629: *Book of Meery Riddles*, Prov. 103.

Peacock hath fair feathers but foul feet, The. 1633: Draxe, 10.

Peacock loudly bawls, When the, Soon we'll have both rain and squalls. 1893: Inwards, *Weather Lore*, 135.

Peacock. *See also* All's well; and Proud.

Peak, To send a wife to the. 1663: Pepys, *Diary*, 19 Jan., My lord did presently pack his lady into the country in Derbyshire, near the Peake; which is become a proverb at Court, to send a man's wife to the Devil's arse-á-Peake, when she vexes him.

Pear and Pears. 1. *After pear wine, or the priest.* 1588: Cogan, *Haven of Health*, 89 (1612), That saying which is commonly used, that peares without wine are poyson. 1608: Harington, *Sch. of Salerne*, sig. B3, Peares wanting wine, are poyson from the tree. 1611: Cotgrave, s.v. " Poire," After a (cold) peare wine, or the priest. 1666: Torriano, *Piazza Univ.*, 201, A pear must have wine after it, and a fig water.

2. *A pear must be eaten to the day, If you don't eat it then, throw it away.* 1886: *N. & Q.*, 7th ser., ii. 506.

3. *A pear year, A dear year.* 1855: *N. & Q.*, 1st ser., xii. 260. 1893: Inwards, *Weather Lore*, 5.

4. *Share not pears with your master, either in jest or in earnest.* 1611: Cotgrave, s.v. " Poire," He that eats peares with his lord picks none of the best. 1732: Fuller, No. 4117.

See also Apple (7).

Pearl on your nail, Make a. 1592: Nashe, *Works*, ii. 78 (Grosart), After a man hath turnd vp the bottom of the cup, to drop it on hys naile, and make a pearle with that is left. 1678: Ray, 88. 1732:

Fuller, No. 3311. 1909: Hackwood, *Inns, Ales, etc.*, 165, The custom of turning upside down the cup, from which the drinker has quaffed the whole contents, to make a pearl, with the last drop left in the vessel, upon his thumb-nail. Cf. Supernaculum.

Pearls before swine, To cast. 1340: *Ayenbite*, 152 (E.E.T.S.), Huerof zayþ ous god ine his spelle. þet we ne þrauwe naȝt oure preciouse stones touore þe zuyn. 1401: in Wright, *Pol. Poems*, ii. 110 (Rolls Ser., 1861), And the presciouse perlis ye strowen to hogges. *c.* 1430: Lydgate, *Minor Poems*, 188 (Percy S.), Men shuld not put . . . perles whight, To-fore rude swyne. 1550: R. Crowley, *Epigr.*, in *Works*, 6 (E.E.T.S.), For before suche swyne no pearles maye be caste. 1606: Day, *Ile of Gulls*, III., To cast eloquence amongst a companie of stinctards is all one as if a man should scatter pearls amongst the hoggish animals ecliped swine. 1848: Dickens, *Dombey*, ch. xxiii. 1905: Shaw, *How He Lied, etc.*, Introducing a fine woman to you is casting pearls before swine.

Peart. *See* Pert.

Pease-field, He is going into the= He is falling asleep. 1678: Ray, 264.

Pease-pottage and tawny Never made good medley. 1659: Howell, 12.

Peckham. *See* All holiday.

Peck of dirt. *See* Eat (39).

Peck of malt. *See* Kiln (2).

Peck of salt. *See* Bushel (3).

Peck of troubles, A. *c.* 1535: in *Archæologia*, xxv. 97 (O.), The said George . . . told hym that Mr. More was in a pecke of trubles. 1569: Grafton, *Chron.*, i. 235 (1809), You bring your selfe into such a pecke of troubles. 1633: Draxe, 37. 1785: O'Keeffe, *Beggar on Horseback*, II. iv., I dare say he's in a peck of troubles. 1857: Hughes, *Tom Brown*, Pt. I. ch. viii., A pretty peck of troubles you'll get into.

Pedlar, A small pack becomes a small. 1611: Cotgrave, s.v. " Mercier," The little pedler a little pack doth serve. 1670: Ray, 143. 1732: Fuller, No. 409.

Pedlar carry his own burden, Let every. 1659 : Howell, 17. 1732 : Fuller, No. 3176.

Pedlar's mare. *See* quot. 1541 : Coverdale, *Christ. State Matrimony*, sig. G2, It is no vntrue prouerbe : She that taketh the pedlers mare must be fayne to haue the pedler himself also at the last.

Pedley, Go pipe at, there's a pescod feast. 1678 : Ray, 78 [" Padley "]. 1790 : Grose, *Prov. Gloss.*, s.v. "Cheshire." 1917 : Bridge, *Cheshire Proverbs*, 62.

Pedley. *See also* Candle (7) ; God help the fool ; I was by ; and Rope (5).

Peep. I see a knave. 1639 : Clarke, 181.

Peeps through a hole may see what will vex him, He who. 1710 : Palmer, *Moral Essays on Proverbs*, 135.

Peewit. *See* Acre.

Peggy behind Margit, To ride. 1917 : Bridge, *Cheshire Proverbs*, 142, . . . To ride one behind the other.

Peg in, To put the = To give no more credit. "A peg of wood above the latch inside . . . effectually locked it." *Ibid.*, 141.

Pelton. *See* quot. 1846–59 : *Denham Tracts*, i. 112 (F.L.S.), They'd come back again like the pigs o' Pelton. Ibid., i. 113, Thicker and ranker, like pigs o' Pelton.

Pen and ink is wit's plough. 1639 : Clarke, 35. 1670 ; Ray, 130.

Pen and ink never blush. 1577 : J. Grange, *Golden Aphroditis*, sig. K2, Better might you haue done it with penne and inke, who (as the prouerbe goeth) neuer blusheth. Cf. **Pens.**

Penance. *See* quot. 1593 : *Tell-Trothes N. Yeares Gift*, 10 (N. Sh. S.), The old saying is, that he which will no pennance doe, must shonne the cause that belongs thereto.

Pence. *See* **Penny.**

Pendle-Hill, As old as. 1659 : Howell, 20. 1670 : Ray, 235. 1790 : Grose, *Prov. Gloss.*, s.v. "Lancs." 1901 : F. E. Taylor, *Lancs Sayings*, 3.

Pendle, Ingleborough, and Penigent, Are the three highest hills between Scotland and Trent. 1586 : Camden,

Britannia, 431, Ingleborrow, Pendle and Penigent are, etc. 1622 : Drayton, *Polyol.*, xxviii., That Ingleborow hill, Pendle, and Penigent, Should named be the high'st betwixt our Tweed and Trent. 1683 : Meriton, *Yorkshire Ale*, 83–7 (1697). 1790 : Grose, *Prov. Gloss.*, s.v. "Yorks," [as in heading, with variant] Pendle, Penigent, and Ingleborough Are the three highest hills all England thorough. 1878 : *Folk-Lore Record*, i. 167 [as in 1790].

Penniless bench, On. 1560–1 : in W. H. Turner, *Select Rec. Oxf.*, 284 (1880) (O.), Item, to . . . for mending the peneles benche [*see* note to 1604 quot.]. 1598 : Greene, *James IV.*, IV. iii., Wee will teach him such a lesson as shall cost him a chiefe place on pennilesse-bench for his labour. 1604 : Middleton, *Black Book*, in *Works*, viii. 27 (Bullen), Pierce should be called no more Pennyless, like the Mayor's bench at Oxford. [Bullen's note : "At the east end of the old Carfax church at Oxford there was a seat for loungers which was known as Penniless Bench. Hence came the proverb 'To sit on Penniless Bench' (=be very poor)."] 1651 : Randolph, *Hey for Honesty*, IV. i., I now must pine and starve at Penniless Bench. 1860 : Warter, *Sea-board*, ii. 43 (O.), Though he have sometimes to sit on the Penniless Bench.

Penny and **Pence.** 1. *A penny at a pinch is worth a pound.* 1639 : Clarke, 45.

2. *A penny earned is better than a shilling given.* 1875 : Smiles, *Thrift*, 163.

3. *A penny for your thought.* 1546 : Heywood, *Proverbs*, Pt. II. ch. iv., Freend (quoth the good man) a peny for your thought. 1594 : Greene, *Frier Bacon*, etc., sc. vi., How cheer you, sir ? A penny for your thought ! 1602 : Marston, *Antonio and Mellida*, II. 1738 : Swift, *Polite Convers.*, Dial. I. 1762 : Hall Stevenson, *Crazy Tales*, Tale II. p. 28, Now, said the Marchioness, and smil'd, I'll give a penny for your thoughts.

4. *A penny in purse will bid me drink, when all the friends I have will not.*

1670 : Ray, 130. 1732 : Fuller, No. 3865 ["make" for "bid"].

5. *A penny in the forehead. See* quots. This alludes to an old game of making a child believe that a coin pressed on its forehead, and surreptitiously removed, is still there. 1658/9 : T. Burton, *Diary*, 9 March, Sir A. Haslerigge turned from the chair, and they called him to speak to the chair. He said, "I am not bound always to look you in the face like children, to see if you have a penny in your forehead." 1740 : North, *Examen*, 324, We may hope better of their abilities than to be wheedled as children with a penny in the forehead.

6. *A penny in the purse is better than a friend at Court.* 1875 : Smiles, *Thrift*, 126 [quoted as "a true saying"]. Cf. **Friend** (3).

7. *A penny more buys the whistle.* 1732 : Fuller, No. 341.

8. *A penny saved is a penny got.* [*c.* 1550 : *Gentleness and Nobility*, in Heywood, *Spider and Flie*, 447 (Farmer), I tell thee plainly, without any boast, A halfpeny is as well saved as lost.] 1640 : Herbert, *Jac. Prudentum*, A penny spared is twice got. *c.* 1686 : in *Roxb. Ballads*, vi. 349 (B.S.), A penny well sav'd is as good as one earn'd. 1711 : Steele, *Spectator*, No. 2, He abounds in several frugal maxims . . . "A penny saved is a penny got." 1733 : Fielding, *Miser*, III. xii. 1852 : Dickens, *Bleak House*, ch. ix.

9. *A penny soul never comes to twopence.* 1859 : Smiles, *Self - Help*, 297 (1869), Narrow-mindedness . . . leads to failure. The penny soul, it is said, never came to twopence.

10. *A penny to serve one's need.* 1637 : in *Pepysian Garland*, 447 (Rollins), The gentle craft doth beare good will, to all kind-hearted tradesmen still, That keepe the prouerbe to fullfill, *a penny to serue their need.*

11. *Better penny in silver than any brother.* 1659 : Howell, *Proverbs: Brit.-Eng.*, 16.

12. *Every one hath a penny for the new ale-house.* 1678 : Ray, 181. 1732 : Fuller, No. 1445.

13. *In for a penny in for a pound.* 1695 : Ravenscroft, *Caut. Guests*, V. i. (O.), Well than, O'er shooes, o'er boots. And in for a penny, in for a pound. 1815 : Scott, *Mannering*, ch. xlvi. 1823 : Byron, *Letters, etc.*, vi. 285 (Prothero). 1877 : S. Butler, in *Life* by Jones, i. 259 (1919), Feeling, therefore, that if I was in for a penny, I might as well be in for a pound, I wrote about your father's book exactly as I should have done about any one else's.

14. *Penny and penny laid up will be many.* 1639 : Clarke, 35. 1670 : Ray, 130. 1732 : Fuller, No. 288.

15. *Penny come quick soon makes two pence.* Ibid., No. 3863.

16. *Penny in pocket is a good companion.* 1659 : Howell, 10. 1670 : Ray, 130. 1712 : Arbuthnot, *John Bull*, Pt. II., ch. iv., I am sure . . . that a penny in the purse is the best friend John can have at last. 1732 : Fuller, No. 3864 ["merry" for "good"].

17. *Penny to bless oneself. See* **Cross** (3).

18. *Penny wise and pound foolish.* 1605 : Camden, *Remains*, 330 (1870). 1631 : Dekker, *Penny-wise, pound-foolish* [title]. 1712 : Addison, *Spectator*, No. 295. 1864 : Mrs. H. Wood, *Trevlyn Hold*, ch. xli. 1878 : Platt, *Business*, 126.

19. *Sometimes a penny well spent is better than a penny ill spared.* 1672 : Walker, *Parœm.*, 32.

20. *Take care of the pence and the pounds will take care of themselves.* Before 1724 : in *Chesterfield Lett.*, 5.2. 1750 (O.). 1834-7 : Southey, *Doctor*, ch. ccxli. 1859 : Smiles, *Self - Help*, 305 (1869). 1924 : *Observer*, 16 March, p. 2, col. 4. Cf. No. 27.

21. *The penny is ill saved that shames the master.* 1736 : Bailey, *Dict.*, s.v. "Shame."

22. *The penny is well spent that gets the pound.* *c.* 1400 : *Beryn*, l. 2244, p. 69 (E.E.T.S.), ffor þere is a comyn byword, yf ye it herd haviþ : "Wele settiþ he his peny, þat the pound [therby] saviþ." 1536 : in *Lisle*

Papers, xiv. art. 40, The old saying,
" Well is spent," etc.

23. *The penny is well spent that saves
a groat*. 1605 : Camden, *Remains*, 332
(1870). 1670 : Ray, 130. 1732 : Fuller, No. 4369.

24. *There is more honesty in a penny
than in five pounds*. 1883 : Burne,
Shropsh. Folk-Lore, 588. [Miss Burne
says that this is an argument for lending
a large sum.]

25. *There's no companion like the
penny*. 1659 : Howell, *Proverbs: Span.-
Eng.*, 13. 1670 : Ray, 21. 1732 : Fuller, No. 4891.

26. *To think one's penny good silver*.
1580 : G. Harvey, *Works*, i. 71 (Grosart),
Euery one highly in his owne fauour,
thinking no man's penny so good siluer
as his own. 1637 : Breton, in *Works*,
ii. *h* 20 (Grosart), There are more
batchelors then Roger, and my penny
is as good siluer as yours. 1732 : Fuller,
No. 3112, Is no coin good silver but
your penny ? Cf. **Farthing**; and **Halfpenny.**

27. *Who will not lay up a penny Shall
never have many*. 1541 : Coverdale,
Christ. State Matrimony, sig. I3, Who
so spareth not the penye shall neuer
come by the pownde. 1670 : Ray,
131 [" keep " for " lay up "]. 1732 :
Fuller, No. 6383. Cf. No. 20.

28. *You may know by a penny how a
shilling spends*. 1678 : Ray, 78. 1732 :
Fuller, No. 5951.

See also **Pennyworth.**

**Penny-weight of love is worth a
pound of law, A.** 1732 : Fuller, No.
343.

Pennyworth, Great. *See* **Great bargain.**

**Pennyworth of ease is worth a penny,
A.** 1605 : Camden, *Remains*, 318
(1870). 1678 : Ray, 130. 1732 : Fuller, No. 344.

**Pennyworth of mirth is worth a pound
of sorrow, A.** 1678 : Ray, 176.

**Pennyworth of poker is worth two of
coals, A.** 1864 : " Cornish Proverbs,"
in *N. & Q.*, 3rd ser., vi. 495.

Penrith, Peerless. 1638 : Brathwait,
Barn. Itiner., 151 (1774), Thence to
Peerless Penrith went I, Which of mer-

chandise hath plenty. 1846–59 : *Denham Tracts.*, i. 182 (F.L.S.). *See also*
Little London.

Pensford. *See* **Stanton Drew.**

Pension never enriched a young man.
1640 : Herbert, *Jac. Prudentum.*

Pens may blot but they cannot blush.
1596 : Harington, *Metam. of Ajax*, vii.
(1814) [quoted as " the old saying "].
1639 : Clarke, 268. Cf. **Pen and Ink.**

Pentecost. *See* **Whitsuntide.**

Penzance, Not a word of. This refers
to the glaring cowardice of the Penzance
men when Cornwall was invaded by the
Spanish in 1595. 1678 : Ray, 350,
Not a word of Pensants. 1750 : Heath,
Scilly and Cornwall, 407. 1906 : *Cornish N. & Q.*, 264.

**People's love is the king's life-guard,
The.** 1738 : *Gent. Mag.*, 475. Cf.
Subject (1).

Pepper. *See* **Snow** (7).

Pepper-gate. *See* **Daughter.**

Pepper in the nose, To take=To take
offence. 1377 : Langland, *Plowman*,
B, xv. 197, And to pore peple han peper
in the nose. *c.* 1500 : Skelton, *Why
Come Ye Nat*, l. 381, For drede of
the red hat Take peper in the nose
[Lest the cardinal take offence]. 1583 :
Greene, *Works*, ii. 52 (Grosart), As old
women are soone angry, she tooke
pepper in the nose at the sharpe reply.
1607 : Marston, *What You Will*, Induction, He's a chollerick gentleman ;
he will take pepper in the nose instantly.
1682 : Bunyan, *Holy War*, ch. x. 1714 :
Ozell, *Molière*, ii. 13, I approve of a
husband's vigilance in this particular ;
but I'm afraid you take pepper i' th'
nose too soon. 1732 : Fuller, No.
2032. Cf. **Snuff.**

**Percys' profit was the Lucys' loss,
The.** 1846–59 : *Denham Tracts*, i. 228
(F.L.S.).

Perseverance kills the game. 1813 :
Ray, 149. 1846–59 : *Denham Tracts*,
ii. 108 (F.L.S.).

**Persuasion of the fortunate sways
the doubtful, The.** 1640 : Herbert,
Jac. Prudentum. 1670 : Ray, 10.

PERT and **PEART:**

(*a*) **Peart as a maggot, As.** Oxfordsh.
1913 : *Folk-Lore*, xxiv. 77.

Peart as a robin, As. [1592 : Warner, *Albion's Eng.*, ch. xxxi. st. 4, As peart as bird.] 1862 : *Dialect of Leeds*, 405. 1901 : F. E. Taylor, *Lancs Sayings*, 3, As peeart as a robin.

Peart as a sparrow, As. 1837 : Mrs. Palmer, *Devonsh. Dialect*, 70, . . . a common phrase for a lively little chit.

Peart as a spoon, As. 1882 : Mrs. Chamberlain, *W. Worcs. Words*, 22 (E.D.S.), . . . means unusually bright and cheerful.

(*b*) Pert as a pearmonger, As. 1564 : Harding, quoted in Jewel, *Defence of the Apol.*, 822 (P.S.), Here pricketh forth this hasty defender, as pert as a pearmonger. 1678 : Ray, 281, As pert as a pearmongers mare. Before 1732 : Gay, *New Song of New Similes*, Pert as a pearmonger I'd be If Molly were but kind. 1738 : Swift, *Polite Convers.*, Dial. I. 1855 : *N. & Q.*, 1st ser., xi. 114, As peart as a pearmonger (Lancs). 1855 : Ibid., 232, " Peart as a pearmonger " does not belong to Lancashire. I have often heard it in Oxon and Bucks.

Pert. *See also* Crouse.

Perverseness makes one squint-eyed. 1640 : Herbert, *Jac. Prudentum.*

Peter of Wood, Church and mills are all his. Cheshire. 1670: Ray, 217. 1852 : *N. & Q.*, 1st ser., vi. 386. 1917 : Bridge, *Cheshire Proverbs*, 103.

Petworth. 1884 : " Sussex Proverbs," in *N. & Q.*, 6th ser., x. 370, Proud Petworth, poor people, High church, crooked steeple. 1911 : A. S. Cooke, *Off Beaten Track in Sussex*, 284, Poor Petworth, proud people, etc.

Physic, *subs.* 1. *He takes physic before he is sick.* 1639 : Clarke, 283. 1670 : Ray, 189.

2. *He that liveth by physicke liveth miserably.* 1588 : Cogan, *Haven of Health*, Epist. Ded. [quoted as " a common saying "].

3. *If physic do not work, prepare for the kirk.* 1678 : Ray, 189.

Physician, heal thyself. 1511 : Colet, *Sermon*, in Dunton's *Phenix*, ii. 8 (1708), 'Tis an old proverb, Physician heal thyself. 1543 : Becon, in *Early Works*, 385 (P.S.). 1579 : Lyly, *Euphues*, 118

(Arber). 1638 : D. Tuvill, *Vade Mecum*, 152 (3rd ed.), First therefore physitian, cure thine own ills. 1692 : L'Estrange, *Æsop*, 205 (3rd ed.) [" cure " for " heal "]. 1781 : Francklin, *Lucian*, ii. 134 *n.*, According to the old adage, " physician, cure thyself." 1875 : Smiles, *Thrift*, 23.

Physicians' faults are covered with earth. 1620 : J. Melton, *Astrologaster*, 17, The sunne doth alwayes behold your good successe, and the earth couers all your ignorances. 1637 : T. Heywood, *Dialogues, etc.*, in Bang, *Materialien*, B. 3, 197, 'Tis said of all physitians What good comes by their physick, the sun sees : But in their art, if they have bad successe, That the earth covers. 1669 : *Politeuphuia*, 175, Physicians are happy men, because the sun makes manifest what good success soever happeneth in their cures, and the earth burieth what fault soever they commit. [As to the Greek original of this saying, by Nicocles, *see N. & Q.*, 8th ser., vi. 246.]

Physicians kill more than they cure. 1703 : E. Ward, *Writings*, ii. 328 [" an old maxim "].

Physicians. *See also* Feastings ; Feed (1) ; Few ; Fool (15) ; God heals ; Good physician ; Hide nothing ; Inward sore ; Old, A (*b*) (7) ; and Patient.

Pick a hole in a man's coat, To. 1588 : *Mar-Prelate's Epitome*, 3 (1843), There is a deuice to fynde a hole in the coat of some of you puritanes. 1639 : Clarke, 80, It's easie to pick a hole in another man's coat, if he be disposed. 1670: Ray, 189. 1745 : *Agreeable Companion*, 105, You have great reason to pick holes in your neighbour's coats. 1808: Manning, *Lett. to Lamb*, 110 (1925), God forgive me if I'm censorious, and pick holes in another man's coat.

Pick a quarrel, To. *c.* 1449 : *Paston Letters*, i. 87 (O.), The seyde parsone . . . hathe pekyd a qwarell to on Mastyr Recheforthe. 1519 : Horman, *Vulgaria*, fo. 128, He begynneth to pyke or fyndeth a quarel of my wordes. *c.* 1550 : *Jacke Jugeler*, 83 (Grosart), Woll sone pike a quarrell, be it wrong or right. 1579 : Lyly, *Euphues*, 107

(Arber). 1669 : Brathwait, *Hist. of Moderation*, 75, Neighbours . . . would be . . . ready to pick any quarrel with her. 1894 : Caine, *Manxman*, V. xiv. 325 (O.), Some of the men began to pick quarrels.

Pick and choose and take the worst. 1884 : H. Friend, *Flowers and Fl. Lore*, 228, We say more colloquially, " Pick and choose," etc.

Pick - pockets are sure traders ; for they take ready money. 1732 : Fuller, No. 3872.

Pickpockets in a fair, They agree like. 1813 : Ray, 178.

Pick up one's crumbs, To = To be convalescent. 1580 : Lyly, *Euphues*, 302 (Arber), What with hir merry sporting, and good nourishing, I began to gather vp my crumbes. 1645 : Howell, *Letters*, bk. i. § ii. No. 1, I . . . am recovering and picking up my crums apace. 1754 : Berthelson, *Eng.-Danish Dict.*, s.v. " Pick." 1886 : Elworthy, *West Som. Word-Book*, 566 (E.D.S.), Our Liz bin ter'ble had . . . but her's pickin' up her crooms again now, like.

Piddinghoe, a Sussex village near Newhaven, in the valley of the Ouse, which has a Gotham-like reputation. *See* quots. 1884 : " Sussex Proverbs," in *N. & Q.*, 6th ser., ix. 401, At Piddinghoe they dig for daylight . . . moonshine . . [and] smoke. 1911 : A. S. Cooke, *Off Beaton Track in Sussex*, 283, More famous Piddinghoe—" where they shoe their magpies"—with its reputed ague and celebrated chalk-pit—" where they hang ponds out to dry." *Ibid.*, 284, Englishmen fight, Frenchmen too : We don't—we live Piddinghoe !

Pie-lid makes people wise. 1678 : Ray, 79. 1875 : Cheales, *Proverb. Folk-Lore*, 114, One can't tell what a pie is till the lid is off.

Pig and Pigs. 1. *A brinded pig will make a good brawn to breed on=*" A red-headed man will make a good stallion " (Ray, 1737). 1678 : Ray, 67.

2. *A pig may fly.* *See* quots. 1732 : Fuller, No. 4350, That is as likely as to see an hog fly. 1872 : De Morgan, *Budget of Paradoxes*, 275, There is a

proverb which says, A pig may fly, but it isn't a likely bird.

3. *A pig of one's own sow.* *c.* 1535 : *Gentleness and Nobility*, sig. A1, v°, That is euyn a pyg of our own sow. 1579 : G. Harvey, *Works*, i. 112 (Grosart), A misshapin illfavor'd freshe copy of my precious poems, as it were, a pigg of myne owne sowe. 1608 : Day, *Humor out of Breath*, III., 'Tis a pig of your owne sow, madam ; and I hope your wit will bestow the nursing of it. 1681 : Robertson, *Phraseol. Generalis*, 1110, 'Tis a pig of your own sow, your own self sold it. 1860 : Reade, *Cl. and Hearth*, ch. xcviii., " Who more charitable than monks ? " " Go to ! They do but give the laity back a pig of their own sow."

4. *A pig of the worse pannier.* 1533 : Heywood, *John, Tyb, etc.*, 89 (Farmer), And, peradventure, there, he and she Will make me cuckold, even to anger me ; And then had I a pig in the worse panyer. 1546 : Heywood, *Proverbs*, Pt. II. ch. xi., He hath a pyg of the worse panier sure.

5. *A pretty pig makes an ugly old sow.* 1732 : Fuller, No. 363.

6. *A red pig for an atchern* [acorn]. 1886 : R. Holland, *Cheshire Gloss.*, 444 (E.D.S.). 1917 : Bridge, *Cheshire Proverbs*, 5.

7. *As happy as a pig in much.* 1828 : Carr, *Craven Dialect*, ii. 43. 1889 : Peacock, *Manley, etc., Gloss.*, 358 (E.D.S.), " As happy as pigs e' muck," means having one's fill of sensual pleasure.

8. *As Irish as pigs in Shudehill market.* Manchester. 1869 : Hazlitt, 65.

9. *Feed a pig and you'll have a hog.* 1732 : Fuller, No. 1517.

10. *He has brought his pigs to a fine* (or *fair*) *market.* 1600 : *Look About You*, sc. xiii., My fa-fa-father has brought his ho-ho-hogs to a fa-fa-fair m-m-market. *c.* 1613 : Rowlands, *Paire of Spy-Knaues*, 9 (Hunt. Cl.), As wise as Iohn of Gotehams calfe : or this fellow brought his hogges to a faire market. 1693 : Urquhart, *Rabelais*, bk. iii. ch. xlv., I have fish'd fair now (quoth Panurge) and brought my pigs to a

fine market. 1713 : C. Shadwell, *Hum.
of Army*, V. ii., Ah, Gemini, I have
brought my hogs to a fair market.
1757 : Murphy, *Upholsterer*, I. iii., Yes,
you've carried your pigs to a fine
market. 1806 : Lamb, *Mr. H—*, II.,
Your Honour has had some morti-
fication, to be sure . . . you have
brought your pigs to a fine market.
1849 : Planché, *Extravag.*, iv. 32 (1879),
To a fine market you have brought
your pigs.

11. *He is teaching a pig to play on a
flute.* 1813 : Ray, 75.

12. *He knows not a pig from a dog.*
1737 : Ray, 206.

13. *He that loves noise must buy a pig.*
1813 : Ray, 143.

14. *Like a pig, he'll do no good alive.*
1589 : L. Wright, *Display of Dutie*, 10,
A noysome hogg, that is neuer profitable till he dye. 1630 : T. Adams,
Works, 452, Like a two-leg'd hog . . .
neuer doth good, till he is dead. 1732 :
Fuller, No. 3226, Like an hog ; he does
no good till he dies. Ibid., No. 5851,
You are like a hog ; never good, while
living. 1828 : Carr, *Craven Dialect*,
ii. 43, " He's like a pig, he'll do no good
alive," said of a covetous man, regard-
less of the happiness of others. 1847 :
Halliwell, *Dict.*, s.v. " Pig."

15. *Like a pig's tail, going all day,
and nothing done at night.* 1865 :
"Lancs Proverbs," in *N. & Q.*, 3rd ser.,
viii. 494. 1901 : F. E. Taylor, *Lancs
Sayings*, 5.

16. *Pigs can see the wind.* 1663 :
Butler, *Hudibras*, Pt. III. can. ii. l. 1105,
Had lights when better eyes were blind,
as pigs are said to see the wind. 1703 :
E. Ward, *Writings*, ii. 271, 'Tis as
natural . . . as 'tis for a hog to see
the wind. 1831 : Hone, *Year-Book*,
29 Feb. [quoted as a common saying].
1890 : *N. & Q.*, 7th ser., ix. 14, That
pigs can see the wind—in particular
the east wind — is a notion pretty
general in the Midlands. 1916 : *N.& Q.*,
12th ser., ii. 358, I have often heard it
said that wind looks like fire to a pig,
and that only a pig can see the
wind.

17. *Pigs fly in the air with their tails

forward.* 1639 : Clarke, 147. 1670 :
Ray, 189. 1880 : Spurgeon, *Ploughman's Pictures*, 32, They say that if
pigs fly they always go with their tails
forward.

18. *Pigs love that lie together.* 1678 :
Ray, 189. 1707 : C. Cibber, *Double
Gallant*, V. ii., You know the old saying,
Sir Solomon, *Lying together makes pigs
love.* 1732 : Fuller, No. 3874.

19. *Pigs play on the organs.* 1639 :
Clarke, 7, A pig playes, etc. 1670 :
Ray, 189. 1685 : S. Wesley, *Maggots*,
22, Why should not other piggs on
organs play, As well as they ? 1732 :
Fuller, No. 3875. Cf. **Hogs Norton.**

20. *The worst pig often gets the best
pear.* 1855 : Bohn, 519.

21. *The young pig grunts like the old
sow.* 1678 : Ray, 184.

22. *There are more ways.* See quot.
1883 : Burne, *Shropsh. Folk-Lore*, 590,
Theer's more ways o' killin' pigs than
chokin' 'em 'ooth [with] butter.

23. *To buy a pig in a poke* [bag].
1546 : Heywood, *Proverbs*, Pt. II. ch.
ix., Ye loue not to bye the pyg in the
poke. 1583 : Greene, *Works*, ii. 121
(Grosart), He is a foole, they say, that
will buy ye pig in the poke. 1631 : F.
Lenton, *Characters*, sig. B11 (1663),
You may perhaps buy a pigge in a poke.
1694 : *Terence made English*, 165, I
don't love to buy a pig in a bag. 1705 :
Steele, *Tender Husband*, III. ii., I
thought it would be proper to see how
I liked you, as not caring to buy a
pig in a poke. 1806 : Lamb, *Mr. H—*,
II., No great harm if you had. You'd
only have bought a pig in a poke.
1920 : Hudson, *Dead Man's Plack*, ii.
20, Athelwold . . . with a friend's
privilege told him not to be so simple
as to buy a pig in a poke.

24. *To drive pigs to market* = To
snore. 1738 : Swift, *Polite Convers.*,
Dial. II., He fell asleep, and snored so
hard, that we thought he was driving
his hogs to market. 1785 : Grose,
Class. Dict. Vulgar Tongue, s.v. " Hog,"
To drive one's hogs, to snore. 1854 :
Baker, *Northants Gloss.*, s.v. " Pigs,"
" To drive your pigs to market." To
snore. 1901 : F. E. Taylor, *Lancs*

Sayings, 16, He were droivin' th' pigs to th' market (He was snoring).

25. *What can you expect from a pig but a grunt?* 1827 : Scott, *Journal*, 10 April ["sow" for "pig," and "grumph" for "grunt"]. 1916 : B. Duffy, *Special Pleading*, 7.

26. *When pigs carry sticks, The clouds will play tricks; When they lie in the mud, No fears of a flood.* 1893 : Inwards, *Weather Lore*, 130.

27. *When the pig is proffered hold up the poke.* c. 1400 : *Douce MS.*, 52, cited in Farmer's *Heywood's Proverbs*, 422 (1906), When me profereth the pigge, open the poghe. 1530: Palsgrave, 594, Whan the pygge is proferd it is good to apen the poke. c. 1580 : Fulwell, *Ars Adulandi*, sig. G1, When pig is proferd, ope the poke. 1670 : Ray, 131. 1732 : Fuller, No. 5601.

28. *You can never make a good shaft of a pig's tail.* 1605 : Camden, *Remains*, 328 (1870), Make a pipe of a pig's tail. 1651 : Herbert, *Jac. Prudentum*, 2nd ed. 1670 : Ray, 104, You can't make a horn of a pigs tail. 1732 : Fuller, No. 5872. 1880 : Spurgeon, *Ploughman's Pictures*, 31, There's sense in choosing your tools, for a pig's tail will never make a good arrow.

See also First pig; Goodyer's pig; Hog; Like the Irishman's pig; More pigs; Pearls; Pelton; Please (6); Sleep, *verb* (9); Snug; Sow; Stare; Subtle; Swine; and Wilful.

Pigeon and **Pigeons.** 1. *Full pigeons find cherries bitter.* 1623 : Wodroephe, *Spared Houres*, 509.

2. *Pigeons are taken when crows fly at pleasure.* 1732 : Fuller, No. 3873.

3. *Pigeons never do know woe But when they do a benting go.* 1609 : T. Ravenscroft, *Deuteromelia*, sig. F3, The pigion is neuer woe, till abenting she goe. 1670 : Ray, 44. 1732 : Fuller, No. 6480. c. 1791 : Pegge, *Derbicisms*, 89 (E.D.S.), Pigeons never know such woe, As when they a-benting go. 1839 : G. C. Lewis, *Heref. Words*, 10. 1842 : Akerman, *Wilts Gloss.*, 5.

4. *To catch two pigeons with one bean.* 1557 : North, *Diall of Princes*, fo. 56, For the prouerbe sayeth, that with one

beane, a man maye take two pigeons. 1577 : J. Grange, *Golden Aphroditis*, sig. E2, In hoping to take two pigeons with one beane you are decyued. 1602 : Chamberlain, *Letters*, 124 (Camden S.), You deserve double thanckes, and serve two pigeons with one beane. 1678 : Ray, 353.

5. *When the pigeons go a benting, Then the farmers lie lamenting.* 1830 : Forby, *Vocab. E. Anglia*, 417. 1866 : Brogden, *Lincs Prov. Words*, s.v. "Benting," When the dove goes a benting, The farmer is lamenting.

See also Children (9) ; and House (20).

Pilchards. 1. *Cream upon pilchards*, said of a smart dress upon a slatternly woman. S. Corn. 19th cent. (Mr. C. Lee).

2. *Heat and pilchards.* Corn. 1869: Hazlitt, 201.

3. *See* quot. 1875 : Cheales, *Proverb. Folk-Lore*, 53, The results of a school of pilchards coming into one of their bays—Meat, money and light, All in one night.

Pilgarlic. Originally a bald head, but became a proverbial name for any unlucky wight, sometimes in self-application. [c. 1400 : *Beryn*, 5 (E.E.T.S.), And yee shull here howe þe Tapster made þe Pardoner pull Garlik al the longe ny3te, til it was nere end day.] Before 1529 : Skelton, in *Works*, i. 122 (Dyce), Ye loste hyr fauyr quyt; Your pyllyd garleke hed Cowde hocupy there no stede. c. 1620 : B. & F., *Hum. Lieut.*, II. ii., There got he a knock, and down goes pil-garlick. 1671 : *Westm. Drollery*, 38 (Ebsworth), Then to the cupboard Pilgarlick must hie, To seek for some crusts that have long lain dry. 1676 : Shadwell, *Virtuoso*, II., Do you think to make a fool of Pilgarlick? 1709 : Centlivre, *Busy Body*, V. iii., So, here's everybody happy, I find, but poor Pilgarlick. I wonder what satisfaction I shall have. c. 1760 : Foote, *Lame Lover*, III., So then it seems poor Pill Garlick here is discarded at once. 1813 : *Life of Pill Garlick, Rather a Whimsical Sort of Fellow* [title]. 1894 : *Punch*, 21 April, 186 (O.), No! 'tis Bull is pilgarlic and martyr.

Pill and Pills. 1. *If the pills were pleasant, they would not want gilding.* 1633 : Draxe, 57, If the apothecaries pilles had a good taste, they would neuer gilde them ouer. 1732 : Fuller, No. 2711.

2. *To give one a pill to swallow* =To tell one something unpleasant. 1567 : Painter, *Pal. of Pleasure*, iii. 52 (Jacobs), The good lady . . . swallowed down that pille without chewing. 1889 : Peacock, *Manley, etc., Gloss.*, 405 (E.D.S.), It'd be a sore pill for him at his time of life.

Pillar to post, From. Often From post to pillar. *c.* 1420 : Lydgate, *Assembly of Gods*, 34 (E.E.T.S.), Thus fro poost to pylour was he made to daunce. *c.* 1532 : R. Copland, *Spyttel Hous*, l. 715, And turmoyleth alway fro pyler to post. 1575 : *Appius and Virg.*, in Hazlitt, *Old Plays*, iv. 151, Thus in hurly burly, from pillar to post, Poor Haphazard daily was toss'd. 1605 : Chapman, *All Fools*, III. i., . . . from post to pillar. 1609 : Dekker, in *Works*, iv. 136 (Grosart), . . . from poste to piller. 1673 : Marvell, in *Works*, iii. 279 (Grosart), . . . hunted from post to pillar. 1777 : in *Garrick Corresp.*, ii. 202 (1832), Your good nature will forgive me, especially when you consider how I am tossed from pillar to post. 1852 : Dickens, *Bleak House*, ch. xxiv., The man was so badgered, and worried, and tortured, by being knocked about from post to pillar, and from pillar to post . . . 1903 : H. James, *Letters*, i. 435 (1902), It all makes me glad I am old, and thereby soon to take leave of a world in which one is driven, unoffending, from pillar to post.

Pilling Moss, Lancs. 1. *God's grace and Pilling Moss are endless.* Lancs. 1846–59 : *Denham Tracts*, i. 180 (F.L.S.).

2. *Once a wood, then a sea, now a moss, and e'er will be.* 1869 : Hazlitt, 305.

Pilsen-pin. *See* Lenson-hill.

Pimlico. *See* quots. *c.* 1680 : Aubrey, *Nat. Hist. Surrey*, v. 221, *To walk in Pimblico* became proverbial for a man handsomely drest ; as these walks [Pimblico-Path, near the Globe Theatre] were frequented by none else. 1863 : *N. & Q.*, 3rd ser., iv. 327, There is a Devonshire proverb, " To keep it in Pimlico," that is, to keep a house in nice order.

Pimpernel. *No heart can think, no tongue can tell, The virtues of the pimpernel.* 1849 : Halliwell, *Pop. Rhymes*, 179. 1878 : Dyer, *Eng. Folk-Lore*, 26. 1910 : *Devonsh. Assoc. Trans.*, xlii. 90, No heart can think nor tongue can tell The virtue there is in pimpernel.

Pin and Pins, *subs.* 1. *A pin a day is a groat a year.* 1712 : Addison, *Spectator*, No. 295. 1738 : Swift, *Polite Convers.*, Dial. I. 1792 : Wolcot, *Works*, ii. 313 (1795). 1829 : Hunter, *Hallamsh. Gloss.*, 21.

2. *He that takes not up a pin, slights his wife.* 1640 : Herbert, *Jac. Prudentum.* 1670 : Ray, 21. 1732 : Fuller, No. 2324.

3. *He that will not stoop for a pin, will never be worth a pound.* 1667–8 : Pepys, *Diary*, 2 Jan., Sir W. Coventry answered : " I see your Majesty do not remember the old English proverb, ' He that will not,' etc." 1732 : Fuller, No. 2355 [with " point " for " pound "].

4. *He that will steal a pin will steal a better thing.* 1537 : R. Whitford, *Werke for Housholders*, sig. D7, The chylde y[t] beginneth to pike at a pynne or a poynte wyl after pyke a penny or a pounde. 1639 : Clarke, 84, He that begins to steale a pin will be hang'd for a pound one day. 1670 : Ray, 145. 1732 : Fuller, No. 6087. 1896 : *N. & Q.*, 8th ser., x. 320, It is a sin To steal a pin has sometimes helped to keep me straight.

5. *Not to care* (or *pass*) *a pin.* *c.* 1410 : *Towneley Plays*, 34 (E.E.T.S.), In fayth thi felowship Set I not at a pyn. *c.* 1555 : in Wright, *Songs, etc., Philip and Mary*, 89 (Roxb. Cl.), Of Goddes ferfull vengance the[y] passyde note a pynne. 1576 : Wapull, *Tide tarrieth no Man*, sig. D3, So that for her mother she cares not a pin. 1642 : in Marchant, *Praise of Ale*, 234 (1888), Yet I care not a pin, for I see no sin . . . 1663 : in *Amanda, Bagf. Ballads*, 480* (B.S.), Let them laugh that win, I care not a pin.

1779 : S. Crisp, in D'Arblay, *Diary*, i. 104 (1876), As to your vexation, child, I don't mind it of a pin. 1856 : in Marchant, *Praise of Ale*, 415 (1888), For whiskey or gin, I don't care a pin.

6. *Pick up pins pick up sorrow.* 1883 : Burne, *Shropsh. Folk-Lore*, 279, Salopians too say, "Pick up," etc. 1913 : E. M. Wright, *Rustic Speech, etc.*, 220, Pick up pins, pick up sorrow, is a saying which is contradicted by other versions such as [*see* Nos. 7 and 8].

7. *See a pin and let it lie, You'll want a pin before you die.* 1843 : Halliwell, *Nursery Rhymes*, 120, See a pin, and let it lay, Bad luck you'll have all the day ! 1872 : *N. & Q.*, 4th ser., x. 477, I have frequently heard the following in Cornwall : "To see a pin and let it lie, You'll want a pin before you die." 1878 : Dyer, *Eng. Folk-Lore*, 270, See a pin . . . All the day you'll have to cry. 1880 : *N. & Q.*, 6th ser., ii. 205. 1913 : E. M. Wright, *Rustic Speech, etc.*, 220.

8. *See a pin and pick it up, All the day you'll have good luck.* 1843 : Halliwell, *Nursery Rhymes*, 120. 1883 : Burne, *Shropsh. Folk-Lore*, 280. 1913 : E. M. Wright, *Rustic Speech, etc.*, 220.

See also Merry pin.

Pin, *verb. To pin one's faith on another's sleeve.* 1599 : *Life of Sir T. More*, in Wordsworth, *Eccl. Biog.*, ii. 149 (1853) (O.), I never intended to pinne my soule to another mans sleeve. 1642 : Fuller, *Holy State :* "Moderation," He never pinned his religion on any man's sleeve. 1656 : T. Ady, *Candle in the Dark*, 4, To pin their opinion upon the sleeve of other mens judgements. 1706 : E. Ward, *Works*, iii. 20, All that pinn'd their faith upon their pastor's sleeve. 1725 : *Matchless Rogue*, 17, With your leave, good Mr. Poet, we must not pin our faith upon your sleeve. 1809 : Pegge, *Anonymiana*, cent. iii. 63, I find now, that the custom formerly was, for people to wear both badges and presents, such as New-year's gifts, on their sleeves . . . Hence, I suppose, the expression *to pin one's faith on another's sleeve.*

Pinch, At a. 1489 : Caxton, *Faytes*

of A., I. xviii. 53 (O.), Corageously at a pynche [he] shal renne vpon hem. 1540 : Palsgrave, *Acolastus*, sig. Aa3, Do nowe helpe me at a pynche. 1564 : Bullein, *Dialogue*, 10 (E.E.T.S.), You are welcome . . . now helpe at a pinche, or els neuer. 1594 : Greene, *Frier Bacon*, sc. v., Helpe, Frier, at a pinch. 1614 : Jonson, *Bart. Fair*, I. 1679 : *Counterfeits*, I. ii., We women seldom fail at a pinch. 1828 : Scott, *Journal*, 4 April, He had not lived so long by the Crown to desert it at a pinch. 1888 : R. L. S., *Black Arrow*, bk. iv. ch. i., It . . . yet might serve him, in a pinch, against Sir Daniel.

Pinch on the parson's side. *See* Parson's side.

Pine wishes herself a shrub when the ax is at her root, The. 1732 : Fuller, No. 4705.

Pinnock to pannock. *See* quot. 1552 : Huloet, *Abced.*, sig. D3, Brynge somethynge to nothynge, as the vulgare speache is, to brynge pynnock to pannock.

Pint of wine to a vintner is but as a pippin to a coster-monger, A. 1659 : Howell, 11.

Pipe in an ivy leaf, You may go = You may do any silly thing you like. *c.* 1370 : Wiclif, *Eng. Works*, 372 (E.E.T.S.), The seculer party may go pipe with an yuy lete for eny lordeschipis that the clerkis wille geue hem agen. *c.* 1386 : Chaucer, *Knight's Tale*, l. 980, That oon of yow, al be him looth or leef, He moot go pypen in an ivy-leef. *c.* 1430 : Lydgate, *Destr. of Thebes*, Pt. II., But let his brother blowe in an horn, Where that him list, or pipe in a reade. *c.* 1547 : in *Ballads from MSS.*, i. 136 (B.S.), They may gowe blowe ther fluett. 1587 : Turbervile, *Trag. Tales, etc.*, 309 (1837), Giue him an iuie leafe in stead of pipe to play, That dreads to bourd a gallant dame for feare she say him nay. 1626 : *Scoggins Jests*, 109 (1864), Unlesse that hee have some man to speake for him, hee may goe pipe in an ivy leafe.

Pipe, No longer, no longer dance. 1605 : Camden, *Remains*, 328 (1870). 1620 : Shelton, *Quixote*, Pt. II. ch. vii.,

It shall not be said, master, for me,
"No longer pipe, no longer dance."
1709: O. Dykes, *Eng. Proverbs*, 197
(2nd ed.). 1806: Scott, *Fam. Letters*,
i. 61 (1894), The vulgar saying of "No
longer pipe, no longer dance," applies
to landlord and tenant, chieftain and
clan . . . in short, to all the relations of
mankind. 1874: *N. & Q.*, 5th ser.,
i. 205.

Piping hot. *c.* 1386: Chaucer, *Miller's Tale*, l. 193, And wafres, pyping
hote out of the glede. 1567: Golding,
Ovid, bk. viii. l. 850, Whote [Hot] meate
came pyping from the fyre. 1595:
Maroccus Extaticus, iii. (Percy S.), A
peece of beefe puld piping hot out of
the furnace. 1638: H. Shirley, *Martyr'd Souldier*, V., I gave her a messe
of porredge piping-hot. 1701: Cibber,
Love Makes a Man, Prol., A ragou, piping hot from Paris. 1766: Garrick,
Neck or Nothing, I. i. 1821: Byron,
Blues, ecl. i. l. 17, I am just piping hot
from a publisher's shop.

Pipkin, She has cracked her. 1681:
in *Roxb. Ballads*, v. 67 (B.S.), For if
you should your pipkin crack, your
credit will away. *c.* 1685: in *Bagford
Ballads*, i. 467 (B.S.), Were not my
pipkin crackt before, I vow I would be
his wife. 1707: *Spanish Bawd*, III. ii.,
If her husband shou'd find out that she
has crackt her pipkin, he'll cut your
throat. 1732: Fuller, No. 4124, She
has broke her pipkin.

**Pirates may make cheap pennyworths
of their pillage.** 1855: Bohn, 474.

Piss on a nettle, To =To be out of
temper. 1546: Heywood, *Proverbs*,
Pt. II. ch. x. 1579: *Marr. of Wit and
Wisdom*, sc. iii. p. 30 (Sh. S.). 1681:
Shadwell, *Lancs Witches*, I. 1714:
Ozell, *Molière*, iv. 255. 1828: Carr,
Craven Dialect, ii. 8, "Thou's p—d of
a nettle this mornin'," said of a waspish,
ill-tempered person.

Pissed his tallow, He has. *c.* 1450:
M. E. Med. Book, 232 (Heinrich), (O.),
Take talow of an hert, suche as he
pysseþ by twene two seynt mary dayes.
1600: Shakespeare, *Merry Wives*, V. v.
1694: Motteux, *Rabelais*, bk. v. ch.
xxviij., Do but see how down o' the

mouth the curr looks : he's nothing but
skin and bones ; he has p—d his tallow.
1737: Ray, 61, . . . This is spoken of
bucks who grow lean after rutting time,
and may be applied to men.

Pitch and pay= Pay ready money.
15th cent.: in Hazlitt, *Early Pop. Poetry*,
ii. 9, Yt ys fule hard bothe to pyche
and paye. 1584: in *Roxb. Ballads*, i. 6
(B.S.), And there was neither fault nor
fray, Nor any disorder any way, But
euery man did pitch and pay. 1599:
Shakespeare, *Henry V.*, II. iii., The word
is "Pitch and Pay": Trust none.
1847: Halliwell, *Dict.*, s.v. "Pitch,"
Pitch and pay, throw down your money
at once, pay ready money.

Pitch. *He that touches pitch shall
be defiled.* [*Ecclesiasticus* xiii. 1. Ex
quo ostenditur noxium esse vivere cum
peccatoribus ; qui enim tangit picem,
inquinatur ab eâ.—St. Jerome, *Comment. in Esai.*, vi. 5.] 1303: R.
Brunne, *Handl. Synne*, l. 6578, Who so
handlyþ pycche wellyng hote, He shal
haue fylþe þerof sumdeyl [in some degree]. *c.* 1380: Wiclif, *Works*, 218
(Matthew, 1880), He that handlith pich
schal be foulid thereof. *c.* 1440: Lydgate, *Fall of Princes*, bk. i. l. 4696, Who
touchith pich, bassay men may see, It
failith nat he shal defouled be. 1579:
Lyly, *Euphues*, 111 (Arber). 1609:
Dekker, *Works*, iv. 198 (Grosart).
1710: S. Palmer, *Moral Essays on
Proverbs*, 249. 1883: R. L. S., *Treasure
I.*, ch. x., "There," John would add,
" you can't touch pitch and not be
mucked." 1922: Weyman, *Ovington's
Bank*, ch. xxxi., You can't touch pitch
and keep your hands clean.

**Pitcher goes often to the well, but is
broken at last, The.** 1340: *Ayenbite*,
206 (E.E.T.S.), Zuo longe geþ þet pot
to þe wetere þet hit comþ to-broke
hom. 1412: Hoccleve, *Regement*, l.
4432, The pot so longë to the watir
goth, That hoom it cometh at the laste
y-broke. 1481: Caxton, *Reynard*, 67
(Arber), A pot may goo so longe to water
that at the laste it cometh to broken
hoom. 1583: Greene, in *Works*, ii. 30
(Grosart), So longe the pitcher goeth
to the brooke, as in tyme it comes

broken home. 1665 : Head and Kirk-man, *Eng. Rogue*, i. 69, I found the proverb verified, The pitcher goes not so often to the well, but that it comes home crackt at last. 1714 : Ozell, *Molière*, vi. 50. 1748 : Smollett, *Rod. Random*, ch. lxiv. 1826 : Scott, *Journal*, 1 Oct., They talk about the pitcher going to the well ; but if it does not go to the well, how shall we get water ? 1926 : J. S. Fletcher, *Massingham Butterfly*, 275, You know the old proverb about the pitcher going to the well ?

Pitchers. *See* **Little pitchers.**

Pitiful surgeon spoileth a sore, A. 1578 : Florio, *First Fruites*, fo. 32, A pitifull physition maketh a scabed wound. 1611 : Cotgrave, s.v. " Mede-cin."

Pity cureth envy. 1732 : Fuller, No. 3876.

Pity is but one remove from love. 1753 : Richardson, *Grandison*, i. 34 (1883). [Nowadays the more usual form is, Pity is akin to love.]

Pity's a poor plaster. 1875 : Cheales, *Proverb. Folk-Lore*, 122.

Pity without relief Is like mustard without beef. Ibid., 122. 1913 : *Devonsh. Assoc. Trans.*, xlv. 90, Pity without relief is like pudding without suet [or] like mustard without beef. Cf. **Sympathy.**

Pity, verb. *He that pities another remembers himself.* 1640 : Herbert, *Jac. Prudentum.* 1748 : Richardson, *Clarissa*, iv. 121 (1785).

Place for everything, and everything in its place, A. 1875 : Smiles, *Thrift*, 66. 1927 : *Evening Standard*, 24 Oct., p. 6, col. 1, He appeals to the more rational view that there is a place for everything, but that everything should be in its place.

Plain as a pack-saddle. 1553 : T. Wilson, *Rhetorique*, 143 (1580) (O.), An honeste true dealyng seruant . . . plaine as a packe - saddle. 1613 : Wither, *Abuses Stript, etc.*, To the Reader, As plaine (as they say) as a pack-saddle. 1670 : Ray, 202. 1736 : Bailey, *Dict.*, s.v. " Plain."

Plain as a (a) pack-staff ; (b) pike-staff. (*a*) 1532 : More, *Works*, 814 (1557). 1542 : Becon, *Early Works*, 276 (P.S.),

He is as plain as a pack-staff. 1589 : Greene, *Works*, vi. 68 (Grosart). 1608 : Middleton, *Family of Love*, V. iii., It shows 'em a flat case as plain as a pack-staff. 1690 : Dryden, *Amphitryon*, III. i. 1881 : Evans, *Leics. Words*, 207 (E.D.S.), The common proverbial simile, " as plain as a pike-staff," is here generally, " as plain as a pack-staff " [the pedlar's staff on which he carries his bundle over his shoulder]. 1886 : Elworthy, *West Som. Word-Book*, 552 (E.D.S.), " So plain's a pack-stave," which literature has corrupted into " plain as a pike - staff." (*b*) 1565 : Shacklock, *Hatchet of Heresies*, fo. 1, They be as playne as a pyke staff. 1591 : Greene, *Works*, x. 21 (Grosart), Plain as a pike - staf. 1664 : Cotton, *Scarronides*, bk. i., Plain as a pike-staff without gilding. *c.* 1750 : Foote, *Knights*, II. 1859 : Dickens, in *C. Dickens as Editor*, 273 (1912), I have read the letter to Evans (which is as plain as a pike staff). 1921 : Hutchinson, *If Winter Comes*, Pt. I. ch. i., Can imagine him riling any wife with wrinkling up his nut over some plain as a pikestaff thing.

Plain as the nose. *See* **Nose** (2).

Plain dealing is a jewel. 1583 : Melbancke, *Philotimus*, Epist. Ded., Plaine dealing is a iewel (though they that vse it commonly die beggers). 1587 : J. Bridges, *Def. of Govt. in Ch. of England*, 124. 1608 : Day, *Law Trickes*, II., *Adam*. . . . thereby grew the prouerbe " plaine dealing is a iewell." *Lu.* But he that vseth it shall die a begger. 1630 : T. Adams, *Works*, 133 [as in 1608]. 1691 : *Merry Drollery*, 81 (Ebsworth) [as in 1608]. 1692 : Congreve, *Old Bach.*, IV. xxii. 1732 : Fuller, No. 3878, . . . ; but they that wear it, are out of fashion. 1775 : Garrick, *Bon Ton*, II. ii.

Plain dealing is dead. 1616 : B. Rich, *Ladies Looking Glasse*, 60, Plaine dealing : honesty is dead. 1732 : Fuller : No. 3879, Plain dealing is dead ; and dyed without issue. 1880 : Spurgeon, *Ploughman's Pictures*, 20 [as in 1732].

Plain dealing is praised more than practised. 1639 : Clarke, 138.

Plain fashion is best, The. 1562 : Heywood, *Epigr.*, No. 201. 1659 : Howell, 7.

Plain of poverty and die a beggar. 1678 : Ray, 191.

Planny. *See* Schemey.

Plants trees, He that, loves others besides himself. 1732 : Fuller, No. 2248.

Plant thorns. *See* Thorn (1).

Play, women and wine undo men laughing. 1659 : Howell, 1. 1670 : Ray, 21. 1732 : Fuller, No. 3884. 1880 : Spurgeon, *Ploughman's Pictures*, 11, Play, women and wine are enough to make a prince a pauper.

PLAY, *verb*:

Play at chess. *See* House (18).

Play at small game before he will sit out, He will. 1605 : Camden, *Remains*, 323 (1870). 1631 : Brathwait, *Whimzies*, 148 (1859). Before 1680 : Butler, *Remains*, i. 253 (1759), The devil himself will rather chuse to play At paltry small game, than sit out, they say. 1732 : Fuller, No. 3882 [" stand out " for " sit out "].

Play Benall, To. Glos. 1639 : in *Berkeley MSS.*, iii. 27 (1885), I must play Benall with you. A frequent speach when the guest, immediately after meat, without any stay departeth.

Play booty, To = To play a treacherous part. 1540 : Palsgrave, *Acolastus*, sig. T4, Shall not I be boty or party felow with the ? 1560 : Awdeley, *Vacabondes*, 9 (E.E.T.S.), They wil . . . consent as though they wil play booty against him. 1692 : L'Estrange, *Æsop*, 116 (3rd ed.), We understand what we ought to do ; but when we come to deliberate, we play booty against our selves. 1707 : Cibber, *Comical Lovers*, II., I believe the Devil plays booty against himself, and tells you of my sins. 1742 : Fielding, *Andrews*, bk. i. ch. ii., He had scornfully refused a considerable bribe to play booty on such an occasion. 1817 : Scott, *Rob Roy*, ch. vii., My uncle is sensible . . . that, were he caught playing booty, he would be disarmed. 1838 : Dickens, *Twist*, ch. ix., Five of 'em strung up in a row, and none left to play booty, or turn white-livered ! 1898 : Weyman,

Shrewsbury, ch. xii., He had played booty, and played the traitor.

Play fast and loose, To. 1557 : *Tottels Miscell.*, 157 (Arber), Of a new maried student that plaied fast or loose. 1580 : Lyly, *Euphues*, 326 (Arber), Thus with the Ægyptian thou playest fast or loose. 1601 : Yarington, *Two Trag. in One*, III. ii., in Bullen, *Old Plays*, iv. 49, Thou . . . dastard fast and loose, Thou weathercocke of mutabilitie. 1629 : in *Pepysian Garland*, 320 (Rollins), But she that wanton is and fond, that fast and loose will play. 1853 : Dickens, *Letters*, iii. 139 (1882), The journal itself is blowing hot and cold, and playing fast and loose in a ridiculous way.

Play for nought as work for nought, As good. 1546 : Heywood, *Proverbs*, Pt. I. ch. xi. 1642 : D. Rogers, *Naaman*, sig. Q6, They had as good sit for nought as toyle for nought. 1714 : Mandeville, *Fable of Bees*, 218, The fellow . . . told him he'd rather play for nothing than work for nothing. 1823 : Scott, *Peveril*, ch. xxv.

Play in summer starve in winter. 1669 : *Poor Robin Alman.*, July.

Play least in sight, To. 1607 : R. West, *Court of Conscience*, sig. D1, Now forasmuch as you play least in sight, That Maister Derrick [the hangman] cannot seize vpon you. 1659 : Howell, 10. 1678 : Ray, 75. 1714 : *Spectator*, No. 616, We had with us the attorney, and two or three other bright fellows. The doctor plays least in sight.

Play on both hands, To = To be guilty of double-dealing. 1530 : Palsgrave, 433, If he ones apperceyve you howe you play on bothe the handes, he wyll never truste you after. 1633 : Draxe, 47, He playeth on both handes.

Play one tune and dance another, They. 1639 : Clarke, 18.

Play racket, To. c. 1374 : Chaucer, *Troylus*, bk. iv. l. 432, Canstow pleyen raket, to and fro, netle in, dokke out ? c. 1387 : Usk, *Test. of Love*, in Skeat's *Chaucer*, vii. 13, " Ye wete wel, lady, eke," quod I, " that I have not played raket, ' nettil in, docke out,' and with the wethercocke waved."

**Plays his money ought not to value it,
He that.** 1640: Herbert, *Jac. Prudentum.*

**Plays more than he sees, forfeits his
eyes to the king, He that.** 1605 : Camden, *Remains*, 324 (1870). 1670 : Ray,
132.

Plays well that wins, He. 1562 :
Heywood, *Three Hund. Epigr.*, No. 230,
He pleyth best that wins. 1640 :
Herbert, *Jac. Prudentum.* 1670 : Ray,
132. 1732 : Fuller, No. 2005.

**Plays you as fair as if he picked your
pocket, He.** 1678 : Ray, 79.

Play the devil for God's sake. *See*
Devil (104).

Play the fool. *See* quots. 1659 :
Howell, *Proverbs: Brit.-Eng.*, 7, If thou
play the fool, stay for a fellow. 1732 :
Fuller, No. 2849, It is a cunning part
to play the fool well.

Play the Good Luck, To = To do
mischief. 1917 : Bridge, *Cheshire Proverbs*, 141.

Play the Jack, To = Query, To play
the knave. 1567 : Golding, *Ovid*, bk.
xiii. 1. 289, Yit durst Thersites bee So
bold as rayle uppon the kings, and he
was payd by mee For playing so the
sawcye Jacke. 1611 : Shakespeare, *Tempest*, IV. i., Monster, your fairy . . .
has done little better than played the
Jack with us. 1670 : Ray, 182.

Play wily beguile, To. 1633 : Draxe,
40, He playeth wily beguile you with
himselfe. 1732 : Fuller, No. 1895, He
hath play'd a wiley trick, and beguil'd
himself. 1737 : Ray, 66, He hath
plaid wily beguiled with himself.

Play with a fool. *See* **Fool** (90).

**Play with boys, you must take boys'
play, If you.** 1732 : Fuller, No. 2779.

**Play with children and let the saints
alone.** 1659 : Howell, *Proverbs: Ital.-
Eng.*, 8, Jest with boyes, and leave the
saints alone. 1710 : S. Palmer, *Moral
Essays on Proverbs*, 322.

**Play with me and hurt me not, Jest
with me and shame me not.** 1582 :
Harvey, *Marginalia*, 188 (1913). 1589 :
Puttenham, *Eng. Poesie*, 261 (Arber)
[quoted as "this common prouerbe,"
but with "Iape" for "Play," and
"Bourde" for "Jest"]. 1591 : Harington, *Orl. Furioso*, bk. xii., Moral.

1630 : Brathwait, *Eng. Gentleman*, 152
(1641). 1656 : F. Osborne, *Advice to
Son*, 34 (Parry), Play with me, but hurt
me not.

**Play with you for shoe-buckles, I'll
not.** 1639 : Clarke, 195, We play not
for shooe-buckles. 1678 : Ray, 347.

Playden, Sussex. *See* quot. 1894 :
A. J. C. Hare, *Sussex*, 63, The proverb—
"Sauket church, crooked steeple,
Drunken parson, wicked people" refers
to Playden, known as Sauket or Saltcot
Street, from the salted cod spread on
its banks to dry.

Pleasant hours fly fast. 1732 : Fuller,
No. 3886.

Please, verb. 1. *He had need rise
betimes that would please everybody.*
1639 : Fuller, *Holy War*, bk. iv. ch. xiv.,
He must rise early, yea, not at all go to
bed, who will have everyone's good
word. 1670 : Ray, 132. 1732 : Fuller,
No. 1854. 1875 : Cheales, *Proverb.
Folk-Lore*, 115, He must rise early that
would please everybody.

2. *He that all men will please shall
never find ease.* 1639 : Clarke, 282.
1692 : L'Estrange, *Æsop*, 325 (3rd ed.),
He that resolves not to go to bed till
all the world is pleas'd, shall be troubled
with the head-ach. 1880 : Spurgeon,
Ploughman's Pictures, 25.

3. *He that would please all and himself too, undertakes what he cannot do.*
1659 : Howell, 5. 1670 : Ray, 132.
1732 : Fuller, No. 6384, . . . what none
could ever do.

4. *If you be not pleased, put your hand
in your pocket and please yourself.* 1678 :
Ray, 79. 1732 : Fuller, No. 2739
["content" for "pleased"].

5. *Please the eye and plague the heart.*
[1611 : Cotgrave, s.v. "Marchandise,"
Please the eye and picke the purse.]
1655 : A. Brewer, *Love-sick King*, III.,
in Bang, *Materialien*, B. 18, p. 38, She
may please your eye a little . . . but
vex your heart. 1754 : *World*, No. 80,
It is a fatal maxim among women, "To
please the eye, though they torment
the heart." 1829 : Cobbett, *Advice to
Young Men*, Lett. III., "Please your
eye and plague your heart" is an adage
that want of beauty invented, I dare

say, more than a thousand years ago.
1913 : *Folk-Lore*, xxiv. 77, (Oxfordsh.)
I'll please my eye if I plague my heart.

6. *Please the pigs*. Before 1704 : T.
Brown, in *Works*, ii. 198 (1760), I'll
have one of the wigs to carry into the
country with me, and please the pigs.
1755 : *Gent. Mag.*, 115, The expression
I mean is *An't please the pigs*, in which
. . . *pigs* is most assuredly a corruption
of Pyx. [This suggested origin of the
phrase is as doubtful as that given in
the 1886 quot. *infra*.] 1790 : *Gent.
Mag.*, 876, 1086–7. 1826–44 : Hood,
Comic Poems: "Report from Below,"
"But please the pigs,"—for that's
her way of swearing in a passion.
1849 : Planché, *Extravag.*, iv. 33 (1879),
You'll have no end of money, please
the pigs. 1886 : Elworthy, *West Som.
Word-Book*, 569 (E.D.S.), Pigs. Contraction of pixies, in the common saying, " Plaze God and the pigs."

7. *When it pleaseth not God, the saint
can do little*. 1670 : Ray, 23.

Pleased as a dog with two tails, As.
1889 : Peacock, *Manley, etc., Gloss.*, 169
(E.D.S.).

Pleased as if the pot was on, As.
Oxfordsh. 1913 : *Folk-Lore*, xxiv. 77.

Pleased as Punch, As. 1854 : Dickens,
Hard Times, bk. i. ch. vi., When Sissy
got into the school here . . . her father
was as pleased as Punch. 1871 : G.
Eliot, *Middlemarch*, ch. xl., I'm as
pleased as Punch, now I've thought of
that. 1901 : F. E. Taylor, *Lancs Sayings*, 3, As pleeos't as Punch.

Pleasing ware is half sold. 1611 :
Cotgrave, s.v. " Chose," Ware that doth
please is halfe sold. 1640 : Herbert,
Jac. Prudentum. 1670 : Ray, 132.
1732 : Fuller, No. 5617, When ware is
lik'd, it is half sold.

Pleasure, *subs.* 1. *Consider not pleasures as they come, but as they go*. 1855 :
Bohn, 339.

2. *Follow pleasure and pleasure will
flee; Flee pleasure and pleasure will
follow thee*. 1546 : Heywood, *Proverbs*,
Pt. I. ch. xi. 1667 : Peacham, *Worth
of Penny*, in Arber, *Garner*, vi. 261
(1883), ["fly" for first "flee," and " be
nigh " for " follow thee "]. 1736 :

Franklin, *Way to Wealth*, in *Works*, i.
445 (Bigelow), Fly pleasures, and they
will follow you.

3. *It is a great pleasure to eat, and
have nothing to pay*. 1855 : Bohn, 427.

4. *Let pleasure overcome thee and thou
learnest to like it*. c. 1320: in *Reliq.
Antiquæ*, i. 110 (1841), "Let lust over-
gon, eft hit shal the lyke," Quoth
Hendyng. 1869 : Hazlitt, 259.

5. *Never pleasure without repentance*.
1605 : Camden, *Remains*, 329 (1870).
1670 : Ray, 21. 1736 : Bailey, *Dict.*,
s.v. " Pleasure."

6. *Pleasure has a sting in its tail*.
1650 : Taylor, *Holy Living*, ch. ii. § 1,
All the instances of pleasure have a
sting in the tail. 1692 : Congreve, *Old
Bach.*, Epil., To think o' th' sting, that's
in the tail of pleasure. Before 1704 :
T. Brown, *Works*, i. 313 (1760), You
know the old saying, pleasure, etc.
1709 : O. Dykes, *Eng. Proverbs*, 172
(2nd ed.), There's a sting in the tail of
all unlawful pleasures.

7. *The pleasures of the mighty are the
tears of the poor*. 1633 : Draxe, 141.
1670 : Ray, 21. 1732 : Fuller, No.
4708, The pleasures of the rich are
bought with the tears of the poor.

8. *Who will in time present from
pleasure refrain, Shall, in time to come,
the more pleasure obtain*. 1546 : Heywood, *Proverbs*, Pt. I. ch. xi.

See also Short pleasure.

**Pledge your own health, You must
not.** 1678 : Ray, 152.

Plentiful. *See* Blackberries.

Plenty breeds pride. 1639 : Clarke, 33.

Plenty is better than a flush, A. 1881 :
Evans, *Leics. Words*, 202 (E.D.S.), I
once quoted the proverb: "A plenty's
better nur a flush," to a farm-labourer,
who answered me with : " Ah, sure !
that's what o'd Bendigo Bilson said
when the yoong masster gen 'im a
chaarge o' rabbit-shot i' the leg."

Plenty is no dainty. c. 1449 : Pecock,
Repr., 184 (O.), Experience wole weel
scheme that plente is no deinte. 1546 :
Heywood, *Proverbs*, Pt. II. ch. iv.
1583 : Melbancke, *Philotinus*, sig. Q2,
I will not be daintie . . . suche guests
as I be plentie. 1678 : Ray, 190.

Plenty know good ale but don't know much after that. N. Corn. 20th cent. (Mr. C. Lee).

Plenty makes dainty. 1732 : Fuller, No. 6375, Tis plenty that makes you dainty. 1869 : Spurgeon, *John Ploughman*, ch. v.

Plenty makes poor. 1590 : Spenser, *F. Q.*, I. iv. 29, Whose plenty made him poor. 1621 : Brathwait, *Natures Embassie*, 269 (1877), She prou'd this true : Much plentie made her poore. 1669 : *Politeuphuia*, 130, Plenty begetteth want ; for he that hath much needs much.

Plenty never wrings its master by the ear. Glos. 1639 : in *Berkeley MSS.*, iii. 31 (1885).

Plenty. *See also* Abundance ; and Peace (2).

Plough, *subs.* 1. *He that by the plough would thrive, himself must either hold or drive.* 1678 : Ray, 191. 1736 : Franklin, *Way to Wealth*, in *Works*, i. 445 (Bigelow). 1860 : A. de Morgan, in *N. & Q.*, 2nd ser., x. 390.

2. *Keep thy plough jogging, so shalt thou have corn for thy horses.* 1659 : Howell, 11, If your plow be jogging, you may have meat for your horses. 1732 : Fuller, No. 3119.

3. *Never let the plough stand to catch a mouse.* 1678 : Ray, 265. 1710 : S. Palmer, *Moral Essays on Proverbs*, 5. 1869 : Spurgeon, *John Ploughman*, ch. i. 1917 : Bridge, *Cheshire Proverbs*, 50, Don't stop the plough to catch a mouse.

4. *The plough goes not well if the ploughman hold it not.* 1639 : Clarke, 92. 1670 : Ray, 132. 1732 : Fuller, No. 4710.

5. *The plough goeth before the oxen =* The cart before the horse. 1571 : *Satir. Poems Reform.*, xxix. 9 (O.), That makis . . . the plewche befoir the oxin go, the best the man to gyde. 1623 : Wodroephe, *Spared Houres*, 501. 1653 : Urquhart, *Rabelais*, 1 (Farmer) (O.), He would put the plough before the oxen.

6. *There belongs more than whistling to going to plough.* 1678 : Ray, 191. 1732 : Fuller, No. 4866 [" a plowman " for " going to plough "].

7. *Where the plough shall fail to go,*

There the weeds will surely grow. 1880 : Spurgeon, *Ploughman's Pictures*, 146.

See also Better have one plough ; Borrowed ploughs ; and Scythe.

Plough, *verb.* 1. *He is ploughing a rock.* 1813 : Ray, 75.

2. *He ploughs the air.* Ibid., 75.

3. *I might as well plough with dogs.* 1611 : Cotgrave, s.v. " Charruë," The plough that a dog drawes is not worth the driving. 1795 : *Gent. Mag.*, Pt. I., 299, I have seen a friendly dame, winding a ravelled skain of thread or yarn, exclaim with a curse, " This is as bad as ploughing with dogs." 1891 : Addy, *Sheffield Gloss. Suppl.*, 44 (E.D.S.), Get on wi' thee ; it's as bad as plewin' wi' dogs. 1917 : Bridge, *Cheshire Proverbs*, 79.

4. *Plough deep while others sleep And you shall have corn to sell and keep.* 1659 : Howell, *Proverbs: Span.-Eng.*, 8, Plow deep, thou shalt have bread enough. 1736 : Franklin, *Way to Wealth*, in *Works*, i. 444 (Bigelow) [" sluggards " for " others "]. 1846 : Denham, *Proverbs*, 14 (Percy S.). 1872 : J. Glyde, jr., *Norfolk Garland*, 158.

5. *Plough or plough not, you must pay your rent.* 1846 : Denham, *Proverbs*, 1 (Percy S.).

6. *To plough the headlands before the butts =* "To begin a thing at the wrong end (as by a suitor applying to the father before the daughter !)." 1883 : Burne, *Shropsh. Folk-Lore*, 597.

7. *To plough the sands.* [Nos tamen hoc agimus tenuique in pulvere sulcos Ducimus et litus sterili versamus aratro. —Juvenal, *Sat.*, vii. 48–9.] Before 1529 : Skelton, *Speke, Parrot*, l. 342, To sowe corne in the see sande, ther wyll no crope growe. 1576 : Pettie, *Petite Pall.*, ii. 95 (Gollancz), So that I plough the barren rocks, and set my share into the shore of the sea. 1587 : Turbervile, *Trag. Tales, etc.*, 404 (1837), And fruitlesse cleane to sowe the barrain sand. 1647 : Stapylton, *Juvenal*, 121, Yet still we plow the shoare and sow the sand. 1894 : Mr. Asquith, *Speech*, 21 Nov., All our time, all our labour, and all our assiduity is as certain to be thrown away as if you were to plough

the sands of the seashore the moment that Bill reaches the Upper Chamber. Cf. **Sow**, *verb* (3).

8. *To plough with the ass and the ox =* To sort things ill. 1813 : Ray, 212.

9. *You must plough with such oxen as you have.* 1678 : Ray, 191, A man must, etc. 1732 : Fuller, No. 5968. 1869 : Spurgeon, *John Ploughman*, ch. i., You know we are obliged to plough with such cattle as we have found for us.

Ploughman. *See* **Bad ploughman**; and **Yeoman**.

Plover. *See* quot. 1655 : T. Muffett, *Healths Improvement*, 98, The gray plover is so highly esteemed, that this proverb is raised of a curious and malecontented stomach : *A gray plover cannot please him.*

Plum as a juggle-mear, As = As soft as a quagmire. Devon. 1670 : Ray, 218.

Plum year, a dumb year, A. 1678 : Ray, 52. 1732 : Fuller, No. 6139. 1856 : *N. & Q.*, 2nd ser., i. 84 [Norfolk]. 1893 : Inwards, *Weather Lore*, 5, A plum year, a dumb year. Kent. In the year when plums flourish all else fails. Devonshire.

Plum. *See also* **Black** (1).

Plumbland Church. 1860 : Whellan, *Cumberland, etc.*, 366, The greatest wonder ever was seen Is Plumbland Church on Parsonby Green.

Plump as a partridge, As. 1678 : Ray, 281. 1694 : *Terence made English*, 62. 1720 : Gay, *Poems*, ii. 278 (Underhill), Plump as a partridge was I known. 1829 : Scott, *Geierstein*, ch. xiii. 1831 : Peacock, *Crotchet Castle*, ch. xiv.

Plum-tree. *See* quots. 1639 : Clarke, 88. The higher the plum - tree, the sweeter the plumme. 1659 : Howell, 17, The higher the tree, the sweeter the plumb ; The better the shooe, the blacker the thumb. 1670 : Ray, 210, The higher the plum-tree, the riper the plum ; The richer the cobler, the blacker his thumb. 1732 : Fuller, No. 6420 [as in 1670].

Plymouth cloak, A = A cudgel. 1625 : Massinger, *New Way, etc.*, I. i., I must tell you if you but advance Your Plimworth cloke . . . 1631 : F. Lenton, *Characters*, sig. F7 (1663), A Plimmouth cloake, otherwise call'd a battoone.

1681 : A. Behn, *Rover*, Pt. II. V. iii. 1855 : Kingsley, *West. Ho!*, ch. vii., " Thou wilt please to lay down that Plymouth cloak of thine," and he pointed to the cudgel.

Plymouth was a furzy down, When, Plympton was a borough town. 1850 : *N. & Q.*, 1st ser., ii. 511.

Pocket a wrong, etc., To = To accept it without protest. 1595 : Munday, *John a Kent*, 28 (Sh. S.), I will not pocket this injurious wrong. 1597 : Shakespeare, 1 *Henry IV.*, III. iii., You will not pocket up wrong. 1638 : D. Tuvill, *Vade Mecum*, 184 (3rd ed.), To pocket up one wrong, is to allure another. 1772 : Graves, *Spirit. Quixote*, bk. vi. ch. xiii., I thought it best to pocket the insult, as well as the money. 1826 : Scott, *Woodstock*, ch. xxiii., The bravest man sacrifices nothing by pocketing a little wrong which he cannot personally resent.

Poets are born, but orators are made. *c.* 1581 : Sidney, *Apologie*, 62 (Arber), Therefore is it an old prouerbe, *Orator fit; Poeta nascitur.* 1600 : Bodenham, *Belvedere*, 55 (Spens. S.). 1669 : *Politeuphuia*, 58.

Poets. *See also* **Painters**.

Poison embitters much sweetness, A little. *c.* 1175 : *Old Eng. Homilies*, 1st ser., p. 23 (Morris), A lutel ater bitteret muchel swete. 1581 : Lyly, *Euphues*, 39 (Arber), One droppe of poyson infecteth the whole tunne of wine.

Poison is poison though it comes in a golden cup. 1630 : T. Adams, *Works*, 705. 1633 : Draxe, 60, In golden pottes are hidden the most deadly poyson.

Pole-cat, To stink like a. 1639 : Clarke, 293, He stinkes like a pole-cat. 1670 : Ray, 207. 1700 : Ward, *London Spy*, 44 (1924), Which made the crooked vermin out-stink a pole-cat. 1740 : North, *Examen*, 172, All which stuff is as rank as a pole-cat. 1889 : J. Nicholson, *Folk Speech E. Yorks*, 22, It stinks like a fummat (pole-cat).

Policy goes beyond strength. *c.* 1590 : G. Harvey, *Marginalia*, 100 (1913), A lytle pollicy præuaileth when a great deale of strength fayleth. Before 1634 : Chapman, *Alphonsus*, II. iii., Policy

help'd above strength. 1666 : Torriano, *Piazza Univ.*, 133. 1754 : Berthelson, *Eng.-Danish Dict.*, s.v. " Policy."
Polperro. *See* quot. 1906 : Q.-
Couch, *Mayor of Troy*, ch. x., The proverb says that a Polperro jackass is
surprised at nothing.

Pomeroy's cat, Hurried in mind, like.
1888 : Q.-Couch, *Troy Town*, ch. xiii.
1908 : *Eng. Ill. Mag.*, Jan., 355.

Pomfret, As sure as a louse in. 1638 :
Brathwait, *Barn. Journal*, Pt. III., A
louse in Pomfrait is not surer, Then
the poor through sloth securer. 1790 :
Grose, *Prov. Gloss.*, s.v. " Yorkshire."
1878 : *Folk-Lore Record*, i. 168, As
" sure as a louse in Pomfret," speaks
ill for that place.

Pompey is on your back. 1869 :
Hazlitt, 317, The *black dog Pompey* is
said to be on a child's back, when he is
fractious. This is a common saying
in some parts of the country . . . In
South Devonshire, they say in a similar
sense, " your tail's on your shoulder."

Pontefract. *See* Pomfret.

Poole, Dorset. 1790 : Grose, *Prov.
Gloss.*, s.v. " Dorset," [three sayings]
(1) If Pool was a fish-pool, and the men
of Pool fish, There'd be a pool for the
devil, and fish for his dish. (2) When
do you fetch the five pounds ? (3)
Shoot zaftly, docy now. [(2) refers
to a story of a never-claimed bequest of
£5 for honesty; (3) refers to a yarn
about a man holding a kettle to receive
shot discharged from guns.]

Poor, *adj.* 1. *A poor beauty finds
more lovers than husbands.* 1640 : Herbert, *Jac. Prudentum.*

2. *A poor man's cow dies, a rich man's
child.* Ibid.

3. *A poor man's debt makes a great
noise.* 1732 : Fuller, No. 355.

4. *A poor man's table is soon spread.*
1633 : Draxe, 136. 1670 : Ray, 132.
1869 : Spurgeon, *John Ploughman*,
ch. v.

5. *A poor man's tale. See* quot.
1639 : in *Berkeley MSS.*, iii. 31 (1885),
A poare mans tale may now be heard :
viz[t] when none speakes the meanest
may (Gloucest.).

6. *A poor man wants some things,*

a covetous man all things. c. 1680 :
L'Estrange, *Seneca's Epistles*, ii., The
poor man wants many things, but the
covetous man wants all. 1732 : Fuller,
No. 356.

7. *A poor spirit is poorer than a poor
purse.* Ibid., No. 358.

8. *A poor wedding is a prologue to
misery.* Ibid., No. 359.

9. *As poor as a church mouse.* [1659 :
Howell, 13, As hungry as a church-
mouse.] 1672 : Corye, *Generous Enemies*, I., All that live with him Are
as poor as church-rats. 1714 : Ozell,
Molière, iv. 38, They're most of them as
poor as church mice. 1778 : T. Cogan,
John Buncle, Junior, ii. 146. 1803 :
Colman, jr., *John Bull*, II. iii. 1841 :
Dickens, *Barn. Rudge*, ch. lxxviii., I
have come back, poorer than a church
mouse. 1901 : F. E. Taylor, *Lancs
Sayings*, 3, As poor as a church-meawse.
1906 : Shaw, *Major Barbara*, V.

10. *As poor as a rat.* 1703 : Ward,
Writings, ii. 120, Whilst men of parts,
as poor as rats . . . 1834 : Marryat, *P.
Simple*, ch. xxxi., He's as poor as a
rat, and has nothing but his pay.
1866 : T. W. Robertson, *Ours*, I., Angus,
a distant cousin, poor as a rat. 1907 :
De Morgan, *Alice-for-Short*, ch. xvi.

11. *As poor as Job.* c. 1300 : Brunne,
tr. Langtoft's *Chron.*, 323 (Hearne), Als
bare was his toure as Job þe pouere
man. c. 1390 : Gower, *Conf. Amantis*,
bk. v. l. 2505, To ben for evere til I
deie As povere as Job. 1560 : T. Wilson,
Rhetorique, 207 (1909), Thou art as
poore as Iob. c. 1640 : in *Roxb.
Ballads*, i. 503 (B.S.), I am backe return'd, as poore as Job. 1700 : Dryden,
Prol. to *The Pilgrim.* 1750 : Smollett,
Gil Blas, iii. 93. 1822 : Scott, *Nigel*, ch.
viii., Who are all as proud as Lucifer,
and as poor as Job. 1850 : Dickens,
Copperfield, ch. vi., Old Mrs. Mell, his
mother, was as poor as Job. 1901 :
F. E. Taylor, *Lancs Sayings*, 3.

12. *As poor as owls.* 1862 : *Dialect
of Leeds*, 405.

13. *Every poor man is a fool.* 1659 :
Howell, *Proverbs : Brit.-Eng.*, 3.

14. *He is not poor that hath little, but
he that desireth much.* 1556 : G. Colvile,

tr. Boethius, 34 (1897), He that fearyth
that he shall lacke, and is not contented
with that he hath, but soroweth for
more, ... is not ryche, but poore.
1637 : A. Warwick, *Spare Minutes*, 4
(1829), Nor her poore that hath but
little, but-hee that wants more. 1640 :
Herbert, *Jac. Prudentum*. 1732 : Fuller,
No. 1937 [" craves " for " desireth "].

15. *He is poor indeed that can promise
nothing.* 1639 : Clarke, 142, He is
poore, can promise nothing. 1670 :
Ray, 132. 1732 : Fuller, No. 1941.

16. *He is so poor that he has not salt
to his porridge.* Ibid., No. 1945.

17. *It's a poor family which hath
neither a whore nor a thief in it.*
1659 : Howell, *Proverbs: Span.-Eng.*, 1,
There's no family but there's a whore
or a knave of it. 1678 : Ray, 9.

18. *It's a poor heart that never re-
joices.* 1834 : Marryat, *P. Simple*, ch.
v., " Well," continued he, " it's a poor
heart that never rejoiceth." He then
poured out half a tumbler of rum.
1841 : Dickens, *Barn. Rudge*, ch. iv.
1850 : Dickens, *Chuzzlewit*, ch. v.

19. *Poor and liberal, rich and covetous.*
1640 : Herbert, *Jac. Prudentum*.

20. *Poor and pert. See* quots.
1887 : T. Darlington, *S. Cheshire Folk
Speech*, 289 (E.D.S.), He's poor an' peeart
[lively], like th' parson's pig. 1913 :
E. M. Wright, *Rustic Speech, etc.*, 11
[as in 1887]. 1917 : Bridge, *Cheshire
Proverbs*, 104 [as in 1887].

21. *Poor and proud, fie, fie!* 1605 :
Camden, *Remains*, 330 (1870). 1670 :
Ray, 132.

22. *Poor and proud, still tailor-like.*
c. 1620 : in *Roxb. Ballads*, ii. 580 (B.S.),
The saying old hath oft beene told, It
plain doth verifie, " Poore and proud,
still taylor-like." Cf. **Tailor** (4).

23. *Poor cook. See* **Ill cook**.

24. *Poor folk fare the best.* 1639 :
Clarke, 205.

25. *Poor folks are glad of porridge.*
c. 1580 : Fulwell, *Ars Adulandi*, sig. G1,
Poore men are pleasde with potage aye,
till better vittailes fall. 1659 : Howell,
4, Poor folks must be glad of pottage.
1732 : Fuller, No. 3892.

26. *Poor in appetite. See* quot.

1653 : R. Brome, *City Wit*, I. ii., It is
rightly said, He that is poor in appetite,
may quickly be rich in purse.

27. *Poor men. See* **Children** (5).

28. *Poor men have no souls.* 1562 :
Heywood, *Three Hund. Epigr.*, No. 167.
1670 : Ray, 21.

29. *Poor men seek meat for their
stomachs; rich men stomachs for their
meat.* 1594 : A. Copley, *Wits, Fits,
etc.*, 105 (1614) [" want " for " seek "].
1678 : Ray, 79 [" walketh to get " for
" seek "]. 1732 : Fuller, No. 3895.
1820 : Scott, in Lockhart's *Life*, v. 44,
The poor man labours to get a dinner
to his appetite, the rich man to get an
appetite to his dinner.

30. *Poor men's reasons are not heard.*
1633 : Draxe, 162, A poore mans tale
cannot be heard. 1640 : Herbert, *Jac.
Prudentum*, The reasons of the poor
weigh not. 1666 : Torriano, *Piazza
Univ.*, 214, The poor mans reasons are
of no weight. 1732 : Fuller, No. 3897.

31. *The poor man's labour is the rich
man's wealth.* 1846 : Denham, *Proverbs*, 6 (Percy S.).

32. *The poor man's shilling is but a
penny.* 1732 : Fuller, No. 4716.

33. *The poor man turns his cake, and
another comes and eats it.* Ibid., No.
4714.

34. *The poor must pay for all.* 1639 :
Clarke, 99.

35. *They are poor whom God hates.*
1633 : Draxe, 162. 1659 : Howell, 11,
Ther's none poor but such as God hates.
1732 : Fuller, No. 2470, He's poor
indeed, whom God hates.

36. *To be in a poor reed* = in poor
condition. 1917 : Bridge, *Cheshire Proverbs*, 126.

37. *To be poor and to look poor, is the
devil all over.* 1913 : *Folk-Lore*, xxiv.
77.

Poorly sit, richly warm. Glos. 1639 :
in *Berkeley MSS*. iii. 30 (1885).

Pope, The. 1. *A pope's bull, a dead
man's skull, and an old trull, are not
all worth a pound of wool.* 1616 :
B. Rich, *Ladies Looking Glasse*, 36.
1647 : Countrym. *New Commonwealth*,
42 [" crooked " for " old," and " fleece "
for " pound "].

2. *If you would be a Pope, you must think of nothing else.* 1855 : Bohn, 422.

Popham. *See* **Horner.**

Poppies. *See* quot. 1880 : *N. & Q.*, 6th ser., ii. 164, The other day I heard a Staffordshire man say " Pluck poppies —make thunder." This was a proverbial saying that was quite new to me.

Possession is (*a*) **eleven,** (*b*) **nine points of the law.** (*a*) 1630 : T. Adams, *Works*, 97, The deuill hath eleuen poynts of the law against you ; that is, possession. 1639 : Fuller, *Holy War*, bk. v. ch. xxix. 1670 : Ray, 132. 1692 : L'Estrange, *Æsop*, 291 (3rd ed.). 1709 : O. Dykes, *Eng. Proverbs*, 213 (2nd ed.), Possession is a mighty matter indeed ; and we commonly say, 'tis eleven points of the law. 1712 : Arbuthnot, *Law a Bott. Pit*, Pt. III. ch. ix., Poor Nic. has only possession ; eleven points of the law ! 1738 : Swift, *Polite Convers.*, Dial. I. 1822 : Peacock, *Maid Marian*, ch. v., In those days possession was considerably more than eleven points of the law. (*b*) 1809 : Malkin, *Gil Blas*, xxi. 20 (O.), She had possession, and that is nine points of the law. 1817 : Scott, *Rob Roy*, ch. xxxvii., Take all necessary measures to secure that possession, which sages say makes nine points of the law. 1923 : J. S. Fletcher, *The Diamonds*, ch. iii., He knew that possession is sometimes more than nine points of the law.

The following is doubtful, but should probably come under (*a*). 1703 : Farquhar, *Twin-Rivals*, II. ii., Upon this you take immediate possession, and so you have the best part of the law on your side.

Post. *See* **Pillar.**

Postern door makes thief and whore, The. 1605 : Camden, *Remains*, 334 (1870). 1670 : Ray, 132. 1732 : Fuller, No. 6176. Cf. **Back door.**

Pot, *subs.* 1. *A pot that belongs to many is ill stirred and worse boiled.* 1732 : Fuller, No. 360.

2. *He's dwindled down from a pot to a pipkin.* Ibid., No. 2457.

3. *Neither pot broken nor water spilt* = No harm done. 1546 : Heywood,

Proverbs, Pt. I. ch. xi. 1619 : B. Rich, *Irish Hubbub*, 16. 1659 : Howell, 14.

4. *Pot and can. See* **Cup** (2).

5. *Pot in the pate. See* **Cup** (1).

6. *The pot calls the kettle black.* 1620 : Shelton, *Quixote*, Pt. II. ch. lxvii., You are like what is said that the frying-pan said to the kettle, " Avant, black-brows." 1639 : Clarke, 8, The pot cals the pan burnt-arse. 1679 : A. Behn, *Feign'd Courtezans*, V. iv., As another old proverb says, do not let the kettle call the pot black-arse ! 1685-6 : Cotton, *Montaigne*, bk. iii. ch. v. *ad fin.*, It is much more easy to accuse one sex than to excuse the other ; 'tis according to the saying, " The pot and the kettle." 1725 : Bailey, tr. Erasmus' *Colloq.*, 365 [as in 1679]. 1732 : Fielding, *Cov. Garden Tragedy*, II. v., Dares thus the devil to rebuke our sin ! Dare thus the kettle say the pot is black ! 1834 : Marryat, *P. Simple*, ch. xxxii., Do you know what the pot called the kettle ? 1920 : G. Lambert, M.P., in *Times*, 27 March, p. 10, col. 3, I would say to my esteemed leaders that the pot calling the kettle sooty doesn't whiten either of them.

7. *To go to pot.* 1546 : Heywood, *Proverbs*, Pt. II. ch. v., The weaker goeth to the potte, we all daie see. 1591 : Harington, *Orl. Furioso*, bk. xxxviii. st. 60, We may assure our selves if any more We take the field, our side goes to the pot. 1649 : in *Somers Tracts*, vii. 88 (1811), Many a wiser man than I hath gone to pot. 1694 : *Terence made English*, 7, If these brains don't help me out at a dead lift, to pot goes Pilgarlick. 1740 : North, *Lives of Norths*, i. 151 (Bohn), It was well for us that we were known there, or to pot we had gone. 1828 : Carr, *Craven Dialect*, ii. 55, " To go to pot," to be reduced to beggary, to suffer.

8. *To make the pot boil.* *c.* 1663 : Davenant, *Play-House to be Let*, V., We'll find out rich husband to make you the pot boil. *c.* 1750 : C. Smart, *Ballads*, No. xiii., She teaches you economy, Which makes the pot to boil. 1864 : Carlyle, *Fredk. Gt.*, XVI. ii. VI. 151 (1872) (O.), A feeling that glory

is excellent, but will not make the national pot boil.

9. *To make the pot with two ears*=To put the arms akimbo. 1675 : Cotton, *Burl. upon Burlesque*, 236 (1765), See what a goodly port she bears, *Making the pot with the two ears !*

10. *When the pot boils over, it cooleth itself.* 1732 : Fuller, No. 5602.
See also Lid ; Little pot ; Pitcher ; and Watched pot.

Potatoes. 1. *A dinner of potatoes and point.* 1825 : J. Neal, *Bro. Jonathan*, i. 75 (O.), The potatoes and point of an Irish peasant. 1864 : " Cornish Proverbs," in *N. & Q.*, 3rd ser., vi. 495.

2. *See* quot. 1893 : Inwards, *Weather Lore*, 23, Plant your 'taturs when you will, They won't come up before April.
See also Bean (5).

Pottage. *See* quots. 1678 : Ray, 70, With cost one may make pottage of a stool-foot. 1732 : Fuller, No. 5796, With cost, good pottage may be made out of a leg of a joint stool. *See also* Broth.

Potterne, Old Ross of. 1659 : Howell, 21, He will live as long as old Russe of Pottern, who lived till all the world was weary of him. 1670 : Ray, 215 [" Ross " for " Russe "].

Pound of butter among a kennel of hounds, What is a? 1670 : Ray, 66. 1732 : Fuller, No. 5498. 1880 : Spurgeon, *Ploughman's Pictures*, 10, His fortune went like a pound of meat in a kennel of hounds.

Pound of care will not pay an ounce of debt, A. 1589 : L. Wright, *Display of Dutie*, 29 [" sorrow " for " care "]. 1590 : Greene, *Works*, viii. 85 (Grosart). 1600 : Dekker, *Shoem. Holiday*, III. v. [" dram " for " ounce "]. 1685 : Meriton, *Yorkshire Ale*, 57, A pund of care'l not pay an ounce of debt. 1732 : Fuller, No. 361.

Pour water into a sieve, To. 1639 : Clarke, 155, You pour, etc. 1670 : Ray, 190. 1732 : Fuller, No. 5979, You pour, etc. 1875 : Smiles, *Thrift*, 169, Putting money into her hands is like pouring water through a sieve.

Poverty breeds strife. Somerset. 1678 : Ray, 354. 1732 : Fuller, No.

6109, Want makes strife Between the good man and his wife.

Poverty comes in at the door, love flies out of the window, When. 1631 : Brathwait, *Eng. Gentlewoman*, 346 (1641), It hath beene an old maxime ; that as poverty goes in at one doore, love goes out at the other. 1732 : Fuller, No. 5565 [" creeps " for " flies "]. *c.* 1810 : C. Dibdin, jr., *My Spouse and I*, Love and poverty they say do not agree ; but the love that flies out of the window at the sight of poverty deserves to have the door shut in his face. 1924 : Divorce Court evidence in *Evening Standard*, 4 April, p. 9, col. 2, She might then realise that poverty might come in at the door and love fly out of the window.

Poverty destroyeth not, There is no virtue that. 1578 : Florio, *First Fruites*, fo. 32, There is no vertue, but pouertie wyl marre it. 1629 : *Book of Meery Riddles*, Prov. 8.

Poverty is an enemy to good manners. 1585 : Sir E. Dyer, in *Writings*, 97 (Grosart) [quoted as " a prouerbe amongst vs "].

Poverty is not a shame, but the being ashamed of it is. 1732 : Fuller, No. 3908. 1869 : Spurgeon, *John Ploughman*, ch. v., Poverty is no shame, but being discontented with it is.

Poverty is no vice but an inconvenience. 1591 : Florio, *Second Frutes*, 105. 1616 : *Rich Cabinet*, fo. 114, Pouertie is no vice : yet a wofull inconuenience. 1666 : Torriano, *Piazza Univ.*, 214. 1781 : Macklin, *Man of the World*, IV., Her poverty is not her crime, sir, but her misfortune.

Poverty is still in suspicion, He that is in. 1629 : *Book of Meery Riddles*, Prov. 73.

Poverty is the mother of all arts and trades. 1666 : Torriano, *Piazza Univ.*, 214.

Poverty is the mother of health. 1377 : Langland, *Plowman*, B, xiv. 298, Pouerte . . . is moder of helthe. 1640 : Herbert, *Jac. Prudentum*. 1748 : Richardson, *Clarissa*, ii. 110 (1785).

Poverty makes strange bed-fellows. 1849 : Lytton, *Caxtons*, Pt. IV. ch. iv.,

I say that life, like poverty, has strange
bed-fellows. 1863 : Thackeray, *Round.
Papers*: " On Some Carp," par. 2, An
illustration of that dismal proverb
which tells us how poverty makes us
acquainted with strange bed-fellows.
Cf. **Misery.**

Poverty parteth fellowship. 1406 :
Hoccleve, in *Minor Poems*, 29 (E.E.T.S.),
Fy! Lak of coyn departith conpaignie.
c. 1470 : G. Ashby, *Poems*, 29 (E.E.T.S.),
It hathe be, and yet is a comyn
sawe, That Poverte departithe felaship.
1546 : Heywood, *Proverbs*, Pt. I. ch. xii.
c. 1650 : in *Roxb. Ballads*, ii. 113 (Hindley). For friendship parts in poverty.
1732 : Fuller, No. 3914, Poverty trieth
friends.

**Poverty very ill, He bears, who is
ashamed of it.** Ibid., No. 1811.

Povey's foot. *See* quots. 1841 :
Hartshorne, *Salopia Ant.*, 535, " Wos
and wos like " [or] " As large as Povey's
foot." 1883 : Burne, *Shropsh. Folk-
Lore*, 594, Worse and worse, like
Povey's foot.

Power seldom grows old at Court.
1651 : Herbert, *Jac. Prudentum*, 2nd ed.

Power weakeneth the wicked. 1659 :
Howell, *Proverbs: Brit.-Eng.*, 6.

Powis is the paradise of Wales. 1662 :
Fuller, *Worthies*, iii. 549 (1840). 1790 :
Grose, *Prov. Gloss.*, s.v. " Montgomery-
shire."

Practice [originally **Use**] **makes per-
fect.** 1340 : *Ayenbite*, 178 (E.E.T.S.),
Uor wone makeþ maister. *c.* 1530 :
Detection . . . of Dice Play, 25 (Percy
S.), For use maketh mastery. 1546 :
Heywood, *Proverbs*, Pt. II. ch. ii.,
Vse maketh maistry. 1560 : T. Wilson,
Rhetorique, 5 (1909), Eloquence was
vsed, and through practise made per-
fect. 1639 : Breton, in *Works*, ii. þ 11
(Grosart), Use makes perfection in
many things. 1766 : Anstey, *New
Bath Guide*, Lett. V., For practice
makes perfect, as often I've read. 1798 :
Morton, *Speed the Plough*, II. ii. 1816 :
Scott, *Antiquary*, ch. xxxv., Use makes
perfect. 1829 : Scott, *Journal*, 27 Jan.,
Use makes perfectness. 1870 : Dickens,
Drood, ch. xxiii. 1920 : P. B. M.
Allan, *Book-Hunter at Home*, 96.

Practice toucheth the quick. 1546 :
Heywood, *Proverbs*, Pt. I. ch. vi.

Practise what you preach. [*c.* 1393 :
Langland, *Plowman*, C, v. 118, Tyl
that lerede men lyue as thei lere and
techen.] *c.* 1426 : Audelay, *Poems*, 31
(Percy S.), A prechur schuld lyve
parfytly, And do as he techys truly.
c. 1680 : L'Estrange, *Seneca's Morals:
" Happy Life,"* ch. ii., We must practise what we preach. 1748 : Richardson,
Clarissa, v. 81 (1785), I love . . . that
the clergy should practise what they
preach. 1840 : Dickens, *Curiosity Shop*,
ch. xxxvii., Divines do not always
practise what they preach.

PRAISE, *subs.*:

Praise is but the shadow of virtue.
Before 1680 : Butler, *Remains*, ii. 118
(1759).

**Praise makes good men better and bad
men worse.** 1659 : T. Pecke, *Parnassi
Puerp.*, 95, Good men are made better ;
bad, worse by praise. 1732 : Fuller,
No. 3918.

Praise of fools. *See* **Fool** (103).

**Praise without profit puts little into
the pot.** 1666 : Torriano, *Piazza Univ.*,
131, Praises fill not the belly. 1732 :
Fuller, No. 3922.

PRAISE, *verb*:

Praise a hill but keep on the plain.
1591 : Florio, *Second Frutes*, 99, Wonder at hills, keepe on the plaine.
1623 : Wodrocphe, *Spared Houres*, 277,
Praise the mountaines, but loue the
plaines. 1640 : Herbert, *Jac. Prudentum*, Praise a hill, but keep below.
1659 : Howell, *Letters*, ii. 666 (Jacobs),
Commend the hills, but keep thyself
on the plains.

Praise at parting, i.e. Praise not too
soon, or Praise not till the entertainment is over. *c.* 1410 : *Towneley
Plays*, 108 (E.E.T.S.), Now prays at
the partyng. *c.* 1440 : *Gesta Rom.*, 39
(E.E.T.S.), " Preyse at the parting,"
seide kny3t, " And bihold wele the
ende." *c.* 1475 : *Rauf Coilyear*, 5
(E.E.T.S.). *c.* 1580 : *Tom Tyler*, l. 667,
p. 19 (Malone S.), It is an old saying,
praise at the parting. 1611 : Shakespeare, *Tempest*, III. iii.

Praise day at night — similar in

meaning to the preceding saying. c.1440:
Lydgate, *Fall of Princes*, bk. ix. l. 2024,
The faire day men do preise at eue.
1605 : Camden, *Remains*, 330 (1870),
Praise a fair day at night. 1637 :
Shirley, *Example*, Epil. [as in 1605].
1681 : Robertson, *Phraseol. Generalis*,
324 [as in 1605]. 1732 : Fuller, No.
3919, Praise not the day before night.
1846 : T. Wright, *Essays on Middle
Ages*, i. 148, We say, " praise the day
when it is over."

Praise no man till he is dead. 1887 :
R. L. S., *Hanging Judge*, III. vi. (iii.).

Praise nor dispraise thyself, Neither ;
thy actions serve the turn. 1640: Herbert,
Jac. Prudentum. 1670: Ray, 21.

Praise not the ford. *See* Ford.

Praise the bridge he goes over, Let
every man. 1678 : Ray, 106. 1740 :
North, *Examen*, 368, It is strange men
cannot praise the bridge they go over,
or be thankful for favours they have
had. 1797 : Colman, jr., *Heir at Law*,
I. i., Well, praise the bridge that carried
you over. 1817 : Scott, in Lockhart's
Life, iv. 59, I am bound to praise the
bridge which carried me over. 1875 :
Cheales, *Proverb. Folk-Lore*, 58, As we
have it—Speak well of the bridge that
carries you over.

Praise the child and you make love to
the mother. 1829 : Cobbett, *Advice to
Young Men*, Lett. IV. [quoted as " an
old saying "].

Praise the sea but keep on land.
1591 : Florio, *Second Frutes*, 99, Praise
the sea, on shore remaine. 1640: Herbert, *Jac. Prudentum*. 1659 : Howell,
Letters, ii. 666 (Jacobs), Commend the
sea, but keep thy self ashoar. 1754:
Berthelson, *Eng. - Danish Dict.*, s.v.
" Praise." 1875 : Cheales, *Proverb.
Folk-Lore*, 83.

Praise the wine before ye taste of the
grape, Ye. 1546 : Heywood, *Proverbs*,
Pt. I. ch. x.

Praiseth himself, spattereth himself,
He that. 1640: Herbert, *Jac. Prudentum*.

Praiseth publicly, will slander privately, He that. 1669: *Politeuphuia*,
140, He that praiseth a man openly
will not stick to flatter him secretly.
1732 : Fuller, No. 2250.

Prate is prate, but it is the duck that
lays the eggs. 1659 : Howell, 13.
1670 : Ray, 215. 1732 : Fuller, No.
3926. Cf. Talk is but talk.

Prate like a parrot, To. 1639: Clarke,
133, He prates like a parrot. 1678:
Ray, 265. Cf. Talk.

Pray, *verb*. 1. *He that would learn to
pray, let him go to sea.* 1660 : Howell,
Parly of Beasts, 9, The common saying
is, that he who cannot pray, must go
to church at sea. 1670 : Ray, 133.
1736 : Bailey, *Dict.*, s.v. " Pray."

2. *Pray for yourself, I am not sick.*
1546 : Heywood, *Proverbs*, Pt. II. ch. vii.

Prayers and provender hinder no
journey. 1640 : Herbert, *Jac. Prudentum*. 1854 : J. W. Warter, *Last of Old
Squires*, 53. 1863 : *N. & Q.*, 3rd ser.,
iii. 258. 1926 : R. A. Knox, *Other Eyes
than Ours*, 182, We're letting luncheon
get cold, ain't we ? I always used to
be told that prayer and provender
hinder no man. Cf. Mass and meat ;
Meals and matins ; and Meat (5).

Prayers are done, my lady is ready,
When. 1611 : Cotgrave, s.v. " Messe,"
When prayers were ended, Madame
ends her pranking. 1640 : Herbert,
Jac. Prudentum.

Prayers bring down the first blessing,
and praises the second. 1659: Howell, 8.

Prayers. *See* quot. 1678 : Ray, 191,
They shall have no more of our prayers
then we of their pies (quoth vicar of
Layton).

Prayers. *See also* Say, *verb* (4) and
(17).

Preach over liquor. *See* Parson
Palmer.

Preacher's wages. Before 1635 : Corbet, *Poems*, in Chalmers, v. 577, Wee
all had preacher's wages, thankes and
wine.

Preaches war is the devil's chaplain,
He that. 1670 : Ray, 27. 1732 : Fuller, No. 2251, He that preacheth up
war, when it might well be avoided, is
the devil's chaplain.

Preaches well that lives well, He.
1620 : Shelton, *Quixote*, Pt. II. ch. xx.
1732 : Fuller, No. 2006.

Precepts may lead but examples draw.
1855 : Bohn, 475. Cf. Example.

Press a stick and it seems a youth.
1640 : Herbert, *Jac. Prudentum.*
· **Preston, Lancs.** 1. *See* quot. 1869 :
Hazlitt, 319, Preston for panmugs,
Huyton for pride ; Childwall for tolling,
and playing beside.
2. *Proud Preston.* 1727 : Defoe,
Tour, iii. 221, The people are gay here,
though not perhaps the richer for that ;
but it has by that obtained the name
of Proud Preston. 1835 : Walker,
The Original, No. xi., Preston, then
always called Proud Preston, because
exclusively inhabited by gentry. 1889 :
N. & Q., 7th ser., viii. 56, Proud Preston,
poor people, Built a church and no
steeple. 1901 : F. E. Taylor, *Lancs
Sayings,* 42, Preawd Presson—poor
people—Eight bells in a crack't steeple !

Prettiness dies first. 1640 : Herbert,
Jac. Prudentum. 1670 : Ray, 21, Prettiness dies quickly. 1732 : Fuller, No.
3930, Prettiness is short-liv'd.

Prettiness makes no pottage. 1678 :
Ray, 192. 1732 : Fuller, No. 3931.

Pretty as paint, As. 1922 : E. V.
Lucas, *Genevra's Money,* ch. xvi., Now,
there's that girl—she's as pretty as
paint.

Pretty fellow. *See* Axle-tree.

**Pretty that have pretty conditions,
They are.** 1633 : Draxe, 15.

Pretty things men make. *See* quots.
c. 1590 : *Plaine Percevall,* 19 (1860), He
spide a Iacke an apes, in a gaie cote.
. . . Good Lord what knacks are
made for money, now adaies. 1594 :
A. Copley, *Wits, Fits, etc.,* 145 (1614),
A cockney seeing a squirrell in a shop,
greatly admir'd it, and said : Jesu
God, what pretty things are made for
money. 1604 : *Jacke of Dover,* 347
(1864), A jack an apes ! quoth she ;
now, Jesus ! what these Fleminges can
make for money !— thinking verily it
had been a thing made by mens hand.
1732 : Fuller, No. 5503, What pretty
things men will make for money, quoth
the old woman, when she saw a monkey.

Prevention is better than cure.
[Venienti occurrite morbo. — Persius,
Sat., iii. 64.] *c.* 1240 : Bracton, *De
Legibus,* bk. v. c. 10, § 14 (Rolls Ser.,
vi. 104), Cum melius et utilius sit in

tempore occurrere quam post causam
vulneratam quaerere remedium. 1630 :
T. Adams, *Works,* 598, Prevention is so
much better then healing. 1685 : in
Somers Tracts, ix. 225 (1811), The
wisdom of prevention is better than
the wisdom of remedy. 1850 : Dickens,
Chuzzlewit, ch. li. 1924 : *Sphere,* 4 Oct.,
p. 2, col. 3, The old copy-book maxim of
prevention being better than cure.

**Pricketh betimes that will be a good
thorn, It.** Before 1500 : in Hill, *Commonplace-Book,* 128 (E.E.T.S.), Sone
hit sharpith, that thorn will be. 1546 :
Heywood, *Proverbs,* Pt. II. ch. ix.
1568 : *Jacob and Esau,* IV. iv., It hath
been a proverb, before I was born,
Young doth it prick, that will be a
thorn. 1590 : Greene, *Works,* viii. 35
(Grosart), Soone prickes the tree that
will proue a thorne. 1670 : Ray, 84, It
early pricks that will be a thorn. 1732 :
Fuller, No. 3043.

**Pride and grace dwell never in one
place.** Ibid., No. 6273.

**Pride and poverty are ill met, yet often
seen together.** Ibid., No. 3933.

**Pride breakfasted with Plenty, dined
with Poverty, and supped with Infamy.**
1736 : Franklin, *Way to Wealth,* in
Works, i. 449 (Bigelow).

**Pride costs us more than hunger,
thirst, and cold.** 1831 : Hone, *Year-
Book,* col. 1612.

Pride feels no frost. 1650 : Fuller,
Pisgah Sight, bk. iv. ch. vi. §7, Some
may plead, pride never feels pain. 1670 :
Ray, 133, Pride feels no cold. 1732 :
Fuller, No. 3935.

Pride goes before, shame follows after.
c. 1440 : *Jacob's Well,* 70 (E.E.T.S.),
For pride goth beforn, and schame
folwyth after. Before 1500 : in Hill,
Commonplace - Book, 128 (E.E.T.S.).
1509 : Barclay, *Ship of Fools,* ii. 164
(1874), Pryde goth before, but shame do
it ensue. Before 1529 : Skelton, in *Works,*
i. 131 (Dyce). 1605 : Chapman, etc.,
Eastw. Hoe, IV. i., Nay, nay, eene let
pride go afore ; shame wil follow after,
I warrant you. 1732 : Fuller, No.
3936.

Pride had rather go out of the way,
than go behind. Ibid., No. 3937.

Pride in prosperity turns to misery in adversity. Ibid., No. 3940.

Pride is as loud a beggar as want, and a great deal more saucy. Ibid., No. 3941. 1736: Franklin, *Way to Wealth*, in *Works*, i. 448 (Bigelow).

Pride is good even in a wild horse, A little. 1864: "Cornish Proverbs," in *N. & Q.*, 3rd ser., vi. 495.

Pride is in the saddle, shame is on the crupper, When. 1647: *Countrym. New Commonwealth*, 26, Lewis the eleventh, King of France, was wont to say, when pride was in the saddle, mischiefe and shame were on the crupper. 1732: Fuller, No. 5566.

Pride is the sworn enemy to content. Ibid., No. 3944.

Pride makes naked side, Overdone. c. 1460: *How the Good Wife*, l. 95, Ouere done pride makythe nakid syde.

Pride may lurk under a thread-bare cloak. 1732: Fuller, No. 3947.

Pride must abide. 1855: Gaskell, *North and South*, ch. xxix., I kept myself up with proverbs as long as I could ; " Pride must abide "—and such wholesome pieces of pith ! 1901: F. E. Taylor, *Lancs Sayings*, 9, Pride mun abide (Upstart people must bear with rebuffs).

Pride of the rich makes the labours of the poor, The. 1639: Clarke, 18.

Pride rides, shame lacqueys, When. 1732: Fuller, No. 5567.

Pride scorns the vulgar, yet lies at its mercy. Ibid., No. 3950.

Pride will have a fall. 1509: Barclay, *Ship of Fools*, ii. 161 (1874), The pryde in them at last sholde haue a fall. Before 1529 : Skelton, in *Works*, i. 131 (Dyce), I have red, and rede I xall, Inordynate pride wyll haue a falle. 1593: G. Harvey, *Works*, ii. 61 (Grosart), Without more circumlocution, pryde hath a fall. 1654: Gayton, *Pleasant Notes Don Q.*, 8, You see pride will have a fall. 1701: Cibber, *Love Makes a Man*, III. ii., So, Pride has got a fall. 1748 : Richardson, *Clarissa*, vi. 258 (1785). 1848: Dickens, *Dombey*, ch. lix., " Pride shall have a fall, and it always was and will be so ! " observes the housemaid.

Pride will spit in pride's face. 1732 : Fuller, No. 3953.

Pride. *See also* Charity ; Fire (4) ; and Love (10).

Priest and Priests. 1. *Priests love pretty wenches.* 1568 : in *Loseley MSS.*, 212 (Kempe).

2. *The priest forgets that he was clerk.* 1533 : Heywood, *John, Tyb, etc.*, 86 (Farmer), But now I see well the old proverb is true ; That parish priest forgetteth that ever he was clerk ! 1587 : Greene, *Works*, iv. 102 (Grosart), Shall the olde prouerbe be verified in thee, that the priest forgets himselfe that euer he was a clerke. 1612 : R. Johnson, *Crown Garland*, 48 (Percy S.), The proverb old is come to passe, The priest when he begins the masse, Forgets that ever clarke he was. 1732 : Fuller, No. 4721.

3. *To know more than the priest spoke on Sunday.* c. 1540 : Bale, *Kynge Johan*, in Manly, *Spec. Pre-Shakesp. Drama*, i. 537 (1903), Clargy, marke yt well, I have more to yow to say Than, as the sayeng is, the prest dyd speke a Sonday. 1595 : *Pedlars Prophecy*, l. 398 (Malone S.), True maid, fie for shame, why do ye sweare ? I know more than the priest spake of a Sunday. 1894 : Northall, *Folk Phrases*, 20 (E.D.S.), More than ever the parson preached about.

4. *To the purpose, as priests praise God in the morning.* 1623 : Wodroephe, *Spared Houres*, 474.

See also Bad priests ; Beware ; Devil (117) ; House (20); Such as the priest ; Three things are unsatiable ; and Woman (59).

Prince that is feared of many must of necessity fear many, The. 1669 : *Politeuphuia*, 79.

Princely mind will undo a private family, A. 1732 : Fuller, No. 364.

Princes' privados. *See* quot. 1662 : *Fragmenta Aulica*, 108, It is an old adage that princes privados and favourites of Kings were like casting counters, which are used in the exchequer or in play to count by, That sometimes they stand for one, sometimes for ten, sometimes for a hundred.

Priscian's head, To break = To speak
or write bad Latin, and, by extension,
bad English. [The *locus classicus* for
the idea that " speaking false Latin "
is equivalent to inflicting violent personal injury on Priscian is Nicodemus
Frischlin's comedy *Priscianus Vapu-
lans* (the preface to which is dated
1 January, 1584).—Prof. E. Bensly, in
N. & Q., 10th ser., ix. 376.] Before
1529 : Skelton, *Works*, ii. 9 (Dyce),
Prisians hed broken now handy dandy.
1589 : Puttenham, *Eng. Poesie*, 258
(Arber), As when we speake false English . . . euery poore scholler knowes
the fault, and cals it the breaking of
Priscians head, for he was among the
Latines a principall grammarian. 1592 :
Shakespeare, *L.L.L.*, V. i., Bon, bon, fort
bon ! Priscian a little scratched : 'twill
serve. 1642 : Fuller, *Holy State:* "Hilde-
gardis," So that throwing words at
random she never brake Priscian's head ;
as if the Latin had learned to make
itself true without the speaker's care.
Before 1680 : Butler, *Remains*, i. 220
(1759), And counted breaking Priscian's
head a thing More capital, than to
behead a king. 1742 : Pope, *Dunciad*,
iii. 164. 1824 : Byron, *Don Juan*, can.
xv. st. 24, 'Gainst rhyme I never should
have knocked my brows, Nor broken
my own head, nor that of Priscian.
1858 : O. W. Holmes, *Autocrat*, v., They
are bound to speak decent English, unless, indeed, they are rough old cam-
paigners . . . in which case, a few
scars on Priscian's head are pardoned
to old fellows that have quite as many
on their own.

Probabilities do not make one truth,
A thousand. 1855 : Bohn, 302.

Proclamations. *See* Head (12).

Procrastination is the thief of time.
1742 : Young, *Night Thoughts*, i. l. 393.
1850 : Dickens, *Copperfield*, ch. xii.

Prodigal robs his heir, the miser himself, The. 1732 : Fuller, No. 4722.

Proffered service stinks. *c.* 1386 :
Chaucer, *Can. Yeoman's Tale*, l. 513,
Ful sooth it is, that swich profred
servyse Stinketh, as witnessen these
olde wyse. *c.* 1480 : *Early Miscell.*, 22
(Warton Cl., 1855), I se proferd serves

stynkit. 1546 : Heywood, *Proverbs*,
Pt. II. ch. iv. 1658 : R. Brome, *New
Academy*, II., She offers up her selfe ;
now may the proverb Of proffer'd
service light upon her. 1710 : Swift,
Journal to Stella, 22 Oct., Is not this
vexatious ? and is there so much in the
proverb of proffered service ? 1809 :
Scott, *Fam. Letters*, i. 139 (1894), It is
vulgarly said that proffered service is
of an evil savour.

Promise and Promises, *subs.* 1. *All
promises are either broken or kept.* 1590 :
Q. Elizabeth, in Dee, *Diary*, 37 (Camden S.), There was never promisse made,
but it was broken or kept. 1641 :
Taylor (Water-Poet), *Last Voyage*, 8,
in *Works*, 2nd coll. (Spens S.). 1692 :
L'Estrange, *Æsop*, 333 (3rd ed.). 1738 :
Swift, *Polite Convers.*, Dial. I., Why,
madam, you know, promises are either
broken or kept.

2. *Promise is debt.* [*c.* 1310 : in
Wright, *Pol. Songs*, 312 (Camden S.),
Promis est dette due, si fay ne seit
oublie.] *c.* 1386 : Chaucer, *Introd.* to
Man of Law's Prol., l. 41, Biheste is
dette. 1412 : Hoccleve, *Regement*, 64
(E.E.T.S.), Of a trewë man, be-heste is
dette. *c.* 1477 : Caxton, *Jason*, 183
(E.E.T.S.), I haue promised hit and
promis is dew. *c.* 1530 : *Everyman*, in
Hazlitt, *Old Plays*, i. 137, Yet promise
is debt ; this ys well wot. 1592 : G.
Harvey, in *Works*, i. 174 (Grosart).
c. 1630 : in *Roxb. Ballads*, i. 201 (B.S.),
For promise is a debt. 1664 : in *Musarum Deliciæ*, ii. 177 (Hotten), If it be
true that promise is a debt.

3. *Promises and pie-crusts are made to
be broken.* [1599 : Shakespeare, *Henry
V.*, II. iii., For oaths are straws, men's
faiths are wafer cakes.] 1706 : Ward,
Hud. Rediv., Pt. 5, can. vii. p. 9, Fair
promises avail but little, Like too rich
pye-crust, they're so brittle. 1738 :
Swift, *Polite Convers.*, Dial. I., Promises
and pie-crust are made to be broken.
1773 : in *Garrick Corresp.*, i. 583
(1831), [as in 1738]. 1828 : Carr,
Craven Dialect, ii. 59. 1860 : Reade, *Cl.
and Hearth*, ch. lxxxi., " Pshaw ! " said
Catherine, " promises are pie-crusts."
1920 : Locke, *House of Baltazar*, ch.

xvi., What about your promise, Mr.
Baltazar ? Pie-crust ?

Promise, verb. 1. *He promises like a
merchant but pays like a man of war.*
1639 : Clarke, 194. 1670 : Ray, 21.
1732 : Fuller, No. 2007.

2. *He promises mountains and per-
forms molehills.* [Maria et montes
polliceri.—Sallust, *C.* xxiii. 3.] 1578 :
Florio, *First Fruites,* fo. 29, He promiseth seas and mountaines. 1629 :
Book of Meery Riddles, Prov. 105. 1880 :
Spurgeon, *Ploughman's Pictures,* 18,
They promise mountains and perform
molehills.

3. *He that promises too much means
nothing.* 1633 : Draxe, 167, He that
promiseth all, deceiueth all. 1732 :
Fuller, No. 2253.

4. *To promise and give nothing is a
comfort for a fool.* 1633 : Draxe, 167,
To promise and giue nought is to comfort a foole. 1670 : Ray, 22. 1732 :
Fuller, No. 5215.

Promising is the eve of giving. 1578 :
Florio, *First Fruites,* fo. 29, The eue to
geue is to promise. 1640 : Herbert,
Jac. Prudentum. 1666 : Torriano, *Piazza
Univ.,* 219, Promise is the eve of the
gift.

**Proof of the pudding is in the eating,
The.** [Exitus acta probat. — Ovid,
Heroid., ii. 85.] *c.* 1300 : *King Alisaunder,* l. 4042, Hit is y-writein, every
thyng Himseolf shewith in tastyng.
1635 : Glapthorne, *Hollander,* III.
1714 : *Spectator,* No. 567. 1828 : Scott,
Fair Maid, ch. vi., The thin soft
cakes . . . were done liberal justice to
in the mode which is best proof of cake
as well as pudding. 1842 : Barham,
Ing. Legends, 2nd ser.: " Black Mous-
quetaire," can. 2.

**Proper that hath proper conditions,
He is.** 1599 : Porter, *Two Angry
Women,* sc. xi. 1670 : Ray, 22.

Properer man the worse luck, The.
1633 : Jonson, *Tale of a Tub,* III. iv.
1670 : Ray, 134, The properer man
(and so the honester) the worse
luck.

**Prospect is often better than posses-
sion.** 1732 : Fuller, No. 3958.

Prosperity. 1. *He who swells in*
prosperity, will shrink in adversity. 1855 :
Bohn, 401.

2. *In time of prosperity friends will
be plenty ; In time of adversity not one
among twenty.* [ἀνδρὸς κακῶς πράσσοντος,
ἐκποδὼν φίλοι.—Menander, *Sent.,* 32.]
c. 1500 : in *Antiq. Repertory,* iv. 398
(1809), In tyme of prosperite remember
adversite. 1659 : Howell, 20. 1670 :
Ray, 11. 1732 : Fuller, No. 6394. 1869 :
Spurgeon, *John Ploughman,* ch. xiv.

3. *Prosperity gets followers ; but adversity distinguishes them.* 1669 : *Politeuphuia,* 176, Prosperity getteth friends,
but adversity trieth them. 1732 : Fuller, No. 3962.

4. *Prosperity lets go the bridle.* 1640 :
Herbert, *Jac. Prudentum.*

Proud as an apothecary. 1639 :
Clarke, 32. 1678 : Ray, 288.

Proud as a peacock. *c.* 1290 : in
Wright, *Pol. Songs John to Edw. II.,*
159 (Camden S.), A pruest proud ase a
po. *c.* 1410 : *Towneley Plays,* 117
(E.E.T.S.), Ther shall com a swane as
prowde as a po. 1513 : Bradshaw, *St.
Werburga,* 69 (E.E.T.S.), Prowde as a
pecocke. 1565 : Shacklock, *Hatchet of
Heresies,* quoted in *N. & Q.,* 2nd ser.,
v. 411. 1681 : Robertson, *Phraseol.
Generalis,* 1030. 1753 : Richardson,
Grandison, iv. 152 (1883). 1869 : Spurgeon, *John Ploughman,* ch. iii.

Proud as Lucifer. *c.* 1394 : in Wright,
Pol. Poems, i. 315 (Rolls Ser., 1859),
They been as proud as Lucifarre. *c.* 1450 :
Partonope, l. 9740 (E.E.T.S.), Be thow
as prowde as Lucifere . . . 1649 : Quarles,
Virgin Widow, V. *c.* 1686 : in *Roxb.
Ballads,* vii. 21 (B.S.). 1764 : Mrs. F.
Sheridan, *Dupe,* III. vii. 1822 : Scott,
Nigel, ch. viii. 1848 : Dickens, *Dom-
bey,* ch. xxvi. 1896 : Conan Doyle,
Rodney Stone, ch. v.

Proud as old Cole's dog. 1834-7 :
Southey, *Doctor,* ch. cxxv., Who was
Old Cole whose dog was so proud that
he took the wall of a dung-cart and
got squeezed to death by the wheel ?

Proud come behind as go before, As.
c. 1565 : Still, *Gam. Gurton,* V. ii., As
proude coms behinde, they say, as any
goes before ! 1605 : Camden, *Remains,*
318 (1870). 1655 : Fuller, *Church Hist.,*

bk. iii. § iii. (5), Pleasing itself that "as
stout came behind as went before."
1732 : Fuller, No. 724. 1853 : Trench,
Proverbs, 76 (1905).

Proud eye, A, an open purse, and a
light wife, bring mischief to the first,
misery to the second, and horns to the
third. 1647 : *Countrym. New Commonwealth*, 35. 1669 : *Politeuphuia*, 281.

Proud folks, for they will not complain, It's good beating. 1639 : Clarke,
31. 1670 : Ray, 133.

Proud heart and a beggar's purse agree
not well together, A. *c.* 1430 : Lydgate, *Minor Poems*, 56 (Percy S.), A
prowde hert in a beggers brest . . . it
accordith nought. *c.* 1532 : R. Copland, *Spyttel Hous*, l. 977, Lo, here one
may see that there is none wors Than
is a proude herte and a beggers purs.
1631 : Brathwait, *Eng. Gentlewoman*,
272 (1641), Wee say there is no good
congruity in a proud heart and a beggers
purse. 1670 : Ray, 133 ["mind" for
"heart"]. 1732 : Fuller, No. 369, A
proud mind and a poor purse are ill
met. Ibid., No. 6386, There's nothing
agrees worse, Than a prince's heart,
and a beggar's purse.

Proud horse that will not bear his own
provender, A. 1546 : Heywood, *Proverbs*, Pt. II. ch. ix. 1597: G. Harvey,
Works, iii. 14 (Grosart), Go too, I say,
he is an ill horse that will not carrie
his owne provender. *c.* 1660 : in *Roxb.
Ballads*, ii. 159 (Hindley). 1670 : Ray,
105 [as in 1597].

Proud look makes foul work in a fine
face, A. 1732 : Fuller, No. 367.

Proud looks lose hearts, but courteous
words win them. 1647 : *Countrym.
New Commonwealth*, 18.

Proud man hath many crosses, A.
1732 : Fuller, No. 368.

Prove thy friend ere thou have need.
c. 1400 : *Cato's Morals*, in *Cursor
Mundi*, p. 1672 (E.E.T.S.), be scarske of
þi louing til hit come to prouing of þi
gode frende. 1546 : Heywood, *Proverbs*, Pt. I. ch. xi. 1670 : Ray, 93.

Provender pricks him. 1546 : Heywood, *Proverbs*, Pt. I. ch. xi., For whan
prouander prickt them a little tyne,
They did as thy wife and thou did both

dote Eche one on other. 1591 : Drayton, *Harmony of Church*, 9 (Percy S.),
That now to lust thy prouender doth
pricke. 1613 : B. & F., *Honest Man's
Fortune*, V. i., But, by my soul, my
provender scarce pricks me. 1716 :
Ward, *Female Policy*, 84, When provender pricks a woman, then she'll
grow knavish.

Proves too much, proves nothing,
That which. 1732 : Fuller, No. 4384.

Provide for the worst, the best will
save itself. 1546 : Heywood, *Proverbs*,
Pt. I. ch. v. 1659 : Howell, 15. 1680 :
L'Estrange, *Citt and Bumpkin*, 6, 'Tis
good however to prepare for the worst,
and the best (as they say) will help itself.

Providence is better than rent. 1640 :
Herbert, *Jac. Prudentum.* 1670 : Ray,
22. 1732 : Fuller, No. 3971.

Providing is preventing. 1883: Burne,
Shropsh. Folk-Lore, 588.

Prudence. *See* Ounce; and Zeal.

Prudent pauses forward business.
1732 : Fuller, No. 3976.

Pry'thee lad, shape. "Shape = set
to work—go on—get along." 1917 :
Bridge, *Cheshire Proverbs*, 104.

Public. *He that does anything for
the public is accounted to do it for nobody.*
1578 : Florio, *First Fruites*, fo. 29, Who
serueth the commons serueth no body.
1611 : Cotgrave, s.v. "Commun," *Ouvrage de commun ouvrage de nul;* All
mens worke is no mans worke ; or that
which is done for many is acknowledged
by none. *Qui sert commun nul ne le
paye, et s'il defaut chascun l'abbaye;*
The service done to a people no man
rewards, the disservices every man
railes at. 1732 : Fuller, No. 2082.
1742 : North, *Lives of Norths*, ii. 120
(Bohn), Which confirms an old lesson,
that "He who serves a community
must secure a reward by his own means,
or expect it from God."

Public reproof hardens shame. 1732 :
Fuller, No. 3977.

Pudding. 1. *A pudding hath two ends.*
1598 : T. Bastard, *Chrestoleros*, bk. iii.
Ep. 12, A podding merits double praise,
a podding hath two ends. 1659 :
Howell, 11, A pudding hath two ends,
but a fool hath none.

2. *A pudding in the fire.* *See* quot.
1659 : Howell, 13, Ther's a pudding in
the fire, and my part lies thereinna.

3. *If it won't pudding, it will froize=*
If it won't do for one thing it will
for another. 1830: Forby, *Vocab. E.
Anglia,* 427. 1872 : J. Glyde, jr., *Norfolk Garland,* 148.

4. *It would vex a dog to see a pudding
creep.* *c.* 1630 : in *Roxb. Ballads,* i. 58
(B.S.), Would not a dog for anger swell
to see a pudding creepe. 1673 : in
Halliwell, *Norfolk Anthology,* 17 (1852).
1738 : Swift, *Polite Convers.,* Dial. II.

5. *Pudding before praise.* 1847 : Barham, *Ing. Legends,* 3rd ser.: " House-
Warming," An old proverb says, " Pudding still before praise ! "

6. *Pudding for a friar's mouth.* *See*
Fit as a pudding.

7. *Pudding is no meat with you.*
1639 : Clarke, 74.

8. *Pudding is poison.* *See* quot.
1738 : Swift, *Polite Convers.,* Dial. II.,
O! Madam, they say a pudding is
poison when it is too much boil'd.

9. *To come in pudding time=*To come
at the right moment. 1546 : Heywood, *Proverbs,* Pt. II. ch. ix., This
geare comth euen in puddyng time
rightlie. 1568 : Fulwell, *Like will to
Like,* in Hazlitt, *Old Plays,* iii. 319.
1596 : Nashe, *Works,* iii. 169 (Grosart),
In pudding time you have spoken.
1604 : Dekker, *Honest Whore,* Pt. I. V.
ii., We come in pudding-time, for here's
the duke. 1663 : Butler, *Hudibras,* Pt.
I. can. ii., l. 865. 1738 : Swift, *Polite
Convers.,* Dial. II. 1769 : Cumberland,
Brothers, II. iv., I want to have a little
chat with you, and thought to have
dropped in at pudding-time, as they
say. 1830 : Colman, jr., in *Hum.
Works,* 421 (Hotten), The good luck of
settling concerns of the greatest consequence, exactly at the critical minute,
is expressed by being " just in pudding
time." 1854 : Baker, *Northants Gloss.,*
s.v., " You've hit pudding-time well,"
is a common salutation to any one who
pops in accidentally to dinner.

See also Cold pudding; and Run (13).
Puff not against the wind. 1605 :
Camden, *Remains,* 330 (1870). 1670 :

Ray, 156. 1846 : Denham, *Proverbs,* 7
(Percy S.).

Pulborough. *See* Chichester.

Pull devil pull baker. 1759 : Colman,
Rolliad, can. ii., Pull Tom, pull Nick,
pull baker, and pull devil. 1831 :
Planché, *Extravag.,* i. 75 (1879),
Orpheus [to Pluto]. But when she
went, it was " pull *you,* pull baker ! "
1881 : in *N. & Q.,* 11th ser., ix. 437,
When the Mayor of Birmingham,
Alderman Baker, tried to unveil the
statue of George Dawson at Birmingham in 1881, the mechanism did not
work. The Mayor tugged at the cord
in vain. In the strained silence was
heard a stage whisper from J. H.
Chamberlain, the architect of the
canopy, " Pull devil—pull Baker ! "
1922 : Ramsay Macdonald in H. of C.,
Times, 14 Dec., p. 8, col. 4, Workmen
and employers must see that the old
game of " pull devil, pull baker " was
not worth the candle.

Pullet in the pen is worth an hundred
in the fen, A. 1869 : Hazlitt, 31.

Pulls with a long rope that waits
for another's death, He. 1640 : Herbert, *Jac. Prudentum.* 1666 : Torriano,
Piazza Univ., 159, He pulls at a long
rope, who longs for another bodies
death.

Pulse beats matrimony, Her. 1678 :
Ray, 265. 1732 : Fuller, No. 2492.

Punch coal. *See* Break (3).

Punctuality is the soul of business.
1869 : Hazlitt, 321. 1878 : Platt,
Business, 95, Punctuality . . . is the
very hinge of business.

Punishment is lame, but it comes.
1640 : Herbert, *Jac. Prudentum.* 1666 :
Torriano, *Piazza Univ.,* 199 [" overtakes " for " comes "]. 1853 : Trench,
Proverbs, 140 (1905).

Purse. 1. *Ask thy purse what thou
should'st buy.* 1732 : Fuller, No. 820.

2. *He hath left his purse in his other
hose.* 1639 : Clarke, 244. 1670 : Ray,
22. 1732 : Fuller, No. 1889 [" breeches "
for " hose "].

3. *He is purse-sick and lacks a physician.* 1546 : Heywood, *Proverbs,* Pt. I.,
ch. xi.

4. *He that shows his purse longs to be*

rid of it. 1639 : Clarke, 176. 1670 :
Ray, 135. 1732 : Fuller, No. 2299, He
that sheweth his wealth to a thief, is
the cause of his own pillage. Ibid., No.
2301 [as in 1639].

5. *His purse and his palate are ill met.*
Ibid., No. 2513.

6. *His purse is made of a toad's skin.*
1678 : Ray, 90.

7. *Keep your purse and your mouth
close.* 1732 : Fuller, No. 3122.

8. *Let your purse be your master.*
1639 : Clarke, 129. 1670 : Ray, 135.
1672 : Walker, *Parœm.*, 47.

9. *The purse-strings are the most common ties of friendship.* 1732 : Fuller,
No. 4727.

10. *To give one's purse a purgation.*
1546 : Heywood, *Proverbs*, Pt. I. ch.
xi., Ye would by my purs, geue me
a purgacion. 1562 : Bullein, *Bulw. of
Defence*, fo. 27, Can giue his masters
purse a purgacion.

See also **Be it better ; Devil** (72) and
(96) ; **Empty** (3)–(7) ; **Heavy purse ;
Less ; Light purse ; Nothing** (4) ; **Proud
eye ; Proud heart ; Silk purse ; Silver**
(2) ; **Two hands ; Wrinkled purses.**

Put, *verb.* 1. *He'll not put off his
doublet before he goes to bed* = He'll not
part with his property before death.
1645 : Howell, *Letters*, bk. i. § iii. No.
xi., This does not suit with the genius
of an Englishman, who loves not to
pull off his clothes till he goes to
bed. 1737 : Ray, 186. 1883 : Burne,
Shropsh. Folk-Lore, 597, To doff one's
shoon before going to bed = to part
with one's property before death.

. 2. *He puts out one of his own eyes, to
put out both of his adversary's.* 1730 :
Bailey, *Eng. Dict.*, s.v. " Solace " [cited
as " the old proverb "].

3. *Never put off till to-morrow what
you can do to-day.* *c.* 1386 : Chaucer,
Melibeus, § 71, " Ther is an old proverbe," quod she, " seith : that the
goodnesse that thou mayst do this day,
do it ; and abyde nat ne delaye it

nat til to-morwe." 1541 : Coverdale,
Christ. State Matrimony, sig. I3, Whatsoeuer thou mayest do to nyght dyferre
it not tyll to morowe. 1633 : Draxe,
41, Deferre not vntill to morrow, if thou
canst do it to day. 1736 : Franklin,
Way to Wealth, in *Works*, i. 444 (Bigelow). 1785 : *Observer*, No. 96. 1869:
Spurgeon, *John Ploughman*, ch. vii.,
These slow coaches . . . take for their
rule an old proverb turned topsy-turvy
—" Never do to-day what you can put
off till to-morrow."

4. *Put in with the bread.* See **Loaf**
(1).

5. *Put no more in the pocket than it
will hold.* 1639 : Clarke, 11.

6. *To be put to one's trumps.* See
Trumps.

7. *To put a churl upon a gentleman.*
1586 : L. Evans, *Withals Dict. Revised*,
sig. D7, Lay not a churle vpon a gentleman, drinke not beere after wine.
1637 : Taylor (Water-Poet), *Drinke and
Welcome*, 20, in *Works*, 2nd coll. (Spens.
S.), And after to drinke beere, nor will
nor can He lay a churle upon a gentleman. 1690: *New Dict. Canting Crew*, sig.
C6. 1738 : Swift, *Polite Convers.*, Dial.
II., *Neverout [offered ale]*, No, faith, my
lord ; I like your wine, and won't put
a churl upon a gentleman ; your
honour's claret is good enough for
me. 1785 : Grose, *Class. Dict. Vulgar
Tongue*, s.v. " Churl."

8. *To put something in the eye.* See
Eye (20).

9. *To put to bed with a shovel* = To
bury. 1859 : in Farmer, *Musa Pedestris*, 160, With shovels they were put
to bed. 1910: *Devonsh. Assoc. Trans.*,
xlii. 68, She callously replied, " Oh, he's
no güde, 'tis taime he were put to bed
wi' a shovel."

10. *To put two and two together.* See
Two and two.

11. *You put it together with an hot
needle and burnt thread.* 1678 : Ray,
350.

Q

Quake like an oven, To. 1670: Ray,
207.

Quality. See quot. 1887: Folk-Lore
Journal, v. 219, To cut an honour for
the trump card is unlucky, for " when
quality opens the door there is poverty
behind."

Quarrel with a knave than with a
fool, It is better to. 1820: Colton,
Lacon, Pt. II. No. 67, These considera-
tions have given rise to this saying,
" It is better," etc.

Quarrel with one's bread and butter,
To. 1738: Swift, Polite Convers., Dial.
I., I won't quarrel with my bread and
butter for all that ; I know when I'm
well. 1748: Richardson, Clarissa, v.
21 (1785). 1833: Planché, Extravag.,
i. 155 (1879). 1869: Spurgeon, John
Ploughman, ch. xix., He who turns up
his nose at his work quarrels with his
bread and butter. 1911: T. Edwardes,
Neighbourhood, 213, Of course I must
not quarrel with my bread-and-butter !

Quartan ague kills the old and cures
the young, A. 1659: Howell, Proverbs:
Ital.-Eng., 15. 1678: Ray, 41. 1732:
Fuller, No. 3991 [in the plural].

Quarter-master where-ever he comes,
He'll be. 1678: Ray, 266. 1732:
Fuller, No. 2414, He would be quarter-
master at home, if his wife would let
him.

Queen Anne's dead. 1722: Ballad,
in Lady Pennyman, Miscellanies, 1740,
He's as dead as Queen Anne the
day after she dy'd. 1738: Swift,
Polite Convers., Dial. I., And pray, what
news, Mr. Neverout? Neverout. Why,
madam, Queen Elizabeth's dead. 1797:
Colman, jr., Heir at Law, I. i., Tell 'em
Queen Anne's dead, my lady. 1840:
Barham, Ing. Legends, 1st ser.: " Look
at the Clock," Mrs. Winifred Pryce was
as dead as Queen Anne ! 1908: Read,
H. & B. in Hants., 353, Portsmouth
offers text and reference for the saying
" Queen Anne is dead."

Queen-apple-tree, To be up the.
1670 : Ray, 198.

Queen Dick. 1667: L'Estrange,
Quevedo's Visions, 50 (1904), This was
well enough in the days of Queen Dick,
when the poor creatures knew no better.

Queen's English. See King's English.

Quern. See Do (39).

Quest. See Wood-pigeon.

Questioneth, He that nothing, nothing
learneth. 1732 : Fuller, No. 2241.

Quey out of a quey, A, Will breed a
byre full of kye. " Quey " = a heifer.
1846 : Denham, Proverbs, 14 (Percy S.).

Quick and nimble ; more like a bear
than a squirrel. 1732 : Fuller, No.
3992.

Quick and nimble 'twill be your own
another day. 1678 : Ray, 345.

Quick as a bee. 1546 : Heywood,
Proverbs, Pt. I. ch. ix. 1595 : Churchyard, Charitie, 16 (1816), As quicke as
bee, seekes honie euery where. 1633 :
Draxe, 172.

Quick as lightning. c. 1440 : Lydgate, Fall of Princes, bk. vi. l. 2114, His
conquest was swifft as wynd or leuene
[lightning]. c. 1623 : B. & F., Love's
Cure, I. i., Swift as lightning he came
on Upon the other. 1763 : Mrs. F.
Sheridan, Discovery, I. ii., I am rather
petulant, flash, flash, flash, as quick as
lightning. 1787 : D'Arblay, Diary, ii.
427 (1876), I turned back, quick as
lightning. 1880 : R. L. S. and Henley,
Deacon Brodie, I. iii. i., I was as quick
as lightning.

Quick as thought. Before 1225 :
Ancren R., 94 (O.), Ase swifte ase is nu
monnes þouht. 1412-20 : Lydgate,
Troy Book, bk. i. l. 1764, By sodeyn
chawnge, hasty as a thought. 1468:
Coventry Mys., 298 (Sh. S.), I am
as whyt [quick] as thought. 1594 :
Zepheria, 30 (Spens. S.), But now (old
man) flye on, as swift as thought.
1620 : Shelton, Quixote, Pt. II. ch. xlviii.

1656 : R. Fletcher, *Ex Otio Negotium*, 84. 1748 : Richardson, *Clarissa*, vi. 13 (1785), Then, as quick as thought . . . 1894 : Northall, *Folk Phrases*, 10 (E.D.S.). 1923 : *Punch*, 10 Jan., p. 29, col. 1, As quick as thought I flung myself forward and snatched at the bridle.

Quick at meat, quick at work. 1611 : Cotgrave, s.v. "Bestes." Ibid., s.v. "Eschauffer," We say, good at meat, good at worke. 1650 : Fuller, *Pisgah Sight*, bk. ii. ch. viii. 1710 : E. Ward, *Nuptial Dialogues*, i. 307, Speedy at victuals, quick at work's an old proverbial saying. 1738 : Swift, *Polite Convers.*, Dial. II. 1829 : Cobbett, *Advice to Young Men*, Lett. III., "Quick at meals, quick at work," is a saying as old as the hills.

Quick baker, A, and a slow brewer. 1732 : Fuller, No. 373.

Quick believers need broad shoulders. 1640 : Herbert, *Jac. Prudentum*.

Quick child is soon taught. *c.* 1320 : in *Reliq. Antiquæ*, i. 110 (1841), "Sely chyld is sone y-lered"; Quoth Hendyng. 1869 : Hazlitt, 322.

Quick landlord makes a careful tenant, A. 1678 : Ray, 165. 1732 : Fuller, No. 3994 [in the plural].

Quick, To the. *See* Touch (2).

Quick with the quick. *See* Live (38).

Quick. *See also* Nimble.

Quickly come, quickly go. 1631 : Mabbe, *Celestina*, 29 (T.T.), Quickly be wonne, and quickly be lost.

Quiet as a lamb. 1362 : Langland, *Plowman*, A, vi. 13, He is as louh [quiet] as a lomb. *c.* 1440 : Lydgate, *Fall of Princes*, bk. i. l. 6934 (E.E.T.S.), Stille as a lamb, most meek off his visage. 1592 : Shakespeare, *Romeo*, II. v., I'll warrant him, as gentle as a lamb. 1694 : *Terence made English*, 180, I can presently make him as quiet as a lamb. 1787 : D'Arblay, *Diary*, ii. 337 (1876), I used to . . . wander about as quiet as a lamb. 1872 : Hardy, *Greenwood*

Tree, Pt. V. ch. i., I walked into the church as quiet as a lamb, I'm sure !

Quiet (or Still) as a mouse. 1656 : Flecknoe, *Diarium*, 9, Was wont to be as still as mouse. *c.* 1670 : in *Roxb. Ballads*, iii. 377 (B.S.), I must be silent as a mouse. 1709 : Cibber, *Rival Fools*, II., I'm mute as a mouse in a cheese. 1772 : Graves, *Spirit. Quixote*, bk. ii. ch. xiv., Tugwell was as still as a mouse during this discourse. 1824 : Scott, *Redgauntlet*, ch. xvi., A place where you will be as snug and quiet as a mouse in his hole. 1894 : R. L. S., *St. Ives*, ch. xi., Both armies lay as quiet as mice. 1923 : *Punch*, 7 March, p. 218, col. 1, If she has her bricks and a pencil and paper she'll be as quiet as a mouse.

Quiet as a 'tatur, As. 1917 : Bridge, *Cheshire Proverbs*, 26.

Quiet sleep feels no foul weather. 1732 : Fuller, No. 3997.

Quiet sow, quiet mow. Devon. 1850 : *N. & Q.*, 1st ser., ii. 512.

Quiet tongue makes a wise head, A. 1562 : Heywood, *Epigr.*, 6th hund., No. 83, Hauyng a styll toung he had a besy head. 1776 : T. Cogan, *John Buncle, Junior*, i. 238, But mum's the word. . . . A quiet tongue makes a wise head, says I.

Quietness is best. *See* quots. 1886 : R. Holland, *Cheshire Gloss.*, 453 (E.D.S.), Quietness is best, as the fox said, when he bit the cock's head off. 1908 : *Eng. Ill. Mag.*, Jan., 357, Quietness is the best noise, as Uncle Johnny said when he knocked down his wife [Cornish]. 1917 : Bridge, *Cheshire Proverbs*, 104 [as in 1886].

Quit bridle, quit tit. 1820 : Scott, *Abbot*, ch. xvii., They are as sharp here north-away as in canny Yorkshire herself, and quit bridle, quit titt, as we say.

Quits his place well that leaves his friend there, He. 1640 : Herbert, *Jac. Prudentum*.

Quoth the young cock. *See* Young (15).

R

Rabbit for a rat, Who will change a ?
1546 : Heywood, *Proverb*, Pt. II. ch. vii.

Rabbit, He's like a, fat and lean in twenty-four hours. 1678 : Ray, 288.

Rabbit-hunting. *See* quot. 1732 : Fuller, No. 5170, To go a coney-catching with a dead ferrit.

Race-horse. *See* **Running horse.**

Race is got by running, The. 1732 : Fuller, No. 4728.

Rack and manger, To lie (or live) at.
c. 1378 : Wiclif, in *Eng. Works*, 435 (Matthew, 1880), It is yuel to kepe a wast hors in stable . . . but it is worse to have a womman wiþ-ynne or wiþ-oute at racke and at manger. 1590 : Greene, *Works*, ix. 178 (Grosart), Mars himselfe hateth to be euer on Venus lappe, he scorneth to lye at rack and manger. 1628 : *Robin Goodfellow*, 10 (Percy S.), Leaped and curveted as nimble as if he had beene in stable at rack and manger a full moneth. 1640 : Shirley, *Love's Cruelty*, III. ii., You think you are at rack and manger, when you divide beans with the horses, and help to foul the stable. 1740 : North, *Lives of Norths*, i. 335 (Bohn), He took divers of them to rack and manger in his family. 1843 : Carlyle, *Past and Present*, bk. ii. ch. i., Tearing out the bowels of St. Edmundsbury Convent (its larders namely and cellars) in the most ruinous way, by living at rack and manger there. 1889 : Peacock, *Manley, etc., Gloss.*, 426 (E.D.S.), To live at rack and manger is to live plentifully ; without stint.

Rag on every bush. *See* quot. 1866 : in *N. & Q.*, 3rd ser., ix. 474, A Rag upon Every Bush.—This saying, or proverb . . . is usually applied to young men who are in the habit of showing "marked attention" to more than one lady at a time. " Oh, he has a rag on every bush."

Ragged as a colt, As. 1863 : Wise,

New Forest, ch. xvi., The proverb of " as ragged as a colt Pixey " is everywhere to be heard, and at which Drayton seems to hint in his *Court of Faerie* : " This Puck seems but a dreaming dolt, Still walking like a ragged colt." 1894 : Northall, *Folk Phrases*, 10 (E.D.S.).

Ragged as a cuckoo, As. Oxfordsh. 1923 : *Folk-Lore*, xxxiv. 329.

Ragged as a sheep, As. 1862 : *Dialect of Leeds*, 405, If the child of a slatternly woman is seen with tattered garments, it is pronounced at once to be " as regg'd as a sheep."

Ragged colt may make a good horse, A. Before 1500 : in Hill, *Commonplace-Book*, 128 (E.E.T.S.), Of a rwgged colte cwmeth a good hors. 1546 : Heywood, *Proverbs*, Pt. I. ch. xi., For of a ragged colte there comth a good horse. 1605 : Chapman, etc., *Eastw. Hoe*, V. [with " prove " for " make "]. 1670 : Ray, 72. 1754 : Berthelson, *Eng.-Danish Dict.*, s.v. " Colt." 1786 : Burns, *Dream*, xi. (O.), Aft a ragged cowte's been known To mak a noble aiver. 1846 : Denham, *Proverbs*, 7 (Percy S.), Of a ragged colt cometh many a good horse.

Ragged colt. *See also* **Scald horse.**

Rags o' th' hob, There'll be. 1917 : Bridge, *Cheshire Proverbs*, 117, . . . There will be a quarrel or unpleasantness.

Rain, *subs.* 1. *A foot deep of rain Will kill hay and grain; But three feet of snow Will make them come mo'* [more]. 1869 : Blackmore, *Lorna Doone*, ch. l. [quoted as " the old saying "]. 1893 : Inwards, *Weather Lore*, 111.

2. *After rain comes sunshine* (or *fair weather*). 1484 : Caxton, *Fables of Æsope*, II. viii. (O.), After the rayne cometh the fair weder. 1597 : C. Middleton, *Chinon of England*, 26 (E.E.T.S.), After showers at length would come a sunne. 1678 : Ray, 194, After rain comes fair weather. 1869 :

Spurgeon, *John Ploughman*, ch. v., After
rain comes clear shining. 1893 : Inwards, *Weather Lore*, 111, After rain
comes sunshine.

3. *A little rain stills a great wind.*
Before 1225 : *Ancren R.*, 246, Eft, me
seiþ, and soþ hit is, a muchel wind aliþ
mid a lutel rein. *c.* 1430 : Lydgate,
Daunce of Machabree, l. 448, And windes
great gon down with litle rein. 1478 :
Rivers, tr. C. de Pisa's *Morale Prouerbes*,
And litle reyne dooth a greet wynd
abate. *c.* 1534 : Berners, *Huon*, 39
(E.E.T.S.), It is sayd that a small rayne
abatyth a grete wynd. 1653 : Urquhart, *Rabelais*, bk. ii. ch. xi. 1732 :
Fuller, No. 410, A small rain may allay
a great storm. Cf. No. 11.

4. *All the rain avore Midzummer
Go'th into the farmer's puss; All the rain
arterwards Is zo much the wuss.* 1891 :
R. P. Chope, *Hartland Dialect*, 20
(E.D.S.).

5. *A sunshiny shower Won't last half
an hour.* 1846 : Denham, *Proverbs*, 8
(Percy S.). 1872 : J. Glyde, jr., *Nor-
folk Garland*, 155. 1893 : Inwards,
Weather Lore, 111, A sunshiny shower
Never lasts half an hour. Bedfordshire.
Sunshiny rain Will soon go again.
Devon. 1899: *N. & Q.*, 9th ser., iv. 165,
There is the rime, Sunshine shower, Rain
half an hour, which children used to
sing-song if caught in a shower on a
summer day coming from school.

6. *Between twelve and two You'll see
what the day will do.* 1872 : J. Glyde,
jr., *Norfolk Garland*, 155.

7. *Bright-backed rain Makes fools
fain.* 1917 : Bridge, *Cheshire Proverbs*,
162, . . . When a rain cloud is succeeded by a little brightness in the sky,
fools rejoice and think it will soon be
fair weather.

8. *For a morning rain leave not your
journey.* Before 1500 : in Hill, *Commonplace-Book*, 131 (E.E.T.S.), He is no
good swayn that lettith his jorney for
the rayn. 1640 : Herbert, *Jac. Prudentum.*

9. *If rain begins at early morning
light, 'Twill end ere day at noon is bright.*
1893 : Inwards, *Weather Lore*, 109.

10. *If the rain comes out of the east,*

'*Twill rain twice twenty-four hours at the
least. c.* 1685 : Aubrey, *Nat. Hist.
Wilts,* 16 (1847). 1830 : Forby, *Vocab.
E. Anglia*, 417, When it rains with the
wind in the east, It rains for twenty-
four hours at least. 1893 : Inwards,
Weather Lore, 109, Rain from the east
Two days at least.

11. *Marry the rain to the wind and you
have a calm.* Ibid., 110. Cf. No. 3.

12. *More rain, more rest.* 1864 :
"Cornish Proverbs," in *N. & Q.*, 3rd
ser., v. 208, More rain, more rest ; more
water will suit the ducks best. 1879 :
N. & Q., 5th ser., xi. 18, Fifty years ago
I read in a book of travels, More rain,
more rest ; Fine weather not the best,
as a saying much used by sailors. 1901 :
F. E. Taylor, *Lancs Sayings*, 41, Mooar
rain—mooar rest : fine weather is no'
awlus th' best. Cf. No. 23.

13. *No one so surely pays his debt As
wet to dry and dry to wet.* Wilts. 1893 :
Inwards, *Weather Lore*, 108.

14. *Plenty rain, plenty sunshine,
Plenty rain, plenty root.* 1899: *N. & Q.*,
9th ser., iv. 165, . . . old hands know
that after an early summer, with nice
rains and hot suns alternating, there
is sure to be abundance of fruit, corn
and root.

15. *Rain before seven, Fine before
eleven.* 1853 : *N. & Q.*, 1st ser., viii.
512. 1888 : Lowsley, *Berks Gloss.*, 30
(E.D.S.), Raain avoor zeven vine avoor
'leven is a very common weather proverb. 1893 : Inwards, *Weather Lore*,
44, Rain at seven, fine at eleven ; Rain
at eight, not fine till eight. 1899:
N. & Q., 9th ser., iii. 317, . . . I have
always heard this proverb with two
additional lines :—If it rains at eleven,
'Twill last till seven.

16. *Rain from the south prevents the
drought; But rain from the west is always best.* 1893 : Inwards, *Weather
Lore*, 109.

17. *Rain has such narrow shoulders it
will get in anywhere.* 1877 : E. Leigh,
Cheshire Gloss., 165. 1917 : Bridge,
Cheshire Proverbs, 105.

18. *Rain long foretold, long last; Short
notice soon past.* 1893 : Inwards, 109. ;

19. *Rain on the green grass, and rain*

on the tree, And rain on the house-top, but
not upon me. 1846 : Denham, Proverbs, 8 (Percy S.).

20. Rain, rain, go away, Come again on
Saturday. 1687 : Aubrey, Gentilisme,
etc., 180 (F.L.S.). 1899 : in N. & Q.,
9th ser., iv. 165 [with " for washing day"
for " on Saturday "].

21. Rain, rain, go to Spain. See quots.
1659 : Howell, 20, Rain, rain, go to
Spain, Fair weather come again. 1837 :
Mrs. Palmer, Devonsh. Dialect, 46, Rain,
rain, go to Spain ; Come again another
day : When I brew and when I bake,
I'll give you a figgy cake. 1864 :
" Cornish Proverbs," in N. & Q., 3rd
ser., v. 209, [as in 1837, plus] and a glass
of brandy.

22. Small rain lays a great dust.
1670 : Ray, 135. 1732 : Fuller, No.
4193. 1846 : Denham, Proverbs, 5
(Percy S.) [" will lay " for " lays "].

23. Some rain some rest. A harvest
proverb. 1678 : Ray, 80. 1893 : Inwards, Weather Lore, 108, Some rain,
some rest ; Fine weather isn't always
best. Cf. No. 12.

24. Sunshine and shower, rain again
to-morrow. Ibid., 111.

25. The farther the sight the nearer the
rain. Ibid., 105.

26. The faster the rain, the quicker the
hold up. Norfolk. Ibid., 109.

27. When the Lizard is clear, Rain is
near. Corn. Ibid., 105.

28. When the rain raineth and the
goose winketh, Little wots the gosling
what the goose thinketh. Before 1529 :
Skelton, in Works, i. 418 (Dyce). 1667 :
Poor Robin Alman., Sept.

29. When the rain's before the win',
'Tis time to take the topsails in, But when
the wind's before the rain, Let your topsails out again. 1875 : A. B. Cheales,
Proverb. Folk-Lore, 27.

Rain, verb. 1. Although it rain,
throw not away thy watering-pot. 1640 :
Herbert, Jac. Prudentum.

2. If it rains before church. See
quots. [16th cent.: in Reliq. Antiquæ,
ii. 10 (1843), Du Dimanche au matin
la pluye Bien souvent la semaine
ennuye.] 1846 : Denham, Proverbs, 11
(Percy S.), If it rains on a Sunday

before mass, It will rain all the week,
more or less. 1881 : in Folk-Lore Record, iv. 130, Rain afore church Rain
all the week, little or much.—Norfolk.
1883 : Burne, Shropsh. Folk-Lore, 261
[as in 1846].

3. If it raineth at tide's flow. See quots.
c. 1685 : Aubrey, Nat. Hist. Wilts, 16
(1847), A proverbial rithme observed
as infallible by the inhabitants on the
Severne side :—If it raineth when it
doth flow, Then yoke your oxe, and goe
to plough ; But if it raineth when it
doth ebb, Then unyoke your oxe, and
goe to bed. 1893 : Inwards, Weather
Lore, 107, If it raineth at tide's flow,
You may safely go and mow ; But if
it raineth at the ebb, Then, if you like,
go off to bed.

4. If it should rain porridge he would
want his dish. [1583 : Melbancke,
Philotinus, sig. Cc3, All the world is
otemeale, and my poke left at home.]
1670 : Ray, 191. 1692 : Poor Robin
Alman., May, What is he better for his
wish, When it rains porridg to want a
dish. 1732 : Fuller, No. 2687. 1895 :
S. O. Jewett, Life of Nancy, 221, " When
it rains porridge hold up your dish,"
said Mrs. Flagg. 1923 : Devonsh.
Assoc. Trans., liv. 136, If it shud be
rainin' porridge, my dish'd sure to be
upside down.

5. It never rains but it pours. 1726 :
Swift and Pope, Prose Miscellanies,
[title of paper] It cannot rain but it
pours. 1755 : Franklin, in Works, ii.
413 (Bigelow), You will say, It can't
rain, but it pours. 1857 : Borrow,
Rom. Rye, ch. xxviii. 1860 : Reade,
Cl. and Hearth, ch. liii. 1904 : Co.
Folk-Lore: Northumb., 171 (F.L.S.), It
does not rain but it pours down.

6. It rains by planets. 1670 : Ray,
45. 1809 : Pegge, Anonymiana, cent.
ix. 48, The common people will say in
the summer-time, it rains by planets.
1828 : Carr, Craven Dialect, ii. 48,
" T" rain faws i' planets," i.e. the rain
falls partially. 1887 : Parish and Shaw,
Dict. Kent. Dialect, 117 (E.D.S.), " It
rains by planets," when showers fall
in a small compass, in opposition to
general rain.

7. *It rains cats and dogs.* 1653 : R. Brome, *City Wit*, IV. i., It shall raine . . . dogs and polecats, and so forth. 1738 : Swift, *Polite Convers.*, Dial. II., He was sure it would rain cats and dogs. 1829 : Scott, *Journal*, 16 April. 1840: Barham, *Ing. Legends*, 1st ser.: " Grey Dolphin.

8. *It rains in summer as well as in winter.* 1732 : Fuller, No. 3044.

9. *To see it rain is better than to be in it.* 1639: Clarke, 278. 1670: Ray, 140. 1732 : Fuller, No. 5223, To see a storm is better than to feel it.

Rain, subs. and verb. *See also* After drought ; Bee (10) ; Cloud ; Devil (111) ; Dew ; Dirt-bird ; Dog-days ; Easter (13) ; Every day in the week ; February ; Fleas ; Friday (6) and (7) ; Frost (6) and (8) ; God will ; Good Friday (2) ; July ; Mobberley ; Peacock ; Rainbow; Red at night ; St. John (1) ; St. Mary ; St. Medard ; St. Peter ; St. Swithin ; St. Vitus ; Smoke (2) ; Snail ; Spring (7) ; Sun ; Whitsuntide ; and Wind, A (a) (1), (13) and (14) ; B (2), (5) and (6) ; D (3) and (5) ; E (1) and (5) ; F (5), (8), (9) and (10).

Rainbow. 1. *A rainbow in the morning and in the evening. See* quots. 1555 : L. Digges, *Prognostication*, sig. B2, If in the mornyng the raynebow appere, it signifieth moysture . . . If in the evening it spend it self, fayre weather ensueth. 1666 : Torriano, *Piazza Univ.*, 13, The evening rainbow portends fair weather. 1825 : Hone, *Ev. Day Book*, i. 670, A rainbow in the morning Is the shepherd's warning ; But a rainbow at night Is the shepherd's delight. 1886 : R. Holland, *Cheshire Gloss.*, 444 (E.D.S.), A rainbow at morn Is a sign of a storm ; A rainbow at night Is a shepherd's delight. 1893 : Inwards, *Weather Lore*, 112, [as in 1825, also as follow] The rainbow in the marnin' Gives the shepherd warnin' To car' his gurt cwoat on his back ; The rainbow at night is the shepherd's delight, For then no gurt cwoat will he lack. *Wilts*. A dog [small rainbow near the horizon] in the morning, Sailor, take warning ; A dog in the night Is the sailor's delight.

2. *A rainbow in the morn, put your hook in the corn; A rainbow in the eve, put your hook in the sheave.* Corn. Ibid., 112.

3. *Go to the end of the rainbow and you'll find a crock of gold.* 1850 : N. & Q., 1st ser., ii. 512, Where the rainbow rests is a crock of gold. 1875 : Parish, *Sussex Dict.*, 31 [given as a " Sussex proverb "].

4. *If the rainbow comes at night, The rain is gone quite.* 1830 : Forby, *Vocab. E. Anglia*, 417. 1893 : Co. *Folk-Lore: Suffolk*, 163 (F.L.S.).

5. *If there be a rainbow in the eve, It will rain and leave: But if there be a rainbow in the morrow, It will neither lend nor borrow.* 1670 : Ray, 43. 1825 : Hone, *Ev. Day Book*, i. 670. 1893 : Inwards, *Weather Lore*, 112.

6. *If two rainbows appear at one time, they presage rain to come.* 1669 : New *Help to Discourse*, 293.

7. *Rainbow to windward, foul fall the day; Rainbow to leeward, damp runs away.* 1893 : Inwards, *Weather Lore*, 112.

Rainy day, To keep something (or To lay up or by) for a. 1582 : Breton, in *Works*, i. a 29 (Grosart), Wise men say Keepe somewhat till a rayny day. 1583 : Stubbes, *Anat. of Abuses*, 115 (N. Sh. S.), Is it not good to lay vp something against a stormie day? 1653 : R. Brome, *City Wit*, IV. i., I hope I had the wit to cozen my husband of somewhat against a rainy day. 1666 : Pepys, *Diary*, 31 Oct., I . . . do provide for it by laying by something against a rainy day. 1690 : Dryden, *Amphitryon*, I. ii. 1705 : Centlivre, *Gamester*, III. i. 1744-6 : Mrs. Haywood, *Fem. Spectator*, i. 113 (1771). 1860 : Reade, *Cl. and Hearth*, ch. lii., So she met current expenses, and laid by for the rainy day she saw coming.

Raise no more spirits than you can conjure down. 1639 : Clarke, 247. 1670 : Ray, 135. 1732 : Fuller, No. 4000. 1754 : Berthelson, *Eng.-Danish Dict.*, s.v. " Raise " [" lay " for " conjure "].

Raise one downstairs, To. 1917 : Bridge, *Cheshire Proverbs*, 142.

Rake gathers, the fork scatters, What the. 1580: Lyly, *Euphues*, 228 (Arber), Youth . . . tedding that with a forke in one yeare, which was not gathered together with a rake, in twentie. *c.* 1630 : in *Roxb. Ballads*, i. 134 (B.S.), Great use he did take, And for me did rake, Which now with the forke I will scatter. 1775 : in *Roxb. Ballads*, vii. 520 (B.S.), What the old folks scrap'd together, I spread it abroad with my fork. 1869 : Hazlitt, 369, The fork is commonly the rake's heir.

Rake hell and skim the devil, you can't find such another man. 1754 : Berthelson, *Eng. - Danish Dict.*, s.v. "Rake."

Rake more than the fork, He uses the. 1670 : Ray, 190, He is better with a rake then a fork. 1732 : Fuller, No. 2375.

Ram. *See* Crooked; and Sheep (8).

Ram [fetid] as a fox, As. [1601: Shake-speare, *Twelfth Night*, II. v., Though it be as rank as a fox. 1693 : D'Urfey, *Richmond Heiress*, I., Red and rank as a fox.] 1828 : Carr, *Craven Dialect*, ii. 69, He's as ram as a fox. 1862 : *Dia-lect of Leeds*, 406. 1889 : J. Nicholson, *Folk Speech E. Yorks*, 20, As ram as an awd fox.

Rame Head. *See* Dudman.

Ramsey the rich. 1662 : Fuller, *Worthies*, ii. 98 (1840). 1708 : *Brit. Apollo*, i., Suppl. Paper, No. 10, col. 4. 1790 : Grose, *Prov. Gloss.*, s.v. "Hunts."

Rancor sticks long by the ribs. 1639 : Clarke, 178. 1659 : Howell, 16.

Rank courtesy when a man is forced to give thanks for his own, It's a. 1670 : Ray, 20. 1732 : Fuller, No. 2871.

Rap. *See* Haste (4).

Rap and rend, To=To seize. 1528 : Roy, *Rede me*, 74 (Arber), To rappe and rende All that commeth in their fingrynge. 1540 : Palsgrave, *Acolastus*, sig. Q2, All that he may gete or laye hande on or rappe and rende. 1817 : Scott, *Rob Roy*, ch. xxvi., Every ane o' them will maintain as mony . . . as he can rap and rend means for. 1866 : J. G. Nall, *Gt. Yarmouth, etc.*, 631, "'A spend everything 'a can rap and rend," i.e. all he can seize and lay hands on.

1866 : Brogden, *Lincs Words*, 163, Rap and rend.—By fair or foul means. 1920 : E. Gepp, *Essex Dialect Dict.*, 29, I've giv ye all I could rap and rend.

Rap and run, To. *c.* 1386 : Chaucer, *Can. Yeoman's Tale*, l. 1422, But wasten al that ye may rape and renne. 1607 : R. West, *Court of Conscience*, sig. E4, When they haue got what they can rap and run. 1742 : North, *Lives of Norths*, ii. 280 (Bohn), All that he could (as they say) rap or run went the same way.

Rare thing to do good, It is a. 1659 : Howell, 9.

Rashness is not valour. 1732 : Fuller, No. 4002.

Rasp [Put aside] the scythe : drink some cyder. S. Devon. 1869 : Haz-litt, 323.

Rat and Rats. 1. *He'd starve the rats, and make the mice go upon scritches* [crutches]. S. Devon. 1869 : Hazlitt, 198.

2. *Rats fly from the falling house.* 1625 : Bacon, *Essays:* "Wisdom for Man's Self," It is the wisedome of rats, that will be sure to leaue a house, somewhat before it fall. 1649 : T. Forde, *Lusus Fort.*, 32, That ill such friends run from, like mice from a falling house. 1663 : Butler, *Hudibras*, Pt. I., can. ii. l. 939. 1672 : Crowne, *Charles VIII.*, V., All vermin from a falling palace run. 1724 : Defoe, *Tour*, Lett. III., 98, The mice and rats have abandoned many [houses] more, as they say they will, when they are likely to fall. 1748 : Richardson, *Clar-issa*, vi. 324 (1785). 1848 : Dickens, *Dombey*, ch. lix., It is a great house still . . . but it is a ruin none the less, and the rats fly from it.

3. *Rats in Ireland. See* Rhyme to death.

4. *The rats may safely play when as the cat's away.* 1611: Cotgrave, s.v. "Rat." .

5. *Too late repents the rat when caught by the cat.* 1591 : Florio, *Second Frutes*, 165, Too late repents the ratt, If once her taile be caught by the catt. 1623 : Wodroephe, *Spared Houres*, 516.

6. *You can't get rats out of mice.* Devon. 1882: *Folk-Lore Record*, v. 159.

See also **Drunk as a rat; Fierce; Poor; Scot (1); Smell (3);** and **Welcome (7).**

Rate thy commodities at home, but sell them abroad. 1611 : Cotgrave, s.v. " Priser." 1666 : Torriano, *Piazza Univ.*, 218, Fix thy rates at home, and in the market sell.

Rather go to bed supperless. *See* **Supperless.**

Raven. Two sayings which = The pot calls the kettle black. 1. *The raven said to the rook, " Stand away, black-coat."* 1732 : Fuller, No. 4729. 1886 : Swainson, *Folk-Lore Brit. Birds*, 88 (F.L.S.).

2. *Thou art a bitter bird, said the raven to the starling.* 1678 : Ray, 195. 1826 : Brady, *Varieties of Lit.*, 38. 1886 : Swainson, *ut supra*, 73.

See also **Black**, *adj.* (7); and **Carcase.**

Raw leather will stretch. 1611 : Davies (of Hereford), *Sc. of Folly*, 46, in *Works*, ii. (Grosart). 1670 : Ray, 136. 1732 : Fuller, No. 4004.

Raw pullen, veal and fish make the churchyards fat. 1611 : Cotgrave, s.v. " Poulet," Raw veale, and chickens, make swelling churchyards. 1678 : Ray, 41.

Read not before you learn to spell. 1639 : Clarke, 4.

Read. *See* quot. 1882 : Nodal and Milner, *Lancs Gloss.*, 225 (E.D.S.), A common Lancashire saying among old folks is " Aw con read [understand] that as ne'er wur printed."

Read, try, judge, and speak as you find, says old Suffolk. 1813 : Ray, 71.

Ready money is a ready medicine. 1611 : Cotgrave, s.v. " Argent." 1651 : Herbert, *Jac. Prudentum*, 2nd ed.

Ready money will away. 1630 : Taylor (Water-Poet), *Works*, 1st pagin., 72, For by long proofe, the prouerbe true doth say, *That ready money euer will away.* 1670 : Ray, 18.

Ready mouth for a ripe cherry, You have always a. 1732 : Fuller, No. 5913.

Ready way to lose your friend is to lend him money, A. Ibid., No. 378.

Reason, *subs.* 1. *Hearken to reason or she will be heard.* 1640 : Herbert,

Jac. Prudentum. 1736 : Franklin, *Way to Wealth*, in *Works*, i. 451 (Bigelow), If you will not hear reason, she will surely rap your knuckles.

2. *Reason governs the wise man, and cudgels the fool.* 1855 : Bohn, 479.

3. *Reason lies between the spur and the bridle.* 1640 : Herbert, *Jac. Prudentum.*

4. *Reason rules all things.* 1633 : Draxe, 175, Let reason rule all your actions. 1659 : Howell, 9.

5. *Reasons are not like garments, the worse for the wearing.* 1599 : Earl of Essex, quoted in *N. & Q.*, 10th ser., ii. 23.

6. *The reasons of the poor.* *See* **Poor** (30).

7. *There's reason in roasting of eggs.* 1659.: Howell, 12. 1681 : Robertson, *Phraseol. Generalis*, 1050. 1762 : Bickerstaffe, *Love in a Village*, III. i. 1855 : Planché, *Extravag.*, v. 145 (1879), But you'll observe he humbly hopes and begs, Some reason in this roasting of her eggs. *c.* 1880 : A. Lang, *Poet. Works*, ii. 205 (1923), " There's wit in poaching eggs," the proverb says.

See also **Rhyme.**

Receiver is as bad as the thief, The. 1650 : Fuller, *Pisgah Sight*, bk. ii. ch. iv. 1668 : Sedley, *Mulberry Garden*, IV. 1734 : Fielding, *Don Quix. in England*, II. xvi. 1830 : Marryat, *King's Own*, ch. xi.

Receiver, No, no thief. 1546 : Heywood, *Proverbs*, Pt. I., ch. xii., Where be no receiuers, there be no theeues. *c.* 1615 : R. C., *Times Whistle*, 89 (E.E.T.S.), For every man this olde saide saw beleeves, " Were no receivers there would be no theeves." 1670 : Ray, 136. 1732 : Fuller, No. 3620. 1884 : Jefferies, *Red Deer*, ch. v., As there are no receivers . . . there are no thieves.

(a) **Reckon without one's host, To.** Also in the form (b) **He that reckons without his host must reckon twice.** *c.* 1489 : Caxton, *Blanchardyn, etc.*, 202 (E.E.T.S.), It ys sayd in comyn that " who soeuer rekeneth wythoute his hoste, he rekeneth twys for ones." 1546 : Heywood, *Proverbs*, Pt. I. ch. viii., Reckners without their host must recken twyce. 1579 : Lyly, *Euphues*, 84 (Arber), He reckoneth without his hostesse. 1605 : Camden, *Remains*, 324 (1870) [as in (*b*)]. 1669 : *Politeuphuia*, 183 [as in (*b*)]. 1709 : O. Dykes, *Eng. Proverbs*, 262 (2nd ed.) [as in (*b*)]. 1766 : Garrick and Colman, *Clandest. Marriage*, III. i., Odso! I had quite forgot. We are reckoning without our host here. 1846 : Planché, *Extravag.*, iii. 140 (1879), Ah, madam, there without your host you reckon! She has deserted us.

Reconciled friend is a double enemy, A. 1732 : Fuller, No. 379.

Recover the horse. *See* **Win** (4).

Red and yellow. *See* quot. 1874 : in *N. & Q.*, 5th ser., i. 219, An old saying is familiar to me—" Red and yellow, Tom Fool's colours." Doubtless the allusion is to the glowing particoloured dress of the Fool or Jester.

Red as a cherry. 1558 : Bullein, *Govt. of Health*, fo. 49, Read as chery. 1577 : Kendall, *Flow. of Epigrams*, 292 (Spens. S.), Her nipples red as cherries. 1614 : *Cobbes Proph.*, sig. D1, (Facs. 1890), When a cup of good sacke . . . Will make the cheeks red as a cherry. 1720 : Gay, *Eclogues*: "Espousal," l. 62, Red as the cherry from the Kentish tree. 1849 : Brontë, *Shirley*, ch. xi., To-day you see them bouncing, buxom, red as cherries.

Red as a ferret. 1690 : *New Dict. Canting Crew*, sig. E4, Eyes as red as a ferret. 1862 : *Dialect of Leeds*, 407.

Red as a rose. *c.* 1260 : *King Horn* (Camb.), l. 16 (Hall), Rose red was his colur. Before 1300 : *Cursor Mundi*, 571 (E.E.T.S.), As rose reed hit is in spring. *c.* 1374 : Chaucer, *Troylus*, bk. ii. l. 1256, " Nay, nay," quod she, and wex as reed as rose. *c.* 1477 : Caxton, *Jason*, 156 (E.E.T.S.), His blood began to chaunge and he woxe rede as a rose. *c.* 1565 : in Huth, *Ancient Ballads, etc.*, 208 (1867), With bloud, I hard saye, as red as a rose. *c.* 1675 : in *Roxb. Ballads*, vi. 244 (B.S.), She stept to him, as red as any rose. 1798 : Coleridge, *Anc. Mariner*, Pt. I., st. 9, The bride . . . Red as a rose is she. 1818 : Austen, *North. Abbey*, ch. x., My cheeks

would have been as red as your roses. 1863 : Kingsley, *Water Babies*, ch. ii.

Red as a turkey - cock. *c.* 1630 : B. & F., *Faithful Friends*, III. ii., The very sight of his scarlet gown made me blush as red as a turkey-cock. 1733 : C. Coffey, *Boarding-School*, sc. ii., Your gills look as red as a turkey-cocks. 1880 : Spurgeon, *Ploughman's Pictures*, 6, Joe . . . came from behind the stack, looking as red as a turkey-cock. 1880 : Courtney, *W. Cornwall Words*, 36 (E.D.S.), As red as a lubber cock [turkey-cock]. 1894 : W. Raymond, *Love and Quiet Life*, 167.

Red as blood. *c.* 1205 : Lay., 15940 (O.), þe oder is milcwhit . . . þe oðer ræd alse blod. 1387 : Trevisa, tr. Higden, i. 123 (Rolls Ser.), þe secunde þre mouþes reed as blood. 1485 : Malory, *Morte d'Arthur*, bk. xvii. ch. iv., Hit was reed as blood. 1594 : *First Part Contention*, 22 (Sh. S.). 1894 : W. Raymond, *Love and Quiet Life*, 246, Wine was dripping into the gutters as red as blood.

Red as fire. *c.* 1310 : *King Horn* (Oxf.), l. 520 (Hall), Red so any glede. *c.* 1489 : Caxton, *Sonnes of Aymon*, 27 (E.E.T.S.), He wexed for grete wrathe as redde as ony fyre in his face. 1567 : Golding, *Ovid*, bk. i. l. 954, At this reproch old Phaëton wax as red as any fire. 1681 : Robertson, *Phraseol. Generalis*, 267, He blusht as red as fire. 1709 : Manley, *New Atlantis*, ii. 87 (1736), I blush'd as red as fire. 1722 : Defoe, *Moll Flanders*, in *Works*, iii. 60 (Bohn).

Red as Martlesham lion=very red. Suffolk. 1892 : *E. Anglian Daily Times* (W.).

Red at night and red in the morning. Several sayings to like effect may be conveniently grouped under this heading. Cf. **Evening.** 1551 : T. Wilson, *Rule of Reason*, sig. M4, The skie was very red this mornyng, Ergo we are like to have rayne or [ere] nyght. 1584 : R. Scot, *Witchcraft*, bk. xi. ch. xv., The skie being red at evening, Foreshewes a faire and clear morning ; But if the morning riseth red, Of wind or raine we shall be sped. Before 1627 :

Middleton, *Anything for Quiet Life*, IV.
i., You shall find her beauty as male-
volent unto you as a red morning, that
doth still foretell a foul day to follow.
1661 : Webster and Rowley, *Cure for
a Cuckold*, III. i., Like a red morning,
friend, that still foretells A stormy day
to follow. 1664 : in *Musarum Deliciæ,
etc.*, ii. 59 (Hotten), When red the sun
goes down, we use to say, It is a signe,
we shall have a faire day. 1696 : J.
Harris, *City Bride*, III. i. [as in 1661].
1831 : Hone, *Year-Book*, 300, If red
the sun begins his race, Expect that
rain will fall apace. 1893 : Inwards,
Weather Lore, 50 [as in 1831]. Ibid.,
53, Sky red in the morning Is a sailor's
sure warning ; Sky red at night Is the
sailor's delight. 1920 : *Punch*, 14 July,
p. 36, cols. 2 and 3, " Red sky at night
shepherd's delight," she quoted. . . .
At dawn Titania looked out of the
window and gave a wild cry. " Red
sky in the morning shepherd's warning,"
she wailed.

Red cap, You shall have the. Said to
a marriage-maker. Somerset. 1678 :
Ray, 352.

Red cow. *See* Cow (4).

Red hair. Several sayings are
grouped hereunder. 1578 : Florio,
First Fruites, fo. 30, If thou meete a
red man, and a bearded woman, greet
them three myle of[f]. 1591 : Florio,
Second Frutes, 99, Beware of red men,
of women that are bearded, and of
such as God hath marked. 1600 : W.
Vaughan, *Directions for Health*, To a
red man reade thy read, With a browne
man breake thy bread. 1615 : R.
Tofte, tr. *Blazon of Iealousie*, 21, The
red is wise, the broun trusty, The pale
envious, and the blacke lusty. Ibid.,
21, [as in 1600, *plus*] At a pale man
draw thy knife, From a blacke man
keep thy wife. 1619 : *Helpe to Discourse*, 153 (1640) [as in the immediately
preceding quotation]. 1623 : Wodroephe, *Spared Houres*, 276, In all
places keepe thee well from redhaired
men, from barded women, and from
them that are marcked in the face.
1659 : Howell, 12, A red beard and a
black head, Catch him with a good

trick, and take him dead. 1659 :
Howell, *Letters*, ii. 666 (Jacobs), Touch-
ing a red-haired man and bearded
woman, salute them a hundred paces
off. 1670 : Ray, 212 [as in first 1659
quot.]. Ibid., 210 [as in second 1615
quot.]. 1732 : Fuller, No. 1915, He is
false by nature that has a black head
and a red beard. 1908 : W. Johnson,
Folk Memory, 57, The old saw puts it
thus, "From a black man keep your wife,
With the red man beware your knife."

Red herring. *See* quot. 1678 : Ray,
52, Red herring ne'er spake word but
een, Broyl my back, but not my weamb
[stomach].

Red man. *See* s.v. Red hair.

Red petticoat. *See* Lass.

Red pig. *See* Pig (6).

**Reeds, Where there are, there is
water.** 1732 : Fuller, No. 5674.

**Refuse with the right and take with
the left, To.** 1639 : Clarke, 149. 1732 :
Fuller, No. 2009, He refuseth the bribe,
but putteth forth his hand.

Regal honours have regal cares.
1855 : Bohn, 479.

Relations. *See* quot. 1858 : R. S.
Hawker, in Byles, *Life, etc.*, 312 (1905),
There is an old English Proverb which
hints thus, Love your relations, but
live not near them.

**Religion is copyhold, and he has not
taken it up, His**=he has none. 1830 :
Forby, *Vocab. E. Anglia*, 427. 1872 :
J. Glyde, jr., *Norfolk Garland*, 148.

**Religion is the best armour in the
world, but the worst cloak.** 1732 :
Fuller, No. 4011. 1827 : Hone, *Table-
Book*, 414.

Religion. *See also* Eye (10).

**Remedy for all things but death,
There is a.** *c.* 1430 : Lydgate, *Daunce
of Machabree*, l. 432, Againes Death
is worth no medicine. 1620 : Shelton,
Quixote, Pt. II. ch. xliii., There is a
remedy for everything but death.
1640 : Mabbe, tr. *Exemp. Novels*, i. 177
(1900). 1712 : Motteux, *Quixote*, Pt. II.
ch. xliii.

**Remedy for everything, could men
find it, There is a.** 1651 : Herbert, *Jac.
Prudentum*, 2nd ed. 1732 : Fuller,
No. 4879.

Remedy, If there be no, then welcome
Pilvall. 1670 : Ray, 189.

Remedy is worse than the disease,
The. [Ingratus L. Sulla, qui patriam
durioribus remediis, quam pericula erat
sanavit.—Seneca, *De Beneficiis*, V. xvi.
4.] 1607 : Bacon, *Essays*: "Counsel,"
The doctrine of Italie, and practize of
Fraunce hath introduced *Cabanett* Coun-
celles, a remedy worse than the disease.
1624 : Massinger, *Bondman*, I. i., The
cure Is worse than the disease. 1697 :
Vanbrugh, *Prov. Wife*, V. 1762 : Hall
Stevenson, *Crazy Tales*, 18 [as in 1624].
1807 : Byron, in *Letters, etc.*, i. 139
(Prothero), Things will therefore stand
as they are ; the remedy would be
worse than the disease. 1898 : Shaw,
Plays Pleasant, etc., i. Pref., xv.

Remove an old tree and it will die.
1570 : A. Barclay, *Mirrour of Good
Manners*, 67 (Spens. S.), An olde tree
transposed shall finde small auauntage.
1605 : Camden, *Remains*, 330 (1870).
1670 : Ray, 22. 1732 : Fuller, No.
4016, Remove an old tree, and you'll
kill it.

Repairs not a part, builds all, He that.
1640 : Herbert, *Jac. Prudentum*.

Repentance always comes behind.
1584 : Robinson, *Handf. Pleas. Delights*,
38 (Arber).

Repentance comes too late. *c.* 1440 :
Lydgate, *Fall of Princes*, bk. iii. l. 915
(E.E.T.S.), Harm doon, to late folweth
repentaunce. 1670 : Ray, 22, Repentance comes too late, when all is con-
sum'd. 1732 : Fuller, No. 5545, When
all is gone repentance comes too late.

Repents is a fool, He that. 1710 : S.
Palmer, *Moral Essays on Proverbs*, 286,
He that repents either was, or is, a fool.
1732 : Fuller, No. 2264, He that repents
of his own act, either is, or was a fool
by his own confession.

Report. *See* Common (7).

Reputation is seldom cured, A
wounded. 1855 : Bohn, 304.

Reputation is the life of the mind, as
breath is the life of the body. 1730 :
T. Saldkeld, tr. Gracian's *Compl. Gent.*,
96.

Reserve the master-blow. 1659 :
Howell, *Proverbs: Ital.-Eng.*, 13, Re-

serve thy master-piece. 1813 : Ray,
20, Reserve the master-blow: i.e. teach
not all thy skill, lest the scholar over-
reach or insult the master.

Resolved mind hath no cares, The.
1640 : Herbert, *Jac. Prudentum*.

Respect a man, he will do the more.
1659 : Howell, *Proverbs: Brit.-Eng.*, 16.

Respect is younger brother to love.
1691 : J. Bancroft, *King Edw. III.*, III.
ii., I have often heard it said, respects
the younger brother sure to love.

Respects not is not respected, He that.
1640 : Herbert, *Jac. Prudentum*.

Rest a while. *See* Sit (6).

Retreat, In a, the lame are foremost.
1640 : Herbert, *Jac. Prudentum*.

Revenged every wrong, Had I. *See*
quots. Before 1500 : in Hill, *Commonplace-Book*, 140 (E.E.T.S.), He that will
venge euery wreth, the longer he levith,
the lesse he hath. 1575 : Gascoigne,
Posies, 147 (Cunliffe), This old sayde
sawe, *Had I revenged bene of every
harme, My coate had never kept me half
so warme*. 1639 : in *Berkeley MSS.*,
iii. 32 (1885), Hee that wreakes himselfe
at every wronge, Shall never singe the
ritch mans songe. 1670 : Ray, 136,
If I had reveng'd all wrong, I had not
worn my skirts so long. 1732 : Fuller,
No. 6462 [as in 1670].

Revenge is sweet. 1566 : Painter,
Pal. of Pleasure, ii. 35 (Jacobs), Vengeance is sweete. 1658 : *Whole Duty
of Man*, Sunday, 16, It is a devilish
phrase in the mouth of men, That revenge is sweet. 1691 : Southerne, *Sir
Antony Love*, IV. iii. 1818 : Byron,
Don Juan, can. i. st. 124. 1864 : Mrs.
H. Wood, *Trevlyn Hold*, ch. lviii., Revenge may be very sweet, but . . .

Reverend are ever before, The. 1640 :
Herbert, *Jac. Prudentum*.

Revess. *See* Rivaulx.

Revolutions are not made with rosewater. In 1789, two months before the
fall of the Bastille, Chamfort, the friend
and confidant of Mirabeau, said to
Marmontel—" Je vois que mes espé-
rances vous attristent : vous ne voulez
pas d'une liberté qui coûtera beaucoup
d'or et de sang. Voulez-vous qu'on
vous fasse des révolutions à l'eau

rose? " — Marmontel, *Mémoires d'un Père*, liv. xiv., in *Œuvres*, ii. 294 (1818–19), 1819 : Byron, *Letters, etc.*, iv. 358 (Prothero), Revolutions are not to be made with rosewater.

Reynard is still Reynard, tho' he put on a cowl. 1732 : Fuller, No. 4033.

Rhubarb and less diet, More. 1655 : T. Muffett, *Healths Improvement*, 8, These addle proverbs, . . . 4. More rubarb and less diet.

Rhyme (and) (nor) (or) reason. [Nec quid nec quare.—Petr., 37. En toy na Ryme ne Raison.—French MS., before 1500, quoted by Skeat, *N. & Q.*, 3rd ser., x. 236.] Before 1529 : Skelton, *Works*, i. 123 (Dyce), Ys ryme yet owte of reson. 1568 : *Jacob and Esau*, II. iii., Ye shall hear him chafe beyond all reason or rhyme. 1601 : Shakespeare, *As You Like It*, III. ii., Neither rhyme nor reason can express how much. 1605 : Jonson, *Volpone*, Prol., Here is rhyme, not empty of reason. 1714 : Ozell, *Molière*, v. 134, This gentleman wou'd find neither rhime nor reason in it. 1764 : Murphy, *Three Weeks after Marriage*, II., There he owns it . . . and without rhyme or reason into the bargain. 1849 : Lytton, *Caxtons*, Pt. IX. ch. iii., A pretty fellow you are . . . to leave me all the morning, without rhyme or reason ! 1920 : P. B. M. Allan, *Book-Hunter at Home*, 87, It does insist most emphatically that there should be a rhyme and a reason for reading any book at any time.

Rhyme, but it accordeth not, It may. Things may be brought together, like riming words, but they will not on that account agree.—Skeat : Note in his *Chaucer*, vii. *c.* 1387 : Usk, *Test. of Love*, in Skeat's *Chaucer*, vii. 51, These thinges to-forn-sayd mowe wel, if men liste, ryme ; trewly, they acorde nothing. *c.* 1430 : Lydgate, *Minor Poems*, 56 (Percy S.), It may wele ryme, but it accordith nought. 1562 : Heywood, *Three Hund. Epigr.*, No. 265, It may rhyme, but it accordeth not. 1633 : Draxe, 45 [as in 1562].

Rhyme to death, as rats in Ireland, To. *c.* 1581 : Sidney, *Apol.*, 72 (Arber), Nor to be rimed to death, as is sayd to be

doone in Ireland. 1601 : Shakespeare, *As You Like It*, III. ii., I was never so be-rhymed since Pythagoras' time, that I was an Irish rat, which I can hardly remember. 1632 : Randolph, *Jealous Lovers*, V. ii., My poets Shall . . . Rhyme 'em to death, as they do rats in Ireland. Before 1680 : Butler, *Remains*, i. 377 (1759), Will rather take thee for an Irish rat-catcher, that is said to rhime vermin to death. 1692 : Temple, *On Poetry*, in *Works*, iii. 418 (1770), The proverb of rhiming rats to death, came I suppose from the same root [Runic incantations].

Ribble, The. *See* Hodder.

Ribchester. 1586 : Camden, *Brit.*, 431, It is written upon a wall in Rome, Ribchester was as rich as any towne in Christendome. 1662 : Fuller, *Worthies*, ii. 191 (1840) [as in 1586]. 1790 : Grose, *Prov. Gloss.*, s.v. " Lancs " [as in 1586].

Rich, *adj.* 1. *A rich man and a miserable.* 1600 : Nashe, *Works*, vi. 99 (Grosart), It is a common prouerbe, Diuesque miserque, a rich man, and a miserable.

2. *A rich man's money hangs him oftentimes.* 1639 : Clarke, 98.

3. *A rich rogue, two shirts and a rag.* 1678 : Ray, 80. 1738 : Swift, *Polite Convers.*, Dial. I.

4. *Always you are to be rich next year.* 1732 : Fuller, No. 787.

5. *As rich as a Jew.* 1720 : Gay, *Poems*, ii. 280 (Underhill), Great as an emp'ror should I be, And richer than a Jew. 1771 : Cumberland, *West Indian*, II., She is as rich as a Jew. 1823 : Scott, *Peveril*, ch. xxvi. 1871 : G. Eliot, *Middlemarch*, ch. xl. 1896 : Shaw, *You Never Can Tell*, I.

6. *As rich as a new shorn sheep.* An ironical saying. [*c.* 1440 : Lydgate, *Fall of Princes*, bk. iii., l. 3262, Bare as a sheep that is but newe shorn.] *c.* 1520 : *Cock Lorells Bote*, 1 (Percy S.), The nexte that came was a coryar, And a cobeler, his brother, As ryche as a newe shorne shepe. 1595 : Churchyard, *Charitie*, 2 (1816). 1637 : Breton, in *Works*, ii. *h* 11 (Grosart). 1681 : Robertson, *Phraseol. Generalis*, 1077. 1732 : Fuller, No. 725.

7. *As rich as Crœsus.* [Superare Crassum divitiis.—Cicero, *Att.*, i. 4 *fin.*] 1577 : Kendall, *Flow. of Epigrams*, 57 (Spens. S.), As riche as Cresus Affric is. 1696 : T. Dilke, *Lover's Luck*, II. i., And I get a patent for it, I shall be as rich as Crœsus. 1724 : Defoe, *Roxana*, in *Works*, xiii. 73 (Boston, 1903). 1850 : Smedley, *Frank Fairlegh*, ch. li.

8. *He is rich enough that needeth neither to flatter nor borrow.* 1669 : *Politeuphuia*, 128, He hath riches sufficient that, etc. 1732 : Fuller, No. 1942.

9. *He is rich enough that wants nothing.* c. 1387 : Usk, *Test. of Love*, in Skeat's *Chaucer*, vii. 88, Is he nat riche that hath suffisaunce? c. 1577 : Northbrooke, *Dicing, etc.*, 48 (Sh. S.), Seneca sayeth : Diues est, non qui magis habet, sed qui minus cupit. He is riche, not that hath much, but that coueteth least. 1637 : A. Warwick, *Spare Minutes*, 4 (1829), Hee is not rich that hath much, but hee that hath enough. 1640 : Herbert, *Jac. Prudentum.* 1732 : Fuller, No. 1943, He is rich that is satisfied. 1875 : Cheales, *Proverb. Folk-Lore*, 101.

10. *He that will be rich before night, may be hanged before noon.* 1692 : L'Éstrange, *Æsop*, 337 (3rd ed.), 'Tis a roguy kind of a saying, that *He that will, etc.*

11. *In a rich man's house the cloth is soon laid.* 1712 : Motteux, *Quixote*, Pt. II. ch. xliii.

12. *Rich men have no faults.* 1732 : Fuller, No. 4036.

13. *Rich men may have what they will.* c. 1630 : in *Roxb. Ballads*, i. 60 (B.S.), Rich people haue the world at will. 1639 : Clarke, 99, Rich men may doe any thing. 1869 : Hazlitt, 325.

14. *The richer the cobbler.* See Cobbler (6).

15. *The rich feast, the poor fast, the dogs dine, the poor pine.* 1630 : T. Adams, *Works*, 39.

16. *They are rich who have true friends.* 1732 : Fuller, No. 4957.

17. *Why should a rich man steal?* 1678 : Ray, 196. 1732 : Fuller, No. 5736.

Riches abuse them who know not how to use them. Ibid., No. 4040.

Riches are but the baggage of fortune. 1580 : Lyly, *Euphues*, 228 (Arber), To bee rich is the gift of fortune. 1659 : Howell, 8. 1732 : Fuller, No. 4042.

Riches are gotten with pain, kept with care, and lost with grief. 16th cent.: in *Reliq. Antiquæ*, i. 208 (1841), Riches are gotten with labor, holden with feare, and lost with greyfe and excessive care. 1732 : Fuller, No. 4043.

Riches bring oft harm, and ever fear. 1546 : Heywood, *Proverbs*, Pt. I. ch. xii. 1633 : Draxe, 180, Riches bring care and feares.

Riches come to him sleeping. 1754 : Berthelson, *Eng.-Danish Dict.*, s.v. " Sleep."

Riches got by craft. See quot. 1589 : L. Wright, *Display of Dutie*, 3, Whereby the prouerbe is verefied, that riches got with craft is commonly lost with shame.

Riches have wings. 1855 : Bohn, 480.

Riches, He is not fit for, who is afraid to use them. 1732 : Fuller, No. 1934.

Riches increase, the body decreaseth, When. 1670 : Ray, 22. 1736 : Bailey, *Dict.*, s.v. " Riches."

Riches rule the roast. 1732 : Fuller, No. 4046.

Riches serve a wise man but command a fool. Ibid., No. 4047.

Riches. See also Money; and Wealth.

Richmond. See Barnard Castle.

Ride a free horse. See Horse (27).

Ride an inch behind the tail, You shall. 1678 : Ray, 266.

Ride as if you went to fetch the midwife, You. Ibid., 266.

Ride post for a pudding, To. Ibid., 79. 1732 : Fuller, No. 5219.

Ride softly that you may get home the sooner. 1678 : Ray, 204, Ride softly, that we may come sooner home. 1732 : Fuller, No. 4050.

Rides well that never falls, He. 1485 : Malory, *Morte d'Arthur*, bk. ix. ch. xxviii., He rydeth wel that neuer fylle. 1732 : Fuller, No. 2011, He rode sure indeed, that never caught a fall in his life.

Ride the dun-horse, To=To dun a
debtor. 1828 : Carr, *Craven Dialect*, i.
123.

Ride the fore-horse, To=To be early,
or to be in the front. 1664 : Etherege,
Comical Revenge, III. v., Palmer [*coming late to duel ground.*] I see you
ride the fore-horse, gentlemen. 1754 :
World, No. 68, " You still love to ride
the fore-horse," alluding to his desire
of being foremost in all parties of
pleasure. 1823 : Scott, *St. Ronan's*,
ch. i., Determined to ride the fore-horse
herself, Meg would admit no helpmate.

Ride the heps, To. 1864 : " Cornish
Proverbs," in *N. & Q.*, 3rd ser., vi. 494,
He is put to ride on the heps. 1880 :
Courtney, *W. Cornwall Words*, 28
(E.D.S.), When a person has been
brought before his superiors and re-
manded, he is figuratively said " to
have been made to ride the heps
[hatch]."

Ride the high horse, To. 1765 : in
Garrick Corresp., i. 205 (1831), Altogether upon the high horse, and blustering about Imperial Tragedy. 1836 :
Marryat, *Easy*, ch. xii., He was determined to ride the high horse—and that
there should be no Equality Jack in
future. 1854 : Baker, *Northants Gloss.*,
s.v. " Horse," " To ride the high horse,"
or " to be on the high horse," is
to assume unbecoming airs, or claim
unacknowledged superiority. 1881 :
Evans, *Leics. Words*, 173 (E.D.S.).

Ride the wild mare, To. 1598 :
Shakespeare, 2 *Henry IV.*, II. iv., [He]
drinks off candles' ends for flap-dragons,
and rides the wild-mare with the boys.
1611 : Cotgrave, s.v. " Asne," *Desfer-
rer l'asne.* To unshooe the asse ; we
say, to ride the wilde mare.

Ride who will, shod is the mare.
1541 : *Sch. House of Women*, l. 572, in
Hazlitt, *Early Pop. Poetry*, iv. 127.

Right as a line. *c.* 1430 : Lydgate,
Minor Poems, 373 (E.E.T.S.), Lede us
thederward as ryght as a lyne. 1546 :
Heywood, *Proverbs*, Pt. I. ch. xi. *c.*1602:
Chapman, *May-Day*, II.

Right as a ram's horn=crooked.
c. 1320 : in *Reliq. Antiquæ*, ii. 19 (1843),
As ryt as rams orn. *c.* 1400 : *Beryn*, 6

(E.E.T.S.), And a red [it] also right as
a rammys hornyd. *c.* 1430 : Lydgate,
Minor Poems, 171 (Percy S.), Conveyde
by lyne ryght as a rammes horne.
Before 1529: Skelton, *Colin Clout*, l.
1201, They say many matters be born
By the ryght of a rammes horne.
1670 : Ray, 207.

Right as a trivet. 1837 : Dickens,
Pickwick, ch. xvi. 1847 : Barham,
Ing. Legends, 3rd ser.: "Blasph. Warning." 1907 : De Morgan, *Alice-for-
Short*, ch. ii., Wait till . . . she's had
time to get sober, and she'll be as right
as a trivet.

Right as my glove. 1816 : Scott,
Antiquary, ch. xxx., Right, Caxon,
right as my glove.

Right as my leg. *c.* 1630 : in *Roxb.
Ballads*, iii. 338 (B.S.), That are as
right's my leg. 1696 : D'Urfey,
Quixote, Pt. III. Act III. sc. ii., And she
as right as is my leg, Still gave him leave
to touze her. 1701 : Farquhar, *Sir H.
Wildair*, I., Are they right ? No Gray's
Inn pieces amongst 'em—all right as
my leg. 1737 : Ray, 225.

Right as ninepence. 1850 : Smedley,
Frank Fairlegh, ch. li., Well, let her say
" no " as if she meant it . . . and then
it will all be as right as ninepence.
1894 : R. L. S., *St. Ives*, ch. xxvii., The
members would all be up and " as right
as ninepence " for the noon-day service.
1901 : F. F. Taylor, *Lancs Sayings*, 1,
As reet as ninepence.

Right as rain. 1894 : W. Raymond,
Love and Quiet Life, 108, " 'Tes so
right as rain, Zir," zes I. 1921 :
Hutchinson, *If Winter Comes*, Pt. III.
ch. v. (viii.), In about a week she'll
be as right as rain and writing me letters
all day.

**Right for the first . . . miles, You
are.** 1678 : Ray, 343. [Apparently the
lacuna might be filled at pleasure.]

**Right hand from his left, He knows
not his.** 1681 : Robertson, *Phraseol.
Generalis*, 1079. 1888 : R. L. S., *Black
Arrow*, Prol., The poor innocent that
cannot tell his right hand from his
left.

**Right, master, right, four nobles a
year is a crown a quarter.** Cheshire.

1670 : Ray, 217. 1917 : Bridge, *Cheshire Proverbs*, 105.

Right mixture makes good mortar. 1732 : Fuller, No. 4052.

Right or wrong, put Bagley in the stocks=Give a dog a bad name, etc. 1883 : Burne, *Shropsh. Folk-Lore*, 590.

Right reckoning makes long friends. 1537 : R. Whitford, *Werke for Housholders*, sig. A6, The commune prouerbe is that ofte rekeninge holdeth longe felawshyppe. 1732 : Fuller, No. 4053. 1760 : Colman, *Polly Honeycombe*, sc. ii. *c.* 1780 : *The First Floor*, I. iii., in Inchbald, *Farces*, vi. 235 (1815).

Right, Roger. *See* Sow, *subs.* (11).

Right side. *See* quots. 1670 : Ray, 195, To take from ones right side, to give to ones left. 1748 : Richardson, *Clarissa*, iv. 321 (1785), What the right side gives up, the left, he says, may be the better for.

Right side, To rise on the. [It was a good omen for the eagle to appear on Priam's right.—Homer, *Iliad*, xxiv. 308–13.] 1540 : Palsgrave, *Acolastus*, sig. M3, Howe happily rose I on my ryght syde to-day. *c.* 1565 : Still, *Gam. Gurton*, II. i., Thou rose not on thy ryght syde, or else blest thee not wel. 1607 : Marston, *What You Will*, V. 1665 : J. Wilson, *Projectors*, I., Certain I rise with the right end upward to-day, I have had such good luck! 1670 : Ray, 191, He rose on his right side. Cf. **Left side.**

Right wrongs no man. 1853 : Trench, *Proverbs*, 8 (1905).

Ring. *Better no ring, than a ring of a rush.* 1732 : Fuller, No. 918.

Ripe. *See* **Beddingham.**

Ripon rowels, As true steel as. 1625 : Jonson, *Staple of News*, I. iii., There's an angel if my spurs Be not right Ripon. 1662 : Fuller, *Worthies*, iii. 398 (1840). 1683 : Meriton, *Yorkshire Ale*, 83–7 (1697). 1790 : Grose, *Prov. Gloss.*, s.v. "Yorks." 1807 : Hogg, *Gilmanscleuch*, in *Mountain Bard*, The rowels of his silver spurs Were of the Rippon steel. 1878 : *Folk-Lore Record*, i. 168, To trustworthy persons the expression has been applied—"As true steel as

Rippon rowels." 1918 : *N. & Q.*, 12th ser., iv. 104.

Rip up old sores, To. 1573 : G. Harvey, *Letter-Book*, 18 (Camden S.), Sutch ripping up of ould matters. 1652 : Walsingham, *Arcana Aulica*, 32 (1694), A hater of those that rip up old offences. 1694 : *Terence made English*, 236, What occasion had you to rip up th' old sore ? 1712 : Arbuthnot, *John Bull*, Pt. I. ch. ix., Such a trial would rip up old sores. 1773 : Garrick, in *Garrick Corresp.*, i. 518 (1831), I am very much hurt to hear that he has ripped up old sores. 1827 : Scott, in Lockhart's *Life*, vii. 90, I am not clear that it is a . . . healthful indulgence to be ripping up old sores.

Rise, *verb.* 1. *As riseth my good so riseth my blood. c.* 1560 : Becon, in *Catechism, etc.*, 599 (P.S.) [quoted as a "common proverb"].

2. *He must rise betimes who will cosen the devil.* 1659 : Howell, 10 (8).

3. *He must rise betimes.* *See* **Please,** *verb* (1).

4. *He must rise early who can*—do this, that, or the other. 1562 : Heywood : *Three Hund. Epigr.*, No. 128(9), Who that shall enterprise This measure from thee, for to gleane, Right erly must he rise. 1593 : Peele, *Edw. I.*, sc. x., She riseth early, Joan, that beguileth thee of a Glocester. 1662 : Fuller, *Worthies*, i. 426 (1840), They must rise early, yea not sleep at all, who over-reach monks in matter of profit. 1681 : Robertson, *Phraseol. Generalis*, 1291, They must rise betimes that go beyond him ; a very wary man. 1791 : R. Jephson, *Two Strings to your Bow*, I. i., Let me alone, he must rise early, brother, who makes a fool of Don Pedro. 1838 : Dickens, *Twist*, ch. xxv., You must get up very early in the morning, to win against the Dodger.

5. *He rises betimes that lies in a dog's lair.* 1860 : Reade, *Cl. and Hearth*, ch. xxiv.

6. *He that riseth betimes hath something in his head.* 1640 : Herbert, *Jac. Prudentum.*

7. *He that riseth first is first dressed.* Ibid.

8. *He who does not rise early never*

does a good day's work. 1633 : Draxe,
142, He that riseth not in the morning,
loseth his iourney. 1659 : Howell,
Proverbs: Span.-Eng., 17, Who riseth
late must trot all the day. 1736 :
Franklin, *Way to Wealth*, in *Works*, i.
443 (Bigelow), He that riseth late must
trot all day, and shall scarce overtake
his business at night. 1846 : Denham,
Proverbs, 5 (Percy S.).

9. *In vain they rise early that used to
rise late.* 1611 : Davies (of Hereford),
Sc. of Folly, 46, in *Works*, ii. (Grosart).
1639 : Clarke, 67, They can't rise early
that use to rise late.

10. *Rise early and you will see; wake
and you will get wealth.* 1846 : Denham, *Proverbs*, 5 (Percy S.).

11. *Rise with an appetite. See* Leave
(6).

12. *To rise with the lark and go to bed
with the lamb. c.* 1555 : in Wright,
Songs, etc., Philip and Mary, 38 (Roxb.
Cl.), And wythe the larke yche day
I ryes. 1580 : Lyly, *Euphues*, 229
(Arber), Goe to bed with the lambe, and
rise with the larke. 1633 : Jonson,
Tale of a Tub, I. iv., Madam, if he had
couched with the lamb, He had no
doubt been stirring with the lark.
1826 : Lamb, *Pop. Fallacies*, xiv., That
we should rise with the lark. xv., That
we should lie down with the lamb.

**Rising of one man is the falling of
another, The.** 1605 : Chapman, etc.,
Eastw. Hoe, I. i., As for my rising by
other men's fall, God shield me! 1633 :
Draxe, 7.

Rising, Norfolk. *See* quots. 1815 :
N. & Q., 1st ser., iii. 206, Rising was,
Lynn is, and Downham shall be, The
greatest seaport of the three. 1865 :
W. White, *Eastern England*, i. 237, Rising was a seaport town When Lynn was
but a marsh ; Now Lynn it is a seaport
town, And Rising fares the worse.

Rivaulx, Yorks. 1754 : *Gent. Mag.*,
426, Near Howden, in Yorkshire, when
a person cannot easily come at a place,
without going a great way about ; or
. . . is forced to make use of several
synonimous words ; or . . . produces
several arguments before he comes to
the main point ; it is a common saying,

that he is going " Round about Revess " [Abbey of Revess or Rivaulx].

River is deepest. *See* Still waters.

River passed and God forgotten, The.
1611 : Cotgrave, s.v. " Sainct," The
danger past our vowes are soon forgotten. 1640 : Herbert, *Jac. Prudentum* [" past "]. 1853 : Trench, *Proverbs*, 68 (1905), In English we say, [as
in 1640].

Rivers need a spring. 1640 : Herbert, *Jac. Prudentum.*

**River will run as it did, A thousand
years hence, the.** 1732 : Fuller, No. 436.

**Riving Pike do wear a hood, If,
Be sure that day will ne'er be good.**
1670 : Ray, 236. 1790 : Grose, *Prov.
Gloss.*, s.v. " Lancs." 1893 : Inwards,
Weather Lore, 101. 1917 : Bridge,
Cheshire Proverbs, 161.

Roach. *See* Sound.

Roast a stone, To= To waste time
and effort. Before 1529 : Skelton, in
Works, ii. 30 (Dyce), They may garlycke
pyll, Cary sackes to the myll, Or
pescoddes they may shyll, Or elles go
rost a stone. 1546 : Heywood, *Proverbs*, Pt. II. ch. ii., I doo but roste a
stone In warnyng hir. 1611 : Davies
(of Hereford), *Sc. of Folly*, 49, in *Works*,
ii. (Grosart), He roasts but a stone.

Roast meat. 1. *He loves roast meat
well that licks the spit.* 1670 : Ray, 137.
1732 : Fuller, No. 1980. 1880 : Spurgeon, *Ploughman's Pictures*, 73, If they
are fond of roast beef, they must needs
suck the spit.

2. *Roast meat does cattle.* 1877 : E.
Leigh, *Cheshire Gloss.*, 63, " Roast meat
does cattle," which means that in dry
seasons cattle, if they can only get at
plenty of water, often milk better than
in cold wet seasons, when there is more
grass. 1917 : Bridge, *Cheshire Proverbs*, 105.

3. *To cry roast meat.* 1605 : Camden, *Remains*, 336 (1870), You cannot
fare well but you must cry rost meat.
1616 : B. & F., *Scornful Lady*, V. iv.,
Cannot you fare well, but you must
cry roast meat ? 1681 : Robertson,
Phraseol. Generalis, 1084 [as in 1605].
1749 : Fielding, *Tom Jones*, bk. iv. ch.
v., They may imagine, that to trumpet

forth the praises of such a person, would, in the vulgar phrase, be crying roast-meat, and calling in partakers of what they intend to apply solely to their own use. 1820 : Lamb, *Christ's Hospital.* 1822 : Scott, *Nigel*, ch. xxxvii. 1894 : Northall, *Folk Phrases*, 27 (E.D.S.), To cry roast meat. (1) to make known one's good luck ; (2) to boast of women's favours.

4. *You are in your roast meat when others are in their sod.* 1639 :- Clarke, 115. 1670 : Ray, 190. 1732 : Fuller, No. 5849.

5. *You give me roast meat. See* **Give** (25).

Rob, *verb.* 1. *He that doth not rob makes not a robe or garment.* 1629 : *Book of Meery Riddles*, Prov. 83.

2. *He that robs a scholar robs twenty men.* 1639 : Clarke, 243. 1670 : Ray, 23. 1732 : Fuller, No. 5716, Who robs a Cambridge-scholar, robs twenty.

3. *To rob Peter and pay Paul.* [Tanquam si quis crucifigeret Paulum ut redimeret Petrum.—12th cent. : Herbert of Bosham, 287.] Before 1384 : Wiclif, *Works*, iii. 174 (Arnold), How schulde God approve þat þou robbe Petur, and gif þis robbere to Poule in þe name of Crist ? *c.* 1400 : Lanfranc, *Cirurgie*, 331 (E.E.T.S.), For sum medicyne is for Peter that is not good for Poul, for the diuersitè of complexioun. *c.* 1440 : *Jacob's Well*, 138 (E.E.T.S.), þe abbot seyde, " To robbe Petyr, and geue it Powle, it were non almesse but gret synne." 1546 : Heywood, *Proverbs*, Pt. I. ch. xi. 1621 : Burton, *Melancholy*, Dem. to Reader, 36 (1836). 1637 : D. Tuvill, *Vade Mecum*, 36 (3rd ed.), To take from Peter, to give to Paul, is meer oppression. 1661 : Heylyn, *Hist. of Reform.*, 121 (1674), The lands of Westminster, so dilapidated by Bishop Thirlby . . . the rest laid out for reparation to the church of St. Paul ; pared almost to the very quick in those days of Rapine. From hence first came that significant By-word (as is said by some) of Robbing Peter to pay Paul. [A baseless guess.] 1768 : Hall-Stevenson, *Works*, i. 27 (1795), I need not steal, like thrifty George, From

Paul, in order to pay Peter. 1882 : J. Platt, *Economy*, 87, Give credit if they will still have it, and charge for it, but cease to rob Peter to pay for Paul.

4. *To rob the spittle* [hospital]. 1639 : Clarke, 6. 1670 : Ray, 191. 1736 : Bailey, *Dict.*, s.v. " Spital."

Robbers. *See* quot. 1750 : Smollett, *Gil Blas*, iv. 12, We got in four days to Oviedo, without meeting with any bad accident on the road, notwithstanding the proverb, which says, that robbers smell the money of travellers afar off.

Robin (redbreast). 1. *As blithe as a robin.* 1639 : in *Berkeley MSS.*, iii. 29 (1885), Hee drew it as blith as a Robin reddocke [redbreast].

2. *He that hunts robin or wren, Will never prosper boy nor man.* 1864 : " Cornish Proverbs," in *N. & Q.*, 3rd ser., v. 208.

3. *If the robin sings in the bush, Then the weather will be coarse ; But if the robin sings on the barn, Then the weather will be warm.* 1830 : Forby, *Vocab. E. Anglia*, 416. 1893 : Inwards, *Weather Lore*, 138.

4. *Robin and wren. See* **Spider** (1).

5. *The robin and the wren are God Almighty's cock and hen. c.* 1555 : *Harmony of Birds*, 10 (Percy S.), Then sayd the wren, I am called the hen Of our Lady most cumly. 1825 : Hone, *Ev. Day Book*, i. 647, [as in heading, *plus*] The martin and the swallow Are God Almighty's bow and arrow (Warwickshire). 1830 : Forby, *Vocab. E. Anglia*, 409 [as in 1825, except that the last of the four lines= " Are the next two birds that follow "]. 1851 : Sternberg, *Dialect, etc., of Northants*, 159, The robin and the wren Be God A'-mighty's cock and hen. 1867 : Harland, etc., *Lancs Folk-Lore*, 142, A Cock Robin and a Jenny Wren Are God Almighty's cock and hen ; A Spink and a Sparrow Are the Devil's bow and arrow. 1879 : Henderson, *Folk-Lore of N. Counties*, 123, Those who say— [as in heading, *plus*] Him that harries their nest, Never shall his soul have rest, add—The martin and the swallow Are God Almighty's bow and arrow ; or, as it runs in some of our midland

counties,—The martin and the swallow
Are God Almighty's birds to hollow.
1883: Burne, *Shropsh. Folk-Lore*, 216,
[as in heading, *plus*] The martin
and the swallow Are God Almighty's
scholars. 1913: E. M. Wright, *Rustic
Speech, etc.*, 219, . . . Other versions of
this rhyme are: Martins and swallows
Are God's teachers and scholars. Robins
and wrens Are God's chickens and
hens. Those who kill a robin or a wren
Will never prosper, boy or man.
    See also **Naked ; One bush ;** and **Pert.**
    Robin Goodfellow. 1. *Robin Good-
fellow was a strange man.* 1639:
Clarke, 69.
    2. *See* quot. 1567: Harman, *Caveat*,
36 (E.E.T.S.), I verely suppose that
when they wer wel waked with cold,
they surely thought that Robin good-
felow (accordingc to the old saying)
had bene with them that night.
    3. *To laugh like Robin Goodfellow.*
1830: Forby, *Vocab. E. Anglia*, 431.
1846–59: *Denham Tracts*, ii. 85 (F.L.S.).
    Robin Hood. 1. *A Robin Hood wind.*
[One correspondent of the *Manchester
City News* suggests that the expression
belongs originally to the neighbourhood
of Rochdale, and refers to the bitter
north and east winds that come from
the direction of Blackstone Edge, a
predominant feature of which hill is
Robin Hood's Bed. The thawing winds
from the south and west are not referred to as " Robin Hood winds."—
N. & Q., 12th ser., x. 378.] *c.* 1855:
Life and Ballads of Robin Hood, ch. ii.,
Every Yorkshireman is familiar with
the observation that Robin Hood could
brave all weathers but a thaw wind.
1870 : H. Fishwick, in *N. & Q.*, 4th ser.,
v. 58, A Robin Hood Wind. In Lancashire this name is given to a wind that
blows during the thawing of the snow.
The reason alleged is, that Robin Hood
said that he could stand any wind except
a thaw wind. 1913 : E. M. Wright,
Rustic Speech, etc., 189 [to the same
effect as 1870 quot.]. 1922 : *N. & Q.*,
12th ser., x. 411, I have frequently
heard in this locality [Clitheroe, Lancs]
not only the saying, " Robin Hood could
stand any wind but a thaw wind," but

also : " All sorts of weather could Robin
Hood bide, But a cold thaw wind off a
high hill side."
    2. *As crooked as Robin Hood's bow.*
Derby. 1889 : *Folk-Lore Journal*,
vii. 291.
    3. *Come turn about, Robin Hood.*
1672 : *Westm. Drollery*, Pt. II. 74
(Ebsworth).
    4. *Good even, good Robin Hood!* Be-
fore 1529 : Skelton, in *Works*, ii. 32
(Dyce).
    5. *Many talk of Robin Hood that never
shot in his bow. c.* 1374 : Chaucer,
Troylus, bk. ii. l. 861, They speken, but
they bente never his bowe. 1401 : in
Wright, *Political Poems*, ii. 59 (Rolls
Ser., 1861), Many men speken of Robyn
Hood, and shotte nevere in his bowe.
1546 : Heywood, *Proverbs*, Pt. II. ch.
vi. 1631 : Brathwait, *Whimzies*, 13
(1859). 1712 : E. Ward, *Poet. Entertainer*, No. 2, p. 7, Yet of religion talks,
as many do of Robin Hood, whose bow
they never drew. 1913 : E. M. Wright,
Rustic Speech, etc., 189, A Yorkshire
proverb runs : Many speak of Robin
Hood . . . i.e. many people talk of
doing great things which they can never
accomplish.
    6. *Robin Hood's choice*—" either this
or nothing." 1623 : *Vox Graculi*,
quoted in J. P. Collier, *Bibliogr. Cat.*,
ii. 481.
    7. *Robin Hood's miles* = more than
ordinary length. 1559 : W. Cunningham, *Cosmogr. Glasse*, 57, quoted in
N. & Q., 12th ser., x. 412.
    8. *Robin Hood's pennyworths.* 1630 :
T. Adams, *Works*, 207, He makes the
world beleeue that he sels Robin-hoods
peny-worths. 1662 : Fuller, *Worthies*,
ii. 569 (1840), " To sell Robin Hood's
pennyworths." It is spoken of things
sold under half their value ; or, if
you will, half sold, half given. 1721 :
Bailey, *Eng. Dict.*, s.v., . . . This proverb is usually apply'd to such as having
gotten any thing dishonestly, sell it at
a price much below the value. 1889 :
Folk-Lore Journal, vii. 293 (Derby.).
1922 : *N. & Q.*, 12th ser., x. 412.
    9. *Tales of Robin Hood are good
among fools.* 1377 : Langland, *Plowman*,

B, v. 402, But I can rymes of Robyn
Hood. 1542: Udall, tr. Erasmus's
Apoph., Pref., xxv (1877), Old wiues
foolish tales of Robin Hoode. 1546 :
Heywood, *Proverbs*, Pt. II. ch. ix.
1600 : Breton, in *Works*, i. *g* 8 (Grosart),
From . . . louing idle tales of Robin
Hood . . . The blessed Lord of heau'n
deliuer me. 1681 : Robertson, *Phraseol.
Generalis*, 1258, Nifles and trifles ; vain
tales of Robin Hood. 1732 : Fuller,
No. 4316 [with " enough for " instead
of " among "].

10. *To go round Robin Hood's barn.*
Robin Hood's " barn " must have been
the surrounding corn lands. 1878 : *N.
& Q.*, 5th ser., ix. 486, It is used thus.
" Where have you been to-day ? "
" All round Robin Hood's barn ! I
have been all about the country, first
here and then there." 1913 : E. M.
Wright, *Rustic Speech, etc.*; 189, To go
round by Robin Hood's barn (Cambridge and West Midlands) is to go a
roundabout way, to go the farthest
way. 1922 : *N. & Q.*, 12th ser., x. 412.

11. *To overshoot Robin Hood.* 1869 :
Hazlitt, 425.

See also May, F (24).

Rochdale. *See* Oldham.

" **Rochester portion, A,** two torn
smocks, and what nature gave." 1690 :
New Dict. Canting Crew, sig. K5. 1735 :
Pegge, *Kent. Proverbs*, in E.D.S., No. 12,
p. 74.

**Rock the cradle empty, If you, Then
you shall have babies plenty.** Sussex.
1879 : Henderson, *Folk-Lore of N.
Counties*, 19. 1913 : E. M. Wright,
Rustic Speech, etc., 266, Rock the cradle
empty, You'll rock the babies plenty.

Rock the cradle in spectacles, To.
1678 : Ray, 69. 1732 : Fuller, No.
5220.

Rod breaks no bones, The. 1633 :
Draxe, 182. 1639 : Clarke, 75. Cf.
Birchen twigs.

Rod for one's own back, To make a.
c. 1374 : Chaucer, *Troylus*, bk. i. l. 740,
For it is seyd, " man maketh ofte a
yerde With which the maker is him-self
y-beten In sondry maner." *c.* 1489 :
Caxton, *Sonnes of Aymon*, 97 (E.E.T.S.),
It is often sayd That men make often

a rodde for them selfe. Before 1529 :
Skelton, in *Works*, i. 186 (Dyce), For
your owne tayle ye made a rod. 1593 :
Tell-Trothes N. Yeares Gift, 35 (N. Sh.
S.), To lock vp ones wife . . . and to
seeke to rule her by correction, when
he cannot gouerne himself with discretion, is to gather a rod to beate his
owne breeche. 1694 : *Terence made
English*, 20, But now he makes a rod
for his own back. 1738 : Swift, *Polite
Convers.*, Dial. I., I am not the first man
has carried a rod to whip himself.

Rod in pickle, To have a. 1553 :
Respublica, III. v., But we have roddes
in pysse for them everye chone. 1606 :
Chapman, *Mons. d'Olive*, I., My little
parcel of wits, I have rods in piss for
you. 1690 : A. Behn, *Widow Ranter*,
III. i., Here's the young rogue that
drew upon us too, we have rods in piss
for him, i' faith. 1784 : O'Keeffe,
Peeping Tom, ad fin., Though you have
as poets see, Rods in pickle steeping ;
Forgive poor Tom of Coventry, And
pardon for his peeping. 1854 : Baker,
Northants Gloss., s.v. " Rod," " Rod in
pickle (or soak)." Punishment in store.

Rod in school. *See* Whip for a fool.

Rodings, The. *See* quot. 1880 : E.
Walford, in *N. & Q.*, 6th ser., ii. 307, A
stupid fellow in Essex is generally said
to come from the " Rodings," or else
from the " sheers "—shires. Cf. **Shires.**

Roger. *See* Sow, *subs.* (11).

Roger Cary's dinner. 1877 : E. Leigh,
Cheshire Gloss.,171, Roger Cary's dinner.
—A saying when the dinner is scanty,
or " just enoo " and nought to spare.
1917 : Bridge, *Cheshire Proverbs*, 87.

Rogue as ever peeped at a speer
[chimney-post], **As big a.** Ibid., 10.

**Rogue, but he's no fool on the march,
He may be a.** 1864 : " Cornish Proverbs," in *N. & Q.*, 3rd ser., vi. 495.

Rogue in grain. *See* Knave.

**Rogue's wardrobe is harbour for a
louse, A.** 1639 : Clarke, 71. 1670 :
Ray, 137. 1732 : Fuller, No. 383.

Roland for an Oliver, A=Tit for tat.
1548 : Hall, *Chron.*, 266 (1809), To
haue a Rowland for an Olyuer. 1659 :
Howell, *Letters*, ii. 665 (Jacobs), She
will alwayes have a Rowland for your

Oliver. Before 1704 : T. Brown, in *Works*, i. 219 (1760), I am resolv'd to give him a Rowland for his Oliver. 1706 : Vanbrugh, *Confederacy*, III. ii. 1790 : Wolcot, *A Rowland for an Oliver* [title]. 1843 : Carlyle, *Past and Present*, bk. ii. ch. xii., Look also how my Lord of Clare, coming to claim his *un-due* " debt " in the Court of Witham, with barons and apparatus, gets a Roland for his Oliver ! 1898 : Weyman, *Shrewsbury*, ch. xvii. 1919 : Barbellion, *Journal of Disapp. Man*, 168, It exasperates me to be unable to give a Roland for an Oliver.

Rolling stone gathers no moss, A. 1362 : Langland, *Plowman*, A, x. 101, Selden moseth the marbelston that men ofte treden. *c.* 1406 : *Book of Precedence*, 39 (E.E.T.S.), Syldon mossyth the stone That oftyn ys tornnyd and winde. 1546 : Heywood, *Proverbs*, Pt. I. ch. xi., The rollyng stone neuer gatherth mosse. 1593 : *Passionate Morrice*, 87 (N. Sh. S.). 1606 : Marston, *The Fawne*, I. ii., Thy head is alwaies working ; it roles, and it roles, Dondolo, but it gathers no mosse. *c.* 1610 : in *Roxb. Ballads*, ii. 512 (B.S.). 1720 : *Vade Mecum for Malt-worms*, 6 (part 2), The proverb says . . . That stones, when rolling, gather little moss. 1776 : Colman, *The Spleen*, I., Well, well ; a rolling stone's always bare of moss, as you say. 1852 : Dickens, *Bleak House*, ch. xxxiv. 1914 : Shaw, "Parents and Children," in *Misalliance, etc.*, lxxxiv, We keep repeating the silly proverb that . . ., as if moss were a desirable parasite. 1917 : Bridge, *Cheshire Proverbs*, 5, A rolling stone gathers no moss, but a tethered sheep winna get fat. (In Sussex they add—" And a sitting hen never grows fat.")

Rome. 1. All roads lead to Rome. *c.* 1380 : Chaucer, *Astrolabe*, Prol., Right as diverse pathes leden diverse folk the righte wey to Rome. 1860 : Reade, *Cl. and Hearth*, ch. xxiv., All roads take to Rome. 1869 : Browning, *Ring and Book*, bk. v. l. 296, Every one soon or late comes round by Rome.

2. *Rome was not built in a day.* [Non stilla una cavat marmor, neque protinus

uno est Condita Roma die.—*c.* 1500 : Palingenius (ps. for Pietro Angelo Manzolli), *Zodiacus Vitæ*, xii. 460 (ed. Tauchn.).] 1546 : Heywood, *Proverbs*, Pt. I. ch. xi., Rome was not built in one daie. 1593 : G. Harvey, *Works*, ii. 133 (Grosart). 1658 : R. Franck, *North. Memoirs*, 258 (1821). 1660 : Tatham, *The Rump*, I. 1763 : Murphy, *Citizen*, I. ii. 1822 : Scott, *Nigel*, ch. xxi. 1849 : Brontë, *Shirley*, ch. vi.

3. *To go to Rome.* There are several old sayings which all appear to mean— to go on a fool's errand. *See* the quots. *c.* 1520 : *Hickscorner*, in Hazlitt, *Old Plays*, i. 168, For if any of us three be mayor of London . . . I will ride to Rome on my thumb. *c.* 1550 : Udall, *Roister Doister*, II. ii., It were better to go to Rome on my head than so. 1600 : Kemp, *Nine Daies Wonder*, Dedn., Me thinkes I could flye to Rome (at least hop to Rome, as the olde prouerb is) with a morter on my head. 1611 : Corbet, *Poems*, in Chalmers, v. 562, No more shall man with mortar on his head Set forwards towards Rome. 1653 : Middleton and Rowley, *Span. Gipsy*, II. ii., A cousin of mine in Rome, I go to him with a mortar.

4. *When at Rome, do as the Romans do.* [Aristo Punico ingenio inter Poenos usus.—Livy, xxxiv. 61. *See also* St. Augustine, Epistle xxxvi., to Casulanus.] Before 1500 : in Hill, *Commonplace-Book*, 130 (E.E.T.S.), Whan thou art at Rome, do after the dome ; And whan thou art els wher, do as they do ther. 1586 : Pettie, tr. Guazzo, *Civil Convers.*, fo. 26, According to the saying, when one is at Rome, to liue as they doe at Rome. 1676 : Cotton, Walton's *Angler*, Pt. II. ch. vi., You know the proverb, "Those who go to Rome must do as they at Rome do." 1712 : Motteux, *Quixote*, Pt. II. ch. liv. *c.* 1780 : *The First Floor*, II. i., in Inchbald, *Farces*, vi. 251 (1815). 1842 : Barham, *Ing. Legends*, 2nd ser.: " Auto-da-fé." 1910 : Lucas, *Mr. Ingleside*, ch. xviii.

Romford, The ready way to = ? 1656 : *Musarum Deliciæ*, i. 31 (Hotten), There is a proverb to thy comfort, Known as the ready way to

Rumford. That, when the pot ore fire you heat, A lowse is better than no meat.

Romford, To ride to. 1738 : Swift, *Polite Convers.*, Dial. II., Well, one may ride to Rumford upon this knife, it is so blunt. 1785 : Grose, *Class. Dict. Vulgar Tongue*, s.v. " Rumford," To ride to Rumford, to have one's backside new bottomed. 1901 : *N. & Q.*, 9th ser., viii. 306, " You might ride to Romford on it." When a youngster I often heard my old grandmother make this remark *à propos* any blunt carving or other knife which failed to come up to expectations.

Romney Marsh. *See* quot. 1911 : A. S. Cooke, *Off Beaten Track in Sussex*, 286, There is an East Sussex saying as to Romney Marsh, which gives the best idea of its area—" The world is divided into five parts, Europe, Asia, Africa, America—and Romney Marsh ! "

Romney Marsh. *See also* **Fairlight Down.**

Roodee, As ronk [rank, rich] **as th'.** 1877 : E. Leigh, *Cheshire Gloss.*, 173. 1917 : Bridge, *Cheshire Proverbs*, 19. [The Roodee is the Chester race-course.]

Rook, The. *See* quot. 1872 : J. Glyde, jr., *Norfolk Garland*, 154, The weather will fine when the rooks play pitch half-penny. That is, if flying in flocks some of them stoop down and pick up worms, imitating the action of a boy playing pitch half-penny. *See also* **Raven.**

Room than your company, I'd rather have your. 1579 : *Marr. of Wit and Wisdom*, sc. iii. p. 27 (Sh. S.), I had rather haue your roome as your componie. 1592 : Greene, *Works*, xi. 255 (Grosart), Let him depart out of this place, for his roome is better than his company. 1615 : Brathwait, *Strappado*, 66 (1878), Whose roome I loue more then his company. 1664: *Witts Recr.*, Epigr. 268. 1798 : T. Dibdin, *Jew and Doctor*, II. i. 1865 : Dickens, *Mutual Friend*, bk. i. ch. vi.

Rootless, must green soon die. *c.*1374 : Chaucer, *Troylus*, bk. iv. l. 770.

Rope, *subs.* 1. *A rope and butter, if one slip the other may hold.* 1678 : Ray,

267. 1732 : Fuller, No. 384 [" will " for " may "].

2. *As meet as a rope for a thief.* 1540 : Palsgrave, *Acolastus*, sig. M2, An host that shalbe as mete for him as a rope is for a thefe. 1579 : *Marr. of Wit and Wisdom*, sc. ii. p. 15 (Sh. S.). *c.* 1625 : B. & F., *Women Pleased*, III. iv., As fit for him as a thief for a halter ! 1671 : *Poor Robin Alman. Prognost.*, sig. C5, A good fire . . . will be now as seasonable as a rope for a thief is at any time.

3. *Give him rope enough and he'll hang himself.* 1639 : Fuller, *Holy War*, bk. v. ch. vii., They were suffered to have rope enough, till they had haltered themselves in a *præmunire.* 1652 : Burroughs, *On Hosea*, iv. 517, As we speak of some, "Give them line enough, and they will quickly hang themselves." 1753 : Richardson, *Grandison*, i. 29 (1883), Give you women but rope enough, you'll do your own business. 1849 : Brontë, *Shirley*, ch. iii.

4. *He puts a rope to the eye of a needle.* 1813 : Ray, 75.

5. *I thought I had given her rope enough, said Pedley, when he hanged his mare.* Yorks. 1670: Ray, 191. 1732: Fuller, No. 2627.

6. *Ropes of sand.* [τὸ ἐκ τῆς ψάμμου σχοινίον πλέκοντες.—Aristides (ed. Jebb, ii. 309).] *c.* 1594: Bacon, *Promus*, No. 778, To knytt a rope of sand. 1649 : T. Forde, *Lusus Fort.*, 31, One shall sooner knit a rope of sand then unite their affections. 1672 : Corye, *Generous Enemies*, II. i., O woman, woman, thy vows are ropes of sand. Before 1680: Butler, *Remains*, ii. 206 (1759), A quibbler . . . dances on a rope of sand. 1712 : in *Somers Tracts*, xiii. 144 (1811), I leave to my said children a great chest full of broken promises and cracked oaths ; likewise a vast cargo of ropes made with sand. 1845 : Carlyle, *Lett. to Emerson*, You have done one very ingenious thing to set Clark upon the Boston booksellers' accounts ; Michael Scott setting the devil to twist ropes of sand. [*See* Scott's *Lay of Last Minstrel*, can. ii. st. 13 *n.*]

7. *Throw the rope in after the bucket.*
1732 : Fuller, No. 5042.

Roper's news, That's = no news.
1879: *Folk-Lore Record*, ii. 203 (Bodmin). 1880 : Courtney, *W. Cornwall
Words*, 47 (E.D.S.), That's Roper's
news—hang the crier.

Rose proveth a thorn, The. 1546 :
Heywood, *Proverbs*, Pt. I. ch. x., I toke
hir for a rose, but she breedth a burre.
1633 : Draxe, 41. 1659 : Howell, *Letters*, ii. 665 (Jacobs), She may prove a
wolf in lambs skinn, instead of a rose
you will have a burr. 1813 : Ray, 155,
For the rose the thorn is often plucked.

Rose. *See also* **Fresh**; and **Red.**

**Rosebery Topping wears a cap, When,
Let Cleveland then beware a clap.** 1610 :
P. Holland, tr. Camden's *Brit.*, 721.
1700 : J. Brome, *Travels*, 164. 1846–
59 : *Denham Tracts*, i. 88 (F.L.S.)
["hat" for "cap," and "Morden-
Carrs will suffer for that"]. 1893 :
Inwards, *Weather Lore*, 101. 1922 :
N. & Q., 12th ser., xi. 25.

Rosemary. *See* quots. 1884 : H.
Friend, *Flowers and Fl. Lore*, 217, The
old saying respecting another equally
popular flower — "Where Rosemary
flourishes the lady rules." 1911 : A. S.
Cooke, *Off Beaten Track in Sussex*,
286, Old sayings . . . are more often
aimed at the weaker sex. "Except
where the missus is master, the rosemary will never blossom," is one such
remark.

Rotheras, Every one cannot dwell at.
1659: Howell, 21. 1700 : J. Brome,
Travels, 19, . . . Rotheras, it having
formerly been a place of too profuse
hospitality. 1790 : Grose, *Prov. Gloss.*,
s.v. "Herefordshire." 1868 : *Quart.
Review*, cxxv. 230, One well known to
Herefordshire men, "Every one can't
dwell at Rotheras " . . . a handsome
mansion near Hereford, requiring, no
doubt, a handsome income to keep it
warm.

Rotten as an asker [newt], **As.** 1917 :
Bridge, *Cheshire Proverbs*, 19, . . . *rotten*
because it can drop its tail off.

Rotten case abides no handling, A.
1598 : Shakespeare, *2 Henry IV.*, IV. i.

Rough as a briar, As. *c.* 1410 :

Towneley Plays, 119 (E.E.T.S.), As rugh
as a brere.

Rough as gorse, As. 1876 : *N. & Q.*,
5th ser., v. 94, The English proverb " As
coarse as gorse " . . . is common in
several parts of England, and about
Nottingham I have often heard it
"As coarse as Hickling gorse." Ibid.,
477, "As coarse as bean-straw" is a
common Lincolnshire saying. 1917 :
Bridge, *Cheshire Proverbs*, 19, As rough
as gorse.

Rough as it runs. 1687 : T. Brown,
in *Dk. Buckingham's Works*, ii. 129
(1705) (O.), If you don't like me rough,
as I run, fare you well, madam. 1813 :
Ray, 231, Rough as it runs, as the boy
said when his ass kicked him.

Rough as a tinker's budget, As. 1659 :
Howell, 18. 1670 : Ray, 207.

**Rough net is not the best catcher of
birds, The.** 1546 : Heywood, *Proverbs*,
Pt. I. ch. ix. 1611 : Cotgrave, s.v.
"Douceur." 1670 : Ray, 125.

Rough with the smooth, To take the.
c. 1400 : *Beryn*, 37 (E.E.T.S.), Take
yeur part as it comyth, of roughe and
eke of smooth. 1900 : Jerome, *Three
Men on Bummel*, 190 (O.), One must
take a little rough with one's smooth.

Rouk-town. *See* quot. 1670: Ray,
52, A rouk-town's seldom a good housewife at home. This is a Yorkshire
proverb. A rouk-town is a gossiping
house-wife.

Round about for the next road, To go.
1917 : Bridge, *Cheshire Proverbs*, 134.

Round as a hoop, As. *c.* 1555 : in
Wright, *Songs, etc., Philip and Mary*,
98 (Roxb. Cl.), Untyll she ryll as rownd
as a hoope. *c.* 1660 : in *Songs and
Ballads*, 132 (Percy S., No. 7), He draws
them up as round as a hoop. 1676 :
Shadwell, *Virtuoso*, I. 1720 : Gay,
Poems, ii. 278 (Underhill), Round as a
hoop the bumpers flow.

Round table. *See* quots. 1623 :
Wodroephe, *Spared Houres*, 483, A
round table yealds no debate. 1666 :
Torriano, *Piazza Univ.*, 132, At a round
table there's no dispute about the place.
1732 : Fuller, No. 824, At a round
table the herald's useless.

Row against the flood. *See* **Strive.**

Rowan tree and red thread Haud the witches a' in dread. 1846–59 : *Denham Tracts*, ii. 329 (F.L.S.).

Row one way. *See* **Look** (7).

Royston horse. *See* **Cambridge.**

Ruan Vean men. *See* quot. 1895 : Jos. Thomas, *Randigal Rhymes*, 61, Like Ruan Vean men — don't knaw and weant be told. [Corn.].

Rub and a good cast. A warning saying, of bowling origin. 1639 : Clarke, 213. 1678 : Ray, 81, Rub and a good cast. Be not too hasty, and you'll speed the better.

Rub on the gall, To. Before 1529 : Skelton, in *Works*, i. 365 (Dyce), Yet wrote he none ill, Sauynge he rubbid sum vpon the gall. 1552 : Latimer, in *Works*, ii. 211 (P.S.), When a thief or a briber heareth this, it rubbeth him on the gall. 1607 : *Barley-Breake*, 27 (Grosart), Forbeare to rub me on that sore. 1710 : T. Ward, *Eng. Reform.*, 147 (1716), I like not rubbing an old sore.

Rubs in the smoothest road, There will be. 1710 : S. Palmer, *Moral Essays on Proverbs*, 364, No way so smooth but it has some rub. 1821 : Scott, *Kenilworth*, ch. xvi.

Rudgwick, Sussex. *See* quot. 1884 : " Sussex Proverbs," in *N. & Q.*, 6th ser., ix. 401, Ridgick for riches, Green [Wisborough Green] for poors, Billingshurst for pretty girls, and Horsham for whores.

Ruffians' Hall, He is only fit for. [Merchant sees his apprentice dressed as a gallant and exclaims: " Hey day, Ruffians' Hall! Sword, pumps, here's a racket indeed!"—1605 : Chapman, etc., *Eastw. Hoe*, I. i.] 1662 : Fuller, *Worthies*, ii. 347 (1840). 1790 : Grose, *Prov. Gloss.*, s.v. " London."

Rugged as a foal, As. 1917 : Bridge, *Cheshire Proverbs*, 19.

Rugged colt. *See* **Ragged.**

Rugged stone grows smooth from hand to hand, A. 1640 : Herbert, *Jac. Prudentum.* 1670 : Ray, 23.

Rule, *verb.* 1. *He that will not be ruled by his dame. See* **He that will not, etc.**

2. *He who will not be ruled by the rudder, must be ruled by the rock.* 1823 :

D'Israeli, *Cur. of Lit.*, 2nd ser., i. 454 (1824) [cited as " a Cornish proverb "]. 1853 : Trench, *Proverbs*, 60 (1905). 1864 : " Cornish Proverbs," in *N. & Q.*, 3rd ser., vi. 494.

3. *Rule lust, temper tongue, and bridle the belly.* 1813 : Ray, 20.

4. *Rule youth well, for age will rule itself.* 1736 : Bailey, *Dict.*, s.v. " Rule."

5. *Rule the roast.* *c.* 1400 : *Carpenter's Tools*, in Halliwell, *Nugæ Poeticæ*, 17, Whatsoeuer ye brage our boste, My meyster yet shall reule the roste. Before 1529 : Skelton, *Colin Clout*, l. 1021, But at the playsure of one That ruleth the roste alone. *c.* 1540 : Heywood, *Four PP.* in Hazlitt, *Old Plays*, i. 361, Nay, if riches might rule the roost, Behold what cause I have to boast! 1593 : Greene, *Works*, ii. 285 (Grosart), If then it be a woman's wish to haue her owne will, and as the common prouerbe saith, to rule the rost after her owne diet. 1606 : Chapman, *Gent. Usher*, V. i., I do domineer, and rule the roast. 1637 : Nabbes, *Microcosmus*, III., I am my ladies cooke, and king of the kitchin, where I rule the roast. 1696 : Vanbrugh, *Relapse*, II. 1736 : Fielding, *Pasquin*, II., They bear the name of power, we rule the roast. 1857 : Borrow, *Rom. Rye*, ch. xxviii., The son a puppy who . . . now rules the roast over his father and mother.

Rule without an exception, There is no. 1620 : Shelton, *Quixote*, Pt. II. ch. xviii. 1738 : Swift, *Polite Convers.*, Dial. I. [with " general " before " rule "]. 1758–67 : Sterne, *Trist. Shandy*, ix. ch. xiii. *Cf.* **Exceptions.**

Run, *verb.* 1. *He is run off his legs.* =He is bankrupt. 1678 : Ray, 89.

2. *He runs far. See* **Go** (10).

3. *He runs far back that means to leap a great way.* 1681 : Robertson, *Phraseol. Generalis*, 480.

4. *He that runs fastest gets most ground.* 1639 : Clarke, 319. 1670 : Ray, 138.

5. *He that runs fast will not run long.* 1855 : Bohn, 392.

6. *He that runs in the dark may well stumble.* 1670 : Ray, 19, He that runs

in the night stumbles. 1732 : Fuller, No. 2271.

7. *He that runs may rally.* Ibid., No. 2272.

8. *I cannot run and sit still at the same time.* Ibid., No. 2590.

9. *If you could run as you drink, you might catch a hare.* 1640 : Herbert, *Jac. Prudentum.*

10. *Ill run that cannot go. See* Ill run.

11. *It runs in the blood like wooden legs.* I heard this saying from the mouth of an Ulsterman, in Surrey, in the sixties of the last century. 1917 : Bridge, *Cheshire Proverbs*, 81. 1924 : *Devonsh. Assoc. Trans.*, lv. III, That rins in fam'lies, like timbern legs.

12. *Run tap run tapster.* 1678 : Ray, 86.

13. *To run as swift as a pudding would creep.* 1608 : Armin, *Nest of Ninnies*, 23 (Sh. S.), They puft and they blowede ; they ran as swifte as a pudding would creepe.

14. *To run at rovers*—To follow wild or random courses. 1528 : More, in *Works*, p. 228, col. 2 (1557), For so shold they nede no such titles at al, nor should nede neither roune at rouers, nor liue in ley mens houses. 1533 : Udall, *Flowers out of Terence*, fo. 191, His hart or mynde, whiche now runneth at rouers in ryot and wantonnes. 1567 : Painter, *Pal. of Pleasure*, iii. 47 (Jacobs), Who I had rather should be somewhat restrayned, than run at rouers to hir dishonour and my shame. 1639 : Clarke, 228, You run at random, shoot at rovers. 1847 : Halliwell, *Dict.*, s.v. "Rovers," *Running at rovers*, having too much liberty.

15. *To run before one's mare to market.* 1709 : R. Kingston, *Apoph. Curiosa*, 79, Taking a great deal of pains for nothing, and with the country proverb, is like running before ones mare to the market.

16. *To run him through the nose with a cushion.* 1672 : Walker, *Parœm.*, 57.

17. *To run over shoes*=To get heavily

in debt. 1598 : *Servingman's Comfort*, in *Inedited Tracts*, 154 (Hazlitt), He is runne ouershooes. Cf. **Over shoes.**

18. *To run with the hare and hunt with the hounds.* c. 1440 : *Jacobs Well*, 263 (E.E.T.S.), Thou hast a crokyd tunge heldyng wyth hownd and wyth hare. 1546 : Heywood, *Proverbs*, Pt. I. ch. x., To holde with the hare, and run with the hound. 1579 : Lyly, *Euphues*, 107 (Arber). 1598 : Greene, *James IV.*, IV. v. 1614 : C. Brooke, *Rich. the Third*, 86 (Grosart), And both could runne with hound, and hold with hare. 1705 : Ward, *Hud. Rediv.*, Pt. 3, can. iv. p. 11. 1893 : R. L. S., *Catriona*, ch. i., The whole thing . . . gave me a look of running with the hare and hunting with the hounds. 1897 : W. E. Norris, *Clarissa Furiosa*, ch. xxxix. 1924 : *Times*, Sept. 19, p. 13, col. 4, His policy of running with the hare and hunting with the hounds is becoming a menace to the general safety.

19. *You run as if. See* **Go** (29).

Running horse is an open sepulchre, A. 1578 : Florio, *First Fruites*, fo. 28 [" graue " for " sepulchre "]. 1611 : Cotgrave, s.v. " Sepulchre." 1666 : Torriano, *Piazza Univ.*, 43. 1732 : Fuller, No. 376 [" racc-horse " for " running horse "].

Rush for him that cares a straw for me, A. 1639 : Clarke, 72.

Rushes. *See* **Green** (9).

Rusty sword and empty purse plead performance of covenants, The. 1670 : Ray, 23.

Rutland raddleman. "Raddleman "= a dealer in raddle=red ochre. 1622 : Drayton, *Polyol.*, xxiii., Little Rutlandshire is termed Raddleman. 1662 : Fuller, *Worthies*, iii. 38 (1840). 1790 : Grose, *Prov. Gloss.*, s.v. " Rutlandshire."

Rye (grain). *See* **December; Good rye ; July** (6); **March** (27) ; **St. Peter** (2); **and Wheat** (2).

Rye (town). *See* **Chichester ;** and **Tenbury.**

Rynt you witch. *See* **Aroint.**

S

Sack. 1. *A short sack hath a wide
mouth.* 1583 : Melbancke, *Philotinus,*
sig. G2.

2. *He has given the sack a turn=*
"He has turned the tables—reversed
the order of things." 1917 : Bridge,
Cheshire Proverbs, 66.

3. *If it isn't in the sack. See* quot.
1911 : *Devonsh. Assoc. Trans.,* xliii. 93,
"If 'tisn't in the sack, 'tis in the pig's
back." This means, you will get, one
way or the other, your money's value.
What you cannot show for it in the
meat left in the sack, you will see in
what you gain for the fat bacon you
have to sell in return for the money
spent on the sack's contents.

4. *Let every sack stand upon its own
bottom.* 1659 : Howell, 4. Cf. **Every
tub.**

5. *Many a sack is tied up before it
be full.* 1607 : Rowlands, *Diog. Lanthorne,* 7 (Hunt. Cl.) [quoted as " the
olde prouerb"]. 1612 : W. Parkes, *Curtaine-Drawer of the World,* 60 (Grosart)
[" knit " for " tied "]. 1671 : Head
and Kirkman, *Eng. Rogue,* ii. 111,
When we fell short at meals . . . he
would put us off with an old proverb,
that *many a sack is tied up before it be
full.*

6. *Sacks to the mill. See* **More sacks.**

7. *There comes nought out of the sack,
but what was there.* 1586 : L. Evans,
Withals Dict. Revised, sig. G1, When
the sacke is opened, it is knowne what
is therein conteined. 1623 : Wodroephe, *Spared Houres,* 489. 1640 :
Herbert, *Jac. Prudentum.* 1869 : Spurgeon, *John Ploughman,* ch. ii., Nothing
comes out of a sack but what was in it.

See also **Broken** (5) ; **Empty** (9) ; **Ill
sack ; Know** (28); **Old,** E (3); **One grain ;**
and **Wish** (7).

Sackworth. *See* **Knipe-scar.**

Sad. *See* quot. 1550 : Udall, *Roister
Doister,* III. iii., *Merry.* . . . Why
speak ye so faintly, or why are ye so

sad ? *R. R.* Thou knowest the proverb
—because I cannot be had.

Saddle, *subs.* 1. *He has a saddle to fit
every horse* = a salve for every sore.
1813 : Ray, 214.

2. *To put the saddle on the right horse.*
1607 : Dekker and Webster, *Westw.
Hoe,* V., How say you wenches, haue I
set the sadle on the right horse ? 1678 :
Dryden, *All for Love,* Pref., I suppose
he would think it a wiser part to set the
saddle on the right horse, and chuse
rather to live with the reputation of a
plain-spoken honest man, than to die
with the infamy of an incestuous villain.
1720 : *Vade Mecum for Malt-worms,*
Pt. I. p. 4, Turn Justice to its proper
course, And place the saddle on the
right horse. 1843 : Carlyle, *Past and
Present,* bk. ii. ch. x., On all sides he
laid about him like a man . . . putting
consequence on premiss, and everywhere the saddle on the right horse.

3. *To set beside the saddle.* 1543 :
Becon, in *Early Works,* 368 (P.S.), Yet
by this means have they obtained their
purpose, and set the other beggarly
fellow besides the saddle. 1630 : T.
Adams, *Works,* 175, Riot iustles and
the wit is turned besides the saddle.
1636 : Taylor (Water-Poet), *Travels,* 52,
in *Works,* 3rd coll. (Spens. S.), Wines
predominant and capitall, To set a
horseman quite beside the saddle.

4. *Where saddles lack better ride on a
pad than on the horse bare-back.* 1546 :
Heywood, *Proverbs,* Pt. I. ch. x. 1605 :
Camden, *Remains,* 335 (1870). 1670 :
Ray, 139. 1732 : Fuller, No. 6464.

See also **Cow** (11) ; **Sow,** *subs.* (12) ;
Win (4).

Saddle, *verb. You saddle to-day and
ride out to-morrow.* 1659 : Howell,
Proverbs: Span.-Eng., 4, He sadleth
to day, and goes to morrow. 1732 :
Fuller, No. 5984.

Saddlewick, or ? **Saddleworth.** *See*
quots. 1670 : Ray, 209, Like the

parson of Saddleworth, who could read
in no book but his own. Cheshire. 1790:
Grose, *Prov. Gloss.*, s.v. " Cheshire " [as
in 1670, but " Saddlewick "]. 1878:
Folk-Lore Record, i. 167, [as in 1790,
plus] is referable to a Yorkshire town.
1917 : Bridge, *Cheshire Proverbs*, 91 [as
in 1790].

**Sadness and gladness succeed each
other.** 1639: Clarke, 326. 1670: Ray,
139. 1732 : Fuller, No. 4063.

Safe as a church, As. 1891 : Hardy,
Tess, ch. xiv., The plain ones be as safe
as churches.

Safe as a crow in a gutter, As. 1639 :
Clarke, 97 [with " sowe " for " crow "].
1670 : Ray, 207.

Safe as a mouse in a cheese, As.
1678 : Ray, 288.

Safe as a mouse in a malt-heap, As.
1639 : Clarke, 47. 1670 : Ray, 207.

Safe as a mouse in a mill, As. 1600 :
Weakest to the Wall, l. 345 (Malone S.),
And all without feare, safe as mouse in
a mill. 1639 : Davenport, *New Trick
to cheat Devil*, III. i., She's safe as mouse
in mill.

Safe as a thief in a mill, As. 1623 :
B. & F., *Maid in Mill*, II. i., The thief
is as safe as in his mill. 1673 : *Vinegar
and Must.*, 20, in Hindley, *Old Book
Coll. Miscell.*, iii., You are as safe as so
many thieves in a mill. 1738 : Swift,
Polite Convers., Dial. I. 1847 : Halliwell, *Dict.*, s.v. " Thief," . . . very
secure. Still in common use. 1889 :
J. Nicholson, *Folk Speech E. Yorks*, 18,
As fast as a thief in a mill. 1901 :
F. E. Taylor, *Lancs. Sayings*, 2 [as in
1889].

Safe as Chelsea, As. Derby. 1889.
Folk-Lore Journal, vii. 291.

Safe as the bank, As. 1862 : Dickens,
Letters, ii. 183 (1880). 1923 : J. S.
Fletcher, *The Diamonds*, ch. xxviii.,
. . . safe as the Bank of England.

Safe bind, safe find. *c.* 1540 : Bale,
Kynge Johan, l. 1897, As the sayinge
is, he fyndeth that surely bynde.
1580 : Tusser, *Husbandrie*, 173 (E.D.S.).
1655 : Fuller, *Church Hist.*, bk. iii. § v.
(6), Sure bind, sure find. 1751 : Fielding, *Amelia*, bk. xii. ch. vii. 1775 :
O'Hara, *Two Misers*, I. 1823 : Scott,

St. Ronan's, ch. xxxvi. 1865 : Dickens,
Mutual Friend, bk. iii. ch. xiv.

**Safe from the East Indies, and was
drowned in the Thames, He came.**
1732 : Fuller, No. 1817.

Safe riding in a good haven, 'Tis.
1659 : Howell, 16. 1732 : Fuller, No.
5083, 'Tis good riding in a safe harbour.

Saffron. *See* quot. 1904 : C. G.
Harper, *Newmarket, Bury, etc., Road*,
110, The very least of the benefits it
[saffron] conferred was the exhilaration
of the spirits, so that the old proverb
for a merry fellow was " He hath slept
in a bag of saffron."

Sage in May. *See* quots. 1588 :
Cogan, *Haven of Health*, ch. xi. p. 32
(1612), In *Schola Salerni* it is demanded,
Cur moriatur homo cui saluia crescit
in horto ? As who should say, such
is the vertue of sage, that if it were
possible, it would make a man immortall. 1635 : Swan, *Spec. Mundi*,
247, Such a desire hath sage to make a
man immortall. 1661 : M. Stevenson,
Twelve Moneths, 23, I shall conclude
with the old proverb, Set sage in May,
and it will grow alway. 1732 : Fuller,
No. 6253, He that would live for aye
Must eat butter and sage in May.
1846 : Denham, *Proverbs*, 44 (Percy S.)
[as in 1732, but omitting " butter
and "].

Said than done, Sooner (or Easier). [Id
dictu quam re, ut pleraque, facilius.—
Livy, xxxi. 38.] *c.* 1534 : Berners,
Huon, 327 (E.E.T.S.), Ye may say your
pleasure, but in the doynge is all the
mater. 1546 : Heywood, *Proverbs*, Pt.
II. ch. v., That is . . . sooner said then
doone. 1595 : *True Trag. Rich. Duke
of York*, 156 (Sh. S.), Tis better said
then done, my gratious Lord. 1681 :
Robertson, *Phraseol. Generalis*, 471,
'Tis more difficult then you think for ;
Sooner said than done. 1766 : Garrick,
Neck or Nothing, I. i., That's easier
said than done. 1850 : Smedley, *Frank
Fairlegh*, ch. li., Easier said than done,
Lawless, unfortunately.

Sail and Sails, subs. 1. *As sails are
to a ship, so are the passions to the spirits.*
1736 : Bailey, *Dict.*, s.v. " Spirit."

2. *Make not thy sail too big for the ballast.* 1732 : Fuller, No. 3322.

3. *To set up a sail to every wind.* c. 1630 : B. & F., *Bloody Brother*, IV. ii., Then he would sail with any wind. 1670 : Ray, 192. 1732 : Fuller, No. 5228. c. 1733 : Swift, *Poems:* "The Storm," He knows to sail with every wind.

Sail, *verb.* 1. *He that will not sail till he have a full fair wind, will lose many a voyage.* 1732 : Fuller, No. 2354.

2. *He that will sail without danger must never come upon the main sea.* 1639 : Clarke, 250. 1670 : Ray, 139. 1732 : Fuller, No. 2353, He that will not sail till all dangers are over, must never put to sea.

3. *Sail, quoth the king; hold, saith the wind.* 1732 : Fuller, No. 4064. 1738 : *Gent. Mag.*, 474.

4. *To sail with wind and tide.* 1580 : Sidney, *Arcadia*, bk. ii. 199 (1893), All men set their sails with the favourable wind, which blew on the fortune of this young prince. 1591 : Florio, *Second Frutes*, 97, For wisdom sailes with winde and tide. 1639 : Clarke, 15, Sayle with the wind and tide. 1783 : Windham, in Boswell's *Johnson*, iv. 201 *n.* (Hill), Set sail, and see where the winds and waves will carry you.

Saint and Saints. 1. *A saint abroad and a devil at home.* 1678 : Bunyan, *Pilgr. Progress*, Pt. I. 81 (1849), Thus, say the common people that know him, *A Saint abroad, and a Devil at home.* 1880 : Spurgeon, *Ploughman's Pictures*, 67, They are saints abroad, but ask their maids what they are at home.

2. *All saint without, all devil within.* 1732 : Fuller, No. 542.

3. *They are not all saints that use holy water.* 1586 : L. Evans, *Withals Dict. Revised*, sig. K6, They be not all saints, of this be you sure, that goe in and out at the churche dore. 1732 : Fuller, No. 4956.

See also **Young** (27).

SAINTS AND SAINTS' DAYS:

St. Andrew, 30 Nov. 1830 : Forby, *Vocab. E. Anglia*, 418, Saint Andrew the King, Three weeks and three days before Christmas comes in.

St. Barnabas, 11 June. *On St. Barnabas Put a scythe to the grass.* 1659 : Howell, *Proverbs: Fr.-Eng.*, 21, At Saint Barnabe the sithe in the medow. 1893 : Inwards, *Weather Lore*, 29. *See also* **Barnaby Bright.**

St. Bartholomew, 24 Aug. 1. *All the tears that St. Swithin can cry, St. Bartlemy's mantle wipes them dry.* 1878 : Dyer, *Eng. Folk-Lore*, 258. 1893 : Inwards, *Weather Lore*, 32 [with "dusty" before "mantle"].

2. *As St. Bartholomew's Day, so the whole autumn.* 1893 : Inwards, 33. 1912 : R. L. Gales, *Studies in Arcady*, 2nd ser., 107, If St. Barthlemy's day be fair and clear, Hope for a prosperous autumn that year.

3. *Bathe your eyes on Bartimy Day, You may throw your spectacles away.* Mon. 1905 : *Folk-Lore*, xvi. 67.

4. *If the wind change. See* quot. 1669 : *New Help to Discourse*, 284, If the winde change on St. Bartholomew's day at night, the following year will not be good.

5. *St. Bartholomew brings cold dew.* 1678 : Ray, 52. 1732 : Fuller, No. 6210. 1893 : Inwards, *Weather Lore*, 33, At St. Bartholomew There comes cold dew.

St. Benedict, 21 March. 1678 : Ray, 52, S. Benedick sow thy pease or keep them in thy rick. 1893 : Inwards, *Weather Lore*, 21 [as in 1678]. 1913 : E. M. Wright, *Rustic Speech, etc.*, 290, Then comes Benedick, if you ain't sowed your beans you may keep 'em in the rick.

St. Catharine, Isle of Wight. *When St. Catharine wears a cap, Then all the Island wears a hat.* c. 1870 : Smith, *Isle of Wight Words*, 61 (E.D.S.).

St. Catherine, 25 Nov. *As at Catherine foul or fair, so will be the next February.* 1893 : Inwards, *Weather Lore*, 37.

St. Chad, 2 March. *Before S. Chad every goose lays both good and bad.* 1678 : Ray, 51. 1732 : Fuller, No. 6163. 1846 : Denham, *Proverbs*, 40 (Percy S.), On or before, etc. *See also* **St. David;** and **St. Valentine** (3).

St. David, 1 March. 1. *David and*

Chad sow pease good or bad. 1659 : Howell, 21 [omitting " pease "]. 1670 : Ray, 43. 1872 : J. Glyde, jr., *Norfolk Garland*, 157, Sow beans and peas on David and Chad, Be the weather good or bad. 1913 : E. M. Wright, *Rustic Speech, etc.*, 290, David and Chad sow your beans be the weather good or bad.

2. *First comes David, next comes Chad, And then comes Winnold* [3 March] *as though he was mad.* 1827 : Hone, *Ev. Day Book*, ii. 284 [quoted as a " traditional West Norfolk proverbial distich "]. 1830 : Forby, *Vocab. E. Anglia*, 418. 1893 : Inwards, *Weather Lore*, 21 [" Winneral " for " Winnold "].

3. *Upon St. David's day, put oats and barley in the clay.* 1678 : Ray, 346. 1846 : Denham, *Proverbs*, 34 (Percy S.). *See also* **St. Valentine** (3).

St. Distaff, 7 Jan. *On St. Distaff's day, Neither work nor play.* 1846 : Denham, *Proverbs*, 23 (Percy S.).

St. George, 23 April. *St. George cries " Goe!" St. Mark* [25 April] *cries " Hoe!"* 1893 : Inwards, *Weather Lore*, 25. *See also* **Always in his saddle**.

St. Gervatius, 13 May. *Who shears his sheep before St. Gervatius' day loves more his wool than his sheep.* Ibid., 28.

St. Giles. 1. *As lame as St. Giles Cripple-gate.* 1662 : Fuller, *Worthies*, ii. 349 (1840). 1790 : Grose, *Prov. Gloss.*, s.v. " London." 1812 : Brady, *Clavis Cal.*, ii. 134.

2. *St. Giles's breed ; fat, ragged and saucy.* 1790 : Grose, *Prov. Gloss.*, s.v. " London."

3. *St. Giles's sweat.* 1869 : Hazlitt, 200, He's in a St. Giles's sweat. *Lancashire.* . . . i.e. He lies in bed, while his clothes are being mended.

St. Hugh's bones = a shoemaker's tools. 1600 : Dekker, *Shoem. Holiday*, II. iii., Yonder's a brother of the gentle craft ; if he bear not Saint Hugh's bones, I'll forfeit my bones. 1637 : L. Price, in *Pepysian Garland*, 445 (Rollins), S. Hughs bones vp we take in hast, both pinsers, punching alle and last. 1700 : Ward, *London Spy*, 139 (1924), So many jolly Crispins in a garret o'er St. Hugh's bones. 1825 :

Hone, *Ev. Day Book*, i. 859. 1917 : Bridge, *Cheshire Proverbs*, 109.

St. Jacob, 20 July. *Clear on St. Jacob's Day, plenty of fruit.* 1893 : Inwards, *Weather Lore*, 32.

St. James, 25 July. 1. *If it be fair. See* quot. 1669 : *New Help to Discourse*, 284, If it be fair three Sundays before St. James's day, corn will be good ; but wet corn will wither.

2. *Till St. James's day be come and gone, You may have hops, or you may have none.* 1670 : Ray, 44. 1732 : Fuller, No. 6469. 1856 : *N. & Q.*, 2nd ser., i. 226 (Herefs.). 1893 : Inwards, *Weather Lore*, 32.

3. *Whoever eats oysters on St. James's day will never want money.* 1846 : Denham, *Proverbs*, 51 (Percy S.). 1864 : Chambers, *Book of Days*, ii. 122.

St. John, 24 June. 1. *Before St. John's Day we pray for rain : after that we get it anyhow.* 1893 : Inwards, *Weather Lore*, 29.

2. *Cut your thistles before St. John, You will have two instead of one.* 1830 : Forby, *Vocab. E. Anglia*, 418. 1893 : Inwards, 30.

3. *Never rued the man That laid in his fuel before St. John.* 1732 : Fuller, No. 6205.

4. *Previous to St. John's Day we dare not praise barley.* 1893 : Inwards, 29.

5. *Rain on St. John's Day, and we may expect a wet harvest.* Ibid., 29.

St. Joseph, 19 March. *Is't on St. Joseph's Day clear, So follows a fertile year.* Ibid., 21.

St. Jude, 28 Oct. *On St. Jude's Day The oxen may play* = wet is expected. Ibid., 36.

St. Keverne's bells, No metal will run within the sound of. Corn. 1887 : M. A. Courtney, *Folk-Lore Journal*, v. 22.

St. Lawrence. *See* **Devil** (28) ; and **Lazy Lawrence**.

St. Leonard's saddle [at Bromley, Essex], **A ride upon**. Spoken to a barren woman. 1659 : Howell, 20.

St. Levan's stone. *See* quot. 1849 : Halliwell, *Pop. Rhymes and Nursery Tales*, 193, When with panniers astride A pack-horse can ride Through St. Levan's stone, The world will be done.

St. Luke, 18 Oct. 1. *On St. Luke's day The oxen had leave to play.* 1732: Fuller, No. 6220.

2. *St. Luke's Little Summer.* 1878: Dyer, *Eng. Folk-Lore,* 260. October the 30th, old St. Luke's Day, often brings with it fine sunny weather, and consequently has received the name of "St. Luke's Little Summer." 1889: Peacock, *Manley, etc., Gloss.,* 455 (E.D.S.), Saint Luke's Summer. A few warm days coming together in October. 1922: Weyman, *Ovington's Bank,* ch. xxii.

St. Margaret, 13 Aug. *St. Margaret's flood.* 1893: Inwards, *Weather Lore,* 33, St. Margaret's flood is proverbial, and is considered to be well for the harvest in England.

St. Mark. *See* **St. George.**

St. Martin, 11 Nov. 1. *If the geese at Martin's day stand on ice, they will walk in mud at Christmas.* 1893: Inwards, *Weather Lore,* 37.

2. *St. Martin's summer.* c. 1591: Shakespeare, 1 *Henry VI.,* I. ii., Expect Saint Martin's summer, halcyon days. 1831: Hone, *Year-Book,* 1343, St. Martin's little summer is a term for the fine days which sometimes intervene about the beginning of November. 1869: A. Dobson, in *Poet. Works,* 26 (1923), For these were yet the days of halcyon weather—A "Martin's summer," when the nation swam . . . 1921: Treves, *Riviera,* 42, In age she was just past the meridian. She was, indeed, the embodiment of St. Martin's summer.

St. Mary, 25 March (Annunciation). *Is't on St. Mary's bright and clear, Fertile is said to be the year.* 1893: Inwards, *Weather Lore,* 21.

St. Mary, 2 July (Visitation). *If it rains on St. Mary's Day, it will rain for four weeks.* Ibid., 30.

St. Mary Magdalene, 22 July. *See* quot. 1884: in *Folk-Lore Journal,* ii. 279, Alluding to the wet usually prevalent about the middle of July, the saiyng is:—"St. Mary Magdalene is washing her handkerchief to go to her cousin St. James's fair" [25 July]. Derbyshire.

St. Matthew, 21 Sept. 1. *Matthew's*

Day, bright and clear, Brings good wine in next year. 1893: Inwards, 35.

2. *St. Matthee shut up the bee.* 1678: Ray, 52. 1732: Fuller, No. 6211. 1893: Inwards, 34.

3. *St. Matthew brings on the cold dew.* 1732: Fuller, No. 6212. 1893: Inwards, 34.

4. *Saint Matthew get candlestick new, Saint Matthi lay candlestick by.* 1830: Forby, *Vocab. E. Anglia,* 418. 1893: Inwards, 35.

St. Matthias, 24 Feb. 1. *If it freezes on St. Matthias' Day, it will freeze for a month together.* 1893: Inwards, 17.

2. *Saint Matthias both leaf and grass.* 1659: Howell, 21. 1893: Inwards, 17 ["sow" before "both"].

3. *St. Matthias breaks the ice; if he finds none he will make it.* 1878: Dyer, *English Folk-Lore,* 253 [by a slip "Matthew" is printed for "Matthias"]. 1893: Inwards, 17.

4. *St. Matthie all the year goes by.* 1678: Ray, 52. 1893: Inwards, 17.

5. *St. Matthie sends sap into the tree.* 1678: Ray, 50. 1893: Inwards, 17.

6. *St. Mattho take thy hopper* [seed-basket] *and sow.* 1678: Ray, 52. 1893: Inwards, 17.

St. Medard, 8 June. If on the 8th of June it rain, It foretells a wet harvest, men sain. Ibid., 29.

St. Michael, 29 Sept. 1. *A Michaelmas rot comes ne'er in the pot.* 1639: in *Berkeley MSS.,* iii. 31 (1885), Michaelmas rott comes short of the pott. 1670: Ray, 44. 1732: Fuller, No. 6215. 1893: Inwards, 35.

2. *If St. Michael brings many acorns, Christmas will cover the fields with snow.* Ibid., 35. *See also* **Michaelmas**; and **Moon** (13) and (17).

St. Michael's Mount. *As formal as the Mount.* Newlyn, Corn. Said of an old-fashioned child. 19th cent. (Mr. C. Lee).

St. Paul's Cathedral. *See* **Paul's.**

St. Paul's Day, 25 Jan. *If St. Paul's be fine and clear, It doth betide a happy year.* 14th cent.: Robert of Avesbury, *Hist.,* 266 (Hearne), Clara dies Pauli bona tempora denotat anni. Si nix vel pluvia, designat tempora

cara. Si fiant nebulæ, morientur
bestia quæque. Si fiant venti, præ-
liabunt prælia genti. Before 1500 :
in R. Hill, *Commonplace-Book*, 134
(E.E.T.S.) [as in first two lines of preceding quotation]. 1584 : R. Scot,
Witchcraft, bk. xi. ch. xv., If Paul th'
apostles day be clear, It doth foreshew
a lucky year. 1658 : Willsford, *Natures
Secrets*, 145, If Saint Paul's day be fair
and clear, It does betide a happy year ;
But if it chance to snow or rain Then
will be dear all kinds of grain : If clouds
or mists do dark the skie, Great store
of birds and beasts shall die : And if the
winds do fly aloft, Then wars shall vex
that kingdome oft. 1725 : Bourne,
Antiq. Vulgares, 160 [a shorter version
of 1658 quot.]. 1753 : *World*, No. 10
[much as in 1658, but omitting the
" clouds or mists " lines]. 1866 : *N. &
Q.*, 3rd ser., ix. 118. To-day, January
25, has been a lovely day, sunny and
mild. A Huntingdonshire cottager said
to me : " We shall have a fine spring,
Sir, There is an old proverb that says :
' If Paul's day is fine, it will be a fine
spring.' " 1893 : Inwards, *Weather
Lore*, 12 [a slightly varied version of
1658 quot.].

**St. Peter le Poor, Where's no tavern,
alehouse, or sign at the door.** 1662 :
Fuller, *Worthies*, ii. 345 (1840), St.
Peter's in the poor, Where, etc. 1790 :
Grose, *Prov. Gloss.*, s.v. " London."

St. Peter's Day, 29 June. 1. *If it
rains on St. Peter's Day, the bakers will
have to carry double flour and single
water ; if dry, they will carry single flour
and double water.* 1893 : Inwards,
Weather Lore, 30.

2. *Peter and Paul will rot the roots of
the rye.* Ibid., 30.

St. Peter's needle, To go through =
To have serious misfortune. 1917 :
Bridge, *Cheshire Proverbs*, 134.

St. Pratt's little summer = the fine
weather that often occurs at the beginning of autumn. "St. Pratt" =
St. Protasius, patron saint of Blisland,
N. Corn. 1908: Heard by Mr. C. Lee.

St. Robert gave his cow, As freely as.
1670 : Ray, 208.

St. Stephen, 26 Dec. 1. *Blessed be St.*

Stephen, There's no fast upon his even.
1659 : Howell, 21. 1670 : Ray, 146.
1846 : Denham, *Proverbs*, 66 (Percy S.).
1925 : *Church Times*, 24 Dec.,
p. 755, col. 1, The old proverb is still
remembered :—Blessed be, etc.

2. *If you bleed your nag on St.
Stephen's-day, He'll work your wark for
ever and ay!* 1528: More, *Works*, p. 194,
col. 2 (1557), On saint Stephens day we
must let al our horses bloud with a knife,
because saynt Stephen was killed with
stones. 1687 : Aubrey, *Gentilisme*, 27
(F.L.S.), On St. Stephen's day the far-
rier came constantly and blouded all
the cart-horses, etc. 1744: *Tusser Redivivus*, 148, About Christmas is a very
proper time to bleed horses in. 1846 :
Denham, *Proverbs*, 66 (Percy S.). 1904 :
Co. Folk-Lore: Northumb., 179 (F.L.S.).

St. Swithin, 15 July. 1. *If it rains on
St. Swithin's it will rain for forty days.*
1599 : Jonson, *Ev. Man Out of Humour*,
I., O here, St. Swithin's . . . why it
should rain forty days after. 1639 :
Taylor (Water-Poet), *Part of Summers
Travels*, 5, in *Works*, 1st coll. (Spens.
S.), Upon Saint Swithin's day, I noted
well The wind was calme, nor any rain
then fell, Which faire day (as old sawes
saith) doth portend, That heav'n to
earth, will plenteous harvest send.
1716 : Gay, *Trivia*, bk. i. l. 183, How,
if on Swithin's feast the welkin lowers,
And ev'ry penthouse streams with hasty
showers, Twice twenty days shall clouds
their fleeces drain. 1846 : Denham,
Proverbs, 52 (Percy S.), St. Swithin's
day, if thou dost rain, For forty days it
will remain : St. Swithin's day, if thou
be fair, For forty days 'twill rain na
mair.

2. *St. Swithin is christening the apples.*
1813 : Brand, *Pop. Antiq.*, i. 342 (Ellis,
1895), There is an old saying that when
it rains on St. Swithin's Day, it is the
Saint christening the apples. 1825 :
Hone, *Ev. Day Book*, i. 960. 1893 :
Inwards, *Weather Lore*, 31. 1912 : R. L.
Gales, *Studies in Arcady*, 2nd ser.,
106.

See also **St. Bartholomew.**

St. Thomas, 21 Dec. 1. *St. Thomas
gray, St. Thomas gray, the longest night,*

and the shortest day. 1859 : *N. & Q.*,
2nd ser., viii. 242.

2. *The day of St. Thomas, the blessed
divine, Is good for brewing, baking, and
killing fat swine.* 1846 : Denham, *Proverbs,* 64 (Percy S.).

St. **Valentine,** 14 Feb. 1. *On St.
Valentine all the birds of the air in
couples do join. c.* 1380 : Chaucer,
Parl. of Foules, l. 309, For this was on
seynt Valentynes day, Whan every foul
cometh ther to chese his make. 1477 :
Paston Letters, iii. 169 (Gairdner), And,
cosyn, uppon Fryday is Sent Volentynes
Day, and every brydde chesyth hym
a make. 1621 : B. & F., *Thierry and
Theod.,* III. i., When you hear the birds
call for their mates, Ask if it be Saint
Valentine, their coupling day. *c.* 1673 :
Roxb. Ballads, vii. 114 (B.S.), There is
an old proverb, that " Birds of a feather
Upon St. Valentine's Day will meet
all together." 1714 : Gay, *Shep. Week,*
Thursday, l. 37, Last Valentine, the
day when birds of kind Their paramours
with mutual chirpings find. 1828 :
Scott, *Fair Maid,* ch. ii., To-morrow
is Saint Valentine's Day, when every
bird chooses her mate. 1830 : Forby,
Vocab. E. Anglia, 418.

2. *On St. Valentine's Day cast beans
in clay, But on St. Chad sow good and
bad.* 1639 : in *Berkeley MSS.,* iii. 33
(1885). 1868 : *N. & Q.,* 4th ser., i. 361,
[Huntingdonshire cottager *loq.*] On
Saint Valentine's day, Beans should be
in the clay. 1913 : E. M. Wright,
Rustic Speech, etc., 290, In Rutland
there is an old saying : Valentine's Day,
sow your beans in the clay.

3. *On Valentine's day Will a good
goose lay; If she be a good goose, her
dame well to pay, She will lay two eggs
before Valentine's day.* 1678 : Ray,
51. 1732 : Fuller, No. 6488. 1882 :
Mrs. Chamberlain, *W. Worcs. Words,* 37
(E.D.S.), By Valentine's day every good
goose should lay ; But by David and
Chad both good and bad.

4. *St. Valentine set thy hopper* [seed-
basket] *by mine.* 1678 : Ray, 52.
1893 : Inwards, *Weather Lore,* 17.

5. *To St. Valentine the spring is a
neighbour.* 1659 : Howell, *Proverbs:*

Fr.-Eng., 21. 1882 : Mrs. Chamberlain,
W. Worcs. Words, 37 (E.D.S.).

See also **Candlemas,** E ; and **March** (22).

St. **Vincent,** 22 Jan. *See* quot.
1584 : R. Scot, *Witchcraft,* bk. xi. ch.
xv., Vincenti festo si sol radiet memor
esto. Remember on St. Vincent's day,
If that the sun his beames display.
1876 : *N. & Q.,* 5th ser., v. 146, [as in
1584, *plus*] 'Tis a token, bright and
clear, That you will have a prosperous
year.

St. **Vitus,** 15 June. 1. *If St. Vitus's
day be rainy weather, It will rain for
thirty days together.* 1846 : Denham,
Proverbs, 49 (Percy S.). 1893 : Inwards, *Weather Lore,* 29.

2. *Oh ! St. Vitus, do not rain, so that
we may not want barley.* Ibid., 29.

Salad. 1. *A good salad may be the
prologue to a bad supper.* 1670 : Ray,
139 [" is " for " may be "]. 1732 :
Fuller, No. 174.

2. *He that sups upon salad goes not to
bed fasting.* Ibid., No. 2322.

See also **Wine** (2).

**Salisbury Plain is seldom without a
thief or twain.** 1659 : Howell, 17.
c. 1685 : Aubrey, *Nat. Hist. Wilts,* 69
(1847) [" never " for " is seldom "].
1790 : Grose, *Prov. Gloss.,* s.v. " Wilts."
1908 : W. Johnson, *Folk Memory,* 280,
Nor, save " a thief or twain " . . .
were there any signs of human life [on
Salisbury Plain a century ago].

Sally Hatch, Dressed to death, like.
1864 : " Cornish Proverbs," in *N. & Q.,*
3rd ser., vi. 6.

**Salmon and sermon have both their
season in Lent.** 1659 : Howell, *Proverbs: Fr.-Eng.,* 21, Salmons and sermons have their seasons in Lent. 1666 :
Torriano, *Piazza Univ.,* 246, A sammon
and a sermon come much of a season.
1670 : Ray, 23. 1917 : Bridge, *Cheshire
Proverbs,* 106.

Salmon. *See also* **Hook.**

Salt, *adj. Salt cooks bear blame, but
fresh bear shame.* 1670 : Ray, 73.
1732 : Fuller, No. 6300.

Salt, *subs.* 1. *Help me to salt, help
me to sorrow.* 1872 : J. Glyde, jr.,
Norfolk Garland, 44. 1879 : Henderson, *Folk-Lore of N. Counties,* 121.

1883 : Burne, *Shropsh. Folk-Lore*, 278.
1910 : *N. & Q.*, 11th ser., ii. 198.

2. *Not worth* (or *Worth*) *one's salt.*
[Non valet lotium suum.—Petr., 57.]
1830 : Marryat, *King's Own*, ch. lii.,
The captain . . . is not worth his salt.
1883 : R. L. S., *Treasure I.*, ch. xviii.,
It was plain from every line of his body
that our new hand was worth his
salt.

3. *Of all smells, bread; of all tastes,
salt.* 1591 : Florio, *Second Frutes*, 53,
Salt no sauour, God no greater. 1640 :
Herbert, *Jac. Prudentum.* 1666 : Torriano, *Piazza Univ.*, 70, Above salt
there's no savour.

4. *Salt seasons all things.* 1591 :
Florio, *Second Frutes*, 53, Salt sauour-
eth, and seasoneth all things. 1659 :
Howell, 9.

5. *To put salt on a bird's tail.* 1580 :
Lyly, *Euphues and England*, 327
(Arber), It is . . . a foolish bird that
staieth the laying salt on hir taile.
1654 : Gayton, *Pleasant Notes Don Q.*,
203, To catch regall birds, by laying
salt upon their tailes. 1704 : Swift,
Tale of a Tub, § vii., As boys [catch]
sparrows with flinging salt upon their
tails. 1806 : Lamb, *Mr. H—*, II., My
name is Finch—Betty Finch . . . you
can't catch me by throwing salt on my
tail. 1858 : Dickens, *Great Expect.*,
ch. iv., Plenty of subjects going about,
for them that know how to put salt upon
their tails.

See also Black, *subs.* (1); Bushel ; and
Neither sugar.

Salve for every sore, There's a. 1542 :
Sch. House of Women, l. 401, A salue
there is for euery sore. 1566 : Gascoigne, *Supposes*, II. i. 1639 : Clarke,
15. 1762 : Smollett, *Sir L. Greaves*,
ch. xv., You must have a little patience,
Crabshaw—there's a salve for every
sore. 1913 : *Folk-Lore*, xxiv. 76 (Oxon.).

**Salve where you got your sore, Seek
your.** 1732 : Fuller, No. 4090.

Sam Babb's pig. *See* quot. 1925 :
Devon and Cornwall N. & Q., xiii. 206,
Like Sam Babb's pig, live 'pon nothing
and get fat in a minute : he had water-
crease broth all the week and essence o'
whip 'pon Sundays (North Cornwall).

Same boat, To be in the. [ταῦτ' ἐμοὶ
ζυγὸν τρίβεις.—Herodas, vi. 12.] *c.* 1594:
Bacon, *Promus*, No. 740, You are in
the same shippe. 1710 : E. Ward,
Nuptial Dialogues, ii. 360, Therefore
the sinner, and the saint, Are often
in the selfsame boat. 1836 : Marryat,
Japhet, ch. lxvi., Well, I will row in the
same boat, and I will be a Quaker as
well as you both. 1922 : Weyman,
Ovington's Bank, ch. xiii., Oh, he's quite
right to speak his mind. We are all in
the same boat—though we do not all
steer.

**Same knife cuts bread and fingers,
The.** 1633 : Draxe, 223, The same
knife cutteth bread and a mans finger.
1659 : Howell, *Proverbs: Span.-Eng.*,
19, The same knife cuts my bread and
my finger.

Sammy Dawkin. *See* quot. 1880 :
Courtney, *W. Cornwall Words*, 48
(E.D.S.), You are a regular Sammy
Dawkin, can't scull a boat. A Padstow
proverb.

**Samson than of Solomon in him,
There is more of.** 1830 : Forby,
Vocab. E. Anglia, 430.

**Samson was a strong man, but he
could not pay money before he had it.**
1659 : Howell, 11 (9), Salomon was a
wise man, and Sampson was a strong
man, yet neither of them could pay
money till they had it. 1732 : Fuller,
No. 4066. 1869 : Spurgeon, *John
Ploughman*, ch. xii.

Sand and clay. *See* England (12).

Sandbach. *See* quot. 1917 : Bridge,
Cheshire Proverbs, 163, A wind from
Sandbach in the East, Blows good to
neither man nor beast.

Sandwich. *See* Deal.

Sandwich Bay (or **Haven**), Conscience is drowned in. 1735 : Pegge,
Kent. Proverbs, in E.D.S., No. 12, p. 74
[an explanatory story].

Sap and heart are the best of wood.
1917 : Bridge, *Cheshire Proverbs*, 106.

Sarum, Secundum usum. 1589 : *Pap
with a Hatchet*, 17 (1844), And for the
winter nights the tales should be told
secundum Vsum Sarum. 1655 : Fuller,
Church Hist., bk. iii. § i. (23), Henceforward the most ignorant parish priest

. . . understood the meaning of *secundum usum Sarum*, that all service must be ordered " according to the course and custom of Salisbury church." *c.* 1685 : Aubrey, *Nat. Hist. Wilts*, 95 (1847), The consistorie of this church [Salisbury] was as eminent for learning as any in England, and the choire had the best method : hence came the saying *secundum usum Sarum.* 1790 : Grose, *Prov. Gloss.*, s.v. " Wilts," It is done, *secundum usum Sarum.*

Satan. *See* **Devil.**

Saturday. 1. *A fine Saturday, a fine Sunday, A fine Sunday, a fine week.* 1893 : *Co. Folk-Lore : Suffolk*, 163 (F.L.S.).

2. *Saturday's flit will never sit.* 1851 : Sternberg, *Dialect of Northants* 169, Thus the saying—Saturday servants never stay, Sunday servants run away. 1854 : Baker, *Northants Gloss.*, s.v. " Flit," " Saturday's flit will never sit," is a proverb of prediction with superstitious servants, who reluctantly enter upon a new service on that day. 1917 : Bridge, *Cheshire Proverbs*, 107, Saturday's flittings, Light sittings. Cf. **Monday** (2).

3. *There is never a Saturday without some sunshine.* 1866 : *New Suffolk Garland*, 166, There is also a saying that " the sun is always seen on a Saturday," and this is firmly believed by many of the country people. 1893 : Inwards, *Weather Lore*, 43.

4. *This is silver Saturday, The morn's the resting day; On Monday up and to't again, And Tuesday push away.* 1846 : Denham, *Proverbs*, 18 (Percy S.).

See also **Friday** (2); and **Moon** (3).

Sauce before you have caught the fish, Make not your. 1732 : Fuller, No. 3324.

Save, *verb.* 1. *He that saveth his dinner will have the more for supper.* 1639 : Clarke, 241. 1670 : Ray, 79. 1732 : Fuller, No. 2288.

2. *He would save the droppings of his nose.* 1567 : Painter, *Pal. of Pleasure*, iii. 299 (Jacobs), As vsurers do God knowes, Who cannot spare the dropping of their nose. 1602 : J. Cooke, *How a Man may choose Good Wife*, sig. G3, It

is such an old snudge, he will not loose the dropping of his nose. 1754 : Berthelson, *Eng.-Danish Dict.*, s.v. " Droppings." 1828 : Carr, *Craven Dialect*, i. 119, "He wad save the vara droppings of his nose," spoken of a penurious person.

3. *Save a thief from the gallows, and he'll cut your throat.* *c.* 1440 : Lydgate, *Fall of Princes*, bk. vi. l. 3253, Who saueth a theef whan the rop is knet Aboute his nekke, as olde clerkis write, With sum fals tourn the bribour wil hym quite. 1484 : Caxton, *Æsope*, ii. 15 (Jacobs), For as men sayen comynly yf ye kepe a man fro the galhows he shalle neuer loue you after. 1583 : Melbancke, *Philotinus*, sig. X4, True is the prouerbe, saue a thief from the gallowes, and he will be the firste shall doe thee a mischiefe. 1622 : Massinger, *Virgin Martyr*, II. iii., She saved us from the gallows, and, only to keep one proverb from breaking his neck, we'll hang her. Before 1704 : T. Brown, in *Works*, ii. 290 (1760). 1771 : Smollett, *Clinker*, in *Works*, vi. 177 (1817). 1820 : Scott, *Monastery*, ch. x., " Save a thief from the gallows," said the Sacristan— " you know the rest of the proverb."

4. *Save at the spigot and let out at the bung-hole.* 1670 : Ray, 193 ["Spare" for "Save"]. 1710 : S. Palmer, *Moral Essays on Proverbs*, 288. 1754 : Berthelson, *Eng.-Danish Dict.*, s.v. "Spare," To spare at the spigot and let it run out of the bung-hole. 1869 : Spurgeon, *John Ploughman*, ch. xvi. [as in 1754]. 1883 : Burne, *Shropsh. Folk-Lore*, 590 ["waste" for "let out"].

5. *Save me from my friends. See* **God defend me.**

6. *Save something for the man that rides on the white horse.* 1639 : Clarke, 129. 1670 : Ray, 139. 1732 : Fuller, No. 4068.

7. *Save your breath. See* **Breath.**

8. *To save a snuff he throws away whole candles.* 1864 : "Cornish Proverbs," in *N. & Q.*, 3rd ser., vi. 495.

9. *To save one's bacon.* 1682 : A. Behn, *City Heiress*, I. i., I go [to church] to save my bacon, as they say, once a month. 1729 : Fielding, *Author's*

Farce, III. iii., No tricks shall save
your bacon. 1742 : North, *Lives of
Norths,* ii. 193 (Bohn). 1829 : in
Farmer, *Musa Pedestris,* 111, I cuts
and runs and saves my bacon.

Saving cometh having, Of. 1633 :
Draxe, 196. 1670 : Ray, 139. 1732 :
Fuller, No. 6102. 1829 : Scott, *Journal,*
April 20, It is saving, not getting, that
is the mother of riches.

Saving is getting. 1666 : Torriano,
Piazza Univ., 265, Saving is the first
getting. 1732 : Fuller, No. 4069. 1828 :
Carr, *Craven Dialect,* i. 3, Saving's good
addlin. 1855 : Robinson, *Whitby Gloss,*
2 [as in 1828].

Saving must equal having, *i.e.* you
must make both ends meet. 1851 :
Gloucester Gloss., 14.

**Sawtrey, by the way, Now a grange,
that was an abbey.** 1568 : in *Loseley
MSS.* 212 (Kempe).

Say, *verb.* 1. *Better say nothing than
not to the purpose.* 1693 : Penn, *Fruits
of Solitude,* No. 132. 1732 : Fuller, No.
921.

2. *He cannot say his Pater-noster.*
1552 : Latimer, *Sermons,* 389 (P.S.),
When we be disposed to despise a man
. . . we say, " He cannot say his Paternoster."

3. *He grants enough that says nothing.*
1611 : Cotgrave, s.v. " Octroyer," He
that sayes nothing yields enough. 1623:
Wodroephe, *Spared Houres,* 476.

4. *He says anything but his prayers,
and them he whistles.* 1732 : Fuller,
No. 2014. 1738 : Swift, *Polite Convers.,* Dial. I., Miss will say anything but
her prayers, and those she whistles.

5. *He who says what he likes shall hear
what he does not like.* 1539 : Taverner,
Proverbs, fo. 2, He that speaketh what
he woll, shall heare what he woll not.
1583 : Melbancke, *Philotinus,* sig. Y1,
Since they say what they liste, they
shall heare what they list not. 1666 :
Torriano, *Piazza Univ.,* 319, Who says
what he lists, hears what is against his
will. 1732 : Fuller, No. 6303, He that
speaks the thing he should not, Shall
hear the thing he would not. 1853 :
Trench, *Proverbs,* 82 (1905).

6. *I will say no more till the day be*

longer. 1562 : Heywood, *Three Hund.
Epigr.,* No. 168.

7. *I will say nought but mum.* 1659:
Howell, 7.

8. *Say as men say, but think to yourself.* 1639 : Clarke, 327.

9. *Say little but think the more.*
c. 1430 : Lydgate, *Minor Poems,* 155
(Percy S.), Take no quarelle, thynk
mekyl and sey nought. *c.* 1490 :
Partonope, 84 (E.E.T.S.), He seyyth
butte lytell, butte more thynckyth he.
c. 1535 : *Pain of Evil Marriage,* 22
(Percy S.), Therfore thynke moche and
saye nought. *c.* 1600 : Deloney, *Thos.
of Reading,* ch. 5, Vpon these words
away went her husband, and though he
said little, hee thought more. *c.* 1640 :
in *Roxb. Ballads,* ii. 97 (Hindley), And
though he said little, yet he thought
the more. 1678 : Ray, 82, Though he
saith nothing, he pays it with thinking,
like the Welchmans jackdaw. 1738 :
Swift, *Polite Convers.,* Dial. I., Miss
says nothing ; but I warrant she pays
it off with thinking. 1836 : Marryat,
Easy, ch. xiv., As for Jack, he said
nothing, but he thought the more.
1886 : Swainson, *Folk-Lore of Brit.
Birds,* 82 (F.L.S.) [as in 1678].

10. *Say nay. See* **Maid** (11).

11. *Say no ill of the year till it be past.*
1640 : Herbert, *Jac. Prudentum.* 1732 :
Fuller, No. 4071. 1846 : Denham,
Proverbs, 1 (Percy S.).

12. *Say nothing when you are dead,*
i.e. be silent. 1678 : Ray, 82.

13. *Say still no, an' ye'll ne'er be
married.* 1738 : Swift, *Polite Convers.,*
Dial. I., But if you always say no, you'll
never be married. 1869 : Hazlitt, 328.

14. *Say well is good but do well is
better.* 1536 : in *Brit. Bibliog.,* iv.
283 (1814), Men say wel that do wel.
c. 1550 : *Six Ballads,* 6 (Percy S., No.
50). 1639 : Clarke, 194, Say well and
do well, end with a letter, Say well is
good, but do well is better. 1640 :
Brome, *Sparagus Garden,* IV. xi. 1732 :
Fuller, No. 6447 [as in 1639]. *c.* 1791 :
Pegge, *Derbicisms,* 137 (E.D.S.). 1852 :
FitzGerald, *Polonius,* 136 (1903) [as in
1639].

15. *Say well or be still. c.* 1480 :

Early Miscell., 63 (Warton Cl., 1855),
Ewyre say wylle, or hold the[e] styll.
Before 1529 : Skelton, in *Works*, i. 17
(Dyce), A prouerbe of old, say well or
be styll.

16. *Say you saw me not. c.* 1520 :
Stanbridge, *Vulgaria*, sig. C2, Yf ony
man aske for me saye thou sawest me
not. 1672: Walker, *Parœm.*, 19, Say
you saw it not. 1681: Robertson,
Phraseol. Generalis, 1097.

17. *To say his prayers backward.*
1678 : Ray, 265. 1846–59 : *Denham
Tracts*, ii. 84 (F.L.S.), Ye're like a witch,
ye say your prayers backward.

18. *You say true, will you swallow my
knife?* 1678 : Ray, 255.

See also Said ; and So said.

Saying and doing are two things.
1546 : Heywood, *Proverbs*, Pt. II. ch. v.
1572 : T. Wilson, *Disc. upon Usury*, 249
(1925), To saye and doe are twoe
thynges. 1678 : Bunyan, *Pilgr. Progr.*,
Pt. I. 82 (1849), I see that *saying* and
doing are two things, and hereafter
I shall better observe this distinction.
1712 : Motteux, *Quixote*, Pt. II. ch.
xxxiv. 1787 : O'Keeffe, *The Farmer*,
I. ii. 1869 : Spurgeon, *John Ploughman*,
ch. xx.

Scabbed. *See* Cuckoo (2).

Scabbed horse abides no comb, A.
c. 1430 : *Pilgr. Lyf. Manhode*, II. civ.
114 (1869) (O.), For riht as a scabbed
beste hateth hors comb. 1611 : Davies
(of Hereford), *Sc. of Folly*, 50, in *Works*,
ii. (Grosart). 1732 : Fuller, No. 1639,
Gall'd horses can't endure the comb.
1869 : Spurgeon, *John Ploughman*, ch.
iii., If any of you get cross over it, I
shall tell you that sore horses cannot
bear to be combed.

**Scabbed horse is good enough for a
scald squire, A.** 1540 : Palsgrave,
Acolastus, sig. M2, For suche a scalde
squier as he is, a scabbed horse. 1562 :
Heywood, *Three Hund. Epigr.*, No. 161.
1732 : Fuller, No. 385 [" scabbed
knight " for " scald squire "]. 1736 :
Bailey, *Dict.*, s.v. " Squire " [" shabby "
for " scald "]. Cf. Scald horse.

Scabbed sheep. *See* Sheep (10).

Scabby heads love not the comb.
1623 : Wodroephe, *Spared Houres*, 516,

A scabbed head doth never loue the
combe. 1732 : Fuller, No. 4072. 1801 :
Wolcot, in *Works*, v. 369 (1801), But
George disliketh much to hear About
his Scottish home ; Thus *scabby heads*,
the proverb says, For ever hate a *comb*.

Scald head is soon broken, A. Before
1500 : in Hill, *Commonplace-Book*, 130
(E.E.T.S.), A skalde manis hede is sone
brokyn. 1598 : Meres, *Palladis*, fo. 302.
1621 : Burton, *Melancholy*, III. ii.
6, 2, p. 589 (1836). 1683 : Meriton,
Yorkshire Ale, 83–7 (1697), A scauld
head is seaun broken.

**Scald horse is good enough for a
scabbed squire, A.** 1546 : Heywood,
Proverbs, Pt. I. ch. xi. *c.* 1580 : Fulwell, *Ars Adulandi*, sig. F4, A ragged
colte may serue a scabbed squire. 1681 :
Robertson, *Phraseol. Generalis*, 1098.
Cf. Scabbed horse.

**Scald not your lips in another man's
pottage.** 1598 : *Servingmans Comfort*,
in *Inedited Tracts*, 99 (Hazlitt), It is
not good to scalde ones lyppes in
other mens pottage. 1696 : D'Urfey,
Quixote, Pt. III. Act II. sc. ii. 1710 : S.
Palmer, *Moral Essays on Proverbs*, 355.
c. 1800 : J. Trusler, *Prov. in Verse*, 58.
1823 : Scott, *St. Ronan's*, ch. viii., I
can tell you, Mr. Meiklewham . . . that
you are scalding your lips in other folks'
kale.

**Scandal will rub out like dirt when it
is dry.** 1732 : Fuller, No. 4076.

Scarborough. *See* Oliver's Mount.

Scarborough warning, A = no warning at all. 1546 : Heywood, *Proverbs*,
Pt. I. ch. xi., Scarbrough warnyng I had
(quoth he). *c.* 1550–70 : in Hindley,
Old Book - Coll. Miscell., i. 40, This
terme, Scarborow warnyng, grew (some
say) By hasty hangyng, for rank robbry theare. 1589 : Puttenham, *Eng.
Poesie*, 199 (Arber). 1593 : G. Harvey,
Works, ii. 225 (Grosart), He meaneth
not to come vpon me with a cowardly
stratageme of Scarborough warning.
1662 : Fuller, *Worthies*, iii. 398 (1840).
1790 : Grose, *Prov. Gloss.*, s.v. " Yorkshire." 1824 : Scott, *Redgauntlet*, ch. xx.,
The true man for giving Scarborough
warning, first knock you down, then
bid you stand. 1913 : E. M. Wright,

Rustic Speech, etc., 189, A Scarborough warning signifies no warning at all. The origin of the saying rests on the statement that in 1557 Thomas Stafford entered and took possession of Scarborough Castle before the townsmen were aware of his approach. [The occurrence of the phrase in 1546, *vide supra*, disproves this theory.]

Scarce of horses. *See* Horse (66).

Scarce of news who told that his father was hanged, He was. 1732 : Fuller, No. 2378. 1852 : FitzGerald, *Polonius*, 40 (1903), He was scant o' news wha tauld his father was hanged.

Scatter with one hand, gather with two. 1659 : Howell, *Proverbs: Brit.-Eng.*, 2.

Sceptre is one thing and a ladle another, A. 1640 : Herbert, *Jac. Prudentum.* 1670 : Ray, 23. 1732 : Fuller, No. 386.

Schemey must louster, He that can't. 1869 : Hazlitt, 482, Yeker that can't scheme must louster. *S. Devon and Cornwall.* 1879 : *Folk-Lore Record*, ii. 203 (Cornwall). 1913 : *Devonsh. Assoc. Trans.*, xlv. 291, A common proverb in Devon is, " He that can't schemey must louster," meaning that he who cannot work with his head must work with his hands. Cf. Work, *verb* (3).

Scholar, A mere, a mere ass. 1639 : Clarke, 151. 1659 : Howell, 3. 1703 : Centlivre, *Stolen Heiress*, I., A meer scholar is a meer—you know the old proverb, father. 1732 : Fuller, No. 322, A mere scholar at Court is an ass among apes.

Scholar as my horse Ball, As good a. 1639 : Clarke, 145.

Scholar may be gulled thrice, a soldier but once, A. 1659 : Howell, *Proverbs: Brit.-Eng.*, 11.

Scholar teacheth his master, The. 1639 : Clarke, 4.

Schoolboys. *See* quot. 1678 : Ray, 81, Schoolboys are the reasonablest people in the world, they care not how little they have for their money.

School-butter = a flogging. 1604 : *Pasquils Jests*, 24 (1864), An unhappy boy, willing to have one of his fellowes taste of such schoole-butter as hee had often broke his fast with. 1607 : R. West, *Court of Conscience*, sig. D4, [Whipper says] When thou hast tasted some of my schoole-butter, Thy limmes will be so hethy thou wilt leap. 1618 : B. & F., *Loyal Subject*, V. iv., He was whipt like a top . . . court schoolbutter ? Is this their diet ? 1690 : *New Dict. Canting Crew*, sig. K8, Schoolbutter, a whipping.

Scilly, Always a feast or a fast in. 1750 : R. Heath, *Acc. of Scilly*, 53, Verifying the proverb, *A feast or a famine in Scilly.* 1864 : " Cornish Proverbs," in *N. & Q.*, 3rd ser., v. 275. 1887 : M. A. Courtney, *Folk-Lore Journal*, v. 38.

Scilly ling is a dish for a king, A. 1864 : " Cornish Proverbs," in *N. & Q.*, 3rd ser., v. 208. 1928 : *Times*, 25 Sept., p. 10, col. 5.

Scoggin's a doctor, Among the common people. 1639 : Clarke, 143. 1670 : Ray, 140.

Scold, subs. *Who hath a scold hath sorrow to his sops.* 1659 : Howell, 15. 1670 : Ray, 23. 1732 : Fuller, No. 5705. Cf. Sorrow.

Scold like a cutpurse, To. 1678 : Ray, 288.

Scold like a wych-waller [salt-boiler], **To.** 1670 : Ray, 208. 1790 : Grose, *Prov. Gloss.*, s.v. " Cheshire." 1836 : Wilbraham, *Cheshire Gloss.*, 91 (2nd ed.), . . . is a common adage. 1917 : Bridge, *Cheshire Proverbs*, 142.

Scold the devil, To. *See* Devil (34).

Score twice before you cut once = Look before you leap. 1688 : Holme, *Acad. of Armory*, bk. iii. cap. vi. p. 292, The point on the back of the shoemaker's pareing knife is to score or trace out the leather before he venture to cut it, according to the saying score twice before you cut once, else they will cut themselves out of doors. 1917 : Bridge, *Cheshire Proverbs*, 107.

Scorn at first makes after-love the more. 1855 : Bohn, 482.

Scornful dogs will eat dirty puddings. 1709 : Mandeville, *Virgin Unmask'a* 32 (1724), Dirty puddings for dirty dogs. 1738 : Swift, *Polite Convers.*, Dial. I.

1816 : Scott, *Antiquary*, ch. xliii., The
messenger (one of those dogs who are not
too scornful to eat dirty puddings) . . .
1824 : Scott, *Redgauntlet*, ch. xii. Cf.
Hungry dogs.

Scorning is catching. [*c.* 1440 : Lydgate, *Fall of Princes*, bk. iii. l. 601
(E.E.T.S.), For it was said sithen go
ful yore, He that reioishith to scorne
folk in veyn, Whan he wer lothest shal
scorned been ageyn.] 1670 : Ray, 140.
1732 : Fuller, No. 4081. 1754 : Berthelson, *Eng.-Danish Dict.*, s.v. "Scornfully," After scorning comes catching.

Scot, *subs.* 1. *A Scot, a rat, and a
Newcastle grindstone, travel all the world
over.* 1662 : Fuller, *Worthies*, ii. 543
(1840), A Scottishman and a Newcastle grind-stone, travel all the world
over. 1790 : Grose, *Prov. Gloss.*, s.v.
"Northumberland." 1821 : in Lockhart,
Life of Scott, v. 99, The old saying,—in
every corner of the world you will find
a Scot, a rat, and a Newcastle grindstone. 1846–59 : *Denham Tracts*, i.
301 (F.L.S.).

2. *A Scot on Scots bank.* 1678 : Ray,
81.

3. *The Scot will not fight till he see
his own blood.* 1822 : Scott, *Nigel*,
ch. i.

4. *We will not lose a Scot.* 1662 :
Fuller, *Worthies*, ii. 542 (1840). 1790 :
Grose, *Prov. Gloss.*, s.v. "Northumberland " [" He " for " We "]. 1846–59 :
Denham Tracts, i. 248 (F.L.S.), We will
not lose a Scot. That is anything,
however inconsiderable, which we can
possibly save or recover.

See also Hard-hearted.

Scotch ordinary, The=The house of
office. 1678 : Ray, 81.

Scottish mist will wet an Englishman
to the skin, A. 1589 : *Pap with a
Hatchet*, Dedn., We care not for a
Scottish mist, though it wet to the
skin. 1639 : Clarke, 11 [" may " for
" will "]. 1641 : in *Harl. Miscell.*, iii.
228 (1744). 1681 : Robertson, *Phraseol.
Generalis*, 1100 [as in 1639]. 1732 :
Fuller, No. 388 [as in 1639]. 1814 :
Scott, *Waverley*, ch. xxv., To beware
of Scotch mists, which, she had heard,
would wet an Englishman through and

through. 1872 : J. Glyde, jr., *Norfolk
Garland*, 150.

Scottish warming-pan, A = A wench.
1678 : Ray, 83. 1685 : S. Wesley,
Maggots, 36, 'Twould better heat a man
Than two Bath faggots or Scotch warming-pan. Note.—Scotch warming-pan
is the hostesses brown daughter. 1785 :
Grose, *Class. Dict. Vulgar Tongue*,
s.v. "Warming-pan." 1826 : Brady,
Varieties of Lit., 40, . . . This saying
arose from the well-known story of a
gentleman travelling in Scotland, who,
desiring to have his bed warmed, the
servant - maid immediately undressed
herself and lay down in it for a while.

Scrambling at a rich man's dole, 'Tis
brave. 1639 : Clarke, 39. 1670 : Ray,
136. 1732 : Fuller, No. 5069.

Scrape and save. *See* quot. 15th
cent.: in *Reliq. Antiquæ*, i. 316 (1841),
Kype [Scrape] and save, and thou
schalle have; Frest [Lend] and leve,
and thou schall crave; Walow and
wast, and thou schalle want.

Scratch a beggar before you die,
You'll = You will be a beggar. 1639:
Clarke, 209, You'l scratch a begger one
day. 1670 : Ray, 164. 1732 : Fuller,
No. 6035.

Scratch a grey head, He will never.
1738 : Swift, *Polite Convers.*, Dial. III.,
I think the countess is very sickly.
Lady Smart. Yes, madam ; she'll never
scratch a gray head. 1901 : F. E.
Taylor, *Lancs Sayings*, 30, He'll never
live for t' scrat a grey yed.

Scratches his head with one finger,
He. 1855 : Bohn, 381.

Scratching. *See* Cat (14).

Scratch me and I'll scratch thee.
[Mutuum muli scabant.—Auson., *Idyll.*,
xii., Praef. Monos.] 1611 : Cotgrave,
s.v. "Contrelouër," To scratch the
back of one who hath already clawed
his elbow. 1694 : D'Urfey, *Quixote*,
Pt. II., Act II. sc. ii., Scratch my back
and I'll claw your elbow. 1706 : E.
Ward, *Works*, iii. 145, Scratch me, says
one, and I'll scratch thee. Cf. Claw (2);
and Ka me.

Scratch where it does not itch, To.
c. 1510 : A. Barclay, *Egloges*, 30 (Spens.
S.), I clawe oft where it doth not itche.

1546 : Heywood, *Proverbs*, Pt. II. ch. vii., Thou makest me claw where it itcheth not. 1578 : Whetstone, *Promos and Cass.*, sig. D3, And straight (through feare) where he clawes it doth not ytch. 1639–61 : in *Rump Songs*, Pt. II. 7 (1662, repr. 1874), 'Twould make a man scratch where it does not itch, To see . . . 1680 : Shadwell, *Woman Captain*, I. *ad fin.*, 'Twould make one scratch where't does not itch, To see fools live poor to die rich. 1737 : Ray, 232 [as in 1680 with very slight variation].

Scythe. *See* quot. 1846 : Denham, *Proverbs*, 17 (Percy S.), Where the scythe cuts, and the plough rives, No more fairies and bee-bikes [nests].

Sea complains it wants water, The. 1639 : Clarke, 6. 1670 : Ray, 192. 1732 : Fuller, No. 4740, The sea complains for want of water.

Sea hath fish for every man, The. 1605 : Camden, *Remains*, 334 (1870).

Sea refuses no river, The. 1703 : E. Ward, *Writings*, ii. 142, The old proverb, The sea and the gallows refuses none. 1732 : Fuller, No. 4741.

Sea, sail, Being on; being on land, settle. 1640 : Herbert, *Jac. Prudentum.* 1670 : Ray, 23.

Sea. *See also* Praise the sea.

Sealed with butter. 1546 : Heywood, *Proverbs*, Pt. II. ch. vii., Euery promise that thou therin dost ytter Is as sure as it were sealed with butter. 1584 : R. Scot, *Witchcraft*, bk. iii. ch. iv., Surely the indentures, containing those covenants, are sealed with butter. *c.* 1625 : Middleton, *Game of Chess*, I. i., I think they have seal'd this with butter. 1634 : S. Rowley, *Noble Soldier*, IV. ii. 1670 : Ray, 198, A warrant seal'd with butter.

Seaman, A. 1. *See* quot. 1670 : Ray, 218, A seaman if he carries a millstone will have a quail out of it. Spoken of the common mariners, if they can come at things that may be eat or drunk.

2. *A seaman is never broken till his neck be broken.* 1671 : Head and Kirkman, *Eng. Rogue*, ii. 194 [cited as a proverb].

Search not too curiously lest you find trouble. 1659 : Howell, 17.

Seasonable. *See* Snow (2).

Second blow makes the fray, The. 1597 : Bacon, *Colours of Good and Evil*, 10. 1642 : D. Rogers, *Matrim. Honour*, 196. 1732 : Fuller, No. 4742. 1875 : Cheales, *Proverb. Folk-Lore*, 107.

Second shaft, Shoot the, and perhaps thou mayest find again the first. 1659 : Howell, 19.

Second thoughts are best. [αἱ δεύτεραί πως φροντίδες σοφώτεραι.—Euripides, *Hippol.*, 438. Posteriores enim cogitationes, ut aiunt, sapientiores solent esse.—Cicero, *Phil.*, xii. 5.] 1586 : Pettie, tr. Guazzo's *Civil Convers.*, fo. 23, The second thoughts are euer the best. 1607–12 : Bacon, *Essays:* "Youth and Age," Generally youth is like the first cogitacions, not so wise as the second. 1681 : Dryden, *Span. Friar*, II. ii. 1715 : Centlivre, *Gotham Election*, sc. ii. 1787 : O'Keeffe, *The Farmer*, I. iii., Indeed, Molly, as second thoughts are best, I'll return to my first design, and have you. 1813 : Byron, *Letters*, etc., ii. 305 (Prothero), In composition I do not think *second* thoughts are the best, though *second* expressions may improve the first.

Second vice is lying, The, the first being that of owing money. 1732 : Fuller, No. 4743. 1736 : Franklin, *Way to Wealth*, in *Works*, i. 449 (Bigelow), . . . the first is running in debt.

Secret, *subs.* 1. *If you would know secrets, look for them in grief or pleasure.* 1640 : Herbert, *Jac. Prudentum.* 1670 : Ray, 23.

2. *Wherever there is a secret there must be something wrong.* 1837 : Lockhart, *Life of Scott*, ii. 42 [cited as " an old saying "].

Secret, *adj.* 1. *A secret foe gives a sudden blow.* 1736 : Bailey, *Dict.*, s.v. "Foe."

2. *See* quot. 1695 : Congreve, *Love for Love*, III. iii., He only is secret who never was trusted ; a satirical proverb upon our sex.

Sedgefield, Durham. Four sayings. *See* quots. 1846–59 : *Denham Tracts*, i. 85 (F.L.S.), (1) I've been as far travelled as Sedgefield, where the folks call strea—STRAW ! (2) Montpellier of the North. To meet with persons here of 80, 90, or even 100 years of age, is no uncommon circumstance. (3) To go at a thing, like a Sedgefield Hunt. Ibid., i. 86, (4) " A Sedgefield Chap "= The knave of clubs.

Sedgly curse. *See* **Devil** (79).

See, *verb.* 1. *I see much, but I say little, and do less.* 1546 : Heywood, *Proverbs,* Pt. I. ch. xi. 1576 : *Parad. Dainty Devices,* in *Brit. Bibliog.,* iii. 86 (1812), The best waie is in all worlds sent, Se all, saie nought, holde thee content.

2. *See for your love, buy for your money.* 1639 : Clarke, 79. 1670 : Ray, 184. 1736 : Bailey, *Dict.,* s.v. "Love."

3. *See me and see me not.* 1546 : Heywood, *Proverbs,* Pt. II. ch. v., If he plaie falsehed in felowship, plaie yee See me, and see me not. 1633 : Draxe, 46. 1639 : Clarke, 289.

4. *To see as far into a mill-stone as another.* 1540 : Palsgrave, *Acolastus,* sig. B3, Or wolde seeme to see farther in a myll stone, than excellent auctours haue done before vs. 1575 : Gascoigne, *Posies,* in *Works,* i. 11 (Cunliffe), They . . . woulde seeme to see verie farre in a mylstone. 1690 : Dryden, *Amphitryon,* V., I am a fool, I must confess ; but yet I can see as far into a mill-stone as the best of you. 1712 : Arbuthnot, *Law a Bott. Pit.,* Pt. IV. ch. v., He can see as far into a millstone as another ! 1778 : Burney, *Evelina,* Lett. xxv. 1911 : T. Edwardes, *Neighbourhood,* 36, I wur allers th' sort as could see through a brick wall fur as most folk.

5. *To see day.* *See* **Day** (13).

6. *We see not what is in the wallet behind.* 1639 : Clarke, 52, Wee see not what sits on our shoulder. 1732 : Fuller, No. 5453.

7. *Who sees thee by day will not seek thee by night.* 1659 : Howell, *Proverbs: Ital.-Eng.,* 2.

Seeing is believing. [Pluris est oculatus testis unus, quam auriti decem.—Plautus, *Truc.,* II. vi.] 1639 : Clarke, 90. 1706 : Farquhar, *Recruiting Officer,* IV. iii. 1850 : Smedley, *Frank Fairlegh,* ch. xxxi., " What an unbelieving Jew it is," said Archer ; " hand

him the list, and let him read it himself. Seeing is believing, they say." 1879 : *N. & Q.,* 5th ser., xi. 157, In this part of the country [Boston, Lincs] we say, " Seeing is believing, but feeling is the truth." 1901 : F. E. Taylor, *Lancs Sayings,* 9, Seein's believin', bu' feelin' 's God's truth. 1923 : A. Bennett, *Riceyman Steps,* Pt. II. ch. iii.

Seek, *verb.* 1. *As good seek nought as seek and find nought.* 1546 : Heywood, *Proverbs,* Pt. I. ch. xi.

2. *He that seeketh findeth.* Ibid., Pt. I. ch. x. 1578 : Florio, *First Fruites,* fo. 34. 1581 : B. Rich, *Farewell,* 128 (Sh. S.), As the proverbe is (he that sekes shall finde). 1633 : Draxe, 185.

3. *He that seeks to beguile is overtaken in his will.* 1578 : Florio, *First Fruites,* fo. 14, Who often seekes others to deceiue, doth rest oppressed and deceyued hym selfe. 1869 : Hazlitt, 186.

4. *He that seeks trouble never misses.* c. 1460 : in *Pol., Rel., and Love Poems,* 69 (E.E.T.S.), Who sechith sorwe, is by [his be] the receyte. 1612 : Shelton, *Quixote,* Pt. I. bk. iii. ch. vi., I heard ofttimes the curate . . . preach that " He which seeks the danger perisheth therein." 1640 : Herbert, *Jac. Prudentum.* 1732 : Fuller, No. 2291.

5. *Seek till you find and you'll not lose your labour.* 1678 : Ray, 200. 1732 : Fuller, No. 4089.

6. *To seek for a thing one would not find.* 1546 : Heywood, *Proverbs,* Pt. II. ch. v., But whan she seemed to be fixed in mynde, Rather to seeke for that she was lothe to fynde. 1591 : Harington, *Orl. Furioso,* bk. xliii., Notes, It is no wisdome to search for that a man would not find. 1659 : Howell, 7, I seek for a thing wife that I would not find.

7. *Who seeks what he should not, finds what he would not.* 1666 : Torriano, *Piazza Univ.,* 44.

Seldom comes a loan laughing home. c. 1320 : in *Reliq. Antiquæ,* i. 113 (1841), " Selde cometh lone lahynde home " ; Quoth Hendyng.

Seldom comes the better. Before 1272 : *MS. Temp. Hen. III.,* in Douce, *Ill. of Shakesp.,* 334 (1839), Seilde comed

se betere. 1519 : Horman, *Vulgaria*,
fo. 299, It is comynly sayd that selde
cometh the better. 1594 : Shakespeare, *Rich. III.*, II. iii. 1622 : Taylor
(Water-Poet), in *Works*, 2nd pagin., 14
(1630). 1740: North, *Examen*, 339,
Change, 'tis true, but seldom comes a
better. 1820 : Scott, *Abbot*, ch. vi., And
for Roland Graeme, though he may be
a good riddance in the main, yet what
says the very sooth proverb, "Seldom
comes a better."

Seldom dieth the ox. *See* **Ox** (6).

Seldom mosseth the stone. *See* **Rolling stone.**

Seldom seen soon forgotten. 1377 : in
Wright, *Pol. Poems*, i. 216 (Rolls Ser.,
1859), Selden seize [seen] and sone
forgete [refrain of song]. *c.* 1450:
in *Reliq. Antiquæ*, i. 25 (1841), She
sayth that she hath seen hit wreten,
That seldyn seen is soon for-yeten.
1546 : Heywood, *Proverbs*, Pt. I. ch. xi.
1620 : Middleton, *World Tost at Tennis*,
Epil. 1670 : Ray, 140. Cf. **Eye** (19);
and **Out of sight.**

Seldom thinks is at ease, He that.
c. 1460 : *How the Good Wife*, l. 85, At
ese he is that seldam thankithe.

Self do, self have. 1546 : Heywood,
Proverbs, Pt. I. ch. viii. 1593 : *Tell-
Trothes N. Yeares Gift*, 7 (N. Sh. S.).
1634 : Ford, *Perkin Warbeck*, I. ii., Self
do, self have—no more words ; win and
wear her. 1674 : Head and Kirkman,
Eng. Rogue, iii. 4. 1748 : Richardson,
Clarissa, i. 222 (1785). 1875 : Cheales,
Proverb. Folk-Lore, 137.

Self first, then your next best friend.
Oxfordsh. 1913 : *Folk-Lore*, xxiv. 76.

Self-love is a mote in every man's eye.
1670 : Ray, 141. 1732 : Fuller, No.
4093.

Self-praise is no recommendation.
1612 : Shelton, *Quixote*, Pt. I. bk. iii.
ch. ii., Which is such that if I do not
praise it, it is because men say that
proper praise stinks ; but my squire
will inform you what I am. 1852 :
Dickens, *Bleak House*, ch. lv. 1865 :
Dickens, *Mutual Friend*, bk. iv. ch. ii.

**Self-preservation is the first law of
nature.** Before 1614 : Donne, Βιαθά-
vaτos, sig. AA (1644) (O.), It is onely

upon this reason, that selfe-preserva-
tion is of Naturall Law. 1675 : Marvell, *Hodge's Vision from Monument*,
Self-preservation, nature's first great
law. Before 1680 : Butler, *Remains*,
ii. 27 (1759). 1720 : C. Shadwell, *Irish
Hospitality*, V. i., Self-preservation
shou'd exert it self, 'tis then indeed
the first principle of nature. 1751 :
Smollett, *P. Pickle*, ch. lvii. 1838 :
Dickens, *Twist*, ch. x.

Sell as markets go, You must. 1584 :
Greene, in *Works*, iii. 224 (Grosart), If
thou bee wise . . . make thy market
while the chaffer is set to sale. 1670 :
Ray, 23, A man must sell his ware after
the rates of ye market. 1732 : Fuller,
No. 5969.

Sell nothing on trust. *See* **Trust,**
subs. (2).

**Sell the bear's skin before the bear
has been caught, To.** 1580 : Lyly,
Euphues, 273 (Arber), I trusted so much
that I solde the skinne before the beast
was taken. 1647 : in *Polit. Ballads*,
20 (Percy S., No. 11), Yet they divide
the skinne Of the beare among them e're
they ha't. 1692 : L'Estrange, *Æsop*,
270 (3rd ed.), He bad me have a care
for the future, to make sure of the bear,
before I sell his skin. 1726 : Defoe,
Hist. of Devil, Pt. II. ch. viii. p. 276
(4th ed.), Indeed the devil may be said
to sell the bear-skin, whatever he buys.
1819 : Scott, *Leg. of Montrose*, ch. iii.,
Somewhat irregular, though, and smells
a little too much of selling the bear's
skin before he has hunted him.

Selsey. *See* **Chichester.**

Selvage showeth the cloth, The.
1611 : Cotgrave, s.v. "Maistre," We
say, the selvidge makes shew of the
cloth. 1670 : Ray, 141 [as in 1611].
1732 : Fuller, No. 4744.

Send, *verb.* 1. *He sendeth to the Eas
Indies for Kentish pippins.* Ibid., No.
2017.

2. *Send a fool. See* **Fool** (91).

3. *Send a wise man. See* **Wise** (33).

4. *Send him to the sea and he will not
get water.* 1683 : Meriton, *Yorkshire
Ale*, 83–7 (1697).

5. *Send not to market for trouble.*
1732 : Fuller, No. 4098.

6. *To send him for yard-wide pack-thread* = To send on a fool's errand. 1813 : Ray, 223.

September. 1. *As on the 8th* [September], *so for the next four weeks.* 1893 : Inwards, *Weather Lore*, 34.

2. *As September so the coming March.* Ibid., 33.

3. *Fair on September 1, fair for the month.* Ibid., 34.

4. *If on September 19 there is a storm from the south, a mild winter may be expected.* Derby. Ibid., 34.

5. *September, blow soft, Till the fruit's in the loft.* 1732 : Fuller, No. 6214. 1893 : Inwards, 34.

See also **Cuckoo** (8) and (12); **July** (10); and **June** (3).

Serjeant is the spawn of some decayed shop keeper, A. 1626: Overbury, *Characters:* "A Sargeant." 1659: Howell, 10.

Serpent by the tail, He holds the. 1813 : Ray, 75.

Serpent. *See also* **Snake**.

Serpents engender in still waters. 1732 : Fuller, No. 4100.

Servant and Servants. 1. *A servant and a cock should be kept but a year.* 1732 : Fuller, No. 389.

2. *A servant is known in the absence of his master.* 1659: Howell, *Proverbs: Ital.-Eng.*, 12. 1732 : Fuller, No. 390.

3. *A servant that is diligent. See* quots. 1590: Greene, *Works*, vii. 311 (Grosart), Whereupon an olde Englishe disticke. A servant that is diligent honest and good Must sing at his worke like a bird in the wood. *c.* 1597: Deloney, *Gentle Craft*, Pt. I. ch. x., It is an old prouerbe. They proue seruants kind and good, That sing at their businesse like birds in the wood.

4. *Don't take a servant off a midden* [dung-heap]. 1917 : Bridge, *Cheshire Proverbs*, 51.

5. *He that would be well served must know when to change his servants.* 1855 : Bohn, 396.

6. *If you pay not a servant his wages, he will pay himself.* 1732 : Fuller, No. 2778.

7. *If you would have a good servant, take neither a kinsman nor a friend.* 1659: Howell, *Proverbs: Span.-Eng.*, 1,

Neither take too young a boy, nor kinsman, nor one that is intreated for thy servant. 1855 : Bohn, 422.

8. *One must be a servant before that he can be a master.* 1633 : Draxe, 18. Cf. **Serve**, *verb* (2).

9. *Servants should put on patience when they put on a livery.* 1732: Fuller, No. 4101.

10. *Servants should see all and say nothing.* 1771 : Smollett, *Clinker*, in *Works*, vi. 3 (1817). 1819: Scott, *Ivanhoe*, ch. ii., Like good servants, let us hear and see, and say nothing. 1820 : Scott, *Abbot*, ch. vi. [as in 1819].

Serve, *verb.* 1. *He serves the poor with a thump on the back with a stone* = He is a miser. 1678 : Ray, 90.

2. *He that hath not served knows not how to command.* 1539 : Taverner, *Proverbs*, fo. 2, No man can be a good ruler, onles he hath bene fyrste ruled. 1578 : Florio, *First Fruites*, fo. 28, Who hath not serued can not commaund. 1629 : *Book of Meery Riddles*, Prov. 81. Cf. **Servant** (8).

3. *He that serves everybody is paid by nobody.* 1611 : Cotgrave, s.v. "Abbayer," He that serves a communaltie is controlled by every one, rewarded by none. 1732 : Fuller, No. 2295.

4. *He that serves well need not be afraid to ask his wages.* 1640 : Herbert, *Jac. Prudentum* [omitting "be afraid to"]. 1670 : Ray, 23. 1732 : Fuller, No. 2296.

5. *Serve God. See* **God**.

6. *To serve two masters. See* **No man can serve**.

7. *To serve two pigeons. See* **Pigeon** (4).

Service is no inheritance. 1412 : Hoccleve, *Regement*, l. 841 (E.E.T.S., Ext. Ser., 72), Seruyse, I wot wel, is non heritage. *c.* 1450: *Songs and Carols*, 22 (Warton Cl., 1856), For servyse is non erytage. 1509: Barclay, *Ship of Fools*, i. 106 (1874), Thus worldly seruyce is no sure herytage. 1600 : T. Heywood, 1 *Edw. IV.*, in *Works*, i. 51 (1874), Seruice is no heritage. 1640 : Herbert, *Jac. Prudentum.* 1712: Centlivre, *Perplex'd Lovers*, I. iii. 1759: Townley, *High Life below Stairs*, I. i. 1776: Mrs. Cowley, *Runaway*, V. i.

1830 : Marryat, *King's Own*, ch. x.
1841 : Dickens, *Barn. Rudge*, ch. lxxx.,
Though she was but a servant, and
knowed that servitudes was no in-
heritances.

Service without reward is punishment.
1604 : Herbert, *Jac. Prudentum*.

Service. *See also* **No service.**

Serving-man. *See* Young (8).

Set a good face on it. *See* **Good face.**

**Set my house afire only to roast his
eggs**, He. 1692 : L'Estrange, *Æsop*,
375 (3rd ed.), These are the people that
set their neighbours houses on fire to
roast their own eggs. 1732 : Fuller,
No. 2018.

Set up one's rest, To. This is a term
taken from the game of Primero. 1576 :
Lambarde, *Peramb. of Kent*, 430 (1826),
She resolved . . . to set up her last
rest, in hope to recover her losses againe.
1590 : Lodge, *Rosalynde*, 50 (Hunt. Cl.),
Aliena resolued there to set vp her
rest. 1592 : Shakespeare, *Romeo*, V. iii.
1653 : Middleton and Rowley, *Span.
Gipsy*, IV. iii., Set up thy rest, her
marriest thou or none. *c.* 1680 : L'Estrange, *Seneca's Epistles*, vii., Teach
me . . . to dispute with Socrates . . .
to set up my rest with Epicurus. 1768 :
Brooke, *Fool of Quality*, iii. 1811, Here
I counted to set up my rest for life.
1840 : Dickens, *Curiosity Shop*, ch.
lxxi., So we . . . will set up our rest
again among our boyish haunts. 1852 :
M. A. Keltie, *Reminisc. of Thought and
Feeling*, 165, As the estate had then to
be sold, it became a question where I
was to set up my rest.

Set up one's staff, To. 1573 : Harvey,
Letter-Book, 4 (Camden S.), He hath
set down his staf, and made his reckning.
1591 : Shakespeare, *Com. of Errors*, III.
i., Have at you with a proverb :—Shall
I set in my staff ? 1766 : Garrick,
Neck or Nothing, I. i., Then my young
master may e'en make a leg to his
fortune, and set up his staff somewhere
else. 1815 : Scott, *Mannering*, ch.
xix., Here, then, Mannering resolved,
for some time at least, to set up the
staff of his rest. 1826 : Scott, *Journal*,
13 Nov., She has set up the whole staff
of her rest in keeping literary society

about her. [In these last two passages,
Scott has curiously combined this and
the preceding proverbial phrase.]

Seven hours' sleep. *See* Sleep, *subs.* (1).

**Seven may be company but nine are
confusion.** 1630 : Brathwait, *Eng.
Gent.*, 178 (1641), Which use was
occasion of that adage, *Septem con-
vivium, novem convitium faciunt*; Seven
make a banquet, nine a riot. 1681 :
Robertson, *Phraseol. Generalis*, 598,
Seven at a feast, nine at a fray. 1732 :
Fuller, No. 4113.

Seven years = any indefinite period.
1362 : Langland, *Plowman*, A, v. 122,
Hit hedde ben vn-sold this seuen yer
so me god helpe ! *c.* 1460 : in Hazlitt,
Early Pop. Poetry, i. 170, For thou may
speke a word to-day That vij ʒer thens
may be for thoʒt. *c.* 1475 : *Rauf
Coilyear*, 25 (E.E.T.S.), Thair suld na
man be sa wyse, To gar me cum to
Parise, To luke quhair the King lyis,
In faith, this seuen yeir ! 1519 : *Four
Elements*, in Hazlitt, *Old Plays*, i. 47,
That is the best dance without a pipe,
That I saw this seven year. 1594 :
Lodge and Greene, *Looking Glasse*,
l. 246, [Thou] shalt not be worth a horse
of thine owne this seuen yeare. 1674 :
J. Howard, *Eng. Mounsieur*, II., I have
not seen you these seven years. *Wel-
bred*. . . . I tell you 'twas not half an
hour ago since you saw me. 1778 :
Burney, *Evelina*, Lett. xxiii., I don't
think I shall speak to you again these
seven years. 1889 : Peacock, *Manley,
etc., Gloss.*, 470 (E.D.S.), Seven-year-
end. A long but indefinite period.
1913 : E. M. Wright, *Rustic Speech, etc.*,
175, A long, indefinite period of time is :
from seven year end to seven year end,
for years long years and donkey's ears.

Severn, River. 1. *Blessed is the eye*.
See quots. 1659 : Howell, 21, Happy
is the eye that dwelleth twixt Severn
and the Wye. 1662 : Fuller, *Worthies*,
ii. 70 (1840), Blessed is the eye, That is
betwixt Severn and Wye. 1790 : Grose,
Prov. Gloss., s.v. " Herefordshire " [as
in 1662]. 1883 : Burne, *Shropsh. Folk-
Lore*, 584, Happy is the eye Between
Severn and Wye, But thrice happy he
Between Severn and Clee.

2. *Fix thy pale in Severn* [with intent to fence out his water], *Severn will be as before.* 1662 : Fuller, *Worthies*, iii. 549 (1840). 1790: Grose, *Prov. Gloss.*, s.v. " Montgomeryshire."

3. *You may as soon sip up the Severn and swallow Mavern* [Malvern]. 1659 : Howell, 20. 1670 : Ray, 258. 1790 : Grose, *Prov. Gloss.*, s.v. " Worcestershire."

Sexton has shaked his shoo [shovel] **at him, The.** 1917 : Bridge, *Cheshire Proverbs*, 120.

Sexton is a fatal musician, The. 1639 : Clarke, 215.

Shade your head and go east. 1864 : " Cornish Proverbs," in *N. & Q.*, 3rd ser., vi. 495.

Shadow, and lose the substance, Catch not at the. 1855 : Bohn, 335.

Shaft or a bolt of it, To make a. 1594 : Nashe, *Works*, iii. 254 (Grosart), To make a shaft or a bolt of this drumbling subiect of dreames. 1644–55 : Howell, *Letters*, I. iii. 24 (1726), The Prince is preparing for his journey ; I shall to it again closely when he is gone, or make a shaft or a bolt of it. 1823 : D'Israeli, *Cur. of Lit.* 2nd ser., i. 448 (1824), None but true toxophilites could have had such a proverb as " I will either make a shaft or a bolt of it" ! 1907 : Hackwood, *Old Eng. Sports*, 103, Hence the old English proverb, " I will either make a shaft or a bolt of it," signifying the determination that a thing shall not go unused.

Shaftesbury and Glastonbury. 1655 : Fuller, *Church Hist.*, bk. vi. § ii. (iv. 14), The country people had a proverb, that " if the Abbot of Glastonbury might marry the Abbess of Shaftesbury, their heir would have more land than the King of England." 1894 : *Somerset and Dorset N. & Q.*, iii. 189, If the Abbot of Glaston could have married the Abbess of Shaston, the King of England would be the poorer man.

Shake a Leicestershire man. *See* **Leicestershire.**

Shake a loose leg, To = To go " on the loose." 1869 : Hazlitt, 430.

Shake the kettle, and it'll sing. Ibid., 332.

Shake your ears, Go. 1573 : G. Harvey, *Letter-Book*, 42 (Camden S.), His Mastership may go shake his eares elswhere. 1601 : Shakespeare, *Twelfth Night*, II. iii., *Maria.* Go shake your ears. 1647 : in *Pol. Ballads*, 69 (Wright, Percy S.), And you may goe and shake your eares, Who had, and could not hold it. 1764: Mrs. F. Sheridan, *Dupe*, I. iii., March off and leave him to shake his ears.

Shall be, shall be, That which. *c.* 1386 : Chaucer, *Knight's Tale*, l. 608, As, whan a thing is shapen, it shal be. *c.* 1390 : Gower, *Conf. Amantis*, bk. i. l. 1714, Bot nede be mot that nede schal. 1546 : Heywood, *Proverbs*, Pt. II. ch. i., That shalbe, shalbe. 1604 : Marlowe, *Faustus*, I. i., What will be, shall be. 1639 : Clarke, 225.

Shame, *subs.* 1. *He has swallowed shame and drank after it* =He has no sense of shame left. 1830 : Forby, *Vocab. E. Anglia*, 433.

2. *He that has no shame has no conscience.* 1732 : Fuller, No. 2148.

3. *It's a shame to steal, but a worse to carry home.* 1639 : Clarke, 190, It's a shame to steale, but a greater shame to bring again. 1670 : Ray, 141. 1732 : Fuller, No. 2875.

4. *Shame in a kindred cannot be avoyded.* 1605 : Camden, *Remains*, 330 (1870).

5. *Shame is as it is taken.* 1534 : More, *Works*, 1253 (1557). 1546 : Heywood, *Proverbs*, Pt. I. ch. ix.

6. *Shame take him that shame thinketh.* Ibid., Pt. I. ch. ix. 1596 : Spenser, *F. Q.*, IV. vi. 61, " Shame be his meede," quoth he, " that meaneth shame." 1596 : Harington, *Metam. of Ajax*, 104 (1814), Wherefore shame to them that shame think. 1605 : Camden, *Remains*, 330 (1870). 1659 : Howell, 9.

7. *'Tis no shame to eat one's meat.* 1611 : Cotgrave, s.v. " Manger," He thats ashamed to eat is ashamed to live. 1672 : Walker, *Parœm.*, 10.

Shameful leaving is worse than shameful eating. 1894 : Northall, *Folk Phrases*, 22 (E.D.S.).

Shameless beggar. *See* **Beggar** (3).

Shameless craving must have a

shameless nay. 1546 : Heywood, *Proverbs*, Pt. I. ch. xi. [with " Shameful " for first word]. 1670 : Ray, 141. 1754 : Berthelson, *Eng. - Danish Dict.*, s.v. " Shameless."

Shameless is graceless, He that is. 1732 : Fuller, No. 2192.

Shankey Hall. *See* quot. 1846–59 : *Denham Tracts*, i. 69 (F.L.S.), Like Shankey Hall, he takes no hints. A highly popular bishoprick [Durham] proverb.

Share and share alike. 1611 : Cotgrave, s.v. " Escot," Whereat every guest paies his part, or, share and share like. 1635 : in *Somers Tracts*, vii. 191, (1811). Not share and share alike, but to every each one the more according to their defects. 1670 : Ray, 218, Share and share like, some all, and some never a whit. *Leonina societas.* 1821 : Scott, *Pirate*, ch. xvii., They say, that a' man share and share equal-aquals in the creature's ulzie. 1914 : Lucas, *Landmarks*, ch. xxxiv., That's the way, Sergison, in married life ; share and share alike.

Sharp as a cobbler's elsin [awl]. 1855 : Robinson, *Whitby Gloss.*, 52.

Sharp as a needle. Before 1000 : *Souls Address*, 120 (O.), ȝifer hatte se wyrm, þe þa eaȝlas beoð nædle scearpran. 1552 : Huloet, *Abced.*, sig. Ee1, Sharpe lyke a nedle. 1566 : Adlington, tr. Apuleius, bk. vii., Sharp thorns, as sharp as needles. 1607 : T. Heywood, *Fair Maide*, in *Works*, ii. 25 (1874). Before 1700 : quoted in *N. & Q.*, 3rd ser., xii. 341, With a stomach as sharp as a needle. 1725 : Bailey, tr. Erasmus' *Colloq.*, 277. 1849 : Lytton, *Caxtons*, Pt. XVII. ch. i. 1872 : Hardy, *Greenwood Tree*, Pt. IV. ch. ii., Lawyer Green—a man as sharp as a needle.

Sharp as a razor. 1519 : Horman, *Vulgaria*, fo. 277, My wodknyfe is as sharpe as a rasur. 1577 : *Misogonus*, IV. i., Take my penknif then, ites as sharpe as a racer. 1694 : D'Urfey, *Quixote*, Pt. I. Act I. sc. ii. 1720 : Gay, *Poems*, ii. 279 (Underhill), Her glance is as the razor keen. 1830 : Scott, *Doom of Devorgoil*, III. ii., Your razor's polish'd, But, as the proverb goes, 'tis

cruel sharp. 1907 : De Morgan, *Alice-for-Short*, ch. viii.

Sharp as a thorn. 14th cent.: *Early Eng. Met. Rom.*, 15 (Camden. S.), Als scharpe as a thorn. *c.* 1480 : *Early Miscell.*, 33 (Warton Cl., 1855), And al here eyrns wer scharpe as any thornus. 1648 : Herrick, *Hesperides*, No. 444, He's sharp as thorn. 1670 : Ray, 207.

Sharp as vinegar. 1631 : Mabbe, *Celestina*, 110 (T.T.), And poure forth words as sharpe as vineger. 1693 : D'Urfey, *Richmond Heiress*, II. i., She's as sharp as vinegar this morning. 1737 : Ray, 225. 1821 : Scott, *Kenilworth*, ch. xxvii., Thou art as sharp as vinegar this afternoon !

Sharper the blast, The shorter 'twill last, The. 1875 : Cheales, *Proverb. Folk-Lore*, 19.

Sharply chides is ready to pardon, He that. 1620 : Shelton, *Quixote*, Pt. II. ch. lxx. 1732 : Fuller, No. 2298 [with " the most " before " ready "].

Sharply too ! says Jack Chumley. 1883 : Burne, *Shropsh. Folk-Lore*, 591.

Sharp's the word. 1709 : Cibber, *Rival Fools*, I., Sharp's the word ! we'll have half ours too. 1720 : *Vade Mecum for Malt-worms*, Pt. II. 24, Cry Sharp's the word, and bite that deepest can. 1854 : Dickens, *Hard Times*, bk. iii. ch. vii., Thay farewell to your family, and tharp'th the word. 1896 : Doyle, *Rodney Stone*, ch. i. 1922 : Weyman, *Ovington's Bank*, ch. xvii., Queer old place, and—sharp's the word, here we are.

Sharp stomach makes short devotion, A. 1639 : Clarke, 272. 1670 : Ray, 142. 1732 : Fuller, No. 4118 [in the plural].

Sheared. *See* quot. 1914 : *Devonsh. Assoc. Trans.*, xlvi. 92, " When it is sheared, it likes to be leared." Used of lambs and then applied as a proverb to persons (Devon).

Shears between them, But a pair of = little or no difference. 1579 : Lyly, *Euphues*, 46 (Arber), And as it were but a paire of sheeres to goe betwene their natures. 1603 : Shakespeare, *Meas. for Meas.*, I. ii. 1611 : Middleton, *Roaring Girl*, III. iii., One pair of shears sure cut out both your coats. 1626 : Overbury,

Characters: "An Apparator," There
went but a paire of sheeres between
him and the pursivant of hell, for they
both delight in sinne. 1633 : Rowley,
Match at Midnight, II. *c.* 1791 : Pegge,
Derbicisms, 120 (E.D.S.), " Only shears
between them," both alike.

She devils are hard to tame. *c.* 1550 :
in Hazlitt, *Pop. Poetry*, iii. 240.

Shed riners with a whaver, To. 1836 :
Wilbraham, *Cheshire Gloss.*, 68 (2nd
ed.), " To shed riners with a whaver "
. . . means to surpass any thing skilful
or adroit by something still more so.
1917 : Bridge, *Cheshire Proverbs*, 143.

Sheen. *See* **Sion.**

Sheep. [There are two groups of
sheep sayings, none of the members of
which occurs elsewhere, and it is a little
doubtful whether they were ever truly
proverbial. It will be convenient to
enter both groups here. A. 1550–3 :
The Decaye of England, 96 (E.E.T.S.),
The more shepe, the dearer is the woll.
The more shepe, the dearer is the
motton. The more shepe, the dearer
is the beffe. The more shepe, the
dearer is the corne. The more shepe,
the skanter is the whit meate. The
more shepe, the fewer egges for a
peny. Before 1641: Best, *Farming Book*
(Surtees S., No. 33), For as the sayinge
is, Sheepe that will live in winter, will
live and thrive in summer ; and sheepe
that growe fleshy with foure teeth, will
growe fatte with eight (p. 3). . . . The
husbandman's sayinge is, that the losse
of an ewe's lambe is as greate as the
losse of a cowe's calfe (p. 5). . . . Hence
ariseth the shepheardes phrase, that
Whiles the grasse groweth, Ewe dryeth,
lambe dyeth (p. 5). . . . The countrey
proverbe is, The man that is aboute to
clippe his sheepe, Must pray for two
faire dayes and one faire weeke (p. 20).]

1. *A black sheep is a biting beast.*
c. 1550 : *Six Ballads*, 4 (Percy S.), The
blacke shepe is a perylous beast. 1598 :
T. Bastard, *Chrestoleros*, bk. iv. Ep. 20,
Till now I thought the prouerbe did
but iest, Which said a blacke sheepe
was a biting beast.

2. *As good be hanged for a sheep as a
lamb.* 1678 : Ray, 350 [" old sheep "

and " young lamb "]. 1748 : Richardson, *Clarissa*, i. 60 (1785), So in for the
lamb, as the saying is, *in for the sheep.*
1841: Dickens, *Barn. Rudge*, ch. liii.,
Others . . . comforted themselves with
the homely proverb, that, being hanged
at all, they might as well be hanged for
a sheep as a lamb. 1920 : O. Onions,
Case in Camera, ii. 42, Not worth while
going home for lunch now. May as
well be hung for a sheep as a lamb. I
wonder if they've got a snack of anything here ? 1924 : Shaw, *Saint Joan*,
sc. ii.

3. *Every time the sheep bleats, it loses
a mouthful.* 1623 : Wodroephe, *Spared
Houres*, 476, The yewe that doth bleate
doth loose the most of her meate.
1666 : Torriano, *Piazza Univ.*, 23, The
sheep that bleats, loseth its pasture.
1732 : Fuller, No. 1471. 1869 : Spurgeon, *John Ploughman*, ch. v.

4. *He loves sheep's flesh well that eats
the wool.* *c.* 1460 : *Good Wyfe wold a
Pylgremage*, l. 71 (E.E.T.S.), He wyll
lowys scheppis flesche, That wettyth
his bred in woll. Before 1500 : in Hill,
Commonplace-Book, 131 (E.E.T.S.), He
loveth well moton, that weteth his bred
in woll. 1546 : Heywood, *Proverbs*,
Pt. II. ch. v. [as in Hill, but with
" sheeps flesh " for " moton "]. 1696 :
D'Urfey, *Quixote*, Pt. III. Act I., He
loves mutton well that can dine upon
the wool. 1732 : Fuller, No. 1979 [as
in 1696, but with " eats " for " can dine
upon "]. 1816 : Scott, *Antiquary*, ch.
xliv., They liked mutton weel that
licket where the yowe lay.

5. *He that hath sheep, etc.* *See* quots.
1523 : Fitzherbert, *Husbandry*, 74
(E.D.S.), For it is an olde sayinge : he
that hath both shepe, swyne, and bees,
slepe he, wake he, he maye thryue.
1634 : C. Butler, *Feminine Monarchie*,
139, The proverb . . . Who so keepe
wel sheepe and bee'n, Sleepe or wake,
their thrift cooms in.

6. *He that makes himself a sheep shall
be eaten by the wolf.* 1583 : Melbancke,
Philotinus, sig. Bb4, He . . . that will
needes be a sheepe, cannot greatly
grudge to be bitten with a fox. 1593 :
Harvey, *Works*, ii. 38 (Grosart), It was

wont to be said by way of a prouerbe ;
Hee that will be made a sheepe, shall
find wolues inough. 1619 : B. Rich,
Irish Hubbub, 4, He that will make
himselfe a sheepe, it is no matter though
the wolues doe eat him. 1651 : Herbert,
Jac. Prudentum, 2nd ed. 1710 : S.
Palmer, *Moral Essays on Proverbs*, 360.
1773 : Franklin, *Works*, v. 86 (Bigelow), There is much truth in the Italian
saying, *Make yourselves sheep, and the
wolves will eat you.* 1869 : Spurgeon,
John Ploughman, ch. iv., He that makes
himself a sheep, will find that the wolves
are not all dead.

7. *It is a foolish sheep that makes the
wolf his confessor.* 1670 : Ray, 23.

8. *It is possible for a sheep to kill a
butcher.* Ibid., 22 [with " ram " for
" sheep "]. 1732 : Fuller, No. 3010.

9. *Let the black sheep keep the white.*
1639 : Clarke, 69.

10. *One scabbed sheep infects a whole
flock.* Before 1500 : Hill, *Commonplace-Book*, 129 (E.E.T.S.), One skabbid
shepe infectith all the folde. 1586 : L.
Evans, *Withals Dict. Revised*, sig. C1.
1593 : Nashe, *Works*, iv. 159 (Grosart).
1630 : Taylor (Water-Poet), *Works*, 3rd
pagin., 59, One scabbed sheep's enough
to spoyle a flocke. 1640 : T. Rawlins,
Rebellion, IV., One tainted sheep mars
a whole flock. 1732 : Fuller, No. 3792,
One scabby sheep is enough to infect
the whole flock. 1796 : White, *Falstaff's Letters*, 16, The tainted wether
doth infect the whole flock. 1846 :
Denham, *Proverbs*, 7 (Percy S.), . . .
will mar the whole flock.

11. *One sheep follows another.* 1816 :
Scott, *Old Mortality*, ch. xxxvi., One
sheep will leap the ditch when another
goes first.

12. *Shear sheep that has them.* 1678 :
Ray, 201.

13. *Shear your sheep in May, And
shear them all away.* 1670 : Ray, 41.
1732 : Fuller, No. 6195. 1893 : Inwards, *Weather Lore*, 26.

14. *The dust raised by the sheep does
not choke the wolf.* 1732 : Fuller, No.
4491.

15. *The lone sheep's in danger of the
wolf.* 1639 : Clarke, 117. 1670 : Ray, 53.

16. *There's a scabby sheep in every
flock.* 1872 : J. Glyde, jr., *Norfolk
Garland*, 150 [more usually a " black
sheep "].

17. *To cast a sheep's eye.* 1577 : J.
Grange, *Golden Aphroditis*, sig. Di, On
whom he many a sheepish eye did cast.
c. 1580 : *Tom Tyler*, l. 124, p. 4 (Malone
S.), If he look but awry ; or cast a
sheeps eye. *c.* 1663 : Davenant, *Play-
House to be Let*, V., On Cleopatra
he has cast a sheep's eye. 1738 :
Swift, *Polite Convers.*, Dial. I., I have
often seen him cast a sheep's eye out
of a calf's head at you. 1855 : Kingsley, *West. Ho!*, ch. ii., What a plague
business had he making sheep's eyes at
his daughter ?

18. *To lose the sheep for a ha'porth of
tar.* Tar is used to protect sores or
wounds in sheep from flies, and the
consequent generation of worms. 1600 :
Day, *Blind Beggar*, V., To him, father ;
never lose a hog for a halfp'north of tar.
1643 : Wither, *Se Defendendo*, 5 (Spens.
S.), Much like the saving of a half-peny
worth of tarre by the losse of a hogge,
jeered in an English proverb. 1749 :
W. Ellis, *Shepherd's Sure Guide, etc.*,
273, That a sheep may not, according
to the proverb, be lost for want of a
halfpennyworth of tar. 1846 : Denham, *Proverbs*, 7 (Percy S.), Lose not a
hog for a halfpenny worth of tar. 1878 :
Smiles, *Lives of Engineers*, iv. 214, He
at length came to the conclusion . . .
that it was better " not to lose a sheep
for a ha'porth of tar."

19. *You have no more sheep to shear.*
1678 : Ray, 344.

20. *You may shear your sheep, When
the elder blossoms peep.* 1893 : Inwards, *Weather Lore*, 153.

See also **Better to give** ; **Crow** (7) ;
Every hand ; **February** (7) ; **Lazy sheep** ;
Leap Year ; **Lion** (1) ; **Many frosts** ;
Naked ; **Ragged** ; **St. Gervatius** ; **Some
good** ; **Soon goes** ; **Stamps** ; **Wolf**,
passim ; **Wool** (5) ; and **You** (7).

Sheep-skin shoe lasts not long, A.
1732 : Fuller, No. 393.

**Sheffield park is ploughed and sown,
When, Then little England hold thine
own.** 1678 : Ray, 340. 1790 : Grose,

Prov. Gloss., s.v. "Yorkshire." 1878 :
Folk-Lore Record, i. 165.

She hath eaten a snake. 1580 : Lyly,
Euphues, 368 (Arber), Therfore hath it
growen to a prouerb in Italy, when one
seeth a woman striken in age to looke
amiable, he saith she hath eaten a
snake.

**Shelter against every storm, 'Tis good
to have a.** 1665 : R. Howard, *Committee*, I. [called "a wise saying"].

**Sheltering under an old hedge, It is
good.** 1674 : *Learne to lye Warm; or,
An Apology for that Proverb, 'Tis good
sheltering under an Old Hedge* [title of
tract]. 1732 : Fuller, No. 2939. 1818 :
Scott, *Heart of Midl.*, ch. xlvi., It's
better sheltering under an auld hedge
than under a new-planted wood. Cf.
Old, E (7).

Shermanbury. *See* **Bolney.**

She that will not. *See* **He that will
not.**

Shew. *See* **Show.**

Shields. *See* quots. 1. 1846–59 :
Denham Tracts, i. 57 (F.L.S.), We'll a'
gan' together like the folks o' Shields.
1892 : Heslop, *Northumb. Words*, 2
(E.D.S.), Aall togither, like the folks o'
Shields.
2. 1846–59 : *Denham Tracts*, i. 46
(F.L.S.), Go to Shields And fish for eels
[a Newcastle phrase].

Shields. *See also* **Newcastle.**

Shilling to ninepence, To bring a.
1546 : Heywood, *Proverbs*, Pt. II. ch.
v., To bryng a shillyng to ix pens
quickely. 1560 : T. Wilson, *Rhetorique*,
185 (1909), But yet, sir, your cunning
was such that you brought a shilling
to nine pence. 1755 : *Connoisseur*, No.
91, The old saying was inverted, and
we lost eleven-pence out of a shilling.

Shilling. *See also* **Penny** (2).

Shin of beef. *See* quot. 1871 : *N.
& Q.*, 4th ser., vii. 9, Useful as a shin of
beef, which has a big bone for the big
dog, a little bone for the little dog, and
a sinew for the cat [an old Shropshire
saying].

Ship and Ships. 1. *As broken a ship
has come to land.* 1732 : Fuller, No.
668. 1800 : Colman, jr., *The Review*,
I. ii., Far more unlikelier ships have

com'd into harbour than this. 1823 :
Scott, *St. Ronan's*, ch. x., As broken a
ship's come to land.
2. *A ship and a woman are ever repairing,* (or *trimming*). 1602–3 : Manningham, *Diary*, 12 (Camden S.), To
furnish a shipp requireth much trouble,
But to furnishe a woman the charges
are double. 1619 : *Helpe to Discourse*,
80 (1640), There are two things that
cannot bee too much trimmed, and
what are they ? A ship and a woman.
1640 : Herbert, *Jac. Prudentum*, . . .
repairing. 1669 : *New Help to Discourse*, 310, A ship and a woman always
trimming. 1732 : Fuller, No. 394, A
ship, a mill, and a woman are always
repairing.
3. *A ship under sail, a man in complete armour, a woman with a great belly
are three of the handsomest sights.* 1659 :
Howell, 2.
4. *Ships fear fire more than water.*
1640 : Herbert, *Jac. Prudentum.* 1670 :
Ray, 24. 1732 : Fuller, No. 4153.
5. *To lose the ship. See* **Sheep** (18).
See also **Woman** (47).

Shipshape and Bristol fashion. 1826 :
Scott, *Chron. of Canongate*, Introd.,
Stretching our fair canvas to the breeze,
all ship-shape and Bristol fashion.
1840 : Dana, *Two Years before Mast*,
ch. xx., Her decks were as white as
snow . . . everything on board "ship-
shape and Bristol fashion." 1914 :
N. & Q., 11th ser., ix. 446, When a seaman wished to speak well of his vessel,
he declared that with her things were
"shipshape and Bristol fashion," although he hailed from another port.

**Shipwreck be your sea-mark, Let
another's.** 1855 : Bohn, 440.

Shires, To come out of the. 1735 :
Pegge, *Kent. Proverbs*, in E.D.S., No. 12,
p. 78, To come out of the Shires. This
is a proverbial saying relative to any
person who comes from a distance.
1875 : Parish, *Sussex Dict.*, 103, The
true Sussex man divides the world into
two parts. Kent and Sussex form one
division, and all the rest is "The
Sheeres." 1882 : *N. & Q.*, 6th ser., v.
496, The natives [of Kent] speak with
contempt of distant compatriots who

live " down in the sheers." Cf. **Rodings.**

Shirt full of sore bones, I will give you a. 1732 : Fuller, No. 2637.

Shirt knew my design, I'd burn it, If my. 1654: *Clarke Papers*, iii. 12 (Camden), (O.), The designe is secrett, knowne to the designer onely, whoe saith if hee thought his shirt knew it hee would burne it. 1732 : Fuller, No. 2695.

Shitten luck is good luck. An unsavoury saying very freely used in the 17th and 18th centuries. 1639–61: in *Rump Songs*, Pt. I. 137 (1662, repr. 1874). 1691: *Merry Drollery*, 261 (Ebsworth). 1709: Ward, *Acc. of Clubs*, 208 (1756). 1785 : Grose, *Class. Dict. Vulgar Tongue*, s.v. " Luck." 1894: Northall, *Folk Phrases*, 22 (E.D.S.).

Shive of a cut loaf, It is safe taking a. " Shive "=slice. 1600 : Shakespeare, *Titus Andr.*, II. i., And easy it is Of a cut loaf to steal a shive, we know. 1670: Ray, 52. 1732: Fuller, No. 3012 [" slice " for " shive "]. 1828 : Scott, in Lockhart's *Life*, vii. 115, " A shave [? misprint for " shive "] from a broken loaf " is thought as little of by the male set of delinquents as by the fair frail. 1901: F. E. Taylor, *Lancs Sayings*, 11, A shoive off a cut loaf's never miss't.

Shive of my own loaf, A. 1670 : Ray, 188.

Shoe and Shoes, *subs.* 1. *His shoe pinches him* = He is drunk. 1745 : Franklin, *Drinker's Dict.*, in *Works*, ii. 26 (Bigelow).

2. *His shoes are made of running leather.* 1575 : Churchyard, *Chippes*, 130 (Collier), My minde could never rest at hoem, My shoes wear maed of running leather suer. 1611 : Cotgrave, s.v. " Divague," Straying, ranging . . . wandring up and downe, whose shooes are made of running leather. 1754 : Berthelson, *Eng.-Danish Dict.*, s.v. " Run." 1831 : Hone, *Year-Book*, col. 1544, This child's shoes are made of running leather.

3. *The shoe will hold with the sole.* 1546 : Heywood, *Proverbs*, Pt. II. ch. v. 1595 : *Pedlars Prophecy*, l. 730 (Malone

S.), Who should hold with the shoe but the sole ? 1605 : Camden, *Remains*, 333 (1870). 1670 : Ray, 142. 1732 : Fuller, No. 4759, The sole holdeth with the upper leather.

4. *Tip at the toe. See* quot. 1885 : J. T. Varden, *E. Anglian Handbook*, 115, A Suffolk rhyme teaches us the significance of the " wear of shoes " :—
Tip at the toe, live to see woe ; Wear at the side, live to be a bride ; Wear at the ball, live to spend all ; Wear at the heel, live to save a deal.

5. *To know where the shoe pinches.* c. 1386 : Chaucer, *Merchant's Tale*, l. 309, I wot best wher wringeth me my sho. 1541: Coverdale, *Christ. State Matrimony*, sig. B5, It maye easely be perceaued where the shoe wryngeth them. 1580 : Lyly, *Euphues*, 413 (Arber), I see that others maye gesse where the shooe wringes, besides him that weares it. 1609: Rowlands, *Whole Crew, etc.*, 4 (Hunt. Cl.), Ah little do you know where my shoo wrings. 1668 : Dryden, *Sir Martin Mar-all*, IV. i., I know where it is that your shoe wrings you. 1693 : Urquhart, *Rabelais*, bk. iii. ch. xxviii., That is not . . . the thing that I fear ; nor is it there where my shoe pinches. 1714: Ozell, *Molière*, vi. 6, Tho' he has not yet told me any thing, I could lay a wager that there the shoe pinches. 1869: Spurgeon, *John Ploughman*, ch. xvi., Those who wear the shoe know best where it pinches. 1922 : Weyman, *Ovington's Bank*, ch. xxxvii., But there, your honour knows best where the shoe pinches.

Shoe, *verb.* 1. *To shoe the colt.* 1828 : Carr, *Craven Dialect*, i. 83, " To shoe the colt " is also a quaint expression of demanding a contribution from a person on his first introduction to any office or employment. 1886 : Elworthy, *West Som. Word-Book*, 664 (E.D.S.), Shoe a colt. To cause to pay colt-ale, or the fine customary on first entering an employment. 1924 : *N. & Q.*, cxlvii. 126, The old custom of " shoeing the colt " still obtains in Hampshire.

2. *To shoe the goose.* c. 1410 : Hoccleve, *Poems*, 13 (1796), Ye medle of al

thyng, ye moot shoo the goos. Before
1529: Skelton, *Colin Clout*, l. 198, What
hath lay men to do The gray gose for to
sho ? 1583 : Stubbes, *Anat. of Abuses*,
117 (N. Sh. S.), But if this [gold in the
lawyer's palm] be wanting, than farewel
clyent ; he may go shooe the goose for
any good successe he is like to haue of
his matter. 1604 : Breton, in *Works*,
ii. *k* 5 (Grosart), And though I be no
great wise man, yet I can doe something
else, then shooe the goose for my liuing.
1801 : Miss Edgeworth, *Lame Jervas*,
ch. iii., " The smith that will meddle
with all things may go shoe the goslings," an old proverb which . . . became ever after a favourite of mine.
1902 : *N. & Q.*, 9th ser., x. 475, . . .
One of the most curious carvings in
the church formerly belonging to the
monastery of St. John at Beverley, in
the East Riding of Yorkshire, repre-
sents a blacksmith in the absurd act of
hammering a shoe on a goose's foot.

**Shoeing-horn to help on his gloves,
He calls for a.** 1732 : Fuller, No. 1816.

Shoemaker. *See* **Cobbler** ; and **Six awls.**

Shoemaker's son is a prince born, A.
c. 1597 : Deloney, *Gentle Craft*, ch. ix.,
Then answeared Vrsula, My Royall
Father, a shoomakers son is a Prince
born. 1637 : L. Price, in *Pepysian
Garland*, 445 (Rollins), Shoemakers
sonnes were princes borne. *c.* 1710 :
Roxb. Ballads, vii. 35 (B.S.).

Shoemaker's stocks, In the = in
shoes too small for the feet. 1678 :
Ray, 347.

**Shoemaker's wife, Who is worse shod
than the?** 1546 : Heywood, *Proverbs*,
Pt. I. ch. xi. 1560 : T. Wilson, *Rhetorique*, 119 (1909). 1593 : *Pass. Morrice*,
69 (N. Sh. S.). Before 1680 : Butler,
Remains, ii. 165 (1759), No man goes
worse shod than the shoemaker. 1690 :
New Dict. Canting Crew, sig. L2. 1772 :
Graves, *Spirit. Quixote*, bk. iii. ch. ii.,
But, says he, the shoemaker's wife often
goes in ragged shoes. 1851 : Borrow,
Lavengro, iii. 191, It is said that the
household of the shoemaker invariably
go worse shod than that of any other
craft.

Shoot, *verb.* 1. *He hath shot his fry.*

1611 : Cotgrave, s.v. " Pouvoir," He
hath shot his frie . . . done the worst
or most he can. 1639 : Clarke, 223.
1828 : Carr, *Craven Dialect*, i. 168, " To
shoot one's fry," to lose the good
opinion of others which he had once
possessed.

2. *He shooteth well that hits the mark.*
1659 : Howell, 20.

3. *He shoots like a crow-keeper.*
c. 1605 : Shakespeare, *Lear*, IV. vi., That
fellow handles his bow like a crow-
keeper. *c.* 1770 : Barrington, *Hist. of
Archery*, quoted in Brady, *Varieties of
Lit.*, 22, So that " to shoot like a crow-
keeper " became a proverb.

4. *He shoots like a gentleman.* 1545 :
Ascham, *Toxoph.*, 150 (Arber), Tel me
somwhat, how I should shoote nere
leste that prouerbe myght be sayd
iustlye of me some-tyme, He shootes
lyke a gentle man fayre and far of.

5. *He shoots wide of the mark.* 1562 :
Heywood, *Three Hund. Epigr.*, No. 184,
He shooteth wyde. 1659 : Howell, 7.
1680 : D'Urfey, *Virtuous Wife*, I., You
are merry sir, and shoot wide o' th'
mark. 1709 : Mandeville, *Virgin Unmask'd*, 134 (1724), The King of France
has several times shot wide of the mark.
1736 : Bailey, *Dict.*, s.v. " Mark," To
shoot wide of the mark.

6. *He that shoots always aright forfeits his arrow.* 1659 : Howell, *Proverbs: Brit.-Eng.*, 34.

7. *He that shoots oft shall at last hit
the mark.* [Quis est enim, qui totum
diem jaculans non aliquando collineat ?
—Cicero, *De Divin.*, ii. 59.] 1551 :
Robinson, tr. More's *Utopia*, 52 (Arber).
1732 : Fuller, No. 2276, He that's
always shooting, must sometimes hit.

8. *I have shot my bolt.* 1826 : Brady,
Varieties of Lit., 21, The implement
shot from the cross-bow is called . . .
by the English a bolt. Hence the saying, " I have shot my bolt." Cf. **Fool**
(24).

9. *To be shot with one's own feathers.*
1587 : Underdoune, *Heliodorus*, bk. ii.
74 (T.T.), That which greeveth me
most, is that (as the proverbe saith)
shee useth mine owne fethers against
mee. 1710 : S. Palmer, *Moral Essays*

on *Proverbs*, 332, We are often shot with
our own feathers.

10. *To shoot at a pigeon and kill a
crow.* 1639: Clarke, 2. 1670: Ray,
189. 1787: Colman, jr., *Inkle and
Yarico*, III. i., But of all the shots, he's
the worst in the art Who shoots at
a pigeon and kills a crow. 1850:
Planché, *Extravag.* iv. 104 (1879).

11. *To shoot at rovers. See Run (14).*

Shorn-bug. *See* quot. 1911: A. S.
Cooke, *Off Beaten Track in Sussex*, 285,
" To eat shorn-bug for dinner " is the
Sussex way of expressing the extremity
of poverty. " Shorn-bug " is a beetle.

**Short acquaintance brings repent-
ance.** 1670: Ray, 142.

Short and sharp. 1546: Heywood,
Proverbs, Pt. II. ch. ii., All thing that is
sharpe is short, folke haue tolde. 1655:
Fuller, *Church Hist.*, bk. ix. § v. (19),
[comment on letter by Lord Burleigh]
Short but sharp. 1926: Phillpotts,
Yellow Sands, III., I see a way—short
and sharp.

Short and sweet. 1539: Taverner,
Erasm. Prov., 68 (1552) (O.), The Eng-
lysh prouerbe is thus pronounced.
Short and swete. c. 1580: Lodge,
Defence of Plays, etc., 28 (Sh. S.),
Shorte and sweete if I were
judge. 1589: Puttenham, *Eng. Poesie*,
68 (Arber). 1593: Peele, *Edward
I.*, sc. viii. 1637: Shirley, *Young
Admiral*, IV. iii. 1778: H Brooke,
Contending Brothers, I. vii., A few words
in full : multum in parvo, short and
sweet ! 1883: R. L. S., *Treasure I.*, ch.
ix. 1901: F. E. Taylor, *Lancs Sayings*,
6, Short an' sweet, like a donkey's
gallop.

Short boughs, long vintage. 1640:
Herbert, *Jac. Prudentum.*

Short counsel is good counsel. 1828:
Scott, *Fair Maid*, ch. vii., " Short rede,
good rede," said the Smith. 1846–59:
Denham Tracts, i. 98 (F.L.S.), Short
counsel is good counsel ; slay ye the
bishop. 1892: Heslop, *Northumb.
Words*, 570 (E.D.S.), The proverb is
specially associated with the death of
Walcher, the first Bishop of Durham
appointed by William the Conqueror.
At Gateshead the bishop had met the

leaders of the people, and on retiring to
the church the cry was raised, " Short
rede, good rede, slay the bishop." The
church was thereupon set on fire, and
the bishop was slain. A.D. 1080.

**Short cut of a way without some ill
way, There is no.** 1732: Fuller, No.
4921.

Shortest answer is doing, The. 1640:
Herbert, *Jac. Prudentum.*

Short harvests. *See* **Harvest (5).**

Short horse is soon curried, A. Before 1500: in Hill, *Commonplace-Book*,
128 (E.E.T.S.). 1571: R. Edwards,
Damon and Pithias, in Hazlitt, *Old
Plays*, iv. 33. 1616: Breton, in *Works*,
ii. *e* 6 (Grosart). 1637: Heywood, *Royal
King*, II., Here's a short horse soone
curryed. 1732: Fuller, No. 395. 1820:
Scott, *Abbot*, ch. xi., A short tale
is soon told—and a short horse soon
curried. 1883: Burne, *Shropsh. Folk-
Lore*, 589. 1917: Bridge, *Cheshire Proverbs*, 4, A little horse is soon wispt,
And a pretty girl is soon kist.

Short life and a merry, A. 1654:
Gayton, *Pleasant Notes Don Q.*, 101,
The indicted cry a merry life and a
short. 1660: Tatham, *Rump*, I., A
short life and a merry life, I cry. 1754:
Connoisseur, No. 50, A short life and a
merry one was their favourite maxim.
1855: Kingsley, *West. Ho!*, ch. xxxii.

Short pleasure long lament. 1468:
Coventry Mys., 32 (Sh. S.), Schort lyk-
yng xal be longe bought. 1556: G.
Colvile, tr. Boethius, 66 (1897), Or as
a man woulde saye : for a lytle pleasure,
longe payne. 1611: Cotgrave, s.v.
" Plaisir," For a short pleasure long
remembrance. 1681: Robertson, *Phraseol. Generalis*, 1001. 1732: Fuller, No.
4155, Short pleasures, long pains.

Short prayer reaches Heaven, A.
c. 1460: *Good Wyfe wold a Pylgremage*,
l. 167 (E.E.T.S.), A schort prayer wyn-
nythe heyvyn. 1493: *Dives et Pauper*,
fo. 74 (1536), It is a common prouerbe,
that a short prayer thirleth [penetrates,
or reaches] heuen. 1666: Torriano,
Piazza Univ., 178, A short prayer
penetrates. 1732: Fuller, No. 397, A
short prayer may reach up to the
Heaven of Heavens.

Short reckonings are soon cleared.
Ibid., No. 4156. 1869: Spurgeon,
John Ploughman, ch. xii., Pay as you
go, and keep from small scores. Short
reckonings are soon cleared.

Short reckonings make long friends.
1831: Hone, *Year-Book*, col. 1417.
1918: Orczy, *Man in Grey :* "Silver-
leg," 2.

Short shooting loseth the game.
1546 : Heywood, *Proverbs*, Pt. II. ch.
ix. [with "your" for "the"]. *c*. 1580 :
Harvey, *Marginalia*, 147 (1913), Let
not short shooting loose yor game.
1670 : Ray, 142. 1732 : Fuller, No.
4157.

Short visits make long friends. Oxfordsh. 1923 : *Folk-Lore*, xxxiv. 329.

Shotley. *See* Axwell Park.

Shoulder of mutton for a sick horse, A.
1541 : *Sch. House of Women*, l. 95, As
holsome for a man is a woman's corse,
As a shoulder of mutton for a sick
horse. 1596 : Jonson, *Ev. Man in
Humour*, II. i., Counsel to him is as good
as ·a shoulder, etc. 1639 : Clarke, 4,
As fit for him as a shoulder, etc. 1678 :
Ray, 236. 1732 : Fuller, No. 1179.

Shoulder out, To put the=To be an-
noyed, to take offence. 1917 : Bridge,
Cheshire Proverbs, 142.

Shouter of Gatley, A. Ibid., 6, A
shaouter o' Gatley. Said of any loud-
spoken boisterous person.

Show a fair (or clean) pair of heels
To. 1546 : Heywood, *Proverbs*, Pt. II.
ch. vii., Except hir maide shewe a fayre
paire of heeles. 1577 : J. Grange, *Golden Aphroditis*, sig. D3, The valyaunt
souldioure hadde rather truste to the
force of hys armes . . . than in the
fielde a fayre payre of heeles to shew.
1630 : T. Adams, *Works*, 55, But for
these shackles, debt would often shew
credit a light paire of heeles. 1698 :
Terence made English, 241 (2nd ed.), I'd
ha' . . . shewn him a fair pair of heels
for 't. 1737 : Ray, 70. 1819 : Scott,
Ivanhoe, ch. xl., Or Folly will show a
clean pair of heels, and leave Valour
to find out his way . . . as best he
may. 1883: R. L. S., *Treasure I.*, ch. ii.,
Black Dog, in spite of his wounds,
showed a wonderful clean pair of heels,

and disappeared . . . in half a minute.
1899 : Dickinson, *Cumberland Gloss.*,
66, When a person runs away through
fear, he shews a pair of clean heels.

Show me the man. *See* quot. 1819 :
Scott, *Bride of L.*, ch. i., The adage
" show me the man, and I will show
you the law," became as prevalent as it
was scandalous.

Shows all his wit at once, He. 1633 :
Draxe, 70. 1670 : Ray, 199.

Shrew and Shrews, *subs.* 1. *A shrew
is better than a sheep.* 1580 : Tusser,
Husb., 157 (E.D.S.), This prouerbe looke
in mind ye keepe, As good a shrew is as
a sheepe, For you to take to wiue.
c. 1600 : *Grim the Collier*, II., 'Tis better
to be a shrew, sir, than a sheep. 1630 :
Taylor (Water-Poet),*Works*, 3rd pagin.,
59. 1659 : *Lady Alimony*, V. iii., I see
one must thank God for a shrew as well
as for a sheep. 1732 : Fuller, No. 873,
Better be a shrew than a sheep. 1880 :
Spurgeon, *Ploughman's Pictures*, 89, A
shrew is better than a slut. Cf. No. 4.

2. *A shrew profitable may serve a man
reasonable.* 1605 : Camden, *Remains*,
317 (1870). 1616 : Breton, in *Works*,
ii. *e* 5 (Grosart) ["is good for" instead of "may serve"]. 1732 : Fuller,
No. 398.

3. *Every man can rule a shrew but
he who has her.* 1546 : Heywood, *Proverbs*, Pt. II. ch. vi. 1596 : Harington,
Metam. of Ajax, 95 (1814). 1621 :
Burton, *Melancholy*, II. ii. 6, 1, p. 364
(1836). 1681 : Robertson, *Phraseol.
Generalis*, 565. 1732 : Fuller, No. 1444
[" tame " for " rule "]. 1883 : Burne,
Shropsh. Folk-Lore, 588, Every one can
manage a bad wife but he who has her.

4. *One shrew is worth two sheep.*
1575 : Gascoigne, *Glasse of Govt.*, III. i.
[quoted as "an olde saying"]. Cf.
No. 1.

5. *When all shrews have dined.* See
quots. 1546 : Heywood, *Proverbs*, Pt. I.
ch. xiii., And when all shrews haue
dind, Chaunge from foule weather to
faire is oft enclind. 1678 : Ray, 243,
It will be fair weather when the shrews
have dined.

Shrewsbury. *See* quot. 1662 : Fuller, *Worthies*, iii. 54 (1840), He that

fetcheth a wife from Shrewsbury, must
carry her into Staffordshire, or else
shall live in Cumberland. 1790 : Grose,
Prov. Gloss., s.v. " Salop " [as in 1662].
1846–59 : *Denham Tracts*, i. 174
(F.L.S.) [as in 1662].

Shrewsbury clock, By. 1597 : Shakespeare, 1 *Henry IV.*, V. iv., We rose both
at an instant, and fought a long hour
by Shrewsbury clock. 1654 : Gayton,
Pleasant Notes Don Q., 183, The Knight
that fought by th' clock at Shrewsberry.
1681 : *Poor Robin Alman.*, March, A
great many people shall feed . . . three
hours together by Shrewsbury Clock.
1783 : Mrs. Cowley, *More Ways than
One*, I. i., My master is as strict, and as
nice, and exact, as Shrewsperry Clock.
1796 : White, *Falstaff's Letters*, 17,
Fifteen minutes, as thou say'st, by
Shrewsbury clock. 1891 : R. L. S.,
Letters, iv. 86 (Tusitala ed.), I remember, when I first saw this, laughing for
an hour by Shrewsbury clock.

Shrink in the wetting, To. 1540 :
Palsgrave, *Acolastus*, sig. V4, Where is
my golden chain become . . . it is
shrunk in the wetynge. 1596 : Lodge,
Divel Coniured, 4 (Hunt. Cl.), Those
conceits are shrunke in the wetting.
1612 : Chapman, *Widow's Tears*, II. iv.,
Then had I been here a fool . . . if for
a lady's frown . . . I should have
shrunk in the wetting. 1639 : Fuller,
Holy War, bk. v. ch. xxii., Who washed
himself in Jordan, and then shrinking
in the wetting returned presently home
again. 1825 : Scott, *Betrothed*, ch. v.,
They [Flemings] are of an enduring
generation, and will not shrink in the
washing.

Shropshire is full of trout and Tories.
1883 : Burne, *Shropsh. Folk-Lore*, 581.

Shropshire sharp-shins. 15th cent.: in
Reliq. Antiquæ, i. 269 (1841), Schrop-
schir, my schinnes ben scharpe. 1622 :
Drayton, *Polyol.*, xxiii., And Shropshire
saith in her, That shins be ever sharp.
1710–12 : Leland, *Itin.*, I am of Shropshire, my shinnes be sharpe. 1883 :
Burne, *Shropsh. Folk-Lore*, 581, " Sharp-
shins " is still applied in Shropshire, 1st
to light heels, 2nd to sharp wits. 1913 :
E. M. Wright, *Rustic Speech., etc.*, 180,

Anciently the Salopian was proverbial
for sharp shins.

Shrove-tide. 1. *Fit as a pancake for
Shrove Tuesday.* 1846 : Denham, *Proverbs*, 27 (Percy S.).

2. *If it thunder upon Shrove Tuesday
it foretelleth winde, store of fruit, and
plenty.* 1669 : *New Help to Discourse*,
283. 1893 : Inwards, *Weather Lore*, 40.

3. *Rejoice Shrove-tide to-day; for to-
morrow you'll be Ashes.* 1732 : Fuller,
No. 4009.

4. *So much as the sun shineth on Pancake Tuesday, the like will shine every
day in Lent.* 1669 : *New Help to Discourse*, 283. 1893 : Inwards, *Weather
Lore*, 40.

5. *When the sun is shining on Shrove-
tide Day, it is meant well for rye and
peas.* Ibid., 40.

Shut not the barn-door. *See* quot.
1860 : Reade, *Cl. and Hearth*, ch. xxxvi,
The law meddles but with men and
women, and these cannot utter a
story all lies, let them try ever so.
Wherefore we shut not the barn-door
(as the saying is), against any man's
grain. Only having taken it in, we do
winnow and sift it.

Shut up shop-windows, He has—He
is bankrupt. 1678 : Ray, 89.

Sick, *adj.* 1. *As sick as a cat.* 1869 :
Spurgeon, *John Ploughman*, ch. xx.,
These great talkers . . . make me as
sick as a cat.

2. *As sick as a cushion.* 1678 :
Ray, 288. 1738 : Swift, *Polite Convers.*,
Dial. I., Poor miss, she's sick as a cushion,
she wants nothing but stuffing.

3. *As sick as a dog.* 1592 : G. Harvey,
Works, i. 161 (Grosart), Now sicke as a
dog. 1599 : Buttes, *Dyets Dry Dinner*,
sig. O4. 1667 : L'Estrange, *Quevedo's
Visions*, 262 (1904). 1766 : Garrick, *Neck
or Nothing*, I. i., I am sick as a dog of being
a valet. 1864 : Mrs. H. Wood, *Trevlyn
Hold*, ch. xx., Folks have never called
him the Squire, though he's as sick as a
dog for it.

4. *As sick as a horse.* 1685 : Meriton,
Yorkshire Ale, 71, It macks me as
seeke as a horse. 1758–67 : Sterne, *Trist.
Shandy*, vol. vii. ch. ii. 1854 : Baker,
Northants Gloss., s.v. "Sick as a horse,"

A common vulgar simile, used when a person is exceedingly sick without vomiting. 1901 : F. E. Taylor, *Lancs Sayings*, 4, As sick as a hawse.

5. *Ever sick of the slothful guise, Loath to bed and loath to rise.* 1639 : Clarke, 292. Cf. **Sluggard's guise.**

6. *He who was never sick, dies the first fit.* 1732 : Fuller, No. 2409.

7. *Sick of the fever lurden.* See **Fever lurden.**

8. *Sick o' th' idle crick, and the belly-wark i' th' heel.* 1678 : Ray, 254.

9. *Sick of the idles.* 1639 : Clarke, 144. 1670 : Ray, 182.

10. *Sick of the Lombard fever.* 1659 : Howell, 11. 1670 : Ray, 215.

11. *Sick of the mulligrubs. c.* 1620 : B. & F., *Monsieur Thomas*, II. iii., Whose dog lies sick o' the mulligrubs ? 1634 : S. Rowley, *Noble Soldier*, IV. ii., The divell lyes sicke of the mulligrubs. 1670 : Ray, 218, Sick of the mulligrubs with eating chop't hay. 1738 : Swift, *Polite Convers.*, Dial. I. [as in 1670].

12. *Sick of the silver dropsy.* 1633 : Draxe, 33, He hath the siluer dropsie. 1639 : Clarke, 40.

13. *Sick of the simples.* 1754 : Berthelson, *Eng.-Danish Dict.*, s.v. "Sick."

14. *Sick of the sullens.* 1580 : Lyly, *Euphues*, 285 (Arber), She was solitary by walking, with hir frowning cloth, as sick lately of the solens. 1596 : Lodge, *Wits Miserie*, 101 (Hunt. Cl.), Rather die sicke of the sullens then tell his griefe. *c.* 1620 : B. & F., *Woman's Prize*, IV. iv., Is fallen sick . . . o' th' sullens. 1828 : Scott, *Journal*, 9 March, I do not know anything which relieves the mind so much from the sullens as trifling discussion . . .

Sickle, subs. 1. *Between the sickle and the scythe, What is born will never thrive.* Derby. 1884 : *Folk-Lore Journal*, ii. 279. Cf. **Marry** (16).

2. *The sickle and the scythe, that love I not to see, But the good ale-tankard, happy might it be.* 1639 : Clarke, 47.

3. *To put one's sickle into another man's corn.* 1387 : Trevisa, tr. Higden, viii. 183 (Rolls Ser.), And seide to hym, "þou hast no leve to sette þyn hook in

oþer men ripe." *c.* 1440 : Anon., tr. Higden, in Ibid., viii. 183, Hit is not lawefull to the to put a sythe into the corne of oþer men. 1576 : Lambarde, *Peramb. of Kent*, 455 (1826), Least I be blamed for thrusting my sicle into another mans harvest. 1602 : Carew, *Surv. of Cornwall*, 211 (1811), I have thrust my sickle overfar into another's harvest. 1681 : Robertson, *Phraseol. Generalis*, 291, You have no business to do there ; Put not your sickle into your neighbours corn. 1732 : Fuller, No. 5218.

Sickness comes on horseback, but goeth away on foot. 1611 : Cotgrave, s.v. "Maladie," Diseases come on horsebacke and return on foot. 1654 : Whitlock, *Zootomia*, 124, Sickness posteth to us, but crawleth from us. 1869 : Hazlitt, 336.

Sickness is felt, but health not at all. 1732 : Fuller, No. 4160.

Sickness is the chapel of devotion, The chamber of. 1633 : Draxe, 190. 1670 : Ray, 24. 1732 : Fuller, No. 4444. 1803 : *The Moralist's Medley*, 1.

Sickness tells us what we are. 1732 : Fuller, No. 4161.

Side pockets. See **Toad.**

Sieve and riddle. *See* quots. 1670 : Ray, 207, As much sib'd [akin] as sieve and ridder, that grew both in a wood together. 1691 : Ray, *Words not Generally Used*, 63 (E.D.S.), No more sib'd than, etc. Prov. Cheshire. 1824 : Scott, *Redgauntlet*, Lett. xiii., Whilk ye are aware sounds as like being akin to a peatship and a sheriffdom, as a sieve is sib to a riddle. 1917 : Bridge, *Cheshire Proverbs*, 98 [as in 1691, but with "sib" for "sib'd "].

Sift him grain by grain and he proveth but chaff. 1633 : Draxe, 46. 1869 : Spurgeon, *John Ploughman*, ch. i., Sift a sluggard grain by grain, and you'll find him all chaff.

Sift night and day, and get nothing but bran, You. 1732 : Fuller, No. 5997.

Sigh not. See **Never sigh.**

Sight of a man hath the force of a lion, The. 1640 : Herbert, *Jac. Prudentum.*

**Sign invites you in ; but your money

must redeem you out, The. 1732:
Fuller, No. 4746.

Silence gives consent. c. 1387 : Usk,
Test. of Love, in Skeat's Chaucer, vii. 36,
Lo eke an olde proverbe amonges many
other : " He that is stille semeth as
he graunted." 1412 : Hoccleve, Regement, st. 442, l. 3093 (E.E.T.S.), And
for he naght ne seith, he his assent
ȝeueþ þerto, by mannës Iugëment.
c. 1490 : Partonope, 467 (E.E.T.S.),
This proverbe was seide full longe a-go :
" Who so holdeth hym still dothe assent." 1591 : Lyly, Endymion, V. iii.,
Silence, madam, consents. 1616 : Jonson, Devil an Ass, I. iii., Let me take
warrant, lady, from your silence, which
ever is interpreted consent. 1638 :
Randolph, in Works, ii. 616 (1875), And
modest silence gives consent. Before
1754 : Fielding, Fathers, II. ii., At least
I shall take your silence for consent.
1768 : Goldsmith, Good - Natured Man,
II. 1821 : W. Combe, Syntax in Search
of Wife, can. xxxv. p. 109, But Ma'am
said nought—though that's consent, He
thought, if but the adage old Does a
decided truth unfold.

**Silence is a fine jewel for a woman,
but it's little worn.** 1732 : Fuller, No.
4166. 1869 : Spurgeon, John Plough
man, ch. vi.

Silence is golden. 1865 : W. White,
Eastern England, ii. 129. 1878 : Gibbs,
Cotswold Village, ch. iv., " Silence is
golden " is the motto here whilst the
viands are being discussed. 1909 : A.
Dobson, in Poet. Works, 403 (1923).
Cf. Speech.

**Silence is the best ornament of a
woman.** 1539 : Taverner, Proverbs,
fo. 50, Silence garnysheth a woman.
1645 : Howell, Letters, bk. i. § iv. No. ix.
1670 : Ray, 24.

Silence is wisdom (or counsel).
c. 1374 : Chaucer, Troylus, bk. iii. l. 294,
These wyse clerkes that ben dede Han
ever yet proverbed to us yonge, That
" firste vertu is to kepe tonge." c. 1470:
G. Ashby, Poems, 85 (E.E.T.S.), Grete
wisdam is, litil to speke. 1540 : Palsgrave, Acolastus, sig. B2, I dare not
. . . saye mum is counseyle. 1546 :
Heywood, Proverbs, Pt. II. ch. v., I

will say nought but mum, and mum
is counsell. 1620 : Two Merry Milkmaids, II. ii., Silence lady is the best
part of wisdome. 1732 : Fuller, No.
4169, Silence is wisdom, when speaking
is folly. 1869 : Spurgeon, John Ploughman, ch. vi.

Silence seldom doth harm. 1630 :
Brathwait, Eng. Gent., etc., 51 (1641),
Silence . . . may doe good, but can doe
little harme. 1670 : Ray, 24. 1732 :
Fuller, No. 4170, Silence seldom hurts.

Silence. See also No wisdom ; Sorrow makes silence ; and Speech.

Silent, adj. 1. A silent woman [is]
better than a double-tongued man. 1659 :
Howell, 11.

2. As silent as death. 1377 : Langland, Plowman, B, x. 136, As doumbe
as deth. 1679 : The Counterfeits, I. i.,
All the houses silent as Death.

3. As silent as the grave. 1604 :
Shakespeare, Othello, V. ii., Ha ! no
more moving ? Still as the grave. 1778 :
H. Brooke, Marriage Contract, I. ii., I
will be silent as the grave, with respect
to your secret. 1829 : Scott, Journal,
1 July, The house . . . then became
silent as the grave. 1893 : R. L. S.,
Ebb-Tide, ch. viii.

4. Beware of a silent dog and a still
water. 1732 : Fuller, No. 1806. 1875 :
Cheales, Proverb. Folk-Lore, 115.

5. He that is silent gathers stones.
1813 : Ray, 159.

**Silk and scarlet walks many a harlot,
In.** 1869 : Hazlitt, 234.

**Silk purse out of a sow's ear, You
can't make a.** 1611 : Cotgrave, s.v.
" Pigeon," A man cannot make a
cheverill purse of a sows eare. 1738 :
Swift, Polite Convers., Dial. II. 1748 :
Richardson, Clarissa, iv. 119 (1785),
Who would expect velvet to be made
out of a sow's ear ? 1806 : Lamb,
Mr. H—, II. 1877 : S. Butler, Life and
Habit, 201, Every man and every race
is capable of education up to a certain point, but not to the extent of
being made from a sow's ear into a silk
purse. 1921 : Times, 18 August, p. 7,
col. 5, A firm of chemists of Cambridge,
Massachusetts, have succeeded in manu-
facturing a silk purse out of a sow's ear.

They admit that it is not yet a commercial proposition, but sufficiently complete and substantial to demonstrate the fallacy of the ancient proverb.

Silks and satins put out the kitchen fire. 1640: Herbert, *Jac. Prudentum*, Silks and satins put out the fire in the chimney. 1736: Franklin, *Way to Wealth*, in *Works*, i. 447 (Bigelow) [with " scarlet and velvets " after " satins "]. 1912: *N. & Q.*, 11th ser., vi. 255, In my childhood in Ulster I often heard the proverb, " Silks," etc.

Silly as a lamb's dad [sheep], **As.** Oxfordsh. 1923: *Folk-Lore*, xxxiv. 329.

Silly fish. *See* Fish (12).

Silly goose. *See* Goose (3) and (21).

Silver, *adj.* and *subs.* 1. *A silver key can open an iron lock.* 1732: Fuller, No. 400.

2. *He that has no silver in his purse, should have silver on his tongue.* [1659: Howell, *Proverbs: Ital.-Eng.*, 5, Who hath not money in his purse, let him have honey in his mouth.] 1732: Fuller, No. 2149.

3. *Silver dropsy.* *See* Sick (12).

4. *Silver hook.* *See* Angle (2).

5. *There is a silver lining to every cloud.* 1634: Milton, *Comus*, 221, Was I deceived, or did a sable cloud Turn forth her silver lining on the night ? 1852: Dickens, *Bleak House*, ch. xviii., I expand, I open, I turn my silver lining outward like Milton's cloud. 1885: Gilbert, *Mikado*, II., Don't let's be down-hearted ! There's a silver lining to every cloud.

6. *To be born with a silver spoon in one's mouth.* [Gallinae filius albae.—Juvenal, xiii. 141.] 1639: Clarke, 39, He was borne with a penny in's mouth. 1712: Motteux, *Quixote*, Pt. II. ch. lxxiii., Every man was not born with a silver spoon in his mouth. 1850: Dickens, *Chuzzlewit*, ch. vi. 1869: Hazlitt, 399, They who are born with silver spoons in their mouths, don't know how to use them. 1922: C. K. Shorter, in *Sphere*, 9 Dec., p. 266, col. 2, Assuredly he was born with a silver spoon in his mouth. He knew none of the struggles and anxieties which some of us have faced.

See also White (18).

Sim steals. *See* Horse (52).

Simondsall sauce. *See* quot. Simondsall is a Gloucestershire farm on high ground. 1639: in *Berkeley MSS.*, iii. 30 (1885), When a man eates little, to say hee wants some of Simondsall sauce.

Simpers as a mare when she eats thistles, She. 1639: Clarke, 120.

Simpers like a bride on her wedding-day, She. 1678: Ray, 288.

Simpers like a furmity kettle, She. 1631: W. Saltonstall, *Picturæ Loquentes*, sig. C5, Makes her simper like a pot that's ready to run o're. 1667: L'Estrange, *Quevedo's Visions*, 136 (1904), This sets the widow a-pinking, and simpering like a furmety-kettle. 1738: Swift, *Polite Convers.*, Dial. I. 1846–59: *Denham Tracts*, ii. 92 (F.L.S.), She simpers like a frummetty kettle at Christmas.

Simpers like a riven dish, She. 1678: Ray, 288.

Simple as a ha'porth o' soap in a washin mug, As. 1917: Bridge, *Cheshire Proverbs*, 19.

Sin and Sins, *subs.* 1. *It is a sin to belie the devil.* *See* Devil (25).

2. *It is a sin to steal a pin.* 1875: Cheales, *Proverb. Folk-Lore*, 129, . . . as we . . . used to be informed in the nursery. 1914: Lucas, *Landmarks*, ch. iv., Certain crusted scraps of nursery wisdom . . . such as . . . " It is a sin to steal a pin."

3. *Our sins and our debts are always greater than we take them to be.* 1659: Howell, *Proverbs: Ital.-Eng.*, 12: Fuller, No. 4179 [" think " for " take "]. 1774: Franklin, in *Works*, v. 291 (Bigelow). 1827: Hone, *Table-Book*, 505, . . . greater than we think of. 1869: Spurgeon, *John Ploughman*, ch. xii. [as in 1732].

4. *Sins are not known till they be acted.* 1640: Herbert, *Jac. Prudentum.*

5. *Sin that is hidden is half forgiven.* 1567: G. Fenton, *Bandello*, ii. 149 (T.T.), Me thinkes a falte don in secrett is halfe perdoned. 1666: Torriano, *Piazza Univ.*, 197, Sin conceal'd, half pardoned.

Sin, *verb.* *See* quot. *c.* 1386:

Chaucer, *Melibeus*, § 29, The proverbe seith : that " for to do sinne is mannish, but certes for to persevere longe in sinne is werk of the devel."

Sinews of war, The. [Pecuniae belli civilis nervi sunt.—Tacitus, II. xxiv. Nervi belli pecunia.—Cicero, *Phil.*, V. ii. 5.] *c.* 1550 : *Disc. Common Weal Eng.*, 87 (1893) (O.), These coins and treasures be not with out cause called of wise men . . . The senowes of warre. 1581 : Stafford, *Exam. of Complaints*, 67 (N. Sh. S.). 1594 : Peele, *Battle of Alcazar*, I. ii., Madam, gold is the glue, sinews, and strength of war. 1623 : Massinger, *Duke of Milan*, III. i., Money is the sinew of the war. 1653 : Urquhart, *Rabelais*, bk. i. ch. xlvi., Coine is the sinews of warre. 1767 : Murphy, *Sch. for Guardians*, II. iii., You have furnished me with the sinews of war. 1838 : Carlyle, *Sartor*, bk. ii. ch. iii., Suppose your sinews of war quite broken ; I mean your military chest insolvent.

Sing, *verb.* 1. *He may sing before thieves.* [Cantabit vacuus coram latrone viator.—Juvenal, x. 22.] *c.* 1230 : in Wright, *Pol. Songs John to Edw. II.*, 35 (Camden S.) [Juvenal's line]. *c.* 1374 : Chaucer, *Boethius*, bk.ii. Pr. v., A pore man, that berth no richesse on him by the weye, may boldely singe biforn theves, for he hath nat wherof to ben robbed. *c.* 1440 : Lydgate, *Fall of Princes*, bk. iii. l. 582 (E.E.T.S.), The poore man affor the theeff doth synge. 1593 : Peele, *Edw. I.*, sc. xii., 'Tis an old said saying . . . a man's purse-penniless may sing before a thief. 1659 : T. Peake, *Parnassi Puerp.*, 21, Clients returning before theefs may sing ; For back from London they can't money bring. 1707 : Dunton, *Athenian Sport*, p. 155, col. 1, The money-less traveller can sing before a thief. 1804 : Mrs. Piozzi, in Hayward, *Mrs. Piozzi*, ii. 263 (1861), The *poor* traveller always sung safely even in company of thieves.

2. *He sings at a deaf man's door.* 1633 : Draxe, 38.

3. *He that sings in disaster* [confesses], *Shall weep all his life-time thereafter.*

1612 : Shelton, *Quixote*, Pt. I. bk. iii. ch. viii., " Here it is quite contrary," quoth the slave, " for ' He that sings once, weeps all his life after.' " 1710 : S. Palmer, *Moral Essays on Proverbs*, 197.

4. *He that sings on Friday, will weep on Sunday.* 1640 : Herbert, *Jac. Prudentum.* 1670 : Ray, 24.

5. *He that sings worst let him begin first. c.* 1410 : *Towneley Plays*, 108 (E.E.T.S.), [Here " worst " is " best "], Who so can best syng Shall haue the begynnyng. 1725 : Bailey, tr. Erasmus' *Colloq.*, 204, According to the old proverb, He that sings worst let him begin first.

6. *Many a one sings that is full sorry.* 1561 : *Queene Hester*, 19 (Grosart), Yᵗ with their mouth thei sing, Though thei wepe in their hart. 1611 : Cotgrave, s.v. " Chanter."

7. *Sing before breakfast, cry before night.* 1530 : Palsgrave, 776, You waxe mery this morning. God gyue grace you wepe nat or nyght. 1855 : *N. & Q.*, 1st ser., xi. 416, If you sing before breakfast, you'll cry before night. 1859 : Ibid., 2nd ser., viii. 484 [Hants]. 1860 : Ibid., 2nd ser., ix. 51, . . . very common . . . in almost every part of Lincolnshire. 1898 : Ibid., 9th ser., ii. 436. 1899 : Ibid., 9th ser., iii. 173 [Northants].

8. *Thou singest like a bird called a swine.* 1678 : Ray, 269. 1732 : Fuller, No. 5230, To sing like, etc.

9. *To sing Lachrymæ* = To be sorry or mournful. *c.* 1610 : in *Roxb. Ballads*, iii. 68 (B.S.), In the prison to stay, Where I sung Lachrima. 1674 : *Poor Robin Alman.*, July, The lawyers shall sing Lachrymæ over Littletons grave.

10. *To sing Placebo* = To be flattering or servile. 1340 : *Ayenbite*, 60 (O.), þe uerþe zenne is þet huanne hi alle zingeþ " Placebo," þet is to zigge : " mi lhord zayþ zuþ, mi lhord deþ wel." *c.* 1540 : Bale, *Kynge Johan*, 30 (Camden S.), By the mas, me thynke they are syngyng of placebo. 1542 : Becon, in *Early Works*, 276 (P.S.), He cannot bear fire in one hand and water in the other. He cannot play *placebo.* 1592 : Nashe,

Works, ii. 50 (Grosart), That poets and good fellowes may drinke, and souldiers sing Placebo. 1618 : Harington, *Epigrams*, bk. ii. No. 56, [entitled] Of a Preacher that sings Placebo.

11. *To sing the same song* (or *one song*). 1580 : Baret, *Alvearie*, E 2, They harpe alwaie vpon one string, they are alwaie in one song. 1639 : Clarke, 8, To sing the old song. 1670 : Ray, 192, To sing the same song. 1681 : Robertson, *Phraseol. Generalis*, 1133. 1736 : Bailey, *Dict.*, s.v. " Tune," You are always in the same tune.

12. *To sing three thrums* = To purr like a cat. 1917 : Bridge, *Cheshire Proverbs*, 143.

13. *Who can sing so merry a note as he that cannot change a groat.* 1546. : Heywood, *Proverbs*, Pt. I. ch. xii. 1594 : Barnfield, *Affect. Sheph.*, 40 (Percy Sh.). 1692 : L'Estrange, *Æsop*, 390 (3rd ed.), . . . the old saying, No man sings a merrier note Then he that cannot change a groat. 1732 : Fuller, No. 6449 [" the cobler " for " he "].

14. *See* quot. 1869 : Hazlitt, 482, Yeow mussent sing a Sunday, becaze it is a sin ; but yeow may sing a Monday, till Sunday cums agin. *Suffolk.*

Singers and ringers are little home bringers. 1893 : *Co. Folk-Lore: Suffolk*, 151 (F.L.S.).

Singing man keeps his shop in his throat, The. 1640 : Herbert, *Jac. Prudentum.* 1670 : Ray, 24. 1732 : Fuller, No. 4747.

Single long, shame at last. 1659 : Howell, *Proverbs: Brit.-Eng.*, 21.

Sink in his own sin, He shall. 1546 : Heywood, *Proverbs*, Pt. I. ch. x., Thou shalte sinke in thine own syn for vs. 1659 : Howell, 15.

Sink or swim, To. *c.* 1386 : Chaucer, *Knight's Tale*, l. 1539, She . . . reccheth neuere wher I synke or fleete [float]. *c.* 1450 : in *Reliq. Antiquæ*, i. 76 (1841), Whedyr she ever flete, or synke. *c.* 1520 : in Skelton, *Works*, ii. 438 (Dyce), But some shall go astraye, And lerne to swyme or sinke. 1594 : Nashe, *Dido*, IV. iii., She cares not how we sinke or swimme. *c.* 1620 : B. & F., *Night-Walker*, III. iii. 1667 : Pepys,

Diary, 4 April. 1709: in *Harl. Miscell.*, i. 206 (1744). 1748 : Richardson, *Clarissa*, vi. 211 (1785), She was determined to get out herself as fast as she could, let me sink or swim. 1818 : Scott, *Heart of Midl.*, ch. xxvi. 1896 : Doyle, *Rodney Stone*, ch. vii., I sink or swim with my friends ! A Whig I started, and a Whig I shall remain.

Sion and Sheen. *See* quots. 1659 : Howell, 21, The nun of Sion, with the frier of Shean, Went under water to play the quean. 1790 : Grose, *Prov. Gloss.*, s.v. " Middlesex," The nun of Sion with the friar of Sheen [=birds of a feather].

Sirrah your dogs ! 1670 : Ray, 192. 1732 : Fuller, No. 6496, Sirrah your dog, but sirrah not me ; For I was born before you could see.

Sit, *verb.* 1. *Better sit idle than work for nothing.* 1642 : D. Rogers, *Matrim. Honour*, 225, Our proverbe saith, better sit for naught, then stir for naught. 1683 : Meriton, *Yorkshire Ale*, 83–7 (1697), Better sit idle than work teaum [for nothing].

2. *Better sit still than rise up and fall.* *c.* 1410 : *Towneley Plays*, 229 (E.E.T.S.). 1546 : Heywood, *Proverbs*, Pt. II. ch. v. 1592 : Warner, *Albion's England*, bk. vii. ch. 37, And rather sit thou safely still, Then for a fall to rise. 1618 : Breton, in *Inedited Tracts*, 190 (Hazlitt), 1732 : Fuller, No. 4181, Sit still, rather than rise and fall down.

3. *He sits not sure that sits too high.* 1611 : Cotgrave, s.v. " Assuré."

4. *He that sits to work in the market-place shall have many teachers.* 1732 : Fuller, No. 2303.

5. *He that sitteth well thinketh ill.* 1578 : Florio, *First Fruites*, fo. 28, Who sitteth wel thynketh yl. 1629 : *Book of Meery Riddles*, Prov. 10.

6. *Sit a while and go a mile.* 1530 : Palsgrave, 436, Rest a whyle and roune a myle. 1639 : Clarke, 235.

7. *Sit by the good, and by the good arise.* 1572 : T. Wilson, *Disc. upon Usury*, 359 (1925) [cited as " an old prouerbe "].

8. *Sit in your place and none can make you rise.* 1611 : Cotgrave, s.v. " Seoir,"

He need not fear to be chidden that sits
where he is bidden. 1640 : Herbert,
Jac. Prudentum. 1670 : Ray, 24.
1732 : Fuller, No. 4180, Sit firm in thy
place, and none can hurt thee. 1853 :
Trench, *Proverbs*, 108 (1905), How ex-
cellently this unites genuine modesty
and manly self - assertion: *Sit in your
place, and no man can make you rise.*

9. *To sit on one's skirts.* 1546 : Heywood, *Proverbs*, Pt. I. ch. v., And also I
shall, to reueng former hurtis Hold
their noses to grinstone, and syt on
theyr skurtis That erst sate on mine.
1598 : Bernard, *Terence*, 58, I will be
reuenged on thee. I will sit on thy
skirts. 1732 : Fuller, No. 2653, I will
stick in your skirts for this. 1816 :
Scott, *Old Mortality*, ch. xliii., " D—n
seize me, if I forgive him for it, though !"
replied the other ; " and I think I can
sit in his skirts now." 1889 : Peacock,
Manley, etc., Gloss., 490 (E.D.S.), To sit
on a person's skirts is to annoy, baffle,
or impede him.

10. *To sit still and pill straws.* 1672 :
Walker, *Parœm.*, 21.

11. *To sit upon thorns. See* **Thorn**
(8).

Sitenhill. *See* **Barton.**

Six awls make a shoemaker. 1670 :
Ray, 216.

Sixes and sevens, At. Originally this
seems to have been a gambling—dicing
—phrase, " To set at six or seven." The
Oxford English Dictionary says—" probably a fanciful alteration of *to set on
cinque and sice*, these being the two
highest numbers." *c.* 1340 : *Avowyne
of Arthur*, st. 65 (Camden S.), Alle in
sundur hit brast in six or in seuyn.
c. 1374 : Chaucer, *Troylus*, bk. iv. l. 622,
Lat not this wrecched wo thin herte
gnawe, But manly set the world on
sixe and sevene. *c.* 1400 : *Towneley
Plays*, 169 (E.E.T.S.), Bot be thay past
me by by mahowne in heuen, I shall,
and that in hy set all on sex and seuen.
1542 : Udall, tr. Erasmus' *Apoph.*, 298
(1877), There is a prouerbe, *omnem
iacere aliam*, to cast att dice, by whiche
is signified, to set al on sixe and seuen,
and at al auentures to ieoperd, assaiyng
the wild chaunce of fortune, be it good,

be it bad. 1596 : Shakespeare, *Rich. II.*,
II. ii., All is uneven, And everything is
left at six and seven. 1630 : Taylor
(Water - Poet), *Works*, 2nd pagin., 71,
Nor carelessly set all at six and seuen.
1670 : Cotton, *Scarronides*, bk. iv., But
like a dame of wits bereaven, Let all
things go at six and seven. 1710 :
Centlivre, *Man's Bewitch'd*, II. iv., Did
he make any will ? . . . No, Sir, he
has left all sixes and sevens. 1768 :
Goldsmith, *Good - Natured Man*, I.,
Haven't I reason to be out of my senses,
when I see things going at sixes and
sevens? 1829 : Cobbett, *Advice to
Young Men*, Lett. III., Leaving books
and papers all lying about at sixes and
sevens. 1920 : Locke, *House of Baltazar*,
ch. xviii., " We're all at sixes and
sevens," cried Weatherley one day in
despair. . . . " Unless we're careful, the
project will drop to pieces."

Six feet of earth make all men equal.
1659 : Howell, *Proverbs: Ital.-Eng.*, 8.
1666 : Torriano, *Piazza Univ.*, 285, Six
foot of earth shuts up every one.

Six o'clock with him, It's welly=He is
failing in health. 1917 : Bridge, *Cheshire
Proverbs*, 86.

Six of one and half a dozen of the
other. 1852 : Dickens, *Bleak House*,
ch. xxiv., Mostly they come for skill—
or idleness. Six of one, and half-a-
dozen of the other. 1859 : Sala, *Twice
Round Clock*, 3 a.m. 1907 : De Morgan,
Alice-for-Short, ch. xvi.

Six score. *See* quots. This is what
is known as the " long hundred."
1647 : in *Somers Tracts* v. 488 (1811),
For in things without heads six score
go to an hundred. 1849 : F. T. Dinsdale, *Teesdale Gloss.*, 111, Five score's a
hundred of men, money, and pins, Six
score's a hundred of all other things.
1881 : Evans, *Leics. Words*, 187 (E.D.S.),
I have often heard quoted the old
rule—[as in 1849]. But the long hundred is now seldom heard of except in piece-work in some few trades.
1889 : Peacock, *Manley, etc., Gloss.*, 330
(E.D.S.) [as in 1849]. 1917 : Bridge,
Cheshire Proverbs, 55, Everything is
counted six-score except men, money
and bricks. *Ibid.*, 96, Naught is

counted six score to the hundred but old women and gorse kids [faggots].

Size cinque will not, If. *See* quot. 1678 : Ray, 348, If size cinque will not and duce ace cannot, then quatre trey must. The middle sort bear public burthens, taxes, etc., most.

Skeer [Rake out] **your own fire.** This is of the family of " Sweep before your own door." 1917 : Bridge, *Cheshire Proverbs,* 109.

Skiddaw. 1. *If Skiddaw hath a cap, Criffel wots full well of that.* In the quotations 1610 to 1709 " Criffel " is given as " Scruffell " ; and in 1790 as " Scuffel." 1610 : P. Holland, tr. Camden's *Britannia,* 767. 1655 : Fuller, *Church Hist.,* bk. xi. § iii. (9). 1709 : O. Dykes, *Eng. Proverbs* (at end). 1790 : Grose, *Prov. Gloss.,* s.v. " Cumberland." 1818 : Scott, *Heart of Midl.,* ch. xl. 1899 : Dickinson, *Cumberland Gloss.,* 54, When Criffel gets a cap, Skiddaw wots well of that.

2. *Skiddaw, Lauvellin and Casticand Are the highest hills in all England.* 1610: P. Holland, tr. Camden's *Britannia,* 767. 1659 : Howell, 21. 1790 : Grose, *Prov. Gloss.,* s.v. " Cumberland."

Skill and confidence are an unconquered army. 1640 : Herbert, *Jac. Prudentum.*

Skimmington, To ride. 1634 : C. Butler, *Feminine Monarchie,* 64, Yet when they have it, let them use poore Skimmington as gently as they may ; especially in publik, to hide his shame. 1714 : E. Ward, *Cavalcade,* 35, That those who knew not the occasion Of such a noisy strange procession, Expected they should find anon The same to be a Skimington. 1825 : Jennings, *Somerset. Words,* 68, To ride Skimmerton, is an exhibition . . . designed to ridicule some one who, unfortunately, possesses an unfaithful wife. 1886 : Hardy, *Casterbridge,* ch. xxxix., Have you seen any gang of fellows making a devil of a noise—skimmington riding, or something of the sort ?

Skin a flint, To. 1640 : Herbert, *Jac. Prudentum,* You cannot flay a stone. 1659 : Howell, 11, To skin a stone for a penny, and break a knife of twelve-pence. 1670 : Ray, 9, No man can flay a stone. 1690 : *New Dict. Canting Crew,* sig. E5, He'll flay a flint, of a meer scrab, or miser. 1754 : Berthelson, *Eng.-Danish Dict.,* s.v. " Skin," He would skin a flint. 1841 : Hartshorne, *Salopia Ant.,* 567, A covetous person, one who, if it were possible, would " skin a flint, to save a penny." 1851 : Sternberg, *Dialect, etc., of Northants,* 97, One who, as the proverb says, will " Skin a flint worth a fardin Spwile [Spoil] a knife worth a grat [groat]." 1901 : *Folk-Lore,* xii. 82, [S.W. Wilts] A would skin a vlint vur a varden and spwile a tenpenny nayl in doin' on't. 1910 : R. L. Gales, *Studies in Arcady,* 335, The writer . . . remembers hearing " to skin a flint, and spoil a shilling knife in doing it."

Skin between the brows. *See* quots. 1575 : Still, *Gam. Gurton,* V. ii., I am as true, I would thou knew, as [the] skin between thy brows. 1599 : Shakespeare, *Much Ado,* III. v., An old man, sir . . . but, in faith, honest as the skin between his brows. 1605 : *London Prodigal,* V. i., She is . . . as true as the skin between any man's brows here. 1696 : D'Urfey, *Quixote,* Pt. III. Act I., I warrant she's as virtuous as the skin between her brows.

Sky falls we shall catch larks, When the. [Quid si ? Redeo ad illos qui aiunt : Quid si coelum ruat ?—Terence, *Haut.,* IV. iii. 41.] Before 1500 : in Hill, *Commonplace - Book,* 128 (E.E.T.S.), And hewin [heaven] fall, we shall hawe mani larkis. 1546 : Heywood, *Proverbs,* Pt. I. ch. iv. [" have " for " catch "]. 1606 : Day, *Ile of Gulls,* V. [" have " for " catch "]. 1638 : Randolph, *Muses' Looking-Glass,* II. ii., . . . Should heaven fall— *Aph.* Why then we should have larks. 1709 : R. Kingston, *Apoph. Curiosa,* 17, When the sky shall fall, and blind men catch larks. 1721 : Bailey, *Eng. Dict.,* s.v. " Sky." 1869 : Spurgeon, *John Ploughman,* ch. xx. 1914 : Shaw, " Parents and Children," in *Misalliance, etc.,* xxx, Just as I do not admit that if the sky fell we should all catch larks.

Slain that had warning, not he that

took it, He was. 1659 : Howell, *Proverbs: Brit.-Eng.*, 3.

Slander, but it is no lie, It may be a. 1546 : Heywood, *Proverbs*, Pt. II. ch. vii.

Slander flings stones at itself. 1732 : Fuller, No. 4183.

Slander is a shipwreck by a dry tempest. 1640 : Herbert, *Jac. Prudentum*.

Slander leaves a scar behind it. 1633 : Draxe, 191, Slander leaueth a skarre. 1670 : Ray, 24 ["score" for "scar"]. 1681 : Robertson, *Phraseol. Generalis*, 1136. 1732 : Fuller, No. 4184 [as in 1670].

Slander one with a matter of truth, To. 1678 : Ray, 269.

Slander that is raised is ill to fell, A. c. 1460 : *How the Good Wife*, l. 25, A slaundrer that is reised is euelle to felle.

Slanderer. *The most dangerous of wild beasts is a slanderer; of tame ones a flatterer.* 1855 : Bohn, 511.

Slapton, Where fools will happen. 1851 : Sternberg, *Dialect, etc., of Northants*, 192.

Slave that cannot command himself, He's a. 1732 : Fuller, No. 2445.

Slavering folks. *See* Snotty folks.

Sleep, *subs.* 1. *Hours of sleep.* 1666 : Torriano, *Piazza Univ.*, 114, Five hours sleepeth a traveller, seven a scholar, eight a merchant, and eleven every knave. 1732 : Fuller, No. 4112, Seven hours' sleep will make a clown forget his design. 1846 : Denham, *Proverbs*, 5 (Percy S.) [as in 1732, but with "the husbandman" for "a clown"]. 1883 : Burne, *Shropsh. Folk-Lore*, 578, Nature requireth five, Custom taketh seven, Idleness takes nine, And Wickedness eleven. 1912 : *N. & Q.*, 11th ser., v. 52, Six hours for a man, seven for a woman, and eight for a fool. The precept seems to be based on the Latin lines : — Sex horis dormire sat est juvenique senique, Septem vix pigro, nulli concedimius octo.—*Collectio Salernitana*, ed. De Renzi, vol. v. p. 7.

2. *One hour's sleep before midnight is worth two after.* 1640 : Herbert, *Jac. Prudentum* ["three" for "two"]. 1731 : in Peck, *Desid. Curiosa*, 226 (1779), As experience it self shews, one hour's rest before twelve of the clock is worth two after. 1829 : Cobbett, *Advice to Young Men*, Lett. I ["worth more than two"]. 1846 : Denham, *Proverbs*, 3 (Percy S.).

Sleep, *verb.* 1. *He hath slept well that remembers not he hath slept ill.* 1732 : Fuller, No. 1897.

2. *He sleeps with his eyes open.* 1586 : Pettie, Guazzo's *Civil Convers.*, fo. 140, Which sleepeth (as they say) her eies being open. 1732 : Fuller, No. 1947, He is so wary that he sleeps like a hare, with his eyes open.

3. *He that sleeps bites no body.* 1567 : *Merry Tales, etc.*, No. xxxvi. p. 50 (Hazlitt), Here by ye maye se, that many thinges passe by them that slepe, and it is an old sayenge : He that slepeth, byteth no body. 1615 : Stephens, *Essays, etc.*, bk. i. No. 21, Hee that drinkes well, sleepes well, and hee that sleepes well thinkes no harme.

4. *I don't sleep to all.* 1593 : G. Harvey, *Works*, ii. 165 (Grosart), Some sleepe not to all : and I watch not to eucryone. 1725 : Bailey, tr. Erasmus's *Colloq.*, 487, You know the old proverb, *I don't sleep to all.*

5. *Sleep without supping, and wake without owing.* 1640 : Herbert, *Jac. Prudentum.*

6. *To sleep as sound as a church.* 1839 : Dickens, *Nickleby*, ch. xxiii., Asleep she did fall, sound as a church. Cf. Fast as a church.

7. *To sleep in a field. See* quot. 1926 : *Devonsh. Assoc. Trans.*, lvii. 152, "You've bin sleepin' in a field wi' the gate open." Said to a man who was fussing about a cold.

8. *To sleep in a whole skin. See* Whole skin.

9. *To sleep like a pig.* 1736 : Bailey, *Dict.*, s.v. "Pig," He sleeps like a pig.

10. *To sleep like a top.* 1668 : Davenant, *Rivals*, III., Or else I shall sleep like a top. 1762 : Hall-Stevenson, *Crazy Tales*, 56, Scolded a while, and slept like any top. 1820 : Byron, *Letters, etc.*, v. 115 (Prothero), I slept like a top. 1855 : Gaskell, *North and South*, ch. xxiii.

11. *To sleep on both ears.* [In aurem utramvis otiose ut dormias.—Terence,

Haut., II. iii. 101.] 1540: Palsgrave, *Acolạstus*, sig. C4, Than truely lyued I lyke one that sleapeth on bothe his eares. Before 1663 : Abp. Bramhall, *Works*, iii. 518 (*Ang.-Cath. Lit.*, 1842-4), Let him set his heart at rest ; I will remove this scruple out of his mind, that he may sleep securely upon both ears. 1754 : Berthelson, *Eng. - Danish Dict.*, s.v. " Sleep."

12. *To sleep without rocking.* 1631 : Brathwait, *Whimzies*, 106 (1859), Hee sleepes soundly without rocking. 1738 : Swift, *Polite Convers.*, Dial. III., I'm sure I shall sleep without rocking.

Sleeping dogs lie, Let. *c.* 1374: Chaucer, *Troylus*, bk. iii. l. 764, It is nought good a sleping hound to wake. 1546 : Heywood, *Proverbs*, Pt. I. ch. x., It is euyll wakyng of a sleepyng dog. 1598: Shakespeare, 2 *Henry IV.*, I. ii., Wake not a sleeping wolf. 1605 : Camden, *Remains*, 326 (1870) [as in 1546]. 1850 : Dickens, *Copperfield*, ch. xxxix., Let sleeping dogs lie — who wants to rouse 'em ? 1898 : Weyman, *Shrewsbury*, ch. xxxii. 1922 : *Sphere*, 5 Aug., 132, It is all very well to let sleeping dogs lie, but in this case the dogs are dogs of war.

Sleeping enough in the grave, There will be. 1736 : Franklin, *Way to Wealth*, in *Works*, i. 443 (Bigelow).

Sleeping lion. *See* Lion (13).

Sleepy master makes his servant a lout, A. [*c.* 1290: in Wright *Pol. Songs John to Edw. II.*, 165 (Camden S.), Mitis prælatus facit ignavos famulatus.] 1640: Herbert, *Jac. Prudentum.*

Sleeveless errand, A. Mr. Warwick Bond, in his edition of John Lyly, quotes (iii. 503) from Lady Charlotte Guest's translation of the *Mabinogion* (" Dream of Mayen Wledig "): " Now this was the guise in which the messengers journeyed : one sleeve was on the cap of each of them in front, as a sign that they were messengers, in order that through what hostile land soever they might pass, no harm might be done them." Mr. Bond adds: " Without the sleeve they might never be able to perform their errand." This seems to

make clear the much disputed origin of the phrase " A sleeveless errand," i.e. a futile, bootless errand. The use of " sleeveless " with this signification naturally spread to other things besides errands. One would have expected to find " sleeveless errand " at an earlier date than the wider uses ; but I have not been able to find examples of the former so early as examples of the latter. There follow illustrations of A, the wider applications of the adjective ; and B, the preciser use in " sleeveless errand."

A. *c.* 1387 : Usk, *Test. of Love*, in Skeat's *Chaucer*, vii. 76, And mesureth his goodnesse, not by slevelesse wordes . . . 15th cent.: in *Reliq. Antiquæ*, i. 83 (1841), Thynke not . . . y schall telle you a sleveles reson. *c.* 1440 : *Jacob's Well*, 181 (E.E.T.S.), Summe in schryfte schal tarye the preest wyth sleueles talys [idle talk] that no-thyng longyth to schryfte. 1593 : *Pass. Morrice*, 65 (N. Sh. S.), So vnmannerly to vse him by sleeueles excuses. 1726 : in Hone, *Ev. Day Book*, ii. 782, Having, under a sleeveless pretence, been deny'd a combat. 1821 : Scott, *Fam. Letters*, ii. 111 (1894), He . . . had no honourable mode of avoiding the sleeveless quarrel fixed on him. 1867 : Waugh, *Tatlin' Mathy*, 18, Single-step doancin', an' sich like sleeveless wark as that.

B. 1546 : Heywood, *Proverbs*, Pt. I. ch. vii., To make . . . a sleeueles errande. 1604 : *Jacke of Dover*, 4 (Percy S.), To whose house I went upon a sleeveles arrand. 1670 : Cotton, *Scarronides*, bk. iv. 1712 : Motteux, *Quixote*, Pt. II. ch. x. 1828 : Carr, *Craven Dialect*, ii. 290, As I've hed a sleeveless earrant.

Slender in the middle as a cow in the waist, As. 1621: Burton, *Anatomy of Melancholy*, III. ii. 3, 1, vol. iii. p. 178 (Shilleto), She stoops, is lame . . . as slender in the middle as a Cow in the waist. 1670 : Ray, 207. 1732 : Fuller, No. 727. 1881 : Evans, *Leics. Words*, 242 (E.D.S.), " As slender," etc. This periphrasis to describe obesity . . . is still in use.

Slight impressions. *See* Impressions.

Slip between cup and lip. *See* Cup (4).

Slip of the foot may be soon recovered, A; but that of the tongue perhaps never. 1732: Fuller, No. 403. Cf. Better the feet slip.

Slip one's neck out of the collar, To. 1583: Golding, *Calvin on Deut.*, cxxv. 772 (O.), Albeit we . . . would slippe our heades out of the coler seeking to shift off yᵉ matter. 1633: Draxe, 189, He draweth his necke out of the coller. 1678: Ray, 350. 1754: Berthelson, *Eng.-Danish Dict.*, s.v. "Slip." 1857: Hughes, *Tom Brown*, Pt. II. ch. vii., If we can slip the collar and do so much less without getting caught, that's one to us.

Slippery as an eel. 1412: Hoccleve, *Regement*, l. 1985, p. 72 (E.E.T.S.), Mi wit is also slipir as an eel. *c.* 1420: Lydgate, *Assem. of Gods*, 31 (E.E.T.S.), Whyche made the grounde as slepyr as an ycle. 1533: Heywood, *Play of Love*, l. 1414 (Brandl, *Quellen*, 204), And coryd [curried (of a horse)] tyll he be slyke as an ele. 1633: S. Marmion, *Fine Companion*, V. ii., He is as slippery as an eel, in love. 1690: Shadwell, *Amorous Bigot*, I. 1740: Richardson, *Pamela*, i. 207 (1883), You'll find her as slippery as an eel, I'll assure you. 1855: Gaskell, *North and South*, ch. xvii.

Sloes. *See* Black, *adj.* (8) ; and Many slones.

Sloe-tree's as white as a sheet, When the, Sow your barley whether it be dry or wet. 1678: Ray, 49. 1732: Fuller, No. 6482. 1825: Hone, *Ev. Day Book*, i. 670. 1893: Inwards, *Weather Lore*, 152.

Sloth breeds a scab. 1546: Heywood, *Proverbs*, Pt. I. ch. iii., Sens we see slouth must breede a scab. 1611: Davies (of Hereford), *Sc. of Folly*, 48, in *Works*, ii. (Grosart).

Slothful is the servant of the covetous, The. 1640: Herbert, *Jac. Prudentum*.

Slothful man is the beggar's brother, The. 1732: Fuller, No. 4748. 1917: Bridge, *Cheshire Proverbs*, 6.

Sloth is the devil's cushion or pillow. 1669: *Politeuphuia*, 306.

Sloth is the key to poverty. 1669: *Politeuphuia*, 306 [with " mother " for

" key "]. 1853: Trench, *Proverbs*, 107 (1905), And to many languages another with its striking image, *Sloth, the key of poverty*, belongs.

Sloth, like rust, consumes faster than labour wears. 1736: Franklin, *Way to Wealth*, in *Works*, i. 443 (Bigelow).

Sloth makes all things difficult, but industry all things easy. Ibid., i. 443.

Sloth turneth the edge of wit. 1579: Lyly, *Euphues*, 126 (Arber). 1670: Ray, 24.

Slow and sure. 1633: Draxe, 111 *bis*, Slownesse is sure. 1639: Fuller, *Holy War*, bk. iii. ch. v., These, though slow, were sure. 1692: L'Estrange, *Æsop*, 337 (3rd ed.), Slow and sure in these cases is good counsel. 1711: Steele, *Spectator*, No. 140, He is rich, and my mother says, As he is slow he is sure. 1768: Goldsmith, *Vicar*, ch. xxi., What significes minding her ? . . . if she be slow she's sure. 1922: Weyman, *Ovington's Bank*, ch. v., Slow and sure is a good rule.

Slow help is no help. 1853: Trench, *Proverbs*, 19 (1905).

Slow worm. *See* Adder.

Sluggard makes his night till noon, The. 1732: Fuller, No. 4749.

Sluggard must be clad in rags, The. 1605: Camden, *Remains*, 333 (1870).

Sluggard's guise. *See* quots. 1639: in *Berkeley MSS.* iii., 32 (1885), Hee is tainted with an evill guise, Loth to bed and lother to rise. 1670: Ray, 143, The sluggards guise, Loath to go to bed and loath to rise. 1732: Fuller, No. 6368 [as in 1670]. 1825: Jennings, *Somerset. Words*, 70, Sluggardy-guise ; Loth, etc. 1842: Akerman, *Wilts Gloss.*, 46, Sluggard's guise Loth to bed And loth to rise.

Sluggard takes an hundred steps because he would not take one in due time, A. 1855: Bohn, 300.

Slut and Sluts, *subs.* 1. *A slut never wants a clout, Whilst her aipernt* [apron] *holds out.* 1880: Courtney, *W. Cornwall Words*, 1 (E.D.S.).

2. *A slut will poison thy gut.* 1685: *Mother Bunch's Closet*, 14 (Gomme, 1885) [quoted as " The old saying "].

3. *Of all tame beasts I hate sluts.*

1678 : Ray, 81. 1732 : Fuller, No. 3697.

4. *Sluts are good enough to make a sloven's porridge.* 1639 : Clarke, 287 [in the singular]. *c.* 1685. : in *Roxb. Ballads*, viii. 869 (B.S.) [as in 1639]. 1732 : Fuller, No. 4190.

See also **Apple** (6).

Small birds must have meat. 1600 : Shakespeare, *Merry Wives*, I. iii., Young ravens must have food. 1639 : Clarke, 292. 1670 : Ray, 63.

Small cheer and great welcome makes a merry feast. *c.* 1600 : Shakespeare, *Com. of Errors*, III. i.

Small choice in rotten apples, There is. 1594 : Shakespeare, *Tam. of Shrew*, I. i. Before 1681 : J. Lacy, *Sauny the Scot*, I. 1875 : Cheales, *Proverb. Folk-Lore*, 116.

Smaller the peas. *See* **Pea** (3).

Small family is soon provided for, A. 1732 : Fuller, No. 405.

Small fish than an empty dish, Better are. 1678 : Ray, 204. 1732 : Fuller, No. 6369.

Small fish to catch a great one, Venture a. 1639 : Clarke, 41. 1670 : Ray, 152. 1732 : Fuller, No. 5348. Cf. **Sprat.**

Small heart hath small desires, A. 1640 : Herbert, *Jac. Prudentum.*

Small house has a wide throat, A. 1865 : " Lancs Proverbs," in *N. & Q.*, 3rd ser., viii. 494. 1901 : F. E. Taylor, *Lancs Sayings*, 7, A smo heawse has oft gétten a wide throttle.

Small invitation. *See* **Beggar** (15).

Small pack. *See* **Pedlar.**

Small pitchers. *See* **Little pitchers.**

Small sore wants not a great plaster, A. 1567 : Fenton, *Bandello*, i. 222 (T.T.), " Like as," sayth he, " small soares require slender medecins." 1732 : Fuller, No. 412.

Small spark. *See* **Spark.**

Small stake makes cold play. *c.* 1597 : in Harington, *Nugae Antiquæ*, i. 205 (1804), I know the saying . . . small stake makes colde play.

Small stomachs, light heels. 1855 : Bohn, 487.

Small sum will serve to pay a short reckoning, A. 1639 : Clarke, 128.

1696 : D'Urfey, *Quixote*, Pt. III. Act V. sc. i. 1732 : Fuller, No. 413. 1753 : Foote, *Taste*, I. i., A paltry affair, a poor ten-guinea job ; however, a small game—you know the proverb.

Smart as a carrot. 1780 : in Farmer, *Musa Pedestris*, 56, I still was as smart as a carrot all day. *c.* 1791 : Pegge, *Derbicisms*, 135 (E.D.S.). 1894 : Northall, *Folk Phrases*, 11 (E.D.S.), As smart as a carrot. Said of one gaily dressed. 1923 : *Folk-Lore*, xxxiv. 329 (Oxfordshire).

Smell, verb. 1. *He smelleth best that doth of nothing smell* [Quoniam optimus odor in corpore est nullus. Seneca, *Epist.* cviii]. 1598 : Meres, *Palladis*, fo. 32, As women do smell well, which smel of nothing. 1607 : *Lingua*, IV. iii. 1619 : *Helpe to Discourse*, 93 (1640), Since as the proverbe is, They smell best that smell of nothing. 1669 : *New Help to Discourse*, 245, They that smell least, smell best.

2. *He that smells the first savour, is the fault's first father.* Glos. 1639 : in *Berkeley MSS.*, iii. 32 (1885).

3. *To smell a rat.* 1533 : in *Ballads from MSS.*, i. 182 (B.S.), For yf they smell a rat. . . . *c.* 1598 : Deloney, *Gentle Craft*, Pt. II. ch. iii., What would you so faine be rid of my company ?—If with Gill I smell a rat. 1608 : Middleton, *Family of Love*, IV. ii., Master Gerardine, disguised and ashore ! nay, then I smell a rat. 1669 : Dryden, *Wild Gallant*, IV. i., Oh, are you there-abouts, sir ? then I smell a rat, i' faith. 1714 : Ozell, *Molière*, i. 102, All these signs betoken no good ; I smell a rat. 1872 : Butler, *Erewhon*, ch. xviii., If they smell a rat about the precincts of a cherished institution, they will always stop their noses to it if they can.

4. *To smell of the lamp.* [The expression ἐλλυχνίων ὄζειν is attributed to Pytheas by Plutarch (*Vit. Demosth.*, c. 8).] 1542 : Udall, tr. Erasmus' *Apoph.*, 379 (1877), The saiyng of Pytheas is commen and muche spoken of, that the oracions of Demosthenes smelled all of the candle, for that the same did in the night season wryte and recorde soche thinges as he had to saye to the

people in the daye time. 1608 : in
Harington, *Nugæ Antiquæ*, ii. 190
(1804), A well-labour'd sermon . . .
that smelt of the candle. 1647 : Howell,
Letters, bk. ii. No. xxi., I thank you
heartily for your last letter, in regard
I found it smelt of the lamp. 1754 :
Connoisseur, No. 3, Our compositions
are so correct that . . . they may be
said to smell of the lamp. 1820 :
Colton, *Lacon*, Pref., Knowledge . . .
will smell of the lamp.

5. *To smell of the oil.* 1577 : J.
Grange, *Golden Aphroditis*, sig. N1, This
litle volume of mine smelleth of the
oyle and candle. 1646 : Browne,
Pseudo. Epi., To Reader, A work of this
nature . . . should smel of oyl, if duly
and deservedly handled. 1883 : Trollope, *Autobiog.*, ch. x., A man who
thinks much of his words as he writes
them will generally leave behind him
work that smells of oil.

6. *Well may he smell fire whose gown
burns.* 1640 : Herbert, *Jac. Pruden-
ium.* 1670 : Ray, 9.

Smell of gain is sweet, The. 1621 :
Brathwait, *Natures Embassie, etc.*, 303
(1877), Smell of gaine makes Labour
sweet. 1659 : Gayton, *Art of Longevity*,
46.

Smile, *verb.* 1. *He smiles like a
basket of chips.* Old Shropshire saying.
Sometimes with the addition " on a
frosty morning." 1871 : *N. & Q.*, 4th
ser., vii. 9.

2. *He smiles like a brewer's horse.*
1659 : Howell, 18.

3. *See* quot. 1702 : Centlivre, *Beau's
Duel.*, Epil., He surest strikes that
smiling gives the blow ; Poets, with
us, this proverb do defy, We live by
smiles, for if you frown we die.

4. *You smile and bite.* 1732 : Fuller,
No. 5999.

**Smiling boy seldom proves a good
servant, A.** 1659 : Howell, 8. 1670 :
Ray, 24. 1852 : FitzGerald, *Polonius*,
60 (1903), An old proverb says, " A
smiling boy is a bad servant."

Smith, *subs.* 1. *A right skilful smith.
See* quot. *c.* 1225 : *Ancren R.*, 52
(Camden S.), Ofte a ful hawur smið
smeoðeð a ful woc knif (Often does a

right skilful smith forge a full weak
knife).

2. *The smith and his penny are both
black.* 1640 : Herbert, *Jac. Prudentum.* 1657 : Gurnall, *Christian in Armour*, Pt. II. v. 15, ch. v. p. 129 (1679).
1737 : Ray, 71. 1875 : J. W. Ebsworth, App. to *Merry Drollery*, 373,
An old proverb says that the Smith
and his penny are both black. So we
need not expect that a Sowgelder's song
will be cleanly. 1875 : Smiles, *Thrift*,
164.

3. *The smith hath always a spark in
his throat,* i.e. he is always thirsty.
1678 : Ray, 90. 1732 : Fuller, No.
4754. 1880 : Spurgeon, *Ploughman's
Pictures*, 39, He is not a blacksmith, but
he has a spark in his throat.

Smithfield bargain, A. 1662 : J.
Wilson, *Cheats*, V. v., Is not this better
than a Smithfield bargain ? 1704 : T.
Baker, *An Act at Oxford*, III. ii., Our
marriage is a perfect Smithfield bargain.
1753 : Richardson, *Grandison*, iii. 434
(1883), The hearts of us women . . .
are apt, and are pleaded with, to rise
against the notions of bargain and sale.
Smithfield bargains, you Londoners call
them. 1775 : Sheridan, *Rivals*, V. i.

Smithfield. *See* **Westminster.**

Smithwick. *See* quot. 1678 : Ray,
291, You been like Smithwick, either
cleui'd [starved] or borsten [replete].
Cheshire. 1917 : Bridge, *Cheshire Proverbs*, 157 [" bin " for " been," and
" bossten " for " borsten "].

Smocks than shirts. *See* quot. Ray
attributes this saying to Chaucer, but
I have failed to find it in Chaucer.
Hazlitt follows Ray, but also gives no
reference. 1678 : Ray, 353, He that
hath more smocks then shirts at a
bucking [washing], had need be a man
of good forelooking. *Chaucer.* 1732 :
Fuller, No. 6427 [as in 1678].

Smoke, *subs.* 1. *Smoke follows the
fairest.* 1639 : in *Berkeley MSS.*, iii. 31
(1885), Smoke will to the smicker. If
many gossips sit against a smokey
chimney the smoke will bend to the
fairest. 1646 : Browne, *Pseudo. Epi.*,
bk. v. ch. xxiii., That smoak doth follow
the fairest, is an usual saying with us

. . . yet is it the continuation of a very ancient opinion, as Petras Victorius and Casaubon have observed, from a passage in Athenæus, wherein a parasite thus describeth himself :—" To every table first I come, Whence Porridge I am call'd by some ; . . . Like smoke, unto the fair I fly." 1687 : Aubrey, *Gentilisme, etc.*, 111 (F.L.S.), That smoak doth follow the fairest is ancient opinion, as is to be observed in Athenæus. 1738 : Swift, *Polite Convers.*, Dial. I., They say smoke always pursues the fair. 1851 : Sternberg, *Dialect, etc., of Northants*, 172, Smoke and dust always follow the fairest.

2. *Smoke, rain, and a very curst wife, Makes a man weary of house and life.* 1647 : *Countrym. New Commonwealth*, 42. 1683 : Meriton, *Yorkshire Ale*, 83–7 (1697), A reeking house and a scawding wife will mack yan weary of his life. 1774 : Colman, *Man of Business*, IV. ii., She would ring it in my ears as long as I live—a smoaky house, and a scolding wife, you know ! I need say no more. —It is a kind of hell to inhabit one, and the devil himself would scarce live with the other. Cf. **Three things drive.**

3. *There is no smoke without fire.* [Flamma fumo est proxima.—Plautus, *Curculio*, I. i. 53.] *c.* 1375 : Barbour, *Bruce*, bk. iv. l. 123, And thair may no man fire sa covir, [Bot] low or reek sall it discovir. *c.* 1440 : Hoccleve, *Minor Poems*, 134 (E.E.T.S.), Wher no fyr maad is may no smoke aryse. 1579 : Lyly, *Euphues*, 153 (Arber), Ther can no great smoke arise, but there must be some fire, no great reporte without great suspition. 1649 : Quarles, *Virgin Widow*, I., There's no smoake without some fire. 1679 : Shadwell, *True Widow*, V. i., 'Sdeath ! there must be some fire under all this smoke. 1757 : Murphy, *Upholsterer*, II. i. 1871 : Planché, *Extravag.*, v. 302 (1879), Where so much smoke is, there must be some fire.

4. *The smoke of a man's own house is better than the fire of another.* 1633 : Draxe, 93. 1670 : Ray, 20. 1732 : Fuller, No. 4756.

5. *To escape the smoke and fall into*

the fire. 1548 : Hall, *Chron.*, 210 (1809), There is an olde sayd saw, that a man entendyng to auoide the smoke, falleth into the fyre. 1639 : Clarke, 250, Shunning the smoake he fell into the fire.

6. *When the smoke goes west, Good weather is past; When the smoke goes east, Good weather comes neist* [next]. 1846 : Denham, *Proverbs*, 17 (Percy S.).

Smoking chimney in a great house is a good sign, A. 1732 : Fuller, No. 415.

Smooth as a carpet. 1678 : Ray, 289.

Smooth as glass. 1580 : Lyly, *Euphues*, 320 (Arber), I see now that there is nothing more smooth then glasse. 1590 : Spenser, *F. Q.*, I. i. 318, Could file his tongue as smooth as glas. *c.* 1660 : in *Roxb. Ballads*, ii. 445 (B.S.), Her skin was as smooth as glass. 1720 : Gay, *Poems*, ii. 279 (Underhill), As smooth as glass, as white as curds. 1821 : Scott, *Pirate*, ch. xxii., The bay . . . seemed almost as smooth as glass.

Smooth as oil. 1716 : E. Ward, *Female Policy*, 51, Her tongue as smooth as oil.

Smooth language grates not the tongue. 1659 : Howell, 5.

Smoothy's wedding, All on one side like. 1864 : " Cornish Proverbs," in *N. & Q.*, 3rd ser., vi. 6. 1888 : Q.-Couch, *Troy Town*, ch. viii.

Snail and Snails, *subs.* 1. *As quick as a snail crawling through tar.* W. Corn. 19th cent. (Mr. C. Lee).

2. *Snailie, snailie, shoot out your horn, And tell us if it will be a bonnie day the morn.* 1893 : Inwards, *Weather Lore*, 144.

3. *The house is blest Where snail do rest.* W. Corn. 19th cent. (Mr. C. Lee).

4. *The snail slides up the tower at last though the swallow mounteth it sooner.* 1580 : Lyly, *Euphues*, 419 (Arber), The slow snaile clymeth the tower at last, though the swift swallowe mount it. 1583 : Melbancke, *Philotinus*, sig. Ff2, Can the sluggish snayle with creeping pace euer reache the castles tower ? 1732 : Fuller, No. 4757.

5. *To go a snail's gallop.* 1546 : Heywood, *Proverbs*, Pt. I. ch. ix., If I shall nedes this viage make . . . I will . . .

thytherward hye me in haste lyke a
snayle. 1670 : Ray, 193, To drive
snails ; A snails gallop. 1681 : Robertson, *Phraseol. Generalis*, 672, Ye go a
snails gallop. 1725 : Bailey, tr. Erasmus'
Colloq., 32, I see what haste you make,
you are never the forwarder, you go a
snails gallop. 1803 : Colman, jr., *John
Bull*, III. i., There he comes, in a snail's
trot. 1821 : Combe, *Syntax in Search
of Wife*, can. xxxvi. p. 120, He, by
degrees, would seldom fail T'adopt the
gallop of a snail. 1866 : Brogden,
Lincs Words, 188, Sneel-gallop.—A
slow pace, compared to the crawl of a
snail.

6. *When black snails cross your path,
Black cloud much moisture hath.* 1893 :
Inwards, *Weather Lore*, 144.

7. *When black snails on the road you
see, Then on the morrow rain will be.*
Ibid., 144.

Snake, *subs.* 1. *If the snake could hear
and the slow-worm could see, Neither
man nor beast should e'er go free.* Norfolk. 1856 : *N. & Q.*, 2nd ser., i. 401.
1871 : *N. & Q.*, 4th ser., vii. 547. Cf.
Adder.

2. *The head of a snake with garlic is
good meat.* 1568 : in *Loseley MSS.*,
213 (Kempe).

3. *There is a snake in the grass.*
[Latet anguis in herba.—Virgil, *Ecl.*,
iii. 93.] *c.* 1290 : in Wright, *Pol. Songs
John to Edw. II.*, 172 (Camden S.), Cum
totum fecisse putas, latet anguis in
herba. 1548 : Hall, *Chron.*, 236 (1809),
But the serpent lurked vnder the grasse,
and vnder sugered speache was hide
pestiferous poyson. 1593 : G. Harvey,
Works, ii. 294 (Grosart), Take heede of
the snake in the grass, or the padd in
the straw. 1677 : Yarranton, *Eng.
Improvement*, 101, Hold, hold, you
drive too fast ; there is a snake in the
bush. 1714 : Ozell, *Molière*, iv. 254.
1777 : in *Garrick Corresp.*, ii. 248 (1832),
There are snakes in the grass, and
you seem to foster them. 1926 : Phillpotts, *Yellow Sands*, I., What cares he
for your wishes—young snake in the
grass !

See also **Thunder** (3).

Snapping so short makes you look so

lean. 1678 : Ray, 345. 1738 : Swift,
Polite Convers., Dial. I., Snap short
makes you look so lean, miss.

Sneck. *See* quot. *c.* 1770 : Pegge,
Derbicisms, 65 (E.D.S.), The sneck is the
latch itself, and not the string. Hence
the proverb : " to put a sneck before
one's snout."

Sneeze, *subs. See* quot. 1732: Fuller,
No. 2436, He's a friend at a sneeze ; the
most you can get of him is a *God bless
you.*

Sneeze, *verb.* 1. *He hath sneezed
thrice, turn him out of the hospital.* 1659 :
Howell, 2.

2. *Sneeze on a Monday, etc. See*
quots. 1867 : Harland, etc., *Lancs
Folk-Lore*, 68, Sneeze on a Monday, you
sneeze for danger ; Sneeze on a Tuesday, you kiss a stranger ; Sneeze on a
Wednesday, you sneeze for a letter ;
Sneeze on a Thursday, for something
better ; Sneeze on a Friday, you sneeze
for sorrow ; Sneeze on a Saturday, your
sweet-heart to-morrow ; Sneeze on a
Sunday, your safety seek, The Devil
will have you the whole of the week.
1878 : Dyer, *Eng. Folk-Lore*, 239, In
Devonshire, it is said that if you—
" Sneeze on Sunday morning fasting,
You'll enjoy your own true love to
everlasting." 1879 : Henderson, *Folk-
Lore of N. Counties*, 137 [much the
same as in 1867, but with the omission
of the Sunday couplet]. 1913 : E. M.
Wright, *Rustic Speech, etc.*, 223 [as in
1867].

Snipe. *See* quots. 1678 : Ray, 344,
The snite needs not the woodcock be-
twite [taunt]. *Somerset.* 1732 : Fuller,
No. 4939, There is winter enough for the
snipe and woodcock too. 1886 : Swainson, *Folk-Lore of Brit. Birds*, 192 (F.L.S.)
[as in 1732]. *See also* **Partridge** (2).

Snotty folks. *See* quot. 1678 : Ray,
204, Snotty folks are sweet, but slavering folks are weet. Others have it,
Slavering folks kiss sweet, but snotty
folks are wise.

Snow, *subs.* 1. *A snow year, a rich
year.* 1580 : J. Frampton, tr. *Mon-
arcles*, ii. 162 (T.T.), For this it is
said, The yeare of snow, the yeare of
fertilitie. 1640 : Herbert, *Jac. Pruden-*

tum, A snow year, a rich year. 1659 :
Howell, *Proverbs : Span.-Eng.*, 21, A
year of snow, a year of plenty. 1732 :
Fuller, No. 416. 1825 : Hone, *Ev. Day
Book*, i. 670. 1893 : Inwards, *Weather
Lore*, 5 ; [also] Snow year, good year.

2. *As seasonable as snow in harvest.*
c. 1568 : Wager, *Longer thou Livest*, sig.
F3, As snow in haruest is untimelie.
1595 : *Pedlars Prophecy*, l. 237 (Malone
S.), As profitable as is snow in harvest.
1605 : Camden, *Remains*, 336 (1870)
[" summer " for " harvest "]. 1670 :
Ray, 202 [as in 1605]. 1732 : Fuller,
No. 5869, You came as seasonably
as snow in summer. 1854 : Baker,
Northants Gloss., s.v., A provincial
sarcasm for want of kindness. " He
looks as cold as snow in harvest."
1894 : Northall, *Folk Phrases*, 34
(E.D.S.), You are come like snow
in harvest, i.e. unexpectedly. 1913 :
Folk-Lore, xxiv. 77, As scarce as snow
in harvest (Oxfordshire).

3. *He roasts snow in a furnace.* 1813 :
Ray, 75.

4. *If February give much snow, A fine
summer it doth foreshow.* 1882 : Mrs.
Chamberlain, *W. Worcs. Words*, 37
(E.D.S.), Much February snow A fine
summer doth show. 1882 : *N. & Q.*,
7th ser., v. 297 ; [also] Snow in
February is the crown of the year.

5. *If there be neither snow nor rain,
Then will be dear all kinds of grain.*
1893 : Inwards, *Weather Lore*, 4.

6. *Snow and geese.* *c.* 1791 : Pegge,
Derbicisms, 138 (E.D.S.), They are pulling geese in Scotland ; so here it snows.
1855 : Dickens, *Holly Tree*, Branch 1,
I don't know when the snow began to
set in ; but . . . I heard the guard
remark, " That the old lady up in
the sky was picking her geese pretty
hard to-day." 1917 : Bridge, *Cheshire
Proverbs*, 121, They're plucking their
geese in Wales and sendin' their fithers
here [said in a snowstorm]. *See also*
Widdecombe.

7. *Snow is white And lieth in the dike,
And every man lets it lie. Pepper is
black, And hath a good smack, And every
man doth it buy.* Before 1500 : in
Hill, *Commonplace-Book*, 128 (E.E.T.S.),

Thowgh peper be blak, it hath a good
smak. *c.* 1520 : Stanbridge, *Vulgaria*,
sig. C1 [as in Hill]. 1546 : Heywood,
Proverbs, Pt. II. ch. iv. 1586 : L.
Evans, *Withals Dict. Revised*, sig. E4
[the full saying reversed—pepper coming first and snow second]. 1633 :
Draxe, 16, Pepper is blacke, and snow
is white. 1659 : Howell, 3. 1681 :
Robertson, *Phraseol. Generalis*, 983,
Pepper is black, yet it hath a good
smack. Ibid., 1142, Snow is white, yet
it lyes on the dike.

8. *Under water, famine ; under snow,
bread.* 1640 : Herbert, *Jac. Prudentum*. 1865 : W. White, *Eastern England*, ii. 32. 1893 : Inwards, *Weather
Lore*, 9 [" dearth " for " famine "].

9. *When snow falls in the mud, it remains all winter.* Ibid., 116.

10. *When now in the ditch the snow
doth lie, 'Tis waiting for more by-and-by.*
Ibid., 116.

11. *When the snow falls dry, it means
to lie ; But flakes light and soft bring
rain oft.* Ibid., 116.

12. *When the snow is in the orchard,
A crab is worth a costard.* 1883 : Burne,
Shropsh. Folk-Lore, 579.

13. *Whether you boil snow or pound it,
you can have but water of it.* 1640 :
Herbert, *Jac. Prudentum*. 1670 : Ray,
24. 1732 : Fuller, No. 5687 [" bake "
for " pound "].

See also **April** (14) and (22) ; **Candlemas**, D and G ; **Last racehorse** ; **March**
(35) ; **May**, F (2) ; **Ram**, *subs*. (1) ; and
White (7), (8) and (14).

**Snowdon will yield sufficient pasture
for all the cattle of Wales put together.**
1662 : Fuller, *Worthies*, iii. 527 (1840).
1790 : Grose, *Prov. Gloss.*, s.v. " Caer-
narvonshire."

Snuff in the nose, To take = To
take offence. 1610 : Rowlands, *Martin
Mark-all*, 34 (Hunt. Cl.), And not by any
means to crosse them, least they take
snuffe in the nose, and so fall together
by the eares. 1661 : Pepys, *Diary*,
6 Oct., Who, I expect, should take in
snuffe that my wife did not come to
his child's christening. 1714 : Ozell,
Molière, i. 83, How very hasty you are.
You take snuff in a minute. 1821 :

Scott, *Kenilworth*, ch. i., But take no snuff in the nose about it. Cf. **Pepper.**

Snug as a bug in a rug. 1769 : *Stratford Jubilee*, II. i., I'll have her, as snug as a bug in a rug. 1772 : Franklin, in *Works*, iv. 525 (Bigelow), Here Skugg Lies snug As a bug In a rug. 1886 : Elworthy, *West Som. Word-Book*, 96 (E.D.S.). 1913 : *Folk-Lore*, xxiv. 77 (Oxfordshire.)

Snug as a pig in pease-straw. 1639 : Davenport, *New Trick, etc.*, III. i., He snores and sleepes as snug As any pigge in pease-straw. *c.* 1662 : in *Bagford Ballads*, i. 198 (B.S.), Like piggs in the pease-straw, intangld they lie.

Soap in a wash tub, They are like a ha'p'orth of. 1855 : Bohn, 525.

Sober as a judge. 1694 : *Terence made English*, 82, I thought my self as sober as a judge. 1712 : Arbuthnot, *John Bull*, Pt. III. ch. vi , Lewis . . . kept himself sober as a judge. 1896 : Doyle, *Rodney Stone*, ch. xvi. 1924 : *Sphere*, 7 June, p. 259, col. 1, A dignitary proverbially " sober as a judge."

Sober man, a soft answer, A. 1659 : Howell, *Proverbs: Brit.-Eng.*, 7.

Soberness. *See* **Drunkenness.**

So cunning. *See* **Weather** (3).

Soft and fair goes far. *c.* 1400 : *Beryn*, 28 (E.E.T.S.), But feir and sofft with ese, homward they hir led. 1542 : Udall, tr. *Erasmus' Apoph.*, 286 (1877), The prouerbe, *spede thee faire and softly*, is a lesson of counsaile. 1583 : Greene, *Works*, ii. 28 (Grosart), Goe as the snaile faire and softly. 1640 : Herbert, *Jac. Prudentum.* 1668 : Dryden, *Sir Martin Mar-all*, II. ii. 1714 : Ozell, *Molière*, ii. 13. 1768 : Goldsmith, *Good-Natured Man*, IV., Soft and fair, young lady. You that are going to be married think things can never be done too fast. 1818 : Scott, *Heart of Midl.*, ch. xlv., " Fair and softly gangs far," said Meiklehose.

Soft as butter. 1567 : Golding, *Ovid*, bk. xiii. l. 937, More soft than butter newly made. 1620 : Shelton, *Quixote*, Pt. II. ch. xii., My lady is as gentle as a lamb and as soft as butter. *c.* 1625 : Wither, *Schollers Purgat.*, 95 (Spens. S.), I found the words of their mouthes

as soft as butter. 1771 : Smollett, *Clinker*, in *Works*, vi. 8 (1817), She is a poor good-natured simpleton, as soft as butter. 1923 : O. Seaman, in *Punch*, 23 May, 482, Soft my words shall be as butter.

Soft as pap. *c.* 1590 : *Plaine Percevall*, Dedn., The first ladlefull had a smacke as soft as pap. 1720 : Gay, *Poems*, ii. 279 (Underhill), As soft as pap her kisses are.

Soft as silk. *c.* 1307 : in *Lyric Poetry*, 36 (Percy S., No. 19), Eythar side soft ase sylk. *c.* 1386 : Chaucer, *Squire's Tale*, l. 605, And strawe hir cage faire and softe as silk. *c.* 1430 : Lydgate, *Minor Poems*, 188 (E.E.T.S.), Hir body, softe as selke. *c.* 1450 : *Partonope*, 66 (E.E.T.S.), Her lees were as softe as sylk. Before 1529 : Skelton, *Philip Sparrow*, l. 1119, And handes soft as sylke. 1555 : S. Hawes, *Past. of Pleasure*, 63 (Percy S.), By her propre hande, soft as any sylke. 1605 : Sylvester, *Du Bartas*, Week II. Day iii. Pt. 1, l. 162. 1782 : Wolcot, *Lyric Odes*, Ode viii., in *Works*, i. (1795), Sweet is the voice of Praise !—oh, soft as silk. 1892 : B. Pain, *Playthings, etc.*, 227, Her cheek was soft as silk.

Soft fire makes sweet malt. Before 1500 : in Hill, *Commonplace-Book*, 128 (E.E.T.S.), A softe fire makith swete malte. 1550 : Udall, *Roister Doister*, I. iii. 1617 : Greene, *Alcida*, in *Works*, ix. 66 (Grosart), The malt is euer sweetest, where the fire is softest. 1694 : D'Urfey, *Quixote*, Pt. I. Act IV. [" Slow " for " Soft "]. 1785–95 : Wolcot, *Lousiad*, can. ii., Soft fires, the proverb tells us, make sweet malt. 1823 : Scott, *Q. Durward*, ch. vii. [" Slow " for " Soft "].

Soft pace goes far. 1598 : Meres, *Palladis*, fo. 259. 1669 : *Politeuphuia*, 182.

Soft wax will take any impression. 1672 : Walker, *Parœm.*, 35.

Soft words and hard arguments. 1670 : Ray, 158. 1732 : Fuller, No. 4203 [" are " for " and "].

Soft words. *See also* **Fair** (31).

Softly as foot can fall. 1530 : Palsgrave, 570, I go as softe as foote maye fall. 1587 : Turbervile, *Trag. Tales*, *etc.*, 30 (1837), There stalkte he on, as softe as foote could tread. 1601 : Shakespeare, *As You Like It*, III. ii. 1681 : Robertson, *Phraseol. Generalis*, 1145.

So got so gone. 1678 : Ray, 349.

So great is the ill that doth not hurt me, As is the good that doth not help me. 1578 : Florio, *First Fruites*, fo. 32 [slightly varied]. 1629 : *Book of Meery Riddles*, Prov. 1.

Sold. *See* quot. Glos. 1639 : in *Berkeley MSS.*, iii. 29 (1885), He hath sold a beane and bought a peaze. He hath sold a pound and bought a penny. He hath sold Bristoll and bought Bedminster.

Soldiers in peace are like chimneys in summer. 1594 : A. Copley, *Wits, Fits, etc.*, 34 (1614). Before 1598 : Lord Burghley, in Peck's *Desid. Curiosa*, 48 (1779). 1611 : *Tarltons Jests*, 11 (Sh. S.), There was a nobleman that asked Tarlton what hee thought of souldiers in time of peace. Marry, quoth he, they are like chimnies in summer. [Tarlton was a plagiarist.] 1670 : Ray, 24. 1732 : Fuller, No. 4207.

Sole is the bread and butter of fish, A. Corn. 1897 : *N. & Q.*, 8th ser., xi. 448.

Sole. *See* Shoe, *subs.* (3).

So like that they are the worse for it, They are. 1678 : Ray, 354. 1732 : Fuller, No. 4959 ["both" for the second "they"].

Solitary man. *See* quots. 1669 : *Politeuphuia*, 137, The solitary man is either a God or a beast. 1732 : Fuller, No. 418, A solitary man is either a brute or an angel.

Solomon. *See* Samson.

Solomon's wise, loath to go to bed, but ten times loather to rise. 1882 : Mrs. Chamberlain, *W. Worcs. Words*, 39 (E.D.S.). Cf. Sluggard's guise.

So long as you'll crowdy [fiddle] they'll dance. E. Corn. 1880 : T. Q. Couch, *E. Cornwall Words*, 82 (E.D.S.).

So many countries, so many customs (or laws). 10th cent.: in *A.-Saxon Gnomic Verses*, i. 17 (Grein), efen—fela bega, þeoda and þeawa [an equal number both of countries and customs].

c. 1320 : in *Reliq. Antiquæ*, i. 109 (1841), " Ase fele [many] thede [countries], ase fele thewes " ; Quoth Hendyng. *c.* 1374 : Chaucer, *Troylus*, bk. ii. st. 6, For thus men seyn eche cuntre hath his lawis. Ibid., bk. ii. l. 28, In sondry londes, sondry ben usages. Before 1634 : Chapman, *Alphonsus*, III. i., So many lands, so many fashions. 1669 : *Politeuphuia*, 224, So many countreys, so many laws. 1670 : Ray, 73, . . . customs. 1732 : Fuller, No. 4196, . . . customs.

So many gipsies, so many smiths. 1846–59 : *Denham Tracts*, ii. 84 (F.L.S.).

So many heads, so many wits, or So many men, so many minds. [Quot homines, tot sententiae. — Terence, *Phorm.*, II. iv. 14.] *c.* 1386 : Chaucer *Squire's Tale*, l. 195, As many hedes, as many wittes ther been. 1539 : Taverner, *Proverbs*, fo. 13, So many men, so many wyttes. 1546 : Heywood, *Proverbs*, Pt. I. ch. iii., So many heds so many wits. 1575 : Gascoigne, *Glasse of Govt.*, II. ii., So many men, so many mindes. 1592 : Greene, *Works*, xi. 44 (Grosart) [as in 1546]. 1610 : Rowlands, *Martin Mark-all*, 6 (Hunt. Cl.) [as in 1575]. 1692 : L'Estrange, *Æsop:* "Life," 18 [as in 1575]. 1753 : Richardson, *Grandison*, iii. 477 (1883), So many persons, so many minds. 1859 : Sala, *Twice Round Clock*, 3 p.m., The proverb reads aright—as many men, so many minds.

So many servants, so many foes. 1539 : Taverner, *Proverbs*, fo. 34, Loke how many bondmen we haue and so many enemyes we haue. 1586: Pettie, tr. Guazzo's *Civil Convers.* fo. 169, According to the saying, We haue so manie enimies as we haue seruants. 1666 : Torriano, *Piazza Univ.*, 257. 1669 : Dudley North, *Obs. and Adv. Œconom.*, 40 ["enemies" for "foes"].

Some are very busy and yet do nothing. 1732 : Fuller, No. 4211.

Some are wise and some are otherwise. 1659 : Howell, 1. 1738 : Swift, *Polite Convers.*, Dial. I. 1748 : Smollett, *Rod. Random*, ch. vi.

Some come, some go ; This life is so. 1732 : Fuller, No. 6340.

Some fish, some frogs. *c.* 1500 : More, *Fortune*, st. 32, in Hill, *Commonplace-Book*, 79 (E.E.T.S.), Lo, in this pond be fishe and froggis bothe. 1579 : Lyly, *Euphues*, 196 (Arber), It is in the courte as in all ryuers, some fish some frogges. 1792 : Wolcot, *Works*, ii. 434 (1795), Whereas it is in Courts, as in a pond, Some fish, some frogs.

Some good, some bad, as sheep come to the fold. 1678 : Ray, 247.

Some have hap [luck], some stick in the gap. 1639 : Clarke, 125. 1659 : Howell, 16, Some have the happ and others sticke in the gapp. 1732 : Fuller, No. 6274. 1846–59 : *Denham Tracts*, i. 296 (F.L.S.).

Some men must love my lady, and some Joan. 1592 : Shakespeare, *L. L. L.*, III. last line.

Somerset. *See* quot. 1622 : Drayton, *Polyol.*, xxiii., Then Somerset says, Set the bandog on the bull.

Somerton ending, A. Somerset. 1678 : Ray, 347. 1790 : Grose, *Prov. Gloss.*, s.v. " Somerset."

Some save-alls do well in a house. 1678 : Ray, 198, Some savers in a house do well. 1732 : Fuller, No. 4217.

Something hath some savour. *c.* 1580: Fulwell, *Ars Adulandi*, sig. C2, Somewhat hath some sauor. 1585 : Sir E. Dyer, in *Writings*, 87 (Grosart) [as in 1580]. 1611 : Davies (of Hereford), *Sc. of Folly*, 43, in *Works*, ii. (Grosart). 1656 : *Musarum Deliciæ*, i. 31 (Hotten), Something, you know, will have some savour. 1738 : Swift, *Polite Convers.*, Dial. I., They say, something has some savour, but nothing has no flavour. 1754 : Berthelson, *Eng.-Danish Dict.*, s.v. " Savour."

Somewhat is better than nothing. 1546 : Heywood, *Proverbs*, Pt. I. ch. x. *c.* 1594 : Bacon, *Promus*, No. 953. 1620 : Shelton, *Quixote*, Pt. II. ch. l., Something is better than nothing. 1659 : Howell, 9.

So much is mine. *See* quots. 1578 : Florio, *First Fruites*, fo. 32, So much is myne as I enioy, or is geue for Gods sake. 1629 : *Book of Meery Riddles*, Prov. 17, So much is mine as I possesse, and give, or lose, for God's sake. 1732 :

Fuller, No. 4198, So much is mine as I enjoy, and give away for God's sake.

Son, *subs.* 1. *A son of the white hen* = a lucky one. [Qui tu gallinae filius albae, Nos viles pulli nati infelicibus ovis ?—Juvenal, xiii. 141.] 1630 : Jonson, *New Inn*, I. i., Yet all, sir, are not sons of the white hen. 1764 : *Poor Robin Alman.*, Feb., For money, like a chick of the white hen, has generally luck on its side.

2. *He is the son of a bachelor*, i.e. a bastard. 1678 : Ray, 66. 1732 : Fuller, No. 1949.

3. *My son is my son till he have got him a wife; But my daughter's my daughter all the days of her life.* 1670 : Ray, 53. 1732 : Fuller, No. 6076. 1851 : Planché, in *Extravag.*, iv. 201 (1879), We lose a son who takes a wife, —Our daughter is our daughter all her life.

Song, A. or An old song = little value. *c.* 1605 : Shakespeare, *All's Well*, III. ii., I know a man . . . hold a goodly manor for a song. 1675 : Cotton, *Burl. upon Burlesque*, 266 (1765), And there's an end of an old song. 1694 : Crowne, *Regulus*, II. i., I bought it for a song. 1704 : Swift, *Tale of Tub*, § ix., Hence comes the common saying, and commoner practice, of parting with money for a song. 1714 : *Spectator*, No. 597, An hopeful youth . . . was forced . . . to resign all for an old song. 1849 : Lytton, *Caxtons*, Pt. XVII. ch. iv., Jack had . . . purchased, on his own account, " for an old song," some barren land. 1919 : J. A. Bridges, *Victorian Recollections*, 187, The inn cost very little to rent ; indeed, he might have bought it for a song if he had cared to.

Soon crooketh the tree that good gambrel would be. " Gambrel" (also " cambrel" and " camock)" = a " bent piece of wood used by butchers to hang carcases on." *c.* 1460 : *Good Wyfe wold a Pylgr.*, The tre crokothe son that good cambrel wyll be. 1546 : Heywood, *Proverbs*, Pt. II. ch. ix., Timely crooketh the tree that will a good camok bee. 1570 : A. Barclay, *Mirrour of Good Manners*, 24 (Spens. S.), Soone crooketh

the same tree that good camoke wilbe.
1670 : Ray, 75. 1676 : W. Lawson,
New Orchard and Garden, 37, The common homely proverb : Soon crooks the
tree That good camrel must be. 1732 :
Fuller, No. 6118.

Soon enough. *See* **Well** (19).

Sooner named sooner come. *c.* 1550 :
Jacke Jugeler, in Hazlitt, *Old Plays*, ii.
116, If I had sooner spoken, he would
have sooner been here. 1581 : Woodes,
Conflict of Conscience, III. ii., I marvel
what doth him from hence so long stay,
Sooner named, sooner come, as common
proverbs say.

Sooner said. *See* **Said.**

Sooner spared than got. 1541 : Coverdale, *Christ. State Matrim.*, sig. I3, A
thinge is soner spared then goten.

**Soon espied where the thorn pricketh,
It is.** Before 1529 : Skelton, in *Works*,
i. 418 (Dyce).

Soonest begun soonest over. 1872 :
Trollope, *Golden Lion*, ch. xx.

**Soon goes the young sheep as the old
to market** (or pot, etc.), **As.** [*c.* 1440 :
Gesta Rom., 364 (E.E.T.S.), The sone
saide, " alse sone deyeth the yong as
the olde . . ."] *c.* 1520 : *Calisto and
Meliboea*, in Hazlitt, *Old Plays*, i. 78, As
soon goeth to market the lamb's fell As
the sheep's. 1546 : Heywood, *Proverbs*,
Pt. II. ch. iv., As soone goth the yonge
lamskyn to the market As tholde
yewes. 1599 : Porter, *Two Angry
Women*, in Hazlitt, *Old Plays*, vii. 302,
Take heed, as soon goes the young
sheep to the pot as the old. 1631 :
Mabbe, *Celestina*, 86 (T.T.), As soone
(lady) dies the young lambe as the old
sheep. 1712 : Motteux, *Quixote*, Pt.
II. ch. vii., As soon goes the young
lamb to the spit, as the old wether.
1819 : Scott, *Bride of L.*, ch. iv., As
soon comes the lamb's skin to market
as the auld tup's.

Soon gotten, soon spent. 1546 : Hey-
wood, *Proverbs*, Pt. II. ch. vi. 1605 :
Camden, *Remains*, 331 (1870). 1732 :
Fuller, No. 4227. 1849 : Brontë,
Shirley, ch. xxvii., " Unless I heard the
whole repeated, I cannot continue it,"
she said. " Yet it was quickly learned."
" Soon gained, soon gone," moralized

the tutor. 1880 : Spurgeon, *Ploughman's
Pictures*, 9, This was a case of . . .
" soon gotten, soon spent."

Soon hot soon cold. *c.* 1450 : Burgh
(and Lydgate), *Secrees*, 60 (E.E.T.S.).
1485 : Malory, *Morte d'Arthur*, bk. xviii.
ch. xxv. 1546 : Heywood, *Proverbs*, Pt.
I. ch. ii., Than perceiue they well, hotte
loue soone colde. 1587 : Greene,
Works, iv. 146 (Grosart). 1617 :
Wither, *Fidelia*, l. 4, Loue that's soon'st
hot, is euer soonest cold. 1732 : Fuller,
No. 4228.

Soon learnt soon forgotten. *c.* 1374 :
Chaucer, *Troylus*, bk. ii. l. 1238, For-
why men seyth, " impressiones lighte
Ful lightly been ay redy to the flighte."
1869 : Hazlitt, 342.

Soon ripe soon rotten. *c.* 1393 :
Langland, *Plowman*, C, xiii. 223, And
that that rathest rypeth roteth most
saunest. 1546 : Heywood, *Proverbs*,
Pt. I. ch. x. 1566 : Harman, *Caveat*,
cap. xxii. 1604 : *Jacke of Dover*, 23
(Percy S.). 1683 : White-Kennett, tr.
Erasmus' *Praise of Folly*, 14 (8th ed.),
Therefore for the curbing of too forward
parts we have a disparaging proverb,
Soon ripe, soon rotten. 1756 : *Gent.
Mag.*, 556. 1889 : Peacock, *Manley,
etc., Gloss.*, 507 (E.D.S.).

Soon todd [toothed] **soon with God—**
an idea which has found expression in
several forms. 1659 : Howell, 4, Soon
todd, soon with God, a Northern proverb, when a child hath teeth too soon.
1670 : Ray, 52, Quickly too'd, and
quickly go, Quickly will thy mother
have moe [more]. Yorksh. Ibid., 26
[as in 1659]. 1879 : W. Henderson,
Folk-Lore of N. Counties, 19, The proverb " Soon teeth, soon toes," shows
another portent of such an event. If
baby's teeth come early there will soon
be fresh toes, i.e. another baby. 1888 :
N. & Q., 7th ser., v. 285, My mother
used always to say, " soon toothed, soon
turfed."

Sooth bourd. *See* **True** (11).

**Sore be healed, Though the, yet a
scar may remain.** 1732 : Fuller, No.
5013.

Sore eyes. 1. *The light is naught for
sore eyes.* 1580 : Lyly, *Euphues*, 394

(Arber), He that hath sore eyes must
not behold the candle. 1663 : Killigrew, *Parson's Wedding*, II. v., *Capt.
. . .* I see you are merry : I'll leave you.
I must go a little way to inquire about
a business. *Wild.* H' has got a sore
eye, I think. 1670 : Ray, 114.

2. *The sight of you is good for sore
eyes.* 1738 : Swift, *Polite Convers.*,
Dial. I. 1893 : Raymond, *Gent. Up-
cott*, ch. iv., It's good for sore eyes to
see you here.

**Sorrow and an evil life maketh soon
an old wife.** 1639 : Clarke, 279. 1670 :
Ray, 144. 1732 : Fuller, No. 6366.

**Sorrow at parting if at meeting there
be laughter.** *c.* 1410 : *Towneley Plays*,
292 (E.E.T.S.), Thus sorow is at partyng
at metyng if ther be laghter.

Sorrow comes unsent for. 1579 :
Spenser, *Shep. Cal.*, May, 159, Sorrow,
ne neede be hastened on : For he will
come without calling anon. 1670 :
Ray, 144. 1732 : Fuller, No. 4230.
1869 : Spurgeon, *John Ploughman*, ch.
v., Sorrows are visitors that come without invitation.

Sorrow ends not when it seemeth done.
1855 : Bohn, 489.

**Sorrow for a husband is like a pain
in the elbow, sharp and short.** 1732 :
Fuller, No. 4241.

Sorrow is asleep, wake it not, When.
1659 : Howell, 16. 1732 : Fuller, No.
5569. *c.* 1850 : Song quoted, *N. & Q.*,
8th ser., xi. 417, When sorrow sleepeth
wake it not.

Sorrow is dry. *c.* 1540 : Bale, *Kynge
Johan*, l. 2459, For heauynesse is drye.
c. 1598 : Deloney, *Gentle Craft*, Pt. II.
ch. iii., Sorrow they say is dry, and I
find it to be true. 1623 : Webster,
Devil's Law-Case, V. iv., 'Tis sorrow
that is very dry. 1667 : Dryden and
Davenant, *Tempest*, II. i. 1714 : Gay,
Shep. Week, Friday, l. 152, Excessive
sorrow is exceeding dry. 1768 : Goldsmith, *Vicar*, ch. xvii., Deborah, my
life, grief, you know, is dry. 1826 :
Scott, *Woodstock*, ch. vii. 1901 : F. E.
Taylor, *Lancs Sayings*, 26, Sorrow will
have ale.

Sorrow is good for nothing but sin.
1659 : Howell, 4. 1732 : Fuller, No. 4232.

Sorrow makes silence her best orator.
1600 : Bodenham, *Belvedere*, 171 (Spens.
S.).

Sorrow rode in my cart. 1830 : Forby,
Vocab. E. Anglia, 429.

Sorrow to one's sops, To have. 1546 :
Heywood, *Proverbs*, Pt. II. ch. viii., I
had sorow to my sops ynough, be sure.
1670 : Ray, 218. 1788 : Grose, *Class.
Dict. Vulgar Tongue* (2nd ed.) (O.),
Sorrow shall be his sops, he shall repent
this.

Sorrow will pay no debt. 1669 : *New
Help to Discourse*, 310, Sorrow quits
no scores. 1670 : Ray, 144. 1736 :
Bailey, *Dict.*, s.v. " Sorrow."

Sorrow. *See also* Lean sorrow ;
Ounce of mirth ; Pennyworth of mirth ;
Sup (4) ; and **Weal** (3).

Sorry, but I can't cry, I am. 1584 :
Three Ladies of London, in Hazlitt, *Old
Plays*, vi. 319, Alas ! Lucre, I am sorry
for thee, but I cannot weep. 1613 : B.
& F., *Knight of Burning Pestle*, I. ii.,
Beshrew me, sir, I am sorry for your
losses, But, as the proverb says, I can-
not cry. 1641 : *Archy's Dream*, 6, in
Hindley, *Old Book-Coll. Miscell.*, iii.,
Archy said he was very sorry, but could
not cry. 1738 : Swift, *Polite Convers.*,
Dial. I. 1827 : Scott, *Journal*, 4 June,
We have lost our Coal Gas Bill. Sorry
for it, but I can't cry.

So said so done. 1594 : Shakespeare,
Tam. of Shrew, I. ii., So said, so done,
is well. 1615 : T. Heywood, *Foure
Prentises*, in *Works*, ii. 200 (1874), So
said, so done, braue lord.

Soulgrove [February] is seldom warm.
1687 : Aubrey, *Gentilisme*, 9 (F.L.S.),
The shepheards, and vulgar people
in South Wilts call Februarie Sowle-
grove ; and have this proverbe of
it : viz. Sowlegrove sil [seldom] lew.
February is seldome warme. 1846 :
Denham, *Proverbs*, 28 (Percy S.),
" Soulegrove sil lew," is an ancient
Wiltshire proverb.

Sound as a bell. 1599 : Shakespeare,
Much Ado, III. ii., He hath a heart as
sound as a bell. 1607 : B. Barnes, *Divils
Charter*, sig. K1. 1607 : Sedley, *Bellamira*, III., I am as sound as a bell, fat,
plump and juicy. 1720 : Gay, *Poems*,

ii. 278 (Underhill), Hearts sound as any bell. 1862 : *Dialect of Leeds*, 406. 1886 : Elworthy, *West Som. Word-Book*, 695 (E.D.S.), " Sound as a bell " is the regular superlative absolute. 1918 : Walpole, *Green Mirror*, bk. i. ch. i., Healthy, happy, sound as so many bells.

Sound as an acorn. 1862 : *Dialect of Leeds*, 407. 1882 : Mrs. Chamberlain, *W. Worcs. Words*, 1 (E.D.S.), " As sound as an ackern " is a local proverb. 1884-6 : Holland, *Cheshire Gloss.* (E.D.S.), As sound as a atchern. 1917 : Bridge, *Cheshire Proverbs*, 20, As sound as an atchern.

Sound as a roach. 1655 : T. Muffett, *Healths Improvement*, 186, According to the old proverb, as sound as a roach. 1668 : Shadwell, *Sullen Lovers*, V. iii. 1697 : Vanbrugh, *Prov. Wife*, V. 1703 : Centlivre, *Love's Contrivance*, I. ii. *c.* 1760 : Foote, *Mayor of Garratt*, I. i., Tar-water and turpentine will make you as sound as a roach. 1881 : Evans, *Leics. Words*, 250 (E.D.S.), Sound as a roach, a common simile.

Sound as a trout. Before 1300 : *Cursor Mundi*, l. 11884, Bi þat þou com þerof oute þou shal be hool as any troute. Before 1529 : Skelton, *Magnyfycence*, l. 1643, I am forthwith as hole as a troute. 1588 : Cogan, *Haven of Health*, 142 (1612). 1599 : Buttes, *Dyets Dry Dinner*, sig. M1. 1678 : Ray, 289. 1828 : Carr, *Craven Dialect*, ii. 219, " As sound as a troot," applied . . . to a person of a sound or good constitution. 1891 : P. H. Emerson, *East Coast Yarns*, 43, Now look at 'em with their red skins and dewy noses, healthy as trout.

Sound love is not soon forgotten. 1894 : Northall, *Folk Phrases*, 23 (E.D.S.).

Sound travelling far and wide, A stormy day will betide. 1893 : Inwards, *Weather Lore*, 106.

Sour ale. *See* Mend (6).

Sour apple-tree. *See* quot. 1670 : Ray, 193, To be tied to the sowre apple-tree, i.e. To be married to an ill husband. 1736 : Bailey, *Dict.*, s.v. " Sour " [as in 1670].

Sour as vargis [verjuice]. 1600 :

Dekker, *Shoom. Holiday*, II. i., He lookt upon me as sowre as verjuice. 1709 : E. Ward, *Works*, iv., *Verse*, 12, And live on small drink that's as sower as varges. 1854 : Baker, *Northants Gloss.*, s.v. " Vargis," Verjuice, " As sour as vargis." 1886 : Elworthy, *West Som. Word-Book*, 798 (E.D.S.), Can't drink this yer stuff, 'tis zo zour's varjis. 1917 : Bridge, *Cheshire Proverbs*, 20, As sour as vargis (or warjis).

Sour as vinegar. *See* Sharp.

Sour as wer [crab-apples]. 1633 : Draxe, 194, As soure as a crab. 1691 : Ray, *Words not Generally Uused*, 73 (E.D.S.), As sour as wharre. 1877 : Leigh, *Cheshire Gloss.*, 225, Sour as wharre. 1917 : Bridge, *Cheshire Proverbs*, 21, As sour as wer (or wharre).

Sour as whig [sour whey]. 1854 : Baker, *Northants Gloss.*, s.v. " Whig," . . . a common proverbial simile.

South Darne. *See* Sutton.

South Molton. *See* Bishop's Nympton.

South Repps. *See* Gimmingham.

South wind. *See* Wind.

Southwold. *See* Walberswick.

Sow (female swine), *subs.* 1. *A barren sow was never good to pigs.* 1855 : Bohn, 281.

2. *A fat sow causeth her own bane.* 1659 : Howell, 7. Cf. **Swine** (1).

3. *An alewife's sow is always well fed.* 1732 : Fuller, No. 578.

4. *As necessary as a sow among young children.* 1678 : Ray, 287. 1732 : Fuller, No. 717 [" an old sow " for " a sow "].

5. *A sow doth sooner than a cow bring an ox to the plough.* Glos. 1639 : in *Berkeley MSS.*, iii. 31 (1885).

6. *A sow to a fiddle.* 1639 : Clarke, 5. 1670 : Ray, 193. 1672 : Walker, *Parœm.*, 53.

7. *As the sow fills the draff sours.* 1639 : Clarke, 113. 1685 : Meriton, *Yorkshire Ale*, 38, For as the sew [sow] doth fill the draffe doth soure.

8. *Every sow to her own trough.* 1678 : Ray, 204. 1712 : Motteux, *Quixote*, Pt. II. ch. xix.

9. *It works like soap in a sow's tail* —and like expressions. 1592 : Lyly,

Mother Bombie, IV. i., This cottons and workes like wax in a sowes eare. 1659 : Howell, 14. 1670 : Ray, 193. Ibid., 216, It melts like butter in a sows tail.

10. *Little knoweth the fat sow what the lean doth mean.* 1546 : Heywood, *Proverbs*, Pt. I. ch. x. *c.* 1560 : Becon, in *Catechism, etc.*, 583 (P.S.), Little wot the full sow, that is in the sty, What the hungry sow aileth, that goeth by. 1670 : Ray, 89. 1732 : Fuller, No. 3257. 1852 : FitzGerald, *Polonius*, xvii. (1903), As when we say " The fat sow knows not what the lean one thinks."

11. *Right, Roger, your sow is good mutton.* 1670 : Ray, 191. 1732 : Fuller, No. 4054. 1864 : " Cornish Proverbs," in *N. & Q.*, 3rd ser., vi. 495, Right, Roger, right ; your sow is very good mutton but better pork.

12. *Sow and saddle. See* quots. 1546 : Heywood, *Proverbs*, Pt. II. ch. i., As meete as a sow to beare a saddle. 1660 : A. Brome, *Poems:* "New Ballad," But the title of knight, on the back of a knave, Is like a saddle upon a sow. 1671 : A. Behn, *Amorous Prince*, IV. ii., These clothes become Thee, as a saddle does a sow. 1732 : Fuller, No. 1972, He looks like a sow saddled. 1762 : Smollett, *Sir L. Greaves*, ch. viii., Lord help his fool's head ! it becomes him as a sow doth a cart-saddle. 1917 : Bridge, *Cheshire Proverbs*, 80, It becomes him as well as a sow does a cart-saddle.

13. *To come sailing in a sow's ear.* 1670 : Ray, 192. 1732 : Fuller, No. 5146.

14. *To grease the fat sow.* 1546 : Heywood, *Proverbs*, Pt. I. ch. xi., What should we (quoth I), grease the fat sow in thars. 1580 : Baret, *Alvearie*, S 411, It is as well bestowed vpon him, as to grease a fatte sowe in the arse. 1639 : Clarke, 10, To grease a fat sow i' th' taile. 1666 : Torriano, *Piazza Univ.*, 243, The more one is rich, the more one may be, usually one greaseth a fat sow in the nose. 1925 : *Times*, 8 Dec., p. 8, col. 3, Mr. Lansbury said that this was only another instance of " greasing the fat sow." Not a single

one of these duties would do any good to the working people.

15. *To have a good nose to be a poor man's sow.* 1530 : Palsgrave, 580, He hath a good nose, etc. 1579 : *Marr. of Wit and Wisdom*, 27 (Sh. S.), I have a good nose, etc. 1670 : Ray, 187 [as in 1530, but with " make " for " be "]. 1738 : Swift, *Polite Convers.*, Dial. I., Colonel, I find you would make a very bad poor man's sow.

16. *You prick up your ears like an old sow in beans.* 1887 : Parish and Shaw, *Dict. Kent. Dialect*, 121 (E.D.S.), A proverbial saying is, " You prick up," etc.

See also Cow (1) and (19) ; Hog ; Pig ; Silk purse ; Still sow ; Swine ; and Wrong (4).

Sow, *verb.* 1. *As you sow so will you reap.* 8th cent. : Cynewulf, *Christ*, l. 84 (Gollancz), Swa eal manna bearn Sorgum sawað swa eft ripað Cennað to cwealme (All the children of men as they sow in sorrow, so afterwards they reap, they bring forth for death). *c.* 1250 : *Owl and Nightingale*, 1037, That man schal erien an sowe Thar he wenth after sum god mowe. *c.* 1270 : in *Old Eng. Miscell.*, 59 (Morris, E.E.T.S.), Hwenne alle men repen schule, that heo ear seowe. *c.* 1420 : Lydgate, *Assem. of Gods*, 37 (E.E.T.S.), But suche as ye haue sowe Must ye nedes reepe. *c.* 1560 : T. Ingelend, *Disob. Child*, in Hazlitt, *Old Plays*, ii. 295, But my son . . . Shall reap in such wise as he did sow. 1609 : Dekker, *Works*, iv. 219 (Grosart), I haue made the olde saying true, who sowes shall reape. 1664 : Butler, *Hudibras*, Pt. II. can. ii. l. 504, As you sow, y'are like to reap. 1766 : Garrick and Colman, *Clandest. Marriage*, I. i. 1836 : Marryat, *Japhet*, ch. xxxi., No, no, Japhet, as I have sown, so must I reap. 1895 : Wilde, *Import. of being Earnest*, II., As a man sows so let him reap.

2. *Forbear not sowing because of birds.* 1640 : Herbert, *Jac. Prudentum*.

3. *He is sowing on the sand.* 1813 : Ray, 75. Cf. Plough, *verb* (7).

4. *He that soweth good seed, shall reap good corn.* 1633 : Draxe, 12.

5. *He that soweth virtue, shall reap fame.* 1629: *Book of Meery Riddles,* Prov. 48.

6. *He that sows iniquity shall reap sorrow.* 1732: Fuller, No. 2306.

7. *He that sows in the highway tires his oxen, and loseth his corn.* 1633: Draxe, 222 ["wearieth" for "tires," and "labour" for "corn"]. 1732: Fuller, No. 2305.

8. *He that sows thistles shall reap prickles.* 1611: Cotgrave, s.v. "Chardon," . . . reaps thornes. 1732: Fuller, No. 2307.

9. *He that sows trusts in God.* 1640: Herbert, *Jac. Prudentum.* 1670: Ray, 24, Who sows his corn in the field trusts in God.

10. *One sows another reaps.* 1709: Dykes, *Eng. Proverbs,* Pref. ii. (2nd ed.)

11. *Sow dry and set wet.* [1580: Tusser, *Husb.,* 101 (E.D.S.), Time faire, to sowe or to gather be bold, but set or remooue when the weather is cold.] 1678: Ray, 49, This rule in gardening, never forget To sow dry, and to set wet. 1846: Denham, *Proverbs,* 11 (Percy S.) ["plant" for "set"]. 1904: *Co. Folk-Lore: Northumb.,* 173 (F.L.S.) [as in 1846].

12. *Sow* [wheat] *in the slop* (or *sop*), *Heavy at top.* 1823: Moor, *Suffolk Words,* 376. 1830: Forby, *Vocab. E. Anglia,* 417. 1872: J. Glyde, jr., *Norfolk Garland,* 154.

13. *Sown corn is not lost.* 1875: Cheales, *Proverb. Folk-Lore,* 126.

14. *The brain that sows not corn plants thistles.* 1670: Ray, 3.

15. *To sow the wind and reap the whirlwind.* 1816: Scott, *Black Dwarf,* ch. xviii., Indiscriminate profusion . . . is sowing the wind to reap the whirlwind. 1895: Purcell, *Life of Manning,* ii. 82, He could no longer call an hour in the day his own. He had sown the wind and was reaping the whirlwind.

16. *To sow wild oats. See* **Wild** (7).

17. *Who sows little mows the less.* Before 1300: *Cursor Mundi,* l. 28831, It was said, "Qua littil saus, þe lesse he mais." 1611: Cotgrave, s.v. "Semer," Little sow little mow. 1846: Denham,

Proverbs, 33 (Percy S.), Sow thin, shear thin.

See also **Quiet sow.**

Sowley hammer. *See* quot. 1863: Wise, *New Forest,* ch. vi., Nothing now remains to tell their former importance [iron-works] but a few mounds . . . and a country proverb, "There will be rain when Sowley hammer is heard."

Space cometh grace, In. 1541: Coverdale, *Christ. State Matrim.,* sig. G8. 1595: *Maroccus Extaticus,* 8 (Percy S.), In space grows grace. 1670: Ray, 144. 1732: Fuller, No. 6167.

Spade a spade, To call a. [τὰ σῦκα σῦκα, τὴν σκάφην δὲ σκάφην ὀνομάσων. — Lucian, *Hist. Conscr.,* 41.] 1539: Taverner, *Garden of Wysdome,* sig. C4, Whiche can call . . . a spade a spade. 1600: Kemp, *Nine Daies Wonder,* in Arber, *Garner,* vii. 34 (1883), That he may, being a plain man, call a spade a spade. 1632: Jonson, *Magn. Lady,* I. *ad fin.,* Faith we do call a spade a spade, in Cornwall. 1668: Shadwell, *Sullen Lovers,* IV. i. 1725: Bailey, tr. Erasmus' *Colloq.,* 181, Who call a fig a fig, and a spade a spade. 1854: Dickens, *Hard Times,* bk. i. ch. vi., There's no imaginative sentimental humbug about me. I call a spade a spade.

Spaniel. *See* **Flattering**; and **Woman** (8).

Spaniels that fawn when beaten, will never forsake their masters. 1732: Fuller, No. 4236.

Span new. *See* **Spick and span.**

Spare at brim. *See* **Better spare.**

Spare not to spend, but spare to go thither. 1659: Howell, 11.

Spare the rod and spoil the child. [ὁ μὴ δαρεὶς ἄνθρωπος οὐ παιδεύεται. — Menander.] *c.* 1000: Ælfric, *Hom.,* ii. 324 (O.), Se ðe spareð his ȝyrde, he hatað his cild. 1377: Langland, *Plowman,* B, v. 41, Who-so spareth the sprynge spilleth his children. 1422: J. Yonge, tr. *Gouern. of Prynces,* 161 (E.E.T.S.), Salamon sayth, Qui parsit virge odit filium, "who sparith the yarde he hatyth the chylde." 1577: *Misogonus,* II. iii., He that spareth the rode, hates the childe. 1692: L'Estrange, *Æsop,* 264 (3rd ed.) [as in

1577]. 1732 : Fuller, No. 4238. 1855 :
Thackeray, *Newcomes*, ch. iii., A brother
to whom my poor mother spared the
rod, and who . . . has turned out but
a spoilt child.

Spare to speak and spare to speed.
c. 1390: Gower, *Conf. Amantis*, bk. i.
l. 1293, For spechëles may noman spede.
c. 1426 : Audelay, *Poems*, 28 (Percy S.),
Whosoever sparys fore to speke sparys
for to spede. Before 1529 : Skelton,
Bowge of Courte, l. 91, Who spareth
to speke, in fayth he spareth to spede.
c. 1597 : Deloney, *Gentle Craft*, ch. xv.
1609 : W. Rowley, *Search for Money*,
24 (Percy S.). 1700 : Congreve, *Way
of World*, IV. iv. 1730 : Lillo, *Silvia*,
I. ix. 1781 : Macklin, *Man of the
World*, V.

Spare well and spend well. 1541 :
Coverdale, *Christ. Stale Matrim.*, sig.
I3, To spare that thou mayest hauc to
spend. *c.* 1600 : in F.E.T.S., Ext. Scr.,
No. 8, p. 71, Spare in tyme, and spend
in tyme. 1869 : Hazlitt, 343.

**Spare when you are young and spend
when you are old.** 1541 : Coverdale,
Christ. State Matrim., sig. I3, Spare
for thyne age. 1611 : Cotgrave, s.v.
" Souper," Hee that spares when he's
young may the better spend when he's
old. 1869 : Hazlitt, 343.

Spare. *See also* Spend.

Sparing is a rich purse. 1541 : Coverdale, *Christ. State Matrim.*, sig. I3.

Sparing is the first gaining. 1580 :
Lyly, *Euphues*, 229 (Arber), Sparing is
good getting. 1629 : *Book of Meery
Riddles*, Prov. 108.

Spark in the throat. *See* Smith (3).

Spark makes a great fire, A small.
1412–20 : Lydgate, *Troy Book*, bk. i.
l. 785, And of sparkys that ben of syghte
smale, Is fire engendered that devoureth
al. *c.* 1470 : G. Ashby, *Poems*, 61
(E.E.T.S.), For of a litle sparkle a grete
fyre comyth. 1509 : Barclay, *Ship of
Fools*, i. 194 (1874), A small sparcle
often tyme doth augment It selfe, and
groweth to flames peryllous. 1607 :
Dekker, etc., *Northw. Hoe*, II., 'Tis a
small sparke giues fire to a beauti-
full womans discredit. 1655 : Fuller,
Church Hist., bk. iii. § ii. (60), What a

great fire doth a small spark kindle !
1748 : Richardson, *Clarissa*, vii. 306
(1785), How soon a little spark kindles
into a flame. 1884 : *Folk-Lore Journal*,
ii. 280, A spark may raise an awful
blaze. *Derbysh.*

**Sparrow-hawk of a buzzard, You can't
make a.** *c.* 1400 : *Rom. Rose*, l. 4033,
This have I herd ofte in seying, That
man [ne] may, for no daunting, Make a
sperhauke of a bosarde.

**Sparrow in hand is worth a pheasant
that flieth by, A.** 1612 : Shelton,
Quixote, Pt. I. bk. iv. ch. iv., For " a
sparrow in the fist is worth more than
a flying bittour." 1732 : Fuller, No.
420.

**Sparrows fight for corn which is none
of their own.** Ibid., No. 4242.

Sparrows. *See also* Pert ; Robin ; and
Two sparrows.

Speak, *verb.* 1. *He cannot speak well
that cannot hold his tongue.* 1666 :
Torriano, *Piazza Univ.*, 279, He can
hardly speak, who cannot hold his peace.
1732 : Fuller, No. 1820.

2. *He never speaks but his mouth opens.*
1639 : Clarke, 133. 1670 : Ray, 193,
You never speak, etc. 1690 : *New
Dict. Canting Crew*, sig. H5.

3. *He speaks as if every word would
lift a dish.* 1732 : Fuller, No. 2024.

4. *He speaks one word nonsense, and
two that have nothing in them.* Ibid.,
No. 2025.

5. *He that speaks ill of his wife, dis-
honoureth himself.* Ibid., No. 2309.

6. *He that speaks lavishly shall hear
as knavishly.* 1670 : Ray, 144. 1732 :
Fuller, No. 6367.

7. *He that speaks me fair and loves
me not, I'll speak him fair and trust him
not.* 1633 : Draxe, 67. 1670 : Ray, 24.

8. *He that speaks, sows, he that hears,
reaps.* 1670 : Ray, 24, He that speaks
doth sow, he that holds his peace doth
reap. 1694 : D'Urfey, *Quixote*, Pt. I.
Act IV. sc. i. [as in 1670, but with
" may " for the second " doth "]. 1732 :
Fuller, No. 2310.

9. *He that speaks well fights well.*
c. 1250 : *Owl and Nightingale*, l. 1070,
Wel fight that wel speath—seide Alvred.

10. *He that speaks without care, shall*

remember with sorrow. 1732 : Fuller, No. 2311.

11. *Some that speak no ill of any, do no good to any.* Ibid., No. 4219.

12. *Speak fair and think what you will.* 1605 : Camden, *Remains,* 331 (1870). 1670 : Ray, 144. 1754 : Berthelson, *Eng.-Dan. Dict.,* s.v. " Speak."

13. *Speak fitly or be silent wisely.* 1611 : Cotgrave, s.v. " Taire," Better no words then words unfitly placed. 1639 : Clarke, 11, Speak to th' purpose or hold your peace. 1640 : Herbert, *Jac. Prudentum.*

14. *Speak no ill of another, until thou thinkest of thy self.* 1629 : *Book of Meery Riddles,* Prov. 92.

15. *Speak of a man as you find him.* 1875 : Cheales, *Proverb. Folk-Lore,* 120.

16. *Speak well of the dead.* 1670 : Ray, 78. 1740 : North, *Lives of Norths,* i. 149 (Bohn), It is fit to be silent, because we should not speak ill of the dead.

17. *Speak well of your friend, of your enemy say nothing.* 1875 : Cheales, *Proverb. Folk-Lore,* 88.

18. *Speak what you will, an ill man will turn it ill.* 1732 : Fuller, No. 6116.

19. *Speak when you are spoken to.* 1639 : Clarke, 20. 1732 : Fuller, No. 4244 [with the addition—" come when you are called "].

20. *To speak as though he would creep into one's mouth.* 1546 : Heywood, *Proverbs,* Pt. II. ch. ix., Ye speake now as ye would creepe into my mouth. 1670 : Ray, 170. 1754 : Berthelson, *Eng.-Danish Dict.,* s.v. " Creep," He is ready to creep into his mouth. Cf. **Creep up one's sleeve.**

21. *To speak ill of others is the fifth element.* 1578 : Florio, *First Fruites,* fo. 29. 1654 : Whitlock, *Zootomia,* 445.

22. *To speak like a mouse in a cheese.* [1631 : Brathwait, *Whimzies,* 70 (1859), He speakes . . . like a frog in a well, or a cricket in a wall.] 1659 : Howell, 4, He speaks like a mouse in a cheese. 1670 : Ray, 186. 1681 : Robertson, *Phraseol. Generalis.,* 1157, You speak, etc. 1732 : Fuller, No. 5233.

23. *To speak like an oracle.* *c.* 1676 : South, *Serm.,* 341 (1715) (O.), He only

now-a-days speaks like an oracle, who speaks tricks and ambiguities. 1738 : Swift, *Polite Convers.,* Dial. II., Colonel, you spoke like an oracle.

24. *Who so speaketh unwisely.* See quot. 1493 : *Dives et Pauper,* fo. 75 (1536), It is a common prouerbe, that who so speakethe vnwysely and vaguely, or in an euylle maner, he speketh to moche.

25. *Who speaks not, errs not.* 1611 : Cotgrave, s.v. " Parler " [" He that " for " Who "]. 1623 : Wodroephe, *Spared Houres,* 507. 1659 : Howell, *Proverbs : Eng.-Fr.,* 11.

26. *You speak in clusters, you were begot in nutting.* 1678 : Ray, 346. 1732 : Fuller, No. 6009.

Spectacles are death's arquebuse. 1640 : Herbert, *Jac. Prudentum.*

Speech is silvern, silence golden. Ibid., More have repented speech than silence. 1924 : *Punch,* 2 April, p. 363, col. 1, Recollect that maxim old, " Speech is silver, silence gold." Cf. **Silence.**

Speech is the index of the mind. 1630 : Brathwait, *Eng. Gent.,* etc. 51 (1641). Ibid., 46, Democritus calls speech εἴδωλον τοῦ βίου, the image of life. 1670 : Ray, 24, Speech is the picture of the mind. 1870 : T. W. Robertson, *Nightingale,* I., Talk ! Ha ! Speech is the index and mirror of the soul.

Speed is in the spurs, All the. 1732 : Fuller, No. 556.

Speed the plough ! originally, **God speed the plough !** 1472 : *Paston Letters,* iii. 50 (Gairdner), God sped the plowghe. *c.* 1500 : *God Spede the Plough* [title]. 1542 : Boorde, *Introd.,* ch. xvii. p. 166 (E.E.T.S.), Yf we do not wel, God spede the plow ! 1604 : Bodley, *Letter,* quoted *Bodl. Quarterly Record,* iii. 48, God speede your plough, I am glad your presse is a-foote, and yow so foreward before. 1661 : in *Harl. Miscell.,* ii. 503 (1744), God speed the plough, plague rooks and crows, And send us years more cheap. 1669 : Dryden, *Wild Gallant,* III. i., Speed the plough ! If I can make no sport, I'll hinder none. 1747 : Garrick, *Miss in her Teens,* I. i., Well, speed the plough !

1798 : Morton, *Speed the Plough* [title of comedy]. 1902 : *N. & Q.*, 9th ser., ix. 12, The saying implies merely a wish for prosperity, in the same way that " God speed the plough " applied to the pursuit of agriculture. [In its later uses " speed the plough " seems to have been little more than an expletive phrase, meaning much the same as " Good luck to you ! "]

Spell for spell is fair play = turn for turn. 1855 : Robinson, *Whitby Gloss.*, 164.

Spend, *verb*. 1. *He that spendeth much*. See quot. 15th cent.: in *Reliq. Antiquæ*, i. 316 (1841), He that spendes myche and getythe nowghte, And owith myche and hathe nowghte, And lokys in hys purse and fynde nowghte, He may be sory, thowe he seythe nowghte. *c*: 1530 : Rhodes, *Boke of Nurture*, 107 (E.E.T.S.) [slightly varied by beginning the second and third lines with " He that "]. 1578 : Florio, *First Fruites*, fo. 104 [as in 1530].

2. *In spending lies the advantage.* 1640 : Herbert, *Jac. Prudentum*.

3. *Know when to spend and when to spare, And you need not be busy; you'll ne'er be bare.* 1732 : Fuller, No. 6437.

4. *Never spend your money before you have it.* 1831 : Hone, *Year-Book*, col. 1612.

5. *Spend and be free, but make no waste.* 1639 : Clarke, 129. 1670 : Ray, 24. 1732 : Fuller, No. 4247.

6. *Spend and God will send.* 1546 : Heywood, *Proverbs*, Pt. II. ch. v. [" shall " for " will "]. 1575 : Gascoigne, *Posies*, 64 (Cunliffe), The common speech is, spend and God will send. 1611 : Cotgrave, s.v. " Manger." 1710 : S. Palmer, *Moral Essays on Proverbs*, 282, There is indeed an unlucky proverb that is often cited on such occasions, Spend, etc. 1869 : Spurgeon, *John Ploughman*, ch. xvi., He must squander it, always boasting that his motto is, " Spend," etc.

7. *Spend not where you may save; spare not where you must spend.* 1678 : Ray, 348.

8. *What we spent we had; What we gave, we have; What we lent is lost.* 1669 : *New Help to Discourse*, 250.

9. *Who more than he is worth doth spend, He makes a rope his life to end.* 1523 : Fitzherbert, *Husb.*, 99 (E.D.S.), He that dothe more expende, thanne his goodes wyll extende, meruayle it shall not be, thoughe he be greued with pouertee. 1670 : Ray, 24. 1732 : Fuller, No. 6397.

10. *Who spends before he thrives, will beg before he thinks.* *c*. 1460 : *Good Wyfe wold a Pylgremage*, l. 151 (E.E.T.S.), He that spendyth more then he gettythe, a beggarris lyfe he schall lede. 1647 : *Countrym. New Commonwealth*, 35. 1732 : Fuller, No. 5720. 1875 : Smiles, *Thrift*, 172, He who spends all he gets, is on the way to beggary.

11. *Who spends more than he should, shall not have to spend when he would.* 1670 : Ray, 25. 1732 : Fuller, No. 6074.

See also **Spare**.

Spice, *subs.* 1. *If you beat spice, it will smell the sweeter.* 1732 : Fuller, No. 2741.

2. *Who hath spice enough may season his meat as he pleaseth.* 1640 : Herbert, *Jac. Prudentum*, He that hath the spice may season as he list. 1670 : Ray, 25. 1732 : Fuller, No. 4140 [" she " for " he "].

Spick and span new; originally **Span new,** which is now found only in dialectal use. *c*. 1300 : *Havelok*, l. 968 (E.E.T.S.), And bouthe him clothes, al spannewe. *c*. 1374 : Chaucer, *Troylus*, bk. iii. l. 1665, His tale ay was span-newe to biginne Til that the night departed hem a-twinne. 1590 : Nashe, *Almond for a Parrot*, 27 (1846), Hee offered her a spicke and spanne new Geneua Bible. 1595 : Munday, *John a Kent*, 52 (Sh. S.), Heeres a coat, spick and span new. 1614 : B. Rich, *Honestie of This Age*, 18 (Percy S.). 1665 : Pepys, *Diary*, 15 Nov. 1712 : Motteux, *Quixote*, Pt. II. ch. lviii., And all, as they use to say, spick and span new, and shining like beaten gold. 1829 : Hunter, *Hallamsh. Gloss.*, 84, Span-new, quite new. 1863 : Kingsley,

Water Babies, ch. i., Some spick and span new Gothic or Elizabethan thing. 1886 : Elworthy, *West Som. Word-Book*, 696 (E.D.S.), Hav'ee zeed our millerd's span-new cart ?

Spick nor crick, There's no. S. Devon. = There is no flaw. 1869 : Hazlitt, 396.

Spider, *subs.* 1. *But for the robin and the wren A spider would o'ercome a man.* c. 1870 : Smith, *Isle of Wight Words*, 62 (E.D.S.).

2. *If you wish to live and thrive, Let a spider run alive.* 1863 : *N. & Q.*, 3rd ser., iii. 262. 1879 : Henderson, *Folk-Lore of N. Counties*, 312, He who would wish to thrive, Must let spiders run alive. 1913 : E. M. Wright, *Rustic Speech, etc.*, 219.

3. *When spiders' web in air do fly, The spell will soon be very dry.* 1893 : Inwards, *Weather Lore*, 147.

See also Bee (17); Swallow, *verb* (1).

Spies are the ears and eyes of princes. 1651 : Herbert, *Jac. Prudentum*, 2nd ed.

Spiggot. *See* Save (4).

Spin, *verb.* 1. *A man cannot spin and reel at the same time.* 1678 : Ray, 205. 1732 : Fuller, No. 2591, I cannot spin and weave at the same time.

2. *She spins well that breeds her children.* 1640 : Herbert, *Jac. Prudentum.* 1732 : Fuller, No. 4137, She spins a good thread that brings up her daughter well.

3. *Spinning out of time never made good cloth.* 1660 : Howell, *Parly of Beasts*, 80 [quoted as " a trite proverb "].

4. *That which will not be spun, let it not come between the spindle and the distaff.* 1640 : Herbert, *Jac. Prudentum.* 1670 : Ray, 25. 1732 : Fuller, No. 2726, If 'twill not be spun, bring it not to the distaff.

5. *To spin a fair thread.* [1412 : Hoccleve, *Regement*, l. 1763, p. 64 (E.E.T.S.), Alasse ! this likerous dampnable errour, In this londe hath so large a threde I-sponne, That wers peple is non vndir the sonne.] 1562 : Heywood, *Three Hund. Epigr.*, No. 228, She hath spun a fair thread. 1595 : *Locrine*, II. iii. (Malone S.), O wife I have spunne

a faire thredde. c. 1625 : B. & F., *Chances*, III. iv., You have spun yourself a fair thread now. 1691.: J. Wilson, *Belphegor*, I. iii., And if I lose my place by the bargain, I have spun a fine thread. 1730 : Lillo, *Silvia*, III. xvii., Ah Lettice, Lettice, what have you been doing ? You've spun a fine thread, truly. 1737 : Ray, 63.

Spit and a stride, A = A short way. 1621 : B. & F., *Pilgrim*, II. ii., Wilt thou take a spit and a stride, and see if thou canst outrun us ? 1676 : Cotton, Walton's *Angler*, Pt. II. ch. ii., You are now . . . within a spit and a stride of the Peak. 1824 : Scott, *Redgauntlet*, ch. xvii., I am to carry you to old Father Crackenthorp's, and then you are within a spit and a stride of Scotland, as the saying is. 1828 : Carr, *Craven Dialect*, ii. 155, Spit and a stride, a very short distance.

Spit, *verb.* 1. *Spit in his mouth and make him a mastiff.* It was an old idea that to spit in a dog's mouth gave him pleasure. 1670 : Ray, 216.

2. *Spit in your hands and take better hold.* 1546 : Heywood, *Proverbs*, Pt. II. ch. iv., Nay, I will spit in my hands, and take better holde. 1577 : J. Grange, *Golden Aphroditis*, sig. H1, Spitte on your handes and take good holde. 1738 : Swift, *Polite Convers.*, Dial. I., I warrant, miss will spit in her hand, and hold fast.

3. *To spit in the church.* See quots. 1591 : Florio, *Second Frutes*, 13, Who sometimes make it a matter of conscience to spitt in the church, and at another time will beray the altar. 1640 : Herbert, *Jac. Prudentum*, Some make a conscience of spitting in the church, yet rob the altar.

4. *Who spits against heaven it falls in his face.* 1557 : North, *Diall of Princes*, fo. 106, As he whiche spitteth into the element, and the spittel falleth againe into his eies. 1640 : Herbert, *Jac. Prudentum.* 1670 : Ray, 13. 1732 : Fuller, No. 4252, Spit not against Heaven ; 'twill fall back into thy own face.

5. *You spit on your own sleeve.* 1639 : Clarke, 54.

Spiteful as an old maid, As. 1732 :
Fuller, No. 730.

Spite of one's teeth, In. 1387 :
Trevisa, tr. Higden, vii. 7 (Rolls Ser.),
What I haue longe desired now I haue
it maugre þyn teeth. *c.* 1489 : Caxton,
Sonnes of Aymon, 109 (E.E.T.S.), Rey-
nawde toke Alarde oute of his enemyes
handes, mawgre theyr teeth. *c.* 1500 :
More, *Juvenile Verses*, in *Works* (1557),
Maugry thy teeth to lyue cause hym
shall I. *c.* 1534 : Berners, *Huon*, 175
(E.E.T.S.), In the dyspyte of his teth
I wyll se my nece. 1567 : Painter, *Pal.
of Pleasure*, ii. 248 (Jacobs), It behoued
to obey, and in despite of my teeth to
do that which the Romane Emperour
commaundeth. 1618 : B. Holyday,
Technogamia, V. vi., I will stand here
in spight of your teeth. 1678 : Otway,
Friendship in Fashion, V. i., She, like
a true wife, may, spite of his teeth, deceive him quite. 1732 : B. Mandeville,
Honour and War, 130, The more I have
perceiv'd and felt the truth of it in
spight of my teeth. 1768 : Walpole,
Lett. to Gray, 18 Feb., He forced himself upon me at Paris in spite of my
teeth and my doors. 1894 : R. L. S.,
Letters, v. 153 (Tusitala ed.), I read over
again . . . and it is good in spite of your
teeth. 1924 : Shaw, *Saint Joan*, sc. vi.

Spite of the cock and his comb. 1613 :
Rowlands, *Paire of Spy-Knaues*, 9
(Hunt. Cl.), He will to London spite of
cock and's combe.

Split hairs, To. 1678 : Ray, 249, To
cut the hair, i.e. to divide so exactly
as that neither part have advantage.
1732 : Fuller, No. 1122, Come, slit me
this hair. Ibid., No. 6457, It's hard to
split the hair, That nothing is wanted,
and nothing to spare. 1846 : Jerrold,
Chron. of Clovernook, 130, Whose keen
logic would split hairs as a bill-hook
would split logs.

Spoil before you spin, You must.
1639 : Clarke, 110. 1670 : Ray, 145.
1732 : Fuller, No. 5970 [with " well "
after " spin "].

Spoke in one's wheel, To put a. 1600 :
Weakest to the Wall, l. 848 (Malone S.),
Ile set a spoake in your cart. 1682 : A.
Behn, *Roundheads*, V. ii., She speaks as

she were Queen, but I shall put a spoke
in her rising Wheel of Fortune. 1712 :
Spectator, No. 498, Tho' indeed I
thought they had clapt such a spoke in
his wheel, as had disabled him. 1848 :
Dickens, *Dombey*, ch. x., Mrs. Dombey,
eh, ma'am ? I think not, ma'am.
Not while Joe B. can put a spoke in
your wheel, ma'am. 1901 : *N. & Q.*,
9th ser., vii. 258, The allusion is to the
pin or spoke used to lock wheels in
machinery ; hence, to put an impediment in one's way.

Spoon or spoil a horn, To make a.
1820 : Byron, *Letters, etc.*, v. 16 (Prothero), I can't cobble : I must " either
make a spoon or spoil a horn." 1824 :
Scott, *Redgauntlet*, ch. i., His voice
faltering, as he replied, " Ay, ay, I kend
Alan was the lad to make a spoon or
spoil a horn." 1910 : *N. & Q.*, 11th
ser., i. 58, A lad showing much promise
was commonly referred to [in the
Border counties] as one who [would
" either make a spoon or spoil a
horn."

Spoon. *See also* Silver (6).

Sport is sauce to pains, Some. 1639 :
Clarke, 191.

Sport is sweetest when no spectators.
1670 : Ray, 145.

Sports and journeys men are known,
In. 1640 : Herbert, *Jac. Prudentum*.

Spot is most seen upon the finest
cloth, A. 1732 : Fuller, No. 421.

Sprained her ankle, She has. 1785 :
Grose, *Class. Dict. Vulgar Tongue*, s.v.
" Ankle," A girl who is got with child
is said to have sprained her ankle. Cf.
Broken.

Sprat to catch a whale, To throw a—
with variants. 1827 : Hone, *Ev. Day
Book*, ii. 1410, It is but " giving a sprat
to catch a herring," as a body may say.
1850 : Dickens, *Chuzzlewit*, ch. viii., It
was their custom, Mr. Jonas said, . . .
never to throw away sprats, but as
bait for whales. 1864 : " Cornish Proverbs," in *N. & Q.*, 3rd ser., vi. 495,
Give a sprat to catch a mackerel.
1869 : Hazlitt, 331, Set a herring to
catch a whale. 1893 : R. L. S., *Letters*,
v. 87 (Tusitala ed.), Baxter . . . will
let you see a proof of my introduction,

which is only sent out as a sprat to catch whales. Cf. **Small fish.**

Spread nets, To. *See* quot. 1630: Taylor (Water-Poet), *Works*, 2nd pagin., 152, The old prouerb neuer failed yet, Who spreads nets for his friends, snares his own feet.

Spring (the season), *subs.* I. *A late spring Is a great bless-ing.* 1846 : Denham, *Proverbs*, 39 (Percy S.). 1893 : Inwards, *Weather Lore*, 6.

2. *A late spring never deceives.* Ibid., 6.

3. *A wet spring, a dry harvest.* 1846 : Denham, *Proverbs*, 32 (Percy S.), A wet spring is a sign of dry weather for harvest. 1893: Inwards, *Weather Lore*, 6.

4. *Better late spring and bear, than early blossom and blast.* Ibid., 6.

5. *He takes the spring from the year.* 1813 : Ray, 75.

6. *If there's spring in winter, and winter in spring, The year won't be good for anything.* 1659 : Howell, *Proverbs: Span.-Eng.*, 22, When there is a spring in winter, and a winter in spring, the year is never good. 1893 : Inwards, *Weather Lore*, 7.

7. *In spring a tub of rain makes a spoonful of mud, In autumn a spoonful of rain makes a tub of mud.* Ibid., 6.

8. *Spring and the daisies. See* quots. 1862 : Chambers, *Book of Days*, i. 312 (1869), Still we can now plant our " foot upon nine daisies," and not until that can be done do the old-fashioned country people believe that spring is really come. 1878 : Dyer, *Eng. Folk-Lore*, 27, " It ain't spring until you can plant your foot upon twelve daisies," is a proverb still very prevalent. 1881 : *Glos. N. & Q.*, i. 43 [as in 1878].

9. *The spring is not always green.* 1846 : Denham, *Proverbs*, 31 (Percy S.). 1893 : Inwards, *Weather Lore*, 6. 1904 : *Co. Folk-Lore: Northumb.*, 175 (F.L.S.).

See also **Blossom** ; **Easter** (9) ; **January** (2) ; and **Thunder** (1) and (4).

Spring at his elbow, He hath a. Said of a gamester. 1678 : Ray, 351.

Sprotborough, near Doncaster. 1869 : Hazlitt, 474, Whoso is hungry, and lists well to eat, let him come to Sprotborough for his meat ; and for a night,

and for a day, his horse shall have both corn and hay, and no man shall ask him, when he goeth away.

Spruce as an onion, As. 1678 : Ray, 289.

Spun. *See* **Spin.**

Spur in the head is worth two in the heel, A. 1670 : Ray, 218. 1694 : Motteux, *Rabelais*, bk. iv. ch. lxv., The horses will perform the better, and that a spur in the head is worth two in flank ; or in the same horse dialect, That a cup in the pate Is a mile in the the gate. 1738 : Swift, *Polite Convers.*, Dial. II. 1854 : Baker, *Northants Gloss.*, s.v. " Spur," " A spur . . ." A common invitation to a person on horseback to take a parting glass.

Spur. *See also* **Horse** (4), (5), (17), (18), (19), (27), and (41).

Spy faults if your eyes were out, You would. 1678 : Ray, 271.

Squirrel, *subs.* I. *See* quot. 1830 : Forby, *Vocab. E. Anglia*, 420, From the general discouragement shewn to this sport [squirrel-hunting on Christmas Day] probably comes the common saying, " Hunt squirrels, and make no noise."

2. *Within a squirrel's jump.* Glos. 1911 : *Folk-Lore*, xxii. 239.

Stable door when the steed is stolen, To shut the. [Ne post tempus praedae praesidium parem. — Plautus, *Asin.*, 294.] *c.* 1390 : Gower, *Conf. Amantis*, bk. iv. l. 901, For whan the grete stiede Is stole, thanne he taketh hiede, And makth the stable dore fast. 1484 : Caxton, *Æsope*, ii. 245 (Jacobs), It was not tyme to shette the stable whan the horses ben loste and gone. 1509 : Barclay, *Ship of Fools*, i. 76 (1874), Whan the stede is stolyn to shyt the stable dore Comys small pleasoure profyte or vauntage. 1579 : Lyly, *Euphues*, 37 (Arber), It is too late to shutte the stable doore when the steede is stolne. 1628 : J. Clavell, *Recantation*, 38, This like shutting vp the stable doore, When as the horse was stolne out before. 1705 : Ward, *Hudibras Rediv.*, Pt. I, can. i. p. 10, And that's but almost like my host, Who stable shuts when steed is lost. 1725 : Bailey, tr. Erasmus' *Colloq.*, 576. 1886: R. L. S., *Kidnapped*, ch. xiv. 1907 : De Morgan, *Alice-for-Short*, ch. xxxv., Nothing I have said would warrant such an absurd mistrust of Providence. Besides, it would be merely shutting the stable-door after the steed had broken loose.

Staff, *subs.* 1. *If the staff be crooked, the shadow cannot be straight.* 1640 : Herbert, *Jac. Prudentum.*

2. *To hold at staff's end. c.* 1374 : *Anel. and Arc.*, 184 (O.), His new lady holdeth him vp 30 narowe Vp by the bridil at the staves ende. 1565 : Shacklock, *Hatchet of Heresies*, fo. 23, They so helde one an other at the staffes end. 1596 : Lodge, *Wits Miserie*, 83 (Hunt. Cl.), The most chollericke and troublesome woman living vpon the earth, shee was alwaies at the staffes end with my father. 1642 : D. Rogers, *Matrim. Honour*, 294–5, Waspish, froward, holding their husbands at staves end. 1816 : Scott, *Antiquary*, ch. xvi. 1889 : R. L. S., *Ballantrae*, ch. ii., Mrs. Henry had a manner of condescension with him . . . she held him at the staff's end.

See also **Stick,** *subs.* (1).

Stafford law=the " law " of the big stick. [*c.* 1400 : *Towneley Plays*, 29 (E.E.T.S.), But thou were worthi be cled In stafford blew [=blue from bruises from beating] ; ffor thou art alway adred.] 1589 : *Hay any Worke*, 10 (1845), That I threatned him with blowes, and to deale by stafford law. 1624 : T. Heywood, *Captives*, III. ii., *Mildew.* Is this lawe ? *Godfrey.* Yes, Stafford's lawe. 1630 : Taylor (Water-Poet), *Works*, 2nd pagin., 156, If it were lawfull for me to examine thee at Staffords Law, I would make thee confesse the receit of ten shillings.

Staffordshire. *See* **Shrewsbury.**

Stale as custom, As. *c.* 1592 : *Sir Thos. More*, 32 (Sh. S.), To vrdge my imperfections in excuse,˙ Were all as stale as custome.

Stalking-horse, To make a person or thing a. 1601 : Shakespeare, *As You Like It*, V. iv., He uses his folly like a stalking-horse. 1604 : Webster, etc., *Malcontent*, IV. i., A fellow that makes religion his stalking-horse. 1642 : D. Rogers,

Matrim. Honour, 55, Pretending that their conscience is the ground, whereas it is but a staulking-horse. 1714 : E. Ward, *Cavalcade*, 3, And Faith . . . Was made a stalking-horse to gold. 1740 : North, *Examen*, 151, To make a stalking horse of the exclusion, to shoot him down. 1855 : Kingsley, *West. Ho!*, ch. xxix., Mary's death was as convenient a stalking-horse to him as to the Pope.

Stamford, As mad as the baiting bull of. 1662 : Fuller, *Worthies*, ii. 268 (1840). 1732 : Fuller, No. 714 [with " baited " for " baiting "]. 1790 : Grose, *Prov. Gloss.*, s.v. " Lincs." 1826 : Brady, *Varieties of Lit.*, 15.

Stamps like an ewe upon yeaning, She. Somerset. 1678 : Ray, 344.

Stand, *verb.* 1. *He stands not surely that never slips.* 1611 : Cotgrave, s.v. " Mescheoir." 1640 : Herbert, *Jac. Prudentum.* Cf. No. 2.

2. *He that stands sure. See* quot. 1412–20 : Lydgate, *Troy Book*, bk. ii. l. 1849, The prouerbe that techeth commounly, " He that stant sure, enhast hym not to meve." Cf. No. 1.

3. *He won't stand keep.* "Said of a person spoilt by prosperity." 1917 : Bridge, *Cheshire Proverbs*, 72.

4. *Stand on one side, John Ball, and let my wife see the bar* [bear]. 1883 : Burne, *Shropsh. Folk-Lore*, 590. 1917 : Bridge, *Cheshire Proverbs*, 44.

5. *To stand buff* = To stand firm. 1693 : D'Urfey, *Richmond Heiress*, I., I have only hedg'd him into this business to stand buff with his purse upon occasion. 1708 : Cibber, *Lady's Last Stake*, III., She . . . stands buff at the head of the mode, without the least tincture of virtue to put her out of countenance. 1777 : Sheridan, *Sch. for Scandal*, II. iii., Ha ! ha ! that he should have stood buff to old bachelor so long, and sink into a husband at last ! 1827 : Scott, *Journal*, 4 Sept., There is no reason why he should turn on me, but that if he does, reason or none, it is best to stand buff to him.

6. *To stand in one's own light.* 1546 : Heywood, *Proverbs*, Pt. II. ch. iv., How blindly ye stand in your owne light.

1635 : in *Somers Tracts*, vii. 188 (1811), If he either stand in his owne light through wilfulnesse . . . 1738 : Swift, *Polite Convers.*, Dial. I., Mr. Neverout, methinks you stand in your own light. 1848 : Dickens, *Dombey*, ch. xxxix., I . . . can't afford to stand in my own light for your good.

7. *To stand upon one's pantofles*, i.e. on one's dignity. 1573 : G. Harvey, *Letter-Book*, 14 (Camden S.), He was altogither set on his merrie pinnes, and walked on his stateli pantocles. 1611 : Cotgrave, s.v. "Bout," To stand upon his pantofles, or on high tearmes. 1631 : Mabbe, *Celestina*, 255 (T.T.), The villaine stands upon his pantofles, and begins to looke big. 1681 : Robertson, *Phraseol. Generalis*, 1031, He is grown very proud ; he stands on his pantofles. 1755 : Walpole, *Letters*, iii. 156 (1846) (O.), I could not possibly to-day step out of my high historical pantoufles to tell it you.

Standers by. *See* **Lookers on.**

Standing pools gather filth. 1639 : Clarke, 144. 1670 : Ray, 145. 1732 : Fuller, No. 4257.

Stanton Drew. *See* quot. 1776 : Stukeley, *Itin. Cur.*, cent. ii. 169, There is an old proverb common in Somersetshire, "Stanton Drew, a mile from Ponsford, another from Chue." 1849 : Halliwell, *Pop. Rhymes and Nursery Tales*, 198 [as in 1776].

Stare, *verb.* 1. *See* quot. 1917 : Bridge, *Cheshire Proverbs*, 143, To stare like a choked throstle. To stare like a throttled earwig *or* cat.

2. *To stare like a stuck pig.* 1694 : Motteux, *Rabelais*, bk. v. ch. ix. p. 41 (O.), Panurge star'd at him like a dead pig. 1720 : Gay, *Poems*, ii. 278 (Underhill), Like a stuck pig I gaping stare. 1789 : G. Parker, *Life's Painter*, 124, Who gape and stare, just like stuck pigs at each other. 1895 : Jos. Thomas, *Randigal Rhymes*, 61.

Starling. *See* **Raven.**

Stars are not seen by sunshine. 1623 : Wodroephe, *Spared Houres*, 503, The starres do not shine at mid-day. 1732 : Fuller, No. 4258. 1846 : Denham, *Proverbs*, 5 (Percy S.).

Stars begin to huddle, When the, The earth will soon become a puddle. 1893 : Inwards, *Weather Lore*, 65.

Starve 'em. *See* quot. 1785 : Grose, *Class. Dict. Vulgar Tongue*, s.v., Starve-'em, Rob'em, and Cheat'em, Stroud, Rochester and Chatham, so called by soldiers and sailors, and not without good reason.

Starve in a cook's shop, To. 1611 : Cotgrave, s.v. "Aimer," He that loves another better than himselfe, starves in a cooks shop. 1630 : T. Adams, *Works*, 565, As the by-word is, staruing in a cookes shoppe, wretched in their highest fortunes. 1738 : Swift, *Polite Convers.*, Dial. II., No, my lord ; I'll never starve in a cook's shop.

Stay, *verb.* 1. *He that can stay obtains.* 1611 : Cotgrave, s.v. "Attendre," He that can stay his time, shall compasse any thing. 1640 : Herbert, *Jac. Prudentum. c.* 1736 : Franklin, in *Works*, i. 455 (Bigelow), He that can have patience can have what he will.

2. *He that stays does the business.* 1640 : Herbert, *Jac. Prudentum.*

3. *She will stay at home, perhaps, if her leg be broke.* 1732 : Fuller, No. 4150.

4. *Stay a little and news will find you.* 1640 : Herbert, *Jac. Prudentum.*

5. *Stay awhile that we may end the sooner.* 1580 : Sidney, *Arcadia*, bk. i. p. 63 (1893), His horse . . . taught him that "discreet stays make speedy journeys." 1651 : Herbert, *Jac. Prudentum*, 2nd ed. 1732 : Fuller, No. 4263, Stop a little, to make an end the sooner. 1823 : D'Israeli, *Cur. of Lit.*, 2nd ser., i. 431 (1824), Sir Amias Pawlet, when he perceived too much hurry in any business, was accustomed to say, "Stay awhile, to make an end the sooner." 1859 : Smiles, *Self-Help*, 271 (1869), A wise man used to say, "Stay a little, that we may make an end the sooner."

6. *Stay till the lame messenger come, if you will know the truth of the thing.* 1640 : Herbert, *Jac. Prudentum.*

Steady as a buggin [ghost] **in a bush, As.** 1917 : Bridge, *Cheshire Proverbs*, 21.

Steal, verb. 1. As good steal a horse
as stand by and look on. 1659: Howell, 5.

2. He has stolen a roll out of the
brewer's basket. 1678: Ray, 87 ["man-
chet" for "roll"]. 1732: Fuller, No.
1900. 1745: Franklin, Drinker's Dict.,
in Works, ii. 23 (Bigelow) [as in
1678].

3. He that steals can hide. 1732:
Fuller, No. 2315.

4. He that will steal an egg will steal
an ox. 1639: Clarke, 148. 1670: Ray,
145. 1875: Cheales, Proverb. Folk-
Lore, 129.

5. One may steal a horse while another
may not look over the hedge. 1546: Heywood, Proverbs, Pt. II. ch. ix., Some
man maie steale a hors better Than
some other may stande and looke vpone.
1591: Lyly, Endymion, III. iii., Some
man may better steal a horse than
another look over the hedge. 1607:
Middleton, Mich. Terme, I. i., Some may
better steal a horse than others look on.
1683: in Harl. Miscell., vi. 62 (1745),
There is an old proverb,—That one may
better steal a steed, than another peep
over the hedge. 1728: Gay, Beggar's
Opera, III. ii. 1772: Garrick, Irish
Widow, I. iii., But an Englishman may
look over the hedge, while an Irishman must not stale a horse. 1921: A.
Bennett, Things that have Interested Me,
315.

6. To steal a goose and give the giblets
in alms. 1659; Howell, 1. 1721:
Bailey, Eng. Dict., s.v. "Steal," He
steals a goose, and gives, etc. Cf.
No. 9.

7. To steal a goose and stick down a
feather. 1546: Heywood, Proverbs, Pt.
I. ch. xi., As dyd the pure penitent that
stale a goose And stack downe a fether.
1608: in Harington, Nugæ Antiquæ,
ii. 200 (1804). 1714: Walker, Sufferings of Clergy, Pt. II. 331, For the
managers of those times thought fit,
when they stole the goose, to stick
down a feather.

8. To steal a pin. See Pin, subs. (4);
and Sin, subs. (2).

9. To steal the hog and give the feet
for alms. 1640: Herbert, Jac. Prudentum. 1670: Ray, 25. 1732: Fuller,

No. 2028, He steals a hog, etc. Cf.
No. 6.

Steed. See Stable door.

Steel to the back. c. 1591: Shakespeare, Titus Andr., IV. iii., We are . . .
steele to the very backe. 1633: Draxe,
87. 1678: Ray, 346. Cf. Mettle.

Step after step the ladder is ascended.
1611: Cotgrave, s.v. "Pas," Step after
step goes farre. 1640: Herbert, Jac.
Prudentum. 1670: Ray, 25. 1732:
Fuller, No. 4260.

Stern chase is a long chase, A. 1836:
Marryat, Easy, ch. xxix., This will be a
long chase; a stern chase always is.
1919: J. A. Bridges, Victorian Recollections, 140, English poetry has had a
start of some centuries, and a stern
chase is proverbially a long one.

Stew in one's own juice. See Grease.

Stick and Sticks, subs. 1. A stick is
quickly found to beat a dog with. 1563:
Becon, Early Works, Pref., 28 (P.S.),
How easy a thing it is to find a staff if
a man be minded to beat a dog. 1594:
First Part Contention, 35 (Sh. S.), A
staffe is quickly found to beate a dog.
1616: Breton, Works, ii. e 6 (Grosart)
["soone" for "quickly"]. 1664: J.
Wilson, Andr. Commenius, II. i., One
need not go far to find A staff to beat a
dog, nor circumstance To make him
guilty that's before foredoom'd! 1721:
Bailey, Eng. Dict., s.v. "Dog," He who
has a mind to beat a dog, will easily
find a stick. 1842: Planché, Extravag.,
ii. 165 (1879), When you wish to lick A
dog, 'tis easy, sir, to find a stick.

2. I gave you a stick to break my own
head with. 1732: Fuller, No. 2595.

3. Sticks and stones. See quots.
1897: N. & Q., 8th ser., xii. 508, I
heard this saying in Warwickshire—
"Sticks and stones may break my
bones; but cruel words can never harm
me." 1898: N. & Q., 9th ser., i. 177,
"Sticks and stones will break my bones,
but scolding will not hurt me," was an
old saw in York thirty years ago.

Stick, verb. 1. To stick by the ribs.
1670: Ray, 194.

2. To stick like burs. c. 1510: A.
Barclay, Egloges, 18 (Spens. S.), Together they cleave more fast then do

burres. 1533 : Heywood, *Play of Love*,
l. 601, I thought her owne tale lyke a
bur Stack to her owne back. 1570 :
Googe, tr. *Popish Kingd.*, 20 (1880), But
fast as burres to wooll they sticke.
1654 : Flecknoe, *Loves Dominion*, IV. ii.,
Still does this burr stick on me. 1720:
Gay, *Poems*, ii. 280 (Underhill), Let us
like burs together stick. 1821 : Scott,
Pirate, ch. xii., He . . . got rid of his
travelling companions, who at first
stuck as fast as burs. 1854 : Baker,
Northants Gloss., s.v. " Burr," Hence
the old adage, " Sticks like a burr to
a beggar's rags." 1925 : *Times Lit.
Suppl.*, 21 May, p. 348, col. 2, Phrases
that stick like burrs in the memory.
Cf. **Cleave.**

Stiff as a poker. 1797 : Colman, jr.,
Heir at Law, III. ii., Stuck up as stiff
as a poker. 1828 : Carr, *Craven Dialect*,
ii. 52, " As stiff as a poker," a proverbial simile generally applied to a
haughty coxcomb. " He's as stiff as
an 'ad swallowed a poker."

Stiff as a stake. *c.* 1566 : *Albion
Knight*, in Malone S.'s *Collns.*, i. 236, As
styffe as a stake Battayle to make.
1697 : T. Dilke, *City Lady*, III. iii., In
the morning he may find himself as
cold as a stone, and as stiff as a stake.

Stiff as Barker's knee. *See* the 1913
quot. 1865 : Hunt, *Pop. Rom. W. of
England*, 88 (1896). 1882 : F. W. P.
Jago, *Gloss. of Cornish Dialect*, 112.
1913 : E. M. Wright, *Rustic Speech, etc.*,
199, Once upon a time there was a miner
called Barker, who was foolhardy
enough to say he did not believe there
were any Knockers [spirits that haunt
Cornish tin-mines]. In revenge for
this insult, a crowd of Knockers way-
laid him, and pelted him with their
tools, causing him a lifelong injury,
whence grew up the proverb : As stiff
as Barker's knee.

Stile, *subs.* I. *He that will not go
over the stile, must be thrust through the
gate.* 1678 : Ray, 206.

2. *You would be over the stile before
you come at it.* 1546 : Heywood, *Proverbs*, Pt. II. ch. ix. 1566 : Gascoigne,
Supposes, II. i., You would fayne leape
over the stile before you come at the

hedge. 1670 : Ray, 184, To leap over
the hedge, before you come at the stile.
1710 : S. Palmer, *Moral Essays on Proverbs*, 188, Don't go over, etc. 1712 :
Motteux, *Quixote*, Pt. I. bk. iii. ch. iv.
[as in 1670]. *See also* **Style.**

Still as a stone. *c.* 1300 : *Havelok*,
l. 928 (E.E.T.S.), Hauelok sette him
dun anon, Also stille als a ston.
c. 1400: *Beryn*, l. 653 (E.E.T.S.), But
lay as styll as ony stone. *c.* 1490:
Partonope, l. 1282 (E.E.T.S.), But
lyethe as stylle as any stone. *c.* 1530:
Thos. of Erceldoune, l. 233 (Lansdowne,
E.E.T.S.), Thomas stode styll as stone.
1768 : Brooke, *Fool of Quality*, iii. 117.
1820 : Scott, *Monastery*, ch. xiv. 1922 :
Weyman, *Ovington's Bank*, ch. xxix.

Still dog. *See* **Dog** (11).

**Stillest humours are always the worst,
The.** 1670 : Ray, 25. 1732 : Fuller,
No. 4768.

Still he fishes. *See* **Fish**, *verb* (3).

Still sow eats up all the draff, The.
1546 : Heywood, *Proverbs*, Pt. I. ch. x.
c. 1580: *Tom Tyler*, l. 521, p. 15 (Malone
S.). 1633 : Jonson, *Tale of a Tub*, III.
v. 1641 : Cowley, *Guardian*, III. viii.
1673: Wycherley, *Gent. Danc.-Master*,
I. ii., The silent sow (madam) does eat
most grains. 1714 : Ozell, *Molière*, iv.
122 [" drinks " for " eats "]. 1865 : *N.
& Q.*, 3rd ser., viii. 7, We have another
pithy proverb [in N. Lancs] which expresses a good deal in little compass :—
" Th' quiet sow eats a' th' draff." 1920:
J. H. Bloom, in *N. & Q.*, 12th ser., vii.
507, A few Warwickshire Folk Sayings:—A sly sow eats all the wash.

Still waters run deep. [Altissima
quaeque flumina minimo sono labuntur.
—Q. Curtius, *De Rebus Gestis Alex.
Magni*, vii. 10.] *c.* 1400 : *Cato's
Morals*, in *Cursor Mundi* (E.E.T.S.),
l. 1672, Ther the flode is deppist the
water standis stillist. *c.* 1430: Lydgate,
Minor Poems, 186 (Percy S.), Smothe
waters ben ofte sithes depe. 1584 :
Lyly, *Sapho and Phao*, II. iv., Water
runneth smoothest, where it is deepest.
1618 : Field, *Amends for Ladies*, III.
ii., Deep'st waters stillest go. 1648 :
Herrick, *Hesperides*, No. 38, Deep
waters noiseless are. 1748 : Richardson,

Clarissa, viii. 146 (1785), The stillest waters is the deepest. 1781 : Macklin, *Man of the World*, I., Smooth water, you know, sir, runs deepest. 1869 : Spurgeon, *John Ploughman*, ch. vi., Still waters are the deepest ; but the shallowest brooks brawl the most.

Still waters, Take heed of, the quick pass away. 1640: Herbert, *Jac. Prudentum*.

Still waters turn no mills. 1907 : F. K. Aglionby, *Life of Bp. E. H. Bickersteth*, 5.

Still. Cf. **Quiet.**

Stink. *See* **Polecat.**

Stinking fish, No man cries. 1664 : J. Wilson, *Cheats*, IV. ii., Did you ever hear a fishwife cry stinking mackarel ? 1708 : tr. Aleman's *Guzman*, i. 278, He won't cry stinking fish, and tell you he has none that's good. 1801 : Wolcot, *Works*, v. 302 (1801), Yet people will in answer say, "'Tis the world's way—We never hear a man cry 'Stinking Fish!'" 1844 : Thackeray, *B. Lyndon*, ch. iii., I replied that I was a young gentleman of large fortune (this was not true ; but what is the use of crying bad fish ?). 1927 : *Sphere*, 26 Nov., p. 366, col. 4, I for one should like to cry truce to everlasting criticism. . . . Let us for a while cry no more stinking fish.

Stir with a knife, Stir up strife. 1910 : *Devonsh. Assoc. Trans.*, xlii. 90. 1917 : Bridge, *Cheshire Proverbs*, 77.

Stitch in time saves nine, A. [Principiis obsta.—Ovid, *Rem. Am.*, 91.] 1732 : Fuller, No. 6291, A stitch in time may save nine. 1845 : Planché, in *Extravag.* iii. 31 (1879), We take a stitch in time that may save nine. 1922 : *Times*, 2 June, p. 5, col. 2, With streets, as with clothes, a stitch in time saves nine.

Stitch your seam before you've tacked it, Don't. 1917 : Bridge, *Cheshire Proverbs*, 50.

Stoat. *See* quot. 1895 : Jos. Thomas, *Randigal Rhymes*, 61, Screech like a whitneck [stoat].

Stocking off a bare leg, It's hard to get a. Spoken of a bankrupt. 1886 : R. Holland, *Cheshire Gloss.*, 451 (E.D.S.). 1917 : Bridge, *Cheshire Proverbs*, 84.

Stockport. *See* quot. Ibid., 155, When the world was made the rubbish was sent to Stockport.

Stockport chaise, A = Two women riding sideways on one horse. 1828 : Carr, *Craven Dialect*, ii. 171, Stopport-Chaise, Two women riding together on horseback. Stopport is the Craven pronunciation of Stock-port. 1917 : Bridge, *Cheshire Proverbs*, 21.

Stoke in the Vale. *See* **Higham.**

Stolen pleasures are sweetest. 1611 : *Bible*, Proverbs ix. 17, Stolen waters are sweet. 1632 : Massinger, *City Madam*, II. i., And, pleasure stolen being sweetest . . . 1636 : Dekker, *Wonder of a Kingdom*, II., Gold barr'd with locks, Is best being stolen. 1671 : Head and Kirkman, *Eng. Rogue*, II., Pref. to Reader, Following the proverb, *that stolen meat is sweetest*. 1696 : Vanbrugh, *Relapse*, III., Nay, I must confess stolen pleasures are sweet. 1709 : Cibber, *Rival Fools*, I., Stolen sweets are best. 1840 : Barham, *Ing. Legends*: "A New Play," Stolen kisses are sweet. 1855 : Gaskell, *North and South*, ch. xxxi., Some one had told you that stolen fruit tasted sweetest.

Stomach. *See* quot. 1605 : Camden, *Remains*, 333 (1870), To have a stomach and lack meat, to have meat and lack a stomach, to lie in bed and cannot rest are great miseries.

Stone and Stones, *subs.* 1. *A stone in a well is not lost.* 1640 : Herbert, *Jac. Prudentum*.

2. *It is evil running against a stone wall.* 1560 : T. Wilson, *Rhetorique*, 189 (1909).

3. *The stone that lieth not in your way need not offend you.* 1732 : Fuller, No. 4770.

4. *Who remove stones bruise their fingers.* 1640 : Herbert, *Jac. Prudentum.* 1670 : Ray, 25. 1732 : Fuller, No. 5715 [with "land-mark" before "stones"].

See also **Still as a stone.**

Stool in the sun. *See* quots. 1659 : Howell, 4, Put a stool in the sun, when one knave riseth another comes. 1670 : Ray, 146 [as in 1659]. 1732 : Fuller, No. 4105 [as in 1659]. 1780 : *Mother*

Bunch, Sec. Part, 27 (Gomme, 1885), Remember the old proverb, Set thy stool in the sun, if a knave goes an honest man may come.

Stoop so low to take up just nothing at all, I will never. 1732 : Fuller, No. 2641.

Stoop that hath a low door, He must. 1678 : Ray, 171. 1732 : Fuller, No. 1995.

Stop, verb. 1. He who will stop every man's mouth, must have a great deal of meal. 1855 : Bohn, 401.

2. Stop stitch. See quot. 1828 : Carr, Craven Dialect, ii. 169, " Stop stitch while I put t'needle in," a proverbial expression . . . when one wishes . . . not to be in a hurry about anything.

3. To stop two gaps with one bush. 1546 : Heywood, Proverbs, Pt. II. ch. ix. c. 1594 : Bacon, Promus, No. 678. 1639 : Fuller, Holy War, bk. v. ch. xxii., These Italians stopped two gaps with one bush. 1681 : Robertson, Phraseol. Generalis, 1174. 1732 : Fuller, No. 5234.

4. To stop two mouths with one morsel. 1639 : Clarke, 45. 1670 : Ray, 197. 1681 : Robertson, Phraseol. Generalis, 1174.

5. Ye will as soon stop gaps with rushes. 1546 : Heywood, Proverbs, Pt. II. ch. ix.

Stopford law, no stake no draw. 1678 : Ray, 301. 1790 : Grose, Prov. Gloss., s.v. " Cheshire." 1917 : Bridge, Cheshire Proverbs, 110, Stopport law, etc. Cf. Lancashire law.

Store is no sore. 1471 : Ripley, Comp. Alch., XII. viii., in Ashm. 186 (1652), (O.), For wyse men done sey store ys no sore. 1553 : Respublica, I. i., The worlde waxeth harde, and store (thei saie) is no sore. 1632 : Jonson, Magn. Lady, II. 1646 : Quarles, Shep. Oracles, Egl. ii. 1720 : C. Shadwell, Sham Prince, II. i. 1776 : Colman, Spleen, I. 1869 : Spurgeon, John Ploughman, ch. xvi., Why not get two or three weeks' supply at once, and so get it cheaper ? Store is no sore.

Storm, subs. 1. After a storm comes a calm. 1377 : Langland, Plowman,

B, xviii. 409, " After sharpe shoures," quod Pees, " moste shene is the sonne." 1590 : Greene, Works, viii. 101 (Grosart), Euerie storme hath his calme. 1618 : Minshull, Essayes, etc., 18 (1821), After stormes calmes will arise. 1630 : Davenant, Cruel Brother, I. 1712 : Motteux, Quixote, Pt. II. ch. xix. 1804 : Byron, Letters, etc., i. 40 (Prothero). 1893 : Inwards, Weather Lore, 75.

2. Always a calm before a storm. 1590 : Greene, Works, viii. 57 (Grosart), Little thinking poore soules such a sharp storme shuld follow so quiet a calme. 1597 : H. Lok, Poems, 208 (Grosart), And stormes insue the calme before that went. 1633 : Draxe, 23, After a calme commeth a storme. 1893 : Inwards, Weather Lore, 75.

3. The sharper the storm, the sooner it's over. Oxfordsh. 1913 : Folk-Lore, xxiv. 76.

4. The sudden storm lasts not three hours. 1893 : Inwards, Weather Lore, 74.

5. To raise a storm in a tea-cup. [Fluctus excitare in simpulo.—Cicero, De Legibus, iii. 16.] 1678 : Ormond, in Hist. MSS. Comm., Ormonde MSS., iv. 292 (O.), Our skirmish . . . compared with the great things now on foot, is but a storm in a cream bowl. 1872 : W. Black, Strange Adv. Phaeton, ch. xix.

Story. See Tale.

Stout, I, and thou stout, who shall bear the ashes out ? " Stout "= proud. 1546 : Heywood, Proverbs, Pt. I. ch. x. ["proud" for "stout"]. 1631 : J. Donne, Polydoron, 44, . . . carry the dirt out? 1732 : Fuller, No. 6284 [as in 1631].

Straight as a line. 1412–20 : Lydgate, Troy Book, bk. ii. l. 6739, The wey hem ladde To the paleis, streight as any lyne. 1587 : Churchyard, Worth. of Wales, 17 (Spens. S.), Upright as straight as line. 1641 : Evelyn, Diary, i. 28 (Bray, 1883), The river, ten miles in length, straight as a line. 1872 : Hardy, Greenwood Tree, Pt. II. ch. iii., I say that we all move down-along straight as a line to Pa'son Mayble's." 1896 : Conan Doyle, Rodney Stone, ch. xv., If I didn't know that he was as

straight as a line, I'd ha' thought he
was planning a cross and laying against
himself. 1901 : Raymond, *Idler Out of
Doors*, 118, This tidal river, in one part
straight as a line . . .

Straight as a loitch [loach]. 1882 :
N. & Q., 6th ser., v. 28, " Straight as a
loitch " . . . has been in common use
in this part of Yorkshire [Batley] from
time immemorial. It is used to express
. . . perfect straightness.

Straight as an arrow. 1592 : Warner,
Alb. England, ch. xxxi., st. 4, As peart
as bird, as straite as boulte. 1682 : A.
Behn, *City Heiress*, II. i., A back as
strait as an arrow. 1713 : Ward, *Poet.
Entertainer*, No. 5, p. 26, As strait as
any arrow. 1817 : Scott, *Rob Roy*, ch.
xxv. 1841 : Dickens, *Barn. Rudge*, ch. i.
1894 : R. L. S., *St. Ives*, ch. xxix. 1924 :
A. Gissing, *Footpath-way in Glouc.*, 114.

Straight as a rush. 1892 : Heslop,
Northumb. Words, 566 (E.D.S.), " Streit
as a rasher " [rush] is a proverbial
expression.

Straight as a yard o' pump water, As.
1886 : R. Holland, *Cheshire Gloss.*, 446
(E.D.S.), . . . Often said of a tall,
lanky girl.

Straight as my leg. 1720 : Gay,
Poems, ii. 279 (Underhill), Straight as
my leg her shape appears. 1738 :
Swift, *Polite Convers.*, Dial. I., Straight !
Ay, straight as my leg, and that's
crooked at knee.

**Straight as the back-bone of a her-
ring.** 1678 : Ray, 289.

**Straight stick is crooked in the water,
A.** 1732 : Fuller, No. 425.

Straight trees have crooked roots.
Ibid., No. 4264.

**Strand on the Green, thirteen houses,
fourteen cuckolds, and never a house
between:**—The father and son lay in
one house. 1659 : Howell, 21. 1790 :
Grose, *Prov. Gloss.*, s.v. " Middlesex."
Cf. **Crafthole.**

**Strange beast that hath neither head
nor tail, It is a.** 1633 : Draxe, 201.
1639 : Clarke, 8.

Stranger's eye sees clearest, A. 1860 :
Reade, *Cl. and Hearth*, ch. lviii. [cited as
"a common saying "]. Cf. **Lookers on.**

Straw and Straws, *subs.* 1. *He gives
straw to his dog, and bones to his ass.*
1813 : Ray, 75.

2. *Straws show which way the wind
blows.* 1802 : Gouv. Morris, in *Life, etc.*,
by Sparks (1832), iii. 166 (O.), Straws
and feathers . . . show which way the
wind blows. 1860 : Reade, *Cl. and
Hearth*, ch. lvi., Such straws of speech
show how blows the wind. 1910 :
Lucas, *Ingleside*, ch. ii. 1922 : Weyman, *Ovington's Bank*, ch. xiii.

3. *Who hath skirts of straw needs fear
the fire.* 1666 : Torriano, *Piazza Univ.*,
184, Who hath his tail of straw is afraid
of fire. 1670 : Ray, 25.

See also **Candlemas, D**; and **Drowning.**

Strawberry. *See* **Oak** (4).

**Stream can never rise above the
spring-head, The.** 1732 : Fuller, No.
4771.

**Stretcheth his foot beyond the blanket,
shall stretch it in the straw, Whoso.**
c. 1240 : Grosteste, *Book of Husbandry*,
quoted Riley, *Memorials of London*, 8,
n. 4, Whoso streket his fot forthere than
the whitel [blanket] will reche, he schal
streken in the straw. 1377 : Langland,
Plowman, B, xiv. 233, For whan he
streyneth hym to streche the strawe in
his schetes. *c.* 1393 : Ibid., C, xvii.
76 [as in 1377, but with " whitel " for
" schetes "]. 1736 : Bailey, *Dict.*, s.v.
" Arm," Stretch your legs according to
your coverlet.

Stretching and yawning leadeth to bed.
1659 : Howell, 17. 1670 : Ray, 216.

Stretton i' th' street [Rutland], **where
shrews meet.** 1678 : Ray, 333.

Strife. *See* **Wife** (10).

Strike, *verb.* 1. *He strikes with a
straw.* 1813 : Ray, 75.

2. *He that strikes with his tongue,
must ward with his head.* 1640 : Herbert, *Jac. Prudentum.* 1670 : Ray, 26.
1732 : Fuller, No. 2319.

3. *He that strikes with the sword. See*
Sword (1).

4. *Strike Dawkin ! See* **Devil** (35).

5. *Strike, or give me the bill* =Mind
what you are about. 1672 : Walker,
Paroem., 37.

6. *To strike while the iron is hot.*
c. 1374 : Chaucer, *Troylus*, bk. ii. l. 1276,
Pandare, which that stood hir faste by,

Felte iren hoot, and he bigan to smyte.
1412-20 : Lydgate, *Troy Book*, bk. ii.
l. 6110, The iren hoot, tyme is for to
smyte. *c.* 1489 : Caxton, *Sonnes of
Aymon*, 136 (E.E.T.S.), Whan the yron
is well hoote, hit werketh the better.
1546 : Heywood, *Proverbs*, Pt. I. ch. iii.,
Whan thyron is hot strike. 1603 :
Dekker, *Works*, i. 100 (Grosart), Seeing
the dice of Fortune run so sweetly, and
resoluing to strike whilst the iron was
hote . . . 1668 : Shadwell, *Sullen Lovers*,
IV. i., Ask no more questions, but to
her, and strike while the iron's hot.
1706 : Farquhar, *Recruit. Officer*, IV. ii.,
c. 1750 : Foote, *Englishm. in Paris*, I.
1841 : Dickens, *Barn. Rudge*, ch. xliv.,
Where's the good of putting things
off ? Strike while the iron's hot ; that's
what I say. 1922 : Weyman, *Ovington's
Bank*, ch. xli.

Strip it. *See* quot. 1678 : Ray, 289,
Thou'lt strip it as Slack stript the cat,
when he pull'd her out of the churn.

Strive against the stream, To. [Diri-
gere bracchia contra Torrentem.—
Juvenal, iv. 89.] *c.* 1270 : *Prov. of
Alfred*, in Morris, *Old Eng. Miscell.*, 110
(E.E.T.S.), Strong hit is to reowe a-
yeyn the see that floweth. *c.* 1311 : in
Wright, *Pol. Songs*, 254 (Camden S.),
Whoso roweth agein the flod, Off sorwe
he shal drinke. *c.* 1390 : Gower, *Conf.
Amantis*, bk. iv. l. 1780, Betre is to
wayte upon the tyde Than rowe ayein
the stremes stronge. *c.* 1480 : *Digby
Plays*, 156 (E.E.T.S.), Ya, I wyll no
more row a-geyn the fflode. Before
1529 : Skelton, in *Works*, i. 418 (Dyce),
He is not wyse ageyne the streme that
stryuith. *c.* 1590 : Greene, *Alphonsus*,
I. i., In vain it is to strive against the
stream. 1694 : *Terence made English*,
207, For what a madness is it to strive
against the stream. 1728 : Fielding,
Love in several Masques, V. xiii. 1822 :
Scott, *Nigel*, Intro. Epistle, No one
shall find me rowing against the stream.
I care not who knows it—I write for
general amusement.

**Stroke at every tree without felling
any, A.** 1855 : Bohn, 301.

**Strokes are good to give, they are good
to receive, If.** 1732 : Fuller, No. 2700.

**Stroke with one hand, and stab with
the other, To.** Ibid., No. 5236.

**Strong affections give credit to weak
arguments.** 1639 : Clarke, 27.

Strong as a horse. *See* **Horse** (24).

Strong as mustard. 1659 : Howell,
18. 1670 : Ray, 207. 1720 : Gay,
Poems, ii. 277 (Underhill), My passion
is as mustard strong.

Stronger house = prison. *See* quot.
1639 : Clarke, 209, You'l be sent to a
stronger house than ever your father
built for you.

Strong man, The. *See* quot. 1871 :
Smiles, *Character*, 16, " The strong man
and the waterfall," says the proverb,
" channel their own path."

Stubble in a fallow field, He seeks for.
Glos. 1639 : in *Berkeley MSS.*, iii. 27
(1885).

Studies his content, wants it, He that.
1611 : Cotgrave, s.v. " Aise," Hee that
studies his contentment overmuch,
ever wants it. 1640 : Herbert, *Jac.
Prudentum*.

Study, In a. *See* **Brown study.**

Stumble may prevent a fall, A. 1732 :
Fuller, No. 424.

Stumble, *verb.* 1. *He that stumbles
and falls not, mends his pace.* 1611 :
Cotgrave, s.v. " Choper," He that
stumbles without falling, gets the more
forward. 1640 : Herbert, *Jac. Prudentum*. 1655 : Fuller, *Church Hist.*, bk. viii.
§ ii. (32), He that stumblteh, and doth
not fall down, gaineth ground thereby.
1732 : Fuller, No. 2316, He that
stumbles and falls not quite, gains a
step.

2. *He who stumbles twice over the same
stone, deserves to break his shins.* 1875 :
Cheales, *Proverb. Folk-Lore*, 114.

3. *To stumble at a straw and leap over
a block.* 1526 : *Hund. Mery Tayles*,
No. xvi. p. 29 (Oesterley), As ye comen
prouerb is they stumble at a straw
and lepe ouer a blok. 1585 : Greene,
Works, v. 90 (Grosart), Tush fond foole,
if thou stumble at a straw thou shalt
neuer leap ouer a blocke. 1630 : T.
Adams, *Works*, 327, Doe they not
stumble at our strawes, and leape ouer
their owne blockes ? 1732 : Fuller,
No. 4270.

4. *To stumble at the truckle-bed.* 1678 : Ray, 81.

5. *To stumble on plain ground.* 1869 : Hazlitt, 432.

Sturdy oak. *See* **Great tree.**

Style toward, A, and a wife forward, are uneasy companions. Glos. I do not understand this saying. Perhaps it should be s.v. " Stile." 1639 : in *Berkeley MSS.*, iii. 32 (1885).

Subject, *subs.* 1.¯ *The subject's love is the King's life-guard.* 1736 : Bailey, *Dict.*, s.v. Cf. **People's love.**
2. *The subject's riches is the King's power.* Ibid.

Subjects. *See* **Wife (19).**

Subtle as a dead pig, As. 1672 : Walker, *Parœm.*, 16. 1681 : Robertson, *Phraseol. Generalis*, 1185, He's as subtle as a dead pig ; Non plus sapit, quam sus mætata.

Subtlety is better than force. 1736 : Bailey, *Dict.*, s.v.

Success is never blamed. 1732 : Fuller, No. 4273. Cf. **Nothing (27).**

Success makes a fool seem wise. 1855 : Bohn, 492.

Such a beginning, such an ending. 1546 : Heywood, *Proverbs*, Pt. II. ch. ix., Such beginnyng, such ende. 1670 : Ray, 3. 1732 : Fuller, No. 4274.

Such a cup, such a cruse. 1549 : Latimer, *Seven Sermons*, 143 (Arber).

Such as the priest, such is the clerk. 1666 : Torriano, *Piazza Univ.*, 1, Such as the abbot is, such is the monk. 1732 : Fuller, No. 4279.

Such a welcome, such a farewell. 1546 : Heywood, *Proverbs*, Pt. II. ch. vii. 1670 : Ray, 28. 1732 : Fuller, No. 4278.

Such beef, such broth. 1598 : Meres, *Palladis*, fo. 218.

Such carpenter, such chips. 1546 : Heywood, *Proverbs*, Pt. II. ch. vii. 1568 : Fulwell, *Like to Like*, in Hazlitt, *Old Plays*, iii. 330. 1670 : Ray, 115, Like carpenter like chips.

Such cup, such cover. 1532 : More, *Confut. of Tyndale*, Pref., sig. Bb1, A very mete couer for such a cuppe. 1565 : Shacklock, *Hatchet of Heresies*, sig. *b*6, As saythe the prouerb, a mete couer for such a cup. 1639 : in

Berkeley MSS. iii., 32 (1885), The cup and cover will hold together. 1642 : D. Rogers, *Matrim. Honour*, 277. 1655 : Fuller, *Church Hist.*, bk. ix. § ii. (20), And became great with the Duke de Alva (like cup, like cover !) . . .

Such saint, such offering. 1581 : T. Howell, *Devises*, 74 (1906), Such saintes, such seruice. 1651 : Herbert, *Jac. Prudentum*, 2nd ed. 1670 : Ray, 115, Like saint like offering.

Such tree, such fruit. Before 1300 : *Cursor Mundi*, l. 38, O gode pertre coms god peres Wers tre, vers fruit it beres. [Of good pear-tree comes good pears Worse tree worse fruit it bears.] *c.* 1370 : Wiclif, *Eng. Works*, 331 (E.E.T.S.), But who shuld preise this lawe therfore ? sith yuel frute witnessith yuel rote. 1402 : Hoccleve, *Minor Poems*, 79 (E.E.T.S.), A wikked tre, gode frute may noon forth bryng ; for swiche the frute ys as that is the tre. Before 1529 : Skelton, *Works*, i. 214 (Dyce), For it is an auncyent brute, Suche apple tre, suche, frute. 1584 : Greene, *Works*, iii. 10 (Grosart). 1611 : Cotgrave, s.v. " Doux," Such as the tree such is the fruit. 1664 : J. Wilson, *Andr. Commenius*, III. iii., Don't we know the tree By its fruit. 1732 : Fuller, No. 4280 [as in 1611]. Cf. **Tree (8).**

Sucked not this out of my fingers' ends, I. 1546 : Heywood, *Proverbs*, Pt. I. ch. xi. 1670 : Ray, 25. 1732 : Fuller, No. 2625.

Sudden friendship, sure repentance. Ibid., No. 4281. Cf. **Sudden trust.**

Sudden glory soon goes out. Ibid., No. 4282.

Sudden joy kills sooner than excessive grief. 1620 : Shelton, *Quixote*, Pt. II. ch. lii., It is usually said that sudden joy as soon kills as excessive grief. 1732 : Fuller, No. 4283.

Sudden rising hath a sudden fall, A. *c.* 1440 : Lydgate, *Fall of Princes*, bk. ix. l. 1211, Sodeyn clymbyng axeth a sodeyn fall. *c.* 1615 : R.C., *Times Whistle*, 39 (E.E.T.S.), And 'tis a saying held for true of all, " A sudden rising hath a sudden fall."

Sudden trust brings sudden repentance.

1669 : *Politeuphuia*, 103. Cf. **Sudden friendship.**

Suds, In the. See **Leave,** *verb* (8).

Suffer. See **Patience** (6).

Sufferance cometh ease, Of. *c.* 1386 : Chaucer, *Merch. Tale,* l. 871, Passe over is an ese, I sey na-more. *c.* 1390 : Gower, *Conf. Amantis,* bk. iii. l. 1672, For suffrance is the welle of Pes [Peace]. 1546 : Heywood, *Proverbs,* Pt. I. ch. ix. 1598 : Shakespeare, 2 *Hen. IV.* V. iv. 1607 : Marston, *What You Will,* Prol., Ile give a proverbe,—Sufferance giveth ease. 1678 : Ray, 207. 1736 : Bailey, *Dict.,* s.v.

Sufferance. See also **Forbearance.**

Suffer and expect. 1640 : Herbert, *Jac. Prudentum.*

Sufferer overcomes. See **Patience** (6).

Suffer the ill and look for the good. 1578 : Florio, *First Fruites,* fo. 33, I suffer the bad, hoping for the better. 1629 : *Book of Meery Riddles,* Prov. 117.

Suffolk cheese—proverbial for hardness. 1661 : Pepys, *Diary,* 4 Oct., I found my wife vexed at her people for grumbling to eat Suffolk cheese. 1662 : *Fragm. Aulica,* 60, He could be glad to have had a suffolke cheese and twelfpeny loafe. 1691 : Shadwell, *Scourers,* V. i., Who snores with fumes from Suffolk cheese and bacon. 1706 : Ward, *Works,* iii. 114, Curse his thin beer, and rail at Suffolk cheese. 1737 : Pope, *Imit. of Horace,* Sat. vi. bk. ii., Cheese such as men in Suffolk make, But wished it Stilton for his sake. 1865 : W. White, *Eastern England,* ii. 176, I forebore to ask him if he liked Suffolk cheese, which . . . is described as hard as grindstones : so hard that even rats and mice refuse it. See also **Hunger.**

Suffolk fair maids. 1622 : Drayton, *Polyol.,* xxiii., Fair Suffolk maids and milk. 1662 : Fuller, *Worthies,* iii. 161 (1840). 1790 : Grose, *Prov. Gloss.,* s.v. " Suffolk."

Suffolk milk. 1622 : Drayton, *Polyol.,* xxiii. *ut supra.* 1790 : Grose, s.v. " Suffolk."

Suffolk stiles = ditches. 1662 : Fuller, *Worthies,* iii. 161 (1840). Cf. **Essex stiles.**

Suffolk whine, The. 1790 : Grose, *Prov. Gloss.,* s.v. " Suffolk."

Suit is best that best suits me, That. 1639 : Clarke, 16. 1670 : Ray, 46 [with " fits " for " suits "].

Suits hang half a year in Westminster Hall ; at Tyburn half an hour's hanging endeth all. 1869 : Hazlitt, 347.

Sulky. See **Bull** (2); and **Cross** (1).

Summer, *subs.* 1. *A cool summer and a light weight in the bushel.* 1893 : Inwards, *Weather Lore,* 8.

2. *A dry summer never begs its bread.* Somerset. Ibid., 7.

3. *A dry summer never made a dear peck.* Ibid., 7.

4. *A dry summer never made a full peck.* 1882 : Mrs. Chamberlain, *W. Worcs. Words,* 38 (E.D.S.).

5. *An English summer.* 1846 : Denham, *Proverbs,* 48 (Percy S.), . . . two fine days and a thunderstorm. 1854 : Doran, *Table Traits,* 27, . . . three hot days and a thunderstorm. 1893 : Inwards, *Weather Lore,* 7, . . . two hot days and a thunderstorm.

6. *Summer in winter, and a summer's flood, Never boded England good.* 1846 : Denham, *Proverbs,* 68 (Percy S.). 1893 : Inwards, 8 [" an Englishman " for " England "].

7. *There's no summer, but it has a winter.* 1846 : Denham, 48. 1904 : *Co. Folk-Lore: Northumb.,* 178 (F.L.S.).

8. *To dream of a dry summer.* 1568 : W. Fulwood, *Enemie of Idlenesse,* 217 (1593), I thinke you dreame of a drie summer. 1639 : Clarke, 64. 1670 : Ray, 172.

See also **One fair day ; Swallow ;** and **Winter,** *passim.*

Sun, *subs.* 1. *A morning sun.* See quots. 1640 : Herbert, *Jac. Prudentum,* The morning sun never lasts a day. Ibid., A morning sun and a winebred child and a Latin-bred woman seldom end well. 1887 : *N. & Q.,* 7th ser., iv. 447, The old proverb in common use in Yorkshire certainly seventy years ago, which runs thus : " A morning without clouds, a child that drinks wine, and a woman that talks Latin seldom come to a good end." 1893 :

Inwards, *Weather Lore*, 48 [as in 1640, first quot.].

2. *A red sun has water in his eye.* 1659 : Howell, *Proverbs: Span.-Eng.*, 22. 1893 : Inwards, 48.

3. *He hath the sun on's face, and th' wind on's back.* 1639 : Clarke, 42.

4. *If red the sun begins his race, Expect that rain will flow apace.* 1846 : Denham, *Proverbs*, 11 (Percy S.). 1872 : J. Glyde, jr., *Norfolk Garland*, 155.

5. *If the sun goes pale to bed, 'Twill rain to-morrow, it is said.* 1893 : Inwards, 52.

6. *If the sun in red should set, The next day surely will be wet; If the sun should set in grey, The next will be a rainy day.* 1838 : Mrs. Bray, *Trad. of Devon*, i. 6. 1865 : Hunt, *Pop. Romances W. of Eng.*, 435 (1896). 1893 : Inwards, *Weather Lore*, 51.

7. *If the sun sets clear, it is a sign of fair weather.* 1754 : Berthelson, *Eng.-Danish Dict.*, s.v. " Clear."

8. *The sun can be seen by nothing but its own light.* 1732 : Fuller, No. 4774.

9. *The sun is never the worse for shining on a dunghill.* 1303 : Brunne, *Handlyng Synne*, l. 2299, The sunne hys feyrnes neuer he tynes thoghe hyt on the muk hepe shynes. *c.* 1386 : Chaucer, *Parson's Tale*, 76, Holy writ may nat been defouled, na-more than the sunne that shyneth on the mixen. 1579 : Lyly, *Euphues*, 43 (Arber), The sunne shineth vpon the dounghill, and is not corrupted. 1732 : Fuller, No. 4776. 1846 : Denham, *Proverbs*, 5 (Percy S.).

10. *The sun shines on both sides of the hedge.* Ibid., 49.

11. *They that walk in the sun will be tanned at last.* 1560 : T. Wilson, *Rhetorique*, Prol. (1909), He that goeth in the sunne shall bee sunne burnt, although he thinke not of it. 1638 : D. Tuvill, *Vade Mecum*, 56 (3rd ed.), Hee that walketh in the sun shall be tan'd. 1670 : Ray, 146. 1732 : Fuller, No. 4986, They that walk in the sun must be content to be tann'd.

12. *Though the sun shine leave not thy cloak at home.* 1640 : Herbert, *Jac. Prudentum.* 1732 : Fuller, No. 5014,

Tho' the sun shines take your cloak. 1846 : Denham, *Proverbs*, 1 (Percy S.) [" coat " for " cloak "].

13. *To set forth the sun with a candle.* 1551 : Robinson, tr. More's *Utopia*, 27 (Arber), They neede not . . . of me to bee praysed, vnlesse I woulde seeme to shew, and set-furth the brightnes of the sonne with a candell, as the prouerbe saieth. 1586 : Whitney, *Emblems*, 107, Bicause it is in vaine, to set a candell in the sonne. *c.* 1594 : Bacon, *Promus*, No. 688, To help the sunne with lantornes.

14. *When the sun is highest he casts the least shadow.* 1732 : Fuller, No. 5607.

15. *When the sun sets bright and clear, An easterly wind you need not fear.* 1846 : Denham, *Proverbs*, 20 (Percy S.). 1893 : Inwards, *Weather Lore*, 51.

16. *When the sun sets in a bank, A westerly wind we shall not want.* 1846 : Denham, 12. 1893 : Inwards, 52 [" lack " for " want "].

17. *When the sun shines, no body minds it; but when he is eclipsed, all consider him.* 1732 : Fuller, No. 5608. 1846 : Denham, 5.

See also **Candlemas**, A and F ; **Christmas** (22) ; **Cloud** (2)–(4) ; **Easter** (7) ; **January** (12) and (14) ; **March** (18), (35), (37), (45), and (46) ; **Red at night** ; **Saturday** (3) ; **Shrovetide** (4) and (5) ; **Sunday** (2) ; and **Wind**, A (*a*) (18).

Sunday. 1. *A wet Sunday, a wet week.* 1830 : Forby, *Vocab. E. Anglia*, 416.

2. *If sunset on Sunday is cloudy, it will rain before Wednesday.* 1893 : Inwards, *Weather Lore*, 43.

3. *Sunday clearing, clear till Wednesday.* Ibid., 43.

4. *Sunday's child is full of grace, Monday's child is full in the face, Tuesday's child is solemn and sad, Wednesday's child is merry and glad, Thursday's child is inclined to thieving, Friday's child is free in giving, Saturday's child works hard for his living.* 1865 : Hunt, *Pop. Romances W. of Eng.*, 430 (1896). Cf. **Monday** (5).

5. *Sunday shaven, Sunday shorn, Better had'st thou ne'er been born!* 1879 :

Henderson, *Folk-Lore of N. Counties*, 18 (F.L.S.).

6. *The first Sunday in the middle of the week* = never. 1883 : Burne, *Shropsh. Folk-Lore*, 596.

7. *When it storms on the first Sunday in the month, it will storm every Sunday.* 1893 : Inwards, *Weather Lore*, 43.

See also **Alike** every day ; **Christmas** (19) ; **Come** (8) ; **Friday** (6), (10), and (12) ; **Monday** (4) ; **Moon** (3) and (14) ; and **Saturday** (1).

Sunderland sowies. *See* quot. 1846–59 : *Denham Tracts*, i. 67 (F.L.S.), This rather coarse and unenviable epithet is, even down to the present day, applied to the fair sex of Sunderland. The meaning of the word sowies, although now nearly forgotten, is evidently the diminutive of sow.

Sunshine but hath some shadow, No. 1658 : R. Franck, *North. Memoirs*, 36 (1821), No sun shines without some cloud. 1670 : Ray, 146. 1732 : Fuller, No. 3631.

Sunshiny rain. *See* **Rain** (5).

Sup, *verb.* 1. *He sups ill who eats up all at dinner.* 1611 : Cotgrave, s.v. " Disner," *Mal soupe qui tout disne:* He sups ill that dines all ; after a gluttonous and disordinate youth, followes a needie and hungrie age. 1732 : Fuller, No. 2030.

2. *He sups who sleeps.* 1860 : Reade, *Cl. and Hearth*, ch. xxiv., It is ill sitting up wet and fasting, and the byword saith, " He sups who sleeps."

3. *Sup, Simon. See* quots. 1607 : *The Puritan*, III. v., Sup, Simon, now ! eat porridge for a month. 1639 : Clarke, 46, Sup Simon 'tis best i' th' bottome [or] here's good broth. 1670 : Ray, 217, Sup Simon, the best is at the bottom. 1738 : Swift, *Polite Convers.*, Dial. II., Sup, Simon ; very good broth. 1854 : Baker, *Northants Gloss.*, s.v. " Sup," " Sup, Simon ! its excellent broth." A common ironical recommendation to any one taking medicine or anything nauseous or disagreeable.

4. *To sup sorrow. c.* 1395 : *Plowman's Tale*, in Skeat's *Chaucer*, vii. 182, Hir servaunts sitte and soupë sorowe ! 1738 : Swift, *Polite Convers.*, Dial. I.,

I'll make you one day sup sorrow for this.

5. *Who sups well sleeps well.* 1666 : Torriano, *Piazza Univ.*, 44.

Supernaculum, To drink = to the last drop. *See* 1813 quot. 1592 : Nashe, *Works*, ii. 78 (Grosart), He is no body that cannot drinke super nagulum. 1617 : T. Young, quoted in Brand, *Pop. Antiq.*, ii. 331 (Bohn), He is a man of no fashion that cannot drinke super-naculum. 1675 : *Mistaken Husband*, IV. vi., Pledge the gentleman—super-naculum. 1682 : A. Behn, *False Count*, IV. i., Your true bred woman of honour drinks all, *Supernaculum*, by Jove. 1709 : Ward, *Acc. of Clubs*, 288 (1756), Here's your old health, To the best in Christendom ; and off it went to a super-naculum drop. 1813 : Brand, *Pop. Antiq.*, ii. 342 (Bohn), To drink *supernaculum* was an ancient custom . . . of emptying the cup or glass, and then pouring the drop or two that remained at the bottom upon the person's nail that drank it, to show that he was no flincher. 1823 : Moor, *Suffolk Words*, 409, Supernaculum. A word well known and occasionally heard in social circles in Suffolk . . . something supercurious. [This is a "supercurious" perversion of the word's meaning.] 1828 : Carr, *Craven Dialect*, ii. 181, Supernaculum. Good liquor of which there is not even a drop left to wet one's nail. Cf. **Pearl.**

Supperless. *Better to go to bed supperless than to rise in debt.* 1659 : Howell, *Proverbs: Span.-Eng.*, 6, 'Tis wholsomer to go to bed without a supper, then rise in debt. 1670 : Ray, 7. 1736 : Franklin, *Way to Wealth*, in *Works*, i. 451 (Bigelow) [" Rather " for " Better "]. 1859 : Smiles, *Self-Help*, 305 (1869).

Supple knees feed arrogance. 1855 : Bohn, 492.

Sure and unsure are not all one. 1639 : Clarke, 29.

Sure as a club. 1577 : *Misogonus*, III. ii., Liturgus bringes him as sure as a clubb. 1584 : R. Scot, *Witchcraft*, bk. iv. ch. ix., Her prophesie fell out as sure as a club. 1656 : Flecknoe,

Diarium, 45, Sure as a club 'twill happen t' ye.

Sure as a gun. 1622 : B. & F., *Prophetess*, I. iii., You are right, master, Right as a gun. 1656 : *Musarum Deliciæ*, i. 94 (Hotten), But when he thought her as sure as a gun, She set up her tail, and away she run. 1693 : Congreve, *Double Dealer*, V. xx. 1734 : Fielding, *Don Quix. in England*, II. viii., As sure as a gun—this is he. 1766 : Anstey, *New Bath Guide*, Lett. viii. 1846 : *Bentley Ballads*, 7 (1876). 1886 : Elworthy, *West Som. Word-Book*, 729 (E.D.S.), Sure or Safe as a gun. Usual similes.

Sure as a juggler's box. 1650 : R. Heath, *Epigrams*, 53, Whom Death hath made sure as his juglers box. 1670 : Ray, 207.

Sure as check = Exchequer pay. 1630 : Taylor (Water-Poet), *Works*, 1st pagin., 85, But those worthy mariners are dead, and an old prouerbe, As sure as Check with them. 1662 : Fuller, *Worthies*, ii. 412 (1840), As sure as Exchequer pay. 1670 : Ray, 207, As sure as Check, or Exchequer pay. This was a proverb in Queen Elizabeths time. 1732 : Fuller, No. 732 [as in 1662].

Sure as death. *c.* 1460 : *Wyse Man taught hys Sone*, l. 93 (E.E.T.S.), For deth, my chyld, is, as y trow, The most ryght sertcyn [thing] it is. 1484 : Caxton, tr. Chartier's *Curial*, 19 (E.E.T.S.), Ne than the deth nothyng more certayn. 1596 : Jonson, *Ev. Man in Humour*, II. i., Nay as sure as death, That they would say. 1606 : Chapman, *Mons. d'Olive*, IV. ii., A love-letter from that lady would retrieve him as sure as death. 1726 : Defoe, *Hist. of Devil*, Pt. II. ch. vi. 232 (4th ed.), Things as certain as death and taxes. 1780 : Burgoyne, *Lord of Manor*, I. i. 1850 : Dickens, *Copperfield*, ch. lii., It is as certain as death. 1926 : Phillpotts, *Yellow Sands*, I., I'll drown to-night sure as death !

Sure as God made little apples. 1894 : Northall, *Folk Phrases*, 11 (E.D.S.). 1911 : *N. & Q.*, 11th ser., iv. 289, . . . I recently heard this saying twice in the same week in the Manchester dis-

trict. 1911 : Ibid., 377, I have always understood that this was a Devonshire or West Country proverb, and that the full rendering was : " As sure as God made little apples on big trees." [Other correspondents at the same reference testify to the use of the saying in the North Midlands, Norwich, and Bristol. The Derbyshire version has " crab " for " little."]

Sure as the coat's on one's back. 1639 : Clarke, 209 [" your " for " one's "]. 1670 : Ray, 208. 1736 : Bailey, *Dict.*, s.v. " Cap," As sure as the cloths on his back.

Sure as the devil is in London. 1752 : Fielding, *Cov. Gard. Journal*, No. 33.

Sure bind. *See* Safe bind.

Surety. *See* Certainty.

Surety for another. *See* quots. 1539 : Taverner, *Proverbs*, 20, Be suretie for an other and harme is at hande. 1633 : Draxe, 199, He that is surety for another must pay. 1651 : Herbert, *Jac. Prudentum*, 2nd ed., He that will be surety shall pay. 1869 : Spurgeon, *John Ploughman*, ch. iv., He who is surety is never sure.

Surgeon must have an eagle's eye, a lion's heart, and a lady's hand, A. 1589 : L. Wright, *Display of Dutie*, 37, In a good chirurgian, a hawkes eye : a lyons heart : and a ladies hand. 1619 : *Helpe to Discourse*, 104-5 (1640) [as in 1589]. 1670 : Ray, 36, A good chirurgion must, etc. *c.* 1671 : in *Roxb. Ballads*, vii. 546 (B.S.), This maid with ingenuity had every surgeon's part, A ladie's hand, an eagle's eye, but yet a lyon's heart. 1732 : Fuller, No. 4292. 1868 : *Quart. Review*, cxxv. 252.

Surgeon. *See also* Pitiful.

Surly as a butcher's dog. 1670 : Ray, 208. 1869 : Spurgeon, *John Ploughman*, ch. iv.

Surly as a cow's husband. 1886 : R. Holland, *Cheshire Gloss.*, 446 (E.D.S.). 1917 : Bridge, *Cheshire Proverbs*, 22.

Suspicion has double eyes. 1597 : Shakespeare, 1 *Henry IV.*, V. ii., Suspicion all our lives shall be stuck full of eyes. *c.* 1680 : in *Roxb. Ballads*, vi. 317 (B.S.), It is a proverb of old, " Suspicion hath double eyes."

Sussex weeds = oaks. 1911 : A. S.
Cooke, *Off Beaten Track in Sussex*, 332,
If you are not quite among the " deep
ghylls " at Hartfield, you are certainly
among the " Sussex weed." The oaks
in Buckhurst Park are a sight to gladden
the eyes.

Sutton. *See* **York.**

Sutton for mutton. *See* quots. The
jingle varies with the county to which
the " Sutton " belongs. The need for
" mutton " to jingle with " Sutton "
in all is obvious. 1790 : Grose, *Prov.
Gloss.*, s.v. " Surrey," Sutton for mutton, Carshalton for beeves, Epsom for
whores, and Ewel for thieves. 1878 :
N. & Q., 5th ser., ix. 88 [another Surrey
version, as in 1790, but with " jades."
for Epsom]. [A Kent version :] Sutton
for mutton, Kirby for beef, South
Darne for gingerbread, Dartford for a
thief. Ibid., 175, [Warwick] Sutton
for mutton, Tamworth for beeves, Brum-
magem for blackguards, Coleshill for
thieves. [Variants for the third line
are, " Walsall for a pretty girl " and
" Walsall for bandy legs " ; and for the
fourth line, " Birmingham for a thief."]
1884 : Walford, *Greater London*, ii. 207,
There is current in the district of West
Kent and East Surrey a couplet which
runs thus :—" Sutton for mutton, Kirby
for beef, Mitcham for lavender, and
Dartford for a thief."

**Sutton-Well and Kenchester are able
to buy all London, were it to sell.** 1659 :
Howell, 20. 1790 : Grose, *Prov. Gloss.*,
s.v. " Herefordshire."

Sutton windmill. *See* quot. 1600 :
Heywood, *Edw. IV.*, Pt. I., in *Dram.
Works*, i. 45 (1874), I am just akin to
Sutton windmill ; I can grind which
way soe're the winde blow.

**Swallow does not make a summer,
One.** [μία χελιδὼν ἔαρ οὐ ποιεῖ.—Aristotle,
Eth. N., I. vii. 16.] 1539 : Taverner,
Proverbs, fo. 25, It is not one
swalowe that bryngeth in somer.
c. 1597 : Deloney, *Iacke of Newberie*,
ch. i., Nay soft (said the widow) one
swallow makes not a summer, nor one
meeting a marriage. 1634 : C. Butler,
Feminine Monarchie, 46. 1784 : *New
Foundl. Hosp. for Wit*, ii. 67, One

swallow does not make a spring. 1850 :
Dickens, *Chuzzlewit*, ch. xliii. 1854 :
J. W. Warter, *Last of Old Squires*, 139
[as in 1784]. 1920 : *Sphere*, 10 April,
p. 27, col. 2, One swallow does not make
a summer, but one gazer inevitably
makes a crowd.

Swallow. *See also* **Robin** and **Snail** (4).

Swallow, *verb.*   1. *He hath swallowed
a spider* = He has been bankrupt.
1659 : Howell, 6. 1670 : Ray, 194.
1754 : Berthelson, *Eng.-Danish Dict.*,
s.v. " Swallow."

2. *To swallow a gudgeon* = To be
gulled.   1579 :   Lyly, *Euphues*, 68
(Arber), Take heede my Philautus, that
thou thy self swallow not a gudgeon.
1584 : Lodge, *Alarum against Usurers*,
44 (Sh. S.), Those gentlemen who have
swallowed the gudgen and have been
intangled in the hooke. 1607 : Dekker
and Webster, *Northw. Hoe*, IV. iv., If
the gudgeon had been swallowed by one
of you it had been vile. 1732 : Fuller,
No. 1902, He hath swallow'd a gudgeon.
1847 : Halliwell, *Dict.*, s.v. " Gudgeon,"
To swallow a gudgeon, i.e. to be caught
or deceived, to be made a fool of.

3. *To swallow an ox.   See* **Ox** (10).

4. *To swallow a stake.   See* **Eat** (31).

5. *To swallow a tavern token.   See*
Tavern token.

Swan sings before death, The.
[Olorum morte narratur flebilis cantus,
falso ut arbitror aliquot experimentis.
—Pliny, *Hist.*, x. 23.] 1398 : Trevisa,
tr. Glanville's *De Propr. Rer.*, XII. ii.,
And whan she [the swan] should dye
and that a fether is pyght in the brayn,
then she syngethe, as Ambrose sayth.
c. 1430 : Lydgate, *Minor Poems*, 157
(Percy S.), The yelwe swan famous and
aggreable, Ageyn his dethe melodyously
syngyng. 1577 : Kendall, *Flow. of
Epigrams*, 61 (Spens. S.), The swanne
doeth sweetely syng Before his death.
1632 : Massinger, *Emp. of East*, V. iii.,
Thus, like a dying swan, to a sad tune
I sing my own dirge. 1681 : Otway,
Soldier's Fortune, V. v., I'll sing a song
like a dying swan. 1712 : Pope, *Rape
of Lock*, v. 66, Thus on Mæander's
flowery margin lies The expiring swan,
and as he sings he dies. 1819 : Byron,

Isles of Greece, st. 16, There, swan-like,
let me sing and die.

Swan. *See also* **Goose.**

Swarston-bridge, He's driving his
hogs over. Derbysh. 1790: Grose,
Prov. Gloss., s.v. " Derbysh." 1889 :
Folk-Lore Journal, vii. 292, He's driving
his hogs o'er Swarson's brig.

Swear, *verb.* 1. *He swears like a
gentleman. c.* 1645 : MS. Proverbs, in
N. & Q., vol. 154, p. 27.

2. *He swears like a tinker, trooper, etc.*
1611 : Cotgrave, s.v. " Chartier," He
swears like a carter (we say, like a
tinker). 1727 : *Devil to pay at St.
James's*, 7, He swears like a trooper.
1754 : Berthelson, *Eng. - Danish Dict.*,
s.v. " Swear," He swears like a tinker.

3. *He that sweareth.* See quots.
c. 1530 : Rhodes, *Book of Nurture*, 107
(E.E.T.S.), He that sweareth tyll no
man trust him, He that lyeth tyll no
man beleeue him ; He that boroweth
till no man will lende him ; Let him
go where no man knoweth him. 1578 :
Florio, *First Fruites*, fo. 104 [as in 1530].
1880 : Spurgeon, *Ploughman's Pictures*,
19 [as in 1530, but prudishly emended
by " promiseth " for " sweareth "].

4. *He that will swear will lie.* 1630 :
Taylor (Water-Poet), *Works*, 2nd pagin.,
189, The prouerbe saies, hee that will
sweare will lie. 1650 : R. Heath, *Epigrams*, 24. 1692 : L'Estrange, *Æsop*,
398 (3rd ed.), Come wife, says he, they
that will swear, will lye.

5. *He who sweareth when he is at play,
may challenge his damnation by way of
purchase.* 1659 : Howell, 2.

6. *If you swear you will catch no fish.*
1607 : Heywood, *Fair Maid of Exchange*, in *Works*, ii. 69 (1874), What are
you cursing too ? then we catch no
fish. *c.* 1630 : B. & F., *Monsieur
Thomas*, I. iii., And next, no swearing ;
He'll catch no fish else. 1790 : Wolcot,
Works, ii. 115 (1795), Besides, a proverb, suited to my wish, Declares that
swearing never catcheth fish. 1830 :
Forby, *Vocab. E. Anglia*, 414, If you
swear, you will catch no fish. 1872 :
E. FitzGerald, in *East Anglian*, iv. 114,
Opinions differ as to swearing. One
captain strictly forbade it on board his

lugger ; but he also, continuing to get
no fish, called out, " Swear away, lads,
and see what that'll do." 1883 :
Burne, *Shropsh. Folk-Lore*, 588, Dunna
swear, or thee'lt ketch no fish.

7. *To swear*—various extraordinary
feats, expressive of rage, perjury, etc.
1658 : R. Franck, *North. Memoirs*, 191
(1821), It's thought they would have
sworn through a double deal-board,
they seem'd so enraged. 1678 : Ray,
271, He'll swear dagger out of sheath.
He'll swear the devil out of hell. Before 1680 : Butler, *Remains*, ii. 363
(1759), He will swear his ears through
an inch-board. [This seems to suggest
the pillory for perjury.] 1731 : Swift,
Poems : " Judas," Some who can per-
jure through a two-inch board. 1917 :
Bridge, *Cheshire Proverbs*, 69, He'll
swear through an inch board. Ibid.,
100, Oo'd [" Oo "—She] swear the cross
off a jackass's back.

Swearing, *verb. subs.* See quot. 1812 :
Brady, *Clavis Cal.*, i. 339, There was
formerly an expression very current,
that " Swearing came in at the head,
but is going out at the tail."

Sweep before your own door. 1650 :
Fuller, *Pisgah Sight*, bk. iii. ch. i. § 5,
How soon are those streets made clean,
where every one sweeps against his own
door. 1684 : *Great Frost*, 20 (Percy S.),
Each one his sins to God confess ; Let
every one sweep clean and neat his door.
1732 : Fuller, No. 4296. 1901 : F. E.
Taylor, *Lancs Sayings*, 22, Thee sweep
up thi own dur-step (Look to your own
faults).

Sweet, *subs.* 1. *All sorts of sweets
are not wholesome.* 1732 : Fuller, No.
543.

2. *He deserves not sweet that will not
taste of sour.* [*c.* 1387 : Usk, *Test. of
Love*, in Skeat's *Chaucer*, vii. 18, For he
is worthy no welthe, that may no wo
suffer.] *c.* 1535 : *Dialogues of Creatures*,
xxi. (1816), Who that desyryth the
swete to assaye, He must taste byttyr,
this is no naye. *c.* 1575 : H. Golding-
ham, *Garden Plot*, 60 (Roxb. Cl.), Indeede he had not deserued thys swete
before he had tasted some sowere.
1611 : in Coryat, *Crudities*, i. 109 (1905),

For he no sweet hath merited (they say) That hath not tasted of the sower by th' way. 1670 : Ray, 25. 1732 : Fuller, No. 1834.

3. *No sweet without sweat.* 1576 : Pettie, *Petite Pall.*, ii. 138 (Gollancz), You . . . live . . . by the sweet of other men's sweat. 1639 : Clarke, 87. 1681 : Robertson, *Phraseol. Generalis*, 1196. 1732 : Fuller, No. 3632 [with " some " before " sweat "]. 1859 : Smiles, *Self-Help*, 305 (1869), No sweat no sweet.

4. *Take the sweet with the sour.* 1546 : Heywood, *Proverbs*, Pt. II. ch. iv. 1560 : T. Wilson, *Rhetorique*, 4 (1909), Both can and will ever, mingle sweete among the sower, be he preacher, lawyer, yea, or cooke.

Sweet as a nut. 1599 : Buttes, *Dyets Dry Dinner*, sig. O4, As sweete as a nutte. 1654 : Gayton, *Pleasant Notes Don Q.*, 34, So have you him uncorrupt . . . sweet as a nut. 1838 : Holloway, *Provincialisms*, 120, We frequently say, " as sweet as a nut."

Sweet as honey. 1506 : Pynson, *Kal. of Shepherds*, 75 (1892), Swete as hony in oure mouth. *c.* 1550 : Udall, *Roister Doister, ad fin.*, Custance is as sweete as honey. 1595 : Churchyard, *Praise of Poetrie*, 41 (1816), As sweete as honie sure. 1612 : Shelton, *Quixote*, Pt. I. bk. iv. ch. v., All those things are as sweet as honey to me. 1716 : E. Ward, *Female Policy*, 51, Her words as sweet as honey. 1844 : Planché, *Extravag.* ii. 310 (1879), Pay me in smiles and kisses, sweet as honey. 1905 : E. G. Hayden, *Trav. Round our Village*, 87, Who'd . . . hand 'ee over 'ee fur a penny, I don't, to put in the bank !

Sweet beauty with sour beggary. 1546 : Heywood, *Proverbs*, Pt. I. ch. xiii.

Sweet discourse makes short days and nights. 1670 : Ray, 7.

Sweetest wine makes sharpest vinegar. 1567 : Painter, *Pal. of Pleasure*, ii. 323 (Jacobs), How mutch the sweter is the wyne, the sharper is the egred sawce thereof. 1579 : Lyly, *Euphues*, 39 (Arber), The sweetest wine tourneth to the sharpest vineger. 1647 : Howell,

Letters, bk. ii. No. xvi., This shews, that the sweetest wines may turn to the tartest vinegar. 1681 : Robertson, *Phraseol. Generalis*, 1196. 1792 : *Looker-on*, No. 2, The sharpest vinegar is made from the sweetest wines. 1852 : Fitz-Gerald, *Polonius*, 11 (1903), " The sweet wine that makes the sharpest vinegar," says an old proverb. 1905 : A. S. Palmer, Note in his ed. of Trench's *Proverbs*, 56, The true meaning is that even the best things may be corrupted and turned to evil, as the sweetest wine makes the sourest vinegar.

Sweet heart and bag pudding. 1659 : Howell, 6. 1670 : Ray, 214.

Sweet heart and honey-bird keeps no house. 1678 : Ray, 57. 1732 : Fuller, No. 4297.

Sweet in the mouth. *See* **Good in the mouth.**

Sweet meat will have sour sauce. *c.* 1400 : *Beryn*, 29 . (E.E.T.S.), ffor " aftir swete, the soure comyth, ful offt, in many a plase." *c.* 1500 : *Colyn Blowbols*, l. 131, in Hazlitt, *Early Pop. Poetry*, i. 98, Sharpe sawce was ordeigned for swete mete. 1546 : Heywood, *Proverbs*, Pt. I. ch. viii. 1620 : T. May, *The Heir*, III., Your sweet meat shall have sour sauce. 1670 : Cotton, *Scarronides*, IV. 1721 : Centlivre, *Artifice*, II. ii. 1769 : Colman, *Man and Wife*, III. [" may " for " will "]. 1771 : Johnson, *Letters*, i. 180 (Hill).

Swell like a toad, To. 1546 : Heywood, *Proverbs*, Pt. I. ch. xi., Streight as she sawe me she swelde lyke a tode. 1672 : Walker, *Parœm.*, 26, She swells like a toad. 1754 : Berthelson, *Eng.-Danish Dict.*, s.v. " Toad."

Swift. *See* **Quick.**

Swift to hear. *See* quot. 15th cent.: in *Reliq. Antiquæ*, i. 92 (1841), Be swyfte to here, and slow to speke, Late to wrathe, and lothe to . . .

Swim, verb. 1. *He can swim without bladders.* 1649 : Howell, *Pre-em. Parl.*, 17 (O.), My whole life (since I was left to myself to swim, as they say without bladders). 1732 : Fuller, No. 1821.

2. *He must needs swim that is held up by the chin.* Before 1500 : in Hill, *Commonplace-Book*, 129 (E.E.T.S.), He

mai lightli swim, that is hold wp by the chin. 1546 : Heywood, *Proverbs*, Pt. I. ch. v. *c.* 1594 : Bacon, *Promus*, No. 473. 1626 : *Scoggins Jests*, 119 (1864). 1732 : Fuller, No. 6088.

3. *I taught you to swim, and now you'd drown me.* Ibid., No. 2626. 1869 : Spurgeon, *John Ploughman*, ch. xiv. [quoted as " the old saying "].

4. *Who swims on sin, shall sink in sorrow.* 1853 : Trench, *Proverbs*, 21 (1905).

Swine, *subs.* 1. *A swine over fat is cause of his own bane.* 1546 : Heywood, *Proverbs*, Pt. II. ch. vii. 1605 : Camden, *Remains*, 318 (1870). 1666 : Torriano, *Piazza Univ.*, 213, A hog over fat is the cause of its own death. 1732 : Fuller, No. 428, A swine fatted hath eat its own bane. Cf. Sow, *subs.* (2).

2. *Swine, women and bees cannot be turned.* 1678 : Ray, 212. 1732 : Fuller, No. 4299. 1875 : Cheales, *Proverb. Folk-Lore*, 6.

3. *The swine has run through it.* 1879 : W. Henderson, *Folk-Lore of N. Counties*, 34, It is unlucky for swine to cross the path in front of a wedding party. Hence the old adage, " The swine's run through it."

See also Hog ; Pig ; Sheep (18) ; and Sow, *subs.*

Sword. 1. *He that strikes with the sword shall be stricken with the scabbard.* 1546 : Heywood, *Proverbs*, Pt. II. ch. vii. 1585 : Sir E. Dyer, *Nothing*, in *Writings*, 83 (Grosart). 1612 : *Cornucopiæ*, 48 (Grosart), The prouerbe still doth threate, Who strikes with sword, the scabbard shall him beat. 1670 : Ray, 147 [with " beaten " for " stricken "].

2. *Sword in madman's hand.* See Ill putting.

3. *Who draws his sword against his Prince, must throw away the scabbard.* 1659 : Howell, 17. 1670 : Ray, 21. 1732 : Fuller, No. 5698.

Sylvester said, As,—fair and softly. 1813 : Ray, 232. Cf. Soft and fair.

Sympathy without relief Is like mustard without beef. 1914 : R. L. Gales, *Vanished Country Folk*, 204. Cf. Pity.

Table   616   Tailor

T

Table robs more than a thief, The.
1640 : Herbert, *Jac. Prudentum.* 1670 :
Ray, 25. 1732 : Fuller, No. 4782, The
table is a great robber.

Tace is Latin for a candle. A humorous hint to be silent. 1676 : Shadwell,
Virtuoso, I., I took him up with my old
repartee ; Peace, said I, *Tace* is *Latin*
for a candle. 1738 : Swift, *Polite Convers.*, Dial. II. 1751 : Fielding, *Amelia*,
bk. i. ch. x. 1824 : Scott, *Redgauntlet*,
ch. xii., There are some auld stories
that cannot be ripped up again with
entire safety to all concerned. *Tace* is
Latin for a candle. 1881 : *N. & Q.*,
6th ser., iv. 157, " Tace is the Latin for
a cat," as I have heard in the north of
England when a hint for silence was
desirable. Cat, candle, or anything else
would do, for *tace* is, of course, the
important word.

Tag, rag and bobtail. The quotations
show the earlier forms of the phrase.
1553 : Bale, *Vocacyon*, in *Harl. Miscell.*,
vi. 459, All the rable of the shippe, hag,
tag, and rag. 1584 : B. R., *Euterpe*,
122 (Lang), To entertayne tagge and
ragge all that would come. 1603 :
Harsnet, *Decl. of Egreg. Popish Impostures*, 50, For all were there tag,
and ragge, cut and long-tayle. 1639 :
Clarke, 236, Tag and rag, cut and long
tayle every one that can eat an egge.
1645 : *Just Defence John Bastwick*, 16
(O.), That rabble rout tag ragge and
bobtaile. 1655 : A. Brewer, *Love-sick
King*, IV., I think there's some match
at foot-bal towards, the colliers against
the whole country cut, and long tail.
1660 : Pepys, *Diary*, 6 March [as in
1645]. 1694 : Motteux, *Rabelais*, bk.
iv. ch. xxxiii., It will swallow us all,
ships and men, shag, rag, and bobtail,
like a dose of pills. *c.* 1740 : Bramston,
Art of Politics, l. 10 from end, Tag rag
and bobtail. 1762 : Smollett, *Sir L.
Greaves*, ch. xvii. [as in 1740]. 1821 :

Byron, *Blues*, ecl. ii. l. 23, By the rag,
tag, and bobtail, of those they call
" Blues." 1907 : Hackwood, *Old Eng.
Sports*, 276, The usual following of the
Rag-Tag-and-Bobtail class.

Tail, *subs.* 1. *His tail will catch the
chin-cough.* Spoken of one that sits on
the ground. 1678 : Ray, 82.

2. *Make not thy tail broader than thy
wings.* 1659 : Howell, 11 (9). 1670 :
Ray, 147. 1732 : Fuller, No. 3323.

Tailor, *subs.* 1. *A tailor's shreds
are worth the cutting.* 1670 : Ray,
147.

2. *Like the tailor that sewed for nothing,
and found thread himself.* 1732 : Fuller,
No. 3237.

3. *Tailor and needle.* *See* quot.
1917 : Bridge, *Cheshire Proverbs*, 160,
If you come on to me, you come on
your sharps, as tailor said when he
showed his needle.

4. *Tailor-like.* Apparently a proverbial phrase. 1601 : Cornwallis,
Essayes, Pt. II., sig. Dd6 (1610), What
is his gaine but the marke of an ideot ?
what his knowledge, but tailor-like and
light ?

5. *Tailors and writers must mind the
fashion.* 1732 : Fuller, No. 4301.

6. *The tailor cuts three sleeves for
every woman's gown.* 1612 : in *Pepysian Garland*, 32 (Rollins), For it is a
common prouerbe throughout all the
towne, The taylor he must cut three
sleeues, for euery womans gowne.
1632 : in Ibid., 412, A taylor that will
liue in peace, cuts out of one gowne
three sleeues.

7. *The tailor makes the man.* 1625 :
Jonson, *Staple of News*, I. i., And thence,
sir, comes your proverb, The tailor
makes the man. *c.* 1630 : B. & F.,
Bloody Brother, III. ii., For though he
[the tailor] makes the man, The cook
yet makes the dishes. 1853 : Planché,
Extravag., iv. 318 (1879), The "tailor

makes the man," we used to say—The tailor makes the manager, to-day.

8. *The tailor that makes not a knot, loseth a stitch.* 1732 : Fuller, No. 4786.

See also Hundred; Miller (10) ; and Nine tailors.

Tainted sheep. *See* Sheep (10).

Take, verb. 1. *A man must take such as he finds, or such as he brings.* c. 1386 : Chaucer, *C. Tales,* A 4129 (Skeat), I have herd seyd, man sal taa of twa thinges, Slyk as he fyndes, or taa slyk as he bringes. c. 1590 : Greene, *George a Greene,* IV. iv., If this like you not, Take that you finde, or that you bring, for me.

2. *He has taken his gears in* = He is dead. 1917 : Bridge, *Cheshire Proverbs,* 67.

3. *It takes all mack to make every mack.* Ibid., 86, . . . " Mack " = sort or kind.

4. *I was taken by a morsel, says the fish.* 1640 : Herbert, *Jac. Prudentum.*

5. *Take a doe. See* Doe.

6. *Take all and pay the baker.* 1678 : Ray, 91. 1732 : Fuller, No. 4303.

7. *Take all, pay all.* 1600 : Shakespeare, *Merry Wives,* II. ii. 1616 : *Jack Drum's Entert.,* I., Rule all, pay all, take all. 1737 : Ray, 273, Take all and pay all.

8. *Take a thorn. See* Thorn (3).

9. *Take away fuel, take away flame.* 1639 : Clarke, 192. 1670 : Ray, 95. 1732 : Fuller, No. 4305, Take away fuel, and you take away fire.

10. *Take away the cause and the effect must cease.* 1620 : Shelton, *Quixote,* Pt. II. ch. lxvii., The cause being removed, the sin will be saved. 1710 : Ward, *Nuptial Dialogues,* ii. 42, For 'tis a maxim that does seldom miss, Remove the cause and the effect will cease. 1734 : in *Walpole Ballads,* 93 (Oxford, 1916).

11. *Take care of the pence. See* Penny (20).

12. *Take, have, and keep are pleasant words.* 1886 : Hardy, *Casterbridge,* ch. xiv. [quoted as " the mediæval saying "].

13. *Take heed is a fair thing.* 1546 : Heywood, *Proverbs,* Pt. II. ch. viii.

1593 : Harvey, *Works,* ii. 166 (Grosart). 1608 : Armin, *Nest of Ninnies,* 29 (Sh. S.).

14. *Take heed is a good reed* [advice]. [c. 1380 : Chaucer, *Troylus,* bk. ii. l. 343, Avysëment is good before the nede.] 1599 : Porter, *Two Angry Women,* in Hazlitt, *Old Plays,* vii. 337. 1670 : Ray, 102. 1732 : Fuller, No. 6315.

15. *Take him in good turn and knock out his brains.* 1639 : Clarke, 150.

16. *Take not counsel in the combat.* 1642 : D. Rogers, *Matrim. Honour,* 199, As the proverbe saith, take not, etc.

17. *Take time by the forelock. See* Time (29).

18. *Take your wife's first advice. See* Wife (20).

19. *To take a dagger and drown one self.* 1678 : Ray, 238.

20. *To take a leaf out of another's book.* 1886 : Hardy, *Casterbridge,* ch. xvi., You should have taken a leaf out of his book, and have had your sports in a sheltered place like this.

21. *To take as falleth in the sheaf.* 1546 : Heywood, *Proverbs,* Pt. II. ch. iv. 1562 : Heywood, *Epigrams,* No. 217, I will take as falleth in the sheaf. 1659 : Howell, 7, I will take it [as] falth in the sheaf where ever it fall.

22. *To take a thing in snuff.* 1592 : Shakespeare, *L. L. L.,* V. ii., You'll mar the light by taking it in snuff. 1681 : Robertson, *Phraseol. Generalis,* 97, He took it in snuff, viz. in anger. Cf. Snuff.

23. *To take a thorn. See* Thorn (3).

24. *To take a venew under the girdle* = To be got with child. 1598 : Chamberlain, *Letters,* 18 (Camden S.), Some say she hath taken a venew under the girdle and swells upon it.

25. *To take counsel of one's pillow.* 1573 : Harvey, *Letter-Book,* 21 (Camden S.), You counsel me to take counsel of mi pillow. 1611 : Cotgrave, s.v. " Conseil," Night gives advice ; We say, take counsell of your pillow. 1676 : Cotton, Walton's *Angler,* Pt. II. ch. ii., I will presently wait on you to your chamber, where, take counsel of your pillow ; and to-morrow resolve me. 1751 : Fielding, *Amelia,* bk. ix. ch. v.,

" I will consult my pillow upon it," said the doctor. Cf. **Night is the mother.**

26. *To take from the right hand and give to the left.* 1732 : Fuller, No. 5241.

27. *To take one a button-hole* (or *peg,* etc.) *lower. c.* 1550 : Becon, *Catechism, etc.,* 561 (P.S.), This doctrine plucketh them down one staff lower than they were before. 1592 : Nashe, *Works,* ii. 77 (Grosart), The hard lodging on the boards [will] take their flesh downe a button hole lower. 1592 : Shakespeare, *L. L. L.,* V. ii., Master, let me take you a button-hole lower. 1633 : Shirley, *Triumph of Peace,* in *Works,* vi. 28c (Dyce), I'd see the tallest beefeater on you all . . . knocking my wife down, and I'll bring him a button-hole lower. 1654 : Gayton, *Pleasant Notes Don Q.,* 234, Had not Daplusse taken him a button lower. 1670 : Ray, 189, To take one a peg lower. 1764 : Mrs. F. Sheridan, *Dupe,* IV. iv., I must take her down a peg or so. 1829 : Peacock, *Misfor. of Elphin,* ch. xiii., I have just brought the abbot this pleasant intelligence, and, as I knew it would take him down a cup or two . . .

28. *To take one's ease in one's inn.* 1546 : Heywood, *Proverbs,* Pt. I. ch. v., To let the world wag, and take mine ease in mine in. 1597 : Shakespeare, *1 Henry IV.,* III. iii., *Falstaff.* . . . Shall I not take mine ease in mine inn but I shall have my pocket picked ? 1620 : Middleton, *World Tost at Tennis,* in *Works,* vii. 185 (Bullen), These great rich men must take their ease i' their inn. 1821 : Byron, *Letters, etc.,* v. 481 (Prothero), The traveller can " take his ease in his inn."

29. *To take one's hands off =* To decline a bargain. 1917 : Bridge, *Cheshire Proverbs,* 143.

30. *To take one up before he is down.* 1583 : Melbancke, *Philotinus,* sig. L1, Thou louest me well that takest me vp before I fall. 1738 : Swift, *Polite Convers.,* Dial. I., You take me up, before I'm down. 1818 : Scott, *Heart of Midl.,* ch. xviii., " Sir, under your favour," replied David, . . . "ye take me up before I fall down." 1880 : Courtney, *W. Cornwall Words,* I

(E.D.S.), He took me up afore I were down.

31. *To take out of one pocket to put in the other.* 1855 : Bohn, 544.

32. *To take pet.* 1669 : *New Help to Discourse,* 252, He thereupon took pet, and so did die. 1706 : D'Urfey, *Stories Moral and Comical,* 57, But at his naming of the net, Venus had certainly took pet. 1732 : Fuller, No. 2325, He that takes pet at a feast, loses it all.

Takeley Street. *See* quots. 1880 : E. Walford, in *N. & Q.,* 6th ser., ii. 307, " All on one side like Takeley Street " . . . the village of Takeley, between Dunmow and Bishop's Stortford, has all the cottages on the one side of the road, and the squire's park on the other. 1896 : *N. & Q.,* 8th ser., x. 475, A common local saying in Essex is " All on one side, like Takeley Street."

Tale, *subs.* 1. *A tale never loses in the telling.* 1633 : Draxe, 177, A tale in the carrying is made more. 1710 : S. Palmer, *Moral Essays on Proverbs,* 177, A story never loses by carrying. 1869 : Spurgeon, *John Ploughman,* ch. vi.

2. *A tale of a tub.* 1538 : Bale, *Three Laws,* Act II., Ye saye they folowe your lawe, And varyee not a shawe, Whych is a tale of a tubbe. 1546 : Heywood, *Proverbs,* Pt. II. ch. ix., A tale of a tub, your tale no truth auouth. 1576 : R. Peterson, tr. *Galateo,* 73 (1892), All thys long babble . . . were but a tale of a tubbe. 1633 : Jonson, *Tale of a Tub* [title]. 1691 : *Merry Drollery,* 225 (Ebsworth), For I think I have told you a Tale of a Tub. 1704 : Swift, *Tale of a Tub* [title]. 1710 : Centlivre, *Man's Bewitch'd,* I. 1714 : Ozell, *Molière,* iv. 125, All is idle talk, trifles, and tales of a tub. 1855 : Kingsley, *West. Ho!,* ch. vii.

3. *A tale twice told is cabbage twice sold.* 1732 : Fuller, No. 429. Cf. No. 5.

4. *Each tale is ended as it hath favour. c.* 1450 : Burgh (and Lydgate), *Secrees,* 51 (E.E.T.S.) [quoted as " a proverbe "].

5. *It ought to be a good tale that is twice told.* 1732 : Fuller, No. 3041. Cf. No. 3.

6. *One tale good. See* **One tale.**

7. *Tell a tale to a mare. See* quots.

1567 : Pickering, *Horestes*, l. 95 (Brandl, *Quellen*, 496), Tell a mare a tale, and shyell gerd out a fart. 1652 : Tatham, *Scots Figgaries*, III. [as in 1567]. 1670 : Ray, 26 [as in 1567]. 1738 : Swift, *Polite Convers.*, Dial. I., Well, miss ; tell a mare a tale . . . 1869: Hazlitt, 351, Tell a tale to a mare and she'll kick thee.

8. *The tale runs as it pleases the teller.* 1732 : Fuller, No. 4783.

9. *To tell tales out of school.* 1530 : Tyndale, *Pract. of Prelates*, 249 (P.S.), So that what cometh once in may never out, for fear of telling tales out of school. 1546 : Heywood, *Proverbs*, Pt. I. ch. x. 1638 : Ford, *Fancies*, I. ii., Beware of the porter's lodge, for carrying tales out of the school. 1679 : Shadwell, *True Widow*, IV. i., Fie, miss ! fie ! tell tales out of school ? 1753 : Richardson, *Grandison*, iii. 110 (1883), Don't tell tales out of school, Emily. 1805 : Mary Lamb, in *Letters*, i. 315 (Lucas), Write us, my good girl, a long, gossiping letter . . . tell me any silly thing you can recollect . . . we will never tell tales out of school. 1854 : Thackeray, *Newcomes*, ch. xii.

See also **Tell**, *verb* (6), (11), (13), and (17).

Tale-bearer is worse than a thief, A. 1736 : Bailey, *Dict.*, s.v.

Tale-bearers, Put no faith in. 1855 : Bohn, 477.

Talk is but talk. 1620 : *Two Mery Milkmaids*, II. ii., But talke's but talke, therefore I vse it not. 1639 : Chapman and Shirley, *Ball*, V. i., You may hear talk ; but give me the man that has measured 'em ; talk's but talk . . . 1678 : Ray, 177, Prate is but prate, its money buyes land. 1681 : Robertson, *Phraseol. Generalis*, 1203 [as in 1678, but with " talk " for " prate "]. 1737 : Ray, 270 [as in 1681]. Cf. **Prate;** and **Words** (13).

Talk, *verb.* 1. *He that talks much of his happiness, summons grief.* 1640 : Herbert, *Jac. Prudentum.*

2. *He that talks to himself talks to a fool.* 1732 : Fuller, No. 2328.

3. *I am talking of hay, and you of horse-beans.* Ibid., No. 2586.

4. *Many talk like philosophers, and live like fools.* Ibid., No. 3358.

5. *Talk not too much of state affairs.* 1659 : Howell, 18.

6. *Talk of camps, but stay at home.* 1732 : Fuller, No. 4319.

7. *Talk of the Devil. See* **Devil** (36).

8. *To talk a bird's* (or *dog's*) *leg off*—and like phrases. 1868 : *N. & Q.*, 4th ser., ii. 488, In Lancashire a loquacious person, whether man or woman, is said to be able to " talk a horse's leg off." Ibid., 591 [also in Norfolk and Midlands]. 1869: Hazlitt, 353, That fellow would talk a horse to death. S. Devon. In the local vernacular : Thilk veller would tell a horse to death. 1893 : Gower, *Gloss. of Surrey Words*, lii. (E.D.S.), I never see sich a fellow to go on, he would talk his dog's hind leg off any day. 1901: F. E. Taylor, *Lancs Sayings*, 34, He'd talk th' leg off a brass pon [pan].

9. *To talk like an apothecary.* 1639 : Clarke, 133, He prates like a poticary. 1670: Ray, 195. 1708: *Brit. Apollo*, i. Suppl. Paper 10, col. 6, Why is a man said, when he speaks at random, to talk like an apothecary ? 1769 : Smollett, *Adv. of Atom*, 65 (Cooke, 1795), Your grace talks like an apothecary.

Talking comes by nature, Silence by understanding. 1875 : Cheales, *Proverb. Folk-Lore*, 86.

Talking pays no toll. 1640 : Herbert, *Jac. Prudentum.* 1732 : Fuller, No. 4317. 1869 : Spurgeon, *John Ploughman*, ch. vi.

Tall, *adj.* 1. *As tall as a hop-pole.* 1788 : Colman, jr., *Ways and Means*, I. ii., Two fine young women . . . tall as hop-poles.

2. *As tall as a may-pole.* 1678 : Ray, 289. 1754 : Berthelson, *Eng.-Danish Dict.*, s.v. " May," He is grown so high, that a man dares not come near him by the length of a may-pole.

3. *He is a tall man of his hands.* 1485: Malory, *Morte d'Arthur*, bk. iv., ch. xvii., He is a passyng goodman of his handes. 1591 : Florio, *Second Frutes*, 117, Is he valiant, and a talle man of his hands ? 1678 : Ray, 82, A tall

man of's hands, He will not let a beast rest in's pocket.

4. *While the tall maid is stooping, the little one hath swept the house.* 1666 : Torriano, *Piazza Univ.*, 108, Whilst a tall Meg of Westminster is stooping, a short wench sweeps the house. 1869 : Hazlitt, 468.

Tamworth. *See* **Sutton.**

Tanfield fools. *See* quot. 1846–59 : *Denham Tracts*, i. 68 (F.L.S.), Tanfield fools, and Anfield lubberts, Hungry Iceton with its empty cupboards. Tanfield, Anfield and Iceton (properly Iveston), are villages and hamlets near the source of the river Derwent.

Tangled skein of it to wind off, I have a. 1732 : Fuller, No. 2603.

Tantera Bobus, who lived till he died, Like. 1864 : " Cornish Proverbs," in *N. & Q.*, 3rd ser., vi. 5. 1882 : Jago, *Gloss. of Cornish Dialect*, 288, Tantra-bobus, or Tantrum-bobus. Term applied to a noisy, playful child. " Oh ! you tantra-bobus ! " 1886 : Elworthy, *West Som. Word-Book*, 737 (E.D.S.), Oh ! I reckon he lived same's Tantara-bobus—all the days of his life. Cf. **Live** (39).

Tantivy and Tantony pig. *See* **Anthony pig.**

Tapster is undone by chalk, The—i.e. by scoring on credit. *c.* 1630 : in *Roxb. Ballads*, i. 71 (Hindley). 1639 : Mayne, *City Match*, IV. vii., You do offend o' th' score, and sin in chalk.

Tapsters and ostlers are not always the honestest men. 1597 : *Discouerie of the Knights of the Poste*, sig. D4.

Tarberry Hill, near Hastings. 1894 : A. J. C. Hare, *Sussex*, 192, " Who knows what Tarberry would bear, Must plough it with a golden share," is a proverb.

Tarleton—the Shakespearean jester. 1813 : Ray, 71, He answers with monosyllables, as Tarleton did one who out-eat him at an ordinary.

Tarring. *See* **Heighton.**

Tarry-long brings little home. 1732 : Fuller, No. 4320.

Taste, *subs. See* quots. 1633 : Draxe, 29, To him that hath lost his taste, sweet is sowre. 1670 : Ray, 26 [as in 1633]. 1732 : Fuller, No. 5182,

To him that has a bad taste, sweet is bitter.

Taste, *verb. See* quot. 1855 : Bohn, 581, You want to taste the broth as soon as the meat is in.

Taunton. *See* **Nertown.**

Taunton Dean—Where should I be born else? 1662 : Fuller, *Worthies*, iii. 91 (1840). 1790 : Grose, *Prov. Gloss.*, s.v. " Somerset."

Tavern bitch, The. *See* quot. 1608 : Middleton, *Trick to Catch Old One*, IV. v., Faith, the same man still : the tavern bitch has bit him i' th' head [he is drunk].

Tavern haunteth, That. *See* quot. *c.* 1460 : *How the Good Wife*, l. 50, That tauerne hauntethe his thrifte forsakithe.

Tavern token, To swallow a = To be drunk. 1596 : Jonson, *Ev. Man in Humour*, I. iv., Drunk, sir ? . . . Perhaps he swallow'd a tavern token, or some such device. 1604 : *Meet. of Gallants*, 17 (Percy S.), Indeed he had swallowed doune many tauerne-tokens, and was infected much with the plague of drunkenness. 1745 : Franklin, *Drinker's Dict.*, in *Works*, ii. 26 (Bigelow), He's swallowed a tavern token.

Teach, *verb.* 1. *He teacheth ill who teacheth all.* 1659 : Howell, 4. 1732 : Fuller, No. 2035.

2. *Teaching of others teacheth the teacher.* Ibid., No. 4323.

3. *Teach your father to get children.* 1659 : Howell, 9 (7). 1754 : Berthelson, *Eng.-Danish Dict.*, s.v. " Father," To teach one's father to get children.

4. *Teach your grandmother to suck eggs*—and perform other feats. 1542 : Udall, tr. Erasmus' *Apoph.*, 380 (1877), A swine to teache Minerua was a prouerbe . . . for whiche we saie in Englishe, to teache our dame to spinne. 1611 : Cotgrave, s.v. " Apprendre," Wee say to teach his grandame to grope ducks. 1659 : Howell, 9 (7), Go teach your granham to grope a goose. 1665 : R. Howard, *Committee*, IV., Pish, teach your grannam to spin. 1670 : Ray, 178, Teach your grandame to gropen her ducks, to sup sowre milk. 1709 : Cibber, *Rival Fools*, II., Go, fools ! teach

your granums : you are always full of
your advice when there's no occasion
for 't. 1732 : Fuller, No. 4321 [as in
1665]. 1738 : Swift, *Polite Convers.*,
Dial. I., You mend it ! go, teach your
grannam to suck eggs. 1749 : Fielding, *Tom Jones*, bk. xii. ch. xiii., A child
may sometimes teach his grandmother
to suck eggs. 1828 : Carr, *Craven
Dialect*, i. 195, The proverb, " Gang
and teach thy granny to sup sour milk
out o' t' ass riddle," is often applied
to a confident person, who would
attempt to teach another, who has more
knowledge than himself.

Teague — an Irishman. 1. *Like
Teague's cocks, that fought one another,
though all were of the same side.* 1732 :
Fuller, No. 3234.

2. *You run like Teague, before your
errand.* Ibid., No. 5983.

Tears are near their eyes, Their.
1864 : " Cornish Proverbs," in *N. & Q.*,
3rd ser., vi. 494.

Tears of the tankard. 1678 : Ray, 82.
1690 : *New Dict. Canting Crew*, sig. M1,
. . . Drops of the good liquor that fall
beside.

Tears. *See also* **Nothing** (8).

**Tees, Escaped the, and was drowned
in the Tyne.** 1846–59 : *Denham Tracts*,
i. 313 (F.L.S.).

Teeth. *See* **Tooth.**

Tell. 1. *He tells me my way and don't
know it himself.* 1732 : Fuller, No.
2036.

2. *He that can tell. See* quot. 1921 :
Devonsh. Assoc. Trans., liii. 162, The
old proverbial saying : " He that can
tell [talk] avore 'a can go 'Ull bring he's
father ta sorrow an' woe."

3. *He that tells a secret is another's
servant.* 1640 : Herbert, *Jac. Prudentum.* 1736 : Bailey, *Dict.*, s.v. " Tell,"
Tell your secret to your servant, and
you make him your master.

4. *He that tells his wife news, is but
newly married.* 1640 : Herbert, *Jac.
Prudentum.* 1670 : Ray, 49. 1732 :
Fuller, No. 2330.

5. *If you tell every step, you will make
a long journey of it.* Ibid., No. 2793.

6. *I tell you my tale and my tales
man* [author]. 1690 : *New Dict. Cant-*

ing Crew, sig. L8. 1738 : Swift, *Polite
Convers.*, Dial. I.

7. *Tell me it snows.* 1639 : Clarke,
8, Fiddle, faddle, tell me it snowes.
1681 : Robertson, *Phraseol. Generalis*,
1142, Tell me it snows ; Piscem natare
doces. 1732 : Fuller, No. 4327.

8. *Tell me news.* 1603 : Raleigh, in
Criminal Trials, i. 408 (1832), All this
while you tell me news, Mr. Attorney.
1639 : Clarke, 303, Tell me what I
know not. 1670 : Ray, 187. 1738 :
Swift, *Polite Convers.*, Dial. I., I know
that already ; tell me news.

9. *Tell me with whom thou goest, And
I'll tell thee what thou doest.* 1586 :
Pettie, tr. Guazzo's *Civil Convers.*,
fo. 22, This common prouerbe sheweth,
Tell me with whom thou doest goe, and
I shall know what thou doest. 1633 :
Draxe, 25. 1667 : L'Estrange, Quevedo's
Visions, 151 (1904), This minded me of
the old saying, " Tell me thy company,
and I'll tell thee thy manners." 1710 :
S. Palmer, *Moral Essays on Proverbs*, 36.
1789 : G. Parker, *Life's Painter*, 137,
"Tell me your company, and I will
describe your manners," is an old
saying.

10. *Tell money after your own father.*
1633 : Draxe, 208, A man must tell
golde after his owne father. 1639 :
Clarke, 90. 1656 : F. Osborne, *Advice to
Son*, 26 (Parry) [" Count " for " Tell "].
1709 : Cibber, *Rival Fools*, V., Always
tell money after your father, sir. 1869 :
Spurgeon, *John Ploughman*, ch. viii.,
Count money after your own kin.

11. *Tell-tale-tit, your tongue shall be
slit, And all the dogs in the town shall
have a little bit.* 1843 : Halliwell, *Nurs.
Rhymes*, 164. 1886 : Elworthy, *West
Som. Word-Book*, 742 (E.D.S.). 1889 :
Peacock, *Manley, etc., Gloss.*, 555
(E.D.S.). 1901 : F. E. Taylor, *Lancs
Sayings*, 43.

12. *Tell truth and shame the devil.
See* **Truth** (3).

13. *Tell you a tale and find you ears.*
1546 : Heywood, *Proverbs*, Pt. II. ch.
ix., He must both tell, etc. *c.* 1594 :
Bacon, *Promus*, No. 673, A man must
tell you tales and find your [*sic*] ears.
1670 : Ray, 195. 1738 : Swift, *Polite*

Convers., Dial. I., What, miss! must I tell you a story, and find you ears?

14. *Tell your cards*. *See* **Cards** (3).

15. *To be able to tell ten*. 1613: B. & F., *Coxcomb*, II. i., He cannot be So innocent a coxcomb; he can tell ten, sure!

16. *Who tells a lie to save his credit, wipes his nose on his sleeve to save his napkin*. 1659: Howell, 1.

17. *You will tell another tale when you are tried*. 1678: Ray, 348.

See also **One Tale**; and **Tale**.

Temperance is the best physic. 1855: Bohn, 495.

Temple-brough. *See* **Winkabank.**

Ten. *See* **Hours**; and **Tell**, *verb* (15).

Tenbury. 1882: Mrs. Chamberlain, *W. Worcs. Words*, 39 (E.D.S.), Sell wheat and buy rye, Say the bells of Tenbury.

Ten commandments = the ten finger-nails. *c.* 1560: in Wright, *Songs, etc.*, *Philip and Mary*, 202 (Roxb. Cl.), Or els her ten commandements She fastens on hys face. 1594: *First Part Contention*, 16 (Sh. S.), Could I come neare your daintie visage with my nayles, Ide set my ten commandments in your face. 1607: Dekker and Webster, *Westw. Hoe*, V. iii., Your harpy that set his ten commandments upon my back. 1814: Scott, *Waverley*, ch. xxx. 1830: Marryat, *King's Own*, ch. xl., Don't put your tongue into your cheek at me . . . or I'll write the ten commandments on your face.

Tender as a chicken. 1678: Ray, 289. 1720: Gay, *Poems*, ii. 280 (Underhill), Till you grow tender as a chick.

Tender as a parson's leman. 1546: Heywood, *Proverbs*, Pt. I. ch. x. 1592: Greene, in *Harl. Miscell.*, viii. 375 (1746), That had a fayre wench to her daughter, as young and tender as a morrow masse priests lemman. 1611: Cotgrave, s.v. "Mol." 1670: Ray, 208.

Tender as Parnell, that broke her finger in a posset-curd. 1678: Ray, 289. 1690: *New Dict. Canting Crew*, sig. M1, Tender-parnel, a very nicely educated creature, apt to catch cold upon the least blast of wind. 1785: Grose, *Class. Dict. Vulgar Tongue*, s.v. "Tender P." ["drink" for "curd"].

1847: Halliwell, *Dict.*, s.v. "Tender" [as in 1785]. 1917: Bridge, *Cheshire Proverbs*, 22.

Ten good turns. I do not understand this dark saying. 1578: Whetstone, *Promos and Cass.*, sig. D2, The prouerbe saies, that tenne good turnes lye dead, And one yll deede, tenne tymes beyonde pretence, By enuious tongues, report abrode doth spread.

Ten pretty. *See* **Twenty** (4).

Tenterden steeple is the cause of Goodwin Sands. 1528: More, *Dialogue*, in *Works*, p. 278, col. 1 (1557) [story of Tenterden steeple being the cause of the choking up by sands of Sandwich harbour]. 1550: Latimer, *Sermons*, 251 (P.S.) [Latimer tells the absurd story]. 1568: in *Loseley MSS.*, 211 (Kempe), Of many people it hath ben said, That Tenterden steeple Sandwich haven hath decayed. 1644: Taylor (Water-Poet), *Crop-Eare*, C. 18, in *Works*, 2nd coll. (Spens. S.), Here is an excellent proofe. Weaker then that of Tenterden Steeple being the cause of Goodwine Sands. 1662: Fuller, *Worthies*, ii. 125 (1840). 1790: Grose, *Prov. Gloss.*, s.v. "Kent."

Testons. *See* **Oxford.**

Tewkesbury mustard. *See* quots. 1598: Shakespeare, *2 Henry IV.*, II. iv., His wit's as thick as Tewkesbury mustard. 1634: *Strange Metam. of Man.*, sig. D10, If he [mustard] be of the right stamp, and a true Tewxbury man. 1662: Fuller, *Worthies*, i. 552 (1840), He looks as if he had lived on Tewkesbury mustard. Before 1704: T. Brown, *Works*, iv. 236 (1760), When Tewksbury mustard shall wander abroad. 1790: Grose, *Prov. Gloss.*, s.v. "Gloucestershire" [as in 1598 and 1662]. 1851: *Gloucestershire Gloss.*, 14 [as in 1662].

Teynham, Kent. *See* **Bapchild**; and **Muston.**

Thakeham, the last place God made. 1884: "Sussex Proverbs," in *N. & Q.*, 6th ser., ix. 402.

Thames on fire, To set the. There is no good ground for connecting "Thames" in this phrase with "temse," a provincial name for a sieve. *c.* 1770:

Foote, *Trip to Calais*, III. iii., Matt Minnikin . . . won't set fire to the Thames, though he lives near the Bridge. 1788: Wolcot, *Works*, i. 509 (1795), Whose modest wisdom, therefore, never aims To find the longitude, or burn the Thames. 1818: J. Austen, *Persuasion*, ch. v., The Baronet will never set the Thames on fire, but there seems no harm in him. 1863: Kingsley, *Water Babies*, ch. viii. 1915: Pinero, *Big Drum*, III.

Thames. *See also* Cast (8).

Thank God that your father was born before you, You may. 1855: Bohn, 579.

Thank you for the next, for this I am sure of, I'll. 1678: Ray, 273.

Thatch, *subs.* *See* Thick as thack; and Wet (5).

Thatch, *verb.* 1. *If a house had to be thatched with muck, there would be more teachers than reachers.* 1762: Smollett, *Sir L. Greaves*, ch. xv., Thatch your house with t—, and you'll have more teachers than reachers. 1917: Bridge, *Cheshire Proverbs*, 76.

2. *When I have thatched his house, he would throw me down.* 1639: Clarke, 170. 1670: Ray, 148. 1732: Fuller, No. 5559, When I had thatch'd his house, he would have hurl'd me from the roof.

3. *Would you thatch your house with pancakes?* Ibid., No. 5829. Cf. Groby pool.

That may happen to many, Which doth happen to any. *c.* 1590: G. Harvey, *Marginalia*, 101 (1913).

That's for that. 1738: Swift, *Polite Convers.*, Dial. I., So much for that and butter for fish. 1880: Spurgeon, *Ploughman's Pictures*, 34, That's for that, as salt is for herrings . . . and Nan for Nicholas.

Th' berrin's. *See* Burying.

There or thereabouts,' as Parson Smith says. 1678: Ray, 343, . . . Proverbial about Dunmow in Essex.

Thetch. *See* Vetch.

They say is half a lie. 1666: Torriano, *Piazza Univ.*, 30, To have heard say is half a lye. 1710: S. Palmer, *Moral Essays on Proverbs*, 261. 1869:

Spurgeon, *John Ploughman*, ch. vi., Hearsay is half lies.

Thick and thin, Through. [Per omne fas ac nefas.—Livy, vi. 14.] *c.* 1386: Chaucer, *Reeve's Tale*, l. 146, And whan the hors was loos, he ginneth gon Toward the fen, ther wilde mares renne, Forth with wehee, thurgh thikke and thurgh thenne. *c.* 1490: *Partonope*, 15 (E.E.T.S.), Alle the day they spare noghte Hym to hvnte thorowe thyke and thynne. 1587: Turbervile, *Trag. Tales, etc.*, 30 (1837), Retchelesse she ran through thick and thin. 1621: B. & F., *Pilgrim*, III. ii., He would run through thick and thin to reach me. 1758–67: Sterne, *Trist. Shandy*, vol. ii. ch. ix., Splashing and plunging like a devil thro' thick and thin. 1857: Borrow, *Rom. Rye*, ch. xxv. 1895: Pinero, *Benefit of Doubt*, II., He would stand by me through thick and thin.

Thick and threefold. 1552: Huloet, *Abced.*, sig. Ii1, Thicke and thre folde. 1577: Kendall, *Flow. of Epigrams*, 103 (Spens. S.), Thicke and threefold frends will flocke. 1650: Fuller, *Pisgah Sight*, bk. ii. ch. ix., Disaster . . . which afterwards fell thick and threefold upon it.

Thick as hail, As. 1205: Layamon, *Brut*, l. 12578, Arwen fluyen ouer wal: al abuten ouer al. swa picke wes heore uæræ: swulc hit hayel wæren (Arrows flew over the wall all about over all: so thick was their flight, as if it were hail). 1566: Painter, *Pal. of Pleasure*, i. 338 (Jacobs), The nomber of shotte, which . . . were bestowed so thicke as hayle, vpon euery part of the fort. 1659: *Crown Garland*, 69 (Percy S.), They discharg'd their shafts So thick as hail from sky. 1720: Gay, *Damon and Cupid*, Men fall as thick as hail. 1819: Scott, *Ivanhoe*, ch. xxix., This heavy discharge, which continued as thick and sharp as hail. 1907: Hackwood, *Old Eng. Sports*, 111, They fell thick and sharp as hail.

Thick as hops, As. 1599: Porter, *Two Angry Women*, sc. xi., Looke, the water drops from you as fast as hops. 1631: Mabbe, *Celestina*, 171 (T.T.), Your presents from all parts . . . came upon me as thicke as hops. 1707:

Dunton, *Athenian Sport*, 19, Fly all
about as thick as hops. 1733 : Swift,
On Poetry, l. 400, The rest pursue as
thick as hops.

Thick as inkle-weavers, As. "Thick"
= close, intimate. 1690 : *New Dict.
Canting Crew*, sig. C3, As great as two
inkle-makers. 1703 : Ward, *Writings*,
ii. 357 [as in 1690]. 1738 : Swift,
Polite Convers., Dial. I., Why, she and
you were as great as two inkle-weavers.
1788 : Cowper, *Letter to Lady Hesketh*,
6 May, When people are intimate, we
say they are as great as two inkle-
weavers. 1822 : Scott, *Nigel*, ch. xxiii.,
We were as loving as inkle-weavers.
1865 : *N. & Q.*, 3rd ser., viii. 130, " As
thick as inkle-weavers."—This saying
is used in some parts of Cheshire and
Lancashire. 1908 : *N. & Q.*, 10th ser.,
x. 186, In my early days at Launceston
. . . and that is now fully seventy-five
years ago [when woollen goods were
made at L.], the proverb " As thick as
inkle-makers " was commonly applied
to great cronies, because inkle-makers
had to work very closely together.

Thick as porridge, etc., As. *c.* 1480 :
Early Miscellanies, 87 (Warton Cl.,
1855), Thyk as pappe. 1828 : Carr,
Craven Dialect, ii. 51, " As thick as
porridge," a proverbial simile frequently applied to beer. 1877 : E.
Leigh, *Cheshire Gloss.*, 200, As thick as
stirrow [hasty pudding]. 1917 : Bridge,
Cheshire Proverbs, 24 [as in 1877].

Thick as thack [thatch], **As.** 1828 :
Carr, *Craven Dialect*, ii. 198. 1889 :
Peacock, *Manley, etc., Gloss.*, 558
(E.D.S.).

Thick as thieves, As. Ibid., 558.
1913 : L. P. Jacks, *All Men are Ghosts*,
213, But I never would have nothing
to do with gypsies ; though his Lordship was as thick as thieves with
'em.

Thick as three in a bed, As. 1820 :
Scott, *Monastery*, Introd. Ep., You twa
will be as thick as three in a bed an
ance ye forgather. 1828 : Carr, *Craven
Dialect*, ii. 201, As thrang as three in
a bed. 1889 : Peacock, *Manley, etc.,
Gloss.*, 558 (E.D.S.). Cf. **Thrunk.**

**Thickness of a sixpence between good
and evil, There is not the.** 1732 : Fuller,
No. 4933.

Thief and Thieves. 1. *All are not
thieves that dogs bark at.* 1633 : Draxe,
48. 1670 : Ray, 56. 1694 : D'Urfey,
Quixote, Pt. II. Act IV. sc. ii. 1865 :
"Lancs Proverbs," in *N. & Q.*, 3rd ser.,
viii. 494. 1901 : F. E. Taylor, *Lancs
Sayings*, 10, They're not o thieves 'at
dogs barken at.

2. *A thief knows a thief, as a wolf
knows a wolf.* 1633 : Draxe, 108, One
thiefe knoweth another. 1732 : Fuller,
No. 430.

3. *He that trusts a thief is a fool.*
c. 1534 : Berners, *Huon*, 706 (E.E.T.S.),
It is sayd in a comen prouerbe that a
man is taken for a foole that putteth
his trust in a thefe.

4. *Of all crafts.* See quot. *c.* 1320 :
in *Reliq. Antiquæ*, i. 115 (1841), " Of
alle mester men mest me hongeth
theves " ; Quoth Hendyng.   1869 :
Hazlitt, 300, " Of all crafts, the thieving
craft is the worst for hanging," quoth
Hendyng.

5. *Set a thief to catch a thief.* [c. 1386 :
Chaucer, *Physic. Tale*, l. 83, A theef of
venisoun, that hath forlaft His likerous-
nesse, and al his olde craft, Can kepe a
forest best of any man (= An old
poacher makes a good gamekeeper).]
1665 : R. Howard, *Committee*, I., According to the old saying, Set a thief
to catch a thief. 1702 : Brown, *Works*,
ii. 244 (1760), Always set a knave to
catch a knave. 1725 : Bailey, tr.
Erasmus' *Colloq.*, 457. 1878 : Jefferies,
Gamekeeper at Home, ch. ix., There is a
saying that an old poacher makes the
best gamekeeper, on the principle of
setting a thief to catch a thief. 1895 :
Pinero, *Mrs. Ebbsmith*, II.

6. *The thief is sorry he is to be hanged,
but not that he is a thief.* 1732 : Fuller,
No. 4788.

7. *Thieves and rogues have the best
luck, if they do but scape hanging.* 1670 :
Ray, 118.

8. *Thieves are never rogues among
themselves. See* **Honour.**

9. *Thieves' handsell ever unlucky.*
1687 : Aubrey, *Gentilisme, etc.*, 120
(F.L.S.).

10. *When it thunders the thief becomes honest.* 1640 : Herbert, *Jac. Prudentum.* 1670 : Ray, 26. 1732 : Fuller, No. 5691, Whilst it thunders, the thief turns honest.

11. *When thieves fall out honest men come by their own.* 1546 : Heywood, *Proverbs*, Pt. II. ch. ix., . . . true men come to their goode. 1600 : Day, *Blind Beggar*, IV. i., When false theeves fall out true men come to their own. 1671 : *Westm. Drollery*, 51 (Ebsworth), True men might have their own, now knaves fall out. 1710 : S. Palmer, *Moral Essays on Proverbs*, 327 [" knaves " for " thieves "]. 1850 : Dickens, *Chuzzlewit*, ch. xlix., last par., Thanks to this quarrel, which confirms the old saying that when rogues fall out, honest people get what they want.

See also **Ask** (3) ; **Call** (1) ; **Careless** ; **Hundred tailors** ; **Miller** (8) and (10) ; **One thief** ; **Rope** (2) ; **Thick as thieves** ; **Too many stairs** ; **True** (12) ; **Two daughters** ; and **War** (6).

Thin as a lath, As. 1744 : *Foundl. Hosp. for Wit*, No. ii. p. 26 (1749), Our hope grows as thin as a lath. 1799 : Dr. Burney, in D'Arblay, *Diary*, iv. 100 (1876), You used to be as thin as Dr. Lind . . . a mere lath. 1828 : Carr, *Craven Dialect*, i. 279. 1862 : *Dialect of Leeds*, 406, As lean as a lat (lath). 1901 : F. E. Taylor, *Lancs Sayings*, 4, As thin as a lat.

Thin as a rasher of wind, As. Oxfordsh. 1923 : *Folk-Lore*, xxxiv. 329.

Thin. *See also* **Lean**.

Thin meadow is soon mowed, A. 1659 : Howell, 3. 1670 : Ray, 26.

Thing and Things. 1. *A thing there was, and done it was, and wise was he that did it, Let no man know who knows it not, nor do so no more that did it.* 1659 : Howell, 3, . . . Of one who mistook his neighbour's wife for his own.

2. *If things were to be done twice, all would be wise.* 1640 : Herbert, *Jac. Prudentum.* 1670 : Ray, 27. 1754 : Berthelson, *Eng. - Danish Dict.*, s.v. " Twice." 1875 : Cheales, *Proverb. Folk-Lore*, 115.

3. *There's a thing in it. See* **Dishclout**.

4. *There's many a thing as belongs to everything.* 1917 : Bridge, *Cheshire Proverbs*, 117.

5. *Things done cannot be undone.* c. 1460 : *Good Wyfe wold a Pylgremage*, l. 119 (E.E.T.S.), When dede is doun, hit ys to lat. 1539 : Taverner, *Proverbs*, fo. 35, The thynge that is done can not be vndone. 1546 : Heywood, *Proverbs*, Pt. I. ch. x. c. 1594 : Bacon, *Promus*, No. 951. 1649 : in Halliwell, *Books of Characters*, 46 (1857), That which is done, cannot be undone. 1718 : W. Taverner, *Artful Wife*, III., Your ladiship knows what's done can't be undone. Cf. **Once done**.

6. *Things present are judged by things past.* 1578 : Florio, *First Fruites*, fo. 30. 1629 : *Book of Meery Riddles*, Prov. 36.

7. *Things well fitted abide.* 1640 : Herbert, *Jac. Prudentum.*

8. *When things come to the worst. See* **Worst** (9).

Think, verb. 1. *He that thinks amiss concludes worse.* 1651 : Herbert, *Jac. Prudentum*, 2nd ed.

2. *He that thinks too much of his virtues, bids others think of his vices.* 1869 : Hazlitt, 188.

3. *He thinks himself as great as my Lord Berkeley.* Glos. 1639 : in *Berkeley MSS.*, iii. 26 (1885).

4. *He thinks not well that thinks not again.* 1611 : Cotgrave, s.v. " Penser," He thinks not well that thinks of all at once ; or thinks not more then once. 1640 : Herbert, *Jac. Prudentum*. 1736 : Bailey, *Dict.*, s.v. " Think," He thinks ill that thinks not twice.

5. *One may think that dares not speak.* 1633 : Draxe, 21. 1670 : Ray, 148. 1732 : Fuller, No. 3783.

6. *They that think no ill are soonest beguiled.* 1546 : Heywood, *Proverbs*, Pt. II. ch. v.

7. *They that think they know everything, know nothing.* 1918 : *Devonsh. Assoc. Trans.*, l. 185, They wat thinks they knows everything, knows nort.

8. *Think and thank God.* 1568 : in *Loseley MSS.*, 207 (Kempe).

9. *Thinking is very far from knowing.* 1855 : Bohn, 528.

10. *Think nothing mean that brings in an honest penny.* 1763: Murphy, *Citizen*, I. ii.

11. *Think of a cuckold.* See **Cuckold** (9).

12. *Think of ease, but work on.* 1640: Herbert, *Jac. Prudentum.* 1670: Ray, 8.

13. *Think on the end before you begin.* Before 1300: *Cursor Mundi*, l. 4379, For qua [who] be-gynne wil any þing euer-mare þink on the endinge. *c.* 1400: *Beryn*, 55 (E.E.T.S.), Who take hede of the begynnyng, what fal shal of the ende, He leyith a bussh to-fore the gap, ther fortune wold in ryde. *c.* 1470: G. Ashby, *Poems*, 39 (E.E.T.S.), In al your maters, er ye bygynne, Thenke what ende wol be the conclusion. 1556: Heywood, *Spider and Flie*, cap. 59, p. 254 (Farmer), This sage saying, the wise have said and say,—Have an eye to the end, ere thou aught begin. 1692: L'Estrange, *Æsop*, 81 (3rd ed.), It is wisdom to consider the end of things before we embarque, and to forecast consequences. 1704: Swift, *Tale of a Tub*, § vii., Thus human life is best understood, by the wise man's rule, of regarding the end.

14. *Think to-day and speak to-morrow.* 1855: Bohn, 528.

15. *Think well of all men.* 1659: Howell, 10.

16. *To think one's farthing, halfpenny, penny, good silver.* See **Farthing**; **Halfpenny**; and **Penny** (26).

Third heir. See **Ill-gotten goods.**

Third time is never like the rest, The. 1875: Cheales, *Proverb. Folk-Lore*, 133.

Third time pays for all, The. 1575: Higgins, *Mirr. for Magis.*, Pt. I.: "Q. Elstride," st. 23, Which I haue prou'd, therefore the sequel vewe, The third payes home, this prouerbe is so true. 1599: *Warning for Faire Women*, II. 1855: Gaskell, *North and South*, ch. xvii., " This is th' third strike I've seen," said she. . . . "Well, third time pays for all." 1922: *Punch*, 20 Dec., p. 594, col. 3, Mrs. Ellison has already been twice married. The third time pays for all, so they say.

Thirty days hath September. See

quots. 1572: Grafton, *Chron.*, sig. Ff2 v°, Thirty dayes hath Nouember, Aprill, Iune and September. February hath xxviij alone, and all the rest have xxxi. 1577: Holinshed, *Chron.*, 119 [as in 1572, with addition: " But in the leape you must adde one "]. 1601: *Ret. from Parnassus*, III. i. 37 (Arber), *S. Rad.* How many dayes hath September? *Im.* Aprill, Iune and Nouember, February hath 28 alone and all the rest hath 30 and one. 1615: A. Hopton, *Concordancy of Yeares*, 60, Thirtie dayes hath September, Aprill, Iune, and November: The rest haue thirtie and one, Saue February alone Which moneth hath but eight and twenty meere, Saue when it's bissextile, or leap-yeare. 1664: *Poor Robin Alman.*, Thirty days hath September, April, June, and November, All the rest thirty and one, as I plainly remember; Onely February hath but twenty and eight for its store, Except when tis leap-year, then it hath one more. *c.* 1703: *Young Man's Companion*, quoted in Denham, *Proverbs*, 19 (Percy S.), Thirty days hath September, April, June, and November; February eight-and-twenty all alone, And all the rest have thirty-and-one; Unless that leap-year doth combine, And give to February twenty-nine.

This is that must neades be, Quoth the good man, whenn he made his wyfe Pine the baskit. 1579: *Marr. of Wit and Wisdom*, sc. iii. p. 27 (Sh. S.).

Thistle and Thistles. 1. *A thistle is a fat salad for an ass's mouth.* 1732: Fuller, No. 435.

2. *Cut thistles.* See quots. 1882: Mrs. Chamberlain, *W. Worcs. Words*, 38 (E.D.S.), Cut thistles in May They grow in a day. Cut them in June That is too soon. Cut them in July, Then they will die. 1883: Burne, *Shropsh. Folk-Lore*, 579, Cut 'em in June, They'll come again soon. Cut 'em in July, They *may* die. Cut 'em in August, Die they *must.* 1893: Inwards, *Weather Lore*, 156 [as in 1883].

See also **St. John.**

Thither as I would go I can go late, Thither as I would not go I know not the gate. 1678: Ray, 296.

Thorn and **Thorns.** 1. *He that goes barefoot must not plant thorns.* 1611 : Cotgrave, s.v. "Pied." 1640 : Herbert, *Jac. Prudentum.* 1670 : Ray, 2, Barefooted men need not tread on thorns. 1732 : Fuller, No. 840, Barefoot must not go among thorns. Ibid., No. 2289, He that scattereth thorns must not go barefoot. 1874 : Waugh, in *Manchester Critic*, 14 March, Barfoot folk shouldn't walk upo' prickles. 1901 : F. E. Taylor, *Lancs Sayings*, 7 [as in 1874].

2. *He that handles thorns shall prick his fingers.* 1616 : Breton, *Works*, ii. e 6 (Grosart). 1694 : D'Urfey, *Quixote*, Pt. I. Act III. sc. ii. 1732 : Fuller, No. 2128, He that handles thorns shall smart for it.

3. *I'll not pull the thorn out of your foot and put it into my own.* 1659 : Howell, *Proverbs : Brit.-Eng.*, 24, I'le never thorn draw from others foot, and having pulld it in mine own put. 1678 : Ray, 273. 1753 : Richardson, *Grandison*, ii. 126 (1883), I should only have taken a thorn out of the foot of another, and put it into my own.

4. *Most men have a thorn at their door.* 1639 : Clarke, 165, Where ever a man dwell he shall be sure to have a thornebush neare his doore. 1670 : Ray, 149 [as in 1639]. 1732 : Fuller, No. 3469. c. 1800 : J. Trusler, *Proverbs in Verse*, 94, Where'er a man dwells, there's a thorn at his door. 1869 : Spurgeon, *John Ploughman*, ch. i., Wherever a man lives he is sure to have one thornbush near his door, and it is a mercy if there are not two.

5. *The thorn comes forth with the point forwards.* 1640 : Herbert, *Jac. Prudentum.* 1670 : Ray, 26.

6. *Thorns make the greatest crackling.* 1732 : Fuller, No. 5031.

7. *Thorns whiten yet do nothing.* 1640 : Herbert, *Jac. Prudentum.*

8. *To sit or stand upon thorns* = To be impatient. 1528 : More, in *Works*, p. 234, col. 1 (1557), I long by my trouth, quod he, and euen syt on thornes tyll I see that constitucion. 1567 : Golding, *Ovid*, bk. iv. l. 385, She thought she stoode on thornes untill she went to him. 1633 : Massinger, *New Way*, III. iii., She . . . sitts on thornes till she be private with him. 1636 : T. Heywood, *Challenge for Beauty*, III., I stand on thornes till I be in action. 1764 : Mrs. F. Sheridan, *Dupe*, I. ii., The captain will be on thorns till he sees me. 1823 : Scott, *Q. Durward*, ch. vii., Lord Crawford . . . sat as it were on thorns at the royal board. 1886 : Elworthy, *W. Som. Word-Book*, 751 (E.D.S.), She has been all upon thorns ever since. 1926 : Phillpotts, *Peacock House*, 222, I was on thorns till us met again.

See also **Candlemas**, B; and **Oak** (3).

Thought, *subs.* 1. *The thought hath good legs, and the quill a good tongue.* 1640 : Herbert, *Jac. Prudentum.* 1670 : Ray, 26. 1732 : Fuller, No. 4790 [" wings " for " legs "].

2. *Thought is free.* c. 1390 : Gower, *Conf. Amantis*, bk. v. l. 4485, I have herd seid that thoght is fre. c. 1490 : *Partonope*, 440 (E.E.T.S.), Therfore this proverbe is seide full truly : Thought to a man is euer fire. Before 1529 : Skelton, *Philip Sparrow*, l. 1201, Thought is franke and fre. 1605 : Camden, *Remains*, 332 (1870), Thoughts are free from toll. 1638 : Randolph, *Muses' Looking-Glass*, III. iv., And yet some think (But thought is free) . . . 1860 : Reade, *Cl. and Hearth*, ch. lii., " I say not that," . . . " You do but think it." " Thought is free."

3. *Your thoughts close and your countenance loose.* 1651 : Herbert, *Jac. Prudentum*, 2nd ed.

Thousand pounds and a bottle of hay, is all one at Doomsday, A. 1659 : Howell, 4. 1670 : Ray, 26. 1732 : Fuller, No. 6398.

Thrash in another man's barn, To. c. 1400 : *Ragm. Roll*, l. 53, in Hazlitt, *Early Pop. Poetry*, i. 72, And whoo so lyst may thressyn in your berne.

Thread, *subs.* 1. *A thread too fine spun will easily break.* 1732 : Fuller, No. 438.

2. *The thread breaks where it is weakest.* 1640 : Herbert, *Jac. Prudentum.* 1670 : Ray, 28. 1732 : Fuller, No. 5647.

3. *Thread is spun.* 1681 : in *Roxb. Ballads*, v. 45, Give them what they

deserve, their thread is spun. 1819 : Scott, *Ivanhoe*, ch. xxiv., Fare-thee-well, I say. My thread is spun out—thy task is yet to begin.

Thread-bare coat is armour-proof against highwaymen, A. 1732 : Fuller, No. 437.

Threatened folks live long. *c.* 1555 : in Collmann, *Ballads, etc.*, 69 (Roxb. Cl.), It is a true prouerbe : the threatned man lyues long. 1599 : Porter, *Two Angry Women*, in Hazlitt, *Old Plays*, vii. 357. 1630 : Taylor (Water-Poet), *Works*, 2nd pagin., 152. 1734 : Fielding, *Don Quix. in England*, II. vi. 1819 : Scott, *Leg. of Montrose*, ch. x. 1870 : Dickens, *Drood*, ch. xiv., " The proverb says that threatened men live long," he tells her lightly.

Threatens many that is injurious to one, He. *c.* 1590 : G. Harvey, *Marginalia*, 101 (1913), He threatenith many, That hurtith any. 1732 : Fuller, No. 2372.

Threats without power are like powder without ball. 1736 : Bailey, *Dict.*, s.v.

Three are too many to keep a secret, and too few to be merry. 1732 : Fuller, No. 5037.

Three bites. *See* Two bites.

Three days. *See* Fish, *subs.* (1).

Three dear years will raise a baker's daughter to a portion. 1678 : Ray, 86.

Three flails and cuckoo. 1917 : Bridge, *Cheshire Proverbs*, 123, A farmer who at the return of the cuckoo can keep three flails at work cannot . . . be otherwise than prosperous.

Three great evils come out of the North, a cold wind, a cunning knave, and shrinking cloth. 1614 : Jonson, *Bart. Fair*, IV. iii., Do my northern cloth zhrink i' the wetting, ha ? 1659 : Howell, 1, Three ills come from the North, a cold wind, a shrinking cloth, and a dissembling man. 1670 : Ray, 19 [as in 1659]. 1683 : Meriton, *Yorkshire Ale*, 83–7 (1697). 1846–59 : *Denham Tracts*, ii. 75 (F.L.S.). Cf. **Cold weather.**

Three-half-pence and twopence = a canter. 1886 : Elworthy, *West Som. Word-Book*, 212 (E.D.S.), Dree-half-pence and two - pence . . . a slow

ambling canter. 1896 : Graham, *Red Scaur*, 35 (W.), They can hear the . . . " three-ha'-pence for tuppence " of a cantering horse.

Three helping one another bear the burden of six. 1640 : Herbert, *Jac. Prudentum.*

Three hungry meals. *See* Two hungry meals.

Three may keep counsel if two be away. 1546 : Heywood, *Proverbs*, Pt. II. ch. v. 1692 : L'Estrange, *Æsop*, 399 (3rd ed.) [" when " for " if "]. *c.* 1736 : Franklin, in *Works*, i. 455 (Bigelow), Thrée may keep a secret, if two of them are dead.

Three merry men. The burden of an old ballad. 1595 : Peele, *Old Wives Tale*, sc. i., Let us rehearse the old proverb : " Three merry men, and three merry men, And three merry men be we ; I in the wood, and thou on the ground, And Jack sleeps in the tree." 1613 : B. & F., *Knight of Burning Pestle*, II. viii., *Mer.* [*sings*] I am three merry men, and three merry men ! *c.* 1630 : B. & F., *Bloody Brother*, III. ii., *Chorus.* Three merry boys, and three merry boys, And three merry boys are we.

Threepence, If you make not much of, you'll never be worth a groat. 1678 : Ray, 210. 1732 : Fuller, No. 2771.

Threepenny planet, To be born under a. *See* quots. 1607 : Dekker, *Knight's Conjuring*, 32 (Percy S.), All such rich mens darlings are either christened by some left-handed priest, or els born vnder a threepenny planet. 1692 : L'Estrange, *Æsop*, 416 (3rd ed.), I'll . . . make good the old saying to you ; *That he that's born under a three-penny planet, shall never be worth a groat.* 1694 : Dryden, *Love Triumphant*, I. i., And yet his good fortune, and my rascally, threepenny planet, make me suspicious without reason. 1738 : Swift, *Polite Convers.*, Dial. I., Egad, I was born under a threepenny planet, never to be worth a groat. 1883 : Burne, *Shropsh. Folk-Lore*, 589 [as in 1738]. 1894 : Northall, *Folk Phrases*, 15 (E.D.S.), He was born under a three-penny planet, i.e. is avaricious, a curmudgeon. 1901 : F. E. Taylor,

Lancs Sayings, 7 [as in 1692, very slightly varied].

Three removes are as bad as a fire. 1736 : Franklin, *Way to Wealth,* in *Works,* i. 445 (Bigelow). 1790 : Grose, *Prov. Gloss.,* s.v. " Flit," Two flittings are as bad as one fire. 1881 : Evans, *Leics. Words,* 237 (E.D.S.), "Thray shifts are as bad as a foire," is the Leicestershire form of the common proverb. 1925 : *Punch,* 11 Nov., p. 505, col. 3.

Three sisters, The. 1662 : Fuller, *Worthies,* iii. 548 (1840), " The three sisters," being a common by-word to express the three rivers of Wye, Severn, Rhiddiall, arising all three in this county [Montgomery].

Three skips of a louse = no value. 1633 : Jonson, *Tale of a Tub,* II. i., I care not I, sir, not three skips of a louse. Before 1674 : in *Roxb. Ballads,* viii. 426 (B.S.), And temper it with three leaps of a lowse. 1700 : Swift, in *Works,* xiv. 57 (Scott), 'Tis not that I value the money three skips of a louse. 1769 : Murphy, in *Garrick Corresp.,* i. 340 (1831), I'd cudgel him back, breast and belly for three skips of a louse!

Three slips for a tester—three counterfeit twopenny coins for a sixpence = to give the slip. 1627 : F. Grove, *A Quip for a Scornful Lasse, or, Three Slips for a Tester* [title of ballad]. 1655 : *Faithful Post,* 7–14 Sept, He wanted agility of body to give them three slips for a tester. 1678 : Ray, 82, Two slips for a tester. *c.* 1685 : *Roxb. Ballads,* vi. 233 (B.S.), *The Forlorn Lover; Declaring how a Lass gave her Love Three Slips for a Tester* [title of ballad], and married another a week before Easter.

Three straws on a staff would make a baby cry and laugh. 1869 : Hazlitt, 403.

Three tailors. *See* **Nine tailors.**

Three things a man may be deceived, In. 1736 : Bailey, *Dict.,* s.v. " Three," In three things a man may be easily deceiv'd, viz. In a man, till known, A tree till down, and the day till done.

Three things are not to be credited. 1616 : B. Rich, *Ladies Looking Glasse,*

34, There are three things that are not to be credited, a woman when she weeps, a merchant when he sweares, nor a drunkard when he prayes.

Three things are nought worth, fayre face in a whore, Great strength in a porter, fine witt in the poore. 1591 : Florio, *Second Frutes,* 191.

Three things are thrown away in a bowling green, namely, time, money and oaths. 1822 : Scott, *Nigel,* ch. xii., Thus making good the saying, that three, etc.

Three things are to small purpose, if the fourth be away. *c.* 1597 : Deloney, *Iacke of Newberie,* ch. i. [cited as " an old saying "].

Three things are unsatiable, priests, monckes, and the sea. *c.* 1560 : in Wright, *Songs, etc., Philip and Mary,* 208 (Roxb. Cl.).

Three things are untameable, Idiots, women and the salt sea. 1875 : Cheales, *Proverb. Folk-Lore,* 8.

Three things cost dear : the caresses of a dog, the love of a mistress, and the invasion of a host. 1855 : Bohn, 530.

Three things drive a man out of his house : smoke, rain, and a scolding wife. [Skeat, in a note on *P. Plowman,* C, xx. 297, says : "Perhaps the original form of this commonly quoted proverb is this : ' tria sunt enim quæ non sinunt hominem in domo permanere ; fumus, stillicidium, et mala uxor'" (Innocens Papa, *de Contemptu Mundi,* i. 18). It is a mere compilation from *Proverbs* x. 26, xix. 13, and xxvii. 15.] 1377 : Langland, *Plowman,* B, xvii. 315, Thre thinges there ben that doth a man by strengthe Forto fleen his owne hous as holywryt sheweth, That one is a wikked wyf that wil nought be chasted ; Her fiere fleeth fro hyr for fere of her tonge. And if his hous be vnhiled and reyne on his bedde, He seketh and seketh til he slepe drye. And whan smoke and smolder smyt in his syghte, It doth hym worse than his wyf or wete to slepe. *c.* 1386 : Chaucer, *Melibeus,* § 15, Of whiche wommen, men seyn that " three thinges dryven a man out of his hous ; that is to seyn, smoke, dropping of reyn, and wikked wyves." *c.* 1530 :

Evyll Maryage, l. 96, in Hazlitt, *Early Pop. Poetry*, iv. 78, And Salamon sayth there be thynges thre, Shrewde wyues, rayne, and smokes blake Make husbandes ofte theyr houses to forsake. 1576 : Gascoigne, *Works*, ii. 227 (Cunliffe), There are three thinges that suffer not a man to abyde in his owne house. Smooke, rayne, and an evil wyfe. 1590 : Greene, *Works*, vii. 249, Foure things driues a man from hys house. 1. Too much smoke. 2. A dropping roofe. 3. A fylthie ayre. 4. And a brawling woman. 1597: Shakespeare, 1 *Henry IV.*, III.i., O, he is as tedious As a tired horse, a railing wife ; Worse than a smoky house. 1619 : *Helpe to Discourse*, 84 (1640), A smoke, a storme, and a contentious wife, Three ils are found, that tire a husbands life : To which, a fourth is by the proverb sed, When children cry for hunger, wanting bread. 1869 : Spurgeon, *John Ploughman*, ch. xii., Poverty is hard, but debt is horrible ; a man might as well have a smoky house and a scolding wife, which are said to be the two worst evils of our life.

Three things that are not to be lent. *See* Lend (5).

Three things that never comes to no good, There be—Christmas pigs, Michaelmas fowls, and parsons' daughters. Mon. 1882 : *N. & Q.*, 6th ser., vi. 246.

Three things there be full hard to be known. 1417 : in *Reliq. Antiquæ*, i. 233 (1841), There been thre thinges full harde to be knowen which waye they woll drawe. The first is of a birde sitting upon a bough. The second is of a vessell in the see. And the thirde is the waye of a younge man. 1486 : *Boke of St. Albans*, sig. f4, Ther be iiii thynges full harde for to know, Wyche way that thay will drawe. The first is the wayes of a yong man. The secunde the cours of a vessayll in the see. The thridde of an edder or a serpent sprent. The iiii of a fowle sittyng on any thyng.

Three things there be which neuer decay whiles the world lasteth, to bake, to brewe, and to powle or sheare, saye the people, or common prouerbe. 1586 : L. Evans, *Withals Dict. Revised*, sig. E4.

Three to one. *See* Two to one.

Three ways—the universities, the sea, the court, There are. 1612 : Shelton, *Quixote*, Pt. I. bk. iv. ch. xii., There is an old proverb . . . and it is this, " The Church, the Sea, or the Court." 1640 : Herbert, *Jac. Prudentum*.

Three women. *See* Woman (35).

Three words, At (or In). *See* quots. 1633 : Draxe, 10, At three words, he is at the top of the house [i.e. he is greatly excited]. 1659 : Howell, 15, In three words she is at the roof of the house.

Thresher take his flail, Let the. *See* quots. 1626 : Breton, *Fantasticks*, 10 (Grosart), It is now November, and according to the old prouerbe, Let the thresher take his flayle, And the ship no more sayle. 1661 : M. Stevenson, *Twelve Moneths*, 51 [as in 1626]. 1675 : *Poor Robin Alman. Prognost.*, sig. C7 [as in 1626]. 1732 : Fuller, No. 6221, November, take flail, Let ships no more sail.

Thrift, *subs.* 1. *Their thrift waxes thin, That spend more than they win.* c. 1460 : *How the Good Wife*, l. 100 [" His " for " Their "]. 1597 : *North. Mothers Blessing*, in *Plasidas, etc.*, 167 (Roxb. Cl.).

2. *Thrift and he are at a fray.* 1546 : Heywood, *Proverbs*, Pt. I. ch. xi., Whan thrift and you fell fyrst at a fray, You played the man, for ye made thrift ren away. 1670 : Ray, 196.

3. *Thrift is good revenue.* 1659 : Howell, *Proverbs : Fr. - Eng.*, 15, Parsimony is the best revenue. 1855 : Bohn, 530.

4. *Thrift is the philosopher's stone.* 1732 : Fuller, No. 5040.

5. *Thy thrift is thy friend's mirth.* c. 1460 : *How the Good Wife*, l. 170, Thi thrifte is thi frendis myrthe.

6. *When thrift is in the town, he is in the field*—or vice versa. 1546 : Heywood, *Proverbs*, Pt. II. ch. ix. c. 1594 : Bacon, *Promus*, No. 675. 1670 : Ray, 196.

Thrive, *verb.* 1. *He that thinketh to thrive by hope, may happen to beg in*

misery. 1647: *Countrym. New Commonwealth,* 23.

2. *He that will thrive must ask leave
of his wife. c.* 1470: *Songs and Carols,*
87 (Percy S., No. 73), Fore he that cast
hym for to thryve, He must ask off hys
wiffe leve. 1523: Fitzherbert, *Husbandry,* 93 (E.D.S.), There is an olde
common sayenge, that seldom doth the
housbande thryue, withoute the leue
of his wyfe. 1669: D. North, *Obs.
and Adv. Œconom.,* 4. 1784: Franklin,
Autobiog., in *Works,* i. 171 (Bigelow).
1875: Smiles, *Thrift,* 144.

3. *He that will thrive must rise at five;
He that hath thriven may lie till seven.
c.* 1590: G. Harvey, *Marginalia,* 102
(1913), [as above, *plus*] He that will
neuer thryuen may lye till aleuen.
1647: *Countrym. New Commonwealth,*
42 [as in 1590]. 1670: Ray, 148.
1732: Fuller, No. 6094. 1750: W.
Ellis, *Housewife's Companion,* vii., To
rise at five is the way to thrive. 1883:
Burne, *Shropsh. Folk-Lore,* 578, Them as
'oon thrive Mun rise at five, Them as
han thruven May lie till seven. 1913:
E. M. Wright, *Rustic Speech, etc.,* 173
[as in 1883].

4. *He thrives well that God loves.
c.* 1460: *How the Good Wife,* l. 10,
Wele thryuethe that God loueth.

Throng [Busy] **as Throp's wife, As.**
1828: Carr, *Craven Dialect,* ii. 201, " As
thrang as Throop wife, when she hang'd
hersell in her garter," a proverbial
simile applied to those who are very
busy in trifling things. 1849: F. T.
Dinsdale, *Teesdale Gloss.,* 134, There is
a phrase, " As thrang as Throp's wife
'at hanged hersell i' t' dish-clout."
1892: *N. & Q.,* 8th ser., i. 12, I have
heard the saying " I'm as throng as
Throp's wife," in Yorkshire, and only
a few days ago. 1900: *N. & Q.,* 9th
ser., v. 414, " As busy as Throp's wife "
—This is a saying current in the dales
of North Derbyshire and West Yorkshire. Ibid., 527, In South Notts
(where " throng "=busy is very common) there is a variant, " As busy as
Beck's wife." Cf. **Thrunk.**

Through stitch, To go=To do a thing
thoroughly. 1579: Gosson, *Sch. of*

Abuse, 68 (Arber), Philippe of Macedon
. . . was not able to go thorowe stitche.
1593: Nashe, *Works,* ii. 205 (Grosart),
What reason haue I . . . but to go
through stitch with you, as well as
him ? 1670: Cotton, *Scarronides,* bk.
iv., Who means to conquer Italy, Must
with his work go thorough stitches.
1712: Motteux, *Quixote,* Pt. I. bk. iii.
ch. xi., If you must needs be knocking
your noddle, to go through stitch with
this ugly job. 1785: Grose, *Class.
Dict. Vulgar Tongue,* s.v., To go thorough
stitch, to stick at nothing. 1828:
Carr, *Craven Dialect,* ii. 169, " To go
through stitch," to accomplish a business completely.

Throw, *verb.* 1. *Don't throw.* See
quot. 1883: Burne, *Shropsh. Folk-
Lore,* 589, Don't throw your property
out through the door with a spade,
while your husband is bringing it in
through the window with a spoon.

2. *He that is thrown would ever
wrestle.* 1640: Herbert, *Jac. Prudentum.* 1732: Fuller, No. 2196.

3. *He who will throw a stone at every
dog.* See quots. *c.* 1555: in Collmann, *Ballads, etc.,* 68 (Roxb. Cl.), Who
flynges a stone at euery dogge, which
barketh in the strete, Shall neuer haue
a iust reuenge, nor have a pacient sprete.
1575: Gascoigne, *Posies,* in *Works,* i. 6
(Cunliffe), He who will throw a stone
at everie dogge which barketh, had
neede of a great satchell or pocket.

4. *Not to have—this or that—to throw
at a dog.* 1546: Heywood, *Proverbs,*
Pt. II. ch. vii., To be unable to give a
dog a loaf. 1600: Day, *Blind Beggar,*
III. ii., I have not a horse to cast at a
dog, man, not I. 1600: Shakespeare,
Merry Wives, I. iv., He shall not have
a stone to throw at his dog. 1607:
Heywood, *Fair Maide,* in *Works,* ii. 54
(1874), I am not furnish'd of a courting
phrase, to throw at a dogge. 1738:
Swift, *Polite Convers.,* Dial. I., Here's
miss, has not a word to throw at a dog.
1765: Bickerstaff, *Maid of the Mill,* II.
i., She was struck all of a heap—she
had not a word to throw to a dog.
1850: Dickens, *Copperfield,* ch. i., It is
nothing to say that he hadn't a word

to throw at a dog. He couldn't have
thrown a word at a mad dog. 1884 :
R. L. S. and Henley, *Beau Austin*, I. i.,
She falls away, has not a word to throw
at a dog, and is ridiculously pale.

5. *Thrown stone or spoken word. See*
quots. 1633 : Draxe, 240, A word and
a stone let goe, cannot be called backe.
1732 : Fuller, No. 485 [as in 1633].
1875 : Cheales, *Proverb. Folk-Lore,* 88
[as in 1633, but with " recalled " for
" called backe"]. 1924 : J. L. Garvin,
in *Observer,* 12 Oct., p. 12, col. 3, Never
more, says the old proverb, comes back
the thrown stone or the spoken word.

6. *To throw snot about* = To weep.
1678 : Ray, 82.

7. *To throw the helve after the hatchet.*
1546 : Heywood, *Proverbs,* Pt. II. ch.
ix., For here I sende thaxe after the
helue awaie. 1587 : J. Bridges, *Def.
of Govt. in Ch. of England,* 90, If the
axe were gone, is this the remedy, to
hurle the helve after it ? 1685-6 :
Cotton, *Montaigne,* bk. iii. ch. ix., I
abandon myself through despair . . .
and, as the saying is, " throw the helve
after the hatchet." 1712 : Motteux,
Quixote, Pt. II. ch. ix. 1829 : Scott,
Journal, 26 April, At night I flung helve
after hatchet, and spent the evening
in reading the *Doom of Devorgoil* to the
girls. 1921 : *Observer,* 10 April, p. 10,
col. 5, The worst of democracy, as Lord
Bryce might admit, is the combination
of power and ignorance. Passion is
born from the imagination of the thing
that is not, and the helve is flung after
the hatchet.

8. *To throw the house out of the
windows. See* **House** (16).

9. *To throw the stone and hide the
hand.* 1732 : Fuller, No. 5246.

10. *To throw water. See* **Cast** (8).

Thrunk [Crowded] **as Chiddle Wakes,
no room areawt, As.** 1917 : Bridge,
Cheshire Proverbs, 24 [" areawt "=out
of doors].

Thrunk as Eccles wakes, As. 1901 :
F. E. Taylor, *Lancs Sayings,* 4.

Thrunk (or **Thrang**) **as three in a bed,
As.** 1828 : Carr, *Craven Dialect,* ii. 201,
Crowded, " as thrang as three in a bed."
1884 : *N. & Q.,* 6th ser., x. 227, In

Yorkshire the expression is " as thrang
as three i' a bed." 1917 : Bridge,
Cheshire Proverbs, 25. Cf. **Thick as
three in a bed** ; and **Throng.**

**Thrush, avoiding the trap, fell into
bird-lime, The.** 1732 : Fuller, No. 4792.

Thrushes. *See* **Wish** (3).

Thumb. *See* **Finger** (2), (8), and (11).

Thunder, *subs.* 1. *Early thunder,
early spring.* 1893 : Inwards, *Weather
Lore,* 7.

2. *If it sinks. See* quot. 1874 :
N. & Q., 5th ser., ii. 184, If it sinks from
the north, It will double its wrath ; If
it sinks from the south, It will open its
mouth ; If it sinks from the west, It is
never at rest ; If it sinks from the east,
It will leave us in peace (Kent). 1893 :
Inwards, 118 [as in 1874].

3. *The first thunder of the year awakes
All the frogs and all the snakes.* Ibid.,
117.

4. *Thunder in spring Cold will bring.*
Ibid., 7.

See also **All Fools' Day** ; **April** (24)
and (26) ; **December** ; **Lightning** ;
March (18), (36), and (48) ; **May,** F (13)
and (25) ; **November** (8) ; **Poppies** ;
Shrovetide (2) ; **Summer** (5) ; and **Winter**
(7) and (13)–(19).

Thunderbolt hath but its clap, The.
1633 : Draxe, 216. 1670 : Ray, 148.
1732 : Fuller, No. 4793, The thunder
hath but its clap.

Thursday. 1. *On Thursday at three
Look out, and you'll see What Friday
will be.* S. Devon. 1893 : Inwards,
Weather Lore, 42.

2. *Thursday come, The week's gone.*
1640 : Herbert, *Jac. Prudentum,* Thursday come, and the week is gone. 1666 :
Torriano, *Piazza Univ.,* 103, The Thursday come, the week lost. 1878 : Dyer,
Eng. Folk-Lore, 241, Working people
are wont to say :—" Thursday come,
The week's gone."

Thynne. *See* **Horner.**

Tib. A generic name for a girl, as Tom
for a boy. *He struck at Tib, but down
fell Tom.* 1639 : Clarke, 1, [with al-
ternative] but struck downe Tom.
1670 : Ray, 196. 1732 : Fuller, No.
2029 [with " Tim " for " Tom "].

Tibberton. *See* quot. 1882 : Mrs.

Chamberlain, *W. Worcs. Words*, 39
(E.D.S.), A stone church, a wooden
steeple, A drunken parson, a wicked
people, is a proverb at Tibberton.

**Tib's eve, neither before nor after
Christmas.** One of the many euphem-
isms for " never." 1785 : Grose, *Class.
Dict. Vulgar Tongue*, s.v. " Tib," He
will pay you on St. Tibbs Eve (Irish).
1854 : Baker, *Northants Gloss.*, s.v.
1861 : *N. & Q.*, 2nd ser., xi. 269, St.
Tib's Eve is used in Cornwall as equivalent to " the Greek Kalends." 1916 :
B. Duffy, *The Counter-Charm*, 8, If you
were boiled in soap from this till Tibb's
Eve, you'd be just as sooty.

Tickhill, God help me. 1850 : *N. & Q.*,
1st ser., i. 247, Can any one tell why
a Tickhill man, when asked where he
comes from, says, " Tickhill, God help
me"? 1888 : S. O. Addy, *Sheffield
Gloss.*, 259 (E.D.S.), In speaking to a
stranger . . . a Bawtry man will say
of a Tickhill man, " Oh, he comes from
Tickhill-God-help-him," as if nobody
need wonder at a Tickhill man's actions.

**Tickle my throat with a feather, and
make a fool of my stomach.** 1678 :
Ray, 210.

Tid, Mid, Misera. *See* quots. 1788 :
Gent. Mag., i. 188, We have in
Northumberland the following couplet,
which gives name to every Sunday in
Lent, except the first : Tid, and Mid,
and Misera, Carling, Palm, and Good-
pas-day. 1825 : Hone, *Ev. Day Book*,
i. 379, Tid, Mid, Misera, Carling, Palm,
Paste Egg Day.

Tide, *subs.* 1. *The tide keeps its
course.* 1659 : Howell, 10.

2. *The tide never goes out so far but it
always comes in again.* 1864 : " Cornish
Proverbs," in *N. & Q.*, 3rd ser., vi.
494.

3. *The tide tarries no man.* *c.* 1440 :
Lydgate, *Fall of Princes*, bk. iii. l. 2801
(E.E.T.S.), The tid abit nat for no maner
man. 15th cent.: in *Reliq. Antiquæ*, i.
268 (1841), Farewele, my frendis, the
tide abideth no man. *c.* 1530 : *Everyman*, in Hazlitt, *Old Plays*, i. 105, For,
wit thou well, the tide abideth no man.
1546 : Heywood, *Proverbs*, Pt. I. ch. iii.
1591 : Lyly, *Endymion*, IV. ii. 1611 :

T. Ravenscroft, *Melismata*, sig. B4.
Cf. **Time** (15).

4. *The tide will fetch away what the
ebb brings.* 1670 : Ray, 26. 1732 :
Fuller, No. 4495, The ebb will fetch off
what the tide brings in.

See also **Rain**, *verb* (3).

Tidings make either glad or sad.
1639 : Clarke, 229. 1670 : Ray, 148.

Tie a knot with the tongue. *See*
Knot (2).

Tied by the tooth. 1917 : Bridge,
Cheshire Proverbs, 124, Sheep and cattle
will not break through fences or try to
wander if the pasture of the field in
which they are grazing is very good.
They are " tied by the tooth."

Tie it well and let it go. 1640 :
Herbert, *Jac. Prudentum*.

Tight as a drum, As. 1720 : Gay,
Poems, ii. 279 (Underhill), No drum
was ever tighter. 1857 : Hughes, *Tom
Brown*, Pt. I. ch. iv., Tom has eaten . . .
till his little skin is as tight as a drum.

Tight boots, To sit in = To be ill at
ease with your host. 1855 : Bohn, 543.

Time, *subs.* 1. *As good have no time,
as make no good use of it.* 1732 : Fuller,
No. 686.

2. *He that has most time has none to
lose.* Ibid., No. 2141.

3. *He that hath time and looketh for a
better time, loseth time.* 1578 : Florio,
First Fruites, fo. 28, Who hath tyme
and tarieth for time, looseth tyme.
1605 : Camden, *Remains*, 323 (1870)
[with " better " omitted]. 1651 : Herbert, *Jac. Prudentum*, 2nd ed., . . .
[ending] time comes that he repents
himself of time. 1732 : Fuller, No.
2162. 1869 : Spurgeon, *John Ploughman*, ch. vii. [as in 1651].

4. *He that hath time hath life.* 1578 :
Florio, *First Fruites*, fo. 28, Who hath
tyme hath life. 1596 : Nashe, *Works*,
iii. 70 (Grosart). 1629 : *Book of Meery
Riddles*, Prov. 14. 1736 : Franklin,
Way to Wealth, in *Works*, i. 443 (Bigelow), Then do not squander time, for
that is the stuff life is made of.

5. *In time of prosperity.* *See* **Prosperity.**

6. *It is time to yoke when the cart comes
to the caples* [horses]. Cheshire. 1670 :

Ray, 48. 1852 : *N. & Q.*, 1st ser., vi. 386. 1917 : Bridge, *Cheshire Proverbs*, 84.

7. *Take time when time cometh, for time will away.* Before 1529 : Skelton, *Works*, i. 137 (Dyce), Take tyme when tyme is, for tyme is ay mutable. 1595 : A. Montgomery, *Cherrie and Slae*, st. 36, Tak time in time, ere time be tint For time will not remain. 1670 : Ray, 149 [" is " for " cometh "]. 1732 : Fuller, No. 4313 [as in 1670]. 1846 : Denham, *Proverbs*, 5 (Percy S.) [as in 1670].

8. *There is a time for all things.* 1399 : Langland, *Rich. the Redeless*, iii. 278, But all thinge hath tyme. 1509 : Bp. Fisher, *Eng. Works*, 174 (E.E.T.S.), Euery thynge hath a tyme. 1591 : Shakespeare, *Com. of Errors*, II. ii. 1605 : Chapman, *All Fools*, V. ii., For as much, Valerius, as everything has time. 1732 : Fuller, No. 1466, Every thing hath its time, and that time must be watch'd. 1861 : Peacock, *Gryll Grange*, ch. xiii., He held that there was a time for all things. 1926 : *Punch*, 28 July, p. 92, col. 2, Nay, nay, there be a time for all things.

9. *There is a time to speak, and a time to be silent.* 1485 : Caxton, *Charles the Grete*, 56 (E.E.T.S.), Thou knowest the comyn prouerbe that sayth that there is a tyme of spekyng and tyme of beyng stylle. 1523-5 : Berners, *Froissart*, ch. cccxlviii., John Lyon . . . sayd, Ther is tyme to be styll and tyme to speke. 1633 : Draxe, 190, There is a time to speake and a time to holde ones peace.

10. *There is a time to wink, as well as to see.* 1732 : Fuller, No. 4885.

11. *Time and chance happen to all men.* 1709 : O. Dykes, *Eng. Proverbs*, 273 (2nd ed.) [cited as " a common saw "].

12. *Time and chance reveal all secrets.* 1709 : Manley, *New Atlantis*, ii. 230 (1736). Cf. No. 24.

13. *Time and patience will wear out stone posts.* 1864 : " Cornish Proverbs," in *N. & Q.*, 3rd ser., vi. 494, . . . stonen postes. 1919 : *Devonsh. Assoc. Trans.*, li. 77, Time and patience wears out most stone paustes.

14. *Time and straw make medlars*

ripe. 1578 : Florio, *First Fruites*, fo. 14, With time and with straw, medlers are made ripe. 1611 : Cotgrave, s.v. " Paille," In time and straw are medlers mellowed. 1712 : Motteux, *Quixote*, Pt. I. bk. iii. ch. vi. 1732 : Fuller, No. 5047, Time and straw ripen medlars.

15. *Time and tide wait for no man.* c. 1386 : Chaucer, *C. Tales*, E 118 (Skeat), For thogh we slepe or wake, or rome, or ryde, Ay fleeth the tyme, it nil no man abyde. Before 1529 : Skelton, *Works*, i. 137 (Dyce), Byde for tyme who wyll, for tyme wyll no man byde. 1596 : Nashe, *Works*, iii. 78 (Grosart), Yet time and tide (that staies for no man) forbids vs . . . 1630 : Brathwait, *Eng. Gent.*, 189 (1641) Whence we commonly say, Time and tide stayeth for no man. 1736 : Bailey, *Dict.*, s.v. " Time," Time and tide will stay for no man. 1822 : Scott, *Nigel*, ch. xxvi. 1850 : Dickens, *Chuzzlewit*, ch. x. Cf. **Tide** (3).

16. *Time cures all things.* 1539 : Taverner, *Proverbs*, fo. 38, Tyme taketh away greuaunce. 1698 : *Terence made English*, 140 (2nd ed.). 1731 : Lillo, *George Barnwell*, V. ii., Time and reflection cure all ills. 1736 : Bailey, *Dict.*, s.v. " Time," Time and thought quells the heaviest grief. 1869 : Hazlitt, 405, Time and thinking tame the strongest grief.

17. *Time fleeth away without delay.* 1639 : Clarke, 308. 1670 : Ray, 149. 1732 : Fuller, No. 6090.

18. *Time is a file that wears and makes no noise.* 1855 : Bohn, 531.

19. *Time is money.* 1607-12 : Bacon, *Essays:* "Despatch," For tyme is the measure of businesse, as money is of wares. 1748 : Franklin, in *Works*, ii. 118 (Bigelow). 1841 : Dickens, *Barn. Rudge*, ch. xxiii. 1875 : Smiles, *Thrift*, 364. 1903 : Gissing, *Henry Ryecroft:* "Winter," xxiv., Time is money—says the vulgarest saw known to any age or people. Turn it round about, and you get a precious truth—money is time.

20. *Time is the father of truth.* 1578 : Florio, *First Fruites*, fo. 32. 1629 : *Book of Meery Riddles*, Prov. 47.

21. *Time is the rider that breaks youth.*

1640 : Herbert, *Jac. Prudentum.* 1670 :
Ray, 26. 1732 : Fuller, No. 5052 [with
" in " after " breaks "].

22. *Time is tickle.* 1546 : Heywood,
Proverbs, Pt. I. ch. iii. 1659 · Howell, 7.

23. *Time lost we cannot win.* c. 1440 :
Lydgate, *Fall of Princes*, bk. iii. l. 2811
(E.E.T.S.), Sumtyme departed, ageyn
men may nat call. c. 1535 : *Pain of
Evil Marriage*, 17 (Percy S.), Tyme
passed wyl not agayne retourne. 1605 :
Camden, *Remains*, 334 (1870). 1659 :
Howell, 10.

24. *Time revealeth all things.* 1539 :
Taverner, *Proverbs*, fo. 37, Tyme dis-
closeth all thynges. 1633 : Draxe, 204.
1736 : Bailey, *Dict.*, s.v. " Time," Time
brings all things to light. Cf. No. 12.

25. *Time stays not the fool's leisure.*
1855 : Bohn, 531.

26. *Time tries truth.* 1546 : Heywood,
Proverbs, Pt. II. ch. v., Let time try!
Tyme tryeth trouth in euery doubt.
1580 : Tusser, *Husbandrie*, 5 (E.D.S.),
Time trieth the troth, in euerie thing.

27. *Time trieth all things.* 1553 :
Respublica, Prol., Yet tyme trieth all.
1599 : Porter, *Two Angry Women*, in
Hazlitt, *Old Plays*, vii. 356, Time and
truth tries all. 1607 : Marston, *What
You Will*, IV. 1633 : Draxe, 204.

28. *Time undermines us.* 1640 :
Herbert, *Jac. Prudentum.*

29. *To take time by the forelock.* 1595 :
Spenser, *Sonnets*, No. lxx., Tell her the
ioyous time wil not be staid, Unlesse
she doe him by the forelock take. 1624 :
T. Heywood, *Captives*, III. iii., Loose
not this advantadge, But take tyme by
the fore-topp. 1708 : Ward, *London
Terræfilius*, No. 5, p. 23, You have
taken Time by the forelock. 1767 :
Brooke, *Fool of Quality*, ii. 252, O, then
we may take good-man time by the
forelock. 1883 : R. L. S., *Treasure I.*,
ch. xii.

30. *When time hath turned white sugar
to white salt.* 1546 : Heywood, *Proverbs*, Pt. I. ch. ii.

See also Nature, time.

Timely blossom, timely fruit. 1639 :
Clarke, 171 [" beare " for " fruit "].
1670 : Ray, 149 [" ripe " for " fruit "].
1732 : Fuller, No. 5057.

Timely crooketh. *See* Soon crooketh.

Tinidal. This is a dark saying. I
cannot identify " Tinidal." 1583 : Melbancke, *Philotinus*, sig. Aa2, It is a
prouerbe in Englande that the men of
Tinidal borderers on yᵉ English midle
marches, haue likers, lemmons, and
lyerbies.

Tinker and Tinkers, *subs.* 1. *A tinker
and a piper make bad music together.*
1639 : Clarke, 5.

2. *A tinker's budget is full of necessary
tools.* Ibid., 72. 1670 : Ray, 149.

3. *The tinker stops one hole and makes
two.* 1576: *Common Conditions* in Brandl,
Quellen, 599, Hoie tiftie toftie tinkers,
good fellowes thei bee, In stoppyng
of one hole thei vse to make three.
1630 : *Tinker of Turvey*, 10 (Halliwell),
Roome for a ioviall tinker, He stop
one hole, and make three. 1692 :
L'Estrange, *Æsop*, 189 (3rd ed.), Till
it comes at last to the tinker's work
of stopping one hole, and making ten.
1738 : Swift, *Polite Convers.*, Dial. I.
1872 : *N. & Q.*, 4th ser., ix. 375, When
I was young it was a proverb in East
Cornwall that the tinkers " repaired one
hole and made two."

4. *Tinker's news.* 1876 : *N. & Q.*,
5th ser., v. 168, In Gloucestershire,
when any piece of information is mentioned that has been heard or told
before, it is called " tinkers' news."
1883 : Burne, *Shropsh. Folk-Lore*, 599,
That's tinker's news ; i.e. stale news.

See also Banbury tinkers ; Cobbler (3);
Merry as tinkers ; Not worth (34);
Rough as a tinker's budget ; and Swear
(2).

Tint for tant=Tit for tat. Hazlitt
suggests derivation from French " *tant*
for *tant.*" The *Oxford Dictionary* suggests " taunt for taunt." 1620 : T.
Granger, *Div. Logike*, 124 (O.), Like for
like, pin driuing out a pin, tint for
taunt, etc. 1672 : Walker, *Parœm.*,
29, Give him tint for tant. 1690 : *New
Dict. Canting Crew*, sig. M2, Tint for
tant, hit for hit, and dash for dash.
1828 : Carr, *Craven Dialect*, ii. 208,
" Tint for tant," a requital similar to
tit for tat.

Tit for tat. [Par pari respondet.—

Plautus, *Truc.*, ii. 47.] 1546: Heywood, *Proverbs*, Pt. II. ch. iv. 1552: Huloet, *Abced.*, sig. Bb6, Requite as tick for tacke. 1611: Cotgrave, s.v. "Beau," A tit for a tat . . . as good every whit as was brought. 1748: Richardson, *Clarissa*, i. 153 (1785), They are resolved to break my heart. And they think you are resolved to break theirs: So tit for tat, Miss. 1898: Weyman, *Shrewsbury*, ch. xvii. 1922: *Observer*, 10 Dec., p. 13, col. 2, They want their tit for tat with Mr. Bonar Law.

Tithe and be rich. 1651: Herbert, *Jac. Prudentum*, 2nd ed.

Tittle, tattle, give the goose more hay. 1659: Howell, 11. 1670: Ray, 214. *c.* 1690: Sedley, *Grumbler*, I. ["Bibble babble" for "Tittle tattle"]. 1732: Fuller, No. 5058.

Toad, *subs.* 1. *The toad and a side-pocket. See* quots. Monkey and dog are variants for the toad. 1785: Grose, *Class. Dict. Vulgar Tongue*, s.v. "Toad," As much use of it as a toad of a side pocket, said of a person who desires anything for which he has no real occasion. 1869: *N. & Q.*, 4th ser., iv. 147, The old fellow said: "I no more wants that than a toad wants side pockets." 1880: *N. & Q.*, 6th ser., ii. 347 ["monkey" for "toad"]. Ibid., 377 ["dog"—Devonsh.]. 1881: *N. & Q.*, 6th ser., iii. 76 ["dog"—E. Riding, Yorks]. Ibid. ["toad" — S.W. England and Northants]. 1888: Q.-Couch, *Troy Town*, ch. x., A bull's got no more use for religion than a toad for side-pockets. Cf. **Cow** (8).

2. *The toad under the harrow. See* quots. [*c.* 1290: in Wright, *Pol. Songs John to Edw. II.*, 166 (Camden S.), Dixit bufo crati, "maledicti tot dominati!"] *c.* 1380: Wiclif, *Select Eng. Works*, ii. 280, Christene men may seye, as the poete seith in proverbe, the frogge seide to the harwe, cursid be so many lordis. 1720: *Vade Mecum for Maltworms*, Pt. I. 33, There says, *He lives like toad beneath a harrow*. 1732: Fuller, No. 3354, Many masters, quoth the toad to the harrow, when every tine turn'd her over. 1817: Scott,

Rob Roy, ch. xxvii., Only muttering between his teeth, "Ower mony maisters . . . as the paddock said to the harrow, when every tooth gae her a tig." 1849: Dinsdale, *Teesdale Gloss.*, 136, "To live like a toad under a harrow," is an expression denoting extreme personal wretchedness. 1854: Baker, *Northants Gloss.*, s.v. "Toad under a harrow." A common simile, applied to any one in a state of mental or bodily disquietude or suffering. 1918: *Devonsh. Assoc. Trans.*, l. 279, The proverbial saying about a man in difficulties, that he is "like a toad under a harrow."

See also **Mulfra**; and **Swell**.

Toasted cheese hath no master. 1678: Ray, 82. 1911: Hackwood, *Good Cheer*, 304.

Toast your bread. *See* quot. 1888: Lowsley, *Berks Gloss.*, 30 (E.D.S.), Two-ast yer bread An' rasher yer vlitch, An' as long as 'e lives Thee'ooll never be rich.

Tobacco. *See* quots. 1678: Ray, 296, Tobacco hic, If a man be well it will make him sick. [Also] Will make a man well if he be sick. 1849: Halliwell, *Pop. Rhymes, etc.*, 180, Tobacco hic, Will make you well If you be sick.

To-day a man, to-morrow a cuckold. 1669: *New Help to Discourse*, 310.

To-day a man, to-morrow a mouse. 1666: Torriano, *Piazza Univ.*, 59. 1732: Fuller, No. 5152.

To-day a man, to-morrow none. Before 1500: in Hill, *Commonplace-Book*, 129 (E.E.T.S.), This dai a man, to-morow non. 1560: T. Wilson, *Rhetorique*, 83 (1909). 1611: Cotgrave, s.v. "Biere." 1633: Draxe, 131.

To-day at cheer, to-morrow in bier. 1611: Cotgrave, s.v. "Chere," To day glad, to morrow dead. 1623: Wodroephe, *Spared Houres*, 476. 1880: Spurgeon, *Ploughman's Pictures*, 67, To-day at good cheer, to-morrow on the bier.

To-day gold, to-morrow dust. *c.* 1500: in *Antiq. Repertory*, iv. 398 (1809), To day a man in golde, to morow closyde in clay. 1869: Hazlitt, 414.

To-day is yesterday's pupil. 1732 : Fuller, No. 5153.

To-day me, to-morrow thee—or vice versa. Before 1225 : *Ancren R.*, 278, And seie . . . " Ille hodie, ego cras " : pet is, " He to dai, ich to morwen." 1596 : Spenser, *F. Q.*, VI. i. 41, What haps to-day to me to-morrow may to you. 1620 : Shelton, *Quixote*, Pt. II. ch. lxv., To-day for thee, and to-morrow for me. 1681 : Robertson, *Phraseol. Generalis*, 427. 1732 : Fuller, No. 5154. 1855 : Kingsley, *West. Ho!*, ch. ix., To-day to thee, to-morrow to me. Addio. 1906 : Doyle, *Sir Nigel*, ch. xv., "It is the custom of the Narrow Seas," said they : "To-day for them; to-morrow for us."

To-day will not, to-morrow may, If. 1732 : Fuller, No. 2725.

Toil of a pleasure, To make a. 1603 : Breton, in *Works*, ii. *j* 7 (Grosart), I doo not loue so to make a toyle of a pleasure. Before 1658 : Cleveland, in *Works*, 267 (1742), And make a toil of's pleasure.

Toil so for trash, what would you do for treasure, If you? 1639 : Clarke, 194.

To it again, no body comes. 1639 : Clarke, 303. 1670 : Ray, 197. 1672 : Walker, *Parœm.*, 53.

Toko for yam. *See* quots. 1823 : John Bee, *Slang Dict.*, Toco for yam.— Yams are food for negroes in the West Indies (resembling potatoes), and if, instead of receiving his proper ration of these, blackee gets a whip (*toco*) about his back, why " he has caught toco " instead of yams. 1855 : Planché, *Extravag.*, v. 124 (1879), Shan't he get toco For yam as surely As I stand here! 1880 : *N. & Q.*, 6th ser., i. 455, This is a common expression among sailors in the navy ; for instance, " He'll get toko for yam," i.e. " he'll get paid out," " he'll be punished."

Toll is more than the grist, The. 1886 : Elworthy, *West Som. Word-Book*, 302 (E.D.S.), Formerly the miller always took his payment in a toll of the corn, and hence one of our most common proverbs : . . . the toll is more than the grist.

Tom All thumbs. *See* All thumbs.

Tom, Dick and Harry. 1566 : Lindsay, *Dial. between Exper. and a Courtier*, sig. A8 (Purfoot), Wherefore to colliers, carters and cokes To Iack and Tom my rime shall be directed. 1604 : James I., in Fuller, *Church Hist.*, bk. x. § i. (22), Then Jack, and Tom, and Will, and Dick shall meet and censure me and my Council. 1622 : J. Taylor, *Sir Greg. Nonsense*, 16, in Hindley, *Old Book-Coll. Miscell.*, iii., I neither care what Tom, or Jack, or Dick said. 1660 : A. Brome, *Poems :* "Royalist's Answer," Though Dick, Tom, and Jack, Will serve you and your pack. 1885 : M. Twain, in *Letters*, 251 (1920), His simple pleasure in the flowers and general ruck sent to him by Tom, Dick and Harry from everywhere. 1921 : B. W. Matz, *Inns and Tav. of " Pickwick,"* 242, He gathered his information from any Tom, Dick or Harry he came in contact with during his wanderings.

Tom Dooley. *See* quot. 1917 : Bridge, *Cheshire Proverbs*, 103, Owd Tum Dooley's note, booath barren and dreigh (said of a barren and dry cow).

Tom Drum. *See* Drum's entertainment.

Tom Fool. *See* More know; and Red and yellow.

Tom Hodges. *See* John Toy.

Tom Long. *See* John Long.

Tum Norton. *See* All worse.

Tom of all trades. *See* Jack of all trades.

To-morrow come never. 1678 : Ray, 343. 1725 : Bailey, tr. Erasmus' *Colloq.*, 34. 1769 : Colman, *Man and Wife*, III. 1825 : Brockett, *Gloss. N. Country Words*, 150, Nivver, never, " To-morrow come nivver—when two Sundays meet together." 1830 : Marryat, *King's Own*, ch. xxvi. 1917 : Bridge, *Cheshire Proverbs*, 141.

To-morrow is a new day. *c.* 1520 : *Calisto and Melibœa*, in Hazlitt, *Old Plays*, i. 86, Well, mother, to-morrow is a new day : I shall perform that I have you promised. 1592 : Lyly, *Mother Bombie*, V. iii. *c.* 1620 : B. & F., *Night-Walker*, II. iii. 1685-6: Cotton, *Montaigne*, bk. ii. ch. iv., To-morrow's

a New Day [title of chapter]. 1712:
Motteux, *Quixote*, Pt. II. ch. lxviii.
1823: Scott, *St. Ronan's*, ch. xxxiii.

To-morrow is untouched. 1846:
Denham, *Proverbs*, 1 (Percy S.).

To-morrow morning I found a horse-shoe. 1620: Shelton, *Quixote*, Pt. II.
ch. xliii., That are as much to the pur-
pose as " To-morrow I found a horse-
shoe." 1732: Fuller, No. 5208. 1926:
Times, 2 Nov., p. 14, col. 7, The eve of
the election finds the Democrats saying,
like the man in the proverb, " To-morrow I found a horse-shoe."

To-morrow. *See also* Put (3).

Tom Prodger's job, A. 1854: Baker,
Northants Gloss., s.v. " Prodger," " A
Tom Prodger's job "; a clumsy piece
of work is so called.

Tom Tell-truth. 1377: Langland,
Plowman, B, iv. 17, Tomme Trewe-
tonge-telle-me-no-tales. 1542: Udall,
tr. Erasmus' *Apoph.*, 202 (1877), (As ye
would say in English) Thom trouth,
or plain Sarisbuirie. 1550: Latimer,
Sermons, 289 (P.S.), Master, we know
that thou art Tom Truth, and thou
tellest the very truth . . . Thou art
plain Tom Truth. 1600: J. Lane, *Tom
Tel-Troths Message* [title]. (N. Sh. S.).
1646: Quarles, *Works*, i. 93 (Grosart).
1681: Robertson, *Phraseol. Generalis*,
1066, So Tom tell-troth talks and re-
ports. 1709: O. Dykes, *Eng. Proverbs*,
p. xxxvi. (2nd ed.), Neither do I
look upon such scraps, as, Latter Lammas . . . Tom Tell-Troth . . . to be
fit for my purpose. 1826: Scott,
Journal, 19 Feb., Yet is he Tom Tell-
truth, and totally unable to disguise
his real feelings. 1869: Spurgeon,
John Ploughman, ch. xviii., Better be
laughed at as Tom Tell-truth than be
praised as Crafty Charlie.

Tom Thumb, A tale of. 1659:
Howell, 14.

Tong, Kent. *See* Bapchild; and
Muston.

Tongue, subs. 1. *A good tongue is a
good weapon.* 1732: Fuller, No. 180.

2. *At one's tongue's end.* 1590: *Tarltons Newes out of Purg.*, 69 (Sh. S.), To
blame those wives whose secrets lay at
their tongues end. 1652: Walsingham,

Arcana Aulica, 18 (1694), Upon whose
tongues-end lay the disposal of his life.
1751: Fielding, *Amelia*, bk. xii. ch. vii.,
Having always at her tongue's end that
excellent proverb . . . 1854: Baker,
Northants Gloss., s.v. " I had it at my
tongue's end," i.e. I was ready to speak,
but on reflection held my tongue.

3. *Her tongue runs on pattens.* 1546:
Heywood, *Proverbs*, Pt. II. ch. vii.
c. 1550: Udall, *Roister Doister*, I. iii., Yet
your tongue can renne on patins as well
as mine. 1611: Davies (of Hereford),
Sc. of Folly, 46, in *Works*, ii. (Grosart).

4. *His tongue goes always of errands,
but never speeds.* 1732: Fuller, No.
2515.

5. *His tongue is as cloven as the devil's
foot.* Ibid., No. 2516.

6. *His tongue is no slander.* 1633:
Draxe, 121. 1670: Ray, 196. 1736:
Bailey, *Dict.*, s.v. " Tongue."

7. *His tongue is well hung.* 1738:
Swift, *Polite Convers.*, Dial. I., I warrant
this rogue's tongue is well hung. 1754:
Berthelson, *Eng.-Danish Dict.*, s.v.
" Hung."

8. *His tongue runs on wheels.* c. 1450:
Partonope, 420 (E.E.T.S.), They haue
no ioy to say the best, Suche mennys
tonges gone euer on whelis. 1738:
Swift, *Polite Convers.*, Dial. I., Why,
wench, I think thy tongue runs upon
wheels this morning. 1828: Carr,
Craven Dialect, ii. 213, " His tongue
runs o' wheels "; i.e. he talks fast.

9. *Let not thy tongue run away with
thy brains.* 1732: Fuller, No. 3190.

10. *That tongue doth lye that speakes
in hast.* 1611: Davies (of Hereford),
Sc. of Folly, 43, in *Works*, ii. (Grosart).

11. *The tongue breaks bones, though
itself has none.* c. 1270: *Prov. of Alfred*, in *Old Eng. Miscell.* 128 (Morris),
For ofte tunge breketh bon theyh heo
seolf nabbe non. Before 1384: Wiclif,
Works, ii. 44 (Arnold), Tunge brekith
boon, al if the tunge himself have noon.
c. 1470: G. Ashby, *Poems*, 64 (E.E.T.S.),
The tonge breketh boon, thaugh he be
tendre. 1546: Heywood, *Proverbs*, Pt.
II. ch. v., Toung breaketh bone, it selfe
hauyng none. 1670: Ray, 26. 1732:
Fuller, No. 4795.

12. *The tongue is ever turning to the aching tooth.* 1586 : Young, tr. Guazzo's *Civil Convers.*, fo. 221, The tongue rolls there where the teeth aketh. 1659 : Howell, *Proverbs : Ital.-Eng.*, 8, Where the tooth pains, the toung is commonly upon it. 1732 : Fuller, No. 4796.

13. *The tongue is not steel, yet it cuts.* 1546 : Heywood, *Proverbs*, Pt. I. ch. x., Her tong is no edge toole, but yet it will cut. 1640 : Herbert, *Jac. Prudentum.* 1732 : Fuller, No. 4797 [with "sorely" after "cuts"]. 1853 : Trench, *Proverbs*, 138 (1905).

14. *The tongue is the rudder of our ship.* 1732 : Fuller, No. 4798.

15. *The tongue of idle persons is never idle.* Ibid., No. 4800.

16. *The tongue talks at the head's cost.* 1640 : Herbert, *Jac. Prudentum.* 1670 : Ray, 26. 1732 : Fuller, No. 4801.

17. *The tongue walks where the teeth speed not.* 1640 : Herbert, *Jac. Prudentum.*

18. *To keep one's tongue between one's teeth.* 1672 : Walker, *Parœm.*, 18, I shall keep my tongue between my teeth. 1692 : L'Estrange, *Æsop*, 271 (3rd ed.), That have the wit yet to keep their tongues betwixt their teeth. 1709 : Cibber, *Rival Fools*, II., If he does not keep his tongue between his teeth, I'll give him a chuck o' the chin, shall chop him in two. 1784 : *New Foundl. Hosp. for Wit*, i. 287. 1821 : Scott, *Kenilworth*, ch. vii., Silence, good neighbours! . . . keep tongue betwixt teeth.

19. *Tongue, whither wilt thou?* 1692 : L'Estrange, *Æsop:* "Life," 11 (3rd ed.) [quoted as " the old proverb "].

20. *Your tongue is made of very loose leather.* 1732 : Fuller, No. 6062.

21. *Your tongue runs before your wit.* c. 1350 : *Pearl*, l. 294, Thy worde byfore thy wytte con fle. 1546 : Heywood, *Proverbs*, Pt. II. ch. iv. c. 1597 : Deloney, *Gentle Craft*, Pt. I. ch. i., Pardon me . . . if my tongue doe outslip my wit. c. 1680 : L'Estrange, *Seneca's Epistles*, i., He will no more speak fast, than he will run, for fear his tongue should go before his wit. 1738 : Swift, *Polite Convers.*, Dial. I. 1822 : Scott, *Nigel*, ch. viii., Blisters

on my tongue, " it runs too fast for my wit."

22. *Your tongue runs nineteen to the dozen.* 1854 : Baker, *Northants Gloss.*, s.v. " Nineteen," A common expression, when any one talks too fast. "Your tongue runs nineteen to the dozen, there is no getting in a word with you." 1901 : Raymond, *Idler Out of Doors*, 123, Whilst she talked nineteen to the dozen.

See also **Heart** (12); and **Long tongue.**

Too big a gun. *See* quots. 1732 : Fuller, No. 1824, He carries too big a gun for me. 1912 : S. Butler, *Note-Books*, 256, This gentleman had a decided manner and carried quite as many guns as the two barristers . . . who sat opposite to us.

Too big for one's fireplace=Beyond one's means. 1893 : Gower, *Gloss. of Surrey Words*, 16 (E.D.S.), I'm much obliged to you for letting me look at the farm ; but I think that it's too big for my fireplace.

Too busy gets contempt, To be. 1640 : Herbert, *Jac. Prudentum.*

Too far East is West. 1853 : Trench, *Proverbs*, 93 (1905), This proverb, *Extremes meet*, or its parallel, *Too far East is West*, reaches very far into the heart of things.

Too free to be fat. 1670 : Ray, 176. 1681 : Robertson, *Phraseol. Generalis*, 641, Too free to be fat ; Promus magis quam condus.

Too good is stark naught. 1738 : Swift, *Polite Convers.*, Dial. II.

Too hasty burnt his lips. 1623 : Wodroephe, *Spared Houres*, 519.

Too hasty to be a parish clerk. 1633 : Draxe, 10 [" priest " for " clerk "]. 1670 : Ray, 180.

Too heavy or too hot. c. 1386 : Chaucer, *Friar's Tale*, l. 138, I spare nat to taken, god it woot, But if it be to hevy or to hoot. 1542 : Udall, tr. Erasmus' *Apoph.*, 359 (1877), As being a taker and a bribing feloe, and one for whom nothing was to hotte nor to heauie. 1607 : *The Puritan*, I. i., Nothing was too hot, nor too dear for me. 1653 : Urquhart, *Rabelais*, bk. i. ch. xxvii., They robbed both men and women, and took all they could catch :

nothing was either too hot or too heavie for them. 1822 : Scott, *Nigel*, ch. viii., Such a sight, sweetheart, will make one loth to meddle with matters that are too hot or heavy for their handling. 1890 : *N. & Q.*, 7th ser., x. 446, " Nothing but what is too hot and too heavy." This sentence is a proverbial saying in North Notts, and its application is in respect of those who . . . are not particular with regard to the manner in which they procure the means for carrying on their mode of living.

Too high for the stirrup, and not high enough for the saddle. Oxfordsh. 1913: *Folk-Lore*, xxiv. 77.

Too hot to hold. 1639 : Clarke, 178. 1678 : Ray, 346.

Too late to grieve when the chance is past, It is. 1605 : Camden, *Remains*, 326 (1870). 1732 : Fuller, No. 5256.

Too late to spare when all is spent. *c.* 1555 : in Wright, *Songs, etc., Philip and Mary*, 30 (Roxb. Cl.), To latte they spare, when all ys goone. 1639 : Clarke, 262. 1721 : Bailey, *Dict.*, s.v. " Spare." 1853 : Trench, *Proverbs*, 112 (1905). 1874 : *N. & Q.*, 5th ser., i. 205.

Too late to spare when the bottom is bare. 1539: Taverner, *Proverbs*, fo. 32, It is to late sparinge at the bottome. *c.* 1590: G. Harvey, *Marginalia*, 102 (1913) [as in 1539]. 1670 : Ray, 144. 1732 : Fuller, No. 6345.

Too light winning makes the prize light. 1855 : Bohn, 545.

Too low for a hawk, too high for a buzzard. 1919 : Max Beerbohm, *Seven Men*, 100, I had done for myself, so far as *those* people were concerned. And now that I had sampled *them*, what cared I for others ? " Too low for a hawk, too high for a buzzard." That homely old saying seemed to sum me up.

Too many cooks spoil the broth. 1662 : Gerbier, *Discourse of Building*, 24. 1732 : Fuller, No. 4657, The more cooks the worse broth. 1778 : S. Crisp, in D'Arblay, *Diary*, i. 84 (1876), In these cases generally the more cooks the worse broth. *c.* 1804 : J. Austen, *Watsons*, 24 (Walkley, 1923). 1855 : Kingsley, *West. Ho!*, ch. xv. 1921 :

Observer, 15 May, p. 13, col. 5, Eleven clever gentlemen have made this jolly entertainment, and, contrary to custom, too many cooks have not spoiled the broth.

Too many stairs and back-doors makes thieves and whores. 1662 : Gerbier, *Discourse of Building*, 14 [cited as " the old English proverb "].

Too much bed makes a dull head. Derby. 1884 : *Folk-Lore Journal*, ii. 279.

Too much breaks the bag. 1666 : Torriano, *Piazza Univ.*, 244 [" sack " for " bag "]. 1670 : Ray, 26. 1732 : Fuller, No. 5259.

Too much consulting confounds. Ibid., No. 5261.

Too much cordial will destroy. Ibid., No. 5263.

Too much cunning undoes. 1659 : Howell, *Proverbs: Brit.-Eng.*, 3.

Too much diligence is hurtful. 1561 : Hoby, *Courtier*, 61 (T.T.), It hath bene a proverbe emonge some most excellent peincters of old time, that To muche diligence is hurtfull.

Too much liberty spoils all. 1611 : Cotgrave, s.v. " Bandon," Much liberty brings men to the gallowes. 1681 : Robertson, *Phraseol. Generalis*, 822. 1694 : *Terence made English*, 123, For too much liberty corrupts an angel.

" **Too much money makes men mad,** the prouerb plaine doth show." *c.* 1640 : in Rollins, *Cavalier and Puritan*, 117 (1923).

Too much of a good thing. 1601 : Shakespeare, *As You Like It*, IV. i., Why then, can one desire too much of a good thing ? 1611 : Cotgrave, s.v. " Manger," A man may take too much of a good thing. 1809 : Syd. Smith, *Works*, i. 175 (1867) (O.), This (to use a very colloquial phrase) is surely too much of a good thing.

Too much of nothing but of fools and asses. 1639 : Clarke, 73.

Too much of one thing is naught (or good for nothing). *c.* 1386 : Chaucer, *C. Tales*, iv. 645 (Skeat), That that is overdoon, it wol nat preve Aright, as clerkes seyn, it is a vyce. *c.* 1450 : *Abce of Aristotill*, in E.E.T.S., Ext. Ser., 8, p. 66, For to moche of on thynge was

neuer holsome. *c.* 1500 : in *Antiq.
Repertory*, iv. 414 (1809), To muche ys
nought of any maner of thynge. *c.* 1554 :
Interlude of Youth, in Hazlitt, *Old
Plays*, ii. 19, Over-much of one thing is
nought. 1591 : Harington, *Orl. Furioso:* "Allegory," 408 (1634), Our English
prouerbe saith, Too much of one thing
is good for nothing. 1634 : C. Butler,
Feminine Monarchie, 170 [as in 1591].
1681 : Robertson, *Phraseol. Generalis*,
877 [as in 1591]. 1725 : Bailey, tr.
Erasmus' *Colloq.*, 39 [as in 1591]. 1751 :
Fielding, *Amelia*, bk. xi. ch. iii. [as in
1591]. 1871 : *N. & Q.*, 4th ser., viii.
506, [Lancs] Too much of ought Is
good for nought. 1901 : F. E. Taylor,
Lancs Sayings, 10, To' mitch ov owt's
good for nowt.

Too much praise is a burthen. 1669 :
Politeuphuia, 140. 1732 : Fuller, No.
5266.

Too much pudding will choke a dog.
1830 : Colman, jr., in *Hum. Works*, 421
(Hotten). 1917 : Bridge, *Cheshire Proverbs*, 141, Too much pudding would
sade [satiate] a dog.

Too much spoileth, too little is nothing.
1659 : Howell, *Proverbs: Ital.-Eng.*, 12,
Too much spoiles, too little doth not
satisfie. 1732 : Fuller, No. 5268.

Too much taking heed is loss. 1640 :
Herbert, *Jac. Prudentum.*

Too old to learn his accidence, He is
now. 1659 : Howell, 11 (9).

Too proud as too slow, As well. 1594 :
Drayton, *Idea*, lix.

**Too proud to ask is too good to re-
ceive, He that is.** 1732 : Fuller, No.
2194.

Too secure is not safe, He that is.
Ibid., No. 2195.

**Too soon, He's up, That's hanged ere
noon.** Ibid., No. 6279.

Too soon wise to be long old. 1592 :
Greene, *Works*, x. 238 (Grosart), The
neighbours saw, I was too soone wise,
to be long olde. 1594 : Shakespeare,
Rich. III., III. i., So wise, so young,
they say, do never live long. 1738 :
Swift, *Polite Convers.*, Dial. I., I fear
Lady Answerall can't live long, she has
so much wit. 1825 : Scott, in Lockhart's *Life*, vi. 134, I should be sorry

the saying were verified in him—" So
wise, so young, they say do ne'er live
long."

Tooth and Teeth, *subs.* 1. *Tooth and
nail* = By all means possible. [Mani-
bus pedibusque.—Terence, *Andr.*, 161.]
1533 : Udall, *Flowers out of Terence*,
fo. 3, He doeth all thynges . . . with
tothe and nayle, as moche as in him
lyeth. 1565 : Calfhill, *Answer to
Martiall*, 228 (P.S.), Defended with
tooth and nail. 1646 : Wither, *What
Peace to the Wicked?*, 2 (Spens. S.),
Some, for themselves, with tooth, and
naile. 1710 : T. Ward, *Eng. Reform.*,
27 (1716), Then fall with tooth and nail
upon 'em. 1766 : Garrick, *Neck or
Nothing*, II. i., She is not to be trusted
. . . tooth and nail against us. 1850 :
Dickens, *Copperfield*, ch. xlii., I've got
a motive . . . and I go at it tooth and
nail.

2. *Your teeth are longer than your
beard.* 1855 : Bohn, 582.

Too too will in two. Cheshire. 1670 :
Ray, 149. 1901 : F. E. Taylor, *Lancs
Sayings*, 10, Too-too will i' two (Friends
who are too intimate are sure to quarrel). 1917 : Bridge, *Cheshire Proverbs*,
141.

Top. *As soon drive a top over a tiled
house.* 1546 : Heywood, *Proverbs*, Pt.
II. ch. v., I shall as soone trie him or
take him this waie, As dryve a top ouer
a tyeld house. 1659 : Howell, 3, You
may drive a toppe over a tylde house
as soon. 1678 : Ray, 291, As good as
ever drave top over til'd house.

Top-heavy, He is = He is drunk.
1678 : Ray, 87. 1736 : Bailey, *Dict.*,
s.v. 1825 : Hone, *Ev. Day Book*, ii.
859, Being top-heavy with liquor.

**Topmost branch is not the safest
perch, The.** 1875 : Cheales, *Proverb.
Folk-Lore*, 103.

Totnes, Devon. *See* quot. 1850 :
N. & Q., 1st ser., ii. 511, Here I sit,
and here I rest, And this town shall be
called Totness. [Said to have been
spoken by Brutus of Troy, when he
landed there!]

Tottenham, Middlesex. 1. *Tottenham
is turned French.* 1536 : Norfolk, to
Cromwell, in *Cal. Lett., etc., Henry VIII.*

ii. No. 233, It is further written to me that a bruit doth run that I should be in the Tower of London. When I shall deserve to be there Totynham shall turn French. 1546 : Heywood, *Proverbs*, Pt. I. ch. vii. 1631 : W. Bedwell, *Briefe Descrip. of . . . Tottenham*, sig. D3, Three prouerbs, commonly by the neighbours vsed and spoken of Tottenham. The first of those is *Tottenham is turn'd French.* 1662 : Fuller, *Worthies*, ii. 314 (1840). 1790 : Grose, *Prov. Gloss.*, s.v. "London."

2. *When Tottenham Wood is all on fire, Then Tottenham Street is nought but mire.* 1631 : Bedwell, *ut supra*, sig. D4. 1662 : Fuller, *Worthies*, ii. 314 (1840). 1790 : Grose, *Prov. Gloss.*, s.v. "London." 1893 : Inwards, *Weather Lore*, 51.

3. *You shall as easily remove Tottenham-wood.* 1631 : Bedwell, *ut supra*, sig. D4. 1790 : Grose, *Prov. Gloss.*, s.v. "London."

Touch, verb. 1. *I would not touch him with a pair of tongs.* 1639 : Clarke, 34, Not to be handled with a pair of tongues. 1658 : *Wit Restor'd*, 159, For without a payre of tongs no man will touch her. 1732 : Fuller, No. 2649, I will not touch her with a pair of tongs. 1854 : Dickens, *Hard Times*, bk. i. ch. iv., I was so ragged and dirty that you wouldn't have touched me with a pair of tongs. 1876 : Blackmore, *Cripps*, ch. iii., As if I would touch him with a pair of tongs, sir! 1901 : F. E. Taylor, *Lancs Sayings*, 33, Aw wouldno' touch him wi' a pair o' tungs.

2. *To touch to the quick.* 1546 : Heywood, *Proverbs*, Pt. I. ch. vi., Practyse in all, aboue all toucheth the quicke. 1567 : Golding, *Ovid*, bk. vi. l. 162, And that did touch Minerva to the quicke. 1602 : Shakespeare, *Hamlet*, II. ii., I'll tent him to the quick. Before 1658 : Cleveland, *Works*, 131 (1742), There I confess I am touched to the quick. 1742 : Fielding, *Andrews*, bk. i. ch. xvii., The last appellation stung her to the quick. 1823 : Scott, *St. Ronan's*, ch. xxix., But when you touch me to the quick . . . you cannot expect me to endure without wincing. 1855 : Kings-

ley, *West. Ho!*, ch. i., Her last words had touched him to the quick.

3. *Touch and take.* 1591 : Florio, *Second Frutes*, 197, Touch and take, take and holde. 1620 : *Two Merry Milkmaids*, IV. ii., I know what the prouerbe saies, touch me and take me. 1662 : Davenant, *Law against Lovers*, IV., My grandam left me nothing at her death But a good old proverb, that's Touch and Take. 1819 : Scott, *Bride of L.*, ch. ix., Touch and try—the gold is good as ever was weighed.

4. *Touch pot, touch penny*=No credit given. 1654 : Gayton, *Pleasant Notes Don Q.*, 83. 1720 : Swift, *Elegy on Mr. Demar*, He touched the pence when others touched the pot. 1772 : Graves, *Spirit. Quixote*, bk. iii. ch. ii., We know the custom at such houses . . . 'tis touch pot, touch penny—we only want money's worth for our money. 1822 : Scott, *Nigel*, ch. xvi., Since touch pot touch penny makes every man equal.

5. *Touch wood, it's sure to come good.* 1906 : *N. & Q.*, 10th ser., vi. 231.

Touch-stone trieth gold, As the, so gold trieth the hearts of men. 1598 : Meres, *Palladis*, fo. 204, As golde is tried by the touchstone, so riches do shew what is in a man. 1669 : *Politeuphuia*, 130. 1732 : Fuller, No. 736 [omitting "the hearts of"].

Tough as leather, As. 1611 : Cotgrave, s.v. "Corias." 1678 : Ray, 290, As tough as whitleather. 1843 : Mrs. Carlyle, *Lett.*, i. 219 (1883) (O.), The "cold fowl" was . . . as tough as leather.

Tow. *To have tow on one's distaff*= To have business on hand, to have "eggs on the spit." *c.* 1386 : Chaucer, *Miller's Tale*, l. 588, He hadde more tow on his distaf Than Gerveys knew. 1412 : Hoccleve, *Regement*, 45 (E.E.T.S.), Tow on my distaf haue I for to spynne, Morë, my fadir, than ye wot of yit. 1533 : Heywood, *Pard. and Friar*, in Hazlitt, *Old Plays*, i. 238, I have more tow on my distaff than I can well spin. 1732 : Fuller, No. 4128, She hath other tow on her distaff. 1818 : Scott, *Fam. Letters*, ii. 4 (1894), I did not much write him *con amore*

. . . above all, I had too much flax on my distaff. 1906 : Doyle, *Sir Nigel*, ch. xxvi., By my ten finger-bones! . . . he found more on his distaff that time than he knew how to spin.

Tower of London. *See* **Fool** (22).

Towers build masons. 1639 : Clarke, 8.

Town-bull is a bachelor, Then the— i.e. as soon as such an one. 1678 : Ray, 66.

Tracies. 1. *The Tracies have always the wind in their faces.* 1662 : Fuller, *Worthies*, i. 552 (1840). 1790 : Grose, *Prov. Gloss.*, s.v. "Gloucestershire." 1897 : Norway, *H. and B. in Devon, etc.*, 378, Who has not heard of the weird of the Tracys, with ever the wind and the rain in their faces. 1905: *N. & Q.*, 10th ser., iv. 335.

2. *See* quot. 1906 : Vincent, *H. and B. in Berks*, 121, "The Tracys, the Lacys, and the Fettiplaces Own all the manors, the parks, and the chases," says the old rhyme.

Trade, *subs.* 1. *A handful of trade is worth a handful of gold.* 1736 : Bailey, *Dict.*, s.v.

2. *A trade is better than service.* 1640 : Herbert, *Jac. Prudentum*.

3. *He that changes his trade.* *See* quots. 1611 : Cotgrave, s.v. "Panier," He that meddles with another mans trade, milkes his cow in a pannier [basket]. 1710 : S. Palmer, *Moral Essays on Proverbs*, 89, He that changes his trade makes soop in a basket.

4. *He that hath a trade.* *See* quot. 1611 : Cotgrave, s.v. "Mestier," He that hath a good trade hath a goodly revenue. 1640 : Herbert, *Jac. Prudentum*, He that learns a trade, hath a purchase made. 1736 : Franklin, *Way to Wealth*, in *Works*, i. 444 (Bigelow), He that hath a trade, hath an estate. 1772 : Franklin, in *Works*, iv. 538, The proverb says, " He who has a trade has an office of profit and honour."

5. *Trade is the mother of money.* 1633 : Draxe, 207. 1670 : Ray, 27. 1732 : Fuller, No. 5271.

See also **Good trade**; **Man** (28); and **Two of a trade.**

Trail a light harrow, To. 1828 :

Carr, *Craven Dialect*, i. 213, " To trail a leet [light] harrow." This expression alludes to the comforts of single blessedness. 1855 : Robinson, *Whitby Gloss.*, 79, He trails a light harrow, his hat covers his family.

Traitors. *See* quot. 1678 : Ray, 82, Are there traitours at the table that the loaf is turn'd the wrong side upwards ? *See also* **Treason.**

Traitors' Bridge [Tower of London], **A loyal heart may be landed under.** 1662 : Fuller, *Worthies*, ii. 347 (1840). 1790: Grose, *Prov. Gloss.*, s.v. " London."

Trap, To understand (or **To be up to**). 1679 : *Counterfeits*, III. i., You're deceiv'd in old Gomez, he understands trap. 1699 : Farquhar, *Love and a Bottle*, III., We understand trap, sir, you must not catch old birds with chaff. 1700 : Ward, *London Spy*, 148 (1924), The rest . . . look'd as if they had understood trap this twenty years. 1821 : Scott, *Pirate*, ch. iv., His good lady (who understood trap as well as any woman in the Mearns) . . . 1828: Carr, *Craven Dialect*, ii. 217, " To be up to trap," to be cunning in business, to be sharp-witted in promoting self-interest. 1854 : Baker, *Northants Gloss.*, s.v. " Trap " [as in 1828]

Trash and trumpery is the highway to beggary. 1678: Ray, 211. 1732 : Fuller, No. 6091.

Travel makes a wise man better, but a fool worse. Ibid., No. 5272.

Travel, *verb.* 1. *He that travels far knows much.* 1639: Clarke, 276. 1670 : Ray, 149. 1732 : Fuller, No. 2335 [with " much " for " far "].

2. *He travelled with Mandeville.* Ibid., No. 2374.

3. *He who travelleth not by sea, knows not what the fear of God is.* 1623 : Wodroephe, *Spared Houres*, 230.

Traveller, *subs.* 1. *A traveller may lie by authority.* 1509 : Barclay, *Ship of Fools*, ii. 68 (1874), There thre sortes be Of people lyuynge, whiche may themselfe defende In lesynge [lying], for they haue auctoryte to lye. The first is pylgrymes that hath great wonders sene In strange countres, suche may say what they wyll. *c.* 1598 :

Deloney, *Gentle Craft*, Pt. II. ch. vi., Trauellers . . . haue liberty to vtter what lies they list. 1630 : Brathwait, *Eng. Gent.*, etc., 77 (1641), Whence it is said, that travellers, poets and lyars, are three words al of one signification. 1683 : Dryden and Lee, *Duke of Guise*, IV. iv., If he has been a traveller, he certainly says true ; for he may lie by authority. 1744–6: Mrs. Haywood, *Fem. Spectator*, iii. 283 (1771), There is a kind of latitude, they say, given to travellers to exceed the truth. 1813 : Byron, in *Letters*, etc., ii. 311 (Prothero), I never have, and never should have, alluded to it on my own authority, from respect to the ancient proverb on Travellers. Cf. **Old**, A (*b*) (14); and **Painters**.

2. *A traveller must have. See* quots. The details of equipment vary. 1591 : Florio, *Second Frutes*, 93, If you will be a traueller . . . haue alwayes the eies of a faulcon . . . the eares of an asse . . . the face of an ape . . . the mouth of a hog . . . the shoulder of a camell . . . the legges of a stagg . . . and see that you neuer want two bagges very full, that is one of pacience . . . and another of money. 1594: Nashe, *Works*, v. 141 (Grosart), A traueller must haue the backe of an asse to bear all, a tung like the tayle of a dog to flatter all, the mouth of a hog to eate what is set before him, the eare of a merchant to heare all and say nothing. 1611 : in Coryat, *Crudities*, i. 44 *n.* (1905), Note reader that a traveller must have the backe of an asse, the mouth of a sow, the eye of a hawke, a merchants eare, etc. 1616 : *Rich Cabinet*, fo. 147, Traueller must haue the head of a philosopher . . . the heart of a lyon . . . the mouth of a swine . . . the eyes of a hawke . . . the backe of an asse . . . the legges of a cammell . . . and the vigilancy of a cocke. 1666 : Torriano, *Piazza Univ.*, 157 [a slightly varied copy of 1591]. 1678 : Ray, 296, To travell safely through the world a must have a falcons eye, an asses eares, an apes face, a merchants words, a camells back, a hogs mouth, and a harts legs.

3. *Much spends the traveller more than the abider.* 1640 : Herbert, *Jac. Prud.*

Treacle Town=Macclesfield. 1917 : Bridge, *Cheshire Proverbs*, 146, No good reason has ever been given why it is so called.

Tread on a worm. *See* **Worm** (3).

Tread one's shoe awry, To = To be guilty of a lapse from virtue. *c.* 1422 : Hoccleve, *Minor Poems*, xxiv. 66 (O.), No womman . . . But swich oon as hath trode hir shoo amis. 1562 : Heywood, *Epigr.*, 6th hund., No. 21, My wife doth euer tread hir shooe a wry. 1590 : *Tarltons Newes*, 75 (Sh. S.), A faire wife, that . . . could not treade right, yet wrincht hir shoe inward . . . as secret as she was false. 1616 : Sharpham, *Cupid's Whirligig*, IV., She hath neuer trode her foot awry. 1639 : D'Urfey, *Richmond Heiress*, II. ii., A foolish female nice and shy, That never yet trod shooe awry. 1710 : Ward, *Nuptial Dialogues*, i. 141, But I defy Your servile spies to prove I've trod awry.

Treason, To love the, but hate the traitor. 1614 : C. Brooke, *Rich. Third*, 109 (Grosart), They loue no traytors, that doe traytors vse. 1683 : Dryden and Lee, *Duke of Guise*, III. i., Hate then the traitor, but yet love the treason. 1692 : L'Estrange, *Æsop*, 172 (3rd ed.), We love the treason but we hate the traytor. 1712 : Motteux, *Quixote*, Pt. I. bk. iv. ch. xii., Who made good to them our Spanish proverb, that the treason pleases, but the traitors are odious.

Treasure is tickle. 1583 : Melbancke, *Philotinus*, sig. E3.

Tree and Trees, *subs.* 1. *A good tree is a good shelter.* 1732 : Fuller, No. 182.

2. *As a tree falls so must it lie.* 1549 : Latimer, *Seven Sermons*, 118 (Arber), Wheresoeuer the tree falleth . . . there it shall rest. 1556 : Heywood, *Spider and Flie*, cap. 88, p. 380 (Farmer), Where the tree falleth there lieth it,— clerks say so. *c.* 1630 : in *Roxb. Ballads*, i. 143 (B.S.), And as he [the tree] falls, so doth he lye. 1820 : Scott, *Monastery*, ch. viii., There lies the faded

tree, and as it fell, so it lies. 1921 : Hudson, *Trav. in Little Things*, ch. iii.

3. *Large trees give more shade than fruit.* 1855 : Bohn, 439.

4. *Set trees poor and they will grow rich, set them rich and they will grow poor.* 1678 : Ray, 350. 1846 : Denham, *Proverbs*, 3 (Percy S.).

5. *The highest tree hath the greatest fall.* 1605 : Camden, *Remains*, 333 (1870). 1670 : Ray, 13. 1736 : Bailey, *Dict.*, s.v. " Tree," The higher the tree the greater the fall.

6. *There is no tree but bears some fruit.* 1616 : Breton, in *Works*, ii. *e* 8 (Grosart), There is no tree but beareth fruit. 1670 : Ray, 149.

7. *The tree falls not at the first blow.* Before 1500 : in Hill, *Commonplace-Book*, 128 (E.E.T.S.), Hit is a febill tre that fallith at the first strok. 1666 : Torriano, *Piazza Univ.*, 48. 1736 : Bailey, *Dict.*, s.v. " Tree " [" stroke " for " blow "].

8. *The tree is known by its fruit.* 1564 : Bullein, *Dialogue*, 86 (E.E.T.S.), You shal know that fruicte by the tree. c. 1630 : in *Roxb. Ballads*, i. 143 (B.S.). 1670 : Ray, 11, A tree is known by the fruit, and not by the leaves. 1719 : Prior, in Peck, *Desid. Curiosa*, 222 (1779). 1861 : Peacock, *Gryll Grange*, ch. v., If you know the tree by its fruit . . . Cf. Such tree.

9. *The tree that grows slowly keeps itself for another.* 1640 : Herbert, *Jac. Prudentum.*

10. *Trees eat but once.* Ibid.

11. *When the tree is fallen, all go with their hatchet.* 1586 : Young, tr. Guazzo's *Civil Convers.* fo. 206, The tree is no sooner fallen downe to the grounde, but euerie one is readie to runne vppon it with his hatchette. 1640 : Herbert, *Jac. Prudentum.* 1732 : Fuller, No. 4804, The tree is no sooner down, but every one runs for his hatchet. 1875 : Cheales, *Proverb. Folk-Lore*, 154, When the tree is down every one runs with his hatchet.

Treelton. *See* Bolsover.

Tregeagle, He roars like. 1864 : " Cornish Proverbs," in *N. & Q.*, 3rd ser., vi. 6. 1865 : Hunt, *Pop. Romances*

W. of Eng., 143 (1896), " Roaring or howling like Tregeagle," is a common expression amongst the vulgar in Cornwall. 1913 : E. M. Wright, *Rustic Speech, etc.*, 196 [Mrs. Wright tells the legend at length].

Tregoney. *See* quot. 1906 : Q.-Couch, *Mayor of Troy*, Prol., The Mayor of Tregoney, who could read print upside-down, but wasn't above being spoken to.

Tre, Pol and Pen, By, You shall know the Cornish men. 1602 : Carew, *Survey of Cornwall*, 149 (1811). 1662 : Fuller, *Worthies*, i. 306 (1840). 1750 : R. Heath, *Acc. of Scilly*, 338, By Tre, Pol, and Pen, Ross, Caer, and Lan, You know Cornish men. 1821 : Scott, *Kenilworth*, ch. i. [" may " for " shall "]. 1864 : " Cornish Proverbs," in *N. & Q.*, 3rd ser., v. 208 [as in 1750, but with " shall " before " know," and " all " before " Cornish "]. 1928 : *Sphere*, 7 Jan., 36, This, of course, is Cornwall . . . the country of " Tre, Pol, and Pen."

Trick, subs. 1. *A trick to catch an old one.* 1608 : Middleton [title of play]. c. 1624 : Davenport, *King John*, IV. iii., 'Twas well yet that the trick has catch'd this old one.

2. *A trick worth two of that.* 1597 : Shakespeare, 1 *Henry IV.*, II. i. 1619 : Chapman, *Two Wise Men*, V. i. c. 1620 : Barnavelt, IV. i., in Bullen, *Old Plays*, ii. 272, I know a trick worth ten o' that. 1772 : Graves, *Spirit. Quixote*, bk. iii. ch. xv. 1879 : R. L. S., *Story of a Lie*, ch. vi.

3. *Trick for trick.* 1659 : Howell, 4, Trick for trick, and a stone in thy foot besides, quoth one pulling out a stone out of his mares hoof, when she bit him upon the back, and he her upon the buttock. 1670 : Ray, 217 [as in 1659]. 1710 : Ward, *Nuptial Dialogues*, ii. 51, Women . . . love to shew us trick for trick. 1730 : Bailey, *Dict.*, s.v. " Quid pro quo," Quid pro quo . . . trick for trick, a Rowland for an Oliver.

Trig as a linnet. 1892 : Heslop, *Northumb. Words*, 744 (E.D.S.), " Trig as a lennard (spruce as a linnet) "—Newcastle proverb.

Trim as a trencher. *c.* 1540 : Bale, *Kynge Johan*, 98 (Camden S.), Trymme as a trencher, havynge his shoes of golde. 1542 : Udall, tr. Erasmus' *Apoph.*, 276 (1877), Filling vp as trimme as a trencher the space that stoode voide, with his own hand. [In the Appendix, Mr. R. Roberts, the editor and publisher of this reprint, says: "A proverbial saying which may still be heard occasionally, in the country, although trenchers have almost entirely disappeared. A new trencher, neatly turned out of sycamore wood, had a particularly clean and wholesome appearance."]

Trimmingham. *See* **Gimmingham.**

Trim tram, like master like man— with variants. 1583 : Melbancke, *Philotinus*, sig. D3, Trim tram, neither good for God nor man. 1653 : Middleton and Rowley, *Span. Gipsy*, IV. iii., Trim, tram, hang master, hang man ! 1681 : Robertson, *Phraseol. Generalis*, 1246. 1714: Ozell, *Molière*, i. 159. 1762: Smollett, *Sir L. Greaves*, ch. xiii. 1785 : Grose, *Class. Dict. Vulgar Tongue*, s.v.

Tring, Wing and Ivinghoe. 1. *See* quots. 1820 : *Gent. Mag.*, ii. 326, Tring, Wing, and Ivinghoe, did go, For striking the Black Prince a blow. *N. & Q.*, 3rd ser., v. 176, The name of Ivanhoe was suggested [to Scott], as the story goes, by an old rhyme recording three names of the manors forfeited by the ancestor of the celebrated Hampden, for striking the Black Prince a blow with his racket, when they quarrelled at tennis . . . "Tring, Wing and Ivanhoe, For striking of a blow, Hampden did forego, And glad he could escape so." [Unluckily for the legend these manors were never in the Hampden family.]

2. *Tring, Wing, and Ivinghoe, Three dirty villages all in a row And never without a rogue or two. Would you know the reason why?* *Leighton Buzzard is hard by.* 1852 : *N. & Q.*, 1st ser., v. 619.

Tripe-broth is better than no porridge. 1732 : Fuller, No. 5274.

Tripe's good meat if it be well wip't. 1678 : Ray, 50.

Trojan, Like a. 1846 : Planché, *Extravag.*, iii. 143 (1879), Upon them ! forward ! charge like Trojans !—go ! 1855 : Dickens, *Holly Tree*, Branch 2, He went on a lying like a Trojan about the pony. 1883 : R. L. S., *Treasure I.*, ch. xviii., He had lain like a Trojan behind his mattress in the gallery.

Trot sire, trot dam. *See* quot. 1560 : Wilson, *Rhetorique*, 119 (1909), Trot sire, and trot damme, how should the fole amble, that is, when both father and mother were nought, it is not like that the childe will proue good. Cf. **Foal.**

Trouble, *subs.* 1. *Let your trouble tarry till its own day comes.* 1732 : Fuller, No. 3200. Cf. No. 2.

2. *Never trouble trouble till trouble troubles you.* Derby. 1884: *Folk-Lore Journal*, ii. 280. 1921: R. L. Gales, *Old-World Essays*, 243 [quoted as a West-Country saying]. Cf. No. 1.

3. *To have one's trouble for one's pains.* *See* **Labour.**

See also **Seek** (4).

Trout. *See* quot. 1893 : Inwards, *Weather Lore*, 142, When trout refuse bait or fly, There ever is a storm a-nigh. *See also* **Chevin;** and **Sound.**

Troy was not took in a day. 1732 : Fuller, No. 5278.

True, *adj.* 1. *All be not true that speak fair.* *c.* 1460 : *How the Good Wife*, l. 65.

2. *As true as a corranto.* 1632 : D. Lupton, *London and Country :* "Country," No. 12, They [news sheets] have used this trade so long, that now every one can say, its even as true as a currantoe, meaning that its all false.

3. *As true as a turtle.* *c.* 1380 : Chaucer, *Parl. of Foules*, l. 355, The wedded turtel with hir herte trewe. *c.* 1440 : Hoccleve, *Minor Poems*, 141 (E.E.T.S.), As treewe as turtle that lakkith hir feere [mate]. *c.* 1470 : *Songs and Carols*, 88 (Percy S.), That women be trew as tyrtyll on tre. 1590 : Spenser, *F. Q.*, III. xi. 2, That was as trew in love as turtle to her make. 1670 : Ray, 203, As true as a turtle to her mate. 1720 : Gay, *Poems*, ii. 280 (Underhill), Tho' seeming as the turtle kind, And like the gospel true.

4. *As true as God is in heaven.* 1737 :
Ray, 226. 1869 : FitzGerald, *Sea
Words and Phrases*, 16, As true as God's
in heaven, here comes Lord Rochford.
1923 : *Folk-Lore*, xxxiv. 329 (Oxfordshire).

5. *As true as steel.* 1303 : Brunne,
Handl. Synne, l. 2338, And to the ded
was as trew as steyl. *c.* 1385 : Chaucer,
Leg. Good Women, ix. l. 21, Pitouse, sadde,
wyse, and trewe as steel. *c.* 1480 :
Digby Plays, 116 (E.E.T.S.), Now, as
thou hast byn trew as stylle. 1553 :
Googe, *Pop. Kingdome*, bk. iv. l. 537,
And sure with no dissembling heart,
for true as steele they bee. 1676 :
Shadwell, *Virtuoso*, III. 1713 : Gay,
Wife of Bath, V. iii. 1824 : Scott,
Redgauntlet, ch. xvi., I am trusty as
steel to owners, and always look after
cargo. 1849 : Brontë, *Shirley*, ch. ix.
1923 : Lucas, *Advisory Ben*, § xxxix.
p. 208.

6. *As true as that the candle ate the
cat*—with variants. 1666 : Torriano,
Piazza Univ., 242, The English say, As
true as that the candle ate the cat.
1700 : Ward, *London Spy*, 230 (1924)
[as in 1666, but with " plain " for
" true "]. 1732 : Fuller, No. 4351,
That is as true that the cat crew, and
the cock rock'd the cradle.

7. *As true as the dial to the sun.* 1663 :
Butler, *Hudibras*, III. ii. 174, True as
the dial to the sun Although it be not
shined upon. 1742 : Fielding, *Andrews*,
bk. i. ch. xviii., She was as true to her
husband as the dial to the sun.

8. *As true as the Gospel.* 1540 : Palsgrave, *Acolastus*, sig. Q3, That is as
trewe as the gospell. 1577 : *Misogonus*, III. i. 1633 : Draxe, 210.
1753 : Richardson, *Grandison*, i. 30
(1883). 1828 : Carr, *Craven Dialect*,
i. 193, " It's as true as t' gospel," a
common asseveration. 1872 : Hardy,
Greenwood Tree, Pt. I. ch. ii., " That's
as true as gospel of this member,"
said Reuben. 1926 : Phillpotts, *Yellow
Sands*, III., Is it true what these old men
be telling ? *Arthur.* True as Gospel!

9. *As true as velvet.* 1608 : *Merry
Devil of Edm.*, IV. i., Thou speakst as
true as velvet. Cf. **Velvet.**

10. *A true friend is known in a doubtful matter.* 1591 : Lodge, *Catharos*,
13 (Hunt. Cl.) [quoted as " an olde
prouerbe "].

11. *A true jest is no jest. c.* 1386 :
Chaucer, *Cook's Prol.*, l. 33, But " sooth
pley, quaad [evil] pley," as the Fleming
seith. 1546 : Heywood, *Proverbs*, Pt.
II. ch. viii., Sooth bourd is no bourd.
1591 : Harington, *Apol. of Poetrie*, par.
9 [as in 1546]. 1633 : Draxe, 99 [as
in 1546]. 1824 : Scott, *Redgauntlet*,
ch. xii., The lady drew up, and the
Provost said, half aside, " The sooth
bourd is nae bourd." 1825 : Hone,
Ev. Day Book, i. 506, To talk now of
" no joke like a true joke " is scarcely
passable.

12. *A true man and a thief think
differently. c.* 1386 : Chaucer, *Squire's
Tale*, l. 529, But sooth is seyd, gon
sithen many a day, " A trew wight and
a theef thenken nat oon."

13. *He is a true friend. See* quot.
Before 1500 : in Hill, *Commonplace-
Book*, 131 (E.E.T.S.), He ys a trew
frend, that loveth me for my love and
not for my good [goods, wealth].

14. *He that is true. See* quots. *c.* 1300 :
King Alisaunder, l. 7367, Who-so is
of dede untreowe Ofte hit schal him
sorë reowe. *c.* 1390 : Gower, *Conf.
Amantis*, bk. vii. l. 1961, The proverbe
is, who that is trewe, Him schal his
while nevere rewe.

15. *It must be true that all men say.*
1546 : Heywood, *Proverbs*, Pt. I. ch.
xi., It must needes be true that euery
man sayth. 1570 : A. Barclay, *Mirrour of Good Manners*, 52 (Spens. S.), It
nedes muste be true which euery man
doth say. 1670 : Ray, 56, That is true
which all men say. 1748 : Richardson,
Clarissa, iv. 118 (1785), What every
one says must be true. 1829 : Scott,
Geierstein, ch. xxii., How should that
be false which all men say is true ?

16. *Many a true word is spoken in
jest. c.* 1386 : Chaucer, *Monk's Prol.*,
l. 76, Ful ofte in game a sooth I have
herd seye. *c.* 1665 : in *Roxb. Ballads*,
vii. 366 (B.S.), Many a true word
hath been be spoke in jest. 1738 : Swift,
Polite Convers., Dial. I. 1892 : Shaw,

Widowers' Houses, I. 1920 : H. Lucy, *Diary of Journalist,* 21.

17. *That's as true as I am his uncle.* 1678 : Ray, 83.

18. *The truest jests sound worst in guilty ears.* 1670 : Ray, 14.

19. *True blood may not lie. c.* 1489 : Caxton, *Sonnes of Aymon,* 248 (E.E.T.S.), But as men sayen "true blood may not lye."

20. *True blue will never stain.* [*c.* 1630 : in *Roxb. Ballads,* iii. 257 (B.S.), That showes a good fellow true blew.] *c.* 1660 : in Ibid., iv. 495 (B.S.), You know true blew will never stain. 1727 : *Harl. MS.,* quoted in *Roxb. Ballads,* iv. 495 (B.S.), True blue was the colour which never will stain. 1732 : Fuller, No. 5279. 1875 : Cheales, *Proverb. Folk-Lore,* 106.

21. *True lovers are shy, when people are by. c.* 1760 : Foote, *Lame Lover,* II. [quoted as " the old proverb "].

22. *True praise roots and spreads.* 1640 : Herbert, *Jac. Prudentum.* 1670 : Ray, 21 [" takes root " for " roots "]. 1736 : Bailey, *Dict.* [as in 1670].

Trugs i' th' Hole or by Brokken Cross, Oather by. 1917 : Bridge, *Cheshire Proverbs,* 99.

Trumpeter is dead, Your. 1729 : Franklin, *Busy-Body,* No. 1, in *Works,* i. 329 (Bigelow), I am cautious of praising myself, lest I should be told my trumpeter's dead. 1854 : Baker, *Northants Gloss.,* s.v. " Trumpeter," Trumpeter. An egotist. . . . Sometimes it is said, " your trumpeter's dead " ; i.e. no one sounds your praises, so you are compelled to extol yourself.

Trumps, To be put to one's. 1559 : *Mirr. Mag. Jack Cade,* xx. (O.), Ere he took me, I put him to his trumps. 1588 : *Mar-Prelate's Epitome,* 13 (1843), It would put a man to his trumps, to answer these things soundly. 1615 : B. & F., *Cupid's Revenge,* IV. i., What is in 't [in a petition] I know not ; but it has put him to his trumps. 1730 : in *Walpole Ballads,* 35 (Oxford, 1916), And for shifts and excuses Sir William he pumps ; Ay, and Bobby the Screen too was put to his trumps. 1825 : Scott, in Lockhart's *Life,* vi. 7, The

great Roman general, Agricola, was strangely put to his trumps at the *Urbs Orrea.*

Trunch. See Gimmingham.

Truro, Cornwall. 1. *Pride of Truro.* 1602 : Carew, *Survey of Cornwall,* 220 (1811), Some of the idle disposed Cornishmen nick their towns with by-words, as . . . " Pride of Truro." 1864 : " Cornish Proverbs," in *N. & Q.,* 3rd ser., v. 275, The Good Fellowship of Padstow ; Pride of Truro ; Gallants of Foy.

2. *See* quot. 1662 : Fuller, *Worthies,* i. 306 (1840), " Tru-ru, Triveth-en, Ombdina geveth Try-ru." Which is to say, " Truru consisteth of three streets ; and it shall in time be said, Here Tru-ru stood."

Trust, *subs.* 1. *In trust is treason. c.* 1460 : *Good Wyfe wold a Pylgremage,* l. 76, Syt not with no man a-loune, for oft in trust ys tressoun. *c.* 1475 : *Mankind,* sc. iii. st. 107. 1575 : Gascoigne, *Posies,* in *Works,* i. 404 (Cunliffe). 1628 : Rous, *Diary,* 30 (Camden S.), In greatest trust is often greatest treason. 1670 : Ray, 149.

2. *This day there is no trust, but come to-morrow.* 1732 : Fuller, No. 4999. 1855 : Bohn, 412, I sell nothing on trust till to-morrow.

3. *Trust is dead, ill payment killed it.* 1666 : Torriano, *Piazza Univ.,* 184. 1911 : T. Edwardes, *Neighbourhood,* 109, [Public-house inscription] Poor Trust is dead : bad pay killed him.

4. *Trust is the mother of deceit.* 1605 : Camden, *Remains,* 332 (1870).

Trust, *verb.* 1. *Do not trust nor contend, Nor lay wagers, nor lend, And you'll have peace to your life's end.* 1732 : Fuller, No. 6351.

2. *He who trusteth not is not deceived.* Ibid., No. 2406.

3. *He who trusts all things to chance, makes a lottery of his life.* Ibid., No. 2407.

4. *If you trust before you try, you may repent before you die. c.* 1560 : in Huth, *Ancient Ballads, etc.,* 221 (1867), Who trusts before he tries may soone his trust repent. 1670 : Ray, 149. 1732 : Fuller, No. 6084.

5. *I'll trust him no farther than I can fling him.* 1618: Harington, *Epigrams*, bk. ii. No. 74, That he might scant trust him so farre as throw him. 1670: Ray, 197. 1732: Fuller, No. 5286, Trust him no further than you can throw him. 1901: F. E. Taylor, *Lancs Sayings*, 33, Aw'd trust him no furr nor aw could throw a bull bi t' tail. 1916: B. Duffy, *The Counter-Charm*, 14, I wouldn't trust her as far as I could throw her.

6. *I'll trust him no farther than I can see him.* 1594: *True Trag. Rich. Third*, 17 (Sh. S.), Ile trust neuer . . . a Duke in the world, further then I see him. 1611: Cotgrave, s.v. "Croire," To trust no man further then he sees him. 1694: *Terence made English*, 91, I'll trust ye no farther than I can see ye. 1869: Spurgeon, *John Ploughman*, ch. xviii., You may trust some men as far as you can see them, but no further.

7. *In whom I trust most.* See quots. c. 1450: *Partonope*, 110 (E.E.T.S.), Ther-fore men saith an olde sawe : He to whom a man do trest Euermore may dysceyve hym best. Before 1500 : in Hill, *Commonplace-Book*, 130 (E.E.T.S.), In whom I trust most, sounest me deseyvith.

8. *I will not trust him though he were my brother.* 1546 : Heywood, *Proverbs*, Pt. I. ch. xi. 1639 : Clarke, 140.

9. *Trusting often makes fidelity.* 1732 : Fuller, No. 5292.

10. *Trust me, but look to thyself.* Ibid., No. 5288.

11. *Trust none better than thyself.* c. 1460 : *How the Good Wife*, l. 125, Leue none better than thi selfe.

12. *Trust not a new friend nor an old enemy.* 1569 : Grafton, *Chron.*, ii. 84 (1809), None of vs I beleue is so vn-wise . . . to trust a newe friend made of an olde foe. Before 1634 : Chapman, *Alphonsus*, I. i., Trust not a recon-ciled friend, for good turns cannot blot out old grudges. 1875 : Cheales, *Pro-verb. Folk - Lore*, 95. Cf. **Reconciled friend.**

13. *You may trust him with untold gold.* 1633 : Draxe, 209, A man may, etc. 1670 : Ray, 197. 1711 : *Spec-*tator, No. 202, His master . . . could trust him with untold gold. 1870 : T. W. Robertson, *Birth*, I., I'd trust him with untold gold.

See also **Try** (2).

Truth, *subs.* 1. *Fair fall truth and daylight.* 1678 : Ray, 211.

2. *In too much dispute truth is lost.* 1659 : Howell, *Proverbs: Fr.-Eng.*, 1.

3. *Tell the truth and shame the devil.* 1552 : Latimer, *Sermons*, 506 (P.S.), There is a common saying amongst us, "Say the truth and shame the devil." 1597 : Shakespeare, 1 *Henry IV.*, III. i. 1616 : Jonson, *Devil is an Ass*, V. v., I will tell truth, And shame the fiend. 1670 : Cotton, *Scarronides*, bk. iv. 1710 : Centlivre, *Man's Bewitch'd*, III. i. 1823 : Scott, *Peveril*, ch. iv., Faith, neighbours, to say truth, and shame the devil, I do not like the sound of it above half. Cf. No. 22.

4. *Truth and sweet oil always come to the top.* 1620 : Shelton, *Quixote*, Pt. II. ch. x., Truth . . . tramples on the lie as oil doth upon water. 1640 : Her-bert, *Jac. Prudentum*, Truth and oil are ever above. 1732 : Fuller, No. 5295 [as in 1640]. 1865 : "Lancs Pro-verbs," in *N. & Q.*, 3rd ser., viii. 494. 1901 : F. E. Taylor, *Lancs Sayings*, 10, Truth an' sweet-oil awlus cum'n to th' top.

5. *Truth fears no colours.* 1732 : Fuller, No. 5296.

6. *Truth finds foes where it should find none.* 1572 : T. Wilson, *Disc. upon Usury*, 188 (1925), It is a common say-ing, *Veritas odium parit*, Truth pur-chaseth hatred. 1660 : Howell, *Parly of Beasts*, 51, Truth, as the proverb runs, begets hatred often times in the minds of those to whom it is spoken. 1670 : Ray, 150, Truth finds foes where it makes none. 1732 : Fuller, No. 5298.

7. *Truth has a scratched face.* 1875 : Cheales, *Proverb. Folk-Lore*, 118.

8. *Truth hath a good face but bad clothes.* 1600 : Bodenham, *Belvedere*, 14 (Spens. S.), Truth most delights, when shee goes meanest clad. 1639 : Fuller, *Holy War*, bk. iii. ch. xix., Truth hath always a good face, though often

but bad clothes. 1670: Ray, 27.
1694: D'Urfey, *Quixote*, Pt. I. Act I.
sc. ii., Truth has a good face, tho the
quoif be torn. 1732: Fuller, No. 5929
[" ill " for " bad "].

9. *Truth hath always a sure bottom.*
1678: Ray, 211 [" fast " for " sure "].
1732: Fuller, No. 5300.

10. *Truth is stranger than fiction.*
1823: Byron, *Don Juan*, can. xiv. st.
101, For Truth is always strange—
Stranger than fiction. *c.* 1890: Gilbert, *Foggarty's Fairy*, II.

11. *Truth is the daughter of Time.*
1736: Bailey, *Dict.*, s.v. " Truth."

12. *Truth is truth to the end of the
reckoning.* *c.* 1581: in *Ballads from
MSS.*, ii. 123 (B.S.), Truth wilbe truth,
in spite of all defame. 1595: Churchyard, *Charitie*, To Gen. Readers, For
truth is truth, when all is saide and
done. 1603: Shakespeare, *Meas. for
Meas.*, V. i.

13. *Truth lies at the bottom of a well.*
[Democritus quasi in puteo quodam sic
alta, ut fundus sit nullus, veritatem
jacere demersam.—Lactantius, *Inst.*,
iii. 28.] 1646: Browne, *Pseudo. Epi.*,
bk. i. ch. v., Truth, which wise men say,
doth lye in a well. 1758–67: Sterne,
Shandy, iv., " Slawkenb. Tale," Whilst
the unlearned . . . were all busied in getting down to the bottom of the well,
where TRUTH keeps her little court . . .
1797: Colman, jr., *Nightg. and Slippers*,
76 (Hotten), And hence the proverb
rose, that truth Lies in the bottom of a
well. 1819: Byron, *Don Juan*, can. ii.
st. 84, You'd wish yourself where Truth
is—in a well. 1852: M. A. Keltie,
Reminisc. of Thought and Feeling, 3,
The thinker . . . who dives below, and
looks for truth in the well wherein she
is said to reside.

14. *Truth lies on the surface of things.*
1824: Maginn, *O'Doherty's Maxims*, 81
(1849), There is not a truer saying in
this world, than that truth lies on the
surface of things.

15. *Truth may be blamed but cannot
be shamed.* 1468: *Coventry Mys.*, 367
(Sh. S.), Trewthe dyd nevyr his maystyr
shame. 1542: *Sch. House of Women*,
l. 6, Wherby the truthe is often blamed,

Yet in no wise truthe may be shamed.
1567: Harman, *Caveat*, 28 (E.E.T.S.).
1655: Fuller, *Church Hist.*, bk. iv. § i.
(56). 1732: Fuller, No. 5307. 1853:
Trench, *Proverbs*, 19 (1905).

16. *Truth needs no colours.* 1519:
Horman, *Vulgaria*, fo. 58, Trewthe
nedeth no peynted or colored termes.
1631: Mabbe, *Celestina*, 94 (T.T.), Because truth needeth no colours.

17. *Truth needs not many words.*
c. 1550: *Parl. of Byrdes*, l. 28, Where is
many wordes the troueth goeth by.
1732: Fuller, No. 5309, Truth needs
not many words ; but a false tale, a
large preamble.

18. *Truth never grows old.* Ibid., No.
5310.

19. *Truths and roses have thorns about
them.* 1855: Bohn, 547.

20. *Truth's best ornament is nakedness.* 1732: Fuller, No. 5314.

21. *Truth seeks no corners.* 1564:
Bullein, *Dialogue*, 81 (E.E.T.S.), Well
man, well ; truth seketh no corners.
c. 1602: Chapman, *May-Day*, IV. iii.,
Why not ? Truth seeks no corners.
1732: Fuller, No. 5311.

22. *Truth shameth the devil.* 1605:
Camden, *Remains*, 334 (1870). 1732:
Fuller, No. 5306, Truth makes the devil
blush. Cf. No. 3.

23. *Truth should not always be re-
vealed.* [*c.* 1380: Wiclif, *Eng. Works*,
270 (E.E.T.S.), Sumtyme it harmeth
men to seie the sothe out of couenable
tyme and euere it harmeth to lie, but
sumtyme it profitith to be stille and
abide a couenable tyme to speke.]
c. 1387: Usk, *Test. of Love*, in Skeat's
Chaucer, vii. 32, Al sothes be nat to
sayne. *c.* 1480: *Early Miscell.*, 63
(Warton Cl., 1855), For soothe may
not alle day be sayd. *c.* 1550: *Parl. of
Byrdes*, l. 36, All soothes be not for to
saye, It is better some be lefte by
reason Than trouth to be spoken out of
season. *c.* 1680: L'Estrange, *Seneca's
Morals:* " Happy Life," ch. vii., The
thing was true ; but all truths are not
to be spoken at all times. 1727: Gay,
Fables, 1st ser., No. 18, l. 24. 1754:
Berthelson, *Eng.-Danish Dict.*, s.v.
" Truth " [as in 1680]. 1827: Scott,

Journal, 16 July, I will erase the passage. Truth should not be spoke at
all times. 1846 : T. Wright, *Essays on
Middle Ages*, i. 140, So again, we say
" Every truth is not to be told."

24. *Truths too fine spun are subtle
fooleries.* 1855 : Bohn, 547.

25. *Truth trieth.* See quot. *c.* 1475 :
Mankind, sc. iii. st. 123, The prowerbe
seyth " the trewth tryith the sylfe."
Alas, I have much care.

26. *Truth will prevail. c.* 1400 :
Beryn, 63 (E.E.T.S.), Ffor, aftir comyn
seying, " evir atte ende The trowith
woll be previd, how so men evir trend."
c. 1580 : Fulwell, *Ars Adulandi*, sig.
E4, Trueth in the ende shall preuayle.
1619 : *Helpe to Discourse*, 98 (1640),
Truth is the strongest of all, which
overcomes all things in the end. 1740 :
North, *Examen*, 170, According to the
proverb, that, *early or late, Truth will
out.*

27. *Truth will sometimes break out,
unlooked for.* 1732 : Fuller, No.
5314.

See also **Follow** (4).

Try, *verb.* 1. *He tries all the keys in
the bunch.* 1633 : Draxe, 189. 1639 :
Clarke, 60.

2. *Try before you trust. c.* 1460 :
Good Wyfe wold a Pylgremage, l. 118
(E.E.T.S.), A-say [Assay] or euer thow
trust. Before 1500 ; in Hill, *Commonplace-Book*, 47 (E.E.T.S.), Geve trust
to them that thow hast preved. 1587 :
Greene, *Works*, iv. 26 (Grosart), From
hence forth trie ere thou trust. 1637 :
T. Heywood, *Dialogues, etc.*, in Bang,
Materialien, B. 3, p. 212, Try ere you
trust. 1639 : Clarke, 31, Try and
trust.

3. *Try your friend before you have need
of him. c.* 1470 : *Songs and Carols*, 28
(Percy S.), Man, beware and wyse in
dede, Asay thi frend or thou last nede.
1564 : Bullein, *Dialogue*, 67 (E.E.T.S.),
It is good trying of friendes before need
do require. *c.* 1600 : in *Roxb. Ballads*,
ii. 573 (B.S.), First trye thy friend
before thou trust. 1659 : Howell, 5.

4. *Try your skill in gilt first, and
then in gold.* 1639 : Clarke, 60. 1672 :
Walker, *Parœm.*, 43.

Tub on its own bottom. *See* **Every
tub.**

Tub to a whale, To throw a. 1748 :
Richardson, *Clarissa*, iii. 51 (1785),
When a man talks to a woman upon
such subjects, let her be ever so much
in *Alt*, 'tis strange, if he cannot throw
out a tub to the whale ;—that is to say,
if he cannot divert her from resenting
one bold thing, by uttering two or three
full as bold ; but for which more favourable interpretations will lie. 1763 :
Mrs. Brooke, *Lady J. Mandeville*, 148
(1820), A wise writer . . . should throw
in now and then an indiscretion in his
conduct to play with, as seamen do
a tub to the whale. 1912 : *Nation*,
29 June, p. 465, col. 2 (O.), He throws
a tub to the High Church whale.

Tum Dooley. *See* **Tom Dooley.**

Tune the old cow died of. *See* **Cow**
(27).

Turk's horse. *See* **Grass** (4).

Turkeys to market, He is driving, i.e.
He cannot walk straight. 1869 : Hazlitt, 165.

Turkeys. *See also* **Hops.**

Turn, *verb.* 1. *He'll turn rather than
burn.* 1639 : Clarke, 222, Rather turne
than burne. 1678 : Ray, 346. 1732 :
Fuller, No. 2432. 1855 : Kingsley,
West. Ho, ch. vii., None that it [the
Inquisition] catches . . . . but must
turn or burn.

2. *It is hard to turn tack upon a narrow bridge.* 1732 : Fuller, No. 2954.

3. *To turn a narrow adlant*=To have
a narrow escape. [1611 : Cotgrave,
s.v. " Charron," A good carter turnes
in a narrow corner. 1616 : *Honest
Lawyer*, sig. E2, He is a cunning coach-
man that can turne well in a narrow roome.] 1879 : Jackson, *Shropsh.
Word-Book*, 3, To " turn on a mighty
narrow adlant " is a proverbial saying
expressive of a very narrow escape.
1917 : Bridge, *Cheshire Proverbs*, 145.

4. *To turn one's copy.* See **Copy** (2).

5. *To turn one's tippet*=To recant
or change one's opinions. 1546 : Heywood, *Proverbs*, Pt. II. ch. i., So turned
they their typpets by way of exchange.
1576 : Pettie, *Petite Pall.*, Pref. Lett.,
You marvel . . . that I should so soon

turn my tippet and recant. 1608 :
Merry Devil of Edm., III. ii., The nun
will soone at night turne tippit. 1659 :
Howell, 5, He hath turned his tippet.
1826 : Scott, *Woodstock*, ch. xxix., A
high reward, and pardon for past acts
of malignancy, might tempt him once
more to turn his tippet.

6. *To turn over a new leaf*. 1548 :
Hall, *Chron.*, 180 (1809), When they
sawe thenglishmen at the weakest, they
turned the leafe and sang another song.
1570 : Ascham, *Scholemaster*, 155 (1743),
Except such men think themselves
wiser than Cicero for teaching of eloquence, they must be content to turn
a new leaf. 1593 : G. Harvey, *Works*,
ii. 328 (Grosart), As may schoole him
to turne-ouer a new leafe. 1687 :
Sedley, *Bellamira*, III., When we are
marry'd I'll turn over a new leaf.
1750 : Smollett, *Gil Blas*, i. 228, I . . .
resolved to turn over a new leaf, and
live honestly. 1895 : Pinero, *Benefit
of Doubt*, I., This . . . has been no end
of a shocker for me. From to-day I
turn over the proverbial new leaf.

7. *To turn with the wind* (or *tide*).
1591 : Harington, *Orl. Furioso*, bk. xxv.
st. 74, Rogero loves to take the surer
side, And turnes his sailes, as fortune
turnes her tide. 1670 : Ray, 197.

8. *Turn about is fair play*. 1891 :
R. L. S., *Wrecker*, ch. xxiv.

9. *Turn-again-Lane. See* 1670 quot.
1531 : Tyndale, *Expos. St. John*, 140
(P.S.), It is become a turn-again lane
with them. 1562 : Heywood, *Epigr.*,
5th hund., No. 69, Find means to take
a house in Turn-again-lane. 1670 :
Ray, 243, He must take a house in
Turn again Lane. This in old records
is called Wind-again Lane, and lieth
in the parish of St. Sepulchres, going
down to Fleet-dike, having no exit at
one end. It is spoken of, and to, those
who take prodigal or other vicious and
destructive courses. 1790 : Grose, *Prov.
Gloss.*, s.v. "London" [as in 1670].

10. *Turn the buckle. See* **Buckle of
belt**.

Turnips like a dry bed but a wet head.
1917 : Bridge, *Cheshire Proverbs*, 147.

Turnips, She has given him = She

has jilted him. 1845 : Ford, *Handbook
Spain*, i. 27 *n.* (O.), This gourd forms a
favourite metaphor . . . she has refused him ; it is the "giving cold turnips" of Suffolk. 1869 : Hazlitt, 333,
She has given him turnips. *Devonshire.*

Turnspits are dry. 1678 : Ray, 83.

Twelfth Day. *See* quots. Ibid., 52,
At twelf-day the days are lengthened a
cock stride. 1867 : *N. & Q.*, 3rd ser.,
xii. 478, On Twelfth Day, the day is
lengthened the stride of a fowl (Surrey). 1868 : Ibid., 4th ser., i. 61, On
Twelfth Day the day is a cock-stride
longer (East Riding).

Twelve. *See* **Hours.**

Twenty. 1. *As good twenty as nineteen*. 1670 : Ray, 150.

2. *I'll go twenty miles on your errand
first.* Ibid., 177.

3. *Twenty sovereigns are worth twenty
acres* = " A bird in the hand," etc.
1917 : Bridge, *Cheshire Proverbs*, 147.

4. *Twenty young. See* quot. 1591 :
Florio, *Second Frutes*, 101, And who is
not [young] at twentie, and knowes not
at thirtie, And hath not at fortie in
store, Will not be while he liues, for to
know vainely striues, And shall neuer
haue anie more. 1882 : Mrs. Chamberlain, *W. Worcs. Words*, 39 (E.D.S.),
Twenty young, Thirty strong, Forty
wit, Or never none.

I find the following manuscript entry,
written in faded ink in an old-fashioned
hand, on p. 232 of my copy of Ray's
Proverbs, 3rd ed., 1737 : "Ten pretty,
twenty witty, thirty strong, if ever
Forty wise, fifty rich, sixty saint, or
never."

Twice boiled. *See* **Colewort.**

Twig. *See* **Bend** (1).

Twineham. *See* **Bolney.**

Twinkling of a bed-post (originally
bed-staff), In the. 1676 : Shadwell,
Virtuoso, I. i., Gad! I'll do it instantly,
in the twinkling of a bedstaff. 1685 :
S. Wesley, *Maggots*, 163, In bedstaff's
twinkling I'll be gone. 1700 : Ward,
London Spy, 264 (1924), She could shake
'em off . . . in the twinkling of a bedstaff. 1834 : Marryat, *P. Simple*, ch.
xxxvi., Won't I get you out of purgatory in the twinkling of a bed-post ?

1847 : Planché, *Extravag.*, iii. 192
(1879), If any one grumbles I'll scuttle
his nob, In the twinkling of a bed post!

Twinkling of an eye, In the. *c.* 1300 :
in *Vernon MS.*, 286 (E.E.T.S.), Ffor in
a twynclyng of an eighe ffrom erthe to
heuene thou maight styghe. *c.* 1400 :
Beryn, 94 (E.E.T.S.), In twynkelyng of
an eye To make a short answer. 1549 :
Latimer, *Seven Sermons*, 117 (Arber),
He maye in the twynkeling of an eye,
saue a man. 1611 : *Bible*, 1 Cor. xv.
52. 1674 : Jas. Howard, *Eng. Mounsieur*, IV. iii. 1704 : Defoe, *The Storm*,
195, The rest of his men . . . in the
twinkling of an eye were drown'd.
1884 : Gilbert, *Princess Ida*, II., I'll
storm your walls, And level your halls,
in the twinkling of an eye.

Twist a rope of sand. *See* **Rope**, *subs.*
(6).

**Twittle, twattle, drink up your posset
drink.** 1670: Ray, 253. . . . This proverb had its original in Cambridge, and
is scarce known elsewhere. 1790 : Grose,
Prov. Gloss., s.v. "Cambridgeshire."

Two anchors. *See* **Good riding.**

Two and two together, To put. 1855 :
Thackeray, *Newcomes*, ch. xlix., Putting two and two together, as the saying is, it was not difficult for me to
guess who the expected Marquis was.
1876 : G. Eliot, *Felix Holt*, ch. xi., You
are men who can put two and two together. 1918 : Orczy, *Man in Grey*:
"M. Vaillant," 5, What that purpose
was it became my business to learn. It
was a case of putting the proverbial two
and two together.

**Two anons and a by and by is an hour
and a half.** 1605 : Camden, *Remains*,
334 (1870). 1670 : Ray, 56. 1732 :
Fuller, No. 5321 [" are " for " is "].

**Two apples in my hand and the third
in my mouth.** 1659 : Howell, 10.

Two are company. *See* **Two is company.**

Two bad paymasters, There are.
1773 : Foote, *Nabob*, II., There are two
bad paymasters ; those who pay before, and those who never pay. 1821 :
Scott, *Pirate*, ch. xxxix., There are two
bad paymasters—he that pays too soon,
and he that does not pay at all.

Two bites of a cherry, To make.
1694 : Motteux, *Rabelais*, bk. v. ch.
xxviii., Nothing is to be got out of him
but monosyllables ; by Jingo, I believe
he wou'd make three bits of a cherry.
1824 : Maginn, *O'Doherty's Maxims*, 69
(1849), The old rule of " never to make
two bites of a cherry " applies with
peculiar emphasis to cherry brandy.
1860 : Reade, *Cl. and Hearth*, ch. xli.

Two blacks will never make a white.
1822 : Scott, in Lockhart's *Life*, v. 162,
To try whether I cannot contradict the
old proverb of " two blacks not making
a white." 1880 : Spurgeon, *Ploughm.
Pictures*, 92.

Two blows. *See* quot. 1883 : Burne,
Shropsh. Folk-Lore, 589, It takes two
blows to make a battle = one swallow
does not make a summer (so used and
explained).

Two buckets. *See* **Buckets.**

Two candles. *See* quot. 1883 :
Burne, *Shropsh. Folk-Lore*, 275, " Two
candles burning And never a wheel
turning," is a saying with which,
though spinning wheels are no more,
careful Staffordshire housewives still
reprove " burning candle to waste."

Two cats. *See* **Two women.**

Two cats in a gutter, They agree like.
1546 : Heywood, *Proverbs*, Pt. II. ch. i.
1589 : L. Wright, *Display of Dutie*, 24,
Agreeing like . . . two cats in a gutter.
1659 : Howell, 3.

Two chimneys. *See* **Chimney** (1).

Two complexions in one face. 1575 :
G. Fenton, *Golden Epistles*, 292 (1582),
A propertie verye familiar with ye
moste of them, to haue two colours to
one meaning, and (as the saying is) to
beare two complexions in one face.

Two cunning knaves need no broker.
1546 : Heywood, *Proverbs*, Pt. I. ch. xi.
[" false " for " cunning "]. 1670 : Ray,
111. 1732 : Fuller, No. 5322.

**Two daughters and a back door are
three arrant thieves.** 1670 : Ray, 51.
1732 : Fuller, No. 5323.

Two determine. *See* **Nought** (3).

**Two dogs fight for a bone, and a third
runs away with it.** 1633 : Draxe, 30,
Two dogs striue for a bone, and the
third whiles that they contend, taketh

it away. 1692 : L'Estrange, *Æsop*, 4 (3rd ed.). 1732 : Fuller, No. 5324. 1880 : Spurgeon, *Ploughm. Pictures*, 85.

Two dry sticks will kindle a green one. 1678 : Ray, 213. 1732 : Fuller, No. 5325.

Two ears. *See* One tongue.

Two eggs a penny. *See* Egg (12).

Two evils choose the least, Of. [Nam quod aiunt, minima de malis, id est, ut turpiter potius quam calamitose : an est ullum maius malum turpitudine.— Cicero, *De Officiis*, 3. 29.] *c.* 1374 : Chaucer, *Troylus*, bk. ii. l. 470, Of harmes two, the lesse is for to chese. *c.* 1440 : *Gesta Rom.*, 10 (E.E.T.S.), The knyyt answerid, and seide, " Sire, hit is wreten, that of too evelis the lasse evill is to be chosyn." 1546 : Heywood, *Proverbs*, Pt. I. ch. v., Of two yls, choose the least, whyle choyse lyth in lot. 1581 : Woodes, *Conflict of Conscience*, IV., Howbeit of two evils the least must be choosed. 1694 : Cibber, *Love's Last Shift*, III. i. 1730 : Fielding, *Temple Beau*, IV. v., Since it is the lesser evil of the two, it is to be preferred. 1913 : Galsworthy, *Fugitive*, II., Of two evils, if it be so—choose the least.

Two executors and an overseer make three thieves. 15th cent. in *Reliq. Antiquæ*, i. 314 (1841).

Two eyes can see more than one. *c.* 1594 : Bacon, *Promus*, No. 946, Two eyes are better than one. 1605 : Camden, *Remains*, 334 (1870). 1681 : Robertson, *Phraseol. Generalis*, 567, Two eyes see better than one. 1732 : Fuller, No. 5326 [" may " for " can "].

Two faces in one hood, To bear = To be double-faced. *c.* 1400 : *Rom. Rose*, l. 7388, And with so gret devocion They maden her confession, That they had ofte, for the nones, Two hedes in one hood at ones. *c.* 1440 : Lydgate, *Minor Poems*, 69 (E.E.T.S.), God lovyd neuer two facys in oon hood. Before 1529 : Skelton, *Magnyfycence*, l. 720, Two faces in a hode couertly I bere, Water in the one hande, and fyre in the other. 1586 : Deloney, *Works*, 462 (1912), With false Iudas you can beare two faces in one hoode. 1668 : Shad-

well, *Sullen Lovers*, IV. i., 'Tis indeed, to be a Pharisee, and carry two faces in a hood, as the saying is. 1754 : Berthelson, *Eng.-Danish Dict.*, s.v. " Face," To carry two faces under a hood. 1841 : Dickens, *Barn. Rudge*, ch. xl., You are a specious fellow . . . and carry two faces under your hood, as well as the best. 1893 : j. Salisbury, *S. E. Worces. Gloss.*, 45 (E.D.S.), Here's vishing the mon may never get fat, as carries two faces under one hat.

Two feet in one shoe Will never do. 1875 : Cheales, *Proverb. Folk-Lore*, 40.

Two folk, To be = To be unfriends. 1631 : Mabbe, *Celestina*, 256 (T.T.), I have nothing to say to him ; as long as I live, he and I shall be two. 1738 : Swift, *Polite Convers.*, Dial. I., Pray, Miss, when did you see your old acquaintance Mrs. Cloudy ? You and she are two, I hear. 1788 : O'Keeffe, *The Toy*, III. ii., Mr. Metheglin, you and I are now two, so good day to you. 1893 : J. Salisbury, *S. E. Worces. Gloss.*, 45 (E.D.S.), Now, Jack, you lazy rascal, uf thee doosn't get on o' thy work, thee un I sh'll be two-folks. 1917 : Bridge, *Cheshire Proverbs*, 127.

Two fools in a house are too many. 1580 : Lyly, *Euphues*, 283 (Arber), For two fooles in one bed are too many. 1732 : Fuller, No. 5328, Two fools in a house are too many by a couple.

Two fools meet, the bargain goes off, Where. Ibid., No. 5679.

Two forencons. *See* quot. 1923 : *Devonsh. Assoc. Trans.*, liv. 136, " You can't 'ave two vorenoons in one day." Meaning you cannot be young more than once.

Two friends have a common purse, one sings and the other weeps, When. 1855 : Bohn, 562.

Two friends with one gift, To make. 1681 : Robertson, *Phraseol. Generalis*, 797 [with " favour " for " gift "]. 1732 : Fuller, No. 5205.

Two good days. *See* Wife (5).

Two good men. *See* quot. 1880 : Spurgeon, *Ploughm. Pictures*, 154, Another saying, " There are only two good men, one is dead, and the other is not born."

Two good things are better than one.
1639 : Clarke, 104. 1678 : Ray, 212.

Two hands in a dish and one in a
purse. 1605 : Camden, *Remains*, 333
(1870). 1639 : Clarke, 218, One hand
in a purse and two in a dish. 1640 :
Nabbes, *Unfort. Mother*, I. iii., Two
hands in a dish, The right Court
Ordinary. 1738 : Swift, *Polite Convers.*, Dial. II.

Two heads are better than one.
[Σύν τε δύ’ ερχομένω.—Homer, *Il.*, x.
224.] 1530 : Palsgrave, 594, Two
wyttes be farre better than one. 1546 :
Heywood, *Proverbs*, Pt. I. ch. ix.
1558 : W. Forrest, *Grisill the Second*,
51 (Roxb. Cl.), This olde sayinge, Twoe
wytts (or moe) to bee better then one.
1638 : Taylor (Water Poet), *Bull, Beare,
etc.*, 28, in *Works*, 3rd Coll. (Spens. S.).
1753 : Foote, *Taste*, II. 1864 : "Cornish Proverbs," in *N. & Q.*, 3rd ser., vi.
494, Two heads are better than one if
only sheeps' heads. 1893 : S. Butler,
in *Memoir*, by Jones, ii. 8 (1919), Two
are better than one : I heard some one
say this and replied : "Yes, but the
man who said that did not know my
sisters." 1894 : Northall, *Folk Phrases*,
32 (E.D.S.), Two heads are better than
one, even if the one's a sheep's. 1917 :
Bridge, *Cheshire Proverbs*, 147 [as in
1864].

Two hungry meals make the third a
glutton. 1546 : Heywood, *Proverbs*,
Pt. I. ch. xi. 1605 : Camden, *Remains*,
331 (1870) [" three " for " two " and
" fourth " for " third "]. 1655 : Fuller,
Church Hist., bk. vi. sect. ii. (v. 13).
1732 : Fuller, No. 5329 [" good " for
" hungry," which makes nonsense of
the saying].

Two in distress Make trouble less.
1875 : Cheales, *Proverb. Folk-Lore*, 32.

Two is company and three is none.
1871 : *N. & Q.*, 4th ser., viii. 506
[" are " for " is "]. 1897 : E. Lyall,
Wayfaring Men, ch. xxiv., "Two is
company, three is trumpery," as the
proverb says. 1907 : De Morgan, *Alice-
for-Short*, ch. viii.

Two kings in one kingdom do not
agree well together. 1586 : B. Young,
Guazzo, fo. 205.

Two knaves well met. 1611 : Cotgrave, s.v. " Chat," *A bon rat bon chat*,
Two knaves well met or matched.
1672 : Walker, *Parœm.*, 54.

Two losses than one sorrow, Better.
1732 : Fuller, No. 936.

Two masters. *See* No man.

Two may keep counsel if one be away.
1579 : Lyly, *Euphues*, 67 (Arber).
1592 : Shakespeare, *Romeo*, II. iv., Did
you ne'er hear say, Two may keep
counsel, putting one away ? 1630 :
Brathwait, *Engl. Gent.*, 158 (1641), One
may keepe counsell, but two cannot.
1753 : Richardson, *Grandison*, ii. 8
(1883), The proverb says, Two can keep
a secret when one is away.

Two mouths. *See* Stop (4).

Two negatives make an affirmative.
1593 : G. Harvey, *Works*, i. 293 (Grosart),
But euen those two negatiues . . .
would be conformable enough, to conclude an affirmatiue. 1647 : Fuller,
Good Thoughts in Worse Times, 173
(1830). 1769 : Smollett, *Adv. Atom*, 20
(Cooke, 1795), In the English language
two negatives amount to an affirmative.

Two of a trade can never agree.
[καὶ κεραμεὺς κεραμεῖ κοτέει καὶ
τέκτονι τέκτων.—Hesiod, Op. 25.]
1630 : Dekker, *Honest Wh.*, Pt. 2, IV.
i., It is a common rule, and 'tis most
true, Two of one trade ne'er love.
1753 : Murphy, *Gray's Inn Journal*,
No. 2, Oct. 8. 1860 : Reade, *Cloist.
and Hearth*, ch. xxxvii.

Two parties to make a quarrel, It
takes. 1732 : Fuller, No. 4942, There
must be two at least to a quarrel.
1838 : Dickens, *Twist*, ch. xv., There
must always be two parties to a quarrel,
says the old adage. 1925 : *Times Lit.
Supp.*, Nov. 5, p. 728, col. 2, It takes
two to make a quarrel, the proverb says ;
it takes the world to make a peace.

Two pigeons. *See* Pigeon (4).

Two removes. *See* Three removes.

Two ride on one horse, one must
sit behind, When. 1599 : Shakespeare,
Much Ado, III. v., An two men ride of
a horse, one must ride behind. 1639 :
in *Berkeley MSS.*, iii. 32 (1885). 1883 :
Burne, *Shropsh. Folk-Lore*, 590, Peggy
behind Marget = inferiors last : when

two ride one horse, one must ride behind. 1927 : *Times*, Feb. 16, p. 10, col. 4.

Two Sir Positives can scarce meet without a skirmish. 1732 : Fuller, No. 5333.

Two slips. *See* Three slips.

Two sorrows of one, Make not. 1546 : Heywood, *Proverbs*, Pt. II. ch. v. *c.* 1580 : Spelman, *Dialogue*, 4 (Roxb Cl.), As the oulde sainge is ; yt is a meere ffollye to make two sorowes of one. 1659 : Howell, 5.

Two sparrows on one ear of corn make an ill agreement. 1651 : Herbert, *Jac. Prudentum*, 2nd ed. 1732 : Fuller, No. 5334, Two sparrows upon an ear of wheat cannot agree.

Two stomachs to eat and one to work, He has. 1869 : Spurgeon, *John Ploughman*, ch. i., Fellows have two stomachs for eating and drinking, when they have no stomach for work. 1882 : *N. & Q.*, 6th ser., v. 266 [Kentish saying], He's got the fever of lurk, Two hearts to eat, and ne'er a one to work. 1889 : Peacock, *Manley, etc., Gloss.*, 598 (E.D.S.), He's two bellies fer eätin' an' noän fer wark.

Two stools, Between. *c.* 1390 : Gower, *Conf. Amantis*, Prol., l. 336, Bot it is seid and evere schal, Betwen two stoles lyth the fal. 1546 : Heywood, *Proverbs*, Pt. I. ch. iii., While betweene two stooles, my tayle go to grounde. 1593 : Giffard, *Dial. on Witches, etc.*, 11 (Percy S.), I perceive your danger is betweene two stooles. 1667–8 : Pepys, *Diary*, Jan. 17, And so, between both, as every thing else of the greatest moment do, do fall between two stools. 1791 : R. Jephson, *Two Strings to your Bow*, I. iii., Well done, Lazarillo ; between two stools they say a certain part of a man comes to the ground. 1864 : Mrs. H. Wood, *Trevlyn Hold*, ch. liii., While he keeps me shilly-shallying over this one, I may lose them both. There's an old proverb, you know, about two stools. 1907 : De Morgan, *Alice-for-Short*, ch. xvi., Charles saw that between the two stools the young couple wouldn't fall to the ground, but would go to the altar.

Two strings to one's bow, To have. [Μηδ᾽ ἐπὶ δυοῖν ἀγκύραιν ὁρμεῖν αὐτοὺς ἐᾶτε. —Demosthenes, *Or.*, 56, 1295 (*fin.*). Nam melius duo defendunt retinacula navim.—Prop., ii. 22, 41.]. *c.* 1477 : Caxton, *Jason*, 57 (E.E.T.S.), I wil wel that euery man be amerous and loue but that he haue ij strenges on his bowe. 1578 : Florio, *First Fruites*, fo. 6, It is alwayes good for one to haue two stringes to his bowe. 1606 : Day, *Ile of Gulls*, II. ii., A wise mans bow goes with a two fold string. 1672 : Wycherley, *Love in a Wood*, I. i. *c.* 1760 : Foote, *Author*, I., I have, I think, at present two strings to my bow ; if my comedy succeeds, it buys me a commission ; if my mistress, my Laura, proves kind, I am settled for life. 1814 : Austen, *Mansfield Park*, ch. viii. 1859 : Planché, *Extravag.*, v. 221 (1879). Cf. Good riding.

Two Sundays come together, When = never. 1616 : Haughton, *Englm. for my Money*, II. ii., Art thou so mad as to turn French ? *Matt*. Yes, marry, when two Sundays come together. 1681 : Robertson, *Phraseol. Generalis*, 1189. 1825 : Brockett, *Gloss. N. Country Words*, 150, To-morrow come nivver— when two Sundays meet together. 1854 : Baker, *Northants Gloss.*, s.v. "Sunday," When two Sundays meet. 1881 : Evans, *Leicest. Words, etc.*, 276 (E.D.S.), To-morrow come never, when theer's tew Soondays in a wik.

Two tailors. *See* Nine tailors.

Two things a man should never be angry at ; what he can help, and what he cannot help. 1732 : Fuller, No. 5335.

Two things doth prolong thy life : A quiet heart, and a loving wife. 1607 : Deloney, *Strange Histories*, 70 (Percy S.).

Two to one is odds at football. 1567 : Pickering, *Horestes*, l. 78, But two is to meyney, the prouerbe douth tell. 1616 : Breton, *Works*, i. *t* 24 (Grosart), Two to one is odds. 1654 : Gayton, *Pleas. Notes Don Q.*, 220, Three to one is odds. 1658 : R. Franck, *North. Memoirs*, 80 (1821), If two to one be odds at football—— 1702 : Brown in *Works*, ii., 25 (1760). 1742 : Fielding, *Andrews*, bk. iii. ch. xii., Who concluded that

one at a time was sufficient, that two
to one were odds. *c.* 1791 : Pegge,
Derbicisms, 138 (E.D.S.).

Two trades. *See* **Man** (28).

Two wants of one, To make. 1738 :
Swift, *Polite Convers.*, i., I don't love to
make two wants of one.

Two will. *See* **Nought** (3).

Two women in one house. *See* quots.
1417 : in *Reliq. Antiquæ*, i. 233 (1841),
Two wymen in one howse, Two cattes
and one mowce, Two dogges and one
bone, Maye never accorde in one.
1486 : *Boke of St. Albans*, sig. F4
["wyues" for "women"]. 1611 : Cotgrave, s.v. "Accorder," Men say, Two
cats and a mouse, two wives in one
house, two dogs and a bone, never agree
in one. 1670 : Ray, 151 [as in 1611].
1732 : Fuller, No. 6095 [as in 1611].
1869 : Spurgeon, *John Ploughman*, ch.
xxi. [as in 1611, but with last line—
"Will not agree long."]

Two words to a bargain. 1598 :
Mucedorus, sig. B2, Tow words to a
bargaine. Before 1625 : Fletcher, *Wild-
Goose Chase*, II. iii. 1696 : Vanbrugh,
Relapse, III. iii. 1734 : Ficlding, *Intrig. Chambermaid*, II. iii., There go two
words though to that bargain. 1822 :
Scott, *Nigel*, ch. xxxi., There gang twa
folk's votes to the unmaking of a
bargain, as to the making of ane.
1860 : Reade, *Clois. and Hearth*, ch.
xxiv. Cf. **More words.**

Two wrongs will not make one right.
1875 : Cheales, *Proverb. Folk-Lore*, 120.

Two year old balk. *See* quot. 1841 :
Hartshorne, *Salopia Ant.*, 314, Hence
as it [land which escapes the plough]
lies fallow has arisen the proverb that
"a two-year-old balk is as good as a
ruck [heap] of muck."

**Twyford, My name is : I know nothing
of the matter.** 1694 : Motteux, *Rabelais*, bk. v. ch. xiii., Hasn't the fellow
told you he does not know a word of the
business ? his name's Twyford. 1732 :
Fuller, No. 3502.

Tyburn. *See* **Newgate** and **Suits hang.**

Tyburn tippet, A = A halter. 1549 :
Latimer, *Seven Sermons*, 63 (Arber),
The byshop of Rome sent hym a
cardinal's hatte, he should haue had
a Tiburne tippet, a halpeny halter.
c. 1570 : in Collmann, *Ballads, etc.*, 115
(Roxb. Cl.), A Tyborne typett a roope
or a halter. 1821 : Scott, *Kenilworth*,
ch. iii., Any one whose neck is beyond
the compass of a Tyburn tippet.

Tympany, To have a two-legged = To
be with child. 1579 : *Marr. of Wit
and Wisdom*, 15 (Sh. S.), I am afraid it
is a timpany with two legges ! *c.* 1685 :
in *Roxb. Ballads*, vii. 28 (B.S.), The
doctor, be sure, is sent for to cure This
two-legged tympany. 1732 : Fuller,
No. 4127, She hath a tympany with
two heels.

Tyne. *See* **Tees.**

Tyrant's breath is another's death, A.
1855 : Bohn, 302.

**Tyrants seem to kiss, 'Tis time to fear
when.** Ibid., 534.

U

Ugly as a witch. 1846–59 : *Denham Tracts*, ii. 84 (F.L.S.).

Ugly as sin. 1821 : Scott, *Kenilworth*, ch. x., Though I am as ugly as sin. 1891 : R. L. S., *Letters*, iv. 75 (Tusitala ed.), All my other women have been as ugly as sin. 1901 : F. E. Taylor, *Lancs. Sayings*, 2, As feaw [ugly] as sin.

Ugly as the devil. 1726 : Defoe, *Hist. of Devil*, Pt. II. ch. vii. p. 249 (4th ed.) [cited as "a proverb in his favour"].

Ugly enough to wean a foal. 1917 : Bridge, *Cheshire Proverbs*, 147.

Unbidden guest knows not where to sit, An. 1546.: Heywood, *Proverbs*, Pt. I. ch. ix. 1612 : Webster, *White Devil*, in *Works* (Dyce), 19, An unbidden guest Should travel as Dutch women go to church, Bear their stools with them. 1732 : Fuller, No. 5395. 1736 : Bailey, *Dict.*, s.v. "Unbidden," An unbidden guest must bring his stool with him.

Unbought hide. *See* **Cut** (11).

Uncle Antony. *See* quot. 1909 : C. Lee, *Our Little Town*, 17, Idle juniors congenically occupied in "helping Uncle Antony to kill dead mice," as the phrase goes.

Uncle Jan Knight, never in the right place, Like. Corn. 19th cent. (Mr. C. Lee).

Uncover not the church to mend the quire = Rob not Peter to pay Paul. 1570 : A. Barclay, *Mirr. of Good Manners*, 30 (Spens. S.), Uncover not the church, therwith to mende the quere.

Under board, To play. 1591 : Florio, *Second Frutes*, 134, Thou haste long hands, and vsest them vnderboord. 1642 : Fuller, *Holy State (Wise Statesman)*, The receivers of such [pensions] will play under-board at the counciltable. 1669 : Donne, *Poems*, i. 102 (Grierson), And often under-boards Spoak dialogues with our feet far from our words. 1669 : Dud. North, *Obs. and Adv. Oeconom.*, 71, While the steward fear to be discovered, if he use

any underboard play. 1681 : Robertson, *Phraseol. Generalis*, 437, That you should not think I ly at catch, or play under board to deceive you.

Under boske. *See* quot. *c.* 1320 : in *Reliq. Antiquæ*, i. 113 (1841), "Under boske [the greenwood] shal men weder abide," Quoth Hendyng.

Understanding and reason cannot conclude out of mood and figure. 1659 : Howell, 19.

Understands ill, answers ill, Who. 1736 : Bailey, *Dict.*, s.v. "Understand."

Under the blanket the black one is as good as the white. 1732 : Fuller, No. 5396.

Under the bungo o' th' moon = to be in difficulties. 1917 : Bridge, *Cheshire Proverbs*, 148.

Under the furze is hunger and cold, under the broom is silver and gold. 1678 : Ray, 348. 1879 : *N. & Q.*, 5th ser., xii. 447. 1885 : *N. & Q.*, 6th ser., xii. 309 ["gorse" for "furze"].

Under the rose. 1546 : Dymocke to Vaughan in *State Papers*, Hen. VIII. ii. 200, The sayde questyons were asked with lysence, and that yt shoulde remayn under the rosse, that is to say, to remayn under the bourde, and no more to be rehersyd. 1639 : Chapman and Shirley, *Ball*, II. iii., Under the rose, if that will do you a pleasure, The lords do call me cousin, but I am——. 1647 : in *Polit. Ballads*, 49 (Percy S.), Any thing may be spoke, if 't be under the rose. 1714 : Ozell, *Molière*, vi. 7, I must tell you (under the rose) that——. 1762 : Bickerstaffe, *Love in a Village*, II. ii., We all love a pretty girl—under the rose. 1862 : Dickens, in *Letters*, ii. 178 (1880), I don't know what their pay was, but I have no doubt their principal complements were got under the rose. 1915 : Pinero, *Big Drum*, IV., I should *puff* you, under the rose—quietly pull the strings——.

Under the weather. 1891 : R. L. S., *Wrecker*, ch. iv., You must not fancy

I am sick, only over-driven and under the weather. 1926 : Phillpotts, *Peacock House*, 222, I've marked you've been a good bit under the weather, and . . . I should like to help you.

Under water. *See* **Snow** (8).

Undone. 1. *As good undone as do it too soon.* 1546 : Heywood, *Proverbs*, Pt. II. ch. v. 1659 : Howell, 3.

2. *Undone as you would undo an oyster.* 1639 : Clarke, 166, He's undone like an oyster. 1672 : ·Walker, *Parœm.*, 34. 1681 : Robertson, *Phraseol. Generalis*, Undone as you would undo an oyster ; Ne salus quidem ipsa servare potest.

Unfinished work, Show not fools nor bairns. 1860 : Reader, *Cloister and Hearth*, ch. lv. [cited as a " byword "].

Ungirt unblessed. *c.* 1477 : Caxton, *Book of Curtesye*, 45 (E.E.T.S.), Vngyrte, vnblyssed. seruyng atte table Me semeth hym a seruant nothing able. 1590 : Spenser, *F. Q.*, IV. v. 18. 1646 : Browne, *Pseudo. Epi.*, bk. v. ch. xxii., As we usually say, they are unblest until they put on their girdle. 1687 : Aubrey, *Gentilisme, etc.*, 43 (F.L.S.), It was accounted before yᵉ civill warres a very undecent and dissolute thing for a man to goe without his girdle in so much that 'twas a proverbe, " Ungirt and unbless't." (*See* Tibullus, *Eleg.*, lib. i. ix. 41, and Pers., *Sat.*, iii. (31).)

Unhardy is unsely. *See* **Cowardly.**

Unkissed unkind. 1584 : Peele, *Arraign. of Paris*, I. ii., And I will have a lover's fee ; they say, unkiss'd unkind. 1897 : Violet Hunt, *Unkist, Unkind* [title].

Unknown, unkissed. *c.* 1374 : Chaucer, *Troylus*, bk. i. l. 809, Unknowe, unkist, and lost that is unsought. 1401 : in Wright, *Polit. Poems* (Rolls S.), ii. 59 (1861), On old Englis it is said, unkissid is unknowen. 1546 : Heywood, *Proverbs*, Pt. I. ch. xi. 1579 : E. Kirke, *Epist. Ded.*, to Spenser's *Shep. Cal.*, Who for that hee is vncouth (as sayde Chaucer) is vnkist, and vnknowne to most men, is regarded but of a fewe. 1670 : Ray, 27. 1732 : Fuller, No. 5403.

Unlikeliest places are often likelier than those that are likeliest, The. 1917 : Bridge, *Cheshire Proverbs*, 120.

Unlooked for often comes. 1875 : Cheales, *Proverb. Folk-Lore*, 133.

Unlucky in love lucky at play. 1738 : Swift, *Polite Convers.*, Dial. III., Well, miss, you'll have a sad husband, you have such good luck at cards. 1868 : T. W. Robertson, *Play*, III. ii., The old proverb is verified in our case, unlucky in love, lucky at play.

Unmannerliness is not so impolite as over-politeness. 1694 : D'Urfey, *Quixote*, Pt. II. I. ii., He that has more manners than he ought, is more a fool than he thought. 1732 : Fuller, No. 5404, Unmannerly a little is better than troublesome a great deal. 1736 : Bailey, *Dict.*, s.v. " Unkind," Better unkind than troublesome. 1831 : Hone, *Year-Book*, col. 1417. Cf. **Better be unmannerly.**

Unminded, unmoaned. 1546 : Heywood, *Proverbs*, Pt. I. ch. ix. 1670 : Ray, 27. 1815 : Scott, *Mannering*, ch. ix., But when folk's missed, then they are moaned.

Untoward boy, or girl, may make a good man, or woman, An. 1548 : Hall, *Chron.*, 12 (1809), Experience teacheth, that . . . of a shrcude boy, proueth a good man. 1592 : Greene, *Works*, x. 239 (Grosart), My mother allowed of my vnhappy parts, alluding to this prophanie and old prouerbe, an vntoward gyrle makes a good woman. 1633 : Draxe, 9, A shrewd boy maketh a good man. 1655 : Fuller, *Church. Hist.*, bk. x., § iv. (52), Verifyed the proverb, that an untoward boy may make a good man. 1670 : Ray, 111, An unhappy lad may make a good man.

Untravelled. *See* **Home-keeping.**

U.P. *See* quots. 1791 : *Gent. Mag.*, i. 327, " U.P.K. spells May goslings," is an expression used by boys at play as an insult to the losing party. 1813 : Brand, *Pop. Antiq.*, i. 219 (Ellis, 1895) [copies the foregoing quotation, with addition——], U.P.K. is " up pick," that is, up with your pin or peg, the mark of the goal. 1854 : Baker, *Northants. Gloss.*, s.v. U.P. spells goslings ! Not an uncommon exclamation when any one has completed or attained an object. 1881 : Evans, *Leicest. Words, etc.*, 282 (E.D.S.), U.P. spells goslins . . . I have heard it not unfrequently, but always as applied to death. " How's Ted going on ? " ." Eh, poor chap, I think it's U.P. spells gos-lins wi' him," meaning, as I always understood, " it is all up with him, and the goslings will soon feed on his grave."

Uphill and against the heart, It goes = It is a hard task. 1883 : Burne, *Shrop-shire Folk-Lore*, 589.

Up horn, Down corn. 1870 : *N. & Q.*, 4th ser., vi. 259, Another proverb in use about thirty years ago was—" Up horn, Down corn " ; meaning that when the price of cattle was " up," that of corn was " down." 1886 : *N. & Q.*, 7th ser., i. 192, The proverb which is common among farmers is generally, " Up corn, Down horn," meaning when corn is dear beef is cheap.

Uppingham trencher, An. 1678 : Ray, 333. 1790 : Grose, *Prov. Gloss.*, s.v. " Rutlandshire.," An Uppingham trencher. This town was probably famous for the art of trencher-making. Here, by a statute of Henry VIII., the standard was appointed to be kept for the weights and measures of this county ; which might induce turners, and other makers of measures, to settle here.

Up the hill favour me, down the hill beware thee. The horse *loq.* 1639 : Clarke, 22. 1670 : Ray, 103. 1732 : Fuller, No. 6276, Up-hill spare me ; Down-hill forbear me ; Plain way, spare me not, Let me not drink,when I am hot.

Up the weather, To go = To prosper. Cf. **Down** (5) for the reverse. 1618 : Breton, in *Works*, ii. *u.* 5 (Grosart), I feare the place you liue in is more costly then profitable ; where, for one that goes vp the weather a number goe downe the winde.

Up to one's gossip, To be = To be aware of a person's designs. 1828 : Carr, *Craven Dialect*, i. 193.

Up to snuff. 1811 : Poole, *Hamlet Trav.*, II. i. (O.), He knows well enough The game we're after : Zooks, he's up

to snuff. 1876 : *N. & Q.*, 5th ser., v. 336, When a man is very acute at a bargain, and " knows a thing or two," he is said to be " up to snuff." 1922 : Weyman, *Ovington's Bank*, ch. xxxvi., Thank ye, but I am up to snuff. If you ask me I think you're a silly set of fools.

Up to the ears. 1594 : Barnfield, *Affect. Sheph.*, 8 (Percy S.), But leave we him in love up to the eares.

Up with it if it be but a devil of two years old. 1639 : Clarke, 202.

Usage. *See* **Custom.**

Use is a great matter. 1672 : Walker, *Paroem.*, 23.

Use is all. 1639 : Clarke, 35.

Use makes perfect. *See* **Prac-tice.**

Use, verb. 1. *He that useth me better than he is wont, hath betrayed or will be-tray me.* 1578 : Florio, *First Fruites*, fo. 28, Who doth vnto me better then he is woont, he hath betrayed me, or els wil betray me. 1589 : Puttenham, *Engl. Poesie*, 295 (Arber), He that speakes me fairer than his woont was too Hath done me harme, or meanes for to doo. 1586 : Pettie, *Guazzo*, fo. 36, Hee which maketh more of thee then he was wont, either hath cousened thee alreadie, or else goeth about to cosen thee. 1629 : *Book of Meery Riddles*, Prov. 12. 1732 : Fuller, No. 2180, He that is kinder than he was wont, hath a design upon thee.

2. *I will use you like a Jew.* 1619 : W. Hornby, *Scourge of Drunkennes*, sig. A4, Ile vse thee like a dogge, a Iew, a slaue. 1662 : Fuller, *Worthies*, ii. 346 (1840), I will use you as bad as a Jew. 1670 : Ray, 209, To use one like a Jew. 1790 : Grose, *Prov. Gloss.*, s.v. " London " [as in 1662].

3. *The used key is always bright.* 1736 : Franklin, *Way to Wealth*, in *Works*, i. 443 (Bigelow).

4. *Use legs and have legs.* *c.* 1582 : Harvey, *Marginalia*, 188 (1913). 1670 : Ray, 153. 1732 : Fuller, No. 5410.

5. *Use not to-day what to-morrow may want.* 1846 : Denham, *Proverbs*, 5 (Percy S.).

6. *Use your wit as a buckler, not a sword.* 1855 : Bohn, 549.

Usual forms of civility oblige no man, The. Ibid., 517.

Usurer is one that tormenteth men for their good conditions, An, viz. The conditions of their bonds. 1659 : Howell, 18.

Usurers' purses and women's plackets are never satisfied. Ibid., 7. 1736 : Bailey, *Dict.*, s.v. " Usurer."

Usury. *See* quot. 1593 : Nashe, in *Works*, iv. 139 (Grosart), It is nowe growne a prouerbe That there is no merchandize but vsury.

Uter Pendragon. *See* Eden.

Vain-glory blossoms but never bears.
1633 : Draxe, 212, Vaine glory is a
floure that beareth no corne. 1732 :
Fuller, No. 5342.

Vale discovereth the hill, The. c.
1594 : Bacon, *Promus*, No. 145 [with
" best " after " vale "]. 1605 : Bacon,
Adv. of Learning, II. xxi. 71, A proverb
more arrogant than sound, " that the
vale discovereth the hill."

**Valiant man's look is more than a
coward's sword, A.** 1640 : Herbert,
Jac. Prudentum.

**Valley, He that stays in the, shall
never get over the hill.** 1633 : Draxe,
42. 1670 : Ray, 152. 1732 : Fuller,
No. 2314.

**Valour can do little without dis-
cretion.** 1670 : Ray, 27. 1732 :
Fuller, No. 5343, Valour is brutish without discretion. Cf. **Discretion.**

Valour that parleys is near yielding.
1640 : Herbert, *Jac. Prudentum.* 1670 :
Ray, 27.

**Valour would fight, but discretion
would run away.** 1678 : Ray, 214. 1732 :
Fuller, No. 5344. Cf. **Discretion.**

Value of money. *See* Money (12).

Varnishing hides a crack. 1732 :
Fuller, No. 5346.

Vavasour family saying. 1659 :
Howell, 21, A sheriff had he bin, and a
Contour, Was no where such a Vava-
sour. An old said saw of that family.

Veal. 1. *In a shoulder of veal there
are twenty and two good bits.* 1678 :
Ray, 83, . . . This is a piece of country
wit. They mean by it, There are
twenty (others say forty) bits in a
shoulder of veal, and but two good ones.
1738 : Swift, *Polite Convers.*, Dial. II.,
They say there are thirty and two good
bits in a shoulder of veal.

2. *Veal will be cheap: calves fall.*
1678 : Ray, 83.

Vein across the nose. *See* quot.
1923 : *Folk-Lore*, xxxiv. 330, If you
have a vein across your nose, You'll
never live to wear your wedding clothes
(Oxfordsh.).

Velvet true heart, He's a. Cheshire.
1678 : Ray, 83. 1852 : " Cheshire
Proverbs," in *N. & Q.*, 1st ser., vi. 386.
1917 : Bridge, *Cheshire Proverbs*, 66,
He has a velvet true heart. Cf.
True (9).

**Vengeance, though it comes with
leaden feet, strikes with iron hands.**
1748 : Richardson, *Clarissa*, iv. 120
(1785). Cf. **God comes.**

Venture it, I'll. *See* quots. 1678 :
Ray, 83, I'll venture it, as Johnson did
his wife, and she did well. 1732 :
Fuller, No. 1367, E'en venture on, as
Johnson did on his wife.

Venture little, hazard little. 1590 :
Tarlton, *Nerves out of Purg*, To the
Readers. Men that venture little,
hazard little. Cf. **Nothing** (30).

Venture not all in one bottom. 1639 :
Clarke, 95. 1672 : Walker, *Parœm.*,
53. 1732 : Fuller, No. 5349. 1831 :
Hone, *Year-Book*, col. 1417, Venture
not all you have at once.

**Venture out of your depth till you can
swim, Never.** 1855 : Bohn, 459.

Ventures too far, loses all, He that.
c. 1534 : Berners, *Huon*, 335 (E.E.T.S.),
Some tyme it fortuneth that it is foly
to aduenture to moche forward and to
late to repent ofter [afterwards]. 1611 :
Cotgrave, s.v. " S'adventurer."

Venus smiles. *See* **Jove laughs.**

Vervain and dill. *See* quots. 1578 :
Dodoens, *Herbal*, quoted in Aubrey's
Gentilisme (F.L.S.), Vervaine and dill
Hinder witches of their will. 1588 :
Cogan, *Haven of Health*, ch. xxii. p. 41
(1612), One olde saying I haue heard of
this herbe, That whosoeuer weareth
verveine and dill, May be bold to sleepe
on euery hill. 1635 : Swan, *Spec.
Mundi*, 250 [as in 1588].

Vessel. *See* **Cask.**

Vetch. *See* quot. 1884 : H. Friend,
Flowers and Fl. Lore, 220, Vetches are
a most hardy grain, according to the
comparison of an old saying—" A
Thetch will go through The bottom of
an old shoe."

Vicar of S. Fools, The. 1562 : Heywood, *Epigr.*, 5th Hund., No. 19, Whens come all these ? from the vicar of sainct fooles. 1565 : Calfhill, *Answ. to Martiall*, 237 (P.S.), Then . . . a dolt with a dawkin might marry together ; and the Vicar of Saint Fools be both minstrel and minister. 1589 : Nashe, *Works*, i. 13 (Grosart), I must needes sende such idle wits to shrift to the vicar of S. Fooles, who in steade of a worser may be such a Gothamists ghostly father. 1659 : Howell, 16, The vicar of fools is his ghostly father. 1670 : Ray, 176 [as in 1659].

Vice, *subs.* 1. *Vice corrects sin.* 1672 : Walker, *Paroem.*, 42. 1693 : Penn, *Fruits of Solitude*, No. 45, But the proverb is just, *Vice should not correct Sin.* 1736 : Bailey, *Dict.*, s.v. " Vice."

2. *Vice is often clothed in virtue's habit.* Ibid., s.v. " Vice."

3. *Vice makes virtue shine.* 1732 : Fuller, No. 5356.

4. *Vice ruleth where gold reigneth.* 1669 : *Politeuphuia*, 271. 1732 : Fuller, No. 5359.

5. *Vices are learned without a master.* 1666 : Torriano, *Piazza Univ.*, 312. 1732 : Fuller, No. 5361.

6. *Where vice is vengeance follows.* 1639 : Clarke, 325. 1670 : Ray, 152. 1681 : Robertson, *Phraseol. Generalis*, 1269, Where vice goes before, vengeance follows after. 1732 : Fuller, No. 5681, Where villainy goes before, vengeance follows after.

See also **No vice.**

Vinegar. *See* quots. 1578 : Florio, *First Fruites*, fo. 30, Beware of vinegar and sweete wine, and of the anger of a peaceable man. 1640 : Herbert, *Jac. Prudentum*, Take heed of the vinegar of sweet wine.

Vine poor, Make the, and it will make you rich, *i.e.* prune it. 1678 : Ray, 350.

Vintner fears false measure, The. 1611 : Davies of Hereford, *Sc. of Folly*, 43, in *Works*, ii. (Grosart).

Viper in one's bosom, To nourish a. 1670 : Ray, 198. 1732 : Fuller, No. 5210.

Virtue. 1. *The virtue of a coward is*

suspicion. 1640 : Herbert, *Jac. Prudentum.*

2. *To make a virtue of necessity.* [*See* Quinct., lib. 1, cap. 8.] Before 1259 : *Matt. Paris* (Record Series), i. 20, Vitam in tantam sanctitatem commutavit, faciendo de necessitate virtutem. *c.* 1374 : Chaucer, *Troylus*, bk. iv. l. 1586, Thus maketh vertue of necessitee By pacience. *c.* 1386 : Chaucer, *Knight's Tale*, l. 2184. 1412 : Hoccleve, *Regement*, 46 (E.E.T.S.), Make of necessite, reed I, vertu. 1584 : *Three Ladies of L.*, in Hazlitt, *O. Plays*, vi. 332, Thus am I driven to make a virtue of necessity. *c.* 1592 : Shakespeare, *Two Gent.*, IV. i. 1618 : J. Taylor (Water Poet), *Pennilesse Pilgrim*, I made a vertue of necessity, and went to breakefast in the Sunne. 1748 : Smollett, *Rod. Random*, ch. xxx., However, making a virtue of necessity, I put a good face on the matter. 1876 : Blackmore, *Cripps*, ch. xxxiv., He resolved to make a virtue of necessity, as the saying is.

3. *Virtue and a trade are the best portion for children.* 1640 : Herbert, *Jac. Prudentum.*

4. *Virtue has all things in* (or *below*) *it self.* 1736 : Bailey, *Dict.*, s.v. " Virtue."

5. *Virtue is its own reward.* [Ut officii fructus sit ipsum officium.— Cicero, *Fin.*, ii. 72.] 1673 : Dryden, *Assignation*, III. i., Virtue, sir, is its own reward : I expect none from you. 1696 : Vanbrugh, *Relapse*, V. 1703 : Farquhar, *Twin-Rivals*, I. ii. 1771 : Smollett, *Clinker*, in *Works*, vi. 158 (1817). 1827 : Scott, *Journal*, Sept. 24, This species of exertion is, like virtue, its own reward. 1850 : Dickens, *Chuzzlewit*, ch. xv. 1919 : Weyman, *Great House*, ch. xviii., " Sometimes," she ventured, " imprudence is a virtue." " And its own reward ! " he retorted.

6. *Virtue is the only true nobility.* 1670 : Flecknoe, *Epigrams*, 50, Vertue is onely true nobility. 1732 : Fuller, No. 5382.

7. *Virtue never grows old.* 1640 : Herbert, *Jac. Prudentum.* 1736 : Bailey, *Dict.*, s.v. " Virtue."

8. *Virtue praised increaseth.* 1560 :

Becon, *Catechism*, 351 (P.S.) [quoted as " the common saying "].

9. *Virtues all agree, but vices fight one another*. 1732 : Fuller, No. 5392.

10. *Virtue which parleys is near a surrender*. 1721 : Bailey, *Dict.*, s.v. " Virtue."

Voice of the people, the voice of God, The. Before 804 : Alcuin, *Opp.*, Ep. cxxvii. t. 1, p. 191, Ed. Froben, 1777, Nec audiendi sunt ii qui volent dicere, vox populi, vox Dei, cum tumultuositas vulgi semper insaniae proxima est. *c.* 1390 : Gower, *Conf. Amantis*, Prol., l. 124, And that I take to record Of every lond for his partie The comun vois, which mai noght lie. 1412 : Hoccleve, *Regement*, 104 (E.E.T.S.), Thus, my gode lorde, wynneth your peples voice ; ffor peples vois is goddes voys,

men seyne. 1575 : Gascoigne, *Posies*, 143 (Cunliffe), Yet could I never any reason feele, To thinke *Vox populi vox Dei est*. 1646 : Browne, *Pseudo. Epi.*, bk. i. ch. iii., Though sometimes they are flattered with that aphorism, will hardly believe, The voice of the people to be the voice of God. 1737 : Pope, *Horace : Epistles*, II. i. 89, The people's voice is odd, It is, and it is not, the voice of God. 1820 : Colton, *Lacon*, Pt. II. No. 266, The voice of the People is the voice of God ; this axiom has manifold exceptions. 1914 : Shaw, " Parents and Children," in *Misalliance, etc.*, lxxii., When an experienced demagogue comes along and says, " Sir : *you* are the dictator : the voice of the people is the voice of God——."

W

Wade's mill. *See* Ware.

Wading in an unknown water, No safe. 1630 : T. Adams, *Works*, 748, It is not safe wading without a bottome. 1670 : Ray, 153. 1732 : Fuller, No. 3627. 1831 : Hone, *Year-Book*, col. 1417, Wade not in unknown waters.

Wager. *See* None but fools.

Wagging of a straw = a trifle. *c.* 1374 : Chaucer, *Tr. and Cr.*, ii. 1745 (O.), In titeryng and pursuyte and delayes The folk deuyne at waggynge of a stre. 1530 : Palsgrave, 468, I can bring hym out of pacyence with the waggyng of a strawe. 1577 : J. Grange, *Golden Aphroditis*, sig. I4, The wagging of a strawe . . . hindreth the flight thereof. 1639 : Clarke, 34, Angry at the wagging of a straw. 1678 : Ray, 75, He'll laugh at the wagging of a straw. 1769 : Smollett, *Adv. Atom*, 7 (Cooke, 1795), He will . . . at the turning of a straw take into his bosom the very person whom he has formerly defamed.

Wait, *verb.* 1. *A waiting appetite kindles many a spite.* 1875 : Cheales, *Proverb. Folk Lore*, 107.

2. *He that waits on another man's trencher, makes many a late dinner.* 1611 : Cotgrave, s.v. "Escuelle," 'Tis long before he be served that waits for another mans leavings. 1670 : Ray, 27. 1732 : Fuller, No. 2339 [" little " for " late "].

3. *Wait meals, flee chars. c.* 1770 : Pegge, *Derbicisms*, 11 (E.D.S.), A chare or jobb of work . . . see . . . the proverb, " Wait meals, flee chars," which I take to be the true reading and not *jars.*

Wakefield, Merry. 1662 : Fuller, *Worthies*, iii. 399 (1840). 1790 : Grose, *Prov. Gloss.*, s.v. " Yorksh." 1878 : *Folk-Lore Record*, i. 161, A similar idea is expressed in the old saying, " Merry Wakefield." [The " idea " alludes to the sixteenth-century Yorkshire song, with chorus—" Yorke, Yorke, for my monie : Of all the citties that ever I see,

For mery pastime and companie, Except the cittie of London." There is probably also a connection with the famous Pindar of Wakefield.]

Waking dog. *See* quot. 1591 : Lyly, *Endymion*, III. i., it is an old saying, madam, that a waking dog doth afar off bark at a sleeping lion.

Walberswick. *See* quot. 1830 : Forby, *Vocab. E. Anglia*, 430, He is a Walberswick whisperer ; you may hear him over to Southwold.

Wales. *See* Knight.

Walk, *verb.* 1. *Walk groundly; talk profoundly; drink roundly; sleep soundly.* 1869 : Hazlitt, 446.

2. *Walk, knave! walk!* 1546 : Heywood, *Proverbs*, Pt. II. ch. iv., Nay (quoth she) walke knaue walke. *c.* 1630 : in *Roxb. Ballads*, i. 55 (B.S.), The parrat pratles " walke, knaues, walke." *c.* 1655 : in Ibid., vi. 211, " Walk, knaue ! " is a parrot's note. *c.* 1685 : in Ibid., viii. 869, And this shall be my last reply Go walk up, out knave ! What care I ?

3. *We must walk before we run.* 1851 : Borrow, *Lavengro*, ii. 15, Ambition is a very pretty thing ; but, sir, we must walk before we run. 1878 : Platt, *Business*, 124, We must learn and be strong enough to walk before we can run.

See also Good walking.

Walking-staff hath caught warmth in your hand, The. 1546 : Heywood, *Proverbs*, Pt. I. ch. x.

Wall, *subs.* 1. *Wall between. See* Hedge (1).

2. *Walls have ears.* 1591 : Harington, *Orl. Furioso*, bk. xxii. st. 32, For posts have eares, and walls have eyes to see. *c.* 1600 : *No-body and Somebody*, l. 177, There is a way : but walls have earrs and eyes. 1633 : Shirley, *Bird in a Cage*, I. i., Take heed what you say . . . walls have ears. 1672 : Wycherley, *Love in a Wood*, III. iii. 1718 : Dennis, *Works*, ii. 298. 1766 : Garrick, *Neck or Nothing*, II. i. 1822 :

Scott, *Nigel*, ch. vi., It is not good to speak of such things . . . stone walls have ears.

Wallington. *See* quots. 1846–59 : *Denham Tracts*, i. 236 (F.L.S.), To teach one the way to Wallington. Show me the way to Wallington. 1890 : *Monthly Chron. of N. Country Lore, etc.*, 421–2, Show me the way to Wallington (title of song).

Walnut-tree : *He who plants a walnut-tree, expects not to eat of the fruit.* 1732 : Fuller, No. 2401.
See also **Woman** (8).

Walsall. *See* **Sutton.**

Walsall clock, You're too fast, like. 1869 : Hazlitt, 491.

Waltham's calf. *See* **Wise** (6).

Wandsworth, the sink of Surrey. 1790 : Grose, *Prov. Gloss.*, s.v. " Surrey," . . . This reproach is in a great measure removed. Formerly the town, which lies low, was one continued puddle.

Wanswell. *See* quot. 1639 : in *Berkeley MSS.* iii. 29 (1885), All the maids in Wanswell may dance in an egg shell. Glos. Cf. **Camberwell.**

Want, *subs.* 1. *For want of a nail, etc.* [*c.* 1390 : Gower, *Conf. Amantis*, bk. v. l. 4785, For sparinge of a litel cost Ful oftë time a man hath lost The largë cotë for the hod [hood].] 1630 : T. Adams, *Works*, 714, The want of a nayle looseth the shooe, the losse of a shoe troubles the horse, the horse indangereth the rider, the rider breaking his ranke molests the company, so far as to hazard the whole army. 1640 : Herbert, *Jac. Prudentum*, For want of a nail the shoe is lost, for want of a shoe the horse is lost, for want of a horse the rider is lost. 1736 : Franklin, *Way to Wealth*, in *Works*, i. 446 (Bigelow) [as in 1640, with " was " for " is," *plus*], being overtaken and slain by the enemy ; all for want of a little care about a horse-shoe nail. 1875 : Cheales, *Proverb. Folk-Lore*, 165 [as in 1736, but ending with " enemy "].

2. *For want of company welcome trumpery.* 1678 : Ray, 69. 1690 : *New Dict. Canting Crew*, sig. M4 [with " good " before " company "]. 1738 :

Swift, *Polite Convers.*, Dial. III. 1830 : Forby, *Vocab. E. Anglia*, 427.

3. *Want goes by such an ones door.* Somerset. 1678 : Ray, 347.

4. *Want is the whetstone of wit.* 1611 : *Tarlton's Jests*, 36 (Sh. S.).

5. *Want makes strife. See* **Poverty** breeds.

. 6. *Want of care admits despair.* 1855 : Bohn, 551.

7. *Want of care does us more damage than want of knowledge.* 1736 : Franklin, *Way to Wealth*, in *Works*, i. 445 (Bigelow).

8. *Want of money, want of comfort.* 1736 : Bailey, *Dict.*, s.v. " Want."

Want, *verb.* 1. *I will not want when I have, and when I haven't too.* Somerset. 1678 : Ray, 344. 1732 : Fuller, No. 2650.

2. *To want a boiled ha'penny:* said of weak or silly persons. 1917 : Bridge, *Cheshire Proverbs*, 146.

3. *What she wants in up and down she hath in round about.* 1678 : Ray, 346.

4. *You want the thing you have.* 1629 : *Book of Meery Riddles*, Prov. 130.

Wanton look. *See* quots. 13th cent. in *Reliq. Antiquæ*, ii. 14 (1843), Lither look and twinkling, Titring and tikeling, Opin breast and singing, theise midoutin lesing, Arin toknes of horelinge. 1869 : Hazlitt, 447, Wanton look and twinkling, Laughing and tickling, Open breast and singing, these without lying, Are tokens of whoring.

War and Wars, *subs.* 1. *He that makes a good war makes a good peace.* 1666 : Torriano, *Piazza Univ.* [" who " for " he " and " obtaineth " for second " makes "]. 1670 : Ray, 28. 1732 : Fuller, No. 2230.

2. *He was saying his war prayers, i.e.* swearing. S. Devon. 1869 : Hazlitt, 194.

3. *War and physic are governed by the eye.* 1640 : Herbert, *Jac. Prudentum.*

4. *War, hunting and love are as full of troubles as pleasures.* 1640 : Herbert, *Jac. Prudentum*, In war, hunting, and love, men for one pleasure a thousand griefs prove. 1670 : Ray, 28 [with " law " for " love "]. 1732 : Fuller, No. 5416, War, hunting, and love have

a thousand troubles for their pleasure.
1846–59: *Denham Tracts*, ii. 109
(F.L.S.) [with " law " for " love "].

5. *War is death's feast.* 1611 : Cotgrave, s.v. " Feste," Warre is the dead
mans holy-day. 1640 : Herbert, *Jac.
Prudentum.* 1732 : Fuller, No. 5417.

6. *War makes thieves, and peace hangs
them.* 1640 : Herbert, *Jac. Prudentum.*
1660 : Howell, *Parly of Beasts*, 117, War
makes the thief, and peace brings him
to the gallows. 1732 : Fuller, No.
5418.

7. *War must be waged by waking men.*
1639 : Clarke, 318. 1670 : Ray, 154.
1732 : Fuller, No. 5419, War must not
be waged by men asleep.

8. *Wars are sweet to those that know
them not.* 1539 : Taverner, *Proverbs*,
fo. 49, Batell is a swete thynge to them
that neuer assayed it. 1560 : E. More,
Def. of Women, l. 239, As warre is
counted pleasaunt to them not tryeng
the same. 1575 : Gascoigne, *Posies*,
147 (Cunliffe), How sweet warre is to
such as knowe it not. Before 1634 :
Chapman, *Revenge for Honour*, I. iii.,
War is sweet to those That never have
experienced it. 1659 : Howell, 11.
1816 : Scott, *Antiquary*, ch. xxviii.,
It's a rough trade—war's sweet to them
that never tried it. 1927 : *Sporting
and Dramatic News*, April 30, p. 361,
The war correspondent in " The Desert
Song," agrees with the proverb that
war is sweet to those who haven't tried
it.

9. *Wars bring scars.* 1670 : Ray,
154. 1732 : Fuller, No. 6096. 1826 :
Scott, *Woodstock*, ch. xxvii., Myself am
in some sort rheumatic—as war will
leave its scars behind, sir.

10. *When war begins Hell opens.*
1736 : Bailey, *Dict.*, s.v. " War."

Wardhall, Cumberland. *See* quot.
1860 : Whellan, *Cumbd. and Westm.*,
290 *n.*, Up now ace, and down with the
traye, Or Wardhall's gone for ever and
aye.

**Ware and Wadesmill are worth all
London.** [1561 : *Queene Hester*, 31
(Grosart), Nowe by wades myll, euerye
mans wyll Is wonderouslye well.] 1588 :
A. Fraunce, *Lawiers Logike*, fo. 27,

Ware and Wadesmill bee worth al
London. 1662 : Fuller, *Worthies*, ii.
39 (1840). 1790 : Grose, *Prov. Gloss.*,
s.v. " Herts."

**Wares are gone, shut up the shop-
windows, When the.** 1612 : Webster,
White Devil, 45 (Dyce), Now the wares
are gone we may shut up shop. 1670 :
Ray, 153. 1732 : Fuller, No. 5609.

Ware skins, quoth Grubber, when he
flung the louse into the fire. 1678 :
Ray, 257. 1732 : Fuller, No. 5420
[with " shins " for " skins " and
" Grub " for " Grubber "].

Warm, *adj.* 1. *As warm as toast.*
See **Hot as a toast.**

2. *As warm as wool.* 1639 : Clarke,
286. 1658 : R. Franck, *North. Memoirs*,
163 (1821), Her body was as warm as
wool. 1692 : L'Estrange, *Æsop*, 411
(3rd ed.), A vengeance on ye, says he,
y'are as warm as wool.

3. *He that is warm thinks all so.*
1640 : Herbert, *Jac. Prudentum.* 1875 :
Cheales, *Proverb. Folk-Lore*, 132.

Warm, *verb.* 1. *He warms too near
that burns.* 1611 : Cotgrave, s.v.
" Brusler," Hee warmes himselfe too
neer that burnes himselfe. 1640 : Herbert, *Jac. Prudentum.*

2. *It is absurd to warm one in his
armour.* Ibid.

Warn, *verb.* 1. *Be warned by others'
harms.* [Feliciter sapit qui alieno peri-
culo sapit.—Plautus, *Merc.*, IV. iv. 40.]
12th cent. in Wright, *Anglo-Latin Sat.
Poets*, i. 145, Foelix quem faciunt, aliena
pericula cautum. Before 1500 : in
Hill, *Commonplace Book*, 132 (E.E.T.S.),
He is wysse, that can beware by an
other manys harme. 1584 : Greene,
Works, iii. 183 (Grosart), It is good
indeed . . . by other mens harmes to
learne to beware. *c.* 1640 : in *Roxb.
Ballads*, i. 371 (B.S.), For happy is he
whom other men's harmes Can make
to beware. 1750 : W. Ellis, *Housewife's Companion*, iii., Happy is he who
by other mens harms learns to beware.
1842 : Barham, *Ing. Legends*, 2nd ser.,
" Misadv. at Margate."

2. *He that is warned. See* **Fore-
warned.**

3. *He that will not be warned by his*

own father, he shall be warned by his stepfather. Before 1500 : in Hill, Commonplace Book, 128 (E.E.T.S.). Cf. He that will not be ruled.

Wary. See Blind, adj. (9).

Wash, verb. 1. For washing his hands none sells his lands. 1640 : Herbert, Jac. Prudentum.

2. He washes his sheep with scalding water. 1813 : Ray, 75.

3. If you would live for ever you must wash the milk off your liver—a toper's saying. 1611 : Cotgrave, s.v. "Laict," Wash thy milke off thy liver (say we). 1670 : Ray, 36. 1732 : Fuller, No. 6073.

4. I will wash my hands and wait upon you. 1678 : Ray, 353.

5. To wash one's face in an ale-clout. 1546 : Heywood, Proverbs, Pt. I. ch. x., As sober as she seemth, fewe daies come about But she will onece wasshe hir face in an ale clout.

6. To wash the head. See Wet, verb. (2).

7. To wash the head without soap = To scold. 1581 : B. Rich, Farewell, 161 (Sh. S.), This olde hag, havyng had her head washed thus without sope [having been well scolded]——.

8. Washing days. See quots. 1865 : Hunt, Pop. Romances W. of Eng., 430 (1896), They that wash Monday got all the week to dry, They that wash Tuesday are pretty near by, They that wash Wednesday make a good housewife, They that wash Thursday must wash for their life, They that wash Friday must wash in need, They that wash Saturday are sluts in deed. 1888 : N. & Q., 7th ser., v. 180, . . . Monday have all the week to dry, . . . Tuesday have let a day go by . . . Wednesday are not so much to blame . . . Thursday wash for very shame . . . Friday wash in fearful need . . . Saturday are filthy sluts in deed. 1910 : Devonsh. Assoc. Trans., xlii. 90, Wash Friday, wash for need, Wash Saturday, sluts indeed.

9. Wash your hands often, your feet seldom, and your head never. 1670 : Ray, 38. 1926 : Inge, Lay Thoughts, 226, A hundred and fifty years ago the maxim for ablutions seems to have been, "Hands often, feet seldom, head never ! "

10. You wash out ink with ink. 1639 : Clarke, 197.

Washington, To give. See quot. 1846–59 : Denham Tracts, i. 92 (F.L.S.), I gave him [or her] Washington. That is, did my work quickly and roughly. But as to whether it alludes to the village of that name in the bishopric [Durham] or the celebrated General Washington I dare not at present decide. The saying is very common in the north of England.

Wasp and Wasps. 1. As angry as a wasp. c. 1350 : Alexander, l. 738, As wrath as waspe. Before 1529 : Skelton, Elyn. Rumming, l. 330, But, Lorde, as she was testy, Angry as a waspy ! c. 1570 : in Hazlitt, E. Pop. Poetry, iv. 194, She is as curste, I dare well swere, And as angry y wis as euer was waspe. 1611 : Davies of Hereford, Sc. of Folly, 45, in Works, ii. (Grosart), " Phryne's as merry as a cricket " sometimes ; But angry as a waspe, when she reads my rimes. 1670 : Ray, 203.

2. As troublesome as a wasp in one's ear. 1732 : Fuller, No. 740.

3. She is as quiet as a wasp in one's nose. 1659 : Howell, 16. 1670 : Ray, 215. 1732 : Fuller, No. 4130 [" ear " for " nose "].

4. To anger a wasp. 1586 : Pettie, Guazzo, fo. 75, It is a perillous thing to mocke and scoffe at others, and, as the saying is, To anger a waspe. 1659 : Howell, Proverbs: Ital.-Eng., 8.

5. Wasps haunt the honey-pot. 1732 : Fuller, No. 5422. 1871 : Smiles, Character, 228, More wasps are caught by honey than by vinegar.

Waste not want not. 1576 : Par. Dainty Dev., in Brit. Bibliog., iii. 88 (1812), For want is next to waste. 1732 : Fuller, No. 5423, Waste makes want. 1872 : Hardy, Greenwood Tree, Pt. I. ch. viii., Taking it across for his own use, on the plea of waste not, want not. 1882 : J. Platt, Economy, 22, " Waste not, want not," is a law of nature. 1907 : De Morgan, Alice-for-Short, ch. ix. Cf. Wilful waste.

Watched pot never boils, A. 1848 : Gaskell, *M. Barton*, ch. xxxi., What's the use of watching ? A watched pot never boils. 1875 : Cheales, *Proverb. Folk-Lore*, 132. 1884 : *Folk-Lore Journal*, ii. 279, Watch pot never boils. Derbysh. 1906 : *Cornish N. & Q.*, 202.

Watch one's water, To. *See* Look, *verb* (26).

Water, *subs.* 1. *As water in a smith's forge, that serves rather to kindle than quench.* 1579 : Lyly, *Euphues*, 61 (Arber), He that casteth water on the fire in the smith's forge, maketh it to flame fiercer. 1639 : Clarke, 158.

2. *As welcome as water in one's shoes* = not welcome at all. 1659 : Howell, 11. 1740 : North, *Lives of Norths*, i. 195 (Bohn), They caressed his lordship very much . . . and talked about a time to dine with him ; all which, as they say, was " water in his shoes." 1880 : Spurgeon, *Ploughm. Pictures*, 47. 1901 : F. E. Taylor, *Lancs Sayings*, 4, As welcome as waytcr i' one's shoon.

3. *As welcome as water into a ship.* 1580 : Lyly, *Euphues*, 381 (Arber), Seeing my counsell is no more welcome vnto thee then water into a ship—— 1605 : Camden, *Remains*, 317 (1870). 1670 : Ray, 203. 1732 : Fuller No. 749, As welcome as water in a leaking ship.

4. *Don't pour water on a drowned mouse.* 1639 : Clarke, 9. 1670 : Ray, 133. 1710 : S. Palmer, *Moral Essays on Proverbs*, 69, . . . Don't add affliction to the afflicted, is the plain English of this proverb. 1738 : Swift, *Polite Convers.*, Dial. I., Take pity on poor miss ; don't throw water on a drowned rat. 1880 : Spurgeon, *Ploughm. Pictures*, 20, I would not be hard on a poor fellow, nor pour water on a drowned mouse.

5. *He seeks water in the sea.* 1813 : Ray, 75.

6. *He wants all the water to run down his own gutter*—said of a covetous person. 1923 : *Devonsh. Assoc. Trans.*, liv. 136.

7. *There's some water. See* quots. 1913 : E. M. Wright, *Rustic Speech, etc.*, 174, There's aye some water where the stirk [heifer] drowns. 1914 : *N. & Q.*,

11th ser., x. 29, " There's some water where the stags drown : "—A friend of mine recently quoted this proverb with the meaning " There is no smoke without fire." She has been familiar with it since her early childhood, which was spent under South Yorkshire and Hampshire influences. [It looks as if " stag " were a perversion of " stirk." Kelly, *Scottish Proverbs*, 309, gives " There's aye some water whaur the stirkie (calf) drouns."]

8. *The water that comes from the same spring cannot be fresh and salt both.* 1732 : Fuller, No. 4817.

9. *To beat water in a mortar.* 1576 : Lambarde, *Peramb. of Kent*, 423 (1826), The house of Yorke had hitherto but beaten water in a mortar, and lost al their former labour.

10. *To carry water in a sieve.* 1591 : Harington, *Orl. Furioso*, bk. xxxii. st 39, Whom your fair speeches might have made beleeve That water could be carrid in a seeve. 1623 : *New and Merrie Prognos.*, 11 (Halliwell), That none may take up water with a sive. 1681 : Robertson, *Phraseol. Generalis*, 1037, It's to no more purpose than to carry water in a riddle. 1716 : Ward, *Female Policy*, 23, Giving presents to a woman to secure her love, is as vain as endeavouring to fill a sieve with water. 1736 : Bailey, *Dict.*, s.v. " Wash," To draw water in a sieve.

11. *To put water in one's wine.* 1567 : Painter, *Pal. of Pleasure*, iii. 364 (Jacobs), Which if he doe after hee hath well mingled water in his wyne, hee may chaunce to finde cause of repentance. 1599 : Chamberlain, *Letters*, 39 (Camden S.), The cheife rebells . . . began to put water in theire wine, and to proceed with more temper. *c.* 1663 : Davenant, *Play-House to be let*, V., Faith, in your wine I perhaps may put water. 1860 : Ld. Acton, in Gasquet, *Acton and Circle*, 149 (1906). (O.) I am afraid you will think I have poured a good deal of water into your wine in " Tyrol " and " Syria."

12. *Under water. See* **Snow** (8).

13. *Water afar off quencheth not fire.* 1586 : Young, *Guazzo*, fo. 191, Water a

farre of doth [not] quench fier that is
nigh. 1640 : Herbert, *Jac. Prudentum.*
1666 : Torriano, *Piazza Univ.*, 1 [" a
neighbouring " before " fire "].

14. *Water, fire and soldiers quickly
make room.* 1640 : Herbert, *Jac.
Prudentum.* 1659 : Howell, 6 [" war "
for " soldiers "]. 1736 : Bailey, *Dict.*,
s.v. " Water " [as in 1659].

15. *Water into the sea.* See Cast (8).

16. *Water into the Thames.* See Cast
(8).

17. *Water is a good servant.* See Fire
(5).

18. *Water is as dangerous as com-
modious.* 1669 : *Politeuphuia*, 184.

19. *Water is a waster.* 1672 : Walker,
Parœm., 27. 1681 : Robertson,
Phraseol. Generalis, 1297.

20. *Water past the mill.* See Miller
(12).

21. *Water trotted is as good as oats.*
1640 : Herbert, *Jac. Prudentum.*

22. *We never know the worth of water
till the well is dry.* 1732 : Fuller, No.
5451. 1832 : J. J. Blunt, *Reform. Eng.*,
140 (O.), We know not, says the proverb, what the well is worth till it is
dry. 1883 : Burne, *Shropsh. Folk-
Lore*, 590, We never miss the water till
the well runs dry.

23. *Where the water is shallow no
vessel will ride.* 1639 : Clarke, 245.
1670 : Ray, 154. 1732 : Fuller, No.
5682.

Water, *verb.* 1. *To water a stake* =
To waste effort or labour. 1681 :
Robertson, *Phraseol. Generalis*, 511,
Why do I thus water a dull and doltish
post ? 1732 : Fuller, No. 5897, You
do but water a dead stake. 1869 :
Spurgeon, *John Ploughman*, ch. i., I am
afraid I have been watering a dead
stake.

2. *To water one's plants* = To weep.
1542 : Udall, *Erasm. Apoph.*, 266 (O.),
When he read the chronicle of Alexander the greate, he could not forbeare
to water his plantes [L. *non tenuit
lachrymas*]. 1557 : North, *Diall of
Princes*, fo. 210 v., They thinke it theyr
dutye to water their plantes with teares.
1560 : T. Wilson, *Rhetorique*, 80 (1909),
So long as my childe liued I fasted, and

watered my plants for my yong boye.
1828 : Carr, *Craven Dialect*, ii. 48.

Wavering as the wind. 1546 : Heywood, *Proverbs*, Pt. II. ch. i., But
waueryng as the wynde : in docke out
nettle. 1672 : Walker, *Parœm.*, 14,
You are as unconstant as the wind ; as
wavering as the weathercock.

**Wavering man is like a skein of silk,
A.** 1736 : Bailey, *Dict.*, s.v. " Wavering."

Waxheads. See Head (4).

Way of all flesh, The. [1611 : *Bible*,
Joshua, xxiii 14, And, behold, this day
I am going the way of all the earth.
Ibid., 1 Kings, ii. 2, I go the way of all
the earth.] 1611 : T. Heywood,
Golden Age, III., If I go by land, and
miscarry, then I go the way of all flesh.
1631 : Heywood, *Fair Maid of West*,
Pt. II. Act IV., She . . . by this is
gone the way of all flesh. 1754 : Ber-
thelson, *Eng.-Danish Dict.*, s.v.
" Flesh." 1829 : Peacock, *Misf. of
Elphin*, ch. vii., Uther Pendragon . . .
went the way of all flesh. 1903 : S.
Butler, *Way of all Flesh* [title].

**Way to be gone is not to stay here,
The.** 1678 : Ray, 72.

**Way to be safe is never to be secure,
The.** 1732 : Fuller, No. 4820.

**Way to bliss lies not on beds of down,
The.** 1639 : Clarke, 16.

**Way to live much is to begin to live
well betimes, The.** 1732 : Fuller, No.
4821.

Weably. See Leominster.

Weak, *adj.* 1. *As weak as a wassail.*
1828 : Carr, *Craven Dialect*, ii. 241, " As
wake as a wassail," is a very common
phrase to denote excessive weakness.

2. *As weak as water.* c. 1320 : in
Reliq. Antiquæ, i. 122 (1841), Y wake
as water in wore. 1545 : Ascham
Toxoph., 28 (Arber), I found my good
bowe clene cast on the one side, and as
weake as water. 1611 : *Bible*, Ezekiel,
vii. 17, All hands shall be feeble, and
all knees shall be weak as water. 1631 :
Shirley, *Love Tricks*, I. 1754 : Berthelson, *Eng.-Danish Dict.*, s.v.
" Weak," He is as weak as water.
1831 : Scott, *Journal*, Oct. 19, I am as
weak as water. 1886 : R. L. S., *Kid-*

napped, ch. xx. 1900 : Pinero, *Gay Lord Quex,* IV., Yesterday I was as firm as a rock ; to-day I'm as weak as water again.

3. *The weaker hath the worse.* 1546 : Heywood, *Proverbs,* Pt. I. ch. x.

4. *The weakest goes to the wall.* 1534 : in *Two Coventry C. C. Plays,* 47 (E.E.T.S.), You mynde nothynge myne age But the weykist gothe eyuer to the walle. 1592 : Greene, *Works,* xi. 252 (Grosart), Howsoeuer the cause go the weakest is thrust to the wall. 1592 : Shakespeare, *Romeo,* I. i. 1609 : Rowlands, *Whole Crew,* 11 (Hunt. Cl.), I know the weakest must vnto the wall. 1689 : Shadwell, *Bury Fair,* III. i. 1712 : Motteux, *Quixote,* Pt. I. bk. iv. ch. 20. 1834 : Marryat, *P. Simple,* ch. v. 1907 : Gairdner, Introd. to *Paston Letters,* IV. ccxxxiv., In times of revolution and tumult the weak must go to the wall.

5. *The weak may stand the strong in stead.* 1577 : Kendall, *Flow. of Epigrams,* 249 (Spens. S.), The prouerbe old doth say : The weake may stand the strong in sted.

6. *Weak food best fits weak stomachs.* c. 1430 : Lydgate, *Minor Poems,* 165 (Percy S.), A proverbe sayde in ful old langage, That tendre browyce made with a marry-boon For fieble stomakes is holsum in potage. 1597 : H. Lok, *Poems,* 302 (Grosart), Weake food best fits weake stomacks—as is sayd.

7. *Weak men had need be witty.* 1639 : Clarke, 42. 1670 : Ray, 154.

8. *Weak things united become strong.* 1732 : Fuller, No. 5460.

Weal, *subs.* 1. *Weal and woman never pan. See* quots. 1639 : Clarke, 118, Weale and women never sam, but sorrow and they can. 1678 : Ray, 355, Weal and women cannot pan, *i.e.* close together, But woe and women can. 1828 : Carr, *Craven Dialect,* ii. 29, We frequently hear it in Craven, "women and weal can never agree." 1889 : *Folk-Lore Journal,* vii. 293 [Derbyshire], Weal and woman never pan But woe and woman can.

2. *Weal and worship.* 1917 : Bridge, *Cheshire Proverbs,* 148, The closing toast

of all Congleton festivities, "May welfare and religion go hand in hand."

3. *Whom weal pricks, sorrow comes after and licks.* 1605 : Camden, *Remains,* 335 (1870).

Wealth, *subs.* 1. *In wealth beware of woe.* c. 1460 : *Proverbs of Good Counsel,* in E.E.T.S., Ext. Ser. 8, p. 69, And ever in welth be ware of woo.

2. *Little avails wealth, where there is no health.* 1659 : Howell, 17.

3. *Wealth is best known by want.* 1732 : Fuller, No. 5463.

4. *Wealth is enemy to health.* c. 1390 : Gower, *Conf. Amantis,* Prol. i. 30 (1857), But in proverbe netheles Men sain : ful selden is that welthe Can suffre is owne estate in helthe. 1586 : Whetstone, *Engl. Myrror,* 14, The rich man's wealth is most enemy unto his health.

5. *Wealth is like rheum, it falls on the weakest parts.* 1640 : Herbert, *Jac. Prudentum.* 1670 : Ray, 28.

6. *Wealth is not his who hath it, but his who enjoys it.* 1659 : Howell, *Prov. Ital.-Engl.,* 13. c. 1736 : Franklin, in *Works,* i. 455 (Bigelow).

7. *Wealth makes wit waver.* 1736 : Bailey, *Dict.,* s.v., "Wealth." 1823 : Scott, *Q. Durward,* ch. xviii., Where much wealth had, according to the ancient proverb, made wit waver.

8. *Wealth makes worship.* 1639 : Clarke, 99. 1670 : Ray, 154. 1732 : Fuller, No. 5464, Wealth wants not for worship.

9. *Where wealth, there friends.* 1855 : Bohn, 564.

See also **Health; Money;** and **Riches.**

Weapon and Weapons, *subs.* 1. *All weapons of war cannot arm fear.* 1578 : Florio, *First Fruites,* fo. 32, All the weapons of London wyl not arme feare. 1629 : *Book of Meery Riddles,* Prov. 15. 1640 : Herbert, *Jac. Prudentum,* All the armes of England will not arme feare.

2. *It is ill putting a weapon. See* **Ill** **putting.**

3. *Weapons bode peace.* Before 1500 : in Hill, *Commonplace-Book,* 128 (E.E.T.S.), Wepin makith pese divers times. 1869 : Hazlitt, 449.

Wear, *verb.* 1. *Ever since we wear*

clothes, we know not one another. 1640 :
Herbert, *Jac. Prudentum.*

2. *He that wears black must hang a
brush at his back.* 1639 : Clarke, 201
[" They " for " He "]. 1670 : Ray, 63.
1732 : Fuller, No. 6298.

3. *He wears a whole Lordship on his
back.* 1639 : Clarke, 262.

4. *Many who wear rapiers are afraid
of goose quills.* 1855 : Bohn, 450.

5. *To wear the breeches. See* Breeches.

6. *To wear the willow.* 1578 : *Gorgeous Gallery*, 84 (Rollins), Which makes
men to weare the willow garland. 1612 :
Field, *Woman a Weathercock*, I, There's
Lucida wears the willow garland for you.
1673 : Davenant, *Siege*, V., I am content To wear the willow now. 1725 :
in Farmer, *Musa Pedestris*, 46, Great
pity 'twas that one so prim, Should ever
wear the willow. 1825 : Hone, *Ev.
Day Book*, i. 1080, The old saying, " She
is in her willows " is here illustrated ;
it implies the mourning of a female for
her lost mate. 1876 : J. W. Ebsworth,
Prelude to Bagford Ballads (B.S.), Lovers
who willow wore. 1907 : De Morgan,
Alice-for-Short, ch. xii., Having given
up wearing the willow on her account,
and consoled himself with inferiority.

7. *Wear a horn and blow it not.* 1639 :
Clarke, 142. 1670 : Ray, 198.

Weasel. *See* quot. 1840 : Barham,
Ing Legends: "Gengulphus," "You
must, be pretty deep to catch weazels
asleep," Says the proverb : that is,
" Take the Fair unawares."

Weather, *subs.* 1. *The weather will
fine. See* Rook.

2. *To talk of the weather, it's nothing
but folly, For when it rains on the hill,
the sun shines in the valley.* 1846 :
Denham, *Proverbs*, 17 (Percy S.).

3. *You are so cunning, you know not
what weather 'tis, when it rains.* 1732 :
Fuller, No. 5859.

Weatherwise. *See* quots. 1735 :
Franklin, *Poor Richard* (1890), 50 (O.),
Some are weather wise, some are other-
wise. 1875 : Cheales, *Proverb. Folk-
Lore*, 18, He who is weather-wise is not
otherwise. 1893 : Inwards, *Weather
Lore*, I, Those that are weather wise are
rarely otherwise. Cornwall.

Weaver. *See* Hundred tailors; and
Miller (10).

Webley. *See* Leominster.

Wed, *verb. He that weds before he's
wise shall die before he thrive.* 1546 :
Heywood, *Proverbs*, Pt. I. ch. viii.
1605 : Camden, *Remains*, 335 (1870).
1685 : Meriton, *Yorksh. Ale, etc.*, 67,
But they that wed before they're wise,
it's said Will dee before they thrive.
1710 : S. Palmer, *Moral Essays on
Proverbs*, 226.

Wedding. *See* Marriage.

Wedding. *See* quot. 1888 : Q.-
Couch, *Troy Town*, ch. iii., When 'tes
over, 'tes over, as Joan said by her
weddin'.

**Wedding and ill wintering tame both
man and beast.** *c.* 1595 : Shakespeare,
Taming of Shrew, IV. i., Thou knowest,
winter tames man, woman and beast.
1639 : Clarke, 328. 1670 : Ray, 47.
Cf. Bad wintering.

**Wedding-ring wears, As your, your
cares will wear away.** 1678 : Ray, 344.
1732 : Fuller, No. 6146, As your wedding ring wears, You'll wear off your
cares. 1831 : Hone, *Year Book*, 78.
1878 : Dyer, *Eng. Folk-Lore*, 192.

**Wedge where the beetle drives it,
There goes the.** 1678 : Ray, 216.
1732 : Fuller, No. 4869.

Wedlock is a padlock. 1678 : Ray,
56. 1732 : Fuller, No. 6261. 1875 :
Cheales, *Proverb. Folk-Lore*, 39, Wedlock is a padlock, and therefore is not
to be lightly entered upon.

Wednesday. *See* Sunday (2), (3),
and (4).

We dogs worried the hare. 1678 :
Ray, 239. 1732 : Fuller, No. 5443, We
hounds kill'd the hare, quoth the lap-
dog. 1846–59 : *Denham Tracts*, ii. 108
(F.L.S.).

Weeds overgrow the corn, The. *c.*
1450 : in *Reliq. Antiquæ*, ii. 240 (1843),
Lest the wede growe over the whete.
1485 : Malory, *Morte d'A.*, bk. vii. ch.
8, It is shame that euer ye were made
knyghte to see suche a ladde to matche
suche a knyghte as the wede ouer grewe
the corne. *c.* 1554 : *Enterlude of
Youth*, in Bang, *Materialien*, B. 12,
p. 17, Lo Maisters here you may see

beforne That the weede ouergroweth the corne. 1638 : D. Tuvill, *Vade Mecum*, 95, (3rd Ed.), But alas ! the tares have overgrowne the corne. 1721 : Kelly, *Sc. Prov.*, 319 (O.), The weeds oergrow the corn, the bad are the most numerous.

Weeds want no sowing. 1732 : Fuller, No. 5466.

Weeds. *See also* Ill weeds.

Week of Sundays, A = A considerable, but indefinite, period. 1876 : Blackmore, *Cripps*, ch. xxxviii., I ain't a been in church now for more nor a week of Sundays. 1894 : Raymond, *Love and Quiet Life*, 164.

Weening is not measure. 1640 : Herbert, *Jac. Prudentum.*

Weep, verb. 1. *I wept when I was born, and every day shows why.* 1654 : Whitlock, *Zootomia*, 31, When first brought forth, we cry ; Each day brings forth its why. 1670 : Ray, 28. 1732 : Fuller, No. 2631.

2. *To weep Irish* = To feign sorrow. 1589 : *Pap with a Hatchet*, 35 (1844), Ile make thee to . . . weep Irish. 1619 : B. Rich, *Irish Hubbub*, 2, Stanhurst, in his History of Ireland [1586], maketh this report of his countreymen ; they follow the dead corpse to the ground with howling, and barbarous outcries, pitifull in appearance, whereof (as he supposeth) grew this proverb, " to weep Irish." 1650 : Fuller, *Pisgah Sight*, II. xii. 15, Surely the Egyptians did not weep-Irish with feigned and mercenary tears. 1681 : Robertson, *Phraseol. Generalis*, 1305.

Weeping Cross = repentance. 1564 : Bullein, *Dialogue*, 78 (E.E.T.S.), In the ende thei go home . . . by weepyng cross. 1610 : Rowlands, *Martin Markall*, 29 (Hunt. Cl.), In the end they come home by weeping crosse, and crie *Peccaui*. 1615 : Braithwait, *Strappado*, 53 (1878), Goe not along, let my aduise enforce, Least thou returne (my boy) by weeping crosse. 1736 : Bailey, *Dict.*, s.v. " Way," The way to Heaven is by Weeping Cross. 1785. Grose, *Class. Dict. Vulgar Tongue*, s.v., To come home by Weeping Cross, to repent. 1869 : Spurgeon, *John Ploughman*, ch.

v., We must needs go to glory by the way of Weeping Cross.

Weigh, verb. 1. *He that weighs the wind must have a steady hand.* 1580 : Lyly, *Euphues*, 222 (Arber), Hee that weighes wind, must have a steadie hand to holde the ballaunce. 1732 : Fuller, No. 2345.

2. *Weigh justly and sell dearly.* 1578 : Florio, *First Fruites*, fo. 33, Weigh iust and sel deere. 1640 : Herbert, *Jac. Prudentum.* 1732 : Fuller, No. 546. Weigh right, and sell dear.

3. *Weigh not what thou givest, but what is given thee.* 1659 : Howell, 12 (10).

Weight and measure take away strife. 1640 : Herbert, *Jac. Prudentum.* 1670 : Ray, 28. 1732 : Fuller, No. 5468, Weight, measure, and tale take away strife.

Weirling, The. *See* quot. 1868 : *N. & Q.*, 4th ser., i. 614 [as in 1886]. 1886 : Swainson, *Folk-Lore of British Birds*, 114 (F.L.S.), In Norfolk there is a saying called " the Wilby warning," frequently quoted by labourers, to this effect :—" When the weirling shrieks at night, Sow the seed with the morning light, But 'ware when the cuckoo swells its throat, Harvest flies from the mooncall's note."

Welcome, subs. *A hearty welcome is the best cheer.* 1611 : Cotgrave, s.v. " Chere," A hearty welcome is worth halfe a feast. 1725 : Bailey, tr. Erasm. *Colloq.*, 429 [cited as " the old proverb"]. 1736 : Bailey, *Dict.*, s.v. " Welcome." Welcome is the best dish upon the table.

Welcome, adj. 1. *As welcome as a storm.* 1732 : Fuller, No. 746.

2. *As welcome as flowers in May.* 1591 : Florio, *Second Frutes*, 55, Welcome Maie with his flowres. 1645 : Howell, *Letters*, bk. i. § vi., No. lx., 'Twas as welcome to me as flowers in May. 1793 : C. Macklin, *Love à la Mode*, I. i., You are as welcome as the flowers in May. 1817 : Scott, *Rob Roy*, ch. viii. 1893 : R. L. S., *Ebb-Tide*, ch. vi. 1911 : *N. & Q.*, 11th ser. iii. 367.

3. *As welcome as snow in harvest.* See **Snow** (2).

4. *As welcome as the eighteen trum-
peters.* 1614 : R. Heyricke, quoted in
N. & Q., 2nd ser., viii. 484, You wryte
how yow reacayved my lettar . . . and
that . . . you esteemed yt as wellcoom
as the 18 trumpytors.

5. *As welcome as water in one's shoes,*
and, *as water into a ship.* See **Water** (2)
and (3).

6. *He that is welcome fares well.* 1736 :
Bailey, *Dict.*, s.v. " Welcome."

7. *Welcome death, quoth the rat, when
the trap fell.* 1659 : Howell, 10, . . .
fell down. 1670 : Ray, 28 [as in 1659].
1732 : Fuller, No. 5469.

8. *Welcome evil, if thou comest alone.*
1640 : Herbert, *Jac. Prudentum.* 1732 :
Fuller, No. 5471 [" mischief " for
" evil "].

Well, *subs.* 1. *If well and them cannot, then ill and them can.* Yorksh.
1670 : Ray, 155.

2. *Well's a fret.* 1853 : *N. & Q.*,
1st ser., viii. 197, It is a very common
practice in Nottingham to say :—
" Well's a fret, He that dies for love
will not be hang'd for debt."

3. *When the well is full it will run over.*
1736 : Bailey, *Dict.*, s.v. " Well."
See also **Truth** (13) ; and **Water** (22).

Well, *adj.* and *adverb.* 1. *He's well
to live* = He is drunk. 1678 : Ray, 87.

2. *He that is well sheltered is a fool if
he stir out into the rain.* 1484 : Caxton,
Æsope, ii. 239 (Jacobs), He whiche is in
a place wel sure is wel a fole to go fro
hit and to putte hym self in grete
daunger and perylle. 1589 : Puttenham, *Eng. Poesie*, 240 (Arber), It is
said by maner of a prouerbiall speach
that he who findes himselfe well shuld
not wagge. 1732 : Fuller, No. 2199.

3. *He that would be well needs not go
from his own house.* 1640 : Herbert,
Jac. Prudentum.

4. *If you would be well served, serve
yourself.* 1869 : J. E. Austen-Leigh,
Mem. of Jane Austen, 35 [quoted as a
homely proverb].

5. *That is well spoken that is well
taken.* 1639 : Clarke, 111. 1685 :
Meriton, *Yorkshire Ale, etc.*, 39, It is
well spoken that is well tane, I've heard.
1732 : Fuller, No. 4364. 1901 : F. E.

Taylor, *Lancs. Sayings*, 9, That's weel
spokken 'at's weel takken.

6. *That which is well done is twice
done.* 1606 : Day, *Ile of Gulls*, V., For,
saies my mother, a thinge once wel done
is twice done. 1682 : A. Behn, *False
Count*, III. ii. [as in 1606]. 1732 :
Fuller, No. 4381.

7. *They are well off that haven't a
house to go to.* This seems perilously
like nonsense. 1846 : Denham, *Proverbs*, 4 (Percy S.).

8. *Well begun is half done.* [Dimi-
dium facti qui coepit habet.—Horace,
Epist., I. ii. 40.] *c.* 1300 : *Prov. of
Hendyng*, st. 2 (Berlin, 1878), God beginning maketh god endynge. *c.* 1430 :
in *Babees Book, etc.*, 48 (E.E.T.S.), And
whanne a thing is weel bigunne, It
makith a good eende at the laste.
c. 1490 : *Partonope*, 438 (E.E.T.S.),
Thing wele ended is wele be-gonne.
1542 : Udall, *Erasm. Apoph.*, 17 (1877),
Laertius ascribeth to hym [Socrates]
this saiyng also : To haue well begonne,
is a thing halfe doen. . . . The saiyng
is halfe a verse of the Greke poete
Hesiodus: ἀρχὴ ἥμισυ παντός, Begynnyng is halfe of the whole. 1607 :
Lingua, II. ii., He that [hath] once
begun well, hath half done. 1680 :
L'Estrange, *Select Coll. of Erasm.*, 208.
1712 : Motteux, *Quixote*, Pt. II. ch. xli.,
A business well begun, you know, is
half ended. 1883 : Burne, *Shropsh.
Folk-Lore*, 273, " Well begun is half
done," is evidently their principle.

9. *Well fare nothing once a year.*
1639 : Clarke, 244. 1659 : Howell, 12.

10. *Well guessed Kath, here's neither
to lack nor to leave.* 1639 : Clarke, 113.

11. *Well horse, winter will come.*
1659 : Howell, 13.

12. *Well is bestowed the meat he eats.*
c. 1300 : *Havelok*, l. 907, p. 33 (Skeat),
Wel is set the mete thu etes.

13. *Well is that well does.* 1736 :
Bailey, *Dict.*, s.v. " Well."

14. *Well paid is well sold. c.* 1630 :
in *Roxb. Ballads*, i. 124 (B.S.).

15. *Well rhymed, tutor, brains and
stairs.* 1639 : Clarke, 70 [" traines "
for " brains "]. 1670 : Ray, 218.

16. *Well thriveth that well endureth.*

c. 1320 : in *Reliq. Antiquæ,* i. 115 (1841),
" Wel abit that wel may tholye," Quoth
Hendyng.

17. *Well to work and make a fire, It
doth care and skill require.* 1670 : Ray,
28. 1732 : Fuller, No. 6246.

18. *Well well, is a word of malice.*
Cheshire. 1670 : Ray, 154. 1917 :
Bridge, *Cheshire Proverbs,* 149.

19. *What is well done is done soon
enough.* 1545 : Ascham, *Toxoph.,* 114
(Arber), Thys wyse prouerbe : *Sone
ynough, if wel ynough.* 1578 : Florio,
First Fruites, fo. 25, That thing is
quickly done, that is done wel. 1598 :
Meres, *Palladis,* fo. 259 [as in 1545].
1605 : Sylvester, *Du Bartas,* Week i.
Day i. l. 489. 1633 : Draxe, 111, *bis,*
Soone enough done, if well done. 1666 :
Torriano, *Piazza Univ.,* 82, That is done
soon enough which is well done. 1730 :
T. Saldkeld, tr. *Gracian' Compl. Gent.,*
126, A thing is soon enough done, if
well done, was one of the antient sage's
maxims.

20. *Where men are well used, they'll
frequent there.* 1659 : Howell, 10.
1670 : Ray, 27. 1732 : Fuller, No.
5649, Where men are kindly used, they
will resort.

Welland, River. *See* Nene.

Wellingborough Fair. *See* quot.
1901 : *N. & Q.,* 9th ser., viii. 421,
" Gone to Wellingborough Fair to blow
their bellows."—This, in addition to
several other curious old sayings, I have
often during recent years heard from a
lady born and bred in Northamptonshire
(1830-51).

Wellington round-heads. 1678 :
Ray, 353. 1790 : Grose, *Prov. Gloss.,*
s.v. " Somerset," . . . A saying,
formerly in use, at Taunton, to signify
a violent fanatic.

Welsh ambassador, The = The cuckoo.
1608 : Middleton, *Trick to Catch,* IV.
(N.), Thy sound is like the cuckoo, the
Welch embassador. *c.* 1630 : in *Roxb.
Ballads,* i. 72 (B.S.), Three dozen of
Welsh embassadors bakt. 1754 : Ber-
thelson, *Eng.-Danish Dict.,* s.v. " Em-
bassador." 1878 : Dyer, *Eng. Folk-
Lore,* 61, In Wales the cuckoo often goes
by the name of " the Welsh Ambassa-

dor." 1917 : Bridge, *Cheshire Proverbs,* 121.

Welsh bait, Give your horse a = a
rest, without any other refreshment.
1662 : Fuller, *Worthies,* iii. 489 (1840).
1790 : Grose, *Prov. Gloss.,* s.v. " Wales."

Welsh blood is up, Her. 1631 :
Shirley, *Love Tricks,* V. iii., *Jen,* . . .
Her Welsh plood is up, look you.
1662 : Fuller, *Worthies,* iii. 488 (1840)
[" His " for " her "]. 1790 : Grose,
Prov. Gloss., s.v. " Wales."

Welsh cousin, A. 1790 : Grose,
Ibid. . . . A relation far removed ; the
Welsh making themselves cousins to
most of the people of rank born in the
country.

Welshman. 1. *The older the Welshman the more madman.* 1659 : Howell,
Proverbs: Brit.-Engl., 31.

2. *The Welshman keeps nothing till
he has lost it.* 1662 : Fuller, *Worthies,*
iii. 520 (1840), " Ni Cheitw Cymbro oni
Gello." That is, " The Welchman keeps
nothing until he hath lost it." The
historical truth thereof is plain in the
British Chronicles, that when the British
recovered the lost castles from the
English, they doubled their diligence
and valour, keeping them more tenaci-
ously than before. 1790 : Grose, *Prov.
Gloss.,* s.v. " Cardiganshire."

3. *The Welshman's jackdaw. See* Say
(9).

See also February (2).

Welsh pedigree, As long as a. 1662 :
Fuller, *Worthies,* iii. 489 (1840). 1790 :
Grose, *Prov. Gloss.,* s.v. " Wales."
1875 : Cheales, *Proverb. Folk-Lore,* 53,
As long as a Welsh pedigree . . . which
Walter Scott in one of his couplets . . .
strikingly illustrates.

Wem, Salop. *See* quot. 1883 :
Burne, *Shropsh. Folk-Lore,* 585, The
women of Wem and a few musketeers,
Beat Lord Capel and all his cavaliers.

Wembury. *See* quot. 1917 : Bridge,
Cheshire Proverbs, 12, As crooked as
Wembury (Wybunbury) steeple.

West Auckland. *See* quot. 1846-
59 : *Denham Tracts,* i. 60 (F.L.S.), By
'grees and 'grees, as the West Auckland
lasses get their fortunes.

West Chester, To be sent to. 1851 :

N. & Q., 1st ser., iii. 353, Passing through a village only six miles from London last week, I heard a mother saying to a child, " If you are not a good girl I will send you to West Chester." 1851 : Ibid., 460, To be sent to *West Chester* [= Chester] (frequently so called in the beginning of the last century) was to be sent into banishment, *i.e.* into Ireland. 1917 : Bridge, *Cheshire Proverbs*, 126.

Westgate, Newcastle-on-Tyne. 1655 : A. Brewer, *Love-sick King*, II., Here did Thornton enter in With hope, a half penny, and a lambs-skin. 1663 : Killigrew, *Parson's Wedding*, II. vii., I have heard of Whittington and his cat, and others, that have made fortunes by strange means, but I scarce believe my son would rise from *Hop, a halfpenny and a lamb's-skin.* 1846–59 : *Denham Tracts*, i. 295 (F.L.S.), At Westgate came Thornton in, With hap [luck], a halfpenny, and a lamb's skin. [Six other slightly varying versions are given at this reference.] Cf. **Hap and a halfpenny.**

Thornton was one of the Bailiffs of Newcastle in 1397, later member of Parliament, and the first Mayor. He became very wealthy.

Westminster : *Who goes to Westminster for a wife, to Paul's for a man, or to Smithfield for a horse, may meet with a whore, a knave and a jade.* 1593 : *Passionate Morrice*, 83 (N. Sh. S.), It is more vncertaine . . . whether a Smithfeelde horse will proue good or iadish. 1617 : Fynes Moryson, *Itinerary*, Pt. 3, p. 53, The Londiners pronounce woe to him that buyes a horse in Smythfield, that takes a servant in Pauls Church, that marries a wife out of Westminster [noted for its stews]. 1658 : Flecknoe, *Enigm. Characters*, 47, That old saying of choosing a horse in Smithfield, and a serving-man in Pauls. 1790 : Grose, *Prov. Gloss.*, s.v. " London."

Westminster Hall. *See* **Suits hang.**

Westmoreland Jury. *See* quot. 1846–59 : *Denham Tracts*, i. 223 (F.L.S.), Wise as the Westmoreland Jury, who found a man guilty of manslaughter who was tried for stealing a grindstone !

Weston. *See* **Holbeach.**

Westridge wood. *See* quot. 1639 : in *Berkeley MSS.* iii. 29 (1885), When Westridge wood is motley, then it's time to sowe barley. Glos.

Westward for smelts. 1603 : *Westward for Smelts, or the Waterman's Fare of Mad, Merry Western Wenches, etc.* [title]. 1607 : Dekker, etc., *Westw. Hoe*, II. iii., But wenches, with what pullies shall wee slide with some cleanly excuse, out of our husbandes suspition, being gone Westward for smelts all night. 1608 : *Great Frost*, in Arber, *Garner*, i. 85 (1877), Say, have none gone " westward for smelts," as our proverbial phrase is ?

Wet, *adj.* 1. *After a wet year a cold one.* 1893 : Inwards, *Weather Lore*, 4.

2. *As wet as a shag* (cormorant). 1838 : Holloway, *Provincialisms*, 150, " As wet as a shag," means very wet. 1875 : Parish, *Sussex Dict.*, 102, . . . is a common expression taken from the idea of a cormorant diving frequently under the water.

3. *As wet as drip.* 1828 : Carr, *Craven Dialect*, i. 119, " As wet as drip " is a common phrase, when a person's clothes are so soaked with rain that it falls off in drops.

4. *As wet as muck.* 1714 : Mandeville, *Fable of Bees*, 219, With his cloaths as wet as dung with the rain. 1883 : Burne, *Shropsh. Folk-Lore*, 595. 1889 : *N. & Q.*, 7th ser., vii. 135, A few years ago such a young woman would have said . . . " It's as wet as muck." 1894 : Raymond, *Love and Quiet Life*, 215, Made him so wet as a muck.

5. *As wet as thatch.* 1889 : Peacock, *Manley, etc., Gloss.*, 604 (E.D.S.), Weet as thack, *i.e.* wet as thatch. 1917 : Bridge, *Cheshire Proverbs*, 26.

6. *As wet as wring.* Ibid., 26 [" wring " perhaps = coarse, rushy grass].

7. *A wet hand will hold a dead herring.* 1580 : Lyly, *Euphues*, 414 (Arber), A wette hande quoth Flauia will holde a dead hearing. 1732 : Fuller, No. 453.

8. *Wet eel.* *See* **Eel** (4).

9. *With a wet finger* = easily, as easily as a wetted finger will turn a page. 1519 : Horman, *Vulgaria*, fo. 195, I wyll helpe all this besines with a wete fynger. 1593 : G. Harvey, *Works*, ii. 32 (Grosart), I hate brawles with my hart : and can turne-ouer a volume of wronges with a wett finger. 1607 : Dekker, etc., *Westw. Hoe*, II. ii., Ile becken, you shal see ile fetch her with a wet finger. 1721 : Cibber, *Refusal*, I., Here's five thousand for you. Mr. Granger. with a wet finger. 1824 : Scott, *Redgauntlet*, ch. xv., He thinks to win them to his turn with a wet finger.

Wet, *verb.* 1. *To wet one's whistle.* [τέγγε πνεύμονας.—Petr., 34]. *c.* 1386 : Chaucer, *Reeve's Tale*, l. 235, So was her ioly whistle wel y-wet. *c.* 1410 : *Towneley Plays*, 119 (E.E.T.S.), Had she oones wett hyr whystyll she couth syng full clere. 1570 : Googe, *Popish Kingdome*, 50 (1880), The meate they go, and all with wine their whistles wet. 1685 : S. Wesley, *Maggots*, 64, Well may I My whistle wet, for sure the subject's dry. 1886 : Hardy, *Casterbridge*, ch. xxxvi., Come in and wet your whistle at my expense. 1926 : Phillpotts, *Yellow Sands*, iii., He'll want a drop to wet his whistle.

2. *To wet the head. See* quots. 1889 : *N. & Q.*, 7th ser., viii. 86, Farmer A., who was on his way from the house of Farmer B., where, said he, "We have been washing the baby's head" [*i.e.* drinking its health]. 1923 : *N. & Q.*, 12th ser., xii. 63, There is a centuries-old custom connected with the first shoeing of a young horse . . . known as "wetting its head." Ibid., 152, The birth of a child frequently afforded an excuse for a drink, on the plea of " wetting its head."

Wettenhall. *See* quot. 1917 : Bridge, *Cheshire Proverbs*, 51, Down Wettenhall long lane, the plovers fly backwards. Said in answer to persistent questions. Imparting information which is of no value.

Weybourne Hoop. *See* **England** (6).

Whale. *See* **Herring** (4) ; **Sprat ;** and **Tub to a whale.**

Whaplode. *See* **Holbeach.**

What again? *See* quots. 1639 : Clarke, 303, "What again?" quoth Paul when his wife made him cuckold the second time. 1659 : Howell, 11, "What again?" quoth Palmer.

What d'ye lack? The traditional cry of the London apprentice, which became a proverbial name for a shopkeeper. 1563 : Newbery, *Dives Pragmaticus*, sig. A3, What lacke ye, sir what seke you, what wyll you bye? 1630 : T. Adams, *Works*, 171, She sits upon the stall, and counts the passengers with a what lacke ye? 1641 : *Stage-Players Complaint*, 3, in Hindley, *Old Book Coll. Miscell.*, iii., I'm persuaded that there's never a *What lack you, Sir*, in all the City, but is sensible of our calamity. 1685 : S. Wesley, *Maggots*, 159, A shop i' th' Change, still damn'd to What d'ye lack !

What greater crime than loss of time? 1732 : Fuller, No. 6324.

What has been, may be. Ibid., No. 5491.

What is she, but what has she, Not. 1621 : Brathwait, *Natures Embassie*, 233 (1877), 'Tis true what th' prouerbe saith, We aske not what he is, but what he hath. 1732 : Fuller, No. 3687. 1738 : Swift, *Polite Convers.*, Dial. I., It is not what is she, but has she now-a-days.

What she wants in up and down. *See* **Want,** *verb* (3).

What's mine's mine own. 1613 : H. Parrot, *Laquei ridiculosi*, bk. i. Epi. 118, 1666 : Torriano, *Piazza Univ.*, 278, The English ever say, That which is mine is my own. 1732 : Fuller, No. 5512, What's mine is my own : what's my brother's is his and mine. 1738 : Swift, *Polite Convers.*, Dial. II., What's yours is mine, and what's mine is my own. 1830 : Forby, *Vocab. E. Anglia*, 430, What's hers is mine ; what's mine is my own, quoth the husband.

What's what, To know. *c.* 1400 : *Ywaine and Gawin*, l. 432 (Ritson), For wa I wist noght what was what. *c.* 1440 : Hoccleve, *Minor Poems*, 138 (E.E.T.S.), And elles woot I neuere what is what. Before 1529 : Skelton,

Works, ii, 60 (Dyce), Yet, whan he toke first his hat, He said he knew what was what. 1542 : Udall, tr. *Erasm. Apoph.*, 239 (1877). 1638 : Ford, *Lady's Trial*, II. i., I know what's what, I know upon which side My bread is butter'd. 1696 : Vanbrugh, *Relapse*, III. 1711 : Steele, *Spectator*, No. 132, This sly saint . . . understands what's what as well as you or I, widow. 1773 : Goldsmith, *She Stoops*, V., I'm an old fellow, and know what's what as well as you that are younger. 1837 : Dickens, *Pickwick*, ch. xxxvii., That 'ere young lady . . . knows wot's wot, she does. 1849 : Lytton, *Caxtons*, Pt. iv., ch. iii.

What the Cheque [Exchequer] takes not, the Church takes. 1660 : Howell, *Parly of Beasts*, 18.

What they want in meat, let them take out in drink. 1598 : Shakespeare, *2 Hen. IV*. V. iii., What you want in meat. we'll have in drink. 1631 : Heywood, *Fair Maid of West*, Pt. I. act ii. [cited as " the old proverbe "].

Wheamow. *See* I.

Wheat. 1. *A good wheat year, a fine plum year.* 1887 : *N. & Q.*, 7th ser., iv. 485, . . . This is a prevailing saying in North Notts.

2. *Good wheat. See* quot. 1860 : R. S. Hawker, in Byles, *Life, etc.*, 323 (1905), The Farmers have a proverb here [Morwenstow] that good wheat in March should cover a sitting hare.

3. *Sow wheat in dirt, and rye in dust.* 1732 : Fuller, No. 4235. 1884 : H. Friend, *Flowers and Fl. Lore*, 219. 1893 : Inwards, *Weather Lore*, 153.

4. *Sow your wheat all in a flood, And it will grow up like a wood.* 1670 : *Poor Robert Alman.*, Sept.

4. *Wheat always lies best in wet sheets.* 1830 : Forby, *Vocab. E. Anglia*, 417.

5. *Wheat is not to be gathered in the blade, but in the ear.* 1732 : Fuller, No. 5528.

6. *Wheat or barley. See* quot. 1886 : Elworthy, *West Som. Word-Book*, 667 (E.D.S.), The old adage about a late season : Wait [wheat] or barley 'll strut [sprout] in June, Nif they baint no higher 'an a spoon.

7. *Wheat will not have two praises* (summer and winter). 1678 : Ray, 348. 1846 : Denham, *Proverbs*, 5 (Percy S.).

8. *When wheat lies long in bed, it riseth with an heavy head.* Gloucest. 1639 : in *Berkeley MSS.*, iii. 28 (1885).

See also **Bark-year** ; **Barley** ; **Bushel** (1) ; **Good elm** ; **March** (27) ; **May** (12); **November** (6) ; **No wheat** ; and **Tenbury.**

Wheelbarrow farmer, A. 1917 : Bridge, *Cheshire Proverbs*, 27, One who rents only an acre or two of land and is supposed to wheel his manure . . . in barrow loads instead of carting it.

Wheels within wheels. [1611 : *Bible*, Ezekiel, i. 16, Their appearance and their work was as it were a wheel in the middle of a wheel.] 1642 : D. Rogers, *Matrim. Honour*, To Reader, This wheele of our conversation . . . including many lesser wheeles in, and under it. 1709 : Mandeville, *Virgin Unmask'd*, Preface, And as a wheel within a wheel, prefixing it to the Preface. 1740 : North, *Lives of Norths*, i. 306 (Bohn), Wheels within wheels took place ; the ministers turned formalisers, and the court mysterious. 1837 : Dickens, *Pickwick*, ch. xl., Veels within veels, a prison in a prison. Ain't it, Sir ? 1867 : Dickens, *Letters*, ii. 304 (1880).

Wheelwright's dog is a carpenter's mate, A = A bad wheelwright makes a good carpenter. 1830 : Forby, *Vocab. E. Anglia*, 427. 1872 : J. Glyde, Jr., *Norfolk Garland*, 148 [" uncle " for " mate "].

When I did well, I heard it never ; When I did ill, I heard it ever. 1732 : Fuller, No. 6414. 1736 : Bailey, *Dict.*, s.v. " When."

When I lent I was a friend, When I asked I was unkind. 16th cent. in *Reliq. Antiquæ*, i. 208 (1841).

When thou dost hear a toll or knell, Then think upon thy passing-bell. 1659 : Howell, 6. 1670 : Ray, 212.

When Tom's pitcher's broken I shall have the shards; *i.e.* Kindness after others have done with it ; or refuse. 1678 ; Ray, 351.

Where a man lives well. *See* **Man** (43).

Where something is found, there look again. 1732 : Fuller, No. 5658.

Whet is no let, A. Before 1628 : J. Preston, *Saint's Daily Exercise*, 32 (1629), (O.), The whetting of the sithe, though there be a stop in the work for a time, yet, as our common saying is, " a whet is no let," and the doing of this is no impediment. 1670 : Ray, 155. 1709 : R. Kingston, *Apoph. Curiosa*, 80, Whetting is no letting. 1732 : Fuller, No. 454, A whet is no let, said the mower.

Whetstone can't itself cut, yet it makes tools cut, A. 1732 : Fuller, No. 455.

Whetstone, To deserve, or, to lie for the. [The tongue compared to a whetstone.—Pindar, *Ol.*, vi. 140.] 1364 : *Liber Albus*, iv. 601 (Rolls), (O.), Juggement de Pillorie par iii heures, ove un ague pier entour soun col, pur mensonges controeves. *c.* 1400 : *Towneley Plays*, 230 (E.E.T.S.), He lyes for the quetstone. Before 1500 in Hill, *Commonplace-Book*, 110 (E.E.T.S), I sawe an ege styng a pye ; geve me drynke, my mowth ys drye ; Yet ys not long syth I made a lye ; I will haue the whetston, and I may. 1580 : Lyly, *Euphues*, 238 (Arber), If I meet with one of Creete, I was ready to lye with him for the whetstone. 1625 : in *Harl. Miscell.*, iv. 87 (1745), Now that this is a lye well worthy of a whetstone, yourself (I hope) will acknowledge. 1732 : Fuller, No. 5991, You shall have the whetstone. 1886 : Elworthy, *West Som. Word-Book*, 828 (E.D.S.), Whetstone. The liar's prize—still used thus. 1926 : *Star*, Feb. 27, p. 5, col. 1, A country amusement of the day [18th century] was " lying for the whetstone."

Which way to London? *See* quots. 1583 : Melbancke, *Philotinus*, sig. 63, God geue you good euen, which is the way to Poclinton, a pokeful of plummes. 1633 : Draxe, 4, Which way to London ? a poke full of plummes. 1639 : Clarke, 19 [as in 1633.] 1666 : Torriano, *Piazza Univ.*, 100, As they say in English, How many miles to London, answer is made impertinently, a poke full of plums.

While men go after a leech— = After

death the doctor. *c.* 1387 : Usk, *Test of Love*, in Skeat's *Chaucer*, vii. 134, While men gon after a leche the body is buryed.

Whim-wham. *See* quot. 1917 : Bridge, *Cheshire Proverbs*, 28, A whim-wham from Yocketon. A whim-wham to wind the sun up. [Answers by old folk to inquisitive young people who interrupt them.]

Whip and whur [whirr] never made good fur. 1550 : Udall, *R. Doister*, I. iii, No haste but good, Madge Mumblecrust ; for whip and whur, The old proverb doth say, never made good fur.

Whip for a fool, and a rod for a school, is always in good season, A. 1613 : S. Rowley, *When you See Me*, sig. F1, A rod in scoole, a whip for a foole, is alwaies in season. 1670 : Ray, 212.

Whip saith the tailor, whit saith the shears, Take a true tailor and cut off his ears. 1659 : Howell, 15.

Whip the cat, To = To be drunk. *c.* 1600 : in *Roxb. Ballads*, ii. 382 (B.S.), But mault made hym the cat to whip. 1611 : Cotgrave, s.v. " Bertrand," To bee drunke . . . to whip the cat. 1807 : *Gent. Mag.*, lxxvii. 1192. 1883 : Burne, *Shropsh. Folk-Lore*, 450 [lines formerly on an inn signboard at Albrighton, Salop.], The finest pastime that is under the sun Is whipping the cat at Albrighton.

Whispering. *See* quots. 1678 : Ray, 348, Where there is whispering there is lying. 1738 : Swift, *Polite Convers.*, Dial. I., There's no whispering, but there's lying. 1753 : Richardson, *Grandison*, i. 196 (1883), Whisperings in conversations are censurable, to a proverb.

Whist, and catch a mouse. 1639 : Clarke, 302. 1670 : Ray, 199.

Whistle, *subs. You'll make an end of your whistle though the cart overthrow.* 1678 : Ray, 276. 1732 : Fuller, No. 6027 [with " for it " added].
See also Wet, *verb* (1).

Whistle, *verb. You can't whistle and drink at the same time.* 1586 : Pettie, *Guazzo*, fo. 137, It is a common saying, that one cannot drinke and whistle altogether. 1659 : Howell, *Proverbs :*

Ital.-Eng., 6, One cannot drink and whistle at once. 1869 : Hazlitt, 484.

Whistling woman. *See* quots. [1721 : Kelly, *Sc. Prov.*, 33, A crooning cow, a crowing hen, and a whistling maid boded never luck to a house.] 1850 : *N. & Q.*, 1st ser., ii. 164, Hence the old proverb often quoted in this district [Northants.] : A whistling woman and a crowing hen, Is neither fit for God nor men. Ibid., 226, A whistling·woman and a crowing hen, Will call the old gentleman out of his den. 1855 : T. Q. Couch, in *N. & Q.*, 1st ser., xii. 37, An old proverb in use here [Cornwall] says : " A whistling woman, and a crowing hen, are two of the unluckiest things under the sun." 1917 : Bridge, *Cheshire Proverbs*, 28, . . . will fear the old lad out of his den.

Whiston. *See* **Bolsover.**

Whist, whist, I smell a bird's nest. 1678 : Ray, 276.

White, *adj.* 1. *As white as a hound's tooth.* 1923 : *Devonsh. Assoc. Trans.*, liv. 137, Of a clean floor : 'Er's so white's a hound's tooth.

2. *As white as a lily. c.* 1310 : *King Horn* (Oxf.), l. 15 (Hall), Whit so any lili flour. 1485 : Caxton, *Charles the Grete*, 90 (E.E.T.S.), Hyr chekys rounde, whyt as the flour de lys. *c.* 1560 : T. Ingelend, *Disobedient Child*, 43 (Percy S.), Your clothes are washte cleane, As whyte as a lylly. 1609 : *Ev. Woman in her Humour*, I. in Bullen, *O. P.*, iv. 319, Thy colour shall be dowlas as white as a lillie. 1682 : A. Behn, *City Heiress*, I. i., The dearest loveliest hypocrite, white as lillies. 1884 : H. Friend, *Flowers and Fl. Lore*, 210, " As white as a lily " has long since passed into a proverb.

3. *As white as a sheet. c.* 1489 : Caxton, *Sonnes of Aymon*, 419 (E.E.T.S.), He . . . becam pale as a white cloth for the grete wrathe that he had. *c.* 1611 : Shakespeare, *Cymbeline*, II. ii., Fresh lily, And whiter than the sheets ! 1751 : Fielding, *Amelia*, bk. vii. ch. viii., He entered the room with a face as white as a sheet. 1834 : Marryat, *P. Simple*, ch. lviii., I turned round to look at the captain ; he was as white as a sheet. 1872 : Hardy, *Greenwood Tree*, Pt. I.

ch. viii., You must be wearied out . . . you'll be as white as a sheet to-morrow. 1922 : Weyman, *Ovington's Bank*, ch. xxxvi., He was in the bank, white as a sheet.

4. *As white as ivory.* (*a*) whale-bone ; (*b*) ivory.

(*a*) *c.* 1307 : in *Lyric Poetry*, 34 (Percy S., No. 19), Hire teht [teeth] aren white ase bon of whal. *c.* 1380 : *Sir Ferumbras*, 80 (E.E.T.S.), That swete thynge as whit as wales bon. 15th cent.: *Torrent of Portyngall*, 29 (E.E.T.S.), Ase whyt ase walles bone. *c.* 1450 : in *Reliq. Antiquæ* i. 28 (1841), And sche be whyte as whales bone. 1590 : Spenser, *F. Q.*, III. i. 15, Whose face . . . through feare, as white as whale's bone. 1592 : Shakespeare, *L. L. L.*, V. ii. 1609 : T. Ravenscroft, *Deuteromelia*, sig. B4, His beard was all on a white a, as white as whale is bone. 1855 : Kingsley, *Westw. Ho*, ch. vii., The lady herself was of an excellent beauty, like a whale's tooth for whiteness.

(*b*) 1592 : Warner, *Alb. England*, bk. vii. ch. 36, Her bodie white as iuorie. 1725 : *The Matchless Rogue*, 83, His teeth were as white as ivory. 1781 : T. Francklin, *Lucian's Works*, ii. 339. 1836 : Marryat, *Midsh. Easy*, ch. v., He showed a row of teeth white as ivory. 1922 : A. Bennett, *Prohack*, ch. xxi. (iii.), The poor lady had gone as pale as ivory.

5. *As white as milk. c.* 1300 : Brunne, tr. Langtoft *Chron.*, 334 (Hearne), In lynen white as milke. *c.* 1380 : *Sir Ferumbras*, 124 (E.E.T.S.), As wyt ase melkys fom. *c.* 1386 : Chaucer, *Prol.* l. 358. *c.* 1400 : *Rom. Rose*, l. 1196. *c.* 1450 : *Partonope*, 66 (E.E.T.S.), And therto whyte as ony mylk. 1555 : S. Hawes, *Past. of Pleasure*, 200 (Percy S.), Whyte as the milke, a goodly garment. *c.* 1650 : in *Poems on Costume*, 119 (Percy S.). 1669-96 : Aubrey, *Lives*, i. 212 (Clark), A long beard as white as milke. 1748 : Smollett, *Rod. Random*, ch. viii., A countenance as pale as milk. 1820 : Byron, *Don Juan*, can. v. st. 77, A slight chemise as white as milk. 1850 : Dickens, *Copperfield*, ch. iii., The walls

were whitewashed as white as milk.
1883 : A. Dobson, in *Poet. Works*, 167
(1923), Her neck is white as milk.

6. *As white as nip. See* **Clean as nip.**

7. *As white as driven snow. c.* 1300 in
Vernon MS., 418 (E.E.T.S.), Als whit
as any dryuen snawe. 1579 : Lyly,
Euphues, 89 (Arber), The fish . . . is
as white as the driuen snow. 1610 :
Shakespeare, *Wint. Tale*, IV. iv., Lawn
as white as driven snow. 1622 : Drayton, *Polyol.*, xxiv., His head and beard
as white as swan or driven snow. 1710 :
Ward, *Nuptial Dialogues*, i. 318, White
as the driven snow or thistly down.
1742 : Fielding, *Andrews*, bk. iv. ch. vi.,
His bosom, when a boy, was as white as
driven snow. 1823 : Byron, *Don Juan*,
can. vi. st. 25, In sheets white as what
bards call " driven snow."

8. *As white as snow. c.* 1000 : *Ags.
Gosp.*, Matt. xvii. 2 (O.), Hys reaf
waeron swa hwite swa snaw. *c.* 1280 in
Vernon MS., 373 (E.E.T.S.), The castel
is whit schinynge So the snowgh.
c. 1360 : Mandeville, *Travels*, 139
(E.E.T.S.), And all ben white as snow.
c. 1440 : Lydgate, *Lyf of our Lady*, sig.
F2 (Caxton), Was whyt in soth as
snowe that falleth newe. 1598 : Meres,
Palladis, fo. 195, The hearbe Moly hath
a flower as white as snow. 1681 :
Rycaut, tr. *Gracian's Critick*, 211, Pipes
of alablaster as white as snow. 1729 :
Coffey, *Beggar's Wedding*, I. iii., Your
head's white as snow. 1883 : R. L. S.,
Treas. Isl., ch. i., The next, bright doctor,
with his powder as white as snow.
1901 : Raymond, *Idler out of Doors*, 5,
Orchards, white as snow in early June.

9. *As white as whale-bone. See* No.
4a.

10. *A white loaf and a hard cheese
never shames the master.* 1659 : Howell,
11.

11. *A white wall is a fool's paper.*
1578 : Florio, *First Fruites*, fo. 32.
1605 : Camden, *Remains*, 319 (1870).
1662 : Fuller, *Worthies*, ii. 191 (1840),
Indeed the Italians have a proverb, " A
wall is the fool's paper," whereon they
scribble their fancies. [The Italian
proverb is *Muro bianco carta da matti.*]
1732 : Fuller, No. 5692, White walls are

fools writing paper. 1868 : *Quarterly
Review*, cxxv. 241, A needful and effec-
tual lesson to wall-scribblers lies in
the saw " Muraille blanche, papier de
fou " (" A white wall is the fool's
writing-paper ").

12. *He has made many a white hedge
black* [? with] *stolen linen.* 1639 :
Clarke, 191.

13. *He is very good at a white-pot* =
custard or baked pudding. Gloucest.
1639 : in *Berkeley MSS.*, iii. 27 (1885).

14. *The filth under the white snow, the
sun discovers.* 1640 : Herbert, *Jac.
Prudentum.*

15. *There's no getting white meal out of
a coal-sack.* 1865 : " Lancs. Proverbs,"
in *N. & Q.*, 3rd ser., viii. 494. 1869 :
Spurgeon, *John Ploughman*, ch. x.,
You cannot get white flour out of a coal
sack, nor perfection out of human
nature. 1901 : F. E. Taylor, *Lancs.
Sayings*, 10, Ther's no gettin' white
meeol eawt of a coal-seck.

16. *To mark with a white stone.* [O
diem lætum, notandumque mihi candi-
dissimo calculo !—Pliny, *Ep.* 6, 11.
Cretâ an carbone notandi ?—Horace,
Sat. II. iii. 246.] 1540 : Palsgrave,
Acolastus, sig. K1, O festyuall daye
. . . . worthye to be marked with a stone
as whyte as snowe. 1548 : Hall, *Chron.*,
8 (1809), This thing is worthy to be noted
with a whitestone. 1632 : Massinger,
Emp. of East, Prol., And, with the
whitest stone, To be mark'd in your fair
censures. 1693 : Dryden, *Persius*, Sat.
ii. l. 2, Let this auspicious morning be
exprest With a white stone. 1748 :
Smollett, *Rod. Random*, ch. lii., He
. . . told me that, in mentioning the
white stone, he alluded to the *dies fasti*
of the Romans, *albo lapide notati.*
1814 : Byron, in *Letters*, etc., lii. 57
(Prothero), I shall mark it with the
" white stone " in my calendar. 1888 :
Marchant, *Praise of Ale*, 581, A day to
be marked for ever by Tom with a white
stone.

17. *White head and green tail. c.*
1386 : Chaucer, *Reeve's Tale*, Prol. l. 24,
For in oure mil ther stiketh ever a nayl,
To have an hoor heed and a grene tayl,
As hath a leek. *c.* 1590 : Sir J. Davies,

in *Poems*, ii. 32 (Grosart), Septimus liues, and is like garlick seene, For though his head be white, his blade is greene. 1598 : Hall, *Satires*, bk. iv. s. iv., The maidens mocke, and call him withered leeke, That with a greene tayle hath an hoary head. 1651 : Cartwright, *Ordinary*, III. i., Mine head is white, but, O, mine taile is green. 1693 : Urquhart, *Rabelais*, bk. iii. ch. xxviii.

18. *White silver draws black lines.* 1598 : Meres, *Palladis*, fo. 151, Silver although it be white, yet it draweth black lines. 1639 : Clarke, 170. 1670 : Ray, 142.

Whitneck. *See* Stoat.

Whitsuntide. 1. *At Whitsun.* See quot. 1659 : Howell, 20, At Witson poke Munday, when peeple shear hogs, viz. Never.

2. *Fine on Holy Thursday, wet on Whit Monday, Fine on Whit Monday, wet on Holy Thursday.* Hunts. 1888 : *N. & Q.*, 4th ser., i. 551. 1893 : Inwards, *Weather Lore*, 41.

3. *If it rains on Pastor Sunday* [second after Easter] *it will rain every Sunday until Pentecost.* 1893 : Inwards, *Weather Lore*, 41.

4. *If Whitsunday bring rain, we expect many a plague.* Ibid., 41.

5. *Rain at Pentecost forebodes evil*, Ibid., 41.

6. *Whitsunday bright and clear Will bring a fertile year.* Ibid., 41.

7. *Whitsunday wet, Christmas fat.* Ibid., 41.

See also **Christmas** (10) and **Easter** (7).

Whittington's College, He has studied at. 1790 : Grose, *Prov. Gloss.*, s.v. " London," He has . . . That is, he has been confined in Newgate, which was rebuilt A.D. 1423 according to the Will of Sir Richard Whittington, by . . . his executors.

Whittlesea mere has foaled. 1865 : W. White, *Eastern England*, i. 255, Among the fenmen the phrase " Whittlesea Mere has folded " (foaled) signified such a flood as drove fish plentifully from the mere into the dykes and rivers.

Who are you for? I am for him whom I get most by. 1855 : Bohn, 565.

Who can help sickness, quoth the drunken wife, when she fell into the gutter? 1732 : Fuller, No. 5696.

Who can hold that they have not in their hand? 1678 : Ray, 155.

Who had that he hath not, would do that he doth not. 1546 : Heywood, *Proverbs*, Pt. II. ch. ix.

Who hath none to still him, may weep out his eyes. 1640 : Herbert, *Jac. Prudentum.* 1670 : Ray, 25.

Who may hold that will away? 1546 : Heywood, *Proverbs*, Pt. II. ch. vi. 1564 : Bullein, *Dialogue*, 121 (E.E.T.S.), Lament no more, good wife, for who can kepe that must needes awaie. 1614 : Jonson, *Bart. Fair*, I. 1640 : Mabbe, tr. *Exemplary Novels*, 196, i. (1900), Keep me not under lock and key, For who can hold what will away ?

Who shall keep the keepers? 1567 : in *Plasidas*, etc., 132 (Roxb. Cl.), In vayne dothe the husbande set kepers ouer her, for who shal kepe those kepers. 1732 : Fuller, No. 5718.

Whole as a fish. Before 1300 : *Cursor Mundi*, l. 8175, As any fisshe thou mades me fere [fair]. *c.* 1350 : *Alexander*, l. 2575, As fast was he fysche-hale. *c.* 1400 : *Mirk's Festial*, 265 (E.E.T.S.), And anon the lepur [leprosy] fel from hym and he was hole as a fyssche. 1486 : *Boke of St. Albans*, sig. A4, She shall be hoole as a fysh. *c.* 1580 : *Tom Tyler*, 19 (1661) (Malone S.), This chafing hath made me as whole as a fish. 1647 : A Brewer, *Countrie Girle*, sig. L2, His flesh as whole as a fish. 1707 : Dunton, *Athenian Sport*, 304, Fishes exceed all creatures in point of health, even to a proverb. Cf. **Sound as a roach**, and, as a trout.

Whole skin, It is good sleeping in a. 1543 : Becon, in *Early Works*, 354 (P.S.), *c.* 1570 : *Merie Tales of Skelton*, xii. in Skelton's *Works*, i. lxv. (Dyce), No, sayde the cobler, I am not afearde ; it is good to slepe in a whole skinne. *c.* 1620 : Day, *Peregr. Scholastica*, 70 (Bullen), As you think it good sleepeinge in a whole skin. 1664 : Etheredge, *Comical Revenge*, IV. i., I heard, poor lady, she wept, and charged you to sleep in a whole skin. 1749 : Fielding,

Tom Jones, bk. xii. ch. iii., If loving to
sleep in a whole skin makes a man a
coward——. 1819 : Scott, *Bride of L.,*
ch. V.

Wholesomest meat is at another man's
cost, The. 1659 : Howell, 19. 1670 :
Ray, 1.

Wholesomest way to get a good
stomach is to walk on thy own ground,
The. 1659 : Howell, 18.

Whore in a fine dress is like a clean
entry to a dirty house, A. 1736 : Bailey,
Dict., s.v. *See also* Once a whore ; and
Young (10).

Whores affect not you but your money.
1670 : Ray, 28. 1732 : Fuller, No.
5726.

Whores and thieves go by the clock.
1678 : Ray, 68.

Whoring and bawdry do often end in
beggary. 1670 : Ray, 28.

Whosoever is king, thou wilt be his
man. 1670 : Ray, 183. 1732 : Fuller,
No. 5734 [" shalt " for " wilt "].

Whoso in youth. *See* quot. 16th
cent. in *Babees Book* 332 (Furnivall),
Who so in youthe no vertu vsith In age
alle honour him refuseth.

Whoso will no evil do. *See* Evil (7).

Why for thy. *See* quot. 1678 : Ray,
345, 'Twill not be why for thy. *Somerset.* Of a bad bargain or great loss for
little profit.

Why hath its wherefore, Every.
1566 : Gascoigne, *Supposes,* I. i., I have
given you a wherfore for this why many
times. *c.* 1590 : Shakespeare, *Com. of
Errors,* II. ii., For they say every why
hath a wherefore. Before 1704 : T.
Brown, *Works,* i. 40. (1760). 1822 :
Scott, *Nigel,* ch. iii. 1869 : Spurgeon,
John Ploughman, ch. xvii.

Wicked, *adj.* 1. *A wicked man is his
own hell.* 1732 : Fuller, No. 460.

2. *A wicked man's gift hath a touch
of his master.* 1640 : Herbert, *Jac.
Prudentum.*

3. *A wicked woman. See* Woman (4).

4. *It is a wicked thing to make a
dearth one's garner.* 1640 : Herbert,
Jac. Prudentum. 1670 : Ray, 6. 1732 :
Fuller, No. 2890.

5. '*Tis a wicked world, and we make
part of it.* Ibid., No. 5063.

Wickedness with beauty is the devil's
hook baited. Ibid., No. 5739.

Widdecombe folks are picking their
geese, Faster, faster, faster. Devon.
Said when snow is falling. 1850 :
N. & Q., 1st ser., ii. 512.

Wide at the bow-hand. *i.e.* the left
hand = Wide of the mark. 1592 :
Shakespeare, *L. L. L.,* IV. i., Wide o' the
bow-hand ! i' faith, your hand is out.
1604 : Dekker, *Honest Wh.,* Pt. I. Act.
I., Y'are wide o' th' bow-hand still,
brother : my longings are not wanton,
but wayward. 1654 : Webster, *Appius,*
III. iv., *First serv.,* I take thee to be an
honest good fellow. *Clown,* Wide of the
bow-hand still : Corbulo is no such man.

Wide ears and a short tongue. 1633 :
Draxe, 190. 1670 : Ray, 8. 1736 :
Bailey, *Dict.,* s.v. " Wide." Wide ears
and a short tongue is best.

Wide quoth Bolton when his bolt flew
backward. 1591 : Florio, *Second
Frutes,* To Reader. 1659 : Howell, 20.
1678 : Ray, 84, Wide quoth Wilson.

Wide will wear but narrow will tear.
1678 : Ray, 217. 1732 : Fuller, No.
6097. 1853 : Trench, *Proverbs,* 19
(1905), Wide will wear, but tight will
tear.

Widow and Widows. 1. *A good
coming in is all in all with a widow.*
1659 : Howell, 7.

2. *A good occasion for courtship is
when the widow returns from the funeral.*
1855 : Bohn, 288. Cf. No. 9.

3. *He that marries a widow and three
children, marries four thieves.* 1669 :
New Help to Discourse, 310 [" Two "
and " three " for " three " and " four "].
1670 : Ray, 51. 1696 : D'Urfey,
Quixote, Pt. III. Act. I. 1716 : Ward,
Female Policy, 69. 1732 : Fuller, No.
2237.

4. *He that will wed a widow must
come day and night.* *c.* 1597 : Deloney,
Iacke of Newb., ch. xi., He that will
wooe a widow, must take time by the
forelocke. 1639 : Clarke, 27.

5. *He who marries a widow will often
have a dead man's head thrown in his
dish.* 1546 : Heywood, *Proverbs,* Pt.
II. ch. vii., For I neuer meete the[e] at
fleshe nor at fishe, But I haue sure a

deade mans head in my dishe. 1605 :
Marston, *Insat. Countess*, I. i., As bold-
faced women, when they wed another
Banquet their husbands with their dead
loves' heads. 1659 : Howell, *Letters*,
ii. 666 (Jacobs), You must also be wary
how you marry . . . a widow, for so
you will be subject to hav a Deaths head
putt often in your Dish. 1736 : Bailey,
Dict., s.v. " Widow."

6. *It is as easy to marry a widow as to
put a halter on a dead horse.* 1883 :
Burne, *Shropsh. Folk-Lore*, 588.

7. *It's dangerous marrying a widow,
because she hath cast her rider.* 1659 :
Howell, *Proverbs: Lett. of Advice*, Be
wary how you marry one that hath cast
her rider . . . I mean a widdow. 1678 :
Ray, 58.

8. *Long a widow weds with shame.*
1659 : Howell, *Proverbs: Brit.-Engl.*, 19.

9. *Marry a widow before she leave
mourning.* 1640 : Herbert, *Jac. Prudentum*. Cf. No. 2.

10. *Widows are always rich.* 1678 :
Ray, 57. Cf. **Wooers.**

11. *Widows' children turn out well.*
1897 : Mrs. Earle, *Pot-Pourri*
(Daughters), There is an old saying that
widows' children turn out well.

See also **Cross a stile** ; **Woo** (1) and
(2) ; and **Wooers.**

Wife and **Wives**, *subs.* 1. *A fair wife
without a fortune is a fine house without
furniture.* 1732 : Fuller, No. 91.

2. *A man's best fortune or his worst is
a wife.* 1670 : Ray, 28.

3. *An obedient wife commands her
husband.* 1732 : Fuller, No. 640.

4. *An unchaste wife. See* quot. 1623 :
Wodroephe, *Spared Houres*, 484, An
unchast wife working mischiefe still, is
oft compared to a foule dung hill.

5. *A wife brings but two good days, her
wedding-day and death day.* [πασα γυνὴ
χόλος ἐστιν ἔχει δ' ἀγαθὰς δύω ὥρας. Τὴν
μίαν ἐν θαλάμῳ, τὴν μίαν ἐν θανάτῳ.—Gk.
Anthol., xi. 381.] *c.* 1560 : T. Ingelend,
Disob. Child, 32 (Percy S.), Who sayde
with a wyfe are two dayes of pleasure ;
The first is the joye of the maryage day
and nyght, The seconde to be at the
wyfes sepulture. 1577 : Kendall,
Flow. of Epigrams, 143 (Spens. S.),

Although all women kinde be nought,
yet two good dayes hath she : Her
marriage day, and day of death, when
all she leaues to thee. 1608 : Middleton, *Fam. of Love*, I. ii. 1745 : *Agreeable Companion*, 44, In every marriage
two things are allow'd ; A wife in
wedding-sheets, and in a shroud ; How
can a marriage-state then be accurst,
Since the last day's as happy as the
first ? 1869 : Spurgeon, *John Ploughman*, ch. xvii., That very wicked
[saying], " Every man has two good
days with his wife—the day he marries
her, and the day he buries her."

6. *Better a portion in a wife than with
a wife.* 1732 : Fuller, No. 868.

7. *Choosing a wife* : various sayings.
See quots. 1546 : Heywood, *Proverbs*,
Pt. I. ch. ii., The best or worst thing to
man, for this life, Is good or ill choosing
his good or ill wife. 1640 : Herbert,
Jac. Prudentum, In choosing a wife and
buying a sword, we ought not to trust
another. 1659 : Howell, *Proverbs :
Span.-Eng.*, 2, Who will have a hansome
wife, let him chuse her upon Saturday,
and not upon Sunday, viz. when she is
in her fine cloaths. 1732 : Fuller, No.
462, A wife is not to be chosen by the
eye only. Ibid., No. 1107, Chuse a
wife rather by your ear than your eye.
1846 : Denham, *Proverbs*, 2 (Percy S.),
Chuse a wife on a Saturday rather than
a Sunday. 1872 : J. Glyde, Jr., *Norfolk Garland*, 150, Choose a wife on
Saturday instead of Sunday.

8. *He that hath a wife and children
must not sit with his fingers in his mouth.*
1732 : Fuller, No. 2158.

9. *He that hath a wife and children
wants not business.* 1640 : Herbert,
Jac. Prudentum. 1670 : Ray, 29. 1732 :
Fuller, No. 2157. 1880 : Spurgeon,
Ploughm. Pictures, 72, Depend on it, he
who has a wife and bairns will never be
short of care to carry .

10. *He that hath a wife hath strife.*
1559 : Bercher, *Nobility of Women*, 127
(Roxb. Cl.), Thear is another common
proverbe. Who hathe no controversye
hathe no wyffe. 1611 : Cotgrave, s.v.
" Noise," He that a wife hath, strife
hath.

11. *He that hath no wife, beateth her
oft.* 1629 : *Book of Meery Riddles,*
Prov. 79. ॒

12. *He that lets his wife go to every
feast, and his horse drink at every water,
shall neither have good wife nor good
horse.* 1591 : Florio, *Second Frutes,* 41,
Who lets his wife go to euerie feaste,
And lets his horse drinke at euerie
puddle, Shall haue of his horse, a starke
iadish beast And of his best wife, a
twang with a huddle. 1623 : Wodroephe, *Spared Houres,* 243 [a variant
of 1591]. 1670 : Ray, 28.

13. *He that loses his wife and sixpence*
(or *a farthing*) *has lost a tester* (=6*d.*) (or
a farthing). 1611 : Cotgrave, s.v.
"Femme," He that loses his wife and
six pence hath some losse by the money.
1678 : Ray, 58, He that loses his wife
and a farthing hath a great loss of his
farthing. 1694 : D'Urfey, *Quixote,* Pt. I.
Act I. sc. ii. [sixpence]. 1699 : Farquhar, *Love and a Bottle,* II. i., Who throws
away a tester and a mistress, loses
sixpence. 1738 : Swift, *Polite Convers.,*
Dial. I. [sixpence]. 1869 : Spurgeon,
John Ploughman, ch. xvii. [as in 1678].

14. *He that marries a wife is happy for
a month, but he that gets a fat benefice
lives merrily all his life.* 1725 : Bailey,
tr. *Erasm. Colloq.,* 27.

15. *He that would an old wife wed,
Must eat an apple before he goes to bed*
[Reverse] 1588 : Cogan, *Haven of
Health,* 88 (1612), Apples . . . are
thought to quench the flame of Venus,
according to that old English saying, He
that will not a wife wed, must eate a
cold apple when he goeth to bed, though
some turne it to a contrarie purpose.
1670 : Ray, 48.

16. *My wife cries five loaves a penny:*
i.e. she is in travail. 1678 : Ray, 71.

17. *Next to no wife a good wife is best.*
1642 : Fuller, *Holy State* "Marriage,"
A bachelor was saying, *Next,* etc.
1659 : Howell, *Letters,* ii. 666 (Jacobs),
next to a single life, a married life is
best. 1732 : Fuller, No. 3539.

18. *Refuse a wife with one fault, and
take one with two.* 1659 : Howell,
Proverbs: Brit.-Eng., 13.

19. *Subjects and wives.* See quot.

Before 1704 : Brown, *Works,* iv. 178
(1760), It justifies the old saying, *that
subjects and wives, when they revolt from
their lawful sovereigns, seldom choose for
a better.*

20. *Take your wife's first · advice.*
1666 : Torriano, *Piazza Univ.,* 51,
Take a woman's first counsel. 1875 :
Cheales, *Proverb. Folk-Lore,* 159, Take
your wife's first advice, and not her
second, is a matrimonial maxim that
is worth remembering.

21. *The cunning wife makes her
husband her apron.* 1670 : Ray, 29.

22. *The death of wives and the life of
sheep make men rich.* 1666 : Torriano,
Piazza Univ., 164, The English say
allusively, If wives fall, and sheep
stand, one must grow rich perforce.
1678 : Ray, 353.

23. *The wife is the key of the house.*
1633 : Drake, 230. 1670 : Ray, 29.
1732 : Fuller, No. 4828.

24. *The wife should be blind and the
husband deaf.* 1539 : Taverner, *Garden
of Wysdom,* Pt. II. fo. 4, Wedded persons
may thus passe ouer theyr lyues quietly
. . . yf the husbande become deafe, and
the wyfe blynde. 1637 : T. Heywood,
Dialogues, etc., in Bang, *Materialien,*
B. 3, p. 227, Then marriage may be said
to be past in all quietnesse, when the
wife is blind, and the husband deafe.
1710 : S. Palmer, *Moral Essays on
Proverbs,* 338, The husband must not
see, and the wife must be blind. Cf.
Husband (1).

25. *The wife that expects to have a
good name, Is always at home, as if she
were lame: And the maid that is honest,
her chiefest delight Is still to be doing
from morning to night.* 1813 : Ray, 49.

26. *Wife a mouse, Quiet house; Wife
a cat, Dreadful that.* 1772 : Garrick,
Irish Widow, I. iii. [quoted as "the old
saying"].

27. *Wife and children are bills of
charges.* 1659 : Howell, 5. 1670 :
Ray, 29.

28. *Wife and children are hostages
given to fortune.* 1732 : Fuller, No.
5742.

29. *Wife and sword.* See **Lend** (5).

30. *Wives and wind are necessary*

evils. 1736 : Bailey, *Dict.*, s.v. " Wife."
Cf. **Woman** (45).

31. *Wives must be had, be they good or
bad.* 1639 : Clarke, 328. 1670 : Ray,
49. 1754 : Berthelson, *Eng.-Danish
Dict.*, s.v. " Whether." 1875 : Cheales,
Proverb. Folk-Lore, 32 [with addition]
and so must husbands.

32. *Wives must have their will.* See
Woman (58).

33. *Wives of clouts.* 1542 : Udall, tr.
Erasm. Apoph., 119 (1877), For which
we saye in our Englishe prouerbe, wiues
of cloutes.

See also **All are good maids ; Commend** (1) ; **Dead** (1) ; **Fair** (9)–(11) and
(49) ; **Fast,** *verb* (2) ; **Good or ill hap ;
Good husband ; Good wife ; Great
need ; Horse** (26), (34), and (36) ;
House (3) ; **Husband ; Nice wife ; No
lack ; Old A** (c) (6)–(8) ; **One good
wife ; Proud eye ; Quartermaster ;
Shrewsbury ; Smoke** (2) ; **Speak** (5) ;
Tell (4) ; **This is that must needs be ;
Westminster ; and Young** (11).

Wigan, Lancs. *See* quot. 1897 : *N.
& Q.*, 8th ser., xi. 187, Can any one
give the origin of a Lancashire saying,
when friends touch glasses before drinking, and say, " Here's to the Mayor of
Wigan, that is, our noble selves " ?

Wight, The Isle of. 1. *An Isle of
Wight parson.* 1838 : Holloway, *Provincialisms*, 150, A shag [cormorant],
from its colour and place of resort, is
called an " Isle of Wight parson."

2. *The Isle of Wight hath no monks,
lawyers, or foxes.* 1607 : Webster,
etc., *Westw. Ho*, III. iii., The Isle of
Wight could not of long time neither
endure foxes nor lawyers. 1610 : P.
Holland, tr. Camden's *Britannia*, 274,
The inhabitants of this Isle [Wight]
were wont merrily to make their boast,
that their case was happier than all
others, because they had neither hooded
monks, nor cavilling lawyers, nor yet
crafty foxes. 1662 : Fuller, *Worthies*,
ii. 5 (1840). 1700 : J. Brome, *Travels*,
251 [as in 1610]. 1790 : Grose, *Prov.
Gloss.*, s.v. " Hants."

Wild, *adj.* 1. *As wild as a buck.*
1639 : Clarke, 287. 1670 : Ray,
208.

2. *As wild as a hawk.* 1820 : Scott,
Abbot, ch. xviii., Thou lookest wild as a
goss-hawk. 1878 : Jefferies, *Gamekeeper
at Home*, ch. vi., Though " wild as a
hawk " is a proverbial phrase, yet
hawks are bold enough to enter gardens.

3. *A wild-goose chase.* [An passim
sequeris corvos testaque lutoque.—
Persius, iii. 61.] 1592 : Shakespeare,
Romeo, II. iv., Nay, if thy wits run
the wild-goose chase, I have done.
1606 : Chapman, *Mons. d'Olive*, I., Let
our wits run the wild-goose chase over
Court and country. 1621 : B. & F.,
Pilgrim, V. i., His anger leads him a
thousand wild-goose chases. 1772 :
Graves, *Spirit. Quixote*, bk. x. ch. xvi.,
Fool enough to . . . ramble about the
country upon such a wild-goose chase.
1868 : Dickens, *Uncom. Trav.*, xxii.,
My mind now began to misgive me that
the disappointed coachmaker had sent
me on a wild-goose errand. 1891 :
R. L. S., *Wrecker*, ch. vi.

4. *A wild goose never lays a tame egg.*
1869 : Spurgeon, *John Ploughman*, ch. i.

5. *He looks like a wild cat out of a
bush.* 1732 : Fuller, No. 1973.

6. *The wild duck.* See quot. 1906 :
E. Peacock, in *N. & Q.*, 10th ser., v.
407, There'll be rain or something waur
When the wild duck swims in the pot-
tery car [Doncaster].

7. *To sow wild oats.* [1542 : Becon,
in *Early Works*, 204 (P.S.), That they
may satisfy the foolish desires of certain
light brains and wild oats, which are
altogether given to new fangleness.]
1577 : *Misogonus*, II. iii., He hath not
yet sowne all his wilde otes. 1600 :
Nashe, *Works*, vi. 152 (Grosart), Youth
ne're aspires to vertues perfect growth,
Till his wild oates be sowne. 1687 :
Sedley, *Bellamira*, III., A certain young
captain . . . ask'd me, if I would never
have sown my wild oats. 1748 :
Richardson, *Clarissa*, iv. 240 (1785),
You are upon the borders of wedlock,
as I may say, and all your wild oats
will be sown. 1836 : Marryat, *Easy*,
ch. xiii., He would have turned out a
shining character as soon as he had
sown his wild oats. 1895 : Pinero,
Benefit of Doubt, I., I'm seven-and-

twenty ; I'm an old woman ; I've sown my wild oats now.

8. *Wild and stout never wants a staff.* 1659 : Howell, *Proverbs: Brit.-Engl.*, 36.

9. *Wildest colts make the best horses.* 1732 : Fuller, No. 463, A wild colt may become a sober horse. 1829 : Cobbett, *Adv. to Young Men*, Lett. 1, These vices of youth are varnished over by the saying, that there must be time for " sowing the wild oats," and that " wildest colts make the best horses." Wiles often do what force can't. 1736 : Bailey, *Dict.*, s.v. " Wile."

Wilful as a pig, As. 1678 : Ray, 291, As willful as a pig, he'll neither lead nor drive. 1732 : Fuller, No. 750 [as in 1678]. 1880 : Spurgeon, *Ploughm. Pictures*, 37.

Wilful man had need be very wise, A. 1732 : Fuller, No. 465. 1736 : Bailey, *Dict.*, s.v. " Wilful." A wilful man should be very wise.

Wilful man must have his way, A. 1816 : Scott, *Antiquary*, ch. vi. 1907 : De Morgan, *Alice-for-Short*, ch. xxxvii.

Wilful man never wants woe, A. 1685 : Meriton, *Yorksh. Ale, etc.*, 49, But wilfull fowkes, duz never want weay [woe] its said. 1732 : Fuller, No. 466. Cf. **Hasty man.**

Wilful waste makes woeful want. Ibid., No. 5755 [" brings " for " makes "]. 1736 : Bailey, *Dict.*, s.v. " Waste."

Wilful will to it. 1829 : Scott, *Geierstein*, ch. xvi., That is as much as to say, wilful will to it. 1875 : Cheales, *Proverb. Folk-Lore*, 103, If wilful will to water, wilful must be drowned.

Will, *subs.* 1. *He may make a will upon his nail, for anything he has to give.* 1732 : Fuller, No. 1986.

2. *To take the will for the deed.* c. 1460 : *Wisdom*, sc. i. st. 28, Wyll, for dede oft ys take ; Therfor the wyll must weell be dysposyde. 1593 : Nashe, *Christs Teares*, Epist. Ded., Christ accepteth the will for the deede. 1694 : Motteux, *Rabelais*, bk. iv. ch. xlix., We'll take the good-will for the deed, and thank you as much as if we had. 1726 : Defoe, *Hist. of Devil*, Pt. II. ch.

iv., To take, as we vulgarly express it, the will for the deed. 1804 : Byron, *Letters, etc.*, i. 47 (Prothero), I dare say he would assist me if he could, so I take the will for the deed. 1852 : Dickens, *Bleak House*, ch. xv.

3. *Where there's a will there's a way.* 1640 : Herbert, *Jac. Prudentum.*, To him that will, ways are not wanting. 1754 : Berthelson, *Eng.-Danish Dict.*, s.v. " Will " [as in 1640]. 1849 : Lytton, *Caxtons*, Pt. XVIII. ch. v., Meanwhile I fall back on my favourite proverb—" Where there's a will there's a way." 1911 : Shaw, *Fanny's First Play*, Pref., Please do not suppose . . . that I do not know how difficult it is . . . But when there's a will there's a way.

4. *Where the will is ready, the feet are light.* 1640 : Herbert, *Jac. Prudentum*, [" your " for " the "]. 1670 : Ray, 29. 1754 : Berthelson, *Eng.-Danish Dict.*, s.v. " Will." Cf. **Willing mind.**

5. *Will buyeth and money payeth.* 1578 : Florio, *First Fruites*, fo. 34, Wyl maketh the market but money maketh payment. 1629 : *Book of Meery Riddles*, Prov. 133.

6. *Will is the cause of woe.* 1639 : Clarke, 253. 1670 : Ray, 155. 1732 : Fuller, No. 5757.

7. *Will will have will though will woe win.* 1546 : Heywood, *Proverbs*, Pt. I. ch. xi. 1605 : Camden, *Remains*, 336 (1870). 1670 : Ray, 29. 1732 : Fuller, No. 5758 [with " its " after " have "].

8. *With will one can do anything.* 1859 : Smiles, *Self-Help*, 7 (1869), Almost to justify, the proverb that " with Will one can do anything."

See also **Wit** (10) and (19).

Will, *verb.* 1. *He that will not be saved, needs no preacher.* 1670 : Ray, 21. 1732 : Fuller, No. 2351 [" sermon " for " preacher "].

2. *That one will not another will.* 1546 : Heywood, *Proverbs*, Pt. I. ch. iii., Sens that that one will not on other will——. 1654 : Gayton, *Pleasant Notes Don Q.*, 75, If one won't another will. 1709 : O. Dykes, *Eng. Proverbs*, 2nd ed., Title-page. If one will not, another will ; or, why was the market

made? 1771 : in *Garrick Corresp.*, i.
410 (1831), Well, if one won't, another
will, they say.
3. *They that will not be counselled cannot be helped.* 1736 : Franklin, *Way to
Wealth*, in *Works*, i., 451 (Bigelow).
4. *Will he nill he. c.* 1220 : *Hali
Meidenhad*, 31 (E.E.T.S.), þat wullen
ha nullen ha. Before 1300 : *Cursor
Mundi*, l. 23729, Nill we, will we, we sal
mete. 14th cent., *Guy of Warwick*, l.
7109 (E.E.T.S.), Gon ich mot, wille y
so nille. 1485 : Malory, *Morte d'A.*,
bk. i. ch. viii., Ye shal ouercome hem
all whether they wille or nylle. 1595 :
Munday, *John a Kent*, 18 (Sh. S.), Will
I, or nill I, all is one to him. 1602 :
Shakespeare, *Hamlet*, V. i., Will he, nill
he, he goes. 1607 : B. & F., *Woman-
Hater*, III. iv., Will she, nill she, she
shall come running into my house.
1740 : North, *Examen*, 67, To which
he was peremptorily bound : Will he,
nill he, that must be. 1872 : Hardy,
Greenwood Tree, Pt. I. ch. viii., Band
played six-eight time ; six-eight chaws
I, willy-nilly. 1909 : De Morgan, *Never
can Happen Again*, ch. xxxviii., Even
my boy is away, and what adds to the
cruelty of the position is that, will I nill
I, I have to feel glad of his absence.
See also **He that will not.**

Willing horse. *See* Horse (20) and
(65).

Willing mind makes a light foot, A.
1629 : Massinger, *Picture*, V. iii., A
willing mind makes a hard journey easy.
1732 : Fuller, No. 467. Cf. Will, *subs.* (4).

Willingly. *See* **Good a will.**

Willow, *subs.* 1. *A willow will buy
a horse before an oak will pay for a saddle.*
1846 : Denham, *Proverbs*, 33 (Percy S.).
1865 : W. White, *Eastern England*, i.
280. 1901 : Raymond, *Idler out of
Doors*, 127, There is a saying that a
willow will buy a horse whilst any other
tree is paying for the halter.
2. *Willows are weak, yet they bind
other wood.* 1640 : Herbert, *Jac.
Prudentum.* 1732 : Fuller, No. 5761.
1917 : Bridge, *Cheshire Proverbs*, 156.

Wiltshire. *See* **Derbyshire.**

Wiltshire moon-rakers. 1790 : Grose,
Prov. Gloss., s.v. " Wilts." 1863 : Wise,

New Forest, ch. xv. *n.*, The expression
of " Hampshire and Wiltshire moon-
rakers " had its origin in the Wiltshire
peasants fishing up the contraband
goods at night.

Wily as a fox, As. 1639 : Clarke,
285. 1670 : Ray, 208.

Win, *verb*. 1. *He's won with a feather
and lost with a straw.* 1732 : Fuller,
No. 2476.
2. *To win and wear.* 1576 : Pettie,
Pet. Pallace, i. 19 (Gollancz), You would
confess, that by force of love I had won
you, and were worthy to wear you.
1607 : T. Heywood, *Faire Maide*, in
Works, ii. 54 (1874), Court her, win her,
weare her, wed her. 1632 : S. Marmion, *Holl. Leaguer*, V. iv., There she
comes ! win her, and wear her. 1825 :
Planché, *Extravag.*, i. 31 (1879), You
. . . shall take your chance with the
rest. Win me and wear me. 1844 :
Thackeray, *Barry Lyndon*, ch. xi., Now
is your time ! win her and wear her
before the month is over.
3. *To win one's spurs. c.* 1425 : Lydgate, *Assembly of Gods*, 980 (O.), These
xiiii knyghtes made vyce that day ; To
wynne theyre spores they seyde they
wold asay. 1523-25 : Berners, *Froissart*, ch. 130, Say to them that they
suffre hym this day to wynne his
spurres. 1580 : Churchyard, *Charge*,
30 (Collier), Perhapps, in winnyng of the
spurres, You maie the horse and saddle
lose. 1642 : D. Rogers, *Naaman*, sig.
G3, I doe not accuse you as if ye sought
to winne the spurres by your parts.
1859 : Smiles, *Self-Help*, 20 (1869),
Lord Mansfield . . . won his spurs by
perseverance, knowledge, and ability,
diligently cultivated.
4. *To win the horse or lose the saddle.*
1546 : Heywood, *Proverbs*, Pt. II. ch.
ix., Recower the hors or leese the saddle too. 1575 : Gascoigne, *Posies*, 169
(Cunliffe), It was my full entent, To
loose the sadle or the horse to winne.
c. 1631 : in *Pepysian Garland*, 383
(Rollins), That either now ile win the
horse Or else the saddle lose. 1700 :
Ward, *London Spy*, 398 (1924), In order
to which, he resolves to win the horse,
or lose the saddle. 1754 : Berthelson,

Eng. - Danish Dict., s.v. " Horse."
1847 : Halliwell, *Dict.*, s.v. " Mare,"
To win the mare or lose the halter, to
play double or quits. 1913 : *Folk-
Lore*, xxiv. 77, I'll win the horse or lose
the saddle. (Oxfordshire.)
  5. *Win at first and lose at last.* 1678 :
Ray, 349.
  6. *Win gold and wear gold.* 1583 :
Melbancke, *Philotinus*, sig. C4, Thou
hast woon goulde, now weare gould.
1605 : Camden, *Remains*, 336 (1870).
1660 : Tatham, *The Rump*, III ., He
that wins gold, let him wear gold, I cry.
1736 : Bailey, *Dict.*, s.v. " Win."
  7. *Win purple and wear purple.*
1650 : Fuller, *Pisgah Sight*, bk. iv. ch.
vi., § 1, Earned with her industry (and
good reason—win purple, and wear
purple). 1853 : Trench, *Proverbs*, 106
(1905).
  8. *Win whoso may.* See quot. *c.*
1386 : Chaucer, *Wife of Bath's Prol.*,
l. 414, Winne who-so may for al is for
to selle.

Winchester. *See* Canterbury (3).

Winchester goose, The = venereal
disease. 1559 : Becon, in *Prayers*, etc.,
284 (P.S.), Making whole of a Winchester goose. 1611 : Cotgrave, s.v.
" Poulain." A botch in the groine,
a Winchester goose. 1730 : Bailey,
Eng. Dict., s.v. " Goose." Winchester
goose, a swelling in the thigh.

Wind. Classification. A. General :
(a) *Literal*, (b) *Metaphorical.* B. East
wind. C. **North wind.** D. **South
wind.** E. **West wind.** F. **Various
combinations of direction.**

A. (a) 1. *After wind comes rain.*
1548 : Hall, *Chron.*, 22 (1809), As the
old prouerbe saith, after winde commeth
rain. 1569 : Grafton, *Chron.*, i. 484
(1908).
  2. *As wroth as the wind. c.* 1350 : in
Reliq. Antiquæ, ii. 95 (1843), Thanne
the kyng wax wrothe as wynde. 1377 :
Langland, *Plowman*, B. iii. 328, Also
wroth as the wynde wex Mede [the Lady
Meed] in a while. *c.* 1400 : *Rich. the
Redeles*, iii. 153, Thei woll be wroth as
the wynde. 1468 : *Coventry Mysteries*,
8 (Sh. S.), As wroth as wynde Is kyng
Herownde.

  3. *A veering wind, fair weather, A
backing wind, foul weather.* 1893 :
Inwards, *Weather Lore*, 71.
  4. *Blow the wind never so fast, It will
fall at last.* 1732 : Fuller, No. 6306.
1869 : Spurgeon, *John Ploughman*, ch.
v. [" lower " for " fall "].
  5. *High winds blow on high hills.*
[Saepius ventis agitatur ingens Pinus et
celsæ graviore casu Decidunt turres.—
Horace, *Carm.* II. x.] Before 1225 :
Ancr. Riwle, 178 (Morton), Vor cuer so
þe hul is more and herre, so þe wind is
more þeron. *c.* 1310 : in Wright, *Pol.
Songs, John to Ed. II.*, 207 (Camden S.),
Summa petit livor, perflant altissima
venti. 1484 : Caxton, tr. *Chartier's
Curial*, 5 (E.E.T.S.), The grete wyndes
that blowe in hye courtes. 1578 :
Gorgeous Gallery, 10 (Rollins), As
highest seates wee see be subiect to most
winde. 1639 : Clarke, 23, Huge winds
blow on high hills. 1670 : Ray, 107
[as in 1639]. 1732 : Fuller, No. 2502.
  6. *If the wind do blow aloft, then of
wars shall we hear oft.* 1855 : Bohn,
418.
  7. *If wind follows sun's course, expect
fair weather.* 1893 : Inwards, *Weather
Lore*, 71.
  8. *Look not, like the Dutchman, to
leeward for fine weather.* Ibid., 69.
  9. *There's no weather ill when the
wind is still.* 1605 : Camden, *Remains*,
334 (1870). 1670 : Ray, 42, No
weather's ill If the wind be still. 1732 :
Fuller, No. 6493. 1825 : Hone, *Ev.
Day Book*, i. 670. 1893 : Inwards, 69.
  10. *The wind keeps not always in
one quarter.* 1670 : Ray, 1156. 1732 :
Fuller, No. 4831.
  11. *The winds of the daytime wrestle
and fight Longer and stronger than those
of the night.* 1893 : Inwards, *Weather
Lore*, 69.
  12. *When the wind backs and the
weather glass falls, Then be on your guard
against gales and squalls.* Ibid., 71.
  13. *When the wind comes before the
rain, You may hoist your topsails up
again; But when the rain comes before
the winds, You may reef when it begins.*
1846 : Denham, *Proverbs*, 20 (Percy S.).
  14. *When the wind is still, the shower*

falls soft. 1814 : Scott, *Waverley*, ch.
xxiv.

15. *Where the wind is on Martinmas
eve there it will prevail through the winter.*
1893 : Inwards, *Weather Lore*, 83, If the
wind is south-west at Martinmas, It keeps
there till after Christmas. 1898 : Gibbs,
Cotswold Village, ch. xvii. 388 (1909),
Last night were Hollandtide [Nov. 11]
eve, and where the wind is at Hollandtide there it will stick best part of the
winter. 1902 : *N. & Q.*, 9th ser., ix.
338, One of our local sayings [Northants.]
is . . . "Where the wind," etc.

16. *Wind and weather do thy worst.*
1678 : Ray, 277. 1732 : Fuller, No.
5743, Wind and weather do your
utmost.

17. *Winds at night are always bright;
But winds in the morning, sailors take
warning.* 1893 : Inwards, *Weather
Lore*, 70.

18. *Winds that change against the sun
Are always sure to backward run* [and]
*When the wind veers against the sun,
Trust it not, for back 'twill run.* Ibid.,
71.

19. *You can't catch the wind in a net.*
1880 : Spurgeon, *Ploughm. Pictures*,
97.

(b) 1. *All this wind shakes no corn.*
1546 : Heywood, *Proverbs*, Pt. I. ch.
xi. 1587 : Turbervile, *Trag. Tales*,
etc., 261 (1837), But al for nought, his
winde did shake no corne. 1604 : *Wit
of a Woman*, sc. viii. (Malone S.). 1670 :
Ray, 199.

2. *As the wind blows you must set your
sail.* 1732 : Fuller, No. 738. 1846 :
Denham, *Proverbs*, 3 (Percy S.).

3. *Is the wind at that door?* c. 1490 :
Partonope, 444 (E.E.T.S.), "What ! "
seith Gaudyn, " stonte the wynde in
that dore ? " 1566 : Gascoigne, *Supposes*, III. i, Is it even so ? is the winde
in that doore ? c. 1600 : Deloney,
Thos. of Reading, ch. 3, What husband
(quoth she) is the winde at that doore ?
1641 : Tatham, *Distracted State*, I.
1737 : Ray, 267, Is the wind in that
corner ? 1817 : Scott, *Rob Roy*, ch.
viii., " Whew ! sits the wind in that
quarter ? " inquired the Justice.

4. *Let this wind over-blow.* 1546 :

Heywood, *Proverbs*, Pt. I. ch. xi. 1659 :
Howell, 7.

5. *The wind in a man's face makes him
wise.* 1640 : Herbert, *Jac. Prudentum*
[" one's " for " a man's "]. 1710 : S.
Palmer, *Moral Essays on Proverbs*, 190.

6. *To know which way the wind blows.*
c. 1380 : *Tale of Gamelyn*, l. 703, in
Skeat's *Chaucer*, iv. 662, To telle him
tydinges how the wind was went. 1546 :
Heywood, *Proverbs*, Pt. II. ch. ix., I know,
And knew, which waie the winde blewe,
and will blow. 1694 : D'Urfey, *Quixote*,
Pt. I. III. ii., Why then I know where
the wind sits. 1766 : Garrick, *Neck or
Nothing*, I. ii., I always listen to reason,
Mr. Stockwell. *Stock.* Well, and which
way does the wind set now ? 1886 :
R. L. S., *Kidnapped*, ch. ix., " Oho ! "
says the stranger, " is that how the wind
sets ? " And he laid his hand quickly on
his pistols. 1906 : Doyle, *Sir Nigel*,
ch. xii., My questions must have shown
him whence the wind blew.

7. *What wind blew you hither?* c.
1374 : Chaucer, *Troylus*, bk. ii. l. 1104,
" Now by your feyth, myn uncle," quod
she, " dere, What maner windes
gydeth yow now here ? " c. 1400 :
Beryn, 51 (E.E.T.S.), Benedicite ! what
manere wynd hath I-brought yewe
here ? c. 1489 : Caxton, *Sonnes of
Aymon*, 106 (E.E.T.S.), Lordes, what ye
be, and what wynde dryveth you
hyther. 1546 : Heywood, *Proverbs*,
Pt. I. ch. x. 1657 : Sir A. Cokain,
Obstinate Lady, II. iii., What wind
brought you hither ? 1713 : Gay,
Wife of Bath, I. 1737 : Dodsley, *Miller
of Mansfield*, I. vi. 1861 : Dickens,
Great Exp., ch. xliv., " And what wind,"
said Miss Havisham, " blows you here,
Pip ? "

B. **East Wind.** 1. *A dry east wind
raises the spring.* Cornwall. 1893 : Inwards, *Weather Lore*, 80.

2. *An easterly wind's rain Makes fools
fain.* Ibid., 80.

3. *An east wind is a lazy wind*—
because it is thin, and will go through
you before it will go round you. 1886 :
R. Holland, *Cheshire Gloss.*, 446 (E.D.S.),
1917 : Bridge, *Cheshire Proverbs*, 7.
1922 : *N. & Q.*, 12th ser., x. 412, I have

often heard a cold piercing wind
described as a " lazy wind "—it is too
lazy to go round, so it goes through one.

4. *A right easterly wind is very unkind.*
1855 : Bohn, 299.

5. *Easterly winds and rain, Bring
cockles here from Spain.* 1846 : Denham, *Proverbs*, 12 (Percy S.).

6. *If it rains when the wind is in the
east, It will rain for twenty-four hours at
least. c.* 1685 : Aubrey, *Nat. Hist.
Wilts,* 16 (1847), A Wiltshire proverb
. . . If the rain comes out of east,
'Twill rain twice twenty-four houres at
the least. 1893 : Inwards, *Weather
Lore,* 79 [as in 1685, but omitting
" twice "]. 1917 : Bridge, *Cheshire
Proverbs,* 163.

7. *If the wind is in the east on Easter
day. See* quot. 1881 : Evans, *Leicest.
Words,* etc., 169 (E.D.S.), A common
Leicestershire saying is : If the wind's
i' the East of Easter-dee, Yo'll ha'
plenty o' grass, but little good hee [hay].

8. *When the wind is in the east, It's
good for neither man nor boast.* 1600 :
R. Cawdray, *Treas. of Similies,* 750,
The east wind is accounted neither good
for man or beast. 1670 : Ray, 41.
1732 : Fuller, No. 6224. 1825 : Hone,
Ev. Day Book, i. 670. 1893 : Inwards,
Weather Lore, 79. 1913 : E. M. Wright,
Rustic Speech, etc., 316.

See also D (1) and F (6) and (9).

C. **North wind.** 1. *A northern air
Brings weather fair* [1611 : *Bible,* Job
xxxvii. 22. Fair weather cometh out
of the north.] 1893 : Inwards, *Weather
Lore,* 77.

2. *A north wind is a broom for
the Channel.* Cornwall. 1887 : M. A.
Courtney, *Folk-Lore Journal,* v. 191.

3. *Fishermen in anger froth When the
wind is in the north; For fish bite the
best When the wind is in the west.* 1893 :
Inwards, *Weather Lore,* 77.

4. *The north wind doth blow, And we
shall have snow.* Ibid., 78.

5. *When the wind is in the north, The
skilful fisher goes not forth.* 1846 :
Denham, *Proverbs,* 17 (Percy S.). 1893 :
Inwards, 77.

6. *When the wind's in the north, You
mustn't go forth.* Ibid., 77.

See also F (6) and (9).

D. **South wind.** 1. *An out* [southerly]
*wind and a fog Bring an east wind home
snug.* 1874 : W. Pengelly, in *N. &
Q.,* 5th ser., ii. 184, I often heard the
following weather-rhymes in Cornwall in
my boyhood :—" An out, etc.—"

2. *A southerly wind and a cloudy sky,
Proclaim a hunting morning.* 1846 :
Denham, *Proverbs,* 8 (Percy S.). 1893 :
Inwards, *Weather Lore,* 81.

3. *A southerly wind with showers of
rain Will bring the wind from west again.*
Ibid., 82.

4. *When the wind is in the south, It
blows the bait into the fish's mouth.* 1653 :
Walton, *Angler,* Pt. I. ch. v., One ob-
serves that " When the wind is south,
It blows your bait into a fish's mouth."
1732 : Fuller, No. 6226. 1825 : Hone,
Ev. Day Book, I. 670. 1893 : Inwards,
Weather Lore, 82.

5. *When the wind is in the south, It's
in the rain's mouth.* 1639 : Clarke, 263.
1670 : Ray, 42. 1732 : Fuller, No.
6225. 1825 : Hone, *Ev. Day Book,* I.
670. 1893 : Inwards, *Weather Lore,* 82,
When the wind's in the south, The
rain's in its mouth.

See also F (5), (6) and (9).

E. **West wind.** 1. *A western wind
carrieth water in his hand.* 1893 : Inwards, 83.

2. *The west wind is a gentleman, and
goes to bed*—i.e. *drops in the evening.*
1846 : Denham, *Proverbs,* 2 (Percy S.), A
west wind and an honest man go to bed
together. 1893 : Inwards, 83. Cf.
F (1).

3. *The wind blows not always west.*
1732 : Fuller, No. 4829.

4. *When the wind is in the west The
weather is at the best.* [1606 : Chapman, *Gent. Usher,* II. i., The wind must
blow at west still or she'll be angry.]
1732 : Fuller, No. 6223. 1893 : Inwards, 83 [" always " for " at the "].
1913 : E. M. Wright, *Rustic Speech,* etc.,
316, The wind in the west Suits every
one best (Lancs.). Cf. F (11).

5. *Wind west Rain's nest.* Devon.
1893 : Inwards, 83. Cf. F (8).

See also C (3) ; D (3) ; and F (6) and (9).

F. **Various combinations of direction.**

1. *An honest man and a north-west wind generally go to sleep together.* 1893 : Inwards, 79. Cf. E (2).

2. *A north-east wind in May, Makes the shotver-men a prey.* 1735 : Pegge, *Kent. Proverbs*, in E.D.S., No. 1270, . . . Shotver men are the mackarel fishers, and a North-east wind is reckon'd at Dover a good wind for them. [Mackerel fishers' nets are called shot-nets.] 1887 : Parish and Shaw, *Dict. Kentish Dialect*, 148 (E.D.S.).

3. *A nor'-wester is not long in debt to a sou'-wester.* 1893 : Inwards, 78.

4. *Do business with men when the wind is in the north-west.* Yorkshire. Ibid., 78.

5. *If the wind is north-east three days without rain, Eight days will pass before south wind again.* Ibid., 78.

6. *North and south the sign o' drouth, East and west the sign of blast.* 1846 : Denham, *Proverbs*, 17 (Percy S.) [in reverse order]. 1893 : Inwards, 77.

7. *North-west wind brings a short storm; a north-east wind brings a long storm.* Ibid., 79.

8. *The zou'-west Is the rain's nest.* 1891 : R. P. Chope, *Hartland Dialect*, 20 (E.D.S.). Cf. E (5).

9. *The west wind always brings wet weather, The east wind wet and cold together, The south wind surely brings us rain, The north wind blows it back again.* 1838 : Mrs. Bray, *Trad. of Devon*, i. 5. 1892 : S. Hewett, *Peasant Speech of Devon*, 29.

10. *Three south-westers, then one heavy rain.* 1893 : Inwards, *Weather Lore*, 83.

11. *When the wind is in the north-west The weather is at its best.* c. 1685 : Aubrey, *Nat. Hist. Wilts*, 16 (1847). 1893 : Inwards, 79. Cf. E (4).

Wind. *See also* **Blow**, *verb* (1) and (5) ; **Candlemas** H (6) ; **Candlemas Eve** ; **Cloud** (3) and (11) ; **Every wind** ; **Fire** (12) ; **Fish**, *subs.* (2) ; **Fog** (1) ; **God tempers** ; **God will** ; **Good wind** ; **Ill wind** ; **March** (4), (9), (13) and (37)–(39) ; **Martinmas** (3) and (4) ; **Moon** (7), (12) and (27) ; **October** (2) and (5) ; **Rain**, *subs.* (3), (11) and (29) ; **Sandbach** ; **Straw** (2) ; and **Sun** (3), (15) and (16).

Windmill. 1. *To have windmills in one's head.* "Windmills" = empty projects, or crotchets. 1612 : Shelton, *Quixote*, Pt. I. bk. i. ch. viii., For they were none other than windmills ; nor could any think otherwise, unless he had also windmills in his brains. 1690 : *New Dict. Canting Crew*, sig. M7. 1737 : Ray, 216. 1869 : Spurgeon, *John Ploughman*, ch. xv., Poor soul, like a good many others he has windmills in his head.

2. *You can't drive a windmill with a pair of bellows.* 1640 : Herbert, *Jac. Prudentum*, You cannot make a windmill go with a pair of bellows. 1670 : Ray, 29. 1732 : Fuller, No. 5880.

3. *Your windmill is dwindled into a nut-crack.* 1678 : Ray, 277. 1732 : Fuller, No. 6064.

Window. 1. *A window wench, and a trotter in streete, is neuer good to haue a house to keepe.* 1623 : Wodroephe, *Spared Houres*, 484.

2. *To come in at the window :* said of a bastard. 1551 : Crowley, *Pleas. and Payne*, 350 (O.), Youe were gladde to take them in, Bycause you knewe that they dyd knowe That youe came in by the wyndowe. 1605 : Chapman, *All Fools*, III., Though he came in at the window he sets the gates of your honour open, I can tell you. 1608 : Middleton, *Family of Love*, IV. iii., Woe worth the time that ever I gave suck to a child that came in at the window. 1664 : Cotton, *Scarronides*, bk. i., Although he had her not by's wife, But by a fishwench he was kind to, And so she came in at the window.

Wine, *subs.* 1. *He cries wine and sells vinegar.* 1659 : Howell, *Proverbs : Span.-Engl.*, 3. 1732 : Fuller, No. 1831.

2. *He that drinks not wine after salad is in danger to be sick.* 1666 : Torriano, *Piazza Univ.*, 308 [slightly varied]. 1670 : Ray, 39.

3. *Of wine the middle, of oil the top, and of honey the bottom is best.* 1659 : Howell, *Proverbs : Ital.-Eng.*, 15, Wine in the middle, oyle aboye, and hony beneath. 1678 : Ray, 41.

4. *The wine is the master's, the good-*

ness is the drawer's. 1639 : Clarke, 204.
1670 : Ray, 29. 1732 : Fuller, No.
5747, Wine is the vintner's ; but the
goodness of it, the drawer's.

5. *When the wine is run out, you'd
stop the leak.* Ibid., No. 5611.

6. *When wine sinks, words swim.*
Ibid., No. 5622. 1736 : Bailey, *Dict.*,
s.v. " Wine."

7. *Where wine is not common, commons must be sent.* 1605 : Camden,
Remains, 335 (1870). 1659 : Howell,
10.

8. *Wine and wealth change wise men's
manners.* 1586 : L. Evans, *Revised
Withals Dict.*, sig. B7. 1639 : Clarke,
33.

9. *Wine and wenches empty mens
purses.* 1586 : L. Evans, *Revised
Withals Dict.*, sig. O2, Women and wine
doe make a man, A doting foole all that
they can. 1639 : Clarke, 28. 1670 :
Ray, 52.

10. *Wine by the savour.* See quots.
1578 : Florio, *First Fruites*, fo. 29,
Wine by the sauour and bread by the
heate. 1611 : Cotgrave, s.v. " Vin,"
Let wine good savour, cloth fresh colour,
have. 1629 : *Book of Meery Riddles*,
Prov. 109, Wine by the savour, bread
by the colour. 1666 : Torriano, *Piazza
Univ.*, 186, Bread by the colour and
wine by the taste.

11. *Wine counsels seldom prosper.*
1640 : Herbert, *Jac. Prudentum.*

12. *Wine ever pays for his lodging.*
Ibid.

13. *Wine hath drowned more men
than the sea.* 1669 : *Politeuphuia*, 299.
1732 : Fuller, No. 5744.

14. *Wine in the bottle quencheth not
thirst.* 1640 : Herbert, *Jac. Prudentum.* 1732 : Fuller, No. 5745 [" hogs-
head " for " bottle "].

15. *Wine in truth out.* 1611 : Cotgrave, s.v. " Mentir," Wine telleth truth
and should not be belied. 1659 : T.
Pecke, *Parnassi Puerp.*, 5, Grant but
the adage true, that truths in wine.
1839 : Dickens, *Nickleby*, ch. xxvii.
1897 : Norway, *H. & B. in Devon, etc.*,
52, The old proverb " In wine there is
truth " might with equal propriety be
applied to brandy.

16. *Wine in, wit out.* See **Drink**,
subs. (1).

17. *Wine is a turn-coat, first a friend,
then an enemy.* 1640 : Herbert, *Jac.
Prudentum.* 1734 : Fielding, *Don Q. in
England*, I. vi., Physic makes you first
sick, and then well ; wine first makes
you well, and then sick.

18. *Wine is a whetstone to wit.* 1736 :
Bailey, *Dict.*, s.v. " Whetstone."

19. *Wine makes all sorts of creatures
at table.* 1640 : Herbert, *Jac. Prudentum.*

20. *Wine makes old wives wenches.*
1639 : Clarke, 192.

21. *Wine neither keeps secrets nor ful-
fils promises.* 1620 : Shelton, *Quixote*,
Pt. II. ch. xliii. 1732 : Fuller, No.
5748.

22. *Wine that costs nothing is digested
before it be drunk.* 1640 : Herbert, *Jac.
Prudentum.* 1670 : Ray, 29. 1732 :
Fuller, No. 5750.

23. *Wine washeth off the daub.* Ibid.,
No. 5752.

24. *Wine wears no breeches.* 1659 :
Howell, 7. 1670 : Ray, 29. 1736 :
Bailey, *Dict.*, s.v. " Breeches." [1781 :
Cowper, *Convers.*, l. 263, When wine has
giv'n indecent language birth.]

25. *Wine, wood, women and water.*
Herefordshire. 1869 : Hazlitt, 476.

26. *Ye praise the wine before ye taste
of the grape.* 1546 : Heywood, *Proverbs*, Pt. I, ch. x.

27. *You cannot know wine by the
barrel.* 1640 : Herbert, *Jac. Prudentum.* 1732 : Fuller, No. 5884 [" cask "
for " barrel "]. 1869 : Spurgeon, *John
Ploughman*, ch. iii., Though you cannot know wine by the barrel, a good
appearance is a letter of recommendation even to a ploughman.

See also **Commend** (1) ; **Drink**, *verb*
(8) ; **Gaming** ; **Good wind** ; **Good wine** ;
Milk (4) ; **Old C.** ; **Play, women** ;
and **Woman** (43), (56) and (65).

Wing. *See* **Tring.**

Wink, *verb.* 1. *All are not blind that
wink.* c. 1570 : in Huth, *Ancient
Ballads, etc.*, 375 (1867), All winkers are
not blind. 1584 : Robinson, *Handf.
Pleas. Delights*, 45 (Arber), Although I
wincke I am not blind. 1615 : J.

Andrews, *Anat. of Baseness*, 32 (Grosart), Tell me, dost thinke that all are blinde that are content to winke ?

2. *He that winketh with the one eye and looketh with the other, I will not trust him though he were my brother.* 1530 : Palsgrave, 782. 1546 : Heywood, *Proverbs*, Pt. I. ch. xi. 1611 : Cotgrave, s.v. "Borgner," To winke with one eye, and looke with another. 1659 : Howell, 8. 1732 : Fuller, No. 6458.

3. *She can wink on the ewe and worry the lamb.* 1546 : Heywood, *Proverbs*, Pt. I. ch. x.

4. *Wink at small faults.* 1639 : Clarke, 108. 1670 : Ray, 156. 1736 : Bailey, *Dict.*, s.v. "Wink," Wink at small faults, unless you can cast the first stone.

5. *You may wink and choose.* 1639 : Clarke, 14, Winke and chuse. 1737 : Ray, 216.

Winkabank and Temple-brough, Will buy all England through and through. 1678 : Ray, 340. 1790 : Grose, *Prov. Gloss.*, s.v. "Yorkshire." 1878 : *Folk-Lore Record*, i. 166.

Winlater, He's a. 1846–59 : *Denham Tracts*, i. 72 (F.L.S.), He's a Winlater. This saying may be illustrated by using the parallel saying of Cumberland, "He's a Bewcastler"—*i.e.* a bad one.

Winter, *subs.* 1. *After a rainy winter follows a fruitful spring.* 1893 : Inwards, *Weather Lore*, 9.

2. *A good winter brings a good summer.* 1633 : Draxe, 12. 1670 : Ray, 29.

3. *A green winter makes a fat churchyard.* 1670 : Ray, 42. 1732 : Fuller, No. 205. 1825 : Hone, *Ev. Day Book*, i. 670. 1893 : Inwards, *Weather Lore*, 8.

4. *An early winter, a surly winter.* 1846 : Denham, *Proverbs*, 61 (Percy S.). 1893 : Inwards, 9.

5. *An early winter is surely winter.* Ibid., 9.

6. *A winter fog will freeze a dog.* Ibid., 9.

7. *Four things. See* quot. 1636 : Breton, in *Works*, ii. *f*.7 (Grosart), Foure things ill for the earth : a winter's

thunder, a summer's frost, a long drought, and a sudden floud.

8. *He that passeth a winter's day, escapes an enemy.* 1670 : Ray, 156.

9. *When winter begins early it ends early.* 1893 : Inwards, 9.

10. *Winter finds out what summer lays up. c.* 1460 : *Good Wyfe wold a Pylgremage*, l. 155 (E.E.T.S.), Wynttur ettythe that somer gettyth. *c.* 1645 ; MS. Proverbs in *N. & Q.*, vol. 154, p. 27, That which summer getts, winter eats. 1678 : Ray, 218, Winter is summers heir. Ibid., 219, Winter finds out what summer lays up. 1732 : Fuller, No. 5753, Winter draws out what summer laid in. 1893 : Inwards, 8.

11. *Winter never died in a ditch.* Ibid., 8.

12. *Winter never rots in the sky.* 1639 : in *Berkeley MSS.*, iii. 33 (1885), Winter never dies in her dams belly. 1655 : Gurnall, *Christ. in Armour*, verse 12, ch. i. p. 61 (1679), May be . . . no cloud to be seen that portends a storm ; but know (as you use to say) Winter does not rot in the clouds, you shall have it at last. 1846 : Denham, *Proverbs*, 23 (Percy S.). 1904 : *Co. Folk-Lore : N'umberland*, 174 (F.L.S.).

13. *Winter's thunder and summer's flood, Never boded Englishman good.* 1732 : Fuller, No. 6479. 1893 : Inwards, *Weather Lore*, 9.

14. *Winter's thunder is a rich man's death and a poor man's wonder.* 1882 : Mrs. Chamberlain, *W. Worc. Words*, 38 (E.D.S.).

15. *Winter's thunder is summer's wonder.* 1605 : Camden, *Remains*, 336 (1870) ["makes" for "is"]. 1611 : Cotgrave, s.v. "Tonner." 1658 : Willsford, *Natures Secrets*, 113, According to the old adigy, Winters thunder is the Sommers wonder. 1731 : Coffey, *Devil to Pay*, I. v. 1846 : Denham, *Proverbs*, 2 (Percy S.). 1926 : *Observer*, Jan. 30, p. 17, col. 3, The old Welsh saying [why Welsh ?] :—Winter's thunder Brings Summer wonder And a great man's fall.

16. *Winter thunder, Poor man's death, rich man's hunger.* 1893 : Inwards, *Weather Lore*, 9.

17. *Winter thunder bodes summer hunger.* 1846 : Denham, *Proverbs*, 3 (Percy S.).

18. *Winter thunder, Rich man's food and poor man's hunger.* 1859 : *N. & Q.*, 2nd ser., vii. 450. 1893 : Inwards, 9 . . . [*i.e.* it is good for fruit and bad for corn.]

19. *Winter thunder, To old folks death, to young folks plunder.* Ibid., 117.

20. *Winter-time for shoeing, Peascod-time for wooing.* 1841 : Brand, *Pop. Antiq.*, ii. 100 (Bohn) [quoted as "an old proverb in a MS." Devon Glossary]. 1846 : Denham, *Proverbs*, 64 (Percy S.).

21. *Winter-weather and women's thoughts change oft.* c. 1450 : *Songs and Carols*, 23 (Warton Cl., 1856), Wynteris wether and wommanys thout, And lordis love, schaungit oft. 1590 : Greene, in *Works*, vii. 293 (Grosart), Wherevnto alludeth our old English prouerbe, Wynters wether, and womens thoght, And gentlemens purposes chaungeth oft. 1670 : Ray, 50. Cf. **Woman** (66).

See also **August** (3) and (6) ; **Autumn** (1) ; **Candlemas, A and B.** ; **Christmas** (19) and (20) ; **Frosty** ; **Leaves** (2) ; **November** (2) and (5) ; **September** (4) ; **Spring** (6) ; **Summer** (6) and (7) ; **Wedding** ; and **Woodcock**.

Wipe, verb. 1 *He that wipes the child's nose.* *See* **Child** (8).

2. *To wipe a person's nose* = To deprive or to cheat. 1577 : Holinshed, *Chron.*, ii. p. 323, col. 2 (O.), Hee deuised a shifte howe to wype the byshoppes nose of some of his golde. c. 1597 : Deloney, *Gentle Craft*, ch. xiv., O John (said Haunce) I have wiped your nose, and Nicks too, you must weare the willow garland. 1639 : Chapman and Shirley, *Ball*, III. ii., Poor gentleman, how is he beguil'd ! *Lam.* your nose is wiped [*aside*]. 1673 : Dryden, *Amboyna*, II. i., There's . . . the Dutchman with my mistress ; my nose is wiped to-day. 1709 : Cibber, *Rival Fools*, I., I durst lay my life thow wipest this foolish knight's nose of his mistress at last. 1737 : Ray, 268, I wip'd his nose on't.

3. *To wipe one's nose on one's own sleeve.* 1436 : *Libell of Engl. Policye*, l. 453, p. 40 (Pauli), And thus, they wolden, if we wil beleve Wipen our nose with our owen sleve. 1546 : Heywood, *Proverbs*, Pt. II. ch. ix., I may . . . make you wype your nose vpon your sleeue. 1577 : Stanihurst, *Descr. of Ireland*, fo. 8, For any recompence he is like to haue at mine handes, he may wype his nose in his sleeue. 1659 : Howell, *Proverbs: French-Eng.*, 22, He wiped his nose with his own sleeve, viz. he cousened him neatly.

Wire-drawer under his work, To sit like a. Yorkshire. 1670 : Ray, 217.

Wisborough Green. *See* **Rudgwick**.

Wisdom. 1. *By wisdom peace, by peace plenty.* 1605 : Camden, *Remains*, 320 (1870). 1670 : Ray, 156.

2. *He hath wisdom at will that brags not of his skill.* 1623 : Wodroephe, *Spared Houres*, 514.

3. *He hath wisdom at will that with angry heart can hold his tongue still.* c. 1460 : *Proverbs of Good Counsel*, in E.E.T.S., Ext. Ser., 8, p. 69, He hathe wysdom at hys wyll that can with angry harte be stylle. 1546 : Heywood, *Proverbs*, Pt. I. ch. xi.

4. *'Tis wisdom sometimes to seem a fool.* 1732 : Fuller, No. 5125.

5. *Well goes the case when wisdom counsels.* 1736 : Bailey, *Dict.*, s.v. "Wisdom."

6. *What is not wisdom, is danger.* 1878 : J. Platt. *Morality*, 34.

7. *Wisdom goes beyond strength.* 1736 : Bailey, *Dict.*, s.v. "Wisdom."

8. *Wisdom is a good purchase, though we pay dear for it.* 1732 : Fuller, No. 5766.

9. *Wisdom is wealth to a poor man.* 1669 : *Politeuphuia*, 45. 1732 : Fuller, No. 5764, Wisdom in a poor man is a diamond set in lead.

10. *Wisdom liketh not chance.* 1568 : in *Loseley MSS.*, 210 (Kempe).

11. *Wisdom sometimes walks in clouted shoes.* 1732 : Fuller, No. 5771. 1869 : Spurgeon, *John Ploughman*, ch. xxiv., Wisdom walks often in patched shoes.

Wise, adj. and *subs.* 1. *As wise as a*

drake. 1560 : *Impac. Pouerte,* in
Bang, *Materialien,* B. 33, p. 27.

2. *As wise as a goose* (or, *gander*).
1528 : More, *Works,* p. 179, col. 2
(1557), And all as wise as wilde geese.
1533 : in *Ballads from MSS.,* i., 230
(B.S.), As wise as a gander. *c.* 1580 :
Tom Tyler, l. 840, p. 23 (1661) (Malone
S.) [as in 1533]. *c.* 1615 : R. C., *Times
Whistle,* 60 (E.E.T.S.), Till they have
made themselves as wise as geese.
1883 : Burne, *Shropsh. Folk-Lore,* 595,
As wise as a sucking gully [gosling].

3. *As wise as an ape.* 1530 : Palsgrave, 591, She hath so insensed him
with folye that he is almoste as wyse as
an ape. *c.* 1568 : Wager, *Longer thou
Livest,* sig. C3, To make him shortly as
wise as an ape. 17th cent. in Hazlitt,
Ined. Poet. Miscell. sig. X1 (1870), And
sometimes it makes them as wise as an
ape.

4. *As wise as a wisp* (or, *wood-cock*).
1533. Heywood, *Play of Love,* l. 319
(Brandl, *Quellen,* 170), I shall proue you
playne as wyse as a woodcocke. *c.*
1560 : T. Ingelend, *Disobedient Child,*
31 (Percy S.), As wyse as a wodcocke,
without any wytte. 1670 : Ray, 203.
1677 : *Poor Robin's Visions,* 61, A fool
to make woodcocks merry. 1720 :
Stukeley, *Memoirs,* i. 135 (Surtees S.),
Lincolnshire proverbs and sayings. As
wise as a wisp.

5. *As wise as Tom a thrum.* Before
1529 : Skelton, *Colin Clout,* l. 284.

6. *As wise as Waltham's calf.* Ibid.,
l. 811, As wyse as Waltoms calfe. *c.*
1570 : in *Bl. Lett. Ballads, etc.* (Lilly),
226, (1867), For Walthams calues to
Tiburne needes must go To sucke a bull
and meete a butchers axe. 1640 : J.
Taylor (Water Poet), *Diff. Worships,* 26,
in *Works,* 1st Coll. (Spens. S.), And each
of them as wise as Walthams calfe.
1667 : L'Estrange, *Quevedo,* 256 (1904),
A senseless puppy to come back to me
with a story of Waltham's calf that went
nine miles to suck a bull. 1732 :
Fuller, No. 751 [as in 1667].

7. *A wise child is father's bliss. c.*
1270 : *Prov. of Alfred,* in Kemble,
Salomon and Sat., 233 (Ælfric S.).

8. *A wise head makes a still tongue.*

1732 : Fuller, No. 469, A wise head hath
a close mouth to it. 1865 : " Lancs.
Proverbs," in *N. & Q.,* 3rd ser., viii.
494.

9. *A wise man begins in the end: a
fool ends in the beginning.* 1732 : Fuller,
No. 471.

10. *A wise man changes his mind, a
fool never will.* 1631 : Mabbe, *Celestina,*
104 (T.T.), A wise man altreth his purpose, but a foole persevereth in his
folly. 1711 : Steele, *Spectator,* No. 78.

11. *A wise man is a great wonder.*
1732 : Fuller, No. 472.

12. *A wise man knows his own.* 1855 :
Bohn, 303.

13. *A wise man never wants a weapon.*
1736 : Bailey, *Dict.,* s.v. " Weapon."

14. *A wise man ought not to be
ashamed to change his purpose.* 1578.
Florio, *First Fruites,* fo. 32. 1629 :
Book of Meery Riddles, Prov. 43
" alter " for " change "]. 1640 : Herbert, *Jac. Prudentum,* A wise man needs
not blush for changing his purpose.

15. *A wise man's thoughts walk within
him, but a fool's without him.* 1732 :
Fuller, No. 478.

16. *A wise man turns chance into good
fortune.* Ibid., No. 475.

17. *A wise man will make more
opportunities than he finds.* Ibid., No.
479.

18. *A wise man will make tools of
what comes to hand.* Ibid., No. 476.

19. *A wise woman. See* **Woman** (5).

20. *He is not a wise man that cannot
play the fool.* 1586 : Pettie, *Guazzo,* fo.
74, To plaie the foole well it behooueth
a man first to bee wise. 1687 : *Poor
Robin Alman.,* July, Sometimes the fool
to play, Is wisdom great they say.
1732 : Fuller, No. 1929 [with the
addition " upon occasion "].

21. *He is not wise that is not wise for
himself.* [Qui ipse sibi sapiens prodesse
non quit nequiquam sapit.—Enn. ap.
Cic., Fam., 7, 6, 2.] 1478 : Rivers, tr.
C. de Pisa's *Moral Proverbs,* Grete
folye is in him, that taketh hede Upon
other and not to his owen nede. 1576 :
Pettie, *Pet. Pallace,* ii. 23 (Gollancz),
Their wisdom is nothing worth which
are not wise for themselves. 1594 :

Lodge and Greene, *Look. Glass*, l. 723.
1615 : Stephens, *Essays, etc.*, bk. i., No.
18, Wise enough to keepe his owne.
1681 : Robertson, *Phraseol. Generalis*,
291, That wise man is little worth, who
is not wise in his own business. 1732 :
Fuller, No. 1954, He is wise that hath
wit enough for his own affairs. 1781 :
T. Francklin, *Lucian's Works*, ii. 132,
After the poet's excellent observation,
" I hate (says he), the wise man, who
is not wise for himself." 1880 : Spurgeon, *Ploughm. Pictures*, 46 [as in
1732].

22. *He is wise enough that can keep
himself warm.* 1546 : Heywood, *Proverbs*, Pt. II. ch. ii., Ye are wise inough
(quoth he) if ye keepe ye warme. 1579 :
Marr. of Wit and Wisdom, 16 (Sh. S.),
Thou art a mery fellowe and wise, And
if thou kepe thy selfe warme. 1607 :
The Puritan, III. vi., Which confirms
the old beldam's saying, *He's wisest, that
keeps himself warmest*. 1670 : Ray, 28.
1820 : Scott, *Abbot*, ch. xviii., " The
child hath wit enough to keep himself
warm," said Adam.

23. *He is wise that follows the wise.*
1852 : FitzGerald, *Polonius*, 132 (1903).

24. *He is wise that is honest.* 1639 :
Clarke, 127. 1670 : Ray, 13.

25. *He is wise that is ware in time.*
1303 : Brunne, *Handl. Synne*, l. 8085,
Yu a prouerbe telle men þys " He wyys
ys, þat ware ys." Before 1500 : in
Hill, *Commonplace Book*, 101, He ys
wyse that ys ware or he harm fele.
1736 : Bailey, *Dict.*, s.v. " Wary."

26. *He is wise that knows when he is
well enough.* 1732 : Fuller, No. 2475.

27. *He seemeth wise with whom all
things thrive.* Ibid., No. 2016.

28. *He was wise that first gave reward.*
c. 1300 : *Havelok*, l. 1635, He was ful
wis that first yaf mede. *c.* 1350 : *Sir
Tristrem*, l. 626, He was ful wise, I say,
That first yave yift in land. *c.* 1390 :
Gower, *Conf. Amantis*, bk. v. l. 4719, For
thus men sein, in every nede, He was
wys that ferst made mede.

29. *If the wise erred not, it would go
hard with fools.* 1640 : Herbert, *Jac.
Prudentum.*

30. *If wise men play the fool, they do

it with a vengeance.* 1855 : Bohn, 419.
1875 : Cheales, *Proverb. Folk-Lore*, 49,
When a wise man errs, he errs with a
vengeance.

31. *It is a wise child that knows its
own father.* [Οὐ γάρ πώ τις ἑὸν γόνον
αὐτὸς ἀνέγνω.—Homer, *Od.*, i. 216.]
1589 : Greene, *Works*, vi. 92 (Grosart),
For wise are the children in these dayes
that know their owne fathers. 1606 :
Day, *Ile of Gulls*, II. i., I am not so wise
a child as you take me for ; I neuer
knewe my father. 1633 : Rowley,
Match at Midnight, I., None but wise
children know their own fathers. 1673 :
Wycherley, *Gent. Danc. Master*, I. i.,
The children of this age must be wise
children indeed if they know their
fathers. 1762 : Goldsmith, *Cock Lane
Ghost*, in *Works*, ii. 472 (Gibbs). 1774 :
Burgoyne, *Maid of Oaks*, I. i. 1823 :
Scott, *Peveril*, ch. xxxiii. 1925 : *Sphere*,
June 6, p. 294, col. 1.

32. *It is a wise father that knows his
own child.* 1595 : Shakespeare, *M. of
Venice*, II. ii. 1606 : B. Rich, *Faultes*,
fo. 28. 1640 : Shirley, *Opportunity*, I. i.

33. *Send a wise man on an errand,
and say nothing to him.* *c.* 1386 :
Chaucer, *Miller's Tale*, l. 412, Men seyn
thus, " send the wyse, and sey no-thing."
1640 : Herbert, *Jac. Prudentum*. 1670 :
Ray, 157.

34. *Some are wise. See* Some.

35. *That is a wise delay which makes
the road safe.* 1659 : Howell, *Proverbs:
Span.-Eng.*, 3, That delay is good which
makes the way the safer. 1855 : Bohn,
495.

36. *The wise and the fool have their
fellows.* 1659 : Howell, *Proverbs: Brit.-
Eng.*, 4.

37. *The wise hand doth not all that the
foolish mouth speaks.* 1640 : Herbert,
Jac. Prudentum. 1670 : Ray, 12.

38. *The wise man, even when he holds
his tongue, says more than the fool when
he speaks.* 1732 : Fuller, No. 4834.

39. *The wise man is deceived but once,
the fool twice.* 1736 : Bailey, *Dict.* s.v.
" Wise."

40. *The wise man must carry the fool
upon his shoulders.* 1623 : Wodroephe,
Spared Houres, 489.

41. *The wise man's tongue. See* **Fool** (27).

42. *They are wise in other men's matters, and fools in their own.* 1672 : Walker, *Parœm.*, 31.

43. *To be wise after the event.* [ῥεχθὲν δέ τε νήπιος ἔγνω.—Homer, *Il.*, 17, 32. Atque illi modo cauti ac sapientes prompti post eventum ac magniloque erant.—Tacitus, *Agric.*, xxvii. Eventus, stultorum iste magister est.—Livy, xxii. 39.] 1609 : Jonson, *Silent Woman*, II. ii., Away, thou strange justifier of thyself, to be wiser than thou wert, by the event. 1875 : Jowett, *Plato*, V. 53 (2nd ed.) (O.), There is no merit . . . in learning wisdom after the event. 1928 : *Sphere*, Jan. 21, p. 93, col. 1, Nor is it a case of being wise after the event.

44. *To be wise behind the hand.* 1820 : Scott, in Lockhart's *Life*, v. 42, The next night, being, like true Scotsmen, wise behind the hand, the bailies had a sufficient force . . . and put down every attempt to riot. 1892 : Heslop, *N'umberland Words*, 9 (E.D.S.), " Ahint yor hand," to have someone to look after your interest in your absence.

45. *Who is wise in the day, can be no fool in the night.* 1659 : Howell, *Proverbs: Ital.-Eng.*, 6.

46. *Wise fear begets care.* 1732 : Fuller, No. 6355.

47. *Wise man if thou art. See* quot. 15th cent. in *Reliq. Antiquæ*, i. 314 (1841), Wyse mon if thou art, of thi god Take part or thou hense wynde ; For if thou leve thi part in thi secaturs [executor's] ward, Thi part non part at last end.

48. *Wise men are caught in wiles. c.* 1250 : Layamon, *Brut.*, 15182, Ac þar nis no man so wis þat me ne mai bi-swike [There is no man so wise that men may not deceive]. 1670 : Ray, 156. 1732 : Fuller, No. 5782, Wise men may chance to be caught.

49. *Wise men care not for what they cannot have.* 1670 : Ray, 29. 1732 : Fuller, No. 5775.

50. *Wise men have their mouths in their hearts, fools have their hearts in their mouths.* 1477 : Rivers, *Dictes and Sayings*, 140 (1877), The tonge of a discrete man is in his herte and the herte of a foole is in his tonge. 1574 : E. Hellowes, *Guevara's Epis.*, 183, The wise man hath his tong in his hart, and he that is a foole and furious, hath his heart in his tongue. 1630 : Brathwait, *Engl. Gent., etc.*, 47 (1641), These are those fooles, which carry their hearts in their mouthes ; and farre from those wise men, which carry their mouthes in their hearts. Cf. **Fool** (27).

51. *Wise men in the world are like timber-trees in a hedge, here and there one.* 1732 : Fuller, No. 5778. 1869 : Spurgeon, *John Ploughman*, ch. ii.

52. *Wise men learn by others' faults, fools by their own. c.* 1380 : Chaucer, *Troylus*, bk. iii. l. 329, For wysë ben by folës harm chastysed. 1591 : Florio, *Second Frutes*, 103, A happie man and wise is he, By others harmes can warned be. 1669 : *Politeuphuia*, 44, By others faults wise men correct their own offences. 1758 : Franklin, *Poor Richard*, in Arber's *Garner*, v. 583 (1882), Wise men, as Poor Dick says, learn by others' harms.

53. *Wise men make proverbs and fools repeat them.* 1710 : S. Palmer, *Moral Essays on Proverbs*, Pref. viii. 1823 : D'Israeli, *Cur. of Lit.*, 2nd ser., I. 449 (1824). *c.* 1860 : R. S. Hawker, in Byles, *Life, etc.*, 82 (1905).

54. *Wise men propose and fools determine.* 1692 : L'Estrange, *Æsop*, 114 (3rd ed.) [quoted as " the old saying "].

55. *Wise men silent, fools talk.* 1639 : Clarke, 5.

56. *Wise men. See also* **Fool,** *passim* ; and **Gotham.**

57. *Wise words and great seldom agree.* 1659 : Howell, *Proverbs: Brit.-Eng.*, 6.

58. *Wise young. See* **Too soon wise.**

59. *You may be a wise man though you can't make a watch.* 1670 : Ray, 29. 1732 : Fuller, No. 5939, . . . and yet not know how to make a watch.

Wisely walketh that doth safely go, He. 1600 : Bodenham, *Belvedere*, 49 (Spens. S.).

Wish and **Wishes,** *subs.* 1. *If wishes were butter-cakes beggars might bite.* 1678 : Ray, 219.

2. *If wishes were horses beggars would ride.* 1736 : Bailey, *Dict.* s.v. " Wish."

3. *If wishes were thrushes beggars would eat birds.* 1605 : Camden, *Remains,* 326 (1870). 1670 : Ray, 157. 1732 : Fuller, No. 2731.

4. *If wishes would bide, beggars would ride.* 1670 : Ray, 157. 1694 : D'Urfey, *Quixote,* Pt. I. Act V. sc. ii. 1732 : Fuller, No. 6098.

5. *The wish is father to the thought.* [Libenter homines id quod volunt credunt.—Cæsar, *De Bello G.,* iii. 18.] 1598 : Shakespeare, *2 Hen. IV.* IV. v, Thy wish was father, Harry, to that thought. 1908 : W. Johnson, *Folk-Memory,* 229.

6. *When a thing is done wishes are too late.* 1736 : Bailey, *Dict.,* s.v. " Wish."

7. *Wishes never can fill a sack.* 1855 : Bohn, 570.

Wishers and woulders are never good householders. c. 1520 : Stanbridge, *Vulgaria,* sig. C6, Wysshers and wolders ben small house holders. 1590 : Greene, *Works,* viii. 64 (Grosart). 1616 : Breton, in *Works,* ii. e 8 (Grosart). 1641 : in *Harl. Miscell.,* i. 483, (1744) Any of those places would suffice you, or myself, but alas ! *Wishers and Woulders,* you know how the proverb runs. 1732 : Fuller, No. 6154.

Wishers want will. c. 1550 : *Parl. of Byrdes,* l. 91, in Hazlitt, *Early Pop. Poetry,* iii. 171, The hawke 'sayd, wysshers want wyll, Whether they speake loude or styll.

Wit. 1. *Better wit than wealth.* 1736 : Bailey, *Dict.,* s.v. " Better."

2. *Bought wit is dear.* 1575 : Gascoigne, *Posies* in *Works,* i. 66 (Cunliffe).

3. *He hath no more wit in his head than thou in both thy shoulders.* 1670 : Ray, 217.

4. *He hath some wit but a fool hath the guidance of it.* 1602-3 : Manningham, *Diary,* 171 (Camden S.), He hath a good witt but it is carried by a foole. 1732 : Fuller, No. 1899.

5. *It is wit to pick a lock and steal a horse, but it is wisdom to let them alone.* 1659 : Howell, 3. 1670 : Ray, 30. 1732 : Fuller, No. 3031.

6. *The wit of a woman is a great*

matter. 1599 : Breton in *Works,* ii. c. 59 (Grosart) [cited as " the common proverbe "].

7. *The wit of you and the wool of a blue dog, would make a very good medley.* 1659 : Howell, 11, The wit of you and the wool of an old dogg, will make a piece of linsay-woolsie. 1732 : Fuller, No. 4836.

8. *To be at one's wits' end.* c. 1420 : Lydgate, *Assem. of Gods,* st. 238, p. 49 (E.E.T.S.), When they were dreuyn to her wyttes ende. c. 1565 : Still, *Gam. Gurton,* IV, ii., And Dame Chat at her wyts ende I have almost set her. 1576 : Pettie, *Pet. Pallace,* i. 172 (Gollancz), Who . . . were at their wits' end what medicine to apply. 1694 : D'Urfey, *Quixote,* Pt. II. Act II. sc. ii., Now is Sancho at his wits-end to know, whether he may believe his eyes and ears or no. 1764 : Mrs. F. Sheridan, *Dupe,* II. iv., I am quite at my wits' end to unriddle it. 1883 : R. L. S., *Treas. Isl.,* ch. xix., They were at their wits' end what to do. 1923 : Lucas, *Adv. Ben,* § xvii. p. 95, Can you tell me what to do ? I'm at my wits' end.

9. *To have wit at will.* c. 1470: *Songs and Carols,* 37 (Percy S., No. 73), If thou have wysdom at thi wyll. c. 1602 : Chapman, *May-Day,* IV. iii., Win her and wear her ; thou hast wit at will. 1738 : Swift, *Polite Convers.,* Dial. I., She's very handsome, and has wit at will. 1772 : Graves, *Spirit. Quixote,* bk. ix. ch. vi., My son says, my lady has wit at will, and will hold discourse with any lord or bishop. 1821 : Scott, *Pirate,* ch. xiv., . . . said Tim, who had wit at will. 1881 : A. R. Ellis, *Introd. to Evelina,* i., The living French writer who has the most wit at will.

10. *Wit and will strive for the victory.* 1736 : Bailey, *Dict.,* s.v. " Wit."

11. *Wit and wisdom are good warison* [possession]. c. 1320 : in *Reliq. Antiquæ* i. 109, (1841), "Wyt ant wysdom is god warysoun," Quoth Hendyng. 1594 : Churchyard, *Mirror of Man,* Wisdome is great wealth.

12. *Wit bought is better than taught.* 1670 : Ray, 157, Wit once bought is worth twice taught. 1875 : Cheales,

Proverb. Folk-Lore, 115. Cf. Ounce of wit.

13. *Wit goes not all by the hair. c.* 1592 : *Sir Thos. More*, 59 (Sh. S.), Why, man, he may be without a beard till he come to mariage, for witt goes not all by the hayre.

14. *Wit is folly unless a wise man hath the keeping of it.* 1813 : Ray, 174.

15. *Wit is never good till it be bought. c.* 1500 : Medwall, *Nature*, Pt. II. l. 1292, Wyt ys nothyng worth tyll yt be dere bought. 1546 : Heywood, *Proverbs*, Pt. I. ch. viii. 1579 : Lyly, *Euphues*, 34 (Arber), It hath bene an olde sayde sawe . . . that wit is the better if it be the deerer bought. 1630 : Randolph, *Conceited Peddler* in *Works*, i. 39 (1875). 1653 : R. Brome, *City Wit*, I. ii. 1678 : A. Behn, *Sir P. Fancy*, II. i., 'Twas a saying of my grandmother's . . . that bought wit was best. 1709 : T. Baker, *Fine Lady's Airs*, IV. ii., My grandmother . . . says bought wit's best. 1732 : Fuller, No. 1011, Bought wit is best, but may cost too much. 1901 : F. E. Taylor, *Lancs. Sayings*, 11, Wit's nowt till its dear bowt. 1917 : Bridge, *Cheshire Proverbs*, 156, Wit's n'er owt [aught] Tin dear bowt [Till dear bought].

16. *Wits are most wily. See* quot. 16th cent. in *Reliq. Antiquæ*, ii. 195, (1843), Wittes are moste wylly where wemen have wyttes, And curtily comethe uppon them by flittes.

17. *Wits have short memories. See* Great wits.

18. *Wit, whither wilt thou?* 1601 : Shakespeare, *A. Y. Like It*, IV. i, A man that had a wife with such a wit, he might say, " Wit, whither wilt ? " 1659 : Howell, 3.

19. *Wit will walk where will is bent.* 1583 : Melbancke, *Philotinus*, sig. Y2.

20. *Wit without learning is like a tree without fruit.* 1647 : *Countrym. New Commonwealth*, 15.

21. *Wit without wisdom. See* quots. c. 1270 : *Prov. of Alfred*, in Kemble, *Salomon and Saturnus*, 229 (Ælfric S.), Wid widutin wisdom is wele ful unwed [wit without wisdom is but little worth]. 1732 : Fuller, No. 5791, Wit without

wisdom cuts other men's meat and its own fingers.

22. *You have wit enough to drown ships in.* 1678 : Ray, 277.

23. *You may truss up all his wit in an egg-shell.* Ibid., 84. 1732 : Fuller, No. 5957.

See also Ounce of wit.

Witch. *See* Burn (6) ; Devil (101) ; Go (4) ; and Rowan-tree.

Witch-wife. *See* quot. 1846–59 : *Denham Tracts*, ii. 81 (F.L.S.), A witch-wife—an evil, Is three halfpence worse than the deevil.

With a mischief. 1533 : Heywood, *John Tib and Sir John*, l. 481, Now go chafe the wax, with a myschyfe. 1541 : *Sch. House of Women*, l. 278, And now God giue the shame at last, Commest drunken home with a mischeef. 1623 : Massinger, *Duke of Milan*, II. i., Pleased, with a mischief ! 1681 : Robertson, *Phraseol. Generalis*, 760, Be gone with a mischief.

With a vengeance. 1533 : Heywood, *John Tib and Sir John*, l. 425, And go with a vengeance. 1593 : Peele, *Edw. I*, sc. ii., Be gone quickly, or my pikestaff and I will set thee away with a vengeance. 1679 : Dryden, *Troilus*, II. ii., Nothing, do you call it ? This is nothing, with a vengeance. 1701 : Cibber, *Love makes a Man*, I., Yes, sir, he has lost with a vengeance. 1778 : Burney, *Evelina*, Lett. xxiii., They'd need to be goddesses with a vengeance . . . for they're mortal dear to look at. 1814 : Byron, *Letters, etc.*, iii. 124 (Prothero), I got in a passion with an ink-bottle, which I flung out of the window one night with a vengeance. 1922 : Weyman, *Ovington's Bank*, ch. xl., They had cooked their goose with a vengeance—no more golden eggs for them !

With a wanion—a proverbial expletive phrase, similar to " With a mischief, vengeance, and witness." *c.* 1568 : Wager, *Longer thou Livest*, sig. G2, Get the[e] hence theefe with a wanion. 1606 : T. Heywood, *If you know not me*, Pt. II, in *Dram. Works*, i. 284 (1874), There's your ten pounds ; tell it out with a wanion, and take it for your pains. *c.* 1627 : in *Pepysian Garland*

(Rollins), 272, Pray let them both packe
with a winion. 1673 : *Vinegar and
Mustard*, 9, in Hindley, *Old Book Coll.
Misc.*, iii., I'll warrant you with a
wannion. 1823 : Scott, *Peveril*, ch. vi.,
Who calls himself a parson, and whom
I hope to fetch down from his perch
presently, with a wannion to him !

With a witness. 1703 : Ward,
Writings, ii. 273, And the Gown often
errs with a witness. 1753 : Richardson, *Grandison*, i. 225 (1883), *Carried* he
should have said ; I was carried with a
witness !

Witham pike. *See* quots. 1611 :
Markham, *Country Contentments*, 65
(1675), The ancient proverb is, Ancome
eele, and Witham pike, In all England
is none sike [such]. 1662 : Fuller,
Worthies, ii. 262 (1840), To return to
our English pikes, wherein this county
[Lincs.] is eminent, especially in that
river which runneth by Lincoln, whence
grew this proverb, "Witham pike
England hath none like." 1874 :
Smiles, *Lives of Engineers*, i. 13 [as in
1662].

**Without danger we cannot get beyond
danger.** 1640 : Herbert, *Jac. Prudentum*.

Wits. *See* **Good wits** and **Great wits.**

**Wive and thrive both in a year, It's
hard to.** *c.* 1410 : *Towneley Plays*, 103
(E.E.T.S.), It is sayde full ryfe, " a
man may not wyfe and also thryfe, And
all in a yere." 1546 : Heywood,
Proverbs, Pt. I. ch. xi. 1580 : Tusser,
Husbandrie, 153 (E.D.S.), It is too much
we dailie heare, To wine and thriue both
in a yeare. 1670 : Ray, 48. 1738 :
Swift, *Polite Convers.*, Dial. I., You can't
expect to wive and thrive in the same
year. 1846 : Denham, *Proverbs*, 5
(Percy S.).

**Wiving and thriving, a man should
take counsel of all the world, In.** 1678 :
Ray, 354.

Wizard Stream, The = The River Dee.
1917 : Bridge, *Cheshire Proverbs*, 121.

Woe, *subs.* 1. *There is no woe to
want.* 1605 : Camden, *Remains*, 332
(1870). 1732 : Fuller, No. 4926.

2. *See* quot. 1509 : Barclay, *Ship of
Fools*, i. 284 (1874), For we fynde in

an olde sayde sawe Wo is hym that to
his maker is vnkynde.

3. *Woe to the house where there is no
chiding.* 1640 : Herbert, *Jac. Prudentum*. 1732 : Fuller, No. 5801.

Wogan. *See* quot. 1659 : Howell,
21, It shall be done when the king
cometh to Wogan, a little village, viz.
an impossibility. 1790 : Grose, *Prov.
Gloss.*, s.v. "Worcestershire" [as in
1659].

Wolf and **Wolves.** 1. *A growing
youth has a wolf in his belly.* 1611 :
Cotgrave, s.v. "Ieune," A youth in
growing hath a wolfe in his guts. *c.*
1625 : B. & F., *Women Pleased*, I. ii.,
This ravening fellow has a wolf in's
belly. 1754 : Berthelson, *Eng.-Danish
Dict.*, s.v. "Dog," To have a dog in
ones belly. 1917 : Bridge, *Cheshire
Proverbs*, 3.

2. *A wolf in sheep's clothing. c.* 1460 :
Wisdom, sc. iii. st. 61, They flatter and
lye as they were woode [mad] ; Ther
ys a wolffe in a lombys skyn. 1509 :
Barclay, *Ship of Fools*, ii. 7 (1874), She
is perchaunce A wolfe or gote within a
lammys skyn. 1584 : Greene, *Works*,
iii. 11 (Grosart), These two . . . had
. . . vnder their sheepes skinnes, hidden
the bloudie nature of a wolfe. 1657 :
Gurnall, *Christ. in Armour*, Pt. II. v. 14,
ch. xvii. p. 67 (1679). The hypocrite
is the wolf clad in the sheeps skin.
1751 : Fielding, *Amelia*, bk. ix. ch. ix.,
There is the meekness of the clergyman.
There spoke the wolf in sheep's clothing.
1876 : Blackmore, *Cripps*, ch. xliv.,
Whose bosom friend is a Jesuit, a
fierce wolf in sheep's clothing. 1926 :
Phillpotts, *Yellow Sands*, III., A wolf in
sheep's clothing—that's what she was.

3. *By little and little the wolf eateth the
sheep.* 1633 : Draxe, 13.

4. *By little and little the wolf eats up
the goose.* 1611 : Cotgrave, s.v.
" Manger."

5. *For the least choice the wolfe tooke
the sheepe.* 1623 : Wodroephe, *Spared
Houres*, 500.

6. *It is a hard winter when one wolf
eats another.* 1579. Lyly, *Euphues*, 78
(Arber). 1643 : Taylor (Water Poet),
Lett. to London, 8, in *Works*, 5th Coll.

(Spens. S.) [" world " for " winter "].
1696 : D'Urfey, *Quixote*, Pt. III. Act V.
sc. i. 1710 : S. Palmer, *Moral Essays
on Proverbs*, 327.

7. *It is hard to have wolf full and
wether whole.* 1374 : Chaucer, *Troylus*,
bk. iv. l. 1373.

8. *The death of a young wolf doth
never come too soon.* 1651 : Herbert,
Jac. Prudentum, 2nd ed.

9. *The death of the wolf is the health of
the sheep.* 1578 : Florio, *First Fruites*,
fo. 31. 1666 : Torriano, *Piazza Univ.*,
132.

10. *The wolf eats counted sheep.*
[Tantum curamus frigora, quantum
numerum (ovium) lupus.—Virgil,
Æneid, 7, 51]. 1611 : Cotgrave, s.v.
" Loup." The wolfe eats counted (and
uncounted) sheepe. 1708 : tr. *Aleman's Guzman*, i. 435, Your Eminence
knows the proverb relating to counted
sheep.

11. *The wolf eats oft of the sheep that
have been warned.* 1651 : Herbert,
Jac. Prudentum, 2nd ed.

12. *The wolf knows what the ill beast
thinks.* 1640 : Herbert, *Jac. Prudentum.*

13. *The wolf must die in his own skin.*
1611 : Cotgrave, s.v. " Loup." 1640 :
Herbert, *Jac. Prudentum.*

14. *To cry wolf* = To give a false
alarm. 1740 : North, *Examen*, 315,
They say the false cry of the wolf made
the neighbours not regard the cry when
the wolf was come in earnest. 1844 :
Planché, *Extravag.*, ii. 288 (1879), Why,
you're cried " Wolf ! " till, like the
shepherd youth, You're not believed
when you do speak the truth.

15. *To have a wolf by the ears.*
[Lupum auribus tenere.—Terence,
Phorm., 3, 2, 21.] 1576 : Lambarde,
Peramb. of Kent, 418 (1826), They had
but a wolfe by the eares, whom they
could neither well hold, nor might safely
let goe. 1642 : Quarles, *Works*, i. 53
(Grosart), A Prince . . . that enter-
taines Auxiliaries, holds a wolfe by the
eares. 1691 : J. Wilson, *Belphegor*, II.
iii., If ever man had a wolf by the ears,
I have one now. 1740 : North, *Lives of
Norths*, i. 211 (Bohn), He found . . .

that it was like a wolf by the ears ; he
could neither hold it nor let it go.

16. *To keep the wolf from the door.*
1546 : Heywood, *Proverbs*, Pt. II. ch.
vii. *c.* 1597 : Deloney, *Gentle Craft*,
Pt. I. ch. x., That we may liue out of
debt and danger, and driue the woolf
from the doore. *c.* 1630 : in *Roxb.
Ballads*, i. 167 (Hindley), Though home
be but homely, and never so poore,
Yet let us keepe, warily, the wolfe from
the doore. Before 1704 : Brown,
Works, iii. 242 (1760), I shall be very
well satisfied if I can keep the wolf from
the door, as the saying is. 1860 :
Reade, *Clois. and Hearth*, ch. lii., And
so the brave girl and the brave soldier
worked with a will, and kept the wolf
from the door. 1921 : Sidney Colvin,
Memories, etc., 48, Fortunately he had
from the first had friends and backers
whose appreciation saved him from any
serious danger of the wolf at the door.

17. *To set the wolf to keep the sheep.*
[Ovem lupo committere.—Terence,
Eun., 5, 1, 16.] 1639 : Clarke, 95, You
have given the wolf the weather to keep.
1694 : *Terence made English*, 89, Oh
you jade, you set the wolf to keep the
sheep. 1736 : Bailey, *Dict.*, s.v.
" Wolf," To give the wolf the weather
to keep.

18. *Who hath a wolf for his mate, needs
a dog for his man.* 1640 : Herbert,
Jac. Prudentum. 1670 : Ray, 30.

19. *Who keeps company with the wolf
will learn to howl.* 1591 : Florio,
Second Frutes, 57, Who is bread among
wolfes, will learne to houle. 1623 :
Wodroephe, *Spared Houres*, 274, Hee
who hantes with wolues doth learne
to houle. 1670 : Ray, 30. 1748 :
Richardson, *Clarissa*, iv. 119 (1785),
Tho' you have kept company with a
wolf you have not learnt to howl of
him. 1871 : Smiles, *Character*, 66,
" Live with wolves," says the Spanish
proverb, " and you will learn to howl."

20. *Who speakes of the wolfe hee seeth
his taile.* 1623 : Wodroephe, *Spared
Houres*, 500.

21. *Wolves lose their teeth but not
their memory.* 1633 : Draxe, 237.
1670 : Ray, 30. 1732 : Fuller, No.

5802, Wolves may lose their teeth, but not their nature.

22. *Wolves never prey upon wolves.*
1576 : Pettie, *Pet. Pallace*, ii. 81 (Gollancz). 1651 : Herbert, *Jac. Prudentum*, 2nd ed., A wolf will never make war against another wolf.

See also **Dog** (1) and (52) ; **Hunger** fetcheth ; **Hungry as a wolf** ; **Law** (3) ; **Man** (52) and (57) ; and **Sheep** *passim*.

Wolf's mouth. *See* **Dark**.

Wolstonbury, Sussex. *See* quot. 1893 : Inwards, *Weather Lore*, 99, When Wolsonbury has a cap, Hurstpierpoint will have a drap.

Woman and **Women.** 1. *A dishonest woman cannot be kept in, and an honest one will not.* 1732 : Fuller, No. 76.

2. *A good woman is worth, if she were sold, the fairest crown that's made of purest gold.* 1623 : Wodroephe, *Spared Houres*, 484. 1880 : Spurgeon, *Ploughm. Pictures*, 88 [omitting " purest "].

3. *As great a pity to see a woman weep as to see a goose go barefoot.* 1526 : *Hund. Mery Talys*, No. x. p. 20 (Oesterley), By thys tale ye may se that the olde prouerbe ys trew that yt is as gret pyte to se a woman wepe as a gose to go barefote. 1621 : Burton, *Melanch.*, III. II. iii. 4, 548 (1836), As much pitty is to be taken of a woman weeping, as of a goose going bare-footed. 1716 : Ward, *Female Policy*, 44. 1830 : Sir H. Taylor, *Virgin Widow*, I. iii. [" gosling " for " goose "].

4. *A wicked woman and an evil is three halfpence worse than the devil.* 1639 : Clarke, 118. 1670 : Ray, 50. 1732 : Fuller, No. 6406. 1875 : Cheales, *Proverb. Folk-Lore*, 4, That coarse old saying A wicked woman and an evil Is some nine parts worse than the devil.

5. *A wise woman is twice a fool.* 1680 : L'Estrange, *Select Coll. out of Erasmus*, 220, I have often heard that *One wise woman is two fools.* 1725 : Bailey, tr. *Erasm. Coll.*, 256.

6. *A woman and a cherry are painted for their own harm.* 1659 : Howell, *Proverbs: Span.-Eng.*, 18, A woman and a cherry paint themselves for their hurt. 1855 : Bohn, 304.

7. *A woman and a glass are ever in danger.* 1640 : Herbert, *Jac. Prudentum.* 1669 : *New Help to Discourse*, 310.

8. *A woman, a spaniel, and a walnut-tree, The more you beat them the better they be.* [Nux, asinus, mulier, simili sunt lege ligati : Haec tria nil recta faciunt, si verbera cessent. 16th cent. : Cognatus, *Adagia*, in Grynæus, *Adagia*, p. 484, col. 1 (1629) (*N. & Q.*, 10th ser., ix. 298).] 1586 : Pettie, *Guazzo*, fo. 139, A woman, an asse, and a walnut-tree, Bring the more fruite, the more beaten they bee. 1589 : L. Wright, *Display of Dutie*, 24, It is sayde that an asse, a walnut-tree, and a woman asketh much beating before they be good. 1596 : Nashe, *Works*, iii. 110 (Grosart), A nut, a woman, and an asse are like, These three doo nothing right, except you strike. 1608 : *Yorksh. Tragedy*, sc. i., For you must note, that any woman bears the more when she is beaten. 1612 : Webster, *White Devil*, V. i., Do you think that she is like a walnut-tree ? Must she be cudgelled ere she bear good fruit ? 1692 : L'Estrange, *Æsop*, 284 (3rd ed.), 'Tis natural for asses, women, and walnut-trees to mend upon beating. 1732 : Fuller, No. 6404. 1878 : Dyer, *Engl. Folk-Lore*, 30 [" whip " for " beat "].

9. *A woman can do more than the devil.* 1559 : Bercher, *Nobility of Women*, 140 (Roxb. C.) [cited as " a common proverbe "].

10. *A woman hath nine lives like a cat.* 1546 : Heywood, *Proverbs*, Pt. II. ch. iv. 1611 : Davies of Hereford, *Sc. of Folly*, 49, in *Works*, ii. (Grosart), Some wiues (some say) haue nine liues like a cat. 1738 : Swift, *Polite Convers.*, Dial. I., They say, a woman has as many lives as a cat.

11. *A woman is an angel at ten, a saint at fifteen, a devil at forty, and a witch at fourscore.* 1620 : *Swetnam the Woman Hater* (Grosart).

12. *A woman is a weather-cock.* 1633 : Draxe, 238, Women are (oft times) weather-cocks. 1636 : W. Sampson,

Vow Breaker, I. iv., in Bang, *Materialien*,
B. 42, p. 22, Faith vncle, i'me a woman,
and they say, a woman is a wethercocke.

13. *A woman is to be from her house
three times; when she is christened,
married and buried.* 1732 : Fuller,
No. 480.

14. *A woman need but look upon her
apron-string to find an excuse.* 1620 :
Westward for Smelts, 17 (Percy S.),
Excuses are never further off women
than their apron strings. 1672 : J.
Lacy, *Dumb Lady*, I., They say when a
woman means mischief, if she but look
upon her apron-strings the devil will
help her presently. 1738 : Swift,
Polite Convers., Dial. III.

15. *A woman's counsel. See* quots.
1620 : Shelton, *Quixote*, Pt. II. ch. vii.,
Woman's advice is but slender, yet he,
that refuseth it is a madman. 1639 :
Clarke, 22, A womans counsell is sometime good. 1659 : Howell, 6, A womans
advice is best at a dead lift. 1875 :
Cheales, *Proverb. Folk-Lore*, 5, A
woman's advice is a poor thing, but he
is a fool who does not take it. Cf. No.
60.

16. *A woman's heart and her tongue
are not relatives.* 1590 : Greene, *Works*,
viii. 90 (Grosart). 1669 : *Politeuphuia*,
31.

17. *A woman's " nay." See* quots. *c.*
1590 : Shakespeare, *Pass. Pilgrim*, xix.,
Have you not heard it said full oft, A
woman's nay doth stand for nought ?
1611 : Davies of Hereford, *Sc. of Folly*,
40, in *Works*, ii. (Grosart), A woman's
nay's a double yea (they say). 1686 :
Loyal Garland, 31 (Percy S.), A woman's
nay is no denial.

18. *A woman's reason—because it is
so. c.* 1591 : Shakespeare, *Two Gent.*,
I. ii., I have no other but a woman's
reason ; I think him so, because I think
him so. 1601 : Lyly, *Love's Metam.*,
IV. i., Women's reasons ; they would
not because they would not. 1634 :
Massinger, *Very Woman*, I. i., Shall I
lose The privilege of my sex, which is
my will, To yield a reason like a man ?
1706 : Farquhar, *Recruiting Officer*, IV.
iii. *c.* 1750 : Foote, *Englishm. in

Paris*, Prol., To contradict you, I know,
is high treason ; For the will of a wife
is always her reason. 1920 : Hudson,
Dead Man's Plack, Preamble, 9, If any
one were to ask me why I dislike him
I should probably have to answer like
a woman : Because I do.

19. *A woman's strength is in her
tongue.* 1560 : Becon, *Catechism*, 345
(P.S.), They shame not to answer :
" A woman hath none other weapon
but her tongue . . ." 1659 : Howell,
Proverbs : Brit.- Engl., 29. 1875 :
Cheales, *Proverbial Folk-Lore*, 8, A
woman's tongue is her sword, and she
does not let it rust.

20. *A woman's tongue is the last thing
about her that dies.* 1612 : Chapman,
Widow's Tears, IV. ii., When a man
dies, the last thing that moves is his
heart ; in a woman her tongue. 1738 :
Swift, *Polite Convers.*, Dial. III.

21. *A woman's work is never done. c.*
1655 : in *Roxb. Ballads*, iii. 302 (B.S.).
1670 : Ray, 50, A womans work is never
at an end. 1732 : Fuller, No. 5810 [in
the plural]. 1825 : Hone, *Ev. Day
Book*, I. 1375 [as in 1732]. 1928 :
Evening Standard, Jan. 3, p. 3, col. 2,
" The old adage that woman's work is
never done should not be tolerated,"
she said.

22. *A woman that is wilful. See*
quot. 16th cent. in *Reliq. Antiquæ*, ii.
195 (1843), A woman thatt ys wylfull
ys a plage off the worste, As good live in
hell, as withe a wytte that is curste.

23. *A woman that loves to be at the
window, is like a bunch of grapes on the
highway.* 1666 : Torriano, *Piazza Univ.*,
74, A woman at a window, as grapes
on the high way. 1869 : Hazlitt, 39.

24. *A woman that paints puts up a
bill that she is to be let.* 1700 : Ward,
London Spy, 420 (1924), For she that
paints will doubtless be a whore. 1732 :
Fuller, No. 481.

25. *A woman that spinnes in vice,
hath her smocke full of lice.* 1623 :
Wodroephe, *Spared Houres*, 484.

26. *Choose not a woman nor linen by
candlelight.* 1578 : Florio, *First
Fruites*, fo. 32, Neither a woman nor
lynnen chuse thou by a candle. 1629 :

Book of Meery Riddles, Prov. 18. 1678 :
Ray, 64, Neither women nor linen by
candle-light. 1928 : *Bystander,* Oct.
17, p. 138, col. 1. Cf. No. 40.

27. *He hath a woman's tongue.* 1630 :
T. Adams, *Works,* 150, The prouerbe
came not for nothing, when we say of a
brawling man, he . . . hath a womans
tongue in his head.

28. *If a woman were as little as she is
good, A peascod would make her a gown
and a hood.* 1591 : Florio, *Second
Frutes,* 175 [in the plural]. 1619 :
Help to Discourse, 55 (1640). 1732 :
Fuller, No. 6446. 1869 : Spurgeon,
John Ploughman, ch. xvii. [" peashell "
for " peascod "].

29. *Let no woman's painting Breed
thy heart's fainting.* 1670 : Ray, 20
[" stomachs" for "hearts"]. 1732 :
Fuller, No. 6243.

30. *Many women many words.* c.
1425 : *Castle of Perseverance,* sc. vi. st.
230, [Where] Ther wymmen arn, are
many wordys. 1542 : *Sch. House of
Women,* l. 482, And where be women,
are many woords. c. 1600 : Deloney,
Thos. of Reading, ch. 12, The old
prouerbe . . . Many women many
words. 1670 : Ray, 214.

31. *One tongue is enough for a woman.*
1678 : Ray, 59. 1738 : Swift, *Polite
Convers.,* Dial. II.

32. *She is a woman and therefore may
be wooed, she is a woman and therefore
may be won.* c. 1591 : Shakespeare,
Titus, Andr., II. i. 1620 : Ford, *Line
of Life,* 59 (Sh. S.), Women were in their
creation ordained to be wooed, and to
be won. 1823 : Scott, *Q. Durward,* ch.
xix., Every woman may be won.

33. *Tell a woman she's a beauty, and
the devil will tell her so ten times.* 1710 :
S. Palmer, *Moral Essays on Proverbs,*
192, Tell a woman she's handsome but
once, And the devil will tell her so fifty
times. 1732 : Fuller, No. 4326.

34. *The more women look in their
glass, the less they look to their house.*
1640 : Herbert, *Jac. Prudentum,* 1670 :
Ray, 50 [in the plural]. 1732 : Fuller,
No. 4669, The more women look into
their glass, the less they look into their
hearts.

35. *Three women and a goose make a
market.* 1586 : Pettie, *Guazzo,* fo. 115,
Doe you not know the prouerbe, that
three women make a market ? 1607 :
Rowlands, *Diog. Lanthorne,* 45 (Hunt.
Cl.), Three women make a market, for
they haue sufficient voyce. 1665 :
J. Wilson, *Projectors,* III., If two women
and a goose make a market, I see no
reason why three may not make a
council. 1738 : Swift, *Polite Convers.,*
Dial. III., Miss, did you never hear, that
three women and a goose are enough to
make a market ? 1865 : W. White,
Eastern England, i. 262.

36. *Where there are women and geese,
there wants no noise.* 1659 : Howell,
Proverbs: Ital.-Eng., 16. 1678 : Ray,
64. 1732 : Fuller, No. 5684, Where
women are and geese, there wants no
gaggling.

37. *Woman's instinct is often truer
than man's reasoning.* 1875 : Cheales,
Proverbial Folk-Lore, 11.

38. *Women and dogs set men together
by the ears.* 1541 : *Sch. House of
Women,* l. 690, The prouerb olde
accordeth right : Women and dogges
cause much strife. 1666 : Torriano,
Piazza Univ., 52, Many women and
dogs cause contention. 1670 : Ray, 50.
1829 : Cobbett, *Adv. to Young Men,*
Lett. iv., Soldiers have leisure, too, to
play with children, as well as with
" women and dogs," for which the
proverb has made them famous.

39. *Women and hens by too much
gadding are lost.* 1611 : Cotgrave, s.v.
" Poule," Women and hennes, that
gad overmuch, are quickly lost. 1666 :
Torriano, *Piazza Univ.,* 10.

40. *Women and linen look best by
candlelight.* 1738 : Swift, *Polite Convers.,* Dial. III. [" shew " for " look "].
1913 : *Folk-Lore,* xxiv. 76 (Oxfordshire).
Cf. No. 26.

41. *Women and music should never
be dated.* 1773 : Goldsmith, *She Stoops,*
III.

42. *Women and their wills are
dangerous ills.* 1613 : S. Rowley,
When you see me, sig. L3.

43. *Women and wine, game and deceit,
Make the wealth small and the wants*

great. 1591 : Florio, *Second Frutes,* 73,
Women, wine, and dice, will bring a man
to lice. 1732 : Fuller, No. 6416. 1736 :
Franklin, *Way to Wealth,* in *Works,* i.
446 (Bigelow).

44. *Women are born in Wiltshire,
Brought up in Cumberland, Lead their
lives in Bedfordshire, Bring their husbands to Buckingham, And die in Shrewsbury.* 1658 : *Wit Restor'd,* 99.

45. *Women are necessary evils.* 1583 :
Melbancke, *Philotinus,* sig. T2, As all
women bee euills, yet necessarie euills.
1591 : Florio, *Second Frutes,* 173,
Women . . . are indeed necessarie, but
euills. 1639 : Clarke, 118. Cf. **Wife**
(30).

46. *Women are saints in church.* See
quots. 1542 : *Sch. House of Women,* l.
658, As holy as saints in church they be,
And in street as angels they were, At
home, for all their hipocrisie, A deuilish
life they lede all the yeer. 1559 :
Bercher, *Nobility of Women,* 127 (Roxb.
Cl.), A woman is a fury and an hurtfull
Spyrite in the house, an angell in the
churche, an ape in the bedd, a mule
vnbrideled in the ffelde and a gote in
the garden. 1560 : E. More, *Defence of
Women,* l. 474, At home lyke dyuelles
they be, abrode lyke aungelles pure.
1589 : Puttenham, *Engl. Poesie,* 299
(Arber), We limit the comely parts of a
woman to consist in foure points, that
is to be a shrewe in the kitchin, a saint
in the church, an angell at the bourd,
and an ape in the bed, as the Chronicle
reportes by Mistress Shore paramour to
king Edward the fourth. 1602 :
Middleton, *Blurt. Master-Const.,* III.
iii., According to that wise saying of
you, [women] be saints in the church,
angels in the street, devils in the kitchen,
and apes in your bed. 1869 : Spurgeon,
John Ploughman, ch. xiii., God save us
all from wives who are angels in the
streets, saints in the church, and devils
at home.

47. *Women are ships and must be
manned. c.* 1630 : in *Roxb. Ballads,* i.
55. (B.S.).

48. *Women be forgetful, children be
unkind.* See quots. *c.* 1470 : *Songs
and Carols,* 34 (Percy S.), Wyves be

rekeles, chyldren be onkynd. Exec-
cuturs be covetys and hold that thei
fynd. Before 1500 : in Hill, *Commonplace-Book,* 138 (E.E.T.S.), Do sum
good, man, by thy lyffe, Whiles thow
hast thy mynde ; Thy children will
for-gete the sone, Thy wyffe will be
unkynd, Thy executours be covytes,
And take all that they fynde ; Yff thow
wilt not, while thow may, They will
bryng the behynde. 1603 : Stow,
Survey of London, 116, I wish men to
make their owne hands their executors
and their eyes their ouerseers, not forgetting the olde prouerbe Women be
forgetfull, children be unkinde, Executors be covetous, and take what they
finde : If anybody aske where the deads
goods became, they answer So God mee
helpe and holydome Hee dyed a poore
man. 1606 : T. Heywood, *If you
know not me,* pt. II. [as in 1603
to " they finde "]. 1632 : Rowley,
Woman never vexed, V. [as in 1603, very
slightly varied].

49. *Women commend a modest man,
but like him not.* 1732 : Fuller, No.
5805.

50. *Women conceal all that they know
not.* 1640 : Herbert, *Jac. Prudentum*
and 1670 : Ray, 50 [both in the singular
number]. 1732 : Fuller, No. 5806.

51. *Women have no souls.* 1566 : L.
Wager, *Mary Magdalene,* sig. E4,
Women have no soules, this sayng is
not newe. *c.* 1610 : Marston, *Insat.
Countess,* V., And lastly, may the
opinion of philosophers Prove true, that
women have no soules ! Before 1680 :
Butler, *Remains,* i. 246 (1759), The souls
of women are so small, That some
believe th'have none at all. 1708 :
Brit. Apollo, Supp. Paper 12, col. 8, I
have often heard say, that the female
sex have no soul, I suppose it to be a
proverbial saying.

52. *Women have two faults.* See
quots. 1606 : B. Rich, *Faultes,* fo. 23,
Amongst women (some will say) there
is but two faults, and those are, they can
neither doe nor say well. 1716 : Ward,
Female Policy, 72, 'Tis said of women,
that they have two faults ; that is, they
can neither say well, nor yet do well.

1875 : Cheales, *Proverb. Folk-Lore*, 13, Men have many faults, poor women have only two, There's nothing right they say, and nothing right they do !

53. *Women in mischief are wiser than men.* 1647 : *Countrym. New Commonwealth*, 11.

54. *Women in state affairs are like monkeys in glass shops.* 1659 : Howell, 12.

55. *Women laugh when they can and weep when they will.* 1611 : Cotgrave, s.v. " Femme." A woman laughes, etc. 1640 : Herbert, *Jac. Prudentum.* 1670 : Ray, 50. 1736 : Bailey, *Dict.* s.v. " Laugh."

56. *Women, money and wine, have their good and their pine.* 1611 : Cotgrave, s.v. " Argent," Money, wine, and women, have good and bad things in them. 1623 : Wodroephe, *Spared Houres*, 484.

57. *Women must have the last word.* 1542 : *Sch. House of Women*, l. 76, Yet wil the woman haue the last woord. 1655 : Fuller, *Church Hist.*, bk. ix. § iii. (7), Whilst women strive for the last word. 1764 : Mrs. F. Sheridan, *Dupe*, Epil., A prating female will have the last word. 1926 : Phillpotts, *Yellow Sands*, III., She was like the rest of your sex, ma'am—she went her own way, and had the last word.

58. *Women must have their wills.* 1547 : Borde, *Brev. of Helthe*, fo. 96, Let her [the wife] haue her owne wyl for that she wyll haue who so euer say nay. 1602–3 : Manningham, *Diary*, 92 (Camden S.), Women, because they cannot have their wills when they dye, they will have their wills while they live. 1616 : Haughton, *Englishm. for my Money*, V. iii., Women will have their will. 1664 : J. Wilson, *Cheats*, V. v. [as in 1616]. 1733 : Gay, Song in *Achilles*, Since woman will have both her word and her way. 1869 : Spurgeon, *John Ploughman*, ch. xvi., But then the proverb says, a wife ought to have her will during life, because she cannot make one when she dies.

59. *Women, priests and poultry never have enough.* 1659 : Howell, *Proverbs: Ital.-Engl.*, 7. 1670 : Ray, 30. 1732 : Fuller, No. 5809.

60. *Women's advice is cold advice. c.* 1270 : *Prov. of Alfred*, in *Old Eng. Miscell.*, 122 (E.E.T.S.), Cold red is quene [woman's] red [advice]. *c.* 1386 : Chaucer, *C. Tales*, B. 4446 (Skeat), Wommennës counseils ben ful oftë colde. [Skeat says " colde " = baneful, fatal.] Cf. No. 15.

61. *Women's jars breed men's wars.* 1642 : Fuller, *Holy State (Wise Statesman).* 1853 : Trench, *Proverbs*, 19 (1905).

62. *Women's tongues wag like lambs' tails. c.* 1597 : Deloney, *Iacke of Newberie*, ch. vii., Considering that womens tongues are like lambs tayles, which seldome stand still. 1612 : *Cornucopiæ*, 7 (Grosart), As womens tongues be like to yong lambs tailes. 1865 : " Lancs. Proverbs," in *N. & Q.*, 3rd ser., viii. 494 [in the singular number].

63. *Women think Place a sweet fish.* 1678 : Ray, 59.

64. *Women want the best first, and the best always.* 1917 : Bridge, *Cheshire Proverbs*, 157.

65. *Women, wealth and wine have each two qualities, a good and a bad.* 1736 : Bailey, *Dict.*, s.v. " Woman."

66. *Women, wind and fortune are given to change.* 1639 : Clarke, 159, A woman's mind and winter-wind change oft. 1670 : Ray, 50 [as in 1639]. 1736 : Bailey, *Dict.*, s.v. " Women." Ibid., A woman's mind is like the wind in a winter's night.

See also All women ; Bad words ; Beware ; Black, *adj.* (3) and (22) ; Dally ; Dead (2) ; Discreet ; Eel (4) ; Every Woman ; Fair, *adj.* (12)–(14) ; Flesh upon horses ; Fool (40) and (47) ; Gaming ; Goose (9) ; Handsome (2) ; Hate (1) ; Honest (7) and (12) ; House (13) ; Love (37) ; Luck (1) ; Man (29) and (58); Many men ; Meat (2) ; Mischief (5) ; Old A(c), D(1) ; One hair ; Ship (2) ; Silence ; Silent (1) ; Swine (2) ; Two women ; Weal (1) ; Whistling ; Winter (21) ; and Wit (6).

Wonder is the daughter of ignorance. 1578 : Florio, *First Fruites*, fo. 32, Maruaile is the daughter of ignorance. 1629 : *Book of Meery Riddles*, Prov. 44, Marvell is, etc. 1677 : *Poor Robin's*

Visions, 24. 1681 : Rycaut, tr. *Gracian's Critick*, 25, Though admiration be the daughter of ignorance. 1732 : Fuller, No. 5811.

Wonders will never cease. 1776 : in *Garrick Corresp.* ii. 174 (1832). 1844 : Jerrold, *Story of a Feather*, ch. xx. 1926 : Phillpotts, *Marylebone Miser*, ch. vii.

Woo. 1. *He that woos a maid must come seldom in her sight, But he that woos a widow must woo her day and night.* 1639 : Clarke, 27, He that will win a maid must seldom come in her sight. 1670 : Ray, 49. 1732 : Fuller, No. 6403.

2 *He that would woo a maid.* See 1669 quot. 1611 : Barry, *Ram-Alley*, II., Do, but dally not; that's the widow's phrase. 1618 : Field, *Amends for Ladies*, IV. i., You have trusted to that fond opinion, This is the way to have a widowhood, By getting to her bed. 1669 : N. Smith, *Quakers Spiritual Court*, 13, He told me that I must observe. the old proverb . . . that he that would woe a maid, must fain, lye and flatter, but he that wooes a widdow . . . must down with his britches and at her. 1670 : Ray, 49 [as in 1669].

3. *To woo is a pleasure in a young man, a fault in an old.* Ibid., 30. 1732 : Fuller, No. 5254 [" phrenzy " for " fault "].

See also Wooing.

Wood. 1. *To be in a wood* = To be puzzled or bewildered. *c.* 1616 : B. and F., *Mad Lover*, IV., Help the boy ; He's in a wood, poor child. 1681 : Robertson, *Phraseol. Generalis*, 369, He is confused ; he has lost himself in a wood. 1786 : D'Arblay, *Diary*, ii. 246 (1876), I assured him I was quite in a wood, and begged him to be more explicit. 1854 : Baker, *Northants. Gloss.*, s.v. " Wood," " All in a wood." In a state of perplexity and bewilderment.

2. *To be unable to see the wood for the trees* = To be unable to take a general or comprehensive view. Heywood, *Proverbs*, Pt. II. ch. iv., Ye can not see the wood for trees. 1581 : Woodes, *Confl. of Conscience*, II. iii., Why, I was in place long before you

came ; But you could not see the wood for the trees. 1630 : Randolph, *Works*, i. 14 (Hazlitt, 1875), We cannot see wood for trees, nor scholars for gowns. 1738 : Swift, *Polite Convers.*, Dial. I., Tom, how is it that you can't see the wood for trees ? 1910 : Hudson, *Shepherd's Life*, ch. ii., There are many more which may not be spoken of, since we do not want to lose sight of the wood on account of the trees.

3. *Wood half burnt is easily kindled.* 1640 : Herbert, *Jac. Prudentum.* 1670 : Ray, 30. 1732 : Fuller, No. 5812 [" half-coal " for " half burnt "].

4. *Woods have ears.* See Fields.

See also Born (6).

Woodcock does not make a winter, One. 1659 : Howell, 11. 1664 : J. Wilson, *Cheats*, I. ii., One woodcock makes no winter. 1736 : Bailey, *Dict.*, s.v. "Woodcock." 1846 : Denham, *Proverbs*, 31 (Percy S.).

Wood-cock. *See* quot. 1921 : R. L. Gales, *Old-World Essays*, 251, " When Daniel's in the lion's den, Then the woodcock comes again." That is of course some time in October.

Wood-cock. *See also* **Partridge** (1) ; **Snipe** ; and **Wise** (4).

Wooden, *adj.* 1. *A wooden dagger in a painted sheath.* 1639 : Clarke, 6.

2. *A wooden leg is better than no leg.* 1732 : Fuller, No. 483.

3. *I'll not wear the wooden dagger.* 1670 : Ray, 198.

4. *The wooden horse* = The gallows. *c.* 1550 : in Hazlitt, *E. Pop. Poetry*, iii. 261, Your happe may be to wagge upon a wodden nagge. 1654 : Gayton, *Pleasant Notes Don Q.*, 119, Others . . . vaile and couch it, when riding the wooden horse. 1680 : D'Urfey, *Virtuous Wife*, II. i., I'de ride the wooden horse e're be troubled with her impertinence.

5. *To get a wooden suit* = To be dead and buried. 1896 : *Folk-Lore*, vii. 377 (Staffs.).

6. *Wooden legs.* See **Run** (11).

Wood Fidley rain. *See* quot. 1863 : Wise, *New Forest*, ch. vii., The Forest proverb of " Wood Fidley rain," that is, rain which lasts all the day.

Wood-pecker. *See* quot. *c.* 1489 :
Caxton, *Blanchardyn.*, *etc.*, 173
(E.E.T.S.), Men saye in a comyn
langage, that " neuer noo wodewoll
[wood-pecker] dyde brede a sperhawke."

Wood-pigeon. *See* quot. 1917 :
Bridge, *Cheshire Proverbs*, 92, Like the
Quest [wood-pigeon], always saying
" do, do," but everybody knows it
makes the worst nest i' th' wood.

Wood's dog. *See* quots. 1732 :
Fuller, No. 3241, Like Wood's dog ;
he'll neither go to church nor stay at
home. 1880 : W. D. Parish, in *N. &
Q.*, 6th ser., ii. 166, " Why," said the
old man [Selmeston, Sussex], " it has
been a say as long ago as I was a child,
Contrairy as Wood's dog, that wouldn't
go out nor yet stop at home." Cf.
Hunt's dog.

Wooers and widows are never poor.
c. 1550 : Udall, *R. Doister*, I. ii. Cf.
Widow (10).

**Woof or warp of any business, To
make.** 1639 : in *Berkeley MSS.*, iii.
30 (1885), Il'e make abb or warp of it
(Gloucest.). 1678 : Ray, 278.

Wooing. 1. *Happy is the wooing that
is not long a-doing.* 1576 : *Parad. of D.
Devices*, in *Brit. Bibliog.*, iii. 71 (1812),
Thrise happie is that woying, That is not
long a doyng. 1606 : *Sir Giles Goosecappe*, III. ii., [" Blest " for " Happy "].
1621 : Burton, *Melancholy*, III. II. vi.
5, 615 (1836), Blessed is, etc. 1707 :
Centlivre, *Plat. Lady*, III. i., They zay
'tis very unlucky to be long a wooing.
1730 : Fielding, *Tom Thumb*, II. ix.
1842 : Barham, *Ing. Legends*, 2nd ser.,
" Sir Rupert."

2. *The wooing was a day after the
wedding.* 1732 : Fuller, No. 4840.

Wool. 1. *He seeks wool on an ass.*
1813 : Ray, 75.

2. *There is no wool so white but a
dyer can make it black.* 1576 : Pettie,
Pet. Pallace, ii. 69 (Gollancz), I see there
is no wool so coarse but it will take some
colour. 1580 : Lyly, *Euphues*, 330
(Arber), There is no wool so white but
the diar can make blacke. 1732 :
Fuller, No. 4927.

3. *To come for wool and go home
shorn.* 1612 : Shelton, *Quixote*, pt. I.

bk. i. ch. vii., Considering how many
there go to seek for wool that return
again shorn themselves ! 1694 :
D'Urfey, *Quixote*, pt. I. IV. i., Several
come for wool that return shorn. 1710 :
Palmer, *Moral Essays on Proverbs*, 148,
Many go to seek wool, and come home
shorn. 1822 : Scott, *Nigel*, ch. xxiii.,
But, lack-a-day ! thou art one of those
that come out for wool, and art sure to
go home shorn.

4. *You may keep wool till it's dirt, and
flax till it's silk.* 1732 : Fuller, No.
5950.

5. *You were better give the wool than
the sheep.* 1670 : Ray, 30.

See also **Warm** (2).

Wool-gathering, His wits are. 1560 :
Wilson, *Rhetorique*, 107 (1909), As
though our wittes and our senses were
a woll gathering. 1580 : Lyly, *Euphues*,
415 (Arber), My witts were not al this
while a wol-gathering. 1665 : Pepys,
Diary, Oct. 5, My mind is run a' wool-
gathering and my business neglected.
1748 : Richardson, *Clarissa*, viii. 220
(1785), That my wits may not be sent a
wool-gathering. 1841 : Dickens, *Barn.
Rudge*, ch. liv., He's so dead scared, he's
wool-gathering, I think.

Woolly fleeces. *See* quots. 1555 :
L. Digges, *Prognostication*, sig. B2, If
thyck clowdes resemblyng flockes, or
rather great heapes of woll, be gathered
in many places, they shewe rayne,
1658 : Willsford, *Natures Secrets*, 125.
When the clouds seem piled upon heaps
like fleeces of wool, it presages wet
weather, and neer at hand. 1831 :
Hone, *Year-Book*, 300, If woolly fleeces
spread the heavenly way, No rain be
sure, disturbs the summer's day [a
flat contradiction to 1555 and 1658].
1846 : Denham, *Proverbs*, 50 (Percy S.)
[as in 1831].

Wool-seller knows a wool-buyer, A.
1670 : Ray, 159. 1732 : Fuller, No.
484.

Worcester. 1. *See* quot. 1882 :
Mrs. Chamberlain, *W. Worc. Words*, 39
(E.D.S.), " It shines like Worcester
against Gloucester " is a very old saying.

2. *Worcester, poor, proud and pretty.*
Ibid., 39, It is proverbial that the

Worcester ladies are " Poor, proud, and pretty." 1894 : Northall, *Folk Phrases*, 33 (E.D.S.)

Word and **Words**. 1. *A word and a blow*. *c*. 1568 : Wager, *Longer thou Livest*, sig. D1, This is manhoode to make thee bolde, Let there be but a worde and a blow. 1592. Shakespeare. *Romeo*, III. i., And but one word with one of us ? Couple it with something ; make it a word and a blow. 1678 : Bunyan, *Pilgr. Progr.*, pt. I. 71 (1849), So soon as the man overtook me, he was but a word and a blow ; for down he knocked me, and laid me for dead. 1720 : C. Shadwell, *Irish Hosp.*, I., Come Ned, let's to my sisters, for my uncle is a country wit, a word and a blow. 1768 : Franklin, in *Works*, iv. 158 (Bigelow), It is said of choleric people, that with them there is but a word and a blow. 1886 : R. L. S., *Kidnapped*, ch. vii., All, as the saying goes, were " at a word and a blow " with their best friends.

2. *A word and a stone*. See **Throw** (5).

3. *A word before is worth two behind*. 1736 : Bailey, *Dict.*, s.v. " Word."

4. *A word spoken is an arrow let fly*. 1509 : Barclay, *Ship of Fools*, i. 108 (1874), A worde ones spokyn reuoked can nat be. 1596 : Lodge, *Divel Coniured*, 83 (Hunt. Cl.), Words are like to arrows, which are easily shot out, but hardly got in again. 1639 : Clarke, 51, A word spoke is past recalling. 1732 : Fuller, No. 486.

5. *A word to the wise is enough*. [Dictum sapienti sat est.—Plautus, *Pers.*, 4, 7, 19.] 1577 : Rhodes, *Boke of Nurture*, in *Babees Book*, 88 (E.E.T.S.), For few wordes to wyse men is best. *c*. 1598 : Jonson, *Case is Altered*, I. i., Presto. Go to, a word to the wise ; away, fly, vanish, 1616 : Haughton, *Englishm. for my Money*, III. i., They say, a word to the wise is enough. 1697 : Vanbrugh, *Esop*, III. 1711 : Addison, *Spectator*, No. 221. 1768 : Sterne, *Sent. Journey*, 157 (1794). 1819 : Scott, *Bride of L.*, ch. vii., But what sayeth the proverb, *verbum sapienti*—a word is more to him that hath wisdom than a sermon to a fool.

6. *Deliver your words not by number but by weight*. 1855 : Bohn, 343.

7. *From words to deeds is a great space*. 1629 : *Book of Meery Riddles*, Prov. 94.

8. *He that sells wares for words must live by the loss*. 1736 : Bailey, *Dict.*, s.v. " Wares."

9. *His word is his bond*. Before 1400 : Chaucer, *Book of the Duchesse*, l. 935, Ne lasse flatering in hir worde, That purely, hir simple recorde Was founde as trewe as any bonde. 1630 : Brathwait, *Engl. Gent.*, 148 (1641). For his word is his gage. 1631 : F. Lenton, *Characters*, sig. G8 (1663), His word is as good as his bond. 1748 : Richardson, *Clarissa*, iv. 239 (1785), You know that my word has always been looked upon as my bond. 1812 : Combe, *Syntax : Pict. Tour*, can. xix. 1886 : R. L. S., *Kidnapped*, ch. iv., I'm a queer man, and strange wi' strangers ; but my word is my bond, and there's the proof of it. 1914 : A. Dobson, in *Poet. Works*, 453 (1923), Fixed our word as our bond has been.

10. *While the word is in your mouth it is your own ; when 'tis once spoken, 'tis another's*. 1646 : A. Brome, in *Roxb. Ballads*, VIII. cix. (B.S.), Our words are our own, if we keep them within. 1736 : Bailey, *Dict.*, s.v. " Word."

11. *Words and feathers are tost by the wind*. 1670 : Ray, 30.

12. *Words are but sands, it's money buys lands*. 1659 : Howell, 11. 1732 : Fuller, No. 6166.

13. *Words are but words*. *c*. 1620 : B. and F., *Little Fr. Lawyer*, I. i.

14. *Words are wind*. Before 1225 : *Ancr. Riwle*, 122, hwat is word bute wind ? *c*. 1390 : Gower, *Conf. Amantis*, bk. iii. l. 2768, For word is wynd. *c*. 1450 : Lydgate, *Secrees*, 39 (E.E.T.S.), Woord is but wynd leff woord and tak the dede. 1509 : Barclay, *Ship of Fools*, i. 207 (1874). 1587 : Greene, *Works*, iii. 102 (Grosart). 1660 : Tatham, *Rump*, V. 1748 : Richardson, *Clarissa*, vi. 212 (1785), Words are wind ; but deeds are mind. 1823 : Scott, *Durward*, ch. xix., " Hard words, or kind ones," said the Zingaro,

"are but wind." 1866: G. Eliot, *Felix Holt*, ch. xi.

15. *Words are women. See* Deeds.

16. *Words cut more than swords—* variously phrased. Before 1225 : *Ancr. Riwle*, 74, Mo sleað word þene sweord. 1594 : Churchyard, *Mirror of Man*, sig. A4 (1816), Sharp words makes more wounds then surgeons can heale. 1621 : Burton, *Melancholy*, I. II. iv. 4, 223 (1836), It is an old saying, a blow with a word strikes deeper than a blow with a sword. 1659 : Howell, 13. 1732 : Fuller, No. 575, An acute word cuts deeper than a sharp weapon. 1871 : Smiles, *Character*, 170, There are words that strike even harden than blows.

17. *Words have long tails; and have no tails.* 1678 : Ray, 221.

18. *Words may pass but blows fall heavy.* 1633 : Draxe, 103, Words are but winde but blowes are vnkinde. 1678 : Ray, 354.

See also Deeds ; Fair (29)–(40) ; Few words ; Good words ; High (6) ; and Soft words.

Work, *verb.* 1. *He that will not work will want.* 1633 : Draxe, 109, He that will not labour must not eat. 1639 : Clarke, 163.

2. *He that works after his own manner, his head aches not at the matter.* 1640 : Herbert, *Jac. Prudentum*.

3. *Those that cannot work. See* quot. 1864 : "Cornish Proverbs," in *N. & Q.*, 3rd ser., vi. 494, Those that cannot work must planny, and those that cannot planny must lowster [hard manual labour]. Cf. Schemey.

4. *To work by the great* = To do piece-work. 1585 : *Nomenclator*, 502, He that vndertaketh to doe a peece of worke vpon a prise, and (as they say) by great. 1626 : Breton, *Fantasticks*, 13 (Grosart), The labourer by great will be walking toward his worke. 1662 : Gerbier, *Disc. of Building*, 26, Let builders put their designs to master-workmen by the great. 1711 : *Spectator*, No. 22, Adv. at end., Any person may agree by the great, and be kept in repair by the year. 1742 : North, *Lives of Norths*, ii. 282 (Bohn), They . . . keep hirelings in garrets, at hard meat,

to write and correct by the great. 1884 : R. Lawson, *Upton-on-Severn Words*, 17 (E.D.S.), Work by the gret, Piece-work. 1917 : Bridge, *Cheshire Proverbs*, 146.

5. *To work for a dead horse. See* Dead (25).

6. *To work for needfire. See* quot. 1879 : Henderson, *Folk-Lore of N. Counties*, 168, The North-country proverb, "to work as if working for need-fire," shows how prevalent this custom [of producing fire, through the smoke of which cattle were passed, by the friction of two pieces of wood] has been in the border counties as in Scotland.

7. *Work to-day, for you know not how much you may be hindered to-morrow.* 1846 : Denham, *Proverbs*, 3 (Percy S.). *See also* Workman.

Work, *subs. If anything stay let work stay.* 1678 : Ray, 278. 1732 : Fuller, No. 2671. Cf. Meat.

Workman. 1. *As is the workman so is the work.* 1611 : Cotgrave, s.v. "Ouvrier," Like workman like work. 1732 : Fuller, No. 702.

2. *It is working that makes a workman.* Ibid., No. 3034.

3. *What is a workman without his tools?* 1546 : Heywood, *Proverbs*, Pt. II. ch. ix. 1559 : Becon, in *Prayers, etc.*, 260 (P.S.). 1670 : Ray, 30. 1732 : Fuller, No. 5494. *See also* Ill workman.

World. 1. *All the world and his wife.* 1738 : Swift, *Polite Convers.*, Dial. III., Pray, madam, who were the company ? *Lady Smart* Why, there was all the world and his wife. 1766 : Anstey, *New Bath Guide*, 130 (1767), How he welcomes at once all the world and his wife, And how civil to folk he ne'er saw in his life ! 1816 : Byron, *Letters, etc.*, iii. 266 (Prothero), In the mean time, I am at war " with all the world and his wife." 1848 : Dickens, *Dombey*, ch. xvii. 1920 : *Sphere*, April, 10, p. 36, col. 1.

2. *A world to see!* = wonderful to see. *c.* 1475 : *Assembly of Ladies*, l. 539, For yonge and olde, and every maner age, It was a world to loke on her visage. 1519 : *Four Elements*, in Hazlitt, *O. Plays*, i. 35, It is a world to see her whirl, Dancing in a round.

1530 : Palsgrave, It is a worlde to se him lowte and knele. 1589 : Nashe, *Works*, i. 149 (Grosart), It is a world to see this world. 1626 : Breton, *Works*, i. *e* 8 (Grosart), Oh what a world it is to see what wiles, A silly foole will finde to gather wealth. 1881 : Evans, *Leicest. Words, etc.*, 292 (E.D.S.), It's a woo'ld to see that theer little un order the big uns to the roight abaout ! A's as marsterful as marsterful !

3. *Had you the world on your chessboard, you could not fit al to your mind.* 1640 : Herbert, *Jac. Prudentum.*

4. *The world is a ladder for some to go up and some down.* 1659 : Howell, *Proverbs: Ital.-Eng.*, 1, The world is like a ladder, one goeth up, the other down. 1732 : Fuller, No. 4841.

5. *The world is a tail and happy is he that gets hold on't.* 1742 : North, *Lives of Norths*, ii. 150 (Bohn) [quoted as " a proverb "].

6. *The world is but a day's walk, for the sun goes about it in twenty four hours.* 1616 : *Rich Cabinet*, fo. 160.

7. *The world is full of fools.* 1627 : in *Harl. Miscell.*, iii. 198 (1744). 1642 : *Discovery of divers sortes of Asses*, sig. A4 [with addition " and asses "].

8. *The world is his who enjoys it.* 1736 : Bailey, *Dict.*, s.v. " World."

9. *The world is his who knows how to wait for it.* 1875 : Cheales, *Proverbial Folk-Lore*, 48.

10. *The world is too narrow for two fools a quarrelling.* 1732 : Fuller, No. 4844.

11. *The world is well amended with him.* 1633 : Draxe, 4, The world is somewhat amended for him. 1672 : Walker, *Parœm.*, 26.

12. *The world runs on wheels.* 1546 : Heywood, *Proverbs*, pt. II. ch. vii. 1592 : Greene, *Works*, x. 203, How is it sweete wench, goes the worlde on wheeles, that you tread so daintily on your typtoes ? 1614 : B. Rich, *Honestie of this Age*, 30 (Percy S.), They were wont to say, the world did runne on wheeles. 1673 : *Vinegar and Mustard*, 9, in Hindley, *Old Book Coll. Misc.*, iii., Now you are come ashore, you think the world runs

on wheels, and that all the world is oatmeal.

13. *The world was never so dull, but if one will not, another will.* 1670 : Ray, 158. 1732 : Fuller, No. 6451.

14. *This is the world and the other is the country.* 1678 : Ray, 84.

15. *This world is nothing except it tend to another.* 1670 : Ray, 31.

16. *To have the world at will.* *c.* 1535 : *Dialogues of Creatures*, cliv. (1816), He that is prosperows and hath the world at wyl. 1586 : Pettie, *Guazzo*, fo. 165, Men hauing the world at will, as he hath, are neuer but merrie. 1629 : *Book of Meery Riddles*, Prov. 52, He that hath the world at will, seemes wise. 1680 : L'Estrange, *Tully's Offices*, 82, Take a wise man, that has the world at will.

17. *To have the world in a string.* See **Have in a string.**

Worm and **Worms.** 1. *He has a worm in his brain.* 1678 : Ray, 278. 1754 : Berthelson, *Eng.-Danish Dict.*, s.v. " Worm," He has got a worm in his head.

2. *To be or to make worms' meat.* *c.* 1430 : Lydgate, *Daunce of Machabree*, l. 640, That wormes food is fine [end] of our liuyng. *c.* 1483 : *Quatuor Sermones*, 28 (Roxb. Cl.), After thyn ende thou shalt be but wormys mete. 1592 : Shakespeare, *Romeo*, III. i., They have made worms' meat of me. 1611 : Cotgrave, s.v. " Estat," Every creature is wormes meat. 1736 : Bailey, *Dict.*, s.v. " State," Every state is worms meat.

3. *Tread on a worm and it will turn.* 1546 : Heywood, *Proverbs*, pt. II. ch. iv., Tread a woorme on the tayle, and it must turne agayne. 1592 : Greene, in *Works*, xii. 143 (Grosart). 1638 : Ford, *Fancies*, V. i., I am, my lord, a worm ; pray, my lord, tread on me, I will not turn again. 1710 : S. Palmer, *Moral, Essays on Proverbs*, 305. *c.* 1800 : J. Trusler, *Proverbs in Verse*, 105. 1816 : Scott, *Old Mortality*, ch. xxvii. 1922 : Weyman, *Ovington's Bank*, ch. ix., The worm will turn, and Thomas . . . did turn.

Worse, adj. 1. *A worse friend.* See **Friend (27).**

2. *There is no worse pestilence than a familiar enemy.* c. 1386 : Chaucer, *Merchant's Tale*, l. 549, For in this world nys worse pestilence Than homly foo, alday in thy presence. 1538 : in *Lisle Papers*, xii. Art. 43, It hath been an old proverbe that there is no worse pestilence than a famylar enemy.

3. *The worse end of the staff.* See **Wrong** (3).

4. *The worse for the rider, the better for the bider.* 1639 : Clarke, 18, Ill for the rider, good for th'abider. 1659 : Howell, 18, A fatt soyl good for the bider, bad for the rider. 1670 : Ray, 43. Before 1680 : Butler, *Remains*, ii. 284 (1759), His discourse is like the road-miles in the North, the filthier and dirtier the longer ; and he delights to dwell the longer upon them to make good the old proverb that says —*they are good for the dweller, but ill for the traveller.* 1735 : Pegge, *Kent. Proverbs*, in E.D.S., No. 12, p. 75, Bad for the rider, good for th'abider. 1865 : W. White, *Eastern England*, ii. 35, The latter . . . still justify in a measure the proverbs—" Bon pays, mauvais chemin," and " The worse for the rider, the better for the bider ? " Cf. **Best** (16).

5. *The worse luck now, the better another time.* 1732 : Fuller, No. 4847.

6. *The worse the passage, the more welcome the port.* Ibid., No. 4848.

7. *Worse things happen at sea.* 1869 : Spurgeon, *John Ploughman*, ch. v.

8. *Worse ware.* See quot. 1762 : Smollett, *Sir L. Greaves*, ch. xvi., Marry hap, worse ware may have a better chap [market], as the saying goes.

Worship, *subs.* *More for worship than for pride.* c. 1460 : *How the good Wife*, l. 90.

Worship, *verb.* *They that worship God merely for fear, Would worship the devil too, if he appear.* 1732 : Fuller, No. 6419.

Worst, *adj. adv.* and *subs.* 1. *He that worst may still holds the candle.* 1546 : Heywood, *Proverbs*, pt. II. ch. ii., Who that woorst maie shall holde the candell. 1576 : Pettie, *Pet. Pallace*, ii. 54 (Gollancz), How unequally it is

provided that those which worst may, are driven to hold the candle ! 1639 : in *Berkeley MSS.*, iii. 32 (1885) [" must hold " for " still holds "]. 1670 : Ray, 159. 1732 : Fuller, No. 2361.

2. *If the worst come to the worst.* 1597 : *Discouerie of Knights of the Poste*, sig. C3. 1620 : Shelton, *Quixote*, Pt. II. ch. lxxiii. 1637 : Shirley, *Example*, II. i. 1682 : A. Behn, *City Heiress*, III. i. 1700 : Congreve, *Way of World*, III. xviii. 1719 : Defoe, *Crusoe*, 234 (1883), If the worse come to the worst. [This is a more reasonable form of the saying than the usual one.] 1886 : R. L. S., *Kidnapped*, ch. i. 1900 : Pinero, *Gay Lord Quex*, III.

3. *The worst can fall is but a denial.* 1546 : Heywood, *Proverbs*, pt. I. ch. xi. If the woorst fell, we could haue but a naie. 1659 : Howell, 14.

4. *The worst dog that is.* See **Dog** (81).

5. *The worst is behind.* 1546 : Heywood, *Proverbs*, pt. II. ch. ii. 1659 : Howell, 6.

6. *The worst piece.* See **All is well.**

7. *The worst spoke in a cart breaks first.* 1678 : Ray, 205. 1732 : Fuller, No. 4851.

8. *The worst wheel of a cart creaks most.* 1586 : Pettie, *Guazzo*, fo. 106, The brokenest wheele of the chariot maketh alwaies the greatest noise. 1611 : Cotgrave, s.v. " Crier." 1666 : Torriano, *Piazza Univ.*, 240. 1869 : Spurgeon, *John Ploughman*, ch. ii.

9. *When things are at the worst they will mend.* 1600 : *Sir John Oldcastle*, l. 1899 (Malone S.), Patience good madame, things at worst will mend. 1691 : *Merry Drollery*, 56 (Ebsworth). 1748 : Richardson, *Clarissa*, iii. 263 (1785). 1824 : Scott, *Redgauntlet*, ch. xii. 1841 : Dickens, *Barn. Rudge*, ch. xx., When things are at the worst they are sure to mend.

See also **Provide.**

Worth, *adj.* and *subs.* 1. *He is worth gold that carries it.* 1732 : Fuller, No. 1956.

2. *The worth of a thing is known by its want.* 1611 : Cotgrave, s.v. " Cogneu," The worth of things is knowne

when they be lost. 1694: D'Urfey, *Quixote*, pt. I. V. ii. 1748 : Richardson, *Clarissa*, iv. 238 (1785), Worth is best known by want ! I know her's now. *c.* 1800 : J. Trusler, *Proverbs in Verse*, 24. Cf. **Water** (22).

3. *The worth of a thing is what it will bring.* 1663 : Butler, *Hudibras*, II. i. 465, For what is worth in any thing, But so much money as 'twill bring. 1847 : Halliwell, *Dict.*, s.v. " Thing."

4. *The worth of water. See* **Water** (22).

5. *To be worth a plum* = To be rich. A " plum " in this sense is usually supposed to be £100,000. 1714 : Mandeville, *Fable of Bees*, 83, If a miser, who is almost a plum and spends but fifty pounds a year—. 1754 : *Connoisseur*, No. 19, I once saw a grave citizen, worth a plum, order a twopenny mess of broth. 1789 : G. Parker, *Life's Painter*, 216, A London merchant worth a plumb.

6. *To be worth one's weight in gold. c.* 1500. Medwall, *Nature*, l. 936, Nay ye ar worth thy weyght of gold. 1587 : Turbervile, *Trag. Tales, etc.*, 45 (1837), So faire a frend is worth her weight in gold. 1698 : *Terence made English*, 224 (2nd ed.), I look upon thee at present to be worth thy weight in gold. 1836 : Marryat, *Easy*, ch. xxxvi., I have [a servant] . . . who is worth his weight in gold. 1891 : Hardy, *Tess*, ch. vi. 1926 : Phillpotts, *Peacock House*, 40.

7. *Whatever is worth doing, is worth doing well.* 1875 : Cheales, *Proverb. Folk-Lore*, 138. 1893 : R. L. S., *Ebb-Tide*, ch. viii. 1915 : Wells, *Bealby*, ch. v. § 8, " If a thing's worth doing at all," said the Professor . . . " it's worth doing well."

See also **Jew's eye.**

Wot, verb. = to know. 1. *I wot well how the world wags.* 1639 : Clarke, 97. 1670 : Ray, 158 [as in 1639, *plus*—], he is most lov'd that hath most bags. 1732 : Fuller, No. 6452 [as in 1670]. 1736 : Bailey, *Dict.*, s.v. " Wag " [as in 1670].

2. *I wot what I wot, though I few words make.* 1546 : Heywood, *Pro-*

verbs, pt. II. ch. vii. 1611 : Davies of Hereford, *Sc. of Folly*, 47, in *Works* ii. (Grosart), I wott what I wott.

Wotton hill. *See* quot. 1639 : in *Berkeley MSS.*, iii. 33 (1885), When Wotton hill doth weare a cap, Let Horton towne beware of that.

Wotton under Wever, Where God came never. 1610 : P. Holland, tr. Camden's *Britannia*, 587. 1662 : Fuller, *Worthies*, iii. 127 (1840). 1790 : Grose, *Prov. Gloss.* s.v. " Staffs " [" comes " for " came "].

Wranglers are never in the wrong. 1633 : Draxe, 243, A wrangler neuer wanteth words. 1670 : Ray, 31, Wranglers never want words. 1732 : Fuller, No. 5833.

Wrapped in mother's smock, To be = To be born lucky—probably connected with the popular idea of the luck attaching to a caul. 1590 : Greene, in *Works*, viii. 198, How should I be vsed, but as one that was wrapt in his mothers smock when hee was borne. 1632 : Randolph, *Jealous Lovers*, II. ii., Did not I tell you, sir, that I was born With a caul upon my face ? My mother wrapp'd me In her own smock. 1661 : Davenport, *City Nightcap*, II. 1707 : Centlivre, *Platonick Lady*, IV. ii., My hero ! adod thou wert wrapt up in thy mother's—Faith thou wert. 1785 : Grose, *Class. Dict. Vulgar Tongue*, s.v. " Wrapt up," He was wrapt up in the tail of his mother's smock, saying of any one remarkable for his success with the ladies. 1813 : Brand, *Pop. Antiq.*, iii. 118 (Bohn), The vulgar saying, " Oh, you are a lucky man ; you were wrapped up in a part of your mother's smock."

Wrath. *See* **Anger** (4).

Wrekin, All friends round the. Shropshire. 1700 : Congreve, *Way of World*, III. xv., You could intreat to be remember'd then to your friends round the Rekin. 1706 : Farquhar, *Recruiting Officer*, Dedn., To all friends round the Wrekin. 1755 : *Connoisseur*, No. 119. 1825 : Lamb, in *Letters*, ii. 680 (Lucas), Love and recollects to all the Wms. Doras, Maries round your Wrekin. 1871 : *N. & Q.*, 4th ser., vii. 9.

Wren. 1. *To bleed a wren according*

to its veins [which are very small] = cut your coat according to your cloth. *c.* 1430 : in *Babees Book, etc.,* 45 (E.E.T.S.), A man must spende as he may that hath but easy good, For aftir the wrenne hath veynes, men must lete hir blood.

2. *Wrens may prey where eagles dare not perch.* 1855 : Bohn, 572.

See also **Eagle** (3) ; **Robin** ; and **Spider** (1).

Wriggle about like a snig [eel] in a bottle, To. 1917 : Bridge, *Cheshire Proverbs,* 146.

Wrinkled purses make wrinkled faces. 1732 : Fuller, No. 5836. 1880 : Spurgeon, *Ploughm. Pictures,* 138.

Write. 1. *He may even go write to his friends.* 1546 : Heywood, *Proverbs,* pt. II. ch. iv., Ye maie wryte to your freendes that ye are in helth. 1670 : Ray, 176, He may even go write to his friends. We say it of a man when all his hopes are gone.

2. *Write down the advice of him who loves you, though you like it not at present.* 1855 : Bohn, 572.

3. *Write with the learned, but speak with the vulgar.* 1732 : Fuller, No. 5837.

4. *You may write on it.* 1901 : F. E. Taylor, *Lancs. Sayings,* 23, Yo' may write on't (you may rest assured of it).

Wrong, *adj.* 1. *To be in the wrong box.* 1546 : Heywood, *Proverbs,* pt. II. ch. ix., And therby in the wrong boxe to thryue ye weare. 1590 : Greene, in *Works,* viii. 88 (Grosart), If . . . thou thinkest . . . thou arte (sweet seruant) in a wrong box, and sittest far beside the cushion. Before 1658 : Cleveland, *Works,* 347 (1742), Faith you were in the wrong box. 1700 : Brown in *Works,* iii. 41 (1760), Some pert critick will tell me now, that I have lost my way in digressions. Under favour, this critick is in the wrong box, for digressions properly belong to my subject. 1838 : Dickens, *Twist,* ch. xvii., I very much question . . . whether the Clerkinwell Sessions will not find themselves in the wrong box before they have done with me. 1849 : Lytton, *Caxtons,* pt. II. ch. iv.

2. *To come on the wrong side of the blanket* = To be illegitimate. 1771 : Smollett, *Clinker,* in *Works,* vi. 381 (1817), My mother was an honest woman. I didn't come on the wrong side of the blanket. 1820 : Scott, *Monastery,* ch. xxxvii., Who, men say, was akin to the Piercie on the wrong side of the blanket. 1901 : F. E. Taylor, *Lancs. Sayings,* 38, He were getten o' th' wrank side o' th' blanket.

3. *To have the wrong end of the stick.* 1534 : in *Two Coventry C.C. Plays,* 49 (E.E.T.S.), He schal be sure, asse God me saue, Eyuer the worse yend of the staff to haue. 1573 : Harvey, *Letter-Book,* 5 (Camden S.), He was faint to put it up quickly bycause he knew he had the wors end of the staf. 1664 : J. Wilson : *Cheats,* I. iv., If at any time you find you have the worst end of the staff, leave off your cause and fall upon the person of your adversary. 1740 : North, *Lives of Norths,* i. 144 (Bohn), He that has the worse end of the staff is very apt to fling off from the point. 1901 : F. E. Taylor, *Lancs. Sayings,* 22, Theaw's getten howd o' th' wrung eend o' th' stick.

4. *To have the wrong sow by the ear.* 1546 : Heywood, *Proverbs,* pt. II. ch. ix., Ye tooke the wrong way to wood, and the wrong sow by theare. 1596 : Jonson, *Ev. Man in his Humour,* II. i., When he is got into one o' your city pounds, the counters, he has the wrong sow by the ear, i' faith. 1664 : Butler, *Hudibras,* II. ii. 580, You have a wrong sow by the ear. 1738 : Swift, *Polite Convers.,* Dial. I. 1798 : T. Dibdin, *Jew and Doctor,* I. ii., If you come to apuse Miss Emily, I tell you, you have got de wrong sow in your ear. 1857 : Hughes, *Tom Brown,* Pt. II. ch. ii.

5. *To rise on the wrong side of the bed.* 1653 : R. Brome, *Court-Begger,* II. [Citwit complains that he has been robbed, and continues]—My watch is gone out of my pocket too o'th right side. *Dai.* You rose o' the wrong side to-day it seemes. 1676 : A. Behn, *Town-Fop,* V. i., Sure I rose the wrong way to-day. I have had such damn'd ill luck. 1824 : Scott, *Redgauntlet,* ch. xx., Thou

art angry this morning . . . hast risen
from thy wrong side, I think. 1828 :
Carr, *Craven Dialect*, i. 29, Thou's gitten
out at wrang side o' th' bed, *i.e.* thou
art peevish and ill-tempered. 1921 :
Hutchinson, *If Winter Comes*, pt. II.
ch. iii. (ii), As a matter of fact that's
why I came back. I got out of bed the
wrong side this morning, didn't I ?

6. *Ye lean to the wrong shore.* 1546 :
Heywood, *Proverbs*, pt. II. ch. ii.

Wrong, *subs. All wrong comes to
wrack.* 1736 : Bailey, *Dict.*, s.v.
"Wrong."

Wryneck. *See* quot. 1879 : Henderson, *Folk-Lore of N. Counties*, 254,
Corresponding with the Lancashire
saying, " He caps Wryneck, and Wryneck caps the Dule," *i.e.* the Devil.

Wybunbury. *See* **Wembury.**

Wye, Kent. *See* **Ashford.**

Wye, River. *See* **Severn.**

Wykin. *See* **Higham.**

Wylam. *See* **Heddon.**

Wyndham. *See* **Horner.**

Wyndy as a w[h]isket [a kind of bas-
ket], **As.** Said of a forgetful person.
1917 : Bridge, *Cheshire Proverbs*, 27.

Y

Yarmouth capon, A = A herring.
1662 : Fuller, *Worthies*, ii. 447 (1840).
1785: Grose, *Class. Dict. Vulgar Tongue*,
s.v. 1886 : J. G. Nail, *Gt. Yarmouth,
etc.*, 579, In England a herring is
popularly known as a Yarmouth capon.
Cf. Norfolk capon.
Yarmouth steeple. *See* quot. 1790 :
Grose, *Prov. Gloss.*, s.v., " Norfolk," You
cannot spell Yarmouth-steeple right.
Year and Years. 1. *A good year will
not make him, and an ill year will not
break him.* 1736 : Bailey, *Dict.*, s.v.
" Year."
2. *As the year is, your pot must seethe.*
1640 : Herbert, *Jac. Prudentum.*
3. *The year doth nothing else but open
and shut.* Ibid.
4. *The year lasts longer than Yule.*
1846–59 : *Denham Tracts*, ii. 92 (F.L.S.).
5. *'Tis year'd*—spoken of a desperate
debt. 1678 : Ray, 344.
6. *Years and years. See* quot. 1913 :
E. M. Wright, *Rustic Speech, etc.*, 34,
Years ago—years and years and
donkey's ears, as the saying is.
7. *Years know more than books.* 1640 :
Herbert, *Jac. Prudentum.*
8. *Year's mind. See* Month's mind.
Yellow, *adj.* 1. *As yellow as a
guinea.* 1852 : Planché, *Extravag.*, iv.
226 (1879), The Japanese have rich
complexions, ninny ! Their sovereign
is as yellow as a guinea. 1901 : Raymond, *Idler Out of Doors*, 3, The white
of his eye turns up yellow as a guinea.
2. *As yellow as a kite's foot.* 1630 :
Davenant, *Just Italian*, I, Yellow as
foot of kite. 1863 : Wise, *New Forest*,
ch. xvi., Forest proverbs . . . such as
" As yellow as a kite's claw." 1880 :
Courtney, *W. Cornwall Words*, 32
(E.D.S.). 20th cent. at Mawgan, W.
Cornwall " Yellow as a kid's foot "
(Mr. C. Lee).
3. *As yellow as a marigold.* 1653 :
Walton, *Angler*, pt. I. ch. v., The
belly of it looked, some part of it, as
yellow as a marigold. 1917 : Bridge,

Cheshire Proverbs, 27, As yellow as a
meadow-bout [Marsh marigold].
4. *As yellow as a paigle* [cowslip].
1735 : Pegge, *Kenticisms*, in E.D.S.,
No. 12, p. 40, As yellow as a pegle. *c.*
1791 : Pegge, *Derbicisms*, 114 (E.D.S.),
Yellow as a peagle. 1854 : Baker,
Northants. Gloss., s.v. " Paigle." Paigle.
The cowslip. Now seldom used except
in the comparison, as " yellow as a
paigle." 1887 : Parish and Shaw,
Dict. Kent. Dialect, 115 (E.D.S.) [as in
1735]. Cf. Blake.
5. *As yellow as gold.* 1552 : Huloet,
Abced., sig. Nn1, Yellow as golde.
1566 : L. Wager, *Mary Magdalene*, sig. C3, 1594 : *First Part Contention*, 22 (Sh. S.). 1631 : Mabbe,
Celestina, 98 (T.T.), Shall make thy
haire as yellow as gold. 1820 : Scott,
Monastery, ch. viii., Not her butter, as
yellow as gold—
6. *As yellow as the golden noble.*
1678 : Ray, 350.
7. *A yellow band and a green wit*—an
allusion to the fashion for yellow starch.
1619 : B. Rich, *Irish Hubbub*, 41 [cited
as " a true proverb "].
8. *He wears yellow stockings* = He is
jealous. 1607 : Dekker, etc., *Northw.
Hoe*, I., Iealous men are eyther knaues
or coxcombes . . . you weare yellow
hose without cause. 1736: Bailey, *Dict.*,
s.v. " Yellow."
9. *Yellow-belly* = a fennan. 1790 :
Grose, *Prov. Gloss.*, s.v. " Lincs." 1866 :
Brogden, *Lincs. Words*, 227, . . . said
to be derived from the eels with which
the fen ditches abound. 1889 : Peacock, *Manley, etc., Gloss.*, 620 (E.D.S.),
He's a real yalla' belly, you maay tell
it by his tung.
Yeoman. *See* quots. 1732 : Fuller,
No. 488, A yeoman upon his legs is
higher than a prince upon his knees.
1736 : Franklin, *Way to Wealth*, in
Works, i. 448 (Bigelow), A ploughman
on his legs is higher than a gentleman
on his knees.

Yesterday will not be called again.
See Call, verb. (3).\

Yew. See quot. 1908 : W. Johnson,
Folk Memory, 354, The New Forest
proverb is almost literally true, " A
post of yew will outlast a post of iron."

Yoke, Irwell, Medlock, and Fame,
when they meet with the Mersey, do lose
their name. 1869 : Hazlitt, 482, . . .
These are the names of small streams,
which flow into the larger one, and so
lose their individuality.

York. 1. As much as York excels foul
Sutton. 1732 : Fuller, No. 715.

2. I cannot be at York and London at
the same time. Ibid., No. 2588.

3. Three P's of York: Pretty, Poor,
Proud. 1869 : Hazlitt, 403.

4. York has the highest rack, but
Durham has the deepest manger. 1846–
59 : Denham Tracts, i. 42 (F.L.S.). Cf.
Canterbury.

5. York, you're wanted. 1816 : T.
Morton, The Slave, II. iv. 1866 : N. &
Q., 3rd ser., x. 355, " York, you're
wanted." This phrase is commonly
used on board a man-of-war when
something goes wrong by reason of the
absence of " the right man " from the
" right place."
See also Lincoln and Oxford.

Yorkshire. 1. A Yorkshire tike, or
bite = A native of Yorkshire. c. 1600 :
Deloney, Thos. of Reading, ch. v., Do
you thinke that any can beare the
flirts and frumps, which that Northerne
tike gaue me the last time he was in
towne ? 1659 : Howell, 21, Yorkshire
tikes. 1762 : Smollett, Sir L. Greaves,
ch. xxii., I'se a poor Yorkshire tyke
. . . . my name is Tim Crabshaw.
1817 : Scott, Rob Roy, ch. iv., Thou
kens I'm an outspoken Yorkshire tyke.
1866 : Brogden, Lincs. Words, 228,
Who respond . . . by calling the people
beyond the Humber " Yorkshire Bites."
1893 : Crockett, Stickit Minister, 268,
The dialect of the " Tykes " of Yorkshire.

2. A Yorkshire way-bit = longer than
a mile. 1639–46 : in Rump Songs,
pt. I. p. 123 (1662), (Repr. 1874), For
'tis (to speak in a familiar style), A
Yorkshire wea-bit, longer then a mile.

1640 : Rous, Diary, 103 (Camden S.),
A Yorkshire way-bit, longer then a mile.
Before 1658 : Cleveland, Works, 27
(1742) [as in 1640]. 1790 : Grose,
Prov. Gloss., s.v. " Yorkshire."

3. He's Yorkshire too. Ibid., s.v.
" Yorkshire," Master's Yorkshire too.
1796 : Wolcot, Works, iv. 102 (1796),
But, hang the fellow, " he was Yorkshire too." 1803 : Kenney, Raising
the Wind, I. i., Aye, and you see I come
fra—Yorkshire. 1878 :   Folk-Lore
Record, i. 174, The saying He's Yorkshire, which is equivalent to " he's a
sharp fellow."

4. To come Yorkshire over one = To
over-reach or cheat. 1700 : Step to the
Bath, 10 (O.), I ask'd what countrey-
man my landlord was ? Answer was
made full North; and faith 'twas very
evident, for he had put the Yorkshire
most damnably upon us. 1757 :
Lancs. Dialect, quoted in Sternberg,
Dialect, etc., of Northants., 127, Yorshar,
to put Yorkshire to a man is to trick
or deceive him. 1839 : Dickens,
Nickleby, ch. xlii., It's not exactly what
we understand by " coming Yorkshire
over us " in London.
See also Bishop Brigg.

Yorkshireman. 1. A Yorkshireman's
coat of arms: a fly, a flea, a magpie, and
a flitch of bacon. 1790 : Grose, Prov.
Gloss., s.v. " Yorkshire." 1846–59 :
Denham Tracts, i. 119 (F.L.S.). 1888 :
N. & Q., 7th ser., vi. 368, . . . a flea,
a fly, and a magpie.

2. Give a Yorkshireman a halter, and
he'll find a horse. 1869 : Hazlitt, 141.

3. Shake a bridle over a Yorkshireman's grave, and he will arise and steal
a horse. 1790 : Grose, Prov. Gloss.,
s.v. " Yorkshire." 1922 : N. & Q., 12th
ser., xi. 499.

You. 1. Since you know all and I
nothing, tell me what I dreamed last night.
1640 : Herbert, Jac. Prudentum.

2. You and I draw both in the same
yoke. 1732 : Fuller, No. 5840.

3. You are a fine fellow to fetch the
devil a priest. Ibid., No. 5841.

4. You are an honest man, and I am
your uncle; and that's two lies. Ibid.,
No. 5845.

5. *You are a sweet nut.* 1583 : Mel-bancke, *Philotinus*, sig. X3, You are a swete nut, the deuill cracke you. 1732 : Fuller, No. 5844, You are a sweet nut, if you were well crackt.

6. *You are not one of our paste.* 1672 : Walker, *Parœm.*, 21.

7. *You cannot tell* [count], *you are naught to keep sheep.* 1607: Wilkins, *Mis. of Enforced Marriage*, in Hazlitt, *O. Plays*, ix. 477, And if you cannot tell, beauty, I take the adage for my reply : You are naught to keep sheep. 1666 : Torriano, *Piazza Univ.*, 172, If you can't tell you are nought to keep sheep.

8. *You see your dinner.* 1546 : Hey-wood, *Proverbs*, pt. I. ch. xi., Ye see your fare (sayd she). 1738 : Swift, *Polite Convers.*, Dial. II., Lady Answerall, pray eat, you see your dinner.

9. *You to the cabbage, and I to the beef.* 1732 : Fuller, No. 6007.

Young, *adj.* and *subs.* 1. *A man may be young in years, and yet old in hours.* Ibid., No. 296.

2. *A young barber and an old physician.* 1578 : Florio, *First Fruites*, fo. 32. *c.* 1594 : Bacon, *Promus*, No. -581. 1666 : Torriano, *Piazza Univ.*, 21.

3. *A young maid married to an old man is like a new house thatched with old straw.* 1659 : Howell, 11 (9).

4. *A young man, a ruler.* See quot. 15th cent. : in *Reliq. Antiquæ*, i. 316 (1841), A yong man, a rewler, recheles ; A olde man a lechowr, loweles ; A pore man a waster, haveles ; A riche man a thefe, nedeles ; A womman a rebawde, shameles. Thes V shalle never thrif blameles.

5. *A young man negligent, an old man necessitous.* 1732 : Fuller, No. 489.

6. *A young man old makes the old man young.* 1659 : Howell, 9 (7).

7. *A young prodigal, an old mumper* [beggar]. 1732 : Fuller, No. 490.

8. *A young serving-man, an old beggar.* 1598 : *Servingmans Comfort*, in *Inedited Tracts* (Hazlitt), 117. 1659 : R. Brome, *English Moor*, III. iii. I am too old to seek out a new master. I will not beg, because Ile crosse the proverb

That runs upon old serving creatures. 1706 : *George-a-Green*, in Thoms, *Early Prose Rom.*, ii., 9 (1828), An old serving-man made a young beggar. 1732 : Fuller, No. 492.

9. *A young trooper should have an old horse.* Ibid., No. 493.

10. *A young whore an old saint.* 1670 : Ray, 155. 1754 : Berthelson, *Eng.-Danish Dict.*, s.v. " Young."

11. *A young wife and a harvest goose.* See quot. *c.* 1400 : in *Reliquæ Antiquæ*, ii. 113 (1843), A yong wyf and an arvyst gos, Moche gagil with both : A man that [hath] ham [= them] yn his clos [possession], Reste schal he wrothe.

12. *If the young man would, and the old man could, there would be nothing undone.* 1736 : Bailey, *Dict.*, s.v. " Would."

13. *Make the young one squeak, and you'll catch the old one.* 1732 : Fuller, No. 3326.

14. *Of young men die many, Of old men scape not any.* 1666 : Torriano, *Piazza Univ.*, 105, Of young people, many dye, of the old none escapes. 1670 : Ray, 127 : 1732 : Fuller, No. 6379. Cf. No. 23.

15. *Quoth the young cock, I'll neither meddle nor make.* 1678 : Ray, 68. 1710 : S. Palmer, *Moral Essays on Proverbs*, 254. 1913 : E. M. Wright, *Rustic Speech, etc.*, 123 [quoted as " the old Berkshire proverb "].

16. *The young are not always with their bow bent, i.e.* under rule. 1678 : Ray, 353.

17. *The young cock crows as he heard the old one.* 1509 : Barclay, *Ship of Fools*, i. 235 (1874), The yonge cok lerneth to crowe hye of the olde. 1589 : Puttenham, *Engl. Poesie*, 199 (Arber), As the olde cocke crowes so doeth the chick. 1615 : Brathwait, *Strappado*, 176 (1878), Since as the old cocke crowes, the young cock learns. 1710 : S. Palmer, *Moral Essays on Proverbs*, 300. 1821 : Scott, *Pirate*, ch. xviii [as in 1615]. 1910 : R. L. Gales, *Studies in Arcady*, 335.

18. *Young birds.* See quot. 1893 : Gower, *Gloss. of Surrey Words*, 2

(E.D.S.), It ain't often that the young birds feed the old 'uns.

19. *Young birds. See also* Small birds.

20. *Young cocks love no coops.* 1605 : Camden, *Remains*, 336 (1870). 1732 : Fuller, No. 6036.

21. *Young courtier. See* Courtier.

22. *Young doth it prick. See* Pricketh betimes.

23. *Young men may die, old men must.* 1534 : More, *Works*, p. 1139, col. 2 (1557), For as we well wot, that a young man may dye soone ; so be we very sure that an olde man cannot liue long. 1605 : Camden, *Remains*, 336 (1870). 1670 : Ray, 126. 1732 : Fuller, No. 6039. Cf. No. 14.

24. *Young men's knocks old men feel.* 1670 : Ray, 38. 1736 : Bailey, *Dict.*, s.v. " Knock." 1748 : Richardson, *Clarissa*, iv. 121 (1785), Nor is that unworthy of his notice, Young men's frolicks old men feel. My devilish gout, God help me—

25. *Young men think old men fools, but old men know the young men are.* 1577 : J. Grange, *Golden Aphroditis*, sig. O2. 1605 : Chapman, *All Fools*, v. i. 1642 : D. Rogers, *Matrim. Honour*, 88, Children will say that old folke dote, and are fooles ; but old ones know that children are so. 1738 : Swift, *Polite Convers.*, Dial. I., You *think* us old fellows are fools ; but we old fellows *know* young fellows are fools. 1901 : F. E. Taylor, *Lancs. Sayings*, 11, Young folk think'n 'at owd folk are foo's, but owd folk know'n 'at young uns are.

26. *Young prodigal in a coach will be old beggar bare-foot.* 1732 : Fuller, No. 6042.

27. *Young saint old devil.* 1493 : *Dives et Pauper*, fo. 34 (1536), It is a common prouerbe yonge saynt olde deuyll. 1552 : Latimer, *Sermons*, 431 (P.S.). 1592 : Greene, in *Works*, x. 239 (Grosart), Fie vpon such as say, young saints, olde devils : it is no doubt a deuillish and damnable saying. 1677 : A. Behn, *Rover*, pt. I. I. ii., There's no sinner like a young saint. 1725 : Bailey, tr. *Erasm. Coll.*, 44, There is an old saying, a young saint and an old

devil. 1846 : T. Wright, *Essays on Middle Ages*, i. 146, We say . . . " young hypocrite, old devil."

28. *Young wenches make old wrenches.* 1639 : Clarke, 174. 1670 : Ray, 51.

Younger brother. 1. *The younger brother hath the more wit.* 1616 : Sharpham, *Cupid's Whirligig*, III., The reason the younger brothers (according to the old wiues tales) alwayes prooued the wisest men. 1678 : Ray, 85.

2. *The younger brother the better gentleman.* 1642 : Fuller. *Holy State.* "Younger Brother," Some account him the better gentleman of the two, because son to the more ancient gentleman. 1738 : Swift, *Polite Convers.*, Dial. I.

3. *To make a younger brother of one.* 1597 : *Discouerie of Knights of the Poste*, sig. C2, Drawer (quoth he) thou must not thinke to make a younger brother of me. 1678 : Ray, 85, He has made a younger brother of him.

Youth. 1. *A lazy youth a lousy age.* 1736 : Bailey, *Dict.*, s.v. " Youth."

2. *If youth knew what age would crave, it would both get and save.* 1611 : Cotgrave, s.v. " Ieunesse," If youth knew what to do, and age could do what it knowes, no man would ever be poore. 1670 : Ray, 160. 1732 : Fuller, No. 6085.

3. *What youth wones* [is accustomed to]. *See* quot. 1303 : Brunne, *Handl. Synne*, l. 7674, Yu a prouerbe of olde englys Tellë men, and soþe hyt ys, " þat yougþe wones, yu agë mones ; þat þou dedyst ones þou dedyst eftsones."

4. *Youth and age will not agree.* 1659 : Howell, 19. 1683 : Meriton, *Yorksh. Ale*, 83–7 (1697), Youth and Age will never agree.

5. *Youth and white paper take any impression.* 1579 : Lyly, *Euphues*, 37 (Arber), The tender youth of a child is . . . apt to receive any forme. 1630 : Brathwait, *Engl. Gent., etc.*, 3 (1641), Youth being indeed the philosophers rasa tabula, is apt to receive any good impressure. 1670 : Ray, 31. 1732 : Fuller, No. 6066. 1820 : Lamb, *South-Sea House*, His mind was in its original state of white paper.

6. *Youth riotously led, breedeth a loathsome old age.* 1588 : Cogan, *Haven of Health*, Epis. Ded., That saying not so common as true : Youth, etc.

7. *Youth will be served.* 1579 : Lyly, *Euphues*, 124 (Arber), We haue an olde (prouerbe), youth wil haue his course. 1633 : S. Marmion, *Fine Companion*, I. vii., Troth, uncle, youth will have his swing. 1851 : Borrow, *Lavengro*, iii. 291, Youth will be served, every dog has his day, and mine has been a fine one. 1896 : Doyle, *Rodney Stone*, ch. x. 1921 : A. Porterfield, "*Youth will be served*" [Story] in *Harper's Mag.*, Nov. 696.

Yule. 1. *A Yule feast may be quit at Pasche* [Easter]. 1846 : Denham. *Proverbs*, 63 (Percy S.).

2. *It is easy to cry Yule at other men's cost.* 1546 : Heywood, *Proverbs*, pt. I. ch. xi. 1736 : Bailey, *Dict.*, s.v. "Yule." 1846 : Denham, *Proverbs*, 62 (Percy S.) [" good " for " easy "].

3. *Yule is come, and Yule is gone, And we have feasted well ; So Jack must to his flail again, And Jenny to her wheel.* 1846 : Denham, *Proverbs*, 67 (Percy S.).

4. *Yule is good on Yule even.* 1639 : Clarke, 307. 1670 : Ray, 44. 1846–59 : *Denham Tracts*, ii. 92 (F.L.S.).

5. *Yule, Yule! a pack of new cards and a Christmas fule.* 1846 : Denham, *Proverbs*, 62 (Percy S.). 1904 : *Co. Folk-Lore: N'umberland*, 179 (F.L.S.).

See also **Bare as the birch ; Christmas ; Dark ; Every day's ; Fool** (78) ; **Martinmas** (1) ; and **Year** (3).

Z

Zeal without knowledge is fire without light. 1732 : Fuller, No. 6069.

Zeal without knowledge is the sister of folly. 1611 : Davies of Hereford,

Sc. of Folly, 42 in *Works*, ii. (Grosart). 1633 : Draxe, 246.

Zeal without prudence is frenzy. 1732 : Fuller, No. 6070.